HANDBOOK OF RESEARCH ON TEACHING

HANDBOOK
OF RESEARCH
ON TEACHING

A PROJECT OF

THE AMERICAN EDUCATIONAL RESEARCH ASSOCIATION

A DEPARTMENT OF THE NATIONAL EDUCATION ASSOCIATION

Edited by N. L. GAGE

RAND McNALLY & COMPANY
Chicago

Preface

Unlike most prefaces, this one was actually written, in good part, in advance of the book. In what follows, I shall draw upon the "Plan of the Handbook," which was sent to all contributors along with the letter of invitation.

Whatever else it may be, teaching is an intriguing, important, and complex process. Because it is intriguing, it attracts scientific attention. Because it is important, it merits careful research. Because it is complex, research on teaching needs many-sided preparation. It is toward this preparation that the *Handbook of Research on Teaching* is aimed.

A handbook is sometimes called a *vade mecum*—a constant companion. Whose companion? For this Handbook, we have primarily in mind the graduate or advanced undergraduate student preparing to do research on teaching. What this student needs by way of intellectual equipment, beyond what his other sources are likely to have given him, this Handbook attempts to provide.

Such students will almost certainly become more numerous in the decades ahead. As public concern with education becomes more insistent, the demand for research on teaching mounts. But the manpower for this research is in short supply. This Handbook is intended as an aid in the training of workers in research on teaching. If it succeeds, it will empower such research workers to begin at a higher level of competence and sophistication, to avoid past mistakes and blind alleys, to capitalize on the best that has been thought and done.

Along with the student, others may find the Handbook useful: the professor of education who prepares teachers and does research; the school administrator concerned with teaching staff; the training specialist in industry or the armed forces; the teacher himself; and the citizen interested in what affects his children.

To serve this audience properly, the Handbook should improve the conceptual and methodological equipment used in research on teaching. Such improvement can result from creative examination of past work and from imaginative appropriation of what related disciplines have to offer. In the half-century since research on teaching began, thousands of studies have been made. It is true that monographs, bibliographies, and reviews have been prepared from time to time to bring this research together. But no full-dress attempt has yet been made to do justice to past research on teaching. To summarize, to critically analyze, and to integrate this body of research are major substantive aims of the Handbook. Our conviction is that much good should come from a long and steady look at what has gone before.

Looking at what is obviously "research on teaching" in retrospection is, however, not enough. In recent decades, such research has lost touch with the behavioral sciences. It has not drawn enough nourishment from theoretical and methodological developments in psychology, sociology, and anthropology. Nor has it recently provided those disciplines with return stimulation, as it did in its earlier period. To remedy this condition—to bring research on teaching into more fruitful contact with the behavioral sciences—is a purpose of this Handbook.

Historical Note

On February 26, 1950, in Atlantic City, at the joint invitation of Warren W. Coxe and Jacob S. Orleans, a group of interested persons met informally, during the annual meeting of the American Educational Research Association, to discuss criteria of effective teaching. At the suggestion of that assemblage, AERA President Arthur Traxler some weeks later appointed a Committee on the Criteria of Teacher Effectiveness, which issued reports in 1952 and 1953.

In 1955, a continuing committee, now named the Committee on Teacher Effectiveness, was appointed by AERA President Francis G. Cornell. The new group adopted as its goal the development of the Handbook. In the 1956 report of that Committee, the conception, purposes, and layout of the Handbook were presented to the AERA Executive Committee. In February 1957, the AERA under President Percival M. Symonds endorsed the project, accepted a subvention offered by

Rand McNally & Company in support of it, and appointed the chairman and members of the Committee on Teacher Effectiveness as Editor and Editorial Advisory Board, respectively.

As editor, I prepared a "Plan of the Handbook," with the criticism and suggestions of the Editorial Advisory Board, and of various consultants—W. W. Charters, Jr., Jacob W. Getzels, R. Stewart Jones, Fred N. Kerlinger, David G. Ryans, Philip J. Runkel, Ray H. Simpson, B. Othanel Smith, and Ralph W. Tyler. The latter subsequently accepted an invitation to join the Board.

Conceptual Framework

A conceptual framework was to provide an orientation for the entire volume, and each chapter was to flow from this framework. At least, that was our hope. This framework for research on teaching specified three major classes of variables: central variables, relevant variables, and site variables.

Central Variables. A central variable in research on teaching is one referring to a behavior or characteristic of teachers. Such variables are central by definition, not as a matter of empirical determination, because they represent the center of our concern.

For an investigation to be "research on teaching" by our definition, it is necessary and sufficient that it deal with such a central variable. Research on teaching is aimed at the identification and measurement of variables in the behavior and characteristics of teachers, at discovering the antecedents or determiners of these central variables, and at revealing the consequents or effects of these variables.

Although a piece of research on teaching must by definition be concerned with at least one such central variable, it will usually also be concerned with noncentral variables, i.e., with variables we shall term "relevant" or "site," to be defined below.

We provided for three categories of central variables: (1) teaching methods, (2) instruments and media of teaching, and (3) the teacher's personality and characteristics.

1. Teaching Methods. The teacher's behavior may be that which is characteristic of a certain definition of the teacher's role, or method; in methods considered as roles, individual differences among teachers are for the moment disregarded. Examples of such roles are "lecturing" and the "project method."

2. Instruments and Media of Teaching. Writers of textbooks, producers of films, programers of teaching machines, or makers of reinforcement schedules all exhibit teaching behavior, no less so because it is "fixed" on a page, film, or tape. And the teacher who uses the textbook or film implicitly incorporates the behavior of the textbook author or film producer into his own. Accordingly, research on teaching must deal with such instruments and media.

3. The Teacher's Personality and Characteristics. When the teacher's behavior is considered to be a reflection of his personality, research attention centers on individual differences among teachers in ability, knowledge, attitude, temperament, and the like. Personality traits are inferences from relatively large samples of behavior. "Intelligence," "knowledge of subject," and "authoritarianism" are examples of dimensions of the personalities of teachers.

A characteristic of teachers is some physical, social, or other nonbehavioral property. Examples of characteristics in this sense are the teacher's age, sex, social class, and years of teaching experience. Characteristics of teachers are generally considered to be involved in research on teaching insofar as they may influence learners directly or are related to teacher behaviors or characteristics that do influence learners directly.

Relevant Variables. Relevant variables are those that refer to antecedents, consequents, or concurrents of our "central" variables. Although they are frequently found in research on teaching, they are neither necessary nor sufficient to characterize a piece of research as research on teaching. Relevant variables are those which research workers typically attempt to relate to central variables. Two loci in which relevant variables cluster are (1) social interaction in the classroom and (2) the social background of teaching.

1. Social Interaction in the Classroom. One group of relevant variables consists in behavior of teachers and pupils which acquires its significance only as social interaction. Interactive variables are those characterizing not the individuals related to each other in teaching but the "field," or relationship, between them. Interpersonal perception, affect, and behavior are examples here. Teacher-pupil relationships in turn become involved with those among pupils themselves, as studied by sociometry and other methods.

2. Social Background of Teaching. Other relevant variables take account of the social background provided by the teaching and administrative staff of the school and school system, by the homes from which learners come, and by the community and society at large. The other persons and social forces in this background affect the teacher's behavior.

Site Variables. Although research is aimed at discovering relationships between variables, not all the variables that enter into any given investigation need to vary. Some variables are typically held constant and are used to characterize the "site," or situation in which other variables are studied. The categories of site variables considered here are (1) grade level, and (2) subject matter.

1. Grade Level. The objectives and procedures of teaching depend on the psychological and social maturity of learners, which are a function of grade level. Therefore, the variables and the relationships between them can be specified in terms of a given grade level, as a "site." Sometimes, of course, grade level is allowed to become a variable in its own right.

2. Subject Matter. Research on teaching has often centered on a given subject matter. That is, we wish to ascertain relationships between variables in teaching a subject matter of particular interest to us. How should one demonstrate a motor skill like handwriting? How should a discussion be led in a class on Shakespeare?

This subject-matter orientation arises almost immediately in research on teaching. Usually such research is concerned with a single subject matter as the "site" in which the teacher's behavior or characteristics are studied as variables. Less often, perhaps, the subject matter is varied, and the relationship between such variations and other variables is the target of investigation.

Other Chapters. Thus far we have laid out the framework of research on teaching in terms of three types of substantive variables: central, relevant, and site. But the Handbook must deal not only with substantive problems and findings; the "complete" investigator also must know something of the historical, philosophical, and theoretical background and even

more about the methodology of research on teaching. These concerns provide the remainder of the Handbook's structure, in which its substantive chapters are embedded.

Editorial Policy

Where does a many-authored book like this one fall on the continuum between freedom and standardization? Did the authors have the kind of freedom possessed by the author of a book written by one person? Or did they submit to the total dominion possessed by the editor of, say, a weekly newsmagazine with anonymous authors? This book falls about midway between these two extremes. No uniform outline or style was imposed on the authors of chapters; they received only the Plan, which contained a one-paragraph sketch of each chapter, and an approximate word allotment. Each author then submitted an outline or a first draft, which was criticized by the editor. The authors developed their themes and approaches with considerable freedom. The author then submitted his final draft, and I edited this as much as seemed necessary. Yet, considerable diversity survived in outline and mode of attack, even in the relatively coordinate chapters (Chapters 15–23) dealing with research on teaching certain grade levels and subject matters.

In my opinion, altogether biased, the ratio between authorial freedom and editorial domination was just about right for the kind of field we were cultivating. Some repetition of references and ideas from one chapter to another still remains, but it seems to be necessary to allow the respective authors to develop their arguments. No chapter, I hope, simply duplicates material to be found in another, without differences in emphasis, point of view, or purpose.

Acknowledgments

After the Plan had been made, we chose and invited the authors. In making the choices, we sought advice from many consultants, including Kenneth E. Anderson, William A. Brownell, Alvin C. Eurich, Chester W. Harris, Virgil E. Herrick, T. R. McConnell, Willard C. Olson, David H. Russell, and Howard E. Wilson; to these advisers, I am grateful.

Many other persons have contributed to the development of the Handbook. At the University of Illinois, a hospitable environment was provided for the kind of long-range and untrammeled work that my many months of commitment to the Handbook required. It is perhaps no coincidence that the University of Illinois also harbored Walter S. Monroe's origination and editing of the first two editions of the AERA's *Encyclopedia of Educational Research*. Various administrative officers of the College of Education, including the late B. L. Dodds, Charles M. Allen, Alonzo G. Grace, Rupert N. Evans, and William P. McLure, have removed many obstacles of time, space, and budget which might have crippled the work. The project owes much to their wisdom and forbearance.

F. Edward Peacock and John Applegath, of Rand McNally & Company, have been unstinting in their understanding and cooperation. Virginia Moser and Maralyn Winter, the publisher's copy editors, worked diligently and effectively.

With awesome patience and ingenuity, Edward G. Holley and Dorothy Miller Black, of the University of Illinois Library, and Enid Olson of the National Council of Teachers of English, helped us find many an obscure reference.

To the many authors and publishers who granted us permission to quote from their work, as indicated in the text, we extend grateful acknowledgement.

My two co-workers in the editorial office carried much of the load. Joyce Fasnacht skillfully retyped many almost illegibly marked-up pages of manuscript, did the work of obtaining permissions to quote, checked most quotations against original sources, prepared the name index, and handled a thousand details. Romayne Ponleithner, in matters of style and expression, gave the writing in this book much of what felicity it may have. Countless major and minor awkwardnesses have disappeared beneath her blue pencil, and every author of this book is in her debt. Her professional contributions in preparing the manuscript and index, in proofreading the galleys and pages, and in simply moving the job along, have made up much of the difference between intention and accomplishment.

N. L. Gage

Champaign, Illinois
August 21, 1962

Contents

PART IV: *Research on Teaching Various Grade Levels and Subject Matters*

CHAPTER 1   Historic Exemplars of Teaching Method

HARRY S. BROUDY
University of Illinois

Once a society becomes self-conscious about schooling its young, the seed of educational theory is sown, and if all goes well, educational practice in time ceases to be blindly empirical and guides its footsteps by the insights of theory.

What sort of teaching theory will command interest during a given period of history depends on what sort of learnings carry a premium in that period. In an age when science and mathematics are richly rewarded, educational theorists strain to formulate new methods for teaching these subjects, and should the time come when it is important to communicate with space creatures, one can be sure that educational thinkers will turn out monographs about this kind of learning to the virtual exclusion of all other kinds.

If these conjectures about educational theorists are not wholly awry, the life style of an age may be discerned in the great teachers of that age. And if, as is likely, each age has its protagonists and antagonists, then one should find the spirit of protest against the values of an age exemplified in great teachers as well.

This chapter constructs a historical set-ting for current concerns with teaching by examining the teaching style of a few great teachers as exemplars of certain periods in the history of Western culture. Protagoras, Socrates, Isocrates, Quintilian, Abelard, the Jesuits, Comenius, Pestalozzi, Froebel, and Herbart were teachers by vocation and without exception believed that they could justify their method by a theory, not only of learning and teaching, but of truth, beauty, and goodness as well. Each man demonstrated how a distinctive set of values was to be embodied in the lives of a new generation by instruction.

These great teachers did not experiment in a way that would edify the researchers of our time; they did not control their variables; they did not quantify their data. They were acute rather than systematic observers, but they did sense the important problems and they did classify human experience into categories which in turn have structured our language and our thinking, and thus even our most current research. Feeling, willing, thinking, remembering, imagining, sensing, perceiving, associating, inhibiting—even the ancients were aware of the phenomenological differences among these processes and the problem of their interrelation. These men also noted that somehow individuals learn different outcomes at different rates and the same outcomes at rates that differ among individuals. They were thoroughly familiar with the problems of selective perception and selective recall and recognized that attitudes and concepts constituted different teaching tasks. But above all, these teachers of the past captured the imagination of the historians so that their names are encountered repeatedly in histories of education.

Standard histories of education cannot linger on a few exemplary figures. Historians feel compelled by the exigencies of historical method to reconstruct the political, intellectual, and economic matrices out of which the educational events in each period are born. Nor is the historian happy unless he can trace every item in a man's thought to its remotest ancestors and to its most recent progeny. A real history of teaching method would, if properly written, be a history of education, and the real history of education would be hard to distinguish from the history of the human race.

Prior to such a systematic study of the history of method it may be of some help to get a more concrete glimpse of these great teachers; to concentrate for a while on what they thought and how they taught, and to postpone for a bit the auditing of their debts to precursors and their contributions to followers. What follows is pretty much like samples of painting, literature, or music that serve to acquaint the student with what is being talked about in the history of art, rather than the history of art itself.

As to the relevance of such an inquiry to current problems of teaching, it is easier to make plausible claims than to make the claims convincing. A rough parallel between the successive phases of differentiation and integration in biological development and in the historical development of

research into educative processes may help to illuminate this relevance.

The teachers of the past analyzed instances of successful and unsuccessful teaching, and like all theoreticians, they ventured hypotheses to take account of the new factors that analysis disclosed. The great difference between their inquiries and modern research is the rate at which differentiations and integrations are made and replicated today.

Part of the acceleration is due to the number of persons engaged in the enterprise, but a more fundamental factor is the invention and refinement of research instruments. For example, the abstraction of the "intelligence" factor is as old as Plato, and the attempt to train it by mathematics is no younger. But nothing really significant in the development of this could occur until tests for intelligence became available and statistical tools were perfected.

With the help of modern instruments, relatively large numbers of researchers distinguished, within intelligence, factors that did not correlate highly with each other, and as the number of these factors increased, the pressure for new integrations increased (Guilford, 1959). Integrations, in turn, triggered research to test the consequences that could plausibly be deduced from the new hypotheses. And so a new round of distinction-making was instituted, to be followed by new integrations.

The connection between our teaching exemplars and current work in educational theory is, therefore, more than genetic and historical. Their interests and modes of inquiry were not different from ours, so far as the analytical phases were concerned. It is not difficult to imagine Socrates, Isocrates, Abelard, and the others teaching in our universities, holding membership in our learned societies, writing articles for educational journals, addressing educational conventions, and perhaps writing chapters for this book.

Methods of teaching, one must suppose, developed historically with beginnings, variations, and continuities that could, theoretically, be dated and documented. This essay does not furnish such a historical account of pedagogy. What follows is historical only in its selection of exemplars of teaching method from great teachers of the past.

A word about the principle of selection may be helpful. An effort was made to find teachers or schools that exemplified a distinctive method or a distinctive phase of method. No attempt was made to prove that these men or schools were the originators of the method. Naturally, teachers whose names are familiar to students of education were chosen over obscure figures, and those presumed to have influence on subsequent educational developments were preferred to those whose influence was slight. Further, the discussion was confined to men who carried on instruction as a principal vocation, thus leaving out Moses, Jesus, and other great religious figures who are known as great teachers.

Selection entailed some problems of taxonomy. For example, whether the Sophists made distinctive contributions to teaching method depends somewhat on whether analysis of the materials of instruction is to be included under the methods of instruction or under research into the structure of language, mathematics, logic, etc. Is mild discipline a part of method or not? Should the Jesuits be studied as exemplars of school administration, curriculum organization, or teaching method?

In this chapter, *method* refers to the formal structure of the sequence of acts commonly denoted by instruction. The term covers both the strategy and tactics of teaching and involves the choice of what is to be taught at a given time, the means by which it is to be taught, and the order in which it is to be taught. The theories of learning that may or may not have suggested the methods, the aims of the total educative process, and the philosophical considerations that might be used to validate them are introduced into the discussion of method, but only as needed to elucidate their nature and import.

It became clear after a preliminary study that teaching methods could be discussed with respect to differences in the following phases of the teaching act: (1) classroom control, (2) presentation of the learning task, (3) inducement of trial responses, (4) correction of trial responses, and (5) institution of test trials for evaluation.

Classroom control refers to the form of activity used to secure attention and to maintain order. Methods of classroom control range from corporal punishment for infraction of rules and disobedience of commands to reliance on the natural goodness of little children. Presentation of the task— the phase of teaching perhaps most frequently coming to mind when method is discussed—varies from the pyrotechnics of the sensational classroom lecturer to the almost casual conversation of Socrates and a companion. Inducement of trial responses might consist of demands that the pupil do problems in arithmetic, recite alone or in chorus, or copy a model composition. Correcting trial responses and instituting test trials likewise have a wide range of variability and exhibit an equally wide range of ingenuity.

Although one can describe methods of teaching without discussing the ultimate aims of education, it is virtually impossible to do so without reference to the more immediate outcomes of instruction. For both Socrates and Isocrates the aim of education was to produce the good Athenian citizen, or more accurately, the good Athenian statesman. But the intervening variable, so to speak, for Socrates was a purgation of character by dialectic, while for Isocrates it was eloquence, and these immediate objectives rather than the ultimate ones differentiated their methods.

In every age the school has been expected to provide, first of all, *linguistic skills,* the basic tool of learning in any well-developed culture. It is not surprising, therefore, that much of the history of pedagogy hovers about the ways and means of teaching language—for the most part, Latin and Greek as foreign languages. Next in the order of expectation was *a stock of knowledge*—whatever knowledge was in vogue: what the poets said, or what the astronomers, astrologers, theologians, physicists, and alchemists certified as truth. Finally, it was expected that instruction would build into the pupil *habits* of using his acquired skill and knowledge in the forum or in the courts of law and kings, as teachers and prelates, princes and ambassadors, doctors, clergymen, lawyers, scientists, and statesmen, or, in later centuries, as tradesmen, workers, and citizens. The immediate goal of pedagogy has been to incorporate the results of instruction into habits of speaking, thinking, acting, and feeling with the hope that they would function reliably in adult life. In short, the practical justification of pedagogy is the promise of transfer. Discerning the logical connection between what is taught and its future use, and the method that actually establishes the connection, constitutes pedagogy's theoretical justification.

Each age, therefore, sought the philosopher's stone—the subject or skill, or the smallest number of them, that would transfer so well and so widely as to provide the key to pedagogical success, e.g., oratory, dialectical skill, Latin grammar, and knowledge about the natural environment. With each shift in emphasis, new theories of learning and new methods of teaching emerged. Once scientific thinking as we know it became important, for example, how people learn to think scientifically became important for learning theory and for pedagogy. And not infrequently the learning theory took its cue from successful teaching methodology rather than vice versa.

Pedagogy has been confronted with a number of challenges: (1) The challenge to train young men for successful political life in democratic Athens and later in republican Rome. The response was the rhetorical curriculum of the Sophists, exemplified at various periods in the persons of Protagoras, Isocrates, and Quintilian.

(2) The challenge to have the pupil introject a particular value schema deeply rooted in metaphysical and religious systems of thought. This challenge occurs in every age, usually as a protest against current school practices that eventuate in the conventional value patterns. Socrates and Froebel exemplify pedagogical responses to this type of challenge.

(3) In the Middle Ages, the challenge to train teachers who could conceptualize all realms of life so as to synthesize Christian theology, ancient philosophy, and science. To deal with the problems of life by faith alone was no longer possible, and to deal with them in terms of empirical science was not yet possible. The *via media* was that of apologetics, and the method was Scholasticism. Abelard is often credited with having ushered in both of these and with them the rise of the universities. With the growth of the universities came the development of a more or less standard method of preparing men for the learned professions and of training the teachers who would conduct such professional education.

(4) The challenge to develop language skill, whose primacy in every age has already been mentioned. The school of the grammarian persisted in one form or another as a preparatory school for the higher education of the rhetor. But mastery of Latin and Greek also became the response of the secondary school of the post-Renaissance—the *Gymnasium,* the *Lycée,* the Latin Grammar school—to the challenge of Classical Humanism. The methodology of these schools is discussed as the contribution of the Jesuits.

(5) The challenge of synthesizing Classical studies with scientific knowledge, created by the rise of modern science and its popularization by Francis Bacon. In Comenius, Pestalozzi, and Herbart, this challenge elicited distinctive pedagogical responses.

(6) The challenge in our industrial and atomic age to combine into a viable whole

scientific knowledge, humane democratic ideals, and the demands on personality that a corporate culture exerts. Other chapters in this volume deal with the pedagogical responses that this challenge has elicited.

TEACHING MEN
TO BE ELOQUENT

Effective oratory sways the hearer either by argument or by arousing his emotions. The cogency of argument depends on the weight of the evidence. Sympathy and antipathy depend on the way language is used to evoke anger, pity, hatred, and love with respect to the object or proposal under discussion. Accordingly, the training of the orator had to provide (1) access to the evidence, (2) skill in argument, (3) facility with the evocative or nonreferential use of language, and (4) a practical command of social psychology.

When, therefore, a Sophist of the fifth century B.C. promised to undertake the training of a young man for three or four years and guaranteed to make of him a successful man of affairs for a fee of 10,000 drachmas, as did Protagoras of Abdera (Marrou, 1956), how did he propose to redeem the promise? Presumably by producing the outcomes listed above.

In order to get students, the ancient Sophist had to advertise himself and his wares. Having no permanent school, he traveled from town to town setting up a temporary base of operations at some house or hall. There he gave a sample lecture on some topic suggested by the audience, or improvised an oration on a theme of his own choosing.

A classic description of such a session is given in Plato's dialogue *Protagoras.* While it was still dark, Hippocrates, an excited young man, roused Socrates from sleep to tell him that three famous Sophists— Protagoras (485–415 B.C.), Hippias of Elis, and Prodicus of Ceos (both living in the fifth century B.C.)—had arrived in Athens and were at the house of the wealthy citizen Callias. Hippocrates wanted Socrates to introduce him to Protagoras and to persuade the famous Sophist to accept him as a pupil.

Socrates and Hippocrates were not the first to arrive at the Callias residence. Protagoras was walking in the portico followed by a "train of listeners" who accompanied him on his travels and a group of distinguished Athenians. In another lobby, Hippias was discoursing on astronomy, while a third knot of admirers surrounded Prodicus, who was still in bed. In the dialogue it is remarked that one could not make out what Prodicus was saying but that he spoke with a booming sound.

Protagoras contains the typical ingredients of the sample lecture: the myth and its interpretation; proof by argument; and the reading or reciting of a Homeric poem or legend together with critical commentaries on it. Several points about these set speeches should be noted: First, they were samples of what the pupil would himself produce on future occasions, i.e., a kind of work sample. Second, requiring a student to reproduce a speech by the master was a major method of teaching eloquence. In the Platonic dialogue *Phaedrus,* for example, Socrates asks Phaedrus to repeat to him the speech he had heard from Lysias.

PHAEDR. What do you mean, my good Socrates? How can you imagine that my unpractised memory can do justice to an elaborate work, which the greatest rhetorician of the age spent a long time in composing. . . .
Soc. I believe that I know Phaedrus about as well as I know myself, and I am very sure that the speech of Lysias was repeated to him, not once only, but again and again;—he insisted on hearing it many times over and Lysias was very willing to gratify him; at last, when nothing else would do, he got hold of the book, and looked at what he most wanted to see,—this occupied him during the whole morning;—and then when he was tired of sitting, he went out to take a walk, not until, by the dog, as I believe, he had simply learned by heart the entire discourse, unless it was unusually long, and he went to a place outside

the wall that he might practise his lesson (Plato, 1927, p. 285).

Third, Homer and other poets were used both as authorities on matters of policy and for literary appeal. They did not ignore other sources of knowledge; they had specialists in mathematics, astronomy, art, and all the other branches, because the legislator who might have to discourse on any topic needed a wide variety of information. Nevertheless, it was literature that celebrated the ethos of the time and it was the medium in which speaker and audience most readily achieved communion (Jaeger, 1943, II, 107 ff.).

The Sophists as Analysts

It is one thing to deliver a brilliant sample speech to bewitch eager young men and another to deliver 10,000 drachmas worth of instruction. To accomplish the latter the Sophists needed a systematic organization of the materials to be taught and an orderly sequence of activities for teaching them.

By analyzing the work of poets and other instances of good writing and speaking, the Sophists were able to formulate rules for effective speaking and writing. Protagoras is credited with the rules for distinguishing the tenses of verbs and for classifying modes of utterance. Prodicus of Ceos studied synonyms in an attempt to clarify the meanings of words. Gorgias of Leontini (483–375 B.C.) is said to have devised the Gorgiac figures of antithesis, balance of clauses, and final assonance (Freeman, 1907; Gomperz, 1912; Marrou, 1956; Moore, 1936).

By the fourth century, when Isocrates (436–338 B.C.), contemporary and rival of Plato (427–346 B.C.), had become the foremost teacher of rhetoric of his time, the analysis of language, its principal parts, inflections, and grammatical rules was well under way. Isocrates charged only 1,000 drachmas for the course of instruction and complained that some teachers would undertake it for as little as 300. He developed the rules of rhetoric to a high degree of perfection and cre-

ated the set speech as an instrument of political action. The influence of Isocrates reached down through Cicero and Quintilian into relatively recent times, and the fact that Isocrates' school turned out many men who made brilliant records in public life did nothing to impair the esteem in which his methods were held.

The analysis of materials into teaching form had to be undertaken by the Sophists in every field they sought to teach: etymology, geography, natural history, genealogy, laws of meter and rhythm, history, mythology, politics, ethics, criticism of religion, mnemonics, logic, tactics, strategy, music, drawing, painting, sculpture, and athletics.

In logic especially, the Sophists had to make a beginning by analyzing rules of debate and argument. Protagoras is said to have formulated eristics, a debating method in which one takes a point conceded by an opponent and uses it as a starting point for further argument. Protagoras' Antilogies were, in a sense, the forerunners of the Socratic dialectic.

By 166 B.C., Dionysius of Thrace had formalized the steps to be followed in presenting a lecture on a literary work:

1. Give the selected passages an exact reading with respect to pronunciation, punctuation, and rhetorical expression.
2. Explain the figures of speech.
3. Explain the historical and mythological references.
4. Comment on the choice of words and their etymology.
5. Point out the grammatical forms employed.
6. Estimate the literary merit of the selection.

This established the form and style of the famous prelection and *exposition de texte* as a mode of instruction, but the point to be made here is that teaching method begins with analysis of the teaching act into a sequence of steps. The Sophists are rightly called the ancestors of the teaching profession, not only because they taught for fees but because they became self-conscious about teaching as an art, and this of necessity led them to the consideration of method.

Analysis and the Teaching of Rhetoric

Even in these days of carefully worked out course syllabi and elaborate instruction in pedagogy, it would be difficult to match the minuteness of analysis that went into the teaching of rhetoric in the schools of Greece and Rome.

I have borrowed extensively from Clark's *Rhetoric in Greco-Roman Education* (1957) to indicate the great detail to which the analysis of both the subject matter and the methodology was carried.

By the fourth century B.C., it was pretty well agreed by Aristotle and others that the teaching of rhetoric involved three factors: nature, art, and exercise. Then, as now, teachers could only wish for a high order of talent and docile temperament. Hence, most of the attention had to be given to art and exercise. The art was summed up in sets of definitions, precepts or rules, and classifications. These were to be learned by heart. The exercises consisted of practice tasks in imitating the best models the instructor could set before his pupils.

An idea of the complexity of the subject can be gained by noting that the art of speaking, and writing as well, was divided by Cicero (*De partitione oratoria,* 46 B.C.; Clark, 1957, pp. 69 ff.) into the following tasks:

inventio: to find out what one should say
dispositia: to arrange what one has found
elocutio: to clothe it with language
memoria: to secure it in one's memory
pronuntiatio: to deliver it

So much for the resources needed by the speaker. As to the oration or speech itself, six divisions were recognized:

exordium: opening
narratio: statement of the facts colored to favor the speaker's argument
divisio: forecast of main points the speaker plans to make

confirmatio: the argument in favor of the speaker's contentions
confutatio: rebuttal of possible objections
peroratio: conclusion or summation

Within these large divisions were numerous subdivisions. Cicero classified 17 sources of arguments for the *inventio.* As to style, Cicero came to be the model par excellence, but models also were sought in other standard Roman authors: Virgil, Horace, Ovid, Lucan, Statius, Persius, Martial, Catullus, Juvenal, and Sallust. Clark quotes Marrou to the effect that Latin was taught as a dead language as early as the days of Jerome and Augustine (Clark, 1957, p. 86; Marrou, 1938, p. 14).

The actual teaching procedure both in the school of the grammarian and in the higher school of the rhetors was as follows:

1. The pupil would memorize the definitions, classifications, and rules as embodied in textbooks.
2. The teacher would analyze the models to be imitated by a prelection.
3. The pupil would apply the precepts and imitate the model in practice declamations or compositions on hypothetical themes.

The imitation which was the heart of the method was obviously not a simple duplication of the model. Good imitation involved:

1. Giving the student the results of careful study of the model by the teacher to reveal how the author achieved his effects. This analysis was offered by the teacher either in a lecture or by assigning material covering this point in a textbook (see Quintilian *Institutio,* II, v. 6–16).
2. Asking the student to write sentences that exhibited the stylistic characteristics of the model: periodic sentences, certain figures of speech, etc. Exercises in imitation included learning by heart, learning by translation from Greek to Latin, and paraphrasing poetry into prose.

Even the exercises in the earlier phases of composition study were not left to chance. There were collections of graded exercises (*progymnasmata*) to guide the writing and speaking practice. Other exercises called for retelling fables, plausible fictions, and stories from history; delivering narrations dealing with persons; amplifying proverbs into a moral essay; refuting an argument; taking a set of facts typical of a class of situations and applying them to a particular case; praising or dispraising a thing or person (one writer treated of this exercise alone in 36 divisions and subdivisions); making comparisons; composing imaginary speeches that might have been given by some historical or mythological figure; describing objects and events vividly; arguing on set questions (e.g., Should a man marry?); and speaking for or against a piece of legislation.

This type of training has long been condemned as highly artificial and formal. In later centuries it deserved many of the hard things said about it, especially when oratory and elegant writing no longer served any significant social purpose. As a method, however, it had its merits.

The Virtues of the Method

In the first place, the method had the virtue of definiteness. At any given moment the pupil had little doubt as to what was expected of him, how he should go about it, and how well he was getting along. As a youngster in the grammar school, he might not be enthusiastic about memorizing definitions he did not understand or the endless writing of dull themes. Wise schoolmasters such as Quintilian understood this and used praise and reproof rather than harsh punishments as a means of class control. Yet routine and clarity of expectation contribute much to psychological security of the pupil and perhaps to the security of the teacher as well. If the teacher cannot be inspired, he ought to be at least intelligent, and if not that, at least methodical, but if he is not even methodical, all is lost. Provided he was not mired in the bewildering classifications and subclassifications, the teacher could always know what to do next and provide a reason to himself and to his pupil for doing it.

The reliance on habituation was almost complete. Quintilian believed that the pupil could form habits of premeditation and even of improvisation. He therefore advised: Have a good stock of thoughts and phrases available. If you have practiced the style of the speech and the order of presentation, you can think ahead of the audible words. The best form of exercise in improvisation, however, is to speak daily before an audience of several persons, or to go over the speech silently, but forming the words. Above all, counseled Quintilian, keep writing: "We must write, therefore, whenever possible; if we cannot write, we must meditate: if both are out of the question, we must still speak in such a manner that we shall not seem to be taken unawares nor our client to be left in the lurch" (Quintilian *Institutio,* X, vii. 3–29).

Though formal and rigid, the method provided for flexibility in at least two ways. For one thing, the goal of the instruction was to give the prospective speaker a set of standardized models for the kind of speaking occasions most likely to occur, e.g., the encomium, pleading a case, or urging legislation. Having perfected these speech- or essay-types, one could discharge any given task merely by filling in the blanks with the right names and circumstances.

Naturally, judgment and acumen would adjust the speech nicely to the occasion; even the rhetoricians realized that there was no way of teaching this systematically. But by learning speech-types the pupil was acquiring flexibility. For example, if the accused had committed a crime that could be brought under the general heading of treason, the well-trained orator had at his disposal a whole store of remarks that could be made on treason: a nest of historical examples, appropriate quotations from the poets and mythology, as well as the utterances of noted men. Moreover, he had probably practiced the "treason" speech often enough to have a go at this one with a high degree of confidence.

Another type of flexibility was provided

by the variety of practice situations. Given enough specificity, the duller student did not have to bother with subsuming particulars under generalizations; "transfer" by identical elements functions even when transfer by generalization does not.

The methods of the rhetor also brought out the role of apprentice teaching or internship training. Because all the exigencies of the concrete speech-making situation could not be anticipated, the student was to select some orator to follow about and imitate. In the law courts and at public occasions, he was to listen to him and then write out his own speeches for the very same cases and occasions (Quintilian *Institutio*, X, v. 19–21). This was a recognition that all professional work is an art as well as a science; that sooner or later the professional operates at the level of the particular. The concrete situation—the sick patient, the unruly classroom, the tense courtroom, the crowd gathered at the funeral—cannot be verbalized without destroying some of its concreteness. Hence, all professional training has to be crowned by practice under a master. This the Rhetoricians realized, as did the universities later on, when the student to a large extent learned by teaching.

Finally, the method presupposed that standards of excellence in speaking, writing, and thinking had already been achieved in the speaking, writing, and thinking of real or fictional characters in the past. To the Rhetoricians, it was a choice between denying the greatness of these products or copying them. Thus Quintilian said:

Is it not sufficient to model our every utterance on Cicero? For my own part, I should consider it sufficient, if I could always imitate him successfully. But what harm is there in occasionally borrowing the vigor of Caesar, the vehemence of Caelius, the precision of Pollio or the sound judgment of Calvus? (*Institutio*, X, ii. 25).

Collections of model speeches were compiled and presumably used, e.g., *The Declamations of Quintilian, Being an Exercitation or Praxis upon His XII Books, concerning The Institution of the Orator* (London, printed by F. R. for John Taylor, 1686). Isocrates also furnished speech models in his *Against the Sophists, Antidosis,* and *Panegyricus,* although they were not written solely for this purpose. Lazarus Piot's *The Orator: Handling a Hundred Several Discourses, in forme of Declamations* is a later sample (Clark, 1957, p. 261).

Imitation is a bad word in contemporary educational language. The abuses of imitation, when speaking and writing degenerated into empty exercises in form, contributed to its bad reputation. Nevertheless, as a method of teaching, imitation has to be evaluated apart from the uses and abuses to which it has been put. Can teaching wholly dispense with it? It is difficult to imagine a test of learning that did not compare the pupil's performance with a model of some sort. Sooner or later the language used by the pupil is compared with that of the scientist, historian, or geographer. If he speaks the way the models do, we hope that he thinks the way they do. If he does not speak as they do, we doubt that he thinks as they do. We cannot be sure in either case, but our doubt is far greater in the latter situation than in the former.

There is a difference, however, between using a model for the testing of learning and using duplication of a model as a means of teaching. In rhetorical education, as described above, exact duplication of material was demanded, especially in the early stages of training, but the final objective could not be exact replication. After all, the case before the court and the trainee was not the case Cicero (the model) had argued. The speaker had to make adjustments to the individuating features of the occasion. What he imitated, therefore, was the *form* of the speech after making a judgment as to which form was appropriate. He had a multitude of formulas from which to choose; he did not have to invent them as he went along. The formulas took care not only of the subject matter but also of the style of composition and delivery. One could, therefore, reduce the art of speaking to a fairly mechanical sequence of selecting and imitating a model. However, mastery in any type of learning means having enough formulas on hand to meet a wide variety of circumstances with a minimum of judgment. Even the complicated reasoning of an engineer, physician, judge, or philosopher approximates this pattern as mastery is achieved.

Advocates of rhetorical methods no doubt believed that they were training memory, observation, imagination, and reasoning as well as forming specific skills. Their methods, unlike those advocated by the doctrines of formal discipline, did not rely on one or two subject matters to train these powers; nor were they indifferent as to what content was used for training. Formal discipline in rhetorical education was literally a discipline of forms, rather than a training of faculties. It relied on a rich stock of widely applicable formulas, not on the strengthening of certain powers. As to creativity, the method did not preclude imaginative maneuvering within the formulas; it encouraged it. The speaker's inventiveness was limited, however, to the turn of phrase or the phrasing of an argument. He was not expected to achieve new solutions to problems, and the method of his schooling did not provide for his learning to produce them (Clark, 1951; McKeon, 1936).

SOCRATIC DIALECTIC

Not everyone was happy with the highly developed methods of rhetorical teaching. Objections to a system of schooling that is enjoying success can be of two sorts. First, one may complain that the ultimate values professed by the school have been abandoned in favor of more immediate values—usually vocational success. Second, within the system there are wide variations in the quality of teaching. At one end of the scale are the teachers who take the professed objectives seriously, who are themselves persons of high cultivation and character, and who use the methods with skill, imagination, and inventive freedom. At the other end of the scale are the men of meager talents who, by becoming versed in the method, achieve a marketable result but leave something to be desired in moral and intellectual quality. One may complain that the inferior practitioners of the art have taken control of the enterprise.

There were those like Xenophon who attacked the Sophists for their fee-taking and their flamboyant claims, charging that they were innovators leading the youth away from the ancient virtues (areté). But Plato's criticism, as expressed in many of his dialogues, raised a more serious objection.

In the person of Socrates, the protest took the following form: In order to teach virtue, as the Sophists claimed to do, they would have to know what virtue really was. Yet on questioning them Socrates found that, instead of a definition of virtue, his respondents were likely to give him examples of conduct or the consequences of conduct conventionally called virtuous.

In the early dialogues, for example, *Laches, Euthyphro,* and the *Meno,* Socrates is portrayed as trying to arrive at a generic definition of virtue or excellence. Although no definition is achieved, each dialogue argues that knowledge is a common element in all the virtues. Virtue, Socrates argued, was a kind of knowledge, but knowledge of what? It was not like knowledge of the stars or common-sense knowledge of the world. To say that it was a knowledge about the norms or standards of conduct is not satisfactory either, because it was obvious that men who knew what they ought to do nevertheless often failed to do it, or did what they acknowledged they ought not to have done. And virtue, if it was knowledge, was action-knowledge. In short, more than ordinary cognition was concerned. It involved a complete reorientation of the personality as a result of which one not only cognized the norms of the true, good, and beautiful, but also introjected them.

Now to impart this sort of education was a far cry from teaching boys how to make good speeches. How could it be brought about? In the works of Plato four methods can be distinguished: exhorting the learner to become concerned about the importance of his achieving these norms; dialectical self-examination; disciplining one's appetites (self-mastery); and a course of intellectual training culminating in dialectics. The first two of these approaches seem to have been characteristic of Socratic teaching; the latter two probably reflect Plato's own elaborate plan for the ideal state and the ideal guardian of that state as set forth in the *Republic*. The real Socrates did not, according to Xenophon, think so highly of mathematical knowledge as did the Platonic Socrates (Jaeger, 1943, II, 304).

Socratic Exhortation

In the *Apology,* Socrates said:
Men of Athens . . . while I have life and strength I shall never cease from the practice and teaching of philosophy, exhorting any one whom I meet and saying to him after my manner: You, my friend . . . are you not ashamed of heaping up the greatest amount of money and honor and reputation, and caring so little about wisdom and truth and the greatest improvement of the soul, which you never regard or heed at all?

The frequent use of exhortation to become concerned about the state of one's values (one's soul) has been noted by Jaeger (1943, II, 39). It is illustrated in the *Protagoras* (313 a–c) when Socrates, accompanying Hippocrates to the house of Callias to hear Protagoras, asks the excited young man:

Well, but are you aware of the danger which you are incurring? If you were going to commit your body to some one, who might do good or harm to it, would you not carefully consider and ask the opinion of your friends and kindred, and deliberate many days as to whether you should give him the care of your body? But when the soul is in question, which you hold to be of far more value than the body, and upon the good or evil of which depends the well-being of your all—about this you never consulted either with your father or with your brother or with any of us who are your companions. But no sooner does this foreigner appear, than you instantly commit your soul to his keeping.

The learner had to be jolted into uneasy anxiety about his soul, just as contemporary man must be scared a bit before he trots off to his periodic medical checkups. Socrates was a past master of irony and enigma. His partner in the dialogue was never sure how literally Socrates was to be taken. He was a provoker and a gadfly, especially to those who were well satisfied with themselves, and his apparent quibbling over words infuriated his opponents.

Socrates usually began with a casual question about something his victim regarded as beyond question: the nature of courage, temperance, or justice. To be shown that one really did not know what seemed so certain, that one's common-sense definitions led to awkward consequences, and that one was, in short, abysmally ignorant precisely where one thought himself to be wise, elicited chagrin, embarrassment, and often anger—usually with Socrates, but occasionally with oneself. When the latter happened, the time was ripe for the positive side of the method, namely, dialectical self-examination.

The resemblance of Socrates' approach to that of the psychoanalyst is striking, and considering the relation of young men to their sponsors in the Greek scheme of things, the analogy is strong indeed. The notion of teaching as a species of love-therapy is an old one.

For Socrates, education and physical healing were closely related. Like the body, the soul when healthy had its order and form. It had its proper excellences as did the body. To teach was to realign the value scheme of the individual so that his list of value priorities, so to speak, corresponded to the value order of the healthy soul. As expounded in the *Republic,* the hierarchical structure was this: reason (the virtue of wisdom) to dominate in all choice; appetite to be willingly subordinated to reason (temperance, the virtue of desire), and spirit (courage, the virtue of will) to be on the side of reason in all its conflicts with appetite. The structure as a whole, when realized, Plato called justice —or the harmonious, naturally functioning, healthy soul. This harmony was the result of self-discipline which, in turn, was produced by intellectual and emotional exercises. To provide emotional training, Plato, in both the *Republic* and *Laws,* prescribed programs of conditioning the young against the temptation of the "unnecessary" pleasures.

Socratic Conversation

Everything in the educational scheme depended on the existence of absolute models of the virtues that could be discerned by human beings. Socrates reasoned that, inasmuch as absolutes of any kind could not be experienced empirically, they were innate. As to why we did not know these from birth, Socrates conjectured that they were forgotten each time the soul was reincarnated in a different body. Hence teaching did not convey these fundamental notions to the learner; it merely prodded him into reminiscing or remembering what he already knew but had forgotten.

To illustrate this point, Socrates in the *Meno* (82a–86b) undertakes to teach a slave boy the proof of the Pythagorean theorem, namely, that the square on the hypotenuse of a right triangle is equal to the sum of the squares on the other two sides. To begin with, it is determined that the slave boy speaks Greek and knows what a square is— that it has four equal sides, and that the lines bisecting the sides of the square are equal. He also can count.

The problem is posed: If the given square has a side equal to two feet, what will be the length of the side of a square twice as large?

The boy answers that it will be four feet. Socrates now draws a square presumably of this form:

and asks the boy what would happen to it if he doubled the side. The figure now looks like this:

By counting the squares the boy sees that doubling the side of a square forms a space not twice as large but four times as large.

Socrates begins again. What length of side would give a square containing eight square feet if a two-foot square gives you four square feet? The boy infers that it will be something between two and four feet and guesses at three, but he admits that he doesn't know how to deal with the problem. He has received the shock and is now ready to begin to learn. Socrates begins again drawing the figure:

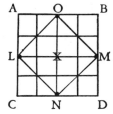

The figure is four times the original one. He draws the diagonals OL, OM, MN, and LN. He asks whether OLNM is a square. Does it have four equal sides? How much space (area) is in this new square?

Boy: I do not understand.

Soc.: Has not each interior line (diagonal) cut off half of the four spaces?

Boy: Yes.

Soc.: How many such half-spaces are there in this division [OLNM]?

Boy: Four.

Soc.: How many in this? [AOXL]

Boy: Two.

Soc.: And four is how many times two?

Boy: Twice.

Soc.: And this space [OLNM] is how many feet?

Boy: Eight feet.

Soc.: And from what line do you get this figure?

Boy: From this. [OL]

Soc.: From the line the learned call the diagonal? Are you prepared to affirm that the double space is the square of the diagonal?

Boy: Certainly, Socrates.

Several points might be noted about this demonstration lesson. A small one is that current interest in teaching mathematics by discovery (Craig, 1956; Haslerud & Meyers, 1958; Hendrix, 1947) is itself a rediscovery. Second, Socrates picked for his demonstration precisely the kind of learning task—a set of deductive relations—that best illustrates the independence of certain conceptual operations from their sources in experience. Because the slave boy had not learned the proof from anyone, Socrates concluded that the boy had been in possession of the criteria of deductive proof all along and had only to be reminded of them. Third, and perhaps most important, Socrates had hit on the touchy problem of how to teach a deductive system of relations, and it was obviously not by rote memorization, not by imitating a model, and not by learning precepts and rules.

The "moment of truth" in this type of learning comes presumably when the learner grasps the nature of the fundamental mathematical relations involved in the proof and "sees" that so-and-so does not merely happen to be the case, but *must* be the case. The insight having occurred, the learner is ready to go on to mastery, i.e., to supplement understandings with the skills of proof and computation. As to what causes the insight, Socrates had his theory of innate ideas and reminiscence—not a convincing theory, to be sure. But is there a convincing theory?

The use of the dialectical conversation or exploration is illustrated in another area by the exchange between Thrasymachus and Socrates in the *Republic* (341–342). Thrasymachus had just argued that a ruler qua ruler makes no mistakes as to what is best for himself, i.e., as to where his own interest

lies. If the ruler is stronger than the ruled, and if it is right to obey the ruler, then right means whatever is in the interest of the stronger.

To attack this "might is right" doctrine, Socrates gets Thrasymachus to admit that in the case of the physician or ship captain the interest or objective of the craftsmen is not to make money or to serve themselves, but rather to serve their clients. They agree also that the craft or art is superior to and stronger than the people it serves (i.e., with respect to the skill involved). In serving the clients, the craft or art therefore serves the interests of the weaker rather than the stronger.

If it is objected that this is quibbling over a term, as Thrasymachus did violently object, then Socrates could and did remind him that earlier in the dialogue Thrasymachus had insisted on dealing with the term "ruler" in its strict meaning in order to prove that a ruler could not be mistaken as to what was in his own interest.

In this selection a definition is tested by applying it to cases where it presumably should apply. The test having failed to confirm the definition, a search has to be instituted for a more adequate definition. A progressive clarification of terms ensues which, according to Plato, can occur only in the dialectical dialogue; hence his distrust of the textbook. Conceptual clarity, he felt, is achieved by an active search on the part of both learner and teacher for a definition that will stand the dialectical test.

The search for such a definition, of course, makes no sense unless one believes that there are real definitions of terms and not merely nominal and conventional ones. All of Plato's metaphysics and epistemology was directed toward proving that by careful abstraction and logical analysis the mind could apprehend the essences or the natures of things, and that these universals had a being independent of the particular minds that happened to entertain them and of the objects that exemplified them. With these considerations in mind, an examination of the phases of teaching method that Plato added to the exhortation and dialectical exploration of Socrates is in order.

Discipline and mathematics. How does one teach the learner to apprehend the most general and absolute norms and at the same time to introject them as imperatives for his thought and conduct?

Two methods were urged by Plato. Today we might call the first a kind of conditioning. By consistent reinforcement of certain behaviors and the punishment of others, the child was to grow up "spontaneously" loving what he ought to love and hating what he ought to hate, i.e., what his elders who had apprehended the absolute norms knew ought to be loved and ought to be hated.

This training was to be carried on not only by the nurse and teacher, but by the whole cultural milieu as well. The music, the fables, the stories of the gods, every facet of social life was to be controlled to keep the reinforcement uniform. So powerful did Plato consider the power of property and family ties in forming value biases that he proposed to do away with both in his scheme for the training of the Guardians (the prospective rulers). The soul was to be made as healthy as the body.

After the future ruler had been ushered into adolescence with sound physiological and emotional habits, he would, if he had adequate mentality, enter upon his secondary education. This consisted of arithmetic, geometry, music, and astronomy, all to be studied in their theoretical aspects rather than in their practical applications.

In the *Republic*, Plato defends this curriculum as training in abstraction. Apart from his belief that the positive, formative principle of the cosmos and of reality in general was measure, i.e., mathematical, he was impressed by the circumstance that mathematics was a system of concepts susceptible of precise definition and rigorous development. The ease with which mathematics could leave the concreteness of objects behind pleased him. To mathematics he gave the second highest rank in knowledge, for it still dealt with hypotheses (or stipulated mean-

ings) and drew necessary conclusions within the rules and limitations of the system of meanings itself. Beyond these stipulations it could not go. In their theoretical phase, music and astronomy also exhibited mathematical structures and therefore qualified as training in abstraction to supplement arithmetic, geometry, and solid geometry. There is reason to believe that this kind of study was carried on at Plato's Academy.

The highest level of knowledge, however, was reserved for dialectic in which the deductive relations characteristic of mathematics were discovered to obtain among "real" concepts, i.e., the scheme of reality itself. If reality were such a deductive system, and if the basic primitive propositions could be intuited, metaphysics would acquire the certainty of mathematics without the arbitrary and contingent nature of a postulational system. Furthermore, the disclosures of metaphysics would not have to be derived from sense experience, but would, on the contrary, furnish the norms for interpreting such experience.

After 10 years of studying the secondary subjects, students who survived the testing were to study dialectics for 5 years. Then they would be drafted for 15 years of public service. What then?

Then, when they are fifty, those who have come safely through and proved the best at all points in action and in study must be brought at last to the goal. They must lift up the eye of the soul to gaze on that which sheds light on all things; and when they have seen the Good itself, take it as a pattern for the right ordering of the state and of the individual, themselves included (Cornford, 1945, p. 261, *Republic*, vii. 540).

Is this merely a poetic flow of language or did Plato mean to say something about the educational process in this paragraph? I believe the latter to be the more plausible alternative. For Plato, all training and study were preliminaries to the act of conversion—a literal turning of the whole individual into a new perspective. Indeed Plato himself said:

Hence there may well be an art whose aim would be to effect this very thing, the conversion of the soul, in the readiest way; not to put the power of sight into the soul's eye, which already has it, but to ensure that, instead of looking in the wrong direction, it is turned the way it ought to be (Cornford, 1945, p. 232, *Republic,* vii. 518).

What the Good is that the philosopher will then see is never made explicit by Plato, but one may speculate that it would have to be a kind of cognition in which the plan of the universe, its scheme of things entire, its axiological structure, would become discernible and would be discerned as so self-authenticating and so necessary as to be irresistible to both mind and heart.

Perhaps that is why Plato believed that the highest education required not only instruction and training but fellowship as well—a way of life, as in a Pythagorean society or perhaps the society of his own Academy—as a condition for achieving the conversion. The kind of man he envisioned as a product of this education could hardly develop in the course of ordinary life, or if he could, it would be with a frequency no greater than that which produced a Socrates. This insight history tends to reconfirm. Even today the scholar is not free from a "conflict of interest" when he has to integrate his scholarly role with the domestic, economic, and political roles into which ordinary life casts him. At another level, we resort to the boarding school as a specially contrived environment for the education of the young, insulating them from the influences of the milieu to which their parents take exception.

From Socrates then comes not the beginning, but rather the high development of the dialogue as a device for clarifying problems by sharpening definitions and testing logically the relations among them. The Socratic midwifery, as he called his teaching, also stressed the psychological notion that the first step in teaching is the incitement of anxiety in the learner about the state of both his knowledge and his being. This puts a heavy burden on the personality of the teacher. Sophists before him had used logical maneuvers to confound and irritate their pupils. But when Socratic performances in the Platonic dialogues are compared with those of the two Sophists in *Euthydemus,* it is clear that Socrates' indirect communication combined artistically, as the others did not, the comic and the tragic, jest and profound seriousness, logic and myth, so as to impress upon his pupil the dialectical nature of both life and learning. Lesser talents tend to neglect the comic and thus become pedantic, or they omit the tragic and become buffoons.

From Plato, more than from Socrates, comes the suggestion that attitudinal and cognitive perfection might be attained by the study of mathematics or the mathematical aspects of certain studies. That an ideational input might of itself indirectly control and shape choice is a hypothesis that has perennial attraction for pedagogical theorists. Another version of this hypothesis was developed in modern times by Herbart; it will be discussed later in this chapter.

The current interest in teaching machines points up an important difference in the way the art of teaching was viewed by Socrates and Plato, on one hand, and by the Rhetoricians on the other. The Rhetoricians regarded teaching pretty much as systematized imitation. By analyzing procedures in great detail and listing numerous alternatives within each class of operations, it was possible to program the "teaching machine" in clearly definable steps for presenting the task, correcting the trial response, and evaluating the test response.

It is quite a different matter with a Socratic dialogue or the Platonic dialectic. The transaction between teacher and pupil and between both of them and a transcendent ideal requires at least two persons; a machine and a person won't do. The outcome of the teaching is not merely a right response but a response plus an attitude with a complex affective aura, an attitude which is not, however, formed once and for all. Perhaps it is this aspect of teaching that restrains many schoolmen from an enthusiastic welcoming of the teaching machine. If teaching is a mechanical process, it probably would be more efficient for an electronic machine to perform it than a human one, and reluctance with respect to use of a machine would be hard to understand and even harder to defend. If such reluctance is justified, it must be on the suspicion that the role of the teacher as a person in the teaching transaction is more real than clear.

That the teacher plays a therapeutic role, a role in group dynamics, a role as father or authority figure—these possibilities have been explored and sometimes deplored. Is there any other role for the teacher? In addition to serving *in loco parentis* and as a substitute analyst, does he perhaps serve as an image of a value system that, *aesthetically* apprehended, conveys to the student in nondiscursive terms certain value norms? What sort of clothes, language, voice quality, amusements, and life style in general would make up such a composite image? What value schema do teachers exemplify as value models? What value schema are teachers perceived by their pupils as exemplifying? Or do students perceive their teachers as the moving pictures and television have pictured them?

A word may be in order about the Platonic faith in mathematics as the road to intellectual, spiritual, and political salvation. The current emphasis in curriculum research on mathematical thinking and the desperate dependence of our culture on mathematics seem to vindicate Plato's prescience. His prescience with respect to teaching method is even more impressive. Consider the extent to which current experimentation with the teaching of mathematics and science is concerned with getting the learner to clarify concepts by stimulating him to distinguish between instances and noninstances of a concept until the principle is intuited (Beberman & Vaughan, 1959). This is the heart of the Socratic and the Platonic dialectic, although, to be sure, their aim was a moral, cognitive, and aesthetic unity of experience that modern mathematics teaching is too modest to profess.

SCHOLASTICISM AS A METHOD OF TEACHING

It was perhaps inevitable that the war between rhetoric and philosophy for the control of education should eventuate in a coalition. Such a unification was exemplified by the movement called Scholasticism, brilliantly foreshadowed by Peter Abelard (1079–1142).

Abelard deserves a place in the history of teaching for a number of reasons. He was a teacher and a teacher of teachers. All his glory and most of his professional difficulties were related to his teaching activity. Second, his teaching employed a method of structuring and presenting materials that helped to set the style for the age of Scholastic education. Third, his personal charm made him one of that fortunate tribe of teachers who need no special devices to motivate their classes. He drew throngs wherever he taught. He exemplified in his teaching a life style that fascinated the would-be scholars of his time. Fourth, Abelard was a prime example, as were Socrates and other great teachers, of how current controversies can dominate the strategy of teaching. Finally, he represented an emphasis on the use and evaluation of knowledge and skill presumably acquired at an earlier period in the student's schooling. This emphasis presumably differentiates higher or advanced teaching from elementary or introductory phases. This distinction, if adhered to, would give a precision to the term "higher" education that it now lacks.

Abelard's great fame came after he was 37 years of age. He attracted students from all parts of the Western world to Paris. After *l'affaire* Héloise he was in more or less continuous battle with his enemies, forever taking refuge in this or that monastery. But despite disgrace and humiliation, Abelard had but to get behind a lectern and students came to hear him. And among them must have been young men of high caliber, because it is reported that 20 of his pupils became cardinals and 50 others became bishops (Rashdall, 1936, I, 58–59).

Controversy and Motivation

It is commonly noted that the medieval ages were agog over the problem of universals, and this is likely to be shrugged off as an aberration much like the question of how many angels could stand on the head of a pin. That we find it difficult to understand the excitement of the medievals over the ontological status of universals or the spatial characteristics of angels is not surprising. However, in an age when sin, redemption, salvation, faith, and God were important to all people, the conceptual apparatus lying at their foundations was as absorbing to intellectuals as are mathematics, physics, atomic warfare, and space exploration to intellectuals now.

To humble men and also to men who were highly sophisticated in secular learning—as were some of the Church Fathers and some of Abelard's contemporaries—the Trinity, Creation, Redemption, and Resurrection were to be taken as part of the Christian revelation vouchsafed to those with a faith in this revelation. Yet, to many intellectuals of the twelfth and thirteenth centuries who were familiar with the teachings of Plato and Aristotle in logic, metaphysics, and other branches of philosophy, a simple faith was impossible. The Christian theology had to be reconciled with philosophy; faith with reason. It so happened that the crux of many of these problems was located in the ontological status of universals, i.e., whether they (1) had independent being (Realism), or (2) were names of classes (Nominalism), or (3) were constructs of the human mind (Conceptualism). How one conceived of the Trinity and the Reincarnation, for example, depended on how the problem of universals was solved.

The tension between the demands of intellectual and doctrinal adequacy paved the way for Scholasticism—the application of philosophical concepts and methods to theology that became the method of the universities in the thirteenth century. It is as precursor of Scholasticism that Abelard is so

important in pedagogy (Harnack, 1896–1899, VI, 42).

The very presumption that an application of rational, secular philosophy could be made to theology at all shocked some of Abelard's famous contemporaries and earned him their sincere enmity. But the tide of the times was with Abelard. The validating sources of Christian doctrine (or, with appropriate variations, of Judaic or Islamic doctrine) were the Scriptures, the writings of the Church Fathers, and official doctrines promulgated by the Church. None of these could be regarded as false—even hypothetically—because they were directly or indirectly divinely inspired.

On the other hand, the validating sources of human thought itself were the principles of logic and the results of philosophy authenticated by logical argument. Thus, for example, *ex nihilo nihil fit* is a principle indispensable to logic and rational thought in general. If the principle is accepted, however, what is one to do with the doctrine of Divine creation? The principles of logic were not hospitable to contradictory statements adduced as evidence for this or that doctrinal position. What was one to do, when, as so often happened, statements from the Scriptures seemed to say contradictory things about important dogmas?

The students of Abelard and at the universities were a heterogeneous lot, but many of them were studying to qualify for the license to teach. That is why Aquinas was to say a bit later: "Because the doctor of the Catholic truth ought not only to teach the proficient but also to instruct beginners . . . we purpose in this book to treat whatever belongs to the Christian religion in such a way as may tend to the instruction of beginners" (Moore, 1938, II, 350).

In *Sic et Non,* Abelard formulated a host of questions about the Trinity, Redemption, the Sacraments, and ethical topics. In one column he placed the "yes" answers from the authorities; in an opposite column the "no" answers, with no attempt to reconcile them. Rules for such reconciliation are given in the Preface. The purpose of the book was to incite students to investigate the truth; it was a teaching device.

Abelard's Dialectic

How were these contradictions to be reconciled?

1. The question having been stated and the incompatible *dicta* lined up, the context of each of them was explored. Read in their context, would the *dicta* still be contradictory? What would enable Abelard to establish these contexts? Only some sort of historical scholarship undertaken by himself or by other scholars in the field. Presumably the new type of teacher would have to include such scholarship in his pedagogical arsenal.

2. Next, textual corruptions should be located and disproved. If the passages cited as evidence had been distorted by copyists, forgers, or accidents of transmission, they would lose their face, evidential value. Hence, textual criticism entailing knowledge of etymology, morphology of grammatical forms, and other elements of linguistic science and history would be brought into play. Precisely such skills were supposed to be imparted in the earlier grammar schools and in the school of Rhetoric (Quintilian *Institutio*, I, vi).

3. The stage was now set to make a judgment as to the *real* meaning of each of the passages cited, as distinguished from the incidental meanings it conveyed. If one compared a passage with others and got help from authoritative glosses, this judgment would not need to be arbitrary.

4. Next, one was to make sure that there was no retraction of the cited passages on record.

5. Finally, one was to search out the facts which led up to the enactment of an ordinance or the making of a decision by the Church or some Council of the Church. These data would help fix the inner meanings or intent of the passage, much as we now try to fix the meaning of certain passages in the United States Constitution by inquiring into the circumstances that led to the writing of the passage in question.

6. If incompatibilities still remained, the rules of the game required one of two conclusions: (1) This was a mystery to be believed, or (2) a theory was needed in the light of which both sides would be correct but only partial views or aspects of the truth. Abelard himself came up with such a formulation in the matter of the universals. He argued that universals exist *before* things in the mind of God; *in* things as their discernible likenesses; and *after* things as likenesses discerned by the learner or by inquiring minds. Thus by making a set of epistemological and ontological distinctions, Abelard could, at least to his own satisfaction, solve some of the problems he had raised.

The resemblance of Abelard's procedure to the Socratic dialectic and to the forensic techniques of the Rhetoricians is fairly obvious. DeWulf (1922, p. 163) calls the method "apologetics." Others believe that Abelard adapted the methods of the canon lawyers to the study of theology (Sikes, 1932, p. 85), and still others refer to his method as something between the Socratic dialogue and the modern case study (Moore, 1938, p. 320). Abelard regarded logic as the method whereby arguments could be discovered to defend the truth of Christian doctrines; dialectic was the means by which contradictions among authorities were to be resolved (Sikes, 1932, p. 88).

The Lecture

The core of Scholastic instruction was the lecture. When books were scarce, the lecture was, to a large extent, the reading of a book by the master while the pupils copied down what he said. Depending on his erudition and the subject, the master might embellish the reading with commentaries and explanations. After Abelard, the lecturer might in his lecture "determine" or argue a question in theology or philosophy by the reconciliation method described above.

Abelard often had to conduct these disputations with one of his doctrinal enemies in public. These were notable occasions. There were, no doubt, many such debates between masters, and what would be more natural than that prospective teachers should try their hand at both the lecture in which they argued a question themselves and a disputation with a real opponent?

This debate—not, strictly speaking, a teaching device—must have done much to establish one's status as a teacher. Dialectical competence became a requisite for all teaching in the higher faculties. Hence, the disputation and the *determinatio* also became features of teacher preparation as well as ingredients of the ceremonies leading to advanced degrees, i.e., licenses to teach.

The lecture form of university teaching put a premium on commentaries, short tracts, and elaborate treatises (*summae*) that provided the teacher with material for his discourses on important issues. There were also collections of *Questiones* containing transcripts of debates or the arguments to be used in debating certain issues, e.g., Peter Lombard's *Sentences*.

By the time of St. Thomas the method of logical demonstration had been perfected. Armed with the mastery of Aristotelian philosophy and the results of theological scholarship, he began with a question, reviewed the authorities, proposed the correct solution, and then systematically refuted all the objections which he thought could be brought against it. In one sense, St. Thomas' method was the culmination of Abelard's subjection of theological questions to rational examination. In another sense, it paved the way for a method of teaching that could dispense with genuine doubt and inquiry and settle for a memorization of St. Thomas' *Summae*. Once an authority of St. Thomas' magnitude gave the answers in a textbook, the temptation to leave out the logical work that went into Thomas' thinking reared its head, and, no doubt, many a master yielded to it.

To put it differently, Scholasticism built reason into its dogma. The effect of this was to make the dogma more rational but also to make a certain type of reasoning dogmatic.

The Disputation

By the end of the thirteenth century, the rules and nature of the disputation had been defined at the University of Paris. Many students at the medieval universities were really apprentice teachers trying to qualify for membership in the teachers' guild—the guild of masters. They often played at being masters before they were old enough to be admitted to the guild. By 1279, playing at giving lectures and disputing a thesis became obligatory before one could qualify for the Chancellor's license to teach. To protect their own reputations and to make sure their students could hold their own in a public disputation, the masters ruled that a prospective determiner or debater must first hold a disputation with a master and then face examiners appointed by their national group. If successful, the student became a bachelor, a sort of assistant teacher (Moore, 1938, II, 362–364).

Rashdall notes (1936, III, 452) that in the higher faculties of the university one encountered a tendency on the part of the doctors to evade the obligation of teaching without surrendering its emoluments, so that the real teaching devolved upon half-trained bachelors; i.e., "in medieval times students were more anxious to learn than the teachers were to teach"—a tendency not without its modern counterpart, one might add.

Bachelors gave lectures modeled after those of the masters and conducted reviews (repetitions). At Bologna a bachelor was required to have given a course of lectures or a repetition and to have completed seven or eight years of study for a degree in civil law or six years of study for a degree in canon law. Sometimes to fulfil the lecturing requirement, the candidate had to bribe students to sit under him. Thus, what probably began as an informal playing at teaching turned into a formal requirement for entrance into the teaching profession.

Here are excerpts from an imaginary reconstruction of such a debate:

The assailant having first denied that *An external world exists,* which is of course asserted by the defender, proceeds to prove his case as follows:

No world independent of consciousness exists; Now, an external world is a world independent of consciousness; Therefore, no external world exists.

DEFENDER: At the major premiss, 'No world independent of consciousness exists,' I take a distinction. No world independent of *all* consciousness? I waive that question. No world independent of *my* consciousness exists? I deny it.—At the minor, 'An external world is a world independent of consciousness,' I counter-distinguish. Of *all* consciousness? I deny it. Of *my* consciousness? I grant that. By this distinction your argument is out of form and inadmissible.

ASSAILANT: But no external world independent of *my* consciousness exists; therefore, your distinction is worthless.

DEFENDER: I deny that.

ASSAILANT: I prove it. Nothing but a modification of myself exists; Now, a world independent of my consciousness is not a modification of myself; therefore, No world independent of my consciousness exists.

DEFENDER: At the major, 'Nothing but the modification of myself exists,' I distinguish. Exists *as my perception?* I admit that. Exists *as the cause* of my perception? I deny it.— As for the minor, 'A world independent of my consciousness is not a modification of myself,' I grant that. So I distinguish the conclusion: 'No world independent of my consciousness exists': *as my perception?* I grant it. *As the cause* of my perception? I deny that.

ASSAILANT: But my perception and the cause of my perception are identical; therefore, your distinction is worthless.

DEFENDER: I deny that.

ASSAILANT: I prove it. What is perceived by me is the cause of my perception; But my perception is what is perceived by me; therefore, My perception is the same as the cause of my perception.

DEFENDER: 'What is perceived by me is the cause of my perception': here I distinguish. What is perceived by me *as something in myself* is the cause of my perception? That I deny. What is perceived by me *as something outside of myself* is the cause of my perception? I grant it.—As for the minor, 'My perception is what is perceived by me,' I counter-distinguish. Is what is perceived by me *as something* in myself? I grant it. Is what is perceived by me *as something outside of myself?* I deny that. By this distinction, your argument is out of form, and inadmissible.

ASSAILANT: But to perceive what is outside of self is absurd; therefore, your distinction is worthless.

DEFENDER: I deny that.

ASSAILANT: I prove it. To have within self what is outside of self is absurd; now to perceive what is outside of self is to have within self what is outside of self; therefore, To perceive what is outside of self is absurd.

DEFENDER: I distinguish your major. To have within self *really* what is *really* outside of self is absurd? That I admit. To have within self *ideally* what is *really* outside of self is absurd? I deny it.—I counter-distinguish your minor. To perceive what is outside of self is to have within self *really* what is *really* outside of self? I deny it. Is to have *ideally* within self what is *really* outside of self? I admit that. By this distinction your argument is out of form and inadmissible (Winterton, 1888, as quoted in Moore, 1938, II, 361–363).

This somewhat bewildering display of dialectical fencing represents in a somewhat exaggerated form the extreme formalizing of the Socratic dialogue. It is far more precise and rigorous than a Socratic dialogue, but it likewise impresses us as being verbalistic and trivial—a kind of word chess—a verbal game.

The formalization was effected first by the rules of the syllogism which the disputant knew by rote and by habit, as well as the fencer or tennis player knows the rules of the game. In other words, he knew just what moves were permitted to invalidate his opponent's argument and to validate his own. In the second place, the distinctions that each made and used throughout the disputation were not invented on the spot; they were as standard as certain gambits in chess. Nevertheless, the rules and the arguments had to be learned and, one might add, understood as well. In addition, there had to be long practice in the use of them in the debating situation.

In later days men passed harsh judgment on these disputations as empty verbalistic exercises. Yet if it is kept in mind that the prospective teacher would one day have to conduct public disputations and give dialectical lectures, their use in the university was a most practical sort of practice teaching. That the masters continued to hold highly formalized disputations long after interest had shifted to other questions is a more serious but a quite different indictment. Pedagogical lag was not, however, peculiar to Scholasticism. It is an indictment of academicians in every age. Course content and classroom procedure are almost never kept abreast of the best knowledge of the time. It is only at the topmost level of graduate instruction that the content of teaching and research converge.

As a method of teacher training, the disputation warrants another glance. To what extent is a high school or college teacher required to use dialectical skill in teaching? Much of what we now try to teach involves the rules of thinking games: the rules of deduction and induction or the rules of evidence in making assertions. This might be called the logic of the subject matter (Smith, 1960, p. 237). To what extent should prospective teachers in their graduate work be given the kind of practice that corresponds to the disputation? Have the potentialities of formal debating really been exploited in this connection? The oral examination on the dissertation is the vestigial remnant of the public disputation. These experiences are not, however, regarded as practice teaching, although in many instances this is about as near to practice in teaching as a prospective college teacher gets during his university career.

Some Observations

The lecture, the repetition, and the disputation constituted the method of the universities. The lecture changed from the mere reading of scarce texts to summarizations of authorities and commentaries upon them; i.e., the lecture became interpretive and critical.

When the commentaries and summaries were themselves put into textbook form, the lecturer had to give new interpretations or explain difficulties, i.e., do something the book did not do. The textmakers seem to be in constant pursuit of the lecturer—intent on making him superfluous and often succeeding without the victim's being aware of it.

Later, at the University of Halle (founded in 1694), the lecture was transformed from a commentary on the text to the systematic presentation of a growing field of knowledge by the research workers or advanced students of the field (Brubacher, 1947, p. 181).

The repetition was not a literal duplication of the lecture, but rather an elaboration of topics and questions growing out of it. At Oxford, lectures were supplemented by *resumpciones,* small informal groups in which scholars were examined by the lecturer or some other master or bachelor on the subject of the lecture (Rashdall, 1936, III, 398–399).

The repetition and the *resumpciones* can be viewed as a trial run to check on the way the student has perceived the materials to be learned. It is a truism that the student hears and reads selectively and that he classifies what he hears and reads in terms of his own categories and his own measures of importance. The teacher never really knows what the student's selection has been until he tests it by a recitation or an examination. Even the most orderly textbooks and the most lucid lectures cannot guarantee of themselves that the student's selection will be the one intended by the teacher. The medieval schoolmen may have erred on the side of overstructuring the selection and perhaps this charge could properly be leveled against all traditional schooling. The other extreme is not without its dangers. One may venture the suggestion that neither extreme is so confusing as the mixture of understructured teaching and overstructured testing. To demand on a test that the pupil reproduce the structure of the text or of the instructor when no particular effort has been made to teach that structure is a strange but not uncommon form of pedagogical irrelevance.

THE JESUITS:
MASTERS OF METHOD

[Humanistic] education, based on the great intellectual inheritance recovered from the ancient world by a relatively small number of Italian scholars, dominated the secondary-school training of the middle and higher classes of society for the next four hundred years (Cubberley, 1920a, p. 263).

The four centuries extended from about 1450 to 1850. Educationally, not the least significant of these recoveries or revivals were Cicero's orations and later a complete copy of Quintilian's *Institutes of Oratory* at St. Gall (Cubberley, 1920a, p. 265). These furnished again the archetype or master model for Latin style and for a method to teach that style.

Because of many factors that cannot be discussed here, the ideal of the cultured gentleman—fit for the demands of citizenship, the new world of commerce, the affairs at court, diplomatic and otherwise—became the educational image of a life style. The Renaissance focused its energies on the revival of the Greek and Roman ideal of human life, an ideal that has a strange, perennial fascination for Western man. It was believed that the literatures of Greece and Rome had everything needed to educate the model man. Battista Guarino put it simply: "I have said that ability to write Latin verse is one of the essential marks of an educated person. I wish now to indicate a second . . . familiarity with the language and literature of Greece" (Cubberley, 1920b, p. 205).

The classic literatures had elegance of style wherewith to make language persuasive, and they provided knowledge to serve as a basis of wisdom in conduct. Milton and Montaigne looked to the classical literature for knowledge and wisdom; others were fascinated by its literary elegance, and still others were willing to settle for formal and verbal conformity to the writings of Cicero, hopeful that by some pedagogical alchemy the powers of the pupil to think, imagine, remember, and judge would flow from the foaming beaker of Latin study.

The spirit of the Renaissance in time permeated the schools. Its spirit and content pervaded such diverse institutions as Johann Sturm's (1507–1589) famous *Gymnasium* in Strassburg, Calvin's colleges in France and Switzerland, Colet's school at St. Paul's, and all the better grammar schools in England. They also pervaded the schools set up by the Jesuits under the influence of Ignatius de Loyola (1491–1556). The Church was challenged by the charm of pagan learning, on one hand, and by the shock of the Reformation, on the other. One of its responses to these challenges was a system of schools which moved Francis Bacon to make the oft-quoted remark: "For the doctrine of school-learning, it were the shortest way to refer it to the Jesuits, who, in point of usefulness, have herein excelled" (*Advancement of Learning*, 1900, p. 207).

The Jesuit schools are selected for discussion not because of their originality in content, form, or even spirit, but because they illustrate how schooling can be organized and systematized to make materials, methods of instruction, and teachers uniformly effective over broad regions of space and time.

The Jesuits systematized every phase of schoolkeeping: Motivational procedures, presentation, practice, and testing were reduced to rules and precepts. These were brought together in the *Ratio Studiorum*, issued first in 1586 and then in revised form in 1599. An example of the thoroughness and definiteness of the directions is afforded by the following quotation:

If an oration or poem is being explained, first its meaning must be explained, if it is obscure, and the various interpretations considered. Second, the whole method of the workmanship, whether invention, disposition, or delivery is to be considered, also how aptly the author ingratiates himself, how appropriately he speaks, or from what topics he takes his material for persuading, for ornament, or for moving his audience; how many precepts he unites in one and the same place, by what method he includes with the figures of thought the means of instilling belief, and again the figures of thought which he weaves into the figures of words. Third, some passages similar in subject-matter and expression are to be adduced and other orators or poets who have used the same precept for the sake of proving or narrating something similar are to be cited. Fourth, let the facts be confirmed by statements of authorities, if opportunity offers. Fifth, let statements from history, from mythology, and from all erudition be sought which illustrate the passage. At last, let the words be considered carefully, and their fitness, their elegance, their number, and their rhythm noted. However, let these things be considered, not that the master may always discuss everything, but that from them he may select those which are most fitting (Fitzpatrick, 1933, pp. 212–213).

Jesuit activity in education also illustrates how a movement not originally established for instruction had to resort to it to achieve its goals. To be a militant force for the Church, the movement needed leaders who could counter the Reformation on intellectual grounds. Such leaders had to be trained, and to secure a considerable number of them, a method of teacher training was indispensable. Under these circumstances it was natural for the problem of method to become an object of deliberate study. It marked another step in the emergence of teaching as a rationally based art.

Rivalry as Motivation

The faith in Classical Humanistic schooling is puzzling to our times. How could young people become enthusiastic enough about ancient Greek heroes and heroines to study Greek language and literature? We can account for this enthusiasm only by the fact that the revival of learning was not merely an intellectual phenomenon, but rather the captivation of an era by a style of life that has managed to fascinate Western man in every era, namely, the Greek ideal of man. When people are thus fascinated they desire to emulate the model, and when the model places high value on individual self-cultivation, on individual excellence, rivalry becomes the mode of school motivation par excellence. In such circumstances schoolboys will compete for whatever the cultural milieu designates as the marks of excellence, provided the school can translate these marks into school behavior.

Rivalry was instituted by the Jesuit schoolmasters between members of a class, between groups within a class, and between classes. Classes were divided into armies, e.g., of Romans and Carthaginians, and pupils were given military ranks. With somewhat incomplete fidelity to the military model, a private who bested an officer in a scholastic exercise assumed the rank of the vanquished.

Even more important methodologically was the use of rivalry as a teaching device. Each pupil had an opposite number charged with catching every mistake he made and correcting it. Not only did the individual's rank depend on alertness and adequate preparation of every lesson, but his team's fortunes also depended on it (Fitzpatrick, 1933, p. 203).

Once a year two or three of the best scholars in a class were matched against a team from the class above it in debating subject matter common to both. It would be interesting to know whether the results of such interclass competition revealed such embarrassing facts about class placement as do our achievement tests.

Public exhibitions of scholastic skill at declamation and debate were encouraged, but only for those who were trained for it. The master polished essays to be given in public although he did not write the essays or compose the speeches himself.

Most important of all was the praise of the teacher, consistently reinforcing every desirable response, and his disapproval, no less consistently discouraging undesirable deviation.

When these methods failed, as with all but angels they occasionally must, there was admonition and punishment. One rule of the *Ratio* points out that it is better for the teacher to pretend not to have seen certain class misdeeds, if it can be done without disadvantage (Fitzpatrick, 1933, p. 206). It takes a long time for the new teacher to realize that not all misdeeds are directed at flouting his authority; that while some are designed to test it, many others merely fill the mysterious need of children to erupt when congregated in classrooms.

Another example of psychological wisdom is the provision that a teacher never strike a pupil but leave such punishment to an official Corrector, "who is not of the Society," i.e., dissociate the punishing act from the teaching act. No less insightful are the injunctions: not to make sarcastic remarks or speak discourteously to pupils; not to call pupils by anything but their right names; not to excuse pupils from class for public exhibitions and plays; not to play favorites; not to speak to pupils outside of class except briefly on serious matters, and not to hold such conversations in the classroom but in an open place; not to use pupils as copyists; and not to permit pupils to spend their own money for the school.

Methods of Presentation and Exercise

The prelection was the chief method of presentation. The teacher, in effect, studied the assignment aloud in front of the class, and the class was expected to repeat his performance as faithfully as possible. The prelection was adapted to the various tasks to be performed: translating Greek materials to Latin or Greek or Latin to the vernacular; criticizing or appreciating a selection from a Latin or Greek author; or giving the directions for writing a composition or expounding a theological question.

Perhaps more significant for method was the way the teacher secured overlapping review. Every segment of instruction was reviewed almost immediately upon its completion. The master's prelection, the week's work, the term's work, the year's work were reviewed. On each Saturday there was a review of the week's work, and for general promotion, students were given a thorough repetition of all the main points of the year's work. It was a methodical attempt to secure learning and overlearning by taking advantage of the curve of forgetting (Fitzpatrick, 1933, pp. 200–201).

Assignments were regular. Written work was to be handed in by all grammar scholars every day but Saturday. In some classes verse exercises in Latin were handed in twice a week and a Greek theme once a week. These exercises were corrected by the master, by pupils exchanging papers, or by the pupil himself from a model furnished by the master. Student helpers were appointed to watch over the pupils and to report faults or defaults in the preparation of lessons.

The disputation was retained in some subjects of instruction. Students were encouraged to make objections to points in the prelection and to raise them with the master or to reserve them for a disputation. With respect to presiding over a disputation, the *Ratio* advised:

. . . preside in such a way that he may himself seem to take part on both sides . . . he shall not keep silent too long, nor yet speak all the time, but let the pupils set forth what they know; he shall . . . not permit an objection which is practically answered to be pressed too far, nor an answer which is unsound to stand too long; after a discussion, he shall briefly define and explain the entire matter (Fitzpatrick, 1933, p. 154).

The Jesuits left little undone to make learning unavoidable, and to frustrate this attempt the pupil would have had to be very stupid or unusually intelligent.

How are the methods of the Jesuits—or more generally, the methods in vogue at the best of the Classical Humanistic schools and colleges—to be evaluated? If well-developed habits of speaking, writing, thinking, and judging are valid objectives, these schools achieved them brilliantly by means of a compact curriculum made up of "the human letters of the different tongues, and logic, natural and moral philosophy, metaphysics, theology, both scholastic and positive, and sacred scripture" (Fitzpatrick, 1933, p. 21).

It was a course of study made up largely of linguistic materials taught for overlearning in a highly prestructured form, but that it resulted in rote learning merely, as has so often been charged, is doubtful. The more just observation is that the materials of the curriculum had a built-in logic and a built-in set of values. Pupils learned words, to be sure, but these words structured their selective processes so that they became *forms* of experience rather than specific responses reinstated on cue. Nor were the words merely logical pigeonholes. The Classical literatures clothed the words with imagery and peopled the boy's experience with a cast of characters who acted out the human drama with impressive directness and vividness.

So long as Western culture conceived excellence in literary terms and in religious categories, the methods of the Jesuits were successful. When success came to be expressed in terms of technology and industrial power —then, literary accomplishments, rhetorical skill, and self-cultivation on the Greek model became anachronistic and with them the school designed to accomplish these results.

While the Classical Humanistic school was flourishing, the learning materials relevant to the new science—new modes of production, new geographical discoveries, and new political forms—were being born in the minds of scholars. But schools, perhaps because they like to believe that they are teaching man as man, are not overly sensitive to cultural changes. New knowledge has to achieve a noncontroversial status before it can find its way into textbooks.

It is a long road from the research front to the classroom. Educationists go back and forth between research and the classroom and while they accelerate the rate of change, they affect its general course less than one might suppose. By this I mean that while the rate at which new materials are incorporated into the textbooks is increased, the rate at which the prime outcomes of instruction are changed is less seriously affected. New material tends to be assimilated to existing objectives. In the centuries after the Renaissance the new materials did knock on the doors of the schools. The emphasis on observation of real objects, usefulness of knowledge in daily life, and personal religious freedom was admitted to the school, but for a long time it manifested itself under the old objectives, namely, to teach Latin and Greek more easily and more effectively. Comenius (1592–1670) is an interesting example of how new forces were put into old bottles, i.e., into Latin schoolbooks, a task "from which he had so often turned in disgust" (Keatinge, 1896, p. 91).

COMENIUS: THE METHOD OF NATURE

In 1658 at Nuremburg appeared *Orbis Sensualium Pictus* with the subtitle: *A World of Things Obvious to the Senses Drawn in Pictures*. It was the first school picture-book ever printed, the historians tell us. It was a huge success, running through many editions with an American edition coming out in New York as late as 1810. Other texts written or projected by John Amos Comenius included:

The *Janua Linguarum Reserata* or *Gate of Languages Unlocked*, the first of the series to be published. The *Orbis* was a simplified version of this book and the *Vestibulum* was supposed to be an introduction to it. The *Janua* was made up of 8,000 or so Latin words arranged in simple sentences with matching vernacular translations in parallel columns. It included information on a wide variety of subjects.

The *Vestibulum,* an introductory first

reader made up of several hundred of the most commonly used Latin words and sentences, each with its translation in an opposite column.

The *Atrium,* an elaboration of the *Janua.* The vocabulary was Latin-Latin rather than Latin-vernacular.

The *Thesaurus,* graded extracts from easy-to-read Latin authors to furnish reading material for the upper three years of the school (Cubberley, 1920a, pp. 412–413).

In *The Great Didactic* (1657) Comenius expounded a system of universal education based on certain principles of learning reared in turn on what he regarded as principles of natural development. Comenius has been praised for being a forerunner of a truly democratic vision of the common school and for an insight into the educational process that was not to be appreciated for generations. But Comenius' influence and fame were measured in his day, at least, by a set of textbooks to be used in teaching the Latin language.

Language and Knowledge

Comenius' texts incorporated some of the new sciences of nature and reflected an interest in the common objects of ordinary experience as against the experience of ancient Greek and Roman figures of exalted station. They also reflected the importance of observation in the new science, which pointed once more to sense perception as the fountain of all genuine, as distinguished from merely verbal, knowledge. *Orbis Pictus,* for example, refers to the world, the heavens, fire, birds, cattle, flesh and bowels, cookery, butchery, eclipses, geometry, printing, and a score of other categories. In the process of learning Latin, the pupil, if Comenius had his way, would also learn *about* his natural environment and the activities of common life. The pictures, of course, were to serve as surrogates for direct perception of the things themselves.

The idea of incorporating content in language study was not new. Even the notion

that the content might be used to engage the interest of the reluctant scholar was tried by Egbert (*c.* 1022–1024), who composed 2,473 lines of verse in his *Fecundia Ratis* to interest boys. The lines were progressively more difficult and touched on material from the Bible, Latin prose, and Latin poetry. In the eleventh century, the authors of Latin readers relied heavily on fables containing many allusions to incidents in the life and manners of the time, e.g., *Fabulae et Parabaloe* of Odo of Cerrington (*c.* 1200), a collection of fables edited by Ernest Voigt (Abelson, 1906, p. 19). It was in the kind and extent of information that Comenius' texts represented an important advance.

Comenius' texts were not merely collections of informational items. For example, in *Orbis Pictus* one section is called "The Barber's Shop." There is a picture of such a shop in which a dozen objects and operations are depicted and numbered. The phrases in Latin and the vernacular paired in parallel columns refer to these objects. Each section had its "core" theme, so to speak.

The Order of Nature

The book was part of a series. The series as a whole and each book in the series embodied certain pedagogical principles fully described in *The Great Didactic.* One such principle was that Nature in its formative processes begins with the universal and ends with the particular. Pedagogically, this was translated by Comenius to mean that instruction ought to begin with such first principles as one can find in a subject and that these should be exemplified in ever-increasing detail. Each topic, accordingly, would be studied at every stage of development, but in ever greater detail. In this way all men could come to know all things (Comenius, 1657, XVI, sec. 45; Keatinge, 1896, p. 274).

Comenius' method leans heavily on the order of nature. Nature has its own reasons, its own timetable, and its own means for bringing the seed to fruition, as anyone familiar with biological change can hardly fail to note. Indeed, the way in which plants and animals follow timetables of development that are impressively uniform for members of the species, and for each species over enormous spans of time, is one of the most formidable obstacles to a mechanical interpretation of nature, because it points to a genic code that limits tolerable variations both in number and degree. Paradoxically perhaps, the more evidence we find for such a code the more sense it makes to speak of living things developing according to a plan or purpose, but a purpose that is encoded "mechanically" by each organism in the genes.

Because the order of development is "natural," i.e., not contrived by any human being, it has the connotation of rightness, as the edict of a power greater than that of any human being. In other words, the natural order is not only descriptive of what does happen, but it is prescriptive of what should happen. Plato and Aristotle incorporated this type of thinking into a theory about the psychic and moral life of the individual and of the good society. With respect to the social order, this prescriptive aspect of Nature is conceived as "natural law."

The theoretical difficulties with this notion are notorious, chiefly because the prescriptions of Nature are so diversely construed by men in different cultures. But whether there can be a science of human behavior if there are no uniformities or invariant relationships in such behavior is a question no less formidable. Comenius was arguing from the analogy between plant life and human life, and insofar as human life is like that of plants, one could expect illuminating suggestions for understanding the growth of children. Unfortunately, the differences between human life and plant life are far more important for the study of mankind than are the resemblances, and this wreaks havoc with the analogy. A few examples of the way Comenius passed from his interpretations of the "natural" to pedagogical analogues show how seductively plausible such thinking can be.

According to Comenius, Nature prepares the materials before she begins to give it form. This principle is transmuted into the pedagogical dictum that knowledge about the appearance of objects should precede the logical classification of them, and that an author's literary work should be studied before grammatical analysis of it is undertaken.

Another natural principle, Comenius notes, is that Nature is not confused in its operations, but proceeds from one point to another. This, pedagogically interpreted, becomes the principle that the scholars shall be occupied with one unit of study at one time (Comenius, 1657, XVI; Keatinge, 1896, p. 271).

Or consider the principle that Nature carefully avoids obstacles and things likely to cause hurt. Aside from the interpretation of the principle itself, it is no small jump to the following pedagogical admonitions: (1) Receive no books but those suitable for their classes; (2) Books should be sources of wisdom, virtue, and piety; (3) Don't allow scholars to mix with bad companions in the school or in the vicinity of the school (Comenius, 1657, XVI; Keatinge, 1896, p. 278).

Understanding versus Imitation

From Comenius comes a strong plea for the understanding of what is learned as against mere memorization of verbal patterns. His plea may have reflected the influence of Francis Bacon's indictment of the literary "delicate" learning and his call for careful induction as a means to reliable and useful knowledge of the world. Comenius urged that learners should not be set to any task until its nature has been thoroughly explained to them and rules for procedure given (Comenius, 1657, XVI; Keatinge, 1896, p. 272). All knowledge, he said, should be deduced from the unchanging principles of the subject in question, and no information should be imparted on bookish authority but should be authorized by actual demonstration to the senses and intellect (Comenius, 1657, XVIII, sec. 28; Keatinge, 1896, p. 302). Everything in science should be taught not only through the senses but also, with reference to its true nature and origin, through its causes (Comenius, 1657, XX; Keatinge, 1896, pp. 341–342). But the examples Comenius gave of causal explanation resemble a genetic account of the phenomenon rather than discourse employed in "proving" a causal hypothesis.

By a general notion of an object he seems to have meant a formal definition of it plus a listing of its parts. To "know" an object was to acquire information about the function and value of the several parts (Comenius, 1657, XX; Keatinge, 1896, pp. 342–343).

In spite of this intellectual and theoretical emphasis on the learning of concepts, rules, and principles, he argued that we learn best by teaching others. Hence, he said, we should let the pupil give the lesson to his fellows, but in giving the lesson, he should repeat the words of the master. He further advised that the clever pupils be called up first (Comenius, 1657, XVIII, secs. 44, 45; Keatinge, 1896, pp. 308–309). Apparently Comenius regarded the ability to repeat the words of the master as evidence of "understanding," for he remarked that frequent repetition will allow even the dullest to grasp it.

The suspicion mounts that Comenius' emphasis upon understanding, demonstration, and the like was really a plea for a change not in the method of teaching and learning, but rather in what was to be imitated and repeated. But is memorizing the law for the expansion of binomials, for example, intellectually a different task from memorizing the steps in explaining a binomial?

Comenius' emphasis on sense perception, his injunctions to correlate words with things, reading with writing, and amusement with serious study all seem to indicate that he was looking for a learning outcome that was not simple memorization. Yet when he justified the use of these approaches it was by the argument that they would facilitate the recall of specific answers to specific questions. Thus he said that, as far as possible, instruction should be given through the senses that it may be retained in the memory with less effort, and that scholars should learn to write down in their notebooks everything they hear or read, for in this way imagination is assisted and it is easier to remember things later on. The dictum: "Nothing should be learned by heart that has not been thoroughly grasped by the understanding," expresses succinctly Comenius' simultaneous loyalty to quite different intellectual processes and the learning outcomes corresponding to them (Comenius, 1657, XVII, secs. 37, 41, 42; Keatinge, 1896, pp. 290–291).

Comenius argued for the use of the same method in the teaching of science, arts, language, and morality, but the methods were essentially those used for skill formation or for perfecting desired responses to selected stimuli. With respect to the arts, the method was imitation of a model with correction on the spot by the teacher. Language teaching was, as has already been indicated, a matter of skill formation. Morality was to be achieved by teaching precepts and by conditioning. Because he felt it was impossible to be so watchful that nothing evil could find entrance, Comenius declared that stern discipline was necessary to keep evil tendencies in check (Comenius, 1657, XXIII, secs. 7–8; Keatinge, 1896, pp. 364–365).

As to class control and motivation, Comenius seemed fully aware that they are not functions of the teacher alone. The parents, civil authorities, the physical plant of the school, the method and content of instruction—all were vectors in the resultant climate of the school. The parents and authorities by pleasant and nonpunitive reinforcement of appropriate pupil behavior, the teacher by following the method of nature, and the school by being a pleasant place with a garden and decorated walls could cooperate to make school and learning attractive (Comenius, 1657, XVII, secs. 17–19; Keatinge, 1896, pp. 283–284).

The Larger Vision

Comenius was a schoolman trying to systematize a dream. The dream was to educate mankind, bring it closer to God, and thus to its own perfection and happiness. His mission was to all people and not merely to the well-born and powerful.

The key was provided by the natural order. The student was led from one bit of knowledge to another in their natural articulation. He was thus put in gear, so to speak, with the cosmic order itself. As his knowledge grew, it approximated the plenitude of nature itself. And if by nature one is to mean the moral and psychical nature of man as well as the constitution of the physical world, growth in moral perfection would proceed *pari passu* with growth in intellectual enlightenment.

Comenius had little choice, however, but to translate the dream into the pedagogical reality of teaching the Latin language. Within the limits of this enterprise, he exploited with great skill the opportunities for emphasizing content other than the content of the classical authors. Both the content and the method of empirical science as they were emerging left their traces on Comenius and his textbooks, as did the conviction that teaching was an art based on knowledge.

ABC'S AND OBJECT LESSONS

Unlike Comenius, the Swiss educator Johann Heinrich Pestalozzi (1746–1827) was not tied to the teaching of Latin as the chief vehicle of schooling. He was able, therefore, to concentrate on methods of teaching the new subjects: arithmetic, geography, nature study, drawing, and music, i.e., the curriculum of the common elementary school that was to take shape in Europe and America.

Like Comenius, Pestalozzi was a strange mixture—a social visionary with a zeal for bringing the new order about through schooling. Like Comenius, but with the benefit of Rousseau's formulation, Pestalozzi looked to Nature as it manifested itself in plant growth for the laws of human development to serve as norms for schooling. The teacher is repeatedly compared to a gardener. Yet the difficulty in interpreting just what Nature says in these matters is illustrated by the different messages received from her by Comenius and Pestalozzi, not to speak of Rousseau, Froebel, and others.

Gabriel Compayré (1908b, pp. 68–69) remarks that for Pestalozzi the outcome of instruction was primarily a clearer and fuller intuition of what was intellectually true, morally right and good, and practically efficient. Put differently, this could mean that the key to efficient learning was a set of images, concepts, or sensorimotor affective patterns that could serve as internal standards for the learner. Once the pupil had a model, it would guide the corrections of his trial responses. Pestalozzi realized that teaching should be concerned with helping the pupil acquire this criterion as rapidly as possible.

The concrete, the immediate, the particular, the familiar objects of experience were, to Pestalozzi, precisely what could furnish these vivid prototype intuitions. So important was immediacy to him that Pestalozzi said:

When I now look back and ask myself, what have I specially done for the very being of education? I find I have fixed the highest, supreme principle of instruction in the recognition of *sense impression as the absolute foundation of all knowledge* (Pestalozzi, 1894, p. 200).

Pestalozzi also recognized that the concrete, particular, familiar objects, although vividly experienced, are confusedly perceived, i.e., are related, by and large, only to immediate use and impulse. They are not, at this stage, related to each other in any logical order and certainly not in the order in which the scholar would arrange them.

By giving names to objects, we make their classification more manageable. Classification is made in terms of some set of observable characteristics and therefore combines observation and judgment. Observation provides the initial clues to the class in which the object might belong, and subsequent judgment verifies the initial classificatory judgment. Observing, counting, and naming objects, accordingly, made up a good deal of the child's learning activity.

Number, form, and *language* are, together, the elementary means of instruction, because the whole sum of the external properties of any object is comprised in its outline and its number, and is brought home to my consciousness through language (Pestalozzi, 1894, p. 89).

As the learner scans class characteristics and objects to be classified and shuttles between universals and particulars, the "concept" becomes richer and more accurate at one and the same time. Seeing the universal in the particular and each particular in its universality constitutes the fuller and deeper intuition mentioned above.

The Logical and Psychological

Pestalozzi reversed Comenius' reading of nature by interpreting the natural order as going from the concrete to the abstract; from the particular to the universal. Pedagogically, Pestalozzi translated this to mean the exploration of the child's immediate environment—physical and moral—to achieve direct sensorimotor-affective models that would serve as touchstones for the "right" response.

At Yverdun he taught geography by direct observation of the surrounding valley and had children make relief maps of what they saw. This method is said to have inspired Carl Ritter's subsequent work in geography (Compayré, 1908b, pp. 90–91). He placed writing after drawing and reading after oral exercise as evidence of his faith in the primacy of the concrete. Even in the moral field he wished the child to experience the sentiments of kindness and love before more verbalized formal instruction in moral precepts was given. How close this is to current advocacy of "guided discovery" and "unverbalized understanding" (Craig, 1956) is hard to estimate, because much of the current interest is with materials that resemble puzzles, the solution to which is embedded in the "given" instances. With Pestalozzi the emphasis was on the directness and immediacy of experience.

This much of his methodology seems to follow directly from the primacy of the concrete and particular over the abstract and the general. When, however, Pestalozzi undertook to organize reading, writing, drawing, and other subjects for instruction, he operated on a somewhat different principle. In reading, for example, the materials were analyzed until the vowel sounds were reached as the basic constituent elements. Points, angles, curves, and lines were the ABC's of drawing. Pestalozzi even hoped to reduce trade training to elementary operations such as twisting, throwing, carrying, and the like. Presumably, by practicing on the elements the pupil learned to synthesize larger units. Or more accurately, learning the elements enabled him both to break up the unknown into the known and to combine the old elements into new combinations as needed.

In the moral life, the constitutive elements were the instinctive feelings or emotions which arose in the infant because of his relation to his mother—a sense of dependence, love, trust, and gratitude as responses to her care and protection. Pedagogy was supposed to transfer these original emotions to mankind and then to God, according to Pestalozzi.

On the one hand, Pestalozzi regarded the concrete particular as easier to learn than the indirect (verbal), abstract, general symbol. On the other hand, he believed that simpler things are easier to learn than complexes. A letter is simpler than a word, and a word simpler than a phrase. But a letter is also more abstract than a word in that it requires an act of abstraction to separate letters or syllables from the concrete experiential whole used in spoken language. Was there a contradiction between concreteness and simplicity as guides to teaching?

Pestalozzi thus became involved in the

distinction commonly drawn between the psychological and logical ordering of subject matter of instruction. By the "logical order" of a subject of study can be meant at least two things:

(1) A subject is "logically" organized if one can relate the statements within it by the rules of deduction or induction, e.g., mathematics or physics.

(2) A subject is "logically" organized when its statements are arranged in some intelligible order, e.g., geography of the town, county, state, nation, continent, hemisphere; or letter, word, phrase, sentence, paragraph, etc.

In the first sense of "logical," the order is a property of the subject matter; in the second sense, the order is more or less arbitrary albeit intelligible. The analysis of materials into their elements is an example of the second kind of order. It is logical in the sense that elements are logically prior to the complexes they make up, but this order may not correspond to the time sequence in which the materials came into the experience of the pupil, e.g., in spoken language the child hears the word long before he hears the names of the letters. The difficulty in learning these elements arises not so much because they are abstract or because they are logical, but rather because they happen to be less familiar than words or phrases.

Materials organized logically in the first sense, for example, as in mathematics or physics, may be difficult to learn because it takes a certain order of mental maturation to comprehend relationships at certain levels of abstraction. Thus, the *elements* of chemistry, history, and cartoons may be perfectly familiar to the immature student, but he may be unable to discern the *relational complex* from which they all derive their meaning or "point."

By the psychological approach, Pestalozzi had in mind the notion of familiarity, on one hand, and simplicity, on the other. The first led him to emphasize sense experience of real objects; the second impelled him to analyze all learning tasks into simple elements, not

quite realizing, perhaps, as has been noted, that the familiarity gained by direct experience was partially canceled out by the analytical approach.

Object Lessons

The object lesson and careful observation of objects provided a fine corrective for empty verbalism and mindless memorization, but where learning consists of an insight into a system of concepts bound together in a logical net, sensory discrimination has a limited usefulness. For example, watching the arcs described by a swinging pendulum, or noting changes in the water level of a vacuum flask inverted in a bowl of water as pressure is varied does not disclose the explanatory principles. They do, however, give data for structuring the problem; they yield clues to the fruitful questions rather than to the answers. It should be remembered that, in Pestalozzi's time, science connoted careful inductions from sense observations rather than rigorous conceptual systems.

Along with the use of a real object, the object lesson combined an interrogation of the class by the teacher that guided the discussion from sense impressions to formal definition of the object under study. It was, therefore, a method of presentation that encouraged concept formation by the learner. The rule, definition, and precept ended the lesson; it did not initiate it. This understandably made demands on teaching that conducting a recitation on previously assigned materials did not. It was a variation of the Socratic dialogue put into the service of teaching the common branches of learning.

The impact of this method on schooling came in large part through such texts as Colburn's *First Lessons in Arithmetic* and through the work of Arnold Guyot (1807–1884) in geography and Lowell Mason (1792–1872) in music. The hosts of visitors to Pestalozzi's schools could copy down the products of his analysis of the various subjects into their ABC's and the sequence in which these were to be presented. They could also observe and duplicate such procedures as visiting the neighborhood and studying its geographical characteristics. They could note how object lessons were prepared and presented, how much time was given to each, and how learners were prompted to recite. Being a schoolmaster, Pestalozzi, like Comenius before him, did not scorn devices. He is credited with introducing the use of slates and pencils, letters of the alphabet fastened on cards, and even more important, simultaneous instruction of a whole class (Eby & Arrowood, 1940, p. 665). At a time when common education was about to expand rapidly in the New World, such methods were precisely what educational reformers could talk about and demonstrate to school officials and to prospective teachers.

DIALECTICAL GARDENING

Froebel wrote of himself:

. . . Nature for more than thirty years . . . has taught me that plants, especially trees, are a mirror, or rather a symbol, of human life in its highest spiritual relations; and I think one of the grandest and deepest fore-feelings that have ever emanated from the human soul, is before us when we read, in the Holy Scriptures, of a tree of knowledge of good and evil; . . . I said my hazel buds gave me the clue of Ariadne. Many things grew clear to me; for instance, the earliest life and actions of our first parents in Paradise, and much connected therewith (Ulich, 1954, p. 527).

The quest for a law of human development, so prominent in Comenius and Pestalozzi, can be said to have achieved theoretical articulateness in Friedrich Wilhelm Froebel (1788–1852), the father of the kindergarten. His method of teaching, correspondingly, was more intimately tied to this notion than were those of his predecessors. Also significant were his extensive studies in natural science and philosophy. For in Kant, Schelling, Fichte, and Hegel, he had available a terminology and set of concepts that lent themselves to his special variant of Absolute Idealism.

Because this chapter is not concerned with the rationale of educational aims, the complicated theoretical apparatus supporting the Froebelian outlook need not be detailed here. A word, however, must be said about a few of the key notions, or the methodology will fail to make any sense at all.

From his philosophical mentor, K. C. F. Krause, Froebel took over the notion of organic unity; a unity in which any given thing is a whole in itself yet a part of a larger whole. The distinctive aspect of this relationship is not simply that of inclusiveness. It is rather that every individual thing exists *only* in its higher unity; e.g., the finger exists *only* in the hand and in that higher unity has a special function. Apart from hands there *are* no fingers. This notion, so fruitful in biology, was extended to the relations between an individual and the social order. In its name everything from moral responsibility to the totalitarian state has found justification.

Froebel was also devoted to the theory of the recapitulation of cultural epochs by each individual, and he believed in the endless progress of man and the race to higher levels of development.

Finally, and perhaps most important for his methodology, is the notion that the developmental process is a swing between opposites toward a synthesis that unites them at a higher level—a process reminiscent of Hegel's dialectic, even though for Froebel it did not confine its operation to Ideas.

The Method of Opposites

Opposition was regarded as a necessary feature of all developmental process. Thus the inner *must* become outer or, as Hegel had said, the Idea must manifest itself; the social *must* have an individual phase, and appearance *must* be an appearance of reality. Methodologically, this principle of opposites means that one looked for causes of behavior not in what resembled this behavior, but rather in what was radically different from it—a procedure not unfamiliar to psychoanalytic theory. "In good education, then, in genuine instruction, in true training, necessity should call forth freedom; law, self-determination; external compulsion, inner freedom; external hate, inner love" (Froebel, 1911, pp. 13–14).

It could be argued plausibly that Froebel formulated what is most distinctive in his method in this law of converse inference. Just as Marx was to use the Hegelian dialectic as a paradigm for the class struggle, so Froebel used it to describe an approach to teaching.

All true education in training and instruction should, therefore, at every moment, in every demand and regulation, be simultaneously double-sided—giving and taking, uniting and dividing, prescribing and following, active and passive, positive yet giving scope, firm and yielding; and the pupil should be similarly conditioned: but between the two, between educator and pupil, between request and obedience, there should invisibly rule a third something, to which educator and pupil are equally subject. This third something is the *right*, the *best*, necessarily conditioned and expressed without arbitrariness in the circumstances. The calm recognition, the clear knowledge, and the serene, cheerful obedience to the rule of this third something is the particular feature that should be constantly and clearly manifest in the bearing and conduct of the educator and teacher, and often firmly and sternly emphasized by him. The child, the pupil, has a very keen feeling, a very clear apprehension, and rarely fails to distinguish, whether what the educator, the teacher, or the father says or requests is personal or arbitrary, or whether it is expressed by him as a general law and necessity (Froebel, 1911, pp. 14–15).

And he continues:

This explains and justifies, too, the next requirement, and indicates, at the same time, the manner of its fulfillment: *The educator, the teacher, should make the individual and particular general, the general particular and individual, and elucidate both in life; he should make the external internal, and the internal external, and indicate the necessary unity of both; he should consider the finite in* the light of the infinite, and infinite in the light of the finite, and harmonize both in life; he should see and perceive the divine essence in whatever is human, trace the nature of man to God, and seek to exhibit both within one another in life (Froebel, 1911, pp. 15–16).

At first blush these passages seem to be a dialectical play on words, and even at a second glance such injunctions as "he should consider the finite in the light of the infinite, and the infinite in the light of the finite, and harmonize both in life" hardly look like prescriptions for a teaching routine. They do not denote behavior that is directly perceptible to the external observer. And yet they do refer to an attitude on the part of the teacher toward the acts of instruction, an attitude that is indirectly but clearly revealed in a gesture, a tone of voice, and general demeanor.

All dialectical teaching utilizes indirect communication, even as did Socrates, its most remarkable exemplar. The use of opposites by the teacher prevents the pupil from resting too quickly or becoming too easily satisfied with himself. Existential situations are so complex that direct indicative language forms never describe them completely. Every proposition that asserts something about any existent leaves out something; to be meaningful it has to be limited. It is always relevant, therefore, when talking about existential situations to say: "On the other hand . . ." or "From another point of view. . . ."

Indeed, as Idealists have long asserted, there is no limit to the number of times one can say, "On the other hand. . ." because every new proposition is itself limited and its opposite has to be invoked to complete it. The process makes it theoretically impossible to say anything that is really true without saying everything about everything. Thus in Hegel, for example, the unity which in the end validates all subordinate propositions is the Absolute in which the distinctions so unavoidable in the direct discourse of propositions are abolished and transmuted (*aufgehoben*). The method of opposites leads to a synthesis which combines the truth of the opposites. The pupil and teacher are unified in their willing subjection to the third higher entity—the right and the best, i.e., the ideal.

Unity

The ultimate unity is God. "All things have come from . . . the Divine Unity, in God alone. . . . It is the destiny and life-work of all things to unfold their essence, hence their divine being, and, therefore, the Divine Unity itself . . ." (Froebel, 1911, pp. 1–2).

Unification, connectedness, relationships were almost an obsession with Froebel. He looked for a unity in organic and inorganic life, and while studying mineralogy tried to unify the laws of crystal formation. As he said of himself:

Chemistry fascinated me. The excellent teacher (Göttling) always demonstrated the true connection of the phenomena under consideration; and the theory of chemical affinity took strong hold upon me. . . . I was always highly delighted with his [Batsch's] expositions, for they suggested ideas to me which bore fruit both in my intelligence and in my emotional nature. Invariably, whenever I grasped the interconnection and unity of phenomena, I felt the longings of my spirit and of my soul were fulfilled.

My stay in Jena had taught me much; by no means so much as it ought to have taught me, but yet I had won for myself a standpoint, both subjective and objective. I could already perceive unity in diversity, the correlation of forces, the interconnection of all living things, life in matter, and the principles of physics and biology (Ulich, 1954, pp. 533–534).

The search for unity in diversity is also characteristic of aesthetic creativity. One criterion of aesthetic value is the degree to which the artist succeeds in unifying a wide diversity of elements so that every element is required by the whole and requires the whole for its own meaningfulness. This resemblance to aesthetic activity is not accidental. The unity so dear to Idealism requires among other unifications the fusing of the true, the good, and the beautiful, i.e., the intellectual, the moral, and the aesthetic. In Froebel every

act of teaching is simultaneously an intellectual, moral, and artistic enterprise, and its goal is a progressively evolving unity of experience for the learner. The harmonious development of heart, hand, and head so devoutly sought by Pestalozzi was given a philosophic foundation and a methodological form by Froebel.

Froebel's metaphysical system seems remote from the problems of teaching school, but his attitude toward the child in school might have been quite different had he not regarded each pupil as an unfolding of God's creative energy. If he had not taken this metaphysical position, he would certainly not have dignified the games and prattle of the little ones by calling them revelations of the Divine nature. Nor would he have taken so seriously the symbolic import of "play" things if they did not signify for him that every act of the child transcended both the childishness and the worldliness of the child's existence.

Froebel held that a third "something," i.e., the right, should rule insensibly over both educator and pupil. This metaphysical injunction suffuses the teacher-pupil relation with a spiritual glow that may explain why some people still insist that teaching, like preaching, is a "vocation" to which one is called by something higher than the need for earning a living.

Furthermore, the doctrine that man is a manifestation of the creative energy of God endows him also with spontaneity and freedom. The notion of "negative" education, i.e., of permitting the child to express himself spontaneously, would not make much sense without such a hypothesis.

Finally, recapitulating the history of the race at various stages of child development would mean little without a theory of evolutionary progress, and progress would make little sense without a criterion of value. The value criterion is the degree of unification of all things in their relations to the unity of the Divine energy.

Perhaps it is because Froebel's metaphysical position was so strong and so elaborately detailed that his methodology was never far from his theory—something that cannot always be said for Comenius and Pestalozzi.

The Symbolic Object Lesson

In Froebel's hands, the Pestalozzian object lesson became more than a focus for perceptual study of sense qualia, number, and shape. Nor was it primarily a trigger to set off conceptualization and verbalization. The object chosen for study was not just an object. It was selected because it had a formal quality that somehow suggested the Divine unity. Thus the cube with its regular angularity and the ball with its regular curvature were symbolic of the way in which Nature develops by opposites. The cylinder mediates between the cube and the ball. How important geometrical properties were to Froebel is illustrated by the following:

Now, since force develops and diffuses itself in all directions equally, freely, and unimpeded, its outward manifestation, its material resultant, is a *sphere*. For this reason the spherical or, in general, the round form is most commonly the first and last form of things in nature. . . . Hence, too, the sphere resembles none of the other natural forms, and yet essentially contains the possibility and the law of all of them; it is, at the same time, formless and the most perfect form (Froebel, 1911, p. 168).

That drawing, clay-modeling, painting, coloring, singing, dancing, hearing dramatic stories, and manipulating blocks, patterns, and cardboard objects were activities suitable to preschool children, it took no Froebel to discover. But it did take a Froebel to endow these activities with the character of "occupations" that were to lead the child to closer identification with the Divine spirit and social unity. It also required a mystical imagination of no mean order to think of the cube and the ball as "gifts" of the Divine spirit, and to say that "play, is the highest phase of child development . . . for *it is a self-active representation of the inner . . . from inner ne-*

cessity and impulse" (Froebel, 1911, pp. 54–55). It would be difficult to find a similar combination of metaphysical imagination and precision of method. History would lead us to expect that the routines of the kindergarten would remain, but that the metaphysical glow would fade from the eyes of Froebel's followers. That this did not always happen may indicate that the people attracted to Froebel's methods already had some of his metaphysical conviction: Mrs. Carl Schurz, Elizabeth Peabody, William T. Harris, and Francis W. Parker, to mention a few of those who introduced the kindergarten to the United States.

Kindergarten work is an unlikely career for anyone who does not love little children and who is not impressed by the symbolic significance of everything they do. For taken at face value and by adult standards, the child is indeed childish—clumsy, ignorant, and never too far from his nonhuman characteristics. Nor are children's potentialities great incentives to love them, because on the basis of experience their future is as pregnant with evil as with good. But when children are seen by a religious light in a transcendent relationship with a higher than human source, they can be treated with that rare blend of patience, love, and tutorial care so characteristic of the pioneer kindergarten teachers.

. . . the school, as such, implies the presence of an intelligent consciousness which, as it were, hovers over and between the outer world and the scholar, which unites in itself the essence of both, holds the inner being of both, mediating between the two, imparting to them language and mutual understanding. This consciousness is the *master* in this art, who is called *master* also because for *most* things he is to point out the unity of things. He is *school*master because it is his business to point out and render clear to himself and others the inner, spiritual nature of things (Froebel, 1911, p. 129).

To be sure, not all the results of Froebel's influence reflected the romantic spirit of the kindergarten. The manual training movement, an extension of the Froebelian gifts and occupations, lost some of it when extended beyond the kindergarten. The same may perhaps be said of the speech, music, modeling, painting, and other motor forms of activity that were to become standard in elementary education. Other modes of justification, largely psychological, took the place of metaphysical romanticism.

INSTRUCTION AS CONSTRUCTION

It is fitting to conclude this survey of teaching method with a consideration of Johann Friedrich Herbart (1776–1841), in whom trends developing since the time of Comenius were brought to explicit formulation.

Herbart was an "educationist" in whatever honorific connotation that term now has. He had a primary, not an incidental, interest in pedagogy. He wrote extensively in the field of professional education, established an experimental school, and systematically related his educational theories to his work in metaphysics, ethics, and psychology. Finally, he was a university professor whose writings had, by the end of the nineteenth century, made his name and teaching method virtually synonymous. His own lectures attracted throngs of students at Königsberg, where in 1809 he took over the most renowned chair in philosophy, that of Immanuel Kant.[1]

Herbart's teaching method has been divided into steps. His followers have transformed Herbart's notions of clearness, association, systematization, and method into the steps of (1) Preparation, (2) Presentation, (3) Association, (4) Systematization, and (5) Application.

As names for teaching procedures, these steps presented little that was new; formulations of them could be found from Isocrates on. The steps interest us because of the conceptual framework used to justify them and because of the specific ways they were to be used in teaching organized bodies of subject matter.

Psychologically, the Herbartian approach is important because it makes cognition the basic psychological activity, with feeling and willing derivative from cognition. Doing away with innate capacities and powers, Herbart believed that he could build up all human experience out of presentations (*Vorstellungen*) that enter experience via the nervous system. Out of the impressions of sense, pain, and pleasure come derived presentations. Those presentations which reflect the idea or thing that caused them develop by comparison, abstraction, and generalization into concepts (indirect sensuous presentations). The child in school has already acquired stocks of presentations from experience and from intercourse with others. The former by instruction eventuates in knowledge, the latter in sympathy (Herbart, 1893, pp. 33–34).

Accordingly, Herbart remarks:

Capacity for culture then, depends not on a relation between several primordially distinct capacities of the soul, but on a relationship amongst each other of presentations already acquired, and again between them and the physical organization. In both respects the pupil will need careful observation (Herbart, 1898, p. 114).

These basic elementary ideas have a power or dynamism of their own that drives them to achieve consciousness. They compete with other ideas or idea clusters for a place in the field of awareness. When driven out of consciousness, they remain latent in the unconscious but always strive to return. In this campaign they can unite with other congruous ideas and summate their separate powers. Congruity among ideas is felt as pleasant; conflict between them as pain. Choice is determined by the nature of the idea clusters dominating the field of consciousness at any given moment.

Pedagogically, Herbart's system is important because in it instruction becomes a

---

[1] It is recounted that he began the manuscript for his *Hauptpunkte der Logic* one mid-day and delivered it to the printers the next noon (Herbart, 1893, p. 16).

controllable process of building idea clusters that make up the apperceptive mass. Each idea cluster can be thought of as carrying a power index, or exponent, so that theoretically, at least, one might have a calculus of probabilities as to what choices the individual will make, given the power values of his ideational components. In a way, Herbart translated the Socratic "Virtue is knowledge" formula into psychological and pedagogical terms. Inasmuch as everything depends on the specific input of ideational material, teaching can be rationalized and methodized.

Turning now to the steps of teaching method, we shall indicate how each one identified an important phase in any teaching method and how it operated in Herbartian pedagogy.

Preparation

Preparation in teaching has two aspects which may be called the motivational and the cognitive. Motivational preparation refers to procedures instituted to arouse and maintain attention of the learner in the learning task. Some motivating devices are extrinsic to the nature of the learning task, e.g., commands, demands, threats, or sudden loud noises. Another type of preparation takes advantage of interests already developed in the learner. For example, knowing that seven-year-old boys are deeply interested in gunfighters and weapons of all sorts, we can secure attention by showing a rusty flintlock to the class. While the first type of preparation is wholly extrinsic to the learning task, exploiting an existing interest may or may not be. The learning task in the example given above might well be related to weapons, but it might also be a dramatic introduction to a lesson on oxidation. Herbartians used both the extrinsic and the more intrinsic types of motivational preparation. They used strict discipline to command attention, but the recapitulation theory enabled them to exploit certain interests that children at various stages of development were supposed to

have as they re-enacted the development of the race. In any event, Herbart advised that "with all instruction which cannot at first be given without some constraint, the chief thing is to make the pupil aware of his own progress as soon as possible" (Herbart, 1898, p. 143).

Herbart believed that the simple social relationships most likely to impress children were to be found in the lives and activities of earlier peoples as expressed in the literature of those people, e.g., the *Iliad* and the *Odyssey* of the Greeks. His followers worked out in great detail the cultural materials appropriate for various age levels, utilizing materials progressing from Mother Goose, to the Old Testament, to epic literature of the Greeks, to the New Testament, to modern literature (Eby & Arrowood, 1940, p. 780).

On the cognitive side, preparation involves "the summoning up of a mental escort into the presence of the newcomer to welcome and introduce him" (Compayré, 1908a, p. 36). Preparation can take the form of the recall of materials similar to those in the learning task, analogous or opposite to it, antecedent to it, a result of it, or in some other way relevant to the learning of it. So the apperceiving presentations have to be inventoried and brought clearly into consciousness. If the old presentations are too few, too confused, or not in the right order to assimilate the new material, the teacher has to make them so.

Part of this preparation the teacher does alone prior to the class meeting. He makes a rough outline of what he can expect to find in the pupils' arsenal of experience. The second part is an interrogation of the class in which the pupils are encouraged to speak freely of everything that in any way relates to the topic. Out of this the teacher selects for summarizing and stress only the most essential notions, i.e., those crucial for apperceiving the new material (Felkin & Felkin, 1898, pp. 108–110).

Naturally, the good teacher is looking for a preparatory procedure that will be both motivationally and cognitively effective. The conventional subject-matter curriculum is hard to motivate intrinsically, i.e., by devices that are intrinsically related to the learning task, while "felt" needs or native interests may not point toward learning tasks that fit into the conventional subjects.

Herbart solved the problem by arguing that the very act of apperception is satisfying in itself and consequently arouses a desire to continue the process, especially if it proceeds with ease. Further, each idea cluster as it developed became "an interest" with power to invade consciousness. Hence, many-sided interest was for Herbart more than a phrase connoting all-round development. It was, rather, a design for instruction so that the empirical, speculative, aesthetic, sympathetic, social, and religious aspects of experience would all receive their due (Herbart, 1898, pp. 147–148).

Presentation

Presentation has for its objective a clear awareness of whatever is to be apperceived as a single object or unit, e.g., a story, a specimen, an experiment, and the like. The emphasis placed on the scrutiny of and absorption in an object apart from all other objects is, of course, witness to the continuation of the belief in the object lesson and the virtues of observation.

Herbart did not idolatrize sense perception as did some of the followers of Pestalozzi. Nevertheless, vividness helped apperception and clarity of perception even more. Presentation was not confined to sense perception; all sorts of verbalizing were encouraged, and Herbart made it clear that the real foe of understanding was not language, but rather unorganized aggregates within the experience of the learner, i.e., the discrepancy between the organizing principle of the pupil and that of the subject matter being taught to him. Hence the great care enjoined by Herbart in both preparation and presentation.

In connection with presentation Herbart spoke of the alternation of concentration (*Vertiefung*) and reflection (*Besinnung*) as

a kind of mental respiration (Herbart, 1893, p. 126n). Pedagogically, this respiration was sustained by having the pupil attend to the new material as an entity with its own characteristics and then allow the several elements within the new material to intermingle and fuse in as many ways as possible.

Association and Systematization

Preparation and association, properly carried out, complete the apperception of a single object or unit of instruction: a poem, an event in history, a geometrical principle. The next step, called association, was designed to enable the student to attain concepts by comparisons and contrasts among instances of the phenomenon being studied. Systematization grouped the information and principles elicited in the lesson, e.g., the various forms of speech would be one such principle of grouping, parts of the body might be another. Or as one commentator put it, "This systematic order is again the parallel to the well-arranged library in which a book can be instantly found" (Felkin & Felkin, 1898, p. 115).

Application

In the last phase, called philosophizing, methodizing, or application, exercises are given to the pupil to test the adequacy of the previous steps. The criteria are (1) the firmness with which the new learning has been incorporated into the apperceptive mass, (2) the number of interest clusters with which it has made connection, and (3) the readiness with which it will function in future learning activities. The series of ideas may be repeated forwards or backwards from different starting points; or the pupil may be asked to give an instance to illustrate a generalization, or to cite the generalization that a given case illustrates. Problems of various sorts are also means of teaching application.

In discussing other methodologies, we have referred to the distinction between the evaluation trial and the practice trial. In the practice trial, teacher and pupil cooperate to correct errors or to reinforce the right performance. In the evaluation trial, help from the teacher is withdrawn and the pupil is asked to recite, write an examination, solve a problem, or imitate a model.

These "payoff" trials are judged by the teacher and sometimes marked or graded. Such judgment and the trial itself are part of the teaching process in a sense that a "life" trial is not. As Herbart said: "Even superficial experience teaches us that the results of an examination are valid only for the day when it is held . . ." (*Brief Encyclopaedia,* sec. 105, as quoted in Ulich, 1954, p. 510).

The application of learning to materials not practiced is a test trial par excellence, especially as a test of generalizations achieved in the previous step. An apt application not only tests the learning, but improves it, because every successful application or even intelligent failure to apply a generalization enlarges or reorganizes the apperceptive mass.

As to life tests, Herbart, as has been noted, placed his faith in the conviction that certain idea clusters would become powerful enough to displace their rivals in the field of consciousness. Thus, the idea cluster representing us as happy with the loot from a bank robbery, if no hindering representation intervenes, and if accompanied by the belief that the bank robbery can be brought off, will result automatically in a try at bank robbery. Everything depends at this juncture on another idea cluster (an idea cluster, let us say, which represents us as jailbirds in disgrace and a strong belief in the probability of being caught) displacing the earlier cluster in consciousness. And this intervening cluster will appear only if it has been built into the experience of the learner in such a way that it has the power at critical points to forge into consciousness.

For this purpose Herbart favored materials from history and literature, because they offered such a rich and vivid source of ideas about moral situations, alternative solutions, and their consequences.

The mechanical aspects of the formal steps tend to obscure the fact that Herbart hoped through them to achieve a flexible use of knowledge, from what he called the "circle of thought."

"Courage," he said, "will then be sustained by the certainty of the *inner* performance, and rightly so, for the external impediments which unexpectedly appear to the foresight of a careful intelligence, can terrify him but little, who knows that, with altered circumstances, he can at once evolve new plans" (Herbart, 1893, p. 213).

SOME OBSERVATIONS

For research on teaching, the survey just completed may have some implications:

1. Instruction has its direct and indirect aspects and outcomes. Skills in arithmetical computation, handwriting, and the conjugation of Latin verbs are more or less direct outcomes, and the methods of instruction can be equally direct. In other words, every segment of the teaching act utilizes the materials that are to figure in the final outcome. No less direct are the methods and outcomes when a given set of concepts and relations is to be learned. In this survey the Sophists, the Jesuits, the Scholastics, Pestalozzi, Comenius, and Herbart were primarily concerned with the direct aspects of method, namely, those that would eventuate in the mastery of certain skills and knowledge. They were hoping that indirectly these studies would contribute to good character, good citizenship, and the good life in general.

In Socrates, Froebel, and Abelard, and to some extent in the others also, the primary emphasis was not on learning a body of knowledge or acquiring skills. Their teaching tried to evoke an attitude or mood toward knowledge, or beauty, or God. The outcome was not so much knowledge of something as becoming something, and it was not aimed at directly. On the contrary, the approach was dialectical and, in the case of Socrates, ironic. Their actual teaching activities—disputation or kindergarten play—were compatible with the outcome, but they were not really samples of it.

It often happens—more often than not—that we can imitate the teaching procedures of the master teacher quite faithfully and yet not achieve his results. The spirit of the method seems to be a vital ingredient in it, and yet it seems detachable from the techniques and devices through which it is expressed.

Educational schemes that profess to produce scientific attitudes, a sense of responsibility, aesthetic sensitivity and creativity may require aspects of teaching method that are indirect and without which the direct procedures are not sufficient to achieve the desired results. The temptation not to aim research at these indirect aspects of method is understandable, but what may be needed are ways of making such aspects of methods "researchable."

2. Research in common with other enterprises has its frontier scouts, solid workers to exploit breakthroughs, and supply forces who run back and forth between the researchers and consumers. There is payoff research that works on problems of immediate concern to society. At the present, for example, we are rightly exercised about how to teach mathematics and science to young people who will forthwith market these learnings in behalf of national defense. We are not concerned with mathematics for peace or for self-cultivation, nor with the appreciative learnings in the humanities and the arts.

The danger in the situation should be apparent. The conditions favorable to rhetoric passed; the premium on logical disputation disappeared; the values of classical learning were undermined. Research needs frontier scouts who can smell a cultural change long before the public senses it. And the first shakings of the earth are usually sensed by the poet, painter, composer, and others who somehow lose their adjustment to the status quo before the masses do.

The shape of things to come, the values

men will prize, the effects of current developments on education—these too should be the concern of educational research. How, for the sake of a speculative example, would we go about giving adults a genuinely liberal education? What would we do if military service became universal and were used by the nation as a time to complete the general education of the young? Would we know how to utilize such an opportunity?

3. Educational outcomes and methods are never completely outmoded. While the heady enthusiasm accompanying the belief that one has hit on something brand new is no mean accelerator of research, perhaps we can make more efficient use of not unlimited research resources if we do not always start all over again on every issue.

The art of speaking well, the art of debating, the art of writing fluently, and the art of thinking correctly have been taught successfully in the history of Western civilization. Is it possible that something in the older methodologies can be salvaged? The current enthusiasm of some researchers for game-playing makes one wonder, for example, whether the medieval disputations at which the apprentice teachers played so assiduously were as barren as they have been made out to be.

4. One other generalization frequently noted in the survey deserves examination for its research potential. It has to do with the tendency for innovations in teaching to be formalized and mechanized so that they become available for mass production and use. Every such step threatens to reduce the value of the individual teacher. Either the role of the teacher will degenerate into machine-tending or, freed from the need to tend machines, the teacher can genuinely aspire to professional status. To approximate the status of engineering or surgery, teaching will have to demonstrate a need for theory and skill-mastery analogous to those of the other learned professions. To this end we need research on clinical teaching, laboratory teaching, and practice teaching in their relations to the theoretical disciplines of psychology,

sociology, and philosophy. Indeed, the further research pushes the mechanization of teaching, the readier we become for the breakthrough to the professionalizing of teaching.

SUMMARY

This chapter, to repeat what was said at the outset, is not a history of teaching method. It is at most a set of highlights of that history selected to illuminate distinctive styles of teaching as responses to various social demands made upon formal schooling.

With the Sophists, the Western world achieved a high order of consciousness about the problems of teaching. The Sophists analyzed subject matter into teachable form. In the schools of Rhetoric of Greece and Rome from Isocrates to Quintilian, elaborate exercises and precepts for achieving success through eloquence were perfected. This type of teaching achieved its goals by a kind of formalism that combined imitation of models with more flexibility than is customarily associated with this approach.

In reaction against teaching virtues through rhetoric, Socrates tried to teach virtue by inciting the pupil through exhortation and dialogue into a search for the ultimate norm of the good, the true, and the beautiful. Socrates saw the teacher as the midwife helping the pupil bring to birth what he had already conceived. Combined with Socrates' emphasis on teaching as a kind of self-examination was Plato's insistence on the study of mathematics and dialectic as the roads to true virtue.

This confrontation of the Sophists and Socrates is repeated whenever debates over the primacy of the direct and indirect aspects of educational strategy occur. The Sophists represent the view that the school should aim as directly as possible at the kind of behaviors to be used in adult life, e.g., arguing in courts of law, declaiming at public functions, persuading legislative assemblies. Socrates represents the view that only by reforming the personality and the cognitive structure of the

individual can he achieve the good life; vocational skills, albeit important, are therefore secondary.

In Abelard and Scholasticism the technical resources of formal logic were used as means to rationalize and intellectualize the creedal and institutional developments of Christianity. In the very process of doing so, Abelard and the Scholastics developed a method of teaching their students to do likewise and in turn to teach others. The lecturing devices of the Rhetoricians, the study of the Scriptures and the writings of the Church Fathers, together with the logical dialectic of Aristotle, in a sense brought together the Sophistic and Socratic emphases in the medieval disputation. One can imagine that when a genuine search for God animated the great debates, the results were as genuine and moving as when Socrates' pupils were animated by genuine yearning for self-discovery; contrariwise, when the motivation was merely to display eristic skill, responsible citizens could hardly be blamed for having reservations about what these young men would come to.

The Jesuit schools were discussed as examples of what system and method could achieve with a curriculum devoted to the Classical literatures and languages, philosophy, and theology pressed into the service of the Ideal of the Catholic Christian gentleman. They utilized the analytical power of the Rhetoricians to order and present their materials, but in a way they systematized and perfected the art of schoolkeeping. They regularized motivational procedures, testing, and correction, and they did not leave the preparation of teaching to chance.

In Comenius, Pestalozzi, and Froebel, schooling took its cue from the conviction that nature, having plotted the course of human development, not only biologically, but cognitively and morally as well, could provide a design for teaching. Not only the natural impulses and activities of children, but also the ordinary objects of daily life and the vernacular languages, were the keys to the good life, the good society, and God. So

the concrete object, sense perception, usefulness in life, came to be recognized in teaching, but whereas in Comenius and Pestalozzi
they were incorporated into the teaching of
languages and information about the world,
in Froebel the tone of the enterprise changed
radically. A metaphysical romanticism in
which the child symbolized the unity of all
things in God created a spirit that was especially friendly to the kindergarten as an
educational institution and child study as a
discipline.

In Herbart, finally, there was a kind of
return to the Sophists. Instruction became
highly methodized and rationalized. Cognitive elements returned to centrality, and affective syndromes were derived from them.
It was a new formula for virtue through
knowledge, not through self-knowledge
alone and not through the semimystical conversion hoped for by Plato, but rather
through the orderly building of idea clusters
from the intellectual resources of the race.
How these idea clusters were to be constructed constituted his theory of method.

The lessons of this survey for the modern
researcher into teaching range from noting
the great age of certain problems in teaching
and learning to reflections on the role of
modern research methods. Research can help
to solve the perennial problems and to provide organized anticipations of the challenges
to teaching in the days to come.

REFERENCES

Abelard, P. *Sic et Non.* In V. Cousin, *Ouvrages inédits d'Abélard.* Paris: Im-primérie Royale, 1836.

Abelson, P. *The seven liberal arts.* New York: Teachers Coll., Columbia Univer., 1906.

Bacon, F. *The advancement of learning* and *Novum organum.* New York: Colonial Press, 1900.

Beberman, M., & Vaughan, H. *High school mathematics.* Urbana, Ill.: Univer. of Illinois Press, 1959.

Brubacher, J. S. *A history of the problems of education.* New York: McGraw-Hill, 1947.

Cicero. *De oratore* and *De partitione oratoria.*

Trans. by E. W. Sutton & H. Rackham. London: Heinemann, 1942. 2 vols.

Clark, D. L. Imitation: Theory and practice in Roman rhetoric. *Quart. J. Speech,* 1951, 37, 11–22.

Clark, D. L. *Rhetoric in Greco-Roman educa-tion.* New York: Columbia Univer. Press, 1957.

Comenius, J. A. *Didactica magna.* In *Opera omnia.* Amsterdam: D. Laurentii de Geer, 1657.

Compayré, G. *Herbart and education by in-struction.* Trans. by M. E. Findlay. London: Harrap, 1908. (a)

Compayré, G. *Johann Heinrich Pestalozzi and elementary education.* Trans. by R. P. Jago. London: Harrap, 1908. (b)

Cornford, F. M. *The Republic of Plato.* New York: Oxford Univer. Press, 1945.

Craig, R. C. Directed vs. independent dis-covery of established relations. *J. educ. Psychol.,* 1956, 47, 223–234.

Cubberley, E. P. *The history of education.* New York: Houghton Mifflin, 1920. (a)

Cubberley, E. P. *Readings in the history of education.* New York: Houghton Mifflin, 1920. (b)

DeWulf, M. *Philosophy and civilization in the Middle Ages.* New York: Dover, 1922, 1953.

Eby, F., & Arrowood, C. F. *The development of modern education.* New York: Prentice-Hall, 1940.

Felkin, H. M., & Felkin, Emmie. *An intro-duction to Herbart's science and practice of education.* Boston: Heath, 1898.

Fitzpatrick, E. A. *St. Ignatius and the Ratio studiorum.* New York: McGraw-Hill, 1933.

Freeman, K. J. *Schools of Hellas.* New York: Macmillan, 1907.

Froebel, F. W. *Autobiography.* Trans. by Emilie Michaelis & K. Moore. Syracuse, N.Y.: Bardeen, 1890.

Froebel, F. W. *The education of man.* Trans. by W. N. Hailmann. New York: Appleton, 1911.

Gomperz, T. *Greek thinkers.* New York: Scribner's, 1901, 1912. 4 vols.

Guilford, J. P. Three faces of intellect. *Amer. Psychologist,* 1959, 14, 469–479.

Harnack, A. *History of dogma.* London: Williams & Norgate, 1896–1899. 7 vols.

Haslerud, G. M., & Meyers, Shirley. The transfer value of given and individually derived principles. *J. educ. Psychol.*, 1958, 49, 293–298.

Hendrix, Gertrude. A new clue to the transfer of training. *Elem. sch. J.*, 1947, 48, 197–208.

Herbart, J. F. *The science of education*. Trans. by H. M. Felkin & Emmie Felkin. Boston: Heath, 1893.

Herbart, J. F. *Letters and lectures on education*. Trans. by H. M. Felkin & Emmie Felkin. Syracuse, N.Y.: Bardeen, 1898.

Isocrates. *Panegyricus, Antidosis,* and *Against the Sophists*. Trans. by G. Norlin. London: Loeb Classical Library, 1929. 3 vols.

Jaeger, W. W. *Paideia: The ideals of Greek culture*. Trans. by G. Highet. New York: Oxford Univer. Press, Vol. I (2nd ed.), 1945; Vol. II, 1943; Vol. III, 1944.

Jowett, B. *The works of Plato*. (3rd ed.) Oxford: Oxford Univer. Press, 1892. 5 vols.

Keatinge, M. W. *The great didactic of John Amos Comenius*. London: Adams and Charles Black, 1896.

Marrou, H. I. *Saint Agustin et la fin de la culture antique*. Paris: E. de Boccard, 1938.

Marrou, H. I. *A history of education in antiquity*. Trans. by G. Lamb. New York: Sheed & Ward, 1956.

McKeon, R. Literary criticism and the concept of imitation in antiquity. *Mod. Philol.*, 1936, 34, 1–35.

Moore, E. C. *The story of instruction*. New York: Macmillan, 1936–1938. 2 vols.

Pestalozzi, J. H. *How Gertrude teaches her children*. Trans. by L. E. Holland & F. C. Turner. Syracuse, N.Y.: Bardeen, 1894.

Plato. *Selections*. R. Demos (Ed.) New York: Scribner's, 1927.

Quintilian, F. B. *Institutio oratoria*. Trans. by H. E. Butler. Cambridge, Mass.: Harvard Univer. Press, 1953. 4 vols.

Rashdall, H. *The universities of Europe in the Middle Ages*. F. M. Powicke & A. B. Emden (Eds.) Oxford: Clarendon, 1936. 3 vols.

Sikes, J. G. *Peter Abailard*. Cambridge: Cambridge Univer. Press, 1932.

Smith, B. O. A concept of teaching. *Teachers Coll. Rec.*, 1960, 61, 229–241.

Ulich, R. *Three thousand years of educational wisdom*. (2nd ed.) Cambridge, Mass.: Harvard Univer. Press, 1954.

Winterton, F. The lesson of neo-scholasticism. *Mind*, 1888, 13, 383–404.

CHAPTER 2

Logic and Scientific Method in Research on Teaching

MAY BRODBECK
University of Minnesota

The analysis of scientific method, or the philosophy of science, is concerned, first of all, with certain fundamental issues common to all sciences. Among these are the principles of concept-formation, the nature of scientific laws, of causality, explanation, and theories. Adequate analysis and understanding of these issues require, in turn, an understanding of certain basic notions of logic. A firm grasp of the nature of logical truth and of valid deduction is indispensable for, among other things, clarifying the nature of definitions and how they differ from laws, the connection between laws, theories, and explanations, as well as between predictions and the testing of theories and hypotheses. I shall here examine these fundamental issues and lay the minimal groundwork by explaining certain relevant, yet quite elementary, logical notions.

Besides these common issues, there are problems that are special to the various sciences. In the social sciences, of which educational research is a part, certain methodological problems arise, for instance, regarding the use of group or institutional concepts. Similarly, how meaningfully to introduce concepts referring to "unobserv-able" states of persons is a perplexing and controversial issue among behavioral scientists. The so-called "problem of reduction" epitomizes a tangled web of issues woven about the controversy regarding the connections among the various social sciences. Further, since virtually all knowledge dealing with persons, groups, and institutions is statistical rather than "deterministic," certain distinctive and limiting features of such knowledge need clarifying. In an area where quantification is achieved with difficulty at best, problems of measurement and the nature and use of models, mathematical and non-mathematical, are particularly acute. In addition to discussing those notions that are common to all sciences, I shall try to clarify some of these issues that are peculiar to the social sciences in general and to educational research in particular.

THE LANGUAGE
OF SCIENCE

Language consists of words and sentences. To the *words* of ordinary speech correspond the *concepts* of science; to the *sentences* its *definitions,* its *statements of individual fact* and *of laws*. Certain sets of sentences constitute the *theories* of science. The distinction between a word and a sentence is so fundamental that it impinges on almost all issues that can be raised within the philosophy or methodology of science. For on the linguistic distinction between words and sentences hangs also the distinction, much more than a matter of language only, between meaning and truth. If the former distinction is blurred, so is the latter; and if the difference between meaning and truth is blurred, then intelligibility itself is forfeit. "Meaning" and "truth" are ponderous yet equivocal terms, for words mean in different ways and there is more than one kind of truth. Language contains two kinds of words and, corresponding to them, two kinds of truth.

The language of science, devoid of greetings, exclamations, questions, and commands, consists wholly of declarative sentences. By means of them, the scientist talks about the world. These sentences may be as simple and qualitative as the statement that ice is cold or as complicated and quantitative as the Newtonian law of attraction. In either case, all such general sentences consist of certain arrangements of two kinds of words. Some of the words in a sentence refer to individual things, either simple or complex, like 'John' or 'Minnesota.' Others refer to the characters or attributes of individual things or to relations among them. All such words are called *descriptive* terms. Those which name not individual things, but their characters and relations, are the *concepts* of science. They may name characters of inanimate physical things, of organisms, or of societies. Thus green is a character of some physical objects, notably grass. Hunger at some time or other belongs to the state of an organism, while totalitarianism is an attribute of some societies. A relation is any attribute requiring two or more individuals for its exemplification, like older, between, more populous, or smarter. These names for characters of things, whether relational or nonrelational, distinguish one area from another—psychology, say, from physics. The subject matter or

content of an area is thus indicated by its descriptive terms or concepts.

Descriptive terms are connected with each other to form statements of individual fact, like 'John is blond' or 'John runs.' As the last example suggests, the "is" or copula of predication is logically superfluous and can always be omitted, as it is in many natural languages, with no more untoward effect than grammatical oddity. 'John blond' may be pidgin English, but it says the same as 'John is blond.' However, when one wants to assert more than a single statement of individual fact, attributing a property to an individual thing or person, certain other kinds of words become indispensable. Sentences are connected with each other to form compound sentences, like 'John is blond and Jim is redheaded.' These compound sentences express connections among individual facts. The words that permit us to express these connections, like 'and,' 'or,' 'if-then,' and 'not,' are called *logical* words or connectives. ('All' and 'some,' though not connectives, are also logical words.) Unlike descriptive words, these do not themselves name or denote anything. Logical words give language its *form* or structure by connecting sentences made up of descriptive words. For example, the sentences 'He is a scholar *and* he is an athlete' and 'He is a scholar *or* he is an athlete' are alike in that they have the same content or subject matter. But their *form* is different. On the other hand, '*If* this is silver, *then* its melting point is *p*' is like '*If* anyone is frustrated, *then* he will be aggressive' in that they share a common form. Their subject matter differs but both statements are conditionals. The logical words are common to all sciences.

The meaning of the descriptive words is given by specifying the individuals, or their properties, or the relations among them to which they refer. The meaning of the logical words is specified by giving the conditions for the truth or falsity of the compound sentences formed by means of the logical words. The truth of the simple component sentences containing no logical words, like

'John is an athlete,' are determined by observation. The truth of a compound sentence is then specified as a function of the truth of its constituents. A conjunction, for instance, is true if and only if both conjuncts are true. Once such conditions are specified for all the connectives, it turns out that, corresponding to the two kinds of words, logical and descriptive, there are also two kinds of sentences, those which are logically true and those which are factually or empirically true. This distinction and its broader implications will be more forcefully seen if we strip compound sentences of their content or descriptive meaning and retain only their form. This may be done by replacing all the simple component statements with letters. Thus 'P or Q,' 'P and Q,' 'If P then Q,' 'not-P,' are the form of a disjunction, conjunction, conditional, and negation, respectively. As they stand, there is no way to distinguish 'P or Q' from 'S or T.' If, however, each letter-variable is replaced by a sentence containing different descriptive words, then the statements say different things though they have the same form. And logic is exclusively concerned with form.

Having stripped the sentences down to their bones or structure, we can then completely specify the meaning of the connectives by Truth Table 1, in which 'T' and 'F' stand for 'true' and 'false.'

Truth Table 1

Sentential Letter-variables		Logical Constants					
P	Q	and	or	if-then	if and only if	not-P	not-Q
T	T	T	T	T	T	F	F
F	T	F	T	T	F	T	F
T	F	F	T	F	F	F	T
F	F	F	F	T	T	T	T

In words, the table tells us that the conjunction of P and Q will be true if and only if both conjuncts are true; the disjunction will be false if and only if both disjuncts are false; the conditional will be false if and only if the

antecedent is true and the consequent is false; the biconditional or 'if and only if' will be true if both components are true or both components are false; and the negation of a sentence will always take the opposite truth-value from the sentence itself. Thus, for all these compound sentences, once we are given the truth-value of the constituent sentences, we know the truth or falsity of the compound. But we must independently know the truth-values of the component sentences. This of course requires observation. Compound sentences, whose truth or falsity depends in this manner upon the truth or falsity of their component parts, are called factual, empirical, contingent, or synthetic, sentences. Their truth depends upon their *content*.

But now let us replace 'Q' by 'not-P.' We then get Truth Table 2 for conjunction and disjunction:

Truth Table 2

Sentential Letter-variable	Logical Constants		
P	not-P	P and not-P	P or not-P
T	F	F	T
F	T	F	T

In words, 'P and not-P' is false while 'P or not-P' is true, no matter whether 'P' is true or false. That is, in order to know that 'P or not-P' is true, we do not have to know independently the truth-value of its constituents, and similarly for the falsehood of 'P and not-P.' 'If P then P,' it can be easily seen, will also be true regardless of whether 'P' is true or false. If 'P' stands for the statement that a judge is elected, then the whole sentence says 'If a judge is elected, then a judge is elected,' which is something less than controversial. All such statements are called logical truths or, also, tautological or analytic. They are also said to be "necessary truths," since they are true no matter what substitutions are made for their component parts, represented by the letter-variables.

Their truth depends only on their *form*.

'Either it will rain or we will go swimming.' If this statement, of the form '*P* or *Q*,' is asserted truly, then we have some factual information, though perhaps it is not as definite as we would like. It will be true if at least one (possibly both) of its disjuncts is true. Appropriate observations will determine its truth or falsity. 'Either it will rain or it will not rain.' This statement, of the form '*P* or not-*P*,' is true regardless of what happens. No observations are required, for its truth is determined by its form alone. Its descriptive words occur vacuously rather than essentially; that is, they make no difference to the truth of the statement. Yet it is a perfectly meaningful and indeed, in its way, an important statement, as are all tautologies or logical truths.

Among other things, they are, as we shall see, indispensable in carrying out logical deductions. Their importance can be assessed by considering that one important subclass of logical or analytic truths is that of mathematics. All arithmetical concepts, like numbers and operations upon them, such as addition, are ultimately definable in terms of logical words alone. The definition is cumbrous and need not concern us here. But, once carried through, it turns out that statements such as $5 + 7 = 12$, as well as those of more abstruse mathematics, are all true by virtue of their form alone. They contain no symbols referring to descriptive properties and relations, and these are irrelevant to the truths of arithmetic. Yet, though they are uninformative about empirical facts, they are clearly both meaningful and remarkably useful assertions.

Some tautologies are as obvious as '*P* or not *P*,' or 'If *P* then *P*.' Others are far from obvious and need long manipulation to reveal their tautological character. Given the structure of our language, as specified by the truth tables for the connectives, the tautologies or logical truths are found—not made—by us.

Definitions are an apparent exception. Since definitions, and the difference between them and factual assertions, are important both in science and in many of the methodological issues discussed in this study, it will be well to be very clear about the logical structure of definitions.

Every science contains a great many defined terms. A definition, no matter how simple or complicated its form, is always a statement about the use of words. It asserts that one or more words may be used as an abbreviation for some combination of several others. Strictly speaking, therefore, definitions are *about* language rather than *within* language. However, it is sometimes useful, particularly for purposes of deduction, to assert the definition as a statement in the language. That is, any *rule about language,* about the use of words, such as " '*A*' means by definition '*B and C*,' " may have a corresponding *sentence within language,* namely, '*A* if and only if *B* and *C*.' Because the rule or definition says that '*A*' is just abbreviatory for '*B and C*,' both the left- and right-hand side of the '—if and only if—' sentence refer to the same thing. This statement therefore has the logical form of '*A* if and only if *A*' or '*B* and *C* if and only if *B* and *C*.'

Within the language, therefore, definitions may be treated as if they were tautologies. They are true by definition, i.e., merely verbal. *Unlike* ordinary tautologies, such as '*P* or not-*P*,' their truth is a matter of convention or stipulation. If this convention had not been adopted, then the corresponding tautology would not occur in our language. Moreover, they are, strictly speaking, logically superfluous, since the defined term can always be replaced by its defining ones. That indeed is why the statement takes the form of a tautology. Ordinary tautologies, however, cannot be eliminated from language. This circumstance is sometimes expressed by saying that tautologies express or reflect the logical structure of the world. *Like* ordinary tautologies, definitions are factually empty and their truth is a matter of their form alone. Both their similarities to and differences from tautologies are crucial for understanding the role of definitions in science.

CONCEPTS, FACTS,
AND LAWS

Some features of the world *stand out,* almost begging for names. Concepts of clouds, thunder, dog, wealth, hunger, child, colors, tastes, and the like, name differentiated slices of reality that willy-nilly impinge on all of us. The concepts of common sense name these obtrusive daily experiences. Other features of the world have to be *cut out,* as it were. They are discerned only by a more subtle and devious examination of nature, man, and society than is made in everyday life. These more covert aspects of experience are named by the concepts of science. Concepts like mass and momentum, IQ and reaction potential, primary group and totalitarianism, name attributes of things that do not stand out as do love and hunger, colors, tastes, and odors.

Much of the language of common sense consists of names for objects of direct experience that need no definition. Anyone who has learned to speak the language and is not born blind knows the meaning of the concept 'blue.' But even in everyday language many terms occur that must be defined before we know what they denote. One who has never seen a gnu must have the term explained to him. We explain it by listing the observable attributes of gnus. 'Gnu' means 'a mammal with an oxlike head, short mane, downward-curved horns, and long tail.' This typical, so-called "nominal" definition tells us by what combination of attributes we shall know a gnu when we see one. It states that one word, gnu, is shorthand for a combination of other words that together denote a certain kind of object. To say that a particular animal is a gnu is the same as saying that the animal is an instance of the concept 'gnu.'

What is 'momentum' or 'bureaucracy' or 'hysteria'? The question in each case is not: What does the concept "really" mean? For it means what we say it does. The question is one of words and is answered in the same way. Words themselves do not "mean." We "mean" by their use. We stipulate what we

mean by them by definitions. 'Momentum' means 'mass times velocity.' But what is 'mass' and what is 'velocity'? We keep exchanging one word for others. On pain of infinite regress or circularity, definition must stop somewhere. It stops where one expects it to, namely, when there is no longer ambiguity or disagreement about the referent of the term.

When is this point reached? In other words, how do we know when we have a good or adequate definition? An adequate definition permits us always to tell when a sentence containing the defined term is true and when it is false. An adequately defined concept is also called "reliable." If a concept is reliable, then different people or the same person at different times always agree about whether or not there is an instance of the concept. 'Velocity' is a highly reliable concept, while 'anxiety' is much less so. What makes the difference? In part, the difference is that one concept is quantified while the other is not. The quantified concept 'melting point' is a much more reliable defining property of a chemical substance than is 'pale yellow.' The color concept is vague in a way in which melting point is not. Since colors shade into each other and lighting conditions affect the color seen, the referent of 'pale yellow' is hard to pin down precisely. But though quantification has many virtues, it is not quantification as such that distinguishes a good definition from a poor one. A nonquantified concept of, say, 'hunger' may be considerably more reliable than the equally nonquantified 'anxiety.' Moreover, a concept like, for instance, 'economic depression,' whose definition would undoubtedly contain many quantified terms, is probably no more reliable than 'anxiety.' Economists are by no means agreed on the defining terms of 'depression.' A difference in reliability is thus not due to counting and measuring alone.

Operational Definitions

In common sense, the meaning of a term referring to a kind of physical object, like a dog or a chair, is given by listing the observable characters of these objects, like barking or shape. The nominal definition of 'gnu' mentioned before is such a definition. In a sense of "abstract" that has no degrees of more or less, both common sense and science use abstract words, that is, concepts or names for properties of things. However, there is a sense in which the character-words of science are more abstract than are the character-words of everyday language. The characteristic abstractness of scientific concepts, like mass or IQ, lies in the fact that these terms cannot be defined by simply listing a cluster of directly observable attributes. Merely by looking at a surface we can tell whether it is red or by looking at an object whether it is a gnu. We cannot so simply tell what the mass of an object or the IQ of a child is. Yet a body has mass as well as color; a child has an IQ as well as blond hair. However, more complicated observations are required to know that a body has a certain mass than to know that it has a certain color. This greater complication is reflected by the way the concepts of science are defined, for scientific definitions are rarely of the simple, dictionary type, illustrated by 'gnu.' They are not, precisely because they name features of the world that can be discerned only under certain conditions. And these conditions are part of the meaning of the concept. They must therefore be included in the defining properties of it. To do this requires an *operational definition*.

A cow is always a cow, but it is not always hungry. It is so only under certain conditions. A political attitude may be a relatively permanent aspect of a man, but, unlike the color of his eyes, he is not always evincing this attitude. Although a man's height needs no stimulus before it manifests itself, certain conditions, like his standing straight, must be met and measurements must be made before we can ascertain this height. At any given moment, a submissive woman need not be submitting, an authoritarian person giving orders, or a malleable piece of iron being bent. Such concepts are called "dispositional," for they refer to the disposition of certain

things or kinds of things to behave in certain ways or exhibit certain characters under certain conditions. We cannot tell merely by direct observation of an individual or thing that it has any of these properties, any more than we can directly see the mass of an object or a child's IQ or his precise height. Yet we must know what to look for in order to tell when a statement that an individual has any of these properties is true or false. To achieve this, scientific terms are defined, not in isolation, as in a dictionary, but by stating the observable conditions under which a sentence containing the term is true or false. Instead of defining the word by itself, as 'gnu' was defined, it is defined by giving the conditions for the truth of a sentence in which the term occurs. Such definitions are called "operational," for they frequently state what must be done in order to make certain observations. For instance, in order to determine a child's IQ, we must first administer a test of a specified kind, then observe his performance on the test, and finally make certain calculations. *All* of these conditions define the meaning of IQ as it appears in the sentence 'John has an IQ of 115.'

More generally, the right-hand side of an operational definition has the form of a conditional or 'if-then' sentence. The antecedent or *if* clause of this sentence states the test or stimulus conditions, or what must be done in order to make certain observations. The consequent or *then* clause states the truth or response conditions, or what must be observed after the test conditions have been imposed. In the case of quantitative concepts, these antecedent or test conditions consist of certain measuring procedures or *operations,* such as weighing on a balance or giving an examination. The truth conditions state what must be observed after these operations have been carried out. Terms referring to personality traits, attitudes, and abilities must also be defined in terms of behavior that is exhibited under certain conditions. All terms requiring the 'if-then' form of definition may be called *dispositional* concepts.

Suppose that a political scientist wishes to

introduce the concept 'conservative.' In order to be quite clear about the kind of individual he is talking about, he defines his term rather than relying upon the vague and varying connotations of common sense to carry his meaning. A conservative, as this political scientist uses the term, is, by definition, an individual who gives a certain pattern of responses to a battery of questions. The questions constitute the antecedent test conditions. The pattern of responses constitutes the consequent truth condition, or what must be observed after the test is given to make the sentence 'X is a conservative' true. The entire conditional sentence, stating a connection between antecedent and consequent conditions, defines the concept. For if a different battery of questions were administered, we would not expect the same pattern of responses. The measuring procedure is part of the meaning of the concept.

A science generally contains both nominal definitions of isolated terms as well as operational definitions of terms as they are used in a sentence. In economics, for instance, the amount of production is defined nominally as the arithmetical sum of the amounts of consumption and accumulation. On the other hand, the concept 'rational man' requires the conditional or operational definition. 'Jones is a rational man' means by definition 'If Jones is presented with certain choices, *then* he orders his preferences transitively.' The only difference between the two kinds of definition is that in the nominal case the term 'production' is eliminated by two other terms and an arithmetical computation, while in the "operational" case, one entire sentence containing the word to be defined is replaced by another sentence not containing this critical word. An operational definition, like any other definition, is thus a statement about the use of words, stating how one term may be eliminated by means of others.

But what others? Definition can proceed indefinitely. As I mentioned before, we can keep on exchanging one word for others. Assuming that we do not run around in a circle, the process must end somewhere. For-

tunately, the connection between language and the world is such that we can say where it must end. Language, we recall, is given its content by descriptive or referential words, those that refer to some thing or kind of thing. 'Gnu' and 'unicorn' are both descriptive words, though there are gnus and there are no unicorns. By their definitions alone we could not know this, for a definition tells us only about words and not about the world. But the defining words must enable us to know an instance of the defined concept when we see one. We must, obviously, know what to look for in order to discover, for instance, whether there are or are not any unicorns. If the defining words do not themselves tell us what to look for, then they must in turn be defined. In this way, a long chain of definitions may be constructed.

Where will this chain stop? Not all descriptive words need be or can be defined. Words that cannot be further defined name directly observable properties of things, like certain colors, tastes, odors, textures, and sounds. Knowledge by direct acquaintance is the kind of knowledge that, for instance, a man born blind cannot have of the meaning of the word "blue." No matter what else he may know by other methods about the physics of color, he does not know the referential meaning of 'blue.' The names for those characters of things, relational or nonrelational, that we either know by direct acquaintance (or, like the blind man, not at all) cannot be further defined. These are the undefinable descriptive words of our language. At this point, therefore, definition stops. If I have finally defined a concept in terms of what anyone can see, feel, hear, and smell, then I shall know how to identify an instance of it. No one can carry definition further.

But even to carry definition this far is, for most scientific purposes, unnecessary. One can, for example, give the meaning of, say, 'table' in terms of objects of direct acquaintance like shape, material, and some further descriptive properties and relations. Generally, the names for physical objects do not require this fine a definition. Science takes over the names of common-sense physical objects. When definition becomes necessary, as of 'thermometer,' the definition is in terms of common-sense physical-object words, as, in the case of 'thermometer,' 'tube,' or 'box.'

Consider, for another example, the concept 'momentum.' It is a label for the product of mass and velocity. In order to be able to say that a body has a certain momentum, we must know how to ascertain its mass and its velocity. But these terms must in turn be defined. 'Velocity' is defined nominally as the distance traveled per unit time. Again, 'distance' and 'time,' as used here, are quantitative notions. Thus they too must be operationally defined by means of rulers and clocks, what we do to them, and what we observe after having done it. But that is as far as we need go. Once the chain of definition has been carried down to the point where all the defining words are names for common-sense physical objects and their directly observable characters, clearly there is no more defining to do. For when this stage is reached, definition has done its job. We know how to tell whether or not we have an instance of the concept and, if the term is quantitative, how much of it is present.

In general, definition in science stops when all descriptive terms in the definition refer either to physical objects, or to some directly observable properties and relations of and among them. To say the same thing differently, definition ends when the defining words are all part of the basic vocabulary of science. In social science, the "physical objects" are people and the characters, among others, their observed behavior. When this basis has been reached, anyone understanding the basic vocabulary can determine whether any sentence containing defined terms is true or false. The longer the chain of definition before this basis is reached, the more "abstract" is the concept being defined.

GROUP CONCEPTS

Research on teaching, and the social sciences generally, are often concerned with the study of people in groups. A tangled web of issues has been woven about the status of group concepts and their relationship to concepts referring to individuals. Intertwined in this controversy are two different issues. One, which I shall discuss now, has to do with the nature of the *terms* or concepts of social science; the other, which I shall discuss later, with the nature of its *laws* and *theories* and their relation in turn to those in other areas. The first issue, with which we are now concerned, is one of *meaning;* the second, of *reduction.*

I mentioned earlier that descriptive characters may be either relational or nonrelational. There are directly observable relations between or among things, like 'taller' or 'louder,' just as there are directly observable properties of individual things, like 'blond' and 'round.' Many terms, such as 'married' or 'mother,' appear grammatically to be properties of single individuals, but, like 'south,' are actually relational—requiring, when defined, reference to two or more individuals. Most of the defined words of science, like 'temperature,' 'distance,' 'force,' 'density,' 'hostility,' 'cohesive,' and 'totalitarian,' turn out, when defined, to be relational concepts.

Descriptive relations are not more important in social science than in other sciences. But to clarify the methodological controversies about the meaning of group concepts, it is important to emphasize that the world consists of descriptive relations *among* as well as descriptive properties *of* individual things. In particular, a group is an aggregate of individuals standing in certain descriptive relations to each other. The kinds of relations exemplified will, of course, depend upon, or determine, the kind of group, whether it be a family, an audience, a committee, a labor union, or a crowd.

Just as the individual John Smith is to be distinguished from his attributes, say, being blond or being tall, so the group must be distinguished from its attributes, such as, say, being numerous or being noisy. It is simple to tell whether a characteristic is being attributed to an individual or to a group. Compare

"Indians are red-skinned" with "Indians are disappearing." In the former, each and every Indian is said to be red-skinned, while in the latter, Indians as a group are said to be disappearing, that is, diminishing in population. When the property is attributed to a group collectively, so that the group itself is logically the subject of the proposition, rather than distributively, in which case "each and every" member of the group could logically be the subject of the proposition, then we have a group property. Group properties, like all others, may be either logical or descriptive. In 'The Apostles are twelve,' for example, 'twelve' is a logical character of the group of apostles, that is, one whose definition can be given in terms of logical words alone, such as 'all,' 'either . . . or,' or 'and,' without recourse to terms having observable referents. The logical definition is cumbrous and need not concern us here. Descriptive terms, which do particularly concern us, may be either physical, in the narrow sense, like 'loud' or 'dirty,' or behavioral, or sociological, like 'efficient' or 'wealthy.'

Clearly there is no issue about the *occurrence* of group characteristics. There is not even any question about the occurrence of behavioral group attributes. No one will deny that it makes sense to say of some groups that they are more efficient or more powerful than others or, of some others, that they are wealthy. The controversial question, or rather one of them, is whether or not there are any such attributes which are undefined or *undefinable,* i.e., whether there are attributes of groups not definable in terms of either the behavior of the individuals composing the group or the relations between these individuals or both.

There are, of course, undefinable terms referring to properties of individual things or persons, like color words or other words referring to directly observable qualities. Are there similarly undefinable terms referring to properties of groups, i.e., properties which can be directly observed but which cannot be defined in terms referring to either the behavior of the individuals constituting the

group or the relations obtaining among them or both? Can we speak, for example, of a "responsive audience" without defining the adjective in terms of the behavior of the individual people in the audience and some more or less precise statistical notion, namely, the percentage of attentive individuals in the group? Do groups or institutions have purposes not definable in terms of individual purposes; do they have purposes of their own, as it were? Similarly, can we meaningfully speak of a "will of the people" which is something different from either the wills of all persons or of the majority of these persons? The question can also be asked about groups themselves. Is there such a thing as the State or a University over and above their constituent individuals and the relations among them? Does this entity itself have attributes? Or, to say it more precisely, are there any undefined terms referring to kinds of groups?

Methodological Individualism

The two questions, about group entities and about undefinable attributes of groups, are obviously not independent. If, for instance, the efficiency of a group is not some function of the behavior of its constituent individuals, then there must be something else that exhibits this efficiency, the group "itself." And if there be such a superentity as, say, a "group-mind," then it will have characteristics of its own: allegedly, it may have political opinions. So there is really only one question. And it can be most economically posed by asking whether or not there are such undefinable descriptive properties of groups.

Let us consider examples. The "cohesiveness" of a group may be defined, say, as the ratio of the number of people within the group with whom its members say they would prefer to be stranded on a desert island to the total number of votes for people within and without the group. Can "crowd hysteria" be similarly defined in terms of individual behaviors or is it rather an undefinable quality of the crowd itself?

The denial that there are such undefinable group properties or such superentities is the view usually known as *methodological individualism*. Its contradictory is *metaphysical holism*. It is called "holism" because its proponents generally maintain that there are so-called wholes, group entities which have undefinable properties of their own. The property of the whole is then also said to be emergent from the properties of its parts. The thesis that there are such properties is accordingly also called "emergentism."

Philosophically, the holistic assumption that there are group properties over and above the individuals making up the group, their properties, and the relations among them, is counter to empiricism. For the latter holds that all terms must ultimately refer to what is observable, directly or indirectly, and that what we observe are people and their characteristics, not supra-individual groups and their characteristics. Or, to say the same thing differently, the antiholist maintains that the behavior *of* groups can be defined in terms of behavior *in* groups.

Culturally, holism is intimately connected with hostility toward the liberal political individualism of the Western tradition. If "States" have wills and purposes of their own, then counting noses is unnecessary and "serving the State" comes to sound like "serving Mr. Jones." Jones's will we know how to ascertain, but who is to divulge the "will of the State"? The answers are, alas, only too familiar. The will and wisdom of the State reside in a privileged class or caste, or they are "embodied" in a charismatic leader. The former is the conservative variant, also called "organicism."

To describe a fact is to state that one or several objects exemplify certain characters, relational and nonrelational or, what amounts to the same thing, that a defin*ed* or undefin*ed* concept has an instance. The occurrence of undefin*able* properties of groups would therefore be emergence at the level of description, or descriptive emergence. The operative word, of course, is "undefinable." For, as already mentioned, no one denies the existence of defined properties of groups, and these properties may well be different from any possessed by the individuals. For instance, they may be inapplicable to individuals because they are statistical aggregates, like the "homogeneity" of a group defined in terms of a standard deviation, or generally like the averaging processes used to arrive at the value of a variable. Since such statistical or aggregative concepts are always derived from information about individuals, they trivially satisfy the requirement of methodological individualism.

Sometimes the actual or possible statistical procedures entailed by the definition of a concept are only implicit or covert in ordinary usage. This appears to be the case in those statements which have been held to refer "anonymously" rather than specifically to individuals. The statement "an increased dividend is anticipated" is interpreted, quite correctly, to be individualistic even though it does not say anything about any particular shareholder. The expectations of the so-called "anonymous" individuals to whom the statement refers would, in the last resort, be ascertained by polling individual shareholders. Thus the "anticipation" is, quite trivially, a statistical concept, even though covertly so in ordinary speech. Similarly, references to, say, "the poor," in statements such as "The candidate received more votes from the poor than from the rich" are implicitly statistical. In neither case is any undefinable group property or group-entity meant or suggested. Neither impersonal, unattached anticipations nor a supra-individual "poor" is implied by the use of these locutions.

Nevertheless, there remains a class of terms frequently used in social science which are not statistical in intent but have not yet been defined in terms of individual behavior. One source of error perhaps peculiar to social science is imprecision in the referents of the terms being measured. Consider the assertion that a boom in trade is followed by a slump and depression. This is imprecise not only with respect to time; its predictive value is also restricted by the nature of its concepts. What exactly are "boom" and "slump" conditions? "Depression"? No doubt in these particular cases there is a large statistical component of the meanings involved. Level of employment, average wealth, and such like are doubtless entailed. But how many such things? What else? At what proportion of unemployment and "other" things will we say depression or boom conditions prevail? Can we be certain when we have one or the other?

Of course, it may be replied, we can't be certain but roughly we can tell. And that is just the point. The roughness results not from inability to determine the facts, statistically or otherwise, but from the fringe of vagueness surrounding the applicability of the terms. There is a common core of meaning—but the boundaries, so to speak, are vague. The definitions within physical science leave no room for this ambience. Prediction or explanation can hardly be precise when, because our terms lack sharp referents, we cannot be sure that we have the initial conditions or the anticipated event, since they are not exactly specified. The more macroscopic the concept, the wider its penumbra of vagueness is apt to be.

Consider next such concepts as 'the Reformation,' 'the Church,' 'capitalism,' 'mercantilism,' 'Cold War,' 'army morale,' and the like. In the meaning of these there is not even an implicit statistical reference. Such nonstatistical "institutional," or "holistic," concepts present difficulties of definition similar to those that face the clinical or, even more, the social psychologist. The precise definition of social attitudes, like pro- or anti-authoritarianism, or of clinical states, like aggression or anxiety, requires one to choose from an almost infinite variety of symptoms those which can be used reliably to define the term in question. This means, of course, not what is *really* anti-authoritarianism or aggression, but how to find a set of symptoms which, without additions or deletions, will enter into laws, that is, enable prediction of other behavior.

Even if we could overcome the difficulty in determining which symptoms should be omitted and which retained in the definition, a further difficulty remains in the case of clinical concepts because the fittingness of a behavioristic definition varies from culture to culture. Just as an "act of war" in one social setting might not be so in another, so what is aggressive behavior for an American might not be so for a South Sea Islander. Thus a definition of, say, aggressive behavior, which does not contain reference to the culture in which the behavior to be called aggressive is displayed, is, in a sense, obviously inadequate.

In the case of institutional concepts like 'the Reformation' or 'capitalism,' an indefinite set of behaviors are loosely encompassed by the term. It is not that certain behaviors are "anonymously" referred to, but that the list of these behaviors cannot yet be sharply terminated. 'Jewish people are cohesive,' as an example of a definable macroscopic term, means 'Jews usually marry Jews, live in close communities, share religious rituals, etc.' The 'etc.' makes my point for me. True, this was only meant to be illustrative. Still, the difficulty of completely spelling out that 'etc.' would also be present in actual scientific usage.

Yet, despite their open-endedness, these institutional concepts are probably just as indispensable to many areas of social science as are clinical concepts to the psychologist. *In principle,* of course, for whatever cold comfort it may provide, all such concepts must be definable in terms of individual behavior. In practice, however, we frequently cannot do this. Are we then prepared to say that in whatever context these terms occur they are wholly ambiguous? I hardly think so. The course of science is not always as smooth as the logical analyst would like. And it seems to me that there are cases in which the best we can do is point out the distinctions and the difficulties. The most that we can ask of the social scientist whose subject matter requires him to use such "open" concepts is that he keep the principle of methodological individualism firmly in mind as a consummation devoutly to be wished, an ideal to be approximated as closely as possible. Adherence to this principle should at least help assure that nevermore will he dally with suspect group-minds and impersonal "forces," economic or otherwise; nevermore will he attribute nonobservable properties to equally nonobservable group-entities. At the same time, he will not by methodological fiat be struck dumb about matters on which there is a great deal to be said, no matter how imprecisely.

LAWS: SIGNIFICANCE VERSUS MEANING

All scientific concepts, then, whether they be physical, psychological, or sociological, about things, persons, or groups of persons, must be defined in terms of observable characters. All good concepts are adequately defined. But not all adequately defined concepts are good ones. Definition is important, but it is by no means the only important thing about a worthwhile concept. Something else is needed before we call a concept "good." Much is made of the need to define one's terms, and rightly so. But definition is only a necessary first step to science's main business, which is, of course, the discovery of truths about the world. Truths state facts, either individual, like "Eisenhower is bald," or general, like "Dogs are carnivorous." The truth of either is ascertained by observation. Statements of fact, either individual or general, are about things. Definitions are merely about words. Statements of fact convey knowledge about the world. Definitions are wholly innocent of any such intent. Even so, it is misleading to say that science is interested in discovering facts and, therefore, the more facts the better. For, though any knowledge is surely better than none, not everything is equally worth knowing. The accumulation of facts or, as it is said, "mere" facts, is often charged, not without justice, with triviality. When is a fact trivial and when is it significant? The answer to this

question reveals what else, besides adequate definition, is needed for a good concept.

Connections between Facts

Bathtub or, less archaically, television-set counting is a much abused occupation—and not without reason. After all, of what significance is it that 90 per cent of the families in a certain city own television sets, 85 per cent own cars, 60 per cent live in their own homes? Useful information, perhaps, for manufacturers or contractors interested in marketing potentialities, but hardly a contribution to knowledge. For that matter, of what use is it to know the proportion of people who vote Republican, the amount of money in savings accounts, the increase in church membership, the decline in heavy-goods production, a certain mother's preference for sons over daughters, Johnny's IQ, or Mary's predilection for married men? Apart from gossip, gratified moral sentiments, or winning bets, what use are all these facts? In and of itself, no statement of individual fact is scientifically interesting. An individual fact, as distinguished from a generalization, refers to the existence of a particular thing, characteristic, event, or kind of event, like Johnny's IQ, Eisenhower's baldness, or the size of the Republican vote. To state a fact, then, is to state that a concept has an instance or a number of instances. 'Eisenhower is bald' says that the concept 'baldness' has an instance and that this instance is the man we call Eisenhower.

Such individual facts are significant only insofar as they are connected with other facts. Connections among individual facts are general facts. Thus, an organism's being a dog is connected with its being a meat-eater. Or, to say it differently, all instances of the concept 'dog' are also instances of 'meat-eater.' The connection is stated by the generalization 'All dogs are carnivorous' or 'If anything is a dog, then it is carnivorous.' The generalization or universal statement 'If there is a rise in wages, then prices increase' states a connection between instances of wage increases and of price increases. The connection is that whenever there is the one, there is also the other. Only "instances" that are connected in this manner with other "instances" are significant.

These generalizations or universal statements connecting individual facts are also called laws. The fact that Johnny's IQ is 110 is significant only if we know a law connecting this fact with some other fact, such as his doing well in school. To find such connections among individual facts is the purpose of counting and measuring, whether one is counting heads or electrons. Counting is sterile only when it is not guided by the attempt to relate by a law what is being counted to something else.

Laws and Hypotheses

Laws express regularities. Just as a concept names what is the same in different individuals, that is, a character they all exemplify, so a law describes another constancy, namely, one instance of a concept always being connected with an instance of another concept, as thunder always follows lightning. A generalization is such by virtue of its form, stating that *all* things having a certain character also have another, or *whenever* we have the first then we also have the second. This form does not depend upon how we come to assert it, whether by the inductive process of generalizing from a finite number of observations, by a hunch, or by a dream. No matter how we happen to hit upon it, a generalization always asserts more than what either has been or can be actually observed and may, therefore, turn out to be false. We do not and, in principle, cannot, test all of a law's instances.

Because this fragility is inherent in all generalizations, laws are also called hypotheses. No matter how these may have been initially arrived at, science is concerned with testing such hypotheses about connections among facts. Science looks for laws because without them neither explanation nor prediction is possible. We shall discuss this in more detail

later, but a few comments now will help. From the fact that Johnny's IQ is 110, nothing at all follows. It is only from this fact about Johnny, in conjunction with the law connecting IQ with school achievement, that we can make a prediction about his future school behavior. Conversely, the law permits us to explain his success by means of his IQ. Without laws or generalizations, no explanation is possible. The mere accumulation of individual facts brings no explanation, hence neither understanding nor control. Facts are trivial, then, only when we do not know their connection with other facts, that is, when we know no laws or generalizations about them.

Meaning and Significance

Concepts are not statements but names or labels. They cannot therefore be said to be either true or false. Yet there are differences between concepts. Just as a fact may be true but not worth knowing, so a concept may be adequately defined, but not worth having. A worthwhile concept is frequently called "meaningful." But only by a play on words can one say consistently that an adequately defined concept is *not* meaningful. Clearly, there is more than one meaning of "meaning." We ask for the meaning of Life, wanting to know why we are here and whither, if anywhere, we are going. We ask for the meaning of an event, like a falling star, wanting to know, perhaps, what it portends. Or, we ask for the meaning of another event, like an election, wanting to know what it indicates about the temper of the people. We search out the meaning of a drama or novel, wanting to know what moral it points for man and his world. Or, more mundanely, we ask for the meaning of words, like 'adze' or 'rubicund,' wanting to know no more than to what they refer.

In the former, more intriguing, questions about "meaning"—such as those about Life and falling stars—we are interested in *significance* in a common-sense use of that term that is generally clear in context. In the last example, however, we are interested in the observable referent of the term. But this referent is also called the meaning of the concept. In asking for "meaning" in the sense of significance, we want to know with what *other* things the events asked about are connected. We know perfectly well what the referent of the concept 'election' is, but are interested in how this referent, namely, voting behavior, is connected with other things, like the people's feelings about foreign or domestic policy. For concepts, "meaning" already has one established use as "referent."

To avoid confusion, therefore, this second kind of "meaning" may better be called *significance*. A concept is significant, then, if it appears in a law connecting it with other concepts. For instance, the concept of a "permissive" teacher is given referential meaning by operationally defining it in terms of responses to a battery of questions. It is a significant concept, however, only if we know something about how being permissive, thus defined, is connected with other characters, say, grade level and subject matter, or how it affects other behavior and attitudes, like giving specific homework assignments or preference for detailed planning of curricular units. These other characters, behaviors, and attitudes, cannot of course be part of the pattern of responses that were used to define 'permissive.' Otherwise, we have not an empirical law, telling us something about permissives, but a tautology, a statement which is true merely by the way we have decided to use the word 'permissive.' If, however, we have true laws, connecting permissiveness with certain other characters, then the concept not only has meaning but is also significant.

Descriptive reference is the primary and indispensable sense in which concepts have meaning. Unless they have this meaning, we cannot even begin to discover whether or not they are significant. A concept may have meaning without significance, but the converse is not true. That is, we may know perfectly well what the *referent* of a term is, yet know nothing *about* it. A good example is the concept 'cephalic index.' This concept can be quite adequately defined operationally in terms of the ratio of the width of a person's head to its length, with the method of measurement precisely stated. Yet, for the psychologist at least, a person's cephalic index is an uninteresting fact. It is not interesting because a person's cephalic index has no connection, as far as we know, with any of his behavior. There are, in other words, no laws connecting it with behavioral concepts. It is, therefore, not a useful concept. Since 'cephalic index' does not enter into laws, the concept is useless for predicting or explaining behavior. It lacks "meaning" in the sense of significance. Consider, on the contrary, that if the folklore generalization about redheads being quick-tempered were true, then the concept 'red-haired' would be significant because the alleged "law" permits us to make certain predictions about redheaded people. Less frivolously, the concept of, say, 'frustration' is significant because we know certain laws that enable us to predict the consequences of frustration. We know that under certain circumstances it leads to aggression.

"Good" Concepts

The reason for a fact's being trivial or not worth knowing is thus the same as that for a concept's not being worth having. Nor is this surprising, since to state an individual fact is to state that a concept has an instance. A law states that two or more kinds of individual facts are invariably connected, that is, whenever there is an instance of one (or more) concept(s), then there are also instances of one (or more) other(s). A concept is significant only if it enters into laws. It is significant, in other words, only if we know something about its referent, know how it is connected with other things. And to know that, in turn, is to know what effects it has, when it occurs, or how it changes. That is why adequate definition is not a sufficient condition for a good concept. Is a certain concept "good" or not? The question is ambiguous. Do you inquire whether the concept is adequately defined or whether it is significant? These are two questions, not one, and each must be answered separately. *A good concept has both meaning and significance.* In other words, a good concept has a reliably identifiable referent (meaning) about which we know one or more laws (significance). The more laws into which a concept enters, the more significant it is, because the more we then know about how it is connected with other things. If we know, for instance, not only that college education is connected with income, but also how it affects social status, success in marriage, political and religious attitudes, then the concept is more significant than if we know only one of these things. It is a more fruitful variable, because, given any instance of it, namely, a college-educated person, the generalizations permit us to say several other things about him.

A Definition of 'Definition'

As we ordinarily speak, the term 'definition' is ambiguous. We sometimes use it to mean only the right-hand or defining side of the whole 'if and only if' statement that, within our language, reflects the rule about the use of the word defined. Usually, this double use of 'definition,' for whole and for part, causes no confusion. With respect to operational or, generally, dispositional concepts, however, this mild ambiguity may cause trouble by adding its bit to the confusions about the connections between definitions and laws.

It will help clarify the subsequent discussion about the criticism of definitions if we are pedantically precise at this point. An operational definition of the concept 'H' has the form 'x is H *if and only if* If x is S then x is R.' That is, x is an instance of H or, what amounts to the same, a statement containing the defined concept 'H' is true if and only if in a given situation, S, certain observations, R, are made. Strictly speaking, the definition consists of the whole thing, left- and right-hand sides together. The right-hand side

alone, 'If x is S then x is R,' elliptically called the definition (of 'H'), is itself neither true nor false, until the name of a specific thing or individual is replaced for the variable x. Whether this right-hand side *alone* is true or false of a specified x depends on whether or not, given S, R always occurs. If it is true (false), then by virtue of the way we have defined 'H,' the left-hand side is also true (false). In either case, the entire if and only if statement, the definition proper, is a tautology or logical truth, since the left-hand side has *no* independent meaning but is only short for what is stated on the right-hand side.

In order for 'H' to be a significant concept, its right-hand defining conditional must enter into a law or generalization. That is, we must know a statement of the form '*If* if x is S then x is R, *then* x is Q.' For instance, if 'H' is 'hungry,' defined dispositionally, then we must know a law such as, say, 'If anyone is hungry (if S then R) *then* he is irritable (Q).' In this case, since irritability is also a dispositional character, 'Q' in turn is defined by an 'If-then' statement, say, 'If S' then R'.' After eliminating the defined terms 'H' and 'Q,' the law connecting hunger with irritability asserts '*If* if S then R, *then* if S' then R'.' Like all laws, this is a synthetic, empirical statement of fact. The referent of 'H' is the complex event that if S then R. If we know some laws about this referent, then and only then is 'H' a significant concept.

The variable x occurring on both sides of the definition of 'H' will of course be replaced by the name of a specific individual or thing to which the defined concept 'H' is being attributed. It is worth noting that in addition to x, the right-hand side of the definition may contain certain "hidden" variables with respect to which this right-hand side will be implicitly generalized. Most frequently, this hidden or implicit variable is "time." For example, a definition of a personality trait, say, vanity, contains an implicit generalization with respect to time. The defining conditional implicitly asserts that *at any time* that an individual x is in certain circumstances, S, then he behaves in the specified way, R. The right-hand side of the definition may thus be generalized with respect to one or more such variables. In particular, concepts referring to traits, abilities, and other such dispositions contain an implicit generalization with respect to time. Similarly, quantified concepts, defined in terms of measuring procedures and their observed results, contain a hidden time variable, implicitly asserting that repetition of the measurement at any time will give the same results. Whether this "reliability" of the concept is true or not is of course an empirical matter to be determined by observation, not something that can be "taken for granted."

Significance and Validity

Meaning or reference is a matter of convention; we make the word (concept) mean what it means. Significance or lawfulness is a matter not of convention, but of fact, that is, of the way things are. We can define any concept we wish to define. But we cannot endow a concept with significance. It either has it or it doesn't have it. If it has significance, social scientists call it "valid." This is a very special technical use of that word. A concept is valid if it yields successful predictions. But prediction is a by-product of lawfulness. Validity, as applied to concepts, is therefore synonymous with significance. In this use, a concept is valid for each variable that it predicts, hence, for each law in which it occurs. Finding laws and establishing the validity of a concept are thus one and the same thing. Concept validity, in this sense, depends on discovery, either by ordinary observation or experiment (Bechtoldt, 1959). Objectivity, on the other hand, depends upon adequate definition. The fruitfulness of a reliable concept is determined by whatever laws we may discover. Finding the laws and finding good concepts are one and the same thing.

Laws, not concepts, are discovered. A concept, after all, is just a name. And names are bestowed, not found. A concept is introduced into language when certain kinds of phenom-ena are selected for attention. The scientist names not, like Adam, for the sake of naming, but only when he has a hunch about a connection between what he names and something else. If his hunch is right, then he has discovered not a concept, but a law. Concepts are not sentences. Only sentences, either of individual fact or generalizations, state that something is or is not the case. Therefore, only sentences are either true or false. Concepts are either well- or ill-defined, significant or useless, good or bad, but they are not true or false. To look for a good concept is to look for a law.

There is no recipe or prescription for finding laws nor, therefore, for finding significant concepts. Scientific method is not a set of rules for discovery, but a certain way of formulating concepts, confirming hypotheses, and constructing theories. We can state the principles of proper concept-formation. We can state the nature of proper scientific evidence for the truth of a hypothesis. But we cannot give any recipes for selecting the concepts and finding the hypotheses to which the method of science is then applied. The scientist in any area needs a firm and broad grasp of already established knowledge and techniques. This he can be taught. The rest is imagination and ingenuity. With these he must be born.

How Concepts are Formulated

However, though we cannot give any recipes for successful research, we can say something about how new concepts often come to be formulated, about how certain features of the world including human behavior come to be selected for attention. When a scientist reflects upon the mass of facts he or others may have accumulated, there are at least three different ways in which these data may suggest new concepts to him. These ways are certainly not exhaustive. There are doubtless others, since we cannot set limits to the power of imagination. Nor are they even mutually exclusive, since all three factors may be operative when a new concept is formed. Nevertheless, these are three distinguishable ways of forming new concepts. Analysis of what is involved in each case may throw some light on the subtle and devious process of finding significant concepts.

Perceiving a common characteristic. Frequently, new concepts arise when the scientist perceives that certain apparently disparate phenomena have a common characteristic. This presumed common character becomes the referent of a new concept. For example, trade unions, large business organizations, and governments are all very different kinds of social groups. Yet the sociologist notices a similarity among them that is not obvious to the naked eye, as it were. He notices that the structure of these groups, the manner in which their various members are related to one another and to the functioning of the organization, is pretty much the same. To this common factor, this similarity, he gives the name 'bureaucracy.' Or he notices that clubs, secret societies, guilds and fraternities of various kinds are all alike in that they are all, as he calls them, 'closed groups.' The political scientist "sees" that a father, the head of a state or of a company, and a teacher, different though their roles are, have in common something he calls "power."

The new concept naming these common features is usually more abstract, in the sense of "highly defined," than are the concepts which stimulated its formulation. The definition of 'bureaucracy' very likely takes longer, as it were, to reach the basis of observable characters than do the definitions of 'trade unions,' 'big business,' and the like. It is, of course, not surprising that this is so, since the new concept incorporates in its definition some of the defining terms of the old concepts.

A new concept, introduced on the basis of features presumed common to several different kinds of things, must "prove itself" in two ways. In the first place, after the concept has been adequately defined, then we must see whether or not the different things actually are instances of it *as it has been defined.*

Do the various organizations actually exhibit the structure newly defined as "bureaucracy"? The concept, if it is adequately defined, must name observ*able* characters. The issue now is, does it name observ*ed* ones? Are there any such things?

If there are, then the second and harder test is yet to come. Is this newly defined pattern of relations itself connected with other things? Is bureaucracy, for instance, lawfully connected with, say, efficiency? If these new concepts do turn out to be significant, then the laws in which they occur will have much greater scope than any laws about the various things which suggested the new concept. Anything that is true about bureaucracies will be true about all and any specific bureaucracies. Once it is established that an organization is a bureaucracy in the sense defined, then by means of the more abstract laws, we know a great deal about that organization without independently studying it. This is one reason why abstract concepts are not only scientifically legitimate but also very valuable. The laws in which they occur provide more knowledge than do the laws in which less abstract concepts occur.

Combining old concepts. New concepts may also be formed by combining those already at hand. The scientist speculates, after making certain observations, that two or more variables act jointly. He therefore forms a new concept out of them. If the original concepts are adequately defined and the new concept is merely some arithmetical function of them, like their product, sum, or quotient, then, of course, the new concept will also be adequately defined.

What decides which concepts shall be combined so as to form a new one? The scientist must have some hypothesis about the significance of the combination he chooses. The ratio of change in velocity to time has a name, 'acceleration,' while the ratio of change in velocity to distance does not. The difference is that there are certain laws about acceleration, while we do not know any about the other quotient. When Galileo introduced the concept of acceleration, he could have defined it, and actually considered so defining it, as the ratio of change in velocity to distance covered rather than to time elapsed. As far as definition goes, this would have been a perfectly adequate concept. But he had a hypothesis that the change in speed of freely falling bodies was proportional only to the time of fall and that the distance covered, like the weight of the bodies, did not affect this. If he were right, this meant that the "acceleration," as he defined it, of freely falling bodies must be uniform or constant, equal intervals of time giving equal increases of velocity. This was itself a hypothesis about acceleration which, if true, would make the concept significant. Moreover, Galileo's law of falling bodies making the distance covered proportional to the square of the elapsed time is true only if acceleration is indeed constant, which it turned out to be. Thus, on the basis of previous knowledge, that freely falling bodies increase their speed as they fall, and a hypothesis about how this change actually occurs, a new, more abstract, concept, defined in terms of concepts already at hand, was introduced. To say that Galileo discovered the "right" concept is simply another way of saying that he discovered a law, that is, something *about* acceleration.

Whenever a concept is thus formed by combination of others, this combination must actually operate jointly in laws. Assume that a concept 'status' is newly defined in terms of a cluster of characters, say, education, income, and occupation. Are these enough or too much? In other words, what should be included and what omitted from the definition in order to discover laws about "status." Suppose that we have some technique for ordering status as higher and lower and wish to test the hypothesis that a person of higher status is always treated deferentially by those of lower status. Given our definition of the concept, this might well be true only of an all-white population. Therefore, if the concept is to be significant for a mixed population, "color," unfortunately, cannot be excluded from the defining terms. Conversely, including "weight" in the concept may well

render it useless, since probably few laws will be found about individuals who share the same weight as well as the other defining attributes of "status." If the component concepts are quantified variables, then we must also know how they combine, whether it is their product, sum, quotient, or some other function that acts jointly. Various research techniques, statistical and otherwise, are at hand to help with the job of deciding whether certain clusters of attributes do in fact go together in a way to justify forming a new concept out of them. The ultimate criterion is significance.

Inferring underlying states, or constructs. If I see a man strike another man, I infer that he is angry. If I notice a child staring into a bakery window, I infer that he would like some of the goodies. A physicist seeing a flash of light on a screen infers the presence of a charged particle. Seeing a husband accidentally spill hot soup on his wife, a psychologist infers unconscious hostility. Hearing someone make certain statements, a social psychologist infers anti-Semitism. Science, like common sense, frequently makes inferences from observations to something not observed. In order to help explain certain manifest behavior, the scientist formulates concepts that name unobserved states of the organism or object exhibiting the observed behavior. He postulates certain lawful connections between these "underlying states" and the observed behavior.

This is a third method of forming concepts or, as the names for such "inferred" characters are often called, constructs. It is widely used and very fruitful. It is also beset with methodological puzzles. From footprints, Robinson Crusoe inferred that he was not alone on the island. He was destined, however, to meet the cause of these footprints face to face. But it may be argued that we cannot meet someone else's anger, hunger, attitude, or ability face to face, as it were. It may be urged further that the operationally defined concepts of attitudes, abilities, and so on, are themselves merely effects of the "unobservables." For example, getting a certain score on an arithmetic test is merely an index of an un-observed ability.

Plausible as all this sounds, it is also puzzling. The statements of an empirical science must be confirmable by observation. How do we confirm statements about these "unobservables"? What, and this amounts to the same question, are the referents of such concepts? Concepts cannot have significance without meaning, yet we seem here to be asserting hypotheses about concepts whose descriptive meaning cannot be stated.

Given the rigorous criteria for good concepts and for what constitutes trustworthy evidence, what are the nature and role of these concepts within science? I shall try to answer this question in two stages. First, I shall discuss a fairly prevalent criticism of definitionalism and a proposed alternative to definition. This will only tell us what will not do, and my reasons for believing that it will not do. Second, a positive answer to the question will be suggested in the context of a more detailed discussion of scientific explanation and theory construction.

CRITICISMS OF DEFINITION

Once a heroic rallying cry in the behavioral sciences, operationism is now everyday good scientific practice there as elsewhere. It is not a special philosophical or methodological position. It merely clarifies the form definitions of scientific concepts must take in order to determine when statements containing these terms are true or false. As the study of man came of age scientifically, it inevitably adopted the practice of defining its terms. In fact, the practice is a necessary condition for such coming of age. Yet this modest proposal for forming empirically meaningful concepts, dignified by the title "operationism," has had its critics.

Criticism from the Right

There has always been criticism from the right, that is, from sources essentially hostile to a science of behavior. Life and space are too short for more than a few brief comments on these last-ditch defenders of lost causes. Their essentially antiscientific plaint is to the effect that definition, operational or otherwise, deprives science of the rich halo of meanings surrounding terms in ordinary use. Far from being a weakness, this is as it should be. A concept means what its definition says it means. If it does not say this clearly so that we know when we do or when we do not have an instance and, if it is quantified, how much of it, then the concept may be criticized legitimately as inadequately defined.

On the other hand, it makes no sense to criticize a concept on the ground that its definition is not "really" what the concept means. It is, for instance, improper to criticize a definition of political 'conservatism' on the grounds that the defining terms do not really capture the "essence" of conservatism, or something of that sort. The scientist's concept is not that of common sense. His concept means only what he says it means. This meaning need not include all or even any of the meanings various people associate with the concept. Generally, in fact, it will include *some* of these associated meanings, since the scientist has picked this particular term and not some other from common sense. But it is unlikely to include all of them and need not include any. The scientist may draw upon the halo surrounding terms which also have a commonsensical use for hunches about laws, but if he wants objective knowledge of behavior, he cannot carry over the vagueness of ordinary use into his technical vocabulary. The concept of IQ, for instance, is by now a classic target for this kind of misplaced criticism. It does not, so the complaint goes, measure intelligence in the common-sense use of that term. Of course not, but the criticism is irrelevant. If IQ is a good concept, it is so not because it is consonant with common sense, but because we can measure it with fair reliability and because we know, with moderately high probability, its connection with other attributes and kinds of behavior. Some of these other things, like general information, success in school, professional achievement, and social adjustment, are part of the meanings commonly associated with "intelligence." But this merely shows that when choosing the ordinary word for their particular concept, the scientists made some rather successful hypotheses about laws connecting performance on certain kinds of tests with some components of the common-sense notion of intelligence. Because certain of its concepts, like 'force' and 'energy,' are also in common sense, physics once had to endure similarly irrelevant criticism. By now, social science remains the only target.

Calls for "Open" Definitions

Such rather transparently obscurantist criticism of definition need not be taken too seriously. Worthier of attention are the criticisms from persons undeniably favorable to a science of behavior. They, too, attack operational definitions as unduly restrictive. Since operational definitions are, after all, just definitions, it is not surprising that, in fact, these critics level their strictures at the whole principle of empiricism, namely, that concepts, to be meaningful, must be defined in terms of observable properties of things. Instead of the narrow criterion of definability, they urge that the meaning of a term must be left *open*. Terms, it is said, should be "introduced" rather than defined. Their openness is gradually filled in, though never closed, as we increase our knowledge. Or, as it is also put, the meaning of a term is given not explicitly by definition, but implicitly by the set of laws in which the term occurs.

What are the arguments for and the merits of the view that meaning cannot be given by explicit definition?

There are several different ways of measuring the length of an object, hunger in a laboratory animal, or the IQ of a child. If the meaning of a term is given explicitly by its definition, all these different antecedent measuring conditions result in different definitions for length, hunger, or IQ. Yet we may have good reason for believing, or even just *feel,*

that these all measure the same thing. Moreover, we may continue to devise new test conditions for the presence or absence of the property in question. Any definition by means of a single test condition for the presence and absence of an attribute, therefore, fails to capture the full meaning of the term. And since we are always adding to the list, the meaning of a concept is never more than partially determined. The group of alternative criteria for the application of the term does not, therefore, literally define it. The unending list of test and truth conditions does not permit the elimination of the term. Accordingly, it is said to be *reduced* to, rather than defined by, the set of 'if-then' sentences about the conditions under which the term is applicable. The latter, in turn, are called reduction sentences and only partially specify the meaning of the term.

Definability was thus liberalized into reducibility. The latter countenanced, if it did not advocate, terminological indefiniteness. It is perhaps not surprising that empirical reference was soon to be drowned in a sea of context. Consider certain clinical and social concepts, like anxiety or group morale. What kinds of observable behavior should constitute the definition of such terms? Answers to a test may give a high anxiety score. But people with identical scores also exhibit many different varieties of behavior. To really know what anxiety means, it seems reasonable to say that one must know not merely the test scores but all the characteristics predictable on the basis of them. Such concepts are also called "constructs" and are considered to be postulated attributes which are *reflected,* but not defined, by the test performance and all other behaviors positively correlated with it.

In particular, "hypothetical constructs," as contrasted with "intervening variables," are said to be among the kinds of terms which are thus "postulated." Their full meaning is given by the set of laws in which they occur. This set of laws is called a nomological network. The more incomplete the network, that is, the less we know, the vaguer are our concepts. Until we know all the laws in which a term occurs, we do not know precisely what it means. It is only partially defined. After we have all the laws, the term is "implicitly defined" by this network.

Few, if any, of the critics of definition hold that *no* terms have meaning apart from a system of laws. The anti-empiricist implications of a holistic view that bases meaning wholly on context at the expense of extrasystematic descriptive reference are too patent. For if one term always "means" another, then language loses all contact with the world. The view is unpalatable both to the scientist who tries to describe the world and to the philosopher who tries to show how the scientist accomplishes this. They grant that some of the terms of the network are definable in terms of observable events. Those which allegedly are not thus definable are held to be connected to these by chains of laws. They are thus also said to be "partially coordinated" to the realm of experience.

Defense of Explicit Definitions

Logical and philosophical technicalities apart, this is the gist of the arguments against explicit definitions. After our preceding discussion of tautologies, definitions, and laws, it should not be difficult to unravel the confusions that give rise to this controversy and to the alleged distinction between hypothetical constructs and intervening variables. Most obvious is the confusion between the two meanings ˙of meaning—reference and significance. Consider, first of all, a trivial example. It is purely verbal or, as one says, a matter of convention that 'dog' refers to a barking rather than to a meowing creature. On the other hand, the generalization or law that dogs are carnivorous is a matter of fact and not a matter of the way we use words. Yet, in the nomological network or implicit definition view, meat-eating is part of the meaning of the concept dog. As we know more about dogs, we expand the meaning of the concept. Obviously, the "meaning" being expanded is what we called significance. But

in order to discover this significance, we must first know the referent of the term. Otherwise, what is it that we are discovering laws *about?*

It is objected, however, that terms referring either to kinds of physical objects, like dogs, or to directly observable characters, like shape and color, are not the real target of the strictures against definability. We can observe that a dog is brown or running, but we do not directly observe its hunger. Or we may see one man strike another, but we do not see his anger. There is a sense, of course, in which no instance of an operationally defined or dispositional concept is directly observable. Unlike names for physical objects and their simple characters, these concepts, as we saw, are defined by means of a conditional or 'if-then' sentence. And we saw, too, that a sentence containing such a concept, like 'soluble,' will be true of a certain substance if and only if a certain conditional is true, namely, that if a sample of this substance is put in water, then it dissolves. And we do not directly observe what conditionals refer to, as we may directly observe the reference of singular statements about, say, Fido being a dog or his being brown. 'This lump of sugar is soluble' thus differs from 'This lump of sugar is white' in that the latter, as a singular statement of individual fact, can be directly observed, while the former, because it contains the dispositional term 'soluble,' requires a more complicated set of observations. (Lest the practical difficulty of repeating the test with a specific lump of sugar confuse the issue, consider instead 'This piece of copper conducts electricity.' Remember the "hidden" time variable that I mentioned earlier. 'Being an electrical conductor' is also a dispositional concept, and the test may be repeated over and over!)

Since to ascribe a dispositional character to anything or anybody is to assert that something will always occur under certain circumstances, dispositional concepts may, like all laws, be called "hypothetical." However, since most concepts in science are of this kind, the term serves no good purpose. More to the point, it is not what the critics of definition mean by calling their constructs "hypothetical." They do not mean merely that, for instance, 'hunger' is defined by an 'if-then' sentence, such as, 'If the organism is presented with food under certain circumstances, then the organism will eat it.' Rather, they insist that these states or traits "underlie" the observed behavior—being given food and eating it—but are not defined by it. They are "postulated," not defined, and this is what makes them "hypothetical." Such postulated or, even, "inferred" entities may be manifested in many ways. Each "manifestation" is a separate law that partially defines the term, whose full meaning is given by all the laws in which it occurs.

Let us take a closer look at what is entailed by saying that the meaning of a term is partially specified by each law in which it occurs. Let 'H' be a simple sentence containing the "postulated" or "inferred" attribute. Let 'If S then R' be the observed behavior by which H is manifested. We then have the following set of "laws":

L_1: If H, then if S_1 then R_1
L_2: If H, then if S_2 then R_2
L_3: If H, then if S_3 then R_3
.
.
.
L_n: If H, then if S_n then R_n

The list of "laws" in which H can occur is, of course, in principle unending. It follows that the full meaning of 'H' can never be specified. But let us assume that we have a small, finite number of such laws. How do we find out whether any one of them, say L_1, is true? All that we in fact observe is that whenever we have S_1 then we have R_1. In each case, only the right-hand side of the conditional containing 'H' as antecedent is ever observed. How do any or all of these justify our asserting that H occurs? More basically still, what exactly is it that we are asserting when we say that H occurs, if it has no mean-

ing independent of the Ss and Rs? These questions simply have no answers.

There is also a peculiar logical difficulty about saying that any of the Ls are either true or false. Since H's "meaning" is partially specified by each law in which it occurs, none of the Ls are logically independent of the others, that is, no L can be true and any other false. For, part of the meaning of 'H' in, say, L_2 is what is expressed by L_1, and so on for each L. If the meaning of 'H' is given by *all* the laws in which it occurs, not only do we not know what 'H' means until science is completed and we have all possible laws, but, when that happy day arrives, the whole batch *must* be true together by virtue of the meaning of 'H.' All of science has become one vast tautology.

Nor are matters helped by saying that the Hs are inferred entities or attributes, in analogy with the way that, say, a physical attribute may be inferred from a law and certain observed conditions. If after pounding on a piece of steel I find that it does not crack, I may infer that it has been tempered. Being tempered is not directly observable, like color, but requires knowledge of some past treatment, namely, having been put in cold water while hot. I infer this unobserved property from a law stating that tempered steel is more malleable than untempered steel. But, in this case, 'being malleable' is not part of the meaning of 'being tempered' and I make an inference from one character to another *different* one. And, I could, in principle and even in practice, confirm the law independently by first tempering a piece of steel and then seeing whether or not it was made more malleable than before. The case of our H differs in two respects. First, since part of the meaning of 'H' is the observed conditional, 'If S then R,' I cannot make an inference from the conditional to something *else*. Second, it is in principle impossible to check L independently because I do not know what 'H' refers to. Yet 'If S then R' is said to be a "predictive property" of H!

Compare all this with the introduction of concepts by definition. Instead of an L, we have, in the first instance, a D, that is, a definition, as follows:

$$D: \text{'}H\text{' means (by definition)}$$
$$\text{'If } S \text{ then } R\text{'}$$

Since 'D' is a rule for the use of 'H,' we may assert within our language the corresponding statement 'If H, then if S then R.' This *looks like L*, but, unlike L, it is, by virtue of the definition, a tautology. Moreover, since it is such only by virtue of the way we have decided to use 'H,' the whole thing is eliminable from the language. This accurately reflects what we mean when we say that such truths are "merely verbal." In principle, they are dispensable. If now 'H' is significant, then we need only use the defining sentence 'If S then R' in the statement of any laws about H. 'H' itself is redundant, hence dispensable, which again reflects what we mean when we say that we have given the referential meaning of one term, that we do *not* understand, in terms of others, which we *do* understand. Since 'L,' on the other hand, is said to be a law and not a definition, then, unlike 'D,' it is not eliminable. Nor is 'H' itself dispensable. Therefore if it is a significant concept, then any law about it would have to include the entire sentence or, rather, set of sentences, 'If H, then if S then R,' all of which contain the term 'H' that we do *not* understand. If 'H' means 'hungry' and we want to assert that hungry men are irritable, we would have to say '*If* if H then if S then R, *then I*.' This, and all other such laws, would contain 'H' as an ineliminable term. Its meaning is not independent of either 'S,' 'R,' or 'I.' For, of course, 'I' is but a term in another law in which 'H' occurs and therefore is also part of the meaning of 'H.' Again, science results in one vast tautology.

To be sure, in one sense of 'meaning,' a concept is more meaningful (significant) to us the more we know about it. But what is the *it* about which we know more and more? Only if we keep in mind our distinction between two different meanings of 'meaning' can this question be answered. As we saw, a term may have meaning or reference without significance, but the converse is not true. Yet, this converse is precisely what the proponents of "implicit definition" are in effect trying to defend.

Can we not add the new things we find out about something to its definition, thus giving more and more "meaning" to the term? Up to a point, we can. Suppose that the results of three different tests for intelligence are found to be correlated. 'Intelligence' is now redefined so that it means not any one of these results, but all three together. The term has been redefined to keep up with our knowledge, but what has been gained by doing so? Suppose 'intelligence' now means a certain level of vocabulary, reading ability, and general information, or perhaps, something presumed common to all three, like linguistic ability. Yet, in order to be able to predict that an individual with high vocabulary is also good at reading, we would still have to state separately the empirical law connecting these attributes. So nothing has been gained by packing everything we know into the meaning of the term. Suppose it happens that the referents of 'status' as initially defined in one way and 'intelligence' as defined in another are found to be correlated. Do we want to coin a new word whose meaning will include both the referent of status and that of intelligence?

This is the logical conclusion to which the notion of partial definition carries us. Yet it leads nowhere. Without independently asserting the empirical law connecting status with intelligence, the new concept is just a word for a cluster of characteristics. Without the statement of the law, we have no justification for stating that members of this cluster uniformly occur together. Nothing follows from definition or meaning alone. Only from laws can we make predictions.

Furthermore, how could we have discovered that intelligence is connected with status unless these terms have independent meaning? Again, what is it that we have knowledge about? In other words, in order to discover the significance of a term, we must first know its meaning. Significance alone will never give us empirical science. If the system of laws is to be about the world— if it is to be a factual, descriptive system—its concepts must also have meaning in the sense of designation or reference.

Nor can laws intelligibly be said to implicitly define their terms. The phrase "implicit definition" is most misleading. If it makes sense at all, it makes sense only when one is speaking of the axioms of a formal system, that is, a system of marks on paper containing expressions like 'If P then Q,' to whose letter variables no meanings have been attached. For such a system, the axioms implicitly define its terms only in the sense that, showing structure though no content, they delimit the range of possible meanings or the interpretations that can be given to the symbols of the system if true statements are to result. Replacing the letter-variables with sentences containing certain descriptive concepts gives true sentences. When these concepts are replaced by others, the resulting sentences will be false. But there may be many alternative sets of descriptive concepts which will give either result.

The uncompleted network of behavioral laws in which the "hypothetical" terms occur will presumably come to include terms referring either to further behaviors, or to neurophysiological events. In any case, these other terms would, if they were not leaning on each other in the curious circular manner of the nomological network, refer to observable attributes. No matter which way you look at it, the behavioral scientist's candidates for hypothetical constructs, like 'hostility,' 'aggression,' 'morale,' and the like, must have *some* referential meaning. If, on the one hand, meaning is confounded with significance and the meanings of these terms are given by the laws in which they occur, then for there to *be* any laws at all, these terms must have independent meaning. On the other hand, if these terms have no independent meaning, their connection to observables can be only verbal or definitional. Their empirical meaning is then given by this defi-

nition, which may, of course, be changed.

Definitions, being merely verbal, are tautologies. Laws are empirical statements. If the latter are absorbed into the former, if everything is made a matter of meaning, we have not an empirical science but a structure of tautologies. This would make nonsense of the whole enterprise. How then does one come to hold this view? I mentioned before, when discussing group concepts, that behavioral scientists often cannot define their terms precisely. When trying to define terms referring to social attitudes or clinical states, the list of behaviors which together enable prediction of other behaviors cannot as yet be sharply terminated. Such terms thus have a fringe of vagueness or openness. To achieve greater reliability and significance, such terms are frequently redefined to include new factors or, for that matter, to drop old ones. Loosely speaking, we say the original definition was only partial. Accurately speaking, we frequently abandon our definitions and propose new ones. The initial vagueness and consequent frequent redefinition is part of the hit-and-miss way a science progresses. But the logic of science is concerned with the principle of good concept-formation. The psychology of discovery is something else again. The purposes of neither science nor logical analysis are served by exalting the vicissitudes of research in a difficult area into a methodological position.

EXPLANATION, PREDICTION, AND THEORIES

As I mentioned briefly before, the scientist looks for laws or connections among facts in order to explain and to predict phenomena. Speaking loosely, we may "explain" the fact that Jones makes more money than Smith by pointing to Jones's superior education. But a man from Mars or anyone else may well wonder why we cite Jones's education rather than, say, his height. Speaking more strictly, we then expand our explanation. To cite a cause as explanation of an event is, implicitly at least, to cite an instance of a law.

Jones's education rather than his height is relevant to his income because we know a law or generalization connecting education with income, while no such law connects height with income. This law and the fact about Jones's education together give a *reason,* in a strict logical sense, for Jones's superior income because they are the premises of a deductive argument from which that fact may be derived. The conclusion may be deduced from the premises because the premises logically imply the conclusion. And the premises logically imply the conclusion because the corresponding conditional, 'If the premises are true, then the conclusion is true,' is a tautology. It is a tautology or logical truth, because the conclusion merely makes explicit what is already implicit in the premises. The fact to be explained therefore *must* be true if the explaining premises are true. That is why explanation is always deductive, no matter how covertly. For otherwise, the statements that purport to do the explaining will fail to explain why what happened should have happened rather than something else. Either the explanation is deductive or else it does not justify what it is said to explain.

Prediction has the same logical form as explanation. In predicting something as yet unknown, we deductively infer it from particular facts and laws that are already known. This deductive, tautological, connection between statements also shows why observations confirm or refute hypotheses. If a prediction inferred from a set of premises turns out to be true, then the generalization is further confirmed. If it turns out to be false, then we know that either the generalization or the individual fact used in making the prediction *must* be false. Since we are less likely to be mistaken about individual facts, in most cases the failure of a prediction means that the generalization is thereby refuted.

It makes no difference whether the premises are statistical or "deterministic," as nonstatistical generalizations are called. If they are deterministic, we may predict an individual event; if they are statistical, only statements about classes of events may be either explained or predicted. Since explanation always seeks to clarify statements by means of other statements, concepts alone have no explanatory or predictive power; only sentences can serve as either premises or conclusion of a deduction. The notion of an "explanatory concept" is simply a confused way of speaking about significant concepts, those about which we know laws permitting explanation and prediction.

An explanation of an individual fact always includes at least one law or generalization among its premises. This law may in turn be explained by deducing it from other laws. The connection between education and income, for instance, may be explained by deducing it from generalizations connecting, say, education, with social mobility and social mobility, in turn, with income. Although all three laws are empirical generalizations which may turn out to be false, the *connection among them* is such that *if* the last two are true, then the law to be explained *must* be true.

A theory is such a deductively connected set of laws. It thus has the logical form of an explanation. Some explanations, those that explain statements of individual fact, contain both laws and statements of individual fact as premises. In a theory, *all* the statements, both explained and explaining, are generalizations. Those that do the explaining are called the *axioms* of the theory. The laws that are explained are the *theorems* of the theory. The axioms are such only by virtue of their place in a theory. Neither self-evident nor otherwise privileged, they are empirical laws whose truth is, temporarily at least, taken for granted in order to see what other empirical assertions, the theorems, must be true if the axioms are true. An axiom in one theory may be a theorem in another. Thus, what is an axiom in Galileo's theory about the free fall of bodies on earth is a theorem in the Newtonian theory of gravitation which explains Galileo's laws. The Newtonian axiom is in turn explained, in conjunction with other statements, by Einstein's theory. Explanation is always relative to a set of premises that logically imply what is to be explained. We stop explaining when we don't know any more. There is no logically "ultimate" explanation.

At the other extreme from those who, confusing meaning with significance, would make all science tautological are those who consider its assertions neither true nor false, but just useful. This confusion, too, is worth dispelling. The theorems of a theory follow deductively from its axioms, though the theorems may be and frequently are known first. This will of course always be the case when the axioms are introduced in order to explain already known laws. Once we have our axioms, then they may also be used to predict new, not yet known, laws. In fact, this is one main purpose of theories. But this functional or instrumental aspect is overemphasized when theories are said to be "merely" instruments for explaining and predicting, and, therefore, like any tool, neither true nor false. This view is at best misleading, at worst false. Looked at as a whole, theories are logically true, for a theory, like any deductive explanation, is a huge, tautological 'if-then' statement. But the *components* of this 'if-then,' the individual premises and conclusions, are themselves (except for dispensable definitions) all empirical laws. Looked at in their parts, therefore, theories are either true or false, since no single statement of the theory, be it axiom or theorem, is a tautology. In this sense, a theory not only explains and predicts, it also describes, for each single statement of the theory states how something is lawfully connected with something else. And a law is a statement of fact, though of course a general, not an individual, fact. No matter how the axioms are arrived at, since they state connections among individual facts, they are general laws. As such, they share the infirmity of other generalizations, namely, contingency. But they also have the merit of other generalizations, namely, that unlike tautologies, they are informative.

A theory, then, as a whole is of course a tautology. But, speaking elliptically, we call a theory true or false. Strictly, this is a way of speaking about its axioms. A theory is false if any of its axioms is false. Otherwise, it is true. A theory can, in fact, be instrumental or useful only if its axioms are true. For, if they are not true, there is no reason why they should give us true predictions. If the axioms of a theory are true, then the theorems must also be true. But if they are false, then the theorems may be either true or false. It has, of course, sometimes happened in the history of a science that false hypotheses by accident have led to true predictions. We now know this historical fact only because such false theories sooner or later betrayed us, as they inevitably will, by permitting us to derive "predictions" that turned out to be false. The predictive or "functional" value of a theory thus derives from the truth of its axioms.

THEORETICAL CONSTRUCTS

Explicit definitions, we recall, have been criticized by some as unduly restrictive. A man may eat not only because he is hungry, but because he is anxious. One man when angry gets red and noisy, another goes white and silent. A clinician may consider many different kinds of behavior "aggressive," even though they have no observable properties in common that could serve to define the term. In general, different psychological states may be manifested by similar behavior, or the same states may be expressed by different people in diverse ways. Explicit definition, its critics claim, cannot take these variations into account. As I tried to make clear, their proposed alternative, so-called "implicit definition," makes statements containing the "introduced" but undefinable concept H unintelligible. Either the statements are empty tautologies because true by meaning, or else we cannot tell whether they are true or false, because we do not know to what H refers. Fortunately, this desperate expedient is not the only recourse open to the behavioral scientist. To explain the intelligible recourse he does have, it will help to say a bit more about the nature of concepts occurring in most worthwhile theories.

A theory not only explains and predicts, it also unifies phenomena. It can perform these functions only because it has a certain structure. An empirical theory is a linguistic structure some of whose component parts say something about the world. It consists therefore of a vocabulary and a set of sentences. The sentences are of three kinds: definitions, axioms, and theorems. Its vocabulary contains, in addition to the logical words common to all science, descriptive words or concepts that, with considerable overlap, distinguish one area from another. A theory contains two classes of descriptive terms: basic, or "primitive," and defined. The basic terms *of* a theory are those that are not themselves defined *within* the theory, but all other descriptive terms of the theory are defined by means of them. The basic terms of a theory *must* occur in its axioms and may also reoccur in its theorems. Its defined terms occur only in the theorems.

The basic undefin*ed* terms of a theory are rarely also undefin*able* descriptive words, that is, terms referring to directly observable characters of things. On the contrary, they tend to be quite abstract, that is, highly defined relative to the undefinable descriptive words of all science. (The only exception is geometry, whose axioms contain such terms as 'point,' 'line,' and 'coincides.') The basic terms of a theory are given referential meaning by appending to them definitions which are not explicitly part of the theory itself. Thus, 'mass' is a basic, undefined, and highly abstract term of Newtonian theory, with, of course, an operational definition appended to it.

Such appended definitions are often called "coordinating" definitions, since they coordinate the basic terms of the theory to observable characters of things. Implicitly, they are part of the theory itself and, indeed, an essential part, since otherwise we would not know what the theory was about. However, they are not explicitly a part of the theory in that they play no role in the deduc-

tion of theorems from the axioms. For this deduction, we need only the definitions of the concepts occurring in the theorems but not in the axioms. And these concepts are defined by means of the basic terms of the axioms. Once the basic terms have been coordinated to what can be observed, then by means of the definitions stated within the theory, the defined terms of the theorems are also automatically coordinated to observable characters of things. We see again how misleading it is to call the axioms of a theory "implicit definitions" just because they contain undefined terms. They are undefined within the linguistic, deductive structure of the theory, but they are not *absolutely* undefined. Their referential meaning is given by the coordinating definitions.

A main purpose of theories is to explain phenomena. The greater the number and variety of phenomena a theory can explain, the greater is its scope. A theory explaining the difference in, say, effectiveness for addition between two teaching methods but not the difference in their effectiveness for multiplication, clearly has less scope than a single theory encompassing both subjects. The greater the scope of a theory, the more comprehensive it is. The more comprehensive a theory is, the greater its ability to unify phenomena, to show that apparently different things are special cases of the same kinds of things. The classic example of a comprehensive, unifying theory is Newton's. From the Newtonian theory, it was possible to derive Galileo's laws for the free fall of bodies on earth, Kepler's laws about the motions of the planets around the sun, the laws about the tides, and a whole host of other previously known but disparate phenomena, as well as to predict new laws not previously known. Newton's theory thus brought the earth and the heavens together by making the laws of each a special case of a more general law.

I mentioned before, when discussing how we sometimes arrive at new concepts, that a concept formulated as a result of finding a common character in many different things, like 'bureaucracy,' is not only more abstract than the terms that suggested it, but also that the laws in which it enters would be more fruitful, i.e., have greater scope. This is, of course, no accident, since the more abstract term incorporates the properties of the less abstract or more "concrete" terms. Similarly, the concepts, like mass and force, occurring in Newton's theory are more abstract than the concepts, like distance and velocity, occurring in the laws of Kepler and Galileo that it explains. In general, the more comprehensive a theory, the more abstract will be the basic concepts in its axioms.

Behavioral scientists want to be able to explain and to predict the great varieties of behavior that people exhibit under the same or different circumstances. A relatively "concrete" definition of a psychological concept in terms of overt behavior alone under specified conditions may be inadequate for either one of two reasons, or both. It may be inadequate because, for the reasons suggested above, it will not be significant. Suppose 'hunger' is defined in terms of quantity of food consumed. If people eat not only when hungry but also when anxious, then no laws are apt to be found about how hungry people, as thus defined, behave. If some aggressive people tend to quarrel, while others exhibit aggression in more devious ways, then a definition of aggression in terms of quarrelsomeness will also most likely not be significant.

The second way in which relatively concrete terms may be inadequate is that though they may well enter into certain laws, these laws will be of rather narrow scope. Most of the laws of simple conditioning, for instance, are of restricted scope. Of course, if we know composition laws that explain how all these elementary behaviors combine, then we can increase the scope of the theory.

One way, perhaps the only way, of trying to find these composition laws and also increase the significance of our concepts is to introduce more abstract concepts. For instance, assume 'fear' is defined in terms of overt behavior like trembling under certain conditions. To explain why one frightened person runs away while another stands his ground, the psychologist may introduce another notion, "underlying" this different behavior, say, 'courage.' This new concept will not be undefined or, what amounts to the same, "implicitly defined," but rather it will be defined in some *other* way besides present overt behavior. This definition may include reference to antecedent conditions such as environment, learning, and family background. Incorporating all these, and possibly other things, the new concept is much more abstract or highly defined than the overt behavior that it is introduced to explain.

In general, in order to introduce a concept referring to a psychological state of an individual which common sense or clinical insight tells us may be manifested in many different ways, the scientist's new concept is defined not in terms of the individual's present behavior alone but also in terms of other people's behavior, like that of the individual's family, environmental and other surrounding circumstances in the past and the present, or some combination of all these things (including his own past behavior). These abstract or highly defined terms may then enter into laws that permit the prediction and explanation of many different kinds of present overt behavior. Within the science of psychology such terms are called "intervening variables," because in the hypotheses formulated about them they appear as intermediary between an observed situation and an overt response.

Of course, it is difficult to hit upon the right combination of antecedent and environmental conditions that defines a significant abstract concept. But this is a practical matter, depending upon the scientist's knowledge and ingenuity, not a matter of principle. Since the abstract terms are introduced in order to find laws that help us explain the more elementary laws of overt behavior, they will appear in the axioms of the theory. For this reason, such concepts are frequently called "theoretical constructs"—"theoretical" because they occur as basic terms in a theory; "constructs" because they are highly defined or abstract. And like the basic terms of Newtonian theory, they will have appended the appropriate complex coordinating definitions. Concepts referring to the behavior to be explained would appear in the theorems.

One feature of the use of abstract terms for "emotional" states may cause some irrelevant resistance to them. Those states directly experienced by a person and named by "concrete" undefinable terms of ordinary speech become for the scientist highly defined or abstract notions. For the individual, his own anxiety, say, is a recognizable, irreducible feeling within himself, just like his experience of being cold. And nothing is more real than our own immediately experienced mental states. While not foolishly denying that there are such things as mental states, the behavioral scientist, qua scientist, eschews them as objects of study, since he cannot observe the other fellow's feelings. His concept of 'anxiety,' therefore, may well be very abstract in contrast to the common-sense notion. The more fruitful his theory, the more abstract and highly defined such "mentalistic" terms are likely to be. But the abstract is just as much a part of the world as the concrete. There are masses in the world as well as colors, though more complicated observations are needed in order to tell that a body has a certain mass than that it has a certain color. Moreover, since for every mental state there is doubtless some corresponding observable state, either physiological or behavioral, for every true statement we can make about ourselves, the scientist can make a corresponding true statement about what he observes.

If behavioral science, as science, knows nothing of our immediate feelings, it is also true that nonscientific common sense knows nothing of these complex states. There is indeed an immediate feeling of love which the psychologist's account omits, but there is also the complex state, compounded of many things in our experience and constitution, which he calls being-in-love, which may explain much of our behavior, including the occurrence of the immediate feeling, but

which in ordinary life we do not discern either in others or in ourselves. It stands to reason that the scientist's highly defined abstract notions for emotional and "mental" states correspond to those unconscious motives and drives which have been suggested by another source. The overt behaviors which these abstract concepts are introduced to explain and predict thus correspond to the conscious components of experience. In any case, by such abstract, defined concepts the scientist can attempt to construct a theory which will explain and predict behavior without sacrificing intelligibility.

CAUSATION

I mentioned before that to cite a cause is, implicitly at least, to assert a law connecting the "cause" with other things. In other words, 'A causes B' says the same as the law 'Whenever A then B.' Yet we are sometimes reluctant to call certain observed regularities "real" laws or causal connections. What is the difference between a causal connection and a merely regular but noncausal conjunction of events? What is the difference between a true and a spurious correlation? (The terms *true* and *spurious* are used here as in Zeisel, 1957, Ch. 9. The term *spurious* is not being used here in the sense that "something other than the tendency of the two variables to vary concomitantly affects the value [of the correlation coefficient] obtained: e.g., the correlation obtained when one of the variables actually includes the other with which it is correlated," English & English, 1958, p. 519.) Despite immediate appearance to the contrary, these turn out to be quite the same question. Researchers accustomed to working with statistical correlations have developed techniques for distinguishing the true from the spurious correlation. A high correlation, for instance, between female marital status and job absenteeism is said to be true, while that between marital status and candy consumption is called spurious. In the latter case, the introduction of an additional factor, age, leads us to abandon the original correlation. In the true case, on the other hand, the introduction of an additional factor, increased housework, is said to confirm the correlation (Zeisel, 1957). Why, in each case, do we treat the original correlations differently after introducing the additional factor?

After all, marriage is statistically correlated with age, thus also with candy-eating. Statistically, therefore, in both cases there actually is a correlation and both are explained by the third factor. Married people eat less candy because they are older; married women are absent more from jobs because they have more housework. We justify saying that the former correlation is spurious and the latter is true, because we analyze the notion of a true correlation in terms of a presumed causal connection. Getting married causes more housework, which in turn causes increased absenteeism; therefore, getting married is truly correlated with absenteeism. Getting older, on the other hand, is a common cause both of marriage and eating less candy. All concomitants of age, like gray hair and paunchiness, would give a high correlation with eating less candy, if age does. They have a common cause, but are not causes of each other. Thus, the difference between true and spurious correlations resolves into a difference between causal and noncausal connections.

Nor does the difference between causal and noncausal conjunctions arise only for statistical correlations. Nonstatistical generalizations, asserting for all things of a certain kind that they are uniformly connected with something else, also raise the same problem. 'All gases expand when heated' states a true causal connection, while 'All the books on my desk are blue' does not. Philosophers have puzzled about how to distinguish the truly causal connections from those which are merely regular. In particular, it has been pointed out that the usual formulation of an empirical law as an 'if-then' statement does not reveal this distinction. Both the causal law and the mere conjunction would each be expressed as conditional statements. If anything is a book on my desk, it is blue; if anything is a heated gas, it expands. The conditional states the observed constant conjunction of these characteristics.

The analysis of statements like 'A causes B' into statements about a uniform conjunction of events, without using the term 'cause,' has been, ever since David Hume, basic empiricist doctrine. This analysis follows from the empiricist criterion of meaning, of which operationism is merely an application. All that we observe is the constant conjunction of the events "A" and "B," not a third thing called a cause.

Using the Subjunctive

Idiomatically, we may distinguish between accidental and causal connections by using the subjunctive mood. If this gas were heated, it would expand. On the other hand, if a book in the bookcase were on my desk, it would not have to be blue. It has, therefore, been suggested that only by means of the subjunctive can we distinguish lawful connections from mere generalizations. 'A causes B' or 'If A then B' is an empirical law only if we can truly assert the corresponding subjunctive, 'If anything *were A,* then it *would be B.*' To put it differently, if the corresponding subjunctive is true, then we have a real connection; otherwise, we have only an accidental generalization. This seems a rather neat solution. Unfortunately, it has some obvious difficulties.

How are we to *know* the truth or falsity of the corresponding subjunctive? Fundamentally, there are only two alternatives. One is that we know it by inductive generalization from observation. But we observe only that whenever we have A, we also have B. The subjunctive, therefore, can be asserted only on the basis of prior knowledge of the indicative conditional. But then the subjunctive is superfluous, since the evidence for it is no different from the evidence for the corresponding indicative conditional. The alternative is that we know the truth of the subjunctive in some special way. The empirical evidence for both the causal connection, or true

empirical law, and the accidental conjunction is never more than a finite number of
instances. There are thus no observations
distinguishing the truth of the subjunctive
from that of the indicative form. If, therefore, the subjunctive says more than the
corresponding indicative and if this excess
meaning is not further analyzable, we must
establish this meaning in some special way.

We must somehow grasp or see that one
subjunctive is true while another is false.
According to the empiricist analysis, a law
of nature is expressed by the indicative
'if-then' form. Rejection of this analysis leads
us down the path of rationalistic intuition or
reason. I mentioned before that one's principle of proper concept-formation or criterion
of meaning was fundamental. We see now
why this is so. If we adopt the unanalyzable
subjunctive view of empirical laws, we are,
in effect, taken back to an unanalyzed notion
of cause and to rejection of the empiricist
criterion of referential meaning. Inductive
generalization gives way to intuitive grasp of
real connections. Is this really the price we
must pay for the ability to distinguish between lawful and accidental uniformities?
Clearly, this is a distinction we should like
to be able to make. Fortunately, this can be
done without sacrificing empiricist views on
meaning and knowledge. But the distinction
cannot be made simply by considering generalizations in isolation.

Looking at the Context

The difference between a law and an accidental conjunction of events is a matter of
fact and not of meaning. For matters of fact,
it is reasonable to point out that we must look
at the context, that is, at the rest of what we
know. Let us reanalyze the difference between the spurious correlation between female marital status and candy consumption
and the true correlation between female
marital status and absenteeism. Why in this
latter case does an additional factor, increased housework, confirm the correlation?
The answer can be given without the use

of cause. Introduction of the third factor,
more housework, leads to two new generalizations: When a woman marries, she has
more housework, and if housework increases, so does absenteeism. From these two
generalizations, the correlation in question
between marriage and absenteeism follows as
a deductive consequence. It is thus explained
by the two generalizations in the only precise
meaning 'explanation' has in science. Because we can explain the correlation by deducing it from other generalizations, we consider it to be a true one.

On the other hand, in the spurious case, the
additional factor, age, does not permit such
deduction or explanation. Again we have
two new generalizations, namely, age correlates with marriage and age correlates with
candy consumption. But from these two generalizations, all that logically follows is that
age is correlated both with marriage and
with candy consumption. We cannot derive
the correlation between marriage and candy
consumption. When we define 'explain' precisely, we see that the new factor, age, does
not explain the correlation. That is why it is
abandoned as spurious.

What all this shows is that we more con-
fidently call a generalization a law if it is part
of a theory. The generalizations serving as
premises are laws because they permit the
derivation, hence the prediction and explanation, of other laws. If a generalization either
predicts or is predicted by other laws, the evidence for it is more than the mere conjunction of its observed instances. It is for this
reason that we state firmly that if a gas were
heated, it would expand. We assert the subjunctive because the law about the expansion
of gases is not established by mere enumera-
tion of instances. On the other hand, neither
is it due to any unanalyzable connection between temperature and expansion. Rather,
we believe this to be more than a mere conjunction because it is part of the theory of
thermodynamics. It both implies and is implied by many other highly confirmed statements. Until we know more about how an
isolated correlation is connected with other

facts and generalizations, we cannot tell whether it is true or spurious, to use statistical jargon. The decision about whether we have a law or an accidental conjunction thus depends upon further empirical knowledge and is not a matter of intuitive insight or grasp of real connections among things.

PERFECT VERSUS IMPERFECT KNOWLEDGE

Suppose that we have a theory of economic behavior, that is, a theory concerned with phenomena such as consumption, income, saving, profits, and the like. Assume that we are given the equations (laws) of this theory, the numerical values of its constant coefficients or parameters, and a set of initial conditions, that is, the observed values of its variables at any particular time or for a specified geographical area. By a leap of imagination, assume moreover that from this system we can predict the future course of all our variables or compute their entire past history; we know how changes in any one variable produce changes in any other; we know to what extent we can bring about desired changes by tinkering with the system, to what extent we are powerless. If we knew all this, either in economics or for that matter in any other social science, there is clearly nothing else we could possibly desire to know, at least as far as these variables are concerned. Such knowledge may therefore be called "perfect."

Given the present state of social science, no doubt the leap required to imagine that we know all this seems to take us far into the realm of fancy, so far, indeed, as to be hardly worth considering. Yet the fact remains that such perfection is not beyond human grasp, since it obtains in certain fundamental branches of physical science, notably celestial mechanics and macroscopic (nonatomic) thermodynamics. Whatever is, is possible. To be sure, what is possible to physics may not be so to social science, yet it will pay us to examine exactly what is requisite for perfection. In this examination I shall follow the more detailed analysis Bergmann (1957) has

given of perfect versus imperfect knowledge.

To summarize, a theory consists of a set of terms or concepts, undefined and defined, and a set of statements, called generalizations or laws, about how the referents of some of the terms affect others. In order to make a prediction about any particular system from the theory—its laws and its definitions—we must add to the theory a set of statements about the state of this system at some specified time, that is, we must know which concepts are or are not exemplified by the system at that time, or, as one says in the case of quantified theories, we must be given the values of the relevant variables.

Assume that prediction is made and, as it happens, is disproved by the course of events. What are the possible sources of error? All theories in all fields are subject to the inherent frailty of empirical science. Inductive generalizations may be overgeneralizations; measurement, too, has its limits and its own kinds of errors. These frailties do not by themselves distinguish the best physical theory from the most poorly confirmed social theory, even though the probability that errors of this kind will pass undetected is, of course, considerably less in the case of a well-confirmed body of laws with a highly developed theory and fine measuring instruments.

In respect to induction and measurement as two sources of error, the difference between the "hard" and the "soft" sciences is only one of degree. This difference in degree is traceable in turn to the characteristic *closure* and *completeness* of certain physical theories, two features which are conspicuously lacking or, at least, still lacking in social science. What makes the difference is (1) whether or not the referents of the terms of the theory interact only among themselves and with nothing else at the time and within the geographical area considered and (2) whether or not any variables that in fact do make a difference have been omitted from the expressions of the theory. These criteria of closure and completeness, respectively, are touchstones for our justifiable feeling that physical science is superior to social science.

And, as we shall see, even this is not the whole story.

Celestial mechanics and nonatomic thermodynamics are two theories within classical physics with nonoverlapping scopes, yet each theory is nearly "perfect" for the variables with which it deals. In the first, mass, velocity, and distance interact only with each other; in the second, volume, temperature, and pressure and a few other variables of this sort do the same. These theories consist of process laws, that is, in each case, the values of *any one* variable at any time can be computed by means of the laws from the values of *all* the others at any other time. Nothing that happens at any time or place other than those being considered affects the behavior of the properties with which the theory is concerned; at worst, we know how to take account of these outside influences in our predictions or computations. The system, in other words, is *closed*. When the planet Neptune was discovered, its presence was predicted from the Newtonian law together with the known "perturbations" of Uranus—its deviations from the predicted path—and of course the state of the sun and the other planets at the time. Logically, this means that the system which had previously been thought to be closed actually was not. The law itself omitted nothing, for Neptune was simply another instance of variables already contained in the law.

The case would be different if, say, the presence or absence of life on the planets was found to affect the laws of motion. In this case, the theory would have omitted variables which in fact make a difference. It would not be *complete*. Newtonian mechanics is complete and we know, in it, the conditions of closure for any system. Because of these features the connections among the variables are reversible or symmetrical. If, in the process theories of physics, a variable x is a function of another y, we know not only that a change in y brings about a change in x, but also that the converse is true. We know, too, what happens to either variable in the absence of the other. In social science, on the other hand, if we know that A causes B, rarely are we in a position to say how changes in B affect A or even what happens to B if A is not present.

The mutual dependency among the variables of classical physics is even more profound than this, marking another item in its perfection. It may be suggested that changes in pressure and volume occur simultaneously, whereas changes in the price of corn come later than the rain. The temporal development presumably marks the irreversibility and consequent utility of the notion of cause. Yet perhaps the most striking feature of process laws is their reversibility with regard to time. Newton's law, for example, permits us to compute the position and velocity of, say, a planet at all times past or future if we know its position and velocity at a single instant. Generally, by means of these characteristic laws of physics, any two states of the system can be inferred from each other, regardless of which comes first in time.

Nor is this reversibility with respect to time all there is to it. The more exactly a prediction can be stated, the more useful it will be both practically and theoretically. There are several dimensions in which a prediction may be more or less exact. Let me revert to the assertion that a boom in trade is always followed by slump and depression. One characteristic restricting the predictive value of such statements, mentioned before, is the vagueness of its concepts. Another is indefiniteness with respect to time. The process laws of physics are extremely specific in this respect. They permit prediction not only to "some" future time, or computation of conditions "sometime" in the past, but for *any* given moment of time, an instant, a day, a year, or a decade before or after the time from which the computation is made. This indeed is what is meant by calling them process laws, for the values of the variables mentioned in the laws are completely determinate for every moment of the temporal sequence. The contrasting imprecision with which slump and depression are said to "follow" a boom hardly needs comment. Exactly when it will follow and how long it will last are not at present within our purview.

Perfection and Social Science

How do the social sciences stand up when measured against the criteria of closure and completeness? A system consists roughly of any group of objects or patterns of behavior remaining constant in time. The planets, identifiable by their masses, the market with its stable procedures for buying and selling, rats in a cage, people in a community identifiable by occupation and income, all constitute systems. Just as velocity and position, changing in time, are the states of a mechanical system, so consumer preferences or political opinions may be the changing states of human systems. To know the conditions for closure of these systems, that is, to know either that nothing outside of the region being considered is affecting it or else to know what is entering or leaving the system, we must first know all the relevant variables; that is, the theory being applied to the system must be complete. No variables that in fact make a difference are omitted from the theory. Since the conditions for closure will in a sense settle themselves if we know all the relevant variables, we can concentrate our attention on the completeness of theories in social science.

(1) *Imperfection and separation of variables.* From the point of view of the physical scientist, a curious characteristic of the social sciences is the division of its terms or variables into two classes. This division is explicit in psychology and theoretical economics, implicit in the other areas. Psychologists distinguish stimulus variables from response variables; economists, the exogenous from the endogenous. Response terms name individual behavior which the psychologist explains in terms of the stimulus variables, that is, the physical and social environment, as well as certain biological states, past habits, and perhaps hereditary factors. The individual's behavior is held to be determined by all these, but, of course, the converse is not true. The stimulus conditions are either given to, or, at least partly manipulated by, the observer, but his theory does not purport to explain them. This is left to other areas of either social, biological, or physical science. The economist's distinction, though not the same, is similar. The economic or "endogenous" variables influence each other and are influenced by the "exogenous," noneconomic, physical, technological, institutional variables, but the converse is not true. The latter are "predetermined" data or conditions in terms of which the economist explains changes in economic factors.

This division among the variables is patently artificial, only a convenient way of speaking, for nothing is in itself either a stimulus or a response, endogenous or exogenous. In neither case is the distinction a hard and fast one. The stimulus conditions may consist in part of one's own and other people's behavior. Similarly, an exogenous factor, say, the imposition of tariffs by Congress, may be affected by economic conditions such as decreasing demand, as well as by political pressures. It is easy to see why this division of the variables reflects a departure from "perfection." Clearly, there is no question here of symmetry between the terms in each class. Changes in the response or economic factors do not generally change the stimulus or noneconomic factors respectively. The category in which a term is placed depends in large part upon how much we know. Tax rates and exports, for example, are exogenous or institutional because determined by political decisions, but if economic causes were found for them, they would be treated as endogenous.

In general, this division of the variables is a reflection of the inadequacy of a given theory, whether in psychology or economics, to account fully for changes in *all* the variables. The sociologist seeking to account for population distribution does not also attempt to explain the geographical formations which may influence where people live. The political scientist does not try to explain the economic factors which may in turn explain the voting behavior in which he is interested. The limited scope of our theories reinforces this distinction while highlighting its artificiality. Given two different theories in an area, the same variable may be either dependent or "predetermined." What is considered exogenous in a business-cycle theory, for example, may not be so in a theory of demand. In psychology, a theory in social psychology may take as stimulus what is response in learning theory.

How does this affect completeness? Let us omit from consideration the physical variables, like rainfall or body-type, in respect to which closure can hardly be expected, since presumably these are to be explained primarily in terms of other physical and physiological variables. Even so, what about the institutional and behavioral variables? It is evident, from all that we now know, that no individual social science can by itself expect to achieve completeness in its terms. Any theory of human behavior will contain references to political, legal, psychological, economic, religious, and other institutional factors in the individual's environment. It is a commonplace by now that these factors all interact, so each social science is to some greater or lesser extent dependent upon the findings of others.

In addition to the division in the variables, there are other clues to an acknowledged lack of completeness. Consider the generalization that, other things remaining unchanged, a new teaching method for a subject causes a change in learning. Incompleteness is signaled here in two ways. First, "teaching method" is an exogenous variable whose imposition is not to be explained by the theory, but in terms of which change in the endogenous variable, learning, is explained. Second, by the phrase "other things remaining unchanged" the researcher hedges his bets that the values of other variables influencing learning—whether mentioned or not mentioned in his theory, whether exogenous, like changes in class size, or endogenous, like motivational level—will remain as they were at the time the teaching method was imposed.

Some, perhaps most, of these changes in the "other things" are not predictable from the theory; hence it is incomplete. To illustrate more obviously perhaps, other things being equal, success is doubtless a function of learning. But probably no change in the learning of a subject like Latin could have prevented its becoming less important to "success in life." Changes in technology and in tastes unpredictable by the theory will have, and, as the qualifying phrase indicates, are expected to have, their effect. Completeness, in the strict sense of exclusive mutual dependency among the terms of the theory, could only be achieved by one vast social science encompassing the entire range of human behavior.

The illustration about the discovery of the planet Neptune suggested that theories may be complete and prediction still fail because the system to which they are applied is not closed. A hypothetical example from social science may bring this closer to home. Suppose an economist wishes to predict the relative demands for butter and white margarine in a state where colored margarine is prohibited. Assume that among the relevant variables he includes people's preferences and in particular their relative preferences for butter over margarine as well as the prices of these products. Assume, quite unrealistically, that he neglects to account for the fact that the region for which he wishes to make his prediction is surrounded on all sides by states where colored margarine is available at the same price as white at home. In this case, closure but not completeness is violated, since individual preference is one of his variables and that between white and yellow margarine would have been taken into account if the alternative were present in the home state. If, again quite unrealistically, individual preferences were entirely omitted from the theory, when in fact they make a difference in demand, then his system is incomplete.

Generally, if nothing is omitted that actually makes a difference in the behavior of the variables with which the theory is concerned, then the theory is complete. If and only if this condition is satisfied, then all other true laws of the area staked out by the terms of the theory follow as deductive consequences from its axioms or fundamental laws.

(2) *Statistics and imperfect knowledge.* Social science has developed much more specific techniques to compensate for lapses in closure and completeness. Here we have a paradox. Statistical knowledge, certainly the kind we have most often in social science, is conspicuously imperfect. Yet, statistics is perhaps the most promising method available for smoothing out the complexities in subject matter which make the road to perfection so rocky. Despite the great gap between what statistical knowledge can tell us and what we would like to know, statistical techniques do suggest, within their limitations, a method for achieving that semblance of closure and completeness which is at once the despair and, as it is for any theory, the *sine qua non* of behavior theory.

Social scientists take the use of statistical techniques so much for granted that they are not always able to articulate clearly just why these techniques are indispensable tools of the trade. The logical basis of this indispensability lies in large part, though not entirely, in the incompleteness of our explanations. The exception is the use of statistical concepts because of errors of measurement. But there is no difference in this respect between the social and physical sciences. The result of a measurement of, say, length, is as much a so-called "chance" or random variable with a frequency distribution determined by the nature of the measurement as is the result of the measurement or computation of an individual's learning ability or a firm's income, though of course neither length nor, for that matter, Jones's 1956 income nor his learning ability are random variables. The latter, unlike "yearly number of automobile accidents," "income of farmers," or "learning ability of five-year-olds," have a single value and not a frequency distribution. But since errors of measurement are not unique to social science, they are not germane to our present preoccu-

pation. The use of random variables, as a consequence of incompleteness, is germane. There are two ways in which the use of statistical concepts betrays incompleteness.

Without some abstraction or selection from all the possibilities the world presents, there can be no science at all. By their very nature scientific laws describe only certain features of the kinds of things or events they hold to be connected. How much can safely be ignored depends upon the way things are. Even in human behavior not everything makes a difference. An individual's taste in music may be a function of many variables, but the color of his eyes is probably not one of them. Even so, the number of different things such as education, age, family background, heredity, special training, and so on, may be so large and so difficult to assign relative importance that we may well despair of formulating an exact functional relationship between such tastes and these other factors.

To say, in consequence, that abstraction is all very well for the physical sciences but will not do for the study of man and society is the counsel of desperation, that is, no solution at all. The social scientist, striving to merit the honorific half of that title, settles for something less than perfection. Completeness has its price and its rewards. Which face will turn up when a die is cast is determined by numerous causes, the center of gravity of the die, the force with which it is thrown, and so on. An attempt to calculate the results of each throw by means of the laws of mechanics is practically hopeless, because of the difficulty in precisely measuring all the initial conditions. Instead, we represent, as it were, this multiplicity of causes by a probability distribution for the attribute in question. The use of the statistical concept marks our ignorance of all the influencing factors, a failure in either completeness or closure or, usually, both.

Similarly, the social scientist, deliberately selecting for study fewer factors than actually influence the behavior in which he is interested, shifts his goal from predicting individual events or behaviors to predicting a random variable, that is, to predicting the frequency with which this kind of behavior occurs in a large group of individuals possessing the circumscribed number of factors. This is the price. The reward, of course, is that instead of helplessly gazing in dumb wonder at the infinite complexity of man and society, he has knowledge, imperfect rather than perfect, to be sure, but knowledge not to be scorned nonetheless, of a probability distribution rather than of individual events. After all, while we might much prefer to know the exact conditions under which cancer develops in a particular person, it is far from valueless to know the factors which are statistically correlated to the frequency of its occurrence.

The relationship between statistical prediction and incompleteness is strikingly explicit in the relatively recent use of so-called "stochastic equations," where "stochastic" means not any statistical concept but a specific form thereof. The probability of success in school, let us say, is expressed as a function of IQ. The observed values of the frequency of such success are affected by errors of observation. If we know the probability distribution of these errors, then we can make a prediction about the probability of success in school for a given IQ or range of IQs. Our predicted attribute is thus a function both of IQ and the distribution of the error. In physics, for example, measured pressure at constant temperature is a function of the volume plus or minus a known error component associated with the measurement of volume—and of nothing else. If there were no errors of observation, then the connection stated between pressure and volume is exact, with no statistical component. In our illustration, however, as in social science generally, even if there were no errors or if our theory of errors permitted us to separate out the error component, we would still be able to predict only a probability distribution and not individual values. There is, as the physicist might say, a systematic component of the error which is not associated with any particular variable but with the asserted connection, an error in the equation itself. Because of a great many other factors, not all children with the same IQ will be equally successful. Just as with measurement errors, all these omitted influences, each one of which may be small in itself, may be expressed as a separate variable. In this case, we may say that the connection holds with a "disturbance." Of course, any two things can be said to be related with a "disturbance," so long as the latter is unspecified.

To rescue these equations from vacuity, to make them empirically meaningful, the disturbances must have a known probability distribution which does not change with changes in the observed variables. Thus, success in school would be expressed as a function of IQ *and* a random variable. This latter probability term would express the aggregate effects of factors as yet unspecified. Thus, incompleteness is explicitly built into the system and, given our ignorance of what these omitted factors are or of how much weight they each carry, at the same time is accounted for in the best possible way. Theoretical economics and, to a much lesser extent, experimental psychology are as yet the only social sciences adapting this technique of further dividing their variables into those which are named by the theory, called "systematic," and those which are only latently expressed, as it were, in the "disturbance."

The lucidity with which stochastic equations betray the incompleteness and consequent statistical character of the theories in which they occur is, of course, not the reason why they are used. I suggested earlier that the two dichotomies, stimulus-response and exogenous-endogenous, were at once recognition of the absence of completeness and an attempt to achieve an approximation to it for the variables of the area, psychology or economics respectively. The split by means of stochastic equations into systematic and disturbance components also serves this purpose. It does so with greater precision by assigning a definite and testable probability to the magnitude of the unknown external factors. Also, packed into the disturbance in the equation may be not only factors which the theory does not seek to explain, such as physical or institutional influences, but also as yet unnoticed variables of the area itself. With increasing knowledge of the sources of error of observation and the improvement in our measuring instruments we are able to reduce the error in the variable due to these factors. In the same way, increasing knowledge may lead to reduction in the amount of error in the equation by analyzing the disturbance into its components, and thus to a greater degree of completeness for the variables of the area.

To illustrate more concretely, assuming perfect observation, let us say that the amount consumed of some commodity is expressed as a function of the price of the commodity and an error factor in the connection. This error, or disturbance, incorporates many other causal factors, both noneconomic, like fashion, and economic, like income. Though there may always remain a residual noneconomic cause of error, with increasing knowledge and accuracy the economic factors influencing the relation may be spelled out and added to the systematic variables, leaving only noneconomic factors in the random variable. In the ideal, all economic variables would be included in the set of systematic variables. Consumption, price, and income, be it noticed, are all economic or endogenous variables. If the disturbance in their connection becomes very small, we may well say that they are relatively autonomous, that is, that they interact primarily only with each other. For complete autonomy, the disturbance would have to be zero and probably only the most extreme economic determinist envisages this as a real possibility. The more comprehensive the social science, say a science incorporating psychological, economic, and sociological phenomena, the greater the degree of autonomy to be envisaged. Since physical, geographical, and physiological factors can be expected to participate in what happens, a wholly autonomous social science, closed and complete by itself, is, to put it moderately,

not likely. But relative autonomy would, again to put it moderately, be no small achievement.

REDUCTION

Closure, completeness, precisely identifiable referents, temporal definiteness of prediction or computation—these then are the ingredients of knowledge at its best. The question about the possibility of an autonomous group science may be precisely stated in the light of these criteria. Is it possible to have perfect knowledge of society, that is, is it possible to have a process theory containing only group variables which will be both closed and complete?

At the beginning of the discussion of group or macroscopic concepts, I mentioned that two different issues were involved. One of them, discussed in that section, has to do with the principle of correct concept-formation in social science. The other issue, which we are now in a position to discuss, has to do with its laws and theories. The first issue is one of *meaning,* the second of *reduction.* Insofar as methodological individualism, which I characterized earlier, is a precept for proper concept-formation, it is a denial of descriptive emergence; that is, it denies that supra-individual group properties can be meaningfully attributed to things or events. The banner of methodological individualism has, however, also been raised in the context of laws and theories. This is a matter of explanation rather than of description. The two are disparate and should not be confounded. The belief that there are no emergent *properties* rests on our criterion of the meaningful. It is thus, broadly speaking, a matter of logic. The assumption that the *laws* of group behavior are or are not, as the case may be, emergent with respect to laws about individuals is a matter of fact, a matter for empirical determination. But for this to be clear, some further distinctions and elaborations are necessary.

The possibility of "reduction" is the issue raised by asking whether the phenomena of one field, say chemistry or psychology, can be explained in terms of the phenomena of another, say physics or physiology, respectively. Explanation *within* a theory is different from explanation *of* a theory. Within a theory, the theorems are explained by deriving them from other laws, the axioms of the theory. The axioms themselves are not explained by the theory, but are the statements that do the explaining. If the axioms of one theory are derivable from the laws of a second theory, then we have an explanation *of* the first theory rather than an explanation *within* it.

Reduction is thus a special case of explanation. Explanation is in fact a major reason for reduction. It is consequently a matter of laws and theories, not of terms or concepts. What is sometimes called "reduction" of terms is, strictly, definition of the kind we discussed earlier. Not all deduction, however, achieves reduction. We explain a law by deducing it from another law or laws. In the classical illustration, we explain Galileo's law of falling bodies by deducing it, as a special case for terrestrial objects, from the Newtonian law of gravitation. But here nothing has been reduced to anything else. Both Newton's and Galileo's laws mention the same subject matter, physical bodies and their spatial-temporal properties. Both laws are in the same area, mechanics. A "psychological" or an "economic" term is one that occurs in the science of either psychology or economics, respectively. One area differs from another in its terms or concepts; these determine its "subject matter." Deduction is also reduction only when the deduced laws are in a different area from those that serve as premises.

But if we have two different theories, one containing only behavioral (psychological or sociological) concepts, the other, say, only physiological concepts, then there can be no deductive connection between their laws. For, clearly, if two laws have no terms or variables in common, then one cannot possibly be a deductive consequence of the other. In order for the laws of one area to be derivable from the laws of another, a logical bridge between the two theories must be constructed connecting the referents of the concepts of the two areas. The nature of the logical bridge permitting the reduction of psychology to physiology is different from that permitting the reduction of sociology to psychology, if we could do either.

The joint occurrence of a psychological event and a physiological event is expressed by a psycho-physiological law. Such laws, stating an observable connection at the same time between two different kinds of events, are called cross-connection laws. They form the logical bridge that is required to make possible the reduction of psychology to physiology. They are not derivable from laws mentioning either only behavioral or only physiological states, but must be independently discovered. If we knew them, then from them, in conjunction with the laws of the physiological theory, the behavioral laws could be deduced. Moreover, from laws about the neurophysiological system together with the laws connecting behavioral and neurophysiological events, we might even be able to derive as yet unknown behavioral laws. The cross-connection laws permit the reduction of psychology to physiology. The behavioral axioms themselves would be deducible from, or explainable by, the physiological theory in conjunction with the cross-connection laws. In this case, the theory itself is explained by another theory. But the laws of the theory which does the explaining are those of an enlarged "mixed" theory and not those of either behavior or physiology alone. Reduction explains one area by means of another. To explain is not to identify. There are still two different areas, so long as the bridge between them is formed, as it must be in the case of psychology and physiology, by empirical cross-connection laws.

Reduction of Group Laws

Group concepts refer, as we saw, to complex patterns of descriptive relations among individuals. Study of the behavior of these complexes results in the formation of laws that we may call macroscopic from the nature of their terms. Such laws are different from laws about the behavior of single individuals. There need not be and in general there is not any similarity between the behavior of a complex and the behavior of the elements of the complex. The behavior of a substance subject to the laws of chemistry differs from the behavior of its particles subject to the laws of mechanics. Groups may be cohesive, which individuals cannot be, and cohesiveness may affect the stability of the group, which is again something that individuals, in this meaning of "stability," cannot have. Both terms in this law, if such it be, refer to congeries of individuals exemplifying descriptive relations, such as choosing each other as friends in the first case and faithfully attending meetings with other members of the group in the second. The law states that whenever a group has the first set of relational attributes, then it also has the second.

Laws may also be found connecting individual behavior or characteristics with those of groups. Ambitious individuals, suppose, are attracted to stratified groups offering opportunity for leadership. This is an example of an *empirical* connection between individual and group attributes. However, since there are no undefinable group entities or properties, every group term will also be *definitionally* connected with a set of (relational) individual behaviors. These latter need not necessarily be "psychological" in the sense that they are technical concepts within the science of psychology. Characteristics which occur in the definitions of macroscopic concepts, such as choosing friends, communicating, buying, or selling, need not be, though of course they may be, accounted for by an existing psychological theory.

It is therefore misleading to say that because group concepts must be defined in terms of individuals they are "really" psychological. Only if "psychological" is broadly defined to include all human behavior is this the case. In this sense, "selling short on the stock market" is psychological. But then the term is so broad as to be virtually useless. Only if this behavior can be explained within the context of a theory in psychology is it significantly called psychological rather than, say, economic.

These considerations should all help to bring into proper focus the issues connected with the possibility of reduction. What then is the logic of the connection between the group sciences and psychology? How, in principle, would the reduction of the one to the other take place?

Process Theories and Composition Laws

A process theory, to repeat, is one permitting the computation of the states of a system at all times from its state at any given time. All such theories contain, in addition to laws for so-called "elementary" situations, another type of law which increases its scope, securing for it a range of widely different systems whose laws are deducible from the theory. The Newtonian law of attraction between two bodies is the elementary law of the system.

One does not independently, however, have to discover the law for three, four, or any larger number of bodies. These are derivable from the two-body law. They are so, not by logical or arithmetical methods alone, nor from the two-body law alone, but by the addition of a special kind of empirical law, the so-called "parallelogram rule." By imaginary decomposition of a system consisting of any number of bodies into pairs of two-body systems, this rule, together with the elementary law, permits us to compute the accelerations of each body in the complex system.

Laws permitting such computation from the elementary to more complex systems may be called composition laws or, a bit misleadingly, composition rules. The latter is misleading because, of course, the "rule" by which the state of a system containing any number of bodies is computed from the law for the elementary, two-body system is itself an empirical generalization or law. The term *vector addition* applied to this particular rule adds to the confusion by making appear purely arithmetical what is an empirical matter, namely, that the resultant of the forces is their vector sum.

Another illustration may help clarify the situation. In chemistry we have the laws for the behavior of hydrogen and laws for the behavior of oxygen. We also have the law of their interaction, that is, the law stating what happens when oxygen and hydrogen occur together under certain conditions. They form water, for instance. Thus we see that the properties of water are predictable from the laws of its elements as well as predictable from the law of their interaction.

Let us take still another example. Airplanes, despite Galileo, often stay up in the air for long periods of time. We know of course that this is not a "violation" of the law of gravity. The fact that they stay up is explained by applying to this situation all the laws involving the variables believed to be relevant to the situation. The rules for combining these laws, which form the subject matter of aerodynamics, are themselves empirical generalizations or regularities.

Such composition rules obviously give to the theories containing them tremendous power and scope. For instance, the prediction of complex human behavior from the laws of learning in psychology waits upon the development of composition laws, that is, laws stating how the laws of the elementary processes combine to result in complex human behavior; e.g., so-called "insight" learning in man may be explained in terms of composition laws based upon the laws of rudimentary trial-and-error learning. If, as there is reason to believe, human behavior consists of complex patterns of elementary processes, the potential scope of such theories is very great. When applied to macroscopic social science, composition laws are, as I shall now try to explain in the following pages, the means by which reduction would take place.

Composition Laws and Group Variables

Macroscopic laws are laws containing group variables. Assume, for instance, that sociologists find a group law to the effect that stratification causes increased efficiency. The kinds of individual behavior, like the giving and taking of orders, who communicates with whom, etc., in terms of which the group variable, stratification, is defined, constitute the undefined terms of the sociological system. But, for two reasons, this definition alone would not enable us to deduce the law from those of psychology. First, as mentioned before, such individual behaviors need not also be terms of an existing psychological theory. Psychologists, in other words, might not have knowledge about the causes and effects of issuing orders, direction of communication, etc. But suppose that these are terms of psychological theory. The definition, though necessary, is still not sufficient to enable us to make the deduction. In addition to elementary laws telling how an individual acts in the presence of one or a few others, we must also have composition laws stating what happens, under certain conditions, as the number of people he is with increases. The latter, of course, state how he behaves in a group.

Assume, more particularly, that we have the elementary laws, none of which mentions stratified groups, about how Jones, that is, an individual with certain characteristics, behaves in the presence of a person like Smith and about how Jones behaves in the presence of a person like Brown. In addition, assume we have a composition law revealing how Jones behaves when he is confronted with both Smith and Brown under the conditions defined as "stratified." We would then know how one individual with certain characteristics behaves as a member of a certain layer of a stratified group. If in addition to these composition laws about the interactions of various kinds of people and the definitions of the group concepts, we are also given the (statistical) description of the initial composition of the group, then we can predict the behavior of the group; that is, we may derive laws of group behavior.

We see now why the reducing area, psychology, is said to be microscopic (molecular) relative to the reduced area. The composition laws state what happens when several elementary situations are combined in specified ways. These combined situations are the macroscopic (molar) complexes referred to by the group terms of the reduced area. The definitions of the group terms provide the common language necessary for the derivation of macroscopic statements from microscopic ones. The composition laws then supply the empirical premises from which the deduction is made. The reduction of group laws to those about individuals thus supplies an explanation *of* group behavior in terms of the behavior of individuals *in* groups. Given the composition laws, the reduction of sociology to psychology is a purely logical matter, following as it does from these composition laws and the definitions.

Or, to say the same thing differently, just as, given the law of vector addition, we do not independently have to discover the law of a three-body system in mechanics, so, given the definitions and the composition laws, we do not independently have to investigate the behavior of groups. And this of course is what we mean by saying that one area has been "reduced" to another. *Definitions* of group concepts in terms of the behavior of individuals in the group *form the logical bridge,* permitting the deduction, between the sociological and the psychological theories. Since all definitions are in principle dispensable and the composition laws contain only psychological terms, there is thus a sense in which there is "really" only one area.

It does not follow, however, that we can scrap the macroscopic social sciences. In addition to the difficulty, already discussed, about the vagueness or openness of group terms, there are even more fundamental reasons, having to do with the nature of composition laws, why the group sciences are probably here to stay.

Reduction: Fact versus Principle

Since these composition laws are empirical generalizations, they may fail at some point. Absurd as physicists might find the idea at this stage of the game, it is nevertheless logically possible that the parallelogram rule would no longer work as one went from a system containing, say, 999 bodies to one containing 1,000. The prediction for the more complex system, made by means of the composition rule, might be proven false. Psychologists similarly might be able to predict the behavior of an individual in groups of a given size, but as soon as another person is added to the group, the prediction might fail.

There are several reasons—apart from the theoretically uninteresting case of errors in induction and measurement—why this might happen. Possibly, but just possibly, there are no laws of human behavior after a certain level of complexity is reached. In this case, the behavior of groups of a certain complexity marks a level of breakdown not only of the composition law, but also of determinism. No sociologist, no matter how fervently devoted to groups he might be, would be happy about this. In fact, if there were any reason to believe indeterminism occurred, his devotion to groups would wane rapidly. More realistically, perhaps we need a different composition law. This new law might be different either because it has a different form or because it contains variables not present in the law for groups of lesser complexity. In our imaginary physical case, for instance, it might be that for systems containing 1,000 or more bodies, the mutual attraction of the bodies turned out to be a function of the cube rather than the square of the distances between them. Or for 1,000-body systems, to pile absurdity upon absurdity, the presence or absence of life might make a difference to the acceleration. Similarly, the composition law about the behavior of individuals in groups might either change in form or some new variable, like fear of being together with large masses of people, might begin to be operative only after the population reaches a given magnitude. The variable is "new" not in the sense that instances of it did not exist before, but because it did not affect the behavior we are interested in predicting; that is, it did not occur in any complete set of relevant variables of a system of lesser complexity. Finally, it might be that even though group behavior is itself lawful, there is no composition rule from which it can be predicted. I shall return to this alternative in a moment.

In any case, for whatever reason, the composition rule might break down. If it should, then we have an instance of *explanatory* emergence. Emergence at the level of explanation should be carefully distinguished from what we earlier called descriptive emergence. The latter phrase refers to the occurrence of a property of groups, like the so-called "group-mind," which is not definable in terms of the individuals making up the group. Explanatory emergence, however, refers to laws of group behavior, which, *even though their terms are defined as they should be,* are still not derivable from the laws, including whatever composition laws there are, about individual behavior.

This is *in fact* the case at present. The anti-emergentist, in the context of explanation, merely denies that *in principle* laws about groups are not derivable from laws about individuals. The emergentist, accordingly, holds that the composition rules necessary for reduction are lacking because on logical grounds there can be no such laws, even though group behavior is itself lawful. This view is held, for instance, by those who maintain that society or history has laws of "its own" for which the behavior of individuals is not relevant. If this were the case, then it would make sense to say that there are *sui generis* laws of the social process.

Two Meanings of Methodological Individualism

Sometimes the phrase *methodological individualism* is applied both to the view that there are no undefinable group concepts and to the view that the laws of the group sciences are in principle reducible to those about individuals. The former is a denial of descriptive emergence; the latter denies that there are any logical grounds for belief in explanatory emergence. Both positions are, indeed, very much a part of the general empiricist tradition. Nevertheless, they are not identical, nor are they equally fundamental. The first, as we saw, is required by the logic of concept-formation within the individualistic, empiricist framework. But, as to the second, whether or not there are composition laws is not something that can be a priori decided.

Descriptive emergence is compatible with and may be used as an argument for the necessity of explanatory emergence. But it is not a good argument. If the alleged emergent properties are lawfully connected with those properties of individuals from which they emerge, as, analogously, psychological properties are lawfully connected with physiological properties, then by means of such cross-connection laws and the microscopic laws, the macroscopic laws could be derived. In any case, the denial of descriptive emergence does not entail the denial of explanatory emergence. The latter is a matter of fact. And matters of fact cannot be legislated into existence. In other words, the empiricist commitment to *definitional* methodological individualism does not logically imply a commitment to *explanatory* methodological individualism, that is, to reduction.

In the context of explanation, methodological individualism is a matter of principle only in that broad sense in which determinism itself is a matter of principle. These issues are often confounded because it is not fully realized that the two alternatives, the successful working of composition rules or their breakdown at some level of complexity, are both "individualistic" in that broad sense of the term denoting a basic metaphysical assumption. As long as it is granted that groups are composed of individuals, and of nothing else, then there is no question of violating this basic assumption. The fact is that we do not as yet and, for all we know, may never have the psychological laws permitting reduction. This does not and cannot in any way militate against that individualism which empiricists are rightly so anxious to preserve. Happily, that frame of reference does not depend, at least not logically, upon the state of our knowledge at any particular moment in history.

Whichever alternative turns out to be the case, the optimistic one that reduction of laws is achievable or its pessimistic contrary, two possibilities still remain for social science. First, whether or not our concepts are defined or, at least, in principle definable, it is still logically possible that a class of group concepts forms a complete set of relevant variables of the social process. A process theory is logically possible with any kind of variables as, for instance, nonatomic thermodynamics demonstrates. It is thus logically possible, even if most unlikely, that we could have a complete theory of psychology with only behavioral, nonphysiological variables. Similarly, it is logically possible that, irrespective of definitional reduction, we may have perfect knowledge of society in the sense of having a process theory whose laws contain only macroscopic or group variables. The reduction of chemistry to physics is by now a fairly well-accomplished fact. At one time chemistry was at a stage analogous to that of the group sciences. The microscopic structure of the molecules in terms of atoms was known, just as we know the composition of our groups, but the laws of quantum physics by which atoms combine into molecules were not known. Once they were known, however, it turned out that the (chemical) laws by which molecules combine could be derived from them. Yet, organic chemistry appears to be here to stay. In principle, the interactions of the complex molecules can be derived from the laws of physics about the fundamental particles. However, the mathematics of the relevant composition laws is so involved that it is much simpler to study directly the behavior of these organic complexes.

Similarly, even if we had reduction, it might still be practically more feasible to study group behavior. Conceivably, there might be a set of macroscopic laws permitting the prediction of the "state" of society (i.e., the values of the group variables) at all times from its state at any given time. This possibility is, to be sure, most implausible. It is implausible not only because the discovery of such a complete set of relevant variables seems a formidable task, but also because it is rather more than likely that changes in the social process do not depend only upon group or macroscopic units, Marxism notwithstanding. People are not like molecules in a gas. Some are different from others and some have more effect upon society than others. It is still a good question whether the October Revolution would have occurred without Lenin. If this variance among individuals makes sufficient difference, then the laws have to take into account the occurrence of a particular kind of individual. In this case, a complete set of variables could not all be macroscopic. The unlikelihood of attaining perfect knowledge on the basis of macroscopic laws alone is probably a source of the mistaken conviction that reduction of laws is *necessary* for empiricist individualism. But, again, it is merely a matter of fact that this possibility is most unlikely.

But if perfect knowledge through experimentation with group variables alone is unlikely, there is still another possibility. It may be that approximate laws of all kinds can be stated in these variables. These laws would of course bear some or all of the marks of imperfection. They would be indefinite with respect to time, hedged in by qualification, and, above all, they would be statistical. The remarkable success of statistical knowledge is a measure of how much can be ignored, particularly of the individual variance, and prediction still be possible. If there be, as in principle there probably are, composition rules from which the behavior of groups may be predicted, they are probably of such complexity and difficulty that it may be well for social scientists to look for whatever imperfect connections may exist among the group variables. These, in turn, may suggest the appropriate composition rules of individual behavior.

MODELS

The term *model* is common in recent social science literature. We encounter models of learning, of rational choice, of communication, of political behavior, of group interaction, and so on, and so on. Yet, what exactly is a model and what purposes does it serve? The fact is that the term model is used most ambiguously. Nor is *mathematical model* any more precise since this term, too, covers different things.

Models as Theories

Broadly speaking, there are two major uses of *model*. The most general use is as a synonym for theory. A theory may be well or ill confirmed, narrow or broad in scope, quantified or nonquantified. *Model* is now frequently used for those theories which are either highly speculative or quantified, or, most likely, both. Thus, a guess about the connections between quantified variables of an area like psychology or economics will frequently be called a mathematical model. Such hypotheses are mathematical only in the sense in which physics is mathematical. That is, they are empirical generalizations whose variables are quantified, so that we can say how much one variable changes with changes in others. They share the virtue of all quantified theories in permitting more precise deduction and prediction.

Quantification, however, is no guarantee of scope. In areas where behavior depends upon many different variables, we may indeed pay for quantification with triviality. But then, nonquantified guesses at theories, like the doctrines of psychoanalysis or speculations about the physiological concomitants of behavior (which are often broader than quantified theories but lack their precision) are also frequently called models. Such speculative theories, whether quantified or not, are after all just theories. The term *model* serves

no particular purpose beyond, perhaps, emphasizing the tentative, unconfirmed nature of the hypotheses in question. This usage would be harmless enough if there were not, as unfortunately there is, another, quite different prevalent use of the term.

Strictly speaking, I should have said two further uses. For in this second meaning of the term two different things are really involved though they have a common feature. This feature I shall now explain. A miniature train is a model of a real train if it is isomorphic with it. Isomorphism requires two conditions. First, there must be a one-to-one correspondence between the elements of the model and the elements of the thing of which it is the model. For every chimney stack, there must be a miniature chimney stack; for every window there must be its replica, and the converse must be true. Second, certain relations must be preserved. For instance, if a door is to the left of a window in the original, their replicas must be similarly situated; also, the model is constructed to scale. If the model works on the same principle as the original—if, for instance, a model steam engine is also steam propelled—the isomorphism is complete.

Extending this notion to theories, we may formulate a precise meaning of *model*. The form of a law is given either by the verbal "if-then" formulation or by an equation. Like all other sentences, quantified laws have a certain form. Many other physical properties besides distance vary as the square of some other characteristic, such as time. The linear equation, $y = ax + b$, represents still another quantified form taken by some laws. The variables might stand for many different things, like weight and height or supply and demand, while the form remains the same. But a quantified empirical law such as $d = 16t^2$ differs from an arithmetic statement like $9 = 3^2$. In the empirical law, the letter variables d and t must be given meaning as distance and time before the truth or falsity of the law can be established. No descriptive terms occur in the arithmetic truths. When letters do occur in arithmetic statements, as in $x + y = y + x$, then it is understood that the letters are to be replaced by numbers. It is a logical truth about numbers that the order of addition does not make a difference. As we shall see later, if the letters do not stand for numbers, then the statement may well be false.

Quantified empirical laws, like $d = 16t^2$, are often called "mathematical." But this term is confusing. A quantified law of empirical science is an empirical or synthetic assertion whose truth or falsity depends upon its descriptive terms. Distance varies as the square of time, but demand probably does not. A statement of mathematics, on the other hand, is analytic. In order to stress the distinction between empirical laws and the tautologies of mathematics, I shall continue to use the term *arithmetic* for the latter. Laws, whether quantified or not, have a certain form, as expressed either by the verbal "if . . . then . . ." or by an equation. Theories differ from each other either in their descriptive terms, in which case they are about different things, or in the form of their laws, or both. For instance, theories within physics and those within sociology presumably differ from each other not only in their descriptive terms but also in the form of the statements connecting these concepts. *Time* and *distance,* for example, are descriptive terms or "variables" of physical theory. The parabola $y = ax^2$, or a differential equation of a certain sort, gives the form of the law connecting these terms. Within sociology, the descriptive terms might be, say, *religious preference* and *political attitude*. A law connecting these attributes might have the form of a nonquantified conditional, like "If anyone is a Catholic, then he is also a conservative." Or it might take the form of a quantified linear equation expressing a statistical correlation between the variables.

Isomorphic Theories

A model train, we saw, is similar to a real one in being isomorphic with it. The isomorphism is complete if both work on the same principles. When extending this notion to theories, we can formulate a precise meaning of *model*. Two theories whose laws have the same form are isomorphic or *structurally similar* to each other. If the laws of one theory have the same form as the laws of another theory, then one may be said to be a *model* for the other. This is the second most general meaning of the term.

How do we discover whether two theories, or parts of them, are isomorphic to each other? Suppose that one area, as indicated by a set of descriptive concepts, for which a relatively well-developed theory is at hand is said to be a model for another area about which little is as yet known. The descriptive terms in the theory of the better-known area are put into one-to-one correspondence with those of the new area. By means of this one-to-one correspondence, the laws of one area are "translated" into laws of the other area. The concepts of the better-known theory are replaced in the laws by the concepts of the new area. This replacement results in a set of laws or hypotheses about the variables of the new area. If observation shows these hypotheses to be true, then the laws of both areas have the same form. The lawful connections are preserved and the two theories are completely isomorphic to each other.

For example, suppose it is wondered whether rumors spread like diseases. That is, can the laws of epidemiology, about which quite a bit is known, be a model for a theory of rumor-transmission? Or, to say the same thing differently, do the laws about rumors have the same form as the laws about diseases? The descriptive concepts in the laws of epidemiology are first of all replaced by letter variables. This reveals the form of the laws. The concepts referring to diseases are put into one-to-one correspondence with those referring to rumors. The letter variables in the epidemiological laws are replaced by the descriptive terms referring to rumors. This results in a set of hypotheses about rumors, which may or may not be confirmed. If, optimistically, these laws are confirmed, then the two theories have the same form.

The notion of *model* as isomorphism of laws is obviously symmetrical. However, when an area about which we already know a good deal is used to suggest laws for an area about which little is known, then the familiar area providing the form of the laws may be called a model for the new area. But once it is found that the laws of both areas do indeed share a common structure, then of course either is a model for the other.

Where knowledge is scarce, speculation abounds. Social science, not surprisingly, witnesses a plethora of speculative "models" or guesses about isomorphisms. A few illustrations will suffice. The notion of society as an organism, though repeatedly discredited, has a way of cropping up in one form or another. In its Spenglerian form, society is likened to a plant, complete with a seasonal life cycle. Like plants, a society has its vernal and autumnal phases. Society is compared to the growth and physiology of man, having like man its own states of development, its organic interrelatedness of parts, and its homeostatic controls. Evolutionary theory is another favorite model, one in the light of which whole societies are seen as engaged in a struggle for survival and subject to natural selection. Within a society, the various institutions and codes of behavior are viewed in the light of their contribution to adaptation and adjustment. Or individual learning is compared with the process of selective survival among random variations. The human brain is compared to an electronic computer. Servomechanisms like the automatic pilot or thermostat are now frequently evoked models for learning and purposive behavior. How does one go about testing these suggested models?

First, it must be possible to state clearly what is in one-to-one correspondence with what. Organisms grow; they increase in size and weight. What is *social* "growth"? What is the autumnal phase of society corresponding to the autumn of a plant? Relatively precise meaning can be given to adaptive and nonadaptive characteristics of organisms within evolutionary theory. Can we give correspondingly precise meanings to these notions for human institutions? What in learning, fitted to the evolutionary model, corresponds to the role of mutations? Second, once clearly defined empirical concepts in one area are made to correspond to the terms of the model, then formal similarities, if any, are sought. Nutrition is connected with growth in biology. Are the social concepts corresponding to nutrition and to growth similarly connected? In other words, not only must the terms of the two areas correspond, but the connections among these concepts must also be preserved, if the model is to be of any use. One area, either part or all of it, can be a fruitful model for another only if corresponding concepts can be found and if at least some of the laws connecting the concepts of the model also can be shown to connect their corresponding concepts in the second area. This implies that the model is from an area better developed than that for which it is used. If very little is known about either field, then to speak of a "model" is hardly more than loose and pointless talk.

Models and Measurement

A third prevalent use of *model* also has something to do with isomorphism, but not with that between the laws of empirical theories. *Mathematical model,* as I just said, may simply mean any quantified theory. On the other hand, it may and frequently does mean any arithmetical structure of a kind I must now explain. We saw before that replacing all the descriptive terms or concepts in the theory of one area by those of a different area results in another theory with the same form but different content from the original. The isomorphic sets of laws, those of the model and of its "translation," are both empirical theories whose truth or falsity depends upon the facts. It is possible, and often highly desirable, to establish another kind of isomorphism, in which the result is not two empirical theories sharing a common structure. Instead, the laws, or some of them, of an empirical theory may have the same form as a set of purely arithmetical truths. If this is the case, then the latter is called an *arithmetical representation* of the empirical theory.

Mathematical model sometimes means just this sort of arithmetical representation of an empirical theory. The laws of arithmetic, rather than those of another empirical theory, may be used as a model. Indeed, only when this is possible can arithmetic be used in empirical science. When laws are quantified, arithmetical tautologies may be used for deducing other laws and facts from them. This is the most important use of such tautologies within science. If, in Galileo's law, $d = 16t^2$, distance is expressed in feet and time in seconds, then from that law in conjunction with the fact that the time of fall was three seconds, we may deduce that the distance was 144 feet. The additional factual premise about the time of fall permits the deduction from the law that the distance is equal to 16 times 3^2. Using the arithmetical tautology $3 \times 3 = 9$ as an additional premise, we deduce that the distance is 16×9. The tautology $16 \times 9 = 144$ permits the final deduction that the distance fallen was 144 feet.

Since the arithmetical statements are tautologies, they may be added as premises without adding any more factual content than is given by the initial empirical premises about distance and time. In such simple calculations or deductions, the arithmetical premises are usually not stated explicitly, but are nevertheless being used. Arithmetic is a subtle and strong logic permitting deductions which, without it, might be quite impossible. What conditions must empirical properties meet before arithmetic can be applied to them?

Consider, first of all, the following three logical truths about numbers. The symbols ">" and "=" have their customary arithmetic meaning.

1. For any three numbers, if $N_1 > N_2$ and $N_2 > N_3$, then $N_1 > N_3$.
2. For any two numbers, at most one of $N_1 > N_2$, $N_1 = N_2$, $N_2 > N_1$ holds.
3. For any two numbers, at least one of $N_1 > N_2$, $N_1 = N_2$, $N_2 > N_1$ holds.

For this set of axioms to be a representation of an empirical theory, a set of descriptive terms must be coordinated to the arithmetic entities and relations. Let the numbers correspond to individual people, the relation ">" to the descriptive relation "higher-in-status" and "=" to "same status." After this coordination, the statements are probably again true, but, if so, they are now empirical truths about the descriptive relation "higher-in-status."

Other descriptive terms can easily be found for which the axioms fail. Let ">" be coordinated to "sibling" and "=" to "same person as." In this case, the second axiom is false. For, of course, if John is Peter's sibling, then Peter is John's sibling and the axiom states that not both of these can hold. The axioms are an arithmetic representation of those descriptive properties which can be ordered. Many other such properties also satisfy the axioms: men and the relationship "taller than," physical bodies and "heavier than," the relative hardness of stones, and students' scores on tests, are a few more candidates for true correspondence with the structure of integers and the relation "greater-than." All true representations of these axioms share a common structure.

The theorems implied by the axioms exhibit still further structure, for instance, irreflexivity and asymmetry. "Irreflexivity" means that an individual cannot have the relation to himself. A person may love himself but he cannot be taller than himself. "Loves" does not satisfy the axioms, so the theorems need not be true of it. "Taller than" does, so it must also be asymmetric and irreflexive.

The axioms and theorems together tell us more than appears at first glance about the structure of whatever satisfies the axioms. Whether or not a descriptive property has this structure is a matter of observable fact. Some things do and, as we have seen, some things do not. Those that do are said to have the structure of what is called a "complete ordering." The possibility of establishing an order of succession among attributes is not an unimportant characteristic, particularly in social science. This possibility is expressed by a set of empirical laws of which these axioms are an arithmetical representation. These empirical laws make ranking possible. There are many descriptive properties which satisfy the first two axioms of order, but not the third. Thus, when the properties of incomparable things are being considered, like food and plays, or musicians and painters, then the relation of "better than" does not satisfy the third axiom. Nor can we order all the people in the world by the relation "ancestor," since, given any two different individuals, one need not be the ancestor of the other. The first two axioms alone therefore express a "partial ordering." Only all three axioms express a completely ordered domain. Insofar as the descriptive concepts of different theories are true representations of some or all of the axioms of order, they share a common structure or form. By virtue of this shared structure, ranking is possible.

For measurement in the strict sense (yielding what Stevens [1951] called *ratio scales*) also to be possible, the descriptive properties must share certain other structural features of arithmetic. In particular, they must also have the same form as axioms like the following three:

4. For any two positive numbers, N_1 and N_2, there is exactly one other, N_3, such that $N_1 + N_2 = N_3$.
5. For any two positive numbers, $N_1 + N_2 = N_2 + N_1$.
6. For any three positive numbers, $(N_1 + N_2) + N_3 = N_1 + (N_2 + N_3)$.

Axiom 4 states that for any two numbers, there is uniquely a third which is their sum. Axiom 5 states that the sum of any two numbers is independent of their order; Axiom 6, that when any three numbers are added, the result is independent of how they are grouped. These axioms state part of the structure of addition. Addition is a binary operation on the elements or members of the set of positive integers, that is, a way of combining two elements of the set to get a third. Note that while these axioms are logical truths about the addition of positive numbers,

they are all false when applied to subtraction of the same elements. If we extend the system of elements to include both positive and negative numbers, then Axioms 5 and 6 do not hold for the operation of subtraction. The kind of elements specified and the kind of operations performed on them determines whether the resulting statements will be logically true or false or, in the case of descriptive entities, empirically true or false.

For these arithmetical truths to be a representation of anything, the number-elements and the arithmetical operations performed on them must be coordinated to descriptive entities and to operations on these descriptive entities. Just as the arithmetical relation "greater-than" can be made to correspond to natural or physical relations like "heavier than," "prefers," "loves," or "higher-in-status," so there must be a natural or physical operation corresponding to addition. As numbers can be added, so things can be put into the same container, glued together, or, even, simultaneously responded to. Suppose that our elements are lumps of sugar, each having a specified weight. Though numbers are assigned to the elements, indicating how much of the property it has, the corresponding operation is performed not on these numbers, but on the elements themselves. Only in the arithmetical representation are the elements themselves numbers. Weight is a measurable property of lumps of sugar because given two lumps of specified weight, the weight resulting from putting them both on the same side of a balance is the arithmetical sum of their individual weights. In other words, the operation of weighing two lumps of sugar has the same structure as the laws of arithmetic.

The sweetness of sugar, on the other hand, is not measurable in the strict sense of ratio scales. For measurable descriptive properties are those having the same form as the addition of numbers. Grinding together two lumps of sugar of equal sweetness, as indicated by some index of sweetness, would not give something twice as sweet. Or the order in which two things are mixed together might make a difference. Not only must a corresponding physical operation be found, but it must satisfy the axioms. If no corresponding physical or natural operation can be found or if it does not satisfy the axioms of addition, then the property cannot be measured. It may be ranked, however, if it satisfies the axioms of order. The measurability of descriptive properties is expressed by a set of empirical laws which are isomorphic to the laws of arithmetic. By virtue of this isomorphism, numbers may be assigned to the properties of things, resulting in quantified empirical laws. All the laws of arithmetic may then be applied to these numbers to derive new empirical laws and facts.

Other parts of arithmetic serving as models for empirical properties are, for example, probability theory and the theory of games. A correspondence is established between the descriptive concepts and those of the arithmetical theory. When a model, either empirical or arithmetical, is used as a source of hypotheses about the connections among the variables of another area, it does not explain these hypotheses. It merely suggests their form. If, however, these new hypotheses are confirmed, they may be used to explain and predict new knowledge.

REFERENCES[1]

Bechtoldt, H. P. Construct validity: A critique. *Amer. Psychologist,* 1959, 14, 619–629.

Bergmann, G. The logic of psychological concepts. *Phil. of Sci.,* 1951, 18, 93–110.

Bergmann, G. Theoretical psychology. *Annu. Rev. Psychol.,* 1953, 4, 435–458.

Bergmann, G. The contribution of John B. Watson. *Psychol. Rev.,* 1956, 63, 265–276.(a)

Bergmann, G. The logic of measurement. In L. Landweber & P. G. Hubbard (Eds.), *Proc. Sixth Hydraulics Conf. Univer. Iowa Stud. Engng,* 1956, 19–33. (b)

Bergmann, G. *Philosophy of science.* Madison: Univer. of Wisconsin Press, 1957.

Bergmann, G., & Spence, K. W. Operationism and theory in psychology. *Psychol. Rev.,* 1941, 48, 1–14.

Brodbeck, May. On the philosophy of the social sciences. *Phil. of Sci.,* 1954, 21, 140–156.

Brodbeck, May. The philosophy of science and educational research. *Rev. educ. Res.,* 1957, 27, 427–440.

Brodbeck, May. Methodological individualisms: Definition and reduction. *Phil. of Sci.,* 1958, 25, 1–22.

Brodbeck, May. Models, meaning, and theories. In L. Gross (Ed.), *Symposium on sociological theory.* Evanston, Ill.: Row, Peterson, 1959. Pp. 373–403.

Brodbeck, May. Explanation, prediction, and "imperfect" knowledge. In H. Feigl & G. Maxwell (Eds.), *Minnesota studies in the philosophy of science,* Vol. III. Minneapolis: Univer. of Minnesota Press, 1962. Pp. 231–272.

Brodbeck, May. Toward a fabric of knowledge—Common elements among fields of learning. *Educ. Record,* 1962, 43, 217–222.

English, H. B., & English, Ava C. *A comprehensive dictionary of psychological and psychoanalytical terms.* New York: Longmans, Green, 1958.

Feigl, H., & Brodbeck, May (Eds.) *Readings in the philosophy of science.* New York: Appleton-Century-Crofts, 1953.

Hempel, C. G. Fundamentals of concept formation in empirical science. In *International encyclopedia of unified science,* Vol. II, No. 7. Chicago: Univer. of Chicago Press, 1952.

Hochberg, H. Axiomatic systems, formalization, and scientific theories. In L. Gross (Ed.), *Symposium on sociological theory.* Evanston, Ill.: Row, Peterson, 1959. Pp. 407–436.

Stevens, S. S. Mathematics, measurement, and psychophysics. In S. S. Stevens (Ed.), *Handbook of experimental psychology.* New York: Wiley, 1951. Pp. 1–49.

Zeisel, H. *Say it with figures.* (4th ed.) New York: Harper, 1957.

---

[1] Some of these references are not cited in the text, as are all the references in most of the other chapters, but are offered for their general value to the reader in further pursuing some of the topics considered in this chapter.

CHAPTER 3   Paradigms for Research on Teaching[1]

N. L. GAGE
University of Illinois[2]

Whatever may have been its status in an earlier period, the term *theoretical* has an attractive connotation now. If it once suggested the opposite of "practical," it now is recognized as referring to the fundamental basis of practice. If "theorizing" once implied an escape from empirical research, it now holds sway as necessary to the planning and interpretation of such research. It is no longer necessary to proclaim, at least as a precept, the thesis that theoretical concerns are centrally significant in any branch of science or technology.

In the physical sciences, every schoolboy knows about the explosive potential of the theoretician's scribblings. In the social sciences, theories were once expected to be overarching world views and master prescriptions, like socialism and the single tax. Now theories are developed for much more modest topics, like learning, leadership, and cooperation, and one need not don a charismatic mantle in order to attempt to theorize.

Despite its present acceptance, the idea of "theory" still keeps many students at a distance. Theorizing is something that they hesitate to attempt. Other aspects of research, like collecting and analyzing data, seem familiar and comfortable in comparison with the task of developing or using theory. As one author put it:

There is no more arcane term in general use among humanists and social scientists than the term "theory." To the graduate student it carries with it a modest prestige suggesting that a person who is a theorist is brighter, deals with "deeper" and more complex material, and has insights which others who identify themselves differently do not have (Lane, 1961, p. 26).

Yet, of course, all men, including graduate students, are theorists. They differ not in whether they use theory, but in the degree to which they are aware of the theory they use. The choice before the man in the street and the research worker alike is not whether to theorize but whether to articulate his theory, to make it explicit, to get it out in the open where he can examine it. Implicit theories—of personality, of learning, and indeed of teaching—are used by all of us in our every-

[1] The author is grateful to B. O. Smith and Philip J. Runkel for criticisms of an earlier draft.
[2] Now at Stanford University.

day affairs. Often such theories take the form of folk sayings, proverbs, slogans, the unquestioned wisdom of the race. The scientist, on the other hand, explicates his theory and goes through procedures that help him approximate the goals that have already been set forth and examined in Chapter 2 of this Handbook.

The present chapter will not examine theory from the point of view of philosophy of science, already taken in Chapter 2. In this chapter, we shall rather display some of the forms that theoretical work has taken in research on teaching and in cognate fields. In the first section, we shall consider the nature of paradigms as working tools in behavioral research, the place of research on teaching in the whole realm of educational research, and the ways in which theorizing fits into the actual working behavior of behavioral scientists, i.e., how theories serve as both ends and means in such research. In a second section we shall consider a few paradigms in fields other than research on teaching, for their illustrative value. In the third section, paradigms designed explicitly for research on teaching will be described and examined as to their implications; this section should be viewed as merely an attempt to initiate the collection and analysis of such paradigms, an attempt that will succeed only insofar as it elicits further effort. The last section considers the possibility of developing a theory of teaching; in order to achieve this, it draws upon various approaches to learning as bases

rather ways of thinking or patterns for research that, when carried out, can lead to the development of theory.

Paradigms derive their usefulness from their generality. By definition, they apply to all specific instances of a whole class of events or processes. When one has chosen a paradigm for his research, he has made crucial decisions concerning the kinds of variables and relationships between variables that he will investigate. Paradigms for research imply a kind of commitment, however preliminary or tentative, to a research program. The investigator, having chosen his paradigm, may "bite off" only a part of it for any given research project, but the paradigm of his research remains in the background, providing the framework, or sense of the whole, in which his project is embedded.

A second characteristic of paradigms is that they often represent variables and their relationships in some graphic or outline form. Events or phenomena that have various temporal, spatial, causal, or logical relationships are portrayed in these relationships by boxes, connecting lines, and positions on vertical and horizontal dimensions. The classical portrayal of Pavlovian conditioning, shown in Fig. 1, illustrates this aspect of a paradigm. The left-hand part of Fig. 1 shows an unconditioned stimulus, S_1, eliciting a response, R. The center part shows S_1 being regularly preceded by another stimulus, S_2. Eventually, as shown in the right-hand part, S_2 alone becomes able to elicit R.

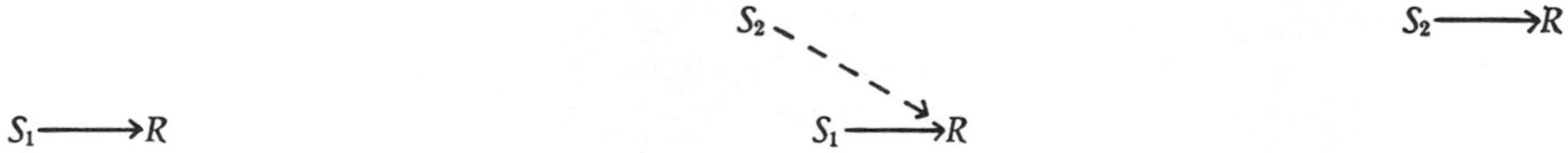

Fig. 1. A Paradigm for Pavlovian Conditioning.

for the formulation of such theory.

PARADIGMS:
THEIR NATURE AND USES

Paradigms are models, patterns, or schemata. Paradigms are not theories; they are

Here, the paradigm's generality implies that the process will occur regardless of the particular kinds of stimuli and responses involved. The stimuli may be bells, food powder, lights, words, electric shocks, the sight of people, an approving "uh-huh" expression, or whatever; the response may be salivation, muscle movement, increased heartbeat, use of the word "I," favorable self-references, or whatever. The paradigm is intended to be general and apply to all of the possibilities. It can serve research by suggesting that various specific instances of the general classes S_1, S_2, and R be tried. Also, various temporal relations between S_1 and S_2 can be explored; thus, the question can be raised whether S_2 must always precede S_1, and whether the interval between S_1 and S_2 affects the conditioning process. In this paradigm, the horizontal (left-right) dimension is a temporal one.

Explicit and Implicit Paradigms and Their Effects

Paradigms, like theories, can be either explicit or implicit. Some have been set forth by their authors in full panoply, with diagrams and elaborations of their connections with completed or projected research. Other paradigms are implicit in what authors have done or proposed by way of research; in these cases, we shall attempt to explicate the paradigm. In either case, we shall seek to use the paradigm as an intellectual tool for examining crucial aspects of research on teaching.

Choice of a paradigm, whether deliberate or unthinking, determines much about the research that will be done. The style, design, and approach of a research undertaking, indeed, the likelihood that it will bear fruit, are conditioned in large part by the paradigm with which the investigator begins. Whether he will perform an experiment, in the sense of actually manipulating one or more variables, or a correlational study, in the sense of studying relationships between variables measured as they occur in nature, may be determined by his paradigm.

Whether he will seek relationships between variables that have some genuine promise, based on logical and empirical grounds, of being related, may be determined by his paradigm. At one extreme, his paradigm may lead him to search for relationships between variables that have a good likelihood of being related. So one investigation may examine the correlation between the teacher's authoritarianism on a verbal, printed test, and the teacher's likelihood of nonpromoting students, because a paradigm (implicit in this case) portrays a connection between these variables; in one investigation the results supported the hypothesis and the paradigm was strengthened. At the other extreme, the paradigm may lead inevitably to negative results. Thus a paradigm may lead to an investigation of the correlation between the teacher's authoritarianism and his effectiveness in producing gain in reading achievement; explication of the paradigm underlying this project might suggest in advance the forlornness of any hope that such a relationship will materialize.

The Definition of Research on Teaching

To insure that the paradigms we shall examine have some bearing on research on teaching, we need a definition of such research. First, however, let us define "research" and "teaching." By research, we mean activity aimed at increasing our power to understand, predict, and control events of a given kind. All three of these goals involve relationships between events or variables. We understand an event by relating it logically to others. We predict an event by relating it empirically to antecedents in time. We control an event by manipulating the independent variables to which it is functionally related. Hence, in the long run at least, research must seek out the relationships between variables.

By teaching, we mean, for the present purpose of defining research on teaching, any interpersonal influence aimed at changing the ways in which other persons can or will behave. The restriction to "interpersonal" influence is intended to rule out physical (e.g., mechanical), physiological, or economic ways of influencing another's behavior, such as pushing him, drugging him, or depriving him of a job. Rather the influence has to impinge on the other person through his perceptual and cognitive processes, i.e., through his ways of getting meaning out of the objects and events that his senses make him aware of.

The behavior producing the influence on another person may be "frozen" (so to speak) in the form of printed material, film, or the program of a teaching machine, but it is considered behavior nonetheless. How the other person "can or will behave" refers to his capabilities for maximum performance, i.e., abilities, or to his modes of typical performance, i.e., habits or attitudes, that constitute the objectives of instruction. The behaviors and intervening variables mediating them (such as abilities, habits, or attitudes) may be classified in many ways, such as the "cognitive," "affective," and "psychomotor" domains of the *Taxonomy of Educational Objectives* (Bloom, et al., 1956).

Having defined *research* and *teaching,* we turn now to *research on teaching.* A useful definition should delimit such research to something more specific than educational research as a whole. Accordingly, we define research on teaching, the subject of our paradigms, as research in which at least one variable consists of a behavior or characteristic of teachers. (Recall that the teacher may be the author of a textbook or program, someone who is not seen by the learner.)

By this definition, many kinds of research potentially relevant to research on teaching are not themselves research on teaching. Some research deals only with behaviors or characteristics of learners, such as their readiness, achievement, or adjustment. Other research may deal with the nature of the objectives, or curriculum—such as knowledge, understanding, or skill—at which teaching may be aimed. An example here would be research on the efficiency of different methods of subtraction. Still other research may deal with relationships between behaviors or characteristics of learners and their attainment of educational objectives. But it is not research on teaching unless it deals explicitly with some behavior or characteristic of teachers.

Variables other than those referring to behaviors or characteristics of teachers are, of course, admissible and desirable in research on teaching. Our definition merely states that behaviors or characteristics of teachers must be involved, not that other kinds of variables may not be involved, in what we shall call research on teaching.

The Basic-Applied Continuum

Educational research, including research on teaching, can range widely along a continuum from the most basic to the most applied. It is useful to display this range so that any specific research undertaking may be located on this continuum. Such positioning should make plain the basic or applied nature of the research, the typical institutional setting of such research, and the connections of the research with investigations at other points on the continuum.

The following sixfold categorization, developed by Clark, Hilgard, and Humphreys,[3] contains "somewhat arbitrary" stages ranging from basic science through actual demonstration of methods in school systems:

1. *Basic scientific investigation, content indifferent.* Here the problems—such as learning, retention, or transfer—may be topically relevant to teaching, but the subjects may be animals or the learning tasks may be nonsense materials and hence not necessarily relevant to school problems. An example is the development of a mathematical model of the relationships between group size, group seating patterns, and communication structures. Game theory might be used to portray in general terms the interaction between one individual behaving according to one set of rules, and a group of individuals governed by another set of rules. Studies of this kind might be made in departments of experimental psychology or mathematics, in

---

[3] D. Clark, E. R. Hilgard, and L. G. Humphreys, Recommendations for committee to be concerned with strategies of research in the improvement of instruction. Unpublished memorandum presented at Conference on the Behavioral Sciences in Education, sponsored by the Social Science Research Council, Cornell University, Ithaca, New York, June 23–25, 1961.

institutes or centers for advanced study, or in basic research laboratories supported by governmental or industrial organizations.

2. *Basic scientific investigation, content relevant.* Here the content would be relevant to something actually taught in schools. The research is basic in that the problem investigated would be posed by the scientist himself out of his own effort to develop systematic knowledge, rather than one stemming from the needs of the educational system; the research is also basic in the sense that laboratory-type, and perhaps somewhat unrealistic, controls and methods may be used rather than those that would be feasible under ordinary classroom conditions. Studies of how children reason, of the early childhood experiences of persons who later become teachers, of how feedback or communication operates in small, classroom-type, laboratory discussion groups, would represent research of this kind. Typically, such research is carried on in institutes for child study, in laboratories for research in group dynamics, and in departments of sociology, anthropology, or psychology.

3. *Investigations of educationally oriented problems.* Here the research setting would be at least a simulated classroom, if not an actual one, and the teaching or learning task would be at least conceptually similar to those found in classrooms. Studies of the effectiveness of the discovery method of teaching mathematics, of the value of feedback from pupils to teachers, of the classroom behaviors of teachers differing in scores on an attitude inventory, would belong here. Work of this kind is typically performed in bureaus of educational research and other departments of university-centered colleges of education.

4. *Classroom experimentation.* Here the research would deal with methods of teaching actual pupils a part of an actual curriculum by methods that seem feasible under actual classroom and school conditions. Trying out a new method of teaching subtraction, giving teachers feedback by a method that seems routinely usable, and determining the comprehensibility of a new diagram of the Wheatstone bridge illustrate this kind of research. Educational research workers in graduate colleges of education, working in experimental or laboratory schools or public schools especially enlisted in the undertaking, carry out such research.

5. *Field testing.* In this kind of research, the new ideas, approaches, methods, or materials are transferred from the especially contrived school setting to a representative set of schools, and the investigator faces the problems of preparing typical teachers to use the new methods or materials, just as in validating tests and gathering norms.

6. *Installing the materials widely.* Here the testing phase is considered finished, and the educational innovator investigates and uses techniques for introducing, gaining acceptance for, and insuring adequate usage of the new methods and materials on the widest basis considered desirable.

As a paradigm of the innovation-installation process, the foregoing analysis represents an idealized conception that has probably been followed in this exact form only rarely. Yet it does portray the kind of division of labor that exists in our society, even if only in an unorganized, haphazard way. The research worker who locates himself in this paradigm should at least have a conception of where he fits in the total enterprise of educational research. The six phases must of necessity interact, as is shown in Fig. 2, and

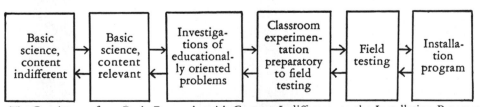

Fig. 2. The Continuum from Basic Research, with Content Indifferent, to the Installation Program.

ideas and problems should flow freely from one phase to another.

Theories as Ends

Research workers use theories as means and also set them up as ends. As ends, or goals, theories are not mere pleasant adjuncts to the facts; rather, they are the *raison d'être* of scientific work, the crux of the matter. Not mere prediction or control, but understanding in the light of theoretical formulation and explanation, is in this view the central aim of science. Prediction may rest on mere empirical correlations that do not necessarily make sense. Control can be achieved with techniques that we actually miscomprehend. We can predict the mean score on achievement tests of the high school seniors of a state from the mean per capita expenditure for alcohol of the teachers of the state; this prediction, although it will have far better than chance accuracy, may not be based on any genuine understanding of the connection between the two variables. Or a medicine man may successfully control the behavior of a fellow tribesman by means of hypnotic suggestion while believing a wildly erroneous explanation of how he achieves his effects.

Similarly, understanding, or theoretical formulation, itself may not enable us to predict or control. We can understand evolution as a natural process although no one has yet been able to predict or control an actual instance of evolution; the same may be said of earthquakes or volcanic eruptions.

Hence, these three objectives of science—understanding, prediction, and control—are to some extent independent and distinct. Theory as an end belongs to the first of the three, namely, understanding. To be able to interrelate a set of variables on the basis of the rules of logic is to have a theory concerning those variables. To build such theory is the goal of many scientists. To build such theory around variables concerning the behavior or characteristics of teachers may be regarded as a prime end of research on teaching.

Theories as Means

As means, or tools, theories allow the research worker to straighten out his thinking, to bring order into his concepts and hypotheses, and perhaps to rationalize what he is doing. As Guba and Getzels (1955) have put it, a theoretical framework sharpens research objectives, suggests what variables should be eliminated as nonmeaningful and hence wasteful, increases the likelihood of significant findings, simplifies the complex task of interpreting results, aids in interpreting meaningful even if nonsignificant results, and makes research cumulative from one study to the next.

How do research workers actually behave in using theory, or in theorizing, as they go about their job? There are at least two views on this question. Sometimes, the research worker is described as proceeding in a logical fashion from established facts and relationships, or premises, to the derivation of new hypotheses, which he then tests empirically. It is even better, in this view, if the research worker states a complex theory, formulating the state of knowledge in his area, rather than merely a "single-idea" theory, based on a single postulate. Accordingly, the research worker carefully reviews the literature, gathering together the various ideas in the field, to reveal the gaps in knowledge. It was in keeping with this view of research behavior that the following advice was offered:

The review of the literature, if it is conducted in the way described here, should provide an overview of the current framework of theory in the area in which it is proposed to undertake an investigation. The student may be expected to abstract from his review of the literature a theory in terms of which he plans to work. A minimum requirement should be that he draw up a statement covering the essential features of the theory, but preferably he should be more ambitious and draft the theory as a set of postulates. He should then show how his hypotheses represent a series of deductions from these postulates. This he will find to be a worthwhile exercise in clear think-

ing (Travers, 1958, pp. 75–76, italics in original).

In contrast with this outlook, we can find experienced research workers testifying that they go through no process so logical and orderly. These workers disclaim any practice of systematically reviewing the literature, designing crucial experiments, collecting data, analyzing results, and drawing conclusions. Instead, they admit to engaging in a somewhat different procedure. Here is how a seminar composed of distinguished, productive research workers in psychology described their working methods:

Actually, the process of doing research . . . is a rather informal, often illogical and sometimes messy-looking affair. It includes a great deal of floundering around in the empirical world. . . . Somewhere and somehow in the process of floundering, the research worker will get an idea. In fact, he will get many ideas. On largely intuitive grounds he will reject most of his ideas and will accept others as the basis for extended work. . . . If the idea happens to be a good one, he may make a significant positive contribution to his science— "may" because between the idea and the contribution lies a lot of persistence, originality, intuition, and hard work. It is in this sort of activity, rather far removed from the public, more orderly and systematic phases of scientific work, that the productive research worker spends much of his time and effort (American Psychological Association, Education and Training Board, 1959, p. 169).

According to these research workers, the more formal picture of research work arose from the logical nature of the finished product. The picture also arose because it is easier to describe the design, statistics, and scholarship aspects of research than the origination, choice, and development of ideas.

The process of getting and developing ideas is undoubtedly a confused mixture of observation, thinking, asking why, cherishing little unformed notions, etc. Some people . . . work very effectively with ideas that have an iceberg quality, that is, most of the content is sub-merged . . . and not made explicit until a very late stage of the research. . . . As a consequence, it is easy in the training of research workers to overemphasize highly formal rigorous theory where the rules of logic can apply. It is equally easy to decry "theory" . . . .

We doubt whether either of these extreme positions, if adopted seriously, can be anything but a hindrance to the research worker. The importance of the vague notion, difficult as it is to explain, should be emphasized. . . . But it should also be emphasized that the notion cannot be allowed to remain forever vague; ideas must eventually achieve clarity and testability if they are to receive serious attention from other researchers (American Psychological Association, Education and Training Board, 1959, pp. 172–173).

In short, the use of theory as a tool in research cannot be reduced to a formula, but it can be accepted as a valuable adjunct to the research process at some stage of the work in one way or another. This chapter is offered on the assumption that some familiarity with the theories of other research workers, and their implicit or explicit paradigms in particular, will make for more sophisticated effort.

Are Paradigms Useful?

As stated earlier, this chapter's justification is that awareness, and even planning, of his choice of a paradigm may help the research worker. As has also been stated, some scientists do not accept this premise. In particular, Skinner (1959), in a witty but earnest case history of himself as a scientist, has thrown doubt on the value of the kind of ideas this chapter presents. In view of his resounding success in research—not only on the behavior of subhuman organisms but in recent years on the teaching of children with machines— his position should be known to any prospective research worker. Only a few quotations of his "unformalized principles of scientific practice" can be given here to intimate the spirit of his approach; the reader must go to the full case history for an adequate grasp of it.

1. "When you run onto something interesting, drop everything else and study it" (p. 81).

2. "Some ways of doing research are easier than others" (p. 82). (For example, automatize the collection of data and administration of experimental variables.)

3. "Some people are lucky" (p. 85). (Good ideas may come through chance occurrences in the laboratory.)

4. "Apparatuses sometimes break down" (p. 86). (The investigator may sometimes discover a new and important experimental variable in what goes wrong.)

This account of my scientific behavior . . . is as exact in letter and spirit as I can now make it. The notes, data, and publications which I have examined do not show that I ever behaved in the manner of Man Thinking as described by John Stuart Mill or John Dewey or in reconstructions of scientific behavior by other philosophers of science. I never faced a Problem which was more than the eternal problem of finding order. I never attacked a problem by constructing a Hypothesis. I never deduced Theorems or submitted them to Experimental Check. So far as I can see, I had no preconceived Model of behavior—certainly not a physiological or mentalistic one and, I believe, not a conceptual one (Skinner, 1959, p. 88).

Skinner's argument needs consideration even beyond the fact that, as he says, "We have no more reason to say that all psychologists should behave as I have behaved than that they should all behave like R. A. Fisher" (p. 99). Apart from his sustained concern with "the eternal problem of finding order," we should note that Skinner must have known some paradigms: the paradigm for Pavlovian conditioning, e.g., as the basis for his own distinction between respondent and operant behavior. Whether the knowledge of the Pavlovian paradigm helped him formulate his own in advance, or rather merely after his research had been done, may not matter. Either as tools or as products, paradigms may be found in Skinner's work. If paradigms are not useful in discovering a new truth, they may at least be useful in communicating it. The recipient of the communication may then find the paradigm serviceable in his own work.

In some ways, of course, Skinner is indisputably right. The research worker should not set up a paradigm in advance and then persist in following it through, come what may. As alleys turn blind, they should be abandoned. As promising leads appear, they should be followed up. What seems to be needed in research, and what Skinner's testimony bears upon, is a kind of artistry about which we still know little. Knowing the paradigm for a concerto will not empower a composer to write one. And knowing his way around paradigms for research on teaching will not empower the research worker to contribute to scientific knowledge about teaching. Yet, even if use of the paradigm is never sufficient of itself to ensure musical composition or fruitful scientific research, it seems plausible that it will usually be necessary, to the composer and research worker alike. Even the antitheoretician will be found to have his theories.

Usages of "Theory"

One widely noted usage of the term *theory* should be distinguished from the one employed here. Skinner (1950) used the term to refer to "any explanation of an observed fact which appeals to events taking place somewhere else, at some other level of observation, described in different terms, and measured, if at all, in different dimensions" (p. 193). With respect to the study of learning, Skinner questioned whether such theories are necessary. Such theories—whether neurophysiological, mental, or conceptual—were considered by Skinner to have the effect of diverting us from the search for and exploration of relevant manipulable variables on which behavior might be dependent. Attributing behavior to a neural or mental event, real or conceptual, tends in Skinner's view to make us forget that we still need to account for the neural or mental event and also to give us an unwarranted satisfaction with the state of our knowledge.

In another sense of the term, however, Skinner does admit the possibility of fruitful theory: "a formal representation of the data reduced to a minimal number of terms" (p. 216). Such theories possess the advantage of generality beyond particular facts but do not refer to another dimensional system and hence do not obstruct the search for functional relations. It is this sense of the term that most writers intend, and it is the one with which this chapter is concerned. Hence Skinner's well-known antitheoretical position does not apply to the kind of theory of teaching considered here.

"Theory" and "Paradigm" in This Chapter

In this chapter, we use the term *theory* in a modest sense—to refer to any systematic ordering of ideas about the phenomena of a field of inquiry. We use the term in antithesis to ad hoc, disorderly planning or interpretation of research, and in contrast to what has been called "dust-bowl empiricism," in which the investigator looks for facts wherever he may find them, with little prior consideration of where it may be most valuable to look and with little idea of how he will interpret what he finds.

There has been much research of the kind against which our concern with theory is aimed. As one committee stated:

Throughout both reports of this Committee has run the conviction that the present condition of research on teacher effectiveness holds little promise of yielding results commensurate with the needs of American education. This condition has two significant characteristics: disorganization and lack of orientation to other behavioral sciences. By disorganization, we mean the condition in which, at present, research too often proceeds without explicit theoretical framework, in intellectual disarray, to the testing of myriads of arbitrary, unrationalized hypotheses. The studies too often interact little with each other, do not fall into place within any scheme, and hence add little

to the understanding of the teaching process (American Educational Research Association, Committee on the Criteria of Teacher Effectiveness, 1953, p. 657).

Our concern with theories and paradigms is therefore aimed at furthering more systematic and orderly approaches to the formulation of the variables and hypotheses that enter into research on teaching. We urge no movement away from facts. It is merely the ill-considered collection of facts against which we argue. We should not aspire to any large-scale deductive system, with theorems rigorously derived from postulates and axioms. But neither should we remain content with mere factual data—averages, differences, or correlations—on which the research worker has imposed little rationale.

PARADIGMS IN RELATED FIELDS

To illustrate the nature of paradigms and further illuminate the ways in which they can serve our field of inquiry, we present a collection of paradigms from other fields. In this section we exhibit paradigms from the fields of statistics, psychopathology, administrative behavior, and group dynamics. Each will be described briefly, with no attempt to portray the elaborations developed by the original authors.

The Tatsuoka-Tiedeman Paradigm for Statistical Methods

In Chapter 4 of this Handbook, Tatsuoka and Tiedeman present a paradigm for classifying statistical techniques in terms of the nature and number of the variables involved. Their classification is based on the following characteristics of variables:

1. Role of the variable: independent (antecedent) or dependent (consequent).
2. Type of scale used in measuring the variables: nominal, ordinal, interval, and ratio.
3. Numbers of independent and dependent variables: 0, 1, and 2 or more.

Using these dimensions, Tatsuoka and Tiedeman organize the whole field of statistical methods, show where available methods fall, and where gaps exist at present. We shall present here nothing more of what is presented in Chapter 4. We merely refer to Table 1 on pages 154–155 of that chapter as an example of a paradigm, whose power for the organization of ideas is made apparent in that chapter.

Bucklew's Paradigms for Psychopathology

Bucklew (1960) has developed a set of paradigms for psychopathologies which are intended for the analysis of case histories. We can present here only a sketch of his method, which is elaborated and applied to more than a score of case histories in his book. Bucklew defined several constructs, each of which is listed and briefly characterized in Fig. 3, along with the graphic symbol, or "diagram element," used for it.

The chronological sequence of the case history reads from the top of the diagram for earlier life to the bottom of the diagram for the personality status at the time the history was recorded. . . . In diagramming cases it is usually easiest to start with symptoms first and then go back to the complex, or else, skipping this step temporarily, to reconstruct earlier life events first, and then the complex as the final step. The visual reconstruction of a case generally follows the order of insights which arise in therapeutic interviewing (Bucklew, 1960, p. 52).

To illustrate Bucklew's purposes and methods, we shall apply them to the fictional case of a teacher suffering from depression; our case is patterned after that of a depressed scientist described by Bucklew (1960, pp. 97–102).

The teacher is a fifty-one-year-old man showing symptoms of severe depression: inability to sleep, feeling exhausted, and frequently weeping. During the past three years he has been absorbed in curriculum development work, during which he has suffered three similar but less severe breakdowns. Soon he will have to present a report on his curriculum development work to the teachers of his school system, and he dreads the occasion. He still needs to write a final report on his project but is unable to bring himself to do so and has asked younger co-workers to take over without even listing him as co-author.

The teacher emphasizes that he has worked not for prestige but for children's welfare. His report is keenly awaited, and he believes no one else can finish the job. Simultaneously, he states his willingness to help his co-workers but wants no credit for doing so.

When the contradictions in his attitudes were pointed out—namely, his former devotion to but present distaste for his work, his wish to serve children and his feeling of indispensability to the job, his lack of desire for recognition—and the possibility that he was repressing some of his motives, the teacher at first resisted these interpretations and was emotionally shaken, but showed some signs of recovery from his depression.

The teacher had been the youngest of six children, had suffered a childhood disease that left him puny and undersized, had been treated as a weakling, and had been overindulged. He was superior to everyone, including his teachers, in handling schoolwork. Once unhappily married, he was now happy and successful in a second marriage and proud of his two children. He was also concerned over a decline in his sexual powers. When the coincidence of his recent intense preoccupation with his work and his decline in sexual vigor was pointed out, and when his feelings of indispensability to his project were related to his earlier competitiveness with teachers and students in the classroom, the teacher seemed to gain increased insight. His adolescent problems were being reactivated by the approach of middle age and, eventually, of retirement.

The diagram of depression in a scientist is presented in Fig. 4. Bucklew would characterize the "complex," i.e., the dotted rectangle, as follows:

Category of Constructs	*Diagram Element*
A. Behavioral unit constructs	Rectangles with rounded edges

1. Ego 2. Role	▢
3. The complex (Inside the rectangles, phrases summarize the leading characteristics of the unit. Right-hand rectangles stand for ego or roles; left-hand rectangles, for ego alien motives.)	▢〰→▢
4. Symptom formation	
5. Anxiety	▢

B. Process constructs	Lines suggesting either motivation or conditions of the units (such as being regressed)

1. Conflict (two arrows pointing at one another)	→ ←
2. Repression (wavy-lined arrow blocked by an opposing line indicating counter motivation)	〰→ ⊢
3. Regression (lines pointing upward)	↑ ↗
4. Fixation (blocked lines pointing down)	⌐ ⌐
5. External conflict	→ ←---

C. Life event constructs	Rectangles with square corners

1. Precipitating events 2. Traumatic events 3. Conditioning events	▭

D. External constructs	

1. Social and legal restrictions	□

E. Developmental sequences	
	/ \

Fig. 3. Chief Constructs and Diagram Elements in Bucklew's Paradigms for Psychopathologies (Adapted from Bucklew, 1960, p. 51).

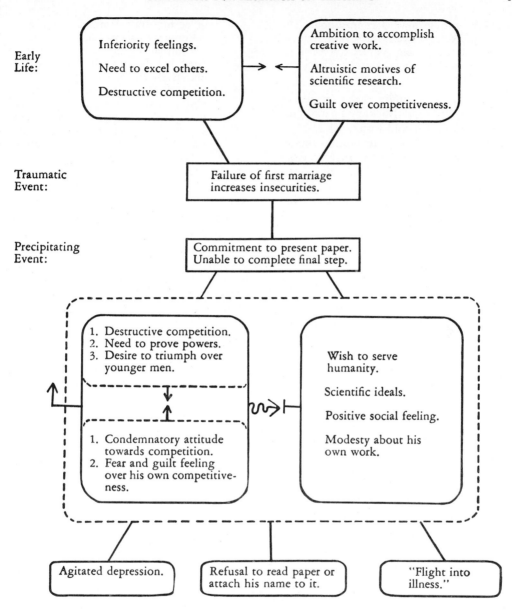

Fig. 4. Depression in a Scientist (Bucklew, 1960, p. 103).

On the side of ego functions we list the man's ideals as a scientist, his desire to help humanity, and his exaggerated desire not to receive recognition for his work. On the side of ego alien motives we first list three motives proper —destructive competition, the increased need to prove his powers, and his desire to triumph over younger competitors. Beneath them we list a counter motive and the feelings that have in the past become associated with it, the condemnatory attitude toward competition. The major conflict is between these two sets of motives, and the whole conflict has been repressed by opposing ego motives (Bucklew, 1960, pp. 102–104).

As a method of bringing order out of the welter of case histories, Bucklew's paradigms may serve well. Case histories, whether of psychopathology or of more normal modes of adjustment, vary in all the myriad ways that human lives vary. Bucklew's conceptual and visual framework for analyzing case histories suggests that similar attempts at schematizing research on teaching can prove helpful.

Halpin's Paradigm for Administrative Behavior

Research on school administration is concerned with behavior that, like teaching, occurs within the institution of education. It is coming somewhat closer to our own interests, therefore, to note that Halpin (1957) has offered a paradigm for research on administrative behavior. The purpose of his paradigm is to provide "the basis for a systematic classification and critique of existent and ongoing research . . . [and] . . . to suggest fruitful lines of inquiry for new research . . . . to spot missing elements in our research knowledge about administration and to achieve a closer integration between empirical findings and theoretical analysis" (p. 155).

As shown in condensed form in Fig. 5, Halpin's paradigm has four "Panels":

Panel I.   The Organization Task: defined in terms of "desirable" *behavior* or behavioral *products*.

Panel II.   Administrator Behavior: the *behavior* of the officially designated leader in his administrative role.

Panel III. Variables Associated with Administrator Behavior: These include behavior on the part of group members other than the leader, products of the behavior of group members, specified conditions under which the administrator and other group members are required to operate, patterns

of administrative organization, and community factors that bear upon the formal organization. It is stipulated that these variables be reported objectively and measured reliably.

Panel IV.   Criteria of Administrator "Effectiveness": Two levels of criteria are postulated: (1) intermediate criteria such as evaluations or ratings of the leader's behavior, and (2) outcomes of behavior measured in terms of organization products and *changes* in these products (Halpin, 1957, p. 174).

In diagraming his paradigm, Halpin assigns variables to different boxes, each designated by a number in parentheses. A time line, omitted in Fig. 5, is extended horizontally across the paradigm, so that each box appears twice to indicate two different points in time.

Panel I contains a box labeled *The Task*, namely, the "desirable" behaviors and products of behavior of the organization.

Panel II, labeled Administrator Behavior, includes three boxes at each point in time: (1) the administrator's perception of the organization's task; (2) his behavior as a decision maker; and (3) his behavior as a group leader. The perception box comes first and is enclosed in dotted lines because it is a slightly different order of behavior in being "less accessible to direct observation" than the other two kinds of administrator behavior.

Panel IV, labeled "Criteria of Administrator 'Effectiveness,' " contains both intermediate criteria, usually in the form of ratings of the administrator's performance as a decision maker and group leader, and ultimate criteria in terms of organization achievement and changes in achievement that can be attributed to the behavior of the administrator. These criteria are measured in respect to the same behaviors and behavioral products that were used to define the Task in Panel I. Ratings are, of course, often invalid against the criterion of changes in the organization's achievement attributable to the administrator. Ultimate criteria are differentiated into those dealing with organizational maintenance and

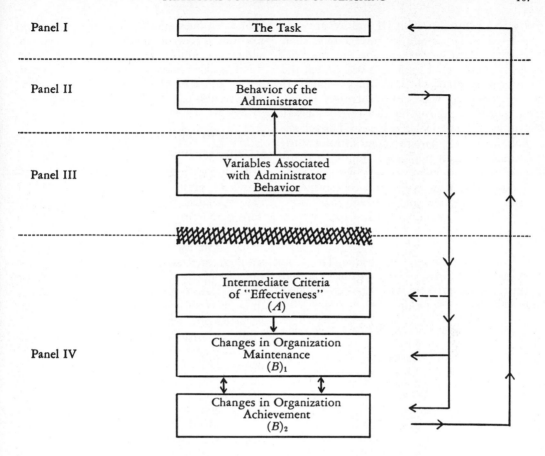

Fig. 5. Condensed Version of Halpin's Paradigm for Research on Administrator Behavior. **Note** that there is no direct connection between Panels III and IV (Halpin, 1957, p. 192).

organizational achievement. The various criteria of the organization's effectiveness may not be unidimensional; for example, superintendents successful in securing salary raises may not spend much time in personal contact with teachers.

The essence of the paradigm is that "the fundamental purpose is to delineate the relationship between the *behavior* of the administrator (Panel II) and *changes* in the Organization's Achievement. . . . *Let it be emphasized again that if one fails to establish the relationship between the behavior of the ad-*

ministrator and syntalic measures of the organization's 'effectiveness,' he evades the most fundamental research issue at stake" (Halpin, 1957, p. 185).

Panel III, labeled Variables Associated with Administrator Behavior, contains variables assumed to affect his behavior, as specified in Panel II, especially those facets of his behavior that are related to pertinent criteria of effectiveness. In Panel III are variables that affect the relationship between the variables in Panels II and IV. Thus, suppose the correlations between Panels II and

III and between Panels III and IV are considered to be zero-order correlations; then partial and multiple regression equations derived from these correlations will permit the determination of which variables in Panel III are associated with either increases or decreases in the correlation between Panels II and IV. The variables in Panel III are classified into three groups: administrator variables (e.g., age, intelligence, training, experience), intraorganization variables (e.g., administrative structure, group cohesiveness), and extraorganization variables (e.g., community pressures, financial support, population increases).

Note the direction of the arrows. The Task defines the purpose of the organization and hence the *change* criteria of the Organization's Achievement are measured in respect to this Task. Hence an arrow points from Panel IV to Panel I. The focus of the research is upon the administrator, and since the purpose is to predict changes in Organization Achievement from his behavior, the arrow from Panel II points to Panel IV. In Panel IV these flow lines have been split to show that it is preferable to go from II to IV-B and that if one goes through IV-A instead, it is still incumbent upon him to demonstrate that there is a significant relationship between IV-A and IV-B. . . . The crux of the problem is to predict events in Panel IV-B on the basis of the variables identified in Panel II. All other relationships are adjuvant.

Panel III variables are studied so as to increase the accuracy of the predictions made from the variables in Panel II. Hence the arrow points from III to II (Halpin, 1957, pp. 191–192).

Halpin's paradigm foreshadows a kind of research on teaching that we shall consider later in this chapter—namely, paradigms based on criteria of teacher effectiveness. In particular, the reader will be reminded of Halpin's paradigm when he comes to Mitzel's paradigm, described on pages 118–120. Whether the "effectiveness" paradigm will prove more fruitful in research on administrator behavior than in research on teachers

is an open question. Whether the partial and multiple regression methods will prove feasible and productive, as Halpin envisages them, is also debatable. Much of what is said below concerning the criterion-of-teacher-effectiveness paradigm also applies here.

Paradigms for Research on Group Dynamics

To provide a conceptual framework for research on group dynamics, Horwitz (1953) developed the paradigm shown in Fig. 6. This paradigm rests on distinctions between (1) individual, (2) group, and (3) institutional systems, the latter including community, societal, and cultural systems for the sake of simplicity. His paradigm consists of a 3 x 3 matrix whose columns specify these three kinds of systems as independent variables and whose rows specify the three kinds of systems as dependent variables. As Horwitz noted, the three cells along the diagonal (A-A', B-B', C-C') represent functional relationships among variables within the *same* system and hence represent the internal dynamics of that kind of system. Similarly, his Cells B-A' and C-B' would contain instances in which a larger system, as the external environment, affects a smaller one. Finally, Cells A-B' and B-C' contain instances in which the smaller system is regarded as part of the larger whole and affects the functioning of the larger unit, "not as external environment, but by directly shaping the properties of the whole" (Horwitz, 1953, p. 311).

Horwitz's levels can be translated readily into categories relevant to research on teaching. The "individual system" becomes the teacher, the "group system" becomes the classroom-group, and the "institutional system" becomes the school as a whole, including the school system and the community. By our definition of research on teaching, only research containing A or A' variables would qualify. Studies of relationships between characteristics and behaviors of teachers as individuals would belong in Cell A-A'.

Upon variables in the:		Effects of variables in the:		
		Individual system A	Group system B	Institutional system C
Individual system	A'	Variables 1 2 . . . n	Variables 1 2 . . . n	Variables 1 2 . . . n
Group system	B'	Variables 1 2 . . . n	Variables 1 2 . . . n	Variables 1 2 . . . n
Institutional system	C'	Variables 1 2 . . . n	Variables 1 2 . . . n	Variables 1 2 . . . n

Fig. 6. Levels and Interrelations of Variables Used in Explaining Social Behavior (Horwitz, 1953, p. 310).

Studies of the relationships between characteristics of teachers, such as teacher morale, and characteristics of classroom-groups of pupils, such as their homogeneity in intelligence, would fall into Cell A-B' or B-A'. Studies of the relationships among characteristics of teachers and those of school systems would fall into Cell A-C' or A'-C.

Jensen and Parsons (1959) presented a paradigm for conceptualizing group phenomena in the classroom. In the top part of Fig. 7 is shown their classification of dependent and independent variables according to whether they represent group structural properties (S), dynamics of functional events in group life (D), and properties of the group-goal region and of members' needs (G). The bottom part of Fig. 7 shows their 3 x 3 matrix "achieved by cross-classifying the independent and the dependent variables in terms of

the S, D, and G categories . . ." (Jensen & Parsons, 1959, p. 344). In their review, Jensen and Parsons found most studies falling into the S → S, D → D, and S → D categories. They also stated that Horwitz's paradigm "may readily be superimposed on . . . [their own], thus permitting the variables in any particular study to be identified not only in terms of their S, D, or G properties but also in terms of their level of complexity as well" (p. 344).

As examples of "structural" variables, Jensen and Parsons cited sociometric status, socioeconomic class, clique formation, rural versus urban residence, and group cohesiveness. Among the "dynamic" variables are conformity to group standards, group-induced attitude change, motives such as need for affiliation or achievement, and cooperative versus competitive management. As studies

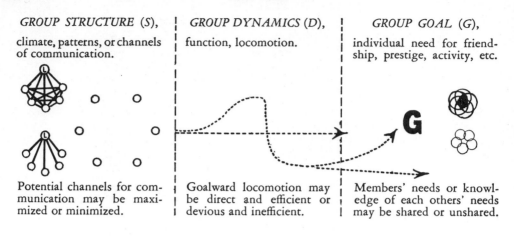

GROUP STRUCTURE (S),	GROUP DYNAMICS (D),	GROUP GOAL (G),
climate, patterns, or channels of communication.	function, locomotion.	individual need for friendship, prestige, activity, etc.

Potential channels for communication may be maximized or minimized.	Goalward locomotion may be direct and efficient or devious and inefficient.	Members' needs or knowledge of each others' needs may be shared or unshared.

PARADIGM CATEGORIES

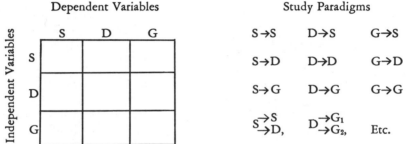

Dependent Variables

Study Paradigms

Independent Variables

	S	D	G
S			
D			
G			

S→S	D→S	G→S
S→D	D→D	G→D
S→G	D→G	G→G

$S{\to S \atop \to D},$　$D{\to G_1 \atop \to G_2},$　Etc.

Fig. 7. A Paradigm for Conceptualizing Group Phenomena in the Classroom (Jensen & Parsons, 1959).

of the S → G type, they mentioned those concerned with the effects of classrooms of differing group structure (teacher-centered, pupil-centered, and group-centered) on instructional outcomes (G variables).

The Altman-McGrath Paradigm for Small Group Research

A "conceptual framework for the integration of small group research information" has been developed by Altman and McGrath (1959). Their work entailed two steps: organizing the information into classes and relating the classes of information to one another. Their unit of classification was the single empirical relationship between two (or more) variables. A research relationship is a statement that $Y = (f)X$, i.e., that the variable Y is some function of, or is dependent upon, the variable X. Such statements are inferred from statements of statistical covariation between indices of the variables. Each such statement of statistical covariation represents a unit relationship in the classification system.

Normally, indices are composites of several items of empirical data. An item of data, which is defined as a single recorded response or judgment about an entity, is a direct abstraction from "reality" based on empirical observation. Indices differ from one another in terms of the classes of data items of which they are composed, and in terms of the ways in which those data items are combined . . . . information contained in each empirical research relationship will be classified at each of three levels:

(1) [The data level—] Classes of data items which form the basis for the indices, X' and Y', of the relationship.

(2) [The index level—] Types of (arithmetic) operations by which data items are combined to form indices X′ and Y′.

(3) [The relationship level—] The direction, degree and form of the statistical covariation between X′ and Y′ (Altman & McGrath, 1959, p. 6).

A syntactical rather than substantive basis of classification is used. That is, the classifications are based on the formal properties (such as whether the data *describe* or, rather, *evaluate* the entity being judged; or whether the data are about a *static* entity or an *action*). This basis should be contrasted with content properties (such as attitudes, personality characteristics, group structure measures, etc.).

How can research relationships and their component parts—after being classified at the data, index, and relationship levels—be related to one another? The basic ordering principle is the concept of "span," defined as the number of classification differences between the two indices involved in that relationship: ". . . the more similar two indices are to one another, the higher their statistical covariation is likely to be" (Altman & McGrath, 1959, p. 8). The span, or difference, between two indices is measured in terms of the number of classification dimensions on which the two indices are classified differently from one another. "The span of relationships can range from zero (both indices being of the same index class) to k (the two indices differing on *all* of the classification dimensions ...)" (p. 9). More refined classification is obtainable by weighting differences on some dimensions.

Let us now examine more closely the various Altman-McGrath classification schemes.

The classification of data. An item of data, defined as a single recorded response or judgment, can be classified in terms of five fundamental properties, or syntactical parameters, as outlined in Fig. 8:

(1) Object, or the referent of the recorded response or judgment;

(2) Mode, or the class of object property being judged;

(3) Judgment task, or the type of response or judgment made about the object;

(4) Source, or the person or instrument recording the response or judgment;

(5) Viewpoint, or the frame of reference from which the judgment is made.

Thus, the five syntactical parameters of data deal with five questions for each item of data: Who (Source) responds in what form (Judgment Task) about what kind of property (Mode) of what entity (Object) from what or whose frame of reference (Viewpoint)? As an illustration of these parameters, the authors cite a measure of "Liking for the group," based on a questionnaire which asks each member to express his attitudes toward the group as a whole. In this instance, a member (Source) evaluates (Judgment Task) a static characteristic (Mode) of his group (Object) from his subjective frame of reference (Viewpoint). Similarly, another variable in this illustration is a measure of member participation in which an investigator (Source) describes (Judgment Task) an action (Mode) characteristic of group members (Object) from an objective frame of reference (Viewpoint).

Objects may be members (member-self or member-other), groups, or surrounds, which are entities or events external to the unit or group and may consist of individuals, groups, or nonhuman aspects of the surrounds.

Modes may be static or action properties of the object; the former provide a summary up to a specified point in time, while the latter occur during a temporal interval.

Judgment Tasks may require descriptions, i.e., specifying the amount of a property possessed by an object, or evaluations, i.e., specifying the distance between an object and some standard. Judgment tasks may also be irrelative or relative to other objects of the same class. Further, irrelative evaluations can be either monotonic or nonmonotonic with respect to the attribute continuum. A monotonic relationship between a preference and attribute continuum occurs when the standard is at one *end* of the attribute continuum, while a nonmonotonic relationship occurs

Parameter 1. Object: the referent of the recorded response or judgment
    a. *Member:* a member of a group
        (1) Member-self: a member responding about himself
        (2) Member-other: a member responding about some other group member
    b. *Group:* the whole unit
    c. *Surround:* entities or events external to that unit
        (1) Individuals
        (2) Groups
        (3) Nonhuman aspects
Parameter 2. Mode: aspect or property of the object being judged
    a. *Static property:* one aspect, as an entity, summarized up to a specified point in time
    b. *Action:* a dynamic property, or an event that occurs during a temporal interval, noncumulative in time
Parameter 3. Task: the type of response or judgment made about an object
    a. *Description:* specifying the amount of a property possessed by the object
        (1) Relative: in terms relative to other objects of the same class
        (2) Irrelative: in absolute terms
    b. *Evaluation:* specifying the distance or discrepancy between the object and some standard with respect to a property
        (1) Relative
        (2) Irrelative
            (a) Monotonic: as to relationship between preference and attribute continuum
            (b) Nonmonotonic: as to relationship between preference and attribute continuum
Parameter 4. Source: the person or instrument recording the response or judgment
    a. *Member*
    b. *Group*
    c. *Investigator:* the individual conducting the experiment
    d. *Investigator Surrogate:* an individual who is not a group member but is acting for the investigator
    e. *Investigator Instrument:* an objective recording device
Parameter 5. Viewpoint: frame of reference from which the judgment is made
    a. *Member-Self:* subjective
    b. *Member-Other:* projective
    c. *Group:* from the viewpoint of the referent group
    d. *Surround:* from the viewpoint of a person or group external to the referent group

Fig. 8. The Altman-McGrath Paradigm for the Classification of Data in Small Group Research (After Altman & McGrath, 1959).

when the standard is not at one end of the attribute continuum.

Sources may be persons or instruments that record the responses or judgments. In small group research, sources may be members, groups, investigators, investigator surrogates, or investigator instruments.

Viewpoints may be judgments of objects from the member-self, member-other, group, or surround points of view, or frames of reference. When an investigator or investigator-surrogate acts as source, only the objective category of the viewpoint parameter can apply.

The classification of indexing operations. Outlined in Fig. 9, this classification refers to the ways in which data items (representing some configuration of Object, Mode, Task, Source, and Viewpoint) are combined by one or more arithmetic operations. Indices may be based on items of the same or of different data classes. The two basic types of indexing operations are *summation* and *discrepancy*. When data items are summed, the resulting

Indexing Operation 1. Summation: arithmetic operations which have as their logical basis the addition of units, and which yield a representative or total estimate (e.g., frequency of occurrence, measures of central tendency, etc.)

Indexing Operation 2. Discrepancy: procedures which yield comparisons among items (e.g., subtraction, estimates of scatter, etc.)

Fig. 9.   The Altman-McGrath Classification of Indexing Operations (After Altman & McGrath, 1959).

index, such as a total score for an individual or the mean of a group, characterizes individual data items or persons; when data items are subjected to some discrepancy operation, such as computing a variance or scatter, the resulting index characterizes the combination of, or relationship between, those items or group members.

The classification of relational terms. Relational terms express the presence, direction, degree, and form of empirical covariations between agent and resultant indices. As outlined in Fig. 10, a statement of the results of a specific statistical test has three parts: the type of statistical test used, e.g., r, chi square, t, or F; the direction and degree of association between the two indices as indicated by the test, e.g., $r = .65$, $F = 3.5$; and a statement of the statistical probability that the obtained relationship is just a chance relationship, e.g., $p < .01$.

The classification of relationships. To classify research relationships, they are put into a matrix in which each resultant index forms a column, each agent index provides a row, and each measure of statistical relationship between the two indices is an entry in the corresponding cell. Each index is listed as both a row and a column, since the agent-resultant classification refers to its functional use in a particular relationship. Empty cells indicate gaps in knowledge, while cells with

many statistically significant relationships indicate well-established empirical findings.

In a later summary of this program, McGrath reported:

The classification system was applied to approximately 250 small group research studies, yielding a detailed set of coded information on nearly 12,000 research relationships contained in those studies. . . . Results of these studies clearly supported the "validity" of the classification system as a means for the systematic ordering of small group research information (McGrath, 1962, pp. 1–3).

Clearly, this paradigm seems adaptable to research on teaching. A similarly massive classification, bibliographic, annotative, cataloging, and coding enterprise in the field of research on teaching could also yield the "systematic ordering of information" which is now claimed for small group research. Such an ordering would indeed not only extract knowledge from the literature more effectively; it would provide that guidance toward fruitful research which is the function of good paradigms.

"CRITERION-OF-EFFECTIVENESS" PARADIGMS

Having considered the nature and uses of paradigms and having examined an illustrative array of paradigms in other fields, we

1. Type of Statistical Test
    a. Tests of association, correlation, or covariation between continuous or discrete indices (e.g., correlation coefficients, chi-square tests)
    b. Tests of difference between two or more subsamples of the data (e.g., t tests, F tests)
2. Degree, Direction, and Form of Association
    a. Degree: 0 to ± 1 (yielded by tests of Type a only)
    b. Direction: $+$ or $-$ (yielded by tests of Type a and b)
    c. Form: rectilinear or curvilinear (yielded by tests of Type a only)
3. Statistical Probability of Association

Fig. 10.   The Altman-McGrath Classification of the Relational Term (After Altman & McGrath, 1959).

come now to our central concern: paradigms for research on teaching. Our effort here has little precedent; there is no literature that goes openly by the name we have adopted for this chapter. Yet we shall not be at a loss for references. Like Molière's bourgeois gentleman, who had been speaking prose all his life without knowing it, research on teaching has inescapably had its paradigms. We shall first examine the kind of paradigm that has overwhelmingly dominated such research: what we call "criterion-of-effectiveness" paradigms. Then we shall turn to a variety of other paradigms that do *not* concern themselves, first and last, with the effectiveness of teachers.

If we ask Anyman, "Why do research on teaching?" his answer is likely to be: "To discover what makes a good teacher." He can easily elaborate on his reply. We need such research in order better to select candidates for teacher training, to design teacher education programs, to provide a basis for teacher certification, to make possible better hiring and promotion policies, to enlighten the supervisors of teachers in service. There is no lack of practical justification for research on the questions of how teacher effectiveness can be measured, predicted, and improved.

Not only the layman has given this answer. Concern with teacher effectiveness has also held almost complete dominion over the conceptions that most research workers have brought to the field of teaching. The major bibliographies, reviews, and summaries of research on teaching (e.g., Barr, 1948; Barr, et al., 1961; Castetter, Standlee, & Fattu, 1954; Domas & Tiedeman, 1950; Mitzel, 1960; Morsh & Wilder, 1954; Ryans, 1960b; Tomlinson, 1955a, 1955b; Watters, 1954) have reflected this concern with the unfailing inclusion in their titles of such terms as "effectiveness," "competence," "evaluation," and "appraisal."

As soon as the idea of effectiveness enters the research, the question of a criterion of effectiveness is raised. The paradigm has then taken the following form: Identify or select a criterion (or a set of criteria) of teacher effectiveness. This criterion then becomes the dependent variable. The research task is then (1) to measure this criterion, (2) to measure potential correlates of this criterion, and (3) to determine the actual correlations between the criterion and its potential correlates. In short, variables in research on teaching conducted according to the "criterion-of-effectiveness" paradigm have typically been placed in two categories: criterion variables and potential correlates. Figure 11 schematizes this paradigm in its simplest form. It is noteworthy that the two articles on "Teacher Effectiveness" in the third edition of the *Encyclopedia of Educational Research* were organized in just this way: "Criteria of teacher effectiveness" (Mitzel, 1960) and "Prediction of teacher effectiveness" (Ryans, 1960b).

Often, for the sake of convenience in exploratory work, the measures of both potential correlates and criteria have been made at about the same time. The resulting correlations are then considered to reflect the "concurrent validity" of the potential correlates. Sometimes the potential correlates have been measured some months or years prior to the measurement of the criterion variable. In such research, the correlations are considered to indicate the "predictive validity" of the potential correlates.

The correlations between other variables and criterion variables need not be simple "zero-order" ones. Partial and multiple correlations may be computed between sets of two or more predictor variables and a criterion variable. Factor analysis (e.g., Schmid,

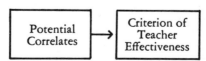

Fig. 11.   The Criterion-of-Effectiveness Paradigm for Research on Teaching.

1961) may be applied to the intercorrelations of whole batteries of variables, consisting of sets of predictor and criterion variables. But, for our present concerns, these are merely elaborations of the same basic criterion-of-effectiveness paradigm.

The reader familiar with personnel selection research will recognize the criterion-of-effectiveness paradigm as indigenous to that field. Whether the purpose has been to select college students or clerical workers, clinical psychologists or airplane pilots, the same paradigm has prevailed: Get a criterion and then find its predictors. The widespread use and practical value of such research has been characterized (Cronbach, 1949, p. 3) as an "outstanding achievement of the social sciences in recent decades." It is easy to understand the devotion to this paradigm—so successful in so many realms—on the part of researchers on teaching.

Types of Criteria of Effectiveness

In research on teaching, as in its other fields of application, the criterion-of-effectiveness paradigm has taken special forms. Apart from the whole question of what potential correlates to try, much analysis has been devoted to the criterion question itself. We turn now to paradigms that have been developed for the criterion problem.

The Wisconsin studies. Perhaps the most extended employment of the criterion-of-effectiveness paradigm was that of Barr, who conducted and led studies of this kind at the University of Wisconsin over several decades (Barr, et al., 1961). As shown in Table 1, Beecher (1961) listed seven categories of criteria of teacher effectiveness used in the Wisconsin studies along with the frequencies with which they were used.

Beecher also presented a table showing the findings on 104 of the 182 "data-gathering devices," or potential correlates, used in the Wisconsin studies. For each correlate, he gave the reliability (as estimated by methods unspecified in the table) and validity in terms of correlation with one of the forego-

TABLE 1

CRITERIA AND THEIR FREQUENCY OF USE IN THE WISCONSIN STUDIES[a]

Criterion	Frequency
I. In-service Rating	
a. By the superintendent	9
b. By the principal	24
c. By other supervisory officials	51
d. By teacher educators	20
e. By departmental personnel in areas of specialization	4
f. By state departmental personnel	11
g. Self rating	11
II. Peer Rating	6
III. Pupil Gain Score	70
IV. Pupil Rating	16
V. Composite of Test Scores from Tests Thought to Measure Teaching Effectiveness	14
VI. Practice Teaching Grades	13
VII. Combination or Composites of Some or All of the Above Criteria	83
Total	332

[a] After Beecher, 1961, pp. 30–31.

ing types of criteria or in terms of mean pupil gain on a measure of achievement. Beecher starred 74 of the 104 measures as having correlated .36 or more with the indicated criteria. In this sense, at least, the Wisconsin studies brought forth positive results. The compendium of findings provided by Beecher impressively displays the fruits of the criterion-of-effectiveness paradigm. This approach to research, in the Wisconsin program alone, apart from many other studies in which it has been used, has not lacked thorough exploitation. Any shortcomings in its scientific and practical yield cannot be attributed to a failure to give it a try.

The Domas-Tiedeman categories. A further paradigm for criteria of teacher effectiveness may be derived from what is implicit in the index of the 1,000-item annotated bibliography prepared by Domas and Tiedeman (1950). Upon analysis, this paradigm turns out to depend primarily on the following distinctions:

1. Between (a) *in-service* and (b) *in-training* teachers;

2. Between criteria based on (a) *pupil achievement*, (b) *judgments* by administrators, teachers themselves, fellow teachers, student teachers, pupils, or laypersons, and (c) *performance on tests* of "teaching ability," etc.;

3. Between pupil achievement criteria (a) "*objectively*" observed and (b) those "*subjectively*" evaluated by administrators or teachers.

Figure 12 shows an organization chart of criteria based on these distinctions. It will be noted that these criteria embody different points on the "ultimacy" and "levels" continua to be described below. The letters and numbers in the boxes in Fig. 12 are those used in the Domas-Tiedeman index.

The "Ultimacy" of Criteria of Teacher Effectiveness

The concept of "criterion of teacher effectiveness" connotes educational or social values of some kind. By teacher "effectiveness" is usually meant the teacher's effect on the realization of some value. Usually, the value takes the form of some educational objective, defined in terms of desired pupil behaviors, abilities, habits, or characteristics. Hence, the ultimate criterion of a teacher's effectiveness is usually considered to be his effect on his pupils' achievement of such objectives. The terms *pupil gain* and *pupil growth* are used to refer to this kind of ultimate criterion. Differences between measures of pupil achievement before and after coming under a teacher's influence have been used to define such gain operationally, and in Chapter 8 some attention is given to the technicalities of using such measures. Ackerman (1954) and Mitzel and Gross (1956) have reviewed studies in which pupil gain criteria of teacher effectiveness have been used.

Many difficulties, both conceptual and practical, beset the use of pupil gain criteria for either research or administrative purposes. These difficulties have been elaborated elsewhere (e.g., Mitzel, 1960; Ryans, 1960a, pp. 44–45). Here we note merely that they have led to the employment in much research of criteria that are not "ultimate." It was the realization that other criteria are seldom entirely escapable in research based on the criterion-of-effectiveness paradigm that led the Committee on the Criteria of Teacher Effectiveness (American Educational Research

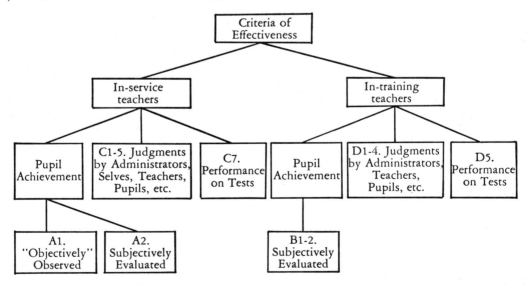

Fig. 12.   Paradigm of Criteria of Teacher Effectiveness Derived from Classification of Annotations by Domas and Tiedeman (1950, pp. 214–215).

Association, 1952) to formulate an ultimacy paradigm for such criteria. This paradigm arranged criteria of teacher effectiveness on a continuum descending from the "ultimate" to the "proximate." At the top of the hierarchy of "ultimacy" might be such a criterion as "the teacher's effect on his pupils' achievement and happiness in life." Next might come "the teacher's effect on his pupils' achievement in subsequent schooling." Third might be "the teacher's effect on his pupils' achievement of current educational objectives." Much lower in the scale would be "parents' satisfaction with the teacher," "teacher's grades in student teaching courses," and "teacher's score on an intelligence test." Figure 13 shows an adaptation of this paradigm.

By this paradigm, each criterion depended for its validity on its correlation, or better, its functional relationship, with criteria higher on the continuum. Much criticism of research on teaching has been based on the critic's dissatisfaction with the position of someone else's criterion on this continuum. The rank of some of these criteria has been hotly argued, as one might expect. For example, some educators have held that the superintendent's satisfaction with the teacher made the big difference in a teacher's career; therefore this criterion should be higher on the scale, and research should be directed toward

the prediction of it. Others have held that, regardless of its "real-life" importance to teachers, this criterion has been shown to be uncorrelated with pupil gain and hence should be disregarded.

"Career Levels" and Criteria of Effectiveness

The list of criteria shown in Fig. 13 applies primarily to teachers already employed. Yet there are other stages of the teacher's career at which criteria are needed in research on teaching by the criterion paradigm. In its second report, the Committee on the Criteria of Teacher Effectiveness (American Educational Research Association, 1953) presented a paradigm of criteria organized on the basis of the different levels, or stages, in the progression from candidate for teacher training to on-the-job operation as a full-fledged teacher. Figure 14 shows this paradigm.

Four different levels, or stages, of a teacher's career were identified: (1) the prospective teacher-in-training; (2) the student in a teacher education program; (3) the student just completing teacher training; and (4) the teacher on the job. Decisions concerning persons at each of these levels take different forms. At Level 1, we make decisions concerning applicants for admission to teacher education programs, or we attempt

ULTIMATE CRITERION

↑ Teachers' effect on:
    pupils' achievement and success in life
    pupils' achievement in subsequent schooling
    pupils' achievement of current educational objectives
    pupils' satisfaction with the teacher
    parents' satisfaction with the teacher
    superintendents' satisfaction with the teacher
Teachers' "values" or evaluative attitudes
Teachers' knowledge of educational psychology and mental hygiene
Teachers' emotional and social adjustment
Teachers' knowledge of methods of curriculum construction
Teachers' knowledge of the subject matter
Teachers' interest in the subject matter
Teachers' grades in practice teaching courses
Teachers' grades in education courses
Teachers' intelligence

Fig. 13.   The Hierarchy of Criteria According to "Ultimacy" (After American Educational Research Association, 1952, pp. 243–244).

ULTIMATE CRITERIA

Changes in pupils (while in school, or upon completion of formal school, or some years later)

IN-SERVICE PREDICTORS

(Teachers' behaviors and characteristics)

[Need for in-service predictors: hiring teachers; granting tenure; selection for special consideration]

IN-TRAINING PREDICTORS

(Behaviors and characteristics in training, achievement in student teaching and professional education)

[Need for in-training predictors: hiring teachers, certification of teachers]

PRE-TRAINING PREDICTORS

(Behavior and characteristics prior to training, achievement in pre-training courses, knowledge, skills, attitudes)

[Need for pre-training predictors: admission to teacher education program; retention in the program, in-training guidance; planning; conduct, and revision of teacher education programs]

Fig. 14. Schematic Representation of Career Levels of Criteria and Their Use (After American Educational Research Association, 1953, p. 649).

---

to provide guidance for high school graduates as to the suitability of teaching as a vocation for them. At Level 2, we make decisions concerning programs for preparing teachers on the basis of evidence or assumptions concerning the hoped-for eventual effects of these programs on the teachers' subsequent effects on pupils; or, we make decisions concerning the guidance of students who are in teacher education programs. At Level 3, decisions as to the certification of teachers or the selection of teachers for jobs from among graduates of teacher education programs are in order.

At Level 4, decisions are made as to the granting of tenure to teachers or the selection of teachers from among teachers who have taught, either for new positions or for special assignments or special treatments, such as salary increases. Obviously, the "predictors" at higher levels can serve as criteria for the predictors at lower levels.

A Refinement of the Criterion-of-

Effectiveness Paradigm

As presented thus far, the effectiveness paradigm has only two classes of variables: predictors and criteria. The "ultimacy" and "levels" paradigms for criteria imply no necessary change on this simple picture. At whatever points on the ultimacy or levels continua the criteria may be chosen, the research worker proceeds with only these two kinds of variables in his paradigm. As Mitzel (1957) put it, ". . . during the past 50 years it has been characteristic of the research on teacher effectiveness to jump directly from predictor variables to the criterion variables . . ." (p. 2).

Research by this paradigm has been abundant; hundreds of studies, yielding thousands of correlation coefficients, have been made. In the large, these studies have yielded disappointing results: correlations that are nonsignificant, inconsistent from one study to the next, and usually lacking in psychological and educational meaning.

Under these circumstances, it was to be expected that research workers would begin to seek refinements in the simple, but relatively fruitless, effectiveness paradigm. One such attempt at refinement, by Mitzel (1957), is presented here to illustrate the lines along which such efforts have been made. This paradigm, illustrated in Fig. 15, contains four types of variables, or "classifications of information." These classifications were identified by Mitzel as necessary concerns of "any investigator who seeks fundamental knowledge in the general research area that is frequently called 'teacher effectiveness' . . ." (p. 1):

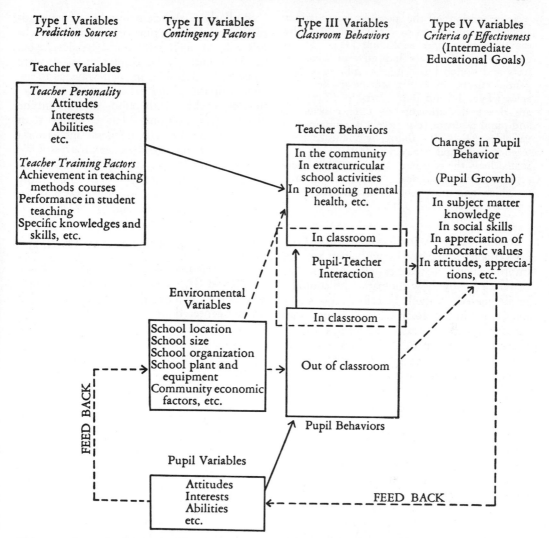

Fig. 15. Generalized Schema for Research in Teacher Effectiveness (Mitzel, 1957, p. 5).

Type I. Human characteristics on which teachers differ and which can be hypothesized to account, in part, for differences in teacher effectiveness.

Type II. Contingency factors which modify and influence the whole complex of behaviors that enter into the educational process. "If Type II variables play a commanding role in the achievement of educational objectives, then we will be required to replicate studies of teacher effectiveness in a great many different situations . . . ."

Type III. Classroom behaviors of teachers and pupils.

Type IV. Criteria or standards, consisting of "intermediate educational goals," i.e., the measurable outcomes at the end of a period of instruction as distinguished from "the ultimate criterion which might be phrased as 'a better world in which to live.' "

Some notion of the possible interrelations among the four types of variables is shown by the connecting lines in Figure [15]. . . . In general, solid lines are indicative of direct effects and dotted lines suggest indirect or tangential effects. In such a scheme teacher variables (Type I) and pupil variables (Type II) are direct determinants of teacher behavior and pupil behavior respectively. Environmental variables (Type II) indirectly influence both teacher and pupil behaviors. In the view presented here, the complex of pupil-teacher interactions in the classroom is the primary source to which one must look to account for pupil growth (Mitzel, 1957, p. 1).

It is through the intercession of his Type III variables that Mitzel saw the best hope of improvement in teacher effectiveness research. To show how the paradigm could be implemented, Mitzel described the study diagramed in Fig. 16, in which various actual measures, or operational definitions, of the variables named in Fig. 15 are entered. The study thus formulated was subsequently published (Medley & Mitzel, 1959).

"Micro-criteria" of Effectiveness

One solution within the "criterion-of-effectiveness" approach may be the development of the notion of "micro-effectiveness." Rather than seek criteria for the over-all effectiveness of teachers in the many, varied facets of their roles, we may have better success with criteria of effectiveness in small, specifically defined aspects of the role. Many scientific problems have eventually been solved by being analyzed into smaller problems, whose variables were less complex.

Physicists did not attempt to predict all aspects of the undulating motion of a feather as it fell in an everyday breeze. They refined the problem into the prediction of the fall of a frictionless body in a vacuum and derived laws for this phenomenon. Such laws, combined with other laws applying to similarly pure situations, can account for the vagaries of the motion of actual objects under field conditions.

Similarly, a sufficient number of laws applying to relatively pure aspects of the teacher's role, if such laws could be developed, might eventually be combined, if it were considered desirable, in such ways as to account for the actual behavior and effectiveness of teachers with pupils under genuine classroom conditions. Hence, rather than studies of teacher effectiveness, and criteria therefor, we may make better progress if we develop "micro-criteria" of effectiveness. At the very least, such an approach would imply that effectiveness be sharply specified in terms of subject matter and grade level.

TEACHING PROCESS PARADIGMS

The foregoing paradigm, with its provision for "Type III," or classroom behavior, variables, provides a transition to paradigms that are not centered on "criteria of teacher effectiveness." Let us first at least mention the reasons for turning away from "effects on pupil achievement" as a criterion: (1) to avoid the inevitable confounding of such criteria with scientifically insoluble questions of values, i.e., to steer clear of the choice described by Levin (1954) as follows: ". . . the ultimate description of the 'good' teacher involves a choice which ideally uses research results but cannot be exclusively determined by them. 'Science can tell us how to get there but not where to go' " (p. 99); (2) to obtain variables of lesser complexity; (3) to circumvent the difficulties of measuring socially desirable but elusive outcomes of education; and (4) to tie research more cleanly to variables that could be attributed to teachers and teaching as against home, community, and pupils' heredity. For all these reasons, research workers have looked away from criteria involved with effectiveness, defined as teachers' effects on pupils' achievement of educational objectives.

Research workers (e.g., Ryans, 1960a, pp. 26–56) continued to use the term *criterion,* but not with the commitment to *effectiveness.* In this sense, *criterion* becomes synonymous with *dependent variable.* Other writers

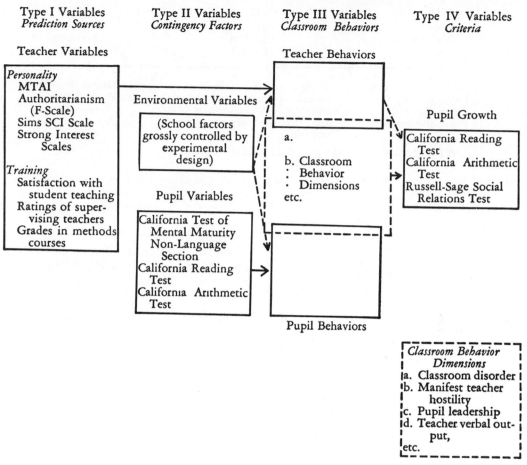

Type I Variables *Prediction Sources*	Type II Variables *Contingency Factors*	Type III Variables *Classroom Behaviors*	Type IV Variables *Criteria*

Teacher Variables

Personality
MTAI
Authoritarianism
(F-Scale)
Sims SCI Scale
Strong Interest
Scales

Training
Satisfaction with
student teaching
Ratings of super-
vising teachers
Grades in methods
courses

Environmental Variables

(School factors
grossly controlled by
experimental
design)

Pupil Variables

California Test of
Mental Maturity
Non-Language
Section
California Reading
Test
California Arithmetic
Test

Teacher Behaviors

a.

b. Classroom
: Behavior
· Dimensions
etc.

Pupil Behaviors

Pupil Growth

California Reading
Test
California Arithmetic
Test
Russell-Sage Social
Relations Test

*Classroom Behavior
Dimensions*
a. Classroom disorder
b. Manifest teacher
hostility
c. Pupil leadership
d. Teacher verbal out-
put,
etc.

Fig. 16. Adaptation of Fig. 15 Concepts in Division of Teacher Education Assessment Program (Mitzel, 1957, p. 6).

(e.g., Mitzel, 1960, p. 1483) used the term *process criteria,* or "aspects of teacher and student behavior which are believed to be worthwhile in their own right," and these were the Type III variables which were included in Mitzel's paradigm, described above. Such process criteria would all fall lower than effects on pupils in the scale of ultimacy described above.

If process variables are to be sought, what orientations can guide the search? Here we come into contact with paradigms of teaching behavior.

Smith's Paradigm

Smith (1960) has offered a paradigm, "which draws upon the psychological paradigm developed by Tolman . . ." (p. 233). As shown in Fig. 17, he classified all the variables involved in and related to teaching into three categories: independent (teaching actions), intervening (learning), and dependent (pupil actions) variables.

In the model, the arrows indicate the direction of causal influences. The teacher's actions are

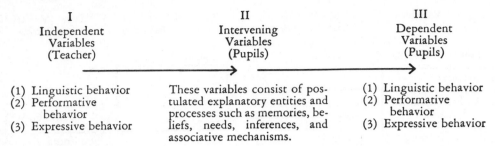

I	II	III
Independent Variables (Teacher)	Intervening Variables (Pupils)	Dependent Variables (Pupils)

(1) Linguistic behavior
(2) Performative
    behavior
(3) Expressive behavior

These variables consist of postulated explanatory entities and processes such as memories, beliefs, needs, inferences, and associative mechanisms.

(1) Linguistic behavior
(2) Performative
    behavior
(3) Expressive behavior

Fig. 17.   A Pedagogical Model (Smith, 1960, p. 234).

followed by postulated states, events, or processes in the pupil and are represented by the intervening variables. Then, as a result of these variables, the pupil behaves in one or more of the ways indicated in the dependent variables column. The teacher can see the pupil's behavior, but he cannot see the postulated events and processes; that is, he cannot observe interests, motives, needs, beliefs, and the like. But these psychological entities and processes are present by implication in the behavior of the pupil. The teacher may therefore infer these psychological factors from the pupil's behavior, and in some instances he actually does infer them, although he may not be aware that he is doing so. Thus the teacher often infers from the reactions of the pupil that he is interested, or that he wants to do so and so, or the contrary (Smith, 1960, p. 234).

To depict the "ebb and flow" of teaching, or the "cycle of giving and taking instruction," Smith extended the model to that shown in Fig. 18,

saying, and so on, as inferred from the teacher's behavior; and R_p is the reaction of the pupil to the actions of the teacher (Smith, 1960, p. 235).

The double vertical lines in Fig. 18 mark off the teaching cycles. The single vertical lines within each cycle mark off "the acts of teaching" from "the acts of taking instruction," the latter of which Smith sharply distinguishes from "learning," since learning may or may not be taking place. On the basis of descriptive studies of classroom teaching by means of analyses of tape recordings of classroom discourse (Meux & Smith, 1961), Smith has stated that "our symbolic schema and verbal performances in the classroom are isomorphic" (1960, p. 235).

Ryans' Paradigms

Lewin's formula for explaining behavior was $B = F(P, E)$, or "behavior is a function

$$\|P_t{\rightarrow}D_t{\rightarrow}R_t|{\rightarrow}P_p{\rightarrow}D_p{\rightarrow}R_p\|{\rightarrow}P_t{\rightarrow}D_t{\rightarrow}R_t|{\rightarrow}P_p{\rightarrow}D_p{\rightarrow}R_p\|$$
$$\rightarrow P_t{\rightarrow}D_t{\rightarrow}R_t|{\rightarrow}P_p{\rightarrow}D_p{\rightarrow}R_p\| \ldots {\rightarrow}\text{achievement,}$$

Fig. 18.   Paradigm of a Series of Teaching Cycles (Smith, 1960, p. 235).

where P_t is the teacher's perception of the pupil's behavior; D_t is the teacher's diagnosis of the pupil's state of interest, readiness, knowledge, and the like, made by inference from the behavior of the pupil; and R_t is the action taken by the teacher in light of his diagnosis; and where P_p is the pupil's perception of the teacher's behavior; D_p is the pupil's diagnosis of the teacher's state of interest, what he is

(F) of the person (P) and of his environment $(E) \ldots$" (Lewin, 1946, p. 791). Ryans (1960a) has applied this formula to the development of a "paradigm illustrating the integration of teacher behavior," shown in Fig. 19. In this paradigm, the boxes on the left-hand side correspond to Lewin's P variables; those on the right-hand side, to Lew-

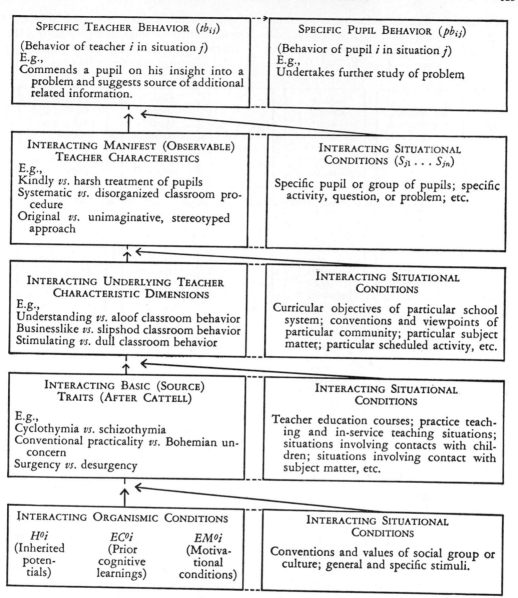

Fig. 19. Paradigm Illustrating the Integration of Teacher Behavior (Adapted from Ryans, 1960a, p. 18).

in's E variables. Ascending, one goes from the most general features, through different levels of generality, to the most specific teacher and pupil behaviors at the top. The dotted arrows connecting the right- and left-hand boxes denote interaction between them. The paradigm shows the various levels of abstraction at which a research worker may operate.

In a second paradigm, stemming from his

"Postulate A: Teacher behavior is social behavior," Ryans (1960a, p. 16) adapted the
schema of "dyadic units" set forth by Sears
(1951), as shown in Figs. 20 and 21. Sears
sonal perception data, Cronbach sharpened
the definition of interaction by noting that
"interpretations dealing with interactions
can be advanced meaningfully only after the

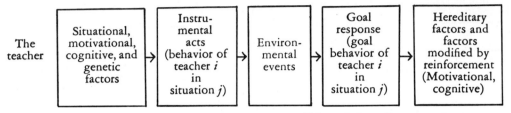

Fig. 20.   The Monadic Instigation, Action Sequence (Adapted from Ryans, 1960a, p. 20, and Sears, 1951).

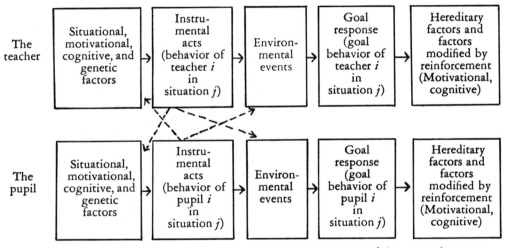

Fig. 21.   The Dyadic Sequence (Adapted from Ryans, 1960a, p. 20, and Sears, 1951).

had shown how a typical learning-theory
model might be expanded to embrace interaction between two persons, each of whose
instrumental acts would influence the factors
antecedent to the other's instrumental acts
and also the consequent environmental
events of the other. In such interaction, by
definition, an individual's behavior can no
longer be accounted for by what we know
about him alone, i.e., his personality and environment, on the one hand, and the consequences of his own acts, on the other; the
acts of another person now also shape these
antecedents and consequences of his behavior.

Applying Sears's conception to interper-
simpler main effects associated with the perceiver or the object of perception have been
given separate consideration" (1958, p. 355).
In teacher-pupil interaction, this caution
means that we should refer to interactional
explanations only after we have exhausted
all the explanatory power of individual
teacher and pupil personality-environment
combinations. An authoritarian teacher's behavior may thus differ when he has "inner-
directed" pupils from what it will be when
they are "other-directed," and the pupils' behavior and learning may also vary according
to the authoritarianism of their teacher. The
dyadic paradigm calls attention to these pos-

sibilities, and research on social interaction in the classroom has been undertaken in pursuance of them (see Chapter 13).

The Stone-Leavitt Paradigm

Still another social interaction paradigm has been prepared by Stone and Leavitt.[4] This analysis suggests that any "interact" between a teacher and a pupil consists of the following steps:

1. *Pupil provides stimuli.* Pupils enter the teacher's environment as sources of stimuli.
2. *Teacher selects stimuli.* The teacher is influenced by a sample of these stimuli. This sample, determined by the teacher's implicit personality theory . . ., by her previous formulation of the pupil's personality, and by her purposes in interacting with the pupil, constitutes the extrinsic basis (input) for the teacher's perception of the pupil.
3. *Teacher perceives pupil.* This input is organized, by the implicit personality theory of the teacher, into a formulation (or reformulation) of the pupil's characteristics and behavior.
4. *Teacher adopts ideal action pattern.* This formulation interacts with the teacher's self-concept and definition of her role so as to result in her ideal pattern of action.
5. *Teacher adopts proposed action pattern.* The teacher's proposed pattern of action is modified by her estimation of the situation (facilities, resources, attitudes of others) so as to result in her proposed pattern of action.
6. *Teacher carries out actual action pattern.* The teacher's proposed pattern of action interacts with the teacher's abilities and the actual situation so as to result in the actual pattern of action.
7. *Teacher provides stimuli.* The teacher's actual pattern of action impinges on the pupil as a source of stimuli.
8. *Pupil selects stimuli.* The pupil is influenced, consciously and unconsciously, by a sample of these stimuli. This sample of stimuli constitutes information (input) which provides the extrinsic basis for the

pupil's perception of the teacher.
9. *Pupil perceives teacher.* This input is organized by the implicit personality theory of the pupil into a perception of the teacher's characteristics and behavior.
10. *Pupil adopts ideal action pattern.* This formulation interacts with the pupil's self-concept and definition of his role so as to result in his ideal pattern of action.
11. *Pupil adopts proposed action pattern.* The pupil's ideal pattern of action is modified by his estimation of the situation (attitudes of others) so as to result in his proposed pattern of action.
12. *Pupil carries out actual action pattern.* The pupil's proposed pattern of action interacts with the pupil's abilities and the actual situation so as to result in the pupil's actual pattern of action.
13. The pupil's actual pattern of action serves as a source of stimuli for the teacher.

In selecting a sample of these stimuli, the teacher may be influenced by a perceived connection between her own action and the pupil's action, *i.e.,* the pupil's action may be seen as "feedback." In any case, at this point the conceptualization of teacher-pupil interaction has come full circle and this specific "interact" is complete.

This process can be completed in a brief instant or can take a much longer time. It can refer to a "molecule" of interaction or to the summation of many such "molecules."

Research can be directed at any one of the phases of this process or at the relationship between any two of them.

Steps 1–7 may be regarded as a sequence of sensation-perception-thought-action on the part of the teacher; Steps 8–13, a similar sequence on the part of the pupil. This analysis is reminiscent of Smith's teaching cycle, but analyzes the behavior on each side more finely. Whether the analysis could be implemented, i.e., assigned operational definitions, is unknown in the absence so far of any attempt to do so. It seems, however, in the light of currently known techniques of observation and measurement, that formidable problems would arise in distinguishing between, say, Step 1 (Pupil provides stimuli) and Step 2 (Teacher selects stimuli), or between Step 2 and Step 3 (Teacher perceives pupil).

---

[4] G. C. Stone and G. S. Leavitt, A schematic analysis of teacher-pupil interaction. Personal communication, 1955.

Runkel's Paradigm

A final example, used by Runkel in his classes, is his "brief model for pupil-teacher interaction,"[5] the steps of which are

listed below, with references to Figs. 22 and 23.

1. The teacher brings to the classroom her own personal needs and goals developed during her *own personal history*. In combination with the particular classroom

[5] P. J. Runkel, A brief model for pupil-teacher interaction. Personal communication, 1958.

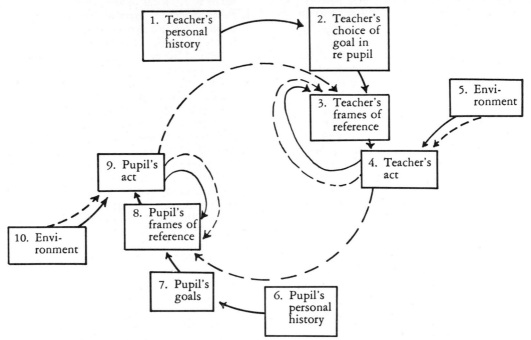

Solid lines represent intrapersonal communication via the nervous system, etc. Dashed lines represent interpersonal communication via vision, speech, etc.

Fig. 22.   A Brief Model for Pupil-Teacher Interaction (P. J. Runkel, personal communication, 1958).

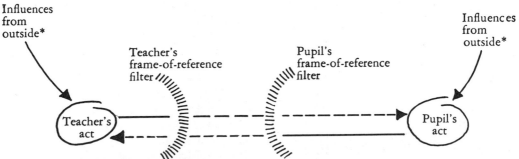

* Influences from outside the immediate interpersonal "system" such as the individual's personal history, the immediate environmental happenings, etc.

Fig. 23.   A Brief Model for Pupil-Teacher Interaction (P. J. Runkel, personal communication, 1958).

situation in which she finds herself, these lead to

2. the *teacher's choice of a goal* involving the pupil. She might want the pupil to learn how to add 3-digit numbers, to appreciate Rembrandt, to be a good boy, to know when Columbus discovered America, to strive valiantly in competitive athletics, etc.

3. The goal chosen by the teacher is circumscribed by her *frames of reference,* and so is the particular series of actions on which she embarks in order to approach the goal. These determinants lead to

4. *the teacher's act.* Examples would be telling the pupils to read Chapter III, sending a boy to the principal's office, explaining how to take square root, taking the class on a trip to the museum, etc. Aside from the influences already listed, however, the particular acts chosen are shaped by

5. the *environment* in which the acts are carried out. The speed of the bus affects the time spent at the museum; the size of the blackboard affects the explanation of square root; the noise of passing trucks affects the remarks made about Rembrandt; the admonitions concerning striving in sports are tempered to suit the respective sizes of the combatants, etc.

The part of the teacher's environment we wish particularly to scrutinize is the pupil. As the teacher chooses the particular actions which mark her path toward her goal, she will devote particular attention to the pupil who is involved in the goal. The pupil's act (Phase 9) therefore appears on the chart separately from other aspects of the teacher's environment (Phase 5). Similarly, the teacher's act (Phase 4) is charted separately from the rest of the pupil's environment (Phase 10).

6. Similarly, the *pupil's personal history*

7. helps determine the *pupil's goals* which he brings with him to the classroom or which he develops there. These, along with his perception of the teacher's act, must fit with a minimum degree of consistency the

8. *pupil's frames of reference.* Having assimilated these extrapersonal and intrapersonal influences, the pupil can now act.

9. The *pupil's act,* like that of the teacher, is also molded by the

10. *environment* in which it takes place.

And the pupil's act, in turn, becomes one of the determinants of the next act on the part of the teacher, after it has been interpreted by the teacher through her frames of reference.

We must also remember that the teacher observes herself acting, and so does the pupil. "Feedback" lines are therefore drawn on the chart from Phase 4 back to Phase 3, and likewise from Phase 9 back to Phase 8. This feedback can accelerate either positively or negatively the existing processes.

The large circle itself represents a feedback circuit, although it is indirect and not self-contained. (It contains "noise.") After the teacher acts (Phase 4), the act has some effect on the pupil (Phases 8 and 9). The pupil's act is in turn perceived by the teacher (via Phase 3), who may then modify her subsequent actions. But the "information" conveyed in this roundabout circuit may be altered in various ways by exterior influences (Phases 1, 2, 5, 6, 7, and 10) and by the intrapersonal feedback.

Common Elements in the Process Paradigms

The reader will by now have noted common elements in the various paradigms of teacher-pupil interaction. As Table 2 shows, it is possible to list the elements in these paradigms in rows cutting across the paradigms, so that each row contains roughly equivalent elements. Each paradigm can thus be seen to begin with (I) an element, or several elements, referring to perceptual and cognitive processes on the part of the teacher. The processes eventuate in (II) action elements on the teacher's part. The teacher's actions are followed by (III) perceptual and cognitive processes on the pupil's part, and these in turn lead to (IV) action elements on the pupil's side.

In one paradigm, i.e., Ryans', the elements of Type I, perceptual-cognitive, are represented by only one inclusive entry. In another paradigm, e.g., Smith's, this type of element is broken down into two parts, perception and

TABLE 2

COMMON ELEMENTS IN PARADIGMS OF TEACHER-PUPIL INTERACTION

Type of Element	Smith	Ryans	Stone-Leavitt	Runkel	Stolurow
I. Perceptual-Cognitive Elements, Teacher	Teacher's perception of pupil's behavior Teacher's diagnosis of pupil's state	Teacher's situational, motivational, cognitive, genetic factors	Pupil provides stimuli Teacher selects stimuli Teacher perceives pupil	Teacher's personal needs and goals, personal history Teacher's choice of a goal Teacher's frames of reference The teacher's environment	4. Comparator unit 6. Collator-recorder 8. Library unit 9. Program 10. Computer
II. Action Elements, Teacher	Teacher's action	Teacher's instrumental acts Teacher's environmental event Teacher's goal response Teacher's hereditary factors and factors modified by reinforcement	Teacher adopts ideal action pattern Teacher adopts proposed action pattern Teacher carries out actual action pattern	Teacher's act	1. Display unit 3. Pacing unit 7. Selector unit
III. Perceptual-Cognitive Elements, Pupil	Pupil's perception of teacher's behavior Pupil's diagnosis of teacher's state	Pupil's situational, motivational, cognitive, genetic factors	Teacher provides stimuli Pupil selects stimuli Pupil perceives teacher	Pupil's personal history Pupil's goals Pupil's frame of reference The pupil's environment	5. Knowledge of results, or feedback
IV. Action Elements, Pupil	Pupil's reaction to teacher's action	Pupil's instrumental acts Pupil's environmental event Pupil's goal response Pupil's hereditary factors and factors modified by reinforcement	Pupil adopts ideal action pattern Pupil adopts proposed action pattern Pupil carries out actual action pattern	Pupil's act	2. Response unit

diagnosis. Similarly, while Smith and Runkel have only one element for the teacher's action, Ryans' paradigm analyzes this rubric into four parts, consisting not only of the act but also of the teacher's subsequent environmental events, goal responses, and reinforcement-induced changes. For the same type of element, Stone and Leavitt have a three-part analysis consisting of ideal, proposed, and actual action patterns.

Despite differences in their terminology, fineness of breakdown of elements in the process, and methods of portraying interaction, all the paradigms have (1) a cyclical, repetitive quality and (2) an oscillatory character. In these paradigms, teacher-pupil interaction is seen, somewhat like tennis, to consist of action first on one side, then on the other. While one side is in action, the other is perceiving, anticipating, getting set.

But these paradigms neglect the fact that the roles of the two sides differ in teaching, if not in tennis. In tennis, each side is identically and competitively motivated, while in teaching, the motivations are, ideally at least, complementary and cooperative. Although each side gets feedback on its actions from the behavior of the other side, these processes are different for teachers and pupils, even if not for two tennis opponents. The paradigms also, in their symmetry, neglect the enormous differences in what is considered appropriate behavior for teachers and pupils. In their excessive generality, these interaction paradigms make teaching and "pupiling" look identical.

None of these models has come to grips with the complication that teachers typically deal with more than one pupil at a time. In classroom lecturing, of course, the pupil side must be "averaged" in some way by the teacher, who engages in most of the action, or overt behavior, shown in the paradigms. In classroom discussion, the pupil on the other side of the "net" from the teacher may change from volley to volley, and stable conceptions of the characteristics of the changing pupil may be hard to envisage.

Finally, let us note that the unit of interaction connoted by these paradigms is a "small" one, a single "interact," analogous to only one complete passage of the tennis ball back and forth across the net. In tennis, of course, significant strategies, like getting one's opponent out of position, or playing to his weak side, often consist of more than one exchange. And the strategy can seldom be described by mere addition, or some similarly simple combination, of several exchanges. Further, the significant outcomes, like winning games and sets, depend on several exchanges, although in this case simple addition of the exchanges may suffice to characterize the outcome. Just how interacts between teachers and pupils should be combined to characterize significant processes and outcomes in the classroom has not been dealt with in the foregoing paradigms. At the present stage of paradigm development, this gap does not seem to be an urgent one. When more experience has been gained in "operationalizing" (i.e., providing operational definitions for) the paradigms, the problem of combining interacts into educationally significant units will become more realistic.

A MACHINE PARADIGM

The design of teaching machines was originally guided by the characteristics and processes of human learners. It is conceivable that this approach can be reversed, i.e., that the design of research on human teachers can be guided by the characteristics of teaching machines. Such an attempt might well be made in accordance with the critical requirements of a teaching machine formulated by Stolurow (1961) and illustrated in Fig. 24. Stolurow's "adaptive teaching machine system" may thus be regarded as a paradigm for research on teaching.

1. The paradigm begins with a *display unit* which presents subject-matter information to the learner. In the machine, this might be done via pages, tapes, discs, slides, films, or recordings; the human teacher may use his voice, a textbook, or the blackboard. The presentation ends with a question or a cue to which the learner is asked to respond.

2. Next there is a *response unit* which receives and implements the learner's action, whether it be a recognition, a recall, a composed sentence, or whatever. In the usual classroom, the response unit might be the pupil's vocal equipment for making an oral reply to a question, or his writing equipment.

3. *The pacing unit* times the intervals between (a) question and correct answer, and (b) each question. Both *a* and *b* intervals

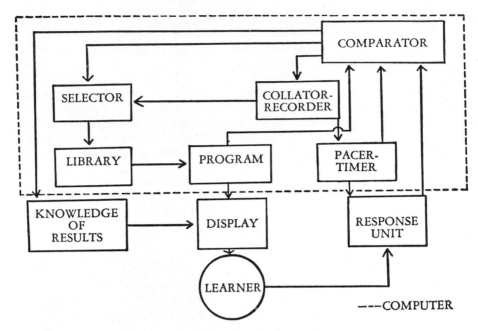

Fig. 24.   Adaptive Teaching Machine System (Stolurow, 1961, p. 7).

may be fixed, both may vary according to the learner's response, or *a* alone may vary while *b* remains fixed. In the classroom, this is merely (a) the teacher's speed of reaction to pupils' responses and (b) his rate of proceeding from one statement-question unit to the next, presumably according to how well his class is learning.

4. *The comparator unit* compares the learner's response with the correct or desired one, either explicitly or merely by presenting the correct response to the learner and letting him make the comparison. The teacher does this by saying to himself, "Right," or "Wrong," or by stating aloud the correct or desired answer.

5. *Knowledge of results or feedback* is then made available to the learner, either through his own inference from his own comparison of his response with the correct response, or by the machine's giving him a correct response, or by the machine's giving him a light or sound or other clue. In the classroom the teacher can allow the pupil to infer his feedback or give it to him explicitly by audibly stating, "Right" or "Wrong."

6. *The collator-recorder* measures and records the learning process, collecting data on number and type of errors, time intervals required for response, etc. The collating unit feeds this information into the part of the unit to which it pertains. In the human situation, the teacher remembers the correctness and style of the pupil's successive responses and uses this memory to make the teaching process more appropriate to the learner's ability and rate of progress.

7. *The selector unit* chooses the next item in the program. Depending on whether the preceding response was wrong or right, it presents the same item or a new one. It may also take into account the learner's whole previous record, as received from the collator-recorder unit. In the classroom, the teacher chooses the next item.

8. *The library unit* stores the information, concepts, etc., to be taught. Its effectiveness depends on its capacity, access time, and form of storage. In the classroom, the teacher's own knowledge, textbooks, and other sources serve this function; how much the teacher knows, or knows how to find,

with what speed, and in what form (books, films, etc.) are the analogous characteristics.

9. *Programing* is the sequence of items, either predetermined (linear, or noninterpretive) or flexible according to the learner's responses (branching, or interpretive). Programing is equivalent to the teacher's implicit or explicit conception of the best pedagogical structure of the discipline being taught, and in the classroom, of course, teachers typically do adapt the sequence of ideas to their pupils, except when lecturing or when individual differences among learners cannot be taken into account.

10. *The computer* is the high-speed electronic digital device that can perform all the functions enclosed in the dotted rectangle in Fig. 24. The teacher's "mind" or thought processes are the best analog of this function in the human teacher.

Note that the components themselves tell much less than the whole story of how teaching machines, and teachers, ideally function according to Stolurow's paradigm. The sources of input and the destinations of output of each component must be considered for any full grasp of what the paradigm represents. These connections among components are shown by the arrows between boxes in Figs. 24 and 25.

Does this paradigm of an idealized teaching machine suggest variables and relationships that have been neglected in research on human teaching? Table 2 shows how the "units" of Stolurow's teaching machine system fit into the previous classification of elements in teacher-pupil interaction paradigms. Appropriately enough, most of the components belong in the teacher's side of the interaction, since this is a *teaching* machine and not a *learning* machine. Stolurow's components are particularly suggestive as to the

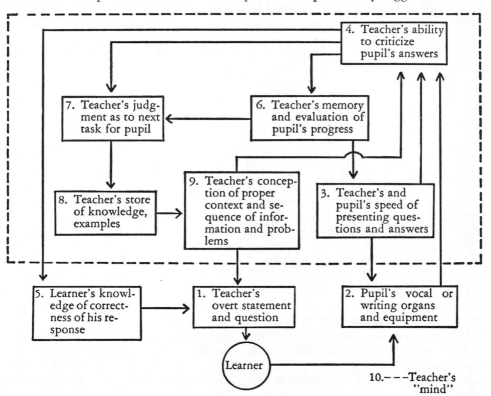

Fig. 25. Human Equivalent of a Teaching Machine System (Based on Stolurow, 1961).

perceptual-cognitive parts of the teaching process.

That is, of the components listed above, it seems that the pacing, comparator, knowledge of results, and collator-recorder functions of teachers have been generally disregarded. How fast teachers proceed, how well they evaluate pupils' responses in the ongoing classroom discussion, how clearly and fully they give pupils knowledge of their own correctness, and how well they keep track of the progress of pupils' learning, are matters that have seldom been variables in research on teaching. When such variables have been used in research, they have been averaged or manipulated over large blocks of behavior, or units of subject matter. Thus, pupils have been given total scores on tests some time after they have taken the test, not knowledge of the correctness of responses to individual items immediately after making each response. If the latter kind of knowledge of results is important to learning, it should be studied as a variable in human teaching as well as machine teaching. Experiments in machine teaching (e.g., Coulson & Silberman, 1960) have called into question the value of some variations of some of Stolurow's components (e.g., branching). Does this imply that research on human teachers' branching, i.e., adaptation of content to individual differences among pupils in learning, would yield the same finding?

The heart of machine teaching is the program, and indeed many of the benefits may be available without any machine at all, e.g., with only a programed textbook. Apart from all the research problems inherent in the programing concept, which are only now beginning to be explored, the teaching machine paradigm suggests that the programs teachers carry around "in their heads" need analysis. Such "implicit programs," or the at least partly unconscious structures and sequences of subject matter that teachers employ, could be revealed with unstructured and open-ended interviewing techniques, among others.

We have made a series of analogies be-

tween teaching machine functions and teachers' behaviors and characteristics. These analogies may serve, more than anything, to reveal the inadequacies of human teachers. Hardly a teacher is alive who can do all the things that teaching machines are supposed to do according to Stolurow's schema. Here lies the reason for the contemporary explosion of interest in teaching machines and programed learning. Systematic comparison of machine functions and those of human teachers, function by function, may reveal the proper and unique role of each. Paradigms for human teaching comparable to those for teaching machines will help in making such analyses.

THEORIES OF TEACHING

The term *theories of teaching* has occurred only rarely in the discussions and research of behavioral scientists. In psychology, a comparable term, *theories of learning,* represents a large and active field of concern. Entire volumes have been written (Estes, et al., 1954; Hilgard, 1956; Thorpe & Schmuller, 1954) to summarize and criticize theories of learning, and courses on this subject are given in most universities.

On theories of teaching there have been no books, courses, symposia, chapters in the *Annual Review of Psychology,* or sections in *Psychological Abstracts.* Books entitled "Psychology of Teaching" turn out to be general educational psychologies. The *Comprehensive Dictionary of Psychological and Psychoanalytical Terms* (English & English, 1958) has 50 entries concerned with "Learning," covering about three pages. On the other hand, "Teaching" has only one entry covering five lines: "the art of assisting another to learn. It includes the providing of information (instruction) and of appropriate situations, conditions, or activities designed to facilitate learning." This difference in the elaboration of the two concepts—learning and teaching—accurately represents the difference in the amount of attention these processes have received from psychologists.

Courses and textbooks in educational psychology deal much more with learning and the characteristics of learners than with teaching and the characteristics of teachers.

Why has theory of teaching been neglected while theory of learning has received so much attention? One answer may be that learning is a much more general phenomenon, as psychologists conceive it, than is teaching. Learning as a subject of scientific study embraces more than what goes on in schools. Rather, it is "the process by which an activity originates or is changed through reacting to an encountered situation, provided that the characteristics of the change in activity cannot be explained on the basis of native response tendencies, maturation, or temporary states of the organism (e.g., fatigue, drugs, etc.)" (Hilgard, 1956, p. 3). Hence, learning is considered to occur in all areas of life, not merely those in the formal educational setting. The effects of propaganda, psychotherapy, child-rearing, social groups, and teachers are seen as explicable in terms of learning, and hence, of theories of learning. If one stops to think about it, he readily concedes that advertisers, psychotherapists, parents, and discussion group leaders may be viewed as teachers. Still, ordinary discourse restricts the term *teaching* to school situations.

Another reason for the relative neglect of theories of teaching may be that they have been seen as unnecessary on strictly logical grounds. This position—itself perhaps a kind of theory of teaching—amounts to saying that, if we have an adequate theory of learning, then the teacher must of necessity act upon that theory, without employing any separate theory of teaching. The teacher, if he is to engender learning, must of necessity do what the theory of learning stipulates as necessary for learning to occur. Teaching must thus be a kind of "mirror image" of learning. This conception of what a theory of learning implies for teaching may explain the neglect of theory of teaching by psychologists.

At any rate, we now take the venturesome path of dealing explicitly with a kind of theory—theory of teaching—which almost may be said not even to exist thus far in behavioral science. In the remainder of this chapter, we attempt to redress this imbalance slightly by examining the case for concern with theories of teaching, and by adumbrating promising directions.

A Case for Theory of Teaching

Let us reply briefly to the contention that if we but had adequate theories of learning, we would not need theories of teaching, that is, if we know how people learn, we will know how to teach them.

Perhaps an analogy will be useful here. Farmers need to know something about how plants grow, and how they depend on soil, water, and sunlight. So teachers need to know how children learn, and how they depend on motivation, readiness, and reinforcement. But farmers also need to know how to farm—how to till the soil, put in the seed, get rid of weeds and insects, harvest the crop, and get it to market. If our analogy applies even loosely, teachers similarly need to know how to teach—how to motivate pupils, assess their readiness, act on the assessment, present the subject, maintain discipline, and shape a cognitive structure. Too much of educational psychology makes the teacher *infer* what he needs to do from what he is told about learners and learning. Theories of teaching would make *explicit* how teachers behave, why they behave as they do, and with what effects. Hence, theories of teaching need to develop alongside, on a more equal basis with, rather than by inference from, theories of learning.

Toward a Theory of Teaching

A general conception of teaching should apply to any grade level, any subject matter, and any situation, whether in school or out. Typically, however, teaching refers to influence by a more accomplished, skilled, or mature person addressed to one who is less so. Further, teaching is typically considered to deal with formal school subject matter or "instructional objectives," in the form of cognitive, affective, or psychomotor behaviors, which the teacher seeks to assist the learner to attain. Also, typically the teaching is considered to go on in situations formally established for that purpose, that is, in schools where the teacher works with a group of learners rather than an individual. But our general conception of teaching should go beyond these typical forms and apply even to their opposites.

Theories of teaching can be of two kinds. First, such a theory can undertake to explain why teachers behave the way they do in their roles as teachers; the teacher's behavior is a dependent variable in such a scheme. This kind of theory of teaching would seek for the behavior of teachers the same kinds of descriptive concepts and explanatory principles that are sought in describing and explaining the behavior of any person. Concepts from social psychology (such as role and personality), or from learning theory (e.g., motivation-cue-response-reinforcement), might be brought to bear on the question of why a teacher behaves the way he does. Ryans' paradigm of teacher behavior as a function of teacher characteristics and teaching situations, shown in Fig. 19, is aimed at this problem.

A second kind of theory of teaching would attempt to explain how it is that the behavior of one person, a teacher, can influence the behavior or learning of another person, a student. This kind of theory would attempt to explain instances of teaching, i.e., of interpersonal influence resulting in learning. All such instances, at whatever age and grade level, in whatever subject matter, and in whatever situation, would constitute the class of problems at which a general theory of teaching would be aimed. It is this second kind of theory with which the Smith, Ryans-dyadic, Stone-Leavitt, and Runkel paradigms are concerned.

Influence by one person on another can take forms other than teaching. Just as not all changes in behavior reflect learning, so not all influences on another's behavior reflect

teaching. Physical coercion, drugs, or denial of rest can be used by one person to change the behavior of another, but their use is not teaching. Rather, the proper definition of teaching must be restricted in the same way as the definition of learning. The influence that one brings to bear on another must enter that person not through his blood stream, either directly as by the injection of a drug or indirectly as by the formation in his muscles of the chemicals that produce fatigue. Nor must the influence be exerted by mere physical forces, whether mechanical energy such as pushing or soundwaves, or radiant energy in the form of electricity or light.

The kinds of force through which a teacher can, by definition, influence a pupil must rather be psychological (perceptual, cognitive, or affective) forces. Thus, the influence from the environment that is allowed conceptually to produce learning must be influence from the environment that the learner perceives. Without going into any detailed consideration of the nature of perception, let us merely say that this influence must not merely operate on the sense organs but must be mediated by the pupil's perceptual apparatus, including sets, prior experiences, and other sources of meaning.

Once the teacher has exerted psychological force on the pupil, by what processes can this force bring about learning? Learning processes must be referred to here, and we shall refer to such conceptions here in only their broadest terms: conditioning, identification, and cognition.

Teaching and Conditioning Theory

The conditioning approach (e.g., Miller, 1957; Mowrer, 1960, especially Ch. 7) sees learning as consisting of the formation through experience of new connections between stimuli and responses. The Pavlovian paradigm of conditioning shown in Fig. 1 still applies, but with refinements. Miller grouped the variables involved in teaching and learning according to the following "fundamental factors":

Drive (motivation)—the student must want something.

Cue (stimulus)—he must notice something.

Response (participation)—he must do something.

Reward (reinforcement)—he must get something he wants (Miller, 1957, p. 63).

Mowrer's two-factor theory, sketched in Fig. 26, was developed to embrace the findings and counter the objections of the half-century of research since Pavlov and E. L. Thorndike. As Mowrer's present version of two-factor theory indicates, the basic distinctions between (1) punishment and reward, (2) primary (unlearned) and secondary (learned) reinforcement, (3) having signals (secondary reinforcements) on or off, and (4) independent and response-dependent stimulation, lead to 12 kinds of reinforcement.

Such a theory may imply that teachers, by manipulating various kinds of reinforcement, can teach pupils to have fear, disappointment, relief, and hope attached to the proper stimulus-response connections. Indeed, this is how people must learn and be educated: (1) be stimulated by something inside or outside themselves, (2) make a covert or overt response, and (3) get some kind of reinforcement that tells them that danger is coming (fear) or going away (relief), or that safety is coming (hope) or going away (disappointment). The stimuli may be arithmetic problems on a blackboard, sentences in a lecture, paragraphs in a textbook, or whatever. The responses may be overt oral or written words or inner efforts to comprehend or think. The reinforcements may be teacher's praise or inner satisfaction with a solution. By the conditioning conception of learning, in any case, teachers can exert teaching force by manipulating the stimuli, responses, and reinforcements in the pupil's environment. Paradigms for research on teaching must then take account of what the teacher does in the sense of manipulating these parts of the learner's environment.

Conditioning theorists have generally agreed that arranging for the learner to make an appropriate response, so that it can be reinforced, is central to the problem of teaching. Kendler (1961), for example, stated, "Once the characteristics of the to-be-learned response are specified, the task becomes one of getting the student to make it, explicitly or implicitly, in the presence of the appropriate stimulus" (p. 37). Similarly, Glaser's (1961) view that "response is the primary object of manipulation in instructional technology" (p. 43), seems at first glance to call for such an emphasis.

On the other hand, Gagné (1962) questioned the assumption that " 'The best way to learn a performance is to practice that performance.' . . . In conditioning, classical or otherwise, one observes learning only *after* the animal has made the first *response*. . .," and one "conceives of what is learned as either a response or an association terminating in a response, in either case established by *practicing the response* (with reinforcement)" (p. 85). This assumption was challenged by Gagné on the ground that "the responses required (turning switches, inserting plugs, moving handles) [in the kinds of training he analyzed] do not have to be learned at all—they are already there in the human's repertoire" (p. 85).

Applying this basic but questionable assumption to the design of effective training situations was found by Gagné to be relatively fruitless. He found that major improvement in gunnery came not from practice of the response but from "informing the learners of the correct picture to be achieved in ranging" (p. 86), i.e., by teaching perceptual aspects of the task. In training men to turn on a radar set, it was the learning of a list of steps—a cognitive structuring—not the practice of the switch-pressing responses, that made for the most effective training. In training men to trouble-shoot complex equipment, there was no single task to be practiced; rather it was the learning of an elaborate set of rules pertaining to the flow of signals through a complex circuit—another cognitive structure—that proved essential.

Types of Reinforcement

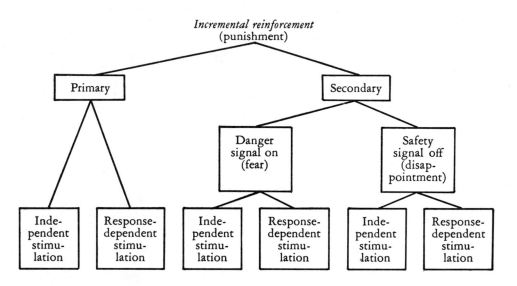

"Here it will be noted that *all* learning is (by implication) conditioning, so that the theory remains "two-factored" only with respect to the forms of reinforcement involved, i.e., incremental and decremental. Since each of these may involve primary drive or either of two forms of secondary drive, there are thus, in effect, *six* operationally distinguishable forms of rein-

Fig. 26, Present Version of Two-Factor Theory (After Mowrer, 1960, p. 213).

Rather than response elicitation and reinforcement, as is implied by at least some interpretations of conditioning theory, the more important principles in training, in Gagné's view, deal with task analysis, intratask transfer, component task achievement, and sequencing. Making responses was less important than learning what and where things are (a cognitive and perceptual task) in turning on a radar set. Acquiring knowledge of rules of signal flow and of the proper use of test instruments represented the major outcomes of task analysis in training troubleshooters; here again the cognitive structure of what was to be learned rather than the response elements proved to be more significant.

In short, Gagné evaluated the fruitfulness of one interpretation of the implications of conditioning theory for teaching and found

these implications wanting. In the present writer's view, conditioning theory can be reinterpreted in more subtle ways, such as those set forth by Glaser (1961), to accord with the lessons of the training programs and research described by Gagné. But Gagné's report indicates that overly direct and simple extrapolations from conditioning theory can mislead research on teaching and draw teachers away from significant variables.

Teaching and the Identification Process

Identification consists in one person's seeking to become like another because of admiration or love for the other. Originally applied by psychoanalysts to the acquisition of the super ego by children through identification with their parents, the concept is also often (e.g., Adelson, 1962; Cronbach, 1954, Ch. 11)

Types of Reinforcement (Cont'd.)

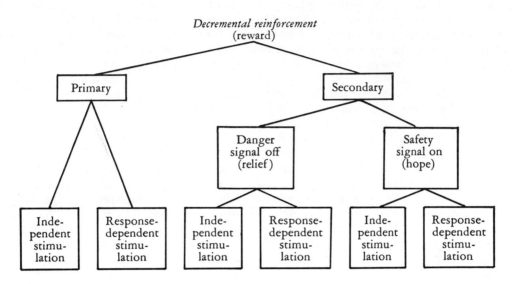

forcement; and each of these may be associated with either independent or response-dependent stimulation. Therefore, if this classification is so defined as to include the nature of the associated stimuli, there are *twelve* "kinds" of reinforcement. The reader is encouraged to test this classification for exhaustiveness."

applied to ways in which students learn from their teachers.

In this conception, teachers can exert force on their pupils by somehow insuring that the pupil has positive attitudes toward the teacher. Although the process of learning through identification is sometimes considered to be merely a special case of conditioning, with the model or teacher serving as a source of secondary reinforcement, a separate literature has grown up around identification and its product, imitation. If conditioning theory is linked by some to the blind formation of habits, identification theory has been considered especially related to the formation of attitudes in the absence of clear, structured, logical, and intellectually compelling bases for attitudes. In matters of taste, appreciation, or values, where the pupil cannot experience any *logically* compelling reason for considering

something good or bad, right or wrong, the process of identification—with, say, a parent or a teacher—takes over.

Heider's theory of balance (Heider, 1958, Ch. 7) holds that people have a tendency to want the same positive or negative relationship to an object—an idea, an attitude, a value, or whatever—as they perceive to be held by another person to whom they see themselves positively related (e.g., liking). They also want a relationship to objects which is opposite to that which they see as held by other persons to whom they see themselves negatively related (e.g., disliking). In any triadic constellation of person *p*, other person *o*, and object *x*, from *p*'s standpoint there will be balance (and psychological comfort) only when the three relationships between *p*, *o*, and *x* are all positive, or when two are negative and one is positive. It follows that, if teachers want pupils to have attitudes similar to their own, they must engender a positive feeling toward themselves on the part of the pupil.

For research on teaching, the implied paradigm has some obvious features. Central in such paradigms must be the affective relationship between teacher and pupil, as seen by the pupil. What teachers do to influence this relationship, and how it shapes learning, will take dominant positions in paradigms built around the notion that teachers teach by exerting the psychological force of identification on their pupils. In this sense, research on teaching will never be replaced by research on teaching machines; it is hard to see the forces of identification operating as pupils work through a cold, impersonal program. Further, some educators' values place what is learned through identification processes at least as high in importance to man and society as what can be learned without such processes.

One problem with the concept of identification is that it can seem to explain too much. How does a pupil choose among competing models the one with whom he identifies? Among the many characteristics and behaviors of his model? How does he fit what he adopts from his model into his already organized personality? What determines how deep or superficial the imitation will be? Complications of this kind, discussed by Adelson (1962), call for investigations built around paradigms that incorporate the identification process.

Teaching and Cognitive Processes

Many educators and psychologists regard conditioning and identification as blind, irrational processes. However powerful, these processes are, in this view, essentially alien to the dignity of man as a thinking animal. The acquisition of the kinds of cognitive knowledge and understanding at which schooling is aimed cannot be reduced, in this conception of the learner and of what is to be learned, to any mere set of stimulus-response connections, no matter how thoroughly elaborated.

Cognitive structure refers to the organization of facts, concepts, and principles. Such a structure is not arbitrary. It is determined partly by how man's mind works and partly by the nature of the subject, i.e., the "intellectual discipline" to be learned. The cognitive structure of logical processes exerts force; it compels assent to a conclusion, for example, once appropriate premises have been stated. Since men are more or less logical beings, it is *not* merely a matter of conditioning that once we accept, say, the mortality of all humans, and the humanness of Socrates, we must—we are compelled to—accept the mortality of Socrates. We can therefore teach another person by manipulating the ideas to which we expose him and thus "force" him to accept, out of greater or less logical necessity, certain other ideas that we wish him to learn.

If the sets of facts, ideas, concepts, principles, and so on, that we want to teach were themselves mere unrelated congeries of items, such an approach to teaching would face severe difficulties. The teacher would have trouble in finding sets of ideas, or cognitive structures, that he could use to apply cognitive force, to compel understanding or acceptance or belief, and produce learning. Fortunately, of course, many subjects taught in schools have highly organized structures. Arithmetic, chemistry, and German are examples at the high extreme of degree of structure. Subjects like literature and history are far from devoid of structure in the views of scholars in these fields. The implication of the cognitive approach to learning and teaching is that maximum advantage should be taken of the cognitive properties of learners and subjects (Bruner, 1960, Chs. 1–2; Luchins, 1961; Schwab, 1961). Properly organized subject matter presented to learners whose cognitive development and processes are correctly understood will produce learning—learning of the best kind, according to the value systems of many educators.

In recent decades, research on teaching has not been much concerned with matters of this kind. Ausubel and Fitzgerald (1961), however, were able to find more adequate attention to cognitive variables in the late 1950's. Their review should be consulted for an introduction to the current upsurge of research on cognitive variables in meaningful learning.

As to paradigms for research on teaching, the cognitive structure variables imply more intensive concern with (1) teachers' own understandings of what they teach and (2) how teachers behave along such dimensions as the "logicality" of their classroom discourse. The first kind of concern is exemplified in Orleans' study (1952) of the understanding of arithmetic processes and concepts possessed by teachers of arithmetic. "Perhaps a major factor in the failure of children to get . . . an understanding of arithmetic . . . is that their teachers are ignorant of the processes and concepts represented . . ." (p. 4). Although he did not test this hypothesis, Orleans did reveal such ignorance on the part of teachers as to throw doubt on their ability to exert the cognitive force that would produce understanding on the part of their pupils. When teachers define, describe, explain, and so on, how well do they conform to the rules of logic? The question is important because the answer should, according to the notion of teaching as the exertion of cognitive forces, tell much about how well the pupils learn from that teacher. A research program directed by Smith has produced a report of work along these lines (Meux & Smith, 1961).

Other cognitive variables should also enter into paradigms stemming from this orientation. The logical organization of content in instructional media, the similarity and also "colinearity" (Runkel, 1956) between teachers' cognitive structures and those of their pupils, and other logical dimensions of teaching behavior should be operationally defined and investigated as to their significance for attaining educational objectives.

REFERENCES

Ackerman, W. I. Teacher competence and pupil change. *Harvard educ. Rev.,* 1954, 24, 273–289.

Adelson, J. The teacher as a model. In N. Sanford (Ed.), *The American college.* New York: Wiley, 1962. Pp. 396–417.

Altman, I., & McGrath, J. E. *A conceptual framework for the integration of small group research information.* Arlington, Va.: Human Sciences Research, Inc., 1959. (ASTIA Doc. No. 212242)

American Educational Research Association, Committee on the Criteria of Teacher Effectiveness. Report of the. . . . *Rev. educ. Res.,* 1952, 22, 238–263.

American Educational Research Association, Committee on the Criteria of Teacher Effectiveness. Second report of the. . . . *J. educ. Res.,* 1953, 46, 641–658.

American Psychological Association, Education and Training Board. (Seminar members: L. Festinger, W. R. Garner, D. O. Hebb, H. F. Hunt, D. H. Lawrence, C. E. Osgood, B. F. Skinner, D. W. Taylor, & M. Wertheimer) Education for research in psychology. *Amer. Psychologist,* 1959, 14, 167–179.

Ausubel, D. P., & Fitzgerald, D. Meaningful learning and retention: Interpersonal cognitive variables. *Rev. educ. Res.,* 1961, 31, 500–510.

Barr, A. S. The measurement and prediction of teaching efficiency: A summary of investigations. *J. exp. Educ.,* 1948, 16, 203–283.

Barr, A. S., et al. Wisconsin studies of the measurement and prediction of teacher effectiveness: A summary of investigations. *J. exp. Educ.,* 1961, 30, 1–155.

Beecher, C. Data-gathering devices employed in the Wisconsin studies. *J. exp. Educ.,* 1961, 30, 30–47.

Bloom, B. S. (Ed.), Engelhart, M. D., Furst, E. J., Hill, W. H., & Krathwohl, D. R. *Taxonomy of educational objectives.* New York: Longmans, Green, 1956.

Bruner, J. S. *The process of education.* Cambridge, Mass.: Harvard Univer. Press, 1960.

Bucklew, J. *Paradigms for psychopathology: A contribution to case history analysis.* New York: Lippincott, 1960.

Castetter, D. D., Standlee, L. S., & Fattu, N. A. *Teacher effectiveness: An annotated bibliography*. Bloomington: Inst. of Educ. Res., Sch. of Educ., Indiana Univer., 1954.

Coulson, J. E., & Silberman, H. F. Effects of three variables in a teaching machine. *J. educ. Psychol.,* 1960, 51, 135–144.

Cronbach, L. J. *Essentials of psychological testing.* New York: Harper, 1949.

Cronbach, L. J. *Educational psychology.* New York: Harcourt, Brace, 1954.

Cronbach, L. J. Proposals leading to analytic treatment of social perception scores. In R. Tagiuri & L. Petrullo (Eds.), *Person perception and interpersonal behavior.* Stanford, Calif.: Stanford Univer. Press, 1958. Pp. 353–379.

Domas, S. J., & Tiedeman, D. V. Teacher competence: An annotated bibliography. *J. exp. Educ.,* 1950, 19, 101–218.

English, H. B., & English, Ava C. *A comprehensive dictionary of psychological and psychoanalytical terms.* New York: Longmans, Green, 1958.

Estes, W. K., et al. *Modern learning theory.* New York: Appleton-Century-Crofts, 1954.

Gagné, R. M. Military training and principles of learning. *Amer. Psychologist,* 1962, 17, 83–91.

Glaser, R. Learning and the technology of instruction. *AV commun. Rev.,* 1961, 9(5), 42–55.

Guba, E., & Getzels, J. W. Personality and teacher effectiveness: A problem in theoretical research. *J. educ. Psychol.,* 1955, 46, 330–344.

Halpin, A. W. A paradigm for research on administrative behavior. In R. F. Campbell & R. T. Gregg (Eds.), *Administrative behavior in education.* New York: Harper, 1957. Pp. 155–199.

Heider, F. *The psychology of interpersonal relations.* New York: Wiley, 1958.

Hilgard, E. R. *Theories of learning.* (2nd ed.) New York: Appleton-Century-Crofts, 1956.

Horwitz, M. The conceptual status of group dynamics. *Rev. educ. Res.,* 1953, 23, 309–328.

Jensen, G., & Parsons, T. The structure and dynamics of classroom groups and educational systems. *Rev. educ. Res.,* 1959, 29, 344–356.

Kendler, H. H. Stimulus-response psychology and audio-visual education. *AV commun. Rev.,* 1961, 9(5), 33–41.

Lane, R. E. *The liberties of wit: Humanism, criticism, and the civic mind.* New Haven, Conn.: Yale Univer. Press, 1961.

Levin, H. A new perspective on teacher competence research. *Harvard educ. Rev.,* 1954, 24, 98–105.

Lewin, K. Behavior and development as a function of the total situation. In L. Carmichael (Ed.), *Manual of child psychology.* New York: Wiley, 1946. Pp. 791–844.

Luchins, A. S. Implications of Gestalt psychology for AV learning. *AV commun. Rev.,* 1961, 9(5), 7–31.

McGrath, J. E. *Integration of small group research information: Program report.* Arlington, Va.: Human Sciences Research, Inc., 1962. (Prepared for Air Force Office of Scientific Research, Contract No. AF 49 (638)-256, Supplemental Agreement No. 5 (62-341).

Medley, D. M., & Mitzel, H. E. Some behavioral correlates of teacher effectiveness. *J. educ. Psychol.,* 1959, 50, 239–246.

Meux, M., & Smith, B. O. *Logical dimensions of teaching behavior.* Urbana: Bur. of Educ. Res., Univer. of Illinois, 1961. (Mimeographed)

Miller, N. E. (Ed.) *Graphic communication and the crisis in education.* Washington, D.C.: National Education Association, 1957.

Mitzel, H. E. *A behavioral approach to the assessment of teacher effectiveness.* New York: Division of Teacher Education, College of the City of New York, 1957. (Mimeographed)

Mitzel, H. E. Teacher effectiveness. In C. W. Harris (Ed.), *Encyclopedia of educational research.* (3rd ed.) New York: Macmillan, 1960. Pp. 1481–1486.

Mitzel, H. E., & Gross, Cecily F. *A critical review of the development of pupil growth criteria in studies of teacher effectiveness.* New York: Board of Higher Education of the City of New York, Div. of Teacher Educ., Office of Res. and Evaluation, 1956. (Res. Ser. 31)

Morsh, J. E., & Wilder, Eleanor W. Identifying the effective instructor: A review of the quantitative studies 1900–1952. *USAF Pers. Train. Res. Cent. (Res. Bull.,* 1954, No. AFPTRC-TR-54-44)

Mowrer, O. H. *Learning theory and behavior.* New York: Wiley, 1960.

Orleans, J. S. The understanding of arithmetic processes and concepts possessed by teachers of arithmetic. New York: Board of Education of the City of New York, Div. of Teacher Education, Office of Res. and Evaluation, 1952. (Publ. No. 12)

Runkel, P. J. Cognitive similarity in facilitating communication. *Sociometry,* 1956, 19, 178–191.

Ryans, D. G. *Characteristics of teachers.* Washington, D.C.: American Council on Education, 1960. (a)

Ryans, D. G. Prediction of teacher effectiveness. In C. W. Harris (Ed.), *Encyclopedia of educational research.* (3rd ed.) New York: Macmillan, 1960. Pp. 1486–1491. (b)

Schmid, J. Factor analysis of the teaching complex. *J. exp. Educ.,* 1961, 30, 58–69.

Schwab, J. J. *Education and the structure of the disciplines.* Washington, D.C.: National Education Association, 1961. (Mimeographed)

Sears, R. R. A theoretical framework for personality and social behavior. *Amer. Psychologist,* 1951, 6, 476–483.

Skinner, B. F. Are theories of learning necessary? *Psychol. Rev.,* 1950, 57, 193–216.

Skinner, B. F. A case history in scientific method. *Cumulative record.* New York: Appleton-Century-Crofts, 1959. Pp. 76–100.

Smith, B. O. A concept of teaching. *Teachers Coll. Rec.,* 1960, 61, 229–241.

Stolurow, L. M. *Teaching by machine.* Washington, D.C.: U.S. Government Printing Office, 1961. (U.S. Office of Education, Coop. Res. Monogr. No. 6. OE-34010)

Thorpe, L. P., & Schmuller, A. M. *Contemporary theories of learning, with applications to education and psychology.* New York: Ronald, 1954.

Tomlinson, L. R. Pioneer studies in the evaluation of teaching. *Educ. res. Bull.,* 1955, 34, 63–71. (a)

Tomlinson, L. R. Recent studies in the evaluation of teaching. *Educ. res. Bull.,* 1955, 34, 172–186. (b)

Travers, R. M. W. *An introduction to educational research.* New York: Macmillan, 1958.

Watters, W. A. Annotated bibliography of publications related to teacher evaluation. *J. exp. Educ.,* 1954, 22, 351–367.

CHAPTER 4

Statistics as an Aspect of Scientific Method in Research on Teaching[1]

MAURICE M. TATSUOKA
University of Hawaii at Hilo[2]

DAVID V. TIEDEMAN
Harvard University

The nature and function of theories in a science have been described in earlier chapters; the nature of experimental method, as applied to research on teaching, is expounded in the next. We start this chapter by considering the interrelationship between theory and experiment, with a view to clarifying the role of statistics in research in general and in research on teaching in particular.

Despite recent developments in the philosophy of science (Hempel, 1952; Popper, 1959, especially pp. 106–111), and despite admonitions by such educational theorists as Smith (1950, pp. 1149–1150) and Travers (1958, Chs. 1 and 2), whose views are consistent with, although not necessarily derived from, these recent developments, the radical empiricist view, namely, that theories are generated inductively from summaries of observational findings, still seems prevalent in some circles. True, it is difficult to find explicit statements of this outmoded view in the contemporary literature, but an implicit adherence to it seems to be reflected in a large bulk of educational research devoted merely to the study of correlations between various pairs of observational variables without, apparently, any theoretical hypothesis in mind —or, at best, with only an ad hoc hypothesis that states no more than the existence of the empirical relationship being studied. One cannot escape the impression that the authors of these studies tacitly hope that, with a sufficient accumulation of such empirical findings, a theory (or a system of "intermeshing" hypotheses) will eventually emerge. According to modern views in the philosophy of science, however, such hopes are foredoomed: Theory-building is a deliberate enterprise.

THE ROLE OF STATISTICS IN THE HYPOTHETICO-DEDUCTIVE-OBSERVATIONAL PROCEDURE

With Hempel (1952), the authors believe that the task of seeking general and reliable principles for predicting and explaining observable phenomena—in short, the "scientific endeavor"—must follow a "hypothetico-de-

[1] The authors are indebted to Henry F. Kaiser for his criticisms of an earlier draft of this chapter and to J. A. Easley for his helpful comments on the present version.

[2] Now at the University of Illinois.

ductive-observational procedure," rather than that of induction:

Guided by his knowledge of observational data, the scientist has to *invent* a set of concepts—theoretical constructs, which lack immediate experimental significance—a system of hypotheses couched in terms of them, and an interpretation for the resulting theoretical network; and all this in a manner which will establish explanatory and predictive connections between the data of direct observation (Hempel, 1952, p. 37; italics ours).

We may schematically represent the procedure characterized above, with some augmentation, in the form of a block diagram as shown in Fig. 1. The augmentation consists

in our having indicated those steps in which we believe statistical techniques can most fruitfully be brought to bear. The omission of such an indication in the first box, representing the stage of collecting "initial observational data," is deliberate. The authors' frank opinion is that the use of statistical techniques at this stage often serves no better purpose than to lend spurious respectability to the study. (Exception must be made for correlational studies which are then followed up, at the second step of "creative invention," by such procedures as factor analysis or discriminant analysis, discussed below.)

Of far greater importance, generally speaking, than statistical analysis at this initial stage is the requirement that the exposure to

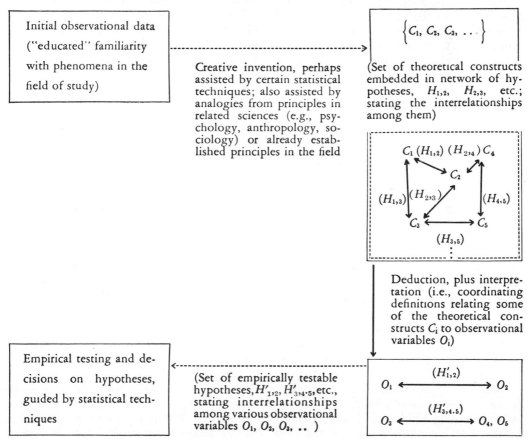

Fig. 1. Hypothetico-Deductive-Observational Procedure, Showing Steps in Which Statistical Techniques Can Be Brought to Bear.

phenomena in the field of study be an "educated" one. In the context of research on teaching, this exposure may well take the form of interviews or participant observation. It is essential, however, that the "participation" take place at two levels, so to speak. First (and this is the customary sense in which "participation" is used in this connection), the observer puts himself in the shoes of the teacher or the pupils. Second, he must actively participate in the process of theorizing even at this stage: he must constantly be formulating "hunches" as to *what to look for* in the classroom situation and he must make observations accordingly. In Popper's (1959, p. 107) words, "Theory dominates the experimental work from its initial planning up to the finishing touches in the laboratory."

The step indicated by the first dashed arrow in Fig. 1—that of "creative invention" of theoretical constructs and hypotheses—is, without doubt, the key step in scientific endeavor and the one which places this endeavor on the same plane of imaginative creativity as that on which artistic and literary endeavors lie. It would take us too far afield to attempt to give anything approaching a complete description of this step. In fact, philosophers of science are not in agreement with one another concerning the feasibility of such a description. For our purposes here, it is sufficient briefly to note that, in general, analogy—both with established principles in the field under study and with those of related disciplines—plays a leading role in the invention of theoretical hypotheses. Our primary concern at this step is with the role which statistical method may sometimes play in the development of theoretical constructs.

The problem of inventing theoretical constructs may alternatively be characterized as that of seeking variables appropriate for use in a theoretical system. Experience in other sciences shows that terms used in everyday discourse or, what is more to the point here, in the workaday classroom situation—for instance, 'reading skill'—will not, in general, be the most appropriate ones for use in a theory. (To give an example from the physi-

cal sciences, the term 'cloud' does not find a place in the *technical* vocabulary of theoretical meteorology.) The problem of finding appropriate variables, therefore, is a crucial one—and, of course, a most difficult one. As a rule, the solution (or attempted solution) of this problem proceeds hand in hand with the development of theoretical hypotheses in whose contexts such variables occur. Speculation, analogy, trial and error, and even sheer luck, all contribute to this dual development of constructs and hypotheses.

Sometimes, however, a potentially useful theoretical construct may be arrived at *relatively* independently of the particular hypothesis in which it eventually functions most successfully. The statistical techniques of factor analysis, discriminant analysis, and certain other species of multivariate analysis described below, are heuristic tools available to the researcher for producing constructs which may prove to be theoretically fruitful. For instance, a factor analysis of a battery of tests may yield (among other things) a "factor" that is somewhat akin to the classroom notion of reading skill and yet possesses greater theoretical relevance. Or, a discriminant analysis performed in order to seek a "dimension," along which a group of "underachievers" and a group of "overachievers" can best be distinguished, may yield a theoretical construct in some way associated with what might be called "motivation." There is no guarantee that these techniques will indeed enable us to discover constructs that will function adequately in a theory. The degree of creative imagination on the part of the researcher in selecting or constructing the psychometric tests for inclusion in either analysis will, to a large extent, determine the fruitfulness of the resulting constructs. In any event, the final test of their fruitfulness will lie in how adequately they function in a theory for explanatory or predictive purposes. So long as this is borne in mind—that these techniques are but heuristic devices—the various statistical techniques of multivariate analysis can serve functions highly useful for the researcher.

Returning now to Fig. 1, the next step (indicated by a solid arrow) in the hypo-thetico-deductive-observational procedure is one of pure deduction followed by *interpretation* (i.e., "translating"—by means of co-ordinating definitions—some of the theoretical constructs into observational variables) in order to derive observable consequences of the theory. The resulting set of empirically testable hypotheses, $H'_{1,2}$, $H'_{3,4,5}$, etc., shown in the next box, requires further discussion.

These hypotheses are statements of inter-relationships which, on the basis of the theory represented in the preceding box, would be expected to hold among the observational variables O_1, O_2, O_3, ... In its simplest form, such a hypothesis (e.g., $H'_{1,2}$ in Fig. 1) may merely state that "O_1 is a function of O_2." More often, the hypothesis would at least specify the *direction* of the functional relationship between O_1 and O_2—that is, whether O_1 increases as O_2 increases or O_1 decreases as O_2 increases.

A slightly more complicated hypothesis (e.g., $H'_{3,4,5}$) would state that "O_3 is a joint function of O_4 *and* O_5." For example, O_3 might refer to a learning outcome (amount learned, degree of mastery achieved, time taken to attain a certain criterion of achievement, etc.); O_4 might be some measure characterizing the teaching method (e.g., relative lengths of time spent on drill and on application of principles), or it might simply specify different teaching methods by labels, say A and B; O_5 might refer to some relevant pupil attribute, such as "average" or "above average" in intelligence. Then $H'_{3,4,5}$ might state, "The amount learned (of a certain material) is a joint function of the teaching method and certain pupil attributes." More specifically, it might state that "For pupils of 'above-average intelligence' Method A will produce greater learning; for pupils of 'average intelligence' Method B will produce greater learning." If we further introduce a variable O_6 referring to teacher attributes, $H'_{3,4,5,6}$ would state a relationship between learning outcome on the one hand and teaching method, pupil attribute, *and* teacher attribute on the other.

The problem of designing experiments or observations for empirically testing such hypotheses (last box of Fig. 1) is discussed in detail in the next chapter. In this chapter we are primarily concerned with pointing out some of the statistical techniques available to help the researcher decide whether the results of his empirical testing tend to confirm or refute his hypothesis. We also wish to describe the general rationale of these various statistical techniques in order to make clear their value and limitations. These techniques, which may generically be referred to as *statistical significance test procedures,* are to be distinguished from those techniques mentioned earlier (factor analysis, discriminant analysis, etc.) that are essentially heuristic tools for discovering potentially fruitful theoretical constructs. In the ensuing discussions, however, these two categories of statistical technique will be discussed side by side, because we find it convenient now to classify the available techniques primarily in terms of the nature and number of variables involved rather than in terms of function of the techniques. Such a classification, the authors believe, will prove to be of greater value to the researcher in selecting a technique (or combination of techniques) appropriate for a particular research problem than would a classification according to function. This classification is especially useful because techniques of both functional categories are often needed for the same problem. The present classification scheme also serves to integrate a large variety of multivariate statistical techniques into a single fold, so to speak, by showing that they may be regarded as different special cases of a single general method known as general regression theory.

We now turn to the task of describing the characteristics of variables that form the basis for organizing our discussion of statistical techniques. At the same time, we define some technical terms which will simplify these discussions and facilitate cross reference.

KINDS OF VARIABLES AND PRELIMINARY DEFINITIONS

In referring to the variables involved in an experimental study, it is convenient to distinguish them, in terms of the role they play, as independent (or antecedent) and dependent (or consequent) variables. The former are those variables which the experimenter manipulates, either by varying the experimental conditions or by selecting subjects with specified characteristics. The latter are those variables which the hypothesis under study asserts are functions of the former. This distinction as to the role of variables in an experiment forms the primary basis on which we classify the several statistical techniques in the ensuing discussions.

Secondly, the type of scale used in making measurements on the variables will generally influence the choice of applicable statistical techniques. Four types of scale—nominal, ordinal, interval, and ratio—were distinguished by Stevens (1946, 1951) on the basis of their algebraic properties and the types of mathematical operations permissible for each of them.

A *nominal scale* merely assigns a numeral, as an identifying label, to each object (or set of objects) under study. Assigning letters instead of numerals would serve just as well. Identifying two teaching methods, say, as Methods 1 and 2 (or A and B) is an example of using a nominal scale.

An *ordinal scale* assigns numerals to objects which are rank-ordered with respect to some characteristic. Thus, if we assign the scale values 1, 2, and 3 to pupils who are, respectively, above average, average, and below average in intelligence, we are using an ordinal scale. Likewise, if we code the responses, "Strongly Agree," "Agree," "Neutral," "Disagree," "Strongly Disagree," to a questionnaire item by assigning them the numerals 1, 2, . . ., 5, we have an ordinal scale.

An *interval scale* is obtained if we can define a unit of measurement such that a difference of one scale value means the same regardless of whether it represents, say, 10–9 or 6–5, etc. Scores on well-constructed intelligence tests may be regarded as approximating an interval scale.

A *ratio scale* is an interval scale which further has an absolute zero point, so that it is meaningful to speak of one scale value being twice (or three times, etc.) as large as another. Ratio scales are rarely, if ever, achieved in psychological and educational measurement, so we will not refer to them in classifying the several statistical techniques below. Thus, so far as type of scale is concerned, our classification will refer only to variables measured on nominal, ordinal, and interval scales.

Finally, the numbers of independent and dependent variables, as well as their respective scale types, make a difference in the available repertoire of statistical techniques. We will distinguish among cases in which the number of each kind of variable is 0, 1, and 2 or more.

Our classification scheme, based on role, scale type, and number of variables, can best be grasped by referring to Table 1 on pages 154–155. Note that the number of *dependent* variables is denoted by k, and the number of *independent* variables by $T - k$, T being the total number of variables.

It was mentioned toward the end of the preceding section that a large variety of statistical techniques concerned with multivariate analysis may be regarded as different cases of *general regression theory*. To see the manner in which these various techniques are interrelated, it is necessary to observe how the total set of T variables is partitioned into the k dependent and $T - k$ independent variables. For this purpose, in turn, it is convenient first to define the *observation matrix*. This is simply a rectangular arrangement of the scores of N individuals on T variables, each row (horizontal array) containing the scores of a particular individual and each column (vertical array) representing a particular variable. If we denote the score of the n-th individual on the i-th variable by X_{ni}

(the first subscript indicating the individual number, the second the variable number), the observation matrix may be written as follows:

$$\begin{bmatrix} X_{11} & X_{12} & \ldots & X_{1k} & \vline & X_{1,k+1} & \ldots & X_{1T} \\ X_{21} & X_{22} & \ldots & X_{2k} & \vline & X_{2,k+1} & \ldots & X_{2T} \\ X_{31} & X_{32} & \ldots & X_{3k} & \vline & X_{3,k+1} & \ldots & X_{3T} \\ \cdot & \cdot & & \cdot & \vline & \cdot & & \cdot \\ \cdot & \cdot & & \cdot & \vline & \cdot & & \cdot \\ \cdot & \cdot & & \cdot & \vline & \cdot & & \cdot \\ X_{N1} & X_{N2} & \ldots & X_{Nk} & \vline & X_{N,k+1} & \ldots & X_{NT} \end{bmatrix}$$

k dependent variables $T-k$ independent variables

Note that the first k columns refer to the dependent variables and the remaining $T - k$ columns to the independent.

Now, associated with this observation matrix with T columns and N rows, we may define a *correlation matrix* of T rows and T columns. This is a square arrangement of the coefficients of correlation among the T variables, the i-th row j-th column entry, r_{ij}, being the correlation between the i-th and j-th variables as numbered in the observation matrix. Corresponding to the partitioning of the observation matrix into two blocks of k and $T - k$ columns, respectively, the correlation matrix may be partitioned into four parts: a square comprising the first k rows and columns which contains the correlations among the dependent variables; the square formed by the remaining $T - k$ rows and columns, containing the correlations among the independent variables; and two rectangular portions, one with k rows and $T - k$ columns, the other with $T - k$ rows and k columns, which contain the correlations between independent and dependent variables. Letting c and p suggest criterion and predictor, respectively, we denote these four parts of the correlation matrix by $\mathbf{R}_{cc}$, $\mathbf{R}_{pp}$, $\mathbf{R}_{cp}$ and $\mathbf{R}_{pc}$, respectively, as indicated at the top of column two.

The correlation matrix is the starting point for several of the multivariate techniques, such as multiple regression, canonical correlation, and most types of factor analysis, discussed below. For other multivariate tech-

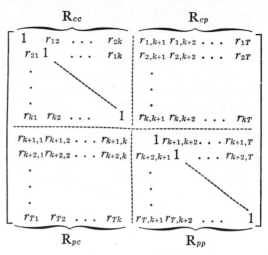

niques, such as discriminant analysis and a certain type of factor analysis, the starting point is not the correlation matrix itself but a related matrix called, interchangeably, the *variance-covariance matrix* or the *dispersion matrix*. The entries (or, technically, the *elements*) of this matrix are of the general form $s_i s_j r_{ij}$, where s_i and s_j are the standard deviations of the i-th and j-th variables, respectively, in the sample of N individuals. These are known as the (sample) *covariances* of the two variables concerned. The diagonal entries (corresponding to the unities in the correlation matrix) are the variances, s_1^2, s_2^2, ..., s_T^2, of the T variables.

Whether it is the correlation matrix or the dispersion matrix that forms the starting point of the particular analysis, the way in which the matrix is partitioned is the distinguishing feature of the technique. That is, the size, k, of the upper left square portion $\mathbf{R}_{cc}$ (or $\mathbf{D}_{cc}$ in the case of a dispersion matrix) characterizes each technique. More particularly, it is whether $k = 0$, $k = 1$, or $k > 1$ that makes the difference. When $k = 0$ (no dependent variable), the matrix is, of course, not partitioned at all, which is the case in factor analysis. When $k = 1$, the "square portion" $\mathbf{R}_{cc}$ degenerates into a single number, 1, and we have the starting point for a multiple regression analysis. With $k > 1$, $\mathbf{R}_{cc}$ is a bona fide square, and the technique in question may be canonical correlation or multiple discriminant analysis. The point is that all these different kinds of multivariate analysis *may* be performed by following essentially similar procedures of matrix algebra that differ only in the absence or presence (and degeneracy or nondegeneracy) of the square submatrix R_{cc} (or D_{cc}). Readers interested in technical discussions of the essential unity of the various types of analysis alluded to above (to which may be added, as a further special case, analysis of variance) are referred to articles by Bartlett (1938, 1947), Guttman (1941a), and Lubin (1950).

Our references in the foregoing to correlations and covariances between pairs of variables despite the fact that we are permitting nominal scales to occur among them may have puzzled the reader. To clarify this point, we note that it is possible to recode a nominally scaled variable into a set of pseudo-quantitative variables, often called *dummy variables,* in the following manner.

Suppose, for specificity, that we have a variable taking four nominal-scale values: A, B, C, D. We can recode the "measurements" on this *single* variable, say X_0, into "measurements" on *three* dummy variables X_1, X_2, X_3, each taking the values 0 and 1, in accordance with the following conversion table:

Score on X_0	Scores on:		
	X_1	X_2	X_3
A	1	0	0
B	0	1	0
C	0	0	1
D	0	0	0

It is readily seen that such recoding can be generalized to a nominal-scale variable with any number of values, say G. We need only define $G - 1$ dummy variables, $X_1, X_2, \ldots, X_{G-1}$, and assign to all individuals having the first nominal score a score of 1 on X_1 and 0s on the other Xs; all individuals with the second nominal score receive 1 on X_2 and 0s on the other Xs; and so on through individuals with the $(G - 1)$-th nominal score, who

receive 1 on X_{G-1} and 0s on the other Xs; individuals with the G-th nominal score receive 0s on *all* the Xs.

In the ensuing discussions, whenever we speak of a multivariate technique involving a correlation or dispersion matrix, we will understand the nominal variables, if any, to have been recoded into the appropriate number of dummy variables, and our total count of variables (T) will be on this basis. On the other hand, in discussing those statistical techniques that do not involve either of these matrices, we will count each nominal variable as a single variable no matter how many different values it may take.

BASIC RATIONALE OF STATISTICAL TESTS AND DISTINCTION BETWEEN PARAMETRIC AND NONPARAMETRIC TESTS

In this section we give a brief description of the rationale underlying statistical significance tests in general. As mentioned earlier, these are procedures that assist the researcher in deciding whether his experimental results tend to confirm or refute his research hypothesis—that is, an assertion that a functional relationship exists between two or more observational variables. One purpose for reviewing this rationale—which should already be quite familiar to most readers—is to bring into focus the essential distinction between traditional parametric tests and the more recently developed nonparametric tests. (Discussions of these latter tests start on page 151.)

As a simple illustration, let us suppose that a certain educational theory leads us to predict that two teaching methods A and B differ in effectiveness, that is, produce different amounts of learning as measured by a suitable test. We call this prediction the *research hypothesis*. To test this hypothesis (and hence the theory from which it is derived), we formulate its negation as our *statistical hypothesis:* that the amounts of learning produced by the two methods are *equal;*

this is known as the *null hypothesis* (H_0). The point is that statistical theory enables us, in general, to anticipate what sort of experimental results we may reasonably expect *if* the null hypothesis is indeed true.

It is trite to say that we would not expect the mean learning scores of two groups taught by the two methods, respectively, to be exactly equal even if the null hypothesis is true. How different must the means of the two groups be before we may reasonably conclude that the null hypothesis is not true (that is, decide to *reject H_0*), and hence infer that our research hypothesis is true? This is the question which statistical theory enables us to answer, provided our experimental procedure has met the appropriate conditions, such as random assignment of subjects to the two groups, or else matching (in terms of such relevant variables as age, IQ, etc.) of each member of one group with one in the other group. The answer, of course, depends, for one thing, on what we mean by "reasonable" when we say "reasonably conclude that the null hypothesis is not true." The notion of "reasonableness" here used is a probabilistic one, and it requires clarification.

In the technical language of statistics the word "reasonable" is not used in the above connection because of its ambiguity. Rather, we speak of the chances or probability of making an erroneous decision to reject the null hypothesis when it is true, or to accept it when it is false. (The tie-in with "reasonableness" is, of course, that we would all agree that it is *not* reasonable to expose ourselves to large chances of making erroneous decisions.) There is an asymmetry between the two kinds of errors just referred to. The probability of erroneously rejecting H_0 when it is in fact true (called *Type I error*) can, in general, be calculated under certain assumptions to be described below. It is this probability that is customarily referred to as the *significance level*. In adopting a certain significance level (such as .01 or .05), we are saying, in effect, that we are willing to expose ourselves to the specified probability of committing a Type I error. On the other hand,

the probability of erroneously accepting H_0 when it is false (*Type II error*) is a more involved concept. It depends, among other things, on *how far wrong* the null hypothesis is. We thus do not have a single numerical value for this probability, but rather a curve showing its values under various degrees of wrongness of H_0.

The above, in very broad outline, are some of the ideas basic to the theory of statistical tests as developed by Neyman and Pearson (1933). Discussions of this theory are available in several textbooks on statistics familiar to the educational researcher, such as those by Walker and Lev (1953, Ch. 2), Edwards (1954, Ch. 13), and McNemar (1955, Ch. 5).

Let us now examine the conditions under which we can calculate the probability of making a Type I error when we decide to reject H_0 upon observing that the difference between the mean scores of our two groups exceeds a certain magnitude. The key to understanding the rationale of such calculations is the idea of *sampling* and *sampling distributions*. The null hypothesis, stating equality of the mean learning scores under the two teaching methods, refers, of course, to the hypothetical populations of all conceivable individuals who might be taught by the two methods, respectively. (More correctly, the reference is to the population of such *scores* and their means.) What we observe are samples from these populations, and the question is, "What is the probability that the sample means will differ by a certain amount or more, given that the population means are equal?"

To answer this question we must know the sampling distribution of differences between pairs of sample means. That is, we need to know what sort of distribution of difference values we would get if (hypothetically) we were to take an infinite series of independent random samples from each of the two populations, calculate the sample means for every sample in the two series, and find the differences of pairs of means in the two series— under the assumption that the respective population means are equal. Once this distribution is known, we can find the proportion of differences which would exceed a given value. This proportion is, by definition, the required probability, which is, in turn, the probability of committing a Type I error when we decide to reject H_0 on the basis of an observed difference exceeding that value. It is the function of mathematical statistics to study such distributions; applied statistics utilizes the results in studying research problems in specific areas.

A different treatment is required depending on how the subjects were assigned to the two experimental groups: at random or by matching. We consider only the first case here. If the scores in question can reasonably be regarded as having normal distributions in the two populations (first assumption), then, provided the sample sizes n_A and n_B are fairly large, it is known that the sampling distribution of the quantity

$$z = \frac{\bar{X}_A - \bar{X}_B}{\sqrt{\dfrac{s_A^2}{n_A} + \dfrac{s_B^2}{n_B}}} \qquad (1)$$

is very nearly the standard normal distribution when H_0 is true ($\bar{X}_A$, $\bar{X}_B$ and s_A^2, s_B^2 are the two sample means and sample variances, respectively). Thus, by referring to a table of normal curve areas, we can find the probability of observing a difference between the two sample means that is equal to or greater than the difference actually obtained, $\bar{X}_A - \bar{X}_B$, if the null hypothesis is true. Hence, if this probability is *smaller* than the significance level we adopted (i.e., the chances of committing a Type I error that we are willing to risk), we would reject H_0.

A further result from mathematical statistics, known as the *central limit theorem,* tells us that, if our samples are *very* large, the quantity z given by equation (1) has a sampling distribution which is *approximately* normal regardless of the kind of distribution our learning scores follow in the populations. In other words, the first assumption mentioned in the preceding paragraph

is not crucial when we are dealing with extremely large samples. Just how large our samples must be for us safely to be able to ignore that assumption is, of course, a debatable point. Fortunately, the scores on many well-constructed psychometric tests, administered to groups for which they were intended, generally yield distributions that are not very far from the normal. Consequently, sample sizes of the order of 100 or even 50 may often qualify as "extremely large."

On the other hand, when we are dealing with very small samples (perhaps 25 or less), the quantity z no longer has a normal (or even nearly normal) distribution *even if* the original score distribution is precisely normal. The trouble lies in the denominator of the expression for z: the variances occurring there should, strictly speaking, be the population variances rather than the sample variances. When the samples are large, the chances are slight that the use of sample variances instead of the population values will introduce large errors, but this is not true when we have small samples. In such a case we can perform a rigorous statistical test only if, in addition to our first assumption (normality of the score distributions in the population), a second one is met: that the variances of the two populations are equal. Their common value need not be known (or assumed); we need assurance only that they are equal, whatever the value may be. It is known that, when both these conditions are met, the quantity

$$t = \frac{\bar{X}_A - \bar{X}_B}{\sqrt{\dfrac{s^2}{n_A} + \dfrac{s^2}{n_B}}}, \qquad (2)$$

where

$$s^2 = \frac{n_A s_A^2 + n_B s_B^2}{n_A + n_B - 2}, \qquad (3)$$

has a sampling distribution called "Student's" t distribution, with $n_A + n_B - 2$ degrees of freedom.

The expressions (1) and (2) are quite similar, the only difference being that, whereas the two sample variances $s_A{}^2$ and $s_B{}^2$ occur individually in the denominator of (1), a single "pooled variance-estimate" (of the common variance of the two populations), defined by equation (3), occurs in (2). But there is a great difference between the role played by the sample variances in (1) and that played by s^2 in (2). In the first case the sample variances are used as *substitutes* for the unknown population variances. How valid the resulting probability of a Type I error is depends, therefore, on how close the sample variances happen to be to their respective population counterparts—which is something we can never ascertain. In the second case, the sample statistic s^2 occurs in its own right: it does not matter how close or how far its value may be from the common variance of the two populations. The validity of the t test depends, instead, on the tenability of the assumption of equal population variances. This assumption can be tested by a separate statistical test, the F test (or variance-ratio test).

The foregoing completes our review of the general rationale of statistical hypothesis testing, with especial emphasis on the underlying assumptions which distinguish parametric from nonparametric methods. Both the large-sample test and the small-sample t test are examples of *parametric* tests. These are statistical tests in which an assumption has to be made concerning the form of the population distribution of scores (normality assumption in our examples) and in which, furthermore, certain conditions regarding population parameters usually have to be met (equality of population variances in the t test). Because such assumptions are often untenable in practice and the requisite conditions on the parameters either are not met or are untestable, increasing attention has been paid recently to statistical tests that do not depend on such assumptions and conditions. These are the *nonparametric* (or distribution-free) tests. Another advantage of nonparametric tests is that they are, for the most part, applicable in situations where the variables are measured on ordinal scales;

some are applicable also to nominal-scale data. Parametric tests typically require at least interval-scale data.

Nonparametric tests may, by and large, be characterized as direct applications of basic principles of probability theory to the problem of calculating the probability of committing a Type I error. The resulting probability values are usually exact, regardless of the form of the relevant population distributions. To illustrate the point, we describe a particularly simple nonparametric test: the sign test for matched pairs.

Suppose, in our earlier example of testing the relative effectiveness of two teaching methods, A and B, that the subjects were assigned to the two groups not at random but by matched pairs. Thus, for each member of Group A, there is a member in Group B who has the same sex, age, IQ, and perhaps other relevant characteristics (such as aptitude for what is to be learned) as his Group A counterpart. To make our discussion specific, let us say there were 20 such matched pairs, one member of each pair being assigned to the group taught by Method A, the other to Group B. Let us further suppose that our research hypothesis this time asserts not just that the two methods differ in effectiveness but that Method A is *superior* to Method B. The null hypothesis appropriate to the sign test is as follows: "The probability that, in any one of the matched pairs, the score of the Group A member will be higher than that of the Group B member is equal to the probability that the opposite will be true, both probabilities having the value $\frac{1}{2}$." The method consists in finding the difference between the Group A member's score and that of his Group B counterpart (always subtracting in the same order, say A — B) and observing how many of these differences are positive and how many are negative.

If H_0 is true, we would expect to find about half of the differences positive and half of them negative. There may, of course, also be some zero differences. If so, they are discarded from the analysis, and the effective sample size is reduced.

Suppose that, of the 20 difference scores, we find 12 to be positive, 4 negative, and 4 zero. Our effective sample size is then 16, and the question is, "What is the probability that we would observe as few as 4 negative differences among the 16 if H_0 is true?" It should be evident that our task is analogous to that of calculating the probability that, out of 16 tosses of an unbiased coin, we should observe *as few as* 4 tails—that is, 4 or fewer. This probability is the sum of the probabilities, respectively, of finding 0, 1, 2, 3, or 4 heads. Each of these can be calculated by making appropriate substitutions in the general formula for the binomial probability distribution, which is

$$P(x) = \frac{n!}{x!\,(n-x)!}\; p^x\,(1-p)^{n-x}, \quad (4)$$

where n is the total number of trials (tosses), x is the number of trials on which the outcome in question (tails) is observed, and p is the probability of that outcome on each trial. Since $p = \tfrac{1}{2}$ under the present null hypothesis, and $n = 16$ in our example, equation (4) becomes

$$P(x) = \frac{16!}{x!\,(16-x)!}\; (\tfrac{1}{2})^{16},$$

in which we take, successively, $x = 0, 1, 2, 3$, and 4 to calculate the probabilities whose sum is the desired probability. The result is

$$(1 + 16 + 120 + 560 + 1820)/65{,}536 = 0.038.$$

Therefore, if we are using the .05 significance level, we would reject H_0 and conclude that the data confirm our research hypothesis.

The sign test, illustrated above, is probably the simplest of all the nonparametric tests. The calculation of the probability of a Type I error is a much more involved process for most other nonparametric tests. Fortunately for the research worker, tables are available for most of the commonly used nonparametric tests. Many of these have been compiled by Siegel (1956) in his highly usable source book for nonparametric techniques written especially for researchers in the behavioral sciences. For each test included in his volume, Siegel discusses its function, rationale, and method, and gives a completely worked out example. Briefer discussions may be found in the following articles and chapters: Moses (1952), Walker and Lev (1953, Ch. 18, by Moses), Mosteller and Bush (1954), McNemar (1955, Ch. 18).

VARIOUS STATISTICAL TECHNIQUES CLASSIFIED ACCORDING TO ROLE, NUMBER, AND SCALE-TYPE OF VARIABLES INVOLVED

We now describe the various statistical techniques listed in Table 1. Each portion of this table that is bordered by double lines will be referred to as a "panel." These are numbered I through IX reading downward and from left to right, in this order.

PANEL I. INTERVAL INDEPENDENT VARIABLES VERSUS INTERVAL DEPENDENT VARIABLES

Case IA. No a Priori Dependent Variable

This is the case of factor analysis, whose starting point, as mentioned above, is the unpartitioned correlation or dispersion matrix. As a heuristic technique, the approach of factor analysis is essentially to obtain a "parsimonious representation" of a complex of variables. That is to say, starting with a set of variables $X_1, X_2, \ldots, X_T$, we determine one or more *linear combinations* (functions of the form $c_1X_1 + c_2X_2 + \ldots + c_TX_T$, where the cs are constants) of the variables that have certain desirable characteristics. What characteristics are deemed desirable for these linear combinations—which, in the present context, are called *factors*—depends on the particular "brand" of factor analysis. One may, for instance, seek *uncorrelated* factors such that the sum of the *factor load-*

ings of the several variables on these factors be a maximum. This is the criterion initially used in Thurstone's (1950) *multiple factor analysis*. Alternatively, one may seek that linear combination which shows greatest variability in the sample—that is, which has the maximum variance under the restriction that the sum of the squares of the coefficients $c_1, c_2, \ldots, c_T$ be unity; one then finds another linear combination which shows greatest variability among those that are uncorrelated with the first factor; and so on, until one has exhausted most of the variability in the original set of variables. This is the approach taken in that type of factor analysis known as *principal components analysis*. Hotelling (1933) is generally acknowledged to be the originator of this method, for, although Kelley (1928) used essentially the same method even earlier, Hotelling developed an ingenious iterative computational procedure for determining the successive principal components.

Of all multivariate techniques, factor analysis is doubtless the best known and most frequently used in educational and psychological research. Since the pioneering work of Spearman (1926), numerous books on mental ability traits, studied via factor analysis, have been written (e.g., Kelley, 1935; Thomson, 1939, 1951; Thurstone, 1935). Personality traits too have been studied by means of this method and recent books in this area include those by Cattell (1957) and Eysenck (1952). Factor analysis has been fruitfully applied to research on teaching (e.g., Ryans, 1960). Interested readers are referred to the books by Thurstone and by Thomson, already cited, and to Harman (1960).

Case IB. One a Priori Dependent Variable

Of the T quantitative variables, one may be designated as the dependent variable from certain a priori considerations and the remaining $T - 1$ variables taken as the independent variables. We then have the familiar (multiple) regression model. As mentioned earlier, the upper left-hand portion, $\mathbf{R}_{cc}$, of the correlation matrix is, in this case, a "degenerate square" of just one number, 1, and the corresponding portion, $\mathbf{D}_{cc}$, of the dispersion matrix is s_1^2.

In multiple regression analysis we are interested in determining a set of $T - 1$ regression weights, $b_2, b_3, \ldots, b_T$, such that the sum of the squared deviations of the dependent variable values X_1 from the linear combination $b_2X_2 + b_3X_3 + \ldots + b_TX_T$ is minimized. Matrix notation facilitates comparison among the several equations we cite in the following and highlights their similarity by virtue of its compactness. (A single matrix equation may represent several ordinary algebraic equations.) We therefore denote the set of regression weights by a $(T - 1) \times 1$ matrix (or a column vector) $\mathbf{b}$, whose elements are $b_2, b_3, \ldots, b_T$. It can then be shown by means of matrix algebra[3] that

$$\mathbf{b} = \mathbf{D}_{pp}^{-1}\, \mathbf{D}_{pc}, \qquad (5)$$

where $\mathbf{D}_{pp}^{-1}$ is the *inverse* of the lower right-hand square submatrix $\mathbf{D}_{pp}$. The familiar multiple correlation coefficient R can be expressed, in matrix notation, as

$$R = \sqrt{\mathbf{D}_{cp}\ \mathbf{D}_{pp}^{-1}\ \mathbf{D}_{pc}}\ .$$

A customary statistical test for this model deals with the possibility that the sample vector $\mathbf{b}$ represents only a random variation from a population vector $\boldsymbol{\beta} = \mathbf{O}$, i.e., the hypothesis that the criterion depends on none of the independent variables and consequently

---

[3] Unfamiliarity with matrix algebra will be no obstacle to the comprehension of the main arguments of this chapter, provided one merely notes the *formal* similarity among certain matrix expressions. For example, it requires no knowledge of matrix algebra to appreciate the similarity between $\mathbf{D}_{cp}\mathbf{D}_{pp}^{-1}\mathbf{D}_{pc}$ and $\mathbf{D}_{pc}\mathbf{D}_{cc}^{-1}\mathbf{D}_{cp}$. Readers who wish to go beyond this will find convenient and adequate introductions to matrix algebra in Thurstone (1950, pp. 1–50) and in Kemeny, Snell, and Thompson (1957, pp. 178–217).

TABLE 1[a]

Statistical Techniques Classified According to the Role,
Scale Type, and Number[b] of Variables Involved

			TYPE AND NUMBER $(T - k)$ OF INDEPENDENT VARIABLES	
			Interval[c]	
			$T - k = 1$	$T - k > 1$
TYPE AND NUMBER (k) OF A PRIORI DEPENDENT VARIABLES	Interval[c]	$k = 0$		Factor Analysis
		$k = 1$	Regression Analysis	Multiple Regression Analysis
		$k > 1$	Multiple Regression Analysis	Canonical Correlation
	Ordinal[c]	$k = 0$	(Transform ordinal variable(s) into either interval or nominal variable(s) and use techniques in Panel I or III, respectively.) OR (Transform interval variable into ordinal and use techniques in Panel V.)	
		$k = 1$		
		$k > 1$		
	Nominal[c]	$k = 0$	Pearson's Resolution of Mixed Gaussian Series	
		$k = 1$	Analysis of Variance (Usually as in Panel VII)	Hotelling's T Mahalanobis's D^2 Fisher's Discriminant Function
		$k > 1$	Analysis of Variance (Usually as in Panel VII)	Rao's V_k Multiple Discriminant Function

[a] Each portion of this table that is bordered by double lines is referred to as a panel; these panels are considered to be numbered I through IX reading downward and from left to right in that order.

[b] The observation matrix is defined in terms of a total of T variables. To determine the number of variables, T, under consideration, add the number of variables in the column under consider-

TABLE 1 (Cont'd.)

STATISTICAL TECHNIQUES CLASSIFIED ACCORDING TO THE ROLE,
SCALE TYPE, AND NUMBER[b] OF VARIABLES INVOLVED (Cont'd.)

TYPE AND NUMBER ($T - k$) OF INDEPENDENT VARIABLES (Cont'd.)			
Ordinal[c]		Nominal[c]	
$T - k = 1$	$T - k > 1$	$T - k = 1$	$T - k > 1$
(Remarks in Panel II apply here as well)			Scores / Scales / Latent Structure Analysis / Typo-dimensions
		Analysis of Variance	
		Multiple Regression Analysis	Multiple Discriminant Function
	Kendall's Coefficient of Concordance(W)		
Spearman's Rank Correlation (ρ) / Kendall's Rank Correlation (τ)		Sign Test / Median Test / Mann-Whitney U Test / Kruskal-Wallis One-way Analysis of Variance	Friedman's Two-way Analysis of Variance
			Chi-square One-sample Test ("goodness of fit")
(See Panel VIII)		Contingency Coefficient / Fisher's Exact Probability for 2 x 2 Tables / McNemar's Test for Significance of Changes / Cochran's Q test for Several Related Proportions / Chi-square Test for Independence / Methods for Maximizing Probability of Correct Classification	
		(None for $k > 1$)	

ation to the number of variables in the row under consideration. The particular cases of 0 and 1 dependent variable and of 1 independent variable are recorded because of their special nature.
[c] Table is cumulative. An ordinal scale may be collapsed to a nominal; an interval, to either an ordinal or nominal.

each of the $T-1$ weights has the value 0. Tests on the centroid of the independent variables based upon a similar model of variation are also available and sometimes used. Rao (1952) made available several other tests which, if used, would add to our understanding of the dependency of the dependent variable. One of Rao's tests applies to the hypothesis that the elements of the column vector β have a common value other than zero (1952, pp. 105–106). A second test assesses the additional predictive value of extra variables (1952, pp. 107–109). A third test deals with the equality of pairs of regression equations with and without an assumption that the centroids of the two sets of points are identical (1952, pp. 112–115). A fourth test is for some a priori assigned regression function (1952, pp. 115–118). Several of these tests have proven useful in studying the reciprocal sensitivity of spouses (Greenwald, 1955).

Case IC. More than One a Priori Dependent Variable

Obviously, we are unnecessarily restricted by a model permitting analyses in terms of only *one* dependent variable. There are instances in research on teaching in which more than one dependent variable is available for study. We may be interested simultaneously in several outcomes of teaching—speed and accuracy of shorthand recording, for example. The criteria might be the grade in a course and the student's satisfaction with the course. In either case, we have several criteria which are frequently analyzed separately or combined into a single criterion on some a priori grounds.

If the several criteria cannot be combined on reasonable a priori grounds, we may seek one or more linear combinations of the criteria that correlate highly with one or more linear combinations of the predictors. This is known as *canonical correlation analysis*. The problem here is to find *two* sets of combining weights—one for the predictor variables, another for the criterion variables. Hotelling (1935, 1936) showed that the sets of weights

that yield the most highly correlating linear combinations are given by the vector solutions, $\mathbf{v}_1$, and $\mathbf{u}_1$, corresponding to the largest scalar solution, μ^2, of the following simultaneous matrix equations:

$$(\mathbf{D}_{pc}\,\mathbf{D}_{cc}^{-1}\,\mathbf{D}_{cp} - \mu^2\,\mathbf{D}_{pp})\,\mathbf{v} = \mathbf{O} \quad (6)$$

and

$$(\mathbf{D}_{cp}\,\mathbf{D}_{pp}^{-1}\,\mathbf{D}_{pc} - \mu^2\,\mathbf{D}_{cc})\,\mathbf{u} = \mathbf{O}. \quad (7)$$

Each μ^2 value which satisfies these equations gives the square of the covariance between the linear combination of predictor variables and the linear combination of criterion variables having as weights the elements of the corresponding vector solutions $\mathbf{v}$ and $\mathbf{u}$, respectively. The number of non-zero values of μ^2 is the smaller of the two numbers k or $T-k$, k being the number of criterion variables.

In the extreme case when there is only *one* independent variable, there is no problem of seeking a set of weights for the single predictor variable, and the canonical correlation analysis reduces to the problem of finding the column vector $\mathbf{u}$ of weights for the $T-1$ criterion variables correlating most highly with the single predictor variable. It is intuitively clear, in this event, that the canonical correlation problem is only a multiple regression problem with the roles of the dependent and independent variables reversed. It can also be shown that equation (7) reduces to

$$k\mathbf{D}_{cp} - \mu^2\,\mathbf{D}_{cc}\,\mathbf{u} = \mathbf{O}$$

in this case. Hence,

$$\mathbf{u} = (k/\mu^2)\,\mathbf{D}_{cc}^{-1}\mathbf{D}_{cp},$$

which is, except for the constant factor k/μ^2, the equivalent of equation (5) with p and c interchanged.

The computational labor involved in the solution of the canonical correlation problem is so great that we have seen few applications of the technique. A monograph by Kelley (1940) presented the idea, emphasizing its importance in vocational guidance and giving several illustrations of its application. In collaboration with Dr. Neal Gross, the authors have experimented with the technique in the study of social sensitivity. The technique was used by Seibel (1955) in a study of the relationship among several predictor variables and several variables reflecting the warmth a practice teacher exhibits in the classroom. O'Hara and Tiedeman (1959) recently made extensive use of the technique in studying the clarification of vocationally relevant conceptions of self in adolescent boys. For the most part, canonical correlation is now of only theoretical interest in educational and psychological research despite the fact that Hotelling considered it to be so important for educators and psychologists that he published his original exposition in the *Journal of Educational Psychology* (1935). This condition may soon change because the cost and labor of high-speed computation are now within manageable bounds. Meanwhile, the technique is of considerable theoretical interest because it enables the unification of regression theory as indicated herein as well as in Horst (1959).

PANEL II. INTERVAL INDEPENDENT VARIABLES VERSUS ORDINAL DEPENDENT VARIABLES

Panel II represents the usual condition in investigations relating predictor variables and course grades. There is no statistical technique specifically designed for this case. The customary way of handling this situation is to change the ordinal dependent variable(s) either into interval variable(s) or into nominal variable(s) by one or another means. Most often, a variable such as course grade is merely *presumed* to approximate an interval scale. Occasionally, however, the more elaborate procedure of using a normalizing transformation is adopted. In either case, the techniques listed in Panel I and discussed above are used. The other extreme, that of converting the ordinal variable into a nominal one, is to force a dichotomy, for example, at the median, or by considering the upper and lower 27 per cents of the cases, etc. The

techniques of Panel III, discussed below, are then applied.

An alternative approach would be to convert the interval variable(s) into ordinal variable(s) and to apply rank-order statistics, which are the most common types of non-parametric tests. (See discussions in connection with Panel V, below.) Such a procedure has been frowned upon as "throwing away information," but in view of the fact that most so-called "interval variables" in educational research are at best ordinal variables that approximate an interval scale, the information thereby lost would not seem to be of any great validity.

PANEL III. INTERVAL INDEPENDENT VARIABLES VERSUS NOMINAL DEPENDENT VARIABLES

Let us turn now to the next panel in Table 1, the panel in which are considered problems involving several interval independent variables and varying numbers of nominal dependent variables.

Case IIIA. No a Priori Dependent Variable

An example of this case is Pearson's treatise (1894) on the dissection of non-normal frequency curves into normal components. Pearson gave equations for estimating the desired means and dispersions (variances and covariances) of two presumably undistinguished groups in terms of the moments of the unresolved series. Although Pearson's method can be generalized to any hypothesized number of components, the computational labor increases so rapidly with increases in the number of groups and variables that the method has been applied only in the simplest case of two groups and one variable. Rao (1952, pp. 300–307) substituted Fisher's system of cumulants[4] for Pearson's system of

---

[4] The cumulants of a distribution are certain functions of the moments that possess properties especially convenient for sampling theory. For example, all but the first two cumulants are zero for the normal distribution.

moments in Pearson's equations for the means and dispersions of the two undistinguished groups; he then proceeded to discuss the trustworthiness of the estimates and proposed an approximate solution for the case of two groups and T independent variables which made use of Penrose's (1947) work on a "size" and "shape" factor in discriminant analysis. Knapp (1959) recently developed a procedure, generalizable to any number of variables, based upon maximization of the kurtosis of the distribution in the unresolved series. Computationally, the method is cumbersome.

Although tests used in research on teaching usually yield (or are made to yield) scores that look as if they are distributed normally in the relevant population at large, there are circumstances in which the resolution of a distribution into a series of normal components is relevant. For instance, Tiedeman and Bryan (1954) found that scores on an interest test differentiated students majoring in various college fields. This result occurred in a test whose scores are ordinarily distributed normally in a college population. The observation, not a unique one, strongly suggests that, even with test scores showing a multivariate normal distribution in a certain population, there still remains the possibility of resolving the over-all distribution into a series of component-distributions which represent various subpopulations. (Strictly speaking, these component-distributions cannot be normal, but they may nevertheless be treated as such as a convenient mathematical model for estimating the required parameters.) Such subpopulations may be called *types* (Tiedeman, 1955).

The development of a nosology of psychological disorders and educational deficiencies is of paramount importance to a science of teaching. A nosology would enable us first to diagnose more accurately and then to be selective in our prescription of a program of education. But little if any research has been done as yet in this direction. Probably for some time to come we will continue to lack a solution for inferring the number of types,

the location of the several centroids, and the several dispersion matrices hidden within an unresolved multivariate set of scores. Our most promising approach for the time being seems to be to establish types on an a priori basis and to study the multivariate distributions of these established types. The information gained from such study may, in turn, provide preliminary estimates of some of the parameters which may guide the researcher when nothing about the types is hypothesized. Research of this nature should lead to isolation of further types for inclusion in the nosology to which we have referred.

Case IIIB. One a Priori Dependent Variable

This case may further be subdivided into those situations in which it is preferable to treat the nominally scaled dependent variable just as it is—i.e., as a set of arbitrarily labeled categories—and those in which it is advantageous to recode it into one or more pseudo-quantitative dummy variables as described on page 148. The familiar technique of analysis of variance is a good example of the first situation. Ordinarily, however, analysis of variance is applied in situations where the *independent* variable(s) is (are) nominally scaled and the *dependent* variable is measured on an interval scale. Accordingly, we will discuss this technique in connection with Panel VII, below. Here we will discuss those techniques which involve a single dichotomous dummy variable.

The situation, then, is formally equivalent to that of the multiple regression problem. Equation (5) yields the set of weights, **b**, for forming the linear combination of the $T - 1$ independent variables that correlates most highly with the dummy criterion variable. The interpretation of this linear combination is distinctive, however, and it can best be seen in terms of Fisher's formulation of the problem in discriminant terms. Fisher (1936) considered the problem of getting a linear combination of $T - 1$ variables which would, better than any other linear combination, discriminate between two chosen groups. By "better discrimination" he meant, specifically, that the ratio of the between-groups sum-of-squares of this linear function to its within-groups sum-of-squares (hereafter called the *discriminant criterion*) would have a larger value than that for any other linear function of the same variables. He showed that the combining weights yielding this optimal linear combination, which he termed the *discriminant function,* are the elements of the column vector $\mathbf{v}$ satisfying the matrix equation,

$$(\mathbf{A} - \lambda\mathbf{W})\,\mathbf{v} = 0. \tag{8}$$

Here W is a $(T-1) \times (T-1)$ matrix whose elements w_{jm} are the sums-of-squares and the sums-of-cross-products, within the two groups, of the $(T-1)$ original independent variables, i.e.,

$$w_{jm} =$$

$$\sum_{g=1}^{2} \sum_{i=1}^{n_g} (X_{igj} - \bar{X}_{\cdot gj})(X_{igm} - \bar{X}_{\cdot gm}); \tag{9}$$

$$(j, m = 2, 3, \ldots, T)$$

and A is a $(T-1) \times (T-1)$ matrix whose elements are the dispersions of the group means about the grand mean, i.e.,

$$a_{jm} = \sum_{g=1}^{2} n_g (\bar{X}_{\cdot gj} - \bar{X}_{\cdot\cdot j})(\bar{X}_{\cdot gm} - \bar{X}_{\cdot\cdot m}); \tag{10}$$

$$(j, m = 2, 3, \ldots, T).$$

The relationship between the matrices $\mathbf{W}$ and $\mathbf{A}$ and the previously defined dispersion matrix $\mathbf{D}$ is that

$$\mathbf{W} + \mathbf{A} = \mathbf{D}_{pp},$$

which is the multivariate analogue of the relationship between "within-groups," "between-groups," and total sums-of-squares in the analysis of variance.

The interesting point is that the discrimi-

nant function weights, $\mathbf{v}$, determined from equation (8) are proportional to the regression weights, $\mathbf{b}$, given by equation (5) for the formal multiple regression problem using the dummy criterion variable to indicate membership in the one or the other group. This fact was shown by Fisher in a 1938 paper, in which he also showed that the difference between the group-means on the discriminant function is proportional to Hotelling's T^2(1931), a generalization of Student's t statistic to multivariate cases, as well as to Mahalanobis' D^2 (1927), a measure of the "distance" between two groups. Because of the relationship of the discriminant function to Hotelling's T^2, Fisher was able to give a firm theoretical basis to his 1936 z test (or the now more common F test) for the null hypothesis of coincidence of the multivariate centroids in the two populations sampled. Further, its relationship with the generalized distance D^2 enables one to use the discriminant function in studies of distances between pairs of group-centroids. Finally, the proportionality to the point-biserial multiple regression function implies a mathematical relation between the value of the discriminant criterion (for the discriminant function) and that of the multiple correlation coefficient.

In 1939 Welch published a short note treating the classification problem from the standpoint of maximizing the probability of correct classification. He showed that Fisher's discriminant function was the best linear discriminator in this probability sense (in addition to being best in the discriminant-criterion sense) when the distributions of the $T-1$ variables were multivariate normal with equal dispersions in the two populations involved. Thus, Fisher's apparently intuitive use of the discriminant criterion in connection with classificatory problems is justified in terms of what is the most natural goal in such problems: to achieve a high probability of correct classification, at least under conditions usually satisfied by the kind of data with which he was primarily concerned.

In the special case of two multivariate normal populations with equal dispersions, it will be noted that the linear discriminant function spans the field, so to speak. While, essentially, it only estimates the *direction* of the difference between populations, it can be used in studying significance, distance, and classification as well, by virtue of its relationships with T^2, D^2, and the likelihood-ratio solution to the classification problem. This versatility of the discriminant function quickly appealed to psychologists, and by 1938, Wallace and Travers had made its first application to psychometric data in their study of specialty salesmen. Travers continued his interest in the linear discriminant function, and first introduced it to the American literature in 1939. Selover (1942) studied the differences between sophomore test scores of graduate concentrators in various fields at the University of Minnesota by means of discriminant analysis. Kuder (1946, pp. 21–25) developed the M-F scale and the Accountant-Auditor Scale for his Preference Record by computing discriminant functions for the respective pairs of groups contrasted. Baten and Hatcher (1944), using a discriminant function based on three measures of cooking ability, differentiated between groups of students taught cooking by two different methods. Harper (1950) used the technique for classifying individuals into normal and schizophrenic groups on the basis of Wechsler-Bellevue subtest scores.

Case IIIC. More than One a Priori Dependent Variable

In research on teaching we frequently wish to study more than two categories of people simultaneously. In developing methods for the guidance of prospective teachers, for instance, the vocational groups under consideration almost always would be more than two in number. While this would still involve only one *nominal* variable as such, its recoding into pseudoquantitative variables requires the use of one less than the number of groups considered, as described on page 148. Thus, given G groups, we will have $k = G - 1$ dummy dependent variables and

$T - k = T - G + 1$ independent variables.

One may analyze such data either by considering the among- and within-groups sums-of-squares of linear combinations of the $T - k$ independent variables (i.e., the analysis of variance approach) or by considering the correlations between linear combinations of the pseudoquantitative dependent variables and the interval-scale independent variables (i.e., the canonical correlation approach). The analysis of variance approach has been the one followed most frequently, so it will be considered first.

Fisher (1938) and Mather (1949) described a method for computing a discriminant function for more than two groups. Equation (8) holds just as well in this case, the only difference being that, in the equations defining the elements of the matrices **W** and **A,** the subscript g, denoting the group, takes the values $1, 2, \ldots, G$ instead of only the values 1 and 2 as previously. There will now exist, in general, $G - 1$ possible vector solutions for **v**, each associated with a permissible value for λ. Of these, Fisher took the **v** associated with the largest value of λ to define the required set of discriminant function weights. The resulting linear combination yields the maximum discriminant criterion, whose value is the corresponding λ value.

While this method does not assume a natural ordering of the groups to start out with, it is clear that, by considering only one linear combination as *the* discriminant function, the method in effect makes a linear ordering of the groups. Consequently, the discriminant function thus defined does not exhaust all the information in the data that is relevant to group-separation, except in the rare case when the population centroids are in fact collinear. Recognizing this, Fisher devised a test of collinearity (1938). A related but more general test-criterion and its distribution were subsequently studied by Tintner (1945). These tests tell us when we can, without appreciable loss of information, use the single discriminant function defined above. When the contrary is true, as will usually be the case, we need to consider more than one discriminant function.

The fact that the matrix equation (8) possesses $G - 1$ solutions was, of course, well known. Thus, Fisher spoke of the "second canonical variate" (1936), and Guttman (1941a) and Tukey (1949) referred to the successive vector solutions of such a matrix equation. The computational difficulty of actually obtaining these successive solutions is so great, however, that no computed example of multigroup discriminant functions qua discriminant functions appeared in the literature until Bryan (1950, 1951) developed a reasonably workable computational routine and also showed that linear combinations defined by these successive vectors have this property: the first (corresponding to the largest λ-value) maximizes the discriminant criterion in Fisher's original sense; the second (whose associated λ-value is the second largest) maximizes the ratio of the *residual* among-groups sum-of-squares to *residual* within-group sum-of-squares after the effect of the first linear combination has been removed; the third maximizes the ratio of the corresponding sums-of-squares after the effects of the first two have been removed; and so forth. Bryan called these successive linear combinations the *multiple discriminant functions*. There are $G - 1$ of these, except in the unusual case when $T - G + 1$ is smaller than $G - 1$, in which case there are $T - G + 1$ discriminants.

While multiple discriminant functions were originally intended primarily to serve as tools in multigroup classification problems, they also permitted the study of *direction* of group differences in precisely those cases of real interest (noncollinearity), which for the single discriminant function constituted "nuisance cases," so to speak. In such studies, the general purpose bears a certain resemblance to that of factor analysis in the sense that a parsimonious description—and perhaps a potentially fruitful one theoretically—is sought, which satisfactorily accounts for the intergroup variations by means of a smaller number of variables than the original

$T - G + 1$. This was illustrated by Tiedeman, Bryan, and Rulon (1951), who obtained multiple discriminant functions, based on the 17 tests of the USAF Airman Classification Battery, for differentiating among eight Air Force specialty groups, and interpreted the first two functions as "factors" representing certain psychological traits.

The other approach to multiple discriminant analysis, using $G - 1$ dummy variables to indicate group membership, is formally equivalent to canonical correlation analysis, discussed above. This method was expounded by Brown (1947). As Tatsuoka (1953) demonstrated, the successive vector roots $\mathbf{v}$ of equation (6), solved in combination with equation (7), are respectively proportional to the corresponding vector roots of equation (8). Solving equation (8) by Bryan's method, mentioned above, is somewhat less tedious than the simultaneous solution of equations (6) and (7), so nothing is gained computationally from the canonical correlation approach. What *is* gained is the knowledge that various significance tests developed in connection with canonical correlation theory can be applied just as well in multiple discriminant analysis. Most of these tests are based upon Wilks's (1932) Λ-ratio, and were developed by Bartlett (1947) and Rao (1948a, 1948b, 1952). One such test permits the determination of the number of multiple discriminant functions to be retained because they represent dimensions of significant intergroup variations, as was illustrated by Tiedeman and Bryan (1954). In case the population centroids are all identical, the number thus determined will of course be zero. Lohnes (1960) has recently noted several cautions that should be considered in using tests of this nature.

PANEL IV. ORDINAL INDEPENDENT
VARIABLES VERSUS
INTERVAL DEPENDENT VARIABLES

This panel is the same as Panel II with the roles of the dependent and independent variables switched around, and all that has been said with regard to Panel II concerning the case of interval independent versus ordinal dependent variables holds just as well for this case.

PANEL V. ORDINAL INDEPENDENT VARIABLES VERSUS ORDINAL DEPENDENT VARIABLES

Case VA. One a Priori Dependent Variable

We deviate from our customary order of discussing the subcases, because the techniques applicable to problems involving one ordinal dependent variable (and one ordinal independent variable) are much better known than the techniques applicable to many ordinal independent variables without any a priori dependent variable.

Spearman's rank correlation coefficient, ρ, is probably too well known to require much discussion. It is simply the Pearsonian product-moment correlation coefficient formally calculated for situations in which we have rank-orders—the prototype ordinal scale—instead of interval scales for the two variables being correlated. Perhaps less well known than the computational formula for ρ is the test of significance of an observed value for ρ. This test is based on the idea that, under the null hypothesis that no relationship exists between the two variables in the population, all possible combinations of rank-orders are equally likely in the sample. A table showing the critical values of ρ (at the .05 and .01 significance levels) for sample sizes up to 30 is given in Siegel (1956, p. 284). For larger sample sizes, an approximate significance test developed by Kendall (1948) is also given in that book.

Another rank correlation coefficient is Kendall's τ, which has the advantage over Spearman's ρ of being generalizable to a partial correlation coefficient that can be applied when it is desired to rule out the possible effects of a third variable. Kendall's τ is based on a count of the number of *pairs* of individuals in the sample for whom the ranks on the two variables are in the same order (i.e., pairs in which the same individual ranks higher than his mate on *both* variables). Observed values of τ, too, can be tested for significance either by an exact method for small samples or an approximate one for large samples.

Case VB. No a Priori Dependent Variable

In research on teaching we sometimes have to rely on expert opinion to judge the relative merits of several individuals or of several groups in terms of some trait or performance. In such cases it would, of course, be desirable to have the opinion of a panel of several judges rather than that of a single person. Then there arises the need to assess the degree of agreement among the several judges, that is, the interjudge reliability. Given T judges, each ranking the N individuals (or groups or objects) in accordance with his opinion of their relative merits, we have a problem involving T ordinal independent variables and no a priori dependent variable ($k = 0$).

Another type of situation in which we need to analyze data on T ordinal variables with $k = 0$ arises when we wish to perform a *cluster analysis* of sets of variables. This is a crude form of factor analysis. We might, for instance, group the T variables into several clusters on a priori grounds, and then wish to test whether those variables which were placed in any one cluster show a higher over-all agreement in rankings than does the entire set of T variables.

In either type of problem alluded to above, we need a measure of over-all agreement among sets of more than two rankings. In principle, we could calculate τs or ρs for all possible pairs of rankings and use the average τ (or ρ) as an over-all measure of correlation. Such a procedure, however, would be extremely tedious unless the total number of variables were very small. Kendall's *coefficient of concordance, W,* is designed for such a situation, and from it can easily be calculated the average ρ, if desired (Kendall,

1948). The coefficient W is the ratio of the variance of the observed sum of the T ranks assigned each individual, to the maximum possible variance of these sums (obtaining under perfect agreement among the T sets of rankings). An exact small-sample test and an approximate large-sample test of the significance of W are available.

Details concerning the techniques listed in this panel are given in Siegel (1956).

PANEL VI. ORDINAL INDEPENDENT VARIABLES VERSUS NOMINAL DEPENDENT VARIABLES

The several techniques listed in Panel VIII may be used for this case with the roles of independent and dependent variables reversed. Alternatively, one may convert the ordinal variables into either interval or nominal variables (as described in connection with Panel II) and use the appropriate technique under Panel III, or Panel IX, respectively.

PANEL VII. NOMINAL INDEPENDENT VARIABLES VERSUS INTERVAL DEPENDENT VARIABLES

This panel is technically the mirror image of Panel III. Certain points of experimental interest concerning cases of this category are, however, worthy of particular notice.

Case VIIA. No a Priori Dependent Variable

Of considerable interest in research on teaching is the situation in which responses of N subjects to a set of T items are available. An interval dependent variable is to be derived from the responses. Although many persons have attacked this problem, Guttman has worked long and consistently at it.

Guttman (1941b) dealt with the problem of quantifying a class of attributes. Three approaches were used: (1) deriving a set of weights for T items which enables a maximal reconstruction of the behavior of the population; (2) deriving a set of scores for the N individuals which will best differentiate individuals who checked an item from those who did not; and (3) deriving simultaneously a set of weights for the T items and a set of scores for the N individuals so that people with similar scores are, by and large, those who have checked subcategories with similar weights.

Guttman demonstrated that the correlation *ratio* approach to the first two problems and the correlation *coefficient* approach to the last problem are identical (1941b, pp. 339–340). His final equations have a form similar to our equations (6) and (7) for canonical correlation. He included a short review of the works of Edgerton and Kolbe (1936), Horst (1936), and Wilks (1938) related to the problem and concluded that "all these solutions for the quantitative case are essentially the major axis of the principal axes solution for multiple factor analysis" (1941b, p. 346) described most fully by Hotelling (1933). Although he noted important distinctions between his solutions and those of the principal axes of factor analysis, Guttman also indicated certain similarities between them; i.e., the matrix to be "factored" in Guttman's procedure comprises the chi-square product-moments between all pairs of the attributes (1941b, pp. 330–332).

Work on the problem of quantifying qualitative attributes has taken great strides since the appearance of Guttman's work (1941b). Lazarsfeld (1950) introduced the notion of latent structure analysis, and both these and other investigators have carried these first tentative notions quite far. McQuitty (1955) initiated description of his notion of typo-dimensions which also deserves attention in any study of this case.

Case VIIB. One a Priori Dependent Variable

The analysis of variance may be regarded as a method for predicting a single quantitative variable from one or more qualitative variables. Thus Lubin wrote, "The simple probability models used in setting up the equations of analysis of variance postulate a quantitative effect for each category of classification. They can, therefore, be regarded as prediction equations" (1950, p. 91).

For instance, in the simplest case of analysis of variance, we have measurements, X, on each of n_1 individuals of Class 1 and on each of n_2 individuals of Class 2, and we use the mean of the Class 1 individuals as an estimate of the measurement, X, of the Class 1 population and the mean of the Class 2 individuals as an estimate of the measurement, X, of the Class 2 population. Discrepancies between actual measurements of members of each class and these estimates for each class indicate the error of these predictions.

When we have only two classes of people, our nominal independent variable can be recoded into a single dummy variable, and our analysis of variance is formally equivalent to an ordinary regression problem. As more groups are introduced, we increase the number of pseudoquantitative independent variables by one for each additional group, following the coding scheme described above. Hence, it is intuitively clear that the problem is one of multiple regression; and this proves to be the case mathematically also. The customary purpose of carrying out an analysis of variance—namely, to test the significance of the over-all difference among several group means—may be accomplished, in this regression approach, by testing the significance of the multiple correlation coefficient thus obtained.

The importance of the analysis of variance technique for research on teaching is now so well known as to need no exposition here.

Case VIIC. More than One a Priori Dependent Variable

When more than one a priori interval variable and one or more nominal independent variables are involved, the problem may be formulated as a multiple regression problem if there is only one nominal in-

dependent variable, and as a multiple discriminant function problem if there is more than one independent variable. This, therefore, is a mirror image of Case IIIC in which the dependent variables of this case play the role of the independent variables of Case IIIC.

Although the technique is the same, there is a difference between the problem of this case and that of Case IIIC. In Case IIIC, we were interested in predicting the *class* to which a person belongs from a set of quantitative measures. In the present case we are interested in predicting the value of each of a set of quantitative measures from a knowledge of the class to which an individual belongs. The first case is exemplified in the guidance situation; the second case in the teaching situation, e.g., how much information is learned from each of two types of cooking instruction (Baten & Hatcher, 1944).

Our information from experiments would be increased considerably if we studied several variables simultaneously, as we can by the multiple discriminant function, rather than by studying them independently of one another as we do in performing several separate variance analyses.

Panel VIII. Nominal Independent Variables versus Ordinal Dependent Variables

A wealth of nonparametric methods is available for use in the situations represented by Panel VIII. Again we refer the reader to Siegel's compendious source book and give here only brief descriptions of a few of the best known and most widely used techniques. All these are applicable only to problems involving one dependent variable ($k = 1$).

The sign test has already been described in some detail on pages 151–152. We point out here that, for samples larger than $N = 25$ (pairs), the normal approximation to the binomial distribution can be used for calculating the probability of a Type I error.

The median test is applied when the two

samples are independent—that is, when individuals are assigned to the two groups at random instead of by matching as in the case when the sign test is applicable. The essential idea of the median test is to compare the numbers of individuals in each group whose scores (or ranks) are above and below the median of the combined group, respectively. If the two groups are samples from populations with equal medians, we would expect about one-half of each group to have scores above the combined median and one-half to have scores below it. An exact test for the significance of an observed departure from this situation is provided by the hypergeometric distribution. An approximate test, for large samples, is based on the chi-square distribution.

The Mann-Whitney (1947) U test is used to test the null hypothesis that two independent groups are samples from the same population. The procedure is quite simple. One simply counts the number of scores in one group that exceed *each* score in the other group. The total of such numbers is the U statistic. Tables are available for finding the probability (under the null hypothesis) associated with each possible value of U for sample sizes up to 8, and for critical U values at selected significance levels for sample sizes between 9 and 20. For samples larger than 20, an approximate test based on the normal curve is available.

The Kruskal-Wallis (1952) one-way analysis of variance is useful in deciding whether several independent groups can be reasonably regarded as samples from the same population or populations with the same median. The method involves ranking the scores in all the groups into a *single* sequence, from smallest to largest. The sum of these ranks is then obtained for *each* group. The test essentially determines whether these sums are so disparate (after allowances are made for differences in group sizes) that they cannot reasonably be regarded as having resulted from samples drawn from the same population. Exact probabilities associated with selected values of the statistic have been tabled for three samples of all possible combinations of sizes up to 5. For larger samples, the test statistic is approximately distributed as a chi square with $G - 1$ degrees of freedom (where G is the number of groups).

A rank-order analysis of variance is also available for the case of two-way classification, or, in our terminology, for problems involving two nominal independent variables. The restriction is that the several groups (which constitute one nominal variable) must each consist of matched individuals. This sort of situation may often arise in research on teaching. The researcher may, for instance, select G groups of N pupils, each group comprising pupils matched on certain relevant variables (IQ, family background, etc.), and assign at random one subject from each of these G groups to a certain experimental condition. The N different conditions constitute the second nominal variable.

The data from such an experiment may be arranged in a matrix of N rows and G columns. The analysis, developed by Friedman (1937), starts out by ranking the scores *within each column* (i.e., group), either from smallest to largest or vice versa. We then have G sets of ranks from 1 to N. The rationale of the test is as follows. If the N experimental conditions (teaching method, etc.) do not differentially affect the learning, then the distribution of the ranks in each *row* would merely be a matter of chance—that is, we would not expect those pupils subjected to any particular one of the experimental conditions to rank consistently high (or consistently low) within their respective groups of matched individuals. If so, the sums of the ranks for the N rows, respectively, would all be approximately equal. Hence, the variance of the N row-totals of the ranks is a measure of the degree of departure from the null hypothesis indicated by the data. Friedman's test statistic is proportional to this variance, and its sampling distribution is, approximately, the chi-square distribution with $N - 1$ degrees of freedom, provided that neither N nor G is too small.

For very small N and G, an exact table is available to indicate probabilities associated with various observed values of the test statistic.

PANEL IX. NOMINAL INDEPENDENT VARIABLES VERSUS NOMINAL DEPENDENT VARIABLES

Relatively few procedures are available for use in the circumstances of this case. Chief among these are the contingency coefficient, the chi-square test of independence, and the related idea of predicting class membership from a knowledge of qualitative independent variables so as to maximize the probability of correct classifications over the situation as a whole. This latter approach has been described by Guttman (1941a).

The contingency coefficient, C, as a measure of strength of association between two nominal variables, is well known and widely used. Since its calculation requires first obtaining the chi-square statistic for testing the independence of the two variables, it has a built-in significance test, so to speak.

Perhaps less widely known is Fisher's exact probability test for 2×2 contingency tables in which the frequencies are so small that the customary chi-square test is not applicable. If the null hypothesis is in fact true, we would expect the cell frequencies to be roughly proportional to the marginal totals. Fisher's test consists in directly calculating the probability, under the null hypothesis, that, given the observed marginal totals, we would get a contingency table which represents as great a departure (or greater) from this proportionality situation as that actually observed. The calculated probability is "one-tailed," since only tables showing greater departure from the null hypothesis situation in the same direction as does the observed table are considered: it is therefore comparable to *half* the probability based on a chi-square test. We note in passing that, although the legitimacy of assuming the marginal totals fixed (over successive sampling) has been questioned in the statistical

literature, the assumption is no different from that implicit in the chi-square test of independence: there the expected cell frequencies are calculated on the basis of the observed marginal totals. We also note that a modification to increase the power of Fisher's test was developed by Tocher (1950).

Two other procedures may be regarded as appropriate to situations represented by this panel: McNemar's (1947) test for significance of changes (i.e., difference between two correlated proportions) and Cochran's (1950) Q test for over-all significance of differences among several correlated proportions.

The prototype situation for which McNemar's well-known test is used is the so-called "before and after" design. That is to say, a single group of subjects is measured on some attribute in terms of a dichotomous nominal scale (such as possessing or not possessing some characteristic, or agreeing or disagreeing with some standpoint) both before and after exposure to some experimental condition. What is determined by the test, which utilizes a chi-square statistic, is whether the change in proportion of positive cases from before to after the experimental treatment is significant.

It should be evident that the above test is equivalent to testing the independence between the variable represented by the experimental condition and that measured on the dichotomous scale. Hence, the test can be applied to other types of designs besides the "before and after." For instance, if two *matched* groups of subjects receive two different experimental treatments and the effects are measured on a dichotomous variable, McNemar's test may be used to test the significance of the difference between the proportions of one category in the two groups. (It should be noted, however, that in this case, unlike a case involving independent groups, it is insufficient merely to find the respective proportions. The data must be arranged in a two-way layout indicating the numbers of pairs in which both members are "positive," both are "negative," the Group

1 member is "positive" while his Group 2 counterpart is "negative," and vice versa.)

Cochran's Q test is essentially a generalization of McNemar's two-related-samples test to the case of G related samples. Suppose we have G matched samples of size N, each placed under a distinct experimental condition. (Alternatively, a single group of N subjects may successively undergo G different experimental treatments.) The responses are, again, measured on a dichotomous scale—"yes-no," "pass-fail," etc. These may be coded into 1s and 0s and arranged into an $N \times G$ matrix. If the null hypothesis (that the probability of, say, "pass" is equal under all G conditions) is true, then the 1s and 0s should be randomly distributed in the rows and columns of this matrix. Working from this fact, Cochran (1950) showed that a certain quantity Q, somewhat akin to the ratio of the variances of the column totals and of the row totals, approximately follows a chi-square distribution with $G - 1$ degrees of freedom.

A NOTE ON CONTROL VARIABLES

With the foregoing we conclude our survey of selected statistical techniques relevant to research on teaching. We have not attempted to be exhaustive. Nor have we tried to make this chapter self-contained as a practical guide to performing the various analyses described. Rather, our twofold purpose has been (1) to impart to the reader a "feel" for the role and function of statistics in scientific research, and (2) to provide him with a theoretical frame of reference from which he can view the various statistical techniques in a more unified and meaningful way.

The particular reference frame we chose— that of classifying the various statistical techniques according to the role (independent and dependent), number, and type (interval, ordinal, and nominal) of the variables involved—may not appeal to all readers. Some readers may find it forced, for instance, to regard a test of significance of the difference between two proportions as a test of independence between two nominal variables. We contend, however, that giving the reader a somewhat unfamiliar viewpoint should broaden his understanding of the statistical techniques suitable to his research problem.

In view of our emphasis on the role played by variables, the lack of mention of *control variables* may, to many readers, seem conspicuous. A few words now about such variables may bridge the gap. In a certain sense, the use of control variables is an admission of defeat: it is tantamount to saying that our theory holds only on condition that certain relevant factors are held in abeyance. To give an example from the physical sciences, Boyle's law states that the volume of a given quantity of gas is inversely proportional to the pressure applied to it, *provided* the temperature is held constant. It says nothing about what would happen if temperature (the control variable) were also permitted to vary. To that extent, it admits defeat. Historically, it has been superseded by (and is a special case of) the general gas law, which states a relationship between the volume, pressure, *and* temperature of a gas. Yet, who can say that the general gas law could have been discovered without the prior discovery of the more restricted Boyle's law (and its companion, Charles' law, stating the relationship between volume and temperature, with pressure held constant)?

In the light of the foregoing argument, it seems that control variables must be accepted as a necessary evil in the course of development of a scientific theory. The most straightforward way to control a variable is, of course, to select samples that are homogeneous with respect to the control variables. The use of matched samples, often referred to in the foregoing, achieves this aim. It is sometimes infeasible, however, to achieve such experimental control. We then have to resort to statistical control in the course of analysis. Most of the parametric techniques, and at least one of the nonparametric techniques (Kendall's τ), described in the foregoing, are susceptible to such statistical control of experimentally uncontrolled variables.

The fortunate circumstance just alluded to should not, however, be permitted to becloud the fact that, by introducing control variables unnecessarily, we restrict our theory unwarrantedly. The alternative of using more independent variables is open to us, provided we familiarize ourselves more with the various techniques of multivariate analysis that are available.

REFERENCES

Bartlett, M. S. Further aspects of the theory of multiple regression. *Proc. Cambridge Phil. Soc.,* 1938, 34, 33–40.

Bartlett, M. S. Multivariate analysis. *J. Royal Statist. Soc.,* 1947 (Supp. 9), 176–190.

Baten, W. D., & Hatcher, Hazel M. Distinguishing method differences by use of discriminant functions. *J. exp. Educ.,* 1944, 12, 184–186.

Brown, G. W. Discriminant functions. *Ann. math. Statist.,* 1947, 18, 514–528.

Bryan, J. G. A method for the exact determination of the characteristic equation and latent vectors of a matrix with applications to the discriminant function for more than two groups. Unpublished doctoral dissertation, Harvard Univer., 1950.

Bryan, J. G. The generalized discriminant function: Mathematical foundation and computational routine. *Harvard educ. Rev.,* 1951, 21, 90–95.

Cattell, R. B. *Personality and motivation: Structure and measurement.* Yonkers, N.Y.: World Book Co., 1957.

Cochran, W. G. The comparison of percentages in matched samples. *Biometrika,* 1950, 37, 256–266.

Edgerton, H. A., & Kolbe, Laverne E. The method of minimum variation for the combination of criteria. *Psychometrika,* 1936, 1, 183–187.

Edwards, A. L. *Statistical methods for the behavioral sciences.* New York: Rinehart, 1954.

Eysenck, H. J. *The scientific study of personality.* New York: Macmillan, 1952.

Fisher, R. A. The use of multiple measurements in taxonomic problems. *Ann. of Eugenics,* 1936, 7, 179–188.

Fisher, R. A. The statistical utilization of multiple measurements. *Ann. of Eugenics,* 1938, 8, 376–386.

Friedman, M. The use of ranks to avoid the assumption of normality implicit in the analysis of variance. *J. Amer. Statist. Ass.,* 1937, 32, 675–701.

Greenwald, H. J. A study of the relation of four social psychological factors to social sensitivity in married couples. Unpublished doctoral dissertation, Harvard Univer., 1955.

Guttman, L. An outline of the statistical theory of prediction. In P. Horst, et al., *The prediction of personal adjustment.* New York: Social Science Research Council, 1941. Pp. 251–311. (a)

Guttman, L. The quantification of a class of attributes: A theory and method of scale construction. In P. Horst, et al., *The prediction of personal adjustment.* New York: Social Science Research Council, 1941. Pp. 321–345. (b)

Harman, H. H. *Modern factor analysis.* Chicago: Univer. of Chicago Press, 1960.

Harper, A. E., Jr. Discrimination between matched schizophrenics and normals by the Wechsler-Bellevue scale. *J. consult. Psychol.,* 1950, 14, 351–357.

Hempel, C. G. Fundamentals of concept formation in empirical science. In *International encyclopedia of unified science,* Vol. II, No. 7. Chicago: Univer. of Chicago Press, 1952.

Horst, P. Obtaining a composite measure from a number of different measures of the same attribute. *Psychometrika,* 1936, 1, 53–60.

Horst, P. *Differential prediction of academic success.* Seattle: Univer. of Washington, 1959. (Mimeographed)

Hotelling, H. The generalization of Student's ratio. *Ann. math. Statist.,* 1931, 2, 360–378.

Hotelling, H. Analysis of a complex of statistical variables into principal components. *J. educ. Psychol.,* 1933, 24, 417–441, 498–520.

Hotelling, H. The most predictable criterion. *J. educ. Psychol.,* 1935, 26, 139–142.

Hotelling, H. Relations between two sets of variates. *Biometrika,* 1936, 28, 321–377.

Kelley, T. L. *Crossroads in the mind of man.* Stanford, Calif.: Stanford Univer. Press, 1928.

Kelley, T. L. *Essential traits of mental life.* Cambridge, Mass.: Harvard Univer. Press, 1935.

Kelley, T. L. Talents and tasks. *Harvard educ. Papers,* 1940, 1.

Kemeny, J. G., Snell, J. L., & Thompson, G. L. *Introduction to finite mathematics.* Englewood Cliffs, N.J.: Prentice-Hall, 1957.

Kendall, M. G. *Rank correlation methods.* London: Griffin, 1948.

Knapp, T. R. Two group classification in the absence of a criterion. Unpublished doctoral dissertation, Harvard Univer., 1959.

Kruskal, W. H., & Wallis, W. A. Use of ranks in one-criterion variance analysis. *J. Amer. Statist. Ass.,* 1952, 47, 583–621.

Kuder, G. F. *Kuder Preference Record: Manual.* Chicago: Science Research Associates, 1946.

Lazarsfeld, P. F. The logical and mathematical foundation of latent structure analysis, and the interpretation and computation of some latent structures. In S. A. Stouffer, et al., *Measurement and prediction.* Princeton, N.J.: Princeton Univer. Press, 1950. Pp. 362–472.

Lohnes, P. A comparison of test space and discriminant space classification models. Unpublished doctoral dissertation, Harvard Univer., 1960.

Lubin, A. Linear and non-linear discriminating functions. *Brit. J. Psychol.* (Statist. section), 1950, 3, 90–104.

Mahalanobis, P. C. Analysis of race-mixture in Bengal. *J. Asiatic Soc. Bengal,* 1927, 23, 301–333.

Mann, H. B., & Whitney, D. R. On a test of whether one of two random variables is stochastically larger than the other. *Ann. math. Statist.,* 1947, 18, 50–60.

Mather, K. *Biometrical genetics.* London: Methuen, 1949.

McNemar, Q. Note on the sampling error of the difference between correlated proportions or percentages. *Psychometrika,* 1947, 12, 153–157.

McNemar, Q. *Psychological statistics.* (2nd ed.) New York: Wiley, 1955.

McQuitty, L. L. A pattern analytic method derived from a theory of individual differences in psychological well-being. In S. B. Sells (Ed.), *Symposium on pattern analysis.* Randolph Air Force Base, Tex.: USAF School of Aviation Medicine, 1955. Pp. 29–41.

Moses, L. E. Non-parametric statistics for psychological research. *Psychol. Bull.,* 1952, 49, 122–143.

Mosteller, F., & Bush, R. R. Selected quantitative techniques. In G. Lindzey (Ed.), *Handbook of social psychology.* Cambridge, Mass.: Addison-Wesley, 1954. Pp. 289–334.

Neyman, J., & Pearson, E. S. The problem of the most efficient tests of statistical hypotheses. *Phil. Trans. Royal Soc.,* A, 1933, 231, 289–337.

O'Hara, R. P., & Tiedeman, D. V. Vocational self-concept in adolescence. *J. counsel. Psychol.,* 1959, 6, 292–301.

Pearson, K. P. Contributions to the mathematical theory of evolution. I. On the dissection of asymmetrical frequency curves. *Phil. Trans. Royal Soc.,* A, 1894, 185, 71–90.

Penrose, L. S. Some notes on discrimination. *Ann. of Eugenics,* 1947, 13, 228–237.

Popper, K. R. *The logic of scientific discovery.* (English ed.) London: Hutchinson, 1959.

Rao, C. R. Tests of significance in multivariate analysis. *Biometrika,* 1948, 35, 58–79. (a)

Rao, C. R. The utilization of multiple measurements in problems of biological classification. *J. Royal Statist. Soc.* (Series B), 1948, 10, 159–193. (b)

Rao, C. R. *Advanced statistical methods in biometric research.* New York: Wiley, 1952.

Ryans, D. G. *Characteristics of teachers.* Washington, D.C.: American Council on Education, 1960.

Seibel, D. W. The prediction of qualities of interaction between apprentice teachers and pupils. Unpublished doctoral dissertation, Harvard Univer., 1955.

Selover, R. B. A study of the sophomore testing program at the University of Minnesota. *J. appl. Psychol.,* 1942, 26, 296–307, 456–467, 587–593.

Siegel, S. *Nonparametric statistics for the behavioral sciences.* New York: McGraw-Hill, 1956.

Smith, B. O. Science of education. In W. S. Monroe (Ed.), *Encyclopedia of educational research.* (2nd ed.) New York: Macmillan, 1950. Pp. 1149–1150.

Spearman, C. *The abilities of man.* London: Macmillan, 1926.

Stevens, S. S. On the theory of scales of measurement. *Science,* 1946, 103, 677–680.

Stevens, S. S. Mathematics, measurement, and psychophysics. In S. S. Stevens (Ed.), *Handbook of experimental psychology.* New York: Wiley, 1951. Pp. 1–49.

Tatsuoka, M. M. *The relationship between*

the canonical correlation and discriminant analysis; and a proposal for utilizing qualitative data in discriminant analysis. Cambridge, Mass.: Educational Research Corp., 1953. (Photo-offset)

Thomson, G. H. *The factorial analysis of human ability.* (5th ed.) Boston: Houghton Mifflin, 1951.

Thurstone, L. L. *The vectors of mind.* Chicago: Univer. of Chicago Press, 1935.

Thurstone, L. L. *Multiple-factor analysis.* Chicago: Univer. of Chicago Press, 1950.

Tiedeman, D. V. On the study of types. In S. B. Sells (Ed.), *Symposium on pattern analysis.* Randolph Air Force Base, Tex.: USAF School of Aviation Medicine, 1955. Pp. 1–14.

Tiedeman, D. V., & Bryan, J. G. Prediction of college field of concentration. *Harvard educ. Rev.,* 1954, 24, 122–139.

Tiedeman, D. V., Bryan, J. G., & Rulon, P. J. *The utility of the Airman Classification Battery for assignment of airmen to eight Air Force specialities.* Cambridge, Mass.: Educational Research Corp., 1951.

Tintner, G. A note on rank, multicollinearity, and multiple regression. *Ann. math. Statist.,* 1945, 16, 304–308.

Tocher, K. D. Extension of the Neyman-Pearson theory of tests to discontinuous variates. *Biometrika,* 1950, 37, 130–144.

Travers, R. M. W. The use of a discriminant function in the treatment of psychological group differences. *Psychometrika,* 1939, 4, 25–32.

Travers, R. M. W. *An introduction to educational research.* New York: Macmillan, 1958.

Tukey, J. W. Dyadic anova, an analysis of variance for vectors. *Human Biol.,* 1949, 21, 65–110.

Walker, Helen M., & Lev, J. *Statistical inference.* New York: Holt, 1953.

Wallace, N., & Travers, R. M. W. A psychometric sociological study of a group of specialty salesmen. *Ann. of Eugenics,* 1938, 8, 266–302.

Welch, B. L. Note on discriminant functions. *Biometrika,* 1939, 31, 218–220.

Wilks, S. S. Certain generalizations in the analysis of variance. *Biometrika,* 1932, 24, 471–494.

Wilks, S. S. Weighting systems for linear functions of correlated variables when there is no dependent variable. *Psychometrika,* 1938, 3, 23–40.

CHAPTER 5

Experimental and Quasi-Experimental Designs for Research on Teaching[1]

DONALD T. CAMPBELL
Northwestern University

JULIAN C. STANLEY
University of Wisconsin

In this chapter we shall examine the validity of 16 experimental designs against 12 common threats to valid inference. By experiment we refer to that portion of research in which variables are manipulated and their effects upon other variables observed. It is well to distinguish the particular role of this chapter. It is *not* a chapter on experimental design in the Fisher (1925, 1935) tradition, in which an experimenter having complete mastery can schedule treatments and measurements for optimal statistical efficiency, with complexity of design emerging only from that goal of efficiency. Insofar as the designs discussed in the present chapter become complex, it is because of the intransigency of the environment: because, that is, of the experimenter's lack of complete control. While contact is made with the Fisher tradition at several points, the exposition of that tradition is appropriately left to full-length presentations, such as the books by Brownlee (1960), Cox (1958), Edwards

(1960), Ferguson (1959), Johnson (1949), Johnson and Jackson (1959), Lindquist (1953), McNemar (1962), and Winer (1962). (Also see Stanley, 1957b.)

PROBLEM AND BACKGROUND

McCall as a Model

In 1923, W. A. McCall published a book entitled *How to Experiment in Education*. The present chapter aspires to achieve an up-to-date representation of the interests and considerations of that book, and for this reason will begin with an appreciation of it. In his preface McCall said: "There are excellent books and courses of instruction dealing with the statistical manipulation of experimental data, but there is little help to be found on the methods of securing adequate and proper data to which to apply statistical procedure." This sentence remains true enough today to serve as the leitmotif of this presentation also. While the impact of the Fisher tradition has remedied the situation in some fundamental ways, its most conspicuous effect seems to have been to

[1] The preparation of this chapter has been supported by Northwestern University's Psychology-Education Project, sponsored by the Carnegie Corporation. Keith N. Clayton and Paul C. Rosenblatt have assisted in its preparation.

elaborate statistical analysis rather than to aid in securing "adequate and proper data."

Probably because of its practical and common-sense orientation, and its lack of pretension to a more fundamental contribution, McCall's book is an undervalued classic. At the time it appeared, two years before the first edition of Fisher's *Statistical Methods for Research Workers* (1925), there was nothing of comparable excellence in either agriculture or psychology. It anticipated the orthodox methodologies of these other fields on several fundamental points. Perhaps Fisher's most fundamental contribution has been the concept of achieving pre-experimental equation of groups through randomization. This concept, and with it the rejection of the concept of achieving equation through matching (as intuitively appealing and misleading as that is) has been difficult for educational researchers to accept. In 1923, McCall had the fundamental qualitative understanding. He gave, as his first method of establishing comparable groups, "groups equated by chance." "Just as representativeness can be secured by the method of chance, . . . so equivalence may be secured by chance, provided the number of subjects to be used is sufficiently numerous" (p. 41). On another point Fisher was also anticipated. Under the term "rotation experiment," the Latin-square design was introduced, and, indeed, had been used as early as 1916 by Thorndike, McCall, and Chapman (1916), in both 5 × 5 and 2 × 2 forms, i.e., some 10 years before Fisher (1926) incorporated it systematically into his scheme of experimental design, with randomization.[2]

McCall's mode of using the "rotation experiment" serves well to denote the emphasis of his book and the present chapter. The rotation experiment is introduced not for reasons of efficiency but rather to achieve some degree of control where random assignment to equivalent groups is not possible. In a similar vein, this chapter will examine the imper-

fections of numerous experimental schedules and will nonetheless advocate their utilization in those settings where better experimental designs are not feasible. In this sense, a majority of the designs discussed, including the unrandomized "rotation experiment," are designated as *quasi*-experimental designs.

Disillusionment with Experimentation in Education

This chapter is committed to the experiment: as the only means for settling disputes regarding educational practice, as the only way of verifying educational improvements, and as the only way of establishing a cumulative tradition in which improvements can be introduced without the danger of a faddish discard of old wisdom in favor of inferior novelties. Yet in our strong advocacy of experimentation, we must not imply that our emphasis is new. As the existence of McCall's book makes clear, a wave of enthusiasm for experimentation dominated the field of education in the Thorndike era, perhaps reaching its apex in the 1920s. And this enthusiasm gave way to apathy and rejection, and to the adoption of new psychologies unamenable to experimental verification. Good and Scates (1954, pp. 716–721) have documented a wave of pessimism, dating back to perhaps 1935, and have cited even that staunch advocate of experimentation, Monroe (1938), as saying "the direct contributions from controlled experimentation have been disappointing." Further, it can be noted that the defections from experimentation to essay writing, often accompanied by conversion from a Thorndikian behaviorism to Gestalt psychology or psychoanalysis, have frequently occurred in persons well trained in the experimental tradition.

To avoid a recurrence of this disillusionment, we must be aware of certain sources of the previous reaction and try to avoid the false anticipations which led to it. Several aspects may be noted. First, the claims made for the rate and degree of progress which would result from experiment were grandi-

[2] Kendall and Buckland (1957) say that the Latin square was invented by the mathematician Euler in 1782. Thorndike, Chapman, and McCall do not use this term.

osely overoptimistic and were accompanied by an unjustified depreciation of nonexperimental wisdom. The initial advocates assumed that progress in the technology of teaching had been slow *just because* scientific method had not been applied: they assumed traditional practice was incompetent, just because it had not been produced by experimentation. When, in fact, experiments often proved to be tedious, equivocal, of undependable replicability, and to confirm prescientific wisdom, the overoptimistic grounds upon which experimentation had been justified were undercut, and a disillusioned rejection or neglect took place.

This disillusionment was shared by both observer and participant in experimentation. For the experimenters, a personal avoidance-conditioning to experimentation can be noted. For the usual highly motivated researcher the nonconfirmation of a cherished hypothesis is actively painful. As a biological and psychological animal, the experimenter is subject to laws of learning which lead him inevitably to associate this pain with the contiguous stimuli and events. These stimuli are apt to be the experimental process itself, more vividly and directly than the "true" source of frustration, i.e., the inadequate theory. This can lead, perhaps unconsciously, to the avoidance or rejection of the experimental process. If, as seems likely, the ecology of our science is one in which there are available many more wrong responses than correct ones, we may anticipate that most experiments will be disappointing. We must somehow inoculate young experimenters against this effect, and in general must justify experimentation on more pessimistic grounds—not as a panacea, but rather as the only available route to cumulative progress. We must instill in our students the expectation of tedium and disappointment and the duty of thorough persistence, by now so well achieved in the biological and physical sciences. We must expand our students' vow of poverty to include not only the willingness to accept poverty of finances, but also a poverty of experimental results.

More specifically, we must increase our time perspective, and recognize that continuous, multiple experimentation is more typical of science than once-and-for-all definitive experiments. The experiments we do today, if successful, will need replication and cross-validation at other times under other conditions before they can become an established part of science, before they can be theoretically interpreted with confidence. Further, even though we recognize experimentation as the basic language of proof, as the only decision court for disagreement between rival theories, we should not expect that "crucial experiments" which pit opposing theories will be likely to have clear-cut outcomes. When one finds, for example, that competent observers advocate strongly divergent points of view, it seems likely on a priori grounds that both have observed something valid about the natural situation, and that both represent a part of the truth. The stronger the controversy, the more likely this is. Thus we might expect in such cases an experimental outcome with mixed results, or with the balance of truth varying subtly from experiment to experiment. The more mature focus—and one which experimental psychology has in large part achieved (e.g., Underwood, 1957b)—avoids crucial experiments and instead studies dimensional relationships and interactions along many degrees of the experimental variables.

Not to be overlooked, either, are the greatly improved statistical procedures that quite recently have filtered slowly into psychology and education. During the period of its greatest activity, educational experimentation proceeded ineffectively with blunt tools. McCall (1923) and his contemporaries did one-variable-at-a-time research. For the enormous complexities of the human learning situation, this proved too limiting. We now know how important various contingencies—dependencies upon joint "action" of two or more experimental variables—can be. Stanley (1957a, 1960, 1961b, 1961c, 1962), Stanley and Wiley (1962), and others have stressed the assessment of such interactions.

Experiments may be multivariate in either or both of two senses. More than one "independent" variable (sex, school grade, method of teaching arithmetic, style of printing type, size of printing type, etc.) may be incorporated into the design and/or more than one "dependent" variable (number of errors, speed, number right, various tests, etc.) may be employed. Fisher's procedures are multivariate in the first sense, univariate in the second. Mathematical statisticians, e.g., Roy and Gnanadesikan (1959), are working toward designs and analyses that unify the two types of multivariate designs. Perhaps by being alert to these, educational researchers can reduce the usually great lag between the introduction of a statistical procedure into the technical literature and its utilization in substantive investigations.

Undoubtedly, training educational researchers more thoroughly in *modern* experimental statistics should help raise the quality of educational experimentation.

Evolutionary Perspective on Cumulative Wisdom and Science

Underlying the comments of the previous paragraphs, and much of what follows, is an evolutionary perspective on knowledge (Campbell, 1959), in which applied practice and scientific knowledge are seen as the resultant of a cumulation of selectively retained tentatives, remaining from the hosts that have been weeded out by experience. Such a perspective leads to a considerable respect for tradition in teaching practice. If, indeed, across the centuries many different approaches have been tried, if some approaches have worked better than others, and if those which worked better have therefore, to some extent, been more persistently practiced by their originators, or imitated by others, or taught to apprentices, then the customs which have emerged may represent a valuable and tested subset of all possible practices.

But the selective, cutting edge of this process of evolution is very imprecise in the nat-

ural setting. The conditions of observation, both physical and psychological, are far from optimal. What survives or is retained is determined to a large extent by pure chance. Experimentation enters at this point as the means of sharpening the relevance of the testing, probing, selection process. Experimentation thus is not in itself viewed as a source of ideas necessarily contradictory to traditional wisdom. It is rather a refining process superimposed upon the probably valuable cumulations of wise practice. Advocacy of an experimental science of education thus does not imply adopting a position incompatible with traditional wisdom.

Some readers may feel a suspicion that the analogy with Darwin's evolutionary scheme becomes complicated by specifically human factors. School principal John Doe, when confronted with the necessity for deciding whether to adopt a revised textbook or retain the unrevised version longer, probably chooses on the basis of scanty knowledge. Many considerations besides sheer efficiency of teaching and learning enter his mind. The principal can be right in two ways: keep the old book when it is as good as or better than the revised one, or adopt the revised book when it is superior to the unrevised edition. Similarly, he can be wrong in two ways: keep the old book when the new one is better, or adopt the new book when it is no better than the old one.

"Costs" of several kinds might be estimated roughly for each of the two erroneous choices: (1) financial and energy-expenditure cost; (2) cost to the principal in complaints from teachers, parents, and school-board members; (3) cost to teachers, pupils, and society because of poorer instruction. These costs in terms of money, energy, confusion, reduced learning, and personal threat must be weighed against the probability that each will occur and also the probability that the error itself will be detected. If the principal makes his decision without suitable research evidence concerning Cost 3 (poorer instruction), he is likely to overemphasize Costs 1 and 2. The cards seem stacked in favor of a conservative approach—that is, retaining the old book for another year. We can, however, try to cast an experiment with the two books into a decision-theory mold (Chernoff & Moses, 1959) and reach a decision that takes the various costs and probabilities into consideration explicitly. How nearly the careful deliberations of an excellent educational administrator approximate this decision-theory model is an important problem which should be studied.

Factors Jeopardizing Internal and External Validity

In the next few sections of this chapter we spell out 12 factors jeopardizing the validity of various experimental designs.[3] Each factor will receive its main exposition in the context of those designs for which it is a particular problem, and 10 of the 16 designs will be presented before the list is complete. For purposes of perspective, however, it seems well to provide a list of these factors and a general guide to Tables 1, 2, and 3, which partially summarize the discussion. Fundamental to this listing is a distinction between *internal validity* and *external validity*. *Internal validity* is the basic minimum without which any experiment is uninterpretable: Did in fact the experimental treatments make a difference in this specific experimental instance? *External validity* asks the question of *generalizability*: To what populations, settings, treatment variables, and measurement variables can this effect be generalized? Both types of criteria are obviously important, even though they are frequently at odds in that features increasing one may jeopardize the other. While *internal validity* is the *sine qua non,* and while the question of *external validity,* like the question of inductive inference, is never completely answerable, the selection of designs strong in both types of validity is obviously our ideal. This is particularly the case for research on

teaching, in which generalization to applied settings of known character is the desideratum. Both the distinctions and the relations between these two classes of validity considerations will be made more explicit as they are illustrated in the discussions of specific designs.

Relevant to *internal validity,* eight different classes of extraneous variables will be presented; these variables, if not controlled in the experimental design, might produce effects confounded with the effect of the experimental stimulus. They represent the effects of:

1. *History,* the specific events occurring between the first and second measurement in addition to the experimental variable.

2. *Maturation,* processes within the respondents operating as a function of the passage of time per se (not specific to the particular events), including growing older, growing hungrier, growing more tired, and the like.

3. *Testing,* the effects of taking a test upon the scores of a second testing.

4. *Instrumentation,* in which changes in the calibration of a measuring instrument or changes in the observers or scorers used may produce changes in the obtained measurements.

5. *Statistical regression,* operating where groups have been selected on the basis of their extreme scores.

6. Biases resulting in differential *selection* of respondents for the comparison groups.

7. *Experimental mortality,* or differential loss of respondents from the comparison groups.

8. *Selection-maturation interaction,* etc., which in certain of the multiple-group quasi-experimental designs, such as Design 10, is confounded with, i.e., might be mistaken for, the effect of the experimental variable.

The factors jeopardizing *external validity* or *representativeness* which will be discussed are:

9. The *reactive* or *interaction effect* of *testing,* in which a pretest might increase or

[3] Much of this presentation is based upon Campbell (1957). Specific citations to this source will, in general, not be made.

decrease the respondent's sensitivity or responsiveness to the experimental variable
and thus make the results obtained for a
pretested population unrepresentative of the
effects of the experimental variable for the
unpretested universe from which the experimental respondents were selected.

10. The *interaction* effects of *selection*
biases and the *experimental variable*.

11. *Reactive effects of experimental arrangements,* which would preclude generalization about the effect of the experimental
variable upon persons being exposed to it in
nonexperimental settings.

12. *Multiple-treatment interference,* likely
to occur whenever multiple treatments are
applied to the same respondents, because the
effects of prior treatments are not usually
erasable. This is a particular problem for one-
group designs of type 8 or 9.

In presenting the experimental designs, a
uniform code and graphic presentation will
be employed to epitomize most, if not all, of
their distinctive features. An *X* will represent the exposure of a group to an experimental variable or event, the effects of which
are to be measured; *O* will refer to some
process of observation or measurement; the
*X*s and *O*s in a given row are applied to the
same specific persons. The left-to-right dimension indicates the temporal order, and
*X*s and *O*s vertical to one another are simultaneous. To make certain important distinctions, as between Designs 2 and 6, or between
Designs 4 and 10, a symbol *R,* indicating
random assignment to separate treatment
groups, is necessary. This randomization is
conceived to be a process occurring at a specific time, and is the all-purpose procedure for
achieving pretreatment equality of groups,
within known statistical limits. Along with
this goes another graphic convention, in that
parallel rows unseparated by dashes represent
comparison groups equated by randomization, while those separated by a dashed line
represent comparison groups not equated by
random assignment. A symbol for matching
as a process for the pretreatment equating of
comparison groups has not been used, because

the value of this process has been greatly
oversold and it is more often a source of mistaken inference than a help to valid inference. (See discussion of Design 10, and the
final section on correlational designs, below.)
A symbol *M* for materials has been used in a
specific way in Design 9.

THREE PRE-EXPERIMENTAL DESIGNS

1. THE ONE-SHOT CASE STUDY

Much research in education today conforms to a design in which a single group is
studied only once, subsequent to some agent
or treatment presumed to cause change. Such
studies might be diagramed as follows:

$$X \quad O$$

As has been pointed out (e.g., Boring, 1954;
Stouffer, 1949) such studies have such a total
absence of control as to be of almost no
scientific value. The design is introduced
here as a minimum reference point. Yet because of the continued investment in such
studies and the drawing of causal inferences
from them, some comment is required.
Basic to scientific evidence (and to all knowl-
edge-diagnostic processes including the ret-
ina of the eye) is the process of comparison,
of recording differences, or of contrast. Any
appearance of absolute knowledge, or intrinsic knowledge about singular isolated
objects, is found to be illusory upon analysis.
Securing scientific evidence involves making
at least one comparison. For such a comparison to be useful, both sides of the comparison should be made with similar care and
precision.

In the case studies of Design 1, a carefully
studied single instance is implicitly compared with other events casually observed
and remembered. The inferences are based
upon general expectations of what the data
would have been had the *X* not occurred,

etc. Such studies often involve tedious collection of specific detail, careful observation, testing, and the like, and in such instances involve the error of *misplaced precision*. How much more valuable the study would be if the one set of observations were reduced by half and the saved effort directed to the study in equal detail of an appropriate comparison instance. It seems well-nigh unethical at the present time to allow, as theses or dissertations in education, case studies of this nature (i.e., involving a single group observed at one time only). "Standardized" tests in such case studies provide only very limited help, since the rival sources of difference other than X are so numerous as to render the "standard" reference group almost useless as a "control group." On the same grounds, the many uncontrolled sources of difference between a present case study and potential future ones which might be compared with it are so numerous as to make justification in terms of providing a bench mark for future studies also hopeless. In general, it would be better to apportion the descriptive effort between both sides of an interesting comparison.

Design 1, if taken in conjunction with the implicit "common-knowledge" comparisons, has most of the weaknesses of each of the subsequent designs. For this reason, the spelling out of these weaknesses will be left to those more specific settings.

2. THE ONE-GROUP PRETEST-POSTTEST DESIGN

While this design is still widely used in educational research, and while it is judged as enough better than Design 1 to be worth doing where nothing better can be done (see the discussion of quasi-experimental designs below), it is introduced here as a "bad example" to illustrate several of the confounded extraneous variables that can jeopardize *internal* validity. These variables offer plausible hypotheses explaining an O_1—O_2 difference, rival to the hypothesis that X caused the difference:

$$O_1 \quad X \quad O_2$$

The first of these uncontrolled rival hypotheses is *history*. Between O_1 and O_2 many other change-producing events may have occurred in addition to the experimenter's X. If the pretest (O_1) and the posttest (O_2) are made on different days, then the events in between may have caused the difference. To become a *plausible* rival hypothesis, such an event should have occurred to most of the students in the group under study, say in some other class period or via a widely disseminated news story. In Collier's classroom study (conducted in 1940, but reported in 1944), while students were reading Nazi propaganda materials, France fell; the attitude changes obtained seemed more likely to be the result of this event than of the propaganda itself.[4] *History* becomes a more plausible rival explanation of change the longer the O_1—O_2 time lapse, and might be regarded as a trivial problem in an experiment completed within a one- or two-hour period, although even here, extraneous sources such as laughter, distracting events, etc., are to be looked for. Relevant to the variable *history* is the feature of *experimental isolation,* which can so nearly be achieved in many physical science laboratories as to render Design 2 acceptable for much of their research. Such effective experimental isolation can almost never be assumed in research on teaching methods. For these reasons a minus has been entered for Design 2 in Table 1 under *History*. We will classify with *history* a group of possible effects of season or of institutional-event schedule, although these might also be placed with *maturation*. Thus optimism might vary with seasons and anxiety with the semester examination schedule (e.g., Crook, 1937; Windle, 1954). Such effects might produce an O_1—O_2 change confusable with the effect of X.

A second rival variable, or class of variables, is designated *maturation*. This term is used here to cover all of those biological or

---

[4] Collier actually used a more adequate design than this, designated Design 10 in the present system.

TABLE 1

SOURCES OF INVALIDITY FOR DESIGNS 1 THROUGH 6

	Sources of Invalidity												
	Internal								External			
	History	Maturation	Testing	Instrumentation	Regression	Selection	Mortality	Interaction of Selection and Maturation, etc.	Interaction of Testing and X	Interaction of Selection and X	Reactive Arrangements	Multiple-X Interference
Pre-Experimental Designs:												
1. One-Shot Case Study X O	−	−				−	−			−		
2. One-Group Pretest-Posttest Design O X O	−	−	−	−	?	+	+	−	−	−	?	
3. Static-Group Comparison X O ---------- O	+	?	+	+	+	−	−	−		−		
True Experimental Designs:												
4. Pretest-Posttest Control Group Design R O X O R O O	+	+	+	+	+	+	+	+	−	?	?	
5. Solomon Four-Group Design R O X O R O O R X O R O	+	+	+	+	+	+	+	+	+	?	?	
6. Posttest-Only Control Group Design R X O R O	+	+	+	+	+	+	+	+	+	?	?	

Note: In the tables, a minus indicates a definite weakness, a plus indicates that the factor is controlled, a question mark indicates a possible source of concern, and a blank indicates that the factor is not relevant.

It is with extreme reluctance that these summary tables are presented because they are apt to be "too helpful," and to be depended upon in place of the more complex and qualified presentation in the text. No + or − indicator should be respected unless the reader comprehends why it is placed there. In particular, it is against the spirit of this presentation to create uncomprehended fears of, or confidence in, specific designs.

psychological processes which systematically vary with the passage of time, independent of specific external events. Thus between O_1 and O_2 the students may have grown older, hungrier, more tired, more bored, etc., and the obtained difference may reflect this process rather than X. In remedial education, which focuses on exceptionally disadvantaged persons, a process of "spontaneous remission," analogous to wound healing, may be mistaken for the specific effect of a remedial X. (Needless to say, such a remission is not regarded as "spontaneous" in any causal sense, but rather represents the cumulative effects of learning processes and environmental pressures of the total daily experience, which would be operating even if no X had been introduced.)

A third confounded rival explanation is the effect of *testing,* the effect of the pretest itself. On achievement and intelligence tests, students taking the test for a second time, or taking an alternate form of the test, etc., usually do better than those taking the test for the first time (e.g., Anastasi, 1958, pp. 190–191; Cane & Heim, 1950). These effects, as much as three to five IQ points on the average for naïve test-takers, occur without any instruction as to scores or items missed on the first test. For personality tests, a similar effect is noted, with second tests showing, in general, better adjustment, although occasionally a highly significant effect in the opposite direction is found (Windle, 1954). For attitudes toward minority groups a second test may show more prejudice, although the evidence is very slight (Rankin & Campbell, 1955). Obviously, conditions of anonymity, increased awareness of what answer is socially approved, etc., all would have a bearing on the direction of the result. For prejudice items under conditions of anonymity, the adaptation level created by the hostile statements presented may shift the student's expectations as to what kinds of attitudes are tolerable in the direction of greater hostility. In a signed personality or adjustment inventory, the initial administration partakes of a problem-solving situation in which the student attempts to discover the disguised purpose of the test. Having done this (or having talked with his friends about their answers to some of the bizarre items), he knows better how to present himself acceptably the second time.

With the introduction of the problem of test effects comes a distinction among potential measures as to their *reactivity.* This will be an important theme throughout this chapter, as will a general exhortation to use *nonreactive* measures wherever possible. It has long been a truism in the social sciences that the process of measuring may change that which is being measured. The test-retest gain would be one important aspect of such change. (Another, the interaction of testing and X, will be discussed with Design 4, below. Furthermore, these reactions to the pretest are important to avoid even where they have different effects for different examinees.) The reactive effect can be expected whenever the testing process is in itself a stimulus to change rather than a passive record of behavior. Thus in an experiment on therapy for weight control, the initial weigh-in might in itself be a stimulus to weight reduction, even without the therapeutic treatment. Similarly, placing observers in the classroom to observe the teacher's pretraining human relations skills may in itself change the teacher's mode of discipline. Placing a microphone on the desk may change the group interaction pattern, etc. In general, the more novel and motivating the test device, the more reactive one can expect it to be.

Instrumentation or "instrument decay" (Campbell, 1957) is the term used to indicate a fourth uncontrolled rival hypothesis. This term refers to autonomous changes in the measuring instrument which might account for an O_1—O_2 difference. These changes would be analogous to the stretching or fatiguing of spring scales, condensation in a cloud chamber, etc. Where human observers are used to provide O_1 and O_2, processes of learning, fatiguing, etc., within the observers will produce O_1—O_2 differences. If essays are being graded, the grading standards may shift between O_1 and O_2 (suggesting the control technique of shuffling the O_1 and O_2 essays together and having them graded without knowledge of which came first). If classroom participation is being observed, then the observers may be more skillful, or more blasé, on the second occasion. If parents are being interviewed, the interviewer's familiarity with the interview schedule and with the particular parents may produce shifts. A change in observers between O_1 and O_2 could cause a difference.

A fifth confounded variable in some instances of Design 2 is *statistical regression*. If, for example, in a remediation experiment, students are picked for a special experimental treatment because they do particularly poorly on an achievement test (which becomes for them the O_1), then on a subsequent testing using a parallel form or repeating the same test, O_2 for this group will almost surely average higher than did O_1. This dependable result is not due to any genuine effect of X, any test-retest practice effect, etc. It is rather a tautological aspect of the imperfect correlation between O_1 and O_2. Because errors of inference due to overlooking regression effects have been so troublesome in educational research, because the fundamental insight into their nature is so frequently missed even by students who have had advanced courses in modern statistics, and because in later discussions (e.g., of Design 10 and the ex post facto analysis) we will assume this knowledge, an elementary and old-fashioned exposition is undertaken here. Figure 1 presents some artificial data in which pretest and posttest for a whole population correlate .50, with no change in the group mean or variability. (The data were

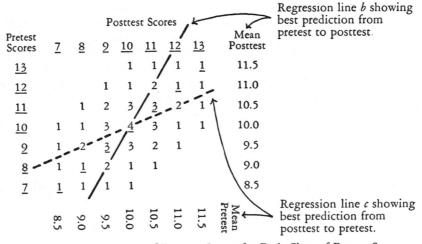

Fig. 1*a*. Frequency Scatter of Posttest Scores for Each Class of Pretest Scores, and Vice Versa.

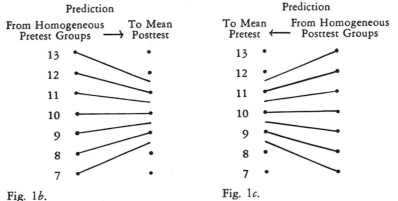

Fig. 1*b*.   Fig. 1*c*.

Fig. 1. Regression in the Prediction of Posttest Scores from Pretest, and Vice Versa.

selected to make the location of the row and column means obvious upon visual inspection. The value of .50 is similarly chosen for presentation convenience.) In this hypothetical instance, no true change has taken place, but as is usual, the fallible test scores show a retest correlation considerably less than unity. If, as suggested in the example initiated above, one starts by looking only at those with very low scores on the pretest, e.g., scores of 7, and looks only to the scores of these students on the posttest, one finds the posttest scores scattered, but in general better, and on the average "regressed" halfway (i.e., the regression or correlation coefficient is .50) back to the group mean, resulting in an average of 8.5. But instead of this being evidence of progress it is a tautological, if specific, restatement of the fact of imperfect correlation and its degree.

Because time passed and events occurred between pretest and posttest, one is tempted to relate this change causally to the specific direction of time passage. But note that a time-reversed analysis is possible here, as by starting with those whose posttest scores are 7, and looking at the scatter of their pretest scores, from which the reverse implication would be drawn—i.e., that scores are getting worse. The most mistaken causal inferences are drawn when the data are presented in the form of Fig. 1b (or the top or bottom portion of 1b). Here the bright appear to be getting duller, and the dull brighter, as if through the stultifying and homogenizing effect of an institutional environment. While this misinterpretation implies that the population variability on the posttest should be less than on the pretest, the two variabilities are in fact equal. Furthermore, by entering the analysis with pure groups of posttest scores (as in regression line c and Fig. 1c), we can draw the opposite inference. As McNemar (1940) pointed out, the use of time-reversed control analyses and the direct examination for changes in population variabilities are useful precautions against such misinterpretation.

We may look at regression toward the mean in another, related way. The more deviant the score, the larger the error of measurement it probably contains. Thus, in a sense, the typical extremely high scorer has had unusually good "luck" (large positive error) and the extremely low scorer bad luck (large negative error). Luck is capricious, however, so on a posttest we expect the high scorers to decline somewhat on the average, the low scorers to improve their relative standing. (The same logic holds if one begins with the posttest scores and works back to the pretest.)

Regression toward the mean is a ubiquitous phenomenon, not confined to pretesting and posttesting with the same test or comparable forms of a test. The principal who observes that his highest-IQ students tend to have less than the highest achievement-test score (though quite high) and that his lowest-IQ students are usually not right at the bottom of the achievement-test heap (though quite low) would be guilty of the regression fallacy if he declared that his school is understimulating the brightest pupils and overworking the dullest. Selecting those students who scored highest and lowest on the achievement test and looking at their IQs would force him by the same illogic to conclude the opposite.

While regression has been discussed here in terms of errors of measurement, it is more generally a function of the degree of correlation; the lower the correlation, the greater the regression toward the mean. The lack of perfect correlation may be due to "error" and/or to systematic sources of variance specific to one or the other measure.

Regression effects are thus inevitable accompaniments of imperfect test-retest correlation for groups *selected for their extremity*. They are not, however, necessary concomitants of extreme scores wherever encountered. If a group *selected for independent reasons* turns out to have an extreme mean, there is less a priori expectation that the group mean will regress on a second testing, for the random or extraneous sources of variance have been allowed to affect the initial scores in both directions. But for a group selected *because* of its extremity on a fallible variable, this is not the case. Its extremity is artificial and it will regress toward the mean of the population from which it was selected.

Regression effects of a more indirect sort can be due to selection of extreme scorers on measures other than the pretest. Consider a case in which students who "fail" a classroom examination are selected for experimental coaching. As a pretest, Form A of a standard achievement test is given, and as a posttest, Form B. It is probable that the classroom test correlates more highly with the immediate Form A administration than with the Form B administration some three months later (if the test had been given to the whole class on each occasion). The higher the correlation, the less regression toward the mean. Thus the classroom failures will have regressed upward less on the pretest than on the posttest, providing a pseudogain which might have been mistaken for a successful remedial-education effort. (For more details on gains and regression, see Lord, 1956, 1958; McNemar, 1958; Rulon, 1941; R. L. Thorndike, 1942.)

This concludes the list of weaknesses of Design 2 which can be conveniently discussed at this stage. Consulting Table 1 shows that there is one more minus under internal validity, for a factor which will not be examined until the discussion of Design 10 (see page 217) in the quasi-experimental designs section, and two minuses for external validity, which will not be explained until the discussion of Design 4 (see page 186).

3. THE STATIC-GROUP COMPARISON

The third pre-experimental design needed for our development of invalidating factors is the static-group comparison. This is a design in which a group which has experienced X is compared with one which has not, for the purpose of establishing the effect of X.

$$\underline{X} \quad \underline{\quad} \quad \frac{O_1}{O_2}$$

Instances of this kind of research include, for example, the comparison of school systems which require the bachelor's degree of teachers (the X) versus those which do not; the comparison of students in classes given speed-reading training versus those not given it; the comparison of those who heard a certain TV program with those who did not, etc. In marked contrast with the "true" experiment of Design 6, below, there are in these Design 3 instances no formal means of certifying that the groups would have been equivalent had it not been for the X. This absence, indicated in the diagram by the dashed lines separating the two groups, provides the next factor needing control, i.e., *selection*. If O_1 and O_2 differ, this difference could well have come about through the differential recruitment of persons making up the groups: the groups might have differed anyway, without the occurrence of X. As will be discussed below under the ex post facto analysis, matching on background characteristics other than O is usually ineffective and misleading, particularly in those instances in which the persons in the "experimental group" have sought out exposure to the X.

A final confounded variable for the present list can be called experimental *mortality,* or the production of O_1—O_2 differences in groups due to the differential drop-out of persons from the groups. Thus, even if in Design 3 the two groups had once been identical, they might differ now not because of any change on the part of individual members, but rather because of the selective drop-out of persons from one of the groups. In educational research this problem is most frequently met in those studies aimed at ascertaining the effects of a college education by comparing measures on freshmen (who have not had the X) with seniors (who have). When such studies show freshman women to be more beautiful than senior women, we recoil from the implication that our harsh course of training is debeautifying, and instead point to the hazards in the way of a beautiful girl's finishing college before getting married. Such an effect is classified here as experimental *mortality*. (Of course, if we consider the *same* girls when they are freshmen and seniors, this problem disappears, and we have Design 2.)

THREE TRUE EXPERIMENTAL DESIGNS

The three basic designs to be treated in this section are the currently recommended designs in the methodological literature. They will also turn out to be the most strongly recommended designs of this presentation, even though this endorsement is subject to many specific qualifications regarding usual practice and to some minus signs in Table 1 under *external validity*. Design 4 is the most used of the three, and for this reason we allow its presentation to be disproportionately extended and to become the locus of discussions more generally applicable. Note that all three of these designs are presented in terms of a single X being compared with *no X*. Designs with more numerous treatments in the Fisher factorial experiment tradition represent important elaborations tangential to the main thread of this chapter and are discussed at the end of this section, subsequent to Design 6. But this perspective can serve to remind us at this point that the comparison of X with *no X* is an oversimplification. The comparison is actually with the specific activities of the control group which have filled the time period corresponding to that in which the experimental group receives the X. Thus the comparison might better be between X_1 and X_c, or between X_1 and X_o, or X_1 and X_2. That these control group activities are often unspecified adds an undesirable ambiguity to the interpretation of the contribution of X. Bearing these comments in mind, we will continue in this section the graphic convention of presenting no X in the control group.

4. THE PRETEST-POSTTEST CONTROL GROUP DESIGN

Controls for Internal Validity

One or another of the above considerations led psychological and educational researchers between 1900 and 1920 to add a control group to Design 2, creating the presently orthodox control group design. McCall (1923), Solomon (1949), and Boring (1954) have given us some of this history, and a scanning of the *Teachers College Record* for that period implies still more, for as early as 1912 control groups were being referred to without need of explanation (e.g., Pearson, 1912). The control group designs thus introduced are classified in this chapter under two heads: the present Design 4 in which equivalent groups as achieved by randomization are employed, and the quasi-experimental Design 10 in which extant intact comparison groups of unassured equivalence are employed. Design 4 takes this form:

$$R\ O_1\ \ X\ \ O_2$$
$$R\ O_3\ \ \ \ \ \ O_4$$

Because the design so neatly controls for *all* of the seven rival hypotheses described so far, the presentations of it have usually not made explicit the control needs which it met. In the tradition of learning research, the practice effects of *testing* seem to provide the first recognition of the need for a control group. *Maturation* was a frequent critical focus in experimental studies in education, as well as in the nature-nurture problem in the child development area. In research on attitude change, as in the early studies on the effects of motion pictures, *history* may have been the main necessitating consideration. In any event, it seems desirable here to discuss briefly the way in which, or the conditions under which, these factors are controlled.

History is controlled insofar as general historical events that might have produced an O_1—O_2 difference would also produce an O_3—O_4 difference. Note, however, that many supposed utilizations of Design 4 (or 5 or 6) do *not* control for unique *intrasession history*. If all of the randomly assigned students in the experimental group are treated in a single session, and similarly the control students in another single session, then the irrelevant unique events in either session (the obstreperous joke, the fire across the street, the experimenter's introductory remarks, etc.) become rival hypotheses explaining the O_1—O_2 versus O_3—O_4 difference. Such an experiment is *not* a true experiment, even when presented, as was Solomon's (1949) experiment on the teaching of spelling, as an illustrative paradigm. (To be fair, we point out that it was chosen to illustrate a different point.) Thinking over our "best practice" on this point may make this seem a venial sin, but our "best practice" is producing experiments too frequently unreplicable, and this very source of "significant" but extraneous differences might well be an important fault. Furthermore, the typical experiment in the *Journal of Experimental Psychology* does achieve control of intrasession history through testing students and animals individually and through assigning the students and experimental periods at random to experimental or control conditions. Note, however, that even with individual sessions, history can be uncontrolled if all of the experimental group is run before the control group, etc. Design 4 calls for simultaneity of experimental and control sessions. If we actually run sessions simultaneously, then different experimenters must be used, and experimenter differences can become a form of intrasession history confounded with X.

The optimal solution is a randomization of experimental occasions, with such restrictions as are required to achieve balanced representation of such highly likely sources of bias as experimenters, time of day, day of week, portion of semester, nearness to examinations, etc. The common expedient of running experimental subjects in small groups rather than individually is inadmissible if this grouping is disregarded in the statistical analysis. (See the section on assigning intact groups to treatments, below.) All those in the same session share the same intrasession history, and thus have sources of similarity other than X. If such sessions have been assigned at random, the correct statistical treatment is the same as that discussed below for the assignment of intact classrooms to treatments. (For some studies involving group testing, the several experimental treatments can be randomly distributed within one face-to-face group, as in using multiple test forms in a study of the effect of the order of difficulty of items. In such cases, the specificities of intrasession history are common to both treatments and do not become a plausible rival hypothesis confounded with X in explaining the differences obtained.)

Maturation and *testing* are controlled in that they should be manifested equally in experimental and control groups. *Instrumentation* is easily controlled where the conditions for the control of intrasession history are met, particularly where the O is achieved by student responses to a fixed instrument such as a printed test. Where observers or interviewers are used, however, the problem becomes more serious. If observers are few enough not to be randomly assignable to the observation of single sessions, then not only should each observer be used for both experimental and control sessions, but in addition, the observers should be kept ignorant as to which students are receiving which treatments, lest the knowledge bias their ratings or records. That such bias tendencies are "dependable" sources of variance is affirmed by the necessity in medical research of the second blind in the double-blind experiment, by recent research (Rosenthal, 1959), and by older studies (e.g., Kennedy & Uphoff, 1939; Stanton & Baker, 1942). The use of recordings of group interaction, so that judges may judge a series of randomized sections of pretest, posttest, experimental, and control group transcriptions, helps to control instrumentation in research on classroom behavior and group interaction.

Regression is controlled as far as mean differences are concerned, no matter how extreme the group is on pretest scores, if both experimental and control groups are randomly assigned from this same extreme pool. In such a case, the control group regresses as much as does the experimental group. Interpretative lapses due to regression artifacts do frequently occur, however, even under Design 4 conditions. An experimenter may employ the control group to confirm group mean effects of *X,* and then abandon it while examining which pretest-score subgroups of the experimental group were most influenced. If the whole group has shown a gain, then he arrives at the stimulating artifact that those initially lowest have gained most, those initially highest perhaps not at all. This outcome is assured because under conditions of total group mean gain, the regression artifact supplements the gain score for the below-mean pretest scorers, and tends to cancel it for the high pretest scorers. (If there was no over-all gain, then the experimenter may mistakenly "discover" that this was due to two mutually cancelling effects, for those low to gain, those high to lose.) One cure for these misinterpretations is to make parallel analyses of extreme pretest scorers in the control group, and to base differential gain interpretations on comparisons of the posttest scores of the corresponding experimental and control pretest subgroups. (Note, however, that skewed distributions resulting from selection make normal-curve statistics of dubious appropriateness.)

Selection is ruled out as an explanation of the difference to the extent that randomization has assured group equality at time *R.* This extent is the extent stated by our sampling statistics. Thus the assurance of equality is greater for large numbers of random assignments than for small. To the extent indicated by the error term for the no-difference hypothesis, this assumption will be wrong occasionally. In Design 4, this means that there will occasionally be an apparently "significant" difference between the pretest scores. Thus, while simple or stratified randomization assures unbiased assignment of experimental subjects to groups, it is a less than perfect way of assuring the initial equivalence of such groups. It is nonetheless the only way of doing so, and the essential way. This statement is made so dogmatically because of a widespread and mistaken preference in educational research over the past 30 years for equation through matching. McCall (1923) and Peters and Van Voorhis (1940) have helped perpetuate this misunderstanding. As will be spelled out in more detail in the discussion of Design 10 and the ex post facto analysis below, matching is no real help when used to overcome initial group differences. This is not to rule out matching as an adjunct to randomization, as when one gains statistical precision by assigning students to matched pairs, and then randomly assigning one member of each pair to the experimental group, the other to the control group. In the statistical literature this is known as "blocking." See particularly the discussions of Cox (1957), Feldt (1958), and Lindquist (1953). But matching as a substitute for randomization is taboo even for the quasi-experimental designs using but two natural intact groups, one experimental, the other control: even in this weak "experiment," there are better ways than matching for attempting to correct for initial mean differences in the two samples.

The data made available by Design 4 make it possible to tell whether *mortality* offers a plausible explanation of the O_1—O_2 gain. Mortality, lost cases, and cases on which only partial data are available, are troublesome to handle, and are commonly swept under the rug. Typically, experiments on teaching methods are spread out over days, weeks, or months. If the pretests and posttests are given in the classrooms from which experimental group and control group are drawn, and if the experimental condition requires attendance at certain sessions, while the control condition does not, then the differential attendance on the three occasions (pretest, treatment, and posttest) produces "mortality" which can introduce subtle sample biases.

If, of those initially designated as experimental group participants, one eliminates those who fail to show up for experimental sessions, then one selectively shrinks the experimental group in a way not comparably done in the control group, biasing the experimental group in the direction of the conscientious and healthy. The preferred mode of treatment, while not usually employed, would seem to be to use all of the selected experimental and control students who completed both pretest and posttest, including those in the experimental group who failed to get the X. This procedure obviously attenuates the apparent effect of the X, but it avoids the sampling bias. This procedure rests on the assumption that no simpler mortality biases were present; this assumption can be partially checked by examining both the number and the pretest scores of those who were present on pretest but not on posttest. It is possible that some Xs would affect this drop-out rate rather than change individual scores. Of course, even where drop-out rates are the same, there remains the possibility of complex interactions which would tend to make the character of the drop-outs in the experimental and control groups differ.

The mortality problem can be seen in a greatly exaggerated form in the *invited remedial treatment* study. Here, for example, one sample of poor readers in a high school is invited to participate in voluntary remedial sessions, while an equivalent group are not invited. Of the invited group, perhaps 30 per cent participate. Posttest scores, like pretest scores, come from standard reading achievement tests administered to all in the classrooms. It is unfair to compare the 30 per cent volunteers with the total of the control group, because they represent those most disturbed by their pretest scores, those likely to be most vigorous in self-improvement, etc. But it is impossible to locate their exact counterparts in the control group. While it also seems unfair to the hypothesis of therapeutic effectiveness to compare the total invited group with the total uninvited group, this is an acceptable, if conservative, solution.

Note, however, the possibility that the invitation itself, rather than the therapy, causes the effect. In general, the uninvited control group should be made just as aware of its standing on the pretest as is the invited group. Another alternative is to invite all those who need remedial sessions and to assign those who accept into true and placebo remedial treatment groups; but in the present state of the art, any placebo therapy which is plausible enough to look like help to the student is apt to be as good a therapy as is the treatment we are studying. Note, however, the valid implication that experimental tests of the relative efficacy of two therapeutic procedures are much easier to evaluate than the absolute effectiveness of either. The only solution in actual use is that of creating experimental and control groups from among seekers of remedial treatment by manipulating waiting periods (e.g., Rogers & Dymond, 1954). This of course sometimes creates other difficulties, such as an excessive drop-out from the postponed-therapy control group. For a successful and apparently nonreactive use of a lottery to decide on an immediate or next-term remedial reading course, see Reed (1956).

Factors Jeopardizing External Validity

The factors of internal invalidity which have been described so far have been factors which directly affected O scores. They have been factors which by themselves could produce changes which might be mistaken for the results of X, i.e., factors which, once the control group was added, would produce effects manifested by themselves in the control group and added onto the effects of X in the experimental group. In the language of analysis of variance, *history, maturation, testing,* etc., have been described as main effects, and as such have been controlled in Design 4, giving it *internal* validity. The threats to *external* validity, on the other hand, can be called interaction effects, involving X and some other variable. They thus represent a potential specificity of the effects of X to some undesirably limited set of conditions. To anticipate: in Design 4, for all we know, the effects of X observed may be specific to groups warmed up by the pretest. We are logically unable to generalize to the larger unpretested universe about which we would prefer to be able to speak.

In this section we shall discuss several such threats to generalizability, and procedures for reducing them. Thus since there are valid designs avoiding the pretest, and since in many settings (but not necessarily in research on teaching) it is to unpretested groups that one wants to generalize, such designs are preferred on grounds of *external* validity or generalizability. In the area of teaching, the doubts frequently expressed as to the applicability in actual practice of the results of highly artificial experiments are judgments about *external* validity. The introduction of such considerations into the discussion of optimal experimental designs thus strikes a sympathetic note in the practitioner who rightly feels that these considerations have been unduly neglected in the usual formal treatise on experimental methodology. The ensuing discussion will support such views by pointing out numerous ways in which experiments can be made more valid externally, more appropriate bases of generalization to teaching practice, without losing *internal* validity.

But before entering this discussion, a caveat is in order. This caveat introduces some painful problems in the science of induction. The problems are painful because of a recurrent reluctance to accept Hume's truism that *induction or generalization is never fully justified logically*. Whereas the problems of *internal* validity are solvable within the limits of the logic of probability statistics, the problems of external validity are not logically solvable in any neat, conclusive way. Generalization always turns out to involve extrapolation into a realm not represented in one's sample. Such extrapolation is made by *assuming* one knows the relevant laws. Thus, if one has an internally valid Design 4, one has

demonstrated the effect only for those specific conditions which the experimental and control group have in common, i.e., only for pretested groups of a specific age, intelligence, socioeconomic status, geographical region, historical moment, orientation of the stars, orientation in the magnetic field, barometric pressure, gamma radiation level, etc.

Logically, we cannot generalize beyond these limits; i.e., we cannot generalize at all. But we do attempt generalization by guessing at laws and checking out some of these generalizations in other equally specific but different conditions. In the course of the history of a science we learn about the "justification" of generalizing by the cumulation of our experience in generalizing, but this is not a logical generalization deducible from the details of the original experiment. Faced by this, we do, in generalizing, make guesses as to yet unproven laws, including some not even explored. Thus, for research on teaching, we are quite willing to assume that orientation in the magnetic field has no effect. But we know from scattered research that pretesting has often had an effect, and therefore we would like to remove it as a limit to our generalization. If we were doing research on iron bars, we would know from experience that an initial weighing has never been found to be reactive, but that orientation in magnetic field, if not systematically controlled, might seriously limit the generalizability of our discoveries. The sources of external invalidity are thus guesses as to general laws in the science of a science: guesses as to what factors lawfully interact with our treatment variables, and, by implication, guesses as to what can be disregarded.

In addition to the specifics, there is a general empirical law which we are assuming, along with all scientists. This is the modern version of Mill's assumption as to the lawfulness of nature. In its modern, weaker version, this can be stated as the assumption of the "stickiness" of nature: we assume that the closer two events are in time, space, and measured value on any or all dimensions, the more they tend to follow the same laws.

While complex interactions and curvilinear relationships are expected to confuse attempts at generalization, they are more to be expected the more the experimental situation differs from the setting to which one wants to generalize. Our call for greater external validity will thus be a call for that maximum similarity of experiments to the conditions of application which is compatible with internal validity.

While stressing this, we should keep in mind that the "successful" sciences such as physics and chemistry made their strides without any attention to representativeness (but with great concern for repeatability by independent researchers). An ivory-tower artificial laboratory science is a valuable achievement even if unrepresentative, and artificiality may often be essential to the analytic separation of variables fundamental to the achievements of many sciences. But certainly, if it does not interfere with internal validity or analysis, external validity is a very important consideration, especially for an applied discipline such as teaching.

Interaction of testing and X. In discussions of experimental design per se, the threat of the pretest to external validity was first presented by Solomon (1949), although the same considerations had earlier led individual experimenters to the use of Design 6, which omits the pretest. Especially in attitude-change studies, where the attitude tests themselves introduce considerable amounts of unusual content (e.g., one rarely sees in cold print as concentrated a dose of hostile statements as is found in the typical prejudice test), it is quite likely that the person's attitudes and his susceptibility to persuasion are changed by a pretest. As a psychologist, one seriously doubts the comparability of one movie audience seeing *Gentlemen's Agreement* (an antiprejudice film) immediately after having taken a 100-item anti-Semitism test with another audience seeing the movie without such a pretest. These doubts extend not only to the main effect of the pretest, but also to its effect upon the response to persuasion. Let us assume that that particular movie

was so smoothly done that some persons could enjoy it for its love interest without becoming aware of the social problem it dealt with. Such persons would probably not occur in a pretested group. If a pretest sensitized the audience to the problem, it might, through a focusing of attention, increase the educational effect of the *X*. Conceivably, such an *X* might be effective only for a pretested group.

While such a sensitizing effect is frequently mentioned in anecdotal presentations of the effect, the few published research results show either no effect (e.g., Anderson, 1959; Duncan, et al., 1957; Glock, 1958; Lana, 1959a, 1959b; Lana & King, 1960; Piers, 1955; Sobol, 1959; Zeisel, 1947) or an interaction effect of a dampening order. Thus Solomon (1949) found that giving a pretest reduced the efficacy of experimental spelling training, and Hovland, Lumsdaine, and Sheffield (1949) suggested that a pretest reduced the persuasive effects of movies. This interaction effect is well worth avoiding, even if not as misleading as sensitization (since false positives are more of a problem in our literature than false negatives, owing to the glut of published findings [Campbell, 1959, pp. 168–170]).

The effect of the pretest upon *X* as it restricts external validity is of course a function of the extent to which such repeated measurements are characteristic of the universe to which one wants to generalize. In the area of mass communications, the researcher's interview and attitude-test procedures are quite atypical. But in research on teaching, one is interested in generalizing to a setting in which testing is a regular phenomenon. Especially if the experiment can use regular classroom examinations as *O*s, but probably also if the experimental *O*s are similar to those usually used, no undesirable interaction of *testing* and *X* would be present. Where highly unusual test procedures are used, or where the testing procedure involves deception, perceptual or cognitive restructuring, surprise, stress, etc., designs having unpretested groups remain highly desirable if not essential.

Interaction of selection and X. While Design 4 controls for the effects of selection at the level of explaining away experimental and control group differences, there remains the possibility that the effects validly demonstrated hold only for that unique population from which the experimental and control groups were jointly selected. This possibility becomes more likely as we have more difficulty in getting subjects for our experiment. Consider the implications of an experiment on teaching in which the researcher has been turned down by nine school systems and is finally accepted by a tenth. This tenth almost certainly differs from the other nine, and from the universe of schools to which we would like to generalize, in many specific ways. It is, thus, nonrepresentative. Almost certainly its staff has higher morale, less fear of being inspected, more zeal for improvement than does that of the average school. And the effects we find, while internally valid, might be specific to such schools. To help us judge on these matters, it would seem well for research reports to include statements as to how many and what kind of schools and classes were asked to cooperate but refused, so that the reader can estimate the severity of possible selective biases. Generally speaking, the greater the amount of cooperation involved, the greater the amount of disruption of routine, and the higher our refusal rate, the more opportunity there is for a selection-specificity effect.

Let us specify more closely just what the *"interaction* of selection and *X"* means. If we were to conduct a study within a single volunteered school, using random assignment of subjects to experimental and control groups, we would not be concerned about the "main effect" of the school itself. If both experimental and control group means were merely elevated equally by this, then no harm would be done. If, however, there were characteristics of the school that caused the experimental treatment to be more effective there than it would be in the target population of schools, this could be serious. We want to know that the interaction of school characteristics (probably related to voluntarism) with experimental treatments is negligible. Some experimental variables might be quite sensitive to (interact with) school characteristics; others might not. Such interaction *could* occur between schools with similar mean IQs, or it could be absent when IQ differences were great. We would expect, however, that interactions would be more likely if the schools differed markedly in various characteristics than if they were similar.

Often stringent sampling biases occur because of the inertia of experimenters who do not allow a more representative selection of schools the opportunity to refuse to participate. Thus most research on teaching is done in those schools with the highest percentage of university professors' children enrolled. While sampling representativeness is impossible of perfect achievement and is almost totally neglected in many sciences (in most studies appearing in the *Journal of Experimental Psychology,* for example), it both can and should be emphasized as a desideratum in research on teaching. One way to increase it is to reduce the number of students or classrooms participating from a given school or grade and to increase the number of schools and grades in which the experiment is carried on. It is obvious that we are never going to conduct experiments on samples representatively drawn from all United States classrooms, or all world classrooms. We will learn how far we can generalize an internally valid finding only piece by piece through trial and error of generalization efforts. But these generalization efforts will succeed more often if in the initial experiment we have demonstrated the phenomenon over a wide variety of conditions.

With reference to the pluses and minuses of Table 1, it is obvious that nothing firm can be entered in this column. The column is presented, however, because the requirements of some designs exaggerate or ameliorate this problem. Design 4 in the social-attitudes realm is so demanding of cooperation on the part of respondents or subjects as to end up with research done only on captive audiences rather than the general citizen of whom one would wish to speak. For such a setting, Design 4 would rate a minus for selection. Yet for research on teaching, our universe of interest is a captive population, and for this, highly representative Design 4s can be done.

Other interactions with X. In parallel fashion, the interaction of *X* with the other factors can be examined as threats to *external* validity. Differential *mortality* would be a product of *X* rather than interactive with it. *Instrumentation* interacting with *X* has been implicitly included in the discussion of *internal* validity, since an instrumentation effect specific to the presence of *X* would counterfeit a true effect of *X* (e.g., where observers make ratings, know the hypothesis, and know which students have received *X*). A threat to external validity is the possibility of the specificity of effects to the specific instruments (tests, observers, meters, etc.) used in the study. If multiple observers or interviewers are used across treatments, such interactions can be studied directly (Stanley, 1961a). *Regression* does not enter as interacting with *X*.

Maturation has implications of a selection-specificity nature: the results may be specific to those of this given age level, fatigue level, etc. The interaction of *history* and *X* would imply that the effect was specific to the historical conditions of the experiment, and while validly observed there, would not be found upon other occasions. The fact that the experiment was done during wartime, or just following an unsuccessful teachers' strike, etc., might produce a responsiveness to *X* not to be found upon other occasions. If we were to produce a sampling model for this problem, we should want the experiment replicated over a random sample of past and future occasions, which is obviously impossible. Furthermore, we share with other sciences the empirical assumption that there are no truly time-dependent laws, that the effects of *history* where found will be due to the specific combinations of stimulus conditions at that time, and thus ultimately will be incorporated under time-independent general laws (Neyman, 1960). ("Expanding universe" cosmologies may seem to require qualification of this statement, but not in ways relevant to this discussion.) Nonetheless, successful replication of research results across times as well as settings increases our confidence in a generalization by making interaction with *history* less likely.

These several factors have not been entered as column headings in Table 1, because they do not provide bases of discrimination among alternative designs.

Reactive arrangements. In the usual psychological experiment, if not in educational research, a most prominent source of unrepresentativeness is the patent artificiality of the experimental setting and the student's knowledge that he is participating in an experiment. For human experimental subjects, a higher-order problem-solving task is generated, in which the procedures and experimental treatment are reacted to not only for their simple stimulus values, but also for their role as clues in divining the experimenter's intent. The play-acting, outguessing, up-for-inspection, I'm-a-guinea-pig, or whatever attitudes so generated are unrepresentative of the school setting, and seem to be qualifiers of the effect of *X,* seriously hampering generalization. Where such *reactive arrangements* are unavoidable, internally valid experiments of this type should by all means be continued. But if they can be avoided, they obviously should be. In stating this, we in part join the typical anti-experimental critic in the school system or the education faculty by endorsing his most frequent protest as to the futility of "all this research." Our more moderate conclusion is not, however, that research should be abandoned for this reason, but rather that it should be improved on this score. Several suggestions follow.

Any aspect of the experimental procedure may produce this *reactive arrangements* effect. The pretesting in itself, apart from its contents, may do so, and part of the *pretest* interaction with *X* may be of this nature, although there are ample grounds to suspect the content features of the testing process. The process of randomization and assignment to treatments may be of such a nature: consider the effect upon a classroom when (as in Solomon, 1949) a randomly selected half of the pupils in a class are sent to a separate room. This action, plus the presence of the strange "teachers," must certainly create expectations of the unusual, with wonder and active puzzling as to purpose. The presentation of the treatment X, if an out-of-ordinary event, could have a similar effect. Presumably, even the posttest in a posttest-only Design 6 could create such attitudes. The more obvious the connection between the experimental treatment and the posttest content, the more likely this effect becomes.

In the area of public opinion change, such reactive arrangements may be very hard to avoid. But in much research on teaching methods there is no need for the students to know that an experiment is going on. (It would be nice to keep the teachers from knowing this, too, in analogy to medicine's double-blind experiment, but this is usually not feasible.) Several features may make such disguise possible. If the Xs are variants on usual classroom events occurring at plausible periods in the curriculum calendar, then one-third of the battle is won when these treatments occur without special announcement. If the Os are similarly embedded as regular examinations, the second requirement is achieved. If the Xs are communications focused upon individual students, then randomization can be achieved without the physical transportation of randomly equivalent samples to different classrooms, etc.

As a result of such considerations, and as a result of personal observations of experimenters who have published data in spite of having such poor rapport that their findings were quite misleading, the present authors are gradually coming to the view that experimentation within schools must be conducted by regular staff of the schools concerned, whenever possible, especially when findings are to be generalized to other classroom situations.

At present, there seem to be two main types of "experimentation" going on within schools: (1) research "imposed" upon the school by an outsider, who has his own ax to grind and whose goal is not immediate action (change) by the school; and (2) the so-called "action" researcher, who tries to get teachers themselves to be "experimenters," using that word quite loosely. The first researcher gets results that may be rigorous but not applicable. The latter gets results that may be highly applicable but probably not "true" because of extreme lack of rigor in the research. An alternative model is for the ideas for classroom research to originate with teachers and other school personnel, with designs to test these ideas worked out cooperatively with specialists in research methodology, and then for the bulk of the experimentation to be carried out by the idea-producers themselves. The appropriate statistical analyses could be done by the research methodologist and the results fed back to the group via a trained intermediary (supervisor, director of research in the school system, etc.) who has served as intermediary all along. Results should then be relevant and "correct." How to get *basic* research going under such a pattern is largely an unsolved problem, but studies could become less and less ad hoc and more and more theory-oriented under a competent intermediary.

While there is no intent in this chapter to survey either good or bad examples in the literature, a recent study by Page (1958) shows such an excellent utilization of these features (avoiding reactive arrangements, achieving sampling representativeness, and avoiding testing-X interactions) that it is cited here as a concrete illustration of optimal practice. His study shows that brief written comments upon returned objective examinations improve subsequent objective examination performance. This finding was demonstrated across 74 teachers, 12 school systems, 6 grades (7–12), 5 performance levels (A, B, C, D, F), and a wide variety of subjects, with almost no evidence of interaction effects. The teachers and classes were randomly selected. The earliest regular objective examination in each class was used as the pretest. By rolling a specially marked die the teacher assigned students to treatment groups, and correspondingly put written comments on the paper or did not. The next normally scheduled objective test in the class became the posttest. As far as could be told, not one of the 2,139 students was aware of experimentation. Few instructional procedures lend themselves to this inconspicuous randomization, since usually the oral communication involved is addressed to a whole class, rather than to individuals. (Written communications do allow for randomized treatment, although student detection of varied treatments is a problem.) Yet, holding these ideals in mind, research workers can make experiments nonreactive in many more features than they are at present.

Through regular classroom examinations or through tests presented as regular examinations and similar in content, and through alternative teaching procedures presented without announcement or apology in the regular teaching process, these two sources of reactive arrangements can probably be avoided in most instances. Inconspicuous randomization may be the more chronic problem. Sometimes, in large high schools or colleges, where students sign up for popular courses at given hours and are then assigned arbitrarily to multiple simultaneous sections, randomly equivalent sections might be achieved through control of the assignment process. (See Siegel & Siegel, 1957, for an opportunistic use of a natural randomization process.) However, because of unique intragroup histories, such initially equivalent sections become increasingly nonequivalent with the passage of long periods of time. *The all-purpose solution to this problem is to move the randomization to the classroom as a unit,* and to construct experimental and control groups each constituted of numerous classrooms randomly assigned (see Lindquist, 1940, 1953). Usually, but not essentially, the classrooms would be classified

for analysis on the basis of such factors as school, teacher (where teachers have several classes), subject, time of day, mean intelligence level, etc.; from these, various experimental-treatment groups would be assigned by a random process. There have been a few such studies, but soon they ought to become standard. Note that the appropriate test of significance is *not* the pooling of all students as though the students had been assigned at random. The details will be discussed in the subsequent section.

Tests of Significance for Design 4

Good experimental design is separable from the use of statistical tests of significance. It is the art of achieving interpretable comparisons and as such would be required even if the end product were to be graphed percentages, parallel prose case studies, photographs of groups in action, etc. In all such cases, the interpretability of the "results" depends upon control over the factors we have been describing. If the comparison is interpretable, then statistical tests of significance come in for the decision as to whether or not the obtained difference rises above the fluctuations to be expected in cases of no true difference for samples of that size. Use of significance tests presumes but does not prove or supply the comparability of the comparison groups or the interpretability of the difference found. We would thus be happy to teach experimental design upon the grounds of common sense and nonmathematical considerations. We hope that the bulk of this chapter is accessible to students of education still lacking in statistical training. Nevertheless, the issue of statistical procedures is intimately tied to experimental design, and we therefore offer these segregated comments on the topic. (Also see Green & Tukey, 1960; Kaiser, 1960; Nunnally, 1960; and Rozeboom, 1960.)

A wrong statistic in common use. Even though Design 4 is the standard and most widely used design, the tests of significance used with it are often wrong, incomplete, or inappropriate. In applying the common "critical ratio" or t test to this standard experimental design, many researchers have computed two ts, one for the pretest-posttest difference in the experimental group, one for the pretest-posttest gain in the control group. If the former be "statistically significant" and the latter "not," then they have concluded that the X had an effect, without any direct statistical comparison of the experimental and control groups. Often the conditions have been such that, had a more appropriate test been made, the difference would not have been significant (as in the case where the significance values are borderline, with the control group showing a gain almost reaching significance). Windle (1954) and Cantor (1956) have shown how frequent this error is.

Use of gain scores and covariance. The most widely used acceptable test is to compute for each group pretest-posttest gain scores and to compute a t between experimental and control groups on these gain scores. Randomized "blocking" or "leveling" on pretest scores and the analysis of covariance with pretest scores as the covariate are usually preferable to simple gain-score comparisons. Since the great bulk of educational experiments show no significant difference, and hence are frequently not reported, the use of this more precise analysis would seem highly desirable. Considering the labor of conducting an experiment, the labor of doing the proper analysis is relatively trivial. Standard treatments of Fisher-type analyses may be consulted for details. (Also see Cox, 1957, 1958; Feldt, 1958; and Lindquist, 1953.)

Statistics for random assignment of intact classrooms to treatments. The usual statistics are appropriate only where individual students have been assigned at random to treatments. Where intact classes have been assigned to treatments, the above formulas would provide too small an error term because the randomization procedure obviously has been more "lumpy" and fewer chance events have been employed. Lindquist (1953,

pp. 172–189) has provided the rationale and formulas for a correct analysis. Essentially, the class means are used as the basic observations, and treatment effects are tested against variations in these means. A covariance analysis would use pretest means as the covariate.

Statistics for internal validity. The above points were introduced to convey the statistical orthodoxy relevant to experimental design. The point to follow represents an effort to expand or correct that orthodoxy. It extends an implication of the distinction between *external* and *internal validity* over into the realm of sampling statistics. The statistics discussed above all imply sampling from an infinitely large universe, a sampling more appropriate to a public opinion survey than to the usual laboratory experiment. In the rare case of a study like Page's (1958), there is an actual sampling from a large predesignated universe, which makes the usual formulas appropriate. At the other extreme is the laboratory experiment represented in the *Journal of Experimental Psychology,* for example, in which *internal validity* has been the only consideration, and in which *all* members of a unique small universe have been exhaustively assigned to the treatment groups. There is in such experiments a great emphasis upon randomization, but not for the purpose of securing representativeness for some larger population. Instead, the randomization is solely for the purpose of equating experimental and control groups or the several treatment groups. The randomization is thus within a very small finite population which is in fact the sum of the experimental plus control groups.

This extreme position on the sampling universe is justified when describing laboratory procedures of this type: volunteers are called for, with or without promises of rewards in terms of money, personality scores, course credit points, or completion of an obligatory requirement which they will have to meet sometime during the term anyway. As volunteers come in, they are randomly assigned to treatments. When some fixed number of subjects has been reached, the experiment is stopped. There has not even been a random selection from within a much larger list of volunteers. Early volunteers are a biased sample, and the total universe "sampled" changes from day to day as the experiment goes on, as more pressure is required to recruit volunteers, etc. At some point the procedure is stopped, all designatable members of the universe having been used in one or another treatment group. Note that the sampling biases implied do not in the least jeopardize the random equivalence of the treatment groups, but rather only their "representativeness."

Or consider a more conscientious scientist, who randomly draws 100 names from his lecture class of 250 persons, contacting them by phone or mail, and then as they meet appointments assigns them randomly to treatment groups. Of course, some 20 of them cannot conveniently be fitted into the laboratory time schedule, or are ill, etc., so a redefinition of the universe has taken place implicitly. And even if he doggedly gets all 100, from the point of view of representativeness, what he has gained is the ability to generalize with statistical confidence to the 1961 class of Educational Psychology A at State Teachers. This new universe, while larger, is not intrinsically of scientific interest. Its bounds are not the bounds specified by any scientific theory. The important interests in generalization will have to be explored by the sampling of other experiments elsewhere. Of course, since his students are less select, there is more external validity, but not enough gain to be judged worth it by the great bulk of experimental psychologists.

In general, it is obvious that the dominant purpose of randomization in laboratory experiments is internal validity, not external. Pursuant to this, more appropriate and smaller error terms based upon small finite universes should be employed. Following Kempthorne (1955) and Wilk and Kempthorne (1956), we note that the appropriate model is urn randomization, rather than sampling from a universe. Thus there is available a more appropriate, more precise, nonparametric test, in which one takes the obtained experimental and control group scores and repeatedly assigns them at random to two "urns," generating empirically (or mathematically) a distribution of mean differences arising wholly from random assignment of these particular scores. This distribution is the criterion with which the obtained mean difference should be compared. When "plot-treatment interaction" (heterogeneity of true effects among subjects) is present, this distribution will have less variability than the corresponding distribution assumed in the usual t test.

These comments are not expected to modify greatly the actual practice of applying tests of significance in research on teaching. The exact solutions are very tedious, and usually inaccessible. Urn randomization, for example, ordinarily requires access to high-speed computers. The direction of error is known: using the traditional statistics is too conservative, too inclined to say "no effect shown." If we judge our publications to be overloaded with "false-positives," i.e., claims for effects that won't hold up upon cross-validation (this is certainly the case for experimental and social psychology, if not as yet for research on teaching), this error is in the preferred direction—if error there must be. Possible underestimation of significance is greatest when there are only two experimental conditions and all available subjects are used (Wilk & Kempthorne, 1955, p. 1154).

5. THE SOLOMON FOUR-GROUP DESIGN

While Design 4 is more used, Design 5, the Solomon (1949) Four-Group Design, deservedly has higher prestige and represents the first explicit consideration of *external validity* factors. The design· is as follows:

$$
\begin{array}{llll}
R & O_1 & X & O_2 \\
R & O_3 & & O_4 \\
R & & X & O_5 \\
R & & & O_6
\end{array}
$$

By paralleling the Design 4 elements (O_1 through O_4) with experimental and control groups lacking the pretest, both the main effects of *testing* and the interaction of *testing* and X are determinable. In this way, not only is generalizability increased, but in addition, the effect of X is replicated in four different fashions: $O_2 > O_1$, $O_2 > O_4$, $O_5 > O_6$, and $O_5 > O_3$. The actual instabilities of experimentation are such that if these comparisons are in agreement, the strength of the inference is greatly increased. Another indirect contribution to the generalizability of experimental findings is also made, in that through experience with Design 5 in any given research area one learns the general likelihood of testing-by-X interactions, and thus is better able to interpret past and future Design 4s. In a similar way, one can note (by comparison of O_6 with O_1 and O_3) a combined effect of maturation and history.

Statistical Tests for Design 5

There is no singular statistical procedure which makes use of all six sets of observations simultaneously. The asymmetries of the design rule out the analysis of variance of gain scores. (Solomon's suggestions concerning these are judged unacceptable.) Disregarding the pretests, except as another "treatment" coordinate with X, one can treat the posttest scores with a simple 2×2 analysis of variance design:

	No X	X
Pretested	O_4	O_2
Unpretested	O_6	O_5

From the column means, one estimates the main effect of X, from row means, the main effect of pretesting, and from cell means, the interaction of testing with X. If the main and interactive effects of pretesting are negligible, it may be desirable to perform an analysis of covariance of O_4 versus O_2, pretest scores being the covariate.

6. THE POSTTEST-ONLY CONTROL GROUP DESIGN

While the pretest is a concept deeply embedded in the thinking of research workers in education and psychology, it is not actually essential to true experimental designs. For psychological reasons it is difficult to give up "knowing for sure" that the experimental and control groups were "equal" before the differential experimental treatment. Nonetheless, the most adequate all-purpose assurance of lack of initial biases between groups is randomization. Within the limits of confidence stated by the tests of significance, randomization can suffice without the pretest. Actually, almost all of the agricultural experiments in the Fisher (1925, 1935) tradition are without pretest. Furthermore, in educational research, particularly in the primary grades, we must frequently experiment with methods for the initial introduction of entirely new subject matter, for which pretests in the ordinary sense are impossible, just as pretests on believed guilt or innocence would be inappropriate in a study of the effects of lawyers' briefs upon a jury. Design 6 fills this need, and in addition is appropriate to all of the settings in which Designs 4 or 5 might be used, i.e., designs where true randomization is possible. Its form is as follows:

$$
\begin{array}{ccc}
R & X & O_1 \\
R &   & O_2
\end{array}
$$

While this design was used as long ago as the 1920's, it has not been recommended in most methodological texts in education. This has been due in part to a confusion of it with Design 3, and due in part to distrust of randomization as equation. The design can be considered as the two last groups of the Solomon Four-Group Design, and it can be seen that it controls for testing as main effect and interaction, but unlike Design 5 it does not measure them. However, such measurement is tangential to the central question of whether or not X did have an effect. Thus, while Design 5 is to be preferred to Design 6 for reasons given above, the extra gains from Design 5 may not be worth the more than double effort. Similarly, Design 6 is usually to be preferred to Design 4, unless there is some question as to the genuine randomness of the assignment. Design 6 is greatly underused in educational and psychological research.

However, in the repeated-testing setting of much educational research, if appropriate antecedent variates are available, they should certainly be used for blocking or leveling, or as covariates. This recommendation is made for two reasons: first, the statistical tests available for Design 4 are more powerful than those available for Design 6. While the greater effort of Design 4 outweighs this gain for most research settings, it would not do so where suitable antecedent scores were automatically available. Second, the availability of pretest scores makes possible examination of the interaction of X and pretest ability level, thus exploring the generalizability of the finding more thoroughly. Something similar can be done for Design 6, using other available measures in lieu of pretests, but these considerations, coupled with the fact that for educational research frequent testing is characteristic of the universe to which one wants to generalize, may reverse the case for generally preferring Design 6 over Design 4. Note also that for any substantial mortality between R and the posttest, the pretest data of Design 4 offer more opportunity to rule out the hypothesis of differential mortality between experimental and control groups.

Even so, many problems exist for which pretests are unavailable, inconvenient, or likely to be reactive, and for such purposes the legitimacy of Design 6 still needs emphasis in many quarters. In addition to studies of the mode of teaching novel subject materials, a large class of instances remains in which (1) the X and posttest O can be delivered to students or groups as a single natural package, and (2) a pretest would be awkward. Such settings frequently occur in research on testing procedures themselves, as in studies of different instructions, different answer-sheet formats, etc. Studies of persuasive appeals for volunteering, etc., are similar. Where student anonymity must be kept, Design 6 is usually the most convenient. In such cases, randomization is handled in the mixed ordering of materials for distribution.

The Statistics for Design 6

The simplest form would be the t test. Design 6 is perhaps the only setting for which this test is optimal. However, covariance analysis and blocking on "subject variables" (Underwood, 1957b) such as prior grades, test scores, parental occupation, etc., can be used, thus providing an increase in the power of the significance test very similar to that provided by a pretest. Identicalness of pretest and posttest is not essential. Often these will be different forms of "the same" test and thus less identical than a repetition of the pretest. The gain in precision obtained corresponds directly to the degree of covariance, and while this is usually higher for alternate forms of "the same" test than for "different" tests, it is a matter of degree, and something as reliable and factorially complex as a grade-point average might turn out to be superior to a short "pretest." Note that a grade-point average is not usually desirable as a posttest measure, however, because of its probable insensitivity to X compared with a measure more specifically appropriate in content and timing. Whether such a pseudo pretest design should be classified as Design 6 or Design 4 is of little moment. It would have the advantages of Design 6 in avoiding an experimenter-introduced pretest session, and in avoiding the "giveaway" repetition of identical or highly similar unusual content (as in attitude change studies). It is for such reasons that the entry for Design 6 under "reactive arrangements" should be slightly more positive than that for Designs 4 and 5. The case for this differential is, of course, much stronger for the social sciences in general than for research on educational instruction.

FACTORIAL DESIGNS

On the conceptual base of the three preceding designs, but particularly of Designs 4 and 6, the complex elaborations typical of the Fisher factorial designs can be extended by adding other groups with other Xs. In a typical single-classification criterion or "one-way" analysis of variance we would have several "levels" of the treatment, e.g., X_1, X_2, X_3, etc., with perhaps still an X_0 (no-X) group. If the control group be regarded as one of the treatments, then for Designs 4 and 6 there would be one group for each treatment. For Design 5 there would be two groups (one pretested, one not) for each treatment, and a two-classification ("two-way") analysis of variance could still be performed. We are not aware that more-than-two-level designs of the Design 5 type have been done. Usually, if one were concerned about the pretest interaction, Design 6 would be employed because of the large number of groups otherwise required. Very frequently, two or more treatment variables, each at several "levels," will be employed, giving a series of groups that could be designated $X_{a1} X_{b1}$, $X_{a1} X_{b2}$, $X_{a1} X_{b3}$, ..., $X_{a2} X_{b1}$, etc.

Such elaborations, complicated by efforts to economize through eliminating some of the possible permutations of X_a by X_b, have produced some of the traumatizing mysteries of factorial design (randomized blocks, split plots, Greco-Latin squares, fractional replication, confounding, etc.) which have created such a gulf between advanced and traditional research methodologies in education. We hope that this chapter helps bridge this gulf through continuity with traditional methodology and the common-sense considerations which the student brings with him. It is also felt that a great deal of what needs to be taught about experimental design can best be understood when presented in the form of two-treatment designs, without interference from other complexities. Yet a full presentation of the problems of traditional usage will generate a comprehension of the need for and place of the modern approaches. Already, in searching for the most efficient way of summarizing the widely accepted old-fashioned Design 4, we were introduced to a need for covariance analysis, which has been almost unused in this setting. And in Design 5, with a two-treatment problem elaborated only to obtain needed controls, we moved away from critical ratios or t tests into the related analysis-of-variance statistics.

The details of statistical analyses for factorial designs cannot be taught or even illustrated in this chapter. Elementary aspects of these methods are presented for educational researchers by Edwards (1960), Ferguson (1959), Johnson and Jackson (1959), and Lindquist (1953). It is hoped, however, that the ensuing paragraphs may convey some understanding of certain alternatives and complexities particularly relevant for the design issues discussed in this chapter. The complexities to be discussed do not include the common reasons for using Latin squares and many other incomplete designs where knowledge concerning certain interactions is sacrificed merely for reasons of cost. (But the use of Latin squares as a substitute for control groups where randomization is not possible will be discussed as quasi-experimental Design 11 below.) The reason for the decision to omit such incomplete designs is that detailed knowledge of interactions is highly relevant to the external validity problem, particularly in a science which has experienced trouble in replicating one researcher's findings in another setting (see Wilk & Kempthorne, 1957). The concepts which we seek to convey in this section are interaction, nested versus crossed classifications, and finite, fixed, random, and mixed factorial models.

Interaction

We have already used this concept in contexts where it was hoped the untrained

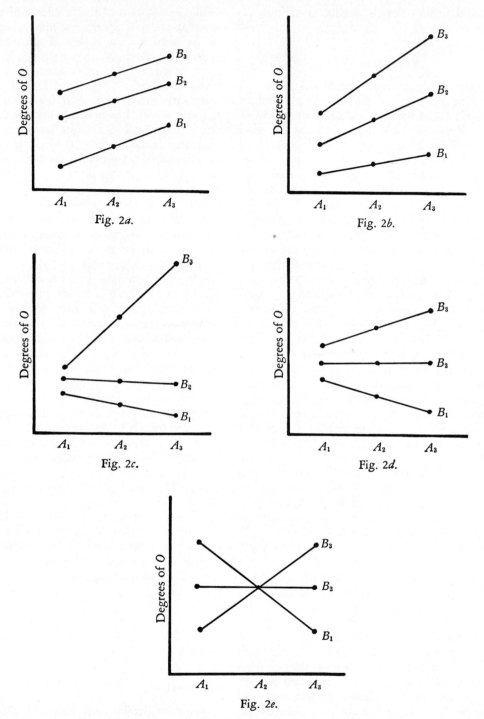

Fig. 2. Some Possible Outcomes of a 3 x 3 Factorial Design.

reader would find it comprehensible. As before, our emphasis here is upon the implications for generalizability. Let us consider in graphic form, in Fig. 2, five possible outcomes of a design having three levels each of X_a and X_b, to be called here A and B. (Since three dimensions [$A, B,$ and O] are to be graphed in two dimensions, there are several alternative presentations, only one of which is used here.) In Fig. 2a there is a significant main effect for both A and B, but no interaction. (There is, of course, a summation of effects—A_3, B_3 being strongest—but no interaction, as the effects are additive.) In all of the others, there are significant interactions in addition to, or instead of, the main effects of A and B. That is, the law as to the effect of A changes depending upon the specific value of B. In this sense, interaction effects are specificity-of-effect rules and are thus relevant to generalization efforts. The interaction effect in 2d is most clearly of this order. Here A does not have a main effect (i.e., if one averages the values of all three Bs for each A, a horizontal line results). But when B is held at level 1, increases in A have a decremental effect, whereas when B is held at level 3, A has an incremental effect. Note that had the experimenter varied A only and held B constant at level 1, the results, while internally valid, would have led to erroneous generalizations for B_2 and B_3. The multiple-factorial feature of the design has thus led to valuable explorations of the generalizability or external validity of any summary statement about the main effect of A. Limitations upon generalizability, or specificity of effects, appear in the statistical analysis as significant interactions.

Figure 2e represents a still more extreme form of interaction, in which neither A nor B has any main effect (no general rules emerge as to which level of either is better) but in which the interactions are strong and definite. Consider a hypothetical outcome of this sort. Let us suppose that three types of teachers are all, in general, equally effective (e.g., the spontaneous extemporizers, the conscientious preparers, and the close super-

visors of student work). Similarly, three teaching methods in general turn out to be equally effective (e.g., group discussion, formal lecture, and tutorial). In such a case, even in the absence of "main effects" for either teacher-type or teaching method, teaching methods could plausibly interact strongly with types, the spontaneous extemporizer doing best with group discussion and poorest with tutorial, and the close supervisor doing 'best with tutorial and poorest with group discussion methods.

From this point of view, we should want to distinguish between the kinds of significant interactions found. Perhaps some such concept as "monotonic interactions" might do. Note that in 2b, as in 2a, there is a main effect of both A and B, and that A has the same directional effect in every separate panel of B values. Thus we feel much more confident in generalizing the expectation of increase in O with increments in A to novel settings than we do in case 2c, which likewise might have significant main effects for A and B, and likewise a significant A-B interaction. We might, in fact, be nearly as confident of the generality of A's main effect in a case like 2b as in the interaction-free 2a. Certainly, in interpreting effects for generalization purposes, we should plot them and examine them in detail. Some "monotonic" or single-directional interactions produce little or no specificity limitations. (See Lubin, 1961, for an extended discussion of this problem.)

Nested Classifications

In the illustrations which we have given up to this point, all of the classification criteria (the As and the Bs) have "crossed" all other classification criteria. That is, all levels of A have occurred with all levels of B. Analysis of variance is not limited to this situation, however.

So far, we have used, as illustrations, classification criteria which were "experimental treatments." Other types of classification criteria, such as sex and age of pupils, could be introduced into many experiments as fully crossed classifications. But to introduce the most usual uses of "nested" classifications, we must present the possibility of less obvious classification criteria. One of these is "teachers." Operating at the fully crossed level, one might do an experiment in a high school in which each of 10 teachers used each of two methods of teaching a given subject, to different experimental classes. In this case, teachers would be a fully crossed classification criterion, each teacher being a different "level." The "main effect" of "teachers" would be evidence that some teachers are better than others no matter which method they are using. (Students or classes must have been assigned at random; otherwise teacher idiosyncrasies and selection differences are confounded.) A significant interaction between teachers and methods would mean that the method which worked better depended upon the particular teacher being considered.

Suppose now, in following up such an interaction, one were interested in whether or not a given technique was, in general, better for men teachers than women. If we now divide our 10 teachers into 5 men and 5 women, a "nesting" classification occurs in that the teacher classification, while still useful, does not cross sexes; i.e., the same teacher does not appear in both sexes, while each teacher and each sex do cross methods. This nesting requires a somewhat different analysis than does the case where all classifications cross all others. (For illustrative analyses, see Green and Tukey, 1960, and Stanley, 1961a.) In addition, certain interactions of the nested variables are ruled out. Thus the teachers-sex and teachers-sex-method interactions are not computable, and, indeed, make no sense conceptually.

"Teachers" might also become a nested classification if the above experiment were extended into several schools, so that schools became a classification criterion (for which the main effects might reflect learning-rate differences on the part of pupils of the several schools). In such a case, teachers would

usually be "nested" within schools, in that one teacher would usually teach classes within just one school. While in this instance a teacher-school interaction is conceivable, one could not be computed unless all teachers taught in both schools, in which case teachers and schools would be "crossed" rather than "nested."

Pupils, or subjects in an experiment, can also be treated as a classification criterion. In a fully crossed usage each pupil gets each treatment, but in many cases the pupil enters into several treatments, but not all; i.e., nesting occurs. One frequent instance is the study of trial-by-trial data in learning. In this case, one might have learning curves for each pupil, with pupils split between two methods of learning. Pupils would cross trials but not methods. Trial-method interactions and pupil-trial interactions could be studied, but not pupil-method interactions. Similarly, if pupils are classified by sex, nesting occurs.

Most variables of interest in educational experimentation can cross other variables and need not be nested. Notable exceptions, in addition to those mentioned above, are chronological age, mental age, school grade (first, second, etc.), and socioeconomic level. The perceptive reader may have noted that independent variables, or classification criteria, are of several sorts: (1) manipulated variables, such as teaching method, assignable at will by the experimenter; (2) potentially manipulable aspects, such as school subject studied, that the experimenter might assign in some random way to the pupils he is using, but rarely does; (3) relatively fixed aspects of the environment, such as community or school or socioeconomic level, not under the direct control of the experimenter but serving as explicit bases for stratification in the experiment; (4) "organismic" characteristics of pupils, such as age, height, weight, and sex; and (5) response characteristics of pupils, such as scores on various tests. Usually the manipulated independent variables of Class 1 are of primary interest, while the unmanipulated independent variables of Classes 3, 4, and sometimes 5, serve to increase precision and reveal how generalizable the effects of manipulated variables are. The variables of Class 5 usually appear as covariates or dependent variates. Another way to look at independent variables is to consider them as intrinsically ordered (school grade, socioeconomic level, height, trials, etc.) or unordered (teaching method, school subject, teacher, sex, etc.). Effects of ordered variables may often be analyzed further to see whether the trend is linear, quadratic, cubic, or higher (Grant, 1956; Myers, 1959).

Finite, Random, Fixed, and Mixed Models

Recently, stimulated by Tukey's unpublished manuscript of 1949, several mathematical statisticians have devised "finite" models for the analysis of variance that apply to the sampling of "levels" of experimental factors (independent variables) the principles well worked out previously for sampling from finite populations. Scheffé (1956) provided a historical survey of this clarifying development. Expected mean squares, which help determine appropriate "error terms," are available (Stanley, 1956) for the completely randomized three-classification factorial design. Finite models are particularly useful because they may be generalized readily to situations where one or more of the factors are random or fixed. A simple explanation of these extensions was given by Ferguson (1959).

Rather than present formulas, we shall use a verbal illustration to show how finite, random, and fixed selection of levels of a factor differ. Suppose that "teachers" constitute one of several bases for classification (i.e., independent variables) in an experiment. If 50 teachers are available, we might draw 5 of these *randomly* and use them in the study. Then a factor-sampling coefficient $(1-5/50)$, or 0.9, would appear in some of our formulas. If all 50 teachers were employed, then teachers would be a "fixed" effect and the coefficient would become $(1-50/50) = 0$. If, on the other hand, a virtually infinite popu-

lation of teachers existed, 50 selected randomly from this population would be an infinitesimal percentage, so the coefficient would approach 1 for each "random" effect. The above coefficients modify the formulas for expected mean squares, and hence for "error" terms. Further details appear in Brownlee (1960), Cornfield and Tukey (1956), Ferguson (1959), Wilk and Kempthorne (1956), and Winer (1962).

OTHER DIMENSIONS OF EXTENSION

Before leaving the "true" experiments for the quasi-experimental designs, we wish to explore some other extensions from this simple core, extensions appropriate to all of the designs to be discussed.

Testing for Effects Extended in Time

In the area of persuasion, an area somewhat akin to that of educating and teaching, Hovland and his associates have repeatedly found that long-term effects are not only quantitatively different, but also qualitatively different. Long-range effects are greater than immediate effects for general attitudes, although weaker for specific attitudes (Hovland, Lumsdaine, & Sheffield, 1949). A discredited speaker has no persuasive effect immediately, but may have a significant effect a month later, unless listeners are reminded of the source (Hovland, Janis, & Kelley, 1953). Such findings warn us against pinning all of our experimental evaluation of teaching methods on immediate posttests or measures at any single point in time. In spite of the immensely greater problems of execution (and the inconvenience to the nine-month schedule for a Ph.D. dissertation), we can but recommend that posttest periods such as one month, six months, and one year be included in research planning.

When the posttest measures are grades and examination scores that are going to be collected anyway, such a study is nothing but a bookkeeping (and mortality) problem. But where the Os are introduced by the experimenter, most writers feel that repeated posttest measures on the same students would be more misleading than the pretest would be. This has certainly been found to be true in research on memory (e.g., Underwood, 1957a). While Hovland's group has typically used a pretest (Design 4), they have set up separate experimental and control groups for each time delay for the posttest, e.g.:

$$
\begin{array}{llll}
R & O & X & O \\
R & O & & O \\
R & O & X & & & O \\
R & O & & & & O \\
\end{array}
$$

A similar duplication of groups would be required for Designs 5 or 6. Note that this design lacks perfect control for its purpose of comparing differences in effect as a function of elapsed time, in that the differences could also be due to an interaction between X and the specific historical events occurring between the short-term posttest and the long-term one. Full control of this possibility leads to still more elaborate designs. In view of the great expense of such studies except where the Os are secured routinely, it would seem incumbent upon those making studies using institutionalized Os repeatedly available to make use of the special advantages of their settings by following up the effects over many points in time.

Generalizing to Other Xs: Variability in the Execution of X

The goal of science includes not only generalization to other populations and times but also to other nonidentical representations of the treatment, i.e., other representations which theoretically should be the same, but which are not identical in theoretically irrelevant specifics. This goal is contrary to an often felt extension of the demand for experimental control which leads to the desire for an *exact* replication of the X on each rep-

etition. Thus, in studying the effect of an emotional versus a rational appeal, one might have the same speaker give all appeals to each type of group or, more extremely, record the talks so that all audiences of a given treatment heard "exactly the same" message. This might seem better than having several persons give each appeal just once, since in the latter case we "would not know exactly" what experimental stimulus each session got. But the reverse is actually the case, if by "know" we mean the ability to pick the proper abstract classification for the treatment and to convey the information effectively to new users. With the taped interview we have repeated each time many specific irrelevant features; for all we know, these details, not the intended features, created the effect. If, however, we have many independent exemplifications, the specific irrelevancies are not apt to be repeated each time, and our interpretation of the source of the effects is thus more apt to be correct.

For example, consider the Guetzkow, Kelly, and McKeachie (1954) comparison of recitation and discussion methods in teaching. Our "knowledge" of what the experimental treatments were, in the sense of being able to draw recommendations for other teachers, is better *because* eight teachers were used, each interpreting each method in his own way, than if only one teacher had been used, or than if the eight had memorized common details not included in the abstract description of the procedures under comparison. (This emphasis upon heterogeneous execution of X should if possible be accompanied, as in Guetzkow, et al., 1954, by having each treatment executed by each of the experimental teachers, so that no specific irrelevancies are confounded with a specific treatment. To estimate the significance of teacher-method interaction when intact classes have been employed, each teacher should execute each method twice.)

In a more obvious illustration, a study of the effect of sex of the teacher upon beginning instruction in arithmetic should use numerous examples of each sex, not just one of each. While this is an obvious precaution, it has not always been followed, as Hammond (1954) has pointed out. The problem is an aspect of Brunswik's (1956) emphasis upon representative design. Underwood (1957b, pp. 281–287) has on similar grounds argued against the exact standardization or the exact replication of apparatus from one study to another, in a fashion not incompatible with his vigorous operationalism.

Generalizing to Other Xs: Sequential Refinement of X and Novel Control Groups

The actual *X* in any experiment is a complex package of what will eventually be conceptualized as several variables. Once a strong and clear-cut effect has been noted, the course of science consists of further experiments which refine the *X*, teasing out those aspects which are most essential to the effect. This refinement can occur through more specifically defined and represented treatments, or through developing novel control groups, which come to match the experimental group on more and more features of the treatment, reducing the differences to more specific features of the original complex *X*. The placebo control group and the sham-operation control group in medical research illustrate this. The prior experiments demonstrated an internally valid effect, which, however, could have been due to the patient's knowledge that he was being treated or to surgical shock, rather than to the specific details of the drug or to the removal of the brain tissue—hence the introduction of the special controls against these possibilities. The process of generalizing to other *X*s is an exploratory, theory-guided trial and error of extrapolations, in the process of which such refinement of *X*s is apt to play an important part.

Generalizing to Other Os

Just as a given *X* carries with it a baggage of theoretically irrelevant specificities which

may turn out to cause the effect, so any given *O,* any given measuring instrument, is a complex in which the relevant content is necessarily embedded in a specific instrumental setting, the details of which are tangential to the theoretical purpose. Thus, when we use IBM pencils and machine-scored answer-sheets, it is usually for reasons of convenience and not because we wish to include in our scores variance due to clerical skills, test-form familiarity, ability to follow instructions, etc. Likewise, our examination of specific subject-matter competence by way of essay tests must be made through the vehicles of penmanship and vocabulary usage and hence must contain variance due to these sources often irrelevant to our purposes. Given this inherent complexity of any *O,* we are faced with a problem when we wish to generalize to other potential *O*s. To which aspect of our experimental *O* was this internally valid effect due? Since the goals of teaching are not solely those of preparing people for future essay and objective examinations, this problem of external validity or generalizability is one which must be continually borne in mind.

Again, conceptually, the solution is not to hope piously for "pure" measures with no irrelevant complexities, but rather to use multiple measures in which the specific vehicles, the specific irrelevant details, are as different as possible, while the common content of our concern is present in each. For *O*s, more of this can be done within a single experiment than for *X*s, for it is usually possible to get many measures of effect (i.e., dependent variables) in one experiment. In the study by Guetzkow, Kelly, and McKeachie (1954), effects were noted not only on course examinations and on special attitude tests introduced for this purpose, but also on such subsequent behaviors as choice of major and enrollment in advanced courses in the same topic. (These behaviors proved to be just as sensitive to treatment differences as were the test measures.) *Multiple Os should be an orthodox requirement in any study of teaching methods.* At the simplest level, both essay and objective examinations should be used (see Stanley & Beeman, 1956), along with indices of classroom participation, etc., where feasible. (An extension of this perspective to the question of test validity is provided by Campbell and Fiske, 1959; and Campbell, 1960.)

QUASI-EXPERIMENTAL DESIGNS[5]

There are many natural social settings in which the research person can introduce something like experimental design into his scheduling of data collection procedures (e.g., the *when* and *to whom* of measurement), even though he lacks the full control over the scheduling of experimental stimuli (the *when* and *to whom* of exposure and the ability to randomize exposures) which makes a true experiment possible. Collectively, such situations can be regarded as quasi-experimental designs. One purpose of this chapter is to encourage the utilization of such quasi-experiments and to increase awareness of the kinds of settings in which opportunities to employ them occur. But just because full experimental control *is* lacking, it becomes imperative that the researcher be thoroughly aware of which specific variables his particular design fails to control. It is for this need in evaluating quasi-experiments, more than for understanding true experiments, that the check lists of sources of invalidity in Tables 1, 2, and 3 were developed.

The average student or potential researcher reading the previous section of this chapter probably ends up with more things to worry about in designing an experiment than he had in mind to begin with. This is all to the good if it leads to the design and execution of better experiments and to more circumspection in drawing inferences from results. It is, however, an unwanted side effect if it

creates a feeling of hopelessness with regard to achieving experimental control and leads to the abandonment of such efforts in favor of even more informal methods of investigation. Further, this formidable list of sources of invalidity might, with even more likelihood, reduce willingness to undertake quasi-experimental designs, designs in which from the very outset it can be seen that full experimental control is lacking. Such an effect would be the opposite of what is intended.

From the standpoint of the final interpretation of an experiment and the attempt to fit it into the developing science, every experiment is imperfect. What a check list of validity criteria can do is to make an experimenter more aware of the residual imperfections in his design so that on the relevant points he can be aware of competing interpretations of his data. He should, of course, design the very best experiment which the situation makes possible. He should deliberately seek out those artificial and natural laboratories which provide the best opportunities for control. But beyond that he should go ahead with experiment and interpretation, fully aware of the points on which the results are equivocal. While this awareness is important for experiments in which "full" control has been exercised, it is crucial for quasi-experimental designs.

In implementing this general goal, we shall in this portion of the chapter survey the strengths and weaknesses of a heterogeneous collection of quasi-experimental designs, each deemed worthy of use *where better designs are not feasible*. First will be discussed three single-group experimental designs. Following these, five general types of multiple-group experiments will be presented. A separate section will deal with correlation, ex post facto designs, panel studies, and the like.

SOME PRELIMINARY COMMENTS ON THE THEORY OF EXPERIMENTATION

This section is written primarily for the educator who wishes to take his research

---

[5] This section draws heavily upon D. T. Campbell, Quasi-experimental designs for use in natural social settings, in D. T. Campbell, *Experimenting, Validating, Knowing: Problems of Method in the Social Sciences.* New York: McGraw-Hill, in preparation.

out of the laboratory and into the operating situation. Yet the authors cannot help being aware that experimental psychologists may look with considerable suspicion on any effort to sanction studies having less than full experimental control. In part to justify the present activity to such monitors, the following general comments on the role of experiments in science are offered. These comments are believed to be compatible with most modern philosophies of science, and they come from a perspective on a potential general psychology of inductive processes (Campbell, 1959).

Science, like other knowledge processes, involves the proposing of theories, hypotheses, models, etc., and the acceptance or rejection of these on the basis of some external criteria. Experimentation belongs to this second phase, to the pruning, rejecting, editing phase. We may assume an ecology for our science in which the number of potential positive hypotheses very greatly exceeds the number of hypotheses that will in the long run prove to be compatible with our observations. *The task of theory-testing data collection is therefore predominantly one of rejecting inadequate hypotheses.* In executing this task, any arrangement of observations for which certain outcomes would disconfirm theory will be useful, including quasi-experimental designs of less efficiency than true experiments.

But, it may be asked, will not such imperfect designs result in spurious confirmation of inadequate theory, mislead our subsequent efforts, and waste our journal space with the dozens of studies which it seems to take to eradicate one conspicuously published false positive? This is a serious risk, but a risk which we must take. It is a risk shared in kind, if not in the same degree, by "true" experiments of Designs 4, 5, and 6. In a very fundamental sense, experimental results never "confirm" or "prove" a theory—rather, the successful theory is tested and escapes being disconfirmed. The word "prove," by being frequently employed to designate deductive validity, has acquired in our genera-

tion a connotation inappropriate both to its older uses and to its application to inductive procedures such as experimentation. The results of an experiment "probe" but do not "prove" a theory. An adequate hypothesis is one that has repeatedly survived such probing—but it may always be displaced by a new probe.

It is by now generally understood that the "null hypothesis" often employed for convenience in stating the hypothesis of an experiment can never be "accepted" by the data obtained; it can only be "rejected," or "fail to be rejected." Similarly with hypotheses more generally—they are technically never "confirmed": where we for convenience use that term we imply rather that the hypothesis was exposed to disconfirmation and was not disconfirmed. This point of view is compatible with all Humean philosophies of science which emphasize the impossibility of deductive proof for inductive laws. Recently Hanson (1958) and Popper (1959) have been particularly explicit upon this point. Many bodies of data collected in research on teaching have little or no probing value, and many hypothesis-sets are so double-jointed that they cannot be disconfirmed by available probes. We have no desire to increase the acceptability of such pseudo research. The research designs discussed below are believed to be sufficiently probing, however, to be well worth employing *where more efficient probes are unavailable.*

The notion that experiments never "confirm" theory, while correct, so goes against our attitudes and experiences as scientists as to be almost intolerable. Particularly does this emphasis seem unsatisfactory vis-à-vis the elegant and striking confirmations encountered in physics and chemistry, where the experimental data may fit in minute detail over numerous points of measurement a complex curve predicted by the theory. And the perspective becomes phenomenologically unacceptable to most of us when extended to the inductive achievements of vision. For example, it is hard to realize that the tables and chairs which we "see" before us are not "confirmed" or "proven" by the visual evidence, but are "merely" hypotheses about external objects not as yet disconfirmed by the multiple probes of the visual system. There is a grain of truth in these reluctances.

Varying degrees of "confirmation" are conferred upon a theory through the number of *plausible rival hypotheses* available to account for the data. The fewer such plausible rival hypotheses remaining, the greater the degree of "confirmation." Presumably, at any stage of accumulation of evidence, even for the most advanced science, there are numerous possible theories compatible with the data, particularly if all theories involving complex contingencies be allowed. Yet for "well-established" theories, and theories thoroughly probed by complex experiments, few if any rivals may be practically available or seriously proposed. This fewness is the epistemological counterpart of the positive affirmation of theory which elegant experiments seem to offer. A comparable fewness of rival hypotheses occurs in the phenomenally positive knowledge which vision seems to offer in contrast, for example, to the relative equivocality of blind tactile exploration.

In this perspective, the list of sources of invalidity which experimental designs control can be seen as a list of frequently plausible hypotheses which are rival to the hypothesis that the experimental variable has had an effect. Where an experimental design "controls" for one of these factors, it merely renders this rival hypothesis implausible, even though through possible complex coincidences it might still operate to produce the experimental outcome. The "plausible rival hypotheses" that have necessitated the routine use of special control groups have the status of well-established empirical laws: practice effects for adding a control group to Design 2, suggestibility for the placebo control group, surgical shock for the sham-operation control. Rival hypotheses are plausible insofar as we are willing to attribute to them

the status of empirical laws. Where controls are lacking in a quasi-experiment, one must, in interpreting the results, consider in detail the likelihood of uncontrolled factors accounting for the results. The more implausible this becomes, the more "valid" the experiment.

As was pointed out in the discussion of the Solomon Four-Group Design 5, the more numerous and independent the ways in which the experimental effect is demonstrated, the less numerous and less plausible any singular rival invalidating hypothesis becomes. The appeal is to parsimony. The "validity" of the experiment becomes one of the relative credibility of rival theories: the theory that X had an effect versus the theories of causation involving the uncontrolled factors. If several sets of differences can all be explained by the single hypothesis that X has an effect, while several separate uncontrolled-variable effects must be hypothesized, a different one for each observed difference, then the effect of X becomes the most tenable. This mode of inference is frequently appealed to when scientists summarize a literature lacking in perfectly controlled experiments. Thus Watson (1959, p. 296) found the evidence for the deleterious effects of maternal deprivation confirmatory because it is supported by a wide variety of evidence-types, the specific inadequacies of which vary from study to study. Thus Glickman (1961), in spite of the presence of plausible rival hypotheses in each available study, found the evidence for a consolidation process impressive just because the plausible rival hypothesis is different from study to study. This inferential feature, commonly used in combining inferences from several studies, is deliberately introduced *within* certain quasi-experimental designs, especially in "patched-up" designs such as Design 15.

The appeal to parsimony is not deductively justifiable but is rather a general assumption about the nature of the world, underlying almost all use of theory in science, even though frequently erroneous in specific applications. Related to it is another plausibility argument which we will invoke perhaps most specifically with regard to the very widely used Design 10 (a good *quasi*-experimental design, often mistaken for the true Design 4). This is the assumption that, in cases of ignorance, a main effect of one variable is to be judged more likely than the interaction of two other variables; or, more generally, that main effects are more likely than interactions. In the extreme form, we can note that if every highest-order interaction is significant, if every effect is specific to certain values on all other potential treatment dimensions, then a science is not possible. If we are ever able to generalize, it is because the great bulk of potential determining factors can be disregarded. Underwood (1957b, p. 6) has referred to this as the assumption of finite causation. Elsewhere Underwood (1954) has tallied the frequency of main effects and interactions from the *Journal of Experimental Psychology,* confirming the relative rarity of significant interactions (although editorial selection favoring neat outcomes makes his finding suspect).

In what follows, we will first deal with single-group experiments. Since 1920 at least, the dominant experimental design in psychology and education has been a control group design, such as Design 4, Design 6, or perhaps most frequently Design 10, to be discussed later. In the social sciences and in thinking about field situations, the control group designs so dominate as to seem to many persons synonymous with experimentation. As a result, many research workers may give up attempting anything like experimentation in settings where control groups are not available and thus end up with more imprecision than is necessary. There are, in fact, several quasi-experimental designs applicable to single groups which might be used to advantage, with an experimental logic and interpretation, in many situations in which a control group design is impossible. Cooperation and experimental access often come in natural administrative units: a teacher has her own classroom avail-

able; a high school principal may be willing to introduce periodic morale surveys, etc. In such situations the differential treatment of segments within the administrative unit (required for the control group experiment) may be administratively impossible or, even if possible, experimentally undesirable owing to the reactive effects of arrangements. For these settings, single-group experiments might well be considered.

7. THE TIME-SERIES EXPERIMENT

The essence of the time-series design is the presence of a periodic measurement process on some group or individual and the introduction of an experimental change into this time series of measurements, the results of which are indicated by a discontinuity in the measurements recorded in the time series. It can be diagramed thus:

$$O_1 \; O_2 \; O_3 \; O_4 X O_5 \; O_6 \; O_7 \; O_8$$

This experimental design typified much of the classical nineteenth-century experimentation in the physical sciences and in biology. For example, if a bar of iron which has remained unchanged in weight for many months is dipped in a nitric acid bath and then removed, the inference tying together the nitric acid bath and the loss of weight by the iron bar would follow some such experimental logic. There may well have been "control groups" of iron bars remaining on the shelf that lost no weight, but the measurement and reporting of these weights would typically not be thought necessary or relevant. Thus it seems likely that this experimental design is frequently regarded as valid in the more successful sciences even though it rarely has accepted status in the enumerations of available experimental designs in the social sciences. (See, however, Maxwell, 1958; Underwood, 1957b, p. 133.) There are good reasons for this differential status and a careful consideration of them will provide a better understanding of the

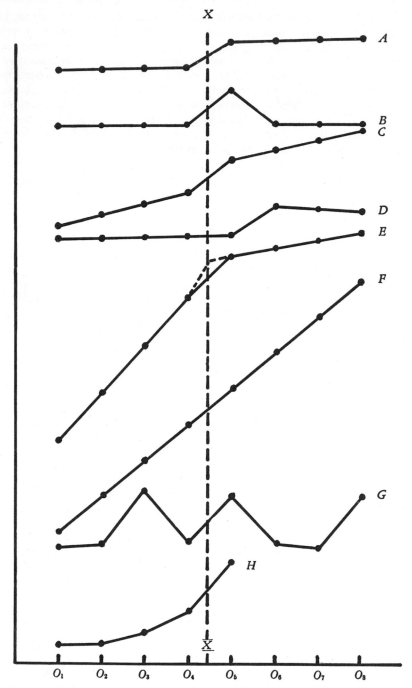

Fig. 3. Some Possible Outcome Patterns from the Introduction of an Experimental Variable at Point X into a Time Series of Measurements, O_1—O_8. Except for D, the O_4—O_5 gain is the same for all time series, while the legitimacy of inferring an effect varies widely, being strongest in A and B, and totally unjustified in F, G, and H.

conditions under which the design might meaningfully be employed by social scientists when more thorough experimental control is impossible. The design is typical of the classic experiments of the British Industrial Fatigue Research Board upon factors affecting factory outputs (e.g., Farmer, Brooks, & Chambers, 1923).

Figure 3 indicates some possible outcome patterns for time series into which an experimental alteration had been introduced as indicated by the vertical line X. For purposes of discussion let us assume that one will be tempted to infer that X had some effect in time series with outcomes such as A and B and possibly C, D, and E, but that one would not be tempted to infer an effect in time series such as F, G, and H, even were the jump in values from O_4 to O_5 as great and as statistically stable as were the O_4 to O_5 differences in A and B, for example. While discussion of the problem of statistical tests will be postponed for a few paragraphs, it is assumed that the problem of internal validity boils down to the question of plausible competing hypotheses that offer likely alternate explanations of the shift in the time series other than the effect of X. A tentative check-off of the controls provided by this experiment under these optimal conditions of outcome is provided in Table 2. The strengths of the time-series design are most apparent in contrast with Design 2, to which it has a superficial similarity in lacking a control group and in using before-and-after measures.

Scanning the list of problems of internal validity in Table 2, we see that failure to control history is the most definite weakness of Design 7. That is, the rival hypothesis exists that not X but some more or less simultaneous event produced the shift. It is upon the plausibility of ruling out such extraneous stimuli that credence in the interpretation of this experiment in any given instance must rest. Consider an experiment involving repeated measurements and the effect of a documentary film on students' optimism about the likelihood of war. Here the failure to provide a clear-cut control on *history* would seem very serious indeed since it is obvious that the students are exposed daily to many potentially relevant sources of stimulation beyond those under the experimenter's control in the classroom. Of course even here, were the experiment to be accompanied by a careful log of nonexperimental stimuli of possible relevance, plausible interpretation making the experiment worth doing might be possible. As has been noted above, the variable *history* is the counterpart of what in the physical and biological science laboratory has been called *experimental isolation*. The plausibility of *history* as an explanation for shifts such as those found in time-series A and B of Fig. 3 depends to a considerable extent upon the degree of experimental isolation which the experimenter can claim. Pavlov's conditioned-reflex studies with dogs, essentially "one-group" or "one-animal" experiments, would have been much less plausible as support of Pavlov's theories had they been conducted on a busy street corner rather than in a soundproof laboratory. What constitutes experimental isolation varies with the problem under study and the type of measuring device used. More precautions are needed to establish experimental isolation for a cloud chamber or scintillation counter study of subatomic particles than for the hypothetical experiment on the weight of bars of iron exposed to baths of nitric acid. In many situations in which Design 7 might be used, the experimenter could plausibly claim experimental isolation in the sense that he was aware of the possible rival events that might cause such a change and could plausibly discount the likelihood that they explained the effect.

Among other extraneous variables which might for convenience be put into *history* are the effects of weather and the effects of season. Experiments of this type are apt to extend over time periods that involve seasonal changes and, as in the studies of worker output, the seasonal fluctuations in illumination, weather, etc., may be confounded with the introduction of experimental change.

TABLE 2

SOURCES OF INVALIDITY FOR QUASI-EXPERIMENTAL DESIGNS 7 THROUGH 12

	History	Maturation	Testing	Instrumentation	Regression	Selection	Mortality	Interaction of Selection and Maturation, etc.	Interaction of Testing and X	Interaction of Selection and X	Reactive Arrangements	Multiple-X Interference
Quasi-Experimental Designs:												
7. Time Series $O\ O\ O\ OXO\ O\ O\ O$	−	+	+	?	+	+	+	+	−	?	?	
8. Equivalent Time Samples Design $X_1O\ X_0O\ X_1O\ X_0O$, etc.	+	+	+	+	+	+	+	+	−	?	−	−
9. Equivalent Materials Samples Design $M_aX_1O\ M_bX_0O\ M_cX_1O\ M_dX_0O$, etc.	+	+	+	+	+	+	+	+	−	?	?	−
10. Nonequivalent Control Group Design $O\ \ \ \ X\ \ \ \ O$ $O\ \ \ \ \ \ \ \ \ \ O$	+	+	+	+	?	+	+	−	−	?	?	
11. Counterbalanced Designs $X_1O\ \ X_2O\ \ X_3O\ \ X_4O$ $X_2O\ \ X_4O\ \ X_1O\ \ X_3O$ $X_3O\ \ X_1O\ \ X_4O\ \ X_2O$ $X_4O\ \ X_3O\ \ X_2O\ \ X_1O$	+	+	+	+	+	+	+	?	?	?	?	−
12. Separate-Sample Pretest-Posttest Design $R\ O\ (X)$ $R\ \ \ \ \ X\ O$	−	−	+	?	+	+	−	−	+	+	+	
12a. $R\ O\ \ \ \ (X)$ $R\ \ \ \ \ \ \ \ X\ O$ $R\ \ \ \ \ \ \ \ \ \ O\ (X)$ $R\ \ \ \ \ \ \ \ \ \ \ \ X\ \ O$	+	−	+	?	+	+	−	+	+	+	+	
12b. $R\ O_1\ \ \ \ \ \ \ \ (X)$ $R\ \ \ \ \ \ O_2\ (X)$ $R\ \ \ \ \ \ \ \ \ \ \ X\ \ \ O_3$	−	+	+	?	+	+	−	?	+	+	+	
12c. $R\ O_1\ X\ \ \ \ O_2$ $R\ \ \ \ \ X\ \ \ \ O_3$	−	−	+	?	+	+	+	−	+	+	+	

Perhaps best also included under *history,* although in some sense akin to *maturation,* would be periodical shifts in the time series related to institutional customs of the group such as the weekly work-cycles, pay-period cycles, examination periods, vacations, and student festivals. The observational series should be arranged so as to hold known cycles constant, or else be long enough to include several such cycles in their entirety.

To continue with the factors to be controlled: *maturation* seems ruled out on the grounds that if the outcome is like those in illustrations *A* and *B* of Fig. 3, maturation does not usually provide plausible rival hypotheses to explain a shift occurring between O_4 and O_5 which did not occur in the previous time periods under observation. (However, maturation may not always be of a smooth, regular nature. Note how the abrupt occurrence of menarche in first-year junior high school girls might in a Design 7 appear as an effect of the shift of schools upon physiology records, did we not know better.) Similarly, testing seems, in general, an implausible rival hypothesis for a jump between O_4 and O_5. Had one only the observations at O_4 and O_5, as in Design 2, this means of rendering maturation and test-retest effects implausible would be lacking. Herein lies the great advantage of this design over Design 2.

In a similar way, many hypotheses invoking changes in *instrumentation* would lack a specific rationale for expecting the instrument error to occur on this particular occasion, as opposed to earlier ones. However, the question mark in Table 2 calls attention to situations in which a change in the calibration of the measurement device could be misinterpreted as the effect of X. If the measurement procedure involves the judgments of human observers who are aware of the experimental plan, pseudo confirmation of the hypothesis can occur as a result of the observer's expectations. Thus, the experimental change of putting into office a new principal may produce a change in the recording of discipline infractions rather than in the infraction rate itself. Design 7 may frequently be employed to measure effects of a major change in administrative policy. Bearing this in mind, one would be wise to avoid shifting measuring instruments at the same time he shifts policy. In most instances, to preserve the interpretability of a time series, it would be better to continue to use a somewhat antiquated device rather than to shift to a new instrument.

Regression effects are usually a negatively accelerated function of elapsed time and are therefore implausible as explanations of an effect at O_5 greater than the effects at O_2, O_3, and O_4. *Selection* as a source of main effects is ruled out in both this design and in Design 2, if the same specific persons are involved at all Os. If data from a group is basically collected in terms of individual group members, then mortality may be ruled out in this experiment as in Design 2. However, if the observations consist of collective products, then a record of the occurrence of absenteeism, quitting, and replacement should be made to insure that coincidences of personnel change do not provide plausible rival hypotheses.

Regarding external validity, it is clear that the experimental effect might well be specific to those populations subject to repeated testing. This is hardly likely to be a limitation in research on teaching in schools, unless the experiment is conducted with artificial Os not common to the usual school setting. Furthermore, this design is particularly appropriate to those institutional settings in which records are regularly kept and thus constitute a natural part of the environment. Annual achievement tests in the public schools, illness records, etc., usually are nonreactive in the sense that they are typical of the universe to which one wants to generalize. The *selection-X* interaction refers to the limitation of the effects of the experimental variable to that specific sample and to the possibility that this reaction would not be typical of some more general universe of interest for which the naturally aggregated exposure-group was a biased sample. For example, the data requirements may limit one to those students who have had perfect attendance records over long periods, an obviously select subset. Further, if novel Os have been used, this repetitive occurrence may have provoked absenteeism.

If such time series are to be interpreted as experiments, it seems essential that the experimenter must specify in advance the expected time relationship between the introduction of the experimental variable and the manifestation of an effect. If this had been done, the pattern indicated in time-series D of Fig. 3 could be almost as definitive as that in A. Exploratory surveys opportunistically deciding upon interpretations of delayed effect would require cross-validation before being interpretable. As the time interval between X and effect increases, the plausibility of effects from extraneous historical events also increases.

It also seems imperative that the X be specified before examining the outcome of the time series. The post hoc examination of a time series to infer what X preceded the most dramatic shift must be ruled out on the grounds that the opportunistic capitalization on chance which it allows makes any approach to testing the significance of effects difficult if not impossible.

The prevalence of this design in the more successful sciences should give us some respect for it, yet we should remember that the facts of "experimental isolation" and "constant conditions" make it more interpretable for them than for us. It should also be remembered that, in their use of it, a single experiment is never conclusive. While a control group may never be used, Design 7 is repeated in many different places by various researchers before a principle is established. This, too, should be our use of it. *Where nothing better controlled is possible,* we will use it. We will organize our institutional bookkeeping to provide as many time series as possible for such evaluations and will try to examine in more detail than we have previously the effects of administrative changes and other abrupt and arbitrary events as Xs. But these will not be regarded as definitive until frequently replicated in various settings.

Tests of Significance for the Times-Series Design

If the more advanced sciences use tests of significance less than do psychology and education, it is undoubtedly because the magnitude and the clarity of the effects with which they deal are such as to render tests of signifi-

cance unnecessary. If our conventional tests of significance were applied, high degrees of significance would be found. It seems typical of the ecology of the social sciences, however, that they must work the low-grade ore in which tests of significance are necessary. It also seems likely that wherever common sense or intuitive considerations point to a clear-cut effect, some test of significance that formalizes considerations underlying the intuitive judgment is usually possible. Thus tests of significance of the effects of X that would distinguish between the several outcomes illustrated in Fig. 3, judging A and B to be significant and F and G not significant, may be available. We shall discuss a few possible approaches.

First, however, let us reject certain conceivable approaches as inadequate. If the data in Fig. 3 represent group means, then a simple significance test of the difference between the observations of O_4 and O_5 is insufficient. Even if in series F and G, these provided t ratios that were highly significant, we would not find the data evidence of effect of X because of the presence of other similar significant shifts occurring on occasions for which we had no matching experimental explanation. Where one is dealing with the kind of data provided in national opinion surveys, it is common to encounter highly significant shifts from one survey to the next which are random noise from the point of view of the interpreting scientist, inasmuch as they represent a part of the variation in the phenomena for which he has no explanation. The effect of a clear-cut event or experimental variable must rise above this ordinary level of shift in order to be interpretable. Similarly, a test of significance involving the pooled data for all of the pre-X and post-X observations is inadequate, inasmuch as it would not distinguish between instances of type F and instances of type A.

There is a troublesome nonindependence involved which must be considered in developing a test of significance. Were such nonindependence homogeneously distributed across all observations, it would be no threat to internal validity, although a limitation to external validity. What is troublesome is that in almost every time series it will be found that adjacent observations are more similar than nonadjacent ones (i.e., that the autocorrelation of lag 1 is greater than that for lag 2, etc.). Thus, an extraneous influence or random disturbance affecting an observation point at, say, O_5 or O_6, will also disturb O_7 and O_8, so that it is illegitimate to treat them as several independent departures from the extrapolation of the O_1—O_4 trend.

The test of significance employed will, in part, depend upon the hypothesized nature of the effect of X. If a model such as line B is involved, then a test of the departure of O_5 from the extrapolation of O_1—O_4 could be used. Mood (1950, pp. 297–298) provides such a test. Such a test could be used for all instances, but it would seem to be unnecessarily weak where a continuous improvement, or increased rate of gain, were hypothesized. For such cases, a test making use of all points would seem more appropriate. There are two components which might enter into such tests of significance. These are intercept and slope. By intercept we refer to the jump in the time series at X (or at some specified lag after X). Thus lines A and C show an intercept shift with no change in slope. Line E shows a change in slope but no change in intercept in that the pre-X extrapolation to X and the post-X extrapolation to X coincide. Often both intercept, and slope would be changed by an effective X. A pure test of intercept might be achieved in a manner analogous to working the Mood test from both directions at once. In this case, two extrapolated points would be involved, with both pre-X and post-X observations being extrapolated to a point X halfway between O_4 and O_5.

Statistical tests would probably involve, in all but the most extended time series, linear fits to the data, both for convenience and because more exact fitting would exhaust the degrees of freedom, leaving no opportunity to test the hypothesis of change. Yet frequently the assumption of linearity may not be appropriate. The plausibility of inferring an effect of X is greatest adjacent to X. The more gradual or delayed the supposed effect, the more serious the confound with history, because the possible extraneous causes become more numerous.

8. THE EQUIVALENT TIME-SAMPLES DESIGN

The most usual form of experimental design employs an equivalent sample of persons to provide a baseline against which to compare the effects of the experimental variable. In contrast, a recurrent form of one-group experimentation employs two equivalent samples of occasions, in one of which the experimental variable is present and in another of which it is absent. This design can be diagramed as follows (although a random rather than a regular alternation is intended):

$$X_1O \quad X_0O \quad X_1O \quad X_0O$$

This design can be seen as a form of the time-series experiment with the repeated introduction of the experimental variable. The experiment is most obviously useful where the effect of the experimental variable is anticipated to be of transient or reversible character. While the logic of the experiment may be seen as an extension of the time-series experiment, the mode of statistical analysis is more typically similar to that of the two-group experiment in which the significance of the difference between the means of two sets of measures is employed. Usually the measurements are quite specifically paired with the presentations of the experimental variable, frequently being concomitant, as in studies of learning, work production, conditioning, physiological reaction, etc. Perhaps the most typical early use of this experimental design, as in the studies of efficiency of students' work under various conditions by Allport (1920) and Sorokin (1930), involved the comparison of two experimental variables with each other, i.e., X_1 versus X_2 rather than one with a control. For most purposes, the simple alternation of conditions and the employment of a consistent time spacing are undesirable, particularly when they may introduce confounding with a daily, weekly, or monthly cycle, or when through the predictable periodicity an unwanted conditioning to the temporal interval may accentuate the difference between one presentation and another. Thus Sorokin made sure that each experimental treatment occurred equally often in the afternoon and the forenoon.

Most experiments employing this design have used relatively few repetitions of each experimental condition, but the type of extension of sampling theory represented by Brunswik (1956) calls attention to the need for large, representative, and equivalent random samplings of time periods. Kerr (1945) has perhaps most nearly approximated this ideal in his experiments on the effects of music upon industrial production. Each of his several experiments involved a single experimental group with a randomized, equivalent sample of days over periods of months. Thus, in one experiment he was able to compare 56 music days with 51 days without music, and in another he was able to compare three different types of music, each represented by equivalent samples of 14 days.

As employed by Kerr, for example, Design 8 seems altogether internally valid. *History,* the major weakness of the time-series experiment, is controlled by presenting X on numerous separate occasions, rendering extremely unlikely any rival explanation based on the coincidence of extraneous events. The other sources of invalidity are controlled by the same logic detailed for Design 7. With regard to external validity, generalization is obviously possible only to frequently tested populations. The reactive effect of arrangements, the awareness of experimentation, represents a particular vulnerability of this experiment. Where separate groups are getting the separate Xs, it is possible (particularly under Design 6) to have them totally unaware of the presence of an experiment or of the treatments being compared. This is

not so when a single group is involved, and when it is repeatedly being exposed to one condition or another, e.g., to one basis for computing payment versus another in Sorokin's experiment; to one condition of work versus another in Allport's; to one kind of ventilation versus another in Wyatt, Fraser, and Stock's (1926) studies; and to one kind of music versus another in Kerr's (although Kerr took elaborate precautions to make varied programing become a natural part of the working environment). As to the interaction of *selection* and X: there is as usual the limitation of the generalization of the demonstrated effects of X to the particular type of population involved.

This experimental design carries a hazard to external validity which will be found in all of those experiments in this paper in which multiple levels of X are presented to the *same* set of persons. This effect has been labeled "multiple-X interference." The effect of X_1, in the simplest situation in which it is being compared with X_0, can be generalized only to conditions of repetitious and spaced presentations of X_1. No sound basis is provided for generalization to possible situations in which X_1 is continually present, or to the condition in which it is introduced once and once only. In addition, the X_0 condition or the absence of X is not typical of periods without X in general, but is only representative of absences of X interspersed among presences. If X_1 has some extended effect carrying over into the non-X periods, as usually would seem likely, the experimental design may underestimate the effect of X_1 as compared with a Design 6 study, for example. On the other hand, the very fact of frequent shifts may increase the stimulus value of an X over what it would be under a continuous, homogeneous presentation. Hawaiian music in Kerr's study might affect work quite differently when interspersed for a day among days of other music than it would as a continuous diet. Ebbinghaus' (1885) experimental designs may be regarded as essentially of this type and, as Underwood (1957a) has pointed out, the laws which he found are limited in their generalizability to a population of persons who have learned dozens of other highly similar lists. Many of his findings do not in fact hold for persons learning a single list of nonsense syllables. Thus, while the design is internally valid, its external validity may be seriously limited for some types of content. (See also Kempthorne, 1952, Ch. 29.)

Note, however, that many aspects of teaching on which one would like to experiment may very well have effects limited for all practical purposes to the period of actual presence of X. For such purposes, this design might be quite valuable. Suppose a teacher questions the value of oral recitation versus individual silent study. By varying these two procedures over a series of lesson units, one could arrange an interpretable experiment. The effect of the presence of a parent-observer in the classroom upon students' volunteer discussion could be studied in this way. Awareness of such designs can place an experimental testing of alternatives within the grasp of an individual teacher. This could pilot-test procedures which if promising might be examined by larger, more coordinated experiments.

This approach could be applied to a sampling of occasions for a single individual. While tests of significance are not typically applied, this is a recurrent design in physiological research, in which a stimulus is repeatedly applied to one animal, with care taken to avoid any periodicity in the stimulation, the latter feature corresponding to the randomization requirement for occasions demanded by the logic of the design. Latin squares rather than simple randomization may also be used (e.g., Cox, 1951; Maxwell, 1958).

Tests of Significance for Design 8

Once again, we need appropriate tests of significance for this particular type of design. Note that two dimensions of generalization are implied: generalization across occasions

and generalization across persons. If we consider an instance in which only one person is employed, the test of significance will obviously be limited to generalizations about this particular person and will involve a generalization across instances, for which purpose it will be appropriate to use a t with degrees of freedom equal to the number of occasions less two. If one has individual records on a number of persons undergoing the same treatment, all a part of the same group, then data are available also for generalization across persons. In this usual situation two strategies seem common. A wrong one is to generate for each individual a single score for each experimental treatment, and then to employ tests of significance of the difference between means with correlated data. While tests of significance were not actually employed, this is the logic of Allport's and Sorokin's analyses. But where only one or two repetitions of each experimental condition are involved, sampling errors of occasions may be very large or the control of history may be very poor. Chance sampling errors of occasions could contribute what would appear under this analysis to be significant differences among treatments. This seems to be a very serious error if the effect of occasions is significant and appreciable. One could, for example, on this logic get a highly significant difference between X_1 and X_2 where each has been presented only once and where on one occasion some extraneous event had by chance produced a marked result. It seems essential therefore that at least two occasions be "nested" within each treatment and that degrees of freedom between occasions within treatments be represented. This need is probably most easily met by initially testing the difference between treatment means against a between-occasions-within-treatments error term. After the significance of the treatment effect has been established in this way, one could proceed to find for what proportion of the subjects it held, and thus obtain evidence relevant to the generalizability of the effect across persons. Repeated measurements and sampling of occasions pose many statistical problems, some of them still unresolved (Collier, 1960; Cox, 1951; Kempthorne, 1952).

9. THE EQUIVALENT MATERIALS DESIGN

Closely allied to the equivalent time-samples design is Design 9, basing its argument on the equivalence of samples of materials to which the experimental variables being compared are applied. Always or almost always, equivalent time samples are also involved, but they may be so finely or intricately interspersed that there is practical temporal equivalence. In a one-group repeated-X design, equivalent materials are required whenever the nature of the experimental variables is such that the effects are enduring and the different treatments and repeats of treatments must be applied to nonidentical content. The design may be indicated in this fashion:

$$M_aX_1O \quad M_bX_0O \quad M_cX_1O \quad M_dX_0O \quad \text{etc.}$$

The Ms indicate specific materials, the sample M_a, M_c, etc., being, in sampling terms, equal to the sample M_b, M_d, etc. The importance of the sampling equivalence of the two sets of materials is perhaps better indicated if the design is diagramed in this fashion:

one person $\Big\{$ Materials Sample A (O) X_0 O
or group $\quad$ Materials Sample B (O) X_1 O

The Os in parentheses indicate that in some designs a pretest will be used and in others not.

Jost's (1897) early experiment on massed versus distributed practice provides an excellent illustration. In his third experiment, 12 more or less randomly assembled lists of 12 nonsense syllables each were prepared. Six of the lists were assigned to distributed practice and six to massed practice. These 12 were then simultaneously learned over a seven-day period, their scheduling carefully intertwined so as to control for fatigue, etc. Seven such sets of six distributed and six massed lists were learned over a period lasting from November 6, 1895, to April 7, 1896. In the end, Jost had results on 40 different nonsense syllable lists learned under massed practice and 40 learned under distributed practice. The interpretability of the differences found on the one subject, Professor G. E. Müller, depends upon the sampling equivalence of the nonidentical lists involved. Within these limits, this experiment seems to have internal validity. The findings are of course restricted to the psychology of Professor G. E. Müller in 1895 and 1896 and to the universe of memory materials sampled. To enable one to generalize across persons in achieving a more general psychology, replication of the experiment on numerous persons is of course required.

Another illustration comes from early studies of conformity to group opinion. For example, Moore (1921) obtained a "control" estimate of retest stability of questionnaire responses from one set of items, and then compared this with the change resulting when, with another set of items, the retest was accompanied by a statement of majority opinion. Or consider a study in which students are asked to express their opinions on a number of issues presented in a long questionnaire. These questions are then divided into two groups as equivalent as possible. At a later time the questionnaires are handed back to the students and the group vote for each item indicated. These votes are falsified, to indicate majorities in opposite directions for the two samples of items. As a post-X measure, the students are asked to vote again on all items. Depending upon the adequacy of the argument of sampling equivalence of the two sets of items, the differences in shifts between the two experimental treatments would seem to provide a definitive experimental demonstration of the effects of the reporting of group opinions, even in the absence of any control group of persons.

Like Design 8, Design 9 has internal validity on all points, and in general for the same reasons. We may note, with regard to external validity, that the effects in Design 9, like those in all experiments involving repeated measures, may be quite specific to persons repeatedly measured. In learning experiments, the measures are so much a part of the experimental setting in the typical method used today (although not necessarily in Jost's method, in which the practices involved controlled numbers of readings of the lists) that this limitation on generalization becomes irrelevant. Reactive arrangements seem to be less certainly involved in Design 9 than in Design 8 because of the heterogeneity of the materials and the greater possibility that the subjects will not be aware that they are getting different treatments at different times for different items. This low reactivity would not be found in Jost's experiment but it would be found in the conformity study. Interference among the levels of the experimental variable or interference among the materials seems likely to be a definite weakness for this experiment, as it is for Design 8.

We have a specific illustration of the kind of limitation thus introduced with regard to Jost's findings. He reported that spaced learning was more efficient than massed practice. From the conditions of his experimentation in general, we can see that he was justified in generalizing only to persons who were learning many lists, that is, persons for whom the general interference level was high. Contemporary research indicates that the superiority of spaced learning is limited to just such populations, and that for persons learning highly novel materials for the first time, no such advantage is present (Underwood & Richardson, 1958).

Statistics for Design 9

The sampling of materials is obviously relevant to the validity and the degree of proof of the experiment. As such, the N for the computation of the significance of the differences between the means of treatment groups should probably have been an N of lists in the Jost experiment (or an N of items in the conformity study) so as to represent this relevant sampling domain. This must be supplemented by a basis for generalizing across persons. Probably the best practice at the present time is to do these seriatim, establishing the generalization across the sample of lists or items first, and then computing an experimental effects score for each particular person and employing this as a basis for generalizing across persons. (Note the cautionary literature cited above for Design 8.)

10. THE NONEQUIVALENT CONTROL GROUP DESIGN

One of the most widespread experimental designs in educational research involves an experimental group and a control group both given a pretest and a posttest, but in which the control group and the experimental group do not have pre-experimental sampling equivalence. Rather, the groups constitute naturally assembled collectives such as classrooms, as similar as availability permits but yet not so similar that one can dispense with the pretest. The assignment of X to one group or the other is assumed to be random and under the experimenter's control.

$$\frac{O \; \_ \; X \; \_ \; O}{O \; \_\_\_\_ \; O}$$

Two things need to be kept clear about this design: First, it is not to be confused with Design 4, the Pretest-Posttest Control Group Design, in which experimental subjects are assigned *randomly* from a common population to the experimental and the control group. Second, in spite of this, Design 10 should be recognized as well worth using in many instances in which Designs 4, 5, or 6 are impossible. In particular it should be recognized that the addition of even an unmatched or nonequivalent control group reduces greatly the equivocality of interpretation over what is obtained in Design 2, the One-Group Pretest-Posttest Design. The more similar the experimental and the control groups are in their recruitment, and the more this similarity is confirmed by the scores on the pretest, the more effective this control becomes. Assuming that these desiderata are approximated for purposes of internal validity, we can regard the design as controlling the main effects of history, maturation, testing, and instrumentation, in that the difference for the experimental group between pretest and posttest (if greater than that for the control group) cannot be explained by main effects of these variables such as would be found affecting both the experimental and the control group. (The cautions about intrasession history noted for Design 4 should, however, be taken very seriously.)

An effort to explain away a pretest-posttest gain specific to the experimental group in terms of such extraneous factors as history, maturation, or testing must hypothesize an interaction between these variables and the specific selection differences that distinguish the experimental and control groups. While in general such interactions are unlikely, there are a number of situations in which they might be invoked. Perhaps most common are interactions involving *maturation*. If the experimental group consists of psychotherapy patients and the control group some other handy population tested and retested, a gain specific to the experimental group might well be interpreted as a spontaneous remission process specific to such an extreme group, a gain that would have occurred even without X. Such a selection-maturation interaction (or a selection-history interaction, or a selection-testing interaction) could be mistaken for the effect of X, and thus represents a threat to the *internal* validity of the experiment. This possibility has been represented in the eighth column of Table 2 and is the main factor of *internal* validity which distinguishes Designs 4 and 10.

A concrete illustration from educational research may make this point clear. Sanford and Hemphill's (1952) study of the effects of a psychology course at Annapolis provides an excellent illustration of Design 10. In this study, the Second Class at Annapolis provided the experimental group and the Third Class the control group. The greater gains for the experimental group might be explained away as a part of some general sophistication process occurring maximally in the first two classes and only in minimal degree in the Third and Fourth, thus representing an interaction between the selection factors differentiating the experimental and control groups and natural changes (maturation) characteristic of these groups, rather than any effect of the experimental program. The particular control group utilized by Sanford and Hemphill makes possible some check on this rival interpretation (somewhat in the manner of Design 15 below). The selection-maturation hypothesis would predict that the Third Class (control group) in its initial test would show a superiority to the pretest measures for the Second Class (experimental group) of roughly the same magnitude as that found between the experimental group pretest and posttest. Fortunately for the interpretation of their experiment, this was not generally so. The class differences on the pretest were in most instances not in the same direction nor of the same magnitude as the pretest-posttest gains for the experimental group. However, their finding of a significant gain for the experimental group in confidence scores on the social situations questionnaire can be explained away as a selection-maturation artifact. The experimental group shows a gain from 43.26 to 51.42, whereas the Third Class starts out with a score of 55.82 and goes on to a score of 56.78.

The hypothesis of an interaction between selection and maturation will occasionally be tenable even where the groups are identical in pretest scores. The commonest of these instances will be where one group has a higher rate of maturation or autonomous change than the other. Design 14 offers an extension of 10 which would tend to rule this out.

Regression provides the other major internal validity problem for Design 10. As indicated by the "?" in Table 2, this hazard is avoidable but one which is perhaps more frequently tripped over than avoided. In general, if either of the comparison groups has been selected for its extreme scores on O or correlated measures, then a difference in degree of shift from pretest to posttest between the two groups may well be a product of regression rather than the effect of X. This possibility has been made more prevalent by a stubborn, misleading tradition in educational experimentation, in which matching has been regarded as the appropriate and sufficient procedure for establishing the pre-experimental equivalence of groups. This error has been accompanied by a failure to distinguish Designs 4 and 10 and the quite different roles of matching on pretest scores under the two conditions. In Design 4, matching can be recognized as a useful adjunct to randomization but not as a substitute for it: in terms of scores on the pretest or on related variables, the total population available for experimental purposes can be organized into carefully matched pairs of subjects; members of these pairs can then be assigned *at random* to the experimental or the control conditions. Such matching plus subsequent randomization usually produces an experimental design with greater precision than would randomization alone.

Not to be confused with this ideal is the procedure under Design 10 of attempting to compensate for the differences between the nonequivalent experimental and control groups by a procedure of matching, when random assignment to treatments is not possible. If in Design 10 the means of the groups are substantially different, then the process of matching not only fails to provide the intended equation but in addition insures the occurrence of unwanted regression effects. It becomes predictably certain that the two groups will differ on their posttest scores altogether independently of any effects of X, and that this difference will vary directly with the difference between the total populations from which the selection was made and inversely with the test-retest correlation. Rulon (1941), Stanley and Beeman (1958),

and R. L. Thorndike (1942) have discussed this problem thoroughly and have called attention to covariance analysis and to other statistical techniques suggested by Johnson and Neyman (see Johnson & Jackson, 1959, pp. 424–444) and by Peters and Van Voorhis (1940) for testing the effects of the experimental variable without the procedure of matching. Recent cautions by Lord (1960) concerning the analysis of covariance when the covariate is not perfectly reliable should be considered, however. Simple gain scores are also applicable but usually less desirable than analysis of covariance. Application of analysis of covariance to this Design 10 setting involves assumptions (such as that of homogeneity of regression) less plausible here than in Design 4 settings (Lindquist, 1953).

In interpreting published studies of Design 10 in which matching was used, it can be noted that the direction of error is predictable. Consider a psychotherapy experiment using ratings of dissatisfaction with one's own personality as O. Suppose the experimental group consists of therapy applicants and the matched control group of "normal" persons. Then the control group will turn out to represent extreme low scores from the normal group (selected because of their extremity), will regress on the posttest in the direction of the normal group average, and thus will make it less likely that a significant effect of therapy can be shown, rather than produce a spurious impression of efficacy for the therapeutic procedure.

The illustration of psychotherapy applicants also provides an instance in which the assumptions of homogeneous regression and of sampling from the same universe, except for extremity of scores, would seem likely to be inappropriate. The inclusion of normal controls in psychotherapy research is of some use, but extreme caution must be employed in interpreting results. It seems important to distinguish two versions of Design 10, and to give them different status as approximations of true experimentation. On the one hand, there is the situation in which the experimenter has two natural groups available, e.g., two classrooms, and has free choice in deciding which gets X, or at least has no reason to suspect differential recruitment related to X. Even though the groups may differ in initial means on O, the study may approach true experimentation. On the other hand, there are instances of Design 10 in which the respondents clearly are self-selected, the experimental group having deliberately sought out exposure to X, with no control group available from this same population of seekers. In this latter case, the assumption of uniform regression between experimental and control groups becomes less likely, and selection-maturation interaction (and the other selection interactions) become more probable. The "self-selected" Design 10 is thus much weaker, but it does provide information which in many instances would rule out the hypothesis that X has an effect. The control group, even if widely divergent in method of recruitment and in mean level, assists in the interpretation.

The threat of testing to external validity is as presented for Design 4 (see page 188). The question mark for interaction of selection and X reminds us that the effect of X may well be specific to respondents selected as the ones in our experiment have been. Since the requirements of Design 10 are likely to put fewer limitations on our freedom to sample widely than do those of Design 4, this specificity will usually be less than it would be for a laboratory experiment. The threat to external validity represented by reactive arrangements is present, but probably to a lesser degree than in most true experiments, such as Design 4.

Where one has the alternative of using two intact classrooms with Design 10, or taking random samples of the students out of the classrooms for different experimental treatments under a Design 4, 5, or 6, the latter arrangement is almost certain to be the more reactive, creating more awareness of experiment, I'm-a-guinea-pig attitude, and the like.

The Thorndike studies of formal discipline and transfer (e.g., E. L. Thorndike & Woodworth, 1901; Brolyer, Thorndike, & Woodyard, 1927) represent applications of Design 10 to Xs uncontrolled by the experimenter. These studies avoided in part, at least, the mistake of regression effects due to simple matching, but should be carefully scrutinized in terms of modern methods. The use of covariance statistics would probably have produced stronger evidence of transfer from Latin to English vocabulary, for example.

In the other direction, the usually positive, albeit small, transfer effects found could be explained away not as transfer but as the selection into Latin courses of those students whose annual rate of vocabulary growth would have been greater than that of the control group even without the presence of the Latin instruction. This would be classified here as a selection-maturation interaction. In many school systems, this rival hypothesis could be checked by extending the range of pre-Latin Os considered, as in a Design 14. These studies were monumental efforts to get experimental thinking into field research. They deserve renewed attention and extension with modern methods.

11. COUNTERBALANCED DESIGNS

Under this heading come all of those designs in which experimental control is achieved or precision enhanced by entering all respondents (or settings) into all treatments. Such designs have been called "rotation experiments" by McCall (1923), "counterbalanced designs" (e.g., Underwood, 1949), cross-over designs (e.g., Cochran & Cox, 1957; Cox, 1958), and switch-over designs (Kempthorne, 1952). The Latin-square arrangement is typically employed in the counterbalancing. Such a Latin square is employed in Design 11, diagramed here as a quasi-experimental design, in which four experimental treatments are applied in a restrictively *randomized* manner in turn to four naturally assembled groups or even to four individuals (e.g., Maxwell, 1958):

	Time 1	Time 2	Time 3	Time 4
Group A	X_1O	X_2O	X_3O	X_4O
Group B	X_2O	X_4O	X_1O	X_3O
Group C	X_3O	X_1O	X_4O	X_2O
Group D	X_4O	X_3O	X_2O	X_1O

The design has been diagramed with post-tests only, because it would be especially preferred where pretests were inappropriate, and designs like Design 10 were unavailable. The design contains three classifications (groups, occasions, and Xs or experimental treatments). Each classification is "orthogonal" to the other two in that each variate of each classification occurs equally often (once for a Latin square) with each variate of each of the other classifications. To begin with, it can be noted that each treatment (each X) occurs once and only once in each column and only once in each row. The same Latin square can be turned so that Xs become row or column heads, e.g.:

	X_1	X_2	X_3	X_4
Group A	t_1O	t_2O	t_3O	t_4O
Group B	t_3O	t_1O	t_4O	t_2O
Group C	t_2O	t_4O	t_1O	t_3O
Group D	t_4O	t_3O	t_2O	t_1O

Sums of scores by Xs thus are comparable in having each time and each group represented in each. The differences in such sums could not be interpreted simply as artifacts of the initial group differences or of practice effects, history, etc. Similarly comparable are the sums of the rows for intrinsic group differences, and the sums of the columns of the first presentation for the differences in occasions. In analysis of variance terms, the design thus appears to provide data on three main effects in a design with the number of cells usually required for two. Thinking in analysis of variance terms makes apparent the cost of this greater efficiency: What ap-

pears to be a significant main effect for any one of the three classification criteria could be instead a significant interaction of a complex form between the other two (Lindquist, 1953, pp. 258–264). The apparent differences among the effects of the Xs could instead be a specific complex interaction effect between the group differences and the occasions. Inferences as to effects of X will be dependent upon the plausibility of this rival hypothesis, and will therefore be discussed in more detail.

First, let us note that the hypothesis of such interaction is more plausible for the quasi-experimental application described than for the applications of Latin squares in the true experiments described in texts covering the topic. In what has been described as the dimension of groups, two possible sources of systematic effects are confounded. First, there are the systematic selection factors involved in the natural assemblage of the groups. These factors can be expected both to have main effects and to interact with history, maturation, practice effects, etc. Were a fully controlled experiment to have been organized in this way, each person would have been assigned to each group independently and at random, and this source of both main and interaction effects would have been removed, at least to the extent of sampling error. It is characteristic of the quasi-experiment that the counterbalancing was introduced to provide a kind of equation just because such random assignment was not possible. (In contrast, in fully controlled experiments, the Latin square is employed for reasons of economy or to handle problems specific to the sampling of land parcels.) A second possible source of effects confounded with groups is that associated with specific sequences of treatments. Were all replications in a true experiment to have followed the same Latin square, this source of main and interaction effects would also have been present. In the typical *true* experiment, however, some replication sets of respondents would have been assigned different specific Latin squares, and the sys-

tematic effect of specific sequences eliminated. This also rules out the possibility that
a specific systematic interaction has produced
an apparent main effect of Xs.

Occasions are likely to produce a main
effect due to repeated testing, maturation,
practice, and cumulative carry-overs, or transfer. History is likewise apt to produce effects
for occasions. The Latin-square arrangement, of course, keeps these main effects
from contaminating the main effects of Xs.
But where main effects symptomatize significant heterogeneity, one is probably more
justified in suspecting significant interactions
than when main effects are absent. Practice
effects, for example, may be monotonic but
are probably nonlinear, and would generate
both main and interaction effects. Many uses
of Latin squares in true experiments, as in
agriculture, for instance, do not involve repeated measurements and do not typically
produce any corresponding systematic column effects. Those of the cross-over type,
however, share this potential weakness with
the quasi-experiments.

These considerations make clear the extreme importance of replication of the quasi-
experimental design with different specific
Latin squares. Such replications in sufficient
numbers would change the quasi-experiment
into a true experiment. They would probably
also involve sufficient numbers of groups to
make possible the random assignment of intact groups to treatments, usually a preferable means of control. Yet, lacking such
possibilities, a single Latin square represents
an intuitively satisfying quasi-experimental
design, because of its demonstration of all
of the effects in all of the comparison groups.
With awareness of the possible misinterpretations, it becomes a design well worth
undertaking where better control is not possible. Having stressed its serious weaknesses,
now let us examine and stress the relative
strengths.

Like all quasi-experiments, this one gains
strength through the consistency of the internal replications of the experiment. To
make this consistency apparent, the main

effects of occasions and of groups should be
removed by expressing each cell as a deviation from the row (group) and column
(time) means: $M_{gt}-M_{g.}-M_{.t}+M_{..}$. Then
rearrange the data with treatments (Xs) as
column heads. Let us assume that the resulting picture is one of gratifying consistency,
with the same treatment strongest in all four
groups, etc. What are the chances of this
being no true effect of treatments, but instead an interaction of groups and occasions?
We can note that most possible interactions
of groups and occasions would reduce or becloud the manifest effect of X. An interaction
that imitates a main effect of X would be an
unlikely one, and one that becomes more
unlikely in larger Latin squares.

One would be most attracted to this design
when one had scheduling control over a very
few naturally aggregated groups, such as
classrooms, but could not subdivide these
natural groups into randomly equivalent
subgroups for either presentation of X or for
testing. For this situation, if pretesting is
feasible, Design 10 is also available; it also
involves a possible confounding of the effects
of X with interactions of selection and occasions. This possibility is judged to be less
likely in the counterbalanced design, because
all comparisons are demonstrated in each
group and hence several matched interactions would be required to imitate the
experimental effect.

Whereas in the other designs the special
responsiveness of just one of the groups to
an extraneous event (history) or to practice
(maturation) might simulate an effect of
X_1, in the counterbalanced design such co-
incident effects would have to occur on separate occasions in each of the groups in turn.
This assumes, of course, that we would not
interpret a main effect of X as meaningful
if inspection of the cells showed that a statistically significant main effect was primarily the result of a very strong effect in but
one of the groups. For further discussion of
this matter, see the reports of Wilk and
Kempthorne (1957), Lubin (1961), and
Stanley (1955).

12. THE SEPARATE-SAMPLE PRETEST-POSTTEST DESIGN

For large populations, such as cities, factories, schools, and military units, it may often happen that although one cannot randomly segregate subgroups for differential experimental treatments, one can exercise something like full experimental control over the *when* and *to whom* of the O, employing random assignment procedures. Such control makes possible Design 12:

$$R \; O \; (X)$$
$$R \qquad X \; O$$

In this diagram, rows represent randomly equivalent subgroups, the parenthetical X standing for a presentation of X irrelevant to the argument. One sample is measured prior to the X, an equivalent one subsequent to X. The design is not inherently a strong one, as is indicated by its row in Table 2. Nevertheless, it may frequently be all that is feasible, and is often well worth doing. It has been used in social science experiments which remain the best studies extant on their topics (e.g., Star & Hughes, 1950). While it has been called the "simulated before-and-after design" (Selltiz, Jahoda, Deutsch, & Cook, 1959, p. 116), it is well to note its superiority over the ordinary before-and-after design, Design 2, through its control of both the main effect of testing and the interaction of testing with X. The main weakness of the design is its failure to control for history. Thus in the study of the Cincinnati publicity campaign for the United Nations and UNESCO (Star & Hughes, 1950), extraneous events on the international scene probably accounted for the observed decrease in optimism about getting along with Russia.

It is in the spirit of this chapter to encourage "patched-up" designs, in which features are added to control specific factors, more or less one at a time (in contrast with the neater "true" experiments, in which a single control group controls for all of the threats to internal validity). Repeating Design 12 in different settings at different times, as in Design 12*a* (see Table 2, p. 210), controls for history, in that if the same effect is repeatedly found, the likelihood of its being a product of coincidental historical events becomes less likely. But consistent secular historical trends or seasonal cycles still remain uncontrolled rival explanations. By replicating the effect under other settings, one can reduce the possibility that the observed effect is specific to the single population initially selected. However, if the setting of research permits Design 12*a*, it will also permit Design 13, which would in general be preferred.

Maturation, or the effect of the respondents' growing older, is unlikely to be invoked as a rival explanation, even in a public opinion survey study extending over months. But, in the sample survey setting, or even in some college classrooms, the samples are large enough and ages heterogeneous enough so that subsamples of the pretest group differing in maturation (age, number of semesters in college, etc.) can be compared. Maturation, and the probably more threatening possibility of secular and seasonal trends, can also be controlled by a design such as 12*b* which adds an additional earlier pretest group, moving the design closer to the time-series design, although without the repeated testing. For populations such as psychotherapy applicants, in which healing or spontaneous remission might take place, the assumptions of linearity implicitly involved in this control might not be plausible. It is more likely that the maturational trend will be negatively accelerated, hence will make the O_1—O_2 maturational gain larger than that for O_2—O_3, and thus work against the interpretation that X has had an effect.

Instrumentation represents a hazard in this design when employed in the sample survey setting. If the same interviewers are employed in the pretest and in the posttest, it usually happens that many were doing their first interviewing on the pretest and are more experienced, or perhaps more cynical, on the posttest. If the interviewers differ on each wave and are few, differences in interviewer idiosyncrasies are confounded with the experimental variable. If the interviewers are aware of the hypothesis, and whether or not the X has been delivered, then interviewer expectations may create differences, as Stanton and Baker (1942) and Smith and Hyman (1950) have shown experimentally. Ideally, one would use equivalent random samples of different interviewers on each wave, and keep the interviewers in ignorance of the experiment. In addition, the recruitment of interviewers may show differences on a seasonal basis, for instance, because more college students are available during summer months, etc. Refusal rates are probably lower and interview lengths longer in summer than in winter. For questionnaires which are self-administered in the classroom, such instrument error may be less likely, although test-taking orientations may shift in ways perhaps better classifiable as instrumentation than as effects of X upon O.

For pretests and posttests separated in time by several months, mortality can be a problem in Design 12. If both samples are selected at the same time (point R), as time elapses, more members of the selected sample can be expected to become inaccessible, and the more transient segments of the population to be lost, producing a population difference between the different interviewing periods. Differences between groups in the number of noncontacted persons serve as a warning of this possibility.

Perhaps for studies over long periods the pretest and posttest samples should be selected independently and at appropriately different times, although this, too, has a source of systematic bias resulting from possible changes in the residential pattern of the universe as a whole. In some settings, as in schools, records will make possible the elimination of the pretest scores of those who have become unavailable by the time of the posttest, thus making the pretest and posttest more comparable. To provide a contact making this correction possible in the sample survey, and to provide an additional

confirmation of effect which mortality could not contaminate, the pretest group can be retested, as in Design 12c, where the O_1—O_2 difference should confirm the O_1—O_3 comparison. Such was the study by Duncan, et al. (1957) on the reduction in fallacious beliefs effected by an introductory course in psychology. (In this design, the retested group does not make possible the examination of the gains for persons of various initial scores because of the absence of a control group to control for regression.)

It is characteristic of this design that it moves the laboratory into the field situation to which the researcher wishes to generalize, testing the effects of X in its natural setting. In general, as indicated in Tables 1 and 2, Designs 12, 12a, 12b, and 12c are apt to be superior in external validity or generalizability to the "true" experiments of Designs 4, 5, and 6. These designs put so little demand upon the respondents for cooperation, for being at certain places at certain times, etc., that representative sampling from populations specified in advance can be employed.

In Designs 12 and 13 (and, to be sure, in some variants on Designs 4 and 6, where X and O are delivered through individual contacts, etc.) representative sampling is possible. The pluses in the selection -X interaction column are highly relative and could, in justice, be changed to question marks, since in general practice the units are not selected for their theoretical relevance, but often for reasons of cooperativeness and accessibility, which make them likely to be atypical of the universe to which one wants to generalize.

It was not to Cincinnati but rather to Americans in general, or to people in general, that Star and Hughes (1950) wanted to generalize, and there remains the possibility that the reaction to X in Cincinnati was atypical of these universes. But the degree of such accessibility bias is so much less than that found in the more demanding designs that a comparative plus seems justified.

13. THE SEPARATE-SAMPLE PRETEST-POSTTEST CONTROL GROUP DESIGN

It is expected that Design 12 will be used in those settings in which the X, if presented at all, must be presented to the group as a whole. If there are comparable (if not equivalent) groups from which X can be withheld, then a control group can be added to Design 12, creating Design 13:

$$
\begin{array}{ll}
R\ O\ (X) & \\
R\quad X\ O & \\
\hline
R\ O & \\
R\quad\quad O &
\end{array}
$$

This design is quite similar to Design 10, except that the same specific persons are not retested and thus the possible interaction of testing and X is avoided. As with Design 10, the weakness of Design 13 for internal validity comes from the possibility of mistaking for an effect of X a specific local trend in the experimental group which is, in fact, unrelated. By increasing the number of the social units involved (schools, cities, factories, ships, etc.) and by assigning them in some number and with randomization to the experimental and control treatments, the one source of invalidity can be removed, and a true experiment, like Design 4 except for avoiding the retesting of specific individuals, can be achieved. This design can be designated 13a. Its diagraming (in Table 3) has been complicated by the two levels of equivalence (achieved by random assignment) which are involved. At the level of respondents, there is within each social unit the equivalence of the separate pretest and posttest samples, indicated by the point of assignment R. Among the several social units receiving either treatment, there is no such equivalence, this lack being indicated by the dashed line. The R' designates the equation of the experimental group and the control group by the random assignment of these numerous social units to one or another treatment.

As can be seen by the row for 13a in Table 3, this design receives a perfect score for both internal and external validity, the latter on grounds already discussed for Design 12 with further strength on the selection-X interaction problem because of the representation of numerous social units, in contrast with the use of a single one. As far as is known, this excellent but expensive design has not been used.

14. THE MULTIPLE TIME-SERIES DESIGN

In studies of major administrative change by time-series data, the researcher would be wise to seek out a similar institution not undergoing the X, from which to collect a similar "control" time series (ideally with X assigned randomly):

$$
\begin{array}{l}
O\ O\ O\ OXO\ O\ O\ O \\
\hline
O\ O\ O\ O\ \ O\ O\ O\ O
\end{array}
$$

This design contains within it (in the Os bracketing the X) Design 10, the Nonequivalent Control Group Design, but gains in certainty of interpretation from the multiple measures plotted, as the experimental effect is in a sense twice demonstrated, once against the control and once against the pre-X values in its own series, as in Design 7. In addition, the selection-maturation interaction is controlled to the extent that, if the experimental group showed in general a greater rate of gain, it would show up in the pre-X Os. In Tables 2 and 3 this additional gain is poorly represented, but appears in the final internal validity column, which is headed "Interaction of Selection and Maturation." Because maturation is controlled for both experimental and control series, by the logic discussed in the first presentation of the Time-Series Design 7 above, the difference in the selection of the groups operating in conjunction with maturation, instrumentation, or regression, can hardly account for an apparent effect. An interaction of the se-

TABLE 3
SOURCES OF INVALIDITY FOR QUASI-EXPERIMENTAL DESIGNS 13 THROUGH 16

| | Sources of Invalidity | | | | | | | | | | | |
| | Internal | | | | | | | | External | | | |
	History	Maturation	Testing	Instrumentation	Regression	Selection	Mortality	Interaction of Selection and Maturation, etc.	Interaction of Testing and X	Interaction of Selection and X	Reactive Arrangements	Multiple-X Interference
Quasi-Experimental Designs Continued:												
13. Separate-Sample Pretest-Posttest Control Group Design	+	+	+	+	+	+	+	−	+	+	+	
13a.	+	+	+	+	+	+	+	+	+	+	+	
14. Multiple Time-Series	+	+	+	+	+	+	+	+	−	−	?	
15. Institutional Cycle Design												
$O_2 < O_1$ / $O_5 < O_4$	+	−	+	+	?	−	?		+	?	+	
$O_2 < O_3$	−	−	−	?	?	+	+		−	?	+	
$O_2 < O_4$	−	−	+	?	?	+	?		+	?	?	
$O_6 = O_7$ / $O_{2y} = O_{2o}$	+							−				
16. Regression Discontinuity	+	+	+	?	+	+	?	+	+	−	+	+

Design 13:

$R \quad O \quad (X)$
$R \qquad\quad X \quad O$

$R \quad O$
$R \qquad\qquad\quad O$

Design 13a:

$R'\left\{\begin{array}{l} R \quad O \quad (X) \\ R \qquad\;\; X \quad O \\ \text{-----} \\ R \quad O \quad (X) \\ R \qquad\;\; X \quad O \\ \text{-----} \\ R \quad O \quad (X) \\ R \qquad\;\; X \quad O \end{array}\right.$

$R'\left\{\begin{array}{l} R \quad O \\ R \qquad\qquad O \\ \text{-----} \\ R \quad O \\ R \qquad\qquad O \\ \text{-----} \\ R \quad O \\ R \qquad\qquad O \end{array}\right.$

Design 14:

$O\ O\ \overline{O X O}\ O\ O$
$\overline{O\ O\ O\ O\ O\ O}$

Design 15. Institutional Cycle Design

Class A X O_1
Class B_1 RO_2 X O_3
Class B_2 R X O_4
Class C O_5 X
[a]Gen. Pop. Con. Cl. B O_6
[a]Gen. Pop. Con. Cl. C O_7

[a] General Population Controls for Class B, etc.

lection difference with history remains, however, a possibility.

As with the Time-Series Design 7, a minus has been entered in the external validity column for testing-X interaction, although as with Design 7, the design would often be used where the testing was nonreactive. The standard precaution about the possible specificity of a demonstrated effect of X to the population under study is also recorded in Table 3. As to the tests of significance, it is suggested that differences between the experimental and control series be analyzed as Design 7 data. These differences seem much more likely to be linear than raw time-series data.

In general, this is an excellent quasi-experimental design, perhaps the best of the more feasible designs. It has clear advantages over Designs 7 and 10, as noted immediately above and in the Design 10 presentation. The availability of repeated measurements makes the Multiple Time Series particularly appropriate to research in schools.

15. The Recurrent Institutional Cycle Design: A "Patched-Up" Design

Design 15 illustrates a strategy for field research in which one starts out with an inadequate design and then adds specific features to control for one or another of the recurrent sources of invalidity. The result is often an inelegant accumulation of precautionary checks, which lacks the intrinsic symmetry of the "true" experimental designs, but nonetheless approaches experimentation. As a part of this strategy, the experimenter must be alert to the rival interpretations (other than an effect of X) which the design leaves open and must look for analyses of the data, or feasible extensions of the data, which will rule these out. Another feature often characteristic of such designs is that the effect of X is demonstrated in several different manners. This is obviously an important feature where each specific comparison would be equivocal by itself.

The specific "patched-up" design under discussion is limited to a narrow set of questions and settings, and opportunistically exploits features of these settings. The basic insight involved can be noted by an examination of the second and third rows of Table 1, in which it can be seen that the patterns of plus and minus marks for Designs 2 and 3 are for the most part complementary, and that hence the right combination of these two inadequate arguments might have considerable strength. The design is appropriate to those situations in which a given aspect of an institutional process is, on some cyclical schedule, continually being presented to a new group of respondents. Such situations include schools, indoctrination procedures, apprenticeships, etc. If in these situations one is interested in evaluating the effects of such a global and complex X as an indoctrination program, then the Recurrent Institutional Cycle Design probably offers as near an answer as is available from the designs developed thus far.

The design was originally conceptualized in the context of an investigation of the effects of one year's officer and pilot training upon the attitudes toward superiors and subordinates and leadership functions of a group of Air Force cadets in the process of completing a 14-month training cycle (Campbell & McCormack, 1957). The restriction precluding a true experiment was the inability to control who would be exposed to the experimental variable. There was no possibility of dividing the entering class into two equated halves, one half of which would be sent through the scheduled year's program, and the other half sent back to civilian life. Even were such a true experiment feasible (and opportunistic exploitation of unpredicted budget cuts might have on several occasions made such experiments possible), the reactive effects of such experimental arrangements, the disruption in the lives of those accepted, screened, and brought to the air base and then sent home, would have made them far from an ideal control group. The difference between them and the experimental group receiving indoctrination would hardly have been an adequate base from which to generalize to the normal conditions of recruitment and training. There remained, however, the experimenter's control over the scheduling of the *when* and *to whom* of the observational procedures. This, plus the fact that the experimental variable was recurrent and was continually being presented to a new group of respondents, made possible some degree of experimental control. In that study two kinds of comparisons relevant to the effect of military experience on attitudes were available. Each was quite inadequate in terms of experimental control, but when both provided confirmatory evidence they were mutually supportive inasmuch as they both involved different weaknesses. The first involved comparisons among populations measured at the same time but varying in their length of service. The second involved measures of the same group of persons in their first week of military training and then again after some 13 months. In idealized form this design is as follows:

$$\text{Class A} \quad X \quad O_1$$
$$\overline{} \;\; \overline{} \;\; \overline{} \;\; \overline{} \;\; \overline{}$$
$$\text{Class B} \qquad\quad O_2 \quad X \quad O_3$$

This design combines the "longitudinal" and "cross-sectional" approaches commonly employed in developmental research. In this it is assumed that the scheduling is such that at one and the same time a group which has been exposed to X and a group which is just about to be exposed to it can be measured; this comparison between O_1 and O_2 thus corresponds to the Static-Group Comparison, Design 3. Remeasuring the personnel of Class B one cycle later provides the One-Group Pretest-Posttest segment, Design 2. In Table 3, on page 226, the first two rows dealing with Design 15 show an analysis of these comparisons. The cross-sectional comparison of $O_1 > O_2$ provides differences which could not be explained by the effects of history or a test-retest effect. The differences obtained could, however, be due to differ-

ences in recruitment from year to year (as indicated by the minus opposite selection) or by the fact that the respondents were one year older (the minus for maturation). Where the testing is all done at the same time period, the confounded variable of instrumentation, or shifts in the nature of the measuring instrument, seem unlikely. In the typical comparison of the differences in attitudes of freshmen and sophomores, the effect of mortality is also a rival explanation: O_1 and O_2 might differ just because of the kind of people that have dropped out from Class A but are still represented in Class B. This weakness is avoidable if the responses are identified by individuals, and if the experimenter waits before analyzing his data until Class B has completed its exposure to X and then eliminates from O_2 all of those measures belonging to respondents who later failed to complete the training. The frequent absence of this procedure justifies the insertion of a question mark opposite the mortality variable. The regression column is filled with question marks to warn of the possibility of spurious effects if the measure which is being used in the experimental design is the one on which the acceptance and rejection of candidates for the training course was based. Under these circumstances consistent differences which should not be attributed to the effects of X would be anticipated. The pretest-posttest comparison involved in O_2 and O_3, if it provides the same type of difference as does the $O_2 - O_1$ comparison, rules out the rival hypotheses that the difference is due to a shift in the selection or recruitment between the two classes, and also rules out any possibility that mortality is the explanation. However, were the $O_2 - O_3$ comparison to be used alone, it would be vulnerable to the rival explanations of history and testing.

In a setting where the training period under examination is one year, the most expensive feature of the design is the scheduling of the two sets of measurements a year apart. Given the investment already made in this, it constitutes little additional expense to do more testing on the second occasion. With this in mind, one can expand the recurrent institutional design to the pattern shown in Table 3. Exercising the power to designate who gets measured and when, Class B has been broken into two equated samples, one measured both before and after exposure, and the other measured only after exposure as in O_4. This second group provides a comparison on carefully equated samples of an initial measure coming before and after, is more precise than the $O_1 - O_2$ comparison as far as selection is concerned, and is superior to the $O_2 - O_3$ comparison in avoiding test-retest effects. The effect of X is thus documented in three separate comparisons, $O_1 > O_2$, $O_2 < O_3$ and $O_2 < O_4$.

Note, however, that O_2 is involved in all of these three, and thus all might appear to be confirmatory just because of an eccentric performance of that particular set of measurements. The introduction of O_5, that is Class C, tested on the second testing occasion prior to being exposed to X, provides another pre-X measure to be compared with O_4 and O_1, etc., providing a needed redundancy. The splitting of Class B makes this $O_4 - O_5$ comparison more clear-cut than would be an $O_3 - O_5$ comparison. Note, however, that the splitting of a class into the tested and the nontested half often constitutes a "reactive arrangement." For this reason a question mark has been inserted for that factor in the $O_2 < O_4$ row in Table 3. Whether or not this is a reactive procedure depends upon the specific conditions. Where lots are drawn and one half of the class is asked to go to another room, the procedure is likely to be reactive (e.g., Duncan, et al., 1957; Solomon, 1949). Where, as in many military studies, the contacts have been made individually, a class can be split into equated halves without this conspicuousness. Where a course consists of a number of sections with separate schedules, there is the possibility of assigning these intact units to the pretest and no-pretest groups (e.g., Hovland, Lumsdaine, & Sheffield, 1949). For a single classroom, the strategy of passing out questionnaires or tests to everyone but varying the content so that a random half would get what would constitute the pretest and the other half get tested on some other instrument may serve to make the splitting of the class no more reactive than the testing of the whole class would be.

The design as represented through measurements O_1 to O_5 uniformly fails to control for maturation. The seriousness of this limitation will vary depending upon the subject material under investigation. If the experiment deals with the acquisition of a highly esoteric skill or competence, the rival hypothesis of maturation—that just growing older or more experienced in normal everyday societal ways would have produced this gain—may seem highly unlikely.

In the cited study of attitudes toward superiors and subordinates (Campbell & McCormack, 1957), however, the shift was such that it might very plausibly be explained in terms of an increased sophistication which a group of that age and from that particular type of background would have undergone through growing older or being away from home in almost any context. In such a situation a control for maturation seems very essential. For this reason O_6 and O_7 have been added to the design, to provide a cross-sectional test of a general maturation hypothesis made on the occasion of the second testing period. This would involve testing two groups of persons from the general population who differ only in age and whose ages were picked to coincide with those of Class B and Class C at the time of testing. To confirm the hypothesis of an effect of X, the groups O_6 and O_7 should turn out to be equal, or at least to show less discrepancy than do the comparisons spanning exposure to X. The selection of these general population controls would depend upon the specificity of the hypothesis. Considering our knowledge as to the ubiquitous importance of social class and educational considerations, these controls might be selected so as to match the institutional recruitment on social class and previous education. They might also be persons who are living away from home for the first time and who are of the typical age of induction, so that, in the illustration given, the O_6 group would have been away from home one year and the O_7 group just barely on the verge of leaving home. These general population age-mate controls would always be to some extent unsatisfactory and would represent the greatest cost item, since testing within an institutional framework is generally easier than selecting cases from a general population. It is for this reason that O_6 and O_7 have been scheduled with the second testing wave, for if no effect of X is shown in the first body of results (the comparison $O_1 > O_2$), then these expensive procedures would usually be unjustified (unless, for example, one had the hypothesis that the institutional X had suppressed a normal maturational process).

Another cross-sectional approach to the control of maturation may be available if there is heterogeneity in age (or years away from home, etc.) within the population entering the institutional cycle. This would be so in many situations; for example, in studying the effects of a single college course. In this case, the measures of O_2 could be subdivided into an older and younger group to examine whether or not these two subgroups (O_{2o} and O_{2y} in Table 3) differed as did O_1 and O_2 (although the ubiquitous negative correlation between age and ability *within* school grades, etc., introduces dangers here). Better than the general population age-mate control might be the comparison with another specific institution, as comparing Air Force inductees with first-year college students. If the comparison is to be made of this type, one reduces one's experimental variable to those features which the two types of institution *do not* have in common. In this case, the generally more efficient Designs 10 and 13 would probably be as feasible.

The formal requirements of this design would seem to be applicable even to such a problem as that of psychotherapy. This possibility reveals how difficult a proper check on the maturation variable is. No matter how the general population controls for a psychotherapy situation are selected, if they are not themselves applicants for psychotherapy they differ in important ways. Even if they are just as ill as a psychotherapy applicant, they almost certainly differ in their awareness of, beliefs about, and faith in psychotherapy. Such an ill but optimistic group might very well have recovery potentialities not typical of any matching group that we would be likely to obtain, and thus an interaction of selection and maturation could be misinterpreted as an effect of X.

For the study of developmental processes per se, the failure to control maturation is of course no weakness, since maturation is the focus of study. This combination of longitudinal and cross-sectional comparisons should be more systematically employed in developmental studies. The cross-sectional study by itself confounds maturation with selection and mortality. The longitudinal study confounds maturation with repeated testing and with history. It alone is probably no better than the cross-sectional, although its greater cost gives it higher prestige. The combination, perhaps with repeated cross-sectional comparisons at various times, seems ideal.

In the diagrams of Design 15 as presented, it is assumed that it will be feasible to present the posttest for one group at the same chronological time as the pretest for another. This is not always the case in situations where we might want to use this design. The following is probably a more accurate portrayal of the typical opportunity in the school situation:

Class A X O_1

Class B_1 RO_2 X O_3
Class B_2 R X O_4

Class C O_5 X

Such a design lacks the clear-cut control on history in the $O_1 > O_2$ and the $O_4 > O_5$ comparisons because of the absence of simultaneity. However, the explanation in terms of history could hardly be employed if both comparisons show the effect, except by postulating quite a complicated series of coincidences.

Note that any general historical trend, such as we certainly do find with social attitudes, is not confounded with clear-cut experimental results. Such a trend would make O_2 intermediate between O_1 and O_3, while the hypothesis that X has an effect requires O_1 and O_3 to be equal, and O_2 to differ from both in the same direction. In general, with replication of the experiment on several occasions, the confound with history is unlikely to be a problem even in this version of the design. But, for institutional cycles of less than a calendar year, there may be the possibility of confounding with seasonal variations in attitudes, morale, optimism, intelligence, or what have you. If the X is a course given only in the fall semester, and if between September and January people generally increase in hostility and pessimism because of seasonal climatic factors, this recurrent seasonal trend is confounded with the effects of X in all of its manifestations. For such settings, Designs 10 and 13 are available and to be preferred.

If the cross-sectional and longitudinal comparisons indicate comparable effects of X, this could not be explained away as an interaction between maturation and the selection differences between the classes. However, because this control does not show up in the segmental presentations in Table 3, the column has been left blank. The ratings on external validity criteria, in general, follow the pattern of the previous designs containing the same fragments. The question marks in the "Interaction of Selection and X" column merely warn that the findings are limited to the institutional cycle under study. Since the X is so complex, the investigation is apt to be made for practical reasons rather than theoretical purposes, and for these practical purposes, it is probably to this one institution that one wants to generalize in this case.

16. Regression-Discontinuity Analysis

This is a design developed in a situation in which ex post facto designs were previously being used. While very limited in range of possible applications, its presentation here seems justified by the fact that those limited settings are mainly educational. It also seems justifiable as an illustration of the desirability of exploring in each specific situation all of the implications of a causal hypothesis, seeking novel outcroppings where the hypothesis might be exposed to test. The setting (Thistlethwaite & Campbell, 1960) is one in which awards are made to the most qualified applicants on the basis of a cutting score on a quantified composite of qualifications. The award might be a scholarship, admission to a university so sought out that all accepted enrolled, a year's study in Europe, etc. Subsequent to this event, applicants receiving and not receiving the award are measured on various Os representing later achievements, attitudes, etc. The question is then asked, Did the award make a difference? The problem of inference is sticky just because almost all of the qualities leading to eligibility for the award (except such factors as need and state of residence, if relevant) are qualities which would have led to higher performance on these subsequent Os. We are virtually certain in advance that the recipients would have scored higher on the Os than the nonrecipients even if the award had not been made.

Figure 4 presents the argument of the design. It illustrates the expected relation of pre-award ability to later achievement, plus the added results of the special educational or motivational opportunities resulting. Let us first consider a true experiment of a Design 6 sort, with which to contrast our quasi-experiment. This true experiment might be rationalized as a tie-breaking process, or as an experiment in extension of program, in which, for a narrow range of scores at or just below the cutting point, random assignment would create an award-winning experimental group and a nonwinning control group. These would presumably perform as the two circle-points at the cutting line in Fig. 4. For this narrow range of abilities, a true experiment would have been achieved. *Such experiments are feasible and should be done.*

The quasi-experimental Design 16 attempts to substitute for this true experiment by examining the regression line for a discontinuity at the cutting point which the causal hypothesis clearly implies. If the outcome were as diagramed, and if the circle-points in Fig. 4 represented extrapolations from the two halves of the regression line rather than a randomly split tie-breaking experiment, the evidence of effect would be quite compelling, almost as compelling as in the case of the true experiment.

Some of the tests of significance discussed for Design 7 are relevant here. Note that the hypothesis is clearly one of intercept difference rather than slope, and that the location of the step in the regression line must be right at the X point, no "lags" or "spreads"

being consistent with the hypothesis. Thus parametric and nonparametric tests avoiding assumptions of linearity are appropriate. Note also that assumptions of linearity are usually more plausible for such regression data than for time series. (For certain types of data, such as percentages, a linearizing transformation may be needed.) This might make a t test for the difference between the two linearly extrapolated points appropriate. Perhaps the most efficient test would be a covariance analysis, in which the award-decision score would be the covariate of later achievement, and award and no-award would be the treatment.

Is such a design likely to be used? It certainly applies to a recurrent situation in which claims for the efficacy of X abound. Are such claims worth testing? One sacrifice required is that all of the ingredients going into the final decision be pooled into a composite index, and that a cutting point be cleanly applied. But certainly we are convinced by now that all of the qualities lead-

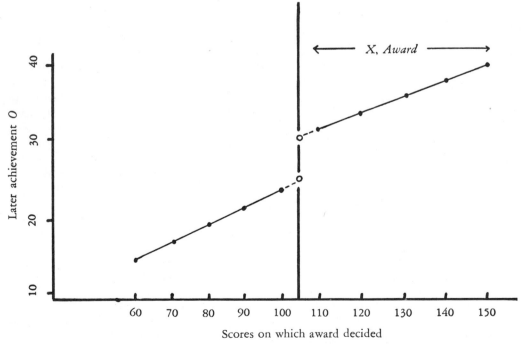

Fig. 4. Regression-Discontinuity Analysis.

ing to a decision—the appearance of the photograph, the class standing discounted by the high school's reputation, the college ties of the father, etc., can be put into such a composite, by ratings if by no more direct way. And we should likewise by now be convinced (Meehl, 1954) that a multiple correlational weighting formula for combining the ingredients (even using past committee decisions as a criterion) is usually better than a committee's case-by-case ponderings. Thus, we would have nothing to lose and much to gain for all purposes by quantifying award decisions of all kinds. If this were done, and if files were kept on awards and rejections, then years later follow-ups of effects could be made.

Perhaps a true parable is in order: A generous foundation interested in improving higher education once gave an Ivy League college half a million dollars to study the impact of the school upon its students. Ten years later, not a single research report remotely touching upon this purpose had appeared. Did the recipients or donors take the specifics of the formal proposal in any way seriously? Was the question in any way answerable? Designs 15 and 16 seem to offer the only possible approximations. But, of course, perhaps no scientist has any real curiosity about the effects of such a global X.

To go through the check-off in Table 3: Because of synchrony of experimental and control group, history and maturation seem controlled. Testing as a main effect is controlled in that both the experimental and control groups have received it. Instrumentation errors might well be a problem if the follow-up O was done under the auspices which made the award, in that gratitude for the award and resentment for not receiving the award might lead to differing expressions of attitude, differing degrees of exaggeration of one's own success in life, etc. This weakness would also be present in the tie-splitting true experiment. It could be controlled by having the follow-ups done by a separate agency. We believe, following the arguments above, that both regression and selection are controlled

as far as their possible spurious contributions to inference are concerned, even though selection is biased and regression present—both have been controlled through representing them in detail, not through equation. Mortality would be a problem if the awarding agency conducted the follow-up measure, in that award recipients, alumni, etc., would probably cooperate much more readily than nonwinners. Note how the usually desirable wish of the researcher to achieve complete representation of the selected sample may be misleading here. If conducting the follow-up with a different letterhead would lead to a drop in cooperation from, say, 90 per cent to 50 per cent, an experimenter might be reluctant to make the shift because his goal is a 100 per cent representation of award winners. He is apt to forget that his true goal is interpretable data, that no data are interpretable in isolation, and that a comparable contrast group is essential to make use of his data on award winners. Both for this reason and because of the instrumentation problem, it might be scientifically better to have independent auspices and a 50 per cent return from both groups instead of a 90 per cent return from award winners and a 50 per cent return from the nonwinners. Again, the mortality problem would be the same for the tie-breaking true experiment. For both, the selection-maturation interaction threat to internal validity is controlled. For the quasi-experiment, it is controlled in that this interaction could not lawfully explain a distinct discontinuity in the regression line at X. The external validity threat of a testing-X interaction is controlled to the extent that the basic measurements used in the award decision are a part of the universe to which one wants to generalize.

Both the tie-breaking true experiment and the regression-discontinuity analysis are particularly subject to the external-validity limitation of selection-X interaction in that the effect has been demonstrated only for a very narrow band of talent, i.e., only for those at the cutting score. For the quasi-experiment, the possibilities of inference may seem broader, but note that the evils of the linear fit assumption are minimal when extrapolated but one point, as in the design as illustrated in Fig. 4. Broader generalizations involve the extrapolation of the below-X fit across the entire range of X values, and at each greater degree of extrapolation the number of plausible rival hypotheses becomes greater. Also, the extrapolated values of different types of curves fitted to the below-X values become more widely spread, etc.

CORRELATIONAL AND EX POST FACTO DESIGNS

One dimension of "*quasi*-ness" which has been increasing in the course of the last nine designs is the extent to which the X could be manipulated by the experimenter, i.e., could be intruded into the normal course of events. Certainly, the more this is so, the closer it is to true experimentation, as has been discussed in passing, particularly with regard to Designs 7 and 10. Designs 7, 10, 12, 13 (but not 13*a*), and 14 would be applicable both for naturally occurring Xs and for Xs deliberately introduced by the experimenter. The designs would be more suspect where the X was not under control, and some who might be willing to call the experimenter-controlled versions quasi-*experiments* might not be willing to apply this term to the uncontrolled X. We would not make an issue of this but would emphasize the value of data analyses of an experimental type for uncontrolled Xs, as compared with the evaluational essays and misleading analyses too frequently used in these settings. Design 15 is, of course, completely limited to a naturally occurring X, and the designs of the present section (even if called data-analysis designs rather than quasi-experimental designs) are still more fully embedded in the natural setting. In this section, we will start again with the simple correlational analysis, then move to two designs of a fairly acceptable nature, and finally return to the ex post facto experiments, judged to be unsatisfactory at their very best.

Correlation and Causation

Design 3 is a correlational design of a very weak form, implying as it does the comparison of but two natural units, differing not only in the presence and absence of X, but also in innumerable other attributes. Each of these other attributes could create differences in the Os, and each therefore provides a plausible rival hypothesis to the hypothesis that X had an effect. We are left with a general rule that the differences between two natural objects are uninterpretable. Consider now this comparison expanded so that we have numerous independent natural instances of X and numerous ones of no-X, and concomitant differences in O. Insofar as the natural instances of X vary among each other in their other attributes, these other attributes become less plausible as rival hypotheses. Correlations of a fairly impressive nature may thus be established, such as that between heavy smoking and lung cancer. What is the status of such data as evidence of causation analogous to that provided by experiment?

A positive point may first be made. Such data are relevant to causal hypotheses inasmuch as they expose them to disconfirmation. If a zero correlation is obtained, the credibility of the hypothesis is lessened. If a high correlation occurs, the credibility of the hypothesis is strengthened in that it has survived a chance of disconfirmation. To put the matter another way, correlation does not necessarily indicate causation, but a causal law of the type producing mean differences in experiments does imply correlation. In any experiment where X has increased O, a positive biserial correlation between presence-absence of X and either posttest scores or gain scores will be found. The absence of such a correlation can rule out many simple, general, causal hypotheses, hypotheses as to main effects of X. In this sense, the relatively inexpensive correlational approach can provide a preliminary survey of hypotheses, and those which survive this can then be checked through the more expensive experimental manipulation. Katz, Maccoby, and Morse

(1951) have argued this and have provided a sequence in which the effects of leadership upon productivity were studied first correlationally, with a major hypothesis subsequently being checked experimentally (Morse & Reimer, 1956).

A perusal of research on teaching would soon convince one that the causal interpretation of correlational data is overdone rather than underdone, that plausible rival hypotheses are often overlooked, and that to establish the temporal antecedence-consequence of a causal relationship, observations extended in time, if not experimental intrusion of X, are essential. Where teacher's behavior and students' behavior are correlated, for example, our cultural stereotypes are such that we would almost never consider the possibility of the student's behavior causing the teacher's. Even when in a natural setting, an inherent temporal priority seems to be involved, selective retention processes can create a causality in the reverse direction. Consider, for example, possible findings that the superintendents with the better schools were better educated and that schools with frequent changes in superintendents had low morale. Almost inevitably we draw the implication that the educational level of superintendents and stable leadership *cause* better schools. The causal chain could be quite the reverse: better schools (for whatever reasons better) might cause well-educated men to stay on, while poorer schools might lead the better-educated men to be tempted away into other jobs. Likewise, better schools might well cause superintendents to stay in office longer. Still more ubiquitous than misleading reverse correlation is misleading third-variable correlation, in which the lawful determiners of who is exposed to X are of a nature which would also produce high O scores, even without the presence of X. To these instances we will return in the final section on the ex post facto design.

The true experiment differs from the correlational setting just because the process of randomization disrupts any lawful relationships between the character or antecedents of the students and their exposure to X. Where we have pretests and where clear-cut determination of who were exposed and who were not is available, then Designs 10 and 14 may be convincing even without the randomization. But for a design lacking a pretest (imitating Design 6) to occur naturally requires very special circumstances, which almost never happen. Even so, in keeping with our general emphasis upon the opportunistic exploitation of those settings which happen to provide interpretable data, one should keep his eyes open for them. Such settings will be those in which it seems plausible that exposure to X was lawless, arbitrary, uncorrelated with prior conditions. Ideally these arbitrary exposure decisions will also be numerous and mutually independent. Furthermore, they should be buttressed by whatever additional evidence is available, no matter how weak, as in the retrospective pretest discussed below. As Simon (1957, pp. 10–61) and Wold (1956) have in part argued, the causal interpretation of a simple or a partial correlation depends upon both the presence of a compatible plausible causal hypothesis and the absence of plausible rival hypotheses to explain the correlation upon other grounds.

One such correlational study is of such admirable opportunism as to deserve note here. Barch, Trumbo, and Nangle (1957) used the presence or absence of turn-signaling on the part of the car ahead as X, the presence or absence of turn-signaling by the following car as O, demonstrating a significant imitation, modeling, or conformity effect in agreement with many laboratory studies. Lacking any pretest, the interpretation is dependent upon the assumption of no relationship between the signaling tendencies of the two cars apart from the influence created by the behavior of the lead car. As published, the data seem compelling. Note, however, that any third variables which would affect the signaling frequency of both pairs of drivers in a similar fashion become plausible rival hypotheses. Thus if weather, degree of visibility, purpose of the driver as affected by time of day, presence of a parked police car, etc., have effects on both drivers, and if data are pooled across conditions heterogeneous in such third variables, the correlation can be explained without assuming any effect of the lead car's signaling per se. More interpretable as a "natural Design 6" is Brim's (1958) report on the effect of the sex of the sibling upon a child's personality in a two-child family. Sex determination may be nearly a perfect lottery. As far as is known, it is uncorrelated with the familial, social, and genetic determinants of personality. Third variable codetermination of sex of sibling and of a child's personality is at present not a plausible rival hypothesis to a causal interpretation of the interesting findings, nor is the reverse causation from personality of child to the sex of his sibling.

The Retrospective Pretest

In many military settings in wartime, it is plausible that the differing assignments among men of a common rank and specialty are made through chaotic processes, with negligible regard to special privileges, preferences, or capabilities. Therefore, a comparison of the attitudes of whites who happened to be assigned to racially mixed versus all-white combat infantry units can become of interest for its causal implications (Information and Education Division, 1947). We certainly should not turn our back on such data, but rather should seek supplementary data to rule out plausible rival hypotheses, keeping aware of the remaining sources of invalidity. In this instance, the "posttest" interview not only contained information about present attitudes toward Negroes (those in mixed companies being more favorable) but also asked for the recall of attitudes prior to the present assignment. These "retrospective pretests" showed no difference between the two groups, thus increasing the plausibility that prior to the assignment there had been no difference.

A similar analysis was important in a study by Deutsch and Collins (1951) comparing housing project occupants in integrated ver-

sus segregated units at a time of such housing shortage that people presumably took any available housing more or less regardless of their attitudes. Having only posttest measures, the differences they found might have been regarded as reflecting selection biases in initial attitudes. The interpretation that the integrated experience caused the more favorable attitudes was enhanced when a retrospective pretest showed no differences between the two types of housing groups in remembered prior attitudes. Given the autistic factors known to distort memory and interview reports, such data can never be crucial.

We long for the pretest entrance interview (and also for random assignment of tenants to treatments). Such studies are no doubt under way. But until supplanted by better data, the findings of Deutsch and Collins, including the retrospective pretest, are precious contributions to an experimentally oriented science in this difficult area.

The reader should be careful to note that the probable direction of memory bias is to distort the past attitudes into agreement with present ones, or into agreement with what the tenant has come to believe to be socially desirable attitudes. Thus memory bias seems more likely to disguise rather than masquerade as a significant effect of X in these instances.

If studies continue to be made comparing freshman and senior attitudes to show the impact of a college, the use of retrospective pretests to support the other comparisons would seem desirable as partial curbs to the rival hypotheses of history, selective mortality, and shifts in initial selection. (This is not to endorse any further repetition of such cross-sectional studies, when by now what we need are more longitudinal studies such as those of Newcomb, 1943, which provide repeated measures over the four-year period, supplemented by repeated cross-sectional surveys in the general manner of a four-year extension of Design 15. Let the necessarily hurried dissertations be done on other topics.)

Panel Studies

The simplest surveys represent observations at a single point in time, which often offer to the respondent the opportunity to classify himself as having been exposed to X or not exposed. To the correlations of exposure and posttest thus resulting there is contributed not only the common cause bias (in which the determinants of who gets X would also, even without X, cause high scores on O) but also a memory distortion with regard to X, further enhancing the spurious appearance of cause (Stouffer, 1950, p. 356). While such studies continue to support the causal inferences justifying advertising budgets (i.e., correlations between "Did you see the program?" and "Do you buy the product?"), they are trivial evidence of effect. They introduce a new factor threatening internal validity, i.e., biased misclassification of exposure to X, which we do not bother to enter into our tables.

In survey methodology, a great gain is made when the panel method, the repetition of interviews of the same persons, is introduced. At best, panel studies seem to provide the data for the weaker natural X version of Design 10 in instances in which exposure to some change agent, such as a motion picture or counseling contact, occurs between the two waves of interviews or questionnaires. The student in education must be warned, however, that within sociology this important methodological innovation is accompanied by a misleading analysis tradition. The "turnover table" (Glock, 1955), which is a cross-tabulation with percentages computed to subtotal bases, is extremely subject to the interpretative confounding of regression effects with causal hypotheses, as Campbell and Clayton (1961) pointed out. Even when analyzed in terms of pretest-posttest gains for an exposed versus a nonexposed group, a more subtle source of bias remains. In such a panel study, the exposure to the X (e.g., a widely seen antiprejudice motion picture) is ascertained in the second wave of the two-wave panel. The design is diagramed as follows:

$$-\left(\frac{O}{O}\right)-\left(\frac{X\ \ O}{\ \ \ \ O}\right)-$$

Two-wave Panel Design (unacceptable)

Here the spanning parentheses indicate occurrence of the O or X on the same interview; the question mark, ambiguity of classification into X and no-X groups. Unlike Design 10, the two-wave panel design is ambiguous as to who is in the control group and who in the experimental group. Like the worst studies of Design 10, the X is correlated with the pretest Os (in that the least prejudiced make most effort to go to the movie). But further than that, even if X had no true effect upon O, the correlation between X and the posttests would be higher than that between X and the pretest just because they occur on the same interview. It is a common experience in test and measurement research that any two items in the same questionnaire tend strongly to correlate more highly than do the same two if in separate questionnaires. Stockford and Bissell (1949) found adjacent items to correlate higher than nonadjacent ones even within the same instrument. Tests administered on the same day generally correlate higher than those administered on different days. In the panel study in question (Glock, 1955) the two interviews occurred some eight months apart. Sources of correlation enhancing those within one interview and lowering those across interviews include not only autonomous fluctuations in prejudice, but also differences in interviewers. The inevitable mistakes by the interviewer and misstatements by the interviewee in re-identifying former respondents result in some of the pretest-posttest pairs actually coming from different persons. The resulting higher X-posttest correlation implies that there will be less regression from X report to the posttest than to the pretest, and for this reason posttest differences in O will be greater than the pretest differences. This will result (if there has been no population gain whatsoever) in a pseudo gain for those self-classified as exposed and a pseudo loss for those self-classified as non-exposed. This outcome would usually be mistaken as confirming the hypothesis that X had an effect. (See Campbell & Clayton, 1961, for the details of this argument.)

To avoid this spurious source of higher correlation, the exposure to X might be ascertained independently of the interview, or in a separate intermediate wave of interviews. In the latter case, even if there were a biased memory for exposure, this should not artificially produce a higher X-posttest than X-pretest correlation. Such a design would be:

$$--\binom{O}{O}\binom{X}{?}\binom{O}{O}--$$

The Lazarsfeld Sixteenfold Table

Another ingenious quasi-experimental use of panel data, introduced by Lazarsfeld around 1948 in a mimeographed report entitled "The Mutual Effect of Statistical Variables," was initially intended to produce an index of the direction of causation (as well as of the strength of causation) existing between two variables. This analysis is currently known by the name of "the sixteenfold table" (e.g., Lipset, Lazarsfeld, Barton, & Linz, 1954, pp. 1160–1163), and is generally used to infer the relative strengths or depth of various attitudes rather than to infer the "direction of causation." It is this latter interest which makes it quasi-experimental.

Suppose that on a given occasion we can classify the behavior of 100 teachers as "warm" or "cold," and the behavior of their students as "responsive" or "unresponsive." Doing this, we discover a positive correlation: warm teachers have responsive classes. The question can now be asked, Does teacher warmth cause class responsiveness, or does a responsive class bring out warmth in teachers? While our cultural expectations prejudice us for the first interpretation, a very plausible case can be made for the second. (And, undoubtedly, reciprocal causation is

involved.) A panel study would add relevant data by restudying the same variables upon a second occasion, with the same teachers and classes involved. (Two levels of measurement for two variables generate four response types for each occasion, or 4×4 possible response patterns for the two occasions, generating the sixteenfold table.) For illustrative purposes, assume this outcome:

FIRST OCCASION

Pupils	Teachers	
	Cold	Warm
Responsive	20	30
Unresponsive	30	20

SECOND OCCASION

Pupils	Teachers	
	Cold	Warm
Responsive	10	40
Unresponsive	40	10

The equivocality of ordinary correlational data and the ingenuity of Lazarsfeld's analysis become apparent if we note that among the shifts which would have made the transformation possible, these polar opposites exist:

TEACHER WARMTH CAUSING PUPIL RESPONSIVENESS

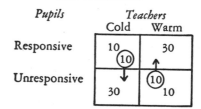

Pupils	Teachers	
	Cold	Warm
Responsive	10 (10)	30
Unresponsive	30	(10) 10

PUPIL RESPONSIVENESS CAUSING TEACHER WARMTH

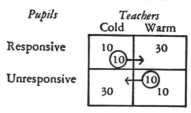

Pupils	Teachers	
	Cold	Warm
Responsive	10 (10)	30
Unresponsive	30	(10) 10

Here we have considered only those changes increasing the correlation and have neglected the inevitable strays. Thus in this diagram, unlike Lazarsfeld's, we present only 8 of the 16 cells in his full sixteenfold table. We present only the four stable types (repeated in both top and bottom diagrams) and the four types of shifters whose shifting would increase the correlation (two in the top and two in the bottom). All four types of shifter could, of course, occur simultaneously, and any inference as to the direction of causation would be based upon a preponderance of one over the other. These diagrams represent the two most clear-cut outcomes possible. Were one of these to occur, then the examination of the character of the shifters, made possible by the panel type of data collection (impossible if different students and teachers were involved in each case), seems to add great plausibility to a one-directional causal inference. For those that shifted, the time dimension and the direction of change can be noted. If the first-shown case held, it would be implausible that students were changing teachers and highly plausible that teachers were changing students, at least for these 20 changing classrooms.

While the sociologists leave the analysis at the dichotomous level, these requirements can be restated more generally in terms of time-lagged correlations, in which the "effect" should correlate higher with a prior "cause" than with a subsequent "cause," i.e., $r_{x_1 o_2} > r_{x_2 o_1}$. Taking the illustration of teachers causing pupils, we get:

| | Teachers Time 1 | |
Pupils Time 2	Cold	Warm
Responsive	10	40
Unresponsive	40	10

| | Teachers Time 2 | |
Pupils Time 1	Cold	Warm
Responsive	20	30
Unresponsive	30	20

In this instance the illustration seems a trivial restatement of the original tables because teachers did not change at all. This is, however, probably the best general form of the analysis. Note that while it is plausible, one probably should not use the argument $r_{x_1 o_2} > r_{x_1 o_1}$ because of the many irrelevant sources of correlation occurring between data sets collected upon the same occasion which would inflate the $r_{x_1 o_1}$ value. It should be noted that the suggested $r_{x_1 o_2} > r_{x_2 o_1}$ gives neither correlation an advantage in this respect.

What are the weaknesses of this design? Testing becomes a weakness in that repeated testing may quite generally result in higher correlations between correlated variables. The preliminary $r_{x_1 o_1} < r_{x_2 o_2}$ may be explained away on these grounds. However, this could not easily explain away the $r_{x_1 o_2} > r_{x_2 o_1}$ finding, unless an interaction or testing effect specific to but one of the variables were plausible.

Regression seems less of a problem for this design than for the two-wave panel study rejected above, since both X and O are assessed on both waves, and classifying in these terms is thus symmetrical. However, for the dichotomous Lazarsfeld-type analysis, regression does become a problem if the marginals of either variable are badly skewed (e.g., 10–90 splits rather than the 50–50 splits used in these illustrations). The analysis of correlations between continuous variables, using all cases, would not seem to encounter regression artifacts. Differential maturation upon the two variables, or differential effects of history, might be interaction effects threatening internal validity. With regard to external validity, the usual precautions hold, with particular emphasis upon the selection-X interaction in that the effect has been observed only for the subpopulation that shifts.

While in most teaching situations Designs 10 or 14 would be available and preferred for the type of problem used in our illustration, there are probably settings in which this analysis should be considered. For example,

Dr. Winfred F. Hill has suggested the application of the analysis to data on parent and child behavior as collected in longitudinal studies.[6]

When generalized to nondichotomous data, the name "Sixteenfold Table" becomes inappropriate; we recommend the title "Cross-Lagged Panel Correlation" for this analysis.

Ex Post Facto Analyses

The phrase "ex post facto experiment" has come to refer to efforts to simulate experimentation through a process of attempting in a Design 3 situation to accomplish a pre-X equation by a process of matching on pre-X attributes. The mode of analysis and name were first introduced by Chapin (Chapin & Queen, 1937). Subsequently this design has been treated extensively by Greenwood (1945) and Chapin (1947, 1955). While these citations come from sociology rather than education, and while we judge the analysis a misleading one, treatment in this Handbook seems appropriate. It represents one of the most extended efforts toward quasi-experimental design. The illustrations are frequently from education. The mode of thinking employed and the errors involved are recurrent in educational research also.

In one typical ex post facto study (Chapin, 1955, pp. 99–124) the X was high school education (particularly finishing high school) and the Os dealt with success and community adjustment ten years later, as judged from information obtained in individual interviews. The matching in this case was done from records retained in the high school files (although in similar, still weaker studies these pre-X facts are obtained in the post-X interviews). Initially the data showed those completing high school to have been more successful but also to have had higher marks in grammar school, higher parental occupations, younger ages, better neighborhoods, etc. Thus these antecedents might have

---

[6] Personal communication.

caused both completion of high school and later success. Did the schooling have any additional effect over and above the head start provided by these background factors? Chapin's "solution" to this question was to examine subsets of students matched on all these background factors but differing in completion of high school. The addition of each matching factor reduced in turn the posttest discrepancy between the X and no-X groups, but when all matching was done, a significant difference remained. Chapin concluded, although cautiously, that education had an effect. An initial universe of 2,127 students shrank to 1,194 completed interviews on cases with adequate records. Matching then shrunk the usable cases to 46, i.e., 23 graduates and 23 nongraduates, less than 4 per cent of those interviewed. Chapin well argues that 46 comparable cases are better than 1,194 noncomparable ones on grounds similar to our emphasis upon the priority of internal validity over external validity. The tragedy is that his 46 cases are still not comparable, and furthermore, even within his faulty argument the shrinkage was unnecessary.

He has seriously *under*matched for two distinct reasons. His first source of undermatching is that matching is subject to differential regression, which would certainly produce in this case a final difference in the direction obtained (after the manner indicated by R. L. Thorndike, 1942, and discussed with regard to matching in Design 10, above). The direction of the pseudo effect of regression to group means after matching is certain in this case, because the differences in the matching factors for those successful versus unsuccessful are in the same direction for each factor as the differences between those completing versus those not completing high school. Every determinant of exposure to X is likewise, even without X, a determinant of O. All matching variables correlate with X and O in the same direction. While this might not be so of every variable in all ex post facto studies, it is the case in most if not all published examples. This error and the reduction in number of cases are avoidable through the modern statistics which supplanted the matching-error in Design 10. The matching variables could all be used as covariates in a multiple-covariate analysis of covariance. It is our considered estimate that this analysis would remove the apparently significant effects in the specific studies which Chapin presents. (But see Lord, 1960, for his criticism of the analysis of covariance for such problems.) There is, however, a second and essentially uncorrectable source of undermatching in Chapin's setting. Greenwood (1945) refers to it as the fact of self-selection of exposure or nonexposure. Exposure is a lawful product of numerous antecedents. In the case of dropping out of high school before completion, we know that there are innumerable determinants beyond the six upon which matching was done. We can with great assurance surmise that most of these will have a similar effect upon later success, independently of their effect through X. This insures that there will be undermatching over and above the matching-regression effect. Even with the pre-X-predictor and O covariance analysis, a significant treatment effect is interpretable only when *all* of the jointly contributing matching variables have been included.

CONCLUDING REMARKS

Since a handbook chapter is already a condensed treatment, further condensation is apt to prove misleading. In this regard, a final word of caution is needed about the tendency to use the speciously convenient Tables 1, 2, and 3 for this purpose. These tables have added a degree of order to the chapter as a recurrent outline and have made it possible for the text to be less repetitious than it would otherwise have been. But the placing of specific pluses and minuses and question marks has been continually equivocal and usually an inadequate summary of the corresponding discussion. For any specific execution of a design, the check-off row would probably be different from the corresponding row in the table. Note, for example, that the tie-breaking case of Design 6 discussed incidentally in connection with quasi-experimental Design 16 has, according to that discussion, two question marks and one minus not appearing in the Design 6 row of Table 1. The tables are better used as an outline for a conscientious scrutiny of the specific details of an experiment while planning it. Similarly, this chapter is not intended to substitute a dogma of *the* 13 acceptable designs for an earlier dogma of *the* one or *the* two acceptable. Rather, it should encourage an open-minded and exploratory orientation to novel data-collection arrangements and a new scrutiny of some of the weaknesses that accompany routine utilizations of the traditional ones.

In conclusion, in this chapter we have discussed alternatives in the arrangement or design of experiments, with particular regard to the problems of control of extraneous variables and threats to validity. A distinction has been made between internal validity and external validity, or generalizability. Eight classes of threats to internal validity and four factors jeopardizing external validity have been employed to evaluate 16 experimental designs and some variations on them. Three of these designs have been classified as pre-experimental and have been employed primarily to illustrate the validity factors needing control. Three designs have been classified as "true" experimental designs. Ten designs have been classified as quasi-experiments lacking optimal control but worth undertaking where better designs are impossible. In interpreting the results of such experiments, the check list of validity factors becomes particularly important. Throughout, attention has been called to the possibility of creatively utilizing the idiosyncratic features of any specific research situation in designing unique tests of causal hypotheses.

REFERENCES

Allport, F. H. The influence of the group upon association and thought. *J. exp. Psychol.*, 1920, 3, 159–182.

Anastasi, Anne. *Differential psychology.* (3rd ed.) New York: Macmillan, 1958.

Anderson, N. H. Test of a model for opinion change. *J. abnorm. soc. Psychol.,* 1959, 59, 371–381.

Barch, A. M., Trumbo, D., & Nangle, J. Social setting and conformity to a legal requirement. *J. abnorm. soc. Psychol.,* 1957, 55, 396–398.

Boring, E. G. The nature and the history of experimental control. *Amer. J. Psychol.,* 1954, 67, 573–589.

Brim, O. G. Family structure and sex role learning by children: A further analysis of Helen Koch's data. *Sociometry,* 1958, 21, 1–16.

Brolyer, C. R., Thorndike, E. L., & Woodyard, Ella. A second study of mental discipline in high school studies. *J. educ. Psychol.,* 1927, 18, 377–404.

Brownlee, K. A. *Statistical theory and methodology in science and engineering.* New York: Wiley, 1960.

Brunswik, E. *Perception and the representative design of psychological experiments.* (2nd ed.) Berkeley: Univer. of California Press, 1956.

Campbell, D. T. Factors relevant to the validity of experiments in social settings. *Psychol. Bull.,* 1957, 54, 297–312.

Campbell, D. T. Methodological suggestions from a comparative psychology of knowledge processes. *Inquiry,* 1959, 2, 152–182.

Campbell, D. T. Recommendations for APA test standards regarding construct, trait, or discriminant validity. *Amer. Psychologist,* 1960, 15, 546–553.

Campbell, D. T. Quasi-experimental designs for use in natural social settings. In D. T. Campbell, *Experimenting, validating, knowing: Problems of method in the social sciences.* New York: McGraw-Hill, in preparation.

Campbell, D. T., & Clayton, K. N. Avoiding regression effects in panel studies of communication impact. *Stud. pub. Commun.,* 1961, No. 3, 99–118.

Campbell, D. T., & Fiske, D. W. Convergent and discriminant validation by the multitrait-multimethod matrix. *Psychol. Bull.,* 1959, 56, 81–105.

Campbell, D. T., & McCormack, Thelma H. Military experience and attitudes toward authority. *Amer. J. Sociol.,* 1957, 62, 482–490.

Cane, V. R., & Heim, A. W. The effects of repeated testing: III. Further experiments and general conclusions. *Quart. J. exp. Psychol.,* 1950, 2, 182–195.

Cantor, G. N. A note on a methodological error commonly committed in medical and psychological research. *Amer. J. ment. Defic.,* 1956, 61, 17–18.

Chapin, F. S. *Experimental designs in sociological research.* New York: Harper, 1947; (Rev. ed., 1955).

Chapin, F. S., & Queen, S. A. *Research memorandum on social work in the depression.* New York: Social Science Research Council, Bull. 39, 1937.

Chernoff, H., & Moses, L. E. *Elementary decision theory.* New York: Wiley, 1959.

Cochran, W. G., & Cox, Gertrude M. *Experimental designs.* (2nd ed.) New York: Wiley, 1957.

Collier, R. M. The effect of propaganda upon attitude following a critical examination of the propaganda itself. *J. soc. Psychol.,* 1944, 20, 3–17.

Collier, R. O., Jr. Three types of randomization in a two-factor experiment. Minneapolis: Author, 1960. (Dittoed)

Cornfield, J., & Tukey, J. W. Average values of mean squares in factorials. *Ann. math. Statist.,* 1956, 27, 907–949.

Cox, D. R. Some systematic experimental designs. *Biometrika,* 1951, 38, 312–323.

Cox, D. R. The use of a concomitant variable in selecting an experimental design. *Biometrika,* 1957, 44, 150–158.

Cox, D. R. *Planning of experiments.* New York: Wiley, 1958.

Crook, M. N. The constancy of neuroticism scores and self-judgments of constancy. *J. Psychol.,* 1937, 4, 27–34.

Deutsch, M., & Collins, Mary E. *Interracial housing: A psychological evaluation of a social experiment.* Minneapolis: Univer. of Minnesota Press, 1951.

Duncan, C. P., O'Brien, R. B., Murray, D. C., Davis, L., & Gilliland, A. R. Some information about a test of psychological misconceptions. *J. gen. Psychol.,* 1957, 56, 257–260.

Ebbinghaus, H. *Memory.* Trans. by H. A. Ruger and C. E. Bussenius. New York: Teachers Coll., Columbia Univer., 1913. (Original, *Über das Gedächtnis,* Leipzig, 1885.)

Edwards, A. L. *Experimental design in psy-*

chological research. (Rev. ed.) New York: Rinehart, 1960.

Farmer, E., Brooks, R. C., & Chambers, E. G. *A comparison of different shift systems in the glass trade.* Rep. 24, Medical Research Council, Industrial Fatigue Research Board. London: His Majesty's Stationery Office, 1923.

Feldt, L. S. A comparison of the precision of three experimental designs employing a concomitant variable. *Psychometrika,* 1958, 23, 335–353.

Ferguson, G. A. *Statistical analysis in psychology and education.* New York: McGraw-Hill, 1959.

Fisher, R. A. *Statistical methods for research workers.* (1st ed.) London: Oliver & Boyd, 1925.

Fisher, R. A. *The design of experiments.* (1st ed.) London: Oliver & Boyd, 1935.

Fisher, R. A. The arrangement of field experiments. *J. Min. Agriculture,* 1926, 33, 503–513; also in R. A. Fisher, *Contributions to mathematical statistics.* New York: Wiley, 1950.

Glickman, S. E. Perseverative neural processes and consolidation of the memory trace. *Psychol. Bull.,* 1961, 58, 218–233.

Glock, C. Y. Some applications of the panel method to the study of social change. In P. F. Lazarsfeld & M. Rosenberg (Eds.), *The language of social research.* Glencoe, Ill.: Free Press, 1955. Pp. 242–249.

Glock, C. Y. The effects of re-interviewing in panel research. 1958. Multilith of a chapter to appear in P. F. Lazarsfeld (Ed.), *The study of short run social change,* in preparation.

Good, C. V., & Scates, D. E. *Methods of research.* New York: Appleton-Century-Crofts, 1954.

Grant, D. A. Analysis-of-variance tests in the analysis and comparison of curves. *Psychol. Bull.,* 1956, 53, 141–154.

Green, B. F., & Tukey, J. W. Complex analyses of variance: General problems. *Psychometrika,* 1960, 25, 127–152.

Greenwood, E. *Experimental sociology: A study in method.* New York: King's Crown Press, 1945.

Guetzkow, H., Kelly, E. L., & McKeachie, W. J. An experimental comparison of recitation, discussion, and tutorial methods in college teaching. *J. educ. Psychol.,* 1954, 45, 193–207.

Hammond, K. R. Representative vs. systematic design in clinical psychology. *Psychol. Bull.,* 1954, 51, 150–159.

Hanson, N. R. *Patterns of discovery.* Cambridge, Eng.: Univer. Press, 1958.

Hovland, C. I., Janis, I. L., & Kelley, H. H. *Communication and persuasion.* New Haven, Conn.: Yale Univer. Press, 1953.

Hovland, C. I., Lumsdaine, A. A., & Sheffield, F. D. *Experiments on mass communication.* Princeton, N.J.: Princeton Univer. Press, 1949.

Information and Education Division, U. S. War Department. Opinions about Negro infantry platoons in white companies of seven divisions. In T. M. Newcomb & E. L. Hartley (Eds.), *Readings in social psychology.* New York: Holt, 1947. Pp. 542–546.

Johnson, P. O. *Statistical methods in research.* New York: Prentice-Hall, 1949.

Johnson, P. O., & Jackson, R. W. B. *Modern statistical methods: Descriptive and inductive.* Chicago: Rand McNally, 1959.

Jost, A. Die Assoziationsfestigkeit in ihrer Abhängigkeit von der Verteilung der Wiederholungen. *Z. Psychol. Physiol. Sinnesorgane,* 1897, 14, 436–472.

Kaiser, H. F. Directional statistical decisions. *Psychol. Rev.,* 1960, 67, 160–167.

Katz, D., Maccoby, N., & Morse, Nancy C. *Productivity, supervision, and morale in an office situation.* Ann Arbor: Survey Research Center, Univer. of Michigan, 1951.

Kempthorne, O. *The design and analysis of experiments.* New York: Wiley, 1952.

Kempthorne, O. The randomization theory of statistical inference. *J. Amer. Statist. Ass.,* 1955, 50, 946–967; 1956, 51, 651.

Kempthorne, O. The design and analysis of experiments, with some reference to educational research. In R. O. Collier & S. M. Elam (Eds.), *Research design and analysis: The second annual Phi Delta Kappa symposium on educational research.* Bloomington, Ind.: Phi Delta Kappa, 1961. Pp. 97–133.

Kendall, M. G., & Buckland, W. R. *A dictionary of statistical terms.* London: Oliver & Boyd, 1957.

Kennedy, J. L., & Uphoff, H. F. Experiments on the nature of extra-sensory perception. III. The recording error criticisms of extra-chance scores. *J. Parapsychol.,* 1939, 3, 226–245.

Kerr, W. A. Experiments on the effect of music on factory production. *Appl. Psychol. Monogr.,* 1945, No. 5.

Lana, R. E. Pretest-treatment interaction effects in attitudinal studies. *Psychol. Bull.,* 1959, 56, 293–300. (a)

Lana, R. E. A further investigation of the pretest-treatment interaction effect. *J. appl. Psychol.,* 1959, 43, 421–422. (b)

Lana, R. E., & King, D. J. Learning factors as determiners of pretest sensitization. *J. appl. Psychol.,* 1960, 44, 189–191.

Lindquist, E. F. *Statistical analysis in educational research.* Boston: Houghton Mifflin, 1940.

Lindquist, E. F. *Design and analysis of experiments in psychology and education.* Boston: Houghton Mifflin, 1953.

Lipset, S. M., Lazarsfeld, P. F., Barton, A. H., & Linz, J. The psychology of voting: An analysis of political behavior. In G. Lindzey (Ed.), *Handbook of social psychology.* Cambridge, Mass.: Addison-Wesley, 1954. Pp. 1124–1175.

Lord, F. M. The measurement of growth. *Educ. psychol. Measmt,* 1956, 16, 421–437.

Lord, F. M. Further problems in the measurement of growth. *Educ. psychol. Measmt,* 1958, 18, 437–451.

Lord, F. M. Large-sample covariance analysis when the control variable is fallible. *J. Amer. Statist. Ass.,* 1960, 55, 307–321.

Lubin, A. The interpretation of significant interaction. *Educ. psychol. Measmt,* 1961, 21, 807–817.

Maxwell, A. E. *Experimental design in psychology and the medical sciences.* London: Methuen, 1958.

McCall, W. A. *How to experiment in education.* New York: Macmillan, 1923.

McNemar, Q. A critical examination of the University of Iowa studies of environmental influences upon the I.Q. *Psychol. Bull.,* 1940, 37, 63–92.

McNemar, Q. *Psychological statistics.* (3rd ed.) New York: Wiley, 1962.

McNemar, Q. On growth measurement. *Educ. psychol. Measmt,* 1958, 18, 47–55.

Meehl, P. E. *Clinical versus statistical prediction.* Minneapolis: Univer. of Minnesota Press, 1954.

Monroe, W. S. General methods: Classroom experimentation. In G. M. Whipple (Ed.),

Yearb. nat. Soc. Stud. Educ., 1938, 37, Part II, 319–327.

Mood, A. F. *Introduction to the theory of statistics.* New York: McGraw-Hill, 1950.

Moore, H. T. The comparative influence of majority and expert opinion. *Amer. J. Psychol.,* 1921, 32, 16–20.

Morse, Nancy C., & Reimer, E. The experimental change of a major organizational variable. *J. abnorm. soc. Psychol.,* 1956, 52, 120–129.

Myers, J. L. On the interaction of two scaled variables. *Psychol. Bull.,* 1959, 56, 384–391.

Newcomb, T. M. *Personality and social change.* New York: Dryden, 1943.

Neyman, J. Indeterminism in science and new demands on statisticians. *J. Amer. Statist. Ass.,* 1960, 55, 625–639.

Nunnally, J. The place of statistics in psychology. *Educ. psychol. Measmt,* 1960, 20, 641–650.

Page, E. B. Teacher comments and student performance: A seventy-four classroom experiment in school motivation. *J. educ. Psychol.,* 1958, 49, 173–181.

Pearson, H. C. Experimental studies in the teaching of spelling. *Teachers Coll. Rec.,* 1912, 13, 37–66.

Peters, C. C., & Van Voorhis, W. R. *Statistical procedures and their mathematical bases.* New York: McGraw-Hill, 1940.

Piers, Ellen V. Effects of instruction on teacher attitudes: Extended control-group design. Unpublished doctoral dissertation, George Peabody Coll., 1954. Abstract in *Bull. Maritime Psychol. Ass.,* 1955 (Spring), 53–56.

Popper, K. R. *The logic of scientific discovery.* New York: Basic Books, 1959.

Rankin, R. E., & Campbell, D. T. Galvanic skin response to Negro and white experimenters. *J. abnorm. soc. Psychol.,* 1955, 51, 30–33.

Reed, J. C. Some effects of short term training in reading under conditions of controlled motivation. *J. educ. Psychol.,* 1956, 47, 257–264.

Rogers, C. R., & Dymond, Rosalind F. *Psychotherapy and personality change.* Chicago: Univer. of Chicago Press, 1954.

Rosenthal, R. Research on experimenter bias. Paper read at Amer. Psychol. Ass., Cincinnati, Sept., 1959.

Roy, S. N., & Gnanadesikan, R. Some contributions to ANOVA in one or more dimensions: I and II. *Ann. math. Statist.,* 1959, 30, 304–317, 318–340.

Rozeboom, W. W. The fallacy of the null-hypothesis significance test. *Psychol. Bull.,* 1960, 57, 416–428.

Rulon, P. J. Problems of regression. *Harvard educ. Rev.,* 1941, 11, 213–223.

Sanford, F. H., & Hemphill, J. K. An evaluation of a brief course in psychology at the U.S. Naval Academy. *Educ. psychol. Measmt,* 1952, 12, 194–216.

Scheffé, H. Alternative models for the analysis of variance. *Ann. math. Statist.,* 1956, 27, 251–271.

Selltiz, Claire, Jahoda, Marie, Deutsch, M., & Cook, S. W. *Research methods in social relations.* (Rev. ed.) New York: Holt-Dryden, 1959.

Siegel, Alberta E., & Siegel, S. Reference groups, membership groups, and attitude change. *J. abnorm. soc. Psychol.,* 1957, 55, 360–364.

Simon, H. A. *Models of man.* New York: Wiley, 1957.

Smith, H. L., & Hyman, H. The biasing effect of interviewer expectations on survey results. *Publ. opin. Quart.,* 1950, 14, 491–506.

Sobol, M. G. Panel mortality and panel bias. *J. Amer. Statist. Ass.,* 1959, 54, 52–68.

Solomon, R. L. An extension of control group design. *Psychol. Bull.,* 1949, 46, 137–150.

Sorokin, P. A. An experimental study of efficiency of work under various specified conditions. *Amer. J. Sociol.,* 1930, 35, 765–782.

Stanley, J. C. Statistical analysis of scores from counterbalanced tests. *J. exp. Educ.,* 1955, 23, 187–207.

Stanley, J. C. Fixed, random, and mixed models in the analysis of variance as special cases of finite model III. *Psychol. Rep.,* 1956, 2, 369.

Stanley, J. C. Controlled experimentation in the classroom. *J. exp. Educ.,* 1957, 25, 195–201. (a)

Stanley, J. C. Research methods: Experimental design. *Rev. educ. Res.,* 1957, 27, 449–459. (b)

Stanley, J. C. Interactions of organisms with experimental variables as a key to the integration of organismic and variable-manipulating research. In Edith M. Huddleston (Ed.), *Yearb. Nat. Counc. Measmt used in Educ.,* 1960, 7–13.

Stanley, J. C. Analysis of a doubly nested design. *Educ. psychol. Measmt,* 1961, 21, 831–837. (a)

Stanley, J. C. Studying status vs. manipulating variables. In R. O. Collier & S. M. Elam (Eds.), *Research design and analysis: The second Phi Delta Kappa symposium on educational research.* Bloomington, Ind.: Phi Delta Kappa, 1961. Pp. 173–208. (b)

Stanley, J. C. Analysis of unreplicated three-way classifications, with applications to rater bias and trait independence. *Psychometrika,* 1961, 26, 205–220. (c)

Stanley, J. C. Analysis-of-variance principles applied to the grading of essay tests. *J. exp. Educ.,* 1962, 30, 279–283.

Stanley, J. C., & Beeman, Ellen Y. Interaction of major field of study with kind of test. *Psychol. Rep.,* 1956, 2, 333–336.

Stanley, J. C., & Beeman, Ellen Y. Restricted generalization, bias, and loss of power that may result from matching groups. *Psychol. Newsltr,* 1958, 9, 88–102.

Stanley, J. C., & Wiley, D. E. *Development and analysis of experimental designs for ratings.* Madison, Wis.: Authors, 1962.

Stanton, F., & Baker, K. H. Interviewer-bias and the recall of incompletely learned materials. *Sociometry,* 1942, 5, 123–134.

Star, Shirley A., & Hughes, Helen M. Report on an educational campaign: The Cincinnati plan for the United Nations. *Amer. J. Sociol.,* 1950, 55, 389–400.

Stockford, L., & Bissell, H. W. Factors involved in establishing a merit-rating scale. *Personnel,* 1949, 26, 94–116.

Stouffer, S. A. (Ed.) *The American soldier.* Princeton, N.J.: Princeton Univer. Press, 1949. Vols. I & II.

Stouffer, S. A. Some observations on study design. *Amer. J. Sociol.,* 1950, 55, 355–361.

Thistlethwaite, D. L., & Campbell, D. T. Regression-discontinuity analysis: An alternative to the ex post facto experiment. *J. educ. Psychol.,* 1960, 51, 309–317.

Thorndike, E. L., & Woodworth, R. S. The influence of improvement in one mental function upon the efficiency of other functions. *Psychol. Rev.,* 1901, 8, 247–261, 384–395, 553–564.

Thorndike, E. L., McCall, W. A., & Chapman, J. C. Ventilation in relation to mental work. *Teach. Coll. Contr. Educ.*, 1916, No. 78.

Thorndike, R. L. Regression fallacies in the matched groups experiment. *Psychometrika*, 1942, 7, 85–102.

Underwood, B. J. *Experimental psychology.* New York: Appleton-Century-Crofts, 1949.

Underwood, B. J. An analysis of the methodology used to investigate thinking behavior. Paper read at New York Univer. Conf. on Human Problem Solving. April, 1954. (See also C. I. Hovland & H. H. Kendler, The New York University Conference on Human Problem Solving. *Amer. Psychologist*, 1955, 10, 64–68.)

Underwood, B. J. Interference and forgetting. *Psychol. Rev.*, 1957, 64, 49–60. (a)

Underwood, B. J. *Psychological research.* New York: Appleton-Century-Crofts, 1957. (b)

Underwood, B. J., & Richardson, J. Studies of distributed practice. XVIII. The influence of meaningfulness and intralist similarity of serial nonsense lists. *J. exp. Psychol.*, 1958, 56, 213–219.

Watson, R. I. *Psychology of the child.* New York: Wiley, 1959.

Wilk, M. B., & Kempthorne, O. Fixed, mixed, and random models. *J. Amer. Statist. Ass.*, 1955, 50, 1144–1167; Corrigenda, *J. Amer. Statist. Ass.*, 1956, 51, 652.

Wilk, M. B., & Kempthorne, O. Some aspects of the analysis of factorial experiments in a completely randomized design. *Ann. math. Statist.*, 1956, 27, 950–985.

Wilk, M. B., & Kempthorne, O. Non-additivities in a Latin square design. *J. Amer. Statist. Ass.*, 1957, 52, 218–236.

Windle, C. Test-retest effect on personality questionnaires. *Educ. psychol. Measmt*, 1954, 14, 617–633.

Winer, B. J. *Statistical principles in experimental design.* New York: McGraw-Hill, 1962.

Wold, H. Causal inference from observational data. A review of ends and means. *J. Royal Statist. Soc.*, Sec. A., 1956, 119, 28–61.

Wyatt, S., Fraser, J. A., & Stock, F. G. L. *Fan ventilation in a humid weaving shed.* Rept. 37, Medical Research Council, Industrial Fatigue Research Board. London: His Majesty's Stationery Office, 1926.

Zeisel, H. *Say it with figures.* New York: Harper, 1947.

CHAPTER 6 Measuring Classroom Behavior by Systematic Observation

DONALD M. MEDLEY
City University of New York

HAROLD E. MITZEL
The Pennsylvania State University

Certainly there is no more obvious approach to research on teaching than direct observation of the behavior of teachers while they teach and pupils while they learn. Yet it is a rare study indeed that includes any formal observation at all. In a typical example of research on teaching, the research worker limits himself to the manipulation or study of antecedents and consequents of whatever happens in the classroom while the teaching itself is going on, but never once looks into the classroom to see how the teacher actually teaches or how the pupils actually learn.

The fact that observations of classroom behavior are so seldom included in investigations in which they should play a central role is easily explained. Research workers point out that observations are expensive in terms of time, money, and the professional skill demanded of observers; that observations constitute an invasion of privacy that teachers and administrators resent and resist (although their pupils do not); that the presence of an observer in a classroom is so disturbing that the behavior seen cannot be regarded as typical of the behavior which goes on when an observer is not present; and,

above all, that most studies in the past which have employed classroom visitation have not been successful in increasing our knowledge about teaching and learning anyhow. Finally they point out that the number of classrooms that it is economically feasible to include in an investigation becomes so small if it is necessary to visit each one that it is better to omit observation and study a larger sample.

That observational data are difficult and expensive to obtain is a fact that cannot be denied. But, in itself, that fact is a poor excuse for omitting observation from a study in which it can play an important part.

That teachers and administrators are reluctant to admit observers to their classrooms is also true. Yet, as the studies reviewed in this chapter demonstrate, this reluctance can be overcome. Teachers and administrators are professionals; once they are convinced that a study is well planned and capable of contributing important knowledge, they will wholeheartedly cooperate. Experience indicates that if the observer is as candid as possible about the type of records to be made and how they will be used, teacher support is usually assured, if it is clear that the use is worth while, and that the participating teachers will remain anonymous.

The objections that past studies have been unsuccessful in contributing to knowledge and that observational studies must usually be made with small samples are valid only if the study is poorly designed. Not every study involving visits to classrooms can properly be called an observational study, and a poor study done with a large sample is still a poor study. Enough examples of significant observational studies done in the past—some with large samples, some with small ones—will be adduced in the pages to follow to show that none of these four objections is insurmountable.

The objection that teachers and pupils may not behave in exactly the same way when observers are present as they behave when no observer is present has no completely satisfactory answer. The problem of comparing observed and unobserved behavior is akin to that of the small boy who turned out the bedroom light but could never quite make it to his bed before the room got dark. To know how teachers and pupils behave while they are under observation seems better than to know nothing at all about how teachers and pupils behave.

If an investigator visits a group of classrooms, he can be sure that, regardless of his presence, he will see teachers teaching and pupils learning; he will see better and poorer teachers, effective and ineffective methods, skillful and unskillful use of theory. If he does not see these things, and measure them, it will not be because these things are not there to see, record, and measure. It will be because he does not know what to look for, how to record it, or how to score the records; in short, he does not know how to measure behavior by systematic observation.

In some studies in the past, classrooms were visited by observers who knew what to look for, how to record it, and how to score what they recorded, i.e., how to measure behavior; such studies have revealed something significant about classroom behavior. The main purpose of this chapter is to extract from a number of such efforts whatever can be learned from them that will be useful in planning future observational studies. Examination of these studies reveals many deficiencies in design and analysis resulting from the well-known lag between precept and practice. This lag is at least as great in observational studies as in any other branch of research on teaching, but, if anything, it is more serious. Because of the difficulty in obtaining observational data, all the information available in the data should be extracted from them. This goal can be attained only if the most powerful statistical methods are used. Many laborious investigations could have yielded far more information than they did had the investigators used modern methods of analysis. A second purpose of this chapter is to study the methods used and call attention to more powerful modern statistical techniques which could have been employed.

The treatment of observational methods in this chapter differs from that in others (Heyns & Lippitt, 1954; Heyns & Zander, 1953; Selltiz, Jahoda, Deutsch, & Cook, 1959, pp. 199–234; Travers, 1958, pp. 161–230; H. F. Wright, 1960) in that it is exclusively concerned with the behavior of teachers and pupils in classrooms. The general principles of observation apply to all sites in which observation may be used, but the present chapter seeks to make the applications to research on teaching specific and explicit rather than leave them implicit or based on analogies.

THE ROLE OF DIRECT OBSERVATION IN RESEARCH ON TEACHING

Direct observation of classroom behavior was first used in research on teacher effectiveness, and it has been used, and misused, most often in such research. Teacher effectiveness must ultimately be defined in terms of effects on pupils, in terms, more specifically, of changes in pupil behavior (American Educational Research Association, 1952, 1953; Mitzel, 1960), but it is widely believed that a trained supervisor or expert of some type can assess the effectiveness of a teacher by watching him teach. It is safe to say that most of the many studies relating one variable or another to teacher effectiveness have used some such judgment as a criterion of teacher effectiveness. None of the procedures so used satisfy the definition of an observational technique presented later in this chapter.

The proper role of direct observation in research on teacher effectiveness would seem to be as a means of learning something about the teaching process and its relationship to pupil learning. In most cases, though, the effects of teaching on pupils cannot be observed directly in normal classroom behavior, but must be assessed by other means. It is thus theoretically possible to distinguish effective teachers from less effective ones without observing them while they teach.

Observation plays its proper role in research on teacher effectiveness when an attempt is made to gain insight into the nature of effective teaching. Some understanding of the nature of effective teaching would seem to be a prerequisite to effective preparation of teachers because of the clues it could afford as to what they should be taught, i.e., as to the repertory of behaviors an effective teacher must possess. Such an understanding would also seem to be important in selecting candidates for teacher training, since it might suggest what personality characteristics such candidates should have.

As research of this type yields fruit, it may also become possible to measure teacher effectiveness in process by direct observation of the teacher. This is not yet possible. Attempts to validate process criteria by correlating them with measured pupil growth have been, on the whole, unsuccessful (Morsh & Wilder, 1954). The identification of patterns of behavior which differentiate effective and ineffective teachers is still a worth-while goal for research employing direct observation of classroom behavior.

Direct observation also has an important role to play in measuring the effectiveness of programs and procedures in teacher education. It is true that the ultimate objective of teacher education is to increase teachers' skill in helping pupils to learn, and that, therefore, the effectiveness of a training program would, in the last analysis, have to be determined by measuring how much is learned by the pupils of the teachers. It turns out, however, that the intermediate objective of teacher education is to get teachers to behave in certain ways while they teach. The ultimate objective—effects on pupils—can only be reached by way of the intermediate one—changes in teacher behaviors. It is impossible to find out whether or not a program is achieving its goal of getting teachers to behave in certain ways without observing the graduates of the program while they teach.

Direct observation should play a crucial part in the most fundamental kind of research on teaching—the search for effective patterns of classroom behavior—the type of research most worthy of the name *methods research*. The latter term is used here to include any study whose purpose is to find out how a teacher should behave in the classroom to achieve more effectively one or more of the goals of instruction.

The classic design for methods research requires that one (or more) classes be taught by an experimental method and one (or more) by a "control" method. The dependent variable is a measure of the gains of pupils in each class on an appropriate test. The classic design does not involve any observation of the teaching in either class to find out whether—and to what degree— the method supposed to be applied actually is applied. If the results of the experiment do not justify rejection of the null hypothesis, there is no way of eliminating the possibility that the failure to find a difference between methods may have been due to the fact that both classes were taught by the same method, despite the fact that the teachers were supposed to use different methods. But if appropriate measurements of the teaching behavior under each experimental condition are made by direct observation, this possibility can be eliminated. If desired, the relationship between the degree to which the method is applied and the amount of pupil gain can be studied directly.

These few examples represent only the most obvious ways in which direct observation can play a role in research on teaching. It seems safe to say that almost any research on teaching and learning behavior can benefit by the use of direct observations of the behaviors, and that in many instances such observations are of crucial importance.

NATURE OF AN OBSERVATIONAL TECHNIQUE

In this chapter, the term *observational technique* will be used to refer only to procedures which use systematic observations of classroom behavior to obtain reliable and valid measurements of differences in the typical behaviors which occur in different classrooms, or in different situations in the same classroom.

A measure is reliable to the extent that the average difference between two measurements independently obtained in the same classroom is smaller than the average difference between two measurements obtained in different classrooms. Unreliability can come about in two ways. Most commonly, it occurs when two measures of the same class tend to differ too much; this may happen because the behaviors are unstable, because the observers are unable to agree on what occurs, because the different items which enter into the measurement lack consistency, or for some other reason.

Unreliability may also result from the fact that differences between different classes are too small; hence, some highly accurate observational procedures may fail to yield reliable measures; we will see some examples of this later in this chapter.

A measure is valid to the extent that differences in scores yielded by it reflect actual differences in behavior—not differences in impressions made on different observers. For an observational scale to be valid for measuring behavior, it must provide an accurate record of behaviors which actually occurred, scored in such a way that the scores are reliable. To be valid for predicting some outside variable, such as teacher effectiveness, the behavior scores would have to correlate with some outside criterion. The present discussion will focus on attempts to measure behavior as such; attempts to score behavior in order to predict something else will be studied to see how well they measure behavior, whether or not they predict the something else.

The validity of measurements of behavior, as the term is used here, depends, then, on the fulfillment of three conditions: (1) A representative sample of the behaviors to be measured must be observed. (2) An accurate record of the observed behaviors must be obtained. (3) The records must be scored so as to faithfully reflect differences in behavior.

The first condition would be fulfilled perfectly if the observed behaviors were a simple random sample of the behaviors to be measured. Unfortunately, it is seldom feasible to obtain a random sample in practice, so it is necessary to use nonrandom samples with care to make them at least appear to be representative.

The second condition—accurate recording of behavior—and the third—meaningful scoring—are interdependent in the sense that how a record may be scored depends on how it is made, but they must be kept separate in using a technique. It is patently impossible to record everything that occurs in a classroom—even with many sound motion picture or television cameras. Barker and Wright (1951) reported an attempt to record everything that happened to an individual child during an entire day. The child was under observation from the time he awoke in the morning until he retired at night, and his behavior was recorded in narrative form: "After picking up a pencil, Raymond opened his English workbook," etc. Scoring was done on transcripts of the record, and consisted in counting the proportion of incidents falling in certain categories such as "Humor," "Restless Behavior," or "High," "Low," or "Medium Intensity." Exhaustive as the record was, it was far from complete, involving considerable selection by the observer as to what to record and what to omit. In the quotation above it may be noted that the observer did not record the color of the pencil, whether the right or left hand was used, the name of the book or the number of the page, etc. A sound film or video-tape recording in color could have yielded a more complete record than this—but of only one pupil's behavior.

The task of the observer is to observe events that take place in the classroom and then to record them in scorable form. The observer should make no attempt to score the behavior before recording an observed event. His crucial function is to serve as an abstractor; to select those aspects of behavior relevant to the scoring process, which occurs later. Abstraction is the principal tool of science, here as well as everywhere else. Abstraction is necessary not only because it is humanly impossible to record everything, but because abstraction makes the phenomena understandable. This abstractive function of the observer takes the form of coding behaviors as they are observed—recording them in categories.

An example of extreme abstraction is a scheme (Harrington, 1955) in which the observer makes a tally each time the teacher smiles during the period of observation, and ignores everything else which occurs. Here it may be said that observed behaviors of the teacher are categorized as "smiling" or "other," and only the one category is recorded.

A less extreme example is a system in which every teacher statement is classified into one of seven categories according to inferred intent (Withall, 1949). Here, only teacher verbal behavior is coded; no other aspects of classroom behavior are scored, so none of them need be recorded. Other aspects may be observed and may affect the coding, but they are not recorded.

The choice of the aspects of behaviors to be recorded in a particular study obviously depends on the purpose of the study. Urban (1943) was interested in the effects of instruction in health and hygiene on classroom behavior of pupils. He was able to ignore the vast majority of classroom behaviors because they were irrelevant to his purpose. Whether pupils whispered or not; how many mistakes in oral English they made; whether they spoke without permission—none of these were relevant, so none of them were recorded. If a pupil sneezed without a handkerchief, chewed a pencil, etc., that behavior was recorded.

The process of selecting the behaviors to be recorded is essentially one of identifying a limited range of behavior relevant to the purpose of the study and of constructing categories or items to be used by the observer. The process is sometimes hampered by the fact that little is known about the variable to be measured. If the purpose of a study is to relate the number of times a teacher smiles to how well he is liked by his pupils, the problem of which behaviors and aspects of behavior are to be recorded practically solves itself. If the purpose is to relate teachers' skill in explaining difficult concepts to pupils' growth in critical thinking, the problem is not so easily solved. It may take considerable prowess to formulate the needed operational definition of "skill in explaining difficult concepts." It was only after Withall had defined classroom climate in terms of teacher statements that it became clear what behaviors needed to be recorded.

It is essential that the behaviors be coded and recorded as soon after they occur as possible. It is known that many factors can affect memory and may seriously distort a record made in retrospect. An instance of such delayed recording is provided by the Teacher Characteristics Study (Ryans, 1960). In this project, the observer, after observing a class for about 50 minutes, made assessments on each of 25 dimensions of the behavior that had occurred and then recorded his assessments in the form of ratings on seven-point scales. Typical dimensions were Apathetic-

Alert (for pupils) and Harsh-Kindly (for teachers).

Each dimension was defined by a "glossary" which specified (to some extent at least) the relevant aspects of behavior upon which the rating was to be based. For "Harsh-Kindly" the following specification was provided (Ryans, 1960, p. 88):

Harsh	*Kindly*
1. Hypercritical; fault-finding.	1. Went out of way to be pleasant and/or to help pupils; friendly.
2. Cross; curt.	
3. Depreciated pupil's efforts; was sarcastic.	2. Gave a pupil a deserved compliment.
4. Scolded a great deal.	3. Found good things in pupils to call attention to.
5. Lost temper.	
6. Used threats.	
7. Permitted pupils to laugh at mistakes of others.	4. Seemed to show sincere concern for a pupil's personal problem.
	5. Showed affection without being demonstrative.
	6. Disengaged self from a pupil without bluntness.

A record containing 25 such assessments based on 50 minutes of observation is not intended as a detailed, objective description of what behaviors actually occurred; rather, it seems designed to provide a record of recollections or general impressions of what went on. The mark made by the observer represents not the classification of some kind of a unit of behavior but a judgment based on many individual behaviors.

If the numbers yielded by these assessments or ratings are to meet the standards of scientific measurement, the task of the rater is equivalent to the following four steps: (1) to observe simultaneously a very large number of specific behaviors (all that are relevant to any of the 25 dimensions); (2) to store these observations in his memory until the end of the period; (3) to weight each separate behavior appropriately by some procedure analogous to that used in a mul-

tiple regression equation; and finally (4) to produce 25 experimentally independent numbers which best summarize all of these data. This seems to the authors to be a task that is extremely difficult and destined to yield questionable results.

So far as this discussion is concerned, procedures for obtaining ratings or assessments based on direct observation of classroom behaviors will not be regarded as observational techniques and will not be reviewed. (Such procedures, among others, are treated in Chapter 7.) Only procedures in which the observer plays no role in the quantification process except to record the frequency of behaviors which fall into certain predetermined categories will be reviewed in this chapter.

The observer should not be required to rate or weight behaviors on any quantitative scale—he should make only qualitative judgments, so far as possible. Suppose, for example, that an observer is using a system for categorizing teacher statements as "pupil supportive," "hostile," etc. When he hears a statement classifiable as hostile, he might be asked to record a single tally if the statement is "mildly hostile," and two tallies if it is "hostile." Since this is tantamount to the use of two categories of hostility in place of one, it would be better to provide two spaces for the two types of hostile statements, and have each hostile statement tallied once in one or the other space. The first scheme, in which the behaviors are weighted *before* recording, although no easier to use, yields a record which contains less information than the record obtained in the second scheme. The distinction between two "mildly hostile" statements and one "hostile" statement is lost. The assigned weights (1 and 2) may not be optimal; if the two kinds of statements have been recorded separately, as in the second scheme, the weights can be changed afterwards on the basis of empirical findings. If the first plan is adopted, they cannot.

The foregoing should not be taken as implying that the observer's function is purely mechanical: On the contrary, the judgment of the observer as to how a behavior should be coded is crucial and may call for great skill. So crucial is the observer's judgment in coding behavior that the major effort in instrument construction is usually devoted to the task of defining categories as unambiguously as possible to make the judgments as easy as possible. For the same reason, considerable pains may be taken in training observers so that they can classify behaviors accurately and swiftly. For this reason alone, it is necessary to free the observer from combining behaviors in his head to arrive at composite ratings, etc.

The ideal is to make the classification act as easy as the purpose of the study will permit. In Urban's study (1943), the observer had only to decide whether or not a pupil chewed a pencil, sneezed without a handkerchief, or the like. How much simpler a task this is, and how much more likely it is to be done correctly, than to rate the pupil's health habits as "Good," "Fair," or "Poor" on the basis of whether or not he chews pencils, sneezes without a handkerchief, etc. In any given study, between the record and the behavior it is supposed to represent should be interposed only the most primitive act of judgment or discrimination possible—the one needed to perceive whether the behavior has occurred or not. No inference about its significance, value, or relationship to other behavior, traits, etc., need be incorporated in the record at this point. That can come later.

The judgment required of Withall's observer as to whether the intent of a teacher's statement is pupil supportive, problem-structuring, neutral, etc., is no doubt much more difficult than the judgment required of Urban's observer. But the discrimination required is the most primitive one that will suffice for measuring what Withall set out to measure. An observer who is to use this method would require considerably more training, no doubt, than one who is to use Urban's.

It is in just such cases as this, when the observer must make difficult discriminations one after the other, that it becomes most important to relieve him of having to do anything else at the same time. Forming the total picture of the teacher's verbal behavior over a period of time, weighting the different categories, and other acts such as these, can be done later, after the behavior has been recorded, when they cannot interfere with the all-important task of securing an accurate record. An inaccurate record cannot be corrected once it has been made. An accurate record scored with the wrong weight can, however, be rescored or at least examined for clues as to what went wrong, since it does tell what happened.

To summarize, then, an observational technique which can be used to measure classroom behavior is one in which an observer records relevant aspects of classroom behaviors as (or within a negligible time limit after) they occur, with a minimum of quantification intervening between the observation of a behavior and the recording of it. Typically, behaviors are recorded in the form of tallies, checks, or other marks which code them into predefined categories and yield information about which behaviors occurred, or how often they occurred, during the period of observation.

Schemes in which the classroom visitor is asked to rate the teacher, class, or pupils on one or more "dimensions," even when the ratings are based on direct observation of specified behaviors, are not included in this definition.

A Note on Reliability Coefficients

Since we shall have a good deal to say in the pages to follow regarding the "reliabilities" reported for the various techniques that have been used, let us establish definitions of some terms before beginning.

We will use the term *reliability coefficient* to refer to the correlation to be expected between scores based on observations made by different observers at different times. The correlation between scores based on observations made by different observers at the same time will be referred to as a *coefficient of observer agreement.* A correlation between scores based on observations made by the same observer at different times will be referred to as a *stability coefficient.*

The true score pertains to the typical behavior that would be observed in a classroom over a period of time, only a sample of which is actually observed. Then a coefficient of observer agreement does not tell us how closely an obtained score may be expected to approximate a true score, because the two measures correlated are based on a single sample of behavior. The true score pertains also to the actual behavior which occurs, rather than to what some particular observer would see. Therefore, a stability coefficient does not estimate the accuracy of a score either, since it is based on a correlation between observations made by a single observer. The coefficient of observer agreement tells us something about the objectivity of an observational technique; the coefficient of stability tells us something about the consistency of the behavior from time to time. But only the reliability coefficient tells us how accurate our measurements are.

ATTEMPTS TO MEASURE CLASSROOM BEHAVIOR

Early Attempts to Measure Pupil Participation

The earliest attempts to obtain objective measurements of classroom behavior seem to have come, naturally enough, from supervisors. A need for objective measures to replace global ratings appears to have been felt before World War I, when Horn (1914) proposed that a small circle be recorded by the classroom visitor in the appropriate space on a seating chart for "each recitation or request for recitation," and a square for each time a pupil responds by doing something. The purpose was to ascertain the distribution of participation by pupils in the lesson. In 1928, Puckett elaborated on the scheme by developing the following set of symbols:

- Pupil raised hand.

⊙ Pupil raised hand and **was called on by** teacher.

⊙ Pupil raised hand, was called on by teacher, and made a single-word response.

⊙- Pupil raised hand, was called on by teacher, and made a fair response.

⊙ Pupil raised hand, was called on by teacher, and made a good response.

-⊙ Pupil raised hand, was called on by teacher, and made a very good response.

☐ Pupil called on when he did not have hand raised.

☐ Pupil called on when he did not have hand raised; made a single-word response.

☐- Pupil called on when he did not have hand raised; made a fair response.

☐ Pupil called on when he did not have hand raised; made a good response.

-☐ Pupil called on when he did not have hand raised; made a very good response.

☐☐ Pupil called on when he did not have hand raised; made no response.

> Pupil asked a question.

| Pupil spoke without being addressed by teacher (Puckett, 1928, p. 210).

Symbols were recorded in squares on a conventional seating plan to indicate which pupil exhibited the behavior.

The plan could be used today, adapted, perhaps, to some other system for classifying pupil contributions to class discussion than the simple quality rating proposed. The recording scheme is particularly ingenious, since each mark made refers to a single behavior or aspect of behavior. When one or more hands go up, one or more dots are recorded. When a pupil is called on, the dot is encircled if the hand was up; if not, a square is drawn. When the pupil responds, the mark indicating the category of response is added. It should be very easy to learn and to use such a system.

Scoring could be done by a clerk, who would count the number of each type of symbol on a chart, the number in each position, the number of seats with no marks, and so on. The counts could be combined and weighted according to whatever plan was desired. This pioneer study illustrates well how convenient a system for recording can be when the recording process is largely divorced from the scoring process. However, it should be noted that, in requiring the recorder to quantify the merit of the pupil's response, the scheme departs from our definition of an ideal observational technique.

Contrast this simple system with one proposed for a similar purpose a few years later by Wrightstone (1934), who used the following code, together with a seating chart:

Directions for use: This code is to be used to denote teacher responses and stimulations arising from the interaction of class or individual pupil personalities with the teacher personality. The activities of the teacher, as they are defined in this code, are to be entered against the name of the pupil who manifestly causes the teacher response or who is the particular recipient of teacher stimulation. If the class group is the recipient of teacher stimulation or response, such activities should be coded in a separate row and that row designated "Class" on the observational record.

Allows pupil to make a voluntary contribution (5a). Enter the code 5a against the name of any pupil whom the teacher, or leader of discussion, allows to volunteer a contribution to the discussion. Regardless of the stimulation that elicits the pupil response or the correctness of response, if the pupil has volunteered a contribution and is allowed to make it, he should receive a code for each such

specific contribution he makes during the periods of observation.

Encourages pupil to make a contribution (5b). Enter the code 5b against the name of any pupil whom the teacher, or leader of discussion, encourages to make a contribution to the discussion. The teacher may encourage a pupil by naming him, pointing to him, or otherwise designating him. He should receive a code for each specific time he is encouraged during observational periods.

Proposes a question or thesis for pupil or class (5c). This type of teacher activity is entered in code in a manner as are previous pupil-teacher interactions. The teacher definitely proposes a question or statement for the reaction of a particular pupil or the class.

Refers pupil or pupils to sources of data or information (5d). Enter in code the same as previous items. This item may be defined as referring of a pupil to any sources of information or data.

Suggests (explains) means, methods, activity, or solution (5e). Enter in code the same as previous items. It may be defined as teacher suggestion of means, methods, activities, or solutions of a problem or situation. This teacher conduct is often stimulated by pupil questions or statements.

Discourages or prohibits a pupil contribution (5f). Enter in code the same as previous items against particular pupil.

Recalls pupil's attention by direct word, look or gesture (5g). Enter in code the same as previous items against particular pupil.

Assignment by teacher of a specific subject-matter or tasks (5h). Enter in code the same as previous items against particular pupil.

Question and answer on assigned textbook subject-matter (5i). Enter in code the same as previous items against particular pupil. This code is used when the recitation is definitely a question and answer on assigned textbook matter. If the response of the pupil is stimulated by a question on assigned textbook matter, code the stimulation 5i, disregarding whether the pupil volunteers or is encouraged to make a contribution. Apply code 5*i* only to such situations (Wrightstone, 1934, pp. 455–456).

Every time the teacher interacts with a pupil, the observer records the appropriate letter on a class roster opposite the name of the pupil involved. Wrightstone suggested that a seating chart with pupils' names in it be referred to by the observer. Since it is unclear how the observer could find time to do this, it seems much better to follow Puckett's lead and record on a blank seating chart, adding pupils' names later, if necessary.

This system of recording would be somewhat more difficult to learn than Puckett's since there is less system to the symbols. Also, it would be more difficult to use as described, since the pupil must be identified and the behavior categorized at the same time. It ought to be possible to combine Wrightstone's more sophisticated categories with Puckett's smoother recording technique so as to get the best of both.

Unlike the study by Puckett, who was not interested in scoring his records, Wrightstone's had the avowed intention of measuring teacher conduct of class discussion. For scoring his record, he suggested a number of possibilities which seem somewhat relevant to his purpose. When it came to estimating reliability, the score he used was the total number of codes of all types recorded after a pupil's name, a separate score being obtained for each pupil in a class.

An estimate of the stability of the records was obtained by dividing each record into two halves (obtained "so far as possible" on different days), correlating the half scores, and then applying the Spearman-Brown formula to estimate the stability of the total record based on about 180 minutes of observation. In 12 classes averaging 35 students each, the coefficients so obtained ranged from .51 to .91, with a median of .83. If these correlations seem high, it should be remembered that they reflect the accuracy of the counts of the total number of interactions

observed, not the accuracy with which they were classified in the nine categories used.

When the system was used by Wrightstone to compare schools using "newer practices" with schools not using them, counts of Items 5*a* through 5*c* were added together to give a score called "Orientation"; counts of Items 5*f* and 5*g* were combined to give a score called "Prohibition"; and 5*h* and 5*i* a score called "Assignment-Quiz." No information is given as to the reliability of any of these scores. Since these scores were used to compare teachers in different rooms, the reliability coefficients given above, which apply to pupils in the same room, seem totally irrelevant.

Wrightstone developed a similar set of categories for recording pupil responses in group situations, which yielded three scores called "Initiative," "Other Items," and "Memory," as follows:

> Directions for Use: This code is to be used when a class is planning, reporting, or discussing units of work, problems, or activities. It is to be used also when a class is reciting on a lesson. It is planned to cover the major types of pupil responses in group recitations and discussions.

Observe the group for the entire period of discussion, if possible. Make an accurate record of the exact number of minutes of the cooperative group planning and discussion. Enter the following codes upon the DATA SHEET FOR SYSTEMATIC OBSERVATIONS as instructed:

INITIATIVE
Initiative in prepared voluntary report or exhibit 3a
Credit each pupil who participates in the preparation or presentation of a voluntary report or exhibit. Examples are: Pupils who voluntarily and independently, either as individuals or as committees, look up information, seek solutions, and make oral or written report to class; or pupils who construct exhibits, models, etc.; who secure pictures, books, samples, and the like.

Initiative in extemporaneous contribution from real experience 3b

Credit each pupil who makes a contribution to discussion gained from excursions, trips to museums, factories, city or country, travel, newspaper, magazine, etc.

Initiative in extemporaneous contributions from vicarious experience 3c
Credit each pupil who makes a contribution to discussion gained from independent reading, pictures, movies, lectures, other persons, friends, etc.—these are credited to pupil.

Initiative in suggesting means, methods, activities, solutions 3d
Credit a pupil 3d each time he makes contributions in suggesting means, methods, activities, solutions, hypotheses, for the problem, project, unit, or topic. The solution must be novel and not reproduced from assigned lesson or reading.

OTHER ITEMS
Responsibility in preparing assigned report or exhibit 3e
If the teacher or the group assigned a report [or] an exhibit, code such reports and exhibits 3e when completed.

Curiosity in asking questions on the topic, unit, or problem 3f
Credit a pupil 3f each time he asks a question or seeks information from others on the problem or topic.

Criticism of a contribution: praise or challenge 3g
Praising or challenging a contribution of some member of the group, including the teacher.

MEMORY
Memory in question-and-answer on assigned academic materials 3h
        (Wrightstone, 1935, pp. 33–34).

As will become apparent in this chapter, the quarter-century since these procedures were introduced has seen little improvement in the form of such items. Improvements have been made, however, in procedures for scoring them. A fresh look at classroom behavior with these old items and new methods of analysis might yield interesting results.

Measuring Effective Teacher Behavior

One direction that research involving systematic observation of classroom behavior can take is toward the identification of patterns of behavior which distinguish effective teachers from ineffective ones. Most classroom visitors go to the classroom with definite preconceptions of what they are looking for. They go to the classroom not to find out what effective teacher behavior is, but to see whether the teacher is behaving effectively, i.e., the way they believe he should behave.

Most such attempts have used ratings on a priori dimensions believed to be related to effectiveness. Such rating approaches have been uniformly unsuccessful in yielding measures of teaching skill. No fallacy is more widely believed than the one which says it is possible to judge a teacher's skill by watching him teach. It is difficult to find anyone, professional educator or layman, who does not think he himself, at least, can recognize good teaching when he sees it. Assuming that the builder of a rating scale knows something about the nature of effective teaching, it may be expected that ratings on his scale will be valid measures of teaching effectiveness.

Dozens of studies in the literature are based on this premise (see Morsh & Wilder, 1954). A smaller number, but quite a few, have tested this assumption by comparing ratings of effectiveness with criteria of teacher effectiveness based on measurements of pupil learning (Mitzel & Gross, 1958). Such criteria have limitations, of course. Some criteria of this kind do not make adequate allowances for factors affecting pupil learning other than the teacher's competence. None of them is complete in the sense of measuring growth toward all objectives of instruction. But if ratings of effectiveness are valid they should show at least moderate correlations even with imperfect criteria.

A reading of these studies reveals uniformly negative results. It may be instructive to quote some typical conclusions as stated by authors of the studies:

Teacher rating scales . . . are only slightly related to the observed pupil growth . . . (Hellfritzsch, 1945, p. 199).

. . . no appreciable relationships exist between rating criteria and pupil attainment criteria (Anderson, 1954, p. 67).

. . . supervision ratings here provided are invalid [as measures of pupil gain] (La Duke, 1945, p. 97).

. . . supervisory ratings . . . seem to lack reliability and validity [as measures of pupil gain] (Jayne, 1945, p. 133).

. . . the criterion of pupil change apparently measures something different from that measured by teacher ratings . . . (Gotham, 1945, p. 165).

The three criteria . . . [pupil gain, pupil evaluations, and a composite of five supervisory ratings] are not related to a greater degree than can be attributed to chance (Lins, 1946, p. 59).

Whatever pupil gain measures in relation to teaching ability it is not that emphasized in supervisory ratings (Jones, 1946, p. 98).

Employers' ratings of teaching ability are not related to pupil gains in information (Brookover, 1945, p. 205).

The fact that ratings of teacher effectiveness have no discernible relationship to effectiveness does not mean that effectiveness cannot be measured in process. Since it may be assumed that whatever effect a teacher has on pupils must result from his behaviors, it is only necessary to identify the crucial behaviors, record them, and score them properly to measure effectiveness in process.

The first study of any magnitude designed to fulfill the purpose with which this section is concerned—the identification of behavior patterns discriminating effective from ineffective teachers—was reported in 1929 by Barr in a monograph entitled, *Characteristic Differences in the Teaching Performance of Good and Poor Teachers of the Social*

Studies. The value of the study was sharply limited by the poorness of the criterion of effectiveness, which was based on supervisory judgment rather than on effects on pupils. But the study is of considerable interest because it marshaled what was probably the greatest variety of behavior data ever brought to bear on the problem of distinguishing these two types of teachers. Data gathered included:

1. *General Observations* which included (a) a record of various kinds of materials and equipment in evidence in the classroom, and (b) detailed records of observable teacher and pupil activities.
2. *Attention* scores using Morrison's chart (H. C. Morrison, 1926, Ch. 8).
3. *Time Chart,* recorded on a sheet of graph paper.
   "The first heavy vertical line on the sheet of graph paper was numbered zero, the next ten (indicating ten seconds of time), the next twenty, and so on across the page to sixty. Thus one heavy horizontal line across the page represents one minute of activity. By the use of a stop-watch and a wavy line the progress of the recitation was recorded. Certain symbols and abbreviations were used to indicate the kind of activity observed: T means teacher; C means teacher's comment; X, teacher's question; Pq, pupil question; V, volunteer; Vc, volunteer comment; W, wait; the numerals followed by H, as $3H$, $5H$, etc., the number of hands raised; the numbers under the short vertical lines indicate the pupil who is reciting (the pupils were numbered); the numbers just above the wavy lines, at ten second intervals, represent the number of pupils attentive; and the various notes under each major horizontal line are explanatory comments upon the activity in progress. Complicated as the record may seem at first sight, practice makes it simple enough" (pp. 24–25).
4. *Stenographic Report.*
5. *Check List,* on which only the major aspects of the recitation were noted.
6. *Time-Distribution Study* covering a pe-

riod of one week. (Adapted from Barr, 1929, pp. 23–26.)

The instruments used to record all of these data are not presented in the published monograph, but it is possible to infer something of their nature from the reported results.

One analysis centered about teachers' comments on pupils' responses to questions. Comments coded on the stenographic records were classified in 20 categories; no significant differences were found between mean numbers per 40 minutes of the "good" and "poor" teachers. Among those showing the largest nonsignificant differences were (poor teachers first):

"Tells pupil to be more specific" 13 vs. 1
"Summarizes discussion"   13 vs. 4
"Unqualified acceptance of
    pupil's answer"   23 vs. 12
                    (Barr, 1929, pp. 48–49).

Results of an analysis of methods used for motivating pupils are shown in Table 1.

TABLE 1

MEANS USED BY GOOD AND POOR TEACHERS
IN MOTIVATING WORK[a]

Means of Motivation	Number of Teachers Using Each Means	
	Poor	Good
1. Little or no motivation in evidence	17	0
2. Indirect means		
a. Competitive devices	3	2
b. Rewards	0	1
c. Penalties	38	47
3. Direct means		
a. Interest appeal of subject matter utilized	6	34
b. Problem-setting and purposeful activity utilized	0	7
c. Interests and experiences of pupils utilized	17	33
4. Total number of teachers in each group	47	47

[a] Adapted from Barr (1929).

Ways in which subject matter was organized were classified into nine categories in four main types—textbook, topical, problem-pupil, and psychological—with some subdivisions when the organization was also partially based on applications, outside reading, etc. Fourteen types of assignments were distinguished. Provisions for individual differences, types of appraisal of pupil response, types of teaching posture, and characteristic actions were noted. An example of the type of data yielded is presented in Table 2.

TABLE 2

CHARACTERISTIC ACTIONS OF GOOD
AND POOR TEACHERS[a]

Type of Activity	Number of Teachers Performing Each	
	Poor	Good
1. Laughs		
a. Little or no laughing	12	1
b. At pupil or class	2	0
c. With class	7	31
d. Laugh mannerism, abruptness, etc.	1	0
e. No report	25	15
2. Smiles		
a. Pleasantly or appreciatively	22	32
b. Sarcastically, critically, etc.	3	1
c. Does not smile	8	1
d. No report	14	13
3. Jokes with class	0	3
4. Giggles	1	0
5. Gestures	19	24
6. Nods to pupil to recite	0	5
7. Nods approval	16	24
8. Points at pupil to recite	3	8
9. Snaps finger for attention	1	0
10. Stamps foot ("hurry up," attention, etc.)	1	0
11. Puts hand on pupil's head, shoulder, etc. to recite	0	3
12. Shakes head (disapproval)	0	2
13. Waves at pupil to sit down	0	1
14. Total number of teachers in each group	47	47

[a] Adapted from Barr (1929).

A time-chart record was made for 67 of the teachers, giving data with respect to the amount of time the teacher talked, length of questions, length of responses, number of hands raised, number of questions asked by the class, number of volunteer contributions by pupils, and proportion of pupils participating in discussion.

Questions were categorized according to the type of answer called for:
1. Recall of facts
2. Memorized judgments
3. Expository question (explain, define, illustrate, etc.)
4. Real judgments
5. Unclassified.

This brief summary presents only a representative selection of the types of data recorded and analyzed in Barr's study. The author did not make it clear in which items the behaviors were coded as observed, and in which the stenographic or other records were coded after they had been made. Most of these sets of categories could, however, be used to classify behavior as it happens, whether or not they were used that way by Barr.

Looking back on this study after more than 30 years, we can make two comments:

(1) The methods used in recording the data were inefficient; a great deal of what was recorded was of no possible use. Such inefficiency is inevitable in a pioneer study when there is not much justification for leaving anything out. There was a need for an exhaustive study like this. Unfortunately, it is difficult to tell from the published results which data were useful and which were not. Data are presented indicating which categories of behavior are seen often enough to be worth including in a new observation schedule and which are not, and which are the ways in which the two groups of teachers differ. But unless the planner of a subsequent study is trying to discriminate the same or similar groups, this information is of little use. What are needed are data on reliability. In what respects were stable differences found between behaviors of different teachers? What are the things all teachers do, and what are the things some do and

some do not do? Whatever important differences there are between teachers must be sought in the second group of things—those in which there is significant variance between teachers.

(2) In regard to this study—and to many other early investigations—it seems unfortunate that the data were not dimensionalized, i.e., that separate items or categories were not intercorrelated or otherwise related to one another to see whether some of them might not be combined into scales homogeneous enough to be called dimensions.

In 1945, Jayne reported two studies attempting to correlate classroom behavior with outcomes. While these studies did not use direct observation, they had implications for studies which do. Sound recordings were made of lessons taught by 38 teachers and then transcribed for analysis. Counts or proportions (or both) of numbers of behaviors in 184 categories were determined for each lesson. The 184 items were selected on the basis of examination of previous analyses of the teaching process (both empirical and theoretical), with the addition of items which occurred to the researcher on the basis of his own observations. Every item found to be observable was used, whether or not it had any apparent relationship to effectiveness. After 100 items which were found too infrequently to merit analysis had been discarded, 84 items were left.

Eleven items which showed some promise were combined into scales called the Index of Meaningful Discussion and the Index of Immediate Recall. The former contained the following seven items:
1. Per cent of fact questions on unprepared material.
2. Per cent of thought questions on unprepared material.
3. Per cent of thought questions dealing with local situations.
4. Number of participations growing out of spontaneous pupil discussion.
5. Number of teacher explanations.
6. Number of times teacher presented factual information.

7. Times teacher raised a question as to correctness of a pupil response.

The Index of Immediate Recall contained four items:

1. Questions demanding recall of specified fact.
2. Number of factual questions on prepared material.
3. Number of thought questions on prepared material.
4. Number of times teacher indicated answer right.

The author concluded:

1. Specific, simple items did not correlate with outcomes, even though many could be reliably recorded.
2. It was possible to combine items into "indices" which did correlate with outcomes.
3. Expert's ratings had low reliability and validity.
4. Behaviors observed should be relevant to the outcomes measured.

Particularly interesting are Conclusions 1 and 2, which point to a generalization confirmed in many other studies: Individual items which do not differentiate between teachers or classes can often be combined into sets of items or scales which do.

Working in an Air Force school, Morsh (1956) conducted a study with a somewhat similar purpose. He pointed out that expert ratings of instructor effectiveness depend for their validity on the skill and experience of the raters, that his purpose was to develop an objective instrument which could be used by airman observers without previous training or experience in rating instructors, and that this goal involved three problems:

1. Determining which behaviors of instructors and their students can be reliably and systematically observed.
2. Determining whether or not instructor behaviors that can be observed tend to be typical and consistent.
3. Determining the relationship between elements of an instructor's or student's behavior and the amount students learn or the manner in which students are graded by their supervisors.

After preliminary observation, Morsh constructed 160 items intended to satisfy four criteria: (1) the observer would need only brief training to observe the behavior, (2) the item would be short enough that all items could be memorized easily, (3) the item might be supposed to be related to effectiveness, (4) the item would require no qualitative judgments. After preliminary tryouts, about 40 items were retained for further study.

A reliability study was carried out at three Air Force bases. At each base, three observers simultaneously observed 10 classes for three periods of 15 minutes each (usually successive) on each of three subsets of items. When observing student behaviors, the three observers agreed upon the selection of 10 students in the class to be observed by all three. Records were synchronized at five-minute intervals. Items not observed at least six times by any observer in 45 minutes of observation of 10 instructors were discarded. Unless at least one of the three interobserver correlations for an item was .70 or higher, the item was rejected.

Three observers then visited each of 10 classes for six 15-minute periods, each using a different section of the instrument. Rank-order correlations were used to estimate stabilities, and, in general, only items with occasion-to-occasion correlations of at least .30 were retained. Table 3 shows the three check lists finally adopted.

The three observers then visited 120 classes together for a period of 30 minutes, each using a different check list. When each list was combined into a single scale, the internal consistency coefficients (estimated by Kuder-Richardson Formula 20) were .28 for Instructor Verbal Behavior, .68 for Instructor Non-Verbal Behavior, and .55 for Student Behavior.

Each item was correlated with various criteria of effectiveness, and multiple regression equations were also set up. It was found that an unweighted composite of the items from a regression equation showed a correlation with the dependent variable about

TABLE 3

ITEMS USED BY MORSH IN OBSERVING
CLASSES IN A SERVICE SCHOOL[a]

Instructor Verbal Behavior
Gives aims
Defines terms
Explains:
  a. Fact
  b. Training aid
Asks:
  a. Designates student, asks question
  b. Asks question, designates student
  c. Class question
  d. For question
Answers:
  a. Own question
  b. Student question
Repeats:
  a. Student answer
  b. Key point
  c. Pet word
Gives example
Gives directions
Calls student:
  a. By name
  b. Other
Threatens, warns

Instructor Non-Verbal Behavior
Stands:
  a. Behind desk
  b. At board
Moves:
  a. Center, rear
  b. Other
Leans on desk
Smiles
Demonstrates:
  a. Training aid
  b. Gestures
  c. At board
Looks at notes, course outline
Uses board:
  a. Key term
  b. Diagram
  c. Erases

Student Behavior
Raises hand
Talks
Answers:
  a. Recognized

Asks question:
  a. Recognized
Looks around
Doodles
Slumps
Yawns, stretches
Class answers
Sleeps or dozes
Ignores instructor
Smiles

[a] Adapted from Morsh (1956).

equal to the multiple R. On this basis, the following key could be used as a measure of a dimension of classroom behavior which correlated $-.58$ with measured student gains, although its internal consistency was only .37:

Student looks around
Student ignores instructor
Student slumps
Student yawns or stretches
Student sleeps or dozes
Instructor asks question, then designates student (negative weight)

It is surprising to see how closely this dimension, which might be named "student apathy" or (if reflected) "alertness," is related to student achievement. It would probably not relate as closely to achievement in public elementary schools, where pupils rarely yawn or sleep in class, however dull the lesson may be. In the public senior high school, this dimension might be valid, although conditions of motivation are so different from those in a service school that no secure generalization is possible. Replication and cross-validation within service schools themselves are obviously needed to substantiate Morsh's findings.

A similarly obtained dimension related to ratings by supervisors contained the following six items of instructor behavior (with signs indicated), had an internal consistency of .54, and correlated $+.46$ with supervisors' ratings of instructor behavior:

Explains training aid $(+)$
Repeats key point $(+)$
Gives directions $(-)$
Stands away from board or desk $(+)$

Looks at notes ($-$)

Demonstrates training aid ($+$)

This finding gives some insight into supervisors' conceptions of effective instructor behavior. Morsh comments as follows: "Supervisors seemed to like formal behavior, . . . behavior which follows the book . . . and to dislike someone who seems not to know his subject" (Morsh, 1956, p. 10).

This workmanlike study might have yielded more interesting information about instruction in this type of school, it would seem, if the author had been less concerned with objectivity (or "observability" as he calls it) in selecting items to try out and with observer agreement in deciding which items to retain. When stability coefficients as low as .30 are permitted, what advantage is there in insisting on observer agreements of at least .70? The instability of behavior from one lesson to another, as Barr long ago pointed out (1929, p. 29), is the dominant component in the unreliability of observations, and the limiting factor on validity. The student behavior dimension described above had a validity coefficient against an outside criterion of .58 but its internal consistency was only .37. Probably observer agreement could be substantially lower than .70, too, without limiting the validity of a scale such as this. It is by no means certain that the items observed most accurately are the ones most likely to prove valid or important. The requirement that observer agreement be at least .70 may well have eliminated many valid items.

Notice that, although the items may appear somewhat trivial by themselves, when a few of them are put together as in the "alertness" scale, it is possible to see a common factor in the items that may not be so trivial. If the six items on the scale are regarded as mere symptoms of some stable characteristic of the class, it becomes clear how items of little intrinsic importance can be used to measure something important—much as a doctor may detect a fatal disease by observing a few individually insignificant symptoms.

These few studies illustrate rather well that it is possible to identify at least some behaviors which differentiate classrooms of teachers of varying levels of effectiveness by the use of objective observational techniques. Some of the studies to be reviewed under other headings will confirm this.

Measuring Classroom Climate

Perhaps the one area of classroom behavior that has received most attention from users of direct observation, and the area in which observation has been applied most successfully, is that referred to as "classroom climate."

We have seen that the earliest attempts to measure classroom behavior grew out of dissatisfaction with existing methods of supervision and developed in the general direction of identifying effective teacher behavior. Other investigators who took an early interest in classroom behavior were social psychologists, whose fundamental interest was in interactions between pupil and pupil, and pupil and teacher.

This line of development seems to have begun with the work of Dorothy S. Thomas and her associates (Thomas, et al., 1929), who made a definite break with ratings and other methods then used in social psychology and carried out a number of highly objective studies of nursery-school behavior. Thomas took the following position, which applies to research in classroom behavior particularly well:

The available data in regard to social behavior consist largely of descriptive accounts—case histories and diary records. These are often very illuminating social behavior documents but they present certain difficulties as material for scientific analysis. The data obtained in such records are, at their best, objective in the sense that they deal with certain verifiable facts, but they are selective, inconsistent, and usually incomparable with other records. This is due to the tremendous complexity of any social behavior act and the consequent recording of different elements of these complex acts at different times. At their worst, these records are such an intermixture of facts and interpretations as to be utterly worthless from the scientific point of view. Even at their objective best, the selection and emphasis are more or less dependent on the recorder. The control of this sort of error in our social data is one of the first problems claiming our attention. In other words, our data must become independent of our observers within a small and predictable range of error.

... The problem seems to be ... to find means of recording the particular stimuli in the uncontrolled environment to which a given individual, at a given moment, reacts overtly— what consistency is observable in his selective responses over a period of time and what variability is shown among different individuals (Thomas, et al., 1929, pp. 3–5).

On the basis of preliminary observations, case studies, and descriptive accounts, Thomas and her co-workers decided to focus on interactions between individuals as contrasted with actions involving material objects or the self.

One technique involved observing a single child and plotting his actual movements on a floor plan of the nursery classroom. At the same time, each new activity of the child and the time spent on it were also recorded. It was found that when both observers timed the same activity, their times correlated from .95 to .98, but that about 9 per cent of the changes in activity were missed altogether by one observer. Agreement on the nature of the activity was described as low.

Thomas noted that when the *numbers* of social contacts were recorded, observer agreement was also "low" (.47 to .80), and attributed this to ambiguity in the definition of contacts, so that when the child approached another the observer used his own judgment in deciding whether a social contact had occurred. She commented: "These low coefficients of correlation are a beautiful example of how unreliability creeps in where interpretation is permitted the recorder" (Thomas, 1929, p. 9).

Another approach used was to record every physical contact made by the child, classified according to the kind of contact (hit, pull, caress, etc.) and kind of response (passivity, cooperation, resistance, flight), and whether given or received. Again the high standard of observer agreement sought was not achieved in recording kinds of contacts and responses, although their number was accurately recorded. A ratio of contacts made to those received was found to be accurately observed but unstable.

A third technique involved stenographic records of the child's vocalizations as well as of everything said to him, and subsequent analysis of transcriptions directed at obtaining indices of the degree to which the child addressed his attention to others, himself, and to material objects. The indices proposed were based on classification of nouns and pronouns according to their referents.

Finally, observations were made of the formation of social groups ("two or more children together, either functionally or spatially, in the same activity"), the times each child spent in the group, the size of the group, etc. Such things as percentage of time spent in social situations and number of social situations entered were accurately observed, but because of the rapidity with which groups were formed, observers had difficulty in observing them all.

These examples give the flavor of the work done by this group. Their concern with accuracy and objectivity of observation set a high standard for subsequent research in the area. One criticism might be made: The group was overly concerned with securing close agreement between observers. Accuracy of observation was (mistakenly) taken as a prerequisite to quantification of any kind. This notion, which runs through almost all of the research in direct observation done since Thomas' day, has already been noted above in the work of Morsh.

In direct line with the tradition of emphasis on objectivity started by Thomas was the work of Anderson and his colleagues on the measurement of dominative and integrative behavior (Anderson & Helen Brewer, 1945; Anderson & J. Brewer, 1946; Anderson, J. Brewer, & Reed, 1946). Their work began with observation of contacts between nursery-school children:

Behavior was recorded as "contacts" and divided into two groups of categories. If a child snatched a toy, struck a playmate, or commanded him, or if he attempted to force him in some way such contacts were included under the term "domination." . . . Other contacts were recorded which tended to increase the interplay of differences. Offering a companion a choice or soliciting an expression of his desires . . . were grouped under the term "socially integrative behavior" (Anderson, J. Brewer, & Reed, 1946, p. 12).

Next, attention was focused on contacts of teachers with children. These were recorded according to the child (or children) involved as individual or group contacts. The two main categories, "Dominant" and "Integrative," were retained but subdivided according to whether or not evidence of conflict or working together was observed. After considerable work, the set of categories shown in Table 4 was evolved.

TABLE 4

CATEGORIES USED BY ANDERSON AND BREWER
TO RECORD TEACHER CONTACTS[a]

DC, Domination, with evidence of conflict
  DC-1, Determines a detail of activity in conflict
  DC-3, Relocates child
  DC-4, Direct refusal or contradiction, evasion of a child's protest or complaint; postponement without expressed reason or consideration
  DC-5, Disapproval, blame, or shame directed toward the child as a person
  DC-6, Warnings, threats, reminders, conditional promises, obstruction, or interruption
  DC-7, Calls to attention or to group activity
  DC-11, Punishment, which includes sending out of room; keeping after school; sending to principal's office; physical attack by T; depriving child of specific material, activity, "right," or privilege

TABLE 4 (Cont'd.)

CATEGORIES USED BY ANDERSON AND BREWER
TO RECORD TEACHER CONTACTS[a]

DN, Domination, with no evidence of conflict; DN (1-8) directive; DN (9-10)
  DN-1, Determines a detail of activity, mostly of a routine sort, with no evidence of conflict
  DN-6, Warnings, threats, reminders, conditional promises, with no evidence of conflict
  DN-7, Calls to attention or to group activity
  DN-8, Makes gratuitous judgment for child, including rationing material
  DN-9, Lecture method: statements
  DN-10, Lecture method: questions

DT, Domination, in working together
  DT-4, Refusal, denial, or contradiction, with explanation; postponement with reason or consideration or with future time set
  DT-13, Selects child for activity on basis of child's expressed interest
  DT-16, Approval of required work
  DT-23, Gives permission

IN, Integration, with no evidence of working together
  IN-18, Extends invitation (always initiated by T, in contrast to IT-18)
  IN-19q, Question regarding possible, though not expressed (in contrast with IT-19q) interest or activity of child
  IN-19s, Statement regarding possible, though not expressed (in contrast with IT-19s), interest or activity of child

IT, Integration, with evidence of working together
  IT-14, Helps child to define, redefine, or advance a problem
  IT-16, Approval, accord, thanks, acceptance of the spontaneous or self-initiated behavior of the child; approval where there can be several answers or new answers
  IT-19q, Questions regarding the child's expressed interest or activity which do not contribute to a problem of the child's (IT-14), or which do not merely express approval (IT-16)
  IT-19s, Statements regarding the child's expressed interest or activity which do not contribute to a problem of the child's (IT-14), or which do not merely express approval (IT-16)
  IT-20, Admits responsibility for own act that is inconvenient, unjust, or unfair to another, or admits own ignorance or incapacity

[a] Adapted from Anderson, Brewer, and Reed (1946, pp. 22–27).

TABLE 5

<small>CATEGORIES USED BY ANDERSON AND BREWER
TO RECORD PUPIL BEHAVIORS[a]</small>

N.H.	Nervous habits
L. Up	Looking up
L. Seat	Leaves seat
F.O.	Playing with a foreign object
P.	Conforming to teacher domination under DC or DN categories of teacher behavior
N-(1-2)	Child domination of other children
N-1	Demands, commands, uses force
N-2	Attacks status
M	Nonconforming to teacher's commands or demands; resistance to teacher domination
L-(1-4)	Response in recitation
L-1	Answers spontaneously
L-2	Holds up hand
L-3	Answers when called upon
L-4	Fails to answer when called upon
K-(1-4)	Problem-solving
K-1	Seeks help
K-2	Plans experiment
K-3	Contributes to own problem
K-4	Contributes to another's problem
J	Social contributions by the child
J-1	Tells experience
J-v-1	Voluntary: initiated by the child
J-r-1	In response to open question or invitation of teacher or others
J-2	Brings something to school
J-v-2	Voluntary: initiated by the child
J-r-2	In response to open invitation or question of teacher or others
J-3	Suggestions
J-v-3	Voluntary: initiated by the child
J-r-3	In response to others
J-4	Offers services
J-v-4	Voluntary: initiated by the child (where problem has not been expressed or help asked for)
J-r-4	In response to others
J-5	Holds up hand
J-v-5	Voluntary: with no evidence of teacher's invitation
J-r-5	In response to open invitation or question (not DN-10) of teacher
J-6	Appreciation
J-v-6	Voluntary
J-r-6	In response to others

[a]Adapted from Anderson, Brewer, and Reed (1946, pp. 27–30).

In the meantime, a method for observing pupil and teacher behavior simultaneously was developed. Pupil behavior was not classified as dominative or integrative in this later work, but rather was used to detect possible effects of teacher behavior on pupils. The categories used are shown in Table 5. Records were made, for a five-minute period, of the behaviors of one child at a time and of contacts between the teacher and him only. Children were listed alphabetically and observed in that order. The observation was continued until 24 observations (two hours) had been made of each child. Each teacher was therefore observed for a number of hours equal to twice the number of pupils in her class. Reliability, studied item by item in terms of observer agreement, was generally very high.

Some steps toward dimensionalization were taken. An over-all score called the I-D Index, the ratio of the total number of Integrative contacts of a teacher to her total number of Dominant ones, was proposed. It and the totals of sets of categories (e.g., DC, DN 1-8, DN 9-10) were used as variables in comparing teachers, classes, and the like.

The principal contribution made by this group is shown in Tables 4 and 5. A system of coding behaviors like this can result only from the creative thinking followed by painstaking trial and error exemplified by this study. The empirical portion of the investigation was intensive; very few teachers were involved—four at most. This small N made it impossible to estimate the reliability of any of the scores proposed for comparing different teachers, different classes, or different occasions in the same class. It also made it impossible to study the internal consistencies of any of the proposed scales. Ample evidence was presented that the behaviors were recorded accurately, and the scales have high intrinsic interest. Evidence of significant differences in the behaviors of the teachers studied suggests that the scores were reliable.

Thomas' group and Anderson's had in common their principal object of observation: interaction, pupil-pupil or pupil-teacher. That classrooms differ markedly in the kinds of interaction which are most common in them was clearly shown by the latter group; that the dimension which they called the I-D Index is related to some characteristic of the teacher's personality was also brought out.

Withall (1949) renamed this dimension Social-Emotional Climate and suggested that it should be possible to measure it in terms of teacher behavior alone. He developed the following set of categories into which teacher statements could be classified on the basis of transcripts of their teaching behavior:

1. *Learner-supportive* statements that have the intent of reassuring or commending the pupil.
2. *Acceptant and clarifying* statements having an intent to convey to the pupil the feeling that he was understood and help him elucidate his ideas and feelings.
3. *Problem-structuring* statements or questions which proffer information or raise questions about the problem in an objective manner with intent to facilitate learner's problem-solving.
4. *Neutral* statements which comprise polite formalities, administrative comments, verbatim repetition of something that has already been said. No intent inferable.
5. *Directive* or hortative statements with intent to have pupil follow a recommended course of action.
6. *Reproving* or deprecating remarks intended to deter pupil from continued indulgence in present "unacceptable" behavior.
7. *Teacher self-supporting* remarks intended to sustain or justify the teacher's position or course of action (Withall, 1949, p. 349).

These seven categories were seen by Withall as lying along a continuum from "learner-centeredness" to "teacher-centeredness," 1, 2, and 3 being learner-centered and 5, 6, and 7 teacher-centered. If more of a teacher's statements fell into Categories 1, 2, or 3 than in 4, 5, or 6, the climate was said to be learner-centered; if more fell in 4, 5, and 6, it was said to be teacher-centered. If more

statements fell into Category 3 than either 1 or 2 combined or 4, 5, and 6 combined, the climate was described as more problem-centered than either of the other two. The ratio of the numbers of 1, 2, 3 statements to the total was called the "Climate Index."

Withall studied classifier agreement, reliability (in the sense of consistency of teacher behavior in different samples of statements), and validity in terms of relationship to Anderson's categories, pupil reactions, and expert ratings. In a later study (1951), Withall followed a group of seventh-grade pupils into classrooms with different teachers and found that different teachers produce a different climate with the same group of pupils. Since, like Anderson's studies, Withall's used very small numbers of teachers, the results cannot be regarded as demonstrating reliability and validity in a statistical sense; however, the results, so far as they went, strongly indicated that the procedure had reliability and validity.

Withall's technique, as used by its author, was not a method for observing and recording behavior in the classroom; rather it was a method for coding typewritten transcripts of sound recordings of classroom behaviors. When Mitzel and Rabinowitz (1953) experimented with the categories in New York, they found that neither sound nor stenographic recordings yielded satisfactory records of teacher behavior because of extraneous noises and other difficulties. They therefore visited classrooms and categorized teacher statements live, as they were made. Together they visited four teachers, two of fourth grade and two of fifth grade, eight times each, i.e., on eight successive Monday mornings. The two observers made independent tallies of teacher statements for about 30 minutes per visit. The proportions of all tallies in Categories 1, 2, 4, 5, 6, and the proportions in 1, 2, and 3 combined were analyzed. (Categories 3 and 7 were used so rarely it was not considered worth while to analyze them separately.)

The original analysis reported by the authors was based on Model I assumptions, which imply that the results obtained are not generalizable to teachers other than those actually observed, times other than those in which the teachers were visited, or observers other than the two who made the observations. An analysis of these data under Model II assumptions was later carried out (Medley & Mitzel, 1958a). Model II assumptions permit generalizing the findings to other teachers, situations, and observers (see Eisenhart, 1947; Medley, Mitzel, & Doi, 1956).

The reliability coefficients obtained from this analysis estimate the correlation between the number of statements classified in a particular category by one observer on one visit on the basis of approximately 100 consecutive statements with the number classified in the same category by a different observer on a different visit.

Coefficients of observer agreement (also based on 100 statements) were also estimated. These coefficients estimate the correlation over teachers between the proportion of 100 statements classified in a given category by one observer and the proportion of the same 100 statements classified in that category by another observer.

Two of the categories failed to show reliabilities significantly different from zero: (4) Neutral and (6) Reproving. One category, (1) Learner-Supportive, had a reliability which, though significantly different from zero, was only .25. The coefficients of observer agreement of these three categories were, respectively, .50, .88, and .90. Except in the case of the Neutral category, it appears that the low reliabilities reflected instability of behavior rather than any difficulty experienced by the observer in using the technique.

The estimated reliability of the Climate Index was .47; the coefficient of observer agreement, .96. The other two categories, (3) Problem-Structuring and (5) Directive, had reliabilities of .50 each, and coefficients of observer agreement of .98 and .97, respectively.

The fact that the observer agreement is typically much higher than the reliability coefficient of a category suggested that sending two observers into a classroom at the same time is more wasteful than sending them in at different times. Two observers watching the same behavior give little more information about what happened than one.

Medley and Mitzel (1958a) estimated what would happen if 12 different observers visited a teacher either (1) at one time or (2) at 12 different times; the amount of observer time would be the same in both cases but the reliabilities would be quite different. The reliability in either case would be the correlation with what 12 other observers would observe (1) on another occasion or (2) on 12 other occasions. Reliabilities of the Climate Index would be, for Plan 1, .50; for Plan 2, .92. Similar differences would be found for the other dimensions. When the number of observers is increased to 12 without increasing the number of visits, observer errors cancel out, but errors due to instability of teacher behavior do not; since the latter errors are much greater than the former, reliability increases only slightly—from .47 to .50. When the number of visits is increased, as well as the number of observers, both types of errors tend to cancel out, and the reliability increases from .47 to .92.

Evidence was also presented that, while the reliabilities of all four scores increase with the number of visits, the rate of increase levels off at around 12 visits, with reliabilities between about .75 and .90.

A later, larger-scale study cast further light on the question of the reliability and validity of the Withall Climate Index. The Observation Schedule and Record technique (OScAR) reviewed below (Mitzel & Medley, 1958b) included, in each half-hour visit, 15 minutes during which teacher statements were classified into the five categories studied by Mitzel and Rabinowitz (1953). The reliabilities of the four categories used (estimated by the methods described in the last section of this chapter) were as follows:

Problem-Structuring	.79
Directive	.51
Reproving	.87
Supportive	.71

A variation on the Withall technique was introduced in this investigation: The observer also classified teachers' expressive nonverbal behaviors as "hostile" or "supportive." Frowns, scowls, glares, and threatening gestures were counted as hostile; smiles, nods of approval, and caresses as supportive. The reliabilities of these categories were, respectively, .81 and .79. This indicated, contrary to expectation, that such behaviors could be classified more reliably than teacher statements.

The Withall categories were combined with other items into two scales as follows:

Manifest Teacher Hostility:

Teacher uses sarcasm

Teacher yells

Reproving statement

Teacher hostile behavior, nonverbal

Supportive Teacher Behavior:

Teacher calls pupil "dear," etc.

Teacher demonstrates affection for pupil

Pupil demonstrates affection for teacher

Supportive teacher behavior, nonverbal

Supportive statement

It should perhaps be pointed out that the first two items on the Manifest Teacher Hostility scale and the first three on the Supportive Teacher Behavior scale were observed at different times than the remaining two on the same scale. Therefore, although the same behavior could be classifiable under two

items, it never was, because the two items were never used at the same time.

The reliabilities of these composite scales were, respectively, .92 and .84. After a factor analysis revealed high communality between them, they were combined (with certain other items) into a dimension called Emotional Climate, which had a reliability of .90.

Some light was shed on the question of the relationship between Emotional Climate and teacher effectiveness by the results shown in Table 6. Emotional Climate appears to be related to supervisors' ratings of a teacher's effectiveness, and to Pupil-Teacher Rapport, measured in terms of pupils' responses to a questionnaire asking for pupils' reactions to the teacher (Medley & Klein, 1957). The zero-order correlation of .32 between Climate and Rapport was not quite significant at the .05 level. (Other data in Table 6 are discussed on page 283.)

Hughes and her associates (Hughes, 1959) developed a comprehensive set of categories for the classification of teacher behavior, shown in Table 7. These categories are similar to Withall's except that Hughes and her associates did not restrict themselves to verbal behavior. For example, Hughes's Controlling Functions are similar to Withall's Directive Statements, and Hughes's Functions That Develop Content resemble Withall's Problem-Structuring Statements.

TABLE 6

RELATIONSHIPS BETWEEN TEACHER EFFECTIVENESS AND CLASSROOM BEHAVIOR[a]

Criterion of Effectiveness	Multiple Correlation	BETA WEIGHTS					
		Classroom Behavior Dimensions			Control Variables		
		Emotional Climate	Verbal Emphasis	Social Organization	Average Mental Maturity	Grade Level	Initial Group Problem-Solving Skill
Average Adjusted Reading Growth	.55	+.20	+.09	0	not used	+.52	not used
Growth in Group Problem-Solving Skill	.26	+.06	−.09	+.09	+.24	not used	−.26
Pupil-Teacher Rapport	.49	+.32	+.28	+.09	not used	−.24	not used
Supervisors' Ratings	.56	+.52	−.01	+.10	+.20	not used	−.32
Teacher's Self-Rating	.48	+.10	0	−.44	+.28	not used	not used

[a] Adapted from Medley & Mitzel (1959).

TABLE 7

OUTLINE OF
UNIVERSITY OF UTAH REVISION
OF THE PROVO CODE FOR
THE ANALYSIS OF TEACHING[a]

Controlling Functions

Structure	Regulate
open	open
closed	closed
intervention	global
sequential	routine
orientation	neutral
ongoing	sequential
public criteria	direction
	public criteria
Standard Set	Judge
recall	direction
teacher edict	punish
group developed	turn back
universal	just

Imposition of Teacher

Regulate self	Inform appraisal
Moralize	Inform
Teacher estimate of need	

Facilitating Functions

Checking	Demonstrate
information	Clarify procedure
routine	
involvement	

Functions That Develop Content

Resource	Clarify
routine	just
child initiative	content
	generalize
	summarize
Stimulate	
one	
three	
	Evaluate
	just
Structure, turn back	negative
	positive
Content-Agree	with discrimination

Functions That Serve as Response

Meets request	Interprets
routine	situation
makes arrangements	feelings
Clarify personal	Acknowledges teacher
problem	mistake
experience	

Functions of Positive Affectivity

Support	Solicitous
just	

TABLE 7 (Cont'd.)

OUTLINE OF
UNIVERSITY OF UTAH REVISION
OF THE PROVO CODE FOR
THE ANALYSIS OF TEACHING[a]

stereotype	Encourage
specific	
	Does for personal

Functions of Negative Affectivity

Admonish	Negative response personal
	public criteria
Reprimand	
public criteria	Verbal futuristic
	public criteria
Accusative	
	Ignore
Threat	

[a]Adapted from Hughes (1959).

The raw data for this study consisted of a detailed, sequential narrative of 30 minutes of teacher behavior as perceived and recorded in shorthand by two trained observers. At the end of each observation period the observers transcribed their notes and collated their separate records. The final record contained only those behaviors which the two observers agreed upon.

A total of 129 distinct half-hour behavior records was obtained on 41 elementary school teachers in this study. Every teacher was observed on three occasions, and a special pilot study group of six teachers was also observed on a fourth occasion. The pilot group of six teachers (four observations each) was initially selected for the project by public school supervisors. The remaining 35 teachers (called the major study group) worked in a large county school system in a West Coast state. Twenty-five of the West Coast teachers, located in five contiguous districts, were judged to be "good" teachers by the central office staff. The remaining 10 were chosen to be a "representative" sample of the teachers in a particular district.

Each of the 129 narrative records was divided into specific teacher acts and these acts were classified according to the 33 teaching functions in seven major categories shown in Table 7. The number of acts on one 30-minute record ranged between 100 and 390; the mean was about 250. Coding was done by two independent workers and checked by a third in conference with the others to eliminate disagreements. Accuracy of coding was assessed by recoding a 20 per cent sample of the more than 1,100 pages of material from 105 observation periods and calculating the percentage of agreement between the two codings.

One outcome of the study was a model pattern for teacher behaviors. According to the authors, the following range of percentages in each of the seven behavior categories produces the optimum interaction pattern for learning in the elementary school:

Controlling Functions	20–40 per cent
Imposition	1– 3 per cent
Facilitating	5–15 per cent
Content Development	20–40 per cent
Personal Response	8–20 per cent
Positive Affectivity	10–20 per cent
Negative Affectivity	3–10 per cent

These challenging conclusions are viewed by the writers as having at present the status of hypotheses concerning the effects of different patterns of behavior upon the quality of children's growth.

Hughes concluded that teachers' behavior patterns are stable through time; that, for example, the number of controlling acts exhibited by a given teacher in different situations does not vary significantly when compared with the interaction between situations and teachers.

This finding held for all seven categories in the observation schedule. It is inconsistent, however, with the findings reported by other investigators using similar instruments. Medley and Mitzel (1958a) and Mitzel and Rabinowitz (1953), for example, found that the variation in teachers' behavior from observation to observation provided a major source of variability. Hughes's conclusion was based on data concerning only six teachers, each observed four times, and hence must be regarded as tentative at best. Regrettably, the same hypothesis was not tested with the data

on the other 35 teachers studied, although they did contain information relevant to the hypothesis.

None of Hughes's seven functions discriminated between the 25 "judged-good" teachers and the 10 "representative" teachers in the major study. This finding, also, is inconsistent with the relationship reported by Medley and Mitzel between classroom climate and principal's ratings, cited above.

Flanders (1960) has developed the most sophisticated technique for observing climate thus far, one which is unique in that it preserves a certain amount of information regarding the sequence of behavior. Using the system of 10 categories shown in Table 8, the observer at the end of each three-second period decides which category best represents the "communication behavior" during that three seconds and writes down the number of that category while observing the next three-second period. (An important part of the training of observers appears to be the development of a certain rhythm in doing this.) The numbers are written in sequence in a column. "When there is a major change in class formation, the communication pattern, or the subject under discussion, a double line is drawn and the time indicated" (Flanders, 1960, Appendix F, pp. 2–3). The series of behaviors between two double lines is called an "episode." Afterwards, anecdotal material is added to aid in classifying the episode.

When the data are tabulated, those referring to any episode or group of episodes may be entered in a 10×10 matrix, each categorization (except the first) being tallied opposite the number of the one just preceding it and below its own number. Thus, if a teacher accepts an idea in one three-second interval and asks a question in the next, so that a 3 is followed by a 4 in the record, a tally would be made in row 3, column 4. If now an 8 follows the 4, a tally would be entered in row 4, column 8, indicating that a teacher question was followed by a student response. In order to ensure that a matrix is symmetrical, a 10 is added at the beginning

TABLE 8

CATEGORIES FOR INTERACTION ANALYSIS[a]

MINNESOTA, 1959

Teacher Talk	Indirect Influence	1.	*Accepts Feeling:* accepts and clarifies the feeling tone of the students in a nonthreatening manner. Feelings may be positive or negative. Predicting or recalling feelings are included.
		2.	*Praises or Encourages:* praises or encourages student action or behavior. Jokes that release tension, not at the expense of another individual, nodding head or saying, "um hm?" or "go on" are included.
		3.	*Accepts or Uses Ideas of Student:* clarifying, building, or developing ideas suggested by a student. As teacher brings more of his own ideas into play, shift to Category 5.
		4.	*Asks Questions:* asking a question about content or procedure with the intent that a student answer.
	Direct Influence	5.	*Lecturing:* giving facts or opinions about content or procedure; expressing his own ideas, asking rhetorical questions.
		6.	*Giving Directions:* directions, commands, or orders to which a student is expected to comply.
		7.	*Criticizing or Justifying Authority:* statements intended to change student behavior from nonacceptable to acceptable pattern; bawling someone out; stating why the teacher is doing what he is doing; extreme self-reference.
Student Talk		8.	*Student Talk—Response:* talk by students in response to teacher. Teacher initiates the contact or solicits student statement.
		9.	*Student Talk—Initiation:* talk by students which they initiate. If "calling on" student is only to indicate who may talk next, observer must decide whether student wanted to talk. If he did, use this category.
		10.	*Silence or Confusion:* pauses, short periods of silence, and periods of confusion in which communication cannot be understood by the observer.

[a] Adapted from Flanders (1960, Appendix F, p. 5).

and end of each episode unless there is a 10 at that place already.

Several episodes may be tallied in a single matrix, as for example, all episodes seen in a single classroom might be combined to give a picture of the over-all pattern of interaction in the class. Although Flanders denies that the categories lie along a scale of any kind, he does conceptualize them as lying along a dimension of "influence." Categories 1 to 4 represent indirect influence in varying degrees—Category 1 allowing the pupil the most freedom, Category 4 the least. Categories 5 to 7 represent increasing amounts of direct influence. Categories 8 and 9 represent different levels of teacher influence as inferred from pupil behavior. Category 10 is an escape category for unclassifiable three-second periods.

Counts of tallies in certain areas of such a matrix provide "scores" of particular interest. Some of these areas are indicated in Fig. 1. The total in Area A measures the amount of teacher talk; that in Area B, the amount of student talk. A large number of tallies in Area D indicates a class in which "indirect influence" statements tend to follow one another relatively often. A tally in Area E occurs whenever a pupil comment follows one by the teacher. Areas F, G, and H are also of particular interest as indicated in Fig. 1.

Coefficients of observer agreement were calculated by a formula proposed by Scott (1955). The coefficient was defined as follows:

$$\pi = \frac{p_o - p_e}{1 - p_e}$$

where p_o is the proportion of agreement, and p_e the proportion of agreement expected by chance. Observers were trained until these "coefficients" were consistently above .85.

Coefficients of observer agreement were calculated only for the totals in Areas A, B, and C of a matrix of the type shown in Fig. 1, and were based (apparently) on one entire visit of unspecified length. Some of the visits made in the study in which the technique was used were one hour long, the others two hours long (Flanders, 1960, p. 48).

For the uses of the technique suggested by Flanders, these reliabilities have limited relevance. Flanders obtained totals in the various areas of Fig. 1, as well as "I/D ratios" (ratios of the number of tallies in Categories 1–3 to the number of tallies in Categories 5–7), based on over-all performances of teachers, to compare one teacher with another. These totals and ratios are also used to compare behaviors of a teacher in one type of situation with behaviors of the same teacher in another type of situation.

For example, given one hour's observation in a secondary class, there may be a separate matrix for each of the following time periods: first, five minutes of routine announcements, getting settled down, taking the roll, etc.; second, fifteen minutes of going over homework and reviewing the assignment of yesterday; third, fifteen minutes for the introduction of some new material and discussion of this material [etc.] . . . (Flanders, 1960, Appendix F, p. 16).

Use of the scores either for comparing dif-

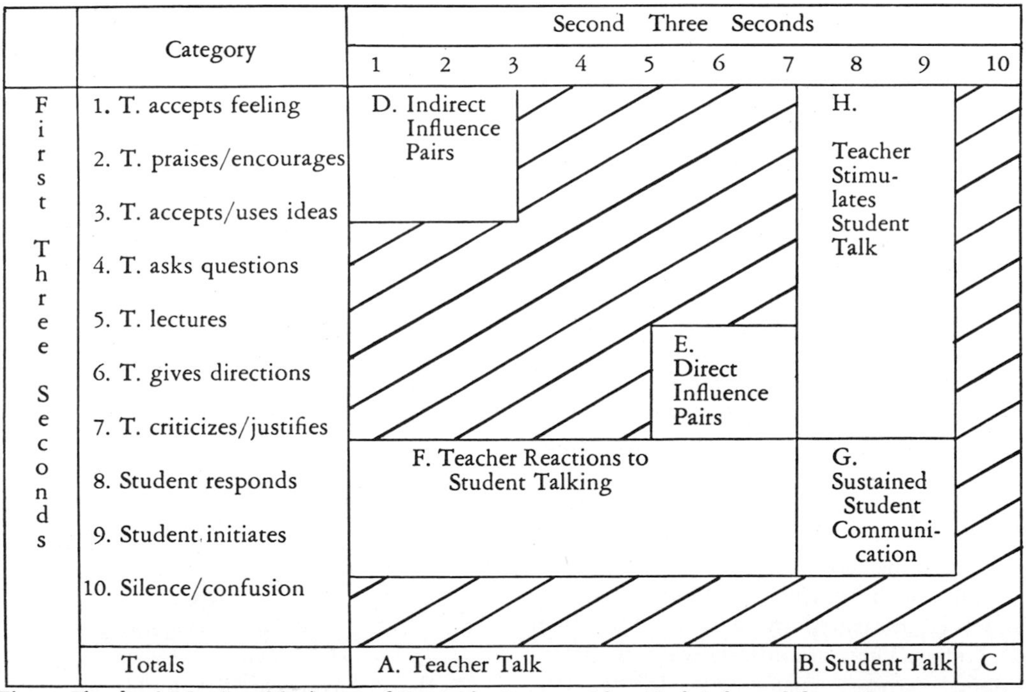

Fig. 1. Flanders' Matrix with Areas of Particular Interest Identified (adapted from Flanders, 1960).

ferent teachers or for studying differences in a single teacher's behavior in these different types of situations implies inferences about unobserved behavior, particularly when behaviors are related to student achievement, attitudes, "dependence proneness," and the like. Satisfactory evidence of reliability of the records and scores based on them would have to show that teacher behavior (within a given type of situation) is stable enough in relation to observed differences between teachers to warrant such inferences.

The absence of appropriate information on reliability does not, of course, call into question any of the interesting findings of Flanders' study—that student achievement in mathematics and social studies is higher in the classes of teachers using more indirect influence, for example, or that teachers who use more direct influence do not vary their behavior in different situations as much as the "indirect" teachers do. A critical ratio justifying rejection of the null hypothesis is de facto evidence that the measuring instrument used had reliability sufficient for the purpose for which it was used. However, anyone contemplating future studies using this scheme would find data on reliability helpful in planning such studies.

Flanders' scheme is extremely ingenious. Every one of the 100 cells in the matrix of Fig. 1 represents a different item of behavior with its own intrinsic interest. Yet the observer needs to learn and use only 10 categories. The idea of categorizing the dominant pattern of a three-second period rather than each statement or other unit of behavior is also ingenious. If, as Flanders says, the observer develops a natural "rhythm" in recording after some training, the task must become at least as easy as that of using Withall's categories after the manner of Mitzel and Rabinowitz.

The dimension of classroom behavior which we have called classroom climate has been measured more successfully than any other. There are differences in the terms applied to the dimension as it has been operationally defined in various studies—domina-tive-integrative, teacher-centered versus learner-centered, hostile-supportive, direct-indirect influence. Yet there is little question that all are referring to highly similar, even identical, dimensions of behavior, reliably measurable, and important in educational theory.

Measuring Multiple Dimensions of Classroom Behavior

We turn now to a group of studies which did not grow out of the efforts of supervisors to identify effective teacher behaviors or the social psychologists' interest in interaction in the classroom, but which are nonetheless heavily indebted to both. These are studies which have tried to measure classroom behavior as such, to describe quantitatively as much as possible of what goes on in the classroom, regardless of its relationship to teacher effectiveness or psychological theory.

A major attempt along this line was made by Cornell, Lindvall, and Saupe (1952). The declared purpose of this attempt was to "measure differences in classrooms as a means of characterizing differences of school systems." The dimensions, defined a priori, were as follows:

A. *Differentiation* . . . the extent to which provision is made for individual differences among students. . . .
B. *Social Organization* . . . the type of group structure and the pattern of interaction among individuals. . . .
C. *Initiative* . . . the extent to which pupils are permitted to control the learning situation. . . .
D. *Content* . . . the source and the organization of the content of learning. . . .
E. *Variety* . . . the extent to which a variety of activities or techniques are used. . . .
F. *Competency* . . . differences in the technical performances of teachers [in] . . . a few selected behaviors. . . .
G. and H. *Classroom Climate* . . . social-emotional climate . . . as it is reflected in the behavior of the teacher [and] . . . the behavior of the pupils (Cornell, Lindvall, & Saupe, 1952, pp. 20–23).

Table 9 shows the "Code Digest" used by the observer as a guide in recording behavior. For Dimensions A, B, C, and D, the number corresponding to the code best describing the state of the classroom was recorded for each

TABLE 9

CLASSROOM OBSERVATION CODE DIGEST

(Used by Cornell, Lindvall, & Saupe, 1952, pp. 53–54)

A. *Differentiation*
1. Identical work—no teacher assistance.
2. Identical work—teacher assistance.
3. Differentiated work—ability basis—few groups—no teacher assistance.
4. Differentiated work—ability basis—few groups—teacher assistance.
5. Differentiated work—ability basis—individual—no teacher assistance.
6. Differentiated work—ability basis—individual—teacher assistance.
7. Differentiated work—ability and interest basis—few groups—no teacher assistance.
8. Differentiated work—ability and interest basis—few groups—teacher assistance.
9. Differentiated work—ability and interest basis—individual—no teacher assistance.
10. Differentiated work—ability and interest basis—individual—teacher assistance.

B. *Social Organization*
1. Single group—teacher leader—no interaction.
2. Multi-group—teacher leader—no interaction.
3. Single group—pupil leader—no interaction.
4. Multi-group—pupil leader—no interaction.
5. Single group—teacher leader—interaction.
6. Multi-group—teacher leader—interaction.
7. Single group—pupil leader—interaction.
8. Multi-group—pupil leader—interaction.

C. *Pupil Initiative*
1. Teacher domination—no pupil participation.
2. Teacher domination—minor pupil participation.
3. Teacher control—major pupil participation.
4. Pupil control—teacher participation.
5. Pupil control—no teacher participation.

D. *Content*
1. One text or workbook.
2. Several texts or similar references.
3. Subject-matter sources other than text.
4. Teacher-designated problems, units, areas.
5. Student-interest problems, units, areas.

TABLE 9 (Cont'd.)

CLASSROOM OBSERVATION CODE DIGEST

(Used by Cornell, Lindvall, & Saupe, 1952, pp. 53–54)

E. *Variety*
1. Teacher lectures or reads.
2. Teacher gives demonstration.
3. Teacher shows movie or slides.
4. Pupils read text at seat.
5. Pupils read other books at seat.
6. Pupils work with workbook at seat.
7. Pupils work problems (not text or workbook) at seat.
8. Pupils study materials other than books at seat.
9. Pupils draw or paint at seat.
10. Teacher questions—pupil answers.
11. Class engaged in discussion.
12. Pupil gives talk or report.
13. Pupils work at blackboard.
14. Pupils read aloud from book.
15. Pupils study charts, drawings, maps.
16. Pupils work experiment.
17. Pupils construct things.
18. Pupils decorate room.
19. Pupils engage in role playing or present play.
20. Class goes on trip.
21. Pupils go to another room to work.
22. Pupils work in small discussion groups.
23. Pupils write test.

F. *Competency*

Positive	*Negative*
1. Suggested aids to learning and study hints.	1. Was inactive.
2. Was thorough in explanation.	2. Was preoccupied; had difficulty keeping attention on activity in progress.
3. Provided for review.	3. Avoided responsibility.
4. Tried to clarify by restating ideas in different contexts; pointed out implications in relationships.	4. Explanation seemed to leave pupils puzzled.
5. Brought in examples and experiences.	5. Answers to pupils' questions were incomplete or inaccurate.
6. Gave complete and satisfying answers.	6. Evidence of limited background in subject taught.
7. Evidence of careful planning and preparation.	7. Evidence of lack of planning for class work.
8. Appears confident and able to meet most situations.	8. Appeared uncertain of self in classroom situation.

TABLE 9 (Cont'd.)

CLASSROOM OBSERVATION CODE DIGEST

(Used by Cornell, Lindvall, & Saupe, 1952, pp. 53–54)

Positive	Negative
9. Shows evidence of good background in subject or in general culture.	9. Allowed discussion to wander from subject.

G. *Climate—Teacher*

Positive	Negative
1. Made courteous remarks.	1. "Laid down the law."
2. Respected public opinion.	2. Was intolerant of pupil suggestions.
3. Gave special evidence of patience.	3. Interrupted speaking pupil.
4. Helped pupil on some nonacademic (personal) problem.	4. Corrected or criticized excessively.
5. Expressed sympathy.	5. Lacked sympathy with pupil failure.
6. Tried to see a pupil point of view.	6. Used threats.
7. Complimented pupil.	7. Was cross; lost temper.
8. Accepted criticism well.	8. Permitted pupils to laugh at mistakes of others.
9. Joked with pupils.	9. Made sarcastic remarks, used ridicule (without humor).
10. Used first-person-plural predominantly.	10. Seemed disturbed in a situation (frowning, tension, distress, etc.).
11. Focused attention on total class.	11. Used first-person-singular predominantly.

H. *Climate—Pupils*

Positive	Negative
1. Responded eagerly in recitation.	1. Were restless, gazed about, doodled, daydreamed.
2. Worked intently with little sign of attention wandering.	2. Were slow in responding to teacher's request.
3. Were prompt in taking part in activities.	3. Were reluctant to recite, did not volunteer.
4. Paid close attention to teacher or other pupil.	4. Whispered or showed other signs of inattention.
5. Made courteous remark.	5. Made rude remark.
6. Received criticism well.	6. Were quarrelsome, irritable.

five-minute period during a one-hour visit. For Dimension E, a check list was provided and each type of behavior observed during a five-minute period was checked. An item on one of these dimensions could be checked no more than 12 times during one visit. Dimensions F, G, and H were recorded only once during a visit, each code being checked if observed once (or more) during the entire hour.

A system of scoring was developed which yielded a single score for each dimension except E, upon which two scores were based: E_1, Diversity (number of different activities seen during a visit) and E_2, Activity Persistency (average number of five-minute periods during which an activity was observed).

A tryout study was conducted during which 32 classrooms were visited three times by six observers in teams of two. On each of the three visits, the two observers recorded the behaviors independently for 30 minutes. The "reliability" coefficients reported in the original monograph (Cornell, Lindvall, & Saupe, 1952, p. 37) are better described as coefficients of observer agreement, since they are, in fact, estimates of the correlations between scores assigned by two different observers to the same performance. They indicate how objective the record of behavior is, but not how well the scores discriminate different classrooms from one another. Reliability coefficients which do indicate the power of the dimensions for discriminating classrooms, as well as coefficients of observer agreement, were estimated in a later study using a slightly modified form of the Cornell technique (Medley & Mitzel, 1958a) in 25-minute visits to 33 classrooms in New York City by six observers in teams of two each. Table 10 summarizes and compares the results of the two reliability studies.

The coefficients of observer agreement reported in the New York study are uniformly lower than those found in the Illinois study. This result is probably due in large part to the greater heterogeneity among the 32 classrooms visited in Illinois. Those classrooms were located in four "rural-urban systems"

TABLE 10

RELIABILITY OF CORNELL DIMENSIONS[a]

| Dimension | Observer Agreement | | Reliability |
	Illinois	New York	
Differentiation	.70	.64	.35
Social Organization	.89	.66	.37
Pupil Initiative	.73	.43	.00
Content	.81	.23	.00
Diversity	.61	.42	.42
Activity Persistency	.78	[b]	[b]
Competency	.42	[b]	[b]
Climate-Teacher	.59	.32	.32
Climate-Pupil	.55	.00	.00

[a] Adapted from Cornell, Lindvall, and Saupe (1952), and Medley and Mitzel (1958a).
[b] These dimensions were not scored in the New York study.

and four "suburban-metropolitan" systems, one class in each system of Grades 4, 6, 8, and 10. The classrooms visited in the New York study were all in the elementary grades and were all in two neighboring schools in one city system. Data on the variability of the measures obtained in the two studies are not available, so that this explanation cannot be verified.

Note that, as usual, the reliability coefficients—correlations between 25-minute records made by different observers at different times—tend to be lower than the coefficients of observer agreement. Three of the former coefficients were not significantly different from zero. It was shown (Medley & Mitzel, 1958a) that the reliabilities of all four scales—Differentiation, Social Organization, Diversity, and Climate-Teacher—would be over .80 if based on 12 visits.

The strengths and weaknesses of an observational technique inhere mainly in the items of which it is composed. The schedule used in this study contained a wide variety of items, some better than others. Consider, for example, these three items from the Climate-Teacher scale:

G2. (+) Respected pupil opinion
G3. (−) Interrupted speaking pupil
G5. (−) Lacked sympathy with pupil failure

All three items are phrased in the past tense,

which suggests that they are to be checked some time after the behavior takes place. The dangers of recording behavior in retrospect have been pointed out already but can be re-emphasized. An item like G2, if marked at the end of a period, becomes a record of a general impression of the teacher's behavior rather than a record of a specific incident; in effect it becomes a rating. This problem is not so serious with an item like G3, which is less ambiguous as to the exact behavior to be looked for, but all three items would be improved if they were changed to the present tense:

G2.' (+) Respects pupil opinion
G3.' (−) Interrupts speaking pupil
G5.' (−) Lacks sympathy with pupil failure

This slight revision, while it makes Item G3 more acceptable, only makes other defects in Items G2 and G5 more obvious. It is easy now to see that G2 does not really refer to a behavior but, at best, it refers to a habit of behaving in a certain way. If it were reworded:

G2.'' (+) Shows respect for pupil opinion
it would more clearly refer to a single incident which happens at a particular moment in time.

If Item G5' refers to an incident at all, it refers to a pupil's failure to do something—to answer a question correctly, perhaps—followed by a teacher's failure to feel sympathy. The observer could watch for an incident in which a pupil fails, and then make a judgment as to whether the teacher feels sympathy, and if the judgment is negative, make a tally. Would it not be much easier to use an item such as "Teacher ridicules pupil for failing" or "Teacher sympathizes with pupil who fails"? Or better, and more simply, "Teacher ridicules pupil" or "Teacher sympathizes with pupil"?

It is much easier to criticize and revise an item than to write one; both steps are useful. Cornell and his co-workers (1952) provided a large number of interesting items (see Table 9) for future researchers to revise and improve.

Medley and Mitzel (1955, 1958b, 1959) did just that when they developed an instrument they called OScAR (Observation Schedule and Record) for use in a follow-up study of teacher education graduates. OScAR was designed to provide quantitative data regarding

Tm_____No. p._____

Tot		I	III	V
	A0 (TP-PT)	X	X	X
	A1 t wks w ind p			
	A2 t wks w sm gp			
	A3 t qu, p ans			
	A4 t ans p qu			
	A5 t ign p qu			
	A6 t lds sng, ex, gm			
	B0 (TP)	X	X	X
	B1 t lctrs			
	B2 t rds, tls sty			
	B3 t tks to cls			
	B4 t illus at bd			
	B5 t illus at mp, cht			
	B6 t dmnstrs			
	B7 t shws fm, sld, plys rcd			
	B8 t pss ppr, bks			
	C0 (T)	X	X	X
	C1 t wrks at dsk			
	C2 t clns, dcrts rm			
	C3 t wrts on, dcrts bd			
	C4 t tks to vstr			
	C5 t lvs, entrs rm			
	Check			

	I	III	V	Tot
D0 (P)	X	X	X	
D1 p rds, stdys at st				
D2 p wrts, mnps at st				
D3 p pnts, cts, drws, etc				
D4 p wks at bd				
D5 p dcrts rm, bd				
D6 p clns rm, bd				
D7 p rsts, has snk				
D8 p lvs, entrs rm				
D9 p pts hnds on hd, etc				
E0 (PP)	X	X	X	
E1 p tks to gp				
E2 p rcts				
E3 p rpts, gvs prpd tk				
E4 p rds ald				
E5 p dmstrs, illus				
E6 p gvs skt, ply				
E7 p sngs, pl instr				
E8 p plys gm				
E9 p interps				
E10 p lds cls				
F0 (PM)	X	X	X	
F1 p ign t qu				
F2 p scfls, fts				
F3 p wsprs				
F4 p lghs				
F5 p pss ppr, bks, mlk				
F6 p tks to vstr				
Check				

Tot	I	III	V	Soc (Gpg) Adm	I	III	V	Tot
				G1 at lst ½ cl in gp w t				
				G2 at lst ½ cl in gp w/o t				
				G3 4 p to ½ cl in gp w t				
				G4 4 p to ½ cl in gp w/o t				
				G5 2-3 p in gp w t				
				G6 2-3 p in gp w/o t				
				G7 p as ind				
				Check				

Fig. 2. Front Side of OScAR 2a (Medley & Mitzel, 1958b).

(Sns)	I	III	V	Tot
S2 t mvs frly				
S3 p mvs frly				
S5 t cls p dr, etc				
S6 t shws afct f p				
S7 p shws afct f t				
S8 p shws ho t t				
S9 p shws ho t p				
S10 t uses srcsm				
S11 t yls				
● Check				

Tot	I	III	V	t　　　(Mtls)　　p	I	III	V	Tot
				L1 Blbd				
				L2 Mp, Cht, Pctr				
				L3 Sld, Fm, etc				
				M Audio Aid				
				N5 Obj				
				N6 Spec Tchg Aid				
				O No Mtls				
				Pl Txt, Wkbk				
				P2 Supl Rdg Mtr				
				Q Wrtg				
				R Hcft, Art				
				Check				

Fig. 2. Front Side of OScAR 2a (Medley & Mitzel, 1958b) (cont'd.).

behaviors of beginning teachers so that the behaviors could be correlated with a number of other variables. It was evolved mainly by modifying and combining items constructed by Cornell, Lindvall, and Saupe (1952) and Withall (1949), on the basis of the results of tryouts of the two techniques (Medley & Mitzel, 1955). Three basic changes were made. The first change was designed to increase observer accuracy by reducing the difficulty of the judgments required, along the lines just pointed out. If an observational technique can be used successfully only by a highly trained observer, it has limited usefulness, and the results of future measurements made with it may be suspect because the observers may not have been adequately trained. For this reason, the categories of both Cornell and Withall were redefined in somewhat simpler terms.

Experience with these two techniques also showed that the often-adopted practice of sending several observers into the classroom together (presumably so that one observer

	II	IV	VI	Tot
K1				
K2				
K3				
K4				
K5				
K6				
K7				
K8				
Chk				

H. Rcp	I1. TI	I2. PD	I3. Tr	J1. DO	J2. NL	J3. RP

Tot	II	IV	VI	(Sbj)	I	III	V	Tot
				T1 Rdg				
				T2 Math				
				T3 Lang Arts				
				T4 Soc St				
				T5 Science				
				T6 Recreation				
				T7 Art, Crafts				
				T8 Music				
				T9 Soc Process				
				T10 Test				
				Check				

REMARKS

Fig. 3. Reverse Side of OScAR 2a (Medley & Mitzel, 1958b).

can record what another misses) is uneconomical. An average score based on observations made by two observers who see a teacher at different times obviously contains more information than one based on observations made by two observers who see the teacher at the same time, because it is based on a behavior sample that is twice as large. The OScAR was therefore designed to be used by a single observer visiting a classroom by himself.

The third change was the separation of the process of scoring from the process of observing teacher behaviors. The OScAR was designed to permit recording of as many possibly significant aspects of what goes on in a classroom as possible, regardless of their relationship to any dimension or scale. The observer's sole concern was to see and hear as much of what was going on as possible and to record as much of it as he could, without assumptions as to its relative importance or relevance to any known dimension.

The front of the card used in recording behaviors is shown in Fig. 2. Behaviors were recorded on this side during the first, third, and fifth five-minute periods of a half-hour visit timed with a stopwatch. As soon as the observer had recorded the necessary identification data, he started his watch and checked in Column I as many items in the "Activity" section (A1 to F6) as he saw.

The observer then concentrated on the Grouping Section (G1 to G7) and checked each type of administrative group (i.e., group apparently set up by the teacher) and each type of social group he observed, a social group being defined as one in which there is pupil-pupil or pupil-teacher interaction.

Next, in the Materials Section (L1 to R), the observer checked the type of instructional materials being used. All through this initial period, the observer kept alert for any type of activity, grouping, or material not already checked and indicated the appropriate term for each one as it occurred. No item on this side of the card was checked more than once during one five-minute period, however. Items in the Signs Section (S2 to S11) were marked with a plus sign if and when they were observed. At the end of five minutes the observer briefly considered each item in this section not already marked, and marked it either plus or zero.

As soon as he had done this, the observer stopped his watch and turned the card over (see Fig. 3). In the Subject Section (T1 to T10) he checked in Column I whichever of the 10 areas of instructional activity listed there had received most attention during the five minutes just ended.

The observer then started his stopwatch again and began to attend to each statement the teacher made in one of five categories— Pupil-Supportive (K2), Problem-Structuring (K3), Miscellaneous (K4), Directive (K5), Reproving (K6)—and to make a tally in

Column II of the Expressive Behavior Section in the line corresponding to the category in which each statement was classified.

At the same time, he watched for changes of expression on the teacher's face, such as smiles, frowns, and scowls, and for expressive gestures such as nods, threatening glances, and body movements. Each time he observed a look or gesture which he judged to express approval of or affection for a pupil, the observer made a tally in Column II after Item K1; each time he observed a look or gesture which he judged to be hostile or reproving he made a tally after K7. Each time a teacher asserted authority he made a tally after K8.

This continued for a second period of five minutes. At the end, the observer stopped his watch again and filled out Column II in the Subject Section just as he had filled out Column I at the end of the first five-minute period. He then turned the card over, started his stopwatch again, and proceeded as in the first period for five minutes more, except that he used Column III rather than Column I. This alternation of sides of the card was continued for six five-minute periods.

The observations which form the primary data of this study were made with OScAR in the classrooms of 49 beginning teachers in public elementary schools in New York City over a period of approximately ten weeks. Of the 49 teachers, 46 were women. The teachers were scattered among 19 schools in four boroughs, the number of teachers in a single school ranging from two to five. Twenty-three of the teachers taught Grade 3; thirteen, Grade 4; nine, Grade 5; and four, Grade 6.

Observers worked in pairs, two observers visiting a school together. In most cases, all of the observed teachers in a school were seen by both observers on the same day, although in no case did two observers visit the same teacher at the same time. No attempt was made to control the type of activity observed; all that was asked was that the teacher and the class be present in the classroom.

After a number of minor shortcomings in the original OScAR were noticed, it was revised to the form described in this report.

The new form was adopted at the beginning of the second round of visits.

The analysis of the data followed four steps. First, the items were combined into 20 "keys," which were scored. Next, a study was made of each key to find out whether there were reliable differences in the mean scores in different classrooms; six keys were discarded as unreliable. Third, a factor analysis of scores on the 14 remaining keys was made. Finally, the keys were combined into three dimensions corresponding to the first three factors (after rotation). Each of these steps is described in the following paragraphs.

Except in the case of a few items that were highly reliable by themselves, each key consisted of a number of items combined on the basis of an a priori judgment that they belonged together. For example, the following three items from the Activity Section:

E1. pupil talks to a group

E5. pupil demonstrates or illustrates

E10. pupil leads the class

were combined into a single key called "Pupil Leadership Activities." The reliability of each key was estimated from a three-way analysis of variance under mixed-model assumptions, teachers and visits being regarded as random effects and items as a fixed effect.

Mixed-model assumptions are used in an analysis of variance when some effects may be regarded as "random" and others as "fixed." A fixed effect is one conceived so that all possible levels are included in the analysis; a random effect is one not so conceived. In this instance, "teachers" and "visits" were regarded as random because the study might just as well have been conducted with other teachers, and the visits could have been made at other times. Since no items other than those on a given key could have been used without changing the nature of the key, "items" was regarded as a fixed effect.

The coefficient of reliability obtained from this analysis estimates the correlation between the mean of all the scores assigned to the teachers by the six observers on the basis of the 12 visits made, and means of scores that would be assigned to the same teachers

by six different observers visiting their classrooms at 12 other times.

Reliabilities of the 14 keys ranged from .605 to .916. The intercorrelations among keys suggested that the differences might be described in terms of fewer than 14 variables, so a centroid factor analysis was made and three factors extracted. The centroid factor matrix was rotated orthogonally twice according to the procedure proposed by Reyburn and Taylor (Thomson, 1951, pp. 146–150). Three "scales" were constructed by combining the keys with largest loadings on each factor. Table 11 shows their reliabilities and the intercorrelations among them.

TABLE 11

INTERCORRELATIONS AMONG THREE FACTOR SCALES BASED ON OScARs OF 49 BEGINNING TEACHERS (RELIABILITIES IN THE DIAGONAL)[a]

Scale	EC	VE	SS
Emotional Climate	(.903)	−.004	−.110
Verbal Emphasis		(.770)	+.028
Social Structure			(.826)

[a] From Medley and Mitzel (1958b, p. 90).

The factors named by Medley and Mitzel were as follows:

Emotional Climate refers to the amount of hostility observable in a classroom; a high score indicates a room in which external manifestations of warmth and friendliness are common and hostile reactions rare. Typical items weighted plus are:

Teacher calls pupil "dear," etc.
Teacher demonstrates affection for pupil
Pupil demonstrates affection for teacher
Teacher makes pupil-supportive statement or gesture

Typical items weighted negatively are:

Teacher uses sarcasm
Teacher makes reproving remark
Teacher frowns, glares, etc.
Pupil ignores teacher's questions
Pupil scuffles or fights
Pupil whispers

Verbal Emphasis indicates the degree to which verbal activities predominate. Typical items include:

Pupil reads or studies at his seat

Pupil writes or manipulates object at his seat

Pupil (or teacher) uses textbook or workbook

Pupil (or teacher) uses supplementary reading matter

Pupil (or teacher) uses writing materials

In addition, such a class was observed to be having a reading lesson relatively often and a social studies lesson relatively infrequently.

Social Organization has to do with the amount of social grouping and pupil autonomy in a class. A class scoring high was one in which it was relatively common to find the class broken up into two or more groups working independently, and in which the teacher talked relatively little (Adapted from Medley & Mitzel, 1959, p. 241).

Data have already been presented showing the relationships of these three dimensions to certain criteria of effectiveness (Table 6, page 269). An attempt to relate some of the preliminary keys to "predictor" data collected while the teachers were still college students was unsuccessful (Rabinowitz & Rosenbaum, 1958). The three dimensions seem to account for some of the differences in teachers with respect to rapport with pupils and to principals' judgments, but not for differences in ability to help pupils learn.

The results of a study of student teacher behavior in high school classes (V. B. Morrison, 1961) confirm some of these conclusions. Morrison was interested in finding out what kind of classroom behavior of teachers and pupils would be rewarded if a system of merit rating were adopted. She made three 15-minute visits to each of 71 student teachers in a laboratory school and recorded what she observed on a slightly modified OScAR. She also obtained ratings of the 71 student teachers from their supervisors on a scale devised by Baxter (1941) and from their pupils on an instrument developed locally. A matrix of 74 OScAR items and the two ratings was subjected to a principal component factor analysis followed by a varimax rotation to approximate simple structure. Twenty-two factors were extracted, and their loadings were studied to ascertain which factors were correlated with the ratings. Table 12 summarizes the relationships between the 22 behavior variables defined by the factor analysis and the two ratings. Again it is clear that emotional climate is an important factor in supervisors' ratings of teacher competence, along with other variables which also seem to be related to pupil-teacher rapport. The pupils' rating scale used here is very nearly the equivalent of the pupil reaction inventory used by Medley and Mitzel (Medley & Klein, 1957), and the results achieved with both are very similar.

A slightly different form of OScAR was used in a study in which 36 student teachers from the University of Minnesota were visited 10 times each by five observers (Wilk, et al., 1960). Each observer saw each teacher once in each of two different classes, once in a lower grade (1–3), and once in a higher grade (4–6), to which the student teacher was assigned. The data were analyzed not in terms of the dimensions described above but rather in terms of subjects taught, materials used, pupil responses, and the following types of activity: teacher-class, teacher-group, teacher-individual, and pupil-class.

Information is not yet available regarding the reliabilities of these measures, but a number of statistically significant findings are reported, indicating that they were reliable. The results indicated that these student teachers taught their classes in traditional ways, with little grouping, and with considerable emphasis on verbal materials and pupil recitation. A teacher tended to use a greater variety of materials, to talk to the pupils more, and to ask more questions when teaching an upper grade (4–6) than she did when she was teaching a lower grade (1–3). The amount of disruptive pupil behavior was negatively correlated with the amount and variety of classroom activities, but did not differ in the different grade levels.

Bowers and Soar (1961) used the OScAR 2a (shown in Figs. 2 and 3) in a study com-

TABLE 12

RELATIONSHIP OF 22 BEHAVIOR VARIABLES DERIVED BY FACTOR ANALYSIS
OF OScAR SCORES OF 71 STUDENT TEACHERS TO RATINGS BY
SUPERVISORS AND PUPILS[a]

Description of Behavior Variable	Ratings Correlated with Variable	Per Cent of Total Variance in Variable
Emotional climate of the classroom	Supervisory-pupil	13.06
Freedom of movement	Supervisory-pupil	8.40
Creative activity	Pupil	7.02
Classroom mobility	None	5.14
Use of audio-visual materials	Pupil	4.72
Pupil disruptive behavior	None	4.54
Pupil oral group participation	Supervisory	4.53
Academic activities	None	4.17
Assistance	None	4.10
Textbook method	None	3.84
Recitation method	None	3.77
Teacher positive control	Supervisory	3.70
Teacher-centered vs. pupil-centered behavior	Supervisory[b]	3.58
Affective rapport	None	3.50
Teacher restriction	None	3.47
Demonstration method	None	3.47
Free activities	None	3.34
Individual attention to pupils	Pupil[b]	3.00
Active vs. inactive contribution	Supervisory	2.85
Teacher uses explanations, facts, information, and miscellaneous statements	None	2.83
Teacher and pupils use audio aid	None	2.79
Teacher hostility vs. pupil hostility	Pupil[b]	2.71

[a] Adapted from V. B. Morrison (1961).
[b] Negative correlation.

paring teachers who had laboratory experiences in human relations with teachers who did not have them. Classes taught by 54 teachers in an unspecified number of Tennessee elementary schools were visited in the spring of 1959 and their behaviors were recorded. A number of personality tests were also administered to each teacher. During the summer of 1959, 25 of the teachers attended summer workshops in human relations; the remaining 29 received no training. During the spring of 1960, the classes then taught by the teachers were visited and behaviors were recorded with the OScAR. It appears (Bowers & Soar, 1961, pp. 184–186) that five visits were made to each class each spring. Each teacher's records were scored on the three dimensions described above.

A summary of all of the results of this study is beyond the scope of this chapter, but we will mention some typical findings as indicating results which can be obtained when objective measurements of classroom behaviors are obtained and related to other data.

One group of findings related personality and attitude test scores to classroom behaviors, all measured during the spring of 1959 (before the workshops were held). Emotional Climate showed a low positive correlation (.29) with scores on the Minnesota Teacher Attitude Inventory (MTAI) (Cook, Leeds, & Callis, 1951). Verbal Emphasis correlated .33 with the Psychopathic Deviate (*Pd*) and .26 with the Schizophrenia (*Sc*) scales of the Minnesota Multiphasic Personality Inventory (MMPI) (Hathaway & McKinley, 1951), and showed significant curvilinear relationships (*etas* of .49 and .41, respectively) with the Psychasthenia (*Pt*) and Hypomania (*Ma*) scales of the same inventory. Social Organization correlated — .51 with the *Pd* scale and — .36 with the *Sc* scale, and had an *eta* of .56 with the *Pt* scale.

The correlation between Emotional Climate and MTAI scores is consistent with the results presented above in Table 6, and the evidence that the MTAI correlates with pupil-teacher rapport presented in the test manual (Cook, Leeds, & Callis, 1951). The results with Verbal Emphasis were interpreted by Bowers and Soar as follows:

Teachers at either extreme on Pt tend to encourage more pupil interaction in their classrooms. Although generally the higher the score on Ma the higher the Verbal Emphasis score, teachers having the very highest Ma scores tend to rely less on Verbal Emphasis. . . . Teachers who might be characterized as impulsive and irresponsible, or withdrawn and lacking in self-confidence tended to rely on written Verbal Methods. . . . Teachers who were just above the mean [on Pt] had the fewest subgroups in their classes. . . . Relatively few subgroups were found in classrooms of teachers characterized either as immature, irresponsible, and asocial (Pd), or insecure and lacking in self-confidence (Sc) (Bowers & Soar, 1961, pp. 72–73).

A comparison of teachers in the experimental and control groups with respect to over-all changes in scores on the three behavior dimensions did not detect any difference between them. But further analysis by the Johnson-Neyman technique (Johnson & Fay, 1950) revealed that the summer workshop experience did have an effect on teacher behavior, but that the nature of the effect was a function of teacher personality as measured by certain MMPI scores.

Figure 4 illustrates how this technique was applied, relating change in teacher behavior along the dimension of Verbal Emphasis to scores on the *Sc* scale of the MMPI. The diagram shows the values of *F* which would be obtained for tests of the hypothesis of equality of mean 1960 (post) Verbal Emphasis scores of experimental and control groups chosen so that the *Sc* and 1959 (pre) Verbal Emphasis scores of all their members were equal to various values in the range of each variable. For instance, if all 54 teachers had had *Sc* scores of 65 and Verbal Emphasis scores of 39 in 1960, the study would have yielded an $F = 4.911$, and the hypothesis that the true difference between the mean Verbal Emphasis scores of the two groups was zero would have been rejected at the .05 level. The line across the chart passes through those values of the 1959 measures for which training would have had no observable effect. Teachers with scores to the left of this line would show higher scores on Verbal Emphasis after training if they had attended the summer workshop, and lower scores if they had not. Groups with scores to the right of the line would show increased Verbal Emphasis if they had *not* had the course, decreased Verbal Emphasis if they had. The curved lines mark off regions in which the differences would be significant at the .05 level.

These results are interpreted as indicating (at the .05 level) that if a teacher's behavior before training earns a low Verbal Emphasis score (below 40) and if her personality is such that she gets a high *Sc* score (above 59), the workshop experience will increase the Verbal Emphasis in her classroom behavior. If a teacher starts out above average on Verbal Emphasis and below about 53 on the *Sc* scale, the workshop experience will decrease the Verbal Emphasis in her classroom. If the purpose of the workshop is to decrease the Verbal Emphasis in teacher behavior, only a teacher above average at the start is likely to profit from it—and then only if her *Sc* score is average or lower.

Similar analyses of the relationships between Verbal Emphasis and other variables, and of the relationship of Social Organization to various measures, yielded similar results. If these findings can be replicated, they may represent a real breakthrough; their

F ratios[a]

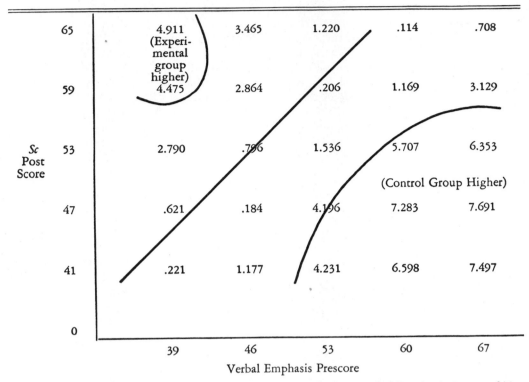

Fig. 4. Results of Johnson-Neyman Test of Significance of Mean Verbal Emphasis Scores of Two Groups of Teachers after One Group Received Human Relations Training, Adjusted to Remove Differences in MMPI Sc Scores and Verbal Emphasis before Training (adapted from Bowers & Soar, 1961).
[a] $F_{.05} = 4.055$; $F_{.01} = 7.225$.

achievement here results from an unusually happy marriage of objective behavior data with the appropriate, powerful statistical technique.

A principal defect in OScAR is its failure to get at any aspect of classroom behavior related to pupil achievement of cognitive objectives. The three dimensions that it measures represent what are probably the most obvious differences among classes—how orderly and relaxed they are, in what ways the pupils are grouped, and the general content of the lessons being taught. To measure these reliably was relatively easy; to measure more subtle and crucial differences which OScAR misses will probably be more difficult. There is no reason to think it impossible, however.

It is possible that important first steps toward the construction of such items have been taken already in two recent studies. The first is a study of logic in classroom discourse reported by Smith (1959). A total of 85 class sessions taught by 17 Illinois high school teachers in five different communities were recorded on magnetic tape. The 17 classes were distributed fairly evenly between the ninth and the twelfth grades, and among four subjects, English, mathematics, science, and social studies. After a class had been chosen and the teacher had agreed to participate, five consecutive class sessions were recorded. Transcripts were carefully prepared, supplemented by a running commentary of notes made by a staff member who was in the classroom at the time the recording was made.

The transcripts were analyzed in terms of two basic units: (1) the *episode,* a verbal exchange between two or more speakers, and (2) the *monologue,* an individualized contribution to class business, or solo performance. Three steps were identified in each episode—an opening phase or entry, a continuing phase, and a closing phase. The bulk of the report deals with the classification of entries or opening phases of episodes. The categories developed for this purpose are presented in Table 13.

TABLE 13

SET OF CATEGORIES FOR CLASSIFYING
ENTRIES (OPENING PHASES OF EPISODES)
FROM TYPESCRIPTS MADE OF SOUND
RECORDINGS IN HIGH SCHOOL CLASSES[a]

1. *Defining.* Entries making up this group are concerned with how words or other symbols are used to refer to objects (abstract or concrete). These entries vary in form and content, but in general they ask, implicitly or explicitly, for the meaning of terms.

2. *Describing.* To describe is to represent something by words or drawing, to tell about something. Thus the entries making up this category mention or suggest something and require that an account of this something be given.

3. *Designating.* To designate is to identify something by name—word or other symbol. The name designates the object (abstract or concrete) to which it refers. Thus this group of entries is made up of items in which something is described or otherwise indicated, and the name used to refer to it or to identify it is asked for.

4. *Stating.* Entries in this group do not ask for names, descriptions, etc., but for things to be stated. They may ask for statements of issues, steps in proofs, rules, obligations, theorems, conclusions, ideas, beliefs, promises, threats, etc.

5. *Reporting.* The entries in this group ask for a report on what a book or document says, for information in the text, or for a summary or review, and the like.

6. *Substituting.* The entries making up this category ask the student to perform a symbolic operation, usually of a mathematical nature.

TABLE 13 (Cont'd.)

SET OF CATEGORIES FOR CLASSIFYING
ENTRIES (OPENING PHASES OF EPISODES)
FROM TYPESCRIPTS MADE OF SOUND
RECORDINGS IN HIGH SCHOOL CLASSES[a]

7. *Valuating.* To engage in valuating is to estimate the worth, dependability, etc., of something. An entry of this type requires that some object, expression, event, action, or state of affairs be rated as to its value, dependability, desirability, and the like.

8. *Opining.* To opine is to express beliefs, usually based on little or no evidence. Such beliefs are about what is possible, what might have been and is not, what might obtain in the future, or the like.

9. *Classifying.* Each entry in this group makes explicit reference to an instance or class (type, sort, group, set, kind) of things or both. The entry requires that a given instance be put in the class to which it belongs, as a subclass.

10. *Comparing and Contrasting.* This type of entry requires that two or more things—actions, factors, objects, processes, etc.—be compared. In some cases, the entry specifies two or more things, and asks that either their similarities or differences be noted with respect to a particular characteristic.

11. *Conditional Inferring.* This category consists of entries, each of which contains an antecedent and a consequent, but never a consequent alone. In all cases where the antecedent alone is given, the entry requires that the consequent—*effect, result, outcome, subsequent behavior*—be supplied as the answer. Some of the entries containing both an antecedent and a consequent ask for value judgments, some ask for statements of result or outcome, and others for descriptions of actions, decisions, and the like.

12. *Explaining.* There are several types of explanation entries, but they all have one thing in common. They give a particular consequent and they require that an antecedent be supplied. There are six kinds of explanation entries, depending upon the sort of antecedent used to account for the consequent. They are mechanical, causal, sequent, procedural, teleological, and normative.

13. *Directing and Managing Classroom.* Many questions asked by teachers have little or no logical significance. They are designed, not to evoke thought, but to keep the classroom activities moving along.

[a] Adapted from Smith (1959, pp. 5:10–5:18).

In their first run through the 85 transcripts, the authors found 3,397 entries. The most numerous categories were Describing (25 per cent), Designating (almost 15 per cent), Explaining (almost 13 per cent), and Classroom Management (9 per cent). Reliability estimates for the classificatory scheme were based upon the percentage of agreements between two pairs of judges, each pair working as a team. The median percentage of agreement was reported by the experimenters to be 67 per cent.

This development—analysis of logical aspects of discourse between students and teachers in high school classes—seems altogether promising. When important between-classroom differences in entries, episodes, etc., are identified, it should be possible to train observers to classify them in the classroom. The differences can then be correlated with other variables, and perhaps used to provide the basis for the development of a theory of classroom instruction.

A second recent attempt to identify behaviors related to pupil achievement has been made by Muriel Wright (1959). After studying the interaction of teachers and pupils in 12 high school algebra classes in metropolitan St. Louis, she classified the content of their verbal exchanges on three dimensions as follows:

A. Ability to think.

B. Appreciation of mathematics.

C. Curiosity and initiative.

Any kind of verbal exchange between teacher and pupils (or pupil and pupil) which did not belong in one of these categories was classified as Neutral.

Wright's system was refined and modified in collaboration with Virginia Proctor (Wright & Proctor, 1961), and the scheme for classifying verbal behaviors in mathematics classes shown in Table 14 was devised by the two of them.

A unique time-sampling arrangement was used in this study. The 45-minute observation period for each class was divided into 15-second intervals identified by means of a stopwatch in the hands of the observer. Ver-

TABLE 14

CATEGORIES USED BY WRIGHT AND PROCTOR IN CLASSIFYING VERBAL BEHAVIORS IN MATHEMATICS CLASSES[a]

A. CONTENT FRAME

Fundamentals: The body of mathematical knowledge at the command of the pupils

1. Structure
   1.1 Fundamental elements, operations, postulates
   1.2 Well-established theory when understanding is apparent
   1.3 Logical principles
   1.4 Strategies of problem-solving
2. Techniques
   2.1 Description and use of mechanical processes or rules where basic mathematical relation is not made apparent
   2.2 Reading of mathematical materials already developed

Relations: The development and statement of "new" relations

3. Deductive
   3.1 Logical proof of new theory
4. Inductive
   4.1 Use of specific examples selected to elicit new generalization or relation
   4.2 Use of graphs, diagrams to make a relation clear
   4.3 Intuitive approach to a relation
5. Statement
   5.1 Statements of new relations
   5.2 Definitions, notation, terminology; mathematical conventions

Applications: The use, place of the mathematical system in specific problems and in historical context

6. Mathematical
   6.1 Solution of mathematical problems
7. Other
   7.1 Brief statement of problem in other field before abstraction essentials
   7.2 Examination of problems in terms of the concepts of the other field
   7.3 References from mathematical history
   7.4 Reference to new topics or different treatment to be met in later courses
   7.5 Humor—when pertinent to mathematical activities

B. PROCESS FRAME

Syllogistic: The syllogistic categories of analyzing and synthesizing require the logical operation of inference. Although synthesizing is often mechanical, it may also be the method of highly creative divergent thinking.

1. Analyzing—from assumption of desired conclusion toward accepted principles

TABLE 14 (Cont'd.)

CATEGORIES USED BY WRIGHT AND PROCTOR IN CLASSIFYING VERBAL BEHAVIORS IN MATHEMATICS CLASSES[a]

1.1 Chain of backward implication—"is implied by"

1.2 Less systematic moving backward from goal, seeking connection with known premises to establish approach to proof

1.3 Justification of a statement

1.4 Moving backward over an argument to discover mistake or clarify meaning

2. Synthesizing—from accepted principles toward desired conclusion

  2.1 Chain of forward implication—"implies"

  2.2 Consolidation of parts into a complete solution

  Classificatory: The classificatory categories of generalizing and specializing include the formulation of generalizations, and the less formal but very necessary heuristic process of problem dissection and focusing on goal.

3. Specializing—the use of significant attributes of a given set in an analogous set, or the application of a given set in a smaller included set

  3.1 Selection of significant parts of a problem—dissection, abstraction

  3.2 Application of a generalization

  3.3 Recognition of relation of corresponding sets

  3.4 Focusing on goal

4. Generalizing—the recognition of significant attributes of a given set and the passing from the consideration of the given set to that of a larger inclusive set

  4.1 Recognizing significant attributes and passing to a larger set

  4.2 Statement of a formula, law, relation, definition to be proved or arising from development or to be examined for meaning

  Relevant: A more static category, the statement of relevant information occurs when mathematical information is presented but belongs to no apparent logical sequence.

5. Relevant

  5.1 Information about specific mathematics

  5.2 Information about more general aspects of mathematics

C. ATTITUDE FRAME

  Teacher or Pupil: The teacher demonstrates or encourages pupil behaviors in each category; the pupils demonstrate the behaviors in each category.

TABLE 14 (Cont'd.)

CATEGORIES USED BY WRIGHT AND PROCTOR IN CLASSIFYING VERBAL BEHAVIORS IN MATHEMATICS CLASSES[a]

1. Curiosity—fresh unusual material; a new direction

  1.1 Teacher statements relating present topic to other areas of mathematics or to other fields, or to more fundamental mathematical concepts or to historical context

  1.2 Teacher encouragement of unusual problem or new direction including positive support of pupil expression of unusual interest

  1.3 Pupils make statements as in 1.1

  1.4 Pupils ask questions about 1.1

2. Independence

  2.1 Teacher open questions or suggestions demanding pupil thinking beyond one carefully structured step

  2.2 Turning of pupil-raised question back to same pupil or to the class

  2.3 Assignment of pupil topics for class demonstration including regular homework questions developed on blackboard by pupil

  2.4 Pupil statements moving problem solution forward more than one step during the interval

  2.5 Responsibility for development taken by pupil sometimes indicated by several steps forward or merely by one powerful step forward in a single interval

  2.6 Pupil initiates discussion by asking a question and noting specific aspects he has considered

3. Receptivity

  3.1 Teacher tells, states, solves problems

  3.2 Teacher asks rhetorical questions or questions limited to one-step often trivial or merely yes–no answers

  3.3 Teacher is responsive to signals that pupils understand, follow the discussion, are interested in the presentation

  3.4 Pupils respond appropriately when called on, but answer is limited to one relatively small step

  3.5 Pupils ask questions without indicating readiness to treat it themselves with teacher's assistance

[a] Adapted from Wright & Proctor, 1961.

bal interactions were observed for 15 seconds running, and then classified during the next

15 seconds, during which interactions were not observed. The third 15 seconds were observed, the fourth used for classifying, etc. Thus, each 45-minute class session yielded two tallies per minute for a total of 90 classifications per session.

Each non-Neutral 15-second period was classified with respect to Control, Process, and Attitude; the "scores" analyzed were counts and proportions in each category, and also of the cross-classifications (Control 1, Process 1, Attitude 1; Control 1, Process 2, Attitude 1; etc.) These latter were called "Triple-Frame Scores." Certain meaningful combinations of categories were also studied; for example, one called "Control-Theory"—structure + deduction + induction + statement. An "Index of Initiative" based on a weighted composite of Curiosity, Independence, Receptivity, and Neutral behaviors was also used.

Observer agreement and stability of class behavior were studied by calculating chi-square values, per cents of agreements, and binomial standard errors. Although the results are not interpretable in terms of reliability coefficients, it appears that observer agreement, though lower than that found with some of the simpler observational techniques reviewed in this chapter, is adequate; and that, when based on observation covering ten class periods, reliability is probably satisfactory as well.

The principal study reported (Wright & Proctor, 1961) involved observation of 12 classes in a 2 × 2 design using degree of mathematical rigor and amount of pupil participation as the two independent variables. The various scores were found highly useful in discriminating the various groups and clarifying differences in the different styles of teaching.

The only problem that emerges clearly from a study of Wright and Proctor's work is the high level of training both in mathematics and in behavior observation required of the observer. Perhaps, as more is learned about the relative importance of the various categories, simpler definitions will be possible, and the discriminations required of the observers will become easier to learn.

Whether or not this ever comes to be, the potential value of this approach to the development of a theory of classroom learning is very great. It is to be hoped that out of the work of B. O. Smith a similar instrument will someday be developed; and that both will be used in new attacks on the old problem of identifying effective teacher behavior.

Systematic Observation in Classroom Experimentation

The remaining observational studies to be examined were all conducted in connection with experimentation in the classroom, with measured behavior functioning as a variable in the study. In some cases, outcomes of treatments were ascertained by observation; in others, measurements of behavior were regarded as independent variables and their relationships to effects on pupils were the object of study.

In a study designed to compare pupil achievement in schools using an "activity" program with schools not using such a program, Jersild and others (1939) compared certain items of pupil behavior in the two kinds of schools. Eight "activity" schools were studied along with eight "control" schools, each chosen to resemble one of the activity schools as closely as possible. It was planned that four classes in each school would be used, although, as opportunity afforded, observations were made (and other data were collected) in additional classes as well. The purpose of the observations was stated as "measuring the broader and less tangible outcomes of an educational enterprise" (Jersild, et al., 1939, p. 166).

Table 15 shows the categories used in coding pupil behaviors. The observer using the categories "endeavored to record, by means of the appropriate coded symbol, each occurrence of any of the activities falling within the scope of any of the categories defined . . ." (Jersild, et al., 1939, p. 169).

It might be argued from the nature of

TABLE 15

CATEGORIES OF BEHAVIOR CODED IN
AN EVALUATION OF THE ACTIVITY
PROGRAM IN NEW YORK CITY[a]

A. *Cooperative Activities*
1. Helping other pupils or teacher with their problems or projects.
2. Offering objects (book, chair, pencil, tool, etc.) to teacher, pupil, or visitor.
3. Responding quickly to requests for quiet, materials, etc.

B. *Critical Activities*
1. Criticizing (praising or challenging) work of others by bringing out good points, suggesting improvements.
2. By defending points of view.
3. By asking pertinent questions of teacher or other pupils.

C. *Experimental Activities*
1. Trying out new things, putting things into new combinations, as in manual, mechanical, or fine arts, or in social studies, natural sciences, mathematics, etc.
2. Creating or constructing an original poem, art form, or subject, a melody, story, chart, diagram, replica, miniature building, instrument, etc.

D. *Leadership Activities*
1. Organizing, directing, or controlling new combinations of persons and things (e.g., setting up plan of procedure, acting as group chairman, etc.).

E. *Recitational Activities*
1. Responding on request, largely from memory, to direct questioning on assigned textbook or subject matter.
2. Voluntarily responding, largely from memory, to direct questioning on assigned textbook or subject matter.

F. *Self-Initiated Activities*
1. Bringing voluntary contributions (clippings, exhibits, books, charts, etc.) for school activities.
2. Submitting voluntarily and orally data or information gained outside of school (observations, trips to buildings, factories, etc.).
3. Presenting a report on a self-directed investigation.
4. Suggesting methods, materials, activities, etc., for developing a project.

G. *Work-Spirit Activities (Negative Activities)*
1. Completing work sooner than others and not using time wisely.
2. Depending upon unnecessary help while working.
3. Not concentrating deeply upon work which requires close attention.

TABLE 15 (Cont'd.)

CATEGORIES OF BEHAVIOR CODED IN
AN EVALUATION OF THE ACTIVITY
PROGRAM IN NEW YORK CITY[a]

4. Not working as efficiently when the teacher leaves the room or is not nearby.
5. Carrying on conversation with neighbors when attention should be given elsewhere.
6. Touching or borrowing property of other children without their permission.
7. Letting materials or paper remain on the floor.
8. Written work not neatly arranged, not legible or free from blots and eraser marks.

[a] Adapted from Jersild, et al. (1939).

these categories that it would be more appropriate (1) to view the results of the observations as indicating whether or not activity schools differed from control schools in respect to the curricular practices supposed to differentiate them, than (2) to use them for the purpose stated by the authors: to measure "the broader and less tangible outcomes of an educational enterprise." Outcomes of an enterprise should be measured after the enterprise is over, not while it is still in process.

Observer agreement was studied by an analysis of a series of 64 half-hour visits to 32 activity classes and 32 control classes made by pairs of observers making independent records of the same half-hour of behavior. To study the stability of the records, records of the first five half-hours and the second five half-hours spent in 51 classrooms were correlated, and the result adjusted by the Spearman-Brown formula to estimate the stability of the total record based on ten visits.

Results are summarized in Table 16. The second column of this table shows the number of behaviors observed in each main category. The number recorded in each period by whichever of the two observers recorded the larger number was used as the estimate of the number of behaviors which occurred. The total of these numbers for all periods was used as an estimate of the total number of behaviors in each category. The third column indicates the number of behaviors

TABLE 16

RELIABILITY DATA ON OBSERVATIONS USED IN AN EVALUATION
OF THE ACTIVITY PROGRAM IN NEW YORK CITY[a]

Activity Category	Number of Behaviors Recorded	Number of Behaviors Recorded by Both Observers	Per Cent Agreement	Reliability Coefficients
Cooperative	429	301	70	.88
Critical	502	351	70	.82
Experimental	579	506	87	.44
Leadership	25	19	76	.90
Recitational	1196	991	83	.68
Self-Initiated	372	287	77	.60
Work-Spirit	47	20	43	.94

[a] Adapted from Jersild, et al. (1939).

recorded by both observers as having occurred at the same time and having been performed by the same pupil. The per cent
which the latter is of the former is taken as
the "per cent of agreement" between observers categorizing the same behavior.

The fifth column shows the estimated
stability of each score, that is, the correlation
between the total number of tallies in a category during 10 half-hour visits and total
number in the same category during 10
more half-hour visits made by the same observer.

There are three highly reliable categories:
Cooperative, Leadership, and Work-Spirit.
Two of these kinds of behavior were rarely
observed. This contradicts a widely held
notion that a behavior must be commonly
or frequently seen if it is to be made the basis
for an observational item. Of the three least
reliable categories, Experimental, Self-Initiated, and Recitational, two are the most
frequently recorded categories of all. Behaviors which the observer has many opportunities to observe are not necessarily measured
more reliably than behaviors which occur
rarely.

It is noteworthy that the category observed
most accurately—Experimental (observer
agreement = 87 per cent)—actually has the
lowest stability ($r = .44$). The most stable
score, Work-Spirit, is the least consistently
observed, with only 43 per cent agreement

between observers. Again it is evident that
reliability of observations depends much
more on consistency of teachers' and pupils'
behaviors from day to day than on accuracy
of observer agreement or frequency of occurrence.

Note that the less frequent activities tend
to have lower observer agreement than those
most often observed. Leadership is an exception to this trend. Such an occurrence as
a pupil's taking charge of or organizing a
group is so conspicuous that, although seldom seen, it is hard to miss when it does occur. But Work-Spirit Activities, apparently
more elusive and transitory, are both infrequent and difficult to recognize when they do
occur.

The type of observer agreement data reported seems irrelevant in any case to the
purpose for which the observations were
made. The scores actually used were simple
totals of the numbers of behaviors in a category without regard to which pupil exhibited
the behavior. So far as these scores are concerned, it made no difference to which pupil
individual behaviors were attributed. Information about how well observers agreed on
who did something is beside the point. The
only important consideration is that the total
number of behaviors marked in a category
by two observers be the same.

A classic example of a study in which
measurements of classroom behavior were

used to measure outcomes of instruction was reported by Urban (1943). A preliminary study of pupils in high school biology classes was made to determine what bad health habits were observable which might be changed by a unit of instruction in communicable diseases. A unit was planned, two forms of an appropriate achievement test were constructed, an interview schedule was prepared, and a list of behaviors to be observed was compiled. Four classes were observed, interviewed, and tested before the unit was begun; two studied the unit in communicable diseases and two studied an unrelated unit. All four classes were tested, interviewed, and observed at the close of the unit. Observations and interviews were also repeated 12 weeks later to check retention. Changes in tests, interviews, and observed behaviors were all studied to assess the effects of the unit. Pupils were observed for three minutes at the beginning of the class period, four minutes during the middle, and three at the end, both in biology and in English. Seven categories were used, and when a behavior fitting into one of them was observed, the category number was written in the appropriate space on a seating plan. The categories were:

1. Puts finger in mouth, gnaws knuckles, puts side of hand in mouth.
2. Puts other objects in mouth.
3. Bites fingernails.
4. Inserts finger in nostril.

5. Rubs eyes with fingers.
6. Coughs without using handkerchief.
7. Sneezes without using handkerchief.

Each pupil's score was the total number of undesirable behaviors he had performed. The correlation between records of two observers observing at the same time was estimated to be .99, and reliabilities estimated by correlations between records made at different times ranged from .86 to .94.

Significant differences in total scores were found in favor of students in the experimental classes; the differences seemed to be retained almost intact for at least 12 weeks.

Somewhat different scores on the last two items were developed. Every time a sneeze or cough was observed, a record was made of whether or not the pupil used a handkerchief. Reliabilities of these scores were not reported, but some typical results obtained with them are shown in Table 17. Notice that the retention scores in this case favored the experimental group more than did the scores obtained immediately after the unit. This was not a consistent pattern, but retention was consistently good. It might also be mentioned that correlations between observed changes in behavior and achievement test scores were low. The pupils who learned the most facts and principles were not the pupils whose health habits improved the most.

Not many behavior changes sought as ob-

TABLE 17

USE OF HANDKERCHIEF WHEN SNEEZING IN ENGLISH CLASSES, EXPERIMENTAL AND CONTROL GROUPS[a]

Group	Number of Pupils Sneezing	Number of Sneezes	Handkerchief not Used	Handkerchief Used	Per Cent Use of Handkerchief
Experimental					
Prestudy	10	14	14	0	0
Poststudy	12	19	10	9	48.4
Retention	13	17	7	10	58.8
Control					
Prestudy	11	16	16	0	0
Poststudy	9	11	10	1	9.1
Retention	9	13	13	0	0

[a] Adapted from Urban (1943).

jectives of the school curriculum are as clear-cut as those of this biology unit. If more objectives were so specifiable, it might be practicable to identify and measure equally observable and apparently relevant behavior items symptomatic of the outcomes of other units. It is true that a pupil needs to learn much more from this unit than to use a handkerchief, keep his fingers out of his mouth, and so on. But, assuming that the pupils and the teacher are unaware that these particular behaviors are being looked for, we can consider the degree of improvement on these specifics to indicate the degree of improvement in other, more important, but less accessible, behaviors. At least, observers should do a better job of measuring behavioral items than scores on conventional paper-and-pencil tests do.

In a methods experiment, observations of the teachers supposed to be using one or another method of instruction can be used advantageously to ascertain whether or not the teachers are playing their assigned role. An example in which this was done is provided by a study conducted at Harvard in an introductory college course in social relations (Wispé, 1951). Eight graduate student instructors who taught sections of the course were first observed while teaching to ascertain which ones were more "directive" and which more "permissive" in their handling of the sections. Then the instructors were divided into groups of the four most directive and the four most permissive. Those in each group were instructed to "sharpen" their natural style for the rest of the term. Students in the sections had been matched on an objective pretest, Scholastic Aptitude Test (SAT) scores, and other variables, and each section contained about 20 students. It appears, although the author does not say so, that about 120 students were studied in all.

Every section meeting (a total of 14) during the semester was observed via a one-way screen by two observers using "an interaction scoring instrument that was the result of an extended period of investigation and four

revisions.... At the conclusion of the study the original observation data were combined so that they would be more compact and more meaningful" (Wispé, 1951, p. 164). Interobserver reliability coefficients were reported to average .91; it is not clear how they were estimated, or on how long a period of observation they were based.

Only those categories which showed differences significant at the .05 level are presented by the authors. They are described as follows, with the scores characterizing directive instructors relative to permissive ones indicated in parentheses after each one.

1. Instructor defines the problem area for discussion. (high)
2. Instructor asks wide-open, reflective-type questions. The subject matter of these questions is usually general, and the target of the question can be either the whole class or one student. The questioner's manner is generally informal. (low)
3. The instructor gives factual information about course-related subjects, or gives administrative orientation about the course. (low)
4. The ratio of the instructor's student-commending behavior to his total commending plus rejecting verbal behavior. (not given)
5. The instructor asks for information, for values, or for the personal experiences of the students. (not given)
6. The amount of general instructor activity, composed of 2, 3, and 4 above. (low)
7. The students ask the instructor for information, for administrative help and/or for personal experiences. (low)
8. The students volunteer information, administrative help, and/or personal experiences. (low)
9. Student humor: students tell humorous stories, laugh, smile, etc. (not given)
10. The amount of general student activity, composed of 7, 8, 9 above. (low)
11. Students give information in response to wide-open or reflective-type questions. (not given)
12. The total amount of student participation disregarding the nature of the

participation. (low) (Adapted from Wispé, 1951)

As the author points out, the significant differences found in these categories provide operational definitions of "directive" and "permissive" teaching as the two styles were formulated in this study and also demonstrate the degree to which the eight instructors were successful in carrying out the roles assigned to them.

As a criterion of achievement in the course, the investigation used the objective portion of a three-hour final examination, whose length in number of items is not reported. Students were divided into two groups: those scoring 601 or above on the SAT, called "good" students; and those scoring 600 or lower, called "poor" students. The mean score on the final examination of the good students was 103, and that of the poor ones was 82. The standard deviation of the total group was about 19 points, which suggests that the test had 160 items or more.

Scores on the final examination were also used as the dependent variable in a multiple regression equation with nine independent variables including a pretest, SAT scores, scores on a number of tests of attitudes and the like, together with two behavior scores: (1) Instructor interaction "composed of the number of informational statements made by the instructor, the number of administrative orientation statements made by the instructor, etc. (High ranks for permissive sections; meaning more instructor 'participation'— not 'guidance.')" (Wispé, 1951, p. 177). (2) Student activity "derived from the number of times students asked for and gave information, administrative help, and personal experience, as well as the number of student jokes, laughter, etc. (High ranks for permissive sections; low ranks for directive ones)" (Wispé, 1951, p. 177).

The beta weights and multiple correlation are shown in Table 18. Apparently, the principal determiners of achievement are aptitude as measured by the SAT, "student participation," and "instructor interactions." The zero-order correlations between the final examination score and the same three variables were, respectively, .48, .07, and .03; the correlation between the final and pretest was .19. The two behavior variables correlated .86 with each other.

It appears, however, that the correlations between the two behavior categories and the final test scores are underestimated because of an error in the use of statistics. Behavior scores which pertain to the instructors are identical for all students in any section, so *within* each section the covariance between behavior scores and test scores must obviously be zero. The only nonzero covariance that can occur must therefore be between sections. Since the sections were carefully

TABLE 18

REGRESSION OF FINAL EXAMINATION SCORES ON CLASSROOM BEHAVIORS AND CERTAIN OTHER VARIABLES OF 120 STUDENTS IN EIGHT SECTIONS OF AN INTRODUCTORY COURSE IN SOCIAL RELATIONS[a]

| | BETA WEIGHTS | | | | | | | |
| | Behaviors | | Tests | | | | | |
Multiple R	Instructor Interactions	Student Participation	Emotions	Attitude toward Instructor	Attitude toward Fellow-Students	Pretest	Attitude toward Sections	SAT
.56	−.45	+.51	−.15	+.20	−.03	+.05	−.19	+.47

[a] Adapted from Wispé (1951).

matched on SAT score, which correlates substantially with the test scores, the between-sections variance of the test scores must be relatively small, and whatever between-sections covariance there is must also be artificially low.

Table 19 shows the "between" and "within" sums of squares and cross-products be-

TABLE 19

BREAKDOWN OF SUMS OF SQUARES AND CROSS-PRODUCTS OF SCORES OF MEMBERS OF SEVERAL GROUPS WHEN SCORES ON ONE VARIABLE (GROUP SCORES) ARE CONSTANT FOR ALL MEMBERS OF THE SAME GROUP AND SCORES ON THE OTHER (TEST SCORES) VARY FOR DIFFERENT MEMBERS OF THE SAME GROUP

Source	Degrees of Freedom	Group Scores	Test Scores	Cross-Products
Between Groups	f_b	a	$b-d$	c
Within Groups	f_w	0	d	0
Total	f_t	a	b	c

tween two sets of scores, one set ("Group" scores) being constant for all members of the same group (or section) and the other ("Test" scores) varying for different members of the same group. Since all scores on the group variable are constant within a group, the sums of squares within all groups must be zero, and so must the sums of cross-products with any other variable whatsoever. This is true because the deviation of any score from the group mean must be zero, so that the sum of squared deviations or sum of squares is also zero and so is the sum of cross-products, since zero times anything is zero. If a and b are the total sums of squares on the two variables and if c is the total sum of products, the total correlation will be r_T where

$$r_T{}^2 = \frac{c^2}{ab}.$$

If the within sum of squares of the test scores is d, then, since the within sums of squares of the group variable and the sum of cross-

products are both zero, the correlation as estimated from between-groups values is r_B where

$$r_B{}^2 = \frac{c^2}{a(b-d)}.$$

Finally, the within-groups correlation is indeterminate since it would equal r_W where

$$r_W{}^2 = \frac{0}{(d)\,(0)}.$$

Since b, d, and $(b-d)$, being sums of squares, must all be positive, b must be greater than $(b-d)$; hence $r_T{}^2$ is always smaller in absolute value than $r_B{}^2$.

In the present instance, the two correlations reported are .03 and .07, calculated by the formula for r_T. Since the behavior scores are group scores, r_B would be the proper formula. The appropriate estimates of correlations must be higher than .03 and .07, but it is impossible to say what they are. Also, each of these correlations would be based on six degrees of freedom, not 118, since the number of independent pairs of scores is only eight.

In view of these facts, it is difficult to say what the reported multiple correlation means. The proper one would relate section *means* to one another, predicting mean achievement of sections from their mean scores in the various variables. With only eight sections available, it would take a multiple R of .912 to be significant at the .05 level, so it is doubtful whether the value obtained would have been statistically significant.

One might also question the use of a product-moment correlation coefficient when the eight sections represent two extremes on the behavior dimensions—directive and permissive.

An analysis of variance and covariance, carried out by Wispé, with SAT scores held constant, failed to find differences in final test scores between directive and permissive sections. The behavior scores measuring the directiveness or permissiveness of each section could, of course, have been incorporated as a second independent variable. An analysis of covariance of the type described in the last section of this chapter could have been used to test the regression of test scores on this measure to see whether the directive-permissive variable was related to achievement. This procedure would utilize all differences among the eight instructors on this dimension, not just the one between the means of the four most directive and the four most permissive ones.

This study has a number of technical faults, the most serious of which have been pointed out above, yet it illustrates the possibilities of interesting findings that arise when observations of behavior are included as variables in a methods study.

Another illustration of how behavioral measures can function in a properly designed experiment is provided by a study (Brown, 1960) purporting to show that classroom climate is positively correlated with pupil achievement in the elementary school. Subjects were 175 boys and 143 girls in 15 third-grade classrooms. The pupils were divided, on the basis of regressions of reading test scores on mental ages, into underachievers, average achievers, and overachievers. Each teacher was observed at least twice; each visit lasted until about 100 statements had been classified by Withall's technique. The Climate Index was computed for each teacher on the basis of all visits.

Pupils were tested in January and in June with the Elementary battery of the Stanford Achievement Test. June scores on four subtests were correlated with teachers' Climate Index scores, January scores on the same subtests being held constant. The results are shown in Table 20.

The error made by Wispé was also made here, with the result that all the partial correlations in Table 20 are undoubtedly too small; some may be considerably underestimated. Each correlation reported is in reality a correlation between 15 teachers' climate scores and the mean achievement of the pupils in their classes. It would take a cor-

TABLE 20

PARTIAL CORRELATIONS BY LEVEL OF ACHIEVEMENT BETWEEN CLIMATE INDICES OF 15 TEACHERS AND JUNE SUBTEST SCORES OF 318 PUPILS WITH JANUARY SUBTEST SCORES HELD CONSTANT[a]

Subtest	Under-achievers	Average Achievers	Over-achievers
Paragraph Meaning	.10	.06	.14
Word Meaning	.17	.01	.17
Arithmetic Reasoning	.32	.19	.31
Arithmetic Computation	.19	.04	.20

[a] Adapted from Brown (1960).

relation of .54 to reach significance at the .05 level. Brown interprets the values of .32 and .31 between arithmetic reasoning and climate as significant, because he is using f_t (from Table 19) instead of f_b as the number of degrees of freedom. The correlations reported would not be significant; but if between-classes correlations had been computed, they would have been larger and might have achieved significance. It is, of course, impossible to tell from the published data what the correct values of r would be.

PLANNING AN OBSERVATIONAL STUDY

The studies described in the preceding section of this chapter represent—at least from a methodological standpoint—the most important yet done. We have attempted to describe each one in sufficient detail to enable the reader to benefit from the experience gained in each investigation. There is at present no well-established, organized theory or methodology for the measurement of classroom behavior. The raw materials for such a theory are, however, present in these studies. As a first step toward the development of such a theory, and in lieu of a summary, we shall offer our view of the major methodological implications of these studies. Despite the fact that these implications are presented in a somewhat dogmatic style, they should be regarded as hypotheses to be investigated further, rather than as established rules.

We have pointed out that there are two phases in the process of measuring classroom behavior: (1) securing a record of a sample of the behaviors to be measured, and (2) quantification of the record. Accordingly, the findings of this chapter will be presented in two phases. First, we shall suggest rules for planning a method of recording classroom behavior; then we shall suggest ways of quantifying such records.

The first problem is that of deciding which behaviors, and which aspects of these behaviors, are to be recorded. The purpose for which a study is undertaken usually determines which behaviors are to be observed by indicating them in greater or less detail. Thus, theory led Withall (1949) to study teacher statements. It also led him to classify them as teacher-, pupil-, or learning-centered. Theory led Flanders (1960) to record interactions and to classify them as reflecting direct or indirect teacher influence.

On the other hand, Jayne (1945) and Morsh (1956) had no clear-cut indication from theory as to the behaviors they should look for in their studies, because theory had little to tell them about the precise nature of effective teacher behavior. As a consequence, both tried out large numbers of items in a "shotgun" approach, hoping to find some that would prove relevant to teacher effectiveness, as reflected in students' learning. Although no doubt guided by hunches or notions that this or that item might function, they used no organized theory which required any particular item to be included or omitted.

Sometimes preliminary informal observations are helpful in identifying promising items for tryout—particularly if teachers high and low on a dimension of interest can be contrasted.

Mechanical recordings can be useful in this process. Transcripts of sound recordings were used by Withall (1949), Hughes (1959), and Smith (1959), in studies already described, in the development of category systems for classifying behaviors. At the time of this writing, a group at Hunter College, in collaboration with the authors, is using kinescope recordings in a similar way. Kinescope recordings are also useful for trying out preliminary forms, for training observers, and for studying reliability. Sound motion picture films could serve the same purposes, but kinescope recordings can record more natural behavior since television cameras are less conspicuous and can be operated without having a cameraman in the classroom.

Howsam (1960) has described in some detail a proposal to "develop kinescopic techniques for recording the actual on-going teaching-learning activities as they occur in classrooms and in other school situations" (p. 10). Such a technique would have distinct advantages in unobtrusiveness, economy, and in making possible the subsequent development and try-out of a variety of methods of analysis of the recordings. Much of what is presented later in this chapter will apply to such kinescopic collection of data with at least as much force as to the collection of data by human recorders using their own eyes and ears.

Two Forms of Items

Two approaches to the construction of items for an observational schedule can readily be distinguished. The first approach is to limit the observation to one segment or aspect of classroom behavior, determine a convenient unit of behavior, and construct a finite set of categories into one and only one of which every unit observed can be classified. The record obtained purports to show, for each period of observation, the total number of units of behavior which occurred and the number classifiable in each category. An approach of this type will be referred to as a *category system*.

The second approach is to list beforehand a number of specific acts or incidents of behavior which may or may not occur during a period of observation. The record will show which of these incidents occurred during a period of observation and, in some cases, how frequently each occurred. An approach of this type will be referred to as a *sign system*.

A category system differs from a sign system primarily in that it is supposed to be exhaustive of behaviors of the type recorded. The Withall (1949) categories are typical. The observer using this system (see page 267) is supposed to record every statement the teacher makes. An example of a sign system would be Morsh's (1956) instrument. An observer using this technique (see Table 3) records only those statements made by the instructor which fall into one of the categories listed. Presumably there will be many statements which will not be recorded at all.

Other techniques using category systems which have been reviewed above include those of Anderson and his colleagues (e.g., Anderson & Brewer, 1946), Flanders (1960), Hughes (1959), Smith (1959), and Wright and Proctor (1961). Other studies using signs include those of Jersild, et al. (1939), Jayne (1945), and Cornell, et al. (1952). Both types of items were used in the OScAR technique (Medley & Mitzel, 1958b).

Category systems have been used more often in studies based on well-developed or elaborated theories purporting to indicate specific behaviors to be looked for and sign systems have been used where theory has not provided much guidance. Studies focused on teacher behaviors related to effectiveness have looked for a wide variety of behaviors. Studies of classroom climate and studies using behavior measurement to strengthen methods experiments have tended to focus more narrowly. The former have typically used signs; the latter, categories.

Observers are likely to feel more comfortable when using a category system than when using signs. Categorizing behaviors along one dimension presents the recorder with a more circumscribed task than watching for signs, since the number of aspects of behavior he must consider is small. As each be-

havior occurs, he makes a decision about it, tallies it, and then forgets it, because by this time another behavior has occurred and another decision must be made, etc. He is kept busy, but not too busy. He has no time to worry about anything but the behavior of the moment.

The recorder looking for signs, on the other hand, must be alert to a much wider range of behaviors, but will record fewer than one who is categorizing. Sometimes there may be a relatively long period during which nothing is recorded at all. It can be disconcerting to see a great many things happening and to record nothing. Observers may become distracted by their uneasiness about whether something has been overlooked or inaccurately observed.

The category system may appear to be naturally superior to the approach using signs —particularly in view of the success achieved with the category approach in measuring classroom climate. This approach is indeed preferable for such a purpose, when there is only one aspect of behavior to be observed. But when several aspects of behavior seem to be of equal importance, or when it is not known which aspects are important and which are not, the sign approach is preferable. The number of different aspects of behavior that can be sampled at one time with this type of item is very large. The observers using OScAR 2a found no difficulty in using about 70 such items at one time. It is doubtful whether a complex function, such as teaching appears to be, can ever be measured by a system for categorizing any one aspect of classroom behavior. In any case, until much more is known about the nature of teaching, it will be impossible to construct such a category system.

Constructing Category Systems

A category system, it will be remembered, provides a set of categories into one and only one of which every behavior of a certain type can be classified. Sets of categories have been described in preceding pages of this chapter for coding teacher statements, teacher-pupil contacts, teacher-student interactions, and social and administrative groupings. Many other aspects of what goes on in a classroom can be coded similarly, so long as classifiable behaviors are relatively common. A system for classifying questions asked by the teacher is more likely to be useful than a system for coding teachers' uses of a filmstrip projector, for the simple reason that there are a lot more data of the first type to work with.

The number of categories into which the behaviors are to be coded should not be too large; few studies have used more than ten. It seems desirable to define the categories so that their average frequencies are roughly equal, but experience has shown that in some instances categories used less than 5 per cent of the time function effectively. There is usually a category with a name such as "Neutral," "Other," or "Unclassified"; the frequency of use of this category should be low. It would probably be preferable to err by having too many categories than too few, since two or more categories can always be thrown together if empirical findings indicate the desirability of doing so.

The unit of behavior to be tallied may be a natural one, such as a statement, contact, or question, or it may be a brief time-unit. When a natural unit is used, each tally represents an *occurrence;* when a time-unit is used, each tally represents a period of time which includes at least one occurrence. The natural unit seems preferable, if only because the results are easier to interpret. A relationship between some variable and the number of reproving statements a teacher makes per hour seems easier to comprehend and use than one between the same variable and the number of five-second periods in which the dominant tone of the teacher's verbal behavior could be described as disapproving. A time-unit should be short, lest the observer begin to respond in terms of a general retrospective impression instead of in terms of behavior that has just occurred, but not so short that the same behavior is likely to be tallied twice because it persists over two time-units.

Categories should be so defined that the discrimination of the observer is as easy and as independent of other judgments as possible. Both of these conditions (particularly the latter) are closely related to the problem of halo, which is discussed on pages 305f. Objectivity is, of course, a function of ease of discrimination, and so is the amount of training the observer needs.

In the search for objectivity and ease of discrimination, some investigators have limited themselves to the most obvious differences among behaviors. Morsh's schedule (Table 3) provides an example. To discriminate among Morsh's four categories, the observer must recognize: first, whether a student or the class is addressed; second, if a student is addressed, whether he is designated before or after the question is asked; third, in some instances only, whether the teacher is asking for questions. Contrast this with Withall's categories on page 267, in which the observer must infer the teacher's intent and discriminate among such intentions as "commending," "conveying to the pupil the feeling that he was understood," "proffering information," etc.

It is clear that Withall's discrimination is much more difficult in the sense that it requires a higher degree of sophistication on the part of the observer and the ability to respond to much subtler cues, than does Morsh's. Yet both systems yield scores that have adequate reliability. Morsh was able to achieve satisfactory reliability using, as observers, airmen without psychological training or experience. Withall's classifying was done by trained psychologists. It was probably almost as easy for them to make the discriminations they had to make as it was for Morsh's observers to make theirs. Difficulty of discrimination is, of course, relative to the skill of the observers.

Objectivity depends not only on the relationship between the difficulty of the judgments required and the psychological sophistication of the observers; it also depends on the degree to which the behavioral basis of the discriminations is spelled out. Just as the intrinsic difficulty of discrimination depends on the *general* background of training and experience of the observers, the degree to which the behavioral basis of an item is explicit depends on the amount of *special* training the observers have had in using the category system. Suppose that teachers' questions are to be classified according to whether they call for the pupil (1) to reproduce previously memorized facts and principles, (2) to apply previously memorized material, or (3) to evolve something not previously learned. Almost any group of observers who could be trained together for a reasonable length of time could learn to agree closely enough in using these categories to remove any limitations on reliability attributable to lack of observer agreement. The categories could therefore be said to have objectivity of a sort. But unless observers who did not sit in on these original training sessions can, after a reasonable amount of training, use the instrument and obtain satisfactory agreement with each other and with the original observers, the item is not truly objective—i.e., the technique is not really a measuring instrument. The categories should be defined clearly enough so that new observers, of comparable sophistication, could learn to use the system merely by practicing it. The descriptions of the categories should specify the behavioral cues to which the observer is to respond in non-esoteric language—language which can be understood by anyone on the same level of sophistication as the original observers. Mitzel and Rabinowitz were able to use a category system in New York that had been developed in Chicago—without having to call on Withall for special training.

What has been learned about constructing category systems may be summarized as follows: There should be a relatively small number of categories, each of which is used an appreciable number of times with some behavior or aspect of behavior that is relatively common. If convenient, the tallies should be based on natural units; if not, the tallies should be based on brief time-units. The behavioral cues on which the discrimi-

nations are to be made should be explicit even to the uninitiated, and the discriminations should be easy for the observers to make.

Constructing Sign Systems

The evolution of a sign begins with the idea that a certain behavior is symptomatic of some dimension of behavior believed to be important, whether it be a personality characteristic of the teacher, an element of classroom climate, or whatever. For example, it is thought that "teacher warmth" is indicated when a teacher uses a term of endearment in addressing a pupil. An item such as "Teacher calls pupil 'dear,' etc." is constructed so that the occurrence of such an incident may be recorded.

A superficial similarity exists between a sign and what Flanagan (1949) has called a "critical incident." The similarity seems great enough, however, to allow the methods he uses in collecting such incidents conceivably to be used in collecting ideas for behavior items. The important difference between the two is that instead of using the reported incidents to get ideas for constructing rating scales, the sign constructor would incorporate the incidents themselves into behavior items on the schedule, so that occurrences of the incidents could be recorded in future observations of teachers. But while Flanagan could use as a critical incident something that might never happen again, the type of incident suitable for use as a sign, although it need not be a common occurrence, must be one that happens at least now and then.

A noteworthy feature of signs is that one recorder can use a relatively large number of them simultaneously. In contrast, he can normally use only one category system at a time. But, if a particular sign must be checked every few seconds, the observer is not going to be able to use many other signs with it. Important behaviors that occur frequently should, if possible, be incorporated into a category system; those that are relatively infrequent should take the form of signs. Suppose, for example, that asking a question answerable with one word (in contrast to a question answerable only by organizing one's thoughts in the form of a sentence) seems to signify some dimension of teacher skill. This kind of "asking behavior" may not appear suitable for a sign item because sometimes a teacher will fire one such question after another for several minutes at a time. It might be best, if possible, to include this as one category in a system for categorizing all teacher statements.

One other stratagem might be as good—or even better: Divide the classroom visit into rather short periods—say three to five minutes each—and perhaps adopt the rule that each sign will be recorded only the first time it is seen during a period. The record will show not how often the behavior occurs, but in how many periods it occurs. In the example under discussion, the record would show in how many periods the teacher had asked this particular type of question one or more times, but not how often. If such a rule is adopted, the frequency of each item is arbitrarily limited to either zero or one per period. With this rule, a behavior like the one under discussion, unsuitable as a sign to be tallied on every occurrence, can still be used. This stratagem seems to be workable for most signs. It was used successfully in OScAR (see pp. 278–283). Its use seems to imply that the number of times a sign occurs over a few hours correlates highly with the number of short time-units in which it occurs at least once.

A sign should pretty well define itself. A category system, with its small number of categories, can have rather detailed descriptions of each. But if an observer is to record, say, 50 or 60 signs simultaneously, and if he needs to understand a paragraph or two exactly defining each sign, the amount of material to be kept in mind might be too great. Moreover, the few types of behavior involved in a category system all occur frequently enough to keep them fresh in the recorder's mind. But the observer recording signs, besides having many more definitions to re-

member, sees each sign occur much less frequently, so that he is more likely to forget one. If, when he sees a behavior, he has to stop to remember a definition—as he almost certainly will if the definitions are lengthy—he may well miss the next behavior that he is supposed to record.

A sign should have three characteristics: present tense, positive occurrence, and singular number. Consider the following item, constructed to lack all three:

Teacher failed to recognize pupils' significant contributions.

This item is in the past tense, it is negative (refers to a behavior's *not* being observed), and it is plural in number. Because it is in the past tense, this sign cannot be recorded during a period. The observer must wait until the end of the period before marking it. Suppose it is therefore changed to the *present* tense:

Teacher fails to recognize pupils' significant contributions.

Now it may appear on the surface that this item can be recorded when it happens; but this is not so. The observer cannot know whether a teacher *fails* to do a thing during a period until the period is over; therefore, he still cannot record the item until the end of the period. Change the item to *positive reference;* thus:

Teacher recognizes pupils' significant contributions.

This item is much better but it is still difficult to use because it is still not clear how many significant contributions a teacher must recognize before a tally is to be made. If the item is revised once more so that it refers to an event in the *singular:*

Teacher recognizes pupils' significant contribution,

then for the first time the item is usable. It is now possible to recognize that the behavior has happened when it happens, to record it, and then to forget it and watch for the next sign. Whether or not it is a good item is, of course, impossible to say without empirical results, but it is at least a usable one.

It might be questioned whether this item

would not be further improved by striking out the word *significant*, on the grounds that significance is a matter of degree, and that there is no indication in the item as to how significant a contribution must be before it is to be recorded as such. Experience suggests that even though this objection may be valid it does not matter much, so long as all the teachers are judged on the basis of records made by the same observer or team. It is the rank-order in which the classes are arranged with respect to an item, rather than the absolute numbers of checks assigned each one, that is important. So long as a teacher who recognizes pupils' significant contributions more often gets a higher score than one who recognizes them less often, the item is doing what it should do, namely, discriminating classes.

A more serious question might be raised with respect to this item: Does the positive statement call for what is important? Failure to recognize pupils' contributions may be symptomatic, but recognizing them may be unimportant. If this is so, the items should be rephrased to get at what is wanted, but in present, singular, and positive terms. For example, this might work:

Teacher ignores pupil's contribution.
Some might say that the distinction between *ignoring* and *failing to recognize* is pretty subtle. So it is. But it is important; a teacher can fail to recognize a contribution without ignoring it. In the former case, he does nothing, perhaps because he does not notice or become aware of the pupil's contribution; in the latter case, he does something, in that he is aware of the contribution and wilfully withholds comment or action upon it. It is far more difficult to observe nothing, and tally it when it doesn't happen than to observe something and tally it when it does.

General Notes on Constructing an Observational Schedule

During the item-writing phase of an observational study, the immediate goal is to prepare an adequate supply of potentially useful items without giving much thought to any practical limitations on the number of items that may be used, or how they will be arranged on the observation form or schedule. Usually there are a number of behavior areas to each of which several items relate, and it is assumed that these areas are the dimensions to be measured. These may be referred to as the apparent dimensions of behavior. Sometimes subsequent analysis of the results justifies the assumption that these dimensions exist, but quite often it indicates that they are illusory, that the behaviors observed cannot be described in these terms. It might seem logical when assembling the items into a schedule to be used by the recorder to group the items from each apparent dimension together. But this is not a good idea. The most important consideration in arranging the items on a schedule is ease in recording; the next most important is minimizing halo effect. Less important are convenience in scoring and ease in forming a subjective impression of what happened from a casual inspection of the record.

Items should, therefore, be arranged, first of all, according to form. Category systems should not be mixed with signs, even if they are to be scored on the same key. Since, as a rule, only one category system is used at a time, a category system might as well be recorded on a sheet separate from any other. Signs may be grouped according to what behavior is to be recorded—those pertaining to pupil behavior separated from those related to teacher behavior, those referring to verbal behavior separated from those related to nonverbal behavior, etc. The best arrangement is the one that makes it easiest for the recorder to locate the sign when he needs to record it.

It seems preferable, whenever possible, to identify different behaviors by changing the position rather than the form of the tallies. That is, it is easier to record items if there is a different space for tallying each item, or, in the case of category sets, each category of an item (see Figs. 2 and 3), than to write down a different number or other symbol. It takes very little practice before the observer's pencil seems to seek out the proper space without conscious effort as soon as the observer recognizes in which category a particular behavior belongs. Flanders (1960) found it necessary to record his data by writing category numbers in order to preserve information about sequence; in such a case no other course was open. Apparently, although less convenient, this method is perfectly feasible.

When the scheme for arranging the items is complete, it may become apparent that one observer cannot record all of the items at once, especially if more than one category system is involved. The possibility of redefining two or more such systems so that they can be combined should be considered. Flanders' system, for example, can be looked upon as combining two—one referring to teacher statements and one to pupil statements. Since only one person at a time is talking, in most instances, this use of the two kinds of items in one system is possible. Medley and Mitzel (1958b) combined a system for classifying teachers' expressive nonverbal behaviors with the Withall (1949) system for categorizing teachers' verbal behaviors. This combination was feasible because the behaviors relevant to the two systems were contiguous in time and space. After all possible combinations of this kind have been made, more than one system of categories may still remain. In that event, either all save one will have to be discarded, or each will have to be assigned to a separate portion or section of the schedule.

Since signs and categories cannot be used simultaneously, signs will have to be placed in still another section. Two sign sections will probably not be necessary unless the number of signs is very large, probably larger than anyone who has never tried it would imagine. One section should suffice, especially if the recommended practice of tallying any given item only once per time period is adopted, and if the items are functionally arranged. Medley and Mitzel (1958b) found no difficulty in using 70 signs on OScAR 2a. But, of course, the only way

to be sure is to try out a preliminary form.

When all the items have been assigned to sections, each containing as many items as one observer can record at one time, it is time to plan the observational procedure. There are at least three basic plans: (1) send a team of observers together into the classroom to be visited, with each observer recording on a different section, (2) send only one observer at a time into the classroom to be visited, with each observer recording on a different section, (3) send one observer at a time into the classroom who tallies on each section in turn for a brief period.

The first plan is the least desirable, especially if the number of sections is very great; it has been shown (see page 268) that for a given amount of observer time spent, the least reliable score is obtained in this way (Medley & Mitzel, 1958a). More important, it is probable that scores obtained by large teams are less valid than scores obtained by solitary visitors, because the sample of behaviors is smaller. Another factor is the fact that when several visitors go in one at a time, the teacher and class have more opportunity to become accustomed to being observed. Subjective impressions reported by observers indicate that after six or eight visits (at the most) even the teacher appears to forget that the observer is there.

The choice between the second and third plans, or a compromise between them, will probably depend mainly on the size of the research staff. If the staff is large enough the second plan might be used, allowing each observer to specialize in one section only. Two design considerations must be borne in mind: (1) It is desirable that every observer record in every classroom on each section he uses; and (2) it is desirable to have two recorders use each section of the schedule, even though this means that each recorder must learn to use two sections, to lessen the effects of bias.

If it does not appear feasible to have every observer visit every teacher in a study before attempting to plan a compromise, it would be wise to consult a good book on experimental designs that includes a section dealing with incomplete blocks designs (e.g., Kempthorne, 1952) or a competent statistician. Balanced incomplete blocks designs, for example, can be adapted successfully only to certain numbers of observers and teachers. It might be disastrous to design such a study without consulting such an expert beforehand, because the results would be unanalyzable.

The text printed on the schedule to guide the observer should be quite unintelligible to anyone else. A sign should be printed *in toto* on the schedule, with abbreviations used to disguise the exact content. Category systems can be represented by letters since the recorder must memorize them anyhow. The reason for the concealment is to prevent a teacher who happens to see the card from unintentionally finding out what items of behavior are being recorded, and possibly modifying his behavior, consciously or unconsciously, as a result.

If the budget allowance for paper will permit, a separate sheet or card should be used for each period during a visit, so that separate records will be more likely to be independent. Even if a particular observer is using only one section of an instrument, the visit should be broken up into separate periods recorded separately. The optimum length of such periods within visits is not known; for signs it should be short, probably not more than five minutes. For categories, it should be longer—at least three minutes. When both signs and categories are used, the length of the period should be a compromise somewhere between those just mentioned.

The total length of a visit to an elementary school classroom is generally between 20 minutes and a half-hour. A visit shorter than 20 minutes hardly seems worth the disturbance of school routine it causes, or the trouble it takes the observer to travel to the school. In the secondary school, it seems logical that a visit should last as long as a regular class period does, usually 40 or 50 minutes.

The Halo Effect

Many of the suggestions made in these pages have had a single purpose: the reduction or elimination of the halo effect—the archenemy of objective observation. The halo effect has been defined as "the tendency, in making an estimate or rating of one characteristic of a person, to be influenced by another characteristic or by one's general impression of that person" (English & English, 1958, p. 236). Although this definition refers specifically to ratings, where halo often has a crippling effect, the potential effects of halo on observational records are equally serious. Consider the rather poor item discussed earlier:

*Teacher failed to recognize pupils'
significant contributions.*

It has already been pointed out that this item calls for an extremely difficult discrimination which must be made at the end of a period of observation. Suppose that by that time the observer has, consciously or unconsciously, formed an impression of the teacher as warm, receptive, and generally the type of person who would recognize pupils' contributions. Now suppose, when he thinks back over a period during which he has observed the teacher, that he is not quite certain whether or not the teacher has failed to recognize pupils' significant contributions. The chances are much higher that he will leave the item blank than that he will check it, regardless of whether the teacher failed to recognize significant pupil contributions. The record on this item may be determined as much, or more, by a general impression based on nobody-knows-what behaviors as by the behavior referred to in the item. The record is no longer a record of behavior but a record of the observer's reactions or opinions.

If this item is grouped with several other equally poor items designed to measure some apparent dimension, the effect of halo will be multiplied because all the items will be recorded in terms of the same general impression. Cronbach (1951) has shown how even a small number of items with one common factor, when combined into a scale, will pile up internal consistency as a measure of this common factor, even though their individual loadings on it are moderate, while the contributions of specific factors to the composite will vanish. Whatever part of the variance of an item on an observational scale is attributable to the specific behavior it refers to will be specific to that item, of course. If halo affects the item's variance appreciably, that part of its variance is likely to be common to all the items, and the scale builds up internal consistency as a measure of the observer's general impression of the teacher. The composite score is no longer sufficiently affected by the specific behaviors to be said to measure behavior at all.

If this is what is happening with a particular observational schedule, it will reveal itself in spuriously high intercorrelations between scales purporting to measure different aspects of classroom behavior. When two scales with manifestly different item content measure the same thing, that thing is almost certain to be halo.

Besides inflating internal consistencies and intercorrelations between scales, halo is also likely to inflate the stabilities and the coefficients of observer agreement of scales affected by it. General impressions tend to persist; if an observer visits a classroom a second time, the impression formed on the first visit will color the record he makes on the second and produce an exaggerated impression of stability in the behavior record. Unfortunately, it also seems that a given teacher tends to impress two different observers in the same way more often than not, regardless of whether both observe the same specific behaviors. Hence, their records will tend to resemble each other, and a spuriously high coefficient of observer agreement will result.

Behavior items in which the effect of halo is not serious can be constructed. This has been demonstrated, most explicitly perhaps in the low intercorrelations reported by Morsh (1956), by Medley and Mitzel (1958b), and by V. B. Morrison (1961). The solution of the problem clearly depends on the construction of the items. In the suggestions presented above an attempt has been made to pull together what can be learned from a half-century of attempts to measure classroom behavior, with a minimum of halo effect, by means of direct observation of it.

Relationship between the Observer and the Observed

One criticism sometimes made of measurements based on direct observations is that they lack validity because the behaviors are not representative of normal classroom behavior. Teachers and pupils, it is argued, behave differently when a visitor is present than when no visitor is present—so much so, presumably, as to render measurements of such behavior, however accurate, worthless.

This argument has merit but should not be taken too seriously. The validity of intelligence tests might be—and very likely has been—questioned on the grounds that people behave differently in a test situation than in a life situation. So might all testing and all laboratory research be questioned. Yet intelligence tests do have validity as predictors of behavior in life situations, and experiments carried out in the psychological laboratory have contributed quite a bit to what is known about human behavior outside of the laboratory. It seems reasonable to assume that, particularly if proper precautions are taken, the resemblance between a classroom with a single observer present and one with no observer present is closer than that between either the test situation or the laboratory situation, on the one hand, and a life situation on the other. Nonetheless, whatever can be done to minimize the disturbing effect of the observer should be done.

A few remarks about possible precautions might be appropriate. Two are most obvious: First, except during the development of a technique, no more than one or, at the most, two visitors should be present in the classroom at the same time. Second, the teacher to be observed, his supervisor, and the observer himself must all three understand clearly the purpose for which the data are to be collected and how they are to be used. It should be understood by all concerned that the study is being conducted to learn more about the behavior of teachers and pupils and its relationship to whatever other variables are involved, and that this purpose can be achieved without any reference being made in public or private to which teacher or pupil did what in which school.

It is perhaps most important of all that this be understood by the observer himself. The implications of such understanding are that he will not discuss what he sees in a particular classroom even in anonymous terms with anyone who might recognize the teacher involved and that he will resist the natural temptation to evaluate what he sees, in terms either of specific incidents or of over-all judgments of the effectiveness of individual teachers.

If the observer himself understands and acts upon these principles, the supervisor will have less difficulty in resisting his urge to "pump" the observer for information or general impressions of the teachers he visits.

Proper attitudes on the part of the observer and the supervisor are necessary if the teacher is to be convinced that the interest of the observer is impersonal and that the teacher's privacy will be respected. The teacher who is insecure will suspect that the observer and the supervisor are getting together and comparing notes. It is important that no confirmation of this suspicion be afforded and that every opportunity of allaying it be taken. This suspicion dies (if it ever does) only after a teacher has been visited several times without any change in his position in the school or his relationships with his supervisor or his peers. This effect on the teacher's adaptation to observers is one of the added advantages of planning to make at least 10 or 12 visits to each teacher in a study.

It may be helpful, if the observers fully understand their roles, for teachers and observers to mingle socially, either informally in the teachers' rooms at the schools, or at the research office in teas or coffee hours especially arranged for orientation purposes.

The teacher, and the supervisor as well, will naturally ask what the observer would like to see during his visit to the classroom. The appropriate answer is, to see the ordinary things that happen in a classroom on an ordinary day. If pressed for specifics, the observer should frankly state that it would not be desirable for the teacher to know exactly what the observer is looking for, because it would make him more self-conscious about those particular aspects of behavior. It may be expedient to plan a meeting after the last visit, at which the teachers will be shown the observational schedule; if so, the teachers may be told at the start that the exact nature of the behaviors to be recorded will not be revealed until then. By the time the meeting is held, probably only half of the teachers will still be anxious enough to attend it.

QUANTIFYING RESULTS OF AN OBSERVATIONAL STUDY

Observational data are perhaps the most expensive to obtain of all the types of data used in research on teaching. Along with the mistaken notion that ratings can serve the same purpose, this high cost is probably the main reason why so few studies have been found that are of sufficient scope and interest to be reviewed in this chapter. It is particularly unfortunate that, with observational data so rare, such primitive methods have been used in analyzing them. The result has been that only a fraction of the information contained in these few data has been retrieved. A lag between methodological development and application is less serious in areas where the accumulation of large masses of data offsets deficiencies of analysis. There is not now, nor is it likely that there will ever be, such an accumulation of data about classroom behavior.

The remainder of this chapter is devoted to some applications of complex analysis of variance and covariance models to the problem of extracting from a set of observational data the maximum amount of information that is relevant to the purpose for which they were collected. Some of the procedures to be described may seem elaborate. But, unless a simpler analysis can yield as much information or more, no analysis can be said to be too elaborate. Obviously, no method of statistical analysis, however refined and elaborate, can extract from a set of data any information not already present in them. It may not be so obvious that, in many cases, no unrefined and unelaborate method of statistical analysis can extract from a set of data all the relevant information present in them. (Compare, for example, Green & Tukey, 1960; Johnson, 1949, pp. 298–324; Stanley, 1957.) No more can be done in this chapter than to point out and perhaps illustrate some of the possibilities.

Dimensionalizing Classroom Behavior

Before proceeding, we may do well to emphasize the potential value of combining items into scales. It has been pointed out in connection with certain studies reviewed above (e.g., Jayne, 1945) that it is unusual to find an individual item which discriminates between classrooms reliably. Such exceptions occur mainly with category systems items like Withall's. Consider a typical sign from OScAR:

E1. pupil talks to a group.

Scores on this item based on, say, 10 or 12 half-hour visits per class, are unlikely to show reliable differences between classes. So many different situations can occur in which a pupil might talk to a class that the item might be checked just about as often in one kind of class as in another. In one class the teacher may have a pupil tell the class a funny story; in another the teacher may have a pupil tell the class what a word means. In a third class there may be several autonomous groups, with pupils in each group discussing plans for a party. Item E1 would be checked in each class once in that period. Although each tally represents a very differ-

ent behavior, they all look alike to the scorer.

Consider two additional items from the same schedule:

E5. pupil demonstrates or illustrates.
E10. pupil leads the class.

These items are also ambiguous—they may occur under such widely different circumstances that a tally could mean many different things.

If the three items are combined into a key so that their tallies are added together, the whole so obtained is greater than the sum of the parts, in its discriminating power at least. Suppose that there are some classrooms in which pupils are given relatively frequent opportunities to share the role usually played by the teacher, and others where such opportunities are rarely afforded the pupils.

In a class of the former type, behaviors on all of these items are likely to have relatively high frequencies, so the class will build up a relatively high composite score. In the second type of class, one or another of the items may be checked, but the total frequency on all three items is not likely to be as high as in the first type of class. The three items will tend to build up in the former, but they will tend to oppose one another or cancel out in the latter. The result is that the three-item composite may discriminate even though the individual items do not. Cronbach's work (1951), showing how items with moderate loadings on a common factor rapidly build up discriminating power while the effects of specific factors tend to cancel out, has already been cited in connection with the halo effect. Here is an illustration of how this phenomenon can help rather than hinder the work of obtaining objective behavior measurements.

Jayne (1945) found that almost none of the individual items he tried out discriminated effective from ineffective teachers, but, when he put a few together into a scale, the composite did discriminate. The same thing happened in Morsh's study (1956) and with the OScAR (Medley & Mitzel, 1958b). It is doubtful that the Cornell-Lindvall-Saupe study (1952) would have yielded significant differences if it had attempted to discriminate schools on individual items rather than on scales. Nor is it likely that research will ever discover many individual objective items of behavior which are crucial to pupil learning (or to any other important variable). The important differences between teachers are more likely to be found in broader patterns of behavior manifested now in one specific behavior, now in another. Any one of these specifics may be observed in the behavior of teachers who do not exhibit the over-all pattern, but all of them may be observed only in those who do. It is a fortunate fact, and one that might not have been foreseen, that a relatively small number of signs will suffice in many cases to measure a broader behavior pattern with satisfactory reliability. This fact holds out the hope that in a reasonable number of visits to a classroom, using a manageable number of items, it is possible to obtain reliable and important measures of important dimensions of teaching behavior.

Progress in the development of scientific knowledge about teaching behavior awaits the development of a set of such dimensions, which are educationally and scientifically significant, so that a substantial portion of the differences between different classrooms can be described quantitatively and related to other variables.

Definition of the Reliability Coefficient

Assume that a given key consists of i items, and that the score of a class on the key for any one visit will be the arithmetic sum of the scores on the individual items. The first step in the analysis will be to study the reliability of each scale in order to decide whether or not it is measuring a dimension of behavior. For simplicity, it will be assumed that a preliminary study or tryout of the schedule is undertaken for this purpose. Before discussing the analysis of the results of such a study, let us define reliability in more rigorous terms.

A sample of classrooms from the population to be studied should be visited by trained recorders using the observational schedule in the same way that it will be used in any subsequent study. Let the number of classes visited be c. To study the objectivity of the items, i.e., how closely observers agree in recording identical behaviors, at least two recorders should be present on each visit, sitting in different parts of the room and making independent records. Suppose that the number of recorders per visit is r. In order to be able to estimate how stable the behaviors are, i.e., how closely two records based on different visits will agree, each classroom should be visited at least twice, so that the behavior will be recorded in at least two different situations. Let the number of situations in which each classroom is visited be s.

Analysis will be vastly simplified if each teacher is visited in the same number of situations s as each other teacher, and if the same r recorders visit each teacher in each situation.

To recapitulate, c teachers are visited in s situations by a team of r recorders. In studying the reliability of a scale with i items on it, the total number of scores to be analyzed will be $cris$.

Much has been written on how reliability should be defined. General agreement has been reached that the form of the definition should be as follows (in terms of population parameters):

$$\rho_{xx} = \frac{\sigma_T{}^2}{\sigma_X{}^2}. \tag{1}$$

The disagreement has had to do with the definition of $\sigma_T{}^2$ and $\sigma_X{}^2$.

There should be no controversy about the definition of $\sigma_T{}^2$ in this case. Suppose that the total score of class c on i items, based on records made by teams of r recorders on s visits, is x_{cris}. If the scale is supposed to measure differences between classes, and if any and all idiosyncrasies of observers, items, or situations are regarded as sources of distortion or error, then the true score of class c would be the mean of all the scores class c could get with any possible combination of i

items, r recorders, and s situations equivalent to the i items, r recorders, and s situations actually used. The symbol $\sigma_T{}^2$ will be used to represent the variance of these true scores about the mean of all such true scores in the population of classes represented by the c classes actually visited.

The definition of $\sigma_X{}^2$ will vary, since it depends on the procedure used in collecting the data of the study. In words, $\sigma_X{}^2$ means the variance of the obtained scores of all of the teachers in the population about their own mean. Obviously, what this variance is depends on how the obtained scores are obtained. It will, for example, be greater if different classes are visited by different observers than if all are visited by the same observers.

In estimating the reliability coefficient appropriate to any situation, the efficient method is the analysis of variance. Most observational studies in the past have studied reliability either in terms of per cent of observer agreement or in terms of an interclass correlation (usually the product-moment, but occasionally the rank-order, coefficient) between two sets of observations.

A per cent of observer agreement tells almost nothing about the accuracy of the scores to be used, mainly because the per cent of agreement between observers is relevant to only a part—and, the evidence indicates, a small part at that—of the reliability problem. The experience with observational studies summarized in this chapter clearly bears out a fact pointed out by Barr in 1929: that errors arising from variations in behavior from one situation or occasion to another far outweigh errors arising from failure of two observers to agree exactly in their records of the same behavior. It is not impossible to find observers agreeing 99 per cent in recording behaviors on a scale whose reliability as defined by Formula (1) above does not differ significantly from zero.

Reliability can be low even though observer agreement is high for a number of reasons. For example, observers might be able to agree perfectly on the number of seats in a room, yet if the number of seats in all rooms is equal, or nearly so, the reliability of seat counts as a measure of differences between classes will be zero. Near-perfect agreement could also be reached about the number of boys in a room wearing red neckties; but if every boy changed the color of his tie every day, the reliability of these counts would be zero. So long as an interclass (product-moment) correlation is based on scores obtained on two different occasions by two different observers, it does estimate ρ_{xx}. But it is not likely to be a very accurate estimate because the number of classrooms c is usually small in observational studies, and the size of c determines the precision of a product-moment correlation coefficient (its standard error varies inversely as the square root of c). In even a rather ambitious study, using 100 classrooms, the 90 per cent confidence interval of ρ_{xx} estimated in this way would be about .33 points wide! If the number of situations or occasions per teacher (s) is increased to more than two, several correlations can be calculated, one between each pair of situations; but since they are not independent, it is difficult to combine all of the correlations into a single best estimate.

A single intraclass correlation can be calculated from an analysis of variance of a set of data collected according to the plan suggested above. Such a single coefficient combines all of the information in the rs independent measurements of each of the c classes. The estimate of ρ_{xx} so obtained is unbiased and is also more precise than any combination of interclass correlations (see Fisher, 1950, p. 216; Medley & Mitzel, 1958a). Moreover, the different reliability coefficients appropriate to the various uses to which the scores might be put can all be estimated from the one analysis of variance.

A General Design for Reliability Estimation

The basic design for analyzing the *cris* scores is a four-way analysis of variance of

TABLE 21

DESIGN FOR RELIABILITY ANALYSIS OF SCORES BASED ON RECORDS MADE BY r RECORDERS OF c CLASSES IN s SITUATIONS ON i ITEMS

Source of Variation	Degrees of Freedom	Obtained Mean Square	Expected Mean Square
1. Class	$c-1$	s_c^2	$ri\sigma_c^2 + is\sigma_{cr}^2 + rs\sigma_{ci}^2 + ri\sigma_{cs}^2 + s\sigma_{cri}^2 + i\sigma_{crs}^2 + r\sigma_{cis}^2 + \sigma^2$
2. Recorder	$r-1$	s_r^2	$cis\sigma_r^2 + is\sigma_{cr}^2 + cs\sigma_{ri}^2 + ci\sigma_{rs}^2 + s\sigma_{cri}^2 + i\sigma_{crs}^2 + c\sigma_{ris}^2 + \sigma^2$
3. Item	$i-1$	s_i^2	$crs\sigma_i^2 + rs\sigma_{ci}^2 + cs\sigma_{ri}^2 + cr\sigma_{is}^2 + s\sigma_{cri}^2 + r\sigma_{cis}^2 + c\sigma_{ris}^2 + \sigma^2$
4. Situation	$s-1$	s_s^2	$cri\sigma_s^2 + ri\sigma_{cs}^2 + ci\sigma_{rs}^2 + cr\sigma_{is}^2 + i\sigma_{crs}^2 + r\sigma_{cis}^2 + c\sigma_{ris}^2 + \sigma^2$
5. $C \times R$	$(c-1)(r-1)$	s_{cr}^2	$is\sigma_{cr}^2 + s\sigma_{cri}^2 + i\sigma_{crs}^2 + \sigma^2$
6. $C \times I$	$(c-1)(i-1)$	s_{ci}^2	$rs\sigma_{ci}^2 + s\sigma_{cri}^2 + r\sigma_{cis}^2 + \sigma^2$
7. $C \times S$	$(c-1)(s-1)$	s_{cs}^2	$ri\sigma_{cs}^2 + i\sigma_{crs}^2 + r\sigma_{cis}^2 + \sigma^2$
8. $R \times I$	$(r-1)(i-1)$	s_{ri}^2	$cs\sigma_{ri}^2 + s\sigma_{cri}^2 + c\sigma_{ris}^2 + \sigma^2$
9. $R \times S$	$(r-1)(s-1)$	s_{rs}^2	$ci\sigma_{rs}^2 + i\sigma_{crs}^2 + c\sigma_{ris}^2 + \sigma^2$
10. $I \times S$	$(i-1)(s-1)$	s_{is}^2	$cr\sigma_{is}^2 + r\sigma_{cis}^2 + c\sigma_{ris}^2 + \sigma^2$
11. $C \times R \times I$	$(c-1)(r-1)(i-1)$	s_{cri}^2	$s\sigma_{cri}^2 + \sigma^2$
12. $C \times R \times S$	$(c-1)(r-1)(s-1)$	s_{crs}^2	$i\sigma_{crs}^2 + \sigma^2$
13. $C \times I \times S$	$(c-1)(i-1)(s-1)$	s_{cis}^2	$r\sigma_{cis}^2 + \sigma^2$
14. $R \times I \times S$	$(r-1)(i-1)(s-1)$	s_{ris}^2	$c\sigma_{ris}^2 + \sigma^2$
15. Residual	$(c-1)(r-1)(i-1)(s-1)$	s^2	σ^2
16. Total Variation	$cris-1$		

the form shown in Table 21. This table gives, under Model II assumptions (see p. 268) the expected mean squares for each line of the table in terms of population parameters related to reliability known as "components of variance."

To obtain a very general expression for ρ_{xx}, it will be assumed that the score x_{cqjt} whose reliability is to be estimated, will be based on q recorders, j items, and t situations, although in the reliability study, scores based on r recorders, i items, and s situations were used. Then it can be shown that the population value of the true score variance as defined above is

$$\sigma_T^2 = (qjt)^2 \, \sigma_c^2 \qquad (2)$$

where σ_c^2 is the first component shown in Line 1 of Table 21 (the component due to differences among classes).

Since the variance of obtained scores may be defined differently for different purposes, it will be necessary to present a general expression, and a rule of thumb for deriving the formula for a particular situation from it. The general expression for q records, j items, and t situations is:

$$\sigma_x^2 = qjt \, (qjt\sigma_c^2 + jt\sigma_r^2 + qt\sigma_i^2 +$$
$$qj\sigma_s^2 + jt\sigma_{cr}^2 + qt\sigma_{ci}^2 + qj\sigma_{cs}^2 +$$
$$t\sigma_{ri}^2 + j\sigma_{rs}^2 + q\sigma_{is}^2 + t\sigma_{cri}^2 +$$
$$j\sigma_{crs}^2 + q\sigma_{cis}^2 + \sigma_{ris}^2 + \sigma^2) \qquad (3)$$

The components on the right are all shown in Table 21, Lines 2–15.

The rule of thumb for adapting this to a particular situation is to *drop out any component all of whose subscripts remain constant in all obtained scores.*

Thus, if the same recorder (or team of recorders) visits all classes, the subscript r will be the same in all scores. Then the expression $jt\sigma_r^2$ would be dropped from Formula (3) above, and what was left on the right side would define σ_x^2 for that study.

If (as is almost always the case) the same items are used in all classes, $qt\sigma_i^2$ will usually be dropped. If the same recorders make all visits using the same items, $jt\sigma_r^2$, $qt\sigma_i^2$, and $t\sigma_{ri}^2$ will all be dropped from Formula (3).

When defining expressions for σ_T^2 and σ_x^2 have been formulated and substituted in Formula (1), ρ_{xx} has been defined. If alternative plans for collecting data are being considered, the reliabilities of the scores which would be obtained by each plan can be defined and compared with one another.

Once ρ_{xx} has been defined in terms of components of variance, the problem of estimating it from the analysis of variance in Table 21 is straightforward. In the third column of the table are symbols representing the numerical mean squares obtained in the analysis. Each of these mean squares is an unbiased estimate of the linear function of parameters shown in the same line of the table under the heading "expected mean square." If each obtained mean square is set equal to its expected value, a set of linear equations is obtained which may be solved

to yield formulas for estimating parameters from sample values. This has been done for all of the components in Table 21, with the results shown in Table 22. These estimates can be substituted in Formulas (1), (2), and (3) to obtain an estimate of the reliability of a particular observational procedure.

Adapting the Design to a Particular Study

The design shown in Table 21 represents a general plan for any study in which i items are recorded in c classrooms in s situations by r recorders. In most applications a simpler design is appropriate. Rules of thumb will now be presented for proceeding from the general plan shown to one appropriate for a

TABLE 22

ESTIMATION OF COMPONENTS OF VARIANCE BASED ON
DESIGN IN TABLE 21

1. $\sigma_c^2 \,(=) \dfrac{1}{ris} \left(s_c^2 - s_{cr}^2 - s_{ci}^2 - s_{cs}^2 + s_{cri}^2 + s_{cis}^2 + s_{crs}^2 - s^2 \right)$

2. $\sigma_r^2 \,(=) \dfrac{1}{cis} \left(s_r^2 - s_{cr}^2 - s_{ri}^2 - s_{rs}^2 + s_{cri}^2 + s_{ris}^2 + s_{crs}^2 - s^2 \right)$

3. $\sigma_i^2 \,(=) \dfrac{1}{crs} \left(s_i^2 - s_{ci}^2 - s_{ri}^2 - s_{is}^2 + s_{cri}^2 + s_{cis}^2 + s_{ris}^2 - s^2 \right)$

4. $\sigma_s^2 \,(=) \dfrac{1}{cri} \left(s_s^2 - s_{cs}^2 - s_{rs}^2 - s_{is}^2 + s_{crs}^2 + s_{cis}^2 + s_{ris}^2 - s^2 \right)$

5. $\sigma_{cr}^2 \,(=) \dfrac{1}{is} \left(s_{cr}^2 - s_{cri}^2 - s_{crs}^2 + s^2 \right)$

6. $\sigma_{ci}^2 \,(=) \dfrac{1}{rs} \left(s_{ci}^2 - s_{cri}^2 - s_{cis}^2 + s^2 \right)$

7. $\sigma_{cs}^2 \,(=) \dfrac{1}{ri} \left(s_{cs}^2 - s_{crs}^2 - s_{cis}^2 + s^2 \right)$

8. $\sigma_{ri}^2 \,(=) \dfrac{1}{cs} \left(s_{ri}^2 - s_{cri}^2 - s_{ris}^2 + s^2 \right)$

9. $\sigma_{rs}^2 \,(=) \dfrac{1}{ci} \left(s_{rs}^2 - s_{crs}^2 - s_{ris}^2 + s^2 \right)$

10. $\sigma_{is}^2 \,(=) \dfrac{1}{cr} \left(s_{is}^2 - s_{cis}^2 - s_{ris}^2 + s^2 \right)$

11. $\sigma_{cri}^2 \,(=) \dfrac{1}{s} \left(s_{cri}^2 - s^2 \right)$

12. $\sigma_{crs}^2 \,(=) \dfrac{1}{i} \left(s_{crs}^2 - s^2 \right)$

13. $\sigma_{cis}^2 \,(=) \dfrac{1}{r} \left(s_{cis}^2 - s^2 \right)$

14. $\sigma_{ris}^2 \,(=) \dfrac{1}{c} \left(s_{ris}^2 - s^2 \right)$

15. $\sigma^2 \,(=) s^2$

particular problem. To make the rules easier to understand, we shall apply them to a specific example.

At the very beginning of the planning of a reliability study, one must decide how many classes will be observed, how often, and how many records will be made. That is, the values of c, r, and s must be set. In the example to be used, 24 teachers were observed by a team of two recorders in five situations each. The key to be analyzed had one item only. Then $c = 24$, $r = 2$, $s = 5$, $i = 1$, and the number of scores to be analyzed is 240.

A second step requires that decisions or assumptions be made regarding the nature of the population of scores which these 240 are regarded as sampling. It must be decided whether this population contains an infinite number of items, recorders, or situations, or whether it contains only i items, r recorders, or s situations. (The population of teachers or classes is always regarded as infinite.)

The principle which should be followed in making each of these decisions is that if other items, recorders, or situations might have been used, then the corresponding populations should be regarded as infinite. The usual effect of assuming that any one of these is *not* infinite is to reduce the error of measurement and increase the reliability considerably, so none of them should be regarded as finite without good reason.

In the example, since only one item was used ($i = 1$), the population of scores was assumed to contain only one item as well. It was assumed to contain an infinite number of situations in which the classes might have been observed and an infinite number of recorders who might have been on the team who observed them, because it is possible to envision having used other recorders who visited the teachers in other situations.

The adaptation of Table 21 proceeds as follows:

Rule 1. Copy the first two columns of Table 21, substituting numerical values for literal values of degrees of freedom, and dropping entirely any line with zero degrees of freedom. Change the name of the source of variation in the last line remaining to "residual" and compute a new total number of degrees of freedom.

In the example, since $c = 24$, $r = 2$, $s = 5$, and $i = 1$, there will be 23 degrees of freedom in the first line (Class), one in the second (Recorder), zero in the third (Item), etc. The third line of Table 21 will be omitted entirely, as will any line with $(i - 1)$ in its second column, since $i - 1 = 0$ in this case. The last line surviving will be that for the interaction $C \times R \times S$, with 92 degrees of freedom. The new total number of degrees of freedom will be 239, since $(crs - 1) = (240 - 1) = 239$.

Rule 2. Copy the expected mean squares for those lines not omitted in Step 1, substituting numerical coefficients for literal ones, and omitting, wherever they occur, all components reflecting sources of variance whose line has been dropped, except σ^2. Drop also the component corresponding to the last line before the total, now called "residual."

The lines to be omitted in the example are those labeled: Item, $C \times I$, $R \times I$, $I \times S$, $C \times R \times I$, $C \times I \times S$, $R \times I \times S$, residual, and total. The last line retained is $C \times R \times S$. Therefore, σ_i^2, σ_{ci}^2, σ_{ri}^2, σ_{is}^2, σ_{cri}^2, σ_{cis}^2, σ_{ris}^2, and σ_{crs}^2 are dropped wherever they are found in Table 21.

For example, here is the expected mean square for "Class" as shown in Table 21 with components to be eliminated enclosed in parentheses:

$$10\sigma_c^2 + 5\sigma_{cr}^2 + (10\sigma_{ci}^2) + 2\sigma_{cs}^2 + (5\sigma_{cri}^2) + (\sigma_{crs}^2) + (2\sigma_{cis}^2) + \sigma^2.$$

The first line of symbols in Table 23 shows the appropriate expected mean square for the same component with all elements involving items omitted. The rest of Table 23 has been similarly derived from Table 21.

TABLE 23

DESIGN FOR A RELIABILITY ANALYSIS WHEN ONE ITEM IS
RECORDED BY TWO RECORDERS IN FIVE SITUATIONS IN 24
CLASSES, ASSUMING THAT THE POPULATION CONTAINS
INFINITE NUMBERS OF RECORDERS AND SITUATIONS BUT
ONLY ONE ITEM

Source of Variation	Degrees of Freedom	Expected Mean Square	Obtained Mean Square
Class	23	$10\sigma_c^2 + 5\sigma_{cr}^2 + 2\sigma_{cs}^2 + \sigma^2$	s_c^2
Recorder	1	$120\sigma_r^2 + 5\sigma_{cr}^2 + 24\sigma_{rs}^2 + \sigma^2$	s_r^2
Situation	4	$48\sigma_s^2 + 2\sigma_{cs}^2 + 24\sigma_{rs}^2 + \sigma^2$	s_s^2
$C \times R$	23	$5\sigma_{cr}^2 + \sigma^2$	s_{cr}^2
$C \times S$	92	$2\sigma_{cs}^2 + \sigma^2$	s_{cs}^2
$R \times S$	4	$24\sigma_{rs}^2 + \sigma^2$	s_{rs}^2
Residual	92	σ^2	s^2
Total	239		

Estimation of Components

$$\sigma_c^2 \ (=) \ \frac{1}{10}(s_c^2 - s_{cr}^2 - s_{cs}^2 + s^2)$$

$$\sigma_r^2 \ (=) \ \frac{1}{120}(s_r^2 - s_{cr}^2 - s_{rs}^2 + s^2)$$

$$\sigma_s^2 \ (=) \ \frac{1}{48}(s_s^2 - s_{cs}^2 - s_{rs}^2 + s^2)$$

$$\sigma_{cr}^2 \ (=) \ \frac{1}{5}(s_{cr}^2 - s^2)$$

$$\sigma_{cs}^2 \ (=) \ \frac{1}{2}(s_{cs}^2 - s^2)$$

$$\sigma_{rs}^2 \ (=) \ \frac{1}{24}(s_{rs}^2 - s^2)$$

$$\sigma^2 \ (=) \ s^2$$

The third rule applies only when the number of items, recorders, or situations in the population is assumed to be equal to i, r, or s, respectively. Suppose, for example, that the five situations had been selected so that each teacher would be observed once teaching each of the five major subjects taught in the school. (Here in place of the word "situation" the word "subject" might better have been used.) Since the total number of subjects taught is five, the population may be assumed to contain only five situations. Then *Rule 3* may be applied.

Rule 3. A source of variation not represented by an infinite number of values in the population will be referred to as "fixed." Examine the components of any expected mean square, and note that each con-

tains all of the subscripts associated with the source of variation named in the same line. All components but the first contain at least one additional subscript. If any of these additional subscripts is "fixed," omit that component from that line. (The first component in a line is never omitted.)

Note that the expected mean square for "Class" in Table 23 contains a component σ_{cs}^2; besides the subscript c, this component also contains the subscript s. Since we are regarding s as "fixed," σ_{cs}^2 is dropped from that line. The same component occurs in the expected mean square for "Situation"; it is not dropped here, however, because the "additional" subscript in this case is c, rather than s, which stands for the source of varia-

TABLE 24

DESIGN FOR A RELIABILITY ANALYSIS WHEN ONE ITEM IS
RECORDED BY TWO RECORDERS IN FIVE SITUATIONS IN 24
CLASSES, ASSUMING THAT THE POPULATION CONTAINS AN
INFINITE NUMBER OF RECORDERS BUT ONLY ONE ITEM
AND ONLY FIVE SITUATIONS

Source of Variation	Degrees of Freedom	Expected Mean Square	Obtained Mean Square
Class	23	$10\sigma_c^2 + 5\sigma_{cr}^2 + \sigma^2$	s_c^2
Recorder	1	$120\sigma_r^2 + 5\sigma_{cr}^2 + \sigma^2$	s_r^2
Situation	4	$48\sigma_s^2 + 2\sigma_{cs}^2 + 24\sigma_{rs}^2 + \sigma^2$	s_s^2
$C \times R$	23	$5\sigma_{cr}^2 + \sigma^2$	s_{cr}^2
$C \times S$	92	$2\sigma_{cs}^2 + \sigma^2$	s_{cs}^2
$R \times S$	4	$24\sigma_{rs}^2 + \sigma^2$	s_{rs}^2
Residual	92	σ^2	s^2
Total	239		

Estimation of Components

$$\sigma_c^2 \ (=) \ \frac{1}{10} \ (s_c^2 - s_{cr}^2)$$

$$\sigma_r^2 \ (=) \ \frac{1}{120} \ (s_r^2 - s_{cr}^2)$$

$$\sigma_s^2 \ (=) \ \frac{1}{48} \ (s_s^2 - s_{cs}^2 - s_{rs}^2 + s^2)$$

$$\sigma_{cr}^2 \ (=) \ \frac{1}{5} \ (s_{cr}^2 - s^2)$$

$$\sigma_{cs}^2 \ (=) \ \frac{1}{2} \ (s_{cs}^2 - s^2)$$

$$\sigma_{rs}^2 \ (=) \ \frac{1}{24} \ (s_{rs}^2 - s^2)$$

$$\sigma^2 \ (=) \ s^2$$

tion named in that line. Table 24 shows the design in Table 23 with situations fixed— after *Rule 3* has been applied.

A Numerical Example

Table 25 shows some data from an unpublished study analyzed under the two sets of assumptions that have been discussed. Notice the effect of a change in assumptions on the estimate of σ_c^2 obtained.

Under the assumption that the population contains an infinite number of situations and recorders, the true score variance for q recorders, t situations, and one item ($j = 1$) is estimated from Formula (2) as follows:

$$\sigma_T^2 = (qjt)^2 \ \sigma_c^2 (=) \ .53(qt)^2.$$

Assuming also that the same q recorders visit all teachers in the same t situations, the variance of obtained scores is estimated from Formula (3) to be:

$$\sigma_X^2 = qt \ (qt\sigma_c^2 + t\sigma_{cr}^2 + q\sigma_{cs}^2 + \sigma^2)$$
$$(=) \ qt \ (.53qt + .01t + 1.41q + .67).$$

The reliability coefficient is then (for q recorders and t visits):

$$r_{qt} = \frac{.53qt}{.53qt + .01t + 1.41q + .67},$$

which may be written

$$r_{qt} = \frac{1}{1 + \dfrac{.02}{q} + \dfrac{2.66}{t} + \dfrac{1.27}{qt}}.$$

TABLE 25

ANALYSIS OF VARIANCE OF PUPIL INTEREST SCORES ON OSCAR 3F

Source of Variation	Degrees of Freedom	Sum of Squares	Mean Square
Class	23	203	8.83
Recorder	1	13	13.00
Situation	4	19	4.75
$C \times R$	23	17	0.74
$C \times S$	92	321	3.49
$R \times S$	4	1	0.25
Residual	92	62	.67
Total	239	636	

Estimation of Components

Situations Not Fixed	Situations Fixed
$\sigma_c^2 \ (=) \ .53$	$\sigma_c^2 \ (=) \ .81$
$\sigma_r^2 \ (=) \ .11$	$\sigma_r^2 \ (=) \ .10$
$\sigma_s^2 \ (=) \ .04$	$\sigma_s^2 \ (=) \ .04$
$\sigma_{cr}^2 \ (=) \ .01$	$\sigma_{cr}^2 \ (=) \ .01$
$\sigma_{cs}^2 \ (=) \ 1.41$	$\sigma_{cs}^2 \ (=) \ 1.41$
$\sigma_{rs}^2 \ (=) \ 0.00^a$	$\sigma_{rs}^2 \ (=) \ 0.00$
$\sigma^2 \ (=) \ .67$	$\sigma^2 \ (=) \ .67$

[a] When the calculated value of a component is less than zero, the component is estimated to be zero because no component can be negative.

Inspection of this formula shows clearly that increasing the number of visits t will increase reliability much more rapidly than increasing the number of recorders q, since the component divided by t only is much larger than the one divided by q only. When $q = 1$ and $t = 5$, for example, $r = .55$; when $q = 5$ and $t = 1, r = .26$.

It has been pointed out that to assume that one of the variables in a study is fixed has the effect of increasing the reliability. If it is assumed that situations are fixed, that the results are to apply only to the five situations in which the teachers were observed, the estimate of true score variance of scores based on 5 visits by q recorders is estimated from Formula (2) as follows:

$$\sigma_T^2 = (qjt) \, \sigma_c^2 = (q \cdot 1 \cdot 5)^2 \, (.81) = 20.25 q^2.$$

The estimated variance of obtained scores is obtained from Formula (3) as follows:

$$\sigma_x^2 = qjt \, (qjt\sigma_c^2 + jt\sigma_{cr}^2 + \sigma^2)$$

$$(=) \, 5q \, (4.05q + .72).$$

Then the reliability (for q recorders) is:

$$r_q = \frac{4.05q}{4.05q + .72} = \frac{q}{q + .18}$$

For $q = 1$ (one recorder), $r = .85$. Contrast this with the reliability estimate of .55 obtained for the same scores when it is assumed that the population contains an infinite number of situations instead of five.

To find out how a reliability of .85 might be obtained under the less restrictive assumptions, substitute .85 for r in the expression for the reliability with q recorders in t situations. Then the following formula is obtained:

$$.09qt = .01t + 1.41q + .67.$$

With one recorder $(q = 1)$, this becomes

$$.08t = 2.08$$

and $t = 26$; this means that 26 visits would have to be made to secure a reliability of .85 with one observer per visit. With two observers $(q = 2)$:

$$.17t = 3.49$$
$$t = 21,$$

so 21 visits would be needed. To achieve a reliability of .85 with only five visits, a team of 18 recorders would have to be present on each visit.

It should be noted that thus far no assumption of normality has been made or used. The estimation of components does not involve any assumptions other than those already stated about the size of the hypothetical population in which the parameters apply (Cornfield & Tukey, 1956).

Quite a bit more can be learned from an inspection of Table 25. The largest components of variation in these observational records are three: σ_c^2, σ_{cs}^2, and σ^2. Variation from situation to situation within the same class (σ_{cs}^2) appears greater than variation in average behavior from one class to another (σ_c^2). In order to measure differences between classes reliably, therefore, it is necessary to observe each class in a number of situations, so that the fluctuations measured by σ_{cs}^2 can cancel one another out.

The large contribution of unexplained sources of variance indicated by the magnitude of σ^2 shows that there are sizable influences affecting behavior records that were not isolated in this experiment.

There is no variation at all which can be attributed to interaction between recorder and situation (σ_{rs}^2), indicating that the observers are not biased in favor of any one situation over any other. The fact that σ_{cr}^2 is estimated to be only .01 reflects the fact that "observer errors" are very slight.

The fact that the estimates of σ_{cr}^2, σ_s^2, and σ_r^2 are all relatively small, but not zero, makes one wonder whether or not they could be neglected, i.e., whether their true values could be assumed to be zero. A decision can be reached by assuming that the factors concerned, as well as residual variation, are normally distributed, and applying the familiar F test to each one. (Remember that, up to now, this assumption has not been used; normality is assumed only when an F test is made.) For example, note in Table 23 that, under the hypothesis that σ_{cr}^2 is zero, the expected mean square for $C \times R$ and that for residual are both equal to σ^2. The ratio of their obtained mean squares should, if this hypothesis is true, be one. Actually, Table 25 shows it to be (.74/.67), or 1.10. According to Snedecor's Table (Johnson, 1949, pp. 362–365), this value is inside the .05 point of the F distribution with degrees of freedom 23 and 92, so the possibility that σ_{cr}^2 is zero cannot be ruled out.

Under the hypothesis that σ_s^2 is zero, the expected value of the mean square for situations and that for $C \times S$ are the same (since $\sigma_{rs}^2 = 0$). The observed mean squares are 4.75 and 3.49, which have a ratio of 1.36. This value also falls inside of the .05 value of the F distribution with degrees of freedom of 4 and 92, so there is no basis for con-

cluding that the average level of pupil interest recorded depends on the situation in which it is observed. The value of σ_r^2, however, cannot be assumed to equal zero; therefore, it may be concluded that recorder biases do exist, although they do not, of course, affect reliability so long as all classes are observed by the same recorders. The results here are typical in that no component involving recorders is significant except the main effect. It would be quite satisfactory in using this scale to employ only one recorder per visit; if more than one competent observer were available, it would be advisable to send them to visit the classes one at a time, so that the number of different situations recorded would be as large as possible.

Measuring Changes in Behavior

Suppose that the data analyzed in Table 25 are based on observations in five situations, two of which occurred before some event or treatment whose effect on the behavior measured by the item is to be studied, and three of which occurred after this event or treatment. A component of variation due to "gains" over this period will be postulated, σ_g^2. The component due to variation from situation to situation either before or after the "treatment" will be called $\sigma_{s(g)}^2$. The subscript g is enclosed in parentheses to indicate that, although the level of gain may be different in different situations, the component does not reflect variation due to such differences.

Interactions involving situations will also have a subscript g in parentheses to indicate this. Table 26 shows the design for analyzing the data under these circumstances. This will be recognized as a three-way design with a nesting or hierarchical classification in one of the dimensions of the design.

A problem arises in the determination of the coefficient of σ_{crg}^2. Ordinarily, this would be s' where s' is the number of situations observed at each level of gain. In this case, however, the numbers are unequal—s' is two for level one, three for level two. In such a

TABLE 26

DESIGN FOR MEASURING CHANGE IN BEHAVIOR

ANALYSIS OF VARIANCE

Source of Variation	Degrees of Freedom	Mean Square Expected	Obtained
Class	23	$10\sigma_c^2+5\sigma_{cr}^2[+4.8\sigma_{cg}^2]+2\sigma_{cs(g)}^2[+2.4\sigma_{crg}^2]+\sigma^2$	s^2
Recorder	1	$120\sigma_r^2+5\sigma_{cr}^2[+57.6\sigma_{rg}^2]+24\sigma_{rs(g)}^2[+2.4\sigma_{crg}^2]+\sigma^2$	s_r^2
Gain	1	$115.2\sigma_g^2+48\sigma_{s(g)}^2+4.8\sigma_{cg}^2+2\sigma_{cs(g)}^2+57.6\sigma_{rg}^2+24\sigma_{rs(g)}^2+2.4\sigma_{crg}^2+\sigma^2$	s_g^2
Situation (within level of gain)	3	$48\sigma_{s(g)}^2+2\sigma_{cs(g)}^2+24\sigma_{rs(g)}^2+\sigma^2$	s_s^2
$C \times R$	23	$5\sigma_{cr}^2[+2.4\sigma_{crg}^2]+\sigma^2$	s_{cr}^2
$C \times G$	23	$4.8\sigma_{cg}^2+2\sigma_{cs(g)}^2+2.4\sigma_{crg}^2+\sigma^2$	s_{cg}^2
$C \times S$	69	$2\sigma_{cs(g)}^2+\sigma^2$	s_{cs}^2
$R \times G$	1	$57.6\sigma_{rg}^2+24\sigma_{rs(g)}^2[+24\sigma_{crg}^2]+\sigma^2$	s_{rg}^2
$R \times S$	3	$24\sigma_{rs(g)}^2+\sigma^2$	s_{rs}^2
$C \times R \times G$	23	$24\sigma_{crg}^2+\sigma^2$	s_{crg}^2
Residual	69	σ^2	s^2
Total	239		

Estimation of Components

$$\sigma_c^2 \ (=) \ \frac{1}{10} \ (s_c^2 - s_{cr}^2 - s_{cs}^2 + s^2)$$

$$\sigma_r^2 \ (=) \ \frac{1}{120} \ (s_r^2 - s_{cr}^2 - s_{rs}^2 + s^2)$$

$$\sigma_g^2 \ (=) \ \frac{1}{115.2} \ (s_g^2 - s_s^2 - s_{cg}^2 - s_{rg}^2 + s_{cs}^2 + s_{rs}^2)$$

$$\sigma_s^2 \ (=) \ \frac{1}{48} \ (s_s^2 - s_{cr}^2 - s_{rs}^2 + s^2)$$

$$\sigma_{cr}^2 \ (=) \ \frac{1}{5} \ (s_{cr}^2 - s^2)$$

$$\sigma_{cg}^2 \ (=) \ \frac{1}{48} \ (s_{cg}^2 - s_{cs}^2 - s_{crg}^2 + s^2)$$

$$\sigma_{cs}^2 \ (=) \ \frac{1}{2} \ (s_{cs}^2 - s^2)$$

$$\sigma_{rg}^2 \ (=) \ \frac{1}{57.6} \ (s_{rg}^2 - s_{rs}^2)$$

$$\sigma_{rs}^2 \ (=) \ \frac{1}{24} \ (s_{rs}^2 - s^2)$$

$$\sigma_{crg}^2 \ (=) \ \frac{1}{2.4} \ (s_{crg}^2 - s^2)$$

$$\sigma^2 \ (=) \ s^2$$

case the coefficient to be used is k, as given by the following formula (Kempthorne, 1952, p. 104), with s_g representing the number of situations within gain level g:

$$k = \frac{s^2 - \Sigma s_g^2}{s(g-1)} = \frac{25 - (2^2 + 3^2)}{5\ (1)} = 2.4.$$

Since only two levels of gain are of interest

—one before and one after the treatment— it may be assumed that the population contains only two levels of gain. Hence, gain is "fixed." *Rule 3* on page 314 should then be applied, and the components enclosed in brackets in Table 26 eliminated. *Rule 3* must be modified slightly: in deciding which components to eliminate on the basis of "fixed" subscripts, all subscripts enclosed in parentheses are ignored. Thus, in the line for "Class," σ_{cg}^2 is dropped because of the subscript g, but $\sigma_{cs(g)}^2$ is not dropped.

Table 27 shows the analysis of the actual data according to the design in Table 26.

TABLE 27

ANALYSIS OF CHANGES IN BEHAVIOR

Source of Variation	Degrees of Freedom	Analysis of Variance	
		Sum of Squares	Mean Square
Class	23	203	8.83
Recorder	1	13	13.00
Gain	1	11	11.00
Situation within Gain	3	8	2.67
$C \times R$	23	17	0.74
$C \times G$	23	48	2.09
$C \times S$	69	273	3.96
$R \times G$	1	0	0.00
$R \times S$	3	1	0.33
$C \times R \times G$	23	9	0.39
Residual	69	53	0.77
Total	239	636	

Estimation of Components

$$\sigma_c^2 \ (=) \ 0.49$$
$$\sigma_r^2 \ (=) \ 0.11$$
$$\sigma_g^2 \ (=) \ 0.09$$
$$\sigma_{s(g)}^2 \ (=) \ 0.00$$
$$\sigma_{cr}^2 \ (=) \ 0.00$$
$$\sigma_{cg}^2 \ (=) \ 0.00$$
$$\sigma_{cs(g)}^2 \ (=) \ 1.60$$
$$\sigma_{rg}^2 \ (=) \ 0.00$$
$$\sigma_{rs(g)}^2 \ (=) \ 0.00$$
$$\sigma_{crg}^2 \ (=) \ 0.00$$
$$\sigma^2 \ (=) \ 0.77$$

The results suggest that most of the postulated components are unnecessary to account for the observed phenomena: the proposed model is unnecessarily elaborate.

Note that since σ_{crg}^2 is estimated to equal zero, the expected mean squares for $C \times R \times G$ and for "Residual" in Table 27 become the same, i.e., σ^2. They can then be combined or pooled by adding their sums of squares together to get a new estimate of σ^2 based on $69 + 23 = 92$ degrees of freedom. (For a discussion of some of the issues involved in deciding when to pool and when

not to pool, see Green & Tukey, 1960.) If all components estimated to equal zero are dropped and all indicated pooling is carried out, only five components remain, and, correspondingly, five obtained mean squares. The analysis simplifies to the form shown in Table 28. The new estimates of the remaining components based on this analysis are more parsimonious and, in some cases, more precise than those in Table 27. Note that if two recorders visited each class in five situations (at the same gain level), the reliability of the scores obtained would be .61. If one recorder only had been used, the reliability would still be as high as .57.

A new possibility comes to mind when it is realized that the reliability of most observations is very nearly as high with one recorder as it is with two. This is the possibility of using two recorders, but having each visit only half of the classes. If this is done, then σ_x^2 must be redefined, since the subscript r will not be the same in all obtained scores. It becomes:

$$\sigma_x^2 = qt \left(qt\sigma_c^2 + t\sigma_r^2 + q\sigma_{cs(g)}^2 + \sigma^2 \right)$$

$$= qt \left(.54qt + .10t + 1.40q + .67 \right).$$

The reliability then drops from .57 to .51 because recorder biases are increasing the error.

Since the study under discussion was supposed to have been undertaken to ascertain whether or not there was any gain between the second and third visit to the classrooms, the question whether the gain component (σ_g^2) of only .06 represents a true gain in the population, or whether it is just a chance occurrence becomes important. To answer this question, it is necessary to make the assumption of normality and test the hypothesis $\sigma_g^2 = 0$. Under the hypothesis that σ_g^2 is zero, Gain and $C \times S$ have the same expected mean square. The hypothesis is tested by comparing the ratio of the two corresponding obtained mean squares (11.00/3.46, or 3.18) with the F distribution with $n_1 = 1$ and $n_2 = 95$. The hypothesis cannot be rejected: the evidence does not indicate that

TABLE 28

SIMPLIFIED ANALYSIS OF CHANGES IN BEHAVIOR

ANALYSIS OF VARIANCE

Source of Variation	Degrees of Freedom	Sum of Squares	Mean Square		F
			Obtained	Expected	
Class	23	203	8.83	$10\sigma_c^2 + 2\sigma_{cs(g)}^2 + \sigma^2$	2.55
Recorder	1	13	13.00	$120\sigma_r^2 + \sigma^2$	19.40
Gain	1	11	11.00	$124.8\sigma_g^2 + 2\sigma_{cs(g)}^2 + \sigma^2$	3.18
$C \times S$	95	329	3.46	$2\sigma_{cs(g)}^2 + \sigma^2$	5.18
Residual	119	80	.67	σ^2	
Total	239	636			

Estimation of Components

$$\sigma_c^2 \,(=)\, \frac{1}{10}\,(s_c^2 - s_{cs}^2) = 0.54$$

$$\sigma_r^2 \,(=)\, \frac{1}{120}\,(s_r^2 - s^2) = 0.10$$

$$\sigma_g^2 \,(=)\, \frac{1}{124.8}\,(s_g^2 - s_{cs}^2) = 0.06$$

$$\sigma_{cs}^2 \,(=)\, \frac{1}{2}\,(s_{cs}^2 - s^2) = 1.40$$

$$\sigma^2 \,(=)\, s^2 = 0.67$$
$$\sigma_T^2 = (qt)^2\,\sigma_c^2$$
$$= .54\,(qt)^2$$
$$\sigma_x^2 = qt\,(q + \sigma_c^2 + q\sigma_{cs(g)}^2 + \sigma^2)$$
$$(=)\, qt\,(.54qt + 1.40q + .67)$$
$$r = \frac{.54\,qt}{.54qt + 1.40q + .67}$$

the treatment has any effect on the behavior measured.

The other three components, σ_c^2, σ_r^2, and $\sigma_{cs(g)}^2$, when tested in similar fashion, are all found to be greater than zero. There are stable differences in behavior in different classes, there are real recorder biases, and the behavior in a particular class does vary from situation to situation.

Analyzing Results of a Methods Experiment

Suppose that the items analyzed in Table 25 were observed in 24 more classes in 10 situations per class, and recorded by one recorder. Suppose also that three different methods of instruction were used, each one being tried out in 8 of the 24 classes (chosen at random), and that the results were as shown in Table 29. This example illustrates a two-way design with a nesting classification in one dimension.

Note that the residual variance ($\sigma^2 = 3.42$) is much larger this time, doubtless because it includes the type of variation isolated in Table 25 and measured by σ_{cs}^2. There seems to be quite a bit more variation resulting from class-to-class differences within methods ($\sigma_{c(m)}^2 \,(=)\, .41$) than results from method differences ($\sigma_m^2 (=)\, .04$); in fact, the interaction between method and situation in the same class ($\sigma_{ms}^2 (=)\, .06$) appears more important than methods. When F tests are run, it is found that only $\sigma_{c(m)}^2$ may safely be regarded as greater than zero. The reliability coefficient of the records would be estimated as follows:

$$\rho_{xx} = \frac{10\sigma_{c(m)}^2}{10\sigma_{c(m)}^2 + \sigma^2} \,(=)\, \frac{10(.41)}{10(.41) + 3.42}$$

$$(=)\, .55.$$

TABLE 29

ANALYSIS OF OBSERVATIONS IN A METHODS EXPERIMENT

Source of Variation	Degrees of Freedom	Sum of Squares	Observed Mean Square	Expected Mean Square
Methods	2	24	12.00	$80\sigma_m^2 + 10\sigma_{c(m)}^2 + 8\sigma_{ms}^2 + \sigma^2$
Classes (within Methods)	21	179	8.52	$10\sigma_{c(m)}^2 + \sigma^2$
Situations	9	33	3.67	$24\sigma_s^2 + \sigma^2$
$M \times S$	18	70	3.89	$8\sigma_{ms}^2 + \sigma^2$
Residual	189	646	3.42	σ^2
Total	239	942		

Estimation of Components

$$\sigma_m^2 \ (=) \ 0.04$$
$$\sigma_{c(m)}^2 \ (=) \ 0.41$$
$$\sigma_s^2 \ (=) \ 0.01$$
$$\sigma_{ms}^2 \ (=) \ 0.06$$
$$\sigma^2 \ (=) \ 3.42$$

It may be concluded that the records were successful in detecting differences between classes taught by the same method, but did not detect any reliable effects of the method on the behavior measurements.

Analyzing the Results of a Survey

The term *survey* is here used to describe an investigation in which, instead of artificially varying conditions as in the experiment described above, the researcher studies natural variation, measuring the variables he is interested in as they occur in a natural situation, and correlating them to see which are related. This method is widely used in observational studies to tease out relationships between classroom behaviors and other variables, e.g., pupil learning, teacher personality, or average IQ of the class (see Barr, 1948). In the past, research of this type has not been highly productive. One reason may well be that, although in almost every such study the teachers are scattered among several schools, no adjustment is made for the effects of school differences in the correlational analysis. It is widely recognized that when pupils in different schools are compared in an analysis of variance, it is essential to make allowance for school effects either by removing variance attributable to

them as a block effect or, if the school effects can be measured, by adjusting for them by analysis of covariance. It does not seem to be recognized that similar allowances should be made in studies correlating variables measured in different schools, and that this can be done readily by proper application of analysis of covariance techniques (see Kendall, 1948, pp. 237–244). At the same time, a number of other meaningful hypotheses not otherwise accessible can be tested.

We will illustrate how this method may be used by applying it to some hitherto unpublished data collected in the OScAR study (Medley & Mitzel, 1958b, 1959). The data consisted of average pupil gain scores of 49 classes in 19 elementary schools and self-ratings on teaching effectiveness of the 49 teachers who taught these classes. Table 30 shows the sums of squares and cross-products and the adjusted sums of squares of average pupil gains of the two variables for each school, as well as the pooled within-schools, between-schools, and total values of each.

Notice that it would be possible to calculate a correlation coefficient between teachers' self-ratings and average pupil gains in each school. These correlations may or may not all be equal. It is also possible to calculate a pooled within-schools correlation, a between-schools correlation—a correlation, that is, be-

TABLE 30

ILLUSTRATIVE DATA BASED ON SCORES OF 49 CLASSES IN 19 SCHOOLS

School Number	Degrees of Freedom	SUM OF SQUARES			Adjusted Degrees of Freedom	Adjusted Sum of Squares of Average Pupil Gain	Correlation Between Self-Rating and Pupil Gain
		Teachers' Self-Rating	Average Pupil Gain	Sum of Products			
1	1	131.2200	102.2450	+115.8300	0	—	
2	3	201.9600	195.6200	− 40.3800	2	187.5464	
3	1	62.7200	23.1200	− 38.0800	0	—	
4	2	53.5200	28.9066	+ 12.5600	1	25.9590	
5	1	25.9200	98.0000	+ 50.4000	0	—	
6	3	501.8400	287.6900	+174.9000	2	226.7343	
7	2	63.3866	45.7266	+ 52.2666	1	2.6292	
8	2	278.7200	260.3400	+200.1600	1	116.5971	
9	1	174.8450	21.1250	+ 60.7750	0	—	
10	1	62.7200	59.4050	+ 61.0400	0	—	
11	1	192.0800	2.6450	− 22.5400	0	—	
12	1	0.0000	141.1200	+ 0.0000	0	—	
13	1	25.9200	4.2050	− 10.4400	0	—	
14	1	332.8200	378.1250	+354.7500	0	—	
15	1	35.2800	134.4800	− 68.8800	0	—	
16	1	188.1800	23.8050	+ 66.9300	0	—	
17	2	91.5466	142.8266	−111.5733	1	6.8456	
18	4	228.9120	149.6480	− 36.6560	3	143.7822	
19	1	151.3800	468.1800	+266.2200	0	—	
					11	710.0938	
Within	30	2802.9702	2567.2128	1087.2823	29	2145.4521	+.41
Between	18	1686.3008	2232.7272	−343.3523	17	2162.8163	−.18
Total	48	4489.2710	4799.9400	743.9300	47	4676.6612	+.16

tween school means on the two variables— and a total correlation based on the 49 pairs of scores.

The conventional study correlating self-ratings and average pupil gains would test one null hypothesis only:

H_0 : The (total) correlation between self-ratings and pupil gain is zero.

This hypothesis may be tested by the F ratio:

$$F_0 = \frac{(47)(.16)^2}{1-(.16)^2} = \frac{1.203}{.974} = 1.24;$$

$$df = 1, 47.$$

This hypothesis cannot be rejected.

There are also two hypotheses which deal with unadjusted means:

H_1 : The self-rating of the average teacher is the same in all schools.

H_2 : The average gain of pupils in all schools is the same.

These are tested, of course, as follows:

$$F_1 = \frac{93.7}{93.4} = 1.00;$$

$$df = 18, 30.$$

$$F_2 = \frac{124.1}{85.6} = 1.45;$$

$$df = 18, 30.$$

Neither hypothesis can be rejected in our example; we find no evidence that schools differ in these respects.

TABLE 31

ANALYSIS OF VARIANCE AND COVARIANCE OF TEACHER SELF-RATINGS AND
ADJUSTED MEAN READING GROWTH SCORES OF THEIR PUPILS

| | | UNADJUSTED ANALYSIS | | | | | ADJUSTED ANALYSIS OF AVERAGE PUPIL GAIN | | | |
| | | Teacher Self-Ratings | | Average Pupil Gain | | Sum of | | | | |
Source of Variation	Degrees of Freedom	Sum of Squares	Mean Square	Sum of Squares	Mean Square	Cross-Products	Source of Variation	Degrees of Freedom	Sum of Squares	Mean Square
							Deviations from Within-Schools Regressions	11	710	64.5 (a)
							Differences among Within-Schools Regressions	18	1436	79.8 (b)
Within Schools	30	2803	93.4	2567	85.6	+1087	Deviations from Pooled Regression Within Schools	29	2146	74.0 (c)
							Deviations of School Means from Between-Schools Regression	17	2163	127.2 (d)
							Difference Between Regressions Between and Within Schools	1	368	368.0 (e)
Between Schools	18	1686	93.7	2233	124.1	− 343	Subtotal between Schools	18	2531	140.6 (f)
Total	48	4489		4800		+ 744		47	4677	

Many more questions can be asked—and answered—about these data, with the aid of an analysis of covariance, as shown in Table 31. Not all of the hypotheses we shall discuss would be tested in any one analysis, of course. One or another may be of interest, depending on the nature of the data, which, of course, will depend on the purpose of the study. However, for illustrative purposes we will test them all in these data.

The analysis shown in Tables 30 and 31 was designed to study the relationships between teachers' self-ratings and the average gain of their pupils. If we have no a priori hypothesis about the nature of this relationship, we can make a conservative test of the following hypothesis:

H_3 : There is no relationship of any type between self-ratings and mean gains

by the following F ratio:

$$F_3 = \frac{(11)\ (4677 - 710)}{(36)\ (710)} = 1.71;$$

$$df = 36,\ 11.$$

The mean square associated with the 11 degrees of freedom estimates the residual variation in average pupil gain not accountable for by any differences between schools or correlation with teachers' self-ratings. This mean square is compared in F_3 with all of the other variation present. We cannot reject H_3 on the basis of this F ratio.

There are, however, some specific hypotheses which may be tested by themselves. We might, for instance, suspect that the degree to which teacher effectiveness, as measured by mean reading growth scores of pupils, can be predicted from teachers' ratings of their own skill varies from school to school, and propose the following null hypothesis:

H_4 : The correlation between self-ratings and pupil gains is the same in all schools.

The test of this hypothesis would employ

$$F_4 = \frac{b}{a} = \frac{79.8}{64.5} = 1.24;$$

$$df = 18, 11.$$

We cannot reject this hypothesis, so let us assume that it is true—that all of the correlations are equal. We then can estimate this correlation from Table 30 to be + .41.

We now ask ourselves whether the population correlation we estimated to be .41 could actually be zero. So we propose another null hypothesis:

H_5 : Teachers' skill, as measured by the average growth of their pupils, cannot be predicted from their ratings of their own skill.

We test it with

$$F_5 = \frac{(11)\ (.41)^2}{1 - (.41)^2} = 2.16;$$

$$df = 1, 11.$$

This hypothesis cannot be rejected either. However, we will not assume that it is true until we have to. For instance, consider this hypothesis:

H_6 : When differences in class mean gains (within schools) predictable from teachers' self-ratings are removed, no differences in school mean gains remain.

If we assume H_5 to be true, that is, that class mean gains cannot be predicted from teacher

self-ratings, H_6 is equivalent to H_2 and has already been tested by F_2. If we do not make this assumption, we can still test H_6 by the ratio.

$$F_6 = \frac{f}{c} = \frac{140.6}{74.0} = 1.90;$$

$$df = 18, 29.$$

Readers familiar with the usual analysis of variance and covariance will recognize that H_6 is the hypothesis of equality of adjusted means which such analyses are usually set up to test. In the present instance we cannot reject H_6.

If we had rejected H_6, it would be reasonable to ask whether the school mean gain scores could not themselves be predicted from the mean self-rating of the teachers in the school. Note that a new element is introduced here: up to now we have suggested only that by comparing self-ratings of different teachers within the same school we might predict differences in average pupil gains for different classes in the same school. Now we are talking about comparing self-ratings from teachers in different schools to predict differences in average pupil gain in different schools, which (as we shall see) may be quite a different thing. Despite the fact that we have no evidence that there are any school differences to predict, we will go ahead. A test of the following hypothesis is available:

H_7 : The regression of school mean gains on school mean self-ratings is linear.

The F ratio is

$$F_7 = \frac{d}{c} = \frac{127.2}{74.0} = 1.72;$$

$$df = 17, 29.$$

We cannot reject this hypothesis, so let us assume it to be true. Our estimate of the correlation between the school means is — .18, which is rather small. So let us propose this hypothesis:

H_8 : There is no correlation between the mean pupil gain score in a school and the mean self-rating of the teachers in that school.

The F ratio is:

$$F_8 = \frac{(17)\,(-.18)^2}{1-(-.18)^2} < 1\,;$$

$$df = 1, 17.$$

We cannot reject this hypothesis—we have no evidence that the means are correlated. Nor have we conclusive evidence that the ratings and gain scores within schools are correlated, since H_5 was not rejected. However, either one or both might be different from zero, but too small for the difference to be detected with so few degrees of freedom available. So we may still raise a question whether the two correlations are equal to each other, and test one more hypothesis:

H_9 : The correlation between teacher self-ratings and pupil gains within schools is equal to the correlation between school means of the same variables.

To test H_9 we use

$$F_9 = \frac{e}{c} = \frac{368.0}{74.0} = 4.97\,;$$

$$df = 1, 29.$$

This hypothesis can be rejected because the probability of the observed F, if the hypothesis is true, is less than .05. We conclude, then, that at least one of the correlations is different from zero; in view of the sample values of $+ .41$ and $- .18$, it is most likely that the within correlation is the one. It appears that differences in effectiveness of teachers in the same school, measured in terms of average pupil gains, can be predicted from the teachers' own self-ratings better than differences in average effectiveness of teachers in different schools can be predicted from such ratings. In fact, the observed negative between-schools correlation suggests that those schools whose teachers rate themselves above average are the ones whose teachers are most likely to be below average in effectiveness.

We have, perhaps, subjected these few data to more statistical analysis than they can be reasonably expected to support. If so, we have probably achieved our purpose in doing so: to demonstrate how much of the information they contain would be lost if the analysis were to stop with the calculation of the total correlation of .16 and the testing of H_0 only.

CONCLUDING REMARKS

A full treatment of the methodology of analysis of behavior measurements is beyond the scope of this chapter. The foregoing examples have been presented merely to suggest the vast potential of the analysis of variance and covariance for solving problems in this area. It has seemed important to emphasize these matters because, as was mentioned earlier, the difficulty of obtaining observational data and their consequent scarcity make it imperative that all usable information be extracted from such data.

Two widespread misconceptions about complex designs should be noted here. One is that a nonparametric method must be used in analyzing behavior data because the assumption of normality does not hold. The minor role this assumption plays has already been pointed out; it has been shown that much information can be extracted from behavior data without making any assumptions about the form of their sampling distribution. Besides, in the experience of the authors it is quite unusual to find behavior data about which the assumption cannot reasonably be made. Finally, the consequences of making this assumption when it is not true are much less serious than many research workers fear.

The second erroneous notion seems to be that one experiment can and ought to shed light on only one hypothesis. This notion reveals itself in a distrust of anything more sophisticated than a "critical ratio" analysis. Some research workers will also admit a *t* test (although the concept of degrees of freedom worries them), and the coefficient of correlation has, of course, the respectability of age. But for some reason, related to the first misconception described, the untrained worker suspects that an elaborate analysis of variance must involve improper assumptions, dubious algebra, or something suspicious; otherwise, it could not possibly yield such a wealth of information.

This attitude has a certain quaint charm and is not difficult to understand. But in anyone charged with responsibility for improving our limited knowledge of the teaching process, it is very difficult to forgive. Any reader who plans to do research in classroom behavior cannot shirk the obligation to learn how to analyze his data properly. Research on classroom behavior is not a pastime for amateurs: it is a full-time occupation for technically competent professionals.

REFERENCES

American Educational Research Association, Committee on the Criteria of Teacher Effectiveness. Report of the. . . . *Rev. educ. Res.,* 1952, 22, 238–263.

American Educational Research Association, Committee on the Criteria of Teacher Effectiveness. Second report of the. . . . *J. educ. Res.,* 1953, 46, 441–458.

Anderson, H. H., & Brewer, Helen M. Studies of teachers' classroom personalities. I. Dominative and socially integrative behavior of kindergarten teachers. *Appl. Psychol. Monogr.,* 1945, No. 6.

Anderson, H. H., & Brewer, J. E. Studies of teachers' classroom personalities. II. Effects of teachers' dominative and integrative contacts on children's classroom behavior. *Appl. Psychol. Monogr.,* 1946, No. 8.

Anderson, H. H., Brewer, J. E., & Reed, Mary F. Studies of teachers' classroom personalities. III. Follow-up studies of the effects of dominative and integrative contacts on children's behavior. *Appl. Psychol. Monogr.,* 1946, No. 11.

Anderson, H. M. A study of certain criteria of teaching effectiveness. *J. exp. Educ.,* 1954, 23, 41–71.

Barker, R. G., & Wright, H. F. *One boy's day.* New York: Harper, 1951.

Barr, A. S. *Characteristic differences in the teaching performance of good and poor teachers of the social studies.* Bloomington, Ill.: Public School Publishing Co., 1929.

Barr, A. S. The measurement and prediction of teaching efficiency: A summary of investigations. *J. exp. Educ.,* 1948, 16, 203–283.

Baxter, Bernice. *Teacher-pupil relationships.* New York: Macmillan, 1941.

Bowers, N. D., & Soar, R. S. *Studies of human relations in the teaching-learning process. V. Final report: Evaluation of laboratory human relations training for classroom teachers.* Chapel Hill: Univer. of North Carolina (U. S. Office of Educ. Coop. Res. Project No. 469), 1961. (Mimeographed)

Brookover, W. B. The relation of social factors to teaching ability. *J. exp. Educ.,* 1945, 13, 191–205.

Brown, G. I. Which pupil to which classroom climate? *Elem. sch. J.,* 1960, 60, 265–269.

Cook, W. W., Leeds, C. H., & Callis, R. *Minnesota Teacher Attitude Inventory.* New York: Psychological Corp., 1951.

Cornell, F. G., Lindvall, C. M., & Saupe, J. L. *An exploratory measurement of individualities of schools and classrooms.* Urbana: Bur. of Educ. Res., Univer. of Illinois, 1952.

Cornfield, J., & Tukey, J. W. Average values of mean squares in factorials. *Ann. math. Statist.,* 1956, 27, 907–949.

Cronbach, L. J. Coefficient alpha and the internal structure of tests. *Psychometrika,* 1951, 16, 297–334.

Eisenhart, C. The assumptions underlying the analysis of variance. *Biometrics,* 1947, 3, 1–21.

English, H. B., & English, Ava C. *A comprehensive dictionary of psychological and psychoanalytical terms.* New York: Longmans, Green, 1958.

Fisher, R. A. *Statistical methods for research workers.* (11th ed.) London: Oliver & Boyd, 1950.

Flanagan, J. C. Critical requirements: A new

approach to employee evaluation. *Personnel Psychol.*, 1949, 2, 419–425.

Flanders, N. A. *Teacher influence, pupil attitudes, and achievement.* Minneapolis: Univer. of Minnesota (U. S. Office of Educ. Coop. Res. Project No. 397), 1960. (Mimeographed)

Gotham, R. E. Personality and teaching efficiency. *J. exp. Educ.*, 1945, 14, 157–165.

Green, B. F., & Tukey, J. W. Complex analyses of variance: General problems. *Psychometrika*, 1960, 25, 127–152.

Harrington, G. M. Smiling as a measure of teacher effectiveness. *J. educ. Res.*, 1955, 48, 715–717.

Hathaway, S. R., & McKinley, J. C. *Minnesota Multiphasic Personality Inventory.* New York: Psychological Corp., 1943. (Rev. ed. of *Manual*, 1951)

Hellfritzsch, A. G. A factor analysis of teacher abilities. *J. exp. Educ.*, 1945, 14, 166–199.

Heyns, R. W., & Lippitt, R. Systematic observational techniques. In G. Lindzey (Ed.), *Handbook of social psychology.* Cambridge, Mass.: Addison-Wesley, 1954. Pp. 370–404.

Heyns, R. W., & Zander, A. F. Observation of group behavior. In L. Festinger & D. Katz (Eds.), *Research methods in the behavioral sciences.* New York: Dryden, 1953. Pp. 381–417.

Horn, E. Distribution of opportunity for participation among the various pupils in classroom recitations. *Teach. Coll. Contr. Educ.*, 1914, No. 67.

Howsam, R. B. *New designs for research in teacher competence.* Burlingame, Calif.: California Teachers Association, 1960.

Hughes, Marie. *Development of the means for the assessment of the quality of teaching in elementary schools.* Salt Lake City: Univer. of Utah Press, 1959.

Jayne, C. D. A study of the relationship between teaching procedures and educational outcomes. *J. exp. Educ.*, 1945, 14, 101–134.

Jersild, A. T., Thorndike, R. L., Goldman, B., & Loftus, J. J. An evaluation of aspects of the activity program in the New York City public elementary schools. *J. exp. Educ.*, 1939, 8, 166–207.

Johnson, P. O. *Statistical methods in research.* New York: Prentice-Hall, 1949.

Johnson, P. O., & Fay, L. C. The Johnson-Neyman technique: Its theory and application. *Psychometrika*, 1950, 15, 349–367.

Jones, R. deV. The prediction of teaching efficiency from objective measures. *J. exp. Educ.*, 1946, 15, 85–99.

Kempthorne, O. *The design and analysis of experiments.* New York: Wiley, 1952.

Kendall, M. G. *The advanced theory of statistics.* Vol. II. (2nd ed.) London: Griffin, 1948.

La Duke, C. V. The measurement of teaching ability. *J. exp. Educ.*, 1945, 14, 75–100.

Lins, L. J. The prediction of teaching efficiency. *J. exp. Educ.*, 1946, 15, 2–60.

Medley, D. M., & Klein, Alix A. Measuring classroom behavior with a pupil-reaction inventory. *Elem. sch. J.*, 1957, 57, 315–319.

Medley, D. M., & Mitzel, H. E. *Studies of teacher behavior: Refinement of two techniques for assessing teachers' classroom behaviors.* New York: Board of Higher Education, City of New York, Div. of Teacher Education, Office of Res. and Evaluation, 1955 (Res. Series No. 28).

Medley, D. M., & Mitzel, H. E. Application of analysis of variance to the estimation of the reliability of observations of teachers' classroom behavior. *J. exp. Educ.*, 1958, 27, 23–25. (a)

Medley, D. M., & Mitzel, H. E. A technique for measuring classroom behavior. *J. educ. Psychol.*, 1958, 49, 86–92. (b)

Medley, D. M., & Mitzel, H. E. Some behavioral correlates of teacher effectiveness. *J. educ. Psychol.*, 1959, 50, 239–246.

Medley, D. M., Mitzel, H. E., & Doi, A. N. Analysis-of-variance models and their use in a three-way design without replication. *J. exp. Educ.*, 1956, 24, 221–229.

Mitzel, H. E. Teacher effectiveness. In C. W. Harris (Ed.), *Encyclopedia of educational research.* (3rd ed.) New York: Macmillan, 1960. Pp. 1481–1486.

Mitzel, H. E., & Gross, Cecily F. The development of pupil-growth criteria in studies of teacher effectiveness. *Educ. res. Bull.*, 1958, 37, 178–187, 205–275.

Mitzel, H. E., & Rabinowitz, W. Assessing social-emotional climate in the classroom by Withall's technique. *Psychol. Monogr.*, 1953, 67, No. 18 (Whole No. 368).

Morrison, H. C. *The practice of teaching in the secondary school.* Chicago: Univer. of Chicago Press, 1926.

Morrison, Virginia B. The relationship of student teacher performance and pupil performance to supervisory and pupil merit ratings. Unpublished doctoral dissertation, Univer. of Michigan, 1961.

Morsh, J. E. Development report—Systematic observation of instructor behavior. *USAF Pers. Train. Res. Cent. Develpm. Rept,* 1956, No. AFPTRC-TN-56-52.

Morsh, J. E., & Wilder, Eleanor W. Identifying the effective instructor: A review of the quantitative studies, 1900–1952. *USAF Pers. Train. Res. Cent. Res. Bull.,* 1954, No. AFPTRC-TR-54-44.

Puckett, R. C. Making supervision objective. *Sch. Rev.,* 1928, 36, 209–212.

Rabinowitz, W., & Rosenbaum, I. A failure in the prediction of pupil-teacher rapport. *J. educ. Psychol.,* 1958, 49, 93–98.

Ryans, D. G. *Characteristics of teachers.* Washington, D.C.: American Council on Education, 1960.

Scott, W. A. Reliability of content analysis: The case of nominal scale coding. *Publ. opin. Quart.,* 1955, 19, 321–325.

Selltiz, Claire, Jahoda, Marie, Deutsch, M., & Cook, S. W. *Research methods in social relations.* (Rev. ed.) New York: Holt, 1959.

Smith, B. O. A study of the logic of teaching: A report on the first phase of a five-year research project. Washington, D.C.: U. S. Office of Education, 1959. (Dittoed)

Stanley, J. C. Controlled experimentation in the classroom. *J. exp. Educ.,* 1957, 25, 195–201.

Thomas, Dorothy S., and associates. Some new techniques for studying social behavior. *Child Develpm. Monogr.,* 1929, 1.

Thomson, G. *The factorial analysis of human ability.* (5th ed.) Boston: Houghton Mifflin, 1951.

Travers, R. M. W. *An introduction to educational research.* New York: Macmillan, 1958.

Urban, J. *Behavior changes resulting from a study of communicable diseases.* New York: Bur. of Publs., Teachers Coll., Columbia Univer., 1943.

Wilk, R. E., Edson, W. H., Davies, D., & Chase, Naomi C. *Student teacher activities and pupil responses: A report to participants.* Minneapolis: Bur. of Educ. Res., Univer. of Minnesota, 1960.

Wispé, L. G. Evaluating section teaching methods in the introductory course. *J. educ. Res.,* 1951, 45, 161–186.

Withall, J. Development of a technique for the measurement of socio-emotional climate in classrooms. *J. exp. Educ.,* 1949, 17, 347–361.

Withall, J. The development of a climate index. *J. educ. Res.,* 1951, 45, 93–99.

Wright, H. F. Observational child study. In P. H. Mussen (Ed.), *Handbook of research methods in child development.* New York: Wiley, 1960. Pp. 71–139.

Wright, E. Muriel J. Development of an instrument for studying verbal behaviors in a secondary school mathematics classroom. *J. exp. Educ.,* 1959, 28, 103–121.

Wright, E. Muriel J., & Proctor, Virginia H. *Systematic observation of verbal interaction as a method of comparing mathematics lessons.* St. Louis, Mo.: Washington Univer. (U. S. Office of Educ. Coop. Res. Project No. 816), 1961.

Wrightstone, J. W. Measuring teacher conduct of class discussion. *Elem. sch. J.,* 1934, 34, 454–460.

Wrightstone, J. W. *Appraisal of newer practices in selected public schools.* New York: Bur. of Publs., Teachers Coll., Columbia Univer., 1935.

CHAPTER 7 Rating Methods in
Research on Teaching

H. H. REMMERS
Purdue University

It is likely that no approach to the measurement of variables in research on teaching has been used more often than the rating method. So widespread and basic has been the use of rating methods in research on teaching that the classification of annotations in the 1,006-item annotated bibliography on teacher competence by Domas and Tiedeman (1950) contained several major headings devoted to various uses of the rating method. Since 1950 the use of rating methods has not diminished in importance or frequency.

The reason for these conditions is readily understood. Many of the variables in research on teaching are so complex that tests, questions, and objective behavior records are either inadequate or too inconvenient. Sometimes we need what only a recording instrument as sensitive, complex, and alert as a human observer can tell us about the behavior or characteristics of another person or object, and then we turn to the methods of recording and communicating such messages called rating scales.

Rating is defined by Good (1959, p. 439) as "an estimate, made according to some systematized procedure, of the degree to which an individual person or thing possesses any given characteristic; may be expressed qualitatively or quantitatively." Good defines *rating scale* as "a device used in evaluating products, attitudes, or other characteristics of instructors or learners. (The usual form is an evaluation chart carrying suggestive points for checking)" (1959, p. 440).

Note that the measuring device is not the paper form but rather the individual rater. Hence a rating scale differs in important respects from other paper-and-pencil devices. In addition to any limitations imposed by the form itself, ratings are limited by the characteristics of the human rater—his inevitably selective perception, memory, and forgetting, his lack of sensitivity to what may be psychologically and socially important, his inaccuracies of observation and, in the case of self-ratings, the well-established tendency to put his best foot forward, to perceive himself in a more favorable perspective than others do.

For various more specific definitions of *rating* and *rating scale,* the entries in Good (1959) are modified by adjectives, e.g., "behavior rating," "efficiency rating," "merit rating," "rank-order rating," for *rating* and "descriptive rating scale," "graphic rating scale," "man-to-man rating scale," "numerical rating scale," "occupational rating scale," "personality rating scale," and "teacher rating scale" for *rating scale*.

The above definition of *rating* requires the term *thing* to be broadly interpreted to include not only individual persons but groups variously defined, e.g., by nationality, race, sex, age, club membership, level of education, vocation, and hundreds of other possible bases. "Things" must also be interpreted to include ideas and concepts of possible concern to the researcher, for, in the absence of a better or more acceptable measuring device, ratings are often used to measure judgments, particularly evaluative judgments, of such "things." Note, for example, such concepts as military service, separation of church and state, lowering the voting age, desegregation of schools, teaching effectiveness, and the like. In nearly all research on teaching, ratings and rating scales have borne a very large part of the burden of proof, particularly as the dependent, or criterion, variable(s) in correlational studies.

The term *scale* is conceptually and operationally ill defined when used with the adjective *rating*. To clear away some of the semantic underbrush, various meanings of the term *scale* as used in measurement (nominal, ordinal, interval, and ratio scales) are reviewed in Chapter 4.

RATING SCALES
AS MEASURING DEVICES

By what criteria can we judge rating scales as measuring devices? The criteria should include at least the following properties of any measuring instrument designated as a rating scale used in research on teaching.

1. *Objectivity*. Use of the instrument should yield verifiable, reproducible data not a function of the peculiar characteristics of the rater.

2. *Reliability*. It should yield the same values, within the limits of allowable error, under the same set of conditions. Since basically, in ratings, the rater and not the record of his response is the instrument, this criterion boils down to the accuracy of observations by the rater.

3. *Sensitivity*. It should yield as fine distinctions as are typically made in communicating about the object of investigation.

4. *Validity*. Its content, in this case the categories in the rating scale, should be relevant to a defined area of investigation and to some relevant behavioral science construct; if possible, the data should be covariant with some other, experimentally independent, index. These requirements correspond to the concepts of definitional, construct, concurrent, and predictive validity (American Psychological Association, et al., 1954).

5. *Utility*. It should efficiently yield information relevant to contemporary theoretical and practical issues; i.e., it should not be so cumbersome and laborious as to preclude collection of data at a reasonable rate.

Rating scales belong logically under the psychophysical heading of "successive intervals," which is described by Guilford as follows:

Essentially, the experimental operation is that of judging each of several stimuli as belonging in one of a limited number of categories differing quantitatively along a defined continuum. No assumption is made concerning the psychological equality of category intervals. It is assumed only that the categories are in correct rank order and that their boundary lines are stable except for sampling errors (Guilford, 1954, p. 223).

While the originators and users of rating scales are usually unaware of the parental role of psychophysics vis-à-vis rating devices, modern psychophysical theory has provided a much better rational basis for psychological measurement, including ratings and rating scales, than was the case not more than three decades ago (Guilford, 1954). William James, were he living today, would certainly not find the literature of psychophysics, all of which he had taxed himself with reading, less rewarding and more futile than counting the stones on a New England farm. Problems of scaling in the behavioral sciences and particularly in psychology have brought forth a formidable, rapidly growing, and highly technical literature.

KINDS OF RATING SCALES

If we take literally the definition of *rating* and *rating scale* given earlier in this chapter, we find ourselves in some semantic confusion. The definition of rating as the psychological operation of making judgments concerning objects would make rating scales of many instruments not usually *called* by that name. A considerable number of self-report instruments variously labeled as personality schedules, problem inventories, interest inventories, preference schedules, attitude scales, opinion questionnaires, and the like, all have in common the essential property of requiring the respondent to make and record judgments concerning himself or some other object. To review within the purview of a chapter on rating scales the vast literature related to these concepts is neither reasonable nor desirable. More profitable for the prospective researcher on teaching is a review of genera and species of rating scales and their properties, and, later, some issues and programs in research on teaching in which rating scales may be or have been applied.

Rating scales have been categorized in various ways. Guilford (1954) gives five major groupings: *numerical, graphic, standard, cumulated points,* and *forced-choice,* but also makes the point that "any such classification must necessarily be a very loose one, based on shifting principles" (p. 263). Guilford's chapter on "Rating Scales" (1954, pp. 263-301)— perhaps the most comprehensive single treatment—is anchored in psychological and psychophysical theory and based on a fairly exhaustive review of the experimental literature (to 1952, the time of his writing). Other references giving some generality of treatment are the various entries under "Rating

Scales" in the *Encyclopedia of Educational Research* (Harris, 1960), in Rummel (1958), and in Remmers (1954, pp. 222–234). Our discussion follows Guilford's (1954) general classification with some modifications and additions.

Numerical Rating Scales

While numerical rating scales have appeared in many varieties, their generic unity stems from their having numbers assigned to the categories, usually on an a priori basis. For example, as a first approximation to valid content of a psychological measuring device, the researcher may collect a large number of statements designed to measure, let us say, teacher morale. He could then ask experts— social psychologists, experienced educators— to evaluate the relevance of the statements under instructions such as the following:

Please rate the following items on their relevance to measuring teacher morale by means of a self-report questionnaire. Write before each item a number to indicate its degree of relevance according to the following scale:

    3 = highly relevant
    2 = somewhat relevant
    1 = irrelevant

Having obtained these ratings from his jury of experts—numbering perhaps eight to twelve—the researcher retains for further experimentation those items which, say, two-thirds or three-fourths of his experts have rated at least a 2. He may also ask these judges or another similarly chosen jury to indicate a scoring scheme of, say, five categories—Agree Strongly, Agree, Uncertain or Indifferent, Disagree, and Strongly Disagree. Or he may instead provide a five-point rating scale for these categories: 5 = Agree Strongly, etc.

Obviously, in such a procedure the investigator is assuming without empirical proof that the intervals on this kind of arbitrarily assigned a priori scale represent equal psychological intervals between adjacent numbers. He can, of course, by suitable psychophysical experimentation determine the validity of his assumption. But in the actual use of numerical rating scales such experimentation is seldom done.

Some "numerical" rating scales actually have no numbers assigned. In the hypothetical example above of the five-point scale, the experts might be asked to respond with one of the verbal categories. The experimenter could then assign the numbers afterwards in scoring and quantifying his results.

ical investigation and revision. Its bipolar terminal verbal anchors (traits), as well as the seven-point numerical scale, are reminiscent of the "semantic differential" described later in this chapter. Each of the terms in this scale was carefully defined in the instructions and training given the raters. Figure 2 shows an excerpt from the Glossary provided the observers for use with the Classroom Observation Record.

Ryans' work in training his observers ex-

CLASSROOM OBSERVATION RECORD

9–22–51

TEACHER CHARACTERISTICS STUDY

Teacher_____ No.____Sex____Class or Subject_____ Date_____

City_____School_____Time_____Observer_____

Pupil Behavior   Remarks:
1. Apathetic	1	2	3	4	5	6	7	N	Alert
2. Obstructive	1	2	3	4	5	6	7	N	Responsible
3. Uncertain	1	2	3	4	5	6	7	N	Confident
4. Dependent	1	2	3	4	5	6	7	N	Initiating

Teacher Behavior
5. Partial	1	2	3	4	5	6	7	N	Fair
6. Autocratic	1	2	3	4	5	6	7	N	Democratic
7. Aloof	1	2	3	4	5	6	7	N	Responsive
8. Restricted	1	2	3	4	5	6	7	N	Understanding
9. Harsh	1	2	3	4	5	6	7	N	Kindly
10. Dull	1	2	3	4	5	6	7	N	Stimulating
11. Stereotyped	1	2	3	4	5	6	7	N	Original
12. Apathetic	1	2	3	4	5	6	7	N	Alert
13. Unimpressive	1	2	3	4	5	6	7	N	Attractive
14. Evading	1	2	3	4	5	6	7	N	Responsible
15. Erratic	1	2	3	4	5	6	7	N	Steady
16. Excitable	1	2	3	4	5	6	7	N	Poised
17. Uncertain	1	2	3	4	5	6	7	N	Confident
18. Disorganized	1	2	3	4	5	6	7	N	Systematic
19. Inflexible	1	2	3	4	5	6	7	N	Adaptable
20. Pessimistic	1	2	3	4	5	6	7	N	Optimistic
21. Immature	1	2	3	4	5	6	7	N	Integrated
22. Narrow	1	2	3	4	5	6	7	N	Broad

Fig. 1. Assessment Blank Employed by Observers (From Ryans, 1960, p. 86, with permission of the author and publisher).

An example of an experimentally refined numerical scale is that developed by Ryans (1960, p. 86) in his extensive research program on teacher characteristics. The content of this Classroom Observation Record (Fig. 1) was determined after considerable empir-

emplifies the principle that the measuring instrument in the rating method is not so much the paper device itself as it is the rater, judge, or observer. His summary of his training procedure is quoted here as an example of a closer approximation to the ideal than

1. Apathetic-Alert Pupil Behavior

Apathetic
1. Listless.
2. Bored-acting.
3. Entered into activities half-heartedly.
4. Restless.
5. Attention wandered.
6. Slow in getting under way.

Alert
1. Appeared anxious to recite and participate.
2. Watched teacher attentively.
3. Worked concentratedly.
4. Seemed to respond eagerly.
5. Prompt and ready to take part in activities when they began.

2. Obstructive-Responsible Pupil Behavior

Obstructive
1. Rude to one another and/or to teacher.
2. Interrupting; demanding attention; disturbing.
3. Obstinate; sullen.
4. Refusal to participate.
5. Quarrelsome; irritable.
6. Engaged in name-calling and/or tattling.
7. Unprepared.

Responsible
1. Courteous, cooperative, friendly with each other and with teacher.
2. Completed assignments without complaining or unhappiness.
3. Controlled voices.
4. Received help and criticism attentively.
5. Asked for help when needed.
6. Orderly without specific directions from teacher.
7. Prepared.

Fig. 2. Excerpt from Glossary for use with Classroom Observation Record (Ryans, 1960, pp. 86–87).

has typically been achieved in this crucial aspect of the rating method:

Observers were trained both individually and in groups, the latter being the more frequent practice. The training procedure consisted of several phases, which may be summarized as follows: (1) the observer trainee met with the senior observer for briefing, review of the Record and Glossary, and discussion of the problems involved in direct observation and assessment; (2) the observer trainee studied the Record and Glossary at length; (3) the trainee and senior observer simultaneously observed a teacher for one class period and made independent assessments on copies of the Record; (4) the trainee met with the senior observer to discuss the observation just completed, to compare assessments, and to clarify the bases for assessments as given in the Glossary; (5) additional simultaneous observations and assessments were made by the trainee and senior observer, followed by further consultation; (6) in the final phase of training, the trainee and the senior observer made forty-five minute observations of the same teachers, but *at different times,*

and subsequently conferred to compare and discuss the assessments made.

During the process of training, correlations between the assessments of the trainee and those of the senior observer were computed as a check upon the training. By the completion of training, observer reliability as measured by correlations of the trainee-senior observer assessments usually were between .8 and .9,* which signified substantial agreement (Ryans, 1960, p. 93).

Another numerical rating scale, similar in format and style to Ryans' but using different bipolar adjectives, was developed by McGee (1955, p. 113) for his research on the classroom behavior correlates of the F scale as a measure of authoritarianism in teachers. Each of the items in McGee's Classroom Observation Record was chosen for its appropriateness "in the sense that it should be related in some dynamic way to one or more of the

* This level of agreement was not usually maintained over an extended series of observations and assessments. Refresher training often was required (Ryans, 1960, p. 93).

variables comprising the authoritarian syndrome" (McGee, 1955, p. 110).

Rating scales designed to measure degree of liking or disliking, approval or disapproval, acceptance or rejection, and the like, assume affectivity to be a linear continuum with a zero-point at indifference, thus leading logically to negative and positive halves of the scale. Negative numbers, however, are a nuisance to the researcher and may be confusing to the respondent. It is best to avoid them.

To anchor an affective scale, i.e., to define its terminals, it seems best at first glance to avoid categories so extreme that no one will use them. Hunt and Volkmann (1937) showed experimentally, however, that the addition of an extreme category at either end makes for greater dispersion of the distribution of ratings.

From the foregoing it is obvious that numerical scales are easy to construct and apply. Processing the data obtained by means of them is also relatively simple. These two properties, of course, account for the exten-

sive use of numerical a priori scales. It is even possible that the numbers assigned to the categories of the scale correspond to psychological reality, although this is unlikely and in any case can only be demonstrated experimentally through psychophysical scaling. Failing that, the researcher's data logically are ordinal in nature, although Michels and Helson (1949) have supported the idea that ratings have the properties of interval and ratio scales even when the categories are not numbered.

Graphic Rating Scales

The graphic rating scale provides a continuous straight line with cues or categories along the line to guide the rater. It appears in many varieties, for it is possible to present the straight line in many ways, with or without descriptive categories and with or without numbers for the scale units. The illustrations shown below indicate how the categories can be either constant or changing.

On many rating scales, the line to indicate

Is this teacher permissive?

| Extremely | Rather | Somewhat | Hardly | Not at all |

Is this teacher business-like?

| Extremely | Rather | Somewhat | Hardly | Not at all |

Is this teacher permissive?

| Permissive in all situations | Usually permissive, rarely authoritarian | Not dependably permissive, sometimes dictatorial | Usually dictatorial | Dictatorial in all situations |

Is this teacher business-like?

| Always orderly and business-like | Usually orderly and business-like | Sometimes unsystematic and unbusiness-like | Usually unsystematic and unbusiness-like | Invariably unbusiness-like and unsystematic |

the continuum of the characteristic is divided into unit distances, usually of equal length. Sometimes numbers are assigned to these units; then scoring across items is often done by summing such numbers on the assumption that the traits are equal in importance.

The horizontal arrangement shown above is by far the most frequent. Some investigators, however, prefer a vertical line. Champney (1941) deplored the fact that the graphic rating scale had its origin in the analogy of the yardstick rather than the thermometer. With a vertical arrangement there is more room for descriptive categories, especially if only one aspect has to be rated on each page, a format which has been urged as a means of controlling, or at least minimizing, contamination of ratings through "halo effect" and other response sets.

The following suggestions for constructing graphic rating scales are based chiefly on common sense rather than on experimental findings, and on some there is divided opinion. If any appear dubious to the reader, some psychophysical experimentation is in order.

1. The line, whether horizontal or vertical, should be unbroken. A broken line may suggest discontinuities or other unwanted assumptions about the complexity of the variables.

2. The line should be five or six inches long—long enough to allow indication of all the discrimination of which the rater is capable. Longer lines may actually decrease the spread of the ratings through the rater's greater tendency to cluster his ratings on a long line.

3. The direction of the lines should be the same; i.e., the socially desirable end should be the same for all the traits or other objects to be rated. It has often been argued that the desirable end should alternate randomly from one line to the next to control response sets, particularly those of halo and leniency. Guilford (1954, p. 268) argues that the fact of such control has never been demonstrated. In experimentation with the ten personal

characteristics of college teachers contained in the Purdue Rating Scale for Instruction, Remmers (1960) found no systematic difference between one arrangement and the other. Students rated their teachers equally well by either.

4. If several objects are to be rated, the arrangement on the page that favors rating all of them on one characteristic before proceeding to another characteristic is best. Again control of halo effect is at issue as well as the fact that it is presumably easier for the rater to rate in this fashion than it is for him to have to change his stance, so to speak, for each response across characteristics for the same object.

5. Guilford (1954) suggests that for unsophisticated raters the "good" end of the line should come first, because, in rating people, the typical rater likes to think of the good qualities first. Putting the "good" end first capitalizes on this tendency. In experimenting with different arrangements of the 10 personality traits of the Purdue Rating Scale for Instruction, Remmers (1960) found it made no difference. With psychologically scaled attitude items, extensive experimentation by Sigerfoos (1936) showed that no arrangement—items randomly distributed, good end first or last—made any systematic difference.

6. Descriptive categories should be as near as possible to the points of the scale they describe.

7. The categories need not be equally spaced. Indeed, if they have been psychologically scaled, the spacing should correspond to the experimentally obtained values.

8. In other than machine scoring, a stencil divided into numbered sections makes a convenient scoring device. In the light of Item 7 above it follows that the "units" need not be equal distances on the line.

9. With segmented lines, Guilford (1954) recommends, "do not call for any finer discriminations than will be used in scoring" (p. 268). In the original version of the Purdue Rating Scale for Instruction, before it was revised and converted to machine scor-

Note to Instructors: In order to keep conditions as nearly uniform as possible, it is imperative that no instructions be given to the students. The rating scale should be passed out without comment at the beginning of the period.

Note to Students: Following is a list of qualities that, taken together, tend to make any instructor the sort of instructor that he is. Of course, no one is ideal in all of these qualities, but some approach this ideal to a much greater extent than do others. In order to obtain information which may lead to the improvement of instruction, you are asked to rate your instructor on the indicated qualities by darkening one of the spaces on the line at the point which most nearly describes him with reference to the quality you are considering. For example, under *Interest in Subject* if you think your instructor is not as enthusiastic about his subject as he should be, but is usually more than mildly interested darken the space indicated thus: Fill the chosen space solidly with the special electrographic pencil; leave no stray marks.

Interest in Subject.............. === === ▉== === === === === === === ===

Always appears full of his subject.	Seems mildly interested.	Subject seems irksome to him.

Name of Instructor _____ Course _____ Date _____

This rating is to be entirely impersonal. Do not sign your name or make any other mark on the paper which could serve to identify the rater.

	Always appears full of his subject.	Seems mildly interested.	Subject seems irksome to him.
1. Interest in Subject..........	Always appears full of his subject.	Seems mildly interested.	Subject seems irksome to him.
2. Sympathetic Attitude toward Students...	Always courteous and considerate.	Tries to be considerate but finds it difficult at times.	Entirely unsympathetic and inconsiderate.
3. Fairness in Grading..........	Absolutely fair and impartial to all.	Shows occasional favoritism.	Constantly shows partiality.
4. Liberal and Progressive Attitude.........	Welcomes differences in viewpoint.	Biased on some things but usually tolerant.	Entirely intolerant, allows no contradiction.
5. Presentation of Subject Matter.........	Clear, definite and forceful.	Sometimes mechanical and monotonous.	Indefinite, involved, and monotonous.
6. Sense of Proportion and Humor.........	Always keeps proper balance; not over-critical or over-sensitive.	Fairly well balanced.	Over-serious; no sense of relative values.
7. Self-reliance and Confidence..............	Always sure of himself; meets difficulties with poise.	Fairly self-confident; occasionally disconcerted.	Hesitant, timid, uncertain.

8. Personal Peculiarities..............

Constantly exhibits irritating mannerisms.   Moderately free from objectionable peculiarities.   Wholly free from annoying mannerisms.

9. Personal Appearance..............

Slovenly; clothes untidy and ill-kept.   Usually somewhat untidy; gives little attention to appearance.   Always well groomed; clothes neat and clean.

10. Stimulating Intellectual Curiosity.......

Destroys interest in subject; makes work repulsive.   Occasionally inspiring; creates mild interest.   Inspires students to independent effort; creates desire for investigation.

Note to Students: Following is a list of factors which are important to many courses but over which the instructor often has little control. You are asked to rate the course on each of the factors by darkening one of the spaces at the right of each statement. Use the special electrographic pencil. Leave no stray marks.

If the course is *extremely poor* with respect to the factor darken space 1, thus:

If the course is *below average* with respect to the factor darken space 2, thus:

If the course is *average* with respect to the factor darken space 3, thus:

If the course is *above average* with respect to the factor darken space 4, thus:

If the course is *excellent* with respect to the factor darken space 5, thus:

For example: If you feel that the course is not contributing very much to the attainment of your ultimate goal; but on the other hand, is not a complete waste of time you would probably respond to item number 20 by darkening space 2, thus:

20. How the course is fulfilling your needs (consider your ultimate as well as your immediate goals)..............

11. Suitability of the method or methods by which subject matter of the course is presented (recitation, lecture, laboratory, etc.)..............

19. Amount of freedom allowed students in the selection of the materials to be studied (considering the subject matter)....

20. How the course is fulfilling your needs (consider your ultimate as well as your immediate goals)..............

12. Suitability of the size of the class (consider the subject matter and type of class —lecture, lab., etc.)..............

13. The degree to which the objectives of the course were clarified and discussed..   5 4 3 2 1

14. The agreement between the announced objectives of the course and what was actually taught..............   5 4 3 2 1

15. Suitability of the reference materials available for the course.............   5 4 3 2 1

16. Suitability of the laboratory facilities available for the course.............   5 4 3 2 1

17. Suitability of the assigned textbook.....   5 4 3 2 1

18. The use made of tests as aids to learning   5 4 3 2 1

21. Range of ability in the class (are there too many extremely dull or extremely bright students?).................   5 4 3 2 1

22. Suitability of the amount and type of assigned outside work............   5 4 3 2 1

23. The weight given to tests in determining the final grade for the course..........   5 4 3 2 1

24. Coordination of the tests with the major objectives of the course.............   5 4 3 2 1

25. Frequency of tests..................   5 4 3 2 1

26. The overall rating of the instructor.....   5 4 3 2 1

Fig. 3. The Purdue Rating Scale for Instruction (Copyright 1950, The Purdue Research Foundation).

ing, each line was divided into 100 segments and scored by means of a millimeter scale. The rationale for this was that since the discriminating power of the raters was unknown, they should have every opportunity to be maximally discriminating so far as the recording device, i.e., the rating scale, was involved.

If the investigator has the use of electronic scoring machines or mark-sensed cards, he can obviously design numerical or graphic rating scales for processing by such machines, thus avoiding the tedium and a good deal of the cost of processing rating scale data. The Purdue Rating Scale for Instruction, as shown in Fig. 3, has been put on an IBM answer-sheet for scoring by means of the IBM Graphic Item Counter.

Cumulated-Points Rating Scales

The cumulated-points method of scoring is common to several rating scale types. By this method, scales are scored in the same way as psychological tests, usually one or zero per item.

The ratings by pupils in the study by Leeds and Cook were made with a 50-item questionnaire entitled *My Teacher,* consisting of items like the following (1947, p. 154):

4. Does this teacher scold
   the pupils a lot? ....Yes No ?
6. Does this teacher explain
   the school work so that
   you can understand it? ...Yes No ?
49. Do you like this teacher? .Yes No ?

The three possible responses to the 50 items were scored 0, 1, or 2 according to their favorability, and the scoring weights of the responses were summed over the 50 items to score each pupil's rating of his teacher. The mean of the pupils' ratings of their teacher was then used in the validation of the teacher-attitude inventory. Typical results with the *My Teacher* rating scale have been reported by Leeds and Cook (1947), Della Piana and Gage (1955), and Mazzitelli (1957); the reliability of the mean of about 20 pupils' ratings is typically about .90, and the means are significantly correlated with such other variables as teachers' scores on the Minnesota Teacher Attitude Inventory.

Check Lists

Lists of items of behavior to be checked according to their occurrence or numbered in order of their occurrence are extensively used not only in educational measurement, but in many other situations. As used in education, a check list typically consists of a list of traits or behaviors, such as work habits or skills, on which one checks those manifested by the individual being considered. Figure 4 illustrates how a check list can be used for rating procedure on the job when a definite sequence must be followed in successful performance (Tyler, 1934). Check lists can be used to provide a record of the time required for successful completion of the task, of the sequence of operations, and of degree of quality.

	Student's Actions	Sequence of Actions
a.	Takes slide	1
b.	Wipes slide with lens paper	2
c.	Wipes slide with cloth	
d.	Wipes slide with finger	
e.	Moves bottle of culture along the table	
f.	Places drop or two of culture on slide	3
	* * *	
ah.	Turns up fine adjustment screw a great distance	
ai.	Turns fine adjustment screw a few turns	
aj.	Removes slide from stage	16
ak.	Wipes objective with lens paper	
al.	Wipes objective with cloth	
am.	Wipes objective with finger	17

Fig. 4. Check List of Student Reactions in Finding an Object under the Microscope (Excerpt from Tyler, 1934).

Multiple-Choice Rating Forms

The alternatives for each item may be arranged in multiple-choice form and the choices weighted a priori according to their "desirability" or degree of representation of a specified dimension of teaching. Such a scale was used as a criterion in developing the Minnesota Teacher Attitude Inventory. Leeds and Cook (1947) correlated teachers' responses to their inventory with ratings of the teachers by an observer (Leeds), by principals, and by pupils. The principals made their ratings on a multiple-choice scale. Leeds, after observing the teachers, also made his ratings with such a rating form adapted from five items of Baxter's Rating Scale of the Teacher's Effectiveness (Baxter, 1941). The first two items of Leeds's form, with the scoring weight indicated for each choice, were the following:

1. In Maintaining Discipline
   - −3 a. Classroom exceptionally quiet; pupils hardly dare move; atmosphere of tenseness; pupils fear teacher who "rules with an iron hand."
   - −2 b. Pupils in classroom appear restless; considerable inattention and noisy behavior; indication of lack of respect for teacher; teacher appears nervous and distraught, unable to control.
   - −1 c. Room fairly quiet; some whispering and inattention, but teacher restores "order" with occasional reprimand or warning look; teacher usually sensitive to minor lapses of conduct.
   - 1 d. Pupils usually attentive to task at hand; teacher usually not on "lookout" for misconduct; work proceeds with little or no interruption.
   - 2 e. Pupils actively interested and busy with school work; atmosphere of room free and natural; usually no question of misconduct even when teacher not present; pupils able to govern themselves.
2. In Creating Friendly Classroom Atmospheres
   - 2 a. Conversational, friendly, and with a sense of humor; seeing pupil point of view.
   - 1 b. Friendly, with an understanding adult point of view.
   - 0 c. Serious, reserved and exacting; stirring competitive effort.
   - −1 d. Aloof, "talking down" to pupils; impatient with interruptions or digression.
   - −2 e. Critical, faultfinding, harsh, definitely unfriendly (Leeds, 1946, Appendix C).

Forced-Choice Rating Scales

The forced-choice rating scale is not an a priori kind of scale but a psychologically scaled instrument requiring considerable experimental work for its construction. A forerunner of forced-choice rating scales is the well-known Kuder Preference Record designed to measure vocational interests. Responses to two members of a triad as best liked and least liked obviously yield a forced ranking of the members of the triad.

One major reason for adapting this technique to rating Army officers during World War II was to counteract the annoying leniency reflected in numerical and graphic rating scales (Sisson, 1948). This leniency was glaringly evident in distributions of such officer ratings on file in the Adjutant General's Office.

The general procedure in constructing a forced-choice scale is briefly as follows. The technician first collects a large number of statements of characteristics relevant to the kind of object (person) to be rated for effectiveness in performance. Second, he obtains experimentally a measure of the degree to which each of these items actually discriminates between good and poor performance—the *discrimination index*. Third, he obtains for each item, again experimentally, a measure of its "social acceptability" or "affect value" or "attractiveness" or "apparent favorableness"—the *preference index*. Statements are then grouped into blocks of dyads, triads, tetrads, or quintads by putting together items in each block with approximately equal favorability indices but different discrimination indices. In choosing the items that apply, the rater will presumably choose those that really describe the ratee rather than socially acceptable ones.

Lanman and Remmers (1954), in reviewing the literature, found considerable confusion in that several quite different indices of favorableness had been proposed, or experimented with, or used. The oldest and most widely used is the average applicability of the item to both the high and low group of ratees. But Lanman and Remmers concluded that the preference index developed by Highland and Berkshire (1951) "seems more compatible with the objective of a favorability or value measurement . . ." (p. 547). The Highland-Berkshire procedure is to secure a separate rating of each statement indicating how favorable the statement appeared when used to describe the group being rated.

Berkshire (1958) investigated the relationship of five different operationally defined forced-choice preference indices to frequency of choice of statements arranged in tetrads within each of which the items were equally discriminating. Three preference indices— "Upper Group Applicability," the "Preference Index," as defined above, and "Face Validity"—correlated about zero with frequency of choice. But the rated "Favorableness" and "Job Importance" of the items yielded significant correlations of .19 and .62, respectively, with actual frequency of choice. The latter index thus emerged as the most useful for the choice of items for forced-choice rating devices.

Hedberg and Baxter (1960) obtained favorability ratings from both applicants and nonapplicants for jobs and found that applicants rated 9 per cent of their items as more favorable than did nonapplicants so that "the changes in value spoiled 40% of the quintads set up on the basis of non-applicant ratings" (p. 472).

An ingenious variation on the forced-choice approach was reported by Cosgrove (1959). To obtain diagnostic measures of teacher performance, he performed a factor analysis and obtained "a general factor of over-all teacher effectiveness, two subgenerals and four specific factors" (p. 201). The four specific factors he labeled:

A. Knowledge and Organization of Subject Matter
B. Adequacy of Relations with Students in Class
C. Adequacy of Plans and Procedures in Class
D. Enthusiasm in Working with Students

His rating scale is shown in Fig. 5 with the four phrases in each set lettered to indicate the factor to which they belong. The phrases in each set are to be ranked from 1 to 4 by the student to indicate how well they apply to his teacher. The score on each factor is obtained by summing the ranks of its phrases across sets. The total factor scores may then be averaged over students, and a four-point profile may be drawn for each teacher rated. It should be remembered that Cosgrove's scale yields "ipsative" data, i.e., judgments about the relative strength of the factors within the teacher, and not about the teacher's standing relative to other teachers. On Cosgrove's scale all teachers have the same total score over all four factors.

That the forced-choice technique largely overcomes the leniency tendency has been well established in the literature previously cited. Norms for the Purdue Instructor Performance Indicator, a forced-choice scale (Snedeker & Remmers, 1960) shown in Fig. 6, could be compared with the norms on the extensively used Purdue Rating Scale for Instruction, a graphic rating scale (Remmers & Elliott, 1960). Both instruments were designed for collecting students' ratings of teachers. The data in each case are from volunteer samples. Figure 7 shows the negative skewness of the distribution of ratings on the graphic rating scale in contrast to the relative symmetry of the distribution for the forced-choice instrument. The negative skewness of the distribution for the Purdue Rating Scale for Instruction is presumably the result of the leniency induced by this type of scale.

Set a
____Always on time
for class   C[a]
____Pleasant in
class   B
____Very sincere
when talking
with students   D
____Well-read   A

Set b
____Contagious en-
thusiasm for
subject   D
____Did not fill up
time with triv-
ial material   C
____Gave everyone
an equal
chance   B
____Made clear
what was ex-
pected of stu-
dents   A

Set c
____Classes always
orderly   C
____Enjoyed teach-
ing class   D
____Friendliness
did not seem
forced   B
____Logical in
thinking   A

Set d
____Encouraged
creativeness   D
____Kept course
material up to
the minute   A
____Never deliber-
ately forced
own decisions
on class   B
____Procedures
well thought
out   C

Set e
____Authority on
own subject   A
____Friendly atti-
tude toward
students   D

____Marked tests
very fairly   C
____Never criticiz-
ed in a destruc-
tive way   B

Set f
____Good sense of
humor   D
____Spaced assign-
ments evenly   C
____Students never
afraid to ask
questions in
class   B
____Well-organized
course   A

Set g
____Accepted stu-
dents' view-
points with
open mind   B
____Increased stu-
dents' vocabu-
lary by own
excellent usage   A
____Students al-
ways knew
what was com-
ing up next
day   C
____Students will-
ingly worked
for teacher   D

Set h
____Always knew
what he was
doing   C
____Appreciated
accomplish-
ment   D
____Did not ridi-
cule wrong an-
swers   B
____Well informed
in all related
fields   A

Set i
____Always had
class material
ready   C
____Covered sub-
ject well   A

____Encouraged
students to
think out an-
swers   D
____Rules and reg-
ulations fair   B

Set j
____Always man-   aged to get
things done on
time   C
____Course had
continuity   A
____Made material
significant   D
____Understood
problems of
students   B

Fig. 5. Scale for Diagnostic Rating of Teacher Performance (Adapted from Cosgrove, 1959).
[a] Capital letters indicate the factors of teacher effectiveness to which the phrase is related.

A valuable source of items is a pool of 900 descriptive phrases assembled by Wherry (1950) to control bias in ratings. It was from this pool that Cosgrove (1959) drew the statements for his scale.

The term *forced choice* is an unfortunate one. During the development of the technique in the AGO Research Section it was evident to the writer and others conducting field trials that Army officers did not take kindly to the technique because they were unable to judge how they were rating their fellow officers. It was precisely this ambiguity, of course, that was the specific intent of the technique.

Spector (1957) judges that forced-choice methods resemble projective techniques, like inkblots, in that the responses have no face validity. Theoretically the forced-choice technique presents the rater with a number of stimuli, all of which appear equally attractive, and gives no clue to the items that will reward the ratee. Isard (1956), experimenting with two forms, one more ambiguous than the other, found higher validity for the more ambiguous form.

One limitation of the forced-choice technique is that the use of rating results in counseling ratees will seriously risk invalidating the scale by making known the discriminating items.

Should the items in forced-choice scales be arranged in blocks of two, three, four, or five? Should statements of undesirable characteristics as well as desirable characteristics be included? Highland and Berkshire (1951) carried out what has come to be a widely cited experiment on these questions. Their major findings were that tetrads containing only statements of desirable characteristics gave most valid results. Specifically they concluded:

Of the six forms used in this project, a form made up of blocks containing four favorable-appearing statements [Form C] from which the rater was asked to choose the two which were most descriptive of the ratee gave generally superior results. This form had high average validity (.68) and satisfactory reliability (.93), was least susceptible to deliberate attempts to give high scores, and was one of the two forms best liked by the raters (Highland & Berkshire, 1951, p. ix).

A number of studies have been concerned with the stability of the preference values. A. L. Edwards (1957), Ghiselli (1954), Gordon (1953), Maher (1959), Rundquist, Winer, and Falk (1950), and Uhrbrock (1950) all report great stability of preference values even over considerable periods of time. The meaning of language, in other words, is pretty constant over time.

Taylor, Schneider, and Symons (1953) carried out experiments on the relationship between length of the forced-choice scale and its validity against a criterion. Comparing two forms, one of 12 and one of 32 tetrads, they found the short form as valid as the longer one. In another study of two forms of 10 and 28 tetrads they obtained validities of .55 and .60, respectively, and judged that the slight loss of validity with the short form was worth the time saved and economy of the shorter form. Snedeker and Remmers (1960) obtained a reliability coefficient of .96 (Kuder-Richardson Formula 20) and a test-retest coefficient of .95 over a three-week interval for 114 college teachers rated by an average of about 70 students per teacher.

The forced-choice technique is still "young"; much more evaluation via research is in order. The considerable amount of time and money involved in developing a forced-choice scale has hampered research. But the research findings warrant some tentative conclusions: (1) The ambiguity of the items has to a considerable degree achieved the original intent of the technique's rationale. (2) Preference values are stable over time. (3) Favorable statements in tetrads appear to yield higher validity than other block designs. (4) Length of the scale is only slightly related to its validity.

SOCIOMETRIC METHODS

The sociometric "test" is a technique for eliciting responses from members of a defined social group about each other. These responses usually have a direction such as like, neutral, or dislike; i.e., they are essentially ratings. These responses, once obtained, are usually presented in some diagramatic or matrix form. A "reader" (Moreno, et al., 1960) has brought together a rich selection of the literature on the theory, methods, and applications of sociometry.

The relevance of sociometric methods to research on teaching arises from the fact that the classroom holds a social group. The structure and dynamics of classroom groups are not too well understood but have recently been the focus of an increasing amount of research. That the social interactions within the classroom have significant bearing on the teacher's effectiveness is well established.

Man's relations with his fellows are crucially important for his personal and social survival. From Aristotle's observation that man is a political (i.e., social) animal, the Christian Scripture's "Ye are members one of another," John Donne's "No man is an Island . . ." to the title of one of the first publications on sociometry, *Who Shall Survive?* it is clear that prophets, poets and thinkers generally have been fundamentally concerned with the problems inherent in these relations. The recent development of sociometric concepts and tools has yielded new and important insight into and understanding of the complex social microcosms that are the classroom and the school (Remmers, in Gronlund, 1959, p. xv).

Name of Instructor_____

Course_____ Date_____

THE PURDUE INSTRUCTOR PERFORMANCE INDICATOR

J. H. SNEDEKER, *Ball State Teachers College* and H. H. REMMERS, *Purdue University*

FORM A

Directions:

This rating scale consists of twelve groups or blocks containing four statements each.

The statements are descriptive of instructors and their teaching behavior or activities.

From each group or block of four statements you are to CHOOSE TWO statements that best describe or apply to the instructor being rated.

Indicate the two statements chosen from each group or block by filling in the pairs of vertical lines to the right of each group.

	A B C D
Sample:	
1A Sincere	‖ ▌ ‖ ▌
1B Speaks Well	
1C Easy to Get Along With	
1D Is Very Diligent	

In this block the answers indicate that we decided that the two statements—"Speaks Well" and "Is Very Diligent" were most applicable to or descriptive of the instructor we were rating. The success of your rating depends on *very careful consideration* of each statement and then deciding which two in the block are most applicable to or descriptive of the instructor you are rating.

Be sure you use the *electrographic pencil.*

Check to see that you have *chosen two statements* from each block.

	A B C D
1A Shows Personal Interest in Student's Work	
1B Likes and Understands Students	
1C Doesn't Make Fun of Student's Response to Questions	‖ ‖ ‖ ‖
1D Has Help Sessions	
2A Is Interested in Subject Matter He (She) Teaches	
2B Connects Lectures with Textbook Used	
2C Willing to Help Those Slow to Learn	‖ ‖ ‖ ‖
2D Uses a Variety of Teaching Techniques	
3A Neat and Clean in Appearance	
3B Good Fellowship Exists Between Him (Her) and Student	
3C Has Confidence in Himself (Herself)	‖ ‖ ‖ ‖
3D Tries to be Fair and has Character and Integrity	
4A Good Use and Command of the English Language	
4B Knows His (Her) Subject	
4C Clear and Pleasant Voice	‖ ‖ ‖ ‖
4D Tries to Find Loopholes in His (Her) Teaching and Correct Them	
5A Keeps Class Attention	
5B Explains Method of Grading	
5C Keeps Accurate Record of Grades	‖ ‖ ‖ ‖
5D Realizes the Complications and Conflicts Met by Students	
6A Keeps Classroom Atmosphere Rather Informal	
6B Has a Sense of Humor	
6C Good Posture	‖ ‖ ‖ ‖
6D Grades Based on Work Done Not Personal Feeling	

THE PURDUE INSTRUCTOR PERFORMANCE INDICATOR (Cont'd.)

		A	B	C	D
7A	Makes Assignments at the Beginning of the Course				
7B	Gives Tests That Are Not Meant to be Tricky				
7C	Presents Materials Interestingly	‖	‖	‖	‖
7D	Encourages Students by Helpful Advice or Praise on Tests				

		A	B	C	D
8A	Talks Slowly Enough for Note Taking				
8B	Lets Students Ask Questions in Class				
8C	Treats Students as Grown Ups	‖	‖	‖	‖
8D	Makes You Earn Grades No Handouts				

		A	B	C	D
9A	Is Loyal to the School and Other Faculty Members				
9B	Writes Difficult Words on Blackboard and Explains Them				
9C	Doesn't Give Same Lectures All the Time	‖	‖	‖	‖
9D	Friendly Outside the Classroom				

		A	B	C	D
10A	Applies Subject to Everyday Life				
10B	Sticks to Subject				
10C	Stimulates Students by Raising Interesting Questions for Discussion	‖	‖	‖	‖
10D	Tutors a Student in His Lessons				

		A	B	C	D
11A	Sticks to the Grade Given				
11B	Grades on a Curve				
11C	Puts Ideas Across Logically and Orderly	‖	‖	‖	‖
11D	Keeps Class a Team, Neglects No Student				

		A	B	C	D
12A	Sticks to the Institution's Grading System				
12B	Well Organized Course and Assignment Sheet				
12C	He (She) is a High Grader	‖	‖	‖	‖
12D	Has Good Discipline				

Fig. 6. The Purdue Instructor Performance Indicator (a forced-choice rating scale).

Sociometric Concepts

The term *sociometry,* as it is read by most psychologists, is probably thought of as analogous to psychometry. Actually, there are certain fundamental differences between psychometry and sociometry. From the make-up of the word we might think of sociometry as being the general enterprise of social measurement. Authors such as Bain, Chapin, Lundberg, Sanderson, and Moreno (Lindzey & Borgatta, 1954, p. 405) have in fact suggested that the term should have such an inclusive meaning. In practice, the term has generally been used in its more restricted sense as applying only to certain techniques developed by Moreno. These include such devices as psychodrama, interaction testing, and the sociometric "test."

The idea of determining the structure of social groups did not originate with Moreno.

Such authors as Olson (1929), Loomis (1931), and Challman (1932) had studied group structure largely on an observational basis. In 1931 Moreno first used the idea of structuring a group according to expressed preference. To Moreno, also, goes credit for the systematic development and promotion of the method of obtaining verbal choice responses and their subsequent representation.

In the process, Moreno and his followers have been vocal and somewhat cultish in advocating the use of the sociometric test and other sociometric techniques in the solution of a great variety of problems. For instance, in referring to his book, *Who Shall Survive?,* Moreno (1953, p. lxvi) said, "It is a new bible, the bible for social conduct, for human societies. It has more ideas packed in one book than a whole generation of books."

By far the larger portion of work with the sociometric "test" has been done by workers

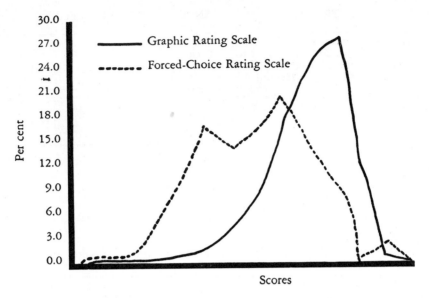

Fig. 7. Students' Ratings of Their Teachers.

associated primarily with Moreno, and most reports of these activities have appeared in *Sociometry,* a journal which until 1956 was apparently under his direct control. The result has been that the sociometric test has failed to take its place in the research repertoire of many social scientists who might otherwise have made good use of it. This fact does not, however, alter the fact that the sociometric "test" is a powerful technique and that much credit must go to Moreno and his followers for its development and use today.

Sociometry has a special terminology which refers to certain phenomena associated with the sociometric test. Hence it is necessary to define certain terms before we proceed further.

The *sociogram* is a method for pictorially or schematically representing the choice pattern obtained with the sociometric test. Various forms which the sociogram can take will be discussed and illustrated later in this chapter.

Tele is the fundamental unit of attraction between members of a group. Tele has two portions—the projective, or outgoing, portion and the retrojective, or returning, portion. Moreno observed that the trend toward mutuality of attraction and repulsion many times surpasses chance possibility. The factor responsible for this is "tele." In a more mathematical discussion of tele, Moreno (1948) described it as being in direct proportion to the number of pair relations and in inverse proportion to the number of unreciprocated relationships.

Transference is a concept related to that of tele. Moreno (1948) describes transference as increasing in direct proportion to the number of unreciprocated relationships and in inverse proportion to the number of pair relations.

Social atom, another concept used extensively by sociometrists, is defined as "the smallest living social unit, itself not further divisible" (Moreno, 1953, p. 291) and further "the smallest living unit of social matter we can comprehend" (p. 317). In relating the concept of the social atom to that of tele, Moreno (1951, p. 23) says, "It is different and more difficult, however, to describe the process which attracts individuals to one another or which repels them, that flow of feeling of which the social atom and the networks are apparently composed. This process may be conceived as tele."

Once the sociometric test has been administered and a sociogram or matrix constructed, several terms serve to describe certain configurations or occurrences within the sociogram. *Star* is used to refer to any person receiving a large number of choices. Lindzey and Borgatta (1954) have suggested the term *overchosen* for the group member who receives a disproportionately large number of choices from other members of the group. They further suggest reserving the term *star* for cases where one individual is chosen from among others who do not distribute a large number of choices among themselves. An *isolate,* on the other hand, is a person who receives no choices and makes no choices. Such an individual differs from the *rejected* person who receives a large number of rejections.

Several terms describe choice configurations within a group. The simplest of these is the *mutual pair,* which consists of two persons each choosing the other. Similarly the *triangle* consists of three people joined by mutual choices. This type of definition can be extended to include various other types of polygons such as hexagons, squares, etc. The *chain* is a somewhat similar device in which individuals are joined by mutual choices except that in the chain there is no cross-over of choices. That is, the individuals in a chain are joined only to the people on either side of them in the chain. Such a chain may be either *open* or *closed.*

Sociometry and Psychometry

The sociometric "test" is functionally a rating, as Lindzey and Borgatta have pointed out:

What other instruments in the psychologists' measurement battery show similarities to sociometric measures? . . . the most important congruence seems to exist in relation to rating scales. . . . It is easy to conceive of the sociometric test as a variety of rating scale—the members of the group are asked to rate or order the other members of the group in terms of their attractiveness or desirability for sharing certain activities.

In spite of an underlying similarity, there are also important differences between these two approaches. Sociometric measures are more limited in the variables they can be used to assess and more restricted in the settings in which they can be employed. On the other hand, there is no need to train raters to engage in sociometric ratings. . . . The rater is asked to apply exactly those particular, unique, and sometimes irrational criteria he has spent a lifetime developing (Lindzey & Borgatta, 1954, p. 406).

For the worker in education the notion of *test* carries with it the conventional notion of validity and reliability. Several authors, however, have pointed out some basic differences between the psychometric test and the sociometric test. Criswell (1949, p. 288) defined sociometric procedures as "those which elicit the pattern of distribution of goal-directed energy in a group, i.e., the strength and direction of inter-individual associations as they occur in the group's orientation toward the achievement of a specified end." She pointed out that psychometric measures do not generate group structure.

Pepinsky (1949) concisely stated the difference between sociometric and psychometric tests by pointing out that it is the function of the sociometric test to "focus on an analysis of the individual as a member of a group rather than on the individual as an entity in isolation" (p. 39). She further stated that the psychometric test makes a frame of reference not always applicable to the sociometric test.

The psychometric test can be considered to resemble the sociometric test insofar as the choices obtained in the sociometric technique can be viewed as ratings or rankings. Here too, however, several authors hasten to remind us that certain differences exist. In line with her concept of the sociometric test, Pepinsky (1949) pointed out that sociometric ratings are not intended to be impersonal evaluations; instead, rater-ratee interaction is intended to play a large part in the ratings. Because of the basic differences between the sociometric test and the psychometric test, Criswell (1949) suggested that the word *technique* be used instead of *test* where the sociometric measure is involved.

Reliability

The application of reliability statistics to sociometric data involves certain difficulties. Several authors point out that the concepts of test-retest reliability and internal consistency can be relatively meaningless and even misleading when applied to sociometric data. The principal difficulty involved in test-retest coefficients lies in the problem of distinguishing between effects of memory and those of real change. If the sociometric test is given in too short an interval, memory will play an important part in increasing the consistency of responses. On the other hand, if the interval is long, there may be real changes in group structure which will lower reliability coefficients. This latter case, Pepinsky (1949) suggested, is akin to clinical reliability in which measured fluctuations are real and related to actual changes in structure. If such fluctuations occur, a low "reliability" coefficient would be more desirable than a high one. Pepinsky suggested that the test-retest reliability coefficient could actually be a measure of fluidity of group structure—a low reliability coefficient indicating merely a group which tends to shift its choice pattern easily. Lindzey and Borgatta (1954) suggested that, if we accept the fact that a group is consistently undergoing change, a high reliability coefficient would indicate an insensitive test that had failed to measure change.

In view of these restrictions and re-interpretations of the test-retest reliability coefficient, Criswell (1949) suggested a guide for using the test-retest approach: where we seek to establish a relationship between a sociometric

test and some criterion, if the test-retest interval is equal to the interval between test and criterion measure, we would obtain through the reliability figure a measure of the extent to which error variance is reducing the test-criterion relationship.

Despite the restrictions mentioned above, several studies have used the test-retest approach (Jennings, 1943, p. 31; Newstetter, Feldstein, & Newcomb, 1938; Zeleny, 1939). These authors, using retest intervals of four days or less, found correlations between choice-status indices ranging from .93 to .96. It would seem that such short intervals would indicate only constancy of memory. But Jennings (1943, p. 57) found correlations of .65 and .66 for positive and negative choices, respectively, over an eight-month interval in her studies.

Internal consistency reliability, too, presents difficulties when applied to the sociometric test. The split-half technique entails the obvious difficulty that random or "equivalent" halves of choice criteria are not both measures of the same thing. But splitting the choosers into random halves, as did Gage and Exline (1953), can yield estimates of the internal consistency of a group in assigning choices to its members.

Pepinsky (1949) suggested that something akin to split-half technique might be used to determine the extent of own-group choices. With such a technique it might be possible to determine when a group gives significantly more choices to its own members than to outsiders. Such a use, however, bears little resemblance to the psychometrician's concept of reliability. It should instead be added to the multiplicity of indices given later in this chapter.

Criswell (1949) suggested that in certain cases the Horst (1949) formula

$$r = 1 - \frac{\dfrac{\sum \dfrac{\sigma_i^2}{n_i - 1}}{N}}{\sigma_M^2}$$

might apply, where

$r =$ an estimate of the reliability of the individual means, M_i,

$N =$ number of persons rated,

$M_i =$ mean of the ratings received by person i,

$n_i =$ number of ratings made of each person i,

$\sigma_i =$ the standard deviation of the ratings of person i,

$\sigma_M =$ the standard deviation of the mean ratings received by the N persons.

As Criswell points out, however, such a formula is most useful in cases where each group member rates all or some of the other group members according to his preference for them in some specified role. Only in such a case could we expect the variance of ratings received within ratees to be less than the variance between ratees. Such a condition would seem to give an estimate of the reliability of ratings rather than that of sociometric choice. In sociometric choices, such a relationship could not be expected to hold. If we are more interested in the reliability of one single person's choice for one other person, such a formula would not apply.

Validity

The task of conceptualizing the validity of the sociometric test also runs into difficulty. Here again the difficulty can be traced to fundamental differences between the psychometric test for which the validity concept was developed and the sociometric test to which we would like to apply it. As Jennings (1943, p. 27) pointed out, in most psychological tests we try to measure some trait by eliciting related responses. In a sociometric test, on the other hand, we actually sample the behavior studied. In effect, under such conditions, the predictor is the same as its criterion. But this is true only if we are not interested in drawing inferences from the behavior observed. Pepinsky (1949) stated that sociometric-choice behavior, once it is used to describe more general traits, should be subject to validation against a suitable criterion.

Pepinsky went on to say that the validity problem in observing the aspect of behavior elicited by the sociometric test lies in being sure that the responses obtained are not falsified. In such a case, validity becomes a function of the rapport between the experimenter and the subjects, and of the subjects' cooperativeness. If we were to follow Moreno's suggestion that the sociometric test should be a prelude to the actual reorganization of the group along lines suggested by the test, and if our subjects were fully aware of this commitment, it seems safe to say that what we have measured is actual behavior and we would be once again at the point where our predictor and criterion are identical.

On the question of face validity for a test, there seems to be agreement that a sociometric test does indeed appear to measure social structure. Criswell (1949) also discussed the problem of "immediate validity." By this she meant, Does a test have "immediate significance" for use as a basis for action? She pointed out that where the action involved is a restructuring of the group, the sociometric test carries a built-in immediate validity.

Fortunately for the purposes of the researcher, Gronlund (1959) reviewed the technical literature on reliability and validity. His chapter on reliability (pp. 117–157) summarizes the rationale and findings of research on the internal consistency, stability over time, and generality over situations, of sociometric results. In general, internal consistency has tended to be high. Stability over time also tends to run high; it varies positively with the age of the individuals in the group and inversely with the time interval. Choices given fluctuate more than those received. Generality over situations, or the correlation between status on one criterion and status on another, is substantial, implying a general social acceptability factor. Further, consistency and stability vary positively with the generality of the criterion of choice, the number of criteria involved in a composite score, the number of choices permitted (three or less yielding lower reliability), the length of time during which the group has been in existence, and the rigidity, as against flexibility, of the procedures used in governing classroom behavior.

As to validity, sociometric results have been found to be significantly related to pupil behavior outside the sociometric testing situation, to teachers' judgments of pupils' choice status, to adults' ratings of pupils' social adjustment, and to pupils' reputations among peers. Sociometric results tend to be more closely related to specific *social* adjustment problems than to those in the realm of *personal* adjustment.

Techniques for Collecting Sociometric Data

Since its beginnings, sociometry has rapidly developed from a relatively simple choice-gathering process to an important quantitative technique for the study of group structure. The purpose of this section and the next one is to review methods for the collection and analysis of sociometric data.

The sociometric test. Moreno (1953, pp. 92–106) placed six stipulations on the sociometric test:

1. The group should be well defined and choices and rejections limited to the members of the group.
2. The subjects should be given a chance to choose or reject as many of the group members as they wish.
3. The subjects should be provided with a definite criterion upon which to base their choices and rejections.
4. The sociometric data should actually be used to restructure the group, and the group members should be informed of this fact.
5. The group members should be allowed to make their choices in private.
6. The questions should be prepared in such a way as to be readily understandable to the group members.

Few of the studies reported in the literature have employed the sociometric test in exactly the way specified by Moreno's six requirements. Variations in several of these requirements have been used. One common variation—in this case, on Moreno's second stipulation—has been to limit the number of choices and rejections to be made by each member of the group. Several investigators have employed the method of partial rank-order. In this technique, described by Northway and Potashin (1946), each member of the group makes a limited number of choices in response to one or more sociometric questions. Group members are then ranked in terms of the total number of times they were chosen. All choices for all questions are weighted equally.

Two methods of securing complete rankings have been developed. The first method is simply to ask the individual to rank all the members of the group except himself in response to some sociometric question. A second method is to use paired comparisons. Koch (1933) applied this method to the measurement of the popularity of preschool children. The method, as applied to sociometry, consists of comparing, in terms of some criterion, each of the n members of the group with every other member. This results in $\frac{n(n-1)}{2}$ pairs of names, and the subject is asked to choose one name from each pair. The number of times each person is chosen determines his rank.

Eng and French (1948) studied the relationships among various methods of securing sociometric data. They found that when the rank-order of the group members, as determined by paired comparisons, served as the criterion, ranks determined on the basis of unlimited choice were more valid than those determined from either two or five limited choices.

Another of Moreno's stipulations which has not always been followed is that well-defined face-to-face groups be used. Lundberg and Steele (1938) studied a small Vermont village in an attempt to determine patterns of social attraction within the population. They interviewed all the families, and, among other things, asked the interviewee, usually the housewife, to name her best friends. It is obvious that, although the village was small, all of its residents were not necessarily acquainted with each other. It would be impossible in this study to define the face-to-face group from which any particular interviewee made his or her choices.

Stewart (1947) introduced another variation when he developed a technique for random cross-sectional sampling of urban groups. In studying "Southtown," a community of about 6,000 people, he interviewed 163 people, representing about 25 per cent of the permanent-resident white families. He concluded that (1) the sociometric configuration of an urban community can be arrived at through interviewing a random cross-section of the adult population; (2) an interview schedule can be devised that will elicit sociometric-type responses on a voluntary basis; (3) an adequate and representative sample can be obtained by this procedure, with refusal bias held at a minimum; and (4) there is no short cut to arriving at the identities of those who have a large measure of interpersonal influence.

In his study of sampling problems in influence studies, Bassett (1948) examined the merits of "wave" as opposed to random sampling. In the wave method, a small random sample is interviewed; then the persons chosen by the members of this random sample are in turn interviewed. This process is continued until a total sample of desired size is obtained. In his study, Bassett found that a 50 per cent wave sample defined 166 mutual choices, whereas a 50 per cent random sample defined only 90. The wave-sampling method, designed to expose the maximum number of mutual choices, is particularly useful in studying this aspect of group structure.

Moreno's stipulation that the group under study must be well defined implies that it must have been in existence for some considerable period. He stressed the need for fairly stable membership so that the members

of the group will have experienced considerable face-to-face interaction. As already indicated, many investigators have seen fit, depending on their purposes, to overlook this restriction. To compare the sociometric patterns of strangers and acquaintances, for example, Barker (1942) confronted 12 college students with sociometric questions at the first class meeting of an educational psychology course. When he repeated the measurement with the same instrument after 36 class meetings, he could consider the students to be acquaintances and then make his comparisons.

Related data-collecting techniques. Many devices similar to the sociometric test have been developed for studying group structure. In many cases they have been designed for use in conjunction with the sociometric test. Moreno (1942) himself has described a sociometric self-rating. Essentially, the subject is asked to rate himself, in regard to some sociometric criterion, as he believes he would be rated by others. Such a test, which can be administered anonymously, may give considerable insight into group members' self-images.

One well-known technique closely related to the sociometric test is the "Guess Who" test developed by Hartshorne, May, and Shuttleworth (1930), which antedated Moreno's *Who Shall Survive?* This test was developed as a means for evaluating an individual's reputation within his group. The following quotation is taken from the test instructions:

Here are some little word-pictures of children you may know. Read each statement carefully and see if you can guess whom it is about. It might be about yourself. There may be more than one picture for the same person. Several boys and girls may fit one picture. Read each statement. Think over your classmates and write after each statement the names of any boys or girls who may fit it (Hartshorne, May, & Shuttleworth, 1930, p. 221).

A typical statement might be:

> *This is someone who controls his temper and never gets angry:* —————

Desirable traits were scored plus one; undesirable traits, minus one. The "Guess Who" technique has been adapted by many investigators to the measurement of social status.

Tagiuri (1952) suggested an important extension of sociometric techniques for the study of group relationships. He pointed out that two types of information are needed to understand interpersonal relationships: "the first of these is the nature of the response of each person to the other. The second aspect consists of the *perception* that each person has of the other person's response toward him" (p. 91).

Standard sociometric procedures yield the first sort of data. Tagiuri proposes the "guessing" or "perceptual" procedure for securing data on the second aspect. In the "guessing" procedure, the subjects are asked to guess who will choose and reject *them*— in addition to making the usual sociometric choices and rejections. The number of choices, guesses of choices, rejections, and guesses of rejection is left unrestricted. The guessing procedure adds the perceptual component (empathetic insight) to the standard sociometric measure. This technique, flexible in its application, has considerable value since it taps a unique aspect of group structure.

Pepinsky, Siegel, and Van Atta (1952) developed a Group Participation Scale for evaluating the outcomes of group counseling. Essentially the scale consists of 24 "guess who" items selected from an original list of 195 such items. Using the Thurstone scaling technique, the authors had these items judged by a group of "experts" and also by a group of students in social psychology. The final 24 items make up a scaled sociometric test with three items at each of eight scale positions, ranging from "least effective" to "most effective" in group participation.

Another variation of the sociometric test is the Group Preference Record. This technique was first developed by Newstetter, Feldstein, and Newcomb (1938) and later used by Zeleny (1939, 1940). The subjects first rank their first five choices of people to belong to the group. Second, they rate each of the group members on a three-point scale: like, indifferent, dislike.

Weschler, Tannenbaum, and Talbot (1952) developed the Multi-Relational Sociometric Survey for use in analyzing interpersonal relationships, particularly in an industrial setting. The authors pointed out that these relationships are specific for various activities and also that various qualitative relationships are defined: prescribed, perceived, actual, desired, and rejected. Activities may be described as goal-directed (such as being given directions or orders, or presenting grievances) or nongoal-directed (such as having lunch with employees or socializing after working hours). The device yields scores for both goal-directed and nongoal-directed activities on the five qualitative relationships listed above. The authors also define a number of indices based on these scores (Massarik, Tannenbaum, Kahane, & Weschler, 1953).

As a result of the difficulties arising from the arbitrary weighting of partial-rank choices, Moreno, Jennings, and Sargent (1940, 1947) suggested the use of time as a measure of choice strength. The test consists of telling the subject that he has a given period of time (perhaps three hours) and that he may do in this time whatever he chooses. He is then asked with whom he would like to spend this time. The period may be divided among as many or as few people as the subject wishes. The amount of time allotted to a given person is taken as an index of the intensity of one's choice of that person.

Another variation on the latter technique was suggested by Stogdill (1949), who pointed out that it is not always practical to ask administrative personnel with whom they would prefer to spend their time. Instead he asked four different groups of naval personnel, "With whom do you spend the most time in getting work done?" A rank-order based on time spent was thus obtained. Although the formal organization of a group may be such that actual time spent and personal preference of the individual may not be equivalent, Stogdill believed that this technique might be useful in studying the interpersonal relationships of work groups.

Techniques for Analyzing Sociometric Data

Having considered the sociometric test and some of its variations, we now turn to developments in the analysis of sociometric data. A review of the literature indicates that these developments are even more impressive than those in the area of data collection. At first sociometrists used primarily graphic, subjective methods for analyzing the results of sociometric tests. Today several quantitative, objective methods of analysis have been invented and the rate of development indicates that more powerful analytical tools may be available in the near future. The techniques described in this section fall into four general categories: graphic analysis, index analysis, statistical analysis, and matrix analysis.

Graphic analysis. The basic method of representing sociometric data is the sociogram (Gronlund, 1959, pp. 68–78). In drawing the sociogram, a circle, square, or some other symbol represents each individual in the group. Different symbols may be used to distinguish various traits or factors such as race, sex, educational level, etc. These symbols are then connected by lines or arrows which represent the choices on the sociometric test. All choices and all rejections may be represented in a similar fashion, or different lines (dotted, broken, etc.) may be used to represent first, second, third, etc., choice or rejection.

Two modifications of the sociogram technique have been suggested by Loomis, Beegle, and Longmore (1947). They used the size of the sociogram symbol to indicate choice status. The more choices received, the larger the symbol. Also they suggested that specific areas of the sociogram be used to designate such factors as class status, race, sex, etc.

A method of determining social distance has been offered by Proctor and Loomis (1951). They suggested that sociometric choice patterns can be placed on a continuum ranging from strong attraction to strong aversion. Six types of interpersonal relationships are possible:

Type A—(i) chooses (j) and (j) chooses (i),
Type B—(i) chooses (j) and (j) ignores (i),
Type C—(i) chooses (j) and (j) rejects (i),
Type D—(i) ignores (j) and (j) ignores (i),
Type E—(i) ignores (j) and (j) rejects (i),
Type F—(i) rejects (j) and (j) rejects (i).

If Type C and Type D are equated, a five-point scale results:

Strong Attraction		Lack of Strong Attraction or Aversion		Strong Aversion
A	B	CD	E	F
1	2	3	4	5

This procedure provides a method for determining the social distance between two individuals. Presumably this distance could be represented graphically on a sociogram.

Northway (1940) developed a basically different method of representing sociometric data and called it the target diagram. She assigned weights to partially ranked choices on several sociometric criteria and derived a status score for the choices received. She drew four concentric circles and used the radius of these circles to represent the distribution of the status scores, the highest score at the center of the circle. Each person is located on the target in terms of his distance from the center as determined by his status score. An arrow is then drawn to the person to whom he gave his highest composite choice.

Later Northway and Quarrington (1946) suggested that separate sectors of the target be used to designate additional factors. This technique has been applied to sex, race, and socioeconomic status.

Bronfenbrenner (1944b) suggested a further modification of the target technique. This involves the use of a chance model in assigning people to the four rings of the target. People who receive more choices than expected by chance at the .02 level of significance are placed in the center ring of the target. Those who receive significantly fewer than chance choices are placed in the outside ring. Rings two and three are used for those people whose choice status is above and below the mean but not significantly high or low. This procedure makes it possible to compare one target diagram with another.

Chapin (1950) pointed out that the traditional two-dimensional representations of sociometric data have certain serious limitations, particularly in the representation of stars or leaders. Most sociograms depict stars as surrounded by a circle of admirers. However, the star does not reciprocate by choosing all those who choose him. This, according to Chapin, means that to some extent the star is an isolate. Since regular sociograms do not take adequate account of this fact, Chapin suggested the use of a three-dimensional representation of the data. The X plane represents social status, the Y plane represents incoming choices, and the Z plane represents outgoing choices. Chapin concluded: "It should be remembered that sociometric diagrams are designed to show clearly the social *direction* of choices, whereas the three-dimensional model is designed to represent usually three variables in a conventional-mathematical space relationship . . ." (p. 267). Here is an adumbration of the concept of semantic space developed by Osgood, Suci, and Tannenbaum (1957), described below.

Index analysis. Throughout the development of sociometry, various authors have suggested indices for use in summarizing sociometric data. The indices listed here are representative of many that have been described. These indices can be used to describe (1) individuals, (2) groups, and (3) subgroups.

The first group of indices (Proctor & Loomis, 1951) presented here are used to describe the choice and rejection pattern of individual i.

$$\text{Choice Status} = CS = \frac{C}{(N-1)},$$

$$\text{Rejection Status} = RS = \frac{R}{(N-1)}, \text{ and}$$

Choice-Rejection
$$\text{Status} = C\text{-}RS = CS - RS$$

where:
C = number of persons choosing i,
R = number of persons rejecting i,
N = number of persons in the group.

In the situation where the individual is allowed an unlimited number of choices:

$$\text{Positive Expansiveness} = PE = \frac{C_i}{(N-1)},$$

$$\text{Negative Expansiveness} = NE = \frac{R_i}{(N-1)}$$

where:
C_i = number of choices i makes,
R_i = number of rejections i makes,
N = number of persons in the group.

The terms *underchosen* and *overchosen* are frequently used in describing an individual's choice-rejection pattern. Jennings (1950) defined these terms as follows: A person is overchosen if the number of choices he received is more than one standard deviation above the mean, underchosen if the number of choices he received is more than one standard deviation below the mean, on the distribution of total choices.

McKinney (1948) asked members of the group to rate each other in terms of choose, reject, indifferent. To describe these data, he developed three indices:

$$\text{Social Status} = SS = \frac{\Sigma I}{(N-1)},$$

$$\text{Compatibility} = C = \frac{M}{(N-1)}, \text{and}$$

$$\text{Sociality (acceptance of others)} = S = \frac{E_g}{N}$$

where:

I = number of acceptances minus number of rejections received by i,

M = number of mutual choices involving i,

E_g = number of choices given by i,

N = number of persons in the group.

Grossman and Wrighter (1948), in their study of sixth-grade children, defined what they called a selection-rejection score as simply the number of acceptances received minus the number of rejections received.

In connection with his development of the Group Preference Record (GPR), Zeleny (1940) defined a social-status ratio and a social-status score.

$$\text{Social-Status Ratio} = SR = \frac{N \times I}{T}, \text{and}$$

$$\text{Social-Status Score} = SS = A + C$$

where:

N = number of acceptances received,

I = average intensity of response (unity); one unit for each acceptance (being rated as liked) plus one unit for each choice (being chosen as a member of a five-member class learning group), the total being divided by the number of persons giving them.

T = total number of acceptances possible,

A = number of acceptances received on GPR,

C = number of choices made on GPR.

Katz (1953) developed an index of social status based upon matrix multiplication by a method too involved to describe here. Raising the choice matrix to higher powers identifies chains which, after having been properly weighted, are added to the direct choices in calculating the index. This method of computing status takes into account not only the number of direct "votes" received by each individual but also the status of each individual who chooses the first, the status of each who chooses these in turn, etc. "Thus the new proposed index allows for *who* chooses as well as how many choose" (p. 39).

We now turn to the consideration of group indices. Many of these indices are merely restatements of the individual indices in terms of the group. Thus we find in Proctor and Loomis (1951, p. 572) that, assuming unlimited choices,

$$\text{Group Expansiveness} = E = \frac{C_t}{N},$$

$$\text{Group Cohesion} = Co = \frac{M}{C_2^N}$$

where:

C_t = total number of choices made by the group,

M = total number of mutual choices,

$C_2^N = \dfrac{N(N-1)}{2}$ = number of possible combinations of N persons taken two at a time (maximum possible number of mutual choices),

N = number of persons in the group.

In her study of reciprocated choices, Criswell (1946) defined indices of group coherence and group integration when the number of choices is limited.

$$\text{Group Coherence} = Icc = \frac{Rq}{Up},$$

$$\text{Group Integration} = I = \frac{1}{(Is)}$$

where:

R = number of reciprocated choices,

U = number of unreciprocated choices,

$p = \dfrac{d}{N-1}$, where d is the number of choices allowed,

$q = 1 - p,$

Is = number of isolates (persons receiving no choices).

The authors of the Multi-Relational Sociometric Survey (Massarik, Tannenbaum, Kahane, & Weschler, 1953; Weschler, Tannenbaum, & Talbot, 1952) described a number of group indices based upon the five relationships measured by the test: prescribed, perceived, actual, desired, and rejected relationships. Using various ratios of the frequencies of these relationships, they obtained an index of understanding (what percentage of the prescribed relationships are perceived), several indices of conformity (e.g., what percentage of the prescribed relationships are actual), and several indices of satisfaction (e.g., what percentage of the prescribed relationships are also desired).

Another group of indices has been developed to describe the relationships between a subgroup and its parent-group. The subgroup is also referred to as the in-group and the parent-group as the out-group. Proctor and Loomis (1951) developed a system of notation described in Table 1.

In this table:

C_{a-a} = choices from members of the in-group to other members of the in-group,

C_{a-b} = choices from members of the in-group to members of the out-group,

C_{b-a} = choices from members of the out-group to members of the in-group,

C_{b-b} = choices from members of the out-group to other members of the out-group,

C_a = total choices made by the in-group,

C_{-a} = total choices given to the in-group,

C_b = total choices made by the out-group,

C_{-b} = total choices given to the out-group,

C_t = total choices made by the in-group and out-group combined,

a = the number of persons in the in-group,

b = the number of persons in the out-group, $(N-a)$,

N = the number of persons in both the in-group and out-group.

$$\text{In-Group Preference} = IP = \frac{C_{a-a}(N-a)}{C_{a-b}(a-1)}$$

(Criswell, 1943),

$$\text{In-Group Cleavage} = IC = \frac{C_{a-a}C_t}{C_aC_{-a}}$$

(Criswell, 1949),

$$\text{In-Group Cohesion} = ICo = \frac{O(C_{a-a}C_{-a})}{aC_a}$$

(Lundberg, 1942),

where:

O = the number of members in the out-group who receive choices from members of the in-group.

TABLE 1

A SYSTEM OF NOTATION FOR DESCRIBING IN-GROUP AND OUT-GROUP RELATIONSHIPS

	Choices Received by Subgroup a	Choices Received by Subgroup b	Total
Choices made by Subgroup a	C_{a-a}	C_{a-b}	C_a
Choices made by Subgroup b	C_{b-a}	C_{b-b}	C_b
Total	C_{-a}	C_{-b}	C_t

In-Group Climate $=$

$$SC = \frac{N(N-1)\ [5A_s + 4B_s + 3(C_s + D_s) + 2E_s + F_s]}{a(a-1)\ [5A + 4B + 3(C + D) + 2E + F]}$$

(Proctor & Loomis, 1951),

where:

the capital letters A, B, C, D, E, and F refer to the six types of interpersonal relationships described by Proctor and Loomis (see page 353);

the subscript s refers to the same interpersonal relationships as they occur in the subgroup.

Jennings (1950) demonstrated the application of sociometric indices. She used six individual indices based on sociometric test results to describe the individual's sociometric profile and six symbols (either pluses or minuses) to represent this pattern. A plus sign indicated that the individual was above the mean in terms of that particular index; a minus sign indicated he was below the mean. The six indices used to describe the "choice-rejection pattern" were (1) choices given, (2) choices received, (3) reciprocated choices, (4) reciprocated rejections, (5) rejections given, and (6) rejections received. Bjerstedt (1952) developed a method of classifying Jennings' choice-rejection patterns. McKinney (1948) also suggested the use of a sociodiagnostic profile for the appraisal of individual students. This profile is made up of indices, previously described, of social status, compatibility, sociality, and personal appraisal.

In using partial ranking to secure sociometric data, the investigator must decide what weights should be assigned to the rankings. Although this problem is only indirectly related to the calculation of sociometric indices, it is worthy of some consideration. In studying the first three choices of children in a summer camp, Northway (1940) arbitrarily assigned five points to first choice, three points to second choice, and two points to third choice.

In discussing the problems of weighting,

D. T. Campbell (1954) suggested that the best procedure is to allow free choice and to use all the choices mentioned in analyzing the data, giving them all equal weights of one.

If, however, ranking is resorted to and normality of distribution of the ranks is assumed, the proper weight for Rank one is determined by finding the value of the area under the normal curve represented by that rank. Thus if there were ten members in the group, the sigma value for Rank one would be at the .05 level or 1.65. Similar calculations could be made for second and third ranks, etc. The sigma value for no mention at all is the mean of the unused area under the curve. In the example above where N is ten and three choices are expressed, the remaining area is the lower 70 per cent of the curve. Its sigma value turns out to be $-.39$. Converting these weights to whole numbers yields ten for first choice, seven for second choice, and five for third choice. Indifference is scored zero.

Statistical analysis. Both statistics and sociometry are young fields. As new statistical methods are developed, attempts are soon made to apply them to sociometric data. One major purpose of statistical analysis is to determine whether or not the obtained data could have resulted by chance. If the decision is that chance cannot account for the data, then statistical procedures also designate what confidence may be placed in this decision. The problem in applying statistics to sociometric data is the construction of adequate chance models for sociometric events. Essentially three methods have been used for this purpose: empirical chance models, binomial probability, and the chi-square technique.

The first attempt to apply the concept of statistical significance to sociometric data was that of Moreno and Jennings (1938), who

tried empirically to develop chance sociometric models. This was done by shuffling
and drawing ballots with fictitious names
and then comparing the chance choices with
actual choices obtained from real groups of
similar size. It seems that real differences did
exist between the chance and actual results,
but tests of significance were not made.

In discussing some of the inadequacies of
ranking and ratio methods, Bronfenbrenner
(1943) suggested that there was need for a
constant frame of reference with which to
compare sociometric data. He proposed the
use of chance models based on the binomial
distribution to define the probability that certain sociometric events would occur. Having
defined these probabilities, Bronfenbrenner
(1944a) surveyed various approximations to
the binomial distribution and suggested that
Pearson's Type III function is the one most
suitable for the analysis of sociometric data.
He concluded that:

The concept of deviation from chance expectancy provides a basis for deriving indices
which may be used for the estimation and
comparison of social status, of the degree of
coherence within social groups, and of the extent of group cleavage on the basis of such
factors as sex, age, race, nationality, or similar
attributes. Definition of sociometric status and
structure in terms of deviation from chance
expectancy (e.g., neglectees and stars) permits
identification of trends otherwise obscured
(Bronfenbrenner, 1944a, p. 70).

But Criswell (1946) considered Bronfenbrenner to be in error in applying the binomial distribution to the case of pairs of
choices. The binomial distribution, she held,
may be used to describe the choices made or
received by a given individual, but when one
is looking at the group as a whole, the chi-
square technique is more applicable. In a
later article, Criswell (1950) also disagreed
with Bronfenbrenner's earlier contention that
percentiles and standard scores were not useful ways of summarizing sociometric data.

D. S. Edwards (1948) also commented
upon the difficulty of securing adequate

mathematical models for dealing with free-
choice data. She not only pointed out inadequacies in Bronfenbrenner's approach but
suggested a modification in the method of
data collection that would make the mathematical model easier to construct. If each
member of the group responds to every other
member in terms of like, indifferent, dislike,
then the binomial expansion and Pearson's
Type III function are applicable.

Loomis and Pepinsky (1948) criticized
Criswell's interpretation of obtained chi-
square values. They are either significant or
they are not; they cannot be taken as indicating gradations of relationship.

Proctor and Loomis have summarized, as
follows, the steps involved in applying any
statistical model to sociometric data:

1. A frame of reference or a model distribution of the relevant characteristics is constructed on the basis of certain either *a
priori* or *a posteriori* assumptions or hypotheses.
2. Relevant to a given characteristic, every
sample which could arise is assigned a certain probability that it could have arisen
from a population which satisfied the assumptions referred to in the preceding rule.
3. The choice pattern of the test population
under investigation is considered as a sample, and the computed probability of its
occurrence, under the previous assumptions,
determines the admissibility of the assumptions.
4. The assumptions are progressively modified
so as to fit more closely the observed data
(Proctor & Loomis, 1951, p. 576).

The analysis of variance, another powerful statistical tool, has been used to a limited
extent in sociometric investigations. Seeman
(1946), in his study of intragroup Negro attitudes, divided two fifth-grade classes into
six groups according to skin color: white,
very light brown, light brown, brown, dark
brown, and very dark brown. He then used
analysis of variance to determine, for each of
the two classes, whether significant differences in friendship choice existed among
several color groups in each class.

French and Mensh (1948) also used analysis of variance in their sociometric study of sorority women. Each sorority member was asked to respond to the following sociometric criteria:

If you were to choose a room-mate at the present time, what three girls now living in the house would you consider *first?*

Under the same conditions, what three girls now living in the house would you consider *last?* (French & Mensh, 1948, p. 338).

These data were used to form three status groups: members of the majority group who received no rejections, members of the majority group who received rejections, and members of the minority or isolate group. In addition, each girl rated herself and each other girl on six traits: punctuality, sociability, fair-mindedness, intelligence, self-confidence, and sense of humor. Analysis of variance was used to determine whether or not significant differences existed among the status groups in ratings on the six traits.

As illustrated in these two studies, the analysis of variance is useful not in evaluating group structure itself but rather in relating group structure to other variables.

Matrix analysis. One of the newest and more promising approaches to the analysis of sociometric data is the use of matrix algebra, first suggested by Forsyth and Katz (1946). As they pointed out, sociometric data can be summarized in an $N \times N$ matrix where N is the number of people in the group. The rows represent the persons choosing or rejecting, and the columns represent the persons chosen or rejected. The main diagonal which represents self-choice is marked with Xs, pluses are used for choices, minuses are used for rejections, and blank cells indicate indifference.

If this original matrix is manipulated by rearranging the rows and columns in such a way that a maximum number of choices fall near the main diagonal, the matrix approaches what might be called standard form. In this form, subgroups can be readily identi-fied. A second result of this manipulation is that closely related people in the group will appear near each other in the margins of the matrix. Groups of rejections will move toward the lower left and the upper right of the matrix. The only restriction on the manipulation of the matrix is that the ordinal position of the rows and columns must be the same.

Moreno (1946) sounded a note of caution. Commenting on the significance of the matrix approach, he pointed out that the matrix is somewhat harder to read than the sociogram. Although he admitted the value of the new approach, he did not feel that it rendered the sociogram obsolete. ". . . I believe that a synthesis between sociogram and sociomatrix is possible" (pp. 348–349).

Forsyth and Katz offered no mathematical way of manipulating the matrix, but other authors soon offered such techniques. Katz (1947) offered further refinement by showing that the optimum ordering of the rows and columns conformed to the principle of least squares. He also suggested the usefulness of the matrix vectors in comparing the choice patterns of individuals within the group. Beum and Brundage (1950) developed a systematic method for maximizing the choices around the principal diagonal.

Luce and Perry (1949) and Festinger (1949) suggested a method for identifying chains from matrix data. Squaring the matrix makes it possible to identify two-step chains. If the original sociometric data indicate the direct relationships between one individual and the other group members, squaring the matrix will reveal other group members to whom he is related indirectly. Raising the matrix to the third power will reveal three-step chains.

If a submatrix containing only the mutual choices expressed in the original matrix is raised to the third power, cliques can be identified. Luce (1950) extended this use of matrix multiplication for the identification of cliques; he defined several types of cliques and showed how they could be identified. Chabot (1950) used some of these techniques in an industrial study. Ross and Harary (1952) pointed out that, in the process of raising a matrix to higher powers, some of the paths which appear between two elements are redundant. They developed formulas for calculating the number of redundant paths that do occur.

Lindzey and Borgatta evaluated the matrix multiplication method:

(1) The limitation to unweighted choices *or* rejections may be found restrictive. (2) The matrix operations are laborious unless done on IBM equipment, and programming for this matrix procedure may be more effort than it is worth. [Since electronic computers have become widely available, this objection has lost point.] (3) Even as extended by Luce, the definitions of structures which may be isolated are restrictive. . . . (4) The holistic view possible with the Forsyth and Katz method and the sociogram approaches is not possible. In favor of the method, it is the only approach available which is relatively unrestricted as to the size of the group which may be examined. . . . In addition, treatment of the data is readily repeatable in the hands of different investigators (Lindzey & Borgatta, 1954, pp. 418–419).

Glanzer and Glaser (1959) reviewed a considerable number of formulas and procedures for the analysis of group structure in their appraisal of the present status of a science of group structure.

One of the major outcomes of the work described above has been to present a set of techniques for simplifying and analyzing the complex data generated by group functioning. These techniques, moreover, involve the translation of the data into mathematical form that permits the application of a wide range of powerful analytic techniques. In addition, these techniques are applicable not only to the original sociometric relations (e.g., "like," "chooses") but also to other relations (e.g., "communicates to," "hands materials to," etc.). They therefore permit the analysis of a much wider variety of organizational relationships than hitherto studied (Glanzer & Glaser, 1959, p. 331).

It may seem that our consideration of sociometry as a kind of rating procedure has taken us far afield from our initial concern with rating methods in research on teaching. Yet this formulation may prove fruitful. In sociometry we do not focus merely on the ratee nor do we regard the rater merely as an approximation to an external, objective measurement device. Rather, sociometry puts the ratee and rater on an even footing, each acting as ratee and rater simultaneously, with respect not just to each other but also to every other member of, say, the classroom group or the teaching staff. The inclusion of sociometry has enormously broadened the scope of our view of rating methods. This broadening should in turn enhance our use of both the rating methods as traditionally conceived and of the sociometric methods that have developed as an almost independent discipline. The marriage of these vigorous lines of methodology should produce still better tools of investigation.

THE SEMANTIC DIFFERENTIAL

A simple-looking but highly sophisticated use of the graphic rating scale has been given the name *semantic differential* by its originator, C. E. Osgood. Its theoretical rationale, properties as a measuring device, and numerous applications have been reported in a volume by Osgood, Suci, and Tannenbaum (1957).

Briefly, it consists of a number of graphic, seven-"unit" rating scales with opposing, or "bipolar," adjectives at each end. These scales set up a "*semantic space,* a region of some unknown dimensionality and Euclidian in character. Each semantic scale . . . is assumed to represent a straight line function that passes through the origin of this space, and a sample of such scales then represents a multidimensional space" (Osgood, Suci, & Tannenbaum, 1957, p. 25). The number of identifiable and reliably measurable independent dimensions, then, set the practical limits of defining semantic space, i.e., the space of differentiable meanings of concepts.

The basic operation of "differentiating" the meaning of a concept can be illustrated as follows. The subject is asked to judge a concept, say *teacher,* against a series of scales. Assigning numbers from 1 to 7 to each of the scale units, we then have for each scale a quantitative value of the concept for each of the scales in relation to the concept under study. Factor analysis of a manageable sample of such bipolar adjectives then yields the factor structure of the concept. The analysis is, of course, done for a sample of the population for whom the meaning of the concept is to be determined. Such factor analyses have yielded three dimensions of meaning: *evaluation* (Items *a–d* in Fig. 8); *potency* (Items

$$D_{il} = \sqrt{\sum_{j} d^2{}_{il}}$$

"where D_{il} is the linear distance between the points in the semantic space representing concepts i and l and d_{il} is the algebraic difference between the coordinates of i and l on the same dimension or factor, j. Summation is over the k dimensions" (Osgood, Suci, & Tannenbaum, 1957, p. 91). Thus, suppose the concepts *teacher* and *pupil* to have the factor scores, as rated by one subject, shown below:

	Evaluation	Potency	Activity
Teacher	3	−3	−3
Pupil	−3	3	−3

Teacher

	(1)	(2)	(3)	(4)	(5)	(6)	(7)	
a. fair	___:	___:	___:	___:	___:	___:	___	unfair
b. clean	___:	___:	___:	___:	___:	___:	___	dirty
c. good	___:	___:	___:	___:	___:	___:	___	bad
d. valuable	___:	___:	___:	___:	___:	___:	___	worthless
e. large	___:	___:	___:	___:	___:	___:	___	small
f. strong	___:	___:	___:	___:	___:	___:	___	weak
g. heavy	___:	___:	___:	___:	___:	___:	___	light
h. active	___:	___:	___:	___:	___:	___:	___	passive
i. fast	___:	___:	___:	___:	___:	___:	___	slow
j. hot	___:	___:	___:	___:	___:	___:	___	cold

Fig. 8. Illustration of a Semantic Differential.

e–g); and *activity* (Items *h–j*). Evaluation accounts for approximately twice the variance of either of the other two, and these two for approximately twice that of any subsequent factors.

The reader should note that with the semantic differential we can measure the meaning, in a given sense, to any individual of literally any concept within his ken—"Of shoes and ships and sealing wax, Of cabbages and kings," as well as me, your father, Miss Jones, my teacher, school, algebra, Democrat, this handbook, paper clip, United Nations, Eisenhower, etc. Then the similarity between any two concepts can be measured by means of the *D* (distance) measure:

D is found by taking the difference between the scores of the two concepts on each factor, squaring the difference, summing the squares over the three factors, and computing the square root of the sum. In the example given, $D = \sqrt{72} = 8.49$. The larger the *D*, the greater the distance or dissimilarity in the meanings of the two concepts to the rater or judge. Difficulties in the interpretation of *D* measures have subsequently been pointed out by Cronbach (1958) and LaForge (1961).

Although Osgood and his associates regard their book as only a progress report, they have progressed far enough to provide a measuring device that is flexible, widely applicable, simple to administer, and in accord with many criteria of an acceptable measuring device. As the "encoder" of information, the rater—the real "measuring device"—can with considerable latitude be controlled as to his accuracy by manipulating the length and variety of the recording device.

Its brief description here will not enable the prospective user to proceed without further orientation. He will need to consult the book and perhaps some of the research literature reporting experimental studies and applications. In addition to the fifty-some studies reported in Osgood, Suci, and Tannenbaum (1957), investigations by others have begun to appear in the literature as this is written. Mention of a few of these to illustrate their variety is appropriate here.

Concerned with the general properties of this device, Mehling (1959) used a nine-point numerical rating with the semantic differential and found that "the semantic differential . . . does measure both the direction and intensity of attitude. Furthermore, this gives added weight to the assumption that the middle (number 4) interval in the scales represents the neutral point in the attitude" (p. 578). Triandis (1959) used the semantic differential to study industrial subjects' perceptions of jobs and people (welder, teacher, vice-president, personnel director, their supervisor's boss, the vice-president of their division, "a fellow at work whom you like," and "an effective manager you have known well and who is not the same as any of the people already rated") (p. 221). He found the hypothesis supported that persons like those who perform their role in society according to the "ideal" expected behavior.

The problem of the similarity of semantic structure for different subjects has been the focus of several investigations. Extremely different subjects have shown highly similar semantic structures. Suci (1952) found high and low scorers on the California F Scale to judge ethnic concepts in similar frames of reference (factor structures) though the meanings of these groups differed significantly. Bopp (1955) reported similar results from

a comparison of the factor structures of normal and schizophrenic subjects.

A few studies have been aimed at answering the question of whether semantic constancy prevails across subjects from different cultural and linguistic backgrounds. Kumata and Schramm (1956) showed equivalent semantic structures for bilingual students from Korea and Japan and for native Americans when the semantic judgments were made in the respective languages. Kumata (1957) extended the generality of the Kumata-Schramm findings with similar findings for American and Japanese monolinguals. Triandis and Osgood (1958) also found that Greek and American monolinguals used similar semantic space. Suci (1960) further extended these findings for Zuni-, Hopi-, Navaho-, Spanish-, and English-speaking subjects in the American Southwest with respect to their evaluative and dynamism dimensions. He was unable to interpret a third factor, highly dissimilar for all groups.

Peters (1957) found the semantic differential to differentiate significantly between delinquent and nondelinquent boys. Ravitz (1958) substantiated the hypothesis that teachers' verbal behavior reflected their concern for self or students.

In summary, the semantic differential, in the light of the rigorous and extensive experimentation that it has so far undergone, appears to be a widely useful research instrument. Of course, it needs further experimental evaluation, research, and development as its originator emphatically states (Osgood, Suci, & Tannenbaum, 1957). Its most obvious shortcoming for the naïve rater is its apparent lack of "face validity." That one can obtain a valid diagnosis of a multiple personality (Osgood & Luria, 1954) against the criterion of a detailed clinical psychiatric diagnosis will possibly impress the unsophisticated observer as bizarre and leave him somewhat skeptical as to the "psychological sense" of such findings. One who accepts the logic of measurement and of factor analysis will be impressed with the convenience, power, and flexibility of the device.

Since the semantic differential is based on the use of graphic rating scales, the cautions given earlier in this chapter for such instruments and for psychological measurement in general apply to it. For example, may response-sets bias results obtained with it? To what extent are its results functions of biases of different cultural and subcultural groups? This problem, of course, is to some extent common to all verbal measuring instruments, since meanings derive from experience. Since no two individuals have identical experience, it follows in strict logic that no two individuals will perceive precisely the same meaning in any given word.

Q-TECHNIQUE RATINGS

In his *Autocrat of the Breakfast Table,* Oliver Wendell Holmes observed that in any dialogue the individual is at least three persons—as he perceives himself, as others perceive him, and as he thinks others perceive him. He might easily have extended this list —as he would like to be, as he would have liked to be, as many individual others (father, mother, teacher) would like him to be. The reader can easily supply many additional frames of reference within each of which the "real" individual would appear somewhat unique. In the systematic, scientific study of individuals or groups within any of these frames of reference, Q technique provides important tools of observation. While any other rating device can be used for these different frames of reference, Q technique has probably been more often so used.

Q technique, developed by Stephenson (1953), originally derived its name from Stephenson's use of the letter Q as the symbol for intra- and interpersonal correlations as distinguished from R, the symbol for correlations between test scores. In a series of papers published over a period of about 20 years, he developed the concept of Q, its rationale, and its possible psychological applications. His book brought all of this together with a considerable tincturing of

polemics as well as experimentation. The versatility of the technique as envisioned by Stephenson is reflected in the fact that his chapters deal with such matters as applications to type psychology, questionnaires, social psychology, self-psychology, personality, projective tests, and clinical psychology.

In using the Q technique, the experimenter originates a number of descriptive statements —perhaps 60 or 100—growing out of some kind of theory, explicit or implicit. The statements can be obtained in a variety of ways: traits mentioned in other rating scales, personality inventories, newspapers, student themes, the literature of psychology, particularly that concerned with personality, detailed characterizations of persons in stories, novels, and plays. When he administers the statements, one on a card, he tells the subject to sort them into a specified number of piles —perhaps seven, nine, or eleven—along a continuum ranging from statements completely applicable to himself or some other person or object to statements completely inapplicable. He also specifies a forced distribution; i.e., the number of cards the subject is to place in each pile is specified so as to yield a roughly normal distribution. Then the ratings, i.e., pile numbers, assigned to the statements by one rater can be correlated with those assigned by another rater. The higher the correlation, the greater the similarity between the raters in the way they judge the statements. The second series of ratings may be made by the same rater as the first, but from a different point of view. For example, the first rating of the statements can indicate how well the rater thinks each statement characterizes his "actual" self; the second rating can be required to indicate how well the rater thinks each statement characterizes his "ideal" self. Then the correlation between these two sets of ratings of the statements may be considered to reflect the rater's personal adjustment. Mowrer (1953) devotes a lengthy chapter to a description, history, and critique of Q technique, one to which the student desiring further orientation will wish to refer. Meehl

(1960) reported a number of studies using Q correlations in a study of cognitive activity of the clinician.

Sheldon and Sorenson (1960) offered four exploratory applications of Q technique to educational problems. To evaluate the effect of a "senior problems course" on personal adjustment, they used Q correlations between each student's Q-sort description of his ideal self and his perceived self. In a course on curriculum development, they investigated Q correlations between administrators' and teachers' conceptions of the curriculum on a subject-centered versus student-centered dimension. For determining change in philosophical position, they prepared a set of statements for Q sorting, each statement representing one of the six possible combinations of realism, idealism, or pragmatism with cognitive or affective content; the lower the Q correlations between sorts at the beginning and end of the course, the greater the change in the student's philosophical position. In a counseling seminar, Q sorts of 40 statements describing counseling interviews were used to determine evaluations of mock interviews by correlating the student's conception of the ideal interview with his Q-sort description of the role-playing interview.

In a comprehensive review of Stephenson's book, Cronbach and Gleser (1954) raised serious questions about some of the devices that have come to be grouped together as Q methodology: The notion of getting responses to questionnaire items from several points of view is considered promising, but the use of card-sorts rather than booklets is of undemonstrated value. The forced distribution is of "dubious value." Q correlations for measuring profile similarity and for factor analysis have major shortcomings. Constructing questionnaire items according to structured designs "is thoroughly relevant to modern personality theory which holds that whether a tendency toward (say) extroversion will be expressed in a given situation depends on the person's other traits" (p. 329). But the use of analyses of variance with such designs, using forced sorts, is incorrect.

In short, Q technique has both virtues and defects; considerable circumspection is required for the researcher to capitalize on the former and avoid the latter. Some research workers, seeing the similarities between Q technique and the semantic differential, have considered the latter to have all the advantages and none of the shortcomings of Q technique. In the semantic differential, one has a single set of items (scales) that are responded to again and again in describing one object after another. Comparisons of the descriptions of the various objects are made (on the semantic differential) with "D" (distance) measure, which is considered to have some advantages over the Pearson correlations used for such comparisons in Q technique. But the forced distribution of Q technique eliminates response sets—such as tendencies toward extremes or neutrality—which can introduce irrelevant variance on the semantic differential. The conclusion must remain that the investigator should take pains to know what he gains and loses when he uses either of these methods.

A SELF-ANCHORING RATING SCALE

While many self-report rating scales are called by such other names as questionnaires and inventories, a development of ipsative scaling grounded in psychological theory is the *self-anchoring rating scale* (Kilpatrick & Cantril, 1960), an outgrowth of transactional theory:

Its key point . . . is that each of us lives and operates in the world and through the self, both *as perceived*. . . . Since each of us behaves in terms of *his* 'reality world,' the only world he knows, it follows that the key to an understanding of human behavior is to take into account the unique reality world of the individual (Kilpatrick & Cantril, 1960, p. 158).

This obviously phenomenological, first-person point of view is opposed to a third-person point of view which rests upon the assumption of an objectively definable reality the same for everyone except for differences due to error.

Self-anchoring scaling, unlike other rating scales, uses no verbal cues attached to the scale. It uses a combination of open-ended, probing interview, content analysis, and nonverbal scaling, on the assumption of real psychological meaning of goal-related variables such as striving, self-evaluation, location of "where one is now," perception of progress, and future expectations. Figure 9, taken from Kilpatrick and Cantril (1960), makes clear the general procedure and possible applications.

card picturing ten steps going up a mountain, with a Bantu on each step. The authors point to the need for (1) the usual checks on the reliability of content analysis and coding, and (2) proper sampling procedures and statistical treatment.

This instrument, obviously highly flexible, invites experimental comparison with the semantic differential in certain situations. Since it requires individual interviewing, content analysis, and coding as used by its authors, it is obviously much less economical for data collection than the semantic differential.

First, the respondent is asked to describe what, for him would be the very best or ideal way of life. Responses are recorded as nearly verbatim as possible, and probing is continued until the respondent indicates that he has nothing further to add to the description. Following this, he is asked to describe what he perceives as the very worst way of life for himself. Verbatim recording and probing are carried out in a similar fashion.

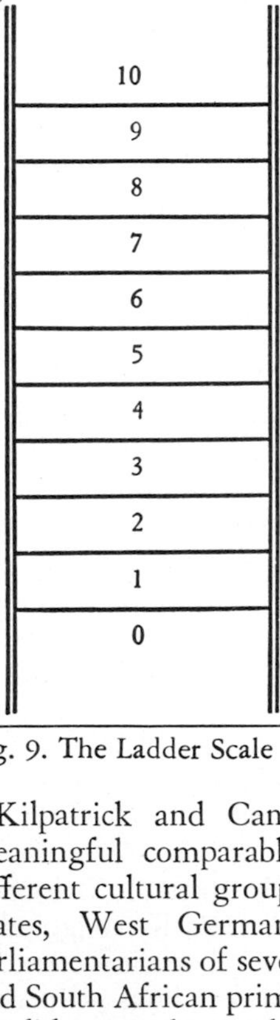

Then, the respondent is handed a pictorial, non-verbal scale, such as the ten-point ladder scale shown in Figure [9]. He is told that the best and worst ways of living he has just described are the end points of the scale, the best at the top and the worst at the bottom. The scale has now been created and is ready for use.

Usually we begin the use of the scale by asking: "Where on this ladder would you say you are now?" (The interviewer records the step number to which the person points.) This "location of the self in the now" provides an additional reference point useful in further scaling and open-ended questioning.

Subsequent scaling and questioning can be carried out in a variety of ways, depending on the purposes of the research. For example, the respondent's sense of progress in overall relation to the pluses and minuses of his own value system may be elicited by asking one, or a series of questions, such as: "Where on this scale were you two years ago?" "Five years ago?" "Ten years ago?" Expectations concerning the future, again in terms of the person's own goal system, may be obtained by asking him where on the scale he expects to be at some time in the future, e.g., five years from now. Content may be explored further by inquiring about differences between scale positions. For example, if a person points to two scale positions higher than his present position as an indication of where he expects to be five years from now, one may inquire: "How will your way of living be different then?" (Kilpatrick & Cantril, 1960, p. 159).

Fig. 9. The Ladder Scale (Reproduced with the authors' permission).

Kilpatrick and Cantril (1960) reported meaningful comparable data from widely different cultural groups within the United States, West Germany, the Philippines, parliamentarians of seven different countries, and South African primitives. Since the Bantu did not understand what a "ladder" was, Sherwood, who collected the data, used a

PRACTICAL AND THEORETICAL MATTERS RELATED TO RATING SCALES

Apart from the theoretical and methodological issues to which this chapter has been devoted, rating methods applied to teachers are involved in certain practical matters in school administration and teaching. Among these matters are merit rating of teachers, students' ratings of their teachers, content of rating scales, matching of personality factors derived from ratings and questionnaires, conceptualization of the classroom as a social system, and bias in ratings. In this section we consider each of these matters in turn.

Merit Rating of Teachers

One current issue closely related to rating scales is merit rating of teachers for the purpose of awarding differential salaries. In general, teachers and their professional representatives in the National Education Association are strongly opposed to such use of ratings. Schoolboard members and some administrators appear to favor the idea. The notion that superior teacher effectiveness should be rewarded by higher pay seems on its face to be eminently sensible. The rub is, of course, that no generally acceptable method of measuring teacher merit is available.

An ambitious attempt to find such a method was that of McCall (1952). In a three-year statewide study the State Department of Public Instruction of North Carolina attempted to find measures usable in merit ratings. The criterion of teacher merit was the proven ability to produce educational growth in pupils as measured by a wide variety of tests. The teachers stimulating the most growth thus were superior teachers, and those stimulating the least growth, the poor teachers. To quote McCall (1952):

Thus, the principals tended to a very slight degree to call good teachers poor and poor teachers good (p. 23) . . . . *The rating of a teacher by her peers showed an index of validity of −11 per cent. In short, there is a tendency for every adult associated with the teachers professionally to misjudge the teachers* (p. 24). . . . All things considered, *this research failed to find any system of measuring teacher merit which the writer is willing to recommend be adopted as a basis for paying the salaries of all teachers* (McCall, 1952, p. 37).

The opposition of teachers has several bases—the possibilities of favoritism, of lowered morale and efficiency among those "passed over," of interteacher tensions, and, above all, the fact that there are no generally accepted criteria of teacher merit. M. V. Campbell (1959) gives one conclusion of his study as follows:

Teacher reluctance to accept the merit rating idea may be due to inability to make self-assessments of effectiveness. In this study practically all of the teachers rated themselves average. Teacher acceptance of the merit rating principle is unlikely to occur if almost all teachers see themselves as average, since they would see little possibility of merit increases for themselves (M. V. Campbell, 1959, p. 4).

Davis (1957) summarized NEA Research Division studies of salary schedules in school districts with more than 30,000 population. She found that 151 districts reported a superior-service maximum salary at some time in the 19 years ended with 1956–1957. But by 1956–1957 only 25 cities of this size still had superior-service maximums in their salary schedules; i.e., 126 of the 151 districts had abandoned such a plan during the two preceding decades.

The NEA Research Division has found examples of at least four procedures in evaluating teachers for merit pay (Davis, 1957):

1. West Hartford, Connecticut, used a formal evaluation procedure with a weighted point scale: Teaching skills and pupil relationships (10 items), 65 per cent; Staff relationships (4 items), 15 per cent; Public relations (3 items), 10 per cent; The teacher as a person (4 items), 10 per cent. Teachers are considered on nomination by others or by themselves. A committee studies the evidence and recommends action on the basis of the foregoing criteria.

2. In Alton, Illinois, formal evaluation with an "unweighted" (equally weighted?) point scale is used. The 26 merit factors are grouped under nine headings—dependability, service, professional consciousness, subject matter, classroom atmosphere, adapt-

ability, personal appearance, emotional stability, and wholesome relationships with fellow teachers. "The rating is developed in a
conference between the classroom teacher
being rated and his principal" (p. 536).

3. Ladue, Missouri, uses a formal evaluation procedure without a point scale. This
procedure specifies continuous evaluation
through conferences and visitations. Principals make recommendations to the superintendent for placement on upper levels of
the salary schedule.

4. Recommendation by the superintendent, without formal evaluation procedure, on
the basis of principals' recommendations to
the superintendent. The principal's recommendation is based, presumably, on recorded
evidence and recommendations made in the
light of all available facts.

Davis (1960) has reviewed other literature
on the subject. In cities with more than 30,000
population, the percentage reporting a "superior-service maximum" has steadily declined
from about 20 per cent in 1938 to about 7 per
cent in 1957. Further, in 1955–1956 and 1956–
1957, "about half of the districts that have
these superior-service provisions do not use
them" (Davis, 1957, p. 535).

What the American Educational Research
Association Committee on the Criteria of
Teacher Effectiveness said in one of its reports (1953) still requires no amend-
ment with respect to procedures usable by a
school administrator for selecting teachers
for merit pay:

. . . the present condition of research on teacher
effectiveness holds little promise of yielding
results commensurate with the needs of American education. . . . after 40 years of research
on teacher effectiveness . . . one can point to
few outcomes that a superintendent of schools
can safely employ in hiring a teacher or granting him tenure (American Educational Research Association, 1953, p. 657).

Student Ratings of Teachers

Robert Burns's invocation *To a Louse,*

Oh wad some power the giftie gie us
To see ourselves as ithers see us!
It wad frae mony a blunder free us
And foolish notion

has been answered with respect to student-
teacher relations. Obviously the kind of feedback a teacher obtains from anonymous ratings by his students is such a "giftie's" boon.
The teacher can see himself as students see
him, at least insofar as the ratings have relevant meaning for him. An experiment by
Gage, Runkel, and Chatterjee (1960) indicated that sixth-grade teachers given such
feedback (pupils' ratings of their actual and
ideal teacher on 12 items) changed in the
direction of their pupils' ideal teacher, as
measured by pupils' subsequent descriptions
of the teachers.

Since about 1927, a considerable body of
research has been done on the Purdue Rating
Scale for Instructors and its revision, the
Purdue Rating Scale for Instruction. This
research has demonstrated that student evaluation is a useful, convenient, reliable, and
valid means of self-supervision and self-
improvement for the teacher. Major generalizations from these researches follow:

1. Reliability of ratings of teachers by students is a function of the number of raters,
in accordance with the Spearman-Brown
prophecy formula (Shock, Kelly, & Remmers, 1927). If 25 or more student ratings are
averaged, they are as reliable as the better
educational and mental tests at present available (Remmers, 1960).

2. Grades of students have little if any relationship to their ratings of instructors who
assigned the grades (Elliott, 1950; Remmers,
1928, 1930).

3. Alumni 10 years after graduation agree
very closely (rank order $rho = .92$) with on-
campus students on the relative importance
of 10 teacher characteristics (Drucker &
Remmers, 1950).

4. Alumni 10 years after graduation agree
substantially (rs ranging from .40 to .68)
with on-campus students in their average
ratings of the same instructors (Drucker &
Remmers, 1950).

5. Halo effect, if present in ratings by such instruments as the Purdue Rating Scale for Instruction, is insufficient to raise the inter-trait correlations to unity when corrected for unreliability of the ratings. Evidence indicates that students discriminate reliably among different aspects of the teacher's personality and of the course (Remmers, 1934).

6. Little if any relationship exists between students' ratings of the teacher and the difficulty of the course (Remmers, 1928).

7. In a given college or university, wide and important departmental differences in teaching effectiveness may exist as judged by student opinion (Remmers, 1928).

8. The sex of student raters bears little or no relationship to their ratings of teachers (Remmers, 1929).

9. The cost in time and money of obtaining student ratings of teachers is low. In fact, it is considerably lower than the cost of administering a typical standardized educational test of some comprehensiveness (Remmers, 1960).

10. Popularity in extraclass activities of the teacher is probably not appreciably related to student ratings of that teacher (Remmers, 1928, 1960).

11. Teachers with less than five years' experience tend to be rated lower than teachers with more than eight years' experience (Remmers, 1929).

12. The sex of the teacher is in general unrelated to the ratings received (Remmers, 1929).

13. There is a low but significant positive relationship ($r = .20$) between the mean objectively measured achievement of an instructor's students (with scholastic ability held constant) and students' ratings of college chemistry teachers (Elliott, 1950).

14. Students are more favorable than instructors to student ratings of instructors, but more instructors than students have noticed improvement in their teaching as a result of student ratings (Remmers, 1960).

Many colleges and universities have used such student ratings. Stecklein (1960), in his review of this topic, cited evidence that 40 per cent of 804 colleges and universities in the United States have used students' ratings of teachers.

A number of factor analyses of students' ratings of teachers have been performed. One example using a fairly carefully drawn sample and intensive analysis of data is the study by Hodgson (1958). This factor analysis of a 41-item numerical scale with five constant alternatives, developed by French (1957), yielded seven factors with variance contributions ranging from 19 per cent to 7 per cent. While sophisticated in its design and analysis, the study is nonetheless based upon a single institution, the University of Washington.

Gupta (1960) factor-analyzed sixth-grade pupils' ratings of their 130 teachers on a 96-item scale combining Leeds' 48-item *My Teacher* inventory (Leeds & Cook, 1947) with a 48-item Teacher Description Inventory developed by Gage and Weitman (1957). Her analysis, analytically rotated to Kaiser's varimax criterion, yielded five recognizable orthogonal factors. These factors, defined on the basis of items with high loadings, were as follows:

I. Affective Merit: Is this teacher usually cross? Is this teacher usually kind to you? Does this teacher think she is always right and the pupil wrong?

II. Cognitive Merit in Motivating Learning: Does this teacher often get you so interested in school work that you read and talk about it outside the school? When the teacher has finished explaining a subject, do you sometimes feel so interested that you want to find out a lot more about it than is in the textbook? Does your teacher make hard subjects seem easier?

III. Cognitive Merit in Promoting Comprehension (Negative Items): Do you feel you are really having trouble learning things in school this term? Is school work harder for you this term? When the teacher has finished explaining a subject, do you often feel you still do not understand it?

IV. Cognitive Merit in Promoting Comprehension (Positive Items): Does your teacher explain your lessons clearly? Does your teacher explain the school work so you can understand it? Does your teacher explain what you don't understand?

V. Disciplinary Ability: Is this teacher able to keep the children quiet in the classroom? Does this teacher know how to keep the class working? Does your teacher let your class waste a lot of time?

The Content of Rating Scales

What should determine the content of rating scales, particularly as it relates to research on teaching? Obviously, the judgment of the originator as to what is relevant and important for his purposes will guide him in choosing the qualities, behaviors, skills, habits, situations, and the like, to be studied. This judgment in turn will be a function of his educational philosophy, his values, and his view of the scientific disciplines relevant to the issue.

That considerable divergence in these matters exists hardly needs elaboration here. To illustrate briefly, it will be enough to point to the controversies around the concepts of "progressive education" and the "life-adjustment" movement.

A rating scale based on a systematic conception of teaching. An excellent example of content based on an explicit conception of the teaching and learning process is the series of 12 rating scales reported by Simpson and Brown (1952). They carried out a study of learning and teaching by means of these scales in eight different colleges. The general directions for students rating classes give the purpose, assumptions, and specific instructions to the raters. Scale A, shown in Fig. 10,

Purpose of the scales: To help the teacher or advanced student or both diagnose significant factors related to effective teaching and learning. Such a diagnosis can provide a framework for systematic improvement in teaching and learning activities in modern schools.

Assumptions underlying the scales: (1) That the student learns only what he practices, and (2) that school experiences should pave the way for continued systematic learning and intelligent problem facing outside the classroom. If these two assumptions are accepted it follows that what the learner needs to experience most in his school work are the types of activities he will need to carry on outside the school.

SCALE A. What is the motivational level on which learners are operating?

1. Learner is antagonistic to procedures and resents teacher efforts to work with him. Does practically no work.

2. Learner sees little or no value in what is done in school and so only does as little as possible to keep from being embarrassed or punished.

3. Learner recognizes goals set up by the teacher, largely rejects them as valueless for him but works because by meeting the teacher's set goals he thinks he can achieve his own goals, such as getting a passing mark for the course or grade.

4. Learner sees goals set up by teacher, accepts them as good, and is working enthusiastically to achieve them.

5. Teacher takes major responsibility for identification and selection of goals and purposes but encourages learners to have minor share in this process.

6. Teacher and learner together assume responsibility for setting up sound goals and purposes and together take responsibility for carrying ahead activities.

7. Learner assumes the major share of responsibility for setting up his goals and for self-improvement; the teacher serves as a guide and at appropriate times checks to see that learning is continuing.

8. None above fits classroom. Situation described on back of rating sheet.

Fig. 10. Excerpts from "Scales for the Psychological Evaluation of Some Course Learnings" (Simpson & Brown, 1952, pp. 9–10).

illustrates the general nature of the scales.

The questions at the head of each scale indicate the nature of the content of the other scales (B through L):

SCALE B. How are assignments handled?

SCALE C. What practice is given in guided problem identification?

SCALE D. What practice is given in guided problem selection?

SCALE E. What practice is given in guided problem solution?

SCALE F. What guided practice is given in trying out possible solutions to problems?

SCALE G. How are evaluative abilities developed?

SCALE H. What opportunities for guided practice of effective record keeping are provided the learner?

SCALE I. What opportunities in learning how better to find resources needed in identifying and solving problems are provided the learner?

SCALE J. What opportunities for learning abilities connected with selecting appropriate resources are given when resources are at hand?

SCALE K. What opportunities are given for practice in democratic group discussion?

SCALE L. What guided practice in purposeful reading to identify, select, and solve problems is being given?

The authors presented results for a total of 1,119 ratings of classes. The average ratings ranged from 2.7 (assignments) to 4.8 (motivation) and show that "the average level on each of the twelve scales is rather low . . ." (p. 37). Feedback to teachers who accept the premises of these scales obviously might provide bases for improvement of the learning-teaching situation.

Consensus of competent judges. Consensus of judges is used in choosing items for many rating scales intended for use in research on teaching. In its early history, shortly after the turn of the century, such consultation of experts tended to yield a large number of trait names whose referents were

assumed to exist as psychological entities in teachers and were hypothesized to be related to teacher effectiveness. Such a rationale is still implicit in many rating scales having to do with teacher effectiveness, although empirical methods of refinement, such as scaling and factor analysis, now provide tools not dreamt of at the turn of the century.

The strategy of the extensive research by Ryans (1960), for example, began with such a rationale: Find the traits and behaviors that yield significant relationships with teacher effectiveness as defined by the consensus of "competent judges." The resulting Classroom Behavior Record was, of course, greatly improved through experimental and statistical refinement.

This strategy, based on time samples of ratings, has not been without its detractors. Turner and Fattu (1960), for example, criticized Ryans:

To construct instruments which are focally related to teaching skill assumes that one knows something about it. It has been one of Ryans' points that much thinking about teaching and, particularly, effective teaching is essentially *a priori,* i.e., it rests upon unestablished assumptions. The authors have no quarrel with the observation that much thinking about effective teaching is *a priori,* but they do diverge from Ryans' position with respect to the strategy for remedying this state of affairs. The strategy which the authors attribute to Ryans is a maximum security strategy. It involves no risk; it inherently involves no theory, although theory may be brought in from external sources; . . . and it accumulates information slowly and in an unsystematic way (Turner & Fattu, 1960, p. 14).

The authors then develop "a strategy which involves a considerable amount of risk and an inherent theory." To review it here, however, is beyond the purview of this chapter, since it does not necessarily involve the use of rating scales.

Critical incidents. A systematic empirical approach related to the use of expert consensus has been proposed and extensively used by Flanagan (1949, 1951) to meet specific personnel problems. To determine significant behavior, he proposed what he called the *critical incidents* technique. This involves asking qualified observers or judges for reports of incidents (behaviors) that were (1) negatively effective or led to failure, and (2) positively effective or led to unusual success. For teacher evaluation, for example, one would ask students, parents, peers, and administrators for such incidents. After assembling a large number of such incidents and noting frequently mentioned behaviors in either the failure or success list, one may infer the psychological traits probably involved and proceed to use these inferentially abstracted traits as a basis for constructing the relevant items for a rating scale.

Ryans (1960, pp. 79–83) has described in some detail his steps in collecting critical incidents, both by informal interview in the early stages and by more formal and systematic procedures in later work, when the participants were carefully instructed:

The final phase of the critical behaviors study, involving sorting the record cards and classifying the reported incidents into appropriate categories, was carried out in the following five steps: (1) identification of the salient features in each incident of teacher behavior reported; (2) derivation of a rough classification scheme for the reported incidents to facilitate ordering of the data; (3) classification of each critical behavior into one of these categories; (4) derivation of a generalized descriptive statement covering each category; and (5) final refinement of the classification scheme and preparation of generalized descriptions of the principal classes of teacher behaviors (Ryans, 1960, p. 81).

Matching Behavior Rating and Questionnaire Personality Factors

A major methodological and theoretical problem involved in personality factor studies is that of identifying personality factors by means of each of three techniques: behavior ratings (*BR* or *L* data in Cattell's writings), questionnaires (*Q* data), and objective tests

(*T* data). This problem has been the focus of considerable research, particularly by Cattell (1957). If the three methods were found to yield the same or similar factor structures, it would provide evidence that the obtained structural model was in better accord with reality than other possible models.

In 1957, Cattell summarized the state of his research on cross-technique factor matching as follows:

The upshot of this cross-media matching is clearly that L and Q factors are far more completely mutually matched than either is with T factors. Only L-data factors J and K, and the factors noted before to be specific to Q-data . . . fail of crossmatching (Cattell, 1957, p. 325).

In a later paper Scheier and Cattell (1958) said:

Factors in the rating and questionnaire realm have been securely linked to each other with all but a few factors now in one realm finding their counterparts in factors in the other realm. . . . Moreover, the linkage between questionnaire and rating realms is so well established that a match to a questionnaire factor is excellent presumptive evidence of a match to a parallel rating factor (Scheier & Cattell, 1958, pp. 608–609).

Becker (1960) reviewed in considerable detail the published quantitative data bearing on the issue and discussed many of the technical, statistical, and psychological issues involved. He also gave suggestions for future research using behavior ratings and questionnaires. But he "challenges assertions made in recent publications by Cattell and his co-workers to the effect that present research has shown in most cases a one-to-one matching of behavior rating and questionnaire factors. A review of the evidence fails to support these assertions" (p. 211). The issue has been discussed in an exchange subsequent to Becker's critique (Becker, 1961; Cattell, 1961).

The Classroom Group as a Social System

A chapter on rating scales might appear to be off-course in discussing "classroom groups as social systems," particularly since so little is yet known about the complexities of such groups. It is inevitable, however, that in the scientific exploration of what until recently was an uncharted sea, rating scales will play a crucial role. Such writings as those in the Fifty-ninth Yearbook of the National Society for the Study of Education (Henry, 1960), particularly Section II on "Sociopsychological Characteristics of Instructional Groups," have carried forward the mapmaking enterprise. The work of a number of others consciously addressed to problems in this area includes in general that of social psychologists concerned with group dynamics and more specifically those using sociometric procedures and rating scales.

The study by Gage, Leavitt, and Stone (1955) may serve as an example of such research in which rating scales played a crucial role. The authors sought to test the proposition that teachers should accurately perceive their pupils. The study, based on 103 teachers and their nearly 3,000 pupils in Grades 4, 5, and 6, involved two rating scales, each employing the same 12 items. Four items were designed to measure pupils' perceptions of each of three kinds of teacher behavior, namely the appropriateness of the teacher's behavior in meeting pupils' cognitive, social, and emotional needs. One scale used the 12 items in an unforced, constant alternative format; the other scale presented the same 12 items in all 66 possible pairs in forced-choice form: "Which is more true of your teacher?" The difficult problem of scoring the latter scale was handled by means of an electronic computer (Illiac).

Davidson and Lang (1960) attempted to test the hypotheses that (1) children's perceptions of their teachers' feelings toward them correlate positively with the children's self-perceptions, (2) favorable perception of teachers' feelings correlates positively with children's academic achievement; and (3) favorable perceptions of teachers' feelings correlate positively with desirable children's classroom behavior. They used a sample of 89 boys and 114 girls attending Grades 4, 5, and 6 in 10 different classrooms in New York City public schools. To measure perceptions and attitudes, they used a check list of bipolar adjectives specially developed for this study and in its final form strongly reminiscent of the semantic differential. Each of the hypotheses was supported. The correlation ($r =$ .82) between (1) favorability of children's perception of themselves, and (2) favorability of children's perception of their teachers' feelings toward them may have resulted, however, from a response set, namely, consistent individual differences in tendency to choose favorable-sounding responses, in describing both one's own perceptions and those of one's teacher. Interpretation of correlations between responses of the same persons to instruments of similar format must always be tempered by suspicions about such instrument-specific tendencies, or sets, unless these have been experimentally controlled.

Forces emanating from patrons and the entire community impinge upon the teaching-learning process in many ways, both subtle and obvious. Doubtless this larger social system will need to be measured in its relevant dimensions to maximize understanding of classroom dynamics. Here again rating scales will be much used.

Bias in Ratings

The human rater, as has already become evident, is imperfectly reliable and often not highly valid in his recorded judgments. What kinds of random and systematic errors have been found to operate in observations recorded by means of rating scales? Such errors must be taken into account in research design and analysis. Brogden and Taylor (1950) classified and discussed some of these.

1. Opportunity bias. In time-sampling observations, there is likelihood of undersampling important behaviors because they may

occur too infrequently to be contained in the time sample.

2. Experience bias. The practice teacher may very well display behavior patterns different from those of the experienced teacher.

3. Criterion distortion. This error may be built into a rating scale by including several similar, substantially correlated behaviors in a rating scale, thus weighting the behavior disproportionately.

4. Rating biases. These include various response sets, such as halo effect; i.e., ratings may suffer from selective perception determined by a general liking or disliking of the rating object by the rater. Various other types of response set have been detected. The leniency error and regression toward the mean, especially in self-ratings, are well-known phenomena.

In a sense, the study of raters and the rating process is equivalent to the study of accuracy of social perception or interpersonal perception, or of empathy, or of social sensitivity, as it has been variously termed. Research on these matters—reviewed by Guilford (1954, pp. 294–296) as "some characteristics of raters," by Bruner and Tagiuri (1954) as the "perception of people," by Taft (1955) as the "ability to judge people," and by Bronfenbrenner, Harding, and Gallwey (1958) as "skill in social perception"—has been abundant. Much of the research has not, however, been methodologically or conceptually valid, as Gage and Cronbach (1955) and Cronbach (1958) have pointed out. Consequently, many of the conclusions reached by earlier workers—e.g., "For certain admirable traits there is a positive correlation between possession and the ability to judge" (Guilford, 1954, p. 295)—are now suspect; artifacts of methodology may possibly account for such findings. Recent trends and points of view in research on person perception have been assembled in the symposium volume edited by Tagiuri and Petrullo (1958). The introduction to that volume is particularly cogent in stressing the "shift of focus from perceptual and cognitive *achievement* to *process*" (Tagiuri & Petrullo, 1958,

p. xvi), and the study of raters and ratings might well profit from the same development.

REFERENCES

American Educational Research Association, Committee on the Criteria of Teacher Effectiveness. Second report of the. . . . *J. educ. Res.,* 1953, 46, 641–658.

American Psychological Association, et al. Joint Committee. Technical recommendations for psychological tests and diagnostic techniques. *Psychol. Bull.,* 1954, 51, Supp.

Barker, R. G. The social interrelations of strangers and acquaintances. *Sociometry,* 1942, 5, 169–179.

Bassett, R. E. Sampling problems in influence studies. *Sociometry,* 1948, 11, 320–328.

Baxter, Bernice. *Teacher-pupil relationships.* New York: Macmillan, 1941.

Becker, W. C. The matching of behavior rating and questionnaire personality factors. *Psychol. Bull.,* 1960, 57, 201–212.

Becker, W. C. Comments on Cattell's paper on "perturbations" in personality structure research. *Psychol. Bull.,* 1961, 58, 175.

Berkshire, J. R. Comparisons of five forced-choice indices. *Educ. psychol. Measmt,* 1958, 18, 553–561.

Beum, C. O., & Brundage, E. G. A method for analyzing the sociomatrix. *Sociometry,* 1950, 13, 141–145.

Bjerstedt, A. A "chess-board sociogram" for sociographic representation of choice directions and for the analysis of "sociometric locomotions." *Sociometry,* 1952, 15, 244–262.

Bopp, Joan. A quantitative semantic analysis of word association in schizophrenia. Unpublished doctoral dissertation, Univer. of Illinois, 1955.

Brogden, H. E., & Taylor, E. K. The theory and classification of criterion bias. *Educ. psychol. Measmt,* 1950, 10, 159–186.

Bronfenbrenner, U. A constant frame of reference for sociometric research. *Sociometry,* 1943, 6, 363–397.

Bronfenbrenner, U. A constant frame of reference in sociometric research. Part II. Experiment and inference. *Sociometry,* 1944, 7, 40–75. (a)

Bronfenbrenner, U. The graphic presentation of sociometric data. *Sociometry,* 1944, 7, 283–289. (b)

Bronfenbrenner, U., Harding, J., & Gallwey, Mary. The measurement of skill in social perception. In D. C. McClelland, A. L. Baldwin, U. Bronfenbrenner, & F. L. Strodtbeck, *Talent and society: New perspectives in the identification of talent.* Princeton, N.J.: Van Nostrand, 1958. Pp. 29–111.

Bruner, J. S., & Tagiuri, R. The perception of people. In G. Lindzey (Ed.), *Handbook of social psychology.* Cambridge, Mass.: Addison-Wesley, 1954. Pp. 634–654.

Campbell, D. T. A rationale for weighting first, second, and third sociometric choices. *Sociometry,* 1954, 17, 242–243.

Campbell, M. V. Teacher-principal agreement on the teacher role. *Admin. Notebook,* 1959, 7 (6), 1–4.

Cattell, R. B. *Personality and motivation structure and measurement.* New York: World Book Co., 1957.

Cattell, R. B. Cattell replies to Becker's "Comments." *Psychol. Bull.,* 1961, 58, 176.

Chabot, J. A simplified example of the use of matrix multiplication for the analysis of sociometric data. *Sociometry,* 1950, 13, 131–140.

Challman, R. C. Factors influencing friendships among preschool children. *Child Develpm.,* 1932, 3, 46–158.

Champney, H. The measurement of parent behavior. *Child Develpm.,* 1941, 12, 131–136.

Chapin, F. S. Sociometric stars as isolates. *Amer. J. Sociol.,* 1950, 56, 263–267.

Cosgrove, D. J. Diagnostic rating of teacher performance. *J. educ. Psychol.,* 1959, 50, 200–204.

Criswell, Joan H. Sociometric methods of measuring group preferences. *Sociometry,* 1943, 6, 398–408.

Criswell, Joan H. Measurement of reciprocation under multiple criteria of choice. *Sociometry,* 1946, 9, 126–127.

Criswell, Joan H. Sociometric concepts in personnel administration. *Sociometry,* 1949, 12, 287–300.

Criswell, Joan H. Notes on the constant frame of reference problem. *Sociometry,* 1950, 13, 93–107.

Cronbach, L. J. Proposals leading to analytic treatment of social perception scores. In R. Tagiuri & L. Petrullo (Eds.), *Person perception and interpersonal behavior.* Stanford, Calif.: Stanford Univer. Press, 1958. Pp. 353–379.

Cronbach, L. J., & Gleser, Goldine C. Review of W. Stephenson, *The study of behavior: Q-technique and its methodology. Psychometrika,* 1954, 19, 327–330.

Davidson, Helen H., & Lang, G. Children's perceptions of their teachers' feelings toward them related to self-perception, school achievement, and behavior. *J. exp. Educ.,* 1960, 29, 107–118.

Davis, Hazel. Where we stand on merit rating as applied to teachers' salaries. *NEA J.,* 1957, 46, 535–536.

Davis, Hazel. Salary schedules. In C. W. Harris (Ed.), *Encyclopedia of educational research.* (3rd ed.) New York: Macmillan, 1960. Pp. 1178–1181.

Della Piana, G. M., & Gage, N. L. Pupils' values and the validity of the Minnesota Teacher Attitude Inventory. *J. educ. Psychol.,* 1955, 46, 167–178.

Domas, S., & Tiedeman, D. V. Teacher competence: An annotated bibliography. *J. exp. Educ.,* 1950, 19, 101–218.

Drucker, A. J., & Remmers, H. H. Do alumni and students differ in their attitudes toward instructors? *Purdue Univer. Stud. higher Educ.,* 1950, No. 70, 62–74.

Edwards, A. L. *The social desirability variable in personality assessment and research.* New York: Dryden, 1957.

Edwards, Daisy S. The constant frame of reference problem in sociometry. *Sociometry,* 1948, 11, 372–379.

Elliott, D. N. Characteristics and relationships of various criteria of college and university teaching. *Purdue Univer. Stud. higher Educ.,* 1950, No. 70, 5–61.

Eng, E., & French, R. The determination of sociometric status. *Sociometry,* 1948, 11, 368–371.

Festinger, L. The analysis of sociograms using matrix algebra. *Human Relations,* 1949, 2, 153–158.

Flanagan, J. C. Critical requirements: A new approach to employee evaluation. *Personnel Psychol.,* 1949, 2, 419–425.

Flanagan, J. C. The use of comprehensive rationales in test development. *Educ. psychol. Measmt,* 1951, 11, 151–155.

Forsyth, E., & Katz, L. A matrix approach to the analysis of sociometric data. *Sociometry,* 1946, 9, 340–347.

French, Grace M. *College students' concepts of effective teaching determined by an analysis of teacher ratings.* Seattle: Univer. of Washington, 1957. (Mimeographed)

French, R. L., & Mensh, I. N. Some relationships between interpersonal judgments and sociometric status in a college group. *Sociometry,* 1948, 11, 335–345.

Gage, N. L., & Cronbach, L. J. Conceptual and methodological problems in interpersonal perception. *Psychol. Rev.,* 1955, 62, 411–423.

Gage, N. L., & Exline, R. V. Social perception and effectiveness in discussion groups. *Human Relations,* 1953, 6, 381–396.

Gage, N. L., Leavitt, G. S., & Stone, G. C. Teachers' understanding of their pupils and pupils' ratings of their teachers. *Psychol. Monogr.,* 1955, 69, No. 21 (Whole No. 406).

Gage, N. L., Runkel, P. J., & Chatterjee, B. B. *Equilibrium theory and behavior change: An experiment in feedback from pupils to teachers.* Urbana: Bur. of Educ. Res., Univer. of Illinois, 1960. (Mimeographed)

Gage, N. L., & Weitman, M. *Teacher Description Inventory.* Urbana: Bur. of Educ. Res., Univer. of Illinois, 1957. (Mimeographed)

Ghiselli, E. E. The forced choice technique in self-description. *Personnel Psychol.,* 1954, 7, 201–208.

Glanzer, M., & Glaser, R. Techniques for the study of group structure and behavior: I. Analysis of structure. *Psychol. Bull.,* 1959, 56, 317–332.

Good, C. V. (Ed.) *Dictionary of education.* (2nd ed.) New York: McGraw-Hill, 1959.

Gordon, L. V. Some interrelationships among personality item characteristics. *Educ. psychol. Measmt,* 1953, 13, 265–272.

Gronlund, N. E. *Sociometry in the classroom.* New York: Harper, 1959.

Grossman, Beverly, & Wrighter, Joyce. The relationship between selection-rejection and intelligence, social status, and personality amongst sixth grade children. *Sociometry,* 1948, 11, 346–355.

Guilford, J. P. *Psychometric methods.* (2nd ed.) New York: McGraw-Hill, 1954.

Gupta, Promila. A study of cognitive merit of teachers. Unpublished doctoral dissertation, Univer. of Illinois, 1960.

Harris, C. W. (Ed.) *Encyclopedia of educational research.* (3rd ed.) New York: Macmillan, 1960.

Hartshorne, H., May, M. A., & Shuttleworth, F. K. *Studies in the nature of character.* Vol.

III. *Studies in the organization of character.* New York: Macmillan, 1930.

Hedberg, R., & Baxter, B. Item favorableness ratings in a forced-choice test: Applicants *vs.* nonapplicants. *Amer. Psychologist,* 1960, 15, 472. (Abstract)

Henry, N. B. (Ed.) The dynamics of instructional groups. *Yearb. nat. Soc. Stud. Educ.,* 1960, 59, Part II.

Highland, R. W., & Berkshire, J. R. A methodological study of forced-choice performance rating. San Antonio, Tex.: Lackland Air Force Base, Human Resources Res. Center, *Res. Bull.* 51–59, May, 1951.

Hodgson, T. F. *The general and primary factors in student evaluation of teaching ability.* Seattle: Univer. of Washington, 1958. (Mimeographed)

Horst, P. A generalized expression of the reliability of measures. *Psychometrika,* 1949, 14, 21–32.

Hunt, W. A., & Volkmann, J. The anchoring of an affective scale. *Amer. J. Psychol.,* 1937, 49, 88–92.

Isard, Eleanore S. The relationship between ambiguity and discriminating power in a forced-choice scale. *J. appl. Psychol.,* 1956, 40, 266–268.

Jennings, Helen H. *Leadership and isolation.* New York: Longmans, Green, 1943, 1950.

Katz, L. On the metric analysis of sociometric data. *Sociometry,* 1947, 10, 233–241.

Katz, L. A new status index derived from sociometric analysis. *Psychometrika,* 1953, 18, 39–43.

Kilpatrick, F. P., & Cantril, H. Self-anchoring scaling, a measure of individuals' unique reality worlds. *J. indiv. Psychol.,* 1960, 16, 158–173.

Koch, Helen L. Popularity in preschool children: Some related facts and a technique for its measurement. *Child Develpm.,* 1933, 4, 164–175.

Kumata, H. A factor analytic investigation of the generality of semantic structure across two selected cultures. Unpublished doctoral dissertation, Univer. of Illinois, 1957.

Kumata, H., & Schramm, W. A pilot study of crosscultural methodology. *Publ. opin. Quart.,* 1956, 20, 229–237.

LaForge, R. Some properties of the D²-statistic. Urbana, Ill.: Dept. of Psychology, Univer. of Illinois (ONR Contract Nonr–1844(11)), Separate Tech. Rept. 2, July, 1961.

Lanman, R. W., & Remmers, H. H. The "preference" and "discrimination" indices in forced-choice scales. *Educ. psychol. Measmt,* 1954, 14, 541–551.

Leeds, C. H. The construction and differential value of a scale for determining teacher-pupil attitudes. Unpublished doctoral dissertation, Univer. of Minnesota, 1946.

Leeds, C. H., & Cook, W. W. The construction and differential value of a scale for determining teacher-pupil attitudes. *J. exp. Educ.,* 1947, 16, 149–159.

Lindzey, G., & Borgatta, E. F. Sociometric measurement. In G. Lindzey (Ed.), *Handbook of social psychology.* Cambridge, Mass.: Addison-Wesley, 1954. Pp. 405–448.

Loomis, A. M. A technique for observing the social behavior of nursery school children. *Child develpm. Monogr.,* 1931, No. 5.

Loomis, C. P., & Pepinsky, H. B. Sociometry 1937–1947, theory and methods. *Sociometry,* 1948, 11, 262–286.

Loomis, C. P., Beegle, J. A., & Longmore, T. W. Critique of social class as related to social stratification. *Sociometry,* 1947, 10, 319–337.

Luce, R. D. Connectivity and generalized cliques in sociometric group structure. *Psychometrika,* 1950, 15, 169–190.

Luce, R. D., & Perry, A. D. A method of matrix analysis of group structure. *Psychometrika,* 1949, 14, 95–116.

Lundberg, G. A. *Social research.* New York: Longmans, Green, 1942.

Lundberg, G. A., & Steele, M. Social attraction in a village. *Sociometry,* 1938, 1, 375–419.

Maher, H. Studies of transparency in forced-choice scales: I. Evidence of transparency. *J. appl. Psychol.,* 1959, 43, 275–278.

Massarik, F., Tannenbaum, R., Kahane, M., & Weschler, I. R. Sociometric choice and organizational effectiveness: A multi-relational approach. *Sociometry,* 1953, 16, 211–238.

Mazzitelli, D. A forced-choice approach to the measurement of teacher attitudes. Unpublished doctoral dissertation, Univer. of Illinois, 1957.

McCall, W. A. *Measurement of teacher merit.* Raleigh, N.C.: State Dept. of Public Instruction, Publ. No. 284, 1952.

McGee, H. M. Measurement of authoritarianism and its relation to teachers' classroom behavior. *Genet. Psychol. Monogr.,* 1955, 52, 89–146.

McKinney, J. C. An educational application of a two-dimensional sociometric test. *Sociometry,* 1948, 11, 356–367.

Meehl, P. E. The cognitive activity of the clinician. *Amer. Psychologist,* 1960, 15, 19–27.

Mehling, R. A simple test for measuring intensity of attitudes. *Publ. opin. Quart.,* 1959, 23, 576–578.

Michels, W. C., & Helson, H. A reformulation of the Fechner law in terms of adaptation-level applied to rating scale data. *Amer. J. Psychol.,* 1949, 62, 355–368.

Moreno, J. L. Sociometry in action. *Sociometry,* 1942, 5, 298–315.

Moreno, J. L. Sociogram and sociomatrix. *Sociometry,* 1946, 9, 348–349.

Moreno, J. L. The three branches of sociometry: A postscript. *Sociometry,* 1948, 11, 121–128.

Moreno, J. L. *Sociometry, experimental method and the science of society.* New York: Beacon House, 1951.

Moreno, J. L. *Who shall survive?* (Rev. ed.) New York: Beacon House, 1953.

Moreno, J. L., & Jennings, Helen H. Statistics of social configurations. *Sociometry,* 1938, 1, 342–374.

Moreno, J. L., Jennings, Helen H., & Sargent, J. Time as a quantitative index of interpersonal relations. *Sociometry,* 1940, 3, 62–80.

Moreno, J. L., Jennings, Helen H., & Sargent, J. Time as a measure of inter-personal relations. *Sociometric Monogr.,* 1947, No. 13.

Moreno, J. L., et al. (Eds.) *The sociometry reader.* Glencoe, Ill.: Free Press, 1960.

Mowrer, O. H. Q technique—description, history, and critique. In O. H. Mowrer (Ed.), *Psychotherapy: Theory and research.* New York: Ronald Press, 1953. Pp. 316–375.

Newstetter, W. I., Feldstein, M. J., & Newcomb, T. M. *Group adjustment, a study in experimental sociology.* Cleveland: Western Reserve Univer., 1938.

Northway, Mary L. A method for depicting social relationships obtained by sociometric testing. *Sociometry,* 1940, 3, 144–150.

Northway, Mary L., & Potashin, R. Instructions for using the sociometric test. *Sociometry,* 1946, 9, 242–248.

Northway, Mary L., & Quarrington, B. Depicting intercultural relations. *Sociometry,* 1946, 9, 334–339.

Olson, W. C. The measurement of nervous

habits in normal children. *Univer. Minnesota Inst. Child Welf. Monogr.,* 1929, No. 3.

Osgood, C. E., & Luria, Zella. A blind analysis of a case of multiple personality using the semantic differential. *J. abnorm. soc. Psychol.,* 1954, 49, 579–591.

Osgood, C. E., Suci, G. J., & Tannenbaum, P. H. *The measurement of meaning.* Urbana: Univer. of Illinois Press, 1957.

Pepinsky, H. B., Siegel, L., & Van Atta, E. L. The criterion in counseling: A group participation scale. *J. abnorm. soc. Psychol.,* 1952, 47, 415–419.

Pepinsky, Pauline N. The meaning of "validity" and "reliability" as applied to sociometric tests. *Educ. psychol. Measmt,* 1949, 9, 39–49.

Peters, J. S. Socio-economic egocentrism in delinquents and non-delinquents. *Purdue Univer. Stud. higher Educ.,* 1957, No. 85, 1–21.

Proctor, C. H., & Loomis, C. P. Analysis of sociometric data. In Marie Jahoda, M. Deutsch, & S. W. Cook (Eds.), *Research methods in social relations.* Part 2. New York: Dryden, 1951. Pp. 561–585.

Ravitz, L. A. Teacher self-acceptance related to acceptance of pupils, in the classroom. Unpublished doctoral dissertation, Univer. of Maryland, 1957. *Dissertation Abstr.,* 1958, 18, 459.

Remmers, H. H. The relationship between students' marks and student attitude toward instructors. *Sch. & Soc.,* 1928, 28, 759–760.

Remmers, H. H. The college professor as the student sees him. *Purdue Univer. Stud. higher Educ.,* 1929, No. 29, 75.

Remmers, H. H. To what extent do grades influence student ratings of instructors? *J. educ. Res.,* 1930, 21, 314–316.

Remmers, H. H. Reliability and halo effect of high school and college students' judgments of their teachers. *J. appl. Psychol.,* 1934, 18, 619–630.

Remmers, H. H. *Introduction to opinion and attitude measurement.* New York: Harper, 1954.

Remmers, H. H. *Manual, the Purdue Rating Scale for Instruction.* West Lafayette, Ind.: University Book Store, 1960.

Remmers, H. H., & Elliott, D. *Manual, the Purdue Rating Scale for Instruction.* (Rev. ed.) West Lafayette, Ind.: University Book Store, 1960.

Ross, I. C., & Harary, F. On the determination of redundancies in sociometric chains. *Psychometrika,* 1952, 17, 195–208.

Rummel, J. F. *An introduction to research procedures in education.* New York: Harper, 1958.

Rundquist, E. A., Winer, B. J., & Falk, G. H. Follow-up validation of forced-choice items of the Army Officer Efficiency Report. *Amer. Psychologist,* 1950, 5, 359. (Abstract)

Ryans, D. G. *Characteristics of teachers.* Washington, D.C.: American Council on Education, 1960.

Scheier, I. H., & Cattell, R. B. Confirmation of objective test factors and assessment of their relation to questionnaire factors: A factor analysis of 113 rating, questionnaire and objective test measurements of personality. *J. ment. Sci.,* 1958, 104, 608–624.

Seeman, M. A situational approach to intragroup Negro attitudes. *Sociometry,* 1946, 9, 199–206.

Sheldon, M. S., & Sorenson, A. G. On the use of Q-technique in educational evaluation and research. *J. exp. Educ.,* 1960, 29, 143–151.

Shock, N. W., Kelly, E. L., & Remmers, H. H. An empirical study of the validity of the Spearman-Brown formula as applied to the Purdue Rating Scale. *J. educ. Psychol.,* 1927, 18, 187–195.

Sigerfoos, C. H. The validation and application of a scale of attitudes toward any vocation. *Purdue Univer. Stud. higher Educ.,* 1936, No. 31, 177–191.

Simpson, R. H., & Brown, E. S. *College learning and teaching.* Urbana: Bur. of Res. and Service, Univer. of Illinois, 1952.

Sisson, E. D. Forced-choice—the new army rating. *Personnel Psychol.,* 1948, 1, 365–381.

Snedeker, J. H., & Remmers, H. H. *Manual, the Purdue Instructor Performance Indicator.* West Lafayette, Ind.: University Book Store, 1960.

Spector, A. J. Forced-choice and projective techniques in attitude measurement. *Personnel Psychol.,* 1957, 10, 55–59.

Stecklein, J. E. Colleges and universities—programs: Evaluation. In C. W. Harris (Ed.), *Encyclopedia of educational research.* (3rd ed.) New York: Macmillan, 1960. Pp. 285–289.

Stephenson, W. *The study of behavior.* Chicago: Univer. of Chicago Press, 1953.

Stewart, F. A. A study of influence in Southtown: II. *Sociometry,* 1947, 10, 273–286.

Stogdill, R. M. The sociometry of working relationships in formal organizations. *Sociometry,* 1949, 12, 276–286.

Suci, G. J. A multidimensional analysis of social attitudes with reference to ethnocentrism. Unpublished doctoral dissertation, Univer. of Illinois, 1952.

Suci, G. J. A comparison of semantic structures in American Southwest culture groups. *J. abnorm. soc. Psychol.,* 1960, 61, 25–30.

Taft, R. The ability to judge people. *Psychol. Bull.,* 1955, 52, 1–21.

Tagiuri, R. Relational analysis: An extension of sociometric method with emphasis upon social perception. *Sociometry,* 1952, 15, 91–104.

Tagiuri, R., & Petrullo, L. (Eds.) *Person perception and interpersonal behavior.* Stanford, Calif.: Stanford Univer. Press, 1958.

Taylor, E. K., Schneider, Dorothy E., & Symons, Nancy A. A short forced-choice evaluation form for salesmen. *Personnel Psychol.,* 1953, 6, 393–401.

Triandis, H. C. Differential perception of certain jobs and people by managers, clerks, and workers in industry. *J. appl. Psychol.,* 1959, 43, 221–225.

Triandis, H. C., & Osgood, C. E. A comparative factorial analysis of semantic structures in monolingual Greek and American college students. *J. abnorm. soc. Psychol.,* 1958, 57, 187–196.

Turner, R. L., & Fattu, N. A. Skill in teaching, a reappraisal of the concepts and strategies in teacher effectiveness research. *Indiana Univer. Sch. Educ. Bull.,* 1960, 36, 1–40.

Tyler, R. W. A test of skill in using a microscope. *Constructing achievement tests.* Columbus: Ohio State Univer., 1934.

Uhrbrock, R. S. Standardization of 724 rating scale statements. *Personnel Psychol.,* 1950, 3, 285–316.

Weschler, I. R., Tannenbaum, R., & Talbot, E. A new management tool: The multirelational sociometric survey. *Personnel,* 1952, 29, 85–94.

Wherry, R. J. Control of bias in rating. (Sub-Project 2) *Instructor rating scales.* Washington, D.C.: Personnel Res. Section, AGO, U. S. Dept. of the Army, 1950.

Zeleny, L. D. Sociometry of morale. *Amer. sociol. Rev.,* 1939, 4, 799–808.

Zeleny, L. D. Measurement of social status. *Amer. J. Sociol.,* 1940, 45, 576–582.

CHAPTER 8 Testing Cognitive Ability and Achievement

BENJAMIN S. BLOOM
University of Chicago

The research worker who wishes to understand teaching and teachers must understand not only the teaching and educational process as it takes place but also the outcomes or effects of the process—the changes that take place in the learners. Is teacher A more effective than teacher B? Is one method of teaching more effective than another method of teaching? Is one set of learning experiences more effective than another set of learning experiences? No matter how the problem is posed, the research worker must have a set of criteria by which to determine more and less, better and worse, effective and ineffective.

The writer takes the position that unless the criteria of effectiveness are related to changes in students, the researcher has avoided the primary criterion and has used only proximate criteria. Thus, we may have a view of what we regard as good teaching and good teachers. We may have a value orientation which helps to define good and poor, and we may have a theory of education which enables us to differentiate the better from the poorer teaching. But even such values and theories must ultimately rest on what we believe or what we know to be the

consequences for the learner. Teaching and learning experiences are not good or poor in their own right. They are good or poor because of the ways in which they affect the learner.

While it may or may not be true that the most important changes in the learner are those which may be described as cognitive, i.e., knowledge, problem-solving, higher mental processes, etc., it is true that these are the types of changes in students which most teachers do seek to bring about. These are the changes in learners which most teachers attempt to gauge in their own tests of progress and in their own final examinations. These, also, are the changes in the learners which are emphasized in the materials of instruction, in the interaction between teachers and learners, and in the reward system which the teachers and the schools employ.

Research on teaching must, in most cases, make use of measures of cognitive achievement to determine whether the teaching method, instructional procedure, or the teacher does produce changes in the learners. Research on teaching makes use of tests of cognitive ability (and achievement) to identify the samples of students being studied and

379

to determine whether there are differential effects of the teaching on the various subgroups. Research on teaching also uses tests of cognitive ability and of cognitive achievement to determine how changes in the cognitive domain are related to changes in other areas.

In the following sections we shall attempt to pose some of the problems that arise in testing for cognitive ability and achievement. We will consider some of the ways in which the attack on these problems must be related to problems of learning and teaching. Research on teaching must take into consideration the development and use of tests of cognitive ability and achievement as well as the relations between the process of testing and the processes of teaching and learning.

TESTING AS A METHOD OF SECURING EVIDENCE

Testing may be viewed as a systematic sampling of an individual's characteristics at a given time under specified conditions. The responses of the individual to given problems, tasks, and questions are summarized to yield one or more index values intended to describe the specified characteristics. Although these index values may be used to represent or describe the individual, the careful worker must recognize that the index value must be kept related to the test or original sample of problems, tasks, and questions. Thus an IQ index based on one intelligence test may be quite different from an IQ based on a different intelligence test. Both the stimuli (the test sample) and the responses (the answers and index values which summarize the answers) must be specified if the results are to have clear meaning.

The research worker must not be confused by the name or title of the test since two tests of general intelligence may sample quite different specific abilities. It is essential in reporting results to specify not only the name of the instrument but also to indicate the abilities being sampled. Furthermore, the researcher must not pool data from several different instruments unless he can demonstrate that the different tests yield much the same measures. For example, if three tests of general intelligence are used to test a sample of students, and one test is used with some of the students while the other tests are used with the remaining students, it would be an error to regard the test scores from the three tests as representing the same ability—unless there was clear evidence that the three tests were highly correlated and equivalent measures of the same ability.

It is important to remember that testing is a sampling operation in which an attempt is made to describe a population of characteristics an individual may possess. That is, although only a limited number of problems, tasks, or questions may be used in a given test, the tester is attempting to draw inferences about the entire population of problems, tasks, or questions which might have been used. Although many problems are involved in specifying the total population of characteristics being sampled, the validity and reliability of the sample take on meaning only as they can be related to an explicitly defined population of characteristics.

With few exceptions, testing involves a limited time-sampling procedure. In some ways this is a strength as well as a weakness of testing operations. In a given amount of time (30 minutes, 60 minutes, etc.), the tester attempts to sample a set of characteristics developed over a much longer period—perhaps even the entire life history of the individual up to that point in time. Thus, a 30-minute vocabulary test may attempt to sample the vocabulary an individual has developed from birth to age 14. To do so represents a difficult problem that can be solved effectively only if the sampling procedures in building the test are well done and the responses of the individual approach the maximum of which he is capable. Most problems of test validity center on this problem of securing a representative sample of the individual's characteristics under the given time-sampling conditions.

One source of difficulty in the use of either

ability or achievement tests is the variability of the students in the schools and the likelihood that a limited sample of tasks may be too easy for some students and too difficult for others. Thurstone (1926) demonstrated that a test yields maximum discrimination when dichotomously scored (right or wrong) test items are at the 50 per cent level of difficulty for the students. It is possible then for a vocabulary sample to approach this level for some students and to be a much less effective test sample for other students. The research worker must recognize that his test may not yield an equally reliable and valid sample for all the students in his study. He may be most confident of the results when he deals with groups of students and when the groups approach the 50 per cent level as the mean score. He should, however, be prepared to regard the extreme scores as less dependable than the scores nearer the mean.

The specified conditions for a test must provide appropriate limits within which it may be regarded as effective. Thus the interaction of the examinee with the test and test material must be of a particular order if the results are to be meaningful. Conditions of rapport, motivation, fatigue (or well-being) are frequently spelled out in great detail for individually administered tests. While these may not be specified as clearly for group-administered tests, results of group tests may be meaningless unless the sample has been secured under appropriate conditions. Since most tests involve the use of language to give directions and to specify the tasks required, one important condition for testing is that the language be appropriate for the subjects to whom the test is given. The arrangement of the tasks must also be planned to insure motivation and rapport and to avoid boredom or extreme frustration.

These considerations are of especial importance when the research worker is studying samples of students with markedly varying cultural and educational backgrounds. Stone (1946) demonstrated that lower-class children may have difficulty not only with the test problems but also with understanding the words used in the directions for answering the test problems. Haggard (1954) demonstrated that the motivation for taking a test may be different in lower- and middle-class children. There is no clear remedy for this except insofar as the research worker recognizes that a particular test may provide a very good index of the ability or achievement of one group of students while the same test may be of only limited usefulness as a measure of the capabilities of a more extreme group.

THE NATURE AND USE OF TEST EVIDENCE

The systematic nature of testing makes it possible to use test evidence for a variety of comparative purposes. If uniformity of testing procedures and conditions is assured, it is possible to summarize the responses of an individual and compare his responses with those of a number of other individuals. The test scores of several individuals can yield an average which may be compared with the distribution of similar scores for an appropriate population of individuals. Normative data make it possible to determine where individuals stand with respect to other individuals who presumably were tested with the same instrument under similar conditions. Such comparisons may make use of so-called raw scores which are relatively simple summations of the original responses, derived scores which transmute the raw scores into positions on a scale (standard scores, percentile scores, mental age, etc.), or judgmental categories which relate the raw or derived score to a qualitative decision (normal-subnormal, passing-failing, good-poor, etc.).

It is also possible to use summaries of test evidence so as to compare the individual with himself. Thus his score on one test may be compared with his score on another test or his score at one time may be compared with his score at another time to determine change, progress, or development.

The way in which the results of tests are

to be summarized must depend, of course, on the use to which the results are to be put. We will refer to this problem at a number of places throughout this chapter. Here it will suffice to point out that economy in the handling of data tends to bias the test constructor and the test user toward the use of a total score of the number of correct responses. If the research worker regards his results as consisting of a two-dimensional table in which one dimension represents the individuals tested while the other dimension represents the responses on each item in the test, he will be prepared to look for more meaningful ways of summarizing the evidence. He should look for part scores which define separable kinds of abilities and achievements. He should also look for patterns and profiles of differentiable performance. If he goes further, he should be able to note patterns of error responses and perhaps even find underlying processes which explain patterns of correct as well as incorrect responses. Finally, he may even find it possible to use item analysis data to understand similarities and differences in both the test questions and in the subgroups of his sample of students.

TESTING TO DETERMINE WHAT THE STUDENT BRINGS TO THE EDUCATIONAL ENTERPRISE

The institutionalization of education in the Western world has brought about a segmentation of the educational process and a specialization of function which brings many teachers into relationships with a single student. The student who completes 12 years in the public school system in a large urban community is likely to have come into contact with 50 to 100 different teachers. Each of these teachers works with a particular group of students for one or two terms and has little to do with the student before or after this time. Knowing little about the student before the particular term in which he teaches him, the teacher tends to look upon him as a standard unit like every other student. Most teachers are likely to regard the student as totally lacking in the particular unit of subject matter or the specific cognitive skills and abilities which the teacher desires to develop.

The fallacy of such assumptions has been amply demonstrated by the work of the past 50 years in the measurement of individual differences. In practically every measurable characteristic, there is a great range of levels of performance from the highest individual in the group to the lowest—where the group is defined by age of its members or the number of years they have attended school (Cook, 1951, pp. 9–15). The magnitude of these differences is difficult to determine because we have very few measurements which can be expressed in absolute units such as we use in the measurement of height or weight. But a quick glance at a set of norms for the different grades on almost any standardized test will convince the reader. Inspecting the norms for a well-known and carefully developed battery of aptitude tests, we note that an average of about 40 per cent of ninth-grade students exceed the scores made by the lowest third of twelfth-grade students. On several of the tests, 50 per cent of the ninth-grade students exceed the lowest third of the twelfth-grade students.

It is also clear that each student brings a unique set of characteristics to the educational enterprise. If one attempts to describe an individual with a battery of tests which yield ten scores or more, it would be difficult to find two identical profiles in a group of 100 persons of the same age or grade level.

While it is clear that there is great variation among individuals on any given characteristic and that each individual is likely to have a relatively unique distribution of characteristics, not all of this variability is directly related to education. If we can accept the assumption that knowledge of the major characteristics of an individual is better than ignorance of these characteristics, we may then ask what characteristics we should know about and what we might do with this knowledge.

Generalized Abilities

The factor analysis research of the past 30 years reveals a general factor (g) underlying a great deal of performance on ability tests. What g is may not be clearly defined, but that there is something which is clearly influencing performance on aptitude as well as achievement tests may be stated without reservation.

General intelligence, g, the IQ, or some other averaged type of generalized aptitude test performance is useful for predicting performance on a great range of intellectual, or cognitive, tasks. The relationship between a general index of intelligence and over-all performance on a battery of achievement tests approaches unity at the elementary school level (Coleman & Cureton, 1954) and drops to about .50 at the college level (Crawford & Burnham, 1946).

It is of interest to note that general intelligence as measured by either an individual intelligence test (e.g., Stanford-Binet, Wechsler-Bellevue) or a group intelligence test becomes relatively constant or stable by about the second or third year of school. Thus, Bayley (1949), Honzik, Macfarlane, and Allen (1948), and Thorndike (1947) have shown that after age eight the correlations between measurements over periods of six to ten years rarely are less than .80 when the same or parallel forms of the same test are used in repeated measurements. This constancy is maintained through the college years (Flory, 1940).

Tests of such generalized abilities may help the teacher to gauge the general rate of student learning and may be useful as one basis for developing subgroups of students for various educational tasks. Perhaps the major difficulty arising from use of such a general index is that it loses value as it is related to more specialized types of educational tasks and processes. An index (IQ, MA, etc.) attached to a single rather general quality is deceptively simple. It has concreteness, apparent quantitative precision, and an authoritative quality which may lead the teacher or research worker to overemphasize it. Such an index may even become a means of rationalizing results and avoiding problems which should be attacked more directly.

Although general intelligence measures have undoubtedly proved useful to teachers over the past 50 years, it should be remembered that intelligence tests were not devised for the specific problems encountered by classroom teachers. Perhaps an analogy is in order here. The physician might find a general index of health to be of some value, but he could hardly depend on it as a very useful piece of information in diagnosing particular ailments or in deciding upon therapeutic procedures. Similarly, the teacher who knows only the general intelligence of the pupil does not have very useful information for determining what the pupil needs or what might be done to help him.

The person doing research on teaching must recognize the increasing stability of a measure of general intelligence and should have less confidence in such a measure when it is obtained at the nursery school and kindergarten level than at later age levels. He must also be prepared to question the value of such an index as a control in his research unless he can demonstrate that it is the best available control for the particular research problem. He must not be misled into using the index of general intelligence in his research primarily because it is so widely available and because it has been so frequently used in the past. Just as the teacher needs more precise and relevant measures for his work with students, so the research worker must seek the most precise and relevant measures for his research problem. The research worker who attempts to understand how teaching and learning may become more effective needs to be alert to the use of more diagnostic measures to help the teachers focus more sharply on the particular needs of the particular students. He must find ways of helping teachers become more clearly aware of the individual differences in students which are most relevant to the learning tasks at hand and which bear most directly on the objectives of instruction.

Specialized Abilities

The factor analysis approach to the study of human abilities has revealed a large number of specialized abilities and skills which have relatively low correlations with each other. Depending upon the statistical criteria employed, the variety of tests used, and the populations studied, the number of factors ranges from six to fifty, or more. Guilford (1959) has presented a logical analysis of mental ability along three dimensions: (1) operations (cognition, memory, divergent thinking, convergent thinking, evaluation); (2) products (units, classes, relations, systems, transformations, implications); and (3) contents (figural, symbolic, semantic, behavioral). The 120 cells resulting from all possible combinations of the $5 \times 6 \times 4$ categories define as many potential factors, many of which have already been exemplified in tests. Undoubtedly, the attempt to find specialized abilities has shaken our confidence in the single general index of intelligence.

In an unpublished study, the writer found that when a level such as the upper tenth of the population was used as a working definition of "giftedness," approximately three-fifths of a particular group of students were found to be in the upper tenth, or "gifted," on one or more of seven primary abilities tests. While this study was done on a group of very able college entrants, it is likely that, in almost any study in which half a dozen or more specialized aptitude tests (which have low correlations with each other) are used, one-half or more of the students are likely to be in the upper tenth on one or more of the tests. The point of this is that instead of one-tenth of the students appearing to be "gifted" on a general intelligence test, one-half or more appear to be "gifted" by being in the upper tenth on one or more of the specialized abilities tested. It is likely that, if enough different tests were used, almost all children would be found to be superior in at least some area measured by the tests.

The consequence of teachers' viewing each individual as possessing unique talents of a high order (in contrast with viewing only a small group—perhaps 10 per cent—as having a high generalized ability) are quite profound. The teacher's appreciation of the unique merits of each child could have important consequences for the ways in which the student and teacher interact as well as for the ways in which the teacher might try to help each student in the learning process.

The basic problem of dealing with specialized talents becomes one of determining which talents and abilities are more relevant to the educational process and which are less relevant. Is a high level of spatial ability relevant to learning in the primary or secondary grades, and if so, in what ways? Verbal ability and numerical ability are, of course, clearly related to learning particular subjects, such as reading and arithmetic. What other abilities should be measured, and how should they be measured, so they can be most effectively used by teachers and research workers? The observation that much of the learning process is mediated by words probably explains why verbal ability is related so highly to most measurements of school achievement. This interpretation suggests that other media of communication must be understood and utilized if the other talents and abilities students develop or possess are to be utilized.

The research of Wilson (1958) in the Portland public schools resulted in the identification of talented students (the upper 10 per cent) in art, music, creative writing, creative dramatics, creative dance, social leadership, and mechanical ability. Wilson developed instruments for selecting students with these very different talents. Getzels and Jackson (1958) also developed instruments for identifying giftedness in qualities other than the usual general intelligence index. In one study they were able to distinguish two mutually exclusive groups, one with a high IQ (upper 20 per cent) and the other with high levels of performance on a battery of creativity measures but not with high IQs. They found the groups equally superior in school achievement, although the two groups differed in many other respects. These research studies suggest a variety of measurable abilities, skills, and talents with which educators must increasingly learn to deal.

What is being suggested here is that it is not enough to utilize specialized talent measurements as bases for guiding students with regard to choices of elective courses and programs. What is needed is to recognize the unique characteristics of individual students and to make use of these characteristics in the learning process. The student who is especially good in spatial visualization may respond well to learning procedures which give him an opportunity to use his spatial talents. Can the learning process be different for the verbally able, the numerically able, and the spatially able? Or, are there ways of describing learners' characteristics which the teacher can utilize more effectively than the factor abilities identified to date? Can the research worker identify the abilities which are most relevant to the learning characteristics and problems he is attempting to understand? Does the possession of certain "talents" and the lack of others affect the learning that students are able to do? In what ways do the patterns of abilities that students bring to the learning situation affect the nature of the teaching process? Do some learning experiences make more effective use of these abilities than others do?

Previous Achievement

While a general intelligence test is, to some extent, a measure of the individual's learning, we may think of an achievement test as a measure which is more closely related to the specific learning that takes place in the school. This distinction, of course, breaks down, since much verbal ability may be learned in the school; also, numerical ability, as measured by some aptitude or factor tests, overlaps considerably with the arithmetic learning which takes place in the school. Still, it is possible to identify and measure the individual's level of competence over material and subject matter explicitly taught in school.

Instead of a numerical ability test we may have an arithmetic achievement test; instead of a verbal ability test we may have a reading comprehension test or even a vocabulary test in which the test content is drawn from the vocabulary emphasized at a particular level of the school. Haggerty (1941); Learned and Wood (1938), and Townsend (1951) have shown a high relationship between previous and later achievement. After Grades 5 or 6, the correlations between measurements of achievement over periods of two to six years are rarely less than .80 when parallel testing procedures are used in repeated measurements. While the relation between intelligence, or aptitude, measurements and achievement measurements tends to become lower at the secondary and higher education levels, the relation between previous and later achievement tends to remain high and even become higher during the secondary and college level.

Hence, the teacher should be able to utilize measures of previous achievement as a basis for sectioning students or finding ways to adapt teaching procedures to the characteristics of individual students. Here again, our ability to predict the final measures of achievement does not mean that we have found the most effective ways of describing the characteristics the students bring to the "new" learning situation. We may find it useful to determine which particular areas of content the student has mastered well and which he has not mastered. But we may also need to summarize his previous achievement in order to determine the kinds of errors he makes and the source of these errors. Attempts to summarize the objectives, or skills and abilities, which he has achieved to a high degree in contrast with those which have been poorly developed may be most useful to the teacher who has a clear view of the objectives as well as content to be stressed in a particular course or program.

Bloom and Allison (1949) reported on the way in which placement tests given at the beginning of a college program differ from the comprehensive examinations taken at the end of each part of the program. These placement tests were used to determine the learning experiences which would be most useful for each student. Such learning experiences might be included in a tutorial program, a remedial program, special selections from parts of the regular program, or the regular course. Dressel (1958, Ch. 7) concluded from his use of comprehensive examinations that about 10 per cent of students could receive a grade of "C" or better on a comprehensive examination in the basic introductory course before enrolling in the course. In a study using pretests which measured knowledge of facts, principles, and concepts, as well as the ability to apply some form of critical thinking, he found that the average student could answer 30 to 50 per cent of the questions correctly before taking the course and an additional 25 to 30 per cent of the questions after completing the course.

The implication for the research worker is that measures of relevant previous achievement are more likely to be useful controls than are measures of general intelligence or of specific aptitudes and abilities. Clues as to the relevant previous achievement may be drawn from an analysis of the objectives of instruction as well as from previous research on pre- and posttest results on instruments which approximate the measures to be employed in the research under consideration. Furthermore, the teacher's awareness or lack of awareness of the ways in which students differ in previous achievement may be an important variable in his teaching and in the ways in which teachers and students interact.

LEARNING EXPERIENCES AS WAYS OF MODIFYING BEHAVIOR

Learning may be conceived of as a change, due to experience, in the students' ways of thinking, feeling, and acting. The effectiveness of the learning process may be thought of in terms of (1) the magnitude of the changes taking place in the individual student or (2) the proportion of the students who have changed significantly in one or more characteristics relevant to the learning process. Thus conceived, education may be regarded as a system of learning experiences which bring about certain desirable changes in students.

This conception of education (Tyler, 1949) requires that teachers (and perhaps learners) be clear about the changes which the learning process should bring about—the educational objectives or goals of the learning process. It also requires that the appraisal or evaluation procedures be so organized and developed that it is possible to determine the changes which the learning process does produce. Finally, it requires that the teachers and curriculum workers find ways of determining what learning experiences are effective in bringing about changes in individual learners or in groups of learners.

From this conception of education and learning, students are seen as coming to the learning process, course, or instruction with particular aptitudes, abilities, and previous achievement. As a result of participating in particular learning experiences, the students are altered, and the degree to which they are altered is theoretically measurable by appraising the extent to which, at the end of the experiences, they have changed from what they were at the beginning of the experiences.

An educational or learning experience may be thought of as an interaction between the learner and the environment—teacher, other students, learning material, and subject matter—which results in some changes in the learner. While learning experiences may include any life experiences which result in changes in the learner, it is clear that not all life experiences are equally likely to bring about desired change in the individual. Day-to-day experiences of life occur as the environment and chance dictate. Some experiences may be too complex for the individual to comprehend or so emotionally overpowering as to affect him adversely. The life experiences of an individual may be so repetitious that later life experiences may not add to or alter what has already been developed from previous life experiences.

Educational experiences have a special character, as contrasted with life experiences, in that they are selected and planned by one person with a view to their impact upon the learning of another. Educational experiences, as planned in the schools, are intended to have a more intense and powerful effect than ordinary life experiences in changing the individual in a given direction. The time and resources of the school are limited and if each educational experience is to have its desired effect, it must be selected or devised with a view to its appropriateness to an individual or to a group of learners; it must be appropriately related to the individual's previous learning experiences (and should have a potential relationship to his future learning experiences), and it must be relevant to the particular subject matter and educational objectives to be "learned."

While the sequence of life experiences may be random, the sequence of educational experiences should be one in which each experience helps the student advance to a greater or lesser extent toward a given set of objectives. Repetition of educational experiences is not desired or intended unless such repetition is likely to help the learner gain additional competence or to foster other desired developments.

Educational experiences must be planned carefully if they are to have the intended effects on the learner. They must start where the learner is and advance him to a new level of competence or maturity. They must

take into full consideration the characteristics of the learner. Planning of an educational experience must be based on an understanding of the learning process as well as the means by which the individual learns.

It should be noted that, throughout the above discussion, learning experiences have been considered effective when they bring about changes in students. The teacher may have a very active role in creating the conditions under which a learning experience takes place, but it is the learner who is having the experience and being affected by it—if it is truly a learning experience. Whether in fact it is a learning experience is determined by changes in the learner. Thus, it becomes important to determine by systematic procedures whether learners have been altered by a set of learning experiences. Have all learners been affected or have only certain learners or types of learners been affected? How much effect has taken place—how much change can be determined?

One function of evaluation is the careful determination of the effects of learning experiences. This requires a clear definition of the conditions presumed to set up the learning experiences, the identification of the changes which have taken place, if any, and, if possible, the range of students and conditions under which significant changes do take place. Thus, we have a post hoc attempt to determine whether a set of experiences did in fact become learning experiences, as well as an attempt to predict whether or not such experiences are likely to become learning experiences in the future under a given set of conditions. Studies of the effectiveness of learning experiences quite frequently become reduced to studies of instructional methods. Perhaps the difference between a study of teachers or teaching and a study of learning experiences is merely one of (1) the degree to which the nature of the experiences is defined, (2) the extent to which the students' roles and interaction with teachers, other students, and material are spelled out, and (3) the extent to which the evaluation evidence is related to changes in the learners directly relevant to the learning experiences.

A study by Chausow (1955) illustrates an attempt to specify in great detail the learning experiences of a group of students in an experimental college social science course. Chausow also obtained evidence on the effectiveness of these learning experiences as contrasted with the effectiveness of a more formal lecture approach to the same subject. It is of special interest to note that Chausow had each of six instructors teach a regular section as well as the experimental section. In each instance, the critical thinking gains made by the students were greater in the experimental section than in the regular section, thus suggesting the importance of the nature of learning experiences as a significant variable even when the instructor variable is held constant. Bloom (1954b) attempted to understand the ongoing interaction between students and a learning situation by using the method of stimulated recall to investigate the thought processes of students in discussion and lecture classes. He found a number of differences in the thought processes in these two situations and suggested the use of this method to investigate the *processes* involved in a particular set of learning experiences in contrast with the more frequent use of pre- and posttests to measure the *products* of the learning experiences.

All too frequently the research worker studies the effects of the teaching process without carefully describing and defining the nature of the learning experiences. He must find ways of penetrating beyond the labels of teaching method (e.g., lecture, demonstration, discussion, team teaching) and move to a more precise definition of what takes place in the learning situation. The research worker must attempt to describe the learning situation not only from the viewpoint of the teacher but also from the viewpoint of the learner. What the teacher intends may be a far cry from what actually takes place when seen through the eyes of the students. Research on "teaching" must also become research on "learning."

Measures of Change

If education is viewed as a process of changing learners, then an appropriate index of the effectiveness of a learning situation is the amount of change which has taken place. We will subsequently deal with the definition of the kind of changes to be studied. Here we will briefly consider some of the problems involved in determining the amount of change.

If we had an absolute scale like height or weight in which there are equal units and a zero point, the difference between the initial and final measures would constitute a satisfactory measure of change. However, measures of aptitude and achievement are relative measures in which little is known about the equality of the units and less is known about the zero point. The difference between derived scores of 30 and 40 may be very different from the difference between derived scores of 40 and 50, even though all the values are based on a single derived score scale with a mean of 50 and a standard deviation of 10.

Dressel and Mayhew (1954, pp. 247–248), in a study of the gains made by college students in critical thinking and attitudes, found a recurring pattern of large gains made by students with low pretest scores and small gains made by students with high pretest scores. They listed several phenomena that could account for this pattern:

1. A "ceiling" effect, i.e., the initially high scores have a reduced possibility for gain.
2. A regression effect, i.e., on retesting, initially low scores tend to move up toward the mean while initially high scores tend to drop rather than gain.
3. A focus-of-instruction effect, i.e., instruction may be aimed at the average or below-average student rather than at the able individual.
4. An effect of familiarity or unfamiliarity with terminology and concepts, i.e., the tests of ability may measure both the ability to do critical thinking and the knowledge of terminology and concepts. The initially

low students may make their gain in the knowledge rather than in the ability to do critical thinking per se, while the initially high students may make their gain primarily in the ability itself.

5. An effect of differential motivation, i.e., able students may be more conscientious at the beginning of the year and may apply themselves when first tested to a greater extent than they do at the end of the year on a test which is not used for grading.

While Dressel and Mayhew did not come to a definite conclusion about these explanations, they believed that the evidence they accumulated supported the first explanation —the ceiling effect.

These problems were considered in some detail by both Lord (1958) and McNemar (1958), who treated the problem as one of distinguishing between true gain and errors of measurement. Both McNemar and Lord proposed statistical formulas to remove the spurious effects resulting from errors of measurements. Lord proposed a rather simple procedure for taking account of the so-called "regression" effect. He suggested giving the pre- and posttests simultaneously at the beginning of the year and then comparing the scatterplot of the two tests with a scatterplot of the results when the pretest is given at the beginning of the year and the posttest is given at the end of the year. Lord took the view that the problem of whether numerically equal gains at different points of the scale are equal is primarily one of test construction. If an experimenter wishes to treat gains at different points of the scale in similar ways he must attempt to build his test in such a way that he can demonstrate at least approximate equality of gains at different points on his own scale.

Mitzel and Gross (1956), after reviewing three methods of dealing with gains (raw gain scores, achievement quotient gains, and regression methods), argued for the use of covariance analysis as the best of the available techniques. They were especially concerned that the research worker match the hierarchy of educational goals of teachers with adequate measuring devices and that research workers recognize the multidimensionality of both teaching competence and learning outcome.

Educational Objectives and Evaluation

From what has been already said about education and educational experiences, it follows that the nature of a particular sequence of educational experiences should be determined by the educational objectives it is designed to further. Educational objectives are statements of desired changes in the thoughts, actions, or feelings of students that a particular course or educational program should bring about. Educational objectives, as they have been used by evaluators, teachers, and curriculum workers, are relatively specific statements of the characteristics the students should possess after completing the course or program. Some have distinguished between educational objectives and the more general statements of aims or goals. Thus, *the development of good citizenship* is so broad and general an aim that it provides little direction for the determination of appropriate learning experiences. Such a general goal also gives little direction for the evaluation process. In contrast, an objective like *the ability to relate principles of civil liberties and civil rights to current events* is more specific and begins to give teachers and evaluators some direction with regard to both the subject *content* and the mental *processes* which the student is expected to develop.

It is in the attempt to clarify and give operational definition to objectives that the construction of examinations is of critical importance. Educational objectives are frequently stated in such a general form that the teacher who claims a particular objective has great difficulty in communicating what is meant by it to others, and perhaps as much difficulty in determining for himself exactly what was intended. At such a level of generality, the consequences for teaching must be almost nonexistent. At any rate, as the

teacher describes the range of behaviors encompassed by the objective, it becomes possible to determine the kinds of observations,
questions, problems, and tasks which it is
appropriate to include in an evaluation instrument. The dialectic involved between the
statement of an objective and the construction of an examination or appraisal procedure is one in which meanings become
clarified. In turn, the evaluation instrument
can become a highly creative development.
Tyler (1934), Dressel and others (1949), and
Furst (1958) have described some of the procedures by which educational objectives are
translated into evaluation procedures as well
as the division of responsibility between
teachers and evaluation workers. All three
would have the teachers assume primary responsibility for stating the objectives. The
further definition and clarification of the
objectives is seen as a joint task involving
teachers and evaluation specialists. The
identification of evaluation models and question types is seen as the task of the evaluation
specialist, while the production and review
of the actual test questions is seen as a joint
task involving both teachers and evaluation
specialists.

It has been noted by several evaluation
workers, including the writer, that with a
little help teachers can translate educational
objectives into evaluation procedures quite
rapidly, but that considerably more time is
required before they can become skillful in
developing learning experiences appropriate
to the objective. In working with secondary
school teachers and university professors, in
this country as well as abroad, the writer has
found that teachers engaged in workshop
activities centering on evaluation procedures
in relation to the instructional objectives were
able to produce highly acceptable evaluation
instruments in a few days. But it seemed
evident that a much longer period of time
would be required before the teachers would
be able to help students develop the kinds
of competence specified by the objective and
further defined by the evaluation procedures.

In the program for modification of the
secondary school curriculum in India (All-
India Council for Secondary Education,
1958), a plan has been adopted under which
a few key objectives are selected in each
subject and then teachers throughout the
country participate in developing evaluation
procedures for use in classroom examining,
as well as in the official external examinations. After evaluation procedures become
available to give relatively precise definition
to the objectives, the teachers work to create
and use learning experiences appropriate to
the key objectives. After two or three years
of work with a few key objectives, the participants select additional objectives and the
procedure of evaluation work followed by
work on learning experiences is repeated
with the new objectives. In this step-wise
fashion, it is anticipated that within a ten-
year period it will be possible to develop a
completely new curriculum in which objectives, evaluation procedures, and learning
experiences are closely related. The pace of
development is intended to be such that the
majority of teachers in service will be able
to participate in the construction and use of
the new curriculum.

The researcher must not be misled into
thinking that the stating and accepting of
educational objectives by teachers means that
these objectives are a determining force in
their actual teaching. As teachers become
clearer about their objectives, they are likely
to become more serious about them and to
attempt to implement such objectives in their
teaching. But it must be recognized that
much teaching is a repetition of instructional
procedures previously used by the individual
teacher. Breaking away from habitual teaching practices requires much more involvement and effort from the teacher than does
the stating of objectives or the use of new
and different evaluation instruments.

Observations and unpublished studies
made by the Examiner's Office of the
University of Chicago indicated that quite
frequently, in the first year in which a group
of instructors accepted and attempted to
teach for a new objective, there was little

evidence that the students had changed in the ways specified by the objective. In fact, in some instances the students did less well on the posttest of the objective than they had done on the pretest of that same objective. As this evidence was made available to the instructors, they questioned the validity of the instruments but they also attempted to modify the relevant learning experiences. With modification in the evaluation instruments and with repeated modifications in the learning experiences, it was usually found that by the second or third attempt on the part of both teachers and examiners it was possible to secure significant evidence that students had grown toward a particular objective.

The point of all this is that the research worker must not expect major modification of teaching practices in a brief period of time. Nor should he expect to secure significant evidence of growth toward new objectives in a single study carried on over a one-year period. If possible, the research worker must plan for two and even three repetitions of a study which actively involves both teachers and evaluators before significant student growth is likely to become evident.

Furthermore, the research worker must recognize that some objectives require learning experiences simultaneously in several parts of the curriculum if growth is to be adequately reinforced. If the ability to apply principles to new problems is the objective in one course, while in the student's other courses the major objective is little more than the remembering of principles, the student is less likely to demonstrate significant growth in application than if the ability to apply principles is stressed in several courses. The research worker must also recognize that significant growth in certain objectives may require a sequence of learning experiences over several semesters.

Little has been done to summarize the literature on the time required and the learning experiences necessary for each type of educational objective. Dressel and Mayhew (1954, p. 206), studying college stu-

dents, found that the largest gains in critical thinking were consistently made in the freshman year. They also noted that institutions having a special course dealing with critical thinking had no advantage over other institutions. In one study, it was found that students in a course in logic made no marked improvement on the Test of Critical Thinking. The largest gains were made by institutions that had well-organized general education experiences for the freshman year. Jacob (1957) also cited evidence that general education programs can have a significant effect on gains in critical thinking. Bloom and Webster (1960) reviewed the recent research on outcomes of college. They cited research showing the effect of college experiences on changes in information, intellectual abilities, and attitudes, as well as more general personality characteristics.

The range of educational objectives which fall in the cognitive domain is illustrated by the *Taxonomy of Educational Objectives* (Bloom, et al., 1956). The *Taxonomy* consists of a classification scheme in which a large number of educational objectives have been classified and the evaluation techniques appropriate to each class and subdivision have been presented and discussed. Comprehensive lists of educational objectives at the elementary and secondary school levels have been compiled by Kearney (1953) and French (1957), respectively. These compilations and classifications of educational objectives serve to show the variation in educational objectives among schools and colleges. If the classifications have, in fact, a basis in learning theory and the psychological process involved in learning, we may expect that educational research will begin to reveal the extent to which similar learning processes are involved in objectives classified under a single subclass.

It may be noted that the emphasis in the foregoing is on "similar learning processes" rather than on similar teaching methods. Different teaching methods may elicit very similar learning processes on the part of students. Thus, the "Knowledge" objectives of the *Taxonomy* may be developed through lecture methods, discussion methods, teaching machines, etc. More complex problem-solving objectives may also be developed through a variety of teaching methods. The research problem is one of how to describe the learning experiences of the student. What is the student doing? What is he motivated to learn? How does the sequence of learning experiences help the student to change? The research task becomes one of looking at the learning situation from the viewpoint of the student rather than exclusively from the viewpoint of the teacher. We are, in effect, proposing that two very different methods of teaching, as viewed by the teacher, may emphasize very similar learning processes (and objectives) when viewed in terms of what the student experiences. Furthermore, we are proposing that two learning situations which appear to be very similar from the teacher's point of view, may, in fact, be very different from the student's point of view.

Future research which makes use of the *Taxonomy* may reveal some of the psychological relations among the different classes of objectives and the extent to which transfer and retention differ among the major types of objectives. It is of interest to note that early research by Tyler (1934) produced evidence that the more complex objectives were retained somewhat better than the less complex objectives.

EFFECT OF EXAMINATIONS ON STUDENTS

Achievement examinations affect the methods of study students use, and they appear to have significant consequences for the learning process. A study by Merkhofer (1954) pointed up the effect of the type of examination on the student's preparation for the examination. Merkhofer investigated study behavior in three subject fields and related the study behavior to both the nature of the subject matter and the nature of the

comprehensive examination which the students were to take. She found that the amount of memorization of material, the extent of rereading of assignments, and the effort to remember facts in contrast with the effort to apply ideas or methods, were related to the nature of the examinations the students expected. She concluded, "Thus the students' behavior preceding and during the examinations—as well as their study behavior during the year—can be partially accounted for by the type of examination the students were given" (p. 369).

Douglass and Tallmadge (1934) found that university students reported that they prepared for objective tests by focusing attention on minute details and the exact wording of the books, while in preparing for subjective tests they favored methods involving organization of material, perceiving relationships and trends, and formulation of personal opinions on the material. Meyer (1935) also found that university students reported that they prepared for an essay test by studying to obtain a general picture of the material while they prepared for objective tests (completion, true-false, and multiple-choice) by studying to learn details. The point to be emphasized is that the type of mental process the student *expects* to be tested will determine his method of study and preparation.

Much more research is needed on this vital aspect of the learning process. What occurs when the learning experiences and the examinations emphasize contradictory objectives? For example, suppose the learning experiences are primarily concerned with complex types of problem-solving and the examinations emphasize only recall of specific information. Is the student able to resolve these differences and develop both, or does he develop only the characteristics required by the examination? In India, the external examinations are the primary means for certifying the students' competence, and these examinations test recall of specific information. There, the students resist learning experiences not in harmony with the examination requirements. Such resistance may be displayed in overt rebellion against the instructor when the students feel that the instruction is not directly preparing them for the examinations. It does seem clear that if the major reward-penalty system is related to examination performance, the students will concentrate on preparation for the examinations by any means at their disposal.

This proposition may be turned around, and the question may be asked, "How can examinations be used to encourage particular types of learning by the students?" If it is desired that students do a great deal of independent study and thinking, how should the examinations be constructed and used to promote such study and thinking? If it is desired that students develop a high degree of creativity in their thinking, research, and writing, how can examinations be developed and used to promote this? Perhaps as we understand how examinations may be used to promote rigid thinking and rote memorization, we will be in a better position to know how to use examinations to prevent this and to develop the characteristics explicitly desired by the objectives of instruction.

The researcher must be aware of the way in which the examination methods used in a school situation promote the achievement of some objectives and retard, and even obstruct, the achievement of other objectives. Anticipation of a particular type of examination may be a more powerful force on the students' learning than is the actual examination. Thus, even though the examination finally used is very different from the one that students anticipated, the learning and preparation have already taken place prior to the examination. The investigator may seek various methods of controlling the effects of the examination on the learning of the students, but he must bear in mind that the nature of the students' previous experiences with examinations is a factor in the teaching and learning.

Effect of Examinations on Teachers and Curriculum

Observation suggests that teachers are also influenced by examinations. This effect is clearly apparent where major decisions are based primarily on the examination performance of students. Thus, as was mentioned previously, the Indian teacher (All-India Council for Secondary Education, 1958) is under great pressure from students, parents, and even educational administrators to prepare the student for the type of official achievement examination to be given. One does not have to go abroad to note the effect of college entrance examinations on teachers and the curriculum at the secondary level.

The above emphasizes the coercive effect of examinations on teachers and the curriculum. There is no doubt that examinations all too frequently have such an effect. But examinations may also have less vicious effects on teachers and instruction. The rather intangible quality of education, the difficulty of determining whether the teacher's efforts have had any effect, and the search for some tangible evidence of the consequences of instruction have frequently led to the use of examinations as a source of evidence and reassurance needed by the teacher. The concreteness of examination performances and the availability of normative data enable the teacher to determine with some precision the effectiveness of his efforts. The teacher's subjective impressions can be verified or corrected by objective evidence.

The "feedback" effect of examinations may help the teacher discover both strengths and weaknesses in the curriculum and in the learning experiences. Education is an exceedingly complex enterprise which rarely can be clearly labeled as success or failure. Although we do use examinations in this crude way, it is far more useful if examination results can be used as a means of diagnosing the strengths and weaknesses of both the students and the learning experiences. This requires that we find alternatives to the total score on an examination (Cook, 1951). Such alternatives may be part scores and item analysis data which will guide the teachers and students. More detailed scoring procedures may help the teachers appraise the appropriate use and effectiveness of particular areas of content, the extent to which particular objectives have been attained, the specific materials and problems which the students have mastered or not mastered, and even the particular kinds of errors students make. If the evidence can be made available to teachers in a form which they can relate to the learning experiences, materials, and content of instruction, and to the sequence of learning experiences, the teachers are likely to make appropriate modifications in the curriculum and organization of instruction (Bloom, 1954a).

It is important in research on teaching to view both teachers and students as operating within a context larger than the classroom. The examinations which teachers use and students take form an intrinsically important part of this larger context. The examinations have a directing force on both teachers and students and this cannot be ignored or controlled simply by changing the examination in a particular piece of research or even by avoiding the use of examinations in a specific study of teaching and learning. The research worker must recognize that the experience that teachers and students have had with examinations, prior to his study, is an important variable in any learning situation. Control over this variable, e.g., changing students' expectations as to the kind of examinations they will take, is especially difficult if the entire pattern of experience with examinations has been quite consistent.

IMPROVEMENT OF THE EFFICIENCY OF ACHIEVEMENT EXAMINATIONS

The educational objective, defined in behavioral terms, is the criterion against which an educational evaluation instrument should be validated. The basic problem in such validation is one of reducing the definition of the objective to a means for gathering evidence. One may distinguish a direct and an indirect (or less direct) way of securing the evidence. The direct way of securing the evidence attempts to secure evidence on the specific behaviors included in the objective by the methods which most directly follow from the statement of the objective and the behaviors. The objective "Skill in the Interpretation of Data" would obviously involve determining how well the student interprets data. This may include presenting the student with new data and asking him to make what interpretations he can, presenting new data to the student and asking him questions about the data, or it may involve observing the student under a variety of conditions to determine how well he interprets data. The objective "Skill in Written Composition" may involve the collection of many samples of the student's writing under a great variety of conditions.

It is likely that the most direct way of securing the evidence will consume a great deal of time on the part of the student and the examiner or observer, and may even require collection of data over a relatively long period of time.

The research worker may then devise less direct techniques of securing evidence which will be highly correlated with the more direct methods. Instead of using the direct ways of determining how well the student makes interpretations of data, it may be possible to present the student with new data as well as possible interpretations of the data and to ask him to judge among the interpretations given. Instead of collecting many samples of the student's writing, it may be feasible to set a few writing tasks which will yield evidence of his writing competence closely approximating that obtained by a more direct method. Smith, Tyler, and others (1942) and Furst (1958) have cited a number of examples of direct and less direct methods of securing evidence.

It may be noted that the direct method of securing evidence has a "face" or "logical" validity, while the less direct method may be validated by determining its relation to the more direct method by both "construct" and "empirical" validation procedures (Cureton, 1951; Remmers & Gage, 1955, pp. 122–131).

Indirect methods are likely to have advantages over direct methods in practicality, ease of scoring and summarizing, and objectivity. The reliability of the less direct instruments, per unit of the examinee's time, is also likely to be higher than that of the direct methods. The basic problem in the use of indirect methods of evaluation is to insure that the relation with the direct method is maintained with new samples of examinees and at different times with the same examinees. It is possible that an indirect method of evaluation may influence the students to prepare for the task involved in this method, and this may be quite different from the kind of motivation and preparation required for the direct method. It may be found that performance on a vocabulary test in French is highly correlated with performance on a test of reading comprehension in French. If a vocabulary test is used as an indirect method of appraising reading comprehension, it is likely that students will emphasize vocabulary in their preparations; over time, the correlation between vocabulary and reading comprehension may become very low. A great deal of research is needed on the relations between indirect and direct methods of evaluation. Under what conditions do the relationships hold constant, and under what conditions do they change?

The use of indirect methods may be necessary in a particular piece of research, and if used for the first time with a particular sample of students, they may have no influence on the students' learning and preparation prior to the administration of the test. However, if similar indirect methods have been used over a period of time with this same sample of students, the investigator must recognize the possibility that the relation between the direct method of appraising the achievement and the indirect method of appraising the achievement may no longer be very high. It may be necessary in some research studies to determine for a small sample of the experimental population the relationship between direct and indirect methods of testing for the same objective.

Improvement of the objectivity and reliability of an evaluation instrument was, for a long time, something of an art. Research on the factors influencing objectivity and reliability and the development of appropriate statistical formulas and item analysis techniques have made it possible to apply "engineering" techniques to the improvement of objectivity and reliability. Objectivity and reliability have increasingly become problems of how a given amount of time of examinees and examiners can be used with maximal efficiency in the collection and processing of evidence (Thorndike, 1951).

CONCLUSION

Examinations are not an end in themselves. The examining process must be viewed as a means of making the educational process more effective. One central problem is that of devising evidence-gathering procedures which can be clearly related to the educational process. Another equally important problem is that of relating the examining process to the teacher and the student so that both can make most effective use of the instruments and evidence.

Research on teaching must take into consideration more than the ways in which examinations may be used as the dependent variable to determine the effects of teaching methods, instructional procedures, and learning experiences. Examinations are also a part of the independent variable, since the kinds of examinations used and the ways in which they are used and regarded by teachers and students (as well as administrators and parents) may have powerful effects on what is learned and how it is learned.

REFERENCES

All-India Council for Secondary Education. *Evaluation in secondary schools*. New Delhi, India: The All-India Council for Secondary Education, 1958.

Bayley, Nancy. Consistency and variability in the growth of intelligence from birth to 18 years. *J. genet. Psychol.*, 1949, 75, 165–196.

Bloom, B. S. Changing conceptions of examining at the University of Chicago. In P. L. Dressel (Ed.), *Evaluation in general education*. Dubuque, Iowa: Wm. C. Brown, 1954. Pp. 297–321. (a)

Bloom, B. S. The thought processes of students in discussion. In S. French (Ed.), *Accent on teaching*. New York: Harper, 1954. Pp. 23–46. (b)

Bloom, B. S. (Ed.), Engelhart, M. D., Furst, E. J., Hill, W. H., & Krathwohl, D. R. *Taxonomy of educational objectives*. New York: Longmans, Green, 1956.

Bloom, B. S., & Allison, J. Developing a college placement test program. *J. gen. Educ.*, 1949, 3, 210–215.

Bloom, B. S., & Webster, H. The outcomes of college. *Rev. educ. Res.*, 1960, 30, 321–333.

Chausow, H. M. The organization of learning experiences to achieve more effectively the objectives of critical thinking in the general social science course at the junior college level. Unpublished doctoral dissertation, Univer. of Chicago, 1955.

Coleman, W., & Cureton, E. E. Intelligence and achievement: The jangle fallacy again. *Educ. psychol. Measmt*, 1954, 14, 347–351.

Cook, W. W. The functions of measurement in the facilitation of learning. In E. F. Lindquist (Ed.), *Educational measurement*. Washington, D.C.: American Council on Education, 1951. Pp. 3–46.

Crawford, A. B., & Burnham, P. S. *Forecasting college achievement*. New Haven, Conn.: Yale Univer. Press, 1946.

Cureton, E. E. Validity. In E. F. Lindquist (Ed.), *Educational measurement*. Washington, D.C.: American Council on Education. 1951. Pp. 621–694.

Douglass, H. R., & Tallmadge, Margaret. How university students prepare for new types of examinations. *Sch. & Soc.*, 1934, 39, 318–320.

Dressel, P. L. *Evaluation in the Basic College at Michigan State University*. New York: Harper, 1958.

Dressel, P. L., & Mayhew, L. B. *General education: Exploration in evaluation*. Washington, D.C.: American Council on Education, 1954.

Dressel, P. L., and others. *Comprehensive examinations in a program of general education*. East Lansing: Michigan State Coll. Press, 1949.

Flory, C. D. The intellectual growth of college students. *J. educ. Res.*, 1940, 33, 443–451.

French, W. *Behavioral goals of general education in high school*. New York: Russell Sage Foundation, 1957.

Furst, E. J. *Constructing evaluation instruments*. New York: Longmans, Green, 1958.

Getzels, J. W., & Jackson, P. W. Meaning of giftedness: An examination of an expanding concept. *Phi Delta Kappan*, 1958, 40, 75–77.

Guilford, J. P. Three faces of intellect. *Amer. Psychologist*, 1959, 14, 469–479.

Haggard, E. Social-status and intelligence: An experimental study of certain cultural determinants of measured intelligence. *Genet. Psychol. Monogr.*, 1954, 49, 141–186.

Haggerty, L. H. An empirical evaluation of the accomplishment quotient: A four-year study at the junior high school level. *J. exp. Educ.*, 1941, 10, 78–90.

Honzik, Marjorie, Macfarlane, Jean W., & Allen, L. The stability of mental test performance between five and eighteen years. *J. exp. Educ.*, 1948, 17, 309–324.

Jacob, P. E. *Changing values in college: An exploratory study of the impact of college teaching*. New York: Harper, 1957.

Kearney, N. C. *Elementary school objectives*. New York: Russell Sage Foundation, 1953.

Learned, W. S., & Wood, B. D. *The student and his knowledge*. New York: Carnegie Foundation for the Advancement of Teaching, 1938.

Lord, F. M. Further problems in the measurement of growth. *Educ. psychol. Measmt*, 1958, 18, 437–451.

McNemar, Q. On growth measurement. *Educ. psychol. Measmt*, 1958, 18, 47–55.

Merkhofer, B. E. College students' study behavior. Unpublished doctoral dissertation, Univer. of Chicago, 1954.

Meyer, G. An experimental study of the old and new types of examination. *J. educ. Psychol.*, 1935, 26, 30–40.

Mitzel, H. E., & Gross, Cecily F. *A critical review of the development of pupil growth criteria in studies of teacher effectiveness*.

New York: Div. of Teacher Education, Office of Res. and Evaluation, Board of Higher Education, City of New York, 1956. (Res. Series 30.)

Remmers, H. H., & Gage, N. L. *Educational measurement and evaluation.* (Rev. ed.) New York: Harper, 1955.

Smith, E. R., Tyler, R. W., et al. *Appraising and recording student progress.* New York: Harper, 1942.

Stone, D. R. Certain verbal factors in the intelligence test performance of high and low social status groups. Unpublished doctoral dissertation, Univer. of Chicago, 1946.

Thorndike, R. L. The prediction of intelligence at college entrance from earlier tests. *J. educ. Psychol.,* 1947, 38, 129–148.

Thorndike, R. L. Reliability. In E. F. Lindquist (Ed.), *Educational measurement.* Washington, D.C.: American Council on Education, 1951. Pp. 560–620.

Thurstone, Thelma G. The relation between the difficulty of a test and its diagnostic value. Unpublished doctoral dissertation, Univer. of Chicago, 1926.

Townsend, Agatha. Growth of independent school pupils in achievement on the Stanford Achievement Test. *Educ. Rec. Bull.,* 1951, 56, 61–71.

Tyler, R. W. *Constructing achievement tests.* Columbus: Ohio State Univer. Press, 1934.

Tyler, R. W. Achievement testing and curriculum construction. In E. G. Williamson (Ed.), *Trends in student personnel work.* Minneapolis: Univer. of Minnesota Press, 1949. Pp. 391–407.

Wilson, R. C. Improving criteria for complex mental processes. *Proc. Invitational Conf. on Testing Problems.* Princeton, N.J.: Educational Testing Service, 1958. Pp. 13–20.

CHAPTER 9 Measuring Noncognitive Variables in Research on Teaching

GEORGE G. STERN
Syracuse University

I believe that teaching is an art, not a science. . . . Teaching is not like inducing a chemical reaction: it is much more like painting a picture or making a piece of music, or on a lower level like planting a garden or writing a friendly letter. You must throw your heart into it, you must realize that it cannot all be done by formulas, or you will spoil your work, and your pupils, and yourself (Gilbert Highet, 1950, pp. vii–viii).

The word *art* has two different meanings. In its most modern usage we think of it in connection with aesthetics. But it also has an older and broader meaning suggesting a carefully developed skill or ability directed toward an end which may be either aesthetic or applied. In this older sense, teaching is an artcraft, clearly one of the useful liberal arts.

Many techniques associated with this applied art have been subjected to formal analysis and research. Psychological theory has not yet proved entirely adequate to the task of developing principles of learning applicable to the full range of classroom processes. But there is considerable empirical evidence bearing on the use of lecture as against discussion methods, massed or distributed practice, and similar technical problems.

It is important to note that these techniques constitute the vehicle for the teacher's act of communication. The study of them is relevant to the development of programs of presentation for teaching machines as much as for live teachers. But live teaching involves an additional element of spontaneous communication between teacher and pupil, a form of self-expression requiring genuine creativity. The product of this creative act has no tangible or enduring shape. In this respect, teaching is more like the improvisation of the jazz musician than the substantiveness of the sculptor. Like the jazz artist, the teacher accepts the discipline of form and structure but begins afresh on each occasion, once having begun must complete the creative act for better or worse within a fixed time interval, innovates with deliberate impulsivity, and never repeats his creation in quite the same way.

The noncognitive aspects of teaching are associated with the teacher's art, as distinguished from his craft. Let us begin by considering the characteristics of this art, and the sense in which such an art form may be made the subject of research as well as of higher criticism.

THE ART OF TEACHING

At first glance the horse which dominates one section of Picasso's "Guernica" is a deformed and scrambled figure. The head, for example, not only resembles no horse in nature but is oddly disjointed within itself. The features are askew, they lie in different planes which seemingly lack relation to one another, and they are grafted for no apparent reason on the same neck. A similar distortion, more romantic than cubist in conception, is found in Picasso's treatment of parts of the human figure in "The Minotaur."

Once these seemingly disparate elements are integrated by the perceiver, however, it becomes clear that Picasso has employed a device for showing us motion in a static medium. The various planes of the horse reconcile themselves into that of a single animal plunging and rearing in an endless paroxysm of terror and pain; the several simultaneous and contradictory representations of the same human figure reflect Pasiphae's passionate response to the embrace of the Minotaur.

Despite its novelty, the technique employed here by Picasso is understandable and reproducible by anyone who may choose to adopt it. What cannot be reproduced again, by Picasso or by anyone else, is the unique understanding which this artist felt for his subject matter at these moments in time, and the unique combination of symbols he employed to communicate this understanding to his audience. The artist is, in this respect, the prototype of the teacher. The artist comments at the same time that he portrays, teaching us to see something in nature in the same way that he saw it. In this way we begin to see beauty where previously there had been only an indifferent and aesthetically neutral experience.

The art of teaching lies similarly in the communication and projection of an essentially private experience. Kahlil Gibran, the Lebanese poet, has expressed this idea eloquently in his verse *On Teaching:*

> Then said a teacher, Speak to us of Teaching.
> And he said:
> No man can reveal to you aught but that which already lies half asleep in the dawning of your knowledge.
> The teacher who walks in the shadow of the temple, among his followers, gives not of his wisdom but rather of his faith and his lovingness.
> If he is indeed wise he does not bid you enter the house of his wisdom, but rather leads you to the threshold of your own mind.
> The astronomer may speak to you of his understanding of space, but he cannot give you his understanding.
> The musician may sing to you of the rhythm which is in all space, but he cannot give you the ear which arrests the rhythm nor the voice that echoes it.
> And he who is versed in the science of numbers can tell of the regions of weight and measure, but he cannot conduct you thither.
> For the vision of one man lends not its wings to another man.
> And even as each one of you stands alone in God's knowledge, so must each one of you be alone in his knowledge of God and in his understanding of the earth (Gibran, 1929, pp. 56–57).

The teacher's unique understanding of his subject matter, and the unique combination of symbols which he employs on some particular occasion to communicate this understanding to his pupils, are the essence of the teacher's art. The art of the teacher is as valid a subject for artistic criticism, or for psychoanalytic interpretation, as is the painter's canvas. But is there any meaningful sense in which we can treat it as an object of experimental research? What if we were to reduce the teacher's understanding of his subject matter to the status of a dependent variable, investigating the impact of various kinds of experience on his subsequent treatment of the same subject matter, for example? Empirical studies of this type are rare, despite the vogue which such an approach now enjoys among biographical writers.

It would seem more profitable to consider the teacher's role as artist as an independent variable in the teaching process, as a possible codeterminant of various educational outcomes. To do this, however, we must first find some way of conceptualizing the teacher as an interpreter of events, and then of transforming such concepts into quantifiable variables.

Among the variables which have been presumed to be related to creative activity are measures of individual differences in attitudes, values, interests, appreciations, adjustments, temperament, and personality. By common usage such variables have been termed *noncognitive* to distinguish them from the more consciously organized conceptual schema associated with measures of intelligence, aptitude, achievement, or performance. This chapter will be devoted to the description of noncognitive variables, the historical trends figuring in their emergence in the behavioral sciences, a summary of techniques involved in their measurement, and a methodology-oriented analysis of current research on the role of noncognitive functions in teaching.

MEASURING NONCOGNITIVE FUNCTIONS

In this section are presented a discussion of historical antecedents in the definition and measurement of noncognitive variables, major approaches to the dynamics of social behavior, an epistemological orientation to "neocognitive" methodology, and certain methodological implications of this orientation.

HISTORICAL ANTECEDENTS

The development of the Stanford-Binet and the Army Alpha in the early part of this century were achievements of considerable significance. For the first time it became possible to grade individuals systematically with respect to their intellectual capacity or learning ability. The performance of a given child could now be compared objectively with that of a representative group of age-mates, supplementing the teacher's limited and subjective evaluation of the child's capacity in relation to that of his classmates. The discovery that various military and civilian occupations could be ordered in terms of the average intelligence test scores of their incumbents, and that this order corresponded to the seeming complexity and social value of these occupations, almost seemed to complete the picture. All that remained to be done was to find the reason for the fact that the intelligence test score was not entirely adequate as a predictor of performance.

For a short time it appeared as if Spearman's distinction between general and specific intelligence might provide the answer. According to this view, performance in any given role was a function of a number of specific mental capacities in addition to the general factor already being measured. Although this gave rise subsequently to the development of a variety of aptitude tests, some of the most important of which proved to be in the areas of mechanical comprehension and manual dexterity, no marked improvement appeared in the correlations between test scores and performance. It was becoming increasingly clear that ability per se did not necessarily correspond with achievement.

A number of factors might account for the failure to obtain better predictions of achievement. The approach through ability tests assumes that the most significant varieties of intelligence have all been isolated, that reliable tests exist for measuring each of them, and that we know exactly which ones are involved in what particular proportions in any given task. These assumptions are far from being fulfilled even today. Nevertheless, many psychologists were inclined to feel that further refinements along these lines would not yield gains commensurate with the effort put into them. These men agreed that important determinants of a noncognitive nature were being overlooked.

Volition

The first of the presumed noncognitive variables to be investigated was that associated with volition or, more specifically, with the will to achieve. Ambition and ability do not always match one another in the same individual, although both are related to performance. The motivation to perform may, under some circumstances, outweigh skill in significance, as in the case of the infantryman whose specific ability as a marksman is less important than his continued presence as a source of firepower. More typically, both aptitude and the need to excel seem to figure in the final performance. But the motivational factor is still presumed to be the more critical of the two, compensating within limits for deficiencies in ability (overachievement) whereas ability without ambition is considered to be the cause of underachievement.

The early efforts of Downey (1924) and others to measure will by means of simple handwriting, sensorimotor, and ideational tests all proved unsatisfactory. The various measures devised for this purpose have been low in reliability and lacking in relationship to one another as well as to external criteria of the strength of volition. Similar difficulties were encountered by Simoneit and the German military psychologists of the 1930's who sought to measure military dependability by means of characterological assessments (Farago, 1942). In the 1940's considerable attention was given to level of aspiration phenomena, involving tasks in which the subject knows how well he is doing and may estimate his future improvement (Lewin, Dembo, Festinger, & Sears, 1944). In more recent years, McClelland and his associates (1953) have been reporting interesting results with a projective approach for measuring the strength of an achievement need.

But none of these attempts to measure volition can be considered comparable in effectiveness with those associated with the measurement of intelligence. The findings have been inconsistent, and these various proposed tests do not appear to be measuring comparable things. The problem may be due in part to the sensitivity of such measures to transitory aspects of the testing situation. The essentially trivial nature of the tasks does not compare favorably with normal life circumstances in which the need for achievement is likely to be elicited. Furthermore, much evidence suggests that the relationship between motivation for achievement and certain forms of measured anxiety is exceedingly complex (Atkinson, 1960) and may constitute still another factor affecting the relationship between performance and aptitude test scores.

Psychopathology

The possible significance of anxiety and other sources of chronic impairment of performance suggested by Freud constitute a second major source of ideas regarding noncognitive determinants of performance. Psychoanalytic formulations provide a rationale for failure regardless of the individual's manifest ability or expressed desire to succeed. Two broad categories of work interference may be differentiated: (1) those resulting from the distracting influence of some incipient pathological process, diverting energy incidentally from more productive employment, and (2) unconscious processes working deliberately toward failure as a goal.

An example of the former may be found in the case of the college freshman so distressed by his enforced separation from home that he can think of nothing save his own helplessness and the depths of his homesickness. The graduate student working sporadically and fruitlessly for years on a dissertation, forever postponing the ultimate transition in status from student to professional, illustrates the second type.

Anamnestic material from interviews and autobiographical essays provides an important source of data for estimating the significance of such processes for a given individual. The Rorschach and other projective tests constitute still another. Use of these techniques requires extensive clinical experience and sensitivity. More conventional measuring devices have also been developed, however, which do not have the broad formulation of a functioning personality as their goal. The earliest of these, published in 1920, was Woodworth's Personal Data Sheet, based on items derived from the symptoms of neurotic patients. Essentially a request for a self-report of symptoms, and depending therefore on the sincerity of the respondent, such a device can elicit an acknowledgment of characteristics similar to those found among many different kinds of pathological conditions. The Bernreuter Personality Inventory, a once widely used instrument of this type, published in 1931, has similar limitations.

Another approach has been employed in the development of the Minnesota Multiphasic Personality Inventory (Hathaway & McKinley, 1943). The statements in this questionnaire have been keyed empirically on the basis of responses from normal adults and from mental patients. The subject's scores are significant therefore not in terms of the superficial face validity or content of the items, but on the basis of their relationship to the actual responses of known groups of deviates.

Unlike the measures of volition, the various attempts to diagnose pathology have enjoyed wide and vigorous application. They have had considerable value in distinguishing abnormal from normal subjects and in differentiating between various types of abnormal processes. As a source of improved accuracy in predicting levels of performance among normal people, however, they have been much less useful.

Several considerations may account for the limitations of these attempts in this respect. To the jaundiced eye of the clinician, nearly everyone reveals some signs of processes which have proved morbid in others. It may be that the significance of such psychic stigmata has been considerably overestimated as a result of their being initially observed in cases of severe disturbance. Perhaps the presumed scars of traumatic experiences are no more than the residue of events vital to mat-uration and growth in our society, rather than symptoms of impending illness.

It has been suggested that the significant factor is not to be found in the signs of repressed conflict, but in the strength of the ego, i.e., its resiliency, or ability to tolerate stress. Since the degree of stress is also a factor, weak egos being as capable as strong ones when the pressures are minimal, this approach also implies the evaluation of a situational or environmental component. Such a conception is at present largely tautological, since levels of environmental stress and of individual stress tolerance are defined by reference to one another. This problem is closely related to the fact that we do not yet know how to evaluate signs of an earlier trauma when they are not accompanied by present afflictions. It is as if we were sometimes able to restore a malfunctioning car to service by repairing the carburetor, knowing at the same time that many cars with carburetors that are just as bad are operating satisfactorily.

Multivariate Assessment

The most recent systematic attempt to improve the prediction of performance from test data takes motivational factors into account as well as pathological processes which may impede their expression. Attributable largely to the innovations of Murray (1938), this approach also contributes a more sensitive treatment of the situational aspects of the performance.

The assessment program conducted during World War II for the Office of Strategic Services (OSS Assessment Staff, 1948) provides a systematic example of this position. It involves an analysis of the performance in terms of its major functional components—intellectual, psychomotor, and interpersonal—and the principal physical and psychological obstacles to the effective fulfillment of these components. On the basis of this analysis, a battery of tests is selected or constructed to obtain relevant evidence regarding the capacities of the individual to meet these various requirements, his involvement in the task and desire to perform well at it, and his ability to withstand the existing or anticipated stresses.

It has been customary to employ a number of different techniques to assess each quality identified in the task analysis; the techniques are administered and interpreted by independent assessment specialists who subsequently pool their information in order to arrive at a joint appraisal of the candidate's potential. Because of the abstract nature of many of these variables, there has been a tendency to rely on global and subjective procedures.

The four major assessment studies conducted since World War II varied in their sympathy for such techniques, but the evidence is clearly against them at the present time (Meehl, 1954; Taft, 1959). The correlations between cross-validated objective test scores and performance ratings have been consistently higher than those obtained from judges using global clinical techniques. The comparison may not be fair, in that the clinical predictions have generally been oriented toward some performance more ultimate than the one from which the criterion measure was derived. It is to be expected that medical school grades, let us say, would be more highly correlated with (1) a set of test items developed originally on the basis of their relationship to medical school grades, than with (2) clinical predictions of potential performance as a physician based on projective or situational test data. The grades may not be a particularly good index of potential performance as a physician, although this is the criterion being predicted by the clinician and not by the objective test.

The studies by Stern, Stein, and Bloom (1956) in particular stressed the fact that the analysis, and prediction, must be directed toward the actual criterion being used rather than toward some hypothetical performance. The unusually high validities reported in these studies have not been tested in large-scale applications, however. Nor has the more important issue—regarding the implications of recruiting or selecting personnel on the basis of criteria derived from performance in training as compared with professional performance—been given adequate consideration (see pp. 421–422, below).

MAJOR APPROACHES TO THE DYNAMICS OF SOCIAL BEHAVIOR

The historical resumé just completed is based on the sequence of events which followed the introduction of large-scale mental testing early in this century, as psychologists sought to develop noncognitive measures to supplement and improve predictions of performance obtained from tests of intellectual ability. This analysis reflected the recognition, first, of motivation as an internal factor influencing performance in a positive direction. This recognition was followed by the discovery of the internal impediments to successful performance represented by psychopathological processes. A decade later saw the beginnings of a synthesis of both of these positions in an approach to personality assessment which also introduced positive and negative situational components into its analysis.

An alternative view of the emergence of noncognitive variables in behavorial research is provided by the major systematic orientations toward the dynamic dispositions underlying social behavior: (1) the sociology of attitudes and values, (2) the measurement school, (3) depth psychology, and (4) neo-Gestalt perceptualism. All four employ the concept of attitudes as a central variable, and each has contributed significantly to the others. Their distinctive orientations throw light on ways, different from those just considered, to study noncognitive variables.

Sociology of Attitudes and Values

The concept of attitudes was first established as a central variable by Thomas and Znaniecki (1918) in their monumental study of people in transition between two cultures. They employed the term as a way of conceptualizing the unifying force which appears to lie behind what would otherwise seem to be discrete and arbitrary overt behaviors. They regarded an attitude as an internalized counterpart of an external object, representing the individual's subjective tendencies to act toward that object.

Subsequent definitions have agreed on four fundamental points:

1. Attitudes are socially formed. They are based on cultural experience and training and are revealed in cultural products. The study of life history data reveals the state of mind of the individual, and of the social group from which he derives, concerning the values of the society in which he lives.

2. Attitudes are orientations toward others and toward objects. They incorporate the meaning of a physical event as an object of potential or actual activity.

3. Attitudes are selective. They provide a basis for discriminating between alternative courses of action and introduce consistency of response in social situations of an otherwise diverse nature.

4. Attitudes reflect a disposition to an activity, not a verbalization. They are organizations of incipient activities, of actions not necessarily completed, and represent therefore the underlying dispositional or motivational urge.

For Thomas and Znaniecki, research on attitudes provided the propaedeutic for the investigation of all sociopsychological processes. They based their work on the analysis of the contents of letters exchanged between Polish peasants and their family members and friends who had emigrated to the United States. The letters were spontaneous documents and more comparable therefore with other forms of uncontrived behavior than with the usual types of self-report solicited by investigators. A good introduction to the techniques of content analysis applicable to such materials may be found in Berelson (1954) and McGranahan (1951).

A source of data like that available to Thomas and Znaniecki is unusual. More typically, the investigator interested in life-history materials must rely on essay or interview data obtained expressly for research purposes. Verbal statements obtained under these conditions have decided limitations and cannot be accepted uncritically since the direct or indirect influence of the investigator himself has become a part of the response process. In a properly conducted interview these artifacts may be minimized but they can never be entirely eliminated. Relevant material on the use of the interview as a social science tool was prepared by Maccoby and Maccoby (1954) and by Sheatsley (1951). A more extended treatment of interviewing techniques may be found in a volume by Kahn and Cannell (1957).

The Measurement School

The techniques of attitude research introduced by sociologists have evolved in a direction closely related to those of psychoanalysis and clinical psychology. But research in this area also underwent an early modification in a substantially different direction as a result of the application of psychological test construction techniques to the development of attitude questionnaires.

One of the earliest efforts in this direction was made by Watson (1925). His test of "fairmindedness" attempts to provide a measure of prejudice on 12 different issues related to religious observance, moral code, and political beliefs. The 12 scores are obtained by adding selected responses from a battery of 300 items arranged in six parts. Each part is constructed in a different way, one presenting a list of opinions to which the respondent indicates his degree of acceptance on a five-point scale ranging from unqualifiedly true (+ 2 points) to unqualifiedly false (− 2 points), another requiring the analysis of the logic employed in a discussion of various ideological issues, etc. Although no longer in use because many of the items are now dated, Watson's test exemplifies a multimethod design that is still of considerable interest (Campbell & Fiske, 1959). By providing a variety of ways for each attitude to be sampled, differing in procedure as well as in item content, Watson enhanced the likelihood that the total score would be a reliable measure of a generalized opinion.

Another scale of the same period was developed by Bogardus (1925) to measure social distance, or the closeness of the relationship to which the respondent is willing to admit members of designated social groups. Bogardus conceived of acceptance in terms of seven steps or points: (1) to close kinship by marriage, (2) to my club as personal chums, (3) to my street as neighbors, (4) to employment in my occupation in my country, (5) to citizenship in my country, (6) as visitors only to my country, and (7) would exclude from my country. A general tolerance score is obtained by averaging the step values (ranging from 1 to 7) assigned by the respondent to each of the groups he has rated.

Four issues arise in evaluating scales of this type when the items are assembled and keyed arbitrarily in accordance with the opinions of the investigator:

1. Are all items relevant to the same measurement continuum?

2. Are the items in fact ordered as steps along that continuum?

3. Is the relative distance between the steps constant?

4. Are the responses actually a function of the attitude the items were intended to sample, rather than of some irrelevant process?

The Bogardus scale pointedly illustrates all four of these considerations: (1) Although most of us would agree with Bogardus that the seven scale items are all logically related to social distance, there is considerable question as to whether they contribute equally to its measurement. (2) The acceptance of an out-group member as a work associate and his acceptance as a fellow citizen are probably steps along the same continuum, but does the first always signify greater acceptance than the second? In 1946, many people in favor of employing the skills of German research workers would nevertheless have rejected the qualifications of these technicians for citizenship. (3) Are the relative distances between the scale steps comparable? There may be much less difference between total exclusion and acceptance as tourists only, on the one hand, or between marriage and close personal friendship, than between employment in the same occupation and acceptance as a neighbor. (4) Finally, what is the relation between the response to these items and "actual" prejudice?

One early attempt to deal with these problems was made by Harper (1927) in a study of the attitudes of educators toward various social issues. Harper asked a panel of experts to judge the relevance of each of his items and indicate how the response should be scored. An extremely important contribution was made during this period by Thurstone and Chave (1929), who used the averages and scatters of judges' ratings of the favorability of a preliminary set of statements to select those with stable means which ranged in value but which were separated by approximately equal intervals.

Despite the methodological elegance of this procedure and the significance of its contribution to test theory, Likert (1932) was able to demonstrate that the arbitrary assignment of response weights, as introduced earlier by Watson, gave essentially the same results as the Thurstone procedure in scales of adequate length at a cost of considerably less effort and time. For many years most scales were constructed on the basis of arbitrary keys and response weights, and then revised in accordance with a statistical analysis of the preliminary results. Such analyses have usually included the computation of the average acceptance of the item and its correlation with the total score. Correlation coefficients like the point biserial and the tetrachoric, relating each individual item to the scale total, have been commonly used along with discrimination indexes like Ebel's (1954), which compares the responses of extreme scorers on the total test with their responses to each item.

Although these simple item analysis techniques continue to be widely employed, the postwar period has seen a number of important new developments. Prominent among these are the more elaborate procedures for scale construction and refinement proposed by Coombs (1952), Guttman (1950), and Lazarsfeld (1950). Coombs (1953) and Green (1954) have each contributed excellent analyses of current methodological problems and developments in the measurement of attitudes. A good general introduction to basic techniques of attitude scale construction is provided by Edwards (1957).

Depth Psychology

The orientation and methods of the clinical psychologist and personologist resemble those of the psychometrician less than they resemble those of the sociologist, at least with respect to research involving noncognitive processes. As has already been noted, both the clinician and the sociologist tend to be concerned with larger, more molar, units of behavior of a complexity more likely to be found in the observation of spontaneous behavior than in responses to a paper-and-pencil questionnaire.

A distinction based on a presumed difference in complexity between this holistic emphasis and what has often been referred to as the atomistic or elementalistic approach of the psychometrician would, however, be misleading. There have been many examples of multimethod tests, similar to Watson's "fair-mindedness" test (1925), described earlier, which use a variety of related tasks to explore the range and depth of the variable in question as well as to increase the reliability of measurement. Multivariate instruments, such as the Minnesota Multiphasic Personality Inventory (Hathaway & McKinley, 1943), referred to previously, also yield a number of scores from which a broadly detailed personality profile may be constructed.

The more significant distinction appears to involve the extent to which the investigator employs inference of underlying process as an analytic tool. Observations of natural behavior, interviews, autobiographies, and projective tests are similar in that they all require interpretations derived from clinical experience if they are to be made meaningful. This is in marked contrast to the empirically derived scales of the psychometrician which provide a score or index number relating the subject's performance to that of various groups of respondents rather than to the construct being measured.

An important exception may be found in the California scales for detecting the authoritarian personality syndrome (Adorno, Frenkel-Brunswik, Levinson, & Sanford, 1950). The authors of these scales began with a conventional scale of self-report items on anti-Semitism. A second scale of general ethnocentrism was found to correlate very highly with the original anti-Semitism scale. In a later attempt to develop an alternative measure of anti-Semitic prejudice containing no explicit references to Jews, they drew first on the general ethnocentrism items, abstracting the broad themes of fear, morality, etc., which seemed to characterize this scale. Then, on the assumption that agreement with items of this type reflected deeper personality needs in addition to the more superficial manifestations of prejudice represented in their substantive content, an entirely new series of items was devised in terms of these hypothesized underlying needs.

The theoretical orientation behind this approach to levels of personality function may be found in the writings of Frenkel-Brunswik (1942) and Sanford, Adkins, Cobb, and Miller (1943). Summaries of methodological problems and relevant research following the appearance of the original volume by Adorno, et al. (1950) may be found in Christie and Jahoda (1954) and Sanford (1956).

The Activities Index (Stern, 1958), the College Characteristics Index (Pace & Stern, 1958; Stern, 1960a, 1960b, 1962a, 1962b), and the High School Characteristics Index (Stern, 1961) are further examples of the impact of depth psychology on psychological measurement. These multivariate self-report instruments were designed in accordance with the need-press schema developed by Murray (1938). The purpose of Murray's constructs is to provide ways of describing dimensions of personality and environment as they are revealed in the characteristic strivings of the individual and in his perceptions of the interpersonal world. As adapted in the Syracuse Indexes, however, they have proved equally useful despite the restrictions of an objectively scorable paper-and-pencil format.

Each of these instruments consists of 300 items distributed among 30 scales of 10 items each. These scales yield a profile of individual needs or of environmental press from which highly detailed elaborations may be made. Simple comparisons may be made with the scores of selected normative groups, but the interscale relationships provide a clinically experienced interpreter with extensive inferential data, at an entirely different level, from which to construct personality and situational descriptions with an apparently high degree of validity.

Neo-Gestalt Perceptualism

An even more indirect approach to the study of attitudinal and personality processes is represented by the perception-oriented studies beginning with Bartlett (1932) and Sherif (1936).

The origins of this approach are to be found in the writings of von Ehrenfels (1890) and the *Gestalt* or configurational school which followed him (e.g., Koffka, 1935). These theorists stressed the role of invariant organizational properties of the perceptual field which transcend the actual physical properties of the stimulus units, as revealed, for example, in the persistence of a melodic phrase regardless of the key in which it is played. Subsequent investigators found analogous field properties suggested by nonphysical perceptual determinants associated with the need and value systems of the perceiver.

Witkin and his associates (1954), for example, reported relationships between personality organization and spatial orientation habits, i.e., a tendency toward field-dependent spatial perception on the part of passive individuals as contrasted with the more independent spatial perception of active personality types. Solley and Murphy (1960) concluded that their data on autistic factors in perception, as well as those obtained by many others, are best understood in terms of a view of perceiving as an active organization of stimuli based on dynamic and affective characteristics of the individual.

A series of articles on various approaches to the study of personality through perception may be found in Blake and Ramsey (1951). A brief discussion of contemporary issues may be found in Klein (1956), as well as in an exceptionally complete and erudite analysis by F. H. Allport (1955).

AN EPISTEMOLOGICAL ORIENTATION TO NEOCOGNITIVE METHODOLOGY

The use of the term *noncognitive* in referring to the various approaches summarized thus far is misleading. The origins of this usage lie in the ancient differentiation between intellectual functions and personality functions as determinants of behavior, the latter presumably incorporating emotional, motivational, and temperamental traits. But, as we have seen, the measurement of such traits has generally involved little more than an extension of ideational structure to incorporate attitudes, values, perceptual sets, and similar indices of conceptual organization and expectation. These developments might be more appropriately described as neocognitive rather than noncognitive, since they contribute to our knowledge of some of the subtleties of the cognitive process rather than introduce genuinely novel factors of an emotional or volitional character.

Neocognitive factors are distinguishable to a degree from their intellective predecessors insofar as they tend to involve mental processes of a less rational character. The sources of these newer ideational elements are also less likely to be available for conscious analysis on the part of the respondent. The distinction is relative, however, and of no particular significance for our present purposes.

The preceding two sections of this chapter have sought to provide some introduction to research on neocognitive processes in terms of a synopsis of historical developments and some major schools of thought. Neither of these modes of analysis does more than highlight relatively arbitrary events. The purpose of this third section is to systematize neocognitive research in terms of the alternative resolutions of two epistemological dilemmas: causal determinism and object generalization. The analysis of these dilemmas provides a basis for organizing research strategies in the study of neocognitive processes.

Determinism: Historic and Ahistoric

All psychologists are agreed that behavior events can be entirely accounted for in terms of their antecedent conditions, at least in principle. What we do not know are the specific antecedents which are relevant to any given behavioral event system, or the relative weights to be assigned to each of several conjoint conditions. We are not even agreed on how large a unit of time should be employed when looking to the past for the experiences which have determined present behavior.

Associationist (S-R) and psychoanalytic theorists alike both tend to stress the role of ontogenetic factors as behavioral determinants. The latter are perhaps more likely to emphasize the peculiar potency of early childhood events for reasons beyond mere primacy or practice, but associationists have introduced concepts like imprinting to account for some of the special qualities of infantile phenomena. The analysts have also tended to press further into the past for relevant antecedent conditions. But prominent associationist counterparts are less difficult to identify for theorists like Federn, who have sought relevant intra-uterine variables, than for those like Jung, who have gone back beyond the immediate biologic origin of the organism into the "racial" history of its species. The re-

jection of Lamarck's hypothesis regarding the inheritance of acquired characteristics tends to make the latter position untenable.

Insofar as early events in the life history of the individual have preceded later ones, it may be said in one sense that they are related. By the same reasoning, however, *all* events which have preceded some designated occurrence are also related to it, from the very beginning of time. One way of avoiding this infinite regression of the present on the past was developed by Dilthey and Spranger around the turn of this century under the name of *Verstehendepsychologie* (see G. W. Allport, 1937; Roback, 1927). These men proposed to restrict the search for meaningful antecedents by disinterestedly incorporating only those prior events which were "fraught with meaning" in relation to the total personality.

The difficulty of selecting these events, and the unreliability of the intuitive act of *verstehen,* was clearly understood at the time by Max Weber, who wrote:

how is the *causal explanation* of an *individual* fact possible—since a *description* of even the smallest slice of reality can never be exhaustive? The number and type of causes which have influenced any given event are always infinite and there is nothing in the things themselves to set some of them apart as alone meriting attention. A chaos of "existential judgments" about countless individual events would be the only result of a serious attempt to analyze reality "without presuppositions." . . . Order is brought into this chaos only on the condition that in every case only a *part* of concrete reality is interesting and *significant* to us, because only it is related to the *cultural values* with which we approach reality. . . . only those causes to which are to be imputed, in the individual case, the "essential" feature of an event. Where the *individuality* of a phenomenon is concerned, the question of causality is not a question of *laws* but of concrete causal *relationships* . . . (Weber, 1949, p. 78).

Elsewhere Weber (1949, pp. 181 ff.) describes the empirical "calculus of probability" by means of which he hoped to isolate the critical causal antecedents of an event, but it is clear that this procedure offers only a refinement of the process of subjective analysis rather than a distinctly objective substitute for it. Lewin, on the other hand, provides a radical solution to the regression paradox by asserting that the only determinants of behavior at a given time are the properties of the field at that particular time. The life space of the individual is an organizational structure which endures through time and is a historical product, but "Any behavior or any other change in a psychological field depends only upon the psychological field *at that time*" (Lewin, 1951, p. 45).

A similar emphasis on the contemporaneity of behavioral determinants has been proposed by phenomenologically oriented personality theorists, represented in this country by Angyal (1941), Kelly (1955), Lecky (1945), and C. R. Rogers (1951). For these men, as for Lewin, the past is of value primarily as a historical clue to the significance of certain aspects of the present system. F. H. Allport (1954), however, has broken completely with any form of temporal analysis, insisting that events are entirely ahistorical and linked in patterns which cut across the conventional and absolute time stream.

Object Generalization: Nomothetic or Idiographic

The paradoxical character of various approaches to causal analysis, ranging between historical all-inclusiveness and ahistorical immediacy, is matched by a paradox regarding the uniqueness of the event under investigation. Freud and Hull were both concerned with the development of *general* laws of behavior. The same might be said of Weber, who was even more explicit in recognizing the significance of the "ideal type" as the object of the analysis, like the "ideal gas" of the chemists, rather than any specific case.

Dilthey and Spranger, on the other hand, were equally insistent on the position that each individual is unique and has meaning only as an isolated and unreproducible complex. They derived this position from Windelband and Rickert (see Kaufmann, 1944), who had distinguished between the cultural and the natural sciences. The former, which include history and psychology, they described as idiographic in character and concerned primarily with the individualization of phenomena. The nomothetic sciences, represented by physics and chemistry, are generalist rather than particularist in orientation.

This argument rests for the most part on the relative lack of equivalence among social science phenomena as compared with physical events. While this difference is not absolute, and does not in any event preclude the derivation of theoretical laws regarding general properties of the individual case, many psychologists have espoused a distinctly idiographic position. This group includes G. W. Allport (1937) and Murray (1938), as well as the phenomenologists referred to previously. The essence of this position has been put quite simply by Murphy (1951, p. xvi): "The conception is that every psychological act is the act of a whole person, and that the first task of psychology is to focus upon the nature of a person."

Although this position has developed steadily in recent decades, it has not been traditional in American psychology. The more characteristic approach to psychological theories of personality or of learning has been directed toward the discovery of general laws governing the relationships between particular conditions of stimulation and associated behavioral responses. These laws are understood to be normative in character, derived from the study of representative samples or cases, and applicable to the individual insofar as he represents an instance of the general case.

METHODOLOGICAL IMPLICATIONS

The crux of the determinism paradox lies in the alternative views of the organism that are implied. Is the organism an agent or an actor? In one sense, the meaning of the individual can be derived only from the past experiences to which he has been exposed. In another sense, the meaning of the past can be derived only from the significance attached to it by the individual himself in the present.

Furthermore, that same individual may be regarded as an absolutely unique phenomenon who is lawfully consistent only in terms of principles peculiar to him. Or we may reject the peculiarities as being of less significance than the communalities between organisms of the same species.

The resolution of each paradox in one way or the other seems more in the nature of a categorical imperative than an objective judgment. The alternatives appear somewhat like forced choices, to be made on the basis of primitive assumptions from which guiding methodological principles may be derived but which are not in themselves the products of a logical derivation. These issues have, moreover, become obscured or confused at times, and are not always clearly identifiable in the work of more eclectic investigators. If the alternatives are viewed as strategies, however, rather than as metaphysical positions, their implications begin to emerge.

The idiographic-nomothetic controversy readily resolves itself in terms of a tactical decision. "Every man is in certain respects (a) like all other men, (b) like some other men, (c) like no other man" (Kluckhohn & Murray, 1953, p. 53). The nomothetic approach is appropriate to the study of those respects in which all (or some) men are alike, whereas idiographic techniques are of value when we have as our purpose the study of intrapsychic relationships in a single personality.

The tactical aspects of historical analysis have also been recognized. Although Lewin, for example, insisted that all the determinants of a behavioral event are to be found in the contemporary situation in which the event occurs, he also conceded that this situa-

tion is not a momentary one wholly lacking in time extension. The total situation, including the antecedent conditions of the specified behavior, extends over a period of time the exact length of which depends on the complexity of the event (Lewin, 1951, pp. 50 ff.).

Sullivan treated one aspect of this conception quite explicitly by recognizing that the events which have survived from the chronological past do not survive unaltered or merely dimmed by time. The "past" events which determine present behavior are in continuous change, at varying rates and magnitudes, as a result of subsequent experience (Sullivan, 1949). Behavior is a process rather than an episode, and the description of any given behavioral event is analogous to the analysis of a segment of a trajectory corresponding to the life-history of the individual. The length of the segment to be abstracted, or of earlier portions of it to be related to the present, depends upon the purpose of the investigation and the kinds of data available.

If the dimensions of the two paradoxes are projected on one another, as in Table 1, they provide a basis for grouping a number of prominent psychological theorists who have adopted distinctive conceptual as well as methodological positions. Each of the four cells in Table 1 may be regarded as representing a strategy for the conduct of research, and the applications of each strategy to research on teaching will be considered briefly.

The Case-Study Method

The combination of historical and idiographic approaches, emphasizing long-term recurrent trends characterizing the isolated individual, leads directly to the case-study method. Life-history techniques are peculiarly suited to the requirements of an approach which stresses the need for a recapitulation of the subject's past in order to better understand his present behavior. G. W. Allport (1937, 1960) has been an especially

TABLE 1

METHODOLOGICAL PREFERENCES OF SOME REPRESENTATIVE PSYCHOLOGICAL
THEORISTS AND RESEARCHERS, AND RELATED EXAMPLES OF STUDIES ON TEACHING

	Nomothetic	Idiographic
Historical	CAUSAL-GENETIC *Examples* Theorist: Dollard & Miller (1950) Research: Blum (1953) Teaching: Waller (1932)	CASE STUDY *Examples* Theorist: G. W. Allport (1937, 1960) Research: Murray (1938) Teaching: Highet (1950)

Ahistorical	PSYCHOMETRIC
	Examples
	Theorist: Thurstone (1951)
	Research: Eysenck (1952)
	Teaching: Ryans (1960)
		SITUATIONAL
		Examples[a]
		Theorist: Lewin (1951)
		Research: Moreno (1953);
		    Cartwright & Zander (1960)
		Teaching: Dahlke & Monahan (1949)
		    Lewin, Lippitt, & White
		    (1939)

[a] See text for clarification of the citations in this cell.

strong advocate of this position, examples of which are to be found in Burton and Harris (1947, 1955), Murray (1938), and R. W. White (1952).

The techniques in these studies may involve the integration of personal documents (G. W. Allport, 1942), interviews, objective test data, and projective responses in some unified formulation of an individual personality. At least two novel procedures have been suggested in recent years. R. G. Barker and his associates (1955a, 1955b) have devised a method (hemerography) for obtaining a detailed analysis and description of the actual life experiences of a person in the course of one day, utilizing a team of observers who take turns observing and recording the subject continuously throughout the day.

A more practicable method for the analysis of sequences has been proposed by Cattell under the name of P technique (1950, p. 280). This provides a method for revealing intrapsychic patterns in the individual case by factoring the matrix obtained by intercorrelating a series of measures yielded by repeated testing of the same individual on many variables daily for a period of several months. Stephenson's (1953) Q technique offers another statistical model which can be used to study interrelationships between various cognitive systems within the same individual. Q technique is not limited to idiographic analyses, however. When employed in the investigation of relationships between persons (as distinguished from relationships between tests), it is capable of yielding very useful nomothetic data on psychological types. (See *Psychometric Methods* below.)

Case-study techniques in educational research have been used mainly for clinical studies of pupils rather than teachers. One exception is to be found in Highet (1950), who uses brief biographical sketches of the lives of outstanding teachers to clarify different aspects of the teaching process. Intensive case studies of individual teachers, or of the interaction between a particular pupil and teacher over a period of time, constitute a source of information about the teaching process which has not been exploited in any way comparable to the clinical studies which have been made of professionals in other fields (see p. 416, below) and deserves further treatment by researchers in the field.

The Causal-Genetic Method

When the purpose behind the study of the individual case is normative rather than biographical, the resulting approach tends to emphasize (1) the common or generalizable elements characteristic of the clinical case or sample, and (2) the general principles which may be derived from the analysis of those elements. When such studies are both nomothetic and historical in orientation, the guiding strategy involves establishing developmental laws relating past events or experiences as causal determinants of the observed syndrome or behavior pattern.

. . . clinical psychology views the mind *genetically*. . . . the significance of any given current mental process is not completely known unless the full genesis of it is also known, unless its predecessors can be traced back in an unbroken chain to the beginnings of mental life in the infant. . . . clinical psychology, following Freud, carries this genetic principle to its logical conclusion and maintains that all our later reactions in life are really elaborations of simpler ones acquired in the nursery. The power to modify the more fundamental types of reaction becomes rapidly less as the child grows, and some of us even think that no fundamental change in character can take place after the fourth year of life (Jones, 1951, p. 117).

Sometimes the prior occurrence of some given condition can be established as having been both necessary and sufficient by means of the direct intervention and manipulation of those conditions by the investigator. The manipulative process involved in such cases is identical with the conventional experimental method of the natural sciences. More often, however, in the study of human behavior direct intervention is impracticable, and the investigator must rely on careful observation and a systematic selection of spontaneously occurring cases which seemingly isolate the causal factors by a process of logical exclusion. This approach is characteristic of research in clinical medicine and, not surprisingly, in clinical psychology.

This approach can be reconciled readily with stimulus-response theories of behavior based on variations of the conditioning paradigm, as demonstrated by the work of Dollard and Miller (1950) on psychotherapy which integrated learning theory and psychoanalysis. Blum (1953) has provided valuable summaries of the research literature bearing on various aspects of psychoanalytic theory. A more eclectic set of investigations using the causal-genetic approach may be found in Kluckhohn, Murray, and Schneider (1953).

Among the comparable types of analysis which bear upon teaching is Waller's classic *Sociology of Teaching* (1932). But, in the main, few clinically oriented studies in teaching have been made.

Psychometric Methods

The one area with no dearth of studies is that characterized by nomothetic-ahistorical strategies. Like the nonexperimental examples of the causal-genetic approach described above, these studies also deal with the analysis of relationships under field conditions for the purpose of arriving at general laws, a similarity noted by Cronbach (1957). A most important distinction resides, however, in the indifference of the psychometrist to the analysis of causal relations in terms of temporal sequence.

Thurstone laid the groundwork for this peculiarly pragmatic approach in 1923 when he wrote:

I suggest that we dethrone the stimulus. He is only nominally the ruler of psychology. The real ruler of the domain which psychology studies is the individual and his motives, desires, wants, ambitions, cravings, aspirations. The stimulus is merely the more or less accidental fact . . . (Thurstone, 1923, p. 364).

Thurstone's subsequent career was devoted to the development and application of the fundamental technique for studying the domain of the individual. But it is clear that the individual being studied by the psychometrist consists of attributes which have become divorced from time; the "individual is simply the point of intersection of a number of quantitative variables" (Eysenck, 1952, p. 18). That point of intersection (which might also be expressed as a profile of test scores) is significant only insofar as it can be shown to coincide with some other dimension of behavior, as in the case of aptitude test scores as predictors of academic or vocational performance.

Applications of the psychometric approach understandably stress the individual case for purposes of selection or categorization, but the underlying purpose of this approach is nomothetic. Indeed, in the absence of normative standards derived from the statistical analysis of group data, it would be impossible to make meaningful evaluations of test scores obtained from the individual case.

The tendency for psychometry to generalize to the entire species, subdivided at best by sex and age levels, is not inherent in this approach. Recent years have seen an increasing development of test tools and analytic models intended to differentiate more homogeneous aggregates of individuals in the total population. Burt (1937) introduced the use of correlations between persons (rather than between tests) for this purpose. The multiple discriminant function (Bryan, 1950) illustrates another approach to the identification of meaningful typological patterns or subvarieties capable of more precise definition than the total group of individuals within which they had been merged. Stephenson's (1953) Q technique can be employed for a similar purpose, as illustrated, for example, in Beck's (1953) use of this procedure to isolate six schizophrenic reaction patterns. These sophisticated nomothetic techniques have sometimes been identified erroneously with the idiographic cause, presumably because they are type- rather than species-oriented, but as G. W. Allport noted long ago, " 'types' are still not individuals, and the method offers no real solution to the problem of the neuropsychic elements in any single personality ..." (1937, p. 247).

One example of the systematic application of the nomothetic-ahistorical approach has already been cited (Eysenck, 1952). Various attempts to assess performance in specialized fields by empirical means have also been characterized by this same orientation (Gough, 1953; Holt & Luborsky, 1958; Kelly & Fiske, 1951). Of the many applications of this approach in research on teaching, the most exhaustive to date may be found in the work of Ryans (1960) on the description and comparison of teachers in terms of observational ratings and test responses.

Situational Methods

The last of the four methodological strategies to be considered results from a combination of idiographic and ahistoric emphases. This position explicitly rejects a nomothetic approach for its limitations in dealing with the individual case:

there is no logical way back from the concept "child" or "abnormal person" to the individual case . . . . What is the value of general concepts if they do not permit predictions for the individual case? Certainly, such a procedure is of little avail for the teacher or the psychotherapist (Lewin, 1951, p. 60).

Unlike the *Verstehende* or *Geisteswissenschaftlich* psychologists referred to previously, the investigators associated with the present position base their analyses wholly on the present situation:

One of the basic characteristics of field theory in psychology, as I see it, is the demand that the field which influences an individual should be described not in "objective physicalistic" terms, but in the way in which it exists for that person at that time (cf. the concept "behavioral environment" of Koffka, . . . [1935]). A teacher will never succeed in giving proper guidance to a child if he does not learn to understand the psychological world in which that individual child lives (Lewin, 1951, p. 62).

Although the phenomenological orientation has had considerable significance as an epistemology for psychotherapy and counseling (see Snygg & Combs, 1949), it has not lent itself readily to application as a research strategy. The primary reason for this, of course, is to be found in the severe tactical restrictions imposed by the idiographic emphasis on the individual case. Nevertheless, as we have seen, there are at least three techniques (Cattell's *P*, Stephenson's *Q*, and Barker's hemerographic analysis) suitable for the study of recurrent temporal sequences in individual subjects.

Sociometry (Moreno, 1953) represents a comparable ahistorical tool of even broader application. The theory and application of sociometry in psychotherapy emphasize situational aspects of role interactions between the patient and significant others in his interpersonal environment. Moreno has developed a number of devices for revealing the parameters of roles characteristically assumed by the subject. Kelly's (1955) work on personal constructs, closely related to Moreno's in several respects, offers a Role Construct Repertory Test of a similar nature designed to elicit information regarding the subject's conceptualization of his relationship to other people. Stephenson's *Q* technique (1953) may also be used in designs involving concurrent multiple responses, according to different sets, by the same subject to arrive at similar types of objectively recorded self-report data regarding the content of significant role configurations.

Sociometric techniques have been used most for assessing the mutual preferences and rejections recorded privately by members of the same group. There is a very extensive literature on this subject, including numerous applications in the formation and structure of classroom groups (see Chapter 7).

Role-playing improvisations and other modifications of the Moreno psychodrama provide an interesting procedure for eliciting essentially spontaneous responses from the subject in a contrived interpersonal situation. Variations of this procedure employed in various personality assessment programs have

been described by Brody and Powell (1947), Harris (1949), and the OSS Assessment Staff (1948). Stern, Stein, and Bloom (1956, p. 103) describe the use of improvisations on teacher-student interactions involving cheating, failure, and poor motivation in a study in an elementary school setting. More formal techniques for the analysis of ongoing interactions have been developed by Bales (1950) and Chapple (1949), among others. A detailed summary of these more systematic observational techniques may be found in Heyns and Lippitt (1954). Applications of observational methods to research on teaching are considered in detail in Chapter 6.

Implicit in these techniques is an acceptance of the individual as he is functioning in the present moment. This further implies a recognition of the significance of the situation acting upon the person. The relevance of these situational components has been the subject of intensive study which, by a happy coincidence, has been largely centered on classroom climates, from elementary school (Lewin, Lippitt, & White, 1939) to college (Stern, 1962a). A summary and analysis of this literature may be found in Chapter 23. Other examples of this approach, reflecting a wider range of techniques and methods, were reported by Cartwright and Zander (1960).

Summary

Three different schemes were adopted here for the purpose of ordering various approaches to the study of neocognitive phenomena. The first of these emphasized the historical sequence in which successive developments in the measurement of such variables first appeared, from their initial emergence after World War I as supplements to intelligence testing in the prediction of performance to the present day. This led us to consider (1) the attempts to measure will or purpose, (2) the measures of negative determinants of performance reflected in psychopathological processes, and (3) the integration of various mechanisms of aid or hindrance to performance in the multivariate assessment procedures of World War II and after.

A second summary attempted to view methods in neocognitive research in terms of some of the major systematic positions or schools into which the literature itself may be organized: (1) the work of the sociologist in studying the development and modification of attitudes, and (2) the subsequent evolution of this interest in the hands of psychometricians. The further modifications introduced by (3) neo-Gestaltists and (4) neo-Freudians, each group contributing its distinctive stamp, were also considered here.

The final scheme was based on alternative resolutions of two major epistemological issues in the analysis of behavior: (1) historical determinism versus ahistorical immediacy, and (2) individualist (*idiographic*) versus normative (*nomothetic*) syntheses of data. The four resulting prototypical approaches were identified as case-study, causal-genetic, psychometric, and situational methodologies. Characteristic theories, research studies, and techniques were discussed to illustrate each of these four approaches.

None of these schemes are offered as definitive, although an obvious personal bias is expressed here in favor of the epistemological analysis. The intent was not to evaluate methods in terms of some external criterion of presumed scientific excellence or efficiency, but only to clarify the various styles, strategies, and methods available for adoption or adaptation. All the analyses of this section were intended to serve as heuristic, rather than explanatory, devices which might guide the reader in selecting procedures of specific tactical significance.

MEASUREMENT AND METHODOLOGY IN NEOCOGNITIVE ASPECTS OF TEACHING

The research literature on neocognitive functions related to teaching may be divided for convenience into (1) studies more or less focused on the teacher in isolation (back-ground, interests, motives, personality characteristics, etc.), and (2) studies of teachers interacting with pupils in the classroom and with adults in the broader social community.

We shall first consider research on two problems that have long intrigued all students of "the teacher" as distinguished from "teaching": (1) factors or variables associated with the choice of teaching as a career, and (2) variables useful in predicting success in teaching. Subsequently we shall turn to studies of the teaching process, including teachers' attitudes toward pupils, attitude change in teachers, and the classroom impact of the teacher. In a third part of this section we take up studies of the learning environment, both in the classroom and in the total school setting. Finally we consider the teacher in relation to the school and the social order.

The approach throughout this discussion will be to summarize the findings relevant to the topic and then to discuss the limitations of the methods employed in these studies of neocognitive variables. Our emphasis will be on the latter—the methodological issues—with the discussion of substantive findings serving primarily to set the stage for those issues.

THE TEACHER

FACTORS IN THE CHOICE OF TEACHING AS A CAREER

Current theories of occupational choice stress a multiplicity of causal factors coming into play at various stages in the developmental history of the individual. Ginzberg, Ginsburg, Axelrod, and Herma (1951), Roe (1956), and Super and Bachrach (1957), for example, have attempted to relate vocational development to the interplay between self-concept, available role models, intelligence, demographic background, status needs, attitudes, values, interests, interpersonal skills, personality dynamics, etc. An unusually succinct and well-formulated statement regarding the integration of "economic" and "psychological" levels of occupational analysis has been made by Samler (1961).

The anthropological, psychological, and sociological thought responsible for these general theories has also contributed to analyses of a number of specific professional and social roles, including bureaucrats (Merton, 1940), business executives (W. Henry, 1949), newspaper publishers (Swanson, 1956), jazz musicians (Hughes, 1951), physicians (Hughes, 1958; Parsons, 1951) and their patients (Schneider, 1947), graduate students (Stern, Stein, & Bloom, 1956) and scientists (Kubie, 1953, 1954; Roe, 1953; Stein, Mackenzie, Rodgers, & Meer, 1955) in various fields, theologians (Stern, 1954), thieves (Sutherland, 1937), and waitresses (Whyte, 1946). Many of the approaches of these studies could be used in studies of the role of the teacher.

By an odd coincidence, the only studies of this type relevant to teaching are of an earlier vintage and were pioneer contributions to the approach just described (Donovan, 1938; Waller, 1932, 1942). Most studies of motives for entering the teaching profession, from Gould's early investigation (1934) to the more recent analyses of Best (1948), Blanchard (1953), Seagoe (1942), and Tudhope (1944) have been limited to tabulations of background characteristics and expressed interests. The limitations of these studies are typified in Ringness (1952), who found that 13 reasons given by students for their choice of teaching as a career were related to teaching success but was unable to verify these findings with alternative techniques for assessing the same reasons.

There is, nevertheless, a substantial core of agreement in these investigations. Levin, Hilton, and Leiderman (1957), in a particularly good study of this type, concluded that the intensity of the "call" to teaching is related to the earliness of choice, family approval, and indifference to low salary. Among elementary school teachers, they found that persistence in teaching was greater for those who had lower socioeconomic status, who were less interested in books or in subject matter, and who were characterized by strong feelings of rapport with children. Low socioeconomic background has also been reported as a factor in the choice of college teaching in studies by Eckert and Stecklein (1958), by Eckert, Stecklein, and Sagen (1959), and by Farber and Bousfield (1958).

Substantial differences in career orientations for men and women have been clearly demonstrated by Mason, Dressel, and Bain (1959). For women the sex role as homemaker is dominant over the occupational role as teacher, although their intention to return to teaching is stronger than it is for men. For the men, teaching is a ladder to other aspects of education, or to other vocations, and their career commitment as teachers is correspondingly limited.

The significance of supportive attitudes toward children for prospective teachers was also reported by Kearney and Rocchio (1955b), who found scores on the Minnesota Teacher Attitude Inventory (Cook, Leeds, & Callis, 1951; Leeds, 1950) to be significantly higher for high school seniors choosing teaching as a career than for those choosing nonteaching occupations. LaBue (1955), working with the Minnesota Multiphasic Personality Inventory (Hathaway & McKinley, 1943), also reported differences between women completing teacher preparation and those applying for admission who did not enroll. Scores on the MTAI are unrelated to the length of teaching experience (Cook & Hoyt, 1952), however, and it has been found that prospective teachers can fake favorable responses to the MTAI without difficulty and seem to do so even under conditions of anonymity (Sorenson, 1956).

A more recent study of faking on the MTAI has been reported by Polmantier and Ferguson (1960). Cook and Medley (1955) have found that high MTAI scores are also associated with high K scores on the MMPI, suggesting the operation of a consistent tendency to refrain from indicating undesirable traits. Other kinds of response set in the MTAI such as tendencies to make extreme and acquiescent responses have been identified by Mitzel, Rabinowitz, and Ostreicher (1956), and by Gage, Leavitt, and Stone (1957) and Gage and Chatterjee (1960).

Shaw, Klausmeier, Luker, and Reid (1952) and Eson (1956) both noted improvement in MTAI scores for students in education courses, but the latter attributed the change to knowledge regarding the desired response rather than to a genuine change in attitude. The positive correlation reported by Fishman (1957) between scores on the MTAI and the level of professional training in education received by his subjects may be a reflection of this same factor. Fishman's findings are consistent with those of Stern, Masling, Denton, Henderson, and Levin (1960), however, who reported that teacher-trainees at a private university were much more pupil-centered, less teacher-centered, than those at a state teachers college, as reflected by scores on their Teacher Preference Schedules.

In an unpublished follow-up of this study by Stern and others, corroboration was found for another aspect of the results obtained by Levin, Hilton, and Leiderman (1957). Scores on the Teacher Preference Schedule scales indicate more practical interests, and less gratification with teaching as a source of status, for teachers who resigned from the Syracuse public school system after less than two years of service than for those who remained. Evans (1952, 1953) and Schultz and Ohlsen (1955) have also noted the relative importance of social as opposed to practical interests among trainees most favorably disposed toward teaching as a career. Unlike the teachers studied by Levin and his associates, the subjects (teacher-trainees) in the Evans and Schultz-Ohlsen studies who were most strongly motivated for teaching also had the strongest academic and scholastic interests. However, Stern (1960b) reported that Activities Index (Stern, 1958) scores on intellectual needs were significantly higher for teacher-trainees than for teachers, although students in three other nonteach-

ing fields were systematically lower in such needs than were corresponding samples of professionals in those fields. Apparently the most academically oriented teacher-trainees do not go on to become elementary school teachers. This is particularly significant in view of the fact that teacher-trainees are lower in scholastic aptitude than other undergraduates to begin with (e.g., Mitzel & Dubnick, 1959; Nothern, 1958), and helps to account for Evans' (1953) report of no correlation between teacher-training marks and intelligence.

Differences between trainees and drop-outs from teachers college on four Kuder scales were found by Stewart and Roberts (1955). Dodge (1943) used a battery of personality inventories in order to describe traits of teachers. Scores reported for independent samples of teachers and trainees on the Edwards Personal Preference Schedule (Jackson & Guba, 1957; Thorpe, 1958), the Guilford-Zimmerman Temperament Survey (Leeds, 1956), and the Stern Activities Index (Haring, Stern, & Cruickshank, 1958; Stern, 1960b) are surprisingly similar in suggesting that those who pursue teaching as a career are essentially cooperative, restrained, lacking in social boldness, friendly, and anxious to please. Peck (1960), on the other hand, found that over half of a sample of women majoring in elementary education suffered from personality disturbances sufficiently acute to have made guidance or therapy advisable.

Methodological Critique

Lack of normative data from other fields. One limitation of studies of this type is the lack of comparable data from other groups to aid in interpreting the results. "Friendliness," for example, becomes meaningful only to the extent that whatever characteristic behaviors are meant by this term for teachers have also been related to similar types of behavior in other known groups of professionals. Interest in intimate interpersonal activities is higher among teachers than among physicists, but considerably lower for either of these groups as compared with theologians, salesmen, engineers, or physicians (Stern, Stein, & Bloom, 1956; Stern, 1960b).

Inferring from practitioners to recruits. A number of other problems arise in connection with these studies of teacher characteristics. As yet there has been no attempt to distinguish between those interests and values which are the consequence of participation in teaching as a career, and those which predispose the individual toward the choice of such a profession. The voice and bearing of the successful teacher are perhaps less striking stigmata than the lung tissue of the coal miner or housepainter, the hands of the tailor, or the stoop of the shoemaker, but they are nonetheless a reflection of experience in the occupation rather than an indication of readiness for it. The stamp of the professions is to be found in the professional attitudes, controls, and morality which the student assimilates during his years of training (Hughes, 1928). As Terrien (1955) has shown, the teaching occupation tends to channel teacher behavior on and off the job into relatively homogeneous kinds of activities, attitudes, goals, patterns of life organization, and beliefs. Comparative studies of people already in a field are in themselves a limited source of data regarding the essential characteristics of those who might aspire to enter it.

Differentiating among kinds of teachers. Furthermore, some evidence suggests that various levels of teaching may involve differences in motivation comparable in magnitude to those between different professions. Levin, Hilton, & Leiderman (1957) noted that women who persisted in secondary school teaching were not as likely to be uninterested in academic matters as were the more persistent elementary school teachers. Wandt (1952) found that secondary school teachers had less favorable attitudes toward their subordinates, peers, and superiors than did elementary school teachers.

At the college level many writers have called attention to the significance of prestige, politics, and power as central variables in faculty affairs, as well as a strong dedication to scholarship (Caplow & McGee, 1958; Riesman, 1958a, 1959a; L. Wilson, 1942). Gustad (1959, 1960), summarizing the results of questionnaires distributed among college teachers in 156 southern schools, concluded that such teachers (1) are highly intelligent, (2) come from middle-class homes in which responsibility, upward mobility, achievement, and hard work are valued, and (3) early in life develop a preference for largely solitary and intellectually stimulating activities in preference to the goals characteristic of their peers. But others have also commented on the excessive caution, constraint, apprehension, and permissiveness of the academic mind in higher education (Jencks, 1960; Lazarsfeld & Thielens, 1958; Riesman, 1959b). The tendency toward polarization of college teachers in terms of liberalism-conservatism, permissiveness-constraint, and subject discipline-university orientation has also been remarked by Gouldner (1957, 1958) in terms of differences between cosmopolitans and locals among the faculty.

Fantasies and ego ideals regarding teaching. It may well be that the increasing participation of young people from Jewish and Catholic families in higher education is the second-choice fall-out from the more highly prized professions, as Riesman (1959a) suggests. Or perhaps this reflects the role of the universities as a way of life which requires no identity card other than that of the detached intellectual relying on his talents, free of the ethnocentric encumbrances of home and parish. Whatever the reasons, there has been no clarification of the selective factors responsible for the recruitment of young people to teaching early in life in any way comparable to that previously cited in relation to the young scientist.

A valuable but neglected source of relevant data is to be found in the fantasies of adolescents regarding teaching as a career (see Beardslee & O'Dowd, 1961; Mead & Metraux, 1957; Remmers & Radler, 1957). As Kubie (1953) pointed out, initial career choices are determined neither by realistic knowledge of the field nor of oneself, since young people have little opportunity to experience the affective meaning of a given occupation in any direct sense.

Consequently the adolescent's and even the college student's anticipation of the quality of life in any future career is dominated by fantasies. To a remarkable degree this is true even of more familiar and humdrum careers. . . . Usually the less familiar the career which a young man chooses, the greater will be the importance of fantasies, both conscious and unconscious, among the forces which determine the initial choice of a career, and also the subsequent adjustment, happiness, and effectiveness in the one selected (Kubie, 1953, pp. 599–600).

Although teaching is one of the few occupations to which all youngsters in our society are persistently and intimately exposed, the nature of that exposure is peculiarly biased. Group sanctions prohibit the future teacher from trying out the role and even from associating too closely with teachers (Grambs, 1952). Furthermore, as H. Miller (1955) noted, the subsequent development of role-awareness is less well defined in teacher-training than, for example, in professional social work. Some evidence suggests that students tend to model themselves after their teachers, even in preference to practicing members of the profession for which they may be in training (Stern & Scanlon, 1958). Yet the circumstances under which this occurs and the factors responsible for the formation of such ego ideals have not yet been studied.

PREDICTIONS OF
SUCCESS IN TEACHING

The lack of historically oriented studies has left us with little information regarding the origins of interest in teaching as a career. But there has been no dearth of empirical attempts to relate some attribute measurable before teacher training to subsequent success. Current concern with the early identification of potentially successful teachers largely reflects the acute shortage of teachers at all levels in our schools.

Correlational Studies

Attempts to measure and predict efficiency as a teacher by means of simple correlational techniques date back to the early part of this century. The first of the Teachers College Contributions to Education, for example, was a study by Meriam (1906), who found no relation between normal school records and the subsequent teaching success of 1,185 teachers.

These early studies varied greatly in sophistication. Boyce (1915) reported high correlations between judges' ratings of 45 personal traits and their ratings of general teaching ability. On the other hand, an exceptionally competent investigation was reported in the following decade by Whitney (1924), who obtained low correlations between intelligence test scores, academic marks, marks in professional courses, marks in secondary courses, chronological age, physical characteristics, judgments of personality, ratings on student teaching, and ratings on teaching success after graduation for 1,156 graduates of 12 reasonably representative state normal schools located in different geographical regions and varying in organization and student body. The highest relationship obtained by Whitney was a multiple R of .25 between six of these variables and teaching success. Tiegs (1928) arrived at a similarly negative evaluation of the contributions made by letters of recommendation, letters of application, photographs, or test performance to the prediction of teaching success.

Summaries of the more recent literature (e.g., Barr, 1948; Barr, Eustace, & Noe, 1955; Getzels, 1955; Keller & Corcoran, 1957) suggest no substantial progress along these lines, despite the marked trend toward the use of more reliable measures of predictor variables. In a few instances, this kind of research has involved measures derived from preprofessional behavior, as in Soderquist's (1935) study of the relationships between participation in extracurricular activities in high school or college and subsequent success in teaching adults. Most investigators today, however, rely on objective test scores for this purpose, often administered at the same time (or even after) the ratings of teacher success are made. Reported results for these postdiction studies have been fairly inconsistent, ranging in success from Bowers (1948a, 1948b), who obtained correlations of .67 to .73 between personality subtests and performance in practice teaching, to Tyler (1954) who could find no basis for predicting student-teaching success from various multivariate analyses of scores on the Minnesota Multiphasic Personality Inventory, the Heston Personal Adjustment Inventory, and the Johnson Temperament Analysis. However, Moore and Cole (1957) reported positive relationships between the MMPI and practice teaching ratings, and promising cross-validations have been reported (Gough & Pemberton, 1952; Gowan & Gowan, 1955) for new scales derived empirically from the MMPI for predicting teaching success.

Clinical Studies

Personality adjustment per se is apparently not a determining factor in teaching performance, whether it is estimated from psychiatric interviews (M. E. Barker, 1948), the Rorschach test (Gough & Pemberton, 1952; Page & Travers, 1953a), or figure drawings (Page & Travers, 1953b). However, the drawing technique ("Draw a picture of a teacher with a class") devised by Rabinowitz and Travers (1953) has been found effective in predicting which student teachers would be judged most competent by their faculty, based on knowledge of faculty expectations regarding student behavior (Page & Travers, 1953b). Stern, Stein, and Bloom (1956) reported similar prognostic success with spontaneous drawings of relevant work situations ("draw a picture of a _____ at

work") for graduate students in teaching, theological school, and physics. They also described the use of the Rorschach and TAT in predicting faculty judgments of student role-fulfillment, in a procedure used with similar effectiveness by Page and Travers (1953a) and by Ohlsen and Schultz (1955) for the same purpose with student teachers.

The Criterion Problem

Supervisors' ratings. In all of these studies projective test data have been employed to detect presumed signs of pathology, as a negative index of performance. But the clinical judgments in these cases were guided by specific criteria—by inferences regarding the extent to which personality characteristics of the students appeared to be reasonably compatible with behaviors implied in the role-expectations of the faculty. This may be the reason for their success.

In the more conventional prediction studies, the faculty ratings or judgments of teaching success have generally been used without further analysis or modification, even though these ratings are transparently imperfect measures of the criterion performance. As Tiegs remarked long ago:

evaluating teaching success has consisted of taking a somewhat arbitrary list of factors, rather general in nature, and undefined either in general terms or in terms of the varying degrees in which evidence of them might be expected to manifest itself, and then guessing at what the answer should be. Under these conditions, it is natural that school officials, with their varied personal equipment, training, objectives, attitudes, and professional environment, should agree neither on the facts of a particular case, nor on the significance of such facts in relation to teaching success (Tiegs, 1928, p. 77).

It is essential to remember that "teaching success" is not in itself an operational criterion. "It is, rather, a *standard of performance* in a specific work situation that some individuals are said to manifest. These judgments are made by significant others in their environment" (Stern, Stein, & Bloom, 1956, p. 32). The basis for these judgments may or may not seem appropriate when viewed from other standards, but they do constitute the only administratively sanctioned empirical target available to the assessor.

In fact, some evidence suggests that supervisors' ratings may even be influenced by factors which are irrelevant, if not actually antithetical, to effective classroom performance. Wandt (1954) found that teachers with most favorable attitudes toward administrators received superior ratings from their principals. Fink (1953) reported a significant correlation between principals' ratings of success and teachers' ethnocentrism scores, suggesting that principals tend to favor more rigid, conforming personalities among their teachers.

Pupils' ratings. Since pupils prefer teachers whose attitudes, as measured by the Minnesota Teacher Attitude Inventory, are receptive and permissive (Kearney & Rocchio, 1955a), it is not surprising to find that principals' ratings of teacher-pupil rapport do not agree consistently with pupils' ratings or with teachers' MTAI scores (Callis, 1953; Leeds, 1952). A number of other investigators have confirmed the lack of correspondence between ratings by supervisors, colleagues, and students (Borg, 1957; Grim, Hoyt, & Mayo, 1954; Willard, 1957). The discrepancy would be even more marked if the student ratings in these studies were further subdivided on the basis of a dimension—pupils' values with respect to teachers—explored by Della Piana and Gage (1955); the correlation between the MTAI and pupil ratings was high ($r = .57$) for pupils with strong measured affective values, but low ($r = .05$) for pupils with strong cognitive values.

A number of statistical studies of student ratings, chiefly factor analytic, have been made in recent years (e.g., Bendig, 1953, 1954, 1955; Coffman, 1954; Gibb, 1955; Lovell & Haner, 1955; Medley & Klein, 1956). Strikingly similar factors have emerged, involving *empathy* (friendly, democratic be-

havior) and *competence* (systematic, organized behavior). These correspond closely to the qualities reported by Hart (1934) from descriptions of best- and least-liked teachers by 10,000 high school seniors. Trabue (1953) found that the responses of 820 college executives to a check list of desirable traits for lower-division college teachers reflected similar values. It seems evident that the verbalized teacher image is a widely shared and extremely stable stereotype. Symonds (1955) noted, however, that the stability of this image is of little help in predicting effective teaching since the great variety of classroom behaviors among effective teachers seems to preclude the use of observation as a tool for distinguishing effective teaching; ". . . the basic determinants are to be found in the personality structure of the teacher rather than in outward behavior" (Symonds, 1955, p. 309).

Training versus in-service criteria. Another source of bias in supervisor ratings has been reported by Seagoe (1957), who found that prospective teachers rejected by a screening board were likely to have higher verbal intelligence as measured by the Miller Analogies Test than those who were accepted, despite the fact that the MAT scores were correlated positively with success in practice teaching. These results illustrate the frequently noted inconsistency between achievement in a teacher-training program and subsequent success as a teacher. The lack of comparability between ratings obtained in the training situation and those made later in the teaching situation has been clearly revealed in a factor analysis of ratings from both sources by Bach (1952), who found that critic teachers and principals emphasized different characteristics to the extent that no relationship could be found between practice-teaching ability and success in the field.

Insofar as judgments of training and of later performance are uncorrelated, there is no justification for assuming that selecting more effective trainees will have the effect of raising ultimate professional standards. At least the effect will not be the same as that of a concerted attempt to screen on the basis of predicted success in actual teaching. The present evidence of bias and inadequacy in administrative judgments of teaching success must be evaluated more carefully, as was done by McCall (1952), in terms of the relationship of such judgments to more objective measures of teacher effectiveness in the classroom. These objective criteria must become in time more compatible with the objectives of teacher-training programs. Otherwise, we shall continue to be confronted by the present anomalous situation in which the practice teachers who are strongest by academic standards are least likely to persist or be viewed favorably by their supervisors on the job.

The development and acceptance of such criteria will, however, bring another problem in its wake. If the screening process becomes too effective, mavericks and dissenters will be eliminated along with other potential academic failures. There is no evidence that nonconformists are likely to make lasting contributions out of proportion to their numbers in any given field. Neither is there evidence that the outstanding students are the greatest source of new developments. It seems likely that we shall always need to maximize variety in training institutions so that some graduates will reflect current values and others will flatly reject them.

THE TEACHING PROCESS

TEACHER ATTITUDES TOWARD PUPILS

Several of the studies just cited suggest that pupils value warmth and friendliness in their teachers. Ryans (1960) found this to be one of three factors characterizing teachers' behaviors, attitudes, and beliefs. Jenkins and Lippitt (1951) also reported this as a dominant theme in teacher interview and questionnaire responses but found that power and control were also a persistent aspect of teacher-pupil relationships, as reported by both teachers and pupils. The conflict felt by teachers between the problem of discipline and the desire to be liked by their pupils appears to be a major source of anxiety for them (Alexander, 1951; Travers, Rabinowitz, & Nemovicher, 1953).

It comes as no surprise then to find that teachers have regarded stealing, cheating, and other forms of extroversive pupil behavior threatening to classroom protocol, as the most serious kinds of behavior problems in children (Hunter, 1957; Mitchell, 1943; Slobetz, 1950; G. A. W. Stouffer, 1956; C. E. Thompson, 1940; Wickman, 1928). The teachers indicate, conversely, that more withdrawn forms of behavior, including hypersensitivity, suspiciousness, and fearfulness, are among the least serious. Teachers evidently codify desirable and problem behaviors in terms of classroom decorum rather than student mental health.

This attitude toward classroom behavior problems is seemingly widespread, being found even in a French study (Xydias, 1956) cited by Coladarci (1958). Some observers have nonetheless reported evidence of increasing teacher sophistication. O. G. Johnson (1956) and Slobetz (1950, 1951) both felt that elementary school teachers were employing constructive remedial procedures in dealing with the withdrawn child. Teachers and students appear to share similar conceptions of educational values (Jervis & Congdon, 1958) and of the ideal student (Brown, 1960; Fager, 1958; Schuhle, 1957). They even prefer students who are also most liked by other students (Gronlund, 1953). Teachers are moderately successful, moreover, in judging how the students themselves feel about one another.

A number of studies . . . [Bonney, 1943, 1947; Gage, Leavitt, & Stone, 1955; Gronlund, 1951, 1955, 1956] have investigated the extent to which teachers are accurate in judging the sociometric status of their pupils. Both student teachers and experienced teachers at the elementary and the secondary school level have been included in the studies. In general, the teachers' judgments have ranged from "near zero" to "near perfect" with an average accuracy score of approximately .60.* Although some teachers seemed to have more ability than others in judging the sociometric status of their pupils, even the best judges made rather large errors in judging individual pupils (Gronlund, 1959, pp. 10–11).

They tend also to underestimate students' desires for self-improvement (Schuhle, 1957), perceive fewer differences between students than psychologists do (Stern, Stein, & Bloom, 1956), and are no better judges than the students themselves when it comes to predicting who is going to leave school or make the honor roll (Ullman, 1957).

The most extensive research on teacher attitudes has involved the differences between teacher- and pupil-centered orientations to teaching. A projective measure for this purpose was developed by Alexander (1950). Attitude questionnaires involving similar dimensions include the Minnesota Teacher Attitude Inventory (Cook, Leeds, & Callis, 1949, 1951; Leeds, 1950), the Teacher Characteristics Schedule (TCS) (Ryans, 1955, 1960), and the Teacher Preference Schedules (TPS) (Stern, Masling, et al., 1960). The TCS also provides measures of teacher responsibility and imaginativeness; the TPS includes nine other areas of teacher motivation and attitude besides dominance.

The California F scale (Adorno, Frenkel-Brunswik, Levinson, & Sanford, 1950), a prototype for much of this work, has itself been used in the study of classroom behavior by McGee (1955). Various modifications of the F scale employing more indirect, non-ideological items (Stern, 1958; Webster, Sanford, & Freedman, 1955) should prove especially useful for future studies of classroom teachers.

ATTITUDE CHANGE

The modification of teacher attitudes in a desirable direction has been the objective of

* This correlation coefficient indicates a moderate positive relationship between the teachers' judgments and the sociometric results . . . (Gronlund, 1959, p. 11).

many training programs. Two studies report modifications of teacher judgments about pupils toward greater accord with those of child specialists, in both cases as a result of closer interaction between teacher and professional in conjunction with specific classroom problems (Haring, Stern, & Cruickshank, 1958; Stern, Stein, & Bloom, 1956). The Haring study reports the use of several specially devised tests for measuring changes in the attitudes of teachers toward exceptional children. The limitations of conventional training programs in modifying teacher attitudes were shown in studies (Travers & Rabinowitz, 1953; Rabinowitz & Travers, 1955) that yielded evidence of improvement in the areas of pupil control, pupil-teacher tension, and mutual pupil-teacher participation after training in a progressive program but not in a conventional or conservative one. No differences between students in the two programs were found before or during the training period.

Test Scores versus Behavioral Changes

These measures of change in test performance are less meaningful, however, than demonstrations of change in actual behavior would be. The possible impact of present-day training programs might be inferred from the fact that young teachers are more personal, informal, and integrative in their role than older teachers (Valenti, 1952). Yet it seems more likely that the idealism of the young teacher becomes tempered with experience. Oliver (1953) reported that elementary school teachers' responses to a check list of educational beliefs were consistent with modern educational philosophy, but classroom observations of the same teachers indicated that these beliefs were not implemented in the classroom. Oliver attributed the discrepancy to a failure to provide teachers with a genuine understanding of principles and of techniques with which to put them into practice. McNassor (1951), however, reported that teachers who attended a summer workshop on teaching methods and interpersonal relationships found neither enthusiasm nor support for new techniques from the local authorities.

The implication of these studies is that training in modern techniques is not as widely acceptable, or as effective, as it ought to be. But there are limits to the capacities of teachers themselves to adapt to the changing requirements of their profession. In an unusual study by Withall (1956), photograph and tape recordings of a teacher presumably skilled in individualizing instruction revealed less than optimal face-to-face interactions, and deliberate efforts to redistribute time and attention were unsuccessful. Willard (1955) suggested that the range of learning experiences provided by teachers is a function of their own maturity as adults, lending further weight to Raths's (1951) recommendations regarding the value of assessing emotional needs in teacher training.

These studies raise provocative questions, but, like much of social science literature, they are more notable as demonstrations that some polemic assumption of the investigator is not controverted by the evidence than as confirmation of formal hypotheses. As demonstrations, however, they are of great value in focusing attention on significant problems.

CLASSROOM IMPACT OF TEACHER ATTITUDES

The basic assumption underlying all these studies is that teacher attitudes are significant for student learning, but direct evidence on this point is surprisingly meager. Several investigators, finding that the more popular and better-adjusted pupils are the better achievers, have concluded that a good classroom climate will therefore promote achievement (Buswell, 1953; Kasper, 1956). A review of educational efforts from a psychiatric orientation has been contributed by Mones (1955). But Hawkes and Egbert (1954) obtained negative results in their attempt to relate empathy to teaching success, and Gage, Leavitt, and Stone (1955) found in Grades 4–6 that teachers' understanding of the intellectual and personal problems of their pupils was not significantly correlated with pupils' ratings; their accuracy in predicting pupils' sociometric choices was, however, moderately correlated ($r = .28$) with pupils' ratings of the teacher on "Does your teacher know which pupils you like best in this class?"

Silberman (1957) reported no relationship between the teacher's use of praise or reproof, or the class's expenditure of time on various subjects, and pupils' gains in reading scores in a classroom setting. In their unpublished follow-up study with the Teacher Preference Schedules referred to previously (Stern, Masling, Denton, Henderson, & Levin, 1960), these investigators could find no relation between teachers' expressed attitudes or gratifications and either pupil behavior, sociometric structure, or performance. But they did find significant correlations between pupil vocabulary and the teachers' Activities Index scores for achievement ($r = .58$), emotionality ($r = .44$), and humanism ($r = .59$). Pupils' spelling level was correlated with teachers' AI scores for achievement ($r = .61$), counteraction ($r = .43$), fantasied achievement ($r = .41$), emotionality ($r = .43$), humanism ($r = .51$), and understanding ($r = .44$). Pupils' IQs were held constant for the several classes and schools included in the study.

A recent study by Heil, Powell, and Feifer (1960) stands alone in relating pupil achievement to the interaction between teacher and pupil personalities. Three teacher and four pupil personality types were identified by means of special instruments. The various teacher-pupil combinations were compared in terms of measures of pupil achievement, teacher knowledge, and classroom ratings. The well-integrated (self-controlling) teachers were the most effective with all types of students, whereas the weakly integrated (fearful) teachers were ineffective with everyone except the "strivers." The third type of teacher (turbulent) identified by these investigators is similar to the defensively intellectual natural scientist described by Kubie (1953, 1954) and Roe (1953) and, even earlier, by Anna Freud (1946, pp. 172 ff.) in relation to intellectualization as a mechanism of defense for the adolescent ego. The turbulent group was found to be effective with children who had been categorized as "conformers" or "strivers," particularly in mathematics and science achievement where these teachers also excelled. They were ineffective with "opposers" and "waverers," two classroom problem types requiring interpersonal skills to which these teachers were totally indifferent.

Other investigators have demonstrated that teachers' attitude scale scores are consistent with their classroom behaviors (Alexander, 1950; McGee, 1955; Ryans, 1960). They have also shown that authoritarian teachers who curtail pupil decisions and expect conformity can readily be distinguished from nonauthoritarian types who encourage the child to make decisions about classroom activities on his own (Anderson & Brewer, 1945). But an extensive analysis by Brookover (1945) showed no advantage for either type in their effectiveness as teachers, as they were judged by pupils, parents, or supervisors.

Methodological Problems in Observation

It may well be that the major problem in this area lies with the limitations of observation of the teacher's classroom performance. Although the various studies just cited all report adequate observer agreement, Mitzel and Rabinowitz (1953) have shown that the presence of the observers may disrupt the classroom. Their observers visited the same classrooms for eight weeks, but the ratings for the first four weeks were treated separately from those for the last four weeks. An analysis of variance of the observation scores indicated good observer agreement, but the teachers actually showed marked fluctuations in behavior from one occasion to the next and the differences between them did not

become clear until the second half of the series. Presumably these later fluctuations reflected the lessened influence of the observers on the teacher. (Other problems in the use and analyses of observation methods are treated in Chapter 6.)

THE LEARNING ENVIRONMENT

Pupil achievement and ratings reflecting student or supervisor satisfaction with the teacher are not the only criteria by means of which to evaluate the effectiveness of a given teacher or attitudinal type. The extensive series of studies of the impact of the teacher's personality in the kindergarten and primary classrooms by Anderson and his associates (Anderson, 1939; Anderson & Brewer, 1945, 1946; Anderson, Brewer, & Reed, 1946) are reviewed and evaluated in Chapter 6.

Sociometry—widely used for describing the pattern of interpersonal relations in small groups—is considered in some detail in Chapter 7. Here it need only be noted that sociometric data have yielded useful indexes of the impact of variations in teaching approach (Cook, 1945; Dahlke & Monahan, 1949; Havighurst & Neugarten, 1957; Hollingshead, 1949).

The impact of specific teachers and their attitudes on student learning, however, has actually been subjected to only limited investigation. On the other hand, a great deal of work has been done in studying the relationship between student learning and classroom techniques presumed to be associated with certain teacher attitudes. The reasons for this oblique approach are largely tactical: It is easier to manipulate contrived teaching roles in an experimental study than it is to sample large numbers of teachers in order to select the few classrooms in which the required roles appear spontaneously. But there are numerous other reasons which account for the particular line of development to which studies of classroom climate have been constrained.

Classroom Climate[1]

The introduction of Rogerian nondirective counseling in the 1940's (Rogers, 1942) laid the groundwork for a new orientation toward teaching which was to have a profound impact in the postwar era. Rogers firmly insisted on the integrity of the client as the initiating agent responsible in every sense for his own destiny. This view struck a responsive chord among educators raised in the Dewey tradition. Nondirective client-centered therapy appeared to offer a point of departure for classroom instruction supported by psychological theory, educational practice, and ethical belief.

Aspects of the Rogerian position were anticipated by several other contemporary personality theorists (Angyal, 1941; Lecky, 1945). The now classic Lewinian studies, done in the late 1930's and recently summarized (White & Lippitt, 1960), demonstrated that acts of student aggression are precipitated by rigid authoritarian leadership but are absent in a democratic classroom atmosphere. The Anderson studies antedated both of these developments. But perhaps the most important factor in support of the new position was the postwar reaction against manipulation and coercion making itself felt in the permissive doctrines of preschool pediatrics.

In some hands the student-centered classroom introduced an exciting forum for the mutual education of student and teacher, contributing to the clarification and reduction of the cultural distance between them (see Jencks, 1960; Riesman, 1959a, 1959b). The theoretical significance of nondirective techniques for educational practice is discussed in Chapters 6, 10, and 23. Here we are concerned with the methodological implications of studies of student-centered classroom climates for research on teaching.

Table 2 classifies the results of 34 studies designed explicitly to measure the differences between student- and teacher-centered instruction in their effect on either the acquisition of information, changes in attitude, or both. These studies vary considerably in procedures, learning tasks, measuring tools, teaching skill, and student characteristics. Nevertheless, some general trends seem evident.

Effect of Teaching Method on Cognitive Achievement

Student-centered achievement. In general, it would appear that the amount of cognitive gain is largely unaffected by the autocratic or democratic tendencies of the instructor. The majority of investigators who have attempted to measure differences in achievement report no particular advantage for either approach. The two exceptions in favor of nondirective teaching are both somewhat ambiguous. Faw (1949) found that a student-centered psychology class had higher grades on three objective examinations administered during the course than either an instructor-centered or alternating-treatment group, but all three sections received lectures along with the special discussion treatment and they were each taught by the experimentalist himself. Thompson and Tom (1957), working with high school students taking vocational agriculture, reported that the student-centered classes were superior in their knowledge of agriculture but not in their ability to solve relevant problems.

The five negative cases are somewhat more convincing, although it is not entirely clear whether the results in these cases are attributable to inappropriate sets rather than to inherent limitations of the nondirective procedures. Asch (1951), for example, compared the performance of his student-centered psychology class on an objective test for which no preparation was required since the students were grading themselves, unlike the control class which took the same test as a final examination.

Other discussion methods. These results resemble those obtained in the many studies of

---

[1] The material in this and the following section has been adapted in part from other publications (Stern, 1960a, 1960b, 1962a, 1962b).

TABLE 2

RELATIVE ADVANTAGES OF NONDIRECTIVE OVER DIRECTIVE INSTRUCTION
IN INFLUENCING TWO TYPES OF LEARNING OUTCOME

Attitude Change (Self or Others)	Gain in Achievement of Cognitive Knowledge and Understanding		
	Negative	No Difference or Unmeasured	Positive
Positive	Asch (1951)[a]	Anderson & Brewer (1946) Anderson, Brewer, & Reed (1946) Anderson & Kell (1954) Bills (1952)[a] Bills (1956)[a] Bovard (1951a, 1951b) Bovard (1952) DeLong (1949)[b] Di Vesta (1954) Flanders (1951)[a] Gross (1948) Lewin, Lippitt, & White (1939)[a] Patton (1955)[a] Wieder (1954)[b]	No cases reported
No Difference or Unmeasured	Brookover (1943, 1945)[c] Burke (1955) Calvin, Hoffman, & Harden (1957) Guetzkow, Kelly, & McKeachie (1954)[b]	Deignan (1955)[a] Eglash (1957) Fersh (1949) Johnson & Smith (1953)[c] Krumboltz & Farquhar (1957) Lagey (1956) Landsman (1950)[c] McKeachie (1954a)[b] McKeachie (1954b) Slomowitz (1955)[a] Ward (1956) R. P. Watson (1956)[c] Wispé (1951)[b]	Faw (1949)[c] Thompson & Tom (1957)
Negative	No cases reported	No cases reported	No cases reported

[a] Expressed student satisfaction with student-centered class.
[b] Expressed student dissatisfaction with student-centered class.
[c] Mixed student reaction to student-centered class.

lecture versus discussion methods. There is apparently little difference between the two, although there may be some slight advantage for the lecture method in promoting mastery of factual materials, and better retention and interpretation associated with discussion (Stovall, 1958; see also Chapter 23 of this Handbook). As Bloom (1953) has shown, however, more relevant student thinking and more passive problem-solving go on during a discussion than during a lecture. These differences should favor discussion (and stu-dent-centered) techniques, but a considerable amount of irrelevant thinking occurs in either type of class as it is typically taught. The extraordinarily superior achievement of the Pennsylvania State University "pyramid plan" classes (Davage, cited by McKeachie, Ch. 23) composed of six freshmen and six sophomores, and led by a faculty-supervised senior with the assistance of two juniors, illustrates what can be accomplished when sufficient care has gone into the planning of any learning experience. The "pyramid plan" students did better on both information and problem-solving tests, worked harder, and became more favorably oriented toward the subject-matter field than did students in a conventional lecture-film-demonstration class.

Attitude Changes in Nondirective Groups

Regardless of whether the investigator was concerned with attitudes toward a cultural outgroup, toward other participants in the class, or toward the self, the results generally have indicated that nondirective instruction facilitates a shift in a more favorable, acceptant direction. Epley (1953) reported that students with positive reactions to their teachers are more likely to grow tolerant than those with negative feelings, presumably because the former are more receptive to the attitudes of their teachers. It will be noted in Table 2 (see footnotes) that most of the studies reporting favorable attitude changes were also accompanied by positive student reactions to nondirective instruction. Other investigators (Bills, 1956; Smith & McGrath, 1948) have called attention to the similarity between student-centered teaching and group therapy in encouraging the self-exploration of emotional attitudes. The effectiveness of these techniques in modifying attitudes is probably attributable to the fact that norms are more readily established in groups characterized by a high rate of communication among the participants. But the latter condition is not necessarily limited to nondirective groups (McKeachie, 1954a, 1958). The group dynamics literature offers a number of other applications regarding group behavior which are relevant to classroom teaching (N. B. Henry, 1960).

Student Reactions to Nondirective Instruction

At least as many students feel dissatisfied, frustrated, or anxious in a nondirective classroom as consider it valuable. Of the 18 coded entries in Table 2 indicating student reaction, nine were predominantly favorable, four unfavorable, and five were mixed. As McKeachie (1951; see also Ch. 23) has noted, these ambiguous results may well reflect the anxiety generated by the lack of formal structure characteristic of the student-centered classroom. Students may place a high value on the social and emotional opportunities offered by such techniques; they also tend to express concern about the adequacy and level of the discussion.

Selective objects of student response. The quality of student-centered instruction encountered by some of these students may in fact have been less than ideal. In its heyday, nondirectivism in the classroom verged on mere leaderless listening. It could be seen as a refuge for those whose feelings of inadequacy as teachers were more readily assuaged by relinquishing than by exercising control. But studies by Wispé (1951) and Patton (1955) both demonstrated that student attitudes toward particular classroom atmospheres were highly selective. Student-centered instruction was preferred by students who reject traditional sources of authority, have strong needs for demonstrating their personal independence, and are characterized by a high drive for academic achievement. These findings are consistent with the findings by Koenig and McKeachie (1959) that flexible, nonauthoritarian women with a high achievement need prefer independent study to lectures and participate more in small groups than do rigid women.

Student preferences for particular types of classroom atmospheres, as demonstrated by these studies, were actually noted but given little significance in an early report by Lewin, Lippitt, and White (1939). They had observed that an Army officer's son was one of the few children to prefer the autocratic climate. Johnson and Smith (1953) found that a member of a student cooperative was the most enthusiastic member of their democratic section. If we can assume that people work most effectively in situations which conform to their preferences (N. Gross, 1959a), then

Wispé's (1951) and Patton's (1955) studies suggest that the absence of clear differences in learning outcome between student-centered and teacher-centered classes may be due to a failure to articulate teaching technique and student need. The particular combination of characteristics continually reappearing here—rebelliousness and intellectuality—suggests that the relevant characteristics are broader and more complex than a mere preference or distaste for group discussion.

Interactions between classroom climate and student personality. Haythorn, et al. (1953, 1956a, 1956b) and Schutz (1955) have shown significant relationships between the characteristic performances of small groups and the essentially autocratic or equalitarian personality traits of the group members. The implications of such relationships among situation, personality, and learning in higher education were investigated initially by Stern, Stein, and Bloom (1956). They found that authoritarianism, as measured by the Inventory of Beliefs, was related to (1) ethnic and religious background, (2) lack of preparation, dislike, and underachievement in the humanities and social sciences, (3) ability to adjust to academic life at the University of Chicago, and (4) vocational choice and preparation. These differences were confirmed in subsequent studies of students at Syracuse University by Gladstein (1957), who also related authoritarianism to kinds of study activity and classroom participation, and by Stern (1960a), who summarized differences in intelligence, grade-point average, family socioeconomic level, geographic origin, political affiliation, and ethnocentric prejudice among authoritarian and antiauthoritarian Syracuse University students.

Stern and Cope (Stern, 1962a) then showed that a group of authoritarian students, segregated in a special section of the citizenship course at Syracuse University but not identified to their instructor, achieved significantly more on a common objective final examination than comparable authoritarian students scattered among conventional sections of the same course. The segregated authoritarian students also did as well as nonauthoritarian students in either conventional sections or in a comparable segregated class taught by the same experimentally naïve instructor. For the nonauthoritarians, the segregation treatment had no effect; they showed no gains and succeeded mainly in demonstrating a competence already enjoyed prior to taking the course. Mayhew (Dressel, 1958), however, reported that a section of nonauthoritarian students in a social science class at Michigan State University, taught by nondirective methods, performed significantly better than the rest of the student body enrolled in the course. But the same methods applied in a section of authoritarian students elicited such violent reactions that the instructor felt impelled to shift to formal lectures.[2] Further support for these findings is implied in the results of studies by Calvin, Hoffman, and Harden (1957), Haigh and Schmidt (1956), McCollough and Van Atta (cited in McKeachie, Ch. 23), and Ward (1956).

THE ACADEMIC ENVIRONMENT

The Stern-Cope study cited above indicated that the pedagogical techniques which proved effective with the authoritarian students—as described in the daily diary maintained by the instructor of the experimental sections (Stern, 1962a)—cannot be categorized as either directive or nondirective. Left to their own devices in a course where they are ill prepared and usually antagonistic, these students would have perpetuated their deficiencies. Assigned en bloc to an instructor prepared to cope with their peculiarities, they came to enjoy and profit from a classroom atmosphere specifically appropriate for them. But the techniques employed by this instructor have no name or classification. Here is a pointed indication of our lack of both (1) a formal system of pedagogical theory and (2) knowledge about the relationships between particular classroom procedures and their educational consequences.

---

[2] Personal communication from L. B. Mayhew.

Significant learning experiences are not limited to events mediated directly by the teacher, nor to the classroom alone. In R. P. Watson's (1956) study of the interaction between student personality and academic climate, the authoritarian and nonauthoritarian students differed most in the type of testing atmosphere each found most congenial. Bendig and Hountras (1959) found that authoritarian students prefer a high degree of departmental control of instruction. Both Moore and Popham (1959; cited in McKeachie, Ch. 23) and Hoehn and Saltz (1956) found that nondirective out-of-class interviews have a greater influence on academic adjustment or achievement than directive ones. The latter study also noted that the effective nondirective interviews were those which became "gripe" sessions and that these helped anxious students but not rigid ones.

Effects on Student Values

Newcomb's (1943) classic study of changes in student values at Bennington was interpreted in terms of faculty impact. The faculty's interest in social and political issues appeared in this case to have been internalized by the juniors and seniors, and especially by the student leaders, thus presenting an exceptionally consistent position to each new incoming class and pulling them from family conservatism to school liberalism. Although other studies bear on the educational implications of close teacher-student identifications (Epley, 1953; Goldsen, Williams, Suchman, & Rosenberg, 1960; J. Henry, 1955; Hughes, 1959; Stern & Scanlon, 1958), the impact of teachers as bearers of new values is not entirely clear. Studies of other institutions suggest weaker and less coherent faculty positions (Jacob, 1957; Lazarsfeld & Thielens, 1958) than Newcomb found at Bennington, and stronger countervailing pressures from the student body.

Waller's (1932) pioneering account of the conflict between the values of the student and the educator, and between the latter and the society outside (see pp. 432–433, below), has been substantiated in a number of recent investigations (Coleman, 1959, 1960, 1961a, 1961b; Cutright, 1960; Gordon, 1955, 1957a). These studies find the adolescent culture antithetical to academic achievement, indifferent to both personal character development and the national welfare, and characterized by privatism and unabashed selfishness (Gillespie & Allport, 1955; Jacob, 1957). But Riesman (1959b) and Jencks (1960) suggest that the seeming docility and uncontentiousness of the student is simply a confirmation of the educator's irrelevance to contemporary student culture, and Heilman (1959) contends that the healthy skepticism and vigorous individualism of contemporary youth are a considerable improvement over the self-conscious nonconformity and tense independence of their critics' generation.

Intellectual Productivity

The picture is not so bleak everywhere. Teachers in some of the elite liberal arts colleges appear to be especially effective in motivating students toward high academic achievement. Knapp and Greenbaum (1953) attributed the high productivity of future scholars and scientists from these schools to the intellectual atmosphere to which the students are exposed. More recently, Jacob (1957) called attention to the "peculiar potency" and distinctive institutional atmosphere of this small minority among American colleges. Dressel and Mayhew (1954) have noted that schools which go the furthest in reducing authoritarian attitudes and increasing critical thinking, as measured by high gains in scores on the Inventory of Beliefs, Critical Thinking in the Natural Sciences, and Critical Thinking in the Social Sciences, have particular characteristics which help to maximize their focus on the student: (1) they are residential; (2) they are based on integrated general education programs with full administrative support; and (3) they give primary emphasis to the intellectual growth of the students. Eddy's (1959) analysis of the colleges with the greatest impact on their students also calls attention to the consistency with which their educational objectives are given expression in other aspects of academic life, including the prevailing level of academic aspiration, the characteristic interpersonal style among students and faculty, the channels available for intergroup communication, and the arrangement of the physical plant.

Analyses of responses to the College Characteristics Index (CCI) from over 6,000 students at 66 colleges (Stern 1960b, 1962a, 1962b) suggested that the teachers at the private liberal arts colleges are unique in the consistency with which they stress intellectual achievement, make themselves available for informal discussion, encourage student efforts toward personal independence and responsibility, and minimize the constraints of custodial personnel practices. Hutchins (1961), working with a modification of the CCI, reported that the faculty at research- and teaching-oriented medical schools stress student independence, in contrast to clinically oriented schools where student compliance is emphasized. Thistlethwaite (1959a, 1959b, 1960) administered another modified version of the CCI to 1,500 National Merit Scholars and Certificate of Merit winners at 327 American colleges and universities, and concluded that:

. . . college environments characterized by faculty affiliation or enthusiasm or faculty emphasis upon achievement, humanism, or independence are associated with increased motivation to seek advanced degrees in the arts, humanities, and social sciences; college environments characterized by a lack of faculty emphasis upon student compliance are associated with increased motivation to seek advanced degrees in the natural and biological sciences (Thistlethwaite, 1960, p. 228).

Superior School or Superior Scholar?

Students majoring in the various sciences describe their most stimulating teachers in terms which are consistent with those they use to describe their respective college environments (Thistlethwaite, 1960). But it has also been noted that there is a significant tendency for students with particular needs to be found at institutions with appropriate press (Stern, 1962a). Even within the same institution there may be subgroups of students with divergent needs and perceptions of press, corresponding to characteristic variations between vocational fields (Siegelman & Peck, 1960; Stern, 1960b).

The strength of the adolescent culture, and the differential representation of this culture in schools at various levels of academic quality, have led some observers to attribute the distinctive ethos of the more productive, high-potency colleges to characteristics of the students rather than the institutions or their faculties (Riesman, 1958b, 1959d). The same position has been adopted by investigators at the Center for the Study of Higher Education at Berkeley (Heist, 1959, 1960; Heist, McConnell, Matsler, & Williams, 1961; McConnell & Heist, 1959). Working with the Omnibus Personality Inventory (Heist & Williams, 1957) and the Study of Values (Allport, Vernon, & Lindzey, 1951), they found support for Holland's earlier (1957, 1959a, 1959b) findings that the highly productive colleges also attract highly motivated students who are more inner-directed, socially independent, receptive to learning, nonauthoritarian, theoretical, aesthetic, unconventional, and creative. They quote Darley as stating that "the merit of certain institutions lies less in what they do to students than it does in the students to whom they do it" (Heist, et al., 1961, p. 362).

The interaction between student personality and teaching effectiveness. It does seem unlikely that the Bennington faculty (Newcomb, 1943) would have had as much influence with *any* group of girls, or could have been as effective even with their own students in an area involving less intellectually provocative material. Liberal attitudes are most marked among girls with social class backgrounds similar to those of the Bennington students (N. Miller, 1958). A comparison of a later generation of Bennington girls with a group of students equally high in academic motivation but attending a Roman Catholic women's college clearly suggested the difficulties the girls at either of these schools would encounter in trying to adapt to the environment described for the other school (Stern, 1960a, 1962a).

Studies of changes in student personality during the college years suggest new criteria of teaching effectiveness (Barton, 1959; Bidwell, 1960; Funkenstein, King, & Drolette, 1957; Heath, 1958, 1959; Sanford, 1959; Sanford, Webster, & Freedman, 1957; Stern, 1960b; and Wedge, 1958). But they also suggest still another significant dimension of the mix of people which contributes to the distinctive character of an institution. Students and staff, with varying social backgrounds, intellectual qualities, and personality characteristics are distributed differentially among American colleges. The particular combination at any given school undoubtedly plays an important role in determining the kinds of educational objectives likely to be stressed and the techniques which will be employed to achieve them.

THE TEACHER IN THE SOCIAL ORDER

The preceding section has touched on one source of conflict in the relationship between the academic subculture of the teacher and the larger culture from which the student comes. The teacher is also a member of this larger culture. Conflicts between school and community are going to be felt most keenly by the teachers themselves. Although some aspects of this conflict are occasionally made overt in our colleges and universities (Lazarsfeld & Thielens, 1958), it is more explicit in elementary and secondary education. The reasons for this difference probably lie in the differences in commitment between faculties in the public schools and those in higher education. The latter are less likely to perceive themselves, or to be perceived, as employees—either of communities or of parents.

A quarter of a century ago, the professional educator tended to see the middle-class background and identification of the public school teacher (Gardner, Gardner, & Loeb, 1942; Havighurst & Taba, 1949; Warner, et al., 1949) as a basis for indicting the schools. Warner, Havighurst, and Loeb (1944) and West (1945) were emphatic in their criticism of the schools as an agency for perpetuating social stratification through the social class biases of teachers, administrators, and the curriculum. Summaries of the literature on class structure and American education have been made by Brookover (1953, 1955a), N. Gross (1953, 1959b), and Havighurst and Neugarten (1957).

The postwar literature continued to provide examples of social class studies and their implications (Becker, 1952a, 1952b; Fisher, 1961; Loeb, 1953; Sims, 1951). There has been, however, an increasing tendency to see the relationship between the schools and society from a broader historical perspective (Floud & Halsey, 1959; Parsons, 1959; Rogoff, 1960). It has become evident, moreover, that the role of the teacher is an ambiguous one. Studies by Getzels and Guba (1954, 1955), S. A. Stouffer (1949), and Washburne (1953) have helped to clarify many of the stresses to which teachers in the public schools are exposed. Robbins (1953) and Brookover (1955a) presented useful summaries of research on social and cultural conflicts in the American public school system.

The teacher looks to the school administrator for support in legitimizing her role vis-à-vis the community (Becker, 1953), and finds satisfaction in her position to the extent that her expectations of the administration are fulfilled (Bidwell, 1955). Hence, it is to be expected that many aspects of the school-community conflict will be felt in the relationship between teachers and principals. An outstanding study of this problem in terms of leadership conflicts in the schools has been contributed by Seeman (1953,

1960). Brookover (1955b) suggested a framework for research on teacher and administrator roles which is also relevant here.

Many students of large-scale organizations believe that patterns in administrative process help determine the character of other organizational activities. Faculty interviews conducted by Caplow and McGee (1958) on personnel practices and by Lazarsfeld and Thielens (1958) on academic freedom are among the few empirical studies which attempt to relate faculty attitudes to administrative practices in higher education. Hemphill (1955) made an unusual study relating leadership style and departmental reputation. But research on the relationships of teachers' behaviors and characteristics to administrative processes, organizational structure, and other aspects of the institutional environment is at a rudimentary stage very little beyond the point to which it was advanced in the classic Western Electric studies (Roethlisberger & Dickson, 1939).

CONCLUDING REMARKS

Anatole France (1918) once wrote:

It is only by amusing oneself that one can learn. The whole art of teaching is only the art of awakening the natural curiosity of young minds for the purpose of satisfying it afterwards; and curiosity itself can be vivid and wholesome only in proportion as the mind is contented and happy. Those acquirements crammed by force into the minds of children simply clog and stifle intelligence. In order that knowledge be properly digested, it must have been swallowed with a good appetite (p. 198).

Although this passage was written before most of the research summarized in this chapter had been done, the problems posed here by France are still central to the study of neocognitive processes in teaching. The fundamental issue is not to amuse the child but to make learning an active, seeking process rather than a passive or even a negative one.

If children were not even entertained, let alone beguiled, the fault was presumed to lie with the teacher. Throughout the 1930's and 1940's mounting evidence appeared to confirm an image of the teacher as someone preoccupied with discipline and classroom decorum, quick to respond to any sign of public disturbance but insensitive to the private varieties, and otherwise rigid and authoritarian in manner. By the 1950's this image had shifted from the teacher to the administrator, reflecting either the success of the teacher-training institutions in inculcating a new set of values, or the success of the preceding generation of teachers as they moved on to positions of higher responsibility in the schools. In the present decade, the picture has shifted still further, from the school to the school board. As we have seen, teachers and administrators are more likely to be viewed sympathetically in the current literature, in contrast to the still unenlightened board member.

Other signs suggest that the pendulum-swing away from primitive authoritarianism has reached its limit and has begun to move back from the extremes of compulsive permissiveness. Taylor (1962) has formulated a basis for seeing such a countercyclical movement in the following terms:

the role of the teacher *is* different from that of the student, and no amount of mutual friendliness between student and teacher will change that role. . . . The teacher does not contribute to student freedom by withdrawal from a going relationship with the student subculture, nor by the older nondirective, permissive approach to students. On the other hand, the alternative to permissive attitudes is not a revival of institutional authority to control the students, any more than the answer to student requests for an examination system, grades, survey courses, and a conventional academic apparatus is to give it to them.

The alternative is to accept, without the edge of disapproval, the plain fact that the contemporary student is different from his predecessors and is at once more mature and less emotionally energetic than the more rebellious ones of the 1930s and 1940s . . . . [and that] the most powerful motivation, positively as well as negatively, lies in the expectations of the faculty for certain attitudes on the part of the students. . . . The danger to be avoided on the one hand is a kind of orthodox liberal piety which by matiness and good fellowship smothers a community with so much tolerance and understanding that everyone becomes a neutered, polite, and conformist liberal. The danger on the other hand is that if there are no clear-cut aims, rules, and procedures with sanctions and authority of some kind against violations, there is endless discussion, ambiguity, confusion, and emotional fatigue from devoting too much energy to discussion and not enough to getting on with the program (Taylor, 1962, p. 802).

Demonstrations in support of this new position may be expected to appear within the next few years. It seems even more likely that the growing emphasis on the need for theoretically oriented research (Guba & Getzels, 1955) will begin to make itself felt. The studies reviewed in this chapter belong by and large to an earlier phase of research, one which might more properly be characterized as polemic rather than experimental (see Good & Scates, 1954; Gordon, 1957b). Recent critiques of educational research by Brim (1958), N. Gross (1959a, 1959b), and Freedman (1960) clearly reflect the growing sophistication.

It is inevitable, however, that ideology should pass for theory in the absence of empirical facts. Basic to many of the issues in American education today is a concern with fundamental purposes: their definition and the means by which they may be achieved. The ferment is more than a reaction to the various charges of inadequacy leveled at education in the 1950's. It arises from anxiety over our ability to meet the unprecedented demands to be made in coming years, and from the realization of our lack of an educational philosophy appropriate to this new situation. John Dewey provided the cement which bound American education for a quarter-century. The conflicting elements held together for a time, even after the ce-

ment keeping them in place had leached away, but have now begun to fall apart. It has become increasingly clear that we need to know more about *what* we do and *how* this affects the student, regardless of the reasons which might be given as to *why* we do them.

Riesman (1958a, 1959c, 1959d) described something of the diversity in American education and called attention to the prevailing lack of information about learning environments and institutions. An adequate taxonomy for the classification of such situations has not yet been developed, although it seems clear that it will include such factors as (1) the need-press relationships of students and staff, (2) levels of academic, intellectual, and socioeconomic achievement, (3) patterns of administrative control and organizational structure, and (4) characteristics of the academic plant and related facilities.

A taxonomic classification of schools is only a step removed from the cataloguing of existing educational practices and the conditions with which they are associated. Such data might be used to develop more meaningful dimensions for the description of teaching than are available at present. The same dimensions would also provide a new basis for describing the institution itself. It would be particularly helpful if benchmarks could be established for institutions with differing types of objectives and clientele, providing measures of teaching relevant to the different needs of different types of institutions.

REFERENCES

Adorno, T. W., Frenkel-Brunswik, Else, Levinson, D. J., & Sanford, R. N. *The authoritarian personality.* New York: Harper, 1950.

Alexander, T. The prediction of teacher-pupil interaction with a projective test. *J. clin. Psychol.,* 1950, 6, 273–276.

Alexander, T. Certain characteristics of the self as related to affection. *Child Develpm.,* 1951, 22, 285–290.

Allport, F. H. The structuring of events: Outline of a general theory with applications to psychology. *Psychol. Rev.,* 1954, 61, 281–303.

Allport, F. H. *Theories of perception and the concept of structure.* New York: Wiley, 1955.

Allport, G. W. *Personality.* New York: Holt, 1937.

Allport, G. W. *The use of personal documents in psychological science.* New York: Social Science Research Council, Bull. 49, 1942.

Allport, G. W. *Personality and social encounter.* Boston: Beacon Press, 1960.

Allport, G. W., Vernon, P. E., & Lindzey, G. *Study of Values.* (Rev. ed.) Boston: Houghton Mifflin, 1951.

Anderson, H. H. Domination and social integration in the behavior of kindergarten children and teachers. *Genet. Psychol. Monogr.,* 1939, 21, 287–385.

Anderson, H. H., & Brewer, J. E. Studies of teachers' classroom personalities. I. Dominative and socially integrative behavior of kindergarten teachers. *Appl. Psychol. Monogr.,* 1945, No. 6.

Anderson, H. H., & Brewer, J. E. Studies of teachers' classroom personalities. II. Effects of teachers' dominative and integrative contacts on children's behavior. *Appl. Psychol. Monogr.,* 1946, No. 8.

Anderson, H. H., Brewer, J. E., & Reed, Mary F. Studies of teachers' classroom personalities. III. Follow-up studies of the effects of dominative and integrative contacts on children's behavior. *Appl. Psychol. Monogr.,* 1946, No. 11.

Anderson, R. P., & Kell, B. L. Student attitudes about participation in classroom groups. *J. educ. Res.,* 1954, 48, 255–267.

Angyal, A. *Foundations for a science of personality.* New York: Commonwealth Fund, 1941.

Asch, M. J. Nondirective teaching in psychology: An experimental study. *Psychol. Monogr.,* 1951, 65, No. 4 (Whole No. 321).

Atkinson, J. W. Personality dynamics. In P. R. Farnsworth & Q. McNemar (Eds.), *Annual review of psychology.* Vol. 11. Palo Alto, Calif.: Annual Reviews, 1960. Pp. 255–290.

Bach, J. O. Practice teaching success in relation to other measures of teaching ability. *J. exp. Educ.,* 1952, 21, 57–80.

Bales, R. F. *Interaction process analysis.* Cambridge, Mass.: Addison-Wesley, 1950.

Barker, M. E. Summary of the relation of personality adjustments of teachers to their efficiency in teaching. *J. educ. Res.,* 1948, 41, 664–675.

Barker, R. G., & Wright, H. F. *Midwest and its children.* Evanston, Ill.: Row, Peterson, 1955. (a)

Barker, R. G., Schoggen, M. F., & Barker, L. S. Hemerography of Mary Ennis. In A. Burton & R. E. Harris (Eds.), *Clinical studies of personality.* New York: Harper, 1955. Pp. 768–808. (b)

Barr, A. S. The measurement and prediction of teaching efficiency: A summary of investigations. *J. exp. Educ.,* 1948, 16, 203–283.

Barr, A. S., Eustace, D. E., & Noe, E. J. The measurement and prediction of teacher efficiency. *Rev. educ. Res.,* 1955, 25, 261–269.

Bartlett, F. C. *Remembering: A study in experimental and social psychology.* Cambridge, Eng.: Cambridge Univer. Press, 1932.

Barton, A. H. *Studying the effects of college education.* New Haven, Conn.: Hazen Foundation, 1959.

Beardslee, D. C., & O'Dowd, D. D. The college-student image of the scientist. *Science,* 1961, 133, 997–1001.

Beck, S. J. The science of personality: Nomothetic or idiographic. *Psychol. Rev.,* 1953, 60, 353–359.

Becker, H. S. Social class variation in teacher-pupil relationship. *J. educ. Sociol.,* 1952, 25, 451–465. (a)

Becker, H. S. The career of the Chicago public school teacher. *Amer. J. Sociol.,* 1952, 57, 470–477. (b)

Becker, H. S. The teacher in the authority system of the public school. *J. educ. Sociol.,* 1953, 27, 128–141.

Bendig, A. W. An inverted factor-analysis study of student-rated introductory psychology instructors. *J. exp. Educ.,* 1953, 21, 333–336.

Bendig, A. W. A factor-analysis of student ratings of psychology instructors on the Purdue scale. *J. educ. Psychol.,* 1954, 45, 385–393.

Bendig, A. W. Ability and personality characteristics of introductory psychology instructors rated competent and empathetic by their students. *J. educ. Res.,* 1955, 48, 705–709.

Bendig, A. W., & Hountras, P. T. Anxiety, authoritarianism, and student attitude toward departmental control of college instruction. *J. educ. Psychol.,* 1959, 50, 1–8.

Berelson, B. Content analysis. In G. Lindzey (Ed.), *Handbook of social psychology.* Cambridge, Mass.: Addison-Wesley, 1954. Pp. 488–522.

Bernreuter, R. G. *Bernreuter Personality Inventory.* Stanford, Calif.: Stanford Univer. Press, 1931.

Best, J. W. A study of certain selected factors underlying the choice of teaching as a profession. *J. exp. Educ.,* 1948, 17, 201–259.

Bidwell, C. E. The administrative role and satisfaction in teaching. *J. educ. Sociol.,* 1955, 29, 41–47.

Bidwell, C. E. *The American college and student personality.* New York: Social Science Research Council, 1960.

Bills, R. E. An investigation of student centered teaching. *J. educ. Res.,* 1952, 46, 316–317.

Bills, R. E. Personality changes during student centered teaching. *J. educ. Res.,* 1956, 50, 121–126.

Blake, R. R., & Ramsey, G. V. *Perception: An approach to personality.* New York: Ronald Press, 1951.

Blanchard, B. E. Some characteristics peculiar to educators. *J. educ. Res.,* 1953, 46, 513–523.

Bloom, B. S. Thought processes in lectures and discussion. *J. gen. Educ.,* 1953, 7, 160–169.

Blum, G. S. *Psychoanalytic theories of personality.* New York: McGraw-Hill, 1953.

Bogardus, E. S. Measuring social distances. *J. appl. Sociol.,* 1925, 9, 299–308.

Bonney, M. E. The constancy of sociometric scores and their relationship to teacher judgments of social success and to personality self-ratings. *Sociometry,* 1943, 6, 409–424.

Bonney, M. E. Sociometric study of agreement between teacher judgments and student choices. *Sociometry,* 1947, 10, 133–146.

Borg, W. R. Personality and interest measures as related to criteria of instructor effectiveness. *J. educ. Res.,* 1957, 50, 701–709.

Bovard, E. W., Jr. The experimental production of interpersonal affect. *J. abnorm. soc. Psychol.,* 1951, 46, 521–528. (a)

Bovard, E. W., Jr. The psychology of classroom interaction. *J. educ. Res.,* 1951, 45, 215–224. (b)

Bovard, E. W., Jr. Clinical insight as a function of group process. *J. abnorm. soc. Psychol.,* 1952, 47, 534–539.

Bowers, H. *Manual descriptive of the aptitude test for elementary school teachers-in-training.* Toronto, Ont.: Dent, 1948. (a)

Bowers, H. The pretraining selection of teachers. *School (Comb. Ed.),* 1948, 36, 490–491, 560–562. (b)

Boyce, A. C. Methods of measuring teachers' efficiency, *Yearb. nat. Soc. Stud. Educ.,* 1915, 14, Part II.

Brim, O. G., Jr. *Sociology and the field of education.* New York: Russell Sage Foundation, 1958.

Brody, W., & Powell, N. J. A new approach to oral testing. *Educ. psychol. Measmt,* 1947, 7, 289–298.

Brookover, W. B. The social roles of teachers and pupil achievement. *Amer. sociol. Rev.,* 1943, 8, 391–400.

Brookover, W. B. The relation of social factors to teaching ability. *J. exp. Educ.,* 1945, 13, 191–205.

Brookover, W. B. Teachers and stratification of American society. *Harvard educ. Rev.,* 1953, 23, 257–267.

Brookover, W. B. *A sociology of education.* New York: American Book, 1955. (a)

Brookover, W. B. Research on teacher and administrator roles. *J. educ. Sociol.,* 1955, 29, 2–13. (b)

Brown, D. R. Non-intellective qualities and the perception of the ideal student by college faculty. *J. educ. Sociol.,* 1960, 33, 269–278.

Bryan, J. G. A method for the exact determination of the characteristic equations and latent vectors of a matrix with applications to the discriminant function for more than two groups. Unpublished doctoral dissertation, Harvard Univer., 1950.

Burke, H. R. An experimental study of teaching methods in college freshman orientation course. Unpublished doctoral dissertation, Boston Univer., 1955.

Burt, C. L. Correlations between persons. *Brit. J. Psychol.,* 1937, 28, 59–96.

Burton, A., & Harris, R. E. (Eds.) *Case histories in clinical and abnormal psychology.* New York: Harper, 1947.

Burton, A., & Harris, R. E. (Eds.) *Clinical studies of personality.* New York: Harper, 1955.

Buswell, M. M. The relationship between the social structure of the classroom and the academic success of the pupils. *J. exp. Educ.,* 1953, 22, 37–52.

Callis, R. The efficiency of the Minnesota Teacher Attitude Inventory for predicting interpersonal relations in the classroom. *J. appl. Psychol.*, 1953, 37, 82–85.

Calvin, A. D., Hoffman, F. K., & Harden, E. L. The effect of intelligence and social atmosphere on group problem-solving behavior. *J. soc. Psychol.*, 1957, 45, 61–74.

Campbell, D. T., & Fiske, D. W. Convergent and discriminant validation by the multitrait-multimethod matrix. *Psychol. Bull.*, 1959, 56, 81–105.

Caplow, T., & McGee, R. J. *The academic marketplace.* New York: Basic Books, 1958.

Cartwright, D., & Zander, A. *Group dynamics.* (Rev. ed.) Evanston, Ill.: Row, Peterson, 1960.

Cattell, R. B. *Personality.* New York: McGraw-Hill, 1950.

Chapple, E. D. The interaction chronograph: Its evolution and present application. *Personnel,* 1949, 25, 295–307.

Christie, R., & Jahoda, Marie (Eds.) *Studies in the scope and method of "The Authoritarian Personality."* Glencoe, Ill.: Free Press, 1954.

Coffman, W. E. Determining students' concepts of effective teaching from their ratings of instructors. *J. educ. Psychol.*, 1954, 45, 277–286.

Coladarci, A. P. Educational psychology. In P. R. Farnsworth & Q. McNemar (Eds.), *Annual review of psychology.* Vol. 9. Palo Alto, Calif.: Annual Reviews, 1958. Pp. 189–212.

Coleman, J. S. Academic achievement and the structure of competition. *Harvard educ. Rev.*, 1959, 29, 330–351.

Coleman, J. S. The adolescent subculture and academic achievement. *Amer. J. Sociol.*, 1960, 65, 337–347.

Coleman, J. S. *The adolescent society.* Glencoe, Ill.: Free Press, 1961. (a)

Coleman, J. S. *Social climate in high schools.* Washington, D.C.: U. S. Office of Education Coop. Res. Monogr., 1961. (b)

Cook, L. A. An experimental sociographic study of a stratified 10th grade class. *Amer. sociol. Rev.*, 1945, 10, 250–261.

Cook, W. W., & Hoyt, C. J. Procedure for determining number and nature of norm groups for the MTAI. *Educ. psychol. Measmt,* 1952, 12, 562–573.

Cook, W. W., & Medley, D. M. The relationship between Minnesota Teacher Attitude Inventory scores and scores on certain scales of the Minnesota Multiphasic Personality Inventory. *J. appl. Psychol.*, 1955, 39, 123–129.

Cook, W. W., Leeds, C. H., & Callis, R. Predicting teacher-pupil relations. In *The evaluation of student teaching.* Lock Haven, Pa.: The Association for Student Teaching, State Teachers Coll., 1949. Pp. 66–80.

Cook, W. W., Leeds, C. H., & Callis, R. *Minnesota Teacher Attitude Inventory.* New York: Psychological Corp., 1951.

Coombs, C. H. A theory of psychological scaling. *Engng Res. Inst. Bull.,* Univer. of Michigan, 1952, No. 34.

Coombs, C. H. Theory and methods of social measurement. In L. Festinger & D. Katz (Eds.), *Research methods in the behavioral sciences.* New York: Dryden, 1953. Pp. 471–535.

Cronbach, L. J. The two disciplines of scientific psychology. *Amer. Psychologist,* 1957, 12, 671–694.

Cutright, Prudence. Students' decision to attend college. *J. educ. Sociol.*, 1960, 33, 292–299.

Dahlke, H. O., & Monahan, T. Problems in the application of sociometry to schools. *Sch. Rev.,* 1949, 57, 223–234.

Deignan, F. J. A comparison of the effectiveness of two group discussion methods. Unpublished doctoral dissertation, Boston Univer., 1955.

Della Piana, G. M., & Gage, N. L. Pupils' values and the validity of the Minnesota Teacher Attitude Inventory. *J. educ. Psychol.*, 1955, 46, 167–178.

DeLong, A. R. The relative effectiveness of two methods of teaching social science at the college level. Unpublished doctoral dissertation, Univer. of Michigan, 1949 (*Microfilm Abstr.,* 1949, 9, 162).

Di Vesta, F. J. Instructor-centered and student-centered approaches in teaching a human relations course. *J. appl. Psychol.*, 1954, 38, 329–335.

Dodge, A. F. What are the personality traits of the successful teacher? *J. appl. Psychol.*, 1943, 27, 325–337.

Dollard, J., & Miller, N. E. *Personality and psychotherapy.* New York: McGraw-Hill, 1950.

Donovan, F. R. *The school ma'am.* New York: Stokes, 1938.

Downey, June E. *The will-temperament and its testing*. Yonkers, N.Y.: World Book Co., 1924.

Dressel, P. L. *Evaluation in the Basic College at Michigan State University*. New York: Harper, 1958.

Dressel, P. L., & Mayhew, L. B. *General education: Explorations in evaluation*. Washington, D.C.: American Council on Education, 1954.

Ebel, R. L. Procedures for the analysis of classroom tests. *Educ. psychol. Measmt,* 1954, 14, 277–286.

Eckert, Ruth E., & Stecklein, J. E. Why teach in college? *NEA J.,* 1958, 47, 120.

Eckert, Ruth E., Stecklein, J. E., & Sagen, H. B. College faculty members view their jobs. *AAUP Bull.,* 1959, 45, 512–528.

Eddy, E. D., Jr. *The college influences on student character*. Washington, D.C.: American Council on Education, 1959.

Edwards, A. L. *Techniques of attitude scale construction*. New York: Appleton-Century-Crofts, 1957.

Eglash, A. Changes in opinionation during a psychology course. *J. educ. Psychol.,* 1957, 48, 164–165.

Epley, D. G. Adolescent role relationships in the dynamics of prejudice. Unpublished doctoral dissertation, Michigan State Univer., 1953.

Eson, M. E. The Minnesota Teacher Attitude Inventory in evaluating the teaching of educational psychology. *J. educ. Psychol.,* 1956, 47, 271–275.

Evans, K. M. A study of attitudes towards teaching as a career. *Brit. J. educ. Psychol.,* 1952, 22, 63–69.

Evans, K. M. A further study of attitude towards teaching as a career. *Brit. J. educ. Psychol.,* 1953, 23, 58–63.

Eysenck, H. J. *The scientific study of personality*. London: Routledge & Kegan Paul, 1952.

Fager, R. E. Student and faculty conceptions of the "successful student." *J. counsel. Psychol.,* 1958, 5, 98–103.

Farago, L. (Ed.) *German psychological warfare*. New York: Putnam, 1942.

Farber, M. L., & Bousfield, W. A. College teaching as a profession. *J. higher Educ.,* 1958, 29, 70–72.

Faw, V. D. A psychotherapeutic method of teaching psychology. *Amer. Psychologist,* 1949, 4, 104–109.

Fersh, G. L. Changes in social beliefs and social values effected by a social studies course based on the problems approach. Unpublished doctoral dissertation, New York Univer., 1949.

Fink, M. Ethnocentrism as it relates to teaching success. *Calif. J. educ. Res.,* 1953, 4, 111–114.

Fisher, R. J. Who is this lower-class child? *J. educ. Sociol.,* 1961, 34, 309–311.

Fishman, J. A. The MTAI in an American minority-group school setting. I. Differences between test characteristics for norm and non-norm populations. *J. educ. Psychol.,* 1957, 48, 41–51.

Flanders, N. A. Personal-social anxiety as a factor in experimental learning situations. *J. educ. Res.,* 1951, 45, 100–110.

Floud, J., & Halsey, A. H. Education and social structure: Theories and methods. *Harvard educ. Rev.,* 1959, 29, 288–296.

France, A. *The crime of Sylvestre Bonnard*. New York: Dodd, Mead, 1918.

Freedman, M. B. Impact of college. *New dimensions in higher education, No. 4*. Washington, D.C.: U. S. Government Printing Office, 1960.

Frenkel-Brunswik, Else. Motivation and behavior. *Genet. Psychol. Monogr.,* 1942, 26, 121–265.

Freud, Anna. *The ego and the mechanisms of defense*. New York: International Universities Press, 1946.

Funkenstein, D. H., King, S. H., & Drolette, M. E. *Mastery of stress*. Cambridge, Mass.: Harvard Univer. Press, 1957.

Gage, N. L., & Chatterjee, B. B. The psychological meaning of aquiescence set: Further evidence. *J. abnorm. soc. Psychol.,* 1960, 60, 280–283.

Gage, N. L., Leavitt, G. S., & Stone, G. C. Teachers' understanding of their pupils and pupils' ratings of their teachers. *Psychol. Monogr.,* 1955, 69, No. 21 (Whole No. 406).

Gage, N. L., Leavitt, G. S., & Stone, G. C. The psychological meaning of acquiescence set for authoritarianism. *J. abnorm. soc. Psychol.,* 1957, 55, 98–103.

Gardner, B. B., Gardner, M. R., & Loeb, M. Social status and education in a southern community. *Sch. Rev.,* 1942, 50, 179–191.

Getzels, J. W. Necessity and innovation in the selection and training of teachers. *Elem. sch. J.,* 1955, 55, 427–434.

Getzels, J. W., & Guba, E. G. Role, role conflict, and effectiveness. *Amer. sociol. Rev.,* 1954, 19, 164–175.

Getzels, J. W., & Guba, E. G. The structure of roles and role conflict in the teaching situation. *J. educ. Sociol.,* 1955, 29, 30–40.

Gibb, C. A. Classroom behavior of the college teacher. *Educ. psychol. Measmt,* 1955, 15, 254–263.

Gibran, K. *The prophet.* New York: Knopf, 1929.

Gillespie, J. M., & Allport, G. W. *Youth's outlook on the future.* Garden City, N.Y.: Doubleday, 1955.

Ginzberg, E., Ginsburg, S. W., Axelrod, S., & Herma, J. L. *Occupational choice: An approach to a general theory.* New York: Columbia Univer. Press, 1951.

Gladstein, G. A. The relationship between study behavior and personality for academically successful students. Unpublished doctoral dissertation, Univer. of Chicago, 1957.

Goldsen, Rose K., Williams, R., Suchman, E., & Rosenberg, M. *What college students think.* Princeton, N.J.: Van Nostrand, 1960.

Good, C. V., & Scates, D. E. *Methods of research.* New York: Appleton-Century-Crofts, 1954.

Gordon, C. W. The role of the teacher in the social structure of the high school. *J. educ. Sociol.,* 1955, 29, 21–29.

Gordon, C. W. *The social system of the high school.* Glencoe, Ill.: Free Press, 1957. (a)

Gordon, C. W. The sociology of education. In J. B. Gittler (Ed.), *Review of sociology.* New York: Wiley, 1957. Pp. 500–519. (b)

Gough, H. G. The construction of a personality scale to predict scholastic achievement. *J. appl. Psychol.,* 1953, 37, 361–366.

Gough, H. G., & Pemberton, W. H. Personality characteristics related to success in practice teaching. *J. appl. Psychol.,* 1952, 36, 307–311.

Gould, G. Motives for entering the teaching profession. *Elem. sch. J.,* 1934, 35, 95–102.

Gouldner, A. W. Cosmopolitans and locals: Toward an analysis of latent social roles. I. *Admin. sci. Quart.,* 1957, 2, 281–306.

Gouldner, A. W. Cosmopolitans and locals: Toward an analysis of latent social roles. II. *Admin. sci. Quart.,* 1958, 2, 444–480.

Gowan, J. C., & Gowan, May S. A teacher prognosis scale for the MMPI. *J. educ. Res.,* 1955, 49, 1–12.

Grambs, Jean D. The sociology of the "born teacher." *J. educ. Sociol.,* 1952, 25, 532–541.

Green, B. F. Attitude measurement. In G. Lindzey (Ed.), *Handbook of social psychology.* Cambridge, Mass.: Addison-Wesley, 1954. Pp. 335–369.

Grim, P. R., Hoyt, C. J., & Mayo, S. T. A study of instruments to appraise teaching competency. *Educ. res. Bull.,* 1954, 33, 69–72, 83–84.

Gronlund, N. E. The accuracy of teachers' judgments concerning the sociometric status of sixth-grade pupils. *Sociometry Monogr.,* 1951, No. 25.

Gronlund, N. E. Relationship between the sociometric status of pupils and teachers' preferences for or against having them in class. *Sociometry,* 1953, 16, 142–150.

Gronlund, N. E. The relative ability of homeroom teachers and special subject teachers to judge the social acceptability of preadolescent pupils. *J. educ. Res.,* 1955, 48, 381–391.

Gronlund, N. E. The general ability to judge sociometric status: Elementary student teachers' sociometric perceptions of classmates and pupils. *J. educ. Psychol.,* 1956, 47, 147–157.

Gronlund, N. E. *Sociometry in the classroom.* New York: Harper, 1959.

Gross, L. An experimental study of the validity of the non-directive method of teaching. *J. Psychol.,* 1948, 26, 243–248.

Gross, N. Social class structure and American education. *Harvard educ. Rev.,* 1953, 23, 298–329.

Gross, N. The sociology of education. In R. K. Merton, L. Broom, & L. S. Cottrell, Jr. (Eds.), *Sociology today: Problems and prospects.* New York: Basic Books, 1959. Pp. 128–152. (a)

Gross, N. Some contributions of sociology to the field of education. *Harvard educ. Rev.,* 1959, 29, 275–287. (b)

Guba, E. G., & Getzels, J. W. Personality and teacher effectiveness: A problem in theoretical research. *J. educ. Psychol.,* 1955, 46, 330–344.

Guetzkow, H., Kelly, E. L., & McKeachie, W. J. An experimental comparison of recitation, discussion, and tutorial methods in college teaching. *J. educ. Psychol.,* 1954, 45, 193–207.

Gustad, J. W. They march to a different drummer: Another look at college teachers. *Educ. Rec.,* 1959, 40, 204–211.

Gustad, J. W. The career decisions of college

teachers. SREB Res. Monogr. Series, No. 2, 1960.

Guttman, L. The basis for scalogram analysis. In S. Stouffer, et al., *Measurement and prediction*. Princeton, N.J.: Princeton Univer. Press, 1950. Pp. 60–90.

Haigh, G. V., & Schmidt, W. The learning of subject matter in teacher-centered and group-centered classes. *J. educ. Psychol.*, 1956, 47, 295–301.

Haring, N. G., Stern, G. G., & Cruickshank, W. M. *Attitudes of educators toward exceptional children*. Syracuse, N.Y.: Syracuse Univer. Press, 1958.

Harper, M. H. Social beliefs and attitudes of American educators. *Teach. Coll. Contr. Educ.*, 1927, No. 294.

Harris, H. *The group approach to leadership testing*. London: Kegan Paul, 1949.

Hart, F. W. *Teachers and teaching*. New York: Macmillan, 1934.

Hathaway, S. R., & McKinley, J. C. *Minnesota Multiphasic Personality Inventory*. New York: Psychological Corp., 1943.

Havighurst, R. J., & Neugarten, Bernice L. *Society and education*. Boston: Allyn & Bacon, 1957.

Havighurst, R. J., & Taba, Hilda. *Adolescent character and personality*. New York: Wiley, 1949.

Hawkes, G. R., & Egbert, R. L. Personal values and the empathic response: Their interrelationships. *J. educ. Psychol.*, 1954, 45, 469–476.

Haythorn, W. The influence of individual members on the characteristics of small groups. *J. abnorm. soc. Psychol.*, 1953, 48, 276–284.

Haythorn, W., Couch, A., Haefner, D., Langham, P., & Carter, L. F. The behavior of authoritarian and equalitarian personalities in small groups. *Human Relations*, 1956, 9, 57–74. (a)

Haythorn, W., Couch, A., Haefner, D., Langham, P., & Carter, L. The effects of varying combinations of authoritarian and equalitarian leaders and followers. *J. abnorm. soc. Psychol.*, 1956, 53, 210–219. (b)

Heath, S. R., Jr. Personality and student development. In *New dimensions of learning in a free society*. Pittsburgh: Univer. of Pittsburgh Press, 1958. Pp. 225–245.

Heath, S. R., Jr. The reasonable adventurer and others—a two-factor model of ego functioning. *J. counsel. Psychol.*, 1959, 6, 3–12.

Heil, L. M., Powell, M., &. Feifer, I. *Characteristics of teacher behavior and competency related to the achievement of different kinds of children in several elementary grades*. New York: Office of Testing and Research, Brooklyn Coll., 1960. (Mimeographed)

Heilman, R. B. Fashions in melodrama. *AAUP Bull.*, 1959, 45, 360–373.

Heist, P. A. Implications from recent research on college students. *J. Nat. Assoc. Women Deans & Counselors*, 1959, 22, 116–124.

Heist, P. Diversity in college student characteristics. *J. educ. Sociol.*, 1960, 33, 279–291.

Heist, P. A., & Williams, P. A. *Manual for the Omnibus Personality Inventory*. Berkeley: Center for the Study of Higher Education, Univer. of California, 1957.

Heist, P., McConnell, T. R., Matsler, F., & Williams, P. Personality and scholarship. *Science*, 1961, 133, 362–367.

Hemphill, J. K. Leadership behavior associated with the administrative reputation of college departments. *J. educ. Psychol.*, 1955, 46, 385–401.

Henry, J. Docility, or giving teacher what she wants. *J. soc. Issues*, 1955, 11, 33–41.

Henry, N. B. (Ed.) The dynamics of instructional groups. *Yearb. nat. Soc. Stud. Educ.*, 1960, 59, Part II.

Henry, W. The business executive—the psychodynamics of a social role. *Amer. J. Sociol.*, 1949, 54, 286–291.

Heyns, R. W., & Lippitt, R. Systematic observational techniques. In G. Lindzey (Ed.), *Handbook of social psychology*. Cambridge, Mass.: Addison-Wesley, 1954. Pp. 370–404.

Highet, G. *The art of teaching*. New York: Knopf, 1950.

Hoehn, A. J., & Saltz, E. Effect of teacher-student interviews on classroom achievement. *J. educ. Psychol.*, 1956, 47, 424–435.

Holland, J. L. Undergraduate origins of American scientists. *Science*, 1957, 126, 433–437.

Holland, J. L. Determinants of college choice. *Coll. & Univer.*, 1959, 35, 11–28. (a)

Holland, J. L. Parental expectations and attitudes about colleges. *Coll. & Univer.*, 1959, 34, 164–170. (b)

Hollingshead, A. B. *Elmtown's youth*. New York: Wiley, 1949.

Holt, R. R., & Luborsky, L. *Personality patterns of psychiatrists*. New York: Basic Books, 1958.

Hughes, E. C. Personality types and the division of labor. *Amer. J. Sociol.,* 1928, 33, 754–768.

Hughes, E. C. Work and the self. In J. H. Rohrer & M. Sherif (Eds.), *Social psychology at the crossroads.* New York: Harper, 1951. Pp. 313–323.

Hughes, E. C. *Men and their work.* Glencoe, Ill.: Free Press, 1958.

Hughes, E. C. Stress and strain in professional education. *Harvard educ. Rev.,* 1959, 29, 319–329.

Hunter, E. C. Changes in teachers' attitudes toward children's behavior over the last thirty years. *Ment. Hyg., N.Y.,* 1957, 41, 3–11.

Hutchins, E. B. The 1960 medical school graduate: His perceptions of faculty, peers, and environment. *J. med. Educ.,* 1961, 36, 322–329.

Jackson, P. W., & Guba, E. G. The need structure of in-service teachers: An occupational analysis. *Sch. Rev.,* 1957, 65, 176–192.

Jacob, P. E. *Changing values in college.* New York: Harper, 1957.

Jencks, C. The academic subculture. In R. Hagan (Ed.), *Character and social structure in America; Selected papers from Social Sciences 136.* Cambridge, Mass.: Harvard Printing Office, 1960. Pp. 93–123.

Jenkins, D. H., & Lippitt, R. *Interpersonal perceptions of teachers, students and parents.* Washington, D.C.: National Education Association, 1951.

Jervis, F. M., & Congdon, R. G. Student and faculty perceptions of educational values. *Amer. Psychologist,* 1958, 13, 464–466.

Johnson, D. M., & Smith, H. C. Democratic leadership in the college classroom. *Psychol. Monogr.,* 1953, 67, No. 11 (Whole No. 361).

Johnson, O. G. The teacher and the withdrawn child. *Ment. Hyg., N.Y.,* 1956, 40, 529–534.

Jones, E. The relation of abnormal psychology to social psychology. In *Essays in applied psycho-analysis.* Vol. 1. London: Hogarth, 1951. Pp. 113–127.

Kahn, R. L., & Cannell, C. F. *The dynamics of interviewing.* New York: Wiley, 1957.

Kasper, A. A. A study of the relationships among classroom climate, emotional adjustment, and reading achievement. *Dissertation Abstr.,* 1956, 16, 1399–1400.

Kaufmann, F. *Methodology of the social sciences.* New York: Humanities Press, 1944.

Kearney, N. C., & Rocchio, P. D. Using the MTAI in counseling prospective teachers. *Personnel guid. J.,* 1955, 34, 159–160. (a)

Kearney, N. C., & Rocchio, P. D. Relation between a teacher attitude inventory and pupils' ratings of teachers. *Sch. Rev.,* 1955, 63, 443–445. (b)

Keller, R. J., & Corcoran, M. Educational psychology. In P. R. Farnsworth & Q. McNemar (Eds.), *Annual review of psychology.* Vol. 8. Palo Alto, Calif.: Annual Reviews, 1957. Pp. 163–184.

Kelly, E. L., & Fiske, D. W. *The prediction of performance in clinical psychology.* Ann Arbor: Univer. of Michigan Press, 1951.

Kelly, G. A. *The psychology of personal constructs.* 2 vols. New York: Norton, 1955.

Klein, G. S. Perception, motives and personality. In J. L. McCary (Ed.), *Psychology of personality.* New York: Grove Press, 1956. Pp. 121–200.

Kluckhohn, C., & Murray, H. A. Personality formation: The determinants. In C. Kluckhohn, H. A. Murray, & D. M. Schneider (Eds.), *Personality in nature, society, and culture.* New York: Knopf, 1953. Pp. 53–67.

Kluckhohn, C., Murray, H. A., & Schneider, D. M. (Eds.), *Personality in nature, society, and culture.* New York: Knopf, 1953.

Knapp, R. H., & Goodrich, H. B. *Origins of American scientists.* Chicago: Univer. of Chicago Press, 1952.

Knapp, R. H., & Greenbaum, J. J. *The younger American scholar: His collegiate origins.* Chicago: Univer. of Chicago Press, 1953.

Koenig, K., & McKeachie, W. J. Personality and independent study. *J. educ. Psychol.,* 1959, 50, 132–134.

Koffka, K. *Principles of Gestalt psychology.* New York: Harcourt, Brace, 1935.

Krumboltz, J. D., & Farquhar, W. W. The effect of three teaching methods on achievement and motivational outcomes in a how-to-study course. *Psychol. Monogr.,* 1957, 71, No. 14 (Whole No. 443).

Kubie, L. S. Some unsolved problems of the scientific career. *Amer. Scientist,* 1953, 41, 596–613.

Kubie, L. S. Socio-economic problems of the young scientist. *Amer. Scientist,* 1954, 42, 104–112.

LaBue, A. C. Personality traits and persistence of interest in teaching as a vocational choice. *J. appl. Psychol.,* 1955, 39, 362–365.

Lagey, J. Does teaching change students' attitudes? *J. educ. Res.,* 1956, 50, 307–311.

Landsman, T. An experimental study of a student-centered learning method. Unpublished doctoral dissertation, Syracuse Univer., 1950.

Lazarsfeld, P. F. The logical and mathematical foundations of latent structure analysis. In S. Stouffer, et al., *Measurement and prediction.* Princeton, N.J.: Princeton Univer. Press, 1950. Pp. 362–412.

Lazarsfeld, P. F., & Thielens, W., Jr. *The academic mind.* Glencoe, Ill.: Free Press, 1958.

Lecky, P. *Self-consistency.* New York: Island Press, 1945.

Leeds, C. H. A scale for measuring teacher-pupil attitudes and teacher-pupil rapport. *Psychol. Monogr.,* 1950, 64, No. 6 (Whole No. 312).

Leeds, C. H. A second validity study of the Minnesota Teacher Attitude Inventory. *Elem. sch. J.,* 1952, 52, 398–405.

Leeds, C. H. Teacher attitudes and temperament as a measure of teacher-pupil rapport. *J. appl. Psychol.,* 1956, 40, 333–337.

Levin, H., Hilton, T. L., & Leiderman, Gloria F. Studies in teacher behavior. *J. exp. Educ.,* 1957, 26, 81–91.

Lewin, K. *Field theory in social science* (Ed. by D. Cartwright). New York: Harper, 1951.

Lewin, K., Lippitt, R., & White, R. Patterns of aggressive behavior in experimentally created "social climates." *J. soc. Psychol.,* 1939, 10, 271–299.

Lewin, K., Dembo, Tamara, Festinger, L., & Sears, Pauline S. Level of aspiration. In J. McV. Hunt (Ed.), *Personality and the behavior disorders.* Vol. 1. New York: Ronald Press, 1944. Pp. 333–378.

Likert, R. A technique for the measurement of attitude. *Arch. Psychol., N.Y.,* 1932, 22, No. 140.

Loeb, M. B. Implications of status differentiation for personal and social development. *Harvard educ. Rev.,* 1953, 23, 168–174.

Lovell, G. D., & Haner, C. F. Forced-choice applied to college faculty rating. *Educ. psychol. Measmt,* 1955, 15, 291–304.

Maccoby, Eleanor E., & Maccoby, N. The interview: A tool of social science. In G. Lindzey (Ed.), *Handbook of social psychology.* Cambridge, Mass.: Addison-Wesley, 1954. Pp. 449–487.

Mason, W. S., Dressel, R. J., & Bain, R. K. Sex role and the career orientation of beginning teachers. *Harvard educ. Rev.,* 1959, 29, 370–383.

McCall, W. A. Measurement of teacher merit. Raleigh, N.C.: State Dept. of Public Instruction, Publ. No. 284, 1952.

McClelland, D. C., Atkinson, J. W., Clark, R. A., & Lowell, E. L. *The achievement motive.* New York: Appleton-Century-Crofts, 1953.

McConnell, T. R., & Heist, P. A. Do students make the college? *Coll. & Univer.,* 1959, 34, 442–452.

McGee, H. M. Measurement of authoritarianism and its relation to teachers' classroom behavior. *Genet. Psychol. Monogr.,* 1955, 52, 89–146.

McGranahan, D. V. Content analysis of the mass media of communication. In Marie Jahoda, M. Deutsch, & S. W. Cook (Eds.), *Research methods in social relations.* Part 2. New York: Dryden, 1951. Pp. 539–560.

McKeachie, W. J. Anxiety in the college classroom. *J. educ. Res.,* 1951, 45, 153–160.

McKeachie, W. J. Individual conformity to attitudes of classroom groups. *J. abnorm. soc. Psychol.,* 1954, 49, 282–289. (a)

McKeachie, W. J. Student-centered vs. instructor-centered instruction. *J. educ. Psychol.,* 1954, 45, 143–150. (b)

McKeachie, W. J. Students, groups, and teaching methods. *Amer. Psychologist,* 1958, 13, 580–584.

McNassor, D. Conflict in teachers who try to learn about children. *Calif. J. educ. Res.,* 1951, 2, 147–155.

Mead, Margaret, & Metraux, Rhoda. Image of the scientist among high school students. *Science,* 1957, 126, 384–390.

Medley, D. M., & Klein, Alix A. *Studies of teacher behavior: Inferring classroom behavior from pupil responses.* New York: Board of Higher Education, City of New York, Div. of Teacher Education, 1956 (Res. Series No. 30).

Meehl, P. E. *Clinical versus statistical prediction.* Minneapolis: Univer. of Minnesota Press, 1954.

Meriam, L. L. Normal school education and

efficiency in teaching. *Teach. Coll. Contr. Educ.,* 1906, No. 1.

Merton, R. K. Bureaucratic structure and personality. *Soc. Forces,* 1940, 18, 560–568.

Miller, H. Role awareness as an objective of group work in teacher education. *J. teacher Educ.,* 1955, 6, 128–133.

Miller, N. Social class and value differences among American college students. Unpublished doctoral dissertation, Columbia Univer., 1958.

Mitchell, J. C. A study of teachers' and mental hygienists' ratings of certain behavior problems of children. *J. educ. Res.,* 1943, 36, 292–307.

Mitzel, H. E., & Dubnick, L. *Comparison of freshman teacher education students with other liberal arts freshmen entering New York City's municipal colleges.* New York: Board of Higher Education, City of New York, 1959.

Mitzel, H. E., & Rabinowitz, W. *Reliability of teachers' verbal behavior: A study of Withall's technique for assessing socio-emotional climate in the classroom.* New York: City Colleges, Div. of Teacher Education, Office of Res. and Evaluation, 1953 (Res. Series No. 15).

Mitzel, H. E., Rabinowitz, W., & Ostreicher, L. M. The effects of response sets on the validity of the Minnesota Teacher Attitude Inventory. *Educ. psychol. Measmt,* 1956, 16, 501–515.

Mones, L. Psychiatric insight and educational effort. *Education,* 1955, 76, 139–151.

Moore, C. H., & Cole, D. The relation of MMPI scores to practice teaching ratings. *J. educ. Res.,* 1957, 50, 711–716.

Moore, Mary R., & Popham, W. J. The role of extra-class student interviews in promoting student achievement. Paper read at joint session of Amer. Assoc. for the Advancement of Science and the Amer. Educ. Res. Assoc., Chicago, Dec., 1959.

Moreno, J. L. *Who shall survive?* (2nd ed.) New York: Beacon House, 1953.

Murphy, G. *Introduction to psychology.* New York: Harper, 1951.

Murray, H. A. *Explorations in personality.* New York: Oxford Univer. Press, 1938.

Newcomb, T. M. *Personality and social change.* New York: Dryden, 1943.

Nothern, E. F. How well do prospective teachers compare with students preparing to enter other occupations? *J. teacher Educ.,* 1958, 9, 387–396.

Ohlsen, M. M., & Schultz, R. E. Projective test response patterns for best and poorest student teachers. *Educ. psychol. Measmt,* 1955, 15, 18–27.

Oliver, W. A. Teachers' educational beliefs vs. their classroom practices. *J. educ. Res.,* 1953, 47, 47–55.

OSS Assessment Staff. *Assessment of men.* New York: Rinehart, 1948.

Pace, C. R., & Stern, G. G. An approach to the measurement of psychological characteristics of college environments. *J. educ. Psychol.,* 1958, 49, 269–277.

Page, Martha H., & Travers, R. M. W. *Relationships between Rorschach performance and student teaching.* New York: City Colleges, Div. of Teacher Education, Office of Res. and Evaluation, 1953 (Res. Series No. 14, pp. 2–9). (a)

Page, Martha H., & Travers, R. M. W. *Use of drawings as a screening device in education.* New York: City Colleges, Div. of Teacher Education, Office of Res. and Evaluation, 1953 (Res. Series No. 14, pp. 41–44). (b)

Parsons, T. M. Illness and the role of the physician: A sociological perspective. *Amer. J. Orthopsychiat.,* 1951, 21, 452–460.

Parsons, T. The school class as a social system: Some of its functions in American society. *Harvard educ. Rev.,* 1959, 29, 297–318.

Patton, J. A. A study of the effects of student acceptance of responsibility and motivation on course behavior. Unpublished doctoral dissertation, Univer. of Michigan, 1955.

Peck, R. F. Personality patterns of prospective teachers. *J. exp. Educ.,* 1960, 29, 169–175.

Polmantier, P. C., & Ferguson, J. L. Faking the Minnesota Teacher Attitude Inventory. *Educ. psychol. Measmt,* 1960, 20, 79–82.

Rabinowitz, W., & Travers, R. M. W. A drawing technique for studying certain outcomes of teacher education. Part 1. The development of the technique and its qualitative uses. In R. M. W. Travers, W. Rabinowitz, Martha H. Page, Elinore Nemovicher, & P. Ventur, *Exploratory studies in teacher personality.* New York: City Colleges, Div. of Teacher Education, Office of Res. and Evaluation, 1953 (Res. Series No. 14, pp. 18–28).

Rabinowitz, W., & Travers, R. M. W. A drawing technique for studying certain outcomes of teacher education. *J. educ. Psychol.*, 1955, 46, 257–273.

Raths, L. E. Emotional needs and teacher training. *J. educ. Sociol.*, 1951, 24, 369–380.

Remmers, H. H., & Radler, D. H. *The American teenager.* Indianapolis: Bobbs-Merrill, 1957.

Riesman, D. *Constraint and variety in American education.* Garden City, N.Y.: Doubleday, 1958. (a)

Riesman, D. The "Jacob Report." *Amer. sociol. Rev.*, 1958, 23, 732–738. (b)

Riesman, D. The academic career: Notes on recruitment and colleagueship. *Daedalus*, 1959, 88, 147–169. (a)

Riesman, D. The influence of student culture and faculty values in the American college. In G. Z. F. Bereday & J. A. Lauwerys (Eds.), *Higher education.* Yonkers, N.Y.: World Book Co., 1959. Pp. 386–404. (b)

Riesman, D. Planning in higher education: Some notes on patterns and problems. *Human Organization*, 1959, 18, 12–17. (c)

Riesman, D. Student culture and faculty values. In M. L. Habein (Ed.), *Spotlight on the college student.* Washington, D.C.: American Council on Education, 1959. Pp. 8–24. (d)

Ringness, T. A. Relationship between certain attitudes toward teaching and teaching success. *J. exp. Educ.*, 1952, 21, 1–55.

Roback, A. A. *The psychology of character.* New York: Harcourt, Brace, 1927.

Robbins, F. G. *Educational sociology.* New York: Holt, 1953.

Roe, Anne. *The making of a scientist.* New York: Dodd, Mead, 1953.

Roe, Anne. *The psychology of occupations.* New York: Wiley, 1956.

Roethlisberger, F. J., & Dickson, W. J. *Management and the worker.* Cambridge, Mass.: Harvard Univer. Press, 1939.

Rogers, C. R. *Counseling and psychotherapy.* Boston: Houghton Mifflin, 1942.

Rogers, C. R. *Client-centered therapy.* Boston: Houghton Mifflin, 1951.

Rogoff, N. Public schools and equality of opportunity. *J. educ. Sociol.*, 1960, 33, 252–259.

Ryans, D. G. Some data on the prediction of observed teacher behaviors from the Teacher Characteristics Schedule. *Amer. Psychologist*, 1955, 10, 390.

Ryans, D. G. *Characteristics of teachers.*

Washington, D.C.: American Council on Education, 1960.

Samler, J. Psycho-social aspects of work: A critique of occupational information. *Personnel guid. J.*, 1961, 39, 458–465.

Sanford, N. (Ed.) Personality development during the college years. *J. soc. Issues*, 1956, 12 (4), 3–72.

Sanford, N. Knowledge of students through the social studies. In M. L. Habein (Ed.), *Spotlight on the college student.* Washington, D.C.: American Council on Education, 1959. Pp. 47–66.

Sanford, N., Webster, H., & Freedman, M. Impulse expression as a variable of personality. *Psychol. Monogr.*, 1957, 71, No. 11 (Whole No. 440).

Sanford, N., Adkins, M., Cobb, E., & Miller, B. Physique, personality and scholarship. *Monogr. Soc. Res. Child Develpm.*, 1943, 8, 1–105.

Schneider, D. M. Social dynamics of physical disability in army basic training. *Psychiatry*, 1947, 10, 323–333.

Schuhle, W. Teachers' understanding of students' academic ideals. *J. higher Educ.*, 1957, 28, 388–408.

Schultz, R. E., & Ohlsen, M. M. Interest patterns of best and poorest student teachers. *J. educ. Sociol.*, 1955, 29, 108–112.

Schutz, W. C. What makes groups productive. *Human Relations*, 1955, 8, 429–465.

Seagoe, May V. Some origins of interest in teaching. *J. educ. Res.*, 1942, 35, 673–682.

Seagoe, May V. A follow-up of 314 students whose fitness for teaching was questioned, 1942–1953. *J. educ. Res.*, 1957, 50, 641–653.

Seeman, M. Role conflict and ambivalence in leadership. *Amer. sociol. Rev.*, 1953, 18, 373–380.

Seeman, M. Social status and leadership. *Educ. res. Monogr.*, 1960, No. 35.

Shaw, J., Klausmeier, H. S., Luker, A. H., & Reid, H. T. Changes occurring in teacher-pupil attitudes during a two weeks guidance workshop. *J. appl. Psychol.*, 1952, 36, 304–306.

Sheatsley, P. B. The art of interviewing and a guide to interviewer selection and training. In Marie Jahoda, M. Deutsch, & S. W. Cook (Eds.), *Research methods in social relations.* Part 2. New York: Dryden, 1951. Pp. 463–492.

Sherif, M. *The psychology of social norms.* New York: Harper, 1936.

Siegelman, M., & Peck, R. F. Personality patterns related to occupational roles. *Genet. Psychol. Monogr.*, 1960, 61, 291–349.

Silberman, H. F. Effects of praise and reproof on reading growth in a nonlaboratory classroom setting. *J. educ. Psychol.*, 1957, 48, 199–206.

Sims, V. M. Social class affiliations of a group of public school teachers. *Sch. Rev.*, 1951, 59, 331–338.

Slobetz, F. Elementary teachers' reactions to school situations. *J. educ. Res.*, 1950, 44, 81–90.

Slobetz, F. How elementary school teachers meet selected school situations. *J. educ. Psychol.*, 1951, 42, 339–356.

Slomowitz, M. A. A comparison of personality changes and content achievement gains occurring in two modes of instruction. Unpublished doctoral dissertation, New York Univer., 1955.

Smith, A. J., & McGrath, F. Parent education and group therapy: An episode. *J. clin. Psychol.*, 1948, 4, 214–217.

Snygg, D., & Combs, A. W. *Individual behavior.* New York: Harper, 1949.

Soderquist, H. O. Participation in extracurricular activities in high school or college and subsequent success in teaching adults. *Sch. & Soc.*, 1935, 42, 607–608.

Solley, C. M., & Murphy, G. *Development of the perceptual world.* New York: Basic Books, 1960.

Sorenson, A. G. A note on the "fakability" of the Minnesota Teacher Attitude Inventory. *J. appl. Psychol.*, 1956, 40, 192–194.

Stein, M. I., Mackenzie, J. N., Rodgers, R. R., & Meer, B. A case study of a scientist. In A. Burton & R. E. Harris (Eds.), *Clinical studies of personality.* New York: Harper, 1955. Pp. 726–767.

Stephenson, W. *The study of behavior.* Chicago: Univer. of Chicago Press, 1953.

Stern, G. G. Assessing theological student personality structure. *J. pastoral Care*, 1954, 18, 76–83.

Stern, G. G. *Preliminary manual—Activities Index, College Characteristics Index.* Syracuse, N.Y.: Psychol. Res. Center, Syracuse Univer., 1958.

Stern, G. G. Congruence and dissonance in the ecology of college students. *Student Med.*, 1960, 8, 304–339. (a)

Stern, G. G. Student values and their relationship to the college environment. In H. T. Sprague (Ed.), *Research on college students.* Boulder, Colo.: Western Interstate Commission for Higher Education, 1960. Pp. 67–104. (b)

Stern, G. G. Continuity and contrast in the transition from high school to college. In N. F. Brown (Ed.), *Introducing entering students to the idea of learning.* Washington, D.C.: American Council on Education, 1961.

Stern, G. G. Environments for learning. In R. N. Sanford (Ed.), *The American college.* New York: Wiley, 1962. Pp. 690–730. (a)

Stern, G. G. The measurement of psychological characteristics of students and learning environments. In S. J. Messick & J. Ross (Eds.), *Measurement in personality and cognition.* New York: Wiley, 1962. Pp. 27–68. (b)

Stern, G. G., & Scanlon, J. S. Pediatric lions and gynecological lambs. *J. med. Educ.*, 1958, 33, Part 2, 12–18.

Stern, G. G., Stein, M. I., & Bloom, B. S. *Methods in personality assessment.* Glencoe, Ill.: Free Press, 1956.

Stern, G. G., Masling, J., Denton, B., Henderson, J., & Levin, R. Two scales for the assessment of unconscious motivations for teaching. *Educ. psychol. Measmt,* 1960, 20, 9–30.

Stewart, L. H., & Roberts, J. P. The relationship of Kuder profiles to remaining in a teachers' college and to occupational choice. *Educ. psychol. Measmt,* 1955, 15, 416–421.

Stouffer, G. A. W. The attitudes of secondary school teachers towards certain behavior problems of children. *Sch. Rev.*, 1956, 64, 358–362.

Stouffer, S. A. An analysis of conflicting social norms. *Amer. sociol. Rev.*, 1949, 14, 707–717.

Stovall, T. F. Lecture vs. discussion. *Phi Delta Kappan,* 1958, 39, 255–258.

Sullivan, H. S. Multidisciplined coordination of interpersonal data. In S. S. Sargent & Marian W. Smith (Eds.), *Culture and personality.* New York: Viking Fund, 1949. Pp. 175–194.

Super, D. E., & Bachrach, P. B. *Scientific careers and vocational development theory.* New York: Bur. of Publs., Teachers Coll., Columbia Univer., 1957.

Sutherland, E. H. *The professional thief.*

Chicago: Univer. of Chicago Press, 1937.

Swanson, G. E. Agitation through the press: A study of the personalities of publicists. *Publ. opin. Quart.*, 1956, 20, 441–456.

Symonds, P. M. Characteristics of the effective teacher based on pupil evaluations. *J. exp. Educ.*, 1955, 23, 289–310.

Taft, R. Multiple methods of personality assessment. *Psychol. Bull.*, 1959, 56, 333–352.

Taylor, H. Freedom and authority on the campus. In R. N. Sanford (Ed.), *The American college*. New York: Wiley, 1962. Pp. 774–804.

Terrien, F. W. The occupational roles of teachers. *J. educ. Sociol.*, 1955, 29, 14–20.

Thistlethwaite, D. L. College environments and the development of talent. *Science,* 1959, 130, 71–76. (a)

Thistlethwaite, D. L. College press and student achievement. *J. educ. Psychol.*, 1959, 50, 183–191. (b)

Thistlethwaite, D. L. College press and changes in study plans of talented students. *J. educ. Psychol.*, 1960, 51, 222–234.

Thomas, W. I., & Znaniecki, F. *The Polish peasant in Europe and America.* Boston: Badger, 1918.

Thompson, C. E. The attitudes of various groups toward behavior problems of children. *J. abnorm. soc. Psychol.*, 1940, 35, 120–125.

Thompson, O. E., & Tom, F. K. T. Comparison of the effectiveness of a pupil-centered versus a teacher-centered pattern for teaching vocational agriculture. *J. educ. Res.,* 1957, 50, 667–678.

Thorpe, J. A. A study of personality variables among successful women students and teachers of physical education. *Res. Quart. Amer. Ass. Hlth Phys. Educ. Rec.*, 1958, 29, 83–92.

Thurstone, L. L. The stimulus-response fallacy in psychology. *Psychol. Rev.*, 1923, 30, 354–369.

Thurstone, L. L. Factor analysis. In M. H. Marx (Ed.), *Psychological theory.* New York: Macmillan, 1951. Pp. 276–284.

Thurstone, L. L., & Chave, E. J. *The measurement of attitude.* Chicago: Univer. of Chicago Press, 1929.

Tiegs, E. W. *An evaluation of some techniques of teacher selection.* Bloomington, Ill.: Public School Publishing Co., 1928.

Trabue, M. R. Judgments by 820 college executives of traits desirable in lower-division

college teachers. *J. exp. Educ.*, 1953, 21, 337–341.

Travers, R. M. W., & Rabinowitz, W. A drawing technique for studying certain outcomes of teacher education. Part II. A quantitative comparison of certain outcomes in two institutions. In R. M. W. Travers, W. Rabinowitz, Martha H. Page, Elinore Nemovicher, & P. Ventur, *Exploratory studies in teacher personality.* New York: City Colleges, Div. of Teacher Education, Office of Res. and Evaluation, 1953 (Res. Series No. 14, pp. 29–40).

Travers, R. M. W., Rabinowitz, W., & Nemovicher, Elinore. The anxieties of a group of student teachers. In R. M. W. Travers, W. Rabinowitz, Martha H. Page, Elinore Nemovicher, & P. Ventur, *Exploratory studies in teacher personality.* New York: City Colleges, Div. of Teacher Education, Office of Res. and Evaluation, 1953 (Res. Series No. 14, pp. 45–51).

Tudhope, W. B. Motives for the choice of the teaching profession by training college students. *Brit. J. educ. Psychol.*, 1944, 14, 129–141.

Tyler, F. T. The prediction of student-teaching success from personality inventories. *Univer. Calif. Publs. Educ.*, 1954, 11, 233–314.

Ullman, C. A. Teachers, peers and tests as predictors of adjustment. *J. educ. Psychol.*, 1957, 48, 257–267.

Valenti, J. J. Measuring educational leadership attitudes. *J. appl. Psychol.*, 1952, 36, 36–43.

von Ehrenfels, C. Über gestaltqualitaten. *Vierteljahrsch Wissenschaft Philosophie,* 1890, 14, 249–292.

Waller, W. *The sociology of teaching.* New York: Wiley, 1932.

Waller, W. The teacher's roles. In J. S. Roucek (Ed.), *Sociological foundations of education.* New York: Crowell, 1942. Pp. 204–222.

Wandt, E. The measurement and analysis of teachers' attitudes. *Calif. J. educ. Res.*, 1952, 3, 10–13.

Wandt, E. A comparison of the attitudes of contrasting groups of teachers. *Educ. psychol. Measmt,* 1954, 14, 418–422.

Ward, J. Group-study vs. lecture-demonstration method in physical science instruction for general education college students. *J.*

exp. Educ., 1956, 24, 197–210.

Warner, W. L., et al. *Democracy in Jonesville.* New York: Harper, 1949.

Warner, W. L., Havighurst, R. J., & Loeb, M. B., *Who shall be educated?* New York: Harper, 1944.

Washburne, C. Involvement as a basis of stress analysis: A study of high school teachers. Unpublished doctoral dissertation, Michigan State Univer., 1953.

Watson, G. B. The measurement of fair-mindedness. *Teach. Coll. Contr. Educ.,* 1925, No. 176.

Watson, R. P. The relationship between selected personality variables, satisfaction, and academic achievement in defined classroom atmospheres. Unpublished doctoral dissertation, Univer. of Michigan, 1956.

Weber, M. *The methodology of the social sciences.* Ed. and trans. by E. A. Shils & H. A. Finch. Glencoe, Ill.: Free Press, 1949. Pp. 50–112.

Webster, H., Sanford, R. N., & Freedman, M. A new instrument for studying authoritarianism in personality. *J. Psychol.,* 1955, 40, 73–84.

Wedge, B. M. (Ed.) *Psychosocial problems of college men.* New Haven, Conn.: Yale Univer. Press, 1958.

West, J. *Plainville.* New York: Columbia Univer. Press, 1945.

White, R. K., & Lippitt, R. *Autocracy and democracy; An experimental inquiry.* New York: Harper, 1960.

White, R. W. *Lives in progress.* New York: Dryden, 1952.

Whitney, F. L. *The prediction of teaching success.* Bloomington, Ill.: Public School Publishing Co., 1924.

Whyte, W. F. (Ed.) *Industry and society.* New York: McGraw-Hill, 1946.

Wickman, E. K. *Children's behavior and teachers' attitudes.* New York: Commonwealth Fund, 1928.

Wieder, G. S. Group procedures modifying attitudes of prejudice in the college classroom. *J. educ. Psychol.,* 1954, 45, 332–344.

Willard, R. A. A study of the relationships between the valued-behaviors of selected teachers and the learning experiences provided in their classrooms. *J. educ. Res.,* 1955, 49, 45–51.

Willard, R. A. Discrepancies in learning experiences reported in classrooms. *Educ. Admin. Superv.,* 1957, 43, 339–348.

Wilson, L. *The academic man.* London: Oxford Univer. Press, 1942.

Wispé, L. G. Evaluating section teaching methods in the introductory course. *J. educ. Res.,* 1951, 45, 161–186.

Withall, J. An objective measurement of a teacher's classroom interactions. *J. educ. Psychol.,* 1956, 47, 203–212.

Witkin, H. A., and associates. *Personality through perception.* New York: Harper, 1954.

Woodworth, R. S. *Personal data sheet.* Chicago: Stoelting, 1920.

Xydias, N. Attitude du corps enseignant de Vienne (Isère) vis-à-vis de divers traits de comportement des écoliers. *Travail hum.,* 1956, 18, 249–256.

CHAPTER 10 Analysis and Investigation of Teaching Methods

NORMAN E. WALLEN
University of Utah

ROBERT M. W. TRAVERS
Western Michigan University

Research on teaching methods is the study of consistencies in the behavior of teachers and the effect of these consistencies on the learning process. For example, teachers differ from one another in the extent to which they allow students to choose classroom activities, in the extent to which they emit information, and in the emphasis they place on grades. Such consistencies of behavior are often grouped together to define what is described here as a pattern of teacher behavior.

The problem of classifying consistent patterns of teacher behavior includes all of the problems of establishing any classification scheme. Consider, for example, the much simpler problem of classifying words which one may wish to set up in developing a dictionary or in teaching a language. Many such classifications of words have been developed, and many more will probably be invented in the future. One way of classifying words is to divide them into short words and long words, a classification which was used to a great extent in developing readers in the last century. Another way is to classify them according to the frequency with which they are used in certain types of literature. This is the classification provided by word counts,

which are used extensively today as a basis of selecting words for elementary school readers.

Grammarians have also developed a number of different ways of classifying words. The traditional grammarians used such classifications as noun, verb, preposition, and so forth; modern grammarians such as C. C. Fries use a different system of classification. Classification systems survive or are abandoned according to their usefulness. A classification is retained if it shows promise of having utility. It is discarded if it lacks that promise. The same is true of teacher behavior. Classifications of behavior should be retained if they have utility in making predictions. They should be discarded if they lack utility. There is no single right or wrong classification—only classifications that prove useful in contrast to those that do not.

PATTERNS OF BEHAVIOR, ROLES, AND TEACHING METHOD

Until the 1950's most attempts to discuss and describe patterns of teacher behavior were made in terms of fairly limited sections of teacher behavior. For example, an extensive literature was developed on permissive versus authoritarian behavior in teachers. Other literature exists on the contrast between teaching according to a project method versus a subject-matter method of learning. Writers in more recent years have attempted to develop more comprehensive and global forms of classification of teacher behavior. This newly evolved and speculative literature concerning the classification of teacher behavior generally uses the term *role* to refer to such classifications.

The term *role* is generally used rather loosely. The term *role,* as it is used within the literature on teaching, does not represent the sophisticated and complex concept which the social psychologist represents by this word. In education, a teacher role is simply a pattern of behavior shared by a group of teachers which is identifiable and generally believed to be related in some way to the learning process. The concept of a teacher role is also related to that of a teaching method. Indeed, the two concepts are often used interchangeably. A teacher role is represented by a pattern of behavior of the teacher in the classroom and so too is a teaching method. Again, both role and method are patterns of behavior believed to be related in some way to the learning process. There is little likelihood that an educator would write about a teaching role which was not believed to be related to the learning process. In most educational writings the use of the two terms is indistinguishable, though in recent years the term *role* has probably had more frequent usage than the term *method.*

The relationship of teacher roles to learning is generally discussed in rather vague terms. Rarely does one read an article in which the behaviors of a teacher within a particular role are discussed in relation to any particular learning theory. Such relationships are commonly discussed in terms of popular theories of learning represented by such vague principles as "one learns by doing." Sometimes role classifications include classifications of teacher behavior outside the classroom as, for instance, the role of the teacher as a member of the community. In the latter case the relationship to the learning process is quite remote, though many writers assume that the behavior of the teacher as a member of the community does have an indirect effect on the pupil.

Examples of the classification of teacher behaviors based on the concept of role have been offered by many contemporary writers on education. For example, Havighurst and Neugarten (1957) provided a classification of teacher behavior in which a separation is attempted between behavior related to other adults in the school system and behavior related to pupils. The classification is as follows:

Roles in relation to adults in school system	Roles in relation to pupils
1. Employee	1. Mediator of learning
2. Subordinate to principal	2. Disciplinarian
3. Adviser to superior	3. Parent substitute
4. Colleague	4. Confidante
5. Follower	5. Surrogate of middle-class morality
6. Leader	

Another classification of roles of teachers was developed by Kinney (1952) and later used as the basis of an extended study by Fishburn (1955). In this classification the teacher is assumed to engage in activity organized with respect to six areas. Each organization of behavior is considered to be a role. The six roles or areas of activity are described as follows:

1. Director of learning,
2. Guidance and counseling person,
3. Mediator of the culture,
4. Member of the school community,
5. Liaison between school and community,
6. Member of the profession.

Kinney assumes that the good teacher will operate with respect to all of these roles. However, there are probably few teachers who can be said to manifest consistency of behavior with respect to all these areas.

In Fishburn's study, evidence was collected to show that the six areas described by Kinney represent fairly distinct areas of activity. A person who was strong in one of these areas of activity was not necessarily strong in the others. In other words, there appeared to be some specialization of role among teachers. Fishburn asked high school teachers to rank these roles in order of importance and arrived at the following order (the one considered most important being given first):

1. Mediator of the culture,
2. Member of a community,
3. Director of learning,
4. Guidance and counseling person,
5. Liaison between school and community,
6. Member of a profession.

School administrators who were asked to perform the same ranking arrived at a considerably different result. The administrators felt that the teacher should be primarily a liaison between school and community, but the teachers ranked this objective fifth. While the teachers felt that the teacher should be primarily a mediator of the culture, the administrators ranked this role sixth. Either administrators and teachers have remarkably different concepts of the role of the teacher or, in discussing these problems, they ascribe different meaning to these roles as they are described by Kinney. In either case there seems to be a need for administrators and teachers to work more closely with one another before they find themselves working at cross-purposes.

The classification of roles by Kinney is broad. It includes teacher behavior outside the classroom as well as teacher behavior within the classroom. Another classification of roles (Nedelsky, 1952) attempts a classification of behaviors in terms of the way in which they are related to interactions with children, but the concept of role which he uses is somewhat different from that which has been considered here and is mainly a classification of the situations in which the teacher operates with respect to pupils. These areas include setting limits of group action, influencing attitudes of the group, teaching basic skills, using and channeling pupil interests, providing a standard of conduct, determining group compositions, and assisting children into the peer group. The writers doubt whether this classification can be considered to represent a classification of patterns of teacher behavior. The mere identification of areas of activity does not mean that behavior in these areas shows any particular integration and hence provides a basis for some kind of consistency.

Swenson and Parton (1953) reviewed some of the literature pertaining to the role of the teacher in the classroom and concluded that the role ordinarily played by the teacher was undergoing a radical change. Specifically, these reviewers believed that the authoritarian role was becoming less frequent and that teachers were becoming more and more accepting of pupil planning activity. The role which is believed to be emerging is that of a teacher who works and plans with pupils. However, this trend may be much more a trend in the literature than a trend in the behavior of teachers.

Despite the extensive use of the term *role* in the discussion of teacher behavior and in the classification of behavior elements, the term seems ill chosen. Current usage of the term in educational literature is often inconsistent with its usage in social psychology. For example, a social psychologist (Sarbin, 1954) defines *role* operationally in the following words:

B performs one of a number of discrete acts which A observes and organizes into a concept, a role. On the basis of this conceptualization of the actions of B, A expects certain further actions from B. . . . Once having located or named the position of the other, A performs certain acts which have been learned as belonging to the reciprocal position; these acts are conceptualized as A's role (Sarbin, 1954, p. 225).

The definition of role requires that it always include a self-other concept. The latter definition has many useful properties, particularly in studying and accounting for the way in which roles develop and interact among the positions in a society, and in including the element of interaction between roles. The latter element introduces complexities which most educational writers ignore when they use the concept of role. Teacher-pupil roles interact, and so do the respective roles of teacher-principal and teacher-parent. Without denying the importance of such interactions and the part which they play in the modification and perhaps in the ultimate stabilization of the role of the teacher, most writers cannot be concerned with phenomena related to the establishment of the teacher's role at this level.

What we are pointing out is that the use of the term *role* in the discussion of teacher behavior is likely to lead only to confusion because it has been generally used with a meaning far different from that assigned to it by social psychologists. For this reason we will abandon the use of the term *role* in further discussion of the classification of teacher behavior in this chapter. In its place we will use the term *pattern of behavior,* a term which involves none of the complexities which social psychologists have injected into the meaning of *role*. A pattern of behavior of a teacher is simply an identifiable grouping of behaviors which occur in the same teacher. No element of expectancy is involved, nor are any of the other connotations which social psychologists have put into their definition of role.

DESCRIPTION OF PATTERNS OF TEACHER BEHAVIOR

A teaching method, or a pattern of teacher behavior (we use the terms interchangeably), may be described and identified in a number of ways. One way is to describe the classroom behavior of an actual teacher who closely approximates the particular pattern. This procedure is not generally adopted because such teachers cannot easily be found. An alternative procedure is to describe the performance of an imaginary teacher who manifests all of the behaviors to be included in the particular pattern. Such a teacher represents a composite picture of the performance of a number of teachers, each one of which represents in his teaching behavior an approximation to the particular pattern. Such an imaginary teacher may be referred to as a *concocted* teacher. Some writers discuss teaching methods in terms of two concocted teachers, one of whom manifests the particular pattern of teaching behavior while the other manifests an antithetical pattern. The latter procedure has merit in that much of the discussion of teaching method revolves around the merit of two contrasting patterns of teaching behavior. For example, during the thirties, the heyday of the Progressive Education Association, the contrast was that between an authoritarian teacher who made all of the decisions and a permissive teacher who delegated decision-making functions to the pupils. More recently, through the influence of the Rogerian school, the contrast has been made between directive and nondirective approaches to teaching.

Behavioral descriptions of teaching methods represent an innovation rather than established practice in this area. The more common practice has been to attempt to describe a particular pattern of teaching behavior in terms of the background of thought or practice on which such patterns are based. For this reason, it is of interest to consider here the conditions that generate particular teaching methods. While such a discussion may appear to be of academic rather than practical significance, such is not the case. The results of research, and the failure of research to produce results favoring any particular pattern, can be understood to some extent in terms of the analysis of the origin of teaching methods which follows.

ORIGINS OF PATTERNS OF
TEACHER BEHAVIOR

The classifications of patterns of teacher behavior discussed up to this point are based mainly on sociological constructs. As tentative explorations of teacher behavior, they have helped to clarify thinking about teacher behavior and to draw attention to its great complexity, particularly in relation to the culture in which it occurs. Few writers, except those concerned with the social class origins of teachers, inquire into the origins of these patterns of behavior, a vital matter which must be explored and understood if control is to be exercised over teacher training. All programs for the training of teachers assume that some knowledge is available concerning the conditions that generate patterns of teacher behavior, despite the fact that this matter is hardly considered in current educational writing. An ideal teacher-training program would be one in which a teaching method, for which teachers would be trained, would be designed in terms of present knowledge of learning. The model would be applied in designing a teacher-training curriculum which would establish in students of education the patterns of behavior which define the teaching method. Teacher training is far from this point at present.

Teaching methods cannot be considered to be, to any great extent, the product of scientific research. They could not have been so in the past because only in the last few years has scientific knowledge begun to reach the point which might permit the systematic design of a pattern of behavior for teachers which would maximize the achievement of the pupil with respect to specific objectives. If teaching methods were to be systematically designed, they would be based on two sources of knowledge. First, they would have to be founded on a theory of ethics which would determine the educational objectives that the method is to achieve. Second, they would have to be built in terms of a theory of behavior which would indicate the conditions under which particular learning could be most effectively produced. In this case, *a theory of behavior* is considered to subsume a series of interrelated laws which have been empirically established.

The fact is that most teaching methods do not have, and, until recently, they could not have, such a foundation. The advanced knowledge of both ethics and the psychology of learning has not existed which would provide the solid foundation needed for the rational construction of teaching methods. The writers can speak only for the latter of these two areas, and concerning that area can say that advances have only in the last decade reached the point where they have begun to provide a suitable basis for the construction of teaching method. Teaching methods of the past had to be designed on foundations other than those which will be used in the future. The sources of past teaching methods have not been, to any great extent, rational and scientific, but some of these sources must be examined to understand what research on teaching methods involves.

The following classification is an attempt to group patterns of teacher behavior in terms of the origin of the patterns. Basically, it is a list of the origins of most of the commonly discussed teaching methods. Each of the main categories will be discussed separately in further sections of the chapter. The presentation of the classification as a whole draws the attention of the reader to the fact that most teaching methods are not mainly derived from an empirical knowledge of learning. That their origin is quite different is an important fact which will help us later in the chapter on the interpretation of research on teaching methods. The following classification of the origin of teaching methods or patterns of teaching behavior is offered:

1. Patterns derived from teaching traditions.
   (Illustration: A teacher teaches as he was taught.)
2. Patterns derived from social learnings in the teacher's background.

(Illustration: A teacher reinforces the behavior of pupils so as to develop a middle-class ideology.)

3. Patterns derived from philosophical traditions.

(Illustration: A teacher teaches in accordance with the Froebel or Rousseau tradition.)

4. Patterns generated by the teacher's own needs.

(Illustration: A teacher adopts a lecture method because he needs to be self-assertive.)

5. Patterns generated by conditions existing in the school and community.

(Illustration: A teacher conducts his classroom in such a way as to produce formal and highly disciplined behavior because this represents the pattern required by the principal.)

6. Patterns derived from scientific research on learning.

What are commonly referred to as teaching methods fall into these categories. So also do less distinctive and less well-recognized patterns of teacher behavior. To understand better the concept of a teaching method, we will now consider patterns of teacher behavior and teaching methods derived from each of the sources which have been listed above.

Patterns Derived from Teaching Traditions

Any visitor who spends time in the schools of a foreign country is impressed by the fact that the behavior of the teachers in that country is different from the behavior of teachers in the United States. Indeed, the first impression of a visitor may be that the teachers in the foreign country differ little from one another. Probably the same impression would be gained by a foreign visitor who spent time in the schools of this country. Teaching reflects the culture and traditions of each country.

A nation's traditional way of teaching is not necessarily that which teacher-training institutions attempt to foster. There may be a broad gap between the cultural condition that prevails and the pattern of teacher behavior that professors of education attempt to inculcate in students of education. The training pattern and the prevailing cultural pattern may even be in opposition to one another. In this country, for example, institutions training elementary school teachers have tended to endorse a pattern of behavior for teachers which differs considerably from that represented by the cultural tradition. The relaxed and quite permissive pattern of behavior endorsed by textbooks on elementary education, with their emphasis on delegating decision-making functions to the child, differs markedly from the pattern typically manifested by elementary school teachers, who control the classroom in the way which has traditionally been expected of them.

Principals commonly voice the opinion that most teachers do not teach in accordance with the pattern prescribed by teacher-training institutions, but rather teach in accordance with the pattern they observed when they were pupils and which they believe is expected of them. This is hardly surprising. Imitation is a well-established phenomenon. The long period of exposure to teachers during the growing years provides a body of experiences and a pattern to imitate which may well serve the new teacher as a guide to action. This rich background of direct experience with teaching probably provides a much more vivid guide to action in the classroom than does the period of teacher-training, which consists so largely of verbal experiences.

A few teacher-training institutions have attempted to develop systematic procedures to counteract the tendency of teachers to imitate the teacher behavior they have previously observed as pupils. A few institutions, for example, require the student of education in the early stages of his training to observe teachers who are considered models of behavior. It is assumed that the observation of these selected teachers will provide a pattern to imitate which will be a positive and desirable influence on their own behavior in the classroom. An imitative process is assumed to occur but the behavior to be imitated is backed up by a cognitive structure which should give it strength and prepotency over the behaviors observed when the trainees were pupils. Whether it is possible by this means to develop imitative tendencies is not known at this time.

Other conditions also tend to give permanence to a particular pattern of teaching within a culture. One of these is the fact that the teaching personnel of most schools cover an age span of 30 or more years, often with a predominance of persons who took their training 20 or more years previously. A new teacher placed in this subculture may be expected to conform to some extent to the modal pattern of behavior manifested by the other teachers, and that pattern inevitably tends to accord with the tradition of the culture.

Patterns Derived from Social Learnings in the Teacher's Background

The writers consider the teacher's own personality prior to the impact of a teacher education program to be the main determinant of teacher behavior in the classroom. Of fundamental importance then is the great complex of factors referred to as social background. Considerable interest has been shown in recent years in these determinants of teacher behavior through work done by Havighurst and his associates at the University of Chicago. Since this matter is discussed in another chapter (Chapter 14), we will say only enough about it to sustain the unity of this chapter.

Interest in how the pattern of behavior of the teacher is determined by his social class affiliation has long been a matter of consider-

able interest to sociologists, social psychologists, and scholars concerned with the American educational system. The interest in this problem stems from the possibility that teachers who represent a particular social stratum in our society will favor pupils who also come from a similar social stratum. In addition, they may be expected to promote in pupils those behaviors which conform to the social mores of the class with which the teacher affiliates and conversely to react with lack of understanding, if not punishment, to behaviors of pupils from a different social class. All of this is, of course, quite speculative. Little is known about what behaviors teachers tend to foster outside of the academic area. Furthermore, while no social class has a monopoly of human virtues, neither does any class have a monopoly of the vices.

One of the earliest studies of the social background of teachers was conducted by Florence Greenhoe (1941), who collected information about the family background of 9,122 teachers in elementary and high schools. By far the largest group of these teachers, 38 per cent, reported that the occupation of their fathers was farming; 18 per cent reported that their fathers worked on a day-to-day basis, and 26 per cent reported that their fathers were engaged in business pursuits. Of particular interest is the fact that only 4 per cent of the teachers reported that their fathers were engaged in professional pursuits. If social background influences teacher behavior, then this influence will be derived mainly from certain sections of the culture.

If the teacher is considered to have even semiprofessional status, then one must regard this group of teachers as one which is moving up the occupational ladder, if not up the class system. What is not clear is whether teachers reflect the social mores and behavior patterns of the class from which they come or the class with which they are identified by those who see them in the community. At least some evidence indicates that the teachers themselves tend to identify with the new social class in which their training and occupation place them. This was illustrated by Becker (1953), who found that teachers in Chicago tended to seek transfers out of schools attended by pupils from lower-class homes and into schools attended by upper-class children. Another explanation of this finding is that teachers may seek out pupils who belong in the same general intelligence grouping as they do. Class-conscious writers in this area are prone to interpret a great range of behavior as resulting from the need of the teacher to establish a position in a particular social class. Much of the behavior may be more easily understood in terms of feelings of compatibility with those pupils who have educational goals similar to their own.

Brookover (1953, 1955) has considered the way in which the pattern of behavior of the teacher may be determined by his class origin and may affect learning in the classroom. In considering this problem, he classifies teachers into four groups: (1) middle-class teachers, (2) established middle-class teachers, (3) striving middle-class teachers, and (4) teachers who are unranked in the social stratification scheme. To each one of these groups of teachers he attributes particular patterns of classroom behavior which are assumed to have particular consequences for the learning process.

Warner, Havighurst, and Loeb (1944) have emphasized the influence that the social class of the teacher may have on the values learned in school and have asserted that these values are likely to be middle class because most teachers are middle class. Yet, while the latter idea is frequently found in recent educational literature, it is speculative rather than founded on fact.

The patterns of teacher behavior discussed in this section must be considered to be postulated rather than established. There seems to be little evidence to support the proposition that class background generates particular teaching methods with corresponding patterns of reinforcement. Some writers on this subject make little distinction between patterns of behavior which are actually demonstrated to exist and patterns of behavior which are postulated to exist under specified conditions. Perhaps research in this area needs to begin by finding out which aspects of such patterns of behavior are real and which are imaginary.

Patterns Derived from Philosophical Traditions

Teacher-training institutions have a long history of associating themselves with particular philosophical traditions. The aim of many teacher-training programs is to develop a pattern of teacher behavior consistent with the particular philosophy that the institution has adopted. Indeed, one of the earliest of teacher-training programs was just an attempt to indoctrinate teachers in a certain philosophical tradition to which were added a number of more or less imaginary laws of development. We refer here to the teacher-training program developed by Froebel in the early decades of the nineteenth century. The conceptual system of Froebel and the methods by which he trained teachers are so similar to those of much more recent times that a brief discussion of his approach to the problem of generating a pattern of teacher behavior is of value here. His problems are also the problems of contemporary teacher training.

From a philosophical point of view, Froebel belongs in the tradition of Rousseau, whose influence is still evident in contemporary American teacher-training institutions. Like Rousseau, he was influenced by the concept that development will proceed harmoniously of its own accord if the child is provided with a suitable environment. Emphasis was placed on the individual worth of each child, and teacher behavior had to be such that it did not do violence to the natural laws of the growing organism. The teacher must be permissive so that the natural process of development will not be violated. Nevertheless, certain activities considered desirable by adults will be accepted naturally by the child if they are properly chosen and are completely harmonious with his own needs and motives at the time. From the point of view of the behavioral sciences, the orientation of Froebel to problems of development was almost mystical. He saw wholeness in nature and a unity in all natural law. The current emphasis in teacher education on the wholeness and unity of the child closely resembles the outlook of Froebel from which it derives. It is not primarily a scientific doctrine but one which stems from religious mysticism and the concept of unity within the soul, a concept which may be extended to that of unity within the universe. It is a doctrine which may lead to respect, if not reverence, for the developing person, but it is also one which presents enormous difficulties when used as a basis for the development of patterns of teacher behavior, since it provides no basis for predicting outcomes of certain behaviors.

Froebel seems to have made the assumption, implicit in much of teacher education, that a correct outlook on educational problems would result in a sound behavior pattern on the part of teachers. Yet there appears to be a growing conviction that teacher education does little to generate appropriate patterns of teacher behavior in students of education. Indeed, there are serious doubts in some quarters whether teacher education can even be considered to generate any teaching patterns. However, this does not mean that much is not accomplished by professional training.

The outlook of Froebel, which is still well represented in many textbooks written for students of education, later found two powerful allies in the form of Gestalt psychology and clinical psychology. Of particular significance in the present context is the assimilation of ideas derived from clinical psychology, for these ideas offered a pattern of behavior for the teacher to manifest in the classroom. This pattern was to be in many respects similar to that of the mental therapist.

Numerous writers on both sides of the Atlantic have suggested that the pattern of behavior of the teacher in the classroom must, first and foremost, foster mental health and provide some degree of therapy. Beginning with the work of Pfister (1917), a long list of writers have expounded this point of view. The list includes such notable names as Anna Freud, Susan Isaacs, Melanie Klein, Karen Horney, Caroline Zachry, Carl Rogers, and Percival Symonds. The viewpoint expressed by these writers has been well accepted by many of those involved in the training of teachers and frequent reference is found to "the mental health role" of the teacher.

Every school of psychotherapy has advocates who suggest that the teacher should adopt the particular patterns of behavior which that school believes to be effective. Questions may be raised whether such suggestions represent an extension of scientifically developed techniques to new areas or whether they are merely attempts to extend the influence of certain schools of thought. It cannot be denied that the various schools of psychotherapy exert a powerful influence on educational thought. A brief discussion of the writings of a few of the proponents of teaching methods based on psychotherapeutic practices is in order here.

Articles by Zweibel (1947) and Seidler (1947) suggest that teachers can become most effective if they study the teachings of Alfred Adler. These teachings are offered as a basis both for understanding child behavior and for action with respect to it. Both articles are more dogmatic assertions of a faith than a set of conclusions based on a careful evaluation of evidence. Writers in this area often make claims that seem excessive. For example, Dreikurs (1959a) claims that the Adlerian approach permits "an immediate understanding of any child" (p. 89), a point of view further expounded in a manual by Dreikurs (1959b). Another proposal (Albrecht & Gross, 1948) is that the teacher acquire the techniques of the nondirective therapist and use them as approaches to teaching, whose outcome will then constitute therapy. Other articles which stress the role of the teacher as therapist and guidance worker are those by Sobel (1948) and Arbuckle (1954). The Division on Child

Development and Teacher Personnel (1945) gloomily pointed out that present courses in educational psychology and child development are limited in scope and do not prepare the teacher for this type of behavior. Anna Freud (1952) pointed out that the teacher is likely to form as close an attachment to the individual child as though it were his own. This attachment is likely to interfere with any therapeutic relationship that may be desirable.

While Melanie Klein (1949) and Anna Freud (1952) have implied that education itself should derive more of its emphasis from psychoanalytic theory, other leaders in the psychoanalytic movement have been skeptical about such possibilities. Some writers, such as Hoffer (1955), suggest that the major applications of psychoanalysis are in the preventive field. At best, the literature in this field can only be described as manifesting a vague and primitive type of theorizing.

Many of the articles referred to here imply that all one has to do is to tell a teacher what pattern to exhibit and that the teacher can then act out this pattern. Such an assumption is, of course, contrary to what is known about the modification of behavior.

Mason (1940), who studied the effectiveness of the teacher in undertaking therapeutic activity by providing opportunities for catharsis, came to a similar conclusion. Among the psychological difficulties encountered by such teachers were (1) their critical nonacceptance of the child's story, (2) a tendency to deal with problems created by the child rather than his internal conflicts, (3) failure to adapt teaching procedures to permit free expression, (4) inability to systematize observations, (5) problems of disrupting regular arrangements, and (6) the development of needs in teachers to pursue and continue therapeutic relationships.

Anna Freud (1952) suggested that the teacher may manifest the patterns of behavior of a mother figure. She also pointed out that the teacher, through constant association with young children, may begin to lose touch with the adult world.

Symonds (1949) thoroughly reviewed the problems that can arise when the teacher assumes the pattern of behavior of the therapist. He pointed out that within limits the two patterns may coincide but that, in some areas of behavior, the teacher cannot carry out the therapeutic pattern. The patterns are similar in that:

1. Teachers and therapists treat children as individuals who are capable of slowly taking over direction of themselves.

2. Teachers and therapists must be warm, friendly, and outgoing.

3. Teachers and therapists must accept the child as he is.

4. Teachers and therapists must be permissive to a degree.

5. Teachers and therapists have a responsibility to understand the child.

6. Teachers and therapists must be sensitive to the feelings of children and must help the child to become aware of them.

On the other hand, according to Symonds, the teacher probably cannot fulfill a complete therapeutic role because:

1. Teachers must be concerned primarily with the world of reality, while therapists must focus their attention on the inner life of the child.

2. A teacher feels love and expresses love, but avoids hate; a therapist does not express either love or hate.

3. The teacher expresses himself directly and boldly, while the therapist plays a much more passive role.

4. The teacher uses rewards and punishments but the therapist does not.

5. The teacher stimulates, directs, and guides, while the therapist finds that these activities interfere with self-determination.

6. A teacher sometimes has to stand firm on an issue but a therapist is not expected to take a stand on any issue.

7. A teacher should have a program (whether it is developed by the teacher himself or by the pupils) and the teacher must give some direction toward the completion of the program. The therapist does not have to be thus tied down.

8. The teacher must work largely through the positive forces in the child's personality which she elicits. Negative forces must be channeled into constructive activities. The therapist, on the other hand, must permit the direct expression of negative forces.

9. The teacher is mainly concerned with conscious mental processes and may have little skill in either handling or recognizing unconscious processes. The therapist is believed to have special skill in recognizing and understanding unconscious forces.

Discussions of the teacher behaving as therapist appear to be based more on optimism and hope than on any performance which is commonly observed among trained teachers. The little information that has been collected on the extent to which teachers do behave in accordance with this pattern indicates that the required behaviors occur rather rarely. Coxe and Anderson (1944) made an interesting study of the extent to which teachers handled 23 common problems in a manner which might have therapeutic value. The authors concluded that "in general in dealing with these twenty-three problem situations the teachers would either defeat their own purposes by making the problem worse, or they would use techniques unrelated to the problem" (p. 544). The ways in which the teachers handled the various kinds of classroom problems which arose was determined both through the reports of the teachers themselves and through the reports of the pupils. Both sets of data substantiated the same conclusion.

The discussion of the teacher functioning as therapist has been pursued, like most other discussions of teacher function, without reference to carefully collected data. The data that have been collected cast considerable doubt on the possibility that the teacher can function successfully in this capacity at the present time. Most writers who discuss this pattern of teacher behavior assume that teachers have extensive and deep understanding of pupils, though how one teacher ever acquires such understanding of 30 or more pupils is never explained. The little evidence available at present suggests that most teachers have relatively little understanding of their pupils and that differences in understanding which occur from one teacher to another have little effect on the learning process. Gage (1958), on the basis of his estimate of his own and other work, concluded that while teachers' understanding of pupils is an objective of just about every teacher-education program, present evidence does not demonstrate that this understanding makes any difference. A conceptual development of the pattern of behavior of the teacher as therapist requires a much clearer conception of what is meant by *understanding* pupils than is found at the present time.

Of course, one must say that most teacher education does not seem to be concerned with the development in teacher-trainees of a method exclusively based on clinical concepts. The major philosophical traditions are still probably far more influential than are the ideas of the leaders of the mental health movement in determining the nature of the teaching method that is advocated. One must also admit that teacher education may actually do little to develop a teaching method in the trainee, though other worth-while goals may be reached.

Some indirect evidence exists that teacher education may exert an effect on the cognitive structures of students of education, an effect related to what teachers should do in the classrooms. Rabinowitz and Travers (1955) studied changes in students of education during teacher training as these changes were manifested in drawings of the students. Students at various stages of teacher training were given a sheet of paper and a pencil and were instructed to "draw a picture of a teacher with a class. Draw as complete a picture as you can. Avoid the use of stick figures. Don't worry about your artistic ability or lack of it; just draw as well as you can" (p. 257). The basic assumption in using this technique was that the drawings are related to the person's concept of how a teacher should perform in a classroom. Evidence is not available to indicate that the representation in the drawing is related to how the person performs in the classroom.

In the study by Rabinowitz and Travers (1955), the drawing test was administered to students of education in two teacher-training programs which had altogether different emphases and attempted to produce teachers with basically different behavioral patterns in the classroom. In Institution A the emphasis was on the intellectual development of the teacher in a rather broad liberal arts tradition. No major in education was offered, so that the emphasis was on liberal arts rather than on professional education. The students in this program did not typically visit public schools, except for practice teaching, and the faculty felt some skepticism concerning the value of having a student observe classes before he acquired the intellectual maturity which might enable him to evaluate what he observed. But the students did have a series of planned visits to community agencies serving children.

In Institution B, professional training was given primary emphasis. While competency in subject matter was expected of the student, he was told that he was being trained primarily as a teacher. In this program, it was assumed that knowledge alone does not ensure that the teacher will manifest a desirable pattern of behavior in the classroom. The student must have the personality characteristics that permit suitable teacher behavior and must also have the opportunity to acquire suitable behavior patterns through observing teachers who are considered to be models. A close relationship between faculty and students made it possible for the faculty to observe closely the development of the student and to eliminate those whose personalities were unsuited to the kind of teaching for which they were being trained.

The drawing test was administered to students in these two programs at various stages of training to compare performance before and after teacher training. The first question to be answered was, How does teacher training affect the extent to which the drawings show activity outside of the control of the teacher and activity showing partial or total pupil control? The drawings were scored for this characteristic after they had been arranged in a random order. The drawings had no identification marks which could indicate their origin to the scorers. Those graduating from Institution B showed a significant change in their drawings over the two-year period while those in Institution A did not. The change in the case of students from Institution B reflected a decreased amount of teacher control over the period of teacher training.

The second question asked was, How does teacher training affect the nature of the pupil-teacher relationships manifested in the drawings? To answer this question, the drawings were first rated for the degree to which they displayed tension in pupil-teacher relationships. Here again, the students were found to be similar in the two institutions at the start of teacher training, but those in Institution B showed a sharp decline in tension during or after teacher training while those in Institution A remained unchanged. A second attempt to answer this question was made by determining the number of drawings in each group which showed teachers and pupils participating together in some activity. The percentage of drawings thus classified showed a marked and statistically significant rise for the students from Institution B over the period of teacher training while the percentage for Institution A did not. Indeed, the latter showed a small but statistically insignificant decline.

In summary, while the students in the two institutions manifested no significant differences in their drawings at the beginning of teacher training, those in one institution showed a marked change during teacher training while the other group did not. The change occurred in that institution which made a deliberate effort to change the students' concepts of what should go on in a classroom.

This study was reproduced by Palmer (1954), who also used a number of other techniques to explore the trainee's conception of the behavior of the teacher in the class-room. In Palmer's study, the subjects were students of early childhood who were pre-paring to be kindergarten teachers. Palmer writes that

the most interesting contrast between the two groups was seen in their picture drawings. The Seniors drew classrooms that were for the most part very informal with a picture of themselves as participating with children in a variety of activities. . . . The drawings made by the Fresh-men showed many more in a formal arrange-ment of furniture and with the teacher standing in front of the room "teaching" (Palmer, 1954, p. 157).

Other results of Palmer's study are of interest. The data indicated that the function of the teacher was generally described as that of an entertainer, friend, and helper. A strong feeling was expressed that children should like and enjoy school. Both the freshmen and seniors in this study expressed the idea that the teacher had an important role to play in relation to parents and that contacts with parents should be actively sought. However, these students did not perceive their function as being that of a mother substitute or a nurse. The pattern of entertainer predomi-nated over these two other patterns.

The idea that patterns of teacher behavior are generated by teacher training and related philosophical traditions is a highly specu-lative one for which it is hard to find evi-dence. Indirect evidence runs counter to this thesis. An appropriate conclusion to this sec-tion is the following attempt to sketch the relationship between teacher training and the development of patterns of classroom behavior:

1. Instructors in teacher-education pro-grams present to the student an outlook on education problems which the student learns by means of a number of different processes, including reinforcement and imitation.

2. As a result of this learning, the student develops an affective response toward each of a number of ideas related to education. For example, he becomes strongly in favor of the idea that pupils should make as many decisions as feasible.

3. The affective responses which he has acquired come to be supported by a cognitive structure. This is evidenced by the fact that the student is able to give reasons for his preference for one set of educational ideas rather than another. At this stage he can speak the language of textbooks of education and has some understanding of the signifi-cance of his verbal behavior.

4. Although it is well known that the de-velopment of affective responses and cogni-tive components related to them may occur without influencing behavior to any great extent, most teacher-training programs do little to develop in the teacher-trainee any action system through which the results of teacher training may be manifested in the classroom. A few programs are based on the assumption that the development of affective responses and cognitive structures is not enough. Programs of the latter type attempt from the earliest stages of teacher training to develop in the student of education an action system through which a philosophy of edu-cation can be expressed. Such programs *may* be effective in generating patterns of teacher behavior related to the philosophy of educa-tion accepted by the teacher-education insti-tution.

Patterns Generated by the Teacher's Needs

Many of the commonly discussed teaching methods appear to be generated largely by the needs of the teachers who promote them. A few examples will help to clarify the origin of some of these patterns of teacher behavior.

Many workers in education advocate that teaching at levels above the elementary school should be conducted by a lecture method in which the teacher speaks and discusses and the pupil listens and thinks. Other students of education, including the writers, hold that, although some learning takes place by this procedure, the lecture method is a rather in-efficient method of producing learning. The concept of "learning by doing" was large-ly a reaction against the lecture-recitation method of teaching which was common in the early part of the century. If the lecture method of teaching is not based on scientific knowledge of learning, then why is it so widely practiced and vehemently defended? One answer which the writers suggest is that some teachers have a need to talk in the class-room and that their best rationalization for their behavior is to insist that a lecture method is a good method of teaching. In large part, the lecture method exists as a recognized teaching method because many teachers like to talk. Of course, in many ways the latter statement tends to be an over-simplification of the matter, for different teachers may like to talk for different reasons. Some talk because they have learned to emit great quantities of verbal behavior. Some talk because this is a means of controlling the pupils. Some talk because this is a way of achieving recognition, and so forth.

Needless to say, many advocates of the lecture method also genuinely hold to the view that lecturing allows the presentation of facts, ideas, cognitive structures, and the like, in ways that are more convenient and compelling than mere reading or other methods of transmission. This view has, un-fortunately, been supported mainly by im-pressionistic evidence.

Other so-called teaching methods may also reflect the need structure of those that pro-mote them. It seems reasonable to hypothe-size that those who advocate a teaching method in which the teacher is highly per-missive would be persons with either a high control need or with a low control need. In the former case the advocacy of this method would represent a reaction against the need. In the latter case it would represent a situa-tion compatible with this aspect of the need structure. One might further hypothesize that the friendly human relationships which form a part of this teaching method would also provide a means of satisfying a high affiliation need.

Probably on no other dimension do teach-ing methods differ more than on the matter of the exercise of control. The pattern of teacher behavior which forms part of the cul-tural tradition is that of the teacher function-ing as an authority figure who maintains or-der in the classroom. The exercise of this kind of authority is often postulated to be a neces-sary condition for learning. What is now known about human need structures suggests that the authoritarian pattern of behavior is highly compatible with the need structure of many who enter teaching and that hence it is a pattern of behavior widely advocated by practitioners in the educational profession. Often teachers advocate an authoritarian pat-tern of behavior in such vigorous terms that the underlying reasons are more than plain.

In this area, as in the others which have been considered, there is little evidence that any of the patterns of behavior advocated have a clear relationship to the learning process itself. Some of the studies suggest relationships which may exist and which should be explored in further research. Studies which attempt to evaluate the ef-fectiveness of some of these patterns of teach-er behavior in producing learning will be discussed in the second half of this chapter.

We turn now to a study (Gordon, 1955) which suggests some of the relationships that may exist between these patterns of teacher behavior and the total milieu in which learn-ing occurs, particularly in the case of a high-ly controlling pattern of behavior. This is one of the few studies of the relation of the teach-er to the authority system, and the pattern of behavior which this relationship usually pre-scribes. This study was undertaken in a four-year suburban high school with a student enrollment of 576 pupils. The pupil popula-tion was derived largely from the lower middle class, but all socioeconomic levels were represented in the school population. According to this study, the pattern of be-havior of the typical teacher in this school system was largely derived from the fact that he was an intermediary between the pupil and the principal in the authority system. The chief threat to the teacher as an authority figure, according to this study, came from interactions within the student group. Such interactions included talking, whispering, inattention, and horseplay. The teacher tolerated such behavior up to the point where it became a challenge to his authority and then took some action to suppress this behavior.

An important matter to note, according to Gordon, is that the point where such interaction was no longer tolerated was not the point where it became a serious competitor with learning but the point where it became a challenge to the status of the teacher. In other words, the need system of the teacher is a crucial factor. This point illustrates the contrast between the situation in the classroom as interpreted by the teacher and as interpreted by the psychologist or sociologist who is sitting there as a disinterested observer. Some data are provided to indicate the nature of the conflict that occurs between the teacher as an authority figure and the student subculture. During a one-year period, a tabulation was made of all pupil offenses which resulted in the pupil's being sent to the principal's office. Of 81 such referrals, 33 were a result of the pupil's being involved in a disturbance in the student group, 27 were for talking without permission, 14 were for talking back to the teacher, 4 for throwing objects, and 3 for other offenses. It is clear that the major threat to the teacher's authority position came from the interaction among the pupils themselves, but the second major threat came from direct verbal aggression of student against teacher.

Other interesting data presented by Gordon show a decline over a three-year period in the number of disciplinary referrals made by teachers to the principal. This decline, it is claimed, was the result of a rumor that the principal graded teachers on the basis of such referrals. It is clear that the success with which the teacher can be expected to function as an authority figure depends to a great extent on the degree to which the principal supports his position.

Gordon pointed out what was also discussed by Becker (1953), namely, that eviction from the classroom represents a serious crisis in student-teacher relationships which may be resolved in a number of ways. Sending the student to the principal is one way. A second way is for the teacher to absorb the conflict by finding some solution to it within the classroom itself. The third way is for the teacher to ignore the problem. Which solution is adopted will depend partly on the behavior exhibited by the principal toward the teacher and partly on the extent to which the teacher can tolerate the threat to his status without seeking support from the outside.

The effectiveness with which the teacher can function as an authority figure depends upon many aspects of his behavior, some of which were considered by Gordon. For example, the teacher should not disregard the fact that he is working with a subculture of pupils which has its own status hierarchy. Not only are there pupils who can be described as isolates from the subculture (27 per cent for boys and 16 per cent for girls, in Gordon's school) but there are also "wheels" within the system whose influence is valuable if it is used. The teacher who is involved in the activity program of the school may be highly sensitive to this social structure. He may become so aware of a need to have the support of certain students that he may violate the ordinary standards of fairness in passing out the rewards under his control. The teacher who is not so involved in the activity program may tread on the toes of the influential student but by so doing may gain status in the eyes of the low status group. Thus, a teacher who is regarded as fair by an underdog group may be regarded with much less esteem by the high status group. The difficulties and tensions produced tend to remain unresolved. For one thing, the problems remain the personal ones of the teachers involved. In the school studied by Gordon, teachers did not discuss their problems with other teachers. The competition for status among the faculty was sufficient to prevent such discussion. Also there was a saying among the faculty that the best teachers do not have problems. Thus to admit having a problem was to admit a weakness. No machinery existed for relieving the teachers of the anxiety which all these factors created.

Two goals would appear to be achieved through the successful exercise of an authoritarian role. First, orderliness of the interactions among pupils may be such that even if learning is not facilitated, at least it is not interfered with. The real issue is whether such orderliness is most effectively achieved through the teacher functioning as an authoritarian figure or by other means. This issue has been central in the numerous comparisons between so-called traditional and so-called progressive teaching which occurred during the 1930's and which will be considered in later sections of this chapter. A second issue is the social development which is likely in children exposed to predominantly authoritarian teachers. Educational folklore suggests that such a role fosters dependency and interferes with what has been rather vaguely described as self-actualization. Psychological analysis does not indicate that this is necessarily so. An authoritarian teacher may still consistently reinforce leadership behaviors in the students, provided they do not conflict with the status of the teacher or the teacher's own leadership.

There is an extensive literature on the merits of the democratic teacher as distinct from the authoritarian teacher. Such literature reached its peak in volume in the late 1930's when much of the discussion of this problem did at least have the merit of being coupled with actual research on the outcomes of teaching under these two conditions. The decrease in such experimentation during the past two decades has returned the literature related to this problem to the exhortatory tones of the past. Brown (1949) presented one such paper, which colorfully presents the old-time phrases advocating the modern "life-centered" school, in which children and teachers live cooperatively and teachers guide pupil growth permissively rather than autocratically. It is unfortunate that an era of research on this important topic should be superseded by a return to a less rigorous level of discourse.

Patterns Generated by School and Community Conditions

The practical school administrator commonly assumes that patterns of teacher behavior in the classroom can be controlled to some extent by the school situation itself. If the school establishes an educational policy requiring a particular pattern of teacher behavior for its execution, the principal is likely to assume that teachers within the school can manifest the required pattern of behavior merely by manifesting cooperation. This position has been taken commonly by educational reformers who assume that, once teachers have seen the merit of manifesting a particular pattern of classroom behavior, the behavior will automatically follow. Similar assumptions have also been made by superintendents and school boards fired with enthusiasm for reform.

A classic case of this tendency was provided by the Board of Education of New York City (Jersild, et al., 1939) of the midthirties which decided to change the curriculum in 69 schools to conform to what was then called an activity curriculum. This changed curriculum required a change in the behavior of the teachers and it was assumed that this change would occur merely by asking the teacher to make the change. That relatively little change did occur in teacher behavior when the new curriculum was introduced was manifestly clear when instruments were applied which were designed to measure the extent of that change. Large numbers of classrooms under the old and socalled traditional curriculum were found to display far more of the features of an activity curriculum than did many of those under the new curriculum. The teachers of the new curriculum were not able to make the substantial changes in their behavior which the new curriculum required. This was not a matter of lack of cooperation, for the difficulties are much more deep-seated than those involved in merely obtaining cooperation. Psychologists know that behavior patterns which are as deeply ingrained as those of teachers with many years of teaching experience cannot be changed overnight. The situation is somewhat analogous to expecting the hardened criminal to change his ways after he had been told by the prison warden that the time has come for a change.

A similar difficulty occurs in the type of teaching method experiment in which each teacher serves as his own control. In this form of experiment, a teacher first teaches a class by one method and then switches the method either with a new class or with the same class. Replications of this design are, of course, necessary with different teachers. The design also makes the assumption that the teacher is able to switch patterns of classroom behavior at will. It is hardly surprising that such experiments rarely result in significant differences between treatments. Even if such classes were to be taught by persons trained in acting, it would be unreasonable to expect that any actor could assume any pattern of behavior. In casting a play, the producer is careful to select actors for specific parts who already manifest some patterns of behavior consistent with the role they are to play. Yet some educational researchers do expect Miss Jones, who has ruled her class with a rod of iron for the last 30 years, to change overnight into a relaxed, permissive teacher who functions mainly as a consultant for a democratically run class.

Any person who visits schools regularly recognizes that teaching patterns vary to some extent from school to school, but little evidence has been forthcoming from research to indicate the extent to which this is so. Indeed, the little evidence that is available indicates that school policy and the pressures of the other members of a teaching group within the school may have only a small influence on the pattern of behavior of the teacher in the classroom.

In addition, the local community sometimes exerts pressures for the teachers to behave in particular ways. A community of professional people is likely to make different demands on the schools than would one consisting of unskilled laboring groups. Often teachers have difficulty in conforming to these community demands, and conflict may result between the teaching group and representatives of the community. Just what teaching patterns result from such pressures is not known at this time.

Patterns Derived from Research on Learning

Research on teaching methods should begin with the design of teaching methods in terms of scientific knowledge of learning. In the previous sections of this chapter we have tried to demonstrate that patterns of teacher behavior and the teaching methods that they represent are mainly the products of forces which have little to do with scientific knowledge of learning. While here and there one can discern some inroad of scientific knowledge as, for example, in the use of controlled vocabularies, most prescribed teaching patterns have been influenced much more by philosophical traditions, cultural traditions, the needs of teachers and of professors of education, and so forth, than they have been influenced by research on learning.

One cannot question the proposition that teaching methods must be built on the basis of an educational philosophy, for different methods are probably required for achieving different values. Nevertheless, once the values to be achieved have been set, the design of a teaching method should be based as far as possible on scientific knowledge of learning rather than on folklore. Why then have the behavioral sciences been so lacking in influence in the design of teaching methods? The reasons are many and complex and cannot be discussed in detail here, but, in passing, we may briefly discuss a few that are of major importance.

First, there has been a tendency in education to pick and choose elements from the behavioral sciences that appear to fit with the philosophical traditions of teacher education.

For this reason Gestalt psychology has enjoyed great popularity among educators. The latter approach to perceptual problems presents a certain harmony with the philosophical tradition of Rousseau, Froebel, and many modern thinkers. The unity of behavior emphasized by Gestalt psychologists bears a close resemblance to the unity both in man and nature which Froebel emphasized. The widespread acceptance of Gestalt psychology by educators represents a selection of those psychological facts which are compatible with a philosophical position. The misfortune is that the discoveries of the Gestalt psychologists provide little of value in the design of teaching methods. As a matter of fact, of all approaches to problems of learning, Gestalt psychology has least to say about the way in which learning conditions should be manipulated if learning is to occur with maximum effectiveness. The consequence is that educators tend to be most unfamiliar with those aspects of the science of learning which have the most to contribute to the scientific design of teaching methods.

Second, within the field of education there has been little place until now for the specialist in the behavioral sciences. A few names stand out as notable exceptions to this generalization, but teachers colleges have tended to close their doors on persons who are primarily the specialists needed for the systematic design of teaching methods. Many such institutions require that all staff members hold a teaching certificate, which necessarily excludes those that are specialists in other disciplines.

It is true, of course, that a few attempts have been made to design teaching methods systematically in terms of modern knowledge of the behavioral sciences. When Carleton Washburne (1932) was at Winnetka, he made a notable effort to do this and developed a curriculum and a related teaching method which became known as the Winnetka Plan. Olson (1959) has also, in a sense, attempted to develop a teaching method on the basis of the findings of a series of scientific studies carried out by him and his associates. The method which derives from the work of Olson is probably different from that which would be constructed on the basis of a broad review of current psychological knowledge.

A new and quite elaborate teaching model has been developed by Woodruff (1959). Based to a considerable extent on his earlier learning model, the teaching model not only lists a set of learning principles which have relevant applications in the classroom but indicates the behavior that the teacher should manifest in order to make effective use of these principles. This raises a point which has been missed by many of those who have concerned themselves with design of teaching methods—a teaching method cannot be designed in terms of a set of laws of learning alone. It must also include a set of laws which should characterize the behavior of the teacher. How such laws should be specified is still a matter for speculation.

THE PRESENT POSITION: TEACHING METHODS AS AN AREA OF SCIENTIFIC INQUIRY

In the first part of this chapter, we have attempted to discuss, first, some of the studies which have been undertaken to define and separate out the patterns of behavior which teachers manifest, some of which are commonly referred to as teaching methods. Second, an attempt has been made to analyze some of the conditions which probably produce particular patterns of teacher behavior. A third part of our discussion dealt with some of the techniques designed to identify particular patterns in the behavior of teachers.

Our first major point, which will structure the rest of this chapter, is that little has been done to develop teaching methods on the basis of scientific knowledge of learning. Most widely advocated teaching methods are based either on a philosophical tradition or on the personal needs of teachers. The progressive education of the 1930's found its roots in the tradition of Rousseau. Little effort has been made to design teaching methods in terms of established principles of learning. Perhaps such an effort has become feasible only within the last two decades, for prior to that time not enough was known to make possible the design of a teaching method in terms of learning principles based on research. Of course, teaching methods of the past have been based in part on ideas about learning, but these have been based on folklore rather than on research. Before the reader jumps to any conclusions based on the latter statements, we must add that many learning principles founded on folklore are probably sound and may ultimately be demonstrated to be sound.

Since teaching methods have arisen largely outside of a scientific context, studies which compare the effectiveness of one with another can hardly be conceived as constituting a program of scientific research. This is a point which has been missed in the numerous reviews of studies of teaching methods which have come to our attention. Most reviewers treat these studies as if they constituted a unified body of scientific knowledge—which they do not. They are comparable to efforts made by a medieval physician to determine which of two herbs had the greater curative value, when he had no knowledge of the chemistry, physiology, or pharmacology involved. Such efforts represent practical head-on attacks on problems which probably cannot be studied by any such direct attack. Such sophistication as these efforts possess stems from the complicated statistical techniques which are often adopted to test hypotheses. Statistical sophistication cannot make up for what may be termed the theoretical naïveté reflected in the concepts which the studies involve.

Studies comparing teaching methods have also lacked scientific sophistication in another sense. The fact that these methods are derived only to the most limited degree from scientific research means that the variables involved reflect few of the properties of well-developed scientific variables. These variables tend to be intuitively derived rather than empirically derived. This difference is important if one is to understand the limited value of the studies that have been undertaken, and, hence, a brief discussion of the matter is in order at this point.

In the early stages of scientific development, the variables are derived from common experience; i.e., they are *intuitively* derived. As science advances, the variables are derived by other means and become less and less related to the world as it is directly perceived. The modern concept of matter with most of the space occupied by a void differs fundamentally from the popular concept of matter which is that solid matter is solid. The layman often has the greatest difficulty in accepting the concepts used by the scientist and may not be easily persuaded that his own concepts are inferior, for many purposes, to those of the scientist. Men did not easily abandon the idea that the world was flat. Popular concepts related to behavior are much less likely to be given up easily. Most persons feel comfortable with intuitively derived concepts. Only very convincing evidence of the superior value of concepts derived by other means will make them abandon their intuitive concepts. This kind of inertia probably accounts for the fact that research on teaching methods is based almost entirely on an intuitive approach.

A second major point which derives from this discussion is that techniques for determining the extent to which particular teaching methods are being pursued are only in the beginning stages of their development. For the most part, studies which supposedly compare the effectiveness of two teaching methods are generally studies which compare two largely unknown conditions. It is hardly surprising then that most such studies cannot be considered to be a major contribution to scientific knowledge, for they compare the effect of one vaguely defined condition with that of another.

Since studies comparing the learning outcomes of two teaching methods have little scientific significance, why have they been carried out? The answer to this question is fairly complex because studies comparing methods derive from many different motives. Some are motivated by a need to justify particular teaching practices in the eyes of the public. Many such studies comparing "progressive" and "traditional" education were carried out between the two world wars. Newer practices in schools were under attack and school authorities had to justify what they were doing. Both large-scale and local studies were directed toward this end. Why present-day attacks on education have not been met by a similar flood of studies is hard to understand. Perhaps educators recognize that the studies aimed at providing a defense of progressive education did little to change public opinion.

Another motive for undertaking minor studies in the area is the production of doctoral and master's dissertations. Since schools of education have often encouraged their graduate students to work on local problems for a thesis or dissertation, the lack of scientific characteristics of most of these studies has not been considered to be of any great disadvantage. From the writers' point of view, this fact highlights the need in schools of education for staff members who have had rigorous scientific training.

THE IDENTIFICATION OF TEACHING METHODS

A teaching method may exist as an abstract concept, that is to say, as a concept of a pattern of teacher behavior. A teaching method may also be manifested as an actual and identifiable pattern of teacher behavior. Methods could be invented for which no concrete examples could ever be found because the method calls for patterns of behavior which persons in our culture could not acquire. All too often the unreasonable assumption is made that, because a teaching method has been described, corresponding patterns of behavior can be, or are, manifested by teachers.

Studies of the differences in the products of different teaching methods all make the assumption that real differences exist in the patterns of behavior manifested by the teachers representing the two methods. This assumption is often a difficult one to justify. What are the different bases used to justify it? These must be understood if studies comparing the outcomes of different methods are to be seen in proper perspective. A brief discussion of the criteria used to justify the assumption that differences exist is appropriate at this point.

Patterns Imposed Ad Hoc

In many studies the experimenter has decided in advance which teacher is to teach according to which teaching method. The assumption is made that a teacher can manifest, at will, one or another pattern of teacher behavior. In a few studies the same teacher may be expected to manifest different patterns of behavior with different classes. For example, a teacher of high school history may lecture to two of her classes, but in two other classes she may be required to run the same course as a sequence of periods of supervised study. The outcomes of the two different teaching methods are then compared, after precautions have been taken either to eliminate or adjust for differences in the ability levels of the four classes. Although the ad hoc assignment of teaching methods to teachers or to the same teacher at different times is a common experimental technique, little evidence has been produced to show that teachers actually switch from one pattern of behavior to another. Indeed, evidence reported earlier indicates that such a switch is far from easy.

Studies in which patterns are imposed ad hoc on a group of teachers or on the same teacher at different times must always be regarded with suspicion, even when some evidence is forthcoming that the teachers were able to modify their behavior according to the experimental design. The possibility always exists that the teachers involved favor one method rather than another. When such is the case one might expect superior results from the favored method. One can hardly expect a teacher to put full effort into the utilization of a teaching method which he does not consider sound or personally congenial. The latter factor may become a much more important determinant of what happens than differences in the prescribed patterns. This basic weakness characterizes all studies that use this particular approach to the study of teaching.

Methods Existing by Reputation

Many studies have been conducted in which a comparison has been made of the outcomes of education in two schools or groups of schools which differ *by repute*. In the 1930's, many studies were undertaken in which outcomes of education in schools reputed to be progressive were compared with those in schools reputed to be more traditional. The independent variable in this instance is not differences in teaching practices but differences in reputation. This distinction has not always been emphasized in studies presenting the results of such investigations. Sometimes such reputations may represent merely the capacity of the school principals to give embellished accounts of their programs. Generally, little is known about the conditions that have generated the reputation of an educational program.

Characteristically, studies which depend on differences in reputation come out with negative results. However, one cannot tell whether these results are due to a lack of difference in actual teaching procedure or to a failure of variation in teaching method to produce differences in learning.

Research workers have not made any vigorous efforts to develop techniques which might be used to determine the actual differences in teaching which accompany differences in reputation. The central difficulty in developing such research techniques is that teaching is a process which cannot be observed without being changed. The problem of the determination of the patterns of behavior which characterize a particular teacher is greatly complicated by many well-established phenomena. For example, a teacher may well show both a particular pattern of behavior and its opposite. A teacher may exert a high degree of control over the class for much of the time but may, at times, develop guilt feelings about her behavior and switch to a pattern which is highly permissive. Soon, however, she may become bored with the situation or perhaps even feel guilty that she is not working hard enough at her job and then revert to a pattern of highly controlling behavior. This vacillation may be very disturbing to a research worker who is attempting to determine the extent to which the teacher is controlling and the extent to which she is permissive. The fact that teachers may manifest many separate and incompatible patterns of behavior makes research in this field particularly difficult. Indeed, the researcher may have to work with only those teachers who have an internally consistent system of behavior patterns.

In a few instances, investigators have made attempts to check on the extent to which different methods are pursued by the two comparison groups used. This may be done through three main approaches. The first technique, which has already been mentioned, is that of observing the teacher directly and determining the extent to which the pattern of behavior conforms more closely to one or the other of the teaching methods being studied.

A second approach is to ask the teachers to describe what they do either by providing a free discussion of their activities or by filling out a questionnaire. This technique has many obvious pitfalls. One is that the teachers, like other persons, probably have only limited insight into what they do and hence will record their concept of how they behave in the classroom rather than what they actually do. Another is that teachers have difficulty in recalling just what they did in the classroom or how much time was devoted to this and that activity.

A third possibility is for the pupils to record what happens in a class conducted by a particular teacher. This technique was adopted in the study of differences between the teachers conducting the activity program and those in the traditional program in the experiment conducted by the New York City system in the late thirties. The questionnaire used for this purpose, developed by McCall, Herring, and Loftus (1937–1938), was intended to yield evidence for the existence of the new educational program as it was defined in the curriculum. (One difficulty with such devices is that they may be threatening to the teachers involved.) Recently, the writers (Travers, Wallen, Reid, & Wodtke, 1961), faced with the same problem, attempted to use the technique of asking children to draw a picture of their class. The usefulness of this technique still remains to be seen.

Rating scales have not been commonly used by observers in assessing the extent to which teacher behavior conforms to certain patterns. Perhaps this is a reflection of the more general fact that direct observation of teachers is rarely undertaken by persons with psychological training. An exception is a study by Manning (1950), who developed a rating scale for the dimension of permissiveness versus control in the classroom behavior of teachers. Manning undertook his study in two 12-year schools and covered the entire range of grade levels. He observed teachers in a number of different situations and concluded that directive behavior was far more common than nondirective. In the least directive situation studied, directive behavior was four times more frequent than nondirective. Directiveness also increased with grade level, indicating, perhaps, that the schools did little to foster self-direction among the pupils. Manning concluded that educational literature about the child-centered school was much more a reflection of talk than of reality.

In Manning's study, as in many others that discuss the control, or authoritarian, dimension, there is considerable obscurity concerning what is meant by the dimension. The tendency is for writers to take the unsophisticated position that a teacher who says to the class "Now turn to page 58 of your book," is exercising control over the pupils, but a teacher who says "You certainly have worked well today" is not. Psychologists know this distinction to be invalid, for it is the last type of statement, considered as a reinforcement, which has the more profound effect in controlling the behavior of pupils. The smile of a teacher may control the behavior of an entire group of children either by offering encouragement, or by reinforcing what they have been doing, or by eliciting similar smiling responses in the pupils. Most of what the teacher does has a controlling effect on the behavior of the pupil, but the teacher is hardly aware of most of the control which he exercises. It is arbitrary though often useful to classify teacher behavior as controlling only when it is deliberately so.

Fishburn (1955) used three techniques to assess the patterns assumed by teachers in the classroom: (1) interviews in which the statements made by the interviewees were later classified, (2) a rating scale in which the importance of various classroom activities was rated by the teachers, and (3) a forced-choice technique in which teachers were asked to choose from blocks of statements those they thought best described effective teachers. In the case of Method 2 the median correlation between patterns was found to be .06. In the case of Method 3 the median correlation between patterns was found to be −.08, indicating independence of the patterns. One should note that in using Method 3 the value of the median correlation may well have been generated by the forced-choice technique, which can only lower one rating by raising another or a combination of others. In the case of the second method the tendency for the correlations between patterns to cluster around zero is not an artifact of the procedure involved. The evidence indicates that one is dealing with fairly distinct variables. While Fishburn reported acceptable reliability coefficients, evidence is needed to determine whether one is dealing with fairly stable characteristics of teachers or whether they show marked day-to-day fluctuations.

Other approaches exist for the identification and study of clusters of behavioral attributes. One alternative is to collect data on the behavior of teachers and then to determine by statistical means how the characteristics observed tend to cluster. The most ambitious attempt to do this has been that of Ryans (1960), whose Teacher Characteristics Study is reviewed in Chapter 11.

It is too early to say whether this empirical approach will lead to the development of variables in terms of which a theory of classroom behavior of teachers may be developed. Any classification of teacher behavior into a pattern system may need to have a certain compatibility with learning theory if it is to be useful. Empirically derived systems of teacher behavior variables are likely to be related to learning variables only by accident, when the data from which they are derived are themselves events related to learning.

RELATIONSHIP OF TEACHING METHODS TO THE OUTCOMES OF EDUCATION

When research on educational methods is viewed in terms of the framework presented in this chapter, it becomes apparent that the vast majority of studies relate to the behavior of the teacher as an authority figure. The authors were unable to locate studies relating teacher behavior to the social-class pattern or to a parent-substitute pattern. A few studies bearing upon patterns of behavior of teachers related to that of the therapist will be considered later. With respect to the authoritarian pattern, it must be emphasized that this grouping of studies does violence to the intent of those researchers who have not always viewed their research in precisely these terms. Furthermore, it will be necessary to delineate clearly the variable as studied by the researcher since the dimensions differ from study to study. Nevertheless, it seems desirable to impose such a structure upon this research in the interest of clarification and organization. The common denominator of these studies is that they all involve as a primary dimension authoritarianism as we define it, i.e., the degree to which some person or persons (in this case, the teacher) exercises control over the behavior of others (in this case, students).

THE AUTHORITARIAN PATTERN

The first evidence to be considered is that deriving from the comparison of "progressive" or "activity" schools with their more traditional counterparts. One of the principal objectives of the progressive education movement was the instigation of classroom procedures wherein the teacher and other adult "authorities" exhibited a less authoritarian pattern, allowing students greater choice of content and procedures as well as greater physical freedom. Research was undertaken to evaluate the merits of this approach as compared to the traditional system.

These studies have followed a classic pattern in educational research. The "progressive" school pupils have been viewed as an experimental group to be compared with the traditional school pupils either directly or by utilizing the norms of standardized tests to represent the "traditional" level of performance. Although this research has focused principally on the academic performance of students, attention has also been given to social and emotional behavior.

The Eight-Year Study

The most extensive of these studies is the so-called "Eight-Year Study" conducted under the auspices of the Progressive Education Association during the period from 1933 to 1939. The following excerpt from the published report summarizes the study:

An intensive study has been made of 2,108 graduates from the Thirty Schools which, under an agreement with more than 300 colleges, had been freed from the necessity of meeting the usual unit or examination requirements for college admission. Of these Thirty Schools' graduates, 1,475 were matched, student for student, with graduates of conventional schools in terms of scholastic aptitude, interests, and socio-economic background. This report deals primarily with these 1,475 matched pairs of college students. In general, these students were fairly representative of the student bodies in most of the colleges where the Study was undertaken.

Four classes were included in the Study: the classes entering college in 1936, 1937, 1938, and 1939. Data were gathered on the first class for four years, on the second for three, on the third for two, and on the last for one year. The follow-up was carried on in 38 colleges of four types: the northeastern men's colleges, the northeastern women's colleges, coeducational endowed colleges and universities, and middle-western state universities.

Success in college, as defined in this Study, included grades earned; certain "intellectual characteristics" which are not necessarily measured by grades; citizenship in the college community as indicated by extent and quality of interest in extra-class activities; and the attainment of personal goals as revealed by the nature of vocational orientation, concern about the contemporary scene, attitudes toward and relation to contemporaries. In effect, these criteria represent success as judged by college standards, by the students' contemporaries, and by students themselves.

Data were gathered from regular interviews with students, questionnaires, records of reading and activities, reports from instructors, official college records, and comments of college officers, house heads, and others who had contact with the students. Summaries were made of grades and of questionnaire responses. In addition each student was judged for each year in college in some 60 separate areas including his quality of thinking, extent of participation in each of a series of organized activities and leisure time interests, personal-social relationships, problems, and a number of others. All available data for each student in a given year were used in arriving at such judgments.

General Findings

A comparison of the 1,475 matched pairs reveals that the Thirty Schools graduates

1. earned a slightly higher total grade average;
2. earned higher grade averages in all subject fields except foreign language;
3. specialized in the same academic fields as did the comparison students;
4. did not differ from the comparison group in the number of times they were placed on probation;
5. received slightly more academic honors in each year;
6. were more often judged to possess a high degree of intellectual curiosity and drive;
7. were more often judged to be precise, systematic, and objective in their thinking;
8. were more often judged to have developed clear or well-formulated ideas concerning the meaning of education—especially in the first two years in college;
9. more often demonstrated a high degree of resourcefulness in meeting new situations;
10. did not differ from the comparison group in ability to plan their time effectively;
11. had about the same problems of adjustment as the comparison group, but approached their solution with greater effectiveness;
12. participated somewhat more frequently, and more often enjoyed appreciative experiences, in the arts;
13. participated more in all organized student groups except religious and "service" activities;
14. earned in each college year a higher percentage of nonacademic honors;
15. did not differ from the comparison group in the quality of adjustment to their contemporaries;
16. differed only slightly from the comparison group in the kinds of judgments about their schooling;
17. had a somewhat better orientation toward the choice of a vocation;
18. demonstrated a more active concern for what was going on in the world.

Some of these differences were not large, but wherever reported, they were consistent for each class. It is apparent that when one finds even small margins of difference for a number of large groups, the probability greatly increases that the differences cannot be due to chance alone.

It is quite obvious from these data that the Thirty Schools graduates, as a group, have done a somewhat better job than the comparison group whether success is judged by college standards, by the students' contemporaries, or by the individual students.

The Thirty Schools differed widely in the extent to which they experimented. A special analysis was therefore made of the graduates of the six schools whose programs differed most sharply from the conventional. A corollary study was made of the graduates from the six schools which departed least from a traditional approach. Each of these groups was contrasted with its respective comparison group.

The graduates of the most experimental schools were strikingly more successful than their matches. Differences in their favor were much greater than the differences between the total Thirty Schools and their comparison group. Conversely, there were no large or consistent differences between the least experimental graduates and their comparison group. For these students the differences were smaller and less consistent than for the total Thirty Schools and their comparison group.

Finally, a study was made of the graduates of two schools which were among the most progressive. Again, these students were contrasted with their matchees. The superiority of these progressive students over their comparison group was greater than any previous differences reported.

Clearly, among the Thirty Schools, the more experimental the school, the greater the degree of success in college. Furthermore, although students of high aptitude seem to have profited most from experimental education, students of low aptitude profited as much from experimental programs as their matchees did from conventional schooling (Chamberlin, Chamberlin, Drought, & Scott, 1942, pp. 206–209).

Before accepting these conclusions we should examine several major criticisms, each illustrative of a recurring problem in experimentation. The first criticism is in terms of what is variously termed "uncontrolled individual variation," "subject error," etc. What is meant is simply that observed group differences, or lack of them, may be attributable to differences between the individuals in the two or more groups, independent of any effect of the different methods. The groups in this study were matched by pairs on several characteristics

known, or thought, to be related to academic success. This procedure is highly desirable because it effectively controls troublesome variables. However, control of all known relevant variables is often difficult and the research worker is seldom, if ever, aware of all individual difference variables related to the dimension studied. This being the case, the important principle of randomization is applied. Simply stated, this principle insures that if the subjects in the comparison groups are placed in the groups on a random basis, all uncontrolled individual difference variables can be assumed to balance out, provided the groups are large enough. In most educational research, a completely random assignment of students to "methods" is not feasible, but one can guard against introducing systematic bias in favor of one group. It is precisely on these grounds that H. C. Johnson (1946) challenged the Eight-Year Study.

In a study such as this, an individual difference variable of paramount importance is that of motivation toward academic goals. The selection of students for college from the progressive schools was based in large part on the recommendation of school authorities, whereas this information was not included in the selection of the matching students from the traditional schools. A result of this selection procedure might have been that the "progressive" group was better oriented toward college goals than the "traditional" group and that this orientation was independent of the progressive-traditional dimension. (If it were largely due to the high school experience, the criticism is of course irrelevant.) Hence, it may be argued that the "traditional" school students were typical of their group, whereas the progressive school group was a select group from among the population of the graduates of these schools who wished to attend college. A similar argument can be offered from a somewhat different point of view. It might be expected that students coming from homes wherein the parents, in the aggregate, approve of curriculum experimentation in the schools, would be exposed to a system of values at home and in the community which would be conducive to academic motivation and hence make them a different group regardless of the nature of the curricular changes. In the absence of more adequate measures of motivation than are available at present, this latter problem cannot be eliminated through matching.

A second criticism of the study has to do with the measuring devices used in matching, particularly the measures of intellectual ability. It is generally accepted that all measures of intelligence are affected at least to some extent by educational experiences. Johnson has argued that a traditional curriculum would better prepare one for such tests than a progressive school experience. Should this be the case, the use of tests given at the end of high school could have the effect of underestimating the "basic capacity" of the progressive school students so that, being a "brighter" group, they would be expected to outperform their traditional counterparts in college. The writers do not feel that this is likely since other studies, though inconclusive, indicate that the progressive school student is not penalized with regard to academic learnings and in fact may undergo experiences advantageous to performance on intelligence tests. It is, nevertheless, pertinent as an illustration of a common problem and highlights the importance of measuring techniques in all such research.

A related issue concerns the rather technical measurement phenomenon of regression of scores. Whenever subjects are selected on the basis of extreme scores, it is to be expected that a retesting would show group performance nearer to the mean than was the case on the first testing. If, as has been argued, test scores were weighted more heavily in selecting students from the traditional schools, this phenomenon could serve to overestimate the relative ability of this group. The extent to which this may be true in the Eight-Year Study has not been determined (and because of absence of the necessary data could not be), though an analysis of previous test scores for a portion of the traditional group suggests that it is not a severe limitation.

A third criticism has to do with the possible confounding of the variable under study. Was the essential difference between the "progressive" and the "traditional" schools the greater student freedom and variety of experiences permitted by the progressive schools' curriculum, or were there also, and perhaps more important, differences in teacher competence and personality or in the enthusiasm engendered in trying something new regardless of the nature of the innovation—the so-called "Hawthorne effect"? This question also cannot be answered within the framework of the Eight-Year Study.

Other "Activity" versus "Traditional" Studies

In addition to the Eight-Year Study, there have been a number of other comparisons of "activity" versus "traditional" procedures. Although less comprehensive, often less rigorous, and subject to the various criticisms previously discussed in connection with the Eight-Year Study, they provide a striking unanimity of results—essentially the same as those of the Eight-Year Study—and extend these findings to the elementary grades.

Whether comparison is made with national test norms (Board of Education, Roslyn, New York, 1938; Hopkins & Mendenhall, 1934; Oberholtzer, 1937; Proctor, 1933) with the performance of students in the same schools before the adoption of "progressive" curriculum changes (Davis & Morgan, 1940; Proctor, 1933), or with students of presumably similar characteristics in traditional schools (Collings, 1923; Helbing, 1940; Jersild, et al., 1941; Pistor, 1937; Sax & Ottina, 1958; Washburne & Raths, 1927), the findings are much the same and can be summarized as follows: In the early grades, students in the progressive curriculum tend to perform somewhat below expectation in reading and arithmetic but overcome their inferiority by about sixth grade; they tend to be average or somewhat superior throughout their school years in achievement areas involving language usage; when moving up to junior high school, they suffer no handicap in dealing with a more traditional curriculum; when compared on tests designed to measure work skills, organizing ability, ability to interpret information, and civic beliefs, they score higher but often not significantly so; they tend to be better informed on current affairs and they tend to be rated higher by high school teachers and independent observers on such dimensions as initiative, work spirit, and critical thinking. In summary, the findings indicate no important differences in terms of subject-matter mastery and a superiority of the progressive students in terms of the characteristics which the "progressive school" seeks to develop.

It is essential, however, that these results be viewed in the light of the criticisms of the Eight-Year Study which, in general, apply to these studies as well, namely, the possibility that the "experimental" students differ initially from the "traditional" with respect to variables related to achievement and the possibility that the experimental variable is confounded with other variables. One last comment with respect to the generality of these findings seems in order. The nature of this research is such that it consists of evaluations of curriculum revisions in schools which have made such revisions. Such schools can hardly be considered typical. They tend to be schools in the socioeconomically more favored communities where the attitudes toward experimentation and toward education itself are more positive than the average and where students are likely to be intellectually superior. The person who generalizes these results to schools in the environmentally deprived sectors of our country is treading on thin ice.

How then is one to evaluate this series of studies? It seems clear that one major conclusion survives the criticisms which have been discussed—namely, that reducing the amount of authoritarian control over students (in some cases rather markedly) does not necessarily result in drastic impairment of their academic skills, contrary to the expectation of many. It seems unlikely, even if one controlled all the possible uncontrolled sources of variation previously discussed which may have worked in favor of the "progressive" schools, that the reduction of authoritarian control would result in a much poorer showing of the "progressive" as compared to the "traditional" students. Certainly it has been demonstrated that many students can and do achieve academically in a less authoritarian school. Once one attempts to push beyond this broad and important conclusion, however, it becomes increasingly apparent that these studies, owing to the nature of the research itself, are not capable of providing answers. To answer questions as to the specific outcomes of less authoritarian procedures, the sources of variation previously discussed *must* be controlled. Furthermore, the actual classroom practices must be spelled out in greater detail if one is to analyze more precisely their relation to student behavior. In addition to reducing the degree of authoritarianism, the progressive school modifications presumably included emphasis on interrelating content areas and on practical problems. Stated in another way, the progressive versus traditional dimension, as this research has studied it, is undoubtedly too complex to prove fruitful in further research and provides only limited evidence as to the effects of authoritarianism per se.

The Lewin-Lippitt-White Studies

The following studies seem to be an advance over studies previously reported in that they have in general attempted a more precise delineation of the dimension studied and have, in at least some cases, varied the dimension experimentally, hence reducing the sources of variation present when the variable is merely observed.

The series of studies originated by Lewin appears to have had a considerable impact upon educators, at least those in university departments of education. We suspect that the Lewin, Lippitt, and White (1939) study is better known to education students than any other single piece of research. (See also White & Lippitt, 1960.) In this study, three boys' club atmospheres were artificially created, one wherein activities were determined by an adult authority figure (five groups), a second employing democratic group-decision processes in which the adult leader acted as one of the group members (five groups), and a third designated as laissez-faire wherein no structure existed and the children were free to do as they pleased (five groups). The children were ten and eleven years old; the groups consisted of five volunteers each and considerable attention was given to matching the groups in terms of sociometric measures obtained in the school classrooms, teacher ratings on social behavior, intellectual performance, physical status, and socioeconomic background. Each of four leaders played both the autocratic and democratic "roles," and as each child was exposed to all three procedures for an equal time, individual variation was controlled. The tasks available to the children were such things as mask making, mural painting, soap carving, model airplane construction, etc. Each group was studied intensively by observations of the incidence of such behaviors as "directive," "compliant," and "objective" responses; sequential analyses of social interaction; continuous stenographic records of all conversations; interviews with the boys and parents; individual Rorschach protocols. In addition, the situation was varied in such ways as having the adult leave the room and, at another time, having a graduate student in the guise of a janitor enter and make derogatory comments about the group's achievements.

The significant differences among the three types of milieu were as follows: The incidence of aggressive behavior under autocratic procedures was either extremely high or extremely low; in the laissez-faire groups it was the highest of all; and in the democratic groups it was intermediate. The low incidence of aggression in some of the autocratic groups was apparently due to fear of reprisal, since it showed a marked rise when

(1) the leader left the room and (2) the group was "in transition" to a different milieu.

A second finding of major importance concerned the amount of time spent in activity judged as productive. With the leader present, the "autocratic" groups spent a higher percentage of time in this way. A further breakdown, however, indicated that this was principally the case with the autocratic groups that exhibited little aggressive behavior. The "rebellious" autocratic group showed approximately the same work output as the "democratic" groups, and the laissez-faire showed the least. When the leader left the room, there was a decided drop in work output in both types of autocratic groups, a very slight drop in the democratic groups, and an increase in the laissez-faire groups, possibly due to an observed tendency for one of the boys to adopt a leadership role. Return of the leader resulted in work output slightly higher than usual in the authoritarian groups, a further slight decrement in the democratic groups, and a more severe decrement in the laissez-faire groups. Thus, it appears that the authoritarian leadership forced output only when the leader was present, whereas the presence of the leader was of little importance in the democratic setting and a hindrance to the laissez-faire groups.

Other data based on the stenographic records and case studies supported the previous findings and led to the following general summary. The "authoritarian role" generated two distinct reactions: (1) a rebellious reaction characterized by a high degree of aggressive behavior, considerable discontent, many demands for attention from the leader, and a constructive work level about the same as for the democratic groups when the leader was present, but a much lower level in his absence; (2) a submissive reaction similar to that noted in (1) except for a higher level of work output with the leader present and less indication of discontent. The democratically led groups showed an intermediate amount of aggression; a moderate level of work output (about 60 per cent of the time was spent constructively, on the average) which was largely independent of the presence of the leader; and generally positive reactions to the leader. The laissez-faire pattern elicited a high level of aggression, the lowest level of work output, and behaviors which seem best interpreted as seeking for some kind of organization.

Once again, limitations must be examined. First, the description of the study suggests that the authoritarian pattern as employed was not only authoritarian, as we have defined it, but also cold, aloof, and threatening. Although the authoritarian pattern was not intended to be an "unfriendly" one, observations indicated that, as played, it manifested many more "disrupting commands," "nonconstructive criticisms," and less "joviality" than the democratic; yet such behaviors need not necessarily accompany authoritarianism.

Other Studies

Another study wherein teachers manifested assigned patterns of behavior is that of Flanders (1951). Using Withall's conception of teacher-centered versus learner-centered teaching, Flanders trained one teacher to manifest each pattern while teaching each of seven one-student "classes" in the interpretation of human behavior. Analysis of teacher statements and of Q sorts by students supported the adequacy of the role-playing. Each student experienced both procedures. In addition to tests of content mastery, student statements were analyzed, and GSR and pulse measures were obtained *during* the class sessions. The student also moved a hidden lever to indicate positive or negative feelings while in the class. The data support the conclusions that the teacher-centered role fostered more negative feelings, a greater concern with interpersonal as opposed to "learning" problems, higher physiological indices of anxiety, and less content mastery. Once again, it is important to note that the teacher-centered role is defined in terms of reproving, disparaging, or disapproving state-

ments by the teacher as well as a high degree of control. Further, the use of only two teachers restricts the generalization which can be made.

It has been frequently alleged that increasing amounts of group work in schools and a concomitant decrease in authoritarianism will greatly increase the productivity, learning facility, problem-solving ability, and the like, of students. These occasionally extravagant claims do not appear to be warranted since the few studies conducted in the public schools are far from conclusive. Rehage (1951) studied the concomitants of teacher-control versus pupil-teacher planning in two eighth-grade social studies classes taught by the same teacher and matched on several tests. No significant differences were found in terms of content mastery though there was a tendency for the less authoritarian group to perform better on measures of problem-solving in the social studies area. One could question the basis for scoring the problem tasks, however, since a higher score was given for certain debatable choices of supporting arguments.

A related finding by Ackerman (1956) indicates that intermediate-grade students taught only one way of solving problems were less flexible and saw fewer alternatives in problem-solving as compared with children taught two alternative approaches, and hence solved fewer problems. However, this group required considerably less time to reach their correct solution than the less "rigid" group. Whether teaching only one approach to problem solution is inferior in terms of subsequent problem-solving skills of students will, it appears, depend upon the nature of the new problems and upon one's criterion of success in solving them. In any case, Rehage's results cannot be generalized beyond the single teacher employed. A similar study by O. E. Thompson and Tom (1957) utilized 22 high school teachers of vocational agriculture. Eleven teachers employed a teacher-centered approach; the remaining 11 used a pupil-centered approach which also involved a greater degree of home responsibility. Interestingly enough, in this instance the pupil-centered group was superior in terms of gain in content but not significantly different with respect to measures of problem-solving in agriculture or attitudes toward farming. Krumboltz and Farquhar (1957) found no differences in mastery of content but did find an interaction between method and teacher with respect to student satisfaction.

Proponents of the intellectual merits of less authoritarian procedures for the public schools have yet to ground their case on research with school children. A good deal of research has been done with adults (Lorge, et al., 1958), however, which in general supports the statement that democratic group procedures have not yet been shown to be the panacea that some have suggested.

A series of studies by Anderson and his associates (1945, 1946a, 1946b) were concerned with the nonintellectual concomitants of dominance. A technique for observing the dominative-integrative dimension was developed which appears to have been quite objective in its application. By applying this procedure to the behavior of children in kindergarten and in the early grades and to the behavior of their teachers, these researchers obtained convincing evidence of what they termed a "vicious circle"—the tendency of dominative behavior to produce dominative behavior in others. The dimension of dominance, as theoretically defined by Anderson, referred to restrictions upon the spontaneous behavior of an individual. As operationally defined, it involved both the dimension of authoritarianism (control) and the dimension of psychological rejection (threats, disapproval, etc.).

In the studies by Anderson and his co-workers, high teacher dominance tended to be associated with a variety of student behaviors which seem undesirable in the learning situation: failure to carry out requests or orders, whispering, playing with foreign objects, etc. Unfortunately, generalization is once again restricted by the fact that in these studies only two teachers were involved. It is of interest that dominative behavior in these two teachers reappeared with new groups of students, whereas dominative behavior in the students changed if the teacher behavior changed.

Throughout this research we have observed a distinct tendency to assume that authoritarianism and rejection are highly correlated; that they form, as it were, a syndrome. Such an assumption seems questionable in the light of several research developments. Work on home climate led to the description of three major dimensions of parent behavior (Baldwin, Kalhorn, & Dreese, 1945). Two of these dimensions correspond closely to authoritarianism and rejection as considered here. These dimensions emerge as separate factors when ratings of parent behavior are factor-analyzed. The democratic home tends to be toward the warm-accepting end of the scale, and the autocratic home tends to be more rejecting, but the dimensions are not identical. One of the 10 common clinical patterns described by these workers has high ratings on warmth and restrictiveness (as well as indulgence). Although the benevolent autocrat has been roundly criticized in the literature, there is at present no evidence to indicate that he has no impact or a negative impact on the learner. Tiedeman (1942) found that some students dislike domineering, authoritarian teachers, but once again we observe the confounding of the authoritarian dimension with rejection.

A relevant contribution of interest in its own right is that of Cogan (1958), who used children's perceptions of teacher behavior rather than trained observers. Three variables of teacher behavior were utilized, corresponding roughly to (1) authoritarianism-rejection, (2) warmth, and (3) technical competence. The extent to which eighth-grade students perceived the teacher as warm and friendly was significantly related to the amount of self-initiated work and amount of required work performed within almost all classes and between composite scores on the same dimensions over all 33 teachers (classes). Furthermore, students agreed quite well as to how friendly the teacher was. The "competence" dimension, as measured, was highly related to the warmth dimension and was also related to the work measures. The dimension of authoritarianism-rejection was *not* related to amount of work performed nor was there a high degree of agreement among students as to teacher placement on this dimension. That the evaluation by principals did not agree with the students' evaluations suggests that perceptions of children, adults, or both may not correspond to the actual behavior of teachers—a state of affairs hardly surprising in the light of research on perception itself.

THE MENTAL HEALTH PATTERN

Few studies have been made which deal with the pattern of teacher behavior in which the teacher seeks primarily to promote the mental health of pupils. The evidence which does exist pertains to three somewhat different approaches to this problem. The first of these has been referred to as the "child study" approach; the second we shall refer to as the "group dynamics" approach; and the third may be termed the "causal orientation" approach. Each of these approaches seems to us to promote a pattern of behavior for the teacher to exhibit. Although the patterns themselves differ (and in fact one can discern subpatterns within the general patterns), they all have as their principal objective the fostering of mental health in the classroom with the assumption that academic learning will be improved in the process.

Child Study

Undoubtedly, the best known advocate of child study as an integral part of the teacher's activities is Prescott (1957), whose program at the University of Maryland has provided extensive in-service training for over 40,000 teachers. Basic to the program is the assertion that the appropriately trained teacher should have information on each child regarding "facts about interpersonal relationships in the home, data about the cultural background and socio-economic status of the family . . ." (Prescott, 1957, p. 428), as well as the more generally accepted information regarding learning ability, subject-matter accomplishment, and health status. This approach avowedly sees the teacher as fulfilling a clinical role, though not before completing a thoroughly planned three-year training program during which teachers systematically gather data on individual students, discuss the data, and formulate hypotheses regarding the child's behavior. Thus, the program is an intensive attempt to train teachers to carry out the behavioral pattern of therapist at least to a degree.

Unfortunately, the only evidence as to the effects of this program is of the anecdotal type. We are told that the training experience of the teachers has a rather profound effect on them, that they feel more comfortable with their students and are better able to create a desirable learning environment. Objective studies of the classroom and nonclassroom behavior of these teachers are needed.

A few studies have dealt with the question of how teachers perform in the mental health pattern. Ojemann and Wilkinson (1939) reported that the students of teachers who were provided with personality analyses and other data on the students showed better performance and more desirable school attitudes and personal adjustment than a control group. However, the teachers did not collect the data or make the analyses. Further, they were provided with psychological assistance in dealing with the students. The findings reflect a program which is broader in scope than one of child study per se. In another study (Hoyt, 1955), one group of teachers was asked to refrain from obtaining data on individual students, a second group was provided with achievement and IQ data only, and a third group was given extensive data which were discussed with the teachers. No differences in achievement resulted, but the attitudes of the students were more favorable toward the teachers having more information.

A study by Gage, Leavitt, and Stone (1955) is pertinent here since it dealt with the question of whether teachers who are best able to predict cognitive, social, and emotional characteristics of their students are in practice more effective in dealing with their students. They chose as their criterion of effectiveness the ratings assigned by students to their teachers on items directly related to the three areas. They found that those teachers making the best sociometric predictions were rated higher by students on their ability to make such predictions. They were not rated higher, however, on such items as "Does your teacher make sure that no pupils get left out of things?" In general, the relationships were insignificant and cast some question on the desirability of teachers' having the ability to "perceive," or make accurate predictions about matters of this kind. However, the measuring devices used in the study, though of considerable interest in their own right, have sufficient limitations of both reliability and validity to make such a conclusion highly tentative. The authors recognized that there are always many possible explanations of "negative results."

Group Dynamics

In essence, this approach, viewed here as a teaching method rather than as a study of group process (though the two are, of course, intimately related), entails discussion among students with considerable attention given to the interplay among the members of the group, their reactions to one another, and so forth. It seems to warrant particular attention because of its current status among educators as a new method.

The principal assumptions of group dynamics, according to Bradford (1958), appear to be the following:

1. "... the [major] target of education is change and growth in the individual and his behavior.... This is a deeper and broader goal than cognitive learning only" (Bradford, 1958, p. 135). Thus, it appears that the emphasis of the group dynamics approach is placed on two points: (1) Much cognitive learning does not reflect itself in general behavior; this is a problem of transfer. Pertinent here are studies frequently labeled "problem-solving," which demonstrate that persons who have acquired given responses frequently do not use them in the problem situation. The major point seems to be that cognitive learnings may not become a part of the individual's general response repertoire but rather remain as isolated responses elicited only by "academic" stimuli (Gross & McDonald, 1958). (2) Schools should place emphasis on, and take responsibility for, other than cognitive learnings. Educators will note the influence of William Kilpatrick in this position.

2. The best way to facilitate the kind of learning which is advocated is through the removal of "learning blocks." It is held that the major inhibitor of learning is the fear on the part of the learner of exposing himself, of opening himself to the possibility of change. Furthermore, in a teaching situation, it is felt that the best way to remove such blocks and hence provide a situation in which learning can occur is to provide experience in expressing personal feelings—discussing the "blocks," etc. It is argued that most teaching situations present too many threats to the individual's self-esteem for him to be able to open himself to change.

There appear to be a number of questions pertinent to this method to which future research can be expected to provide answers:

1. To what extent do students, after experience with this method, become better able to attend to problems, content, etc.?

2. To what extent do participants in such a method become more sensitive to the behavior of other persons and particularly to the effects of their own behavior on others? Since such sensitivity is held to play a vital role in a good learning situation and since a primary goal of the method is the development of this characteristic, this question seems of paramount importance. A study by Gibb and Gibb (1952) provides some indirect

support for this contention in showing that students who had participated in such groups tended to be rated higher than other students in likableness and group-membership skills.

3. To what extent do groups of this type and individuals within such groups actually learn and perform in a superior fashion? An answer to this question will undoubtedly have to take into account a number of dimensions related to group membership (age, education, etc.) as well as the history of the group.

Causal Orientation

In this approach an attempt is made to develop in teachers and subsequently in their students a causal orientation which is defined as "an understanding and appreciation of the dynamic, complex, and interacting nature of the forces that operate in human behavior. It involves an attitude of flexibility, of seeing things from the view point of others as well as an awareness of the probabilistic nature of knowledge ... and that there are alternative ways of solving social problems" (Muuss, 1960, p. 122). The basic assumption of the program is that the person possessing the causal orientation is better able to solve his own problems and to meet social situations.

As a pattern of teacher behavior, this approach entails modifications in both curricular content and general classroom behavior. Content modifications include stories which emphasize the relationships of cultural background to a person's behavior, direct teaching of the "causal" point of view through the use of pamphlets and similar media, exercises emphasizing alternative explanations of behavior, etc. The desired pattern of teacher behavior is not spelled out in detail; rather, it seems to be assumed that the causally oriented teacher will behave in ways consistent with the over-all theory—presumably in being less "judgmental," having better relationships with students, and fostering the causal orientation through his own behavior.

The research which has been reported thus far gives considerable support to this program. The studies give every indication of having been carefully conducted. Muuss (1960) reported that fifth- and sixth-graders scoring high on paper-and-pencil tests of causal orientation obtained lower scores on the Children's Manifest Anxiety Scale (questionnaire) and had a lower "lie" score. They also were less insecure, as measured by ratings based on systematic observation of the child's behavior in school. Further, students who had experienced the "causal" curriculum had significantly higher scores on the measures of "causality." Very similar results were reported by Bruce (1958). There appears then to be some support for the effectiveness of the program in developing the causal orientation in children as well as for the postulated relationships between this orientation and the domain of anxiety-insecurity. It seems to us, however, that the reported research does suffer from three principal weaknesses. First, little is known of the actual classroom behavior of the "causal" teachers; second, it appears that a very small number of teachers have been involved in the various studies (perhaps as few as four if all studies are based on the same teachers), and third, a great reliance is placed on paper-and-pencil measures. It is to be hoped that research workers in the "causal" orientation will employ additional measures, similar to the rating scale of insecurity, in future studies.

PATTERNS DERIVED FROM TEACHING TRADITIONS

Over the years a number of general teaching methods have evolved which imply particular patterns of teacher behavior as well as modifications in objectives and content. Among the best known of these methods are the recitation method (study and recite), the lecture method, the discussion method, the laboratory or project method, and the problem-solving method, as well as the activity method previously considered. With the exception of the comparison of lecture versus discussion methods, which has been the focus of considerable research at the college level, there has been little research on the various methods. The research which has been done has produced results which follow the pattern noted in the activity method studies; i.e., the slight differences found usually favor whatever is designated as the "experimental" method. It is our opinion that lack of specificity of the variables involved has been a major limiting factor in such studies.[1]

The Lecture Method

On first thought, what constitutes the lecture method would appear obvious. One envisions the teacher talking to a group of students, who are presumably listening. On second thought, however, one may note that many variations of the lecture are possible. Many teachers who consider themselves lecturers encourage questions on the part of students, or ask questions themselves. About the most definitive statement one can make about the lecture method is that during most of the time the instructor is "talking to" the students. Evaluation of the lecture method has consisted almost entirely of comparison with the discussion method.

The Discussion Method

Once again, we find no consistent definition of this method either by proponents of the method or in research related to it. As contrasted with the lecture method, a greater degree of active participation (talking) on the part of the students is the salient characteristic. Actual practices may vary from a largely unstructured situation in which the instructor plays a noncommittal, mediating role to one in which the instructor asks and answers questions. Varying degrees of student control of class activities are also found.

[1] The reader may wish to refer to the following reviews of teaching methods: Barr (1951); Birney & McKeachie (1955); Eckert (1960); Informal committee appointed by the Progressive Education Association (1941); Jersild, Thorndike, Goldman, and Loftus (1939); Ruja (1953); Stovall (1958); Wingo (1960); and Wispé (1953).

Thus we note that one man's "lecture" may be another man's "discussion."

With these limitations in mind, what does research have to say? With respect to immediate mastery of factual information, most studies find no significant differences between lecture and discussion methods (Asch, 1951; Bane, 1931; Bills, 1952; Carlson, 1953; Casey & Weaver, 1956; Deignan, 1956; Eglash, 1954; Gerberich & Warner, 1936; Haigh & Schmidt, 1956; Husband, 1951; D. M. Johnson & Smith, 1953; Lifson, Rempel, & Johnson, 1956; Maloney, 1956; Slomowitz, 1955; Wispé, 1951; Zeleny, 1940). But a few studies do report differences, usually in favor of the lecture (Burke, 1956; Guetzkow, Kelly, & McKeachie, 1954; Remmers, 1933; Ruja, 1954; R. B. Spence, 1928), but not always (Faw, 1949).

The more important question of retention of material has been seldom investigated. Of three studies which have dealt with this question, two (Bane, 1931; Rickard, 1946) found retention of material to be superior in groups taught by the discussion method and one found no difference (Eglash, 1954). Ward (1956) found greater retention of "understanding-type" learning among students with greater academic ability under discussion procedures but found greater retention of such material under the lecture method with students of lower ability. Further, students of less ability showed greater immediate recall of information under the lecture method whereas the "method" made little difference in such performance on the part of the more able students. It should be noted that all of these studies have been undertaken at the college level.

Inasmuch as proponents of discussion methods have characteristically claimed advantages in problem-solving, application of knowledge, etc., it would seem appropriate to evaluate the method primarily in terms of its success in these areas. There is, however, little direct evidence. Smith (1955) found no difference among three classes differing in degree of "directiveness." There is some evidence of greater acceptance of responsibility for learning on the part of students in discussion classes (Patton, 1955) and some indication of greater use of psychological knowledge (Bovard, 1951; McKeachie, 1954; Perkins, 1950). For a more extensive treatment of these studies and for a review of an "ego-involving" educational program involving group discussion as one aspect (the Pyramid Plan), see pages 427–428, 1139.

Although they focus on aspects of the learning process rather than on "outcomes," the following two studies seem to us particularly interesting. Bloom (1953) played back tapes of classroom activity to groups of college students and asked them to recall what they were thinking about at the time. He found that students in lecture classes as compared to students in discussion classes reported significantly more thoughts classified as "irrelevant" and "simple comprehension," and significantly fewer thoughts classified as relating to "self," "other persons," and "problem-solving." There were no significant differences in "attempts to apply material" or "evaluating and considering meaning." Edmiston and Braddock (1941) had trained observers record the level of attention shown by a large sample of secondary school students to nine types of teacher activity. The mean percentage of students attending ranged from 81 per cent for laboratory activities to 88 per cent for student report. Student discussion was 85 per cent and lecture 84 per cent. The most interesting findings are the high percentage paying attention to all "methods" and the slight differences among them. In a related study, Brinkley (1952) asked college students to rate 10 academic activities as to the extent to which they elicited "mental activity." He found great variability among students. He also found that a composite ranking remained much the same for groups of students over a 20-year interval. Group discussion was ranked second and lecture eighth in the composite ranking.

Another purpose for which discussion techniques are advocated is that of changing attitudes, interpersonal relations, and self-con-

cept. There is some evidence, primarily from nonschool settings, that discussion methods are more effective in achieving change on these dimensions (Asch, 1951; Faw, 1949; Levine & Butler, 1952; Lewin, 1958; Radke & Klisurich, 1947). Furthermore, it would appear that such techniques permit types of social learnings not possible in a lecture.

In view of the interest in group procedures in general, we present the major conclusions which we feel derive from a comprehensive review of studies on this topic by Lorge, Fox, Davitz, and Brenner (1958). Several types of groups are distinguished:

1. Interacting, face-to-face group involving discussion. Such groups vary on a continuum from the ad hoc group arbitrarily formed to serve immediate purposes to the "traditioned" group having a defined role and history and presumably a common goal.

2. Noninteracting face-to-face group involving physical meeting but no discussion. An example would be the individual working alone but in the presence of other persons—as in a highly formalized classroom or study hall.

3. Noninteracting nonface-to-face group involving no meeting and no discussion. An example is the averaging of several individual performances to obtain an average "group" performance. Such groups are of less interest with respect to educational problems but have frequently been studied in other contexts.

A pertinent point raised by the reviewers is that generalizations based on one form of group, e.g., "ad hoc," must be applied with caution to other groups, e.g., "traditioned." The following generalizations are those applying to Groups 1 and 2 above:

1. Judgments based on group consensus are not necessarily more accurate than the average judgment by the individual members of the group but are likely to be so when the material is unfamiliar or there is a great range of individual judgments.

2. Group problem-solving is not necessarily superior to the average solution by the individual members of the group but is likely to be so when individuals are previously

familiar with the type of problem and bring with them skills which are pertinent to the problem. Group solutions are likely to be inferior to the best individual solution.

3. The advantage of groups in problem-solving appears to be more in facilitating rejection of incorrect approaches than in providing more approaches to the problem.[2]

4. Group interaction is likely to be of most benefit to those persons making poorest individual judgments or solutions to problems.

5. Group superiority, where found, is a function of the quality of the individual contributions of members. It is suggested that group solution to a problem is likely only if at least one individual in the group could have solved the problem alone.

6. If evaluated in terms of man-hours to solution, group process is generally, and often strikingly, less efficient.

7. The mere presence of other persons has an effect on individual performance. The effect appears to be beneficial if the other persons are "working," but deleterious if they are observing the individual or if they constitute an "audience."

8. Group process appears more effective than direct attack in changing expressed attitudes and certain aspects of behavior, e.g., in instituting changes in procedures for rating subordinates.

9. With respect to productivity on routine tasks, such as those assessed in industrial settings, group discussion of changes in procedures, goals, etc., appears markedly superior to arbitrary procedures.

[2] This generalization may require modification when applied to the particular group activity called "brainstorming," wherein participants are instructed to emit every notion which occurs to them regardless of its apparent merit. Parnes and Meadow (1959) report significantly more "good-quality" ideas pertaining to the solution of the Hanger and Broom problems from the AC test of creativity, which requires subjects to list uses of these objects, from a brainstorming group than from a group required to present only "good" ideas. A study by Taylor, Berry, and Block (1958) suggests, however, that it is the instruction to "let go" and express all ideas which is crucial and that doing so in a group may actually have a deleterious effect on the process.

Other Teaching Methods

In addition to the lecture and discussion methods, several other teaching methods should be mentioned. The *laboratory method* emphasizes direct experience with materials pertinent to the area of study. Thus, it includes "field experience," such as trips to local industries and courts, as well as the more common laboratory techniques associated with science teaching. Present research is of little help in evaluating outcomes of this method. Early research was generally favorable to it (Briggs, et al., 1938). More recent studies at the college level have found the usual contradictory results (Balcziak, 1954; J. R. White, 1945).

The *project method* has as its predominant characteristic the acceptance of an assignment by the student, who is then free to fulfill the requirements independently, with help from the teacher when necessary. Research evidence, though meager, is not particularly favorable (Goldstein, 1956; Novak, 1958). Once again, however, the principal measuring devices emphasize mastery of facts—hardly one of the objectives of this method. When devices attempting to measure "scientific attitude," independence of study, etc., have been included, no differences have been found between this and the "lecture" approach (Novak, 1958; Timmel, 1955). Dawson (1956), however, did report superior skills in solving directly related problems. A study by Corman (1957) illuminates the complexities of providing an appropriate amount of guidance.

The *recitation method,* characterized by assignment, study, and report, was—according to a study which surveyed teaching practices in 200 secondary school classrooms (Dale & Raths, 1945)—the most common "method" employed. This method is, in the public schools, considered to be the "traditional method." Thus the method has tended to be the one with which other methods are compared. As has been indicated, there is little experimental support for this method or its competitors as a general teaching method.

Approaches to Teaching
Critical Thinking

An oft expressed educational objective, critical thinking appears to be receiving renewed attention. Here again there are differences among conceptions of what behaviors constitute critical thinking. The critical thinker is variously described as possessing the following attributes, which are often assumed to go together: (1) use of scientific methods, including emphasis on evidence and the nature of hypotheses; (2) the tendency to be inquisitive, critical, and analytical with respect to issues, personal behavior, etc., including lack of susceptibility to propaganda, (3) use of correct principles of logic. The emphasis is on the development of that elusive philosophical ideal, the rational man.

With respect to methods of fostering critical thinking, two major approaches have been advocated. The first is "progressive education." Critical thinking is presumed to be but one of the objectives which are fostered by a greater degree of self-determination, flexibility of curriculum, and freedom of behavior. The results of the Eight-Year Study discussed previously provide some support for this position. Further support of an indirect type is provided by studies which indicate that questioning and critical behaviors are less likely to occur in rigid, highly formalized situations wherein deviation is punished (Carpenter, 1956).

The second approach emphasizes the tools rather than the attitude of critical thinking. Thus, emphasis is placed on acquainting students with the principles of logic and experimentation and with their use. The most extensive study of this approach is that conducted in three Illinois high schools (Henderson, 1958). Thirty-six teachers and approximately 1,500 students in English, geometry, science, and social studies participated. It appears that the study was carefully conducted and that the students taught by the experimental method showed greater gain on measures of critical thinking than the control group without showing impairment in mastery of course content. Whether or not the students will carry their new-found skills beyond an academic, paper-and-pencil test situation is a question which awaits further study.

A LEARNING MODEL FOR ANALYZING TEACHING METHODS

What conclusions may be drawn from the research on teaching methods? The first impression is likely to be that there has not been much research. In view of the quantity of heated debate over these issues, one might have expected more. A second impression is that teaching methods do not seem to make much difference, or to phrase it more appropriately, there is hardly any direct evidence to favor one method over another. Perhaps one should not have expected research to discover consistent differences between methods in the first place.

In the introductory sections of this chapter, emphasis was placed on the fact that teaching methods have not been designed systematically in terms of what is known about the learning process but rather have been products of other trends in thinking. The conditions which most commonly generate teaching methods are unlikely to produce patterns of teaching behavior markedly more effective than those that have been produced in the past. A consequence of this is that research on teaching methods bears little resemblance to scientific research which systematically builds up knowledge of a particular phenomenon. To some persons, administrators in particular, this has often been interpreted to mean that research has had little to offer and that they are justified in basing curriculum decisions either on personal experience or on some vague philosophical or psychological theory. At present, one is compelled to agree. It does not follow, however, that one cannot look to research for help on these matters in the future. There is no question but what educational research has, in the past, been extremely helpful on such specific issues as appropriate word difficulties for beginning reading books. Further, educational research shows signs of entering a new and more sophisticated era; the old "shotgun" studies, useful as they may have been in their time, are giving way to studies formulated in such a way as to provide clear-cut evidence on sharply defined problems.

Research in this area shows a lack of integration between descriptions of teaching procedures on the one hand and learning models on the other. This is hardly surprising, for most teaching methods did not become established because they fitted a psychological model of the learning process. Their origins are entirely different. The teacher who represented the progressive education movement of the 1930's supposedly had a pattern of behavior that reflected many of the teachings of the eighteenth-century philosopher Rousseau. Its only relationship to the learning theory of the 1930's was that it included a small element of rebelliousness against associationist doctrines and offered a certain amount of lip service to the then popular Gestalt psychology. One cannot, however, point to particular practices of the "progressive" teachers of that period and state that these practices are those suggested by Gestalt psychology. On the other hand, one can point to some practices and state that Rousseau recommended them.

The time has come for teaching methods to be based on a learning model stemming from psychological research. Only in this way can such methods be expected to show greater value than those they replace. Perhaps the tendency for research comparisons of two methods to show, in general, only small differences in terms of measured outcomes reflects the fact that methods are not generally based on knowledge of learning phenomena. This is hardly surprising, for knowledge which could be used for the design of teaching methods has only recently been acquired and postdates much of the research we have considered.

The systematic design of a teaching method involves two steps. First, a set of identifiable conditions related to learning must be specified. The importance of these conditions must have been established by empirical research; i.e., their relevance to the learning of children must have been either directly established or there must be other compelling reasons for believing that the conditions have an important relation to classroom learning. The ideal case is one in which studies involving the experimental manipulation of the condition with classroom children had demonstrated that the condition was related to the achievement of particular educational objectives.

A second step in the design of teaching methods involves the design of teacher behavior. This has to be so designed that it generates the learning conditions which have already been specified. This set of specifications is probably more difficult to draw up than is the listing of the conditions that are assumed to favor learning. Where several alternative patterns of behavior on the part of the teacher are likely to be equally successful in producing the desired learning condition, then that one which is most easily generated in teachers should be specified in the method. In this type of design activity, there is always a danger of designing teacher behaviors which teachers are not capable of performing. However desirable it might be for teachers to reinforce the desirable responses of each child, say 100 times per hour, the physical impossibility of a teacher's performing this amount of reinforcing activity means that teacher behavior with this specification should not be included in the design. Sometimes a design of teacher behavior may specify that certain equipment be available so that a learning condition may be satisfied. A design might specify that the teacher use certain equipment such as teaching machines in order to compensate for deficiencies in teacher behavior such as the limited amount of reinforcing behavior that the teacher alone can successfully perform.

The design of a teaching method is a task of tremendous magnitude which cannot be undertaken as a part of this chapter. The most that can be done here is to provide a general sketch of a learning model such as might be used in the design of a teaching method and then to sketch in some of the aspects of teacher behavior which might be hypothesized to produce the conditions related to learning which the model requires.

Many recent textbooks in educational psychology present models of learning similar to the one given below. These models are at a gross rather than a detailed level of development. At this stage they have to be. They do not give precise operational definitions of the variables involved in the learning process nor do they attempt to provide equations which will show the relationship between the variables. They generally do provide a number of broad classifications of the variables involved in learning and some information concerning ways in which the teacher may manipulate these variables in order to improve the efficiency of the learning process. A brief discussion of such a model seems appropriate here since it provides a medium for discussing some of the problems of designing teaching methods. Our first step will be to list the broad classes of variables that are involved.

The variables in any learning model can be classified as dependent and independent. The dependent variable in any learning model must be a response variable, and it will be considered first.

Response Variables,
the Dependent Variables

Response variables are derived from any publicly observable behavior. Variables which fall into a dichotomous classification, such as "ignores student," are of considerably less value than are classifications of responses on a continuum which permits the assignment of scores. Examples of such response variables derived from classes of responses which have been commonly included in educational research are scores derived from paper-and-pencil tests, check lists filled in by observers, and self-report forms of various kinds filled in by the pupils themselves. Many of these response variables are based on a trait concept where the variables represent emitted behavior. Such an approach tends to neglect stimulus-response sequences. For example, although there appears to be a general trait of honesty which characterizes some children, one is likely to make poor predictions concerning the honesty of a particular child's behavior unless one has a knowledge of the situation in which the prediction is to be made.

Some response variables involve a classification of response, as for instance, when the responses of a child are classified as either honest or dishonest. Other response variables involve simple characteristics of the response itself, such as latency. For example, a student learning to type is expected to acquire a certain speed of typing after a given amount of instruction and practice. Speed of typing is a latency variable; that is to say, it measures the speed of the response.

While a curriculum may be designed to produce changes in central psychological processes, the evidence that the curriculum actually produces such changes must come from the responses of the student. While it is often desirable to think of educational objectives as being concerned with changes in central processes such as perception, neural sets, attitudes, and so forth, the operational definition of these internal conditions requires that they be defined in terms of both the antecedent conditions that produce them and the consequent conditions, namely, the behaviors through which they are manifested. The specification of a teaching method requires that the objectives, or internal conditions, to be achieved through the method be adequately tied to both the antecedent and consequent conditions.

The response variables should be defined as part of the design of a teaching method. This step is necessary if evaluation procedures are to be built into the design. At this stage in the development of disciplines related to education, it is inconceivable that a teaching method could be designed without building into it techniques for the evaluation of pupil progress.

Independent Variables

These are the variables, related to the learning process, that the teacher may be able to manipulate. By doing so, the teacher may be able to exercise some control over the efficiency with which the learning process takes place. This is not an appropriate place to begin to enumerate in detail the variables which have been identified as the independent variables in the learning process. All that can be done here is to indicate the general classes of independent variables in the learning process which must be taken into account in the design of a teaching method.

Situation characteristics. By situation is meant the external stimuli capable of affecting the learner during a given interval, for example, a one-hour class period. It is immediately apparent that one cannot usefully work with *all* the possible stimuli which may affect the learner's sense organs during this interval. It is assumed, however, that one can deal with certain classes of stimuli of major importance and ignore the rest. Thus, one may describe the situation of the student in terms of teacher behaviors, work materials, behaviors of other students, etc., and ignore such things as the color of the walls, street noises, etc. It is, of course, necessary that no "important" classes of stimuli be omitted, though one can determine what is important only through experimentation. For example, such extraneous stimuli as street noises appear to be of major importance in the classroom "situation" of brain-injured persons.

A first point to be noted is that the situation is defined in terms of observables, though such observables are themselves abstractions. For example, once an observer is acquainted with the class of teacher behaviors described as "autocratic," he can observe teachers and assign them much the same position on a scale as will another trained observer. In the process, we should recognize that a structure is imposed on the behavior of the teacher—we are looking for "autocratic" behaviors while ignoring others. Another observer, trained differently, or not trained at all, might well impose a different structure on the behavior of the teacher. Once one moves beyond isolated behaviors, one can find only what one looks for, and, of course, one can find it only if it is there. Thus, a description of the situation for a learner consists of statements describing certain classes of stimuli which can affect him, the classes themselves being largely a matter of theoretical preference.

A second point to be noted is that this approach does not include the notion of the "situation-as-perceived" by the learner. It is important to emphasize this distinction because of the currency in educational circles of the Lewinian and Rogerian definition of the "situation" as those stimuli which the person responds to or is "aware of." It is assumed in the present model that the situation as objectively described will have an impact on the learner which can be usefully analyzed.

Motivation. It is assumed that all learners are capable of being "aroused" or energized toward certain activities and that an optimum energizing level exists for facilitating learning. It is further assumed that some energizers are, as it were, built into the learner—such things as hunger, sex, etc. As a result of experience, persons come to develop other internal conditions, such as "need for approval," which serve as energizers. In any case, it is assumed that motivation is of prime importance in learning, and further that events external to the learner interact with internal states so as to arouse greater activity. It is further assumed that, although the learner may be aware of the arousing conditions and his own motivational states, this is not necessarily the case. Unconscious motivation is an accepted phenomenon. Interesting issues in present-day psychology involve such questions as the number and nature of innate or nonenvironmentally produced motives (or need, or drive, as they are often denoted), the conditions under which motives are learned (if they are) and maintained, and the most profitable way of conceptualizing motivation. Although such unresolved issues are of paramount importance in psychology and have profound implications for education (as, for example, whether aggression as a drive is innate or acquired), the present state of knowledge is sufficient to suggest many fruitful lines of educational research, some of which will be discussed later.

Reinforcement. Closely allied to the concept of motivation is that of reinforcement. In simplest terms, reinforcement refers to a state of affairs following a given response, or series of responses, which makes the future occurrence of that response or series more probable. Some theorists attempt a more restrictive definition in terms of a decrease in motivation, but this theoretical position has recently suffered a number of setbacks (see, for example, Cofer, 1959) and is not a necessary part of the concept. It is, nevertheless, often useful to think of reinforcers as related to motivation. Other theorists believe the essential characteristic of a reinforcer is that it changes the stimulus situation. Originally expounded by Guthrie (1952), this view is achieving renewed currency through the writings of Hebb (1958).

Readiness. This construct refers to the likelihood that the individual can make the response in which we are interested. Readiness is dependent, in turn, on capacity (taken here to mean the limiting conditions set by the nature of the learner's physiological system) and on previously learned behaviors.[3] Limitations due to capacity are considered to arise through the influence of heredity, maturation level, and physical injury. Thus, some behaviors, such as the solution of calculus problems, are considered to be beyond the capacity of subhuman species, the mentally retarded, young children, or persons with certain forms of brain injury. Although the

possibility of assessing capacity directly (perhaps through direct observation of the nervous system) is remote at present, it is often necessary to make inferences as to capacity since situational arrangements should obviously be different for the learner whose deficiency is due to this variable than for the learner whose deficiency is due to lack of previous learnings. Such inferences are typically made after observing samples of behavior which reflect previous learnings as well as capacity, and hence they must be regarded as fallible inferences.

Limitations on readiness which result from inadequate prior learnings are more easily assessed. The important question of the basis for the failure to acquire the prerequisite responses remains, as, for example, when we predict that a student's reading skills are so poor that he is unlikely to acquire the responses required at the college level, but next want to know whether the lack of necessary skill is due to lack of capacity or lack of opportunity to learn the skill. Nevertheless, recognition of the importance of previous learning in any given learning situation has resulted in the development of many measuring devices of proven value to teachers. An opportunity for significant educational research has recently evolved from the demonstration (Hebb, 1958) that many responses acquired during the first two or three years of life must be learned and that they require situations which facilitate such learning. Perhaps educational experiences could be provided at these ages which would greatly facilitate typical first-grade learnings. Though nursery school experience has not been shown to fulfill this function, the difficulty may lie in the nature of the situational arrangements.

Mediating response. This concept has had a controversial history. Due in part to a desire to avoid constructs smacking of metaphysics, many psychologists have preferred to do without the notion of *mediating response* though there have always been objections to the omission. Perhaps the easiest way to introduce this notion is to examine briefly the learning paradigm based only on the con-

---

[3] Readiness is sometimes defined more broadly as the likelihood of the behavior occurring, in which case the construct includes motivation and interpretation as well as the variables included in the present definition.

structs previously discussed. In such a model, if one wishes to obtain certain responses to certain situations, he would (1) describe the situation and desired response in detail; (2) obtain as much information as possible as to the ability of the organism to respond as desired (readiness); (3) make inferences as to the motivations of the organism and, through manipulation of the situation, arouse an optimal level of motivation; (4) either manipulate the situation so as to facilitate the occurrence of the desired response or wait for it to occur, and then reinforce it. The word "manipulate" is used advisedly—this is an attempt to manipulate the situation so as to obtain certain behaviors.

It has become increasingly apparent, however, that even simple responses in relatively simple subhuman species are not this easily controlled. For example, even the most "mechanistic" of laboratory experimentalists find that much of animal behavior subsequent to a given learning experience cannot be predicted from information on situation, readiness, response, motivation, and previous reinforcement alone. To account for such behavior, theorists have invoked a variety of constructs often called mediating responses. The point is that one must add another construct to those previously discussed in the learning model. Many other instances could be cited to illustrate this point, including "insightful" behavior of the sort emphasized by Köhler, problem-solving behavior, and new and productive, i.e., "creative," responses to novel situations.

Perhaps the best known example of the point we are making is the emphasis on perception which is popular in education today. From this point of view, the important thing to study in any learning situation is not the objective situation or the reinforcements which may be administered, or other aspects of our original model, but rather how the learner perceives the situation. To the extent that such an approach specifies perceptual variables which may be inferred from behavior and studied in terms of their relation to learning, it is likely to be fruitful.

Some writers (Prescott, 1957; Snygg & Combs, 1949) have concluded that perception is all-important, and hence that there is little point to exploring further the other aspects of the model presented here. The present state of knowledge about learning does not, however, justify such a position. To cite an example, we may refer to certain recommendations for curriculum modification. Viewed in terms of our model, the curriculum which is advocated consists of providing the learner with a very complex and relatively unstructured situation, usually presented as a problem to be solved. Little attention is given to ways of altering the situation or controlling reinforcement so as to facilitate the learning of desired behaviors; rather, reliance is placed on the perceptual reorganization of the person which is expected to result in "insight" or the sudden emergence of responses which are successful in solving the problem. Granted that insight may not take place, it is contended that this approach is nonetheless the one most likely to result in insight.[4]

Although it is true that both theory and research in learning support the notion that creative, novel, insightful behavior cannot be rigidly controlled or predicted at this time (a proposition comforting to psychologists as well as educators), present evidence suggests rather strongly that insight is more likely to result when certain appropriate responses have been previously acquired and that the development of such responses may be taught directly. It has been shown (Birch, 1945) that apes placed in the classic "insight" situation of Köhler do not show insightful behavior if they have not had previous experience with sticks, which must be used to solve the problem. Further, Harlow (1949) has shown how the controlled development of ways of responding to discrimination problems great-

---

[4] It should be mentioned that advocates of this position emphasize problem-solving and complex learnings as the only truly important learnings. Not everyone shares their view as to the objectives of education. This is another problem, however, and we are here concerned with learning per se.

ly facilitates "insightful" solution of new problems. The implication for education is obvious, but the spelling out of the responses which are likely to facilitate insight in various situations is a task which has hardly been begun.

Relationship of the Classes of Variables to Teacher Behavior

The previous section described a number of broad categories of variables which would have to be represented in a learning model to be used as a basis for the design of a teaching method. In the actual design procedure, the variables within each one of these categories would have to be defined, and this necessary step would have to be undertaken prior to the construction of a pattern of teacher behavior intended to implement the model. All that can be done here is to indicate some of the relationships that might be developed between teacher behavior and the learning model.

A major portion of the ultimate product of teaching model development would be a set of laws of teacher behavior which would follow the general form

$$T = f(R_g, R_i).$$

This symbolic representation has the following meaning. The behavior of the teacher T is a function of the goals to be achieved R_g and the present behavior of the pupil R_i. The design of a teaching method may have to assume that a response system of the teacher T can be developed which is appropriate and efficient for achieving R_g.

What is the possibility of defining the lawfulness of teacher behavior, which is a requirement of a particular teaching method, in terms of equations into which can be placed the values of the variables involved? Such a possibility is still remote. It involves not only the problem of measuring the variables but also that of determining the values of the constants which the system of equations would inevitably require. Such an approach to the problem of defining a teaching method is now merely an ideal rather than a format which can be adopted at this time. In the discussion that follows we will not even remotely approximate this format, if only because we have not yet even reached the point of defining the variables that would enter into the equations.

To indicate the general direction which we believe model-building should take in the area of planning teaching procedures, we shall now consider the problem of relating (1) the categories of learning variables previously outlined to (2) the teacher behavior which constitutes the method. These relationships will be considered category by category:

The independent variables. The last quarter of a century has seen an increasing emphasis in educational literature on the need for teachers to be able to identify the response characteristics that are to be considered evidence of desired learnings. This emphasis was necessary because the behavior of teachers indicated that a large percentage of them had little conception of what the product of the learning process was to be. Once teachers are aware of educational goals stated in concrete terms and accept the goals as inherently worth while, then whatever classroom procedures are actually effective in achieving the goals will be reinforced. One suspects that, unless teachers have such awareness, the reinforcements provided by the classroom for teacher behavior will reinforce the wrong teacher behaviors, i.e., those which have little relevance for the learning process. For example, if a teacher has some vague goal, such as "self-realization," then any hint that something in this direction may have been achieved will reinforce her behavior. Many of these "hints" may be quite unrelated to the learning process and may hence reinforce behavior which has little relevance to the learning process. Indeed, one suspects that some teacher behavior is closely similar to the "superstitious" behavior of pigeons (Skinner, 1948) who acquired peculiar mannerisms through the action of randomly distributed reinforcements.

To achieve the goal of coordination with learning variables, a model of teacher behavior will have to show certain definite relationships to the independent variables of the educational process. One of these relationships involves the capacity of the teacher to discriminate between the observables of pupil behavior and the unobservables that, presumably, determine his behavior. The capacity to make such a discrimination should do much to eliminate the error, commonly made by teachers, of assuming that certain internal changes have occurred in the pupil even though there are no observable manifestations of the change. In other words, teachers may introduce unobservables into educational concepts only if the unobservables are operationally defined in terms of observable antecedents and consequents.

Another lawfulness of teacher behavior that might constitute an important component of most teaching methods is that the behavior of a teacher should be systematic in collecting evidence and properly use the rules of logical inference in making deductions from the evidence.

Situational variables. Numerous laws of teacher behavior with respect to the physical environment of the educational process have to be specified for any particular teaching method. Since the teacher is the major manipulator of the educational environment of the child, the relationships of the teacher's behavior to this environment are obviously many and complex. For this reason, there may be merit in attempting to classify the relationships through the use of a simplified model. For example, let us consider the teacher as the primary source of stimulus control for the pupils. Here, the term *stimulus control* is used in a technical sense and does not have the same significance as the term *controlling teacher behavior,* as it is commonly used in educational literature.

In the model under consideration, the teacher does not retain stimulus control throughout the teaching day but delegates such control to various other aspects of the environment. In the project method of Kilpatrick, stimulus control is delegated to a great range of material objects in the environment related to the execution of a project. These include reference books and other sources of information as well as aspects of the community itself which the pupil goes out to explore. In a more traditional educational program, the teacher delegates stimulus control to a textbook or a workbook. In most classrooms today this aspect of teacher behavior shows considerable lawfulness which might be stated in such terms as "Teachers tend to delegate stimulus control to textbooks and workbooks which maintain control of pupil behavior until the teacher determines that some other source of control will take over." We are not, of course, at this time evaluating this practice but are merely pointing out a typical lawfulness which characterizes teacher behavior within the teaching methods currently found in schools.

The advent of teaching machines introduces a new element in the educational environment to which the stimulus control of the pupil may be delegated. If a teaching method were to utilize such equipment, it would have to specify the behavior of the teacher in relation to such equipment and the conditions under which the teacher would delegate stimulus control to the machine.

The teacher is an element of central importance in the educational environment of the child. Hence a teaching method must specify with as great a degree of precision as possible the behaviors related to the programing and planning of learning and the behaviors which involve teacher-pupil interactions.

Here again, we must point out that our illustrations do not represent an attempt to specify a particular teaching method. Rather, we are attempting merely to explore some of the problems entailed in specifying a teaching method.

In a sense, of course, all of the conditions that the teacher ever manipulates in order to facilitate the learning process are situational variables. Some of the conditions that are manipulated have such a well-established bearing on the internal processes of the pupil that they will be considered separately. Teaching activities that relate to the motivation of the pupil, reinforcement, and the development of mediating processes in the pupil are three such categories which must now be considered.

The motivation of the pupils. Teaching methods have differed considerably in the extent to which they have assumed that the motivation of the pupil is "teacher-generated" from without or "pupil-generated" from within. The Rousseau tradition assumed that motivation was generated from within and that the main effect of external influences, if any, was an inhibiting one. This position assumes lawfulnesses in pupil behavior which subsequent research has failed to demonstrate. Teacher behavior in relation to the motivation of the pupil, as in all other aspects, must have a pattern that is consistent with empirically established knowledge. The tradition of Rousseau is not consistent with such knowledge, although it still influences some teachers who assume that their function is to prevent the natural high motivation of children from being inhibited. Yet the practice of supposedly "progressive" teachers shows numerous activities which would have the inevitable effect of increasing the "arousal" level of the pupils. Such teachers commonly introduce numerous sources of stimulation through the establishment of displays—a science table, an art table, wall charts, exhibitions of pupil products. At least there is strong presumptive evidence that these materials will influence the level of arousal of the pupil. A design for teacher behavior would have to specify the extent to which the teacher should manipulate the environment of the child in order to raise his level of arousal.

The trend in theory of motivation is to suggest that, as the individual grows older, arousal can be triggered by more and more specific and identifiable classes of stimuli. For example, suppose a person is said to manifest a high level of achievement need.

The implication would be that his arousal system is activated by situations in which he has an opportunity to excel. If the function of the teacher is to raise the level of arousal of the pupil to an optimum level, then he must be able to introduce into the environment those stimuli which will have arousal value for particular pupils. Specifications for a teaching method should describe with some precision samples of the arousal cues that the teacher might manipulate and introduce into the classroom. The cues introduced for this purpose will be determined to some extent by the educational objectives of the teaching method.

Reinforcement. Discussion by psychologists of "new" teaching methods often begins with the idea that the teacher does not provide the reinforcements needed for effective learning and hence that teaching practices should be so modified that adequate reinforcements are introduced into the learning process. At present, there are difficulties in determining whether this assertion is true because in most current teaching patterns the reinforcers are extremely difficult to identify. Also, relatively little is known about who is reinforced by what in a typical classroom which has children with a great variety of backgrounds and abilities. The design of a teaching method assumes that knowledge is available concerning the reinforcements that are effective in a particular classroom.

As we accumulate knowledge of the value of various reinforcements that can be introduced in the classroom and also of individual differences with respect to what reinforces, the design of teacher behavior in relation to this set of learning conditions will become more and more a practical possibility. As far as one can see at present, almost any method that is systematically designed will have to allow for the delegation of some reinforcing functions to equipment, such as workbooks and learning machines, and to pupil-pupil relationships. Whether equipment can provide adequate reinforcements for all pupils or whether the teacher has unique properties as a reinforcing agent for some pupils remains to be seen. Some teaching methods have assumed that the social reinforcements provided by the teacher are more valuable for promoting learning than those provided by, say, workbooks.

Readiness to learn. This aspect of the learning process requires that the teacher develop the skills necessary to determine the degree of readiness of a particular pupil for a particular learning activity. The present state of the art is such that one can specify without too much difficulty the skills that are needed in estimating readiness for reading and for a number of other activities. The lawfulnesses of teacher behavior defined by a teaching method must specify the conditions in the classroom which evoke the diagnostic skills of the teacher. The application of these skills at times when they are inappropriate is obviously not the kind of lawful behavior that a teaching method would prescribe.

Mediating processes. Almost every theory of education takes the position that a major objective of teaching is the development of mediating processes in the pupil. These may be discussed either in terms of such constructs as perceptual reorganization and cognitive structure or in terms of nonphenomenological constructs. A major difficulty in prescribing patterns of teacher behavior which will facilitate the development of effective mediating processes in the pupil is that the learning processes involved have not yet been well identified except for certain cases. That is, the laws of learning in this area have not been developed to the point where much can be done to define the facilitating patterns of teacher behavior.

Certain exceptions to the latter statement can be made. Extensive knowledge does exist concerning the conditions under which "learning sets" may be developed. The work of Harlow (1949) with both human and animal subjects has provided extensive knowledge concerning the teaching conditions that must exist in order for learning sets to be developed. This knowledge is sufficient to indicate the pattern of teacher behavior that

is likely to be effective in developing such mediating processes and also some of the teacher behaviors that should be avoided. For example, the work of Harlow suggests that simple demonstration is wholly inadequate for teaching the student how to learn to solve a whole class of problems. Rather, the teacher must provide opportunities for the pupil to solve problems in a particular kind of sequence.

This area of learning is one about which educational reformers take great delight in speculating. Numerous attempts have been made to design teaching methods which will achieve such varied objectives as critical thinking, creativity, problem-solving ability, and so forth. Such methods have generally been stated in only the vaguest terms largely because knowledge on which they could have been built has been lacking.

An Overview of Problems of Research on Teaching Method

Research on teaching methods which will contribute to an organized body of scientific information requires that teaching methods themselves be designed systematically in terms of empirically established learning principles. The design of teaching methods represents a branch of educational technology which is still in its infancy, but the development of this technology is necessary for the advancement of educational practice. Worthwhile research on teaching methods cannot be carried out opportunistically. Past research bears little resemblance to what the scientist does. Much of it is an attempt to justify new practices, and much of it represents the ill-designed research of the graduate student. Most attempts to design teaching methods provide only the flimsiest foundation for subsequent research on their effectiveness. These attempts have not been based on a comprehensive set of principles of learning but rather are based on other considerations. Too often the designer of a teaching method has based an entire method on a single appealing principle. Such behavior is analogous to that of the engineer who, in designing a machine, attended only to the laws of friction and neglected all other established laws of physics. The faults of design make it futile to conduct studies comparing them with other teaching methods which are just as poorly designed. Such research merely reveals that all the methods compared are approximately equal in their ineffectiveness.

What of the future? The era of research involving the comparison of one teaching method with another seems to be coming to a close. At the public school level, few studies have been undertaken during the last two decades, perhaps because the "disappointing" results have failed to reinforce the behavior of investigators. Studies at the college level seem to be having a similar history, with an initial burst of enthusiasm for classroom research producing anticlimatic results. Research workers must surely go back, take stock of their position, and realize that the starting place must be the systematic design of teaching methods.

RELATIONSHIP OF SOME TEACHING METHODS TO SOME PRINCIPLES OF LEARNING

The two previous sections of this chapter have been devoted to the design of teaching methods and the general nature of the procedures that should be followed. Although, in the past, knowledge available for the planning of teaching methods has been very meager, there are reasons for doubting that available knowledge has been used systematically. If teaching methods from the past are evaluated on their consistency with current knowledge of learning, they appear even more inadequate. But the interesting task of making such a comprehensive analysis would require major research. Nonetheless, to indicate the general lack of relationship between teaching methods and current knowledge of learning, a less extensive analysis will be presented. In this analysis, we shall not attempt to list a comprehensive set of widely accepted principles of learning and then study the extent to which each of a number of methods utilizes the principles involved. Rather, we will limit our discussion to six principles, as against the broad categories of variables used in our earlier discussion. The six principles are sufficient to illustrate the limitations of most teaching methods and perhaps also the difficulties involved in designing a method consistent with many principles.

Principle 1: Behavior which represents the achievement or partial achievement of an educational objective should be reinforced.

Significance of the principle for classroom learning. This principle means that there are known events which, if they occur subsequent to a response, facilitate the learning of the response, at least for some learners. The principle has great potential importance for education, because many of the common reinforcers are at least partially under the control of the teacher. Beginnings have been made in research on the identification of reinforcers. That such research is likely to be fruitful is evident from the studies that have been undertaken on the effects of praise and blame (Forlano & Axelrod, 1937; G. G. Thompson & Hunnicutt, 1944), a simple classification of potential reinforcers. These studies suggest that although praise may, in most cases, be a better reinforcer, blame is better for some students, and that the efficiency of each type can be predicted with some accuracy even with a fairly crude questionnaire measure of student personality. It is also known that certain kinds of information may serve as reinforcers, at least under some conditions.

A special class of reinforcers is described by the phrase "knowledge of results." Whenever the learner has a clearly defined goal toward which he is striving, and when the attainment of the goal depends upon the comparison of the learner's behavior with some kind of standard, such comparisons may function as reinforcers. This aspect of reinforcement, easily demonstrated in the laboratory, has also been demonstrated in educational settings.

Despite the excellent beginnings that have been made in research in this area, little is known about the reinforcing effect of the following practices which are frequently observed in schools:

1. Public display of the accomplishments of the student.

2. Providing new problems to be solved after the student has shown some skill in solving a particular class of problem.

3. Physical contact with the teacher.

4. Praising a child for good behavior but with an implied reprimand for the other children.

5. The smiles or laughter of the teacher.

6. Gestures of approval from fellow students.

7. Meeting standards set by the pupil himself.

8. Disagreement of the teacher with the student.

Utilization of the principle by different teaching methods. Teaching methods show substantial differences in the presumed reinforcers which they introduce and also in the extent to which they recognize and utilize reinforcement at all. For example, what is commonly referred to as the lecture method of teaching assumes that information can be communicated without making any provision for reinforcement. The transmission is strictly an intellectual process. Other traditional forms of teaching rely upon grades, release from the learning situation ("You may go as soon as you have the right answers"), reduction in anxiety, or the promise that the results of learning will be appreciated later in life. Recitation methods appear to rely either on direct approval as a reinforcer or on silence, as when the teacher indicates only when a pupil is wrong and moves on to the next question when he is right. Newer methods rely more upon "intrinsic" reinforcers which are assumed to derive from the learning activity or the response itself. Group approval, teacher approval, and self approval are also mentioned

as reinforcers in some descriptions of modern teaching methods. Skinner (1958) used a concept similar to that of "intrinsic" reinforcers when he stated that some activities are self-reinforcing. Discussion methods of conducting classes, in which the pupils interact with one another, would appear to rely upon social conditions such as approval of another's response.

Since we do not know which set of reinforcers or which combination is most effective, differences in method must represent differences in personal preferences. Perhaps a person is likely to recommend the use of those reinforcers which are effective for him.

Principle 2: The introduction of cues which arouse motivation toward the achievement of an educational objective will increase the effectiveness with which that objective is achieved.

Significance of the principle for classroom learning. An important corollary should be added to this principle—*an optimum level of motivation exists at which learning is facilitated to a maximum degree.* Motivation energizes action and also gives direction to action. Many who have studied the problems of effective teaching hold that the main function of the teacher is to arrange conditions so that the pupil directs his energies toward worth-while goals. The doctrine of interest which preceded modern conceptions of motivation recognized that some objects in the environment were more capable than others of arousing a positive affective response, but the relationship between affective responses and goal-directed action systems was never clear. Implicit in most discussions of interest was the idea that pupils learn most when they like what they do. The doctrine had difficulty in coping with the fact that a pupil will sometimes voluntarily devote large amounts of time to distasteful activities which enable him to achieve a goal important to him. Modern conceptions of motivation have overcome this basic difficulty in the doctrine of interest, though many other difficulties remain. Of special interest to the understanding of classroom behavior are the concepts of motivation developed by McClelland, Atkinson, Clark, and Lowell (1953) and by Spence and Taylor (1951). McClelland's type of theory recognizes that the level of motivation depends partly on the cues provided by the environment and partly on internal capacity to respond to those cues. It implies that teachers may be able to supply cues which arouse activity, but also that the structures which permit these cues to operate may not exist in all pupils. The theory does not exclude the possibility that all environmental stimuli or variations in such stimuli may have arousal properties.

Of particular importance is the variable denoted "anxiety." Although defined in various ways, it generally connotes a condition of observable agitation accompanied by such physiological observables as sweating palms, increased heartbeat, etc., and verbal statements of "unpleasantness." In short, "anxiety" connotes a response pattern similar to what is often called fear. Although it was once fashionable to speak of anxiety as unequivocally undesirable in an educational setting, present thinking and research do not support this generalization. Excessive anxiety may indeed hinder learning; a great body of evidence shows that extreme, persistent anxiety hinders at least certain types of learning in both subhuman species and man. Yet some data suggest that anxiety facilitates very simple forms of learning, wherein previously learned responses are of slight importance. Furthermore, some theorists consider reinforcement—in this case anxiety reduction—to be the crucial variable. They argue that the deliberate arousal of anxiety is desirable (particularly if it can, through learning, come to be elicited by any problem situation) provided that the anxiety is reduced subsequent to certain behaviors. Perhaps activity directed at the problem can itself become reinforcing—such would seem to be the case with at least some scientists. From this point of view, the undesirable features of anxiety result when anxiety is allowed to persist too long (Bugelski, 1956,

pp. 460–463). It is also possible that excessive motivation may hinder learning when the motivation is other than anxiety.

Despite the growing body of knowledge about motivational conditions related to learning, we lack much information vitally needed for the design of teaching methods. No method exists for determining which cues will produce arousal in a particular child. A clear picture of the development of motives is lacking. What to do about the child who typically shows a very low level of arousal or a very high one is still largely speculative. Numerous other problems could be listed.

Utilization of the principle and its corollaries by different teaching methods. The state of knowledge in this area is unsatisfactory. The fact that the most significant work is of recent origin is reflected in the vague and confused thinking about motivation which characterizes most teaching methods. The methods which derive from the Rousseau tradition are based on the assumptions that the world surrounding the child is full of cues adequate to arouse motivation and that the teacher must take great care not to remove these cues or inhibit their effect. The progressive education movement after World War I followed this tradition and attempted to fill the classroom with objects and materials which would raise the level of arousal. Individual differences in the arousal produced by different classes of cues were taken into account by the variety provided. Visitors to such classrooms generally agreed that they witnessed a high level of activity among the pupils, though some would question whether it was directed toward desirable goals.

Traditional education has tended to adopt the reverse policy of avoiding distracting elements in the classroom so that the pupil would devote more attention to either the teacher or his books. Where the moving-about of the pupils was restricted, as it was in such classrooms, a rich range of materials would have little value. In this situation great reliance was placed on the arousal value of the teacher and the printed materials. In some cases the teacher was able to perform this arousal function with great success, but in others the teacher had to fall back on the utilization of anxiety as a motive. To some extent, the policies of the progressive education movement represented a revolt against the use of anxiety as a motive manipulated by the teacher.

Other teaching methods disregard to a great degree the operation of motivational variables. The typical lecture method assumes that a lecturer can transmit information and that whatever motivation is necessary has to be inherent in the student. Still, even the most ardent protagonist of the lecture method would agree that some lecturers are much more capable than others of "arousing interest." How a lecturer is to do this is not generally specified. Advocates of self-selection teaching methods (Olson, 1959) assume that a rich environment will provide cues which arouse a pupil in such a way that worth-while long-term goals are eventually achieved.

Undoubtedly, the designer of a teaching method may have considerable choice concerning what motives to invoke. The same educational goal may be achieved through the operation of many different motivational variables. Choice may depend also on factors other than the efficiency of the learning process. Objections to the use of anxiety as a motive are based more on ethical than on psychological issues.

Principle 3: Practice in applying a principle to the solution of problems will increase the probability of transfer of training to new problems which require the use of the same principle for their solution.

Significance of the principle for classroom learning. This is the principle which emerges from the work on learning sets conducted by Harlow (1949) and his associates. Most educators would agree that the learning of principles such as Newton's laws of motion cannot be considered an end in itself, and that the importance of the learning lies in

the possibility that the principles may be applied to the solution of numerous problems. Just how such transfer of training was to take place was a complete mystery until Harlow demonstrated that transfer to novel situations would occur most readily if certain training practices were followed. These demonstrations do not imply that all is known concerning the most effective ways of teaching broad problem-solving skills. A particularly important problem is whether principles which are "self-discovered" are better retained and more easily transferred than those which have been handed to the student. That relationships of learning conditions in the area of problem-solving to subsequent performance are complex is well illustrated in a study by Kersh (1958). In this study three groups learned the "rules" necessary for solving mathematical problems. The groups consisted of a "no help" group which was supposed to discover the rules, a rule-given group, and a group given an intermediate amount of assistance. The "no help," or "self-discovery," group developed a greater postexperimental interest in the problems than either one of the other two groups. But the intermediate group was superior to the other two groups in application of the rules to new problems.

Utilization of the principle by different teaching methods. Long before current knowledge of methods of teaching problem-solving, the protagonists of particular teaching methods adopted policies for teaching problem-solving skills. Some of these practices were based on practical experience and have subsequently been justified by research. For example, teachers of mathematics in a traditional framework of education commonly gave their students large numbers of problems to solve related to each principle that was studied. Physics teachers have done likewise. Experience in teaching in these areas seems to justify this practice, and it is also largely in accordance with recent research on problem-solving. In contrast, the project method of Kilpatrick assumed that the kind of problem-solving involved in working on large projects would develop the required problem-solving skills. Furthermore, lecture and demonstration methods of teaching problem-solving assume that the process can be learned efficiently by vicarious experience, though in fairness one must state that lecture methods have often been coupled with problem-solving assignments given as homework. In recent years, those who have proposed that teaching be centered around the use of teaching machines have seen the possibility of exposing the pupil to carefully planned programs of problems. Mechanized teaching equipment offers the possibility of developing learning sets much more systematically than is possible with the typical recitation method. Indeed, they are ideally suited to making use of the operation of this particular principle.

Principle 4: Since learners differ in their capacity to make the responses to be acquired, learning will be most efficient if it is planned so that each learner embarks on a program commensurate with his capacity to acquire new responses.

Significance of the principle for classroom learning. The principle is stated in general terms and could be stated in a series of separate and distinct principles, each specifying some known variable which is related to the capacity of the individual to acquire or manifest particular categories of response. This principle excludes variables in the motivational and affective categories. Under ideal conditions a teacher should be able to measure the capacity of each child to learn a range of responses before instruction is initiated. In the absence of such a procedure, the possibilities of individualized teaching are limited. If individual differences are to be taken into account, the only alternative to systematic assessment is the adoption of some procedure for the study of the child under conditions as they exist in the school. Despite the widespread claim that child-study methods are going to solve this problem, the failure of the leaders of this movement to evolve any set of validated tech-

niques for observing children under typical school conditions has led to skepticism about the value of this approach to the assessment of individual differences.

While much research has already been undertaken on the intellectual capacities related to individual differences in the capacity to learn, many fundamental issues still have to be explored. For example, little is known about the generation of the various psychological "factors" that have been demonstrated to represent measurable variables related to learning in the young adult. To what extent early learning, in the sense used by Hebb (1958), generates some of the "factors" that are measured is an important question which still needs to be investigated.

Utilization of the principle by different teaching methods. Emphasis on individual differences and on differences within the same individual over a period of time has been largely responsible for the development of many of the "methods" mentioned previously, such as the activity, progressive, and laboratory approaches. Carried even further, it has led to the propagation by Olson (1959) of an interesting approach to teaching method called "self-selection." In essence, the child is allowed a great deal of freedom in structuring his learning situation whether it be in terms of books to read, arithmetic workbooks, or presumably the broader areas of what responses are to be learned. This approach places great reliance on the child's seeking those experiences which will develop desired responses. Thus, the role of the teacher, according to Olson (1959, p. 404), is to "guarantee that every classroom situation, or its immediate surroundings, will have in it tasks which are interesting in terms of the intrinsic content, and which also cover a range of difficulty as great as the variability in the human material with which he deals." Research with this technique is virtually non-existent, though Olson does mention a study in arithmetic at the third- and fourth-grade level which, he believed, indicated that on the whole the children were sound in the judgment of their abilities and that the gains under a considered self-selection plan seemed somewhat better than under a more laissez-faire procedure maintained in previous years. Inasmuch as this technique assumes that arousal of motivation and reinforcement will occur without any specific planning by the teacher and that the student will adequately assess his readiness—assumptions which many psychologists would not be willing to grant—further research is imperative.[5]

Principle 5: If a pupil has had training in imitation, then he is capable of learning by observing demonstrations of the skills to be acquired.

Significance of the principle for classroom learning. The nature of imitative activity and the conditions under which it occurs have long been matters of interest to education. The frequently voiced notion that the teacher should set a good example and perhaps behave according to standards far above those demanded of other members of the community is based upon the assumption that children will imitate teachers. In the classroom many teachers have doubted the efficacy of imitation as a mechanism for development of skills. Little was known about the phenomenon of imitation until it was systematically studied by Miller and Dollard (1941) within a framework of reinforcement learning theory. Their research with animal and human subjects showed that imitation is a learned behavior tendency, and without the learning of the tendency, imitation does not occur. This finding suggests that there may be individual differences in the ability to imitate produced by differences in previous training in imitation. Insofar as this is the case, the teacher may either have to develop imitative skills in some children or plan for them a learning program which does not involve imitation. Certainly, the inability of many children in kindergarten or first grade to learn from demonstrations suggests that substantial individual differences do exist in this area.

Utilization of the principle by different teaching methods. Few teaching methods have been clear in the application of this principle. Despite general agreement that many attributes of character are learned by an imitative process, there is little agreement that intellectual skills are learned by a similar process. Indeed, the concept that has found its way more and more into education during the last half-century has been that learning is most effective when the learner performs directly the response to be learned. One claim of progressive education was that traditional education involved learning by vicarious experience and that greater activity on the part of the learner was desirable. In the new education, learning by imitation was not to be a central method of intellectual development. A similar emphasis is seen in many "plans" such as the Winnetka Plan and the Morrison Plan. Such approaches to education and the teaching methods which they imply leave little place for the application of the principle under consideration. Perhaps the "learning by doing" concept of education has had an undue influence on educational planning. Certainly other methods of learning have value and these include learning by imitation and learning by being shown, as when the teacher takes the hand of a child and guides it in the writing of his name. The latter process, studied in a variety of situations, has been shown to produce learning, sometimes of a kind that is hard to produce by other means.

Principle 6: The learner will learn more efficiently if he makes the responses to be learned than if he learns by observing another make the response or makes some related response.

Significance of the principle for classroom learning. This principle does not exclude the

---

[5] Since the writing of this chapter, *Summerhill,* by A. S. Neill, has appeared and requires comment. Although not a research report, this description of the techniques and results of 40 years of experience with self-selective procedures in a small residential school is a persuasive argument for their effectiveness. It is to be hoped that further work meeting the more rigorous definition of research advocated here will be done and reported.

possibility that learning may be accomplished by imitation, i.e., by means other than doing. It does emphasize the importance of the learner's own attempt to make the response to be learned. As has been emphasized in the discussion of the principle involving imitation, there are circumstances under which the learner may profit by observing the performance of another. Nevertheless, the actual performance of the learner permits aspects of learning to take place which are not, and often cannot be, acquired by vicarious means. This has led many psychologists, notably Skinner (1958), to emphasize the importance of the learner's making the full and complete response. A distinction must also be made between the learner's making the full response and the learner's making certain substitute responses, often of a verbal nature. A child's expressing his attitude toward, say, religious or racial minorities in a classroom situation may differ vastly from what emerges in a real problem situation.

Utilization of the principle by different teaching methods. Many traditional forms of teaching relied heavily on learning occurring through the learner's observing the response of another. In the lecture method, as it has been used in teaching mathematics and the physical sciences, the teacher often solves a problem in front of the class and expects the pupils to learn thereby the problem-solving technique. Doubts concerning the efficiency of this approach were highly influential in bringing about educational change during the first half of the present century. Another common approach to education has been for the pupil to make, not the response to be learned, but some substitute or related response. Thus the student may discuss how he would behave in certain situations involving moral issues and indicate the moral stand he might take. For years, Sunday schools relied upon this method of teaching moral values. The assumption was that verbal behavior which reflected high moral values would be followed by other forms of behavior which reflected the same

values. The classic research of Hartshorne and May (1930) demonstrated that this assumption was not sound. The project method of Kilpatrick was an attempt to abandon the method of learning by indirect experience or by substitute verbal responses. Some educators trained in group dynamics have also suggested teaching methods where the learner practices responses or aspects of responses to be learned rather than practicing verbal responses. The danger of designing a teaching method around single principles is seen in many of these efforts to apply a "learning by doing" concept of education, to the neglect of other approaches to learning or other variables.

Implications for Research and Practice

The preceding discussion is not a comprehensive analysis of the relationship of learning principles to teaching methods. Only a few principles of learning have been discussed. Teaching methods have been discussed in terms of broad categories, and particular viewpoints within these categories have been overlooked. The object has not been to present a complete blueprint of these relationships; rather it has been to show that different teaching methods emphasize different principles and neglect others. Since this is the case, there is little likelihood that any one is superior to any other when the over-all effects of teaching are appraised. The best one might hope for would be slight differences in teaching effectiveness within narrow aspects of the learning process, and this is roughly what is found by empirical research.

The writers see the great need at the present time for an attempt to design a teaching method which makes as much use as possible of a wide range of learning principles. When this is done, there may be some hope of finding a teaching method which is definitely and markedly superior to others which have not been thus systematically designed. There is a possibility that many different teaching methods might be designed which would make full use of many principles, differences between them being a product of the objectives that each is designed to achieve. Also, the same goals may be achieved with equal efficiency by each one of a number of different teaching methods, efficiency being measured as a function of learner time. These are problems which will have to be explored before research of a scientific nature can be expected to make a major contribution.

REFERENCES

Ackerman, W. I. Presentation of alternatives and its relation to set in problem solving. Unpublished doctoral dissertation, Harvard Univer., 1956.

Albrecht, M., & Gross, L. Nondirective teaching. *Sociol. soc. Res.*, 1948, 32, 874–881.

Anderson, H. H., & Brewer, J. E. Studies of teachers' classroom personalities. I. Dominative and socially integrative behavior of kindergarten teachers. *Appl. Psychol. Monogr.*, 1945, No. 6.

Anderson, H. H., & Brewer, J. E. Studies of teachers' classroom personalities. II. Effects of teachers' dominative and integrative contacts on children's classroom behavior. *Appl. Psychol. Monogr.*, 1946, No. 8. (a)

Anderson, H. H., Brewer, J. E., & Reed, Mary F. Studies of teachers' classroom personalities. III. Follow-up studies of the effects of dominative and integrative contacts on children's behavior. *Appl. Psychol. Monogr.*, 1946, No. 11. (b)

Arbuckle, D. S. The classroom teacher's role in guidance. *Rev. educ. Res.*, 1954, 24, 181–189.

Asch, M. J. Nondirective teaching in psychology: An experimental study. *Psychol. Monogr.*, 1951, 65, No. 4 (Whole No. 321).

Balcziak, L. W. The role of the laboratory and demonstration in college physical science in achieving the objectives of general education. *Dissertation Abstr.*, 1954, 14, 502–503.

Baldwin, A. L., Kalhorn, J., & Dreese, F. H. Patterns of parent behavior. *Psychol. Monogr.*, 1945, 58, No. 3 (Whole No. 268).

Bane, C. L. *The lecture in college teaching.* Boston: Badger, 1931.

Barr, A. S. (Chairman). Classroom dynamics. *J. educ. Res.*, 1951 (special issue), 45, 81–160, 161–204.

Becker, H. S. The teacher in the authority system of the public school. *J. educ. Sociol.*, 1953, 27, 128–141.

Bills, R. E. An investigation of student centered teaching. *J. educ. Res.*, 1952, 46, 313–319.

Birch, H. G. The relation of previous experience to insightful problem solving. *J. comp. physiol. Psychol.*, 1945, 38, 367–383.

Birney, R., & McKeachie, W. The teaching of psychology: A review of research since 1942. *Psychol. Bull.*, 1955, 52, 51–68.

Bloom, B. S. Thought-processes in lectures and discussions. *J. gen. Educ.*, 1953, 7, 160–169.

Board of Education, Roslyn, N.Y. *The Roslyn elementary schools.* Roslyn, N.Y.: Board of Education, 1938.

Bovard, E. W., Jr. The psychology of classroom interaction. *J. educ. Res.*, 1951, 45, 215–224.

Bradford, L. The teaching-learning transaction. *Adult Educ.*, 1958, 8, 135–145.

Briggs, T. H., et al. *Laboratory techniques of teaching.* New York: Teachers Coll., Columbia Univer., 1938.

Brinkley, S. G. Mental activity in college classes: Student estimate of relative value in ten learning situations. *J. exp. Educ.*, 1952, 20, 373–378.

Brookover, W. B. Teachers and the stratification of American society. *Harvard educ. Rev.*, 1953, 23, 257–267.

Brookover, W. B. A research on teacher and administrator roles. *J. educ. Sociol.*, 1955, 29, 2–13.

Brown, M. S. The role of the teacher today. *Childh. Educ.*, 1949, 26, 70–73.

Bruce, P. Relationships of self-acceptance to other variables with sixth-grade children oriented in self-understanding. *J. educ. Psychol.*, 1958, 49, 229–238.

Bugelski, B. R. *The psychology of learning.* New York: Holt, 1956.

Burke, H. R. An experimental study of teaching methods in a college freshman orientation course. *Dissertation Abstr.*, 1956, 16, 77–78.

Carlson, C. R. A study of the relative effectiveness of lecture and directed discussion methods of teaching tests and measurements to prospective Air Force instructors. *Dissertation Abstr.*, 1953, 13, 1112–1113.

Carpenter, F. Educational significance of studies on the relation between rigidity and problem solving. *Science Educ.,* 1956, 40, 296–311.

Casey, J. E., & Weaver, B. E. An evaluation of lecture method and small group method of teaching in terms of knowledge of content, teacher attitude, and social status. *J. Colo.-Wyo. Acad. Sci.,* 1956, 4, 54.

Chamberlin, C. D., Chamberlin, Enid, Drought, N. E., & Scott, W. E. *Adventure in American education.* Vol. IV. *Did they succeed in college?* New York: Harper, 1942.

Cofer, C. N. Motivation. In P. R. Farnsworth (Ed.), *Annual review of psychology.* Vol. 10. Palo Alto, Calif.: Annual Reviews, 1959. Pp. 173–202.

Cogan, M. L. The behavior of teachers and the productive behavior of their pupils. *J. exp. Educ.,* 1958, 27, 89–124.

Collings, E. *An experiment with the project curriculum.* New York: Macmillan, 1923.

Corman, B. R. The effect of varying amounts and kinds of information as guidance in problem solving. *Psychol. Monogr.,* 1957, 71, No. 2 (Whole No. 431).

Coxe, Grace B., & Anderson, H. H. A study of teachers' responses to problem situations in school as reported by teachers and students. *Amer. J. Orthopsychiat.,* 1944, 14, 528–544.

Dale, E. & Raths, L. E. Discussion in the secondary school. *Educ. res. Bull.,* 1945, 24, 1–6.

Davis, P. R., & Morgan, M. E. *A balanced educational program for Santa Monica.* Santa Monica, Calif.: Board of Education, 1940.

Dawson, M. D. Lecture vs. problem-solving in teaching elementary social sciences. *Science Educ.,* 1956, 40, 395–404.

Deignan, F. J. A comparison of the effectiveness of two group discussion methods. *Dissertation Abstr.,* 1956, 16, 1110–1111.

Division on Child Development and Teacher Personnel, Commission on Teacher Education. *Helping teachers understand children.* Washington, D.C.: American Council on Education, 1945.

Dreikurs, R. Do teachers understand children? *Sch. & Soc.,* 1959, 87, 88–90. (a)

Dreikurs, R. *Psychology in the classroom.* New York: Harper, 1959. (b)

Eckert, Ruth E. Colleges and universities—Programs. In C. W. Harris (Ed.), *Encyclo-pedia of educational research.* (3rd ed.) New York: Macmillan, 1960. Pp. 268–285.

Edmiston, R. W., & Braddock, R. W. The study of the effect of various teaching procedures upon observed group attention in the secondary school. *J. educ. Psychol.,* 1941, 32, 665–672.

Eglash, A. A group discussion method of teaching psychology. *J. educ. Psychol.,* 1954, 45, 257–267.

Faw, V. A psychotherapeutic method of teaching psychology. *Amer. Psychologist,* 1949, 4, 104–109.

Fishburn, C. E. Teacher role perception in the secondary schools of one community. *Dissertation Abstr.,* 1955, 15, 1798–1799.

Flanders, N. A. Personal-social anxiety as a factor in experimental learning situations. *J. educ. Res.,* 1951, 45, 100–110.

Forlano, G., & Axelrod, H. C. The effect of repeated praise or blame on the performance of introverts and extroverts. *J. educ. Psychol.,* 1937, 28, 92–100.

Freud, Anna. The role of the teacher. *Harvard educ. Rev.,* 1952, 22, 229–234.

Gage, N. L. Explorations in teachers' perceptions of pupils. *J. teacher Educ.,* 1958, 9, 97–101.

Gage, N. L., Leavitt, G. S., & Stone, G. C. Teachers' understanding of their pupils and pupils' ratings of their teachers. *Psychol. Monogr.,* 1955, 69, No. 21 (Whole No. 406).

Gerberich, J. R., & Warner, K. O. Relative instructional efficiencies of the lecture and discussion methods in a university course in American national government. *J. educ. Res.,* 1936, 29, 574–579.

Gibb, L. M., & Gibb, J. R. The effects of the use of "participative action" groups in a course in general psychology. *Amer. Psychologist,* 1952, 7, 247. (Abstract)

Goldstein, A. A controlled comparison of the project method with standard laboratory teaching in pharmacology. *J. med. Educ.,* 1956, 31, 365–375.

Gordon, C. W. The role of the teacher in the usual structure of the high school. *J. educ. Sociol.,* 1955, 29, 21–29.

Greenhoe, Florence. *Community contacts and participation of teachers: An analysis of the community relationships of 9,122 public school teachers.* Washington, D.C.: American Council on Public Affairs, 1941.

Gross, R. E., & McDonald, F. J. Classroom methods. III. The problem solving approach. *Phi Delta Kappan,* 1958, 39, 259–265.

Guetzkow, H., Kelly, E. L., & McKeachie, W. J. An experimental comparison of recitation, discussion, and tutorial methods in college teaching. *J. educ. Psychol.,* 1954, 45, 193–207.

Guthrie, E. R. *The psychology of learning.* (Rev. ed.) New York: Harper, 1952.

Haigh, G. V., & Schmidt, W. H. Learning of subject matter in teacher centered and group centered classes. *J. educ. Psychol.,* 1956, 47, 295–301.

Harlow, H. The formation of learning sets. *Psychol. Rev.,* 1949, 56, 51–65.

Hartshorne, H., & May, M. A. A summary of the work of the Character Education Inquiry. *Religious Educ.,* 1930, 25, 607–619, 754–762.

Havighurst, R. J., & Neugarten, Bernice L. *Society and education.* Boston: Allyn & Bacon, 1957.

Hebb, D. O. *A textbook of psychology.* Philadelphia: Saunders, 1958.

Helbing, M. E. Evaluation of the procedures of a modern elementary school in terms of the subsequent adjustment of its pupils. *Calif. J. elem. Educ.,* 1940, 8, 137–146.

Henderson, K. B. The teaching of critical thinking. *Phi Delta Kappan,* 1958, 39, 280–282.

Hoffer, W. *Psychoanalysis: Practical and research aspects.* Baltimore: Williams & Wilkins, 1955.

Hopkins, L. T., & Mendenhall, J. E. *Achievement at Lincoln School.* New York: Bur. of Publs., Teachers Coll., Columbia Univer., 1934.

Hoyt, K. B. A study of the effects of teacher knowledge of characteristics on pupil achievement and attitudes toward class work. *J. educ. Psychol.,* 1955, 46, 302–310.

Husband, R. W. A statistical comparison of the efficiency of large lecture versus small recitation sections upon achievement in general psychology. *J. Psychol.,* 1951, 31, 297–300.

Informal committee appointed by the Progressive Education Association to report on evaluation of newer practices in education. *New methods versus old in American education.* New York: Bur. of Publs., Teachers Coll., Columbia Univer., 1941.

Jersild, A. T., Thorndike, R. L., Goldman, B., & Loftus, J. J. An evaluation of aspects of the activity program in New York City public elementary schools. *J. exp. Educ.,* 1939, 8, 166–207.

Jersild, A. T., et al. A further comparison of pupils in "activity" and "non-activity" schools. *J. exp. Educ.,* 1941, 9, 303–309.

Johnson, D. M., & Smith, H. C. Democratic leadership in the college classroom. *Psychol. Monogr.,* 1953, 67, No. 11 (Whole No. 361).

Johnson, H. C. Weakness in the Eight Year Study. *Sch. & Soc.,* 1946, 63, 417–419.

Kersh, B. Y. The adequacy of "meaning" as an explanation for the superiority of learning by independent discovery. *J. educ. Psychol.,* 1958, 49, 282–292.

Kinney, L. B. *Measure of a good teacher.* San Francisco: California Teachers Association, 1952.

Klein, Melanie. *The psychoanalysis of children.* (3rd ed.) London: Hogarth, 1949.

Krumboltz, J. D., & Farquhar, W. W. The effect of three teaching methods on achievement and motivational outcomes in a how-to-study course. *Psychol. Monogr.,* 1957, 71, 14.

Levine, J., & Butler, J. Lecture versus group decision in changing behavior. *J. appl. Psychol.,* 1952, 36, 29–33.

Lewin, K. Group decision and social change. In Eleanor Maccoby, T. Newcomb, & E. Hartley (Eds.), *Readings in social psychology.* (3rd ed.) New York: Holt, 1958. Pp. 197–211.

Lewin, K., Lippitt, R., & White, R. K. Patterns of aggressive behavior in experimentally created "social climates." *J. soc. Psychol.,* 1939, 10, 271–299.

Lifson, N., Rempel, P., & Johnson, J. A comparison between lecture and conference methods of teaching physiology. *J. med. Educ.,* 1956, 31, 376–382.

Lorge, I., Fox, D., Davitz, J., & Brenner, M. A survey of studies contrasting the quality of group performance and individual performance. *Psychol. Bull.,* 1958, 55, 337–372.

Maloney, R. M. Group learning through group discussion: A group discussion implementation analysis. *J. soc. Psychol.,* 1956, 43, 3–9.

Manning, D. An analysis of the relative directiveness of instruction in selected situations as indicated by a refined observation technique. *Indiana Univer. Sch. Educ. Stud. Educ.,* 1950, No. 2, 81–85.

Mason, H. Teachers' use of cathartic methods. *Fort Hays, Kan., State Coll. Stud. Clin. Psychol.,* 1940, No. 2.

McCall, W. A., Herring, J. P., & Loftus, J. J. *School practices questionnaire.* New York: Laidlaw Brothers, 1937.

McCall, W. A., Herring, J. P., & Loftus, J. J. Measuring the amount of activity education in activity and control schools. *Teachers Coll. Rec.,* 1937–1938, 39, 230–240.

McClelland, D. C., Atkinson, J. W., Clark, R. A., & Lowell, E. L. *The achievement motive.* New York: Appleton-Century-Crofts, 1953.

McKeachie, W. J. Student-centered vs. instructor-centered instruction. *J. educ. Psychol.,* 1954, 45, 143–150.

Miller, N. E., & Dollard, J. *Social learning and imitation.* New Haven, Conn.: Yale Univer. Press, 1941.

Muuss, R. E. The relationship between "causal" orientation, anxiety, and insecurity in elementary school children. *J. educ. Psychol.,* 1960, 51, 122–129.

Nedelsky, R. The teacher's role in the peer group during middle childhood. *Elem. sch. J.,* 1952, 52, 325–334.

Neill, A. S. *Summerhill.* New York: Hart, 1960.

Novak, J. D. An experimental comparison of a conventional and a project centered method of teaching a college general botany course. *J. exp. Educ.,* 1958, 26, 217–230.

Oberholtzer, E. E. *An integrated curriculum in practice.* New York: Bur. of Publs., Teachers Coll., Columbia Univer., 1937.

Ojemann, R. H., & Wilkinson, F. R. The effect on pupil growth of an increase in teacher's understanding of pupil behavior. *J. exp. Educ.,* 1939, 8, 143–147.

Olson, W. C. *Child development.* (2nd ed.) Boston: Heath, 1959.

Palmer, Josephine S. Role concepts of prospective teachers of young children. Unpublished doctoral dissertation, Columbia Univer., 1954.

Parnes, S. J., & Meadow, A. Effects of "brainstorming" instructions on creative problem solving by trained and untrained subjects. *J. educ. Psychol.,* 1959, 50, 171–176.

Patton, J. A. A study of the effects of student acceptance of responsibility and motivation on course behavior. *Dissertation Abstr.,* 1955, 15, 637–638.

Perkins, H. V. The effects of climate and curriculum on group learning. *J. educ. Psychol.,* 1950, 41, 268–286.

Pfister, O. *The psychoanalytic method.* Trans. by C. R. Payne. New York: Moffat, Yard, 1917.

Pistor, F. A. Evaluating newer type practices by the observational method. *Nat. elem. Principal,* 1937, 16, 377–389.

Prescott, D. A. *The child in the educative process.* New York: McGraw-Hill, 1957.

Proctor, W. M. *The six-four-four plan of school organization in Pasadena, California.* Pasadena, Calif.: Board of Education of the Pasadena Schools, 1933.

Rabinowitz, W., & Travers, R. M. W. A drawing technique for studying certain outcomes of teacher education. *J. educ. Psychol.,* 1955, 46, 257–273.

Radke, Marian, & Klisurich, D. Experiments in changing food habits. *J. Amer. Diet. Ass.,* 1947, 23, 403–409.

Rehage, K. J. A comparison of pupil-teacher planning and teacher directed procedures in eighth grade social studies classes. *J. educ. Res.,* 1951, 45, 111–115.

Remmers, H. H. Learning, effort and attitudes as affected by three methods of instruction in elementary psychology. *Purdue Univer. Stud. higher Educ.,* 1933, No. 21.

Rickard, P. B. An experimental study of the effectiveness of group discussion in the teaching of factual content. Northwestern Univer., *Summaries of doctoral Dissertations,* 1946, 14, 72–77.

Ruja, H. Experimenting with discussion in college teaching: Survey of recent research. *Educ. Admin. Superv.,* 1953, 39, 321–342.

Ruja, H. Outcomes of lecture and discussion procedures in three college courses. *J. exp. Educ.,* 1954, 22, 385–394.

Ryans, D. G. *Characteristics of teachers.* Washington, D.C.: American Council on Education, 1960.

Ryans, D. G., & Wandt, E. A factor analysis of observed teacher behaviors in the secondary school. *Educ. psychol. Measmt,* 1952, 12, 574–586.

Sarbin, T. R. Role theory. In G. Lindzey

(Ed.), *Handbook of social psychology.* Cambridge, Mass.: Addison-Wesley, 1954. Pp. 223–258.

Sax, G., & Ottina, J. R. The arithmetic achievement of pupils differing in school experiences. *Calif. J. educ. Res.,* 1958, 9, 15–19.

Seidler, R. Alfred Adler and the teacher. *Indiv. psychol. Bull.,* 1947, 6, 51–53.

Skinner, B. F. "Superstition" in the pigeon. *J. exp. Psychol.,* 1948, 38, 168–172.

Skinner, B. F. *Science and human behavior.* New York: Macmillan, 1958.

Slomowitz, M. A comparison of personality changes and content achievement gains occurring in two modes of instruction. *Dissertation Abstr.,* 1955, 15, 1790.

Smith, H. C. Team work in the college class. *J. educ. Psychol.,* 1955, 46, 274–286.

Snygg, D., & Combs, A. W. *Individual behavior.* New York: Harper, 1949.

Sobel, F. S. Remedial teaching as therapy. *Amer. J. Psychother.,* 1948, 2, 615–623.

Spence, K. W., & Taylor, J. Anxiety and strength of the UCS as determiner of the amount of eyelid conditioning. *J. exp. Psychol.,* 1951, 42, 183–188.

Spence, R. B. Lecture and class discussion in teaching educational psychology. *J. educ. Psychol.,* 1928, 19, 454–462.

Stovall, T. F. Lecture vs. discussion. *Phi Delta Kappan,* 1958, 39, 255–258.

Swenson, E. J., & Parton, D. General aspects of instructional method. *Rev. educ. Res.,* 1953, 23, 162–170.

Symonds, P. M. Education and psychotherapy. *J. educ. Psychol.,* 1949, 40, 1–32.

Taylor, D. W., Berry, P. C., & Block, C. H. Group participation, brainstorming, and creative thinking. *Admin. sci. Quart.,* 1958, 3, 23–47.

Thompson, G. G., & Hunnicutt, C. W. The effect of praise or blame on the work achievement of "introverts" and "extroverts." *J. educ. Psychol.,* 1944, 35, 257–266.

Thompson, O. E., & Tom, F. K. T. Comparison of the effectiveness of a pupil-centered vs. a teacher-centered pattern for teaching vocational agriculture. *J. educ. Res.,* 1957, 50, 667–678.

Tiedeman, S. C. A study of pupil-teacher relationships. *J. educ. Res.,* 1942, 35, 657–664.

Timmel, G. B. A study of the relationship between methods of teaching a college course in mental hygiene and change in student adjustment status. *Dissertation Abstr.,* 1955, 15, 90.

Travers, R. M. W., Wallen, N., Reid, I., & Wodtke, K. H. *Measured needs of teachers and their behavior in the classroom.* Salt Lake City: Univer. of Utah, 1961. (Mimeographed)

Ward, J. N. Group vs. lecture-demonstration method in physical science instruction for general education college students. *J. exp. Educ.,* 1956, 24, 197–210.

Warner, L., Havighurst, R. J., & Loeb, M. B. *Who shall be educated?* New York: Harper, 1944.

Washburne, C. W. *Adjusting the school to the child.* Yonkers, N.Y.: World Book, 1932.

Washburne, C. W., & Raths, L. E. The high school achievement of children trained under the individual technique. *Elem. sch. J.,* 1927, 28, 214–224.

White, J. R. A comparison of the group-laboratory and the lecture-demonstration methods in engineering instruction. *J. engng Educ.,* 1945, 36, 50–54.

White, R. K., & Lippitt, R. *Autocracy and democracy; An experimental inquiry.* New York: Harper, 1960.

Wingo, M. Methods of teaching. In C. W. Harris (Ed.), *Encyclopedia of educational research.* (3rd ed.) New York: Macmillan, 1960. Pp. 848–861.

Wispé, L. G. Evaluating section teaching methods in the introductory course. *J. educ. Res.,* 1951, 45, 161–186.

Wispé, L. G. Teaching methods research. *Amer. Psychologist,* 1953, 8, 147–150.

Woodruff, A. D. *Fundamental concepts of teaching.* Minneapolis: Burgess Pub. Co., 1959.

Zeleny, L. D. Experimental appraisal of a group learning plan. *J. educ. Res.,* 1940, 34, 37–42.

Zweibel, A. D. Re-educating parents and teachers. *Indiv. psychol. Bull.,* 1947, 6, 54–57.

CHAPTER 11 | The Teacher's Personality and Characteristics[1]

J. W. GETZELS
University of Chicago

P. W. JACKSON
University of Chicago

The personality of the teacher is a significant variable in the classroom. Indeed, some would argue it is the most significant variable. The educational impact of an Ichabod Crane or a Mark Hopkins, of a Mr. Chips or a Socrates, is surely not due solely to what he knows, or even to what he does, but in a very real sense to what he is. There has always been a concern with the personal qualities of teachers, and recently this concern has become the basis for a growing body of research. The present chapter attempts to review this research.

The studies legitimately falling within the scope of this chapter are too numerous for individual mention, much less for adequate treatment. Fortunately, there are already three relevant bibliographies: Barr (1948), Domas and Tiedeman (1950), and Morsh and Wilder (1954). The Domas and Tiede-

man bibliography alone contains some 1,000 titles. Because these sources ably survey the field prior to 1950, the focus here will be on the work done since then.

Accordingly, with 1950 as a starting date, we compiled a list of more than 800 references and applied three general criteria toward the selection of a manageably representative sample of studies. Preference has been given to published work, to work appearing in American rather than foreign publications, and to quantitative and experimental investigations rather than case reports or anecdotal accounts. Even within these limits we could not be exhaustive, and many valuable studies have been regrettably but unavoidably omitted.

Gordon Allport (1937) listed some 50 meanings of the term *personality,* and no doubt even this list is not all-inclusive. The term *personality* derives from the Latin *persona,* or theatrical mask, and one meaning of personality is the *appearance* (even false appearance) of the individual as socially perceived. As used in *dramatis personae,* personality has another meaning, that is, the *role* or function an individual has in a group. In this sense, the personality of the teacher

[1] The authors wish to express their appreciation to Miss Barbara McGill for her invaluable assistance in compiling the bibliography. Appreciation is also due Dean Francis S. Chase of the Graduate School of Education, University of Chicago, for generously supporting this project. Parts of this chapter were written while the first-named author was at the Center for Advanced Study in the Behavioral Sciences, Stanford, California.

would be defined narrowly by what he does as a teacher. In a third and broader sense, personality means the person as a psychological or unique whole, and refers to the dynamic organization of motives within the individual. We adopted this broad meaning of the term for our guidance in the selection and discussion of studies on the teacher, although, to be sure, some of our studies tend inescapably to shade off into the other concepts of personality as well.

We attempted to apply to the mass of studies we selected a number of possible alternate frameworks within which to organize our discussion. Among the schemes we tried were:

1. *Chronology.* That is, we tried to order the studies in time sequence in the hope that this would bring into view possible developmental trends in the concepts, methods, and findings in research on teacher personality. We were forced to abandon this framework because the time span with which we were dealing was so short (or change so slow) that few worth-while developmental trends came to light.

2. *Teacher subgroups.* We examined the studies by the particular sample of teachers serving as subjects, e.g., elementary versus secondary, male versus female, mathematics versus English. We rejected this framework because it tended to focus on the differences among teachers as an occupational group at the expense of possible communalities.

3. *Teacher-effectiveness criteria.* We asked the question, What personality variables are related to what kinds of ratings by students, supervisors, observers, etc.? This would have been useful, but it tended to place too much emphasis on what is at present the very ambiguous concept of teacher effectiveness.

4. *Research instruments.* We could have turned to a simple grouping of the studies by the research instrument used, or the major variable (like masculinity-femininity) measured, say, in some alphabetical or other convenient order. This would have provided a ready reference for the findings with the various instruments, but this scheme, although clearly useful, does not lead anywhere conceptually or theoretically.

5. *Personality theory.* We attempted to classify the studies according to the dominant personality theory underlying each one, e.g., trait theory, need theory, psychoanalytic theory, etc. On a priori grounds this seemed to us potentially the most fruitful framework for a chapter of this sort. Regrettably, the greater number of studies were so atheoretical that we were forced to abandon this plan.

It was, however, possible to organize the studies according to a number of current psychological concepts relevant to the dynamic definition of personality, such as attitude, value, adjustment. Even this plan presented some difficulties. Some studies used the same concept but differed so greatly in procedure that it was questionable whether the concept had the same meaning in the different investigations. Though the basic element in the structure of the chapter is personality or motivational concept, it was necessary to separate investigations using radically different instruments. In order to fill out the portrait of the teacher as a functioning individual, we added to the review of these studies of motivational variables a brief account of research dealing with the cognitive abilities of teachers. Accordingly, the studies reviewed in this chapter are organized under the following headings:

1. Attitudes
2. Values, Interests, Favored Activities
3. Adjustment, Needs
4. Personality Factors
5. Projective Techniques
6. The Teacher Characteristics Study
7. Cognitive Abilities
8. Conclusion.

One final word: There is a temptation in an undertaking of this sort either to be only descriptive, reviewing the relevant studies without any critical evaluation, or to be aggressively didactic, using the studies primarily as examples of what should have been or what should be done. In the first case, there is, we think, a shirking of responsibility; in the second case, often only a demonstration of the merits of hindsight, or worse, of the academic game of intellectual sharp-shooting. We have tried to avoid both extremes, on the one hand by writing critically about *general lines* of theory and method rather than second-guessing single studies, and on the other hand by describing rather fully the studies we mention, thus enabling the reader to make his own evaluations.

ATTITUDES

THE MINNESOTA TEACHER ATTITUDE INVENTORY

By far the most popular instrument for the measurement of teacher attitudes is the Minnesota Teacher Attitude Inventory (MTAI). More than 50 research studies using this instrument are reported in the literature. The MTAI was developed at the University of Minnesota, and the Manual published in 1951 states:

Investigations carried on by the authors over the past ten years indicate that the attitudes of teachers toward children and school work can be measured with high reliability, and that they are significantly correlated with the teacher-pupil relations found in the teachers' classrooms. The *Minnesota Teacher Attitude Inventory* has emerged from these researches. It is designed to measure those attitudes of a teacher which predict how well he will get along with pupils in interpersonal relationships, and indirectly how well satisfied he will be with teaching as a vocation (Cook, Leeds, & Callis, 1951, p. 3).

Norms are given for various types of high school and college students, for teacher-trainees, and for experienced elementary and secondary school teachers.

Although a number of publications relating to the MTAI appeared prior to publication of the Manual, it is the monograph by Leeds (1950), based on a dissertation completed in 1946, that presents most fully the rationale, procedures, and basic findings on which the final form of the MTAI was established. The construction and validation of the instrument (originally called the Teacher Pupil Inventory) and the results obtained by Leeds may briefly be described as follows:

1. Selection of items for preliminary tryout. On the basis of the literature on teacher-pupil behavior, 378 opinion statements representing teacher reactions to children and pupils were compiled and a Likert-type scale constructed. Sample items were: "Children should be seen and not heard," "The boastful child is usually over-confident of his ability," "Without children life would be dull." He then rewrote these statements into two forms, one positive and the other negative in wording, thus establishing a pool of some 700 items.

2. Validation and scoring of the try-out items. A purely empirical rationale was applied. Validity was defined as the degree to which each of the selected items would discriminate between those teachers having the desired and those having the undesired types of relations with pupils. Two such criterion groups were established by asking principals of 70 elementary and secondary schools in Pennsylvania and Ohio to designate several of their teachers who were "superior" and several who were "inferior" in their ability to maintain "harmonious relations" in the classroom as evidenced by "(1) Ability to win the affection of his pupils, (2) Fondness for, and understanding of children, (3) Ability to maintain a desirable form of discipline" (Leeds, 1950, p. 7). One hundred "superior" and one hundred "inferior" teachers completed two forms of the instrument, each containing about 380 items, a month apart, being assured on each occasion of complete anonymity. The forms bore surreptitious identification so that the responses could be collated, and chi square was computed to determine the extent to which each item discriminated between the two groups. One hundred and sixty-four items were chosen for use in the final inventory, and weighted and simplified scoring systems for the five responses to each item were developed on the basis of this empirically established differentiation.

3. *Validity of the Inventory as a whole.* Having thus constructed and empirically validated these teacher-attitude items, Leeds then posed the crucial question: Would the Inventory as a whole differentiate among a random sample of teachers? Accordingly, he administered the instrument in the established "anonymous" fashion to 100 teachers in Grades 4–6, inclusive, and correlated their scores with the following three criteria of teacher-pupil rapport: (1) Ratings of the teachers by their principals, (2) Classroom ratings of the teachers by Leeds himself on a modification of Baxter's Rating Scale of the Teacher's Personal Effectiveness, (3) Ratings of the teachers by their pupils on a 50-item "My Teacher" questionnaire. The correlations between these principal, observer, and pupil ratings and the Inventory were .434, .486, and .452, respectively, all significant at the .01 level. A combination of the three criteria gave a validity coefficient of .594. A multiple correlation of .595 between the Inventory and the three ratings was also obtained. The split-half reliability (with the Spearman-Brown correction) was .909.

Changes Related to Training and Experience

The Leeds study certainly seemed to demonstrate that teacher-pupil relations in the classroom were associated with the kinds of teacher attitudes measured by the Inventory. However, little was known about the effect of training and experience on these attitudes. Accordingly, Callis (1950) investigated the changes that occur during teacher training and early teaching experience, using "a slight extension" of the Leeds Inventory that correlated .95 with the original. In effect, this study, as developed by Callis, was designed "to determine in a general way the stability of the attitudes being measured" (Callis, 1950, p. 719) by comparing the test-retest scores of four groups of subjects: (1) Controls—57 first-quarter juniors in the College of Education tested and retested at one-week or ten-day intervals; (2) Juniors—175 first-

quarter juniors in the College of Education tested at the beginning of the school year and again six months later; (3) Seniors—147 first-quarter seniors in the College of Education tested at the beginning of the school year and again six months later; (4) Beginning teachers—137 teachers from the College of Education tested just before graduation and again after they had been teaching for six months.

The results were quite straightforward:

1. All groups, including the Controls, showed a significant change in mean Inventory scores between the first and second testing.

2. For the Controls, Juniors, and Seniors this change was an increase from first to second testing; for the Beginning Teachers, it was a decrease.

3. When the change in score of the Experimental groups was compared with the change of the Control group, the following was found: (a) For the Juniors, the increase was significant at the .01 level; (b) For the Beginning Teachers, the decrease was significant at the .01 level; (c) For the Seniors, the increase was not significantly different from the increase for the Controls.

4. The correlation coefficient between the first and second testings for the three Experimental groups was .71 for the Juniors, .74 for the Seniors, and .66 for the Beginning Teachers.

5. Analysis of the effect of training and early teaching experience on each of the 239 items of the Inventory revealed that the first six months of professional training produced significant changes in the desired direction in 20 per cent of the attitudes (items), while the first six months of experience produced significant changes in the undesirable direction in 11 per cent of the attitudes (items). The investigator concluded: *"the attitudes measured by the Teacher Attitude Inventory are of sufficient stability to warrant further investigation as to their efficiency in predicting teacher-pupil relations and in pre-training selection of teacher[s]"* (Callis, 1950, p. 725).

Major Curricular Groupings
of Education Students

Callis (1950) also examined the teacher-attitude scores of education juniors and seniors when the students were classified into three major curricular groupings: (1) Early childhood education majors—nursery to elementary; (2) Academic field majors; (3) Special field majors—art, home economics, industrial, music, physical education. He found significant differences among the three groups, with the early childhood education majors scoring highest and the special field majors scoring lowest in about the same magnitude both at the junior and senior

item instrument. Using the published form of the Inventory, Leeds (1952) again investigated the relation between teacher attitudes and teacher-pupil rapport as measured by principal, observer, and pupil ratings. The procedures were essentially the same as in the original validity study. One hundred randomly selected teachers of Grades 4–6—this time in South Carolina instead of Ohio and Pennsylvania—were given the MTAI. The same principal, observer, and pupil rating scales were used, and Inventory scores were correlated with each rating scale and in combination. The results were very much the same as those of the first study. The relevant present and comparable 1950 data are given

TABLE 1

CORRELATIONS BETWEEN INVENTORY SCORES AND TEACHER RATINGS
BY STUDENTS, SUPERVISORS, AND OBSERVERS IN FOUR STUDIES

Factors Correlated	Leeds (1950) $N=100$	Leeds (1952) $N=100$	Callis (1953) $N=77$	Chappell & Callis (1954) $N=82$
Inventory vs. Pupils' (Students') Ratings	.45	.31	.49	−.05
Inventory vs. Principals' (Supervisors') Ratings	.43	.46	.19	.18
Inventory vs. Observers' Ratings	.49	.59	.40	.11
(Combined equal weights)	.59	.59	.46	.11
Inventory vs. Three Validating Criteria (combined multiple weights)	.60	.63	...	...

levels, i.e., at the beginning and at the end of professional training.

The MTAI and
Experienced Teacher Ratings

The final form of the Minnesota Teacher Attitude Inventory—the form used in all subsequent studies to be reviewed here—was constructed on the basis of the experimental work reported in the preceding investigations (among others). Of the 150 items in the published MTAI, 129 were taken from Leeds's 164-item instrument and 21 from Callis' 239-

in Table 1.

Callis (1953) conducted a similar study, using a version of the MTAI that varied in "a few minor details only" from the published form. The sample consisted of 77 teachers from central Missouri. The over-all procedure and the principal, observer, and pupil rating scales were essentially the same as those used by Leeds, except that: (1) the teachers were from a wider range of grades (4–10 rather than 4–6), and (2) ratings were made by two observers rather than by one. The results were somewhat less clear cut than in the preceding studies but still largely confirmatory of a significant relationship between Inventory scores and teacher-pupil rapport as measured by the indicated ratings. The relevant data are presented in Table 1.

In 1954, Chappell and Callis attempted another replication with the same design, this time with 82 instructors at the Naval Air Technical Training Center at Jacksonville, Florida. Seventy-six of these instructors were noncommissioned officers in the Navy or Marine Corps and six were PFC's in the Marine Corps. Modifications of the preceding principal (supervisor), observer, and pupil (student) rating scales were used, and the MTAI was administered in both standard and slightly modified form. For this group of instructors the MTAI was not significantly related to any of the ratings singly or in combination. The investigators concluded that there is a difference between "teaching" children and "training" adults as conceived in the military situation. The relevant data are presented in Table 1.

The MTAI and
Ratings of Student Teachers

The preceding studies were concerned with experienced teachers. The study by Stein and Hardy (1957) was concerned with student teachers. Three samples of student teachers from the University and the Normal School in Manitoba were utilized. Two samples of 50 subjects each were in the elementary schools and the third, of 26 subjects, in the secondary schools. MTAI scores were correlated with four types of classroom measures: (1) ratings by pupils on an adaptation of the Leeds scale called "Our Student-Teacher," (2) ratings by pupils of the student teacher's lessons apart from his personality, (3) adviser ratings, (4) a combination of the three ratings. Of eight correlations reported, six were significant at or beyond the .05 level. One provocative finding is the difference in the relationship between the MTAI and pupil ratings of the student teacher's personality on the "Our Student-Teacher" scale and the

pupil ratings of the student teacher's lessons themselves. The former gave a significant correlation of .507, the latter a nonsignificant correlation of .282. The combined ratings gave a correlation of .39 for the elementary student teachers and .56 for the secondary student teachers. The investigators concluded from these findings that student teacher attitudes are measured by the MTAI with a "fair degree of both validity and reliability" (p. 326).

But other investigations adduce quite contradictory results. Sandgren and Schmidt (1956) divided a sample of 393 student teachers into an upper, middle, and lower group on the basis of their MTAI scores. No significant relationship between the MTAI score and the critic teacher's rating of teaching effectiveness was obtained no matter how the student teachers were further subdivided (male versus female, elementary versus secondary, or according to the curriculum followed). The investigators concluded, "... because there was no apparent relation between MTAI scores and critic teachers' ratings the MTAI cannot be used to predict probable success in teaching if the ratings made by public school critic teachers on the Student Teaching Report are used as a criterion of success" (Sandgren & Schmidt, 1956, p. 679).

Oelke (1956) examined the relationship between the MTAI scores of 44 senior student teachers and the ratings given them by their supervisors, and similarly found no significant relationship. Fuller (1951), in an earlier study of 74 senior student teachers in a nursery-kindergarten-primary teacher-training curriculum, also found no systematic relationship between MTAI scores and supervisors' ratings and concluded unequivocally, "Therefore, while the MTAI may serve a highly useful purpose in selecting students from the general population for training in early childhood education, or even for refinement of selection policies within subdivisions of the College of Education, it does not identify the ablest or weakest student teachers within the experimental group" (Fuller, 1951, p. 682).

The MTAI and Selected Teacher Characteristics

There have been numerous studies of the relation between the attitudes measured by the MTAI and observed teacher characteristics. As has already been indicated (p. 510), Callis quite early demonstrated with the 239-item experimental version of the Inventory that there were significant mean score differences for students majoring in different educational curricula. Similar studies using other teacher characteristics were undertaken with the published version.

1. *Teacher-training institution.* Kearney and Rocchio (1956) examined the relationship of MTAI scores to the type of teacher-training institution attended by elementary school teachers. The subjects were 291 teachers in a large Midwestern city who had earned a bachelor's degree from one of the following types of institutions: (1) liberal arts college ($N = 51$); (2) teachers college ($N = 88$); (3) university ($N = 152$). Significant differences in MTAI scores were found for the three groups, the respective means being 34, 51, and 56. The investigators concluded:

... it seems reasonable to expect that a teacher who is educated in an institution endorsing the viewpoint that a thorough background in liberal arts is essential for effective teaching will differ from one educated in an institution which emphasizes that knowledge alone does not guarantee that the teacher will manifest a desirable pattern of behavior in the classroom. ... The MTAI is the only known instrument that discriminates between teachers educated in various types of institutions—liberal arts colleges, teachers colleges, and universities. It will be to the advantage of both prospective teachers and their pupils if these institutions find it possible to build curriculums in reference to improvement on MTAI scores (Kearney & Rocchio, 1956, pp. 704–706).

However, the findings, recommendations, and arguments adduced for the obtained differences in this study do not seem to hold in a second study with secondary school teachers

as subjects. Cook, Kearney, Rocchio, and Thompson (1956) reported the following data: Secondary school teachers who took their training in liberal arts colleges ($N = 114$) had a mean MTAI score of 27; those in teachers college ($N = 66$) had a mean MTAI score of 26; those in a university ($N = 279$), a mean score of 42. Although the authors presented the two sets of data, they attempted no explanation for the variation in the findings.

2. *Sex, teaching level, experience, etc.* Beamer and Ledbetter (1957) examined the MTAI scores of various types of educational personnel. The subjects were 212 students enrolled in graduate courses at North Texas State College, subdivided into male and female, elementary and secondary school teachers, guidance workers, administrators, and inexperienced education majors. Of the experienced personnel, guidance workers ($N = 27$) had the highest mean scores (84), and administrators the lowest (56). The inexperienced education majors ($N = 48$) had a higher mean score than experienced teachers ($N = 164$)—90 versus 70; female teachers ($N = 104$) a higher mean score than male teachers ($N = 60$)—76 versus 61; elementary teachers ($N = 87$) a higher score than secondary teachers ($N = 54$)—74 versus 70. Data were also reported for the elementary and secondary school teachers subdivided by years of teaching experience, although the number of teachers in each experience group became very small. In the elementary school group, teachers with over 15 years' experience ($N = 14$) had the highest mean score (81), teachers with 2 to 5 years' experience ($N = 32$) the lowest (69); in the secondary school group, teachers with one year of experience ($N = 10$) had the highest mean score (69), teachers with from 2 to 5 years' experience ($N = 28$) the lowest (60). Size of the system in which teachers work had no effect on Inventory scores. Number of hour credits in child development courses had no effect on Inventory scores. Regrettably, the sample size was small; no analysis of the possible interaction

effects among, for example, sex, level of teaching, and experience was undertaken and no rationale for the findings was offered.

3. *Nature of the subject matter taught.* Kearney and Rocchio (1955) studied the differences in MTAI scores between 587 elementary school teachers who taught all subjects to the same pupils (self-contained classrooms) and 52 teachers who taught different pupils in art, home economics, industrial arts, music, and physical education (specialist classrooms). The respective MTAI scores for the two groups were 41 and 28, differing significantly at the .01 level. The investigators explained the findings as follows:

Teachers who have pupils for longer periods during the day are interested not only in the pupil's acquisition of subject matter, but also are concerned with the pupil's whole personality which demands knowledge of the pupil's home background, his physical and mental health, and his outside activities. On the other hand, teachers of "special" subjects think in terms of the subject matter to be covered rather than the development of a self-directing personality in their pupils (Kearney & Rocchio, 1955, p. 359).

But an equally tenable explanation might well be that individuals who choose to teach special subjects are basically different in attitude structure from the other teachers. Indeed, the study by Callis cited earlier (see p. 510, above) shows just this. College juniors majoring in special field subjects, like the teaching of art, music, or physical education, even before they have had any teaching experience have lower MTAI scores than college juniors without teaching experience who major in early childhood education or in the teaching of academic subjects.

4. *Teachers' failure of pupils; liking of teachers by pupils; effect of pupils' values.* Rocchio and Kearney (1956b) examined the relationship between the MTAI score and the rate at which teachers gave failing grades to pupils, using as subjects 395 secondary school teachers in a large Midwestern city.

Since sex, age, and subject-matter field might affect both the failure rate and its relation to the MTAI score, separate analyses of these factors were carried out. Failure rates were found not to be significantly different for teachers within the academic (English, mathematics, science, social studies) or nonacademic (arts and crafts, commercial, industrial arts and homemaking, music, physical education) classification of subject-matter fields. Nor was there a significant difference in mean failure rate by age within the academic and nonacademic categories, or for male and female teachers within each subject-matter classification. When the teachers were separated into academic and nonacademic categories, and relationship between MTAI scores and failure rates estimated, the correlation coefficients were found to be $-.38$ for the academic group and $-.23$ for the nonacademic group, both significant at the .01 level. Further, an examination of the correlation in each of the nine subjects for both male and female teachers shows that even though they are not all significant in the "statistical" sense, 15 of the 18 coefficients are in the same direction, i.e., there is a negative relationship between the MTAI score and the failure rate of the teachers. The investigators concluded:

The high school teacher with undesirable teacher-pupil relations, who creates an atmosphere of fear and tension, and thinks in terms of the *subject matter to be covered* rather than in terms of what the pupils need, feel, know, and can do, is more likely to fail pupils than a teacher who is able to maintain harmonious relations with his pupils and who is interested in pupils as *pupils* (Rocchio & Kearney, 1956b, p. 251).

Cook, Kearney, Rocchio, and Thompson (1956) reported the results of a study in which pupils in the tenth and twelfth grades of four high schools were asked to name the subjects taken during the year with the two teachers they liked best and with the two teachers they liked least. There was no difference in the sex or age of the teachers most often liked and disliked but the difference in the MTAI scores was pronounced, the mean of the liked group ($N = 50$) being 39 and the mean of the disliked group ($N = 50$) 18.

In one of the few theoretically oriented studies in this group, Della Piana and Gage (1955) argued that classroom behavior is a function of both teacher characteristics and pupil values and needs, and that, therefore, the values of pupils are factors in the effectiveness of teachers. Within this framework, they hypothesized that pupils' liking of teachers is a function of the interaction between pupil values and teacher attitudes. That is, the significant positive relationship (corroborated in this study) between teacher scores on the MTAI and ratings of the teacher by their pupils should change predictably as pupils' value orientations are varied. The subjects for the study were 97 of the 98 teachers of Grades 4 to 6 and their 2,700 pupils in a Midwestern city. The teachers took the MTAI, and the pupils filled out several inventories including the Leeds "My Teacher" rating scale and a forced-choice values instrument measuring how much pupils want teachers with cognitive merit (effectiveness in helping pupils achieve intellectual objectives) as against affective merit (effectiveness in helping pupils satisfy their social-emotional needs).

The general hypothesis was tested in a number of ways, and in each case it was found that for the pupils who have stronger affective values, the teachers' MTAI scores correlated more highly with how much they were liked by the pupils. For example, the correlation between the MTAI scores and the Leeds "My Teacher" ratings in the 20 most cognitively oriented classes was .05, while in the 20 least cognitively oriented classes it was .57, a difference significant at the .05 level. The investigators concluded from these results that this study supports the interactional point of view in the understanding of teacher-pupil relationships. With respect specifically to the MTAI, they said,

... the MTAI will vary in validity for teacher effectiveness according to the values of the pupils interacting with the teacher. Teachers scoring high on the MTAI will probably be better liked by pupils who have strong affective values concerning teachers. If the pupils have strong cognitive values, the teacher's MTAI will make less difference (Della Piana & Gage, 1955, p. 178).

5. *The effect of special courses, practice teaching, and amount of education.* In addition to the initial investigation by Callis on attitude change and teacher training (see p. 509, above), several other studies have dealt with aspects of this problem. Rocchio and Kearney (1956a) posed the question, Does a course in mental hygiene affect MTAI scores? The subjects were 1,175 elementary and secondary school teachers representing 92 per cent of the personnel of a public school system in a large Midwestern city. Each teacher completed the MTAI and indicated whether he had completed a recent course in mental hygiene. A statistically significant difference beyond the .01 level in MTAI means was obtained between both elementary and secondary school teachers having the course and those not having the course. However, when the upper 25 per cent of the MTAI distributions of the two groups were compared, no significant difference was found. That is, when the highest fourth of the MTAI distribution of teachers having a mental hygiene course and the highest fourth of the MTAI distribution of teachers not having a mental hygiene course were considered, the means were essentially the same. Having a course in mental hygiene had not improved MTAI attitudes at the higher levels. Although the investigators did not examine the possible effect of the test ceiling on their data, they did consider several alternate explanations for their results, and on the basis of their best judgment concluded, "Apparently, the attitudes measured by the MTAI are basic and deeply rooted in the personality of the teacher. Such attitudes are not changed by a course in mental hygiene" (Rocchio & Kearney, 1956a, p. 93).

Sandgren and Schmidt (1956) investigated the problem: Do the attitudes of teachers change as a result of practice teaching and do these attitudes correlate with ratings of teaching proficiency? The subjects were 393 seniors in elementary, secondary academic, and secondary nonacademic education, and other types of seniors at a Midwestern teachers college who took practice teaching during one or more of the three 12-week terms of the school year. The MTAI was administered at the beginning and again at the end of this practice-teaching experience, and critic teachers' ratings on the Student Teacher Report for each student teacher were obtained. Comparisons were made between the two MTAI scores, and between the second MTAI score and the critic teacher's rating. The findings were quite straightforward. The mean for the entire group of 393 student teachers was 43 before practice teaching and 54 at the end of practice teaching, a statistically significant increase. On a subgroup basis the changes upward were noticeable in every group in which there were at least 10 persons. However, as has already been indicated above (see p. 511), there was no relationship for any of the groups between the MTAI score and the critic teacher's rating on teaching proficiency.

Cook, Kearney, Rocchio, and Thompson (1956) described a study investigating the relationship between MTAI scores and the "amount of education" of teachers. (A portion of this study is reported in greater detail by Rocchio and Kearney, 1955.) They reported that elementary school teachers with two years of college education ($N = 238$) obtained a mean MTAI score of 21, those with four years ($N = 291$) obtained a mean of 51, those with five or more years ($N = 73$) obtained a mean of 66; secondary school teachers with four years ($N = 287$) obtained a mean of 52. Several interpretations of the results are offered, among which are: (1) The teachers with only two years of college may have realized they did not have teaching aptitude and discontinued their preparation; or (2) They may have

been subjected to less comprehensive training in such things as child growth and development; or (3) Teachers who acquire more college education may be a superior group to begin with, or (4) The superiority of the MTAI scores was directly affected by the increased richness of a full college education. Incidentally, this report by Cook and his associates provides an excellent summary of a number of the studies in this section, although regrettably it does not give the bibliographical references to the original sources.

The MTAI and Other Personality Measures

Attempts have been made to relate the attitudes measured by the MTAI to other personality variables, notably those measured by the Minnesota Multiphasic Personality Inventory (MMPI), the Guilford-Zimmerman Temperament Survey (GZTS), and the Kuder Preference Record, Vocational (Kuder).

Cook and Medley (1954) used the standardization data of the MTAI to identify two groups of teachers differing sharply in their attitude scores. The MMPI was administered to these two groups, and 212 completed inventories were obtained, 112 representing approximately the 8 per cent of teachers scoring highest and 100 the 8 per cent scoring lowest on the MTAI. From these returns, the investigators developed two new keys for the MMPI using items that discriminated significantly between teachers scoring high and teachers scoring low on the MTAI. The Ho (Hostility) scale (50 items) reveals a type of person characterized by a dislike and distrust of others. The Pv (Pharisaic Virtue) scale (50 items) reveals a type of person preoccupied with morality and ridden by fears. A Ta (Teacher Attitude) scale, combining the Ho and Pv scales, was also prepared. When administered to a rather homogeneous group of graduate education students, all experienced teachers, the $Ho, Pv,$ and Ta scales correlated $-.44$, $-.46$, and $-.50$, respectively, with the MTAI. A second study done elsewhere (Stein & Hardy, 1957) using 89 prospective teachers in the Faculty of Education at the University of Manitoba found the following correlations for the same variables: —.297, —.257, —.315.

Using the same standardization data of the MTAI, Cook and Medley (1955) also studied the relationship between the MTAI and certain scales of the MMPI. The following conclusions were reported: (1) Teachers high on MTAI tend to have high K scores, teachers low on the MTAI do not; (2) Teachers high on MTAI score higher than those low on MTAI on the "subtle" items of the Hysteria, Psychopathic Deviate, and Paranoia scales; (3) The MTAI lows tend to score higher on the Depression scale and "obvious" items in general; (4) The highest MMPI score of an MTAI high is likely to be on the Hysteria or Psychopathic Deviate scales; the highest MMPI score of an MTAI low is likely to be on the Hypochondriasis, Depression, or Social Introversion scales.

Since an elevated K score was designed to represent a generalized "set" to mark items in a socially acceptable way more often than the average person does, the finding that "Teachers scoring high on the MTAI tend to have extremely high K scores, while those scoring low tend to have K scores near the mean of normal adults" (Cook & Medley, 1955, p. 125) bears careful attention. The investigators argue that no matter what the reason for this high relationship between the MTAI and the K scale, "there can be no question of the validity of the MTAI, which was developed and evaluated by strictly empirical methods" (Cook & Medley, 1955, p. 128). Accordingly, they feel that it is "worthwhile" to look at some of the other relationships between the MTAI and the MMPI. Unfortunately, no explanation for these relationships is given. Why, for example, should a high MMPI score on the Hysteria or Psychopathic Deviate scale be related to "desirable" rather than to "undesirable" teacher-pupil relations, i.e., to high rather than to low MTAI scores? It is the explanatory vacuum here as elsewhere in work with the

MTAI which is disturbing. In any event, despite the empirical findings that are given, the investigators end their report with: "Because of the prominent role of the set factor measured by the K scale, no conclusions are justified regarding personality differences between teachers who have high rapport with their pupils and teachers who do not have high rapport with their pupils on the bases of the results of this study" (Cook & Medley, 1955, p. 129). We shall return later in this chapter (pp. 540–541) to the meaning of K scores for teachers.

Leeds (1956) studied the relationship between the MTAI and the Guilford-Zimmerman Temperament Survey (GZTS). The MTAI and the GZTS were administered to 300 teachers in one of South Carolina's largest cities, and a mean of 29 with a standard deviation of 43 was obtained for the MTAI. The correlation coefficients between the MTAI and the 10 temperament measures ranged from —.07 in Thoughtfulness to .52 in Personal Relations, all coefficients except General Activity, Restraint, and Thoughtfulness being significant at the .01 level. The investigator concluded that teachers who get along well with pupils tend to be cooperative, friendly, objective, and emotionally stable, and to a lesser degree, manifest sociability, social ascendancy, and masculinity in emotions and interests. Those who do not have high rapport with pupils tend to be critical and intolerant, hostile and belligerent, hypersensitive, depressed, and emotionally unstable, and to a lesser degree, they tend toward submissiveness, shyness, seclusiveness, and femininity. Leeds suggests that "to a certain extent, the MTAI score is an indirect measure of these temperament traits" (Leeds, 1956, p. 334). An attempt was made to explain the results by reference to item analysis, but the possible effect of the "set to score good," i.e., the elevated K score found for the high MTAI teachers by Cook and Medley was not considered.

Beamer and Ledbetter (1957), in a study cited previously (see p. 512, above), investigated the relationship between the MTAI and Social Service preferences as measured by the Kuder, feeling that this is the one interest area that might be related to teacher attitudes. The MTAI and the Kuder were administered to 164 experienced teachers attending North Texas State College. The mean MTAI score was 70 with a standard deviation of 29. The mean Kuder Social Service score was 57 with a standard deviation of 10. The correlation between the two measures was .35. However, there were variations for male and female, and for elementary and secondary school teachers. Although male teachers scored lower than female teachers on the MTAI, they scored higher on the Kuder; although secondary school teachers scored somewhat lower than elementary school teachers on the MTAI, they scored somewhat higher on the Kuder. No interaction effects between sex and teaching level were given, and no over-all rationale for the findings offered, but the investigators concluded, "If these tests are valid, then this study strongly indicates that many persons are now engaged in teaching who do not exhibit the two essential characteristics of teachers [interest in social service and permissive attitudes toward children] mentioned by Snygg and Combs" (Beamer & Ledbetter, 1957, p. 661).

Studies of the MTAI Itself

Since the MTAI has been so widely used for the study of teacher attitudes and personality, and since it has been so frequently recommended for selecting prospective teachers, a number of investigations have been devoted to examining the character of the instrument itself. Among the questions posed are: What psychological factors do the attitudes represent? To what extent are the results due to response sets? How liable is the Inventory to faking?

Factor analysis. Ferguson, Brown, and Callis (1954), following up a preliminary cluster analysis study by Callis and Ferguson (1953) which was unable to discover meaningful psychological categories for the obtained clusters, did a factor analysis of the clusters and included tests of known psychological content to help interpret the results. The factor analysis showed that there were no significant factor loadings among any of the MTAI clusters and those of the remaining scales of the battery. Instead, the clustering of the items was found to be a function of the *strength of the expressed attitudes* of the teacher rather than of the substance or content of the items. The investigators concluded, "In terms of content, the evidence obtained so far suggests a single positive attitude factor is measured by the MTAI" (Ferguson, Brown, & Callis, 1954, p. 7).

This finding corroborates other evidence regarding the influence of test-taking tendencies of respondents on the variance of the MTAI. Cook and Medley, in data already cited (see p. 516), found a significant positive relationship between a high score on the K scale of the MMPI and a high score on the MTAI. The same relationship between the K scale and the MTAI was found by Tanner (1954).

Response sets. Perhaps the most comprehensive study of response sets and the MTAI is the work of Mitzel, Rabinowitz, and Ostreicher (1955). MTAI data for 204 superior and 204 inferior teachers selected by principals and superintendents on the criterion of "ability to get along with pupils," were analyzed, and three response sets identified: *Positive intensity,* defined as the ratio of "Strongly Agree" to all positive responses; *Negative intensity,* defined as the ratio of "Strongly Disagree" to all negative responses; and *Evasiveness,* based on the number of "Undecided" responses given by the teachers. The negative intensity response set was found to influence the test scores in such a way that test validity was increased by its presence. Positive intensity was found to exert very little effect on MTAI validity. Evasiveness was found to be an attenuating influence on the validity of the MTAI. The investigators suggest, "From the standpoint of interpretation, the validity of the MTAI that is due to the content of the items should be kept separate from the validity that is accounted for by response set" (Mitzel, Rabino-witz, & Ostreicher, 1955, pp. 20–21).

Also concerned with the problem of response sets and MTAI performance were Budd and Blakely (1958), who asked two direct questions: (1) Is the scoring on the MTAI biased in favor of the extreme response positions? (2) What is the relationship between scores on the MTAI and the tendency of subjects to choose either extreme or moderate response positions on the Inventory? A simple tabulation was made of the number of extreme (Strongly Agree or Strongly Disagree) response positions and of moderate (Agree or Disagree) response positions classified as correct or incorrect in the scoring key given in the Manual. The result was striking: For the extreme response positions, 110 responses were keyed "correct," 97 "incorrect"; for the moderate response positions, 112 were keyed "correct," 168 "incorrect." What is, of course, noteworthy in this tabulation is the large number of moderate responses keyed "incorrect." From this the investigators concluded that persons taking a moderate position on the items of the Inventory would necessarily tend to receive lower scores.

To examine this empirically, the MTAI was administered to 225 teacher-education students, mostly juniors, and each answer-sheet was scored in three ways: (1) standard scoring of rights minus wrongs; (2) scoring only the two extreme response positions for rights; (3) similar scoring for only the two moderate positions. Two subsamples of 24 subjects each were drawn, one of individuals who were at the top of the distribution on score No. 2, the other of individuals who were at the top of the distribution on score No. 3. The two groups were then compared on score No. 1, i.e., the actual MTAI score. In addition, the groups were compared on the basis of the ACE Psychological Examination gross scores to see if ability was a factor.

The results were straightforward and compelling. The mean MTAI for the first group was 59; for the second group it was 23.

The difference of over 35 points was significant at the .01 level. The difference between the ACE scores was not significant. The correlation between the MTAI score and score No. 2 (extreme response positions) for the total sample of 225 subjects was .56; the correlation between the MTAI score and score No. 3 (moderate response positions) was −.26. The investigators modestly concluded, "These data help to confirm the hypothesis that high scores on the MTAI are associated with the tendency to prefer extreme response positions to moderate response positions when taking this inventory" (Budd & Blakely, 1958, p. 709).

Gage, Leavitt, and Stone (1957) recognized that the MTAI, like the F Scale, is "loaded with acquiescence set," but argue that acquiescence itself may belong to the family of "authoritarian" and "conformity" dispositions. In that case, the agree-disagree format and high loading with negative items —those expressing authoritarian opinions— of the F Scale and the MTAI make a positive contribution to the validity of these instruments. On the basis of this reasoning, they stated the hypothesis that negative items have greater validity than positive items for the measurement of authoritarianism—more specifically in the present context, the negative items of the MTAI would be more valid than the positive items.

To test this hypothesis, the MTAI was given to 97 of the 98 teachers of Grades 4 to 6 in a Midwestern city. The criterion ratings of the teachers were furnished by their 2,700 pupils, who responded to Leeds's "My Teacher" rating scale. The correlation between the MTAI's 38 positive items and the criterion was .13. The 112 negative items were divided into three random sets of 38, 38, and 36 items to make the scores on negative items comparable in length of test with scores on the positive items. The three sets of negative items correlated .30, .22, and .22 with pupil ratings. The mean correlation was .25. The t value of the difference between the correlations of .13 and .25 was 1.64, and the one-tail level of significance almost .05. When all 112 negative MTAI items were combined, the score correlated .31 with the pupil ratings. This correlation was higher than the correlation of .26 for the entire 150-item MTAI. The investigators concluded, "Thus, the score based only on negative items is more valid than the entire inventory" (p. 101), and they went on to point out that since both the F scale and the MTAI used a preponderance of negative items, "It appears, with the hindsight provided by the present data, that the authors of the F scale and the MTAI built better than they knew" (p. 102).

This study contained certain weaknesses in that it used the highly selected positive and negative items of the published version of the MTAI, and when Gage and Chatterjee (1960) tried three replications of the preceding findings with similar data, the results were nonsignificant. However, it was argued that a more appropriate test of the hypothesis would compare the validity of positive and negative items not previously selected on the basis of their validity. Such a comparison was carried out using 738 items originally written by Leeds in the process of constructing the MTAI. Two forms of the test, each consisting of positive and negative items in approximately equal proportions, had been administered by Leeds to 200 teachers, 100 of whom had been identified by their principals as superior in maintaining a good classroom atmosphere, the other 100 as inferior in this respect. The findings for both forms were consistent with the hypothesis: the proportion of the negative items with validities above average was very significantly higher than that of the positive items.

Fakeability. The susceptibility of self-report personality instruments to faking is, of course, well known. Accordingly, a number of studies were undertaken to determine the fakeability of the MTAI. Perhaps the earliest of these investigations was by Callis (1950) in a study already cited (see p. 509, above). He administered the MTAI to several groups of juniors in the University of Minnesota College of Education, first with standard instructions, and after an interval of

several weeks with instructions to "get as high a score as possible." Relevant types of controls such as sequence of testing and test-retest gain or loss were used. The investigator concluded that "the Inventory was found to be only slightly susceptible to attempts to fake good" (Callis, 1950, p. 725).

Since the preceding finding may have been due to the naïveté of the students in training who were the subjects, Coleman (1954) used 76 experienced teachers in his experiment. The MTAI was administered twice, first with standard instructions, and five to seven days later with instructions to fill out the Inventory "as you might in applying for a teaching position in a school system known for its permissive atmosphere and pupil-centered point of view . . ." (Coleman, 1954, p. 235). A mean gain of 12.42 points, significant at the .01 level, was obtained between the two scores. The investigator states, "Use of the M.T.A.I. as a major factor in hiring a teacher or accepting a student for teacher-training would not seem warranted in light of the instrument's susceptibility to faking" (Coleman, 1954, p. 236).

Stein and Hardy (1957) referred to the two preceding studies and concluded that neither investigation established "categorically whether or not the Inventory is significantly susceptible to faking" (p. 326). They, therefore, investigated the problem also. Three random samples of 25 education students were drawn at the University of Manitoba, and the MTAI was administered to these prospective teachers before and after the mid-year recess. The first testing was based on standard instructions for all three groups. In the second testing one group ("controls") was again given the standard instruction. The second group was given the Coleman instructions, namely a "progressivist" point of view. The third group was given instructions based on the extreme opposite of the Coleman instructions, namely, a "traditionalist" point of view. The "control" group registered a significant gain in mean score with an *increase* of 9.92 points; the "progressivist" group registered a mean *increase* of 68.84

points; the "traditionalist" group a mean *decrease* of 141.68. The correlations between scores for the two testings for the three groups were .88, .09, and .15.

Despite these findings, the investigators argued that "this does not mean that the test is susceptible to faking, it means rather that the test is adequate in revealing a biased or prejudiced attitude toward children from either extreme position" (Stein & Hardy, 1957, p. 329). To demonstrate further that the MTAI is not susceptible to faking, the same investigators returned to the initial experimental design by Callis and administered the Inventory to two groups of student teachers, a control group of 36 subjects and an experimental group of 22 subjects, with standard instructions and with the instructions to "fake good" as used by Callis. The following findings are reported: (1) Only the control group increased its score significantly; (2) The variance of the control group increased from 840 to 931, that of the experimental group from 660 to 1,082; (3) The correlation between the two testings for the control group was .92, for the experimental group .69; (4) The difference between the correlations was significant at the .01 level. Since there was no difference in the mean scores of the experimental group, the investigators suggested that "faking instructions only served to confuse the subjects" (Stein & Hardy, 1957, p. 331), and implied that the Inventory is not susceptible to faking.

On the basis of the data presented, it is perhaps equally possible to entertain another hypothesis. The reason for no difference is not that the instrument is not susceptible to faking but that since the instructions to fake did not specify whether the hypothetical superintendent was "traditional" or "progressive," the subjects guessed in opposite directions, thus increasing the variance but keeping the mean the same.

Rabinowitz (1954) was critical of the Callis design on somewhat different grounds. He argued that people tend in general to think of their own attitudes and good attitudes as identical. To ask a subject to take the MTAI under instructions to secure as high a score as possible provides him with an explicit set which does not differ greatly from the set which, under standard instructions, he provides for himself. Accordingly, Rabinowitz used a design quite similar to the one later used by Stein and Hardy, administering the Inventory to 74 female upper juniors and lower seniors in a large metropolitan college under standard instructions, instructions to fake in a "permissive" direction, and instructions to fake in an "authoritarian" direction. The crucial relevant result is that for both the "permissive" and the "authoritarian" groups there was a significant difference between the two testings, in the first case an increase of 15.16 points and in the second a decrease of 94.58 points. Of course, neither this study nor the others tell us the extent to which the MTAI *would* be faked in an actual selection setting. It is, however, important to note, as the investigator suggested, "Although the MTAI has been recommended for teacher selection purposes . . ., the evidence presented here would argue against this use of the test. . . . The subject with some knowledge of the viewpoint endorsed by the selection agency could, in most cases, reflect this viewpoint in responding to the MTAI" (Rabinowitz, 1954, p. 663).

In addition to the problem of faking, the question of whether or not the respondent identifies himself is crucial to the interpretation of MTAI responses, especially when it is recalled that the initial validation of the MTAI was based on anonymous responses. Sorenson (1956) examined not only the issue of fakeability but simultaneously the effect of asking subjects to sign or not to sign their names when responding to the MTAI. The Inventory was administered to 406 prospective teachers. Half of the subjects were told to sign their names; the other half were told that they need not do so. A comparison of the unsigned and the signed answer-sheets produced the following data: For the 204 subjects who did not sign their answer-sheets, the original mean score was 41 with a standard deviation of 29, and the fake score was 70 with a standard deviation of 28. For the 202 subjects who did sign their names, the original mean score was 46 with a standard deviation of 28, and the fake score was 71 with a standard deviation of 29. The difference between mean original scores was significant at the .05 level; the difference between the mean fake scores was not significant. The effect of signing one's name versus not signing one's name was further checked by an analysis of the difference in gains from standard instructions to faking instructions for the two groups. The difference was 7.1 points, significant at the .01 level. The investigator's answer to both the question "Can prospective teachers fake the MTAI?" and the question "Does signing the answer-sheet make a difference?" was affirmative.

In addition to the problems raised by the preceding studies of the MTAI itself, there are numerous unresolved issues with respect to the nature of the findings provided by research using this instrument. For example, studies using similar groups of subjects come up with substantial differences in mean score —differences for which no explanation is given (Callis, 1953; Leeds, 1952). Studies attempting to predict success in teacher training result in contradictory findings, one study reporting satisfactory predictive relationships (Stein & Hardy, 1957), another stating flatly, "the MTAI cannot be used to predict probable success in teaching . . ." (Sandgren & Schmidt, 1956, p. 679).

We have already called attention (p. 512) to the unexplained differences in MTAI scores between elementary and secondary school teachers classified according to type of teacher-training institution attended. As was also indicated above (p. 514), one study found MTAI scores unchanged by a course in mental hygiene. But another study reports a direct relationship between MTAI scores and education (Cook, et al., 1956). Or again, one study says, "the Inventory was found to be only slightly susceptible to attempts to fake good" (Callis, 1950, p. 725), but another concludes, "Use of the

M.T.A.I. as a major factor in hiring a teacher or accepting a student for teacher-training would not seem warranted in light of the instrument's susceptibility to faking" (Coleman, 1954, p. 236).

Empirical versus logical scoring. To call attention to these unresolved issues is not to condemn the MTAI and other instruments like it out of hand. But it is crucial to note that the MTAI is a particular kind of instrument. It is an empirically constructed scale, with a scoring key that is essentially atheoretical, not permitting any logical explanation of the responses that are "right" and the responses that are "wrong"—other than that teachers selected on some a priori ground as "good" give the one, the teachers selected on some a priori ground as "bad" give the other. Why they give the one or the other, or how the one response or the other is related to good or bad teaching, is not considered relevant, for the problem posed is not rational understanding but pragmatic prediction. Here, for example, is the first item of the scale: "Most children are obedient." If a respondent says Strongly Agree, he gets $+1$; if he says Agree, -1; if he says Uncertain, he gets 0; if he says Disagree, he gets -1 (the same as if he had said Agree); and if he says Strongly Disagree, he gets 0 (the same as if he had said Uncertain). Or, here is another item: "A teacher should not be expected to do more work than he is paid for." If the respondent says Strongly Disagree, he gets $+1$; if he says Disagree, he gets -1; if he says Uncertain, he gets -1; if he says Agree, he gets 0; and if he says Strongly Agree, he gets -1 (the same as if he had said Uncertain or Disagree). As Gage says,

It is difficult to make psychological sense out of such scoring weights. The general direction or trend of the weights for all items does indeed assign positive weights to a permissive, child-centered orientation. But the non-monotonic weights defy any such conceptualization. And they imply that dimensions other than degree of agreement with the items are relevant to the test's purpose (Gage, 1957, p. 213).

Gage shows that a logical scale can be constructed on the basis of the present MTAI, thus increasing slightly both the reliability and validity of the instrument. But what is more to the point, when this is done, as Gage says, "the MTAI's meaning becomes relatively easy to formulate" (Gage, 1957, p. 215). The importance of understanding teacher attitudes would certainly justify any efforts to make the MTAI more meaningful.

THE AUTHORITARIANISM (F) SCALE

"Authoritarian personality structure", is surely one of the more provocative social-psychological concepts, and the California F Scale based upon this concept one of the most widely used instruments of the past decade. A number of studies have applied the scale to teachers. Remmers (1954) studied the relationship between the F-Scale scores of 180 graduate students in education, "practically all" of whom were either teachers or administrators, and nine other variables: social class identification, attitude toward church, sex, age, church attendance, home discipline, political party preference, race, and religion. A number of significant but small correlations were reported.

Levin, Hilton, and Leiderman (1957) reported a study by Stuart still in progress in which the F Scale was related to teacher behavior in the classroom. Sheldon, Coale, and Copple (1959), in a study described below (see p. 559), found a significant relation between scores on the so-called "warm teacher scales" and scores on the F Scale, subjects scoring high on the "warm teacher scales" being lower in "authoritarianism." Piers (1955) gave a correlation of −.38 between MTAI and the F Scale and reported confirmation of the hypothesis "that authoritarian tendencies in teacher-pupil relationships are related to the so-called 'anti-democratic' or 'authoritarian' personality type in general, and that more permissive tendencies are related to the more liberal or 'democratic' personality types" (Piers, 1955, p. 247). It may

of course be, as Gage, Leavitt, and Stone (1957) point out (see p. 518 above), that these effects are obtained because both instruments are "loaded with acquiescence set."

However, these are only scatterings and in many ways not too dissimilar from the atheoretical, empirical-predictive emphases of the attitude studies examined in the preceding section. The study by McGee (1955) is of another order. Placing the essential issues of teacher personality within the domain of psychological as well as psychometric theory and seeking not only empirical prediction but logical understanding, McGee took as his premise that

personality is a more or less enduring organization of forces within the individual which helps to determine response in various situations. The forces of personality are not responses, but readiness for response, and it is largely to them that consistency of behavior—whether verbal or physical—is attributable. Whether or not *readiness* will issue in overt expression depends not only upon the situation of the moment but upon what other readinesses stand in opposition to it (McGee, 1955, p. 138).

Within this framework, he argued further that among the readinesses of special relevance in the classroom are the authoritarian or equalitarian attitudes of the teacher, and he posed his major hypothesis for research as follows: ". . . verbal responses of teachers to statements on an opinion-attitude scale for measuring authoritarianism and teachers' overt behavior toward pupils in the classroom are positively correlated" (McGee, 1955, p. 93).

To attack this problem required methods for describing and measuring (1) underlying authoritarian trends in the personality and (2) manifestations of these trends in overt action. Available for the first requirement was the F Scale with apparently demonstrated reliability and validity in estimating antidemocratic potential. For the second requirement, it was necessary to construct instruments to catch not only surface expressions of authoritarian behavior, but the more covertly expressed evidences of underlying tendencies as well.

The trends in authoritarian character structure thought of as forming the F syndrome were: Conventionalism, Authoritarian Submission, Authoritarian Aggression, Anti-Intraception, Superstition and Stereotypy, Power and "Toughness," Destructiveness and Cynicism, Projectivity, and Exaggerated Concern with Sex. The selection of behavior categories for observation was based on hypotheses as to how the specific behaviors in the classroom might be connected with these generalized authoritarian trends. For example,

when it was observed that a teacher was severe; the teacher grabbed, shook, or otherwise 'manhandled' a child; the teacher was abusive; the teacher was 'personal' in praise and criticism of the work of each pupil; or the teacher ridiculed a pupil or depreciated a pupil's efforts, one interpretation was that this individual had a particularly strong concern with anti-weakness (McGee, 1955, p. 109).

A full account of the construction and content of the Classroom Observation Record and Glossary is contained in the report. The final form of the Record had an interscorer reliability of .90 for 150 cases, and the investigator commented (not without justification), "the construction of an instrument designed to give qualitative estimates of authoritarian behavior in the classroom is one of the major contributions of the present study" (McGee, 1955, p. 121).

Classroom observations and F-Scale scores were obtained for 150 relatively young (not over 32 years of age) and relatively inexperienced men and women teachers (not more than three years of experience) in public elementary and secondary schools in Oakland, California. Analysis of the data yielded the following results:

1. The over-all correlation of .58 between the independent variable (the F-Scale score) and the dependent variable (the assigned behavior score) is highly significant (.005

level), thus confirming the major hypothesis of the study, i.e., a positive relationship between a measure of antidemocratic potential and a measure of teachers' overt authoritarian behavior in the classroom.

2. The over-all mean F-Scale score per item of 2.89 is almost one point lower than the mean score of 3.81 for the normative sample of middle-class adults, supporting the hypothesis that teachers as a group are less authoritarian than other adults of similar status.

3. No significant differences in means or correlations were obtained for any subgroupings of teachers, except that men were found to be significantly lower than women on both the F-Scale and Classroom Observation measures of authoritarianism.

In concluding his study, the investigator interpreted his specific findings within the theory of *The Authoritarian Personality* (Adorno, Frenkel-Brunswik, Levinson, & Sanford, 1950), offered a number of implications for countering authoritarianism in teachers, and finally suggested that *"teachers' classroom behavior on an Authoritarian-Equalitarian dimension can be predicted with fair accuracy from scores on the F-Scale"* (McGee, 1955, p. 144).

OTHER ATTITUDE STUDIES

In addition to the teacher attitude studies using the widely disseminated and standardized MTAI and F-Scale instruments, there are, of course, teacher attitude investigations —too numerous to cite—using other types of instruments. A sampling may be described here by way of illustrating the range and variety of problems, methods, and findings of these studies.

Lindgren and Patton (1958) tested the hypotheses that (1) the attitudes of high school teachers are less favorable toward children and toward current educational theory and practice than are the attitudes of teachers in the lower grades, and (2) that male teachers are likewise less favorably disposed than female teachers. A 50-item questionnaire dealing with teacher-child relationships and based in part on a previous study of effective and ineffective teachers was administered to 216 elementary and secondary school teachers. When the questionnaire was scored with a key based on favorable attitudes toward children and acceptance of current educational theory and practice, both hypotheses were supported at the .05 level of significance, i.e., nonhigh school teachers scored higher than high school teachers, and women scored higher than men. An item analysis was also made, and the investigators remarked that "the items on which teachers were in most disagreement with the key should give administrators and educational psychologists food for thought" (Lindgren & Patton, 1958, p. 83). They cited as instances: Only 25 per cent of the teachers gave the keyed response to the item "Most boys and girls who present extreme cases of 'problem' behavior are doing the best they can to get along with other people" (keyed response is Agree); only 37 per cent gave the keyed response to "An activity to be educationally valuable should train reasoning and memory in general" (keyed response is Disagree) (p. 84).

Cottle, Pownall, and Steimel (1955) reported the last of a half-dozen studies designed to develop an attitude scale which would differentiate between the responses of counselors and of teachers to items derived from personality inventories. The scale was administered to 236 female counselors and to 236 "matched" teachers. Fifty-three items differentiated the two groups: one category of 10 items dealt with activities connected with counseling; a second category of 14 items dealt with relations to others; and a third category of 29 items dealt with personal adjustment. Although the report itself draws no general conclusions regarding the personality differences, an examination of items seems to indicate that counselors are "better adjusted" than teachers (e.g., "I have periods of such great restlessness that I cannot sit long in a chair"—counselors more frequently responded False; "I have frequent ups and downs in mood, sometimes without apparent cause"—counselors more frequently responded False). It may be, of course, that counselors are more aware of the nature of personality instruments and give more guarded responses.

Wandt (1952) argued that a knowledge of teachers' attitudes toward the various groups contacted in the schools would provide information helpful in assessing the total teacher personality. As part of the Teacher Characteristics Study (described in detail below), he undertook to: (1) construct scales measuring teachers' attitudes toward the various groups contacted in the schools; (2) study the interrelationships of these attitudes; (3) study the relationship between teachers' attitudes and various other factors, e.g., experience; (4) study the relationship between teachers' verbalized attitudes and various overt behaviors; (5) develop disguised measures of teachers' attitudes.

Scales were constructed to measure teachers' attitudes toward administrators, supervisors, pupils, parents, nonteaching employees, democratic classroom procedures, and democratic administrative procedures. Returns from 240 teachers (stratified by experience and grade level) yielded three oblique (correlated) factors: (1) attitude toward administrators; (2) attitude toward adult nonadministrative groups; (3) attitude toward pupils. Significant differences were found between the elementary and secondary school teachers, the elementary group having the more favorable attitudes. No differences were found at various grade levels or for various experience groups.

Since the foregoing self-report scales can be faked, it seemed advisable to investigate the extent to which disguised and structured items could be used to reveal the same attitudes measured by the nondisguised structured scales. A questionnaire was devised requiring subjects to respond to items as if the questions had a factual answer (see Hammond, 1948). For example, one item was: "What per cent of teachers say that their principals do a good job? a. 20%, b. 40%, c. 60%, d. 80%." A significant relationship (r not given) was found between scoring high on the nondisguised instrument and choosing the greater percentages. The teachers with favorable attitudes toward administrators chose response "d" (80%) more than ten times as frequently as the teachers with unfavorable attitudes toward administrators. The investigator concluded that "it is obvious that such items can be used to measure teachers' attitudes" (Wandt, 1952, p. 119). Brief summaries were also given for sections of the research for which the analysis of the data was not yet complete, including one section which appears to show a significant relation between the scale scores of teachers and their observed behavior in the classroom.

Wandt (1954) also studied the attitudes of superior and inferior teachers toward various groups of persons contacted in the schools. Three teacher attitude scales described in the previous report were used: Scale P, measuring attitudes toward pupils; Scale A, measuring attitudes toward administrators; Scale N, measuring attitudes toward other teachers and nonteaching groups. Six hundred principals of a nationally representative sample of elementary and secondary schools nominated one teacher in their school who deviated significantly above, and one teacher who deviated significantly below, the typical or average teacher in over-all teaching effectiveness. Each principal gave the scales to the teachers nominated for his school, who then returned them unsigned directly to the investigator, the answer-sheets of the high and low groups being distinguished only by color coding. Returns were received from 41 high and 26 low elementary teachers; from 82 high and 67 low English-social studies teachers; and from 80 high and 69 low mathematics-science teachers. The results for all groups were strikingly similar. The high teachers were significantly more favorable in their Pupil and Administrator attitudes. There was no difference in their attitudes on the N scale. The investigator concluded that the results "strongly indicate that teaching behavior (as measured by principals' judgments) and teachers' attitudes toward pupils and administrators are related" (Wandt, 1954, p. 422).

VALUES, INTERESTS, FAVORED ACTIVITIES

THE ALLPORT-VERNON-LINDZEY STUDY OF VALUES

The Study of Values, originally published in 1931 and revised in 1951, aims to measure the relative prominence of six basic interests or motives in personality: the theoretical, economic, aesthetic, social, political, and religious. In the test manual accompanying the 1951 revision (Allport, Vernon, & Lindzey, 1951), the authors presented data for various occupational groups, including a group of 68 male graduate students in education. Compared with the male college students ($N = 851$) on whom the norms were based, the men in education were higher on aesthetic and social values and lower on economic and religious values. On none of the value scores, however, were men in education extreme. Although their highest score, for example, was in social values, it was not as high as the average score of theological students. Although their lowest score was in religious values, it was not as low as the score of engineering students. Comparable data for women education students do not appear in the manual, nor is it specified whether the men in question all had teaching as their goal.

A much more detailed picture of the responses of education students to the Study of Values appears in MacLean, Gowan, and Gowan's descriptive study of 1,700 teaching candidates at UCLA (1955). Because of the large sample, the researchers were able to present mean scores for both sex and teaching specialty subgroups. With respect to the male education students ($N = 658$), the California sample confirms two of the differences reported in the test manual; i.e., the men in education were lower in economic and higher in social values than were men in general. Differences on the other value scores were negligible. Women education students ($N = 1,066$) shared one important characteristic with the men. They too were lower on economic values than were the norms for their sex. In addition, the education women were higher in theoretical and lower in religious values than were women in general.

Although the differences between the education students and the norms are noteworthy, they are not nearly so illuminating for the understanding of teacher personality as are the differences between various teaching specialties. For example, comparing majors in kindergarten-primary education with those in home economics (all women), the former are noticeably higher in aesthetic and social values but lower in economic values. Or, again, comparing majors in theater arts with those in physical education (each group about equally divided between men and women), the former are considerably higher in aesthetic and theoretical values, but correspondingly lower in religious, political, and economic values. In none of the six value areas were the subgroups of education students consistently above or below the population mean. For each value, the difference among the various subject-matter groups was greater than the difference between the mean for the entire education student sample and the population norms.

Finally, the UCLA data contain one striking example of the interaction between sex, teaching specialty, and values. In the case of physical education majors, large differences between men and women appeared on all six value scores, each of the critical ratios being 3 or greater. No other teaching specialty revealed such sex differences and, indeed, in the case of theater arts and arts majors, sex differences in value scores were virtually nil.

Using the UCLA norms, Gowan (1958) presented correlation coefficients between the scores of 240 students on the Study of Values and their scores on two Teacher Prognosis scales derived from the MMPI (see p. 542 for a description of these scales). Although none of the coefficients exceed .25, two of the value scores—Social and Aesthetic —do show significant positive correlations with the Teacher Prognosis scales ($r = .21$

and .25, respectively), and a third—Economic —shows a significant negative correlation ($r = -.25$).

A more direct examination of the power of the Study of Values to discriminate between successful and unsuccessful teachers was made by Seagoe (1946), who correlated the scores of 31 students with ratings of their student-teaching success made two years later. She also collected "field success" scores (principal's ratings) on 25 of these students made two years after their graduation and correlated these with their original value scores. Thus, there was a two-year and a four-year time lapse between the administration of the Study of Values and the collection of teacher-effectiveness ratings.

The correlations reported by Seagoe were small but interesting. Economic and Aesthetic values showed the highest correlations with effectiveness ratings. The former correlated negatively ($r = -.33$) with student-teaching success and the latter correlated positively ($r = .26$) with field success. Neither, however, shows a consistent relationship with both success criteria. In fact, there was a tendency for almost all the value scores to relate to one criterion or the other, but not to both. It is as if the values indicative of the good student teacher bear no relationship to the values characteristic of the successful practicing teacher.

Another attempt to relate values to teaching effectiveness was made by Tanner (1954), who studied two groups of education students labeled "superior" ($N = 44$) and "inferior" ($N = 22$) on the basis of faculty ratings and MTAI responses. The superior women were significantly lower on economic and higher on social values than were the inferior women. Differences between superior and inferior men were not significant.

In sum, research with the Study of Values suggests that significant differences in values exist between teachers in different subject-matter areas. Indeed, some of these differences, such as those between physical education majors and theater arts majors or kindergarten-nursery-primary majors and home economics majors, invite additional exploration. Further, there is evidence that in at least two of the value areas—Economic and Social—teachers, as a group, might be distinguished from the general population. Despite these differences between teacher groups and population norms, the usefulness of this instrument for discriminating between good and poor teachers on the criterion of classroom performance still needs to be established.

THE KUDER PREFERENCE RECORD

The manuals of both the Strong Vocational Interest Blank and the Kuder Preference Record, Vocational, report data regarding the vocational preferences and interests of teachers. The Kuder Manual (1953, p. 14) gives the following percentile profile (against the male norms) for 225 male secondary school teachers: Outdoor 59, Mechanical 28, Computational 52, Scientific 51, Persuasive 35, Artistic 40, Literary 63, Musical 51, Social Service 68, Clerical 48. For 476 female secondary school teachers the following profile (against the female norms) is given: Outdoor 49, Mechanical 45, Computational 52, Scientific 46, Persuasive 48, Artistic 56, Literary 59, Musical 53, Social Service 50, Clerical 40. For 544 female primary and kindergarten teachers the profile (against the female norms) is: Outdoor 54, Mechanical 42, Computational 49, Scientific 35, Persuasive 40, Artistic 63, Literary 56, Musical 62, Social Service 65, Clerical 38.

It is evident from the data presented in the Kuder manual that the given norms for otherwise undifferentiated groups of teachers are not very discriminating. Indeed, the female secondary school teachers' profile seems about as "flat" as any in the manual. When, however, the total teacher male and female groups are divided into subject-matter subgroups, notable differences are obtained. For example, on the Scientific scale, the percentile score for male teachers of commercial subjects is 32, of mathematics 81, of social studies

41; on the Clerical scale, the respective percentiles are 86, 33, 38; on the Computational scale, the percentile score for teachers of commercial subjects is 76, for teachers of English 36, home economics 45, language 29, mathematics 91; on the Literary scale, the respective scores are 45, 88, 49, 76, 35. And so on. In effect, it seems that the Kuder vocational preference categories are not so much distinctive of teachers qua teachers as of teachers in specific subject areas.

In view of these data, it would seem that studying "good" teachers versus "poor" teachers by way of the Kuder would not prove very profitable, at least not unless the teachers were subdivided into subject-matter areas. Nonetheless, a number of investigations compare the vocational preference profiles of inferior and superior teachers. From 840 beginning students in secondary education, Hedlund (1953) studied some 150 who failed to complete the program satisfactorily, 54 who became "effective" teachers, and 54 who became "ineffective" teachers (based in both cases on observer, supervisor, and pupil judgments). He reported that those who became good teachers could be differentiated from those who became poor teachers and also from those who failed to complete the program satisfactorily as follows: Females scored lower in Literary preferences and higher in Social Service preferences. In addition, the good teachers could be differentiated from the poor teachers as follows: Males *and* females scored higher in Persuasive interests; females scored lower in Musical interests. No reasons were advanced for these findings. Surely, it is not immediately understandable why good teachers have lower interests in music than poor teachers, or for that matter why this characteristic should be true of female teachers but not of male teachers.

Gowan (1957) reported the Kuder profiles of 20 outstanding female elementary school teachers who were at the 90th percentile or better on each of the criterion judgments of teacher effectiveness used in the Teacher Characteristics Study (see p. (see p.

566 below). These teachers had a median age of 39 with a range from 23 to 56. About half had master's degrees; most had taken training beyond the B.A. On the Kuder, their mean percentile profile (against the female norms) was: Mechanical 43, Computational 23, Scientific 48, Persuasive 64, Artistic 58, Literary 59, Musical 23, Social Service 93, Clerical 43. As compared with the norm group of teachers in the Teacher Characteristics Study, these teachers were significantly less interested in the Mechanical, Computational, Scientific, and Clerical areas, and significantly more interested in the Social Service area. As compared with elementary school teacher controls, they were less interested in the Computational and Clerical areas, and more interested in Persuasive and Social Service matters.

The Kuder has also been used in attempts to discriminate among "promising" and "other" students in education. Tanner (1954), in a study already described (see p. 526, above), examined the vocational preference profiles of 44 student teachers rated "superior" and 22 rated "inferior" on the basis of practice-teaching and MTAI scores. No difference in preferences was observed for the male students; among the female students, the superior group had a significantly greater score in Social Service.

Stewart and Roberts (1955) examined the Kuder profiles of 124 entering female freshmen at George Peabody College for Teachers, of whom 66 left the institution by the second year. The investigators reported that those who stayed and planned to become teachers were significantly lower in Persuasive and Clerical interests and higher in Mechanical and Outdoor interests. Although the normative groups were not exactly comparable, it is interesting to recall that Gowan (see p. 527), in his investigations of 20 of the outstanding teachers participating in the Teacher Characteristics Study, found them significantly less interested in the Mechanical area, and significantly more interested in the Persuasive area. Nearly everyone argues that his Kuder data might be wisely used for guidance purposes, but no one gives any reason for the nature of his particular findings, or any reason why his findings are different from those of others.

THE STRONG VOCATIONAL INTEREST BLANK

Strong (1943) argued that individuals engaged in a particular occupation have not only a characteristic pattern of preferences with respect to a particular vocational area but a characteristic pattern of likes and dislikes in other more general interest areas such as habitual activities, amusements, hobbies, people, and so on. Strong's Vocational Interest Blank measures how nearly a person's interests coincide with those of the average person sucessfully engaged in a given occupation. It is assumed that if a person likes and dislikes the same things that people who are successful in a given occupation like and dislike, he will feel at home in that occupational environment and be more effective there than elsewhere.

The norms for the scale for elementary school women teachers were based on 238 teachers rated superior by superintendents of schools in Missouri, Nebraska, Kansas, and Iowa. Analysis of the responses one must make in order to attain a high score on this scale, i.e., to be similar to these "superior" teachers, is most illuminating of the "normative" elementary school teacher personality, at least as seen through this instrument. For example, with respect to liking and disliking particular groups of people, to like "Optimists," "Religious people," "Fashionably dressed people," and "Teetotalers," and to dislike "Pessimists," "Irreligious people," "People who are unconventional," "Women who smoke," "Carelessly dressed people," and "People who tell you their troubles," increases one's score, i.e., indicates similarity to the normative female successful elementary teacher. But to like "Emotional people," "People who are unconventional," "Foreigners," "Negroes," "Independents in politics," "Women who smoke," and "People who take chances on situations of doubtful outcome," and to dislike "Thrifty people," "Religious people," and "Teetotalers" decreases one's score, i.e., indicates dissimilarity from the normative female successful elementary school teacher.

Similar analyses may be made for occupations, amusements, and activities. For example, liking the following items is given a high positive score: such occupations as "Governess" and "Civil service employee" instead of "Dramatist" or "Surgeon"; such amusements as "Movies," "Women's pages," *Good Housekeeping, Ladies' Home Journal, Reader's Digest,* instead of "Plays," "Financial pages," or "Detective stories"; such activities as "Attending church," "Looking at shop windows," "Regular hours of work" instead of "Discussion of politics," "Studying the latest hobby, e.g., Einstein's theory, Freud, etc." or "Continually Changing Activities."

This is surely not the place for an exhaustive item analysis of the Strong as such, but one additional striking feature of the scoring weights must be noted—the limited intellectual interests attributed to the elementary school teacher. The nature of the preferred occupations, amusements, and activities illustrated above is one sign of this apparent nonintellectualism. But even when the teacher is offered the opportunity to choose specifically between an intellectual and a nonintellectual interest, she appears most frequently to reject the intellectual interest as against any other. For example, given a choice between "Reading a book" or "Going to the movies," a teacher who chooses the former is penalized two points (a nurse is penalized only one); given a choice between "Physical activity" and "Mental activity," the successful teacher expresses no preference for one or the other; asked which features are most important to her in her work, she gains a point if she says "Salary" and another if she says "Steadiness and performance of work"; but she loses two points if she says "Opportunity to make use of all of one's knowledge and experience."

The interests of secondary school teachers differ greatly from those of elementary school teachers. The correlation between scores for, say, a female high school teacher of English and a female elementary school teacher is .05 (Strong, 1943, p. 161). It is even more noteworthy that, within the secondary school teacher group, the kind of subject taught is a more significant differentiating factor than teaching itself. For example, male high school teachers of mathematics and physical science belong in Group IV (Farmer, Carpenter, Printer, Mathematics–Science Teacher, Policeman, Forest Service), but male high school teachers of social science belong in Group V (YMCA Physical Director, Personnel Manager, YMCA Secretary, Social Science Teacher, School Superintendent, Minister). The correlation between scores for the two kinds of interests is only .13. As Strong commented,

The theory upheld by most departments of education that all teachers should be interested in teaching young people first and only secondarily interested in their subject matter may possibly be a worthy ideal. But the facts of the case are that these two types of men teachers have quite different interests. The former correlate .49 with masculinity-femininity, the latter —.40. The same situation holds true with respect to women high-school teachers. . . . Evidently teaching per se, like managing per se, is less significant than the specific kind of teaching or managing. Whatever one may wish to believe regarding the proper function of teaching, he must recognize that today teachers of mathematics and science have interests that are quite distinct from those of teachers of the social sciences (Strong, 1943, pp. 161–162).

It is, of course, no surprise to find studies attempting to apply the Strong to discriminating between "good" and "poor" teachers. Thus, Schultz and Ohlsen (1955), using the criterion of team judgments by student-teacher supervisors, selected 28 of the "best" and 29 of the "poorest" men students, and 22 of the "best" and 19 of the "poorest" women students, representing all secondary teaching fields and the elementary field with the exception of special education. Form M of the Strong was given to men, and Form W to women. The two groups of men students gave responses significantly different at the .05 level of confidence for 18 of the 400 items, and the two groups of women gave responses significantly different at the .05 level of confidence for 24 of the 400 items. In both cases, the number of significant items could be accounted for by chance, and the investigators suggested that "this seems to give evidence that the Strong is not a suitable instrument for predicting teaching success when all items are considered together" (Schultz & Ohlsen, 1955, p. 108).

When the differentiating items were examined alone, however, a number of noteworthy relationships were found. The "best" students appeared to be interested in working with people, selecting occupations involving teaching, and pursuing intellectual interests. The "poorest" students tended to avoid occupations related to teaching and to select those offering personal gain. They were also inclined to consider salary most important in selecting occupations and failed to identify themselves with interests requiring considerable intellectual ability. In many ways these findings seem to be quite contrary to the scoring key provided for elementary teachers. The authors concluded that there is "need for much additional research before the value of the Strong as a predictive instrument can be determined" (Schultz & Ohlsen, 1955, p. 112).

Using faculty ratings and MTAI scores as criteria, Tanner (1954) selected for study 13 men and 31 women "superior" teachers and 14 men and 8 women "inferior" teachers. The only differences he found on the Strong were for the men on the Interest-Maturity scale, and for the women on the YWCA Secretary scale; in both cases the "superior" teachers had the greater score.

Sixty-three men and 37 women undergraduates enrolled at the University of Wisconsin School of Education were used in a study by Ringness (1952). A number of questionnaires asking questions about the choice of teaching as a profession were administered. A year later, when the subjects were beginning teachers, 16 men and 18 women were rated by university observers and school superintendents on their teaching efficiency and acceptability to the school system. The Strong was also administered at this time. In the investigator's words, "The Strong Vocational Interest Blank results were found to have little or no relationship to teaching success in terms of the treatment used in this study.... Little relationship was found between factors of the Strong blank and factors found in this study, except for interest in 'Welfare, or Uplift' factors" (Ringness, 1952, p. 50).

Although the use of the Strong as a predictor of teaching success seems contraindicated by the preceding research studies, the general formulation by Strong regarding the nature of teaching interests cited above (p. 529) was substantially confirmed by Blum (1947). This investigation dealt with the interests and personality traits of 125 University of Wisconsin male students, 25 each in the School of Education, School of Law, School of Journalism, Medical School, and the College of Engineering. A number of personality instruments including the Strong were administered, and the differences and similarities among the groups examined. A central finding of special relevance to the present inquiry was that "the greatest differences between the five groups of professional students were in their vocational and non-vocational interest tendencies rather than in personality traits" (Blum, 1947, p. 65), although, to be sure, these differences in interest patterns were not "clear cut." Blum also found a correlation of .62 between Masculinity-Femininity and Group IV (Mathematics, Physics, Science Teacher), and a correlation of −.21 between Masculinity-Femininity and Group V (Social Science High School Teacher). He concluded, ". . . on the secondary level at least there are sharp differences in the interests of various subject matter teachers. Any unity of interest which their common participation in teaching should include is not revealed" (Blum, 1947, p. 55).

This finding, and of course Strong's own formulation, give a clue to the essential futility of attempting to use the Vocational Interest Blank to predict success and failure in teaching qua teaching. Researchers often assume teaching to be a unitary interest and do not differentiate prospective teachers by subject matter or by teaching level. They indiscriminately lump students in education without regard to their teaching objectives and pool the obtained data, thus averaging out differences in interests that might exist. Why Strong's often reiterated findings about intrateacher group variations are not heeded remains a mystery.

OTHER STUDIES

The Allport-Vernon-Lindzey, the Kuder, and the Strong are the most widely used instruments in the field of values, preferences, interests, and favored activities. Numerous other devices and studies can only be sampled here to illustrate the general nature of the work. Kreitlow and Dreier (1955) constructed a scale for measuring the preferences of teachers for Academic, Progressive, and Community school philosophies. The authors claim a high reliability for the scale, and although no systematic data are presented, they suggest it measures the indicated preferences of teachers.

Dilley (1957) studied the preferences and values held by education students by means of a paired-comparison scale including such items as "Marriage and children," "A personal library of selected books," "A trip to Europe," "Contact with children and/or adolescents." The scale was administered to 266 future teachers and to 90 future engineers. Among the findings were: (1) The desire for marriage and children ranked highest for both male and female teachers and for the engineers; (2) Contacts with children and/or adolescents were considered more important by the future teachers than

by the future engineers; (3) None of the groups of students placed much importance on a personal library of selected books— actually a library ranked fifteenth and sixteenth out of a possible ranking of seventeen for male teachers and male engineers respectively, lower, for example, than "a new automobile" or "a trip to Europe"; (4) The distinguishing personal values of college students who enter teacher education are: "Desire for contacts with children and/or adolescents" and "Desire for opportunities to help other people."

Fisher (1958) studied the professional reading patterns of 50 teachers in relation to such possible influences as interest in reading, experience and education, accessibility of materials, and curriculum committee work. She found that teachers with higher degrees and teachers who participated in committees did more reading than teachers without these characteristics.

Koile (1955) pointed out that although interest in counseling activities has been mentioned frequently as important in the selection of school counselors, there was no instrument for assessing teachers' interests in counseling activities. Accordingly, he developed an instrument for identifying college teachers' interests in student personnel work. Three series of statements representing a teacher's potential activities were written, viz., primary teaching preferences (classroom teaching interests), secondary teaching preferences (committee and research interests), and faculty counseling preferences (student personnel interests). Forced-choice triad items were then constructed, including one statement from each of these preference categories, and a Professional Activity Inventory for College Teachers was developed. The scoring system based on the logic of discriminant analysis was highly effective in discriminating between teachers interested in counseling activities and teachers with little or no interest in this work. A cross-validation of the Inventory proved highly successful, and the author concluded with admirable caution, "The inventory should be a useful aid in identifying and selecting for counseling duties those college teachers who are similar to the faculty counselors who participated in this investigation" (Koile, 1955, p. 56).

Standlee and Popham (1958) studied the leisure-time interests and activities of public school teachers as related to five variables: sex, marital status, teaching level, salary, and type of graduating institution. The subjects were 880 Indiana public school teachers, including all those employed during the 1956–1957 academic year who were 1954 graduates of 24 Indiana colleges and universities. Of these, 84 per cent responded to the questionnaire. Female subjects reported more school-related, organization, entertainment, and hobby activities; male subjects, greater participation in sports activities. Married subjects reported greater participation in daily living and hobby activities; single subjects, greater participation in entertainment activities. Subjects in higher teaching levels reported greater participation in out-of-school employment, daily living, and sports activities; subjects in lower teaching levels, greater participation in profession-related, school-related, organization, entertainment, and hobby activities. Subjects with higher salaries reported greater participation in profession-related, school-related, daily living, organization, and hobby activities. No systematic relationships were found between the type of college from which subjects had been graduated and the types of leisure-time activities in which they participated.

In a companion study, Popham and Standlee (1958) explored the relationship between the teachers' favored out-of-school activities and their professional performance, as measured by (1) principals' ratings of overall teaching effectiveness, and (2) teachers' attitudes toward pupils as reflected on the MTAI. The research sample was the same as in the preceding study. Among the findings were significant positive relationships between the following pairs of variables: (1) current enrollment in college courses for credit and principals' ratings, but not MTAI scores; (2) attendance at professional meetings and MTAI scores, but not principals' ratings; (3) the number of professional books read and both MTAI scores and principals' ratings; (4) the number of hours spent by teachers viewing television and MTAI scores, but not principals' ratings; (5) the extent of participation in leisure organizations (dramatic club, country club, band, etc.) and principals' ratings, but not MTAI scores; (6) the number of hours spent doing housework and both MTAI scores and principals' ratings; (7) the extent of participation in religious organizations (church, Sunday school, etc.) and principals' ratings; this kind of participation was negatively related to MTAI scores. Attendance at school events such as athletic contests, musical programs, etc., was negatively related to MTAI scores but not to principals' ratings. More generally, the authors concluded that teachers' professional performance as measured by the MTAI and principals' ratings yielded differing patterns of relationships with teachers' out-of-school interests and activities. As measured by the MTAI, a teacher's school performance seems to be related to his professional out-of-school activities; as measured by principals' ratings, it seems to be related to his nonprofessional organization and sports out-of-school activities. No rationale is provided for the specific findings—why, for example, viewing television should be positively related to MTAI scores, or why there are differences between principals' and MTAI ratings.

A persistent issue underlying all studies of teacher personality is whether the same teacher, no matter what his personality, will affect all students in the same way. The assumption is made that there is an "ideal" teacher equally effective with all students. But common observation suggests that the effect of one individual upon another is a function of the personality structure of *both* individuals. A recent study deals explicitly with this issue in the classroom setting.

Washburne and Heil (1960) posed the following hypothesis: teachers who deal with children all day long throughout the year have a definite and determinable influence on the intellectual, social, and emotional growth of children, and this influence is conditioned by both the type of teacher and the kind of children with whom she is dealing. They argued that if they could categorize children and distinguish among types of teachers, they should be able to determine what kinds of teachers have what kinds of effects on what kinds of childen.

Fifty-five fourth-, fifth-, and sixth-grade teachers and their pupils served as subjects for the study. All children were given the Stanford Achievement Test early in the year and another form of the test near the end of the year. They were also given the Ohio Social Acceptance Scale at the beginning and the end of the year. This instrument is a sociometric test showing the degree of friendliness of one child for another. Toward the end of the school year, all children were given the Otis Group Intelligence Test, Form AS, and another instrument called "Assessing Children's Feelings." The latter instrument was designed especially for this study and classifies children as Conformers, Opposers, Waverers, and Strivers.

All teachers were rated on the Teacher Observation Scale, which provides ratings on 17 polar categories like Democratic-Authoritarian. Also, the teachers took the Teacher Education Examination (Educational Testing Service) and the Manifold Interest Schedule. The latter instrument consists of 420 activity statements (e.g., Attending parties where I meet new people; Writing a petition and collecting signatures), to each of which the teacher may respond "Like," "Dislike," or "Indifferent." On this basis the teachers in the experiment tended to fall into three categories: "the turbulent teacher," "the self-controlling teacher," and "the fearful teacher."

The results were quite illuminating. On the negative side, (1) there was no significant relation between teachers' scores on the Teacher Education Examination and any kind of growth on the part of their pupils;

and (2) there was no significant relation between teachers' scores on the Teacher Observation Scale and children's progress. On the positive side, there was one striking finding with the Manifold Interest Schedule. There was clear evidence that the teacher's personality has a marked and measurable effect on the progress of her pupils academically and socially. There appeared also to be an interaction between the type of teacher and her children's emotional adjustment as shown on the children's feeling test.

Although Washburne and Heil do not cite specific data, their conclusion is noteworthy:

The results verified the major hypothesis of the study—that different kinds of teachers get varying amounts of achievement from different kinds of children. The self-controlling teacher got the most achievement from the several different kinds of children; the fearful teacher got the least achievement. The turbulent teacher got almost as much achievement as the self-controlling teacher from children classified as conformers and strivers but less than half as much achievement from children classified as opposers and waverers. Although the fearful teacher got the greatest achievement with strivers, the amount of such achievement did not differ appreciably from that obtained by the self-controlling teacher and the turbulent teacher.

In terms of growth in friendliness, the fearful teacher actually got more gain than either the turbulent teacher or the self-controlling teacher from children categorized as waverers (Washburne & Heil, 1960, p. 425).

This study illustrates the methodological, theoretical, and empirical complexities encountered in the move from the naïve search for the "ideal" teacher. But its findings also illustrate the value of such an approach. The issue is not whether the particular typology suggested by Washburne and Heil is the optimal one. Rather, it is whether efforts such as these will enable us to shift from studying the personal qualities of teachers as if there were an ideal teacher to an analysis of the interaction between the personalities of students and teachers.

ADJUSTMENT, NEEDS

MINNESOTA MULTIPHASIC PERSONALITY INVENTORY (MMPI)

Among personality inventories, the Minnesota Multiphasic stands out as prominently as does the Rorschach among projective techniques or the Binet among intelligence tests. Few, if any, psychological questionnaires have been as widely used by researchers. Evidence of the MMPI's popularity is given by the 689-item bibliography covering its use over the 14-year period following its development in 1940 (Welsh & Dahlstrom, 1956). Nor does this popularity appear to be decreasing. Over half of the publications listed appeared in the last four years of the period covered, and at the time that bibliography was completed, MMPI articles were appearing at the rate of 100 per year. A more recent bibliography containing some 780 references is to be found in Buros (1959). Given this evidence of research interest, therefore, it is hardly surprising to find that the MMPI has been widely used in the study of teacher personality.

In its first published form the MMPI provided scores on nine scales that were shown empirically to discriminate between "normal" subjects and various types of psychiatric patients. The scales were: (1) *Hs*—Hypochondriasis; (2) *D*—Depression; (3) *Hy*—Hysteria; (4) *Pd*—Psychopathic Deviate; (5) *Mf*—Masculinity-Femininity; (6) *Pa*—Paranoia; (7) *Pt*—Psychasthenia; (8) *Sc*—Schizophrenia; and (9) *Ma*—Hypomania. In addition, three correction or control keys (*?, L, F*) were used to identify protocols made invalid by evasiveness, carelessness, or faking to produce either "good" or "bad" responses.

As work with the instrument progressed, many new scales were developed to further its usefulness—e.g., *Si*—Social Introversion scale (Drake, 1956); *Pr*—Anti-Semitic Prejudice scale (Gough, 1956); *Es*—Ego-Strength scale (Barron, 1956)—so that by 1954 more than 100 scoring keys were available (Welsh & Dahlstrom, 1956).

Teachers Compared with Other Groups

Shortly after the MMPI was published, it was used by Lough (1946) in a study of education students. The two guiding questions were whether the original nine scales would discriminate between women preparing to be music teachers (*N* = 111) and those preparing to be elementary school teachers (*N* = 74), and whether both of these groups could be distinguished from the general MMPI norms. With reference to the last question, Lough wanted to know also whether MMPI scores would give evidence that her subjects might develop "those types of maladjustments which have been claimed to be predominant in various studies of school teachers" (Lough, 1946, p. 241).

An analysis of mean scores showed no significant differences between the two curriculum groups or between the total sample and the published norms. On Scale 9—Hypomania, a slight difference appeared between the students and the normative group.

In a second study, Lough (1947) administered the MMPI to 115 women students in a liberal arts college. Sixty-one of the subjects were preparing for nursing; the remaining 54 were in the general liberal arts program. Lough compared the mean scores of these two groups and the education students tested earlier. Again no statistically significant differences between students enrolled in the four different curricula appeared on any of the scales.

Failing to find differences in mean scores, Lough examined the percentages of women in the four curriculum groups who had *T* scores above 70 on any of the scales. The number of subjects meeting this criterion was so small, however, that it was difficult to draw conclusions from the data. Nonetheless, the very fact that this number was small led Lough to conclude that her subjects were "on the whole, normal and stable" (Lough, 1947, p. 443). This conclusion provides an interesting contrast to estimates of the psychological health of teachers and student teachers based upon other assessment procedures (see, for example, the section on projective techniques, p. 554).

In view of the paucity of her findings, Lough stated, "On the basis of this study . . ., the MMPI has little or no value in educational selection; it is not a useful instrument for differentiating between those who are more suited for one occupation than another" (Lough, 1947, p. 444).

The value of the MMPI in differentiating students preparing for different occupations, including teaching, was also studied by Blum (1947). The subjects were 125 male students enrolled in five professional training programs—education, law, journalism, medicine, and engineering. In addition to the original nine scales of the MMPI, Blum included Drake's Social Introversion-Extroversion scale. Again, however, the MMPI yielded only minor differences between the students in the various curricula. Analyses of variance of the five mean scores resulted in a significant (.05 level) F ratio on only three of the ten scales—Hysteria, Schizophrenia, and Social Introversion. (By comparison, the Strong interest inventory yielded significant differences on 13 scores for the same subjects.) The mean of the education students was extreme—lowest of the five groups—on only one of these three scales (Hysteria) and even then the difference between this mean and the next highest (journalism students) was too slight to be of psychological significance.

When compared with the general norms, education students showed few deviations worthy of comment. Their greatest divergence was on the Masculinity-Femininity scale; their interests were more feminine than those of the normative group. Again, however, their score of 40.9 was hardly distinctive, for students in journalism had a score of 39.4, in medicine 44.5, in law 44.8; only students in engineering had the substantially different score of 54.6.

Finally, Blum commented, as did Lough, on the relative inferiority or superiority of education students as compared with students in other professional programs. He stated: "The fact that the differences in personality traits between education students and students in law, medicine, mechanical engineering, and journalism are so small as to be statistically insignificant refutes any implication that education students are inferior in personality traits to other groups" (Blum, 1947, p. 65).

Extensive MMPI norms, which may be of great value for the study of teacher personality, have become available as the result of a teacher selection study at the University of California at Los Angeles. Entering education students at UCLA were required to take a battery of tests including the Cooperative English Test, the American Council on Education Psychological Examination, the Allport-Vernon-Lindzey Study of Values, the MMPI, and others. The first published report of this testing program provided general norms for more than 1,700 students (MacLean, Gowan, & Gowan, 1955). For the standard MMPI scales these norms indicated that both men and women tend to be slightly high on the Hysteria, Psychopathic Deviate, Schizophrenia, and Hypomania scales. Concerning these differences, the researchers commented, "perhaps this is a reflection of the teacher's self-control, absence of social fear, scholarly withdrawal, or idealism and energy" (MacLean, Gowan, & Gowan, 1955, p. 672). In addition, the men appear feminine in interests, though women score near the general norm. Other comparisons of the sexes show the men to be higher on the Psychopathic Deviate scale and the women to be higher on the Hypochondriasis, Hysteria, Psychasthenia, and Responsibility (Re) scales. No significant differences were reported between students specializing in different teaching areas.

At least one study has applied the MMPI to a college faculty. Appleby and Haner (1956) studied the majority of faculty in a small college with the MMPI. Fifty-three faculty men and 13 faculty women participated, as did 23 male and 13 female education students. The male faculty group was significantly above (.05 level) the MMPI normative mean on the Depression, Hysteria, Masculinity-Femininity, and Paranoia scales and significantly below the mean on the Psychopathic Deviate, Schizophrenia, and Psychasthenia scales. Faculty women were similarly below the normative mean on the Psychopathic Deviate and Schizophrenia scales but showed no other significant differences from the norms. MMPI profiles were remarkably similar for the education students and the faculty members. It may be noted that at least two of the above differences for the faculty group (low Schizophrenia and low Psychopathic Deviate scores) are reversals of the differences reported for education students at UCLA.

In the Appleby and Haner study the most marked departure from the normative data (a mean almost two standard deviations above the normative mean) occurred with the Masculinity-Femininity scores of faculty men. An examination of the feminine-keyed items tends to explain why the male college teachers scored high in femininity. The researchers state:

It is scarcely surprising that faculty men should respond "yes" to such questions as "I like poetry," or "I liked 'Alice in Wonderland' by Lewis Carroll," or to reply "no" to the question "I believe there is a devil and hell in afterlife." Nor is it surprising that faculty men in music and language and literature should be more feminine in their replies than scientists, and that the physical education group should be the most masculine of all the groups. Even this small group, however, is decidedly feminine, falling one standard deviation above the normative mean (Appleby & Haner, 1956, pp. 608–609).

Blum's data (see above), showing that men in mechanical engineering and medicine are even more "feminine" in their interests than are men in education, offer empirical support to Appleby and Haner's criticism of the Masculinity-Femininity scale.

Considered as a group, the five studies reviewed in this section seem to offer little encouragement to researchers seeking to discriminate between teachers and nonteachers with the standard MMPI scales.

The MMPI and Teaching Success

Even though efforts to distinguish between teachers and nonteachers were relatively unsuccessful, there remained the possibility that the MMPI would be useful in identifying correlates of teaching success. LaBue (1955) attempted to discriminate between students who showed a "persistent" interest in teaching and those who did not. A persistent interest in teaching was defined as completion of a teacher-training program and acceptance of a teaching position. Students at Syracuse University who applied for the program but did not enroll were said to exhibit a "nonpersistent" interest in teaching. LaBue's final sample consisted of 50 "persistent" women, 49 "non-persistent" women, 47 "persistent" men, and 28 "non-persistent" men.

Numerous differences appeared between the two groups of women; "persistent" women were significantly lower on the Hypochondriasis, Psychopathic Deviate, Psychasthenia, Schizophrenia, and Hypomania scales. Only one scale differentiated between the two groups of men: "persistent" men were lower on the Psychopathic Deviate scale. Significant point biserial correlations for the total group paralleled these differences. All of the correlations, however, were quite small (the order of .25), a fact that led LaBue to conclude that "it seems evident that the real value of the MMPI is in clinical rather than in vocational diagnosis" (LaBue, 1955, p. 365).

A more popular question, i.e., one asked more frequently, than the one examined by LaBue, is whether the MMPI may be used to discriminate between students who go on to become effective teachers and those who do not. This question was the focus of a cooperative study involving 840 education students from 18 colleges in New York State (Hedlund, 1953). Beginning in 1949 these colleges administered the MMPI (and other assessment devices) to applicants in one- and two-year training programs for secondary school teachers. The purpose of the project was to develop a predictive index for identifying applicants who might fail in the program or become ineffective teachers. Measures of teaching effectiveness, obtained at the end of the students' first year of teaching, were based upon composite ratings by the teacher's supervisor (generally the principal), an "expert" observer, and the teacher's pupils. The student teachers were rated on the quality of disciplinary control in their classrooms as well as on general effectiveness. The positive findings were disappointingly few. A low Paranoia score was the only MMPI variable that differentiated those who became good teachers from those who became poor teachers and also from those who failed to complete the program satisfactorily. In addition, the lie score (L) distinguished those who became good teachers from those who did not, the former receiving lower L scores.

Gough and Pemberton (1952), in a somewhat more intensive examination of MMPI responses and teaching success, combined the traditional analysis of mean scores with a "configural and intuitive" approach. Composite success ratings of 147 practice teachers (89 males; 58 females) were used to divide the sample into high, average, and low groups. In addition to the nine original MMPI scales, the researchers scored the protocols for Re (Social Responsibility), Do (Dominance), St (Status), Sp (Social Participativeness), Pr (Prejudice), Ac (Academic Achievement), Ds (Dissimulation), Psy (Psychological Aptitude), Ie (Intellectual Efficiency), and Si (Social Introversion).

The first step of Gough and Pemberton's analysis was the customary one of comparing the mean scores of the three effectiveness groups on each of the MMPI variables. For the female sample, none of the scales yielded a significant F ratio. For the males, three of the scales showed "some promise." The successful male practice teachers scored lower on Hy (Hysteria) and Pd (Psychopathic Deviate), and higher on Psy (Psychological Aptitude).

Disappointed with these results, Gough and Pemberton began to look more "intuitively" at the MMPI protocols. There followed, "first, a great deal of free association and ratiocination about the signs and clues involved in the intuitive sortings; and second, an attempt to write simple indices and functions summarizing them" (Gough & Pemberton, 1952, p. 308). This process gave rise to eight "signs" that appeared to be related to success in practice teaching. When reapplied to the original records used in their detection, the two most "powerful" (i.e., most discriminatory) of the signs were: (1) a Paranoia T score between 50 and 56; and (2) a Hypomania score between 48 and 60.

It is instructive here to recall Hedlund's findings. In his study, a low Paranoia score characterized the good teacher; Gough and Pemberton, however, reported that an above-average Paranoia score is a "sign" predictive of success in practice teaching. Since no attempt was made in either case to explain the findings, one can only conclude that one set of results is as "sensible" as the other.

Using five of the original eight "signs," Gough and Pemberton attempted a "cross-validation" study. The subjects were 160 practice teachers divided into two rating categories: high and low. The number of "signs" in the protocols was again shown to be related to success in practice teaching. Oddly enough, however, the relationship did not appear to be linear. The signs seemed more effective in identifying better practice teachers than poorer ones. In fact, as the authors pointed out, subjects with very few "signs" (0 or 1) received slightly higher success ratings than did those with a moderate number of "signs." The authors said that they would not expect this phenomenon to occur if all eight signs were used instead of only five. They pointed out, however, that no evidence existed to support their expectations.

Reviewing their work, Gough and Pemberton concluded,

the method of profile interpretation advocated here does possess validity for predicting success in practice teaching. Its practical efficiency may not be high, but the empirical confirmation of the methodology indicates that a systematic and diligent search for signs and patterns might well yield predictors of practical utility. . . . Certainly the results highlight the error involved in concluding that the MMPI does not "work" because single scale analysis fails (Gough & Pemberton, 1952, p. 309).

The gradual departure from single-scale analysis was further illustrated in a study by Schmid (1950), who applied factor analytic techniques to a battery of test and rating data obtained from 102 education students (51 men; 51 women). Without presenting any rationale for the selection, Schmid chose the following MMPI scales for his analysis: Ma—Hypomania; D—Depression; Mf—Masculinity-Femininity; and Si—Social Introversion. Other variables in the study included two personality inventories (the Washburne Social Adjustment and the Mooney Problem Check List), grade-point averages, practice-teacher ratings, professional attitudes tests, and the like. Data were treated separately by sex.

The factor analysis of the female data yielded four common factors, one of which, labeled "Introversion," contained three of the four MMPI variables together with practice-teaching ratings. Low practice-teaching ratings were associated with low Hypomania scores, high Depression scores, and high Introversion scores. Concerning this factor the author stated:

Apparently, the three MMPI scales are measuring similar areas of personality rather than independent areas. Lack of teaching ability as measured by . . . [practice-teaching ratings] agrees with the MMPI scales because teaching requires an extrovertive individual. Accordingly, the interpretation that this factor primarily is related to introversion may be accepted (Schmid, 1950, p. 315).

For female teachers, the only other factor on which an MMPI variable appeared was labeled "Professional Maturity" and was characterized (on the negative side) by "youthfulness, undifferentiated interest pattern, poor professional educational judgment, and low grades in education courses" (Schmid, 1950, p. 314). The MMPI Mf (Masculinity-Femininity) scale appeared with a high loading on this factor in a direction suggesting that feminine interest patterns were associated with good professional judgment. On the basis of this finding the author stated, "The masculinity-femininity interest pattern of an individual might prove to be a valuable clue in selecting, guiding, and counseling prospective teachers" (Schmid, 1950, p. 314).

When Schmid turned to his factor analysis of the male data, however, the value of the MMPI in teacher selection was not supported. In place of the four common factors for the females, the male data yielded only two. The first of these factors, labeled "Social and Educational Adjustment," contained grade-point averages, practice-teaching ratings, "good" educational attitudes, and three scores from the Washburne inventory. No MMPI variable had a high loading on this factor. The second factor, labeled "Personality-Psychological Factor," was comprised of a cluster of personality variables (including two MMPI scores—D and Si) but contained no variables directly related to teaching or academic success. The author concluded that for males, "none of the education measures seem related to the tendency to respond to stated problems or abnormal psychological traits" (Schmid, 1950, p. 318). Of course, the small Ns in Schmid's study cast some doubt on his findings.

It will be recalled that for female subjects a low Social Introversion score was found to be associated with practice-teaching success. This finding is contradicted in a later study by Singer (1954), who reported a positive correlation between Social Introversion and over-all ratings of teacher effectiveness for a group of 41 in-service teachers in 18 Wisconsin senior high schools. Since, however, Singer failed to report the sex of his subjects, it is impossible to say whether this finding is in direct contradiction to the Schmid findings.

How a combination of rated success in teaching and MTAI scores is related to MMPI scores was investigated by Tanner (1954). His "superior" teachers (13 men; 31 women) were rated as superior by one or more faculty members and, in addition, scored above the 45th percentile on the MTAI. "Inferior" teachers (14 men; 8 women) were rated as inferior by one or more faculty members and, in addition, scored below the 40th percentile on the MTAI. These experimental groups were chosen from a total population of approximately 575 students who had had practice teaching in elementary and secondary schools. Psychological inventories administered to the experimental groups included the MMPI, the Strong Vocational Interest Blank, the Allport-Vernon-Lindzey Study of Values, the Kuder Preference Record, and a biographical inventory.

Two of the MMPI scales (D—Depression; and Pt—Psychasthenia) differentiated between Tanner's superior and inferior female teachers. The superior women teachers were lower on both scales. Neither of the scales, however, also distinguished both groups from the population in general. The mean score of inferior women teachers on the D scale was very close to the general average as was the mean score of superior women teachers on the Pt scale.

A small number of researchers have attempted to use the MMPI in a "global" fashion. Moore and Cole (1957), for example, administered the MMPI to 127 elementary school student teachers whose teaching performance was rated by supervisors, and found (without reporting significance tests) that the mean scores on *all* the MMPI scales were somewhat lower for the top 10 per cent of the student teachers than for the bottom 10 per cent. This finding led the researchers to sum the T scores across all the MMPI scales to obtain a "total T-score." As might be expected, this score was greater for poor students than for good students in the class.

The findings suggest that a wide variety of maladjustments may be involved in poor practice teaching performance. The solution for the candidate who is "unsuccessful" in practice teaching may not be in finding a more suitable major, but rather in seeking counseling and psychotherapy, which may aid him in overcoming his emotional difficulties and hence in becoming more suitable for a wide variety of potential vocations (Moore & Cole, 1957, p. 715).

Given the lack of independence of the various MMPI scales, the meaning of this "total T-score" metric is ambiguous.

A second study that focused more upon the total instrument than upon any single scale was made by Nagle (1955), who administered the MMPI to 61 education students before and after student teaching. Nagle considered possible change in the MMPI scores to be an indicator of growth in "emotional maturity and mental health" occurring during the student teaching experience. There were no significant changes although the author points out that the differences in the two administrations "were in the desired direction for the goal of emotional maturity and mental health" (Nagle, 1955, p. 713). Since there was no control group, it may, of course, be that the observed differences were a function only of test-retest effects.

The heterogeneity of the findings with respect to the nine original MMPI scales may be seen in Table 2, which summarizes five studies reviewed in this section. Each of the scales seems to have "worked" for at least one of the researchers. On only three of the scales are the findings of one study supported by the findings of another. Focusing on these three instances of agreement, it appears that the successful teacher is lower on the Depression, Psychopathic Deviate, and Psychasthenia scales than is the unsuccessful one. Finally, in the case of at least one scale (Hypomania) the research findings seem to disagree. LaBue's results (1955) associate a low

TABLE 2

ORIGINAL NINE MMPI SCALES RELATED TO SUCCESS IN TEACHING

MMPI Scales									Researcher
Hs	D	Hy	Pd	Mf	Pa	Pt	Sc	Ma	
low F	...	...	low	...	...	low F	low F	low F	LaBue (1955)
...	...	...	...	...	low	...	...	...	Hedlund (1953)
...	...	low M	low M	...	50–56[a]	...	...	48–60[a]	Gough & Pemberton (1952)
...	low F	...	...	high F	...	...	...	high F	Schmid (1950)
...	low F	...	...	...	...	low F	...	...	Tanner (1954)

Note: Cell entries give the direction of the scores of "successful" subjects. Letters indicate whether the finding concerns male (M) or female (F) teachers. Where no letter appears, the same finding was reported for both sexes.

[a] Range of scores characteristic of successful student teachers. Only the two most "powerful" signs are reported here.

Hypomania score with a "persistent interest in teaching"; Schmid's (1950) associate a high Hypomania score with general success in practice teaching. While these two findings are not in direct conflict with each other, they disagree sufficiently to raise questions concerning the predictive value of the individual MMPI scales when used with teachers.

The K Scale and
Teacher Personality

A major technical innovation in the development of the MMPI was the construction of a fourth control score, K (the other three being $?$, F, and L), to be used in correcting for the tendency of respondents to be defensive (plus-getting) (Meehl & Hathaway, 1946). Although the K scale was not designed to be of psychiatric significance, subsequent research has shown it to be of interest in its own right, apart from its function as a correction score. Indeed, the studies to be reviewed here offer evidence that the K scale has particular relevance for the study of teacher personality.

In three of the studies discussed above, the researchers found K scores to have as much, if not more, discriminatory power as any of the MMPI scales. MacLean, Gowan, and Gowan (1955), for example, found high K scores to be among the most salient characteristics of their education students. "Both men and women have high K scores, indi-

cating defensiveness; perhaps this is a teacher characteristic and perhaps a function of the testing conditions" (MacLean, et al., 1955, p. 672).

Similarly, Tanner (1954) found that the K scale was the only MMPI variable that discriminated between superior and inferior male teachers. Not only were these two groups quite dissimilar in their mean K scores (68 and 57, respectively), but both groups were considerably above the mean of the general population. Thus the K scale had a double discriminatory power. It separated superior and inferior male teachers, and it also distinguished both of these groups from the norms.

The findings for females were in agreement with those reported for males. Again, the K scale differentiated between superior and inferior female teachers and also distinguished both of these groups from the population in general. Means for the superior and inferior females were 66 and 57, respectively.

A third study pointing to the significance of the K scale for teachers was that of Moore and Cole (1957) described above. For 127 elementary school student teachers, the mean T score on the K scale was 62.6. No other MMPI scale yielded a mean score above 55 for the total group.

Cook and Medley, in a study already described, reported on the unexpected prominence of the K scale in their search for MMPI variables that would discriminate between high and low scorers on the MTAI. Again the K scale was found to be the most discriminating variable of the MMPI scales, with high scorers on the MTAI also high on K. Viewing the alternate interpretations that could be attached to this finding, Cook and Medley stated:

Concluding that this set factor is discriminating high- and low-rapport groups indicates either that this is a contamination in the MTAI when used as a criterion of teacher-pupil rapport, and we are actually studying two groups of teachers with different attitudes toward personality tests instead of with different attitudes toward their pupils, or that this difference in set is a real difference between the two types of teachers as important as any other (Cook & Medley, 1955, pp. 127–128).

The discriminatory power of the K scale observed in these four studies was reported at a time when numerous other investigators were beginning to question the meaning of scores on this scale. The authors of the scale offered evidence supporting the effectiveness of the K variable in identifying attempts to fake a "bad" profile, but its effectiveness in identifying corresponding attempts to fake a "good" profile was questioned (McKinley, Hathaway, & Meehl, 1956). They also reported that university students have a relatively higher mean on K as contrasted with the norms for their age range. From other research (Sweetland & Quay, 1953) came suggestions that high K scores were related to positive psychological qualities such as "healthy emotional adjustment" and "personality integration."

An attempt to synthesize the growing literature on the K scale, particularly as it concerned teachers, was made by Gowan (1955). Reviewing a number of studies including the ones mentioned above, he stated,

. . . each of these researchers, justifiably cautious in his conclusions because the K scale was devised as a control of test-taking attitude, has contented himself with claims which are over-conservative with regard to the meaning and significance of K, and has therefore missed the full implication of the K scale. It seems evident that K represents much more than a validating key, and that *high scores on it have intrinsic significance for positive personality integration in general and for teaching prognosis in particular, over and above the test-set factor* [italics added] (Gowan, 1955, p. 209).

Gowan presented correlational and factor analytic evidence from the UCLA testing program regarding the relation between the K scale and a number of other psychological variables. Positive correlations of .4 or higher were found between the K scale and such variables as the Good Impression, Tolerance, and Honor Point Ratio scores on the California Psychological Inventory; the Emotional Stability, Objectivity, Friendliness, and Good Personal Relations scores on the Guilford-Zimmerman; and the Gowan Teacher Prognosis Scale (to be discussed below). In the factor analysis of the correlations, Gowan found that the K scale also had high loadings on a factor called General Teaching Adjustment.

Drawing on the findings, Gowan stated,

These facts argue for a picture of the high K individual as tending to be responsible, conscientious, conforming, controlled and friendly, with a strong ego and good performance in interpersonal relations. He thinks well of others, as he tends to see the best in everyone, himself included. Rather than pointing to an absence of basic problems, this delineation indicates some degree of social anxiety overlaid with a reaction formation in which emphasis is directed towards control of self and adaptation to the needs and demands of others (Gowan, 1955, p. 210).

He concluded that "Moderate $(t = 65)$ elevation of K, characteristic of college students in general and teaching candidates in particular, is no indication of an attempt to 'fake good,'" and that "This sign is a valid and widely reported test indicator of teaching potential" (Gowan, 1955, p. 212).

The MMPI and
Teacher Prognosis Scales

One recent development in the use of the MMPI with teachers has been the construction of scales made up of specific items shown to discriminate between groups of effective and ineffective teachers or student teachers. At present, four attempts to develop such "teacher prognosis" scales have been published: Cook and Medley (1954), Michaelis (1954), Tyler (1954), and Gowan and Gowan (1955a).

As has already been indicated (see p. 515 above), the Cook and Medley Ta (Teacher Attitude) scale resulted from efforts to develop an MMPI scale to "measure a person's ability to get along well with others" (Cook & Medley, 1954, p. 414). The Ta scale comprised two subscales, Ho reflecting "generalized hostility" to people, and Pv reflecting "Pharisaic Virtue." When administered to a group of graduate students in education, all of whom were experienced teachers, the Ho, Pv, and Ta scales correlated $-.44$, $-.46$, and $-.50$, respectively, with the MTAI.

Despite the promising results obtained by Cook and Medley, the value of their scales for discriminating between good and poor teachers, or even between teachers who score high on the MTAI and those who score low, was questioned by Chappell and Callis (1954). These researchers administered the MMPI and the MTAI to 82 Navy instructors who had been rated on teaching effectiveness by an observer, students, and a supervisor. The three effectiveness ratings were considered both singly and as a composite estimate of the instructor's teaching ability. Neither the Hostility nor the Pharisaic Virtue scale correlated significantly (.05 level) with any of the three effectiveness ratings. The highest correlation was $-.19$ between scores on the Hostility scale and supervisor's ratings. It is even more noteworthy that both scales failed to correlate significantly with the instructors' MTAI scores, the variable used in the empirical derivation of the scales. While Navy instructors probably differ in important ways from the teacher group used in the construction of the Cook and Medley scales, the failure of the scales to relate to their "parent" variable raises doubts concerning their general validity.

A similar attempt to devise an MMPI scale for teachers was made by Gowan and Gowan (1955a). Four criterion groups, each containing 50 highs and 50 lows, were selected as follows: Group A—Males only, selected as "able" or "weak," either by counselor's interview impression or by practice teacher's grades; Group B—Females only, selected by the composite of two practice-teaching grades; Group C—Females only, selected by counselor's interview impression based on full analysis of test data, health record, speech check, and an hour's interview; Group D—Females only, experienced teachers, selected on the basis of ratings by their principals and superintendents. Thus, combined totals of 200 highs and 200 lows were obtained. MMPI items discriminating between the total groups of highs and lows and in a consistent direction for each of the four criterion groups were identified.

This procedure resulted in a 98-item instrument called the Teacher Prognosis Scale. Three "suggestive but not comprehensive" validity studies using parts of the total scale are described and these indicate that the scale does in fact discriminate between teachers judged to be effective and teachers judged to be ineffective. One validity study of particular significance suggests that the scale can be used to discriminate between very effective teachers and those who are "normally successful." This study puts the scale to a rather stringent test since in validation studies the extremes are generally used as criterion groups.

In addition to the data cited above, Gowan presented correlations between the Teacher Prognosis Scale and scores on numerous other tests including the ACE, Allport-Vernon-Lindzey Study of Values, MMPI, California Psychological Inventory, and the Guilford-Zimmerman. Among many significant relationships, the most salient are positive correlations, ranging from .48 to .64, between the Teacher Prognosis Scale and each of the following: (1) K scale of the MMPI; (2) Tolerance, Intellectual Efficiency, and High School Academic Achievement of the California Psychological Inventory; and (3) Emotional Stability and Objectivity of the Guilford-Zimmerman.

Some evidence regarding the predictive validity of the Gowan scale is offered by Seagoe (1957), reporting on a follow-up study of students in the UCLA program whose fitness for teaching was questioned. Faculty decisions regarding these students were classified into three broad categories: rejected, action deferred, and approved. Gowan Teacher Prognosis scores were available for 57 of the 314 students considered by the faculty committee. The Gowan scale, more clearly than any other test data, distinguished between those whose fitness for teaching was questioned and those whose fitness was not. The scale also showed a difference between students finally rejected and those approved. Rather surprisingly, however, students on whom faculty action was deferred received lower Teacher Prognosis scores than did those who were rejected. In view of this contradiction and of the lack of a detailed report on procedures, the promise of the positive findings must be qualified.

Twenty-nine items are common to both the Gowan scale and the Cook and Medley scale. Given this overlap, it is hardly surprising to find, as did Sheldon, Coale, and Copple (1959), high correlations (above .5) between the two measures. In all instances but one, the scoring on the overlapping items is the same. The item on which there is disagreement is: "My speech is the same as always (no faster or slower, or slurring; no hoarseness)." A subject saying "yes" to this item would be giving evidence of good teaching potential according to Gowan, and of poor teaching potential according to Cook and Medley.

Although Cook and Medley's and Gowan's findings seem encouraging, the success of such empirically derived scales is far from

assured, as the research of Tyler (1954) and of Michaelis (1954) shows. Tyler, in a study to be discussed more fully below, identified 46 items from the MMPI and the Heston Personal Adjustment Inventory (HPAI) that discriminated between criterion groups of good and poor student teachers. The correlation between the derived teacher scale and the student-teaching success of the group on which it was standardized was .55. When the scale was applied to a similar group for validation purposes, however, the correlation was −.10. Essentially the same finding is reported by Michaelis (also discussed below), who identified 38 items (28 on the MMPI and 10 on the HPAI) that discriminated between good and poor student teachers. The correlation between scores on the scale and student-teaching success of the criterion group was .53. This correlation was .13 when a validation group was used. The shrinkage in these rs from the group on which the scale was empirically derived to the cross-validation group exemplifies the importance of cross-validation. Spuriously inflated validity coefficients always result from using the same subjects both in (1) deriving a scoring key or selecting a test battery, and in (2) checking its validity.

The MMPI and the Problem of Prediction

The majority of MMPI studies reviewed thus far had as a goal, either explicitly or implicitly, the use of personality variables to predict teacher and student-teacher effectiveness. Few of these studies, however, have been carried to the point of prediction, that is, to the point of testing the accuracy of classification that could be achieved with the predictor variables. Most have stopped after showing a significant difference between "good" and "poor" teachers, or after reporting a significant correlation between concurrent personality and criterion variables.

At least two investigators (Michaelis, 1954; Tyler, 1954), however, have intensively examined the problem of predicting from personality instruments like the MMPI to teacher effectiveness. Tyler (1954) used as subjects 189 male candidates for the secondary teaching credential, all of whom were beginning graduate study at the time of testing. Three personality tests were administered: the MMPI, the Heston Personal Adjustment Inventory, and the Johnson Temperament Analysis. The latter instrument was eliminated from the analysis because of relatively low reliability. Most of the MMPI scores were also eliminated for the same reason. Only three scales that yielded an odd-even or random split reliability of .90 were retained. These were Psychasthenia, Hypochondriasis, and Schizophrenia.

During their student-teaching experience, all subjects were rated by their supervisors on four characteristics: (1) personal relations with students and teachers; (2) command and use of subject matter; (3) use of teaching procedures; and (4) class management. Criterion groups of high, average, and low were formed in three ways: first, by using the "personal relations" ratings alone; second, by summing ratings on the last three characteristics to form a "teaching skill" score; and third, by using the sum of all four ratings as a measure of "teaching efficiency." The total sample was further split into two parts, an "empirical group" ($N = 131$) used in the original identification of differences, and a "validation group" ($N = 58$) used to test the replicability and predictive power of the original findings.

Tyler's first step was the customary one of testing for differences between the means of the high and low subgroups within each of the criterion groups. Regarding MMPI variables, he concluded that students who had superior "teaching skills" were less psychasthenic than those with inferior skills; also, students with higher ratings on "teaching efficiency" were less psychasthenic and schizophrenic.

In the more refined analysis that followed, however, the promise of predictability implicit in these differences failed to materialize. Using a number of multivariate techniques—

including multiple regression equations, discriminant functions, generalized distance functions, and multiple critical scores—Tyler attempted to combine variables in ways that would lead to the most successful prediction of the subgroups within each criterion group. Combinatorial procedures that showed promise with the empirical group were repeated with the validation group. In general, the results were disappointing. No combination of variables, for example, successfully distinguished the "high" from the "average" students in any of the criterion groups. No combination of variables yielding greater-than-chance predictive accuracy in the empirical group did so when applied to the validation group. One MMPI variable, Psychasthenia, in combination with Sociability and Confidence scores from the Heston Personal Adjustment Inventory, succeeded in discriminating between "high and low" and "average and low" teaching-effectiveness groups. This combination of variables led to 67 per cent accuracy in the prediction of teacher effectiveness for the empirical group. When applied to the validation group, however, the prediction accuracy dropped to 54 per cent, a value not significantly different from chance.

Tyler concluded his report with a critique of the studies designed to predict teacher effectiveness. Most relevant to this chapter is his argument that despite the professed goal of the prediction of teacher efficiency, few if any researchers carry their investigation to the point of prediction per se. Tyler pointed out that, "The fact of a significant difference between two groups or the existence of a positive correlation between the criterion and a series of variables gives no evidence on accuracy of classification or prediction" (Tyler, 1954, p. 290). After commenting on the lack of cross-validation studies and the inappropriate statistical procedures that mar many studies of teacher effectiveness, Tyler concluded: "Indeed, it might be argued that at least up to the time of ... [Barr's] review [1948], there had not been a single complete investigation concerned with the *prediction* of teaching efficiency" (Tyler, 1954, p. 282).

Following the general pattern set by Tyler, Michaelis (1954) conducted a similar study of women student teachers. With respect to the MMPI, Michaelis' study differed from Tyler's by adding nine new clinical scales to the original nine scales. Also, a single criterion group (teaching effectiveness) replaced the three criterion groups used by Tyler. Like Tyler, Michaelis eliminated those MMPI scales that failed to yield a split-half reliability coefficient of at least .80. Thus, only five of the 18 scales were studied further: Psychasthenia, Schizophrenia, Intellectual Functioning, Social Introversion, and Dissimulation. Only one of these, Schizophrenia, discriminated at the .05 level between the extremes of the criterion group. More successful students received a higher score on this scale than did less successful students. (It may be recalled that for Tyler's male students this scale discriminated in the opposite direction.) Noticeable but nonsignificant differences between extreme criterion groups were also observed on the Psychasthenia and Intellectual Functioning scales, and Michaelis retained these for use in multivariate analysis, "even though they would not be effective predictors if used as separate measures" (Michaelis, 1954, p. 440).

The results of the various multivariate techniques applied by Michaelis (at least those involving the MMPI) were as disappointing as those reported by Tyler. Michaelis concluded: "None of the scales included in the MMPI . . . were found to have a significant relation to rated success of university graduate students enrolled in elementary school student teaching" (Michaelis, 1954, p. 473).

It is perhaps significant that Michaelis ended his rigorously empirical paper with a plea for more theory. He stated:

There is need for a theoretical analysis of teacher personality. One drawback in personality theory is the lack of basic information about personal traits and characteristics of normal persons who choose teaching as a profession. An analysis of theoretical considerations oriented toward teaching may give clues to the development of predictors that will prove more valuable than the approaches that have been employed in the past (Michaelis, 1954, p. 477).

OTHER PERSONALITY INVENTORIES

In addition to the MMPI, numerous other personality adjustment inventories have been applied through the years to the study of teacher personality and teacher effectiveness (Goodenough, Fuller, & Olson, 1946; Rostker, 1945; Seagoe, 1946; Ward & Kirk, 1942). Although such instruments as the Bell, the Bernreuter, the Washburne, the Thurstone, and the Mooney may still be found in occasional studies (Carlile, 1954; Jarecke, 1952; Ryans, 1951; Schmid, 1950), their use is rapidly decreasing. Perhaps the study by Carlile (1954) is illustrative of recent findings with these instruments. He correlated scores on the Allport A-S Reaction Study with the grades in student teaching for 44 subjects and obtained a coefficient of .035; he correlated the Home Adjustment, Health Adjustment, Social Adjustment, and Emotional Adjustment scores on the Bell with the grades in student teaching for 53 subjects and obtained the following coefficients: —.026, .013, .035, .083; he correlated the Neurotic Symptoms, Self-Sufficiency, Dominance-Submission, and Social Adjustment scores on the Bernreuter with the grades in student teaching for 92 subjects and obtained the following coefficients: .073, —.014, .168, .044.

A more current personality inventory is the 225-item forced-choice Edwards Personal Preference Schedule (EPPS). This instrument attempts to assess the relative strength of 15 "manifest needs" originally identified by Murray: (1) Achievement; (2) Deference; (3) Order; (4) Exhibition; (5) Autonomy; (6) Affiliation; (7) Intraception; (8) Succorance; (9) Dominance; (10) Abasement; (11) Nurturance; (12) Change; (13) Endurance; (14) Heterosexuality; and (15) Aggression (Edwards, 1959).

Shortly after the instrument appeared, it was used by Jackson and Guba in a study of 366 public school teachers in the Midwest (1957). In the first phase of their analysis Jackson and Guba subdivided their sample into elementary school teachers (196 women; 27 men) and high school teachers (52 women; 91 men) and compared the teacher groups with the norms provided in the Edwards manual (based on the responses of 1,509 liberal arts students). For two of the need measures, Deference and Heterosexuality, there were significant differences between all four teacher groups and the norms. With the exception of the male elementary school subgroup, the teachers also scored significantly higher than the normative group on Order and Endurance but lower on Exhibition. The authors concluded: "These five needs thus appear to be more or less typical of teachers in general, at least insofar as the teacher occupational group may be differentiated from liberal arts students" (Jackson & Guba, 1957, p. 178).

In the second phase of their study, Jackson and Guba divided their sample into three groups (males and females separately) on the basis of teaching experience: 0–3 years; 4–9 years; and 10 or more years. Among the comparisons made, one of the most provocative dealt with the relative similarity of need structure between the "novice" teachers (0–3 years) and the "veteran" teachers (10 or more years). For men, this comparison of the need profiles yielded a correlation coefficient of .32; for women the equivalent correlation was .71. Thus it appeared that young female teachers more closely resembled their older, more experienced, counterparts than did males.

One major limitation of the Jackson and Guba findings (and of the findings of many teacher personality studies that use commercial instruments) arose from the fact that the norms with which teachers were being compared were not contemporaries but liberal arts students significantly younger than the teachers. Regarding this limitation the authors stated:

For example, the factor of low heterosexuality is considerably more pronounced in veteran teachers, as one might expect in view of the fact that experienced teachers are generally older and therefore subject to the usual sexual decline accompanying aging. Or, again, the relatively high deference score may be a function of the (presumed) low age of the normative group, . . . If it might be hypothesized that low deference characterizes an adolescent or young adult group in its general revolt against adult standards or authority, the validity of the high deference scores of teachers becomes somewhat dubious. Lacking an equivalent adult group with which to compare teachers, the conclusions must remain limited (Jackson & Guba, 1957, p. 190).

The recent appearance of extensive adult norms for the Edwards PPS (1959) shows the researchers' concerns to have been well founded. Compared with college-educated adults of the same age, the teachers no longer differed on many of the need measures that distinguished them from liberal arts students. Female high school teachers, for example, were consistently higher on Heterosexuality than were college-educated females of the same age.

The Edwards PPS was also the principal instrument in a study of teacher-trainees made by Guba, Jackson, and Bidwell (1959). The researchers compared female education students in a state university ($N = 124$); a private teachers college ($N = 35$); a Southern Negro university ($N = 100$); and a private university ($N = 28$) with the liberal arts norms provided in the Edwards Manual. Their findings indicated that education students in a professional school such as a teachers college display personality configurations resembling those of practicing professionals far more than do education students in multipurpose institutions. Concerning this finding the authors stated:

It seems probable then that for those students who choose to enter teachers' colleges, the choice of a training institution is secondary to the decision to become a teacher. Those who want the most "direct" route to the public-school classroom have the opportunity in a teachers' college of becoming acquainted early with professional problems and techniques; . . . Since such persons seem to be more "profession oriented" than are those who enter multi-purpose institutions, there is a strong possibility that in many respects they closely resemble practicing professionals. Indeed the resemblance between their personality structure and their perception of the teaching task may have been a major factor in their original decision to teach (Guba, Jackson, & Bidwell, 1959, p. 5).

Sheldon, Coale, and Copple (1959), in a study considered in greater detail below (see p. 559), obtained EPPS data from students with high ($N = 10$) and low ($N = 10$) scores on a series of scales such as the MTAI "that purport to be helpful in selecting teachers and candidates to become teachers. . ." (p. 37). They used six of the EPPS need measures in this analysis: Affiliation, Nurturance, Aggression, Dominance, Succorance, and Abasement. Those high on the "warm teacher scales" (i.e., potentially good teachers) had significantly higher scores on Affiliation and Dominance and significantly lower scores on Aggression, Succorance, and Abasement than did those low on the "warm teacher scales." The researchers stated:

The direction of the significant differences found in this study will not be surprising to those familiar with public education. It would be expected that friendly teachers and teacher candidates when compared to unfriendly ones would . . . have a higher need for affiliation, and a lower need for aggression, succorance and abasement (Sheldon, Coale, & Copple, 1959, pp. 38–39).

Published studies using the EPPS with teachers are as yet too few to justify any conclusions concerning the ultimate usefulness of the instrument in studying teacher personality. One obvious advantage of the instrument is that it was derived from a well-known conceptual formulation (Murray's need system) to which the empirical findings may readily be related.

PERSONALITY FACTORS

GUILFORD PERSONALITY INVENTORIES

The main objective of the inventories by Guilford and his co-workers has been to provide scores for separate factors or primary traits of personality. The most recent form of this series, the Guilford-Zimmerman Temperament Survey, comprises 300 items designed to assess the following personality traits: G—General Activity; R—Restraint versus Rhathymia; A—Ascendance; S—Sociability; E—Emotional Stability; O—Objectivity; F—Friendliness; T—Thoughtfulness; P—Personal Relations; and M—Masculinity. As might be expected, Guilford's tests, in their various forms, have been applied to populations of teachers and student teachers. Studies using these instruments with teachers, while not as numerous as those involving the MMPI, for example, do contribute to the total picture of teacher personality.

As with most commercially available tests, the simplest, and frequently the first, question raised by researchers is whether or not special populations of subjects differ significantly from the norms provided by the test-maker. This question provided the focus of a study by Clark (1950), who administered the Guilford-Martin Inventory to 181 female elementary school teachers in a Midwestern city. Significant differences (.01 level) between the teachers and the norms were found on 9 of the 13 Inventory traits. Teachers were above average in Objectivity, Agreeableness, and Cooperativeness. They were less introversive in their thinking, showed fewer signs of Depression and Cycloid Disposition, and had lower scores on General Activity and Ascendance-Submission than did the normative group. From the standpoint of "mental health," and considering only the surface meaning of the traits in question, the teacher group appears "better" than the normative college students. Indeed, one of Clark's primary objectives was to compare the "mental health" of teachers with that of the normative group. Clark concluded, "these data appear to indicate that the subjects selected for this study had comparatively good mental health, as measured by the Guilford-Martin Inventories" (Clark, 1950, p. 4).

A more extensive application of the Guilford tests to a teaching population was made by Gowan and Gowan (1955b). As part of a testing program already described (see p. 542 above), these researchers administered the Guilford-Zimmerman Temperament Survey to 337 candidates for teaching credentials (of whom about two-thirds were women). Their subjects, like Clark's, were significantly higher than the norms on a majority (seven out of ten) of the traits in the Guilford instrument: Restraint, Ascendance, Sociability, Emotional Stability, Objectivity, Friendliness, and Personal Relations.

Clearly there are significant points of agreement between Clark's description of in-service teachers and the Gowans' description of teachers-in-training. Despite slight differences in the two instruments (the Guilford-Zimmerman is, in one sense, a modernized version of the Guilford-Martin), a comparison of some of the subscores common to both does not seem inappropriate. Both researchers, for example, found their subjects to be above average in Objectivity, Agreeableness (Friendliness), Cooperativeness (Personal Relations), and Emotional Stability (low Depression and Cycloid Disposition). The major disagreement involved Ascendance. Clark's in-service teachers were significantly less ascendant (i.e., described themselves as possessing fewer leadership habits, tended toward submissiveness rather than self-defensiveness, etc.) than were the college norms; the Gowans' student teachers were more ascendant than were subjects in the normative group.

In a study dealing principally with the meaning of MTAI scores, Leeds (1956) administered the Guilford-Zimmerman Temperament Survey to 300 public school teachers in a Southern city. Leeds's findings are strikingly similar to those reported by Clark and by Gowan and Gowan. Again, the teachers were significantly higher than the norms on Restraint, Objectivity, Friendliness, Personal Relations, and Emotional Stability. Leeds's teachers were also below average on Ascendance and General Activity—a finding that agrees with Clark's description of in-service teachers but conflicts with the Gowans' description of student teachers.

In combination, the studies by Clark, the Gowans, and Leeds produce a picture of the teacher, or teacher-in-training, as a restrained, friendly, and agreeable person more likely than the college student to be optimistic and cheerful rather than pessimistic or gloomy. At least in the case of the in-service teacher, this person is also more likely than is the college student to be submissive and to avoid leadership roles. Finally, the teacher portrayed in this composite picture is also less "on the go" than is the college student. The important question left unanswered by these comparisons is whether the results yield a description of teachers qua teachers or whether the same differences might be found when any population of adults is compared with a college sample. Some of the traits involved—general energy expenditure (General Activity), for example, or serious-mindedness (Restraint)—might well show developmental shifts distinguishing adults in general from college students. Guilford (1959), in a summary of research with his instruments, offers evidence suggesting that other occupational groups differ from the norms in ways that teachers do not.

If comparison with general norms is the first step in research with a commercially available test, the next most obvious procedure is to use the instrument to discriminate between experimentally chosen criterion groups. In research on teacher personality the most "natural" criterion groups are "good" and "poor" teachers.

Jones (1956) offered a mildly affirmative answer to the question whether the Guilford tests can be used to distinguish between "good" and "average" teachers. She measured 46 female high school teachers on five traits assessed by the Guilford-Zimmerman

Temperament Survey (General Activity, Restraint, Ascendance, Sociability, and Emotional Stability). Numerous other tests were included. Using a composite criterion involving practice-teaching grades, placement bureau ratings, and principals' ratings, Jones divided her subjects into two equal groups of "good" and "average" teachers. The single Guilford score discriminating between the two groups was General Activity. This score correlated .46 with a composite criterion of teaching success, and Jones stated, ". . . good teachers would appear to be characterized as liking a rapid pace rather than a slow and deliberate one; they may be further characterized by a liking for quickness of action and production and efficiency" (Jones, 1956, p. 178). Jones's finding is noteworthy in view of the findings by Clark and by Gowan and Gowan that teachers were lower in General Activity than the normative group.

Another attempt to distinguish between good and poor teachers with the Guilford-Zimmerman was made by Bendig (1955). Although his sample was small ($N = 15$ men; 1 woman), Bendig's research is worth noting because it deals with a relatively unstudied population—college instructors. In this study the subjects—introductory psychology instructors—were rated by their students on the Competence and Empathy scales of the Purdue Rating Scale for Instruction. None of the correlations between these ratings and the 10 trait scores on the Guilford-Zimmerman were statistically significant. The only significant correlates of competence ratings were reading comprehension scores ($r = .58$); empathy ratings were significantly related ($r = .55$) only to the instructors' expression of interest in clinical psychology.

A step removed from the use of a test for the direct comparison of criterion groups is the attempt to relate a test to other tests that in turn are related to an important criterion variable. At least three studies with teachers have used the Guilford-Zimmerman Temperament Survey in this fashion.

Gowan (1958) presented intercorrelations among all the instruments given to the teaching candidates in the UCLA testing program. Of particular relevance here are the correlations between the 10 Guilford-Zimmerman scores and two Teacher Prognosis Scales developed by Gowan. (These were the positive and negative sections of the scale discussed on page 542, above. The positive section consisted of items where the percentage of subjects making the common response was near mid-range, with a promising difference between high and low groups. The negative section consisted of items eliciting an unusual response, which less than 10 per cent of the subjects in any one criterion group gave, but to which the ineffective teacher always made the unusual response.) As the scales are scored, a prognosis of good teaching is given by a high positive score on one and a high negative score on the other.

Only three of the GZTS scales—General Activity, Thoughtfulness, and Masculinity—failed to correlate significantly with one or both of the Teacher Prognosis Scales. Each of the seven remaining scales correlated positively with the Teacher Prognosis Scale that was positively scored. In addition, four of the scales showed significant negative correlations with the negatively scored prognosis scale. The four Guilford scales that showed both consistent and significant correlations with the prognosis scales were: Emotional Stability, Objectivity, Friendliness, and Personal Relations. It should be noted that in the studies reviewed above these same four scales consistently discriminated teachers or teaching candidates from Guilford's norms. In a subsequent factor analysis of a matrix including the Guilford-Zimmerman, the California Psychological Inventory, and the Teacher Prognosis Scales, four of the Guilford scores—Ascendance, Stability, Friendliness, and Personal Relations—were found to have high loadings (.76, .89, .65, and .85, respectively) on the first rotated factor which Gowan labeled General Teaching Adjustment.

In the study by Leeds (1956) described above (see p. 548), the crucial research question was whether the Guilford inventory could be used to clarify "those factors in personality and temperament that the MTAI is measuring" (p. 333). Seven of the ten Guilford scores correlated positively with the MTAI scores of the 300 teachers in Leeds's sample. The three exceptions were General Activity, Restraint, and Thoughtfulness. Again the same four as in Gowan and Gowan's study—Emotional Stability, Objectivity, Friendliness, and Personal Relations—yielded the highest correlations (.36, .44, .36, and .52, respectively) with the MTAI scores.

While the correlations between the Guilford-Zimmerman and the MTAI reported by Leeds are encouraging, apparently they are partially dependent upon the type of population studied. In a study using 117 practice teachers (91 women; 26 men), Ferguson (1954) reported much lower correlations between the Guilford scores and the MTAI than did Leeds. In Ferguson's study the highest correlation coefficient was .28 between Guilford's Personal Relations and MTAI score. Emotional Stability, with a correlation of .21, was the only additional Guilford variable to yield a coefficient significant at the .05 level.

In the field of testing, new psychological instruments continually evolve from the old. One research practice that seems to speed this evolutionary process is to treat a prepared test as a collection of items from which new scores or scales may be empirically derived. This procedure, characteristic of much MMPI research, was applied by Gowan (1960) to the Guilford-Zimmerman using the same method that he had used in developing the Teacher Prognosis Scales with the MMPI (see p. 542, above). The resulting scale included 30 of the Guilford-Zimmerman items, approximately two-thirds of which (19 items) were originally scored for the personality factors of Friendliness and Personal Relations. The remaining 11 items were originally divided about equally among four of Guilford's factor scores: General Activity, Restraint, Emotional Stability, and Objectivity. One item came from the Masculinity scale. The prominence of Friendliness and Personal Relations items in the Teacher Prognosis Scales is not too surprising, given the consistently higher mean scores of teachers and teacher-trainees on these scales.

In summary, results with the Guilford instruments are somewhat more consistent than those with other instruments—the MMPI, for example—although the relatively small number of studies reduces considerably the possibility of conflicting findings. Interpreted at their face value, the results add support to a psychologically favorable picture of the teacher. Name a psychological "good"—sociability, emotional stability, friendliness, good personal relations—and teachers seem to have "more" of it than do nonteachers, and effective teachers "more" of it than ineffective teachers. Although Guilford warns users of his tests that a person may be too good on a number of the subscales—that a very high score on Friendliness, for example, may have some negative implications—the warning is difficult to apply in interpreting the mean score of groups. One is left, therefore, with the conclusion that, on the whole, teachers as a selected group are more likely to obtain "good" scores on the Guilford instruments than a random group. Reassuring as this may be, it does not seem to lead directly to a conceptual formulation of teacher personality.

CATTELL'S SIXTEEN PERSONALITY FACTOR QUESTIONNAIRE (16 P.F. TEST)

Of all the psychological instruments developed in the Laboratory of Personality Assessment and Group Behavior at the University of Illinois, only Cattell's 16 P.F. Test has created noticeable activity among researchers in teacher personality. Even this instrument, however, has not been used nearly as extensively as have most of the other questionnaire-type tests discussed thus far. The 16 P.F. Test does differ from other factorially structured questionnaires in a way that might make its use less appealing to researchers oriented toward "practical" outcomes. The 16 factors which the test is designed to assess carry labels relatively free of obvious connotations of "good" and "bad." Indeed, Cattell's most recent labeling of these factors makes abundant use of neologisms in order, among other reasons, to avoid value-laden terms. For example, it is difficult to say whether it is better to be high or low on his Autia-versus-Praxernia, or his Parmia-versus-Threctia factors. Technical considerations aside, it is hardly surprising to find that, in a field dominated by the practical concerns of teacher selection and recruitment, instruments such as Cattell's might be passed over in favor of those promising to yield measures of general adjustment or good personal relations.

Cattell's hopes for the application of his questionnaire to research on teacher personality were made clear in an editorial (1948) published about two years after the appearance of his 16 P.F. Test. He stated:

I have been interested now for years in the description, measurement, and evaluation of personality factors. On the basis of this work I would suggest that experimental designs now being planned in teacher personnel research should include measures of at least six of the ten or twelve personality factors we already find to be reasonably confirmed by two or more researchers (Cattell, 1948, pp. 718–719).

Cattell proceeded to offer some speculative hypotheses concerning the role of personality factors in teacher behavior:

The general clinical knowledge of cyclothyme-schizothyme tendencies suggests that the cyclothyme tendency would be favorable to teaching success. Surgency almost certainly would contribute to the ability to deal quickly with the behavior and other problems of children. . . . However, these hypotheses are at present somewhat speculative and the important thing is that researchers get together with an experimental design large enough to satisfy these statistical criteria and objective enough to provide real measures of personality. Upon such a foundation, studies leading to cumulative

increases in knowledge could be built up (Cattell, 1948, p. 719).

At least four researchers, excluding Cattell himself, have responded to his suggestion by applying the 16 P.F. Test to groups of teachers. Lamke (1951) used a very small sample; he compared the scores of 10 "good" teachers and 8 "poor" teachers on the 16 P.F. Test. Teachers were assigned to groups on the basis of a composite rating by their principal and two observers. The two groups differed on three of the factor scores involved. Lamke's good teachers were above average and his poor teachers were below average on Cattell's source traits F (Surgency-Desurgency) and H (Parmia-versus-Threctia). Concerning this finding Lamke stated:

Using Cattell's terminology for source trait F, the good teachers are more than usually talkative, cheerful, placid, frank, and quick; whereas the poor teachers are below average in these respects. . . .
For the source trait H, the good teachers are above average in their tendencies to be gregarious, adventurous, frivolous, to have abundant emotional responses, strong artistic or sentimental interests, and to be interested in the opposite sex. The poor teachers are below average in these respects . . . (Lamke, 1951, p. 243).

Lamke's good teachers also were average or slightly below average on source trait N (Shrewdness-versus-Naïveté), while his poor teachers were far below on this trait. In this regard he stated, "good teachers are approximately average in their tendencies to be polished, fastidious and cool, while poor teachers are definitely below average in these respects" (Lamke, 1951, p. 243). Despite these findings, Lamke was cautious in the claims he made for the predictive value of the 16 P.F. Test. He concluded, "certain elements of some response patterns have been identified, but complete patterns have not been identified. A given subject could not be categorized as a good or poor teacher on the basis of his responses to the 16 PF Test on the basis of the information so far available" (Lamke, 1951, p. 247).

A sample of about 60 teachers was used in a study by Erickson (1954) in which scores on parts of the 16 P.F. Test were correlated with nine different measures of teaching effectiveness. Among the 144 correlation coefficients, however, only 14 reached the .05 level of significance. Four of the factor scores yielded significant correlations (.05 level) with at least two of the nine effectiveness criteria. These were:

Factor G—Positive Character versus Immature Dependent Character (later renamed Super-Ego Strength) correlated positively with supervisor's ratings ($r = .26$) and with pupil evaluation ($r = .27$).

Factor M—Bohemianism versus Practical Concernedness (later renamed Autia-versus-Praxernia) correlated negatively with principal's ratings ($r = -.29$) and with pupil evaluation ($r = -.28$).

Factor O—Worrying Suspiciousness versus Calm Trustfulness (later renamed Guilt Proneness-versus-Confidence) correlated negatively with teacher's ratings by an outside agency ($r = -.27$) and with teacher's self-ratings ($r = -.27$).

Factor Q_3—Will Control and Character Stability (later renamed Self Sentiment Control) correlated positively with acceptability to principal ($r = .28$), with principal's rating during the second year of teaching ($r = .28$), and with teacher's self-evaluation ($r = .38$).

After factor-analyzing his data, Erickson concluded:

The low correlations of the several temperament, personality, and achievement variables, as here measured, with the nine estimates of teaching success and the three "composites" [composite estimates of teaching success] seems to indicate. that the relationship of these measures to teaching success as here measured has not been definitely established (Erickson, 1954, p. 36).

In a study that partially confirmed and

partially contradicted the findings reported above, Hadley (1954) administered the 16 P.F. Test to the entire graduating class (number and sex not reported) at a state teachers college in Pennsylvania. He then compared students who received a practice-teaching grade of "A" with those whose grade was "C." Three of the 16 factor scores discriminated between the two groups at the .05 level or better. Students who received an "A" grade, as compared with those who received a "C," were more likely to be low on Factor F—Surgency versus Desurgency—and high on Factor G—Positive Character versus Immature Dependent Character. The former finding contradicts and the latter confirms the findings of Lamke reported above. In addition, the "A" students were low on Factor N—Sophistication versus Rough Simplicity. For the total sample the three Factors, F, G, and N had correlations of .33, .32, and .27, respectively, with student marks.

It is interesting that Cattell himself has apparently modified his original expectation that teachers would be high in Surgency. More recently he commented, "The many sociometric votes which the F [high Surgency] person gets in group dynamics situation[s], his being voted a good speaker, and his tendency to get elected as a leader, should apparently not be taken as evidence of actual effectiveness in leadership . . ." (Cattell, 1957, p. 187). Commenting on Hadley's study, Cattell continues, "Hadley . . . found in student teachers that those with A grades were more desurgent . . . than those with C grades, presumably due to press of misdirected talk in the latter" (Cattell, 1957, p. 187). Or again, "The association of surgency with sociometric popularity and success in an immediate group, but with lower performance in long-term 'serious' undertakings, is consistently found" (Cattell, 1957, p. 113).

Montross (1954), studying 35 high school teachers (16 male; 19 female), correlated scores on Cattell's 16 P.F. Test with two composite ratings of success in teaching. The first was a summation of four ratings given by the principal and two outside raters during the subject's first year of teaching. The second comprised all the ratings included in the first plus an additional one made by the principal during the subject's second year of teaching. (Because of teacher drop-out, the second composite rating was available for only 25 of the teachers.) None of the correlation coefficients between scores on the 16 P.F. Test and the first composite reached the .05 level of significance. Only one of the 16 factor scores—Factor A (Cyclothymia versus Schizothymia)—correlated significantly (r = .40) with the second composite rating. The researcher concluded that "the Cattell 16 P.F. Test seemingly fail[s] to identify aspects of temperamental behavior which are related to success in teaching as measured in this investigation" (Montross, 1954, p. 96).

In a study using a rather unusual sample, Cattell and Drevdahl (1955) administered the 16 P.F. Test to 294 eminent scientists. The subjects represented three fields—biology, physics, and psychology—and within each were further divided into three groups —administrators, teachers, and researchers.

As compared with researchers, the teaching scientists were significantly higher on Factor A—Cyclothymia versus Schizothymia —and lower on Factor Q_2—Self Sufficiency. It is particularly noteworthy that in a later discussion of Factor A, Cattell pointed out that "The factor seems identical with the Thurstone schedule F (Friendly) which is a simple structure combination of Guilford's scales for Objectivity, Agreeableness, and Cooperativeness" (Cattell, 1957, p. 178). This similarity would bring Cattell's finding into line with a number of the studies that used the Guilford-Zimmerman Temperament Survey with teachers (see p. 547 above). Concerning Factor Q_2—on which the teachers were lower than the researchers—Cattell stated that the high Q_2 individual

Would rather work with one or two assistants than with a committee, prefers reading to classes, does not avoid doing things that might make him seem odd, would rather be an artist than a secretary, is not afraid of his own ideas just because they are odd. . . . (The Q_2 individual avoids society because it wastes time, not because of any emotional rejection, and because experience has told him his thinking is well enough organized to solve problems for himself) (Cattell, 1957, pp. 210–211).

When the teaching scientists in Cattell and Drevdahl's sample were compared with administrators, they showed a greater number of differences than when they were compared with researchers. The teachers were significantly higher (.05 level or better) than the administrators on five factors—Factor L (Paranoia); Factor M (Bohemian Unconcern); Factor O (Free Anxiety); Factor Q_1 (Radicalism); and Factor Q_4 (Psychosomatic Anxiety). They were significantly lower than the administrators on Factor H (Adventurous Cyclothymia). Since the last-named difference is the most sizable one, it is perhaps instructive to note Cattell's description of the low H person: "His greater conscientiousness, application to school work and regard for authority are part of the tendency to more fearful reactivity, i.e., of the belief that 'life is serious,' so lacking in the H (+) [high H] person" (Cattell, 1957, p. 130). The high H person, on the other hand, ". . . is not bothered socially by self-conscious shyness; has no difficulty starting up conversations with people; prefers spouse who will command admiration, rather than religious person; . . . thinks people like to see him coming; . . . is not troubled by sense of inferiority" (Cattell, 1957, p. 193).

Too little has been done with the 16 P.F. Test, with teachers as subjects, to accept without question the results that have appeared and to make possible a comprehensive evaluation of the method. In some cases the findings of the several studies contradict one another. Nevertheless, the instrument has at least two specific advantages (aside from purely technical considerations). First, by providing scores on factors that are not purely evaluative (i.e., psychologically "good" or "bad"), the test encourages the use of hypotheses that are more sophisticated than those linking "adjustment-maladjustment" or some such dichotomous variable to the complex phenomena of teaching and of teaching effectiveness. Second, the instrument derives from an extensive program of both theoretical and empirical work carried out by Cattell and his associates over a number of years (Cattell, 1957). The resulting body of concepts and findings would seem of considerable heuristic value for investigators intending to use the 16 P.F. Test for studies of teacher personality.

PROJECTIVE TECHNIQUES

The term *projective technique* has been applied to a wide variety of data-gathering procedures ranging from such classic instruments as the Rorschach and the TAT to such less widely used procedures as sentence completions, word association tests, and picture drawing. While the "correct" usage of the term may occasion theoretical argument, general usage labels "projective" those techniques that require a person to bring structure to an unstructured test stimulus without knowing how his response will be evaluated. In this general sense, all of the studies reviewed in this section may be said to use projective techniques in the analysis of teacher personality.

THE RORSCHACH

Although the Rorschach stands foremost among the clinician's diagnostic devices, its use in studies of teachers and student teachers has been limited. The obvious explanation for the relatively infrequent use of the Rorschach in research on teacher personality lies in the technical difficulties of administration and scoring. Nonetheless, it is likely that these difficulties (which are considerably diminished by the development of group Rorschach techniques and scoring check lists) would be surmounted if studies in which it had been used demonstrated its theoretical or practical value when applied to teachers. Unfortunately, the research literature offers conflicting testimony regarding

the advantages of viewing teacher personality via the Rorschach.

Johnson (1955) administered the Rorschach to 13 secondary school teachers in a group session and scored each protocol according to the Klopfer system. The protocols were checked for the presence or absence of 17 "adjustment signs" used as a "measure of potentiality for adjustment." The correlation between these "adjustment scores" and teaching efficiency (as judged by two classroom observers) was .61. When two other predictors of teaching effectiveness were used (age and TAT scores), however, the contribution of the Rorschach to the multiple correlation coefficient was insignificant. Johnson concluded that the Rorschach score did not add appreciably to the accuracy of prediction of teaching success. He contended, however, that it is an important measure since it gives an indication of the teacher's adjustment potential. His report ended with the suggestion that a minimum of 9 of the 17 adjustment signs be obtained for teachers and for prospective teachers. Although Johnson's results appear promising when compared with other Rorschach research, his small sample and the need to know more about many technical aspects of the study make an evaluation of this research difficult. His conclusions must be viewed with caution.

A second study reporting a significant relationship between Rorschach variables and a criterion of teaching effectiveness is that of Cooper and Lewis (1951). From a sample of 225 secondary school teachers and student teachers rated by their pupils, these researchers identified two extreme groups: (1) 30 most favorably rated and (2) 29 least favorably rated. The Rorschach was administered individually to each teacher and the protocols analyzed using the Miale and Harrower-Erickson list of psychoneurotic signs plus the Munroe Checklist. In addition, the responses of the two groups were compared for the kind of determinants used, the median number of human movement responses, the degree of introversiveness and extratensiveness, and emotionality.

A positive tetrachoric correlation of .52 was found between the absence of neurotic signs and favorable pupil ratings. (The use of tetrachoric r with extreme groups is, of course, questionable.) The Munroe Checklist did not show significant differences between the two experimental groups, nor did the examination of determinants, human movement responses, and degree of introversiveness and extratensiveness. Emotionally impulsive persons were found with equal frequency in both groups, but emotionally constricted persons were more often found among the least-liked teachers.

Regarding the single significant relationship using the Miale and Harrower-Erickson list, the investigators called for caution. They pointed out that the extent of overlapping on this measure in the two experimental groups precludes high accuracy in individual predictions. They conclude that quantified Rorschach data are not as yet dependable for differentiating between liked and less-liked teachers. Cross-validation studies are needed.

It is instructive to note that in both of the Rorschach studies reviewed above, the researchers commented tangentially on the amount of psychological maladjustment in their samples of teachers. Cooper and Lewis, for example, reported that 42 per cent of the least-liked and 47 per cent of the best-liked teachers were seriously maladjusted! Using somewhat different criteria, Johnson suggested that a minimum of nine Rorschach adjustment signs be considered appropriate for teachers and prospective teachers, yet the average for his experimental group of teachers was *below* nine. These data must, of course, be considered in the light of recent suggestions that projective techniques, and especially the Rorschach, tend to make clinicians see more maladjustment than do other instruments.

At least one researcher applied the Rorschach directly to the task of estimating the amount of maladjustment among teachers. Blair (1946) used the Multiple Choice Rorschach Test with a sample of 205 experienced teachers and 152 prospective teachers.

A cutting point of 15 poor answers (from among 30 possible) served as an indicator of serious disturbance. Blair found that 8.8 per cent of experienced teachers and 2.0 per cent of prospective teachers were maladjusted—a statistically significant difference. Equally notable was the difference between Negro and white teachers. Of the Negro teachers, 21.4 per cent were maladjusted; 6.8 per cent of the white teachers were maladjusted. Negro males showed the highest per cent (33.3) of maladjustment.

The variability in the estimates of maladjustment reported in the three studies is puzzling. Perhaps a partial explanation may be found in the different sample-selection procedures used. In both the Johnson and the Cooper and Lewis studies, for example, all the subjects were volunteers. A number of teachers contacted did not participate. Blair, on the other hand, recruited his subjects from graduate and undergraduate classes in education and reported that all members of these classes participated in the study.

The effect of different selection procedures upon Rorschach protocols and its implications for the study of teacher personality became, rather unexpectedly, the subject of an investigation by Page (1953). The initial purpose of Page's study was to compare the Rorschach responses of students preparing to teach ($N = 64$) with those of noneducation students at the same college ($N = 26$). The education students were contacted by the education department, which made a strong effort to have all student-teaching candidates sign up for the test. The noneducation group, on the other hand, was composed of volunteers from among 80 students selected at random. Page, who personally administered the Rorschach, reported that she soon noticed that the noneducation group contained many persons with a strong need to find out if they were "normal" or to discuss their personal problems with someone. She stated that this attitude contrasted sharply with the reaction of the majority of education students. The latter, it seems, were concerned with being personally charming and exhibited no strong need to bring up personal problems, even when given the opportunity. Page attributed the "cautious" responses of the education students to the fact that they were aware of being scrutinized by the faculty.

In addition to the above differences, Page reported that the volunteer group had more responses than the education students, and indeed more than the average quoted in the literature. Since many of the Rorschach scores depend upon the number of responses the subject gives, Page cautioned against making interpretations or characterizations of nonpathological groups without taking into account the subject's feelings about the test and the possible ways in which these feelings affect the protocol. She pointed out that without taking these factors into account, the blind interpretation of the Rorschach protocols of the education students would emphasize their shock behavior, their high level of ambition, and the lack of richness in their thinking. Paradoxically, many students with Rorschachs of this sort did creative student teaching, according to the observations of responsible and critical supervisors.

In a second study using the same group of education students, Page and Travers (1953a) compared the subjects' Rorschach performance with their student-teaching evaluation. Elementary and secondary school student teachers were considered separately. No relationship was found between adjustment scores derived from the Munroe Checklist and desirable behavior as judged by supervisors. Among the elementary education students, the researchers did find a pattern of three Rorschach scores that discriminated between "highly desirable" and "undesirable" student teachers. This triad of scores consisted of two or more whole responses (W) to one human movement response (M), the weighted sum of color responses (C) greater than human movement responses (M), and color-form plus color responses (CF + C) greater than form-color responses (FC). The researchers interpreted this pattern as reflecting a strong

drive, the desire for achievement, emotional outgoingness, an outward orientation with interest in environment and people, lability, and suggestibility. It was pointed out that these qualities are closely associated with the kinds of behavior seen as desirable by supervisors. Page and Travers properly urged caution in accepting these findings since they still required cross-validation.

Among the secondary school student teachers no Rorschach response patterns were consistently associated with any of the supervisors' evaluations. The investigators suggested that the personality characteristics apparently important in elementary education may be subordinate in secondary education to situational factors such as the intellectual level of the work, the maturity and greater independence of the pupils, and the shorter time spent with pupils. The absence of differences between good and poor secondary school teachers disagrees, of course, with the findings of Johnson reported above.

A similar lack of positive findings, this time with elementary school teachers, was reported by Callis and others (1953), who administered a "Rorschach Content Test" to 42 grade-school teachers and correlated scores on Anxiety and Hostility with pupils', observers', and principals' ratings of the teachers' effectiveness. None of the correlation coefficients were statistically significant.

Perhaps the most optimistic view of the potential value of the Rorschach in teacher research was presented by Symonds and Dudek (1956). On the basis of interviews, observation of classroom practice, and information made available by supervisors and principals, Symonds ranked 19 teachers in order of teaching effectiveness "according to his judgment." Rorschach protocols of the subjects were scored and interpreted by Dudek, who also ranked the teachers on effectiveness using her "blind" Rorschach interpretations. The correlation between these two sets of ranks was .60. A third researcher who was aware of the Rorschach factors that appeared to discriminate between effective and ineffective teachers (according to the results of the first correlation) also ranked the Rorschach protocols, and this ranking correlated .54 with Symonds' original ranking. As an explanation of their relative success, the authors pointed out that Rorschach reports—total personality descriptions—were used rather than individual signs. A search for Rorschach signs that would discriminate between the five best and the five poorest teachers was unsuccessful. They concluded that "the significance in the Rorschach cannot be found by a mere counting of signs, but by an attempt to interpret the character of the responses both from their formal qualities and the nature of their content" (Symonds & Dudek, 1956, p. 232).

Symonds and Dudek also provided an analysis of the three cases showing the greatest discrepancies between the Rorschach rankings and the effectiveness ranking. This analysis was offered as support for the conclusion that "the trouble is not with the Rorschach which presents a faithful picture of the many sided aspects of personality, but of knowing which of the aspects are crucial in determining the kind of teacher a person will be." And finally, the authors stated, "A person who both knows the Rorschach and also the qualities that make for successful teaching should undoubtedly be able to predict teaching success corresponding to a correlation of well over .60" (Symonds & Dudek, 1956, pp. 233–234). The value of the Rorschach for studying teacher personality would be greatly enhanced by an empirical corroboration of Symonds and Dudek's conclusion.

THEMATIC APPERCEPTION TEST

Although Murray's Thematic Apperception Test is second only to the Rorschach in popularity among personality researchers, this is not evident from a study of the literature on teacher personality. Modifications of the original TAT, however, have been used in some research on teaching.

One TAT-type instrument that has been used in several studies of teacher personality is the Adult-Child Interaction Test (ACI) developed by Alexander (1950, 1952). The original form of this instrument contained eight pictures of children and adults about which the subject was asked to tell or write stories. Using data obtained from 25 elementary school teachers, Alexander analyzed the stories according to the degree to which they implied acceptance of the following characteristics of children: (1) fun-making, (2) aggression, (3) dependence, (4) nonachievement, (5) disorder in activities or living spaces, (6) sexuality. In addition, he analyzed the respondent's willingness to offer affection to children. These criteria were rated on a three-point scale ranging from little acceptance to much acceptance for the first six and from "offering little" to "offering much" for the seventh. Each teacher was also visited by classroom observers who rated her on the same scales used in the analysis of the ACI. The research question was whether the ratings of the stories agreed with the ratings of classroom behavior. For six of the seven categories Alexander found the agreement between the two sets of ratings to be significantly greater than chance. The category that failed to show agreement was that of acceptance of disorder in children's activities or living spaces. The author concluded that responses to the ACI may be used to predict certain types of teacher behavior and that these predictions are in "close agreement" with observed behavior in the classroom.

Like many researchers who use projective techniques with teachers, Alexander commented tangentially about the over-all adjustment of his subjects. He reported the existence of psychosexual difficulties, high levels of anxiety, and immaturity in affective development. This negative picture was balanced somewhat by the additional comment that some teachers seemed not to have severe conflicts or high levels of anxiety but met the problems of their environment in a mature manner. The proportions of the sample that fit these two categories were not reported.

Ohlsen and Schultz (1955) used five of Alexander's pictures in an attempt to discriminate between good ($N = 49$) and poor ($N = 49$) student teachers. The students, most of whom were teaching in high school, were judged on effectiveness by their supervisors. A "blind" analysis of the students' protocols was made in order to obtain an over-all evaluation of their personal adjustment. This evaluation failed to show significant differences between good and poor student teachers. Ohlsen and Schultz reported that 15 students in each group probably could profit from counseling, and that 5 others in the "best" group and 2 in the "poorest" were seriously disturbed. Thus, over one-third of the total sample showed a need for some sort of therapy, and this was no greater for "poor" than "good" student teachers.

Failing to find differences in general adjustment, Ohlsen and Schultz proceeded with a content analysis of the students' stories. This analysis made use of 16 questions (e.g., Does the story take place in a school setting? Does the subject identify with the child in the story?), 8 of which yielded answers that successfully discriminated between the experimental groups. Good student teachers, as compared with poorer ones, were more likely to: (1) attribute to children in the pictures extreme attitudes (either positive or negative) toward school; (2) provide a school setting for the action in the pictures; (3) introduce characters not depicted in the pictures themselves; (4) write complete, straightforward stories; (5) describe, rather than interpret or evaluate, human behavior; (6) identify with the child figure in the picture; (7) depict the central characters in a problem setting and attribute decision-making power to these characters; and (8) reveal the central characters' attitudes toward life in general. From these differences the authors concluded, "all we can say is that this approach merits further study. The right combination of the content analysis questions may prove to be very useful in selecting teacher-education candidates" (Ohlsen & Schultz, 1955, p. 26).

Although Ohlsen and Schultz avoided discussing the differences between their experimental groups in general terms, it is perhaps instructive to note that the fantasy productions of their good student teachers contained more "school-oriented" elements than did those of the poorer group. This phenomenon, although admittedly somewhat vague, serves to introduce a theme that gains in insistence as the findings from studies using other projective techniques are examined (see p. 565, below).

The modifications of the TAT procedure (ACI) used by Ohlsen and Schultz reappeared in a study by Oelke (1956). Using a test-retest technique, Oelke examined the changes in the ACI protocols of 44 student teachers after they had completed seven weeks of teaching. A group of 59 junior education students who did not have teaching experience served as controls. In addition, Oelke searched for changes in the protocols that might discriminate between "best" ($N = 6$) and "poorest" ($N = 7$) student teachers.

The results of this study are somewhat surprising. As judged by changes in the stories, students who did *not* have teaching experience became more accepting of children's dependency upon adults over the seven-week period. The same group also increased more in acceptance of nonachievement as normal behavior of children. Students who *had* the teaching experience became more optimistic, but also showed less tendency to select the child as the most-liked person in their stories. Although the latter finding is tempered somewhat by the fact that the "best" student teachers expressed a greater liking for children than did "poor" student teachers, an essential contradiction remains between the findings of this study and commonly held expectations concerning the effect of student teaching.

A somewhat puzzling use of a TAT-type instrument was reported by Johnson (1955, 1957). Thirteen secondary and 26 elementary school teachers who had been rated on classroom effectiveness by two observers were shown 10 pictures involving children and asked to react to each picture as an "educational psychologist." Subjects were required to identify and solve "the most significant problem" depicted in each picture. Responses were scored on the basis of the subject's ability to identify a "significant" problem (five-point scale) and upon the quality of the "solution" offered. These two scores were summed over the 10 pictures to provide a total score. Johnson reported a scoring reliability coefficient of .91 when the responses were scored independently by two clinicians.

For the secondary group Johnson found a correlation coefficient of .75 between scores on the TAT-type instrument and ratings of effectiveness. The equivalent coefficient for the elementary teachers was .54. As in the case with the Rorschach, Johnson's success in relating the results of a projective test to ratings of teaching effectiveness stands in rather marked contrast to the prevailing trend of research findings.

A further modification of the TAT was reported by Sheldon, Coale, and Copple (1959). Their goal was to examine the concurrent validity of a number of empirically developed scales such as the MTAI and the MMPI K scale—labeled "warm teacher scales"—that had been used to discriminate between "good" and "poor" teachers. In essence, these researchers argued that if the "warm teacher scales" are in some way measuring a particular personality structure, then individuals with high scores on a number of these scales ought to differ on certain other psychological measures from individuals with low scores on these scales. From among 176 college freshmen, 10 students with the highest (Group A) and 10 with the lowest cumulative scores on the teacher scales (Group B) were chosen for further testing. Of the many tests used, two are of interest at this point—a modified version of the TAT and the Edwards Personal Preference Schedule.

Ten of Murray's TAT cards were administered and scored in a manner developed by Friedman (1957). This scoring procedure required the subject to describe the hero of each of his TAT stories by sorting a 60-item Q sort designed to obtain measures of the need for affiliation, nurturance, aggression, dominance, succorance, and abasement. Measures purporting to assess the same six needs were obtained from the Edwards Personal Preference Schedule. (See p. 545 for a more complete description of the Edwards instrument.) In support of their expectations the researchers found that students in Group A demonstrated a higher need for affiliation and a lower need for succorance on both the TAT and the Edwards instrument.

There were, however, certain unexpected findings. On the TAT measure, Group A had a significantly lower need for dominance than did Group B. On the Edwards, this finding was reversed. Again, on the TAT, Group A showed a higher need for aggression than did Group B. With the Edwards data, however, this finding was exactly reversed. It is perhaps sufficient to express mild surprise at these reversals, as do the researchers, and to dismiss them with some remarks about the dangers of comparing results from different types of testing procedures. Nonetheless, if the same labels are given to the scores obtained from two instruments, the appearance of opposite findings cannot be treated lightly. Contradictions such as this point to the need for a guiding theoretical structure against which inconsistencies of findings may be tested, if not resolved.

WORD ASSOCIATION AND SENTENCE COMPLETION METHODS

Despite their long history in psychological research, word association procedures have been neglected by researchers studying teacher personality. The results of at least one study, however, suggest that this neglect is unwarranted. Goodenough, Fuller, and Olson (1946) used a list of 238 stimulus words to which subjects responded by writing the first word that came to them after reading the stimulus. Approximately 200 female student teachers specializing in nursery school and kindergarten-primary education and an equal number of female students in a liberal arts college served as subjects. The purpose of the research was twofold: (1) to distinguish between education students and liberal arts students with the use of the Word Association Test, and (2) to distinguish between student teachers who received high ratings from their supervisors and those who did not.

Using the established scoring systems for the Word Association Test, Goodenough, Fuller, and Olson failed to distinguish between the experimental groups. However, an empirically derived scoring system based on a subsample of the total population did produce differences that separated education from noneducation students and successful students from nonsuccessful ones. This system focused only upon the responses the subjects made, without considering the stimulus word (except in those cases where the meaning of the response was dependent upon it). Weights were given to categories of responses that discriminated between education and noneducation students in the subsample.

The following types of responses were at least five times as frequent among student teachers as among liberal arts students: (1) reference to children's activities (test examples: block—building; skip—hop; blow—bubbles); (2) favorable adjectives referring to ability or behavior (test examples: mind—bright; conduct—good; pupil—smart); and (3) references to music (test examples: play—piano; beat—drum). References to children or babies (test examples: rattle—baby; pupil—child; poor—little boy) were at least three times as frequent among student teachers as among liberal arts students.

Three categories of responses were at least twice as frequent among student teachers as among liberal arts students. These were: (1) references to neatness (test examples: put—away; pick—up; handle—carefully); (2) opposites, except those with unfavorable or unpleasant connotation (test examples: right

—left; host—guest; round—square); and (3) coordinates (test examples: pink—green; bat—ball; orange—lemon). Using these categories, the researchers successfully discriminated between the total group of education and liberal arts students as well as between a subsample of superior and inferior student teachers who had also been part of the group on whom the scoring weights were established. The correlation between pooled supervisors' ratings and the weighted scores for these categories was .26. It is also worthy of note that a high score on this instrument was a better prognosis of success in student teaching than a low score was of failure. No significant relationships appeared between scores on the Word Association Test and scores on the Bell Adjustment Inventory, the Army Alpha, or the Miller Analogies Test.

Hilton (1955) used an interesting modification of classic word association methods in a study of 130 teacher-trainees. His instrument, called the Word Completion Form, contained 108 items, each consisting of a series of connected letters from which several common words could be made by adding letters (e.g., GOA___; CHI___). Twenty of the items were designed to elicit words regarded as pertinent to education (e.g., teacher, children, school, testing). The score on the instrument was the number of "education" words used as completions. Within his theoretical framework, the author used this measure of accessibility of education words as a reflection of the subject's ego-involvement in teaching.

The aim of Hilton's study was to examine the relationship between scores on the Word Completion Form and an index of involvement in teaching, supervisors' ratings of practice-teaching performance, and MTAI scores. For all groups except women preparing to teach in secondary schools, there were significant correlations, ranging from .30 for 35 men preparing to teach secondary school to .50 for 31 women preparing to teach elementary school, between Word Completion Form scores and scores related to their willingness to remain in teaching. For 38 women students preparing to enter primary and elementary school teaching there were significant positive correlations between their Word Completion scores and both supervisors' ratings ($r = .24$) and MTAI scores ($r = .29$). Although the relationships were not strong, they pointed to the potential fruitfulness of searching for "educational" content in the unrestricted cognitive products of teachers.

The sentence completion method was used with 104 high school teachers in a study by Reed (1953). Students and administrators rated the teachers on three scales designed to assess (1) the teacher's general effectiveness; (2) the teacher's attitude toward students; and (3) the ease with which the teacher went about his teaching. In addition, 71 of the teachers used the same three scales in completing a self-evaluation report. The Sentence Completion Test (SCT) contained 91 items measuring the subject's "attitude of acceptance" of himself and his environment. Scoring difficulties reduced the original 91 items to 40, of which 27 were scored on a seven-point scale. High scores were given to responses indicating a self-accepting attitude (e.g., "When people contradict me—*I don't mind it too much*"); low scores to responses indicating a self-rejecting attitude (e.g., "When people contradict me—*I stop talking*"). Scores on the remaining 13 items were based on an examination of the responses of effective and ineffective teachers (as judged by students) in one of the schools. Thus, Reed's scoring procedure involved a combination of theoretically and empirically derived standards. In the analysis of the data the results of the two scoring procedures are presented separately and in combination.

Before computing correlation coefficients between SCT scores and effectiveness ratings, Reed further reduced his sample of 40 items by eliminating all those that did not discriminate between the 10 most and 10 least effective teachers (as judged by students). Twenty-six items, each of which had been shown to be related to some criterion of effectiveness, remained. Reed noted that as a result of this procedure the correlation coefficients between SCT scores and effectiveness ratings were "slightly improved." Since the degree of this improvement can only be conjectured, it is impossible to judge the significance of his findings. Suffice it to say that most of the correlations between students' evaluations and SCT scores for two cross-validation samples are fairly substantial, ranging between .23 and .78. However, relatively few (4 out of 24) of the coefficients involving administrators' ratings reach the .05 level of significance. Reed concluded his study by reporting significantly greater self-acceptance (SCT scores) for married than single teachers; for academic than nonacademic teachers; and for young than old teachers.

In a study of the anxieties of 120 student teachers, Travers, Rabinowitz, and Nemovicher (1953) administered a 21-item sentence completion test at the beginning and the end of a semester course in student teaching. Three of the sentence stems (I hope my class never __; I shall expect the pupils in my class __; and, When I become a teacher I suppose my greatest problem will be ____) were used in the analysis of the data. The major sources of anxiety were the problem of discipline and the question whether the pupils would like the student as a teacher. The researchers noted that these two dominant concerns might imply a potential conflict for teachers. They pointed out that teacher conduct that endears a teacher to pupils is often incompatible with teacher conduct that produces a well-disciplined class. The salience of these concerns was emphasized by the finding that the student teachers' responses did not vary much during the time period studied. The authors concluded, "It seems safe to say that student-teaching for this group provides an experience which does not greatly alter original anxieties concerning teaching . . . " (Travers, Rabinowitz, & Nemovicher, 1953, p. 50).

Guba and Getzels (1955), in a theoretically oriented article, reported the use of a 50-item sentence-completion test with a population of approximately 200 Air Force instructors. Two forms of the instrument were used. The first, called the "direct" form, contained the personal pronoun "I" in the sentence stem. The second, called the "projective" form, contained proper names in place of the pronoun "I." Responses to each form of the instrument were scored for the number of "negative" endings (aggressive, morbid, depressive). A third score, obtained by subtracting the score on the "direct" from the score on the "projective" form served as an indicator of the disparity between the public and private perceptions of the respondents.

These three scores were used to discriminate between the instructors described as effective by their superiors and peers and those described as ineffective ($N = 30$ or more in each group). Guba and Getzels hypothesized that high negative scores on the projective form of the instrument and high disparity scores would relate to ineffective ratings among the instructors. They further hypothesized that negative scores on the direct form of the instrument would not relate to effectiveness. Each of these hypotheses was substantiated. The researchers used their data primarily to argue the merits of "theoretically-oriented research" over "traditional, normative research," but their findings may be viewed independently as additional evidence of the relationship between the inner subjective world of the teacher and his teaching performance as seen by others.

In a study by Peck (1959), sentence completion responses and biographical data from teachers were clinically analyzed to yield predictions of principals' ratings. Principals in five schools named teachers who were high, average, and low on each of five ratings: (1) organizing and communicating information and skills; (2) creating a healthy relationship with pupils; (3) creating good relations with other teachers; (4) building good relations in the community; and (5) supervisor's personal evaluation. The 49 teachers named completed a biographical information form and a 90-item sentence completion test. Using these data, the researcher

attempted to duplicate the ratings of the principals on each of the five scales. This attempt yielded significant correlations on three of the scales ("good relations with other teachers," "good community relations," and "supervisor's personal evaluation"). Because the Ns were small in each of the groups, Peck warned that his positive findings can only serve to encourage further research.

DRAW-A-TEACHER TEST

Among the most provocative findings to come from projective studies of teacher personality are those obtained by researchers at the City College of New York using a drawing test (Mitzel, Ostreicher, & Reiter, 1954; Travers & Rabinowitz, 1953). The technique requires students to "draw a picture of a teacher with a class." Aside from cautioning the subject to avoid using stick figures and to forget his artistic ability or lack of it, no further directions were given.

In the first study using this technique, Rabinowitz and Travers (1953) commented on the extreme variability found in the drawings. Using a case-study approach, they attempted to show that the changes in the drawing of a single student paralleled changes in interview material obtained during various stages of training. In a second study, Travers and Rabinowitz (1953) examined more intensively the phenomenon of change in the drawings over time. The subjects were students at different levels of training in two colleges that varied greatly in their educational outlook ($N_1 = 65$; $N_2 = 57$). The program of teacher education in the first college was described as conservative in character. The emphasis was on the liberal arts rather than professional education, and students had very limited contact with the public schools until they began practice teaching. The program of the second college placed much greater emphasis on professional education, and students were provided with opportunities to observe in selected schools from the earliest weeks of their professional training.

Drawings from these students were rated "blind" by three judges according to whether the following criteria were present or absent: (1) activity outside the control of teacher (e.g., some pupils studying by themselves while the rest are listening to the teacher); (2) situations in which there was partial or total pupil control; (3) tension in the relationship between pupil and teacher; and (4) teacher and pupils working together on some project. Significant differences were found on each of these criteria between beginning students and those who had completed their student teaching, the former producing far more teacher-dominated pictures than the latter. Even more striking, however, were the differences between seniors at the two colleges. In the conservative institution, seniors were much *less* likely than were those from the teaching-oriented institution to draw pictures in which teacher control was relaxed and tension was absent. On each of the four criteria the drawings of the "conservative" group portrayed a more restricted, teacher-dominated classroom. This finding is all the more significant since beginning students in the two institutions did not differ on any of the drawing criteria.

Although Travers and Rabinowitz cautioned their readers against assuming that these differences imply corresponding differences in teaching behavior, their findings challenge the argument that "Methods and procedures learned during college preparations may influence teaching superficially but they do not determine the nature of the relation of a teacher to his pupils or the teacher's basic attitude toward teaching" (Symonds, 1954, p. 83).

Page and Travers (1953b) used the Draw-a-Teacher technique somewhat differently to test the hypothesis that the amount of pathological disturbance evident in the drawings is related to disturbed behavior in teacher training. Drawings of 175 students in elementary education were rated by three judges on a five-point scale of psychological disturbance. Faculty members were asked to identify the students possessing personal

qualities that would seriously interfere with their adequacy as teachers. It was suggested to the faculty that approximately 10 per cent of the students might fall into this category.

The difference between the means of the selected and unselected students on the psychological disturbance ratings was not significant. An examination of the standards used by the faculty in rating the students revealed, however, that these standards were quite different from those used by the psychologists in rating the drawings. Whereas the latter looked for signs of emotional disturbance and psychopathology, the former were more concerned with whether the student displayed well-organized work habits, leadership ability, receptivity to new ideas, enthusiasm, and the like. When the drawings were rejudged by the psychologists using a set of characteristics based on the faculty's standards, significant differences were found between the means of the selected and unselected students.

The results of the Page and Travers study are instructive not only for what they say about the potential value of a new projective device. They also contribute to understanding of the recurrent conflict between judgments of psychological health and judgments of teaching efficiency. It is becoming increasingly evident that, extremes aside, the relationship between conventional criteria of teaching effectiveness and conventional criteria of psychological disturbance is weak at best. It is entirely possible, as the Page and Travers study suggests, that the clinician's view of the teacher differs in its essentials from the view of those whose job it is to evaluate teaching behavior. Ever since the classic study by Wickman, educators have been aware of the different frames of reference used by psychologists and teachers when viewing the behavior of children. Perhaps it is necessary to recognize a similar difference in orientation between psychologists and those who judge the effectiveness of teachers if we are to understand the lack of agreement between the two sets of judgments. This position does not imply that personality variables per se are unrelated to teacher behavior; it does imply that the variables traditionally used to define psychopathology may not be the most fruitful ones for exploring this relationship.

A more refined analysis of the Draw-a-Teacher technique appears in a study by Mitzel, Ostreicher, and Reiter (1954). These researchers analyzed the drawings of approximately 700 student teachers in order to identify specific scorable dimensions that might be related to other educational variables. Each picture was rated on five dimensions: (1) relative teacher emphasis; (2) teacher initiative; (3) psychological distance of teacher from pupils; (4) traditionalism in classroom arrangement; and (5) artistic quality. The researchers evaluated each dimension on a five-point scale and obtained a high degree of interscorer reliability. The relative independence of the scoring dimensions was indicated by the low intercorrelations. When, however, the five drawing scores were related to other attitudinal variables—the MTAI and an authoritarianism scale—no significant relationships appeared. All the drawing scores correlated negatively with the MTAI and positively with the authoritarianism scale, but none of these coefficients reached the .05 level of significance.

Stern, Stein, and Bloom (1956) obtained support for the effectiveness of the Draw-a-Teacher technique. Using a small sample of 10 teacher-trainees—ranked by faculty judges on their degree of success in a training program—these researchers reported that successful and unsuccessful trainees differed quite sharply in their drawings. The successful trainees drew pictures in which teacher control and domination were de-emphasized, whereas the opposite was true of unsuccessful students. These differences closely resemble those that Travers and Rabinowitz reported in their study of a "conservative" and a "teaching-oriented" training program. Stern, Stein, and Bloom concluded that the drawing test was one of the most valuable techniques in their study of teacher-trainees.

MISCELLANEOUS PROJECTIVE PROCEDURES

To the list of projective techniques especially designed or modified for use with teachers can be added the Cartoon Situations Test (CST) developed by Shapiro, Biber, and Minuchin (1957). This test consists of seven cartoons depicting teachers, children, and parents in a variety of situations. For example, a principal is seated at her desk when a teacher—hair awry and sleeve torn—carries in a screaming child. The teacher says, "Miss Gaffney, may he visit with you until he calms down?" Analysis of the responses makes use of categories such as: quality of expressive tone, quality of emotional identification with characters, modes of aggressive expression, and the like. The test was administered in group sessions to 65 students in a teacher-training program who were also rated by faculty members on a number of qualities relating to their success in student teaching. Responses on the CST were compared with these ratings.

The researchers report a number of "significant" relationships. Unfortunately, only the probability levels of the findings are given, with no indication of the method used to obtain them. The following examples illustrate the general tenor of the results. Subjects who identified with children on the CST seemed to overidentify with them in student-teaching situations and were rated as least prepared to teach. Subjects who expressed least hostility on the CST seemed better able to establish "empathic" relations with children and to "conceptualize and to enact the control role in a balanced, realistic way..." (p. 180). Subjects who assessed the dilemmas in the cartoons less realistically seemed to have uncertain future development as teachers and were less able to form empathic relationships with children. A composite score on the CST separated subjects who were "ready for teaching responsibility at the end of the training year" from those who were not, but the same score failed to distinguish between those having high and low "teaching potential"

(Shapiro, Biber, & Minuchin, 1957, p. 181).

The precariousness of specific results from projective studies of teacher personality is illustrated by a contradiction between the findings of Shapiro, Biber, and Minuchin using the CST and those of Ohlsen and Schultz using a modification of Alexander's ACI. Shapiro found that identification with the children in the cartoons is a "bad" sign; i.e., it is positively related with certain unfavorable ratings by faculty supervisors. Ohlsen and Schultz (1955), on the other hand, found that identification with children in a TAT-type picture is a "good" sign; i.e., it is positively related to favorable ratings by faculty supervisors. Now the dangers of comparing results from two different assessment procedures are well known. Nonetheless, it is disheartening to find two projective instruments yielding results couched in almost precisely the same language but opposite in direction.

A well-known projective instrument, the Rosenzweig Picture-Frustration Study, was used in the study by Guba and Getzels cited above. These researchers found several hypothesized differences between effective and ineffective Air Force instructors, as judged by peers and superiors, on a number of scores derived from the Rosenzweig test. In brief, their findings showed greater intropunitiveness and more intense need persistence (i.e., focusing on the solution to the problem presented) among effective instructors and greater extrapunitiveness among ineffective instructors.

Compared to more direct data-gathering procedures, projective tests as yet occupy a secondary position in the literature on teacher personality. Although their use appears to be increasing, the impetus for this increase seems to come more from encouraging results in other areas of psychological inquiry than from demonstrated success in studying teacher personality. In the latter realm, projective devices have probably done more to unsettle prematurely stable conceptions regarding teachers than to uncover consistent empirical relationships.

An example of the unsettling effect of projective studies upon stereotypic notions about teachers may be found in the recurring mention of psychological disturbances in the groups studied and the relative independence of these disturbances and measures of teacher effectiveness. If, on the one hand, one accepts the validity of Rorschach and TAT-type material as indicators of psychological health, the incidence of malfunctioning reported by Alexander (1950), Blair (1946), Cooper and Lewis (1951), and Ohlsen and Schultz (1955) is disturbingly high. If, on the other hand, one accepts the validity of the effectiveness criteria used in these studies, the relationship between psychological malfunctioning and teaching effectiveness reported by Page and Travers (1953a) and by Ohlsen and Schultz (1955) is surprisingly low. There are, to be sure, a group of studies (Cooper & Lewis, 1951; Guba & Getzels, 1955; Johnson, 1955, 1957) that indicate a somewhat stronger relationship between adequacy of psychological functioning and teacher effectiveness. But methodological and sampling problems prevent one set of results from gaining ascendancy over another.

Naturally, the task of interpreting such equivocal findings requires a more intensive examination of technical research questions than can be given in this summary. Perhaps the safest statement to make is that the findings seriously disturb, if not destroy, any naïve assumptions concerning a positive, linear relationship between psychological health, as assessed projectively, and teaching behavior, as reflected in the judgments of supervisors and peers.

To search for persistent or common themes in these projective studies is perhaps naïve in view of the variety of procedures and findings. Nonetheless, a small but important group of researches (Goodenough, Fuller, & Olson, 1946; Hilton, 1955; Ohlsen & Schultz, 1955) do bear interesting relations to each other. These studies suggest, each in its own way, that the unrestricted cognitive products of teachers (or potential teachers) contain more "educational elements" than do comparable products from a nonteacher group. Further, the presence of these "educational elements" seems also to distinguish those rated successful in teaching from those rated unsuccessful.

The phenomenon common to these studies may be conceptualized in many ways. On the one hand, one might simply (and perhaps cynically) point out that the findings show that teachers think about teaching, and that better teachers think more about teaching and children than do poorer teachers. This observation, it may be argued, is trite. If, on the other hand, one stresses the spontaneous, unpremeditated quality of these projective responses, one might view them as more than mere reflections of the teacher's preoccupation with teaching. Rather, they suggest that teachers characteristically view their world—provide it with structure and meaning—in ways that distinguish them from nonteaching groups. Further, this perceptual mode appears related to measures of the teacher's effectiveness. The fact that students in training show this perceptual tendency suggests that it is not merely a product of teaching experience. The findings of Seagoe (1942) are suggestive in this regard. She reported, in a study of the childhood experience of prospective teachers and nonteachers, that those who chose to enter teaching enjoyed playing school as a child more than did those preparing for some other profession. Gowan (1957) reported a similar finding in an intensive study of 20 effective teachers. The role that such a perceptual orientation might play in the decision to become a teacher seems worthy of further research. A recent theoretical statement by Stephens (1960) argues for just this point of view.

THE TEACHER
CHARACTERISTICS STUDY

The Teacher Characteristics Study directed by Ryans (1960) is the single most extensive study of teachers to date. In many ways it is representative of the aims, methods, and findings of work on teacher personality and be-

havior of this period. Three major objectives guided the Study: (1) The identification and analysis of some patterns of classroom behavior, attitudes, viewpoints, and intellectual and emotional qualities which may characterize teachers; (2) The development of paper-and-pencil instruments suitable for the estimation of certain patterns of classroom behavior and personal qualities of teachers; (3) The comparison of various groups of teachers. The ultimate purposes of the study are given as follows:

The Teacher Characteristics Study was conducted with two possible uses of the results in mind: first, by school systems as an aid in identifying teachers who, at the time of selection for employment or perhaps in connection with promotion, have characteristics similar to those deemed important and desirable by the particular school system and the culture it represents; and, second, by teacher education institutions as an aid to a better understanding of teacher characteristics and associated conditions, which would contribute to improved procedures for selecting teacher candidates and to the improvement of professional courses and curricula (Ryans, 1960, p. 11).

During the more than six years of the major study, approximately 100 separate research projects were carried out, and more than 6,000 teachers in 1,700 schools and about 450 school systems participated in the research. Many of the studies involved classroom observation by carefully trained and retrained observers to discover patterns of teacher behavior and associated pupil behavior. A number of paper-and-pencil inventories were developed and related to patterns of observed classroom behavior. Other investigations surveyed teacher activities, preferences, and attitudes. Still others compared groups of teachers along these observational, inventory, and survey dimensions (e.g., elementary teachers versus secondary teachers, married teachers versus unmarried teachers, teachers in progressive school systems versus teachers in traditional school systems).

Although the Study was not directed specifically at the problem of teacher effectiveness, the issue was not ignored. For example, one investigation deals with certain characteristics of teachers who were classified as high, average, or low with respect to patterns of observed classroom behavior. Another compared the characteristics of teachers nominated by principals as superior or inferior. Still another, involving the pre- and posttest measurement of pupils in a study relating observed teacher behavior to pupil change, could not be completed because of unexpected difficulties.

Obviously, neither the specific procedures nor the numerous separate findings of the Study can be given here. Nevertheless, several of the more general outcomes may be noted briefly.

Three patterns of teacher behavior stood out in separate factor analyses of observational data:

Pattern X_o—warm, understanding, friendly versus aloof, egocentric, restricted teacher behavior.

Pattern Y_o—responsible, businesslike, systematic versus evading, unplanned, slipshod teacher behavior.

Pattern Z_o—stimulating, imaginative, surgent versus dull, routine teacher behavior.

Sample comparisons of groups of teachers with respect to these patterns were: (1) Among elementary school teachers, the Patterns X_o, Y_o, and Z_o were highly correlated and each also seemed to be highly correlated with pupil behavior in teachers' classes. Among secondary school teachers, the intercorrelations were less high, and much less highly correlated with pupil behavior. (2) Among elementary school teachers, Patterns X_o, Y_o, and Z_o tended to be higher for married than for single teachers. Among secondary school teachers the patterns tended to be higher for single than for married teachers. (3) The patterns did not vary significantly with scores on the Minnesota Multiphasic Personality Inventory and the Allport-Vernon-Lindzey Study of Values. However, X_o (warm, friendly) and Z_o (stimulating) varied positively with the Impulsive, Dominant, and Sociable scales of the Thurstone Temperament Schedule.

Certain dimensions of teacher attitudes, verbal understandings, educational viewpoints, and emotional stability were investigated by paper-and-pencil instruments. Among the trends in the data were: (1) The attitudes of elementary school teachers toward pupils, administrators, fellow teachers, and nonadministrative personnel were markedly more favorable than were similar attitudes of secondary school teachers. (2) Actual pupil behavior in the classroom (based upon observers' assessments) did not appear to be related to the attitudes held by teachers. (3) The educational viewpoints expressed by secondary school teachers were more traditional, while those of elementary teachers were more permissive. (4) The verbal understanding scores (based on vocabulary and verbal analogy items) of secondary school teachers were significantly higher than those of elementary school teachers, and English and foreign language teachers excelled all other subject-matter groups within the secondary school. (5) Male teachers at both the elementary and secondary school levels appeared to be markedly more emotionally stable than female teachers.

The actual sampling of teachers' classroom behavior is usually inconvenient and frequently impossible, and the employment of direct-question inventory methods may result either in intentional or unintentional falsification of critical responses. Accordingly, an alternative approach to the estimation of teacher characteristics and classroom behavior was undertaken—that of attempting to predict teacher traits and behaviors, as Ryans puts it, from correlates, or symptoms, of those behaviors and traits. Much of the Teacher Characteristics Study was devoted to determining these *correlates* of teacher classroom behavior. Materials were selected and assembled into an instrument known as the Teacher Characteristics Schedule, an omnibus self-report inventory, made up of 300 multiple-choice and check-list items referring to personal preferences, self-judg-ments, activities, biographical data, and the like. Using observer assessments and scores on the direct-response scales as criteria, hundreds of item analyses were carried out and scoring keys for the Teacher Characteristics Schedule were derived for a large number of teacher groups. Reliability coefficients fell between .70 and .80. Concurrent validity coefficients were typically between .20 and .50; predictive validity coefficients were similarly positive but low, seldom exceeding .20; cross-validation coefficients of teacher attitudes, viewpoints, verbal ability, and emotional stability were typically between .40 and .60.

The Schedule yielded scores for the following characteristics of teachers (Ryans, 1960, p. 388):

X_{co}—warm, understanding, friendly vs. aloof, egocentric, restricted classroom behavior.

Y_{co}—responsible, businesslike, systematic vs. evading, unplanned, slipshod classroom behavior.

Z_{co}—stimulating, imaginative vs. dull, routine classroom behavior.

R_{co}—favorable vs. unfavorable opinions of pupils.

R_{1co}—favorable vs. unfavorable opinions of democratic classroom procedures.

Q_{co}—favorable vs. unfavorable opinions of administrative and other school personnel.

B_{co}—learning-centered ("traditional") vs. child-centered ("permissive") educational viewpoints.

I_{co}—superior verbal understanding (comprehension) vs. poor verbal understanding.

S_{co}—emotional stability (adjustment) vs. instability.

The third major objective of the Study was to compare the characteristics of teachers who had been classified with regard to various conditions—to take a look, as Ryans says, at a cross-section of American teachers during the first half of the decade beginning in 1950. For the most part, the subjects were the samples used in the other parts of the study.

Illustrative findings are presented according to some of the characteristics studied:

1. *Age and experience.* Among 60 different F tests computed, 45 of the sets of differences were significant at or beyond the .05 level. Generally, the scores of the older teachers (55 years and above) show the group to be at a "disadvantage" compared with the younger teachers except from the standpoint of Y_{co} (systematic and businesslike classroom behavior) and B_{co} (learning-centered, traditional educational viewpoints). And, as might be expected, trends with regard to extent of teaching experience are not substantially different from those noted when teachers were classified according to age.

2. *Sex.* At the elementary school level, men and women teachers differed in only four of the personal-social characteristics studied; men were less responsible and businesslike in classroom behavior and more favorable toward democratic classroom practices, more inclined toward permissive, child-centered educational viewpoints, and more emotionally stable than women. At the secondary school level, differences between the sexes were fairly general and pronounced with women tending to attain significantly higher scores on the seven scales measuring friendly, responsible, stimulating classroom behavior, favorable attitudes toward pupils, democratic classroom practices, permissive educational viewpoints, and verbal understanding. Men teachers scored significantly higher in emotional stability, however.

3. *Marital status.* There are systematic differences between married and unmarried teachers with respect to various classroom behaviors and attitudes, but these differences often vary according to school level, grade, and subject taught. For example, at the elementary school level, the married group attained more favorable scores in businesslike classroom behavior and child-centered educational viewpoints; at the secondary school level, the single group attained more favorable scores on the same variables. Ryans suggested that, despite general trends, it is

probably more important to recognize the interaction of marital status with grade or subject taught when considering the teaching characteristics under study.

4. *Undergraduate college and academic achievement.* Very few significant differences were found with respect to type of school attended. The only two worthy of note were that teachers from large universities attained higher scores on stimulating classroom behavior and child-centered educational viewpoints. With respect to academic achievement, teachers who reported having been outstanding students scored higher than other groups on most scales including friendly, responsible, stimulating classroom behavior, and favorable attitudes toward pupils, democratic school practices, and the like. The only exception to this trend had to do with emotional stability.

5. *Influences affecting choice of teaching, and activities during childhood.* Teachers who said they entered the profession because of its intellectual nature, because they had liked school, and because of its social service character, generally scored higher on most of the teacher characteristics under study; teachers who entered the profession because they were advised to do so, or because of the desirable position in the community and favorable prospects for advancement scored lower. Teachers who reported such childhood and adolescent activities as "playing school," "reading to children," and so on, attained higher scores on such scales as friendly, responsible, stimulating classroom behavior, favorable attitudes to pupils, democratic classroom procedures, and the like, than teachers who did not report such activities. It is suggested that participation in school-like activities during childhood and adolescence may offer significant clues to the characteristics of teachers.

6. *Teacher characteristics in relation to size of school, size of community, socioeconomic status of community, geographic area in which teaching is performed.* Teachers in larger schools scored significantly higher than teachers in smaller schools on scales measur-

ing friendly and stimulating classroom behavior, favorable attitudes toward administrators, verbal understanding, and emotional stability. As might be expected, the trends held also when teachers were classified by size of community. Teachers from smaller communities attained lower mean scores than those from large communities—at least up to and including communities of 500,000 to 1,000,000 population. But teachers from the largest cities (1,000,000 and over) scored relatively low (about as low as teachers from the very small communities) on most characteristics, verbal understanding being a notable exception.

Ryans suggested that the teacher-selection procedures in large cities (e.g., written and oral examinations) may identify verbal understanding but not other characteristics relating to personal and social qualities. When teacher characteristics were studied in relation to socioeconomic level of the community in which the schools were located, the lowest scores in friendly, stimulating classroom behavior, favorable attitudes toward democratic classroom practices, verbal understanding, and emotional stability, and the most traditional educational viewpoints were attained by teachers in communities of average socioeconomic level. The relationships between socioeconomic level and several of the characteristics seem curvilinear, high scores being attained in both socioeconomically low and high (but not average) communities. Teachers whose schools were located in the Middle Atlantic states and on the West Coast scored higher in stimulating classroom behavior, verbal understanding, and permissive educational viewpoints. The Midwestern states tended to be lowest in stimulating classroom behavior; the Mountain and Southern states lowest in verbal understanding; the East-Southern and Southern states lowest in emotional stability. The Midwestern and East-Southern teachers were more traditional in educational viewpoints; the Middle Atlantic and West Coast teachers were more permissive in educational viewpoint when compared with other groups.

7. *Characteristics of teachers assessed as generally high and generally low in certain types of observed classroom behaviors.* Three groups of teachers were identified, one group comprising teachers with observer ratings a standard deviation or more above the mean on each of the three central classroom behavior dimensions of the Study (friendly versus aloof, systematic versus slipshod, stimulating versus dull), the second group comprising teachers with observer ratings at the mean on each of the three dimensions, the third group comprising teachers with observer ratings a standard deviation or more below the mean on each of the three dimensions. Distinguishing characteristics of the groups were determined by responses to the Teacher Characteristics Schedule. The more notable differences between the high and the low teachers are given as follows:

There was a general tendency for high teachers to: be extremely generous in appraisals of the behavior and motives of other persons; possess strong interest in reading and literary affairs; be interested in music, painting, and the arts in general; participate in social groups; enjoy pupil relationships; prefer nondirective (permissive) classroom procedures; manifest superior verbal intelligence; and be superior with respect to emotional adjustment. On the other hand, low teachers tended generally to: be restrictive and critical in their appraisals of other persons; prefer activities which did not involve close personal contacts; express less favorable opinions of pupils; manifest less high verbal intelligence; show less satisfactory emotional adjustment; and represent older age groups (Ryans, 1960, pp. 397–398).

Taken as a whole, the Teacher Characteristics Study is a most impressive research undertaking, but it is, of course, clear that many of the issues raised with respect to the methods and findings in preceding sections also apply here.

COGNITIVE ABILITIES

It seems eminently reasonable to expect that teaching should attract persons of relatively high intelligence and, further, that within the profession itself differences in intellectual ability should be related to success or effectiveness. Numerous researchers have set out to test the validity of these expectations. As is the case with much of the work on teachers, the results of these investigations are far from clear cut.

There is ample evidence, to be sure, that teachers as a group score appreciably higher on tests of intellectual ability than does the general population. In a comprehensive survey of college students and graduates, Wolfle (1954) reported an average score of 117 on the Army General Classification Test (AGCT) for students specializing in education. The average for the general population is 100. Similar findings based on different instruments have been reported by Clark and Gist (1938), Learned and Wood (1938), Powell (1950), and many others.

When, however, teachers and students preparing to teach are compared with other professional groups, the comparison is not nearly so favorable. Students of education consistently rank near the bottom. On the AGCT, for example, graduating seniors specializing in education obtained a mean score that is equaled or surpassed by students in all other major fields with the exception of home economics and physical education (Wolfle, 1954, p. 199). The latter two fields are also comprised largely of students expecting to teach. The relatively low ranking of education students on the AGCT is corroborated by the results of the Selective Service College Qualification Test, which show that college men going into teaching score lower as a group than do men entering most of the other professions (Lieberman, 1956, p. 231).

It should of course be noted that reliance on mean scores alone can be deceiving, particularly since the overlap among students majoring in various fields is great. For example, the average AGCT score of graduate students in medicine is exceeded by approximately 35 per cent of the graduate students in education. Nonetheless, the rather consistent differences in mean scores attest to the fact that teachers as a group are significantly above average in intellectual ability when compared to the general population but somewhat below average when compared to most other professional groups.

Relatively little is known concerning the relationship between the cognitive ability of teachers and general demographic variables such as subject matter taught, grade level taught, years of teaching experience, size of school, and the like. One of the most extensive studies providing at least preliminary data on such relationships was part of the Teacher Characteristics Study (Ryans, 1960) described in the preceding section. As a measure of "verbal understanding," Ryans used 11 vocabulary and verbal analogy items which were included in a questionnaire taken by more than 700 elementary and 900 secondary school teachers. If scores on these items are accepted as a rough measure of cognitive ability or intelligence, Ryans' findings would indicate a slight superiority in verbal understanding on the part of female teachers as against male teachers; single and widowed teachers as against married teachers; secondary school teachers as against elementary school teachers; graduates of liberal arts or women's colleges as against graduates of state or teachers colleges; foreign language and English teachers as against business education and boys' physical education teachers; teachers of Grades 7 and 8 as against teachers of Grades 1 and 2; teachers in large cities as against those in small communities; teachers from schools of high or low socioeconomic status as against teachers from schools of middle socioeconomic status; private school teachers as against public and parochial school teachers; teachers from "traditional" schools as against those from "progressive" schools (descriptions made by the teachers themselves); and teachers from the Middle Atlantic and West Coast states as against those from the Southern and Mountain states.

Although all the differences reported by Ryans meet the traditional criteria of statistical significance, few if any of them seem large enough to be of much psychological or predictive significance. In most instances, the overlap between the groups is too great to allow any definitive statement concerning cognitive differences among various groups of teachers. Moreover, the question of how cognitive abilities are related to demographic variables among teachers seems to be of less theoretical consequence than the question of how these abilities are related to criteria of teaching effectiveness.

Even before standardized intelligence tests became generally available, researchers were attempting to relate intellectual power to success in teaching. For example, Boyce (1912) asked 27 administrators to rank 328 secondary school teachers according to (1) their general merit as teachers and (2) the administrator's estimate of their intellectual capacity. The correlation coefficient between the two rankings was .71. Other researchers, using similar methods and also neglecting the possible operation of the "halo effect," reported similarly high relationships. When more objective measures of intelligence were substituted for personal judgments, the promising findings of the earlier investigators failed to be corroborated.

Between 1912 and 1950 numerous tests of intelligence were administered to teachers and related to one measure or another of teaching effectiveness. Morsh and Wilder (1954) reviewed 55 studies appearing between 1927 and 1952 in which intelligence test scores were related to effectiveness measures. In general, the results are disappointing. Relatively high correlations do appear occasionally (in 16 of the 55 studies reviewed by Morsh and Wilder, the correlation coefficient exceeded .30), but these are balanced by many instances in which no relationship was found and by at least 15 investigations reporting negative correlations between intelligence test scores and measures of teaching effectiveness.

Faced with these relatively discouraging findings, researchers have seemed less willing in recent years to include measures of general intelligence in their studies of teacher effectiveness. When such measures are included, the findings are typically inconsequential. One researcher, for example, included among his instruments the Detroit Advanced Intelligence Test and the Henmon-Nelson Test of Mental Ability. The correlation coefficients between these two tests and the practice-teaching grades of approximately 80 students were .28 and .23, respectively (Carlile, 1954, pp. 657–658). Shea (1955) administered the National Teacher Examination and the American Council on Education Psychological Examination (along with tests of reading comprehension and subject-matter mastery) to 110 graduates of a four-year teachers college program. The correlations of practice-teaching grades with the NTE nonverbal reasoning and the ACE *L* and *Q* scores were .00, −.08, and −.17, respectively. The respective correlations of Wisconsin M-Blank ratings of teacher effectiveness with the same mental ability measures were .06, .34, and .29 (Shea, 1955, p. 20). After an extensive factor analysis of his data, Shea stated:

> On the basis of the data used in this study, it must be concluded that none of the standardized tests, with the possible exception of the subtests that measure general information or current events of the day, are factorially related to marks obtained by the subjects on Practice Teaching, and On-the-job Rating. . . . Teaching Success, Practice Teaching Grade, and Academic Average all came out on one factor which is not related to what these tests measure (Shea, 1955, p. 36).

It seems highly unlikely that future researchers using global measures of intelligence and conventional criteria of teaching success will tell us much more than we now know about the relationship between general ability and teaching efficiency. However, two approaches remain to be fully explored. First, different types of cognitive functioning, in addition to those currently assessed by tests of general ability, might be more closely related to teaching efficiency. Second, attitudinal and behavioral correlates of cognitive ability may be as important in understanding

teaching efficiency as are abilities per se.

The growth in our understanding of cognition has led to the realization that many types of intellectual processes are not adequately assessed by conventional tests of intelligence. Guilford explicitly recognizes this fact when he states:

> Briefly, the most important implication for us to note here is the great richness of human resources that exists in the general domain of intellect. . . . Those who search for simple answers and for a single key to unlock the door to the understanding of intellect will be disappointed. . . . As for testing practices, no longer should we favor one or two of the abilities, letting them determine our impression of the total intellectual stature of an individual. No longer should we fail to respect talents other than those emphasized in verbal-intelligence tests (Guilford, 1959, p. 395).

At least one study points to the value of examining cognitive factors other than general intelligence among teachers. Knoell (1953) administered nine tests of word fluency to 38 teachers, and one year later obtained for each of his subjects three measures of teaching efficiency (a rating of general acceptability by the principal and an outside observer, a rating by the principal on the Wisconsin M-Blank, and a rating by two outside observers on the Wisconsin M-Blank). Two of the nine measures were significantly related to all three criteria of teaching success, the correlation coefficients ranging from .28 to .46. These two measures dealt with "ideational fluency," which has been defined by Guilford as a divergent-thinking factor characterized by "the ability to call up many ideas in a situation relatively free from restrictions, where quality of response is unimportant. . ." (Guilford, 1959, p. 382). One of the tests required the subject to "write all the adjectives which could be used to describe a house," the other to "list all the things that are round or could be called round." Performance on each test was limited to four minutes.

Although the correlations reported by

Knoell are only moderately high, they are at least as high as most of those obtained with measures of general intelligence. Also it should be remembered that these correlations are based on performance on brief four-minute tests given a full year before collecting the teaching efficiency measures. From the standpoint of theory development, what is perhaps more important than the magnitude of the correlations is the fact that the types of cognitive process observed by Knoell seem to lend themselves more readily to a conceptualization of the teaching process than do many of the abilities included in most measures of general intelligence. It is easier to understand, for example, why the "ability to call up many new ideas in a situation relatively free from restrictions" should be related to the teacher's efficiency in the classroom than to understand why her "ability to memorize digits" should be so related.

Psychologists have long noted that ability measures are reflected in personality variables. Groups differing greatly in intelligence are also found to differ in attitudes, values, and interests. The identification of psychosocial correlates of ability and the relationship between these attitudinal correlates and teaching behavior has been explicitly attempted by Ryans (1960) and his associates in the Teacher Characteristics Study. Using the 11 verbal understanding items described above, Ryans identified a series of attitudinal and behavioral statements that were correlated to the extent of .15 or greater with the ability items. Thus, for example, a person scoring high on the verbal understanding items, as contrasted with a person scoring low on the same items:

1. Prefers *Harper's Magazine* to the *American Magazine* or *Popular Mechanics*. (elementary and secondary teachers)

2. During the past year read books and magazines. (elementary teachers)

3. Thinks learning is accomplished more successfully by reading a book or article dealing with a topic than through class or group discussion. (secondary teachers)

4. Interest in books was a factor contributing to choice of teaching as a career. (secondary teachers)

Conversely, teachers scoring low on the verbal understanding items tended to agree with the following statements:

1. Would like being a scientist *less* than being president of a large industrial concern. (elementary teachers)

2. Is strongly in agreement with the statement, "Cleanliness is a more valuable human trait than curiosity." (elementary teachers)

3. Thinks a majority of high school classes (about 65 per cent) are disruptive in that students frequently "get off the subject" either intentionally or unintentionally. (secondary teachers)

4. Thinks disorderliness and noise is more indicative of a poor class than listless student performance, hesitancy on part of student, or dependency of students. (secondary teachers) (Ryans, 1960, pp. 222–223).

The over-all relationship between the correlates of verbal understanding and principals' ratings of general teaching effectiveness was found to be nil. For a combined sample of 113 elementary and secondary teachers the correlation coefficient was .01 (Ryans, 1960, p. 258). When, however, a relatively large group of principals were asked individually to nominate one superior and one inferior teacher, the difference between the superior and the inferior groups in the verbal understanding correlates was significant at the .05 level.

The relationship of the verbal understanding correlates of various types of teacher behavior and pupil behavior, as judged by observers, was relatively low, the 31 coefficients reported ranging between —.18 and .32. The highest correlation, .32, was obtained with 117 secondary school teachers of foreign languages. Among this group, teachers who agreed with the statements associated with high verbal understanding tended to have classes whose behavior was judged to be alert, responsible, and confident. Teachers who were low on the verbal understanding correlates tended to have classes whose behavior was judged to be more apathetic, dependent, and obstructive. As might be expected, the verbal understanding correlates were more closely associated with other clusters of attitudinal elements among the teachers than they were with either classroom behavior or measures of teaching effectiveness.

Despite its attractiveness as a hypothesis, the proposition that very high cognitive ability is a *sine qua non* of the good teacher has relatively little empirical support. The relevance of general intellectual ability to success in teaching (within the range set by those who enter the profession) is small at best and is certainly of little value for predictive purposes. The role played by different types of abilities (e.g., divergent thinking) and by attitudinal correlates of ability has yet to be fully explored. If linked to an adequate conceptualization of teaching, these two types of inquiry may lead us closer to an understanding of how intellectual power contributes to the teacher's behavior and effectiveness in the classroom.

CONCLUSION

Despite the critical importance of the problem and a half-century of prodigious research effort, very little is known for certain about the nature and measurement of teacher personality, or about the relation between teacher personality and teaching effectiveness. The regrettable fact is that many of the studies so far have not produced significant results. Many others have produced only pedestrian findings. For example, it is said after the usual inventory tabulation that good teachers are friendly, cheerful, sympathetic, and morally virtuous rather than cruel, depressed, unsympathetic, and morally depraved. But when this has been said, not very much that is especially useful has been revealed. For what conceivable human interaction—and teaching implies first and foremost a human interaction—is not the better if the people involved are friendly, cheerful, sympathetic, and virtuous rather than the opposite? What is needed is not research leading to the reiteration of the self-evident

but to the discovery of specific and distinctive features of teacher personality and of the effective teacher (Getzels, 1955).

But this desideratum is more easily asserted than achieved, for a number of serious obstacles face the research worker in this area. To mention only three, there is first, the problem of definition; second, the problem of instrumentation; third, the problem of the criterion.

There are profound differences in what is meant by the term personality. Despite its widespread use—surely no psychological term is more popular—personality is an inordinately elusive concept. Definitions are often contradictory, and observations based on one definition will contradict observations based on another definition. In general, the more common definitions may be classified into three main categories: (1) *behavioral* definitions, that is, personality is the totality of a person's usual behavior; (2) *social-stimulus* definitions, that is, personality is defined by the response made by others to the individual as a stimulus; (3) *depth* definitions, that is, personality is the dynamic organization within the individual that determines his unique behavior. The problem is not that there are different conceptions of personality but that researchers fail to distinguish one conception from another, and the data obtained in terms of one definition are not differentiated from the data obtained in terms of another (Getzels, 1953).

A second issue facing the researcher is the choice of instrument. What devices are available for assessing personality, and from these how is one to choose the most appropriate measure? The number of instruments available is legion, and indeed most have been tried in one study or another. If there is a test that promises anything at all, it has probably been administered to some group of practicing or prospective teachers. But the data provided by one instrument called a personality test are not necessarily the same as the data provided by another instrument also called a personality test. For example, data from self-report instruments are likely to represent a behavioral concept of personality; data from rating scales a social-stimulus concept; data from projective techniques a depth concept. The use of tests on the basis of availability ("Here's a new test; let's try it on teachers") rather than on relevant personality concepts ("Are the definition and measure appropriate to the issue under study?") has led to a "shotgun" type of research yielding outcomes that are often inexplicable.

Perhaps the most intransigent of the difficulties is the matter of the criterion. Although teacher effectiveness need not be involved in the study of teacher personality, it usually does enter, at least indirectly. Ultimately, the results of teacher personality research are presumed to be relevant to the problem of selection and prediction, and the crucial question cannot be avoided: What are we selecting for and predicting to? How does one define the effective teacher in some distinctive and characteristic way?

The most frequent criterion of teacher effectiveness studies is the rating. Teachers and student teachers are rated by critic teachers, supervisory teachers, principals, superintendents, pupils, the experimenters themselves, or almost anyone else who is for one reason or another believed capable of expressing an opinion. The pitfalls of this method are obvious. For one thing, these ratings are frequently highly unreliable. For another, what is good teaching in the opinion of a principal or a superintendent may be poor teaching in the view of a pupil or another teacher (or for that matter of another principal or superintendent). In fact, there is evidence showing just this: teachers, students, and supervisors tend to differ on what constitutes teacher effectiveness.

To get away from these so-called "subjective ratings," some researchers have proposed pupil gain as the criterion of teacher success. But although this is apparently a more "objective" criterion, it has some striking and especially pernicious shortcomings all its own (Ryans, 1960, pp. 44–46; Tyler, 1954). The point is that the question of the

criterion cannot be handled arbitrarily and without relation to some framework of school objectives and the total social and psychological context within which the child functions.

In addition to these general conceptual limitations, there are a number of specific experimental limitations. For example, there is the limitation of treating teachers—male and female, young and old, primary grade and intermediate grade, teachers of English and of science—as a single group. Often this is done even though differences within the teaching profession may obscure the very differences that need to be revealed. Or, to mention just one other obvious but serious limitation, there is the problem of varied teaching situations. Variations in the teaching situation from one school to another may exist in such factors as educational viewpoints, nature of the student body, conditions in the community related to teacher status, and so on, but little provision is made for taking into account the effect of such situational variables on the experimental results. Investigators seem for the most part content to take their subjects where they can find them, implying that a teacher is a teacher whether his school is in the country or in the city, in Mississippi or in California, in an upper-class suburb or in a lower-class slum.

The single most general reason for these conceptual and experimental limitations on research on teacher personality as well as on teacher effectiveness was given most directly by the Committee on the Criteria of Teacher Effectiveness of the American Educational Research Association (1952, 1953). The Committee's contention is simply that research in this field is conducted in a theoretical vacuum. When studies are not engaged in merely "trying out a test," they are busy seeking ad hoc solutions to immediate problems with little regard to the theoretical meaning or long-range fruitfulness of the findings. Hypotheses are based upon an oversimplification of teacher personality and the teaching situation, leading both to inadequate methodology and to conclusions which make neither psychological nor sociological nor common sense. The Committee concluded that only by working within the context of sound theory can one hope for useful, relevant, and widely applicable findings. They suggested that any teacher characteristic involved in a research study should be submitted to the question: "On what grounds in learning theory or social-psychological theory (or any other body of theory) can we justify hypothesizing that this characteristic of teachers is related to a given effect?" (American Educational Research Association, 1952, p. 255).

The application of theory to research on teacher personality (or indeed to any research) has several distinct advantages over the empiricism currently typical of the field (Guba & Getzels, 1955). The initial tendency of the worker in a new research area is to observe. "Get the facts" is a familiar exhortation. But what "facts"? The researcher surely cannot begin by getting all the facts. He must make a selection from among the phenomena and ascribe weightings of relative importance to the various elements which he does select. But theory does more than provide the dimensions within which a workable research design may be formulated. A theory is not only taxonomic; it is relational. It attempts not only to describe but to explain. And precisely because it contains such relational elements, theory leads to hypotheses, and ultimately the findings resulting from tests of these hypotheses serve not only a descriptive function but also, and more vitally, an explanatory function.

Finally, theory provides a framework for interpreting observations already made and data already collected. Without such framework, any observation that seems "significant" must be accepted at face value, and two contradictory observations cannot be resolved except on an ad hoc basis. Theory acts in two ways here: first, by flashing a "caution" signal when data that do not make sense are uncovered, and second, by serving as a guide to attempts to resolve apparent inconsistencies. This is not to say that theory

will inevitably be taken as correct and observations that contradict theory as wrong. Of course not. It does mean that when such inconsistencies occur, they will be apparent, and further conceptual and empirical inquiry will be indicated. As has been suggested:

Pure empiricism is a delusion. A theorylike process is inevitably involved in drawing boundaries around certain parts of the flux of experience to define observable events and in the selection of events that are observed. Since multitudinous events could be observed and an enormous number of relationships could be determined among all of these events, gathering all the facts with no bias from theory is utterly impossible. Scientists are forced to make a drastic selection, either unconsciously on the basis of perceptual habits and the folklore and linguistic categories of the culture, or consciously on the basis of explicitly formulated theory (Miller, 1959, p. 200).

REFERENCES

Adorno, T. W., Frenkel-Brunswik, Else, Levinson, D. J., & Sanford, R. N. *The authoritarian personality.* New York: Harper, 1950.

Alexander, T. The prediction of teacher-pupil interaction with a projective test. *J. clin. Psychol.,* 1950, 6, 273–276.

Alexander, T. The Adult-Child Interaction Test: A projective test for use in research. *Monogr. Soc. Res. Child Develpm.,* 1952, 17, No. 2 (Whole No. 55).

Allport, G. W. *Personality: A psychological interpretation.* New York: Holt, 1937.

Allport, G. W., Vernon, P. E., & Lindzey, G. *Study of Values: A scale for measuring the dominant interests in personality.* (1951 rev.) New York: Houghton Mifflin, 1951.

American Educational Research Association, Committee on the Criteria of Teacher Effectiveness. Report of the . . . . *Rev. educ. Res.,* 1952, 22, 238–263.

American Educational Research Association, Committee on the Criteria of Teacher Effectiveness. Second report of the . . . . *J. educ. Res.,* 1953, 46, 641–658.

Appleby, T. L., & Haner, C. F. MMPI profiles of a college faculty group. *Proc. Iowa Acad. Sci.,* 1956, 63, 605–609.

Barr, A. S. The measurement and prediction of teaching efficiency: A summary of investigations. *J. exp. Educ.*, 1948, 16, 203–283.

Barron, F. An ego-strength scale which predicts response to psychotherapy (*Es*). In G. S. Welsh & W. G. Dahlstrom (Eds.), *Basic readings on the MMPI in psychology and medicine.* Minneapolis: Univer. of Minnesota Press, 1956. Pp. 228–234.

Beamer, G. C., & Ledbetter, Elaine W. The relation between teacher attitudes and the social service interest. *J. educ. Res.*, 1957, 50, 655–666.

Bendig, A. W. Ability and personality characteristics of introductory psychology instructors rated competent and empathetic by their students. *J. educ. Res.*, 1955, 48, 705–709.

Blair, G. M. Personality adjustments of teachers as measured by the multiple choice Rorschach test. *J. educ. Res.*, 1946, 39, 652–657.

Blum, L. P. A comparative study of students preparing for five selected professions including teaching. *J. exp. Educ.*, 1947, 16, 31–65.

Boyce, A. C. Qualities of merit in secondary school teachers. *J. educ. Psychol.*, 1912, 3, 144–157.

Budd, W. C., & Blakely, Lynda S. Response bias on the Minnesota Teacher Attitude Inventory. *J. educ. Res.*, 1958, 51, 707–709.

Buros, O. K. (Ed.) *The fifth mental measurements yearbook.* Highland Park, N.J.: Gryphon Press, 1959.

Callis, R. Change in teacher-pupil attitudes related to training and experience. *Educ. psychol. Measmt*, 1950, 10, 718–727.

Callis, R. The efficiency of the Minnesota Teacher Attitude Inventory for predicting interpersonal relations in the classroom. *J. appl. Psychol.*, 1953, 37, 82–85.

Callis, R., & Ferguson, J. L. *Cluster analysis of the Minnesota Teacher Attitude Inventory.* Columbia: Univer. of Missouri, 1953 (Rep. No. 2, ONR 649(00)).

Callis, R., et al. Studies in the effectiveness of teaching. Cited by F. P. Frutchey, *Differential characteristics of the more effective teachers: A summary report of nine studies.* Washington, D.C.: U.S. Dept. of Agriculture, Extension Service, Division of Field Studies & Training, 1953. Pp. 5–6.

Carlile, A. B. Predicting performance in the teaching profession. *J. educ. Res.*, 1954, 47, 641–658.

Cattell, R. B. Clinical versus statistical measures of teaching ability. *J. educ. Res.*, 1948, 41, 718–719.

Cattell, R. B. *Personality and motivation, structure and measurement.* Yonkers, N.Y.: World Book Co., 1957.

Cattell, R. B., & Drevdahl, J. C. A comparison of the personality profile of eminent researchers with that of eminent teachers and administrators. *Brit. J. Psychol.*, 1955, 46, 248–261.

Chappell, T. L., & Callis, R. *The efficiency of the Minnesota Teacher Attitude Inventory for predicting interpersonal relations in a naval school.* Columbia: Univer. of Missouri, 1954 (Rep. No. 5, ONR 649(00)).

Clark, C. D., & Gist, N. P. Intelligence as a factor in occupational choice. *Amer. sociol. Rev.*, 1938, 3, 683–694.

Clark, E. J. The mental health of elementary school teachers as measured by the Guilford-Martin Personality Battery. Paper read at National Council on Measurements used in Education, Atlantic City, March, 1950.

Coleman, W. Susceptibility of the Minnesota Teacher Attitude Inventory to "faking" with experienced teachers. *Educ. Admin. Superv.*, 1954, 40, 234–237.

Cook, W. W., & Medley, D. M. Proposed Hostility and Pharisaic Virtue scales for the MMPI. *J. appl. Psychol.*, 1954, 38, 414–418.

Cook, W. W., & Medley, D. M. The relationship between Minnesota Teacher Attitude Inventory scores and scores on certain scales of the Minnesota Multiphasic Personality Inventory. *J. appl. Psychol.*, 1955, 39, 123–129.

Cook, W. W., Leeds, C. H., & Callis, R. *The Minnesota Teacher Attitude Inventory.* New York: Psychological Corp., 1951.

Cook, W. W., Kearney, N. C., Rocchio, P. D., & Thompson, A. Significant factors in teachers' classroom attitudes. *J. teacher Educ.*, 1956, 7, 274–279.

Cooper, J. G., & Lewis, R. C. Qualitative Rorschach factors in the evaluation of teacher effectiveness. *J. educ. Res.*, 1951, 44, 703–707.

Cottle, W. C., Pownall, J. E., & Steimel, R. J. Counselors and teachers take the Experimental Attitude Scale. *Personnel guid. J.*, 1955, 33, 374–378.

Della Piana, G. M., & Gage, N. L. Pupils' values and the validity of the Minnesota Teacher Attitude Inventory. *J. educ. Psychol.,* 1955, 46, 167–178.

Dilley, N. E. Personal values held by college students who enter a teaching education program. *J. teacher Educ.,* 1957, 8, 289–294.

Domas, S. J., & Tiedeman, D. V. Teacher competence: An annotated bibliography. *J. exp. Educ.,* 1950, 19, 99–218.

Drake, L. E. Scale O (social introversion). In G. S. Welsh & W. G. Dahlstrom (Eds.), *Basic readings on the MMPI in psychology and medicine.* Minneapolis: Univer. of Minnesota Press, 1956. Pp. 181–184.

Edwards, A. L. *Edwards Personal Preference Schedule: Manual.* (1959 rev.) New York: Psychological Corp., 1959.

Erickson, H. E. A factorial study of teaching ability. *J. exp. Educ.,* 1954, 23, 1–39.

Ferguson, J. L., Brown, K. B., & Callis, R. *Factor analysis of the Minnesota Teacher Attitude Inventory.* Columbia: Univer. of Missouri, 1954 (Rep. No. 4, ONR 649(00)).

Fisher, Helen. Teacher differences in professional reading. *Educ. Admin. Superv.,* 1958, 44, 282–289.

Friedman, I. Objectifying the subjective—A methodological approach to the TAT. *J. proj. Tech.,* 1957, 21, 243–247.

Fuller, Elizabeth M. The use of teacher-pupil attitudes, self-rating and measures of general ability in the pre-service selection of nursery school–kindergarten–primary teachers. *J. educ. Res.,* 1951, 44, 675–686.

Gage, N. L. Logical versus empirical scoring keys: The case of the MTAI. *J. educ. Psychol.,* 1957, 48, 213–216.

Gage, N. L., & Chatterjee, B. B. The psychological meaning of acquiescence set: Further evidence. *J. abnorm. soc. Psychol.,* 1960, 60, 280–283.

Gage, N. L., Leavitt, G. S., & Stone, G. C. The psychological meaning of acquiescence set for authoritarianism. *J. abnorm. soc. Psychol.,* 1957, 55, 98–103.

Getzels, J. W. Methods used to study personality. *J. Nat. Ass. Deans Women,* 1953, 16, 154–158.

Getzels, J. W. Educational news and editorial comment (Necessity and innovation in the selection and training of teachers). *Elem. sch. J.,* 1955, 55, 427–434.

Goodenough, Florence L., Fuller, Elizabeth M., & Olson, Edna. The use of the Good-

enough Speed-of-Association test in the pre-service selection of nursery school–kindergarten–primary teachers. *J. educ. Psychol.,* 1946, 37, 335–346.

Gough, H. G. A personality scale for anti-Semitic prejudice (*Pr*). In G. S. Welsh & W. G. Dahlstrom (Eds.), *Basic readings on the MMPI in psychology and medicine.* Minneapolis: Univer. of Minnesota Press, 1956. Pp. 205–211.

Gough, H. G., & Pemberton, W. H. Personality characteristics related to success in practice teaching. *J. appl. Psychol.,* 1952, 36, 307–309.

Gowan, J. C. Relation of the "K" scale of the MMPI to the teaching personality. *Calif. J. educ. Res.,* 1955, 6, 208–212.

Gowan, J. C. A summary of the intensive study of twenty highly selected elementary women teachers. *J. exp. Educ.,* 1957, 26, 115–124.

Gowan, J. C. Intercorrelations and factor analyses of tests given to teaching candidates. *J. exp. Educ.,* 1958, 27, 1–22.

Gowan, J. C. A teacher prognosis scale for the Guilford-Zimmerman Temperament Survey. *J. educ. Res.,* 1960, 53, 345–348.

Gowan, J. C., & Gowan, May S. A teacher prognosis scale for the MMPI. *J. educ. Res.,* 1955, 49, 1–12. (a)

Gowan, J. C., & Gowan, May S. The Guilford-Zimmerman and the California Psychological Inventory in the measurement of teaching candidates. *Calif. J. educ. Res.,* 1955, 6, 35–37. (b)

Guba, E. G., & Getzels, J. W. Personality and teacher effectiveness: A problem in theoretical research. *J. educ. Psychol.,* 1955, 46, 330–344.

Guba, E. G., Jackson, P. W., & Bidwell, C. E. Occupational choice and the teaching career. *Educ. res. Bull.,* 1959, 38, 1–12.

Guilford, J. P. *Personality.* New York: McGraw-Hill, 1959.

Guilford, J. P., & Zimmerman, W. S. *The Guilford-Zimmerman Temperament Survey: Manual of instructions and interpretations.* Beverly Hills, Calif.: Sheridan Supply Co., 1949.

Hadley, S. T. A study of the predictive value of several variables to student teaching success as measured by student teaching marks. *Teach. Coll. Bull., State Teachers Coll., Indiana, Pa.,* 1954, 60 (3), 1–10.

Hammond, K. R. Measuring attitude by error-choice: An indirect method. *J. abnorm. soc. Psychol.*, 1948, 43, 38–48.

Hedlund, P. A. *Cooperative study to predict effectiveness in secondary school teaching: Third progress report.* Albany: Univer. of State of New York & State Education Department, 1953.

Hilton, T. L. Ego-involvement in teaching: Its theory and measurement by a word completion technique. Unpublished doctoral dissertation, Harvard Univer., 1955.

Jackson, P. W., & Guba, E. G. The need structure of in-service teachers: An occupational analysis. *Sch. Rev.*, 1957, 65, 176–192.

Jarecke, W. H. Evaluating teaching success through the use of the teaching judgment test. *J. educ. Res.*, 1952, 45, 683–694.

Johnson, G. B., Jr. An evaluation instrument for the analysis of teacher effectiveness. *J. exp. Educ.*, 1955, 23, 331–344.

Johnson, G. B., Jr. An experimental technique for the prediction of teacher effectiveness. *J. educ. Res.*, 1957, 50, 679–689.

Jones, Margaret L. Analysis of certain aspects of teaching ability. *J. exp. Educ.*, 1956, 25, 152–180.

Kearney, N. C., & Rocchio, P. D. The relation between the Minnesota Teacher Attitude Inventory and subject matter taught by elementary teachers. *Educ. Admin. Superv.*, 1955, 41, 358–360.

Kearney, N. C., & Rocchio, P. D. The effect of teacher education on the teacher's attitude. *J. educ. Res.*, 1956, 49, 703–708.

Knoell, D. M. Prediction of teaching success from word fluency data. *J. educ. Res.*, 1953, 46, 673–683.

Koile, E. A. A measure of interest for selecting faculty counselors. *Educ. psychol. Measmt*, 1955, 15, 47–57.

Kreitlow, B. W., & Dreier, W. R. A scale for measuring teachers' beliefs about children, schools and teaching. *Elem. sch. J.*, 1955, 55, 325–330.

Kuder, G. F. *Examiner manual for the Kuder Preference Record, vocational form-C.* (5th ed.) Chicago: Science Research Associates, 1953.

LaBue, A. C. Personality traits and persistence of interest in teaching as a vocational choice. *J. appl. Psychol.*, 1955, 39, 362–365.

Lamke, T. A. Personality and teaching success. *J. exp. Educ.*, 1951, 20, 217–259.

Learned, W. S., & Wood, B. D. *The student and his knowledge.* New York: Carnegie Foundation for the Advancement of Teaching, 1938.

Leeds, C. H. A scale for measuring teacher-pupil attitudes and teacher-pupil rapport. *Psychol. Monogr.*, 1950, 64, No. 6 (Whole No. 312).

Leeds, C. H. A second validity study of the Minnesota Teacher Attitude Inventory. *Elem. sch. J.*, 1952, 52, 396–405.

Leeds, C. H. Teacher attitude and temperament as a measure of teacher-pupil rapport. *J. appl. Psychol.*, 1956, 40, 333–337.

Levin, H., Hilton, T. L., & Leiderman, Gloria. Studies in teacher behavior. *J. exp. Educ.*, 1957, 26, 81–91.

Lieberman, M. *Education as a profession.* Englewood Cliffs, N.J.: Prentice-Hall, 1956.

Lindgren, H. C., & Patton, Gladys M. Attitudes of high school and other teachers toward children and current educational methodology. *Calif. J. educ. Res.*, 1958, 9, 80–85.

Lough, Orpha M. Teachers college students and the Minnesota Multiphasic Personality Inventory. *J. appl. Psychol.*, 1946, 30, 241–246.

Lough, Orpha M. Women students in liberal arts, nursing, and teacher training curricula and the Minnesota Multiphasic Personality Inventory. *J. appl. Psychol.*, 1947, 31, 437–445.

MacLean, M. S., Gowan, May S., & Gowan, J. C. A teacher selection and counseling service. *J. educ. Res.*, 1955, 48, 669–677.

McGee, H. M. Measurement of authoritarianism and its relation to teachers' classroom behavior. *Genet. Psychol. Monogr.*, 1955, 52, 89–146.

McKinley, J. C., Hathaway, S. R., & Meehl, P. E. The K scale. In G. S. Welsh & W. G. Dahlstrom (Eds.), *Basic readings on the MMPI in psychology and medicine.* Minneapolis: Univer. of Minnesota Press, 1956. Pp. 112–123.

Meehl, P. E., & Hathaway, S. R. The K factor as a suppressor variable in the MMPI. *J. appl. Psychol.*, 1946, 30, 525–564.

Michaelis, J. U. The prediction of success in student teaching from personality and attitude inventories. *Univer. Calif. Publs Educ.*, 1954, 11, 415–481.

Miller, N. E. Liberalization of basic S-R concepts: Extension to conflict behavior, motivation and social learning. In S. Koch (Ed.), *Psychology: A study of a science.* Vol. 2.

General systematic formulations, learning and special processes. New York: McGraw-Hill, 1959. Pp. 196–292.

Mitzel, H. E., Ostreicher, L. M., & Reiter, S. R. *Development of attitudinal dimensions from teachers' drawings.* New York: City Colleges, Div. of Teacher Education, Office of Res. and Evaluation, Publ. 24, 1954.

Mitzel, H. E., Rabinowitz, W., & Ostreicher, L. M. *Effects of certain response sets on valid test variance.* New York: City Colleges, Div. of Teacher Education, Office of Res. and Evaluation, 1955 (Res. Series No. 26).

Montross, H. W. Temperament and teaching success. *J. exp. Educ.,* 1954, 23, 73–97.

Moore, C. J., & Cole, D. The relation of MMPI scores to practice teaching ratings. *J. educ. Res.,* 1957, 50, 711–716.

Morsh, J. E., & Wilder, Eleanor W. Identifying the effective instructor: A review of the quantitative studies, 1900–1952. *USAF Pers. Train. Res. Cent. (Res. Bull.,* 1954, No. AFPTRC-TR-54-44).

Nagle, L. M. Effects of an internship upon selected goals of the program. *J. educ. Res.,* 1955, 48, 711–714.

Oelke, M. C. A study of student teachers' attitudes toward children. *J. educ. Psychol.,* 1956, 47, 193–196.

Ohlsen, M. M., & Schultz, R. E. Projective test response patterns for best and poorest student-teachers. *Educ. psychol. Measmt,* 1955, 15, 18–27.

Page, Martha H. Effects of mental set on certain aspects of Rorschach performance. In R. M. W. Travers, W. Rabinowitz, Martha H. Page, Elinore Nemovicher, & P. Ventur, *Exploratory studies in teacher personality.* New York: City Colleges, Div. of Teacher Education, Office of Res. and Evaluation, 1953 (Res. Series No. 14, pp. 11–17).

Page, Martha H., & Travers, R. M. W. Relationships between Rorschach performance and student-teaching. In R. M. W. Travers, W. Rabinowitz, Martha H. Page, Elinore Nemovicher, & P. Ventur. *Exploratory studies in teacher personality.* New York: City Colleges, Div. of Teacher Education, Office of Res. and Evaluation, 1953 (Res. Series No. 14, pp. 2–9). (a)

Page, Martha H., & Travers, R. M. W. Use of drawings as a screening device in educa-

tion. In R. M. W. Travers, W. Rabinowitz, Martha H. Page, Elinore Nemovicher, & P. Ventur, *Exploratory studies in teacher personality.* New York: City Colleges, Div. of Teacher Education, Office of Res. and Evaluation, 1953 (Res. Series No. 14, pp. 41–44). (b)

Peck, R. F. Predicting principals' ratings of teacher performance from personality data. *J. educ. Psychol.,* 1959, 50, 70–74.

Piers, Ellen V. Effects of instruction on teacher attitudes: Extended control group design. *Abstracts of dissertations for the year 1954.* Nashville, Tenn.: Peabody Coll. for Teachers, 1955. Pp. 245–249.

Popham, W. J., & Standlee, L. S. Out-of-school activities and professional performance of teachers. *Indiana Univer. Sch. Educ. Bull.,* 1958, 34 (4).

Powell, H. F. Characteristic differences in certain attributes of teachers in various teaching fields. Unpublished doctoral dissertation, Univer. of Michigan, 1950.

Rabinowitz, W. The fakability of the Minnesota Teacher Attitude Inventory. *Educ. psychol. Measmt,* 1954, 14, 657–664.

Rabinowitz, W., & Travers, R. M. W. A drawing technique for studying certain outcomes of teacher education: Part I. The development of the technique and its qualitative uses. In R. M. W. Travers, W. Rabinowitz, Martha H. Page, Elinore Nemovicher, & P. Ventur, *Exploratory studies in teacher personality.* New York: City Colleges, Div. of Teacher Education, Office of Res. and Evaluation, 1953 (Res. Series No. 14, pp. 18–28).

Reed, H. J. An investigation of the relationship between teaching effectiveness and teacher's attitude of acceptance. *J. exp. Educ.,* 1953, 21, 277–325.

Remmers, H. H. Relationships between eight variables and *F* test scores of teachers. *J. educ. Psychol.,* 1954, 45, 427–431.

Ringness, T. A. Relationships between certain attitudes towards teaching and teaching success. *J. exp. Educ.,* 1952, 21, 1–55.

Rocchio, P. D., & Kearney, N. C. Using an attitude inventory in selecting teachers. *Elem. sch. J.,* 1955, 56, 76–78.

Rocchio, P. D., & Kearney, N. C. Does a course in mental hygiene help teachers? *Understanding the Child,* 1956, 25, 91–94. (a)

Rocchio, P. D., & Kearney, N. C. Teacher-pupil attitudes as related to non-promotion of secondary school pupils. *Educ. psychol. Measmt,* 1956, 16, 244–252. (b)

Rostker, L. E. The measurement of teaching ability: Study number two. *J. exp. Educ.,* 1945, 14, 6–51.

Ryans, D. G. A study of the extent of association of certain professional and personal data with judged effectiveness of teacher behavior. *J. exp. Educ.,* 1951, 20, 67–77.

Ryans, D. G. *Characteristics of teachers.* Washington, D.C.: American Council on Education, 1960.

Sandgren, D. L., & Schmidt, L. G. Does practice teaching change attitudes toward teaching? *J. educ. Res.,* 1956, 49, 673–680.

Schmid, J. Factor analyses of prospective teachers' differences. *J. exp. Educ.,* 1950, 18, 287–319.

Schultz, R. E., & Ohlsen, M. M. Interest patterns of best and poorest student teachers. *J. educ. Sociol.,* 1955, 29, 108–112.

Seagoe, May V. Some origins of interest in teaching. *J. educ. Res.,* 1942, 35, 673–682.

Seagoe, May V. Prediction of in-service success in teaching. *J. educ. Res.,* 1946, 39, 658–663.

Seagoe, May V. A follow-up of 314 students whose fitness for teaching was questioned, 1942–1953. *J. educ. Res.,* 1957, 50, 641–653.

Shapiro, Edna, Biber, Barbara, & Minuchin, Patricia. The Cartoon Situations Test: A semi-structured technique for assessing aspects of personality pertinent to the teaching process. *J. proj. Tech.,* 1957, 21, 172–184.

Shea, J. A. The predictive value of various combinations of standardized tests and subtests for prognosis of teaching efficiency. *Cath. Univer. of Amer. Educ. Res. Monogr.,* 1955, 19, No. 6.

Sheldon, M. S., Coale, J. M., & Copple, R. Current validity of the "warm teacher scales." *J. educ. Psychol.,* 1959, 50, 37–40.

Singer, A., Jr. Social competence and success in teaching. *J. exp. Educ.,* 1954, 23, 99–131.

Sorenson, A. G. A note on the "fakability" of the MTAI. *J. appl. Psychol.,* 1956, 40, 192–194.

Standlee, L. S., & Popham, W. J. Participation in leisure time activities as related to selected vocational and social variables. *J. Psychol.,* 1958, 46, 149–154.

Stein, H. L., & Hardy, J. A validation study of the MTAI in Manitoba. *J. educ. Res.,* 1957, 50, 321–338.

Stephens, J. M. Spontaneous schooling and success in teaching. *Sch. Rev.,* 1960, 68, 152–163.

Stern, G. G., Stein, M. I., & Bloom, B. S. *Methods of personality assessment.* Glencoe, Ill.: Free Press, 1956.

Stewart, L. H., & Roberts, J. P. The relationship of Kuder profiles to remaining in a teachers' college and to occupational choice. *Educ. psychol. Measmt,* 1955, 15, 416–421.

Strong, E. K., Jr. *Vocational interests of men and women.* Stanford, Calif.: Stanford Univer. Press, 1943.

Sweetland, A., & Quay, H. A note on the K scale of the Minnesota Multiphasic Personality Inventory. *J. consult. Psychol.,* 1953, 17, 314–316.

Symonds, P. M. Teaching as a function of the teacher's personality. *J. teacher Educ.,* 1954, 5, 79–83.

Symonds, P. M., & Dudek, Stephanie. Use of the Rorschach in the diagnosis of teacher effectiveness. *J. proj. Tech.,* 1956, 20, 227–234.

Tanner, W. C., Jr. Personality bases in teacher selection. *Phi Delta Kappan,* 1954, 35, 271–277.

Travers, R. M. W., & Rabinowitz, W. A drawing technique for studying certain outcomes of teacher education. Part II. A quantitative comparison of certain outcomes in two institutions. In R. M. W. Travers, W. Rabinowitz, Martha H. Page, Elinore Nemovicher, & P. Ventur, *Exploratory studies in teacher personality.* New York: City Colleges, Div. of Teacher Education, Office of Res. and Evaluation, 1953 (Res. Series No. 14, pp. 29–40).

Travers, R. M. W., Rabinowitz, W., & Nemovicher, Elinore. The anxieties of a group of student teachers. In R. M. W. Travers, W. Rabinowitz, Martha H. Page, Elinore Nemovicher, & P. Ventur, *Exploratory studies in teacher personality.* New York: City Colleges, Div. of Teacher Education, Office of Res. and Evaluation, 1953 (Res. Series No. 14, pp. 45–51).

Tyler, F. T. The prediction of student-teaching success from personality inventories. *Univer. Calif. Publs Educ.,* 1954, 11, 233–313.

Wandt, E. The measurement of teachers' attitudes toward groups contacted in the schools. *J. educ. Res.,* 1952, 46, 113–122.

Wandt, E. A comparison of the attitudes of contrasting groups of teachers. *Educ. psychol. Measmt,* 1954, 14, 418–422.

Ward, L. B., & Kirk, S. A. Studies in the selection of students for a teachers college. *J. educ. Res.,* 1942, 35, 665–672.

Washburne, C., & Heil, L. M. What characteristics of teachers affect children's growth? *Sch. Rev.,* 1960, 68, 420–428.

Welsh, G. S., & Dahlstrom, W. G. (Eds.) *Basic readings on the MMPI in psychology and medicine.* Minneapolis: Univer. of Minnesota Press, 1956.

Wolfle, D. *America's resources of specialized talent.* New York: Harper, 1954.

CHAPTER 12 Instruments and Media of Instruction

A. A. LUMSDAINE
University of California, Los Angeles[1]

There are perhaps three purposes to which a chapter on research on instruments and media of instruction might be addressed: (1) to aid the research worker in sharper, more useful delineation of problems; (2) to analyze the current status of research-based knowledge in the more important problem areas; and (3) to consider methodological techniques and pitfalls in order to improve the incisiveness and efficiency of future research.

All three of these objectives have influenced the selection of material and the emphases adopted in preparing this chapter. No attempt has been made to catalog all past research on instructional films and other visual aids or to cover comprehensively the wide range of related research on conditions that influence the efficiency of learning. However, an attempt has been made to deal with a number of studies which illustrate points that can help us assess the current state of the art, in terms of both methodology and the formulation of research problems. In attempting to do this, the author has drawn occasionally from related research in the field of learning which, though not necessarily conceived to deal directly with instructional tools and ma-

terials, nevertheless contributes to the research area with which this chapter is concerned.

No attempt is made to analyze or criticize in detail all the methodological aspects of each study mentioned. Rather, only those aspects of methodology are discussed in particular studies that appear most relevant to the formulation, design, or execution of future studies.

[1] The author also serves as Advisor for Educational Media to the American Institute for Research. Portions of this paper were presented at an Invitational Working Conference on Training Research, February 1–3, 1960, at the University of Pittsburgh, under sponsorship of the Office of Naval Research and the University of Pittsburgh Department of Psychology (see Glaser, 1962). The author also wishes to express his appreciation to Professor Glaser for use of abstracts and summaries of literature prepared for the book, *Teaching Machines and Programmed Learning: A Source Book* (A. A. Lumsdaine and R. Glaser, Editors), sponsored and published by the Department of Audio-Visual Instruction, National Education Association. Some of the materials for this chapter were prepared in conjunction with research projects at the American Institute for Research sponsored by the Air Force Office of Scientific Research, the Office of Naval Research, and the Educational Media Branch of the U.S. Office of Education; and at the University of California, Los Angeles, by the U.S. Office of Education, Educational Media and Cooperative Research Branches.

The chapter deals primarily with instructional media *as objects of experimental research,* and in particular with the kinds of experimental research which can result in improved prediction and control of the effects of instructional media in attaining specific outcomes. It does not deal, except incidentally, with attempts by educators or psychologists to provide expert judgments or guidelines for the use or design of instructional media on the basis of educated guesses or rational analyses. It deals only incidentally with curriculum studies and content analyses of instructional instruments or communications conducted to divine the objectives of their authors.

The omission of these efforts and activities from primary consideration here is in no way meant to deprecate the service that they may provide. Rather, it reflects an orientation, for the purposes of this Handbook, toward research as empirical inquiry which obtains new *behavioral data*—data obtained and used either for specific applied (technological) purposes or to contribute toward principles and methods. These principles and methods represent, on the one hand, a science of instruction firmly grounded in experimental findings and, on the other hand, a technology of research methods that can be used to improve specific instructional instruments.

INSTRUCTIONAL INSTRUMENTS AND MEDIA AS OBJECTS OF RESEARCH

The word "instructional," as employed here, embraces many of the connotations of the terms *training* and *education. Instruction* is used as a generic term referring to any specifiable means of controlling or manipulating a sequence of events to produce modifications of behavior through learning. It is applicable whenever the outcomes of learning can be specified in sufficiently explicit terms to permit their measurement. These outcomes may include changes in attitudes, interests, motivations, beliefs, or opinions as well as in knowledges, skills, and other performance capabilities, so long as they are defined in terms which identify specific, observable behaviors agreed to be manifestations or indications of these outcomes. Use of the word *outcomes* rather than *objectives* does not preclude consideration of *any* outcome, whether anticipated, desired, or otherwise; however, our main concern is naturally with the attainment of objectives which are chosen in advance to represent the purpose of the instruction.

As used in this chapter, *instructional media* refers to a class of instructional resources, e.g., films, or to a group or subset of such a class. An instructional *instrument* generally refers to a particular member or instance of this class, e.g., a particular film. The terms *instruments* and *media* can include both instructional materials prepared for teaching a particular subject matter or the combination of equipment and associated materials—e.g., a film and projector, or a teaching machine and the program of materials presented by it.

Instructional resources which can aid in the learning process include, in addition to the teacher, a wide variety of tools, devices, materials, and other "aids." Broadly speaking, these either present, or help to present, information to the learner, or afford opportunities for him to make responses which help him to learn or indicate what he has learned. The so-called "audio-visual" media of instruction comprise an important and widely used class of such instructional resources, generally employed to present information. Other tools include instruments which permit the student to make relevant responses (e.g., workbooks, self-scoring test forms, and other manipulanda) which can aid the learning process. Teaching machines or "auto-instructional" devices—another important class, partly overlapping with "audio-visual" instruments—serve an information-presenting function and also afford a means for the student to make appropriate responses to the material presented.

Auto-instructional devices (teaching machines) imply an individually determined rate of presentation and response and permit the student to proceed for an appreciable time without the intervention of a teacher. This latter characteristic also applies to many forms of audio-visual media, e.g., sound films, in which the student is supposed to learn from the audio-visual presentation without the continuous intervention of the teacher, just as he is expected to do when pursuing independent study of a textbook or reference source. Some other visual and audio-visual "aids," by contrast, are used by the teacher as adjuncts to his other activities, rather than as independent devices of instruction.[2]

Sequenced and Reproducible Presentation

The instructional media considered in this chapter are primarily those presented in some predetermined sequence. The sequence is determined either by the structure of the instructional instruments, by well-defined procedures and constraints in the way they are used, or by the mechanical arrangements used to present them. The instruments thus generate events whose occurrence is more or less predictable in terms of sequence or pacing. The sequencing and pacing need not be fixed, but they do depend on clearly specifiable factors in the learning situation. A specifiable factor does not mean merely the activities of an instructor, nor the decisions of a student in whose hands materials are placed.[3] The events generated by instruc-

tional media are also reproducible events in that they may be repeated (as in the case of a film) or be duplicated (as in the case of instructional television) at a number of locations simultaneously.

In concrete terms, the materials dealt with here include motion picture films, tape recordings, filmstrips, and self-instructional programs for presentation by a teaching machine or some related device. These materials do not, for the most part, include, as such, charts, diagrams, models, or isolated photographs or drawings, except when they represent elements in a predictable pattern of instruction governed by a relatively well-defined procedural sequence. The latter can be regarded only as tools or components for instructional acts or instruments; a complete instrument consists of the aid plus the activities of the teacher. This restriction is necessary if we are to consider instructional media and instruments as specifiable events which are amenable to scientific research, which can deal only with reproducible events.

As the writer has pointed out elsewhere (Lumsdaine, 1960), single ·visual displays represent only an isolated and incomplete fragment of a total instructional stimulus pattern. Thus, except when they are considered as a component of other specified instruction, it is difficult to control or predict their practical effects on instruction. When they are considered alone, it is difficult to partial out their contribution from other unspecified factors in the instructional situation. Perhaps this is why little significant experimental research has been done on nonsequenced, isolated visual aids, and why little is likely to be done in the future. Most of the studies excluded are demonstrational tests of specific devices showing that their use did or did not contribute to training, and they provide little in the way of potentially generalizable findings.

In terms of the criteria set forth above, textbooks represent a borderline case.[4] The

---

[2] All instructional instruments and the media they represent can properly be considered "aids" to *learning*. However, not all need be considered aids to the teacher, since some, e.g., self-instructional programs, or, in a sense, textbooks, are clearly capable of instructing without the teacher's direct intervention.

[3] This does not mean that their presentation may not require the activity of a teacher or assistant (e.g., film projectionist). It does mean that the student is expected to learn something from a previously prepared sequence of instruction even though the teacher is not present or active at the moment. Instructional media, as the term is used here, provide acts of instruction, not merely the wherewithal to effect such acts.

[4] Despite the venerability of the textbook as a medium of instruction, a case may be made for the position that it actually has two quite distinct functions—

usual textbook does not control the behavior of the learner in a way which makes it highly predictable as a vehicle of instruction or amenable to experimental research. It does not in itself generate a describable and predictable process of learner behavior, and this may be the reason why there has been very little experimental research on the textbook.[5] In any case, the textbook, and its cousin, the training manual or training syllabus, is not treated explicitly here as a primary object of research.

A few studies (Hovland & Weiss, 1951; Hovland, Janis, & Kelley, 1953; Klare, Mabry, & Gustafson, 1955a, 1955b; Klare, Nichols, & Shuford, 1957; Klare, Shuford, & Nichols, 1957, 1959) are included, however, in which the format or content of printed textual material has been experimentally manipulated in a situation involving supervised reading for a fixed interval or a similarly structured situation. A further potential exception might be envisaged in a large-scale field experiment in which the experimental factor is the *availability* of text or reference materials in two or more clearly differentiated alternative forms. Such a study would require a considerable sampling of classes or schools, and teachers. It would pose the question: Does placing one kind of text in the hands of teachers or students result (despite probable wide variations in the conditions of

that of a reference source of information and that of a sequenced medium of instruction or learning. The basic requirements for these two functions differ fundamentally, as, for instance, in the need for sequencing and redundancy of information. With the development of programed self-instructional media and concomitant improvement in the information-retrieval utility of handbooks, and similar reference sources, it seems possible that the next decade or so may witness the decline, if not the demise, of the textbook, as now conceived, in favor of programed instructional material on the one hand and of the well-designed reference handbook or source book on the other.

[5] The paucity of experimental research on the characteristics of textbooks was noted by C. R. Carpenter at the Western Regional Conference on Title VII of the National Defense Education Act, held in Sacramento in 1960. Carpenter indicated that there were no known experimental comparisons of the effectiveness of alternate versions of text material.

its use) in differences in achievement? No such studies on conventional textbooks are known to the author, though studies of "programed" textbooks such as the one by Klaus and Lumsdaine (1960), described later, follow this pattern.

Stimulus Control

As objects of controllable experimentation that may generate usable research findings, instructional media possess an important characteristic that distinguishes them from instructional methods or procedures. It can be very misleading to reify a specific medium or category of instruments—such as "films," "television," or "graphic aids"—and to invest it with class properties. Nevertheless, a *particular* instrument or specific set of instruments, as distinguished from a method or procedure of instruction, constitutes a tangible product or *thing*. This property of concreteness or thingness has important consequences with respect to constancy, specifiability, and reproducibility which affect the degree to which experimental manipulation of the properties of instruction can be defined and specified.

On the one hand, we can control and specify the experimental stimulus to a degree not often possible when we experiment with the properties of a method or procedure of instruction. In the case of a film, for example, we can point to, display, and describe very concretely what the experimental stimulus is. The same is true for a self-instructional program designed for a teaching machine, or for a tape recording used in language instruction. The extent to which we can reproduce the stimulus material in constant fashion is, despite possibly important variations in the conditions and context of its use, still far greater than the reproducibility of most so-called methods or procedures of instruction used by a classroom teacher. It is obvious that such constancy, if not a *sine qua non,* at least greatly facilitates successful research on instruction.

Dealing with the properties of a concrete

product can, furthermore, give us much greater control of the application of research findings than we have for research findings that pertain to a procedure or method. *Products*—things—can be made the subject of *specifications;* specifications can be checked, and specified products in the form of devices and materials have, in turn, an inherent constancy and predictability which can scarcely be expected in using a method or procedure.

Another consequence of the reproducibility of materials and devices is the fact that their production involves fewer people than does the implementation of procedures or methods by a multitude of instructors. This group of individuals is likely to be less dispersed geographically and hence more accessible to influence than are individual instructors. One film produced by a relatively small group of individuals is used hundreds of times; there is one *act* of production, on the part of this small group, which needs to be influenced— to implement a demonstrably superior technique of presentation—on only one occasion, instead of having to insure use of this technique by hundreds of instructors over an indefinite period of time. Similarly, self-instructional programs for a teaching machine, being capable of indefinite reproduction, are relatively easy to control because they are the product of a small group of individuals who can be given specialized training in such skills as sequencing materials, to a degree that would be impractical for a multitude of individual teachers. It can thus be argued that, in terms of likely payoff, higher priority can justifiably be accorded to research on the controllable properties of instructional media than to similar research on abstract methods or procedures of instruction.

Control of Student Response

So far we have discussed stimulus properties. What about the response side as a factor in learning? Disregarding such questions as the exact role of reinforcement in learning and the mechanics by which unitary response acts are integrated into complex sustained performances, it may be agreed that learning involves development of capabilities for responses that could not be elicited, prior to learning, by a given stimulus. In a broad sense, this notion applies whether we are speaking of response "shaping" or are bringing an already well-defined response under the control of a new set of stimuli. We may also agree, regardless of differences in interpretation, that to acquire new stimulus-response contingencies, the responses to be learned must occur in some form during the course of learning or acquisition—regardless of whether these responses are implicit or overt, simple or complex, unitary or integrated, symbolic or otherwise, mediating or terminal.

In this sense, the responses made by the learner comprise a crucial class of independent variables that influence the outcomes of learning experiences. In another sense, however, student response is never an independent variable; it is, rather, a mediating one. This is true because we never can manipulate responses *as such;* we can manipulate only the stimulus conditions that govern responses. In this sense, external control over the process of learning reduces to the control of stimuli. But this by no means implies that the response factors in learning are to be ignored. On the contrary, the writer believes that the most productive orientation for research on instructional media is to look for ways in which responses of the student, overt and implicit, can be controlled by stimulus conditions. To a considerable extent, the content of this chapter reflects this orientation.

It should be clear that control of student response can reside in considerable part in the instructional materials, and particularly in the way in which they call for or prompt response elements of the to-be-learned behavior. To an appreciable extent, however, occurrence of appropriate student response may depend on the physical opportunities provided for writing, pressing keys, or other manipulation. One reason for special interest in the instructional potentialities of teaching machines, as opposed to the usual forms of films and other audio-visual media, is that the requirement for overt response is inherent in the instructional situation and thus forces us to pay attention to the control of student response.

CURRENT STATUS OF
MAJOR INSTRUCTIONAL MEDIA

Instructional Films and Related Media

"Teaching films," "educational films," "training films" (the military and industrial term) all are terms indicating the notion that material can be presented by motion picture film for instructional purposes. Most instructional films are produced as 16 mm. sound films, frequently in color. They present an enormous variety of instructional materials, including film-recorded lectures, surrogate field-trip visits (the travelogue and other films which aim primarily to "bring the world to the classroom"), demonstrations, dramatic or theatrical presentations of literary or historical events, and dramatized expositions which depict students being taught by a teacher or parent.

In addition, two quite different kinds of "demonstrational" films can be identified: (1) demonstrations of phenomena which depict events or characteristics of the animate or inanimate world, and (2) procedural demonstrations which teach the performance of a specific sequence of acts. Aside from the latter category, sometimes referred to as "nuts-and-bolts" training films, the instructional objectives of films are often stated imprecisely, if at all. When not characterized as "telling a story about" a subject matter or "presenting" the "content" of a lesson (without specifying precisely what is to be learned), films are often described as creating a general familiarity, understanding, background, or "knowledge about" the subject treated. Because of this vagueness of objective, typified by the question, "What might this film be used for?" (not unlike the question asked by the graduate student, "I wonder what experiment I could do with this piece of apparatus"), it is often difficult to define the appropriate criteria for evaluating instructional films. That the same vagueness of objective characterizes other forms of instruction is perhaps less obtrusive because nonmedia instruction is less often the subject of experimental evaluation.

Instructional sound films are produced either with synchronized sound recorded concurrently or with narration and other sound added separately. Their high cost when commercially produced can sometimes be greatly reduced by local, short-cut production techniques such as those described by Greenhill (1955). Often the content and sequencing are governed as much by practices and traditions borrowed from the field of theatrical motion pictures as by considerations of pedagogy. The respects in which films are likely to differ instructionally from kinescopes or video-tape recordings of "live" televised instruction probably lie more in philosophy and practice of production than they do in inherent media differences.

Television not prefilmed or recorded by video tape or kinescope is, of course, transitory and not temporally repeatable. Aside from minor differences in grain or resolution (which are considerable in terms of physical measurement but seldom important from an instructional standpoint), the televised instructional lesson, kinescope recording, or video-tape recording differs instructionally from the sound motion picture primarily in screen size and in the potentiality for using color, except where immediacy of presentation is important. Even this difference is more a matter of tradition and logistics than of inherent properties, however, since motion picture film can, by special equipment, be processed and projected within a matter of seconds after an event is photographed. For most instructional purposes, then, the inherent instructional properties of film and of recorded television presentations can be considered substantially identical, both consisting of a series of moving or sequenced still pictures accompanied by recorded sound. In many instances, only an expert can detect the difference between prefilmed or taped and live television presentations, or between films photographed directly on a photographic emulsion and those in which the original action was picked up by a television camera.

At the present time, however, films and televised instruction differ considerably because of traditional factors—the budgets and time schedule for their production and the practice of filming television-linked films "straight through" instead of shooting one scene at a time and later combining the bits and pieces by a careful job of editing. This difference in tradition appears to be weakening, however, with the increasing use of prefilming for both instructional and entertainment television, and of so-called "straight through" or "television-style" techniques for making instructional films. The feasibility of the latter is somewhat enhanced by the so-called "telecam" technique in which the same image is picked up concurrently on film and over a video circuit, enabling on-the-spot direction and editorial decisions to be made, and at the same time preserving a high-quality film original for subsequent reproduction.

Aside from these questions of production technique, most of the variation in cost as well as in instructional properties results from what is placed in front of the camera. It may also be noted (see the study by Lumsdaine and Sulzer, 1951, described on p. 631) that reproducible, carefully planned instruction, as represented by film and its television cousins, can be valuable even where the visual material is largely static. Similar instruction can often be provided by a sound-accompanied series of still pictures requiring simpler equipment and less expensive materials. Some devices for sequenced still-picture projection are not only capable of regulating the timing of successive frames or scenes by automatic signals from the accompanying sound recording, but also of changing frames rapidly enough to simulate motion, pop-on effects, and other characteristics of motion picture presentation. When one considers also

the absence of motion, and frequent lack of need for it, in many sequences in the "motion picture" film, it is evident that the distinction between "film" and "filmstrip" media is a hazy and shifting one, clear only in the extremes, and better specified in terms of specific stimulus properties of motion and transition, than by characterization in terms of "media" properties.

For group-presented, pre-paced (as well as pre-sequenced) presentation, it is true, however, that presentation by motion picture film has maximum flexibility in that it permits any combination of still and motion presentation. On the other hand, sometimes the motion picture is at an important cost disadvantage where motion is not utilized effectively for considerable periods of the instruction. In addition, flexibility is lost since, with most existing forms of motion picture projection equipment at least, the pacing or timing of the instructional material cannot be guided by the reactions of an individual learner. Thus far, this has not been considered a disadvantage because film presentation has generally been used as a group medium. With the advent of teaching machines, however, increasing use will undoubtedly be made of individually presented films with flexible start-stop characteristics (see Lumsdaine, 1959c, pp. 175–177).

It is difficult to obtain firm data on the prevalence of film usage; no exact counts are readily available on the number of educational films in use in our schools and colleges, nor on the number of showings or pupil-hours of film viewing per year. The number of films available, however, is very large; the most comprehensive catalogue, Wilson's, lists over 10,000 films in the 1954–1958 edition and subsequent supplements. Teachers have increasingly been trained and encouraged to use films, as well as the simpler visual aids to instruction; some states require teachers to have had at least a one-unit laboratory course in the operation of film projection and related equipment.

Guidelines for the use of films have stressed their role as *aids* to teaching, rather than as self-contained instruments of instruction. Teachers are encouraged to preview films, to provide introduction to them for students, to conduct follow-up discussions, and less commonly, to intersperse question-and-answer sessions or other class participation exercises between sections of a film. Although these practices are useful in many instances, it is not necessary to regard the film merely as an adjunct to other instruction, and there has been an increasing tendency to construct films which can stand alone, if necessary, as independent instructional media. A well-known example is the Harvey White physics series, which was initially filmed on the basis of a series of televised lessons. One suspects that the emphasis on using films as mere aids is slowly decreasing as better and more comprehensive films become available. Reluctance to depend on films in the past was rooted partly in the knowledge that many films were ill equipped to stand as independent acts of instruction, and partly in apprehension lest the film displace the teacher. Recently, however, more films have been perceived as carrying the main burden of instruction with the classroom teacher aiding the film presentation, rather than using the film as an aid to instruction organized by the teacher. An advantage of the "self-sufficient" televised or filmed lesson is that its use makes it possible to offer courses of instruction on a wide variety of subjects in small schools where qualified teachers are not available for all subjects.

Television

Instructional television has tended, even more than films, to assume a primary role in conveying instruction; even where a teacher is present, his role is often a supporting rather than a supported one. Where complete half-hour or hour-long lesson periods are transmitted by television, the classroom teacher may provide follow-up or preparatory activities; or, the televised instruction may be the only instruction the students get. Whatever disadvantages may be pointed out

in the latter pattern, it exists, and may represent an increasing trend. However, closed-circuit television has also been used as an aid —for example, in the use of the overhead television camera to replace slide projection and other forms of projected aids (see Wade & Bretz, 1960) or to transmit demonstrations, e.g., in science and medicine, including surgical operations, so that more students can get a good view of the demonstration. Nonetheless, the primary role has been that of televising a complete lesson, and the increasing tendency to record these lessons—and the obvious wastefulness of not doing so when extensive preparation and resources have gone into their production—make it further apparent that, for many purposes, televised instruction and equivalent instructional films are identical media. Certainly, research on factors that make for effective presentation of information on a film screen should, in most particulars, apply to equivalent instruction projected on a television screen.

In addition to the "educational" programs transmitted over television for public information or general enlightenment, many class hours of instruction are being transmitted over educational stations in the United States. Approximately 50 stations are licensed at the present time as educational stations on UHF or VHF channels, and many of these devote considerable time, particularly during the school day, to televised lessons for use in school classrooms or as extension credit courses. For example, WQED in Pittsburgh and its UHF affiliate, WQEX, together currently transmit over eight hours a day, including lessons in subjects ranging from shorthand to physics and providing basic course content for approximately 10 courses in addition to supplemental programs for numerous other subjects. Extensive coverage is also provided by an increasing number of closed-circuit installations operated by school systems (e.g., Hagerstown, Maryland, and Anaheim, California). The advent of an airborne television facility designed to blanket a wide geographic region with televised courses further dramatizes the increasing utilization of transmitted instruction and emphasizes the importance of research on presentation characteristics.

TV as an aid. As noted above, the use of television is not limited to transmitting an entire lesson or series of lessons over a closed-circuit or open-circuit (broadcast) channel; it may also be employed as an aid to an instructor in a classroom. Bretz, at the University of California, Los Angeles, has developed a portable installation which can be quickly set up in most classrooms and which employs an overhead camera at the instructor's podium to substitute for a variety of other projection facilities and to eliminate the need for special transparencies. Textbook illustrations, charts, drawings, and other visual material which the instructor wishes to use in a lecture are simply placed on the desk under the camera and are projected on one or more monitor screens in the classroom. The use of a Zoom lens on the overhead camera permits adaptation to materials of different sizes and increased magnification for showing detailed portions of a display. (See Wade & Bretz, 1960.)

Audio Instruction

Unquestionably the major current use of audio instruction in most schools is for teaching foreign languages. Although a number of recorded lectures have been made available to schools, their use and that of radio-presented instruction has never caught on in the United States as the use of films and televised instruction has. Thus far, less attention appears to have been paid to making well-designed instructional recordings available than to the installation of language laboratory equipment, the assumption evidently being that the teacher would prepare materials locally for use with the equipment. Hundreds of such language laboratory installations have been made, generally including a magnetic recording system employing tapes or, occasionally, discs. Students listen to recorded material in the foreign language and then attempt to reproduce it. A number of the systems allow recording of the student's efforts so that he may compare them with the master recording he has imitated. The effectiveness of such instruction depends not only on the availability of recorded materials, but also on the characteristics of the equipment. In some instances, this permits the student to proceed at his own pace, using an individual recording. In other instances, the group is lock-stepped to a common master recording. In some systems, the student is able to play back a comparison of his own vocalization efforts immediately in comparison with the model; in other systems playback and comparison must be delayed for an appreciable period, perhaps for as long as the completion of a half-hour recording. The latter system would appear to be much less efficient. A comprehensive survey of the use of recorded materials in language instruction is provided by Oinas (1960); it provides instructive comments on the existing differences and potential similarities between language laboratory instruction and instruction by teaching machines. (See also Chapter 21 in this Handbook.)

Auto-Instructional Methods

The development of teaching machines and programs for self-instruction requiring the participation of the student has proceeded rapidly during the past few years. Many proponents of teaching machines believe that the auto-instructional concept and its implementation are likely to have very important implications for the conduct of instruction, and may even revolutionize education. Basically, teaching machines present sequences of programed instruction to the student, requiring his active response at frequent intervals or, in many instances, almost continuously, and providing him with prompt feedback in the form of correction or confirmation for each response. By allowing individuals to proceed at their own rate through a program of materials, these devices permit students to proceed as rapidly as their abilities permit. The obvious economy of really doing something about individual differences in education (other than merely measuring them) has, in itself, potentially revolutionary significance, not only for the efficiency of instruction, but for the organization of classes and schools. The literature describing development activities and a certain amount of research on auto-instructional techniques extends back to the mid-1920's following the development of Pressey's first teaching machine. The relatively small stream of papers stemming from Pressey's work expanded enormously following publication of Skinner's 1954 paper in the *Harvard Educational Review,* and papers based on further research are appearing constantly.

Virtually all of this literature up to mid-1960 is either reproduced in full or abstracted in the recent book of readings edited by Lumsdaine and Glaser (1960). The extent of the work summarized in this compilation and in the briefer compendium edited by Galanter (1959), comprising a total of nearly a thousand pages of literature, indicates the emphasis being placed on development in this area at the present time. The work that has been reported deals with the development of mechanical devices and programed materials, rationale and theory, and experiments designed either to evaluate the educational effects of programed auto-instructional materials or to investigate specific factors related to their effectiveness. In the opinion of the writer, auto-instructional methods may represent the most important innovation in education since the advent of the textbook. One reason for this opinion is the fact that the development of programed self-instructional material is closely tied to the use of empirical data obtained from students' responses as a basis for program revision.

EXPERIMENTAL RESEARCH ON INSTRUCTIONAL MEDIA

Since this chapter is concerned primarily with experimental research on the effects of instructional media, many kinds of research

connected with instructional media are not covered here, including problems of distribution logistics, curriculum analysis, ways of increasing use of instructional media, and library "research" on material used as content for instructional instruments. In addition, relatively little attention is given to non-experimental methods, such as the collection of reviews and "evaluations" from preview groups, or the results of surveys that infer effects from essentially correlational data. A word about this last exclusion will help to define what is meant by experimental studies of the effects of instructional media.

Experimental Manipulation versus Correlational Comparison

The effects of an instructional instrument's use can usually be established only through measurements made in connection with the controlled administration of that instrument. By "controlled" we mean, basically, that the instructional instrument is administered arbitrarily to a given group of students, in order to reveal the effects it produces—without the contamination of spurious factors which could lead to erroneous attribution of "effects" to the instrument. In particular, comparison of the knowledge possessed by those individuals *who happen to have been exposed* to a particular film (or other instrument of instruction) with that of other individuals not thus exposed is regarded as a method of correlational or "survey" research rather than experimental research. The primary basis for ruling out this source of data as a sound basis for identifying the effects of instructional media is that it inevitably leaves open the confounding effects of "self-selection" and related sources of contamination, thus confusing correlation with causation. (Chapter 5 of this Handbook contains an extended treatment of this problem.)

The fact that those who have seen a particular film know more about the content than those who have not seen it obviously does not mean that the difference in knowledge is necessarily the result of having seen the film. This can be concluded only when the film was arbitrarily administered to one group of individuals and withheld arbitrarily from another group. Otherwise, there is, for example, no way to preclude the possibility that those who saw the film already knew more about the content than those who did not, or that the observed superiority results from the fact that they chose, or were chosen, to see it because of their greater interest in, and correlated knowledge of, the subject. Despite various attempts at matching and equating to insure that those who saw the film are "otherwise comparable" with those who did not, there is in general no way to rule out the adventitious correlates of self-selection, even though the groups compared are made "comparable" with respect to a host of selection variables. Thus, the first essential of the experimental identification of the effects of an instructional instrument is that of arbitrary administration of the instrument. The word *arbitrary,* as used here, implies, for rigorous experimentation, some form of randomization. The role of randomization in eliminating systematic bias from experimental "effects," and in providing a defensible, unbiased estimate of error, is further discussed herein in connection with statistical and sampling problems (p. 656 ff.).

Statistical Significance

A second requirement is that some method be available to assess whether the observed effects are great enough, in relation to the variability in performance associated with the imperfect reliability of the measuring instrument, not to be attributed to chance variations. This requires a defensible method of assessing experimental error, in order to demonstrate the statistical significance of the differences which purport to reflect the effects of an instrument (or the difference between the effects achieved by two instruments). Statistical significance is a necessary but not sufficient condition to support the claim that the effects of an instrument have been re-

vealed. Thus, effects of an instrument are indicated only if a significant difference between measurements is obtained under the conditions of a controlled experiment, as characterized above.

Some departures from the requirements of controlled experimentation may be appropriate in the experimental development of instructional materials, where inputs from the responses of students are used as a basis for an instructional sequence to be incorporated in an instrument. Thus, in the case of the immediate effects of a segment of an instructional instrument—e.g., a single "frame" of a self-instructional program—we may be dealing with a single response by a single individual who is under such close observation and control as to make it reasonable for us to conclude that his reponses can be taken as effects of the sequence, even though no formal controlled comparison is employed. Such evidence may be deemed adequate cause for revising the frame or sequence, even though it would not suffice to document a general proposition about instructional effects.

PURPOSES AND TYPES OF EXPERIMENTAL RESEARCH

Within the field of experimental research on the effects of instructional instruments or media, two broad purposes need to be distinguished. They may be characterized broadly as technological and scientific. The two classes of research that correspond, respectively, to these purposes, have been characterized by Hovland, Lumsdaine, and Sheffield (1949) as "evaluative" experiments and as scientific experiments involving controlled manipulation of specific factors.

Evaluative experiments and scientific experiments are both concerned with measuring the effects of instructional media, and they share many of the requirements for valid experimental design, including an adequate basis for randomization or sampling, adequate insurance of sensitivity and validity of the measuring instruments used, and adequate safeguards against contaminating influences. However, the two classes differ fundamentally in purpose. The latter seeks to test propositions or hypotheses to build a usable science of instructional effects; that is, it seeks to develop a tested body of propositions or theory to be used as a basis for predicting the effects of other instruments, or for selecting methods of presentation in designing subsequent instruments.

Experiments with a technological purpose, on the other hand, are those which seek to assess or improve a particular instrument. They may be either formal quantitative experiments designed to reveal statistically significant effects of an instrument on the learning of a group of individuals or, as noted above, they may consist of small-scale, informal, exploratory experiments carried out with a few subjects or only a single subject to obtain suggestions for revisions in the content or mode of presentation of an instrument.

EVALUATIVE STUDIES

Hovland, Lumsdaine, and Sheffield (1949) have made a useful distinction between the evaluation of a *single* film (or other single instructional instrument) and the evaluation of a *class* of instruments taken as representative of a particular medium. It is important to be quite clear as to the kinds of conclusions that are possible from these categories of research.

Evaluation of a Particular Instrument; Comparison of Two Specific Instruments

The experimental question posed here may be simply: How much did a particular instrument (e.g., film) teach? This requires a way of determining the "before" and "after" status—and hence the change from before to after—of those who were given the instruction. Alternatively, if the evaluation is one in which the effects of two instruments are compared, a comparison of the "after" status resulting from the use of each will suffice for some purposes (provided initial compara-

bility of the two groups of students is assured), though a more complete picture is, of course, provided if a "before" baseline is also provided.

An important variant of this kind of comparison is one in which the attainments effected by a particular instrument are compared with those effected by some alternative form of instruction characterized as "conventional" or "currently used" instruction—where the latter is not mediated by a specifiable single alternative instrument. The severe restrictions on interpretation of such a comparison arise from the lack of specificity of the instruction with which the instrument is compared; the same kinds of restrictions apply to a considerable degree in the comparison of two classes of media, and are discussed subsequently in that connection.

The restrictions on interpretation which inhere in evaluative studies can be identified by considering the purposes of such studies. These purposes include, first, the basis for some over-all assessment of the instrument—to determine, for example, whether anything has been learned through its use, or to determine, in comparison with some implicit or explicit standard of reference, or basis for expectations, whether enough is learned through its use to warrant its adoption for some future instructional purpose. Such a decision can be made on the basis of an over-all assessment of effects—for example, total amount of gain on a relevant test. Where the evaluation made in over-all terms is a comparative one involving two alternative instruments or presentations, the purpose may be to determine which of these two specific instructional instruments (e.g., two specific films) to adopt. (A legitimate purpose is *not* the determination of whether similar instruments of the same general class should be accepted for further use in the future; see below.)

Diagnostic Evaluation

Aside from over-all assessment in terms of some total score, a very important class of evaluative experiments are those conducted for "diagnostic" purposes, in which specific effects of the instrument on a number of specific points are separately measured. If the instrument is an orientation film, for example, these might include points of factual information and a variety of specific opinions which, it is hoped, will be influenced by the film. Here one would pay attention not only to the total score but to the amount of information learned on each specific test question or point. To achieve adequate sensitivity or stability of results, this diagnostic purpose may, of course, require a larger sample than would be required to detect differences of the same magnitude in an over-all score.

Data on the instructional effects achieved (and on those of the desired outcomes which fail to be achieved) by the use of a particular instrument are useful primarily in deciding whether to use or further develop a particular instrument. If the instrument is one which had been completed (say, a completed and released instructional film), then the use of information is limited to indicating whether it is worth while to use the instrument and, if so, what specific additional instruction may be needed to achieve the defined goals. Such results can, for example, show the teacher or curriculum supervisor which points of subject matter to devote special attention to in subsequent classroom instruction, as distinguished from those which can be achieved simply by showing the film.

One of the most important uses of such diagnostic evaluative experiments is realized when they are carried out on a preliminary version of an instrument, or on an instrument which is to be revised. The results can then be used in modifying or redesigning the instrument. As pointed out by Hovland, Lumsdaine, and Sheffield (1949), such studies should be carried out in the early stages of production and repeated after each major stage of revision so that, by successive correction and re-evaluation, the desired instructional goals can be achieved in a satisfactory manner. In the case of group media of instruction such as films, such evaluative test-

ing and successive revision have long been advocated (e.g., Carpenter, 1948; Lumsdaine, 1947) but have seldom been carried into practice. One exception is the recent series of studies of television programs by Gropper and Lumsdaine (1961). This approach is also being pursued vigorously in the development of materials for use in teaching machines or as "programed text" material.

An Air Force study reported by Zuckerman (1954) explored the possibility of using preliminary filmstrips, based on "story board" sketches, as media for predicting the effectiveness of films prior to their completion. In this study, a comparison was made between a preliminary filmstrip with accompanying narration and the finished sound motion picture, "Flight Capabilities of the F-86A." After viewing the filmstrip or the film, the subjects (Air Force pilot students) were tested on specific points of information presented in the films. The data were analyzed in terms of the performance of each group on each test item. The results showed a high degree of correspondence between percentages of answers given correctly by the film group and by the preliminary filmstrip group on each point of information—e.g., those test items best learned from the film tended also to be the ones best learned from the filmstrip. This correspondence between film and filmstrip was also present for the more difficult items. Based on all test items, the correlation between percentages of correct answers for the two groups exceeded .80.

Although Zuckerman's study established the feasibility of predicting the degree to which different points would be learned from a finished presentation, it did not go on to demonstrate how such data from a preliminary form of presentation could be used to improve a revised version. This was done in a later study by Gropper and Lumsdaine (1961). Two lessons, one on "heat" and one on "chemistry," were prepared by two different television instructors. These lessons were scheduled as a part of a regular junior high school science series. Before being shown on the air to the entire population of classes that ordinarily watch the lessons, a preview showing of the "heat" and "chemistry" lessons was transmitted (on a UHF channel during nonpeak hours) to a few sample classes. Following the program, students were given a quiz to determine which points in the lesson had been communicated effectively and which had not. As anticipated, item-by-item analysis of the test results indicated that, while certain points in the lesson were fairly well understood, certain other points were much less well learned. The television instructors then revised their presentations to attempt to remedy the specific weaknesses of the lesson as revealed by empirical data.

To test the improvement in effectiveness resulting from this try-out and revision procedure, the original and revised versions were telecast simultaneously to eight matched classes over WQED-WQEX, a unique two-channel educational facility in western Pennsylvania. Following the simultaneous telecast, students were tested on their comprehension of principles as well as their knowledge of facts presented in the lesson. Students who watched the revised lesson tended, in general, to acquire a better understanding of the concepts presented. This was true for both the "heat" and the "chemistry" lessons. Students who watched the revised version of the heat lesson averaged 9.5 points higher on a 90-point test than those who watched the original. For the chemistry lesson, the students who watched the revised version averaged 12.9 points higher on a similar test than those who watched the original. Both differences were statistically significant.

The results of this study support the notion that student responses on achievement tests administered following a preliminary showing of a lesson may be used to provide useful feedback to the television instructor. The information about students' responses helps the instructor to adjust his presentation to the level of his audience, thus providing a substitute for the "live" responses he might get in a small classroom. Student test responses can inform him about common misconceptions and misunderstood points, as well as about points which got across well. The instructor then need only revise those points which students fail to understand.

Evaluation of a Class or Classes of Instruments

As has been pointed out repeatedly (e.g., see Hovland, Lumsdaine, & Sheffield, 1949, p. 5), conclusions from an evaluative study of a single instrument apply only to that particular instrument, and the generalization of the results to other instruments of the media it represents have, at most, the status of untested hypotheses. Many studies based on measuring the effects of a single instrument, such as a film, have unfortunately had the purpose of wider generalizability rather than the limited technological purpose of evaluating a single product but nevertheless have conformed to the pattern for the more specific technological studies and have had the same limitations on generalizability. In the extreme case, it should be obvious that the effects of a single film cannot be used to "determine the utility of films as educational devices."

Roshal (1960) has delineated two broad classes of studies which, it is contended, have dominated all too much of the history of research on instructional films. These involve evaluative studies in which the permissible conclusions are really limited to the evaluation of the particular film or set of films studied, but which were conducted for the broader purpose of evaluating the capabilities of films in general. Roshal's characterization may be generalized to other instructional media, including instructional television presentations, which comprise loosely defined, broad classes of instructional instruments or materials. Often these have been grouped together as particular media on the basis of some class property which has historical significance, or which characterizes a production or distribution process but which does not define their specific instructional-stimulus properties.

As in the case of experiments on single instruments, these studies are often "controlled experiments" in that the paraphernalia of control groups, pre- and postmeasurements, and the like are introduced. Sometimes the methodology of measurement or experimental design is impeccable, ingenious, or both. Whether this was the case in a given experimental demonstration obviously affects the tenability of the direct conclusion that the particular instructional instrument tested did or did not produce the learning claimed by the experimenter. But whether this was true or not, the experimental results contribute little, as such, to our knowledge of the specific instructional factors that may have been responsible for the observed effect, and thus, per se, they add next to nothing to a science of instruction.

One class of evaluative experiments identified above seeks to compare the merits of two media or classes of media, or to compare a given medium or device with something loosely defined as "conventional methods." The latter has usually meant some unspecified combination of presentation by some instructor, plus perhaps some unspecified use of some text or other study material. The crucial weakness of such experiments has been characterized by Roshal (1960). In the case of comparisons involving the instructional film, he pointed out that "it was *some* film, not the best possible film nor a representative (in the sampling sense) film but *some* film compared with some other instruction; not the best possible teacher nor a representative teacher, but *some* teacher" and that "neither the film nor the compared medium is specified analytically or chosen by a sampling technique which lends itself to determination of an estimate of error" (p. 115, italics added) so that little or nothing can be concluded that permits any scientifically useful generalization to be drawn.

A similar type of study, most often conducted when a device or medium is introduced, may be called the evaluative demonstration experiment. It asks, in essence, the questions, Can films teach? or Can television teach? or Can device X teach? More specifically, it may go on to inquire, Can medium X (or device type Y) be used to attain a specific class of instructional outcome? Thus, can X teach motor skills, teach factual information, produce changes in opinion, etc.?

The status of this kind of study has been described as follows:

For example, a study may be done to determine the effectiveness of films in teaching a particular subject, such as general science. Even if an adequate sample of existing films of this type were used and compared with an adequate sampling of other instructional devices, the conclusion would apply only to *existing* films of this type and would not determine how effective such films *could* be (Hovland, Lumsdaine, & Sheffield, 1949, p. 6).

Nevertheless, a seemingly endless series of studies falling in one or the other of these two classes has been conducted and reported. Studies documenting that films can teach this or that were reviewed at length by Hoban and Van Ormer (1950), who also summarized numerous studies presenting evidence that a particular film was shown or failed to be shown superior to some alternative instruction in terms of some level of confidence. More recently, Allen (1960) has marshaled extensive citations of similar results not only for films, but also for instructional television and other forms of audiovisual presentation.

No attempt will be made here to describe or even to cite most of these experimental demonstrations that "X can teach," that "X can teach A," or that "X_1 taught a bit more than Y_1" while "X_2 taught a bit less than Y_2," though "X_3 and Y_3" were not shown to differ significantly (regardless of whether X was a film, a television lesson, or the use of some other instructional medium or device). In the case of films, television, and related media, the interested reader can refer to the reviews by Allen and by Hoban and Van Ormer. A few comparisons of this type have been cited elsewhere by the writer (Lumsdaine, 1960, pp. 91–92), who also character-

ized the status of such device-device or media-media comparisons as follows:

Comparisons between existing devices, procedures, or media that represent mixed aggregates of characteristics can be useful as a
basis for making a specific, practical choice
between two existing alternative devices or
sets of material. It seems apparent, however,
that most such "evaluative" comparisons are
not likely to improve our understanding of any
one of the several specific factors that happen
to have been thrown into any one "pot" (device), nor to give us a valid basis for deciding
what characteristics future devices should
have. . . .

The inherent weaknesses of such media-vs-
media or device-vs-device comparisons have
long been recognized as relatively unproduc-
tive in terms of any direct scientific contribution (Hovland, Lumsdaine, & Sheffield,
1949, pp. 120–121, and pp. 179–181; Lumsdaine, 1953, pp. 85–90). Little can be contributed to the applied science of human learning by adding to the already large number of
so-called "evaluational" experiments that have
been conducted to try to compare "media" or
"device types."

These past experiments have, all too often,
been foredoomed to failure (so far as any permanent scientific contribution is concerned).
Though sometimes . . . painstakingly executed
experimental designs were used, the *things compared* represented *undefined or adventitious
combinations of characteristics*. It was thus impossible to isolate the specific factors to which
any differences obtained could be unambiguously attributed (Lumsdaine, 1960, pp. 91–92,
italics added).

Can device-versus-device, media-versus-
media, or media-versus-"conventional" experiments ever have utility? As a basis for
scientific generalizations, no. Their utility as
a basis for choice between two existing alternatives has been indicated above, but the
logic and consequences of this basis for decision are exactly the same as if the choice is
merely between two specific representations
of the *same* medium—i.e., the question, Is
Filmstrip A better than Film B? does not

differ in scientific status from the even more
obviously ungeneralizable question, Is
Smith's film (A_1) better than Brown's film
(A_2)?

Under certain circumstances, comparison
of two nonanalytically defined media may be
defended, despite the foregoing, but primarily for purposes other than that of providing
scientific generalizations. These purposes
may be propagandistic, in the interest of gaining support for more incisive research and
development, or may represent other heuristic aims, such as testing the worth of a general approach before proceeding; or to provide *experiences* or hypotheses about specific
factors that may be a useful background for
planned future experiments; or to establish
that a sufficient range of effects can be
achieved, to insure that a methodology can
profitably be further pursued along similar
lines; etc.

However, it can be contended that such
media-versus-media experiments are justified
only under rare circumstances which could
include meeting all five of the following conditions.

First: Either:
   a. There is a very confident a priori basis
      for expecting that a new medium, X,
      will show sizable achievement that is
      grossly superior (not just reliably supe-
      rior in terms of a statistical-significance
      criterion) to some other medium, Y (or
      to some aggregate of "conventional"
      procedures); *or*
   b. There is a firm basis for expectation,
      based on prior estimates of the potency
      of X and Y *and* of the sensitivity of the
      measuring instruments that, where X
      is considerably and consistently cheaper
      than Y, X will show a *somewhat* supe-
      rior achievement to Y at a significant
      confidence level; *or*
   c. X and Y have a considerable and con-
      sistent difference in cost, and there is
      some defensible basis for stipulating that
      a difference of less than a specified
      amount on a standardized criterion

measure is of less importance than the difference in cost.[6]

Second: Either:

   a. X and Y are both represented by a reasonable sampling of instances X_1, X_2, . . . X_N from a well-defined population class; *or*

   b. Y is thus represented in sampling terms, and X is defined analytically so as to specify its properties, and/or the principles it is designed to embody, in generalizable form. (A necessary condition for this is that, were X and Y *both* so defined, comparison of X and Y would constitute a scientific experiment to test a hypothesis concerning a single, specified characteristic with respect to which they differed.)

Third: The status of the experimental comparison as an evaluative comparison is clearly recognized and its lack of generality is explicitly stated.

Fourth: The propagandistic or other heuristic purpose of the experiment could not be served as well or better (1) by a less expensive method, or (2) by some alternative (such as rational argument) less likely to invite spurious generalization of the results, or (3) within feasible limitations of resources, by an analytic experiment capable of yielding generalizable findings about the operation of specific variables.[7]

Fifth: No similar experiment involving substantially the same media comparison (e.g., television versus live instruction) has been performed which is substantially the same in purpose, concept, general method, and class of training outcome, despite differences in specific subject matter, branch of government or other institution conducting the experiment, or other such adventitious factors. Application of this condition would, for example, counterindicate all or nearly all of the recent "television-can-teach" experiments after the *first* one.

It can be recommended that evaluative media-media comparisons not fulfilling all five of these conditions be largely, if not wholly, discontinued in favor of experiments employing controlled variation of specific factors (see below). Even if there are other extenuating circumstances under which such media comparisons might be warranted, this proscription would probably do much to improve research in the study of instructional media. Much, indeed, could have been accomplished had such a proscription been enforced during the decade 1949–1959.

Because of the restrictions on generality that apply to evaluative studies, only two studies, dealing with the newer, self-instructional media, will be summarized. The first of these studies (Porter, 1959) was concerned with teaching spelling to elementary school children. Porter used a simple write-in type of teaching machine (see Lumsdaine & Glaser, 1960). The materials were printed as a series of frames on paper fed through the machine, and required the student to respond by writing directly on the sheet through an open window in the machine. The student then moved a lever which moved the paper up one line; this placed the student's written answer under a sheet of transparent plate where he could no longer change it and also exposed the correct answer so that he could check the correctness of his answer before proceeding to the next item. Teaching ma-

---

[6] This condition is seldom if ever realized at present. It may be realized if the difference in criterion score can be directly translated into costs of operational consequences; this translation can hardly ever be made in academic situations and seldom even in operational training. Where this condition is realized, it should, at least in principle, be possible to formulate the problem in a decision-theory paradigm rather than a null-hypothesis rejection paradigm, requiring a rational basis for setting the probability values for both Type I and Type II errors. This amounts to an ability to make valid estimates of the utility of a given achievement outcome (see W. Edwards, 1956, and p. 667 ff.).

[7] See the dual experiment reported by Hovland, Lumsdaine, and Sheffield (1949, pp. 130 ff. and 201 ff.) in which a media-media comparison ("dramatic" versus "documentary" radio programs) was made a vehicle, in a four-program 2 x 2 design, for an analytic experiment on presentation of "one-sided" versus "two-sided" arguments.

terials paralleled, as closely as possible, standard lessons in textbooks used by a conventionally taught control group. The words taught were the same as those taught to the control group.

Spelling programs (see Porter, 1959, pp. 86–87) were used by sixth- and second-grade pupils for about 20 weeks of a normal academic year's work in spelling. Results, measured by standardized achievement tests, showed the experimental group to be "significantly superior" to the control groups at both the second- and sixth-grade levels. For the sixth-grade level, time required for the machine program was reported to be only about a third of the time required for the usual class instruction. Porter's report, however, gives no basis for determining how typical the "conventional" instruction may have been, nor does it indicate whether the significance tests reported took class-to-class variability into account (see pp. 656–658).

Klaus and Lumsdaine (1960) were concerned with the effectiveness of applying self-instructional techniques as supplements to ongoing instruction. Their specific objective was to determine the contribution made to achievement in high school physics by providing self-tutoring materials in the form of programed textbooks. The self-tutoring materials covered approximately six weeks of instruction in the second semester of high school physics and comprised approximately 3,000 individual question-and-answer "frames." Results were appraised with comprehensive examinations administered to approximately 450 students in 15 schools in western Pennsylvania which regularly utilized a filmed physics course telecast daily over station WQED in Pittsburgh. These tests were constructed by an independent agency and were not seen by the program writers until after the programs were completed.

Comparison of results for experimental classes who received the self-instructional materials to supplement the physics course (as compared with control classes who did *not* receive them) demonstrated that the self-

tutoring materials made a significant contribution to the level of achievement of the students. The units of sampling and corresponding units of statistical analysis were intact class groups.

Other Uses of Evaluative Experiments

Despite the foregoing caveats, the measurement methodology and some aspects of experimental design employed in evaluative studies are often useful in studies which employ controlled variation of specific factors. In addition, the analysis of effects on individual points of content, associated with particular features of presentation in the instrument being studied, can frequently provide leads concerning the factors at work. Sometimes, indeed, using different techniques several times within a film for specific subject-matter topics provides comparisons, relating size of effect to technique employed, which may represent the best evidence available on a particular kind of presentation.

Examples are found in the detailed evaluative studies by May and Lumsdaine (1958) of science films on osmosis and the causes of seasonal change, and in the orientation-film evaluation studies by Hovland, Lumsdaine, and Sheffield (1949). In these cases the results were not limited to over-all assessment, but included analyses of the specific effects associated with various points of content within the films. Comparisons between large and small effects generated for different aspects of the subject matter by contrasting techniques are correlational in the sense that they only permit statements of the form, "That which was presented by technique X yielded larger measured effects than that which was presented by technique Y." However, such statements, though correlational in nature, should be distinguished from correlational findings of the "those who" type, previously mentioned, which only show a relationship between the effects produced on different groups of persons. The "that which" statement at least involves an association between contrasting techniques, whereas the "those who" statement only shows an association of outcomes which may have been due entirely to predisposing factors.

Although correlational associations relating technique to size of effects are obviously less desirable than controlled manipulation of content, they are fairly efficient as a source of leads about the value of alternative techniques. This is particularly true when contrasting findings about size of effect are found within a single experiment on the effects of a particular instrument. Here the audience is constant, and at least it cannot be disputed that the difference in size of effects is associated with some difference in presentation technique or aspect of subject matter. Even though the presentation technique and subject-matter differences are, strictly speaking, confounded, gross differences in effects can suggest plausible hypotheses about the effects of contrasting presentation techniques. (See Hovland, Lumsdaine, & Sheffield, 1949, Chs. 2 and 3, for examples.)

It should also be noted that in some instances it is possible to produce minor experimental variations on several different points within a study originally designed for evaluation. Thus, within a single instrument involving a range of subject-matter items which can be regarded as substantially independent, one can conduct several "little experiments" by varying the technique of presentation of specific aspects of subject matter. Sometimes, also, it is possible to make "experimental" comparisons where the difference lies not in the instructional materials but rather in the test used. An example is found in May and Lumsdaine (1958, p. 252), where inferences are drawn concerning the degree of transfer resulting from a particular kind of presentation. The inferences are based on the use of alternative test items that required different degrees of transfer from the kind of depiction used in the instructional instrument.

Analyses of this type may considerably extend the usefulness of data from evaluation studies, and thus might seem to counterindicate the proscription proposed above. How-ever, such analyses can also be conducted using data from experiments of the controlled-variation type, in which, as argued below, the over-all comparisons provided also make potentially useful contributions to a more rigorously documented body of generalizable principles. The fact that something valuable can be salvaged from the data of evaluative studies thus should not necessarily imply that they be conducted, but only indicates the potential value of the data they may sometimes yield when the data can be analyzed for purposes other than over-all comparison.

CONTROLLED VARIATION OF SPECIFIC FACTORS IN DESIGN AND USE OF INSTRUCTIONAL MEDIA

The Study of Specific Factors

If the arguments of the preceding section are accepted, it becomes clearer what kinds of experiments are most needed to construct a usable science of instructional media. What is needed are experiments which seek to reveal the influence of specific factors in the design characteristics of the media. These factors should define reproducible stimulus and response characteristics that can be implemented in future instructional materials and devices. In this way we can obtain experimental data to support the validity of generalizations on which to base future design decisions about media.

It can well be argued also that the precision and applicability of experimental findings are likely to be augmented to the extent that the specific factors chosen for manipulation are defined in terms of theoretically oriented variables, and not solely in terms of gross physical characteristics of instructional media. As pointed out by Hovland, Lumsdaine, and Sheffield (1949, p. 8), definition in terms of theoretical variables seems likely to afford a better base for generalization of results and is also likely to identify variables which have a consistent influence on the outcomes of instruction.

Emphasis on manipulation of single, defined factors in experimentation is not meant to minimize the importance of interactions or cumulative effects of several variables; quite the contrary (see below). But such interaction effects can be established only through analytic experiments in which each specific factor is independently covaried, not through over-all comparisons of an aggregate of factors.

It is, of course, true that it is not always easy to recognize which variables should be regarded as elementary or primary. Thus, results of an experiment on the effects of a single procedural element may have to be refined by further experimental analysis to isolate the primary factors at work. This will be illustrated presently. It should also be recognized that in some instances there may be a tactical advantage in confounding several theoretically related factors in an initial experiment in order to maximize the chances of establishing a palpable effect on instructional outcomes before proceeding with further attempts to isolate more specific primary variables. This tactic might insure a favorable experimental setting for more refined analysis, including adequate sensitivity of measurement to make more precise experimental definition worth while.

Studying the influence of specific factors in instruction by the method of controlled variation should be sharply contrasted with attempts to study such influences by comparing classes of instruments. For example, if the question were, Which is more effective for a particular educational purpose, color film or black-and-white film?, the specific factor or variable would be the presence or absence of color in the film. Such a question *could* conceivably be attacked by collecting examples of color and black-and-white film, trying to assure that they are "comparable" in other respects, and comparing one group of films with the other to determine their "relative effectiveness." As stated by Hovland, Lumsdaine, and Sheffield (1949, pp. 6–7), "The results of this mode of attack have doubtful generality. At best, they could only give the typical effects of the variable as usually employed; when the sampling of films [or other instruments] is small, as is usually the case, even this conclusion cannot be drawn."

The effects of a particular variable should, instead, be studied by manipulating the variable experimentally by controlled variation. This requires constructing or obtaining alternative versions of a particular instrument, which differ only with respect to the specific factor under investigation. Two general classes of such experiments can be distinguished—experimental investigation of a single variable by controlled variation, and experimental analysis of two or more variables in combination.

Variation of a Single Factor

In this approach, all factors are held constant except the one being investigated. This requires the use of two presentations, e.g., films, which have exactly the same content but differ with respect to the specified variable. An example is the use of a color film and an achromatic print of the same film to investigate the effect of color. Here, the experimental and control forms of the instrument are constructed so as to be comparable with respect to all factors except one. In the case of many variables, however, it may be difficult to achieve comparability with respect to all variables except one, because differences in content are likely to be associated with differences in technique of presentation.

Even when such difficulties are overcome, a major problem arises in drawing useful conclusions from studies in which only one factor is varied, because of the difficulty of assuring an adequate basis for generalization of the findings. Inherently, experiments which manipulate only a single variable without respect to other variables fail to take account of the possible interaction of the experimental variable and other factors which might influence its operation. For example, the use of color might be an aid to learning under some conditions and not under others, or the effectiveness of review procedures might depend on the characteristics of the original presentation. An unqualified conclusion drawn from a single-variable study thus ordinarily needs to be checked with a variety of instruments and under a variety of conditions before its generality can be determined.

Experimental Analysis of Two or More Variables in Combination

The case for multivariable experimentation is stated by Hovland, Lumsdaine, and Sheffield as follows:

As suggested above, it seems likely that with the complexity of variables present there would be few empirical generalizations that would hold up for all educational films, all audiences, and all conditions for using the films. Variables would be expected to interact so that the effects of any one variable would have to be differentially designated according to the accompanying variables. Accordingly, the result of an attempt to determine the generality of a conclusion about a single variable would lead to a series of principles rather than a single principle.

Because of this likelihood, the type of research that will probably result in the broadest generalizations for the field of educational films and related media is research studying the controlled variation of several variables in combination. The qualifications on the generalizations are thus determined, and generalizations may be stated in the form: "Under condition A, result 1 is obtained, whereas under condition B, result 2 is obtained" (Hovland, Lumsdaine, & Sheffield, 1949, p. 8).

A number of the experiments subsequently discussed involve simultaneous variation of two or more factors to afford a basis for this kind of contingent generalization. As noted by Lumsdaine (1953), however, such variation need not involve highly complex experimental designs. One of the simplest designs— the so-called "2 × 2" factorial design—is especially attractive because it provides an economical basis for observing the effect of a given variable under each of two conditions with respect to another variable.

Classes of Independent Variables

The categories of independent variables used in experimental analysis can be classified in a variety of ways. One useful classification, introduced by Hovland, Lumsdaine, and Sheffield (1949), distinguishes among population variables, film variables, and external variables. Population variables are "sorting" variables reflecting characteristics of the students (e.g., intelligence, age, and previous knowledge of the subject matter), and thus are not capable of experimental variation. Nevertheless, manipulation of characteristics of instruction through creation of two versions of a film, for example, can be studied in relation to population variables so as to obtain information about the generality of the results for two or more subgroups of the population.

Film variables, or media variables, more generally, usually included among the primary variables in an experiment, may relate to either content or manner of presentation, or both. "External variables" may be manipulated, either singly or in interaction with media variables, so as to reveal the effects of these variables as such, or to investigate their influence on the effects of media variables. Such variables may include conditions of use, special instructions given in conjunction with the teaching, physical conditions, and the like. In addition, time can be considered an external variable when, for example, it represents the interval between instruction and testing, and thus permits assessment of the effects of a particular media variable (or another procedural variable) not only in terms of retention immediately after completion of the instruction, but also after a longer period.

As will be noted in relation to procedures for fostering student response to instructional instruments, and also in the case of other instructional variables, a particular instructional characteristic may be implemented either as a media variable or as an external variable. For example, question-and-answer pauses might be provided by the instructor between segments of an instructional film or they might be built into the film. Similarly, attention-directing indicators or pointers might be built into a film by means of overlay animation, or the teacher might perform the pointing and indicating functions during the showing of the film. Thus, from the standpoint of instructional psychology, some variables may be implemented either as media variables or as utilization variables (external variables) with no difference in their psychological status. Other variables are, however, by their nature, either media variables (e.g., the use of color versus black and white in an instructional film) or external variables (e.g., time of day or room temperature).

Simple versus Complex Experimental Designs

Despite the above-noted emphasis on multivariable experiments, the research methods discussed in this chapter are, in general, relatively simple ones. Although several multigroup experiments are described, highly complex designs have, for the most part, been avoided. This reflects, in part, a prejudice of the writer that, in general, the simpler, more straightforward designs are better calculated, in the present state of the art, to reveal important causal relationships. A carefully formulated problem—though it may deal with different effects of media variables as a function of other variables (such as differences in the intelligence of the learner or in the conditions of use)—generally leads to a relatively simple design affording a few specific comparisons. The author feels that such experiments have generally been more productive than "shotgun" multifactorial experiments that are less sharply focused on specific hypotheses.

Similarly, highly complex analyses, including analysis of covariance, are not stressed here. Granted the necessity of employing these refined and laborious methods on occasion, their use may often be occasioned by the fact that the experiments to which they **are** applied were not cleanly designed or

properly conducted in the first place. Frequently, more attention to the simpler aspects of design and, in particular, to proper randomization in the design of an experiment will obviate the need for highly refined methods of statistical analysis.

In any event, the primary purpose of this chapter is to contribute to a sound orientation toward *fundamentals* of research technique in the experimental study of instructional media. This purpose may be better served if the methods discussed are not obscured by complex analyses which most students will have to accept without genuine understanding. (For an amusing commentary on this point by an eminent statistician, see Kendall, 1959.)

Methodology and Rationale in This Chapter

The next major section of this chapter presents a survey of selected studies on the effects of instructional instruments of various media, primarily audio-visual media. This survey is devoted primarily to a picture of the current status of research on a variety of problems and, in general, does not deal intensively with details of methodology. In addition to indicating major research problem areas and findings, however, this survey is also intended to provide a background for a more systematic identification of methodological problems enumerated subsequently. In some instances, however, for the sake of convenience, methodological points are discussed as they arise in connection with the studies.

Descriptive Categories for Research

Reviews of research on instructional materials have commonly been organized in terms of media categories—films, filmstrips, television, recordings, teaching-machine programs, and the like. The author believes that this organization is less likely to reveal communalities than an organization in terms of the stimulus features and response provisions of instructional sequences, regardless of the mechanics of presentation of a given sequence. Accordingly, the present survey is organized in terms of stimulus and response features of an instructional sequence, however presented. Thus, for the most part, we shall deal with the specific physical media used in producing or disseminating instructional material only as they have an explicit bearing on describable stimulus and response variables.

Some illustrative categories of research on the effects of specific factors or variables in instruction, to be considered below, include: (1) techniques for elicitation of active learner response and its role in learning from sequenced instruction; (2) methods for guiding and prompting learner responses; (3) the character of response required of the learner; (4) knowledge of results, feedback, and reinforcement; (5) the organization and content of practice, and of repetition and review sequences; and (6) factors of sequencing, rate, and pacing in verbal instruction. An advantage of utilizing psychologically defined categories such as these rather than classifying studies by media is that findings having potential generalizability are brought together, regardless of their source in terms of the particular media utilized in obtaining them.

The results of a particular "study" or "article" have not always been reported in one place within this chapter, particularly where a study deals with several variables and where the results can be treated more meaningfully in relation to a particular class of variables. Thus, some of the results of a study by Michael and Maccoby (1953, 1961) are reported in relation to the importance of active response (Topic 1, above), and other results from the same study are reported in relation to Topic 4 (knowledge of results, feedback, and reinforcement). Similarly, some of the results of a recent study by Coulson and Silberman (1959) bear particularly on the question of response mode and are discussed in relation to other studies bearing on this question, while other data from the same study

are discussed in relation to the organization and "size of steps" in an instructional sequence.

In general, we shall stay within the purview of "training" and "education" studies, directed toward specific problems that enter directly as variables into practical instruction. However, dealing with psychological rather than media categories can also facilitate the introduction of relevant "pure" research on learning from academic psychological laboratories.

STATUS OF RESEARCH AND DEVELOPMENT ON VARIOUS MEDIA

As noted above, the main discussion of experimental problems that follows will be organized in terms of categories of psychologically or pedagogically defined variables affecting learning, rather than grouped in terms of media. Accordingly, to provide perspective in relation to more usual media-oriented discussions, a brief overview of the research which has been conducted using the major classes of media is presented here.

Self-Contained Instructional Presentations

a. Instructional films and related media. By all odds the most extensive experimental research on the effects of instructional media has been conducted with motion pictures. Motion pictures and the sound filmstrip are particularly amenable to research in that they present a sequenced, paced presentation package, complete with visual material (still or moving) and accompanying sound consisting of either dialogue, narration, music, and sound effects, or some combination of these. The earliest studies were necessarily, of course, conducted with silent motion pictures. Research on silent and sound films spans a period of over four decades, from around 1918 to the present. Most of the earlier studies were directed toward evaluation of the effects of particular films as indicative of the educational capabilities of motion pictures; analytic experiments on specific factors did not start to appear in any volume until the period beginning with the World War II studies of Hovland, Lumsdaine, and Sheffield (1949). Those who are interested in the interaction between psychology and education in the development of an instructional technology (see Lumsdaine & Glaser, 1960, pp. 94–98 and 563–572; Melton, 1959) may note that though most of the research conducted during the 1920's and 1930's was carried out by individuals within the field of education, one of the earliest extensive studies (Lashley & Watson, 1922) was the work of two psychologists. Research workers with backgrounds in experimental psychology have also been largely responsible for the increasing number of analytic experimental studies conducted during and since World War II.

A major summary of the research on instructional films from 1918 to 1950 was provided by Hoban and Van Ormer (1950) under the Navy-sponsored instructional film research program at Pennsylvania State University. (See Lumsdaine, 1953, 1, 176–184.) Roughly two-thirds of the Hoban and Van Ormer volume was devoted to evaluative studies and approximately one-third to analytic studies of specific factors. Later reviews have concentrated more heavily, though not exclusively, on analytic studies. Several major programs of intensive research on the characteristics of instructional films have been carried out since 1940. The first of these is the series of studies conducted in the Information and Education Branch of the Office of the Chief of Staff of the War Department during World War II and subsequently reported by Hovland, Lumsdaine, and Sheffield (1949). The latter report can be considered a major resource on experimental research on the effects of instructional films.

Another sizable program of research, conducted at Yale University from 1946 to 1949, was subsequently reported in a volume by May and Lumsdaine (1958) which also represents a major reference. The most extensive single program of experimentation dealing with instructional films was that conducted under sponsorship of the Office of Naval Research at Pennsylvania State University, under the direction of C. R. Carpenter, between 1947 and 1954. This work, which dealt with a wide range of film topics, experimental variables, and types of experimental design, has been reported in more than 50 mimeographed reports issued by the U.S. Naval Training Device Center and available from the Office of Technical Services, U.S. Department of Commerce. These mimeographed reports were later collected in two bound volumes (*Instructional Film Research Reports,* and *Instructional Film Research Reports,* Vol. II), issued by the same organization, although no summary of them has as yet appeared in a regularly published, widely available volume.

A fourth major program of research was conducted through an in-service and contract program of the U.S. Air Force, under the direction of A. A. Lumsdaine, from 1950 to 1953, and was continued, less intensively, in the context of research on other forms of training aids and devices, from 1954 to 1957. Reports on this work, in addition to a number of journal articles and papers presented at professional meetings, have thus far been largely confined to mimeographed reports of limited circulation, issued by the Air Force Personnel and Training Research Center and predecessor organizations. (See Lumsdaine & Glaser, 1960, pp. 574–579, in regard to the availability of these and related government reports.) A central group of these Air Force studies, dealing with active student response procedures used in conjunction with instructional films, has been edited for publication under a project sponsored by the National Research Council (Lumsdaine, 1961b). A number of the analytic experimental studies discussed below derive from this Air Force research program.

Abstracts and summaries of a number of the studies conducted under the Navy Instructional Film Research Program at Pennsylvania State University and under the Air Force program have appeared in the *Audio-*

Visual Communication Review and in *Contemporary Psychology*. Some of the findings have also been discussed in other works, of which the three principal ones are the volume by N. E. Miller and his associates (1957), an excellent summary by Cook (1960), and the readily accessible, less theoretically structured, summaries by Allen (1956, 1960). The summary by Cook and the second part of the report by Miller and his associates, dealing systematically with specific variables, are both organized in terms of factors grouped under the headings of "Drive," "Cue," "Response," and "Reward." The Allen summary employs the major headings of "Effectiveness of Audio-Visual Materials" (evaluative studies of motion pictures, television, and other audio-visual media), "Audience-Learner Characteristics," "Characteristics of the Learning Environment," and "Instructional Use of Audio-Visual Materials," with most of the studies of specific variables summarized under the first, second, and fourth of these topics.

b. Audio instruction. Relatively little research has been conducted using purely audio presentation, although a considerable number of the research studies on audio-visual media have used transcriptions or tape recordings as accompaniments to a sequence of visual materials presented by filmstrip, by a series of slides, or, occasionally, by booklet materials, (e.g., Kimble & Wulff, 1953; Newman & Highland, 1956). Somewhat wider use has been made of purely audio materials in studying the variables underlying the effectiveness of persuasive communications—for example, the reports by Hovland (1957), Hovland, Lumsdaine, and Sheffield (1949, Ch. 8), Hovland, Janis, and Kelley (1953), and Lumsdaine and Janis (1953). An interesting series of experiments dealing with utilization of electronic speech compression techniques was reported by Fairbanks, Guttman, and Miron (1957a, 1957b, 1957c). These attempted to improve the effectiveness of audio-recorded instruction by compressing more information into a given period of time.

Some pilot experimentation on the use of audio-recordings for on-the-job instruction was reported by Hoehn and Lumsdaine (1958). Also to be noted is the literature dealing with recordings for language instruction, including their use in the "language laboratory." Almost all of this literature, however, is of a descriptive sort, and hardly any controlled experiments on specific factors governing the effectiveness of the instruction are to be found as yet.

c. Instructional television. The rapidly growing literature of experimental studies on instructional television is similarly loaded with descriptive articles, with several very detailed accounts of "experimental" programs introduced into school systems by closed-circuit or open-circuit television. In many instances, no data are presented other than information about the content of the lessons, cost factors, etc. However, a considerable number of experimental evaluation studies have also appeared.

Interesting accounts of the development and utilization of techniques for televised instruction in the military services are presented in the series of articles by Kanner and others (e.g., Kanner, 1960). Major reports of the development of televised instruction in public schools and colleges include reports of the experiments at Hagerstown, Maryland (Weiss, 1957), Pennsylvania State University (Carpenter & Greenhill, 1955, 1958), San Francisco State College (1958a, 1958b), Los Angeles City School Districts (1959), and the National Workshop (1959).

A number of analytic experiments on specific factors in instructional presentation by television have been initiated under projects supported by Title VII of the National Defense Education Act. At the time of writing, relatively little has been published on results of these studies. Gropper and Lumsdaine (1961) have reported a series of experiments oriented toward the importance of (1) methods of lesson preparation and try-out, which can utilize student responses as a basis for revising a television lesson; (2) methods of eliciting active student response during instruction to increase the efficiency of learning;

and (3) methods of encouraging student follow-up activity as a manifestation of active interest in the subject matter stimulated by the television presentation.

d. Self-instructional programs and devices. It should be emphasized that the control of learner behavior and feedback which is provided by the continuous record of student response from auto-instructional programs may afford the most promising vehicle yet developed for the analytic experimental study of variables affecting human learning (as well as for the incorporation of research findings in improved instruments). In view of this possibility, it is somewhat disconcerting that relatively few analytic experiments in self-instructional learning programs have thus far been published. These experiments are summarized in the following pages, along with experiments in other research enterprises that throw light on similar problems.

Evaluative research aimed at product improvement is an inevitable concomitant of the development of auto-instructional materials if one accepts the position adopted by most workers in this field. Several examples of such empirical development of materials in which student responses to self-instructional frames were used as a basis for program sequence revision have been reported. Thus, Meyer (1960) and Klaus and Lumsdaine (1960) made immediate, cumulative revision based on a relatively small number of cases. Holland (1960b), on the other hand, obtained responses from a considerably larger group to an already completed program, which was later revised on the basis of his data. In the study by Klaus and Lumsdaine, step-by-step revision was based on misconceptions discovered in the responses of even a very few students. This procedure permitted a cumulative revision which, in some instances, might be more useful in product development than a longer-deferred, larger-scale study.

Use of student-response data as a basis for product revision should be distinguished from the collection of more extensive data for over-all assessment or evaluation of the product. In the study by Holland, extensive response data for a considerable population of students actually served both purposes—program evaluation and program revision. On the other hand, in Holland's work, the data reported were limited to student responses to the program itself rather than responses to an independent criterion test, as in the evaluation reported by Klaus and Lumsdaine, and thus cannot be regarded as an independent assessment of the program's effectiveness.

Adjunctive or Nonprogramed Materials

As indicated previously, materials such as graphic aids, charts, the chalkboard, isolated slides, models, and mock-ups lend themselves to experimental research only if they are considered elements that are integrated, sequenced, and governed by an instructor's presentation, recorded or otherwise. (Several studies of such presentations are mentioned below in relation to specific variables studied experimentally.) When visual aids are used in this integrated fashion, there is some evidence to indicate that their contribution can easily be exaggerated (see Swanson, Lumsdaine, & Aukes, 1956). An analysis of types of mock-ups, models, and other graphic aids used both as self-contained training devices and (with appropriate programing) as aids to lectures has been presented by Lumsdaine (1960). Several attempts to evaluate classes of devices have been made; an example is the study by Torkelson (1954), who compared the effectiveness of a mock-up, a cutaway, and projected charts in teaching nomenclature and equipment function, and found no evidence for large or significant differences among these "classes" of visual aids.

The extensive literature dealing with textbooks (see the summary by Buckingham, 1960) contains, as previously indicated, relatively few experimental studies of effects; empirical research in this field is mostly limited to content analyses and readability studies (e.g., Flesch, 1949) which, in almost all cases, have used correlational comparisons rather than experimental manipulation of a particular piece of instructional content. (In contrast, see the experimental study of the "readability" of film commentary reported by Gladstone, 1958.) The most extensive series of studies in which factors affecting comprehension were experimentally manipulated was that conducted by Klare and his associates (Klare, et al., 1955a, 1955b, 1957, 1959). Controlled reading of text presentation has also been compared experimentally, as a "control" baseline, with "programed" text materials of the self-instructional sort (Goldbeck, 1960; Holland, 1960a).

The other line of laboratory investigation pertinent to the design of textbooks, and other forms of visual materials for instruction, is the study of the legibility of type faces, such as the work done by Tinker and Paterson (1940). This and related lines of investigation dealing with visual display characteristics are summarized in the report by Saul and others (1954) and in a technical memorandum by Stolurow and Lumsdaine (1956); these also deal with a number of other factors, including color and layout in the design of graphic training aids.

Nonexperimental research on printed materials was reviewed by Otto and Flournoy (1956) under three headings: (1) analysis of textbook content, including interest factors, textbook presentation and format, and physical layout characteristics of printed materials; (2) textbook uses; and (3) magazine and textbook adoption policies and practices. The main empirical research discussed had to do with factors in readability and legibility. (See also Buckingham, 1960.)

Characteristics of Capital Equipment

Some instructional materials require capital equipment (in the form of projectors, transcription players, response-registering equipment, and other apparatus) in order to be converted from inert material into functioning instructional media. Hence, experimental research on the characteristics of this associated equipment would appear to be a legitimate concern. In some instances the functional characteristics of the media are intimately bound up with specific features of the presentation equipment, as has been noted previously. With a few exceptions, however (e.g., Ash & Jaspen, 1953), relatively little experimental research has been devoted directly to the functional or physical characteristics of equipment. Implications for functional characteristics of start-stop, daylight loading, automatic-threading film projection equipment emerge (see Lumsdaine, 1959c) directly from some of the studies by Maccoby and Sheffield (e.g., 1958) and others on alternate film demonstration and practice, though these studies were not aimed directly at determining projection equipment characteristics. There is an intimate connection between the content of self-instructional programs and the equipment features related to provision of prompts and, particularly, to response mode and automaticity of feedback in the case of teaching machines. Accordingly, an increasing stream of work has been oriented directly toward the equipment characteristics of auto-instructional methods.

EXPERIMENTAL ANALYSIS OF SPECIFIC FACTORS AND VARIABLES

ACTIVE STUDENT RESPONSE

Concern with active, explicit, student response as an object of experiment stems in part from the emphasis on "learning by doing" espoused by Dewey and elaborated in behavioral terms by Guthrie (1935) and others. Experimental studies of the value of active student response, recitation, "participation" exercises, and the like derive in part from early positive findings of Witasek (1907) and Gates (1917). The further finding of Gates that increasing the proportion of time spent in recitation was more important for learning rote material than for learning from prose should be kept in mind in relation to subsequent experimentation reported below. This finding is also of interest in the light of current concern with programed self-instructional materials that stress overt responding in learning connected-discourse subject matter.

Active, overt student response is of great interest for two reasons: (1) Procedures which foster active student response are generally, though not uniformly, favored by experimental evidence over procedures which do not. (2) More important, overt responses by definition can readily be observed, can be checked and, potentially, can be effectively controlled. The sufficiency of covert or implicit responding to mediate learning effectively is obvious, else no one would gain anything from reading a book without reading it aloud, from watching a film without mimicking its actions, or from listening to a lecture without chorusing echoing responses. But only by getting a response to occur overtly can we utilize its direct consequences to guide the course of learning. For example, it is the overt responses of the student which are utilized by a good tutor or coach to regulate instruction so that the right response gets made, to guide its elicitation, to provide specific, unit-by-unit reinforcement for successes, and to initiate prompt redirection of error tendencies.

Effectiveness of Overt Active-Response Procedures

Allen (1957, 1960) has summarized a number of studies in which active student response was used in conjunction with presentation of content by films. Studies summarized by Allen include those of Ash and Carlton (1951), Gibson (1947), Hovland, Lumsdaine, and Sheffield (1949), Jaspen (1950), Kurtz and Hovland (1953), Michael and Maccoby (1953, 1961), and others. The results and conclusions of the studies are reported by Allen pretty much as presented by the authors and are summarized under the headings of verbalization of response, perceptual motor responses, knowledge of results, mental practice, and note taking. The follow-

ing discussion extends Allen's by analyzing some of these findings in more detail and by presenting the results of additional studies.

The potential advantages of incorporating active-response procedures in instructional media have been studied in a number of experiments performed in military training research. The earliest and most widely cited of these, performed during World War II, was reported by Hovland, Lumsdaine, and Sheffield (1949, pp. 228–246). A film was used to teach the military phonetic alphabet, Able for A, Baker for B, and so forth (plus some related information). Two forms of the film were compared to study the effect of using active review, or so-called "audience participation."

The sole difference between the two forms was in the review sequences which followed the presentation of the letter-word equivalents. The control film used a standard, "passive" form of review, in which letters were presented along with their phonetic equivalents. In the active review, the letters only were presented, and the audience members were instructed to try to call out the correct equivalents for each letter. The fact that the correct equivalents had been recently presented provided the basis for their being emitted during the review. Feedback via further "prompts," confirmation, or correction was provided by the fact that the whole group had to call out each response aloud. Since someone almost always gave a correct answer audibly, prompts were almost always thereby provided for those who had not yet responded, and a form of confirmation or correction was provided for those who responded more promptly.

Data presented by Hovland, Lumsdaine, and Sheffield (also reproduced in Hovland, 1951, and in Lumsdaine, 1959a) showed consistent superiority of the active over the passive group on various criteria of recall-promptness in oral tests given at the end of the training. In connection with a replication of the experiment, Lumsdaine and Gladstone (1958) found that performance for the active group could be raised to near-perfect by increasing the amount of repetition of the response sequences. Further analysis of the data by Hovland, Lumsdaine, and Sheffield showed that the difference in favor of the active-response and feedback procedure appeared to be least where least needed and most where most needed—that is, it was greatest for less motivated, slower students in learning the more difficult portions of the material, and least for brighter, highly motivated students in learning the easier portions of the material.

The replication by Lumsdaine and Gladstone (1958) used the same subject matter but differed in experimental procedure and criterion measures employed. Details of this study are described later (pp. 632–633). The results on active response corroborated the previous findings, indicating superiority for active-response procedure over passive review. (In addition, the results showed that a simple, straightforward verbal presentation of the subject matter was more effective than one in which various audio-visual embellishments had been used in an attempt to make the presentation more interesting and to provide mnemonic associations; see pp. 632–633.)

In these experiments, the subject matter was verbal and the task was a matter of simple one-to-one association between paired terms. Such tasks are of considerable prevalence and importance, as in learning a foreign language vocabulary (see Kopstein & Roshal, 1954, 1961), learning nomenclature, pairing names and faces, matching commodities and prices, etc. Thus, direct application of the method in many practical learning situations is possible, in addition to the more general theoretical interest of the results. The function of active response procedures in insuring explicit rehearsal of correct associations is of increased interest in the light of experimentation performed since the study by Lumsdaine and Gladstone. The applicability of the active-recitation principle has been studied experimentally for film-based teaching of other kinds of tasks, including learning of facts and principles (e.g., Michael & Maccoby, 1953, 1961), procedural

skills such as equipment assembly (Maccoby & Sheffield, 1958), intellectual skills such as reading slide-rule scales (Kimble & Wulff, 1953, 1961b). More important, from further experiments on this kind of procedure has come considerable information on which to base principles concerning specific conditions that influence the effectiveness of active response interspersed in expository or demonstrational instruction. The evidence obtained with respect to several specific variables is discussed in the next section. Although some of these studies have been reviewed by Allen (1957, 1960) and by Cook (1960), many of them have not been available previously outside of government reports with limited circulation. Full reports on a number of these have recently been published, however, by the National Academy of Sciences–National Research Council, in the volume edited by Lumsdaine (1961b). Some of the studies have been concerned with simple rote identification of isolated paired associates, others with acquisition of more complex response patterns.

Time as a Variable

One aspect of the above-cited experiments that deserves comment is the expenditure of instructional time. There are two questions which can be asked about the contribution of a specific factor to learning: First, does it help? and Second, is it a more effective way to spend instructional time than some alternative way? Although the first question may provide useful leads for both theory and practice, even where additional time is spent in introducing an instructional factor, the clearest translation into practical recommendations obviously lies in those cases in which the time factor is explicitly taken into account. This consideration generally involves either showing that a given criterion can be attained in less time by one means than by an alternative means, or that the first means produces a higher level of achievement in a constant period of time than does the alternative. In the experiment by Hovland, Lumsdaine, and Sheffield (1949, pp. 228–246), time was controlled in the latter fashion, since both active and passive review procedures took the same amount of time.

Time allocation for active-response procedures in other experiments has not always been similarly controlled. In a 1946 experiment at Yale University (see Lumsdaine, May, & Hadsell, 1958), for example, use of pupil participation questions, with the correct answer given after pupils had responded, increased significantly the substantive information learned from a film on the heart and circulation of the blood. (It was noted that such devices could be used by producers in making new films, or in revising old ones at very little expense. This and related studies also suggest that, for teaching purposes, more liberal use could be made of titles, questions, and other printed words. As noted by the authors, "There is no reason why the verbal aspect of a teaching film should be exclusively auditory" [p. 82]). These questions, which did not replace any sections of the basic film, added some 4.5 minutes to the film-showing time of 8.5 minutes. However, it was also found that showing the film *twice,* which took about 17 minutes, did not yield appreciably higher scores than the single showing with active-response exercises, which took less time (13 minutes).

A similar situation was encountered in the later experiment by Michael and Maccoby (1953, 1961); substantial gains were obtained by adding student participation questions which, however, also added about 3 minutes to the basic instructional time of about 14 minutes for the subject matter (defense against atomic attack). The primary purpose of the Michael and Maccoby experiment and of several other later experiments was not, however, to show that active student response is effective but to investigate more specific factors which, with a fixed amount of time for recitation activity, bear on its effectiveness. (See below.)

Some small-scale experiments, in which the time factor also enters, were reported by Evans, Glaser, and Homme (1959). These experiments included a comparison of conventional textbooks with "programed" texts that sequenced the material in small steps and required active student response at each step. An awkward question for interpretation is posed in some of these experiments by the fact that the somewhat higher mean achievement with the programed materials was accompanied by an increase in the time spent in study. (See p. 664.)

Factors other than time expenditure by students, such as the cost of preparing instructional materials, obviously enter into the total cost of instruction. For example, the disadvantage of a quick, lower-cost production method resulting in less than optimal effectiveness might be offset in part by the introduction of an active response procedure. In this case, the additional instructional time would have to be weighed against the decreased cost of producing the materials. An instance of this kind is found in a study by Duva and Lumsdaine (1956), in which the relatively poor quality of learning resulting from a quick, kinescope method of reproducing an instructional film was offset by introducing student participation procedures; the kinescope version of an instructional film not utilizing student participation procedures was less effective than a superior-quality motion picture version of the film using quality production methods, but this differential was eliminated when relatively brief student participation sessions were added to the kinescope version.

In situations in which total time spent is fixed, the amount of time may also influence the effectiveness of procedures that introduce overt, controlled learner response. For example, a few experiments have been conducted in which students tried to carry out active-practice exercises *during* the showing of a filmed demonstration. Roshal (1949, 1961) used this procedure for some of his experimental subjects while they viewed a film on how to tie knots. The active-practice group did not show a significant increase in proficiency as compared with groups that did not practice actively during the film.

The lack of effectiveness was attributed by Roshal to the fact that the students had insufficient time for effective practice, and that their attention was divided between trying to watch the demonstration and trying to practice tying the knot.

Results of a later experiment by Jaspen (1950) lend some support to Roshal's explanation. Jaspen's experiment was concerned with the influence of several variables on the effectiveness of a procedural film designed to teach the assembly of the breech-block of an anti-aircraft gun. In this experiment, active practice by the students during the film was effective with a version of the film that proceeded slowly enough to allow the students to perform the actions demonstrated and still be able to attend to the demonstration as it proceeded. With a faster-paced film, however, Jaspen's data, like that of Roshal, showed no significant improvement as a consequence of attempted practice during the film showing. These findings are paralleled by those obtained with a different kind of task in the experiment by McGuire described later (p. 618), and have an obvious bearing on the results of Ash and Carlton (1951), who found no advantage for note-taking during a film when notes were collected and tests were administered immediately after the showing. With a film deliberately planned to allow enough time for effective note-taking or with provision for using notes for review, it seems likely that a different result would be obtained.

The feasibility of obtaining gains in instructional effectiveness through active student response has been shown in the case of televised instruction in recent studies by Gropper and Lumsdaine (1961). In one experiment, a 25-minute television lesson dealing with physical, chemical, and nuclear changes was prepared by a science teacher in accordance with a detailed statement of lesson objectives. The same set of objectives was used as the basis for an experimental television presentation covering substantially the same material. It differed from the standard or controlled lesson in that it provided numerous occasions for students to make active, explicit responses as the lesson proceeded, and the sequencing of the lesson was organized to maximize the likelihood that correct responses could be made at each point. The active-response lesson was shown to be significantly more effective in an experiment using six classes at the seventh- and eighth-grade levels.

Half of the children within each class, matched for intelligence, were randomly assigned to one of two rooms. One room received the experimental version of the lesson on a UHF TV channel, and the other received the standard version on a VHF channel. Both versions were telecast simultaneously. In the experimental version, active response was provided for by having the lecturer pause at strategic places in the lesson to allow students time to complete a statement he had begun. Students were instructed to think of the correct completion before the lecturer told them what it was. At other points, incomplete sentences were shown on the screen, and the students were instructed to fill in the missing word or words on blanks that had been distributed to them before the correct answer was flashed on the screen. Instructions thus encouraged anticipation of correct answers as well as competition with the instructor. Observers in the experimental classrooms uniformly reported that the students did, in fact, anticipate answers—that is, they wrote them down before they were flashed on the screen.

Although the content was not as closely controlled in this television experiment as in some of the experiments previously reported, later experiments reported by Gropper and Lumsdaine revealed positive effects of the active-response precedures, even when all aspects of lesson content were controlled except for active versus passive review sequences. Time was also controlled in these experiments, in that the control and experimental lessons both were telecast simultaneously and were of equal duration.

Other studies on the use of active-response procedures have been reported by Hirsch

(1952) and by Kurtz, Walter, and Brenner (1950). These investigations utilized a variety of questioning procedures and provided some further information on conditions that influence the effectiveness of such techniques. Despite these positive findings, the advantages of active, explicit student response are not clear-cut in all instances. Not only have such experiments as those of Michael and Maccoby (1953) and Cook and Spitzer (1960) indicated, for some instructional situations, that "covert" or "mental" responses were as effective, or more effective, than overt responses (see pp. 617 ff.), but also the study by Goldbeck (1960) (see p. 618) found that, for some kinds of material, merely reading passages in which key words were underlined could be at least as effective as having students make the active, explicit response of filling in the blanks mentally or in writing.

Amount of Active Response

Two different questions can be asked about the amount of practice or amount of active response. How much repetition or practice (whether overt or implicit) is enough? What proportion of a constant amount of time should be devoted to active, explicit responding or recitation, as against reading or similar implicit-response activities? The latter was the original question posed by Gates in 1917, and it is disconcerting to find little direct evidence on this question from experiments reported since his time. (Recent studies on overt versus covert or implicit responding have generally compared them in all-or-none fashion rather than varying the proportions devoted to each.)

Gates compared the effectiveness of various allocations of total learning time between merely reading the material and attempted recitation, both for discrete, paired-associates material and for prose or "connected discourse" material. His data, reproduced by Hovland (1951, p. 642), are in Table 1.

Although the amount learned increased

TABLE 1

INFLUENCE OF DIFFERENT AMOUNTS OF RECITATION UPON LEARNING (FROM GATES, 1917)

Percentage of Total Time Spent		Materials Learned	
In Reading	In Recitation	Syllables	Biographies
100	0	65.4	87.8
80	20	92.2	94.6
60	40	99.7	105.0
40	60	105.5	105.5
20	80	137.3	106.8

progressively with increasing amount of time spent in recitation or active responding, the effect was much more marked for the isolated syllables than for the prose material (biographies). In discussing these results, Hovland noted that Woodworth (1938) attributed the relatively slight gains due to active responding in the case of prose material to the fact that, in rereading such material repeatedly, the student is likely to anticipate what is coming and consequently engages in recitation while reading. Such implicit recitation during the course of reading may occur also, of course, even during a first reading if the material is structured, as it is in many auto-instructional programs, so that gaps left in the material could readily be filled in, covertly or overtly, by the learner. The theory of implicit anticipatory responses during reading is not only of great potential importance as a lead to understanding the nature of reading behavior, but is suggestive as an explanatory factor in experiments, later described, in which overt response to auto-instructional programs has been compared with covert or implicit responding (see p. 617).

One unpublished study addressed to this problem included two experiments by Kimble and Wulff (1961a). They used a combination of booklets and tape-recorded instruction to present instruction on reading slide-rule scales. The booklets contained examples which were either accompanied by explanation (expository examples) or required the student to determine the answer (participation examples). After four basic examples were given, the proportion of the remaining 16 examples which were presented as participation examples was varied, for different experimental groups, from 0 to 100 per cent. From the results, the experimenters concluded that the optimal proportion of active-response or participation examples was probably between 50 per cent and 75 per cent. However, differences significant at a satisfactory level of confidence were obtained in the analyses presented by the experimenters only in comparing the 50 per cent and 100 per cent levels of practice, in one experiment, and in comparing 50 per cent and more with 25 per cent or less in the other experiment.

Another experiment, by Kurtz, Walter, and Brenner (1950), compared a larger with a smaller number of questions interspersed in sections of factual content presented by a film, but results for different groups were inconsistent and the results generally inconclusive. The question of optimum frequency of overt response involves the dual question of the relative importance, under various circumstances, of the role of response as (1) a motivational factor, and (2) a factor involving direct practice of a to-be-learned response (see below). These questions are of considerable interest in relation to current philosophies of programing auto-instructional material.

As Lumsdaine (1961a) has pointed out, the approaches to programing associated with Crowder (1960), on the one hand, and with Skinner (e.g., 1958) and his many followers, on the other hand, differ not only in the use of program branching and form of response required, but also in the frequency with which overt responses are required—or amount of explicit response as compared with the implicit responses involved in reading. This difference in response frequency is associated with the difference in the emphasis placed on the two roles of response. In Crowder's programs, the role of response is

primarily one of testing to check on the knowledge which the student is supposed to have acquired through implicit responding in the course of reading a lengthy frame. Skinner and his followers assume, on the other hand, that the elicitation of appropriate overt responses by the student, with explicit reinforcement or confirmation of these responses thereby made possible, are per se a means by which the responses will be learned more effectively.

Direct-Practice Effects versus Side Effects

One objective of the above-cited experiment by Michael and Maccoby was to assess the direct effects of practice versus possible motivational effects that would show up in better attention and hence better learning of material not specifically practiced. Indirect evidence from the original experiment by Hovland, Lumsdaine, and Sheffield suggested that both kinds of effects would operate; that is, the superiority of active over passive review groups was less when added external motivation was provided, by announcing that a test would be given after the lesson, than when the test was not announced. Michael and Maccoby gave practice through use of active-response questions on only half of the material covered in the film. They found marked gains on the material practiced, but no appreciable gains on the other half of the material. (A similar result was found by Kanner and Sulzer [1956, 1961] in a later study using phonetic alphabet material as subject matter.) These results pointed to practice as the key factor. The effect was believed by the investigators not to be limited to wholly "rote" learning, however, since in a later experiment reported by Maccoby, Michael, and Levine (1961) the practice effects held even though test-question wording differed considerably from practice-question wording. A later replication of this experiment reported by these investigators used less interesting subject matter and found gains both on practiced and nonpracticed material for groups who did not have the extraneous incentive of being told they would be tested. The latter gains attributed to motivational or incentive effects tended, however, to be smaller than the direct-practice effects.

One motivational function that may be served by overt practice, especially when accompanied by prompt reinforcing feedback, is that of keeping a student working at the learning task when time spent is on a voluntary basis. This effect obviously cannot be observed in a fixed study-time experiment. Well-controlled experiments on this question are badly needed, even though positive results (more learning through more time spent in study) would raise the complicating question of where the time taken for the added study comes from. If it came from time otherwise wasted, the positive effect would be an important and clearly desirable one. If the added time used were "stolen" from other studies or other essential activities, however, a problem involving difficult value judgments would be brought into focus.

FACTORS INFLUENCING THE
EFFECTIVENESS OF
ACTIVE-RESPONSE PROCEDURES

Form of Overt Response in Verbal Learning

In connection with the design of teaching machines, Skinner (1958) has emphasized his conviction that the learner should compose his answer rather than merely recognize it from a set of alternatives. This position is based on the assumption that there is low transfer from selective to constructive responding and that the presence of plausible distractors in a multiple-choice question will strengthen unwanted responses for some learners. This issue has important consequences for the design of teaching machines because of the much greater difficulty and expense in instrumenting a constructive-answer device that provides automatic answer discrimination. Skinner and others believe the latter to be desirable, even though they have compromised thus far, primarily through using the learner as the comparator in devices for teaching complex verbal subject matter. It should be noted, however, that a straight comparison between existing free-response devices using student-compared answers versus multiple-choice devices with automatically compared answers would confound mode of response with type of feedback.

Two recent experiments have compared constructive and multiple-choice responding. The first of these was reported by Coulson and Silberman (1959), who also introduced experimental variation in the number of steps included in a program, and in the use of branching to vary program content depending on the subject's performance. Constructive-response frames in the teaching program (which was a portion of a Harvard program on behavior) required the subject to fill in blanks in the sentences presented by each frame. For multiple-choice responding, the subject chose one out of the two to five alternatives supplied for each blank. In either case, the correct answer to each item was revealed to the subject after he had responded. Multiple-choice responding took significantly less time (44 minutes on the average) than constructive response (54 minutes). No significant over-all differences were obtained using either multiple-choice or constructive-response criterion tests. However, with a criterion test requiring constructive responses, the constructive-response programs were superior under the nonbranching condition. No analysis was presented to test the significance of this difference as related to the increased time required for constructive responding.

In the second experiment on response mode, reported by Fry (1960), paired-associate materials (16 English-to-Spanish words and phrases) were used rather than continuous-discourse materials. There were three conditions, differing in the way time was controlled, and two criterion tests. Scores on multiple-choice criterion tests (either immediate or delayed) approached perfect for all groups and hence showed no significant differences. The results with constructive-answer criterion tests showed the following significant results for both immediate and delayed tests: (1) under the first condition, working to a criterion of two correct responses at their own rate, students using constructive responses in training did better on the test than those using multiple-choice responses, but the students took considerably more time (14 minutes versus 8 minutes) to finish the program. These results have the same ambiguity as those of Coulson and Silberman. However, (2) when time was controlled by letting students work at their own rate but giving them equal working time (Condition 2), or by arbitrarily keeping time per frame constant (Condition 3), use of constructive answers in training also produced significantly better results than multiple-choice responding.

One other interesting finding bearing on the response-mode problem was reported by Zeaman (1958). For multiple-choice responding in teaching retarded children, he reported better results when only two choices were provided than when three or more were used.

Overt and Covert Responding

In ordinary reading, listening to a lecture, or watching a film, responses are implicit rather than being explicitly evoked by specific questions or gaps which the student is directed to fill in. Experiments dealing with stimulus factors calculated to influence unidentified implicit or perceptual responses are described in a later section (pp. 628 ff.). Explicit responding on cue need not, however, be overt (e.g., written or oral) but can be performed covertly or mentally. In this chapter, the term "covert response" is used to designate response acts which, unlike implicit responding to a text or lecture, are deliberately made as explicit answers to a question or other express invitation for response, but which are not performed overtly. Such responses may serve as active symbolic practice but afford a less clear basis for differential feedback to the student from an instructional program or teacher (and vice versa) than do overt responses.

A second factor studied by Michael and Maccoby (1953, 1961) was overt versus covert responding to the same set of questions. Time allowed for the two kinds of responses did not differ. They obtained no significant difference between the effects of the two kinds of responses, even though the experimental conditions were sufficiently sensitive to detect fairly small differential effects. This finding was confirmed in some later studies (e.g., Kanner & Sulzer, 1961).

A recent small-scale experiment reported in papers by Evans, Glaser, and Homme (1959) compared overt and covert responding to a self-instructional program in music fundamentals. No significant difference in later test scores was found. (Any differences would have had to be quite gross, however, to be significant with the small Ns used.) In this experiment, time was not controlled, and one result cited (though it was also reported as not significant statistically) was that the covert-response group took less time to finish the program. This finding again raises the question of time control from a formal control standpoint. It also suggests the importance of deciding under what circumstances more learning in more time is preferable to faster but less complete learning. The question cannot be answered in this form, of course, but it is not necessarily a trivial question, especially where the time saved may otherwise be wasted and where the more time-consuming program is one which students will voluntarily finish (see p. 664).

In a further experiment, Evans (1960) designed programs to teach the construction of short deductive proofs, employing 15 rules similar to those used in symbolic logic. Several experimental versions of this two- to three-hour program were developed in order to investigate several programing variables, including overt (written) versus covert (mental) responding. Experimental variations in mode of responding significantly affected learning time; subjects not required to make an overt response to each item completed the learning program in about 65 per cent of the time required for composed or multiple-choice responding. Criterion performance in terms of error scores was not significantly affected by differences between overt and covert responding. Subjects who did not respond overtly to learning programs took significantly more time on performance tests which immediately followed the program than did subjects who made their responses overtly. Such differences disappeared, however, in a retention test after one week.

One of the most interesting experiments on covert response was performed by McGuire (1955a, 1961a). As in the above-cited Jaspen experiment, two rates of presentation were used, though rate was better defined in the experiment of McGuire, who compared overt responses with explicitly occasioned specific covert ones rather than overt participation versus no explicit response. McGuire's subjects were given six practice trials in naming mechanical parts that were displayed and named in six presentation trials. The presentations lasted two seconds for each part per trial at the fast rate, and four seconds each at the slow rate. Time for the *practice* trials was constant for all subjects. Overt-responding subjects wrote the names of the parts; covert-responding subjects merely named them mentally. The interesting finding was that, despite the lack of any significant difference for the two forms of responding at the slower rate, *covert* responding was significantly better at the faster rate. One interpretation of these results is interesting: if instruction has not adequately prepared the learner to respond correctly, forced overt responding may lead to distracting anxiety, to practicing errors, or both.

Another recent experiment concerned with response mode in research on auto-instructional devices was conducted by Goldbeck (1960) to determine the effects on learning of three modes of response in combination with variation in the level of difficulty of learning the responses. The three response modes used were *overt response* (students were required to write responses to fill in the blanks in incomplete statements), *covert response* (students were asked to think of the response to fill in the blank), and *implicit response* (there were no blanks, and the student read the key responses, which were underlined). Three "levels of difficulty" were established by varying the cues and prompts given to suggest the response word. (The "better-cued" versions were also considerably longer, however.) The learning material consisted of a series of discrete items, each written to teach a single fact. A total of 63 subjects from two seventh-grade classes completed a learning booklet of 35 "frames" (items) at a self-paced rate of speed and immediately took a quiz of 35 questions paralleling the 35 learning frames. They were randomly assigned to one of the nine cells representing each mode of response at each level of difficulty.

One criterion took time to learn into account. Learning efficiency scores, obtained by dividing test score by learning time, showed that the implicit (reading) response condition produced significantly more efficient learning than the overt-response condition. The covert-response condition fell between the other two conditions with respect to this measure.

A second criterion did *not* take time to learn into account. A statistical test of quiz-score results, using a reading maturity test in a covariance analysis, showed that the overt-response group performed significantly less well than the other response-mode groups at the easy level of difficulty; however, performance of the overt-response group improved significantly at the intermediate-difficulty level to the extent that it exceeded the performance of all other groups. Goldbeck states that these results cast doubt upon the assumption that the best learning is achieved by using easy items and requiring written constructed responses.

Results of recent experiments described by Holland (1960a) and by McCollough and Van Atta (1960) in a symposium at the 1960 convention of the American Psychological Association have also indicated that, with carefully programed continuous-discourse materials, the performance of overt-responding students did not necessarily exceed that of students who read the same material with the blanks filled in. (In Holland's study, performance superior to straight reading was obtained only when the response blanks were chosen to represent the responses considered most relevant and were also well cued so that the student could readily come up with the correct response.) In commenting on these findings, the symposium discussant, F. S. Keller, said that the data must be explained by assuming the occurrence, in the implicit-response version, of covert "textual behavior" and "built-in textual reinforcement." Though such an explanation is necessary to account for the data in S-R learning theory terms, it is obvious that such an explanation will be unsatisfactory to many until a better theory of the functioning of implicit and other forms of covert responding is formulated in a way that can be subjected to experimental test. The experimental results to date certainly indicate the need for further analysis of the conditions under which overt and explicit responding result in optimal learning.

Feedback, Reinforcement, and Knowledge of Results

Despite the voluminous literature on the effects of reinforcement and variations in its scheduling on learning by infrahuman species, relatively few studies have experimentally manipulated reinforcement factors as they operate in practical instruction. Where this has been done, the role of reinforcement as a variable presumed to strengthen directly the effects of immediately preceding practice (in a Skinnerian, Hullian, or Thorndikean sense) has seldom been disentangled from other functions of response feedback. Among these other functions are indirect or cognitively mediated consequences of "knowledge of results." In general, differences in the ways that knowledge of results functions have not been clearly analyzed either, particularly in verbal learning.

In the previously cited experiment by Michael and Maccoby (1953, 1961), half of the groups who were required to give active, explicit responses—overt (written) or covert—after a slight pause for responding, were told the correct answer to the question they had just been asked. This information was termed "feedback" in a preliminary report and "KCR" (knowledge of the correct response) in the reports cited. The other half of the actively responding groups was not given KCR. Instructional time, item by item and over-all, was identical for the two sets of groups. The results showed slight though significant gains for the active-response procedure without KCR, but more marked gains (as expected, of course) when KCR was provided.

The results thus progressed to some degree toward isolation of several components involved in earlier experiments in which feedback was invariably confounded with active response. However, the precise functions of the KCR procedure still were not fully clarified, since, as Michael and Maccoby pointed out, the procedure not only had potentially reinforcing properties (confirmation of initially correct responses) but also provided an opportunity for correction of errors and, in effect, *for an additional implicit-practice trial* in which covert practice of the correct response doubtless occurred. This ambiguity is also present in current use of a correct-answer panel, revealed after the student's response to each frame, in teaching-machine programs where the student serves as his own comparator, as noted above.

Some evidence on the importance of the

latter mechanism is found in the results of Hirsch (1952), who compared several forms of "knowledge of results" in connection with questions posed to students as a participation procedure used with films. Hirsch concluded that there was less effect when students were simply told "Right" or "Wrong" than when the correct answer was also presented. The best results were found when this correct answer was presented in the context of repeating the question—a condition which should strengthen the "added practice trial" function, and stresses the information-feedback rather than the reinforcement-reward aspect of a KCR procedure. The results were far from clear cut, however, because the gains were small and the variability large.

The kind of "feedback" involved here does not seem to be quite the same as the differential feedback provided by the "knowledge of results" in a motor skill. In dart-throwing (Judd, 1905) or in marksmanship, the knowledge of results varies with the degree of correctness or accuracy of the antecedent response, and is used to redirect the subsequent overt practice trial; the immediate perceptual response to this information does not in itself appear to provide a close surrogate for overt practice. Also, the question of whether the kind of KCR or knowledge of results provided in a Skinner teaching machine or through the procedures employed by Hirsch, by Michael and Maccoby, and others, provides *differential* feedback or invariant feedback is not an easy one to answer; the physical stimulus or information provided in giving KCR is the same regardless of whether the student responded correctly or incorrectly, but its interpretation differs in the sense that it is either confirmation or correction. The ambiguous role of KCR-feedback also figures in the theoretical interpretation of experiments on prompting and confirmation, which will be discussed shortly.

Truly differential feedback *is* provided in the teaching-machine programs, such as those of Crowder (1959), which employ branching contingent on each response, through so-

called "intrinsic programing," and also in other devices in which an automatic intra-machine comparator is used, as in several of Pressey's devices (1926, 1927, 1950) and other devices (e.g., Briggs, 1958; Skinner, 1954) which provide automatic answer discrimination. Here the feedback given depends on the response made, and in some cases the difference results in an alteration of the instructional sequence. The same is true in the feedback pattern provided by Rath, Anderson, and Brainerd (1959) in simulating a teaching machine by using a digital computer; any error changes the program, pushing the student back to review antecedent material which, if mastered, should have prevented the error from occurring. (No data were presented by Rath, Anderson, and Brainerd on the effectiveness of this procedure.)

In general, little experimental research seems to have been reported which makes a clear experimental analysis of the factors in the different kinds of response consequences; the tendency seems to be to lump them all under the heading of "Knowledge of Results," "Reinforcement," "Confirmation," or some similar blanket term, potentially confounding several factors. However, one clearer comparison of the effects of the different kinds of feedback provided by Hirsch's experiment has been reported by Irion and Briggs (1957) and by Briggs (1961a). They used a 20-alternative multiple-choice teaching machine called the "Subject Matter Trainer" (SMT) for both paired-associate and serial learning, and employed various modes of training for each task for a fixed period of 20 minutes per task. Several repetitions of the material were allowed, depending on each student's rate of working. In both tasks, giving complete knowledge of results (showing the correct answer after each attempt) was significantly better than giving partial knowledge of results (a mere right-wrong indication).

An earlier study by Stephens (1953) compared three conditions for learning paired associates with a four-alternative multiple-choice device. In one condition, complete knowledge of results was given by using the so-called "Retained" method in which the student keeps trying on each item until he gets the correct answer. This was compared with no KCR and also with partial KCR (giving right-wrong information only before proceeding to the next item). In Stephens' experiment, three trials on each set of material were used, and time required varied with the method used. The "Retained," or trial-and-error, method (full but not immediate KCR) was best, but it also took the longest.

In the better controlled Irion and Briggs experiment, which used a constant time period, the try-till-right method was better than the one-try method (with incomplete KCR: right-wrong feedback only) for serial learning but not for paired associates. Of the two methods of providing full KCR used by Irion and Briggs, identifying the correct answer immediately rather than by trial and error was only slightly (not significantly) superior. The earlier noted consistent superiority of this immediate and complete KCR over *partial* KCR appears to reflect the avoidance of practicing more than one overt error per trial, and of immediately following each overt response by opportunity for correct implicit practice. Even more complete control of errors in practice is afforded by various forms of prompting given before the student makes his overt response to each item. (Experimental data on this kind of procedure is discussed in a following section.)

An experiment by Angell (1949) was designed to determine the effect of immediate and delayed knowledge of quiz results on three types of learning outcome in freshman chemistry: knowledge of facts and principles, application of facts and principles in nonquantitative problems, and application of facts and principles in quantitative problems. Students in the experimental group obtained immediate knowledge of quiz results by means of a punchboard developed by Angell and Troyer (1948). Delayed knowledge of

results was obtained through the use of IBM answer-sheets which were scored and returned to the students at the meeting following the taking of the quiz. Differences between scores on a final examination were statistically significant in favor of the experimental group that used the punchboard and received immediate knowledge of results.

A critical commentary on some related experiments by Angell and Troyer (1948), Little (1934), J. C. Peterson (1931), and Pressey (1950) was presented by Porter (1957). Porter indicated that, in some of these previous experiments, "immediacy of reinforcement of the punchboard groups was not responsible for their *superiority,* but lack of knowledge of results in the control groups was responsible for their *inferiority*" (p. 138). As Porter further pointed out: "A crucial test of the value of immediate reinforcement has to meet the following, so far unattained, criteria: (1) Provide both experimental and control groups with knowledge of results, making sure that both groups receive equivalent information about the correctness of their responses. (2) Reinforce subjects in the experimental group as quickly as possible after a response has been made. (3) Delay reinforcement of the control group" (p. 139).

Guidance, Cueing or Prompting

Prompting to achieve "small steps." A basic principle underlying the design of most teaching-machine programs, as well as other instruction that employs a fixed-sequence program, is that of building up mastery through small, easy steps, so that the learner is kept performing correctly from the outset of training. Techniques by which this can be done in learning verbal material have been elaborated by Skinner (1958) and other writers. Basically, they consist of giving the learner a great deal of help initially through prompting cues, which are gradually reduced or "vanished" to free the learner from depending on them. To date, there is more evidence on the value of prompting as such than on the value of "vanishing."

Prompting just prior to each reponse. An early experiment on the use of semantic prompts in verbal learning was that of Pan (1926), who found that semantic hints indirectly suggesting the response term facilitated paired-associates learning of arbitrarily paired terms. For less artificial tasks, one of the clearest pieces of evidence on the value of partial prompting (response guidance to control errors in practice) comes from a study by Kimble and Wulff (1953, 1961a). They used a combination of filmstrips and workbooks to teach reading of slide-rule scales. Students were given a practice schedule that alternated short practice exercises with short segments of audio-visual exposition and demonstration. Students did practice exercises in workbooks in which slide-rule scales were reproduced. Responses consisted of finding a specified value on the scale. All groups were given the same exposition and the same amount of practice. The main experimental variable was the use of various forms of prompts. For example, when asked to locate a particular scale value, the prompted group was provided with a constraint cue which limited the possible responses, though without specifying exactly the correct answer. By withholding such prompts, the experimenter allowed the no-guidance group to make more errors. (In all cases, the students had already been told how to do a similar exercise.) The results showed a clear margin of superiority for the subjects in the prompted group. They did better, on a later test, not only on the items used in practice but also in transferring to other similar items. The margin of superiority was greater on hard items than on easy ones and was greatest where the prompts had been chosen to help the student avoid the most common types of errors.

Indirect techniques for insuring correct practice. Emeson and Wulff (1957) reported several small experiments to explore the rationale that with difficult learning tasks one must be concerned not only with insuring active practice but with setting up training conditions that will foster appropriate or useful practice. (A later report on this study is given by Wulff and Emeson, 1961.) The former is easy; the latter is difficult. Wulff and Emeson used relatively difficult paired-associate learning tasks requiring students to learn the names of eight electrical circuits. The eight circuits consisted of four pairs, and the members of each pair were almost identical, and thus highly confusable. In an initial experiment, unstructured study by oneself was compared with formalized associate learning procedures in which the circuit diagrams were presented one at a time and the learner selected the correct name from a list of eight; the order of presentation and name arrangement in the list was changed from trial to trial, and an immediate correction procedure used on each trial. Both self study and this formalized paired-associate training were relatively inefficient, but learning was considerably more rapid under conditions of unstructured self study than under the organized paired-associate method. These results, like Newman's (1957), emphasized the necessity of analyzing a learning task and providing appropriate practice and cueing in a formalized set of learning materials, if an attempt to develop and apply a science of teaching is to yield better performance than is attained by the individual's own modes of learning.

Several subsequent experiments also reported by Wulff and Emeson (1961) attempted to throw light on critical factors in the requirements for effective learning materials, so as to improve the basic paired-associate technique. Because of the confusability of pairs of elements, the authors decided that the learner would have to acquire a reliable differentiating cue for each item before he could consistently give a correct name response. The second critical requirement was practice in responding to reliable cues. Accordingly, in one experiment a card-sorting procedure was used, prior to paired-associate training, in which the student sorted the stimulus terms into boxes and concurrently learned a number corresponding to the position of each sorting box. The paired-associate training which followed utilized these number cues. This resulted in considerably better performance, in terms of time required to learn, than simple paired-associate procedures.

In another experiment, two paired-associate procedures were compared, which differed only in that, for one experimental group, the stimulus materials were arranged *in a fixed order* to provide associative support through position cues used during early stages of training. The students using these materials performed better at later stages of practice in which the standard paired-associate arrangement was used (with scrambled order) than did the students who used the scrambled-order arrangement throughout the entire period of practice.

Prompting in procedural and motor learning. Experiments reported by Maccoby and Sheffield (1958) on optimal distribution of demonstration and practice are closely related conceptually to the question of prompting. Their finding (see pp. 625 ff.) that practice immediately following short segments of demonstration was better than deferring practice until a larger section of demonstration had been completed is interpretable as favoring strong (temporally proximal) over weaker (temporally more remote) prompting in the case of procedural skills. The role of coaching in demonstrational teaching of motor skills is further discussed below (pp. 625 ff.).

The "Prompting versus Confirmation" Issue

No other experiments with direct, controlled manipulation of prompts just preceding each response have yet been reported for the learning of meaningful symbolic or continuous-discourse verbal material. However, several experiments on paired-associates training have shown superiority for more complete prompting of responses as compared with nonprompting.

Cook and Kendler (1956; see also Cook, 1961a) used letters as stimulus terms and nonsense drawings as the required responses in comparing training procedures they termed "prompting" and "confirmation." On "prompting" trials they showed the correct response pattern after exposing the stimulus letter but *before* the students were asked to respond to it. On "confirmation" trials, the subject was told to respond before being prompted by exposure of the correct response figure; then, after he had been allowed time to respond, the response pattern was exposed. The "confirmation" procedure thus provided either verification or correction of the response. The condition using prompting trials was clearly superior both in the original experiment and in varied replications reported by Cook (1958) and by Cook and Spitzer (1960) in which, with both procedures, an unprompted and unconfirmed test trial was given by the experimenters after each three training trials. To account for their results, Cook and Kendler proposed a theory that learning individual paired-associate items is, in general, a two-stage process; first the learner learns the unfamiliar response terms as such, and then he learns to associate each of them with the corresponding stimulus term. The authors hypothesize that "this process is mediated by the stimulus properties of the implicit responses S [the subject] makes to the two terms constituting a paired-associate item" (p. 98).

In interpreting the findings of these experiments which favor prompted responses and hence a higher proportion of correct responses during a training program, we should note that the response used in the experiments was fairly difficult to learn (a nonsense drawing which had to be imitated accurately) rather than one (such as learning English equivalents of foreign words) where the response term is already familiar and merely has to be hooked to the proper stimulus equivalent. Another significant aspect of the procedures used in the two later experiments (Cook, 1958; Cook & Spitzer, 1960) illustrates the difficulties of experimentation in which the process of measurement may alter the learning conditions it is designed to assess: the use of test trials interspersed after every three prompted trials in these experiments meant that the prompting procedure was actually a mixture of prompted and unprompted trials (the latter used for measurement purposes, but obviously influencing the total learning program also). Theoretical considerations, however, would suggest that a mixture of prompted trials (to get the correct response elicited) and unprompted trials (to give practice in the unprompted test situation) would be the best condition. This condition was, in fact, actually present in the prompting condition used in Cook's 1958 experiment because of the frequent test trials.

Clarification of the conclusions of Cook and his collaborators (see Cook, 1958, 1961b) is provided in an experiment by Angell and Lumsdaine (1960, 1961). This experiment was aimed at clarifying the results of Cook and others and was an initial investigation of the efficacy of partial or incomplete prompting. (Some further experiments in this area have been reported by Israel, 1960, using variably blurred cues; see also Lumsdaine, 1959b.) In the experiment by Angell and Lumsdaine, incompleteness or partialness of prompting was a matter of the frequency of the prompting rather than of the degree of prompting provided on any one trial. The basic comparison in this case was between two groups, one of which received the prompting on all trials in learning a set of paired associates, and one of which practiced responding without prompting on every fourth trial. The paired-associate learning materials used and intratrial stimulus-response time intervals were substantially the same as those employed by Cook (1958). The results of the Angell-Lumsdaine experiment indicated that learning was more efficient under incomplete prompting (prompting on three-fourths of the trials) than under complete prompting (prompting on every trial). This result accords with the theoretical predictions outlined by Lumsdaine (1959b), and it also contradicts the interpretation, derived from previous studies, that maximum prompting represents the optimal condition.

Interaction of Prompting and Overt Responses

A further experiment was undertaken by Cook and Spitzer to discover some reasons for the superiority of prompting over confirmation that was shown by the Cook and Kendler (1956) experiment and also in a later study by Cook (1958). Using the same materials as were used in these two previous experiments, Cook and Spitzer (1960) employed a 2×2 design consisting of the following four conditions: (A) Prompting—No overt practice; (B) Confirmation—No overt practice; (C) Prompting—Overt practice; and (D) Confirmation—Overt practice. Subjects were 35 male undergraduates per condition. Practice was continued until mastery was achieved. As in previous experiments by Cook and his associates, there was an unprompted test trial after every 3 of the 27 training trials.

The results, in terms of the number of correct items on test trials, bore out the experimenters' predictions that Condition A would be best (because of a short S-R delay and no intervening practice to interfere) and that Condition D would be worst (because of a long S-R delay and because of the interfering effect of overt practice during the S-R delay interval). The relative positions of Conditions B and C were not predicted.

Overt responding and the use of the delay interval (Confirmation Condition) also affected adversely the number of different legitimate responses—excluding duplicates—that subjects produced on test trials. (A "legitimate response" means any one of the response terms used in the experiment, whether it is elicited by its proper stimulus or by some other one.) The conclusions drawn by Cook and Spitzer were that: (1) Overt practice interfered both with learning the response term as such and with connecting it with its proper stimulus; (2) S-R delay interfered with the process of connecting a response to its proper stimulus, but had no consistent effect upon learning the response term as such.

Results favoring straight prompting over confirmation-correction were found in the experiment by Irion and Briggs (1957; see also later report by Briggs, 1961a) using the Subject Matter Trainer. The several previously described methods of feedback following the student's response in each trial were compared to a condition in which direct prompting prior to response was given on all trials. The results showed the prompting condition to be significantly superior to limited (right-wrong) feedback following the response, for both paired-associate and serial learning, and superior to all of the feedback conditions for the paired associates.

Another complicating factor in the support given by these experiments to the use of maximum prompting is that the time intervals used did not preclude anticipatory responding before the prompting cue was given. This objection is somewhat weakened, however, by the results of a study by Kopstein and Roshal (1955, 1961). In learning paired associates (giving Russian names for common objects), they compared simultaneous presentation of S and R terms versus "staggered" presentation in which the response term joined the stimulus term after an interval of about two seconds. Overt responses to these presentations were not required; acquisition was measured by test trials interspersed after every third presentation of the paired terms. The results clearly favored the simultaneous presentation, especially during the early stages of acquisition. The interpretation in favor of immediate cueing to head off incorrect anticipatory responses is not unambiguous but it is certainly suggestive. The authors speculated that the difference favoring the immediate prompting afforded by the simultaneous presentation may drop out or even reverse in later stages of acquisition, but their data do not permit a check on this possibility.

One of the few attempts to study a transition from more prompting early in training to less in later stages in verbal learning was made in a follow-up to the experiment by Irion and Briggs (1957; see also Briggs,

1961a). A prompting condition was followed, for different groups, by each of several unprompted conditions. The lack of significant differences was attributed to the fact that a high level of learning had already been attained by the end of the initial prompted period of practice. Further, no condition was included in which the prompted mode of practice was used throughout. Evidence on the theoretically important question of transition from more to less prompting in verbal learning is thus not provided; see, however, the study by Maccoby and Sheffield (1958) reported below.

Organizational and Sequencing Factors

Several experimental investigations concerning the utilization and design of filmed demonstrations for procedural training were conducted under an Air Force contract at Boston University by Maccoby, Sheffield, and their associates. Most of these studies dealt with methods of interspersing motion picture demonstration and overt practice in serial learning of mechanical assembly or construction tasks. However, the principles utilized and tested in the studies are considered common to any case of complex sequential learning where demonstration is coupled with practice. The theoretical factors involved include the cueing and prompting of correct responses during practice (see above) and the integration and consolidation of elements into total task performance. The experiments also provide some evidence on the question of "vanishing," or reduction in cue supports as learning progresses.

Optimal lengths of demonstration and practice segments. One study by Maccoby and Sheffield (1958, 1961) was designed to test concepts relating to the optimal lengths of demonstration and practice for learning sequential tasks. A filmed demonstration of the assembly of a 30-part ignition distributor was divided into four segments. Each segment had been empirically determined to be a "small step" of such difficulty that approximately 75 per cent of subjects could correctly perform it immediately after seeing it demonstrated. Four training procedures were used. These differed solely in the length of the filmed demonstrations used by the learners before practice. They were (1) short-segment practice, in which the learner viewed a demonstration of one step and then practiced this short segment before going on to the next segment; (2) larger-segment practice, in which the units of demonstration and interpolated practice were two steps in length; (3) whole practice, in which demonstration of a complete task was followed by practice of a complete task; and (4) transition, in which the learner first used one-step practice, then larger-segment practice, and then whole practice. Each procedure was repeated three times, and each required the same amount of demonstration time.

Results were expressed in terms of mean "performance rate" (number of correct assembly responses per unit of time). They showed that the poorest performance, both during practice and on later tests, was obtained when the entire task was demonstrated before it was practiced. In most of the experiments, the best performance resulted when demonstration of a segment was followed by practice of just that segment before the next segment was demonstrated. Results of a related experiment indicated that it was even better to start the students with small demonstration steps, changing to larger steps in later trials. For superior students, the best results were obtained with a self-pacing procedure (Briggs, 1961b; see p. 627, below) in which the student himself regulated the length of the demonstration segment. Under these conditions, the superior students tended to adopt the transitional pattern spontaneously, i.e., starting with short, easy steps on the first trial but ending with the whole practice by the last trial.

Repetitive versus continuous demonstration and practice. Two studies were conducted by Margolius, Sheffield, and Maccoby (1957a, 1957b, 1961a) to compare a procedure in which each of several subassemblies was demonstrated and practiced twice before the student moved on to the next subassembly, with a procedure in which a subassembly was demonstrated and practiced only once by the student before demonstration of the next segment, and then the entire demonstration-and-practice sequence was repeated. The first of these treatments is referred to as Repetitive; the second is called Continuous. Two different mechanical assembly tasks were used. The results obtained with the first task substantiated the hypothesis that learning a lengthy serial task can be facilitated by breaking it into "natural" (contextually similar) units and emphasizing adequate separate practice on the individual units rather than practice of the task as a whole. On the other hand, with the second task, no significant difference between the treatments was noted. In interpreting this result, the experimenters point out that the potential advantages of the Repetitive procedure stem from its tendency to reduce intraserial interference. The second task appeared to be intrinsically well organized already. Hence, there may have been too little room for improvement by minimizing intraserial interference between elements of the separate subtasks. In general, the Repetitive procedure seems to have an advantage, but the extent of its contribution to acquisition is a function of the intrinsic organizational characteristics of the task being demonstrated.

Other Experiments on "Size of Step"

In the first of the Maccoby-Sheffield procedural studies, step size was varied in terms of the length of demonstration before each segment of practice. In this case, the larger segments provide more remote cueing for the steps of the procedure; the steps preceding practice are thus smaller and less difficult. Amount of instructional material was constant. In verbal learning, the "difficulty of steps" has been varied by decreasing the number of steps and thus the amount of instructional material. In a recent study using verbal learning, Evans, Glaser, and Homme (1959) varied the number of steps required to get through programed lessons on number theory. Data for a small number of cases indicated that, with smaller steps, less time per step (though more total time) was required, and fewer errors occurred in the course of the learning. Beyond a certain point, however, increasing the number of steps in a sequence did not seem to result in improved performance.

One other study of long, numerous-step programs (thus those having easier, or "shorter," steps) in connected-discourse verbal subject matter was recently reported by Coulson and Silberman (1959). They also varied "step size" by deleting certain steps from the program to yield fewer steps with larger gaps separating them. Smaller and more numerous steps gave better learning scores, but these results, like those of Evans, Glaser, and Homme, are difficult to interpret because the small-step program (1) provided more practice on varied examples, and (2) took considerably more time.

It is evident from the preceding examples that resolution of the question of "size of step" and number of steps to be used in an instructional sequence involves factors which need to be disentangled. Not only more experimentation, but also better formulation of factors and hypotheses, is needed to permit precise statements about the advantages of "proceeding by small steps" in automated learning programs for verbal learning.

Self-Pacing of Practice

Briggs (1961b) has described a study (also distributed earlier as a mimeographed report by Briggs, Plashinski, and Jones, 1955) in which self-pacing in the presentation of self-instructional materials (the subject works at his own rate, as in the usual teaching-machine situation) was compared with controlled or automatic pacing (in which the instructional items or frames were presented at a fixed rate, determined in advance by the experimenter). Lumsdaine and Glaser

(1960) summarized this experiment as follows:

Two groups of subjects of approximately 30 subjects each were given about 13 minutes practice on a 20-item paired-associate learning task with the Subject-Matter Trainer (see Briggs, 1958), employing the "single-error-permitted mode." For the self-paced group, the number of trials (repetitions of the material) varied from one to seven in the time allowed, depending on the speed at which the individual subject worked. The automatically-paced group received three trials, with the paired associates presented at a fixed 13-second interval. The test scores of the automatically-paced group were not significantly different from those of the self-paced group; in fact, the means for the two groups on a test given at the conclusion of training were almost identical ($t = .23$). However, an interesting finding was that the automatically-paced group was significantly poorer in terms of accuracy on the first practice trial ($t = 5.4$), though this difference washed out on subsequent trials. The authors' interpretation is that it takes a while for a subject to adjust to the automatic, externally-paced procedure (Lumsdaine & Glaser, 1960, p. 592).

It may be of interest to speculate on the relationship of the factor of self-pacing, involved in this experiment and that of Maccoby and Sheffield, to other aspects of pacing or rate in the presentation of material, e.g., the experiment by McGuire (see p. 618, above), and experimentation by Zuckerman (1949) and Fairbanks, Guttman, and Miron (1957a, 1957b, 1957c) on variation in narration rate.

Teaching-Machine Instrumentation

Eigen and Komoski (1960) reported one of the relatively few experiments on specific factors in teaching-machine instruction. The experiment was concerned with the relative effectiveness of mechanical teaching machines and programed textbooks as teaching devices and also with the effect of grade level on learning by means of these auto-instructional materials. Write-in machines of the type developed by Skinner were used to present a mathematics program on sets, relations, and functions, consisting of about 700 self-instructional frames. The two experimental conditions differed in several respects, including control of sequencing, "cheat-proof" features, ease and reliability of operation, and, probably, novelty and interest factors.

On the day following completion of the program, students were given a test which included transfer items not specifically covered in the program. Results failed to show a statistically significant difference in the amount of learning produced by presenting the teaching sequence mechanically and in programed-text format. The mean score of the machine group was somewhat lower than that of the programed-text group. The mean time which the machine group required to finish the program exceeded that of the programed-text group by more than 37 minutes; however, this difference was attributed to mechanical difficulties in the machine. With either form of material, no significant differences among Grades 9, 10, and 11 were found on direct-learning items, although the performance of the students in the higher grades was superior on transfer items. The experiment used 74 subjects (25 ninth-grade, 23 tenth-grade, and 26 eleventh-grade); thus the lack of statistically significant differences cannot be attributed to the lack of sufficient cases to reveal moderate differences in effects.

STIMULUS-CONTROL FACTORS IN PRESENTATION OF MATERIAL

The Concept of Stimulus Control

The preceding two sections have dealt with procedures designed to regulate or control active or explicit student response (overt or covert) on predetermined occasions during instruction. A stimulus-response conception of the learning process implies that, aside from such explicit, instructed responses, learning is mediated through a concatenation of implicit or unidentified covert responses

by the student during the course of reading, listening, or watching a demonstration. Even when such responses remain unidentified and unspecified, it can be presumed that they are governed in one way or another by the deliberate or intuitive manipulation of stimulus events which the designer of the medium has provided. That the nature of the implicit responses involved in reading, watching, or listening is not well understood does not preclude our studying the terminal effects of the stimulus manipulations in the content, sequencing, or organization of an instructional instrument, or the factors of display, emphasis, and mode of delineation. These stimulus properties govern the momentary perceptual or cognitive responses that, we assume, mediate the development of skills, knowledges, understandings, discriminations, beliefs, or other sought-for outcomes of instruction.

The basic posture adopted in this chapter is that the most productive approach to the experimental manipulation of instructional factors is to view these stimulus factors as instrumental in the control of student response, whether explicit or implicit. It follows that the treatment of all or most variables in instruction, other than those concerned with manipulation of explicit, specifically occasioned student responses, can be viewed as methods of providing suitable, effective control of implicit responses that are presumed to be mediating learning throughout any instructional sequence. It may be useful to keep this orientation in mind in relation to the variables discussed in this section, whether they are identified solely in terms of stimulus factors (e.g., repetition, content organization, pictorial quality factors) or whether they are identified in terms that have more direct implicit-response overtones (e.g., attention-directing, familiarization, or perceptual-discrimination factors).

Cueing Implicit Responses

Question-posing techniques. An example of the use of "prompts" calculated to induce active if not overt student response and, to some extent to direct it, is found in an experiment by Hall (1936), who reported that flashing relevant questions on the screen during a silent film increased the amount of learning. Similar results were reported by May and Lumsdaine (1958) for "motivating" questions to which students were not asked to respond explicitly.

The experiment reported by May and Lumsdaine (1958, Ch. 6) showed that the teaching effectiveness of existing film materials could be improved somewhat by the simple device of splicing in "thought-provoking" questions designed to "arouse curiosity," but without calling for explicit responses. Such questions were helpful in addition to questions which fostered explicit practice of material to be learned. The use of questions preceding rather than following segments of the film to which they referred was also found, in an unpublished 1954 study later reported by Maccoby, Michael, and Levine (1961), to be less effective than practice questions following the expository sections of the film. (See p. 616, above.) The use of a set of questions preceding a section of the film to direct pupils' attention to particular aspects of the film to be shown is discussed in a later section. (See p. 640.)

A further study by May and Lumsdaine (1958, Ch. 3) used two narrated versions of a film on causes of seasonal change. One form of narration was purely expository, while the other made liberal use of rhetorical questions. Fifth-grade pupils showed only a slight tendency to improve through the use of the rhetorical questions (which they were not asked to answer). These results, of course, do not rule out the possibility of profitable use of rhetorical questions in a film script. But, in conjunction with findings of other studies (e.g., Lumsdaine, May, & Hadsell, 1958; Michael & Maccoby, 1953, 1961), they do strongly suggest that the value of introducing questions may be more readily gained if the pupil is enabled, by virtue of the preceding content, to give an immediate, explicit correct response. Both this

experiment and one on live-dialogue versus off-stage narration (see p. 638) suggest ways in which further development of dialogue and narration techniques might increase relevant implicit responses by pupils. As yet, most of these possibilities have not been followed up experimentally. One unpublished small-scale study by D. N. Michael made an unsuccessful attempt to demonstrate gains in learning by stimulating anticipatory implicit rehearsal during the showing of a procedural film depicting a complex geometric construction.

"Perceptual blueprinting." In discussions of theory bearing on the learning of organizable sequences, Sheffield (1957, 1961) described the formation of "perceptual blueprints" as a means of providing cues for learning lengthy sequential tasks. The essential concept is illustrated in an experimental technique called the "implosion" method, devised for use in filmed demonstrations of assembly tasks. This method consists of a display of the parts, followed by a rapid succession of "stills" of each part placed in its appropriate place in the assembly, so that the parts appear to "jump into place" in sequence. This technique was evaluated experimentally using a filmed demonstration of a complex assembly (Sheffield, 1957; Sheffield, Margolius, & Hoehn, 1961). It was found that the "implosion" device, which required only a very short amount of additional time, made a significant contribution in the teaching of the lengthy mechanical task. The sizable gains from using the "implosion" method seem particularly striking in view of the already highly organized nature of the demonstration; an even greater effect would be anticipated with an inferior, less-organized demonstration.

Task representation from the learner's point of view. Depicting a to-be-imitated performance so that the learner observes the task from the same aspect which he will face when he comes to perform the task is commonly held to be preferable to having the demonstrator face the learner so that the task performance is reversed left-to-right. Experimental data verifying this reasonable but frequently ignored assumption were obtained in a Navy experiment performed by Roshal (1949, 1961) with a film on how to tie knots. Two camera angles were used—the "zero-degree" camera angle and the "180-degree" camera angle. With the "zero-degree" or "subjective" angle, the camera is placed in the position from which a student would be viewing the knot if he were tying it himself. With the "180-degree" angle, the demonstration is shown from the angle from which the student would be looking if he were watching an instructor show him how to tie the knot with the instructor facing the student. The "zero-degree" angle was found to produce reliably better results than the "180-degree" angle in terms of knot-tying proficiency gained from the films. Although the reasons for the superiority of the "zero-degree" angle have not been fully explored, it may be noted that the "zero-degree" angle presents to the learner exactly the same cues he will have to respond to when he is actually tying the knot.

Implicit imitation of motor skills. A special form of implicit responding occurs when the learner, either spontaneously or by direct instruction, "imagines" himself performing a response he is seeing demonstrated. Presumably some such implicit subthreshold responding takes place whenever the witnessing of a demonstrated activity is effective as the basis for later transfer into overt performance. Harby (1952) reported a study on the use of repeated film demonstrations in learning basketball tossing from a demonstrational film-loop. Students who were instructed to "mentally practice" while watching these films several times a day for two weeks showed some evidence of improvement, though the evidence is not clear cut; other groups who "practiced" for longer or shorter times did not.

The previously cited experiments by Maccoby and Sheffield suggest that translating the perceptual response into overt practice after a short delay is better than deferring practice for a longer period. However, it may be noted that these experiments, concerned as they were with contrasting two reasonable alternative procedures, did not attempt to separate out the factor of delay per se from the additional, interfering, factor of presenting additional demonstration before the overt practice was attempted. It is likely that both the delay before practice and the interfering effect of additional material operated to place the longer demonstration segments at a disadvantage.

Slow-motion photography. Another factor which may affect the adequacy of implicit perceptual responses for guiding later practice is the adequacy of the original perception. A special case is the learning of motor-coordination skills where the skilled act may occur too swiftly to permit formation of a stable perceptual pattern. Here, the use of slow-motion photography would seem to be especially useful, yet hardly any experiments have been completed on this stimulus factor, which represents one of the few really unique capabilities of motion pictures. The limited evidence on comparative effectiveness of slow-motion and normal-speed photographic depiction comes mainly from a study by McGuire (1955b, 1961c), who compared them as aids to learning pursuit-rotor performance. The differences obtained favored use of slow motion.

Moving pictures versus still pictures. The principal evidence here comes from the experiment by Roshal (1949, 1961), who compared a moving-picture demonstration of how to tie three knots with a parallel presentation which used the same narration and a series of still pictures that showed the various key stages in tying the knots. The movie version was significantly better in teaching the subjects (Navy basic trainees) how to tie the knots. It would appear that the advantage of actual motion depiction depends largely on the kind of task and on the frequency of transition and rapidity of change of the successive stills. Further data on this question are very much in order, particularly in view of their direct implications for equipment that differs greatly in cost, and especially when demonstrational aids are contemplated as individually available teaching machines rather than budgeted on a mass-viewing basis. Also needed are basic data on the perception of motion in still pictures (see O. W. Smith & Resnick, 1953), i.e., the simulation of motion through successive stills, and on the utility of blending and multiple-image techniques and the like.

Static versus moving ("animated") transparencies. The use of "animated" visual aids as compared with static representations in accompanying verbal instruction on weapons was studied by Silverman (1958). Verbal instruction in controlled form was given by means of a tape-recorded lecture supervised by one instructor for all experimental groups. The animated transparencies covered a considerable range of complexity, as reflected in the number of moving parts in each. Performance tests, as well as multiple-choice and fill-in verbal tests, were employed as criterion measures. With the verbal tests, no significant differences were observed in the effectiveness of animated and static transparencies. Significant differences were, however, revealed by performance tests, although no clear relationship was reported between the degree of animation employed (number of moving parts) and the effectiveness of the animated displays.

Multiple Cues Provided by Animation Techniques

A study of animation techniques (Lumsdaine & Sulzer, 1951; see later report by Lumsdaine, Sulzer, & Kopstein, 1961) is of interest both methodologically and in relation to general questions in the analysis of visual-depiction factors. A special aspect of the latter is that of how we may guide perceptual responses by focusing attention on specific aspects of the material presented and showing the interrelationship of the various aspects of the visual presentation. Student attention was directed to relevant cues by visual indicators accompanying narration within the instructional film sequence at appropriate

intervals. (See also the study reported by Wulff & Kraeling, 1961.) This form of attention-directing differs from the attention-arousing devices in the study by Neu (1950) in terms of the function served by the attention devices. This use of attention-directing devices within the film contrasts also with methods of directing attention through prior testing or instructions, such as those reported by May and Lumsdaine (1958, Ch. 7) and several other studies in which preinstruction tests were used to indicate the points to which the student was expected to attend.

In the animation study reported by Lumsdaine, Sulzer, and Kopstein (1961), 32 intact classes of Air Force basic trainees were tested to assess their ability to read micrometer settings after seeing one of several specially prepared films on micrometer reading. The films employed simple animation devices, such as pop-on labels, moving arrows, etc., superimposed on the pictorial material. For example, in an illustrative sequence, the narration stated: "The reading is determined by first referring to the scale on the barrel of the micrometer. The figure 7 . . . [at this point an animated arrow pops in indicating the figure 7 on the barrel scale of the micrometer] indicates seven-hundred thousandths . . . [at this point the arrow moves down and points to a blank space under the micrometer, where the figure .700 pops on to the screen]." The narration then continues: "Two more graduations are seen on the barrel scale . . ."; two arrows pop in to point these out, and similar indicators are used as the exposition goes on, describing the further components of the reading and the way they are summated. Control films were identical in narration and in other respects, except that the animation devices in the key sequences in the film were omitted. As predicted, the animated films were superior.

In general, little experimental study has been made of the specific characteristics of animation techniques, and it should be recognized that the present study did not deal with more complex sorts of animation, e.g., figure animation as used in animated cartoons. It was, instead, restricted to the use of simple pop-in labels, moving arrows, and the like, employed primarily to help the learner visualize and pay attention to salient portions of the pictorial material. Definition of the experimental variable in film-production terms ("animation") is thus less appropriate, from the standpoint of learning, than is defining it in terms of attention-directing or implicit-response cueing functions of the animation devices used. The lack of specificity as to response-cueing functions evident in the descriptive use of such a blanket variable as "animation" parallels that in the similar studies of "participation." The blanket designation of a global procedure or production "variable" does not identify the precise functions of the devices experimentally studied, and hence does not provide a very useful basis for identifying the implications of the result.

It may be remarked that an equivalent pointing and labeling function could have been provided by live action—and it is doubtful that the results would have differed had this been done. The procedural variable was, as is often the case, a compound one; the results thus do not differentiate whether it was the pointing function or the labeling of the numerical values that mainly contributed to the superior efficacy of the animated films.

In the animation study reported by Lumsdaine, Sulzer, and Kopstein (1961), the joint use of both visual and oral presentation of verbal material was also appraised. The effects of two different presentations used in an introductory section of the film were also compared as to their relative effectiveness in teaching the nomenclature of the micrometer. The first kind of presentation (Technique "A") employed pop-on arrows to indicate the parts of the micrometer named orally by the narrator, while the second (Technique "B") used, in addition, a more complex animation arrangement in which printed labels were also popped on, and the various portions of the micrometer identified by the arrows and labels were differentially stressed by fade-in techniques. Technique "B" was appreciably more effective, resulting in about 30 per

cent mean correct naming of parts of the micrometer on the postfilm test, as against only 15 per cent for Technique "A."

Further analysis of these data illustrates how results of an experiment may be differentially analyzed, in relation to other variables, so as to provide additional information. The hypothesis tested in this analysis was that the additional stress and stimulus value provided by the more elaborate technique would be of advantage primarily for nomenclature items that did not recur frequently in later portions of the film. The advantage of the more elaborate technique was only 4.5 per cent (27.2 per cent correct answers for Technique "B" versus 22.7 per cent for Technique "A") for terms occurring frequently in other parts of the film, whereas the advantage of the more elaborate Technique "B" was 25.8 per cent (32.8 per cent correct answers for Technique "B" versus only 7.0 per cent correct for Technique "A") for terms that occurred infrequently elsewhere in the film and hence were taught only in the introductory nomenclature section.

Pictorial and auditory "embellishments." The producers of the original version of the phonetic alphabet slide film used in the study by Hovland, Lumsdaine, and Sheffield (see pp. 610–611) evidently believed that the musical accompaniment and the humorous cartoons and comments employed in the film would make it a better teaching device than unadorned presentation of the material. (For a description of these "embellishments," see Hovland, Lumsdaine, & Sheffield, 1949, p. 229, and May & Lumsdaine, 1958, pp. 58–63.) This intended improvement could have been achieved if (1) there were a need for a general interest-getting function which these features might have served; (2) if these features had served to direct attention to relevant cues related to the learning task; or (3) if such features had been designed to serve as memory aids (mnemonics) to association of cue (letter) and required response (phonetic name). The results reported by Lumsdaine and Gladstone (1958) showed, however, that the "fancy" presentation using the pictorial and auditory embellishments was actually *less* effective than a "plain" version in which the letters and equivalent phonetic names were merely presented starkly on a plain background with neither pictorial nor auditory adornment. These results indicate either that none of the three hypothesized functions was operative or else that they occurred to such a small extent that, for the training conditions found in the experiment, they were overbalanced by other, detrimental effects.

It may be asked why music and humorous effects should have any detrimental effects. The hypothesis that immediately suggests itself is that though they may indeed serve as attention-getters, their net effect is to draw attention away from rather than toward the essentials of the learning task. That is, they may distract the learner from implicitly or subvocally rehearsing to himself the association between cue (letter) and response (phonetic word) that must be established to master the task as defined. The possible positive effects of the embellishments would, then, to be worth while, have to more than offset this distracting influence. Under certain conditions this could easily happen. In particular, if attention to what is being presented (insuring "exposure" to the learning materials) is the most critical requirement, the presence of the entertaining material might well make the difference between exposure (watching) and nonexposure (e.g., turning the television set to another channel or going to sleep). Under these circumstances the interest-gaining use of embellishments could result in effecting *some* learning— even if it were not very efficient—rather than no learning at all. But for the captive audience found in any reasonably well-motivated classroom situation, this minimum guarantee of mere exposure is already taken care of, and the superior efficiency of the uncluttered, simple materials is likely to show up as the determining factor.

Even for well-motivated learners, however, it is possible that pictorial aids somewhat like those used in the film might be advan-

tageous mnemonically, if differently employed. Studies of simple association-formation by Lumsdaine (1949; see May and Lumsdaine, 1958, Ch. 10) and by Kopstein and Roshal (1954, 1961; see also Kale and Grosslight, 1955) have shown that in learning paired associates, pictures are more effective than words as stimulus terms (though less effective as response terms). The question arises why this superiority of pictorial cues did not operate in the "fancy," pictorialized version of the film studies by Lumsdaine and Gladstone. The answer is probably that the pictures with the stimulus letters, in order to serve an effective mnemonic function after their initial presentation and association with the phonetic response words, would have to be used on one or more subsequent trials, presumably without presentation of the response words. An opportunity would thus be afforded for them to mediate recall and permit practice of the correct responses. With skill in implementing this approach, using materials selected to minimize distracting aspects and maximize mnemonic value, pictures might be used effectively as mnemonics or partial cues. In the films used in the Lumsdaine-Gladstone study, where each picture appeared only once, such an effect was very unlikely.

Other Visual-Perceptual Factors

Pictorial "quality." May and Lumsdaine (1958, Ch. 2) reported an experimental comparison of a crude, preliminary pencil-sketch version versus a finished, regular, color version of an elementary science film on the causes of seasonal change. In this study, as the authors pointed out, the content of the two versions was not entirely parallel. Hence, the study could not afford the basis for generalization that is obtainable from an experiment in which there is controlled variation of the pictorial presentation factor and content is held constant. A comprehensive test given to parallel groups after seeing each film failed to show an appreciable difference between the effectiveness of the two. Because of the imperfect control of content, these results can be interpreted, at most, only as showing that a crude presentation *may* at least equal in teaching effectiveness a polished color film costing more than ten times as much to produce. The results do not demonstrate that technical quality is an unimportant factor in the effectiveness of an instructional film; the virtual equality in effectiveness of the two versions may have been due to a cancellation of factors. For example, superiority of the crude version in some points of pedagogy or the kind of visualization devices employed might have offset an actual disadvantage due to the crudity of the photographic material. This superiority could have occurred at some point in the exposition, even though educational and film experts had tried to improve the teaching effectiveness of each preproduction version. However, this hypothesis is weakened by the fact that no differences in any of ten content-area subscores included in the two films even approached significance in favor of the pencil-test version. These results, together with evidence from other studies that attest to the wide variation in effectiveness that a given film can have on different aspects of the content presented, thus at least suggest that for teaching conceptual material the contribution made by polished visualization is likely to be minor in comparison with other influences affecting learning.

A later study in which pictorial quality figured was conducted under the Air Force audio-visual research program, described by Lumsdaine (1953). This study was reported by Zuckerman (1954) and by P.N. Smith, Aukes, and Lumsdaine (1954). In this study, a storyboard-based filmstrip of about 250 frames was used. This filmstrip closely paralleled a finished film (for familiarizing jet pilots with flight characteristics of the F-86A fighter aircraft) and was prepared, after the fact, to match the final narration and picture point for point. As in the May-Lumsdaine study, the visuals in the filmstrip were relatively crude sketches, as contrasted with the combination of live action and elaborate animation used in the final color film. This Air Force study had the quite different purpose of determining whether point-by-point effectiveness of the final film could be predicted from the filmstrip mock-up. (See p. 595.) However, the results also confirmed those of the May-Lumsdaine study in showing not only that there were wide variations within each version in the effectiveness with which it conveyed specific points of content, but also that the polished color version had no material over-all superiority over the crude visual presentation provided by the parallel filmstrip mock-up of the film.

One of the few other studies of the alleged technical superiority of the film as a factor in learning is an unpublished experiment by Duva and Lumsdaine (1956) which compared the amount learned from a motion picture version of a film (on how to read vernier scales) with the amount learned from kinescope reproduction of the same film. In this case, the purely physical characteristics of technical quality were manipulated so as to vary in rather extreme fashion; in the "poor" version, not only was the print fuzzy, but some of the relevant material was obliterated by being left out of frame when the kinescope print was made from the original film.[8] The results of the study by Duva and Lumsdaine showed the motion-picture version (better quality) to be reliably superior to the inferior-quality kinescope, regardless of whether the kinescope version was labeled as such or as a motion picture. The inferiority of the kinescope was not offset by preceding it with a briefing which cautioned the subjects to try to compensate for the poor quality of the film by paying careful attention. How-

---

[8] In addition, preconceptions of the medium by individuals were manipulated, in some instances, by telling them it was a TV kinescope and in other instances by telling them it was a film. This study was made during the relatively early days of television, when some glamor might have attached to the TV designation. Jackson (1952) had earlier reported that telling students that a film they were seeing was a TV kinescope somewhat increased the amount learned. This effect was not found in the later study by Duva and Lumsdaine (1956).

ever, a variation of the kinescope version that permitted active practice in reading vernier scales during the showing apparently did make up for inferior quality; this variation was reliably superior to the other kinescope versions shown, and did not differ significantly from the higher-quality motion picture version in the amount of learning produced. (The mean scores were 10.78 for the film version, 7.51, 6.34, and 7.52 for the kinescope without active-response procedures, and 11.73 for the kinescope that incorporated the active-response feature.)

Color. No really definitive studies have been made on specific ways in which color may contribute to learning from instructional media. The principal experiments (May & Lumsdaine, 1958; VanderMeer, 1952) have compared black-and-white versus color prints of the same instructional films. These studies failed to show significant differences in learning in favor of the color films, though some of VanderMeer's data indicated slightly superior retention for some of the color films he used. The negative findings, of course, pose the usual problems in interpretation, and as May and Lumsdaine (1958, p. 30) point out, "All that can really be concluded from the evidence is that the effects, if any, of color were not large enough to show up as the significant difference that would be predicted by some producers and educators." Nevertheless, their report did attempt to cope with some of the possible questions about negative results on procedural grounds as well as the inevitable logical ones. They summarized the situation as follows:

In explaining this lack of substantial advantage, several possible objections can be ruled out. The lack of differences was *not* an artifact due to lack of effective learning, as shown by substantial before-after differences for both versions. Nor was it due to lack of fairly good sensitivity in the measurements, as shown by gross score differences between grade levels and among different content areas within the film. The most reasonable interpretation is that color as a general factor in effectiveness of films is easily overrated and

that, except in special instances where color cues have crucial or specialized advantages, color contributes, if anything, much less than do other aspects of presentation to the instructional value of a classroom film (May & Lumsdaine, 1958, p. 30, italics added).

These two experiments lend little support to those who argue for producing classroom teaching films in color in order to achieve greater educational effectiveness. But neither do they justify the conclusion that color is wholly irrelevant to learning, even in films which have no intrinsic color content to be learned. As noted by the writer:

Color in some places in a film may facilitate learning—in other places it may inhibit learning. Furthermore, an exciting color film on a dull subject shown to tired pupils on a dull rainy afternoon might well result in more learning than would a black-and-white print of the same film shown to a control group at the same time. Under such circumstances, the presumably more attractive nature of color might exert a positive influence because other factors were very unfavorable to attention (May & Lumsdaine, 1958, p. 29).

The writer has summarized the general status of the color versus black-and-white issue as follows:

The clearest case for use of color is . . . where color cues are essential for a discrimination that is to be learned—for example, in learning signal code flags, certain types of insignia, identification of minerals, flora and fauna, etc. In films and printed materials color differentiation is also obviously advantageous when multiple color codes keep otherwise confusing visual elements separable and readily followed (as in complex electrical schematic diagrams). But the evidence suggests strongly that any general value of color for increasing learning through increased strikingness or attractiveness has probably been overrated. The importance attributed to color may have been influenced by the demonstrated value of color in magazine advertising, where there is not the captive audience that one can assume in the classroom use of teaching films, and where color thus can help determine *what is looked at* (May & Lumsdaine, 1958, pp. 29–30).

Studies in pictorial perception: (1) Distance judgment in photographs. It seems evident that the design of media depending heavily on pictorial presentation would benefit from improved understanding of basic factors in the perception and associative stimulus value of pictures. Of the relatively few experimental studies completed in this area, several have been concerned with optimal viewing distance. O. W. Smith and Gruber (1958) and O. W. Smith (1958) demonstrated, for example, that apparent distances between points in a photograph increase when the photograph is placed farther from the eye. Results of a study by O. W. Smith, Smith, and Hubbard (1953) indicated that judgment of distances in drawings was determined primarily by linear perspective and was but little influenced by the amount of detail or shading used in the drawing. An interesting finding by P. C. Smith and O. W. Smith (1961) was that rather good accuracy in tossing a ball at a target could be achieved when subjects who believed that they were looking at an actual scene actually aimed on the basis of a photograph of the scene. Several further studies by O. W. Smith and his associates have been conducted to investigate factors affecting perception of photographic representations, but the total amount of evidence, especially on problems other than distance perception, is still quite slight.

(2) *Depiction of motion.* Considering the economic differences between using motion pictures and successive stills for instruction, it is surprising that little research has been done on the representation of motion in still pictures. One of the few studies is that by O. W. Smith and Resnick (1953), who showed that untrained observers were able (1) to differentiate fairly reliably between live drawings of human figures excerpted from a motion sequence and those where the figure was not moving, and (2) to judge speed of motion with some reliability, but with only fair accuracy.

The well-controlled but isolated study by Roshal (see p. 630), together with Silverman's (1958) study (see p. 631, above), furnishes the main evidence comparing still with moving depiction. No systematic experiments appear to have been done on the effectiveness of "swish lines," multiple exposures, and other devices calculated to delineate motion in a still picture, nor on speed or frequency of cutting from one still to the next, as these affect perception or imitability of demonstrated operations.

Pictures versus words in paired-associate learning. A theoretically oriented study comparing the functioning of pictures and words as associative cues and as response prompts was conducted by Lumsdaine (1949, 1958). Four kinds of pairs were used to present the paired terms to be learned: picture-picture, picture-word, word-picture, and word-word. In all cases, the subjects (audience) had to learn, after repeated exposure to the pairs, to name the second or "response" object of each pair in answer to the test-presentation of the first (or "stimulus") member of the pair. The question was whether use of pictures or of words made for better learning, (1) in presenting the first or stimulus object in the pair, and (2) in presenting the second or response term. The results showed rather conclusively that the use of pictures to represent the first object of the pair was better than verbal presentation, but that verbal presentation (printed words) was definitely superior to pictorial presentation for the *second* ("response") term of the pair. This was true for both college and grade-school learners, for individual as well as classroom presentation, for brighter learners as well as slower ones, and held regardless of a number of systematic variations in conditions of presentation.

This finding, which would seem to have interesting implications for learning such tasks as lexical equivalents, was replicated by Kopstein and Roshal (1954, 1961) with Russian-English vocabulary. They also found that *learning* (practice) under the picture-word condition tended to produce better performance when verbal as well as pictorial stimuli were subsequently used in testing the outcomes of the learning.

Other visual-display factors. In a widely cited study by Swanson (1954),[9] several different devices were used as visual aids supplementing lectures to familiarize Air Force mechanics with complex subsystems of the B-47 medium bomber. Live lectures for various groups were similar, but visual aids depicting the same equipment differed markedly. These consisted of mock-ups, two-dimensional symbolic diagrams, and realistic pictorial charts. No significant differences were found among the mean final test scores of the groups; the author concluded that, as a supplement to a well-prepared lecture for instruction of skilled technicians, complex and expensive training aids may be no more effective than less complex and less expensive aids. A basis for questioning this conclusion arose when data on a later control group (lecture with *no* visual aids) indicated that, for the experienced mechanics at least, the test used showed no significant contribution for any of the visual aids.

A later experiment by Swanson, Lumsdaine, and Aukes (1956) was conducted as a follow-up to Swanson's experiment, using inexperienced airmen as subjects and two training aids from the earlier experiment (the mock-up and diagram for the rudder-control system of the B-47). Subjects were divided into two groups, which received identical tape-recorded lectures but different visual supplementary aids (mock-up and symbolic diagram). A third (control) group heard the lectures without visual aids. On the hypothesis that different visual aids were appropriate for different objectives, effects were assessed by three achievement tests. On a parts-recognition test, the mock-up group achieved superiority; on a test of functional interconnec-

tions, the diagram group was superior; and on the third test (verbal knowledge), there were no significant differences among the three groups. The conclusion was that the effectiveness of each training aid depends on specific instructional objectives. Of methodological interest was the better control on verbal content achieved by tape-recorded lectures than by live lectures and the more analytical comparison afforded by using two kinds of visual tests as well as the original type of verbal test. Unfortunately, no group was tested with realistic photographs in place of the expensive mock-ups, but it seems likely that the photographic depictions would have served as well as a basis for parts identification.

A gain from the use of visual aids along with a recorded lecture was also shown by an experiment by Aukes and Simon (1957) on the learning of system data flow by inexperienced trainees. Aukes and Simon were concerned in part with the possible distracting role of irrelevant cues furnished by material extraneous to the point under consideration. Air Force personnel, unskilled in aircraft maintenance, were divided into equivalent groups and given instruction by a tape-recorded lecture on the B-47 rudder power control system. A standard equipment display used as a visual aid to a lecture was compared with an "add-a-part" display in which only those portions relevant to each major point of the lecture were present during discussion of that point. The latter was significantly superior. Comparison of two experimental groups led to the conclusion that when a series of conditions or subsystems is involved, a device which eliminates irrelevant materials for each condition or presents only the information relevant to each condition is more effective than an over-all device which presents all the information at all times. Comparison with a control group that had the same lecture without visual aids also showed a significant difference. The results of this experiment led to the conclusion that, in teaching a system of at least moderate complexity to relatively unskilled stu-

[9] A more detailed report on this study is given by Swanson and Aukes (1956). See also the report by Swanson, Lumsdaine, and Aukes (1956) on this and a follow-up experiment, and the similar though less extensive comparisons by Torkelson (1954), Murnin (1955), and Murnin, VanderMeer, and Vris (1954).

dents, a device that provides a visual map of the system flow and component relationships can significantly increase the amount of learning.

Data tending to cast doubt on the necessary superiority of pictorial or graphic presentation over verbal or symbolic presentation in a different kind of application were obtained by Vernon (1950), who reported little difference in ability of British grammar school students to graph the results of comparisons in vital statistics when presented by pictorial chart, graph, or numerical table, with or without printed text material. A later experiment (1952) by the same investigator failed to reveal any gains from the use of pictorial charts to accompany, precede, or follow the reading of text material. As in the original Swanson experiments, however, the results do not show that visual aids "are of no value," but rather are mainly of value in engendering a skeptical, "show-me" attitude toward graphic or pictorial presentation as a short-cut to learning, and in focusing the attention of the researcher on the question of what kind of visual presentation is helpful in achieving specifically defined instructional outcomes.

Positive results on differential ease of reading graphs of differing styles were reported by V. Peterson and Schramm (1954), who tested basic airmen with eight types of graphs (circle, disc, single bar, multiple bar, multiple cylinder, multiple square columns, multiple-area columns, and "partial cosmograph") constructed to represent the same five proportions. The similarity in content depicted by the graphs was concealed by giving each graph a different title and presenting test graphs in random fashion among decoy graphs. Subjects were asked to estimate the five percentages of each graph to complete the experiment. They found significant differences in the accuracy of reading different forms of graphs. The circle graph was most accurately read, the multiple-area column graph was least accurately read, and the remaining six types comprised a middle group.

"Live Action" and Realism

Narrated versus dialogue films. In an experiment reported by May and Lumsdaine (1958, Ch. 3), a nonprotagonist version of a film on the causes of seasonal change was produced by using animation scenes and edited demonstrational sequences from the footage shot for an original live-action version of the film. An offstage narrative commentary covering the same instructional points as the dialogue of the original version was prepared.[10] Fifth- and ninth-grade classes were each divided at random into two groups which saw the two different versions, and learning was tested by a 56-item test. The differences between the mean test scores of the two groups were too small to be reliable, although the fifth-graders did express significantly higher interest in the story-dialogue form of the film. This comparison exemplifies a situation where relative instructional effectiveness is not the whole issue in deciding on the method of choice in designing instructional media. Except where the use of live-dialogue film can be shown to have marked superiority in meeting particular educational objectives, the narrated film has great practical advantages. These include its much lower initial cost and the ease with which it can be produced, without complex equipment, to meet local needs. A further important advantage is that it may be easily modified for revision or for making alternate versions—for experimental study or other purposes—at minimal additional cost. These variations can include foreign language versions or changes in the style or difficulty of narration such as the ones that were studied

---

[10] This comparison also involved, to some extent, minor but largely irrelevant content differences associated with use of the story form and expository form of presentation. In contrast to the "dramatic versus documentary" comparison of restricted "evaluative" status described by Hovland, Lumsdaine, and Sheffield (1949, Ch. 5), the present study can be regarded as involving controlled variation of the single, if somewhat loosely defined, "variable" of narrated commentary versus dialogue, both used in parallel expositions of the same basic content.

by May and Lumsdaine (1958, Chs. 3–4).

Live versus filmed instruction. A study by Shettel and his co-workers (1956) was concerned with the practical question of whether filmed recordings of lectures could serve as substitutes for, or supplements to, the more expensive and cumbersome mobile training devices then commonly used by the Air Force for training mechanics. In each of three replications, live-lecture groups were compared with corresponding filmed-lecture "control" groups on a verbal test immediately after training and on a test given six to eight weeks later. The three lectures were one on the rudder-control system of the B-47, using a nonoperating equipment mock-up, one on the same system using symbolic diagrams, and one on the B-47 fuel system using an operating mock-up.

On the immediate test, two of the live-lecture groups scored higher than the corresponding filmed-lecture groups, but the differences, though reliable, were small. On the delayed test, scores were much lower, and no reliable differences were found between any of the live and filmed-lecture groups. However, for one of the replications, the film was reshown, as a demonstration experiment, just prior to the delayed test. The fact that this predictably produced a reliable improvement in the scores on that test was used to emphasize the logistic advantage that, unlike the live lectures, the filmed ones could be kept available for periodic review, and could readily be scheduled immediately prior to the time their content was needed in operations, thus avoiding large decrements due to forgetting over the period between instruction and application on the job.

Filmed demonstrations were compared with live instruction in an athletic skill by Harby (1952). The live instruction was reported to be superior, but the difference was attributed to the effect of coaching which accompanied the live instruction; coaching was confounded with the difference in mode of depiction, so that interpretation solely in terms of superiority of live demonstration was not possible.

Three-dimensional depiction. For some instructional purposes, live demonstration might well be superior to the usual form of film depiction, particularly if depth perception requirements were such that binocular disparity or convergence cues were critical. One comparison has been reported in which such cues might have been helpful. In this comparison, reported by Cogswell (1952), stereoscopic films were compared with standard films used to teach the assembly of 20 mm.' anti-aircraft gun breech-blocks. No significant superiority for the "3-D" film was obtained.

Filmed test instructions. One situation in which filmed instruction could well be superior to live is that in which live-instruction variability is high or competent instructors are scarce. One instance is in giving standardized test instructions to large groups. Here visual demonstration of answer-sheet marking is also desirable. Without separating out these possible contributing factors, McClure and Peterman (1956) demonstrated the potential superiority of filmed instructions over "live" instructions on how to mark the answer-sheet in a machine-scored test in decreasing the incidence of mismarked answer-sheets. Each half of eight flights of about 50 men was randomly assigned either to a treatment in which live instruction on how to mark was given or to a treatment in which the instruction was given by means of a film. Both treatments were then given the same two machine-scored tests. The filmed instructions yielded a significant decrease in rated amount of mismarking on test papers.

Visual and Auditory Channels

Cheatham (1950) provided an analysis of the variables affecting the probable efficiency of visual and auditory modalities considered from the standpoint of their utility as communication channels for exchange of information. His conclusions and the survey of research literature bearing on this problem by Day and Beach (1950) make it apparent that the problem is a complex one that involves a number of variables. In limiting cases where the visual channel is crowded, it is no surprise to find, as in a pilot study reported by Hoehn and Lumsdaine (1958), that audio task instructions can be much more efficient than printed ones. But in the more complex situation of class instruction on complex subject matter, it is unlikely that either modality would be consistently superior; any stable advantage would almost certainly depend on other specified variables in the nature of the task and learning situation. The inconsistent results obtained by Nelson and Moll (1950) in comparing presentation by audio and visual elements of several existing films are not surprising. Nor is it likely that a consistent advantage for one or the other modality would be found to have much generality beyond the specific films (and tests) used. Needed are studies that test specific, hypothesized advantages for one or the other modality as a function of other instructional variables.

CONTENT AND ORGANIZATION OF INSTRUCTION

Preinstruction Tests or Procedures

The value of using a prefilm test to identify points which are to be learned in a film has been studied by several investigators. In the animation study reported by Lumsdaine, Sulzer, and Kopstein (1961), a brief prefilm test of five sample micrometer readings significantly increased the amount learned from the film. Several experiments reported by May and Lumsdaine (1958, Ch. 7) also show that the amount learned from certain aspects of a film can be increased substantially by directing the attention of students to these aspects before an instructional presentation. This was done by oral or written instructions, by giving a prefilm test, and by pointing out the "hardest" questions on a postfilm test before giving a second showing of a film. However, the increase in amount learned from the material covered by the pretest

tended to be offset by losses in the material not covered.

In an unpublished 1952 study using a film on various types of map projection, A. K. Romney also reported that instructions designed to induce a "set" to learn facts significantly increased the scores on factual items, whereas inducing a set to learn "principles" resulted in nonsignificantly higher scores on "principle" items. (Less intelligent subjects tended to gain more from fact-set instructions, and more intelligent subjects gained more from principle-set instructions.)

Giving a relevant prefilm test thus can have a selective attention-directing function, stressing certain aspects of content differentially. On the other hand, merely announcing that a test of some sort will be given following instruction can have a general motivating function which, in the phonetic alphabet study by Hovland, Lumsdaine, and Sheffield (1949, Ch. 9) significantly increased learning. This effect was also of interest because of its possible interaction with other variables, e.g., the active-response procedure. The procedure of announcing a test did not work, however, when Michael and Maccoby (1953, 1961) tried to use it for a similar purpose (probably because, unlike the Army subjects of Hovland, Lumsdaine, and Sheffield, their students were already about maximally motivated), and hence no opportunity was afforded to test the expectation that motivational effects of the active-response procedure would be greater with no external test motivation.

Another study which showed increased learning by use of prefilm tests was that by Stein (1952). Using full-length prefilm tests, Stein obtained significant gains, however, only when the prefilm test procedure incorporated "knowledge of results" that, in effect, provided additional instruction; though this was naturally effective, Stein's main results thus seem more nearly akin to those on active practice previously reported than to attention-focusing phenomena. In the experiment reported by Lumsdaine, Sulzer, and Kopstein (1961) on animation techniques, controlled use of a short (five-item) prefilm test, with no knowledge of results, was introduced as an incidental feature of the study. Comparison with a control group that did not get this pretest showed that the test helped emphasize the critical instructional objective (learning how to read the micrometer) as differentiated from other information (e.g., use and care of the micrometer) presented in the film. This effect appears to be one of focusing attention, similar to the effects produced in the May-Lumsdaine experiments (1958, Ch. 7). A similar effect for a pretest preceding a film designed to teach reading of meters and gauges was found in an unpublished study by Peterman and Bouscaren (1954). More general attention-intensifying functions were probably involved also in the effect of the motivating questions used to introduce various sections of a film in the study reported by Lumsdaine, May, and Hadsell (1958).

The lack of effect on material not covered by participation questions has been noted in the study by Michael and Maccoby (1953, 1961), in a similar study by Kanner and Sulzer (1956, 1961), and also in one of the attention-directing experiments reported by May and Lumsdaine (1958, Ch. 7). This lack is in contrast with the results of an introductory orientation exercise used in an experiment comparing introductory and summarizing exercises by Hovland, Lumsdaine, and Sheffield (1949, Ch. 5). The instruction afforded by the introductory exercise in the latter experiment was shown to have positive effects on the material not expressly covered as well as on that specifically covered. The same was found for between-showings tests used by May and Lumsdaine (1958, Ch. 7), where students were told, prior to a reshowing (on the day after the first showing) which test questions had been most often missed. It appears that in these cases, as in the experiment reported by Maccoby, Michael, and Levine (1961; see p. 616, above), a general motivational effect was produced in addition to specific alerting effects or reiteration effects on material that

was covered in the auxiliary student exercises.

Effects of tests interpolated between two sections of film instruction for set-producing or motivational purposes were reported by Kimble (1955b). The experimental groups were given a test (without provision for correcting errors, or any specific knowledge of results) on reading slide-rule scales. This test was given after preliminary film instruction on the subject and prior to a follow-up film that gave instruction both on scale reading and on use of the slide-rule for multiplying and dividing. Kimble reported that the results of the interpolated test were specific, as compared with control groups who had no interpolated test: the experimental groups showed greater gains on the content covered by the test (scale reading) but no appreciable effect on the content not covered (arithmetical operations).

The psychological basis of the effectiveness of utilizing prefilm or intershowing tests to direct attention to particular types of content or even to specific elements of a subject matter seems to be closely related to the more localized attention-focusing effects that can be produced by devices used within the film presentation—e.g., the animated arrows and labels used by Lumsdaine, Sulzer, and Kopstein (1961) to direct attention to key aspects of the picture and to interpret the significance of cues. In either case, gains in effectiveness seem to depend on using some means for focusing attention on particular aspects of the material being presented—or about to be presented—so as to make those aspects stand out from possible competing perceptions. On the other hand, Neu (1950) failed to find any significant effects for "attention" devices which were evidently calculated merely to arouse attention in a general way, rather than to direct it expressly to relevant cues or specific aspects of content.

Familiarization

A number of studies have been conducted on the value of various forms of so-called "familiarization" training. Most of these (e.g., Stein, 1952; Weiss & Fine, 1955) merely show that additional time devoted to some form of familiarization produces beneficial results, without showing that using it in familiarization activity is more effective than using it in some other way. Weiss and Fine, for example, found that prior familiarization training on key terms in a sound filmstrip on the structure and functions of the United Nations yielded scores on a post-filmstrip test that did not differ significantly from those achieved by the about equally time-consuming procedure of giving two showings of the filmstrip (though they were reliably superior to those produced by a single showing of the filmstrip).

One exception, which also deals with specific cue factors involved in familiarization procedures, is a study by Wulff, Sheffield, and Kraeling (1954; see later report by Wulff and Kraeling, 1961). This experiment involved the notion that generally it is not necessary for the learner to attend to *all* of the features of a task to be learned, but rather that he needs to learn to attend only to certain features important in performing it. The rationale for the experiment made the assumption that "familiarization" procedures designed to teach the learner to focus attention on the important features of each part in a mechanical assembly would facilitate learning to assemble the parts properly. It was hypothesized that students not given such "familiarization" training would be very likely to attend to irrelevant features during a demonstration of the assembly, and would thus be handicapped when they subsequently attempted to assemble the mechanism. Using the assembly of an automobile ignition distributor as a training task, the investigators compared two training procedures providing familiarization (and also with training without familiarization).

One kind of familiarization required training subjects to attend to important features of all mechanical parts before any assembly training; the other familiarization procedure (which took less time) involved pointing to the same important features of each part just before the assembly of each part was shown. Assembly training was accomplished by means of a 16 mm. black-and-white sound film especially prepared for the experiment. During subsequent testing of ability to assemble the entire mechanism, time as well as assembly errors and errors in the selection of parts were scored. Both familiarization procedures were shown to be effective in reducing both kinds of errors; however, the most interesting finding was that the group that was given all familiarization prior to assembly training performed less well, with respect to both selection errors and assembly errors, than the group that used the other familiarization procedure (which took less time). The results support the conclusions that (1) a procedure which directs the learner's attention to important features will facilitate training in the manipulation of complex task elements in which only some features are important, and also that (2) such familiarization is more effective if given in the context of, and just prior to, training in the utilization of each task element than if given as a completely separate, prior procedure.

The writer believes that such specifically oriented studies as the preceding one are likely to be more rewarding than general evaluative studies of less well-defined "introductory" or "summary" sequences. The latter kind of sequence was compared in an early study by Hovland, Lumsdaine, and Sheffield (1949, Ch. 5). Later studies have compared the relative effectiveness of summaries and introductions to several films or asked the equally ungeneralizable question, "Do introductions help?" Cook (1960) summarized the results of several such studies as follows:

. . . a study by Lathrop (1949) got conflicting results, using three films with and without an introduction. For two of the films the version with an introduction proved to be slightly superior; however, for the third film, the version without an introduction yielded higher learning scores. In a similar study by Norford (1949) using three other films, very small differences were found in favor of the versions which included the summaries. Only one of these differences was statistically significant. The previously mentioned massive experiment by Peterman and Bouscaren (1954) using a motivational sequence, a "familiar example" sequence and an "essential steps" sequence to a film on *Reading Meter Scales* showed that any one or any combination of these three introductory sequences failed to increase significantly the amount learned from the film (Cook, 1960, p. 94).

Repetition and Redundancy

Amount. Although it is clear that learning may occur in a single trial, as stressed by Guthrie (1935), the need for repetition of material to assure mastery is well established by the experimental literature (see Hovland, 1951); the concern of psychologists with "learning curves" or "acquisition curves" is in itself evidence of this general phenomenon. Experiments on the factor of repetition in instructional media have reflected a prevalent educational philosophy which tends to grade students on how much they learn in a given time rather than addressing itself, as has been not uncommon in laboratory psychology, to the length of training (e.g., "number of trials") necessary, for instance, to achieve some predetermined criterion of mastery. (This conception is being increasingly challenged in work on auto-instructional methods; see, for example, Skinner, 1958.) As a corollary, these experiments have, also, generally dealt with mean scores, attained through equal experience of all members of a classroom group, rather than with data obtained by adjusting the time spent in accordance with the needs of individual students.

For these reasons, experimental data have, in general, reflected varying degrees of incompleteness of learning resulting from various degrees and forms of repetition. If used without supplementation, instructional films seem to be designed with insufficient repetition (or too fast a "pace" or "rate of development") to enable most students to approach mastery on specific knowledge or skills. Jaspen (1950), for example, found that a "succinct" treatment, chosen as representative of

the pace and level of repetition commonly employed in many "nuts and bolts" films, was far from adequate to teach an assembly task. As Cook (1960, p. 99) has remarked, "The consensus of the findings is that audiences can usually profit from a greater number of repetitions than they are generally given. The person who creates an audio-visual demonstration is usually so familiar with the material that it may be difficult for him to believe that people cannot learn it in one trial." The common finding that students achieve far from perfect scores on criterion tests after seeing an instructional film has led several experimenters to study the effects of repeat showings of a film *in toto,* and a few experiments have been conducted on varied amounts or arrangements of repetition within an instructional film.

Repeat showings have sometimes been used as a comparative control on time expended for other instructional procedures (e.g., Lumsdaine, May, & Hadsell, 1958; Weiss & Fine, 1955) as well as a focus of study per se. Typical findings, predictably, are that two showings teach more than does just one (e.g., Kurtz, Walter, & Brenner, 1950). Additional showings may or may not show significant further gains. McTavish (1949) found that little or no further gain was produced after one repeat: ". . . the contribution made by repetition of showings fell off rapidly after the first repetition. . . . Only the increment attributable to the first repetition is statistically significant" (p. 7). McTavish's study and the later study by Lumsdaine, Sulzer, and Kopstein (1961) thus indicate the predictable existence of a "saturation point," although the latter study dealt with repeated demonstration within a film and the former with repeated showings of films. The important thing, however, is not the mere existence of a "saturation point"; rather, it is the question of what determines where this point will occur.

The obvious fact that there is no fixed, low value for the number of repetitions that can be usefully employed is illustrated in comparing McTavish's work with that of

Kendler, Cook, and Kendler (1956, cited in Cook, 1961a), who used films on map symbols with one, two, and three repetitions of a key review portion of the film. Their results showed benefits with up to three repetitions though improvement decreased with additional repetitions. (This study employed both passive- and active-response forms for the reviews; the latter was more effective but showed a similar decrement in the gain achieved by successive repetitions.) A. K. Romney, in an unpublished 1952 study on the effects of "learning set" instructions, also found evidence to indicate that with a set to learn specific factual material, three repetitions of a film appeared to be superior to two. On the other hand, McGuire (1961c), in experimentally varying the length of a filmed demonstration designed to teach pursuit-rotor tracking, found no significant difference between the effectiveness of a long film which contained four repetitions of each instructional point and that of a shorter film which presented only two repetitions of each point. The two groups seeing the films achieved significantly higher scores, however, than those of a no-film control group.

One difficulty in studies of the effect of redundancy (e.g., varied repetition) on substantive content of a presentation is that, as opposed to standardized presentation of paired-associates material, the unit of presentation, and hence, of repetition, is difficult to define cleanly. One form of redundancy that can be defined with little equivocality is the use of examples illustrating a procedure or parallel instances of the application of a principle. Lumsdaine, Sulzer, and Kopstein (1961) studied the effect of the number of examples in films on micrometer reading. From three (the number included in a standard "training film") to ten examples were employed using a combination of films and filmstrips. In this study, the potency of repetition was evidenced by the fact that adding only *three* additional examples produced roughly twice as much gain as did the use of overlay animation techniques employed in the original film (see p. 631, above). Six or seven examples were much better than three; ten examples were somewhat better than six or seven. Gains from using added examples were understandably greater for more difficult aspects of the subject, as shown by post-film test data for the harder-to-read kinds of settings. Perhaps less predictably, the value of adding more examples was greater for the more intelligent students than for the less intelligent. It might be thought that repetition would help only the less intelligent, that the more intelligent would not profit from it. On the contrary, it was the more intelligent who benefited most from further repetition.

However, the apparent contradiction disappears as soon as a distinction is made between *need* for repetition and *ability to profit from it*. The data showed that the less intelligent men needed more repetition than did the brighter men in order to reach a certain level of accomplishment—say, 40 per cent correct readings. But at the same time, the gains from a given amount of repetition were greater for the brighter men. The latter did not need as much repetition to reach a minimum level of performance, but they were better able to profit from a reasonable amount of further repetition, especially on the difficult material.

Interaction between amount of review and use of active student response, noted above in the study by Kendler, Cook, and Kendler (1956), also entered into a study by Rothkopf (1960). He was concerned with varying the amount of review as a function of student performance in a teaching-machine-like arrangement for teaching paired-associate material. Rothkopf (see also Stephens, 1953) compared the efficiency of dropping out items in the list of paired associates after one correct anticipation by the student and after two correct anticipations, and found little difference between the two procedures.

One way of introducing more repetition within a given time is through a speeded-speech technique used in several experiments reported by Fairbanks, Guttman, and Miron (1957a, 1957b, 1957c). Time was saved by compressing audio instruction through an electronic-chopping technique. Compression by 50 per cent was used; no attempt was made to approach the 250 per cent level of compression found feasible for discrete words (with less than 10 per cent intelligibility loss) by Garvey and Henneman (1950). The attempt to squeeze in more learning through two full repetitions of instruction in a given time period was unsuccessful; scores for students who had one uncompressed presentation did not differ significantly from those who had two successive 50 per cent time-compressed presentations. Attempts to use the time saved by compression to introduce selective repetition of key points resulted in better learning of those particular points but at the expense of other points that were not repeated, and no evidence was found for a net over-all gain.

Type of repetition. The question of the relative merits of varied as against identical repetition was investigated in a study by Kanner and McClure (1956), using films on micrometer reading somewhat similar to those used in the study by Lumsdaine, Sulzer, and Kopstein (1961). Kanner and McClure compared the use of four examples seen twice with the use of eight different examples. They performed two experiments. In the first experiment they failed to find a statistically reliable difference between the two treatments immediately after training, but did find a reliable, though small, difference in favor of the varied-repetition treatment for the more able when subjects were tested a week after training. In the second experiment, no statistically reliable differences of any kind were found.

Results of an experiment by Rimland (1955), on the other hand, showed a consistent advantage for two identical repetitions over two different presentations (of about equal separate effectiveness) in teaching a perceptual-motor skill (knot-tying) by filmed demonstration. However, since a *specific* skill was being taught here, this finding is not necessarily incompatible with a hypothesis of greater effectiveness for varied examples in tasks, such as micrometer reading, which require generalization from examples used to teach a conceptual or procedural pattern.

Distribution of review. A study by Miller and Levine (1952) investigated two different ways of employing review sequences. It was concerned with the relative advantages of spacing the review sequences through a film, so that they followed each major topic, and of "massing" the review at the end of the film. The film used in this experiment dealt with Ohm's law. In the massed-review condition, the entire film was shown and then it was all reviewed. In the spaced-review condition, each of the four sections of the film was reviewed immediately after it was shown and then it was not mentioned again. The comparisons showed massed-review to be superior at the .01 level to the spaced review.

The authors offered two alternative but not mutually exclusive explanations for the superiority of massed review. The first explanation was that the condition of spaced review may be described as a massed-practice situation (since review of each section follows immediately its initial presentation), while the condition of massed review may be regarded as a spaced-practice condition (since review of each section is separated from its initial presentation by intervening material). The second explanation involves the recency factor: it is possible that performance on the test, which was given immediately after the film, was facilitated by the recency of the massed review in summarizing the main points of the film.

A later replication with military subjects using the same films failed to achieve significant differences, but the high degree of variability and low level of learning (probably due to adverse motivational conditions) would have prevented any but very gross effects from showing up. A further replication used another, more interesting film ("Pattern for Survival," a film on atomic attack) with high school classes as subjects. Eight classes were assigned to a no-review condition, eight classes to the spaced-review condition, and seven classes to the massed-review condition. For the spaced-review condition, the film was divided into four sections, and each section was reviewed by means of recorded narrations and colored slides before proceeding to the next section. For the massed-review condition, the entire review was deferred until the end of the film.

The massed-review condition was found to be superior to the spaced-review condition at the .05 level. (The spaced-review condition was found to be superior to the no-review condition at the .01 level.) However, a still further varied replication once more yielded no significant differences. Here an "active-participation" type of review was substituted for passive review. An explanation may lie in the fact that, despite the use of KCR, the potential benefits of spaced practice in the massed-review condition may have been negated by the effect of the students' practicing more errors in this condition (which was less well prompted because temporally more remote from the corresponding first presentation of each topic).

Structure and Organization of Sequences

Fatigue and distribution of effort. Some of the factors in the programing of instruction have been discussed earlier (pp. 625–626) in relation to conditions governing the efficient arrangement of practice sequences. The variable of spaced versus massed distribution of review sequences as just considered (p. 645) is not only related (inversely) to the massing or spacing of *practice,* but is also related to a variable occasionally confounded with the latter in the literature, namely, distribution of *effort.* Practice refers to the relative concentration of repeated trials; effort refers to concentration of successive units of relatively dissimilar material.

An experiment on distribution of effort in the context of instructional media was reported by Ash (1949). Using two film series, each consisting of four 15-minute silent films, Ash failed to find significant differences in effectiveness between showing all four films in a single, one-hour session and showing the films in two 30-minute sessions or in four 15-minute sessions. Effects were assessed in terms of retention one or two weeks later.

A different picture, however, is seen in the results of Faison, Rose, and Podell (1955), who showed that the effectiveness of a single 20-minute film during a single showing could be increased by rest breaks to increase audience attentiveness. An experiment utilizing infrared photography as an audience-observation technique indicated that the insertion of three very short (30-second) rest pauses in a 20-minute film led to reliable increases in an index of audience attentiveness. The underlying relation between duration of the film showing and audience attentiveness was exhibited in a progressive gradual decline in attentiveness for the "straight-through" showing, as contrasted with the abrupt rise in attentiveness following the rest pauses under the experimental condition. The introduction of the rest breaks led in turn to reliably greater learning as measured by a postfilm test than did a continuous showing of the same film.

The disparity between these results and those of Ash remains to be reconciled, perhaps taking into account differences in sensitivity of measures, of duration of the instructional periods (a total of 20 minutes versus one of about an hour), and of motivational factors related to subject matter and showing conditions, which were quite adverse in terms of temperature and ventilation in the study by Faison, Rose, and Podell (1955).

Structuring in relation to student practice. The use of rest pauses in the above-mentioned experiment by Faison and his co-workers and the use of active-response exercises interspersed between instructional sequences may serve the additional function of structuring or organizing the content. The importance of this function may, as suggested by the study of Margolius, Sheffield, and Maccoby (1957c, 1961b), interact with optimal use of student practice and may depend on the extent to which the task is inherently well structured. The purpose of this study by Margolius, Sheffield, and Maccoby was to test the hypothesis that, in learning a lengthy mechanical assembly task by joint use of demonstration and overt practice, the optimum placement of overt practice is at the completion of each "natural unit" of a total assembly task. A "natural unit" was defined as a portion of a task sequence which has its own distinctive context cues, such as a separate subassembly. Two methods for selecting demonstration-practice segments were compared: (1) use of overt practice at the end of such "natural units," and (2) use of overt practice at the end of arbitrarily defined segments of the task which match the "natural units" in their temporal length. Results for the film that was used showed no effects of the difference in treatment. The explanation which the experimenters offer is that if a task is inherently well organized, as this one appeared to be, there may be little to gain from additional procedures designed to enhance the organization.

Structuring by subtitles and outlines. In the previously described study by Miller and Levine (1952) on spaced versus massed distribution of review, a second question was how the effectiveness of the film might be affected by frequent subtitles designed to identify, set off, and structure the various topics and subtopics (electrical current, voltage, resistance, and Ohm's law) taken up successively in the film. Two degrees of structuring, employing (1) major subtitles only, and (2) "complete" subtitling for each subtopic, were compared with (3) a control film with no subtitles in which each sequence of material followed the next without a break. No significant differences were found among these three treatments, though, as previously noted, significant differences were found between different distributions of review. This may have been due to the fact that the material in the film on Ohm's law was already well structured in terms of its logical organization. In a later study by Northrop (1952),

significant differences were obtained favoring film versions in which structuring organizational outlines were employed as compared with similar films lacking these aids to organization.

Sequencing to Facilitate Discrimination

Several studies conducted in military training situations have an important bearing on the sequencing of material, particularly paired-associate materials, and may also have implications for the sequencing of connected discourse material in auto-instructional programs or other instructional instruments. A good example is the paper by Wulff and Stolurow (1957, 1961) dealing with "class-descriptive" cues that differentiate subgroups of materials which a trainee must learn to identify. The task used in this study was the standard code system by which aircraft rivets are coded, by color markings, etc., in terms of four properties: length, diameter, head shape, and material. Two forms of organization were used in sequencing the instruction. A series of training cards was used to teach the code for rivets. "Class organization" displays showed all the items in relation to one class of differentiating cues, e.g., rivet-head silhouettes or rivet-head markings that indicated diameter. "Item organization" displays gave the same information, but with all features about a given item presented at one time, e.g., a single rivet with each of the four coded characteristics depicted. By presenting many different individual rivets, one at a time, the application of the code was illustrated and taught. The latter method made it theoretically unlikely that the learner could utilize class cues effectively during learning, and thus it was predicted that class organization would be more effective. However, presentation and organization of information in existing handbooks and technical manuals were found to differ in practice according to the stylistic preferences of authors and editors for "class organization" or "item organization." The results supported the theoretical analysis; that is, the method of presentation which fostered utilization of class cues proved reliably superior to the other method.

A second study on sequencing of materials, by Detambel and Stolurow (1956), was concerned with a problem-solving situation in which the trainee was supposed to discover during the course of successive trials on which a varying display was presented (1) which of the components of the display was relevant to the decisions he had to make, and (2) which variation in the relevant component indicated that a particular decision was required. Two different training sequences were used. In one sequence the displays were arranged to provide minimum synchrony and in the other to provide maximum synchrony. *Synchronous* sequences were those with trial-to-trial relationships in which a relevant and an irrelevant component either *both maintained* their value or *both changed* value. Changes with respect to relevant and irrelevant aspects of the display, occurring concurrently (synchronously) were thus confounded so as to provide no way for the subject to isolate relevant from irrelevant features. But when either a relevant stimulus component changed and the irrelevant one did not, or vice versa (irrelevant component changed and relevant one did not), this relationship was described as asynchronous (having minimum synchrony), since in this case the relevant changes were isolated from the irrelevant ones.

Minimum synchrony between relevant and irrelevant components produced significantly larger proportions of solvers, but only at the lower ability levels. Under the maximum synchrony sequence the percentage of solvers increased regularly with increased ability; with minimum synchrony the percentage of solvers was about equal regardless of ability. The authors concluded that the principle of minimum synchrony should be used in arranging stimulus materials for training purposes. This would mean that, to the maximum extent possible, displays should be sequenced so that when a relevant component changes from display to display, the irrelevant component does not change; similarly, when the relevant component does not change, the irrelevant ones do change. Presumably such a rule would be applicable in programing displays for training devices such as simulators, instructional films, and programs for concept-learning tasks.

A third study on sequencing of material for discriminative learning is that of Rothkopf (1958), who performed several experiments employing Morse code signals as stimulus terms, and their appropriate alphabetic or numeric equivalents as response terms. The first experiment compared practice orders involving the maximal separation of similar stimuli with orders involving maximal clustering of similar stimuli. Other experiments compared four different methods of arranging practice orders: (1) maximal separation of similar stimuli; (2) successive presentation of similar stimuli; (3) successive presentation of relatively dissimilar stimuli; and (4) random stimulus presentation. The results indicated that the maximal separation of similar stimuli in the practice order produced the most efficient learning.

These results contrast with those of an earlier study by Gagné (1950), who found that successive presentation of similar stimuli was the most effective practice sequence in a paired-associate task which employed nonsense figures as stimulus terms and nonsense syllables as response terms. The reversal of the Gagné findings by Rothkopf's results indicates the complexity of factors governing optimum sequence in programing, which are likely to operate differently as a function of such factors as (1) the susceptibility of stimulus materials (as in Gagné's but not Rothkopf's) to utilization of mediating descriptive responses, and (2) the amount of response-term learning required and the resulting relative frequency of substitution errors (high for Rothkopf's conditions, low for Gagné's) and nonsubstitution errors.

Differences in sequencing instructional material could, in principle, be fully specified by sequencing rules with paired-associate tasks, as in the case of the three preceding studies. In the case of substantive, continuous-discourse materials, similar rules may also potentially be used to govern the programer's activities. One of the few studies in which different sequences generated in the latter sense have been compared experimentally is that of Evans (1960), who compared a program constructed by the "Ruleg" programing system with one constructed by a less systematic procedure. The former, in which more or less systematic relationships are observed between the introduction of principles or rules, in complete or incomplete form, and examples also in complete or incomplete form, was reported to produce a "comparable degree of learning but in less learning time." For details on the "Ruleg" system, see Homme and Glaser (1959) and Evans, Homme, and Glaser (1960).

Some of the studies previously mentioned in other contexts are also related to the problem of sequencing or programing. Examples are the familiarization study reported by Wulff and Kraeling (1961), in which advance familiarization with discriminative cues was found less effective than "in situ" familiarization, and the study by Miller and Levine (1952) on the spacing of review sequences.

Changes in Effects with Passage of Time

Effects of instruction usually change or dissipate with lapse of time, the familiar phenomenon being that of decreased retention due to "forgetting." The practical advantage of reproducible media such as films and self-instructional programs is that their initial use, or use for review, can be arranged so as to reduce forgetting by employing them at the most expedient point in time, shortly before the material learned is to be put to use. This advantage was brought out in the demonstration experiment by Shettel, et al. (1956), in which most of the material learned from conventional instruction had been forgotten after an interval of several weeks.

This loss was prevented or offset by showing the filmed version of the instruction just before its use in testing or practical application was demanded.

How long after instruction should its effects be measured? There is little evidence to guide the experimenter in this decision. Frequent practice is to test immediately or shortly after instruction and to retest for delayed retention after an interval of days or weeks. The prevailing pattern of results is a decrease in knowledge or skill for all forms of instruction, and, not infrequently, the finding that differences originally found between alternative treatments have "disappeared" or can no longer be demonstrated as significant statistically. Often this merely indicates that forgetting has reduced scores to such a low level that only very gross residual effects could be detected. For this reason, as well as on grounds of validity, the use of "savings" or relearning techniques for measuring retention might be preferable to the usual recall test; however, this technique appears not to have been used to any appreciable extent in nonlaboratory studies of learning from instructional media.

There are few instances in which the relative superiority of different instructional treatments has been found to change with passage of time. One possible exception is the earlier cited results of VanderMeer (1952), who found significant differences between some color and black-and-white versions, but only for delayed retention tests, not for immediate tests. An important exception to the general expectation of diminishing effects with passage of time is the finding by Hovland, Lumsdaine, and Sheffield (1949, Ch. 7) that some of the effects of films on attitudes or opinions showed an *increase* with passage of time, in contrast to effects on factual knowledge, which showed the usual phenomena of forgetting.

As factors in the sequencing and organization of instruction are attacked in more thoroughgoing fashion by study of alternative programing techniques, other instances will probably be found in which the immediate superiority of a particular instructional-sequence treatment may not necessarily be predictive of its relative effectiveness in later or transfer testing. Such an instance might well be found, for example, with respect to distribution of review (see the discussion of the 1952 Miller and Levine results on pp. 645–646).

SOME VERBAL FACTORS IN INSTRUCTION

"Readability" of Printed and Recorded Material

Despite the wide attention attracted by so-called readability formulas propounded by Flesch (1946, 1949), Dale and Chall (1948), and others, relatively little effort has been devoted to studying experimentally the utility of simplifying language to increase the effectiveness of learning from instructional media. Most studies (e.g., Park, 1945; Chall & Dial, 1948) have compared existing prose passages selected in terms of external criteria as exemplifying differences in level of difficulty, rather than manipulating material by application of the "rules" and then experimentally comparing the comprehension of the resulting simplified version with a more difficult version.

An interesting exception is the study by Gladstone (1958), who, rather than dealing with printed presentation, constructed alternative forms of the narration for a 20-minute instructional film by invoking rules for style simplification.[11] The two commentaries had the same factual content. The easier commentary was at the fourth-grade level of difficulty according to the Flesch formula, and at the sixth- to seventh-grade level according to the Dale-Chall formula; for the harder commentary, the corresponding levels were ninth- to tenth- and tenth- to twelfth-grade. An interesting aspect of the design was the use of two "split" versions, each with half the content in the difficult and half in the easier style. This design was used to control for individual differences because it was necessary, in this experiment, to use a relatively small number of intact classes rather than split the classes into comparable halves (see p. 657, below) or use unit-sampling statistics (see pp. 657–658). The experimental comparison substantiated, in general, the expectation that more factual material would be learned from the easier commentary. Much further experimentation would be needed, however, even to determine what aspects of the simplification procedures used were the effective ones, much less to validate general propositions about the factors that most strongly affect understandability of recorded or printed exposition. A factor analysis of materials differing in difficulty level has been performed by Stolurow and Newman (1956) to suggest factors that differentiate various difficulty levels.

Role of Verbalization

Some studies of the contribution of audio accompaniment to instructional films are difficult to interpret because the assignment of information to audio or visual modes is rather arbitrary in the first place. Thus, the findings of Nelson and Moll (1950) concerning the relative amounts of learning attributable to picture and sound track in certain films are of questionable generality because they can be taken as reflecting how much of the information tested by the experimenters happened to be given in the picture and in the sound track in those particular films. Demonstration of motor skills with or without accompanying commentary is perhaps less ambiguous because the appropriate content for visual and auditory components is more clearly generated by the nature of the task itself. McGuire (1955b, 1961c), using a demonstrational film designed to teach pursuit-rotor skill, found that groups trained by film scored significantly higher than a no-film (control) group, and also that film plus descriptive narration produced reliably better

---

[11] A similar study was made by Allen (1952), who covaried interest and difficulty levels of the commentary independently and found results generally similar to those of Gladstone.

results than the filmed demonstration alone. An experiment by Thomson (1944) reported by May (1946, 1958) studied verbalization as an aid to learning an assembly task, finding that guided verbalization of steps by the learner facilitated performance if the verbalization was relevant, but hindered it if the verbalization was irrelevant. The report by May is noteworthy for its trenchant, theory-based prescriptive guidelines for demonstration teaching. The rules given represent reasonable hypotheses, some of which are susceptible of experimental test. The same is true of the similar guidelines given by Sheffield and Maccoby (1961).

That the relevance of verbal labels makes a difference is also shown in studies on the utility of teaching nomenclature. Wulff (1955) found that, in terms of selection time, prior familiarization with the parts of the assembly (the same task as that used in the study reported by Wulff and Kraeling, 1961) was significantly better when the parts were named, than was prior familiarization when the parts were not named. This finding may be compared with the earlier results of Jaspen (1949), who found no significant improvement in performance on an assembly task when he required the audience to learn the technical nomenclature of the parts.

Cook (1960, p. 94) has suggested that these data on the use of nomenclature "suggest that people have individual ways of symbolizing objects to themselves. They make implicit perceptual responses to the objects—they may even apply names to them that are at variance with the correct technical nomenclature, but which are quite effective in guiding their selection of parts. [Such a procedure was recommended and employed by Sheffield and Maccoby (1961).] Perhaps requiring them to learn correct technical names interferes with these implicit symbolization responses." A related formulation is suggested by the results of Saltz and Newman (1960), who used the conceptualization of instructions as a serial list of cues. Saltz and Newman performed an experiment to test the following hypotheses: (1) if the symbols used in the

instructions are to be meaningful, they must be connected to the appropriate acts and to the equipment components for which they are referents (component-name learning); and (2) if the symbols are to aid performance, they must be connected to each other in the order that corresponds to the assembly sequence (order-of-name learning). The criterion task consisted of having Air Force recruits indicate the order in which the components of a pressure regulator fitted into the main shell of the regulator. The amount of component-name learning and the amount of order-of-name learning were manipulated independently. Results indicated that: (1) if there was any previous component-name learning, greater order-of-name learning resulted in increasingly better assembly performance; (2) if there was any previous order-of-name learning, greater component-name learning resulted in increasingly better assembly performance; (3) if there was no previous component-name learning, order-of-name learning had no effect on assembly performance; but (4) if there was no order-of-name learning, small amounts of component-name learning facilitated assembly, whereas large amounts of component-name learning produced decrements in assembly performance.

We may conclude that one way in which nomenclature can be used effectively is to utilize its cue properties, making sure that a way is provided for them to operate effectively. For example, in facilitating assembly, sequential ordering of the verbal cues appears necessary if the cues are to function effectively in guiding sequential performance. This ordering can be assured either by an explicit training procedure, as in the Saltz and Newman experiment, or by selecting verbal cues that already possess an inherent order, as in the study by Thomson (reported by May, 1946, 1958) in which numbering the parts in the order of their use in the assembly considerably facilitated performance. Evidence on the role of verbalization in other kinds of learning tasks is found in a study by Kurtz and Hovland (1953). They presented familiar objects to elementary school children and asked one group to locate and circle the appropriate object on a sheet of *pictures* and the other half to circle the appropriate object on a sheet of *names* and pronounce each name aloud. When tested for retention a week later, the group that verbalized at the time of presentation recalled significantly more items correctly and made fewer incorrect responses.

Several studies have investigated "rate" of verbalization and other factors in the style of verbal commentary accompanying demonstration films. Jaspen (1950) and Zuckerman (1949) varied the rate of verbalization in commentary accompanying assembly and knot-tying demonstration films, respectively, and concluded that a "medium" (90–130 words per minute) rate of verbalization was preferable. Unfortunately, rate was, to some extent, necessarily confounded with content and redundancy, as the commentary-rate variation was in the context of a fixed-pace demonstration. It is thus not altogether clear what the effective variable was in these experiments. A reasonably clear and obvious implication is that a commentary may contain either too little or too much information, but the specific rate that would be optimal could vary considerably, depending on the informational requirements of the task. Zuckerman also compared various modes of narration differing in voice and mood and concluded that imperative instructions were superior to passive-voice descriptions of the steps in the task being demonstrated. For another study of commentary variations, see Nelson and VanderMeer (1955).

Typographic Variations in Printed Material

Numerous studies of type-print legibility by Tinker and Paterson (e.g., 1940) and others are of at least passing interest in designing instructional instruments and in preparing materials where the focus is on legibility and readability rather than on learning and retention. A recent study in this category is that of Anderson, Novick, and Braunstein (1960). Standards of print size for verbal material in projected form based on acuity and resolution factors have been presented by the Eastman Kodak Company (1955), Stolurow and Lumsdaine (1956), and others. Several experimental studies of the effects of conventional and novel typographic arrangements on short-term learning and retention of verbal material have also been performed, the most extensive series being those reported by Klare and his co-workers (1955a, 1955b, 1957, 1959). However, the applicability of the findings to date for the design of instructional instruments appears to be rather slight.

Persuasive Communications

Although somewhat peripheral to the design of specifically instructional materials, at least a brief mention should be made here of experiments on factors in the sequencing of verbal material in persuasive communications. The most impressive group of studies in this field is that of Hovland and his co-workers (e.g., Hovland, 1957; Hovland, Janis, & Kelley, 1953). These studies illustrate the evolution of findings and redelineation of problems for research in a programatic effort centered in a particular problem area in the effectiveness of verbal communication. It seems to the writer, moreover, that as behavior and communication theories evolve in the light of experimental inquiry, some crucial theoretical substructure for effective practice in *persuasive* communication is likely to show many points of close similarity or even identity with that underlying communication designed to influence knowledges and skills. Even at a superficial level, for example, there is an interesting parallel between (1) the assumptions used in sequencing arguments in the communications used to study one-sided and two-sided arguments (Hovland, Lumsdaine, & Sheffield, 1949, Ch. 8; Lumsdaine & Janis, 1953) and (2) the rationale used in anticipating and heading off errors in the construction of small-step teaching-machine programs. In view of such parallels, the student and research worker concerned with purely instructional media need to become informed not only on methodological points in research on persuasive communication, but also on substantive findings and theoretical developments in this field.

MOTIVATION-INCENTIVE-INTEREST FACTORS

Interest and Motivation as Variables

Interest, motivation, and incentive factors may figure in the objectives and design of instructional media both as independent and dependent variables. In the former sense we ask how procedural or content aspects of an instructional instrument which are believed to have motivational properties can be manipulated to increase the extent to which desired instructional objectives (of whatever sort) are attained. In the latter sense, we ask how manipulations of instructional variables (of whatever sort) affect not only direct instructional outcomes in knowledge and skills, but also influence motivations, interests, or other outcomes desired for their indirect value in facilitating or stimulating further learning.

An example of a study where the latter emphasis predominates is that reported by May and Lumsdaine (1958, pp. 31–45), who compared two versions of a film presenting a scientific explanation of the causes of seasonal change. One version of the film used live dialogue and the other version used narration. Fifth-grade students tended to prefer the live dialogue version to the narration version, and those who were shown the live-dialogue version expressed somewhat greater interest in the subject matter of the film than those who were shown the narration version. However, the amounts learned from the two versions were not found to be significantly different.

Experiments on the relationship between interest in an instructional presentation and amount learned from it have not pinned the question down very closely. The experiment by Hovland, Lumsdaine, and Sheffield (1949, Ch. 5) is an example of a study in which an "interesting" kind of presentation (dramatic) was compared with a more straightforward, presumably less interesting, kind of presentation. No genuinely analytic definition of the specific variables involved was provided in this experiment, which yielded no significant difference favoring one treatment over the other. VanderMeer (1953) made a somewhat similar comparison of the effect of two versions of a film on personal hygiene. This experiment is one of the relatively few studies in which motivated nonverbal behavior—in this case personal hygiene habits—has been measured as a criterion variable. VanderMeer compared a straight lecture film with one which has been described as "a jazzed up version with folk music in elaborate Hollywood style" (Cook, 1960, p. 92). Both versions appeared to produce some change in personal hygiene behavior and appeared to be "about equally effective" (p. 92). Aside from the usual difficulties in the interpretation of negative results (see pp. 664 ff., below), these two studies must be considered as semi-evaluative ones in which two films representing approaches that presumably differed with respect to some factor (in this case, interest) were compared, but without precise manipulation of specific, identifiable factors and close control over other aspects of content.

Twyford (1951) found a negative correlation between how much students liked a film and how much they were reported to have learned from it. This interpretation requires clarification and represents an interesting methodological question. Cook (1960) interpreted the findings of VanderMeer (1953), Twyford (1951), and May and Lumsdaine (1958) as justifying the conclusions that "interest in a film is not the same as interest in the subject matter of the film; the amount of interest in the film does not predict the amount that will be learned from it, and as a rule technical slickness does not increase the amount learned from a film" (p. 92).

Manipulation of Incentive
and Motivational Factors

The use of feedback to students of test results in the May-Lumsdaine experiment (1958, Ch. 7) involved motivational as well as informational functions. An experiment in which reports of test results were confined to motivational aspects was one reported by Kimble (1955a). The effects of praise and reproof were compared for student performance on a test covering preliminary phases of an instructional topic. Praise and reproof had no significant effect, in terms of subsequent test performance, on material learned before the administration of praise or reproof. But on material taught *after* the administration of praise or reproof, there were significant effects; the reproved group scored highest, the praised group next, and a no-incentive-comment group lowest. The differences were significant, and thus call into question the generalizability of the widely cited results of the early study by Hurlock (1925), which have generally been advanced as evidence favoring the use of praise rather than reproof as a motivating agent.

A superficially quite different manipulation of incentive-reward factors in an instructional presentation was that employed by McGuire (1961b). In using a film to teach pursuit-rotor tracking, he found that items nearer to a "reward sequence" (a film sequence demonstrating the beneficial effect of a particular instructional point) were learned significantly better than those more remote from the reward sequence. However, these findings may be more closely related to the phenomena of attention-directing, studied by May and Lumsdaine and others (see p. 640, above), than to a generalized motivational effect.

In investigating the effect of films on subsequent student activity, May and Lumsdaine (1958, Ch. 13) found no evidence that showing a film version of a novel induced pupils to read the book or even to withdraw it from the classroom library. Later, May and Jenkinson (1953, 1958) demonstrated that showing interesting but incomplete filmed episodes from a novel did significantly increase the number of pupils who withdrew the book from the library, though the evidence was less clear that many of them then read the novel and remembered the content.

Two experiments have dealt with attempts to increase drive, and hence learning, by producing anxiety. In the first of these, Kendler, Kendler, Desiderato, and Cook (1953) attempted to utilize the effects of anxiety to increase the amount learned from a film on safety measures for reducing the likelihood of injury in automobile accidents. A color filmstrip with sound accompaniment depicting results of automobile accidents was shown preceding a film demonstration of safety measures. The filmstrip was intended to heighten anxiety in the audience, so as to increase drive and, in turn, the amount learned from the film on safety measures. However, it produced no discernible effect on scores on a test that followed the safety-demonstration film.

The second experiment, by Feshbach and Janis (1951), was more successful. As part of instruction on care of the teeth, three groups of subjects were given anxiety-producing communications such as close-up shots of decaying teeth and diseased gums. Three versions of the anxiety-stimulating material were used, designed to evoke high, medium, and mild degrees of anxiety. Although one might expect that the higher the drive, the greater the learning, this was not found; rather, the lowest degree of anxiety was most effective. The results may be interpreted in terms of the hypothesis that although the high-anxiety group may have been given a high degree of drive, the need to reduce their anxiety led them not to pay attention or think about their teeth at all. A lesser degree of anxiety, however, presumably was helpful because it stimulated attention and learning of the desired habits without being so aversive as to cause subjects to avoid thought that could lead to desired habits in the course of reducing anxiety.

METHODOLOGICAL PROBLEMS IN EXPERIMENTS ON INSTRUCTIONAL MEDIA

A number of methodological points in the rationale, design, and execution of experiments on instructional instruments have been noted in discussing the research evidence. A full treatment of the methodological considerations in such experimentation would carry us far beyond the space available for the present chapter.

GENERAL CONSIDERATIONS

Some of the methodological problems and issues arising in the studies discussed above are, however, briefly discussed in the following pages. The problems selected for discussion are those which may arise in any educational experimentation, but are particularly likely to enter into the design of experiments on instructional media.

It is neither possible nor necessary here to give any complete treatment of the design of experiments on instructional media and instruments. As a general source, the reader is referred to Chapter 5 of this Handbook. In addition to standard texts such as Lindquist (1953), and A. L. Edwards (1954), the chapter by Mosteller and Bush (1954) can be very helpful in planning experimental tests of hypotheses concerning instructional media. For a more detailed treatment of research methods oriented specifically to problems in research on instructional media, see the guidebook prepared for the Educational Media Branch of the U.S. Office of Education (Lumsdaine & Roshal, 1962). A useful reference on problems not systematically or concisely treated in more general works is provided by Hovland, Lumsdaine, and Sheffield (1949). Among the factors they discuss in describing specific experiments are the questions of anonymity of response in experiments on attitudes, interests, motivations, or opinions, and ways in which experimental design and procedures can be arranged to retain anonymity even while allowing for matching of "before" and "after" responses, on the basis of demographic data and handwriting (see Hovland, Lumsdaine, & Sheffield, 1949, pp. 28 ff.). These writers also discussed various measurement procedures not commonly dealt with in textbooks on experimental method. For an elementary discussion of the use of objective tests in assessing effects in experiments with instructional media, the reader is referred to Chapter 18 of May and Lumsdaine (1958).

Various appendices in Hovland, Lumsdaine, and Sheffield (1949) are devoted to common methodological problems encountered in their experiments: (1) measurement in terms of percentage changes based on amount of room for change, a problem which arises frequently in one form or another in comparisons of media effects on groups with unequal initial baselines—e.g., two groups differing in intelligence or in initial attitude; (2) the problem of correction for guessing with use of multiple-choice test items; (3) the comparative advantages and disadvantages of (a) experimental designs incorporating before-after measures obtained from the same individuals, and (b) "after-only" designs in which the "before" level is obtained by measurements of a separate control group; (4) the often valuable analysis of "internal" shifts in the responses of individuals which can be identified, of course, only in the paired-measures "before-after" design; (5) the tricky and often ignored problem of regression, due to unreliability of the measuring instrument, as it enters into analysis of the effects of a communication. This latter discussion bears especially on tests of hypotheses which predict effects in opposite directions for subjects differing in terms of initial response or in terms of characteristics correlated with initial response. It demonstrates that, in general, a valid analysis for testing such hypotheses must include paired before-after measures not only for the experimental groups but also for a control group. The control group is needed to serve as an index of the amount of downward change from higher scores and upward change from lower ones. That is, although the direction of such changes is a foregone conclusion, their extent is generally unpredictable without a control group, in the case of repeated observations with measuring instruments of less than perfect reliability.

SOME STATISTICAL AND SAMPLING PROBLEMS

Individual and Group Sampling

Many experiments on instructional instruments such as films are conducted in real classroom situations. This means that often the experimental treatments are assigned to *class groups* rather than randomized among *individuals*. This procedure poses serious difficulties in obtaining a valid measure of experimental error and, in some cases, in assuring that the groups compared are "comparable" in the sense that the comparison is not affected by factors other than the experimental variable.

One way of handling this situation—though it is never really satisfactory except as an adjunct to some appropriate randomization procedure (see below, and cf. Chapter 5 of this Handbook, *passim*)—is to seek comparability (elimination of bias) by use of equating or by covariance analysis employing background or prediction variables to match the groups so as to assure that they are "equivalent" except for the effect of the experimental variable(s). When matching is to be used, matching the groups by selective discarding of cases may be less efficient than use of covariance in terms of purely statistical efficiency. This less efficient method may be preferable nevertheless, especially where many cases are available and when there are a number of prediction variables in terms of which to match the groups. It is usually preferable to match groups by distribution categories rather than solely in terms of means. However, groups may be quite dissimilar with respect to certain background variables without affecting the outcome if these variables are uncorrelated with

—and hence irrelevant to—the criterion variable (see Hovland, Lumsdaine, & Sheffield, 1949, pp. 324–325). Use of selective-discard matching (to even up the distributions with respect to several stratifying variables) rather than employing covariance may save labor when the number of dependent criterion variables is large, as in the case of detailed evaluation studies (e.g., Hovland, Lumsdaine, & Sheffield, 1949, Chs. 2, 3; May & Lumsdaine, 1958, Appendices A and B), since one process of equating suffices for any number of dependent variables (e.g., 100 points of information to be conveyed by an instructional film). For efficiency, it is necessary, of course, that the matching variables be relevant to this whole class of criteria.

The use of matching or analysis of covariance to equate preformed groups may, if carefully carried out, result in demonstrably close "comparability" of the groups to be compared, e.g., in terms of very close similarity on a relevant pretest. *Sole* dependence on matching to compensate for lack of individual sampling, however, still leaves the experimenter without a rigorous basis for assessing experimental error. Such a basis should derive clearly from the operations performed in the assignment of experimental treatments. The investigator who would use matching as a sole basis for "comparability" runs the hazard that he must assume the matching will result in group composition that does not differ materially from what would have been obtained had random assignment to experimental treatments been employed. Such "let's not and say we did" procedures can never be as satisfying from the standpoint of experimental rigor as can procedures in which a random manner of assigning experimental treatments directly generates (1) the method of computing the measure of experimental error and (2) the test of significance that is used to determine whether the differences in criterion measures represent dependable, nonchance effects of the treatments. Accordingly, matching or analysis of covariance procedures should be resorted to only when administrative factors preclude the setting up of a true experiment, in which the unit entry that contributes one degree of freedom to the error estimate (be it a person, a classroom, a school, or a city) in the statistical analysis has a one-to-one relationship to the unit of random assignment by which subjects are allocated to experimental treatments.

There are two general ways in which this condition may be attained. The first is by sampling (assignment to treatments) of individual subjects rather than groups. The second, where assignment to treatments must be made in terms of intact, preformed groups, e.g., classrooms, rather than in terms of individuals, is to use the group rather than the individual as the unit of statistical analysis. (See Hovland, Lumsdaine, & Sheffield, 1949, p. 327, and Lindquist, 1953, Ch. 7, for further discussion of the rationale.) A good example of the use of the unit-sampling technique is found in the study by Lumsdaine and Gladstone (1958). In either case, the essential condition for a rigorous experimental test, as emphasized by Fisher (1947, pp. 33–40), is that the estimate of experimental error·be based on the operations that actually determine experimental error, with degrees of freedom based on the number of independent acts of randomization. In practical terms, this means that spurious attribution of effects will not result from the not infrequent situation in which group-to-group, e.g., school-to-school, variability grossly exceeds what would result from random sampling of equivalent-sized groups.

A special advantage of "unit sampling, unit variance" designs is that the measure of error derived from group-to-group variability takes into account not only the fluctuations due to individual-difference (population) variables, but also properly reflects the influence of variations in conditions for different classroom groups, e.g., time of day, instructor, behavior, procedural irregularities, etc. A more secure basis for generalization of results is thus afforded than is obtained even from individual sampling and assignment of subjects, unless the experimental instruction

and testing is also performed individually. On the other hand, if individually sampled students are assembled for instruction and testing en masse, procedural irregularities common to the assembled group can still represent important sources of error variance which may not be adequately randomized or may not be adequately reflected in error estimates. What to do about the group in which the projector temporarily broke down during the experimental film is a case in point. If all, or a sizable proportion of, the subjects for an experimental condition were in this group, the experimenter would be in real trouble, and the fact that subjects were randomly assigned to that group would be of little help to him. But if subjects were run individually or in a number of groups, each of which is treated as one experimental observation, he is much better off. He can afford to throw out the procedurally aberrant group if the aberration is considered serious (in terms of predetermined criteria, applied so as not to bias the comparison); or, he can retain the group with the assurance that the effect of the aberration will be safely reflected in his estimate of experimental error.

Administrative conditions may require that the experimental instruction be performed in groups. In that event, random assignment of individuals to treatments may still be feasible. If so, this procedure may be greatly preferable to the block assignment of intact classroom groups because it reduces unwanted variability due to population variables not randomly distributed in the intact groups. This procedure is often much more feasible in two-group (two-treatment) experiments than in cases where a larger number of treatments are employed, particularly if the experimental variation is introduced only for a single lesson or class period. Under these circumstances, students in a given classroom may be assigned randomly to two alternative groups, each of which is then instructed (and tested also, perhaps) in a separate room with one of the alternative experimental instruments. Examples of this design are found in the study of live dialogue versus offstage narration reported by May and Lumsdaine (1958, Ch. 3), in which the two subgroups saw alternate versions of a film, and in several experiments by Gropper and Lumsdaine (1961) in which the two subgroups saw alternate versions of TV lessons presented simultaneously over two channels.

When the experimental variations are implemented by means of printed, verbal, or pictorial materials, used alone or with a constant audio-recorded explanation, within-class sampling of more than two experimental treatments, if desired, may be readily implemented within a single classroom (e.g., Hovland & Weiss, 1951; Kimble & Wulff, 1961b). Such an arrangement can be very advantageous from the standpoint of experimental economy. The same advantage obviously applies to experimentation using individually paced auto-instructional materials.

In this case, as well as in instances where both assignment and experimental instruction are done individually, the assignment of individuals need not be *wholly* random: some stratification may be introduced to reduce error variance further, with the experimenter then randomly assigning individuals to the treatments within stratification categories (see Ch. 5, p. 196). Such categories may, in the extreme case, be pairs of individuals; for example, an efficient procedure that is often administratively workable is to obtain a class roster in advance and assign one member of each adjacent pair on the roster to each of two experimental treatments (alternative versions of a film or other instructional instrument). If the roster has been arranged in random order, assignment of every other person to one of two experimental treatments will, of course, produce two random halves of the group; if the roster is alphabetical, similar assignment will also generally produce substantially random halves. However, if the roster has first been arranged according to a stratifying variable (e.g., intelligence test score) that is well correlated with criterion test performance, variability of the halves of classes will be materially less than random. In such a case, the experimenter must of course modify his statistical analysis if he wishes to take advantage of this fact to increase the sensitivity of the comparisons; this modification can be achieved automatically when the split-class division is replicated in a large enough number of classrooms (e.g., half a dozen or more) if, despite the individual assignment of subjects, the experimenter uses the pairs of experimental-administration groups as the units of statistical analysis, as suggested above for the group-sampling case. As noted previously, this procedure has the advantage that variance due to group-linked differences in instructional conditions (time of day, etc.) enters appropriately into the error estimate. If unit analysis, with *df* based on number of pairs of instructional groups rather than number of individual subjects, is employed to achieve this desideratum, random or stratified-random assignment of individuals rather than classes to treatment groups still has the advantage of reducing error variance and thus rendering experimental comparisons potentially more sensitive.

Sampling of Subject Matter

Brunswik (1947) is noted for having called attention to the importance, in psychological or educational experiments, of having not only an adequately representative sampling of people but also an adequate sampling of materials or subject matter. This point is important because of the danger of unsound generalization of results from experiments using only a single restricted set of materials.

Granted that some sampling of materials is always desirable, the fact is that it is often difficult and costly to sample a wide range of material. It is therefore well to recognize that the importance of sampling subject matter may differ depending on the experiment, and that replication of findings with respect to subject matter may be sought in several ways, some of which are less costly and difficult than others. Sampling subject matter reflects an effort to take account of the principle that the generalizability of any finding depends on the number of *independent* observations on which the sampling is based.

Independent in what respects? From the standpoint of maximum generalizability of results, the ideal experiment on educational media would provide an explicit basis for generalization in which N, the number of observations on which experimental inference is based, would represent N *completely independent* observations, alike only in that they provided instances of the operation of the hypothesis being tested. This condition would be very well approximated if a sign test were applied to the outcomes of N experimental tests of a hypothesis, each conducted with different subjects, a different subject matter, and different experimenters in different locations, possibly using different experimental designs. Under these ideal conditions we could be reasonably sure that rejection of a null hypothesis did not result from experimental artifacts or peculiarities of the specific sampling of subjects or learning materials. Somewhat less formal assurance that this is the case is provided when several more or less independent replications of an experiment are conducted, and each yields a significant difference with respect to the factor manipulated in all the replications.

Within any one experiment, the security and breadth of the basis for generalizing the findings can, in a sense, be assessed from the degree to which the observations (equal in number to N in the tests of significance employed) are independent with respect to relevant factors. In rare instances, such as the experiments by Sheffield (1946) and Lumsdaine (1949, 1958), degrees of freedom can be based on observations each of which represents an independent sampling of learners each of whom learns an independent sample of material drawn from some more or less well-defined populations of learners and materials. Unfortunately, this is generally not done, and N is most commonly based on the number of independently assigned learners— or, in some cases (see p. 192, above), independently assigned groups of learners. Here, sampling of subject matter or material is rarely taken explicitly into account, although

for some kinds of experimental designs it is more appropriate to base degrees of freedom on number of subject-matter items than on number of individual learners tested. For example (see Lumsdaine, 1958), suppose a design is employed in which each subject (learner) "serves as his own control" by learning one set of material under Experimental Condition I and a different set of material under Experimental Condition II. Then valid comparisons of I and II *must* take the sampling of subject-matter items explicitly into account in estimating error. It is obvious that no matter how large the number of subjects, differences between I and II could depend solely on differences in the sample of material assigned to each. Certainly, no significance test not basing N on the number of items sampled could assess the likelihood that a given difference could have arisen by accident of differences arising from item sampling.

But in most experiments, subject matter is "controlled," i.e., content is presumably the same for the two or more experimental treatments (experimental conditions). In these instances, even though we should ideally proceed as above and base df on the number of independent replications of subjects and materials, we generally settle instead for basing df only on sampling of persons, leaving the generalizability to new subject matter up to faith or at most replicating with one or two subject matters to provide one or two df on which to satisfy ourselves as to this generalizability. Some further considerations with respect to replication are discussed below.

REPLICATION IN RESEARCH DESIGN

Old Variables in New Experiments

An increase in generalizability can be sought in the replication of experiments. Beyond this, a special advantage is often gained in replicating, in an experiment on a variable not previously studied, one or more variables whose effects have already been assessed as significant in a previous experiment. For example, one purpose of including the active-versus-passive review variable in the Lumsdaine-Gladstone (1958) experiment on pictorial and auditory embellishments was to replicate the previous findings of Hovland, Lumsdaine, and Sheffield (1949) under slightly varied conditions. This scientifically healthy practice is almost routine in the physical sciences but, unhappily, is the exception in educational experimentation. There was also an additional methodological purpose in including this variation of active-passive review in a study in which the primary (new) variation was manipulation of the entertaining embellishments. This purpose was to provide a yardstick against which effects of the primary variable could be assessed.

Since absolute values of the kind of scores used here have little meaning, the coexistence within an experiment of two experimental factors can indicate, at least in rank-order terms, the relative potency or importance of the two factors. This comparison is the more informative if one of the factors is known in advance to have a sizable effect, and especially if data exist (as was true in the study by Lumsdaine and Gladstone, 1958, on the basis of the previous study) as to its importance in comparison with other variables, such as ability. In the present example, we might wish to hazard the tentative conclusion that the adverse distracting effect of this type of embellishing device has less potency—i.e., may account for less variation—than the positive effect of overt practice provided by a good active-review procedure.

A secondary factor that predictably turns out to make a significant difference is, perhaps, even more desirable when manipulation of the primary factor shows no significant effect. With such negative results—which occur in a considerable proportion of the experimental studies in audio-visual education —the problem of interpretation is almost always difficult (see below). The auxiliary variable that does show a sizable influence provides reassurance that the experimental circumstances were sensitive enough to re-veal potent causes of real variation. This advantage relates to the more general problems of experimental sensitivity and the logic of interpreting negative results, discussed below.

Replication of Subgroups and Covaried Experimental Treatments

Another interesting aspect of methodology in the animation study by Lumsdaine, Sulzer, and Kopstein (1961) was the use of a factorial design which, in effect, permitted independent replicative comparisons to be made for different subgroups of the audience. Thus, the animated films produced better learning than the nonanimated films, regardless of whether (1) the film was preceded by a preliminary quiz which oriented men to the nature of the material to be learned; (2) longer films with six instructional examples or shorter films with only three examples were used; (3) a supplementary slide film was used following the film showing; and under all possible combinations of these three conditions. Other comparisons indicated that the animated films were superior to the nonanimated ones regardless of whether the films were shown under favorable temperature conditions (morning showings) or under extremely humid conditions (afternoon showings) in the indoctrination training center, regardless of variations in the size of the audience and the distance men sat from the screen, and regardless of whether proficiency in micrometer reading was strictly scored in terms of fully correct answers or more leniently scored with credit also given for partially correct answers.

Similarly, analyses were made to ascertain whether the differential effect was a function of the mental ability as measured by the Air Force qualifying examination. This kind of analysis is often worth making because, in some cases, it has been shown that effect of a particular instructional variable may differ considerably according to the intelligence of the learner (see Hovland, Lumsdaine, &

Sheffield, 1949, Chs. 6–9). In the animation study, the effect of animation on the ability to read micrometer settings was shown by the difference between 72 per cent mean correct answers for the animated films and 66 per cent for the nonanimated films, in the case of the more intelligent men, while for the less intelligent men the mean scores were 41 per cent correct for the animated films and 28 per cent for the nonanimated films. Analysis of the data for learning of nomenclature showed that the beneficial effect of the animation devices also held for groups of trainees differing in intelligence and educational level.

"Replicative" Criterion Measures

The advantage for animation devices in the study just noted also held regardless of whether knowledge of nomenclature was strictly scored (correct spelling of terms) or loosely scored (credit given for a reasonably close approximation to the correct name). This suggests that the advantage of using labels is not limited merely to providing the correct spelling of the terms. Experimental findings may, however, often be questioned because of the arbitrariness of a particular criterion variable. For example, in studies of attitude change (e.g., Hovland, Lumsdaine, & Sheffield, 1949, Ch. 2), some criterion questions may show significant effects and others may not. In a World War II experiment on the persuasive effects (on men's estimates of how much longer the war would last) of presenting one side versus both sides of a controversial question (Hovland, Lumsdaine, & Sheffield, 1949, Ch. 8), "internal-change" measures indicating the net percentage who changed their opinions to any extent furnished a more sensitive indicator than did percentages based on shifts in marginal distributions or changes in mean values of men's estimates. The same may be true of test items used to measure instructional effects. Furthermore, some of the ways in which criterion measures may be derived from such items may be sensitive to differen-

tial effects of alternative treatments and others may not be. Consequently, confidence that a result does not depend on peculiarities of a particular measure, as well as confidence that an experiment is sensitive enough to reveal any effects that took place, may be increased by examining each of several independent indicators, or even each of several ways of summarizing the data. As an illustration, in the study of animation devices by Lumsdaine, Sulzer, and Kopstein (1961), the experimental results were examined in terms of several criteria deriving from the same performance. For example, mean scores (expressed as mean per cent of correct reading) showed a mean of 56 per cent correct for the animated version as opposed to 47 per cent for the unanimated version. In addition, the relative effectiveness of the two versions was also observed by comparing the results for the two groups in terms of the percentages of men who achieved various criteria of proficiency. For example, 72 per cent of the men who saw the animated film answered at least three test questions correctly, but only 57 per cent of the nonanimated film group were able to do so. Similarly, 59 per cent of the animated group got more than half the test questions correct, while only 46 per cent of the nonanimated group did this well. Thus, the results were consistent in direction, with variation in the absolute magnitude of "effects" according to the method of expressing the results. A further advantage of showing results for several different measures is that the specific numerical values used to indicate the "amount of superiority" of one experimental version over another will sometimes vary widely, depending on how the results were expressed. In some instances, indeed, different conclusions may be arrived at, depending on which measure is selected as the criterion. Thus, conservatism is served by examining several different measures. When, as in this case, all of the measures lead to the same conclusion, the experimenter can rightly claim more confidence for his conclusions than when they are based on only a single measure of effect.

GROUP VERSUS INDIVIDUAL TESTING WITH VERBAL AND PICTORIAL MATERIALS

The question of whether to administer criterion tests individually or in groups is often confounded with the related question of group versus individual sampling or assignment to experimental treatments. When we are considering individual assignment to groups, we may recognize that individual *administration* of an experiment often carries with it individual testing of subjects' achievement. However, the questions of group versus individual *sampling, experimental instruction, testing,* and *application of results* are by no means synonymous. In theory, one might employ any one of the 16 possible combinations of four dichotomous alternatives: (1) sampling by individuals versus sampling by preformed groups, (2) administration of the experimental instruction in a group or individually, (3) testing achievement in a group or individually, and (4) application of the conclusions to later instruction in a group or in an individual situation. For example, in the Hovland-Lumsdaine-Sheffield study of active versus passive review (1949, Ch. 9), both group and individual testing were employed, though sampling was on an individual basis and experimental administration of instructional treatments was done in groups. Here, however, the applicability to an individual-instruction situation of findings favoring active review was limited by the fact that the active-review procedure employed oral group responses that provided interperson feedback. On the other hand, the general principles favoring active response, as exemplified in written-response procedures used in later experiments such as that of Michael and Maccoby (1953, 1961), would also be applicable to individual instruction using teaching machines or other devices.

Sometimes, regardless of whether sampling, experimental instruction, or desired application is by individual or by group, individual testing may have advantages with respect to sensitivity, reliability, or demonstrability of consistency in the results. For example, in the experiment on active review by Hovland, Lumsdaine, and Sheffield (1949, Ch. 9), individual-test results were found to be more sensitive and useful for most of the analyses than were group-test results. The individually administered, one-item-at-a-time tests controlled the amount of time devoted to each item in a way that group-administered paper-and-pencil tests did not and also allowed measurement of individual reaction time. The individual tests permitted comparison of correct responses given promptly with those given more hesitantly. (See Fig. 3 in Hovland, Lumsdaine, and Sheffield, 1949, p. 235.) On the other hand, the group tests provided a more economical source of data for analyses of differential effects on population subgroups. In a later replication of this experiment by Lumsdaine and Gladstone (1958), the advantage of item-exposure control (though not the availability of reaction time data) was realized, together with the economy of group administration, by using projected slides to present test items one at a time to a group for a predetermined interval. The interval could, of course, be varied as desired from item to item by the instructor to conform to his purposes.

Another useful aspect of projected visual test materials is seen in the study of animation technique (Lumsdaine, Sulzer, & Kopstein, 1961), in which criterion test performance was closely related to the criterion behavior which the film was designed to teach, namely, the reading of micrometer settings. Although actual performance tests with real micrometers were not employed, the effective stimulus that would be encountered in an actual performance test was realistically simulated by means of slides, each showing micrometer settings which the trainees were required to read. Fifteen different settings were used in the test, given after exposure to any one of the experimental films. (In addition, other test questions were used to test effects on knowledge of nomenclature, construction, and principles of operation of the micrometer.) In testing ability to read micrometer settings, each slide was projected on a screen for a fixed interval, and the trainees were instructed simply to write down the value of the settings on a test blank. This test had high face validity, and, furthermore, preliminary experimentation had indicated that if men could read the pictured settings, they could also read the settings given in actual micrometers.

The writer has devised an interesting variant of this procedure used in connection with a later study by Kanner and Sulzer (1956), in which objective scoring was employed without eliminating the advantage of having constructed, rather than recognition, responses by the examinees. A picture of a micrometer setting was projected for an appreciable period of time, during which the examinee had to figure out the reading and write it down. Then four possible numerical values for the setting were flashed on the screen, for an interval so brief that the examinee had time only to determine which one (if any) of the four possible settings matched the one he had "constructed" (figured out) for himself. The four values were arranged horizontally and coupled with "boxes" that simulated the spaces of the IBM answer-sheet on which the student recorded his answer by indicating a, b, c, d, or "none of these."[12]

---

[12] This technique is similar to the method described by Gilbert (1958) and others for use in self-instructional devices to permit semi-automatic, relatively cheat-proof comparison of constructed responses (rather than judgmental right-wrong assessment by the student). In this case, constructed responses are compared with possible answers which are subsequently revealed, whereupon the student indicates which answer, if any, matches his own—an assessment action which does not necessarily reveal the correct answer to him at once but which can be made the basis for objective comparison by the machine (and for scoring or program branching). This technique has also been used experimentally in self-instructional programs for teaching basic job knowledge to SAGE-system operators. (See Shettel, Angell, & Lumsdaine, 1961.)

THE RATIONALE OF EXPERIMENTATION

Formal and Informal Experimentation

Gilbert (1960) recently took a position which implies that the use of student-response data in revision of a specific self-instructional program may be the only defensible use of empirical data in the study of learning. Gilbert decries the conduct of systematically controlled experiments to test particular hypotheses. Instead, he feels, the laboratory should be the scene of informal, developmental "tryout and discovery." He admonishes us to "resist the temptation to design formal experiments," on the supposition that "you don't want to know whether one method teaches better than another; you want to know what method teaches best."

Although the way in which one discovers the latter without the former is not clear in terms of formal logic, Gilbert does make the valid point that an efficient method of teaching can display itself in a controlled experimental study only if the truly efficient method of teaching is used in the experiment. But his contention also leads us to consider the utility of "applied-development" versus "basic research" (defined as the testing of potentially generalizable propositions) and, perhaps more cogently, the order in which research and development should proceed. One can argue that until an effective method of teaching has been evolved by informal trial and error in a particular situation, comparison of specific factors may be conducted at such a low level of over-all efficiency that the influence of variables manipulated may be distorted. On the other hand, in formal experiments to test hypotheses, it is sometimes difficult to reveal the influence of a particular variable efficiently if other factors in the situation are so favorable that it cannot account for much variance. An example is found in the study by Maccoby, Michael, and Levine (1961) following up the study of Michael and Maccoby (1953), in which it was found that, in order to reveal motivational effects of active student response (as distinct from direct-practice effects), it was necessary to operate at a very low level of over-all motivation.

Even if we dissent from Gilbert's seemingly serious abandonment of the scientific method as a way of arriving at valid inductive generalizations about the operation of specific factors, it must be admitted that the optimum strategy in improving instruction is often far from clear regarding the balance and timing of effort between informal, "tryout" experimenting and more formal experimentation. We can perhaps agree that observations deriving from informal experimenting, even if based on only one or two students, may be helpful as a basis for revision of a particular instructional sequence without constituting acceptable proof of inductive generalizations which may be useful in the future. Perhaps also it will be agreed that both informal, practically oriented try-out and more formal experiments have an important role to play in the combined research and development effort needed to develop a genuine instructional technology.

Time as a Variable in Comparing Instructional Treatments

A special problem in experimental rationale mentioned previously at several points is the problem of the interpretation to be placed on the expenditure of instructional time. This problem has been commented on with respect to the studies of Coulson and Silberman (1959), Fry (1960), and Evans, Glaser, and Homme (1959). The most obvious specific dilemma is that posed when, as in the results of Coulson and Silberman, a measure of time spent in learning favors one group, whereas a measure of achievement favors the other group. Such troublesome problems of interpretation do not, of course, arise directly so long as experimentation is confined to fixed-pace instructional instruments in which total time is "controlled" at the same value for both of the alternate presentations.

There are, however, two general problems concerning time which, though not peculiar to auto-instructional media, are brought into sharper focus by the potentiality of these media for adjusting time spent to the capabilities of the learner. First, is it more relevant to ask how high a score (less than perfect) is achieved by the end of a fixed, preset period of instruction (often fixed by administrative considerations), or to ask how long it will take, by one form of instruction or another, to get students up to some preset minimum level of proficiency? Though there is no simple answer to this question, it interacts intimately with the philosophy and organization of education, and it has drastic implications for techniques of assessing instruction, as well as for the design of instructional programs. How, for example, do we design the test sequences of an auto-instructional program to provide a valid indicator that criterion level has been reached for a particular portion of the subject matter—especially when it is implicit in the criterion that the capabilities achieved will be retained over an extended period?

Second, how should we determine or even estimate reliably the "payoff" value of achievement scores as compared with time expenditure devoted to instruction? Use of some relative measure, such as amount learned per unit of time (see Goldbeck, 1960), may help us evade the question for a while, but its fundamental importance will persist. What are the relevant bases for choosing between two instruments when one produces a higher achievement at the cost of more instructional time? The answer to this question requires some defensible, uniform way of assessing the utility of instruction.

The Null Hypothesis and Interpretation of "Negative Results"

It is well known that the logic of statistical inference underlying most experiments, whether in instructional media or in the behavioral and biological sciences more generally, is one in which the data are analyzed with reference to a null hypothesis which asserts that two or more samples of data are in fact random samples from a common population. That is, the null hypothesis supposes that there are no differences between the data that result from two or more experimental treatments, e.g., two forms of instructional presentations, and the experimenter then proceeds to test the feasibility of this hypothesis. He does so by reference to appropriate tabulations or calculations which indicate the probability that, if the null hypothesis were in fact true, differences as large or as consistent as those he observes could occur simply as a consequence of random sampling fluctuations. If this probability is lower than some value (such as .01) agreed on conventionally as an acceptable level of statistical "significance," he rejects the null hypothesis. In doing so, he concludes that it is preferable to accept the alternative conclusion that the observed difference resulted from some nonrandom causal factor. This factor, in a well-controlled experiment, he will normally identify as the difference in the experimental treatments he employed.

There are many elaborations and sophisticated statistical details in the application of the null-hypothesis rationale, but all of them involve the basic argument just stated. When "positive" results are obtained—i.e., when the data are shown, as above, to be "incompatible" with a null hypothesis of no difference—the interpretation generally seems clear cut, and the experimenter rightly regards his data as having shown that a "significant difference" is present. That is, he has a convincing case for claiming that a nonchance difference has been demonstrated, since his statistical test has shown that it is very unlikely that his data would result if no systematic difference were present.

But difficulty arises when the data do not afford a basis for rejecting the null hypothesis at a level of confidence which has been agreed on as significant. The root of the trouble in this case is that there is then no logically defensible basis for drawing any conclusion about the true state of affairs. As R. A. Fisher long ago pointed out, the null hypothesis can only be disproved; it cannot be proved. This is because any set of data compatible with a null hypothesis of *no* difference is also compatible with a number of alternative hypotheses that some difference *does* exist, even though it is not gross enough, in relation to the variability of the data, to be significant.

Logically, therefore, failure to disprove the null hypothesis leaves the experimenter, and those who wish to interpret or utilize his results, no defensible position except that of suspended judgment. Of course, this position is uncomfortable for a person who has to make a practical decision, and for the experimenter who has toiled in the hope of arriving at some definite conclusion. The temptation is great, therefore, to translate the only defensible statement of findings—namely, that the results merely fail to show evidence that there was a significant difference—into some more equivocal and more palatable form, e.g., that "no significant difference was found to exist," or that "there is no significant difference between the treatments" (with a semantic shift on the meaning of significant), or simply that "the two treatments did not differ significantly" (with the last word often deleted in the final summary written for the man who just wants the results and doesn't care how they were arrived at).

That this often unintentional verbal legerdemain, which translates inconclusive results into definitive-sounding "negative results" (that are then cited to show that a particular factor is unimportant or "makes no difference") is denounced by logicians seems to have little effect on those who are wont to accept such negative conclusions. Aside from wish-fulfillment, ignorance, or sloppy thinking, there are perhaps two reasons why such unsupportable conclusions are not more often successfully challenged. The first reason is that plainly there must be variables that are relatively unimportant in influencing any outcome, and it would often be as helpful to identify these as it is to identify those variables which do have an important influence. The second reason is that, in an extended series of experiments on a number of relevant factors, we should expect that, by and large, the more important or more potent sources of variation would be those that show up as statistically significant, and that, by and large, the unimportant or weak sources of variation would not. But this expectation will be borne out if and only if one crucial condition is fulfilled—namely, *that the experiments are of comparable sensitivity, so that equally potent factors in the different experiments have about the same chance of showing up as significant.* The fact that this condition is, in general, not fulfilled over the range of educational experiments creates a morass of ambiguity and inconsistency which has led some, including the writer, to wonder whether it is worth doing experiments until some basis for achieving comparable sensitivity from experiment to experiment is achieved.

The basis for this grave concern can be seen more clearly by considering four hypothetical, but perhaps not atypical, experimental situations. Experiment I sets out to test the influence of a variable which, in the knowledge of an omniscient deity, is of finite though trivial importance (though the experimenter does not know this). The experiment is, however, executed with great precision—because optimally sensitive measures are employed, because many cases are tested, and because extraneous sources of variation are under tight procedural control. The difference between treatments, though small, is found to be highly significant. Experiment II is concerned with assessing the effects of another variable, also of small actual potency, but is conducted with less precision, and leads to a conclusion of no significant difference. Experiments III and IV exactly parallel Experiments I and II, respectively, with respect to their precision and their outcomes, but they have dealt with experimental variables which, the deity knows, are in fact important, potent sources of variation. This fact does not show up as a significant difference in Experiment IV, however, because of the insensitivity of the experiment. The upshot is that, when the results are duly reported, the determination of which factors "made a significant difference" and of those which "had no significant effect" depends solely on the differential sensitivity of the several experiments and not at all on the real importance of the factors investigated.

Now, of course, the situation as it exists over the range of experiments actually conducted on factors in instructional media (or on other factors studied in psychological and educational research) is not quite this bad. But a close look at the literature suggests that it may well be nearly this bad, and, in the absence of suitable, uniformly applicable criteria of experimental sensitivity, it is nearly impossible to know just how bad it is. Certainly, in many a reported experiment the absence of significant differences is readily attributable to the insensitivity (due to one or more causes) of the experimental situation. Certainly, in some instances (perhaps less frequent), attention has been unduly focused on a factor found to produce significant effects because it has been studied in an experimental situation possessing high precision or sensitivity.[13] It is clear that the dismal hypothetical picture outlined above exists, to some degree, and will continue until either (1) some way is found to set standards of experimental sensitivity that take into account all the main sources of differential sensitivity, or (2) we can abandon the null-hypothesis paradigm, perhaps in favor of a paradigm yielding a workable estimation statistic which can indicate, within specifiable limits of error, the proportion of total relevant variation

---

[13] The author is conducting a census of the experimental literature of instructional media from this standpoint. He has, however, only limited hopes for it because of the difficulties encountered in comparing experimental sensitivity across experiments. These difficulties arise from the lack of any consistently applicable standards of sensitivity as well as from the frequent gaps in relevant information available under current research-reporting practices.

in attainment, loosely speaking, which is attributable to each factor studied. Reaching even a rough approximation of a solution for the dilemma in research interpretation posed by the undetermined-sensitivity dilemma would be exceedingly difficult. But the author believes that explication of this dilemma should be accorded the highest priority.

Pending some basic advance in this respect, the author recommends: (1) that experimenters address themselves primarily to studying the interactions of factors they strongly suspect will produce significant differences in experiments of reasonable precision; (2) that they try to design their experiments to incorporate one or more factors which, it is known in advance, should make a difference (see pp. 659–660, above), as a basis for establishing that at least minimal sensitivity has been realized; (3) that when nonsignificant differences are obtained, they try to refrain from indicating anything except that the findings are inconclusive; (4) that all data and circumstances which might reasonably be found relevant to an assessment of experimental sensitivity be reported in full; and (5) that a determined effort be made to impress on those who use and interpret research findings the limitations imposed by current methodology on the interpretations that can be made from experimental results. These limitations should include the fact that at present we (1) can establish (at any agreed-upon level of confidence) that a difference exists; (2) may, however, find this claim to be erroneous if already known methodological safeguards (e.g., see the above discussion on group sampling) are not used; (3) have little basis for consistent statements about the magnitude, potency, or importance of obtained significant differences; and (4) have *no* way at present to establish flatly that a given factor does *not* make a difference, e.g., to show that two educational procedures or instruments are "equally effective." It seems obvious that merely to state the last stricture emphasizes the importance of methodological advances beyond the customary null-hypothesis rationale.

Possible Solutions to the Methodological Dilemma

Decision-theory approaches. One approach to the problem of interpreting negative results in experiments is, of course, the use of fiducial limits to permit a conclusion that the difference, if any, resulting from the two methods is no greater than some specified amount. Though this approach is straightforward, it is seldom used and does not help with the basic problem of deciding what the "specified amount" ought to be (see below). A more thoroughgoing approach would be to formulate questions of the comparative effectiveness of educational media in terms of a decision-theory rationale. Cronbach and Gleser (1957) have discussed the applicability of decision-theory paradigms to problems of personnel selection, and W. Edwards (1956) has illustrated the theory of statistical decision functions (see Chernoff & Moses, 1959; Wald, 1950) in choosing between two training methods. Edwards presents an interesting hypothetical example in which calculations based on an appropriate model may be used to decide which of two competing methods is economically preferable. The example is worked out in such a way as to identify requirements that would have to be met to make utilization of this approach possible in a practical experimental situation. Perhaps the most significant aspect of his analysis is that it brings one face to face with our general inability to make reasonable estimates of the costs and, particularly, the anticipated payoff of educational procedures. The ability to do so, directly or indirectly, is a crucial requirement for any decision-theory solution to the problem. Hence, while decision-theory approaches may ultimately provide the best rationale for comparison of educational instruments or procedures, a prior task would seem to be the exploration of ways to estimate educational costs and payoffs. Perhaps the first question should be whether it is possible to agree on what constitutes an educationally worth-while difference in the effectiveness of two compared alternatives The latter question can also be discussed per se, without explicit reference to its utilization in decision-function calculations. Some aspects of the problems involved can, in fact, be perceived in attempting to set standards of sensitivity for experiments following a null-hypothesis rationale, as discussed briefly in the following section.

"Improving" the null hypothesis. If we are not yet in a position to supersede the null-hypothesis rationale for experiments, and since the null hypothesis cannot be proved, we may ask how its application to the design and conduct of educational experiments can be *improved*. How, that is, can we agree on standards for the sensitivity of differences and for deciding which magnitudes of effects shall be regarded as negligible and which as educationally noteworthy, so as to diminish the confusion and inconsistency which at present attend the interpretation of experimental findings? The following suggestions are offered in addition to the experimental and reportorial recommendations suggested above (pages 666–667). Of necessity, these suggestions are tentative, incompletely formulated, and therefore offered with hesitation. It is the author's belief, however, that at least some of them may afford one basis for making some much-needed improvements in the state of the art in educational experimentation. Such possibilities ought at least to be considered by the prospective experimenter who seeks to discover laws and principles concerning the operation of factors that regulate the effectiveness of instructional media.

A first step that can apply in any experiment is to decide *in advance* how small a difference in the criterion measure the experimenter is willing to regard as of negligible importance, and then to design the experiment so that any actual differences larger than this value will show up as significant. A clear, unequivocal, initial statement of where this just detectable difference has been set would, in some cases, lead to a decision not to do the experiment; in other cases, it would lead the experimenter to increase the

sensitivity of his experiment (perhaps, in the interests of economy, sometimes through a sequential set of replications); in all cases, it would probably clarify the interpretation to be placed on negative results, fostering statements such as "the difference if any is less than such and such" rather than "no difference exists." Insistence by editors of technical publications on reportorial scrupulousness in this respect might help; further, it would be worth trying to see if standardized phraseologies for different kinds of experimental outcomes might not be agreed on and enforced.

A second step that might be useful in extended programatic research would be the adoption of a few standard subject matters, coupled with criterion tests of known, consistent properties. Several such subject matters might be chosen to represent various classes of learning problems, e.g., a standard set of language materials, a standard science subject, a standard motor-skill task. Despite some obvious disadvantages in doing this, the practice would minimize the extent to which results were governed by subject-matter–linked differences in experimental sensitivity. Use of a rather restricted set of standard experimental subject matters would also facilitate agreement on an acceptable value for just detectable differences.

Another probably useful practice would be to discourage the reportorial convention of merely dichotomizing results as significant or nonsignificant, and to encourage the reporting of actual probability levels obtained, stipulating in each case whether one-tail or two-tail values are being reported. Doing so would not only indicate that experimental results represent varying degrees of confidence but might also encourage suspended judgment and, it is hoped, the tendency to replicate "borderline-significance" results.

A fourth helpful tendency might automatically accompany increased study of contingent propositions rather than global assessments and the introduction of covaried experimental factors previously found to be effective (see pp. 659–660). It is, of course, possible to demonstrate that one difference is less than another even though one cannot demonstrate that the first is zero.

Probably the most difficult and fundamental direction of progress, however, is to develop rationales more satisfactory than an individual experimenter's arbitrary judgment for deciding on the magnitude of a just detectable difference. Several possibilities, all of them far from satisfactory, may be suggested.

(1) We might try to select experimental subject matter in terms of criterion variables that seem to yield the most tangible immediate educational payoff. Experiments on instruction used in vocational training are perhaps closest to meeting this need.

(2) As one means to this end, we might try to increase the proportion of experiments in which time to reach a fixed criterion of proficiency is the criterion variable, rather than scores arrived at in a fixed time interval. Difficult as it may be to translate instructional time into economic payoff (at least in general education), it is probably less difficult than making this translation for differences in test scores.

(3) We might make a uniform practice of trying to obtain estimates from several presumably qualified judges, at least, as to how large a difference in test scores (or in instructional time) can reasonably be left undetectable. At least such estimates might give a reliable basis, if one of unestablished validity, that would be preferable to purely arbitrary decision by one experimenter. We might also see whether more meaningful judgments would result if the just detectable difference were expressed in terms of grade norms (e.g., the experiment should at least be able to detect as significant the difference between an "A" and a "B"), or age norms (the experiment might be regarded as unsatisfactorily insensitive if incapable of detecting the difference between average fifth- and seventh-grade pupils).

(4) The foregoing procedure might be more meaningful if test-score differences were equated to instructional-time differences. (For how large a test-score difference would we be willing to increase instructional time by 10 per cent?)

(5) We could try to agree on minimal detectable differences in relation to population variation in the criterion measure, perhaps agreeing that no experiment should be conducted that will probably not detect as significant a difference of, say, one-half of a standard deviation in the distribution of some standard student population.

(6) For a considerable range of subject matters, we might similarly specify minimal satisfactory sensitivity as the ability of an experiment to reveal differences associated with prediction variables, e.g., that the experiment should be capable of detecting a difference as large as that between students differing by 15 IQ points.

Finally, and most generally, we might—and indeed must—make a determined effort to see what agreement can be obtained by these or, it is hoped, better approaches on *some* standard for the sensitivity of our experiments, whereby we can begin to report on a more consistent, describable basis the grounds for paying more attention to "significant" than to "nonsignificant" experimental results.

CONCLUDING REMARKS

The experimental work reported in this chapter, even though quite extensive, clearly represents only a beginning in the effort to develop the technology of instructional method which such research can ultimately generate. Study of the work to date should stimulate more incisive investigation, invention, and discovery, both substantive and methodological. Only in this way can educational psychologists achieve the explicit identification of variables and functional relationships which most potently influence the modification of behavior through instruction, and thus play a crucial role in far-reaching improvements in the effectiveness and economy of instruction. The reproducibility of instructional materials, and the consequent multiplication of the acts of instruction for which they can function, carry important implications for the amount of research and development resources that should be devoted to the perfection of the product. These implications bear upon the range and complexity of the displays used, the level of the instructional personnel employed in preparing instructional instruments, and the amount of development time, try-out, and revision that can be expended on perfecting them. A given instructional instrument may be used for only a few minutes of any one student's time, but the cost of perfecting it can be prorated in terms of a denominator representing thousands of students for whom the perfected instrument can be used.

These considerations impinge on the question of implementing research findings. Often the researchers do not deserve serious consideration by the practitioner because of deficiencies in their conception or execution which have rendered their conclusions meaningless or misleading. But this is beside the point at the moment, for even sound research products have not generally met with enthusiastic adoption and wide-scale implementation. However, even this may be partly related to the deficiencies of much research. The practitioner may sometimes be smarter than we think. Sensing the uselessness or absurdity of some conclusions enunciated by researchers and lacking a technical basis for discriminating good from poor research, he is sometimes not to be blamed for resisting *all* research implications for the conduct of his trade.

Travers (1962) has presented a penetrating and disconcerting analysis of reasons why the results of research (and the products of invention) may fail to find their way into educational or training practice. It is possible that the results of research or innovation are likely to be translated into improved practice only when they become embodied in concrete devices, materials, or other usable products. To a lesser extent, research findings may affect practice when they generate specifica-

tions for such tangible products, devices, or materials, particularly if these specifications have been embodied in prototypes shown to be useful. It seems likely that research on instruction will be applied much less frequently when its sole product is principles, conclusions, or scientific laws.

This is not an argument against basic research—far from it. We need much more basic research to identify and manipulate fundamental factors with a significant influence on the effectiveness of learning. But we should not expect the conclusions and principles derived from such research to find their way into educational and training practice unless we make the translation ourselves or develop a systematic technology through which such translation may be effected (see Melton, 1959). By all odds, the most direct way to accomplish this translation is through embodying what we find out through research in devices and materials which will be bought, be put to use, and thus engender a demand for more of such devices and materials. Conversely, the decisions encountered in the design of concrete devices and materials often represent the most useful point of departure from which needs for basic research can be identified in terms that will lead to findings which can eventually be fed back into practice.

Informal try-out as a basis for product improvement is likely to be particularly useful in small-step programing of self-instructional materials. If a film, or TV lesson, or lecture, or textbook is seen by subsequent tests to have partly failed, there is, ordinarily, no way to know at what point the student went astray. In the small-step auto-instructional program, however, the student's response at each point tells us whether or not we have constructed the program in a way that has enabled him to add that small step of competence to his repertoire before proceeding to more advanced material. In a real sense, the student helps write the program.

Basic research also seems especially promising in the field of self-instructional media, both because of the close control of the learning situation which teaching machines can provide, and because of the directness with which inductive generalizations can be translated into practice. This research needs to be aimed at a number of central problems, including those of response form, program organization, branching, size of steps, display characteristics, types of correction or feedback provided, difficulty level for optimum progress, and a number of other factors (see Lumsdaine, 1959b). Such research is not easy to perform, and definitive results are hard to come by. No major question can be answered by a single experiment.

Finally, before research on all forms of instructional media can progress more rapidly toward achieving its potentialities, it is essential that variables and experimental problems be defined more incisively, and that crucial methodological advances be made. We need, at a minimum, a rationale for coping with the dilemma of instructional time and payoff, an improvement on the null-hypothesis paradigm of experimentation, and a set of standards for the sensitivity of experiments.

Meanwhile, it is important to insure that research effort produces studies which are, by and large, technically as good as current knowledge permits. This goal in no way precludes the exercise of ingenuity in trying out new approaches, but it does suggest the need for better training of, and communication among, research workers.

REFERENCES[1]

Allen, W. H. Readability of instructional film commentary. *J. appl. Psychol.,* 1952, 36, 164–168.

---

[1] All references preceded by (LG) are reprinted in A. A. Lumsdaine & R. Glaser (Eds.), *Teaching machines and programmed learning: A source book.* Page numbers in brackets refer to that volume. "TMPL abstr." indicates that that volume contains an abstract of the study after which the notation appears. All references preceded by (L) are chapters in A. A. Lumsdaine (Ed.), *Student response in programmed instruction: A symposium.* Chapter numbers are in parentheses.

Allen, W. H. Audio-visual materials. *Rev. educ. Res.,* 1956, 26, 125–156.

Allen, W. H. Research on film use: Student participation. *AV commun. Rev.,* 1957, 5, 423–450.

Allen, W. H. Audio-visual communication research. In C. W. Harris (Ed.), *Encyclopedia of educational research.* (3rd ed.) New York: Macmillan, 1960. Pp. 115–137.

Anderson, Nancy S., Novick, L., & Braunstein, M. An evaluation of the human readability and recognition of a specialized font. Yorktown Heights, N.Y.: IBM Research Center, 1960. (IBM Res. Memo. RC–219)

Angell, D., & Lumsdaine, A. A. *Prompted plus unprompted trials versus prompted trials alone in paired-associate learning.* Pittsburgh: American Institute for Research, 1960. (See also Angell & Lumsdaine, 1961.)

(L) Angell, D., & Lumsdaine, A. A. Prompted and unprompted trials versus prompted trials only in paired-associate learning. (Ch. 24) 1961.

Angell, G. W. Effect of immediate knowledge of quiz results on final examination scores in freshman chemistry. *J. educ. Res.,* 1949, 42, 391–394.

(LG) Angell, G.W., & Troyer, M. E. A new self-scoring test device for improving instruction. *Sch. & Soc.,* 1948, 67, 84–85. [66–68]

Ash, P. *The relative effectiveness of massed versus spaced film presentation.* (Pennsylvania State Univer. Instructional Film Research Program) Port Washington, N.Y.: U.S. Naval Training Device Center, Office of Naval Research, Tech. Rept. No. SDC 269-7-3, 1949.

Ash, P., & Carlton, B. J. *The value of notetaking during film learning.* (Pennsylvania State Univer. Instructional Film Research Program) Port Washington, N.Y.: U.S. Naval Training Device Center, Office of Naval Research, Tech. Rept. No. SDC 269-7-21, November, 1951.

Ash, P., & Jaspen, N. *Optimum physical viewing conditions for a rear projection daylight screen.* (Pennsylvania State Univer. Instructional Film Research Program) Port Washington, N.Y.: U.S. Naval Training Device Center, Office of Naval Research, Tech. Rept. No. SDC 269-7-37, 1953.

Aukes, L. E., & Simon, G. B. *The relative effectiveness of an Air Force training device used intact versus with isolated parts.* Lackland Air Force Base, Tex.: Air Force Personnel and Training Res. Center, Res. Rept. AFPTRC-TN-57-77 (ASTIA Doc. No. 131429), June, 1957.

(LG) Briggs, L. J. Two self-instructional devices. *Psychol. Rep.*, 1958, 4, 671–676. [299–304]

(L) Briggs, L. J. Prompting and confirmation conditions for three learning tasks employing the Subject-Matter Trainer. (Ch. 23) 1961. (a)

(L) Briggs, L. J. Self-pacing versus automatic pacing in paired-associate learning. (Ch. 25) 1961. (b)

Briggs, L. J., Plashinski, D., & Jones, D. L. Self-pacing versus automatic pacing of practice on the Subject-Matter Trainer. Air Force Personnel and Training Res. Center, Unpublished Lab. Note ASPRL-LN-55-8, September, 1955. (TMPL abstr., pp. 591–592). (Mimeographed) (See Briggs, 1961b.)

Brunswik, E. *Perception and the representative design of psychological experiments.* Berkeley: Univer. of California Press, 1956.

Buckingham, B. R. Textbooks. In C. W. Harris (Ed.), *Encyclopedia of educational research.* (3rd ed.) New York: Macmillan, 1960. Pp. 1517–1523.

Carpenter, C. R. A challenge for research. *Educ. Screen,* 1948, 27, 119–121.

Carpenter, C. R., & Greenhill, L. P. *An investigation of closed-circuit television for teaching university courses.* University Park: Pennsylvania State Univer., Instructional Television Res. Rept. No. 1, 1955.

Carpenter, C. R., & Greenhill, L. P. *An investigation of closed-circuit television for teaching university courses.* University Park: Pennsylvania State Univer., Instructional Television Res. Rept. No. 2, 1958.

Chall, Jeanne S., & Dial, H. E. Predicting listener understanding and interest in newscasts. *Educ. res. Bull.,* 1948, 27, 141–153, 168.

Cheatham, P. G. *A comparison of the visual and auditory senses as possible channels for communication.* Wright-Patterson Air Force Base, Ohio: U.S. Air Force Air Materiel Command, A.F. Tech. Rept. No. 5919, May, 1950.

Chernoff, H., & Moses, L. E. *Elementary decision theory.* New York: Wiley, 1959.

Cogswell, J. F. *Effects of a stereoscopic sound motion picture on the learning of a perceptual-motor task.* (Pennsylvania State Univer.

Instructional Film Research Program) Port Washington, N.Y.: U.S. Naval Training Device Center, Office of Naval Research, Tech. Rept. No. SDC 269-7-32, September, 1952.

Cook, J. O. Supplementary report: Processes underlying learning a single paired-associate item. *J. exp. Psychol.,* 1958, 56, 455. (TMPL abstr., pp. 601–602)

Cook, J. O. Research in audio-visual communication. In J. Ball & F. C. Byrnes (Eds.), *Research, principles, and practices in visual communication.* East Lansing: Michigan State Univer., National Project in Agricultural Communications, 1960. Pp. 91–106.

(L) Cook, J. O. From audience participation to paired-associates learning. (Ch. 21) 1961. (a)

(L) Cook, J. O. Response analysis in paired-associate learning experiments. (Ch. 22) 1961. (b)

Cook, J. O., & Kendler, Tracy S. A theoretical model to explain some paired-associate learning data. In G. Finch & F. Cameron (Eds.), *Symposium on Air Force human engineering, personnel, and training research.* Washington, D.C.: National Academy of Sciences–National Research Council, Publ. No. 455, 1956. Pp. 90–98.

Cook, J. O., & Spitzer, M. E. Supplementary report: Prompting versus confirmation in paired-associate learning. *J. exp. Psychol.,* 1960, 59, 275–276. (TMPL abstr., pp. 604–605)

(LG) Coulson, J. E., & Silberman, H. F. *Results of an initial experiment in automated teaching.* Santa Monica, Calif.: System Development Corp., 1959. [452–468]

Cronbach, L. J., & Gleser, Goldine C. *Psychological tests and personnel decisions.* Urbana: Univer. of Illinois Press, 1957.

Crowder, N. A. Automatic tutoring by means of intrinsic programming. In E. H. Galanter (Ed.), *Automatic teaching: The state of the art.* New York: Wiley, 1959. Pp. 109–116.

(LG) Crowder, N. A. Automatic tutoring by instrinsic programming. In A. A. Lumsdaine & R. Glaser (Eds.), *Teaching machines and programmed learning: A source book.* Washington, D.C.: National Education Association, 1960. Pp. 286–298.

Dale, E., & Chall, Jeanne S. A formula for predicting readability: Instructions. *Educ. res. Bull.,* 1948, 27, 37–54.

Day, W. F., & Beach, Barbara R. *A survey of the research literature comparing the visual and auditory presentation of information.* Wright-Patterson Air Force Base, Ohio: U.S. Air Force Air Materiel Command, A.F. Tech. Rept. No. 5921, 1950.

Detambel, M. H., & Stolurow, L. M. Stimulus sequence and concept learning. *J. exp. Psychol.,* 1956, 51, 34–40.

Duva, J. S., & Lumsdaine, A. A. The influence of image quality on the teaching effectiveness of the kinescope. U.S. Air Force Human Factors Operations Research Labs., Unpublished HFORL Report, March, 1956.

Eastman Kodak Company. *Legibility standards for projected material.* Rochester, N.Y.: Kodak Pamphlet No. S-4, 1955.

Edwards, A. L. *Statistical methods for the behavioral sciences.* New York: Rinehart, 1954.

Edwards, W. The use of statistical decision functions in making practical decisions. In G. Finch & F. Cameron (Eds.), *Symposium on Air Force human engineering, personnel, and training research.* Washington, D.C.: National Academy of Sciences–National Research Council, Publ. No. 455, 1956. Pp. 115–124.

Eigen, L. D., & Komoski, P. K. *Research summary number 1: Automated teaching project.* New York: Collegiate School, 1960. (Mimeographed)

Emeson, D. L., & Wulff, J. J. *The relationship between "what is learned" and "how it's taught."* Air Force Personnel and Training Res. Center, Maintenance Lab., Tech. Memo. ML-TM-57-32, December, 1957. (See also Wulff & Emeson, 1961.)

Evans, J. L. An investigation of teaching machine variables using learning programs in symbolic logic. Unpublished doctoral dissertation, Univer. of Pittsburgh, 1960. (TMPL abstr., pp. 618–619)

(LG) Evans, J. L., Glaser, R., & Homme, L. E. A preliminary investigation of variation in the properties of verbal learning sequences of the "teaching machine" types. 1959. In A. A. Lumsdaine & R. Glaser (Eds.), *Teaching machines and programmed learning: A source book.* Washington, D.C.: National Education Association, 1960. Pp. 446–451.

Evans, J., Homme, L. E., & Glaser, R. *The Ruleg (Rule-Example) system for the construction of learning programs.* (A report prepared under the Cooperative Research Program of the U.S. Office of Education)

Pittsburgh: Dept. of Psychology, Univer. of Pittsburgh, 1960. (TMPL abstr., pp. 619–620) (Mimeographed)

Fairbanks, G., Guttman, N., & Miron, M. S. Auditory comprehension in relation to listening rate and selective verbal redundancy. *J. speech hear. Dis.,* 1957, 22, 23–32. (a)

Fairbanks, G., Guttman, N., & Miron, M. S. Auditory comprehension of repeated high-speed messages. *J. speech hear. Dis.,* 1957, 22, 20–22. (b)

Fairbanks, G., Guttman, N., & Miron, M. S. Effects of time compression of connected speech. *J. speech hear. dis.,* 1957, 22, 10–19. (c)

Faison, E. W. J., Rose, N., & Podell, J. E. A technique for measuring observable audience reactions to training films. Air Force Personnel and Training Res. Center, Training Aids Research Lab., Unpublished Lab. Note TARL-LN-55-45, December, 1955. (Mimeographed) (Summary in Lumsdaine, 1961b)

Feshbach, S., & Janis, I. L. An experimental study of the effects of anxiety-arousing appeals in mass communication. Paper read at Eastern Psychol. Ass., New York, March, 1951.

Fisher, R. A. *The design of experiments.* (4th ed.) London: Oliver and Boyd, 1947.

Flesch, R. *The art of plain talk.* New York: Harper, 1946.

Flesch, R. *The art of readable writing.* New York: Harper, 1949.

(LG) Fry, E. B. A study of teaching machine response modes. In A. A. Lumsdaine & R. Glaser (Eds.), *Teaching machines and programmed learning: A source book.* Washington, D.C.: National Education Association, 1960. Pp. 469–474.

Gagné, R. M. The effect of sequence of presentation of similar items on the learning of paired associates. *J. exp. Psychol.,* 1950, 40, 61–73.

Galanter, E. H. (Ed.) *Automatic teaching: The state of the art.* New York: Wiley, 1959.

Garvey, W. D., & Henneman, R. H. *Practical limits of speeded speech.* Wright-Patterson Air Force Base, Ohio: U.S. Air Force Air Materiel Command, A.F. Tech. Rept. No. 5917, May, 1950.

Gates, A. I. Recitation as a factor in memorizing. *Arch. Psychol., N.Y.,* 1917, 7 (40).

Gibson, J. J. (Ed.) *Motion picture testing and research.* (Army Air Forces Aviation Psychology Program) Washington, D.C.: Government Printing Office, Res. Rept. No. 7, 1947.

Gilbert, T. F. Some recent attempts at the partial automation of teaching. A report to the University of Georgia, 1958. (TMPL abstr., pp. 635–636) (Unpublished, mimeographed)

(LG) Gilbert, T. F. On the relevance of laboratory investigation of learning to self-instructional programming. In A. A. Lumsdaine & R. Glaser (Eds.), *Teaching machines and programmed learning: A source book.* Washington, D.C.: National Education Association, 1960. Pp. 475–485.

Gladstone, A. The readability of the commentary. In M. A. May & A. A. Lumsdaine, *Learning from films.* New Haven, Conn.: Yale Univer. Press, 1958. Pp. 46–57.

Glaser, R. (Ed.) *Training research and education.* Pittsburgh: Univer. of Pittsburgh Press, 1962.

Goldbeck, R. A. *The effect of response mode and learning material difficulty on automated instruction.* Tech. Rept. No. 1. Contract No. Nonr-3077(00). Pittsburgh: American Institute for Research, 1960.

Greenhill, L. P. *A study of the feasibility of local production of minimum cost sound motion pictures.* (Pennsylvania State Univer. Instructional Film Research Program) Port Washington, N.Y.: U.S. Naval Training Device Center, Office of Naval Research, Tech. Rept. No. SDC 269-7-48, 1955.

Gropper, G. L., & Lumsdaine, A. A. *The use of student response to improve televised instruction: An overview.* Report No. 7 (Summary of six prior reports), *Studies in televised instruction.* Pittsburgh: American Institute for Research, Rept. No. AIR-C13-61-FR-245 (VII), 1961.

Guthrie, E. R. *The psychology of learning.* New York: Harper, 1935, 1952.

Hall, W. H. A study of three methods of teaching science with classroom films. *Sch. Sci. Math.,* 1936, 36, 968–973.

Harby, S. F. *Evaluation of a procedure for using daylight projection of film loops in teaching skills.* (Pennsylvania State Univer. Instructional Film Research Program) Port Washington, N.Y.: U.S. Naval Training Device Center, Office of Naval Research,

Tech. Rept. No. SDC 269-7-25, 1952.

Hirsch, R. S. *The effects of knowledge of test results on learning of meaningful material.* (Pennsylvania State Univer. Instructional Film Research Program) Port Washington, N.Y.: U.S. Naval Training Device Center, Office of Naval Research, Tech. Rept. No. SDC 269-7-30, September, 1952.

Hoban, C. F., Jr., & Van Ormer, E. B. *Instructional film research, 1918–1950.* (Pennsylvania State Univer. Instructional Film Research Program) Port Washington, N.Y.: U.S. Naval Training Device Center, Office of Naval Research, Tech. Rept. No. SDC 269-7-19, 1950.

Hoehn, A. J., & Lumsdaine, A. A. *Design and use of job aids for communicating technical information.* Lackland Air Force Base, Tex.: Air Force Personnel and Training Research Center, Tech. Rept. AFPTRC-TR-58-7 (ASTIA Doc. No. AD 152109), January, 1958. (TMPL abstr., p. 639)

Holland, J. G. A teaching machine program in psychology. In E. H. Galanter (Ed.), *Automatic teaching: The state of the art.* New York: Wiley, 1959. Pp. 69–82.

Holland, J. G. Program design and use. Paper read at American Psychol. Ass., Chicago, 1960. (Unpublished, mimeographed) (a)

(LG) Holland, J. G. Teaching machines: An application of principles from the laboratory. In *Proc. ETS invitational Conf.* October, 1959. Princeton, N.J.: Educational Testing Service, 1960. [215–228] (b)

(LG) Homme, L. E., & Glaser, R. Problems in programming verbal learning sequences. Paper read at American Psychol. Ass., Cincinnati, September, 1959. [486–496]

Hovland, C. I. Human learning and retention. In S. S. Stevens (Ed.), *Handbook of experimental psychology.* New York: Wiley, 1951. Pp. 613–689.

Hovland, C. I. (Ed.) *The order of presentation in persuasion.* New Haven, Conn.: Yale Univer. Press, 1957.

Hovland, C. I., & Weiss, W. The influence of source credibility on communication effectiveness. *Publ. opin. Quart.,* 1951, 15, 635–650.

Hovland, C. I., Janis, I. L., & Kelley, H. H. *Communication and persuasion: Psychological studies of opinion change.* New Haven, Conn.: Yale Univer. Press, 1953.

Hovland, C. I., Lumsdaine, A. A., & Sheffield,

F. D. *Experiments on mass communication.* Princeton, N.J.: Princeton Univer. Press, 1949.

Hurlock, E. B. An evaluation of certain incentives used in school work. *J. educ. Psychol.,* 1925, 16, 145–159.

Irion, A. L., & Briggs, L. J. *Learning task and mode of operation variables in use of the Subject-Matter Trainer.* Lackland Air Force Base, Tex.: Air Force Personnel and Training Research Center, Tech. Rept. AFPTRC-TR-57-8 (ASTIA Doc. No. AD 134252), October, 1957. (TMPL abstr., pp. 642–643) (See Briggs, 1961a)

Israel, M. L. Variably blurred prompting: I. Methodology and application to the analysis of paired-associate learning. *J. Psychol.,* 1960, 50, 43–52.

Jackson, R. *Learning from kinescopes and films.* Port Washington, N.Y.: U.S. Naval Training Device Center, Office of Naval Research, Tech. Rept. No. SDC 20-TV-1, 1952.

Jaspen, N. Contribution of especially designed sound motion pictures to the learning of skills: Assembly of the breech block of the 40 mm. antiaircraft gun. Unpublished doctoral dissertation, Pennsylvania State Univer., 1949.

Jaspen, N. *Effects on training of experimental film variables, Study II: Verbalization, "how-it-works," nomenclature, audience participation, and succinct treatment.* (Pennsylvania State Univer. Instructional Film Research Program) Port Washington, N.Y.: U.S. Naval Training Device Center, Office of Naval Research, Tech. Rept. No. SDC 269-7-11, March, 1950.

Judd, C. H. Practice without knowledge of results. *Psychol. Monogr. Suppl.,* 1905, 7, No. 1, 185–198 (Whole No. 29).

Kale, S. V., Grosslight, J. H., & McIntyre, C. J. *Exploratory studies in the use of pictures and sound for teaching foreign language vocabulary.* (Pennsylvania State Univer. Instructional Film Research Program) Port Washington, N.Y.: U.S. Naval Training Device Center, Office of Naval Research, Tech. Rept. No. SDC 269-7-53, August, 1955.

Kanner, J. H. Army television research activities. *AV commun. Rev.,* 1960, 8, 74.

Kanner, J. H., & McClure, A. H. Varied versus identical repetition in filmed instruction on micrometer reading. Air Force Per-

sonnel and Training Research Center, Training Aids Research Lab., Unpublished Lab. Note TARL-LN-56-11, April, 1956. (Mimeographed) (Summary in Lumsdaine, 1961b)

Kanner, J. H., & Sulzer, R. L. Overt and covert rehearsal of 50% versus 100% of the material in film learning. Air Force Personnel and Training Research Center, Training Aids Research Laboratory, Unpublished Staff Memorandum TARL 56-12, 1956. (See Kanner & Sulzer, 1961.) (Mimeographed)

(L) Kanner, J. H., & Sulzer, R. L. Overt and covert rehearsal of fifty per cent versus one hundred per cent of the material in film learning. (Ch. 28) 1961.

Kendall, M. G. Hiawatha designs an experiment. *Amer. Statistician,* 1959, 13, 23–24.

Kendler, H. H., Kendler, Tracy S., Desiderato, A. H., & Cook, J. O. *An investigation of the effect of audio-visually induced anxiety on learning and performance.* New York: New York Univer., 1953.

Kendler, Tracy S., Cook, J. O., & Kendler, H. H. An investigation of the interacting effects of repetition and audience participation on learning from films. Air Force Personnel and Training Research Center, Training Aids Res. Lab., Unpublished Lab. Note TARL-LN-56–2, January, 1956. (Paper presented at American Psychol. Ass., Cleveland, Ohio, September, 1953; see also abstract in *Amer. Psychologist,* 1953, 8, 378–379; and Cook, 1961a.)

Kimble, G. A. The effect of praise, reproof, and no incentive on the value of a training film. Air Force Personnel and Training Research Center, Training Aids Research Lab., Unpublished Lab. Note TARL-LN-55-7, 1955. (Mimeographed) (Summary in Lumsdaine, 1961b) (a)

Kimble, G. A. The value of an interpolated test in increasing the effectiveness of a training film. Air Force Personnel and Training Research Center, Training Aids Research Lab., Unpublished Lab. Note TARL-LN-55-10, 1955. (Mimeographed) (Summary in Lumsdaine, 1961b) (b)

Kimble, G. A., & Wulff, J. J. *Response guidance as a factor in the value of audience participation in training film instruction.* Washington, D.C.: U.S. Air Force Human Factors Operations Research Lab., HFORL Memo. Rep. No. 36, 1953. (See Kimble & Wulff, 1961b.)

(L) Kimble, G. A., & Wulff, J. J. The effectiveness of instruction in reading a scale as influenced by the relative amounts of demonstration and problem-solving practice. (Ch. 16) 1961. (a)

(L) Kimble, G. A., & Wulff, J. J. "Response guidance" as a factor in the value of student participation in film instruction. (Ch. 15) 1961. (b)

Klare, G. R., Mabry, J. E., & Gustafson, L. M. The relationship of patterning (underlining) to immediate retention and to acceptability of technical material. *J. appl. Psychol.*, 1955, 39, 40–42. (a)

Klare, G. R., Mabry, J. E., & Gustafson, L. M. The relationship of style difficulty to immediate retention and to acceptability of technical material. *J. educ. Psychol.*, 1955, 46, 287–295. (b)

Klare, G. R., Nichols, W. H., & Shuford, E. H. The relationship of typographic arrangement to the learning of technical training material. *J. appl. Psychol.*, 1957, 41, 41–45.

Klare, G. R., Shuford, E. H., & Nichols, W. H. The relationship of style difficulty, practice, and ability to efficiency of reading and retention. *J. appl. Psychol.*, 1957, 41, 222–226.

Klare, G. R., Shuford, E. H., & Nichols, W. H. The relationship of format organization to learning. *Educ. res. Bull.*, 1959, 38, 49–50.

Klaus, D. J., & Lumsdaine, A. A. *An experimental field test of the value of self-tutoring materials in high school physics: An interim report of progress and preliminary findings.* Pittsburgh: American Institute for Research, 1960. (Mimeographed)

Kopstein, F. F., & Roshal, S. M. Learning foreign vocabulary from pictures versus words. *Amer. Psychologist,* 1954, 9, 407–408. (Abstract) (See Kopstein & Roshal, 1961).

Kopstein, F. F., & Roshal, S. M. Method of presenting word pairs as a factor in foreign vocabulary learning. Paper read at American Psychol. Ass., San Francisco, September, 1955. (Abstract in *Amer. Psychologist,* 1955, 10, 354; see Kopstein & Roshal, 1961.)

(L) Kopstein, F. F., & Roshal, S. M. Verbal learning efficiency as influenced by the manipulation of representational response processes: Pictorial-verbal and temporal contiguity factors. (Ch. 20) 1961.

Kurtz, A. K., Walter, J. S., & Brenner, H. R. *The effects of inserted questions and statements on film learning.* (Pennsylvania State Univer. Instructional Film Research Program) Port Washington, N.Y.: U.S. Naval Training Device Center, Office of Naval Research, Tech. Rept. No. SDC 269-7-16, September, 1950.

Kurtz, K. H., & Hovland, C. I. The effect of verbalization during observation of stimulus objects upon accuracy of recognition and recall. *J. exp. Psychol.*, 1953, 45, 157–164.

Lashley, K. S., & Watson, J. B. *A psychological study of motion pictures in relation to venereal disease campaigns.* Washington, D.C.: U.S. Interdepartmental Social Hygiene Board, 1922.

Lathrop, C. W., Jr. An experiment to determine the effectiveness of the film introduction in presenting instructional sound motion pictures. Unpublished master's thesis, Pennsylvania State Univer., 1949. (See Lathrop & Norford, 1949).

Lathrop, C. W., Jr., & Norford, C. A. *Contributions of film introductions and film summaries to learning from instructional films.* (Pennsylvania State Univer. Instructional Film Research Program) Port Washington, N.Y.: U.S. Naval Training Device Center, Office of Naval Research, Tech. Rept. No. SDC 269-7-8, 1949.

Levine, S. The role of motivation in the effects of "active review" on learning from a factual film. *Amer. Psychologist,* 1953, 8, 388–389. (Abstract; cf. Lumsdaine, 1961b)

Lindquist, E. F. *Design and analysis of experiments in psychology and education.* New York: Houghton Mifflin, 1953.

(LG) Little, J. K. Results of use of machines for testing and for drill, upon learning in educational psychology. *J. exp. Educ.,* 1934, 3, 45–49. [59–65]

Los Angeles City School Districts. *An experiment in instructional TV in the Los Angeles junior colleges.* Los Angeles: Div. of Extension and Higher Education, 1959.

Lumsdaine, A. A. Experimental research and the improvement of teaching films. *Educ. Screen,* 1947, 26, 254–255.

Lumsdaine, A. A. Ease of learning with pictorial and verbal symbols. Unpublished doctoral dissertation, Stanford Univer., 1949.

Lumsdaine, A. A. Audio-visual research in the U.S. Air Force. *AV commun. Rev.,* 1953, 1, 76–90.

Lumsdaine, A. A. Cue and response functions of pictures and words. In M. A. May & A. A. Lumsdaine, *Learning from films*. New Haven, Conn.: Yale Univer. Press, 1958. Pp. 123–149.

Lumsdaine, A. A. Partial and more complete automation of teaching in group and individual learning situations. In E. H. Galanter (Ed.), *Automatic teaching: The state of the art*. New York: Wiley, 1959. Pp. 147–166. (a)

(LG) Lumsdaine, A. A. Response cueing and "size-of-step" in automated learning programs. Paper read at American Psychol. Ass., Cincinnati, September, [Printed in TMPL under title, "Some issues concerning devices and programs for automated learning": 517–539] 1959. (b)

(LG) Lumsdaine, A. A. Teaching machines and self-instructional materials. *AV commun. Rev.*, 1959, 7, 163–181. [Reprinted in TMPL under title "Teaching machines: An introductory overview": 5–22] (c)

Lumsdaine, A. A. Graphic aids, models, and mockups as tools for individual and classroom instruction. In G. Finch (Ed.), *Educational and training media: A symposium*. Washington, D.C.: National Academy of Sciences–National Research Council, Publ. No. 789, 1960. Pp. 69–113.

Lumsdaine, A. A. Some differences in approach to the programming of instruction. In J. P. Lysaught (Ed.), *Programmed learning: Evolving principles and industrial applications*. Ann Arbor, Mich.: Foundation for Research on Human Behavior, 1961. Pp. 37–52. (a)

Lumsdaine, A. A. (Ed.) *Student response in programmed instruction: A symposium*. Washington, D.C.: National Academy of Sciences–National Research Council, Publ. No. 943, 1961. (b)

Lumsdaine, A. A., & Gladstone, A. Overt practice and audio-visual embellishments. In M. A. May & A. A. Lumsdaine, *Learning from films*. New Haven, Conn.: Yale Univer. Press, 1958. Pp. 58–71.

Lumsdaine, A. A., & Glaser, R. (Eds.) *Teaching machines and programmed learning: A source book*. Washington, D.C.: National Education Association, 1960.

Lumsdaine, A. A., & Janis, I. L. Resistance to counter-propaganda produced by one-sided and two-sided propaganda presentations. *Publ. opin. Quart.*, 1953, 17, 311–318.

Lumsdaine, A. A., May, M. A., & Hadsell, R. S. Questions spliced into a film for motivation and pupil participation. In M. A. May & A. A. Lumsdaine, *Learning from films*. New Haven, Conn.: Yale Univer. Press, 1958. Pp. 72–83.

Lumsdaine, A. A., & Roshal, S. M. *Experimental research on educational media*. Los Angeles: Univer. of California, 1962.

Lumsdaine, A. A., & Sulzer, R. L. *The influence of simple animation techniques on the value of a training film*. Washington, D.C.: U.S. Air Force Human Factors Research Lab., HRRL Rept. No. 24, 1951. (See Lumsdaine, Sulzer, & Kopstein, 1961.)

(L) Lumsdaine, A. A., Sulzer, R. L., & Kopstein, F. F. The effect of animation cues and repetition of examples on learning from an instructional film. (Ch. 17) 1961.

(L) Maccoby, N., Michael, D. N., & Levine, S. Further studies of student-participation procedures in film instruction: Review and preview covert practice, and motivational interactions. (Ch. 19) 1961.

Maccoby, N., & Sheffield, F. D. Theory and experimental research on the teaching of complex sequential procedures by alternate demonstration and practice. In G. Finch & F. Cameron (Eds.), *Symposium on Air Force human engineering, personnel, and training research*. Washington, D.C.: National Academy of Sciences–National Research Council, Publ. No. 516, 1958. Pp. 99–107.

(L) Maccoby, N., & Sheffield, F. D. Combining practice with demonstration in teaching complex sequences: Summary and interpretation. (Ch. 5) 1961.

(L) Margolius, G. J., & Sheffield, F. D. Optimum methods of combining practice with filmed demonstrations in teaching complex response sequences: Serial learning of a mechanical assembly task. (Ch. 3) 1961.

Margolius, G. J., Sheffield, F. D., & Maccoby, N. *Repetitive versus continuous demonstration and practice in the learning of a serial mechanical assembly task I*. Air Force Personnel and Training Research Center, Maintenance Lab., Tech. Memo. ML-TM-57-11, September, 1957. (See Margolius, Sheffield, & Maccoby, 1961a.) (a)

Margolius, G. J., Sheffield, F. D., & Maccoby, N. *Repetitive versus continuous demonstra-*

tion and practice in the learning of a serial mechanical assembly task II. Air Force Personnel and Training Research Center, Maintenance Lab., Tech. Memo. ML-TM-57-12, September, 1957. (See Margolius, Sheffield, & Maccoby, 1961a.) (b)

Margolius, G. J., Sheffield, F. D., & Maccoby, N. *Timing of demonstration and overt practice as a function of task organization*. Air Force Personnel and Training Research Center, Maintenance Lab., Tech. Memo. ML-TM-57-13, September, 1957. (See Margolius, Sheffield, & Maccoby, 1961b.) (c)

(L) Margolius, G. J., Sheffield, F. D., & Maccoby, N. Repetitive versus consecutive demonstration and practice in the learning of a serial mechanical-assembly task. (Ch. 6) 1961. (a)

(L) Margolius, G. J., Sheffield, F. D., & Maccoby, N. Timing of demonstration and overt practice as a function of task organization. Ch. 7) 1961. (b)

May, M. A. The psychology of learning from demonstration films. *J. educ. Psychol.,* 1946, 37, 1–18.

May, M. A. Verbal responses to demonstrational films. In M. A. May & A. A. Lumsdaine, *Learning from films.* New Haven, Conn.: Yale Univer. Press, 1958. Pp. 168–180.

May, M. A., & Jenkinson, Nelle L. Developing interest in reading with film. *AV commun. Rev.,* 1953, 1 (3), 159–166.

May, M. A., & Jenkinson, Nelle L. The reading of a book based on a film. In M. A. May & A. A. Lumsdaine, *Learning from films.* New Haven, Conn.: Yale Univer. Press, 1958. Pp. 195–203.

May, M. A., & Lumsdaine, A. A. *Learning from films.* New Haven, Conn.: Yale Univer. Press, 1958.

McClure, A. H., & Peterman, J. N. Filmed instructions for marking machine-scored test forms. Air Force Personnel and Training Research Center, Training Aids Research Lab., Unpublished Lab. Note TARL-LN-56-7, January, 1956. (Mimeographed)

McCollough, Celeste, & Van Atta, L. The use of miniature programs to supplement conventional teaching techniques. Paper read at American Psychol. Ass., Chicago, 1960.

McGuire, W. J. The relative efficacy of overt and covert trainee participation with different speed of instruction. Air Force Personnel and Training Research Center, Training Aids Research Lab., Unpublished Lab. Note TARL-LN-55-46, December, 1955. (See McGuire, 1961a.) (Mimeographed) (a)

McGuire, W. J. Studies of factors influencing the effectiveness of demonstrational film for teaching a motor skill: II. Slow motion, added narration and distributed showings. Air Force Personnel and Training Research Center, Training Aids Research Lab., Unpublished Lab. Note TARL-LN-55-50, December, 1955. (See also McGuire, 1961c.) (Mimeographed) (b)

McGuire, W. J. Studies of factors influencing the effectiveness of demonstrational films for teaching a motor skill: III. Serial position and proximity to reward within the film. Air Force Personnel and Training Research Center, Training Aids Research Laboratory, Unpublished Lab. Note TARL-LN-55-51, December, 1955. (See also McGuire, 1961b.) (Mimeographed) (c)

(L) McGuire, W. J. Audience participation and audio-visual instruction: Overt-covert responding and rate of presentation. (Ch. 27) 1961. (a)

(L) McGuire, W. J. Effects of serial position and proximity to "reward" within a demonstrational film. (Ch. 14) 1961. (b)

(L) McGuire, W. J. Some factors influencing the effectiveness of demonstrational films: Repetition of instructions, slow motion, distribution of showings, and explanatory narration. (Ch. 13) 1961. (c)

McTavish, C. L. *Effect of repetitive film showings on learning.* (Pennsylvania State Univer. Instructional Film Research Program) Port Washington, N.Y.: U.S. Naval Training Device Center, Office of Naval Research, Tech. Rept. No. SDC 269-7-12, November, 1949.

Melton, A. W. The science of learning and the technology of educational methods. *Harvard educ. Rev.,* 1959, 29, 96–106.

(LG) Meyer, Susan R. Report on the initial test of a junior high-school vocabulary program. In A. A. Lumsdaine & R. Glaser (Eds.), *Teaching machines and programmed learning: A source book.* Washington, D.C.: National Education Association, 1960. Pp. 229–246.

Michael, D. N., & Maccoby, N. Factors influencing verbal learning from films under varying conditions of audience participation. *J. exp. Psychol.,* 1953, 46, 411–418.

(L) Michael, D. N., & Maccoby, N. Factors influencing the effects of student participation on verbal learning from films: Motivating versus practice effects, "feedback," and overt versus covert responding. (Ch. 18) 1961.

Miller, J., & Levine, S. *A study of the effects of different types of review and of "structuring" sub-titles on the amount learned from a training film.* Washington, D.C.: U.S. Air Force Human Resources Research Lab., HRRL Memo. Rept. No. 17, March, 1952. (Summary in Lumsdaine, 1961b)

Miller, N. E., et al. Graphic communication and the crisis in education. *AV commun. Rev.,* 1957, 5 (3) (Special Issue).

Mosteller, F., & Bush, R. R. Selected quantitative techniques. In G. Lindzey (Ed.), *Handbook of social psychology.* Cambridge, Mass.: Addison-Wesley, 1954. Pp. 289–334.

Murnin, J. A. *Comparison of training media: Transfer of principles involved in a manipulative skill; operation of the aircraft load adjuster slide rule.* (Pennsylvania State Univer. Instructional Film Research Program) Port Washington, N.Y.: U.S. Naval Training Device Center, Office of Naval Research, Tech. Rept. No. SDC 269-7-103, September, 1955.

Murnin, J. A., VanderMeer, A. W., & Vris, T. *Comparison of training media: Trainee manipulation and observation of functioning electrical systems versus trainee drawing of schematic electrical systems.* (Pennsylvania State Univer. Instructional Film Research Program) Port Washington, N.Y.: U.S. Naval Training Device Center, Office of Naval Research, Tech. Rept. No. SDC 269-7-101, June, 1954.

National Workshop. *The national program in the use of television in the public schools.* New York: The Fund for the Advancement of Education, 1959.

Nelson, H. E., & Moll, K. R. *Comparison of the audio and video elements of instructional films.* (Pennsylvania State Univer. Instructional Film Research Program) Port Washington, N.Y.: U.S. Naval Training Device Center, Office of Naval Research, Tech. Rept. No. SDC 269-7-18, November, 1950.

Nelson, H. E., & VanderMeer, A. W. *The relative effectiveness of differing commentaries in an animated film on elementary meteorology.* (Pennsylvania State Univer. Instructional Film Research Program) Port Washington, N.Y.: U.S. Naval Training Device Center, Office of Naval Research, Tech. Rept. No. SDC 269-7-43, June, 1955.

Neu, D. M. *The effect of attention-gaining devices on film-mediated learning.* (Pennsylvania State Univer. Instructional Film Research Program) Port Washington, N.Y.: U.S. Naval Training Device Center, Office of Naval Research, Tech. Rept. No. SDC 269-7-9, 1950.

Newman, S. E. Student vs. instructor design of study method. *J. educ. Psychol.,* 1957, 48, 328–333.

Newman, S. E., & Highland, R. W. *The effectiveness of four instructional methods at different stages of a course.* Lackland Air Force Base, Tex.: Air Force Personnel and Training Research Center, Tech. Rept. AFPTRC-TN-56-88, June, 1956.

Norford, C. A. Contributions of film summaries to the effectiveness of instructional sound motion pictures. Unpublished master's thesis, Pennsylvania State Univer., 1949. (See also Lathrop & Norford, 1949.)

Northrop, D. S. *Effects on learning of the prominence of organizational outlines in instructional films.* (Pennsylvania State Univer. Instructional Film Research Program) Port Washington, N.Y.: U.S. Naval Training Device Center, Office of Naval Research, Tech. Rept. No. SDC 269-7-33, 1952.

Oinas, F. J. (Ed.) Language teaching today. *Int. J. Amer. Linguistics,* 1960, 26 (4), Part II.

Otto, H. J., & Flournoy, Frances. Printed materials. *Rev. educ. Res.,* 1956, 26, 115–124.

Pan, S. The influence of context upon learning and recall. *J. exp. Psychol.,* 1926, 9, 468–491.

Park, J. Vocabulary and comprehension difficulties of sound motion pictures. *Sch. Rev.,* 1945, 53, 154–161.

Peterman, J. N., & Bouscaren, Nancy. A study of introductory and summarizing sequences in training film instruction. Air Force Personnel and Training Research Center, Training Aids Research Lab., Unpublished Staff Research Memo., 1954. (Mimeographed)

(LG) Peterson, J. C. The value of guidance in reading for information. *Trans. Kan. Acad. Sci.,* 1931, 34, 291–296. [52–58]

Peterson, V., & Schramm, W. How accurately are different kinds of graphs read? *AV commun. Rev.*, 1954, 2, 178–189.

(LG) Porter, D. A. A critical review of a portion of the literature on teaching devices. *Harvard educ. Rev.*, 1957, 27, 126–147. [114–132]

Porter, D. A. Some effects of year long teaching machine instruction. In E. H. Galanter (Ed.), *Automatic teaching: The state of the art.* New York: Wiley, 1959. Pp. 85–90.

(LG) Pressey, S. L. A simple apparatus which gives tests and scores—and teaches. *Sch. & Soc.*, 1926, 23, No. 586, 373–376. [35–41]

(LG) Pressey, S. L. A machine for automatic teaching of drill material. *Sch. & Soc.*, 1927, 25, No. 645, 549–552. [42–46]

(LG) Pressey, S. L. Development and appraisal of devices providing immediate automatic scoring of objective tests and concomitant self instruction. *J. Psychol.*, 1950, 29, 417–447. [69–88]

Rath, G. J., Anderson, Nancy S., & Brainerd, R. C. The IBM Research Center teaching machine project. In E. H. Galanter (Ed.), *Automatic teaching: The state of the art.* New York: Wiley, 1959. Pp. 117–130.

Rimland, B. *Effectiveness of several methods of repetition of films.* (Pennsylvania State Univer. Instructional Film Research Program) Port Washington, N.Y.: U.S. Naval Training Device Center, Office of Naval Research, Tech. Rept. No. SDC 269-7-45, May, 1955.

Romney, A. K. Effects of selected "set"-inducing instructions upon learning from multiple film showings. Unpublished manuscript, Boston Univer., September, 1952. (Summary in Lumsdaine, 1961b.)

Roshal, S. M. *Effects of learner representation in film-mediated perceptual-motor learning.* (Pennsylvania State Univer. Instructional Film Research Program) Port Washington, N.Y.: U.S. Naval Training Device Center, Office of Naval Research, Tech. Rept. No. SDC 269-7-5, 1949. (See Roshal, 1961.)

Roshal, S. M. The instructional film. In G. Finch (Ed.), *Educational and training media: A symposium.* Washington, D.C.: National Academy of Sciences–National Research Council, Publ. No. 789, 1960. Pp. 114–121.

(L) Roshal, S. M. Film-mediated learning with varying representations of the task: Viewing angle, portrayal of demonstration, motion, and student participation. (Ch. 11) 1961.

Rothkopf, E. Z. Signal similarity and optimal signal arrangement of lesson and drill orders in alphabetic Morse code training. In G. Finch & F. Cameron (Eds.), *Symposium on Air Force human engineering, personnel, and training research.* Washington, D.C.: National Academy of Sciences–National Research Council, Publ. No. 516, 1958. Pp. 188–193.

Rothkopf, E. Z. Automated teaching devices and a comparison on two variations of the method of adjusted learning. Murray Hill, N.J.: Bell Telephone Laboratories, 1960. (Mimeographed)

Saltz, E., & Newman, S. E. The effect of prior learning of symbols on performance in reasoning. *Amer. J. Psychol.*, 1960, 73, 91–99.

San Francisco State College. *An experimental study of college instruction using broadcast television.* Project No. 1. San Francisco: San Francisco State Coll., 1958. (a)

San Francisco State College. *An experimental study of college instruction using broadcast television.* Project No. 2. San Francisco: San Francisco State Coll., 1958. (b)

Saul, E. V., et al. *A review of the literature pertinent to the design and use of effective graphic training aids.* Port Washington, N.Y.: U.S. Naval Training Device Center, Office of Naval Research, Tech. Rept. No. SDC 494-08-1, 1954.

Sheffield, F. D. The role of meaningfulness of stimulus and response in verbal learning. Unpublished doctoral dissertation, Yale Univer., 1946.

Sheffield, F. D. *Perceptual mediation in the learning of organizable sequences: Theory and experiment.* Air Force Personnel and Training Research Center, Maintenance Lab., Tech. Memo. ML-TM-57-14, September, 1957. (See Sheffield, 1961.)

(L) Sheffield, F. D. Theoretical considerations in the learning of complex sequential tasks from demonstration and practice. (Ch. 2) 1961.

(L) Sheffield, F. D., & Maccoby, N. Summary and interpretation of research on organizational principles in constructing filmed demonstrations. (Ch. 9) 1961.

(L) Sheffield, F. D., Margolius, G. J., & Hoehn, A. J. Experiments on perceptual mediation in the learning of organizable sequences. (Ch. 8) 1961.

Shettel, H. H., Angell, D., & Lumsdaine, A. A. *Self-instructional programs for SAGE system operators: The development, use, and evaluation of two prototype self-instructional programs covering basic job knowledge for SAGE track monitor and intercept director operator positions.* Air Force Rept. No. ESD-TR-61-17. Pittsburgh: American Institute for Research, April, 1961.

Shettel, H. H., Faison, E. J., Roshal, S. M., & Lumsdaine, A. A. An experimental comparison of "live" and filmed lectures employing mobile training devices. *AV commun. Rev.,* 1956, 4, 216–222.

Silverman, R. E. *The comparative effectiveness of animated and static transparencies.* (Pennsylvania State Univer. Instructional Film Research Program) Port Washington, N.Y.: U.S. Naval Training Device Center, Office of Naval Research, Tech. Rept. No. NAVTRADEVCEN 78-1, April, 1958.

(LG) Skinner, B. F. The science of learning and the art of teaching. *Harvard educ. Rev.,* 1954, 24, 86–97. [99–113]

(LG) Skinner, B. F. Teaching machines. *Science,* 1958, 128, 969–977. [137–158]

Smith, O. W. Comparison of apparent depth in a photograph viewed from two distances. *Percept. mot. Skills,* 1958, 8 (2).

Smith, O. W. & Gruber, H. Perception of depth in photographs. *Percept. mot. Skills,* 1958, 8, 307–313.

Smith, O. W., & Resnick, L. Impressions of movements from static line drawings of human figures. Ithaca, N.Y.: Cornell Univer., 1953. (Unpublished)

Smith, O. W., Smith, Patricia C., & Hubbard, D. Perceived distance as a function of mode of representation. Ithaca, N.Y.: Cornell Univer., 1953. (Unpublished)

Smith, Patricia C., & Smith, O. W. Ball throwing responses to photographically portrayed targets. *J. exp. Psychol.,* 1961, 62, 223–233.

Smith, P. N., Aukes, L. E., & Lumsdaine, A. A. (Eds.) *Conference report.* Air Force Personnel and Training Research Center, Training Aids Research Lab., Tech. Memo. TARL-TM-54-1, 1954.

Stein, J. J. *The effect of a pre-film test on learning from an educational sound motion picture.* (Pennsylvania State Univer. Instructional Film Research Program) Port Wash-

ington, N.Y.: U.S. Naval Training Device Center, Office of Naval Research, Tech. Rept. No. SDC 269-7-35, 1952.

(LG) Stephens, A. L. Certain special factors involved in the law of effect. *Abstr. doctoral Dissertations, Ohio State Univer.,* 1953, 64, 505–511. [89–93]

Stolurow, L. M., & Lumsdaine, A. A. *Training characteristics for illumination of animated classroom trainers.* Air Force Personnel and Training Research Center, Training Aids Research Lab., Tech. Memo. TARL-TM-56-1, April, 1956.

Stolurow, L. M., & Newman, R. J. A factorial analysis of objective features of printed language presumably related to reading difficulty. *Amer. Psychologist,* 1956, 11, 403. (Abstract)

Sulzer, R. L., Lumsdaine, A. A., & Kopstein, F. F. *The value of using multiple examples in training film instruction.* Washington, D.C.: U.S. Air Force Human Resources Research Lab., HRRL Rept. No. 25, May, 1952. (See Lumsdaine, Sulzer, & Kopstein, 1961.)

Swanson, R. A. *The relative effectiveness of training aids designed for use in mobile training detachments.* Lackland Air Force Base, Tex.: Air Force Personnel and Training Research Center, Res. Rev. AFPTRC-TR-54-1, March, 1954.

Swanson, R. A., & Aukes, L. E. *Evaluation of training devices for B-47 fuel, hydraulic and rudder power control systems.* Lackland Air Force Base, Tex.: Air Force Personnel and Training Research Center, Res. Rept. AFPTRC-TN-56-2, January, 1956.

Swanson, R. A., Lumsdaine, A. A., & Aukes, L. E. Two studies in evaluation of maintenance training devices. In G. Finch & F. Cameron (Eds.), *Symposium on Air Force human engineering, personnel, and training research.* Washington, D.C.: National Academy of Sciences–National Research Council, Publ. No. 455, 1956. Pp. 267–275.

Thomson, Louise. The role of verbalization in learning from demonstrations. Unpublished thesis, Yale Univer., 1944. (Reviewed in *J. educ. Psychol.,* 1946, 37, 1–12, by M. A. May.)

Tinker, M. A., & Paterson, D. G. *How to make type readable.* New York: Harper, 1940.

Torkelson, G. M. *The comparative effectiveness of a mockup, cutaway, and projected* charts in teaching nomenclature and function of the 40 mm. antiaircraft weapon and the Mark 13 type torpedo. (Pennsylvania State Univer. Instructional Film Research Program) Port Washington, N.Y.: U.S. Naval Training Device Center, Office of Naval Research, Tech. Rept. No. SDC 269-7-100, March, 1954.

Travers, R. M. W. A study of the relationship of psychological research to educational practice. In R. Glaser (Ed.), Training research and education. Pittsburgh: Univer. of Pittsburgh Press, 1962. Pp. 525–558.

Twyford, L. Film profiles. (Pennsylvania State Univer. Instructional Film Research Program) Port Washington, N.Y.: U.S. Naval Training Device Center, Office of Naval Research, Tech. Rept. No. SDC 269-7-23,1951.

VanderMeer, A. W. Relative effectiveness of color and black and white in instructional films. (Pennsylvania State Univer. Instructional Film Research Program) Port Washington, N.Y.: U.S. Naval Training Device Center, Office of Naval Research, Tech. Rept. No. SDC 269-7-28, 1952.

VanderMeer, A. W. Training film evaluation: Comparison between two films on personal hygiene: TF8-155 and TF8-1665. (Pennsylvania State Univer. Instructional Film Research Program) Port Washington, N.Y.: U.S. Naval Training Device Center, Office of Naval Research, Tech. Rept. No. SDC 269-7-50, October, 1953.

Vernon, M. D. The visual presentation of factual data. Brit. J. educ. Psychol., 1950, 20, 174–185.

Vernon, M. D. A further study of visual perception. London: Cambridge Univer. Press, 1952.

Wade,. W. L., & Bretz, R. A report on the experimental use of TV in the UCLA School of Education during 1959–60. Los Angeles: Univer. of California, Univer. Extension, Educational TV, 1960.

Wald, A. Statistical decision functions. New York: Wiley, 1950.

Weiss, J. K. Teaching by television in Hagerstown. Sch. Rev., 1957, 65, 466–473.

Weiss, W., & Fine, B. J. Stimulus familiarization as a factor in ideational learning. Air Force Personnel and Training Research Center, Training Aids Research Lab., Unpublished Lab. Note TARL-LN-55-48, 1955. (Mimeographed) (Summary in Lumsdaine, 1961b)

(L) Weiss, W., Sheffield, F. D., & Maccoby, N. Combining practice with demonstration in teaching complex sequences: Serial learning of a geometric-construction task. (Ch. 4) 1961.

Witasek, S. Über lesen und rezitieren in ihren beziehungen zum gedachtnis. Z. Psychol., 1907, 44, 161–185.

Woodworth, R. S. Experimental psychology. New York: Holt, 1938.

Wulff, J. J. The teaching effectiveness of a filmed mechanical assembly demonstration with supplementary nomenclature training. Air Force Personnel and Training Research Center, Training Aids Research Lab., Unpublished Lab. Note TARL-LN-55-8, 1955. (Mimeographed) (Summary in Lumsdaine, 1961b)

(L) Wulff, J. J., & Emeson, D. L. The relationship between "what is learned" and "how it's taught." (Ch. 30) 1961.

(L) Wulff, J. J., & Kraeling, Doris G. Familiarization procedures used as adjuncts to assembly-task training with a demonstration film. (Ch. 10) 1961.

Wulff, J. J., Sheffield, F. D., & Kraeling, Doris G. "Familiarization" procedures used as adjuncts to assembly task training with a demonstration film. Air Force Personnel and Training Research Center, Training Aids Research Lab., Unpublished Staff Res. Memo., 1954. (See Wulff & Kraeling, 1961.) (Mimeographed)

Wulff, J. J., & Stolurow, L. M. The role of class descriptive cues in paired-associates learning. J. exp. Psychol., 1957, 53, 199–206.

(L) Wulff, J. J., & Stolurow, L. M. The role of class-descriptive cues in paired-associate learning. (Ch. 29) 1961.

Zeaman, D. Comments on the automation of teaching. Paper read at American Psychol. Ass., Washington, D.C., August, 1958.

Zuckerman, J. V. Commentary variations: Level of verbalization, personal reference, and phase relations in instructional films on perceptual-motor tasks. (Pennsylvania State Univer. Instructional Film Research Program) Port Washington, N.Y.: U.S. Naval Training Device Center, Office of Naval Research, Tech. Rept. No. SDC 269-7-4, December, 1949.

Zuckerman, J. V. Predicting film learning by pre-release testing. AV commun. Rev., 1954, 2 (1), 49–56.

CHAPTER 13 Social Interaction in the Classroom

JOHN WITHALL
University of Wisconsin

W. W. LEWIS
University of Wisconsin

Our concern in this chapter is with the interactions, the behavioral transactions, between the human beings in the school learning situation. We shall focus attention on the cognitive and affective interactions between teachers and learners, and learners and learners, and on the research that has been done to assess and quantify these acts. The phenomena are overt and may be verbal or nonverbal. It is assumed that observation and analysis of these overt behaviors will enable us to make some inferences about the covert dynamics of these interactions. In contrast to the methodological focus of Chapter 6, which deals with some of the same literature, the present chapter gives primary attention to substantive problems and findings.

Social interaction is, of course, a relation between persons such that "the behavior of either one is stimulus to the behavior of the other" (English & English, 1958, p. 270). Sears (1951) defined a related concept, the dyadic unit, as "one that describes the combined actions of two or more persons" (p. 479). It is sometimes important in using the concept of interaction that the referent differ from anything that can be ascribed to the participants in the interaction considered alone. Cronbach explained it as follows:

The term *dyadic* therefore may be applied to any study which compares descriptions of, statements about, or actions by two persons. These studies test hypotheses about interactions between two sets of data; their principal difficulty is that interpretations dealing with interactions can be advanced meaningfully only after the simpler main effects associated with the perceiver or the object of perception [or any two components of an interaction] have been given separate consideration (Cronbach, 1958, p. 355).

Cronbach's proviso has not always been observed in research on social interaction. The literature considered in this chapter has handled the interaction concept less rigorously than such a stipulation would allow. Often the research merely deals with how people behave in relation to other people, e.g., how teachers treat pupils, without distinguishing "simpler main effects" from interactions. It will be useful to the reader to keep in mind, however, the distinction between the loose and rigorous conceptions of interaction.

We shall trace the historical background of current trends and indicate the several stages through which research on social interaction in the classroom has moved. These stages appear to have concentrated in turn on teacher qualities or traits, child development, sociometric relationships, and, currently, socio-psychological phenomena. Attempts at assessment of classroom interaction have moved from the rating and opinionnaire stage, through the observation and analysis of perceptions by pupils and teachers of their interpersonal relations, to analyses of some of the specific variables in the socio-psychological content of the instructional process. We shall cite some of the major research to substantiate our thesis regarding the several stages through which the research seems to have progressed. Finally, we shall offer a summary and prognosis derived from what we have examined.

HISTORICAL PERSPECTIVE

From a historical perspective, three principal streams of influence, arising from educational, clinical, and social psychology, have shaped research on social interaction in the classroom. Although these are three somewhat independent areas of concern, workers in each have been aware of what the others have been doing. In recent years especially, each group has incorporated aspects of the others' work into its own. Each of the three areas of interest has reflected a somewhat different set of assumptions. Further, each has witnessed an upsurge of interest and has had its main impact upon public school practices at different points in time.

The first of these influences, coming naturally enough from within the field of education, reflected a concern with the conditions under which effective classroom learning can take place. Studies of classroom learning can be divided according to their concern with three kinds of conditions: characteristics of teachers which make for effective learning by pupils, characteristics of children which make some kinds of learning experiences more effective than others, and characteristics of the mechanical aspects of the learning act. A second kind of influence

came from what has been called the mental hygiene movement, more specifically from clinical psychologists and psychiatrists who elaborated their concepts of mental illness to include concepts of mental health, and who saw the public schools as one institutional vehicle for promulgating mental health. The third and most recent influence has been the effort of social psychologists and sociologists to study the behavior of groups—especially small, relatively permanent, face-to-face groups like those in classrooms.

The Influence from within Education

In most studies by educators on the effectiveness of learning, it has been assumed that there is probably a straightforward cause-and-effect relationship between the conditions or ingredients present in any learning situation and the quality of learning produced in that situation. Educators are practical people with a job to do, and much of their research reflects this practical turn of mind. Without saying it in so many words, they have seemed to use the "black box" paradigm in classroom learning research; i.e., the processes of teaching and learning in themselves have been left unexamined. Researchers have looked for consistent relationships between what was put into the "black box," the conditions of learning, and what came out of the "black box," the outcomes of learning, without looking into the classroom process itself.

Teacher characteristics. One obvious condition of learning is, of course, the classroom teacher, to whom the major responsibility for devising the learning experiences is given. The researcher assumes here that the "right" combination of personality traits, attitudes, and background characteristics on the part of the teacher will enable her to provide the "right" kinds of learning experiences for her pupils. This approach has an obvious implication for recruitment of new members of the teaching profession: On the one hand, if there are certain permanent human qualities that good teachers must have, then candidates who do not have these qualities must be screened out; on the other hand, if the necessary qualities can be learned, then provision for learning them should be included in teacher education curricula.

As reflected in research on teaching, interest in discovering these characteristics of the good teacher dates back to the early 1920's and continues to the present. Initially, the teacher characteristics studies dealt with easily obtained demographic variables—type of training, scholarship, and so on. More recently, subtler variables, such as attitudes and personality, have appeared in these studies. But, in spite of more sophisticated measurement and design techniques, the basic assumption has remained unaltered: the teacher is the primary ingredient in the learning process, and the characteristics of good teachers should be identified in order to provide more good teachers and fewer poor ones.

Child development. Another way of viewing the conditions of learning which go into the "black box" is to look at the qualities brought to the situation by the learner. Here the assumption again seems reasonable and practical: Since children obviously differ in the skills they bring to a learning situation, the most effective learning will take place when the material to be learned is most appropriate to whatever skills the child is currently able to muster. One primary outcome of the interest in child-conditions in learning has been the evolving body of research in child development, beginning in the early 1930's and continuing to the present.

These studies have dealt with a variety of kinds of behavior including intellectual, linguistic, social, and motor. But two dominant themes have been relevant to the education of children: (1) the concept of development itself, comprising lawful and predictable stages of growth, emphasizing the similarities between different children at the same stage of development and the dissimilarities between different stages of development of the same child; and (2) the

existence of a relationship between the developmental, or maturational stage of the individual and his readiness for certain kinds of learning activities, such that too early or too late introduction of experiences results in inefficient learning. In combination, these concepts led to (1) curricula designed to fit the average abilities and interests of children at different ages and (2) an emphasis on understanding the unique needs of individual children through personal contact. In either case, educators have continued to assume that the most effective learning experiences will result from adapting the curriculum to the developmental level of the individual learner.

Impersonal conditions of learning. Still another way of looking at the conditions of learning in the classroom is to relate outcomes to the method of presentation, the sequence, or the timing of experiences, aside from the teacher and pupils as persons. The assumption in this approach is that, given an "average" teacher and class, the arrangement of the learning experiences would be crucial to obtaining good outcomes.

Many concepts currently taught in educational psychology courses reflect the findings of research on such conditions of learning. The earliest research on learning reflected the educator's practical concern with the most efficient methods of getting information and skills incorporated into the behavioral repertoire of learners—the advantages of distributed practice over massed practice, of whole over part learning, of arranging for transfer of training, and so on.

Most questions raised in this kind of research appeared to have a direct relevance for classroom learning and were incorporated into the subject matter to be learned by prospective teachers during their training. Investigators of the conditions of learning made a concerted attempt to evolve precise relationships among independent and dependent variables in learning; for example, the independent variable of similarity of performance required in two situations and the dependent variable of transfer of training from one to the other. But the search for increased precision in studying the conditions of learning has led to the investigation of systematic, quasi-mathematical concepts that seem to have decreasing relevance for classroom learning. The most recent formulations of Hull, Guthrie, or Tolman, for example, have few direct implications for the practices of the classroom teacher. Nonetheless, these approaches provided the first systematic attempts, regardless of the directions they eventually pursued, to formulate and test relationships relevant to the learning process.

The Influence of the
Mental Hygiene Movement

Although most clinical workers in the mental hygiene professions have been interested primarily in the treatment of mental illness, they quickly recognized that a child's school experiences probably have, next to his family experiences, the most influence on his emotional well-being. The clinical workers were also quick to suggest, on the basis of individual cases handled in clinics, that a child's emotional well-being could have a striking effect on his progress in school. The interests of educators and mental hygienists seemed to overlap naturally. Two rather different assumptions seem to be implicit in much of the writing which connects clinical concepts with educational experiences: (1) a child must be in a reasonable state of adjustment to make optimum use of school learning experiences, and (2) a child's state of adjustment is subject to modification as a result of what happens to him in school.

Probably because clinical workers usually deal with single individuals in a one-to-one situation, much of the writing in this field satisfies only a loose definition of research. Studies often report findings and develop concepts based on a single case. But since the findings on each case tend to be rather elaborate and detailed, the arguments for the interdependence of emotional well-being and learning are often quite convincing. To many educators, the concepts dealt with—emotion-

al blocks to learning, transference, unconscious motivation, and the like—have seemed somewhat vague, and at times ridiculous, when applied to the classroom situation. Clinical conceptualizations of human behavior have, however, focused the attention of educators on the continuous, interactive nature of the learning process. However inarticulately the concepts were formulated, learning was taken out of the "black box" and exposed to daylight. Learning was conceived as determined not by a set of prior conditions but by a series of ongoing interactions between two or more human beings with feelings as well as ideas and skills. The influence of mental hygiene workers in helping conceptualize learning as a complicated and continuous interaction served to raise new questions, rather than to answer the older questions previously raised in the research of educators.

The Influence from
Studies of Group Life

The most recent influence on studies of social interaction in the classroom—namely, studies of group life—has proceeded independently but concurrently with much of the educational research and has only recently become incorporated in the educational literature (e.g., Glidewell, 1959; Henry, 1960). Studies of group life by sociologists and social psychologists, beginning particularly with the Lewinian studies of group climate in the 1930's, have evolved concepts relevant to the ways in which group members in different roles influence each other. The concepts of group influence, problem-solving, and decision-making did not entirely overlap with the educator's concepts of learning in the classroom. Yet both the social psychologist and the educator were concerned with changing behavior elicited in a group situation.

The assumption of mutual interest to educators and students of group life is that interactive influences emanating from the group itself bring about changes in the behavior of individual members of the group. The earliest studies of group life looked for independent variables of an antecedent nature, for example, the autocratic versus the democratic leader. But such studies soon shifted to a concern with the interaction of variables during group process. Like the mental hygiene sources, the group process studies seem to demand that classroom learning be conceptualized as a resultant of mutual influences in a dynamic process.

FRAMEWORK OF EARLY RESEARCH

Most human learning occurs in a social context. The neonate is in contact with, dependent on, and nurtured by the physician, nurse, and mother as soon as it emerges from the uterus. From that moment on, most of the individual's knowledge, ideas, feelings, goals, values, and ways of behaving are developed in interaction with other persons. Most of the knowledge any one of us possesses derives from direct or vicarious interaction with our fellows in the psychological and social context of "objective reality."

In the preschool years, youngsters learn—through social interaction with their parents or parent surrogates, siblings, peers, and other human beings—the meaning of the world around them and ways of behaving toward that world. The meaning is obviously colored by the cultural, socioeconomic, moral, and ethical values or mores of the key persons in the child's environment (Barker, Kounin, & Wright, 1943; Blair, 1946; Dollard, 1937; Hollingshead, 1949; Murchison, 1933). For example, of the studies included in the book edited by Barker, Kounin, and Wright, six are directly concerned with cultural influences on the development of children. The kinds of influence investigated were social class differences (Skodak, pp. 259–278; Davis, pp. 607–620), longitudinal trends (Macfarlane, pp. 307–328), group leader roles (Anderson, pp. 459–484; Lippitt & White, pp. 485–508), and "primitive" culture (Dennis, pp. 621–636).

The process of socializing and acculturating the individual has been institutionalized in our society by setting up schools. Here, trained workers deliberately utilize social interaction to bring about changes in the knowledge, skill, and attitudes of the youth put into their charge. For many years it was imagined that social interaction was confined merely to traffic in ideas between an adult teacher and younger learners. Closer examination of the process soon revealed that classroom learning inevitably involved traffic in feelings as well as ideas. Also, the traffic was not limited to lines running from teacher to learner but extended to channels among all the individuals in the classroom.

The earlier view of classroom interaction as confined to a learner and the teacher was exemplified best by the efforts of researchers and writers to identify the teacher traits, qualities, and behaviors hypothesized to facilitate learning. Thus, by means of rating scales and questionnaires completed in the early days of such research, by administrators and subsequently completed by pupils as well, attempts were made to identify the specific teacher traits that ultimately spelled success in terms of pupil achievement.

These efforts hardly constituted research on social interaction in the classroom; that is a relatively recent development. The studies focused on the behavioral or professional qualities of teachers deemed to make them "effective." Such a study may be an indirect way of assessing social interaction, but it is hardly a frontal attack on the problem. For instance, if the teacher is not continued in his job, then we might conclude that the teacher-pupil relationship had not been conducive to the intellectual, emotional, social, or physical development of the learners in his charge.

However, the early research did not put the problem in this framework. Rather, the question asked in early investigations was: What contributes to teacher effectiveness? The criterion for judging "effectiveness" was frequently the simple one of ascertaining whether the teacher retained or lost his job.

A number of studies (James, 1930; Morrison, 1927; Nanninga, 1924) used this criterion, along with the opinions of teachers, superintendents, school board members, and, eventually, of students, to identify the factors that contributed to the teacher's failure to be reappointed. James (1930) employed what he labeled the "case method." This involved interviewing principals and others and inquiring whether they personally knew of a teacher who had "failed," i.e., had not been reappointed. The interviewees were asked to describe the case they knew of and to tell the salient details, including reasons for dismissal. These descriptions afforded the researcher a list of 10 factors entering into teacher-failure. Freshman students, teachers, and principals were then asked to rate these factors in terms of the contribution each was believed to have made to a teacher's being dismissed. Poor discipline headed the list in all cases. Another high-ranking problem was too much dating. Intimacy with pupils also ranked high. Lack of knowledge of subject matter was placed midway by all groups of raters.

Morrison (1927) reported that he used "a careful record of forty interviews," without, however, specifying how the record was kept or how the interviews, once "recorded," were analyzed. The interviewees in this study were school superintendents and members of school boards. The results of analyzing these interviews permitted Morrison to indicate the frequency of causes for failure and to offer a composite picture of the teacher who "fails." The resulting composite picture indicated that the teacher who didn't get reappointed was a poor disciplinarian, contributed to school gossip, made an unwise choice of associates, lacked teaching skill, had no desire to grow professionally, left the classroom immediately at dismissal time, and reported late for duty. Morrison's final sentence, both hopeful and highly inferential, stated: "These facts show quite definitely that many of the causes which lead to. failure can be controlled" (p. 105).

The careful study by Nanninga (1924)

made use of a questionnaire sent to superintendents of schools in cities having a population of 2,500 or more in Oregon, Washington, Kansas, and Nebraska. Of 143 questionnaires sent out, 55 per cent were returned. The questionnaire contained only two items: (1) the number of teachers employed in the high school and their sex; (2) the number of teachers who had been dismissed or resigned and the reason for the "failure." Like the other studies cited, Nanninga's reported that poor discipline, lack of cooperation, and poor instruction were most often mentioned as reasons for "failure." Poor discipline, it appears, headed the list of causes in nearly all studies. Questionnaires and rating scales, based on traits or qualities which superintendents and supervisors considered necessary and desirable, controlled the field at this stage of the research movement. A refinement was added later as students' opinions of teachers and their desirable qualities were used to assess the teacher's effectiveness.

In this wilderness of ratings and questionnaires appeared Wickman's study (1928). It, too, relied on opinionnaires to assess teachers' attitudes regarding children's behaviors. The instruments Wickman used were no more refined than those used by other researchers at that time. He made some attempt, however, to identify items that were more discriminating by using a more methodical approach and a somewhat larger population of teachers from whom the items were derived Furthermore, he sought to assess the perceptions of teachers themselves of children's behaviors in the classroom. In addition, some basic statistical tests were used in processing the data. Neither the instruments nor the techniques used in Wickman's study, however, caused it to stand out. It was rather the inferences he drew concerning the kinds of individuals needed in teaching, the importance of the methods they used in dealing with their private emotions and needs, and most significant of all, the kind of teacher education program that would cultivate the qualities, attitudes, and skills needed by teachers for working with children most effectively. This less well-known aspect of Wickman's study is not to be confused with his well-publicized finding that teachers and mental hygienists tend to view children's school behaviors quite differently. The latter difference, as Wickman was at pains to emphasize, was a function, in part, of the kind of question put to each professional group.

Barr (1935) summarized the outlook of the professionally unsophisticated by quoting from the Twenty-Third Yearbook of the National Society of College Teachers of Education, published in 1935:

all graduate schools and research divisions ... should be encouraged to develop a measure or measures of teaching merit. . . . A hoped-for result from these investigations would be the discovery of one or two tests—simple, short, inexpensive, easily administered, quickly and accurately scored, reliable, and obviously related to teaching—which will measure a teacher's success. With such a measure many troublesome issues could be removed from the controversial group (Barr, 1935, p. 561).

Barr went on to demonstrate the forlornness of this hope. He reported a study on 99 elementary school teachers in Grades 2–7. Nineteen instruments were applied to these teachers and the pupils they taught. These instruments included the Moss-Hunt-Omwake Social Intelligence Test, A.C.E. Psychological Examination for High School Graduates and College Freshmen; the Morris Trait Index; the New Stanford Arithmetic Test; an informal 10-point scale for assessing personality; the Strong Vocational Interest Blank; and the Standard Achievement Test. The criteria of teaching success were (1) a composite of gains in test scores made by pupils on the Stanford; (2) a composite of ratings of teachers by superintendents on seven rating scales used twice; (3) a composite of scores by teachers on nine measures of qualities such as health, intelligence, personality, knowledge of subject matter, and professional interest, and (4) a composite of all the foregoing measures. Barr reported that the "values calculated were ex-

ceedingly low . . . most . . . in terms of coefficients of correlations, falling between 0 and .35" (p. 565). He concluded that such results are "disappointing." In light of the use of rating scales of questionable validity and reliability, and in view of the shakiness of personality assessments by pencil-and-paper tests and the highly tenuous nature of the several variables being assessed, it is not astonishing that low coefficients of correlation were derived. Barr explained that the negative results were due to the "minuteness of the contribution made by the different aspects of teaching measured when compared with the whole of teaching ability" (p. 566). He concluded that qualities, such as knowledge of subject and mastery of teaching skills, that are readily measured are overshadowed by the difficult-to-measure and subtler variables of the teacher's philosophy, personality, interpersonal relationships, and the whole area of teacher-pupil relationships. He argued that we "need functional tests measuring the teacher in action" and that the "ultimate criterion of teaching success will have to be found in the changes produced in pupils . . ." (p. 568).

Melby (1936) set forth a similar view:

there is greater need than ever for technics of describing the learning activities of children. . . . If we can devise methods for describing the learning activities of children we can at least know how children live while they are learning even though we cannot measure all that is learned (p. 333). . . .
We can only say that in a given situation certain things were done and here is a picture of what happened. If we have a large number of such cases, certain generalizations will be possible (Melby, 1936, p. 335).

Despite the weight of evidence and despite the eloquence of the pleas for more reliable and valid techniques for measuring one facet of social interaction, i.e., teacher-pupil relationships in the teaching-learning process, the dependence on rating scales, questionnaires, and opinionnaires persists. But some effort is being made today to utilize observational instruments which can quantify relevant observable behaviors and interactions in vivo.

As it became more and more evident that superintendents', principals', supervisors', and board members' ratings of teachers showed very little reliability and little relationship to one another's assessments, the researchers on teacher behaviors in the classroom began assiduously to collect student ratings of teachers. A more realistic attitude began to appear, one which held that student ratings might be merely "taken purely as an accumulation of opinion without raising any question of how valid that opinion may be. The views of the students may be prejudiced, mistaken, superficial, immature, but, whatever their validity, they exist and exert a powerful influence on the effectiveness of the course" (Bryan, 1933, p. 296, quoting from Wilson, 1932, p. 79).

Our reservations and skepticism regarding rating scales can be summed up in the following strictures. It appears that ratings encourage inferences and extrapolations beyond the observed behavior, in that large, global, undifferentiated segments of behavior are rated in terms of private, unstated criteria of the rater. Gage and Cronbach (1955) have stressed the importance of considering *"degree of extrapolation* or inference required between Input and Outtake" (p. 412). Requiring much extrapolation of this kind, as is often the case in the kinds of ratings made of teachers, makes ratings lack comparability in that each rater has his own private frame of reference and tends to select those aspects of the global behavior which particularly suit his frame of reference. Sociometric devices, if viewed as rating instruments (as in Chapter 7, especially on pp. 345–360), deliberately exploit this fact of the uniqueness of individual perceptions and predilections to get a picture of the peculiar perceptions of each of the participants in a group. Ratings of qualities, global behaviors, traits, and skills (frequently not defined specifically), on the other hand, are usually tossed into the hopper on the basic assumption that the same behavioral phenomena were assessed and that the criteria governing each individual's rating were similar and comparable.

Sociometry and the Teacher's Verbal Control of Children's Behavior

Parallel with the burgeoning interest in students' ratings of their teachers as a means of assessing teacher impact on learners came Moreno's *Who Shall Survive?* (1934) and its exposition of a new device for measuring relationships within groups. The fact that rating scales had been used and found wanting made it inevitable that, when educators became acquainted with the sociometric devices of Moreno, they would see the value of them for their purposes. It took a little while, however, as it often does with a promising and useful device, for Moreno's devices to be discovered and used in schools.

A number of worth-while sociometric studies of social relationships in the classroom appeared in the 1940's (Bonney, 1947; McLelland & Ratliff, 1947; Young, 1947) along the lines laid down by Jennings (1947, 1948). Bonney sought to ascertain how effectively teachers could identify students who have the most and the least friends. He asked 291 students to rate their best friends on a personality scale. He also asked 13 teachers to check in one of four columns (High, Middle, Low, and Unable to Judge) how they thought each student ranked in number of friends. Teachers appeared to overrate students who were active in formal class and student activities, who were amenable to teacher directions, who were socially inhibited, and who had desirable personality traits, but who were looked on as outsiders as far as other students were concerned. Teachers underrated students who were academically inept but who had good interpersonal relationships with their own clique and who were apt to disregard teacher regulations but were well liked by their peers.

To collect data on the social relationships of a group of 41 seventh-graders, Young (1947) used controlled interviews about the school, the Ohio Social Acceptance Scale, and a "guess-who" technique, in addition to a standard sociometric test requesting the subject to pick someone to sit with, play on his team, go on a picnic, and be his best friend. A rank-order correlation of .90 was obtained between the sociometric test and the Ohio Social Acceptance Scale. It appears that the same factors which enter into a child's choice of friends influence his selecting them for his team and as president of his class.

Planned change was initiated through small-group activities in which social relationships would be encouraged and developed in a study by McLelland and Ratliff (1947). They asked 35 ninth-graders to indicate someone (1) with whom they'd like to go to a show; (2) with whom they'd like to study; (3) whom they'd like to have at home as a guest; and (4) with whom they'd rather share a secret. After isolates and rejectees were identified, the experimental treatment was applied. Follow-up sociometric tests indicated that social acceptance was more widespread. These investigations represented attempts to assess the interpersonal relationships of pupils with their peers by collecting data on social relationships directly from the members of the class group under study.

One tack pursued in the interim was that of analyzing the behaviors of teachers in the situation. This marked a considerable advance over attempts to assess a teacher's relationships with her pupils by out-of-classroom ratings. Johnson's study (1935) demonstrated that positive, directive, and approving verbal communication to pupils ensured a greater degree of complying with requests and directions by learners, as compared with directions or requests to learners that were negative, nonspecific, and reproving. She used two groups of 38 children each and asked them one at a time to perform simple tasks, solve problems, and to inhibit certain activities. One type of positive verbal direction was used with the "experimental" group with explicit directions and requests, e.g., "Cut it in the corner to save the paper." Negative and unexplicit directions, such as

"Don't waste paper," were given to the "control" group. The "Do" type of directions appeared more effective than the "Don't," in that consistently larger percentages of the experimental group children than of control group children succeeded in performing tasks assigned them (cutting a paper circle). Johnson pointed up the greater number of successes in the one group where "more positive, unhurried, specific and encouraging types of directions" were given, as compared with the situation where "more negative, general, hurried and discouraging verbal directions" were given (p. 204).

Olson and Wilkinson (1938) examined the same question by a time-sampling technique and substantiated Johnson's findings that directive, approving, specific statements are more efficacious in obtaining compliance and cooperation than negative, blanket, and nonspecific statements or requests. They recorded during each five-minute period just one reaction by the student teacher to marked inattention or restlessness on the part of the children. The student teacher's verbal behavior was labeled positive if she suggested "Do this"; it was labeled negative if she said "Don't do that or else you'll suffer"; and finally, "blanket" responses were identified when one child's behavior was reprimanded by such statements as: "We should all be working right now" or "Pupils in my class don't run." In addition, "gestural" responses, i.e., movements of head, hands, and shoulders were noted. The researchers sought an answer to the question, Does the type of language and the control technique of the teacher indicate his probable teaching efficiency? On the basis of ratings by the principal and critic teacher, it was found that quantity of control was unimportant but that quality of control was important (see Kounin & Gump's recent work, 1958, 1961). Furthermore, it appeared that "blanket" responses were used by the least efficient teachers, while abler teachers used more discriminating and varied control procedures and a larger proportion of directing and approving statements. The percentage of positive language used correlated .59 with the Haggerty-Olson-Wickman rating scale.

The work of Anderson and his collaborators (Anderson & Helen M. Brewer, 1945; Anderson & J. E. Brewer, 1946; Anderson, Brewer, & Reed, 1946), Jersild and others (1939), Thorndike, Loftus, and Goldman (1941), as well as the descriptions, analyses, and summaries of the then current research and its implications by various writers (e.g., Jones, Conrad, & Murphy, 1939; Leonard & Eurich, 1942; Ohio State University, University High School Class, 1938; and Stoddard, 1939), pushed still further the examination of teachers' and children's classroom behavior. This type of research may have become prominent, in part, because of the international political currents then running and because a developing sensitivity to mental hygiene principles encouraged educators and researchers to view the teacher's behaviors in terms of their controlling or facilitating influence.

The work of Anderson and his co-workers was reported fully in a series of *Applied Psychology Monographs*. These researchers worked from the basic postulate that the main direction of influence in the classroom is from teacher to pupil. To measure this, Anderson developed teacher-behavior categories, and Brewer developed child-behavior categories. With these categories they were able to determine the extent to which teacher behavior influenced the behavior of the pupils and the psychological atmosphere of the classroom. Their subjects were teachers and pupils in kindergarten and the primary grades.

Anderson developed 26 categories for the classification of teacher behavior. These categories embraced two main types of teacher behavior vis-à-vis the child: "dominative" and "integrative." The dominative teacher behaviors were further divided into three kinds: (1) dominative with conflict; (2) dominative without conflict; and (3) dominative with evidence of working together. Integrative teacher behaviors were divided into two kinds: (1) integrative contacts without working together; (2) integrative contacts with evidence of working together. Nonverbal as well as verbal behavior of the teacher was sampled by means of the categories. Contacts of the teacher with each pupil individually or with the group as a whole were recorded on a standard observation blank developed by Anderson and Brewer. Some examples of dominative behaviors by teachers included (1) telling a child to move to another part of the room; (2) using warnings, threats, and reminders; (3) punishing by sending out of room; (4) making gratuitous judgment, and (5) calling to attention. Integrative behaviors included (1) questioning to obtain information regarding possible interest of child; (2) helping child to define, redefine, and solve a problem; (3) approving, commending, and accepting the spontaneous self-initiated behavior of the child; and (4) asking questions regarding the child's expressed interests.

The reliability of the observers was determined by computing percentages of agreement between the simultaneous, independent observations of two categorizers. The mean percentages of agreement for two observers were 90 per cent for teacher behavior and 95 per cent for child behavior. It appeared that identifiable teacher behaviors could be categorized so that teachers could be differentiated on the basis of the relative number of their integrative and dominative contacts with children. Furthermore, concomitant differences in pupil behavior were found to be consistent with the classroom personalities of the teachers. Children with more integrative teachers showed significantly lower frequencies of distracted and nonconforming behavior, and significantly higher frequencies of spontaneous, cooperative, and self-directed behavior. In order to assess further the validity of the instruments, a study was made of the same groups of children who had been observed in Grade 2 after they moved into Grade 3. It was found, using Brewer's categories, that the pupils' behavior in Grade 3 was different from what it had been in Grade 2. These behavior differences were consistent with the behaviors of the Grade 3 teachers as identified by Anderson's categories. Another follow-up study, made on the Grade 2 teachers, found that those teachers, although working with new groups of children, maintained virtually the same patterns of behavior that they had exhibited the previous year and that the new second-graders reacted with behaviors that were highly similar to those of their predecessors.

The studies of Anderson and his co-workers tended to demonstrate that the teacher's classroom personality and behaviors influenced the behavior of the children she taught. Teachers who used dominative techniques produced in their pupils aggressive and antagonistic behaviors which were expressed toward both their teachers and their peers. On the other hand, teachers who used socially integrative behaviors appeared to facilitate friendly, cooperative, and self-directive behaviors in the children.

Jersild, Thorndike, Goldman, and Loftus (1939) set out to assess the influence of "activity" programs in selected schools in New York City. They developed procedures for recording pupil behaviors, and measured the learning outcomes with pencil-and-paper tests of work-skills, over-all achievement, intelligence, and social beliefs and attitudes. Pupils in eight "activity" schools and eight "control" (traditional) schools comprised the Ss. The youngsters studied were elementary school children (Grades 1–6), most of them in Grades 4, 5, and 6. The behavioral data were collected through coded observations of seven major types of activities: (1) cooperative; (2) critical; (3) experimental; (4) leadership; (5) recitational; (6) self-initiated; and (7) negative work spirit. The quantified data of the coded observations were supplemented by anecdotal observations. Detailed notes of behaviors of particular youngsters were related to the coded observations of the same youngsters. Concurrent but independent observations in the same classroom by two observers yielded median percentages of agreement between observers ranging from 70 to 97 per cent when the coded records were compared item by item. However, the problem of obtaining adequate reliability and agreement when specific behaviors have to be recorded is demonstrated by the median corrected split-half coefficient of .47 obtained in assessing the reliability of coded observation scores of single individuals, where correlations were computed between first and second periods of observation for each of 1,833 pupils in 51 classes. On the other hand, a median coefficient of .97 was obtained between class averages assigned to the same records by two sets of two independent raters of 76 classes when rating the global data of anecdotal observation.

This study demonstrated that behaviors of children in activity programs differed from those of children in traditional classes. The activity children participated more in planning and directing activities, were able to capitalize more on their interests and aptitudes, gave more outward appearance of self-direction, utilized their greater freedom constructively, and engaged in more diverse activities in the classroom. Nonetheless, the pencil-and-paper tests indicated that children under the activity regime did less well on the Comprehensive Achievement Test and lagged behind the control groups in certain tool subjects—mainly arithmetic and spelling. Jersild and his co-workers suggested that the paper-and-pencil instruments used to measure the learning of the activity program youngsters were not adequate to the task of measuring outcomes in the activity classes.

To determine the immediate values, or the ultimate benefits of the various performances in which the activity children surpassed the controls would require more intensive study. More intensive investigation likewise would be required to determine the extent and nature of other learnings and performances that were not measured by the methods so far employed, and to explore the extent to which such learnings might offset, or outweigh, the somewhat greater degree of competence that the control pupils meanwhile had gained in certain academic subjects . . . (Jersild, et al., 1939, p. 206).

Thorndike, Loftus, and Goldman (1941) reported in more detail the development of the categories used in recording the behaviors of the children studied in the New York City "activity" investigation. The differences in the behaviors of the two groups were spelled out, and the disappointingly low percentages of agreement (around 50 per cent) were highlighted.

Child Development and Group Climate

Two other mainstreams of influence—research on child growth and development (Blos, 1941; Prescott, 1938; Zachry & Lichty, 1940) and the assessment of group life and climate by Lippitt (1940)—began to influence research at about this time. Ojemann and Wilkinson (1939) conducted a study to ascertain whether teachers became more effective when they made a careful study of children's behavior and the bases for it. Their study represents an attempt to assess the value of the child-development point of view in the learning situation. The question asked was: If the teacher is helped to develop a comprehensive understanding of how children grow and develop, will not the children's learning and personal-social development be enhanced? The writings of Dearborn and Rothney (1941), Prescott (1938), Rothney and Roens (1949), and the Division on Child Development and Teacher Personnel (1945) consistently exemplify this orientation. Ojemann and Wilkinson's study can be viewed as the prototype of studies concerned with the teacher's understanding of child development and behavior as a determiner of her ability to facilitate learning and enhance personality development. Their method consisted of selecting experimental and control groups of 33 children each in a ninth grade. The groups were matched on chronological age, intelligence scores (Otis Group Test), school achievement, and home background. The teachers of the experimental group received and discussed the comprehensive data gathered on each child from tests, home interviews, and school records. Suggested procedures were developed from these discussions on the planning of daily classwork and ways of conducting the class. One of the investigators in this study dropped in occasionally to discuss the experimental group's progress with their teachers. The experimental group made a significantly greater gain academically, differed significantly from the control group in its attitudes toward school, and seemed to manifest fewer personality conflicts and psychological disturbances than pupils in the control group. It was concluded that teachers are more effective guides of children's learning when they know about the youngster's abilities, home environment, emotional problems, and attitudes.

In an experiment somewhat resembling that of Ojemann and Wilkinson, Burrell (1951) attempted to test the effectiveness of a deliberate effort on the part of teachers to meet the emotional needs of youngsters who were evincing learning problems and blocks. The researcher's question was: Can learning be facilitated if the teacher makes a concerted effort to meet the child's emotional needs? She selected two schools in Brooklyn, New York, and within School A chose three classes in the intermediate grades as the experimental subjects. School B provided three classes of control subjects. The six teachers (three control and three experimental) were asked to identify five students in each class who were having learning difficulties. The Wishing Well Test, Ohio Social Acceptance Scale, Otis-Pintner, Stanford Achievement Tests, and Wetzel Grid were administered to both the control and experimental pupils. Beyond collecting the data on the control subjects, nothing else was done with that group. The teachers working with the experimental groups were instructed to try to meet the emotional needs of the five youngsters in each of their classes who were having learning difficulties. Statistical analyses indicated that the experimental subjects manifested improved learning (as judged by results on posttests), improved social relationships, diminished deviate behavior, improved work habits, and reduced truancy; furthermore, the experimental teachers' attitudes toward the youngsters improved.

One question raised by experiments of the kind done by Ojemann-Wilkinson and Burrell is: To what extent can the results be explained by the "Hawthorne effect"? Thus, it may have been the superior motivation, due to the additional attention given to teachers and pupils by the investigators, rather than the teachers' superior understanding of their pupils, that produced the greater gains in the experimental group. More adequately designed experiments (see Chapter 5) are needed to rule out this rival hypothesis.

Brookover's study (1940) on the relationship of measured person-to-person interactions between teachers and pupils and the ratings of pupils and administrators epitomizes the many studies of its kind. To measure the "person-person interaction" of the teacher and her pupils, Brookover carefully developed a nine-item multiple-choice scale. The scale appears to have measured the pupil's impression of the pleasantness of his relationships with his teacher. Teachers with high ratings by their pupils on this instrument were also rated high ($r = .64$) as instructors by pupils using the Purdue Rating Scale for Instructors. This correlation probably reflects the strong operation of social desirability factors in both instruments. In a sense, both get at the degree to which the student likes the teacher, and it is little wonder that they correlate substantially. Furthermore, the students' mean ratings of their teachers on the Interaction Scale correlated only $-.08$ with the ratings of the teachers by a single administrator. Finally, the ratings by two groups of principals and administrators of their teachers' effectiveness on the Purdue Rating Scale correlated only .24.

Another study in student-teacher relationships at this time (Bush, 1942) examined the relevance—to the teacher's effectiveness—of such variables as the teacher's social beliefs, the student's opinion of the teacher's fairness, the teacher's personal liking for students, and the teacher's opinion of the student's thinking ability. Bush decided to explore the nature of effective teacher-pupil relationships "by focusing upon the student-teacher relationship rather than upon only the teacher, or the student, or the teaching method" (p. 645). His subjects in the ninth grade and up were drawn from a private boys' school. The relationships between nine social science teachers and the students in their classes were his basic concern. Tests, rating scales, anecdotal records, interviews, questionnaires, and regular school records were all used as sources of the basic data. He found that the more discriminating variables for assessing student-teacher relationships were similarity of social beliefs between teacher and students, mutual personal liking of student and teacher, the teacher's skill in developing harmonious relations with students, the teacher's effectiveness in counseling, and the teacher's belief that he has an effective relationship with a student. Nondiscriminatory variables were the teacher's appearance and possession of more knowledge than the student.

A useful summary of the major research up to this time was made by Tiedeman (1942). He collated materials dealing with pupil-teacher relationships based on child development studies (e.g., Meek, 1940; Prescott, 1938) and students' ratings of teachers (e.g., Jersild & Holmes, 1940; Remmers, 1934).

A study resulting in the development of an inventory to measure the attitudes of teachers relevant to teacher-pupil relationships (Leeds & Cook, 1947) is a good example of research based on psychometric tools and approaches. (This work is also considered in Chapter 11.) Judgments by principals were used in the selection and identification of the two extreme groups on the criterion of rapport with students; against this criterion, about 150 attitude statements were validated and selected. The principals rated a subsequent group of teachers on a six-item scale, Leeds himself used Baxter's rating scale for assessing the same teachers, and a 50-item "My

Teacher" scale was used by the pupils to rate their teachers. It is not surprising to learn that "the single validating criterion showing the highest correlation (.486) with the Inventory was the writer's rating of the teacher's classroom behavior" (p. 155). Since the researcher had developed the inventory within a certain orientation and framework for observing the teachers' behaviors, this finding seems to indicate that the same orientation and framework guided him in making on-the-spot classroom observations. The correlations of the inventory with the principal's rating and the pupils' mean rating of the teacher were .43 and .45, respectively. Such variables as the sex, marital status, or parental status of the teacher and such matters as size of school and subjects taught had little or no relationship to the teachers' inventory scores or to ratings by pupils of their teachers.

Social-Emotional Climate in the Classroom

The Iowa studies. Lewin, Lippitt, and White's work (1939) on interpersonal interactions of children in differing social climates opened up, as did the techniques of sociometry, new horizons for the study of social interaction in learning situations. Recently presented in book form (White & Lippitt, 1960), this work reflected, implicitly at least, the concern with values stemming from the international situation and the expansion of totalitarianism in the 1930's.

The early work on the effect of social climate and of leadership roles on group life and productivity is best represented by Lippitt's Iowa investigation. He organized four clubs of five boys each. The boys were eleven years old and drawn from public school populations. Each club met for six weeks under a leader who implemented a specified style of leadership. Thus, in a consecutive 18-week period the four clubs each had three different leaders who employed either a democratic, autocratic, or laissez-faire leadership style. The leadership styles were rotated among the

several leaders so that personality might be partialled out as a biasing factor. Two clubs met concurrently in adjoining rooms and were headed by leaders implementing two different leadership methodologies according to stated criteria. Two sets of observers recorded (1) quantitative running accounts of social interaction between the five boys and the leader; (2) a continuous stenographic record of the conversation of the six persons in each club; (3) activity subgroupings and activity goals of each; (4) a running account of psychologically interesting interactions in each group; and (5) an account of interclub contacts. The mean percentage of agreement between two investigators categorizing the verbal behavior was 80 per cent. Other data included interview material secured from each club member; interview data from the parents of the boys at the end of the experiment; ratings by parents of a boy's cooperativeness, hobbies, and developmental history; information on the boy filled out by his classroom teacher; and, finally, the results of a Rorschach test given to each child. Analyses were made of the verbal behavior of the six individuals in each club. Their social behavior was analyzed in terms of (1) ascendant, (2) fact-minded, (3) submissive, and (4) ignoring categories.

The social climate resulting from different leadership styles produced significant differences among the several groups in amount of expression of discontent, out-of-group-field conversation, and work-centered conversation. At the same time, it was demonstrated that club personnel (as distinguished from leadership style) produced somewhat less significant differences among the groups in amount of expression of discontent, friendliness, group-mindedness, and out-of-group-field conversation.

Lippitt's major conclusions were (1) that different styles of leader behavior produce differing social climates and differing group and individual behaviors; (2) that conversation categories differentiated leader-behavior techniques more adequately than did social-behavior categories; (3) that different leaders playing the same kind of leadership roles displayed very similar patterns of behavior and that group members reacted to the same kind of leadership style in strikingly similar and consistent fashion; (4) that group members in a democratic social climate were more friendly to each other, showed more group-mindedness, were more work-minded, showed greater initiative, and had a higher level of frustration tolerance than members in the other groups; (5) that leader-behavior categories represent the important parameters to which the children reacted.

The significance of Lippitt's work lies in the fact that it is the earliest, major, successful attempt to observe and control objectively the climate variable in group life. Subsequent work in the area has been influenced and helped by his concepts and methodology. His clear demonstration of the influence of the leader on group life and productivity had strong implications for teachers and education.

Subsequent to Lippitt's work, the entire complex or network of relationships in learning groups began to be examined. Such concepts as the socio and psyche group (Jennings, 1947) were offered as one way of organizing the data with which the researcher has to be concerned in understanding social interaction in group situations—whether in the classroom or elsewhere. Jennings conceptualized group life and interaction as fulfilling two major groups of needs of individuals, i.e., (1) the friendship, or psyche, needs and (2) the task or work, or socio, needs. Usually, different social groups serve one of these functions much more adequately and efficiently than the other, though all groups tend to serve both sets of needs to a lesser or greater extent (Thelen, 1960b, pp. 114–121). The bridge club, golf foursome, or recreational group where the individual is prized and accepted for himself and not for his role may be seen as the epitome of the psyche group. Work groups, task-oriented organizations such as medical teams including doctors, nurses, and technicians, and task forces of all kinds, where the individual is prized for the roles or functions he can perform to achieve the group's work goals, constitute socio groups. It appears, however, that the psyche needs of man are pre-eminent, regardless of whatever formal or informal group in which he finds himself, since subgroups to meet individual needs come into being even in the most work-centered situations. Where individuals have similar interests and social-emotional needs which they perceive the other can fulfill, they gravitate to each other as they work on the substantive problem and thus sustain and affirm each other's unique, individual worth apart from their role and responsibilities in the task-centered operation.

The Chicago studies. In the late 1940's, Thelen (1951) and others at the University of Chicago began to capitalize on several streams of thought: Lewin's field theory; the work of Prescott, Havighurst, and Tryon in child study and development; Rogers' client-centered therapy; and group dynamics. They sought to develop a theory of instruction which utilized constructs drawn from child development, field theory, and psychotherapy.

The Chicago research was interdisciplinary and both theoretically and empirically oriented. Hypotheses were derived from analysis of time-lapse pictures, recordings, and observations in the classroom by sensitive and trained educators. The earliest of a train of researches that is still continuing (Flanders, 1959; Thelen, 1959a, 1959b) was that of Withall (1949). In his study, social-emotional climate was treated as a group phenomenon determined primarily by the teacher's verbal behavior taken as representative of her total behavior. He developed an instrument, called the Climate Index, for categorizing and quantifying the verbal behavior of the teacher in any class. The procedure involved making an intensive study and analysis of tape recordings of daily classroom sessions of some junior high school classes. Teacher statements within the context of students' questions, responses, and statements were analyzed. The emotional tone and inferred dominant intent of each teacher verbalization were assessed with considerable care. At first, 25 kinds of teacher statements seemed identifiable, but further analysis of the records showed that the types identified were not mutually exclusive. Thirteen types were then identified. These 13 kinds of statements in turn were consolidated into seven categories. The seven categories into which all teacher verbalizations appeared to fall encompassed statements or questions by the teacher which (1) commended or approved the learner (learner-supportive); (2) conveyed understanding or acceptance of the learner (clarifying or acceptant); (3) gave information to or asked questions of fact vis-à-vis the learner (problem-structuring); (4) comprised "chit-chat" and routine administrative items (neutral); (5) limited or controlled the learner's behavior (directive); (6) deprecated or disapproved (disapproving or reproving); (7) defended or supported the teacher (teacher-supportive).

It seemed that the first three categories (1, 2, and 3) could be viewed as learner-supportive and the last three (5, 6, and 7) as teacher-supportive. In categorizing a statement, the categorizer was asked at the outset to determine whether the dominant intent of the statement was to sustain the teacher or the learner. Once the dominant intent had been determined, the decision had to be made as to which one of the first three or last three categories was represented by the statement.

The objectivity and reliability studies involved computing correlations (tetrachoric) between the judgments of five categorizers. The median correlations between categorizers on three discrete samples of data were .84, .76, and .93. Contingency coefficients computed on the same data ranged between .76 and .89. The validation of the instrument involved (1) a comparison of the categorizations of the Climate Index with Anderson's (1946) Integrative-Dominance Ratio secured on the same data; (2) pencil-and-paper assessment of their classroom situation by pupils on the basis of seven standardized questions; and (3) the use of an electrical graph mechanism for recording pupils' positive and negative feelings expressed by their pushing one of two buttons while they were exposed to experimentally varied "learner-centered" and "teacher-centered" social-emotional climates (Thelen & Withall, 1949).

The development of a Climate Index with demonstrable reliability and validity (see Mitzel & Rabinowitz, 1954) spotlighted several issues for further research. One crucial question was how learning and achievement were influenced in the classroom by the nature and quality of the teacher-pupil interaction. Flanders (1949) undertook an investigation of this problem. Psychological and physiological measures (GSR and heartbeat measures) were made of seven high school students exposed to standardized, 25-minute learning experiences under two experimental climates. The student was placed in two different learning situations having reasonably equivalent learning tasks. The social-emotional differences between the two situations were created by the role of the teacher. In a teacher-centered (TC) situation, the behavior of the teacher tended to support himself first, the problem second, and the student third. As a consequence, it was difficult for the student to operate efficiently in the situation, and, as a result, interpersonal anxieties were created. In a learner-centered (LC) situation, the behavior of the teacher tended to support the student first, the problem second, and the teacher third. As a consequence, the student was able to clarify his position in the structure of the interaction, and his interpersonal anxiety remained within tolerable limits. Thus, an experimental sequence of events was organized which permitted the student to participate in the TC and LC learning sessions, then to distribute 121 statements (Q sort) into 11 categories of student feelings about and perceptions of the teacher with reference to the learning periods just experienced and, finally, to participate in a postlearning interview. Pre- and posttesting of mastery of content and principles to be learned was carried out. With the climate treated as an independent variable, measured by Withall's Climate Index, it was demonstrated that student behavior reflecting interpersonal anxiety took precedence over behavior oriented to the objective problem and learning content. It appeared, too, that demanding, directive, and deprecating teacher behavior vis-à-vis pupils resulted in withdrawal, apathy toward the achievement problem, aggressiveness, and hostility on the part of the pupils. On the other hand, teacher behavior which was oriented to the problem, analytical of student procedures according to publicly stated criteria, and generally learner-centered elicited less interpersonal anxiety, more problem-solving behavior, and a degree of emotional integration.

Rehage (1948), with matched eighth-grade social studies classes, investigated the quality of social interaction in pupil-teacher relationships in the planning stages of classroom work. He also investigated the similarities and dissimilarities in problem-solving and knowledge of the two matched classes. The experimental group planned its own program in social studies problems with particular attention to democratic values and institutions in the nearby community. The plans and activities developed by the experimental group were utilized by the social studies teacher as the program for the control group, which was given no opportunity to participate in planning its program or identifying its goals. In group problem-solving and group planning skill, as well as in flexibility of the network of social relations in the classroom, the differences revealed by the investigation favored the experimental group.

Perkins (1949) investigated the influence of social interaction at the adult level, i.e., with in-service teachers. He compared learner-centered and teacher-centered classes as differentiated by Withall's Climate Index. The study demonstrated that the variable of learner- versus teacher-centeredness of classroom "climate" makes a remarkable difference in problem-orientation, in attitudes toward other persons, in learning of facts, and in human relations skills. The evidence he cited included the following: as compared with leader-centered groups, study groups in which the leader was learner- or group-centered made markedly superior use of evidence to substantiate their ideas and interpretations of child behavior and gave more evidence of useful insights and sound reasoning. Learner-centered study groups revealed greater objectivity and warmth in their attitudes toward children, whereas leader-centered groups were more conventional and cold. Finally, more child development concepts were expressed in group- or learner-centered climates. All of these findings, based on a content analysis of group members' verbalizations in the in-service study groups, favored the learner-centered groups.

The studies of Glidewell (1951), Singletary (1951), and subsequent co-workers with Thelen in the Human Dynamics Laboratory at the University of Chicago represent a trend toward examining the dynamics of social interaction at the overt level of teachers' and learners' observable behaviors and at the same time trying to relate these behaviors, as observed and interpreted by the "actors" themselves, to the inferred covert dynamics. Glidewell raised the question of how effective a teacher's leadership can be when she denies her own feelings. To answer this he set up controlled group situations involving four experienced role-players and the subject (leader). The group situations were arranged so that both acceptable and unacceptable feelings could be engendered in the leader-subject. It appeared obvious from the analysis of the recorded discussions and the statistical relationship between predictions of ratings and actual ratings by six observers, that "denial of feelings by the leader was accompanied by a reduction of leadership effectiveness; acceptance, by an increase of effectiveness" (p. 126). "The most effective teacher can be seen as one who seeks, through her feelings as one medium, the reality of her own needs and those of her students [the psyche aspect] with an eye toward a need-meeting group learning activity" [the socio aspect] (p. 120). This approach is founded on the view that group processes are geared to the resolution of the psyche (emotional) as well as the socio (problem-solving) needs of the individual and of the total group.

Singletary (1951), by means of interviews and questionnaires directed to administrators and teachers in one school, sought to get at teachers' and administrators' perceptions of pupils and of each other with respect to expectations, demands, group relations, and social organization. The data were assessed for their impact on the interactions and roles of pupils, teachers, and administrators. The findings included the fact that a group's social organization depends on its perceptual consistency. Fundamental differences in perception existed between teachers and administrators regarding the basic expectations that the administrators have for pupils. Teachers and administrators were most consistent in perceiving the things that teachers do which administrators like and dislike, and the things that pupils do that teachers like and dislike.

Thelen and his colleagues went beyond the efforts of Moreno and others who examined the dynamics of groups in terms of the observed behaviors and the stated perceptions of the actors. Thelen drew on the theory-based inferences and hypotheses of an external observer to test the validity of the interpretations and perceptions of the participants in the group. Moreno managed to demonstrate the complexity of lines of communication and interaction in groups at one level. The Chicago group went ahead to relate the observable complex of interactions—and the interactors' interpretations of those interactions—to theory-based inferences. For instance, teachers' behaviors can be hypothesized to determine to a large extent the quality of the teacher-student interaction and the learning that takes place in an instructional situation. Flanders' (1949) study dealt with this inference, which was based on a developing socio-psychological theory of school learning. From the same theoretical foundations, Rehage's (1948) study assessed the effect of having teachers and learners jointly plan

the instructional process and identify goals. Finally, the needs of the teacher in the learning situation would appear to be as pertinent to the learning process as those of the learners, and the teacher's ability to recognize and accept these needs may be hypothesized to have considerable significance for her effectiveness in guiding the pupils' learning. This is the issue to which Glidewell (1951) addressed himself.

A widely applicable system of observation of group interaction was developed by Bales (1950). Although his original intention was to provide a method of analyzing the behavior of small work groups, the categories he used seem appropriate to describe the behavior of a teacher or pupils in a classroom. The recording is done "live," that is, by an observer in the actual situation. The observer takes the point of view of the "generalized other," or recipient of the behavior being recorded. He records every discriminable act of the group members in one of 12 categories: (1) shows solidarity, (2) shows tension release, (3) agrees, (4) gives suggestion, (5) gives opinion, (6) gives orientation, (7) asks for orientation, (8) asks for opinion, (9) asks for suggestions, (10) disagrees, (11) shows tension, and (12) shows antagonism.

RESEARCH ON SOCIAL INTERACTION IN THE CLASSROOM SINCE 1950

About 1950, a number of statements signaled the beginning of heightened activity in research on social interaction in the classroom. In this section we shall review developments of the past decade, beginning with a review of various programmatic and theoretical statements. Then we shall consider, in turn, research on interpersonal perception in school settings, on social climate, and on teaching styles.

Programmatic and Theoretical Statements

The statement by Thelen and Tyler

(1950) that "realization of the very great influence of the classroom group upon individual learning follows from a consideration of the implications of much of the recent research in social psychology" (p. 307) can be regarded as a kind of prologue to the period in which educational research began to capitalize on a view of the classroom group as a social milieu in which learning and instruction occurred. They identified four functional interrelationships between the individual and the group in which the classroom group helps the individual to learn, to progress toward self-realization, to test social concepts and conduct, and to adapt to his culture.

Thelen's (1950) impressive monograph elaborated even more pointedly on concepts and principles that could help in understanding, predicting, and controlling teacher-pupil interaction. The major concepts specified by Thelen were "experiencing" (in the sense of the term used by John Dewey), "interdependence," and "conflict." Conflict he dubbed the "most significant social psychological phenomenon." He offered nine principles to guide the study of classroom teaching and learning. These principles asserted that classroom learning experiences (1) serve to meet the psyche (affective, interpersonal) and socio (achievement) needs of the learner; (2) have potency for the learner to the extent they help him meet his needs; (3) deal with the basic problem of learning the experimental method; (4) when structured and planned, provide goals and limits for the learner; (5) are highly susceptible to anxiety pressures arising from interpersonal conflict; (6) are only a fraction of the total life of the learner; (7) can provide reinforcement to the culturally approved sides of student ambivalence; (8) can best be guided through an assessment of group affect and group problems; and (9) will be most effective when governed by the "Principle of Least Group Size" (see Thelen, 1949). These papers emphasized the need to examine and understand the individual learner's frame of reference within the context of the group values

and pressures in the classroom situation. This understanding requires the development by the teacher of ability to hypothesize the internal frame of reference of each learner (a kind of "empathy" or interpersonal perception), and to ascertain how she can use group forces and group problem-solving mechanisms to bring about learning.

These kinds of analyses of educational processes from the vantage point of research in social psychology led into a kind of three-dimensional investigation of (1) the teacher's actual behaviors in the classroom and her comprehension of the learners' self and social perceptions, (2) the learners' perceptions of the instructional activities, and (3) the group-life context in which the teacher and learner interacted. This view added up to a much more complex process than had heretofore been spelled out. Classroom processes comprised a much more dynamic interaction of learner and teacher, along with content to be learned and the over-all learning environment, including the material resources (books, films, pictures, and audio-visual aids) and the human resources.

Cunningham and her associates (1951) attempted to tie up a whole series of insights in one neat bundle. The authors related the curriculum—defined as meaningful experiences for the learners—to the group interaction process in the classroom which determines the development of social skills, creativity, democratic skills, and subject-matter mastery. The development of these outcomes is governed in turn by the learner's desire for maximum individual development and for the development of social interaction skills. Cunningham and her associates, viewing all learning as problem-solving, believed the teacher can best fulfill her function in the classroom group as a skilled practitioner of evocative leadership. The teacher would help learners to identify common goals, common values, and roles of members, and also to develop institutionalized methods of problem-solving and evaluating goal achievement.

Jenkins (1951) pointed up the interdependent nature of the pupil-teacher relationship by asserting that learning will be more effective not only when the pupil's emotional needs are met in the classroom, but also when learners are made aware of their part in helping teachers fulfill some of the teachers' legitimate emotional needs in the classroom, e.g., the needs to become more effective in fulfilling their professional responsibilities and to achieve a sense of adequacy and worthwhileness.

Wright, Barker, Nall, and Schoggen (1951) delineated the rationale of a somewhat different research. They urged the value of field observations of teachers and learners in identifying the "psychological habitat" of each person, so that better prediction and control of the learning process might be assured. They indicated that "an adequate psychological ecology of the classroom must describe the psychological habitats that *are* brought about in this setting and the particular behaviors which these habitats engender" (p. 190). As a beginning point for spelling out the psychological ecology of a classroom, they suggested keeping an anecdotal record which would give a naturalistic description of a child's behavior in the learning process. In addition to behavior episodes such as making a May basket, drawing a picture on the chalkboard, and listening to the teacher telling a story, the raw behaviors observed in a classroom would be noted, ordered, and categorized. Furthermore, if behavior categories within these episodes such as direction of action, form of interpersonal activity, and outcome of action are developed, then the task of assessing, analyzing, and predicting classroom behavior will be facilitated. Data on "Raymond" were cited to demonstrate how a description of this child's psychological habitat in the classroom could be used to interpret and predict his overt behaviors in the instructional situation.

Jensen (1955) formulated a rationale for assessing the social structure of the classroom which sums up one aspect of the methods of analyzing classroom interaction. He specified the needs of class members as individuals and as group members. Like Thelen, he emphasized the close interdependence of personal needs and group needs, and the fact that fulfillment of the one kind depends directly on the satisfaction of needs of the other kind. Individuals in the learning situation have to help ensure the satisfaction and resolution of group needs if their private personal needs are to be met optimally. Furthermore, unless individuals are relating effectively to one another in a class, the achievement, or socio, problems cannot be dealt with.

Jensen identified seven dimensions of interaction (problem-solving, authority-leadership, power, friendship, personal prestige, sex, and privilege) under which the two problems of group productivity and group cohesiveness fall. These "dimensions" are conceptualizations of critical variables which must be taken into consideration in developing an effective learning situation. For example, the authority-leadership dimension focuses attention on the importance of how decisions are arrived at—what the task goals will be, who will carry out different parts of the assignment, and how the work is to be evaluated. An adequate description of any of these activities, however, should take into consideration other dimensions, such as power, for an individual's ideas must be attractive to other members of the group if he is to have a role in group decision-making, and this attractiveness is dependent upon the others' regarding him as having superior resources or ability. Jensen suggested:

The conceptual framework also indicates to the practitioner that the productivity of a class, the achievement of its members as individuals, and the member-satisfaction with life in the class is a function of the relationships within and between the seven different dimensions. This is "how" a classroom group must be conceived in order to analyze or diagnose effectively the conditions that upset class productivity and class cohesiveness (Jensen, 1955, p. 374).

In evidencing concern with the public, or socio, problems of the classroom group, and the psyche, or interpersonal relationship, problems of the group, Jensen focused the attention of teachers on two dimensions of the situation with which they inevitably have to concern themselves.

Trow (1960a), in the third edition of the *Encyclopedia of Educational Research* and elsewhere (Trow, Zander, Morse, & Jenkins, 1950; Trow, 1960b), set forth the group dynamics rationale for group process in education. He distinguished a group from a mere collection of human beings in one place, in that the latter, although it may have some qualities in common, has no genuine interaction. A group, on the other hand, is characterized by the interaction of its members in such a way that each person is changed by the group and changes as the group changes. A collection of individuals becomes a group as members accept a common purpose, become interdependent in implementation of this purpose, and interact with one another to promote its accomplishment—whether that purpose be to get a car out of a mudhole, or to organize a lobby, or to fulfill individual needs. Trow discussed group climate, autocratic versus democratic control, the questions of group morale and group structure, the importance of position and role, and the nature of various roles in a group. His discussion of leadership goes into the question of power relationships, where the superior-subordinate relationship of teacher to learner is emphasized. In describing the roles teachers are expected to fulfill, Trow mentions "therapist," "controller," "democratic strategist," and "instructor." The controversial nature of the therapeutic role is brought out, while the general acceptance of the appropriateness of the other roles is noted.

Interpersonal Perceptions of Teachers and Students

The postwar *zeitgeist* in social psychology and perception made it seem almost inevitable that research workers would turn to interpersonal perception as a realm of phenomena in which to seek improved understanding of social interaction in the classroom.

The study by Jenkins and Lippitt (1951) of teachers', students', and parents' interpersonal perceptions took a naturalistic, descriptive approach resembling somewhat that of the psychological ecologists. They asked all three groups in one community a series of open-ended questions about "What do (teachers, parents, pupils) do that you (parents, pupils, teachers) like (or dislike)?" Coding and tabulating the replies made it possible to describe how each group saw the school setting through the eyes of the others. There was no attempt in this study to measure "variables" such as accuracy of interpersonal perception, or to relate these to other variables such as effectiveness in interpersonal relations. The Jenkins-Lippitt study was a piece of "action research," in tune with the times, with only limited and modest theoretical pretensions.

In contrast, Gage and Suci (1951) sought to determine the accuracy of the teachers' perceptions of pupils' attitudes as one variable in the intricate dynamic interactions of teachers and learners. They tested the hypothesis that teachers who perceive their pupils' attitudes more accurately will be regarded more favorably by their pupils. They asked 20 teachers to estimate the percentage of 200 pupils in a small high school who would respond affirmatively to a set of opinion items. The items had to do with scholastic, recreational, and student government issues. In addition, they used a preliminary form of the Minnesota Teacher Attitude Inventory. Their conclusion was that a teacher's accuracy of social perception was positively related ($r = .50$) to the pupils' mean favorability toward the teacher.

A study by Bush (1954) was involved with interpersonal "knowledge" as well as many other variables. Working in several schools with a total of over 650 students, he measured the amount of knowledge about the pupils possessed by the teachers and found no direct linear relationship between such knowledge and satisfactoriness of interpersonal interactions between teachers and pupils. He also assessed teacher-pupil relationships on the dimension of liking for each other by pupil and teacher and found little significant relationship in the mutuality of such liking. The correlation between the teacher's liking for the pupil and the pupil's liking for the teacher was .28 for 150 cases at School A, and .25 for 500 cases at Schools B and C. Yet, it seemed reasonable to Bush to assume that pupils must like teachers if they are to learn most effectively.

Bush's study raised important questions about the dimensions of teacher-learner compatibility that influence the learning process, the kinds of information the teacher ought to possess about individual learners, and the legitimacy of expecting the teacher to be all things to all students. The study also identified some factors that may be relevant to the teacher-pupil relationship: the teacher's and learner's selective knowledge about each other, the manner in which the teacher fulfills her leadership role, the teacher's own appraisal of her effectiveness with the learners, and the student's need for a balance between freedom and limits in the learning situation.

Whether interpersonal perception, and variables derived from it, has implications for teaching is still questionable. Gage's review (1958) of his own varied approaches in the search for such implications yields an impression of unfulfilled promise in this area.

Our own negative results should cause us to look more closely at what we mean by "understanding of pupils." Such understanding is a basic objective of teacher education curricula. . . . It is indeed highly plausible as a desideratum for teachers. Yet up to now, in our own . . . and in others' research, support for this proposition has been hard to come by (Gage, 1958, pp. 100–101).

Sociometry in the Classroom

The general utility of sociometric assessments by the classroom teacher as a means of enhancing pupil growth is persuasively presented by Gronlund (1959), whose book is primarily intended as a practical manual for classroom teachers. But one major section of the book is devoted to an extended review and interpretation of the literature on the reliability and validity of sociometric choices (see Ch. 7 of this Handbook) and the relationship of these choices to personal and social factors. The conception of classroom learning as an interactional process involving the reciprocal interplay of person upon person is reflected in studies of the significance of sociometry and sociodrama for teacher-pupil rapport (Dysart, 1952).

Just how sociometric differentials arise in the classroom has not been as well studied as the differences in status themselves. It is plausible that the teacher helps determine which pupils become over- and under-chosen by their peers. But how does the teacher do this? Withall's study (1956) shed some light on the process. He offered, at a rather specific level, objective evidence, through the use of time-lapse photography, concerning a way of measuring teacher-pupil interaction in terms of the proximity of learners to the teacher, i.e., in terms of whether the learner was within a 36-inch radius and facing toward the teacher. It seemed that within the limits of this approach there were gross variations in the amount of attention bestowed on each learner by the teacher. More interesting still, it was extremely difficult—even after the teacher had been alerted to the discrepancies in attention she gave to differing pupils—for her to redistribute her attention in the light of the inferred needs of each learner.

In a study on a similar phenomenon, Polansky (1954) examined eight classrooms in terms of the group social climate and the teacher's supportiveness of group status systems. Using the Wrightstone "Pupil-Teacher Rapport" scale and the learner-supportive, teacher-supportive, and neutral categories of the Withall Climate Index, she found that teachers in "good climate" classrooms supported the group status system, whereas teachers in "poor climate" classrooms did not.

If the pupil's acceptance by his peers depends in part on the amount and kind of attention he receives from the teacher, and if that attention varies with different pupils, it is reasonable to suppose that the teacher's values should be related to sociometric status. Among other things, what the teacher values, it is safe to assume, is the pupils' achievement of the objectives of schooling. At this point of the argument, a study of relationships between achievement and sociometric status becomes relevant. Buswell (1953) used a population of 300 fifth-grade pupils and a number of standardized tests including the Stanford-Binet, the Iowa Test of Basic Skills, the Ohio Social Acceptance Scale, and a sociometric test of best-liked peers to find out whether there was any relationship between how a learner performs intellectually in class and his relationships with his peers. The highly accepted group, as identified and perceived by their peers, were significantly higher than the rejected group in mean achievement. It appeared that achievement is related to social acceptability and, in fact, that acceptability by peers is founded in many instances on the learner's achievement.

Interpupil relationships are significant not only to a pupil's social adjustment but also to his achievement of skills in working with others. Such skills have long been upheld as important objectives of education for living in a democracy. Until recently, however, no convenient and standardized method was available for measuring the achievement of such objectives by a classroom group. With considerable ingenuity, Damrin (1959) has remedied this lack. Her Russell Sage Social Relations Test, intended to measure the competence of elementary school pupils in group planning and group work, provides three construction-type problems with miniature blocks. The problems are given in turn to the small subgroups that are set up within a classroom. The task involves a Planning Stage, in which the group decides how it is going to construct the figure, and an Operations Stage, in which the figure is constructed. No

time limit is set on the planning period; a 15-minute limit is allowed for the implementation session. During both the Planning and Operations Stages an observer keeps a record of behavior, using standardized observation sheets.

Seven types of groups have been identified by Damrin through studying the learners at work during the Planning Stage. These groups have been labeled (1) mature, (2) dependent, (3) immature, (4) semicontrolled, (5) semirestrained, (6) uncontrolled, (7) restrained. Nine types of groups have been identified in the Operations Stage: (1) mature, (2) immature, (3) disinterested, (4) rollicking, (5) excited, (6) rowdy, (7) suppressed, (8) bickering, (9) quarreling. The promise of the instrument lies in the fact that it draws on socio-psychological concepts and focuses on specific, observable learner behaviors in the classroom setting.

Teacher-Centered versus Learner-Centered Instruction

One recurrent theme in much research on social interaction has been the differential effects of conducting classroom work in teacher-centered and learner-centered styles. The teacher-centered style is typically defined as one in which the teacher does most, by far, of the talking, directing, explaining, goal-setting, assignment-making, and evaluation. In the learner-centered style, these activities are all permitted by the teacher to devolve to a far greater extent upon the learners. Although terminology and various details of execution have varied, a number of significant studies in this tradition have enough in common to bear examination as a group. We turn now to such studies, representative of many others.

In a study that sought to point up the value of taking into consideration the emotional and intellectual needs of college students, Wispé (1951) provided either directiveness or permissiveness according to the needs and expectations of the students. He selected eight instructors who utilized one of two styles of teaching, i.e., directive or permissive. The instructors, selected on the basis of "what came naturally" to them, were given training to sharpen up these teaching proclivities. Eight sections of 20 students each were organized, matched in terms of a pretest on content mastery, Scholastic Aptitude Test (SAT) scores, secondary school background, and year in college. The course was an elementary one in social relations. The end-of-semester tests included (1) a TAT-type test using pictures of teaching situations; (2) Stein's Sentence Completion Test; (3) a 25-item questionnaire on attitude toward sections, on interests, and on feelings of students in sections; (4) a three-hour final examination, containing both essay and multiple-choice items. It appeared that the majority of the students preferred the directive sections, and that the teaching styles had no effect on the final examination scores of the brighter (high SAT score) students, whereas the less able students did better in the directive sections. Wispé identified three types of students through analysis of their questionnaire responses: (1) a want-more-direction group, (2) a want-more-permissiveness group, and (3) a satisfied group. He was interested in the intensity of the desires for either directiveness or permissiveness and noted that one-third of those already receiving directive teaching wanted more directiveness, and one-third of those already in the permissive teaching sections indicated a desire for more permissiveness. One of his major conclusions was that students who do less well on the SAT benefit more from directive-type teaching. To Wispé, this indicated that the student's emotional and intellectual needs should be taken into consideration in determining the kind of instruction he is to receive. (Methodological criticisms of Wispé's study are made in Chapter 6.)

In a similar study of the interaction between teaching style and student intelligence, Calvin, Hoffman, and Harden (1957), although modest in their claims, found indications that the mere creation of a permissive climate is not a sufficient, though it may be a necessary, condition of more effective teaching and group problem-solving. Their research, somewhat similar in direction to Wispé's, indicated that permissiveness with individuals of high intelligence yielded better learning than did a traditional teaching-learning situation with bright students or a permissive situation with average students. In fact, the permissive situation tended to handicap subjects with average intelligence.

In a study by Maier and Maier (1957), small groups of college students were placed in "permissive" and "developmental" group problem-solving situations. (In the latter, the leader helped the group break down the problem into subparts.) A significant difference was obtained between the two groups; 40 per cent of the "developmental" discussion groups reached high-quality decisions as against 19 per cent of the "free" or "permissive" groups.

Haigh and Schmidt (1956) concerned themselves with a similar question, How much subject matter is mastered by learners in so-called teacher-centered and group-centered classes? The students were placed in the teacher-centered and group-centered sections on the basis of stated preferences, and the amount of subject matter learned was assessed. The students in the group-centered class did not derive their grade from a final examination, although they and the control group were both given the Horrocks-Troyer test on knowledge of facts and principles in adolescent development. There was no significant difference between the two classes in knowledge of subject matter.

In an experiment on attitude change as a function of teaching by these two socially different styles, McKeachie (1954) assessed the conformity of individuals to the attitudes and norms of their classroom groups. He set up six sections comprising 25–35 undergraduates each and had each of three instructors teach two sections, each by a different method: leader-centered and group-centered. The hypothesis was that the individual tends to adopt attitudes corresponding to those of the group with which he is currently associated or identified. McKeachie suggested that certain attitudes learned in key primary groups, such as the family, are not easily superseded by attitudes espoused by a classroom group. Congruence of perceptions of group standards and values was *not* consistently higher in liked class groups than in nonliked groups. He explained this by pointing out that, in liked groups, a higher degree of rapport permitted verbalized disagreement to be accepted, encouraged, and sustained more readily than in nonliked groups, where pressure was applied to ensure greater conformity of all members to the same norms and attitudes.

In a report of work altogether nonexperimental in any rigorous sense, but rather clinical, anecdotal, and observational, Moustakas (1956) started with the proposition that the most effective learning occurs in the educational situation where threat to the learner's self is minimal. He proceeded to indicate, by descriptions of specific teachers and their methods of relating to children, the kinds of teacher behavior that he judged necessary for learning and growth. To him, the resulting interpersonal relationship was one

where there was freedom of expression within the limits of the classroom, where each person could state himself in terms of himself without fear of criticism or condemnation, where feelings were expressed and explored, where ideas and creative thinking were treasured, and where growth of self was the most important value (Moustakas, 1956, p. 259).

To make operational this global conception of the conditions of teacher-learner interaction which were most conducive to learning and development, Moustakas narrated the ways in which the teachers he observed implemented these ideas. He described (pp. 110–120) an "experiment" intended to help second-grade youngsters face and express their feelings openly. To introduce them to the procedure, the teacher invited the children in her class to discuss some of their common feelings. The youngsters tended to

dwell in this discussion on "anger." "Constructive" ways of expressing angry feelings were identified.

Later he arranged a number of sessions in which both structured and unstructured procedures were used. During the structured periods, directions were given by the teacher and all the children did the same thing. During the unstructured sessions, the children were told "to do as they pleased" as long as they were fairly quiet and did not bother one another or children in other rooms. On these occasions they tended to talk with the teacher or told about pictures they were encouraged to draw. The teacher showed interest in and complete acceptance of what the children were doing and saying. Of the 26 children involved in the study, 14 followed a definite pattern, such as drawing and talking about fighting and war, and adhered to it throughout. Seven of them said little at first but were quite vocal at the end of the experience and revealed their feelings and attitudes quite clearly. Five children, after drawing their pictures, described them without expressing much feeling. We are told that the angry and unsettled youngsters tended to reflect these qualities in their pictures and stories.

Moustakas emphasized that many of these children were aggressive and unsettled. This program, he felt, provided an acceptable outlet for their hostility, enabled the children to understand that it helps to express one's feelings even in imagination and fantasy, and thus reduced their impulse to act out tensions in everyday life.

At the high school level, Moustakas reported (pp. 202–204) on a program which a teacher carried out with a group of 30 twelfth-grade students. The class met twice a week for one hour over a period of one semester. The teacher told the group that they were free to present any concepts, ideas, and problems for discussion. A number of problems in human relationships including dating, petting, early marriage, child-rearing, parental authority, and independence were discussed. The teacher asked each member of the class to keep a journal of his reactions to the sessions, and explained that the journal need not, but could, be turned in to her.

Toward the end of the semester the teacher gave the group an opportunity to write a paper exploring personal experience. No one was required to write the paper but every student decided to, and each turned it in to the teacher. The teacher "felt that the explorations showed considerable growth in self-understanding on the part of several members of the group" (p. 204).

THE SOCIAL-INTERACTION VIEW OF CLASSROOM PROCESSES

Until very recently, the approach to the analysis of teacher-pupil and pupil-pupil interaction in the learning situation was that of examining and quantifying certain "monadic" variables, such as the teacher's training and experience, the learners' socioeconomic status and intellectual capacities, the goals of the school and community, and the materials provided to help achieve those goals. The examination of such variables has tended to be unrewarding and sterile. Researchers thus tried to examine social processes and interactions through static means. It was long believed that if we manipulated one or two variables, we could create conditions that would ensure both predictability and control of the quality and type of learning. Much experience has shown that this expectation is unsupported, that variables in the learning situation interact with each other in kaleidoscopic complexity, and that specification of the interactions and outcomes is extremely difficult.

We have known for a long time (but have not accepted the implications of this knowledge) that groups of learners are vehicles for fulfilling the personal goals and needs of the learners—not to mention those of the teachers (Jenkins, 1951)—as well as for ensuring attainment of content-mastery goals. In recent years we have begun to examine the group forces in the instructional situation

that mediate fulfillment of both cognitive and affective needs.

Along with this trend has emerged the realization that examination of these phenomena requires a rationale and instrumentation adequate to the "motility" of the data being treated. Getzels and Thelen (1960) describe the image of the classroom that should guide our research:

It is not the image of a social system in equilibrium. It is rather the image of a system in motion or, if you will, in dynamic disequilibrium. It is the image of a group continually facing emergent complexity and conflict (if not confusion) and dealing with these realities, not in terms of sentiment but in terms of what the complexity and conflict suggest about the modifications that have to be made in the goals, expectations, needs, and selective perceptions of the teachers and learners. It is through this experience of recognizing and dealing with complexity, conflict and change in the classroom situation that we can educate children to take their places as creative and autonomous participants in the other social systems that constitute the larger social order (Getzels & Thelen, 1960, p. 82).

Jensen (1960) has pointed out that the way a group is organized derives from the efforts of members of the group (1) to develop need-meeting relationships with others and (2) to establish working relationships necessary for the attainment of work goals. The result of the interrelationship of the need-meeting and work-doing activities seems to be a gratification-deprivation ratio which makes it possible for the needs of some members to be met and prevents the needs of others from being met. In Jensen's view, this situation has significance for the whole matter of motivation, progress, individual achievement, class morale, and discipline.

Jenkins (1960) delineated areas of conflict that emerge as the individuals in a class work toward achievement of both subject-matter mastery and personal goals. He also offered principles for the resolution of these conflicts including the following: The teacher should (1) accept the full responsibility that devolves upon him because of the power and authority the school and community vest in him; (2) define, with the class, the authority and behavioral limits that will guide both his and the learners' activities; (3) permit decision-making by the students within predefined limits; (4) be open to influence by the students so as to be amenable, within mutually defined and acceptable limits, to their point of view. If these things are done by the teacher, Jenkins argued, the full potential of group forces in the classroom can be harnessed to enhance both the fulfillment of personal needs and the mastery of subject matter.

It would seem, however, that we need to look beyond this objective of mastery of subject matter to the development of the skills of problem-solving and inquiry. Thelen (1960a) has outlined the general procedures required for modern education, including (1) relating learning activities to the developmental processes of learners and to their current and immediate interests and needs, and (2) utilizing evaluation procedures that support rather than contradict our efforts to develop democratic individuals skilled in co-operative activity, question-raising, and problem-solving.

Much of the early research on classroom learning was set in the stark framework of the given conditions in an educational situation. Given a group of children with standard physical, intellectual, and psychological equipment, and given some subject-matter content, what are the characteristics of the teacher who can effectively arrange a meeting of the two? Research effort was directed toward identifying the traits, skills, and personal qualities needed by teachers, toward identifying the instructional procedures, motivational techniques, and disciplinary methods to be used, and toward finding correlates of effective instruction in such extra-class variables as marital status, age, and experience. It seems that the researchers of the 1920's and the mid-1930's sought to analyze the process of teaching in terms of the conditions brought to it by the teacher as a professional worker. She was presumed to be devoid of any personal needs, purposes, or idiosyncrasies. The other actors in the classroom, i.e., the learners, were even more taken for granted. The independent variables were the teacher's skills, abilities, and traits; the dependent variables were the pupils' learnings.

At the other end of the channel lay the goals of education. These objectives were relatively fixed and predetermined without regard for differences among individual learners in physiological organization, family background, and community resources. The conditions represented by teacher competencies have been manipulated to see which ones produce specified educational outcomes most efficiently, usually in the language of achievement tests. The identification or construction of satisfactory criteria of teacher effectiveness has been a persistent problem, but it is, of course, primarily a question of values rather than one to be resolved by empirical research. In any event, supervisors' ratings, students' opinions, and psychometric assessments all have, in their own way, shortcomings as serious as those of achievement tests in the evaluation of teaching.

A way out of the single-criterion impasse has been suggested by the combined influence of the mental health and group dynamics viewpoints. In both these points of view, attention is focused on complicated patterns of interaction and molar concepts of influence, rather than single indices of effectiveness, such as the mean reading achievement of children in a classroom. The studies on experimentally induced social climate (Lewin, Lippitt, & Escalona, 1940) provide an example of a more molar approach to the assessment of group-life phenomena. Procedures for analyzing the patterns of interactive process in the classroom have been slowly developed and utilized. The problems indicated here may stem, in part, from the harnessing of educational activity to predetermined educational objectives used to guide classroom instruction at all levels, and from the ambiguity with which such objectives must be surrounded in order to be applicable to millions of children of varying ages and abilities.

Some consistent trends can be discerned in the pattern of research reported in this chapter. With some misgivings, we may project these trends to form expectations as to the directions that future research will take. Some of the most significant of these trends seem to come under the rubric of philosophy of science, the rules for formulating questions and finding answers. Operationism, with its procedures for defining sets of theoretical constructs, has had an impact on educational research, just as it has influenced research in other social sciences. One important ramification of this impact is the slow abandonment of the search for a "philosopher's stone" of teacher effectiveness. Although the research pattern of establishing a single, easily measured criterion of effectiveness has been persistent, it is gradually being replaced by a more complicated construct-making approach to multiple criteria (see Jahoda, 1958). Instead of assuming that some effectiveness criterion would be available if one were only clever enough to discover it, current research tends to lower its sights to less evaluative concepts, such as classroom control, communication patterns (Withall, 1962), achievement of specified goals, and so on. These concepts most often serve as summaries for several kinds of behaviors, or conversely, several different kinds of behaviors serve as operations defining the concepts. In either event, the concepts in current use are less abstract and are pointed more directly toward behavioral referents; research workers are less likely to ask an observer to make a global judgment about the effectiveness of the teacher. Rather, they now ask him to record physical movement of the teacher in the room or the dominant intent of individual statements of teachers (see Lewis, Newell, & Withall, 1961) and children, and to relate these operations to an organizing concept like classroom control or climate.

Accompanying the change away from the single-criterion study has been a change in conceptualizing the significance of behavior in the classroom. Earlier studies attempted to isolate qualities or traits of a relatively permanent nature in the teacher's personality or conduct that would hold regardless of the group with whom she was working. More recently, what happens in the classroom has been viewed more as a function of a constellation of factors, not all of which reside in the teacher, and as part of some kind of over-all change process rather than as a permanent cause-and-effect relationship. A study of classroom control, for example, would probably not be conceived in terms of permissiveness or punitiveness of the teacher, but in terms of some complex pattern of inferences regarding initiation of a sequence of behavior by the teacher, responses by her students to her cues, and so on to the end of the sequence. The inferences made would probably not include generalizations to all of her teaching behavior, e.g., "She is a permissive teacher," but attempt to specify under what circumstances she is permissive and under what circumstances she may be controlling or punitive.

These brief references to current concerns suggest that future research on social interaction in the classroom may give increasing attention to careful development of theories of the classroom interaction as a dynamic process in which the teacher is an important participant but is not the total determiner of the outcomes of learning. The theories, taking the lead from group dynamics studies, may be miniature systems rather than attempts to encompass all behavior, and may contain sets of related concepts referring directly to behavioral events defined in the language of operations performed by participants in or observers of a process. What the content of these theoretical systems will be, we can only guess, but prevailing interest in applying concepts from group dynamics, social psychology, psychotherapy, and information theory to classroom interaction suggests a general direction that may be taken by research on teaching in the immediate future.

REFERENCES

Anderson, H. H., & Brewer, Helen M. Studies of teachers' classroom personalities. I. Dominative and socially integrative behavior of kindergarten teachers. *Appl. Psychol. Monogr.,* 1945, No. 6.

Anderson, H. H., & Brewer, J. E. Studies of teachers' classroom personalities. II. Effects of teachers' dominative and integrative contacts on children's classroom behavior. *Appl. Psychol. Monogr.,* 1946, No. 8.

Anderson, H. H., Brewer, J. E., & Reed, Mary F. Studies of teachers' classroom personalities. III. Follow-up studies of the effects of dominative and integrative contacts on children's behavior. *Appl. Psychol. Monogr.,* 1946, No. 11.

Bales, R. F. *Interaction process analysis.* Cambridge, Mass.: Addison-Wesley, 1950.

Barker, R. G. Kounin, J. S., & Wright, H. R. (Eds.) *Child behavior and development: A course of representative studies.* New York: McGraw-Hill, 1943.

Barr, A. S. The measurement of teaching ability. *J. educ. Res.,* 1935, 28, 561–569.

Blair, A. W. Social and personal integration during later childhood. Unpublished doctoral dissertation, Harvard Univer., 1946.

Blos, P. *The adolescent personality: A study of individual behavior.* New York: Appleton-Century, 1941.

Bonney, M. E. Sociometric study of agreement between teacher judgments and student choices: In regard to the numbers of friends possessed by high school students. *Sociometry,* 1947, 10, 133–146.

Brookover, W. B. Person-person interaction between teachers and pupils and teaching effectiveness. *J. educ. Res.,* 1940, 34, 272–287.

Bryan, R. C. A study of student ratings of college and secondary-school teachers. *Educ. Admin. Superv.,* 1933, 19, 290–307.

Burrell, Anna P. Facilitating learning through emphasis on meeting children's basic emotional needs. *J. educ. Sociol.,* 1951, 24, 381–393.

Bush, R. N. A study of student-teacher relationships. *J. educ. Res.,* 1942, 35, 645–656.

Bush, R. N. *The teacher-pupil relationship.* New York: Prentice-Hall, 1954.

Buswell, Margaret M. The relationship between the social structure of the classroom and the academic success of the pupils. *J. exp. Educ.,* 1953, 22, 37–52.

Calvin, A. D., Hoffman, F. K., & Harden, E. L. The effect of intelligence and social

atmosphere on group problem solving behavior. *J. soc. Psychol.,* 1957, 45, 61–74.

Cronbach, L. J. Proposals leading to analytic treatment of social perception scores. In R. Tagiuri & L. Petrullo (Eds.), *Person perception and interpersonal behavior.* Stanford, Calif.: Stanford Univer. Press, 1958. Pp. 353–379.

Cunningham, Ruth, & Associates. *Understanding group behavior of boys and girls.* New York: Bur. of Publs., Teachers Coll., Columbia Univer., 1951.

Damrin, Dora E. The Russell Sage Social Relations Test: A technique for measuring group problem-solving skills in elementary school children. *J. exp. Educ.,* 1959, 28, 85–99.

Dearborn, W. F., & Rothney, J. W. M. *Predicting the child's development.* Cambridge, Mass.: Sci-Art Press, 1941.

Division on Child Development and Teacher Personnel, Commission on Teacher Education. *Helping teachers understand children.* Washington, D.C.: American Council on Education, 1945.

Dollard, J. *Caste and class in a southern town.* New Haven, Conn.: Yale Univer. Press. 1937.

Dysart, J. M. A study of the effect of in-service training in sociometry and sociodrama on teacher-pupil rapport and social climate in the classroom. Unpublished doctoral dissertation, New York Univer., 1952.

English, H. B., & English, Ava C. *A comprehensive dictionary of psychological and psychoanalytical terms.* New York: Longmans, Green, 1958.

Flanders, N. A. Personal-social anxiety as a factor in learning. Unpublished doctoral dissertation, Univer. of Chicago, 1949.

Flanders, N. A. Teacher-pupil contacts and mental hygiene. *J. soc. Issues,* 1959, 15, 30–39.

Gage, N. L. Explorations in teachers' perceptions of pupils. *J. teacher Educ.,* 1958, 9, 97–101.

Gage, N. L., & Cronbach, L. J. Conceptual and methodological problems in interpersonal perception. *Psychol. Rev.,* 1955, 62, 411–422.

Gage, N. L., & Suci, G. J. Social perception and teacher-pupil relationships. *J. educ. Psychol.,* 1951, 42, 144–152.

Getzels, J. W., & Thelen, H. A. The classroom group as a unique social system. In N. B.

Henry (Ed.), *Yearb. nat. Soc. Stud. Educ.*, 1960, 59, Part II, 53–82.

Glidewell, J. C. The teacher's feelings as an educational resource. *J. educ. Res.*, 1951, 45, 119–126.

Glidewell, J. C. (Ed.) Mental health in the classroom. *J. soc. Issues*, 1959, 15, No. 1.

Gronlund, N. E. *Sociometry in the classroom.* New York: Harper, 1959.

Haigh, G. V., & Schmidt, W. The learning of subject-matter in teacher-centered and group-centered classes. *J. educ. Psychol.*, 1956, 47, 295–301.

Henry, N. B. (Ed.) The dynamics of instructional groups. *Yearb. nat. Soc. Stud. Educ.*, 1960, 59, Part II.

Hollingshead, A. B. *Elmtown's youth.* New York: Wiley, 1949.

Jahoda, Marie. *Current concepts of positive mental health.* New York: Basic Books, 1958.

James, H. W. Cause of teacher failure in Alabama. *Peabody J. Educ.*, 1930, 7, 269–271.

Jenkins, D. H. Interdependence in the classroom. *J. educ. Res.*, 1951, 45, 137–144.

Jenkins, D. H. Characteristics and functions of leadership in instructional groups. In N. B. Henry (Ed.), *Yearb. nat. Soc. Stud. Educ.*, 1960, 59, Part II, 164–184.

Jenkins, D. H., & Lippitt, R. *Interpersonal perceptions of teachers, students, and parents.* Washington, D.C.: Division of Adult Education, National Education Association, 1951.

Jennings, Helen H. Leadership and sociometric choice. *Sociometry*, 1947, 10, 32–39.

Jennings, Helen H. Using children's social relations for learning. *J. educ. Sociol.*, 1948, 21, 543–552.

Jensen, G. E. The social structure of the classroom group: An observational framework. *J. educ. Psychol.*, 1955, 46, 362–374.

Jensen, G. E. The sociopsychological structure of the instructional group. In N. B. Henry (Ed.), *Yearb. nat. Soc. Stud. Educ.*, 1960, 59, Part II, 83–114.

Jersild, A. T., & Holmes, F. B. Characteristics of teachers who are "liked best" and "disliked most." *J. exp. Educ.*, 1940, 9, 139–151.

Jersild, A. T., Thorndike, R. L., Goldman, B., & Loftus, J. J. An evaluation of aspects of the activity program in the New York City public elementary schools. *J. exp. Educ.*, 1939, 8, 166–207.

Johnson, Marguerite W. The influence of verbal directions on behavior. *Child Devlpm.*, 1935, 6, 196–204.

Jones, H. E., Conrad, H. S., & Murphy, Lois B. Emotional and social development and the educative process. In G. M. Whipple (Ed.), *Yearb. nat. Soc. Stud. Educ.*, 1939, 38, Part I, 361–389.

Kounin, J. S., & Gump, P. V. The ripple effect in discipline. *Elem. sch. J.*, 1958, 59, 158–162.

Kounin, J. S., & Gump, P. V. The comparative influence of punitive and non-punitive teachers upon children's concepts of school misconduct. *J. educ. Psychol.*, 1961, 52, 44–49.

Leeds, C. H., & Cook, W. W. The construction and differential value of a scale for determining teacher-pupil attitudes. *J. exp. Educ.*, 1947, 16, 149–159.

Leonard, J. P., & Eurich, A. C. *Evaluation of modern education.* New York: Appleton-Century, 1942.

Lewin, K., Lippitt, R., & Escalona, Sibylle K. Studies in topological and vector psychology. *Univer. Iowa Stud. Child Welf.*, 1940, 16, No. 3.

Lewin, K., Lippitt, R., & White, R. K. Patterns of aggressive behavior in experimentally created social climates. *J. soc. Psychol.*, 1939, 10, 271–299.

Lewis, W. W., Newell, J. M., & Withall, J. An analysis of classroom patterns of communication. *Psychol. Rep.*, 1961, 9, 211–219.

Lippitt, R. An experimental study of the effect of democratic and authoritarian group atmospheres. Studies in topological and vector psychology. *Univer. Iowa Stud. Child Welf.*, 1940, 16, No. 3, 43–195.

Maier, N. R. F., & Maier, R. A. An experimental test of the effects of "developmental" vs. "free" discussions on the quality of group decisions. *J. appl. Psychol.*, 1957, 41, 320–323.

McKeachie, W. J. Individual conformity to attitudes of classroom groups. *J. abnorm. soc. Psychol.*, 1954, 49, 282–289.

McLelland, F. M., & Ratliff, J. A. The use of sociometry as an aid in promoting social adjustment in the ninth grade home room. *Sociometry*, 1947, 10, 147–153.

Meek, Lois H. *The personal-social development of boys and girls.* Washington, D.C.: Progressive Education Association, 1940.

Melby, E. O. Supervision. *Rev. educ. Res.*, 1936, 6, 324–336.

Mitzel, H. E., & Rabinowitz, W. Assessing social-emotional climate in the classroom by Withall's technique. *Psychol. Monogr.,* 1954, 67, No. 18.

Moreno, J. L. *Who shall survive?* Washington, D.C.: Nervous and Mental Disease Publ. Co., 1934.

Morrison, R. H. Factors causing failure in teaching. *J. educ. Res.,* 1927, 16, 98–105.

Moustakas, C. E. *The teacher and the child: Personal interaction in the classroom.* New York: McGraw-Hill, 1956.

Murchison, C. (Ed.) *Handbook of child psychology.* Worcester, Mass.: Clark Univer. Press, 1933.

Nanninga, S. P. Teacher failures in high school. *Sch. & Soc.,* 1924, 19, 79–82.

Ohio State Univer., Univer. High Sch. Class, 1938. *Were we guinea pigs?* New York: Holt, 1938.

Ojemann, R. H., & Wilkinson, Frances R. The effect on pupil growth of an increase in teacher's understanding of pupil behavior. *J. exp. Educ.,* 1939, 8, 143–147.

Olson, W. C., & Wilkinson, N. Muriel. Teacher personality as revealed by the amount and kind of verbal direction used in behavior control. *Educ. Admin. Superv.,* 1938, 24, 81–93.

Perkins, H. V. The effects of social-emotional climate and curriculum on learning of in-service teachers. Unpublished doctoral dissertation, Univer. of Chicago, 1949.

Polansky, Lucy. Group social climate and the teacher's supportiveness of group status systems. *J. educ. Sociol.,* 1954, 28, 115–123.

Prescott, D. A. *Emotion and the educative process.* Washington, D.C.: American Council on Education, 1938.

Rehage, K. J. A comparison of pupil-teacher planning and teacher-directed procedures in eighth-grade social studies classes. Unpublished doctoral dissertation, Univer. of Chicago, 1948.

Remmers, H. H. Reliability and halo effect of high school and college students' judgments of their teachers. *J. appl. Psychol.,* 1934, 18, 619–630.

Rothney, J. W. M., & Roens, B. A. *Counseling the individual student.* New York: Dryden, 1949.

Sears, R. R. A theoretical framework for personality and social behavior. *Amer. Psychologist,* 1951, 6, 476–483.

Singletary, J. Teacher-administrative leader perceptions of pupils. *J. educ. Res.,* 1951, 45, 126–132.

Stoddard, G. D. Child development: A new approach to education. *Sch. & Soc.,* 1939, 49, 33–38.

Thelen, H. A. Group dynamics in instruction: Principle of Least Group Size. *Sch. Rev.,* 1949, 57, 139–148.

Thelen, H. A. Educational dynamics: Theory and research. *J. soc. Issues,* 1950, 6, 5–95.

Thelen, H. A. (Ed.) Experimental research toward a theory of instruction. *J. educ. Res.,* 1951, 45, 89–136.

Thelen, H. A. Classroom grouping of students. *Sch. Rev.,* 1959, 67, 60–78. (a)

Thelen, H. A. Work-emotionality theory of the group as organism. In S. Koch (Ed.), *Psychology: A study of a science.* Vol. III. *Formulations of the person and the social context.* New York: McGraw-Hill, 1959. Pp. 544–611. (b)

Thelen, H. A. The triumph of "achievement" over inquiry in education. *Elem. sch. J.,* 1960, 60, 190–197. (a)

Thelen, H. A. *Education and the human quest.* New York: Harper, 1960. (b)

Thelen, H. A., & Tyler, R. W. Implications for improving instruction in the high school. In N. B. Henry (Ed.), *Yearb. nat. Soc. Stud. Educ.,* 1950, 49, Part I, 304–335.

Thelen, H. A., & Withall, J. Three frames of reference: The description of climate. *Human Relations,* 1949, 2, 159–176.

Thorndike, R. L., Loftus, J. J., & Goldman, B. Observations of the behavior of children in activity and control schools. *J. exp. Educ.,* 1941, 10, 138–145.

Tiedeman, S. C. A study of pupil-teacher relationships. *J. educ. Res.,* 1942, 35, 657–664.

Trow, W. C. Group processes. In C. W. Harris (Ed.), *Encyclopedia of educational research.* (3rd ed.) New York: Macmillan, 1960. Pp. 602–612. (a)

Trow, W. C. Role functions of the teacher in the instructional group. In N. B. Henry (Ed.), *Yearb. nat. Soc. Stud. Educ.,* 1960, 59, Part II, 30–50. (b)

Trow, W. C., Zander, A. F., Morse, W. C., & Jenkins, D. H. Psychology of group behavior: The class as a group. *J. educ. Psychol.,* 1950, 41, 322–338.

White, R. K., & Lippitt, R. *Autocracy and democracy: An experimental inquiry.* New York: Harper, 1960.

Wickman, E. K. *Children's behavior and*

teachers' attitudes. New York: Commonwealth Fund, 1928.

Wilson, W. R. Students rating teachers. *J. higher Educ.,* 1932, 3, 75–82.

Wispé, L. G. Evaluating section teaching methods in the introductory course. *J. educ. Res.,* 1951, 45, 161–186.

Withall, J. The development of a technique for the measurement of social-emotional climate in classrooms. *J. exp. Educ.,* 1949, 17, 347–361.

Withall, J. An objective measurement of a teacher's classroom interactions. *J. educ. Psychol.* 1956, 47, 203–212.

Withall, J. A symposium on conceptual frameworks for analysis of classroom interaction: Introductory comment. *J. exp. Educ.,* 1962, 30, 307–308.

Wright, H. F., Barker, R. G., Nall, J., & Schoggen, P. Toward a psychological ecology of the classroom. *J. educ. Res.,* 1951, 45, 187–200.

Young, L. L. Sociometric and related techniques for appraising social status in an elementary school. *Sociometry,* 1947, 10, 168–177.

Zachry, Caroline B., & Lichty, Margaret. *Emotion and conduct in adolescence.* New York: Appleton-Century, 1940.

CHAPTER 14 The Social Background of Teaching

W. W. CHARTERS, JR.
Washington University

The teaching-learning process is affected and shaped by a tremendous variety of forces originating in the social environment. Major philosophical movements, changing child-training practices, urbanization and industrialization, economic and social crises, legislation regarding school attendance or teacher liability, technological developments such as the automobile or television—all are vital aspects of the context of the teaching-learning process in our society. The forces affecting the teaching situation defy classification; they encompass virtually every field of the social sciences, social history, and educational practice.

This review cannot attempt to cover the vast array of knowledge concerning the effects of the environment on the teaching-learning process. Our area of inquiry must be severely delimited if our presentation is to be reasonably coherent and systematic. The following paragraphs describe the rationale by which we have circumscribed this review.

SCOPE OF THE REVIEW

Our interest will be limited to the educative process as it occurs within the American

public school and will draw principally upon the research literature of educational sociology, social psychology, and education proper. We will not consider anthropological and sociological materials relating to general processes of socialization of youth in society outside the school, or the educative processes occurring in colleges and universities, the government and the armed forces, industrial schools and the host of adult and specialized trade schools across the nation. By narrowing our attention to the public elementary and high schools of the United States, we exclude comparative materials from other societies.

These limitations rule out three major areas of contemporary scholarship which study the interdependency between society and the educative process—the history of education, comparative education, and cultural anthropology. All three view the educative process as shaped by and, simultaneously, as shaping, the social order of which it is a part. All agree that the educative process cannot be regarded apart from the social and cultural context in which it is embedded or from the historical events which have formed it.

Scholars in the three areas have addressed

715

themselves mainly to the task of describing the congruities between the educative process and the environing social and cultural order. Thus, the burden of both Butts' (1947) volume on the history of education and of Kandel's (1955) monograph on comparative education is to demonstrate the ways in which the educational system of a society "fits" the cultural configuration of that society. The two volumes differ principally in their selections of societies for the demonstration. Ethnographic materials of the cultural anthropologists have provided the same kind of documentation with respect to the entire socialization process in small, homogeneous societies (C. Kluckhohn, 1949). For the most part, these disciplines have contributed knowledge about particulars of time and place phrased in terms which are rarely abstract enough to suggest hypotheses applicable to other times or other societies, especially to such complex and changing societies as our own. To document the congruities between the educative process and the environing society is to concentrate on forces of stability. Consequently, incongruities or dysfunctions which promote and help to understand change are ignored. Even the anthropologists, most experienced of the three in formulating issues in terms of the processes of stability *and* change (cultural dynamics), have seldom turned their attention to education in changing societies. We shall refer in later sections to a few who have.[1]

This review is circumscribed· in another way: we consider only those social and cultural forces of the environment which are introduced into the teaching-learning process by the teacher. The person who occupies the position of teacher becomes, in effect, the intervening variable in our inquiry—intervening between the environmental forces, on the one hand, and the teaching-learning process, on the other. We can state the paradigm

for our review in the form of a question: What social and cultural forces operating in the environing society affect teachers in ways which are relevant to the teaching-learning process? By concentrating on those forces transmitted to the teaching-learning process by way of the teacher we hope to avoid an unmanageable task.

This paradigm carries several implications which should be made explicit. First, it restricts our review to the impact of the social environment upon the educative process; it excludes consideration of the impact of education upon society, or the reciprocal relationships between the two.

Second, the impact of environmental forces upon the teaching-learning process (by way of the teacher), *not* their impact upon the school or the institutional structure of education, occupies our attention. This distinction is not easy to maintain. The teaching-learning process of the classroom is, in a very real sense, subordinate to the social system of the school which, in turn, is only one of the components of the institutional structure of education. Forces which affect the school affect the conduct of the teaching-learning process. Thus, shifts in community opinion concerning the school may decide the fate of a school tax referendum which could determine the number of pupils with whom the teacher must cope in the teaching situation. Similarly, social forces operating upon the larger institutional structure of education, such as those shaping the enactment and enforcement of the state school law, often have a direct bearing upon the teaching process. It is impossible, however, to trace out all such chains of relationship in this review.

Third, we are interested only in those consequences of social and cultural forces for teachers which are clearly relevant to the conduct of teaching. Unlike Chapter 11, this chapter deals with the operation of social and cultural forces upon occupants of the teaching position, not with enduring personal attributes of teachers as they affect the teaching-learning process. The two chapters should illumine one another but they do

---

[1] Contributions of cultural anthropologists to modern education are not fully covered in this review. Brameld and Sullivan (1961) provide a comprehensive bibliography of recent literature in the field.

represent two discrete bodies of research literature.

Organization of the Chapter

This chapter is organized around the conception that the person who enacts the role of teacher in the teaching-learning process also participates in other systems of social relations within the society and thus is exposed to patterns of influence which may shape his performance as a teacher. This conception is consistent with a sociological point of view which holds that each member of a society occupies a variety of social "statuses" which link him to the general social system in distinct ways and which, in large measure, define him as a social person.

. . . the structure of even the simplest primary society, such as a primitive village, is by no means simple or homogeneous. The individuals who compose such a society are classified and organized in several different ways simultaneously. Each of these systems has its own functions as regards relating the individual to culture, and he occupies a place within each of them (Linton, 1945, p. 75).

Each person, Linton points out, has a place in the age, sex, and prestige systems of the society and belongs to some family or kinship unit and one or more formal and informal association groups. In heterogeneous societies such as our own, important statuses are associated with social class and caste, with ethnic derivation, with religious affiliation, and with position in the societal division of labor.

The various statuses of a person are not independent of one another. They all come to bear on the particular individual, of course, and he is obliged to organize the rights and duties, the rules of conduct, the expectations associated with each into a more or less coherent whole by which he can order his life. In the simple societies, the person's statuses tend to be mutually consistent and reinforcing; in complex and transitional societies, inconsistencies and conflict more frequently pose problems for the individual. The various statuses are interdependent in another sense: A person's occupancy of one status may affect his opportunities to attain other statuses or participate in other segments of society. Belonging to a minority group in the American caste system generally precludes attainment of a broad spectrum of occupational, associational, and prestige statuses. In modern industrial society, occupational status is of key importance. To know a person's occupation —as a taxi-cab driver, a grocer, or a high school teacher—is to know a great deal more about him than just his economic function. It specifies with reasonably high probability the segments of society from which he originated, the extrinsic rewards he commands, the prestige he enjoys, and the social circles in which he travels.

The four sections of this chapter treat different systems of social relationships in which teachers participate and which afford them social statuses. Our selection of the four is governed by the existence of a tradition of scholarly conjecture, if not always a body of empirical evidence, that the environing systems have a definitive influence upon teachers' participation in the teacher-pupil relationship. The four are (1) the social structure of American society, (2) the structure of the teaching occupation, (3) the social system of the community, and (4) the social system of the school.

Social and cultural forces impinge upon occupants of the teacher status, and thereby upon the teaching-learning process, in two distinct ways: by determining who engages in the teaching occupation and by affecting directly those persons so engaged. These two modes of impact, the selective and the formative, are not independent of one another since the same social force may be regarded as having both kinds of consequence. The "low prestige" often attributed to the teaching occupation, for example, is believed to discourage certain kinds of people from entering or remaining in it, on the one hand, and, on the other, to demoralize or otherwise reduce the efficiency of those who remain.

The first section of the chapter is distinguished from the other three sections largely by the relatively heavy emphasis upon selective as opposed to formative modes of influence.

The form of our presentation is dictated by the character of the research literature in the field. Little of the research is explicitly directed toward the question we posed above regarding the impact of social and cultural forces on the teaching-learning process. Typically, researchers assume that these forces are significant—that certain consequences for teachers and for teaching will follow from them. Data collection serves not to test the assumptions but to describe the array of forces at a particular time and place. The study which deliberately tests the assumptions concerning cause-effect relationships is unusual. Our plan of presentation is governed accordingly. Normally, we will first discuss the descriptive data, attempting at the same time to make explicit the often implicit assumptions regarding their consequences for the teaching-learning process. Following this, we will report on the studies, if any, which bear upon the underlying assumptions. The greater part of our review is devoted to explication of the rationale of research rather than to a report of definitive research findings.

THE TEACHER'S POSITION IN THE AMERICAN SOCIAL STRUCTURE

Who is the American teacher? That is to say, how is the teacher linked to the social structure of American society? What are the consequences of who he is for his performance in the teaching-learning situation? These are the questions to which we turn in this section.

SOCIAL COMPOSITION OF THE TEACHING OCCUPATION

A wealth of information is available to describe the American teacher in terms of his nonoccupational statuses, especially the more readily ascertainable statuses of age, sex, marital status, educational attainment, and the like. The U.S. Office of Education, the Research Division of the National Education Association, and the U.S. Bureau of the Census regularly publish population statistics for the teaching occupation. Data also have been assembled through the years in survey studies of the "social composition" or the "social and economic status" of teaching. Some of these surveys were specifically directed to the problem which concerns us here. Thus, the earliest studies of social composition were predicated on the belief that knowledge of the social origins and characteristics of teachers would illuminate teaching "efficiency" in the classroom; the same rationale underlies some surveys today. Many surveys of teacher characteristics and conditions, however, were motivated by other interests, especially the desire for information regarding teacher supply and demand. Discovery of the societal sources of teacher supply and of the social and economic circumstances in which teachers work is presumed to suggest ways in which more and better teachers may be attracted to and retained in the profession. Whatever the purpose of the surveys, the fund of data is large and, in some cases, highly dependable.

Population Characteristics of Teachers

Age, sex, and marital status. The modal American teacher, in the late 1950's, was a married woman between the ages of 46 and 55 years, representing approximately 19 per cent of the total occupational group (National Education Association, 1957). Teaching clearly draws heavily from the female population. Currently, slightly less than three-quarters of the teachers are women, a figure which has varied substantially during the past 100 years. Most teachers, both male and female, are married or previously married (the "old-maid school teacher" now represents only about 11 per cent of the teaching force), but the married woman in teaching is a recent phenomenon. In 1931, married women constituted less than one-fifth of the total teaching group. Today, male teachers are predominantly young, female teachers middle-aged.

Community origins. There is a persistent belief that teachers are drawn heavily from small town and rural communities. L. A. Cook and Cook (1950, pp. 438–439) argued strongly in this vein, citing data from Greenhoe's (1941) national survey just before World War II. Greenhoe reported that about one-half of the responding teachers had been born in areas with populations of 2,500 or less and had spent most of their life in such places. More recently, McGuire and White (1957) found that nearly three-quarters of the Texas teachers they studied had been born in communities of less than 20,000. Tabulations from a national sample of the teaching population in 1957 (National Education Association, 1957) showed that 32 per cent of the teachers came from farm homes. An agrarian or small town background certainly is strongly represented in the present teaching group, but this group, with a median age of around 40 years, also represents an earlier generation when urbanization of our society was considerably less marked. Whether teacher recruits today are being drawn disproportionately from "provincial" backgrounds is an unanswered question. An inadequately controlled study of a group of Detroit teachers (Wattenberg, 1957b) suggests a changing pattern: Where 20 per cent of the teachers over 40 came from farm families, only 2 per cent of the younger teachers had a farm origin.

Educational attainment. Whatever may be the American teacher's provincial origins, he has, with relatively few exceptions, been exposed to the liberalizing experience of four years of college education. In 1957, over three-quarters of all teachers held at least a bachelor's degree, and one-quarter of them a master's degree. Six out of every seven beginning teachers in the fall of 1954 were college graduates (National Education Association, 1956). The college graduate in teaching, like

the married woman teacher, is a phenomenon of the last 20 or 30 years. In 1931 only one-third of the public school teachers had four years of college education (Evenden, Gamble, & Blue, 1933).

Nativity, race, and religion. Dependable national statistics regarding the nativity, the race, and the religious affiliation of public school teachers are less abundant, but it is probably safe to say that the overwhelming majority of American teachers today are native-born, white, and Protestant. The 1950 census, for example, reported that Negro and other nonwhite races constituted less than 7 per cent of the teaching population (U.S. Department of Commerce, 1952).

Social Class Origin and Mobility

In the last 20 years, a growing interest in the relationship between social stratification and education, stimulated by the community research of W. Lloyd Warner and his colleagues, has resulted in a number of studies of the social class origins of teachers. "The overwhelming proportion of teachers in the grammar schools and high schools are middle-class, often lower-middle-class," Warner concluded in one of his commentaries on the subject (Warner, 1953, p. 176). He estimated that 94 per cent of American teachers were members of the middle class. This figure was based upon three intensive community studies—Yankee City in the East, Old City in the Deep South, and Hometown (Elmtown) in the Midwest. The detailed social class distributions of teachers in the three communities are shown in Table 1. Warner, Havighurst, and Loeb noted, with respect to the *differences* in social class distributions displayed in Table 1.

In the East and the South, where class lines have been established longer, the teachers are usually in the upper-middle class, and many of them have risen from lower-middle class families. In the Middle West and the West, the teachers are usually lower-middle class, and many of them have risen from lower-class families (Warner, Havighurst, & Loeb, 1944, p. 101).

TABLE 1

SOCIAL CLASS DISTRIBUTION OF TEACHERS

(WHITE TEACHERS ONLY)[a]

	Hometown	Yankee City	Old City
	%	%	%
Upper upper	0	2	2.5
Lower upper	0	1	2.5
Upper middle	26	76	72.5
Lower middle	72	21	20.0
Upper lower	2	0	2.5
Lower lower	0	0	0.0

[a] Warner, Havighurst, and Loeb (1944, p. 101).

Because conclusions based on these data have been so widely cited, they are worth considering more fully. First, it is apparent that Warner's data refer to the social class position *attained* by teachers, not their social class *origins*. With this in mind, a subsequent passage in the Warner, Havighurst, and Loeb volume raises the question of how the social class position of teachers was established:

The social position of teachers is indefinite. Their social participation is often limited to their own professional group. . . . The unmarried Hometown female teachers live together in groups of two to five, either boarding or renting apartments. Where social participation is used as the test of social status [as Warner does], the teachers are difficult to locate in the social structure because they participate so little in the social life of the community (Warner, Havighurst, & Loeb, 1944, p. 103).

Second, Warner's conclusions are generalizations from three communities, none of them metropolitan. Only Yankee City, a town of 17,000 inhabitants, approximates a modern, industrialized city; Old City (13,-000) and Hometown (6,000) are small, agrarian communities relatively untouched, at the time of the studies, by the sweep of urbanization and suburbanization in our society. In light of massive changes in the composition of the teaching population since World War II, we question the wisdom of resting conclusions on such limited and dated studies.

Finally, the *particular* figure Warner offers

for the proportion of middle-class teachers might well be questioned. While other research bears out the concentration of teachers in the middle class, the conclusion that nearly 19 out of 20 are so located may be misleading. Data on the occupation of teachers' fathers go back as early as 1911, and a number of surveys have been conducted subsequently. [2] In the early studies, the majority of teachers were found to come from families of farmers, an occupational group which falls largely outside the social stratification schemes of Warner and other students. Thus, Coffman (1911) reported that at the time of his study 52 per cent of the nation's teachers derived from farm families.

A substantial percentage of teachers with labor backgrounds is shown in many of the studies. Of Coffman's teachers, 26 per cent had fathers whom he classified as "artisans" and "laborers," and 22 per cent had fathers who were professionals, businessmen, and public officials (p. 74). Thirty years later, Greenhoe's (1941) national survey of teachers showed 18 per cent whose fathers were day-laborers. Of 198 Detroit teachers taking in-service training in mid-1950, 29 per cent had fathers in unskilled or semiskilled labor occupations, a proportion especially pronounced among the younger teachers in the group (Wattenberg, 1957b). While occupational classification is not strictly comparable to Warner's scheme for social class placement, Warner's distinction between the middle and lower social classes corresponds, by and large, to a distinction between the white-collar and blue-collar or manual worker. A study of Texas teachers offered data more

[2] Most studies on occupational background have surveyed teachers-in-training, not teachers on the job. Generalizing from such data to the teaching population at large is hazardous. Aside from the fact that substantially less than 100 per cent of these students enter teaching, a fact which introduces the possibility of unknown bias, several studies have demonstrated important differences among types of college in background characteristics of their students. Teacher-trainees in the small teachers colleges, for example, are more likely to come from agricultural and laboring families than teacher-trainees in liberal arts colleges or the larger universities (Evenden, Gamble, & Blue, 1933; Kiely, 1931; McGuire & White, 1957).

closely comparable to the Warner classification: of 100 elementary and secondary school teachers sampled from in-service training programs, 18 per cent had their origins in lower-class families (exclusively the upper-lowers), 79 per cent in middle-class families (predominantly the lower-middles), and 3 per cent in upper-class families (McGuire & White, 1957).

Thus, to conclude that teaching is virtually monopolized by persons of middle-class origin is probably to overstate the case. It may hold in some locales, but available research suggests that there may be variation from one type of community or school system to another, and a number of the surveys of teacher origin going back to the early 1900's show that a small but significant proportion of teachers came from the working class. It would be no exaggeration to conclude that the teaching occupation draws heavily from the middle ranges of the American social class structure: the lowest and highest classes are under-represented in the profession.

As to the social class *mobility* of teachers, Warner frequently cites the generalization that teaching is an avenue for moving upward in the class structure and that large numbers of teachers are, indeed, upward mobile. The generalization is based principally on case studies of teachers which, of course, provide no evidence regarding the prevalence or frequency of upward mobility. But the one study directly examining teacher mobility does support the generalization; McGuire and White (1957) compared the social class positions attained by teachers and other school personnel (counselors and administrators) in Texas with the social class position of their parents and found that slightly over one-half of the sample of 150 had moved upward.

Summary and a Qualification

We have sought to describe the American teacher in terms of the societal statuses he occupies in addition to his occupational status. We find that American teachers may be characterized as predominantly college-edu-cated, native-born, Protestant, white, middle-aged, married females of middle-class and possibly rural or small-town origin. The modal description is based upon the occupational group as it is currently constituted and does not necessarily represent the kinds of people now being recruited into teaching.

Such a characterization of the teaching population in America, however, is over-drawn. Not only does it discount variations from the norm, a danger inherent in any modal description, but in this case it hides the *systematic nature* of such variations. In particular, the detailed statistics often show remarkable differences in social composition between rural and urban school districts, between elementary and secondary schools (and, within the secondary school, among teaching fields), between Negro and white schools (where segregated), and among states or regions of the nation. When these dimensions are cross-classified with one another (yielding, for example, rural, white, elementary schools of New England or urban, white, elementary schools of the South), the differences in the social characteristics of teachers are of such magnitude as to suggest that the various "teaching situations" represent discrete occupational categories with social compositions shaped by distinct arrays of forces.[3]

In the school year of 1930–1931 (for which unusually comprehensive statistics are available), the median age of elementary school teachers in the open country schools of Connecticut was 23 years; in similar California schools it was 32 years, a nine-year difference (Evenden, Gamble, & Blue, 1933). Elementary school teachers in the large city schools of these two states were substantially older— 29 years old in Connecticut and 36 in Cali-

---

[3] Mobility of teachers from one teaching situation to another does not contradict the presumption of "discrete occupational categories." The movement of teachers from rural to urban schools or from elementary to secondary schools is probably no longer the important avenue of vertical mobility it once was. But, to the extent that such mobility does exist, it is in itself a selective process which shapes the social characteristics of teachers in schools on all levels of the mobility ladder.

fornia. Senior high school teachers (unspecified by community size) were older still—32 and 37 years, respectively. The same data showed even more dramatic variations in sex distribution. For example, the percentage of male teachers in elementary schools ranged from 2 per cent in New Hampshire, Connecticut, and Maine to a high of 41 per cent in Indiana.

Within the secondary school, differences among teaching fields may be equally impressive. Some fields, such as home economics and vocational agriculture, are clearly sex-typed, others less obviously so. Wattenberg (1957b) reported that his Detroit teachers with laboring class backgrounds principally supplied the fields of physical education, industrial education, home economics, and social studies, although his data do not make a strong case. Research on personal attributes of high school teachers, such as interest patterns, personality characteristics, values, and so on, supports the observation of differences among teaching fields (Lieberman, 1956, pp. 219–220; Ryans, 1960, pp. 322–327).

Besides variations among teaching situations, major changes in social composition have occurred over the years, possibly at different rates in different teaching situations. Within recent years, teaching has undergone a transformation so great as to render obsolete many popular conceptions of the occupation. We have already alluded to a few of these. While the data are scanty, it is reasonably clear that the social forces shaping occupational composition have never been constant for any extended period in our history. The sex distribution is a case in point. The teacher in the colonial period and through the first half of the nineteenth century typically was a male, though this fact depended, as Elsbree (1939) carefully pointed out, upon region of the country and type of school. From the latter part of the nineteenth century until 1920, the proportion of males declined steadily to 14 per cent; since then it has climbed, with setbacks during war periods, to the present figure of 26 per cent.

Variations of these kinds should be viewed as evidence of phenomena to be understood, not hidden by modal descriptions. Fortunately, data on certain teacher characteristics are abundant in the files and reports of the Office of Education, the Research Division of the National Education Association, and the Bureau of the Census. Many national and local surveys reporting the "general status" of teachers are scattered through the professional literature, some of them dating back to 1905. Betts, Frazier, and Gamble (1933) provided an exhaustive bibliography of such studies covering the first two decades of this century. Conceivably, the very act of summarizing data on changes over the years in teacher characteristics in the various teaching situations would illuminate the nature of forces operating on the social composition of the teaching occupation. In turn, the variations in social composition offer an opportunity to examine and test the effects of these forces on the teaching-learning process.

THE CONSEQUENCES OF POSITION IN THE SOCIAL STRUCTURE

How is the teaching-learning process influenced by the positions teachers occupy in the American social structure? When we turn to this question, we meet far more conjecture than research. Nevertheless, it may be of some value to summarize the major assumptions, bringing to bear, where possible, the research studies relating to them.

With a few exceptions, the modes of reasoning have been of two major kinds, one representing an educational tradition and the other an anthropological approach. In both, a person's position in the social structure is viewed as having a formative influence, as producing certain enduring attributes which he carries into the classroom and which affect his teaching behavior.

In the tradition of educational studies of social composition, assumptions are made as to what social statuses are likely to produce the *best* teachers. These assumptions entail two sets of subsidiary assumptions concerning, first, the particular personal attributes necessary for effective performance as a teacher and, second, those segments of society which produce persons with the "proper" attributes.

The emphasis of the anthropological approach is different. Position in the social structure is regarded as shaping the general value orientations which affect a teacher's behavior in the classroom rather than as a determiner of the specific cognitive abilities, pedagogical skills, or attributes of personal and moral character deemed necessary for effective teaching. Thus, the anthropological approach goes beyond the issue of teaching effectiveness to the more general question of the impact of teacher values on the teaching-learning process.

Teaching Effectiveness and Societal Position

In the educational studies of social composition, assumptions regarding the connection between societal position and effective teaching have been little more than the embodiment of popular conceptions or stereotypes. The personal attributes deemed necessary for teaching effectiveness and presumed to be formed by societal statuses are varied but may be roughly ordered as (1) cognitive competencies, skills, and abilities exercised in teaching, (2) character traits and personality attributes expressed in teaching, and (3) "appropriate" motivations for performing in the teaching role.

Coffman's early survey of teacher characteristics (1911) offers a convenient way to illustrate the rationale in these various realms. He based his study on over 5,200 questionnaires returned by teachers in 17 states, chiefly in the East. From them he sought information on such things as age, sex, salary, education, teaching experience, nativity of subjects and parents, parental occupation and income, and number of siblings. The following paragraphs contain, in germinal form at least, most of the assumptions on which 50 years of subsequent research on the social composition of teaching has been based:

The kind of people we have in teaching necessarily affects the kind of teaching we get. Differences in race must make a vast difference in customs, traditions, moral and religious ideals, language habits, and originality. Differences due to social class, to economic station, to intellectual maturity, to academic and professional training, and the like, must likewise be important factors affecting public opinion of the merits of the teacher and his work. . . .

If we knew the class of people which is contributing the teachers, its fecundity, its ambitions and its outlook, its possibilities for refinement, for culture, and for personal improvement, we could, with the aid of modern science, tell something of the intellectual grade of people we are getting. If we knew the motive that impels teachers to choose it as a vocation, the preparation they make for it, and their recognition of its opportunities for social service, we would have some measure of how far there is a craft-spirit, a spirit of professional ethics dominating the body of workers (Coffman, 1911, pp. 14–15).

Assumptions regarding cognitive competencies. In the realm of cognitive competencies, skills, and abilities, Coffman spoke of "originality," of "intellectual grade," or of "intellectual maturity." How do these attributes tie up with societal positions? In part, Coffman exhibited a strong genetic bias, common in his day, implying an inherent superiority among the "favored" classes in the virtues necessary for teaching. Thus, he expected the higher social classes "naturally" to contain more intellectually capable persons than the lower social classes. This genetic bias, however, has been left by the wayside since Coffman's time; the alleged superiority of the higher classes is now more likely to be attributed to the influences of the social environment. Coffman included this in his rationale too: "The formative influence of any body of workers must always be in terms of their social class. Their strengths and limitations are determined not merely by their immediate ancestry but also by their social position" (p. 54).

Thus, cognitive attributes are shaped by social position, but, in keeping with contemporary sociological doctrine, Coffman saw the impact of the environing social structure as a restricting one as well. Thus, after showing that teachers come from very large families (4 to 5 siblings) with very low incomes, Coffman wrote: "This condition means that the population that teaching selects is restricted as to its opportunities for personal improvement and for liberal culture, that in the main it must enter the field of teaching with little or no professional preparation" (p. 79). Position in the social structure, then, is regarded as limiting or enhancing the life chances of the person. Low "economic station," especially, limits the opportunity for academic and professional training, which in turn affects the development of cognitive attributes.

The presumption that educational attainment, or more specifically, academic and pedagogical training, produces the cognitive competencies and skills requisite for teaching has become firmly embedded in the rationale underlying surveys of teacher characteristics in the ensuing years. Indeed, the presumption has been firmly institutionalized in the American educational system in teacher certification requirements, in criteria for accrediting schools, in salary promotion schedules, and in teacher-training programs. The presumption no longer is a matter of debate, except in regard to what kind of education is needed.

Societal statuses other than educational attainment and social class origins have also been seen as associated with the knowledge, skills, and abilities appropriate to teaching. Arguments concerning the suitability for teaching of males and females (their comparative ability to control, and ability to understand, children), the young and the older (fresh ideas versus tried methods), and the married and unmarried (maturity of judgment and experience in handling children) have waxed and waned with the decades. Such arguments often seem directed toward issues other than classroom performance, such as increasing the prestige of the occupational group, or enhancing the likelihood of

professional commitment to the occupation, or increasing the stability of school staffs.

Assumptions regarding character traits and motivations. In the realm of character traits and personality attributes, Coffman spoke of "customs," "moral and religious ideals," "language habits," and the like. A review of subsequent writings would extend the list of attributes almost indefinitely to include the whole range of traits commonly associated with leadership capacity, congenial personal relations, devotion to study, and refinement of manners and taste. Such social statuses as religious affiliation (that is, activeness of membership, not particular affiliation), community of origin, and social class background typically are seen as playing a part in fostering these attributes.

The rural and small town origins of teachers are said to forge a "parochial outlook" among them, especially when their normal occupational mobility fails to carry them into the broader world (L. A. Cook & Cook, 1950). In the early studies, lowly social class origin was in itself a mark of defective character. Or it was conceived to limit the opportunity for personal mobility in society, which in turn supports one's parochial outlook and values; it reduces the possibilities for "refinement" through contact with "cultural" or "broadening" experiences; it restricts opportunity for academic and professional training. Lieberman (1956) expressed this mode of reasoning in the more recent vein:

The majority of teachers are coming from homes which are culturally unpromising if not impoverished. They are coming from homes in which light popular books and magazines or none at all are the rule. If the future teacher's family subscribes to any magazines, it is likely to be *Colliers, Saturday Evening Post,* or the *Reader's Digest.* It is not likely to be *Harper's, Atlantic Monthly, Freeman, Saturday Review of Literature, American Mercury, Reporter,* or any other periodical devoted to serious writing on political, social, or cultural topics. The families from which teachers come are generally inactive both politically and in community affairs. Their social activities are likely to be confined to fraternal orders and lodges such as the Masons, Shriners, Order of Eastern Star, Elks, Moose, International Order of Odd Fellows, or Knights of Columbus. Families in the upper lower and lower middle classes usually have rather limited experience in the fine arts such as music or painting. Attending movies, playing cards, listening to radio and watching television, and visiting the neighbors are the most popular recreational outlets for these classes (Lieberman, 1956, p. 466).

(He tempers the extremity of his assertion in the subsequent paragraph by pointing out that the "impoverishment" is characteristic of the classes from which teachers are drawn, not necessarily of the teachers themselves.)

Moffett's (1929) survey of the social and "cultural" worlds of teachers college students in the 1920's epitomizes the line of reasoning which connects social class and community background with character attributes requisite for good teaching. From student reports in 15 training institutions, she describes the typical students in terms such as these: father is owner or manager of small business or farm, and family is unbroken by death or divorce; reared in a rural community or small town; recreation restricted to the resources of a small community; little participation in formal organizations and even less leadership experience; small group from which to select associates, and contact with people has been limited; no creative activities; "cultural standards" those of her community associates rather than those "generally held best" in her high school or college.

Finally, in the realm of motivations appropriate to the teaching status, the implicit assumptions are not strikingly different from the foregoing. Incentive for "personal improvement," embodiment of the "craft-spirit," and commitment to "social service" are some of the appropriate motives which Coffman mentioned. These are commonly seen to inhere in the "better" social classes or among males.

Empirical tests. Research support for the various sets of implicit assumptions is virtually nonexistent. Some investigators, in the context of research on teacher effectiveness, have sought to establish relationships between social structure variables and teacher performance in the classroom. Since the findings, like those on teacher effectiveness generally, are either inconclusive or contradictory, only a few illustrations will be presented here. Herda (1935) found no differences between males and females in effectiveness as measured by a teachers' examination and by pupil ratings. Age showed a slight positive correlation with effectiveness when measured by supervisors' ratings (Odenweller, 1936), a slight negative correlation when the criterion was the Professional Test for Elementary Teachers (Bathurst, 1929), and a curvilinear relationship when the criterion was pupil gains on a history examination (Brookover, 1945). Peters' (1934) exhaustively controlled study of married and single females showed a slight advantage for married teachers on criteria of pupil achievement and mental growth, but, in accord with a previous study (Waits, 1932), no advantage on a criterion of supervisors' ratings. The teacher's socioeconomic status was found to be unrelated to teaching effectiveness as measured by supervisors' ratings (W. S. Phillips, 1935), by tests of teaching ability (Greene & Staton, 1939), or pupil gains (Brookover, 1945).

The Teacher Characteristics Study (Ryans, 1960) exemplifies a more direct approach to measures of performance and describes their relationships to various teacher statuses. In this study, teachers were scored on a number of dimensions of classroom behavior from ratings provided by trained observers and data furnished by responses of teachers to questionnaire items. Two of the bipolar dimensions, for example, were "warm, understanding, friendly teacher behavior" versus "aloof, egocentric, restricted teacher behavior" and "responsible, businesslike, systematic teacher behavior" versus "evading, unplanned, slipshod teacher behavior." But simple relationships between the performance dimensions and age, sex, marital status, and extent of religious participation were not discernible. These statuses interacted in complex ways with teaching level and teaching field to produce different patterns of performance scores for teachers.

It is too much to expect, perhaps, that empirical relationships would support the unsophisticated assumptions of studies in the social composition tradition. The logical chain connecting the teacher's position in the social structure and performance in the classroom is long and tenuous, especially when performance is restricted to preconceptions of attributes necessary for effective teaching. Furthermore, decades of empirical research have failed to identify unequivocally the *behaviors* which *define* "effective teaching," much less to establish an association between such behaviors and enduring personal attributes of teachers. If the problem cannot be anchored on the "proximal" end, it can hardly be pursued fruitfully at the "distal" end.

Value Orientations of Teachers

The second major mode of reasoning regarding the consequences of the teacher's position in the social structure is associated with the work of social anthropologists and sociologists. In this approach, the social environment is seen to shape the generalized value orientations by which a person lives and works. Simple societies with relatively homogeneous, internally consistent, unchanging patterns of culture present no complex "educational" problems. The educational issue in simple societies, if it is an issue at all, is one of providing the means of "teaching" most suitable for inducting the youth into the values dominant in the society.[4] But contemporary industrial societies consist of differentiated groups, or subcultures, each

with a propensity to develop a different set of values in its members. Moreover, the groups may be hierarchically ordered with respect to prestige or power, which introduces further complexities into relationships among persons with different values. Nor are the value systems unchanging. The changes occurring in the dominant value system of the society proceed at different rates in the several groups and subcultures, producing, in another way, dislocations of value orientations among the society's members.

From this point of view then, the significant aspect of the teaching-learning process in the classroom is the transmission of value orientations from teacher to pupil. It proceeds not so much through didactic teachings as through the reward and punishment system and other subtleties of the flow of interaction, a point illustrated vividly in Henry's (1955b, 1957) accounts of interaction in elementary school classes. Which values will be transmitted depends upon the teacher's own value orientation, which, in turn, is determined by his position in the groups and subcultures of the social structure. Problems arise in those cases where classroom participants (teachers and pupils) are located at different points in the larger social structure and enter the classroom with conflicting value orientations.

Margaret Mead, in her analyses of American education (1946, 1951), postulates three distinct value orientations which teachers stress in the teaching situation. These she derives from her cross-cultural observations of the role of different age groups in inducting the young into society. One is a stress on conservatism and preservation of tradition, where the function of education is to transmit the accumulated wisdom of the society. This function, appropriate to highly stable preliterate societies, is performed by the elders, in what Mead calls the "grandparent role."

The second value orientation emphasizes the immediacy of the here and now, unfettered by concerns for the future or constraints of the past. In some societies it is the child's

---

[4] Henry's (1955a) provocative essay, distinguishing a number of characteristics of the instruction process in terms of communication theory, specifies in detail how instruction is suited to particular societies.

world of fantasy, of direct bodily expression, or communication by gesture and touch which is valued. Here the function of education is to preserve for society these resources of childhood; it is accomplished by relegating the socialization process to the older siblings who, themselves, have not emerged from the child's world. This is Mead's "child nurse role."

The third value orientation, appropriate to a society in the throes of rapid change, stresses the preparation of youth for the future, but for a future which cannot be comprehended in terms of the past, or, indeed, in terms of the present generation of parents. Parents can only raise their children to succeed them, to become the next possessors of a world still unknown and uncharted, and they find an ally in the school teacher who assumes the "parent role."

In contemporary American society, teachers assume these differing roles, depending upon the requirements of the school, according to Mead. Thus, the "grandparent role" is epitomized by the teacher in schools of small, provincial communities where he merely saves the time and energy of parents in teaching what the parents themselves could just as well teach. It is also epitomized by teachers in the academies (private high schools) and by high school teachers of mathematics, science, literature, and other classics who convey to pupils a sense of the relatedness of life.

The "child nurse role" is manifested in the nursery school and kindergarten where the upper middle-class girl, concerned less with verbal facility than material objects, allies herself with the world of the child and encourages the child's self-expression and self-indulgence.

Finally, the "parent role" is epitomized by teachers of middle-class suburbia, by teachers of modern history, current events, and scientific methods of exploration, and by teachers of the city schools charged with acculturating the flood of immigrants reaching our shores (e.g., the Puerto Ricans of the 1950's in New York City). These teachers convey to youth what their parents cannot. They represent the future as different from the past and induce youth to move beyond their parents. In order to do so, the youth are taught the virtues of sacrifice, of impulse restraint, of industry, and the wisdom of ignoring those traditions which block success.

Mead suggests that the teachers conveying these value orientations are drawn from, and have their values formed in, different sectors of the American society. Teachers in the city schools and in suburbia, for example, are selected from among urbanites raised in the midst of cultural diversity and change, from among middle and lower middle-class persons who, themselves, are seeking to transcend their past. Teachers in traditional communities are recruited from similar communities and are able to convey the provincial values with ease. Academy teachers and teachers of the academic subjects in public high schools tend to be drawn from the downward mobile sectors of the population, from persons who are clinging to the past. Thus, the value orientations transmitted in the classroom are reflections of the teachers' own societal circumstances, and an occupational selection process sorts them into school situations to which their value perspectives are congenial.[5] Mead's substantive propositions, however, have not been subjected to direct empirical check, either in terms of the societal positions of teachers in the various school situations or in terms of their characteristic value perspectives as manifested in teaching.

Spindler's (1955) conceptualization, in

---

[5] There is a parallel between Mead's three teacher roles and the time dimension of societal value orientations proposed by Florence Kluckhohn (1953): value systems may emphasize the past ("grandparent role"), the present ("child nurse role"), or the future ("parent role"). Kluckhohn's analysis similarly tied differences in time orientation directly to social class position: the upper class adheres more to a past than a future orientation, the middle class more to a future orientation, and the lower class more to a present orientation. This observation has produced a number of empirical investigations which, however, are outside the field of education and beyond the scope of the present review.

much the same vein as Mead's, provides a more fruitful base for empirical research in that his hypotheses are more explicitly formulated and his key variables are more readily operationalized. Spindler conceived of a major change occurring in the core values of American society, a change associated with our recent, unsettling history—our engagement in global wars, our experience with a "boom or bust" economy—and with the insecurities generated by an atomic age and its portent of cataclysm. In the present ethos, the *traditional values* which founded our society no longer serve, and they have tended to give way to a new value system, which Spindler calls the *emergent values*. Specifically, the traditional values of puritan morality, work-success ethic, individualism, achievement orientation, and future-time orientation are being supplanted by such emergent values as sociability, a relativistic moral attitude, consideration of others, conformity to the group, and a hedonistic present-time orientation.[6]

Three principal societal statuses help to determine a person's value orientation. One of these is social class. Spindler regarded the middle and the lower middle class as a stronghold of moral respectability, the work-success ethic, and, generally, the traditional value system. Another is position in the community power structure. Persons so located, Spindler suggested, have a vested interest in the status quo and, hence, support traditional values. The third societal status is age. Assuming that value orientations are acquired early in life, we can say that the older generations, acculturated during a period when traditional values prevailed, are more likely to exhibit the traditional values today than are the younger generations. One further subculture enters Spindler's analysis

as a determinant of values—the education profession itself, especially as represented in teacher-training institutions. The cultural force in schools of education, Spindler observed, is clearly in the direction of emergent values.

On the basis of these determinants, then, Spindler hypothesized that the various participants in the school and community will array themselves in the following order, from the traditional to the emergent pole on a value orientation continuum:

School board members
General public and parents
Some students
School administrators
Older teachers
Younger teachers
Other students

School board members are most traditional by virtue of their advanced age and the fact that they represent community power groups. Spindler's "general public and parents" refers particularly to the vocal critics of the school; others may well range over the entire continuum. Students are located in two places on the range, depending upon the location of their families. School administrators are in the middle, literally and figuratively, inasmuch as they must face the demands of persons with conflicting values. Older teachers differ from the younger teachers principally by virtue of the fact that they grew up and acquired their values at a time when the system was more traditional.

Spindler used this continuum to imply that the severity of value conflict increases as the difference in status of participants increases. For purposes of this review, it is especially noteworthy that the teacher, young or old, may well be faced with value conflicts within the classroom. Even the young teacher who finds close kinship in outlook with some students can still be confronted by other students from families whose basic value orientations diverge greatly from the teacher's.

---

[6] Spindler is by no means alone in noting a major shift in the dominant values of American society or the implications it holds for education or socialization patterns generally. While the details and emphases differ, his observations are closely similar to those of such writers as Getzels (1957), Riesman (1950), Swanson and Miller (1958), and Whyte (1956).

Spindler's immediate interest in presenting his analysis was to uncover the roots of the conflict between the school and its public. The present-day ethos of anxiety leads to societal demoralization, disorganization, and conflict, he argued; the hostile feelings which result are vented in attacks of one group upon another, in attacks by persons with traditional values on other persons and institutions representing the emergent system of values, and vice versa. But Spindler's analysis goes beyond the school-community conflict. He suggested that conflicts may arise between participants in the school institution holding dissimilar values and, more important, within individual participants exposed to divergent cultural pressures during formative periods of their lives.

Spindler reserved special attention for teachers in his discussion of internal value conflict. He proposed that teachers typically are drawn from the middle and lower middle classes and, further, that within these classes the teaching occupation is selective of the more puritanical element, of those who emphasize self-denial, altruism, and a moralistic self concept—all adding up to a strong commitment to traditional values. But in their training, teachers encounter a new culture with a strong press toward emergent values, and they experience a discontinuity in their acculturation process.

The value conflict which ensues in teachers has one of three consequences: ambivalence, compensation, and adaptation. The ambivalent teacher is one prone to vacillation in matters of classroom discipline and authority, vacillation between laissez-faire and authoritarian relations with pupils. The compensating teacher goes to either the emergent or the traditional extreme in his classroom performance. At the emergent extreme are those thoroughly committed to the social adjustment movement and the "groupthink" cult; at the traditional extreme are those teachers who are downright authoritarian in their dominance over pupils and enter into formal, rigid relations with them. The adaptive teacher is one who manifests either of the preceding mechanisms of conflict resolution but in far less severe form.

Several empirical studies have given a modicum of support to Spindler's hypotheses regarding differential value orientations of participants in the school institution. Prince (1957) developed a 64-item forced-choice questionnaire designed to distinguish persons in their positions on the traditional-emergent continuum and administered it to principals, teachers, and students in 22 high schools. He reported that older teachers were significantly more traditional in their value orientations than young teachers, and that older principals were more traditional than younger principals.

Using the same questionnaire, McPhee (1959) studied 600 respondents in eight Midwestern communities, mainly citizen-members of a variety of civic organizations but also some school personnel. He, too, found greater traditionalism among the older respondents but no significant difference between teachers and laymen. Nor could he report differences in value orientations associated with occupation, income, educational attainment, home ownership, the school attended by the respondents' children, or participation in school elections.

Abbott's (1960) study of school board members and superintendents in 40 Midwestern school districts showed board members to be significantly more traditional than superintendents. But, in contrast to the other studies, he found among the superintendents a negative relationship between traditional value orientation and age. The older superintendents were more emergent in their values than the younger superintendents. Abbott found no relationships among board members between value orientations and occupation or type of community in which they were reared. From the brief published reports of these studies, it would appear that McPhee and Abbott examined only the first-order relationships between value scores and respondents' social characteristics. In Spindler's reasoning, the agent responsible for a person's value orientation is the cultural group in which he was raised and trained; social characteristics are but rough indicators of this prime variable. A faithful test of Spindler's hypotheses requires more sensitive analyses than Prince, McPhee, or Abbott provided. It should be noted, however, that none of them designed his study as a direct test of Spindler.

Value Orientations:
The Case of Social Class

Sociologists and anthropologists associated with Warner's theory of social stratification regard the social class strata as the most important set of subcultures in American society. In this view, the social class structure consists of a series of loosely formed groups larger than the friendship circle but smaller than the entire community and ordered on a scalar dimension of prestige.[7] Personal interaction tends to be limited between members of the different classes but relatively intense within class strata, a circumstance which favors the emergence of unique culture patterns and value systems within each class. A child born to a family within a particular stratum is acculturated by means of unique patterns of child training and then comes to internalize the appropriate value orientations. Nevertheless, personal movement from one stratum to the next is not uncommon in American society. Indeed, exponents of this theory of social class consider the aspiration to enhance one's social standing (or to maintain a favorable standing) as an extremely important human motivation. Movement from one stratum to another is never easy, and in some cases, for example, when the host stratum excludes those without a proper family lineage or those without white skin

---

[7] The Warner theory of social stratification departs in a number of important respects from classical Marxian theory and other sociological theories. Since educators are inclined to regard it as *the* theory of social class, the author recommends to them the excellent, authoritative review of contemporary social class theories by Mayer (1953) which places the Warner theory in perspective.

color, it is impossible. To be mobile, a person must acquire the value orientations, attitude, language habits, manners, and other cultural trappings appropriate to the host stratum, and this frequently requires him to renounce the values and way of life of the stratum from which he moves, running the risk, consequently, of alienating himself from his family and earlier friends.

In the view of the theorists, the school assumes a highly significant function in the stratification system of twentieth-century America (Warner, Havighurst, & Loeb, 1944). On the one hand, the school is one of the few remaining avenues of upward mobility from the lower to the middle classes or, within the middle class, from its lower to its higher reaches. Formal educational training is a *sine qua non* of membership in higher social strata. Not only is educational attainment itself a criterion for membership but it is a prerequisite for more "respectable" occupational or professional opportunities and higher or more secure incomes. Moreover, the theorists propose that the public school is a middle-class institution in the sense that it embodies the middle-class culture and thereby serves the upward mobile child of the lower class as a secondary acculturating agency, a place where he can assimilate the values, customs, morals, and manners essential to acceptance in the higher strata.

On the other hand, the school preserves the stability of the stratification system by limiting upward mobility to those youth who are willing and able to play within the rules of the game or, more specifically, to acquire the value orientations and motivations appropriate to middle-class membership. The public school serves as a sifting and sorting mechanism which differentiates between those who go to college and those who do not. Among those who do not go on to college, the school makes differential allocations to the various levels of occupational opportunity in the community; among the college-bound, to the various types of advanced training. As one analyst recently suggested

(Parsons, 1959), the sorting process begins as early as the elementary school.

Our purpose is not to assess the adequacy of the social class theory nor to review the research which serves as its underpinning. Our discussion is offered as background for the task of examining the research pertinent to the impact of the teacher's social class position upon the teaching-learning process in the classroom. In undertaking such an examination, we will identify and elaborate on the main links in the chain of reasoning which connects the teacher's social class origins to his classroom performance. Given the fact that teachers derive principally from the middle class, one can draw certain conclusions concerning how the degree of success pupils will experience in the classroom and school will depend on the pupils' own social class position. But these conclusions can be drawn from the given fact only if three basic assumptions, or tenets, also hold. These tenets relate to (1) social class differences in values, (2) teachers' internalization of middle-class values, and (3) the manifestation of middle-class values in the classroom interaction process.

Social class differences in values. The first basic tenet is that persons raised in middle-class families (or upper-class families) will hold values in their adulthood differing in certain critical respects from those held by persons raised in lower-class families. Two implications of this statement demand elaboration and some qualification. The statement reflects the strong emphasis social class theorists place on childhood as the formative period of adult character. While theorists of the Warner school do not disregard the influence on the adult's behavior of his contemporary social class position or of his social class aspirations and mobility, they are inclined to stress the enduring attributes of personality acquired during the early acculturation period. Hence the significance of their research on class differences in child training practices. The statement also posits major differences in value orientations and cultural patterns among the social strata of American

society. This assumption has been abundantly supported by empirical research over the years, especially regarding differences between the middle and lower classes. Such demonstrated differences, however, do not preclude the existence of a dominant or core value system in American society, more or less internally consistent, more or less integrative of the variant values and ideologies in the several social strata and other subcultures.

At the risk of oversimplifying the research findings, we will outline some of the more important differences in ideology and value orientation between the middle class (representing most closely what Warner and others call the "common man" or lower middle class) and the lower (or working) class.[8] Orientation of the middle class is toward sacrifice of immediate gratifications to attain future rewards, together with long-term planning to tie future goals to instrumental acts of the present; orientation of the lower class is toward immediate impulse gratification and "getting by" in the present rather than "getting ahead." This difference in orientation is related to several other divergences, including the valuation of expressions of "raw" emotions. In the middle class, strong taboos are associated with the direct expression of aggressive or sexual impulses; such impulses are neither controlled nor denied in the lower class but, rather, are rewarded when prowess is displayed. In the middle class, money, property, and material goods are things to be accumulated and cared for; in the lower class, they are regarded as things to be used. Personal "ownership" is a concept less applicable to goods in the lower class; in the middle class, the distinction be-

---

[8] It is impossible in the space available here to cite the supporting evidence regarding social class differences in culture patterns, and the literature *summarizing* the evidence is, perhaps, more voluminous than the research itself. In the following sketch we have drawn heavily upon the systematic schematization of value orientations presented by C. Kluckhohn and Kluckhohn (1947). The reader wishing to pursue the evidence should consult a standard textbook on sociology or social stratification.

tween "your" possessions and "mine" is taught early and reinforced by sanctions.

Schooling, study, and academic achievement, in the middle class, are viewed as instrumental to the attainment of occupational aspirations and "success"; in the lower class, they are either irrelevant or only vaguely instrumental, representing primarily a delay in entering the labor market and in establishing one's status as a nondependent adult. The person who is "too educated" is a misfit in the lower-class community. In the middle class, respect for a person depends on the extent of his conformity to standards of propriety, including proper forms for eating, address, greetings, exchange of gifts, expression of sympathy, offering of apology, language usage, and standards associated with tidiness of person, apparel, and possessions. In the lower class, respect is accorded on the basis of attributes of the person, such as being a "good fellow" or a "good-hearted woman," unmediated by conformity to many formal conventions. In the middle class, value is associated with the nuclear, but not the extended, family, with participation in formal organizations, and with allegiance to and respect for institutionalized authority. In the lower class, the extended family is the proper base of one's associations, and institutionalized authority of the law and courts, of the school, and of formal community organizations is feared or treated opportunistically, not respected.

The preceding sketch, as well as the evidence on which it is based, describes modal value orientations of the middle and lower classes in the aggregate. Even when the social strata are broken down into five or six divisions, or when classification is made on the basis of self-identification rather than objective placement, characterizations of the various classes represent modal tendencies distilled, in effect, from comparisons of statistical averages. Inspection of the original data reveals sizable departures from the modal tendencies within each stratum, due in part to the crudity of measurement. Such intrastratum variability is probably due in larger part, however, to differences among stratum members in their exposure to a wide gamut of value-forming experiences other than social class. This point becomes relevant as we examine the second tenet of the social class reasoning.

Social class values of teachers. The second basic tenet is that teachers are drawn from the middle stratum of the American social class structure and, therefore, hold middle-class value orientations. Evidence for the first part of this tenet has been reviewed earlier. It is almost certainly true that a majority of the families of persons currently teaching are from the middle class. The second part of the tenet, however, does not necessarily follow from the first part. Does teaching select those middle-class members who hold the value orientations of the middle class? Is the teacher a member of the middle class who is fully imbued with the notions of sacrifice of present desires and denial of emotional expression, fraught with taboos regarding sex and aggression, conventional and proper, convinced of the instrumental worth of education? According to the popular stereotype, the answer would be yes, but the answer must be sought in facts. Other possibilities are open. In any event, empirical investigation relating to the latter half of the second tenet is meager.

Few studies of class-related attitudes or values have been conducted so as to permit either (1) comparison of teachers with the general population from which they are drawn or (2) comparison among teachers of different social class memberships. The most relevant is Sims's (1951) study of several hundred public school teachers attending a summer session at the University of Alabama. Sims asked these teachers the six questions Centers (1949) had asked a nationwide sample five years earlier to assess positions on a "conservatism-radicalism" dimension of politico-economic attitudes. The questions were of the following kind: Do you agree or disagree that America is truly a land of opportunity and that people get pretty much what's coming to them in this country? In strikes and disputes between working people and employers, do you usually side with the workers, or with the employers? (Sims, 1951, p. 332).

Centers had found a substantial positive relationship between degree of conservatism, as derived from responses to these questions, and social class membership, when measured either by self-placement or by objective placement. The distribution of attitude scores for the Alabama teachers showed them to be more conservative, on the average, than any of Centers' occupational categories except businessmen; they were more conservative in scores than the white-collar workers whom they would most closely approximate in social-class position.

Sims's study is far from definitive in regard to the issue of social class selectivity. One would anticipate higher conservatism scores from a Deep South sample, whether or not composed of teachers, than from a cross-sectional sample of the nation. Moreover, the Alabama summer session teachers almost certainly were largely composed of nonurban persons, a factor which Centers showed was associated with conservatism. Nevertheless, to the author's knowledge, Sims's study remains the most direct attempt to test the second tenet of the social class theory.

A test of the proposition that middle-class teachers internalize the value orientations of their social class might be sought in research, such as Wickman's (1928), on the kinds of pupil behavior teachers regard as serious problems. If teachers' standards of conduct were found to correspond to the values associated uniquely with the middle class, the hypothesis would be supported, assuming, of course, that the teachers studied were principally of middle-class origin. Among the 12 problems most frequently cited as serious by 511 elementary school teachers in Wickman's (1928) study, three related to sex taboos (heterosexual activity, masturbation, obscene notes and pictures), two related to disrespect for property (stealing, destroying school materials), two related to disrespect for authority (impertinence and defiance, disobedi-

ence), and one related to unbridled aggression (cruelty and bullying). Two of the remaining might also be regarded as class-typed standards—truancy, unreliability, and irresponsibility—but the last two might better be considered as related to core values of American society—untruthfulness and cheating.

As evidence for the second tenet, however, Wickman's data are highly equivocal. There is no assurance that social class differences would be shown *on these particular items*. Furthermore, certain variations appear in Wickman's data where no variations in social class of teachers would be expected, and no variations appear where differences in social class might be expected. In Wickman's study (1928, pp. 246–247), 35 teachers in three villages in Minnesota and New York State (probably not varying substantially from the urban teachers in social class position) regarded selfishness, smoking, and profanity as among the most serious behavioral problems, matters of considerably less concern to the teachers of New York City, Cleveland, and Newark. These differences may be more closely associated with the puritanical code of the rural areas than with social class mores. In his data from experienced teachers enrolled in college classes, Wickman observed that the departure of their ratings from the public school sample in some instances could be attributed to the course instruction and its emphases (pp. 105, 108–109). This would suggest that teachers' norms with respect to pupils are affected by professional training. Finally, Wickman obtained ratings from 10 male teachers in a private academy near Cleveland; these teachers, conceivably of a higher social class than the remainder of the public school sample, nevertheless rated pretty much the same problems as the most serious (pp. 106–107).

Several replications of the Wickman study in the 1940's and 1950's supported the contention that influences other than social class membership affect standards of judgment regarding undesirable pupil behavior (Mitchell, 1943; Schrupp & Gjerde, 1953; Stouffer, 1952). While the same kinds of behavior problems that appeared in 1926 (when Wickman's data were collected) still appeared in the top ranks of seriousness—such as heterosexual activity, stealing, cruelty, obscenity, and lying—certain subtle shifts in ranking were observed. Mitchell (1943), for example, reported that such nonaggressive behaviors as sullenness, unhappiness, and resentfulness increased in rank between 1926 and 1940. Where the correlation between teacher rankings and the rankings by mental hygiene experts had been — .08 in the Wickman study, Mitchell's teachers and mental hygienists in 1940 agreed to the extent of a .70 correlation. Mitchell, however, gave his mental hygiene experts different instructions from those Wickman had given, and the two studies were hence not strictly comparable.

Schrupp and Gjerde (1953) exactly replicated the Wickman study and found a correlation of .56 between the rankings of teachers and of mental hygienists in 1951. These authors showed that it was the teachers and not the experts who had changed their rankings in the intervening 25 years. Stouffer's (1952) study provided very similar evidence.

It is reasonable to attribute the shifts in teachers' judgments of behavior problems to changes which occurred in professional education in this period and even to the Wickman study itself. The Wickman research appeared just at the time the mental hygiene point of view was gaining a foothold in teacher-training curricula, and the conclusion widely drawn from Wickman's data, rightly or wrongly, that teachers do not appreciate the significance of withdrawal and autism as symptoms of personality disturbance in children, became a point of departure for mental hygiene courses and textbooks. There is no doubt that the generations of teachers trained after 1930 have been sensitized during their training to problems of personal and social adjustment far more than were earlier generations of teachers.

The simple fact is that no definitive conclusion can be drawn from existing data regarding the extent to which teachers internalize the value orientations unique to their social class position. One might anticipate considerable variation among teachers here, but the empirical tests have not been made.

Manifestation of values in teaching. The third basic tenet, completing the connection between the teacher's social class position and the teaching-learning process, is embedded in the following statement: "Since the teachers' judgments of the children and of standards of performance are inevitably based on their own personal standards, buttressed by those set up by the school as an institution, the lower-class child is at a disadvantage when competing with children from the middle classes" (Warner, 1953, p. 177).

The key phrase here is that teachers' judgments of pupils are "inevitably based on their own personal standards," meaning, in the context of the paragraph, on their own *social class* standards. Thus, the tenet states that teachers guide their classroom behavior according to the general cultural values of the social stratum in which they were raised. This is a critical assumption, for it could very well be that, even though a teacher had thoroughly internalized the value orientations of his social class, his performance in the role of teacher is governed by frames of reference and value orientations other than those of his social class, such as those provided by his specialized occupational training, by the core values of society, or by requirements of the social organization of the learning process. Dahlke (1958) poses the latter alternative forcefully:

A current interpretation of the public school is that it merely reflects and upholds middle-class values. The norms apparently support this idea, but continuity of school and middle-class norms is incidental. Many of the norms and even value emphases occur not because of middle-class influence but because the school is a group. Emphasis on work, punctuality, getting the job done, control of aggression, avoidance of conflict, and being relatively quiet are necessary conditions if any group is to persist (Dahlke, 1958, p. 253).

Nevertheless, the assumption that the performance of teachers in the classroom is governed by their middle-class values is central to the line of argument. Davis and Dollard (1940, Ch. 13) used this reasoning in the most thoroughly detailed analysis of the operation of social class standards in the teaching-learning process available to us. In accord with the learning theory developing in the Yale Institute of Human Relations at the time (Miller & Dollard, 1941), Davis and Dollard proposed that behavioral responses of human beings are reinforced when accompanied by reward, especially the social rewards of privilege and approval, or when they reduce anxiety produced by the threat of punishment or of social disapproval. To understand the classroom situation, it is necessary to consider the teacher's distribution of social rewards and punishments and to examine the behavioral responses of pupils with which they are associated. Davis and Dollard argued that, initially at least, the teacher distributes rewards on the basis of the child's social class membership, not on the basis of his classroom performance.

[Children of middle- or upper-class membership] begin to receive favors and status privileges . . . as soon as they enter school. They must work, as their parents and teachers demand, but they are also immediately rewarded. Their anxiety is thus reduced, and they are reinforced in repeating those actions which have pleased the teacher. Before long, the person of the teacher, her smile or praise, become subgoal responses in themselves. The average lower-class child, however, who on status grounds is systematically punished by his teacher, becomes a sullen, hostile child. Anger, overt or repressed, is a barrier to effective learning. . . .
He sees the upper-class and upper-middle-class children being accorded preference, not only in classroom recitations but also in school entertainments and in intimate friendship relations with the teacher. He finds that he is not granted these privileges; instead, he is stigmatized by teachers and their favored students on grounds of the "ignorance" of his parents, the dialect which he speaks, the appearance of his clothes, and, very likely, the darkness of his skin. It does not take him long to discover that something is wrong and that the teacher's "pets" of high status are the only ones who can make the prestige goal responses. If there is no reward for learning, in terms of privilege and anxiety-reduction, there is no motive for work (Davis & Dollard, 1940, pp. 281–285).

The lower-class child is "systematically punished" for what he *is* and not for what he *does*. It is thereby impossible for him to learn which behavioral responses are instrumental in obtaining reward or in avoiding punishment. The case of the child of higher social class position is different. Initially, he is favored for what he is, but he is also "reinforced in repeating those *actions* which have pleased the teacher." This means that the teacher differentially rewards the behavioral responses of the middle-class child but not those of the lower-class child. This phase of the Davis and Dollard argument is rather awkward, for it leaves unexplained why in the one case reward and punishment remain attached to the class membership of the child and in the other case they are transferred to the behavioral responses of the child. But whether it is the child's social position as such or whether it is the propriety (by middle-class standards) of his behavior which inclines the teacher's actions, the fact remains, Davis and Dollard would argue, that lower-class children monopolize the punishments, higher-class children the rewards.

Reward and punishment, according to the underlying learning theory (Miller & Dollard, 1941), have very different consequences for the pupil. In brief, the middle- and upper-class child learns how to succeed in school while the lower-class child learns how to escape punishment in school. There are, of course, many ways of escaping punishment besides becoming a success. And, as the quoted passage intimates, punishment induces anger and aggressive impulses which not only interfere with cognitive learning but also, when overtly expressed, are likely to bring further punishment. A "circular reinforcement" process is instituted in the interaction between teacher and pupil which over time stabilizes the teacher's inclinations to favor the higher-class child and to discriminate against the lower-class child. The social reinforcement which a favored child receives from his teacher has consequences for the child and also for the teacher. In the first place, the acts of the teacher in praising the pupil and granting him dominant relationships to his fellow students diminishes the pupil's anxiety and thus reinforces him in learning his lessons and in maintaining good "deportment." At the same time, the student's successful learning reinforces the teacher in continuing her acts of preference toward him. The teacher is herself a member of the class system. She is rewarded by the behavior of the good student, first, because his habits are evidence that she is a proficient teacher, and, second, because through the child she is able to gain the approval of his upper middle-class or upper-class parents (Davis & Dollard, 1940, pp. 281–282). The upshot of the analysis by Davis and Dollard is that the social class value orientations of the teacher enter the teaching-learning process in two ways: by governing the teacher's distribution of reward and punishment, and by determining what kinds of pupil behavior will be rewarding to the teacher.

A markedly different form of analysis was offered by Brookover (1953) in which he centered his concern less on how the teacher's values govern his classroom behavior than on what the teacher's values and social class position represent to the pupil.[9] In so doing, he proposed four ideal types of teacher which he called "upper-class," "established middle-class," "striving middle-class," and "unranked" teachers. These teacher types vary not only in the behavior patterns and beliefs they manifest but in such attributes as their sense of security in the stratification system, their capacity to appreciate, understand, and communicate with pupils of various social

[9] Getzels (1957) has approached the matter of value learning in much the same way as Brookover, emphasizing the process of the pupil's *identification* with the teacher.

class levels, and their ability to provide the skills and incentive for upward mobility. Depending upon the social class position of the pupils involved, each type of teacher differs both in the kind of behavioral model he provides the pupil and in the likelihood that he will serve as a model at all. The pupil's identification with a given type of teacher is a major determiner of the pupil's own orientation to the social class structure. While Brookover advanced a number of specific hypotheses on these themes, none of them have been tested to date.

Classroom studies of manifest social class values. What of the research evidence for the assumption that teachers govern their classroom behavior in accordance with the cultural orientations of their social class? Direct evidence on the issue is scanty, entailing, as it must, classroom observations of teacher-pupil interaction; we will shortly review the one study which bears precisely on the issue. Some circumstantial evidence is available in teachers' reports about their pupils and, as in studies of the Wickman type cited above, about the behavior of pupils which distresses them. We will first look at a few studies of teacher reports on pupils and pupil behavior, beginning with Becker's sociologically oriented investigation.

During interviews with 60 teachers in the Chicago public schools about the problems of teaching, Becker (1952b) found them spontaneously making evaluations in terms of the social class of the pupils they taught. (Becker presented no evidence regarding the incidence of these evaluations.) Problems with pupils centered in three areas, each varying in severity and kind with the pupils' social class. The first area was the problem of performing the task of teaching successfully. As Becker said, "The teacher considers that she has done her job adequately when she has brought about an observable change in the children's skills and knowledge which she can attribute to her own efforts . . ." (p. 453). In this respect, pupils in the "better neighborhoods"—i.e., of the upper middle class—furnished the teacher with the greatest reward, and those of the "slum" schools—i.e., the lower lower class—offered the least reward. "Ambivalent feelings are aroused by children of the middle group. While motivated to work hard in school they lack the proper out-of-school training . . ." (p. 455). The second area related to problems of discipline. "Slum" children were considered the most difficult to control, but those of the "better" neighborhoods were also hard to handle in some respects by virtue of their disinclination to submit to the authority of the teacher. The middle group was regarded as the least difficult to discipline.

Neither of the preceding two problem areas, however, directly implicates teachers' middle-class values. Indeed, they suggest that the occupational role of teacher induces standards of evaluation quite apart from the general cultural standards of the social stratum. The third area, on the other hand, directly involves social class standards—the problem of the moral acceptability of the students. Becker offers a variety of instances in which teachers were concerned with pupil transgressions against deeply felt moral standards, especially those of "health and cleanliness, sex and aggression, ambition and work, and the relations of age groups" (p. 461). The most severe instances involved children of the "slum" schools, but again children of the "better" neighborhoods often violated teachers' standards regarding smoking, drinking, and respect for their elders. "Children of the middle group present no problem at this level, being universally described as clean, well dressed, moderate in their behavior, and hard working" (p. 461).

Kaplan (1952) summarized annoying forms of pupil behavior as those which either violated the teachers' personal standards or challenged the teachers' authority in the classroom. He had asked elementary school teachers to write freely on "What problems or situations disturb or annoy you in your work and life as a teacher?" About one-half of the responses of teachers related to pupil behavior; others related to problems of school organization, professional status, and out-of-school obligations and pressures. From these free responses he prepared a 100-item check list and administered it to 250 experienced elementary school teachers in an Oregon summer school. Those pupil behaviors which two-thirds or more of the teachers agreed were "very disturbing" or "greatly annoying" referred to such matters contravening the teachers' sense of morality as stealing, lying, cheating, aggression, and destruction of property—items reminiscent of the Wickman list. Teachers also agreed on the annoying character of such matters as inattentiveness, indifference to school work, reluctance to work except under compulsion, nonconformity, and refusal to follow regulations, which Kaplan regarded as challenges to the teachers' roles as "leaders, disciplinarians, and instructors." A similar theme is found in Clark's (1951) report, but his conclusion—that teachers are more annoyed by behavior disruptive of classroom decorum than by behavior personally threatening to them—is not warranted by his data.

Teachers' ratings of the personal or social adjustment of particular pupils have been found to correlate with the social class position of the pupils in a number of studies. Objective measures of adjustment, however, often indicate that lower-class pupils are indeed less well adjusted. Hence, it is more parsimonious to attribute the correlation to veridical estimations by the teacher rather than to a "social class bias" on their part. A recent study (Glidewell, Gildea, Domke, & Kantor, 1959) demonstrated that teachers tend to see a lower incidence of adjustment problems among middle-class pupils than among either upper- or lower-class pupils, but the data they obtained simultaneously from parents led them to reject the "social class bias" explanation.

Thus, the ratings and reports of teachers about pupil behavior are not substantial evidence regarding the operation of social class values within the teaching-learning situation. More convincing would be investigations of the flow of classroom interaction, especially in terms of the privileges, favors, and attention accorded by the teacher to his pupils.

The study by Hoehn (1954) is the only systematic test made along this line to determine the extent of teachers' "unconscious discrimination against lower-class children." [10] Using a modification of the Anderson-Brewer schedule of dominative-integrative teacher behavior, he recorded the frequency and kinds of teacher contact with children high and low in social class position in 19 third-grade classrooms in central Illinois. The teachers were all middle class, Hoehn reports, but were heterogeneous with respect to age, experience, and marital status. He found no relationship between the frequency of teacher contacts, regardless of kind, and social class position of the child; children of low social class position were just as likely to receive the teacher's "attention" as those of high social class position. With respect to the *kind* of contact involved, however, some differentiations were noted. The proportion of "domination with conflict" contacts was greater for low social class children than for high social class children. The proportion of "integration with evidence of working together" contacts was greater for high than for low social class children, and the ratio of integrative to dominative contacts favored the higher class children.

Hoehn introduced a note of caution in interpreting these results: He had studied the relationship between teacher contact and the achievement level of the pupils, measured by the Progressive Achievement Test. He reported that the low achievers received a greater share of the teacher contacts but also a greater proportion of the "less favorable" kinds of contact (dominative and conflictful) than the high achievers. The question was

raised by Hoehn as to whether the teachers' discrimination against the lower-class children is not simply a reflection of their discrimination against low achievers, since the two are highly correlated. If we take the Davis and Dollard analysis seriously, though, we would expect to find a relationship between teacher discrimination by social class and discrimination by pupil achievement. Discrimination by social class leads to differential learning success which, in turn, stabilizes the teacher's social class discriminations (Davis & Dollard, 1940).

A more important qualification is found in Hoehn's remark that the absolute magnitude of the differences in teacher behavior toward low- and high-class pupils was small. (His presentation of data does not show the amount of difference; it only shows the number of the 19 classrooms in which differentiation occurred in *some* degree and the direction of such discrimination.) Hoehn was considerably more impressed by the variation *among teachers* in the extent of their discriminatory behavior. On the basis of his inspection of the data, he noted that some teachers did not discriminate consistently between either group of pupils, other teachers consistently favored the high social class children, and in one of the classrooms the teacher consistently favored the low social class pupils with the greater proportion of integrative and the smaller proportion of conflict contacts. Recall that all of these teachers, nominally at least, were members of the middle class.

Hoehn's study ties in with a long line of research on the implications of teacher-pupil interaction for promoting a healthy learning environment for pupils. Some of these studies, like Hoehn's, find teachers directing their promotive acts principally at high achieving pupils and their disruptive acts at the low achievers. Recording interaction in four New York State classrooms by means of a Teacher Approval-Disapproval Scale, DeGroat and Thompson (1949) found that children who received many approval responses but few disapproval responses from

---

[10] Hoehn cited a dissertation by Clifton (1944) in which observations of the dominative-integrative behavior of teachers in second-grade classrooms were reported. The classrooms were located in three different socioeconomic areas. According to Hoehn, Clifton found little difference between the classrooms in the nature of teacher contacts with pupils, but there were somewhat fewer conflict contacts and somewhat more integrative contacts in the schools of the highest socioeconomic area.

the teacher were significantly higher in intelligence test scores and in achievement than were those who received few approval but many disapproval teacher responses.

Subsequently, Meyer and Thompson (1956) recorded a sex discrimination in teachers' interactions with pupils in three sixth-grade classrooms: boys received a substantially greater proportion of the (female) teachers' disapproval responses than girls. No strong sex difference appeared in the approval responses. The authors interpreted the sex discrimination in terms of an interplay between the middle-class values of teachers and the societal definition of the male and female roles, especially as it regards assertive behavior. Boys are expected to be more aggressive, they argue, and in fact they are more aggressive in the classroom than girls. But this aggressive behavior of boys is unacceptable to teachers on the grounds of their middle-class standards, and the teachers consequently direct more disapproval toward the boys. The authors fail to explain, however, why teachers do not share in the societal expectations of differences in the male and female roles.

The key assumption of Warner and his followers—that teachers' middle-class standards inevitably determine their classroom responses—stands virtually untested at the present time. Persuasive as the illustrative anecdotes of writers may be, provocative as the indirect evidence may be, one central question remains unanswered: Do teachers with value orientations of the lower or the upper class behave differently in the classroom than those professing middle-class values? Affirmative evidence respecting relationships between teachers' social class and their distributions of reward and punishment, or respecting the value premises underlying their classroom actions and communication, would be compelling. To generalize, we submit that the greatest fruit will be borne by research which pits the assumption that middle-class values determine teacher behavior against one or more competing assumptions concerning the source of

teachers' classroom standards. Such research would require specification of distinct points of discontinuity or conflict between middle-class values and professional values, or between middle-class orientations and orientations of the "core culture" of American society, or between middle-class standards and standards imposed by the requirements of social order in the classroom. Where conflict or discontinuity can be specified, observation in the classroom can be directed toward assessing the relative potency of the opposing forces acting on the teacher. Research can be set the task of delineating the conditions which predict which force will ultimately govern the teacher's performance in the teaching-learning situation. If, on the other hand, it is found impossible to specify points of discontinuity, serious doubt would be cast upon the conceptual stature of the social class argument.

Social class differences in pupil "success." The final link in the chain of reasoning concerning the teacher's position in the social class structure remains to be stated explicitly, although we have alluded to it throughout our discussion. Recall our three basic assumptions: (1) that persons raised in middle-class families hold values in their adulthood differing from those held by persons raised in lower-class families, (2) that teachers are drawn from the middle stratum of the American social class system and thereby hold those values characterizing the middle class, and (3) that teachers guide their classroom behavior according to the values of their social stratum. Given these three basic tenets, it is proper to conclude that pupils of the lower classes will experience frustration and failure and pupils of the higher classes will experience gratification and success in their educational experiences. The evidence supporting this conclusion is overwhelming.

To categorize youth according to the social class position of their parents is to order them on the extent of their participation and degree of "success" in the American educational system. This has been so consistently confirmed by research that it now can be regarded as an empirical law. [11] It appears to hold, regardless of whether the social class categorization is based upon the exhaustive procedures used in Elmtown (Hollingshead, 1949) or upon more casual indicators of socioeconomic status such as occupation or income level. It seems to hold in any educational institution, public or private, where there is some diversity in social class, including universities, colleges, and teacher-training institutions as well as elementary and secondary schools. Social class position predicts grades, achievement and intelligence test scores, retentions at grade level, course failures, truancy, suspensions from school, high school drop-outs, plans for college attendance, and total amount of formal schooling. It predicts academic honors and awards in the public school, elective school offices, extent of participation in extracurricular activities and in social affairs sponsored by the school, to say nothing of a variety of indicators of "success" in the informal structure of the student society. Where differences in prestige value exist in high school clubs and activities, in high school curricula, or in types of advanced training institutions, the social class composition of the membership will vary accordingly.

The predictions noted above are far from perfect. Inasmuch as social class position rarely accounts for more than half the variance of school "success," the law holds only for differences in group *averages,* not for differences in individual success. The relationship in some instances may be curvilinear rather than linear, but the data rarely have been assembled to test this possibility. Finally, there are a few cases in the literature in which the expected relationships have failed

to emerge. Nevertheless, positive findings appear with striking regularity.

The weight of evidence supporting the conclusion of the chain of argument does not, however, necessarily justify the assumptions from which the conclusion is drawn. To infer that it does is to commit the logical fallacy of affirming the consequent. Conditions other than the teacher's position in the social class structure may account equally well for the relationship between the pupil's social class position and his degree of success in the educational system. The complexity of the situation was well recognized by Warner and his associates. In discussing the correspondence between social class and high school dropouts, Warner drew this conclusion:

We believe this is a two-way relationship. On the one hand, the class culture of the child provides him with certain beliefs and values about the high school and what it has to offer. On the other [hand], the institutional values of the school, represented by the Board of Education, the professional administrators and teachers, as well as the students, develop differential attitudes toward persons in different positions in the social structure which act as attractive or repellent agents to keep the adolescent in, or to force him out of, school (Warner, et al., 1949, p. 206).

During the 1950's, research efforts moved strongly in the direction of explaining school success in terms of the motivational structure and cultural experiences provided by the pupil's family rather than in terms of the "bias" of the educational institution. Representative studies include those of Davie (1953), Douvan and Adelson (1958), Drews and Teahan (1957), Girard and Bastide (1955), Hieronymus (1951), Hyman (1953), Kahl (1953), and Toby (1957).

CONCLUSION: THE CONSEQUENCES OF OCCUPATIONAL SELECTIVITY

It is obvious that teachers are drawn selectively from various statuses in the American social structure. At the same time, assumptions have been made regarding what this

[11] We cannot undertake to document each of the following statements separately. The reader is referred to the bibliographies of Dixon (1953) and Gordon (1957b), to the various community studies in the social class tradition, especially Hollingshead on Elmtown (1949), and Warner, Havighurst, and Loeb's (1944) monograph on education, to the comprehensive selection of readings in Stanley, Smith, Benne, and Anderson (1956, Part 2), and to the competent summaries of Brookover (1955b, Ch 5) and Havighurst and Neugarten (1957, Chs. 10, 11).

selectivity means for the teaching-learning process; some of these assumptions have been naïve and some sophisticated. In either case, research which tests the veridicality of the assumptions is meager, and what findings there are suggest that the assumptions are gross oversimplifications of the processes involved. We submit that the absence of positive findings regarding the relationship between societal statuses and performance in the teaching-learning situation is attributable in large part to the fact that programs of research and theoretical development have not concentrated on this problem as such. The research we have had to draw upon has more often emerged as a by-product of other research movements, such as those aimed at specifying the qualities of the "good teacher," the conditions under which more and better teachers may be induced to enter the teaching occupation, the mental hygiene implications of the classroom behavior of teachers, or the relation of social stratification to societal stability and change. Conceptualizations developed for these other purposes may be highly provocative for the problem of the relationship between occupational selectivity and the teaching-learning process, yet they are not necessarily adequate for the task. Indeed, they are almost bound to be partial accounts of the relationship. If and when the relationship in question is itself taken as a problem for investigation, theoretical models will almost certainly arise which will be capable of accounting for the complexities of the interdependence between the teacher's statuses in society and his conduct in the classroom. Such theoretical models, however, will also have to come to terms with other environmental forces acting on the teacher, including those to which we now turn.

FORMATIVE INFLUENCE OF THE TEACHING OCCUPATION

In American society, the occupational status is a key one for adults. A person's entry into the social world about him is affected profoundly by the kind of job he holds or the work he does. His occupation has direct effects on his income, possessions, place of residence, associates, leisure, amount of expenditures, and, in general, the kind of privileges and disadvantages which make up his daily experiences. The importance of one's vocational status is shown by the fact that even nonprofit vocations, such as the ministry, supply the basis of classification for one's place in the community. Thus, it appears that occupation gives the most general basis of classification for men, so far as it pertains to their reciprocities in community life (Hiller, 1947, pp. 339–340).

A number of social theorists carry this further. Not only does one's occupational pursuit affect his participation in other segments of society, but the nature of the work itself is seen to leave a deep and lasting impression upon the very person of the worker. Thorstein Veblen was an outstanding proponent of this thesis.

His guiding principle, reiterated insistently in his various writings, may be stated as follows: In human life the great agencies of habituation and mental discipline are those inherent in the kind of work by which men live and particularly in the kind of technique which that work involves. Here, above all, must be sought the influences which shape men's thoughts, their relations with one another, their culture and institutions of control (MacIver, 1937, p. 453).

Sorokin (1947) put it in these words:

A durable occupational work molds the body, mind, and behavior of its members. . . . When the same occupational operations are performed from day to day for many years, they effectively modify the mental, moral, social, physiological, and anatomical properties of their members in accordance with the nature and requirements of the occupational work. Each occupation tends thus to remake its members in its own image. And the longer an individual stays in the same occupation the deeper is the transformation (Sorokin, 1947, p. 211).

To what extent do these contentions regarding the impact of occupation on the experiences of the worker hold for teachers? And if the vocational status does carry definitive consequences, what is their bearing upon the processes of teaching and learning in the classroom setting? These are the questions we take up in this section of the chapter, insofar as empirical research can carry us. We will investigate particularly (1) the prestige which accrues to a person by virtue of his teaching position, (2) the impact of induction into the teacher's role, (3) career patterns of the teacher, and (4) the teacher stereotype.

The Occupational Category of Teaching

Before moving into these matters, let us consider an issue of some moment for the following discussion: the extent to which teaching is a part-time occupation. In either a cross-cultural or historical comparison, the teaching occupation in the United States today clearly constitutes a bona fide niche in the division of societal labor. Mead (1942) noted that preliterate societies infrequently separate the teacher's role from that of all other adults who induct the young into the cultural standards of the group. "Furthermore, when we do find explicit and defined teaching, in primitive societies we find it tied in with a sense of the rareness or the precariousness of some human tradition" (Mead, 1942, p. 219). At another point (1943), she suggested that "teacher," as we conceive of the term, is a misnomer for the role of those who instruct in preliterate societies. The initiative for instruction comes from the one who would learn, not from the one who would "teach." The "teacher" is passive if not reluctant in initiating the relationship and must be induced to enter the relationship by suitable and attractive exchanges. Even in sacred matters of the society, where the initiative for instruction may rest with the elders, only the young of that society are sought for instruction; the "teachers" are entirely indifferent to those beyond the bounds of the tribe.

The point at which the teacher's role, in the active sense in which we understand it, becomes differentiated is when members of a group develop the conception that their set of cultural beliefs is superior to another, according to Mead. When a group asserts, for example, the infallible superiority of its own religious system, instruction becomes a matter of concern to those who teach rather than to those who learn.

In a different vein, Batten (1953) observed that the teacher's function in preliterate society is very different from his function in industrial society, where he not only transmits the culture to each new generation but encourages development, change, and progress. "Progress" is a concept which has no counterpart in the isolated, traditional societies. [12] Znaniecki (1951), writing from a historical point of view, saw the teaching occupation as having evolved from the apprenticeship relation, used for training the young in the specialized occupational skills of the society, and, Znaniecki noted, still widely used today.

But gradually, as we know, the education of candidates for certain specialized roles considered valuable for society as a whole began to be carried on cooperatively in organized

---

[12] Interestingly enough, according to anthropological accounts, some educative processes in preliterate societies are not profoundly different from those of industrial societies. Hart (1955) observed that the initiation rites of puberty, where youth are instructed in the sacred traditions of their group, in some tribes entail the removal of youth from their homes and familiar surroundings for lengthy periods of time to the custody of adults who are virtually strangers to them. The child is "exposed to a series of social situations in which friendship counts for naught, crying or whining gets one no place, whimsy or charm of boyish attractiveness pays no dividends, and friends, pull, and influence are without effect" (Hart, 1955, pp. 141–142), situations not unfamiliar in our own public education system. As Hart points out, specialized training schools are not unknown in primitive society, viz., the wood-carving schools of Polynesia and the African "bush schools" for training in metal-working. These involve the same universalistic attributes and emphases on achievement that are associated with the American public schools—unfamiliar and nonintimate teachers, standardized curricula, and examinations for promotion (Watkins, 1943).

schools by groups of educators recognized as authorities in their respective fields, and eventually such education became standardized by professional associations. This is the most significant trend in the evolution of education. It started with the education of priests in schools controlled by associations of priests, extended first to medicine and law, later with increasing rapidity to every branch of science, natural and cultural, to all kinds of engineering—military, civil, industrial, agricultural—to art and music, military strategy and tactics, higher bureaucratic functions, banking and commerce, social work, diplomacy, journalism, industrial management, "personnel management," "home economics," advertising, propaganda. . . .

Among the social roles which have become professionalized as a consequence of this new trend are the roles of *educators* whose function is to prepare children and adolescents not for special occupations, but for active participation in society at large (Znaniecki, 1951, p. 77).

During the American colonial period and the early years of the Republic, teaching had not emerged as a full-time calling (Elsbree, 1939, Chs. 5, 18). The short duration of the school term, often less than one-half the year even at the time of the Civil War, made it impossible for a person to occupy himself throughout the year exclusively as a teacher. With the gradual extension of the school year, it has become more possible to devote oneself fully to teaching, but a report for 1956 showed that over one-half of the nation's male teachers were employed in work outside the school, either during the summer months or after school hours during the academic year (National Education Association, 1957). Less than one in ten of the female teachers, however, held outside work. Detailed investigations, local and national in scope, indicate that the occupational status of teaching still does not claim the full-time efforts of all its practitioners (Moore & Burke, 1960).

In another sense, too, teaching is less than a full-time calling. Many persons spend only a small part of their productive lives in teaching, leaving the occupation for other forms of gainful employment or, in the case of females, in favor of domestic life. Little direct evidence is available, though, on the occupational "longevity" of teachers. Two recent surveys of teachers' *intentions* of continuing to teach until retirement gave widely divergent figures, even allowing for differences in populations sampled and questions asked (Mason, Dressel, & Bain, 1958; National Education Association, 1957). The more "optimistic" of the two surveys showed about 57 per cent of the nation's teachers intending to commit the remainder of their productive lives to teaching. Estimates of changes through time in the occupational "longevity" of teachers are equally difficult to make, based as they usually are on data from cross-sectional surveys of teacher composition.

It is clear from these studies, however, that at any point in time American schools have had to rely upon relatively inexperienced personnel. Elsbree presented data for Pennsylvania teachers in 1865 showing that well over one-quarter of them were in their first year of teaching (1939, p. 294). By 1931 the least experienced quarter of the nation's teachers had somewhat greater experience: the first quartiles of "years of experience" were roughly 3, $5\frac{1}{2}$, and $4\frac{1}{2}$ years for rural elementary, urban elementary, and secondary school teachers, respectively (Evenden, Gamble, & Blue, 1933, Table 8). More recent figures indicate that one-quarter of the teachers across America have been teaching for four years or less (National Education Association, 1957).

Little reliance can be placed on figures of the sort reported here to reveal the extent to which teaching may constitute a lifetime career, reflecting as they must such incidental factors as expansions and contractions in the demand for new teachers from one time to another. On logical grounds, however, it would seem that teaching today is considerably more conducive to a lifetime commitment than it was even 20 years ago. Extension of training requirements for teacher certification results in a heavier time and money investment in the occupation by prospective teachers and simultaneously reduces opportunities of preparing for alternative occupations. With the barriers against married women abandoned, women have the option of combining marriage and teaching.

Our consideration of the extent to which the occupational lives of teachers are, in fact, encompassed by teaching has import for some of the matters to which we now turn. If a person shares his status as teacher with other occupational statuses or if he is in this occupational status for a brief period only and, perhaps, never fully committed to it, the consequences which are presumed to ensue from teaching, especially those which are said to have an enduring effect on his personal attributes, may have neither a clear field nor sufficient time to exert their formative force.

THE PRESTIGE OF TEACHING[13]

Teaching, like any occupational status, supplies one important basis upon which extrinsic valuation of a person is made. Because of its importance in this respect, occupation is a key status in our society. This valuation —the amount of honor, deference, or prestige —accorded an occupation is derived from the culture at large and, in general, applies to the incumbent regardless of his competence

---

[13] With reluctance we have substituted the term *prestige* for the more common term *social status* in this section to refer to the rank of an individual or an occupational group in the stratification system of society. We have already used the term *status* in another sense to refer to a societally defined position around which rights and obligations of the position-holder are organized, and used in this sense it carries no implication of placement within a hierarchy. The educational literature reveals a third common use of the term *status*, in this case as a synonym for *current state*. Thus, studies of the *social status* or *general status* of teachers refer to descriptions of a variety of attributes—age, sex, salary, experience, and so on—as they exist at the present time. Because of the different usages of the term, we have sought consistency in terminology in this review even at the expense of some awkwardness, such as the present example, where we have departed from the more customary usage.

or capacity to perform the work. Sociologists' measures of social class, while admitting other bases of valuation, rely heavily on occupation to place the individual.

Warner's Index of Status Characteristics, a short procedure he devised as an alternative to the time-consuming, exhaustive system of social class ranking used in his community studies, weights occupation above any of the other three items which form the index. If a teacher derives his income principally from his salary, it is impossible, in Warner's index, for him to be ranked above the middle class and virtually impossible (unless he lives in a slum) to be ranked in the lower class (Warner, Meeker, & Eells, 1949). Other indexes of "socio-economic status," similarly, depend upon occupation in conjunction with educational attainment and/or income level to place persons in the prestige or class system.

By virtue of the assumptions on which such indexes are constructed, teachers can hardly fall elsewhere than in the middle ranges of the system. One consequence of the close dependency of general social standing upon occupation represented in the sociological indexes is that the indexes of social class cannot be used to compare the prestige of teaching from one time to another or one place to another. Evidence regarding the prestige attached to teaching must be sought elsewhere.

Bases for Prestige Estimates

Investigators have drawn inferences regarding the prestige of teaching from a variety of sources. One of the more popular sources is the comparison of income levels among occupational groups. On this basis, teacher salaries are shown to be at about the level of *all* persons working for wages and salaries in the United States—roughly comparable with the earnings of employees in manufacturing establishments but substantially below the income of fee-taking professionals, such as physicians, lawyers, and dentists (Lieberman, 1956, Ch. 12; Ruml & Tickton, 1955). Comparisons of income level, however, are unusually difficult to make. Fee-taking professionals, in contrast to teachers, must provide their own quarters, equipment, and assistants, and their professional preparation normally is more expensive; on the other hand, the tax structure tends to favor them. Married female teachers, who constitute a large proportion of the teaching population, often supplement the family income rather than provide full support, in contrast to male factory workers. As an index of prestige, salary level is not entirely satisfactory. It is in part the *discrepancy* between salaries realized by teachers and some other cultural valuation of what teachers "ought" to have because of the work they do which leads observers to decry the plight of the teacher. Income level may be closely correlated with social standing in the United States, but it is not perfectly correlated with social standing, as the cases of artist, minister, bartender, and school teacher attest. Other bases of valuation obviously exist.

Another basis for inferring the prestige rank of teaching is the social standing of those who enter it. Is teaching for the "successful" or the "unsuccessful" members of society? Is it populated by the intellectuals and scholars of society, by members of the working class, by persons of agrarian derivation, by the civil servant class, or members of the business community? "The social status of any profession," Richey wrote, "can usually be determined to some extent by the type of people who seek to enter it" (Richey, 1953, p. 224). Our discussion of the social class origins of teachers in the previous section, of course, bears on this issue. The occupations of American teachers' fathers cover a broad range—farmers, skilled workers, clerks, business and professional men—but they are concentrated roughly in the middle class. Extremes of the social and economic scale contribute relatively few individuals to teaching.

The occupations in which teachers engage when not teaching provide another clue to their rank. Male teachers who reported earning money during the summer months of 1955 occupied themselves as follows (National Education Association, 1957, p. 22):

Professional and semi-professional worker	31%
Skilled or semi-skilled worker	27
Unskilled worker	15
Clerical or sales worker	13
Farmer	7
Managerial or self-employed	7
Total	100%

Again the occupations cover a relatively broad spectrum, giving only a rough indication of the rank of teaching in the prestige system.

Faced with a paucity of data in the historical records, Elsbree devised several ingenious devices for estimating the deference accorded the colonial schoolmaster, including, in addition to wealth, the assignment of pews in the congregational meetinghouses, the use of titles in addressing the teacher, and the order of listing on the rosters of classes at Harvard and Yale (arranged not alphabetically but in order of the social rank of the students' fathers) (Elsbree, 1939, Ch. 10). Although the evidence he produced was equivocal, suggesting that the teachers' esteem may have varied more with personal qualities than with occupational status, his approach had a forthrightness which could well be emulated by scholars working with contemporary data. Gummere (1960), also using historical records, described the prestige of eighteenth-century school teachers of the Middle Atlantic region in this way: "The majority had come into Philadelphia or Baltimore from England as indentured servants to be sold to the highest bidder. Significantly, a school teacher did not bring as high a price as a shoemaker, a cooper, a mason, a carpenter, or a barber" (Gummere, 1960, p. 117).

Ratings of Occupational Prestige

The most direct approach to the question of the prestige associated with teaching has entailed asking a number of people to rank occupations according to their general social standing. Spawned by educators, this line of research has been extended significantly by sociologists. In the first of such studies, Counts (1925) collected ratings of 45 occupations, including college professor, school superintendent, high school teacher, elementary school teacher, and rural school teacher, from various groups of high school students, college students, and teachers. Each of the teaching occupations appeared above the midpoint (locomotive engineer) of the final ranking, but they were notably separated from one another, showing, at least for 1925, that "teaching" could not be considered a unitary occupational category. High school teaching ranked tenth, elementary thirteenth, and rural elementary nineteenth in Counts' list of 45 occupations. The Counts' study demonstrated in incipient form what has subsequently emerged as one of the most remarkable findings from this line of research: the high order of agreement in rankings among diverse kinds of judges. Counts found correlation coefficients of above .90 among his groups of judges, even though they varied in social background and in the section of the country in which they lived.

Hartmann (1934) found no tendency for adult judges to distort their rankings by raising the level at which they rated their own occupations, although later studies have challenged this (Coutu, 1936; National Opinion Research Center, 1953). Many studies have demonstrated the marked stability of the rank-ordering of occupations through time. Deeg and Paterson (1947), for example, replicated Counts's study in 1947 with 25 occupations from the original list and found virtually no changes; Richey, Fox, and Fauset (1951) found close similarity between Hartmann's order in 1934 and their own.

Two studies dealing exclusively with female occupations contain no surprises. Teachers were roughly on the same level as nurses and social workers but well below physicians and lawyers (Baudler & Paterson, 1948; Menger, 1932). Perhaps the most remarkable finding of all is the high agreement in occupational prestige across national boundaries. Inkeles and Rossi (1956) compiled results of ranking studies from the United States, Germany, Great Britain, Japan, New Zealand, and the Union of Soviet Socialist Republics, which showed, in 12 of the 15 pairings of nations, correlation coefficients of .90 or higher. The position of teacher was virtually standard across the six nations, ranking slightly below such occupations as certified public accountant and army officer, slightly above farm owners and operators, and well above skilled craftsmen.

The many studies of occupational prestige in the United States, well summarized by Davies (1952), have been small in scope in comparison with the study carried out by the National Opinion Research Center in 1947. The NORC interviewing staff reached a representative sample of the entire adult population of the United States, nearly 3,000 people in all, to ask for their ratings of 90 occupations (National Opinion Research Center, 1953). Highly consistent rankings were derived from this procedure. The composite scores ranged from a low of 33 (shoe shiner) to a high of 96 (U.S. Supreme Court Justice). The public school teacher was thirty-fifth from the top with a composite score of 79, just below the economist and building contractor, just above the railroad engineer and the county agricultural agent. Two different titles were given to the same occupation in a few instances as a methodological check. Thus, "instructor in the public schools" and "public school teacher" were both presented the respondents at different points in the interview, and the resulting ranks were identical. Substantial agreement was found among people regardless of their section of the country, the size of their community, their occupation, sex, age, and so on, although a number of disparities also were noted. For example, those 40 years of age and over tended to rate the educational occupations (college professor, public school teacher, and playground director) higher than did the younger respondents.

The occupational ranking studies locate the teacher more precisely in the prestige hierarchy than do the estimations based upon salary comparisons or upon teacher origins, but two important reservations must be noted. Several students have questioned whether prestige of occupations can be ordered on a single dimension in a given society or whether several overlapping hierarchies are involved (Caplow, 1954, Ch. 2; Hatt, 1950). The question is still an open one. Another reservation has to do with the ranking of "teacher," as though this were one unitary occupational category. In those studies, beginning with Counts (1925), in which the high school teacher is listed separately from the elementary school teacher, the prestige of the latter invariably is the lower (W. F. Anderson, 1954). It is unfortunate, but understandable, that distinctions between different kinds of teaching have not been maintained in the occupational lists of the major studies. In their historical and comparative sketch of teacher prestige, Hall, Hans, and Lauwerys (1953, Ch. 1) were obliged to discuss elementary and high school teachers as two entirely separate occupational categories. "Nor could anyone have foreseen that the time would come when primary school teachers, secondary school masters, and academic teachers would all be thought of as belonging to the same profession: for this is a modern idea" (p. 5). It may well be that the prestige gap between elementary and secondary school teachers is closing, but unless the occupational distinction is maintained in the investigations we may never know for certain.[14]

[14] It is beyond the scope of this review to treat the cross-cultural and cross-national reports on teacher prestige in detail. The interested reader is advised to consult the observations of Henry (1960), Mead (1951), and the analyses contained in the introduction to the *Yearbook of Education 1953* (Hall, Hans, & Lauwerys, 1953). In this same volume, an especially

Consequences of the Prestige of Teaching

The crucial question in our discussion of the prestige accorded teachers in American society has to do with the consequences it holds for the teaching-learning process. The educators who have studied and written on the prestige of teaching rarely take this question as a central one. Their prime interest, rather, is to illuminate the processes of occupational selectivity and, in the long run, to discover ways of recruiting or holding in teaching more "able" persons. The prestige accorded teaching, so the argument runs, determines the kind of person attracted to the occupation. Where the prestige and rewards of teaching are low, only those unable to compete for great success in the society will find teaching attractive, but where the prestige is high, the services of many kinds of persons will be offered and the most competent can be chosen. Not only does occupational prestige determine the kind of person attracted to the occupation, but the kind of person seeking to enter the occupation determines, in its turn, the level of occupational prestige. To the extent that both of these arguments are true, they imply a stable equilibrium, unable to change without the intervention of external forces. Neither theoretical analysis nor empirical research has developed in education at this level, nor have propositions specifying the "kinds" of person attracted under conditions of high and low prestige been made in detail sufficient to suggest empirical tests. It is hoped that future research will do this.

The prestige of teaching may operate not only as a selective force—by attracting certain people and "driving out" other people—but as a force affecting directly the performance of incumbents. Again, this has not been explored systematically. Casual observations of the following sort have appeared in the educational literature: (1) The incumbent's

sensitive analysis of the sources of prestige accorded the teacher in tribal communities is presented by Batten (1953).

motivation for fulfilling the functions of teacher in the classroom and school is depressed by low prestige; (2) Independence of thought and freedom of action in the teaching situation is lower for those without esteem; (3) Where prestige of teaching is low, the teacher lacks the influence or authority which, presumably, is essential to the success of the teaching-learning process; (4) Persons realizing low prestige and reward from their occupation divert their energies and interests away from fulfillment of their occupational functions toward, for example, activities designed to enhance their economic subsistence. These observations rarely appear in the form of researchable propositions and at the present time remain untested.

Grambs (1949) offered a speculative, sociological analysis in which she proposed that the low esteem of teaching leads to personal problems of adjustment in much the same way that membership in minority groups in our society does. It interferes with the teacher's ability to cope with the normal frustrations he encounters in his personal and work situations. Like the Negro or Jew, the teacher is inclined to reject his membership group—to disidentify himself with his occupation—a matter made more difficult, Grambs observed, by the "conspicuousness" of his status. The teacher is likely to belittle the accomplishments of education and to take a cynical attitude toward his work, the school system, and educational ideas and ideals. Grambs suggested that teachers are extremely sensitive to public appraisal of themselves and their occupation.

While Grambs's conclusions are extreme, a recent study of 40 teachers in two high schools brings some data to bear on several of her central points (Rettig & Pasamanick, 1959). The investigators reported that, indeed, the teachers were more concerned with their standing in the general public than members of four other professional groups simultaneously studied—psychiatrists, psychologists, social workers, and nurses. They also showed that the teachers accorded a lower standing to their own occupation than

did a group of 110 laymen; in Grambs's terms, the teachers were self-disparaging. Moreover, when asked what standing they *thought* laymen accorded them, the teachers seriously underestimated it. The investigators extended Grambs's analysis in an interesting way by showing that the standing they felt they *ought* to be accorded as an occupational group was markedly higher than that aspired to by the other professionals. The unrealistically high prestige aspirations of the teachers are unfortunate for them, the investigators asserted, since they tie in with job satisfaction. Rettig and Pasamanick demonstrated that the greater the discrepancy between the standing which the teacher thinks is accorded him and that which he feels ought to be accorded him, the lower his job satisfaction. Analyzing such consequences for job satisfaction, however, is as close as the investigators come to examining the effects of occupational prestige upon the teacher's performance in the classroom, and the implications are indirect at best. In short, no definitive knowledge exists regarding the impact of teaching's prestige on the teaching-learning process.

INDUCTION INTO THE TEACHING OCCUPATION

All teachers in this day and age must go through a training period before receiving a license from the state permitting them to teach. This period is no longer a casual, informal experience. Over the last 100 years and even the last 10 or 20 years, more and more stringent requirements have been imposed on teachers-to-be, and the induction process has become a deliberate, formal, and highly rationalized procedure. Havighurst and Neugarten (1957) summarize the present situation in these terms:

Compared with other occupations (although not with other professions) teaching involves a relatively long period of preparation. Four years of college culminating in a bachelor's degree is increasingly becoming the minimum requirement for teachers. Preparation is followed at once by full membership in the profession. A teacher takes on full status with his first regular teaching assignment, and, while informally he may be regarded as a novice for a few years by his older and more experienced colleagues, there is no formal period of apprenticeship once the first job placement is made, nor a period when participation and responsibility are only partial (Havighurst & Neugarten, 1957, p. 433).

A vast number of surveys of pre-service programs, in-service programs, and other procedures for teacher preparation and induction have appeared in the educational literature through the years to add infinite detail to the above summary. The topics covered in these surveys have been nearly as diverse as the practices themselves, and we will make no effort to review them here.

The effects assumed to flow from such programs and practices, to the extent that they are articulated at all, almost universally have to do with the enhancement of the teacher's cognitive competence and skill in classroom performance. The questions which arise in this realm relate to the value of particular programs and practices—fifth-year programs, provisions for student teaching, schemes for orienting new teachers to the school, courses and course patterns, and so on—and studies designed to evaluate particular programs are not uncommon. The ubiquitous investigations of teacher effectiveness, too, frequently search for relationships between effectiveness measures and length and kind of teacher training, years of teaching experience, success in student teaching, and similar variables relating to the induction process. The notable feature of all these studies, however, is the absence of definitive results and fruitfully cumulative findings. This is partly due, we believe, to the fact that educational researchers have been concerned with aspects of the induction process which are institutionally and programatically important but theoretically barren. Examination of the various issues of the *Review of Educational Research* on "Teacher Personnel," for example, reveals that research is normally formulated around such problems as "in-service training," "fifth-year programs," "student teaching," and "teacher orientation plans." These are not simply convenient categories for summarizing the research; they are the guiding concepts in the formulation of the research studies. Such distinctions, however, are purely on the phenotypical level, to use Kurt Lewin's term (Lewin, 1935, Ch. 1). They deal with superficial differences among phenomena and thereby disguise the fundamental, or genotypical, similarities and differences among the programs and practices. The educational researchers' reliance upon gross, programatically defined concepts rather than upon penetrating concepts from the behavioral sciences which could tie diverse realms of phenomena together in an analytical system is what the critics mean when they charge that educational research is atheoretical.

In any event, it is another consequence of the induction process which interests us here —the kind that ensues from the teacher's participation in the system of social relationships which comprise the training institutions and programs. These relationships shape the teacher's role conceptions and his attitudes and values concerning himself, his colleagues, his clients, and the teaching-learning process. Unfortunately, research conducted on the teacher induction process from the framework of role learning is still in its incipient stages. Our knowledge about the process comes from studies conducted in professional schools for lawyers, nurses, physicians, and the like (Becker & Carper, 1956; Becker & Geer, 1958; Lortie, 1959; Merton, Reader, & Kendall, 1957). As a result, our discussion of this topic will be brief.

Adult Socialization and Attitude Change

When teacher training is conceived as a period of role learning, one can see that it is not unlike the period of socialization of the young child. Indeed, some of the same psychological and social mechanisms undoubtedly are operative, such as identification, internalization of expectations, reformulation of the self concept, and so on.

. . . the technical term socialization designates the processes by which people selectively acquire the values and attitudes, the interests, skills, and knowledge—in short, the culture—current in the groups of which they are, or seek to become, a member. It refers to the learning of social roles. In its application to the medical student, socialization refers to the processes through which he develops his professional self, with its characteristic values, attitudes, knowledge, and skills, fusing these into a more or less consistent set of dispositions which govern his behavior in a wide variety of professional (and extraprofessional) situations. Socialization takes place primarily through social interaction with people who are significant for the individual—in the medical school, probably with faculty members above most others, but importantly also with fellow-students, with the complement of associated personnel (nurses, technicians, caseworkers, etc.), and with patients. Since the patterns of social interaction of medical students with these others are only similar and not identical, the variations result in different kinds of medical men emerging from what may at first seem to be the "same" social environment of the medical school (Merton, Reader, & Kendall, 1957, p. 287).

From the perspective of adult socialization and role learning, the significant aspects of teacher-training programs lie not so much in the formal programs and practices as in the ideology and value systems to which the trainee is exposed, in the student's informal relations with his peers, and in those aspects of his institutional experience which usually are regarded as incidental to his training.

For as with all educational institutions, it is natural for those far removed from the details of life and work in the medical school to assume that the great bulk, and the most significant part, of what the student carries away with him is learned through formal instruction —an assumption which many members of medical faculties reject as remote from the actual facts of the case. It is clear that not all

which is taught in medical school is actually learned by students and that not all which is learned is taught there, if by teaching is meant didactic forms of instruction. Students learn not only from precept, or even from deliberate example; they also learn—and it may often be, most enduringly learn—from sustained involvement in that society of medical staff, fellow-students, and patients which makes up the medical school as a social organization (Merton, Reader, & Kendall, 1957, pp. 41–42).

Teacher-training institutions have not been studied from this perspective yet, but the recent development of social psychological research on higher education (Sanford, 1962) makes such an institutional analysis imminent. Spindler (1955), whose work we reviewed earlier, called attention to the value orientation of teachers colleges and the stress created when the "traditionally" reared trainees came face to face with the "emergent values" of the college. Pace and Stern devised a means for measuring the environmental *press* exerted by colleges on their students (Pace & Stern, 1958), have applied it systematically to a wide variety of American colleges and universities (Pace, 1960), and have sought to relate differences in press to needs of students (Stern, 1960). In recent years, peer group relations among college students have captured research attention (Newcomb, 1961), as well as those among high school students (Coleman, 1961; Gordon, 1957a).

As to the effects of the training program, a few longitudinal studies of student attitudes conducted during the 1950's departed from the predominant concern with the acquisition of knowledge and skills. Callis (1950) used an early version of the Minnesota Teacher Attitude Inventory (MTAI) to demonstrate a significant increase in favorable-toward-children, permissive, and supportive attitudes among University of Minnesota students during their junior year in the College of Education, but he found no change over a six-month period among seniors exposed in the interim to the student teaching experience. He also noted a significant downward trend in attitude scores among graduates after six months of teaching. Since other evidence showed scores on the Inventory to be negatively correlated with length of teaching experience, Cook and his co-workers sought to eliminate this relationship in the final form of the MTAI but with equivocal success (W.W. Cook & Hoyt, 1952; W. W. Cook, Hoyt, & Eikaas, 1956).

Subsequently, Day (1959) demonstrated that MTAI scores of Florida State University seniors were lower immediately after the student teaching experience. There was a dramatic drop among graduating seniors after one year of teaching experience. The scores of graduates who did not enter teaching showed no significant change. The decline in attitude scores was confirmed, in this case after three years of teaching experience, by another pair of investigators (Rabinowitz & Rosenbaum, 1960) among graduates of the four New York City municipal colleges. Exploring their data further, they discovered that the most severe decline in MTAI scores occurred among graduates whose teaching experience was in the schools of New York City as opposed to those who took jobs outside the city. But, at least for those within New York City, the magnitude of decline was not related to the "difficulty" of the teacher's assignment as measured by three indicators of the quality of students in the school. Item-by-item inspection of the Inventory responses suggested that the greatest decrease came in items relating to classroom discipline and academic standards.

Taken at face value, the changes in response indicate that in the three years between testings the teachers became less concerned with pupil freedom and more concerned with establishing a stable, orderly classroom, in which academic standards received a prominent position. The change was accompanied by a decline in the tendency to attribute pupil misbehavior or academic difficulty to the teacher or the school. . . . Items that seem to reflect cynicism, hostility, or punitiveness showed little change; the generally accepting view the student teachers expressed toward pupils

seemed stable (Rabinowitz & Rosenbaum, 1960, pp. 317, 319).

The investigators also found the teachers at the end of three years making fewer extreme endorsements of the items, a tendency which would reduce the total score when the customary scoring key for the Inventory is employed.

Both Eson (1956) and Sandgren and Schmidt (1956) reported "improvement" in MTAI scores. Improvement was associated in the first case with an educational psychology course, and in the second case with student teaching. Eson, however, was skeptical of the changes in MTAI scores he found, noting that they were of the same magnitude the test authors had found for subjects instructed to "fake good." He believed his subjects simply learned to recognize the "right" responses during the course. (Learning to associate the appropriate feeling tone with the occupational jargon, of course, is one part of role learning, but it is not attitude change.)

But even if attitude "improvement" of this sort did occur, would it have any bearing upon the student's performance as a teacher in the classroom? Evidence is sketchy on this point but generally suggests that a person's attitude has some bearing upon his style of teaching. Oliver (1953) found no relationship between elementary school teachers' professed acceptance of certain "principles" of teaching and the practices they were observed to use in the classroom. On the other hand, McGee (1955) employed the F Scale developed by Adorno, Frenkel-Brunswik, Levinson, and Sanford (1950). He noted a correlation of .58 between authoritarian trends in teachers' personalities, as assessed by the F Scale, and observations of authoritarianism in their classroom teaching. Ryans (1960), too, reported a number of modest relationships between teachers' attitudes toward pupils and administrators, as well as their educational viewpoints, and observations of their style of classroom behavior. Willard (1955) found several relationships between teachers' values and the absence or presence of 20 learning experiences they provided in their elementary classrooms. Those teachers who "positively" valued new experience, security, workmanship, personal freedom, helpfulness, and the like, as measured by their choices among alternative courses of action in written and photographic depictions of classroom episodes, provided substantially more of the 20 learning experiences than teachers who "negatively" valued one or more of the behaviors in children. None of the teachers who "negatively" valued new experience offered pupils first-hand learning experiences or used community resources as standard parts of their classroom instructional practices. Unfortunately, the Willard report displays few methodological details and no significance tests.

The kind of effects of the induction process which have been examined are still limited, as the studies cited above testify. One would hope that the scope of research would be broadened to include the effects of training experience on the student's clarification of his aspirations and occupational goals, on the redefinition of his self concept to incorporate the new occupational status he is acquiring (Chansky, 1959), on his investment in or motivation to fulfill the teacher's role (Levin, Hilton, & Leiderman, 1957), on his processes of interpersonal perception (Ojemann, Levitt, Lyle, & Whiteside, 1955; Perkins, 1958), on his modes of relating to other persons, and on the development and articulation of his general perspective on his world.

The Transition from Student to Teacher

At what point in the induction process do the crucial role learnings occur? Is it during the early years of academic training, or during the student teaching experience, or is it not until the first job? For some, of course, it may be a gradual process beginning long before college. But for others the effective role learning may not occur until the teacher experiences the "reality shock" of the first

position (Wagenschein, 1950). The fact that educators have devoted so many surveys over so long a time to the problems of the beginning teacher suggests that this is a particularly critical time (Archer, 1960, p. 704), and the dramatic decline in MTAI scores associated with the early years of teaching (Day, 1959; Rabinowitz & Rosenbaum, 1960) points in the same direction. Warren has proposed that the transition from college student to teacher entails a drastic role reversal for the individuals involved: from concern with abstract principles to concern with concrete application, from the rights and duties of a student to the reciprocal rights and duties of a teacher, from free and easy sociality to a position of isolation, from personal freedom to control, from a liberal to a conservative environment, and from semi-anonymity and limited responsibility to a highly visible position as a responsible adult in the community.[15] This analysis is based in part upon circumstances of teaching which today hold true only in the more provincial communities. Nevertheless, it points up the general theoretical issue of role discontinuity and its psychological conflict which Ruth Benedict (1938) outlined many years ago. Warren's analysis also raises a question of some import in teacher education: To what extent and under what circumstances does student teaching, particularly in off-campus locations, ease the transition from the role of student to the role of teacher? This, like the general question regarding the time of role learning among teacher-trainees, has yet to be investigated.

CAREER PATTERNS OF THE TEACHER

Any specialized occupation in society confronts its practitioners with more or less standardized and limited ways for them to pursue their careers within it. In some instances, as in the highly bureaucratized or-

---

[15] From my notes on an unpublished manuscript prepared by Roland L. Warren, *ca.* 1948, Ch. 6, "The Social Role of the High School Teacher."

ganization, career lines are established as a matter of formal policy which specifies the mode of progression through a series of positions or ranks in the organization. In other cases, career lines are little more than typical patterns of progression informally regarded among the practitioners as customary or proper (Hughes, 1958, p. 128). Around these career phases and sequences, the practitioners organize their aspirations and define their occupational goals; it is in accordance with movement along the career line that they gauge their own and their colleagues' attainment of occupational success. And more broadly, "a career is the moving perspective in which the person sees his life as a whole and interprets the meaning of his various attributes, actions, and the things which happen to him" (Hughes, 1958, p. 63). By institutionalizing certain sequences of experiences to which practitioners typically are exposed, the occupation potentially exerts a formative influence upon those who follow it.

The career patterns of American teachers are almost exclusively matters of common knowledge rather than of accurate, statistical description. The most frequently cited observations in this corpus of common knowledge are the following. With respect to *vertical* mobility, "The normal line of advancement in public school work is to department head, the principalship (possibly several), and superintendencies" (Morris, 1957, p. 253). But beyond the elementary school principalship, this is an avenue for males only. One might also regard movement from one grade level to another as a form of vertical mobility. "The typical direction is to move from lower to higher grades within the elementary school, and from elementary to high school teaching" (Havighurst & Neugarten, 1957, p. 437). With respect to *horizontal* mobility, from one school system to another or from one school to another within a large system, Havighurst and Neugarten have this to say:

Although teachers move from one place to another for a variety of reasons—to leave or to return to their families, to gain new experience, and so on—the most typical direction of movement has been from smaller to larger communities. In general, with added academic training and added years of experience, teachers tend to go from an orbit of small towns to small cities to large cities; such moves are usually accompanied by increased salary, increased security, or increased prestige in the profession (Havighurst & Neugarten, 1957, p. 437).

Reliance upon common knowledge instead of accurate description of career patterns leaves us unable to assess the magnitude of alterations in the above patterns which certainly have occurred in recent years. A number of factors can reasonably be assumed to affect career patterns in teaching, among them the general economic conditions and the oversupply or undersupply of teachers, the extent of the disparity in salary levels among various teaching positions, and local hiring policies with respect to such questions as previous experience, marital status, or place of residence. Marked changes have occurred in these factors in the last two decades (Morris, 1957, pp. 250–257).

Consequences for Teachers and Teaching

When the educational literature touches on the career patterns of teachers, it is usually in the context of manpower utilization and the ability of the occupation to retain competent personnel. The literature abounds in proposals designed to make the career more "attractive," thereby reducing the difficulties of recruiting or of holding competent persons in the occupation. Implicitly it is argued that career experiences other than those typifying teaching would induce different and presumably better kinds of persons to serve in the nation's classrooms. Two additional kinds of effect on the teaching-learning process occasionally appear as frameworks for research or discussion in the literature, one regarding the formative influence of career experiences on the teacher and another regarding the direct impact of teacher turnover on classroom processes. We shall discuss these in turn.

Greenhoe (1941) and her co-workers (L. A. Cook, Almack, & Greenhoe, 1938; L. A. Cook & Greenhoe, 1940) were interested in part in the effects of transiency in the occupation on certain facets of the teacher's personality. Their data had shown that while teachers in the late 1930's changed jobs frequently, they rarely moved very far.

By taking a 50-mile radius and eliminating no-response totals one can include from over a fourth to more than a half of all the moves listed. . . . Moreover, as case materials show, not many of these changes are the kind that bring new mental stimulation. In the main, they are moves within similar worlds, such as from village to village within the same locality. While there is movement toward bigger places, it is of far less consequence than the trend just indicated. Thus the principle most descriptive of teacher mobility is that of *limited circulation,* and implications for teacher personality, for school, and the community relations are fairly evident (L. A. Cook & Cook, 1950, p. 440).

While the implications of the limited circulation principle may be "fairly evident," they have been neither specified in testable form nor certified by subsequent empirical research. Yet in its general form the hypothesis is potentially a fruitful one. It does not rest literally upon the extent of a teacher's geographical mobility, which certainly has increased in the last 20 years, but upon the extent of his mobility from one "social world" to another. Thus, a long move in terms of statute miles, from Iowa to California, for example, does not necessarily imply a move from one social world to another for the teacher; and a short move, geographically speaking, from, say, a "slum" school to a school in a lower middle-class neighborhood, may constitute a dramatic change in social worlds for the teacher (Winget, 1952). If variations in teacher circulation of this order are demonstrable, their associated consequences for "mental stimulation" or other aspects of attitude and personality are eminently researchable issues.

The most direct attack on the formative influence of the teaching career was made by Becker (1952a) in his study of the Chicago public school teacher. The burden of his investigation (at least, that part which relates to the present issue) was to demonstrate the interplay between the demands of the work situation and the teacher's mode of adjustment to them. Indeed, it is the teacher's search for favorable work circumstances which, in Becker's view, gives rise to teacher mobility and standardized career patterns. While this view was hardly novel, Becker systematically developed it by specifying the particular problems of work faced by the Chicago teachers and the work circumstances in which these problems were least aggravated or most susceptible to solution. The basic problems of work which Becker found among the 60 Chicago teachers whom he interviewed at length revolved around the "important categories of people in the structure of the school: children, parents, principal, and other teachers" (Becker, 1952a, p. 471). The teacher's severest problems involved his interaction with pupils, particularly in the realms of teaching, discipline, and moral acceptability. (See pp. 736–737, above.) Problems in his interaction with parents, principals, and colleagues were primarily those of preserving autonomy in his work or, as Becker called it, his "authority" (Becker, 1953). Chicago teachers found these various problems most heavily concentrated in the lower-class schools where they typically began their teaching careers. Here the problem of gaining intrinsic reward from teaching—i.e., producing change in the pupils' skills and knowledge which can be attributed to one's own efforts—the problem of maintaining order and discipline, and the problem of moral acceptability appeared in their severest forms (Becker, 1952a, pp. 471–472). Consequently, teachers in the "slum" schools began early to seek transfers to schools in "better" neighborhoods, giving rise, in Chicago at least, to a centrifugal pattern of career movement—from the center of the city outward. Winget's (1952) companion study quantitatively documented the pattern, adding the condition that teacher transfers normally reduced the distance between their homes and their places of work. Becker, then, regarded mobility as one mode of adjustment to the problems of work.

Another mode of adjustment discussed by Becker is especially relevant. Some Chicago teachers found it impossible to transfer quickly from the "slum" schools. Rather than adjusting by changing schools, these teachers discovered two ways of adapting themselves to the basic problems of work in the difficult schools. First, the teacher developed techniques and outlooks in his relations with pupils which enabled him to cope directly with these problems. Thus, the teacher reduced his aspirations as to the amount of pupil change he regarded as signifying success; he learned disciplinary techniques workable with the "slum" children; and he found grounds for evaluating the actions of children other than his previously moralistic ones. Second, the teacher capitalized on the fact that the "slum" schools offered a comparatively satisfactory place to cope with the other problems of work besides those involving pupils. He found, for example, that by remaining in the high-turnover "slum" school he quickly established a position of influence and prestige in the informal structure of colleague relations; as he built up enduring relationships with the lower-class families, he found a teaching situation singularly free of parental threat to his authority. The extent of change in the *person* of the teacher which such adaptation required appears impressive from Becker's discursive analysis. His conclusion regarding the adaptation is especially provocative: The techniques and outlooks the teacher develops to suit the requirements of one teaching circumstance may be entirely inappropriate for another teaching circumstance. Teaching routines, disciplinary techniques, and aspiration levels suitable to the "slum" school, once they become established facets of the teacher's

occupational repertoire, make him a misfit in schools in the "better" neighborhood.

She is tied to the school by the routine she has developed to suit its requirements and by the relationships she has built up with others in the school organization. These very adjustments cause her, at the same time, to fear a move to any new school, which would necessitate a rebuilding of these relationships and a complete reorganization of her work techniques and routine (Becker, 1952a, p. 475).

Thus, Becker specified in some detail the kinds of occupational experiences which may affect the teacher. While his study was based upon a limited number of teachers in the Chicago school system, the propositions developed in his investigation are general enough to guide investigation in other settings. This, of course, is necessary before the propositions may be regarded as established. Becker's own study and his anecdotal documentations have *produced* the hypotheses; systematic research is required to *test* them.

Occupational mobility may have direct consequences for the teaching-learning process quite apart from any formative influence it may exert on the teacher. From the standpoint of the pupil, there is roughly one chance in five each year (depending on the size of the school system) that he will be faced with a teacher new to the school (Mason & Bain, 1959). Despite widely held assumptions as to why such turnover should be detrimental to the teaching-learning process, the consequences of turnover for the teacher's classroom performance have not been investigated. It is commonly assumed, for example, that a teacher's effectiveness in instruction requires him to "know" or "appreciate" the home background and family circumstances of his pupils. Similarly, it is assumed that the new teacher must spend several months or even years "learning the ropes" of the school, familiarizing himself with instructional materials and facilities, and so on, before he can perform smoothly and surely in the classroom. These are plausible assumptions but they need to be examined empirically if only to determine how much of the variance they account for in the classroom interaction patterns of teachers.

THE TEACHER STEREOTYPE

No discussion of the formative influence of an occupation would be complete without reference to the concept of *stereotype,* a term introduced into the vocabulary of social psychology in the early 1920's to represent the oversimplified, widely shared, often derogatory images which man holds of his fellow man (Lippmann, 1922). The term was a happy one for social scientists of the day. Although it has been superseded by other concepts more general in application and more systematically wedded to psychological theory (see, for example, Krech & Crutchfield, 1948, pp. 171–172), it captured central ideas germinating in such diverse fields of psychology as perception, cognition, and public opinion.

Stereotypes have been empirically studied most often in the realm of prejudice and intergroup relations—in describing the beliefs people hold about ethnic, racial, and nationality groups (Harding, Kutner, Proshansky, & Chein, 1954, pp. 1023–1025)—but occasional studies have been directed toward stereotypes of occupational groups, including teachers. In many of these investigations the prime interest has been purely descriptive—to portray and, perhaps, to deplore the stereotype as it is found to exist. Yet some of the studies have had a distinct analytical bent. They have attempted to demonstrate the stability of stereotypes over time or to account for changes in stereotypes associated with major public events; they have investigated the way stereotypes are learned by children, the role of objective experience in stereotyped beliefs, the relationship between tendencies to stereotype and other psychological variables, and so on. The advances in understanding which have come about through these investigations, however, have all dealt with the psychology of the person who stereotypes. Aside from theoretical discussions, social science has bypassed the social psychological consequences for the person who is stereotyped.

Descriptive Studies of Teacher Stereotypes

Empirical studies of the teacher stereotype have been devoted exclusively to describing the characteristics people attribute to teachers, without giving serious attention to how widely shared the attributions are. The usual procedure is to elicit from a group of subjects descriptive phrases or adjectives which they associate with "teacher." Those phrases elicited most frequently are regarded as components of the teacher stereotype. Jones's (1957) dissertation is a convenient summary of the writings of educators and sociologists on the teacher stereotype.

McGill (1931), in his oft-cited study, had University of Nebraska students guess the occupations of unidentified men and women in a series of photographs; then he asked students their reasons for making their estimates. He listed (virtually verbatim) the descriptive terms the students used in explaining why they identified some of the photographs as "teachers" and compared the frequency with which the various terms were mentioned. Terms describing facial characteristics as "stern, dignified, or reserved" were mentioned 20 times by the 130-odd students as they explained their reasons for identifying one or more of the photographs as "teachers." The phrases "intelligent, capable" appeared a total of eight times, "vinegar drinker" once, and so on. McGill apparently felt his purpose was met when he combined the phrases appearing most frequently into a description of the teacher "stereotype." Unanswered was the question of whether or not this statistically constructed description corresponded to an image which any individual literally held of the teacher or, if it did, how widely shared such an image was. His published data provide no definitive test, but they do suggest that the agreement among students was not overwhelming.

The persistence of this almost journalistic interest in portraying the substance of teacher images is exemplified by Rogers (1950) and Saltz (1960). Gainsaying the free-response approach of McGill, Rogers confronted 120 teachers and teachers-to-be with a list of 21 adjectives, asking them to underline "any of the adjectives that the public might use in describing the typical school teacher" (p. 482). Her depiction of the teacher "stereotype," then, was based upon those adjectives most frequently underlined. Saltz (1960) asked 37 Chicago housewives to reply to the Edwards Personal Preference Schedule as they thought the majority of teachers would. Their responses were compared against data compiled by P. W. Jackson and Guba (1957) from elementary and high school teachers. Those personality attributes on which the housewife subjects scored above or below the teacher mean became components of the teacher "stereotype" held by the public. Saltz's conclusion is worth quoting in full, since it well illustrates the journalistic emphasis of studies of the teacher stereotype.

The picture that emerges is one of an ambitious, domineering, managing, fussy, tyrannical woman who has powers that enable her to see more of people's motives than they wish to reveal. She has few friends; she is not interested in people's problems; social mingling is not to her liking. When things go wrong she rarely blames herself. Set in her ways, bound up in routine, she hesitates to do the unconventional (Saltz, 1960, p. 109).

Walker's Australian investigation (1958) provided modest information concerning the extent of agreement among people in their images of teachers (as well as of other occupational groups). Following the procedures developed in the 1930's by Katz and Braly (1958), Walker's college student subjects checked five adjectives from a list of 112 to describe members of each of 10 occupational groups. For each occupation, Walker computed the Katz and Braly "clarity index," a measure which shows the extent to which the subjects agree on the adjectives used to characterize members of a group. (The lower the index number, the higher the agreement; in Walker's case, perfect agreement would yield an index of 2.5, perfect disagreement an index of 56.) The occupational stereotypes on the whole were about as strong as the ethnic and nationality stereotypes studied by Katz and Braly and by Gilbert (1951), when measured by the clarity index.

Among Walker's occupational groups, greatest clarity was registered for the medical doctor (7.9) and the factory owner (8.5), and least for the trade union leader (15.5). The school teacher, described as well-educated, intelligent, tolerant, fair-minded, and friendly, was intermediate in clarity of stereotype (11.7). This figure is not substantially different from those reported by Whiteford (1955), which were based on Illinois school administrators' descriptions of teachers in five subject-matter areas. She found clarity indexes ranging from 8.6 for social studies teachers to 10.0 for home economics teachers. (Interstudy comparisons of clarity measures, however, must be interpreted with care since differences in the number of adjectives, in the adjectives themselves, or in the number of choices permitted subjects may influence the magnitude of the index number in unknown ways.)

Whiteford's (1955) study was one of a pair conducted in Illinois comparing stereotypes concerning female high school teachers in different subject-matter areas as held by principals and superintendents and, in the second study (Barkley, 1956), as held by high school students. Whiteford asked several hundred administrators to check the 5 of 90 phrases which best characterized female teachers of home economics, business education, English, social studies, and physical education. Her results showed that the administrators' choices of phrases for each of these teachers were far more heavily concentrated on a few phrases than one would expect on the basis of chance. Some of the frequently endorsed phrases were common to all teachers, suggesting either a general "female high school teacher" stereotype or a response set among the administrators. Thus, all five kinds of teachers were seen as "conscientious," "enthusiastic," "capable," "resourceful," and "poised." Phrases attributed more uniquely to teachers in the several areas follow:

Home economics: orderly, wholesome, appropriately dressed.
Business education: exacting, orderly, precise.
English: dramatic, academic, intellectual, well read.
Social studies: democratic, academic, intellectual, well read.
Physical education: robust, mannish, aggressive, wholesome.

Whiteford applied the Osgood-Suci *D* statistic to compare the extent of similarity between profiles (across all 90 phrases) describing the teachers. Profiles for the home economics and the business education teacher were highly similar, as were profiles for the English and the social studies teacher, but these two pairs were quite dissimilar. The profile for the physical education teacher was the most distinctive of the five, sharing a modest degree of similarity only with that for the home economics teacher.

The second investigation (Barkley, 1956) was an interesting departure from the normal stereotype studies in that the investigator put to empirical test stereotypes she had constructed in advance, in this way attempting to preserve the coherence of the stereotype content. Asch (1952) had criticized the typical adjective check-list methodology of stereotype studies in these terms:

The procedure is summative; it breaks down a subject's view of a group into a series of discrete, abbreviated responses. These are then combined statistically to produce the equivalent of a composite photograph, which may not correspond to the view of any one individual. The results do not give us the concrete representation of any one group held by any one individual (Asch, 1952, p. 234).

Barkley tried to meet this objection with-

out forgoing entirely the advantage of the check-list procedure in processing quantitative data. First, she constructed statements of the stereotypes of home economics, business education, English, and physical education teachers by reading through a large number of protocols provided by high school students, attempting to discern the core underlying the descriptions in the protocols. The students had freely responded to such questions as, "Describe in your own words the picture that comes to your mind when you hear the word 'home economics teacher,'" and, "If you see a group of women teachers in the hall the first day of school, and you do not know any of them, how can you guess which is the English teacher? the physical education teacher?" and so on. The dominant image of the business education teacher, for example, seemed to be organized around the "career girl" type. She was described as self-confident and efficient, brisk and systematic in the classroom, rather impersonal in her relations with students and adults alike, and crisp and well-tailored in her appearance. The English teacher descriptions seemed to reflect many components of the "old-maid school teacher," while the physical education teacher image was of the "outdoor girl" and the home economics teacher image was of the "motherly" type. In the latter two cases, Barkley saw alternative themes running through the descriptions and was unable on the basis of the protocols to decide between them. Thus, there was some indication that the image of the home economics teacher might tend toward the "TV home economist"—young, enthusiastic, attractive, and original—rather than toward the plump and matronly, old-fashioned, but easygoing "motherly" type. Similarly, some of the protocols suggested that the physical education teacher was conceived in a less heterosexually oriented image than that of the energetic, physically attractive, all-around "outdoor girl." As an alternative, Barkley proposed an image of the physical education teacher organized around what she called the "playmate" type—the girl's girl, a confidante of students, husky and mannish in appearance, whose interests lie rather exclusively in games and sports.

To test the adequacy of these hypothesized stereotypes, Barkley then selected what seemed to be key phrases from each of the organized conceptions and pooled them, along with some neutral phrases, to form three check lists, one on appearance, another on classroom behavior, and a third on personal relations of teachers. Some 800 eleventh- and twelfth-grade students in 25 Illinois high schools were asked to check the phrases on the lists most descriptive of the typical home economics teacher, business education teacher, and so on. (In another part of the inventory, Barkley included a number of forced-choice questions to allow her to choose between the alternative themes for the home economics and the physical education teacher.)

Her results showed that the keyed phrases distinguished rather well among the four kinds of teachers, although they were not consistently the most frequently checked phrases for a given teacher as she had predicted they would be. Some of the keyed phrases (e.g., "Is a happy and enthusiastic person") were attributed to all teachers, while other phrases, especially those carrying a negative connotation, were rarely attributed to any of the teachers. Clearly, the phrases in the check lists evoked a response set among the respondents which obscured the findings. Nevertheless, her data confirmed the image of the physical education teacher as the "outdoor girl" type; the home economist appeared to the high school students more like the "TV home economist" then like the "motherly" type. The business education teacher was seen as the brisk, efficient "career girl," but more personable and informal in her classroom relations than originally envisioned.

Key elements in the "old-maid school teacher" image of the English teacher, however, did not appear as predicted. She was not seen, for example, as elderly or as prim and prissy; rather, the outstanding features in the descriptions were intelligence, culture and refinement, formality in classroom relations, but a keen interest in students, a composite suggesting more of a "scholar" type. The Osgood-Suci D measure of profile similarity confirmed Whiteford's (1955) findings in certain respects: the physical education teacher profile was the most distinctive of the four, showing a kinship with only the home economics teacher profile, and then only with respect to their modes of personal relations. But the most similar pair of profiles were for the business education and the English teacher, not for the business education and the home economics teacher, as Whiteford had found from the administrator descriptions.

While this is not the place to criticize the stereotype studies in detail, it is worth noting that the research methods usually employed in the studies yield an operational measure of stereotype which has little correspondence to its conceptual definition. Theoretical discussions using the term presuppose at least three properties of *stereotype*. First, the term refers to an abbreviated but psychologically coherent image or conception of a category of persons held by an individual. We have already cited Asch's (1952) comments regarding the synthetic character of stereotype descriptions arising from the typical check-list procedure, and only in the Barkley (1956) study has an attempt been made to preserve the psychological unity of stereotype content.

Second, theoretical discussions presume that the stereotype held by an individual actively enters into and governs the interaction between him and members of the category. No measures of stereotype certify this. Indeed, the usual research methods force subjects to respond in stereotyped terms even though their manifest behavior in interaction with others may not in the least be governed by stereotypes.

Third, most conceptual definitions of *stereotype* specify that the image must be widely shared in some finite group or society. Attempts to meet this specification are rare and, at best, oblique. Occasionally, an investigator will take the pains to test the distribution of responses against a chance distribution (Whiteford, 1955), but agreement exceeding chance is hardly the same as wide agreement. Occasionally, too, investigators apply the Katz and Braly "clarity index" as an indicator of agreement (Barkley, 1956; Walker, 1958; Whiteford, 1955), yet both this and the procedure of testing against a chance distribution do not take into account the high level of agreement which can be generated artificially by response sets (e.g., favorability) of subjects with respect to a particular list of phrases. Because of these methodological shortcomings, about the only similarity existing between the operational measure and the conceptual definition of *stereotype* lies in the word itself.

Effects of the Teacher Stereotype on Teaching

In what ways can the teacher stereotype—the widely shared image in people's heads—exert an influence upon the teaching occupation? Although little stereotype research has directly attacked this question, some investigators have implicitly asserted that the stereotype does have a significant effect. Their reasoning follows one of two courses.

One course of argument holds that the teacher stereotype enters into and helps to determine the career decisions of young people, thereby shaping the composition of the occupational group. From this viewpoint, occupational stereotypes are a form of "vocational information" furnished by the culture and used by youth to weigh the suitability or attractiveness of various life pursuits. The argument asserts that an unfavorable or derogatory stereotype of an occupational group renders that occupation less attractive to potential recruits and limits the membership to those persons with few alternative opportunities. The form of this argument is identical to that reported earlier regarding the consequences of occupational prestige. (See above, p. 747.)

A subtler phrasing of the same argument proposes that the occupational stereotype provides a "model" of the kind of person who typifies the occupational category. The potential member, as he makes his career choice, can match his own self-image and self-aspirations against this model. In the event that his image of the occupational type corresponds to his conception of the kind of person he wants to be, the occupation will attract him. This line of reasoning, especially in the subtler form, entails an interesting corollary: the stereotype is self-reinforcing. Cronbach (1944) developed this point in connection with his study of stereotypes of college sorority houses.

The significance of the stereotype lies not in its accuracy as a description of a group—it is often erroneous—but in its effects on the house. Whether voiced or not, the stereotype influences the members of the house and the ways the campus reacts to them. This is especially important during rushing. The newcomer to the campus cannot know each house in reality, but it is easy to sense the esteem in which a house is regarded. The rushee cannot test her ability to fit into a given group, but she can readily compare herself with its stereotype. . . . This fact makes stereotyping a vicious circle; as a house acquires a label, be it true or false, it attracts girls who fit the label (Cronbach, 1944, p. 215).

In the same way, as an occupational group acquires a stereotype, it attracts recruits who fit the image; this, in turn, reinforces the popular stereotype. There are, of course, many influences shaping vocational choice and occupational composition other than the stereotype, a fact which prevents a perfect equilibrium from being established.

The second course of argument holds that the teacher stereotype exerts its effect directly on members of the occupational group by means of the teachers' interaction with persons in their social worlds (including other teachers) who share the stereotyped image.

The man on the street carries in his mind images of numerous occupational personality types. When a person speaks of the secretary, salesman, or teacher, his comments reflect the image which he has of each and call out similar images in the minds of his listeners. . . . Such concepts of personality types are generally superficial and incomplete, but they are the basis on which people interact with persons occupying various positions in any society. . . . Although these are stereotyped images, each person reacts to the teacher, salesman, or secretary as if the image were real (Brookover, 1955b, p. 263).

Or, in Waller's words:

Much of social interaction rests upon stereotypes. The interaction of intimates largely escapes the influence of the stereotype, and so does naive experience for which no model exists in one's social world. But a very wide range of social interchange is affected by the presence of more or less definite stereotypes, sometimes stereotypes which have currency in an entire group (this is the best use of the term) and sometimes constructs of our own relating to particular persons or classes of persons. This is possible because in many kinds of relations we do not respond to another person directly, but always to a more or less veracious construct of him in our own minds (Waller, 1932, pp. 415–416).

As a consequence of such interaction, the teacher eventually comes to internalize the common image of himself. Given a world in which "everyone" interacts with him as though he were a certain kind of person, the teacher finds it expedient, if not necessary, to respond as though he were, indeed, that kind of person. In time, so the argument runs, the line between make-believe and reality fades, and the teacher begins to regard himself as manifesting the foibles and virtues so universally attributed to him. The image becomes his self concept. Standards by which he judges himself and his fellow teachers are the standards he has unwittingly incorporated from the significant others with whom he interacts. "When the teacher has internalized the rules which bind him, he has become truly a teacher" (Waller, 1932, p. 420).

This course of reasoning, rooted in the turn of the century work of C. H. Cooley and G. H. Mead, today constitutes the intellectual basis of a prominent branch of social psychology roughly denoted as *role theory*. Over the years, Lippmann's concept of *stereotype* has been subsumed by the more general and more flexible concept of *role expectation*. The convergence of role theory and the phenomenological theory of personality in psychology (e.g., Sarbin, 1954) has offered scholars a systematic framework for coming to terms with the consequences of stereotypes for the person who is stereotyped. However, the analysis and the research is no longer carried on in the name of stereotype but in the name of role-taking. We will return to this in a later section.

CONCLUDING COMMENT: WORK AND PERSONALITY

In the present section we have limited our review to topics which have stimulated a number of empirical studies in the educational setting. By this limitation we have omitted several provocative expositions detailing the processes by which "occupational work molds the body, mind, and behavior of its members." It may be worth while to remark briefly on some of the currents of thought concerning these processes.

For some writers, such as Sorokin, cited early in this section, the formative process lies in the activities required of man by his work. The particular tasks and demands of the daily job require the practitioner to focus attention on certain kinds of objects and issues, to exercise certain kinds of skills and thought processes, and to manifest repeatedly certain patterns of response. In time the response patterns become habitual, the perceptual and cognitive organizations imposed by the circumstances of work become deeply ingrained in the practioner's personality and are expressed both within and without the occupational setting. Waller put it this way:

Those who follow certain occupations are continually thrown into certain kinds of social situations. These social situations call for, or are best met by, a certain kind of reaction on the part of the professional. The individual thus plays certain roles and shows certain attitudes habitually, and there is a tendency for him to distort other social situations until they conform to a pattern which can be met by his habitual roles and attitudes. . . . Training an individual for the practice of such a profession often consists in teaching him what he is expected to do or say upon certain occasions, as when the minister offers the consolations of religion to a bereaved family, a teacher assigns a lesson, a doctor enters a sick room, or a lawyer threatens suit. Long practice in the social techniques enjoined upon one in a profession makes those the deepest grooves, and at length they grow so deep that there is no getting out of them (Waller, 1932, p. 376).

Waller's (1932) penetrating development of this and related points is unparalleled in the educational literature, in spite of the fact that his illustrative materials and his grim view of the teacher's life harken back to an earlier era. The teacher is formed, he said, in the social situations imposed by his job, but especially in the nature of his relationship to students. This relationship basically is one of covert generational conflict—between teachers who bear the culture of the society of adults and youth who accede to the inculcation of the culture only with reluctance.

The characteristic mode of social interaction of the school, an interaction centered about the giving and receiving of instruction, determines the political order of the school. The instruction which is given consists largely of facts and skills, and of other matter for which the spontaneous interests of students do not usually furnish a sufficient motivation. Yet teachers wish students to attain a certain mastery of these subjects, a much higher degree of mastery than they would attain, it is thought, if they were quite free in their choices. And teachers are responsible to the community for the mastery of these subjects by their students. The political organization of the school, therefore, is one which makes the teacher dominant, and it is the business of the teacher to use his dominance to further the process of teaching and learning which is central in the social interaction of the school (Waller, 1932, p. 8).

The teacher-student relationship is sus-

tained by the teacher's exercise of institutional authority, but uneasily so. The authority is constantly subject to challenge by the students and exposed to regulation and interference by the community of parents. To use Waller's phrase, the social order of the school is in a "state of perilous equilibrium." Out of the peculiar demands of the classroom relationship, out of the circumstances of the teacher's work, buttressed by the particular character of community and colleague relationships, emerges the teacher type—dignified, reserved, conservative, unbending, and intellectually impoverished. These are traits which have survival value for the teacher. They are the modes, as Waller elaborated in detail (pp. 381–409), by which the teacher adapts to the demands of the work. Embodied in a concrete teacher, these attributes of the teacher type work back on the classroom from which they arose to channel the conduct of the teaching-learning process.

The substance of Waller's analysis unquestionably is overdrawn, presupposing as it does that universal teacher-student conflict ensues from the absence in the student of intrinsic motivation to learn. The absence of intrinsic motivation is a special case, holding in less degree in neighborhoods where such motivation is furnished in the home or by teachers skilled in harnessing the tasks of learning to the spontaneous interests of students. Where the force toward learning is the student's own, induction of force by the teacher is less necessary and, if we follow Waller, the political order of the school would be modified accordingly. By viewing Waller's analysis as an elaboration of the consequences of the special case, his thesis is brought into proper perspective, and his remarkable observations concerning "What Teaching Does to Teachers" (1932, Chs. 22, 23) stand in less danger of being rejected outright.

Another current of thought, extending from the foregoing, was expressed by Hughes (1958) and reflected by Becker (1952a, 1952b, 1953). Where Sorokin, Veblen, and, to an extent, Waller emphasized the formative power of the techniques and materials of the practitioner's work, albeit they are "human materials" in the case of teaching, Hughes preferred to emphasize the influence of the social relations into which the practitioner's work throws him. A person's work presents him with a unique configuration of personal crises and problems which he has to meet or solve. Foremost among the problems are those involving such sociogenic needs as maintaining positive self-regard, preserving a sense of autonomy and self-determination, avoiding extreme psychological involvement in the tribulations of clients, and so on. As practitioners of the same occupation face similar problems and develop practices and procedures to cope with them, the solutions become institutionalized as part of the occupational culture. The presence of the teacher's desk or lectern in the college classroom, for example, helps him regulate the social distance between himself and the students, a problem which may otherwise be difficult when the age of his students approaches or exceeds his own. At the point where the cultural solutions to occupational problems are manifested in the practitioner's behavior and attitudes and in his relationships to others, they define the occupational personality.

Still other writers emphasize mechanisms of social control—the imposition of role prescriptions and the exercise of sanctions against those who deviate—as the prime force shaping practitioners of an occupation. "Success" is realized at the point where the practitioner internalizes the desires and beliefs of the controlling group so completely that he never feels the yoke of control; role prescriptions become self-imposed (Brookover, 1955b, pp. 60–71). We have touched on this matter in our previous discussion of the teacher stereotype and will again in the section which follows.

These currents of thought are not sharply distinguishable from one another in the major expositions devoted to the formative influence of the teaching occupation (Brookover, 1955b; Terrien, 1955; Waller, 1932). They blend in the analyses, and differences among authors are differences in emphasis only. None of them, however, has generated the body of empirical research which could clarify and specify the processes by which the occupation exerts its influence and point up the different conceptual issues which each invokes.

In closing this section, we must point out one aspect of the teacher's occupational life which has not supported sufficient empirical research to warrant a review. This is the teacher's membership in occupational organizations and associations. Aside from historical accounts, critical evaluations (Lieberman, 1956), or occasional membership surveys, the education associations have completely escaped serious investigation. It may well be true that for a large proportion of the teachers enrolled in, say, the National Education Association, membership is merely token, carrying little personal significance. On the other hand, there is no question but what the associations are viable social systems, providing intricate career channels, offering role models of the "professional teacher," and promulgating their respective ideologies and belief systems. An organization or association may serve as a reference group for some teachers, providing a source of psychological sustenance and social support offsetting the influences of the community and school in which they work. The significance of education associations in these ways, however, will not be known until appropriate investigations have been undertaken.

THE COMMUNITY ENVIRONMENT OF TEACHING

In American society, we have suggested, a person's occupational status plays a key part in determining the nature and extent of his relationships with others in his social world, quite apart from the relationships in which he is immediately and necessarily implicated by his occupational role. The teacher status potentially locates the person in a series of interlocking role relationships in the social system of the community and specifies his mode of entry into community life. How far and in what manner does occupational status, in fact, govern the teacher's social participation in the community, and what are the consequences for the teaching-learning process? These are the questions to which we now turn.

Implications from Previous Sections

Previous sections of this chapter carry certain implications concerning the teacher's social relationships in the community. The stereotype literature implies (although the studies do not demonstrate) that members of a community respond to the teacher not as an individual person but as a member of a category and attribute to him all the characteristics associated with the category. Thus, if a citizen regards teachers as prudes, he interacts with the particular teacher as though he were a prude, regardless of the individuality of the teacher. For the teacher, then, in the context of stereotypes, interaction with community members is unreal; his individuality enters not at all into the interaction process. Interaction is only a discourse between a citizen and the citizen's stereotyped image; the teacher is involved merely as a bystander who triggers the image. Whether the stereotype is complimentary or disparaging, the mode of interaction is disconcerting to the teacher because of its complete impersonality. The stereotype studies, as we noted, do not offer any empirical tests of these implications, and we suspect that the implications hold only under highly special circumstances, if at all. These circumstances will be discussed below.

The research on social class position and on the prestige of teaching also implies certain kinds of relationships between the teacher and community members. In rough perspective, these studies suggest that the American teacher inhabits the lower-middle or, sometimes, the upper-middle strata of our society. If we followed Warner's analysis of stratification, we would expect the teacher's most

intimate and personally meaningful relationships to be among members of the community occupying the same stratum and his social intercourse with community members remote from his own social class to occur infrequently. (The reader may recall, however, that Warner and his colleagues found so little participation by teachers in the social fabric of the small communities they studied that they had difficulty in locating them in the class structure.) (See p. 720, above.) Wattenberg (1957a, pp. 67–68) observed that one consequence of greater heterogeneity in the social class origins of teachers is an expansion in the number of community strata linked to the school. Working-class teachers can become "human bridges" between the school and segments of the community never before adequately connected with the school. But, he warns, this will depend upon the teacher's concern with social mobility. The upward mobile teacher of the working class may reject his heritage and cut himself off from the groups from which he arose; other teachers of the working class may resent the comparative financial success of friends who did not enter teaching and withdraw "into professional groups which boast higher standards of taste or knowledge" (Wattenberg, 1957a, p. 68).

THE TEACHER IN THE SACRED COMMUNITY

The materials bearing most directly upon the teacher's community relations were mainly produced by educational sociologists during the 1930's. These students were appalled by the strict social controls imposed upon teachers, especially in the more provincial communities of America, and they proceeded to record them as best they could. They wrote their impressionistic observations in the sociological style of the day, offering as evidence carefully selected anecdotes or lengthy extracts from autobiographical documents furnished by teachers. These materials shortly became *the* definitive description of the teacher's position in the American community and, to a certain extent, they continue to be today.

Today, we can see that these writers had in mind a community of a special type—the culturally homogeneous small town or village relatively untouched by urbanization and industrialization. The city and the suburb were ignored in the educational sociologists' descriptions of the modes of social relations between teacher and community. Thus, their implicit model was a community at the sacred end of what sociologists have called the sacred-secular continuum (Dewey, 1960; Miner, 1952). The secular (or urban) community is characterized by a high degree of division of labor, anonymity, social heterogeneity, and impersonality in relationships; the sacred (or folk) community is economically undifferentiated, socially homogeneous, tradition-bound, and the relationships among its members are highly personal. In the sociological conception, communities fall on a continuum whose extremes are defined by the sacred and secular types. The period in which the educational sociologists were writing was, of course, prior to the massive programs of school district reorganization of the late 1940's and 1950's, and American schoolhouses were located preponderantly in just such sacred communities as they envisioned.

Despite their obvious limitations as analytical research, the writings of this period call attention to a mode of social and cultural influence operating on the teacher which has been largely ignored in the research reviewed up to this point—the influence accompanying social interaction between the teacher and other adults in his immediate environment. For this reason and because these materials have made a profound impression on discussions and research in subsequent years, it may not be amiss for us to reconstruct the description of the teacher-community relationship as presented in them. Our description will be put explicitly in the frame of reference of the sacred community, where the cultural values are homogeneous or dominated by a single controlling group; the frame of reference is at best implicit in the original writings.

The Descriptive Model [16]

The outstanding features of the teacher's relations in the sacred community are (1) the unusual degree to which relationships are lacking altogether, and (2) the highly constrained nature of those relationships which are present. Occupational status is not just one of the key statuses of teachers but *the* key status in the small town. Other statuses which might connect the person to the social structure of the community are denied him. Contractual provisions typically preclude marriage, at least by females, so the teacher cannot enter into the social fabric of the community as a householder, a neighbor, a parent, and so on. Strict codes of conduct enforced by the community with respect to recreation, entertainment, and courtship prevent the unmarried, young teacher from entering into the role relationships normally associated with his age-sex status. And, we might add, the fact that the teacher often is female and young makes it unlikely that she would be integrated in the community by virtue of positions of civic responsibility, which are reserved for mature male adults. The teacher's migration from community to community makes his only connection with the local system of relationships come from his occupational identity. Highly visible in the small town, he is always "the teacher." He can only escape his identity by withdrawing completely from the town, and even this is prohibited except during summer vacations. (The hometown teacher's plight is not so desperate, tied as he is by kinship and friendship statuses, but these ties bring other difficulties.) Observations such as these led Waller (1932, pp. 62–63) and L. A. Cook (1938, pp. 308–311) to invoke Simmel's concept of "the stranger" to describe the teach-

---

[16] The portrait of the teacher in the sacred community presented in the following paragraphs is a composite from a number of sources, the more comprehensive of which are Beale (1936), Brookover (1955b), L. A. Cook and Cook (1950), Dahlke (1958), Grambs (1952), Greenhoe (1941), Havighurst and Neugarten (1957), Lieberman (1955), and Waller (1932).

er's role in the community. The teacher is a socially unattached and psychologically detached person.

The occupational identity is a trying one. The teacher is a public servant, and his life is public property. His time is demanded for Sunday school teaching, for charity bazaars, for sponsorship of youth activities, and for other innocuous enterprises well removed from the realms of decision and power. At the same time, he loses freedom of choice as to where he takes residence, where he buys his clothes and groceries, where and how he entertains himself, and so on. Codes of conduct cover a wide range of deportment, both public and private, from matters of personal adornment to smoking, drinking, and card-playing. In the activities he is expected to undertake as well as in those he is obliged to forgo, the teacher stands as a symbol of the sacred values of the community. He is a breed apart. The gulf between him and other men is maintained by strained and artificial forms of interaction, by the embarrassed silences, by the inane and stereotyped conversations he encounters in his day-by-day contacts with the citizenry. Wherever he goes in this closed and homogeneous society, the teacher sees his unique status mirrored back at him.

Most public of all is the teacher's performance in the classroom. Close surveillance is exercised by board members and citizens to insure not merely that he succeeds in his teaching but that his means of attaining success conform to the local image of proper teaching, to insure not only that he teaches what he is expected to teach but that he teaches nothing that is unexpected or "controversial."

As the educational sociologists viewed it, the prime function of the restrictive role into which the teacher is cast is to preserve intact the sacred values of the culturally homogeneous community and to defend the status quo of the prevailing social order. To these the teacher poses an imminent and ever-present threat as he attempts to provide his pupils with an adequate education.

Coming from the outside world, the teacher is the bearer of new ideas and new action patterns . . . . he touches the local area at its most sensitive spot, its children. Children are the carriers of the locality culture. If these forms and norms of area life are to survive, they must do so *via* the children. Naturally a teacher is viewed with mixed feelings (L. A. Cook, 1938, p. 308).

Teachers are selected for their positions and dismissed from their positions not on the grounds of their technical merit as teachers but on the degree of threat they pose to the sanctity of the local value system. Pacifists, militarists, radicals, Communists, Catholics, and Jews are *persona non grata*. Teachers from the provinces are preferred over those from the city; those trained at the nearby normal school are preferred to those from the university. School board interviews with teacher candidates probe character, not competence. Constant vigilance is demanded to certify that persons from whom the children would learn alien ways of life do not get in or stay in the local schools.

The literature is replete with instances of subtle as well as overt reprisals against teachers who overstep the narrow boundaries of conduct "befitting a teacher." As a group they command no bargaining power and are vulnerable to arbitrary actions of employing officials; lacking community ties, they have no means of mobilizing sentiment or power on their own behalf. Yet recourse by local citizens to punitive action or the threat of it is rarely necessary in the sacred community for two reasons. Informal mechanisms of social control—the lifted eyebrow, the unexplained coolness of acquaintances, the circulation of rumor and gossip, all arts in which the community members are well versed—frequently suffice to correct the teacher in his transgressions. Further, the teachers selected for service in the provincial community normally are unmotivated to conduct themselves in any way other than that prescribed by their role. "Although there are some teachers who feel the yoke of control," Brookover wrote, "many have so completely internalized the desires and beliefs of the controlling group that these attitudes are clearly their own" (Brookover, 1955b, p. 69). The internalization of community expectations occurs by virtue of two processes: "interaction and identification with people in the schools who hold such values and beliefs; and ... the desire for the security, status, and approval which those in control are in a position to give" (1955b, p. 69). In any event, internalization of the community's role expectations makes the imposition of external constraints on the teacher superfluous.

The implications of this model of the teacher's community relations for the teaching-learning process are readily specified. The teacher is a pawn, a passive agent, of community forces and exercises only the narrowest band of discretion in the classroom. No points of discontinuity exist between classroom and the environing community. As the community, so the teaching. If the dominant community values are those of the business ethic or those of religious fundamentalism, they are immediately reflected in the content and method of teaching. If the community is torn by factional strife, the conflict is played out in school and classroom. What the student learns, how he learns it, and the social order in which he learns it are all in keeping with the status quo.

Systematic Documentation

In the latter half of the 1930's, L. A. Cook and his students launched a series of questionnaire surveys designed to document the prevailing conceptions of the teacher's community relations. The studies, abundantly reported in the professional literature (L. A. Cook, Almack, & Greenhoe, 1938; L. A. Cook & Almack, 1939; L. A. Cook & Greenhoe, 1940; Greenhoe, 1939, 1940, 1941), made a lasting impression on the field. Interest centered in five areas: the geographical mobility of teachers (discussed earlier in this chapter, page 754), community selection of teachers for employment, the participation of teachers and pressures on them to participate in community activities, the codes of conduct applied to teachers, and teacher reactions to community controls. Questionnaires regarding these matters were distributed to teachers, school board members, laymen, and students in a variety of ways—by direct mail, by circulation at professional meetings, and through college professors, state departments of education, and school administrators. Nationwide distribution was sought in some cases, but other distributions were restricted to certain Midwestern states. One suspects that a strongly rural bias was present in some of the distributions, although it is difficult to determine this in the various survey reports. Where the investigators relied on voluntary questionnaire returns, the reply rates hovered around 50 per cent, and at one point Cook reported a total failure of board members to respond to a nationwide mailing (L. A. Cook & Cook, 1950, p. 441). All in all, the various samplings offer an extremely hazardous base for making estimates about any known population.

The Cook and Greenhoe results. Be that as it may, the survey results were regarded as broadly confirming the impressionistic observations of previous writers. Thus, school board members as well as other respondents (including teachers) were discovered to be extremely reluctant to hire Negroes, radicals, Communists, and persons in bad health. They were least "prejudiced" against Protestants but showed decreasing favor toward native-born persons with foreign names, non-local residents, city-reared persons, and out-of-state residents, in that order.

As to participation in community activities, over 95 per cent of the teachers reported membership in at least one community group (typically in four or five), but these were principally religious, professional, and relief and welfare organizations; less than one-eighth of them belonged to political groups, patriotic societies, and economic groups. The percentage of teachers who were officers in these groups ranged up to 22 per cent (in religious organizations), with men showing somewhat higher office-holding rates than women teachers. High school teachers were reported to be more active than elementary school teachers, and the amount of community participation among all teachers varied inversely with community size. One-half of the 622 responding teachers in Ohio indicated that pressures were brought to bear upon them to take part in community activities, especially to participate in the Parent-Teachers Association and in church and Sunday school work. Males and high school teachers reported such pressures more frequently than females and elementary school teachers.

As to conduct, teachers, board members, students, and laymen were asked to indicate their approval or disapproval of teachers engaging in a variety of behaviors (for male and female teachers separately), and in one study, teachers were asked to estimate the probable reaction of the community to teachers who engaged in such behaviors. Owing to the wide disparity among respondents in the various reporting groups, it is unfair to make cross-group comparisons, and only the grossest findings are worth noting. The most universally disapproved forms of teacher behavior among the reporting groups were drinking alcoholic liquor and dating students. Running for political office and making political speeches tended to be disapproved. Of perhaps greater interest are the forms of behavior which were approved or on which there were no clear normative expectations: dating a town person or another teacher, leaving the area over the weekend, buying clothes outside the area, joining a teachers' union, smoking in private, dancing, and even teaching controversial issues (mildly disapproved by board members). These, as the reader will note, are forms of behavior at variance with the descriptive model of the teacher in the sacred community. Expectations on the female teacher in a few areas were more restrictive than on the male teacher, particularly with respect to smoking and playing pool and billiards; board members were indifferent about the male teacher's failure to attend church but

strongly disapproved of failure in female teachers.

A final feature of the nationwide survey was a question put to teachers regarding their reactions to community control over their out-of-school conduct. They were permitted to indicate whether they accepted, rebelled against, protested, or evaded community control, or sought to educate the community to greater tolerance. No option was provided the teacher who denied the premise of the question, namely, that the community sought to control out-of-school conduct. The most popular category of response (about one-half of the teachers) was "accept," and the next two most popular were "educate" and "no reply." Cook's interpretation of this finding—"The most significant fact is the high percentage of teachers who frankly report an acceptance of community control over their out-of-school conduct" (L. A. Cook & Cook, 1950, p. 448)—failed to take account of the fact that the questionnaire wording virtually precluded any other finding.

As we said earlier, the surveys by Cook and his students were designed to document, not to question, the prevailing conceptions of the teacher's community relations. Unless carefully formulated and analyzed, descriptive data of the sort they collected can give comfort to any point of view one adopts. One may take delight, for example, in the fact that two-thirds of the teachers visited regularly in pupils' homes, or he may despair over the one-third who did not. He may find joy in the 95 per cent who belonged to community groups or be discouraged by the "small" number who were officers in these groups. In drawing their conclusions, Cook and his colleagues were inclined to emphasize the pessimistic view:

Findings [with respect to conduct codes] indicate that community concern may readily go beyond the bounds of common sense and necessity, and when such is the case many worthy young people must certainly turn to pursuits other than teaching (Greenhoe, 1939, p. 511).

Faced with the data reported, some education majors think for the first time about the teacher's life in the community, wondering if they are fitted for it. Others are for the moment too disturbed to do much thinking, saying that they will withdraw from the training program. Still others refuse to face the facts, claiming that conditions cannot be as bad as painted. . . . A few, by contrast, . . . will show a willingness to accept community controls, however narrow and senseless such "blue laws" may be, believing that this adjustment is either compulsory or else will make them better teachers (L. A. Cook & Cook, 1950, pp. 449–450).

The reader is encouraged to compare Cook's discussion of the teacher in the community in the 1938 and in the 1950 editions of his text, one written before and the other after the survey data were collected (L. A. Cook, 1938, Ch. 17; L. A. Cook & Cook, 1950, Ch. 18). The tenor of the discussion is identical. Both chapters close with a summation of the teacher's role as a stranger—a person *in* the community but not *of* it. Although the 1950 chapter was completely rewritten, its basic argument was neither modified nor refined by the data accumulated in the intervening period. Nothing is made, for example, of the curious observation that participation in community activities varied inversely with community size. Does this mean that teachers are more likely to be accepted in the smaller towns as full-fledged members, or does it mean that the pressures on the teachers to participate are greater in the smaller towns? Intent as they were on documentation, Cook and Greenhoe rarely raised questions such as this and were insensitive to data discrepant with the prevailing view of the teacher in the sacred community.

Results of subsequent surveys. Numerous studies of teacher participation, pressures, and conduct codes patterned after the work of Cook and Greenhoe have been reported since 1940. Their findings are neither surprising nor particularly significant:

1. Teachers participate in a variety of community organizations. Although one-half of Callaway's (1951) Missouri teachers belonged to neither civic nor social organizations, the figure for nonmembership more often has been in the neighborhood of 10 per cent (Griffin, 1953; National Education Association, 1957). Contrary to Cook's data, the frequency of organizational membership among the nation's beginning teachers (National Education Association, 1956) varied directly, not inversely, with community size. This, the writers pointed out, may have been due to the larger proportions of hometown teachers in the larger communities, since other analyses show higher participation rates among persons beginning to teach in their home towns than among those beginning in new towns. Memberships are reasonably well distributed among community organizations (National Education Association, 1956, 1957) following rather closely the pattern reported by L. A. Cook and Cook (1950, p. 444): Teachers are not significantly represented in political, business, and patriotic organizations. Unanswered in the various studies are questions such as these: Do teacher participation rates differ from the rates for nonteachers who are comparable with respect to age, sex, marital status, length of residence in the community (see Grobman & Hines, 1957, p. 141)? If the teacher participation rate is comparatively high, is it because teachers are obliged to participate or because they "want to"?

2. Some teachers report that they are expected to participate in community activities. Two-thirds of Lichliter's (1946) small town teachers believed they were "expected to" participate in extracurricular school activities, 33 per cent to attend church, and 29 per cent to engage in community activities. Only one-fifth of nonmetropolitan Missouri teachers (Callaway, 1951) reported social pressures on them to attend church, although 40 per cent of M. R. Thomas' (1954) Idaho teachers indicated they were subjected to "unwarranted" pressures to participate in community activities. Teacher reports of "expectations" or of "pressures," however, are open to varying interpretations. Do the reports reflect more closely the realities of the

situations they face or the autistic fears and moods of the teachers themselves? This we will discuss shortly. Further, unless questions are carefully worded on this subject, it is impossible to distinguish between responses indicating an *obligation* to participate and those indicating *permission* to participate. Thus, Terrien (1953) reported that 92 per cent of his sample of New London, Connecticut, citizens replied "yes" to the question, "In your opinion, *should* teachers join in community activities?" (p. 152). Is this an affirmation of an obligation, an affirmation of permission, or a denial that participation is forbidden to teachers? The question is unanswered in these studies as to whether or not the expectations, where they exist, apply to teachers as teachers or as responsible adults in the community.

3. Some people feel that teachers should not drink alcoholic beverages or date high school students. These restrictions on teacher conduct receive the highest endorsement of all in the several surveys of conduct codes, but even then the consensus is hardly overwhelming. About one-half of a group of citizens in Washington State would not employ teachers who drink, and smaller proportions of them objected to smoking, dancing, and drinking (Jaynes, 1951). Half of Lichliter's (1946) teachers believed they were forbidden to drink and to date their students; negligible proportions said they were forbidden to dance, play cards, wear rouge, or spend weekends away from the community. Lichliter was impressed by the fact that 27 per cent of these small town teachers reported no restrictions of any kind. Again, are the codes for teachers, where they exist, different from the codes applicable to any citizen, male or female? Or are teachers' transgressions of the codes more severely sanctioned? The survey studies do not tell.

4. Most teachers do not feel that pressures are applied to them regarding their out-of-school conduct. Only one-fourth of the Missouri teachers felt "some pressures" on their personal habits (Callaway, 1951). The National Education Association's (1957) comprehensive national survey showed 65 per cent of the teachers reporting no restrictions on their personal lives, 33 per cent reporting "some restrictions, but not serious," and 2 per cent reporting serious restrictions. Higher frequencies of restrictions appear among teachers in the smaller communities.

Two problems of interpretation arise in these data. First, the inclination to report pressures may well be more indicative of the teacher's lack of commitment to teaching than of the objective circumstances. Thus, older teachers reported restrictions less frequently than younger teachers; restrictions were reported with decreasing frequency as one proceeded from single men (highest frequency), to married men, to married women, and to single women (lowest frequency); and of those reporting no restrictions, 77 per cent also reported that they would enter teaching again (National Education Association, 1957). It is impossible to trace out the cause-effect relations in these data, but the suspicion remains that variations in reports of this nature are more closely associated with respondent characteristics than with situation characteristics.

The second problem of interpretation arises from an entirely different source. If we take Brookover's analysis seriously (see pp. 766–767) and assume that teachers are likely to internalize the role prescriptions of the communities in which they work, we would anticipate that few of them would feel or report external pressures. Hence such internalization would make it impossible to measure community role prescriptions in terms of teachers' reports of restrictions or pressures to which they are subjected.

Criticism of the studies. We are forced to conclude this brief review of the empirical data regarding teachers' community relations on a severely critical note. The findings are mundane: Teachers participate in a variety of community activities; some teachers say they are expected or pressed to participate in them; some people believe teachers should not drink, date students, smoke in public, and so on, or, at least, some teachers think people believe this; and most teachers do not feel that pressures are applied to them by the community with respect to forms of out-of-school conduct. These findings are also equivocal in their implications. It is impossible, further, to compare the results of one study with those of another: The populations of subjects from whom responses were obtained are not comparable, and, even if they were, the questions to which the subjects responded differ (usually in an indeterminate way) in meaning. Finally, the questionnaire surveys beginning with the Cook study offer little in the way of evidence either to support or to deny the prevailing conceptions of the teacher's relationship to the community, except as one chooses to emphasize certain findings and ignore others. Concentrating as they do on description, lacking an explicit theoretical framework, their findings are little more than unassimilated bits of intelligence.

These criticisms of the line of studies instigated by the Cook and Greenhoe surveys are not intended as an indictment of these early investigators. They were, after all, opening a new area to empirical investigation, and they conducted their studies at a time when the methodology of survey research was poorly developed. The criticisms, rather, are intended to warn contemporary students against accepting their data unequivocally. Nor is this an empty warning. A recent research article on the teacher's role begins with these words: "It is safe to say that there are more constraints and demands upon the teacher than upon almost any other member of the community" (Getzels & Guba, 1955, p. 30). Even the recent textbooks in educational sociology tend to describe the teacher's community relations much as Waller did in 1932, citing the Cook surveys as evidence (Brookover, 1955b; Dahlke, 1958; Havighurst & Neugarten, 1957). While some of these contemporary writers (Grobman & Hines, 1957; Havighurst & Neugarten, 1957) remark on the loosening of community constraints on the teacher, attributable, they suggest, to the teacher shortage and to changes in general cultural standards, the model

which still dominates scholarship in the field is that of the teacher in the sacred community. That some teachers are (or were) subjected to severe community constraints cannot be doubted without denying the authenticity of the autobiographical documents introduced as evidence in numerous writings, and this we do not propose to do. It is the universality of this situation which we question and which the empirical evidence fails to support.

Effects of Community Constraints on the Classroom

Earlier we pointed to one of the implications of the teacher's supposedly marginal position in the community: his lack of autonomy in carrying out the teaching functions within the classroom. To the degree that he is submissive in the face of community demands, the teacher does not figure as a variable in the equation linking community forces to the conduct of the teaching-learning process. This view of the teacher as a passive agent is similar in some respects to that implied in educational research devoted to academic freedom and to pressures of organized interest groups. Understandably concerned with attacks on the public schools, educators have devoted considerable energy to documenting instances of infringed academic freedom. The obvious presumption is that public outcry against the schools or against certain of its teachings instills fear in the hearts of teachers and constrains their pursuit of educational goals in the classroom. Considerable effort has been devoted to documenting the means by which the special pleadings of organized interest groups are introduced into the classroom and curricula of the schools.[17] The implicit conceptual

---

[17] We cannot attempt to cite even the more prominent studies in this line of educational research. The reader is advised to refer to the *Review of Educational Research,* especially the issues treating school-community relations, where the research literature is periodically reviewed (Jenson & Staub, 1961; Naslund & Brown, 1958).

model is more optimistic in this line of investigation, however, than in writings on the teacher's community relations. On the one hand, it is presumed that teachers and other school personnel can mobilize their own resources to defend themselves and the school against attack and even to forestall destructive criticism. Thus, part of the literature in this realm furnishes school personnel with factual evidence to refute critics of public education and offers advice on means of developing a popular base of support for the schools in the local community. Further, it is presumed that if teachers can be made aware of or sensitized to the pleadings and pressures of the special interest groups, they will abandon their compliant role and no longer transmit the pleadings. Odell's (1957) empirical study of teachers' awareness of propaganda in teaching materials is notable in this connection, not for its merits as an investigation but because it raises the question of the extent to which teachers passively comply with such pressures.

Several additional implications also underlie the prevailing conception of community-imposed constraints on the teacher insofar as they are presumed to affect the teaching-learning process. One of these is the influence of information about the teacher's "sad plight" in shaping the composition of the occupational group and, thus, in determining the kind of person who confronts students in the classroom. A number of studies, of which B. N. Phillips' (1955) is an example, have surveyed the opinions of high school students regarding the teacher's community life, reasoning that foreknowledge of the constraints on the teacher discourages the more promising young persons from choosing teaching as a career. In the same vein, much of the voluminous literature on job satisfaction and teacher turnover is predicated on the assumption that the imposition of community constraints is one of the factors driving "better" persons out of the teaching corps. Studies by Martindale (1951) and Pepper (1954) are typical examples.

Another kind of implication arises from a

different source. On the assumption that "good teaching" requires teachers who know fully the social and cultural conditions within which their students live and who are familiar with the problems as well as the resources of the community, the teacher's transient or marginal community position is said to militate against classroom competency (Greenhoe, 1941, pp. 73–74). Such teachers are unable to integrate the academic curriculum with issues of vital and immediate concern to the students.

Of all these implications, only the last has been tested, and then in only one serious study (Brookover, 1945). No significant correlations were found between teaching ability, measured by pupil gains in knowledge of history, and such indicators of teachers' community position as length of residence, extent of community participation, or extent of acquaintanceships in the community. No attempt was made in this study to examine the mediating variables between community position and "good teaching," viz., the teacher's knowledge of local conditions and his interest or ability in effecting integration with academic subject matter, as specified in the basic assumption.

Secularization of the School Community

In the absence of definitive evidence as to how universal community constraints on the teacher were at any previous point in time, it is difficult to verify the observation of some writers that they have relaxed in recent years. A case can be made in favor of such an observation, however, on the basis of circumstantial evidence. Strongest evidence for this case is the fact that fewer and fewer schools today are located in communities approximating the pure type of the sacred community. This is a consequence not only of the increasing secularization of American society but of the trend toward relocation of the schools, through consolidation and district reorganization, in more secular communities. With social differentiation and cultural heterogeneity in the secular community, and, indeed, with the demise of the community itself as the organizing base for values and beliefs, expectations on the teacher are likely to be multiple rather than unitary, ill defined rather than sharply drawn. If it *were* necessary, the teacher could escape his occupational identity in the relative anonymity of the secular community. Thus, the urbanized setting offers the person a variety of statuses which are not principally dependent upon his occupational classification, and the recent massive extension of the teaching corps to include persons with cross-cutting social statuses, such as married females, diminishes the likelihood that teachers will be responded to exclusively as teachers.

The case becomes stronger as we trace out the implications of the lengthened period of occupational preparation, of the growth in the number and significance of professional associations, and of the undersupply of teachers in recent years. The latter fact not only signifies that employing officials probably find it wiser not to impose unpopular restrictions on members of the school faculty. It also means that teachers no longer must look to these community agents so exclusively for "security and approval" which, in Brookover's analysis, leads to the teacher's internalization of the desires and beliefs of the controlling group. The lengthened period of teacher training and the growth in the significance of professional associations suggest that more teachers internalize and find social support for role definitions other than those defined by laymen.

The point of these comments is not so much to argue that community controls on the teacher have loosened in recent years as to stimulate analyses of the conditions under which constraints are likely to arise within the community and to affect the teacher. We have attempted to generalize the descriptive model of the teacher's community relations and transform it into an analytical model capable of generating research questions of more than passing moment. As limited as the attempt is, it may help to offset the prevailing approach to the teacher's position in the community which is our legacy from an earlier generation.[18]

ROLE ANALYSIS AND COMMUNITY EXPECTATIONS

During the 1950's, an increasing number of studies introduced a different formulation of the research problem of the teacher's community relations. The earlier studies were purely descriptive ones in which the responses of teachers or other informants were taken at face value to reveal the realities of the teacher's situation. Such studies began to give way to those in which these same responses were taken as problematic in their own right. In place of the research question, "How extensive *are* the constraints on the teacher?" another question was asked, "What is the significance of the fact that respondents do not uniformly agree in describing the constraints?" To an extent this shift was forced on investigators by incongruities in the data from the descriptive surveys. Manwiller (1958, p. 318), for example, was piqued by the fact that an earlier investigator, who had interviewed more than one teacher in a given community about constraints on them, found a lack of agreement among them on the extent and nature of restrictions.

A more prominent factor in the shift, however, was the entry into educational research of the concepts of role theory. This influential framework, developed in social psychology and related disciplines, takes the view that expectations are products of group interaction, that different groups of people, including teachers, may define expectations in different ways, and that a person's perception of the expectations in even his own group are not necessarily veridical. Problems of consensus and conflict in expectations on the teacher and problems of the veridicality of perceptions of expectations came to be taken

[18] For a similarly inspired analysis of the community from the point of view of an anthropologist, see Gillin's (1955) discussion.

as the focus of research in a number of studies. The major empirical task in such studies was that of tracing out the causes and consequences of role consensus or conflict in the school setting. From the standpoint of role analysis, the community is but one of a larger number of sources from which role expectations emanate to form a kind of social environment for the teacher. Other sources of expectations are his colleagues or the administrative officers in the school. In any event, formulations in terms of role theory tend to subordinate the research area of the teacher's community relations to the more general problem of role expectations on the teacher, whatever their source. The role expectations on the teacher are, in turn, a special case of the still more general problem of expectations on any status occupant, whether student, superintendent, principal, in or out of the educational institution. While there are profound advantages in this assimilation to a more general level of theory, we are obliged to point out that the particular mode of abstraction in role analysis is, in practice if not in principle, limited to *expectations* held by those in the teacher's milieu. Research to date has tended to ignore the extent and nature of the status occupant's *interaction* with the persons constituting his social environment, a matter which was at the heart of the educational sociologists' formulation of the teacher's community relations in previous years. In this sense, shifts to role analysis have not represented pure gain.

An attempt to review the literature on community expectations from the standpoint of role analysis confronts us with problems of presentation. First of all, the most significant educational literature on role analysis per se deals with role expectations on the superintendent, the school board, and other officials (Gross, Mason, & McEachern, 1958), or with expectations on the teacher from a variety of sources (Getzels & Guba, 1957), not specifically from the community. Hence, much of the material falls outside the scope of our review altogether or belongs more appropriately in the final section. Second, since

the small amount of appropriate literature has focused on such a heterogeneity of issues, findings are not cumulative or comparable. Finally, role analysis, and especially the analysis of role agreement and of role conflict, is beset by intricate methodological and conceptual problems to which many investigators have been oblivious. Recognition of these problems has come about in education only in very recent years (Biddle, Rosencranz, & Rankin, 1961, Vol. 1; Gross, Mason, & McEachern, 1958), and a review of the research literature must discuss some of the more salient methodological issues.

Our solution to these difficulties is to discuss at this point only the studies specifically relevant to community role expectations and to reserve for a later section a more detailed treatment of role concepts and methodological problems. We similarly postpone a thorough consideration of the presumed impact of role expectations upon the teacher and, through the teacher, on the teaching-learning process. Only a few comments directly arising from the studies under review will be introduced in the present context.

Empirical Research on Community Role Expectations

The now classic study by Jenkins and Lippitt (1951), centering on the teacher-parent, the teacher-student, and the parent-student relationships in a Massachusetts junior high school, is a logical point of departure for our discussion. These investigators obtained free-response data bearing upon all three relationships from teachers, from parents, and from students. Each group was, of course, directly involved in two of the relationships but was an outside observer of the third. Each respondent was asked for his own reactions and for his estimates of the opposite party's reactions regarding the two relationships in which he was involved; regarding the relationship which he only observed, he was asked for his estimate of the reactions of each party to the other. For example, each teacher was asked what he liked and did not like about the way parents behaved toward him as a teacher and about the way students behaved toward him as a teacher. He was also asked to estimate what parents and what students liked (and did not like) about the way teachers behaved toward them. Finally, the teacher was asked to estimate the likes and dislikes of parents concerning the behavior of their children toward them as parents and to estimate the likes and dislikes of students concerning their parents' behavior. Similar data were collected from parent respondents and from student respondents.

In analyzing these complex data, the investigators first had to establish categories of "likes" and "dislikes" to use in coding the free-response material. The free-response format required a different kind of data analysis than that involved in the customary check-list format. Given freedom to mention any like or dislike which came to mind, respondents did not always express themselves on the same matters. Consequently, the major burden of the Jenkins and Lippitt analysis was carried by comparisons of the relative frequency with which specific kinds of likes and dislikes were mentioned by the various respondents.

Not surprisingly, the dominating concern in the teacher-parent relationship, to which we will confine our summary (Jenkins & Lippitt, 1951, Ch. 3), was the relation of the adults to the third party—the student. In this realm, the data suggested that some severe misunderstandings existed among the teachers regarding the interests of parents. Nearly one-half of the teachers believed that the parents wished them to give special attention to their own child, to be interested in the child as an individual, and to help students with their personal problems, whereas fewer than one-quarter of the parents actually mentioned these as things they liked teachers to do. Taken at face value, it seemed that many teachers *inaccurately* perceived parents as making demands on them which they could fulfill only with difficulty. The authors raised the question, however, as to whether this was really a misunderstanding

on the part of teachers or whether parents were reluctant to admit such feelings to interviewers. Whichever was the case, it signified a problem confronting teachers.

A second major conclusion of the study is aptly summarized in this statement: "Whereas the parents see their major contact with the teacher arising from their common interest in the child, the teachers express a strong need for a relationship based on adult-adult contacts" (Jenkins & Lippitt, 1951, p. 50). Several pieces of evidence undergirded this conclusion. While the relation of adults to students was the dominating concern of the teacher-parent relationship, as we noted above, it was more strongly expressed by parents than by teachers. That is to say, when parents described what they liked and disliked about the behavior of teachers, it usually was about the way teachers behaved toward students, not toward them as parents. When teachers estimated parents' likes and dislikes regarding their behavior as teachers, again the teachers were concerned about the way teachers behaved toward students. But when teachers reported their own likes and dislikes about the behavior of parents, they usually dealt with the way parents behaved toward them as teachers, not toward the child. Relatively high proportions of teachers said they liked parents who appreciate the teacher's efforts, who are friendly with the teacher, who are sincere to the teacher and not "hypocritical or gushy," and who are fair in their criticisms of the teacher. Yet, virtually none of the parents attributed such interests to the teacher; they apparently saw the teachers' interests as entirely consumed by their classroom relations with students.

The Jenkins and Lippitt findings, though provocative, must be taken as strictly tentative. Aside from the question of how far they can be generalized beyond the Massachusetts school, the conclusions harbor a certain indeterminacy arising from the free-response format of the study. Just because a respondent did not mention a particular like or dislike in the interview or questionnaire does not certify that he had no feelings about it or was unaware of others' concerns with it. Had parents, for example, been queried directly on the issue of teachers' desires for adult contacts with them, their perceptions may well have proved to be more accurate than the Jenkins and Lippitt data allow. Theirs was an exploratory, hypothesis-producing study, the conclusions of which must be tested by more rigorous methods.

Several recent studies provided data bearing upon the general problem of misperceptions which Jenkins and Lippitt raised. Doyle (1956) found that the teaching functions which elementary school teachers believed were expected of them by parents, board members, and administrators did not correspond to what these groups in fact expected of them. In a similar vein, Biddle, Rosencranz, and Rankin (1961, Vol. 5) reported a persistent tendency of respondents (predominantly parents and pupils) to attribute to "people in general" expectations of the teacher which they themselves did not hold. The respondents saw "people in general" as wanting teachers to be disciplinary and directive and to exercise close control over pupils, to participate in community activities and attend Parent-Teachers Association meetings, and to perform menial and other nonteaching chores. The investigators could find no evidence that any group actually held such restrictive expectations. But whether the attributions were correct or incorrect, the fact that respondents believed their own definition of the teacher's role was so different from the definition of "people in general" led the investigators to propose that persons apply a double standard to their own behavior toward teachers.

There exist startling and persistent disparities between roles for the teacher held by respondents and attributed (mistakenly) by respondents to others. . . . This suggests that many persons operate on two levels with regard to judgments made about the public school teacher, a private and a public one. When a school official, for instance, interacts with a teacher in a situation structured as "private," he may be able to apply standards for conduct which he, himself, holds. On the other hand, when the situation is "public," he will be likely to utilize standards which he attributes (however incorrectly) to "the public" (Biddle, Rosencranz, & Rankin, 1961, Vol. 5, p. 93).

Biddle's findings throw serious doubt on a fundamental assumption of the educational sociologists: that respondents can report accurately on the expectations held by other people around them. Can we trust the reports by teachers of what "the public" expects of them to coincide with reality? Can we count on the reports of parents on what "parents" expect of teachers to approximate what parents do, in fact, expect of teachers? It is even more difficult for informants to report accurately when there is no consensus in "the public" or among "parents." And of the absence of consensus on role definitions in some communities, there can be no doubt (Gross, Mason, & McEachern, 1958; Manwiller, 1958). Extensive evidence, most of it beyond the scope of this review, suggests that we place faith in the accuracy of informants on such matters only at our peril. Biddle would suggest, more specifically, that when we do, we may see the constraints as more prudish and more restrictive than they really are.

Some role studies, such as those cited above, concentrate on the amount of *agreement* between sets of expectations. The agreement may be that within a given population (Manwiller, 1958), between expectations from two or more populations, between definitions of role attributed by one party to another and the actual definitions of the other party (Doyle, 1956; Jenkins & Lippitt, 1951), or between definitions of role attributed by one party to another and the attributors' own role definitions (Biddle, Rosencranz, & Rankin, 1961, Vol. 5). Other role studies concentrate on *conflict* in expectations, a distinction which will be elaborated on in a later section.

Getzels and Guba (1955) made a prominent study of conflict in expectations. They confronted teachers in six Midwestern school systems with some 70 statements, each of which referred to a stressful or logically incompatible demand which community members could make on the teacher, and asked them to rate the statements as to the proportion of teachers in their schools who would agree that such demands existed and the extent to which the demands troubled them personally. The statements reflected three aspects of conflict in the teacher's role: (1) between expectations on the teacher to maintain a middle-class standard of living and a salary too small to allow him to conform to the expectations, (2) between the teacher's status as a responsible, adult citizen and constraints placed upon him qua teacher, and (3) between the presumption of the teacher's professional competence and expectations that he will submit to the encroachments of others on his field of expertness. A statement illustrating the third aspect of role conflict follows:

While many parents expect the teacher to discipline their children as well as to educate them, these same parents are often resentful of the disciplinary methods employed, even when those methods are justified (Getzels & Guba, 1955, p. 32).

Results of teachers' reports on the incidence of conflicting demands showed some understandable variations from one school system to another. Thus, demands on the teacher to maintain a middle-class standard of living on an inadequate salary were most commonly acknowledged in the school system with the lowest salary schedule; conflicts between the citizen and teacher role were most frequently acknowledged "by the teachers of a rural secondary school in a relatively isolated community where teacher visibility is quite high"; and "conflicts arising from restraints placed upon teachers with respect to marriage, is scored highest in the teaching situation whose contracts include a provision forbidding the teacher to marry while in the employ of that community" (Getzels & Guba, 1955, pp. 36, 37). The teachers who reported themselves to be the most troubled personally by the demands were those who also reported themselves to be alienated from or marginal to the teaching occupation and the community in which they taught. Teachers with the higher conflict scores had relatively few friends in the community, felt their relations with the administration were not satisfactory, believed other teachers had more influence with the administration than they, and felt that teaching was a wrong occupational choice for them. It is impossible, however, to determine the direction of causation from the data—to determine whether alienation was the consequence of role conflict or whether acknowledgment of conflict was simply another form in which respondents expressed their alienation. This kind of indeterminacy is especially problematic in studies where measures of both the dependent and independent variables are based upon data furnished by the same respondents.

The Effects on Teaching of Discrepancies in Expectations

We will pause only briefly here to note the effects of role disagreement and role conflict propounded in the literature which we have reviewed, reserving for a later section (pp. 797–800) a detailed treatment of the matter. For the most part, the arguments are similar to those associated with earlier studies of community constraints on the teacher. Disagreement or conflict in role definitions is a form of occupational disadvantage, driving the more competent persons out of the ranks of teaching and leaving behind those who are the most compliant and submissive or, perhaps, those who are most able to tolerate ambiguity and cope with conflict. Discrepancies in expectations, too, are presumed to be frustrating to the teacher, reducing his effectiveness in the teaching situation.

The rationale of the Jenkins and Lippitt (1951) study also was expressed in terms of the effects of misperceptions on the satisfaction of participants in the role relationships, but it was more closely articulated with social psychological theory.

The importance of accurate interpersonal perceptions lies in the fact that people are dependent upon each other for the fulfillment of psychological as well as physical needs. Because of their interdependence, individuals find it necessary to make some adjustments to each other. Their working relationship is established most satisfactorily when each is willing to recognize the needs of the other and both work together to satisfy their respective needs. If, however, either individual fails to make the necessary adjustments, or through inappropriate behavior fails to meet adequately the needs of the other, maladjustment seems bound to result. The second person may retaliate by failing to meet adequately the needs of the first or, at the very least, he will have to search elsewhere to find satisfactions for needs which legitimately should be met by the first individual. In either case the productivity of the individual and the harmony between these two persons will be affected (Jenkins & Lippitt, 1951, pp. 20–21).

Specifically for teachers, Jenkins and Lippitt noted (but did not test) the following kinds of consequence of divergence in interpersonal perceptions:

1. Teachers become insecure in their jobs and "need a greater amount of recognition and attention from their students" when parents fail to satisfy their needs (Jenkins & Lippitt, 1951, p. 23).

2. Cleavage increases between the parties, further reducing their ability to communicate with one another and, hence, their opportunity for common understanding.

3. Relationships within the teacher group deteriorate when the needs of teachers are not met satisfactorily by members of other groups; the common frustrations may "result in aggressions among the group members themselves, reducing their ability to get on with their own task efficiently" (Jenkins & Lippitt, 1951, p. 24).

In the second point, above, the authors refer to communication as a key condition determining whether participants in a role relationship will avoid misperceptions. Their observation regarding the spiraling effect of communication breakdown and misperceptions—where communication barriers lead to misunderstandings, which lead, in turn, to further barriers to communication—is reminiscent of Newcomb's (1947) autistic hostility hypothesis. Significantly, their observation provides a link between the literature on teacher role expectations and the educational sociologists' discussions regarding restrictions on the teacher's participation in the sacred community. To the degree that barriers to parent-teacher communication exist, and especially barriers preventing free communication about their feelings toward one another, disagreements in role perceptions are likely to arise (Jenkins & Lippitt, 1951, pp. 86–88). This is not just a matter of the frequency of occasions for teachers and parents or other community members to interact, but of the nature of the communication which transpires among them when they do. If the interaction is confined to stereotyped or formalistic communication, as the sociologists allege it is in the sacred community, it will not be adequate to prevent misperceptions. Formalistic interaction is a most insidious barrier to communication, in Jenkins and Lippitt's terms. Hence, in the sacred community, or wherever any kind of barrier to spontaneous self-revelatory communication exists, role misperceptions, disagreements, or even conflict will arise.

OTHER ASPECTS OF THE COMMUNITY ENVIRONMENT

Social and cultural forces from the community influence occupants of the teacher status and thereby affect the teaching-learning process in many ways other than those we have discussed so far. For example, the climate of public opinion regarding the schools, be it a climate of indifference, or overprotectiveness, or antagonism, certainly is sensed by the teacher and may well affect what he attempts to do in the classroom. Other features of the community—its wealth, is geographical location, its attractiveness as a place to live—help to select the kind of person who will serve as a teacher in its schools. But in the absence of systematic research suggesting how these forces are translated into observable influence on the teacher or classroom, we have left them unmentioned.

It is fitting, then, to close the present section with reference to the logical model proposed by Paul Mort (Mort, 1954; Mort & Furno, 1960) to describe the way in which community characteristics come to bear upon the educational program of the local schools. This model, called the Sequential Simplex, is an outgrowth of nearly 30 years of programatic research on school adaptability conducted by Mort and his colleagues. By *adaptability* is meant the extent to which a given school system incorporates the educational practices regarded as desirable by leading professional educators. Operationally, it is measured by an elaborate rating form, sometimes self-administered and sometimes administered by trained observers, on which the presence or absence of a wide range of educational practices in the classrooms or in the school at large is noted. Ratings of the separate practices are numerically weighted and combined to yield an adaptability score. The early instrument, the Mort-Cornell Guide, painstakingly constructed for a statewide study of Pennsylvania school systems during the 1930's (Mort & Cornell, 1941), has since appeared in several modified forms (Mort & Pierce, 1947; Ross, 1958, Appendix B). While there may be disagreement as to whether adaptability scores measure "good education," the fact remains that extensive application of these instruments to school systems has revealed major variations among schools which are meaningfully related to a variety of community measures. Adaptability is found to correlate with such characteristics of school and community as population size and growth, property value, tax rate and tax leeway, occupational composition and level of educational attainment of the population, pupil-teacher ratio, teacher salary level, trends in postal receipts, and opinion poll responses (Ross, 1958, Part 3). On this wide assortment of correlates of adaptability the Sequential Simplex model seeks to impose logical order.

The model sorts the characteristics known to be correlated with adaptability into four clusters, or *panels,* logically arranged according to the remoteness of their effect upon the criterion, school "quality" or adaptability:

> Characteristics of the immediate school
> School system policy
> Educational climate of the community
> Community characteristics.

The forces acting to produce school quality may be looked upon as a series of concentric spheres or as an onion with its layers of leaves. At the core is the criterion measuring school quality. The innermost sphere, having the most direct and immediate influence upon quality is "The School" itself with its staff of educators. The next sphere or level of remoteness from the product is "The School System Policy" including such considerations as salaries, numbers of staff, and adequacy of supplies. Moving another minute away from quality (in time but not in impact) is "The Educational Climate" as determined by the expenditure level and socio-economic factors in the community. The encompassing sphere is "The Community Characteristics," represented by such factors as wealth and certain socioeconomic and physical considerations (Mort & Furno, 1960, pp. 13–14).

This arrangement of clusters introduces *by assumption* a sequential flow of causation from the most remote through the less remote clusters to the adaptability criterion.

The resources of the community (natural, technical, human, and cultural) set the tone of "The Educational Climate," primarily expenditure level. These two combine to shape "The School System Policy" (salaries, staffing patterns, supply purchases, and so on). The vector of the first three spheres largely determines the quality of personnel hired. The personnel are the ones that deal directly with the pupils, thus through their skills (or lack of skills) the quality of the educational product is determined (Mort & Furno, 1960, p. 14).

The characteristics forming each of the four clusters were assembled by statistical rather than rational considerations. For any given characteristic, the statistical question was asked, does it enhance the predictive power of the cluster? If the answer was yes, if its inclusion increased the multiple correlation between the measures in the cluster and the adaptability criterion, it was regarded as a member of that cluster. In this way, it was possible for a given characteristic to meet the statistical requirement in two or more clusters; opinion poll responses, for example, enhanced the predictive power of all four clusters and were included in each. Each cluster, in the end, was found to correlate between .7 and .8 with the criterion. The clusters, however, are independent of one another in the sense that "little improvement is made in the relationship with the criterion if the four panels are combined in a multiple correlation. In other words, each panel measures approximately the same thing, but at different levels in the time sequence" (Mort & Furno, 1960, p. 15). They are not independent in the sense of being orthogonal to one another.

The Sequential Simplex is an attempt to bring order out of diversity by introducing assumptions regarding the direction of causality into an array of correlational data. The statistical manipulations which locate given characteristics in their appropriate clusters in no sense test the assumptions; they merely follow from the assumptions. The test of the assumptions and of the model in which they are encompassed lies, first, in its capacity, in comparison with other models, to order the relevant knowledge and, second, in its fruitfulness in generating new knowledge. In this respect, of course, it does not differ from any other scientific theory.

THE TEACHER IN THE SCHOOL

The most immediate environment for the teacher and the teaching-learning process is, of course, the school and the system of social relationships of which it consists. We may view the school as an organization of roles designed expressly to educate successive generations of children of the community. The roles are goal-oriented in that the activities and social relationships they specify are those, and only those, believed to contribute to the organization's purpose. Also, the roles are formal and impersonal in the sense that the activities and interactions expected of role incumbents do not change when the incumbents change; the claims and obligations of incumbents on one another are defined without regard for who they happen to be. The behavior of a particular teacher, caught up in the system of interlocking roles, is bounded by the fact that he is dependent upon the role performance of other school personnel and they are dependent upon his. The interdependent relationships of school personnel exist even in the absence of direct, personal interaction among them; the interdependency is inherent in the way their tasks are organized.

The teacher's involvement in this system of relationships has important consequences for him and for his conduct of the teaching-learning process. Some of these consequences are so patent that we often fail to appreciate their significance. Knowing only the formal definition of a person's role in the school and certain salient attributes of the organization of work, one can determine with a high degree of precision what behaviors that person will engage in at what times, at what places, and with what material resources, with whom he will communicate on what subjects, with what other persons his crucial relationships will be established, and among what group of persons he will find companionship. All this without reference to his motives, moods, feelings, or whims. The prevailing "human relations" emphasis in educational literature inclines us to lose perspective on these less personalized effects of the teacher's entry into the social system of the school. Nevertheless, the "human relations" approach has pointed to influences emanating from the social relationships in the school which are not as obvious as the foregoing.

The great preponderance of the empirical research has been restricted to two central relationships of the teacher, the teacher-administrator relationship and the teacher-pupil relationship; the latter of these is reviewed elsewhere (see especially Chapter 13) in this Handbook. Curiously, one of the most significant of the teacher's relationships—the informal colleague relationship—has been virtually ignored in educational research. Nor has the teacher's involvement in the *system* of social relationships been investigated in many studies, although batteries of relevant concepts, such as *power, group norms, communication network,* have begun to appear in the discursive, if not the empirical, literature of education.

STYLES OF ADMINISTRATIVE BEHAVIOR

The teacher in the American public school typically stands in relation to some officer who is responsible, at least nominally, for the teacher's instructional activities. The precise location of this office within the school's administrative structure and the nature of the supervisory responsibilities associated with it are by no means firmly established at the present time. The unsettled disposition of supervisory responsibilities seems to center on the distinction between "administration" and "supervision" which is drawn and even institutionalized in American education. Responsibility for the supervision of classroom teaching typically rests in the hands of the principal, or the district superintendent in smaller units. But the demands on these officers to perform managerial functions in their increasingly complex organizational units often cause them to neglect their supervision responsibilities. The strain toward autonomy of the teacher, associated with the general increase in the level of teacher training and technical competence over the years, fortifies this tendency. As a matter of fact, the specialized competence and training of some teachers exceeds that of their generally trained administrative officers, thereby altering the relative position of the teacher and the person who would supervise him. In some larger school systems, the responsibility for classroom supervision is separated from administrative officers and placed in the hands of a corps of specialists variously called "supervisors," "consultants," "coordinators," and so on. But whatever the disposition of responsibilities may be, the teacher-administrator relationship is an especially sensitive one in the public school.

Some of the earlier studies were concerned with the absence or presence of a supervisory relationship; these studies compared pupil achievement under supervised and unsupervised teachers.[19] But educators have been far more engrossed in the character or style of that relationship, especially as its tone is set by the administrative officer in the school.

Autocratic and Democratic Leadership Styles

As the reader is well aware, the most popular way of talking about leadership in education—whether with respect to the classroom, the school, or the community—is in terms of the autocratic-democratic dimension. Originating in the "group atmosphere" studies of Kurt Lewin and his associates in the late 1930's (White & Lippitt, 1960), the dimension rapidly entered into educational ideology. Hardly a textbook on school administration fails to invoke the distinction between autocratic and democratic leadership, but educational research in which the distinction is applied is relatively scarce. For the most part, the empirical basis of discussion in education consists of extrapolations from a few prominent studies conducted in other settings. A detailed treatment of the autocratic-democratic dimension would carry us into the social psychological literature on leadership and related topics well beyond the scope of this review, so we will discuss the distinction only as it appears in research on the administrator-teacher relationship.

---

[19] Readers wishing to pursue this research should consult Barr's summary, which cites 12 studies "testifying to the general worth of supervision" (Barr, 1950, p. 1372).

The following descriptions of autocratic and democratic leadership styles bring out the central features of this typology.

[The hardboiled autocrat] is the supervisor who believes that he must constantly check up on everyone to keep up production. He gives the orders and employees carry them out. He believes that the only way to get conscientious performance is to expect and secure discipline and immediate acceptance of all orders. He is careful not to spoil the employee with too much praise, believing that because the employee is paid to work he needs nothing else. It is the employee's place to carry out directives, not to question or always understand them. This supervisor is usually very conscious of his position and authority and believes that employees cannot be trusted very long on their own initiative. . . .

The democratic supervisor endeavors wherever possible to share with his group the decision-making about work planning, assignment and scheduling. Where a decision must be made by him, he helps the group to understand clearly the basis for his decision. He is careful to develop as much participation, opinion-giving and decision-making as possible, and a feeling of responsibility for the success of the work on the part of everyone. He is concerned that each employee clearly understand his work and have opportunities for success in it. His praise and criticisms are always delivered objectively in terms of work results and never personally in terms of what he may or may not like. He encourages worthwhile suggestions and the development of new procedures (Bradford & Lippitt, 1945, pp. 143–145).

Bradford and Lippitt also described the "laissez-faire" style of leadership and a variant of the autocratic style, the "benevolent autocrat."

Several education studies have attempted to distinguish between autocratic school officials on the basis of the administrative practices they employ. Weber (1943) examined leadership techniques used by building principals in in-service training programs for teachers, although he referred to the styles as "traditional" and "cooperative." A series of studies conducted at the University of Florida, summarized by Hines and Grobman (1956) and by Wiles and Grobman (1958), applied the autocratic-democratic differentiation most forthrightly to the administrative practices of principals. As these investigators conceptualized the continuum, it contained most of the features of the Bradford-Lippitt descriptions cited above. These included such matters as the extent to which administrators arrange for teacher participation in decision-making, maintain free channels of communication, exercise influence so as to enhance and not reduce the personal security of teachers, manifest attitudes of respect for the dignity of the individual, and attempt to minimize status distinctions between themselves and teachers (Hines, 1956). To construct a measure of principals' leadership style, judges were asked to order on the autocratic-democratic continuum each of a variety of operational procedures which principals had been found to use in meeting on-the-job problem situations. (The judges' ratings, incidentally, corresponded closely to a second rating of the operational procedures on the basis of what they regarded as "good practices.") Scores were obtained for principals by asking their teachers and the principals themselves to report how they typically met the various problem situations.

Investigators sought relationships between democratic leadership style of elementary and high school principals and such variables as the incidence of curriculum change in the schools (number of added and modified courses, changes in daily schedules, in guidance procedures, and so on), faculty attitudes toward curriculum change, principals' own attitudes toward curriculum change, and measures of personality of the principal. A significant correlation was found between democratic style and incidence of curriculum change and, in elementary schools only, between democratic style and faculty attitudes toward, or "readiness for," change, but the reports give no assurance that the correlation could not be attributed to uncontrolled variables (Wiles & Grobman, 1958). The personality measures were unrelated to administrative style (Hines, 1956).

The conceptual similarity between autocratic administrative style and authoritarian personality structure has not escaped the notice of educational researchers, and, indeed, one of the measures used by Hines was the California F Scale, a measure of authoritarian tendencies in basic personality make-up (Adorno, et al., 1950). Some investigators have used the F Scale to distinguish between "authoritarian" and "non-authoritarian" school officials (Lambert, 1955) or to relate authoritarianism to expectations on the administrator's role (Wilcox, 1957), and some, like Hines (1956), have examined the relationship between authoritarian personality tendencies and manifest administrative style. At this point, however, it is not clear in what ways high and low F-Scale scores among administrators affect the instructional process of teachers.

Staff participation in decision-making. A central ingredient of the "democratic" as opposed to the "autocratic" style of administrative behavior, as previous paragraphs suggest, is the engagement of subordinates in the formulation of policy decisions, especially on matters of policy affecting them and their work. This aspect of democratic school administration has been the topic of much doctrinaire discussion, some controversy, and a little empirical investigation. Several mailed-questionnaire studies of teachers showed relationships between teacher reports on the extent of their participation in policy formulation and the extent of their satisfaction with the school (Chase, 1952) or between the agreement in their statements of who should and who does make decisions, on the one hand, and their satisfaction with the school, on the other (Sharma, 1955). Although widely quoted in the educational literature, these studies could not certify that participation caused satisfaction rather than the reverse or that the relationships were not spurious concomitants of other variables. The same observations apply less severely to Griffiths' (1952) study, in which he found greater staff partici-

pation in decision-making in school systems under superintendents rated as "most successful" than under superintendents rated as "least successful." At least Griffiths' measures on his variables came from independent sources.

The most sophisticated studies of teacher participation in decision-making were conducted by a group of investigators in four farm belt school districts in Illinois, following an articulated model of administrative behavior and teacher performance (Bey, 1956; Cornell, 1954a, 1954b, 1955; Inabnit, 1954). One version of the model (Cornell, 1954a) corresponds closely to the general framework we have used throughout this chapter and asks, in this case, how the organizational climate affects teacher behavior with respect to decision-making and how this behavior affects teacher performance in the teaching-learning process. The effects are seen to be mediated by differences in individual teacher characteristics. More specifically, the amount of time and energy devoted by teachers to participation in the solution of school system problems was conceived as the joint product of administrative arrangements for and expectations of *effective* decision-sharing, on the one hand, and such individual teacher variables as length of service in the system, amount of training, degree of professionalization (Minnesota Teacher Attitude Inventory), and personality characteristics (Thurstone Temperament Schedule). *Effective* decision-sharing meant, among other things, that teachers were accorded a high order of responsibility in formulating policy recommendations and that their recommendations carried significant weight in the final decisions. Data regarding administrative arrangements for effective decision-sharing were obtained from the teachers themselves, unfortunately, and more literally represent teacher *perceptions* of expectations, responsibility, and influence in decision-making. In any event, the actual amount of time teachers spend participating in decision-making was regarded as affecting their level of satisfaction with the school and their performance in the classroom. Teaching performance measures were obtained from pupil reports of classroom activities in terms of the "degree of departure from the conventional, regimented, assign-study-recite, classroom routine" (Cornell, 1955, p. 220).

Results of the analyses, however, showed the various relationships to be more complicated than anticipated by the model. Thus, the amount of teacher participation in decision-making was found to be unrelated to measures of teacher performance in the classroom and only slightly, although significantly ($r = .22$), related to teacher morale. Teacher morale and classroom performance were, themselves, modestly correlated. The most important influence operating on teacher satisfaction was not the extent to which the teacher actually participated in decision-making but, rather, his conception of its significance if he were to participate. That is, teacher perceptions of administrative arrangements for and encouragement of effective decision-sharing contributed heavily to a multiple regression on teacher satisfaction; the amount of time devoted to participation contributed negligibly to it. The interactive effects of individual teacher characteristics were interesting. When teacher morale scores were examined in pairs of systems whose administrators were classified as *most* and *least* inclined to share decisions, it became apparent that the morale of only the more professionalized teachers (above-average MTAI scores) was related to decision-sharing opportunities. That is, while administrative encouragement of decision-sharing enhanced morale, and administrative discouragement depressed morale among the more professionalized teachers, the level of morale among the less professionalized teachers remained the same regardless of the administrator's disposition with respect to decision-sharing. While the findings of the Cornell-Inabnit-Bey analyses must be replicated in other school systems, they strongly suggest that the relationship between staff participation in decision-making and teacher morale or teacher performance in the classroom is more intricate than the

educational literature has generally conceded it to be.

One additional study, also limited in scope, sought to relate administrative style in implementing curriculum revision to consensus among teachers and among administrators in their reports about and evaluations of the curriculum revision program (D. M. Jackson, 1957). Jackson selected four urban and suburban secondary schools for the investigation. In two schools, responsibility for program planning was widely shared among teachers and administrative personnel. In another two, responsibility was restricted to a few teachers directly involved in the core areas. (Involvement of administrative personnel in the latter two schools also varied substantially: The impetus for curriculum revision in one school was sustained largely by administrators and supervisors rather than even the core teachers, while in the other school, active administrative support for program revision seems to have been withdrawn altogether upon a change in the principalship.) Jackson found that consensus among administrative personnel, among core teachers, and among noncore teachers was greater in the first pair of schools ("group pattern of administrative procedures") than in the second pair. It is impossible, of course, to decide from this study whether consensus arose from the broad participation in program planning or whether the broad participation was possible because of the consensus among school personnel. Either alternative is consistent with social psychological theory.

Democratic administration and the teaching process. Much good is presumed to flow from a democratic style of leadership in schools. It enhances the motivation of teachers with respect to their work, inducing them to use their initiative and creativity and to apply themselves to the task at hand without undue concern for the teacher-administrator relationship per se. In this way, it brings about a high quality of performance in teaching, and it makes teachers better able to cope with emergencies and to adjust to new situations. Democratic leadership has a salutary effect on the interpersonal relations among teachers. These relationships become supportive and integrative, lacking the divisive tensions and incipient, if not overt, aggressions common under the autocratic leader. The relationships are task-oriented; teamwork is enhanced. For the individual teacher, democratic leadership and the cohesive, supportive group of colleagues that it produces promote self-respect, personal security, a feeling of belongingness, a sense of success, and generally an aura of well-being and satisfaction.

Decision-sharing is believed to have many of the same effects. Cornell (1954b) analyzed the popular arguments for involving teachers in policy-making in these terms:

Some authorities on the subject of school administration tell us that "those affected by a decision should participate in making it." Some imply that "the more sharing of teachers in the making of policy" the better. Some of the positions held seem to be simply appeals to the gallery; others are accompanied by supporting arguments. Although few writers on the subject draw upon all of them, the arguments for increasing teacher involvement in the formation of policy run something like this:
1. It results in more democratic administration.
2. It improves the quality of decisions; the more talents brought into the process, the better the thinking and the better the solution.
3. It improves morale (however this may be defined).
4. It creates more effective execution of policy; sharing permits an understanding and develops a "sense of joint responsibility."
5. It achieves greater effectiveness of teachers in their jobs as teachers by stimulating adaptability and change necessary to improve instruction (Cornell, 1954b, p. 43).

To an extent, these merely repeat the advantages seen for democratic administration generally, of which subordinate involvement in policy formation is a central ingredient, but the two-way communication involved in decision-sharing also is presumed to improve the quality of decisions and to increase teachers' understanding of policies.

The evidence produced by educators on these assertions is slim and, for the most part, untrustworthy. As we have reported above, researchers specifically have related administrative style to the incidence of curriculum change, to teacher "readiness for change," to teacher satisfaction, or morale, to consensus in perceptions of curriculum revision programs, and to teacher performance in the classroom. The best we can say is that the studies show the assertions to be oversimplified. But perhaps we can expect no more from concepts as value-laden as "autocratic" and "democratic" administration. After all, research on central components of an ideological system is not likely to be impartial.

Other Styles of Administrative Behavior

Several investigators have developed conceptualizations of administrative style from theoretical systems or from theoretical and empirical analyses rather than from ideological premises. One of the more influential of such conceptualizations was derived from the Ohio State Leadership Studies (Hemphill & Coons, 1950) and is associated in educational administration with the work of Halpin (1956). According to this conception, administrative behavior varies on two principal dimensions—*initiation of structure* and *consideration*. These dimensions resulted from an extensive series of studies, mostly outside of education, on detailed descriptions of the behavior of leaders and factor analyses of these descriptions. In the course of these studies, Halpin and Winer (1952) found a parallel between results of the statistical analyses and the social psychological concepts of *goal achievement* and *group maintenance,* two necessary but not always compatible functions which must be served if a cooperative system is to persist.[20]

---

[20] As Halpin pointed out (1956, pp. 4–6), this pair of functions is found under one set of labels or another throughout the theoretical literature on the operation of social systems.

Initiating Structure refers to the leader's be-havior in delineating the relationship between himself and members of the work-group, and in endeavoring to establish well-defined pat-terns of organization, channels of communica-tion, and methods of procedure. Consideration refers to behavior indicative of friendship, mutual trust, respect, and warmth in the re-lationship between the leader and the members of his staff (Halpin, 1956, p. 4).

Measures of the frequency with which an ad-ministrator manifests behavior on each di-mension lead to a profile of administrative style for that person. An administrator may be high or low on both Initiating Structure and Consideration, or he may be high on one and low on the other.

Some emphasize group goal achievement even to the detriment of group maintenance. Others follow an opposite pattern and stress group maintenance to such an extent that they sacri-fice goal achievement. These styles obviously do not fall into a neat dichotomy. Various combinations occur. Accordingly, the two leader-behavior dimensions may be conceptual-ized best as a pair of co-ordinates with refer-ence to which any leader's behavior (or leader-ship ideology) may be described . . . (Halpin, 1956, p. 9).

Halpin hypothesized that effective leader-ship requires high performance on both di-mensions of leader behavior. [21]

A severe methodological problem has in-truded upon the attempts by Halpin (1956) and others (Hunter, 1959; Seeman, 1958) to describe the leadership style of school officials, using the Leader Behavior Description Ques-tionnaire (LBDQ). The procedure followed in the studies was to ask those who presum-ably were in a position to know the official—his superiors, his subordinates, and the official himself—to check each of 30 LBDQ items concerning the frequency with which the official "does personal favors for staff mem-bers," "emphasizes the meeting of deadlines," and the like. Fifteen items are scored for Initiation of Structure and 15 for Considera-tion. The studies showed, however, that the various informants did not agree in their de-scriptions of how the official behaves. In con-sequence, a difficult choice is posed for the investigator in deciding whose word to take on specifications of the official's administra-tive style.

A second prominent conceptualization of administrative style was developed by Getzels and his associates at the University of Chi-cago (Getzels & Guba, 1957; Guba & Bidwell, 1957). Drawing from the sociological writ-ings of Talcott Parsons, they constructed a theoretical framework for the analysis of so-cial systems such as the school and described three styles of administrative behavior con-sonant with the theory. They referred to the three types as the *nomothetic* leader, the *idio-graphic* leader, and the *transactional* leader.

The nomothetic leader stresses the require-ments of the institution and the conformity of role behavior to expectations at the expense of the individual personality and the satisfac-tion of needs. He perceives authority to be vested in his office, and he maintains the scope of his interactions with his subordinates in as diffuse a manner as possible. He places heavy emphasis on universalistic rules and procedures, and he imposes extrinsic sanctions whenever feasible. Effectiveness is his major standard of follower excellence.

The idiographic leader, in contrast, stresses the demands of the individual's personality, his need structure, and need-motivated be-havior. Here organizational requirements tend to be minimized. This leader views his author-ity as delegated, and he tends to maintain higher specific interactions with his subordi-nates. His relationships to others are, in general, particularistic, tailored to each indi-vidual's personality, and he places major re-liance upon intrinsic sanctions. Efficiency is his major standard of follower excellence (Guba & Bidwell, 1957, p. 11).

The transactional leader is an intermediate type lying between the nomothetic and idio-graphic extremes. He achieves a balanced per-

---

[21] Subsequently, Halpin presented an elaborate para-digm for assessing the contributions to organizational effectiveness uniquely associated with administrative behavior (Halpin, 1957); this paradigm is described in Chapter 3 of this Handbook.

spective on the demands of the institution and the requirements of the people who inhabit it, and he is capable of shifting his emphasis from one to the other as the occasion arises. The nomothetic-idiographic concepts bear a close resemblance to Halpin's concepts of Initiating Structure and Consideration in that they both distinguish between leaders principally oriented to the institution and the task and leaders oriented to personal relationships. The schemes are similar, too, in that they regard the effective leader as the one who can reconcile the fundamental conflict between the requirements of the system and the needs of the individuals. In Getzels' terms, such a person is the transactional leader; in Halpin's terms, he is the leader high in both Initiating Structure and Consideration.

Investigators who seek to measure the nomothetic-idiographic-transactional leadership styles of school officials apparently face the same problem which confronted Halpin: The parties providing the information about the official do not agree. Guba and Bidwell (1957) measured administrative style of principals in terms of the expectations held by the principal of his teachers. Thus, it was the principal's expectations of teachers which could classify him as nomothetic, idiographic, or transactional. To obtain the information, they asked principals to respond to a check list of teacher behaviors according to their own (the principals') expectations of teachers; they also asked teachers to report on what they believed their principals expected of them. While the investigators do not report the extent of agreement, it would seem from their data that it was not high. Commenting on the items for which the greatest divergence in reports occurred, they said:

Thus it appears that the principals are perceived as more idiographic and/or nomothetic than they themselves are able or willing to report. On the other hand. . . . the principal reports a larger number of transactional expectations than teachers are able or willing to perceive. To put it another way, the principals' expectations appear less transactional to teach-ers than the principals would like to believe (Guba & Bidwell, 1957, p. 57).

Moreover, when the investigators related the measures of administrative style based on principal reports and those based on teacher reports to outside variables, the pattern of relationship with the outside variables differed. Specifically, they found significant positive correlations between the extent to which teachers perceived their principals as transactional and teachers' self-reports of confidence in the principals' leadership, of their effectiveness as teachers, and of their satisfaction with the teaching situation. (Teacher perceptions of nomothetic leadership correlated negatively and perceptions of idiographic leadership correlated indifferently with the same outside variables.) But when the measure of administrative style was based upon principals' own reports, no correlations with teacher confidence, effectiveness, or satisfaction appeared. This difference reflects the fact that it is easier to find correlations between variables when their measures are not methodologically independent than when they are. We should point out, however, that for purposes of the Getzels theory, the absence of agreement on reports of administrative style is largely irrelevant. Most of the hypotheses which investigators have tested using this triad of administrative styles (Guba & Bidwell, 1957; Moser, 1957) deal not with the consequences of variations in administrative style per se but with the consequences of divergences of perceived style from desired style, of one's own behavior from perceived expectations of one's own behavior, and the like. In a sense, the very departures from agreement have been taken as the problem for investigation.

A number of additional concepts and measures of administrative style have been used in research during the last few years, some of which are but variants of the ones cited above. Like the concepts noted above, most of these were developed and used as a basis for measuring role agreement rather than as a means of examining the effects of one administrative style as opposed to another. Hence, we shall simply mention a few of them, referring the reader to the original sources for their detailed descriptions. As noted earlier in the review, Prince (1957) adapted Spindler's (1955) traditional and emergent values concepts to the administrative situation. Other distinctions include the leader-centered and follower-centered styles (Moyer, 1955), the formal-impersonal and informal-personal styles (Congreve, 1957), the hierarchic, democratic, and outer-oriented styles (Bidwell, 1957), and the more elaborate set offered by Sweitzer (1958) including the authority-centered, the inner-directed, the work-group–oriented, the individual-centered, and the other-directed administrative styles.

ROLE ANALYSIS

The analysis of the teacher's environment in terms of role is a topic we have touched on at several earlier points. The concept of *role* represents the social scientist's acknowledgment of certain uniformities observable in human behavior which are specific to situations. One may observe, for example, that a person who is a school teacher for part of his day, a bowling companion for another part, and a family man for another may behave in quite different or even contradictory ways in these various situations. Or, a number of individuals of quite different personal dispositions may show strikingly uniform modes of behavior, despite their disparate personality organizations, when all are teaching school, bowling, or enjoying the comforts of home. It is with these situationally specific uniformities in behavior that *role* and related concepts deal. The concept of *role* originated in several disciplines of the social sciences to serve somewhat different theoretical purposes, and the usage of the term is by no means consistent at the present time. Moreover, as role analysis has been put to empirical use in recent years, such a remarkable proliferation of related concepts has occurred that it is impossible to use the terms definitively. The reigning confusion can be illustrated by the fact that what

one author (Cameron, 1947, p. 90) means by *role* is what a second author (Newcomb, 1950, p. 228) means by *role behavior,* and not at all equivalent to what this second author means by *role.* Or, what one author (Gross, Mason, & McEachern, 1958, pp. 58–59) means by the distinction between *expectation* and *anticipation* is identical to what another (Biddle, Rosencranz, & Rankin, 1961, I, 3) means by the distinction between *norm* and *expectation,* respectively. We will attempt neither an exhaustive account of the development of role concepts nor a clarification and synthesis of terminology. The reader will find the exposition of Gross, Mason, and McEachern (1958, Ch. 2) a useful introduction to such matters. But we can point out certain general features of role analysis, especially as applied in educational research, and discuss a number of methodological problems associated with its research application.

Generally speaking, then, the concept of *role* stresses the influence of contemporaneous forces arising in the person's immediate social environment to impress his behavior. It designates, in particular, the force constituted by *expectations* (Getzels & Guba, 1957; Gross, Mason, & McEachern, 1958) on a person which are held by significant others in his milieu. The person lives in an environment in which other people around him expect him to be (and not be) a certain kind of person or expect him to behave (and not behave) in certain ways, and these expectations vary systematically from one situation to another in which he and other people are enmeshed. In the sociologically oriented role theories, the expectations are regarded as culturally patterned and as attached to the statuses, or positions, a person occupies rather than immutably to the person himself. In any event, the force of expectations is transmitted to the person during interaction between himself and the significant others. The force is effective, however, only as the person perceives, or cognizes, the expectations. Role theorists in education are inclined to the view that perceived expectations constitute the behaviorally influential environment for the person, although other theoretical positions on the matter are tenable and, possibly, more fruitful. Heider (1958), for example, holds that a theory of interpersonal relations must take account of the influence others may exercise over a person's behavior by manipulating his opportunities to perceive.

Role theorizing in education takes one of two directions. Either it emphasizes the conditions and consequences of role definitions existing at a given point in time, or it emphasizes the process by which role definitions are formed and modified in interaction through time. Only the former has produced empirical research in education. Role theorizing which stresses the interplay between the conceptions that interacting parties have of one another, of themselves, and of their behavior toward one another during their interaction, although more consonant with underlying social psychological theory, nevertheless requires a mode of empirical research relatively unfamiliar in education. It requires that detailed observations be made of a restricted range of events through time, even a short period of time, such as the course of interaction episodes in the teacher-parent conference. On the other hand, theorizing which stresses the consequences of agreement, disagreement, or conflict in role definitions is more amenable to the massive data-assembling procedures of the cross-sectional survey so familiar to educational researchers. But whatever may be the reasons for differences in research productivity, the fact is that conceptualizations of role-taking as a process occurring through time and in the course of person-to-person interaction remain in an undeveloped and unsupported state. We shall pursue this form of role analysis no further but direct the reader's attention to its most succinct educational presentation, the paradigm offered by Brookover (1955a, pp. 2–7).

The Nomothetic-Idiographic Dimension of Social Systems

The most influential role theory in education of the first sort mentioned above is asso-ciated with the work of Getzels. It was set forth definitively in an article by Getzels and Guba (1957) and a publication by Guba and Bidwell (1957). Recently, Getzels and Thelen (1960) applied it to the classroom group. It is not literally a theory of roles but rather a theory of social system functioning in which *role* is one of the central concepts. In this theory, social systems, particularly those which carry out specialized functions in society, are conceived as consisting of two distinct but interactive dimensions of human activity—the *nomothetic* dimension and the *idiographic* dimension.

The nomothetic dimension has three principal aspects, arranged here in order of increasing generality: role *expectations,* which specify the normative rights and duties associated with a status, or position, and which taken together define *role;* roles are complementary, each deriving its meaning from other related roles; taken together, they comprise the most important units of *institution.* The nomothetic dimension, then, describes those aspects of social relationships which are oriented exclusively to goal attainment by the social system.

The idiographic dimension, on the other hand, describes those aspects of human activity which are oriented exclusively to fulfillment of personal needs or expression of personal characteristics among those who happen to "people" the social system at a given time. Like the nomothetic dimension, the idiographic dimension has three aspects, also arranged in order of increasing generality: *need-dispositions,* which specify tendencies to act in certain ways and which, taken together, define *personality;* personality represents a unique mode of reaction to the environment and constitutes the relevant characteristic of the *individual.*

The nomothetic and idiographic dimensions jointly govern observed behavior within the social system. Role expectations and need-dispositions both have a quality of demand, the one derived from the sanctions of legitimate authority within the institution and the other associated with tension reduction within the individual. Behavior is a product of the two sets of demand, varying in relative magnitude from one role to another and from one personality to another.

Up to this point the theory is definitional. Theoretical derivations follow when two general propositions are added to the definitions, the first of which has to do with the conditions for goal attainment by the social system.

> The actions of members of the enterprise . . . must be contained within limits set by the nature of the specific task of the enterprise. From this fact arises the necessity of the restrictive nature of the organizational expectations. A staff member's behavior must conform, within fairly narrow limits, to those specifications which will enable the enterprise to move toward its goals. Equally important, his behavior must be co-ordinated with the actions of the other members of the organization. Conflicting actions lead to organizational impotence (Guba & Bidwell, 1957, p. 7).

This proposition holds that goal attainment by the social system occurs only when the behavior of the various members corresponds to role expectations. The proposition probably should be taken as specifying a necessary rather than a sufficient condition for goal attainment inasmuch as the theory does not treat the question of how differences in the organization of roles and differences in the substance of role expectations facilitate goalward movement. At any rate, the teacher's contribution to goal achievement, according to the proposition, is a function of his conformity to the institutionally prescribed role, whatever it may be.

A second general proposition relates to conditions which produce psychological tensions within the individual. "If the institutional demands are contradictory to, or irrelevant to, the demands of personality, then the individual is presented with a conflict and is strongly driven to act in ways which will be personally fulfilling, to the detriment of organizationally useful behavior" (Guba & Bidwell, 1957, p. 8). Thus, a tensionless state, or satisfaction,

as the writers refer to it, occurs when role expectations and need-dispositions are congruent. A quasi-empirical corollary of this proposition holds that institutional demands can never be congruent with the needs of all members of a social system because of the uniqueness of individual personality structures. In any real situation "the attempt to structure expectations congruent with the needs of one role incumbent will produce results at least partially unsuitable for another incumbent" (Guba & Bidwell, 1957, p. 9). When expectations and needs are not congruent, the individual must choose between meeting the institutional demands and forgoing his personality demands (defined as *effective* behavior), or satisfying his personal needs at the peril of bringing institutional sanctions to bear upon him (defined as *efficient* behavior), or fashioning some working combination of the two. But whatever mode of conflict resolution the individual chooses, psychological tension will not be entirely assuaged.

Empirical research following the Getzels theory would require observations of (1) institutional demands made on role incumbents, (2) personality dispositions among them, and (3) their manifest behavior. Data would also have to be taken with respect to (4) goal attainment by the social system, predicted from the congruity or disparity between *1* and *3,* and (5) psychological tension arising from the nonfulfillment of personality demands or from the risk of invoking institutional sanctions, predicted from the congruity or disparity between *1* and *2.*

Several complicating features, however, have severely hampered empirical inquiry. For one thing, no satisfactory criterion of *4*—goalward movement of a social system—has been developed. For another, the institutional demands, *1,* have been operationalized in terms of role expectations held by a wide assortment of people—school board members, citizens, superintendents, principals, fellow-teachers, and so on—and disagreement among these agents is the rule. Hence, an unambiguous criterion of role as institutionally defined has not been achieved. Added to this is a third complication: It is the expectations as perceived by the role incumbent that, according to the theory, comprise the influential force in the institutional demands, not the expectations actually held by any of the defining agents. Operational measures of *1,* then, have become role incumbents' perceptions of expectations on them as held by school board members, citizens, superintendents, and so on. Not only are these perceptions highly variable from one incumbent to another, but any given incumbent is likely to perceive expectations differentially from one set of defining agents to another. These complications have led the empirical research into seemingly endless comparisons and cross-comparisons which, though they occasionally yield interesting information, rarely constitute direct tests of the propositions in the theory.

Some Methodological Issues

Whatever conceptual propositions are at stake, the empirical operations in role analysis nearly always entail comparison of two sets of data respecting a single issue—data from two sets of respondents or two sets of data from the same respondents. The comparison gives rise to a measure describing the amount of agreement-disagreement (convergence-divergence) or describing the existence of conflict on the issue, and this measure is related to other variables in the research. Some investigations conducted in the name of role analysis, however, end at the point where the measure of agreement level or of conflict is derived, without attempting to relate it to other variables. This makes it exceptionally difficult to make a clear distinction between role studies and other forms of investigation in the educational literature. For years, educational researchers have surveyed the opinions held on an issue by two or more categories of respondents and have compared the distributions of responses so obtained. Bowman (1955), for example, asked Oregon superintendents and principals the same questions regarding personnel administration practices that had been asked of classroom teachers in other parts of the nation in two other surveys five and ten years previously. The burden of his study was carried by an item-by-item "comparison of teachers' and administrators' opinions" on the practices, to quote the title of his report. This kind of study could become a role study if the investigator wished to label it as such. While role studies presumably are limited to the particular issue of *expectations* held of a status occupant, this concept turns out to be so broad that, at the operational level, opinions regarding the personnel practices which should be employed in schools are indistinguishable from expectations that school officers should employ these practices.

Two kinds of methodological problems are acutely involved in studies of the role expectations which constitute the teacher's environment. One of these has to do with the nature of the data which are to be compared to discern the level of agreement or the existence of conflict. It has to do, as suggested above, with the theoretical definition of role expectations. Detailed analysis of the concept recently (Biddle, Rosencranz, & Rankin, 1961, Vol. I; Gross, Mason, & McEachern, 1958) has demonstrated its multifaceted character and the necessity of adding distinctions to the terminology. A second problem has to do with the particular comparisons which are made and from which arise the measures of agreement and conflict. This, too, is a far more complex and troublesome matter than it would appear to be. Although we cannot treat these two kinds of problems in depth, we here point out some of the salient issues associated with each, if only to indicate why an extended review of the empirical research findings is not yet a fruitful undertaking.

The data to be compared. As we said earlier, role analysis nearly always entails a measure of the extent to which two sets of parallel data are somehow alike or different. While data comparisons assume many forms, the principal types include comparisons between (1) two sets of expectations on a status occupant, (2) expectations on and the actual (or perceived) behavior of a status occupant, and (3) expectations attributed to another and the expectations actually held by the other. It is apparent that, if statements regarding the agreement or disparity in roles are to arise from such comparisons, the assembled sets of data must indeed be parallel. Following are a few basic distinctions which examination of the concept of role has revealed.

1. Normative versus predictive beliefs. Although it is not always recognized in empirical studies, beliefs which imply that a behavior "should" or "should not" occur are quite distinct from those which imply that a behavior "will" or "will not" occur. The former are normative, or evaluative, beliefs in the sense that they incorporate a moral standard; the latter are evaluatively neutral, referring only to the probability of an event occurring. Gross distinguishes between these beliefs with the terms *expectation* and *anticipation,* respectively (Gross, Mason, & McEachern, 1958, pp. 58–59), Biddle with the terms *norm* and *expectation* (Biddle, Rosencranz, & Rankin, 1961, I, 3). But whatever the terms used, the response of a person who answers questionnaire or interview questions from the one frame of reference is not comparable with that of a person who answers from the other frame of reference. The most severe difficulty arises when questions in an investigation are ambiguous as to the frame of reference which is demanded.

2. Direction and intensity of beliefs. Any given expectation is measurable in both its direction and its intensity (Gross, Mason, & McEachern, 1958, pp. 59–60). With respect to direction, an expectation on the behavior of a status occupant may be a prescription or a proscription—a requirement that the teacher behave in a particular way or one that prohibits certain teacher behavior. If we conceive of these two directions as the two extremes of a single continuum, as many do, the middle range of the continuum is said to consist of "permitted" or "allowed" behavior (Newcomb, 1950, pp. 281–282).

A second dimension of expectation refers to the intensity of the respondent's conviction regarding the prescribed or proscribed behavior. For example, a school board might prescribe that its superintendent *absolutely must* attend school board meetings or, in another case, that he *preferably should* attend board meetings. An expectation, then, is said to vary on a continuum ranging from the mandatory, through the preferential, to the completely permissive, independently of the direction of the expectation.[22] Two members of a population defining the role of a status occupant may agree on direction but not on intensity or, conversely, on intensity but not on direction. To confound the matter, both the intensity and the direction of an expectation may differ at what Biddle calls the *scale points* of an expectation, i.e., on the amounts of the behavior in question (Biddle, Rosencranz, & Rankin, 1961, Vol. I). For example, a person may believe that teachers absolutely should not drink alcoholic beverages regularly but, at the same time, may have no objection to their taking an occasional drink. A high level of agreement regarding the direction or intensity of an expectation may be found among members of a defining population at one scale point but a low level of agreement may be found at another scale point for the behavior in question.

3. Level of situational specificity. A role

---

[22] As the reader may note, direction and intensity are not entirely independent dimensions. If the direction dimension is conceived as a continuum anchored at one end by "must" and at the other end by "must not," with the middle range designated as "permitted" behavior, this middle range is equivalent to the lower end of the intensity dimension where there is neither demand nor preference for the behavior. An expectation which falls at the low end of the intensity continuum or in the middle range of the direction continuum produces conceptual embarrassment in another way. Gross and his colleagues (1958) found, for example, a high level of agreement among school board members that superintendents *may or may not* smoke. In what sense is this an expectation on the superintendent? Consensus at the low end of the intensity continuum may be more in the nature of agreement that the behavior or attribute in question is a matter of indifference. Greater conceptual clarification is in order with respect to these two dimensions.

definer's expectations may apply to teachers' behavior in a particular situation or to teachers' behavior regardless of the situation. Investigators have not always been careful to elicit responses from a defining population so that this distinction could be maintained. If respondents are asked, "Should teachers smoke?" it is not possible to discern unambiguously the intent of a "No" answer. It could mean, "No, teachers should not smoke under any circumstances," or it could mean, "No, teachers should not smoke as teachers, on the school premises or in sight of students." The significance of the situational designation is shown by the Cook and Greenhoe surveys (L. A. Cook & Cook, 1950, p. 447) where substantially different responses were obtained to questions about "smoking in public" and "smoking in private." It is rather obvious that, at least among some members of the defining population, what is expected of a teacher will differ according to whether the teacher is in the classroom guiding discussion, in the teachers' lounge with colleagues after school hours, or attending a party in the home of a school board member. Confronted with a question which is not situationally specific in its phrasing, respondents must reply in terms of whatever situation they happen to read into the question. If they employ heterogeneous frames of reference, the level of agreement in the defining population will be low.

4. The orientation of expectations. On what aspects of status occupants are expectations held? In our previous discussion, we used the phrase, "expectations of behavior," but some writers distinguish between expectations on *behavior* and expectations on more enduring *attributes* of status occupants—between what status occupants *should do* and what they *should be* (Gross, Mason, & McEachern, 1958, p. 63). Biddle (Biddle, Rosencranz, & Rankin, 1961, Vol. I) carries the same distinction a step further with the concepts of *behavior, feature,* and *pseudofeature.* In theoretically slanted conceptualizations of social role, as opposed to the operationally slanted conceptualizations

of Gross and Biddle, the aspects of status occupants relevant to social role are often more narrowly restricted. Role expectations are limited to those expectations bearing upon the mode of *interaction* between incumbents of particular statuses. Thus, it is the interlocking expectations between a status occupant and occupants of particular counterstatuses—the rights of one which are the duties of the other—which constitute the proper subject matter of role expectations from this point of view. The role associated with the status of teacher exists only with respect to the role of student, the role of parents, the role of principal, and so on (Gross, Mason, & McEachern, 1958, pp. 48–56). If this conceptualization were followed through in empirical studies, as it rarely is, only those expectations on status occupants would be measured which were involved in reciprocal relationships with persons in adjacent statuses. This limitation, too, would help to resolve the issue of situational specificity discussed in the preceding paragraph.

5. Expectations on detailed behaviors versus general functions. It is reasonable to believe that the level of generality at which expectations are assessed has a bearing upon the likelihood of finding agreement within a defining population (Gross, Mason, & McEachern, 1958, p. 74). In some investigations, expectations are sought with respect to the general functions fulfilled by teachers, for example, as "directors of learning" as opposed to "mediators of the culture," and so on (Fishburn, 1955). In other investigations, expectations are measured with respect to highly detailed behaviors—"The teacher pays bills but not promptly," "The teacher holds dances for teenagers in own home" (Manwiller, 1958). If it is true that people agree more upon general functions than upon ways of fulfilling the functions (Sweitzer, 1958), or even if the reverse is true, interstudy and intrastudy comparisons of expectations must take account of differences in the level of generality at which expectations are sought.

6. The attribution of role expectations. The preceding distinctions in concepts of

role expectation suggest the delicacy required in ascertaining whether two or more members of a defining population are alike or different in their expectations on a status occupant. If the matter is complex up to this point, then the complexity is compounded when studies involve the attribution of expectations by one party to another, or, as some writers would say, of a person's perceptions of role expectations. Empirically, investigation of the accuracy or inaccuracy of a person's attribution of role expectations to another person requires two sets of information, one from the first party regarding his estimation of the other's expectations and a second from the other party regarding what his expectations actually are. This is a straightforward procedure so long as a subject is asked to furnish estimations for each of a few, specifically designated, other persons. Of course, it is of the utmost importance that the subject be asked to estimate precisely the same aspect of expectations that the investigator assesses for each of the other persons. It could be misleading, in assessing a person's accuracy in perceiving role expectations, to compare his estimate against a criterion he was not intending to estimate in the first place. In another sense, however, such comparisons can be enlightening. For example, we can compare attributions of expectations to principals with the actual expectations of parents. The similarity here would reveal the degree to which parents' pressure would support or conflict with that seen as coming from principals. Or, attributions to others can be compared with the subject's own opinions to yield measures of "assumed similarity" (Fiedler, 1958).

The difficulties begin to mount when a subject is asked to estimate the expectations among a number of persons as a whole. "How would you say citizens in your community feel about teachers smoking in public?" If subjects took this question literally, many of them would be unable to answer it, recognizing that "citizens" would not be in full agreement on the matter. Neither subjects nor investigators, normally, take the question literally. Rather, they take it to mean, how do "most citizens" or how does "the typical citizen" feel about teachers smoking? And, of course, the investigator may deliberately include this kind of phrasing in his questions. Under the circumstances, then, the subject's attribution is compared for its accuracy against the average of the expectations in the defining population. But when is a subject accurate in his estimation? Is he as accurate in saying that "most citizens would approve" when the distribution shows that 51 per cent of the citizens "approve" as when it shows that 95 per cent of them "approve"? And what about the respondent who recognizes an absence of consensus on the issue but who, nevertheless, is confronted by a request that he report how "most citizens" feel.

These problems sometimes are met in the empirical research by asking the subject to estimate the level of agreement, or the per cent agreeing, in the defining population. "What proportion of the citizens in your community would you say objected to teachers smoking in public?" In one instance, an elaborate extension of this idea was used to measure the accuracy of school superintendents' estimates of educational viewpoints held in their communities (DeGood, 1959). The superintendents made their estimates by choosing from among 80 distribution curves displayed by the interviewer the one which they believed would most closely correspond to the distribution obtained through measurements of viewpoints in the communities.

The point at which investigators are most likely to overlook the noncomparability of estimates of expectations and measured expectations occurs in connection with the boundaries of the defining population, an issue we discuss more fully in the succeeding paragraphs. When a teacher replies to the question, "How would you say other teachers feel about a teacher visiting at the superintendent's home?" it is possible for him to have in mind an entirely different population of "other teachers" than the one from which the investigator obtains criterion responses. The respondent may implicitly answer in terms of "the other teachers whom I know best," while the investigator may compare his estimation against responses from a random sample of teachers in the school system. The empirical procedures may show the teacher to be quite inaccurate, whereas, in terms of the question which he implicitly answered, the teacher may be highly accurate. This difficulty can be avoided only by specifying precisely for which concrete population the teacher is to make an estimate and then measuring all, or a painstakingly drawn sample of, members of that population and no others. This amount of care is rarely exercised or even approximated in empirical studies of role perceptions.

The comparisons to be made. A number of methodological and conceptual problems arise as the investigator compares the data he has taken from respondents to measure agreement or conflict.

1. Conflict as distinct from disagreement. The two basic purposes of comparing responses in role analysis, to establish the level of agreement in expectations and to designate the existence of conflict in expectations, are conceptually and operationally distinct problem areas. Conceptually, conflict refers to expectations which are not simply different but which are, in some way, incompatible and mutually contradictory. A low level of agreement in expectations in no way certifies the existence of conflict between them. While agreement and conflict both entail comparisons between the expectations of two or more individuals, to establish the fact of conflict the investigator must be able to show that a role incumbent, in conforming to one set of expectations, behaves in contradiction to the other set of expectations.

Some role theorists define role conflict as a subjectively experienced incompatibility in expectations rather than an objectively demonstrated incompatibility. In this event, the investigator needs to take data only from the status occupant himself and need not measure the expectations held by other individuals or groups. The investigator may make no comparisons of responses at all, relying instead upon the report of his subjects that they are or are not exposed to conflicting demands of particular kinds (Getzels & Guba, 1955). On the other hand, he may elicit from subjects the expectations they attribute to each of two or more parties and, by comparing these responses, identify instances of conflict. Gross, Mason, and McEachern (1958, Ch. 15), for example, required school superintendents to indicate which of two contradictory expectations they attributed to each of a variety of groups and individuals in their communities, and wherever a superintendent reported an expectation of one group to be different from (and hence, incompatible with) an expectation of another group, it was inferred that he experienced role conflict. That he did in fact experience it as conflict was confirmed by the interviewer in follow-up questioning. But in any case, the problem of role conflict is a different one from the problem of role agreement and disagreement.

2. Role consensus. One basic issue in the measurement of role expectations involves what Gross and his colleagues have called the postulate of role consensus (1958, Ch. 3). This is the assumption, common to many formulations of social role, that full agreement exists among members of some defining population on the expectations they apply to occupants of a social status. Operationally, agreement is determined by measuring the expectations held by each member of the defining population and then showing low variance in the array of population scores. Needless to say, only in rare (or trivial) cases in empirical research is the variance zero, indicating full agreement. Usually the variance approaches zero in widely varying degrees, suggesting different levels of agreement. But even if the investigator relaxes his insistence on full agreement as the criterion for social role, there still remain a number of difficulties in establishing the fact of agreement at any lesser degree.

3. The defining population. Another difficulty is that of determining the boundaries

of the defining population within which agreement is to be sought. Theoretically, role definers may be single individuals (where, of course, no issue of agreement arises), they may be members of a social *group* in the sociological sense of the term (persons in interaction), they may be members of a *collectivity* (persons sharing a body of social norms but not in direct interaction), or they may be elements of a social *category* (persons with like social characteristics but not in interaction nor necessarily sharing a body of social norms) (Merton, 1957, p. 299).

As the boundaries of the defining population extend, its members become more heterogeneous and the likelihood of discovering agreement diminishes. There may be high agreement, for example, in expectations on the teacher among board members in School District M and high agreement among board members in School District N, each of which is a sociological group, but when their expectations are pooled to measure the level of agreement in the social category, say, of city school board members in the state of Ohio, the variance almost certainly will increase. It cannot decrease.

Empirical studies of role expectations on the teacher rarely consider the question of what social unit their populations of respondents represent. The normal procedure has been to attract questionnaire responses from available subjects specified in no greater detail than "principals," "school board members," "high school teachers," and the like, leaving the possibility open that the populations may be groups, collectivities, or social categories. Differences in role expectations on the teacher from one study to another or from one population to another within a given study may well be attributable to variations in the boundaries of the defining populations unless great care is given to assuring equivalence in the social units from which measurements are taken.

4. Types of conflict and agreement. The number of ways in which either agreement or conflict can be sought empirically is so great that it defies exposition. Usage of the

concept of *conflict* in the social sciences has covered not only conflicts between role definers but conflicting expectations held by a single role definer, conflicts between expectations and personality needs, and conflicts between expectations and behavior. Writers have combined the various conceptual elements in such ways as to construct still other types of conflict (Getzels & Guba, 1957; Gross, Mason, & McEachern, 1958, Ch. 15; Sarbin, 1954; Seeman, 1953).

With respect to agreement, the possible kinds of comparison are also numerous. In studies of the teacher's role, four or five counterstatuses usually are regarded as significant defining populations—parents, the "general public," school board members, principals, superintendents, and pupils. To these may be added the status occupants themselves, as teachers, or subdivided as elementary teachers, academic or vocational teachers, high school teachers, and so on. Agreement may be sought within any of these populations or between any pair of populations. Thus, five defining populations give rise to 15 sources of agreement. A variation on this was illustrated in Manwiller's (1958) study in which he examined the agreement within each of 30 boards of education in comparison with the level of agreement across all board members in his study. He made a similar analysis for teachers. In effect, he compared the amount of agreement within sociological groups with the amount of agreement within the social category, i.e., comparisons between different kinds of population units. If interest centers on the individual and the expectations he holds, still further comparisons are permitted. Agreement may be sought between his expectations and the modal expectations in the defining population of which he is a member or in each of the other defining populations investigated. The number of such comparisons can be multiplied by the number of respondents from whom data are taken.

If data are taken not only on expectations held but on expectations attributed to one or more defining populations by members of one or more defining populations, the number of possible comparisons becomes altogether inordinate. To list a few, measures may be derived showing (1) level of agreement on attributed expectations within each population, (2) agreement between individuals' own expectations and attributions, (3) differences between individuals' attributions to one as opposed to another population, (4) accuracy of expectations attributed to Population A by members of Population A, and (5) accuracy of expectations attributed to Population A by members of Population B, calculated either by comparing the average attributions among members of Population B against average expectations held in Population A or by comparing the expectations attributed by each individual in Population B against the average expectation held in Population A.

It may seem that we have engaged in a purely academic expansion on the virtually limitless number of empirical operations which can be performed on role data. The fact is, however, that our discussion reflects the studies now available in the literature. We could cite at least one empirical study for every combination illustrated in the preceding paragraphs.

Moreover, there are complexities in data-reduction operations found among the role studies which we have not taken time to discuss.

Many of the methodological issues in the analysis of role data resemble those that have been raised in research on interpersonal perception. In the latter area, judges have typically been asked to predict the responses of others, whose own responses are then used as the criterion for the accuracy of the predictions. Accuracy in turn has been interpreted as empathy with, or understanding of, the others. Or, in obtaining measures of "assumed similarity," the judges' self-descriptions have been compared with their predictions. Many variations on these themes can be played (Cronbach, 1953), and many of the theoretical and methodological problems of this kind of research have been explicated

(Gage & Cronbach, 1955). Apart from merely calling attention to problems that are common to research on role analysis and on interpersonal perception, we emphasize here the importance of (1) considering statistical breakdowns (Cronbach, 1955) or intermediary keys (Gage, Leavitt, & Stone, 1956) for analyzing the components of measures of similarity and difference between two sets of responses and (2) insuring that "dyadic" measures, those involving comparisons of descriptions or statements by two persons, are employed "only after the simpler main effects associated with the perceiver or the object of perception have been given separate consideration" (Cronbach, 1958, p. 355).

One purpose of our expatiation on these matters is to signalize the essentially noncomparable, noncumulative nature of much of the research thus far conducted in the name of role analysis. The deceptively simple operations for collecting role data have induced investigators to outrun the theoretical formulations which would bring order to the data and allow them to see the significance of their various comparisons.

Consequences of Role Expectations for Teachers

If the expectations which others hold of the teacher constitute an important aspect of the teacher's environment, as role theorists would assert, in what ways is this environmental force exerted on the teacher and with what effect? Some social psychological theories would stress the teacher's identification with significant others around him and the impress of their expectations, experienced in the interaction situation, upon his own self concept and definition of role. Other theories would stress the function of group norms in providing frames of reference, or the "social reality" in ambiguous situations, for perceiving and judging oneself and others who internalize the norms. Even if the role makes no lasting impression upon the teacher, there would be, according to these theories, a direct effect of others' role definitions upon the teacher's more or less public modes of performance in the classroom. Since we must limit ourselves to the reasoning employed in educational research on the teacher's role, we cannot pursue these social psychological formulations. It is worthy of note, however, that a reasonable and straightforward proposition emerges from these formulations which has never been explored in the educational research literature, viz., definitions of the teacher-pupil role relationship held among persons known to be important to a particular teacher shape the manner in which the teacher enters into the classroom relationship.

Where the above proposition points to the similarity between the expectations held by a few significant others and the teacher's performance in a given relationship, the line of reasoning common in the educational literature focuses on the congruity or disparity among personality needs, perceptions of behavior, desires for (or expectations of) behavior, attributions of expectations, and the like. Congruity is seen to lead to a tensionless state of harmony and satisfaction; disparity is said to create tension and dissatisfaction. Although rarely studied empirically, congruity and disparity are presumed to determine the effectiveness with which an individual or a social system pursues its goals.

Role agreement and goal attainment. The theoretical connection social psychologists posit between role agreement and the individual's effectiveness in pursuing his goals can be stated concisely (Jenkins & Lippitt, 1951, Ch. 1). A person cannot be indifferent to how others perceive him when he must interact with them in order to attain his goals. It is only in the reasonably predictable environment, interpersonal or otherwise, that the individual can effectively pursue his goals. To maximize the predictability of the environment, not only must he strive for accuracy in discerning how others view him and the situation but he must be willing to conform to some degree to the expectations that others have of him. If he enters the situation as an unpredictable participant, under nor-

mal circumstances he, in turn, will be unable to predict the responses of the other participants to him. There are, of course, other reasons a person may have for being concerned with what others expect of him, not the least of which is the ego rewards which group members may furnish him for his compliance with their expectations. Also, such concern enables the person to avoid the sanctions which may accompany noncompliance. But quite apart from these, it is to the person's advantage in pursuing his goals, whether they be goals jointly shared with others or idiosyncratically defined for himself, to estimate accurately the expectations which others hold of him.

For goal achievement by social systems, the Getzels theory regards congruity between role and member behavior as a *sine qua non.* (See pp. 789–790, above.) Bidwell (1955) developed the theme in a vein not unlike the reasoning of Jenkins and Lippitt:

Role-expectations allow alter to predict the behavior of ego and act toward ego in an appropriate way. It is impossible for an integrated social system to function unless such predictions are possible, since, there being no secure basis for his actions toward ego, such action becomes difficult at best. . . . One source of disturbance . . . is perception by teachers of administrative behavior other than that defined by the role-expectations. The teachers will be unable to predict accurately the behavior of their administrators, and they will be unable to act effectively toward them in the administrative situation (Bidwell, 1955, p. 41).

The normal procedure when a person does not behave in conformity with expectations, Bidwell argued, is for other persons to apply negative sanctions, but in the superior-subordinate relationship it is not entirely safe for the subordinate, the teacher, to attempt to exercise sanctions against his superior.

The teacher thus finds himself in a situation in which he has no basis for a coherent system of action and loses his orientation toward his administrators. He finds himself frustrated in his attempts to apply sanctions to remedy the tension-producing situation, heightening the degree of tension (Bidwell, 1955, p. 42).

Bidwell predicted, then, that teacher job satisfaction (an indicator of tension) would vary directly with the degree to which administrator behavior was perceived by the teacher to accord with the teacher's expectations on the administrator.

Bidwell held that disparity creates tension and dissatisfaction, and he elaborated no further on the matter of effective goal achievement. The same course of reasoning appears in theory based on the nomothetic-idiographic distinction (Guba & Bidwell, 1957). Its proponents did not dwell long on social system effectiveness, and when the term *effectiveness* is used in a propositional sense or appears in operationalized form, it is as a kind of individual satisfaction—a congruency between need-dispositions and role demands.

Role agreement and teacher satisfaction. The central prediction in studies of role agreement which attempt to examine consequences for status occupants is well stated as follows:

. . . when the perceptions of the expectations of participants in an administrative interaction overlap, the participants feel satisfied with the work accomplished no matter what the actual behavior or accomplishment; when the perception of the expectations does not overlap, the participants feel dissatisfied (Getzels, 1958, p. 160).

A number of investigators have attempted to test this proposition or some variant of it in the educational setting (Bernstein, 1959; Bidwell, 1955, 1957; Campbell, 1958; Ferneau, 1954; Guba & Bidwell, 1957; Moyer, 1954). These investigators, and others whose work we have not cited, have found consistently that subjects who report agreement in expectations also report relatively high levels of satisfaction. Since most of the studies are correlational, we can turn the finding around to say that subjects who report high levels of satisfaction are inclined to perceive agreement in role expectations. As our reversal of

the finding suggests, the direction of causality is equivocal. Moreover, since indexes of agreement are customarily constructed from data furnished by the same subjects who report their levels of agreement, the writer suspects that the correlations are created by both constant and random errors in the measurement process (Selltiz, Jahoda, Deutsch, & Cook, 1959, pp. 149–154). This suspicion is strengthened when one notes that the correlations are inclined to vanish when indexes of agreement are constructed from data furnished by methodologically independent sources. We have encountered this issue before in this review and will not belabor it further.

Even if role congruity enhances the job satisfaction of teachers, as it may well do despite this reviewer's qualms respecting the empirical demonstrations, the question remains as to what effect job satisfaction in teachers has upon the teacher's classroom performance. We will return to this question immediately following a brief consideration of the effects of conflict in expectations upon teachers.

The consequences of role conflict. Role conflict by definition means trouble for the individual. Choosing between two incompatible demands on behavior means gaining the advantages of the one and forgoing the advantages of the other or avoiding the disadvantages of the one and risking the disadvantages of the other. Theoretical discussions of role conflict have dealt largely with typologies of conflict situations—i.e., the various ways in which conflict in role behavior may arise—while the empirical investigations have been purely descriptive or have concentrated upon the various strategies of conflict resolution (Gross, Mason, & McEachern, 1958, Ch. 17). Less attention has been given to the relatively enduring consequences of role conflict for the teacher or to the consequences which would carry definite implications for the teacher's entry into the teaching-learning process. Nevertheless, it is commonly assumed in research studies that role conflict is disruptive, tension-inducing, and, over a period of prolonged exposure, productive of anxiety. Only an occasional educational investigation has tested this assumption (Gross, Mason, & McEachern, 1958, pp. 274–280). Seeman (1953) explored the possibility that role conflict induced ambivalence in the behavioral responses of those subjected to it.

Merton (1957, p. 376) observed that role conflict may reduce rather than increase the problems of role incumbents, as, for instance, when those who impose incompatible demands on the status occupant become aware of their respective impositions.

As long as members of the role-set are happily ignorant that their demands upon the occupants of a status are incompatible, each member may press his own case upon the status-occupants. The pattern is then many against one. But when it is made plain that the demands of some members of the role-set are in full contradiction with the demands of other members, it becomes the task of the role-set, rather than the task of the status-occupant, to resolve these contradictions, either by a struggle for exclusive power or by some degree of compromise. As the conflict becomes abundantly manifest, the pressure upon the status-occupant becomes temporarily relieved (Merton, 1957, p. 376).

Where the contest between the demanding groups is a stand-off, the consequence for the status occupant—the professional personnel of the school, for example—is to allow him to pursue his own course. Role conflict under these conditions would not produce tension, anxiety, or dissatisfaction.

JOB SATISFACTION AND THE TEACHING-LEARNING PROCESS

Many of the lines of reasoning on which we have reported throughout this review converge upon teacher satisfaction as the important consequence, the prime dependent variable, of the forces impinging from the teacher's social environment. Indeed, studies of teacher "morale," "job satisfactions," "annoyances," and "problems" have comprised one of the more vigorous areas of educa-

tional research over the years. Although these studies often touch upon the same environmental forces to which we have referred in our discussions, the typically primitive research procedures and hazy conceptualizations make it unwise to review the studies here. At this point, rather, we offer some observations concerning the widespread assumption that whatever affects teacher satisfactions thereby affects the teaching-learning process—that a high level of teacher morale has a salubrious effect upon the teacher's participation in the teaching-learning process.

In the first place, while it is not unreasonable to assume that "happy" teachers behave differently in the classroom than "unhappy" teachers, the issue has rarely been conceptualized beyond this kind of statement. In what particular ways does satisfaction manifest itself in the teacher's classroom performance other than to make him vaguely a "better" or "poorer" teacher? The concepts of satisfaction and morale, too, have come under conceptual scrutiny only on rare occasions (Getzels & Guba, 1957; Guba, 1958). Industrial social psychologists discovered many years ago that these are multidimensional concepts (Morse, 1953), a discovery seldom reflected in the educational literature. Thus, the assumption that teacher satisfaction level has a significant effect upon relevant aspects of the teaching-learning process is sorely in want of conceptual specification. That it has not received such attention may be the consequence of its being an implicit rather than an explicit assumption or of its being regarded as so "obvious" that it is conceded without further question.

In the second place, the few admittedly inadequate studies which have sought a relationship between teacher satisfaction and "proficiency" have not provided consistently positive evidence. For example, L. W. Anderson (1953) found that teachers in high schools in which students ranked high on an achievement examination were more inclined to report satisfying teacher-community relations than were teachers in high schools ranking lower in student achievement. But

Knox (1956) found no significant correlations between various efficiency ratings of teachers and their reports of satisfaction.

Finally, strong evidence from industrial situations, where many morale investigations have been carried out, indicates that morale is not necessarily related to productivity on the job (Brayfield & Crockett, 1955). Dubin (1959) was led by the evidence regarding the absence of relationship between morale and organizational effectiveness to take the position that, "Under many circumstances, therefore, it may be that high morale is not an important organizational goal, and authority holders need to give little conscious attention to its development and maintenance" (Dubin, 1959, p. 363). Dubin's position may be extreme, especially in the light of dangers which inhere in extrapolations from industrial and business organizations to educational organizations. But Halpin (1957), too, was impressed by these data. In the following paragraph he summarizes our own reservations regarding the connection between morale and the course of the teaching-learning process.

[Morale] is an emotionally charged term that means quite different things to different people. . . . First, whatever it is, it is not a unidimensional concept. It has more than a single component, and each component can be defined best only in respect to the operations by which it is measured. High "morale" in respect to one component does not guarantee high "morale" in respect to another. Secondly, there is no necessary relationship between high "morale" and high productivity. An increase in "morale" may or may not be accompanied by an increase in productivity, and even where both rise together it is extremely difficult to establish a causal relationship. Does higher productivity, for example, increase "morale"; or is it improved "morale" that makes higher productivity possible? (Halpin, 1957, pp. 165–166).

In short, if there is a connection between the teacher's level of satisfaction and his influence on the course of the teaching-learning process, it is bound to be a more complex connection than we generally have assumed.

Another way in which satisfaction level could affect the teaching-learning process is through its operation as a selective factor. As we have observed in earlier sections, it is commonly assumed that environmental forces which affect the satisfactions of members of an occupation thereby determine who will enter or remain in the occupation and who will choose to pursue his career elsewhere. In thé same vein, it is often proposed that community circumstances or organizational arrangements which minimize teacher satisfactions induce all but the most marginal members of the teaching staff to leave the school district and, perhaps, the occupation altogether. But the research on occupational choice and on teacher turnover (Charters, 1956) shows the intervention of a number of variables quite apart from satisfaction or morale. March and Simon (1958, pp. 47–52, 93–108) went into extensive theoretical detail to specify (1) the alternatives open to a dissatisfied employee other than leaving the organization, and (2) a variety of conditions, other than satisfaction, which govern the decision to leave. Hence, this assumption, too, covers an issue which is considerably more intricate than it appears on the surface.

THE SYSTEM OF INFORMAL RELATIONS

A conception of the teacher as enmeshed in and influenced by the *system* of social relationships among teachers, administrators, parents, pupils, noncertificated personnel, and others constituting the social world of the school has never been part of the main current of educational thought. Until the 1950's, researchers ignored the most intimate aspects of the teacher's social environment. This is not entirely surprising, of course, since, as Shils (1951) pointed out in his review of the primary group concept, the sociologists themselves have only gradually come to an appreciation of the informal system of social relationships. But even where research or theorizing on the teacher's informal relations has appeared in the educational literature, the central issue has not been how these group processes bear upon the conduct of the teaching-learning process. Consequently our treatment of this topic will be highly abbreviated.

As for general commentaries, Waller's (1932) treatment of the social and cultural order of the school was two decades ahead of its time (see above, pp. 761–762), and few subsequent essays surpass his contribution in either insightfulness or scope. Brookover's textbook (1955b) and Becker's (1953) study of the Chicago public school teacher owed a heavy debt to Waller's formulations. Other recent treatments (Conrad, 1952; Dahlke, 1958, Ch. 17; Jensen, 1954; Washburne, 1957), however, derived less from the Waller tradition than from the sociological approaches to organization and bureaucracy. The Getzels theory, discussed above, represents the most systematic formulation of the latter approach to educational affairs. During the late 1940's and early 1950's, the influence of Lewin's approach to the dynamics of group process made itself felt not only in the realm of autocratic and democratic administrative styles but in the realm of staff relationships, especially as they related to the issue of curriculum change (Benne & Muntyan, 1951). The significance of the informal social order of the school was sufficiently established by 1956 for a major textbook in school administration to be organized around such topics as motivation, perception, communication, power, and the like (Griffiths, 1956), but it outran the educational research literature and was obliged to rely heavily upon extra-education sources.

Empirical research on the social system of the school has reflected or, at least, paralleled the approach of social anthropology in the emphasis upon the intensive case study by means of observational methods, including, in some instances, participant observation (Boyan, 1951; Conrad, 1951; Gordon, 1955). Beyond the methodology, the influence of social anthropology on the social systems concepts employed was apparent in the studies of Atwood (1960) and Iannaccone (1958). Congreve's (1957) investigation, however, departed from the single-case approach. He selected two schools with principals who manifested contrasting leadership styles and directed his observations toward differences in the modes of teacher-to-teacher interaction.

The communication network in the school has been singled out for especial attention by several investigators. Berner (1957) and McCleary (1957) both described methods by which communication processes could be investigated in school faculties, and Charters (1957), using base line data collected by McCleary, demonstrated high stability of the basic communication pattern over a six-month period despite an intervening staff turnover of 50 per cent. A quasi-experimental study by Rollins (1958) examined the rate of diffusion of planted information among staff members in four high schools with well and poorly articulated communication networks.

We must point out again that the bearing of the informal relationships in the school upon the teacher in ways relevant to the teaching-learning process has not been the prime issue in any of these investigations. It is clear that the teacher's informal relations are presumed to have an important influence on his attitudes, or sentiments, regarding issues of vital significance for him, including his orientation to the task of teaching. Some of the studies have specifically investigated the connection between patterns of interaction and the sentiments of staff members. But the central question of our review has not been fully delineated by this area of educational research.

CONCLUDING REMARKS

We began this review with the question, What social and cultural forces operating in the environing society affect teachers in ways relevant to the teaching-learning process? We have referred to a variety of forces at work on the teaching occupation and its practitioners. Some of these forces emanate from the society at large to shape the composition of the occupational group, some from the conditions of training and work in the occupation, others from the community in which the teachers work, and still others from the social system of the teacher's school.

These forces, as we have seen, impinge upon the teaching-learning process in two distinct ways—by determining who will occupy the teaching status and by affecting those who occupy it. Not infrequently, the same environmental variable is considered to operate in both ways. Nevertheless, the distinction must be borne in mind, for the processes which mediate the impact of the environmental forces will differ in the two cases. For example, the processes by which occupational prestige is brought to bear upon those engaged in teaching so as to affect their participation in the classroom necessarily differ from those which shape the career decisions of those who would enter teaching. Of the two ways in which social and cultural forces impinge upon teaching, the selective has been a more common theme than the formative in the research we have examined. Let us inspect this more closely.

A Dominating Theme and Its Implications

Running through the research on the social background of teachers is a predominating concern with "up-grading" the teaching corps. This is the *raison d'etre* for many of the studies we have examined. The principal question which seems to motivate those who investigate the impact of social and cultural forces on teaching is this: *How do these forces affect the probability that capable people will enter or remain in teaching?* We hold that dedication to this question has limited research to a narrow spectrum of problems formulated in an overly restrictive fashion. The limitation has come about, first, by the conceptions invoked by the tacit question and, second, by the research strategy commonly employed in attacking the question.

Conceptual limitations. When the above question motivates research, a great deal hinges on the conception of *capability*. The difficulty with this concept is not just in specifying what attributes are necessary for competency in the classroom or in specifying what "effective teaching" is, although this is a difficult problem in itself. The more severe difficulty lies in its implication that, of all the ways in which people differ from one another, only the one dimension of capability-incapability (competence-incompetence, effectiveness-ineffectiveness) is of cardinal importance. Investigators are inclined to reduce virtually every variation among individuals to this one dimension. Thus, in the social composition studies, the significance of age and sex differences is sought in what they mean for teacher "effectiveness." Research on the geographic mobility of teachers and the Cooks' (L. A. Cook & Cook, 1950) principle of *limited circulation* are held to be significant for illuminating the "quality" of classroom teaching. The teachers' opportunity to participate in community affairs is regarded as important insofar as it encourages or discourages "capable" people in a commitment to a teaching career. In the reduction to a single dimension of quality or capability, other variations in the way people might participate in the teaching-learning process tend to be ignored. Perhaps the dedication of research to such a narrow concern is appropriate for an applied science, such as education, but it inhibits our understanding of a more comprehensive range of problems in the educative process.

A certain genetic bias seems to be bound up in the underlying conception, too. Many investigators appear to regard an individual's potential or manifest capability in teaching as a relatively enduring, relatively immutable attribute which is somehow fixed in early childhood and remains basically unaffected by subsequent experience. Even teacher training, in which most researchers have a vested interest, and teaching experience, in which educators similarly have a strong faith, tend to be seen as ways in which people acquire the techniques and tools of the trade, not as ways of altering the fundamental level of capability itself. But whatever its source, the conception of capability turns investigators toward the formative influences of the past and away from the contemporary influences of the present. Thus, greater interest is shown in the motives which once propelled teachers into the occupation than in how the motives are transformed by more immediate social circumstances. More research is conducted on the social origins of teachers than on their present social relations. This we believe is a consequence of the undue concentration on the question of how capable people are attracted to and retained in teaching.

Where investigators do focus on contemporaneous forces, the same overweening question of capability often lurks in the background to restrict, again, the scope of research. It is customary to examine the current circumstances of the teacher in terms of what they imply for his satisfaction. This satisfaction-dissatisfaction dimension is presumed to be related in a one-to-one fashion with the probability of capable teachers continuing in the occupation. Salary levels and work load, the social standing of the occupation, the presence of role conflict, the press of community constraints, the opportunity to participate in policy-making—each is seen as affecting the teacher's job satisfaction. Why should the investigator be interested in teacher happiness? Because unhappiness is presumed to drive him out of teaching or to depress his level of competence in the classroom. We do not intend to deny the reasonableness of the basic research issue here but only to point out that the teacher's general level of satisfaction is just one of the characteristics with which he enters the teaching-learning process and, perhaps, not a very significant one at that. Preoccupation with "up-grading" the teaching corps has encouraged investigators to formulate the dependent variable of research in terms of a single, value-laden dimension of satisfaction-dissatisfaction and, thereby, to ignore other

fruitful variations among teachers which bear upon the conduct of the educative process in the classroom.

Lest our remarks be misunderstood, we should emphasize that we are describing the tendencies in research on the social background of teaching as we discern them, not characterizing all of the research which we have reviewed. Important countermovements exist in the research literature. Thus, Becker (1952a) was interested in the modes of adjustment of the teacher to his different work situations without making a prejudgment regarding the consequences of adjustment needs for teacher satisfaction or for leaving the occupation. The social class studies were conducted to suggest the operation in the classroom of different kinds of value systems, again without initial concern for the quality of teaching. Ryans (1960), and a number of other students we have not discussed, have introduced more highly differentiated conceptions of the teacher's participation in the classroom than those which immediately refer to "good" teaching or "bad" teaching. Getzels' nomothetic-idiographic formulation entails choices between two forms of a dilemma, neither of which is necessarily "desirable." Other countermovements could be cited.

Limitations in research strategy. Part of the restricted character of the knowledge growing out of the literature on the social forces affecting teaching is, we believe, attributable to the research strategy so commonly employed in the studies. Let us designate the social and cultural forces as A, the teacher presumably affected by these forces as B, and the conduct of the teaching-learning process as C. On this basis, the most frequent study is one in which A and only A is observed, and the connections between A and B and between B and C are taken as self-evident. No observations are taken on either B or C; hence, the assumed connections are not subjected to empirical examination. This characterization, of course, describes the format of the so-called status study, or survey. One obvious result of the strategy is that our ignorance on the crucial matters is unabated or even rendered more profound, since the untested assumptions can continue to spawn further surveys until their very number is taken as demonstrating the assumptions' tenability. Another result is less obvious. When faced with the task of taking observations on a variable, the investigator is likely to find himself forced into conceptual differentiation of that variable. Or conversely, so long as the investigator is not obliged to measure a variable, he may entertain highly simplified, nonoperational conceptions of it. It is in this way that a strategy of research which calls for no observations on the B and C variables is able to reinforce other tendencies which have restricted the range of problems studied in the social background of teaching. Simply for researchers to take observations on a variable, however, does not certify that they will conceptualize it more thoroughly, a fact attested to by the decades spent in measuring intelligence and teacher effectiveness. Required for this purpose and for the general purpose of freeing research in this area from its bonds is the development of theoretical frameworks which attempt to come to terms with the *functional connections* between the A and B variables, the effects of social and cultural forces on the teacher, and between the B and C variables, the operation through the teacher of these forces on the teaching-learning process. Required are programs of research to test, amend, and extend the propositions of theory.

REFERENCES

Abbott, M. G. Values and value-perceptions in superintendent-school board relationships. *Admin. Notebook,* 1960, 9(4), 1–4.

Adorno, T. W., Frenkel-Brunswik, Else, Levinson, D. J., & Sanford, R. N. *The authoritarian personality.* New York: Harper, 1950.

Anderson, L. W. Teacher morale and student achievement. *J. educ. Res.,* 1953, 46, 693–698.

Anderson, W. F. Attitudes of parents of differing socio-economic status toward the teaching profession. *J. educ. Psychol.,* 1954, 45, 345–352.

Archer, C. P. In-service education. In C. W. Harris (Ed.), *Encyclopedia of educational research.* (3rd ed.) New York: Macmillan, 1960. Pp. 702–710.

Asch, S. E. *Social psychology.* New York: Prentice-Hall, 1952.

Atwood, M. S. An anthropological approach to administrative change. Unpublished doctoral dissertation, Columbia Univer., 1960.

Barkley, Margaret K. The concept of the home economics teacher held by high school students. Unpublished doctoral dissertation, Univer. of Illinois, 1956.

Barr, A. S. Supervision. In W. S. Monroe (Ed.), *Encyclopedia of educational research.* (Rev. ed.) New York: Macmillan, 1950. Pp. 1371–1373.

Bathurst, J. E. Relation of efficiency to experience and age among elementary teachers. *J. educ. Res.,* 1929, 19, 314–316.

Batten, T. R. The status and function of teachers in tribal communities. In R. K. Hall, N. Hans, & J. A. Lauwerys (Eds.), *The yearbook. of education 1953.* Yonkers, N.Y.: World Book Co., 1953, Pp. 76–94.

Baudler, Lucille, & Paterson, D. G. Social status of women's occupations. *Occupations,* 1948, 26, 421–424.

Beale, H. K. *Are American teachers free?* New York: Scribner's, 1936.

Becker, H. S. The career of the Chicago public schoolteacher. *Amer. J. Sociol.,* 1952, 57, 470–477. (a)

Becker, H. S. Social-class variations in the teacher-pupil relationship. *J. educ. Sociol.,* 1952, 25, 451–465. (b)

Becker, H. S. The teacher in the authority system of the public school. *J. educ. Sociol.,* 1953, 27, 128–141.

Becker, H. S., & Carper, J. The development of identification with an occupation. *Amer. J. Sociol.,* 1956, 61, 289–298.

Becker, H. S., & Geer, Blanche. The fate of idealism in medical school. *Amer. sociol. Rev.,* 1958, 23, 50–56.

Benedict, Ruth. Continuities and discontinuities in cultural conditioning. *Psychiatry,* 1938, 1, 161–167.

Benne, K. D., & Muntyan, B. (Eds.) *Human relations in curriculum change.* New York: Dryden, 1951.

Berner, M. K. Development of procedures and techniques for the analysis of the relationships between the formal organization of high school systems and the informal communication structures within these systems. Unpublished doctoral dissertation, Univer. of Illinois, 1957.

Bernstein, Mildred R. H. A study of teachers' role-expectations and role-perceptions of a principal, superintendent and board of education, and the relationship between convergence and divergence of role-expectation and role-perception and teacher morale. Unpublished doctoral dissertation, New York Univer., 1959.

Betts, G. L., Frazier, B. W., & Gamble, G. C. *Selected bibliography on the education of teachers.* Washington, D.C.: U.S. Dept. of the Interior, Office of Education, Bull. 1933, No. 10, Vol. 1.

Bey, D. R. A further study in school organization. *Phi Delta Kappan,* 1956, 37, 217–221.

Biddle, B. J., Rosencranz, H. A., & Rankin, E. F. *Studies in the role of the public school teacher.* Columbia: Soc. Psychol. Lab., Univer. of Missouri, 1961.

Bidwell, C. E. The administrative role and satisfaction in teaching. *J. educ. Sociol.,* 1955, 29, 41–47.

Bidwell, C. E. Some effects of administrative behavior: A study in role theory. *Admin. sci. Quart.,* 1957, 2, 163–181.

Bowman, E. W. A comparison of teachers' and administrators' opinions on personnel administration practices. *J. educ. Res.,* 1955, 49, 229–233.

Boyan, N. J. A study of the formal and informal organization of a school faculty. Unpublished doctoral dissertation, Harvard Univer., 1951.

Bradford, L. P., & Lippitt, R. Building a democratic work group. *Personnel,* 1945, 22, 142–152.

Brameld, T., & Sullivan, E. B. Anthropology and education. *Rev. educ. Res.,* 1961, 31, 70–79.

Brayfield, A. H., & Crockett, W. H. Employee attitudes and employee production. *Psychol. Bull.,* 1955, 52, 396–424.

Brookover, W. B. The relation of social factors to teaching ability. *J. exp. Educ.,* 1945, 13, 191–205.

Brookover, W. B. Teachers and the stratification of American society. *Harvard educ. Rev.,* 1953, 23, 257–267.

Brookover, W. B. Research on teacher and administrator roles. *J. educ. Sociol.,* 1955, 29, 2–13. (a)

Brookover, W. B. *A sociology of education.* New York: American Book Co., 1955. (b)

Butts, R. F. *A cultural history of education.* New York: McGraw-Hill, 1947.

Callaway, A. B. Some environmental factors and community influences that are brought to bear upon the personal lives of Missouri teachers and administrators. Unpublished doctoral dissertation, Univer. of Missouri, 1951.

Callis, R. Change in teacher-pupil attitudes related to training and experience. *Educ. psychol. Measmt,* 1950, 10, 718–727.

Cameron, N. A. *The psychology of behavior disorders.* Boston: Houghton Mifflin, 1947.

Campbell, M. V. Self-role conflict among teachers and its relationship to satisfaction, effectiveness, and confidence in leadership. Unpublished doctoral dissertation, Univer. of Chicago, 1958.

Caplow, T. *The sociology of work.* Minneapolis: Univer. of Minnesota Press, 1954.

Centers, R. *The psychology of social classes.* Princeton, N.J.: Princeton Univer. Press, 1949.

Chansky, N. M. The self-concept and the perception of values of teachers. *Human Relations,* 1959, 7, 358–366.

Charters, W. W., Jr. What causes teacher turnover? *Sch. Rev.,* 1956, 64, 294–299.

Charters, W. W., Jr. The communication structure of school staffs. Paper read at Amer. Sociol. Soc., Washington, D.C., August, 1957.

Chase, F. S. The teacher and policy making. *Admin. Notebook,* 1952, 1(1), 1–4.

Clark, E. F. Teacher reactions toward objectionable pupil behavior. *Elem. sch. J.,* 1951, 51, 446–449.

Clifton, D. E. Dominative and socially integrative behavior of twenty-five second grade teachers. Unpublished doctoral dissertation, Univer. of Illinois, 1944.

Coffman, L. D. The social composition of the teaching population. *Teach. Coll. Contr. Educ.,* 1911, No. 41.

Coleman, J. S. *Social climates in high schools.* Washington, D.C.: U.S. Dept. of Health, Education, and Welfare, Office of Education, Coop. Res. Monogr. No. 4, 1961.

Congreve, W. J. Administrative behavior and staff relations. *Admin. Notebook,* 1957, 6 (2), 1–4.

Conrad, R. The administrative role: A sociological study of leadership in a public school system. Unpublished doctoral dissertation, Stanford Univer., 1951.

Conrad, R. A sociological approach to public school administration. *Educ. Admin. Superv.,* 1952, 38, 385–392.

Cook, L. A. *Community backgrounds of education.* New York: McGraw-Hill, 1938.

Cook, L. A., & Almack, R. B. The community participation of 2,870 Ohio teachers. *Educ. Admin. Superv.,* 1939, 25, 107–119.

Cook, L. A., & Cook, Elaine F. *A sociological approach to education.* (2nd ed.) New York: McGraw-Hill, 1950.

Cook, L. A., & Greenhoe, Florence. Community contacts of 9,122 teachers. *Soc. Forces,* 1940, 19, 63–72.

Cook, L. A., Almack, R. B., & Greenhoe, Florence. Teacher and community relations. *Amer. sociol. Rev.,* 1938, 3, 167–174.

Cook, W. W., & Hoyt, C. J. Procedure for determining number and nature of norm groups for the Minnesota Teacher Attitude Inventory. *Educ. psychol. Measmt,* 1952, 12, 562–573.

Cook, W. W., Hoyt, C. J., & Eikaas, A. Studies of predictive validity of the Minnesota Teacher Attitude Inventory. *J. teacher Educ.,* 1956, 7, 167–172.

Cornell, F. G. Some aspects of teacher participation in administrative decision-making. Paper read at Amer. Educ. Res. Ass., Atlantic City, N.J., February, 1954. (a)

Cornell, F. G. When should teachers share in making administrative decisions? *Nation's Sch.,* 1954, 53(5), 43–45. (b)

Cornell, F. G. Socially perceptive administration. *Phi Delta Kappan,* 1955, 36, 219–223.

Counts, G. S. The social status of occupations. *Sch. Rev.,* 1925, 33, 20–21.

Coutu, W. The relative prestige of twenty professions as judged by three groups of professional students. *Soc. Forces,* 1936, 14, 522–529.

Cronbach, L. J. Stereotypes and college sororities. *J. higher Educ.,* 1944, 15, 214–216.

Cronbach, L. J. Correlation between persons as a research tool. In O. H. Mowrer (Ed.), *Psychotherapy: Theory and research.* New York: Ronald Press, 1953. Pp. 376–389.

Cronbach, L. J. Processes affecting scores on "understanding of others" and "assumed similarity." *Psychol. Bull.,* 1955, 52, 177–194.

Cronbach, L. J. Proposals leading to analytic treatment of social perception scores. In R.

Tagiuri & L. Petrullo (Eds.), *Person perception and interpersonal behavior.* Stanford, Calif.: Stanford Univer. Press, 1958. Pp. 353–379.

Dahlke, H. O. *Values in culture and classroom.* New York: Harper, 1958.

Davie, J. S. Social class factors and school attendance. *Harvard educ. Rev.,* 1953, 23, 175–185.

Davies, A. F. Prestige of occupations. *Brit. J. Sociol.,* 1952, 3, 134–147.

Davis, A., & Dollard, J. *Children of bondage.* Washington, D.C.: American Council on Education, 1940.

Day, H. P. Attitude changes of beginning teachers after initial teaching experience. *J. teacher Educ.,* 1959, 10, 326–328.

Deeg, M. E., & Paterson, D. G. Changes in the social status of occupations. *Occupations,* 1947, 25, 205–208.

DeGood, K. C. Can superintendents perceive community viewpoints? *Admin. Notebook,* 1959, 8(3), 1–4.

DeGroat, A. F., & Thompson, G. G. A study of the distribution of teacher approval and disapproval among sixth-grade pupils. *J. exp. Educ.,* 1949, 18, 57–75.

Dewey, R. The rural-urban continuum: Real but relatively unimportant. *Amer. J. Sociol.,* 1960, 66, 60–66.

Dixon, N. R. Social class and education: An annotated bibliography. *Harvard educ. Rev.,* 1953, 23, 330–338.

Douvan, Elizabeth, & Adelson, J. The psychodynamics of social mobility in adolescent boys. *J. abnorm. soc. Psychol.,* 1958, 56, 31–44.

Doyle, L. A. A study of the expectancies which elementary teachers, school administrators, board members and parents have of the elementary teachers' role. Unpublished doctoral dissertation, Michigan State Univer., 1956.

Drews, Elizabeth M., & Teahan, J. E. Parental attitudes and academic achievement. *J. clin. Psychol.,* 1957, 13, 328–332.

Dubin, R. Human relations in formal organizations. *Rev. educ. Res.,* 1959, 29, 357–366.

Elsbree, W. S. *The American teacher.* New York: American Book Co., 1939.

Eson, M. E. The Minnesota Teacher Attitude Inventory in evaluating the teaching of educational psychology. *J. educ. Psychol.,* 1956, 47, 271–275.

Evenden, E. S., Gamble, G. C., & Blue, H. G.

Teacher personnel in the United States.
Washington, D.C.: U.S. Dept. of the Interior, Office of Education, Bull. 1933, No.
10, Vol. 2.

Ferneau, E. Role-expectations in consultations.
Unpublished doctoral dissertation, Univer.
of Chicago, 1954.

Fiedler, F. E. *Leader attitudes and group
effectiveness.* Urbana: Univer. of Illinois
Press, 1958.

Fishburn, C. E. Teacher role perception in the
secondary schools of one community. Unpublished doctoral dissertation, Stanford
Univer., 1955.

Gage, N. L., & Cronbach, L. J. Conceptual
and methodological problems in interpersonal perception. *Psychol. Rev.,* 1955, 62,
411–423.

Gage, N. L., Leavitt, G. S., & Stone, G. C.
The intermediary key in the analysis of interpersonal perception. *Psychol. Bull.,* 1956,
53, 258–266.

Getzels, J. W. Changing values challenge the
schools. *Sch. Rev.,* 1957, 65, 92–102.

Getzels, J. W. Administration as a social
process. In A. W. Halpin (Ed.), *Administrative theory in education.* Chicago: Midwest Administration Center, Univer. of
Chicago, 1958. Pp. 150–165.

Getzels, J. W., & Guba, E. G. The structure
of roles and role conflict in the teaching
situation. *J. educ. Sociol.,* 1955, 29, 30–40.

Getzels, J. W., & Guba, E. G. Social behavior
and the administrative process. *Sch. Rev.,*
1957, 65, 423–441.

Getzels, J. W., & Thelen, H. A. The classroom
as a unique social system. *Yearb. nat. Soc.
Stud. Educ.,* 1960, 59, Part II, 53–82.

Gilbert, G. M.. Stereotype persistence and
change among college students. *J. abnorm.
soc. Psychol.,* 1951, 46, 245–254.

Gillin, J. The school in the context of the
community. In G. D. Spindler (Ed.), *Education and anthropology.* Stanford, Calif.:
Stanford Univer. Press, 1955. Pp. 62–72.

Girard, A., & Bastide, H. Orientation et selection scolaires: Une enquète sur les enfants
à la sortie de l'école primaire. *Population,*
1955, 10, 605–626.

Glidewell, J. C., Gildea, Margaret C. L.,
Domke, H. R., & Kantor, Mildred B. Behavior symptoms in children and adjustment in public school. *Human Organization,*
1959, 18, 123–130.

Gordon, C. W. The role of the teacher in the
social structure of the high school. *J. educ.
Sociol.,* 1955, 29, 21–29.

Gordon, C. W. *The social system of the high
school.* Glencoe, Ill.: Free Press, 1957. (a)

Gordon, C. W. The sociology of education.
In J. B. Gittler (Ed.), *Review of sociology:
Analysis of a decade.* New York: Wiley,
1957. Pp. 500–519. (b)

Grambs, Jean D. Teachers as a minority
group. *J. educ. Sociol.,* 1949, 22, 400–405.

Grambs, Jean D. The sociology of the "born
teacher." *J. educ. Sociol.,* 1952, 25, 532–541.

Greene, E. J., & Staton, T. F. Predictive value
of various tests of emotionality and adjustment in a guidance program for prospective
teachers. *J. educ. Res.,* 1939, 32, 653–659.

Greenhoe, Florence. The community contacts
and participation of 9,122 public-school
teachers selected as a national sample. *Sch.
& Soc.,* 1939, 50, 510–512.

Greenhoe, Florence. Community contacts of
public-school teachers. *Elem. sch. J.,* 1940,
40, 497–506.

Greenhoe, Florence. *Community contacts and
participation of teachers.* Washington, D.C.:
American Council on Public Affairs, 1941.

Griffin, J. F. Community relationships of business teachers in the high schools of Illinois
(excluding Chicago). Unpublished doctoral
dissertation, Northwestern Univer., 1953.

Griffiths, D. E. An evaluation of the leadership of the school superintendent. Unpublished doctoral dissertation, Yale Univer.,
1952.

Griffiths, D. E. *Human relations in school administration.* New York: Appleton-Century-
Crofts, 1956.

Grobman, Hulda G., & Hines, V. A. Private
life of the teacher. In L. J. Stiles (Ed.), *The
teacher's role in American society.* New
York: Harper, 1957. Pp. 132–145.

Gross, N., Mason, W. S., & McEachern, A. W.
*Explorations in role analysis: Studies of the
school superintendency role.* New York:
Wiley, 1958.

Guba, E. G. Morale and satisfaction: A study
in past-future time perspective. *Admin. sci.
Quart.,* 1958, 3, 195–209.

Guba, E. G., & Bidwell, C. E. *Administrative
relationships.* Chicago: Midwest Administration Center, Univer. of Chicago, 1957.

Gummere, R. M., Jr. Prestige and the teacher.
Sch. & Soc., 1960, 88, 117–118.

Hall, R. K., Hans, N., & Lauwerys, J. A. (Eds.) *The yearbook of education 1953.* Yonkers, N.Y.: World Book Co., 1953.

Halpin, A. W. *The leadership behavior of school superintendents.* Columbus: School-Community Development Study Monogr. Series, No. 4, Ohio State Univer., 1956.

Halpin, A. W. A paradigm for research on administrator behavior. In R. F. Campbell & R. T. Gregg (Eds.), *Administrative behavior in education.* New York: Harper, 1957. Pp. 155–199.

Halpin, A. W., & Winer, B. J. *The leadership behavior of the airplane commander.* Columbus: Ohio State Univer. Res. Found., 1952.

Harding, J., Kutner, B., Proshansky, H., & Chein, I. Prejudice and ethnic relations. In G. Lindzey (Ed.), *Handbook of social psychology.* Cambridge, Mass.: Addison-Wesley, 1954. Pp. 1021–1061.

Hart, C. W. M. Contrasts between prepubertal and postpubertal education. In G. D. Spindler (Ed.), *Education and anthropology.* Stanford, Calif.: Stanford Univer. Press, 1955. Pp. 127–145.

Hartmann, G. W. The prestige of occupations. *Personnel J.,* 1934, 13, 144–152.

Hatt, P. K. Occupation and social stratification. *Amer. J. Sociol.,* 1950, 55, 533–543.

Havighurst, R. J., & Neugarten, Bernice L. *Society and education.* Boston: Allyn & Bacon, 1957.

Heider, F. *The psychology of interpersonal relations.* New York: Wiley, 1958.

Hemphill, J. K., & Coons, A. E. *Leader behavior description.* Columbus: Personnel Res. Bd., Ohio State Univer., 1950.

Henry, J. Culture, education, and communications theory. In G. D. Spindler (Ed.), *Education and anthropology.* Stanford, Calif.: Stanford Univer. Press., 1955. Pp. 188–207. (a)

Henry, J. Docility, or giving teacher what she wants. *J. soc. Issues,* 1955, 11(2), 33–41. (b)

Henry, J. Attitude organization in elementary school classrooms. *Amer. J. Orthopsychiat.,* 1957, 27, 117–133.

Henry, J. A cross-cultural outline of education. *Curr. Anthropol.,* 1960, 1, 267–304.

Herda, F. J. Some aspects of the relative instructional efficiency of men and women teachers. *J. educ. Res.,* 1935, 29, 196–203.

Hieronymus, A. N. Study of social class motivation: Relationship between anxiety for education and certain socio-economic and intellectual variables. *J. educ. Psychol.,* 1951, 42, 193–205.

Hiller, E. T. *Social relations and structures.* New York: Harper, 1947.

Hines, V. A. F Scale, GAMIN, and public school principal behavior. *J. educ. Psychol.,* 1956, 47, 321–328.

Hines, V. A., & Grobman, Hulda G. What a principal does, matters. *Phi Delta Kappan,* 1956, 37, 308–310.

Hoehn, A. J. A study of social status differentiation in the classroom behavior of nineteen third grade teachers. *J. soc. Psychol.,* 1954, 39, 269–292.

Hollingshead, A. B. *Elmtown's youth.* New York: Wiley, 1949.

Hughes, E. C. *Men and their work.* Glencoe, Ill.: Free Press, 1958.

Hunter, O. N. Relationship between school size and discrepancy in perception of the superintendent's behavior. Unpublished doctoral dissertation, Washington Univer., 1959.

Hyman, H. H. The value systems of different classes: A social psychological contribution to the analysis of stratification. In R. Bendix & S. M. Lipset (Eds.), *Class, status, and power.* Glencoe, Ill.: Free Press, 1953. Pp. 426–442.

Iannaccone, L. The social system of an elementary school staff. Unpublished doctoral dissertation, Teachers Coll., Columbia Univer., 1958.

Inabnit, D. J. Characteristics of teacher participation in decision-making functions of public school administration. Unpublished doctoral dissertation, Univer. of Illinois, 1954.

Inkeles, A., & Rossi, P. H. National comparisons of occupational prestige. *Amer. J. Sociol.,* 1956, 61, 329–339.

Jackson, D. M. Administrative procedure in curriculum revision. *Admin. Notebook,* 1957, 5(6), 1–4.

Jackson, P. W., & Guba, E. G. The need structure of in-service teachers: An occupational analysis. *Sch. Rev.,* 1957, 65, 176–192.

Jaynes, B. L. Public attitudes in the State of Washington on important characteristics and salaries and personal practices of public school teachers as related to certain socio-economic factors. Unpublished doctoral dissertation, Washington State Coll., 1951.

Jenkins, D. H., & Lippitt, R. *Interpersonal perceptions of teachers, students, and parents.* Washington, D.C.: Division of Adult Education Services, National Education Association, 1951.

Jensen, G. E. The school as a social system. *Educ. res. Bull.,* 1954, 33, 38–46.

Jenson, T. J., & Staub, W. F. School-community relations. *Rev. educ. Res.,* 1961, 31, 406–416.

Jones, H. E. Some aspects of an occupational stereotype: The American public school teacher. Unpublished doctoral dissertation, Claremont Graduate School, 1957.

Kahl, J. A. Educational and occupational aspirations of "common man" boys. *Harvard educ. Rev.,* 1953, 23, 186–203.

Kandel, I. L. *The new era in education: A comparative study.* Boston: Houghton Mifflin, 1955.

Kaplan, L. The annoyances of elementary school teachers. *J. educ. Res.,* 1952, 45, 649–665.

Katz, D., & Braly, K. W. Verbal stereotypes and racial prejudice. In Eleanor E. Maccoby, T. M. Newcomb, & E. L. Hartley (Eds.), *Readings in social psychology.* (3rd ed.) New York: Holt, 1958. Pp. 40–46.

Kiely, Margaret. Comparison of students of teachers colleges and students of liberal arts colleges. *Teach. Coll. Contr. Educ.,* 1931, No. 440.

Kluckhohn, C. *Mirror for man.* New York: McGraw-Hill, 1949.

Kluckhohn, C., & Kluckhohn, Florence R. American culture: Generalized orientations and class patterns. In L. Bryson, L. Finkelstein, & R. M. MacIver (Eds.), *Conflicts of power in modern culture.* New York: Harper, 1947. Pp. 106–128.

Kluckhohn, Florence R. Dominant and variant value orientations. In C. Kluckhohn & H. A. Murray, & D. M. Schneider (Eds.), *Personality in nature, society, and culture.* (2nd ed.) New York: Knopf, 1953. Pp. 342–357.

Knox, W. B. A study of the relationships of certain environmental factors to teaching success. *J. exp. Educ.,* 1956, 25, 95–151.

Krech, D., & Crutchfield, R. S. *Theory and problems of social psychology.* New York: McGraw-Hill, 1948.

Lambert, P. Interaction between authoritarian and non-authoritarian principals and teach-

ers. Unpublished doctoral dissertation, Univer. of California, 1955.

Levin, H., Hilton, T. L., & Leiderman, Gloria F. Studies of teacher behavior. *J. exp. Educ.,* 1957, 26, 81–91.

Lewin, K. *A dynamic theory of personality.* New York: McGraw-Hill, 1935.

Lichliter, Mary. Social obligations and restrictions placed on women teachers. *Sch. Rev.,* 1946, 54, 14–23.

Lieberman, M. *Education as a profession.* Englewood Cliffs, N.J.: Prentice-Hall, 1956.

Linton, R. *The cultural background of personality.* New York: Appleton-Century, 1945.

Lippmann, W. *Public opinion.* New York: Harcourt, Brace, 1922.

Lortie, D. C. Laymen to lawmen: Law school, careers, and professional socialization. *Harvard educ. Rev.,* 1959, 29, 352–369.

MacIver, R. M. *Society: A textbook of sociology.* New York: Farrar & Rinehart, 1937.

Manwiller, L. V. Expectations regarding teachers. *J. exp. Educ.,* 1958, 26, 315–354.

March, J. G., & Simon, H. A. *Organizations.* New York: Wiley, 1958.

Martindale, E. F. Situational factors in teacher placement and success. *J. exp. Educ.,* 1951, 20, 121–177.

Mason, W. S., & Bain, R. K. *Teacher turnover in the public schools, 1957–58.* Washington, D.C.: U.S. Dept. of Health, Education, and Welfare, Office of Education, Circular No. 608, 1959.

Mason, W. S., Dressel, R. J., & Bain, R. K. *The beginning teacher.* Washington, D.C.: U.S. Dept. of Health, Education, and Welfare, Office of Education, Circular No. 510, 1958.

Mayer, K. The theory of social classes. *Harvard educ. Rev.,* 1953, 23, 149–167.

McCleary, L. E. A study of interpersonal influence within a school staff: The development and trial of a method of analyzing influence within established networks of communication. Unpublished doctoral dissertation, Univer. of Illinois, 1957.

McGee, H. M. Measurement of authoritarianism and its relation to teachers' classroom behavior. *Genet. Psychol. Monogr.,* 1955, 52, 89–146.

McGill, K. H. The school-teacher stereotype. *J. educ. Sociol.,* 1931, 4, 642–650.

McGuire, C., & White, G. D. Social origins

of teachers—in Texas. In L. J. Stiles (Ed.), *The teacher's role in American society.* New York: Harper, 1957. Pp. 23–41.

McPhee, R. F. Individual values, educational viewpoint, and local school approval. *Admin. Notebook,* 1959, 7(8), 1–4.

Mead, Margaret. An anthropologist looks at the teacher's role. *Educ. Method,* 1942, 21, 219–223.

Mead, Margaret. Our educational emphasis in primitive perspective. *Amer. J. Sociol.,* 1943, 48, 633–639.

Mead, Margaret. Teachers' place in American society. *J. Amer. ass. univer. Women,* 1946, 40, 3–5.

Mead, Margaret. *The school in American culture.* Cambridge, Mass.: Harvard Univer. Press, 1951.

Menger, Clara. The social status of occupations for women. *Teachers Coll. Rec.,* 1932, 33, 696–704.

Merton, R. K. *Social theory and social structure.* (Rev. ed.) Glencoe, Ill.: Free Press, 1957.

Merton, R. K., Reader, G. G., & Kendall, Patricia L. (Eds.) *The student physician: Introductory studies in the sociology of medical education.* Cambridge, Mass.: Harvard Univer. Press, 1957.

Meyer, W. J., & Thompson, G. G. Sex difference in the distribution of teacher approval and disapproval among sixth-grade children. *J. educ. Psychol.,* 1956, 47, 385–396.

Miller, N. E., & Dollard, J. C. *Social learning and imitation.* New Haven, Conn.: Yale Univer. Press, 1941.

Miner, H. The folk-urban continuum. *Amer. sociol. Rev.,* 1952, 17, 529–537.

Mitchell, J. C. A study of teachers' and mental hygienists' rating of certain behavior problems of children. *J. educ. Res.,* 1943, 36, 292–307.

Moffett, Mary L. *The social background and activities of teachers college students.* New York: Bur. of Publs., Teachers Coll., Columbia Univer., 1929.

Moore, H. E., & Burke, J. E. Staff—economic status. In C. W. Harris (Ed.), *Encyclopedia of educational research.* (3rd ed.) New York: Macmillan, 1960. Pp. 1367–1374.

Morris, C. N. Career patterns of teachers. In L. J. Stiles (Ed.), *The teacher's role in American society.* New York: Harper, 1957. Pp. 247–263.

Morse, Nancy C. *Satisfactions in the white-collar job.* Ann Arbor: Survey Res. Center, Univer. of Michigan, 1953.

Mort, P. R. School and community relationships to school quality. *Teachers Coll. Rec.,* 1954, 55, 201–214.

Mort, P. R., & Cornell, F. G. *American schools in transition.* New York: Teachers Coll., Columbia Univer., 1941.

Mort, P. R., & Furno, O. F. *Theory and synthesis of a sequential simplex.* New York: Inst. of Admin. Res., Teachers Coll., Columbia Univer., Study No. 12, 1960.

Mort, P. R., & Pierce, T. M. Measuring community adaptability. *Sch. Executive,* 1947, 66, 35–36.

Moser, R. P. The leadership patterns of school superintendents and school principals. *Admin. Notebook,* 1957, 6(1), 1–4.

Moyer, D. C. Teachers' attitudes toward leadership as they relate to teacher satisfaction. Unpublished doctoral dissertation, Univer. of Chicago, 1954.

Moyer, D. C. Leadership that teachers want. *Admin. Notebook,* 1955, 3(1), 1–4.

Naslund, R. A., & Brown, C. A. The school and the community. *Rev. educ. Res.,* 1958, 28, 16–28.

National Education Association, Research Division. First-year teachers in 1954–55. *NEA res. Bull.,* 1956, 34, No. 1.

National Education Association, Research Division. The status of the American public-school teacher. *NEA res. Bull.,* 1957, 35, No. 1.

National Opinion Research Center. Jobs and occupations: A popular evaluation. In R. Bendix & S. M. Lipset (Eds.), *Class, status, and power.* Glencoe, Ill.: Free Press, 1953. Pp. 411–426.

Newcomb, T. M. Autistic hostility and social reality. *Human Relations,* 1947, 1, 69–86.

Newcomb, T. M. *Social psychology.* New York: Dryden, 1950.

Newcomb, T. M. *The acquaintance process.* New York: Holt, Rinehart, & Winston, 1961.

Odell, W. C. Are teachers aware of propaganda in sponsored teaching aids? *J. educ. Res.,* 1957, 51, 81–88.

Odenweller, A. L. Predicting the quality of teaching. *Teach. Coll. Contr. Educ.,* 1936, No. 676.

Ojemann, R. H., Levitt, E. E., Lyle, W. H.,

Jr., & Whiteside, Maxine F. The effects of a "causal" teacher-training program and certain curricular changes on grade school children. *J. exp. Educ.,* 1955, 24, 95–114.

Oliver, W. A. Teachers' educational beliefs *versus* their classroom practices. *J. educ. Res.,* 1953, 47, 47–55.

Pace, C. R. Five college environments. *Coll. Bd Rev.,* 1960, 41, 24–28.

Pace, C. R., & Stern, G. G. An approach to the measurement of psychological characteristics of college environments. *J. educ. Psychol.,* 1958, 49, 269–277.

Parsons, T. The school class as a social system: Some of its functions in American society. *Harvard educ. Rev.,* 1959, 29, 297–318.

Pepper, J. N. Factors involved in the recruitment and retention of teachers in Michigan. Unpublished doctoral dissertation, Wayne State Univer., 1954.

Perkins, H. V., Jr. Teachers' and peers' perceptions of children's self-concepts. *Child Develpm.,* 1958, 29, 203–220.

Peters, D. W. The status of the married woman teacher. *Teach. Coll. Contr. Educ.,* 1934, No. 603.

Phillips, B. N. Community control of teacher behavior. *J. teacher Educ.,* 1955, 6, 293–300.

Phillips, W. S. An analysis of certain characteristics of active and potential teachers. *Peabody Coll. Contr. Educ.,* 1935.

Prince, R. Individual values and administrative effectiveness. *Admin. Notebook,* 1957, 6(4), 1–4.

Rabinowitz, W., & Rosenbaum, I. Teaching experience and teachers' attitudes. *Elem. sch. J.,* 1960, 60, 313–319.

Rettig, S., & Pasamanick, B. Status and job satisfaction of public school teachers. *Sch. & Soc.,* 1959, 87, 113–116.

Richey, R. W. The United States. In R. K. Hall, N. Hans, & J. A. Lauwerys (Eds.), *The yearbook of education 1953.* Yonkers, N.Y.: World Book Co., 1953. Pp. 203–228.

Richey, R. W., Fox, W. H., & Fauset, C. E. Prestige rank of teaching. *Occupations,* 1951, 30, 33–36.

Riesman, D. *The lonely crowd.* New Haven, Conn.: Yale Univer. Press, 1950.

Rogers, Dorothy. Implications of views concerning the "typical" school teacher. *J. educ. Sociol.,* 1950, 23, 482–487.

Rollins, S. P. A study of the diffusion of information within secondary school staffs.

Unpublished doctoral dissertation, Washington Univer., 1958.

Ross, D. H. (Ed.) *Administration for adaptability.* (2nd ed.) New York: Metropolitan School Study Council, 1958.

Ruml, B., & Tickton, S. G. *Teaching salaries then and now.* New York: Fund for the Advancement of Education, 1955.

Ryans, D. G. *Characteristics of teachers.* Washington, D.C.: American Council on Education, 1960.

Saltz, Joanne W. Teacher stereotype—Liability in recruiting? *Sch. Rev.,* 1960, 68, 105–111.

Sandgren, D. L., & Schmidt, L. G. Does practice teaching change attitudes toward teaching? *J. educ. Res.,* 1956, 49, 673–680.

Sanford, R. N. (Ed.) *The American college.* New York: Wiley, 1962.

Sarbin, T. R. Role theory. In G. Lindzey (Ed.), *Handbook of social psychology.* Cambridge, Mass.: Addison-Wesley, 1954. Pp. 223–258.

Schrupp, M. H., & Gjerde, C. M. Teacher growth in attitudes toward behavior problems of children. *J. educ. Psychol.,* 1953, 44, 203–214.

Seeman, M. Role, conflict and ambivalence in leadership. *Amer. sociol. Rev.,* 1953, 18, 373–380.

Seeman, M. Social mobility and administrative behavior. *Amer. sociol. Rev.,* 1958, 23, 633–642.

Selltiz, Claire, Jahoda, Marie, Deutsch, M., & Cook, S. W. *Research methods in social relations.* (Rev. ed.) New York: Holt, 1959.

Sharma, C. L. Who should make what decisions? *Admin. Notebook,* 1955, 3(8), 1–4.

Shils, E. A. The study of the primary group. In D. E. Lerner & H. D. Lasswell (Eds.), *The policy sciences.* Stanford, Calif.: Stanford Univer. Press, 1951. Pp. 44–69.

Sims, V. M. The social-class affiliations of a group of public school teachers. *Sch. Rev.,* 1951, 59, 331–338.

Sorokin, P. A. *Society, culture, and personality: Their structure and dynamics.* New York: Harper, 1947.

Spindler, G. D. Education in a transforming American culture. *Harvard educ. Rev.,* 1955, 25, 145–156.

Stanley, W. O., Smith, B. O., Benne, K. D., & Anderson, A. W. (Eds.), *Social foundations of education.* New York: Dryden, 1956.

Stern, G. G. Student values and their relationship to the college environment. In H. T. Sprague (Ed.), *Research on college students.* Boulder, Colo.: Western Interstate Commission for Higher Education, 1960. Pp. 67–104.

Stouffer, G. A. W., Jr. Behavior problems of children as viewed by teachers and mental hygienists. *Ment. Hyg., N.Y.,* 1952, 36, 271–285.

Swanson, G. E., & Miller, D. R. *The changing American family.* New York: Wiley, 1958.

Sweitzer, R. E. The superintendent's role in improving instruction. *Admin. Notebook,* 1958, 6(8), 1–4.

Terrien, F. W. Who thinks what about educators? *Amer. J. Sociol.,* 1953, 59, 150–158.

Terrien, F. W. The occupational roles of teachers. *J. educ. Sociol.,* 1955, 29, 14–20.

Thomas, M. R. Extra-school community activities of high school teachers with implications for the community school. Unpublished doctoral dissertation, Univer. of Utah, 1954.

Toby, J. Orientation to education as a factor in the school maladjustment of lower-class children. *Soc. Forces,* 1957, 35, 259–266.

U.S. Department of Commerce, Bureau of the Census. *Census of Population: 1950.* Vol. 1. *Number of Inhabitants.* Washington, D.C.: U.S. Government Printing Office, 1952.

Wagenschein, Miriam. "Reality shock:" A study of beginning elementary school teachers. Unpublished master's dissertation, Univer. of Chicago, 1950.

Waits, L. A. A study of the comparative efficiency of single and married women as teachers. *Educ. Admin. Superv.,* 1932, 18, 630–633.

Walker, K. F. A study of occupational stereotypes. *J. appl. Psychol.,* 1958, 42, 122–124.

Waller, W. *The sociology of teaching.* New York: Wiley, 1932.

Warner, W. L. *American life: Dream and reality.* Chicago: Univer. of Chicago Press, 1953.

Warner, W. L., et al. *Democracy in Jonesville.* New York: Harper, 1949.

Warner, W. L., Havighurst, R. J., & Loeb, M. B. *Who shall be educated?* New York: Harper, 1944.

Warner, W. L., Meeker, Marchia, & Eells, K. *Social class in America.* Chicago: Science Research Associates, 1949.

Washburne, C. The teacher in the authority system. *J. educ. Sociol.,* 1957, 30, 390–394.

Watkins, M. H. The West African bush school. *Amer. J. Sociol.,* 1943, 48, 666–675.

Wattenberg, W. Social origins of teachers and American education. In L. J. Stiles (Ed.), *The teacher's role in American society.* New York: Harper, 1957. Pp. 61–70. (a)

Wattenberg, W. Social origins of teachers— A Northern industrial city. In L. J. Stiles (Ed.), *The teacher's role in American society.* New York: Harper, 1957. Pp. 13–22. (b)

Weber, C. A. Reactions of teachers to in-service education in their schools. *Sch. Rev.,* 1943, 51, 234–240.

White, R. K., & Lippitt, R. *Autocracy and democracy: An experimental inquiry.* New York: Harper, 1960.

Whiteford, Emma M. B. Administrators' stereotype of the high school home economics teacher. Unpublished doctoral dissertation, Univer. of Illinois, 1955.

Whyte, W. H., Jr. *The organization man.* New York: Simon and Schuster, 1956.

Wickman, E. K. *Children's behavior and teachers' attitudes.* New York: Commonwealth Fund, 1928.

Wilcox, R. T. Authoritarianism and expectations of leadership. Unpublished doctoral dissertation, Univer. of California, 1957.

Wiles, K., & Grobman, Hulda G. The role of the principal in curriculum development. *Educ. Admin. Superv.,* 1958, 44, 10–14.

Willard, Ruth A. A study of the relationship between the valued-behaviors of selected teachers and the learning experiences provided in their classrooms. *J. educ. Res.,* 1955, 49, 45–51.

Winget, J. Teacher inter-school mobility aspirations of elementary teachers, Chicago Public School System, 1947–48. Unpublished doctoral dissertation, Univer. of Chicago, 1952.

Znaniecki, F. The scientific function of sociology of education. *Educ. Theory,* 1951, 1, 69–78, 87.

CHAPTER 15 Research on Teaching in the Nursery School

PAULINE S. SEARS
Stanford University

EDITH M. DOWLEY
Stanford University

Upon being asked at what age the education of a child should begin, Oliver Wendell Holmes is said to have replied: "One hundred years before the child's birth." This chapter is concerned with problems and findings in relation to a kind of education which does not go quite so far back in the child's history, but represents the earliest education given him in a setting which might be called a "school." Recent work by ethologists (Hess, 1959), as well as personality theory developed by psychoanalysts and later by their learning theory protagonists, has forcibly raised questions concerning the possibility of critical periods early in the child's life and their influence on later development. The evidence as to the importance of primacy effects as compared with later situational determinism is by no means complete; nonetheless educators would do well to examine the evidence concerning influences on children's behavior potentials at the early as well as the later ages, in the interests of determining how best to achieve their purposes in the education of children.

The nursery "school" has had a short history compared to schools for children beyond the age of six. Its aims have always differed from those of schools for older children. In varying degrees, traditional, subject-centered curricula, as against child-centered, emergent curricula, have been present here as at higher levels. Slow building, by habit training, of routines for toilet, rest, and tying shoelaces, have their counterparts in the sequential teaching of arithmetic fundamentals to youth of other ages. More recently, nursery educators have advocated watching and waiting for the child's needs to emerge and determine the timing of different activities, as compared to having adults make decisions as to the scheduling of activities of a group of children of a given age.

In examining the present state of knowledge with respect to the relationships of teaching methods, materials, environment, personality, and the like, to demonstrable effects on the children exposed to teaching, it is necessary to have a certain background with reference to the kinds of teaching which have been going on and the apparent societal reasons motivating changes in methods and program. Therefore, this chapter begins with a short history of the nursery school movement in this country, continues with a representative list of objectives for nursery education, and then goes on to the experimental results on relationships of methods and environment to effects on children.

HISTORY OF OBJECTIVES IN NURSERY SCHOOL TEACHING

A survey of the objectives of nursery education over the past 40 years reveals many interesting trends and changes. The first nursery schools in the United States were for the most part connected with universities and colleges and had as their purpose the discovery and demonstration of "better" ways of caring for young children. Their objectives varied from one nursery school to another according to whether the sponsoring college department was home economics, education, psychology, or medicine. The curricular objectives of most of these schools were, however, primarily concerned with habit training and with promotion of physical health.

During the depression years of the 1930's, the nursery school movement experienced its first spurt in growth when federal legislation and support were instrumental in establishing nursery schools throughout the country under the WPA program. The primary objective of these schools was to provide employment for teachers who were out of work. The curriculum of these nursery schools continued to stress physical health with a strong emphasis on nutrition. Surplus foods were made available to children in federally supported nursery schools in abundant supplies as a by-product of a government program of economic supports for farmers. The teaching of "good" eating habits was consequently emphasized, along with habits of sleeping, dressing, washing, and elimination. Teachers whose training was deficient in child development found security and confidence in teaching these specific learnings, and their objectives were for the most part concerned with the acquisition of efficient, routine habits.

The war years brought another spurt in the growth of nursery schools. The Lanham Act provided funds for day-care centers for young children in order to allow mothers to work in strategic war industries and help meet the manpower shortage. The quality of these schools varied with the qualifications of the teaching personnel. Continued emphasis on routines with longer periods of so-called "free play" brought little change in the expressed aims or objectives, but teachers became more aware of their own needs for skills and techniques in handling child behavior. Longer hours at nursery school and disturbances in parent-child relationships as the result of separation from the father (Stolz, et al., 1954) and employment of the mother often showed up in nursery school in an increase of emotional difficulties among children. Teachers were therefore forced to look for improved ways of working with children, and the search often led to revision of their objectives, the program, and the school environment for learning.

The postwar years saw the growth of nursery education take another direction in the popular, fast-growing parent cooperative nursery school movement. Parents recognized the value of nursery schools in providing group experiences for children and in furnishing the parents themselves with opportunity for learning. Many good programs for young children have resulted from these cooperatives. Their primary objective, however, was the guidance and education of parents rather than good education for young children.

This brief sketch discloses that, throughout the history of nursery education in the United States, the primary objective of the nursery schools has often been the welfare of persons other than the children. Preparental education of high school and college students, teacher training, and research have been added to parent education, teacher employment, and the provision of custodial care for children of employed mothers as the main objectives of nursery schools. The natural result has been less emphasis on the child as an individual.

Some teachers tend to look at nursery school as an extension of the elementary school downward. The term "preschool" is used to indicate getting ready for kindergarten and first grade, and the learning experiences presented to children are structured in terms of segregated age groups. Conformity to the wishes of the adult or to demands of the group of children is expected, with the rationale that such conformity is a necessary step in socialization.

Other teachers think of the nursery school as an extension of the child's home outward —a supplement to the experiences and relationships he has known within his family. Recognition of the child as an individual with a need to discover, experiment, and explore the world outside his home determines the objectives of his learnings. Conformity is less emphasized.

During the 1940's the writings of J. E. Anderson (1947), Frank (1938), Gesell (1940, 1943), and Spock (1946) influenced the thinking of nursery educators and caused them to re-evaluate their aims and objectives. Gesell presented, in great detail, hundreds of developmental characteristics which, he believed, follow a more or less consistent pattern in all children during the first five years of life. Spock gave new strength to the concept that growing and learning proceed more smoothly if permitted to occur in the child's own way and time. Anderson pointed out that learning occurs within a relationship and stressed the significant role of the environment in effecting learning. Frank analyzed the necessary learnings of early childhood in relation to the child's fundamental needs as a feeling, responding individual. He cautioned teachers against the dangers of expecting too much too soon and at too great cost to the child in his personal, social, and cultural maturing. In his view, the role of the nursery school teacher is not only educational but clinical.

The goals of teaching in nursery schools are usually of two kinds: those that concern the learnings of nursery school children as a *group* and those concerned with the modification and direction of the behavior of *individual* children. Both are found to some extent in every nursery school curriculum. Some teachers, however, tend to think more in terms of *group* expectations, while others do their day-to-day and long-term planning with the specific purpose of making a curriculum for each *individual* child.

In the first case, the emphasis is usually on the efficient learning of routines, of ability to follow directions in a group, of acceptance of authority, and of attitudes conducive to harmony between individual children's wishes and the needs and wishes of the group. Such group goal objectives usually predominate in nursery schools where children are taught in homogeneous age groups. The teacher sets goals in accordance with norms established for three-, four-, or five-year-olds and judges teaching effectiveness in terms of how children measure up to the norms of the next age group. This kind of teaching expectation assumes that some learnings are worth while for all children at a given age and therefore that all children can and probably should learn them together.

Doing things together such as resting, napping, going to the toilet, washing, dressing, and eating, have been traditional practices in many nursery schools since their beginnings. In addition, there have been "set" times for outdoor play, stories, music, and working with creative materials. The value of predictable regularity for children has been stressed. The assumption that group learnings are more palatable to a child than individual guidance in terms of level of physiological development was no doubt a justification for perpetuating practices which were originally aimed at economy of adult supervision. The value of many of these group practices is now questioned, and the trend is toward more individualization of routines. For example, Read, in the third edition of *The Nursery School,* stated: "Naps or rest periods are individual rather than group affairs and can usually be managed better at home than at school" (1960, p. 25). Her first edition, however, advocated a 15-minute rest on cots for all children (1950, p. 24).

The value of learning to rest or nap in

groups at nursery school is questionable in comparison with that of other learnings. Bach (1945) suggested that children consider rest and nap periods an interference with their play activities and regard the nursery school teacher as the agent of that interference. Using a doll-play technique to determine the quantity and types of young children's fantasies, he found that children subjected to the frustration of longer nap routines displayed more fantasy aggression and more aggression involving the teacher than children who had only a brief rest routine. On elimination learning, Read said that "a set schedule for going to the toilet has the disadvantage of not meeting individual needs, or not meeting changing needs in the same individual." She advocated, however, the wisdom of suggesting a toilet period before lunch for all children (1960, p. 137).

Less emphasis is placed today, it seems, on teaching dressing and undressing in nursery school. The improvement of children's clothing by manufacturers and more enlightened parent attitudes toward the selection of garments worn by children may account for this. Read warned that since a child finds "great satisfaction in doing a thing [dressing] unaided," the nursery school teacher should avoid "helping him needlessly" (1960, p. 152). Some differences in emphasis are noted between schools in mild climates and those which experience long periods of cold weather. Langford (1960), noting that teachers of young children are sometimes called "snow-suit stuffers," stressed the responsibility of adults for helping children gain independence and self-confidence in dressing and undressing. She devoted an entire chapter to principles and methods of guidance in relation to buttons, zippers, shoelaces, and other dressing skills.

Learning to master routines as an objective for nursery school children was often regarded as "learning for life" and therefore deemed to be of such tremendous importance that most of the child's time in nursery school was devoted to perfecting routine habits. The fact that a child may repeat certain behavior over and over does not necessarily mean that it will become fixed. Behavior that is suited to one level of maturity and frequently repeated does not necessarily establish a habit that will carry over to a later level (Jersild, 1960, p. 27). Teachers who invested much time in teaching the proper techniques of handwashing before lunch, for example, were disappointed to find that when children left nursery school there was no voluntary carry-over of this learning. Unfortunately, children whose teachers felt fundamentally obliged to teach routines were left to educate themselves in social and play techniques even though early studies suggested that children at any age level would benefit from training in handling social situations and in skills which would increase their resources (Murphy, Murphy, & Newcomb, 1937, p. 403). Thompson's (1944) work confirmed the value of such training.

Although research is scarce in the area of motor and manipulatory behavior, nursery schools have always advocated development of the large muscles through an abundance of outdoor play. Children use play in a wide variety of ways. In attempting to understand his environment, the child experiments with it. He solves problems by using his strength and his intelligence. Research does not give much guidance as to the amount of time a child should engage in active physical play nor as to the effectiveness of various sorts of equipment. The skilled teacher is guided by the child's choice of activity and the equipment he seeks to satisfy his developing interests (Gutteridge, 1947, p. 218). Children develop motor and manipulatory skills in an environment in which they are (1) encouraged to move about freely, (2) challenged to try new and increasingly complex activities, and (3) motivated by personal and social success.

During the nursery school years, children acquire many of the basic manipulatory skills such as sorting, buttoning, tying, drawing, and cutting. Proficiency is related to both developmental age and practice. Nursery schools generally provide a variety of materials and equipment for fostering and furthering development. Puzzles, blocks, construction toys, sand, clay, paints, crayons, scissors, hammers, and saws contribute to the development of eye-hand coordination and finger dexterity. The acquisition of skills frees the child from the dominance of the situation (J. E. Anderson, 1947) and gives him time for other desirable activities.

Some nursery schools put great stress on learning to sit still and listen to stories and music in groups. Often the story or the music *will* hold the attention of the group for several minutes. By nature, however, the young child is active, and concerned with his own ego and its needs. The child's realization of himself as a member of a group can only come gradually, and it must be built on a foundation of personal security. Although adjustment and conformity to the group make the running of a nursery school easier, they often demand of a child sacrifices which are not easy and which may have little value for him. Research on the effect of early subordination to group membership and on children's interests in group stories or other presentations is very much needed (Wolffheim, 1953). The inability of young children to share an important adult with many others, children's obvious needs for bodily activity, and the great individual differences they manifest in length of attention span (Olson, 1959) and in story interests make it difficult to believe that large groups of children will take part in structured group activity day in and day out unless they are subjected to external force.

Some observers feel that today the nursery school places too much emphasis on the group and too little on the individual. This loss of individuality is disheartening insofar as two-, three-, and four-year-olds are learning to become good group members at the expense of discovering themselves as individuals (Martin, 1960–1961).

Studies of the effects of nursery school experience on children at elementary school age found that the personality difficulties and strengths which individual children had revealed in nursery school tended to follow them into the later school years. Van Alstyne

and Hattwick (1939) held that one aim of nursery school teachers should be to help children to deal with the difficulties they are showing in nursery school which are likely to persist through life. According to another study (Jersild & Fite, 1939), mere attendance at nursery school will not necessarily provide individual children with what they need. The benefits they derive from nursery school will probably be influenced to a large degree by the personality and competence of the teacher (Jersild, 1960). There is need for more research of the type done by Thompson (1944), whose work is described below, to help teachers set goals and make plans to modify children's social and emotional development by means of certain amounts, kinds, and timings of teacher guidance.

Other contemporary aims and objectives of nursery school teaching, as expressed in the literature of child development and nursery education, fall into several categories. Some are general aims such as meeting needs and providing scope for growth (Stone & Church, 1957). Developing self-possession, security, and self-confidence and the lessening of the child's guilt feelings "must be the aim of all education" according to Wolffheim (1953). Gardner (1957) held that physical, emotional, and social needs are fundamental and predominant, but intellectual needs are vital, too.

Most writers feel that learning to play is extremely important in the preschool years. An understanding of how play develops (Parten & Newhall, 1943) and what it means to the child is helpful in goal-setting for this learning. When teachers find children in nursery school who, for some reason or other, have not yet developed their play interests and play skills, they speak of a need for "play-tutoring" these children.

Learning to get along well with others is another important objective for individual children in nursery school. This objective involves the encouragement or modification of ascendance in the behavior of children to accord with what is judged acceptable (Chittenden, 1942; Mummery, 1947). Children need guidance in asserting their own rights as well as in respecting the rights of others. Learning the balance between give and take in social relationships is important for young children. The guidance of children in learning how to manage their emotional reactions to anger, frustration, fear, and grief (Frank, 1938); in learning controls from within (Redl & Wineman, 1952); and in learning acceptable social techniques (Langford, 1960) are also among major aims of nursery education.

To this list of objectives have been added learning to understand adults (Langford, 1960), learning to respect the personal and property rights of others, and acceptance of and respect for authority (Frank, 1938).

Learning to share has always been mentioned as one of the objectives of nursery education. The experiences, equipment, materials, and furniture of nursery schools have been systematically designed in the light of the significance of learning to share in early childhood. The Forty-Sixth Yearbook of the National Society for the Study of Education (Part II, *Early Childhood Education*) included a comprehensive coverage of the research literature on sharing (Chittenden, 1947); very little can be added to that chapter.

One other important group of aims for nursery educators revolves about the concept of identification. Nursery school teachers are growing increasingly aware of the importance of identification models for children in the preschool period. The predominance of feminine models in young children's lives and the limited amount of time fathers in certain occupation groups—servicemen, commuters, pilots, students, for example—can spend with their children today (Stolz, et al., 1954) have made teachers increasingly aware of the need for masculine models in the nursery school. Some teachers have found ways of bringing men into the nursery school to serve in a variety of capacities ranging from teacher to casual visitor. Fathers are now participating regularly in some nursery school groups, as mothers have been doing for the last 15 years. In recent years an increasing amount of attention has been given to investigating the

ways in which children learn their appropriate sex behavior, incorporate their moral and ethical concepts, and develop the ability to judge rightness or wrongness in relation to their own and others' behavior. Since these learnings begin early in a child's life (P. S. Sears & Levin, 1957), nursery school teachers need to understand what is known about the process of identification. Erikson (1950) speaks of the ages three, four, and five as a time when the child tries to find out what he will be like when he grows up. Nursery school teachers are aware of the tremendous amount of role-playing that goes on in nursery school at this age, provided children can find the necessary "props" for their dramatic play, the freedom to "try on" these roles without being interrupted or made to feel self-conscious about them, and the appropriate models in their everyday lives with whom to identify (Bandura & Huston, 1961; P. S. Sears & Levin, 1957; Stoke, 1954; Vitz, 1961).

Teachers no longer think in terms of helping children to avoid all guilt feelings in relation to behavior. Instead, they are concerned with the appropriate amount and kind of guilt and the ways children handle feelings of guilt in the development of a healthy conscience (R. R. Sears, 1960–1961).

The nursery school has traditionally stressed the importance of language learning for the preschool child. The content of his speech is significant not only in relation to his growth in language and to his interests but also as a measure of his personality development (Breckenridge & Murphy, 1958). Language serves many important functions for the child. By means of the spoken word he makes known his feelings and desires; he secures and imparts information; he develops his imagination through narration and role-play; he increases the amount and variety of his social contacts; and he expresses complex thought and abstract reasoning (Dawe, 1947). Nursery school provides opportunities for developing the language of children through the choice and arrangement of materials, equipment, furniture, and program. Books, pictures, stories, walks, and trips contribute topics for thought and conversation (McCarthy, 1954).

In recent years the participation of his parents in a child's nursery school has been thought to accelerate his learning because of the increased opportunity it affords for discussion and thinking about their shared experiences.

Much of the literature on learning in nursery school is devoted to the environment, situations, equipment, materials, and methods for effecting emotional, social, and personal adjustment; in fact, it would almost appear that the intellectual development of children was of minor concern to preschool educators. This impression is, however, unwarranted. Many writers see the nursery school as both a place to adjust and a place for cognitive learning. For example, Roeper (1959) advocated paying more attention to cognitive and intellectual development in nursery school. Speaking for many others, she held that a good nursery school program can arouse the curiosity of the child and develop his ability to think logically. The nursery school curriculum normally includes simple, basic, quantitative, scientific, creative experiences through which a child learns concepts of space, time, size, weight, shape, balance, age, texture, temperature, and the distinction between animate and inanimate, to name only a few.

In addition, the child is encouraged to develop his creative abilities. Although much current writing is concerned with the study of creativity, little has been directly applicable to the nursery school. However, the materials which encourage the child's creative expression, such as paints, clay, finger paints, blocks, and collage materials are almost always found in nursery schools together with the freedom to use them and to develop individual ideas and expression.

Some writers have recognized that children can and often do learn more subject matter than is usually included in the nursery school curriculum. Apart from the young child's interest in the exploration of materials and processes, language, music, dramatics, and social contacts, he often has a real awareness of society's respect for knowledge, skill, and the ability to produce. Parents frequently feel that their four- and five-year-olds should be learning to read, print, and do simple arithmetic. Throughout the country there are private nursery schools and kindergartens which offer subject-matter teaching as a part of the curriculum. Public criticism of the academic achievement of high school graduates has not only led to demands for revision of the elementary school curriculum in some places but has suggested a revision of the nursery school curriculum as well.

No systematic studies on learning to read during the nursery school years have been found. The well-established doctrine (e.g., Olson, 1959) that children grow at different rates and have different aptitudes for learning implies that early instruction in reading will not necessarily create readiness or develop skill but may result in lack of interest and avoidance on the part of the child. "Reading," Olson points out, "does not occur without instruction and practice. . . . Most children [will] practice eagerly and almost continuously when the opportunity is present and the child is mature enough. . . . If he is ready and the people around him value reading as an accomplishment, nothing can stop him" (1959, p. 144). Hence, many learnings provided by nursery schools seem to take precedence over the learning of the three R's. Baruch (1939) and Forest (1949, p. 190) pointed out how certain practices and experiences in nursery school develop reading readiness and the basic foundations for quantitative learnings and handwriting skills. On page 845 is reported some recent experimentation with teaching of reading.

The bibliography of nursery education included with this chapter appears imposing both in length and breadth. Yet, on looking over the references used in preparing this section on objectives in nursery school teaching, one is impressed with the dearth of contemporary entries. The bulk of research in early childhood education was carried on in the 1920's and 1930's when nursery education was just getting started in this country. Those years saw the elaboration and implementation of the scientific approach to the education of the young child in such newly established research centers as those at Iowa, Yale, Minnesota, Columbia, and Toronto. The same years witnessed the initiation of growth studies at such places as Harvard, Stanford, Michigan, California, and Chicago. Various other programs throughout the country were devoted to the study of child development and family life (Fuller, 1960). The nursery school became a valuable setting for research efforts, and enthusiastic leaders in child development published a sizable body of scientific information about learning in the preschool years.

World War II probably turned the attention of nursery educators to the more immediately pressing problems of housing and staffing nursery day-care programs. During the postwar years, research on child development seemed to focus on parent-child relations and child-rearing practices because of the wider dissemination of psychoanalytic concepts and the influence of anthropological cross-cultural studies. In recent years, as the result, at least in part, of apparent Russian superiority in certain areas of science and engineering, the emphasis has swung back somewhat to a critical scrutiny of our educational practices. This history may account in part for the gap between those references with dates in the thirties and those in the late fifties and early sixties.

An Overview of the Trends

In sum, the history of the nursery school movement, as we know it, covers only some 40 years. Those have been years of tremendous scientific and social change. Two world wars and an economic depression, the great movement of populations from one part of the country to another, the G.I. education bill, our sudden and dramatic entrance into a nuclear age, and the beginnings of space exploration have changed life in the United States. These changes are reflected in the philosophy and practices of nursery education.

The postwar years have drawn parents closer into the nursery school picture. The trend toward families with larger numbers of children born closer together, and the crowded living conditions of suburban, city, and university village living, have sharpened the need for greater knowledge concerning children. Young parents, as a result of their postwar relocations, often lost contact with their own family traditions in child-rearing. Consequently, parents formed groups to share common concerns and problems in the education of their young children under the guidance of professional educators. Parent education, through adult education programs as well as through parent-organized cooperatives, has spread throughout the country.

As parents and teachers have shared their ideas and convictions, many nursery school practices once held precious have been modified. There has been a tendency, for example, to shift from very small groups to somewhat larger numbers of children. Nursery school teachers, as a result of this trend, have relinquished some of their protective, often proprietary, feelings about their nursery school children and have recognized the value to preschoolers of having in the nursery school a variety of adults with different personalities and skills working together as a team. The pendulum, too, has swung from the overly permissive attitude in child-rearing to one based on mutual consideration, cooperation, and respect for the child's ability to accept reasonable, comfortable limits. The former attitude based on a philosophy that love alone can accomplish almost anything often resulted in much frustration and guilt on the part of parents and reinforced their feelings of inadequacy.

A Classification of Objectives

Although trends are noticeable, no universal philosophy of nursery education has emerged. In fact, little or no attempt to integrate a set of theoretical concepts is evident. In a survey of objectives such as this one, we can discern only common concerns related to areas of child learning and growing. In addition to the general aims of meeting needs and providing scope for growth, the specific aims seem to fall under the following headings:

1. Meeting organic needs and establishing routine habits: Eating, elimination, sleeping, washing, dressing, undressing.

2. Learning motor skills and confidences: Climbing, running, jumping, balancing; learning to use the body effectively.

3. Developing manipulatory skills: Using scissors, crayons, paste, paints, clay, dough, etc.; building with blocks, working with puzzles, beads, tying, buttoning.

4. Learning control and restraint: Listening to stories, sitting still, reacting to music, etc.

5. Developing appropriate behavior: Independence-dependence in adult-child relations; coping with fear, angry feelings, guilt; developing happy qualities, fun, humor, healthy optimism.

6. Psycho-sexual development: Identification, sex role learning, formation of conscience.

7. Language development.

8. Intellectual development: Cognitive learning; concept formation; self-understanding and self-esteem; creativity; academic subject matter.

TEACHING METHODS

In this section we shall review the literature and research on the effects of different teaching methods in the nursery school. Such methods are regarded as behavior characteristic of a teaching *role*.

1. What kinds of *behaviors* of adults, interacting with nursery school children in a teaching situation, have been studied?

2. What have been the effects, if any, on children exposed to these different teaching behaviors?

Note that such behaviors may or may not be stable characteristics of the teacher's personality. Teachers in some of the studies to be cited have consciously altered their methods, behaviors, and materials to suit ex-

perimental purposes; it is known also that teachers can be influenced and trained to use certain methods in preference to others. While there is, no doubt, interaction between the stable characteristics of the teacher's personality and the teaching methods adopted, i.e., while personality influences behavior, our first question is whether changes are observed in children's behavior in association with specific teacher behaviors. Our consideration of personality characteristics per se will come later.

The teaching methods on which we have some experimental evidence include the following:

Warmth, nurturance, giving of attention to children

Dominative-integrative behavior of teachers

Amount of active guidance with respect to individual children

Discipline techniques: control and restraint

Frustration conditions, imposed by an adult or by the environment

Small-group training procedures

Attendance at nursery school versus nonattendance; attendance at various types of nursery schools.

In the sections which follow, descriptions of available studies are grouped under those headings.

Warmth, Nurturance, Giving Attention

The early history of nursery education was influenced strongly by the psychology of Watsonian behaviorism. Consequently, much stress was put on training children to become independent of adult help. There are advantages, certainly, in the child's acquiring skills and competencies which increase his feelings of adequacy, if his self-sufficiency in one area does not deprive him of access to further learning. In teaching independence, the behaviorists de-emphasized warmth and affection in the learning relationship and stressed efficiency. The goal of learning was to become an independent, mature human being as early as possible.

The process of socialization begins when the infant learns to look to others for help and then learns effective means of getting help. Socialization is, then, first learning to be dependent and then learning to be independent (Heathers, 1955). The nursery school teacher finds it difficult to help the child to grow and learn when the child does not allow her to help him, rejects her comfort when he is hurt, or rejects her friendly acceptance of him as a person. On the other hand, prolonged dependency on the teacher by a child may be difficult to handle indefinitely and may result in rejection of the child by the teacher.

In more recent years, it has been emphasized that nursery school teachers should behave in a warm and friendly fashion to the young children in their charge. The nursery school child has been regarded as having a need for emotional security with the adults working with him; in the absence of such security, it has been thought, learning and personality development will progress less effectively. This point of view probably stems from psychoanalytic doctrine.

Until recently, no attempt had been made to test the effects on children of varying amounts of warmth or nurturance. Since 1948, however, attention has been directed toward the problems of *nurturance* as a behavior employed by adults in their relations to children, and *succorance* or the seeking of nurturance by young children. There is now a respectable literature of experimental studies of these factors. Some of the work has been oriented toward parental practices in this regard, and others, using preschool children as subjects, have utilized adult experimenters, whose behavior could be considered very similar to that of nursery school teachers. In this review the studies involving parents and child-rearing practices continuing over years of the child's life will be, for the most part, omitted.

Preschool educators have generally considered emotional dependence in children to be a normal manifestation of their development. All nursery school teachers have observed wide individual differences in emotional dependence, and children who at a later preschool age are still clinging and needing the reassurance of adult presence or attention are often considered to be immature in their development. One aim of preschool education, as cited earlier in the section on objectives, is the achievement by the child of some emotional independence of adults, without undue side effects such as anxiety or insecurity.

Dependence of children. Hartup's study (1958) is a good example of the type of experiment which relates directly to methods of nursery school teachers. His design was aimed at determining the relationship between one specific form of non-nurturance— the withdrawal of nurturance—and young children's acquisition of responses which elicit adult approval. This relationship was studied in the laboratory, where some manipulation of the relevant antecedent conditions was possible.

The first step was to define categories of "dependent" behavior in the child, so that children could be assigned to experimental conditions on the basis of initial high or low dependency (Hartup, 1955). Children observed in a natural preschool situation were categorized as to the amounts of the following behaviors:

(1) Seeks recognition and approval.
(2) Seeks unnecessary help.
(3) Seeks necessary help.
(4) Seeks physical contact.
(5) Seeks to be near.
(6) Seeks positive attention.
(7) Seeks negative attention.

In addition, the children were rated by their preschool teachers on these kinds of dependence, and behavior-sampling observations were made of the children in the laboratory setting. Parenthetically, it is interesting to find that the correlation between dependence on the experimenter in the laboratory situation and dependence on the preschool teacher in the natural classroom situation was .40. This correlation, while not high, was significant at beyond the .05 level and indicated that the laboratory setting represented a fair sample of the child's typical behavior in relation to teachers in the classroom setting; thus the results may properly be generalized, with appropriate caution, from the laboratory to the child's behavior in other settings.

Using the data gained through these observations and teacher ratings, Hartup set up two subgroups of preschool children, counterbalanced as to sex and initial dependency. The age of the children ranged from three years ten months to five years six months, and they came from a typical laboratory nursery school population. Two young women served as experimenters for the laboratory procedures. Each experimenter worked with a randomly assigned half of the subjects in each group. Since the experimental procedure in this study was similar to others which will be reported later, it will be given in some detail.

Each child was brought individually to the laboratory room for the experimental session. This room was equipped with one-way mirrors for observation and was furnished with a child's table and chairs, an adult-sized table with comfortable chair, and a large bench. The experimental session proceeded as follows:

1. For a period of five minutes, the experimenter interacted nurturantly with the child while the child played with toys. For purposes of this experiment nurturance consisted of adult behavior which rewarded, encouraged, supported, or showed affection to the child; during this five-minute period the experimenter attempted to maximize these qualities in her behavior toward the child. Children in both experimental groups experienced this period of nurturant interaction with the experimenter.

2. Children in the consistent-nurturance group (hereafter called group C) then immediately experienced a second five-minute period like the first.

3. The second five minutes for the nurturance-withdrawal group (group NW) were marked by the experimenter's behaving non-nurturantly toward the child. She ceased to interact with the child, withdrew from his proximity, and did not reward any of the child's supplications beyond telling him that she was "busy." The experience of children in group NW, having first a period of nurturant interaction, then a period of non-nurturance from the experimenter, has been called "nurturance-withdrawal."

4. Children in both experimental groups were then asked by the experimenter to learn two tasks, the reward for which was the verbal approval of the experimenter. Task I consisted of learning a simple position concept in an arrangement of two blue and two red one-inch blocks. The task was presented to the child as a guessing game. The experimenter placed the blocks on the floor first in this order (reading from the child's left): red, red, blue, blue. She then said: "I'm thinking of one of the blocks and I want to see if you can guess which one it is. Point with your finger to the one you think is right and I'll tell you if it's the right one." The child's first guess was always unsuccessful, as was his second. The third guess was always successful. This introductory procedure was followed to eliminate chance successes on the first guess. On each succeeding trial the arrangement of the blocks was changed through all the possible order-permutations. The correct block was always the block in the same position in the row as the one which the child chose on his third guess. The performance criterion was three consecutive correct trials. Task II consisted of copying from memory a row of adjacent blue, red, and yellow one-inch cubes which were shown to the child for five seconds per trial. Six blocks were arranged in the following order: red, yellow, blue, blue, yellow, red. The performance criterion was one perfect reproduction of the arrangement completed by the child from his own supply of blocks. Measures used in the subsequent analysis of the data were: (a) number of errors to criterion on task I; (b) number of trials to criterion on task I; (c) number of errors to criterion on task II; (d) number of trials to criterion on task II. Error- and trial-scores were correlated .93 on task I, .96 on task II (Hartup, 1958, pp. 192–193).

The data from the learning tasks were studied by the triple classification analysis of variance technique for unequal cell entries.

The three independent variables in this analysis were (1) sex of child; (2) dependency ratings obtained from the teacher—high dependency and low dependency; (3) experimental treatment, consistent nurturance versus nurturance withdrawal. Four analyses of variance were completed for each trial or error score from the learning tasks, one for each summary dependency score described above. The results were as follows:

The findings for girls uniformly support the hypothesis that nurturance-withdrawal is associated with more efficient performance on the learning tasks than consistent nurturance. The results for boys, however, showed that there were no differences between the nurturance-withdrawal and the consistent nurturance groups. Actually, the results for boys were not so clearly negative. When the boys' groups were divided according to the measures of dependence, *highly* dependent boys were found to respond much as the girls while *low* dependent boys responded in the reverse fashion. Thus, highly dependent boys (who may be assumed to be generally anxious concerning their relationships with adults) did learn more efficiently when the experimenter withdrew her nurturance. The boys in the low dependency group who were consistently nurtured learned more efficiently than boys in this group who experienced nurturance-withdrawal. Although the number of cases in these subgroups was small, this trend in the data suggests support for the hypothesis concerning the influence of nurturance-withdrawal for highly dependent boys as well as for the girls (Hartup, 1958, p. 199).

Hartup went on to consider possible explanations for the fact that the findings for boys were more equivocal than those for girls. In this experiment the adult in the situation was a female, as are nearly all nursery school teachers. Much research work at the present time is concerned with the theoretical effects of identification by the child with an adult of the same sex as compared to an adult of the opposite sex. The behavior of the adult is thought to differ depending on the sex of the adult. Here we become involved with the theoretical literature on identifica-

tion, child-rearing antecedents of dependency, and the effects of nurturers of different sexes. Currently, the implications of this fascinating area for teaching methods are not by any means clear, and they will not be discussed in detail. Interested readers are referred to Beller (1955), Gewirtz (1956), Heathers (1955), R. R. Sears, et al. (1953), and Stendler (1954). Maccoby (1959) has also developed a theory of role-taking in childhood and its consequences for social learning. In this chapter we will be concerned less with the origins of dependence than with the effects of certain types of nurturance and dependency behaviors adopted by adults in their interaction with children.

Learning of children. Whereas Hartup (1958) called upon tasks of concept formation and memory to test the effects of nurturance and nurturance-withdrawal, Rosenblith (1959) used the Porteus Maze Test, a well-standardized and frequently used test of cognitive function. Her subjects were divided not on the basis of degree of dependency, as were Hartup's, but according to ability in performing the maze test initially. Her experiment utilized four experimental treatments of the subjects. An adult model, who performed the same task asked of the child, was introduced as one variation. Second, the sex of that adult model, considered especially in relation to the child's sex, was varied. Third, nurturance and nurturance-withdrawal were treated essentially as by Hartup. Fourth, Rosenblith was able to look for interaction between the "sex of model" and "treatment" (namely, nurturance and withdrawal of nurturance) variables. Here the adult model provided the nurturance, acting like a friendly adult interested in the play of a child, and under certain conditions, withdrew nurturance. He (or she) first played with the child for five minutes and then either played for another five minutes (consistent nurturance conditions) or said, at the end of five minutes, "I'm sorry I can't play with you anymore, I have to read a book for five minutes."

At the end of the ten-minute period for both groups, the experimenter said, "I'm ready to play the game now." The adult model and the child moved to the experimenter's table, and the adult model was given the first turn at the game. The adult was given the first maze which the child had failed previously and the same instructions that the child had received. The adult model did the maze correctly at a rather slow pace and paused at choice points while engaging in some visual search. The child watched during this period and then was given a turn at the same maze. The scores of the children, tested under the varying conditions mentioned, were the number of passes at mazes of increasing difficulty in the second (experimental) session.

Rosenblith (1959) summarized the results of this experiment as follows:

In general, having a model was more effective than merely having additional trials. There were important differences between the effectiveness of the male leader and the female leader. The male leader was, in general, more effective. There were also important differences between boys and girls. Boys showed more improvement. Girls seemed less sensitive to the experimental manipulations. There was a tendency for attention to be more effective than withdrawal of attention except in the case of boys with a male leader (Rosenblith, 1959, p. 79).

Since these findings are contrary in some details to those of Hartup's study, replication with comparable procedures is necessary before clear conclusions can be drawn. Rosenblith's (1959) experiment utilized one male and one female adult model. Hartup (1958) used two females and found no significant differences between them. Before sex of the adult model is called the significant variable here, we must have evidence that it is not the personality characteristics of the particular man or woman adult model, rather than the sex role behaviors, which are influencing the child.[1]

---

[1] It is amusing occasionally to observe the male adult who is behaving like the female nursery school teacher in his efforts to learn her methodology. Often his adoption of her gentleness in action and her manner of speaking is incongruous.

Thus, it has been demonstrated that a warm and attentive adult, operating on the same task required of the child, can clearly produce better performance on the child's part than is produced in a situation where the child has merely additional trials at the task himself, without the advantage of observing the adult's performance. If this warm adult is a male, the results are more striking than when a female adult model is used. Rosenblith (1959) suggests that possibly the whole nursery school situation represents, to the children, social deprivation of adult male companionship.

Incidental learning. Whereas the experiments just reported have been concerned with children's learning of assigned tasks, and in the case of the Rosenblith (1959) experiment, direct observation of the performance of an adult model on the same task, Bandura and Huston (1961) performed an ingenious experiment testing effects on the child's imitation of attitudes and patterns of behavior which the adult model never directly attempted to teach or to show. It has long been hypothesized that emotional identification with adults may induce incidental learning of adult behaviors, that is, learning which apparently takes place in the absence of an induced set or an *intent* to learn specific behaviors or activities. As the child grows through the nursery school years, the range of cues displayed by the adults in his immediate environment is obviously tremendous. Some of these may be intentionally displayed as cues to "good" behavior. Many others are undoubtedly displayed unintentionally by the teacher, or adult model, as he behaves in his customary fashion during the school day. Bandura and Huston's experiment was intended to get at the effect of such incidental cues. Thus the main hypothesis tested in this experiment was that nursery school children, while learning to solve problems, also learn to imitate certain of the experimenters' behaviors which are totally irrelevant to a successful performance of the required task.

In this experiment the subjects were divided into two groups for different treatment conditions. The groups were matched individually on the basis of sex and ratings of dependency behavior. Each group contained 20 subjects. In the *non-nurturant* condition, the adult model (in this experiment there was one female model for all children under all conditions) brought the subject to the experimental room and after instructing the child to play with the toys that were spread on the floor, busied herself with paper work at a desk in the far corner of the room. During this period the model avoided any interaction with the child.

In contrast, during the *nurturant* sessions the model sat on the floor close to the subject, responded readily to the child's bid for help and attention, and in other ways fostered a consistently warm and rewarding interaction. These experimental social interactions, which preceded the imitation learning, consisted of two 15-minute sessions separated by an interval of approximately five days.

The task given the children was a two-choice discrimination problem. Inside of one of two small boxes, a reward was placed, consisting of a small picture of animals or flowers. The child's task was to discover in which box the picture sticker was contained. Performance on this task was, however, only incidental to the experiment; the main aim was to observe the imitation by the child of the adult model's irrelevant behavior in approaching the task. Thus, when the child and the model came into the experimental room, with the model given the first turn at playing the game, the model performed a number of actions which were completely irrelevant to the performance of the discrimination task toward which the subject's attention was directed. For example, the model began by saying clearly "Here I go," and then marched slowly toward the box containing the stickers repeating, "March, march, march." On the lid of each box was a small rubber doll which the model knocked off aggressively when she reached the box. She then paused briefly, remarked "Open the box," removed one sticker and pasted it on a pastoral scene which hung on the wall immediately behind the boxes, and then terminated the trial by replacing the doll on the lid of the container. When the child subject then took his turn, the number of these irrelevant behaviors which he reproduced was recorded.

With a control group, the adult model walked to the box, choosing a highly circuitous route along the sides of the experimental room, lifted the doll gently off the container and left the doll on the floor at the completion of the trial. While walking to the boxes the model repeated, "Walk, walk, walk." The control group had the same nurturant and non-nurturant experiences as the experimental group.

Results of this experiment on the amount of imitative behavior displayed by subjects in the experimental and control group showed the following:

Of the experimental subjects, 45 per cent imitated the marching of the adult model; no control subjects did so. Of the control subjects, 75 per cent took the circuitous route to the boxes, in imitation of the adult model, while no experimental subjects did so.

On the other types of responses given by the adult models under the experimental and control conditions, the results were similar. There was practically no overlap between the imitative behavior displayed by the two groups. They imitated the adult model behavior despite the fact that it had nothing to do with success at obtaining the reward.

The effects of nurturance on this imitation, as predicted, showed that subjects who experienced the rewarding and warm interaction with the adult model manifested considerably more imitation than did the subjects who experienced the rather cold and distant relationships. One exception to this generalization is that aggression (knocking off a doll laid on top of one of the boxes) was readily imitated by subjects regardless of the quality of the model-child relationship. Thus, *nonaggressive* behaviors were imitated more readily if the relationship between the adult and the child had been warm and nurturant, and *aggression* was imitated regardless of whether the relations had been warm. Nurturance did not seem to influence the actual discrimination choices subjects made. In this case boys and girls in both control and experimental groups did not differ in the number of trials on which they imitated the model's choice of box in the discrimination problem, or in the number of trials required before the first imitative discriminational response was made.

The results of this study generally substantiate the hypotheses that children display a good deal of social learning of an incidental imitative sort, and that nurturance is one condition facilitating such imitative learning. It is interesting to recall the data described by Milner (1951), who found that mothers of children receiving high reading readiness scores were more verbal and affectionately demonstrative in their interactions with their children than were the mothers of subjects in the low reading ability group.

The stability of these imitative patterns remains to be tested. Milner's (1951) experiment showed that reading readiness was related to length of the period of nurturant interaction with the mother. The Bandura-Huston experiment was based on two rather brief sessions of warm and nurturant interaction with the experimenter. Nevertheless, the finding that these irrelevant and functionless behaviors of the model were imitated by the child is rather startling. It suggests that teachers should give thought to their mannerisms and behavior which, however irrelevant to the learning task, may influence the child's general learning as much as the teacher behaviors intentionally directed toward helping the general growth of the child along socially accepted and planned-for lines.

Social availability of adults; dependence of children. A series of papers by Gewirtz and others (Gewirtz, 1956; Gewirtz & Baer, 1958a, 1958b; Gewirtz, Baer, & Roth, 1958) relate primarily to the dimensions and antecedents of emotional dependence in children. Behaviors which apparently are employed by children to gain such positive social responses from other persons as attention, approval,

affection, reassurance, and nearness, are the major foci of these researches. Because Gewirtz employed varying conditions of social availability of an adult, the results are of interest to us here in relation to the teacher's social availability to the child in a nursery setting. Low availability of the adult and previous deprivation effected similar increases in the incidence of children's seeking social reinforcers from the adults. Attention-seeking was greater under low availability than under high availability. Acting in such a way as to demand approval was reliably increased by the social deprivation condition as compared with the nondeprivation condition.

Interpretation. Warmth and nurturance, given by adults to young children, clearly affect performances by children on concept formation, memory, maze performance tasks, and imitation of adults' irrelevant behavior. Nurturance, and subsequent withdrawal of nurturance, appears generally to yield the strongest effects. Possibly children interpret the withdrawal as a threat to the warm relationship, and hence are motivated to greater effort in an attempt to win back the rewarding warm interaction. The effects have been tested only over short periods of time; it will be valuable to pursue these relationships over longer periods. For example, under what conditions will the child internalize some of his need for attention and nurturance, permitting self-motivation of behavior and less pressing and immediate need for nurturance from adults in the environment?

Sex of child and sex of the warm adult are probably involved in these relationships, but the current experiments do not provide conclusive data on these factors. Male experimenters and models appear in some cases to produce more effect than women. Rosenblith (1959) suggests, following Gewirtz and his co-workers (1956, 1958, 1958a, 1958b), that possibly the nursery school child, relatively "deprived" of interaction with men, responds with more strength to the male experimenter. If this is true, reduction of deprivation by longer contact with men might reduce differences possibly attributable to sex of adult.

Furthermore, it should be noted that Rosenblith's (1959) experiment utilized only one adult model of each sex. Personal characteristics, aside from sex, may be the relevant variable. In this connection an experiment by Borstelmann (1961) may be of interest as a model. His experimental variable was the sex of the experimenter, and his dependent variable was score for sex-typed behavior. He measured the sex-typed behavior of nursery children by doll-play procedures, varying and also holding constant the sex of experimenter. Four men and four women acted as experimenters, thus presumably reducing the effect of individual personal characteristics. The results did not support the hypothesis of influence of sex of experimenter; sex-typing scores were stable on retest when sex of experimenter varied, and intercorrelations between different measures of sex-typing were high regardless of sex of experimenter.

Dominative and Integrative Behavior of Teachers

Between 1937 and 1946, a distinguished series of naturalistic studies of teachers' methods in relation to children, and the effects on these children, was carried out under the leadership of H. H. Anderson. Others involved in these studies were Helen M. Brewer, J. E. Brewer, and Mary F. Reed. The original articles are listed in the references (H. H. Anderson, 1937, 1939a, Reed, 1946); however, the reader may find Anderson's chapter in Barker, Kounin, and Wright (1943), or his chapter with Gladys L. Anderson (1954) in the *Manual of Child Psychology* easier to obtain. These studies are distinguished by the idealism of their theoretical orientation toward mental hygiene for the child and also by the care and rigor of the methodology used. The studies were initiated at the preschool and kindergarten levels, and these will be the ones reported here. Later studies, with improved methodology, were done mainly at the primary grade levels, but the results were much the same.

The theory on which these studies are based divides behavior, whether the behavior is by teacher or by child, into *dominative* and *integrative* categories. *Dominative* behavior is characterized by

rigidity or inflexibility of purpose, by an unwillingness to admit the contribution of another's experience, desires, purposes or judgment in the determining of goals which concern others.... [It] attempts to make others behave according to one's own standards or purposes.... [*Integrative* behavior] is said to be an expression not so much of pursuing one's own unique purposes as attempting to discover and get satisfactions through common purposes. ... It makes allowance in one's own behavior for differences in others (H. H. Anderson, 1939a, pp. 123–124).

Generally speaking, integrative behavior is similar to "democratic" ways of operating with others, and dominative behavior to "autocratic" ways of interacting with others.

Anderson's theory goes on to state the concept of "circular behavior," thus:

1. Domination incites resistance, which itself is dominative.
2. Integrative behavior induces cooperation or integrative behavior in a companion.
3. Domination is not only different from, but where a potential avenue of escape is left open, it is dynamically unrelated to integrative behavior.... [The main distinction seems to be as to whether] *conformity by the child* [is asked for] versus *joint participation by the child or by the group*. Did the teacher tell them or ask them? Did she base decisions on her own desires or judgment or did she allow some measure of interplay for the child's desires, the child's judgment? (H. H. Anderson, 1939c, pp. 74–75).

Domination in these studies included social contacts in which the activity of the child or the group is determined by the experience or judgment of the teacher. Such a contact is psychologically different from the contact in which there is a democratic interplay, in which the determination of the child's activity comes from a broader experiential base that includes the judgment or choices of the child himself.

The methodology of these studies entailed observation and recording of contacts between teacher and child, type of contact (dominative-integrative), and the person who initiated it, whether teacher or child. Teachers were shown to vary considerably in the number of both dominative and integrative contacts they made. Children also varied in the contacts they initiated toward the teacher. The observers' records were checked for reliability by consecutive and simultaneous records. It is noteworthy that the observation records were more reliable for dominative contacts than for integrative contacts; this finding is in harmony with a great deal of literature which suggests that when active aggression and suppression of another person's wishes is the object of study, the observations and measurement can be made with considerable accuracy. More positive, constructive aspects of behavior are difficult to observe and record in a reliable way. Possibly, positive forms of behavior are more idiosyncratic than negative forms.

The results of the Anderson (1937, 1939a) studies are complex and do not lend themselves to easy generalizations. The main hypothesis of the studies—that there is a circular reaction, with domination inciting domination and integration inciting integration—can probably be said to have been confirmed. Yet the individual differences between teachers and between children, and the interaction of these two, are extremely intricate. Educational research has suffered in the past from over-easy generalizations from the results of experimental studies, and the results of these studies should not suffer this fate. In fact, the careful reader will be forced into caution in generalization by the sheer complexity of the data.

Among kindergarten children, a positive correlation of .57 appeared between teachers' domination, initiated by the teacher, and teachers' domination following an initiation by a child. This correlation suggests that those children who tended to be on the receiving end of domination started by the teacher, tended also to encounter domination when they themselves approached the teacher. Some children, during a number of hours of observation, had almost no individual contacts with the teacher; others averaged as high as 55 contacts per hour. The children with the more dominating teacher showed significantly higher frequencies of behavior which was nonconforming to teacher domination. This finding supports the authors' hypothesis that domination incites resistance and is reminiscent of the hypothesis that "frustration instigates aggression."

Further, the authors found that integration was not used with children who had themselves been more dominative; this finding is interpreted by these authors to mean that the teacher was failing to "cut the vicious circle" of domination and resistance. "The teachers would thus be failing to use systematically the most effective technique for giving the misbehaving children status in the room and making them feel that they belong, and that they have a part to play and a contribution to make" (H. H. Anderson & G. L. Anderson, 1954, p. 1192).

In summarizing their work with these kindergarten children and their teachers, the authors stated the following conclusions:

. . . that these kindergarten teachers had higher mean frequencies of dominative than integrative contacts; that, *among the contacts initiated by the teacher, two out of three were dominative;* that, on the other hand, *among teacher contacts which resulted from the child's initiative, six out of seven were integrative.* It was revealed, however, that these teachers were meeting aggression with aggression; that they were systematically inciting resistance and not systematically cutting the vicious circle (Anderson & Brewer, 1945, p. 156).

The correlations indicating stability of the teachers' positions in ratio of dominative to integrative contacts were high, and teachers' ratios remained rather stable from year to year (Reed, 1946). However, the behavior of the children in a second grade showed practically zero relationship with that of the same children in the third grade a year later under another teacher. Thus the stability of the teachers' behavior comes out strongly, and much less stability appears in the behavior of the children. The children behaved dominatively in interaction with one teacher, but not dominatively in interaction with another one. Teachers differed in the respect with which the domination on their part was met by domination in the children. Teachers also differed in their domination-integration ratios with respect to different children.

How shall we evaluate these inspiring, laborious, and methodologically sound observations of childrens' and teachers' behaviors in a naturalistic situation? Our judgment is that the concepts of dominative and integrative behavior, while interesting and useful as a first approach, probably do not take into account a sufficient number of variables, either in the teacher's behavior, or in the effects on the children, to encompass the complexity of the interpersonal relationship between teacher and child. This conclusion is strengthened in the Anderson (1937, 1939a) studies by the differences between teachers and by the differences in effects among children exposed to the same teaching methods.

These studies provided strong impetus to the naturalistic investigation of social interaction between teachers and children in the classroom. Subsequent investigators were able to utilize the experience of these workers to provide more precision and breadth in the observation of teacher behavior, and, also, to examine a wider variety of effects on children due to varying types of teacher behavior. It must be said that the observational method of measuring teacher-child interaction has considerable difficulties. Adequate time must be assured to establish (1) a proper sampling of teacher behavior, and (2) the stability of that behavior. The interaction between variables existing within the child and the methods the teacher employs with that child, as well as with other children of differing characteristics, makes the problem a complex one. If we approach such observation with the idea that certain teacher behavior is "good," from a mental hygiene standpoint,

we will probably omit from consideration the variety of individual differences in both teacher and child. Yet it is these individual differences which lower the relationships found when antecedent-consequent relationships are examined over a period of time.

Such observational work is going on at Harvard and at Stanford. The plans for these studies are described in an early article by one of the present authors (P. S. Sears, 1957); the experimental results will be reported in future work. Chapter 6 of this Handbook is devoted to the methodology of observation in the classroom.

Teachers' Active Guidance of Individual Children

A study by Thompson (1944) is unique in research on teaching in the nursery school. His research design involved the careful planning of two different curricula for children; the children, in matched groups, were then exposed to these two different programs for eight months. Examination of the effects on the children at the end of the period showed strong differences between groups. Since this study utilized a number of valuable experimental controls and since it was actually carried out in a naturalistic classroom rather than in a laboratory setting, it will be reported in some detail.

One curriculum was planned as:

a "group atmosphere" in which the teacher made of her own initiative a minimum of contacts with the children, permitting the latter to work out their own plans for the school day and giving assistance to them only upon request. The teachers were to intervene in the children's activities only when undue danger was threatened toward the children or the equipment. The children responding to this curriculum will be designated in this research as "Group A" or "the group with little teacher guidance."

In constructing the other curriculum, B, it was thought feasible to make plans for a "group atmosphere" in which the teacher would attempt to become a warm friend, a guider, and in general would more actively participate in the children's play experiences as an interested and helpful adult.

Both curricula A and B were constructed to be responsive to the children and to insure the children's physical safety. The two fundamental differences between the two curricula were: 1) in curriculum B the teacher was instructed to develop a particularly warm friendship with each child; in curriculum A such a cultivation of friendship with the children was not to be emphasized; and 2) in curriculum B the teacher was instructed to stimulate the children's activities by her skillful arrangement of the play materials and to help the children develop their self-initiated activities by giving them information and help whenever she felt that such information and help would be to their advantage; in curriculum A the amount of teacher participation in the children's play experiences was to be dependent on the children's requests for help and information from the teachers (Thompson, 1944, p. 2).

The steps taken and controls instituted in this experimental design are of interest for their thoughtful consideration of variables extraneous to the effect of the programs.

The experimenter essayed to do the following things in this study:

1. To set up two preschool programs that differed, theoretically, in terms of the number and types of contacts the teachers had with the children in each curriculum; and to equate for the two groups other known variables that might influence social and emotional growth such as:

   a. teachers (two of the teachers, the head teacher and one of the assistants, spent an equal amount of time in each group)

   b. play materials (the same play materials were available to both groups)

   c. time of exposure to the program (the children were exposed to the two "group atmospheres" the same length of time, a few days over eight months)

   d. socio-economic status of the parents

   e. the social and emotional stati of development of the children in the two groups (the children were equated in the two groups at the beginning of the experiment by ratings of general personality characteristics . . . as determined by the initial measurements of social and emotional development)

   f. intelligence and chronological age (the children were equated in the two groups on chronological age and on IQ; for the latter, IQ scores were available at the time the groups were formed for only those children who had attended preschool the previous year and had been given intelligence tests . . .).

2. To instruct the teachers as to their behavior in the two programs (this was done through a series of conferences with the head teacher and her assistants).

3. To measure both at the beginning and at the end of the preschool year the social and emotional development of the two groups of four-year-old children exposed to the different curricula . . . .

4. To measure the differences between groups A and B during the school year in the number and types of teacher contacts with the children and the number and types of other-children's contacts with an observed-child . . . .

5. To point out the differential constituents of the two "group atmospheres" that seem to be related to differentials in group development in the social and emotional areas (this is to be done by showing which measured environmental impacts are significantly different for the two groups and which types of social and emotional development are significantly different for the two groups) (Thompson, 1944, p. 3).

The children were equated for personality traits on a number of measures:

1. Constructiveness when faced with possible failure scored with the techniques used by Keister (1943), which are described on page 843 of this chapter. Briefly, these techniques involved presenting the child with a very difficult test situation and during 15 minutes observing the occurrence of the following types of behavior: attempting to solve the problem alone; no overt attempt; asking another to solve; asking help; stops trying; destructive behavior; rationalization, plus some types of emotional behavior.

2. Ascendance as measured by the Jack (1934) technique, reported on page 841. Pairs of children were introduced to a room con-

taining a few toys, and observed for five-minute pairings with five different children. The ascendance score was the total number of times in these pairings that the one child attempted to secure play materials from his companion, attempted to direct or criticize his companion, was successful in directing, in providing a pattern of behavior for his companion, or in defending his own play materials.

3. Social participation as measured by the method for observation of social participation during free play devised by Parten and reported by Parten and Newhall (1943).

4. Leadership behavior, scored according to the scheme also devised by Parten, the records for leadership being taken at the same time as the records for social participation. A time-sampling procedure of observation was used for these measures 3 and 4.

5. Nervous habits, scored by observation after Carr's (1938) modification of Olson and Hughes's (1940) method.

6. Chronological age.

7. Intelligence quotient.

8. Socioeconomic position of the parents.

While the experimenter and the preschool staff attempted to make certain, through discussion with the teachers involved, that all teachers understood the differences to be provided in the two curricula, observations were also made to see whether this desired group atmosphere was actually promoted and maintained by the teachers. Observational procedures over the entire year, on a sample of occasions, showed that the teachers of Group B were reliably higher than those of Group A on a number of categories, called "extensive" teacher contacts. These included the teacher's giving information, giving help, making structuring suggestions, asking leading questions, and behaving in a friendly fashion. On all these categories the teachers of Group B were significantly higher, or more "extensive," in their behavior.

Another type of teacher behavior was termed "restrictive" in aims. No difference was found between Group A and Group B in these restrictive contacts with the children.

These categorizations included such teacher behaviors as being ascendant to the child in order to stop undesirable behavior, behaving in a stern fashion, and ignoring the child's approach. Note that these categories closely resemble H. H. Anderson's (1937–1946) integrative-dominative behaviors. Observational checks on the behaviors of the teachers in Groups A and B thus showed that the teachers were in fact able to carry out rather different contacts with the children under the two experimental programs.

Another factor of group atmosphere in the nursery school stems from the attitudes and behaviors of other children in the group. Thompson (1944) admitted that he was not able to instruct the other children in their behavior in order to promote differing group atmospheres! However, observation of what happened in the two settings showed that there were no significant differences between the two groups in what was called "extensive other child contacts." This category included one child's giving another information, giving help, giving materials, complying with a child's wishes, and developing a social situation with other children. On only one of these behaviors did the difference between Groups A and B approach significance; this difference was in the amount of giving help, which was shown to be greater in Group B at a .10 level of confidence.

On the frequency of occurrence of "restrictive contacts with other children," the differences between Groups A and B were significant. Thus Group B was found to be lower than Group A on rejection of a child by other children; refusing or ignoring of a child by other children; being hit, shoved, or grabbed at by other children; being persecuted by other children; and being threatened by other children. In all of these, Group A, the group with little teacher guidance, showed more restrictiveness in the children's behavior toward one another.

At the end of the eight-month period, the children of both groups were tested for a number of outcomes of their experiences during the year under different types of programs. The measures on which they were tested were the same, in a good many instances, as those on which they were initially equated. Thus Groups A and B were compared for the change over the year's period, having started the year approximately equal. Analysis of covariance was used to determine the significance of differences between the two groups on the final scores, thus taking account of some minor lack of equivalence in the initial scores.

The measures on which the children were finally tested were constructiveness when faced with possible failure, ascendance, social participation, leadership, number of nervous habits, IQ changes, and certain observed behavior of a nonconstructive and destructive type.

The results showed that Group B, the highly guided group, (1) was more constructive, when faced with possible failure, than Group A; (2) was more ascendant than Group A; (3) showed more participation; (4) showed more leadership; and (5) was significantly lower than those of Group A in destructive behavior.

No differences were found between the two groups in number of nervous habits; in IQ changes; in making rationalizations; in number of conflicts over property rights; and in getting equipment for the equipment's sake.

Thompson was careful to point out that his findings were limited to populations of teachers and children resembling those in his experiment. The preschool used in the experiment had experienced teachers with advanced training in preschool education, flexible and abundant play materials, children above average in intelligence, drawn from the upper two socioeconomic strata of a university city, and parents who had attempted to apply modern child development principles in rearing their children.

While results found here may not be applicable to other situations, this study is noteworthy for its careful control of the teaching method involved and the clear effects it revealed on the children experiencing these two environments. The children who were exposed to a personal guidance type of teacher method surpassed the children who had less personal guidance in the numerous ways mentioned.

The stability of this effect on the children was not investigated. It would be asking too much of the author of this detailed, careful, and laborious study to give us data on these same children as they went on through a year or two years with other teachers. H. H. Anderson's work, earlier described, suggested that the effects demonstrated here after one year might not show up when children moved to a different teacher and teaching environment. Experiments of this sort will have to be done before we know whether such teacher methods have lasting significance in the development of children. In Lippitt and White's (1943) classic experiment on autocratic and democratic group atmospheres, groups were switched from one atmosphere to another in order to determine the stability of the observed effects. Thompson's experiment involved the participation of numerous people, and the wholehearted support of those responsible for preschool education at the institution where the experiment was performed. Such conditions are extremely difficult to duplicate, and it is not surprising that experiments of this kind are rare in the educational literature. This experiment is comparable, at the nursery school level, to the Eight-Year Study (Chamberlin, Chamberlin, Drought, & Scott, 1942) at the high school level and to studies by Jersild and his co-workers (1939, 1941) on activity group programs in nursery and elementary schools.

Discipline Techniques: Control and Restraint of Aggression

Occasions arise in the social interchange in the nursery school setting in which both children and teachers feel angry and ready to show aggression. Generally, teachers have advocated external calm and restraint of aggression as rational methods of dealing with emotion, with striving toward understanding how the other person feels. What are the effects on children of this sort of teaching method? Under what conditions do children learn to control the primitive expressions of aggression and operate according to more socialized and adult patterns of behavior?

Aggressive and nonaggressive adults as models. In a study resembling Bandura's work described in the section on warmth, Bandura, Ross, and Ross (1961) investigated the occurrence of aggression (and inhibition of aggression) through imitation of adult models, i.e., the generalization of imitative response patterns involving aggression to new settings in which the model is absent. Thus this study approximated the situation in which some stability of the child's behavior is observed over a period of time and transfer to other situations is considered.

Twenty-four preschool children were assigned to each of three conditions. One experimental group observed an adult aggressive model; a second observed an inhibited nonaggressive model; and subjects in a control group had no exposure to the models. Half the subjects in the experimental conditions observed a model of the same sex, and half viewed a model of the opposite sex. Subjects were then tested for amount of imitative as well as nonimitative aggression performed in a new situation in the absence of the model.

Subjects exposed to the aggressive models reproduced a good deal of aggression resembling that of the model, and their mean scores were clearly higher on aggression than those of subjects in the nonaggressive control groups. Subjects in the aggressive condition also exhibited significantly more partially imitative and nonimitative aggressive behavior and were generally less inhibited in their behavior than subjects in the nonaggressive condition.

Imitation was found to be differentially influenced by the sex of the model, with boys showing more aggression than girls following exposure to the aggressive male model; the difference was particularly marked on

highly masculine-typed physical aggression behavior such as hitting and punching a Bobo doll.

Subjects who observed the nonaggressive models, especially the subdued male model, were less aggressive in their behavior than the controls. When later exposed to play material with no model present, these subjects spent more than twice as much time as the subjects who had observed the aggressive models, in simply sitting quietly without handling any of the play materials. Exploratory play, of aggressive and nonaggressive sorts, seemed to be inhibited by the effect of the subdued model. Thus the general range of behavior emitted by the subjects, including generally approved and nonaggressive exploratory behavior, seemed to be decreased. This study had only one adult model of each sex, and hence cannot clearly distinguish between personal characteristics of the models and the role variable of sex. Yet it is interesting that in the case of a highly masculine-typed behavior such as physical aggression, both male and female children tended to imitate physical aggression in the male model to a greater degree than the female model. It is as if the children were shocked by the display of *physical* aggression in the aggressive female model and were not receptive to her influence.

Both boys and girls imitated the *verbal* aggression of the adult model of their same sex. The children's spontaneous comments in some cases gave hints as to their feelings about what is sex-appropriate behavior. For example, after exposure to the adult female aggressive model, children made such comments as:

Who is that lady. That's not the way for a lady to behave. Ladies are supposed to act like ladies. . . ." "You should have seen what that girl did in there. She was just acting like a man. I never saw a girl act like that before. She was punching and fighting but no swearing. . . ." Aggression by the male model, on the other hand, was more likely to be seen as appropriate and approved by both the boys ("Al's a good socker, he beat up Bobo. I want to sock like Al.") and the girls

("That man is a strong fighter, he punched and punched and he could hit Bobo right down to the floor and if Bobo got up he said 'Punch your nose.' He's a good fighter like Daddy.") (Bandura, Ross, & Ross, 1961, p. 581).

The quantitative results of the experiment, supported by these spontaneous comments by the children, suggest that female nursery school teachers might create some surprise and perhaps unfavorable effects in their children by expressing physical aggression. Evidently these middle-class children, by the time they came to preschool, were sufficiently indoctrinated in "lady-like" and "masculine" behavior to be critical of behavior which seemed contrary to these ideas.

Presence of adults and children's aggression. According to results of the research studies just reported and others existing in the child development literature, aggression seems to be normally inhibited in children by most adults with whom the children come in contact. Yet a considerable reservoir of impulse in this direction seems to remain. Will children show aggressive impulses more frequently in the presence or absence of an adult? The initial hunch is that children would restrain aggression in the presence of an adult because of the general inhibiting effect to which they have been exposed by adults in the past.

Siegel and Kohn (1959) offered a somewhat different hypothesis: In the presence of a *permissive* adult, a child's aggression may be expected to *increase* because (1) he will infer from the behavior of the adult that this is a setting in which aggression is suitable or appropriate, and (2) with experience he will undergo a progressive decrease in inhibition based on fear of punishment. In the absence of any adult, these workers predicted, a child's aggression may be expected to decrease as time goes on. Lacking adults to define the social situation and to express expectations of his behavior in it, the child will, after an initial "release" or testing of the limits, rely increasingly on his own learned standards of conduct. In the middle-class child, these standards will typically render

aggression unacceptable in any social play.

The experiment by Siegel and Kohn used pairs of boys taken from a university nursery school. Each pair participated in two play sessions occurring two days apart. The two boys were asked to come to the playroom so that the experimenter could read a story to them and then let them play with some special toys. The experimenter read the story and then invited the children to play as they wished with any of the toys in the room. For the pairs in the Adult-Present condition, the experimenter sat quietly in a chair at one side of the playroom during the two sessions in which the boys played. Her attitude was friendly, acceptant, interested, but nonintrusive. She did not initiate any conversation, and she replied only briefly and noncommittally to any initiation from a child.

For the pairs in the Adult-Absent condition, the experimenter followed her invitation to play with another statement, indicating that she had to leave the room for a while to work at her desk. She explained that they were to stay in the room until she returned for them. She said that she would knock on the door before entering the room upon her return, and that during her absence they would be alone and their privacy would not be disturbed. Each pair remained in the room for a 14-minute play period. During this period their play was observed by an observer behind a one-way vision mirror on one wall of the room. Aggression was scored on the basis of the observational records.

The results showed that two-thirds of the subjects in the Adult-Present session were more aggressive in the second than in the first session, and that all the subjects in the Adult-Absent session were less aggressive in the second than in the first session. Thus, when the two sessions are considered together, the total incidence of aggression is not shown to vary with presence or absence of the adult. Rather, subjects with an adult present initially showed less aggression and later, more; the subjects with the adult absent initially showed more aggression, and, at the second session, less.

This result is interpreted by the authors as showing spontaneous establishment of ego-control by the children themselves when they did not have a permissive adult present to observe their play in a friendly way. The presence of the friendly adult, an accepting authority figure, may have given these subjects a flow of support and a strengthened perception of rules and regulations consonant with their behavior. The authors suggested that a technique for assessing a child's ego-strength or maturity of controls would be to compare his behavior in the two settings of Adult-Absence and Adult-Presence, and especially to observe the swiftness and ease with which the child's own ego function of vigilance on his aggressive behavior comes into play in the absence of an adult.

For nursery school teaching, this study yielded interesting suggestions as to the effect of the generally warm figure of the adult teacher. It is possible that the development of children's own egos and defenses against impulsive behavior will not occur as rapidly if there is a warmhearted and permissive adult present to whom they can, in effect, allocate some of the control of their own behavior. In the absence of such a figure the child may be put on his own and may have to institute his own controls. We have much more to learn about optimum periods at which this transfer of control from the adult to the child himself can be done without damaging anxiety to the child. Redl and Wineman's (1952) material on older, but seriously disturbed, children is interesting in this respect.

Aggression in the nursery school setting. Further light on adult responses to children's aggression comes from a naturalistic study in a nursery school classroom by Jersild and Markey (1935). They found that in about a third of the children's conflicts, the teachers took steps to stop or settle disputes. In a majority of such instances the teachers decided the issue against the children who were most aggressive and who "won" a high proportion of their conflicts when left to themselves. Frequently this seemed justified, but such fa-

voritism toward the less aggressive child sometimes went so far as to leave him the winner in a dispute in which he was not the guiltless one. It has also been noted (Fite, 1940) that an adult, coming abruptly upon a fracas between children, can easily make a wrong judgment concerning the underlying issue. Two children are involved, for example, in a tug of war over a small box. On the surface, it seems that only the box is at stake and that a reasonable solution can be found; actually, however, the struggle for the box may be only incidental to an effort by one combatant to "get even" with the other.

Jersild and Markey (1935) also studied two groups of children in two different naturalistic settings, finding that the teachers in one group normally interfered in aggression between children more than the teachers in another group. In addition, there was more "presence of adults" since three or four teachers were present in the one group as compared with only one or two in the other group. During the year, as these conditions of Teacher-Presence and Teacher-Interference prevailed, the much-interfered-with children had fewer fights than did the children who had more freedom to settle their disputes in their own way. But the following year when children from both groups moved on into two kindergartens, in which the teachers interfered relatively little with the children, the reverse was true. The children who had previously shown little fighting in the presence of many teachers now doubled the frequency of their conflicts. On the other hand, the children who had had fewer teachers and little interference with conflicts in nursery school declined in fighting behavior slightly over their records of the previous year, even though in the kindergarten situation they were allowed considerable freedom in this respect. Aggressive fighting by children has generally been shown to decline with age, as evidenced by comparisons between nursery school- and kindergarten-age children, but this study shows that the methods employed by the teacher, and the actual number of teachers present, may have an effect on the outward expression of children's aggression. The amount of interference, or more constructively put, guidance, of children by the adult, is evidently a factor to be considered in relation to the age and experience of the children being worked with. Further discussion of these factors appears in a later section of this chapter, when variables of environment are considered.

"Discipline." The concept of *discipline* is not much used in nursery education. In the public schools, however, beginning with kindergarten, the idea is often in the minds of beginning teachers as well as of administrators and parents. Kounin and Gump (1958) studied the reaction of *"watching* kindergarten children," i.e., of children who were merely looking on, to the teacher's control of a misbehaving child. They termed this reaction the "ripple effect," or the influence that control techniques have—not on the children who are being disciplined—but on the other children who are watching and listening.

Undergraduates observed situations in 26 public school kindergartens in Detroit, making note of disciplinary incidents. The data consisted of 406 such incidents, occurring in the first days of the school year. They were classified as to (1) the control technique itself, (2) the behavior of the watching child before the incident, and (3) the behavior of the watching child after the incident.

The results are quoted:

To the extent that we can generalize on cause and effect, the study indicates that the reaction of watching children to a teacher's control of a misbehaving child is related to at least three factors.

First, the newness of the situation. On the first day in kindergarten, watching children showed the strongest responses.

Second, the behavior of the watching children. Pupils who were themselves misbehaving or interested in children who were misbehaving were more likely to show the strongest reactions; the particular response was most likely to be vacillation.

Third, the disciplinary technique itself, that is, the clarity, the firmness, and the roughness of the technique.

When the teacher made it clear what behavior she objected to or what behavior she expected, the watching children responded with increased conformance and decreased non-conformance.

If the teacher's behavior conveyed firmness, the watching children sometimes responded with increased conformance and decreased non-conformance. This reaction occurred if the watching children had been misbehaving or interested in a child who was misbehaving.

If the teacher used rough techniques, the children showed behavior disruption but not conformance or non-conformance.

It should be kept in mind that clarity in the teacher's directions led to greater conformance and less non-conformance in a new and unstructured situation. When children are new to kindergarten or to the teacher, they may be especially sensitive to his directions and desires. As the child feels more at home in kindergarten and more at ease with the teacher, we would expect clarity to be less important (Kounin & Gump, 1958, p. 161).

Finally, we note that Maccoby (1959) proposed that "a child acquires a repertoire of actions by practicing covertly the actions characteristic of the adults with whom he interacts most frequently and who control the resources that he needs" (p. 251).

Influences on aggression. Aggression and fighting in children have been shown to be influenced by several factors: (1) Direct interference by teachers, which may cause fighting to decline for a time, only to reoccur when the interference is less strong. (2) Presence of a permissive adult, which seems to increase the freedom with which aggression is shown, as if the children watch for cues of disapproval from adults and permit themselves the luxury of expression of aggression when they feel it will not be disapproved. (3) Seeing an adult behaving aggressively, which makes children more likely to imitate him, particularly if the adult is a male; female adults do not seem to carry the same stimulus properties as males in the case of aggression. (4) Finally, viewing the behavior of an inhibited and nonaggressive adult, which makes children's behavior become much subdued, even to the extent of apparent reduction in exploratory and socially approved types of interaction with the environment.

These findings point to the importance of the teacher's own behavior as a model and strong influence on the behavior of children. In this chapter we illustrate other types of methods which the teacher may follow—mitigating frustrations in the environment and stimulating constructive explorations on the part of children, as well as warmth, nurturance, guidance, and integrative behavior.

Frustration by Adults or Environments

Teaching methods which involve frustration of the child are generally considered undesirable in accomplishing the aims of nursery education. Yet the child must be socialized, learn to live harmoniously in his group, and show cooperation and agreeable social behavior with adults and other children. An important question for teaching methods is the extent to which the frustration of socially desirable behavior may result in child behavior of a disruptive sort. Many studies have demonstrated that aggression is heightened in situations in which the child feels frustration and failure. Regression is another kind of response which has been studied in relation to frustration. Reports of experimental, rather than naturalistic, induction of frustration follow.

Experimental studies of children's behavior following frustrations. Several experimental studies which utilized experimentally produced frustrations will be cited here. Yarrow (1948) observed preschool children in two half-hour doll-play sessions, during which they were allowed to play freely with the dolls and tell stories about their behavior. Aggression in the doll play depicted by the child was scored. Three groups of children were used. The "failure" group was given difficult tasks to perform just previous to the doll-play session. This gave them experiences of failure and frustration. The "satiation" group

was not given failure but was given a boring and dull task and kept at it for 20 minutes just previous to the doll-play session. A control group had neither frustration nor satiation experiences before the doll play.

The results showed clearly that both the frustration and satiation conditions increased the amount of aggression shown in the children's play with the dolls as compared to aggression shown by the control group. Thus the children who were in a state of frustration utilized the doll-play session to express their feelings of frustration and boredom.

A classic experiment by Barker, Dembo, and Lewin (1941, 1943) involved the study of constructiveness of play in children who had undergone frustration. The children were first tested in a free play situation in which they played alone for half an hour in a room which contained a standard set of play materials. The behavior was observed and categorized in terms of its constructiveness. For example, one end of the scale (a low level of constructiveness) involved simply a superficial examination of the toys. The highest score on constructiveness was given to a highly original and elaborate game or story involving the toys. Older children and brighter children made higher constructiveness scores. Thus the scale was related to mental and chronological age.

With scores established for each child on constructiveness of play, the next steps were to provide a frustration experience and then examine the constructiveness of play following this experience. Frustration was induced in the following way: The child was brought into the experimental room where he found the same toys he had used in the standard testing situation earlier. To these toys, however, a number of large, elaborate, and highly desirable toys were added. After the child had started his play with these new toys, the experimenter collected the less desirable, standard toys and put them in another part of the room. He then asked the child to come with him to that section of the room and lowered a wire screen between the child and the highly desirable toys. The child could see those toys through the screen but could not get to them. For 30 minutes the child was observed, and his behavior in play with the less desirable play materials was categorized for constructiveness. When the score obtained during this period following frustration was compared with the original scores, it was found that constructiveness of play had decreased strongly after frustration. This decrease was interpreted by the authors as "regression" or primitivization of play. When the scores were translated into mental-age equivalents (there being a strong positive correlation between mental-age and constructiveness scores in the original situation), the regression amounted to over 17 months. This result suggests that environmental frustration, represented by the refusal of the experimenter to permit the child to play with the desirable toys which he had seen, produced a reduction in the level of maturity in the play.

An interesting variation on this study was performed by Wright (1942). The same frustration situation was used, and constructiveness of play was measured as before. The variation was that children were brought in pairs to the playroom, and these pairs were varied as to whether they were good, close, and strong friends or whether they were only casual friends. All children reacted less constructively under conditions of frustration, but the children who were paired with a good friend showed less decrease in the constructiveness of play than those who were paired with a casual friend.

Another study by Wright (1943) showed that when close friends were put into another frustrating situation, they reacted with less aggression toward one another than did casual friends, but worked cooperatively together to express hostility toward the experimenter who was the source of their frustration.

Strength of child's ego-control and frustration. Block and Martin (1958) replicated the study of Barker, Dembo, and Lewin (1941, 1943), adding as a variable the child's strength of ego-control. Ego-control was measured with two types of tests: (1) delay of gratification, and (2) the co-satiation experiment. In the former, the experimenter gave each child the opportunity to accumulate as much candy as he wished, with the proviso that once he stopped to taste a piece of candy he could no longer accumulate more. The candy was placed by the experimenter, one piece at a time, in a cart of a toy known as a "coke loader." The child cranked a handle which raised the cart until it tipped, emptying its contents into a large glass jar. It was explained to the child that he could put as many pieces of candy into the jar as he wished and that when he was all through playing the game, the candy was his to eat. He was also told that when he ate any candy, the game was over. The delay of gratification score was simply the number of pieces of candy accumulated in the jar at the time the child chose to eat the candy.

The co-satiation experiment was based on the theory that, with strong ego-control, satiation of one need system will have little effect upon the satiation of another need system. The more immature, undercontrolling individual was seen as one who would be easily satiated in a second area as a result of satiation in the first. In this case a spool-packing task was used. Spools were placed on a rectangular rack on top of a box. By sliding the rack to one side, the spools fell through a hole into the box below, and the rack was then available for refilling. The child did this task until he became tired of it, and at this point the experimenter said that he could now take some colored blocks and make them fall into the box below. The score was the number of times the child packed the colored blocks after having become tired of the spool-packing; i.e., if he tired quickly of packing blocks, he was scored as weak in ego-control.

The results of the experiment, in general, supported the hypothesis that low ego-control in children is associated both with decrement in play constructiveness under conditions of frustration and with a tendency to direct behavior toward the barrier causing the frustration. The children who were judged to be undercontrolling could not adequately control the feelings engendered by the frustrating situation. They were unable to play constructively with the substitute toys and freely "acted out" their feelings of frustration by frequent and sometimes violent attacks upon the barrier. On the other hand, children toward the overcontrolling end of the ego-control continuum were able to maintain integrated play performance following frustration. They showed less tendency to direct their behaviors to the barrier, the cause of frustration. Seemingly, these children were not affected by their desires to play with a more attractive toy and were able to inhibit expression of feelings. They patiently played and only occasionally would refer to the other side of the barrier.

Punishment for aggression and frustration. Chasdi and Lawrence (1958) were concerned with frustration and punishment for aggression as they occur in the home and in the experimental situation. On the basis of the investigators' interviews with the mothers, the children in this experiment had been assigned to groups of high and low home punishment for aggression and high and low home frustration. The children were observed in doll play, and the frequency of aggression shown by them in doll play was recorded. At certain prescribed times, the experimenter "punished" the child's expression of aggression in doll play by saying, "No, John, don't you know that nice boys shouldn't do a thing like that?" (p. 443).

The results showed that children who were experimentally "punished" for doll play aggression were significantly less aggressive in doll play than nonpunished children. Under conditions of permissive doll play, a significant increase in aggression from the first to the last session was found regularly. The home variables of high punishment and frustration appeared to intensify these effects. Punishment of aggression thus decreased the frequency of aggression in the situation in which the punishment occurred, but it increased the frequency and intensity of aggression in situations distinctly unlike that in which the punishment occurred. That is, home punishment *increased* doll-play aggression. Thus the effect of the strict teacher (or mother) of a child may be to decrease the expression of aggression by the child in the current situation, but this aggression may come out again in other situations and with increased strength.

In short, children frustrated by the environment, or by an adult in the environment, react with both aggression and regression—the latter shown by a decrease in the constructiveness of play. Aggression may not come out directly toward the frustrating adult, but may appear, in a displaced form, in other situations less fraught with danger for the child. The presence, in the frustrating situation, of a good friend of the child provides support in the expression of aggression directly toward the frustrating adult.

Small-Group Training Procedures

A series of experiments on training procedures in preschool education, carried out at the Iowa Child Welfare Research Station during the 1930's, was concerned with the extent to which the social and personality characteristics of children could be modified by training procedures aimed at the direct and purposeful development of skills. The experiments were carried out either in individual sessions with the subjects or in small groups. The modifications looked for in the children included increases in leadership in initially submissive and "following" children, cooperation, maturity of reactions to frustration, singing ability, and language, motor, and art skills.

Modification of ascendant behavior. Jack (1934) developed a technique for testing ascendance in children. These tests were based on observations of a pair of children playing for five minutes, with the interactions of the pair observed and "leading" or "following" reactions recorded. When each child had been paired with each of 10 other children, selected according to a prearranged order, the score for ascendance was found to be reliable.

Training procedures were used with the five children who showed the lowest ascendance scores. When initially tested, these children were dominated by others, were unable to pursue their own purposes against interference, and were unable to direct the behavior of others. Training sessions were carried out individually in which the subject was taught all the knowledge and skills necessary to master three tasks (picture puzzles, mosaics, recalling a story). Then the children were again paired, for test purposes, in situations resembling those in the training, with a number of children who were originally more ascendant. The children who had had the special training showed considerably more leadership at this testing; they instructed their companions in use of the materials and spent more time in the leading role. After a period of several weeks, the trained children were again paired in the original experimental situation with 10 other children. The tests here were those used for the initial testing, and they differed considerably from the materials on which the training had been carried out. Yet the trained children again showed, in the different situations, evidence of ability to direct the behavior of others and to lead. Thus transfer in ascendance was demonstrated from the training to the different setting of the original test situation.

Page (1936) found that a similar sort of training in ascendance was followed by increased ascendance in free play activities in the normal nursery school setting. Not all these gains in ascendance were, however, considered to be desirable for the child's total personality development. Mummery (1947) utilized training procedures of the same kinds, designed to increase children's security and self-confidence. Afterwards, these children were shown to be more ascendant in a number of categories. Some of these categories were socially acceptable and others were not, as judged by experts. For example, the trained children showed selfish and hos-

tile responses to others as well as "constructive" self-assertive reactions.

Increase in cooperative behavior. Chittenden (1942) followed up on these experiments to see whether cooperative behavior could be increased by training. She selected initially dominating and uncooperative children, as determined from testings in which each child was paired separately with each of five other children, placed for five-minute periods in a room containing only one toy. Domination and cooperation scores were derived from observations of the children's behavior in this situation.

The training used for the most dominating children, who were selected as the experimental group, consisted of a number of individual periods with the experimenter in which two dolls were used. The experimenter told the child a story in which the dolls got into conflicts and showed uncooperative behavior toward one another. The child and the experimenter talked over the situation and tried to decide upon good ways of solving the difficulties. After each of 10 children had had 11 such doll-play periods, the experimental and control subjects were again tested in the original situation, that is, paired with another child in the room with only one toy. The children who had undergone the experimental training showed at this time considerably more cooperation and less domination of their companion than they had at the original testing period. The children in the control group, who had originally shown as much domination as the experimental group but had had no training, were also tested, and their behavior was not changed; they were as dominating as before. The trained group was tested again after a month's time had elapsed, and the decrease in domination was still present. Also, while these children were now acting more cooperatively and less dominatively, they were not more submissive, and they were still actively engaged in the normal play of preschoolers. These findings suggest that it is possible to develop in the child approved ways of interaction with others without stamping out or inhibiting his general sociability and participation.

Modification of children's reactions to failure. Since children in the process of growing up must meet many situations that are difficult for them, the experience of failure is a frequent one in the nursery school child's life. As they mature, children generally discover and use more effective ways of reacting to failure. Some nursery-age children continue, however, to show immature and undesirable responses to difficult situations. Keister (1943) tested a number of preschool children on two very difficult tasks. One was having to get toys out from under a box weighted down with 96 pounds of weights. The second was trying to place some puzzle objects in a box so that the lid could be closed; this task was difficult even for adults, and all children failed on it.

The categories of immature and undesirable response to these difficult situations included the following:

1. Giving up almost at once or without exploring many of the possibilities of solution.

2. Repeated and numerous requests for help (more than one-half the total time of the test).

3. Aggression and destructive behavior.

4. Rationalizing the failure.

5. Exaggerated emotional responses, such as crying, sulking, yelling, and angry responses.

The next step was to select, out of a large number of children, 12 who had shown strongly immature and undesirable responses to failure. An additional 12 children were used as a control group but were not exactly equivalent to the experimental children, because they were somewhat more mature in their reactions to failure. One might therefore have expected more change in the experimental group than in the control in the normal course of events. The experimental group was then given special training designed to teach each child to persist longer in the face of tasks that were difficult for him, to depend less on an adult for help in solving the problem, to give fewer rationalizations in the face of failure, and to attack a problem and see it through with composure. The training method consisted of introducing a child to a series of problems of puzzle variety which increased in difficulty. The subjects were given difficult problems only after they had experienced success at simpler ones. During a six-week training period, the experimenter met with each child in individual sessions, encouraged the child to work at the picture puzzles, and praised independent behavior in the child. The experimenter did not help the child directly but continued to encourage and reward him for independent work. The control group had no such training.

After completion of the training, the children were again tested in a difficult puzzle box experiment similar to the original one. Now the trained group made significantly more "attempts to solve alone" and mature responses than they had in the original tests. Rationalization and exaggerated emotional responses had declined. The control group, which had not had the special training, did not show significant improvement in handling the frustration. The methods employed in this study, which were successful in modifying the undesirable responses to failure, consisted in general of two things: (1) training on materials which were initially easy but became more difficult, and (2) an experimenter attitude of leaving the task to the child, encouraging his independent efforts, but not providing direct assistance in the task. Planning materials for the child's learning which are sufficiently challenging to capture his attention, but not so difficult as to provoke withdrawal and emotional reactions, and encouraging independent work, are methods which can be and frequently are used in nursery school teaching.

Training of singing ability and interest. Jersild (1932) trained three-year-old children to sing tones and intervals not already included within their vocal range. Practice and control groups were employed. A number of factors were studied, including ability to sing tones, intervals, and songs, the effect of training on this ability, and the range and content of children's spontaneous vocalizations during their free play. Nineteen children enrolled in a nursery school were given the training in groups of two and sometimes three. The training consisted of drill and singing songs containing notes within and beyond the child's pitch range. The policy of grouping a relatively superior with a less competent child was used during training. The children were rotated so that the same two children did not sing together on successive days. Training was continued over a period of approximately six months, with a total of 40 training periods, each lasting ten minutes.

In comparison with the control group which had had no specific training, the trained group showed substantial advantage. This advantage was maintained on a retest after summer vacation. The following quotation from Jersild (1932) illustrates his conclusions:

A child's tonal range often represents only a part of what he actually can produce, the particular tones which he employs may reflect the beginnings of a vocal habit, originating in a more or less fortuitous manner; the development of proficiency in the use of a wide tonal range is similar in many ways to the acquisition of a new skill . . .; by means of early training a child may be able to sing tones quite beyond his accustomed range; it is possible that early training may give a child a lasting advantage over other children, with similar · original endowments, whose efforts to improve upon their accustomed ranges are not begun until a later age when old habits interfere with the establishment of new skill in the use of the voice (Jersild, 1932, p. 61).

A study in the Iowa series (Updegraff, Heiliger, & Learned, 1937) also involved an attempt to improve the ability and interest in music of children at ages three, four, and five. After being tested for a variety of aspects of singing ability, a group of young children were given training for about 40 days, in small groups, in which the sing-

ing was made enjoyable and children had practice in increasing their tonal ranges and other musical skills. The training probably increased the child's self-confidence in his musical abilities, and gave him increased motivation in attempting to learn.

A control group was tested for musical ability and interest without having the training periods. The trained group clearly surpassed the control group in musical ability at the end of 40 days. Furthermore, interest in music, as observed and scored in the natural environment of the nursery school classroom, was found to have increased over the training period in the experimental group, while remaining at approximately the same level in the control group.

Training in motor skills. This treatment of special training would not be complete without the classic experiment on motor skills by Hilgard (1932). She equated two groups of 10 children, two and three years old, on various factors, including initial abilities in three skills: buttoning, cutting with scissors, and climbing. The practice group was given 12 weeks of practice, and the control group, without special practice during this time, was tested at the end of the 12-week period, and then given four days of intensive practice. After the 12 weeks of practice, the practice group exceeded the performance of the control group on all the tests, but one week of practice by the control group was sufficient to bring the scores of the two groups to similar levels. The rapid gains of the control group were interpreted as indicating that factors other than specific training contributed to the development of these three skills, factors which may be partly accounted for by maturation and partly by general practice in related skills.

Training of art skills. Dubin (1946), utilizing a control group matched for age, sex, IQ, and interest in art, attempted to develop the complexity of children's drawings by a discussion technique. The experiment was done over a period of three quarters of a school year. During the fall, the children's spontaneous drawings were categorized and scored according to a scale of complexity. During the winter quarter, each child in the experimental group was taken out of class individually by the experimenter, who proceeded to discuss the child's drawings with him. The child was encouraged to verbalize about them, to relate the whole to the parts, and to develop conceptualizations relating to his drawings. During the spring, the children's drawings were again categorized in the same way as before, and a distinct improvement in complexity was found in the experimental group. The drawing skill seemed to have improved as a result of the stimulation given the children to handle information and conceptualization more effectively and to translate it into their drawings.

Training in language and concepts. To compensate for the meager language environment of a group of orphanage children who had few conversations with adults, little experience in reading aloud, and low levels of experience outside the orphanage grounds, Dawe (1942) instituted a program which included the following types of training:

1. Training in understanding words and concepts.
2. Looking at and discussing pictures.
3. Listening to poems and stories.
4. Going on short excursions.

Emphasis was not on "stuffing" children with words but on real comprehension of the words and concepts. Especial care was taken to see that no direct coaching on test items was included in the training program.

At the end of the training period (about 50 hours), the experimental group had made significantly greater gains than the control group (which had no special training) in vocabulary, information about home living, and general science information. Readiness for reading was significantly better, and IQ (with the exception of scores on the performance tests) had increased significantly.

A sociologist at Yale, Moore (*Time,* 1960), has developed a theory of language development which he carries over into a technique for the teaching of reading. He has tried this technique with some children of nursery school age. Two-year-olds, for example, "play" with an electric typewriter, so arranged that the child produces a letter only when he places the right finger on the right key for touch typing. The child himself controls most of the learning; little teaching is done by the instructor. What lures the child on, according to Moore, is the sense of discovering rules for himself. So far the data reported from this study have been chiefly anecdotal. Some young children have learned to read by this method, he reports, but more systematic evaluative data are not yet available.

The meaning of the small-group training studies. The studies cited in this section represented deliberate attempts to modify children's behavior in small-group or individual training sessions, as compared with the natural nursery school classroom which normally contains 15 or more children. The small-group studies were, in effect, attempts to ascertain whether certain changes can be induced under very special conditions of intensive training. The answer here is yes, for the results cited here are positive. This does not, however, mean that these intensive methods can or should be taken over and put into effect by the teacher of the normal-sized nursery school group. Such a teacher is a *group* worker who at times, perhaps briefly, utilizes individual or small-group techniques but always needs to recall her responsibilities to the total group.

It would be quite possible to devise studies of the naturalistic classroom whole-group setting comparable to those of Thompson (1944) and H. H. Anderson (1937–1946) earlier cited in which (1) initial tests are made of children's behavior, (2) measurements of various teachers' behaviors and methods are made, and (3) final tests are made of children's behavior after a period of association with a given teacher. Such studies would suggest the kinds of changes which may occur under different teacher methods in the whole-group setting. Studies of this type logically grow out of the small-group type which we have considered in this section.

One further point is of interest. The intuitive assumption represented by the foregoing argument is that when behavior can be deliberately changed in an individual or small-group training procedure, the teacher operating in the whole-group situation may or may not be able to accomplish the same thing; i.e., she is at a disadvantage compared with the small-group experimental training worker. This disadvantage may hold for certain types of learnings, but it is probable that the "large"-group teacher has a positive advantage for other types. *Which* learnings occur under *which* types of teaching is the real question.

Effects of Nursery School Attendance

Nursery school education has never been a part of the public system of education. Attendance is not required by law, as it is for elementary and other levels of schooling. Most frequently, nursery schools are privately supported and are independent of the legally constituted school districts which are supported by public taxation. (In most states, but not all, kindergartens are now a part of these school districts.) This means that the choice of whether or not a child attends nursery school is largely up to the parents, and in many cases the parents must pay tuition for their child, or provide services themselves, as in the parents' cooperative nursery schools.

What benefits accrue to the child from attendance at nursery school? A number of studies have attempted to evaluate consequences of nursery school attendance, to determine whether some of the objectives of nursery school named in the first section of this chapter are better achieved by children in the nursery school setting than by children who remain at home during the nursery school period. These studies have utilized children, generally matched in groups for age and socioeconomic background of the parents, who did and did not attend nursery school.

It should be noted that since the decision on attendance or nonattendance is up to the parent, it is very likely that the parents of children attending nursery school have somewhat different attitudes toward and relationships with their children than those who do not attend. It would be interesting to have researches on parental reasons for choosing to send or not to send a child to nursery school. One reason for desiring nursery school attendance for their child might be that the parents value the development of social skills and believe that the nursery school will facilitate this development in their child. If a group of parents who did not send their children to nursery school held different values with relation to the development of social skills from a group that did, one would expect that these parental values would influence the child's development in any case. It may also be that parents who send their children to nursery schools are more highly achievement-oriented than parents who do not. We have considerable evidence that such parental attitudes are influential in the development of children. Similarly, mothers who wish to be free of child care in order to pursue other interests of their own may be more interested in providing nursery school for their children than mothers who enjoy child care. Thus, comparisons between children who have and who have not gone to nursery school may be as dependent on the reasons of the parents for sending them to school as on the school experience itself. One group may very well not represent an adequate control for the other.

Changes in social behavior with nursery school attendance. What changes in children's behavior are observable over a period of time in nursery school? Walsh (1931) selected two matched groups of children, one group attending nursery school and one group not attending, and had them rated on a series of behavior items at the beginning of the school year and again six months later. During the six months, those attending nursery school gained more than the other children in initiative, independence, self-assertion, self-reliance, curiosity, and interest in the environment.

Studies by Hattwick (1937), Joel (1939), and Kawin and Hoefer (1931) have shown that children attending nursery school eliminated more "undesirable" infantile and dependent habits during the year than a matched group of peers who did not go to nursery school. Independence of adults seems to develop faster in children attending nursery school. Hattwick's study (1937) compared two matched groups of children—one with an average of nine months' attendance in nursery school and one having attended nursery school only a few weeks. Those who had been in the school for the longer period showed considerably better routine habits and social adjustments, but were *not* superior in freedom from emotional behaviors such as "cries easily, fears animals, twitches, sulks, temper tantrums, thumb-sucking." Similarly, Andrus and Horowitz (1938), studying various types of "insecurity" behavior and length of nursery school attendance, obtained generally negative results. The insecurity feelings, like the emotional reactions studied in the Hattwick experiment, did not seem to be influenced by the preschool experience.

Jersild and Fite (1939) studied social participation in children who had attended nursery school for a previous year and children who were starting nursery school for the first time. Those who had been in nursery school longer were more sociable at the beginning, but the new children made rapid gains in social participation. By the end of the school year the two groups were equal in social activity, as judged by the time spent in cooperative play, sharing, and conversation.

When a child is increasing his social participation in the nursery school environment he is not necessarily becoming a conformist. Caille (1933) showed that children's scores on "resistance" (the number of times they refused by word or deed to carry out the demands of others, to yield ground to another, and so on) were more closely related to the length of time they had spent in nursery school than to their chronological age.

Ezekiel (1931) found that children who were initially timid and unaggressive became more aggressive with nursery school experience and showed increasing skill at making themselves the center of activity. Initially aggressive children continued to be aggressive.

Vitz (1961) studied children over an eight-week period in a nursery school summer session, observing antisocial aggression, defined as any expression of anger or destructiveness, either physical or verbal, e.g., hitting, fighting, shoving, threatening to hit, yelling names or threats, cutting or critical remarks, kicking, or damaging school equipment or the toys of another. Note that antisocial aggression is only one type of aggression and is less globally defined than Ezekiel's. Vitz also examined adult-like ("grown-up") behavior of such types as the following: taking an adult role in any way, e.g., playing mother or father, cowboy, etc.; giving advice or stating facts in an adult manner; helping or assisting another; comforting another child. His results showed that the antisocial aggression steadily decreased from the second to the eighth and final week. During the second week of school the children (boys and girls taken together) showed antisocial aggression during 8.9 per cent of the observed time. During the final week of the session, this figure was 5.6 per cent of the observed time. The decrease is close to 40 per cent of the initial figure. Adult-like behavior steadily increased from 13.5 per cent to 18.5 per cent; this is also a change of close to 40 per cent. This finding is descriptive of what happened to the children while they were attending nursery school. Without a comparable group who had not attended nursery school, the result cannot be attributed solely to the nursery school attendance.

Checking on former nursery school children as they went into the early school grades in the Winnetka schools, Van Alstyne and Hattwick (1939) used a rating scale to study (1) leadership, defined as being willing to lead or follow according to the necessities of the play situation, and (2) being unselfconscious. They compared children who had attended nursery school with children who had not attended, and also compared ratings of the nursery school children in grade school with ratings of their behavior obtained two years previously in nursery school. The most conclusive finding was that children who were leaders in nursery school also tended to show leadership in grade school. The evidence that nursery school attendance contributes to the development of leadership was less strong, but the authors indicated that there was a tendency in this direction.

Bonney and Nicholson (1958) reviewed various studies of the effects of preschool training on children in later life, including three original studies done in Texas. One study in a college nursery school found that sociometric scores of former nursery school pupils (now in kindergarten, first grade, second grade, or third grade) were significantly higher than those of their age mates who had not attended nursery school.

In a second study, done in a public elementary school in a predominantly lower middle-class neighborhood, the children were in Grades 1–6. Questionnaire data from the parents were used to ascertain whether or not the children had had preschool training. The nursery schools attended varied widely and probably were not as good as the college nursery school mentioned previously. None of the differences between children who had and had not attended nursery school were found to be significant, either on the sociometric test or on the basis of teacher evaluation. A third study utilized sixth-grade classes; here again no difference related to nursery school attendance was found in social adjustment. The authors suggested that the quality of the preschool training may be a factor; the first study cited here supports the possibility that a certain quality of preschool education is necessary to produce a difference between children who attended nursery school and those who did not.

A study by Allen and Masling (1957) asked similar questions. They gave a battery of five near-sociometric questions to 34 children with nursery school experience and 82 children without nursery school experience. The children were pupils in the kindergarten, first, and second grades in a school in Syracuse, New York. The two groups were equated in terms of scores on the Vineland Social Maturity Scale, extent of parents' education, age, and sex. The fathers of the nursery school children had significantly more prestigeful occupations than the parents of the other subjects, but the data revealed no relationship between fathers' occupation and near-sociometric choices received.

When the mean number of nominations received was computed for each group on each of the five questions in each of the three grades, it was found that the nursery school group had received the higher mean in 14 out of 15 comparisons. The difference between the two groups was not statistically significant in the kindergarten or first grade, but significant differences were recorded in the second grade. The nursery school subjects were seen by their classmates as being more prestigeful, more spontaneous, and more intelligent.

Changes in intellectual development with nursery school attendance. It is curious that in the stated aims and purposes of the nursery school, intellectual development of the child has been very little considered. The review of objectives cited in the literature hardly refers to these cognitive aspects of a child's development. Yet, since intelligence depends upon the observing, thinking, and conceptualizing that the child carries on, it is reasonable to assume that contact with professionally trained adult teachers, providing a rich and stimulating environment for children, should foster the conceptual development and intellectual activity of children. During the 1930's and early 1940's, Wellman and others at the Iowa Child Welfare Research Station made a number of studies of changes in children's IQs in the especially enriched environment provided by a well-organized nursery school.

The early studies in this series had defects in experimental design and analysis. In the later studies, these defects were remedied, and these studies are summarized in Wellman (1943).

An interesting study by Olson and Hughes (1940) found that nursery school children from privileged backgrounds did not differ significantly in their intellectual growth from a matched sample of non-nursery school children; this result suggested that the home background of the children they studied was already of such a nature that the nursery school could add little to it. The statement of Jones (1954) in his review of the literature on environmental influences on mental development is of interest here: "It is quite reasonable to expect some IQ gains among children released from a static and unstimulating environment, whether this release is provided by nursery school, a foster home, or other environmental change" (p. 682). And, since children raised in such static environments often have low IQs to start with, one must be certain that gains on retest are attributable to more than simple regression effects.

Earlier mentioned was a study by Walsh (1931) in which nursery school children were shown to have more curiosity and interest in their environment.than non-nursery school children. Other things being equal, one would expect the child with such qualities to develop his intellectual resources more effectively than the child who is more apathetic and passive in relation to his environment. If the nursery school, by the use of environmental resources, stimulates curiosity, then we should expect conceptual development to progress more favorably with nursery school attendance than in a home situation which may provide less stimulation. Hunt (1961, pp. 27–33) succinctly reviewed the research on the effects of nursery school on intelligence. While finding that existing evidence does not show large IQ gains attributable to attendance at nursery schools, organized as they now are, he also looks to the future increase of our knowledge in this area: "Various bits of the evidence reviewed hint that if the manner in which encounters with the environment foster the development of intellectual interest and capacity were more

fully understood, it might be possible to increase the average level of intelligence within the population substantially" (p. 346).

Effects of nursery school attendance on language development. Young (1941) took samples of language in four different nursery school situations. Each child was observed for six hours in periods of 10 minutes each during about 15 days. The situations studied were outdoor play, indoor play, dinner, and a period in which the children were looking at picture books. It was found that the *setting* in which the responses were collected had a marked relation to talkativeness. Young stated:

The amount of comprehensible verbal behavior varies significantly from setting to setting. The Outdoor and Picture situations were the scenes of the largest amounts of speech. The results indicate that in order to secure truly representative samples of the language of preschool subjects it is important to procure records in several relatively distinct types of environmental situations. If this is impossible the setting which is used should be carefully described and the limitations recognized (Young, 1941, p. 127).

In a study by Van Alstyne (1932), it was found that over half the time preschool children tended not to talk to other children while working with play materials. Certain materials appeared to have considerably more "conversation value" than others. Doll play, blocks, crayons, and clay ranked high in the percentage of time during which their use was accompanied by conversation, whereas painting, scissors, and books were low in conversation value.

In another study (Smith, 1935), children were shown to use longer sentences and to use more advanced patterns of language, during a situation in which they conversed with an adult as compared to a situation involving conversation with other children. McCarthy (1954) has suggested that probably for most children of upper socioeconomic levels, nursery school experience results in more child contacts and fewer adult contacts than is the case for children who are not attending nursery school. Adult patterns of speech might thus be *slower* to develop in children attending nursery school.

It will be remembered from the section on small-group training procedures that Dawe (1942) was able to foster language and conceptual growth in a group of orphanage children. These children had very little contact with adults as compared with children living in their own homes. The planned program, involving definite training in the use of linguistic symbols which serve as intellectual tools, did produce significant changes over and above those found for a control group.

Readiness for first grade. An interesting series of articles from the Merrill-Palmer Institute (Brenner, 1957; Brenner & Samelson, 1959; Hofman, 1957, 1958) considered characteristics of kindergarten children which indicate degree of readiness for first grade, as well as the kinds of expectations and requirements which schools set up for children.

One of these (Brenner & Samelson, 1959) examined early kindergarten behavior in its relation to first-grade achievement. Sixteen children in a private school class were ranked by their first-grade teacher in terms of functioning in first grade and preparedness for second grade. The five most successful and the five least successful children were chosen for case-study analysis. Data were drawn from extensive classroom observations made during the first six weeks of kindergarten attendance. The 10 children were described in their transactions with objects, verbal symbols, peers, the teacher, and other adults. From these case descriptions, generalizations emerged regarding different styles of child-school relationship that are characteristic of children who are likely to be highly successful in first grade and of children who are likely to be less successful. The interested reader will want to go to original sources for these thoughtful analyses, based on a few cases carefully studied.

The effect of nursery schools. It is clear that attendance at nursery school, in and of itself, does not radically alter personalities of children. The evidence suggests, but not strongly, that certain social participation skills are enhanced by a good nursery school experience and that in certain cases these effects can be observed several years later. Language and intellectual development may be influenced, apparently, particularly if the home or out-of-school environment of the child is meager in stimulating qualities.

Trends in research in this area include analysis of the dyadic and reciprocal effects on one another of children with certain personality characteristics. Studies are also being made of children's gratifying or nongratifying interactions with teachers and peers.

Some children fit immediately into the school situation, like it very much, and generally continue to receive and provide reinforcement to others as they go from grade to grade. Others lack these characteristics of readiness; their experiences are less gratifying to themselves and to others. What is needed is more study of changes, as a function of varying teaching methods, in these less happy and less successful children. To what extent, with what methods and what timing, can the unsuccessful trend be reversed or ameliorated in the nursery school or kindergarten setting?

TEACHING MATERIALS AND ENVIRONMENT

The presence or absence of certain conditions or objects in the nursery school environment influences the behavior and learning of children. For example, Body (1955) was impressed with the possibility that important influences which differentiated the patterns of aggression of two groups of nursery school children were situational and environmental differences in the physical plants and equipment of the schools.

Henry and Sharpe (1947) compared the behavior of children from two nursery school environments: (1) a city nursery school housed in a big public school building which imposed many restrictions upon children's activities—including a rigid daily schedule, almost no outdoor play, and a high degree of adult direction and supervision; and (2) a college nursery school which encouraged spontaneous social interchange. Children in the college school were observed to make twice as many aggressive responses as the city school children. The children in the city school, however, showed less social interchange of any kind, and when they were invited to play in an experimental permissive play situation, many of them found it so threatening to their security that they refused to remain.

Nursery school teaching relies heavily on a carefully planned environment to minimize frustration and conflict as well as to stimulate a wide variety of learnings appropriate to the developmental levels of preschool children. Teachers learn by experience to avoid combining certain materials or equipment in the nursery school which might suggest undesired experimentation on the part of the children. For example, books arranged next to crayons and scissors, or hammers placed near windows may often, indeed, provide the sight of means to do ill deeds! On the constructive side, blocks combine well with toy cars, animals, or people; paints available near a supply of large sheets of white paper encourage creative expression. The teacher "sets the stage" (Beyer, 1958) in the nursery school to facilitate play, encourage creativity, and promote learning. Teachers' concerns about the environment are concerns with space, materials, equipment, the ratio of children to teachers, the grouping of children, and the amount and kind of teacher-child interaction.

Space

Many writers speak of the desirability of ample play space in the nursery school. Jersild and Markey (1935), in a study of conflicts between preschool children, compared nursery school situations in different types of buildings. They found that where play space was most restricted (as in a school with its play area on the roof), conflicts were greatest in number. The least conflict was found in the school with a large outdoor playground. Murphy (1937) also found that the nursery school group which had the greatest number of conflicts had a much smaller play space in proportion to the number of children. Markey (1935), in studying the imaginative behavior of three groups of children, discovered that the play space of the group with the highest degree of creativity (highest imaginative behavior score) was five times as large as the area of the other two groups.

Equipment

The selection and placement of equipment in nursery school are often determined by such considerations as health and safety, age and maturity, nursery school tradition, and recommendation by educational authorities. Available research evidence for including or rejecting equipment is meager.

Amount and arrangement of equipment. Equipment can affect behavior in nursery school. Johnson (1935) observed a group of nursery school children on a playground under two conditions—with all the toys and movable equipment removed, and with all the equipment replaced. When only the stationary equipment was available, children played with sand and dirt and devised games of their own. They also engaged in more quarrels and required more teacher intervention and direction. Landreth (1941) reported that 75 per cent of the incidents of crying in a nursery school setting were due to conflicts over toys and play equipment. Murphy, Murphy, and Newcomb (1937) suggested that "a large supply of simple materials available to everyone may focus attention on what can be created out of the materials, whereas an equally large supply of more complicated toys, but with only one or two of each kind available, is likely to stimulate competition and quarreling over materials" (pp. 344–345). Children who have been restricted in the use of toys and materials may need to be encouraged to handle them (Henry & Sharpe, 1947).

Equipment for motor behavior. Gutteridge (1939) obtained teacher ratings and observations of the motor performances of 1,973 children, two to seven years of age in 33 different schools. Although she was impressed with the wide individual differences in achievement in any activity, her data revealed that young children show motor control and proficiency far in advance of what is commonly believed possible or traditionally expected. Furthermore, she found that children progressively subordinate motor performance to its social purposes. She found, however, that after age four or five, children had exhausted the equipment provided for them in some motor activities. This, she felt, accounted for the slowing down of the median curve of achievement after three years of age. She suggested increasing the variety and complexity of climbing apparatus and other motor play equipment included in nursery schools. A search of the available literature did not produce a follow-up study.

However, a survey of the catalogues of leading manufacturers and distributors of educational toys, materials, and playground equipment reveals a remarkable awareness of the developmental needs and interests of children at different maturity levels. The manufacturers' insight must be the result of careful, detailed research in child growth and behavior. Nursery schools have increased and are continuing to increase the variety and complexity of their motor play equipment as well as their equipment for dramatic play and creative expression.

Equipment and social learnings. Equipment such as sand boxes, sleds, wagons, housekeeping toys in the doll corner, tea sets, slides, and tricycles with footholds on back for hangers-on stimulated cooperation, according to L. B. Murphy (1937). She also recommended swings for promoting cooperation in play since few children of nursery school age could adequately "pump" in the swings. Updegraff and Herbst (1932) found that cooperation behavior in two- and three-year-old children occurred more frequently during play with clay than during play with blocks. Sand and blocks were most frequently used in imaginative activities according to Markey (1935). As noted (p. 849), Van Alstyne (1932) rated some equipment higher in "conversational value" than others.

Equipment and materials preferences of preschool children. Blocks are standard equipment in nursery schools and are rated by various researchers at both the high and the low ends of the preference scale. Boys' preferences for blocks over other equipment are consistently greater than girls'. Moyer and Gilmer (1956) analyzed the preferences of 87 three-, four-, and five-year-old children for various block shapes and sizes used and reused in building construction. They concluded that selection and use of blocks is not necessarily related to chronological age but that children's "preferences for block shapes and sizes were made on the basis of their utility in being combined together for building" (p. 9). Individual differences in the design of structures were just as great within any age bracket as the differences found between different age groups.

Paints, crayons, and clay are also usually found in nursery schools. Studies of color usage in the painting performance of young children tend to show that selection of color is less a function of choice than a result of the arrangement of colors presented to them. Corcoran's study (1954) of color usage by 20 three-year-olds in a university nursery school gave evidence that three-year-old children use colors at an easel in the order in which they are presented. Corcoran noted that the approach of three- and four-year-olds to painting "is to apply the color without conscious deliberation and to react to the color as it is spread out on the paper." He felt that this approach accounts "for the overlaying of color and painting out [of] previously colored areas . . . so commonly observed among preschool children" (p. 113). Middle-class children, according to Alper, Blane, and Abrams (1955), prefer crayons to finger paint and show less tolerance for getting or staying dirty, and for the products they produce while dirty, than lower-class children.

Grouping Children in
Nursery School

Nursery schools differ in whether they group children into narrow, homogeneous age groups or into wider age ranges (such as the range from 2½ years to the age of kindergarten entrance). G. Murphy, L. B. Murphy, and Newcomb (1937) suggested that a group of 20 two-year-olds with the same interests and without mature capacity for cooperation may produce a high degree of tension and competition. They recommended splitting a large group into smaller subgroups to help counteract the effects of a narrow age range in a small group. L. B. Murphy (1937) found that "the presence of markedly younger children, that is, two-year-olds, in a group of children from three and a half to four years, stimulated a variety of big-brother behaviors, some affectionate, some putting the younger child in his place, some showing him how to handle things, some which were philanthropic efforts to entertain the younger child, or to take care of him" (p. 75). She also found more competitive pressure among children in narrow age-range groups.

Markey (1935) suggested some disadvantages of the narrow age-range group. The child who deviated considerably from the modal age of such a group, she observed, was likely to have fewer social contacts in his play, whereas a member of a heterogeneous group had more social contacts. She found a higher correlation between mental age and imaginative behavior than between chronological age and imaginative behavior. A younger child in a group of wide age-range exhibited more imaginative behavior than a child of the same age and sex in a group of limited age-range. The companionship of older siblings tends to increase imaginative behavior among younger children.

More samples of aggressive behavior both verbal and physical were recorded in the group with less variability in age (Body, 1955). This group also received a higher activity level rating. All the research seems to lead to the advocacy of heterogeneous grouping, but this policy is rarely practiced (Goodlad & Anderson, 1959).

Number of Teachers and
Amount of Teacher Interaction

Jersild and Markey (1935), as previously cited on pages 837 and 851, observed that aggressive responses occurred more frequently in a nursery school where there were only a few teachers; where many teachers were present, fewer aggressive interactions were allowed to develop. These authors were convinced that teachers often interfere in children's conflicts which the children themselves could resolve. Many times teachers decide against the aggressive child without knowing the reason for his aggressive act (Fite, 1940). Some teachers in nursery school commonly used what Appel (1942) called "ending" techniques rather than "teaching" techniques which help children learn ways of getting along in their play.

Markey (1935) advocated more active participation by adults in the games of nursery age children to help the children form clearer concepts in their imaginative behavior and to develop techniques for social and emotional adaptation to other members of the play group.

THE NURSERY SCHOOL
TEACHER'S PERSONALITY
AND CHARACTERISTICS

There is little research literature on characteristics of nursery school teachers. We have nothing like the monumental work by Ryans (1960), whose long-term and comprehensive study did not include nursery school teachers as part of the experimental samples.

Several research workers at the University of Minnesota (Goodenough, Fuller, & Olson, 1946; Fuller, 1951; and others) made a series of studies of nursery school and kindergarten primary teachers. Fuller (1951) correlated measures of ability and general adjustment with ratings of nursery school student teachers. A. C. E. Psychological Examination and Miller Analogies Test scores showed no relationship with the ratings. No significant correlation was found between the ratings and high school grades, Cooperative General Culture Test scores, Bell Adjustment Inventory scores, or students' self-ratings.

The failure of any of these variables to predict quality of student teaching can be explained in at least three ways: (1) Possibly intelligence, personal adjustment, and academic accomplishments in general studies are *not* related to success in preschool teaching. (2) Since a certain level of aptitude is necessary for admission to college, the range of scores was already curtailed before these students began their college work. (3) Rating success in preschool teaching, as in other levels of teaching, is difficult and seldom done with any degree of validity. Reliability estimates on the ratings by different supervisors were not incorporated in this report, but the author does suggest that further critical examination of the methods of rating teachers is much needed.

The one variable which did produce positive results in prediction of success at student teaching was the honor-point ratio for grades earned in professional subjects during the junior and senior years of the students' preparation. This correlation was .62, suggesting at first that the best prediction of success as a nursery school teacher comes from one's success in methods courses and other course work closely related to the teaching itself. But a more pessimistic interpretation of this correlation is that the ratings of student teaching were contaminated by the rater's knowledge of the student teacher's grades in other courses or by irrelevant halo effect.

Goodenough, Fuller, and Olson (1946) made an interesting study using a word association test, scored with reference to categories which differentiated between students preparing for nursery school teaching and students who were not enrolled in this nursery-kindergarten-primary curriculum. A scoring key was developed empirically on the basis of the extent to which response words differentiated between the two groups of students. The significant categories suggest what kinds of associations are foremost in the thinking of students who are planning to go into nursery-kindergarten-primary work. The categories which obtained the largest weights on this basis were as follows: (1) references to children's activities; (2) references to music; (3) favorable adjectives referring to ability or behavior; (4) references to children and babies; (5) references to neatness; (6) references to holidays, including birthdays. The following additional categories which differentiated do not seem to have the same clear relationship to nursery school teaching: opposites of the stimulus word, except those with unfavorable or unpleasant connotation; coordinates of the stimulus word; and active, present-tense verbs. No hypotheses are presented by the authors to account for the differentiating power of these latter associations.

The internal consistency of the word association test, scored according to these categories, is indicated by a corrected odd-even correlation of .76. The test-retest correlation over a 10-month interval was .55. When scores on this test were correlated with the judgment of supervisors on success in student teaching, the correlation was only .30. However, the extremes on success in student teaching were fairly well differentiated, i.e., poor teachers and excellent teachers seemed to be moderately well identified by this test. The authors stated that the test was not sufficiently accurate in its prediction to be used as a selection device, but that it is promising and interesting in its suggestion of semantic differentiation of patterns of thinking among teachers and nonteachers.

A by-product of this study was that the preschool teaching students scored definitely more "feminine" on a masculinity-femininity test than other young women of corresponding age and education. Coupled with the pattern of responses to which weights could be given for nursery school student teachers, this finding suggests that nursery school teachers have an especially positive orientation to children's activities and to the training of children in warm and favorable ways.

The Minnesota Teacher Attitude Inventory (Cook, Leeds, & Callis, 1951; Leeds, 1950) is designed to measure those attitudes of a teacher which predict how well he will get along with pupils in interpersonal relationships. Tables of norms for students differentiate between students in early childhood, elementary, and secondary education. For both beginning juniors and graduating seniors, the scores obtained by teachers-in-training at the early childhood and elementary school levels are considerably higher (warmer in relation to children) than scores obtained by those at the secondary school level. The students who go into teaching of younger children appear to respond to this Inventory in a way showing greater permissiveness and greater desire for rapport with children. Self-selection on the basis of such attitudes is no doubt operating to make these students choose the teaching of younger, rather than secondary age, pupils. It is likely that role-learning, i.e., the teacher's rapid adoption of attitudes appropriate to the role she is entering, also accounts for the differences in inventory scores between nursery school teachers and other teachers.

When one considers the possible influence of various personality characteristics of teachers on nursery school children attending school under their guidance, the numerous experimentally manipulated variables cited in the section on teaching methods become relevant. It was shown there that imitation of an adult model occurs frequently among children, suggesting that personality characteristics and expressive styles may be "caught" by children through imitation. Nurturance given by an adult has been shown to affect children's learning and concept formation. Positive uses of language have been taken over by children exposed to teachers using such forms.

The sex of the teacher seems to make a difference in the behavior of children. Dominative or integrative patterns of teacher behavior are associated with reciprocal behavior in children. The amount of guidance given by the teacher affects children's later behavior. Frustration, delay of reward, punishment for aggression, and so on have been shown to be effective. If any of the variables appear as personality characteristics which the teacher displays over and over again throughout her teaching, then we should expect such effects to be cumulative and to be shown in the development of the children exposed to them.

"Catching," or incidental learning, of certain language forms was studied by Dowley (1935). She investigated the character and quantity of language of 92 children in nursery school, kindergarten, and the first, second-third, and third-fourth grades of a university laboratory school to find out to what extent their language patterns resembled those of their teachers. The teachers in that school were trained in the use of positive, constructive, directive, encouraging language in the control of children's behavior. The majority of the children in the upper grades had been in attendance since nursery school and had therefore been exposed to the positive language patterns for as many as 10 semesters.

Using a time-sampling technique (16 one-minute samples per child) and teacher rating scales, Dowley found that at the four age levels there was a slight increase with age in the amount of positive constructive language within each grade group and in the combination of all of the groups with length of attendance at school. Although girls at all age levels studied tended to talk more than boys, boys showed a tendency to be more constructive and positive in their language than girls. The lack of a control group weakens the study since it does not take into account the language quality of children whose teachers were not trained.

Hilton (1955) investigated "ego-involvement" in teaching by a word completion form, a type of testing somewhat similar to Goodenough's (Goodenough, Fuller, & Olson, 1946) word association test. Hilton's pencil-and-paper device presents the subject with 108 items, each consisting of a series of connected letters from which several common words could be made by adding additional letters. For instance, "GOA—" is one of the items. From these letters, *goat, goal, goad, goatee,* and several less common words can be made. The form included 20 items deliberately designed to elicit as possible completions a series of words which were regarded as pertinent to education, such as *teacher, children, goal, education, school, mental,* and *testing.* These "education" items were spaced randomly throughout the form. Using an a priori scoring of the "education words" as an initial criterion, an analysis of all the items in the form provided the final scale of items from which a so-called "education score" was computed for each subject. This score is essentially the number of certain education words which are used as completions. For student teachers in the elementary and early childhood groups, this education score had substantial internal consistency. It also correlated with scores derived from another index of "ego-involvement in teaching." It thus appears to measure, like Goodenough's association words (Goodenough, Fuller, & Olson, 1946), the accessibility of words in the semantic category of education words. This score correlated .24 with ratings of teaching performance, .29 with Minnesota Teacher Attitude Inventory scores, and .18 with professional grades in the Harvard Graduate School of Education.

One part of a large project at Harvard (Levin, Hilton, & Leiderman, 1957) included obtaining ratings on emotionally warm teacher behavior in the classroom by well-trained raters. The categories of classroom behavior considered to be relevant to emotional warmth were (1) the use of praise and rewards, (2) the offering of encouragement and support, (3) affectionate physical contacts with pupils, (4) movement about the classroom, (5) noninstructional service to pupils, (6) compliance with suggestions made by pupils, (7) solicitation of suggestions, and (8) the use of humor. The student teachers rated themselves on these categories also, and in the early childhood and elementary school group of student teachers the self-ratings were significantly higher than those of the secondary school student teachers, although there were no significant differences between the groups on the supervising teachers' ratings. Thus the group of student teachers working with younger children perceived themselves as having warmer relations with children than did the secondary teachers. The self-rating was best predicted by the observer's rating on the amount of physical contact the student teacher had with the student; the second best predictor was the observer's rating on the amount of her movement about the classroom. Of other types of measures used to predict self-ratings of warmth, it was found that scores on the Miller Analogies Test should be weighted negatively, and scores on the Minnesota Teacher Attitude Inventory, positively.

An interesting finding was that the *change* in Minnesota Teacher Attitude Inventory scores between the beginning and the end of the academic year was more predictive than either of the separate scores. If the change was in the direction of more permissive attitudes toward children, the student teachers were likely to show more physical contact, more movement about the classroom, provide more support, give more reward, etc.

The prevalence of certain types of teacher-child interaction was also measured by Landreth and her co-workers (1943) in a university-operated nursery school and in a WPA nursery school. In the latter the teachers were inadequately trained for the most part. In their interactions with children the WPA teachers, compared with the university teachers, showed more commanding behavior and more compulsion. The university teachers operated more with suggestions, questions, information, and encouragement. The amount of giving of physical assistance was the same for both groups. Interestingly, the WPA teachers more often petted and fondled the children than did the university teachers. These differences probably reflect a composite picture of the differences between the professional, trained teacher's role, as seen in 1943, and lay people's conceptions of their adult role in relation to children.

A report from the U.S. Office of Education (Davis, 1947) showed that 65 per cent of nursery and kindergarten teachers had from four to eight years of educational preparation for teaching. The remaining 35 per cent had three years or less. More than half had at least one professional degree.

A questionnaire on theory and practice in nursery school teaching was used by Moustakas and Berson (1956) with teachers at 222 nursery schools and 90 day-care centers (a 72 per cent return). Four types of attitudes were distinguished: democratic, child-centered, authoritarian, and laissez-faire. Comparisons were made between responses to questions involving theory and those involving practice.

The most prevalent pattern of response, not surprisingly, was child-centered *theory* and authoritarian *practice*. Apparently, a considerable gap exists between what nursery school teachers believe and what they report themselves as doing. Presumably, a study of what they actually are doing would show the gap to be wider still. It is as if the teachers proclaim what they know to be "right" but find it difficult or impossible, in practice, to do what is right.

A clue to reasons for this is found in Callis (1950). With repeated administration of the Minnesota Teacher Attitude Inventory, he found students' scores increasing (changing toward attitudes of greater warmth and understanding of children) as they took more professional courses in education. After six months of full-time teaching, however, scores decreased significantly; the decrease suggests that the students may have become disillusioned with the ideals they had held before teaching full time.

CONDUCTING RESEARCH IN NURSERY SCHOOLS

University nursery schools have always been the scene of research. Such schools generally have as one of their purposes the provision of an experimental laboratory for university students and teachers in training. Nonetheless, the objectives of the teachers who plan for the education of children and the objectives of the research workers have not always coincided. Parents have sometimes wondered whether the research procedures were actually in the best interests of their children.

In Mussen's *Handbook of Research Methods in Child Development,* Baldwin (1960) has discussed some of the problems and contributions of research conducted in nursery schools. Among others, the ethical problems of working with children are discussed.

One of the present authors (Dowley, 1960) has presented the case history of a large research project at Stanford University and described how this project fitted into the ongoing program of a nursery school. The preparatory work and the communication between teachers, parents, and researchers are reported. A second article, by R. R. Sears (1960–1961) goes into the involvement of parents in such a research project; it includes the actual report which was sent to the parents involved in one summer research project. A third article, by Rowe (1960–1961), discusses the nursery school teacher's part in a research project.

Conclusions from the Stanford project and its evaluation, as described in the three articles just cited, suggest that even a massive research program, involving a large staff of research workers, can operate successfully in a nursery school, with good results for the children, stimulation for the teachers, and cooperation from the parents. Several important points can be made: (1) It is the nursery school teacher who sets the stage, in an atmosphere of relaxed informality, in such a way that the environment directs, guides, and determines the limits for child behavior. The teacher makes available a wide variety of carefully selected materials and experiences and encourages the children to choose their own activities rather than follow a predetermined program. (2) There is some dependability and orderliness in the sequence of daily events, but at the same time children are protected from overdemanding time schedules and from arbitrary conformity to group desires and activities. (3) The requests by the research team for alteration of schedule and of environment must not typically be drastic ones. A few such drastic requests were made in the Stanford project, but the nursery staff was able to adapt to them and make the program arranged for the children a valuable one in spite of this. In fact, the head teacher felt that these exigencies alerted the staff to discover more ingenious ways to make the environment stimulating for the children.

Relationships with the parents were kept open and free through communication both with the research director and with the head teacher. The research workers were introduced into the life of the nursery school and genuinely adopted the role of friendly adults interested in the children's welfare and supportive of the teaching staff. Children were given freedom of choice to decide whether to go with an experimenter at a given time or not, but the head teacher made sure that the time schedule of the research was not unduly hampered by delays in the use of the experimenters' time. The professional stimulation of having research go on in a school setting, the increased insights into children's behavior, and the presence of other people also interested in and respectful of children, all were felt to be decided assets in this particular project.

SUMMARY AND EVALUATION

What is the current state of the field of research on nursery school teaching? Readers of this chapter may be surprised at the length and number of research articles which bear in some way on the teaching process and its effects. When gathered together, the literature constitutes a considerable body of knowledge bearing on the problems of teaching. A number of variables have been isolated, defined, and tested for their effects. Relationships between certain events have been shown to appear with some predictable regularity.

Yet, the body of knowledge is spotty and difficult to organize and integrate. Interesting small facts abound but often are not clearly related to other facts in the same area. A picture begins to emerge in certain areas, perhaps, but it is shadowy and blurred. We cannot speak of the teaching process with the certainty which we would like.

The present authors suggest several reasons for this state of affairs; these may apply to research on teaching at all grade levels but they apply with particular cogency to the nursery school level:

1. There is the perennial complaint that we lack theory for the teaching process. This lack certainly presents a handicap. Fragmentation of knowledge is bound to result in the absence of a coherent and integrating set of theoretical concepts. In certain areas reported in this chapter, the advantages accruing from the presence of theory appear—for example, in the work on nurturance, on frustration, and on dominative-integrative interaction. In these areas it is possible for one study to take off from the findings of another, to pursue, refine, and clarify the influence of certain independent variables. Note that the initial impetus for these studies has not been the study of the teaching process per se. Interpersonal relations, particularly those involving adult-child relations, have been the original focus. Teaching is one important form of adult-child interaction, but the theory and findings of the research apply also to parent-child relations and other types of adult-child relations. When we apply these theoretical constructs to the teaching process, we are rooting that process where it belongs—solidly in the area of social psychology and behavioral science. This orientation is entirely proper and will result in more fruitful directions of research on the teaching process itself.

2. Nevertheless, it is necessary to pursue or follow up these more general findings in

the actual nursery school environment before firm applications to nursery school *teaching* can be made. Teachers are not parents of the children they teach; roles of teachers are different from roles of parents, and the objectives of the nursery school are different in some respects from the over-all objectives of parents. Teachers are different, also, from adult research workers, and the impact of their interaction with the child may well be somewhat different for the two groups for a variety of reasons. Prominent among such reasons is the child's expectation concerning teachers as compared to other adults in his environment.

3. Very few studies have carried the same variables and procedures utilized in the controlled experimental situation into the less controlled naturalistic setting of the actual nursery school group and environment. Some notable exceptions have been cited here—the work of H. H. Anderson, Thompson, Jersild, and some others—but they are few indeed. Yet it is precisely here that we get the biggest payoff in knowledge of effects of teaching.

4. Furthermore, it is not impossible that teachers themselves, as hypothesis-makers and action researchers, can provide insights and leads to more carefully controlled research. As we improve the quality of teacher training it is expected that teachers will more and more be able to function as stimulators of solid research.

5. There appears to be a great reluctance among most researchers to replicate, even in modified form, the work of others. Since the methods available for tests of interpersonal influence are crude at best, and since much depends on particular characteristics of children used as experimental subjects, it is essential that findings be confirmed on other groups and by other experimenters before they can be considered true and replicable facts. The desire for originality and creativity among researchers can be carried too far; promotion of sound scientific knowledge requires some sacrifice of individuality in the interests of building on rock rather than sand. Longitudinal or follow-up studies should test the stability of effects and the amount of transfer to other situations.

6. Finally, it should be mentioned that firm knowledge of the effect of teaching methods or roles cannot be gained without taking into account characteristics of the children toward whom the methods are directed. It is clear by now that a "method" cannot be abstracted from the interpersonal setting; methods are employed by teachers having certain characteristics and they are directed toward children with certain characteristics. Shorn of these factors, statements about a method must necessarily be stated in such tentative terms that they are of little value.

REFERENCES

Allen, G. B., & Masling, J. M. An evaluation of the effects of nursery school training on children in the kindergarten, first, and second grades. *J. educ. Res.,* 1957, 51, 285–296.

Alper, Thelma G., Blane, H. T., & Abrams, Barbara K. Reactions of middle- and lower-class children to finger paints as a function of class differences in child training practices. *J. abnorm. soc. Psychol.,* 1955, 51, 439–448.

Anderson, H. H. Domination and integration in the social behavior of young children in an experimental play situation. *Genet. Psychol. Monogr.,* 1937, 19, 341–408.

Anderson, H. H. Domination and social integration in the behavior of kindergarten children in an experimental play situation. *J. exp. Educ.,* 1939, 8, 123–131. (a)

Anderson, H. H. Domination and social integration in the behavior of kindergarten children and teachers. *Genet. Psychol. Monogr.,* 1939, 21, 287–385. (b)

Anderson, H. H. The measurement of domination and of socially integrative behavior in teachers' contacts with kindergarten children. *Child Develpm.,* 1939, 10, 73–89. (c)

Anderson, H. H. Domination and socially integrative behavior. In R. G. Barker, J. Kounin, & H. F. Wright (Eds.), *Child behavior and development.* New York: McGraw-Hill, 1943. Pp. 459–484.

Anderson, H. H., & Anderson, Gladys L. Social development. In L. Carmichael (Ed.), *Manual of child psychology.* (2nd ed.) New York: Wiley, 1954. Pp. 1162–1215.

Anderson, H. H., & Brewer, Helen M. Studies of teachers' classroom personalities. I. Dominative and socially integrative behavior of kindergarten teachers. *Appl. Psychol. Monogr.,* 1945, No. 6.

Anderson, J. E. The theory of early childhood education. *Yearb. nat. Soc. Stud. Educ.,* 1947, 46, Part II, 70–100.

Andrus, R., & Horowitz, E. L. The effect of nursery school training: Insecurity feeling. *Child Develpm.,* 1938, 9, 169–174.

Appel, M. H. Aggressive behavior of nursery school children and adult procedures in dealing with such behavior. *J. exp. Educ.,* 1942, 11, 185–199.

Bach, G. R. Young children's play fantasies. *Psychol. Monogr.,* 1945, 59, No. 2 (Whole No. 272).

Baldwin, A. L. The study of child behavior and development. In P. Mussen (Ed.), *Handbook of research methods in child development.* New York: Wiley, 1960. Pp. 3–36.

Bandura, A., & Huston, Aletha C. Identification as a process of incidental learning. *J. abnorm. soc. Psychol.,* 1961, 63, 311–318.

Bandura, A., Ross, Dorothea, & Ross, Sheila A. Transmission of aggression through imitation of aggressive models. *J. abnorm. soc. Psychol.,* 1961, 63, 575–582.

Barker, R. G., Dembo, Tamara, & Lewin, K. Frustration and regression: An experiment with young children. *Univer. Iowa Stud. Child Welf.,* 1941, 18, No. 1, 1–314.

Barker, R. G., Dembo, Tamara, & Lewin, K. Frustration and regression. In R. G. Barker, J. Kounin, & H. F. Wright (Eds.), *Child behavior and development.* New York: McGraw-Hill, 1943. Pp. 441–458.

Baruch, Dorothy W. *Parents and children go to school.* Chicago: Scott, Foresman, 1939.

Beller, E. Dependency and independence in young children. *J. genet. Psychol.,* 1955, 87, 25–35.

Beyer, Evelyn. *Nursery school settings—Invitation to what?* Chicago: National Association for Nursery Education, 1958.

Block, Jeanne, & Martin, B. Predicting the behavior of children under frustration. In J. Seidman (Ed.), *The child: A book of readings.* New York: Rinehart, 1958. Pp. 453–461.

Body, Margaret K. Patterns of aggression in the nursery school. *Child Develpm.,* 1955, 26, 3–11.

Bonney, M. E., & Nicholson, Ertie Lou. Comparative school adjustments of elementary school pupils with and without preschool training. *Child Develpm.,* 1958, 29, 125–133.

Borstelmann, L. J. Sex of experimenter and sex-typed behavior of young children. *Child Develpm.,* 1961, 32, 519–524.

Breckenridge, Marion, & Murphy, Margaret. *Growth and development of the young child.* Philadelphia: Saunders, 1958.

Brenner, A. Nature and meaning of readiness for school. *Merrill-Palmer Quart.,* 1957, 3, 114–135.

Brenner, A., & Samelson, Nancy M. Kindergarten behavior and first-grade achievement: A case study exploration. *Merrill-Palmer Quart.,* 1959, 5, 140–155.

Caille, R. K. Resistant behavior of preschool children. *Child Develpm. Monogr.,* 1933, No. 11.

Callis, R. Change in teacher-pupil attitudes related to training and experience. *Educ. psychol. Measmt,* 1950, 10, 718–727.

Carr, V. S. The social and emotional changes in a group of children of high intelligence during a program of increased educational stimulation. Unpublished master's thesis, Univer. of Iowa, 1938.

Chamberlin, D., Chamberlin, Enid, Drought, N. E., & Scott, W. E. *Did they succeed in college?* New York: Harper, 1942.

Chasdi, Eleanor H., & Lawrence, Margaret S. Some antecedents of aggression and effects of frustration in doll play. In J. Seidman (Ed.), *The child: A book of readings.* New York: Rinehart, 1958. Pp. 442–453.

Chittenden, Gertrude E. An experimental study in measuring and modifying assertive behavior in young children. *Monogr. Soc. Res. Child Develpm.,* 1942, 7, No. 1.

Chittenden, Gertrude E. Experiences in which young children may learn to share. *Yearb. nat. Soc. Stud. Educ.,* 1947, 46, Part II, 179–193.

Cook, W. W., Leeds, C. H., & Callis, R. *Minnesota Teacher Attitude Inventory: Manual.* New York: Psychological Corp., 1951.

Corcoran, A. L. Color usage in nursery school painting. *Child Develpm.,* 1954, 25, 107–113.

Davis, M. D. *Schools for children under six.* Washington, D.C.: U.S. Office of Education Bull., 1947, No. 5.

Dawe, Helen C. A study of the effect of an educational program upon language development and related mental functions in young children. *J. exp. Educ.,* 1942, 11, 200–209.

Dawe, Helen C. The child's experiences in communication. *Yearb. nat. Soc. Stud. Educ.,* 1947, 46, Part II, 193–208.

Dowley, Edith. The effect of teachers' verbal direction on the language of young children. Unpublished master's thesis, Univer. of Michigan, 1935.

Dowley, Edith. Doing research in a nursery school. *J. nursery Educ.,* 1960, 16, 22–25.

Dubin, E. R. The effect of training on the tempo of development of graphic representation. *J. exp. Educ.,* 1946, 15, 166–173.

Erikson, E. *Childhood and society.* New York: Norton, 1950.

Ezekiel, L. F. Changes in egocentricity of nursery school children. *Child Develpm.,* 1931, 2, 74–75.

Fite, M. D. Aggressive behavior in young children and children's attitude toward aggression. *Genet. Psychol. Monogr.,* 1940, 22, 151–319.

Forest, Ilse. *Early years at school.* New York: McGraw-Hill, 1949.

Frank, L. K. Fundamental needs of the child. *Ment. Hyg., N.Y.,* 1938, 22, 353–379.

Fuller, Elizabeth M. The use of teacher-pupil attitudes, self-rating, and measures of general ability in the pre-service selection of nursery school-kindergarten-primary teachers. *J. educ. Res.,* 1951, 44, 675–686.

Fuller, Elizabeth M. Early childhood education. In C. W. Harris (Ed.), *Encyclopedia of educational research.* (3rd ed.) New York: Macmillan, 1960. Pp. 385–396.

Gardner, D. E. M. *The education of young children.* New York: Philosophical Library, 1957.

Gesell, A., et al. *The first five years of life: A guide to the study of the preschool child.* New York: Harper, 1940.

Gesell, A., et al. *Infant and child in the culture of today: The guidance of development in home and nursery school.* New York: Harper, 1943.

Gewirtz, J. L. A program of research on the dimensions and antecedents of emotional dependence. *Child Develpm.,* 1956, 27, 206–221.

Gewirtz, J. L., & Baer, D. M. The effect of brief social deprivation on behaviors for a social reinforcer. *J. abnorm. soc. Psychol.,* 1958, 56, 49–56. (a)

Gewirtz, J. L., & Baer, D. M. Deprivation and satiation of social reinforcers as drive conditions. *J. abnorm. soc. Psychol.,* 1958, 57, 165–172. (b)

Gewirtz, J. L., Baer, D. M., & Roth, Chaya H. A note on the similar effects of low social availability of an adult and brief social deprivation on young children's behavior. *Child Develpm.,* 1958, 29, 149–152.

Goodenough, Florence L., Fuller, Elizabeth M., & Olson, Edna. The use of the Goodenough Speed-of-Association Test in the pre-service selection of nursery school-kindergarten-primary teachers. *J. educ. Psychol.,* 1946, 37, 335–346.

Goodlad, J. I., & Anderson, R. H. *The nongraded elementary school.* New York: Harcourt, Brace, 1959.

Gutteridge, Mary V. A study of motor achievements of young children. *Arch. Psychol., N.Y.,* 1939, 34, No. 244.

Gutteridge, Mary V. The child's experiences in bodily activity. *Yearb. nat. Soc. Stud. Educ.,* 1947, 46, Part II, 208–222.

Hartup, W. W. Nurturance and nurturance-withdrawal in relation to the dependency behavior of preschool children. Unpublished doctoral dissertation, Harvard Univer., 1955.

Hartup, W. W. Nurturance and nurturance-withdrawal in relation to the dependency behavior of preschool children. *Child Develpm.,* 1958, 29, 191–201.

Hattwick, Berta W. The influence of nursery school attendance upon the behavior and personality of the preschool child. *J. exp. Educ.,* 1937, 5, 180–190.

Heathers, G. Emotional dependence and independence in nursery school play. *J. genet. Psychol.,* 1955, 87, 37–57.

Henry, Myra M., & Sharpe, Doris F. Some influential factors in the determination of aggressive behavior in preschool children. *Child Develpm.,* 1947, 18, 11–28.

Hess, E. H. The relationship between imprinting and motivation. In M. R. Jones (Ed.), *Nebraska symposium on motivation, 1959.* Lincoln: Univer. of Nebraska Press, 1959. Pp. 44–77.

Hilgard, Josephine R. Learning and maturation in preschool children. *J. genet. Psychol.*, 1932, 41, 40–53.

Hilton, T. L. Ego-involvement in teaching: Its theory and measurement by word completion technique. Unpublished doctoral dissertation, Harvard Univer., 1955.

Hofman, H. Behavioral patterns in kindergarten and first grade. *Merrill-Palmer Quart.*, 1957, 3, 136–144.

Hofman, H. Children's drawings as an indication of readiness for first grade. *Merrill-Palmer Quart.*, 1958, 4, 165–179.

Hunt, J. McV. *Intelligence and experience.* New York: Ronald Press, 1961.

Jack, Lois M. An experimental study of ascendant behavior in preschool children. *Univer. Iowa Stud. Child Welf.*, 1934, 9, 7–65.

Jersild, A. T. Training and growth in the development of children. *Child Develpm. Monogr.*, 1932, No. 10.

Jersild, A. T. *Child psychology.* (5th ed.) Englewood Cliffs, N.J.: Prentice-Hall, 1960.

Jersild, A. T., & Fite, M. D. The influence of nursery school experience on children's social adjustments. *Child Develpm. Monogr.*, 1939, No. 25.

Jersild, A. T., & Markey, F. V. Conflicts between preschool children. *Child Develpm. Monogr.*, 1935, No. 21.

Jersild, A. T., & Meigs, Margaret F. Direct observation as a research method. *Rev. educ. Res.*, 1939, 9, 472–482, 597–599.

Jersild, A. T., Thorndike, R. L., Goldman, B., Wrightstone, J. W., & Loftus, J. J. A further comparison of pupils in "activity" and "nonactivity" schools. *J. exp. Educ.*, 1941, 9, 303–309.

Joel, W. The influence of nursery school education upon behavior maturity. *J. exp. Educ.*, 1939, 8, 164–165.

Johnson, Marguerite W. The effect on behavior of variation in the amount of play equipment. *Child Develpm.*, 1935, 6, 56–68.

Jones, H. E. The environment and mental development. In L. Carmichael (Ed.), *Manual of child psychology.* (2nd ed.) New York: Wiley, 1954. Pp. 631–696.

Kawin, Ethel, & Hoefer, C. *A comparative study of nursery-school vs. non-nursery school group.* Chicago: Univer. of Chicago Press, 1931.

Keister, Mary E. The behavior of young children in failure. In R. G. Barker, J. Kounin, & H. F. Wright (Eds.), *Child behavior and development.* New York: McGraw-Hill, 1943. Pp. 429–440.

Kounin, J. S., & Gump, P. V. The ripple effect in discipline. *Elem. sch. J.*, 1958, 59, 158–162.

Landreth, Catherine. Factors associated with crying in young children in the nursery school and the home. *Child Develpm.*, 1941, 12, 81–97.

Landreth, C., et al. Teacher-child contacts in nursery schools. *J. exp. Educ.*, 1943, 12, 65–91.

Langford, Louise M. *Guidance of the young child.* New York: Wiley, 1960.

Leeds, C. H. A scale for measuring teacher-pupil attitudes and teacher-pupil rapport. *Psychol. Monogr.*, 1950, 64, No. 6 (Whole No. 312).

Levin, H., Hilton, T. L., & Leiderman, Gloria F. Studies of teacher behavior. *J. exp. Educ.*, 1957, 26, 81–91.

Lippitt, R., & White, R. K. The "social climate" of children's groups. In R. G. Barker, J. Kounin, & H. F. Wright (Eds.), *Child behavior and development.* New York: McGraw-Hill, 1943. Pp. 485–508.

Maccoby, Eleanor E. Role-taking in childhood and its consequences for social learning. *Child Develpm.*, 1959, 30, 239–252.

Markey, F. V. Imaginative behavior of preschool children. *Child Develpm. Monogr.*, 1935, No. 18.

Martin, W. E. An armchair assessment of nursery education. *J. nursery Educ.*, 1960–1961, 16, 90–96.

McCarthy, Dorothea. Language development in children. In L. Carmichael (Ed.), *Manual of child psychology.* (2nd ed.) New York: Wiley, 1954. Pp. 492–630.

Milner, Esther. A study of the relationship between reading readiness in grade one school children and patterns of parent-child interaction. *Child Develpm.*, 1951, 22, 95–112.

Moustakas, C. E., & Berson, M. P. *The young child in school.* New York: Morrow, 1956.

Moyer, K. E., & Gilmer, B. Experimental study of children's preferences and use of blocks in play. *J. genet. Psychol.*, 1956, 89, 3–10.

Mummery, D. V. An analytical study of ascendant behavior of preschool children. *Child Develpm.*, 1947, 18, 40–81.

Murphy, G., Murphy, Lois B., & Newcomb, T. M. *Experimental social psychology.* (Rev. ed.) New York: Harper, 1937.

Murphy, Lois B. *Social behavior and child personality; An exploratory study of some roots of sympathy.* New York: Columbia Univer. Press, 1937.

Olson, W. C. *Child development.* (2nd ed.) Boston: Heath, 1959.

Olson, W. C., & Hughes, B. O. Subsequent growth of children with and without nursery school experience. *Yearb. nat. Soc. Stud. Educ.,* 1940, 39, Part II, 237–244.

Page, M. L. The modification of ascendant behavior in preschool children. *Univer. Iowa Stud. Child Welf.,* 1936, 12, No. 3.

Parten, Mildred B., & Newhall, S. M. Social behavior of preschool children. In R. G. Barker, J. Kounin, & H. F. Wright (Eds.), *Child behavior and development.* New York: McGraw-Hill, 1943. Pp. 509–526.

Read, Katherine H. *The nursery school: A human relationships laboratory.* (3rd ed.) Philadelphia: Saunders, 1960. (1st ed., 1950).

Redl, F., & Wineman, D. *Controls from within.* Glencoe, Ill.: Free Press, 1952.

Reed, Mary F. Consecutive studies of the schoolroom behavior of children in relation to the teachers' dominative and socially integrative contacts. *Appl. Psychol. Monogr.,* 1946, No. 11, 15–100.

Roeper, Annemarie. Nursery school—A place to adjust or a place to learn. *Child Study,* 1959, 36, No. 2, 3–9.

Rosenblith, Judy F. Learning by imitation in kindergarten children. *Child Develpm.,* 1959, 30, 69–80.

Rowe, P. A nursery school teacher's part in a research project. *J. nursery Educ.,* 1960–1961, 16, 65–70.

Ryans, D. G. *Characteristics of teachers.* Washington, D.C.: American Council on Education, 1960.

Sears, Pauline S. Problems in the investigation of achievement and self-esteem motivation. In M. R. Jones (Ed.), *Nebraska symposium on motivation, 1957.* Lincoln: Univer. of Nebraska Press, 1957. Pp. 265–339.

Sears, Pauline S., & Levin, H. Levels of aspiration in preschool children. *Child Develpm.,* 1957, 28, 317–326.

Sears, R. R. Reporting research to parents. *J. nursery Educ.,* 1960–1961, 16, 25–32.

Sears, R. R., Whiting, J. W. M., Nowlis, V., & Sears, Pauline S. Some child-rearing antecedents of aggression and dependency in young children. *Genet. Psychol. Monogr.,* 1953, 47, 135–234.

Siegel, Alberta E., & Kohn, Lynette G. Permissiveness, permission, and aggression: The effect of adult presence or absence on aggression in children's play. *Child Develpm.,* 1959, 30, 131–142.

Smith, M. E. A study of some factors influencing the development of the sentence in preschool children. *J. genet. Psychol.,* 1935, 46, 182–212.

Spock, B. *Common sense book of baby and child care.* New York: Duell, Sloan, & Pearce, 1946.

Stendler, Celia B. Possible causes of overdependency in young children. *Child Develpm.,* 1954, 25, 125–146.

Stoke, S. The concept of identification. In W. Martin & Celia Stendler (Eds.), *Readings in child development.* New York: Harcourt, Brace, 1954. Pp. 227–239.

Stolz, Lois M., et al. *Father relations of warborn children.* Stanford, Calif.: Stanford Univer. Press, 1954.

Stone, L. J., & Church, J. *Childhood and adolescence.* New York: Random House, 1957.

Thompson, G. G. The social and emotional development of preschool children under two types of education programs. *Psychol. Monogr.,* 1944, 56, No. 5 (Whole No. 258).

Time. OK's children. 1960, 76 (19), 103.

Updegraff, Ruth, & Herbst, Edithe K. An experimental study of the social behavior stimulated in young children by certain play materials. *J. genet. Psychol.,* 1932, 42, 372–391.

Updegraff, Ruth, Heiliger, Louise, & Learned, Janet. The effect of training upon singing ability and musical interest of three-, four-, and five-year-old children. *Univer. Iowa Stud. Child Welf.,* 1937, 14, 85–129.

Van Alstyne, Dorothy. *Play behavior and choice of play materials of preschool children.* Chicago: Univer. of Chicago Press, 1932.

Van Alstyne, Dorothy, & Hattwick, LaBerta A. A follow-up study of the behavior of nursery school children. *Child Develpm.,* 1939, 10, 43–72.

Vitz, P. Some changes in behavior of nursery school children over a period of seven weeks. *J. nursery Educ.,* 1961, 16, 62–65.

Walsh, M. E. The relation of nursery school training to the development of certain personality traits. *Child Develpm.,* 1931, 2, 72–73.

Wellman, Beth L. The effects of preschool attendance upon intellectual development. In R. G. Barker, J. Kounin, & H. F. Wright

(Eds.), *Child behavior and development.*
New York: McGraw-Hill, 1943. Pp. 229–
243.

Wolffheim, Nelly. *Psychology in the nursery
school.* New York: Philosophical Library,
1953.

Wright, M. E. Constructiveness of play as
affected by group organization and frustration. *Character & Pers.,* 1942, 11, 40–49.

Wright, M. E. The influence of frustration
upon social relations of young children.
Character & Pers., 1943, 12, 111–122.

Yarrow, L. J. The effect of antecedent frustration on projective play. *Psychol. Monogr.,*
1948, 62, No. 6 (Whole No. 293).

Young, Florene M. An analysis of certain variables in a developmental study of language.
Genet. Psychol. Monogr., 1941, 23, 3–141.

CHAPTER 16 Research on Teaching Reading

DAVID H. RUSSELL
University of California

HENRY R. FEA
University of Washington

Research on reading instruction comprises more material than does research in any other part of the curriculum. In one of his summaries of such research, W. S. Gray (1960) estimated that some 4,000 careful, scientific studies of the sociology, psychology, and teaching of reading are available. Other interpretive and descriptive writing would at least double this number of reports. Material in such quantities is a mixed blessing; it provides not only a wealth of fact and opinion to guide teachers' and pupils' procedures, but it also creates the problem of organizing and focusing these findings so that current knowledge can be comprehended and the needs for further research laid bare. The reading field illustrates as well as any the influences which may affect teaching methods. These influences include opinions of parents or of the teacher next door, personal experiences of the teachers themselves, hortatory articles in professional journals, accounts of action research or "how we did it" in a particular situation, careful descriptions of applied research in classroom and individual situations, and scholarly accounts of basic investigations in laboratory and other settings. The amount and variety of material available in this area make evaluation of the research and practice doubly necessary if an adequate basis for fruitful new research on reading is to be laid.

In view of the broad scope of the literature on reading and the purpose of this Handbook, this chapter is necessarily delimited. It focuses on reading instruction in classroom, group, and individual situations and therefore omits a considerable body of research on reading. The chapter largely ignores research on the physiology and psychology of the reading process, which dates back at least to the 1880's but which is not the specific concern of most teachers. It largely bypasses a considerable body of knowledge on the sociology of reading including such topics as the rise of literacy, the reading habits of adults, and the effects of the mass media on the citizen's communication behavior. It contains only minor reference to theories of language and such studies as linguistics which have possible implications—still largely unrealized—for the use of phonics and other approaches in reading instruction. Instead of reporting evidence on these topics, the chapter centers on the methods and materials of teaching reading.

HISTORICAL BACKGROUND OF READING INSTRUCTION

As suggested above, the teacher of reading may be influenced by many factors. The practices of a successful teacher of reading in the primary grades, for example, are sometimes the result of historical influences rather than of specific research studies. We teach, at least in part, because of tradition. In the United States the teaching of reading dates back over 250 years. In that time skillful teachers and textbook writers have developed materials and methods which have greatly influenced reading instruction, usually without making any careful study of either the material or the method in the modern sense of experimental try out. When teachers do not have scientific justification for their teaching methods, they often have a precedent of successful practice to which they can point. Resourceful teachers sometimes use reading materials and teaching methods which work well for them before a careful evaluation of these procedures has been made. In one sense, such people are experimenting at a demonstration or action research level, and the initiative displayed by these highly motivated teachers is to be encouraged. The writers feel, however, that such efforts can be advantageously combined with carefully designed research studies. Classroom procedures can be evaluated more critically, and research can be conducted in meaningful settings on problems important to teachers. Furthermore, because individual writing and teaching may depend upon specific or local circumstances and may be swayed, for example, by dynamic qualities of the teacher, the writers urge that a scientific study of materials and methods be included in every kind of demonstration or new operation.

Despite this emphasis, it is important for research workers and teachers to know that current methods and materials in reading instruction are often based, not on careful research, but on trial and adaptation by able teachers through many generations. When a teacher explains methods in reading instruction to a parent, for example, he should be aware that his procedures are not the product of his own invention or the recipe of one teacher's manual, but rather that they are usually the resultant of long use by many teachers and children.

Reading instruction in the United States has always been strongly influenced by the character of the materials available. The content of these materials has usually reflected the dominant mores of the day. For example, the religious views of colonial times were reflected in the famous schoolbook of the period, *The New England Primer*. This compendium of catechism, hymnal, speller, and reading book was published about 1690 and for a hundred years was the chief schoolbook of the time. It was found in most homes and its total sale in various editions is estimated at over three million copies. It introduced reading by the alphabet method; children were expected to learn their letters, put them together in syllables such as *ab, ac, ad, af, eb, ec, ed,* etc., and gradually work up to words and sentences.

The second "best-seller" in the reading field was Noah Webster's *Elementary Spelling Book,* published in 1783 and better known as the *Blue-Back Speller*. This book emphasized the word method and was used for reading instruction as well as for spelling. Words were presented in long lists which had to be memorized. Webster's book was successful at least partly because English books were unavailable during the Revolutionary War. Together with his *Dictionary of the English Language,* it established American spellings for certain words which differed from the English spellings, but it probably did not go far enough in simplifying spelling generally. It is estimated that one hundred million copies of the *Blue-Back Speller* have been printed. In aiming to establish American English, Webster was more concerned with "correct" pronunciation in oral reading and in speaking than with methods of learning to read as such.

A third great success in the reading field started, like Webster, with word lists but gradually shifted to phonetic aids to word recognition. The first set of McGuffey readers appeared between 1836 and 1844 and, with later editions, dominated the field for some 50 years. The content of these books included many extremely conservative social and political ideas (Mosier, 1947). The McGuffey readers have been praised for the ethical values they propounded, but actually they included less material illustrating values such as courage, honesty, and loyalty than do certain modern readers (P. S. Anderson, 1956). One of McGuffey's lasting contributions was his careful gradation of material in a series which provided one reader for each grade of the elementary school. By modern standards, the series contained small amounts of reading material at each level of difficulty, but it did not include a beginning level corresponding to modern preprimers and primers. Its content reflected the rural character of much of the life of the day. The books presented such virtues as thrift and obedience although, as indicated in the section on "The Teacher Encourages Interpretation," below, there is little conclusive evidence on the effects of reading on conduct.

A historical account of these and more recent materials and methods of instruction has been given by N. B. Smith (1934). By the end of the nineteenth century, different publishers had produced readers and reading programs which, like McGuffey's, emphasized some variety of the phonics approach in word recognition. Around 1915 a reaction against "The fat cat sat on the mat" type of literature led some teachers to the "whole" method of having children learn more interesting words, sentences, and even nursery rhymes in initial stages of reading. About 1925, this system was supplemented by the "experience approach," sometimes associated with "progressive education," in which children read charts and other materials growing out of their daily activities (Lamoreaux & Lee, 1943). A little later, Gestalt psychology was used as a theoretical basis for learning word "wholes," a practice not entirely justified by the facts (Morris, 1959).

By the 1930's, many teachers were using a combination of different methods and materials, often adopting an "experience approach" leading to the use of some basal reading program or programs, supplemented by individual books or series as more material written for children became available. In the 1930's and 1940's, as research findings became better known and as more instructional materials became available, differences in theory and practice were evident in such aspects of reading instruction as the readiness program, the use of grouping for instruction, and the place of oral reading. The most prominent criticism of instruction in the 1940's and 1950's centered around the place of phonics in the teaching of reading. Toward the end of the period, one conspicuous problem was the extent of use of individualized procedures rather than group or class instruction in reading.

All of these somewhat controversial matters are considered in some detail in the sections below. This list of topics of concern to teachers and research workers illustrates how thinking in the field has moved away somewhat from an either-or point of view about one method or set of books to a realization that different children learn in different ways, that the processes of learning to read and reading are more complex than we once thought, and that the issues in reading instruction are many-sided. Unfortunately, the work of the teacher with 30 children in a class is not as simple as the authors of some reading "systems" suggest. From the scientific point of view, we must regard as false prophets those who advocate one method or one type of material for all children regardless of whether they are at different stages of learning to read or whether they are reading for different purposes. As suggested below, some methods and materials are better than others, but there seems to be no "best" method for all children learning to read.

TEACHING IDENTIFICATION
AND RECOGNITION

All methods of instruction mentioned above give considerable place to learning to recognize symbols. In essence, the reading act is divisible into two processes: (1) identifying the symbol, and (2) obtaining meaning from the recognized symbol. Without both processes, the reading act is incomplete. When a child is beginning to read, the teacher's main task is to assist him to identify and recognize letters, syllables, words, phrases, and perhaps even short sentences. This twofold identification-recognition process may involve meaning. Most students of linguistics feel they can describe language adequately without reference to meaning, but this approach seems incomplete in a reading situation which assumes communication of ideas from author to reader. Meaning can assist identification-recognition and vice versa, but there is no one-to-one relationship between them (Betts, 1953). Taylor (1958) discovered that recognition of nonsense syllables was not enhanced by arbitrary association with meaningful pictures. J. A. Holmes (1953) suggested that word discrimination, word sense, and span of recognition contribute 56 per cent of the variance in speed and power of reading, while factors such as vocabulary-in-context, intelligence, and perception of verbal relationships may account for 77 per cent of the variance in power of reading. It can be seen that the relationship of meaning to recognition is far from clear. A number of writers have suggested that an empathetic response to a symbol establishes meaning and a stimulus-response connection establishes recognition (I. H. Anderson & Dearborn, 1952).

The identification-recognition process is further complicated by the sensory approaches used to establish it. It is possible that all identification-recognition is multisensory. But the relative influence of sight, hearing, touch, smell, and taste, in the production of percepts for identification and recognition, is difficult to measure. The influence of one avenue of learning as compared with another

alters with the situation and the learner (Dvorine, 1958), although emphasis on one sensory modality in the reading process is implicit in such labels as "Sight Words" and "Phonic Method." Diverse as such labels indicate it to be, the learning process may proceed without the multisensory approach to identification-recognition and meaning: "After he goes to school the bulk of the child's vocabulary is learned without any handling or smelling or seeing at all" (LaBrant, 1949, p. 15).

In perceptual learning, not only the relative importance of the senses, but also the organization which leads to perception—and thus to identification and recognition—is not clearly understood. D. H. Russell (1956, p. 66) stated: "It is not a simple case of sensation plus past experience, but rather the result of sensory processes organizing themselves in some fashion in the cerebral cortex into an experience variable." Various writers have suggested three stages in the development of a percept: (1) vague response to the general situation, (2) analysis of the situation with some elaboration of sensory elements, (3) synthesis of the sensory elements to form a new pattern or percept. It has been suggested that perception is like a flashlight in a dark room—at any one time it can select but a small portion of the environment. When a child begins to read, the recognition process may require his whole attention, but as he gains proficiency, the recognition process may shift to a subcortical level of performance (Dvorine, 1958). Other than the brief explanation offered in this paragraph, theories of perception and cortical organization are beyond the province of this chapter: An examination of the relation of various senses to reading is more relevant to research on the teaching of reading.

Visual Perception

For a physiological exploration of visual perception, the reader is referred to J. A. Holmes (1957). Others may differ in detail, but Holmes's theory concerning the work of the brain in the discrimination and appraisal of symbolic meanings seems to agree in principle with the work of other modern writers such as D. E. P. Smith (1958), who developed the synaptic transmission theory of perception, and Gilbert (1959a, 1959b), whose work on the after-image and memory-after-image appears to support Smith's theory. Though we will not discuss the nature of visual perception itself, we will consider two aspects of it: (1) visual perception in reading, and (2) development of visual perception in the child.

In considering visual perception in reading, some psychologists have attempted to classify perceivers, or perception, others have formulated psychological theories of perception, and still others have attempted to discover what the reader sees of print which enables him first to identify it and later to recognize it.

Among those who attempted to classify perceivers were M. C. Petty (1939), Goins (1958), and D. E. P. Smith (1958). Petty, from a study of eidetic imagery and susceptibility to illusion, concluded that children who had high reading but low drawing ability exercised a highly synthetic method of perception. Children who had high drawing but low reading ability succeeded in drawing because of attention to detail, but did not succeed in reading because they were inconsistent in selecting detail. She believed that such children used a highly analytic method of perception. She classified perceivers, in agreement with previous investigations, as subjective readers (who recognized words from total character) and objective readers (who recognized words from details). Goins, from observations of how children studied picture squares, believed that some children looked at the pictures as wholes, while other children matched details to determine similarities in pictures. This conclusion agreed with Petty's. The work of Rudisill (1956) on differences in recognition rate for flashed digits and flashed phrases added further confirmation. Smith classified children in placid, hyperactive, and alexic groups. The placid child sees letters clearly but cannot shift atten-

tion rapidly enough to blend the unfolding sequence of letters into a word. The hyperactive child can blend easily, but his attention remains on each stimulus letter for such a short time that it makes no impression. The alexic group has both difficulties. Smith believed that his classification reflected differences in the amount of cholinesterase present in the neurons of the perceiver.

Goins (1958) attempted to classify perception rather than perceivers. On the hypothesis that perception is a primary mental ability, she sought to determine the relationship between competence in visual perception and reading achievement in first-grade children. By use of a variety of visual perception tests and intercorrelational techniques, she identified a general factor of visual perception related to reading. Further, she identified two components: (1) ability to hold in mind a perceptual Gestalt during rapid (timed or forced) perception (She noted that this had been designated in previous studies as "speed of perception," and that it called for simple discriminations of likenesses and differences.); and (2) ability to keep in mind a configuration against distraction (This component she termed "strength of closure."). Goins stated that if more discriminating measures had been available, "strength of closure" might have been differentiated into (a) strength of closure and (b) facility in achieving closure in an unorganized field.

Perhaps we should conclude that whether perceivers or perception can be placed in separate classes remains to be proven and that, in agreement with Betts (1953), Vernon (1959), and Fleming (1959), the process of perception in reading is extremely complex— the stimulus of the visual form of the written word is but a small part of the total stimulus situation.

Before it is possible to consider what the reader sees of print which leads to the identification-recognition process, we must consider some theories of perception. One issue is whether individuals see by "whole" or by "parts," although some writers have indicated a belief that the processes are not dichotomous. The "wholes" view, or Gestaltist theory of perception, was endorsed by Goins (1958) and A. J. Harris (1956). (Implicit in Harris' discussion of a child's omission of detail is the probability that the child does not see the detail.) Coleman (1953), perhaps the strongest proponent of the Gestaltist view, claimed that perception has its own sequence of ontogenetic development—from perception of the crude whole through differentiation of details to integration of the differentiated parts into an articulate whole.

Morris (1959) questioned the validity of applying Gestalt principles of perception to reading. She claimed, with justification, that the "meaningful whole" of the Gestaltist did not apply to a written word but to human experience, that many Gestaltists tended to demonstrate phenomena rather than conduct rigorous research, and that if the tendency to perceive "wholes" did apply to words, it would prove a source of confusion in learning to read. I. H. Anderson and Dearborn (1952) suggested that stimulus-response psychology might offer a more valid explanation of perception in reading. The possibility that both "whole" and "parts" serve as perceptual cues for the identification-recognition process seems to be implied by Vernon (1959, p. 3): "Nevertheless, it is clear that some aspect of the word and its letters must be perceived, if only in skeleton fashion, before the remainder of the word, and of the other words in the sentence not directly perceived, can be inferred."

From this brief consideration of theories of perception as they apply to reading, we may next proceed to consider what the reader sees of print which makes possible the identification-recognition process. Here, during the past decade, there have been excellent summaries and interpretations of research (I. H. Anderson & Dearborn, 1952; W. S. Gray, 1956, 1960; Morris, 1959). Theories of perception as applied to reading form the basis for classification here. The broadest and most popular classification is the "analytic-synthetic" which parallels the "whole-parts" classification in perception. The term *analytic* is used to refer to methods of perception which begin with recognition of wholes as units of meaning from which their elements may be analyzed: the story method, sentence method, phrase method, and word method. The term *synthetic* is used to refer to methods of perception which build to a recognition of wholes from the constituent parts: the alphabet method, phonic method, syllable method. The question to be answered at all times is: What cues are used by the reader for his perception? The following discussion of the various methods is necessarily brief, and the reader is referred to the four summaries listed above for thorough consideration of the research.

Synthetic-letter. This includes alphabet methods and phonic methods. I. H. Anderson and Dearborn (1952) thoroughly considered the research in this area. Their review included studies on the legibility of different letters of the alphabet, the dominant features of letters which determine their perceptive weight, the determining letters (ascenders and descenders), and the position of letters in a word. Anderson and Dearborn emphasized that most of the research was done with adults and was concerned with controlled rapid-exposure perception. One example of research in this area is that of Berger (1956), who demonstrated that the distance threshold of word recognition (distance between eye and word) is equal to the mean distance threshold of recognition of the constituent letters. This finding would seem to show that the reader uses all the letters of the word as cues to recognition.

Synthetic-groups of letters. This method includes the use of syllables, affixes, double letters, small known parts of words, and small words within larger unknown words. Again, Anderson and Dearborn (1952) have provided an excellent summary. They quoted research to show that the first part of the word has the most influence in recognition and that known syllables or parts in long words may be misleading as well as helpful. Thus, Miller, Bruner, and Postman (1954) concluded that the number of letters perceived correctly by tachistoscopic exposure was not a measure of the amount of information received from the exposure since such a measure failed to include redundancy. They indicated, further, that if the redundancy factor could be controlled, identification scores for familiar and unfamiliar sequences of letters would be equivalent. This seems to indicate that the reader does not see by groups of letters but by individual letters. Morris (1959) implied a similar conclusion by her assertion that the chief weakness of synthetic methods lay in the inability of the reader to synthesize, not in his inability to recognize or sound individual letters.

Analytic-words. Here the word shape is the cue to perception. Morris (1959) and W. S. Gray (1960) summarized research in this area. Research by Solomon and Postman (1952) appeared to add proof that frequency of usage of words reduces the recognition threshold for them and thus indicates that the "pattern" is the perceptual unit. Forgays (1953) arrived at similar conclusions. Morris (1959), while endorsing findings of research on "word" methods, warned that whole-word methods should precede synthetic methods, because synthetic methods require greater maturity in the pupil. Further, she criticized the exclusive use of the word method and suggested that probably teachers do not use it in the pure form recommended by some investigators. Finally, she suggested that word methods were not intended to replace other methods but merely to introduce the learning of reading to the pupil. Mention should be made here of perceptual or reading methods which seem at first to be neither analytic nor synthetic, but which, on further examination can be seen to fall in one of these general classifications. Two examples are the "non-oral method" (McDade, 1937) and the "film" method (McCracken, 1954); both of these are word methods.

Analytic-phrases. W. S. Gray (1956) expounded this method, emphasizing the value to the reader of perceiving several words or a "thought-unit" as a unit. If a "thought-unit" is considered as the goal, this heading would include phrases, sentences, and larger units such as paragraphs or stories. Perhaps the work of Forgays (1953), indicating decrease in recognition threshold for certain positions of words in peripheral vision, would serve as evidence for such "thought-unit" reading. If this is true, training in extending the field of vision might assist the child in learning to read.

Multiple factor. Few writers would suggest the exclusive use of any one method. W. S. Gray (1956) used the term *eclectic* to designate various combinations in which meaning and context supplemented various combinations of the methods considered above. Morris (1959) and D. H. Russell (1944) found teachers using and recommending various combinations to produce multiple-factor methods. Sparks and Fay (1957) concluded, from experimenting with two teaching methods, that exclusive use of any one method is probably unwise.

Development of visual perception. The second aspect of visual perception to be considered in this chapter is the development of visual perception in the child. I. H. Anderson and Dearborn (1952), Vernon (1959), and Morris (1959) have written excellent interpretations of research on the development of perception in children. Three factors of perceptual development are pertinent to reading: (1) shape or pattern, (2) orientation, (3) sequential order. The following discussion will be limited to these three factors.

As suggested by Morris (1959), visual discrimination of object shape must precede discrimination of symbol shape, but this subject has not been adequately investigated. There is some evidence that children can perceive simple pictures and differentiate simple geometric shapes by the time they are two years old. But to copy a simple outline of a geometric shape does not seem possible for a child until he is five. This sequential development from object to picture, to shape, to word, has been accomplished before the child can recognize words, but little is known of this process. Malter (1948), in his experiments with children interpreting diagramatic materials, emphasized that children's ability to identify pictured objects has not been investigated. Dolch (1946) stressed the need to teach children to read pictures, suggesting that at first only the familiar is seen in a picture. McCracken (1954), experimenting with the use of films in teaching reading to school children, used projected pictures and words. His use of life-size pictures may have helped the children make the transition from reality to the symbol. Feldman, Merrill, and MacGinitie (1960) have suggested making the transition from reality to the picture by the use of three-dimensional color transparencies. There is some evidence that the ability of a child to recognize a shape as a whole depends upon the "goodness" of that shape. (This may be another way of inferring his familiarity with the variations of such a shape.) If it is not possible for him to recognize the symbol from general shape, he may, instead, recognize a dominant detail or details. This development seems to conform to the idea that there are certain "dominant" letters in a word, as discussed by I. H. Anderson and Dearborn (1952). A. J. Harris (1956) felt that perception of detail follows perception of the general shape. Vernon (1959) concluded that perhaps length, outline, and the presence of dominant detail are all of use in visual perception of the child. Although Vernon did not suggest that development follows that sequence, the research of others seems to indicate that it does. Hill's (1936) study of errors in word discrimination of children beginning to read produced evidence that general shape and the beginnings and ends of words provided the majority of cues.

It has been suggested that skills in discrimination should be taught (H. M. Robinson, 1958, 1959). Vernon (1958), however, questioned the desirability of "readiness" activities, because research has not demonstrated their value in learning to distinguish letters and words. She held that children cannot infer the course of action in a picture until they are nine or ten years of age.

All investigations to date agree that children find orientation of shape very difficult.

Primarily, the child confuses a word or letter with its mirror image. Thus, Potter (1949) showed that mirror-error in perception correlated negatively with reading readiness.

The sequential order of shapes—the letters in a word—is another source of difficulty for children. Vernon (1959) considered this kind of discrimination more difficult than orientation. Again, this skill may not be well developed until the child is nine or ten years of age. Hill (1936) indicated that when letters and configurations or words remained the same, differences in the order of letters gave rise to a large number of errors.

Evidence on how and when children perceive words and letters has been limited to studies of the errors in word-recognition made by children with some schooling (Hill, 1936). However, it is common knowledge that children are letter-conscious at an early age, as shown by their attempts to trace or write upper-case letters of the alphabet. One study (Nicholson, 1958) used matching of upper- and lower-case letters as indications of reading readiness. Studies have demonstrated that children distinguish words by length, by general shape, and by arresting detail (Hill, 1936). The consensus seems to be that general shape is the first clue, although some studies have cast doubt upon the existence of a sequential order of perceptual clues. All writers on the subject agree that children should profit from instruction in sequence convention—the left-to-right direction of reading. Stevenson and Robinson (1953) experimented with hand preference in children in Grades 1 and 2 and concluded that teachers must give practice to children in left-to-right movements to insure this habit. Burton and Richards (1949) suggested the use of a limited number of alphabetic letters for beginning reading, selected to avoid orientation confusion. In general, investigators are divided on the value of perceptual training per se, but agree that training in the shape orientation and sequence of words and letters should be of value. Such conclusions are a far cry from those of Meriam (1930), who believed that environment and motivation were all that a teacher needed to provide to teach reading.

Auditory Perception

The reader is referred once again to J. A. Holmes (1957) for a physiological explanation of auditory perception, together with an explanation of the dimensions of hearing which has been given fully in several sources (e.g., Miller, 1951). Two aspects of auditory perception will be discussed: (1) auditory perception in reading, and (2) development of auditory perception in the child.

A number of excellent evaluations of research are available on the relationship between reading and listening (Berg, 1955; Witty & Sizemore, 1958, 1959). It is generally agreed that reading and listening ability are closely related—two skills which contain from 30 to 80 per cent of a general language ability; a number of studies have shown listening and reading ability to be related to such factors as intelligence and age. (There is no reading ability to compare with listening ability when the child is very young, but ability to learn through either medium is equal in the intermediate grades for certain conditions and materials. In adults, reading ability is probably greater.) However, listening ability is difficult to measure, so that many of the studies contradict other studies. Fiedler (1949) found that primary-grade children with hearing loss had difficulty in reading, spelling, and phonics. Other investigators showed similar relationships between reading and listening in children of different ages (Durrell & Murphy, 1953). Reynolds (1953) found no relationship between auditory abilities and reading at the fourth-grade level. Blewett (1951) found only a moderate relationship between listening comprehension and reading comprehension among university students, but J. D. Young (1953) reported greater gains in reading vocabulary scores by university students who practiced reading materials aloud than by those who listened only. Perhaps part of the reason for the conflict in results was revealed by Poling (1953). She found that in poor readers 8 through 13 years of age auditory acuity and word discrimination were not related; auditory memory span and word discrimination were not related; but when auditory factors (auditory acuity and memory span) were treated as related rather than discrete, they had a significant relationship to word discrimination. It may be that different investigators are exploring different elements of auditory discrimination.

Turning to the part which auditory perception plays in the learning of reading, we might well examine, first, auditory perception versus visual perception. It is safe to state that the role of auditory perception is a minor one since, in theory at least, it is possible to see, to recognize, and to understand (i.e., to go through the complete reading process) without auditory perception, but reading without visual perception is a negation of the term. Duggins (1958), in considering the relative contribution of the two kinds of perception, stated that together the two become the basis for comprehension of ideas in reading. She believed that both the mechanics and meaning of reading must be complete before vocal production is possible, and that auditory perception makes possible discrimination and generalization before the sound pattern of the visual symbol becomes a percept. Others differ with this view. The work of J. D. Young (1953), referred to previously, indicated that university students who vocalized tended to gain more than those who read silently. A. J. Harris (1956) suggested that listening ability can be used as a potential of reading ability, but other investigators have indicated that reading ability is superior to listening ability in adults. The latter finding seems to agree with that of Duggins.

Since there is lack of agreement on the relative contribution of auditory and visual discrimination to reading, the two could be considered in relation to the task of the beginner in learning to read. Here, the two have not yet become fused, since the visual stimuli for words have not yet developed. Duggins (1958), adhering to her theory of auditory perception and reading, was firm in her contention that auditory images must precede visual. She stated that in the beginning stages of learning to read, the learner should listen and not look, as auditory images must come first and visual images will interfere with formation of clear auditory images. It is, she claimed, wrong to believe that beginning reading is based on speech; rather, she believed, it is based on listening. To support her contention, she explained that the child's imitations in speech are not necessarily synonymous with those he has heard, and that, although it is possible for a child to produce all of the sounds of a language from a very early age, the sight-sound association may prove very difficult for him. She maintained that the child must learn "to listen to print" rather than to people: Vocal responses should be held to a minimum, and the child should be directed to listen.

H. M. Robinson (1955) agreed with Duggins in holding that auditory discrimination is necessary for early success in reading. She stated that auditory discrimination appears basic to success with phonics and that the influence of auditory and visual discrimination together is greater than that of intelligence in learning to read. Hildreth (1954) took a more moderate position than Duggins. Although the two writers might agree on the relative value of auditory perception, they differed in their application of auditory discrimination. Hildreth stated that the visual form and context usually supply the word for the reader, but if they do not, the reader can pronounce the sounds of the letters. She believed that clues make recognition of the word possible to the reader by the process known as "clang association." Hildreth stated, further, that blending the individual sounds provides a more valid auditory stimulus, but that some children cannot blend. Research by Lantz (1956) revealed a factor which might account for difficulty in blending—the possibility that individuals listen either to the content of a speech or to the method of delivery and that concentration on one causes decreased perception of the other. It is possible that the

child, concentrating on hearing the sounds of the separate letters, cannot hear the blend of letters, and that because he does not hear it, he cannot produce it. Generalizing still further (in perception), we might conclude that the child who concentrates on visual perception cannot attend to auditory perception. (Duggins would agree with this.) According to results of many studies, however, use of more than one avenue of perception increases learning (J. D. Young, 1953); hence, it seems that, if a proper balance of attention can be maintained, cumulative learning is possible.

Results of tests of reading and listening are positively correlated. An investigation of common factors in vocabulary (I. H. Anderson & Fairbanks, 1937) yielded such a correlation. As reading requires visual and auditory discrimination, comparison will always reveal some degree of positive relationship. Studies of visual recognition of words have generally agreed that length of word per se is not a factor in word recognition. Apparently the same can be said of auditory recognition, according to F. J. Holmes (1934). Further, comparison of visual and auditory discrimination after practice in identification led Postman and Rosenzweig (1957) to conclude that prior training improves recognition for either sense, but that the transfer effects from visual training to auditory recognition are more pronounced than the converse. This indicates that auditory discrimination may be present as part of visual discrimination, but that the converse is not possible.

Auditory perception may be present in reading in the following degrees, though there is no research to support such a rank order.

(1) The learner hears sounds uttered by others.
(2) The learner hears sounds self-uttered.
(3) The learner hears blends of sounds self-uttered.
(4) The reader vocalizes—to use visual and auditory cues.
(5) The reader subvocalizes—(reduction of auditory cues).

(6) There is no measurable vocalization but a trace remains in all reading as an auditory cue.

At this point we shall consider what the reader "hears" of print which aids the identification-recognition process. Summaries and interpretations have been made by I. H. Anderson and Dearborn (1952), Witty (1953), Witty and Sizemore (1958, 1959), and Morris (1958). In terms of the analytic-synthetic classification, the use of names or sounds of letters (or groups of letters) as auditory perception clues in reading is synthetic and is usually subsumed under the title of "phonics." Discussion of auditory perception clues in a whole-word or analytic method is rare.

The alphabet methods. I. H. Anderson and Dearborn (1952) discussed the historical significance of alphabet methods, concluding that such techniques of word analysis might be admirable as methods of spelling, but that ability to spell words should not antedate ability to read words. There is fairly widespread endorsement of this view that letter names provide a poor basis for word identification and recognition, but a minority opinion has been voiced by Daniels and Diack (1959), who contended that an alphabetic letter is a written instruction to the reader, and that sequence of letters indicates time-order for sounds. Teaching "the meaning of letters" rather than the meaning of words is a novel approach. Daniels and Diack suggested further that reading is the process of converting the "undifferentiated whole" into the "differentiated whole."

Support for the practice of teaching the names of the letters and their sounds, though not necessarily for the theory expounded by Daniels and Diack, is provided by studies by Linehan (1958) and Nicholson (1958) and interpretation by Durrell and Palos (1956). These investigators concluded that most difficulties which pupils develop in learning to read could have been prevented by early instruction in letter names and sounds, and that tests of letter names made with children entering school predict later reading ability. It is possible, as suggested by H. M. Robinson (1959), that uncontrolled variables such as teacher enthusiasm were responsible for such results; that is, the teacher's impression of the child who knows the alphabet leads him to approve more of all the child's efforts from then on. It would seem more fruitful to inquire into home situations which caused some children to learn the names of the letters and their sounds.

Phonics methods. In phonics methods, the sounds of single letters or groups of letters are auditory clues to word identification-recognition. Probably more has been written on phonics in the past five years than on any other aspect of the teaching of reading. The resulting volume of literature is enormous, selection is difficult, condensation is imperative, and organization arbitrary. The present writers justify their selection from the literature as representative, their condensation as method-oriented, and their organization— according to the "why, when, where, what, and how" of phonics—as convenient.

Why teach phonics? Justification is found in opinion, practice, and research. D. H. Russell (1955) obtained the opinions of teachers on a number of issues on teaching phonics. The replies left no doubt that teachers believe phonics to be a necessary part of the reading program. Since 98 per cent of the teachers indicated that they taught phonics, they apparently practiced what they believed. Further evidence of practice was revealed in investigations of teaching methods by Morris (1958), who found that all teachers in 60 primary schools in Kent, England, were giving phonic instruction.

The many "phonics versus whole-word" experiments in teaching have contained uncontrolled variables. Experiments designed to determine the relative effectiveness of different amounts of phonics, or the value of phonics at different maturational levels, have been more successful. Gates and Russell (1938) investigated word analysis factors in beginning readers in New York. They concluded that a program containing little or no phonetic analysis was not as good as one which contained moderate amounts of informal word analysis. On the other hand, a program containing moderate amounts of informal word analysis was better than one containing substantial amounts of drill-type phonics. Tate, Herbert, and Zeman (1940) used methods of instruction which differed slightly from those of Gates and Russell, but their results were substantially the same. Agnew (1939), working with primary school children in North Carolina, obtained inconclusive results: Large amounts of phonic training seemed detrimental in Grades 1 and 2, but beneficial in Grades 1 and 3. Agnew performed a later experiment with a similar group and concluded that large amounts of phonics were beneficial. Tiffin and McKinnis (1940) correlated the reading ability and phonetic ability of children in Grades 5–8 and concluded that phonic knowledge is of value in reading (the correlation coefficients were positive, varying from .5 to .7) and thus, that moderate amounts of phonics should be taught in elementary grades. Results of other studies have agreed with those of Tiffin and McKinnis (Mulder & Curtin, 1956; Rudisill, 1957). Perhaps it can be concluded that, although differences in maturity level of subjects and in method of presentation produce great variations in results, knowledge of moderate amounts of phonics is helpful in reading.

When should phonics be taught? Readiness for phonics has been the subject of much opinion and some research. Linehan (1958), Nicholson (1958), and Durrell and Palos (1956) favored early instruction in letter sounds and names, suggesting that it would prevent most reading difficulties. H. M. Robinson (1958) questioned such findings. Dolch and Bloomster (1937), in a study of the relationship of phonics and mental ability, concluded that higher mental ability was required to apply phonic principles than to memorize sight words. Children with a mental age below seven failed in tests of phonic ability. From a study of 220 experienced teachers in 33 different states, D. H. Russell (1955) found that many teachers believed that phonics should be emphasized in Grades 2 and 3—24 per cent favored emphasis in Grades 1 and 2, and 36 per cent favored emphasis in Grades 2 and 3. Morris (1958) concluded, in a review of research, that for normal children, phonics should be deferred to the second or third grade, and that for children of high intelligence and good cultural background, phonics in an earlier grade seemed appropriate, although research here is meager.

Where should phonics be taught? Few investigators would disagree that: (1) phonics should be part of the thought-getting process of reading; and (2) phonics should be but one of the word-recognition techniques known and used by the pupil. Research by Gates and Russell (1938) and Tate, Herbert, and Zeman (1940), previously referred to, indicates that isolated drill is inferior to phonics which is intrinsic to the reading process. Teacher statements (D. H. Russell, 1955) indicated that the majority of teachers: (1) do not use separate phonic workbooks; (2) do teach phonics as one of a group of word-attack skills, and (3) do relate phonic instruction directly to the reading program through the use of teachers' manuals of a basal reader series.

Perhaps the words of Burrows (1951, p. 9) best express the feeling of most educators: "Apparently, only *if* phonics teaching is part and parcel of the thought-getting activity, only *if* the phonetic analysis is an immediate means to an immediate end, is it helpful to children ...."

What phonics should be taught? Research to discover what phonic elements are of most value to pupils is rare. Oaks (1952) listed vowels and vowel combinations in primary basal readers and indicated the levels at which they began to appear frequently in the text. Further, she listed eight phonetic rules for primary-grade readers. Opinion and experience are valuable guides. It is safe to assume that elements such as the sound of *a* in "cat" will be of great value, and that the sound of *ough* in "dough" represents the point of extremely diminished returns. W. S. Gray (1948) noted phonetic elements to be taught and established a sequence for teaching them. A. J. Harris (1956, p. 351) compiled a refined list of elements to be taught.

How should phonics be taught? Studies of different methods of teaching phonics are also rare and have frequently been conducted by enthusiastic proponents of one of the methods. Fundamental differences between the methods have seldom been explored; rather, comparisons of mere superficialities have usually been undertaken. Although the categories are somewhat arbitrary, it appears to the present writers that phonic methods might be classified as follows.

(1) The traditional method. This method uses an individual-letter sound and then a blend as an approach to word synthesis. The approach is deductive; that is, the teacher presents the new phonic element, asks the child to pronounce it, uses it in a nonsense blend or three-letter word, and then transfers it to words. Hay and Wingo (1948) adapted this approach, emphasizing that attack in pronunciation must always be through the initial blend. An initial blend is a "combination of one or more consonants with a vowel at the beginning of a word or syllable, such as *ca* in *catch,* or *thi* in *thick,* that, when pronounced together and added to the remaining letters of the word or syllable, enable the pupil to determine the pronunciation" (Good, 1945, p. 47).

(2) The blend method. Here, the child is taught to recognize blends rather than individual-letter sounds. Blends are more difficult to recognize than individual letters, but the resultant sounds more closely approximate the sound of the word. Thus, Cordts (1953) suggested that the word "sand" should be sounded "sa"..."nd" rather than "s - a - n - d."

(3) The multiple-sense method. This method emphasizes speech, listening, kinesthetics, or a combination of these. Durrell, Sullivan, and Murphy (1945) began with the sound elements of the child's spoken vocabulary, gradually transferring them to the visual form. An even more ambitious approach was used by McCrory and Watts (1947), who held that the perceptual skills of speech, vision, hearing, and feeling are interrelated in word-recognition activities. The "phonic-word" method of Daniels and Diack (1959) is the most recent. Workbooks were written to conform to graded phonic complexity, and a constant relationship was established between visual and sound symbol. Daniels and Diack explained that other methods led to "part-seeing" and "whole-saying" which resulted in many errors. Therefore, their program taught the child to see and obtain meaning from each letter of every word and thus to recognize the "differentiated whole" from the "undifferentiated whole."

(4) Chart method. Although it may be inappropriate, the term *chart method* refers to those phonic systems which begin with classifications into syllables, series of prefixes, phonic charts, phonic designs, etc. One classification of phonetics is Dolch's (1945). He used five categories: (1) single-letter sound combinations, (2) two-letter sound combinations, (3) helpful-letter sound combinations, i.e., combinations which are not essential but do assist the reader—*ng* being an example, (4) rules, and (5) syllables. There are more elaborate plans in which phonograph recordings, charts, colored sticks of wood with phonic elements printed on them, etc., are employed.

(5) Basal-reader method. Under this method, the phonetic element is always introduced in the context of a reading lesson, and instruction is always inductive. In manuals which accompany basal readers, editors inform teachers when pupils have met at least three words containing a phonetic element and when the fourth word containing such an element is to be introduced. The teacher expects pupils to know the three sight words, and expects to assist the pupils in generalizing from the presence of the phonetic element in known sight words. An example of such an approach is that of McCullough (1955).

From the research on phonics, some useful

generalizations can be made. One list which may prove of value to research workers evaluating methods is that of D. H. Russell (1961):

(1) Phonetic analysis is only one of several good methods of word recognition. . . .
(2) A program of phonetic analysis must be intrinsic [to the total program of instruction]. . . .
(3) Readiness for phonetic analysis must be established as for other reading activities. . . .
(4) Since phonics is a series of generalizations about words, the teacher will teach inductively. . . .
(5) Teachers must plan carefully when they will introduce word-analysis techniques into a lesson. . . .
(6) Lessons should be designed so that children have a chance to practice and synthesize various methods of recognizing new words. . . .
(7) Teachers should have a systematic approach in teaching the use of phonetic analysis (D. H. Russell, 1961, pp. 309–312).

Whole-word methods. The "look-and-say" approach has been used widely for many years. In general, the pupil is supposed to concentrate upon the visual aspects of the word and simultaneously listen as the teacher pronounces the word. In theory, audio-visual perception clues should result. Following the "look-and-listen" phase, the pupil concentrates upon the visual aspects of the word while he pronounces it aloud. Whether this is the response to the original audio-visual stimulus, or to a later audio-visual stimulus (in that the child can hear his own pronunciation) or both, has not been determined. Duggins (1958) holds the first view; Hildreth (1954), the second. Descriptions of the method, with slight variations, are to be found in most modern basal-reader manuals.

Development of auditory perception. The second aspect of auditory perception to be considered in this chapter is development of auditory perception in the child. In summarizing and interpreting research on the development of auditory perception, Witty and Sizemore (1958, 1959) considered research comparing development of auditory and visual perception. It is common knowledge that from a very early age children learn through auditory perception. The characteristics of the development of such early auditory perception have not been investigated. In part, this may be due to the lack of research on picture interpretation by children (Malter, 1948). If the picture is not used as a visual symbol, in comparison with the spoken word as an aural symbol, research must wait until the child can utilize written words as visual symbols.

In general, there are indications, from rather meager evidence, that (1) auditory perception develops at a rate comparable to visual perception; (2) auditory perception is an important prerequisite for learning to read; and (3) auditory memory is used to a greater extent than visual memory in younger children, but before adolescence visual memory becomes dominant. Evidence for such tentative conclusions is found in studies by R. D. Russell (1928), who discovered that resultant retention is increased if material is read to pupils in the fifth grade, but that pupils in the ninth grade retain more after reading the material themselves. Investigation by W. E. Young (1936) produced results which agreed in principle with those of Russell. Evidence that auditory perception is a prerequisite for reading is to be found in a study by Harrington and Durrell (1955) which showed that auditory and visual discrimination and phonic ability are more important than mental age for learning to read.

Kinesthetic Perception

It is recognized that the movement of the eyes and the vocal cords in reading also produces kinesthetic stimuli and percepts, but with reference to learning to read, the term has been restricted historically to percepts resulting from (or to some extent the result of) movements of the hand and arm in writing or drawing. One aspect of kinesthetic perception will be discussed here: kinesthetic perception in reading. It is usually considered secondary to visual and auditory perception, and will be discussed only briefly.

The chief proponents of the kinesthetic method of teaching reading were Fernald and Keller (1921) and Schonell (1951). The "Fernald method" consisted of having the child write a word in sand from a copy while saying the word aloud. Thus, the child learned through visual perception, auditory perception, and kinesthetic perception. Fernald believed that all children could profit from such a method of learning to read.

Other investigators and educators believed that the kinesthetic method should be reserved for those who could not learn to read through visual and auditory perception. Roberts and Coleman (1958), investigating the role of kinesthetic factors in reading failures, showed that those who fail have poor visual perception and are helped by kinesthetic learning, but that normal readers do not get help from kinesthetic experience. H. M. Robinson (1948) pointed out that children who lack visual efficiency will not be able to distinguish likenesses and differences in pictures and forms and suggested that teachers use a kinesthetic approach. French (1953) devised a test for kinesthetic recognition—a maze of different shapes for children 8 to 10 years of age who were having difficulty with reading. French concluded that children retarded in oral reading, where the retardation could not be attributed to known extrinsic or intrinsic factors, were inferior in kinesthetic recognition. He suggested that kinesthetic recognition may be related to the normal process of learning to read.

In a summary of research, Morris (1958) stated that kinesthetic methods reinforced other sensory impressions of words, developed consistent left-to-right direction in reading, and encouraged careful and systematic observation. However, she criticized exclusive use of such methods because they do not provide an independent word-recognition technique, they develop arm and lip movements hampering later speed and fluency progress in reading, and they require individualized instruction. Eberl (1953, p. 143) stated: "We find that the child begins to build his world close about him. He uses his mouth, his eyes, and his hands for this purpose and in that order." While Morris and Eberl acknowledged the value of kinesthetic factors in learning, they doubted their usefulness in learning to read. It is possible that kinesthetic approaches should be used by teachers only when concrete objects are involved. When a kinesthetic method is employed with symbols, it may encourage visual and auditory attention—or it may detract from them by dividing the child's attention. Further, tracing the outline of an object in a picture may impress the sensation of a slick surface rather than the shape of the object itself. The same question can be raised relative to the use of kinesthetic factors with any form of symbolization.

Multisensory Perception

In reality, there can be no single sensory approach to reading for normal children since visual perception in oral reading always involves a degree of auditory perception. The methods of teaching reading which we have considered up to this point were designed to stress learning to read through one sense. On the other hand, the "experience approaches" to reading were designed deliberately to use several of the senses.

In the experience approaches, a common, shared experience is used as a means of introducing children to reading matter. The most extensive discussion of the principles and methods involved is to be found in Lamoreaux and Lee (1943), and an excellent criticism appears in I. H. Anderson and Dearborn (1952). The experience approaches were designed to emphasize meaning in reading rather than identification-recognition, but the two are related, and any use of such methods involves some degree of learning of identification-recognition.

The experience approaches involve four steps: (1) sharing an experience (a meaningful activity), (2) discussing the experience (oral language), (3) dictating the experience story (written language), (4) reading the experience story (reading). Thus, this approach makes clear to the child how the material gets written and what its relationship is to reality. Anderson and Dearborn (1952) believed that the chief value of such an approach lies in the formation of a context (experience) to enable the reader to test his attempts at word recognition and interpretation of reading material. They warned, however, that this is not reading—that it is, instead, a meaningful approach to reading. Some identification-recognition is involved, but the great variety of words and the small amount of repetition required create a situation that does not provide the practice necessary to memorize symbols. Finally, they estimated that an experience method is probably the most popular means of initiating children into an understanding of the meaning of the reading process.

As a method of teaching reading per se, the experience method is an extension of the sentence method and requires provision for word repetition to build identification-recognition. It also requires some provision for limiting the range of vocabulary involved (Lamoreaux & Lee, 1943).

Justification for the experience approach to reading is found in the theoretical position that (1) sense organs and nervous system are stimulated from a number of sources simultaneously so that children react to patterns of sensations, and (2) concepts are percepts with greater organization, including sensation, images, and a name. Further justification is to be found in experimental results of Bradley (1956) and Dice (1942). Bradley compared two methods of preparing children for reading—the control, where children were introduced early to reading, versus the experimental, which provided a stimulating environment, materials for various types of activity, and situations relating language to experience. According to Bradley, by the end of the third year the experimental group equalled the control group in reading ability and surpassed it in word-study skills, basic language skills, and basic arithmetic skills. The experiment by Dice (1942) seems at first

to contradict that of Bradley. Dice matched readiness, as usually taught in schools, against immediate teaching and found that immediate teaching was of greater value in teaching reading. However, the immediate teaching was actually a closely knit sequence of experiences with reality, leading through pictures to words. Thus, the results supported the experience approach and perhaps indicated the need for a method of teaching for greater transfer in such an approach. The research of others (Almy, 1949; Fast, 1957) supports that of Bradley by showing that children with kindergarten experience had greater success in first-grade reading. Readiness research (e.g., Welshinger, 1948) provides further support.

In short, with regard to identification-recognition and the experience approach to reading, it appears that the main job of the teacher is to help the child supply the label or symbol for the real object or experience and then to assist him to recognize that label when he meets it again.

Implications for Teaching and Research

From this discussion of perception, perhaps a few generalizations and suggestions relative to pupils and the identification-recognition process are in order.

Visual perception. There is no doubt that visual perception is learned; therefore teachers can assist pupils in learning such perception. However, opinion is divided on the value of learning through perception of other than printed symbols.

As to the perception of objects, if Petty (1939) and others are right in their classifications of perceivers, tests of ability to draw might guide teachers in determining which children would learn best from an analytic approach to reading and which would learn best from a synthetic approach. If A. J. Harris (1956) is right in his contention that children look at general characteristics of objects and tend to ignore detail, teachers can arrange the environment so that important detail becomes the center of attention. Since the child will see what he is prepared to see, the teacher must prepare him to see what the teacher wants him to see by telling him what to look for in his observation. Perhaps removal of distractions in the perceptual field or intensification of essential features would lead to more efficient perception. Use of such items as felt boards and opaque projectors may help focus attention but cannot be classed as methods.

As to the perception of pictures, some research in art indicates how children look at pictures generally, but teachers must remember that, as Malter (1948) indicated, little is known of the way in which a child perceives a picture in relation to reading. Dolch (1946) suggested that a habit of taking more time to examine a picture must be established and that a pattern of exploration of a picture can be taught. Vernon (1958) indicated that although children enjoy pictures, they may fail to notice what the adult sees in a picture, and they cannot infer course of action from a picture until they are nine or ten years of age.

Bergman and Vreeland (1932) compared a "visual method" (sight approach) and "picture-story" method of beginning reading. The "picture-story" method built sight vocabulary from pictures and parts of pictures. The "picture-story" method produced superior results in word recognition. This seems to agree with results obtained by Dice (1942). Teachers may have been using pictures to teach meanings without realizing their possibilities for promoting word recognition.

H. M. Robinson (1958) believed that visual discrimination for likenesses and differences in words could be increased through consistent attention to likenesses and differences in pictures. As this would seem to substantiate the findings of Bergman and Dice only under certain rigid conditions, research is necessary in this area.

With respect to the perception of symbols in general, it can be said that all teachers run the danger of believing that the child perceives what they themselves perceive. D. H. Russell (1956) and Goins (1958) held that the teacher must make sure that the child perceives at least in part what the teacher perceives. The best ways for accomplishing this must be found. Because the whole process of symbolization is complex, teachers must be aware of the complexities inherent in the process and diversify their methods of helping the child to perceive. For example, the child who plays with an orange crate, pretending that it is an airplane, is perhaps exercising ability for symbolization far greater than the child who plays with a toy plane which is an authentic reproduction of the original. Teachers strive for authenticity of environment: Is it possible that an earlier use of symbols, as soon as the child is capable of thinking with them, would assist him more in learning to read?

Fleming (1959) and others have discovered that small cooperating groups of pupils accomplish more in learning to read than pupils who work alone. Is it possible that children in groups help one another to perceive because they can sense the perception problems of their age-group readily? Fleming (1959) also discussed teaching word recognition by means of machines. Many suggestions for automation in teaching are a direct result of the work of Skinner (1954), but insufficient work has been done to apply automation to teaching of reading. Perhaps teachers can look to machines to supply much of the drill in word-recognition techniques now supplied by seatwork exercises.

Let us now consider perception of the printed symbols of reading. Fleming (1959) suggested that perhaps teachers must be helped to start more simply and look more deeply into the complicated process of reading, because children are presented with words, phrases, letters, and other symbols simultaneously. There is no certain knowledge as to what effect this conglomeration has on the child. Dvorine (1958) raised a question concerning the child's efforts to identify a symbol: If the child has his whole attention on learning to identify the word "legs," of what value is the teacher's question, "What is it that a dog has four of?"

Perhaps the teacher should give more thought to that which might interfere with the identification-recognition process. D. H. Russell (1956) emphasized that a clear and final pattern is necessary if the child is to be capable of future recognition and that the teacher must arrange the environment so that a clear, definite, unified pattern is possible for the child. Concerning how this is to be done, the question raised by Schubert (1953) must be in the mind of every good teacher: What is the best brand of teaching reading? Children are visually, auditorily, or kinesthetically oriented concerning ability to learn. Perhaps teachers need diagnostic devices to determine which avenue of learning is the best for an individual child, so that a clear, definite, unified pattern of a symbol is possible for that child.

As to perception of single letters of the alphabet, W. H. Burton and Richards (1949) showed that teachers can help their pupils avoid confusion in perception by selecting letters of the alphabet which have few similarities. This principle could be pursued further. For learning the perception of words, the "word" method, or teaching pupils to perceive unanalyzed whole words, has been advocated. Exclusive use of the "word" method was the real objection to its use. But as D. H. Russell (1955) and Morris (1958) found, few teachers use it exclusively today. According to Harrington and Durrell (1955), the visual discrimination required for "look-and-say" reading is more important as an indicator of reading readiness than of mental age. Perhaps teachers can select words which are dissimilar in general shape for children who have difficulty distinguishing likenesses and differences. This practice would accord with a suggestion of H. M. Robinson (1948). The tachistoscope, or some other form of limited-time exposure device, has been suggested as a means of assisting children to acquire identification-recognition techniques. Proponents of the tachistoscope claim that it aids the child in rapid and accurate perception. However, in the beginning, the interval between exposure and recogni-

tion is long; thus the technique may not be useful until the pupil has considerable facility in word recognition. Buswell (1947) believed that tachistoscopes help by changing the character of perceptual experience but warned that perception by tachistoscope is not equivalent to perception in reading.

The differences of opinion over "whole" and "part" methods of perception of words must be resolved before the teacher can translate theory into practice. Coleman (1953) indicated that the processes of differentiation and integration can be taught. Perhaps the teacher can demonstrate the process repeatedly, with language, until the pupil achieves insight. Betts (1953) suggested that the printed word is not the only factor in the reading situation; the pupil's awareness of his need and his ability to reconstruct the symbolization are also involved. Teachers must be aware of the complexity of the process. D. H. Russell (1944) added a reassuring note. Although there was considerable difference of opinion among a group of experts on reading methods, the group generally favored a combination method involving sentence, word, and phonics.

Goins (1958) indicated that two types of perception were involved in reading—ability to distinguish likenesses and differences, and "strength of closure." As seen by Goins (1959), reading readiness workbooks were designed primarily to promote the first, but much of the discrimination they elicit is gross discrimination requiring nothing of the pupil other than busywork. Many excellent exercises for building sight vocabulary have been designed, and teachers should be aware both of the exercises and of the principles involved in their construction (Sutton, 1953). Word lists, sharing periods, games, charts—all can contribute to building a sight vocabulary.

Many techniques have been devised to help children learn to read by phrases or thought units. A detailed account of these techniques (Dolch, 1949; Gates & Cason, 1945) would, however, be inappropriate here.

Auditory perception. If Duggins (1958)

is right in contending that the child learns through listening rather than through speech, teachers must plan for much more listening to words in their reading lessons for beginners and for clear auditory patterns for their pupils to identify with printed symbols. According to A. J. Harris (1956), listening ability is a better predictor of reading potential than IQ. There is some controversy as to the importance of having children know the names and sounds of the letters of the alphabet when they enroll in school or soon thereafter. Perhaps this issue should be investigated. It might be of value for teachers to help pupils become aware of the significance of the letters of the alphabet and of the instructions they bear implicitly to convert the silent symbol to an oral one (Daniels & Diack, 1959).

Several check lists for phonic readiness may be of value to teachers (A. J. Harris, 1956; Hildreth, 1954). As Hildreth noted, sounding the letters of a word does not unlock the word for the pupil. Teachers must teach the "trick" of listening to these sounds and considering their context to enable the pupil to make a promising attack on the word. Various writers such as Burrows (1951), Hildreth (1954), and D. H. Russell (1961) have suggested guides for phonic instruction based on research. These should prove of value to teachers who are not sure of their responsibility for phonic instruction. Apparently, much of value in word recognition can be accomplished with a tape recorder (Daniel, 1953). It may serve either as a diagnostic instrument when a teacher studies a pupil's word-recognition techniques or as a means of allowing a pupil to listen to his own attempts at phonetic analysis. Rogers (1938) showed a relationship, at the college level, between inability to pronounce a word and ignorance of its meaning. But it is apparent that teachers are not aware of the value of phonics above the primary and intermediate grades. Triggs (1952) discovered that little growth occurs in word-recognition skill, as measured by ability to match auditory and visual phonic symbols, above the sixth grade. Per-

haps teachers should continue practice and application of phonics in grades above the elementary level.

Kinesthetic perception. It is apparent that teachers must give practice in left-to-right eye movements to insure this habit (Stevenson & Robinson, 1953). Kinesthetic approaches may be used to supplement methods stressing visual and auditory practices. Perhaps kinesthetic techniques can be used effectively with difficult tasks regardless of the ability of the pupil. For example, Baker (1945) showed that oral and written spelling of words aided the recognition of certain difficult words on the Dolch list.

TEACHING MEANING

Word recognition is a prerequisite to reading, but it does not guarantee understanding. Comprehension requires knowledge not only of the meaning of words but of their relationships in sentences, paragraphs, and longer passages. It involves understanding of the intent of the author and may go beyond literal recorded facts to hidden meanings or implications. As with identification-recognition, the exploration of meaning may be multisensory. J. A. Holmes (1953) listed vocabulary-in-context, intelligence, and perception of verbal relations as factors affecting the acquisition of meaning in reading. Accordingly, this section is concerned with (1) percepts (sensations and images), (2) concepts (symbolization of meaning), (3) verbals (standardization of symbols), and (4) relationships of verbalized concepts (multiple-meanings, denotation-connotation, figurative language, grammar-syntax).

Percepts

Although perception is extremely complex and its relationship to reading incompletely understood, certain definitions and relationships must be considered if the process of comprehension in reading is to be understood sufficiently to enable teachers to improve the process. The materials of thinking (in contrast to the processes) are the instruments of meaning, according to D. H. Russell (1956, p. 69), and are "sensations, images, percepts, memories, concepts, and generalizations." Although the materials of thinking may be considered separately, thinking remains an entity.

Sensations have been extensively explored by psychologists. For the present discussion, the following explanation of sensation will suffice: Each of the senses is susceptible to stimulation by factors within and outside the body. The stimulation generates electrical impulses which result in the appropriate sensation in the cortical area. Difference in order of stimulation is produced by frequency modulation in impulse. The sensation, being a product of multisensory stimulation, is a product of degree of sensory affectation and ratio of involved senses. Organized patterns of sensations form percepts.

"A *percept* may be defined as what is known of an object, a quality, or a relationship as a result of sensory experience" (D. H. Russell, 1956, p. 66). A percept may be considered to be the organized pattern of sensations at any given moment. Since sensations may be present from various senses, the percept may be a product of multisensory stimulation. Many explanations of percept development have been offered. Psychologists agree that percepts are learned, but the method of learning is open to question. Two widely accepted theories are discussed by T. R. McConnell (1942). The first theory is synthetic, holding that percepts are formed through association of stimulus and response until this relationship is learned. The second theory is analytic, holding that the learner reacts first to a vague pattern, then to parts of the pattern, and finally integrates a new pattern. In either case, perception is the process whereby sensations are apprehended and reorganized.

While much experimentation has been done on sensation and perception, only conclusions relative to how pupils learn meaning through reading are pertinent here. Briefly, they are as follows:

1. Only direct experience in building percepts will assure the successful building of concepts (Serra, 1953). No meaning can result without a foundation of direct experience.

2. The learner will do what he "perceives" as being done; thus imitation is important in learning to read just as it is in other learning.

3. Various studies have demonstrated that part of a stimulus pattern may eventually evoke the whole pattern. Thus cue reduction is important in reading.

4. Where a stimulus pattern is complex, some analysis of stimulus relationships seems to aid perception.

5. The importance of giving a child many types of associated sensory experience seems evident, but only if the child sees the relationships involved. Many simple percepts, such as those of number and form, can be improved with practice (Gibson, 1953).

6. Some clear, integrated pattern is imperative if the child is to have a memory of the percept at some future time (L. Gray, 1951; D. H. Russell, 1956).

The necessity for a clear pattern, favorable to future memory of the percept, invites consideration of both images and memory. The image, like the percept, is centrally aroused; it differs from the percept in that it is aroused in the absence of the original sensations. Images are of two general classes—afterimages and memory images. The afterimage is similar to that of the television screen. In most individuals it disappears quickly and is replaced by the memory image. Sharp mental images could be antagonistic to habits of highly generalized, abstract thought—a clear image of one chair might hamper a generalized concept of chair. If such is the case, a learner would be aided by assistance in making an appropriate meaningful response to the reality represented by the symbol and hindered by exhortation to form a clear mental image of the represented reality.

Experiments on memory have led to the following generalizations: (1) Logical memory (reproduction of meaningful relations) is usually of more value than rote memory (exact reproduction). (2) The more meaningful, organized, and emotion-saturated (within limits) the experience, the greater will be the learning. (3) Memory becomes more selective and more accurate as the learner matures.

Concepts

Many writers have discussed the nature, development, and importance of concepts. Concepts emerge from percepts and memories. In forming concepts, the individual does not usually distinguish clearly between percepts and memories. One definition of a concept is: "A symbolic response to the members of one group or class of stimulus patterns." Since the definition indicates no action for the teacher, the following illustration may serve that purpose: A unification of a unique shape, odor, and color forms a pattern in a learner's mind. The pattern acts as a symbol for that class of objects. It may be organized on various levels of complexity, and the complexity increases with experience. The pattern is always symbolized, sometimes verbalized, but the existence of the pattern is revealed by the individual's behavior toward the class of objects (Serra, 1953). The usual symbol is a word. Using the word "orange" as an example, we see that a child distinguishes the fruit by the characteristic color, odor, shape. The symbol he uses for unified characteristics is the word "orange." A rose is a characteristic color, form, and odor. "Democracy" may serve as another example. The child attaches the symbol to certain procedures, countries, values.

Research on concept development was summarized by Smoke (1946), Vinacke (1951), and D. H. Russell (1954). Each of them noted the importance of concept development. Russell (1956) stated that the completeness and clarity of a child's concepts are the best measure of his ability to learn. It is obvious that concepts develop frequently and easily in human beings. When attempts are made to establish a sequence of development, however, it becomes apparent that concepts have many dimensions. Therefore, a linear sequence of development is difficult to establish. D. H. Russell (1956, p. 249) described the process thus: "They seem to move along a continuum from simple to complex, from concrete to abstract, from undifferentiated to differentiated, from discrete to organized, and from egocentric to more social." In the development of understanding of relationships among members of a class, the sequence appears to be: the idea of order, of classification, and of hierarchy.

While the consensus is that concepts are formed by the complementary processes of abstraction (in the sense of "taking from") and generalization, attempts to demonstrate such formation have resulted in single-facet experiments on multiple-facet phenomena. Experiments to show the multidimensionality of concept development have been infrequent.

Piaget (1932), perhaps the best known investigator of concept development, has supplied a partial answer to the question of what meaning for children lies behind the symbol in such areas as number, time, space, and scientific phenomena. In one of a series of studies, Heidbreder (1934) worked with college students in a memory situation in which subjects were required to evolve nine concepts—three concrete objects, three spatial, and three number. Students were divided into two groups, the first working with pictorial materials, the second with typewritten materials. Verbal definition of a concept was considered as proof of learning. Heidbreder observed that concepts were more easily evolved from pictorial material and that a concept was frequently applied correctly when the subject was unable to define it verbally. For pictorial material, concepts of concrete objects were mastered with least difficulty and those of number with greatest difficulty. No consistent order of difficulty was discernible with verbal material. An investigation by Wenzel and Flurry (1948) confirmed Heidbreder's findings.

Amen (1941) studied the reaction of nursery school children to picture material. She found three major patterns of interpretation:

(1) simple identification, (2) description in terms of overt activity, and (3) psychological inference. The first pattern of interpretation was characteristic of two-year-olds, the last of four-year-olds.

Welch (1947), from experimental evidence, suggested the following levels of abstraction: Level one—concrete object such as "this dog"; Level two—collie; Level three—dog; Level four—animal; Level five—living substance; Level six—substance.

Curti (1950), considering development from percept through concept, suggested the following levels of conceptualization: (1) presymbolic state, in which the infant reacts to objects; (2) preverbal symbolic state, in which the child has an idea but not the concept (he says "mama" to the door through which she has passed); (3) implicit generalization state, in which the idea of a class is there, but it is vague (the child says "horsie" to most four-legged creatures, and some with two legs); (4) explicit generalization state, in which the child forms fragmentary but true concepts.

Lorge and Feifel (1950) investigated successive stages of concept development in children as revealed by their verbal responses to the vocabulary test of Form L of the Revised Stanford-Binet Scale. Responses were classified as synonyms, description, explanation, demonstration (repetition, illustration, and inferior explanations were included here), and error. Subjects were 900 pupils 6 to 14 years of age. Results revealed that no particular type of response was exclusively found on a particular age level, but that younger children made more frequent use of description, demonstration, and inferior explanation. Older children employed synonyms and explanation. Younger children saw words as concrete ideas and emphasized an isolated aspect of them rather than categorical or class features. Their descriptions were more personal than symbolic.

Other than sequence, what developmental characteristics of concepts are worthy of consideration from the viewpoint of instruction and learning? Because understanding of specific words and phrases is basic to understanding a paragraph or chapter, a few further factors in concept development may be mentioned.

1. Concrete concepts, concerned with objects and their functions, are probably the first to be acquired and are basic to the formation of other concepts (Carner & Sheldon, 1954). Objects can be examined and manipulated; therefore direct experience with objects seems vital in early stages of concept development. The more direct the experience, the greater the learning (Serra, 1953). It follows that the school must not prevent sensory investigations (LaBrant, 1949). Most concept development requires a background of experience (G. L. Bond & Wagner, 1960), and the immediate and personal will be learned first. The integration which results in concept formation is an outcome of sensory impression, muscular activity, motor manipulation, and problem-solving (D. H. Russell, 1956). No one can give the learner his concepts; he must construct them actively, out of his own experiences (G. L. Bond & Wagner, 1960; W. A. Brownell & Hendrickson, 1950). Teachers who watch children examine and manipulate objects, plants, animals, and machines should realize the potential value of such experience in learning (T. L. Harris, 1948). Concepts learned solely from textbooks are often only superficially understood because direct experience is not usually involved (Diederich, 1944).

2. Concept development in children is primarily a product of intelligence. It is not experience but the ability to profit from experience which largely determines concept development (McCullough, 1959), although at times the relationship between concept development and chronological age seems to be closer than that between concept development and mental age (D. H. Russell, 1956).

3. Vicarious experience is important in the development of concepts. Although direct experience is vital as a foundation for other experiences, it is not, after the initial foundation has been laid, necessarily the best ex-

perience for concept development. It is impossible to develop all needed concepts by direct experience alone (Serra, 1953). Picture interpretation, oral language, dramatization, demonstration, and experimentation all have their place in the development of concepts.

In some reading lessons, three-dimensional pictures using stereoscopic color transparencies can stimulate learning (Feldman, Merrill, & MacGinitie, 1960), and two-dimensional motion pictures are of value in concept development (T. L. Harris, 1948). Gorman (1951) found that films and film-readers aided primary-grade children in understanding concepts which had previously caused difficulty. Teachers found films valuable in building a common background of experience for readers in the second grade (Witty & Fitzwater, 1953). The film appeared to define new words to the extent that little discussion was required for clear understanding.

Flat pictures have been used extensively to build concepts. They may serve to reinforce the spoken explanation or dramatization (I. H. Anderson & Dearborn, 1952), or they may be used alone. Dolch (1946) suggested five ways in which pictures may aid growth of understanding. The observer sees (1) new things which are just variations of phenomena formerly observed (an animal which differs in color from that previously seen); (2) new combinations of that which has been understood already (the howdah is a combination of the familiar box on the familiar elephant); (3) more of the familiar (by longer or more frequent study); (4) something previously overlooked (object or relationship, such as size comparison of previously observed horse and rider); (5) the completely new (by having someone call it to his attention). Further, Dolch suggested techniques for teaching with pictures: (1) Pictures must be studied, not given a cursory glance; (2) A slow reading habit must be formed for reading pictures; (3) A habit of exploration must be established, so that the picture is examined piece by piece; (4) A habit of discussing pictures must be formed, or the child will look at but not think of what he sees.

Relief maps, maps, charts, diagrams, and other representations which do not contain identifiable pictorial elements can aid in concept development (T. L. Harris, 1948). Examination of research on the ability of children to interpret such illustrative material led Malter (1948) to conclude that no one has thoroughly investigated the ability of children of various ages to identify pictured objects, to read graphs, or to read maps. Wagner (1953) came to similar conclusions concerning the map-reading ability of sixth-grade children. Although vicarious methods of concept building are of great value, they run greater risk of permitting misinterpretation than does direct experience. A child's concept of a train from a picture may be very different from that which he builds from the real object. Experience combining pictured objects with the objects pictured can aid perception and concept formation. Osburn, Huntington, and Meeks (1946) worked with kindergarten children in an effort to build concepts of relationships among objects. The relationships taught were: A is smaller than B, A is part of B, A belongs with B, A is made of B, A is a kind of B, A is the opposite of B. No control group was used, but the children made scores on reading readiness tests which showed gains superior to average as a result of this training.

4. Teachers can aid concept development by controlling the environment. W. A. Brownell and Hendrickson (1950) stated that readiness for learning in any area was maintained by providing a graded series of experiences. A child needs help when the patterns are complex. He must combine previously acquired concepts, word meanings, and direct experience to extend meaning. The child employs, or may be helped to employ, naming, counting, measuring, discriminating, abstracting, and generalizing. His thinking may be inductive, deductive, creative, or a combination of these (D. H. Russell, 1956), if the teacher provides the appropriate experiences. The child must build

concrete concepts, chronological concepts, spatial concepts, numerical concepts, and social concepts (Carner & Sheldon, 1954). The teacher must learn to listen for evidence of existing concepts and concept errors (I. H. Anderson & Dearborn, 1952), then perform two duties (T. L. Harris, 1948): (1) identify and clarify types and degrees of experience children possess, and (2) enrich and extend experiences essential to new learning. This can be done by providing an abundance of experience which is varied rather than repetitive and by attempting to control the emotional factors associated with the experiences.

Verbals

"In all probability, an inadequate vocabulary is the greatest single cause for failure to read with comprehension, in either general or technical fields" (Cole, 1946, p. 40). Concepts are symbolized, but the symbols are frequently not verbals. Verbals are usually considered to be those standardized oral and written symbols which form the vocabulary of a language. "Reading is concerned with verbalized concepts . . . . Through general agreement, certain sounds, symbolized in writing by certain combinations of letters, are called 'words,' and certain meanings are attached to certain words. The question is simply whether a child is aware of, and in accord with, the common agreement concerning each word" (Serra, 1953, p. 275). As Pei (1949) indicated, in English the written language follows the spoken language, symbolizing sounds or words. Learning to read is easier if the learner is aware of this relationship.

An even more important relationship is that between meaning and written symbols. Many writers have stated that reading is primarily for meaning and that the reading process is one of obtaining meaning from printed symbols. Saale (1950) stressed the relationship between previous knowledge and symbols. I. H. Anderson and Dearborn (1952) acknowledged that meaning rests on experience, that meaning comes through

empathy, through response to the symbols rather than the symbols themselves, and that the job of the teacher is to make the child's experiences verbal through reading. Similar opinions have been expressed by others (Eberhart, 1945; Gates, 1950). Cole (1946) considered the difficulty experienced by the child, in accepting written words as representatives of realities, to be the basic difficulty in learning the first few words.

Before proceeding with discussion of verbals, we should mention three considerations:

1. The "meaning vocabulary" and "concept knowledge" of a child are not necessarily the same. Serra (1953) noted the tendency of investigators of children's concepts to regress to meanings which children have of words. D. H. Russell (1954) resolved the dilemma by suggesting that if total word knowledge is considered—depth and breadth—the result must differ but slightly from the knowledge of the concept represented by the symbol. It is possible that there is always a concept symbol prior to the verbal symbol.

2. Investigators and educators make a distinction between a word in context and the same word in isolation, implying that meaning is more easily derived from a word in context. It is probably safe to assume that a word is *always* in context, not necessarily heard or seen in context, but at least understood to be in context. Many problems of investigating word meaning are resolved if such a position is accepted. For example, I. H. Anderson and Dearborn (1952) explained that in attempting to read an experience chart, the child has the previously experienced activity as context to aid his word-recognition and comprehension. To an experienced reader, the text supplies context or his memory supplies context, but both are dependent upon previous experience.

3. Reading involves deriving meaning from a symbol of a symbol, since the printed word usually represents for the child not the concrete object, but the oral symbol of the concrete object.

Research on "verbals" has also been concerned with the following problems: (1) Total meaning vocabulary (where a word is considered to have but one meaning): (a) measures of vocabulary, (b) size of vocabulary, (c) methods of building vocabulary; (2) Breadth and depth of vocabulary: (a) multiple meanings, (b) implied meaning, e.g., denotation-connotation, figures of speech; (3) Word order: (a) grammar and syntax, punctuation, (b) contractions, initials, formulas; (4) Verbalism.

Total vocabulary. Attempts to measure segments and estimate totals of children's vocabularies have been numerous during the past 75 years. Among the summaries of this research are those of McCarthy (1946), D. H. Russell (1954), and Dale and Reichert (1957). Such sources indicate that teachers can distinguish among a child's understanding, speaking, reading, and writing vocabularies.

1. Measures of vocabulary. Research workers should know some of the problems involved in measuring vocabulary, methods which have been found effective for measuring vocabulary, and sources of word lists used in vocabulary estimates.

Two problems in measures of children's vocabularies are that (1) they are measures of limited samples of vocabulary from which the true vocabulary can only be estimated; and (2) investigators cannot agree as to what evidence indicates that the word is "known" by the child. D. H. Russell (1954) concluded that measures of children's vocabularies were usually confined to simple recognition of a synonym in a multiple-choice situation. Kelley (1933), from research on a number of methods of measuring children's knowledge of word meaning, concluded that matching and multiple-choice tests correlated most highly with pupil ability to use words in sentences. Hurlburt (1954), working with pupils in Grades 9 and 11, concluded that recall and recognition techniques must both be used to measure precise knowledge of word meaning. His research showed a limited number of common factors in results of the two measures. In his study, recall was

measured by sentence completion, recognition by multiple-choice questions; words were selected from Roget's *Thesaurus.*

Reasons for lack of agreement among these studies are perhaps suggested by LaBrant (1949), who maintained that a young child has one meaning for each word and cannot conceive of it as having another. LaBrant considered language to be always but partially learned—words are partially pronounced, partially understood—and held that, at best, words have the meaning implied by the context in which they were learned. It is important that the teacher not believe or impart the idea that what is known by the child is total learning. As to errors in estimates of a child's vocabulary, McCullough (1959) listed factors which affect children's vocabularies: socioeconomic status, television viewing, experience background, intelligence, sex. Since it is difficult to know the relative influences of these factors for any group of children, the validity of any sample of children must be considered.

Some studies have been made of the measures of vocabulary that have been used. Kelley (1932) analyzed standard vocabulary tests and isolated 26 item forms which were in use at that date. Larrick (1953) suggested the following methods for estimating the size of children's vocabularies: (1) counting different words used in a natural oral-language situation, (2) counting different words used in a natural written-language situation, (3) counting different words in a free-association situation, (4) counting different words in a stimulus-response situation, (5) estimating vocabulary from words recognized on a selected list. The most current list of standard vocabulary tests is to be found in Buros (1959). The two most commonly used lists for estimate of total vocabulary are a random sample from an unabridged dictionary and a sample from *The Teacher's Word Book* (Thorndike & Lorge, 1944).

2. Size of vocabulary. How large are children's vocabularies? It is not surprising that this question is difficult to answer when one considers the difficulties encountered in esti-

mating them. Different samples, different sampling situations, an adequate number of samples, methods of evaluating meaning—each contributes a problem in obtaining evidence on the size of children's vocabularies. There have been many studies and many opinions. The weight of research and opinion seems to support somewhat smaller numbers than the estimate by M. K. Smith (1941) of 24,000 words for the total vocabulary of the average first-grade pupil, and by Seashore and Eckerson (1940) of 155,000 words for the vocabulary of the average college student. These estimates are based on recognition of synonyms in a multiple-choice situation. Most other estimates, based on different methods of sampling, are lower.

Of what value is such knowledge to teachers? Perhaps most obvious is the fact that the reading vocabulary requirements of children are very small in comparison to total vocabulary. Perhaps the value of such evidence lies in suggesting other questions which should be answered by research: Has television increased the total meaning vocabularies of children? Are children given opportunity to use the extensive oral vocabularies which they apparently possess or could possess and which could be used as an indirect means of extending meaning vocabularies? Are teachers continuously extending their own meaning vocabularies?

3. Methods of building vocabulary. What methods have been used to build children's meaning vocabularies? The methods used to build children's concepts also apply to children's meaning vocabularies. The only distinction between the two situations is that, in vocabulary building, only words can constitute the symbol to complete the concept. Direct experience, experiences with film and still pictures, and conversation to clarify meaning can all be used in conjunction with the word-symbols for which meaning is to be built. Gates (1950) and I. H. Anderson and Dearborn (1952) demonstrated the values of direct experience in clarifying meaning; Dolch (1946) did the same for pictures; Myers (1957), for listening and conversation

with pictures and models; Reid (1958), for film; Cole (1946), Gates (1950), Serra (1953), and McCullough (1959) for language activities. It is reasonable to hypothesize that teachers help build vocabulary to the degree that they listen carefully for clues to errors in word meaning, ask questions which reveal the extent of the meaning of words to children, insist that children use words accurately, and write and speak so that children obtain accurate oral and written information concerning words.

In analyzing the development of meaning in words, Dolch (1953) distinguished four separate processes: (1) expanding vocabulary without increasing meaning (adding nutrition as a synonym for food), (2) obtaining new meanings from old meanings (sharper distinctions such as *nutrition* for food that builds and *sustenance* for food that sustains), (3) undergoing new experiences that yield new meanings, (4) learning incidental vocabulary (from discussion and reading).

Turning to expansion of vocabulary in reading, specifically, investigators recognize three ways in which vocabulary is built in relation to reading: (1) wide reading, (2) direct instruction, and (3) incidental instruction in building meaning vocabulary.

Wide reading is universally recommended as a method of building vocabulary. To consider one example, Alm (1957, p. 14) stated: "The best single means of increasing one's vocabulary is, of course, to read widely." However, most experimental evidence in support of wide reading is indirect, merely indicating that vocabulary and comprehension are closely related. Dunkel (1944) concluded that ability to determine precise meaning was related to ability to read with comprehension. Research by Hunt (1953) and Reed and Pepper (1957) yielded approximately the same result.

Direct research on the value of reading in increasing meaning vocabulary has yielded disappointing results. Traxler (1938) found that mere reading did not appear to build the vocabulary of high school pupils. Sachs (1943) revealed substantially the same with college freshmen. There was a low correlation between frequency of appearance of a word in assigned reading and percentage of correct definitions. Perhaps one reason for the discouraging result is to be found in the reading situation presented to the pupil. Many teachers and pupils believe that it is possible to learn unfamiliar context and new vocabulary from the same reading. It is obvious that if the context is unknown, it cannot furnish clues to unfamiliar words. Wide reading in a familiar context containing some unfamiliar words is necessary to build meaning vocabulary.

Direct vocabulary instruction entails selecting appropriate words to be taught and then teaching association of meaning by various techniques. McCullough (1957b, p. 477) defined it as follows: "The direct approach is one in which lists of words or sentences containing words are studied deliberately for the development of word power...." She stressed the importance of vocabulary study, particularly in high school. But which words? And what methods should be used to assist students in vocabulary study? Cole (1946), McCullough (1957b), and D. H. Russell (1961) referred to research and practice in support of direct vocabulary instruction, and Alm (1957) warned that much of what is termed "word study," writing definitions of words from supplied lists, out of context, is of little value. The words must be those which the pupil has an opportunity to use.

A number of useful word lists have been compiled. Examples are those of Thorndike and Lorge (1944), a frequency count of the 30,000 most frequently used words, and thus a general vocabulary list; Kyte (1953), a general vocabulary list of 663 words compiled as a core vocabulary; Cole (1940), a technical vocabulary designed for high school subjects; Brown (1952), a list of words containing frequently used prefixes, suffixes, and roots; Thorndike (1941), a list of English suffixes necessary for efficient word meaning analysis; Stauffer (1942), a list of important prefixes from *The Teacher's Word Book* (Thorndike & Lorge, 1944).

The literature contains few examples of methods of word study which have been scientifically proven valuable. The following studies illustrate typical problems investigated and typical results. Haefner (1932), working with university summer students, exposed them to one word each day for 20 days by writing word and definition on the chalk board. A test before and after the experiment showed much improvement. Traxler (1938) found drill effective in building vocabulary at the junior high school level. Reasonably permanent gains were achieved by studying definitions and composing sentences containing the words to be learned. Pond (1938) found that a study of Latin was of little value in increasing the meaning vocabulary of high school pupils. Since Latin is a prime source of affixes and roots, there would seem to be little transfer to English vocabulary.

Miles (1945) investigated the residual benefits of one semester of word study. Ten minutes per day was devoted to discussing the meaning, use, and grammatical classification of words. Emphasis was placed on making the new words a part of each pupil's speaking vocabulary. Significant gains remained after two and one-half years. Miles estimated, from his and similar studies, that the effect of direct word study is approximately three times that of incidental word study. Otterman (1955) taught prefixes and roots to 20 Grade 7 classes for 30 days, 10 minutes per day. Pupils were tested by ability to interpret meaning of unfamiliar words containing the elements. Only those of high intelligence showed a statistically reliable gain in ability to interpret the new words. There was no measurable improvement in general vocabulary or reading comprehension. Brown (1952) compiled a list of words rich in affixes and frequently used roots and suggested the following procedure: (1) First look up the word in the dictionary and check its prefix. (2) List 10 other words containing the prefix. (3) List 10 other words containing the root. No evidence was submitted as to the value of this method.

There have been a number of attempts to increase vocabulary by teaching the history of words. Moir (1953) outlined a unit on the history of the English language for the eighth grade. Funk and Lewis (1954) and Jespersen (1955) compiled similar material. Serra (1953), from a survey of research results, concluded that a method whereby the teacher supplies a definition, explains, and gives illustrations is superior to one by which the child uses the dictionary for himself.

McCullough (1957b) suggested two procedures for assisting children with vocabulary building: (1) Determine initial vocabulary inventory, including words and word relationships, both in and out of context. (2) Determine ability to analyze the form of a word. She concluded that careful pronunciation of the word is important; multisensory impressions of the word are superior to a unisensory approach; meaning, structural analysis, and comprehension are closely related, as noted by others (Hunt, 1953; Reed & Pepper, 1957); classifying words increases appreciation of relationships among them and thus increases meaning; knowledge of roots and affixes may be helpful, but prefixes have many conflicting meanings, and knowledge of them frequently does not lead to exact definition. Dale (1958) listed suggestions similar to those of McCullough. In addition, he suggested that students should be made aware of the four stages in which vocabulary grows: (1) The reader is positive he has never before seen the word. (2) He has seen the word previously but does not know its meaning. (3) He can place the word in a broad classification. (4) He knows the word accurately. Price (1957) worked out methods of practice in dictionary skills for those who are not efficient with a dictionary.

Incidental instruction to build meaning vocabulary is often a combination of wide reading and direct instruction. Teachers have not yet solved the problem of the degree to which word study should be assisted by them or should be unaided, although most studies agree that a teacher should guide word study. There seems to be no doubt among investigators that pupils must be taught to use context. This view is supported by Strang (1944), McCullough (1957b), Alm (1957), and others.

A definition of the incidental method of word study has been given by McCullough (1957b, p. 477): "the casual or incidental approach involves the study of words as they happen to occur in material the students are about to read or are currently reading." McCullough added that both this method and the direct method of vocabulary study are valuable and that probably neither should be used to the exclusion of the other.

The following are examples of research on the teaching of meaning vocabulary by incidental study: Traxler (1934), working with seventh-grade pupils and university students, found rate of reading and speed of association to be slightly and positively related. Both may be related to speed of obtaining meaning from context. W. S. Gray and Holmes (1938) used control and experimental groups to evaluate methods of building meaning vocabulary. Their study demonstrated that specific direct help brings the greatest vocabulary growth; that vocabulary growth is stimulated if the author defines and illustrates when new vocabulary is introduced; that discussion of new units of work by the teacher is of some value; and that, when specific guidance is not given, the context forms the chief clue to meaning.

Tate, Herbert, and Zeman (1940) conducted a two-year experiment to evaluate a nonphonetic approach to reading. For primary-grade children who were not taught phonics, every attempt was made to supply contextual clues to aid word recognition. The techniques used in this study could be used to teach meaning of words, although this was not the purpose of the study. Teachers referred to illustrations, reviewed the story to the point where difficulty occurred, reread several lines preceding the point of difficulty, asked two or three pertinent questions, suggested a known word of opposite meaning, used a synonym, referred to an analogous experience, asked such questions as, "It could not be anything but . . .," and pantomimed the meaning.

Morgan and Bailey (1943) used a story with an artificial vocabulary and compiled a dictionary by which university students were expected to learn the meanings of the artificial words. An equivalent group was supplied with the artificial vocabulary but no story content and, thus, no context clues to meaning. The experimental group completed exercises more rapidly and made less use of the dictionary. Since results were conflicting, no conclusion could be drawn. Morgan and Bailey surmised that time and dictionary use would be reduced by use of context clues but that guessing meaning from context might introduce serious error.

Strang (1944) conducted an exploratory study of the characteristic reactions of high school and college students to unfamiliar words in context. Students were asked to keep detailed records of their procedures and to evaluate the effectiveness of the procedures. Among the procedures reported by the students were the following: ask someone in the immediate vicinity; use the dictionary; guess, then use the dictionary; use context; use affixes and roots (if the student had a foreign language background); use small words in the larger unknown word; use memory association; use a combination approach. Strang concluded that the students had only a vague notion of the types of context clues or techniques for using them to ascertain the meaning of a word; that even mature readers had small success in using roots or affixes; that serious inadequacies in one of the most important aspects of reading were revealed; that unsystematic or casual word study had little value.

Hovious (1945) suggested a simple plan for teachers to use in any subject where pupils were required to read material containing unfamiliar words. The plan was twofold. The teacher marked the essential words before assigning the reading and then presented them, anchoring them to the pupils' experience through demonstrations, visual aids, discussions, contrasts, and implications.

Saale (1950) reviewed research indicating that amplification of reading material helps students obtain meaning from context. The extensive reading which results from amplification enables students to gain the background of information needed to learn word meaning from context. This suggests that it may be helpful to expand materials by use of teacher's and students' writing.

Werner and Kaplan (1950) investigated the processes underlying acquisition of word meaning through context. Twelve series of six sentences each were constructed using artificial words embedded in sentences. A reader arrived at the meaning of an artificial word by progressing through sentences which increased in definiteness of clues. An example was the artificial word *corplum* and the six phrases: (1) A _____ may be used for support. (2) _____ may be used to close off an open space. (3) A _____ may be long or short, thick or thin, strong or weak. (4) A wet _____ does not burn. (5) You can make a _____ smooth with sandpaper. (6) The painter uses a _____ to mix his paint. When the sentences were submitted as exercises for children between the ages of 8 and 13, results were as follows: (1) Correctness was closely related to conventionalization of word meaning used in a given context. (Thus if a child gave a "correct" meaning for an artificial word, it showed his power of logic, his experience, and his mastery of the English language.) (2) For pupils to succeed in these exercises, it was necessary for them to realize that words have a relatively stable and self-contained meaning apart from any sentence. (3) Meaning was expressed through linguistic media. (Lack of grammar or syntax made it difficult for a pupil to distinguish the lexical entity of a word.) (4) For pupils to succeed, it was necessary for them to discover that a verbal symbol could stand for object, situation, or relationship, and could vary from instances where there was a direct relation between symbol and referent (as in onomatopoetic words) to those where relation of symbol to referent was indirect.

Heavey (1954) studied word meaning in newspaper contexts and formulated the following procedure for use by pupils in acquiring meanings: (1) Guess the meaning from context. (2) Obtain the pronunciation from dictionary. (3) Name the part of speech. (4) Compose an original sentence using the word. Ragle (1956) worked with eleventh- and twelfth-grade pupils, using contemporary magazines and newspapers. Pupils were asked to record words encountered in context and to consult the dictionary for meaning. Ragle claimed that his procedure increased student interest in word meaning, especially when the students were asked to locate, in contemporary reading, unknown words which had occurred in literature assignments.

McCullough (1958), from a review of research on word study in context, concluded that pupils must be helped to understand that context clues extend beyond the sentence in which the unknown word appears. In some cases the nature of an entire book must be understood in order to understand the specific meaning of an unknown word used in a specific setting in the text. McCullough listed context clues which should be taught by teachers as follows: (1) experience clues, (2) comparison-contrast clues, (3) synonym clues, (4) summary clues, (5) definition clues, (6) clues of familiar expression, and (7) presentation clues (word order).

In concluding the discussion of total meaning vocabulary, we present a number of suggestions by W. S. Gray (1951) for guidance in vocabulary development. Each of these suggestions may be regarded as a hypothesis: (1) Reading vocabulary becomes permanent vocabulary only it if is transferred to writing, speaking, and thinking vocabularies. (2) Teachers should constantly direct pupil attention to words—to appropriateness of the author's choice of words, to accuracy of meaning, to the power of words in appealing to the various senses. (3) Teachers should offer two choices when a word is required so that pupils may practice selecting the exact word. (4) Reading material must contain unknown words to afford practice in extending word meaning, but the number of new words should not be great, and material with numerous context clues should be used. (5) Pupils should be encouraged to build their own lists of technical words. (6) Pupils should learn the meanings and pronunciations of words used on television and radio.

Breadth and depth of vocabulary. LaBrant (1949, p. 14) said, "The young child has one meaning for every word, and to him that's the only meaning of the word." This is the situation which exists despite the fact that the world of language presents the child with the problem of using more than one word as symbol for an object and using one word as symbol for different objects or situations. Confusion and rejection may result when the one-to-one relationship of one reality to one symbol is violated. Children may react in different ways in attempting to reconcile this violation of the simple law of communication. Do they attempt to avoid the confusing symbol? Do they experiment with the confusion, such as telling riddles in which the less common meaning of the word forms the riddle?

1. Multiple meanings. A number of writers have discussed the problem of multiple meaning in vocabulary growth. McKee (1945), McCullough (1957b), and G. L. Bond and Wagner (1960) believed that study of multiple meanings is rewarding and should be undertaken by pupils with teacher assistance, but they cited no research to support their opinions. Betts (1949, 1959) cited no research relative to teaching multiple meanings of words, but discussed the problem thoroughly. He listed different situations in which a child meets multiple meaning: another word may be used with no change in meaning apparent to the child (use of "dwelling" for "house"); language may imply a unity which does not correspond to experience ("foot" for human and for bed); experience is infinite while language is finite (thus the necessity for using the same words for several things); a word's meaning depends on its context (isolated words mean different things to different in-

dividuals); the individual must structure his experience in reading so that it conforms with the situation described by the author; words may shift meaning without a reason which is apparent to the child (the word "is" can be used to mean "exist," but one level of abstraction cannot exist at another level of abstraction).

The following three studies indicate how little is known about multiple-meaning development: Foster (1943), working with written compositions of eighth-grade pupils, tabulated the frequency of words with multiple meanings. The tabulation revealed that words with the greatest number of different meanings were used more frequently and with more different meanings than other words. This seems to indicate that pupils have acquired multiple meanings for many words by the eighth grade. Further, it suggests that teachers should be aware of the number of meanings of some common words ("take," for example, has 106 meanings) and use some method of direct instruction on multiple meanings before the eighth grade.

Gammon (1952) tabulated the occurrences of multiple-meaning words in primary readers. When the various meanings were presented in context to primary-grade children, those in Grade 1 responded incorrectly to one-quarter of the situations, those in Grade 2 to one-third, and those in Grade 3 to one-quarter. Apparently the problem exists even in the primary grades.

D. H. Russell (1954) attempted an exploration of vocabulary breadth, depth, and height for pupils in Grades 4–12. Multiple meanings for words were investigated by a test designed specifically for the purpose, in which pupils were required to select one of a number of words to suit a specific context. Results did not correlate highly with those of measures of general vocabulary. Girls scored higher than boys on this test—which was not true of the other tests. Both boys and girls showed considerable gains on this test in intermediate grades, and their rate of gain declined at the high school level. It seems that this test was measuring a factor not common to general vocabulary tests, that multiple meanings are of primary concern about the time pupils are in intermediate grades, and that many have successfully coped with the problem by the time they reach high school. Perhaps they could be assisted more efficiently; research is needed in this area.

2. Implied meaning. In addition to increase of vocabulary by multiple meaning, the pupil must learn to cope with increase of vocabulary by implied meaning. Obviously, a reader faces a difficult task in obtaining meaning which is only implied (W. S. Gray, 1951). Three types of presentation imply meaning; (1) connotation, as compared to denotation of the symbol; (2) figurative language; (3) meaning generated from a broad context such as the setting of the material or the reflection of the mood of the writer.

The problem of denotation-connotation of words has been discussed by a number of writers. Betts (1949) considered the problem of shortening the distance between high-level abstractions (fictions), which are primarily connotative, and experience. Such words may be charged with emotion, and misinterpretation of them has disastrous effects on communication. Kincheloe (1951) discussed connotative aspects of propaganda.

Concerning figurative language, Betts (1949) acknowledged the metaphor to be a compact, useful means of communication, but stated that the reader must have a background of experience in evaluating a metaphor, or communication breaks down. McKee (1945) suggested that pupils in intermediate grades should receive several lessons on interpreting figures of speech.

Meaning may be implied in a still more diffuse manner—in the broad context of the whole communication, setting, tone, mood. "Broader context" was defined by H. A. Anderson (1951, p. 111) as "those factors largely outside the text itself which influence interpretation of what is read." He listed, as such factors, character of the time, locale, experience of the writer, reader's background, audience the writer had in mind, and mood or tone of the text. Each, according to Anderson, presents a problem in communication. Kincheloe (1951) noted the difficulties faced by readers in persuasive language, in telescoped descriptions, and in that which is left unsaid.

The only investigations of methods of instruction in the use of figurative language are "action research," i.e., classroom investigations where variables are subject to little control, and therefore more detailed study is needed in this area. Gill (1954) stressed the importance of teaching figurative language to pupils, because such language is increasing as writers attempt to explain an increasingly complex world. Gill explained that the figures of speech are, themselves, very complex. She categorized them as follows: (1) contrived figures, those built on existing ones (bamboo curtain), built on opposites (cold war), based on clichés (brow like a mountain); (2) omissions—elliptical (the wolf and pig struggled in his face), allusion (busman's holiday), implication (dollar diplomacy); (3) language in which figures are expressed in obsolescent words (dog in manger), in unfamiliar words (perils), in words with multiple meanings (horns); (4) figures having unfamiliar references (squeaking wheel). She suggested acting out appropriate figures for clearer understanding. I. B. Williams (1954) attacked the same problem and discovered that students could be encouraged to look for figures of speech in their conversations.

A number of writers have discussed difficulties in communication which arise because of meaning which lies in the broader context of written materials. Although research has not been conducted here, all of these writers stress the importance of teaching students to observe closely, to study the text to obtain meaning from the broader context. N. B. Smith (1950) stressed the need to observe words with multiple and changing meanings, trends in word formation (such as the tendency to add endings and beginnings to old words to produce new words), and invented words. The teacher needs models, illustrations, discussions, films, and exhibits to clari-

fy these words. LaBrant (1958) listed clues in the context which supply meaning with reference to such factors as the time and setting of the writing. Such "setting" clues may be famous names, methods of transportation, buildings, clothing, methods of food storage, or occupations that are mentioned in the piece of prose. She suggested that junior high school teachers might ask pupils when and where the story occurred and then have pupils answer the questions by a search for context clues. Cook (1959) discussed the same topic, stressing close observation of very difficult clues such as the use of idioms.

Word order. In addition to meaning conveyed by selection of words, the English language conveys meaning by syntax, grammar, and punctuation. Pei (1949) explained that in English the sentence is the unit of thought, because vocabulary, morphology, and syntax all bear the burden of meaning. Further, he stated that those who need precise linguistic distinctions have little scope within the simple morphology of English, but boundless resources in involved English syntax. Teachers must remember that pupils have difficulty with syntactical problems in literary and scientific writing.

1. Grammar, syntax, and punctuation. Cook (1959) criticized methods of teaching grammar, syntax, and punctuation in schools. He stressed the fact that understanding of language as an instrument of communication has progressed enormously in the past half-century, but grammar is still taught as a set of rules instead of as a factor in interpretation of meaning. Both grammar and punctuation may be taught as part of interpretation in teaching reading. Other writers such as McKee (1945) and Ebbitt (1951) have expressed similar convictions. Others have suggested a structural approach in the teaching of reading (Warfel & Lloyd, 1957).

Research on effects of knowledge of syntax or grammar on reading ability is rare. Strom (1956) noted the frequency with which subject and predicate agreement, juxtaposition of adjective or adverb with word modified, and concord of pronoun with antecedent were held to be important for understanding context. She analyzed the syntax and grammar of poetry and literary prose which college students were required to read for comprehension. She found little, if any, relationship between student comprehension and ability to classify crucial elements of grammar and syntax in the passages. Her conclusions imply that if grammar and syntax were taught as aids to meaning in reading, her experiment would have demonstrated a significant relationship.

2. Contractions, initials, formulas. While no mention is made of it in research studies, the recent custom of using first letters to replace words (NEA, AERA, CARE, etc.) may cause difficulties for those who read material containing them. Formulas (which are of the same general nature) may cause similar communication problems. We need further studies on increasingly abstract symbolization in the following hierarchy: reality —picture—word—formula.

Verbalism. A discussion on verbals would be incomplete without mention of verbalism and vocabulary control. Verbalism is a constant threat to communication, and a constant problem for the teacher. There is no intrinsic connection between concept and concept symbol. The child may use the symbol with little meaning or wrong meaning. This phenomenon is termed "verbalism." Scott and Myers (1923) and others over the ensuing years have demonstrated the lack of meaning which common historical and geographic terms have for children. Serra (1953) criticized placing emphasis on vocabulary building without reference to the dimensions of the supporting concepts. Cole (1946) listed composition habits of authors which lead to verbalism: use of abstract terms; figures of speech; varied wording; squeezing in too many ideas; and failure to supply context clues, concrete illustrations, or hints concerning the relative importance of facts.

Two devices for reducing verbalism were suggested by Helmkamp (1951)—the Triangle of Reference and the Abstraction Ladder. The Triangle of Reference is a triangle with "Object" and "Word" at the corners of the base and "Thought" at the apex. The pupil is told that communication is a two-way process. The writer sees the object, which causes a thought, which produces the word. For the reader the process is reversed. Since the change is from specific to general to abstract, the possibility of misunderstanding is great. The Abstraction Ladder demonstrates visually for the pupil the linguistic process of classifying objects according to similar characteristics while ignoring variations. For example, canned peas are classified as canned vegetables, canned vegetables as canned goods, canned goods as groceries, groceries as commodities, commodities as national wealth. The higher the words are on the ladder, the more abstract they are and therefore the less likely to produce similar thoughts in the reader. Helmkamp (1951, p. 102) suggested that pupils should analyze prose passages in terms of levels of abstraction and check written definitions to make sure that words used to define were lower on the ladder than the word defined: "A meaningful definition of a word must point down the abstraction ladder. It must give specific examples in terms of observable behaviors."

Perhaps the best hope for reduction of verbalism lies in uncovering a fallacy and adopting a process. The fallacy is the naïve belief that students can read material with content which is unfamiliar and contains words with unknown meanings, and learn content and word meanings by so doing. The process to be adopted involves assigning students material containing no unfamiliar words (words taught beforehand) if the content is unfamiliar and familiar content (simple material) if new word meanings are to be derived from context.

Vocabulary control was suggested as a partial answer to verbalism—i.e., adding unknown words at a rate which would assure understanding and familiarity. Control of syntax and vocabulary are usually considered under the heading of readability. Chall (1958) discussed the problem thoroughly, stressing the assumption underlying control of syntax and vocabulary, i.e., that reduction in readability level will lead to reduction of communication difficulty. Further, she noted that the readability of material for use by pupils can be controlled by altering the ratio of familiar to unfamiliar words and the number of repetitions of unfamiliar words once they have been introduced. Chall expressed the current doubts concerning vocabulary control: What is the optimum vocabulary load for a grade? Is there danger of hampering growth of meaning vocabulary? Are frequency-of-use lists a wise basis for vocabulary control? Does use of a formula to build written materials interfere with normal language learning? Research answers to these questions are lacking.

Research by Michaelis and Tyler (1951) on reading ability and readability estimated the readability of United Nations publications and measured the reading ability of high school pupils. Their study showed that formulas underestimate reading difficulties. Saale (1950) cited research which indicated that amplification of materials increased its meaning for students. Dale (1956) stated, from his experiments on technical vocabulary, that estimates of the size of pupil vocabulary have been too optimistic.

Discussions of vocabulary control have been pessimistic. Diederich (1944) maintained that meaning for the reader is little enhanced by simplifying sentences and substituting more familiar words. Saale (1950) stressed the many shades of meaning of words and the impossibility of maintaining unaltered meaning if words are substituted. Carner and Sheldon (1954) concluded that the nature of concepts and the limitations of the reader had more effect on meaning than familiarity of the words. They cited as examples the facts that chronological concepts soon go beyond human experience, spatial concepts are multidimensional, numerical concepts transcend human experience, and social concepts are extremely involved. Effectiveness of learning through reading depends on the extent to which relationships among such concepts are grasped. Martin (1955) analyzed almost a century of concept studies and concluded that the concept load of subject-matter textbooks makes understanding a very difficult task.

How can teachers help pupils cope with heavy concept loads and language difficulties in materials which they should read? Guilfoile (1951) suggested that teachers can help the pupil increase his command of language, supply material within the limits of his comprehension, and give specific training in coping with legitimate language difficulties. Teachers must select texts that are written to assist learning and study them to familiarize themselves with the language barriers which the pupils will meet.

COMPREHENSION ACCORDING TO THE PURPOSES OF THE READER

Since comprehension of the ideas expressed is often the chief outcome of the reading act, it may be repeated that the teacher can help pupils work for comprehension in three main ways. The previous sections dealt with the perception and comprehension of words, phrases, and sentences. This section is based on the concept of comprehension in terms of the reader's purposes, and the next section is organized in terms of comprehension of content in the various curriculum areas. These are obviously overlapping concerns. For example, in reading sentences or paragraphs the pupil may be skimming to get some specific facts (purpose) and he may be reading social studies materials (content). By the time the child has reached the primer or first-reader level of reading ability, he may need the teacher's suggestions about efficient ways of reading one sentence in contrast to reading a whole story (unit of material), reading a paragraph for main idea rather than specific details (purpose), and distinguishing between factual and fictional materials (content). Despite this overlapping of types of comprehension in reading, there may be some value in presenting samples of the research or practice in each of the three main divisions as a guide to the research worker who wishes to study problems of teaching children engaged in specific reading activities. As in the case of other kinds of teaching, research on teaching reading must always take into account each of the specific ends toward which teaching and learning are aimed.

As suggested above in the discussion of comprehension of various verbal units, the teacher who is concerned with comprehension in terms of purpose has clear direction from research that specific reading techniques vary with purpose. The child who reads carefully for detailed recall is not necessarily the child who reads best for the main idea of a passage, and the child who recognizes clearly the sequence in a chapter in a history textbook is not necessarily the one who masters his facts in a chapter on science. From some of the studies of eye movements reported by Buswell, Judd, and others around 1920, there is evidence that the poor reader goes about various reading tasks in the same inflexible way, whereas good readers adapt their rate and method to the purpose at hand. In an early study, Pressey and Pressey (1921) concluded that a good silent reader of one type of material may be an average or poor reader of other material. Later, Shores and Husbands (1950) found that speed of reading depends upon both the purpose of the reader and the characteristics of the printed materials. These investigators and others, such as Fay (1950), give strong support to the idea that reading is not a unitary skill. The capable teacher is the one who helps children recognize various purposes for reading and then gives them opportunities to improve their abilities to read for these somewhat distinct and separate purposes. The question of which specific abilities to develop is answered in various sections below after a few references have been made to general studies of comprehension.

M. S. Johnson (1949) summarized studies of comprehension up to the middle 1940's and found comprehension related to characteristics of the reader and readability of the materials. She believed that most tests of comprehension are measures of "word knowledge and recall of facts" and do not evaluate higher-level comprehension abilities. In a much quoted study, Davis (1944) factor-analyzed the results of nine reading tests and found such components of reading ability as word knowledge, verbal reasoning, and ability to focus on specific statements, to use context, and to determine the author's purpose. In a later analysis of the same data using Spearman's unidimensional method of analysis, Thurstone (1946) found that the intercorrelations of test results could be accounted for by a single common factor which he termed simply "reading ability" and concluded that we need further evidence about "the components of the complex that we call reading ability" (p. 188).

Another type of study more closely related to classroom situations was made by Bell (1942) with fifteen-year-olds in Scotland. He found that comprehension questions ranged from easy to difficult as follows: (1) questions of direct reference, whose answers can be found in the text in the same words; (2) questions of indirect reference whose answers can be found in the text in slightly different words; (3) questions demanding easy inferences that are not stated in the text but can be inferred from it and may range from easy to difficult; (4) comprehension involving qualifying phrases such as "largely," "alone," "chief," "only," "full," and similar words; and (5) questions demanding difficult inferences with emphasis on ideas rather than words. This order may differ somewhat with younger children. A study by Keneally (1939) illustrated just how difficult it may be to acquire skills like grasping the main idea and organizing a passage. By controlling the relative difficulty of passages, she found that only the following percentages of a group of sixth-graders performed various tasks correctly:

Task	Percentage Correct
1. Supplying minor ideas in an outline which lists the major ideas	65
2. Selecting the statement which best summarizes a paragraph	50
3. Putting a list of topics in the sequence in which they occur	39
4. Matching headlines or topics with paragraphs	23
5. Supplying major topics in an outline in which minor ideas are given	16
6. Writing original headlines or topics for paragraphs	10

The studies by Bell and Keneally indicate that when teachers ask different kinds of questions about the same passage, pupils will find some types of questions more difficult than others. McNaughton (1960) found that the written responses of seventh-graders to selections containing concrete historical materials could be categorized on five levels: (1) copied facts, (2) qualified facts, (3) concrete concepts, (4) abstract concepts, and (5) generalizations. In free responses about the most important ideas in a passage, the pupils tended to answer at the level of facts and concrete concepts. When given further chances to answer other questions, they responded more at the level of abstract concepts and generalizations. The kind of question asked is an important determiner of the level of children's responses to reading materials.

N. B. Smith (1952) reviewed 11 studies showing that different reading purposes are used in different subject-matter fields and that specialized reading skills can be improved with direct instruction. What are some of the specific skills related to the reader's purpose? Some 15 purposes have been identified, four of which are discussed below.

1. *Reading for the main idea.* This skill is often acquired, in part, in the first grade. It is sometimes used by children and adults in casual reading, such as going over the newspaper when one is not deeply concerned with the news items. Pupils practice the skill when the teacher asks them, "Tell in one sentence what the paragraph is about" or "Choose the best title for the story." McCullough (1957a) showed that children can grasp the main idea of story material as early as the readiness level. Although there was a positive relationship among skills in different types of reading at the second and fourth grades, there was some evidence the children tested were better at reading for specific facts than at reading for main idea or drawing conclusions. Broening (1941), in an analysis of the reading abilities of a large group of secondary school students, concluded that reading to grasp the central idea is based on three skills: (1) noting key words and topic sentence as clues; (2) differentiating between main points and supporting details; and (3) knowing the meaning of relational words such as *but, therefore,* and *consequently.*

2. *Reading for sequence.* This skill often begins in first grade with the ability to follow the main events of a story, an ability also related to reading readiness (Gates, Bond, & Russell, 1939). Children may be encouraged to check word clues such as *then, next,* or *after some time* in establishing sequence. Adults reading a continued story in a magazine employ skills in remembering sequence. In school, the skill is needed in reading social studies (Thorndike, 1941), in following the plot of a story, and in outlining in many areas.

3. *Reading to follow directions.* This skill may involve detailed reading, but it seems to require an additional factor of translating printed symbols into some sort of action. As such it may also involve sequence, as in the steps for conducting an experiment or making a cake. Although many teachers spend much of their school day giving directions, a psychology of direction-giving has not been developed. Some studies of listening ability have dealt with such factors as interference

and redundancy (Hovland, 1954), but little help is available to teachers in the use of printed directions. Many children acquire some of these abilities in following workbook directions and the requirements of study-type exercises. This type of reading is probably close to the reading of verbal problems in arithmetic, which is discussed below. Carroll (1926) has shown that reading directions improves with specific practice.

4. *Reading to draw conclusions.* Such reading may be defined as picking up ideas explicitly stated by the author, rearranging them as needed, and coming to some fresh or original generalization about them. It occurs, for example, when children take the actions of a character in a story—what others say about him, what he says—and come to some conclusion about the kind of person he is. Such reading is sometimes described as problem-solving, especially when the problem is presented to the child by other persons or circumstances, or it may be included under the broader label of "creative reading" discussed below. Clark (1958) analyzed some of the skills needed by sixth-graders in reading as a basis for predicting various outcomes and found they could be taught successfully in the form of self-explanatory materials. He found a correlation of .52 between general comprehension ability and scores on his experimental test of ability to predict.

Critical Reading

In a world of conflicting opinion, propaganda, high-pressure advertising, and specialized points of view, a reasonable aim of the language arts program is teaching children to evaluate critically what they read and hear. The tendency of curriculum workers in previous years to postpone such activities at least to junior high school has been superseded by the opinion that critical thinking can be taught in the primary grades (W. Petty, 1956) or even as early as the reading readiness program (M. S. Johnson, 1953). Research has not yet clarified, however, just what critical reading is and what activities are most useful for teaching it at the various grade levels.

The terms *critical thinking* and *critical reading* have been used with many different meanings by different writers. Glaser (1941) summarized points of view up to 1940. B. S. Bloom and others (1956) included the term and examples of relevant test items in their *Taxonomy of Educational Objectives.* D. H. Russell (1956) and Sochor (1959) listed some of the many activities included under the "critical" rubric. Many writers have equated it with the problem-solving approach to reading. Hayakawa (1950) spoke of "recognizing stereotypes as substitutes for thought." Kottmeyer (1944) said that it occurs when "the reader projects his own judgments, attitudes, and appreciations into juxtaposition with the reading material." Triggs (1959) wrote of finding the facts, determining their accuracy, and interpreting them in new understandings. Pingry (1951) indicated that the term *critical thinking* has been used in at least five ways.

A few studies have shown that critical reading may be distinguished from literal comprehension in reading. Shores and Husbands (1950) found no reading tests at the elementary school level which measured the ability to think critically about printed materials. McCullough (1957a) found correlations between various tests of literal comprehension and "creative reading" (which included drawing conclusions and making judgments) that ranged from .26 to .63, with a median of .47. She believed that such tests may measure a common factor of fact-getting ability but that the different abilities should be practiced and tested separately. Maney (1958) found a correlation of only .11 between general reading ability and critical reading scores in science (with intelligence partialled out). Similarly, Sochor (1958) found a correlation of only .23 between literal comprehension and critical reading scores on social studies materials (with intelligence partialled out). Such results suggest that there are certain critical reading abilities which may be distinguished from factual reading and which the teacher, accordingly, should present specifically to a reading group.

Factors affecting children's ability to read critically have not been studied in detail except in the area of the reader's attitude. Crossen (1948), Groff (1955), and McKillop (1952) have all shown that the attitude which the reader brings to the content of a passage affects his comprehension of it. This attitude affects not so much his comprehension of facts stated specifically in the passage as it does his ability to make an inference, as in critical reading. Other factors which may affect critical reading are the nature of the materials (the message), the setting in which they are read (the situation), and other characteristics of the reader himself (the receiver). Hovland (1954) summarized the research on the influence of such factors from the point of view of the social psychologist. More specific studies of children, individually and in groups, are needed. An example of the investigation needed in many related areas is Gans's (1940) study of fourth-grade children's abilities to distinguish between relevant and irrelevant materials. She found that the ability to select material pertinent to a specified problem is not usually taught in the intermediate grades and is not tested in the ordinary tests of reading comprehension. Her study suggested the importance of the pupil's having a clear purpose for reading.

Gans's study also suggested that there are specific reading abilities which may be included under the term *critical reading* and that these should probably be practiced directly. Kottmeyer (1944) described three units used in the upper elementary school grades which dealt with propaganda analysis, reading newspaper editorials, and interpretation of cartoons. Nardelli (1954) found that, in a specially designed six-week unit, sixth-grade pupils made better gains in ability to detect propaganda than in some forms of creative reading. J. A. Brownell (1953) found gains in ability to read critically in the social studies after 28 weeks of instruction in the ninth grade, although the evidence was not conclusive that the greater gains in the experimental group could be attributed to training in reading alone. Artley (1956) analyzed the abilities needed for critical reading in various content areas.

The studies cited above suggest that the curricular aim of developing critical reading abilities is generally accepted, but that teachers, curriculum specialists, and research workers still need to define critical reading adequately for teaching and research purposes. Through most definitions runs the idea of not accepting as true everything that one sees in print, but, instead, trying to judge or evaluate the source, the ideas, the argument, and the conclusions in the light of one's other experiences. This idea may be presented as early as the first grade and should probably be given a specific place in reading instruction at all subsequent grade levels. Most standardized reading tests do not include measures of critical reading ability. Therefore, the research worker must rely on his own ingenuity in making such measures or consult additional sources, such as B. S. Bloom, et al. (1956), some tests used with specific basal series of readers, or some of the research noted above. Suggestions for the development of critical reading abilities are available in the manuals of some basal reading series (G. Williams, 1959) and in studies of the kind mentioned above.

Creative Reading

The adjective *creative* may be overused these days, and some writers reject the term when applied to reading. The writers of this chapter believe, however, that reading instruction for the modern world cannot be restricted to word-recognition techniques and literal comprehension. Emerson once wrote, "Tis the good reader that makes the good book," and most writers on literary matters agree today upon the importance of the reader's reactions to a piece of literature. The present use of the term extends the idea beyond literature to include any worth-while writing. Interpretation and appreciation which involve the characteristics and experience of the reader himself are part of high-level creative reading. Even the young child may have an individual and original response to a story or passage and thus may be said to read creatively.

The term *creative reading* may involve *critical reading,* but it ordinarily includes a wider range of activities. In general, it is applied to any reading in which the reader combines or uses the ideas of the writer in a fresh, original way. The reader "creates" from the ideas presented on the printed page. Creative reading thus goes beyond literal comprehension of ideas explicitly stated by the author to "reading between the lines" or to an individual, uncopied, novel response to the material. In reading a story or poem about a farm, a group may respond in such ways as, "I liked the sounds of some of the words," "I saw a picture of the farm," or "That farm was different from the one I visited last summer." Reading the same selection evokes individual responses which go beyond mere responses to the facts directly stated. The main varieties of creative reading may be classified as (1) finding meanings implied by the author, (2) inferring beyond the facts stated or the intent of the author, (3) appreciative reactions such as enjoying beauty or responding to imagery, and (4) critical evaluations as described above.

Some of the research support for concern with such creative reading is given below under the heading "The Teacher Encourages Interpretation." The more general topic of creative reading goes beyond interpretation to include problem-solving and description of the process. For example, Bedell (1934) found that, for eighth- and ninth-graders reading science materials, ability to infer from the facts differed from ability to recall the facts. Artley (1943) and McCullough (1957a) found median correlations in the high .40s between various tests of literal comprehension and creative reading, such as seeing relationships, drawing conclusions, and evaluating arguments, but both concluded that the two main types represented

abilities requiring separate, specific practice. Similarly, Clark (1958), in the study mentioned on page 901, identified abilities in reading to make predictions. He found that two tests of ability to predict correlated positively with one another but were somewhat independent of ordinary measures of vocabulary and comprehension.

There are many technical skills and methods of acquiring accurate literal impressions from reading which must be taught. Creative reading must be based on such accurate, exact, reading. As television for large groups, self-administering printed materials, and teaching machines are developed more fully, perhaps word recognition and literal comprehension will be taught in these ways, and the teacher will be able to concentrate more on developing creative reactions to good literature and other prose containing important ideas. The same paragraph may be read for specific facts or it may be read creatively, e.g., to determine sequence and make original inferences. D. H. Russell (1961) has suggested 20 specific reading-thinking abilities which result in fresh, individual ideas and which, therefore, may be labeled creative reading.

Most research on creative reading has been included under the rubric "interpretation" in relation to literary materials, but it has also had a wider scope, as in the factual materials used in such studies as those of Arnold (1938), Crosscup (1938), and Nardelli (1954). Some of its components have been listed in Burkhart's (1945) analysis of expert opinions on the reading process, and Piekarz (1956) has shown that children must be able to read a passage with reasonable ease before they can go into its implied meanings. In some of these and other studies, the terms *critical reading* and *creative reading* have been used in overlapping senses, partly because of confusion in definition, and partly because the more general term *creative reading* may include critical thinking as one of its parts, as when a new idea or product is evaluated. Reading is creative when the reader uses his background of experience to criticize or interpret. Evaluating and using ideas gained in reading may be considered a part of the total reading process, and pupils should be encouraged to judge the value of ideas, make interpretations, and organize ideas into fresh concepts and generalizations. Critical and creative reading can be taught.

COMPREHENSION ACCORDING TO SUBJECT-MATTER FIELDS

A discussion of the teacher's work in improving reading in subject-matter fields necessarily overlaps with one on reading according to purpose. The reader's purpose is often centered in one or more curricular or recreational areas, and purposes may differ widely in various areas. The child's reading of a geography text to get some idea of the size of the South Pacific area is not the same as his reading for fun, for general impression, or for visualizing the scene in a Robert Louis Stevenson poem.

Although each subject-matter area makes separate demands on the reader, investigators have found positive, even if low, correlations between reading abilities in different areas. Such correlations suggest that some verbal or reading abilities are common to most reading situations. The evidence is not clear whether general or specific factors are more important in the lower grades, but in the ninth grade, E. Bond (1938) found clear differences in reading ability in such areas as history, science, and foreign language. At the sixth-grade level, Fay (1950) found that scores on a group of reading tests correlated highly with achievement in the social studies and in science, when the tests measured understanding of precise directions and general comprehension. However, with CA and MA controlled, the particular tests used were not related to achievement in mathematics. In another study, F. P. Robinson and Hall (1941) found that reading scores in different content areas at the college level, such as art, fiction, geology, and history, were not highly correlated even when the selections were written under one editorship. Whether dif-

ferentiation of abilities increases with age has not been established but, in another article, Fay (1954) recommended that specific instruction in reading for content should be given in all grades beyond second grade.

The demands of subject-matter areas may differ because (1) vocabulary and concept are specific to a field, (2) different organizations or thought patterns occur in the printed materials of each field, and (3) specific devices, symbols, and illustrations are unique to each content area (D. H. Russell, 1961). Each of these factors probably calls for specific teaching. Distinctive techniques are required for such tasks as reading an arithmetic problem, studying a chapter in history, following directions for an experiment in science, and utilizing library resources such as encyclopedias or card catalogs. All are examples of functional reading for getting work done, but all involve somewhat specific skills such as those mentioned below.

Social Studies

Michaelis (1956) listed some 10 main types of material which the child must read in social studies. Some of the research showing relationships between reading and achievement in social studies has been summarized by Horn (1937, pp. 151–205), W. E. Young (1941), and Witty (1950). In a study of two groups of eighth-grade children, Rudolf (1949) found that instruction in reading skills over a five-month period produced superior knowledge of social studies information and superior test scores in study skills and reading comprehension without requiring additional class time. She gave the group practice in comprehension and interpretation of social studies materials, reference work, note-taking, outlining, and summarizing. Howell (1950) commented on the values of special instruction in the use of references and in reading maps, graphs, charts, and tables. Culbertson and Powers (1959) found vertical bar graphs somewhat easier to interpret than horizontal bar graphs and both of these easier than line graphs. Labels and symbols on graphs seemed somewhat easier to interpret than cross-hatching and keys. Edgerton (1954) found that articles in well-known children's encyclopedias were often at the seventh- or eighth-grade levels of difficulty.

One aim of social studies instruction, often cited in courses of study, is that of developing habits of critical reading or thinking, as described in the section above. Although not based directly on research, a list of criteria suggested by Tiegs and Adams (1959), for the evaluation of social studies materials which require critical thinking, might improve the selection of items to be placed in the pupils' hands. The criteria included authorship, philosophy, organization, content, readability, illustrations and physical features, and the use of other teaching aids and accessory materials.

Mathematics

Spencer (1960) stated that "mathematical reading occurs whenever quantity or relationships of a quantitative nature are experienced" (p. 204). Mathematical symbolism is one type of language which each child must acquire, at least in part, and understanding of meaning is essential in both mathematics and reading. Skills required in reading arithmetical materials were discussed by McKee (1948), by G. L. Bond and Wagner (1960), and others. Research on the role of reading in solving verbal problems was summarized by D. H. Russell (1960). This research has revealed a low relationship of arithmetical achievement to general reading ability but a closer relationship to specific vocabulary and to selected reading skills such as ability in noting details, drawing inferences, and integrating scattered ideas. For example, H. C. Johnson (1944) found that a seventh-grade group instructed in mathematical vocabulary not only gained in arithmetic vocabulary but made significant advances in ability to solve problems which included the vocabulary taught. Treacy (1944) found that, with the effect of mental age removed, there was little relationship between problem-solving abil-

ities and such reading abilities as predicting outcomes, comprehending at a particular rate, getting the central thought, and interpreting the content. On the other hand, success in problem-solving was related to mathematical vocabulary, ability to perceive relations, ability to note details clearly, and ability to combine dispersed ideas. In other words, ability in problem-solving is related to some reading-thinking abilities but not to others. Again, research on some focus for reading instruction by the mathematics teacher is indicated. In the article mentioned above (D. H. Russell, 1960), 12 specific researchable suggestions were given for classroom practice on the basis of our knowledge of research in reading and in problem-solving.

Science

Although the reading of science textbooks is common in both the elementary and secondary grades, such books do not constitute a complete program in science, for reading must be combined with observation and experiment. However, reading can be useful in building up a background of information on such matters, for instance, as the lives of scientists or methods used in studying weather. It may have additional values in developing attitudes, focusing observations, or preparing for experimentation. As in the case of mathematics, not all kinds of reading are used in these activities. Swenson (1942) found that scores on tests of ability to read science materials and on standardized general reading tests were substantially correlated but that rate of reading was not highly correlated with achievement in science classes. Shores (1943) found, for ninth-graders, that good reading in science was related to power (level) in reading comprehension and to vocabulary knowledge but not to abilities in locating information or comprehending the general meaning of a passage. In a later study, Shores and Saupe (1953) found that results of a test of reading ability in science materials, given in Grades 4, 5, and 6, suggested the existence of specific abilities in reading different materials for different purposes.

English

Most developmental reading programs are based largely on fiction or literary and semi-literary materials. In the primary grades, a story enlivened by characterization, conversation, and description is probably easier to read than a factual passage with a high idea-density. The specific nature of reading abilities described above, however, suggests that basal or developmental reading programs should include practice in reading social studies, mathematics, and science after some of the first difficulties in learning to read have been hurdled. Furthermore, the reading tasks in the field of literature are themselves specific and perhaps unique. A child must learn to read poetry with its specific format, imagery, and compression of ideas. He must acquire some techniques in reading material in the form of drama and must learn how to read whole books and novels. Many books on the teaching of English, such as *The English Language Arts in the Secondary School* (National Council of Teachers of English, 1956) and the volume by Hook (1959) for junior and senior high schools, give recommendations, based on investigation, for developing such specific abilities. Two sound motion picture films (Ruth Strang, consultant) on this subject, entitled *How to Read Novels* and *How to Read Poetry* (Coronet Instructional Films), make suggestions which can be subjected to experimental research.

In reading fiction, the child or adult may want to get a general impression, predict the outcome of a story, form sensory impressions (as in comparing *flowing, rushing, trickling,* and *gushing*), enjoy humor, follow a plot, or understand character. Some of the research on these more creative aspects of reading has been mentioned above and will be noted below in the discussion of interpretation in reading.

The above summary of research in subject-matter areas suggests that the teacher can develop general reading abilities which apply to several fields; it also suggests, however, that both teacher and researcher should identify and give practice in the specific reading abilities peculiar to certain purposes and substantive areas. The studies further suggest that children often need help in pinpointing a purpose and in adapting reading procedures to the material in hand. Research has not given much help so far in identifying or developing differentiated skills, appropriate attitudes, or flexibility in attack. Carrillo and Sheldon (1952) discussed flexibility in reading rate, and Letson (1960) developed an informal test of flexibility. At the college level, McDonald (1958) and Ward (1956) described tests yielding a versatility or flexibility score, and Ward concluded that flexibility should be considered as part of a total comprehension score. The area would seem to be a fruitful one for further study.

THE TEACHER ENCOURAGES INTERPRETATION

Much of the reading described in the two preceding sections under purposes and content fields is labeled "work-type" or "functional" reading. In addition to these workaday uses of reading, the teacher may have goals in the realm of developing interests, appreciations, and tastes. Such outcomes may be achieved in reading a chapter in history or a description of a scientific experiment. In addition, the teacher attempts to encourage the achievement of these outcomes through reading literature. Even in juvenile books, the child may find humor, plot, excitement, and insight into human behavior. In both factual and fictional materials he can begin to understand the "big ideas," the values held in our culture in such realms as truth, honesty, beauty, and courage. In meeting these ideas, he makes a start on high-level understanding, on appreciations and tastes, and on interests which may persist for the rest of his life.

Research on such effects of reading, often labeled the "intangibles," has been neither abundant nor rigorous. Research on reading interests is extensive but is usually limited to lists of favorite titles or of types of stories preferred by different groups of children and adolescents. A classic investigation in the area is that of Terman and Lima (1935). More recent reports are those of Norvell (1950, 1958) on the interests of secondary and elementary school pupils. A few studies such as those of Rudman (1955) and Jefferson (1958) have attempted to get at factors affecting interests. In the subtle and complex area of developing appreciations and tastes for good literature, and assessing the influence of literature on values and conduct, the evidence is scanty.

One hypothesis about reading interests is that children will become avid and permanent readers as reading meets some of their deepest needs or helps them fulfill important purposes. Curiosity and excitement influence the start on reading; more enduring benefits are needed for lifetime habits. One group of studies about such benefits depends upon the insecure evidence of personal testimony. For example, N. B. Smith (1948) found that 61 per cent of elementary school pupils reported changes in attitudes as a result of reading, especially of reading stories about people and animals; 30 per cent reported changes in concepts and understandings, but only 9 per cent indicated changes in behavior as a result of reading. Similarly, as a result of direct questions, Weingarten (1954) reported that, in reading, adolescents found some understanding of themselves, a worthy concept of self, recognition of personal qualities or behavior to be emulated, and some understanding of the meaning of life. He concluded that teachers, librarians, clinicians, and counselors should guide youth to books which combine interest and value for personal and social development.

Some study has been made of the conditions under which reading affects the reader and of the kinds of effects that may occur. D. H. Russell (1958) summarized some 70 sources and concluded that the impact of reading depends upon (1) the "noncontent"

characteristics of the material read—author prestige, physical format, etc.; (2) the content of ideas contained in the message; and (3) the personal characteristics of the reader. Some overt responses to reading, that is, the kinds of effects that reading had, were also summarized. Examples of the relation of effect to the first two factors, the characteristics of the material read, are found in the classic study by Richards (1930), who found difficulties due to the reader's inability to comprehend the author's meaning in relation to feeling, tone, intention, and imagery. The second factor, content of ideas, has been utilized in studies of the mass media and in such books as McConnell's (1956) analysis of 24 biographies for children and Child, Potter, and Levine's (1946) evaluation of third readers in basal reading series.

Examples of the influence of the reader himself on comprehension are evident in the studies by McKillop (1952) and Loban (1954), who found that previous attitudes affected comprehension, not so much in literal understanding as in interpretation of the materials. Other studies of types of response include the early qualitative one by Waples, Berelson, and Bradshaw (1940) and Squire's (1956) coding of responses of adolescents to four short stories with themes of personal development. A study in England by Whitehead (1956) indicated that the content of the book was a more potent determiner of response than were age, sex, teacher, or school for a group of 1,800 children between ages 11 and 16. Characteristics associated with the effectiveness of novels were easy language, relatively immature emotional problems, possibilities of easy identification, and open-endedness of plot conducive to interpretation on the basis of wish fulfillment.

Studies like the one by Squire may be said to deal with reactions sometimes described as reflecting "appreciation" and "taste." Early (1960) described possible stages in the growth of literary appreciations, and Rosenblatt (1960) underlined the importance of the reader himself in developing these. Tests of appreciation were used by Hartley (1930),

D. L. Burton (1952), and E. D. Williams, Winter, and Woods (1956). Williams and his co-workers found some appreciation "in primitive form" in children at an early age but little response to literary devices (structure, aptness of simile, etc.) before they were 12 years of age. Sussams (1949) found considerable dislike of poetry among children aged 11 to 14. Avegno (1956) studied poetry choices of intermediate-grade children, and Britton (1954) concluded that such choices could be improved by reading poetry and returning to it from time to time. In an interview study of third- and fourth-graders, Fennema (1959) found that pupils' imagery could be divided into five categories: nonaction, action, place, color, and combinations of these. The amount of such imagery correlated negatively with some of the usual measures of reading comprehension. One city school system (Oakland Board of Education, 1960) issued bulletins suggesting poems for primary and intermediate grades that might be used in developing five levels of appreciation: (1) enjoyment of rhythm, of melody, and of story; (2) recognizing one's own experiences mirrored in poetry; (3) projection into a world other than that in which one lives; (4) understanding of symbolism and hidden meanings; and (5) sensitivity to patterns of writing and to literary style.

The evidence about the subtler effects of reading on personality and beliefs is even more scattered, and much of it, such as support for the process of bibliotherapy (D. H. Russell & Shrodes, 1950), is found in reports of case studies rather than in experimental literature. Perhaps this absence of experimental evidence will always prevail. Because the impact of a passage or story must be largely idiosyncratic, the evidence of impact must be related to one or to a few individuals. In a second-reader story, one child may identify with a picture of a happy family, another may be attracted by a boy who was "bad," and a third may dismiss the story as "baby stuff" compared to the account of space travel he has just been enjoying. In interpretive reactions, especially those involved with

autistic thinking or personality factors, there is probably no one right answer to questions about plot or character, and it is therefore difficult to predict the effects of the material on individuals. Examples of the use of bibliotherapy to improve emotional and social adjustment are found in studies such as those of Shrodes (1949) and Herminghaus (1954). Applications to groups in a typical classroom are largely untried.

The evidence cited above is given in some detail, not because it represents a large body of research, but because it illustrates facets of a topic usually neglected in discussions of alphabet, phonics, or literal interpretation. Interpretation differs from one child to the next because the youngsters themselves differ in reading ability, in background of experience, and in attitudes and expectancies. Interpretation varies because of the piece of literature itself. Some literature, for example, can evoke images in seeing, hearing, or feeling. Symbols such as the lion or Abraham Lincoln may lead to an understanding of such values as courage and compassion. Interpretation varies with defined purpose for reading, that is, with "set." With older children it may be narrational or associational, illustrate self-involvement, or stress literary and prescriptive judgments (Squire, 1956). In years to come, as some of the more mechanical learnings in reading are taken care of by television or by teaching machines, research on teaching reading should probably give more attention to the ways in which interpretation can be fostered, especially at the elementary school level.

CLASSROOM ORGANIZATION

Any discussion of research on classroom organization for teaching reading should begin with a list of the various types of behavior needed in the habits, skills, interests, and attitudes characteristic of efficient reading. From this list of behaviors it should be possible to formulate hypotheses as to the ideal classroom organization for each. Research on methods of classroom organization should be considered against a framework of desirable outcomes. This arrangement is attempted in the following paragraphs.

Each item in this classification begins with reading objectives, progresses to situational requirements, and concludes with hypotheses as to the ideal organization as follows:

1. Reading habits

(a) Of concentration on meaning: The reader must learn to be oblivious to all but the reading material and his thoughts; ideally, the learner should be alone, without distraction of any kind.

(b) Of application of what is learned: The reader must learn to speak of and overtly apply that which he read; ideally, the learner should be with others who are interested in his application and who are at the same level of learning.

2. Reading skills

(a) Of word recognition—sight association–word-recognition techniques: The reader learns words at sight by looking at and saying words or parts of words or sounds (or hearing others say them). Ideally, the learner should work with a teacher or with a small group in which his speech and listening are active. For practice of these skills, a monitor could replace the teacher, or teams could be used. Any group here should be of the same level of development. For diagnosis, the pupil and teacher should not feel the pressure of a waiting class, but one pupil and one teacher may mean inefficient use of the teacher's time.

(b) Of word meaning—dictionary skills and context clues: The reader learns by being told or by reading definitions or by study of context. Ideally, if learning is by hearing or seeing, association of background experience is necessary. Therefore, any size of group is satisfactory, so long as the experience background is there and the words have immediate use. Dictionary work requires the teacher to check on individual work as soon as possible. Context study improves through wide individual reading and through periodic oral work with a group to *widen* the individual pupil's exploration of context.

Here, the group members should be of varying ability in skill, but all should be interested in the same topic.

(c) Of interpretation—reading in subject-matter fields for various purposes: Oral interpretation requires a climate of acceptance, then practice, then an audience situation. Ideally, oral practice should take place within a small, flexible group, with good rapport, so that criticisms come easily and oral turns come quickly. The size of the listening group is unimportant as long as the members of the group are interested in the subject.

3. Reading interests and attitudes: Silent interpretation is of the "study-type" and brooks no interruption except an occasional check with the teacher. These attitudes are built through success with reading material and through enthusiasm of others. Ideally, individual library situations in which the child is free to enjoy reading build good attitudes and interests. A chance for the child to discuss reading informally with his peers does the same. Group size is unimportant, so long as all are interested and feel free to participate further and have the opportunity to discuss and to cooperate in using the ideas and facts gathered in their silent study.

Purposes of Grouping

M. A. Robinson (1960) summarized opinion concerning the purposes of grouping by stating that any system of grouping is an attempt to reduce the range of achievement within the group so that the teacher can come closer to the individual pupil. Questions arise when practices are examined. Are innovations achieving the purposes of grouping? McCullough (1954) and others (Botel, 1960; N. B. Smith, 1957) have expressed doubts.

Doubts, confusion, and innumerable innovations in classroom organization may be the result of one influential factor. That is, as Betts (1958, p. 562) stated, "The key to the problem of class organization is the professional competence of the teacher." The importance of this factor becomes obvious when suggested practices for efficient grouping are examined—all depend on advanced teaching skills. Dolch (1954) and others (A. J. Harris, 1956; McCullough, 1957b) stressed the fact that the extent of individual differences will be approximately the same in any typical classroom group as in the total elementary school population.

Whipple (1953) listed practices to insure efficient learning in groups: flexibility (use of activities beyond the boundaries of the subgroup, i.e., including the whole class); purposeful, self-directed activities (self-responsibility of each pupil); activities under direct teacher guidance (guidance of discussion beyond the basic reader selection); guidance through grouping (good grouping helps the child succeed through effort); supervision (efficient supervision makes grouping succeed). Tinker (1952) and W. S. Gray (1957) produced similar lists. Sheldon (1960, p. 26) stated: "Organization should facilitate and never hinder the development of a well organized, well integrated, sequential reading program." It is interesting to speculate whether teacher ability may not be the only factor in determining the success of any organizational pattern.

Advantages and disadvantages of grouping have been discussed by many writers. Advantages of grouping were considered by Dawson (1955) to be philosophical, i.e., equality of opportunity to learn, and psychological, i.e., opportunity for success in learning. W. S. Gray (1957) listed the following advantages: In grouped classes, materials can be limited as to difficulty and interests and provide a closely integrated program for teacher guidance, development of common skills is promoted, group dynamics provides motivation, and discussion produces breadth and depth of interpretation. One disadvantage in grouping was considered by Dawson (1955) to be of a sociological character, in that it could lead to segregation or be used for such a purpose. Strang, McCullough, and Traxler (1955) recognized the danger and suggested that special grouping at the high school level could be avoided by having small classes,

skillful teachers, plenty of materials, and interclass grouping, defined on page 911. Canfield (1957) and Crosby (1960) noted the time-consuming preparations necessary when ability grouping is used, the stigma usually attached to the lowest group, and the difficulty in providing individual instruction with grouping.

Types of Grouping

There are three general types of grouping (M. A. Robinson, 1960): homogeneous groups, heterogeneous groups, and individualized programs. Within the homogeneous and heterogeneous types, groups can be organized on at least four bases: pupil achievement, mental ability, special needs, and pupil interests.

Currently advocated plans for grouping and the characteristics of each plan are as follows:

1. Total class. Here the whole class is considered to be one group. In good reading programs, no matter what pattern of grouping is used, some activities involve the entire class (A. J. Harris, 1956): audience situations, common learnings, choral reading, "open text" sessions, current events. Dolch (1954) discussed two practical applications. In the first application, each member of the class reads a different book, but each has the same topic. Library materials can be "unitized" for such a procedure. Efficient listening and contributing are crucial to the success of this scheme. In the second application, each member of the class has the same reader. The initial step entails discussion of pictures and learning new words as a group. The selection is presented orally by a reading committee which has prepared the material beforehand. All pupils participate in reading passages to answer questions.

Ungraded systems resemble total-class organizations. By this method of organization, children are segregated according to achievement in reading and rate of growth (Brearley, 1954; Goodlad & Anderson, 1959). The main advantage of ungraded plans is the break in rigid grade promotion, but a high degree of professional cooperation from teachers and principals is required for efficient operation.

M. A. Robinson (1960) suggested team teaching as a method of total-class organization. Teachers of adjoining rooms plan and work jointly so that pupils have a home room teacher and a reading teacher. The Joplin Plan (Floyd, 1954), by which pupils in Grades 4, 5, and 6 are regrouped into three groups according to reading achievement, is an example of this kind of total-class organization.

2. Interclass grouping. Such a plan of organization can be either homogeneous, subdividing classes according to rate of learning, achievement in one field, interests, or special needs (M. A. Robinson, 1960) or heterogeneous where no attempt has been made to reduce the range of differences. A homogeneous group of pupils is one in which the range of differences has been substantially reduced. Under the heading of homogeneous grouping by achievement, Dolch (1954) suggested a "Two-Group" plan for teachers who find a whole class unwieldy. Green (1953) suggested the same grouping for high school classes. Dolch noted the unfortunate designation of one group as a "slow" group.

A "Three-Group" plan has been widely used. A. J. Harris (1956) stressed that, under a three-group organization, materials and methods should be adapted to each group. Further, he stated that although the three-group plan was designed to produce homogeneous instructional groups, no system of grouping did so. Dolch (1954) and others (e.g., Hester, 1957) suggested grouping by invitation, in which each pupil has materials suitable to three reading lessons. In theory, bright pupils should drift away from the simple materials and slow pace designed for slow learners, and vice versa.

Betts (1958) suggested that, within each of the three instructional levels, five kinds of reading levels exist: an independent reading level, an instructional level, a comprehension level, an interest level, and a reading-study level. It is essential for teachers to estimate levels and guide pupils toward independent reading. In spite of its being intended to produce homogeneity, such grouping by levels results in groups with wide ability and interest ranges, requiring enormous variety in materials if individual differences are to be satisfied.

Special-need groups are flexible. Formed to work intensively with the teacher on some special skill, they are disbanded as soon as proficiency increases (McCullough, 1957b). Sometimes such groups form part of a complex class organization, as illustrated by the high school grouping described by Pellett (1957); in this scheme, total-class grouping for developmental reading was on four levels according to rate of learning, with a multiple-materials approach, subgrouping within subject-matter classes, and a special-needs group of readers needing remedial work.

Heterogeneous interclass grouping may be arranged to provide for study of special subject-matter areas, in which all pupils at work on the project are considered to be a group (McCullough, 1957b). Materials are allotted according to ability. It is more common to make heterogeneous interclass groupings according to interests. To be effective, such grouping requires careful planning and evaluation by the class (Betts, 1958). Since self-selection of material is a part of such a grouping plan, a pupil must be aware of his own limitations in reading and of his contribution to the group. Wide variation in material is essential.

3. Team grouping. In practice, this organization consists of two or three pupils working without the teacher, or tutorial groups with one pupil acting as teacher for several others (McCullough, 1957b). Durrell and Palos (1956) noted a need for research on the values of team learning, suggesting that possible advantages might be greater adjustment in levels of learning, security in learning, and group responsibility; disadvantages might be the possibilities that one pupil would do most of the work, distraction would occur because of high noise level, and an ex-

cessive burden might fall upon the teacher who must keep track of a large number of teams.

4. Individualized organization. This can be considered the complete absence of grouping or the ultimate in grouping. The recent resurgence of individualized approaches to teaching reading may be attributed to dissatisfaction with current reading outcomes, including the failure of pupils to develop permanent interest in reading (Witty, 1959b). Modern individualized programs embody three dominant concepts—"seeking, self-selection, and pacing"—which were used by Olson (1952) to explain child growth. The basic skills of reading are corrected, improved, and sometimes taught in a social setting which involves only the individual learner and teacher. Many variations have been suggested by Veatch (1959) and others (Bonney & Hanigan, 1955; Darrow & Howes, 1960; Fox & McCullough, 1958; Kirby, 1957; Lazar, 1957; Parkin, 1956). Two critical summaries and evaluations of individualized reading are those of Witty (1959b) and Sartain (1960a); a more favorable statement is that of Veatch (1960). Opinions on the value of individualized reading programs are conflicting. Possible advantages are those of paying individual attention to learners, producing high motivation, removing the stigma of being in the low group, and improving individual learning rate. Possible disadvantages are those of basing reading upon present interests (since the teacher should extend interests), having no goal for the reading but pupil interest, and making demands for careful time scheduling, intimate knowledge of each child, and vast information concerning books; these demands may be greater than the average teacher can meet.

In summary, it can be stated that different reading goals and activities probably require different class organizations (Betts, 1958; W. S. Gray, 1957). Research on class organization is sparse, and results are conflicting. Four factors are worthy of mention before we consider experiments in class organization.

1. Since measures of reading development were designed primarily to measure skills, and different organizational patterns have not been designed to improve skills, the use of the tests to measure the effectiveness of the patterns may yield conflicting results. For example, if grouping was designed to assist the teacher in working with an unwieldy number, it does not follow that a test of reading skill should show greater achievement because groups have been formed.

2. What is a group? It may be a mere collection of individuals, a collection of individuals with some measure of homogeneity (such as grade), a collection of individuals who interact to the extent that each personality is changed by the relationship. It becomes obvious that an experiment which purports to compare "grouping" and "individualized instruction," when the groups are of the first variety mentioned, is only comparing a small amount of individual instruction with a larger amount of individual instruction.

3. Research has demonstrated the following effects, which must be considered in evaluating groups: (1) If a group is failing, an individual member evaluates his own performance less accurately. (2) Failure causes a greater feeling of inadequacy if the individual identifies with the group. (3) If roles are not clear, the low-status individual feels ineffectual. (4) Group "cohesiveness" is increased by increasing the desirability of being a member of the group. (5) A highly cohesive group is less anxious but not necessarily more productive. (6) Failure reduces the cohesiveness of a group. (7) Cooperative situations usually lead to increased cohesiveness; competitive situations produce the opposite effect. (8) A group member will work for group rather than personal goals if he understands the nature of the group goals and how his behavior will help the group to attain them.

4. Research has compared undifferentiated classroom instruction in heterogeneous classes with the same in homogeneous classes, showing no advantage for either (A. J. Harris,

1956). If instruction and materials are selected to suit the type of organization, results may be more clear-cut.

Experiments in Grouping

In considering the following examples of experiments in "group" and "individualized" organization, the reader should keep in mind that "at the present time there is no real proof that one pattern of organization is superior to another in the primary grades" (Sheldon, 1960, p. 25)—or in any other grades.

Experiments in grouping for reading may be classified as those in which grouping on the basis of reading achievement was evaluated and those which considered other factors. The former kind of experiment includes a study by Bigelow (1934). Intermediate-grade pupils were grouped into three groups according to reading achievement. The best group was given a program of extensive library reading; the poorest group, a mechanics and vocabulary development program. The average reading comprehension grade equivalent score increased from. 3.6 to 6.2, representing a gain of 2.6 grades in comprehension in seven months. We must infer that grouping was advantageous in comparison with previous progress. D. H. Russell (1946) investigated a similar situation in which intermediate-grade children were regrouped in different rooms and each group subdivided for reading instruction. After two years of such grouping no reliable differences could be discerned. Another experiment in grouping elementary-grade pupils according to reading achievement was that of Carlson and Northrup (1955), who used three groups and differentiated methods. Evaluation showed the homogeneous groups to be slightly superior to intact, ungrouped grades. The investigators believed that grouping for reading reduced pupil tension and was conducive to greater differentiation of instruction. They concluded that cooperation among teachers must be superior and that correlation of reading with other subjects was difficult in the grouped classes. A. Bloom (1959) reported on a three-year experiment in ungraded primary grouping according to reading achievement and rate of learning. Ungraded primary programs in two schools showed approximately one year of superiority over control schools in reading ability. Bloom listed other apparent advantages which could not be measured by standard tests.

A number of miscellaneous experiments on grouping may be noted. Edmiston and Benfer (1949) investigated the relationship between group achievement and the range of abilities within the groups, using two groups of intermediate-grade pupils, one with a wide range of abilities, the other with a narrow range. According to a standard test of reading, the wide-range groups made superior gains. This suggests that the goal of homogeneity of groups is perhaps not a desirable one. Delacato and Delacato (1952) attempted to use permissive group environments with previously unsuccessful individual reading cases. Attitude and progress both improved, according to the investigators, who attributed the improvement to the effects of group process on personality.

Lazarus (1955) compared interest-grouping with ability-grouping by selecting special English classes on the basis of high ability or superior interest. The interest-selected group made higher scores on a standardized English test, read more books, and did more creative writing.

Rittenhouse (1960), working with pupils in Grades 1–4, investigated grouping by invitation. She concluded that slight but significantly superior gains were made when children were grouped by invitation in Grades 1, 2, and 4. Teachers who took part in the experiment stated that the most valuable outcome of grouping by invitation was in growth of the child's ability to assess his own strengths and weaknesses. From a review and evaluation of research, Wrightstone (1957) estimated that actual reduction in range of ability when three groups are formed in a classroom is 15 to 17 per cent, and 7 to 10 per cent if two groups are formed. Wrightstone held that most pupils in ungrouped programs were better adjusted socially and academically than their peers in grouped classes and that at the end of the three-year ungrouped period there is likely to be less retardation among these children than in a grouped situation.

Individualized Programs

Research in individualized programs has been largely of the "testimonial" type. Although the sincerity and industry of individuals initiating individualized approaches is not in question, the situations contain too many variables for evaluation of results. Examples of such activities are those of Duker (1957) and Jenkins (1957). Continuing studies of various phases of independent reading in primary grades were reported by Schatz, et al. (1960), and in junior high school by Fisher (1958).

Research in individualized organization for reading by Anderson, Hughes, and Dixon (1956) compared a laboratory school individualized program with a basal reader program in another school. The basal reader group achieved higher levels of competence. Kaar (1954) reported results of reading instruction in third grades in two communities, one individualized and one using groups. The group procedure yielded slightly greater gains in vocabulary and comprehension after six months. Walker (1957), in a study of two groups of intermediate-grade children matched for reading ability, IQ, and socioeconomic status, and taught by supervised student teachers, reported no significant differences between the children taught in groups and those taught by an individualized approach.

Bohnhorst and Sellars (1959) reported a study of individualized instruction in the primary grades of one school. The first half of the year was devoted to group work followed by eight weeks of individualized instruction. Although no significant differences appeared, gains were somewhat higher during group instruction; teachers who participated were of the opinion that individualization might benefit the more able readers. Sartain (1960b) investigated the relative merits of teaching Grade 2 pupils for three months by an ability-group (basal-reader) approach or an individualized self-selection approach, and then reversing methods for the next three months. Except in advanced word recognition, significantly greater gains were made during the first three months regardless of method. The only significant difference between methods of organization was found for individuals of lower ability whose gains on word-recognition tests under grouping were superior to those under an individualized approach.

Safford (1960) studied the results of seven elementary classes which had been taught by individualized methods of self-selection and instruction. Presumably the classes were representative or "normal" in ability level, but no evidence was cited on this matter. Results of reading tests showed the seven classes had made gains considerably below national or district norms. Safford also found that individualized programs resulted in no significant difference in growth between reading vocabulary and reading comprehension and that individualized programs showed no significantly different results with superior pupils than with average pupils.

In conclusion, studies of class organization have had three weaknesses: The number of uncontrolled variables has made any assigning of a specific cause for an effect a matter of conjecture; the objectives of organization have not been defined, and therefore it is difficult to determine what is being evaluated; and the various organizational patterns have many common factors (i.e., grouping is used in individualized programs, and individual instruction is used in grouping). Perhaps a more fruitful subject for investigation would be the proper class organization for the different behaviors required for reading, as was suggested at the beginning of this section. It might be revealed that growth in different reading abilities is dependent upon versatility of class organization.

EMERGING PROBLEMS IN RESEARCH ON TEACHING READING

The research on teaching reading cited in the preceding sections is impressive in bulk and variety, and it also has a certain dynamic character which suggests that new ideas are being tested continuously. As in other curricular areas, much of the frontier activity occurs in the classrooms of capable, creative teachers, and the try-outs of novel procedures must be labeled "operational" or "action" research rather than rigorous experimentation. Such try-outs of new ideas, in turn, may stem from advances outside the classroom, such as the improved technology of audio-visual teaching devices. Detailed, definitive research on these and other devices and methods necessarily lags behind initial utilization, but many new problems, or old problems reconsidered, face the teacher and research worker in reading instruction today. It is difficult to forecast, but we can discern a few of the emerging problems that will face teachers of reading and research workers.

The Growth of the Mass Media

Some writers believe that the ubiquity of radio, films, magazines, pictures, and television means "the twilight of the printed book." Witty (1959a), for example, having recorded the amount of children's televiewing over at least a decade, has found that elementary-school children prefer TV to almost any other activity and spend, on an average, something like three hours a day watching it. This amount decreases in adolescence. In a study of factors affecting use of the mass media, Bailyn (1959) found, for children in the fifth and sixth grades, that high exposure to the pictorial media is associated with lack of parental restriction, low IQ, fathers with worker or service occupations, and certain types of religious affiliation. These and other writers find that television viewing may cut into time spent on reading the comics but does not seem to affect more serious reading; rather, children and adults may be categorized as low, medium, and high users of all kinds of verbal communication materials. The teacher's problem would seem to be that of helping children find a genuine place for reading in a world of words and of developing tastes and standards so the children can select from a wide range of material. Such studies as *Maturity in Reading* (W. S. Gray & Rogers, 1956) may help determine long-range goals for a school system's reading program, including junior college or even college reading. The book is concerned not with the mass media but with the habits and tastes which must be established in a context which includes the mass media of communication.

Television

Problems of television relate not only to the effects of commercial television on children's reading habits and tastes but to the more specific question of educational television for direct teaching of reading abilities. The sparse literature on the topic suggests no revolutionary methods for such instruction but usually ties it to audio-visual devices used in classrooms, such as tachistoscopes and reading-rate controllers, and to teachers' hints on skimming, organizing, and other ways of reading. Flierl (1957) and Fea and Fletcher (1960) have reported on the planning, production, and results of instruction in reading by television. The latter study distinguished between casual viewers and a second group of over 600 students and adults who purchased syllabuses and whose progress was evaluated by a perception test, a test of reading rate, and a questionnaire. Reports of small-group and large-group instruction in typical elementary and secondary school classrooms are still to come.

Other Audio-Visual Devices

Mechanical aids to reading improvement have been in use for over 30 years, especially in adult courses, in reading clinics, and in remedial instruction. The various tachistoscopes and rate-controllers seem to have some value in classroom instruction, especially for stimulating interest in those who have been failing in reading, but their efficiency is no greater than that of careful help from a teacher (A. J. Harris, 1956, pp. 525–538). The recent interest in teaching machines has extended the range of mechanical materials available for students' practice. Finn (1960, p. 17) placed the kinds of audio-visual equipment designed for individual or near-individual operation in five categories on "an ascending scale of sophistication: (1) individual reading pacers and similar devices, (2) individual viewing and listening equipment for existing slides, filmstrips, motion pictures and recordings, (3) language laboratories of all types, (4) specifically programmed printed materials such as scrambled textbooks ... and (5) true teaching machines of the Skinner or Pressey type ...." He stated also that a combination of certain of these types is the next immediate step in applying technology to learning.

Modern interest in teaching machines may be traced to the work of S. L. Pressey and B. F. Skinner. Skinner, for example, stated that "there is no reason why the schoolroom should be any less mechanized than, for example, the kitchen" (Skinner, 1959, p. 157). The Pressey (1927) machines were of the multiple-choice type, with wrong items repeated until they are twice chosen correctly. Skinner believes that pupils should compose their own responses, not merely select them. Because of his espousal of the importance of reinforcement, he is suspicious of the effect of wrong answers in a multiple-choice situation. Thus Skinner has the pupil propose his own answer in numbers or letters or write his answer in an appropriate space. Some of the early machine materials dealt with arithmetic and spelling, but up to 1960 few experimental attempts had been made to teach reading with machines (Fry, Bryan, & Rigney, 1960). Skinner himself has given little attention to the understanding that is a part

of comprehension in reading, but future programing of materials may remedy this lack. Problems of transfer to new reading situations and of varied programs for different learners have not yet been attacked experimentally, but the field is rapidly expanding. Particularly for some of the basic skills, such as word-recognition techniques, teaching machines hold enough promise to warrant their experimental try-out in various classroom situations.

Individualization of Instruction

Reading is learned by individuals. Provision for individual differences in learning to read is probably more advanced than in most other curricular areas, notably in flexible grouping for instruction and in providing varied materials. Explorations in the use of teaching machines and individualized reading are only two examples of current interest in do-it-yourself activities. Making children independent in word-attack skills, in ability to use the library, and in recreational reading continues to be the aim of all good teachers, an aim stimulated by the expanded production in recent years of easy-to-read books and the potentialities of the programed textbook. This trend probably means that teachers must help pupils more in learning how to learn (Buswell, 1959).

Some of the research on individualized reading has been reviewed above with the suggestion that it is not so much a revolutionary method in its own right as a desirable part of a total reading program. Earlier research on systematic versus incidental approaches to reading gave the advantage to the systematic development of abilities, but the later studies indicate high pupil and teacher interest in an individualized program. Some studies of group action indicate that there may be learnings in a group situation which are difficult to obtain in an individual activity. This may be especially true in critical reading and the appreciative aspects of creative reading. More research is needed on the kinds of learning that occur best in individual, small-group, and large-group situations. Teachers, too, can experiment with different types of bridges between teacher-directed reading activities and individual experiences.

Reading Readiness Reconsidered

Another type of provision for individual differences is the use of the reading readiness program. The doctrine of readiness, originating in research on child development, has been extremely influential in reading instruction. During the first three decades of studies in child development, most of the data about children (their physical growth, interests, concepts, etc.) were interpreted as restricting what teachers can do. Recent changes in social life, however, have affected the characteristics of five-year-olds who start to school. Their experiential background now usually includes several years' exposure to television and may include considerable knowledge of children's books, gleaned perhaps from the 25-cent variety their mothers buy at the supermarket. Perhaps American children are ready to read somewhat earlier, on the average, than they once were. A report by Bruner (1960) on the deliberations of a group of scholars, mostly scientists, offered the sweeping "hypothesis that any subject can be taught effectively in some intellectually honest form to any child at any stage of development" (p. 33), providing attention is paid to the psychological development of the child. Recent experiments in presenting scientific and mathematical material to young pupils have given striking evidence of children's ability to acquire some abstract ideas, but this does not mean the second-grader can read Darwin's *Origin of the Species* or Shakespeare's *Antony and Cleopatra*. Yet, in a changing climate of opinion about the optimum time for beginning reading or the study of certain types of reading materials, the problem of reading readiness should be considered.

More specifically, Alsup (1956) has collected problems of teachers in applying research and has given judgments of readiness programs which will help a teacher or school system evaluate its readiness practices. He considered existing programs for "teaching" readiness to be stronger if they (1) use basic readiness material, (2) use grouping, (3) use readiness tests, (4) use an extended program for slow learning children, (5) require a physical examination for entrance to first grade, (6) provide for parent-teacher conferences, (7) call for visual and auditory discrimination activities, and (8) use juvenile literature. He considered readiness programs to be weak if they (1) provided inadequate visual and auditory screening, (2) made ineffective use of intelligence test data, (3) lacked an enriched readiness program for accelerated learners, and (4) reflected lack of understanding of procedures to use in helping a child adjust socially and emotionally to school situations. Alsup also listed specific problems faced by teachers in promoting growth in initial reading abilities. His lists should be interpreted in the light of the situation in a particular school and of the newer knowledge of social conditions affecting children.

The Role of Parents

Much of the writing on the place of parents in children's reading development is hortatory and inspirational rather than grounded in research. Some researchers, such as Almy (1949), relate early reading progress to home conditions. Pressnall (1956) collected parents' opinions about reading programs, and Artley (1956) and McConnell (1957) analyzed the questions parents ask. The importance of parental language in influencing early language development and of parental knowledge in introducing children to nursery rhymes and stories is generally acknowledged. It seems reasonable to suggest that many parents can be helpful to the third- and fourth-grade child as he makes a transition from closely directed reading to wider reading activities. There is also clear evidence from the study of reading interests that the type of home is influential in determining the reading habits of older children.

Most activities in the area of home-school cooperation must be regarded as desirable projects rather than rigorous experiments, and continuation and expansion of such projects should undoubtedly be encouraged. From the research point of view, more studies are needed which give specific data about the influence on reading achievement of parents' activities and educational aspirations. Studies such as those of Jefferson (1958) and Rudman (1956), which showed some specific relationships between parents' and children's choices in juvenile literature, exemplify the more exact investigations needed. An evaluation of methods of communication and of ways schools can assist parents, such as that presented by Fea (1958), may be more effective in demonstration-action situations than in more carefully controlled experiments.

This sampling of emerging problems could be extended by adding such topics as applications of linguistics to reading instruction, problems of giftedness in language abilities, neurological factors in reading performance, and the training of teachers and specialists in the reading field. Such topics, explored but not thoroughly researched, are omitted here.

In the first section of this chapter, we noted the large amount of research on the teaching of reading available today. We have offered only a sampling from this body of work. The studies noted were not selected because of their research technique and sophistication, but rather because they suggest the wide variety of studies that have been made, and they have implications for teachers and research workers. So wide and varied is the relevant literature that students of reading instruction may well find some highly respected study missing from our discussion. Students will find here, it is hoped, a representative sample of the work done or underway. Work underway is important because, as has been obvious in this chapter, many important problems in reading instruction re-main. It is equally evident that the teacher and research worker do not have to rely entirely on tradition, the opinions of the teacher next door, or personal experience. The studies reported in this chapter give many leads to fruitful research and practice in the realm of classroom procedures and materials for developing competent readers.

REFERENCES

Agnew, D. C. *The effect of varied amounts of phonetic training on primary reading.* Durham, N.C.: Duke Univer. Press, 1939.

Alm, R. S. Teaching reading is our business. *Engl. J.,* 1957, 46, 11–19.

Almy, Millie. *Children's experiences prior to first grade and success in beginning reading.* New York: Bur. of Publs., Teachers Coll., Columbia Univer., 1949.

Alsup, R. F. A study of the procedures used and the problems encountered in promoting growth for initial reading. *Dissertation Abstr.,* 1956, 16, 76–77.

Amen, E. W. Individual differences in apperceptive reaction: A study of the responses of preschool children to pictures. *Genet. Psychol. Monogr.,* 1941, 23, 319–385.

Anderson, H. A. Influence of the broader context in interpretation. In *Promoting growth toward maturity in interpreting what is read. Supp. educ. Monogr.,* 1951, 74, 111–115.

Anderson, I. H., & Dearborn, W. F. *The psychology of teaching reading.* New York: Ronald Press, 1952.

Anderson, I. H., & Fairbanks, G. Common and differential factors in reading vocabulary and hearing vocabulary. *J. educ. Res.,* 1937, 30, 317–324.

Anderson, I. H., Hughes, B. A., & Dixon, W. R. The relationship between reading achievement and the method of teaching reading. *Univer. Michigan Sch. Educ. Bull.,* No. 27, 1956, 104–108.

Anderson, P. S. McGuffey vs. the moderns in character training. *Phi Delta Kappan,* 1956, 38, 53–58.

Arnold, D. L. Testing ability to use data in the fifth and sixth grades. *Educ. res. Bull.,* 1938, 17, 253–259.

Artley, A. S. The appraisal of reading comprehension. *J. educ. Psychol.,* 1943, 34, 55–60.

Artley, A. S. What do parents' questions mean? *Reading Teacher,* 1956, 10, 17–20.

Avegno, T. Sylvia. Intermediate-grade children's choices of poetry. *Elem. Engl.,* 1956, 33, 428–432.

Bailyn, Lotte. Mass media and children: A study of exposure habits and cognitive effects. *Psychol. Monogr.,* 1959, 73, No. 1 (Whole No. 471).

Baker, Norma. Confusion in word recognition. *Elem. sch. J.,* 1945, 45, 575–577.

Bedell, R. Relationship between the ability to recall and the ability to infer in specific learning situations. *Science Educ.,* 1934, 18, 158–162.

Bell, H. Comprehension in silent reading. *Brit. J. educ. Psychol.,* 1942, 12, 47–55.

Berg, P. C. Reading in relation to listening. *4th Yearb., Southwest Reading Conf. Coll. and Univer.,* 1955, 52–60.

Berger, C. Grouping, number and spacing of letters as determinants of word recognition. *J. gen. Psychol.,* 1956, 55, 215–228.

Bergman, W. G., & Vreeland, W. Comparative achievement in word recognition under two methods of teaching beginning reading. *Elem. sch. J.,* 1932, 32, 605–616.

Betts, E. A. Reading: Semantic approach. *Education,* 1949, 69, 527–555.

Betts, E. A. Visual perception in reading. *Education,* 1953, 73, 575–582.

Betts, E. A. Developing basic reading skills through effective class organization. *Education,* 1958, 78, 561–576.

Betts, E. A. Reading is thinking. *Reading Teacher,* 1959, 12, 146–151.

Bigelow, E. B. Improvement in reading as shown by standard tests. *Educ. Method,* 1934, 13, 258–263.

Blewett, T. T. An experiment in the measurement of listening at the college level. *J. educ. Res.,* 1951, 44, 575–585.

Bloom, Alice. *Report on continuous growth program.* Bellevue, Wash.: Bellevue Public Schools, 1959.

Bloom, B. S., Engelhart, M. D., Furst, E. J., Hill, W. H., & Krathwohl, D. R. *Taxonomy of educational objectives.* New York: Longmans, Green, 1956.

Bohnhorst, B. A., & Sellars, Sophia N. Individual reading instruction vs. basal textbook instruction: Some tentative explorations. *Elem. Engl.,* 1959, 36, 185–190, 202.

Bond, Eva. Reading and ninth grade achievement. *Teach. Coll. Contr. Educ.,* 1938, No. 756.

Bond, G. L., & Wagner, Eva B. *Teaching the child to read.* (3rd ed.) New York: Macmillan, 1960.

Bonney, Jill, & Hanigan, L. B. Individualized teaching of reading. *Nat. elem. Principal,* 1955, 35, 76–82.

Botel, M. We need a total approach to reading. *Reading Teacher,* 1960, 13, 254–257.

Bradley, Beatrice E. An experimental study of the readiness approach to reading. *Elem. sch. J.,* 1956, 56, 262–267.

Brearley, H. C. Are grades becoming extinct? *Peabody J. Educ.,* 1954, 31, 258–259.

Britton, J. N. Evidence of improvement in poetic judgment. *Brit. J. Psychol.,* 1954, 45, 196–208.

Broening, Angela M. Abilities which contribute to effective reading. *Education,* 1941, 62, 11–17.

Brown, J. I. *Efficient reading.* Boston: Heath, 1952.

Brownell, J. A. The influence of training in reading in the social studies on the ability to think critically. *Calif. J. educ. Res.,* 1953, 4, 28–31.

Brownell, W. A., & Hendrickson, G. How children learn information, concepts, and generalizations. *Yearb. nat. Soc. Stud. Educ.,* 1950, 49, Part I, 92–128.

Bruner, J. S. *The process of education.* Cambridge, Mass.: Harvard Univer. Press, 1960.

Burkhart, Kathryn H. An analysis of reading abilities. *J. educ. Res.,* 1945, 38, 430–439.

Buros, O. K. (Ed.) *Fifth mental measurements yearbook.* Highland Park, N.J.: Gryphon, 1959.

Burrows, Alvina T. *What about phonics?* Washington, D.C.: International Association for Childhood Education, 1951.

Burton, D. L. The relationship of literary appreciation to certain measurable factors. *J. educ. Psychol.,* 1952, 43, 436–439.

Burton, W. H., & Richards, I. A. New proposals concerning beginning reading. *Elem. Engl.,* 1949, 26, 461–464.

Buswell, G. T. Perceptual research and methods of learning. *Scient. Mon.,* 1947, 64, 521–526.

Buswell, G. T. Helping children learn how to learn. In *Learning and the teacher. Yearb., Ass. Superv. curric. Dev.,* 1959, 145–155.

Canfield, J. K. Flexibility in grouping for

reading. *Reading Teacher,* 1957, 11, 91–94.

Carlson, Esther S., & Northrup, Joyce. An experiment in grouping pupils for instruction in reading. *Nat. elem. Principal,* 1955, 35, 53–57.

Carner, R. L., & Sheldon, V. D. Problems in the development of concepts through reading. *Elem. sch. J.,* 1954, 55, 226–229.

Carrillo, L. W., & Sheldon, W. D. The flexibility of reading rate. *J. educ. Psychol.,* 1952, 43, 299–305.

Carroll, R. P. An experimental study of comprehension in reading, with special references to the reading of directions. *Teach. Coll. Contr. Educ.,* 1926, No. 245.

Chall, Jeanne S. What about controlled vocabulary? *Reading for effective living. Proc. Internat. Reading Ass. Conf.,* 1958, 3, 177–186.

Child, I. L., Potter, E. H., & Levine, Estelle M. Children's textbooks and personality development: An exploration in the social psychology of education. *Psychol. Monogr.,* 1946, 60, No. 3 (Whole No. 279).

Clark, C. M. Teaching sixth-grade students to make predictions from reading materials. Unpublished doctoral dissertation, Univer. of California, 1958.

Cole, Luella. *The teacher's handbook of technical vocabulary.* Bloomington, Ill.: Public School Publishing Co., 1940.

Cole, Luella. *The elementary school subjects.* New York: Rinehart, 1946.

Coleman, J. C. Perceptual retardation in reading disability cases. *J. educ. Psychol.,* 1953, 44, 497–503.

Cook, Luella. Language factors involved in interpretation. *Reading Teacher,* 1959, 12, 152–157.

Cordts, Anna D. Functional phonics for power in reading. *Elem. Engl.,* 1953, 30, 91–94.

Crosby, Muriel. Organization for reading instruction. *Elem. Engl.,* 1960, 37, 169–173.

Crosscup, R. B. Experimental exercises in learning to interpret reading. *Education,* 1938, 59, 20–31.

Crossen, Helen J. Effects of the attitudes of the reader upon critical reading ability. *J. educ. Res.,* 1948, 42, 289–298.

Culbertson, H. M., & Powers, R. D. A study of graph comprehension difficulties. *A.V. commun. Rev.,* 1959, 7, 97–110.

Curti, Margaret W. Child development: X. Concepts. In W. S. Monroe (Ed.), *Encyclo-pedia of educational research.* (Rev. ed.) New York: Macmillan, 1950. Pp. 175–177.

Dale, E. The problem of vocabulary in reading. *Educ. res. Bull.,* 1956, 35, 113–123.

Dale, E. How to improve your vocabulary. *The News Letter* (Ohio State Univer. Bur. Educ. Res.), 1958, 23, No. 7.

Dale, E., & Reichert, D. *Bibliography of vocabulary studies.* (Rev. ed.) Columbus: Bur. of Educ. Res., Ohio State Univer., 1957.

Daniel, W. C. Some experiences with a tape recorder. *Elem. Engl.,* 1953, 30, 427–428.

Daniels, J. C., & Diack, H. The phonic word method. *Reading Teacher,* 1959, 13, 14–21.

Darrow, Helen F., & Howes, V. M. *Approaches to individualized reading.* New York: Appleton-Century-Crofts, 1960.

Davis, F. B. Fundamental factors of comprehension in reading. *Psychometrika,* 1944, 9, 185–197.

Dawson, D. T. Some issues in grouping for reading. *Nat. elem. Principal,* 1955, 35, 48–52.

Delacato, Janice F., & Delacato, C. H. A group approach to remedial reading. *Elem. Engl.,* 1952, 29, 142–149.

Dice, L. Kathryn. An experimental study of two methods of teaching beginning reading. *Johns Hopkins Univer. Stud. Educ.,* 1942, No. 32.

Diederich, P. B. Relationships among experience, language, and reading. In *Reading in relation to experience and language. Supp. educ. Monogr.,* 1944, 58, 12–15.

Dolch, E. W. How a child sounds out a word. *Elem. Engl.,* 1945, 22, 275–280.

Dolch, E. W. Reading pictures. *11th Yearb., Claremont College Reading Conf.,* 1946, 183–186.

Dolch, E. W. Phrase perception in reading. *Elem. sch. J.,* 1949, 49, 341–347.

Dolch, E. W. Vocabulary development. *Elem. Engl.,* 1953, 30, 70–75.

Dolch, E. W. Groups in reading. *Elem. Engl.,* 1954, 31, 477–484.

Dolch, E. W., & Bloomster, M. Phonic readiness. *Elem. sch. J.,* 1937, 38, 201–205.

Duggins, Lydia A. Theory and techniques of auditory perception as an approach to reading. In O. S. Causey (Ed.), *The reading teacher's reader.* New York: Ronald Press, 1958. Pp. 35–39.

Duker, S. Effects of introducing an individualized reading approach by student teachers. *Reading in action. Proc. Internat. Reading Ass. Conf.,* Vol. 2. New York: Scholastic, 1957. Pp. 59–62.

Dunkel, H. B. Testing the precise use of words. *Coll. Engl.,* 1944, 5, 386–389.

Durrell, D. D., & Murphy, Helen A. The auditory discrimination factor in reading readiness and reading disability. *Education,* 1953, 73, 556–560.

Durrell, D. D., & Palos, Viola A. Pupil study teams in reading. *Education,* 1956, 76, 552–556.

Durrell, D. D., Sullivan, Helen B., & Murphy, Helen A. *Building word power.* Yonkers: World Book Co., 1945.

Dvorine, I. What you should know about sight: Parts I and II. *Education,* 1958, 78, 381–382, 471–475.

Early, Margaret. Stages of growth in literary appreciation. *Engl. J.,* 1960, 49, 161–167.

Ebbitt, Wilma R. Problems caused by the grammatical, logical, and rhetorical structure of what is read. In *Promoting growth toward maturity in interpreting what is read. Supp. educ. Monogr.,* 1951, 74, 91–95.

Eberhart, W. Discovery of meaning—childhood's greatest adventure. *Educ. res. Bull.,* 1945, 24, 152–162.

Eberl, Marguerite. Visual training and reading. In *Clinical studies in reading, II. Supp. educ. Monogr.,* 1953, 77, 141–148.

Edgerton, R. B. How difficult are children's encyclopedias? *Elem. sch. J.,* 1954, 55, 219–225.

Edmiston, R. W., & Benfer, J. G. The relationship between group achievement and range of abilities within the groups. *J. educ. Res.,* 1949, 42, 547–548.

Fast, Irene. Kindergarten training and grade I reading. *J. educ. Psychol.,* 1957, 48, 52–57.

Fay, L. C. The relationship between specific reading skills and selected areas of sixth grade achievement. *J. educ. Res.,* 1950, 43, 541–547.

Fay, L. C. What research has to say about reading in the content areas. *Reading Teacher,* 1954, 8, 68–72.

Fea, H. R. For parents—On reading. *Univer. Washington Coll. Educ. Rec.,* 1958, 24, 40–47.

Fea, H. R., & Fletcher, J. E. Formal instruction by television in reading improvement. *Univer. Washington Coll. Educ. Rec.,* 1960, 26, 17–29.

Feldman, Shirley C., Merrill, Kathleen K., & MacGinitie, W. H. An effective aid for teaching reading. *Reading Teacher,* 1960, 13, 208–211.

Fennema, Elizabeth H. Mental imagery and the reading process. *Elem. sch. J.,* 1959, 59, 286–289.

Fernald, Grace M., & Keller, Helen. The effect of kinesthetic factors in the development of word recognition in the case of nonreaders. *J. educ. Res.,* 1921, 4, 355–377.

Fiedler, Miriam F. Teacher's problems with hard of hearing children. *J. educ. Res.,* 1949, 42, 618–622.

Finn, J. D. Automation and education: III. Technology and the instructional process. *A. V. commun. Rev.,* 1960, 8, 5–26.

Fisher, J. A. Individualizing junior high school reading instruction. In O. S. Causey (Ed.), *The reading teacher's reader.* New York: Ronald Press, 1958. Pp. 84–89.

Fleming, C. M. What's happening in reading in Great Britain? *Reading Teacher,* 1959, 12, 176–180.

Flierl, Nina T. Planning and producing TV programs in reading. *Reading Teacher,* 1957, 11, 17–22.

Floyd, C. Meeting children's reading needs in the middle grades: A preliminary report. *Elem. sch. J.,* 1954, 55, 99–103.

Forgays, D. G. The development of differential word recognition. *J. exp. Psychol.,* 1953, 45, 165–168.

Foster, H. K. The semantic variations of certain high frequency words in written compositions of eighth grade pupils. *J. exp. Educ.,* 1943, 11, 293–297.

Fox, L. K., & McCullough, Constance M. Individualized reading. *NEA J.,* 1958, 47, 162–163.

French, E. L. Kinesthetic recognition in retarded readers. *Educ. psychol. Measmt,* 1953, 13, 636–654.

Fry, E. B., Bryan, G. L., & Rigney, J. W. *Teaching machines: An annotated bibliography.* Washington, D.C.: Department of Audio-Visual Instruction, National Education Association, 1960.

Funk, W., & Lewis, N. *30 days to a more powerful vocabulary.* New York: Funk, 1954.

Gammon, Agnes L. Comprehension of words with multiple meanings. *Calif. J. educ. Res.,* 1952, 3, 228–232.

Gans, Roma. Study of critical reading comprehension in the intermediate grades. *Teach. Coll. Contr. Educ.,* 1940, No. 811.

Gates, A. I. *The improvement of reading.* (3rd ed.) New York: Macmillan, 1950.

Gates, A. I., & Cason, E. B. Evaluation of tests for diagnosis of ability to read by phrases or thought units. *Elem. sch. J.,* 1945, 46, 23–32.

Gates, A. I., & Russell, D. H. Types of material, vocabulary burden, word analysis and other factors in beginning reading. *Elem. sch. J.,* 1938, 39, 27–35, 119–128.

Gates, A. I., Bond, G. L., & Russell, D. H. *Methods of determining reading readiness.* New York: Bur. of Publs., Teachers Coll., Columbia Univer., 1939.

Gibson, Eleanor J. Improvement in perceptual judgments as a function of controlled practice or training. *Psychol. Bull.,* 1953, 50, 401–431.

Gilbert, L. C. Saccadic movements as a factor in visual perception in reading. *J. educ. Psychol.,* 1959, 50, 15–19. (a)

Gilbert, L. C. Speed of processing visual stimuli and its relation to reading. *J. educ. Psychol.,* 1959, 50, 8–14. (b)

Gill, Naomi B. "Depth" reading. II: The figures. *Engl. J.,* 1954, 42, 297–303.

Glaser, E. M. An experiment in the development of critical thinking. *Teach. Coll. Contr. Educ.,* 1941, No. 843.

Goins, Jean T. Visual perceptual abilities and early reading progress. *Supp. educ. Monogr.,* 1958, 87.

Goins, Jean T. Visual and auditory perception in reading. *Reading Teacher,* 1959, 13, 9–13.

Good, C. V. (Ed.) *Dictionary of education.* New York and London: McGraw-Hill, 1945.

Goodlad, J. I., & Anderson, R. H. *The nongraded elementary school.* New York: Harcourt, Brace, 1959.

Gorman, H. Adventure with film-readers: How motion pictures plus correlated film-story books help young readers read. *Educ. Screen,* 1951, 30, 13–15.

Gray, Lillian. Making it their own. *NEA J.,* 1951, 40, 405–406.

Gray, W. S. *On their own in reading.* Chicago: Scott, Foresman, 1948.

Gray, W. S. Reading and understanding. *Elem. Engl.,* 1951, 28, 148–159.

Gray, W. S. *The teaching of reading and writing.* Chicago: Scott, Foresman, 1956.

Gray, W. S. Role of group and individualized teaching in a sound reading program. *Reading Teacher,* 1957, 11, 99–108.

Gray, W. S. Reading. In C. W. Harris (Ed.), *Encyclopedia of educational research.* (3rd ed.) New York: Macmillan, 1960. Pp. 1086–1135.

Gray, W. S., & Holmes, Eleanor. *The development of meaning vocabularies in reading.* Chicago: Univer. of Chicago Laboratory School, 1938.

Gray, W. S., & Rogers, Bernice. *Maturity in reading: Its nature and appraisal.* Chicago: Univer. of Chicago Press, 1956.

Green, R. M. Grouping for reading in the secondary schools. *J. Educ.,* 1953, 136, 77–78.

Groff, P. J. Children's attitudes toward reading and their critical reading abilities in four content-type materials. Unpublished doctoral dissertation, Univer. of California, Berkeley, 1955.

Guilfoile, Elizabeth. Training pupils to cope with language difficulties in interpreting what is read: In grades four to six. In *Promoting growth toward maturity in interpreting what is read. Supp. educ. Monogr.,* 1951, 74, 96–101.

Haefner, R. Casual learning of word meanings. *J. educ. Res.,* 1932, 25, 267–277.

Harrington, Sister Mary J., & Durrell, D. D. Mental maturity versus perception abilities in primary reading. *J. educ. Psychol.,* 1955, 46, 375–380.

Harris, A. J. *How to increase reading ability.* (3rd ed.) New York: Longmans, Green, 1956.

Harris, T. L. Making reading an effective instrument of learning in the content fields. *Yearb. nat. Soc. Stud. Educ.,* 1948, 47, Part II, 116–135.

Hartley, Helene W. Tests of the interpretive reading of poetry for teachers of English. *Teach. Coll. Contr. Educ.,* 1930, No. 433.

Hay, Julie, & Wingo, C. E. *Reading with phonics.* Chicago: Lippincott, 1948.

Hayakawa, S. I. Recognizing stereotypes as substitutes for thought. *Etc.,* 1950, 7, 208–210.

Heavey, Regina. High school students build vocabularies. *Reading Teacher,* 1954, 7, 229–231.

Heidbreder, Edna. A study of the evolution of

concepts. *Psychol. Bull.,* 1934, 31, 673. (Abstract)

Helmkamp, Eunice. Training pupils to cope with language difficulties in interpreting what is read in grades seven to ten. In *Promoting growth toward maturity in interpreting what is read. Supp. educ. Monogr.,* 1951, 74, 101–105.

Herminghaus, E. G. The effect of bibliotherapy on the attitudes and personal and social adjustment of a group of elementary school children. Unpublished doctoral dissertation, Washington Univer., 1954.

Hester, Katherine B. Grouping by invitation. *Reading Teacher,* 1957, 11, 105–108.

Hildreth, Gertrude. The role of pronunciation and sounding in learning to read. *Elem. sch. J.,* 1954, 55, 141–147.

Hill, Margaret B. A study of the process of word discrimination in individuals beginning to read. *J. educ. Res.,* 1936, 29, 487–500.

Holmes, F. J. Syllabic length, recognition, and immediate recall. *J. appl. Psychol.,* 1934, 18, 831–841.

Holmes, J. A. *The substrata-factor theory of reading.* Berkeley: California Book, 1953.

Holmes, J. A. The brain and the reading process. *22nd Yearb., Claremont Coll. Reading Conf.,* 1957, 49–67.

Hook, J. N. *The teaching of high school English.* (2nd ed.) New York: Ronald Press, 1959.

Horn, E. *Methods of instruction in the social studies.* New York: Scribner's, 1937.

Hovious, Carol. What words mean. *Clearing House,* 1945, 19, 403–407.

Hovland, C. I. Effects of the mass media of communication. In G. Lindzey (Ed.), *Handbook of social psychology.* Cambridge, Mass.: Addison-Wesley, 1954. Pp. 1062–1103.

Howell, W. J. Work-study skills of children in grades IV to VIII. *Elem. sch. J.,* 1950, 50, 384–389.

Hunt, J. T. The relation among vocabulary, structural analysis, and reading. *J. educ. Psychol.,* 1953, 44, 193–202.

Hurlburt, D. The relative value of recall and recognition techniques for measuring precise knowledge of word meanings—nouns, verbs, adjectives. *J. educ. Res.,* 1954, 47, 561–576.

Jefferson, B. F. Some relationships between parents' and children's preferences in juvenile literature. *Elem. sch. J.,* 1958, 58, 212–218.

Jenkins, Marian. Self-selection in reading. *Reading Teacher,* 1957, 11, 84–90.

Jesperson, O. *Growth and structure of the English language.* (9th ed.) Garden City: Doubleday, 1955.

Johnson, H. C. Effect of instruction in mathematical vocabulary upon problem solving in arithmetic. *J. educ. Res.,* 1944, 38, 97–110.

Johnson, Marjorie S. Factors in reading comprehension. *Educ. Admin. Superv.,* 1949, 35, 385–406.

Johnson, Marjorie S. Readiness for critical reading. *Education,* 1953, 73, 391–396.

Kaar, H. An experiment with an individualized method of teaching reading. *Reading Teacher,* 1954, 7, 174–177.

Kelley, V. H. Techniques for testing word meaning knowledge. *Elem. Engl. Rev.,* 1932, 9, 102–105.

Kelley, V. H. Experimental study of certain techniques for testing word meanings. *J. educ. Res.,* 1933, 27, 277–282.

Keneally, Katherine G. A study of the relative order of difficulty of several types of study skills. Master's thesis, Boston Univer., 1939.

Kincheloe, I. Promoting growth in interpreting what is read in the light of its broader context in grades 11–14. In *Promoting growth toward maturity in interpreting what is read. Supp. educ. Monogr.,* 1951, 74, 133–138.

Kirby, Margaret. Tête-à-tête lessons develop independent reading. *Elem. Engl.,* 1957, 34, 302–303.

Kottmeyer, W. Classroom activities in critical reading. *Sch. Rev.,* 1944, 52, 557–564.

Kyte, G. C. A core vocabulary in the language arts. *Phi Delta Kappan,* 1953, 34, 231–234.

LaBrant, Lou. A genetic approach to language. *14th Yearb., Claremont Coll. Reading Conf.,* 1949, 5–29.

LaBrant, Lou. The larger context: Setting. *Reading Teacher,* 1958, 11, 234–238.

Lamoreaux, Lillian A., & Lee, Doris M. *Learning to read through experience.* New York: Appleton-Century-Crofts, 1943.

Lantz, W. C. An experimental study of listener's perception of speech content as compared with delivery. *Speech Monogr.,* 1956, 23, 94.

Larrick, Nancy. How many words does a child know? *Reading Teacher,* 1953, 7, 100–104.

Lazar, May. Individualized reading: A dynamic approach. *Reading Teacher,* 1957, 11, 75–83.

Lazarus, A. L. Grouping based on high interest versus general ability: A senior high school teacher's viewpoint. *Calif. J. sec. Educ.,* 1955, 30, 38–41.

Letson, C. T. Building an informal flexibility test. *Education,* 1960, 80, 537–539.

Linehan, E. A. Early instruction in letter names and sounds as related to success in beginning reading. *J. Educ.,* 1958, 140, 44–48.

Loban, W. *Literature and social sensitivity.* Champaign, Ill.: National Council of Teachers of English, 1954.

Lorge, I., & Feifel, H. Qualitative differences in the vocabulary responses of children. *J. educ. Psychol.,* 1950, 41, 1–17.

Malter, M. S. Children's ability in reading diagrammatic materials. *Elem. sch. J.,* 1948, 49, 98–102.

Maney, Ethel S. Literal and critical reading in science. *J. exp. Educ.,* 1958, 27, 57–64.

Martin, F. W. Concept development through reading: What research says. *J. Educ.,* 1955, 137, 24–26.

McCarthy, Dorothea. Language development in children. In L. Carmichael (Ed.), *Manual of child psychology.* New York: Wiley, 1946. Pp. 476–581.

McConnell, G. A. Criteria for juvenile biographies. *Elem. Engl.,* 1956, 33, 331–335.

McConnell, G. A. What do parents want to know? *Elem. sch. J.,* 1957, 58, 83–87.

McConnell, T. R. Introduction: The purpose and scope of the yearbook. In N. B. Henry (Ed.), *Yearb. nat. Soc. Stud. Educ.,* 1942, 41, Part II, 3–13.

McCracken, G. The Newcastle reading experiment. *Elem. sch. J.,* 1954, 54, 385–390.

McCrory, Mae, & Watts, Pearl. *Phonetic skill texts.* Columbus: Charles Merrill, 1947.

McCullough, Constance M. Groping or grouping. *Elem. Engl.,* 1954, 31, 136–138.

McCullough, Constance M. An inductive approach to word analysis. *Education,* 1955, 75, 583–587.

McCullough, Constance M. Responses of elementary school children to common types of reading comprehension questions. *J. educ. Res.,* 1957, 51, 65–70. (a)

McCullough, Constance M. What does research reveal about practices in teaching reading? *Engl. J.,* 1957, 46, 475–490. (b)

McCullough, Constance M. Context aids in reading. *Reading Teacher,* 1958, 11, 225–234.

McCullough, Constance M. Implications of research on children's concepts. *Reading Teacher,* 1959, 13, 100–107.

McDade, J. E. A hypothesis for non-oral reading: Argument, experiment and results. *J. educ. Res.,* 1937, 30, 489–503.

McDonald, A. E. A reading versatility inventory. In *Significant elements in college and adult reading improvement. 7th Yearb., Nat. Reading Conf. Colleges and Adults,* 1958, 48–53.

McKee, P. Reading for meaning in the intermediate grades. *Educ. Digest,* 1945, 10, 51–53.

McKee, P. *The teaching of reading in the elementary school.* Boston: Houghton Mifflin, 1948.

McKillop, Anne S. *The relationship between the reader's attitude and certain types of reading responses.* New York: Bur. of Publs., Teachers Coll., Columbia Univer., 1952.

McNaughton, A. H. The ability of seventh grade children to infer meaning and to generalize from two selections of written history materials. Unpublished doctoral dissertation, Univer. of California, Berkeley, 1960.

Meriam, J. L. Avoiding difficulties in learning to read. *Educ. Method,* 1930, 9, 413–419.

Michaelis, J. U. *Social studies for children in a democracy.* (Rev. ed.) New York: Prentice-Hall, 1956.

Michaelis, J. U., & Tyler, F. T. A comparison of reading ability and readability. *J. educ. Psychol.,* 1951, 42, 491–498.

Miles, I. W. An experiment in vocabulary building in high school. *Sch. & Soc.,* 1945, 61, 285–286.

Miller, G. A. *Language and communication.* New York: McGraw-Hill, 1951.

Miller, G. A., Bruner, J. S., & Postman, L. Familiarity of letter sequences and tachistoscopic identification. *J. gen. Psychol.,* 1954, 50, 129–139.

Moir, W. A world of words. *Engl. J.,* 1953, 42, 153–155.

Morgan, C. L., & Bailey, W. L. The effect of

context on learning a vocabulary. *J. educ. Psychol.,* 1943, 34, 561–565.

Morris, Joyce. Teaching children to read. *Educ. Res.,* 1958, 1, 38–49.

Morris, Joyce. Teaching children to read. *Educ. Res.,* 1959, 1, 61–75.

Mosier, R. D. *Making the American mind.* New York: Columbia Univer., King's Crown Press, 1947.

Mulder, R. F., & Curtin, J. Vocal phonetic ability and silent reading achievement. *Educ. Digest,* 1956, 21, 46–47.

Myers, G. C. Reading to babies and young children. *Education,* 1957, 77, 576–579.

Nardelli, R. R. A study of some aspects of creative reading. Unpublished doctoral dissertation, Univer. of California, Berkeley, 1954.

National Council of Teachers of English, Commission on the English Curriculum. *The language arts in the secondary school.* New York: Appleton-Century-Crofts, 1956.

Nicholson, A. Background abilities related to reading success in the first grade. *J. Educ.,* 1958, 140, 7–24.

Norvell, G. W. *The reading interests of young people.* Boston: Heath, 1950.

Norvell, G. W. *What boys and girls like to read.* New York: Silver Burdett, 1958.

Oakland Board of Education. *Time for poetry.* (Supp. to Curriculum Guide, Elementary, No. 2.) 2 vols. Oakland, Calif.: Board of Education, 1960.

Oaks, Ruth E. A study of the vowel situations in a primary vocabulary. *Education,* 1952, 72, 604–617.

Olson, W. C. Seeking, self-selection, and pacing in the use of books by children. *Packet.* Boston: Heath, 1952.

Osburn, W. J., Huntington, Mirriel, & Meeks, Viola. The language of relativity as related to reading readiness. *J. educ. res.,* 1946, 39, 583–601.

Otterman, L. M. The value of teaching prefixes and root-words. *J. educ. Res.,* 1955, 48, 611–616.

Parkin, Phyllis. An individual program of reading. *Educ. Leadership,* 1956, 14, 34–38.

Pei, M. *The story of language.* Philadelphia: Lippincott, 1949.

Pellett, Elizabeth A. New approaches to grouping in high school. *Reading Teacher,* 1957, 11, 109–115.

Petty, Mary C. An experimental study of cer-

tain factors influencing reading readiness. *J. educ. Psychol.,* 1939, 30, 215–230.

Petty, W. Critical reading in the primary grades. *Elem. Engl.,* 1956, 33, 298–302.

Piaget, J. *The language and thought of the child.* (Trans. by M. Gabain) New York: Harcourt, Brace, 1932.

Piekarz, Josephine A. Getting meaning from reading. *Elem. sch. J.,* 1956, 56, 303–309.

Pingry, R. E. Critical thinking: What is it? *Math. Teacher,* 1951, 44, 466–470.

Poling, Dorothy. Auditory deficiencies of poor readers. In *Clinical studies in reading, II. Suppl. educ. Monogr.,* 1953, 77, 107–111.

Pond, F. L. Influence of the study of Latin on word knowledge. *Sch. Rev.,* 1938, 46, 611–618.

Postman, L., & Rosenzweig, M. R. Perceptual recognition of words. *J. speech hear. Dis.,* 1957, 22, 245–253.

Potter, Muriel C. Perception of symbol orientation and early reading success. *Teach. Coll. Contr. Educ.,* 1949, No. 939.

Pressey, Luella C., & Pressey, S. L. A critical study of the concept of silent reading ability. *J. educ. Psychol.,* 1921, 12, 25–31.

Pressey, S. L. A machine for automatic teaching and drill material. *Sch. & Soc.,* 1927, 25, 549–552.

Pressnall, H. E. Parents' opinions of reading instruction. *Elem. Engl.,* 1956, 33, 29–33.

Price, Devona M. Everything with a name is in the dictionary. *Education,* 1957, 77, 266–269.

Ragle, J. W. Something old, something new, something borrowed—A vocabulary program. *Engl. J.,* 1956, 45, 208–211.

Reed, J. C., & Pepper, R. S. Interrelationship of vocabulary, comprehension and rate among disabled readers. *J. exp. Educ.,* 1957, 25, 333–337.

Reid, Florence. Films provide a rich source of vocabulary study. *J. educ. Res.,* 1958, 51, 617–623.

Reynolds, M. C. A study of relationships between auditory characteristics and specific silent reading abilities. *J. educ. Res.,* 1953, 46, 439–449.

Richards, I. A. *Practical criticism: A study of literary judgment.* New York: Harcourt, Brace, 1930.

Rittenhouse, Gloria G. An experiment in reading by invitation in grades one through four. *Reading Teacher,* 1960, 13, 258–261.

Roberts, R. W., & Coleman, J. C. Investigation of the role of visual and kinesthetic factors in reading failure. *J. educ. Res.*, 1958, 51, 445–451.

Robinson, F. P., & Hall, Prudence. Studies in higher-level reading abilities. *J. educ. Psychol.*, 1941, 32, 241–252.

Robinson, Helen M. Special difficulties in word perception as revealed in clinical studies. In *Basic instruction in reading in elementary and high schools. Supp. educ. Monogr.*, 1948, 65.

Robinson, Helen M. Factors which affect success in reading. *Elem. sch. J.*, 1955, 55, 263–269.

Robinson, Helen M. Development of reading skills. *Elem. sch. J.*, 1958, 58, 269–274.

Robinson, Helen M. Methods of teaching beginning readers. *Elem. sch. J.*, 1959, 59, 419–426.

Robinson, Margaret A. Differentiating instruction to provide for the needs of learners through organizational practices: In grades 4–6. In *New frontiers in reading. Proc. Internat. Reading Ass. Conf.*, 1960, 5, 29–32.

Rogers, Maurine V. Phonic ability as related to certain aspects of reading at the college level. *J. exp. Educ.*, 1938, 6, 381–385.

Rosenblatt, Louise M. Literature: The reader's role. *Engl. J.*, 1960, 49, 304–310.

Rudisill, Mabel. Flashed digit and phrase recognition and rate of oral and concrete responses: A study of advanced and retarded readers in the third grade. *J. Psychol.*, 1956, 42, 317–320.

Rudisill, Mabel. Interrelationships of functional phonic knowledge, reading, spelling, and mental age. *Elem. sch. J.*, 1957, 57, 264–267.

Rudman, H. C. Informational needs and reading interests of children in grades IV through VIII. *Elem. sch. J.*, 1955, 55, 502–512.

Rudman, H. C. Parents and their children's reading interests. *Reading Teacher*, 1956, 10, 26–32.

Rudolf, Kathleen B. The effect of reading instruction on achievement in eighth grade social studies. *Teach. Coll. Contr. Educ.*, 1949, No. 945.

Russell, D. H. Opinions of experts about primary-grade basic reading programs. *Elem. sch. J.*, 1944, 44, 602–609.

Russell, D. H. Inter-class grouping for reading instruction in the intermediate grades. *J. educ. Res.*, 1946, 39, 462–470.

Russell, D. H. The dimensions of children's meaning vocabularies in grades four through twelve. *Univer. Calif. Publs Educ.*, 1954, 11, 315–414.

Russell, D. H. Teachers' views on phonics. *Elem. Engl.*, 1955, 32, 371–375.

Russell, D. H. *Children's thinking.* Boston: Ginn, 1956.

Russell, D. H. Some research on the impact of reading. *Engl. J.*, 1958, 47, 398–413.

Russell, D. H. Arithmetic power through reading. In *Instruction in arithmetic. 25th Yearb., Nat. Council Teachers Math.*, 1960, 208–223.

Russell, D. H. *Children learn to read.* (2nd ed.) Boston: Ginn, 1961.

Russell, D. H., & Shrodes, Caroline. Contributions of research in bibliotherapy to the language-arts program. *Sch. Rev.*, 1950, 58, 335–342.

Russell, R. D. A comparison of two methods of learning. *J. educ. Res.*, 1928, 18, 235–238.

Saale, C. W. The role of meaning in reading. *15th Yearb., Claremont Coll. Reading Conf.*, 1950, 19–33.

Sachs, H. J. The reading method of acquiring vocabulary. *J. educ. Res.*, 1943, 36, 457–464.

Safford, A. L. Evaluation of an individualized reading program. *Reading Teacher*, 1960, 13, 266–270.

Sartain, H. W. A bibliography on individualized reading. *Reading Teacher*, 1960, 13, 262–265. (a)

Sartain, H. W. The Roseville experiment with individualized reading. *Reading Teacher*, 1960, 13, 277–281. (b)

Schatz, Esther E., & others. *Exploring independent reading in the primary grades.* Columbus: Ohio State Univer., 1960.

Schonell, F. J. *Psychology and teaching of reading.* (3rd ed.) Edinburgh: Oliver & Boyd, 1951.

Schubert, D. G. Whose brand of reading is the best buy? *Clearing House*, 1953, 27, 266–267.

Scott, F., & Myers, G. C. Children's empty and erroneous concepts of the commonplace. *J. educ. Res.*, 1923, 8, 327–343.

Seashore, R. H., & Eckerson, L. D. Measurement of individual differences in general English vocabularies. *J. educ. Psychol.*, 1940, 31, 14–38.

Serra, Mary C. How to develop concepts and their verbal representations. *Elem. sch. J.*, 1953, 53, 275–285.

Sheldon, W. D. Differentiating instruction to

provide for the needs of learners: 1. In primary grades; a. Through organizational practices. *New frontiers in reading. Proc. Internat. Reading Ass. Conf.*, 1960, 5, 23–26.

Shores, J. H. Skills related to the ability to read history and science. *J. educ. Res.*, 1943, 36, 584–593.

Shores, J. H., & Husbands, K. L. Are fast readers the best readers? *Elem. Engl.*, 1950, 27, 52–57.

Shores, J. H., & Saupe, J. L. Reading for problem solving in science. *J. educ. Psychol.*, 1953, 44, 149–159.

Shrodes, Caroline. Bibliotherapy: A theoretical and clinical-experimental study. Unpublished doctoral dissertation, Univer. of California, Berkeley, 1949.

Skinner, B. F. The science of learning and the art of teaching. *Harvard educ. Rev.*, 1954, 24, 86–97.

Skinner, B. F. *Cumulative record*. New York: Appleton-Century-Crofts, 1959.

Smith, D. E. P. A new theory of the physiological basis of reading disability. *Reading for effective living. Proc. Internat. Reading Ass. Conf.*, 1958, 3, 119–121.

Smith, Mary K. Measurement of the size of general English vocabulary through the elementary grades and high school. *Genet. psychol. Monogr.*, 1941, 24, 311–345.

Smith, Nila B. *American reading instruction.* New York: Silver Burdett, 1934.

Smith, Nila B. Some effects of reading on children. *Elem. Engl.*, 1948, 25, 271–278.

Smith, Nila B. Reading: Concept development. *Education*, 1950, 70, 548–558.

Smith, Nila B. Utilizing reading opportunities in the entire curriculum. *Education*, 1952, 72, 579–589.

Smith, Nila B. Classroom organization: An age-old problem with new slants. *Reading Teacher,* 1957, 11, 73–74.

Smoke, K. L. Concept formation. In P. L. Harriman (Ed.), *Encyclopedia of psychology.* New York: Philosophical Library, 1946. Pp. 97–100.

Sochor, Elona E. Literal and critical reading in social studies. *J. exp. Educ.,* 1958, 27, 49–56.

Sochor, Elona E. The nature of critical reading. *Elem. Engl.*, 1959, 36, 47–58.

Solomon, R. L., & Postman, L. Frequency of usage as a determinant of recognition thresholds for words. *J. exp. Psychol.,* 1952, 43, 195–201.

Sparks, P. E., & Fay, L. C. An evaluation of two methods of teaching reading. *Elem. sch. J.,* 1957, 57, 386–390.

Spencer, P. Perspective in mathematical reading. In *Instruction in arithmetic. 25th Yearb., Nat. Council Teachers Math.*, 1960, 202–207.

Squire, J. R. The responses of adolescents to literature involving selected experiences of personal development. Unpublished doctoral dissertation, Univer. of California, Berkeley, 1956.

Stauffer, R. G. A study of prefixes in the Thorndike list to establish a list of prefixes that should be taught in the elementary school. *J. educ. Res.*, 1942, 35, 453–458.

Stevenson, Lillian P., & Robinson, Helen M. Eye-hand preference, reversals, and reading progress. In *Clinical studies in reading, II. Supp. educ. Monogr.*, 1953, 77, 83–88.

Strang, Ruth M. How students attack unfamiliar words. *Engl. J.*, 1944, 33, 88–93.

Strang, Ruth, McCullough, Constance M., & Traxler, A. E. *Problems in the improvement of reading.* (2nd ed.)-New York: McGraw-Hill, 1955.

Strom, Ingrid M. Does knowledge of grammar improve reading? *Engl. J.*, 1956, 45, 129–133.

Sussams, T. W. *Poetry and the teacher.* London: Nelson, 1949.

Sutton, Rachel S. The effect of vocabulary building on reading skills. *Elem. sch. J.,* 1953, 54, 94–97.

Swenson, Esther J. A study of relationships among various types of reading scores on general and science materials. *J. educ. Res.,* 1942, 36, 81–90.

Tate, H., Herbert, T., & Zeman, J. Non-phonetic primary reading. *Elem. sch. J.,* 1940, 40, 529–537.

Taylor, Janet A. Meaning, frequency, and visual duration threshold. *J. exp. Psychol.,* 1958, 55, 329–334.

Terman, L. M., & Lima, Margaret. *Children's reading.* New York: Appleton-Century, 1935.

Thorndike, E. L. The teaching of English suffixes. *Teach. Coll. Contr. Educ.,* 1941, No. 847.

Thorndike, E. L., & Lorge, I. *The teacher's word book of 30,000 words.* New York: Bur. of Publs., Teachers Coll., Columbia Univer., 1944.

Thurstone, L. L. Note on a reanalysis of

Davis' reading tests. *Psychometrika,* 1946, 11, 185–188.

Tiegs, E. W., & Adams, Fay. *Teaching social studies—A guide to better citizenship.* Boston: Ginn, 1959.

Tiffin, J., & McKinnis, M. Phonetic ability: Its measurement and relation to reading ability. *Sch. & Soc.,* 1940, 51, 190–192.

Tinker, M. A. *Teaching elementary reading.* New York: Appleton-Century-Crofts, 1952.

Traxler, A. E. The relation between rate of reading and speed of association. *J. educ. Psychol.,* 1934, 25, 357–365.

Traxler, A. E. Improvement of vocabulary through drill. *Engl. J.,* 1938, 27, 491–494.

Treacy, J. P. The relationship of reading skills to the ability to solve arithmetic problems. *J. educ. Res.,* 1944, 37, 86–98.

Triggs, Frances O. The development of measured word recognition skills, grade four through the college freshman year. *Educ. psychol. Measmt,* 1952, 12, 345–349.

Triggs, Frances O. Promoting growth in critical reading. *Educ. Digest,* 1959, 25, 42–44.

Veatch, Jeannette. *Individualizing your reading program.* New York: Putnam's, 1959.

Veatch, Jeannette. In defense of individualized reading. *Elem. Engl.,* 1960, 37, 227–234.

Vernon, Magdalen D. Development of visual perception in children. *Education,* 1958, 78, 547–549.

Vernon, Magdalen D. The perceptual process in reading. *Reading Teacher,* 1959, 13, 2–8.

Vinacke, W. E. The investigation of concept formation. *Psychol. Bull.,* 1951, 48, 1–31.

Wagner, Louise D. Measuring the map-reading ability of sixth-grade children. *Elem. sch. J.,* 1953, 53, 338–344.

Walker, Clare. An evaluation of two programs of reading in grades four, five, and six of the elementary school. Unpublished doctoral dissertation, New York Univer., 1957.

Waples, D., Berelson, B. R., & Bradshaw, F. R. *What reading does to people.* Chicago: Univer. of Chicago Press, 1940.

Ward, L. R. Measuring comprehension in reading. *Coll. Engl.,* 1956, 17, 481–483.

Warfel, H. R., & Lloyd, D. J. Structural approach to reading. *Sch. & Soc.,* 1957, 85, 199–201.

Weingarten, S. Developmental values in voluntary reading. *Sch. Rev.,* 1954, 62, 222–230.

Welch, L. A behaviorist explanation of concept formation. *J. genet. Psychol.,* 1947, 71, 201–251.

Welshinger, D. M. Summary of reading readiness research. *Educ. Admin. Superv.,* 1948, 34, 372–376.

Wenzel, Bernice M., & Flurry, Christine. Sequential order of concept attainment. *J. exp. Psychol.,* 1948, 38, 547–557.

Werner, H., & Kaplan Edith. The acquisition of word meanings: A developmental study. *Monogr. Soc. Res. Child Develpm.,* 1950, 15, No. 51.

Whipple, Gertrude. Good practices in grouping. *Reading Teacher,* 1953, 7, 69–74.

Whitehead, F. The attitudes of grammar school pupils towards some novels commonly read in school. *Brit. J. educ. Psychol.,* 1956, 26, 104–111.

Williams, E. D., Winter, L., & Woods, J. K. Tests of literary appreciation. *Brit. J. educ. Psychol.,* 1938, 8, 265–284.

Williams, Gertrude. Provision for critical reading in basic readers. *Elem. Engl.,* 1959, 36, 323–331.

Williams, Ida B. Figuratively speaking. *NEA J.,* 1954, 43, 51.

Witty, P. A. Reading of social studies materials. *Elem. Engl.,* 1950, 27, 1–8.

Witty, P. A. Phonic study and word analysis I and II. *Elem. Engl.,* 1953, 30, 296–305, 373–383.

Witty, P. A. A tenth yearly study and comments on a decade of televiewing. *Elem. Engl.,* 1959, 36, 581–586. (a)

Witty, P. A. Individualized reading—A summary and evaluation. *Elem. Engl.,* 1959, 36, 401–412, 450. (b)

Witty, P. A., & Fitzwater, J. P. An experiment with films, film readers, and the magnetic sound track projector. *Elem. Engl.,* 1953, 30, 232–241.

Witty, P. A., & Sizemore, R. A. Studies in listening. *Elem. Engl.,* 1958, 35, 538–552; 1959, 36, 59–70, 130–140.

Wrightstone, J. W. What research says about class organization for instruction. *NEA J.,* 1957, 46, 254–255.

Young, J. D. An experimental comparison of vocabulary growth by means of oral reading, silent reading, and listening. *Speech Monogr.,* 1953, 20, 273–276.

Young, W. E. The relation of reading comprehension and retention to hearing comprehension and retention. *J. exp. Educ.,* 1936, 5, 30–39.

Young, W. E. Recent research on reading in social studies. *Education,* 1941, 62, 18–26.

CHAPTER 17 Research on Teaching the Social Studies

LAWRENCE E. METCALF
University of Illinois

This chapter will review and critically analyze research on teaching the social studies. No attempt has been made to treat the literature exhaustively, partly because of the availability of recent summaries, considered in the first section of this chapter, and partly because of the sterility of much of that literature. Instead, the chapter has been focused on an approach to teaching the social studies, the reflective method, which serves as a point of vantage for examining the major issues. Empirical studies of reflective method and its cognates are considered at some length. Finally, the chapter turns to analytic history, with an extensive discussion of the problem of teaching historical explanation, and to recent formulations of concept analysis.

RECENT SUMMARIES

Within the past few years three summaries of research on teaching the social studies have appeared. Only one of these, an encyclopedia article by Gross and Badger (1960), purported to be a complete summary. An unpublished bibliography by McPhie (1959) listed doctoral dissertations for the past 25 years and annotated some of them. The pam-

phlet by McLendon (1960), one of a series entitled *What Research Says to the Teacher,* was not offered as a complete summary but, in the author's words, "attempted to draw from research material on the social studies the items which promise to be of most help to classroom teachers" (p. 2). All three authors reported great difficulty in ascertaining what the research has been. The social studies field is broadly and vaguely defined, and no systematic practice has been set up in collating studies in this field.

McLendon's Pamphlet

McLendon was at his best when he summarized the research on trends in objectives as follows:

Research has revealed several clear but not always favorable characteristics of objectives in social studies: (a) an excessive number of objectives stated; (b) marked uniformity among various localities, grades, and subjects; (c) frequently nebulous statements; (d) a time lag in reflecting social trends; (e) increasing emphasis on social (as distinguished from individual) values; (f) apparent lack of rating according to importance; and (g) little evi-

929

dence of application of research that has attempted to formulate more specific statements of objectives (for example, by answering the question, "What is a good citizen?" through detailed analysis of adult activities) (McLendon, 1960, pp. 7–8).

He did not specify the research that has revealed these characteristics of objectives, and the reader, therefore, is in no position to verify his claims by turning to the original studies. He also omitted from his list the tendency of teachers to list inconsistent objectives. His recommendation that one answer the question, What is a good citizen? through detailed analysis of adult activities suggests the question of where objectives originate. Such analysis could surely reveal to some extent what adult citizens *do* but fails to consider what adult citizens *should do.*

McLendon's assertion about the excessive number of nebulously stated objectives in the social studies is well taken. Earlier, Horn (1937) had described studies which revealed that American history teachers claimed to pursue 1,400 different objectives; one junior high school course of study began with 47 mimeographed pages of objectives. After considering such studies, Horn suggested for the social studies a single objective cast as a biblical injunction: "*Finally, brethren, whatsoever things are true, whatsoever things are honest, whatsoever things are just, whatsoever things are lovely, whatsoever things are of good report, if there be any virtue, and if there be any praise, think on these things*" (Horn, 1937, p. 4).

As a further example of the proliferation of objectives, we may consider Wesley as quoted by Griffin (1942). To a list suggested by Charles Beard which included nine skills, seven habits, eleven attitudes, eight qualities, and a separate category called "Information," Wesley (1942) added 17 objectives of his own for history, and another 36 to be shared with economics, geography, civics, and sociology. His objectives included such familiar expressions as "to develop an appreciation of our social heritage," "to acquire

a perspective for understanding contemporary issues," "to develop a love of historical reading," and "to promote international understanding." He then, said Griffin, "warns teachers against the danger of trying to 'analyze every step in order to state the specific purpose for taking it,' because to do so might lead to 'the obscuring of the larger and more fundamental objectives' ..." (Griffin, 1942, p. 20).

Wesley did not state the larger and more fundamental objectives, unless his own list is to be so taken. In any case, Griffin correctly described the social studies as moving toward the statement of larger, more numerous, and more glittering objectives. Indeed, the social studies have tended to appropriate all the objectives of general education. Almost none of the stated objectives could be taken as peculiar to the social studies. At the level of objectives, general education can hardly be distinguished from the social studies. In mathematics and science, it has become customary to list objectives that more or less state the potential uses of an intellectual discipline. Workers in the social studies, however, have tried to define the good life, and then have assumed that they are its sole guardian. Equal time and thought have not been given to how one may achieve so many worthy objectives. Consequently, the actual program has always been inferior to the stated objectives. With purposes much better than their means, social studies educators, therefore, need research to develop means adequate to their purposes.

An example of high purpose and mean program is the situation in the teaching of critical thinking. Critical thinking is a frequently stated objective in social studies, yet teachers are seldom satisfied with results in this area. The social studies are not alone in emphasizing critical thinking as a process to be taught. But the teaching of this process in the social studies is hindered by barriers not usually present in mathematics or science. Research in social studies might indicate what the barriers are and how a classroom teacher of social studies might overcome them. McLendon (1960) devoted two full pages to critical thinking without, however, suggesting what it is, or how it might be taught, or even, indeed, whether it can be taught. His treatment leaves one with the unhappy impression that social studies research may have nothing to say on a matter as crucial as the teaching of critical thinking.

McPhie's List of Dissertations

McPhie's list (1959) purported to include all doctoral dissertations in social studies education for the preceding 25 years, and it is doubtful that he overlooked a single major study. This writer found listed and annotated everything of significance that has ever come to his attention, and much that had not. The quality of the annotation varies with the dissertation, and McPhie did not indicate whether he or the original author was responsible for each annotation.

McPhie's list indicated indirectly the research interests and methods of professors of social studies education, and therein is one of its major values. Graduate students are not always capable of identifying the problems of their specialty, and even when they are, it is usually sensible for them to explore problems in which their advisers are interested and capable of advising.

The list reflects no sustained concern with building and clarifying theory for teaching the social studies. The empirical studies have also not been the kind likely to contribute to theoretical knowledge. Dissertations have resulted in teaching manuals, course outlines, trend identification, status studies which are soon out of date, surveys of local peculiarities, controlled experiments of dubious design, historical studies, and textbook analysis. Many studies are local and dated in nature, and no attempt has been made to relate them to the larger, abiding questions in teaching the social studies.

Analyses of textbooks to identify biases have been abundant. McPhie listed 46 dissertations, written in the period 1936–1956, which studied textual materials. The concern with bias is revealed in such titles as "A Study of Bias in the Treatment of Nullification and Secession in the Secondary School History Textbooks of the United States"; "The Treatment of the Negro in American History School Textbooks"; and "The Treatment of the Immigrant in American History School Textbooks."

Almost every possible kind of bias that might appear in social studies instructional material has been studied. The value of such studies has not, however, been exactly specified or closely questioned. Some of the studies belong properly to the history of education rather than to the theory or practice of social studies education. A typical study is one in which the author examined 87 high school American history textbooks used between 1895 and 1950 to see whether the treatment of Japan and people of Japanese descent had moved toward a world point of view, such as that expressed in certain UNESCO materials.

It is difficult to see how a knowledge of bias in materials contributes to a theory of teaching social studies. Even if it were known how teachers use such material, it would still be necessary to develop a theory of method which would suggest how a teacher could use material for learning purposes regardless of the biases or purposes of those who produce materials of instruction. It makes no difference to the building of such a theory whether materials originate with responsible publishers, skillful propagandists, well-meaning administrators, conservative boards of education, or misinformed scholars. Neither does it make any difference to such theory-building whether the dominant biases are pro or con an international point of view, because a sound theory will indicate how any bias may be handled by teachers who favor conceptual or any other kind of learning.

McPhie's valuable list of dissertations would have been even more useful if it had included an introduction clarifying how the list was compiled and how the annotations were made. Only then could a reader judge the completeness of the list and the authenticity of the annotations. The National Council for the Social Studies, through its research committee, should systematize the annual compilation of such a list and the writing of critical evaluations of current doctoral studies in social studies education.

Gross and Badger's Encyclopedia Article

Gross and Badger (1960), in their encyclopedia article, mentioned 274 studies in the social studies. They did not mention a dissertation by Griffin (1942), listed without annotation by McPhie, which in this writer's judgment ranks among the most significant studies of the past 20 years. Gross and Badger's bibliography is nonetheless the most complete this writer has seen. Since these writers mentioned most of these many studies, they were unable to deal at length with any of them. Gross and Badger treated a broad range of topics, as is perhaps appropriate for an encyclopedia article. This writer would have preferred an attempt to organize the studies around different theories to show the extent to which each theory had been examined in the research, and to reach some conclusion as to the status of various theories. Instead, they covered such headings as the curriculum, objectives, problems of instruction, evaluation, and the social studies teacher. The history of the social studies, the curriculum, the courses offered, enrollment in each, and course trends are especially well treated.

Interpretations of results or critiques of research designs, especially negative evaluations, are largely absent. Their comment on Devitt's study (1957) follows:

Devitt . . . attempted to help delimit the content of the course [American history] by gathering a comprehensive list of basic concepts to be taught; he submitted 938 concepts to three separate juries on a national level to validate the generalizations. Such a list organized in order of importance can be an aid to those attempting to build better courses (Gross & Badger, 1960, p. 1302).

But Devitt's study listed facts more often than concepts. The list consisted of statements, most of which were of the order: "Columbus discovered America in 1492." It is questionable whether Devitt sorted out the basic concepts to be taught in American history or even whether he distinguished concepts from facts. Concepts are usually defined as categories, or laws, as in Bruner, et al. (1956), but seldom as facts, or singular statements, even though facts are necessary to teaching certain kinds of concepts, i.e., those that have some empirical grounding.

Gross and Badger did criticize some findings, but not the studies, i.e., the purposes, conceptual framework, or design of the studies. For example, they had this to say about one study:

Anderson and Phelps' survey of discussion techniques used by 110 social-studies teachers in 15 high schools showed that, although all teachers used some discussion, they varied greatly in the types of discussion situations provided and thus in the number of students involved. . . . The distressing finding here was that in 55 percent of the classes students had no preparatory instructions or had little help from the teachers in planning for their panels or reports (Gross & Badger, 1960, p. 1306).

Gross and Badger's competent history of the social studies and comparisons of such figures as the percentage of high school students taking economics today with the percentage 30 years ago nonetheless lacked a curriculum theory for interpreting the figures. They did take to task those who label the social studies "social slush," without making it clear whether they oppose those who would substitute courses in history, political science, geography, economics, and sociology for various fused or correlated offerings. They also omitted any comment on a perhaps more significant issue—whether there is too much history and not enough behavioral science in the social studies curriculum.

Gross and Badger, like McLendon, treated technique without reference to a guiding theoretical framework. Gross has indicated in some of his other writings a leaning toward problem-solving as a method, but although the encyclopedia article treats it and controversial issues in consecutive sections, that discussion does not hint that one is intrinsically a part of the other. Their concept of problem-solving does not give a higher priority to the "hot" issues than to personal problems. In economics, for example, they might give attention to problems of personal finance before they would concern themselves with analysis of unemployment, economic growth, fiscal policy, and other so-called adult problems.

The three summaries suggest that research on teaching the social studies has not been guided by a framework or theory that would make possible a distinction between basic and trivial investigations. It is desirable to avoid a dogmatic or closed system, but it does not follow that objectivity means neutrality, or that one can prove his neutrality by taking an antitheoretical position, or that one should conduct empirical studies which have no relationship to the clarification of theories.

If there has been any bias in the research, it has been a faint-hearted and confused preference for problem-solving as a method of teaching. Some investigators have looked upon problem-solving as adequate for certain purposes, while favoring other methods for other purposes, without apparent need to have consistent purposes. A common point of view was expressed by Gross and Badger: "A teacher may state six aims of equal importance and find that socialized discussion is better in reaching three of them, while question-and-answer recitation brings better attainment of the other three" (1960, p. 1305). Yet, of course, the six aims of this teacher may lack internal consistency and hence may to some extent be self-defeating.

The same theme appears in the frequently expressed preference for a variety of teaching methods. Gross and Badger commented that "the teacher should not use one or two methods to the exclusion of all others; a variety of techniques, each of which fits certain special purposes or situations, probably will yield the highest returns in learning" (pp. 1305–1306). Here again technique is not related to any particular theory of method.

REFLECTIVE THEORY OF METHOD

In contrast to a position that seems to favor variety of technique for its own sake within a general preference for problem-solving is the solid theoretical work on method by Dewey (1910, 1933), Bayles (1950), and Hullfish and Smith (1961). These writers treat reflective thinking as a method by which to foster conceptualization in learning skills, attitudes, habits, information, and understandings at all grade levels and in all subjects. Those who hold this concept of method have been accused of stretching their concept beyond recognition in a futile attempt to encompass all educational purposes, and of confusing epistemological method with pedagogical. In the latter instance, it is argued that although reflective thought is adequate for discovering new knowledge, it is inappropriate for teaching that which is already known and systematized. These quite fundamental criticisms have not been put to any experimental test by any social studies research known to the writer.

Since Dewey's influence on social studies has been pervasive, research should have been expected to emphasize the testing, clarification, and refinement of his theory. Yet only a few studies have attempted to do so, and the rest cast no light on his, or any other, theory of how a teacher might expect to perform his chief intellectual function, the direction of a process by which to assist students in concept attainment. Because the summaries by McLendon (1960), McPhie (1959), and Gross and Badger (1960) have not had this focus, this chapter will attempt to sum up our present position in relation to the practice and theory of conceptual teaching. This attention to conceptual teaching follows from an assumption that intellectual development of the young is the chief function of all education, including social studies education, and that intellectual development consists in the formation and attainment of concepts.

First, we shall outline the reflective theory of teaching the social studies; then we shall consider the few empirical studies which purport to test and clarify this theory. The general theory was stated by Dewey (1933). Although the fact has not been generally recognized, Griffin (1942) stands almost alone in his attempt to elaborate in practical and theoretical terms what reflective theory means for teaching history and for the subject-matter preparation of high school history teachers. He has developed his theoretical position more completely and precisely than has any other student of method. Studies of the adequacy of problem-solving methods must take his position into account.

It is significant that Griffin never used the term *problem-solving* in his discussion of method. He probably wished to divorce himself from a term that has often been interpreted in ways that stifle opportunities for reflection in a classroom. It is also significant that his view of reflection was not limited to questions of method but also included the selection and organization of content and the curriculum of teacher education. His main contribution has been to pedagogical method, however, and it would be proper to view his theory as a psychological-logical model for teaching conceptual learning. His dissertation, rich in concrete illustrations of this model at work in history classrooms, ranks as a major intellectual achievement in social studies education within the past two decades, with a quality of writing and thought seldom found in a dissertation.

The following propositions and definitions, stated or implied by Griffin, are presented here in summary form to set forth in broad outline his proposals for achieving conceptual learning in the social studies:

1. Reflective thought is the active, careful, and persistent examination of any belief, or purported form of knowledge, in the light of the grounds that support it and the further conclusions toward which it tends.

2. Although reflective thought is widely regarded as a method of ascertaining truth—even authoritarian societies make this admission—the survival of democracy in present times depends upon our recognition of reflection as *the* method of determining truth.

3. Societies are democratic in the degree to which they refrain from setting limits upon matters that may be thought about. It is a corollary that such societies place their faith in knowledge and actively promote occasions for doubt on the ground that doubt is the beginning of all knowledge.

4. Authoritarian societies achieve social cohesion by (1) instilling preferred values and beliefs, (2) holding such values and beliefs above or beyond question, and (3) carefully keeping out of people's experience any knowledge which might cast doubt upon the soundness of any preferred belief. Suppression of occasions for doubt becomes a necessary means to a stable, orderly, social unity possessed of purpose and continuity. Doubt can be fully eliminated only if all children learn the same beliefs and if their beliefs are consistent with the central values of the state. It follows, therefore, that the specific content of a child's early beliefs is crucially important to the maintenance of an authoritarian society.

5. Democracies also need order, stability, unity, purpose, and continuity. For them the solution cannot take the form of instilling specific beliefs in all children. Democracies cannot justify the suppression of knowledge, and if they consider doubt to be the beginning of all knowledge, they must positively encourage occasions for doubt. A reliance upon knowledge rather than hallowed belief means that reflection, as the only means of ascertaining belief, becomes the central, all-embracing value.

6. All culture patterns, democratic or authoritarian, have central and directing values. Democracy is not so much concerned with the specific character of the directing values as with the way in which central values are maintained and modified.

7. The earliest beliefs of children are not and cannot be acquired reflectively, although some writers have urged that they can be. Early beliefs are taken on uncritically and are often the consequence of conditioning or animal preference. The uncritical acquisition of early beliefs takes place in all societies, democratic or authoritarian, and a child need be no more ashamed of those beliefs than he is of his ancestry. Both are beyond his capacity to choose.

8. The development of children into adults who can steadily modify their beliefs in terms of their adequacy for explaining a widening range of experience requires two things: (1) improving and refining the reflective capacities of children, and (2) breaking through the hard shell of tradition which encases many deeply rooted and emotionally charged beliefs.

9. Many areas of belief in American culture are not subject to reflective examination. Our beliefs about race and sex are more open to study than they once were. Religion and economics remain particularly difficult to examine, even though conflicting traditions exist in both of these areas.

10. Two conceptions of learning are resident in the culture of teachers. It makes a difference in the development of human intelligence whether children *learn to say that* something is true, or whether they *learn that* something is true. A parrot could learn to say that Columbus discovered America in 1492, but only a human being could learn that such was the case. The latter is what is meant by conceptual learning.

11. Content may be viewed in two ways. These two ways, if analyzed, clarify what is sometimes meant by functional information. One kind of content, the pattern-of-action kind, is functional if we know what we want to do, or are set to act in a certain way. For example, the person who wants to vote would regard a knowledge of how to mark a ballot as functional. Unfortunately, this is the only concept of functional content known to some teachers. Such teachers, before teaching any information, want to know whether children are ready to make use of it. It is difficult, if not impossible, to justify the teaching of history if one's criterion is functional education of the pattern-of-action kind.

Another kind of content is the kind that may function as data in the testing of beliefs. This kind is just as functional as the pattern-of-action kind, and acceptance of it opens the way to teaching history.

12. Information can be the result of reflection as well as data for reflection. When an individual is in a situation that is unclear, either because no appropriate way of acting is readily suggested by the situation, or because mutually exclusive responses are implied, then he has a chance, and some reason, to reflect. Reflection takes the form of trying to figure out what is blocking action, to hypothesize some ways out of the difficulty, to elaborate in imagination the probable consequences of each, and to accept that hypothesis which is seen as solving the problem. Once this clearly accepted hypothesis has been learned, it can even be viewed as a habit that will govern behavior when future situations are seen to be of the same kind as the one that gave rise to the hypothesis. This learning of a new belief and a new habit includes learning those facts relevant to testing the hypotheses which the learner formulated for solution of the problem.

13. The beliefs used to rationalize a particular attitude constitute a cognitive basis that supplements whatever emotional basis there may be. Reflective examination of these rationalizing beliefs may or may not result in attitudinal change. It follows that reflection cannot guarantee that attitudes will change in a particular direction. The attempt to promote specific changes in attitude would, of course, be undemocratic since it would require a rejection of reflective thought as the sole basis for conceptual learning.

14. A generalized change in attitudes, however, may occur. Students taught by the reflective method would become more conscious of their attitudes, what they mean, and their interrelationships in a field of consequences.

Griffin's theory of teaching, addressed to the service of a large social purpose, has as its central concern the analysis of student beliefs. It assumes that historical data can function as evidence for testing such beliefs, though not necessarily the historical data found in standard schoolbooks, if indeed these books include any data at all. His proposal no doubt calls for sweeping revisions in course content. The specific nature of the revisions is not treated in his study, except by implication. The many studies of textbooks reported by McPhie (1959) do not bear upon this problem. Griffin does indicate that the beliefs of young people can be reliably inferred from studies of American culture, and there have been many of these studies. A significant implementation of Griffin's theory would entail the development of new teaching materials containing facts relevant to the testing of commonly held American beliefs. The development of such materials would render more explicit a practical side of his theory, a step toward its eventual testing.

It should be said in passing that the absence of such instructional materials from present-day schools does not constitute a basis for rejecting Griffin's theory. Rather, any such lack in the schools becomes a deficiency in practice—if the theory is sound—and means that the schools rather than the theory are impractical. Likewise, the idea that Griffin's proposal is impractical because the absence of academic freedom in public schools makes it unlikely that teachers will risk their jobs by exposing student prejudice, and, by implication, community prejudice, is not relevant to the soundness of his theory. If history teaches anything, it teaches that many theories, sound and unsound, have been unacceptable to powerful undemocratic forces in American culture.

Griffin was well aware of the opposition to permitting students in public schools to reflect upon basic beliefs. Hence, he urged teachers not to act in terms of his theory without a full realization of the risks involved. He would also have the teacher consider fully the risks of not acting in terms of a reflective

theory of teaching. It is one of the dilemmas imposed by his theory that the kind of content most likely to stimulate reflection in students is also the content likely to arouse the opposition of authoritarian groups. Such groups are more desirous of instilling particular beliefs than of teaching students how to modify any belief intelligently. There have been no recent studies of intellectual freedom in our public schools comparable to the study by Lazarsfeld and Thielens (1958) of how college teaching of social science was influenced by the pressures of McCarthyism.

At no time in recent years has anyone been sure in his judgment of the status of intellectual freedom in the public schools. The last study to investigate this question was made by Beale (1936). In place of studies, there have been expressions of opinion ranging from one extreme to another. One extreme says that there is no academic freedom in the public schools. Another extreme is represented by the statement that "teachers who understand how to teach democratically [reflectively] and do so in a competent way are likely to have *less* trouble with a community than other teachers and will probably be able to stay in their jobs as long as they wish to do so" (Bayles, 1956, p. 32).

Because Griffin's theory is concerned with concepts and how they are taught and learned, it confronts one with a basic rather than a trivial proposal. Experiments which would establish the truth or falsity of his theory would provide teachers with answers to those difficulties that lie at the heart of any program in citizenship education that has intellectual development as its chief concern. Bruner and his co-workers (1956) correctly pointed to concept formation and attainment as the basis for all thinking and cognition. It makes no difference whether the teacher is teaching an understanding, appreciation, skill, attitude, explanation, description, interpretation, definition, or valuation—all of which have been identified by Smith (1960) as daily operations of many teachers. Whatever his objective, the teacher's task is largely conceptual in nature. His endeavors will meet with success only if they are rooted in sound theory. Yet most research in the social studies has been irrelevant to testing Griffin's or any other theory of conceptual teaching. It is therefore not surprising that there have been no studies of academic freedom or other institutional prerequisites to the practice of reflective teaching. If there had been widespread interest in testing, clarifying, and refining a theory of teaching, the practice of which required a social-educational climate favorable to reflection, it is likely that attempts would have been made to measure the extent to which such an atmosphere prevailed in the public school system.

The Uncertain Status of Methods

A few attempts have been made to test a reflective theory of teaching. Feeble and awkward though some attempts have been, the literature of social studies abounds with references to their significance. Studies by Bayles treat reflection as an important variable, but most studies concentrate on the manipulation of less basic factors. Searles (1952) reported that college courses in methods of teaching social studies stress group discussion, group reports, use of current materials, individual reports, and unit approaches over other methods. This list suggests that college teachers of method are confused in their conception of method. It is difficult to understand, for instance, how one could label as method such very different entities as discussion, use of current materials, and unit approaches. Only discussion seems to qualify as a method, and then only if one locates it within a theoretical framework.

The conception of method reported by Jewett (1958) is evidently rare. In his methods class, Jewett confronts students with three questions: (1) What is reflection? (2) What is the role of social science data within a reflective process? and (3) By what techniques can a teacher hope to induce the use of reflection by students of social studies? If we compare Jewett's conception of method with that held by most college teachers in Searles'

study, we discover that they are not talking about the same problem. Most teachers would list discussion, lecture, and recitation as methods, while Jewett would be more likely to list reflection as a characteristic element to be found in any classroom technique that fosters conceptual learning.

Hunt and Metcalf (1955, pp. 53–59) referred to intuition, revelation, reason, and other nonreflective approaches to truth. It is difficult to see how a teacher could use revelation as a method of testing any proposition, and therefore using it as a method of teaching, although he can teach content that is said to be revealed. If it is *assumed,* however, that reflection is the only way by which anyone knows anything, then such approaches as revelation, reason, and intuition, although treated by the culture as approaches to truth, cannot be accepted as methods by which to attain knowledge. This interpretation would be consistent with Griffin's view that a technique such as discussion is no more effective than the amount and quality of the reflection it induces.

A reflective theory of method is never put to test by experiments that compare lecture, let us say, with discussion, unless the experiment takes under control the extent to which one of the techniques used is more reflective than the other. Since this control of reflection as a variable has almost never been present in experiments with technique, the conflicting results obtained through use of any technique, whether it be discussion or some other, are easily explained. Adams (1954) concluded from his survey that it is impossible to state which technique is most effective. A similar conclusion was reached by Jacob (1957, pp. 88–99) in his study of techniques of college teaching. This conclusion should be expected, according to Griffin's theory of method. A class taught by lectures that induce and improve reflection should produce better results than one taught by unreflective discussion. Similarly, reflective discussion should be more effective than conventional lectures. Reflection, its amount and quality, is the one variable that has seldom been controlled, because few investigators have recognized reflection as a significant variable. Even if they did so recognize it, investigators might not know how to control it. Hence, conflicting conclusions are bound to appear. Teachers, whether they know it or not, vary in their understanding and valuing of reflection. Teachers with the best understanding of reflection do not necessarily prefer discussion to any other technique of teaching.

Because research on the outcomes of any given technique has yielded conflicting results, many educators consider the teacher and his personality to be more important than his technique. It is assumed that different teachers using the same technique get different results because some personalities are more compatible with the given technique. The position that a teacher should use a technique that fits his personality is fairly popular even though research on the interactions between personality and teaching techniques is fairly rare.

A related assertion is the notion that teachers should use a variety of techniques. McLendon expresses the common view that "in general, research confirms the judgment of most authorities that no single method is best for all teachers, classes, and subject matter. Each classroom teacher needs to utilize a variety of techniques in order to develop the varying abilities, interests, and backgrounds of his students" (McLendon, 1960, p. 16). He does not cite his "authorities" or their research, and he neglects to develop in even a summary fashion a theory of teaching method within which variety of technique would be an essential ingredient. Although Griffin argued that students might easily tire of the same technique, if used day after day, and that therefore some variety is tactically appropriate, the larger strategical question is whether the techniques used contribute to students' conceptual learning by promoting some phase of the reflective process.

Statements that assign more importance to teacher personality and variety of technique than to any other factors will probably be made until research on technique brings under control variables as basic as the amount and quality of reflection taking place in classrooms. A resort to teacher personality as an explanation of learning is a tempting conclusion when not much is known about the relationship between how a teacher teaches and the learning that results.

The Bayles Studies

Bayles (1950) has indicated in his theoretical writings a grasp of reflective method. He reported (1956) on six studies (Avery, 1941; Droll, 1940; Johnston, 1941; Reader, 1953; Sailer, 1942; Trefz, 1941) completed during the period 1940–1953 which were intended to test the effects of reflection. Of these six studies, all master's theses written under his direction, three dealt with American history, one with American government, one with fifth grade, and one with sixth grade. Bayles has never claimed that the teachers in these studies were fully reflective in their approach. In fact, all but two of the studies were made by teachers who were trying out this method for the first time. According to Bayles (1956, p. 1), Trefz (1941) and Reader (1953), two teachers who were not entirely unfamiliar with reflective method by the time their studies were completed, both felt that "a teacher can gain competence in such teaching as she or he gains experience in it" and that "the change-over is gradual rather than abrupt."

In the six studies, both formal and informal data were collected. The formal data resulted from use of standardized achievement tests. The informal data were supplied by teachers who offered testimony on their own teaching. Since the teachers were recent converts to reflective method, one should read their testimony with considerable reservation. Writers of master's theses of this kind may sometimes want an experiment "to come out right" and this frequently means that a hypothesis is rationalized rather than tested.

The experimental groups were compared

with much larger groups used in building norms for the standardized tests. In commenting upon the absence of control groups, Bayles said:

It may be well at this point to anticipate a criticism which is likely to be raised with reference to this and the following studies. It may be objected that no control groups were used which would furnish a basis for comparison and thereby for judging experimental results. It is our considered opinion that such a criticism is ill-founded and will not stand careful scrutiny . . . .

The major control in each of these investigations was the group which furnished the standardizing base for each of the tests used. If the standardizing base was reported as representative of the nation as a whole, it was assumed that normal expectation for a normal class conventionally taught would be the standard norm for the test; sometimes the median, and sometimes the percentile ranks. Class median scores on intelligence examinations were compared with national medians for the grade levels in question, such as eleventh or twelfth, in order to reach a conclusion as to whether a given class was approximately above, equal to, or below the standard group. Thus, a group with IQ's approximately equal to those of the standardizing group would normally be expected to make scores approximately equal to standard on the achievement tests, and variations above or below would be interpreted accordingly (Bayles, 1956, pp. 6-7).

Bayles defended this design as against one in which the same teacher would teach both control and experimental groups. He felt that any teacher is likely to prefer one method to another, and that this preference could influence results in favor of the preferred method. He also opposed the use of a control group taught by a teacher other than the one who taught the experimental group on the ground that differences in teachers' capacities could contaminate results. He preferred to compare his experimental teachers with a larger group of teachers that, he was willing to assume, used conventional teaching methods.

The teachers who made these studies did not use the more advanced statistical procedures and concepts which we would now expect of such research. According to Bayles, these advanced techniques were not available at the time that all but one of the investigations were made. Bayles did not regard this deficiency as a serious criticism of the experimental design because the obtained differences were so large as to make refined measures unnecessary, or as he put it: "A butcher does not need an extremely accurate chemical balance to weigh out a pound of beef steak" (p. 7). In all the studies reported by Bayles, the students in experimentally taught classes scored higher on achievement tests than the students around the nation who were presumably taught less reflectively. Most of the items of the tests required mere recall of facts and therefore did not test the adequacy of a reflective approach for teaching concepts. Some of the tests, however, required more conceptual responses than did others, and Bayles considered it significant that the reflectively taught classes always scored higher on the average than the students in the "normal" group.

Two additional conclusions were drawn by Bayles. Superior achievement was found in conventional curriculums and courses, demonstrating to his satisfaction that a reflective approach is adaptable to standard curriculums. Second, it was concluded that teachers grew considerably in their mastery of a reflective approach over a period of years. As teachers acquired this method, it apparently produced increasingly strong effects on learning.

Such a "multiplier effect" was exemplified most dramatically in the Trefz study (1941), in which the teacher, described by Bayles as mature and experienced, found that her students' scores on a standardized achievement test improved steadily over a six-year period. That is, although the master's thesis covered only a seven-month period, Bayles continued to receive follow-up reports, covering a six-year period, on group intelligence and achievement test scores collected by this teacher.

One interesting aspect of the study is that Trefz conducted her seven-month experiment with a group whom she had taught in a conventionally factual manner during its enrollment in the fifth grade. When this class completed the fifth grade, it was somewhat below the achievement norm for beginning sixth grade. During the summer Trefz studied Bode, Dewey, Wheeler, and Kilpatrick, and then decided to make her first effort at reflective teaching. The gains in achievement by her pupils exceeded normal expectations.

During her second year of experience with reflective teaching, Trefz had a group of 30 pupils with a median IQ of 105 and a range from 63 to 127. In October, median achievement was exactly at grade level, namely 6.1. In April, seven months later, median achievement was 12 months higher, i.e., five months above the then expected grade level. The largest gain for any pupil was 15 months.

Trefz continued to take measurements of achievement and intelligence in her classes for the next four years. Each year she used one form of a test battery in the fall, and another form in the spring, six or seven calendar months later. Sometimes she used the Stanford Achievement Test, and sometimes the Metropolitan Achievement Test. Each year she sent reports to Bayles. In her third year, 1941–1942, the tests were given six months apart. The median grade placement in October was 5.8, three months below the grade standard, 6.1. In March the median achievement was 7.8, or 11 months above the standard grade placement, 6.7. Bayles's comment on this third year was:

Thus we note that, in her third year of reflective teaching, this teacher—a mature and experienced teacher at the outset—made a large gain over her second year, an average gain of three times normal expectation or eighteen months' improvement in six (Bayles, 1956, p. 22).

For the fourth and fifth years, Trefz continued to report results far beyond normal expectations. In the sixth year, she made her final report to Bayles. Tests were again administered six months apart. The reported average gains were as follows: Although the class began the school year two months below standard grade placement, at the end of six months the median grade placement was 11 months above standard.

Because these test results were obtained from standardized tests which measured recall rather than reflective understanding, there is some doubt that the study put Griffin's theory to a sufficiently relevant test. Trefz was aware of this problem, for she commented:

Because of the nature of the tests, being of the multiple choice type of objective tests, they required mostly recognition-level thinking (understanding) and not reflection-level thinking. As a result, we believe that the outcomes of some of our best work are not reflected in our test results at all (Trefz, 1941, pp. 61–63).

Bayles evidently encouraged Trefz and the others who made studies of reflective teaching to use standardized achievement tests in order to prove that students were not "hurt" by reflection. To show that students were helped, Bayles relied heavily upon the testimony of the six teachers who made studies. They reported that the students were more interested, made greater voluntary use of library facilities, showed a greater interest in current national affairs, and a greater tendency to question statements made by fellow students and teachers. Judgments of this kind have subjective aspects, but Bayles has expressed some confidence in the teachers' objectivity. His confidence would be more convincing to a neutral observer if these judgments had not been made by teachers who were recent converts to a new method of teaching. Bayles himself admitted that the teachers did not fully understand reflective teaching. This lack of understanding often meant that teachers were naïve or given to irrelevant observation, such as "Pupils and teachers found it very interesting," or "We found changed attitudes," or "Radio news of the day was sometimes discarded as propaganda," or "The children enjoyed the privilege of discussion." These reported consequences cannot be taken as evidence of the success of reflective teaching because it is quite possible that children in unreflective groups would make similar impressions on their teachers.

Before we dismiss entirely the strength of the test results in the Trefz and other studies, it should be freely granted that a response that is unreflective for one person may be quite reflective for another. It is conceivable that the students in Trefz's classes responded more reflectively than students in the norm-setting groups even though they made many of the same responses. This is consistent with Griffin's distinction between *learning to say that* and *learning that*. A response that is merely mechanical for those students who have been placed in a conventional learning environment may reflect profound insight when made by students in a more critical environment.

About all that can be concluded from the test scores is that reflective teaching enhanced conventional learning; that is, pupils learned to say what the teacher wanted them to say and they learned to say it in greater amounts. To establish that pupil responses are conceptual in quality, we need evidence more conclusive than teacher testimony. Since the Bayles studies, advances have been made in the study of conceptual teaching. Bruner and his co-workers (1956) studied the process of concept attainment in a person trying to locate the defining attributes of nonverbal concepts. Their work may yield methods of securing evidence on whether a student is attaining verbal concepts, although the application of Bruner's clinical findings to classroom experiences with verbal concepts will not be easy. Studies by Smith (1960) indicated that tape recordings of classroom teaching can provide evidence not only on teaching procedures but also on the conceptual processes of students. Bruner's model for concept attainment could conceivably be used as one basis for interpreting transcriptions

of classroom discussions. Bayles and his teachers cannot be criticized for failing to use resources not available in the 1940's, but it would be appropriate now to investigate reflective teaching in the light of recent advances in research method.

The Reflective Model in Teaching History

It is clear that Bayles and Griffin worked from much the same model. The following excerpts, one from Bayles, and the other from Griffin, indicate how similar is their approach to teaching history. Bayles described a cut-and-dried recitation in which the class moves along in a conventional fashion. The teacher pursues a line of questioning intended to create in students enough doubt to provoke investigation of what meaning can be given to the typical social studies response, "Columbus discovered America in 1492":

When was America discovered and by whom? The answer which is practically sure to come is that America was discovered by Columbus in 1492. The teacher rather thoughtfully gives assent and, without changing expression, responds, "Ye-e-e-es. And what did he find when he got here?" Numerous things will perhaps be enumerated, such as a sandy beach and trees. And then people will be mentioned. The teacher inquires about the people, asking what kind they were. The name Indians will probably come into the discussion and the teacher may ask at once how Columbus knew that they were Indians. However, that question can well come a little later. The immediate next question can then be, "Now, if Columbus found Indians here, why do you say that Columbus discovered America? Why not give the Indians credit for discovering America? If we should give the Indians credit for discovering America, when was America discovered anyway?" In this way information will be gathered regarding the prehistoric human migration probably from northeastern Asia, across the shallow water and mostly land connections to Alaska, thence downward across the Americas. This would put the discovery of America at perhaps 25,000 B.C.

It might then be asked how Columbus knew they were Indians, and the circumstances causing Columbus to give them that name would be forthcoming. This, of course, would bring out salient features of Columbus' efforts to get his expedition going. But it finally has to be concluded that we do not give the Indians credit for discovering America because they were not Europeans and therefore did not count.

This conclusion, however, causes the teacher with feigned innocence to ask why, if we are going to give credit to Europeans, we leave out Leif Ericson. Then comes the story of the Vikings and their actual settlement within what is now continental United States about 1000 A.D. Why not count Leif Ericson? Apparently because he was not a southern European. He was a *Nordic*. Since our ancestors came from further south, we have not seen fit to give credit to the Nordics. Obviously, at this point the present-day attitude regarding Nordic supremacy—not confined to Hitler alone—may come in for a bit of discussion.

After a time, however, the teacher says, "All right. We give Columbus credit because he was from southern Europe. But what did Columbus discover? Where did he land?" Here is where the facts of Columbus' actual discoveries can enter, why he called the islands the West Indies, etc. Columbus' whole story may well be introduced here, rather than earlier. And the point might be made that, although occasionally we refer to our land as Columbia, we do not normally use that name.

The teacher then asks, therefore, if Columbus did not discover America, who did? Now comes the intriguing story of Americus Vespucius and how, although he was merely a passenger on the ship, he has become immortalized in the name America; how it became known as Americ's Land, perhaps because his letter home was the first to announce the discovery of a great continent. Again, however, the teacher asks what continent Americus saw. It comes out that it was South rather than North America and that the time was 1498 rather than 1492.

In this way, the class is essentially forced to the interesting conclusion that the original and almost universally accepted answer to the question is correct except that it was Vespucius rather than Columbus, that it was South America rather than North, and it was 1498 rather than 1492.

The study can then take various turns. The one suggested by Roberts is why the discovery that actually took hold of the attention of Europe came in 1492 rather than 1000 A.D., 1200, 1300, or later than 1492. Thus, the conditions in Europe at those various periods come in for study, out of which arises an understanding of how the period of American discovery and colonization was brought about by European developments during the fifteenth century. History, business, and politics thereby become integrated in the minds of students (Bayles, 1950, pp. 223–225).

We can quarrel, as we should, with some of the historical interpretations in the above passage, but the tone is essentially reflective, and also it compares with Griffin's treatment of the election of 1800 in the following passage:

Let us suppose that a class is reading what the text-book has to say about the election of 1800. There will surely be something on the bitterness of the campaign, and on the horrible consequences predicted for the country if Jefferson, "a radical and an atheist," were elected.

A teacher may cut in here, in discussion, to raise the question, "Do you suppose these people—Dwight, for example—believed what they said? Or did they just make those things up for the election?" Groups will divide sharply on this question, some insisting that the sheer extravagance of the Federalist charges (the teacher may have to augment these, since texts often go easy at this point) reveals them as propaganda, while others insist that men like Adams and Hamilton would not deliberately be false to what they thought.

Now suppose that the teacher injects a new question: "If men really believe that this election of a given candidate will ruin the country, how far are they justified in going, out of sheer patriotism, to prevent his election?"

Some ideas will emerge here toward which the example of Hamilton's famous letter to Jay may be addressed. "Suppose, for the sake of argument, that Hamilton was perfectly sincere in believing that Jefferson's election would be disastrous. Now consider this: among the papers of John Jay (time out for 'Who remembers Jay? What did he do?' etc.) was a letter from Hamilton, written just before this election of 1800. It asks Jay, as Governor of

New York, to juggle the election laws (time out for, 'Have you ever heard of that before? Tell about it. What's a gerrymander? What happened recently to Congressman Eliot of Massachusetts?' etc.) in such a way as to insure a Federalist victory no matter what the people wanted (time out for 'How could he do that?' discussion of electoral college, etc.). Now, then, what do you think of Hamilton's proposal? If he was trying to save his country from a horrible fate, wasn't he justified (time out for fairly heated forensics, largely ungrounded)?"

After a while, the teacher interjects, "Jay left a note on the envelope of that letter. It said, 'A proposal for party purposes which it would ill become me to consider.' How do you react to that?"

The point must be made clear that Jay agreed with Hamilton as to the character and extent of the disaster Jefferson's election would cause. It should also be made clear that the Federalists, being in power rather generally, could have followed Hamilton's suggestion with some success, and driven Jefferson's followers to submission or revolution as their only alternatives. Secondary school students probably cannot formulate the difference between Jay's outlook and Hamilton's, but they sense it readily and show some insight into its quality. They rarely condemn Hamilton out of hand, though; they seem to understand how loyalty to a set of fixed standards may compel that kind of behavior.

Other aspects of the same situation may be used in the same direction. Dwight was trying to save the country from the horrors of an atheist president. Has an atheist a right to run for president? Does the freedom of religion we are fighting for include the freedom to have no religion? Did Americans of the eighteenth century feel more friendly toward atheism than people do today? Why wouldn't Philadelphia permit a statue to Tom Paine? What kind of president did Jefferson turn out to be? What were the religious views of Benjamin Franklin? Of George Washington? (This last is perhaps *too* risky—if the youngsters find out, they'll probably bubble over in the wrong places. However, only the very diligent are likely to find out anything on this point until many years later).

Some reference in this connection to the practice in many states of barring certain political parties from the ballot may also be related to the Hamilton-Jay business. The economic make-up of the Federalist party also has utility here, and a quick look back over Adams' administration, emphasizing the alien and sedition laws and Adams' immigration policy, will yield quantities of evidential material.

One may treat the election of 1800 in scholarly and thorough fashion without upsetting anyone and without doing more than skirt the edges of controversy. One may even promote a fair amount of thinking that way. But the intent to develop, through thinking, a frame of reference that *relies on* thinking, will make certain ideas and events seem almost to pop out of the pages of the text or out of our own remembered reading (Griffin, 1942, pp. 194–198).

The quotation from Bayles, which he took from Roberts (1941), indicates the extent to which the latter teacher started from the same verbal model as Griffin. It is apparent that not all the teachers who experimented under Bayles were as close to Griffin in their models, but probably they were more so than the run-of-the-mine teacher. In the absence of transcribed classroom discussion, nothing more can be said at this point in our consideration of these matters about the probability that these experimental teachers could translate their newly acquired theory into classroom teaching acts.

Attitude Education

It is not easy in the area of attitudes to provoke conceptual responses in pupils. We note that Griffin, in his discussion of attitudes and their relationship to beliefs, raised points which suggest how difficult, if not impossible, it would be to test his theory with conventional measuring devices. His theory classifies attitudes into three kinds—those held below the level of consciousness, those held consciously but involving only the emotions, and those consciously held attitudes that possess both cognitive and emotional content. The first two kinds are closed, autonomous systems with which publicly accessible evidence cannot interact. The third kind consists not only of emotional postures but of the beliefs or propositions used in their rationalization. This kind of attitude *may or may not* shift as related beliefs undergo a reflective test. Griffin put it as follows:

If we assume that the propositional statement represents a genuine belief to which the student is fully committed and about which he *cares* deeply, it is safe to say that, as a result of its reconstruction, further significant change in the individual is likely to go forward. If, on the other hand, the statement of belief is given offhand and is regarded as trivial by the student who offers it, the outcome may well be of no consequence. A lot of superficial sparring, in which nobody cares much about any of the points allegedly at "issue," goes on in the name of promoting reflective thinking (Griffin, 1942, p. 153).

In other words, a group of students who discuss any issue may offer reasons for taking a certain position, some of which are genuine, but many of which are spurious. In a discussion of whether it is democratic to segregate Negroes, one can expect any group of students to be split in its position. Those who favor segregation can be expected to make certain statements about the attributes and potentialities of Negroes. Those who oppose segregation will offer different beliefs about Negroes as reasons for their position. The fact that group members will differ in their stereotyped opinions of Negroes is enough to provoke some doubt in reasonable youngsters, but the teacher in the kind of situation we have described could produce a greater basis for doubt by placing each youngster in disagreement with himself as well as in conflict with other youngsters. The use of what Hunt and Metcalf (1955, p. 116) have called the subject-matter switch is a promising technique for getting a maximum number of students to feel puzzled over what to believe.

Griffin maintained that if the expressed beliefs about Negroes are seriously held by students who offer them, then any change in

those beliefs might be accompanied by change in related attitudes. A belief structure constructed and offered as a rationalization for a purely emotional preference does not *remove* the irrational basis for the attitude, and therefore feelings are not automatically abolished by breaking down the beliefs used in their sanction. For this reason, it is not possible to predict or guarantee specific changes in attitude as a consequence of cognitive learning.

Although specific change cannot be expected, it is probable that generalized change in attitudes will take place as a consequence of reflective testing of the consciously held beliefs that function as the rational basis for certain attitudes. The character of this change cannot be measured by typical attitude scales. In fact, the kind of change to be expected is not easy to evaluate by any means. The magnitude and complexity of this problem was suggested by Griffin:

Reflection will not guarantee that one acquires "desirable" attitudes if we mean by desirable a set of values at which we want youngsters to arrive, or . . . a set of attitudes toward specific matters which we want them to adopt. Once thinking starts, nobody knows what will happen to values and to attitudes. . . . [But attitudes will be better in the sense that the individual will be] more conscious of the values he holds and of their relationships to one another in a widening range of experiences (Griffin, 1942, pp. 156–157).

He held a similar view respecting the very beliefs which function as rationalization for an attitude. He indicates this view when he distinguishes between authoritarianism and democracy in the manner indicated above on page 934.

Griffin would accept a belief as "right" or "correct" only if it represented knowledge. If data conflict with it, or if it is expressed in nonpropositional form, thus rendering it immune to evidential test, or if it amounted to an expression of emotional preference—all these he would not take as "correct" no matter how fundamental or central their status might be within the cultural traditions of a group. A shift in responses on an attitude scale, for example, from "conservative" to "liberal," would not be evidence with which to test the adequacy of his teaching theory. A growing consistency in attitudes is an expected consequence of reflective teaching. Since such consistency can also be achieved through brainwashing or indoctrination, however, it cannot be concluded from growth in consistency that reflection has taken place and that the consistency expressed is conceptual in quality.

The Stanford Social Education Study

Another empirical investigation of a reflective method of teaching social studies was the Stanford Social Education Study (Quillen & Hanna, 1948). Three approaches to teaching American history were compared, the chronological, topical, and problem-solving. The chronological approach, so common in the schools, is clear to everyone. The difference between problems and topics, however, is not so easy to discern.

Their list of *topics* (Quillen & Hanna, 1948, p. 120) includes the following:

1. What has been the influence of revolutions on social changes?

2. How did medieval man deal with social problems similar to those today?

3. What has determined the rise of nationalism?

They then list the following as *problems* (pp. 135–136):

1. What should be the role of the United States in international affairs?

2. How can we safeguard our civil liberties during war?

3. How can we prevent war in the future and establish a peace that will be just for all nations?

4. How can we more intelligently use our school environment?

The two lists do not make explicit the criteria by which to decide whether a question deals with a topic or a problem. In their discussion of criteria, Quillen and Hanna said:

Characteristics of the problems approach.— There are two essential characteristics of a problem: (1) it is an area of concern producing tensions which can be resolved only by solution of the problem, and (2) it involves the choice of a course of action from among two or more possible solutions. "What role should the United States play in international affairs?" becomes a real problem according to these criteria. This problem has not been solved; adolescents as well as adults are vitally concerned in seeing that the United States follows the right course of action, and they feel confused or blocked in not knowing which course is best (Quillen & Hanna, 1948, p. 124).

It is not clear whether Quillen and Hanna meant that a student can have a problem only if he has a question no one can answer. Their statement that a real problem "has not been solved" could be interpreted to mean that the teacher is as ignorant as the student, but one cannot be sure that this is the meaning they intended. Their meaning for the term *concern* is also unclear. When they say that both adolescents and adults are concerned whether the United States is following the right course of action, it is not clear whether "concerned" means "interested in" or "affected by."

But enough is clear in their discussion to make it certain that Griffin would define a problem differently than they would. Griffin would hold that many of the topics listed by Quillen and Hanna could become problems without any change in the wording of the questions. If a student is puzzled and concerned over the meaning and truth of a proposition, then, according to Griffin, he has a problem. The psychological elements of doubt and concern rather than the content of a question determine whether the question is viewed or felt as a problem. Quillen and Hanna, the chief architects of the Stanford Social Education Study, may have investigated a reflective theory of conceptual teaching, but it was not the theory developed by Griffin.

Griffin's difference from Quillen and Hanna is seen in a passage from Griffin's dissertation which indicates a reflective approach to content that Quillen and Hanna would insist, by their criteria, was topical:

By way of illustration, let us suppose a world history classroom in which students have encountered, during the reading of an assignment, the statement used in Chapter V to illustrate the extreme of apparently useless information: "Alexander crossed the Hellespont with 35,000 men and began the series of conquests that quickly made him master of Darius' empire."

In the actual course of events, this statement would be "believed" in the limited sense of "not doubted," but nobody would be likely to care much one way or the other about it, except on the off chance that an examination question might call for its regurgitation. Nevertheless, for what it is worth, the students have seen the words and are able after a fashion to visualize some sort of event not inconsistent with them, which is about all the "knowledge of events" anyone ever does get out of a high school text-book.

Suppose, however, that the teacher raises the question, "Could that sentence be a misprint? Surely it doesn't sound reasonable that 35,000 troops could conquer a land containing many millions of people."

That much is enough to get the flow of student hypotheses started. "Maybe there weren't so many people in those days." Investigation will bear this out, but not in sufficient degree to explain Alexander's conquests. "Maybe his army increased as he went along." Investigation supports this also—at least, a student can readily find out that Alexander trained some 30,000 of his conquered subjects in Macedonian military techniques,— but again the explanation is quantitatively inadequate. "Maybe the people had no weapons." But Macedonian weapons were not particularly complicated, as the student can easily discover. Vast numbers of people armed with only equipment for hunting, farm implements, clubs, and stones could make a fair showing against a small army. However, a new question could be introduced by the teacher, namely, "Why didn't Darius see to it that every household contained the simple weapons of his day?" . . . .

Sooner or later, someone will discover that the ordinary inhabitant of an Asiatic empire never took part in wars at all—that he apparently cared not at all who ruled over him. By the time a student has found out why, and has come to compare the passive hopelessness of the natives of Persia with the vigorous self-defense against Persia carried on by the Greek cities a century and a half earlier, and perhaps even to wonder what had enabled Alexander to conquer those same Greek cities, the comparison with the present scene will have become painfully obvious. The state of affairs in India, in Burma, in Egypt, in Malaya, will have become relevant to the idea under discussion, which is no longer Alexander but rather the proposition, "People who believe that they have no stake in their government will not fight to maintain it. . . ." (Griffin, 1942, pp. 179–181).

We have in this passage an example of how a class may reflect upon a past event in an attempt to explain its occurrence. The problem of how Alexander was able to conquer a vast territory with an army much smaller than its population, and to do this with very simple and primitive weapons, is a problem already solved by a good many people. Certainly, many research historians possess an answer, and no doubt the teacher in the example also had an answer. The fact that the problem had been solved somewhere by someone does not make it impossible for students to have the problem and to seek and find an answer reflectively.

That Quillen and Hanna did not hold this conception is indicated by the following comment:

It is obvious that problems which have already been solved or which have ceased to be troublesome do not produce a tension, and therefore are no longer problems. Thus, problems which are selected for class consideration should be contemporary, because a present-day problem usually presents a genuine issue in which adolescents have a real interest and vital concern (Quillen & Hanna, 1948, p. 125).

Quillen and Hanna seem to adhere to what has been disparaged as "contemporaneity."

This concern makes it doubtful that problem-solving as they conceive it could ever be applied to the teaching of history. In fact, it is doubtful that "contemporaneity" could be applied to the teaching of any school subject. Certainly, their point of view clashes with the theory of teaching which Bruner has attributed to the new teaching of physics, chemistry, biology, and mathematics in the various experimental curriculums he has described (1960). Bruner commented as follows on these programs and the teaching that characterizes them:

. . . intellectual activity anywhere is the same, whether at the frontier of knowledge or in a third-grade classroom. What a scientist does at his desk or in his laboratory, what a literary critic does in reading a poem, are of the same order as what anybody else does when he is engaged in like activities—if he is to achieve understanding. The difference is in degree, not in kind. The schoolboy learning physics *is* a physicist, and it is easier for him to learn physics behaving like a physicist than doing something else. The "something else" usually involves the task of mastering what came to be called at Woods Hole a "middle language" —classroom discussions and textbooks that talk about the conclusions in a field of intellectual inquiry rather than centering upon the inquiry itself. Approached in that way, high school physics often looks very little like physics, social studies are removed from the issues of life and society as usually discussed, and school mathematics too often has lost contact with what is at the heart of the subject, the idea of order (Bruner, 1960, p. 14).

The Quillen-Hanna conception of a problem makes the problems approach difficult to apply to teaching school subjects. Their conception becomes usable only at the frontier where knowledge is actually in doubt for everyone. The fact that each student has his own frontiers, and that these are not always the same as the frontiers of a discipline, is overlooked. Perhaps this is why Quillen and Hanna concluded that "all three approaches to social education...have unique advantages" (p. 139). They agree with the teachers

in the Stanford Study that "no one approach should be used to the exclusion of the other two" (p. 139).

Quillen and Hanna held that whether a teacher should use a problems approach depends somewhat upon his objectives and taste. It follows that a teacher who "likes" the chronological approach will be more effective with it than with any other approach, regardless of his objectives. Yet they felt that certain objectives such as skill in critical thinking, interest in current events, and sensitivity to a wide range of social problems can best be achieved through use of a problems approach. Quillen and Hanna suggested no solution for the teacher who "likes" chronology but "wants" his students to improve in their thinking processes. Whether Griffin's conception of a problem or that of Quillen and Hanna is "correct" is not the point at issue. They are different, and an experiment carried through under the leadership of one is not likely to put the other's theory to a test.

The Stanford Study concluded that the problems approach, although not clearly superior to the chronological approach, was better than the topical approach in fostering such outcomes as critical thinking, good study habits, work skills, knowledge and understanding of the subject, knowledge of contemporary affairs, and consistency of attitudes. The significance of this difference is not clear since the difference between a topic and problem was never adequately developed.

In a list of some 45 problems presented by Quillen and Hanna, all but one are like the following: What should the United States do about the international situation? How can we best secure our democracy within our country? How can we provide adequate leisure and recreation for all? All of these deal with policy questions, or put another way, all ask the question, What policy is desirable to attain a certain end? The single exception in the total list of 45 is the one that reads: "How, in earlier times, has our nation provided for defense against foreign enemies and how can we now provide for national defense?" (Quillen & Hanna, 1948, p. 135).

It should be noted that this last question consists of two parts, and that one of these parts is like the other 44 questions. Therefore, all but one of the listed problems have in common an orientation to the future and deal with policies to be chosen to bring about a desirable state of affairs. Presumably, each would require normative analysis should there be any question over the desirability of the intended consequences of a policy. None of the problems on the Quillen-Hanna list deals directly with problems of definition or explanation. None is directly concerned with understanding past events. Presumably, the policy questions stated in their list could not be answered without recourse to definition of terms, verification of beliefs, clarification of values, and study of history; yet, all such exercises in logic are mentioned only by implication. The Quillen-Hanna conception of a problem is limited to a present-day uncertainty in choosing policy; moreover, their problem must be a policy question that is puzzling to everyone. Conceivably, a knowledgeable teacher, who knew or thought he knew the answer to many policy questions, would be handicapped in his use of a problems approach.

Quillen and Hanna also considered a problem-solving experience to be incomplete if it is not followed by some action, a view that Griffin did not share. They granted, as did Griffin, that an action need not be overt and direct, but their distinction between overt and other kinds of action is not always clear:

There are many complex problems of national and international scope about which older adolescents are deeply concerned but about which they can do little in the way of direct action. Such problems should not be eliminated for this reason. Action in these cases can take the form of utilizing opportunities to exert some influence with reference to the solution. It means that every student in a given group should be increasingly sensitive to the problem. He can discuss it with his agemates and adult friends; he can help clarify

the thinking of people who have not studied it. The group can submit recommendations and memorandums to senators and representatives in Washington. There are thus many ways by which students can apply the conclusions which they have drawn, by which they "can do something about it" even when the problems they have been considering are national and international in scope (Quillen & Hanna, 1948, pp. 125–126).

They then summed up their position by saying:

Thus, all problems selected for study should lead to some form of action. When school and community problems are studied, the action may be overt and direct; but when the problem is a complex one of national or international scope, the action may take some other form. The drawing of a conclusion from a number of possible solutions plus the "doing something about it" after the solution is reached are features of the problems approach which distinguish it from both the topical and chronological approaches (Quillen & Hanna, 1948, p. 126).

One point that is clear in all the above is that "drawing a conclusion" is not enough for a problem-solving experience to be complete.

Griffin conceived action in much broader terms. " 'Action' as here used need not refer to any large or complex task in process; it may refer to as simple a matter as attempting to express oneself clearly in an informal conversation" (Griffin, 1942, pp. 171–172). He included reading and listening as forms of action. It is apparent that he would regard achievement of a sounder basis for a particular belief as sufficient purpose for problem-solving. Whatever action took place, whether it was listening, reading, speaking, writing, or lobbying, would be important only in further testing a belief. If action of any kind were followed by other than expected consequences, doubt would again be raised as to the meaning or truth of the beliefs upon which action had been based. Griffin's objective is better grounded belief, not with action of some kind, no matter how broadly conceived. The intent of reflection, as he saw it, was revealed in his statement, "Anything that renders belief at all uncertain is a sufficient occasion for reflection" (Griffin, 1942, p. 172).

Gross, a leading interpreter of problem-solving and the Stanford Study, has not commented directly on the question of action, but in his discussion of levels of problem-solving (Gross, Zeleny, et al., 1958), he expressed a preference for the kind of problem which Quillen and Hanna believed can most easily result in solutions that include action of a direct or overt kind. In speaking of problems that are "personal, school, and community problems," Gross observed that

Motivation is much more easily attained where the students are so directly involved. "What are my potentialities for my chosen vocation?" "In what ways can we improve human relations in our school?" or "How can our school contribute more effectively to neighborhood well-being?"—these are examples of problems which are favorites with pupils in civics and problems classes. Some leaders in the problem-solving movement have claimed that this is the only kind of problem-solving that is really effective and deserving of the title (Gross, Zeleny, et al., 1958, pp. 362–363).

The underlying causes of the American Revolution, or the effect of materialism upon moral standards, were labeled by Gross as adult problems, or unsolvable issues. These problems are so intellectual that students may not feel deeply involved in them. They *can* have a real sense of involvement in such problems, but the teacher must strive mightily to see to it that students feel concerned about these "adult problems." If a teacher fails to do this, the students' problem-solving "can become merely another stereotyped series of lessons to 'get through'" (p. 362). But personal problems, the kind that can be followed by direct action, are intrinsically such that no serious problem in motivating pupils confronts the teacher.

This view of student interest clashes with the view held by subject-matter specialists who are leading current reforms in the curriculums of science and mathematics. According to Bruner (1960), students are more interested in ideas of the most theoretical kind than many educators have assumed. The new curriculums in science and mathematics are based on the proposition that a study of ideas increases students' interest in school and results in greater retention and transfer of what is taught than is the case when science students work diligently on such practical problems as making soap or toothpaste.

It follows, from Bruner's view, that students who are bored with a study of school discipline, eating habits in the cafeteria, or how to get a job as an airline stewardess, will come to life quickly when social studies classes deal with ideas that are controversial in their community or are fundamental to an understanding of a social theory.

There is a sharp conflict, not often explicitly stated, between subject-matter specialists and certain interpreters of problem-solving. Gross and Quillen and Hanna glossed over the conflict in holding that problem-solving should be used as a method of teaching more commonly than it is, but not to the exclusion of other approaches. Gross, for example, after his discussion of three levels of problem-solving, attributed to Harold Rugg a conception of problem-solving which combines all three levels into a fourth level that incorporates the best features of the other three. Yet, Gross held, even this eclectic conception should not become the only, or even dominant, method of instruction in the schools, for many important objectives can best be achieved by other means. The conflict is one between the value placed on knowledge by the subject-matter specialist, including knowledge of the process of intellectual inquiry, and the unsound psychology practiced by certain advocates of problem-solving, including the assumption that pupils lack genuinely intellectual interests.

The Kight-Mickelson Study

The concern of some educators with personal problems and direct action may be considered to reflect this anti-intellectualism. Kight and Mickelson (1949), in a study of problem-solving significantly entitled "Problem vs. Subject," gave evidence that preference for action over knowledge does occur in the problem-solving movement. They investigated the differing effects of problem-solving and subject-centered instruction upon the learning of factual information, the learning of rules of action, the ratio of rules of action learned to factual information, and the connecting of specific facts with their corresponding rules of action (Kight & Mickelson, 1949, p. 4). In a most revealing comment upon their findings, they recommended that classroom presentation should make "doing rather than knowing primary in the presentation" (p. 7).

The fact that this comment is restricted to methods of teaching does not lessen its import for those who believe that methods of thinking constitute an important part of all content. The notion that doing is more important than knowing, like the belief that basic ideas are "caught rather than taught," may be traced to a certain misinterpretation of John Dewey, who is usually regarded by all advocates of the problem-solving method, regardless of their internal differences, as their leader. Yet, in a discussion of learning as insight, Bayles commented: "The statement, 'We learn to do by doing,' is usually credited to John Dewey, though doubtless erroneously. The writer has followed Dewey's writings rather carefully and has never yet discovered such a statement made by him" (Bayles, 1950, p. 81).

According to Bayles, this cliché about a relationship between learning and doing is a shorthand expression of Dewey's definition of experience in his *Democracy and Education,* and the shorthand has been taken literally by people who perhaps have not read the original statement. Dewey spoke of experience as having both an active and passive side. The individual does something (active) and then undergoes consequences (passive). If he sees a connection between what he did, and what he underwent—if, in short, he sees

consequences as consequences—he has had an experience. Obviously, the individual is not always aware of the consequences of his acts, and "In the degree to which the outcomes [of an act] are unknown [to him], the doing fails to constitute experience and fails to promote learning" (Bayles, 1950, p. 82). The individual learns by doing something, noting its consequences, and then by modifying his subsequent doing in the light of those consequences. It should be noted also that doing is defined in the broad terms that Griffin brings to his definition of action. Noting relationships between what is done and what flows back as consequence is possible or likely only as one reflects upon what he is doing. A more adequate slogan than "we learn to do by doing" would be that "we learn to do by reflecting upon what we are doing." Certainly, this appears to be Dewey's meaning, and those interpreters of problem-solving who prefer doing to knowing cannot in any accurate sense cite Dewey as their authority.

Kight and Mickelson studied 24 teachers and their 1,415 students in English composition, English literature, science, and social studies classes. These teachers taught, in rotation, problem- and subject-centered units. The design of their study differed radically from that used by Bayles's students in their six studies. Kight and Mickelson wanted to exclude from their results variations due to teacher competence, while Bayles wanted to exclude from his results any differences owing to a teacher's preference for one method over another. Bayles simply assumed that the experimental and nonexperimental teachers were equally favorable to whatever method they used, and equally competent.

Kight and Mickelson concluded that pupils learned more factual information in problem-centered units—a conclusion that Bayles also reached—but that the difference, for a number of the classes, was not great. They also concluded that problem-solving groups were markedly superior in helping students learn rules of action in all four subjects—science, literature, composition, and social studies.

The studies by Bayles, Quillen and Hanna,

and Kight and Mickelson fell short of testing the main propositions in Griffin's theory. Bayles relied too much upon standardized tests, but in doing so he proved that reflective method does not hurt a student's achievement of knowledge of facts. Quillen and Hanna defined a problem differently than did Griffin, to the degree that the latter's theory could not have been applied in their study except by accident. Quillen and Hanna, in their definition of a problem, emphasized that problems should deal with questions that have not yet been solved and should have an orientation to the future and to values; they placed much emphasis upon action rather than grounded belief as an outcome of reflection. Kight and Mickelson are theoretically quite close to Griffin in their conception of what outcomes to expect from reflection— the learning of rules of action together with the data that support these rules. They reveal a theoretical weakness, however, in their view of action as a necessary method by which to acquire knowledge.

We have not learned, then, from these representative empirical studies, very much more than was known at the time that Griffin wrote his dissertation. In the meantime, theoretical developments, not without empirical support, have further refined Griffin's theory and have indicated more precisely what would be involved in rigorous testing of it.

ANALYTIC HISTORY

One refinement in the basic theory of reflection is now being made in the field of history. This development is particularly important to a theory of teaching the social studies because it is history, more than any other school subject, that has dominated the social studies curriculum. The methodology of history is now undergoing something of a revolution, paralleled and supported by developments in philosophy, semantics, and logic.

The work of David Potter perhaps best exemplifies what is happening to the research methods of historians. His study, *People of Plenty* (1954), is significant on two scores—

for its revision of Turner's frontier thesis, and for its borrowing of research methods from the behavioral sciences. He distinguished between description and explanation as research problems in history, and compared historical research with related and more precise studies in sociology and anthropology.

He pointed out that the national character of the American people has been discussed by Henry Steele Commager, Allan Nevins, Arthur M. Schlesinger, Samuel Eliot Morison, James Truslow Adams, Charles and Mary Beard, Vernon Parrington, Ralph H. Gabriel, Merle Curti, Albert Bushnell Hart, and Louis Hacker, to mention only a few. These names constitute a distinguished roster in historical scholarship. All have described and interpreted American national character. One would expect to find the idea of an American national character clarified and refined by their efforts. "Yet the fact is," said Potter, "that historians have done very little either to clarify or to validate this concept which they employ so freely. The looseness with which the term 'national character' is used and the inconsistent meanings which attach to it are striking evidence of the lack of adequate analysis" (p. 8). For most historians, this term, like many others in their stock of intellectual tools, lacks the precision of a scientific concept. Literary expression and common sense rather than genuine concepts of a logical and scientific nature constitute much of the content of history. The difference between Potter and his less scientific colleagues is a manifestation of that more general difference discussed by C. P. Snow (1959) in his study of two cultures.

Potter believes that behavioral scientists such as Margaret Mead, Ruth Benedict, Geoffrey Gorer, Karen Horney, and Abram Kardiner have made significant contributions to a delineation of American national character. In contrast, the research of professional historians appears to be almost totally empty of meaning. Concluding that the methodology of the behavioral sciences would be useful in any study of the past,

Potter applied that methodology, in the second half of his book, to an appraisal and study of Frederick Jackson Turner's frontier thesis. He concluded that economic abundance, rather than a physical frontier, accounts for much of what American national character has become, and this factor of abundance continues to shape the character of the American people to this very day, long after the disappearance from American geography of a physical frontier.

Many historians, and not only those who prefer literature to science, will disagree with Potter's interpretation of Turner. But his suggested reforms in historical method can be appraised without regard to this substantive conclusion. It would appear that Potter's reconstruction of research method is parallel to certain developments in psychology and philosophy. Potter indicated in his study, for example, a preference for the kind of careful analysis of concepts illustrated by Bruner and his co-workers (1956). Potter also distinguished between description and explanation, as did Hempel (1959) and Oppenheim and Hempel (1953).

The Problem of Explanation

Hempel (1959) has argued the strength of one kind of explanation—the model used in the natural sciences. In these sciences an event is explained when it is subsumed under a general law or theory. He discussed and urged the application of this model to historical events. The failures and mistakes of Buckle, Marx, and Toynbee constitute no argument against use of the model. Their failures simply indicate how difficult historical research is. These failures also raise questions about the degree to which historians possess scientific knowledge. Are there precise and meaningful criteria by which to choose between conflicting interpretations or explanations?

The Hempel model for an explanation is triadic and syllogistic. It consists of a general law or hypothesis which functions as a major premise in a syllogism. The minor premise

describes what Hempel calls the boundary or antecedent conditions for the event to be explained, according to the general law stated by the major premise. The minor premise simply states the presence of these boundary conditions within a certain state of affairs existing in space and time. The conclusion of the syllogism, then, is a description of the event to be explained. It is significant to note that Hempel's explanation contains a great deal of what historians would call description, but the description functions within a logic of explanation, and any description that is irrelevant to any part of the syllogism is omitted. This use of description differs from the practice of those historians who define explanation merely as more detailed description.

Many historians will argue against the use of Hempel's model on the ground that there are no discoverable laws in history. Hempel, for example, in an attempt to explain a given revolution, would first try to decide what type of revolution it is. This attempt would take him into what Bruner would call concept analysis. Hempel would then try to find out whether certain social conditions are always antecedent to the occurrence of revolutions of a certain type. If no such relationship has been established by historical research, Hempel would simply conclude that there is no scientific explanation for revolutions of that type. The historians who claim that they have an explanation even though it is not very scientific would simply be opening up the question of whether all knowledge is scientific.

Even though many historians deny that there are laws in history, they do not hesitate to make generalizations, any one of which may be taken by an unreflective student to be a law. The application of Hempel's model to the explanations offered by any historian would help a student to reflect upon the adequacy of those explanations. If any explanation were to imply a law, or something like a law, the use of Hempel's model would make the implication quite explicit. Having the idea in the open, so to speak, would enable a student to determine whether it is testable, what it might mean, and, if testable, rather than merely clever and literary, to inquire whether there were grounds for accepting it. This procedure, highly reflective as it is, could not help but make history clearer, even to the slowest student, and would reveal in a given case precisely whether a historian knew what he was talking about.

Students who take this approach to their reading and study of history will understand it better and become less susceptible to the pitfall of easy familiarity.

History Textbooks and Explanation

The pitfall of easy familiarity originates to a considerable degree in the way textbooks in history are manufactured. The conditions surrounding textbook manufacturing practically guarantee that the textbook content will be conceptually empty at the same time that students, particularly the bright ones, will be led to believe that they are learning great and significant truths.

Over the years a standard content has been established in American and world history. An American history text that fails to mention the Emancipation Proclamation in both index and body runs the risk of losing customers among those who believe the book to be seriously incomplete because of this omission. But a book that is complete must also be up to date. If it fails to mention the more recent events, particularly those that have been admitted to the field of history since competing texts were published, it will lose customers among those who want a "new" or "modern" or "different" book. But a book that is complete and up-to-date must also be portable if it is to be used in schools that make use of a platoon system (in which two groups of pupils, called platoons, alternate in studying the tool subjects and in engaging in activities in special rooms) or homework, both of which require students to carry their books about. The requirement of portability places some general limit upon number of pages and weight.

The general requirement, then, of any textbook writer in the field of high school history is to write about more and more within roughly the same number of pages. Any modern tendency to make a book attractive and "teachable" by including charts, tables, pictures, and end-of-chapter teaching aids cuts into precious space. The only solution is for the writer to express himself in generalities, leaving out all the detail that would give these generalities meaning. He proceeds to violate a "law" laid down by William James who said that no one sees any further into a generalization than his knowledge of detail extends.

What does this practice of confronting students with other people's generalizations mean? How does it make students victims of the pitfall of easy familiarity? First, it must be recognized that a writer turns to generalities because he can use them as a kind of shorthand, a language that helps him to compress a great deal of information into a few words. Second, if he understands his own generalizations, it is because he possesses the information upon which they are based. Third, students won't understand what he is saying unless they also possess his information, and they seldom do. Fourth, they will be most aware of their ignorance only if the generalities are cast in technical language, the most effective of all shorthand. Fifth, history does not possess a technical language, such as is found in sociology or economics, but uses instead the abstractions of popular language. Because history uses a nontechnical language, students may feel that they are learning more than they are. Hence, they become victims of easy familiarity. The student in an economics course who is perplexed by the abstraction *marginal utility* may learn nothing. The student in history who reads the term *Manifest Destiny* may learn nothing but believe that he has learned something. A little analysis, which takes time and information, would help him learn the extent to which historical content is "true" as against the extent to which it is merely clever in its language and phrasing.

A knowledge of the kinds of explanatory sketches presented in textual materials is not available in the studies of bias listed by McPhie (1959), perhaps because the distinction between explanation and description was not a common one at the time most of these studies were made. We do not know at this time the extent to which explanations offered by social studies textbooks are descriptive, pseudo, teleological, or incomplete. Neither have studies been made of the logical or empirical adequacy of the explanations offered by textual materials. As pointed out below, Swift (1958) has suggested certain criteria for the evaluation of any explanation —the presence of lawlike statements, the testability of such statements, their truth, and finally, internal validity, that is, whether the statement describing or naming the event to be explained follows logically from the reasons stated in the major and minor premises.

One doctoral study has examined explanations in high school social studies textual material. Palmer (1960) studied 27 textbooks in world and American history to test the hypothesis that "high school history textbooks, by the explanations of social change they provide, contribute significantly to an understanding of the process of social change" (p. 187). His conception of an explanation was a broad one, not limited to Hempel's model or Swift's criteria. To test his hypothesis, he asked two questions: What is the nature of the explanations of social change which appear in high school history textbooks? and Do these explanations give promise of contributing significantly to the reader's understanding of the processes of social change?

Palmer used a jury to judge the adequacy of the explanations, rather than relying upon his own opinion alone. He found a high correlation between his and the jury's opinion. Only 5 of the 27 books, or 18 per cent, were rated as contributing significantly to the students' understanding of the process of social change. This percentage might well have been lower if Palmer had used the rigorously logical and empirical criteria implicit in Hempel's model. Of the books in his sample, 41 per cent were rated as contributing little or nothing to the readers' understanding of social change; 80 per cent were judged "inadequate" in their treatment of social change.

A study that reveals the theoretical inadequacies of textual material is more useful to teachers whose purpose is conceptual learning than are studies of bias in textbooks. A teacher of conceptual learning will approach biased or unbiased material in the same way; but the teacher who finds that the material lacks conceptual content, and emphasizes instead merely factual offerings, has a problem that may best be solved by not using that material at all except for reference purposes.

The Study and Teaching of Explanation

Swift (1958, 1959, 1961) has examined the teaching of explanation as one aspect of instruction in critical thinking. His research suggests the kinds of classroom procedures in which teachers should be educated if they are to teach students how to make reflective tests of the explanations offered by present-day teaching materials in history. He has suggested that a historical explanation along Hempel's model may be "a deductive argument in which the premises have empirical content" (Swift, 1958, p. 16).

The adequacy of an explanation, according to Hempel's model, would be determined by a reflective test that included analysis of concepts, empirical testing of major and minor premises, and deduction of conclusions from logically related premises. The criteria for an adequate explanation, according to Swift's interpretation of Hempel's model, would be: (1) the presence of a major premise that is lawlike, testable, and true, (2) the inclusion of a minor premise, testable and true, that states the presence of antecedent conditions, and (3) a description of the event to be explained.

It may be recalled that Griffin's study referred to a hypothetical class that sought the reasons why Alexander was able to conquer an immense territory with a small army. This class hypothesized that a people will not fight to maintain a government in which they have no voice. This generalization can be treated as a major premise in a possible explanation. It would run as follows:

Major Premise: If a population of a country has no voice in its government, it will not fight to defend that government or country against foreign attack, and a small army could conquer such a country even though the country's population might be quite large.
Minor Premise: At the time that Alexander invaded Persia with an army of no more than 35,000 troops, the people of Persia had little or no voice in the government headed by Darius.
Conclusion: Alexander conquered Persia with an army much smaller than the total population of that country.

It will be argued that a reflective test of the major premise, if it is to mean anything, would require a student to learn so much more history than he could ever be expected to learn in four years of high school that he would be well advised not to make or test any generalizations at all for fear that he might begin to believe certain ones without sufficient ground for doing so. This is a calculated risk that may be much less dangerous than the risk taken by those teachers who expose students to written history without requiring criticism from the student.

Hempel believes, for example, that many of the explanations in historical writings are pseudo, or incomplete. Unless the student receives help from his teacher in analyzing explanations, he will not be able to judge the adequacy of these explanations. The danger that he will reach wrong conclusions seems greater in a straight, chronological, descriptive course than in one that emphasizes analysis. In the latter kind of course he may learn to label as pseudo explanation any explanation whose premises are untestable. These are the explanations that explain "the achievements of a person in terms of his 'mission in history,' his 'predestined fate,' or similar notions" that are metaphorical rather than lawlike in their content and language. Such explanations "convey pictorial and emotional appeals instead of insight into factual connections" (Hempel, 1959, p. 347). These pseudo explanations may be logical in their connections between premises, but this fact only makes the explanation valid, not true.

An incomplete explanation, or, as Hempel calls it, an explanation sketch, omits some part of the triad, usually the major premise. A typical example would be a passage that lists and discusses reasons for the occurrence of an event. In explaining a fire, it may be said that the barn burned down because someone dropped a cigarette in the hay. A political movement, it is said, gained adherents because of widespread racial prejudice. The following passage from a popular high school text in American history is a typical explanation sketch:
"During the war, industry had begun to spread into the South and West, so there was increased sentiment for protection in these agricultural areas."

This appears to be a plausible explanation for a change in public sentiment toward tariffs. At least, high school students are not likely to be critical of such an explanation unless their teacher encourages and helps them. Students who read this "explanation" and commit it to memory may actually feel that they have learned; but a translation of this passage so that it reads like a syllogism changes its appearance and may even bring students to wonder about its truth.

Major premise: If an agricultural region begins to acquire industries, an initial effect is an increased public sentiment favorable to tariffs which would protect new industries from foreign competition.
Minor premise: During World War I new industries began to develop in southern and western United States, two regions traditionally agricultural.
Conclusion: During World War I, the sentiment in favor of protective tariffs increased in southern and western United States (Metcalf, 1960, p. 29).

The use of Hempel's model enables us to look carefully at the major premise, precisely defining its key terms, and examining empirically its probable truth or falsity. Hempel calls this process "filling in" an explanation sketch. The sketches are clearer as a consequence of this "filling in," and the student is more certain as to whether he has learned the true antecedents of an event.

Not every sketch needs to be filled in. Neither Hempel nor Swift indicates clearly what criteria he would use in deciding whether to submit a sketch to thorough analysis. Swift's only direct contribution on this point is his comment that

Answers to some why-questions will necessarily be dealt with at the level of common-sense familiarity. If the question arises, Why did Americans migrate in large numbers to California in 1848–49?, it can be met in the incomplete form by the answer: Because gold was discovered there. The generalization that people will flock to areas where minerals are newly discovered, or simply that many people are attracted by prospective riches, is probably not a new insight into social phenomena for most students. Here, the process of detecting it as an assumption and formulating it as a generalization is not worth the time (Swift, 1958, p. 16).

Obviously, teachers will tend to push their students into a somewhat thorough analysis of those sketches which in their view lack validity or truth. In this way they hope that their students will avoid the learning of error. But good teachers would not want to limit analysis to sketches that are wrong, for a student can learn just as much from analysis of sketches that are right and, at the same time, the teacher can avoid giving the impression that the only purpose of analysis is the destruction of belief.

Griffin proposed that students re-examine beliefs in the closed areas of American culture. A closed area has been defined as "a segment of culture which traditionally has been largely closed to reflective examination, and within which many superstitions and rationalizations may be identified" (Hunt & Metcalf, 1955, p. xi). Students pick up beliefs unreflectively from all segments of their cul-

ture; these beliefs are acquired willy-nilly very early in life. Beliefs dominant in such closed areas as sex, social class, religion, patriotism, and economics are most likely to be fuzzy and invalid because it is in such areas that emotions run high. Maximum social insight might be fostered if teachers used the closed area criterion as a basis for deciding which explanation sketches to require their students to fill in. This criterion would then become the standard for selecting content as well as for deciding whether to submit an explanation sketch to analysis.

Hempel has observed that historians sometimes use an empathetic method of explanation. They ask their students to put themselves in the place of a person who participated in some historical event.

The historian . . . imagines himself in the place of the persons involved in the events which he wants to explain; he tries to realize as completely as possible the circumstances under which they acted, and the motives which influenced their actions; and by this imaginary self-identification with his heroes, he arrives at an understanding and thus at an adequate explanation of the events with which he is concerned (Hempel, 1959, p. 352).

This method can be fruitful in generating explanatory hypotheses, but it does not test the adequacy of any hypothesis. It is also possible to arrive at hypotheses without recourse to empathy, as in the case of a sane teacher who hypothesizes about the behavior of mentally disturbed persons. At best, this method is a device for getting ideas, and it serves this purpose without putting ideas to a logical or experimental test.

Another contribution by Swift is his careful distinction between explanation, on the one hand, and description, interpretation, and chronology, on the other. These are useful categories for a study of teaching. It would be revealing to know the extent to which teachers describe or interpret rather than explain. To what extent do they use a chronological or genetic approach to the process of explanation? To what extent do teachers rely upon the psychology of an empathetic approach rather than the logic of Hempel's model? To what extent do they use what Swift has called the teleological explanation? Thus, how many teachers teach that the Pilgrims came to America because they desired religious freedom, and how do such teachers "prove" the motives of the Pilgrims? Are motives simply attributed, or do the teachers approach the problem of motive in much the same way in which a court of law would approach it?

In a further study of how the teaching of explanation may foster development of critical thinking in the social studies, Swift (1959) identified different types of explanation and classified them according to their logical rigor. First, he distinguished between relational and nonrelational explanations. Nonrelational explanations amount to descriptions or interpretations. In a nonrelational explanation a teacher may ask students to "explain separation of powers in American federal government," or "explain the use of a map scale," or "explain how to locate a biography of Jackson in the school library." Swift comments on these examples:

The expected response in instances like these is a series of statements cataloging information, naming certain symbols, describing characteristics of especially constituted governmental branches, or describing a series of actions supplemented with particular items of information (Swift, 1959, p. 14).

The student who "explains" separation of powers usually names the branches of government, the operations of each, and then describes the procedures and criteria by which governmental functions are divided among the branches. The teacher may then ask the student to illustrate the meaning of separation of powers by tracing a bill through Congress and showing what can happen in case of a presidential veto or Supreme Court decision which invalidates an act of Congress. Running throughout this conception of explanation is an emphasis upon sheerly descriptive information which places no de-

mands upon the logic of teacher or student. No doubt most teachers equate explanation with description, particularly if they define learning as memorization and rely upon recitation as the only reliable "method" of teaching. Actually, empirical studies of teachers' conceptions of explanation have not been made, so one can only guess at the number of them who have a nonrelational conception.

Swift mainly upholds the value of relational explanation, which he defines as one that explains an "affair in terms of some other affair, condition, or situation" (p. 124). He then classifies relational explanations into two types, rational and nonrational. Nonrational relational explanations, although sometimes logical, are never both logical and empirical in their criteria. Anthropomorphic explanation is one example of a nonrational relational explanation. A teleological explanation, if it refers to some ultimate purpose, was classified by Swift as nonrational relational.

The major part of Swift's study was devoted to rational relational types, each of which satisfies his four criteria for judging the adequacy of an explanation. Swift identified and discussed five types of rational relational explanation: (1) the dispositional, (2) the psychological, (3) the genetic, (4) the causal, and (5) the historical.

Types (1) and (2), dispositional and psychological explanations, refer to some inner state of the individual, such as purpose, need, or tension, but oddly enough Swift did not classify them as teleological. He appeared to reserve this term for inner states that are said to express the ultimate purpose of God, nation, or universe. The logic for this distinction between immediate and ultimate purposes is not always clear.

Swift granted that teachers who ask apparently teleological questions may have in mind a concept other than purpose, human or divine. The teacher who asks, "What is the purpose of the Federal Communications Commission?" may be trying to find out whether the class can list the *functions* given to this commission by Congress. When he asks about the purposes for dropping an atomic bomb on Hiroshima, he may have *effects* in mind. But some questions of a teacher do refer to purpose, such as "What was Wilson's purpose in going to Europe?"

The latter question, which Swift would classify as an attempt by the teacher to elicit a rational explanation from his students, causes one to wonder whether individual purposes in history are any more accessible than so-called ultimate purposes of the universe. It is possible to learn from a study of letters and other documents what Wilson's stated purposes were for going to Europe, but everyone knows that stated purposes are not always the same as motivating purposes. Some people lie about their purposes; others do not know their purposes well enough to state them; still others do not understand their purposes well enough to pursue them with appropriate means. If the policies or behavior of an individual are inconsistent with his stated purposes, it does not follow that he is a liar. Other inferences are more charitable and just as reasonable. The reasons for inconsistency between what people say and what they do are not always accessible to empirical investigation, and one may be restricted in his analysis to concluding no more than whether behavior and stated purpose are consistent. Despite this limitation, Swift would treat all teleological explanations, except those which deal with ultimate purposes, as rational in type. He prefers the terms *dispositional* or *psychological* to *teleological* for any explanation that relies upon some judgment of an individual's inner state or purpose. The possibility that all such judgments make some use of an empathetic method is never mentioned by Swift.

His rejection of explanations that deal in ultimate rather than immediate or stated purpose is summarized in an incisive discussion of Manifest Destiny:

At least two kinds of objections have been raised against teleological explanations of events—the objection that they attribute human characteristics to nonhuman entities, and the objection that the terms which name the entelechy or the force are in the last analysis undefinable with reference to a set of observable characteristics. Concerning undefinability, the difficulty can be seen in a claim that America expanded to the Pacific because it was her Manifest Destiny to do so. . . . the expression "Manifest Destiny" is not susceptible of precise definition to the extent of being able to assert what is and what is not an instance of it. The actual population movement is traceable through such sources as land office records and the Bureau of the Census, and hence the expression "expansion to the Pacific" can be defined in terms of density of population and coverage of territory. But the term "Manifest Destiny" as a characteristic of a nation offers considerable difficulty (Swift, 1959, pp. 57–58).

In Swift's discussion, the only difference between dispositional and psychological explanations is that the former refers to purpose at the level of human action while the latter refers to any inner state of purpose, belief, tension, and the like. As long as a purpose is not claimed to be ultimate, Swift has no trouble with it. "Why is he driving to the city? Because he wants to do some shopping," is offered as an example of dispositional explanation. In defining psychological explanation, Swift says that the thing to be explained is a human action, and the reason for the action is some internal condition of the organism. In psychology the latter is called an "intervening variable." He then offers the following as an example of a psychological explanation:

For example, Custer's defeat by the Sioux on the Little Big Horn may be explained in terms of relationships of numbers of men, of distance between his troops and possible reinforcements, as well as in terms of his temperament and his knowledge about the whereabouts of the Sioux, i.e., his military intelligence. . . . When particular explanations are offered which emphasize the internal conditions of the actor rather than the antecedent conditions of the external environment, the explanation sketch on occasion is described as "psychological" rather than as "physical" or "natural" (Swift, 1959, p. 66).

The problem of formulating dispositional and psychological explanations as rational types comes into the open when one casts either into Hempel's syllogistic form. If one were to explain an action of Lincoln's by reference to an inner state, the syllogism might be:

Major Premise: Lincoln as President of the United States, in decision situations affecting national policy on the Civil War issue, followed the line of action he thought would contribute to the strength and cohesiveness of the Federal Union.
Minor Premise: Lincoln thought that freeing the slaves would contribute to the strength and cohesiveness of the Federal Union.
Conclusion: Lincoln issued the Emancipation Proclamation.

Regardless of whether "strength and cohesiveness of the Federal Union" was one of Lincoln's immediate or ultimate purposes, how is one to know his innermost desires? A radical behaviorist would say that one could never know.

In any event, it appears that an explanation that relies upon observable instead of inner elements would have more rigor. Griffin, in his analysis of beliefs, ignores inner, or private, states. A person who says that he does not like Negroes may very well express a personal belief, but it is the kind of belief that cannot be tested with publicly accessible evidence. Whether a person dislikes Negroes cannot be established from anything that a person says or does, for the evidence on how he feels is inside the speaker. Not even his overt behavior can be taken as evidence one way or the other because people who like Negroes often behave no differently from people who dislike Negroes. Only a statement such as "many Negroes, according to present-day intelligence tests, are more intelligent than many white persons" qualifies as a testable belief. It can be tested by reference to publicly available evidence, and one need pay no attention to inner belief in order to confirm or disconfirm this kind of assertion.

Swift rejects as pseudo explanation the kind of teleology expressed in the statement that "the element of purpose may be viewed as a remote future condition or state of affairs which in some manner is supposed to control the shape of developments through extended periods of time, or it may be viewed as a process of change influenced by a purposing agent which is superpersonal rather than human" (p. 55). He does not include in this rejection explanations "in which the reason is a statement about the aims or objectives of a person in a decision-making capacity. . ." (p. 56). He does not clarify the exact process by which he would verify the purposes of a decision-maker. He refers vaguely to documents, statements, and the like, all of which suggests that he would take stated purposes at face value.

Type (3), as we have seen, consists of the chronological or genetic type of explanation. The genetic explanation answers a *why* question by listing a series of events or stages, and each item in the series is said to lead up to the next item. The relationship of item to item is at least temporal, and teachers who ask pupils to "trace" something probably approach explanation problems with chronology rather than science or logic as their major intellectual tool. Unless we can show that events such as A, B, and C, under certain conditions, always result in an event such as D, we have not explained D, according to the Hempel model. Without the protection of Hempel's model, the genetic method of explanation may lead into the *post hoc, ergo propter hoc* fallacy. The genetic approach also assumes that the past makes the present, yet Smith (1938) has proved that it would be equally reasonable to argue that the past is a construct of the present.

Type (4), causal explanations, are offered by Swift as another example of rational explanation of a relational type. Such explanations name certain events as the cause of other events, and as in genetic explanations, the relationship of events may be no more than temporal. Explanations that list causes are logically no different from those that list reasons. They are incomplete, and "filling in" is their most essential need. A causal explanation is typically divided into three parts, the causes of an event, the event itself, and the effects of the event. Typically, the teacher who asks for causal explanations will, in his treatment of the Civil War, require the student to name at least three causes of the war, to describe major events in the war, and then list results of the war.

Swift maintained that an analysis of causal explanations requires a teacher to distinguish, or help his students to distinguish, between necessary causes, and causes that are both necessary and sufficient. It is very doubtful that most teachers actually do so, since their education seldom provides them with the necessary instruction in logic. It appears that some casting of causal explanation into a subsumptive form would help a teacher and his students to draw the distinction between necessary and sufficient historical explanation.

Type (5), historical explanation, is the last example considered by Swift. Its chief feature is the assumption that historical events are unique and nonrecurring. Emphasis is upon accounts of the past, without predictions of the future. Prediction, like subsumptive explanation, requires events to be classified, and the assumption that everything is unique can be interpreted so as to deter one from classification. Bruner has observed sagely that classification does not deny the uniqueness of events (Bruner, et al., 1956), and therefore those who argue for uniqueness could succumb to logic and classification without giving up uniqueness as a value and a criterion. No two civil wars are exactly alike, and neither are any two cases of measles or mumps, but there is intellectual advantage to grouping wars *of a certain kind* and treating them *as if* they were the same, despite the differences that make each unique. In fact, it is not possible to know that an object is a unique example of its kind ex-

cept as we know differences between it and other objects of the same kind. Certainly, when a person says that his cat is unique, he means very little and communicates even less except as he can clearly indicate the attributes shared by all cats, pointing out also that his cat possesses these as well as a few others that comprise its uniqueness. Those who limit explanations to the historical type generally search out the uniqueness of events rather than their generality, and this factor accounts for much of their style of history teaching.

It is clear not only that Swift prefers relational explanations to nonrelational, and rational to nonrational, but also that his four criteria lead to a further conclusion—that the subsumptive or scientific explanation, has more rigor than any other type of rational relational explanation. Its rigor places one in a position to determine how much scientific knowledge a particular historian has and the extent to which he relies upon opinion or literary expression as a substitute for knowledge. If there is any flaw in Swift's reasoning, it is in his willingness to treat dispositional or psychological explanations as essentially different from those teleological explanations that assume cosmic intent; this is not a serious flaw, however, as long as he confines his "knowledge" of human purpose to the realm of stated purposes and their consistency with what people do.

Swift's research suggests one direction for research on teachers, their methods, and materials. One would expect teachers to differ in usages and conceptions of explanation, and that some, but not all, of the differences would be related to the context of the teaching—grade level, subject matter, ability of student, community climate, and so on. One would also expect teachers to be confused as to differences between description, classification, interpretation, explanation, and justification. Probably their explanations would lack logical or empirical rigor. But the actual state of affairs is not known, because these features of classroom teaching have not been studied except in an exploratory sense by

Smith (1960). We do not know whether teachers appraise an explanation by asking appropriate questions about the meaning of terms, about generalizations and the assumptions they imply, about empirical data related to testing a generalization, or about the validity of conclusions in relation to premises.

Regardless of what teachers are now doing, it is clear from Swift's analysis of explanation as one aspect of critical thinking that the training of teachers should prepare them not only to make explanations but also to teach students about the general nature of explanation and the problems that an explanation may be expected to solve. Swift suggests that instruction in explanation as a process should require teachers to raise questions such as the following:

1. Is this an explanation or a description?
2. What kind of thing is being explained?
3. What are the word clues that show it is an explanation?
4. What are the reasons offered in the explanation sketch?
5. How complete is the explanation? (Swift, 1959, p. 130).

Swift's approach to teaching history emphasizes use of logic and scientific method; it does not assume that there is a "logic of history," nor does it express any doctrine of "historical necessity" or "historical inevitability." Some philosophers of history— Geyl and Collingwood—have attributed authoritarian orientations to any approach to history that is concerned with making and testing lawlike generalizations. Possibly the same critics would regard a method of teaching that is largely rational as similarly authoritarian in its effects. The weakness of these criticisms seems to be that they identify any attempt to generalize with a tendency to be doctrinaire. Actually, Swift's analysis, to the extent that it is a refinement of those of Dewey, Griffin, Bayles, and others who have written on the nature and value of reflective teaching, strengthens our defenses against doctrinaire interpretations of any kind, regardless of their source.

THE PROBLEM OF CONCEPT ANALYSIS

Bruner, Goodnow, and Austin (1956) offered a refinement of Griffin's conception of a concept. Griffin seems to define a concept as any idea cast in propositional form and does not distinguish between a concept and a generalization. Bruner makes this distinction when he defines a concept as a category or classification. The act of categorization renders "discriminably different things equivalent," or "groups the objects and events and people around us into classes," so that one can "respond to them in terms of their class membership rather than their uniqueness" (Bruner, Goodnow, & Austin, 1956, p. 1).

Categories are invented, not discovered. "Science and common-sense inquiry alike do not discover the ways in which events are grouped in the world; they invent ways of grouping" (Bruner, Goodnow, & Austin, 1956, p. 7). If one decides to group things differently in science from the way they have been grouped in the past, it is because one expects to be able to make more accurate predictions as a result of this change in categories. As soon as one recognizes that categories are invented rather than discovered, he no longer falls into the error of trying to prove that his categories are true or right. Definitions are recognized as definitions, and not treated as propositions.

Bruner and his co-workers further refined the meaning of a concept by describing the various types. Most people assume that the conjunctive type—one defined in terms of common elements—is the only kind. The assertion that "all men are mortal" is conjunctive, although a conjunctive concept may have more than one common attribute. Bruner has learned that the strategies that are successful for learning conjunctive concepts will not work as well with other kinds of concepts.

Another kind of concept is disjunctive; this kind is defined in terms not of common elements but of alternative attributes. A strike in baseball, for example, may be a pitch that passes over the plate within a certain zone, or it may be a pitch that the batter swings at and misses, or it may be a ball hit into foul territory when the count on the batter includes fewer than two strikes. If one studies all instances of a strike in baseball, and if he assumes conjunctivity, he may not learn the concept, or he may learn it incompletely.

The incomplete learning of a concept that results from taking a conjunctive stance toward a disjunctive concept may be illustrated by the concept of citizen. This concept may be viewed as either conjunctive or disjunctive. If a citizen is defined as a person born in this country, or as a person who has passed certain examinations, or whose parents were born in this country, the concept of citizen is disjunctive. But if one defines a citizen as a person who can vote and hold public office, the concept is conjunctive. Assuming that this concept is disjunctive would probably enable us to learn the concept more completely than assuming that it is conjunctive. The scientific tradition in our culture predisposes everyone to assume all concepts to be conjunctive. If Bruner is correct in his analysis, teachers need to be ready to help students who approach all concepts as if they were conjunctive.

A third kind of concept is the relational. This type expresses a certain relationship among the attributes of a concept. Full employment, as the economist defines it, is probably a relational concept. It expresses at the very least a relationship between size of labor force and number of unemployed. But it also includes length of work week, productivity per man-hour, and value of the product. Since technological change, price fluctuations, and monetary policy affect these factors, full employment is a dynamic concept as well as a relational one. A relational concept, to the extent that it expresses a relationship that is empirical rather than definitional, amounts to a generalization. Thus the identity of concept and generalization in Griffin's original theory, as mentioned above (see page 961), is once more before us.

Bruner has identified strategies followed by subjects in a clinical environment as they pursued the learning of nonverbal concepts. Strategies vary with type of concept, cognitive strain, order of presentation, and other factors.

The significance for teaching of the work of Bruner and his colleagues is not entirely clear. There is no doubt of its significance as a psychological study, although it suggests only in broad ways what may be involved in the analysis of a concept by teachers and students alike.

CONCLUDING REMARKS

This summary of research on teaching concepts and a process of reflective thought in the social studies suggests that division of labor among research workers may have disadvantages. One group of investigators has worked on building a comprehensive theory of social studies education. This group has pretty much rejected controlled experimentation as a research tool. It claims, however, that its theory is not in conflict with well-established facts. Another group has gathered and counted facts without weighing their significance for basic theoretical problems. There has been notably little interaction or communication between the two groups. Each has worked independently of the other. Each probably always will be, unappreciative of the other's conception of research.

A few studies have attempted to test the effectiveness of a problem-solving method of teaching. The group that carried out these studies was not anti- or nontheoretical in its research interests and conceptions. But their studies, with the exception of those done under Bayles, have not shown a sufficient understanding of the more comprehensive theory of problem-solving as developed by Dewey and Griffin, and as refined and extended by the related work of Swift and Bruner. The net result is that the research findings of this group are largely irrelevant to an experimental testing of the comprehensive theory.

There are many reasons why the kind of theory that Griffin has developed has not been experimentally tested. The most likely reason is that it will never be a popular theory among the many interest groups that shape and influence educational policy. An experiment that tested this theory might find its teachers criticized by the community for engaging in seemingly subversive activity. Any teacher who creates student doubt about dominant community beliefs, no matter how obvious his commitment to democratic ideals and reflective process, runs some risk of community displeasure or misunderstanding.

A second reason is that even our best prepared teachers have not been well trained in logic and scientific method. Moreover, their acquisition of content from college courses has seldom been reflective in quality. It is one of Griffin's claims that a teacher can best use content reflectively if he acquired it that way. The tendency of college professors to use methods other than the method of reflection is well established. College courses are concerned with dissemination of content and little concerned with methods of inquiry.

One large question raised by Griffin's theory is whether organized content and methods of inquiry can be learned in the same course. It is a question that so far has not been investigated experimentally by professional workers in departments of educational research. Griffin's proposition that "the reflective examination of any proposition tends to develop skill in the use of the method" (p. 193), if true, would settle part of the matter. Students would simply reflect upon their beliefs, using organized content as a basis for reaching conclusions, and this practice of reflection would develop their reflective capacity. There would be the question of whether a student who reflected upon his beliefs would necessarily learn subject matter as a logical structure, but this question could be answered through experimentation.

There is some doubt, however, as to the truth of Griffin's proposition. This doubt is expressed by Griffin in the following statement:

A formal course in reflective thinking *as a beginning point* would be absurd; but the need *at some point* to pull the process out and look at it is an implication of the intent to develop teachers who can promote reflection not only through habitual ways of handling materials, but *on purpose* (Griffin, 1942, p. 214).

For purposes of teacher training, then, it is not enough to have teachers take courses in which content is covered and learned reflectively. Occasionally, the professors who teach teachers must stop what they are doing and have their students make a direct study of what has been taking place. By implication, teachers of high school social studies should do the same thing if their students are to understand and appreciate the connection between reflective process and the survival of democratic values.

To say that students must at some point in a history course, let us say, pause in their study of history in order to take up a study of historical method as an example of reflective thinking suggests that content and reflection cannot be learned at one and the same time, except to the degree that reflection is learned through practice. To what extent can reflection be learned through practice? To what extent can reflection be studied directly within a course that has other goals, largely goals in substantive content? Can students who reflect upon their beliefs acquire organized content in the sense of coming to understand the basic structure of an intellectual discipline, and is knowledge of the structures of disciplines a necessary part of general education? These are some of the unanswered questions in Griffin's theory of social studies teaching which research has so far neglected to explore.

Research and theory in teaching the social studies have reached a point where no further progress is possible without a marriage of one to the other. So far, the two parties involved have been largely incompatible in their conceptions of research. Unless the research model and techniques of the professional research worker in education can be applied to testing and clarifying some of the more comprehensive theories of social studies educators, the present impasse is bound to continue.

REFERENCES

Adams, J. A. A survey of controlled experiments in social studies. Unpublished master's thesis, Florida State Univer., 1954.

Avery, T. C. An experiment with teaching a class in American history according to the pragmatic theory. Unpublished master's thesis, Univer. of Kansas, 1941.

Bayles, E. E. *Theory and practice of teaching.* New York: Harper, 1950.

Bayles, E. E. Experiments with reflective teaching. *Kansas Stud. Educ.,* 1956, 6, No. 3.

Beale, H. K. *Are American teachers free? An analysis of restraints upon the freedom of teaching in American schools.* New York: Scribner's, 1936.

Bruner, J. S., Goodnow, Jacqueline J., & Austin, G. A. *A study of thinking.* New York: Wiley, 1956.

Bruner, J. *The process of education.* Cambridge: Harvard Univer. Press, 1960.

Devitt, J. J. The relative importance of United States history concepts in general education programs at the secondary school level. Unpublished doctoral dissertation, Boston Univer., 1957.

Dewey, J. *How we think.* Boston: Heath, 1910, 1933.

Droll, Helen A. A study of a semester's work in government at the high school level, presented in accordance with the Dewey-Bode point of view. Unpublished master's thesis, Univer. of Kansas, 1940.

Griffin, A. F. A philosophical approach to the subject-matter preparation of teachers of history. Unpublished doctoral dissertation, Ohio State Univer., 1942.

Gross, R. E., & Badger, W. V. Social studies. In C. W. Harris (Ed.), *Encyclopedia of educational research.* (3rd ed.) New York: Macmillan, 1960. Pp. 1296–1319.

Gross, R. E., Zeleny, L. D., & others. *Educating citizens for democracy.* New York: Oxford Univer. Press, 1958.

Hempel, C. G. The function of general laws in history. In P. Gardiner (Ed.), *Theories of history.* Glencoe, Ill.: Free Press, 1959. Pp. 344–356.

Horn, E. *Methods of instruction in the social studies.* New York: Scribner's, 1937.

Hullfish, H. G., & Smith, P. *Reflective thinking: The method of education.* New York: Dodd, Mead, 1961.

Hunt, M. P., & Metcalf, L. E. *Teaching high school social studies.* New York: Harper, 1955.

Jacob, P. E. *Changing values in college.* New York: Harper, 1957.

Jewett, R. A social studies methods course. *Soc. Educ.,* 1958, 22, 293–294.

Johnston, Laura C. An experiment with the problem-raising and problem-solving method of teaching American history. Unpublished master's thesis, Univer. of Kansas, 1941.

Kight, S. S., & Mickelson, J. M. Problem vs. subject. *Clearing House,* 1949, 24, 3–7.

Lazarsfeld, P. F., & Thielens, W. *The academic mind.* Glencoe, Ill.: Free Press, 1958.

McLendon, J. C. *Teaching the social studies.* Washington, D.C.: American Educational Research Association, National Education Association, 1960. (Pamphlet)

McPhie, W. A comprehensive bibliographic guide to doctoral dissertations in social studies education. Research Committee, National Council for the Social Studies, 1959. (Unpublished)

Metcalf, L. E. Teaching economic concepts in the social studies. *Illinois Councilor,* 1960, 21, 24–30.

Oppenheim, P., & Hempel, C. G. The logic of explanation. In H. Feigl & May Brodbeck (Eds.), *Readings in the philosophy of science.* New York: Appleton-Century-Crofts, 1953.

Palmer, J. R. The treatment of social change in high school history textbooks. Unpublished doctoral dissertation, Univer. of Illinois, 1960.

Potter, D. M. *People of plenty.* Chicago: Univer. of Chicago Press, 1954.

Quillen, I. J., & Hanna, Lavone A. *Education for social competence.* Chicago: Scott, Foresman, 1948.

Reader, Edna C. L. An experimental study of reflective teaching in a fifth-grade classroom for a two-year period. Unpublished master's thesis, Univer. of Kansas, 1953.

Roberts, L. M. Ten units in American history formulated in accordance with the pragmatic theory of teaching. Unpublished master's thesis, Univer. of Kansas, 1941.

Sailer, R. L. A third experiment in teaching a semester of American history in accordance with the Roberts plan. Unpublished master's thesis, Univer. of Kansas, 1942.

Searles, J. E. The social studies methods course in the training of high school teachers. Unpublished doctoral dissertation, Stanford Univer., 1952.

Smith, B. O. Is history a prerequisite to the study of social problems? *Soc. Studies,* 1938, 29, 206–210.

Smith, B. O. A study of the logic of teaching. Urbana: Bur. of Educ. Res., Univer. of Illinois, 1960. (Mimeographed)

Snow, C. P. *The two cultures and the scientific revolution.* Cambridge, Eng.: Cambridge Univer. Press, 1959.

Swift, L. F. The teaching of explanation in history. Paper read at Nat. Assoc. Coll. Teachers of Educ., Chicago, February, 1958.

Swift, L. F. Explanation as an aspect of critical thinking in secondary school social studies. Unpublished doctoral dissertation, Univer. of Illinois, 1959.

Swift, L. F. Explanation. In B. O. Smith & R. H. Ennis (Eds.), *Language and concepts in education.* Chicago: Rand McNally, 1961.

Trefz, Ida R. An experimental study of teaching a sixth-grade class for seven months employing a pragmatic program. Unpublished master's thesis, Univer. of Kansas, 1941.

Wesley, E. B. *Teaching the social studies.* Boston: Heath, 1942.

CHAPTER 18

Research on Teaching Composition and Literature

HENRY C. MECKEL
San Jose State College

A review of research pertaining to teaching composition and literature should recognize that any conceptual framework for interpreting and evaluating studies must take account of recent educational controversies. The national debate on education has been sharpened by a number of factors, among them the new interest in the quality of education, the increase in the percentage of secondary school graduates entering colleges and universities, and the increased skill in composition and acquaintance with literature demanded of more and more high school graduates. Whereas, in the early years of this century, the forces operating to create increased enrollments in the public schools appeared to indicate that college preparation was to be only a minor function of the American secondary school, influences today suggest that college preparation has become a major function. Modifications of the high school program also affect the curriculum of the elementary school. Public school English instruction is consequently undergoing a period of transition characterized by efforts to redefine aims and content and skills.

In states where junior colleges exist to any extent, every high school student becomes, at least in theory, a college preparatory student. As a result, more students are expected to develop a higher degree of competency in language skills and literature than ever before, for the learning activities of colleges and universities require higher levels of such competencies than do most of the adult activities of life. Development of language skills requires long periods of carefully planned sequential instruction. The present state of American education, therefore, strongly emphasizes the importance of curricular sequence from elementary school through college and suggests that the framework for considering problems of teaching must be formulated on somewhat different premises from those which we have inherited from the first quarter of this century.

Another factor affects interpretations of research in the teaching of composition. Among the important scholarly accomplishments of our century is a substantial body of linguistic research, particularly research on the English language (Bloch & Trager, 1942; Bloomfield, 1933; Chomsky, 1957; Fries, 1941, 1952; Hockett, 1955; Jesperson, 1933; Kurath & Bloch, 1939–1943; Malmstrom, 1959; Roberts, 1956; Sapir, 1921; and Trager

& Smith, 1951). New insights into the nature and structure of the language have caused many of the studies on the teaching of composition to lose the significance attributed to them in the past. This fact is especially true of the research relating to grammar and usage.

RESEARCH ON TEACHING COMPOSITION

Although much educational practice emphasizes that effective instruction in composition must be related to instruction in literature, the research reported in this chapter has been organized into two separate divisions: The first section of the chapter treats research on teaching composition; the second major section deals with research on teaching literature.

Objectives of Teaching Composition

Research on teaching any subject necessarily operates within a framework of assumptions about the basic educational purposes of that subject. All teachers of English will agree that the major purpose of teaching composition is to develop the skills that are important in writing. Disagreements arise concerning the purposes which writing skill is to serve, the priority of certain purposes over others, and the nature and relative importance of the specific enabling skills associated with certain general purposes. Through the first quarter of this century, objectives in composition, particularly in the secondary school, were influenced by the classical tradition of the liberal arts of grammar and rhetoric (Hosic, 1917). As industrial democracy developed in this country and with it a system of universal education, pragmatic conceptions began to affect theory and practice in teaching English—a development which paralleled more general changes in American education. The National Council of Teachers of English has been highly influential throughout the past 50 years in developing and promulgating pragmatic conceptions of the English curriculum. The historical influence of the Council in attempting to broaden the curriculum in writing to meet the needs of all kinds of students is evident in such publications as *Reorganization of English in Secondary Schools* (Hosic, 1917), *An Experience Curriculum in English* (1935), *The English Language Arts* (1952), *Language Arts for Today's Children* (1954), and *The English Language Arts in the Secondary School* (1956).

The National Council has viewed objectives for the teaching of composition primarily from the point of view of the situations which require written language either in school or in adult life. This approach was given direction in an early study by R. I. Johnson (1926, 1932), who sought to identify "functional centers" of language activity to serve as a basis of curriculum planning and teaching.

In harmony with traditional Council theory, language activities such as the following would constitute a curriculum of functional language experiences (Hudelson, 1923; National Council of Teachers of English, 1935, 1952): writing directions, announcements, and minutes of a meeting; writing reports on reading; summarizing data from reading, oral and written reports, and class discussions; communicating personal experiences; writing imaginative compositions; writing letters for both social and business purposes; writing for the school magazine or newspaper; writing which requires special competencies in the organization and development of ideas. These various written language activities require skills in mechanics, sentence structure, diction, paragraph construction, and planning and organization. The experience curriculum suggested by National Council publications has emphasized the desirability of teaching such skills in a functional way—by relating them to the composition activities which require their use.

The objectives of composition have been clarified by work in the evaluation of composition skill by the Armed Forces Institute and by the Educational Testing Service (1957, 1958; V. White, 1947). Both organizations have utilized the experience and opinions of teachers, supervisors, and other leaders in the field of English instruction to determine the objectives which should serve as the basis for achievement tests in composition. Recent tests developed by such a procedure (Educational Testing Service, 1957, 1958) illustrate the following four principles as criteria for determining the objectives of a sequential program of composition in a school system: (1) the objectives should represent a range of writing situations, so that the total writing process receives attention in the curriculum; (2) the objectives should represent the range of performances typical of pupils at different stages of development—particularly with reference to general sophistication, vocabulary, and organization; (3) the objectives should represent the range of skills which constitute competence in specific writing situations believed to be important; (4) the objectives should represent those phases of skill in which there should be continuous sequential growth.

The items comprising such a test, developed as they are in accordance with the above principles, suggest composition objectives that may be regarded as deserving wider acceptance within the schools. The tests are designed on the assumption that students should have experience with the following types of writing: a friendly letter, a letter applying for a job, an announcement of an event for a newspaper, a discussion of a problem, a narrative report of a personal experience, directions, an answer to an essay question, a personal opinion, answers to a questionnaire, a description, the minutes of a meeting, the draft of a speech, a paragraph summarizing the most important concepts resulting from a study, an evaluative comment on a radio or television program or on a play or book, an editorial. To illustrate the degree of writing skill that represents reasonable performance at different grade levels, extensive samples of student work were examined. The aspects of writing skill con-

sidered included logical expression; ability to organize materials in a whole paper, in a paragraph, and in a sentence; ability to write effectively in terms of such matters as clarity, emphasis, exactness of word choice; ability to use conventions of writing.

As more and more students continue education beyond high school, a greater degree of skill in expository writing is being required of a larger percentage of high school students. Groups of college teachers have from time to time issued statements regarding the priority and value of certain kinds of writing both in the elementary and the secondary school (*The Basic Issues in the Teaching of English,* 1958; Departments of English, etc., [1959]; Grommon, 1953; Ward, 1956–1957). In general, such statements stress the importance of expository writing and warn against overstress on the writing of personal experiences, imaginative compositions, letters, or other forms of composition. These statements recommend that college preparatory students be given continuous practice in writing that requires greater skill in thinking, planning, organizing, and composing, especially writing that requires the extended development of a single idea or point of view. Such statements often urge more recognition of the relationship between writing and literature and more attention to the examination of language structure in literature. Quite recently, at the high school level, there has been some evidence of a return to the older idea that the study of rhetoric would strengthen the composition program of college preparatory students.

Methods of Teaching Composition

In this review, research on methods of teaching composition has been classified according to whether it is (1) indirectly or (2) directly concerned with teaching methods. The "indirect" classification includes studies directed toward discovering interrelationships among specific language skills, including (a) studies of language in relation to such factors as the early environment, intelligence, and personality characteristics of children, and (b) studies of language development as a phase of growth and maturity. Such investigations have important implications for teaching procedures in the classroom: Conclusions from such research may affect the organizational structure of the English curriculum, may strongly influence the attitudes of teachers toward the composition problems and difficulties of their students, and may determine the kind of instruction and guidance which teachers of composition give to individual pupils. The teacher's knowledge of such research and his ability to apply this knowledge must be regarded, therefore, as variables associated with the effectiveness of his methods of teaching composition. These variables become increasingly significant in a culture that progressively emphasizes higher degrees of language skill.

The "direct" classification includes studies which bear directly on classroom method: the effectiveness of instruction in formal grammar, the utility of so-called "functional" grammar, and the effectiveness of methods of instruction that do not involve traditional grammatical approaches. This classification also includes research concerned with composition assignments, the teacher's treatment of the students' papers, the teaching conditions required for effective instruction in composition, and the preparation of teachers of composition.

Interrelationships Among Language Skills

Much current opinion emphasizes that English language skills should be taught so that specific skills reinforce one another. The National Council of Teachers of English, for example, takes the position that "the curriculum in the language arts should be so organized as to provide experiences which involve all facets of language in their normal relations" (National Council of Teachers of English, 1952). This statement was sharply critical of teaching methods devoting separate semesters, parts of semesters, or days of the week to grammar and composition, to reading and literature, or to speech activities, in an unrelated fashion. A more recent statement growing out of a consideration of basic issues in the teaching of English referred to the "absolute impossibility of divorcing the consideration of writing from reading. . ." (*An Articulated English Program,* 1959, p. 16). A state survey of secondary school practices in teaching composition suggested the importance of reading as a source of ideas for writing, and stressed the value of writing as a means of clarifying, organizing, and applying ideas gained from both reading and discussion (Meckel, Squire, & Leonard, 1958).

A major problem in interpreting research concerned with interrelations among language skills was noted by McCarthy (1954). Such research is obviously dependent on the measures used to appraise language development. McCarthy pointed out that while a wide variety of measures have been employed in such studies, the methods of analysis used and the statistical results obtained do not allow comparison outside of the framework of the particular studies themselves. Among the most widely used measures, for example, have been those of vocabulary and length of sentence; the latter, according to McCarthy, has proved to be perhaps the most objective and reliable single index of language development. McCarthy noted further that comparatively little has been done to determine the relative importance of the different aspects of linguistic development or to arrive at any single index of development in the tremendously complex phenomena of language behavior.

The patterns of language development of the individual, moreover, and the constellation of skills which characterize him as a person do not necessarily follow group patterns. McCarthy regarded language as an area of a child's development in which more striking degrees of individual variation can be observed than in almost any other phase of growth. McCarthy's comments, made after an extensive and thorough examination of the reports of research, suggested the difficulties in generalizing about relations among such gross categories of language skill as reading, writing, speaking, and listening.

Language and the early environment of children. Artley and his associates (1954) pointed out that interrelations among language skills are indicated by the relations of language skills to common factors which influence language development. Especially important among such factors are those which affect the early oral experiences of children, help to set the basic patterns of oral expression, influence readiness to learn to read and write, and appear to affect later linguistic performance. Such factors include the very early environment of children, the socioeconomic status of their families, and the extent to which patterns of social intercourse with families encourage language expression. The teacher's knowledge of these factors is usually regarded as of major importance in elementary school teaching (Artley, et al., 1954). In research on methods of instruction in composition at elementary or secondary school levels, such factors have to be considered in determining the equivalence of experimental and control groups.

Studies of the language development of children reared in institutional, orphanage, or hospital environments have revealed that such children have deficiencies in speech sounds, vocabulary, and language organization (McCarthy, 1954). Children from families of upper socioeconomic status have been found to have linguistic advantages over children from lower social class groups with respect to vocabulary, sentence structure, and usage (E. A. Davis, 1937; Day, 1932; Lloyd & Warfel, 1956; McCarthy, 1954). Several studies have indicated that an environment which broadens a child's experience is also likely to increase his vocabulary (McCarthy, 1954). Studying first-grade Negro children, Milner (1951) examined patterns of family life of children making high and low scores on language items on the California Test of Mental Maturity. She found that children with high scores tended to come from families where the patterns of interaction between parents and children encouraged parent-child conversations and involved habitual overt expressions of affection.

After a child enters school, the curriculum and the teaching staff are highly influential in determining the extent to which language privations due to early environment persist or whether the experiences of the school help the pupil overcome his early handicaps. Research is needed to determine the merit of teaching procedures that accomplish such purposes. Pupils with problems in composition might profitably be studied, therefore, from the point of view of their linguistic history.

Composition skill and intelligence. Intelligence is often regarded as a common factor in various language behaviors. The close relationship between reading ability and scores on intelligence tests is partly accounted for by the nature of the tests. McCarthy (1954) concluded, after a careful review of research, that individual differences in language development closely parallel the differences which exist in intellectual development. The nature of the relation of intelligence to writing skill is complicated, however, by the complexity of intelligence itself and of the skill involved in composition. Diederich (1957) reported studies which indicated that the vocabulary sections of intelligence tests have superior value in predicting composition skill. Lorge and Kruglov (1950) designed an experiment to test the hypothesis that both the structural and conceptual aspects of written composition are indicative of the general intellectual level. Frogner's data (1939) supported the hypothesis that maturity rather than intelligence affected the percentage of sentences containing dependent clauses.

Composition skill and personality characteristics. Personality characteristics are also thought to be related to various forms of language behavior. Some sort of relationship between the personality of a writer and his writing is usually taken for granted. Attempts are commonly made in literary studies, for example, to establish connections between the characteristics of a writer and his personality. Teachers of composition have usually regarded the relationships among teacher, student, and the student's writing as highly personal. A composition, consequently, is felt by both teacher and student to be an especially personal and creative product; in fact, whenever the problem of reading, correction, or criticism of a composition is carefully considered by a teacher, he realizes that a personal factor is involved that he must handle with understanding and finesse (Confrey, 1927; Dusel, 1955b).

The content of compositions, as well as the language structure, is thought to reflect the personality of the writer. Teachers of composition have long believed, in fact, that a pupil's writing may serve guidance purposes as well as purely linguistic ones. Articles on this subject appeared early (J. Davis, 1912). A survey of composition practices (Meckel, Squire, & Leonard, 1958) suggested that, through his writing, a pupil may project information about himself that can aid the teacher in guiding his learning. As examples, the survey listed evidence of (1) a pupil's feelings of insecurity, including such feelings toward the language activities of reading and writing and speaking; (2) other feelings and attitudes, including those directed toward language skills; (3) the pupil's sense of belonging or his sense of isolation; (4) fantasies and daydreams; (5) thoughts, beliefs, and ideas; (6) life history; (7) personal problems; (8) interests; (9) adjustment to school; (10) relationships to peers; (11) relationships to adults; (12) relationships within his family; (13) dominant value patterns.

Russell (1953), however, after reviewing over 250 references pertaining to the interrelationship of the language arts and personality, summarized his major conclusions as follows:

. . . although language activities and personality are theoretically close, research evidence about their relationships is frequently spotty and vague. Certain topics such as interrela-

tionships of language arts difficulties and personality difficulties have been rather thoroughly explored. Other areas, such as the positive contribution of language abilities to personality development or the relationships between certain types of personality and different forms of language activity, have been relatively untouched (Russell, 1953, p. 167).

Most studies pertaining to language and personality difficulties have been done in the fields of speech, reading, and spelling. Fewer studies throw light on the personality factors that may be related to the composition problems of a student. Several studies, however, have suggested approaches to the relationship. Free association-type stories told as responses to pictures have been widely utilized in the Thematic Apperception Test as projective material for personality study (Murray, 1938). Content analysis of writing in terms of the symbols and themes which occur and reoccur has been regarded as yielding possible clues to personality predispositions (R. White, 1947).

Patten (1950), as a result of work in a college writing clinic, became interested in exploring relationships between personality factors and written expression. He obtained four diverse samples of writing from each of 60 first-semester freshmen and administered the Minnesota Multiphasic Personality Inventory to each subject. Eight of the nine clinical subscales of the Inventory were used in his statistical treatment, the Masculinity-Femininity scales being omitted. The writing was analyzed in terms of 15 categories: handwriting control, manuscript neatness, spelling, quantity, organization, use of extraneous material, topic coverage, sentence complexity, sentence clarity, sentence directness, use of qualifying expressions, word appropriateness, use of imagery, and word omission or repetition. Patten then examined differences in pattern on the personality inventory between groups of students segregated on the basis of the various writing criteria. He found significant differences between groups compared on the basis of quantity, organization, use of qualifying expressions, and topic coverage. No other groupings on single or combined writing criteria yielded statistically significant results.

Mann's quantitative study (1944) illustrates another approach to the study of the relationship between personality factors and written language. She compared samples of written language of 24 university freshmen with those of 24 psychotic patients diagnosed as schizophrenic but similar in intelligence. There were no differences between the groups in terms of most frequently used words, but her normal subjects used more different words and appeared to have "a more highly differentiating language structure." They used more adjectives per noun and more adverbs per verb, and had higher "adjective-verb quotients," a variable explored by Boder (1940). Mann interpreted her findings as indicating that her normal persons were distinguished from her schizophrenic persons in that the former define, modify, and restrict their language in such a way as to make it more accurately representative of the actualities which they are attempting to symbolize. Mann's research, apart from the hypotheses it suggests, has methodological value for research on teaching composition.

The term *personality* denotes a complicated organization of human characteristics and behaviors. Complicated also are the particular responses of any human being to his writing tasks, especially to the writing assignments which the school or his social relationships impose upon him. In a certain sense, the language patterns and style of a person may be regarded as an intrinsic part of his personality. There is great need, therefore, for case studies that will throw light on the relationships of different facets of personality to writing behavior, particularly on the dynamics of such relationships and on the dominant patterns of personality involved.

Some of the significant questions are the following: (1) Are fluency and quantity of writing related to certain facets of personality? (2) Is the amount of detail used by a writer to add specificity to writing associated in any way with his personality character-istics? Is considerable detail, for example, likely to be associated with spontaneity of personality? Is paucity of detail associated with structured and rigid kinds of personality? (3) Is skill in organization associated with propensity for organization as part of the functioning structure of personality? In what ways does the creative process of writing depend on perception of organization in its various stages? Do personality factors have a relationship to the organizational structure demanded by certain types of writing such as narration, description, or exposition? (4) Is the tendency to use active rather than passive forms of verbs associated with certain personality traits? (5) What personality predispositions function in writing situations? Specifically, what patterns of attitude and emotion function in school writing situations? (6) What relationships do security and insecurity as general personality traits have to certain aspects of writing?

Written and oral language. Relationships between written language and oral language are of special importance for the elementary school teacher, because the speech patterns of children are the foundation upon which the teacher develops composition skill. According to Anderson (1941), the significant period for acquiring spoken language is from age two to eight. While vocabulary continues to increase, and additional skills in the use of sentences appear after age eight, the essentials of spoken language are present by that age. Hockett (1950) believed that the fundamental speech habits of the individual are firmly established by the age of puberty and that the most important force shaping the dialect is the speech of other children. E. A. Davis (1937) concluded from her research that the child's mastery of articulation relates closely to other phases of language development, and that faulty articulation, if unduly prolonged, may become an obstacle to adequate command of language in more general respects. Shire (1945), in studying the relation of speech patterns of children to progress in first-grade reading, found that children making unsatisfactory progress in reading also showed linguistic immaturity with respect to absence of elaborated sentences, shortness of sentences, lack of connectives, and lack of variety in their vocabularies. Heider and Heider (1941) demonstrated the close relationship between written sentence structure and oral experience by comparing the written compositions of deaf and hearing children. The language patterns of deaf children, they found, resembled the language patterns of younger children with hearing ability. The importance of oral teaching of language patterns was suggested by D. V. Smith (1938). The success of the U.S. Army in teaching foreign languages by auditory methods suggests that oral methods can be useful in developing sensitivity to patterns of language and stylistic devices at different levels in the school program. Such teaching methods are clearly indicated by the research already mentioned, yet few controlled studies of oral methods in teaching composition have appeared in the literature (Moyer, 1958).

Composition and reading skill. The most significant research on the relationship of writing skill to reading skills has been done under the sponsorship of the College Entrance Examination Board. Reporting on a phase of this research, Diederich (1957) maintained that good measures of reading ability have turned out to be the most trustworthy indicators of writing ability. The verbal score on a scholastic aptitude test was found to be more highly correlated with teachers' ratings of pupils' composition skills than was any other measure. The teachers doing the rating were known by other data to be especially good judges of student writing, and their ratings were based on samples of student writing done at various times over a period of a year.

Composition Skill and Maturity

Language skill is affected by maturity, as well as by the environmental factors mentioned in the previous section. Thus, the teacher's knowledge and use of those factors of language structure related to growth and development are also variables that should be considered in research on teaching composition. McCarthy (1954) summarized many studies on the language development of younger children. Most such studies have been made with preschool children. Dimensions of language growth which have been studied include the amount and rate of talking, growth of vocabulary, sentence structure, and grammatical form. Among the problems in such research are the difficulties of getting adequate samples of normal language performance, determining adequate categories and methods to use in the analysis of language samples, and managing the variables that are related to language behavior. Perhaps the most significant generalization supported in different studies pertains to sex differences. Girls show a slight superiority over boys in nearly all aspects of language that have been studied (McCarthy, 1954).

Studies of the written language development of children have been made of pupils in Grades 1–12. Studies by Bear (1939), Frogner (1933), LaBrant (1933), and Watts (1944) have involved intensive examinations of samples of writing of different groups of pupils. The writer knows of no longitudinal studies of written language growth patterns of individual children made over long periods of time. The group studies which have been reported appear to warrant the following generalizations: Length of sentences tends to increase with age and maturity (Bear, 1939; Frogner, 1933; LaBrant, 1933; Watts, 1944). Sentence completeness is a persistent problem; it is related to the complexity of sentence patterns and thought processes (Frogner, 1933; LaBrant, 1933). The run-on sentence becomes more frequent in the middle grades, apparently because pupils are attempting more complicated expression (Bear, 1939). Use of the complex sentence increases with age and progress through school, and this increase is associated with increased use of subordinate clauses (Bear, 1939; Frogner, 1933; LaBrant, 1933).

Watts's study (1944) indicated that phrase

subordination may represent a more mature aspect of language skill than clause subordination. Increase in subordination is paralleled by increasing exactness in the use of connectives (LaBrant, 1933). Subordination appears to have a closer relationship to chronological age than to mental age (Frogner, 1933; LaBrant, 1933). Frogner (1933) reported that (1) greater increase in frequency of sentences with dependent clauses occurs between Grades 9 and 11 than between Grades 6 and 9; (2) adverbial clauses are most frequently used by pupils, and noun and adjective clauses rank second and third in frequency of use; (3) more sentence fragments involve the adverbial clause than the adjective clause, noun clauses being seldom written as fragments; (4) the more intelligent students use fewer clauses of time and cause and more of manner and concession. For some, growth in language skill, as measured by kinds of clauses used and by length and complexity of the clauses themselves, proceeds far beyond the level attained by most high school students (LaBrant, 1933).

The Relation of Grammar
to Composition Skill

That an understanding of grammar is related to the development of skill in speech and writing has been one of the most consistently held beliefs in the history of education, originating in the philosophical and educational theories of the Greeks. In current practice, also, most teachers appear to assume that teaching grammar and usage is an important phase of teaching composition, for surveys of classroom methods have confirmed the fact that grammatical analysis and terminology receive a great deal of attention in English classrooms throughout the nation (Pooley, 1957). In fact, if findings of surveys in Wisconsin (Pooley & Williams, 1948) and Georgia (Farmer & Freeman, 1952) are typical of practices elsewhere, such instruction receives a very large proportion of classroom time—much more than is allotted for practice in writing.

To determine prevailing attitudes of teachers concerning instruction in grammar, Pooley polled 20 leaders in public school English instruction in different parts of the United States—teachers and supervisors whose professional activities brought them closely in touch with teachers and classrooms (Pooley, 1957). The following view of grammar represented the opinion of a majority of teachers at the time of the survey:

Grammar is the means to improved speech and writing. Because it explains usage, grammar must be learned to support usage instruction. Grammar skills are best gained by learning the parts of speech, the elements of the sentence, and the kinds of sentences. These skills are usually all taught before the end of the ninth year. Drill and practice from textbooks and workbooks establishes grammar, which will then function in composition (Pooley, 1957, p. 51).

In an earlier analysis of textbooks, Pooley concluded that nearly all the concepts of grammar are still taught before the end of the eighth grade, and that grammar taught in Grades 9 through 12 is merely repetition of what has been taught, though generally not learned, in the junior high school (Pooley, 1933).

Reviews of educational research, however, have continually emphasized that instruction in grammar has little effect upon the written language skills of pupils. The interpretations and curricular applications of this general conclusion have ranged from the view that grammar and usage should not be taught in isolation from written composition (Searles & Carlsen, 1960) to the position that formal grammar merits little or no place in the language arts curriculum (Shattuck & Barnes, 1936).

Studies related to the teaching of composition through the use of grammar may be classified in seven categories: (1) those in which the emphasis is on the transfer value of knowledge of definitions of grammatical terms and the ability to parse; (2) those aimed at determining the transfer value of diagramming; (3) those attempting to ascertain the value of grammatical knowledge for skill in punctuation; (4) those designed to identify critical items of usage and the so-called "functional" principles of grammar associated with them; (5) those primarily concerned with the determination of phrases of sentence structure in which pupils most need instruction; (6) those attempting to appraise the efficiency of methods of instruction which emphasize the relation of grammatical structure to the adequate expression of ideas; and (7) those which emphasize that practice in writing is superior to all else.

In appraising research related to the transfer value of grammar, it is important to consider the particular phases of grammatical understanding with which studies were concerned. Tests used in grammar research have measured the following kinds of achievement:

1. Knowledge of the parts of speech at any of the following levels of understanding: at a level of mere memorization and recall of definitions; at a level that involves conceptual understanding of these definitions; at a level represented by the ability to designate the part of speech of words in sentences of varying degrees of complexity.

2. Ability to define and recognize structural elements of sentences, such as subjects, predicates, complements, modifiers, including single-word modifiers and phrase and clause modifiers.

3. Ability to choose preferred forms of usage, particularly of pronouns, verbs, adjectives, adverbs.

4. Extended knowledge of grammatical terms such as *case, number, voice, tense, mood, agreement, comparison.*

5. Ability to diagram sentences.

6. Ability to recognize sentence faults associated with parallelism, predication, pronoun reference, tense sequence, placement of modifiers.

In reporting their studies, experimenters have frequently applied the term *formal grammar* to any of the above kinds of specific achievement, and reviewers under pressure of space limitations have tended to report the general conclusions of experimenters without specifying the particular grammatical abilities involved in specific pieces of research. In this chapter, therefore, an attempt has been made to identify the specific grammatical abilities involved in the various studies.

Knowledge of grammatical terminology and ability to parse. Hoyt (1906) tested 200 first-semester ninth-grade pupils in grammar, composition, and ability to interpret a poem, using essay tests which were graded on a scale basis by two readers. The grammar test consisted of four stanzas from Gray's *Elegy Written in a Country Churchyard,* with questions that called for (1) diagramming the last two lines of each stanza; (2) identifying types of sentences, phrases and clauses, the parts of speech, the case of nouns, and voice, mood, tense, and number of verbs; and (3) understanding the use of adjectives and verbals. Hoyt concluded, after correlating scores on the essay test in grammar with scores on a composition test and an essay test on interpretation, that (1) about the same relation exists between grammar and composition, and grammar and interpretation, as exists between any two totally different subjects, such as grammar and geography; (2) grammar is of little avail in strengthening one's power to use language; (3) grammar should either be omitted from the elementary school curriculum and left to the high school, or else the character of grammatical instruction should be changed.

Briggs (1913), interested in challenging claims for the value of grammar as mental discipline, set up two comparison classes of seventh-grade pupils at Columbia University's Horace Mann School, taught the grammar himself, and compared his test results with scores on the same test given to pupils in five Illinois public schools. Pupils in experimental classes had formal grammar for three 30-minute periods a week for three months—a total, apparently, of only 18 or 20 hours. Briggs's tests were designed to measure a fairly high degree of grammatical knowledge: ability to explain syntax and the use of words and groups of words in sentences, application of grammatical definitions, ability to parse, and ability to recognize types of sentences. Among Briggs's conclusions were these: (1) Despite the general interest of the children in classroom work, they learned just enough grammar to be a disappointment and source of vexation to teachers in the high school. (2) Whatever be the truth about the amount of transfer, it is a question whether, under ordinary conditions, elementary school children can learn enough of formal grammar to justify its study.

Boraas (1917) reported finding a lower correlation between knowledge of grammar and ability in composition than he found between knowledge of grammar and knowledge of history and arithmetic.

Using tests devised by Starch (1915), Asker (1923) made correlational studies of test scores and grades of 295 freshmen at the University of Washington. His grammar test measured ability to identify the parts of speech, the case of nouns and pronouns, and the tense and mood of verbs. His test of sentence correctness was a scale purporting to measure judgment of correct sentences on the basis of usage items and faults in parallelism, predication, tense sequence, pronoun reference, and placement of modifiers. Asker reported the following correlation coefficients: between grammatical knowledge and ability to judge correctness of sentence, .23; between grammatical knowledge and grades in freshman composition, .37; between freshman composition and grades in all subjects, .63.

Segel and Barr (1926) reported a correlation of .48 between a test of "formal grammar" and ability to choose correct forms, which was called "applied grammar."

The utility of diagramming. Even if teaching definitions of grammatical terms and the ability to parse sentences has little transfer value in improving composition skills, does the method of diagramming have utility, focusing, as it does, on visual representation of structural elements of sentences? Studies on diagramming were reported by Greene (1947), who sponsored the research at the University of Iowa. Using roughly equated groups of ninth-grade pupils in a preliminary experiment lasting six weeks, Barghahn (Greene, 1947) found no evidence that diagramming contributed to the more rapid acquisition of English correctness. Following the same experimental design, but using more carefully paired pupils in two tenth-grade classes and extending the instructional period to twelve weeks, Barnett reached the same conclusion (Greene, 1947).

The most thorough study in this field, however, was done by Stewart (1941). In terms of instruments of measurement and experimental design, the Stewart study represented a distinct advance over earlier research: It involved approximately 1,000 pupils in 22 randomly selected school systems whose pupils had not previously received instruction in diagramming. Comparisons were· made between groups of pupils taught by the same teacher. The classes designated as control groups and experimental groups were also chosen on a random basis. The training period on which results were based was eight weeks. Data were treated by analysis of covariance.

Stewart's purpose was to determine the effectiveness of sentence diagramming as a method of teaching usage, capitalization, punctuation, grammatical information, and sentence structure. Experimental classes were taught methods which largely utilized diagramming; control classes were taught the same language skills, but by writing original sentences and rewriting poor sentences. Results were measured by use of the Iowa Every-Pupil Test in English Correctness (1939 and 1940 editions); a test utilizing items selected from forms of the Iowa Grammar Information Test; a special diagramming test; and a test of skill in sentence construction which required the students to combine short sentences into long sentences. The results led Stewart to conclude that diagramming had no superiority in instructional value over direct use of composition exercises.

Grammar and punctuation. Butterfield's

study (1945) involved 831 sixth-grade, seventh-grade, and eighth-grade pupils from 19 Midwestern city school systems. Using an experimental design and statistical procedures similar to Stewart's, she attempted to secure information about the effect of a knowledge of certain grammatical elements on acquisition and retention of punctuation skills. Thirty-five items of grammar were selected on the basis of previous studies, an analysis of courses of study, textbooks, and workbooks, and the judgments of three well-qualified teachers. Control classes received instruction in which grammar was related to instruction in punctuation; experimental classes received instruction in which emphasis was placed on use of punctuation marks as aids to the reader in clarifying thought and meaning. Butterfield concluded that (1) pupils taught grammar improved in knowledge of grammar, but grammatical knowledge did not transfer appreciably to skill in punctuation, and (2) superior results were obtained by the method stressing thought and reasoning.

Determination of critical items of usage. As the doctrine of formal discipline was displaced and as the proportion of noncollege students in the secondary schools increased, interest shifted to a determination of the most functional phases of grammar. Until quite recently, four kinds of data were regarded as pertinent to the determination of items of usage that required "functional" grammatical explanation:

1. Errors in students' writing, represented by the research of Charters and Miller (1915), R. E. Johnson (1917), O'Rourke (1934), and Stormzand and O'Shea (1924).

2. Opinions of experts about specific items of usage, represented by Leonard's *Current English Usage* (1932).

3. Facts about specific items of usage based upon the usage of writers and dictionary evaluations, represented by the work of Marckwardt and Walcott (1938).

4. Facts about items of usage as revealed by analysis of adult usage, represented by Fries's *American English Grammar* (1941).

In its earlier stages, the functional grammar movement was closely associated with the doctrine of linguistic correctness. According to this theory, there are correct and incorrect ways of speaking and writing. Grammar is a means of correcting errors by reference to rules; *functional* grammar refers to those rules of grammar governing the items of usage with respect to which pupils most often make mistakes. This doctrine of correctness is being abandoned as new knowledge about language is gained from descriptive studies of actual usage.

Especially significant with respect to the status of studies of errors in usage have been the findings of linguistic atlas studies which have been completed in certain sections of the country (Kurath & Bloch, 1939–1943) and are currently in progress in other sections. Linguistic atlas studies represent attempts to *describe* usage patterns as they are actually found in the speech of people in different areas of the nation. Such studies suggest, according to Malmstrom (1959), that we need a five-dimensional model to describe American usage, a model that includes social, situational, methodological, temporal, and regional factors. For example, in marked contrast to the superficial characterization of an item of usage as grammatically correct or incorrect, a description of usage based upon linguistic atlas research would point out that either standard or nonstandard forms of language (social) may be used, on formal or informal occasions (situational), in either speech or writing (methodological), by either young speakers or older speakers (temporal), in either isolated rural areas or urban centers of culture, in any given dialect area (regional).

Another phase of the functional grammar movement has been the proposal to simplify and perhaps standardize terminology and to omit unessential content so that students may gain maximum understanding of those phases of grammar with the greatest utility (Rivlin, 1930). In certain instances, however, the disciples of functional grammar seem to have taken the point of view that there should be no systematic study of grammar at all, *systematic study* being regarded as synonymous with *formal* or "nonfunctional" grammar. The untenability of such a point of view is suggested in an article by Roberts (1960), who indicated the extent to which knowledge of any particular grammatical structure depends on knowledge of other grammatical structures. We cannot, he pointed out, really define the concept *sentence* short of describing English grammar. In the opinion of this writer, the term *functional grammar,* with its overtones of practicality, has given many teachers and administrators an unwarranted confidence in the usefulness of scraps of grammatical information.

That textbooks used in the school are extremely conservative and even in error with respect to usage, and that teachers tend to be both conservative and uninformed about recent linguistic research seems to be clear from the research of Malmstrom (1959), Womack (1959), and a recent survey on the preparation of English teachers (National Council of Teachers of English, 1961).

Faults in sentence structure. A number of studies have been focused on faults of sentence structure in student writing. Potter (1922), in an early study of the writing of entering university freshmen, reported that the number of errors in sentence structure was equal to the number of errors in grammatical usage and diction combined; that 32 per cent of all errors in sentence structure were due to statements in which clauses were unclear; that 14 per cent of sentence structure errors were caused by omission of words needed for understanding; and that 12 per cent of the errors were caused by faulty reference of pronouns.

Pressey (1925) studied the comparative frequency of errors in sentence structure in papers written by pupils in Grades 7–12 and classified them into two types: (1) errors in which pupils failed to make proper sentence division (fragments, stringy sentences, and omission of words accounted for half of such errors), and (2) errors of pronoun reference and redundancy. Symonds and Daringer

(1930) analyzed errors in sentence structure, in compositions selected from composition scales and calibrated to the Hillegas Scale, to show the improvement in sentence structure as one progresses to writing of better quality. They reported weak, broad, or divided reference of pronouns as the most prominent error in sentence structure throughout the whole school program, called attention to the persistent prominence of the "comma blunder" in all grades, and emphasized the greater prominence of misplaced modifiers as the cause of inadequate sentences in the higher grades.

Symonds and Hinton (1932), following the same procedure, analyzed grammatical errors and concluded that they were among the least serious difficulties in poorer compositions. Grammatical errors were of less consequence, for example, than the choice of words; the order in which words and phrases are presented; omitted words; incomplete, jumbled, and run-on sentences; sentences with little or no idea worth expressing; broad and uncertain reference; and wrong use of words.

Frogner (1933) studied problems of sentence structure in compositions of pupils in Grades 7, 9, and 11 and found the run-on sentence to be the greatest source of error in all grades. She reported that sentence errors seemed to be much more frequently made by some pupils than others and suggested the importance of individual methods of instruction.

The efficiency of methods. A number of studies have been made of the efficiency of methods of improving composition. Many of them have attempted to compare grammatical approaches with nongrammatical approaches.

Symonds (1931), using sixth-grade classes in different New York schools and without any attempt to equate groups, investigated the following six methods for improving language usage: (1) oral drill with written drill sheets on correct forms; (2) oral drill with written drill sheets in which correct and incorrect forms were printed side by side;

(3) study of definitions, rules, and principles of grammar; (4) grammar analysis in which pupils were given instruction in determining parts of speech and usage in the sentence; (5) practice in choosing the correct usage to fill a blank; (6) a method that incorporated all the previous procedures.

The findings indicated that: (1) Use of a combination of methods was most effective. (2) Practice in correct and incorrect forms was almost as effective as the combined methods. (3) Practice in choosing correct form was next in effectiveness. (4) Students receiving grammatical instruction made gains but only about half the gain that was made after receiving necessary instruction with correct and incorrect forms. (5) Drill on correct forms was least effective, and when prolonged it appeared to have negative results. (6) Brighter pupils appeared to profit most from grammatical approaches.

Using seventh-, eighth-, and ninth-grade pupils in three West Virginia schools, Ash (1935) attempted to ascertain the effectiveness of what he called a *stylistic approach* in teaching written composition. This approach emphasized sentence structure, paragraph-building, diction, unity, coherence, sequence, emphasis, clearness, exactness of expression, rhetorical fluency, creativeness, and avoidance of monotony. Experimental groups were taught the stylistic approach through units; classes in two other schools, used as controls, received the regular instruction prescribed by the state course of study, which was largely grammatical. The experiment was conducted during a single semester. Progress of pupils was estimated on the basis of 23 selected items which included the mean form values of compositions according to the Willing Composition Scale and the mean content values of the compositions according to the Hudelson Typical Ability Composition Scale. At the end of the experiment, the experimental group exceeded the control group in percentage gains on 19 of the 23 items and exceeded the control group at each grade level in percentage of reduction of errors. Evidence was most marked in the seventh grade; here the experimental group began the experiment with lower scores than the control classes, but was able to reduce errors by 60 per cent as compared with reductions of 3 per cent and 11 per cent in the other two schools. Ash concluded that the formal elements needed by junior high school pupils are fewer than hitherto supposed and that many of the formal elements of written composition can be secured by emphasizing content through its application in written thought.

Cutright (1934), in a study with children in Grades 4, 5, and 6, found the writing of correct forms followed by oral reading of sentences to be superior to other methods for securing correct language usage.

Catherwood (1932) reported that, of 93 per cent of students in the seventh grade who could correct a grammatical mistake, only 8 per cent could state the grammatical rule involved and that the correlation between knowledge of subject and predicate and the ability to correct sentences for completion was .41.

Crawford and Royer (1935), in a series of eight lessons, compared the value of oral drill with that of studying the grammatical explanations of errors and found the oral method slightly inferior.

Evans (1939), in studying methods of teaching punctuation, compared the progress of pupils taught by the same teacher in 19 city schools in the Midwest—one class receiving instruction in grammatical approaches to punctuation and the other using an approach which emphasized thought and meaning. Superior results were obtained by use of the nongrammatical approach.

Frogner (1939) compared two methods of teaching sentence structure for one semester. The "thought approach" utilized meaning and thought exclusively; the "grammar approach" supplemented this approach with grammatical terminology and drill. Using 47 pairs of pupils in Grade 9 and 60 pairs in Grade 11, she developed units emphasizing coordination and subordination of ideas in clauses, subordination of ideas in phrases, recognition of sentences, reference of pronouns, sequence of tenses, parallelism, and sentences with faults caused by omission of words. She reported the following findings: (1) Results of unit tests in the individual elements of sentence structure given immediately at the close of each unit favored neither approach. (2) The "thought approach" appeared to result in longer retention of the abilities acquired; all observed differences in general tests given at the end of the experiment favored the "thought" group, and three of these differences were statistically significant at the "upper level." (The exact levels of confidence were not given.) (3) The "thought approach" in both Grades 9 and 11 was superior to the grammar approach for all pupils with an IQ below 105, all differences satisfying the "lower level of statistical significance." (Exact level of confidence was not indicated.) (4) There was little difference between the two methods among superior pupils, though there was an observable tendency for students with IQs of 114–129 to profit more from the grammar method. (5) Investigation showed that even in grammar classes pupils used thought aids more than grammatical reasoning. (6) Pupils in the grammar classes learned more grammar than those in the thought classes. (7) The thought approach required approximately 80 per cent of the time required by the grammar method.

The transfer value of grammar. Eleven studies are commonly cited as documenting the uselessness of formal grammar in building composition skill. The grade levels of these studies are shown below:

Grade Level	Study
6	Butterfield, 1945; Cutright, 1934
7	Ash, 1935; Briggs, 1913; Butterfield, 1945; Catherwood, 1932
8	Butterfield, 1945
9	Ash, 1935; Catherwood, 1932; Frogner, 1939; Greene, 1947; Hoyt, 1906; Rapeer, 1913; Stewart, 1941
10	Frogner, 1939; Segel & Barr, 1926
11	Segel & Barr, 1926
College freshman	Asker, 1923

It is evident that the majority of these studies attempted to test the transfer value of grammar at the junior high school level. Yet, at this level, according to considerable research, grammar is not mastered to any extent. In this connection a study by Macaulay (1947) is pertinent. Although carried on with Scottish children, Macaulay's findings generally accord with the conclusions of at least three writers in this country (Briggs, 1913; Catherwood, 1932; Pooley, 1957). To secure data on the extent to which children acquired the ability to recognize the part of speech of a word by its use in a sentence, Macaulay constructed a test consisting of sentences; he set the passing of 50 per cent of the items as a standard of achievement. Administering the test to 131 students who had completed primary school and who had averaged 30 minutes of grammatical instruction per day over a period of four years, Macaulay found that only one student met his standard. While 37 per cent of the students passed half the items involving nouns, and 21 per cent passed half the items concerned with verbs, only 5 per cent passed half the items involving adjectives and 4 per cent the items pertaining to adverbs. Administering the same test to 400 boys and girls in the junior secondary school, who had been instructed in grammar for at least six years, Macaulay found that only four pupils out of 397 scored at least 50 per cent on all five parts of speech involved in the test. After testing students completing the highly selective senior secondary school, which admits only the top fifth of the graduates of the junior secondary school, Macaulay found that only 42 per cent of these students were able to pass 50 per cent of the items, even though they had had three additional years of grammatical instruction.

These data suggest one reason why studies of the transfer value of grammar have shown so little evidence of transfer: The pupils in the various studies had apparently acquired little knowledge that could be transferred. The research indicates that none of the studies of transfer have extended beyond an experimental period of one semester—a time span much too short to permit development of the degree of conceptualization necessary for transfer to take place.

The studies appear to justify the additional observation that the problem of transfer has been conceived in the wrong way. If, as certain writers believe, the value of grammar is largely editorial, then grammatical knowledge would be expected to function most efficiently in situations in which pupils are recasting the structure of a sentence or paragraph, revising first drafts of their own papers, or reading and discussing papers of their fellow students to help them make revisions.

Since transfer of learning appears to be a function of a pupil's intelligence and his ability to generalize (Stephens, 1960), it appears that the value of grammatical knowledge would be best tested in an experiment that utilized intelligent pupils who had received instruction to the point of mastery of principles. No studies of the transfer values of grammar appear to have been made in which students who have demonstrated knowledge of grammar have been compared with students of the same intelligence and socioeconomic background who have little grammatical knowledge.

The psychology of the transfer of training suggests that transfer of learning is achieved when there is similarity between the training situation and the situations to which learning is to transfer. The methods of instruction suggested by structural linguists have come closer to fulfilling this requirement than have customary methods. The structuralist emphasizes that the acquisition of grammatical knowledge must involve an awareness of language structures. Such awareness can result from practice exercises in creating different language structures and in applying this skill to all writing experiences.

The present situation in research on transfer of grammar to composition skill may be summarized as follows:

1. There is no research evidence that grammar as traditionally taught in the schools has any appreciable effect on the improvement of writing skill.

2. The training periods involved in transfer studies have been comparatively short, and the amount of grammar instruction has frequently been small.

3. There is no conclusive research evidence, however, that grammar has *no* transfer value in developing composition skill.

4. More research is needed on the kind of grammatical knowledge that may reasonably be expected to transfer to writing. For example, commonly accepted principles of transfer of training would not lead an experimenter to expect much transfer value from knowledge of grammar which has not included the knowledge and ability to apply grammatical principles to the construction of the pupil's own sentences (Stephens, 1960).

5. Research does not justify the conclusion that grammar should not be taught systematically. In some appraisals of research there has been a confusion between the term *formal grammar* as used to denote systematic study and mastery and the term as used to mean grammar taught without application to writing and speaking. Systematic study does not preclude application.

6. There are more efficient methods of securing *immediate* improvement in the writing of pupils, both in sentence structure and usage, than systematic grammatical instruction.

7. Improvement of usage appears to be more effectively achieved through practice of desirable forms than through memorization of rules.

8. The items of usage selected for inclusion in the curriculum should be determined not only by "errors" made in students' papers but also by descriptive studies of national usage by linguistic experts.

9. In determining what grammar is functional and what is not, teachers cannot safely rely on textbooks used in schools but must depend on the expert opinion of linguists based on modern studies of the usage and structure of the language.

Discounting present practices in the schools and considering only the substantial body of recent linguistics research and theory, much of the earlier research on teaching grammar must be regarded as no longer of great significance outside the period in educational history which it represents. There is, therefore, great need at present for new and differently conceived studies. These studies might profitably concern themselves with such questions as: (1) What specific items of grammatical knowledge hold the greatest promise for improving composition skill? (2) What degree of mastery of this knowledge is required before we may reasonably expect transfer to writing skill? (3) What constitutes a desirable learning sequence of grammatical understandings? (4) How much knowledge of grammar is appropriate at any particular level of the school system in terms of the maturity of students and of assisting them to learn to write effectively? (5) To what degree is grammatical knowledge merely a factor contributing to writing skills, along with other factors such as intelligence, reading experiences, and amount of guided practice in writing?

The Relation of Structure to the Expression of Ideas

If grammatical terminology is reduced to a minimum and principles of sentence structure are formulated in terms of their relationship to the idea being expressed, what conditions are likely to facilitate the improvement of writing? An experiment by Kraus (1959) suggested conditions such as the following: Pupils must be given opportunities to write; instruction should be focused on the sentence structure errors on which pupils most need help; opportunities for individualized instruction should be increased; pupils should

be helped to assume initiative and responsibility for self-instruction; pupils should be taught to apply principles in correcting and improving their own work.

Using experimental classes of eleventh-grade pupils in Oregon, Kraus (1959) compared three methods of teaching sentence structure. She developed teaching materials designed to improve completeness of sentences, coordination, clarity, emphasis, variety, and conciseness; her method of instruction emphasized the relation of structure to the adequate expression of ideas.

Six classes, each representing a random sample of the entire junior class, were used during an 11-week experimental period. Two instructors were involved, each teaching three classes, and each of the three classes received instruction in a different method. Students in Method I classes were taught principles of sentence structure but did no writing. Students in Method II classes were taught the same principles, but wrote themes once a week on topics of their own choosing. Themes were marked, graded, and returned, but no follow-up instruction was given on errors. Students in Method III classes received instruction based solely on errors made in papers written in connection with a literature unit, worked in small groups on specific errors, were referred to specific pages of a handbook, and helped one another correct errors before returning corrected themes to a teacher. The Method I class received a total of 30 hours of instruction in sentence structure; the Method II class, 24 hours; and the Method III class, 10 hours.

Analyses of variance and covariance revealed that all classes made significant gains in reduction of errors and in ability to detect weaknesses in sentence structure. Gains were greatest in the Method III class, however, and were achieved in one-third of the time.

The Effects of Practice

Teachers of composition believe that the development of skill in writing is most closely related to the amount of practice pupils have in writing. But experimental evidence on the relation of practice to skill is meager. Lokke and Wykoff (1948) increased the number of themes required in two small experimental freshman classes from 16 to 32 a semester. They concluded that the added practice in writing reduced failures 66 per cent and produced a 60 per cent improvement in grades. Dressel, Schmid, and Kincaid (1952) asked 2,400 freshmen how much writing they did in all courses during an academic year and compared the improvement of students doing the most writing with that of students doing the least. They concluded that mere practice in writing will not improve composition skills unless attention is given to the quality of writing.

Using two groups of randomly selected remedial students, Maize (1954) compared a control class which followed a workbook drill on grammar, punctuation, and spelling and wrote 14 weekly themes corrected by the instructor, with an experimental group which wrote 40 themes. The instructor did not read or correct any of the writing of the experimental group outside regular class hours; instead the instructor and students analyzed and commented on the themes in the writing laboratory. The experimental group showed greater improvement in all scores on the Rinsland-Beck Natural Test of English Usage except vocabulary.

The Composition Assignment

An important phase of teaching composition is the making of adequate composition assignments. Many excellent suggestions for making such assignments are published in books, pamphlets, and magazine articles on teaching methods. Such suggestions come mainly from creative teachers whose understanding of children and adolescents is derived from much experience with student writing. Only a few research studies, however, have been done in this field, and they have limited value because of the many uncontrolled variables involved. The literature on teaching composition suggests that assignments should (1) be appropriate to the age of children, (2) be based on consideration of previous experiences in writing, (3) be in harmony with composition objectives at different grade levels, and (4) be suitable, in subject matter and skills required, to pupils' needs. The success of some assignments appears to be closely related to the topics chosen and the success of others appears to be linked to the source from which stimulation for writing comes. Many assignments depend entirely on the success of the teacher in developing interest and motivation. Little is known about the precise effects of blocks to expression stemming from feelings of insecurity, hostile attitudes, or lack of knowledge or skill, yet effective assignments should take such matters into consideration.

Some attempts have been made to compare compositions on assigned topics with those initiated in some other way.

In an early study, Sofell (1929) compared three compositions written on self-chosen topics with three written on assigned topics, using 304 pupils in Grades 4–6. Ratings on the Hillegas Scale favored the compositions on self-chosen topics. The assigned topics were (1) What Can I Do To Promote Safety? (2) A Narrow Escape, and (3) How I Should Like to Spend My Vacation.

Howell (1955), working with 24 seven-year-old children, compared 240 written and dictated compositions that grew out of shared learning experiences with compositions on assigned topics. Compositions were analyzed in terms of number of running words, number of different words, and number of generalizations. She found that children wrote more running words and used more different words about a shared experience but dictated more on assigned topics.

Edmund (1958) compared pupils' stories about direct experiences and their stories about experiences derived from books, radio, television, and other sources. Fifth- and seventh-grade pupils wrote compositions of higher creative quality when the writing was based on derived experiences, but there were no differences in the ninth grade papers.

Clark (1954), working with 36 sixth-grade children for a year, studied the writing of these pupils in 21 different kinds of writing situations and some additional voluntary assignments. He found that when pupils wrote compositions involving their own feelings and emotions, they responded more freely and their writing had better quality and interest. Impersonal subjects were handled better when the writer told his feelings about the subject. In highly personal writing, children wrote longer sentences and used more dependent clauses. It should be pointed out, however, that objectivity in writing and the use of illustration and proof naturally place more responsibility on the writer and call for greater effort and control than does the expression of feelings and opinions. Skill in such writing, even though more difficult to attain, has to be learned; the real instructional issue involves judgment as to when instruction should begin and to what extent it should be interspersed with assignments calling for less demanding writing.

E. Smith (1944) studied procedures used to encourage writing in 40 elementary school systems. She analyzed the responses of teachers to questionnaires; observed classroom writing activities; interviewed teachers, pupils, and administrators; and analyzed samples of children's writing. On the basis of these studies, she identified 10 procedures as most useful in encouraging creative writing. Many of these procedures suggest factors related to making effective composition assignments, especially at the elementary school level: (1) providing attractive classrooms rich in materials; (2) encouraging pupils to write from their own interests and needs; (3) providing rich experiences about which a child can express himself; (4) developing sensitivity to good writing which in turn helps a child to improve his own experience; (5) using real needs of children or helping them to develop new ones; (6) providing freedom from fear and helping pupils gain confidence in their ability to create; (7) providing abundant time and opportunity for writing in many areas and in many forms;

(8) developing skill in mechanics without sacrificing spontaneity; (9) sharing the end products of writing; and (10) evaluating the writing in terms of the total growth of the child.

Meckel, Squire, and Leonard (1958) analyzed reports of composition practices secured from every junior and senior high school English teacher in California through an official state survey. Teachers were asked to describe a successful writing assignment. They reported that such assignments developed from literature, personal experiences, classroom discussions, pictures, phonograph recordings, and films. Comparatively few teachers reported getting outstanding papers from routine book reports. Meckel and his co-workers concluded that these teachers' assignments, while designed to stimulate imaginative powers and certain types of verbal skill, did not appreciably require the thought processes, evaluative skills, or skills of organization necessary in writing an expository essay dealing with contemporary issues—the kind of writing typically required of freshmen for placement purposes by the colleges and universities of the state.

In commenting on studies of writing assignments at the elementary school level, Burrows and her associates (1952) pointed out that existing research encourages teachers to use a variety of techniques. Perhaps the most useful insights available, at least at the elementary school level, are those suggested by Burrows' own case studies.

The present status of research on composition assignments indicates that:

1. There is little merit in attempting to determine further whether students write better on assigned topics or unassigned topics. The real issues are whether assignments do or do not facilitate responses reflecting feeling, imagination, or ideas appropriate to the maturity of pupils; whether assignments assist the pupils with the aspects of mechanics, vocabulary, or structure which are involved; and whether assignments motivate students to put forth their best efforts.

2. Expectations of teachers with respect to

standards of achievement must be carefully adjusted to the abilities of pupils so that the standards become goals for improvement rather than obstacles to effort and expression. Additional research on this point would be helpful. From the point of view of the teacher, variables to be considered include accurate knowledge of the difficulty of the composition task and the enabling skills involved in various kinds of writing; knowledge of the characteristics of average, below-average, and superior performance at various grade levels in different kinds of writing; and knowledge of the emotional factors and attitudes involved in the composition process.

3. At the junior and senior high school levels, pupils can be taught procedures for preparing a composition: preview or planning, writing a first draft, proofreading, self-criticism, and revision (Lyman, 1931). Experimentation is needed to ascertain effective methods of incorporating such procedures into assignments.

4. Length of assigned compositions needs additional study. A recent survey, for example, showed that, in some secondary schools, students wrote 10,000-word term papers (Meckel, Squire, & Leonard, 1958). Sometimes, merely writing a series of carefully worded phrases may provide beneficial practice in writing description. Practice in careful generalization may involve writing a carefully and accurately worded sentence. Watts (1944) suggested that three-sentence compositions have certain values. Certain skills can be learned through writing a single paragraph; others require a longer paper. Research might provide helpful answers to the following questions: Can short assignments be devised that will yield improvement in skill? When does length cease to be useful for teaching how to plan and organize? When does it become an obstacle? Are carefully prepared shorter papers more suitable for teaching research techniques than papers of considerable length?

5. More specific knowledge is needed on the relation of planning to the writing process. Such knowledge would be useful in ascertaining (1) what maturity pupils should possess at certain grade levels, and (2) what types of planning are most helpful in teaching different types of writing. What kinds of plans facilitate writing? When is formal outlining helpful and when is it restrictive? When should assignments involve assistance in planning? When should students not be given such assistance?

6. How can the assignment stimulate the imagination of the pupil so that it becomes a creative force arousing him to discover the possibilities of an assignment and helping him develop ideas?

Marking and Evaluating Student Writing

The teacher's treatment of student writing is an important aspect of teaching composition. Principles important at the elementary school level have been outlined by Strickland (1960), who emphasized the importance of adjusting criteria and methods of evaluation to the level and needs of the individual and class. Children's first compositions are dictated to the teacher to write. At this level, said Strickland, the teacher should evaluate the quality of the child's ideas, the evidence they present of the richness or meagerness of his background, and his potentialities for expression. Comments should encourage the child, help him clarify his thinking, and help him express his meaning. These same values should continue to be paramount as the child begins to write for himself, and gradual attempts should be made to develop independence through the use of word lists for vocabulary and spelling, picture dictionaries, models, and guide sheets. Security, interest, and constructive attitudes are important for the child at this stage of development, and Strickland emphasized that grading papers and assigning marks are, therefore, inappropriate at this stage.

In the middle grades Strickland recommended class discussion of writing quality, and attention to the effectiveness of beginnings, conclusions, paragraphs, and plots.

Instruction in manipulation of sentences with suggested changes in the position of words or phrases helps to develop knowledge and skill in sentence structure. Proofreading of rough drafts and revision for a final copy help the child to learn the process of preparing an adequate piece of written work.

For a study of creativity in the writing of elementary pupils, Carlson (1959) devised a scale to be used in scoring original stories.

The development of the student's ability to judge his own work is also an important aspect of evaluation. Lyman (1931) sought to determine the extent to which pupils in Grades 6–9 could be taught to discover and correct language errors in their own compositions; he attempted to establish a work pattern for writing compositions. This pattern included planning, writing a first draft, proofreading and revision, and writing a final copy. He found that pupils could be taught to discover and correct three-fifths of their own errors.

In a survey of practices at the secondary school level (Meckel, Squire, & Leonard, 1958), teachers reported success with the following procedures in teaching pupils to judge and evaluate their compositions: use of a check list of standards developed through discussion with pupils; small-group procedures, especially for reading and discussing first drafts; exhibits of papers showing progress from first drafts to finished manuscripts; reading a paper aloud to a friend; use of student editors; and teacher-student conferences.

Teachers customarily resort to three procedures to improve the quality of compositions: marking errors and writing criticisms on individual papers, reading and discussing individual papers in class, and holding conferences with individual pupils. Because of the number of students for whom one teacher is responsible, conferences cannot be held frequently. Only a few papers can be read and discussed during a class hour. The written comment of the teacher on themes becomes, therefore, a chief method of guiding and directing improvement of writing.

Two studies have been concerned with this phase of composition teaching. Confrey (1927) investigated the comments made by 40 instructors in first-year college English in 11 different colleges and universities. Comments were classified in five categories according to their effectiveness in promoting better writing: worthless, encouraging but not directive, encouraging and directive, condemnatory and not directive, condemnatory and directive. Of the comments studied, 36 per cent were regarded as worthless and 45 per cent as not helpful, so that less than 20 per cent gave the students any direction that would improve their writing.

Dusel (1955b) devised a 12-point scale to be used in discriminating among desirable and undesirable marking practices of teachers. This scale included criteria such as noting clear errors; concern for content as well as errors and form; making appreciative comments; focusing the pupil's attention on important points to work on in the next paper; explaining needed changes in a reasonable, rather than an authoritarian, manner; and making suggestions to the student about necessary corrections rather than making all corrections for him. In commenting on the marking procedures of 200 teachers, Dusel raised questions about the semantic and psychological phases of theme correction as a method of instruction. He warned that young persons attributed varied meanings to terms frequently applied to their writing, such as "awkward," "clumsy," "weak," "disorganized," "confused," and "incoherent."

There appear, however, to have been no actual investigations of student attitudes and responses to teachers' comments on papers. Consequently, research might well be directed to students' semantic and psychological interpretations of theme correction as well as to the effectiveness of methods of handling papers. LaBrant (1951) suggested the following criteria: keep the pupil writing without causing him to fear writing; help him reduce errors without causing him to fear them; encourage him to communicate his feelings and responses to life; and help him accept increasing responsibility for the expression of his ideas.

The adequacy of the teacher's marking of compositions was shown by Dusel (1955a) to be a major determiner of his teaching load. This load was affected by the number of students assigned to him, the amount of practice in writing required of them, and the way in which the teacher marked compositions. Dusel submitted a sample composition of 250 words to 430 teachers with the request that they mark the composition as they marked papers written by their own pupils and then report the exact time required to do so. He then computed the average time required when teachers read papers (1) merely to assign a grade (3.5 minutes), (2) to indicate faults, but not correct them (5.9 minutes), (3) to correct mistakes (5.9 minutes), and (4) to give suggestions designed to teach writing and thinking (8.6 minutes). A teacher with 150 students, who assigned one 250-word composition a week, would have to spend at least 21.5 hours a week reading the papers if he were interested in giving pupils suggestions to improve writing. Since graded compositions glanced at by the pupil and thrown away, or rewritten incorrectly, are of little educative value, Dusel also ascertained the amount of time required to check a pupil's corrections or revisions. He found that an average of seven additional hours a week would be required for a class of 150 students. Thus, for a class of 150 students a total of 28.5 hours a week would be required on an average to read papers adequately and supervise corrections.

The teacher's treatment of his students' papers is related to questions about validity that arise in using essay tests to measure writing ability. Whenever the teacher grades a composition, he in a sense ceases to be a teacher and becomes a judge, often a harsh judge from the point of view of the student. Thus the teacher who reads his pupils' papers with an awareness of the needs of individual writers and the intent of guiding improvement in writing skill assumes a somewhat different role from that of the teacher who acts as an examiner seeking to measure composition skill with accuracy.

The validity and reliability of measurement become of great importance in required writing courses in which students must earn a satisfactory grade. The validity and reliability of measurement become important, also, in research when essay tests are used as one of the measures of gains or losses in skill which are to be attributed to experiments in teaching methods.

During the first quarter of the century, as a result of interest in scientific approaches to teaching, a number of efforts were made to develop composition scales. These scales were described by Hudelson (1923), and Monroe (1923) severely criticized their reliability. Greene (1950), while feeling that such scales had some value, also called attention to their limitations with respect to validity and reliability.

A number of attempts have been made recently to develop handbooks for analysis of composition (California Association of Teachers of English, 1960; Dressel & Mayhew, 1954; Dressel, Schmid, & Kincaid, 1952; *Evaluating ninth-grade themes,* 1953; Grose, Miller, & Steinberg, 1958; Thomas, 1955). While many of these publications present typical compositions scaled according to excellence, the scales have not been subjected to rigorous statistical treatment. The intent of such publications has been to help teachers become aware of phases of writing skill that should receive attention at different levels of instruction, to help them read compositions with more adequate perspective, and to assist them in guiding the writing skill of their pupils. Such guides for theme analysis have often been developed as supervisory devices; they have provided a supervisor, a curriculum director, or a director of a study project with assistance in directing the in-service education of a group of composition instructors.

The major problem of grading essays lies in variation in grades assigned by different readers. Such variation occurs especially when readers do not discuss criteria before reading and marking papers. Diederich (1957), commenting on the difficulties involved, pointed out that when 10 readers read a set of 20 papers without discussing standards, chances are high that papers of average quality will receive every grade from "A" to "F" and that no paper will receive a range of less than three grade points out of a possible five. When two teachers, who are members of a mature and stable composition staff but have no special training in grading, grade each essay independently without knowledge of who wrote the papers, the average correlation between the grades they assign is usually about .55. The correlation between readers, as the Stalnakers (1934, 1937) pointed out, can be raised by carefully training the readers. According to Diederich (1957), outstanding teachers operating under strict rules of grading and careful supervision can raise the correlation to about .70.

Diederich suggested the following three criteria for judging tests of writing ability: (1) The writing assignment must not be extremely unlike the writing pupils will do in the normal course of events—an explanation, a persuasive argument, a single narration of a sequence of events such as one might write in a letter, for example. (2) The paper should not be graded for accuracy and completeness of the writer's knowledge of the subject. (3) The topic must be within the student's comprehension. Difficult subjects increase possibilities of lack of organization, vagueness of statement, and poor sentence structure.

Reliability is influenced by the fact that quality of writing varies from one form of writing to another. Samples of writing done over a semester are obviously a better index of writing ability than any single essay. Diederich (1957) suggested the following procedures to increase reliability in grading papers: (1) All students should write on the same topic. (2) The topic should not be so easy that levels of excellence cannot be determined. (3) All papers should be based on a common set of materials. (4) Readers must be highly competent teachers, especially trained in marking practices, and especially

prepared for grading any specific set of papers by discussing standards and selected papers. (5) Names should be removed from all papers. (6) Two sets of readers should be used, if possible; their grades will make possible calculation of a reliability coefficient which can be checked against research results. (7) Any paper that will make a difference in students' grades should be read twice under conditions that do not permit one reader to know the marks of the other; in case of disagreement, the mean of both readers' marks should be used. (8) If possible, at least two samples of writing should be obtained from each student at different sessions and the grades averaged.

Particularly helpful is Diederich's suggestion that papers be sorted first into five piles in terms of quality, then re-sorted on a second reading into nine piles or stanine groups in order to give special attention to the borderline papers.

Huddleston (1954) reviewed research on the reliability of essay tests in reporting studies conducted by the College Entrance Examination Board on the measurement of ability in English composition. She pointed out that while reader reliabilities of .85 or higher have occasionally been reported, such high correlations are not representative of those usually obtained, and when test-item reliability is considered along with reader reliability, the essay test becomes too unreliable an instrument to measure composition skill as a basis for determining admission to college. An objective English examination developed by the College Board and the verbal score on the Board's Scholastic Aptitude Test have each been demonstrated to be superior to the essay test, the verbal score being most closely related to writing ability. Huddleston concluded that careful statistical analysis of multiple correlations appears to show that measurable "ability to write" is no more than general verbal ability and that this ability can be most reliably measured by a typical verbal-ability test.

A factor-analytic study involving 53 readers from six different professional areas was made by Diederich, French, and Carlton (1961). Resting on a very extensive factual base, results of this study alter somewhat the conclusions drawn by Huddleston. The more recent study revealed five "schools of thought," emphasizing:

I. *Ideas:* relevance, clarity, quantity, development, persuasiveness;
II. *Form:* organization and analysis;
III. *Flavor:* style, interest, sincerity;
IV. *Mechanics:* specific errors in grammar, punctuation, etc.;
V. *Wording:* choice and arrangement of words.

No standards or criteria for judging the papers were suggested to the readers. Instead, they were told to use "whatever hunches, intuitions, or preferences you normally use in deciding that one paper is better than another." They sorted the papers into nine piles in order of "general merit." The only restriction was that all nine piles must be used, with not less than 4 per cent of the papers in any pile.

The five reader-factors or "schools of thought" were identified by a "blind" classification of 11,018 comments written on 3,557 papers that were graded high (7-8-9) or low (1-2-3) by the three highest and three lowest readers on each factor. The person who classified the comments did not know the standing of any reader on any factor. In addition to the reader factors, three College Board tests taken by these students formed a separate "test-factor" that had practically zero correlations with all reader-factors except Mechanics (.50) and Wording (.45).

It was not the purpose of this study to achieve a high degree of unanimity among the readers but to reveal the differences of opinion that prevail in uncontrolled grading—both in the academic community and in the educated public. To that end, the readers included college English teachers, social scientists, natural scientists, writers and editors, lawyers, and business executives. Nonetheless, it was disturbing to find that 94 per cent of the papers received either seven, eight, or nine of the nine possible grades; that no paper received less than five different grades; and that the median correlation between readers was .31. Readers in each field, however, agreed slightly better with the English teachers than with one another (Diederich, French, & Carlton, 1961, Abstract).

The Preparation of Composition Teachers

The preparation of the teacher of language and composition merits more research. Several recent studies have been concerned with this problem. The National Council of Teachers of English (1961) summarized statistical information from a number of surveys. Because of a rapidly increasing school population, the demand for English teachers has increased faster than the number adequately trained. The Council's report revealed that one-fourth of all elementary school teachers were not college graduates, that more than three-fifths of the colleges preparing elementary school teachers did not require their candidates to complete course work in grammar and usage, and that 80 per cent of the colleges training elementary school teachers did not require their elementary school trainees to complete course work in composition beyond the freshman level. The report stated further that only 41 per cent of all colleges require candidates for secondary school teaching to complete a course in advanced composition, only one-fourth of them require a course in the history of the English language, and only 17 per cent of them require a course in modern English grammar.

Nordberg (1949) surveyed research on teaching grammar, usage, composition, and spelling and constructed a test to measure knowledge of the findings of such research. After administering the test to a group of student teachers, he concluded that they were not well acquainted with such research findings.

Scofield (1955) studied younger teachers to determine the extent to which they employed methods in the classroom which they had been taught in methods courses. She found not only that the teachers did not use many of the procedures which they had been taught, but that after being in the classroom, they tended to adopt routine procedures often contrary to those they had been taught during their training.

RESEARCH ON TEACHING
LITERATURE

Research on teaching literature has been mainly of the following kinds: studies of the reading interests of pupils, including both spontaneous reading interests and patterns of interest resulting from classroom activities and teacher guidance; studies of the merit of extensive as opposed to intensive teaching of literature; observations and surveys of classroom practices; studies of responses of pupils to determine the impact made by the reading and discussion of literature; studies of the factors in comprehension of literature made to enable construction of more valid and reliable tests. Before turning to these kinds of research, however, we shall consider the objectives of instruction in literature.

The Objectives of
Instruction in
Literature

Research on teaching literature, like research on teaching composition, must be interpreted in terms of the changing character of American education, especially at the secondary school level. In the early years of this century, the literature program of the secondary school was influenced by reading lists prepared by the National Conference on Uniform Entrance Requirements in English, which suggested aims for English study as well as standards of achievement for college entrance examinations. The purpose of such lists was to encourage the reading of a common body of literary materials.

As a result of the increasing number of noncollege students in the secondary school and the consequent discontent of teachers and students at having to meet college requirements, a national movement for the reorganization of secondary school English was started at the Boston meeting of the National Education Association in 1910. The meeting led to the organization of the National Council of Teachers of English and the publication of a statement (Hosic, 1917),

prepared by a joint committee of the National Council and the Commission on the Reorganization of Secondary Education of the National Education Association. This report sought to free the high school curriculum from the restrictions of college-preparatory reading lists and set forth the following objectives:

1. To broaden, deepen, and enrich the imaginative life of the student.
2. To provide materials out of which may be created worthy and lasting ideals of life and conduct.
3. To raise the level of appreciation and enjoyment in reading.
4. To provide intellectual and spiritual stimulation.
5. To encourage development of intellectual faculties: sensitivity, imagination, thinking, and interpretation.

During the next three or four decades, the reaction against the influence of the colleges and the type of literary study recommended by college entrance committees led to experimental programs of extensive reading and to programs that emphasized literature as a means of education rather than as an end in itself (D. V. Smith, 1933).

During the years between 1917 and the Second World War, objectives in teaching literature were influenced by three factors: (1) publications of the National Council of Teachers of English (1935, 1936), particularly *An Experience Curriculum in English* and *A Correlated Curriculum,* (2) curriculum studies sponsored by the Eight-Year Study of the Progressive Education Association (e.g., Rosenblatt, 1937), and (3) research on reading interests.

An Experience Curriculum in English (National Council of Teachers of English, 1935) maintained that the literature curriculum should "consist of experiences with and through stories, poems, plays, essays, and books of information or discussion addressed to the general reader," that literary selections must be within the intellectual and emotional range of pupils at the time they are read, that much of the classwork as well as the home reading must be entirely individual, and that discussion of literature in the classroom should be limited to such matters as main events and impressions, larger phases of character, and theme—the classroom taking on the atmosphere of a literary club in which the teacher is the most experienced member.

A Correlated Curriculum (National Council of Teachers of English, 1936) suggested means for correlating literature with other school subjects, propounded methods of teaching in which literature and the arts might be combined in certain curricular experiences, and called attention to the possibilities of a humanities course in which literature, art, and music were combined with history.

Among the publications associated with the Eight-Year Study was *Literature as Exploration* (Rosenblatt, 1937), which emphasized the dynamic nature of the literary experience as an interaction between the stimuli present in the literary work and the mind and emotions of the reader. To teach literature from this point of view was essentially to promote exploration of human experience. The student was to choose literary materials that had potentialities for significant interaction with his personality. Through literature, the reader, according to this theory, may explore his own nature, the world in which he lives, other personalities, and other ways of life.

Another significant outcome of the Eight-Year Study was an analysis of the objective of literary *appreciation* in terms of typical pupil behaviors that could be observed or inferred by the teacher and thus serve as a guide for classroom practice (Smith & Tyler, 1942). Experiments in measuring reading interests during the Study led to the formulation of categories to describe desirable dimensions of growth. Generally, the 30 high schools which participated in the Eight-Year Study attempted (1) to promote more individualized instruction in literature, (2) to encourage wide reading, and (3) to develop patterns of interest in books that would lead to desirable

lifelong reading habits. The development of school libraries through the cooperation of English teachers and librarians was recognized as an important phase of such programs (LaBrant, 1936).

Studies of the reading interests of children and adolescents have influenced the content of anthologies, have affected reading lists for children and adolescents, have been utilized by librarians in developing school library collections, and have affected the supplementary reading programs in the junior and senior high school.

During the Second World War, the War Department contracted with the University of Chicago Board of Examinations to construct tests to determine the amount of credit to be given servicemen for work taken under special programs or by correspondence. White and Enochs (1944), for purposes of test construction, worked with a group of specialists in English instruction from various sections of the country and developed objectives for the teaching of high school literature based on the suggestions of their consultants. These objectives were statements of desirable outcomes for teaching the reading and interpretation of literature in Grades 10, 11, and 12. The emphasis in these objectives was not on the student's acquaintance with particular literary works, but on his ability to read and interpret. The major objectives included abilities and skills in (1) getting the "plain sense" of the material; (2) reading *critically,* with attention to the relationship of ideas and the quality of writing; (3) going beyond the written word to implications, points of view, and future actions of characters; (4) reacting emotionally and imaginatively, as in identifying with situations, or being sensitive to and enjoying artistry of expression; (5) incorporating reading experiences into one's self, so as to develop an understanding of man, society, and institutions, or refine one's personal-social philosophy, or develop new interests and habits; and (6) becoming acquainted with an increasing number of the books and authors that have made significant contributions to our culture.

Recognizing the need for re-examination of the English program at all levels of instruction, the Commission on the English Curriculum of the National Council of Teachers of English (1952, 1954, 1956) published three volumes suggesting objectives and curricular designs for the elementary and secondary school. The Commission has contended that literature, as the imaginative interpretation of human experience, should have a significant place in the curriculum and should not be neglected in favor of reading that is merely informative and factual; that the teaching of literature must bring books and readers together in a way that will have meaning, bring satisfaction, and arouse a desire for further reading; that while occasional reading in common by all members of a class may help to introduce a unit of study, to transmit ideas, or to bring about shared aesthetic enjoyment, different materials must be provided for individuals and groups within a class; that experience in choosing books is necessary for the development of standards for personal reading; that discerning reading of magazines and newspapers should have a place in the school and college program; and that radio, motion pictures, and television contribute to the study of literature (National Council of Teachers of English, 1952).

Recent developments have made it clear that teachers of English do not at the present time agree as to what the curriculum in literature should be. The national debate over education is reflected in a disagreement as to basic issues in the teaching of literature (*An Articulated English Program*, 1959; *The Basic Issues in the Teaching of English*, 1958). After keeping themselves remote from public school instruction for most of the century, college and university professors are now assessing the secondary school curriculum. They are especially concerned with the increase in the number of college preparatory students in the high school. Recent statements on the literature program by professors of English are alike in several respects: They emphasize the critical importance of literature as a *humane* study, stress the need for a common literary background if the cultural and humanistic heritage is to be a part of education, and argue for the development of a sequence of instruction in representative literary works, especially for the more capable students (Kitzhaber, Gorrell, & Roberts, 1961; San Francisco Curriculum Survey Committee, 1960). The most recent developments with respect to the objectives of literature teaching suggest in part, then, a return to the philosophy of instruction dominant in the first part of the century prior to the democratization of secondary education.

Reading Interest Studies

As an area of research, the study of reading interests involves two questions: What do people read, and Why do they read it? To secure information on what pupils read, teachers and researchers have used questionnaires, check lists of titles, reading records, records of library use and circulation, and interviews. The validity of data obtained by such instruments always depends on the availability of reading material and the extent of freedom of choice. That is, data showing what pupils read is not a true reflection of interests unless pupils have been able to select from a variety of books and unless they have had freedom of choice (Carnovsky, 1934). Changes in the type of books published may affect book collections in schools and public libraries and likewise affect the preferences of children (Rankin, 1944). This source of change affects current fashions in the themes of adolescent fiction, especially as the writing and publishing of books for children and adolescents develops into a business.

Studies of the reading interests of children have revealed that patterns of interest may vary with maturity, sex, and intelligence (Gray, 1955; Norvell, 1958; Robinson, 1955; Russell, 1949). Studies have variously described reading interests in terms of the types of literature read (Kangley, 1938; Norvell, 1950, 1958; Smith & Tyler, 1942); in terms of the characteristics of literature which have interest value (Kangley, 1938; Krieg, 1943; Shepard, 1959); and in terms of satisfactions derived by the readers (Dunkel, 1947).

On the assumption that interests are a primary source of pupil motivation, research on reading interests has had significant implications for teaching method, especially in suggesting points at which instruction should begin in the literature class. While some teachers have regarded interest patterns as the major criterion for determining content and teaching procedures, it also seems necessary that the goals of the teacher be focused on the development of new interests. Estimates of the effectiveness of teaching in improving reading interests have used categories such as the following: (1) increase in the amount of reading, (2) variety of subjects read about or literary types, and (3) maturity of books read (Meckel, 1948; Smith & Tyler, 1942). In some cases, reading records have been designed to provide information concerning sources from which students obtain books; such information helps the teacher or researcher estimate the relative influence of classroom, school library, community library, home, or newsstand (Smith & Tyler, 1942). Reading records have also been designed to supply information about the general reaction of the student to different books (National Council of Teachers of English, 1956).

Extensive and Intensive Teaching of Literature

Since it has been assumed that the teaching of literature in school should affect the reading habits and interests of pupils after they leave school, the attitudes of pupils and individualization of instruction have both been regarded as of great significance in the English class. Closely associated with the problems of attitudes and individualized reading has been the issue of extensive and intensive teaching of literature. It has been assumed customarily that intensive study and analysis have an adverse effect on attitudes and interests, but this assumption obscures certain basic principles: (1) that pupils need litera-ture-reading experiences that develop depth of insight, (2) that unless pupils do considerable reading that is enjoyable, they are not likely to have sufficient practice in reading to develop reading skill or to acquire the habit of reading, and (3) that improvement in literary taste is not likely to develop either in an atmosphere that permits no choice or in a setting that provides no guidance.

The most careful attempt to compare the results of extensive and intensive teaching of literature was an early experimental study carried on for a year in eleventh-grade classes by Coryell (1927). Experimental and control classes were divided into superior, average, and low groups according to previous achievement in English, Terman IQ, and reading-age and reading-quotient as measured by the Thorndike-McCall Reading Scale. Three classes were taught by extensive methods and three by intensive methods; three other classes were used as controls.

To develop criteria for judging the relative success of the two methods, objectives were formulated for each type of literature taught. Specific objectives, based upon a summary prepared by a national committee on reading, were ranked in importance by five teachers. The average rankings favored such objectives as grasping the meaning of a selection as a whole, reacting to mood, and interpreting by relating to one's own experience. Rankings did not favor objectives related to formal aspects of literature, such as style, technique, literary history, form and details, vocabulary, and information. The objectives so ranked were then used to determine content for a series of tests on specific literary works. The tests consisted of multiple-choice, true-false, and matching items.

To ascertain the superiority of one method over another, the following procedures were used: (1) Achievement was compared on the basis of mean scores of the different groups on objective tests on literature; on a battery of tests consisting of the Thorndike-McCall Reading Scale, the Lagosa-McCoy Tests in Appreciation of Literature, the Abbott-Trabue Exercises in Judging Poetry, and the

Thorndike Tests of Word Knowledge; and on the uniform school examination in literature and the Regents Examination in Literature. (2) Stenographic reports of 12 lessons were analyzed quantitatively according to the specific objectives implicit in the teaching, and comparisons were made between the experimental classes and the controls. (3) Students' written comments on their year's work in English were analyzed and rated according to a seven-point scale in terms of enthusiasm or displeasure.

The major findings evident in the Coryell data were as follows: (1) There were no statistically significant differences in achievement between the extensive and intensive groups on any of the tests. (2) The low extensive reading group, however, made gains on the Thorndike-McCall Reading Scale that were significantly higher than the low intensive study group, suggesting that the greater amount of reading practice and the type of class work were of special assistance to the less capable readers. (3) The extensive reading group read and discussed six times as much literature as did the intensive group. (4) Quantitative analysis of stenographic reports of recitations showed that, in the extensive reading group, objectives deemed to be of greatest importance by judges were given three times as much emphasis as in the intensive group. (5) Pupils' comments on their English work at the end of the year showed greater enthusiasm on the part of pupils taught by the extensive method. (6) Pupil activity in terms of discussion was greater in the extensive reading classes. (7) Although given no suggestions, pupils in the extensive reading groups commented on the value of wide reading and mentioned the effect of the year's work in English on their reading habits.

Norvell (1941), using 24 experimental classes, each matched with a control class and taught by the same teacher, also attempted to ascertain the merits of instruction which emphasized extensive reading as compared with instruction emphasizing the intensive study of a few works of literature by all members of a class. Classes were matched on the basis of

scores on the Thorndike-McCall Reading Scale for Understanding of Sentences. A second form of the same test was used at the end of the experiment to measure gains, and scores on the Regents Examination were compared. Norvell found small but significantly greater gains on these measures for the students in the extensive group. Superior pupils taught by the extensive method made greater gains than weak students, who progressed about equally under the two methods.

LaBrant's survey (1961) of the merits of extensive reading is the only study of which the writer is aware that attempts to appraise the teaching of literature in terms of its effects on lifelong reading habits. The LaBrant survey consisted of interviews with members of a high school class 20 years after graduation. The program of extensive reading in the school emphasized individualized reading by the students and was characterized by a high degree of interest in the students and their individual needs on the part of the teachers and librarian. The high school program stressed personal contact and discussion between teachers and individual students, careful guidance in the selection of books and periodicals, and the development in the students of a sense of responsibility for their own progress. LaBrant's study indicated that adult reading patterns were sufficiently superior to warrant satisfaction on the part of the school; moreover, members of the class appeared to be applying the basic principles used in the school in guiding the reading of their own children.

Surveys of General Classroom Practice

Several surveys have been made recently of the status of the teaching of literature in certain parts of the nation. In Wisconsin, for example, Pooley and Williams (1948) visited several hundred classrooms in elementary schools. Their reports indicated that (1) at the elementary school level little classroom time is given to literature and, although students are encouraged to read books, many schools, especially those in rural areas, have poor book collections; (2) in Grades 7 and 8, literature from anthologies is studied, but not in a way that develops appreciation; and (3) in Grades 11 and 12, while literature occupies half the teaching time, factual details are stressed at the expense of insight and understanding of literary values, and there is a tendency to have pupils study works beyond their comprehension.

In Georgia, Farmer and Freeman (1952) found that (1) in elementary schools, only 4 per cent of the classroom time was devoted to literature, and (2) in high schools, literature was given approximately 25 per cent of the total time devoted to English.

In California, the State Department of Education (*English Language Arts in California Public High Schools,* 1957) collected information about teachers' opinions on the organization of literature teaching in the secondary school. Organization of literature by themes, or topics, ranked first in the preferences of teachers and that by literary types second. Of the teachers surveyed, 16 per cent thought literature should be separated from composition or oral instruction and taught in different courses, 29 per cent thought literature should be taught in separate units, and 30 per cent thought that separate days of the week should be devoted to literature, composition, and oral instruction.

In Portland, Oregon, a survey of the high school curriculum was conducted by consultants from college and university English departments, who visited classrooms, examined textbooks and study guides, and conferred with teachers (Kitzhaber, Gorrell, & Roberts, 1961). The report of this survey is significant in indicating how the public school English program is appraised from the perspective of college teachers of literature. The college teachers viewed the high school program in terms of its value for college preparation and its relation to the curricula of college English departments. They did not consider its value as general education for all kinds of high school students. The college consultants criticized the lack of literary merit of many of the books on reading lists, the small amount of common reading done in classes, and the absence of a sequential pattern of instruction, particularly in the ninth and tenth grades.

Responses to Literature

Studies of responses to literature are of special significance for research on teaching. Waples, Berelson, and Bradshaw (1940), defining the scope of reading behavior as an area of research, pointed out that any model for research must include not only an analysis of the impact or effect of the reading act, but also analyses of the content of the reading matter and of the predispositions of the reader. Russell (1958), reviewing over 73 studies on the impact of reading, found four variables mentioned: the form of materials, their content of ideas, the reader himself, and the setting or matrix in which overt responses are made. Russell concluded that, while we are beginning to get clues about the kinds of reactions we can expect from individuals of different backgrounds, interests, and personality patterns, it is difficult to disentangle the influences of reading from those of other activities.

Emotional responses to literature are complicated and individualistic. Many motives cause a person to read, even in a single reading experience. Waples and his associates (1940) maintained that people read to gain prestige, to escape from the pressures of reality, to get respite, to find security for their beliefs and behavior, to find reinforcement for their beliefs and attitudes, to get information, and a few, to enrich their aesthetic experience. In attempting to determine the satisfactions college students derive from reading fiction, the staff of the Co-operative Study in General Education devised the following categories: (1) relaxation and pastime; (2) escape; (3) associational values, such as being reminded of past experiences and pleasant episodes; (4) information, including that relevant to personal needs and concerns; (5)

technical-critical satisfactions, including reactions to technical aspects of fiction and aspects of criticism; (6) "self-development," including satisfaction of desires for status or personality improvement (Dunkel, 1947).

The study of responses to literature is further complicated by the fact that what may appear to be purely literary responses or intellectual judgments, may, in terms of subconscious motivations, be actually quite another kind of response. Thus, an adequate description of responses to literature requires analysis not only in terms of literary components or surface motivations, but also in terms of the insights of clinical psychologists into human personality. This requirement holds especially for the dynamic mechanisms involved in identifications made by readers with characters in fiction, in reactions to emotional situations, and in responses to content involving emotionally charged attitudes such as social sensitivity or prejudice. Consequently, research on responses to literature should be designed to use case studies of subjects about whose personality organization and emotional patterns much is known. Such research still remains to be done.

Since responses to literature cannot be directly observed or adequately measured during the reading act, the nature of such responses has to be inferred. A number of studies of students' responses to literature have been conducted in teaching situations. The methods used to secure data have included the questionnaire (Dunkel, 1947), objective-test items (Loban, 1954), analysis of freely written responses (Meckel, 1946), analysis of class discussions (Loban, Ryan, & Squire, 1961; Taba, 1955), and examination of recorded interviews (Squire, 1956). Data have been obtained by these methods after students have read certain pieces of literature and, in some studies, at certain stages during the reading.

A major problem in such research has been to determine a conceptual framework in terms of which questionnaires may be designed, objective-test items constructed, or a scheme developed for analysis of written responses, discussions, or interviews. Such a framework is likely to be affected by the objectives of literary instruction (Loban, 1954; Lodge, 1956; Meckel, 1946; Squire, 1956; Taba, 1955), by the fact that literary responses are both intellectual and emotional in quality, by the psychological orientation of the researcher (Muller, 1942; Waples, Berelson, & Bradshaw, 1940), by the type of literature involved (Loban, 1954; Lodge, 1956; McConnell, 1952; Meckel, 1946; Richards, 1930; Squire, 1956), and by the nature of the ideas, plot situations, and characters which are potential stimuli within a particular literary work (Loban, 1954; Meckel, 1946; Squire, 1956).

General procedures for content analysis have been described by Berelson (1952). Richards' study (1930) of interpretation suggests categories for analysis of pupils' reactions to poetry. McConnell (1952) developed a scheme for analyzing biographies for children and young adults. Krieg (1943) worked out categories to be used in analyzing fiction in terms of its potential sources of appeal for younger readers. Taba (1955) suggested categories for analyzing responses to fiction, when the latter was used by teachers to promote sensitivity to human problems, values, and feelings. Meckel (1946) and Squire (1956) developed schemes for content analysis that attempted to take account of both intellectual and emotional responses to fiction. White (1947), a psychologist, devised a system of psychoanalytic categories for studying the dominant value system of a writer as projected through his work. Such a scheme could be adapted also to analysis of responses to literature that might occur by written discourse, recorded interviews, or discussions.

An unguided reading response is likely to be quite personal and often not in the direction desired by the teacher. This fact has been substantiated by a number of studies. Irion (1925), for example, secured information on reading comprehension difficulties of pupils in the study of literature. Crossen (1948), Jackson (1944), and McCaul (1944) demonstrated the effects of prejudices and attitudes on comprehension. Waples and his colleagues (1940) have pointed out that readers prefer material that reinforces their own beliefs and feelings and tend to be dissatisfied with or even openly dislike material at variance with their own beliefs and feelings.

Richards' study (1930) of the interpretation of poetry by Cambridge students showed how students may err in attempting to grasp the meaning of a poem. He called attention to the misleading effects of the reader's memories of some personal scene or adventure; of erratic associations and stereotyped responses; of confusion caused by doctrinal dispositions of the reader, especially when his beliefs conflict with those presented in a poem; and of the effect of general critical misconceptions and technical judgments. Meckel (1946) suggested that in emotionally unpleasant reading situations, the reader tends to reject content that suggests, or is dynamically related to, areas of experience in which he has emotional tension and also tends to suppress or resist identification with characters associated with such content.

Loban (1954), in his study of literature and social sensitivity, found that mere exposure to stories read aloud to adolescents did not bring about any apparent change in the group of students rated as having least social sensitivity; discussion was necessary for the students to achieve desired insights. Taba (1955) found that factual restatement of what transpired in a story was the main type of response made by upper elementary-grade pupils 'in discussion, that only about 12 per cent of the students generalized beyond the immediate facts of the story, but that group discussion appeared to push the thinking to levels which pupils as individuals ordinarily did not attempt. Squire's data (1956) showed that factual retelling of story content in interviews, without attempts to interpret or generalize, was a characteristic response of students of lesser reading ability.

The Discussion Method

Since pupils left to their own resources are likely not to acquire the insights desired by the teacher, the discussion method becomes of great significance in the effective teaching of literature. Through discussion, the teacher can lead pupils to perceptions and discoveries that they are not likely to apprehend or understand without his guidance.

Heaton and Lewis (1955) held that discussions of literature are much more effective if the teacher plans a sequence. Sequence should be planned, they maintained, both in terms of the concepts the teacher wishes students to learn and in terms of the discussion process itself. They suggested the following steps as being psychologically effective in discussing fiction which is used to develop social sensitivity: Step 1. Telling what occurred in the story itself in order to identify incidents, feelings, and relationships under discussion. Step 2. Analyzing what happened in terms of feelings of characters, such as shifts in relationship or changes in behavior. Step 3. Identifying similar incidents in experiences of pupils or experiences of characters in other stories. Step 4. Exploring the consequences of certain behavior or feelings. Step 5. Coming to a conclusion or generalizing so that conceptualization is sharp and effective.

While the effectiveness of the Heaton-Lewis discussion pattern has been demonstrated in classrooms (Taba, 1955), research is still needed to define psychological phases of the discussion process when literature is used for different purposes, when literary types other than fiction are involved, and when different kinds of concepts are emphasized by the teacher.

Methods of evaluating the effectiveness of classroom discussions of fiction were described by Taba (1955). Statements made by pupils were coded and classified into four main categories: (1) projections, including statements that represented attempts to understand the story, to explain and evaluate behavior, or to suggest courses of action for characters; (2) generalizations, representing interpretations carried beyond the immediate facts of the story; (3) self-references, or applications of story content to personal experiences, and (4) irrelevancies, i.e., statements unconnected with the story being discussed. Through coding, the researcher saw patterns of individual responses in discussion and described patterns of thinking of the group.

On the basis of the patterns of readers' responses in discussions of fiction, Taba believed it was possible to distinguish types of readers: (1) readers who enter into a story freely and rather spontaneously, but who do not generalize from it or relate it to previous experience; (2) readers in whom a story touches off associations with their own experience so strongly that they appear to get meaning from stories primarily through such experiences; (3) readers who can project their thinking into the situations, motivations, and actions of characters, for example, and can generalize so as to attain new insights.

Squire (1956), however, considered responses to vary so much with individual pieces of literature and the individual reading response to be such a complex of differently balanced factors that it was impossible to construct a typology of this kind. The responses of his students to short stories were described by the following categories: (1) literary judgments, which were direct or implied judgments on the story as a story; (2) interpretational responses, in which the reader generalized and attempted to discover the meaning of the story, the motivational forces, or the nature of the characters; (3) narrational reactions, in which the reader repeated words, details, or incidents without attempting to interpret or generalize; (4) associational responses, in which the reader associated characters, ideas, events, or places in the story with his own experiences; (5) self-involvement responses, in which the reader associated himself with the behavior and emotional reactions of characters by identification or rejection; and (6) prescriptive judgments, responses in which the reader prescribed a certain course of behavior for characters.

Factors in Comprehension of Literature

The intellectual components involved in the interpretation of literature have been studied mainly in connection with test construction. Irion (1925) designed tests to measure five aspects of comprehension: (1) "broad" reading comprehension, (2) fact comprehension, (3) expression comprehension, (4) word knowledge, and (5) general comprehension. Cavins (1928) prepared poetry tests to measure comprehension of central thought and understanding of factual background, diction, involved imagery, narrative thread, vocabulary, symbolism, allusions, and historical connections. Hartley (1930) constructed tests to measure four aspects of the comprehension of poetry: (1) meanings conveyed by figures or symbols; (2) meanings conveyed through sense impression; (3) meanings conveyed by suggestion or implication, as through word values or rhythm; (4) literal expression in passages that are condensed or structurally irregular.

F. B. Davis (1944) factor-analyzed tests embodying concepts of reading comprehension held by specialists in reading. He identified nine skills, some or all of which may be involved in the comprehension of literature: (1) knowledge of word meanings, (2) ability to select the appropriate meaning for a word or phrase in the light of its context, (3) ability to follow the organization of a passage and to identify antecedents and referents in it, (4) ability to select the main thought of a passage, (5) ability to answer questions that are specifically answered in a passage, (6) ability to answer questions that are answered in a passage but not in the words in which the questions are asked, (7) ability to draw inferences from a passage, (8) ability to recognize the literary devices used in a passage and to determine tone and mood, and (9) ability to determine a writer's purpose, intent, and point of view.

Harris (1948) reported another important factor analysis of literary comprehension. He conceived of literary comprehension as involving four kinds of operations: (1) translating, which includes attempts to get meaning from a passage which is obscure because of unfamiliar words, uncommon terms, figuratively used terms or groups of terms, or difficult structures of word patterns; (2) summarizing, including such behaviors as combining specific details in a passage with other passages or with other literary works; (3) inferring tone, mood, and intent; (4) relating techniques and meaning. This analysis led Harris to specify seven components of skill in the comprehension of literary materials:

1. Recognition of synonyms or equivalents for uncommon words and groups of words as they are used in the context.
2. Recognition of equivalents for words and groups of words that are used figuratively or as symbols.
3. Recognition of antecedents of pronouns, of subjects and predicates in loosely organized statements or in statements with inverted or uncommon word order, and of missing parts of elliptical statements.
4. Recognition of summaries of ideas expressed or implied, including the main idea as well as subordinate ideas, the subject of the discourse, the situation being discussed or described, etc.
5. Recognition of summaries of characteristics of persons or characters described in the passage, including their actions, motives, attitudes, etc.
6. Recognition of the author's attitude toward his subject, his characters, etc., of his mood or emotion, and of his intent or purpose.
7. Recognition of the relationship between technique and meaning, including the function of images, illustrations, and the like, the function of comparisons, the function of sentence structure and word choice, etc. (Harris, 1948, p. 332).

Harris constructed tests of the above skills and found one general factor running through all seven. He found, moreover, no evidence to support the contention that the comprehension of poetry and of prose demands different abilities.

Promising Research Areas

Past research on teaching literature and current articles on teaching English suggest three important areas of investigation: research problems suggested by the statement of the Joint Committee on Basic Issues established by the Modern Language Association, the College English Association, the American Studies Association, and the National Council of Teachers of English; studies of the kinds of classroom atmosphere and learning conditions that generate valid responses to literature; and investigations concerned with effective uses of audio-visual aids.

Implications of the Basic Issues statement. The statement of the Joint Committee is predicated on the conception that the major educational value of literature is to transmit the humanistic and cultural heritage. The Joint Committee asks whether or not there are certain literary works that ought to be known by all educated men and women (*An Articulated English Program,* 1959; *The Basic Issues in the Teaching of English,* 1958). From the point of view of curriculum design, at least three important problems follow: identification of these works, their placement in an effective instructional sequence, and development of teaching methods. Research might profitably investigate, therefore, the nature of responses of pupils of different levels of ability to particular pieces of literature, the grade levels where desirable responses are most likely to occur, and the approaches and methods that elicit most effective pupil responses.

Classroom atmosphere and approach. A promising area for research on teaching literature is the kind of classroom atmosphere and teacher-pupil relationship that encourages fortuitous experiences with literature. Rosenblatt (1937) discussed phases of teaching that suggest hypotheses for such research. She emphasized that teachers of literature are primarily concerned with "transactions between readers and books," not books per se. The atmosphere in the classroom, she explained, must permit a personal response

by the student. Frank expressions of boredom or even of rigorous rejection are more
valid starting points for learning than docile
attempts to say or feel what the teacher
wants. To lay the basis for lifelong personal
relationships with books, according to Rosenblatt, students need classroom situations that
(1) provide literature for which pupils have
emotional and experiential readiness, (2) encourage personal integrity in relationships to
literature, and (3) offer pupils a chance to
share and compare literary reactions and follow a personal bent. These ideas suggest important problems for investigation.

Audio-visual teaching devices. The extensive use of audio-visual equipment in the
training programs of the armed services has
greatly stimulated the use of such equipment
in public school instruction over the past two
decades. Research is greatly needed, however, to demonstrate the usefulness of audio-
visual techniques in teaching literature, particularly as they apply to learning problems
resulting from the differences in abilities of
students. The literature on audio-visual methods mainly describes classroom procedures,
not research.

1. Recorded literature. Some types of literature, such as plays and poetry, are written
for oral presentation. Recordings of such literature by professional readers or actors can
be used to heighten the student's awareness
of artistic and literary values. Moreover, some
pieces of literature that are difficult to comprehend when read silently may be more
teachable when students can hear the same
works through records. Qualities of style and
form which frequently elude a student in
silent reading might be more easily analyzed
if approached first through recordings.

2. The tape recorder. In addition to its use
for presenting professional recordings, the
tape recorder offers special opportunities for
oral interpretations of literature which further comprehension and appreciation. Such
oral readings by students may be straight
reproductions of literary works, productions
of dramatized versions, or interpretations
which require pupils to study a work for
editing or script-writing purposes.

3. Films. Films may be used by the teacher
of literature for a number of purposes. Plot
changes in a film version of a work may help
students to understand such concepts as the
motivation of characters, plausibility of incident, and outcome of plot. Films also may
assist students in understanding artistry of
form, the effectiveness of selected details and
incidents, and devices for suggestion of
meaning, such as symbolism.

4. Television. Programs of literary productions, especially of plays, panel discussions
of specific literary works by critics, and lectures on television may be used by teachers
to encourage students to make use of these
programs as part of their homework assignments.

Such questions as the following suggest
needed research:

1. What methods of using recordings and
films are most effective?

2. Do students whose classroom experiences include professional recordings of literary works make greater gains in knowledge and appreciation than those who study
the same works without recordings? What
differences in attitude and in reading habits
are involved? Are there differences in the
permanency of learning?

3. To what extent can the quality of literature appreciated by less able readers be
improved by the use of recorded literature?
To what extent can the use of recorded literature make possible the teaching of a common body of significant literature to all
students?

4. Does the use of recorded literature make
possible more effective discussions of literature for average and below-average students?

5. If school libraries were equipped with
listening equipment, to what extent could
classroom experiences be supplemented by
outside listening? Over a period of several
years, what is likely to be the cumulative
effect of such a program on the student's
acquaintance with significant literary works?

6. How can concepts of characterization,
plot, and style be effectively taught through
the use of supplemental aids such as recordings and films?

7. What results can be obtained from effective use of the combined resources of recordings, films, and home television?

REFERENCES

Anderson, J. E. Principles of growth and maturity in language. *Elem. Engl. Rev.*, 1941, 18, 250–254, 277.

An articulated English program: A hypothesis to test. *Publ. Mod. Lang. Ass. Amer.*, 1959, 74, 13–19.

Artley, A. S., Hildreth, Gertrude, Townsend, A., Berry, A., & Dawson, M. *Interrelations among the language arts*. Champaign, Ill.: National Council of Teachers of English, 1954.

Ash, I. O. An experimental evaluation of the stylistic approach in teaching written composition in the junior high school. *J. exp. Educ.*, 1935, 4, 54–62.

Asker, W. Does knowledge of formal grammar function? *Sch. & Soc.*, 1923, 17, 109–111.

The basic issues in the teaching of English. American Studies Association, College English Association, Modern Language Association, National Council of Teachers of English. Champaign, Ill.: National Council of Teachers of English, 1958.

Bear, Mata V. Children's growth in the use of written language. *Elem. Engl. Rev.*, 1939, 16, 312–319.

Berelson, B. *Content analysis in communications research*. Glencoe, Ill.: Free Press, 1952.

Bloch, B., & Trager, G. *Outline of linguistic analysis*. Baltimore: Waverly Press, 1942. (Published for Linguistic Society of America)

Bloomfield, L. *Language*. New York: Holt, 1933.

Boder, D. P. The adjective-verb-quotient: A contribution to the psychology of language. *Psychol. Rec.*, 1940, 3, 310–343.

Boraas, J. Formal English grammar and the practical mastery of English. Unpublished doctoral dissertation, Univer. of Minnesota, 1917.

Briggs, T. H. Formal English grammar as a discipline. *Teachers Coll. Rec.*, 1913, 14, No. 4, 1–93.

Burrows, Alvina, Ferebee, June, Jackson, Dorothy, & Saunders, Dorothy. *They all want to write*. (Rev. ed.) New York: Prentice-Hall, 1952.

Butterfield, Clair J. The effect of a knowledge of certain grammatical elements on the acquisition and retention of related punctuation skills. Unpublished doctoral dissertation, Univer. of Iowa, 1945.

California Association of Teachers of English. *A scale for the evaluation of high school student essays*. Champaign, Ill.: National Council of Teachers of English, 1960.

Carlson, Ruth K. Stimulating children in grades four, five, and six to write original stories. Unpublished doctoral dissertation, Univer. of California, 1959.

Carnovsky, L. A study of the relationship between reading interest and actual reading. *Lib. Quart.*, 1934, 4, 76–100.

Catherwood, Catherine. A study of relationships between a knowledge of rules and ability to correct grammatical errors and between identification of sentences and knowledge of subject and predicate. Unpublished master's thesis, Univer. of Minnesota, 1932.

Cavins, L. *Standardization of American poetry for high school purposes*. Chicago: Univer. of Chicago Press, 1928.

Charters, W. W., & Miller, Edith. *A course of study in grammar based upon the grammatical errors of school children of Kansas City, Missouri*. Univer. of Missouri Bull., 1915, 16, No. 2, Educ. Ser. No. 9.

Chomsky, N. *Syntactic structures*. 'S-Gravenhage: Mouton, 1957.

Clark, G. R. Writing situations to which children respond. *Elem. Engl.*, 1954, 31, 150–155.

Confrey, A. An investigation of the comments made by forty instructors upon students' themes. *Cath. educ. Digest*, 1927, 24, 335–340.

Coryell, Nancy G. An evaluation of extensive and intensive teaching of literature: A year's experiment in the eleventh grade. *Teach. Coll. Contr. Educ.*, 1927, No. 275.

Crawford, C. C., & Royer, Madie M. Oral drill versus grammar study. *Elem. sch. J.*, 1935, 36, 116–119.

Crossen, Helen J. Effects of the attitudes of the reader upon critical reading ability. *J. educ. Res.*, 1948, 42, 289–298.

Cutright, Prudence. A comparison of methods of securing correct language usage. *Elem. sch. J.*, 1934, 34, 681–690.

Davis, Edith A. *The development of linguistic skill in twins, singletons with siblings, and only children from age five to ten years.* Minneapolis: Univer. of Minnesota Press, 1937.

Davis, F. B. Fundamental factors of comprehension in reading. *Psychometrika,* 1944, 9, 186.

Davis, J. Vocational and moral guidance through English composition in the high school. *Addresses and Proceedings, NEA,* 1912. Pp. 713–718.

Day, Ella. The development of language in twins: I. A comparison of twins and single children. *Child Develpm.,* 1932, 3, 179–199.

Departments of English, Ball State Teachers College, Indiana State Teachers College, Indiana University, and Purdue University. *Joint statement on freshman English in college and high school preparation.* Terre Haute: Indiana State Teachers College [1959].

Diederich, P. The problem of grading essays. Princeton, N.J.: Educational Testing Service, 1957. (Mimeographed)

Diederich, P. B., French, J. W., & Carlton, S. T. Factors in judgments of writing ability. Res. Bull. Series RB-61-15. Princeton, N.J.: Educational Testing Service, 1961. (Mimeographed)

Dressel, P., & Mayhew, L. (Directors) *Handbook for theme analysis.* Communications Committee, Cooperative Study of Evaluation in General Education, American Council on Education. Dubuque, Iowa: Wm. C. Brown, 1954.

Dressel, P., Schmid, J., & Kincaid, G. The effect of writing frequency upon essay-type writing proficiency at the college level. *J. educ. Res.,* 1952, 46, 285–293.

Dunkel, H. *General education in the humanities.* Washington, D.C.: American Council on Education, 1947.

Dusel, W. J. Determining an efficient teaching load in English. *Illinois Engl. Bull.,* 1955, 43, No. 1. (a)

Dusel, W. J. Some semantic implications of theme correction. *Engl. J.,* 1955, 44, 390–397. (b)

Edmund, N. The relationship between prior experiences and the creative quality of stories of fifth grade children. *Elem. Engl.,* 1958, 35, 248–249.

Educational Testing Service. Sequential tests of educational progress: A brief. Princeton, N.J.: Author, 1957, 1958.

English language arts in California public high schools. Sacramento: California State Department of Education Bull., 1957, 26, No. 7.

Evaluating ninth-grade themes. *Illinois Engl. Bull.,* 1953, 40 (3), 1–35.

Evans, J. W. The social importance and the pupil control of certain punctuation variants. Unpublished doctoral dissertation, Univer. of Iowa, 1939.

Farmer, P., & Freeman, Bernice. *The teaching of English in Georgia.* Atlanta: Georgia Council of Teachers of English, 1952.

Fries, C. *American English grammar.* New York: Appleton-Century, 1941.

Fries, C. *The structure of English.* New York: Harcourt, Brace, 1952.

Frogner, Ellen. Problems of sentence structure in pupils' themes. *Engl. J.,* 1933, 22, 742–749.

Frogner, Ellen. Grammar approach versus thought approach in teaching sentence structure. *Engl. J.,* 1939, 28, 518–526.

Gray, W. S. Summary of reading investigations, July 1, 1953 to June 30, 1954. *J. educ. Res.,* 1955, 48, 401–442.

Greene, H. A. Direct versus formal methods in elementary English. *Elem. Engl.,* 1947, 24, 273–285.

Greene, H. English—language, grammar, and composition. In W. S. Monroe (Ed.), *Encyclopedia of educational research.* (Rev. ed.) New York: Macmillan, 1950. Pp. 383–396.

Grommon, A. Preparing high school students for college composition. *Calif. J. sec. Educ.,* 1953, 28, 113–118.

Grose, Lois, Miller, Dorothy, & Steinberg, E. *Suggestions for evaluating junior high school writing.* Pittsburgh: Association of English Teachers of Western Pennsylvania, 1958.

Harris, C. W. Measurement of comprehension of literature. *Sch. Rev.,* 1948, 56, 280–289, 332–343.

Hartley, Helene W. Tests of the interpretative reading of poetry for teachers of English. *Teach. Coll. Contr. Educ.,* 1930, No. 433.

Heaton, Margaret, & Lewis, Helen B. *Reading ladders in human relations.* Washington, D.C.: American Council on Education, 1955.

Heider, F., & Heider, Grace M. Comparison of sentence structure of deaf and hearing children. *Volta Rev.,* 1941, 43, 364–367, 536–540, 599–604.

Hockett, C. F. Age grading and linguistic change. *Language,* 1950, 26, 449–457.

Hockett, C. F. *A manual of phonology.* Bloomington: Indiana Univer. Res. Center in Anthropology, Folklore, and Linguistics, Publ. 11, 1955.

Hosic, J. F. (Compiler) *Reorganization of English in secondary schools.* Washington, D.C.: U.S. Government Printing Office, 1917. (Dept. of the Interior, Bur. of Education Bull. 1917, No. 2)

Howell, Miriam. The control of mechanics of expression and the quality of preceding experiences as differentiating factors in certain aspects of compositions of seven-year-olds. Unpublished doctoral dissertation, Univer. of Wisconsin, 1955.

Hoyt, F. S. The place of grammar in the elementary curriculum. *Teachers Coll. Rec.,* 1906, 7, 1–34.

Huddleston, Edith. Measurement of writing ability at the college-entrance level: Objective vs. subjective techniques. *J. exp. Educ.,* 1954, 22, 165–213.

Hudelson, E. English composition, its aims, methods, and measurement. *Yearb. nat. Soc. Stud. Educ.,* 1923, 22, Part I.

Irion, T. W. H. Comprehension difficulties of ninth grade students in the study of literature. *Teach. Coll. Contr. Educ.,* 1925, No. 189.

Jackson, Evalene P. Effects of reading upon attitudes towards the Negro race. *Lib. Quart.,* 1944, 14, 47–54.

Jesperson, O. *Essentials of English grammar.* New York: Holt, 1933.

Johnson, R. E. Persistency of error in English composition. *Sch. Rev.,* 1917, 25, 555–580.

Johnson, R. I. *English expression: A study in curriculum-building.* Bloomington, Ill.: Public School Publishing Co., 1926.

Johnson, R. I. Functional centers of expression. *Engl. J.,* 1932, 21, 275–280.

Kangley, Lucy. Poetry preferences in the junior high school. *Teach. Coll. Contr. Educ.,* 1938, No. 758.

Kitzhaber, A. R., Gorrell, R. U., & Roberts, P. *Education for college.* New York: Ronald Press, 1961.

Kraus, Silvy. The teaching of written composition in the public schools: A summary of research. *Univer. Oregon Curr. Bull.,* 1959, 15, No. 190.

Krieg, Laurel. A suggested method of analyzing children's fiction reading. Unpublished master's thesis, Univer. of Chicago, 1943.

Kurath, H., & Bloch, B. *Linguistic atlas of New England.* Providence, R.I.: Brown Univer., 1939–1943.

LaBrant, Lou L. A study of certain language developments of children in grades four to twelve, inclusive. *Genet. Psychol. Monogr.,* 1933, 14, 387–491.

LaBrant, Lou L. *An evaluation of the free reading in grades ten, eleven, and twelve.* Columbus: Ohio State Univer. Press, 1936.

LaBrant, Lou L. *We teach English.* New York: Harcourt, Brace, 1951.

LaBrant, Lou L. The use of communication media. In Margaret Willis, *The guinea pigs after 20 years.* Columbus: Ohio State Univer. Press, 1961. Ch. 8.

Leonard, S. *Current English usage.* Champaign, Ill.: National Council of Teachers of English, 1932.

Lloyd, D. J., & Warfel, H. R. *American English in its cultural setting.* New York: Knopf, 1956.

Loban, W. *Literature and social sensitivity.* Champaign, Ill.: National Council of Teachers of English, 1954.

Loban, W., Ryan, Margaret, & Squire, J. R. *Teaching language and literature.* New York: Harcourt, Brace, 1961.

Lodge, Helen C. The influence of the study of biography on the moral ideology of the adolescent at the eighth grade level. *J. educ. Res.,* 1956, 50, 241–255.

Lokke, V. L., & Wykoff, G. S. "Double writing" in freshman composition—An experiment. *Sch. & Soc.,* 1948, 68, 437–439.

Lorge, I., & Kruglov, L. Relationship between the readability of pupils' composition and their measured intelligence. *J. educ. Res.,* 1950, 43, 467–474.

Lyman, R. L. A cooperative experiment in junior high school composition. *Sch. Rev.,* 1931, 39, 748–757.

Macaulay, W. J. The difficulty of grammar. *Brit. J. educ. Psychol.,* 1947, 17, 153–162.

Maize, R. Two methods of teaching English composition to retarded college freshmen. *J. educ. Psychol.,* 1954, 45, 22–28.

Malmstrom, Jean. Linguistic atlas findings versus textbook pronouncements on current American usage. *Engl. J.,* 1959, 48, 191–198.

Mann, Mary B. The quantitative differentiation of samples of written language. *Psychol. Monogr.*, 1944, 56, No. 2, 41–74 (Whole No. 255).

Marckwardt, A. H., & Walcott, F. G. *Facts about current English usage.* New York: Appleton-Century, 1938.

McCarthy, Dorothea. Language development in children. In L. Carmichael (Ed.), *Manual of child psychology.* (2nd ed.) New York: Wiley, 1954. Pp. 492–630.

McCaul, R. The effect of attitudes upon reading interpretations. *J. educ. Res.,* 1944, 37, 451–457.

McConnell, G. A. An analysis of biographical literature for children. Unpublished doctoral dissertation, Univer. of California, Berkeley, 1952.

Meckel, H. C. An exploratory study of responses of adolescents to situations in a novel. Unpublished doctoral dissertation, Univer. of Chicago, 1946.

Meckel, H. C. Evaluating growth in reading. *Yearb. nat. Soc. Stud. Educ.,* 1948, 47, Part II, 251–275.

Meckel, H. C., Squire, J. R., & Leonard, V. T. *Practices in the teaching of composition in California public high schools.* Sacramento: California State Department of Education Bull., 1958, 27, No. 5.

Milner, Esther. A study of the relationships between reading readiness in grade one school children and patterns of parent-child interaction. *Child Develpm.,* 1951, 22, 95–112.

Monroe, W. The unreliability of the measurements of ability in written composition. *Yearb. nat. Soc. Stud. Educ.,* 1923, 22, Part I, 169–171.

Moyer, H. Does ear training help? *Research in the three R's.* New York: Harper, 1958.

Muller, H. Two approaches to the social psychology of reading. *Lib. Quart.,* 1942, 12, 1–28.

Murray, H. A. *Explorations in personality.* New York: Oxford Univer. Press, 1938.

National Council of Teachers of English, Curriculum Commission. *An experience curriculum in English.* New York: Appleton-Century, 1935.

National Council of Teachers of English, Committee on Correlation. *A correlated curriculum. Engl. Monogr. No. 5.* New York: Appleton-Century, 1936.

National Council of Teachers of English, Com-

mission on the English Curriculum. *The English language arts.* New York: Appleton-Century-Crofts, 1952.

National Council of Teachers of English, Commission on the English Curriculum. *Language arts for today's children.* New York: Appleton-Century-Crofts, 1954.

National Council of Teachers of English, Commission on the English Curriculum. *The English language arts in the secondary school.* New York: Appleton-Century-Crofts, 1956.

National Council of Teachers of English. *Cumulative reading record.* (1956 rev.) Champaign, Ill.: National Council of Teachers of English, 1956.

National Council of Teachers of English, Committee on the National Interest. *The national interest and the teaching of English.* Champaign, Ill.: National Council of Teachers of English, 1961.

Nordberg, H. O. The awareness among student teachers regarding research in the language arts. Unpublished doctoral dissertation, Univer. of California, Berkeley, 1949.

Norvell, G. W. Wide individual reading compared with the traditional plan of studying literature. *Sch. Rev.,* 1941, 49, 603–613.

Norvell, G. W. *The reading responses of adolescents.* Boston: Heath, 1950.

Norvell, G. W. *What boys and girls like to read.* Morristown, N.J.: Silver Burdett, 1958.

O'Rourke, L. J. *Rebuilding the English-usage curriculum to insure greater mastery of essentials.* Washington, D.C.: Psychological Institute, 1934.

Patten, J. Personality patterns related to written expression. Unpublished doctoral dissertation, Stanford Univer., 1950.

Pooley, R. C. Grammar and usage in textbooks on English. Madison: Bur. of Educ. Res., Univer. of Wisconsin, 1933, Bull. No. 14.

Pooley, R. C. *Teaching English grammar.* New York: Appleton-Century-Crofts, 1957.

Pooley, R. C., & Williams, R. D. *The teaching of English in Wisconsin.* Madison: Univer. of Wisconsin Press, 1948.

Potter, H. E. Abilities and disabilities in the use of English found in the written composition of entering freshmen at the University of California. Berkeley: Bur. of Res. in Educ., Univer. of California, 1922, No. 12.

Pressey, S. L. A statistical study of children's

errors in sentence structure. *Engl. J.,* 1925, 14, 529–535.

Rankin, Marie. Children's interests in library books of fiction. *Teach. Coll. Contr. Educ.,* 1944, No. 906.

Rapeer, L. The problem of formal grammar in elementary education. *J. educ. Psychol.,* 1913, 4, 125–137.

Richards, I. A. *Practical criticism: A study in literary judgment.* New York: Harcourt, Brace, 1930.

Rivlin, H. N. Functional grammar. *Teach. Coll. Contr. Educ.,* 1930, No. 435.

Roberts, P. *Patterns of English.* New York: Harcourt, Brace, 1956.

Roberts, P. The relation of linguistics to the teaching of English. *Engl.,* 1960, 22, 1–9.

Robinson, Helen M. What research says to the teacher of reading: Reading interests. *Reading Teacher,* 1955, 8, 173–177.

Rosenblatt, Louise M. *Literature as exploration.* New York: Appleton-Century, 1937.

Russell, D. H. *Children learn to read.* Boston: Ginn, 1949.

Russell, D. H. Interrelationships of the language arts and personality. *Elem. Engl.,* 1953, 30, 167–180.

Russell, D. H. Some research on the impact of reading. *Engl. J.,* 1958, 47, 398–413.

San Francisco Curriculum Survey Committee. *Report.* San Francisco: San Francisco United School District, 1960.

Sapir, E. *Language.* New York: Harcourt, Brace, 1921.

Scofield, Alice F. G. The relationship of teaching methods in language arts used in the classroom to those advocated in method courses in language arts. Unpublished doctoral dissertation, Stanford Univer., 1955.

Searles, J., & Carlsen, G. English: Language, grammar, and composition. In C. W. Harris (Ed.), *Encyclopedia of educational research.* (3rd ed.) New York: Macmillan, 1960. Pp. 454–470.

Segel, D., & Barr, Nora R. Relation of achievement in formal grammar to achievement in applied grammar. *J. educ. Res.,* 1926, 14, 401–402.

Shattuck, M. E., & Barnes, W. *The situation as regards English.* Washington, D.C.: Dept. of Supervisors and Directors of Instruction, National Education Association, 1936.

Shepard, J. P. The treatment of characters in popular children's fiction. Unpublished

master's thesis, Univer. of California, Berkeley, 1959.

Shire, Sister Mary Louise. The relation of certain linguistic factors to reading achievement of first grade children. Unpublished doctoral dissertation, Fordham Univer., 1945.

Smith, Dora V. *Instruction in English.* Washington, D.C.: U.S. Government Printing Office, 1933. (U.S. Office of Education Bull. 1932, No. 17)

Smith, Dora V. English grammar again. *Engl. J.,* 1938, 27, 643–649.

Smith, E. R., & Tyler, R. W., and others. *Appraising and recording student progress.* New York: Harper, 1942.

Smith, Ethel. Procedures for encouraging creative writing in the elementary school. Unpublished doctoral dissertation, Northwestern Univer., 1944.

Sofell, C. A comparison of the use of imposed with self-chosen subjects in composition of elementary children. Unpublished master's thesis, Univer. of Pittsburgh, 1929.

Squire, J. R. The responses of adolescents to literature involving selected experiences of personal development. Unpublished doctoral dissertation, Univer. of California, Berkeley, 1956.

Stalnaker, J. Essay examinations reliably read. *Sch. & Soc.,* 1937, 46, 671–672.

Stalnaker, J., & Stalnaker, Ruth C. Reliable reading of essay tests. *Sch. Rev.,* 1934, 42, 599–605.

Starch, D. The measurement of achievement in English grammar. *J. educ. Psychol.,* 1915, 6, 615–626.

Stephens, J. M. Transfer of learning. In C. W. Harris (Ed.), *Encyclopedia of educational research.* (3rd ed.) New York: Macmillan, 1960. Pp. 1535–1543.

Stewart, J. The effect of diagraming on certain skills in English composition. Unpublished doctoral dissertation, State Univer. of Iowa, 1941.

Stormzand, M. J., & O'Shea, M. V. *How much English grammar?* Baltimore: Warwick and York, 1924.

Strickland, Ruth G. Evaluating children's composition. *Elem. Engl.,* 1960, 37, 321–330.

Symonds, P. M. Practice versus grammar in the learning of correct usage. *J. educ. Psychol.,* 1931, 22, 81–95.

Symonds, P. M., & Daringer, Helen F. Studies in the learning of English expression. IV.

Sentence structure. *Teachers Coll. Rec.,* 1930, 32, 50–64.

Symonds, P. M., & Hinton, E. M. Studies in the learning of English expression. V. Grammar. *Teachers Coll. Rec.,* 1932, 33, 430–438.

Taba, Hilda. *With perspective on human relations.* Washington, D.C.: American Council on Education, 1955.

Thomas, Ednah. *Evaluating student themes.* Madison: Univer. of Wisconsin Press, 1955.

Trager, G. L., & Smith, H., Jr. *An outline of English structure.* Norman, Okla.: Battenburg Press, 1951. ("Studies in Linguistics," Occasional Papers No. 3)

Waples, D., Berelson, B., & Bradshaw, F. *What reading does to people.* Chicago: Univer. of Chicago Press, 1940.

Ward, W. S. (Ed.) Principles and standards in composition for Kentucky high schools and colleges. *Kentucky Engl. Bull.,* 1956–1957, 6, 295–367.

Watts, A. F. *The language and mental development of children.* Boston: Heath, 1944.

White, R. *Black Boy:* A value analysis. *J. abnorm. soc. Psychol.,* 1947, 42, 440–461.

White, Verna. Measuring achievement in high school English. *Sch. Rev.,* 1947, 55, 474–483.

White, Verna, & Enochs, J. B. Testing the reading and interpretation of literature. *Engl. J.,* 1944, 33, 171–177.

Womack, T. Teachers' attitudes toward current usage. *Engl. J.,* 1959, 48, 186–190.

CHAPTER 19 Research on Teaching Secondary School Mathematics

KENNETH B. HENDERSON
University of Illinois

Teaching can be conceived as the ternary relation: x teaches y to z. Expressed in the notation of relation theory, this becomes $(x, y)T z$, or more generally, $T(x, y, z)$. As popularly conceived, the domain of 'x' is the set of persons who act as teachers; the domain of 'y' is a set of knowledge, beliefs, or skills selected by a teacher; and the domain of 'z' is a set of individuals—humans and other animals capable of modifying their behavior as a result of experience—who are taught by a teacher. To continue the popular conception (which undoubtedly would not be expressed by means of the symbols being used), values of 'z' exist such that $x = z$, for on occasion we hear a person characterized as "self-educated" or "self-taught."

With some modifications, this conception is a useful one for analyzing research on teaching secondary school mathematics. The proposed modifications follow. When one stops to think about teaching, he realizes that the teacher is not the significant factor. It is what the teacher does, in other words, his behavior, that becomes significant for research. Hence, the domain of 'x' in '$T(x, y, z)$' is more fruitfully regarded as sequences (sets) of verbal and nonverbal behavior the teacher

manifests. Such a conception enables us to consider a person whose voice and image appear on a television screen and one whose voice emanates from a loud-speaker to be teachers if their objective is to produce learning in a group of people. Moreover, it allows us to consider a machine or a textbook to be a teacher if its function is the same as that of a human being who teaches. In all these cases, values of 'x' in '$T(x, y, z)$' are sequences of actions.

When we compare sequences of teacher behaviors, we find that they are not random but ordered so as to accomplish an objective of the teacher, usually to help a student learn some items of subject matter. Moreover, we find that the sequences can be classified into sets in terms of the common properties which characterize the set. The pattern, that is, the set of common properties that a set of behavior sequences manifests, will be called a *method*. This is in keeping with the conventional use of this term, for we speak of "the lecture method," "the supervised study method," "the discovery method," and others, having in mind a sequence of acts which a teacher performs.

It seems reasonable to hypothesize that a

method maximizes certain factors and minimizes others. For example, writing terms, mathematical sentences, and rules for changing the form of expressions on the chalkboard maximizes time; that is, it takes longer to write these on the chalkboard than it does merely to say them, but it minimizes the cognitive effort that the student must expend to remember the expressions. Discouraging questions from the students minimizes the time required to cover a topic, but it probably also minimizes the student's understanding and maximizes his frustration. To determine which factors are maximized and which are minimized by a certain method is the function of research on teaching methods.

We shall say, therefore, that methods—patterns of sequences of teacher behavior—will be the values of $'x'$ in $'T(x, y, z)'$. A distinct advantage of this point of view is that it allows textbooks and so-called teaching machines to be considered as "teachers." The people who design them can build in certain methods which then become values of the independent variable $'x'$.

As in the case of the variable $'x'$, it is the behavior the student manifests rather than the student per se which is the significant factor for research, e.g., what he does in the face of temporary blocking, to what extent he can apply what he has learned to new problems, whether he sees a pattern in a set of problems, to what extent he exhibits behavior which inclines us to say that he is interested in the study of mathematics, whether he passes or fails in college, and so on. Hence, the domain of $'z'$ in the teaching relation $T(x, y, z)$ is profitably taken as the behaviors of those taught.

The concept of a student's knowledge about a subject fits into this model. Knowledge is an inferred entity rather than an observed one. Typically, we infer concerning a student's knowledge about values of $'y'$ from (his) values of $'z'$; that is, we observe him do or say something and from this behavior we infer how much he knows about the subject.

One kind of research on teaching second-ary school mathematics focuses on the binary relation ySz abstracted from the ternary relation $T(x, y, z)$. Research of this kind studies the relation between subject matter taught a student and his behaviors subsequent to having been taught it and which are considered relevant to it. This kind of research may be thought of as curricular research. In its pure form, it attempts to identify members (y, z) of the relation which are invariant with respect to values of $'x'$. That aspect of the work of the School Mathematics Study Group which culminates in selecting subject matter for various grades and mathematics courses may be considered research of this kind. This group has not sought to study any methods of teaching the subject matter they select. But by allowing the teachers who use their text materials to employ any methods they choose, the "methods" variable is randomized. By the definition of the function of this Handbook, we shall not be concerned with this kind of research.

A second kind of research focuses on the binary relation xRz abstracted from $T(x, y, z)$. Research of this kind studies the relation between the methods a teacher (person, text, or machine) employs and those behaviors of a student which under various hypotheses are related to the methods. It tries to identify members (x, z) of the relation which are either invariant with respect to values of $'y'$, viz., items of subject matter, or depend on values of $'y'$, the nature of the dependence being the subject of research.

THEORETICAL PROPOSALS FOR TEACHING SECONDARY SCHOOL MATHEMATICS

This chapter considers the kind of research defined in the previous paragraph. But before considering this body of research, we shall review briefly some theoretical proposals concerning the teaching of secondary school mathematics. This review seems appropriate because a theory makes a difference in the research attempted. For example, a theory which regards mathematics primarily as a tool for the housewife, businessman, and scientist, will dispose a researcher to ask different questions from those theories which conceive of mathematics primarily as a study of properties of a logical structure, e.g., an ordered field, a group, or a function, will dispose him to ask. Whatever the theory, it is a source of hypotheses amenable to empirical testing. A fruitful theory suggests many hypotheses. If few hypotheses are suggested by a theory, it either is an uninterpreted one or consists of ideas which have few implications. Findings from empirical studies, in turn, test the theory, either confirming it or demanding some revision to explain the findings. Implication, therefore, operates in two directions: from the basic propositions of a theory to researchable problems and from the findings of the research to the basic propositions of the theory.

The Report of
the National Committee on
Mathematical Requirements

The proposal taken as the springboard for this section is the report of the National Committee on Mathematical Requirements appointed in 1916 by the Mathematical Association of America. Initially the Committee consisted only of professors of mathematics, but it broadened its membership, as instructed, by adding high school teachers of mathematics representing the associations of teachers of mathematics in various regions, viz., New England, the Middle States and Maryland, and the Central States.

The Committee's report—the outcome of more than five years of careful study—gave formal expression to many ideas for improving the teaching of secondary school mathematics which had been voiced earlier by distinguished professors of mathematics. Moore (1926), for example, recommended in his 1902 presidential address to the American Mathematical Society that the existing organization of mathematics courses, e.g., algebra, plane geometry, solid geometry, and

trigonometry, be altered to create unified courses which would portray the interrelation of these particular bodies of knowledge. Klein (1908) of Germany had advocated a similar organization using the concept of a function as the unifying idea. He also had argued that some psychological considerations should be taken into account in organizing and teaching the subject matter, and he was particularly interested in the training of secondary school teachers of mathematics. Perry (1901) of Great Britain, like Moore and Klein, advocated a broader study of mathematics than was provided by the narrowly conceived courses offered in his country at the time. Finally, the Committee's report had the backing of its sponsor and several other professional organizations which were given an opportunity to read the preliminary report and offer suggestions.

For the present chapter, two conceptions or recommendations of the National Committee on Mathematical Requirements are noteworthy. One was its conception of the aims of mathematical instruction: (1) practical—the usefulness of a fact, method, or process of mathematics in the workaday world; (2) disciplinary—the training of certain intellectual skills like the ability to analyze a complex problem into simpler parts, to recognize logical relations between interdependent factors, and to discover and state a general law (the Committee eschewed the extreme of formal discipline and also the extreme of disbelief in any transfer of training); and (3) cultural—the aesthetic satisfaction accruing from an understanding of logical structure, precision of statement, and the power of mathematics. In expressing the last aim, the Committee approached mysticism: "mention should be made of the religious effect, in the broad sense, which the study of the permanence of laws in mathematics and of the infinite tends to establish" (Mathematical Association of America, National Committee on Mathematical Requirements, 1921, p. 8).

The second noteworthy conception was the Committee's point of view on instruction: Formal demonstration (proof) should be preceded by "a reasonable amount of informal work of an intuitive, experimental, and constructive character" (p. 9), and drill on the manipulation of symbols should be kept in perspective as a means of improving speed and accuracy after understanding has been developed.

Reports of the Joint Commission of the Mathematical Association of America, and the National Council of Teachers of Mathematics

In 1940 two major publications expounded theory on teaching mathematics in secondary schools: (1) the report of the Joint Commission of the Mathematical Association of America and the National Council of Teachers of Mathematics (1940) entitled *The Place of Mathematics in Secondary Education* and (2) *Mathematics in General Education* (Committee on the Function of Mathematics in General Education, 1940), one of a series of reports for the Commission on the Secondary School Curriculum of the Progressive Education Association. There was some overlapping of membership in the two groups that wrote these reports. But, while all members of the Joint Commission were either college or high school teachers of mathematics, some members of the PEA's Committee were not mathematics teachers.

Both reports considered the function of mathematics against the backdrop of the general function of secondary education in the United States and the contributions mathematics can make to both general and specialized education. Both provided a conceptualization of the organization of the subject matter to be taught. The Joint Commission (1940, p. 61) proposed (1) a subdivision according to major subject fields, viz., number and computation, geometric form and space perception, graphic representation, elementary analysis (algebra and trigonometry), logical (or "straight") thinking, relational thinking, symbolic representation and think-

ing, and (2) a subdivision of each of the fields into categories, viz., basic concepts, principles and terms, fundamental processes, fundamental relations, skills and techniques, and applications. The Committee on the Function of Mathematics in General Education (1940, pp. 59–63) proposed a set of seven major concepts or understandings, viz., formulation and solution, data, approximation, function, operation, proof, and symbolism.

A reader of both reports probably would have regarded the Joint Commission's point of view as more practicable than that of the Committee on the Function of Mathematics in General Education (1940). The Committee frankly stated that the efficacy of its theory would "require experimentation, both extensive and intensive, over a period of years" (1940, p. 14). This may even be the case today, particularly for classroom teachers. But the Committee's theory that major concepts could be used as the basis for the articulation of mathematics courses has continued to command interest. Moreover, the consensus concerning the particular concepts is remarkable. For example, Fawcett (1942) proposed number, operation, proof, symbolism, measurement, and function as a set. The committee that wrote *The Growth of Mathematical Ideas: Grades K–12* (National Council of Teachers of Mathematics, 1959) selected number and operation, relations and functions, proof, measurement and approximation, probability, statistics, and language and symbolism as its set.

Both reports offered recommendations concerning methods of teaching. The Joint Commission recommended "overviews" and motivating discussions, periodic summaries and reviews, practice aimed at promoting insight, and "spaced learning." It set forth principles for determining a sequence of presentation of topics of study. It also offered specific suggestions for teaching talented and retarded students. The Committee offered fewer explicit recommendations. Its theory of methodology might be stated in two principles: (1) Students should have many and varied experiences related to each of the seven major concepts named above. (2) Their attention should then be directed to the process per se, e.g., formulation and solution, proof, or symbolization or to the idea, e.g., data, function, or operation—presumably so that the students might abstract from their experiences and generalize about the process. (Some educators describe the latter principle as intellectualizing or internalizing the experiences.) In a chapter on understanding the student, the Committee discussed implications for teaching which were oriented to the emotional aspect of the student's personality.

Reports of the Commission on Post-War Plans

In 1944 the National Council of Teachers of Mathematics created a commission to provide leadership for mathematics teaching in secondary schools in the postwar period. One reason for the appointment of the Commission was the revelation during World War II of the small number of mathematicians and scientists in the United States and of the inadequate mathematical proficiency of the general run of inductees.

The Commission on Post-War Plans (1944, 1945) issued two reports; the second of these set forth the Commission's theory in 34 theses. These pertained to the function of arithmetic and secondary school mathematics, the essentials of functional competence in mathematics, the organization of the program of studies in mathematics, and methods of teaching. The latter theses stressed the desirability of teaching which fosters meaning and understanding. At one point the Commission stated:

Consider as a case in point the common practice of giving children rules instead of *developing* them; for example, of telling children where to write quotient figures in division, instead of helping them to see that their positions are predetermined by the principles of place value; or, of telling children to invert and multiply (a short cut) when

they divide by a fraction, instead of developing, first, a rational explanation through the use of the common denominator (Commission on Post-War Plans, 1945, p. 201).

Although the illustration is made in the context of arithmetic, the principles implied are germane to teaching at other levels.

Conclusions about Pedagogical Theory

It is useful to compare the several theoretical proposals on two grounds: (1) their substance—what is said, and (2) the nature of pedagogical theory, at least in the area of mathematics teaching. Comparing the substance of the theories, which have spanned a period of almost 50 years, one finds some remarkable agreements. The idea of using major mathematical concepts as the organizational basis has been pervasive. It resisted the trend in the 1930's when general educational theory became both narrowly utilitarian and overly oriented to the social studies. Also pervasive has been a belief in the efficacy of a methodological sequence in which the teacher starts the students working informally with concrete objects or ideas which they understand and then guides their activities and thoughts so that they discover relations, principles, and procedures, rather than stating these relations, etc., as the initial step in the sequence. Drill is regarded as having a place in teaching but as being best used to speed up routine computations and manipulations only after meaning and understanding have been instilled in students. Finally, there has been continuing stress on the desirability of choosing subject matter to be taught and methods of teaching it in terms of the ability of the students involved.

We now turn briefly to the nature of pedagogical theory and subsequently to some proposals for theory construction. One does not have to read much pedagogical theory before he realizes that such theory is essentially normative. Builders of pedagogical theory are interested primarily in influencing institutional practices regarding mathematics education or the classroom behavior of mathematics teachers. Hence the language of the theory (more accurately—theories) is primarily advisory rather than descriptive. *Should* and *ought,* which are explicitly monitory, are freely used. Rating words like *good, right, important, significant,* and *satisfactory,* which in a context of choice are implicitly monitory, are also freely used. Misled by an ancient theory of grammar which admits only a few categories of sentences—declarative, interrogative, etc.—many persons have considered sentences containing such words as statements having a truth-value.

More recent linguistic theory (e.g., Hart, 1952; Nowell-Smith, 1954; Strawson, 1956; Urmson, 1953) classifies sentences in terms of their use. Sentences declarative in form are not necessarily used to make statements. 'Feedback in teaching is important' may not be used to describe a state of affairs but rather to rate a procedure in teaching. If 'Teaching should emphasize discovery'[1] has a truth-value,[1] the rules for assigning the truth-value are certainly different from those used to assign a truth-value to 'Teaching does not emphasize discovery' or 'For every natural number $n, n \cdot 1 = n$'. It seems more profitable conceptually to regard the function of sentences containing *should, ought, right, good,* etc., as giving advice in a context in which choices have to be made.

In essence, pedagogical theory is a set of proposals or recommendations, together with a justification of them. The justification is based on three bodies of knowledge or belief. One is a matrix of *contingent generalizations* about states of affairs in society, how students

learn, what student behavior is correlated with certain actions of teachers, and what subject matter can be learned by students of certain degrees of maturity. These facts emanate from reliable research or from extensive, though perhaps not as carefully controlled, personal experience. The facts about students' learning are embedded in a mesh of propositions constituting a theory of learning.

A second body of knowledge or belief is the *value* matrix. Here are included beliefs about the rights and obligations of man and the nature of the good life, and corresponding beliefs about the obligations of society and the primary function of formal education relative to these rights and the good life. The Joint Commission considered the primary function of formal secondary education and pointed out the contribution of mathematics toward performance of this function. The Committee on the Function of Mathematics, using the philosophy of education of its parent commission, the PEA's Commission on the Secondary School Curriculum, described what mathematics courses can do to implement that philosophy.

The third body of knowledge or belief on which a theory of teaching mathematics is based is a conception of the *nature of mathematics.* The role of this knowledge (belief) usually is implicit. It is nevertheless significant in shaping recommendations, particularly concerning what should be taught, and, often, how it should be taught. It seems apparent, for example, that someone who conceives of mathematics as "schemes of languages of multiordinal relations capable of exact treatment at a given date" (Mendenhall, 1939, p. 87) and at another point says, "The *meaning* of a mathematical sentence is found in its *form* or *structure* though the *truth* of the sentence depends on empirical verification" (p. 100), will teach mathematics in a way different from one who believes the following:

One of the characteristic features of mathematics is its special symbolism. This had led

---

[1] It is doubtful that this sentence has a truth-value. To be sure, we often reply to 'Teaching should emphasize discovery' by 'true' but 'true' is used in the sense of 'I agree' or 'Yes, that is a desirable thing to do'. It is not used to imply that the sentence is a reliable description of an existing state of affairs or that it follows by an agreed-upon rule of inference from a set of statements which arbitrarily have been assigned the truth-value 'true'.

some people to say that mathematics *is* a language . . . . [Yet] the view that mathematics is a language involves the confusion of symbols and their use. Mathematics, like any other discipline, has special terms and symbols, but mathematics is the subject that is expressed by these symbols and not the symbols themselves . . . . Mathematics is the collection of known abstract, axiomatic, consistent theories. That is, mathematics is the set to which an object belongs if and only if it is a theory that is abstract (in the sense of having multiple interpretations), axiomatic (logically organized), and consistent (having at least one application or example . . .) (May, 1959, pp. 581–583).

A quite explicit connection between a conception of a structure of mathematics and propositions on how to teach it was demonstrated by Austin (1927) when he said:

[Geometry is] essentially an experimental science, like any other, and . . . it should be taught observationally, descriptively, and experimentally . . . . the inherent nature of the subject-matter demands a scientific and experimental treatment; . . . the child to whom the subject is to be taught is fundamentally a scientist, who lives and learns by experimentation and observation in a wonderful world laboratory . . . (Austin, 1927, p. 286).

We find that theorists who speak of modern mathematics also stress the idea of mathematical structure, i.e., a set, rules or postulates for operating on the set and its subsets, and the properties of the set which are implied by the postulates. It is not unexpected, then, to find these individuals advocating teaching that helps students discover patterns; e.g., that $sin^2 x + cos^2 x$ is like $a^2 + b^2$, that multiplying 26×38 in the usual way is an instance of the distributive principle of multiplication over addition, that for every real number $n, n \cdot 1 = n,$ and that the one model $x - y = z$ can be used to find "how much is left," "how much more is needed," and "how much larger." Nor is it unexpected to find them urging that students understand the logic of variables and parameters, for these help discover and describe patterns.

EMPIRICAL STUDIES

We turn now to various empirical studies bearing on the relation xRz whose orientation to a theory of teaching mathematics is recognizable even though it is not made explicit by the experimenter. The implications of the findings of these studies for theory of teaching mathematics will be discussed in a subsequent section.

Research on methods of teaching mathematics seems to be of three kinds. One kind tests the existence hypothesis, that is, whether or not the set $R(x, z)$ or xRz is empty where the hypothesis of the research defines 'xRz'. In other words, the experimenter seeks to exhibit the conjunction of an identifiable method and certain behaviors of a student which may reasonably be considered related to the method employed. He is interested in finding a method which is a *sufficient* condition for manifestation of certain behavior by the student. If there are enough experiments to demonstrate that the conjunction is independent of the subject matter taught, we conclude that the method is the sufficient condition for the student's behavior. Then, if a person wants that kind of behavior on the part of the student, he employs that method which is the sufficient condition for the behavior.

A second kind of research tests the uniqueness hypothesis. A researcher shows that a pattern of behavior by students is associated only with a certain method the teacher employs. The method then becomes a *necessary* condition for the student behavior in question. Or the researcher shows that a certain method is not a necessary condition for the manifestation of a certain pattern of student behavior.

The third kind of research attempts to find that method which is both *necessary and sufficient* for certain behavior on the part of a student to occur. This is the most exciting kind of research; it is also the most difficult. We turn first to research that tests the existence hypothesis that a certain method produces certain behavior.

Telling Methods versus
Heuristic Methods

One pervasive issue in teaching secondary school mathematics has been that of determining the consequences of using two methods, or rather, members of two sets of methods, known as "tell-and-do" and "heuristic." The former consists of the following steps:

1. Stating the item of knowledge to be taught.

2. Clarifying, if necessary, the meaning of the sentence used to express the knowledge.

3. Justifying the item, i.e., establishing the truth of the item if it has a truth-value, or arguing that it is a means to some acceptable end if it is a prescription.

4. Clinching the understanding of the item. (This is often done by having the students work problems based on the knowledge being taught.)

5. Making a transition to the next item to be taught.

If one of the five steps is omitted, the sequence may be regarded as another distinct method subsumed under the general rubric, "tell-and-do." In case Step 3 is omitted, the method is called the *drill method* by some educators. Omission of Step 4 would dispose some educators to call the method the *lecture method*. Any of these methods becomes a value of 'x' in the relation xRz.

The second set of methods—variously called *heuristic methods* or, more vaguely, *the discovery method*—calls for the teacher (person, textbook, or machine) to direct the student's attention to some data. The student then infers from these data. If his inference, as evidenced by his verbal or nonverbal behavior, is correct, the method terminates. If his inference is incorrect, the teacher utilizes the same method with new data or selects another heuristic method which will allow the student to converge on the correct knowledge. But the teacher does not state the item of knowledge; the student discovers it. Henderson (1958, 1959) and Robinson (1960) have described various heuristic methods available to the teacher.

Characteristic of the heuristic methods is the feedback from the student's behavior to the teacher. The teacher's responses are determined in part by the inferences he draws from the student's behavior, both verbal and nonverbal, which he observes. It is this feedback which so dramatically distinguishes these methods from the tell-and-do methods. In fact, the role of the teacher who employs heuristic methods is closely similar to the role of a student in the teacher's class. Both entertain hypotheses from the data available to them—the student from the data which the teacher brings to his attention, the teacher from what the student does and says. Both test these hypotheses, rejecting or accepting them in terms of new data which become available. Both converge on an acceptable conclusion—the student on the item of knowledge the teacher has selected, the teacher on an inference concerning the student's state of knowledge. The signal difference between the two kinds of problem-solving is the relative assurance the student has that his discovery will not be wrong, because the teacher will not allow this to happen. But for his own "discovery" the teacher has no one who is to him as he is to his student. Hence he cannot have the same confidence that his methods are efficacious in attaining his goal.

Inductive methods. The heuristic methods may be divided into two groups which, for the purpose of discussion, will be called the *inductive methods* and the *deductive methods*. The inductive method follows:

1. Presenting instances of the item of knowledge to be taught in order to enable the students to form hypotheses.

2. Presenting evidence—perhaps more instances—serving either to confirm or disconfirm the various hypotheses students state or appear to be acting on.

3. Stating or having a student state the item of knowledge which is a warranted inference from Steps 1 and 2.

If one uses the teaching model $T(x, y, z)$, these activities or a subset of them become values of 'x'.

Some advocates of the inductive method omit Step 3. Hendrix (1947), for one, urges the omission of Step 3 for quite some time. She calls her method the *unverbalized awareness method*.

Values of 'z' considered worth studying when comparing the two methods are behaviors denoted by the terms *problem-solving, transfer of knowledge,* or *application of knowledge.*

Hendrix's research (1947) bears on both the comparison of the tell-and-do and inductive methods and the necessity of including Step 3 of the inductive method defined above. Hendrix studied the problem, *"To what extent, if any, does the way in which one learns a generalization affect the probability of his recognizing a chance to use it?"* (1947, p. 197). The generalization, The sum of the first n odd numbers is n^2, was taught by three methods to different groups of students. It was not indicated whether the groups were made equivalent by matching or by random assignment. One method generally followed the tell-and-do model; the generalization was stated first, then illustrated, and then applied to new problems. In the *unverbalized awareness method,* the students were asked to find the sum of the first two odd numbers, the sum of the first three odd numbers, the sum of the first four, and so on. As insight came, the students began to give succeeding answers rapidly, more rapidly than would be expected if they were laboriously summing the terms. The third method, called *conscious generalization,* proceeded as the second did, except that the students were asked to state the rule they had discovered. By means of counterexamples, Hendrix gradually got the students to state the rule correctly.

Two weeks after learning the generalization, the three groups were given a test in which were scattered several items which could be answered readily by applying the generalization. Hendrix found that in each of the three replications the highest transfer effects were achieved by the students taught by the unverbalized awareness method and the lowest transfer effects achieved by the students taught by the tell-and-do method. The transfer effects achieved by the students taught by the conscious generalization method were between those achieved by the other two groups. From these findings Hendrix ventured three hypotheses:

1. For generation of transfer power, the unverbalized awareness method of learning a generalization is better than a method in which an authoritative statement of the generalization comes first.
2. Verbalizing a generalization immediately after discovery does not increase transfer power.
3. Verbalizing a generalization immediately after discovery may actually decrease transfer power (Hendrix, 1947, p. 198).

She concluded, "Important as symbolic formulation must be for verification and organization of knowledge, it is *not* the key to transfer. That key is a sub-verbal, internal process—something which must happen to the organism before it has any new knowledge to verbalize" (Hendrix, 1947, p. 200).

Hendrix's findings were confirmed by Haslerud and Meyers (1958), who tested the hypothesis "that principles derived by the learner solely from concrete instances will be more readily used in a new situation than those given to him in the form of a statement of principle and an instance" (Haslerud & Meyers, 1958, p. 294). The principles, i.e., the values of 'y' in $T(x, y, z)$, were those describing a particular decoding and encoding. On the basis of their findings, the experimenters accepted their hypothesis.

Two studies (Luchins, 1942; Luchins & Luchins, 1950) which point out some possible consequences of the tell-and-do method will be discussed jointly. While the values of 'y' in $T(x, y, z)$ for these studies were not items of knowledge conventionally taught in secondary school mathematics, the implications are clear enough to merit consideration in this chapter.

In one experiment, Luchins gave his subjects seven problems in which they were asked to find a stated volume of water by using three containers of different volumes. For example, suppose the students had an empty two-quart jar, an empty five-quart jar, and a ten-quart jar full of water and were asked to use the jars so as to secure one quart. They would fill the five-quart jar once and the two-quart jar twice, thereby leaving one quart in the ten-quart jar. All the seven problems were solved by this same formula, $a - b - 2c$, but the formula was not told the subjects.

As the subjects worked the seven "practice" problems, insight was demonstrated by a sudden drop in the time required to arrive at the answer. Thereupon the subjects were given five "test" problems which, though resembling the former seven problems, could be solved only by the formulas $b - c$ or $b + c$. Luchins found that many subjects persisted in using the formula $a - b - 2c$ even though it was obvious this would not work. A second group not trained by the first set of seven problems did not manifest the rigidity of the first group when presented with the five "test" problems. Additional findings were (1) the greater the success on the practice set, the greater was the impact of the *Einstellung* (mechanization or rigidity); (2) all age groups were affected; (3) subjects of the three categories of intelligence Luchins used were affected; (4) education, as measured by the number of years of schooling, had no significant effect in reducing the *Einstellung;* and (5) the phenomenon of *Einstellung* was manifested for abstract content, e.g., in geometry, as well as for the concrete manipulation of the jars.

Among the conclusions drawn by Luchins and Luchins were the following:

They [the students] were accustomed to the use of isolated drill in arithmetic, wherein in order to "learn" a method or formula they practiced it in a series of similar problems— a situation quite similar to our experimental setup. They were accustomed to being taught a method and then practicing it; to have to discover procedures was not only quite foreign to them in arithmetic but also in most school

subjects. It seems to us that the methods of teaching to which they had been subjected tended to develop, not adaptive responses, but fixations, so that a child might know methods and formulas and yet not know where to apply them or how to determine what method best suited a particular problem. Our schools may be concentrating so much on having the child master the habits that the habits are mastering the child (Luchins & Luchins, 1950, p. 286).

Miller (1957) investigated more carefully the relation between intelligence and E effects (*Einstellung* effects). His experiment was carried on in a British integrated secondary-modern-technical school. He felt that he was therefore better able than Luchins to hold constant such influential factors as the physical surroundings, teacher's personality, and the socioeconomic status of the parents of the students. The boys in the technical school were preparing for examinations or apprenticeships; those in the modern school were without such clear objectives. As Miller put it, in many cases the latter "would not have been regretful when schooling ceased" (p. 128). The same teachers taught both groups of subjects, but varied their methods, using drill more extensively in the classes in the modern school.

Miller's design was better than that of Luchins in that he was able to minimize the effect of some factors (e.g., teacher personality and socioeconomic status of the parents of the students) not so readily controlled by Luchins. One of Miller's findings confirmed one of Luchins'; in the middle IQ group there was a statistically significant difference between the performance of the modern school students (who were drilled) and that of the technical school students. However, unlike Luchins, Miller found a significant negative correlation between IQ and E effects. He concluded that teaching methods are a major influence in inducing E effects: "It seems likely that in being trained to utilise sure methods of work, the pupils [those in the modern school] tend to approach all new situations in this way, thus failing to show the same flexibility in attack as do other pupils in whose formal training emphasis is placed on finding alternative methods of solution" (Miller, 1957, p. 132).

Some mathematics educators cite the findings and conclusions of research like this in arguing for a de-emphasis on drill and an emphasis on teaching which demands the forming and testing of hypotheses. This position appears consistent with the findings of Frick and Guilford (1957) that most of the nonchance variance in the performance of their subjects on a test (an adaptation of Luchins' water-jar test) designed to induce an *Einstellung* was accounted for by such factors as general reasoning and logical evaluation and very little by adaptive flexibility, the opposite of rigidity.

Obliquely related to inductive discovery are the theory of Wertheimer (1945) and his research, on which the theory is grounded. (Wertheimer's ideas probably stimulated the Luchins research, which has many similar elements.) Wertheimer was interested in that kind of thinking which some people call problem-solving. He directed himself to the following questions: What takes place in this process? Whence the flash of insight? What conditions and attitudes seem associated with it? Why are some individuals good at productive thinking and others not? How can productive thinking be improved? From the reports of Wertheimer's studies, it is clear that his research does not fit any of the canonical designs. Apparently making no attempt to control certain relevant variables, he relied instead on his intuition. Relevant to the teaching of mathematics were his studies on finding the area of a parallelogram, on the proof of the theorem on the equality of vertical angles, and on finding the sum of the measures of the angles of a polygon. The protocols presented in these studies, one of the better features of the research, provide ideas concerning methods of teaching, in addition to performing their main function of supporting the theory of learning and teaching Wertheimer advocates. In this theory the concept of structure (pattern) is central.

Thinking involves search for a structure or the imposition of a known structure on the problem. The thinker tries to reorganize, regroup, or restructure the "given" until he sees some meaning (pattern) and proceeds from there. Wertheimer's evidence is particularly impressive when visual structures are concerned. When he extrapolates to structures in general, his differences with other theoreticians seem to be semantic.

Additional evidence on the consequences of the tell-and-do method and a heuristic method was supplied by Nichols (1956). He formed a group of 42 pairs of students in a high school, the members of each pair matched insofar as possible as to score on a geometry test, IQ, age, and sex. The "criterion" geometry test measured knowledge of the meaning of a set of geometric terms, ability to think critically, ability to solve a geometric problem, and skills in using a ruler and protractor for mensuration. The matching permitted the assumption that the two groups had a common population variance on the first three of these variables. Both groups were taught the same 15 "basic geometric principles" (theorems) for the same length of time. One group was taught by a "dependence approach" and the other by a "structured search approach." The experimenter described these as follows:

Students taught by the Dependence Approach depended on the teacher for statement of assumptions, theorems, definitions, and verbalization of principles. Direct student participation and involvement in the development of new topics was encouraged only to the extent of ascertaining that the students were not "lost." The method of presentation was highly verbal and abstract. Students were required to keep a notebook in which they recorded statements of assumptions, definitions, proofs of theorems, and other significant statements, written by the teacher on the blackboard. . . . The teacher was directed in his presentation by a guide . . . prepared by the writer, containing references to "Basic Geometry" by Birkhoff and Beatley.

Students taught by the Structured Search Approach discovered every relationship, which was presented by the teacher to the Dependence Group, through a series of concrete experiences with drawings of geometric figures and through mensuration. A verbalization of each relationship thus discovered was made by each student. The experiences leading to discoveries of these relationships were structured through teaching materials, divided into units, called experiments, prepared by the writer. The students were required to have individual portfolios in which they kept all the experiments for future reference (Nichols, 1956, pp. 14–15).

Nichols concluded that the two approaches were equally effective, in terms of the criterion test in geometry, for high school freshmen whether of average or superior IQ; there was no statistically significant difference between students taught by the two approaches in performance on the criterion test.

Michael (1949) studied the relative effectiveness of what he called "inductive" and "deductive" methods for teaching the fundamental operations on real numbers. The inductive method was characterized as follows:

[This method] emphasized the use of exercises in thinking, with the exercises built around familiar situations involving time, money, directions, temperature, and others of the type commonly used in textbooks in algebra. Through the use of these exercises, the pupil was expected to discover and understand the fundamental principles and relationships to be learned. The use of numerous practice exercises to bring about efficiency in the operations was supposed to follow the discovery and understanding brought about inductively by the learning exercises. While pupils undoubtedly came to generalize for themselves individually at various times during the experimental period, no statement of the rules of operation was made by teachers or pupils in teaching, reteaching, or pupil discussion (Michael, 1949, p. 83).

The deductive method, on the other hand,

. . . emphasized the use of authoritative statements of the rules of operation combined with extensive practice or drill. No attempt was made, before practice with the respective processes was begun, to explain why the rules operated to give the correct results. Through the process of working with the rules in many exercises the pupil was expected to gain operative efficiency and to acquire understanding of the principles and relationships in the area under consideration (Michael, 1949, p. 83).

It seems reasonable to conclude from Michael's description that the latter method departs from the tell-and-do method in that no attempt was made to justify, other than pragmatically, the rules presented.

Michael used a design based on analysis of covariance, with an unspecified number of pupils in Grade 9 algebra. Three criterion tests measured in turn (1) accuracy of computation, (2) ability to use generalizations, and (3) attitudes toward algebra and toward mathematics in general. The tests were administered before and after the teaching program so that measures of growth could be obtained.

Comparisons of mean adjusted posttest scores in accuracy of computation favored the inductive method; however, the difference was not significant at the .05 level. The difference in ability to use generalizations favored the deductive method; here the difference was significant at the .05 level. Differences in the teaching methods produced no significant difference in attitudes toward mathematics in general, but a significantly (.01 level) more favorable attitude toward algebra was associated with the inductive method.

When the students were grouped in three levels of mental ability, as measured by the California Short-Form Test of Mental Maturity, no differences between teaching method groups significant at the .05 level were found on any of the criterion tests.

It should be noted that, in Michael's test of ability to use generalizations, the "generalizations" were open sentences. The concept of a generalization implied by the items in the test is not in accordance with the concept found in logic, that is, an explicit quantification using either '∀' (for all) or '∃' (for some) or their equivalent names in English.

In light of the different values of 'z' in 'xRz', namely, performances on the three criterion tests which Michael used and on those which Hendrix (1947) and Beberman (1958) used, a conclusion that the findings of these researches are contradictory is not warranted. Yet one cannot quarrel with Michael's final conclusion:

It can be said with safety that the results of the study are such as to throw doubt upon the advisability of making broad assertions regarding the best methods of teaching topics in high school algebra unless a body of supporting evidence from classroom experimentation has been accumulated (Michael, 1949, p. 87).

Deductive methods. It was pointed out earlier in this section that heuristic methods can be classified into two groups: inductive and deductive. We now turn to a consideration of the latter.

It is more difficult to analyze the deductive discovery method of teaching and arrive at a detailed structure like those presented above. Suppose a teacher wishes to teach an item of subject matter q. In general, a teacher who uses the deductive discovery method to teach q operates in such a way as to get a student to consider in juxtaposition two or more propositions $p_1, p_2, p_3, \ldots$ which imply q. The teacher then relies on the student's inferring q. As in the case of the inductive discovery method, the teacher accepts appropriate nonverbal or verbal behavior by the student as evidence that he has made the inference.

An example of the deductive discovery method, while fictitious, may clarify the method. Suppose a student says, "You can't add 2 and $\sqrt{3}$." His statement implies 'There exists no real number which is the sum of 2 and $\sqrt{3}$'. The teacher might ask, "Is it true that *every* pair of real numbers has a unique sum?" The student, assuming that he recognizes this as the closure postulate for addition for the field of real numbers, would say "Yes." The teacher would

then ask, "Are 2 and $\sqrt{3}$ real numbers?" The student, if we may assume that he knew that they are (and if he did not know this, the teacher could use the deductive discovery method to convince him that they are), would again say "Yes." The teacher would then confront him with his pair of contradictory statements which may be paraphrased as "You can't add 2 and $\sqrt{3}$" and "You can add 2 and $\sqrt{3}$." Since the student cannot defeat the argument whose conclusion is the latter, he must abandon his claim of the former.

Another fictitious example of the deductive discovery method, given by Hendrix (1959), illustrates how this same method can be used at greater length. It is possible to argue either that the Socratic questioning technique (which Hendrix's fancied episode also illustrates) is an example of the deductive discovery method, or vice versa. This technique consists of asking questions or making statements which enable the other participant in the dialogue—in the present context, the student—to correct his belief or answer the question he originally asked.

Both inductive and deductive heuristic methods are employed in the extensive research being conducted by the University of Illinois Committee on School Mathematics (UICSM). This research may be regarded as an existence proof that certain values of 'x' in 'xRz'—among which are heuristic methods (UICSM calls these "discovery")—are associated with certain values of 'z'. (The research being conducted by UICSM is also curricular research in that it seeks to study the relation ySz. Distinctive subject matter becomes values of 'y', the independent variable, and values of 'z', the dependent variable, are described. This aspect of the UICSM's research is fully as significant as that being considered in this Handbook.)

We turn first to a description of the discovery method which UICSM uses. When the inductive discovery method is used, UICSM delays the verbalization of the item of knowledge discovered by the student. In one report on the project, Beberman (1958) said, "This technique . . . of *delaying* the verbalization of important discoveries is characteristic of the UICSM program, and differentiates our discovery method from other methods which are also called 'discovery methods' but which always involve the immediate verbalization of discoveries" (p. 27).

This principle is employed in the Exploratory Exercises often used by the UICSM (1960) in introducing a topic in their text, *High School Mathematics*. Consistent with this principle is the UICSM's policy of insisting that the student become aware of a concept before a name is assigned the concept. As an example of this, Beberman stated,

Through a series of activities and exercises in which a student becomes quite familiar with graphs of sets of ordered pairs (advancing from finite domains and ranges to infinite ones), the student builds for himself the concept that a set of ordered pairs is an entity and that membership in the set can be expressed by means of a graph, and, in some cases, by means of a simple sentence (Beberman, 1958, p. 34).

Deductive discovery characterizes the method of some of the teachers in the UICSM Project. Illustrations of this appear in the set of films developed as part of the UICSM Project.

A second distinctive characteristic of the UICSM method is precision in the use of language. The text distinguishes between numbers, numerals (names of numbers), and pronumerals (variables replaceable by names of numbers). It uses linguistic signals like single quotation marks and displays (i.e., varying arrangements of lines) to indicate clearly when a term is being mentioned rather than used. Use of the quantifiers '$\forall$' and '$\exists$' clarifies the meaning of expressions like '$x + 2 = 6$', '$x + y = y + x$', and '$y < y + 1$'. As Beberman (1958) stated in his Inglis Lecture,

One can give a defense of the language used in conventional courses by saying that many of the usages are colloquial or elliptical, and that such idiomatic modes of expression

are helpful in facilitating informal communication. We grant the importance of using colloquialisms and elisions, but we also insist that students know what is being idiomatized. For example, if a student says that "You can add 3x and 5x", we want him to understand that he means that the distributive and commutative principles can be used to transform the expression '3x + 5x' to '8x', and that he does not mean that 3x and 8x can be added because you can add "like numbers." If he says '$\angle ABC = 30°$', we want him to intend this as an abbreviation for 'the degree-measure of $\angle ABC = 30°$' or for '$\angle ABC$ belongs to the magnitude 30°'. He may talk about the line '3x + 5y − 7 = 0' but he should understand that he means the line which is the set of all ordered pairs (x,y) such that 3x + 5y − 7 = 0 (Beberman, 1958, pp. 20–21).

Values of 'z' in 'xRz' which, the UICSM reports, are associated with the methods (values of x) described above are interest in mathematics, power in mathematical thinking, and versatility in applying mathematics in new problems (Beberman, 1958, p. 38). Hendrix has observed that students in classes in which these methods are used seem better able to tolerate that period of time between the posing of a problem and their getting a hunch on how to solve it.[2] They are not as likely as other students to give up or say, "We haven't had a problem like that." Some psychologists might be inclined to consider the UICSM students' behavior as evidence of a feeling of security in the face of a threatening situation.

Conclusions. Before turning to other kinds of research on teaching secondary school mathematics, let us consider what can be concluded about the consequences of tell-and-do methods versus heuristic methods. One conclusion is that the evidence is not conclusive. But as soon as this is said, we should point out that no agreed-upon criteria exist which enable all persons to decide—and agree— whether a conclusion is warranted in a probable inference. And the significant inferences in the empirical research described above are

_____
[2] Personal communication.

probable inferences. Hence 'conclusive' in the context of the first part of this paragraph is used, not to describe for the reader an existing state of affairs, but to offer advice concerning how much confidence he should put in the findings of the research studies. It should be realized that to say the findings are not conclusive is to talk explicitly about the findings and implicitly about the values of the writer.

One is tempted to admonish the reader to draw his own conclusions about the findings and conclusions of the various experimenters. But more than this can be offered even if it is negative in tone. If the consequences of being wrong are serious, one should be wary of adopting one method rather than another *on the basis of the evidence available.* If the consequences of being wrong are not serious, one is freer to choose. For example, if thousands of dollars are to be committed to writing textbooks which employ Method X with the possibility that the books will not sell, or if thousands of man-hours are to be committed to redesigning teacher-training curricula to eliminate Method X, the consequences of being wrong are serious. It is hard to believe that a steel mill, for example, would alter a process it has used for some time solely on the basis of evidence on a new process no greater than that available on any of the teaching methods discussed above. Nor is it reasonable to believe that therapy for a serious disease would be altered because of evidence equivalent to what we have on any of the teaching methods.

The Unit Plan and Supervised Study as Methods

In some proposals for teaching, it is argued that a unit plan should be used instead of a daily recitation plan. Hunziker and Douglass (1937) compared the effect of these two plans. Two groups of students studying elementary algebra and two groups studying plane geometry were used. All groups were in the same high school and were taught by the same teacher. Students were dropped from the experiment (though not from

membership in the classes) to make the groups approximately equivalent with respect to IQ, chronological age, and initial scores on the tests administered at the end of the experiment. The two methods were interchanged at the end of the first semester, i.e., the groups that had been subjected to the unit plan were then subjected to the daily recitation plan, and conversely.

The experimenters described the unit plan as follows:

. . . unit assignments of from four to twenty days were employed. One to three days were spent in making the assignment and preparing the class to attack it. This state was then followed by several days of supervised study in which for the greater part silent individual study was employed though occasional class discussion was used. Each unit was concluded by a 'recitation' in the form of an oral discussion or an oral or written quiz over the unit (Hunziker & Douglass, 1937, p. 122).

The daily recitation method was described as follows: "the students covered the same materials though the assignments were not always the same, the recitation plan group being given daily assignments involving work to be done outside of class. They had no time for supervised study" (p. 122).

By administering the same tests before and after the use of the two methods, Hunziker and Douglass were able to compute gains. These were the measures of the dependent variable, viz., achievement in the subject studied.

At the end of the first semester, there was a difference in the gains favorable to the supervised study method, but the difference was not significant ($p < .14$). At the end of the second semester, the difference between the gains was highly favorable to the daily recitation method and the difference was significant ($p < .01$). The findings were invariant as to the intelligence of the students. The experimenters concluded:

with pupils trained in the daily recitation method for years and with little experience in the large unit plan of supervised [study], the daily recitation plan in the hands of at least some teachers of mathematics if not a majority of them, will yield better results as measured by gains on written examinations than the large unit plan of supervised study employed by Mr. Hunziker (Hunziker & Douglass, 1937, p. 124).

Douglass (1928) attempted to study the relative effect during a class period of having students recite first and then study (presumably the next assignment) or study first and then recite on what they had studied. He does not describe the recitation; hence one must infer from how the term 'recitation' is ordinarily used. It is usually used to denote the teacher's quizzing the students to see whether or not they have "learned" what was assigned. The quizzing may consist of oral questioning by the teacher or having students display on the chalkboard their solutions to problems in the assignment.

Douglass attempted to select pairs of students, with the members of each pair matched on initial knowledge of the mathematics involved (e.g., arithmetic or algebra), intelligence (Otis), and chronological age. The group of first members of each pair followed one sequence, e.g., study, then recite, and the group of second members of each pair followed the reverse sequence. Classrooms, times of classes, and teachers were assigned so as to control the influence, if any, of these factors. While there was some variation in what the students did during the study period, most of them used it for silent study. The dependent variable was gain in score on an achievement test sampling what was taught during the time covered by the experiment.

Douglass found that, for two of his three replications of the experiment, the recite-study sequence was significantly associated ($p < .12$) with the greater average gain in achievement. In the third replication, the difference was in the same direction, but less significant statistically ($p = .44$). His design did not employ analysis of variance or covariance. While he attempted to match the

students using the two sequences, he reported no facts concerning the variance within each group.

Schunert's extensive study (1951) was concerned in part with the method of supervised study. We shall review his entire study at this point. Schunert investigated the relation between mathematical achievement and certain factors associated with teaching, the teacher, the pupil, and the school. That part of his study which investigated the relation of certain methods of teaching and mathematical achievement is relevant to this chapter.

The variables in teaching method Schunert studied were: (1) type of assignment, i.e., identical assignment for all students or differentiated assignments (Schunert did not name the factors with respect to which the differentiation was made); (2) frequency of testing, i.e., once a week, more than once a week, or less than once a week; (3) use of supervised study, i.e., less than an average of 20 minutes a day, or more than an average of 30 minutes a day; (4) use of workbooks, i.e., used a workbook or did not use a workbook; and (5) use of reviews, i.e., frequently or infrequently (Schunert did not define "frequently" and "infrequently").

The dependent variable was measured by tests which Schunert constructed. These tests purported to place approximately equal emphasis on knowledge of mathematical concepts and principles, mathematical skills, and application of mathematical knowledge and skills to the solution of practical problems. The tests were judged valid by a jury. Their reliability (Hoyt) was in the range .89 to .94. To control differences among the various groups of students in initial achievement on the mathematics test and on the Otis Quick-Scoring Mental Ability Test, analysis of covariance was used.

The following teaching methods were found to be significantly (.05 level) and positively associated with achievement in algebra: regular use of differentiated assignments rather than identical assignments, reviews occurring more frequently than once a month rather than not more frequently than once every six weeks, and 20 to 30 minutes of supervised study each day rather than less. No significant relationship was found between achievement in algebra and amount of assigned homework or frequency of testing.

The following practices were found to be significantly (.05 level) and positively associated with achievement in geometry: requiring more than 30 minutes of supervised study each day rather than less than 20 minutes, and testing more frequently than once a week rather than less frequently. No significant relationship was found between achievement in geometry and the type of assignment used, the amount of homework assigned, and the use of a workbook.

Schunert's analysis of variance also yielded significant interaction variances which enabled him to conclude that these findings were not invariant as to (1) size of school in enrollment, (2) kind of school organization, viz., four-year schools versus six-year and three-year schools, (3) years of experience of teachers, (4) kind of college from which the teacher graduated, viz., state universities or private colleges versus teachers colleges, and (5) class size. Hence it is hazardous to generalize from his findings.

Gadske's findings (1933) were inconsistent with those just given. Gadske compared two methods of teaching first-year algebra: One method was "a unit method in which instruction and progress were strictly individual within each unit and the assignments were unit assignments" (pp. 635–636). The assignments stated the purposes of the unit, presented a preview of it, stated the work to be done by the student, e.g., pages to be read and problems to be solved. During the period of study of the unit, students worked individually, and the teacher provided whatever help he deemed necessary. The class convened only when the unit was introduced and at the end for a test. The second method was one "where the pupils progressed as a group through lectures, demonstrations, recitations, daily assignments, tests, and group remedial instruction" (pp. 636–637).

The dependent variable, acquisition of knowledge about algebra, was measured by two written tests—one given at the end of each of the two semesters of the experiment. Intelligence (IQ), knowledge of arithmetic, and reading ability were controlled by matching pairs of students. Twenty-three pairs were obtained from the 100 students taking first-year algebra. These pairs became the *de facto* subjects in the study.

Gadske found that greater achievement in algebra was significantly (difference in means > three times standard error of the difference) associated with the unit method. This was true for both semesters. Although the students with lower IQs also had greater achievement under the unit method, the difference was not as great for them as for the superior students. The slower students subjected to the unit method were also less discouraged with their progress, even though it was slow, than were the slower students taught by the other method.

Gadske's findings are consistent with those of Williams (1932), Eilberg (1931), and Hare (1923). Williams used a modified form of the Winnetka Contract Plan for his unit method; his study was in second-year algebra. Eilberg and Hare used plane geometry for the subject matter. The dependent variable in all cases was acquisition of knowledge about the subject studied.

Two plans of supervised study were compared by Stallard and Douglass (1935). One method, in essence, was the unit method described by Gadske. In the other method each daily class period was divided into two halves; the first half was devoted to recitation, discussion, and giving the assignment, and the second half to supervised study of the assignment in which the teacher behaved in the conventional manner, i.e., provided individual help, etc. The experimental groups were matched as to means and standard deviations in chronological age, IQ, and knowledge of arithmetic. The dependent variable was knowledge of the algebra taught. The experimenters found that the large unit of supervised study was associated with greater achievement by the superior students involved. The difference in the two methods was not associated with a difference in achievement for average students.

Other Studies

In plane geometry and also in solid geometry, as these subjects are usually taught, students spend a lot of time proving theorems, be they so labeled or called "original exercises." Almost no time is spent disproving generalizations. Moreover, little or no time is spent getting students to think of generalizations on their own. Hence, it is likely that students get no feeling for how a mathematician works. They do not create; they tread a narrow path carefully laid out for them by the author of their textbook so that it has no cul-de-sacs, and do not try to prove a universal statement to be a theorem when it is not.

Heinke (1953, 1957) sought to develop a way of teaching which would help students discover new (to them) generalizations which could then be tested to see whether they were theorems. Heinke's research showed that if a teacher encourages students to change the hypotheses (given conditions) or conclusions of a theorem, the students will tend to discover new (to the students) statements of related properties. Some of these statements turn out to be universally quantifiable over a domain, hence theorems; others do not. Students get experience in disproving as well as proving statements. Variation of the hypotheses can be accomplished by deletion, addition, or substitution of one or more conditions in the hypotheses, viz., p_1, p_2, p_3, ... in 'If p_1 and p_2, and p_3, ... then q_1, and q_2 and q_3 ...', or similar changes in the conclusion, viz., q_1, q_2, q_3, ... One class of possible changes consists of forming converses or partial converses, inverses or partial inverses, and contrapositives. Success with this particular method has also been reported by Allen (1950). The method is based on the logical analysis of Lazar (1938), who suggested uses of partial converses and partial inverses.

Although both Heinke and Allen restricted their conclusions to the teaching of geometry, their technique is general enough to be applied to any mathematics course in which proofs of theorems are presented. Since a trend in the teaching of secondary school mathematics is toward more proofs in the algebra studied, the technique should prove widely effective, if it can be assumed that the results are invariant as to the subject matter taught. Acceptance of the truth of this assumption does not seem hazardous. But it should be recognized that we have little evidence to support the assumption. Hence, many persons will be unwilling to pass from the findings of this research to an inference normative in form—for example, that a teacher should have students permute the conditions in the hypothesis and conclusion —even if they value the kind of student behavior Heinke and Allen found associated with this method.

Much has been written about the use of instructional aids like models, films, and filmstrips. How effective are these? In one of the better studies of these media, Johnson (1949) investigated the relative effectiveness of sound motion pictures and filmstrips in promoting learning in geometry. The learning he considered was acquiring and retaining information, applying the information in new situations, and acquiring and retaining certain skills. The high schools participating in the study were selected at random, as were the geometry classes within those schools which were selected as the experimental classes. Such relevant factors as the subject matter studied, the time of study, the teacher, and the tests used were controlled. The design made possible 15 replications and employed analysis of variance and covariance.

Most of Johnson's findings were negative; that is, there were no significant differences between media, and there were no significant differences between using a medium and not using one. The one outcome for which results were consistently in favor of the experimental groups was in the retention of learning in those classes using three filmstrips and three sound films (the greatest number employed) for the study of the geometry of the circle. A possible explanation of the results may be inferred from one of Johnson's conclusions:

It appears that audio-visual aids which are developed for use in mathematics classes might be more effective as aids to learning if they were designed to supplement rather than repeat the type of instruction which the students have in the typical mathematics classroom (Johnson, 1949, p. 372).

A study based on systematic classroom observation of verbal interaction in mathematics classrooms was conducted by Wright and Proctor (1961). The investigators first designed a technique for making observations of the nature of mathematical content considered, the psychological processes involved, and the sociological attitudes manifested by the students. The mathematical content and psychological processes were analyzed according to the schema shown on pp. 288–290 in Chapter 6.

The three attitudes considered were curiosity, independence, and receptivity. These were regarded as functionally determined by the social environment in which the teaching-learning was carried on and hence were termed *sociological attitudes*.

After the technique was refined and the two observers trained until the reliability of observation was satisfactory, the technique was employed to compare types of mathematics classrooms selected in terms of the rigor of mathematical argument presented and the amount of participation by the students. Four types were selected: high rigor, high participation; low rigor, high participation; low rigor, low participation; and high rigor, low participation.

Wright and Proctor found that an increase in rigor, with participation held constant, and an increase in participation, with rigor held constant, were associated with an emphasis on structure without loss of technical skill. Moreover, increase in student participation was associated with greater emphasis

on strategies in solving problems, with the students making occasional halting attempts at playing the role of a teacher, and did not limit unduly the amount of subject matter covered.

The conceptualization underlying the Wright-Proctor technique is sound, the factors on which the observation is focused are significant, and the observational method is carefully described. It appears to provide one way of analyzing and studying the relation between methods of teaching and associated student behavior.

THE PRESENT CONDITION AND SOME PROSPECTS

After considering the research reviewed above, one is inclined to accept Dodes's conclusions:

The teacher can not depend upon any special type of lesson, such- as "supervised study," to guarantee success in teaching and learning . . . . There is no decisive proof that any particular method of teaching (inductive, deductive, individual, group) or any particular philosophy of teaching (teacher-dominated lesson or socialized lesson) will guarantee better results than any other method or philosophy, so far as achievement is concerned (Dodes, 1953, p. 163).

These conclusions are warranted if one sets as an expectation generalizations universally quantified over the domains of subject matter, teachers, students, and schools. There are two reasons for this. One is that there have not been enough studies sampling the domains named to generate much confidence in the findings. The second is that the findings are not always consistent even for a particular domain.

The conclusion seems inescapable: Teaching, as of 1963, is an art, not a science. For it to move toward becoming a science, we need much more empirical research to test current theories. But we also need new theoretical concepts or orientations that will provoke different questions to be asked of nature, so to speak. We turn to each of these matters in turn.

Just about all the research done uses as values of 'z' in $T(x, y, z)$ behavior of students, which is closely associated with values of 'x' in point of time. For example, a method (value of 'x') is employed to teach some subject matter (values of 'y'). The value of 'z' studied is the students' acquisition of the subject matter. This certainly is valid; the results of this research are worth while. But the justification given for some methods, e.g., some heuristic methods and their characteristics, such as precision in the use of language, is that the greater intellectual power produced will result in greater creativity and enhanced success in subsequent mathematics courses in high school and college. Such hypothesized outcomes can be defined in terms of behavior of students. It will be recognized that these behaviors (values of 'z') are separated considerably in point of time from the teaching. Research studies can then be designed to test these justifications or implied hypotheses. This kind of research is needed to enable us to attach a truth-value to the statements purporting to justify using a certain method.

As Ausubel (1961) pointed out in a carefully documented analysis, there is insufficient empirical evidence to support the claims for the unverbalized awareness method if universal quantification over domains (e.g., all teachers, all items of knowledge, all students) is held as a criterion. (It may be, however, that if a domain is restricted, e.g., to a particular teacher, the claims are warranted.) On the other hand, no published research counters the claims for this method. The advocates of this method do not object to having the student verbalize his discovery; they simply urge that the teacher not press for verbalization "too soon." But how is a teacher to know whether or not his asking for a verbalization is "too soon"? The facetious definition of a civil engineer is relevant. A civil engineer is a person who can tell, *before* a train passes over a bridge he has designed, whether or not the bridge will collapse. After the train has passed over the bridge, anyone can tell. Similarly, a skilled teacher is one who can tell *before* he asks for the verbalization whether or not the student will have difficulty making it. Once the student attempts the verbalization, anyone can tell. But to be able to predict, we need research which will identify cues a teacher can use. There seems to be no research of this kind.

Associated with such research should be research to determine whether or not the kind of language used to express the verbalization is influential.

It has been suggested by David Page, as a result of his research on teaching arithmetic, that three kinds of language appear to be used in the mathematics classroom.[3] One is the language used by novices. It is full of imprecision and ambiguity and employs a lot of gestures and pointing. One student might say to another, in talking about multiplying two rational numbers, "You multiply across the top and you multiply across the bottom." "Cross multiplying," "inverting the divisor," "dropping the denominator," and other inexact expressions may belong to this language.

At the other extreme is the precise language that mathematicians can employ when they choose to do so. To this language belong numerals, variables, symbols for relations, quantifiers, and such symbols as '$+$', '$-$', '$\times$', '$\div$', '$=$', '$<$', 'ε', '$\cap$', '$\cup$', '$\sim$', '$\wedge$', '$\vee$', '$\Rightarrow$', et al. In this language, the statement the student made about multiplying rational numbers would be '$\forall$ a, b $\neq$ o, c,

$$d \neq o, \frac{a}{b} \times \frac{c}{d} = \frac{ac}{bd}.$$

Between these two languages is a middle language. To this language belong *sum, addend, subtrahend, minuend, quotient, dividend, multiplier, multiplicand, denominator, numerator, mixed number, improper fraction,* etc. As Page points out, the principal characteristic of the middle language is that

---

[3] Personal communication.

it can be avoided with no loss in communication—except by a teacher who knows nothing else.

If this theory of languages is correct, one might speculate that verbalization should be easiest in the first language and most difficult in the middle language. Most teaching, whether by a person in front of a class or by a textbook, is done in terms of the middle language. When a teacher seeks a verbalization, he may predispose his student to use the middle language. Let us suppose the student cannot state the generalization correctly. Would he experience as much difficulty if he were encouraged to use variables, quantifiers, and logical constants? Research to provide the answer is needed.

Research on the utilization of methods by machines has great potentialities. These machines may be classified into two kinds: (1) those which have no "memories" and hence are incapable of feedback, i.e., selection of instances in terms of student reponses so as to converge on the generalization to be learned, and (2) those which do have "memories" and hence are capable of feedback. Research utilizing the latter kind of teaching machines is especially promising. Robinson (1960) has provided one theoretical model which can be used to program such a machine. Probably the chief obstacle to such research will be expense. But for certain values of $'y'$ in $T(x, y, z)$, it is reasonable to argue that a machine like some of the data processors now in existence (and others more powerful which even now are realizable) servicing an individual viewing screen for each student would be more effective than many teachers.

We turn now to a consideration of theory construction. In many theories the concepts of generalizing, abstracting, explaining (in the sense of telling why), inferring (discovering is subsumed under inferring), intuiting, and insight are employed. Relying on psychological theory, research workers consider generalizing, abstracting, and the others to be processes. It seems reasonable, then, to study these processes psychologically. But such study has not yielded any substantial growth of knowledge about these processes.

Another approach utilizes modern logical theory rather than psychological theory. Space permits only a brief sketch of an approach using this theory. Ryle (1955, Ch. 5) points out the difference in the logic of process words like *run, search, listen, think,* and *study* and achievement words like *win, choose, find* (an object), and *hear.* In applying an achievement word, we assert that over and beyond the performance there is a state of affairs distinct from the performance. For a runner to win, he must not only run, he must "hit the tape" before any of the other runners. Winning, in a sense, is not something he *does;* it is something that *happens* to him. Whereas process words have a present continuous tense, achievement words do not. For example, it makes sense to say, "Tom is running." It makes no sense to say, "Tom is winning," even though Tom is twenty yards ahead of his nearest rival and the finish line is only a yard away.[4] As Ryle says, achievement words, unlike process words, can be dated but not timed.

Applying this distinction to certain concepts used in talking about learning, we find it fruitful to propose that 'generalizing', 'discovering', 'abstracting', etc., are achievement words. One does not generalize until the generalization appears, abstract until the abstraction is made, infer until the inference is made. While it makes sense to say, "I am thinking, reading, studying...," it makes no sense to say, "I am inferring, discovering,

---

[4] To be sure, people *do* say, "Tom is winning," but anyone who hears this readily converts it into "Tom is ahead and probably will be the winner." Language is a tremendously flexible instrument. We do not always have to say what we mean for people to know what we mean. Mathematics is replete with examples to confirm this. "Invert the divisor and multiply" and "change the sign of the subtrahend and add" are mathematical nonsense, inasmuch as symbols are distinct from numbers, but students and teachers respond appropriately with respect to them. The point is that when we analyze what is said—not what is *meant*—the illogical nature of the sentence readily becomes apparent.

generalizing, ..." Uses such as "I am discovering that people with meager mathematical training are limited in vocational opportunities" are not counterexamples. They simply indicate an impoverished vocabulary or mental lethargy in hunting for a proper word. It follows that educational psychologists, in attempting to study inferring and generalizing as *processes,* are misguided and might be better off to study the achievements.

Modern logic allows such a study. Explaining, defining, inferring, etc. are relations; e.g., *x* explains *y*, *s* is an abstraction from *t*, *m* is inferred from *n*. So, also, are other relations; e.g., *x* means *y*, *x* means the same as *z*, and *x* means *y* to *p*, which are not appropriately subsumed under processes. It might be enlightening and profitable for research to consider each of these as a set of ordered *n*-tuples and to apply whatever principles of the theory of relations are appropriate. Would there then be fewer cases of bad syntax like 'meaningful experiences' and 'meaningful teaching' (Is meaning a property of anything other than symbols?) which either mirror confused thinking or warrant only the inference that, whatever the experience or teaching is, the speaker is favorably disposed to it?

Mathematics educators have command of logical theory which can clarify many of the concepts employed in discussing teaching and learning. It seems reasonable to hypothesize that if semantic confusion is reduced, the theory will be more productive of questions worth asking—questions to which research may produce answers in the form of statements universally quantified over a certain well-defined domain. There seems little to lose by this approach, for the sterile theories of educational psychology which have squeezed all logic from theories of methodology provide few new questions.

REFERENCES

Allen, F. Teaching for generalization in geometry. *Math. Teacher,* 1950, 43, 245–251.

Austin, C. A. The laboratory method in teaching of geometry. *Math. Teacher,* 1927, 20, 286–294.

Ausubel, D. P. *Learning by discovery: Rationale and mystique.* Urbana: Bur. of Educ. Res., Univer. of Illinois, 1961.

Beberman, M. *An emerging program of secondary school mathematics.* Cambridge, Mass.: Harvard Univer. Press, 1958.

Commission on Post-War Plans. The first report of the . . . . *Math. Teacher,* 1944, 37, 226–232.

Commission on Post-War Plans. The second report of the . . . . *Math. Teacher,* 1945, 38, 195–221.

Committee on the Function of Mathematics in General Education. *Mathematics in general education.* New York: Appleton-Century, 1940.

Dodes, I. A. The science of teaching mathematics. *Math. Teacher,* 1953, 46, 157–166.

Douglass, H. R. Study or recitation first in supervised study in mathematics. *Math. Teacher,* 1928, 21, 390–393.

Eilberg, A. The Dalton Plan versus the recitation method in the teaching of plane geometry. Unpublished doctoral dissertation, Temple Univer., 1931.

Fawcett, H. A mathematics program with an emphasis on general education. *Sch. Sci. Math.,* 1942, 42, 25–31.

Frick, J. W., & Guilford, J. P. An analysis of a form of the water-jar test. *Amer. J. Psychol.,* 1957, 70, 427–431.

Gadske, R. E. A comparison of two methods of teaching first year high school algebra. *Sch. Sci. Math.,* 1933, 33, 635–640.

Hare, J. S. An experimental study of two types of teaching procedure in geometry. Unpublished master's thesis, Ohio State Univer., 1923.

Hart, H. L. A. The ascription of responsibility and rights. In *Logic and language.* (1st ser.) Oxford: Blackwell, 1952. Pp. 145–166.

Haslerud, G. M., & Meyers, Shirley. The transfer value of given and individually derived principles. *J. educ. Psychol.,* 1958, 49, 293–298.

Heinke, C. H. Discovery in geometry through the process of variation. Unpublished doctoral dissertation, Ohio State Univer., 1953.

Heinke, C. H. Variation—A process of discovery. *Math. Teacher,* 1957, 50, 146–154.

Henderson, K. B. Strategies for teaching by the discovery method. *Updating Math.,* Section IV, November, 1958.

Henderson, K. B. Strategies for teaching by the discovery method. *Updating Math.,* Section IV, April, 1959.

Hendrix, Gertrude. A new clue to transfer of training. *Elem. sch. J.,* 1947, 48, 197–208.

Hendrix, Gertrude. Variable paradox: A dialogue in one act. *Sch. Sci. Math.,* 1959, 59, 461–464.

Hunziker, C. W., & Douglass, H. R. The relative effectiveness of a large unit plan of supervised study and the daily recitation method in the teaching of algebra and geometry. *Math. Teacher,* 1937, 30, 122–124.

Johnson, D. A. An experimental study of the effectiveness of films and filmstrips in teaching geometry. *J. exp. Educ.,* 1949, 17, 363–372.

Joint Commission of the Mathematical Association of America and the National Council of Teachers of Mathematics. The place of mathematics in secondary education. *Yearb. nat. Counc. Teachers Math.,* 1940, 15.

Klein, F. *Elementary mathematics from an advanced standpoint.* Vol. 1. Trans. from 3rd German ed. (1908) by E. R. Hedrick & C. A. Noble. New York: Dover Publications, 1939.

Lazar, N. The importance of certain concepts and laws of logic for the study and teaching of geometry. *Math. Teacher,* 1938, 31, 99–113, 156–174, 216–240.

Luchins, A. S. Mechanization in problem solving, the effect of Einstellung. *Psychol. Monogr.,* 1942, 54, No. 6 (Whole No. 248).

Luchins, A. S., & Luchins, Edith H. New experimental attempts at preventing mechanization in problem solving. *J. gen. Psychol.,* 1950, 42, 279–297.

Mathematical Association of America, National Committee on Mathematical Requirements. *The reorganization of mathematics in secondary education.* Washington, D.C.: U.S. Government Printing Office, 1921. (Dept. of the Interior, Bur. of Education Bull. 1921, No. 32)

May, K. O. *Elements of modern mathematics.* Cambridge, Mass.: Addison-Wesley, 1959.

Mendenhall, C. B. Mathematics in general education. Unpublished doctoral dissertation, Ohio State Univer., 1939.

Michael, R. E. The relative effectiveness of two methods of teaching certain topics in ninth grade algebra. *Math. Teacher,* 1949, 42, 83–87.

Miller, K. M. Einstellung rigidity, intelligence and teaching methods. *Brit. J. educ. Psychol.,* 1957, 27, 127–134.

Moore, E. H. On the foundations of mathematics. In C. A. Austin (Chairman), A general survey of progress in the last twenty-five years. *Yearb. nat. Counc. Teachers Math.,* 1926, 1, 32–57.

National Council of Teachers of Mathematics. The growth of mathematical ideas: Grades K–12. *Yearb. nat. Counc. Teachers Math.,* 1959, 24.

Nichols, E. D. Comparison of two approaches to the teaching of selected topics in plane geometry. Unpublished doctoral dissertation, Univer. of Illinois, 1956.

Nowell-Smith, P. H. *Ethics.* London: Penguin, 1954.

Perry, J. Discussion on the teaching of mathematics. *Proc. Brit. Ass. Mtg.* Glasgow: British Association for the Advancement of Science, 1901.

Robinson, G. A. Strategies for the teaching and learning of concepts: An analysis by symbolic logic. Unpublished doctoral dissertation, Univer. of Illinois, 1960.

Ryle, G. *The concept of mind.* London: Hutchinson House, 1955.

Schunert, J. The association of mathematical achievement with certain factors resident in the teacher, in the teaching, in the pupil, and in the school. *J. exp. Educ.,* 1951, 19, 219–238.

Stallard, B. J., & Douglass, H. R. An experimental study of two plans of supervised study in first year algebra. *J. exp. Educ.,* 1935, 4, 17–19.

Strawson, D. F. On referring. In A. G. N. Flew (Ed.), *Essays in conceptual analysis.* London: Macmillan, 1956. Pp. 21–54.

University of Illinois Committee on School Mathematics. *High school mathematics.* Urbana: Univer. of Illinois Press, 1960.

Urmson, J. O. On grading. In A. G. N. Flew (Ed.), *Logic and language.* (2nd ser.) New York: Philosophical Library, 1953. Pp. 159–186.

Wertheimer, M. *Productive thinking.* New York: Harper, 1945.

Williams, G. B. A controlled experiment to determine the efficiency of the contract method of teaching second-year algebra to normal and superior pupils. Unpublished master's thesis, Pennsylvania State Coll., 1932.

Wright, E. Muriel J., & Proctor, Virginia H. *Systematic observation of verbal interaction as a method of comparing mathematics lessons.* St. Louis: Washington Univer., 1961. (U.S. Office of Education Coop. Res. Project No. 816)

CHAPTER 20 Research on Teaching Science

FLETCHER G. WATSON
Harvard University

Research on the relations between the behavior of science teachers and other variables, such as behaviors of their pupils, is meager. The scarcity of such research on science teaching is especially unfortunate, for the structure of science and its continuous contact with manipulatable objects offer numerous opportunities for clear and diversified appraisal of pupil behaviors, This lack of research also seems inconsistent with the numerous "grand" objectives of science education spelled out from time to time. Achievement of such objectives does appear to be amenable to operational definition, and therefore to experimental study as a function of teacher behavior (Henry, 1947). While selection of instructional objectives may be distinguished from the instructional act itself, it does result in stressing certain pupil behavior, so that even this selection may be regarded as an act of the teacher.

The relative scarcity of research on science teaching in relation to pupil behavior arises from at least two factors: the persistent focus upon knowledge in the sense of ability to recall, and the orientation of those few individuals who might be expected to carry out most of the research. Most of the research involving pupil behavior has utilized pupil gain on achievement tests as the sole or primary description of changed pupil behavior. Such tests have been concerned mainly with recall and recognition behaviors and with application of principles to what Nedelsky (1949) called "academic problems" similar to those used during class instruction. Actually, these achievement tests explore only a small portion of the cognitive domain (Bloom, et al., 1956) and disregard the affective and psychomotor domains. Even if such achievement tests are valid for their narrow purpose, there is small basis for asserting that they have any relevance to the more general objectives claimed for instruction in science. Although the whole realm of affective behavior has been neglected, in our post-Sputnik concern for the identification and nurturance of more scientists, the emotional impacts of instruction and learning are of basic importance. Numerous reports from scientists (Brandwein, 1955; Cole, 1956; Knapp & Goodrich, 1952; Super & Bachrach, 1957; Terman, 1954), to the effect that one teacher often turned a student toward science as a career, make it imperative to study the affective influence of science teachers.

Tests potentially useful in such studies have recently become available. The Test of Knowledge about Science and Scientists (Educational Testing Service) was initiated by the Cincinnati School Department for appraising the impact of their television instruction. Subsequently modified by the Educational Testing Service, its standardization data are still inadequate, although they may be improved in the future.

As a reaction to the images of scientists and of science as a vocation found by the Purdue Opinion Panel (Heath, Maier, Remmers, & Rodgers, 1957) and by Mead and Metraux (1957), a Test on Understanding Science for use with upper-grade pupils in high school was prepared by Cooley and Klopfer (1961). Its three subscales were concerned with pupils' images of (1) scientists (18 items), (2) the scientific enterprise (18 items), and (3) the methods and aims of science (24 items) (Educational Testing Service).

Nearly all individuals in a position to conduct research on teaching science were originally committed to natural science and its teaching, rather than to the behavioral sciences. Obliged to maintain some comprehension of explosively growing scientific knowledge, and involved in teacher training and retraining through courses and numerous institutes, such individuals have had little time or inclination to become competent in the aspects of behavioral science research needed to study the consequences of various forms of teacher behavior. To acknowledge this is not to find fault with science educators, but rather to make clear why contributions to research on teaching science have been so meager. Forthright acknowledgement of past omissions may spur increased research activity in this field.

Be that as it may, most studies related to teacher and student behavior in science courses have been made by behavioral scientists. Free to choose the site of their experiments, few research workers have centered upon science as a field of instruction. Some have involved science teachers among others, but have failed to report results separately for the various groups of teachers involved; see, for example, Jones (1946) and Lins (1946). Also, the issues and potentialities unique to instruction in science have generally been overlooked. As Ackerman (1954) emphasized, much research has proceeded on the bland assumption that teacher effectiveness was one-dimensional, while surely it is multidimensional. If we take seriously the evidence about the individual differences of pupils, we should expect "different kinds of effectiveness for different kinds of teachers, pupils, programs or situations" (Ackerman, 1954, p. 285). We might add: different kinds of objectives and different types of content.

Perhaps the difficulty here is not lack of awareness of the multidimensional interaction of teachers, content, and pupils, but the magnitude of the study that would be required to provide statistically reliable evidence. If this has been a major block to multidimensional studies, adequate funds and staff for such an inquiry surely should be sought. It is naïve to assume that we can find some single *general* attribute of teacher behavior that would account for a significant portion of the subsequent pupil behaviors.

The diversity of teacher behaviors that might have some significance was well conveyed by the work of Van Denberg (1937). He reported on a project begun in 1933 to establish a rating scale for high school teachers of biology in New York City. Forty-five supervisors of biology teachers (including department chairmen) were involved in the study for three years. When they were asked what a superior teacher did, ranked from "always" to "never," their list of behaviors totaled 5,000! Of these, 1,100 behaviors were recorded as "always did." By eliminating some overlap, this list was cut to 500 items. Then, with the cooperation of 200 teachers and supervisors, the list was cut to 199 items. After this list had been used by three to five judges to rate 50 teachers, a final list of 118 observable behaviors was distilled. Even a shortened check list of this magnitude is very difficult to use. No further report about its use, or analysis of results obtained with it, has been found.

Van Denberg's paper points up the hopelessness of completely empirical approaches to the description of teacher behavior. His study, which absorbed many hours of many persons, lacked any theoretical framework relating teacher characteristics to subsequent behaviors of pupils. Surely many of Van Denberg's teacher behaviors would prove to be marginal or trivial in terms of subsequent pupil behaviors. While Van Denberg and his associates labored some years ago, and for their own purposes, the lack of studies based on theoretical deductions continues today, not only regarding the teaching of science, but regarding teaching in general (Herriott, 1960). Since it is unlikely that specialists in the subject fields will have the time to explore various psychodynamic theories deeply, team research involving specialists on different aspects of the problem is needed.

In the sections to follow, we shall appraise early research based upon supervisors' ratings and research using pupil descriptions of teacher behavior. These sections deal with the literature immediately pertinent to individual differences in teacher behavior, i.e., to teacher personality. Three sections on "methods" of instruction are then presented, followed by a general summary and suggestions for future research.

In the literature on science teaching, the term *method* is often used to refer to the use of laboratory work, among other things. While this use of the term does not identify the behaviors of the teacher, at least some teacher behaviors are implicit in it. More recently, attention has been given to the use of films and of television, separately or together, as a means of providing instruction, and recent papers on their use are reviewed here. Just on the horizon is programed instruction, with or without some form of teaching machine; this too merits discussion. In conclusion, an effort is made to appraise the total research on the teaching of science and to suggest some important lines of study in this area.

A REVIEW OF SELECTED PAPERS

While early investigations suffered from the lack of adequate statistical techniques, some of these will be mentioned to characterize beginning phases in the long history of this area of inquiry.

In 1912, Mayman (cited in Curtis, 1926) completed a thesis at New York University comparing the results of instruction in introductory physics by a book method, a lecture method, and two procedures with demonstration equipment. The experiment continued through two terms of the school year. About 500 boys in Grades 7 and 8 in one school in New York City were involved. The results found were:

On the basis of efficiency as measured by *percental attainment,* by *lasting impression* on the minds of elementary school pupils, by *persistence in memory* [up to 56 days], by *encouragement of independent thought and self reliance,* and by *popularity among the pupils,* the three methods rank . . . *experiment method, lecture method, book method.* . . . Carefully written note-book work and neatly drawn diagrams of scientific apparatus do not increase pupils' knowledge of elementary science . . . . The work in elementary science must be concrete and must be based on daily experiences and observations of pupils. . . . Elementary science in the elementary schools should be largely, if not entirely, qualitative, and not quantitative (Mayman, cited in Curtis, 1926, pp. 32–33).

More than 20 years later, Davis (1934) published a thesis entitled "The Use of High School Examinations as an Instrument for Judging the Work of Teachers." He used results on the Minnesota State Board Tests of Pupil Achievement as his criterion data. Included in the study were 107 teachers of chemistry, 175 of general science, and 180 of biology. The prime question was whether there were more failures on Board tests among the pupils studying with "qualified" or with "unqualified" teachers. Davis' definitions of these categories were ambiguous; he defined "qualified" teachers as those having a "major" or "minor" in the subject taught, or in any of the other natural sciences. Since collegiate programs for majors or minors differ considerably in amount and kind of study required, Davis' definition tells us little about the technical preparation of the teachers. Separately for "qualified" and for "unqualified" teachers, the mean rate of failure on a test in a science subject was subtracted from the mean failure rate of the school (presumably on the tests in all subjects). Then, by subject, he computed a second difference, that between the mean differences, of qualified and unqualified teachers. As might be expected, the second differences were small. Since Davis included no information about the scatter of the differences in failure rates, no further study of the significance of his results can be made.

Davis' study has been described in some detail because it raises several persistent problems. First, in what way does the technical competency of a teacher influence his pupils' success on examinations? Second, how much and what kind of technical competency in the teacher produces what kinds of pupil behaviors? Third, to what extent, if any, can external examinations be properly used as measures of "teacher competency"?

The first and second questions relate to the structure of programs of teacher training and retraining. The National Science Foundation is underwriting numerous institutes designed to help teachers gain greater technical competency in science and mathematics. The assumption is that greater "command of the subject" by the teacher will ultimately result in "better" performance by the pupils. We shall assume that no teacher can work effectively in a subject which he does not understand. But what is meant by this "understanding"? It implies such a familiarity with the assumptions, the evidence, and the concepts in a subject that the teacher can play freely with their interrelationships and restructure the instruction in many ways. This competence requires time and experience beyond what usually is available in a first introduction to the subject. Yet there is

now great haste to "update" science instruction, which means to utilize in schools quite recent interpretation of complex and current experimentation. Frequently this interpretation is novel to the teacher who has been out of school for some years. He is struggling to comprehend these new results and ideas. Will he then be competent to handle them flexibly in his teaching? Or is he likely to present them merely as the latest scientific dogma from the authorities?

Also, one can raise questions about the kind of performance of the pupils which would be used as evidence of achievement. Will this evidence be restricted to recall and performance on "academic" problems, or to subsequent grades in collegiate science courses? Or other evidence? Such questions parallel those raised by any consideration of the preparation of future science teachers. The whole topic of teacher training is fraught with questions needing careful analysis and research.

The third question opens another Pandora's box. So long as pupil accomplishment and, inevitably, teacher success are defined in terms of narrowly conceived achievement examinations, teachers will center their explicit instructional purposes around the limited kinds of tasks required in these examinations. Or conversely, they will not be willing to invest much effort in other types of objectives. For this reason, such instruments as the Test of Knowledge about Science and Scientists and the Test on Understanding Science should be used to probe further into the affective domain. It is regrettable that the Test of Developed Abilities in Science of the College Entrance Examination Board, used in an early form by Neivert (1955), has not become available. This test was designed to go beyond recall into more general behaviors in the cognitive domain (Brandwein, Watson, & Blackwood, 1958). Apparently it did not predict college grades more effectively than existing tests—the grades being awarded, of course, by teachers oriented toward the kinds of achievement measured by existing tests. Had the Test of Developed Abilities become available, it would have influenced the emphasis and intent of teachers toward more general pupil behaviors than those that are now of major concern.

Use of Supervisors' Ratings

A number of studies, mostly of an early vintage, have attempted to find relationships between supervisors' ratings of teachers and subsequent pupil behaviors. Such efforts have become rarer as the unreliability and invalidity of such ratings have become increasingly apparent (see, for example, Morsh, Burgess, & Smith, 1956; Morsh & Wilder, 1954; Webb & Nolan, 1955).

Seyfert and Tyndal (1934) selected the "best" and the "poorest" teacher from seven general science teachers involved in Rulon's (1933) study of the use of motion pictures. They made this selection on the basis of observations by superintendents, principals, and supervisors. Both teachers had used the control material provided for groups not seeing the films. The subject taught was initially unfamiliar to the students. From several classes of each teacher, a group of 73 girls was selected. The girls taught by one teacher were equated with those taught by the other teacher on age and for Terman IQ. On the Ruch-Popenoe General Science Test, given prior to instruction, the girls with the "best" teacher scored significantly higher. After the instruction they took the special test prepared by Rulon on the materials discussed. The group with the "best" teacher again scored significantly higher. On the Terman test the raw scores of the girls with the "best" teacher were lower than those of the girls in the other group, but not significantly so. The authors concluded that the group with the "best" teacher learned more. This conclusion is, however, questionable since this group also scored significantly higher on the pretest of general science knowledge. A covariance adjustment for pretest scores and perhaps also for Terman scores might have eliminated the significant difference on the posttest.

Supervisors' ratings were also used by Bim-son (1937). His study, carried out in Lincoln, Nebraska, involved 25 teachers, including 9 general science teachers with 266 pupils. The pupils' academic progress during one semester was measured with the Cooperative General Science Test, Form 1934. To shorten the testing, odd-numbered items were used for the pretest and even-numbered items for the posttest. IQs were based on three different tests, unspecified in the report. Teachers in the whole study were ranked from 1 to 25 on the basis of supervisors' ratings made from two to five times each year for three years. The rating device with 34 five-choice items was not included in the published report. The distribution of the ratings for science teachers among the 25 teachers was not given either. But two groups called "good" and "poor" teachers were formed. In addition to the gain scores, the "progress quotient" (change in score divided by IQ), as used by Barr, was examined. For the entire group of pupils, the differences in mean gain scores and mean progress quotients between the pupils of "good" and "poor" teachers were very small. Among two groups, one with IQs above 110, and one with IQs below 90, the low IQ group with the "good" teachers showed rather larger gains both on raw score and progress quotient. Unfortunately, no tests of statistical significance were made, and the absence of information on the dispersion of the scores precludes further analysis of the results. As in other studies, we are given no information on the behaviors of the teachers which caused them to receive "good" or "poor" ratings. Further, the "progress quotient," like the ill-reputed "accomplishment quotient," incorporates the incorrect assumption that there is a perfect correlation between gain and IQ. Because the correlation is far from perfect, such quotients are susceptible to artifacts and should not be used.

Here, and in studies to be mentioned later, we encounter the difficulties imposed by the "test ceiling." Most tests include some relatively easy items, numerous moderately difficult items, and a few very difficult items. As a consequence, it is difficult for a competent student with a fairly high pretest score to make much of a gain. But the less able student with low original score encounters numerous items of only slightly greater difficulty than he could initially answer correctly. This difficulty plagues all studies which utilize typical tests. Another reason why those students whose pretest scores or IQs are below the mean of the group tend to gain more on the posttest is the well-known regression effect. Any group below the mean on one variable will probably not be as far below the mean on another variable which is imperfectly correlated with the first. This phenomenon is explicated in Chapter 5, pages 180–182.

Another effort to relate pupil-gain scores to teacher characteristics was made by Anderson (1950). On biology and chemistry tests he made for the Minnesota State Board he included items dealing with four objectives: acquisition of factual information, use of principles of science, use of scientific method, and acquisition of scientific attitudes. He did not spell out what kinds of items were used to elicit these attributes, or the number of items in the tests that were related to each of the four areas of appraisal. The tests were, however, pretested and designed with attention to their reliability and validity.

Anderson intended to investigate three kinds of problems: (1) factors in the teaching situation which contributed to achievement of the four types of objectives, (2) relations between the four types of objectives, and (3) the practices and attributes of teachers. Despite the variety of the objectives spelled out in the tests, all but one of the analyses eventually made were based upon total test scores. Therefore, no subscores for the various objectives were presented and the interrelations between achievement of the four objectives could not be examined.

The study, made in 1944–1945, involved a random sample of high schools in Minnesota, stratified according to population in the school district, rather than pupil distribution within the state. Most of the 56 schools in the study had small total enrollments. We may conclude that these schools also had small faculties, were in rural areas, paid relatively low salaries, and were staffed by relatively inexperienced teachers. Of the 56 schools, only 6 were in towns with populations over 5,000, while two more schools were in large cities.

In the analyses of variance and covariance, adjustments were commonly made for Otis IQ and for pretest scores. Although the nature of the pretests is not made clear in the report, presumably they were the same as or equivalent to the posttest. The study involved 1,980 biology students and 1,352 chemistry students. Generally, biology was a required subject and chemistry an elective.

Anderson compared different attributes of the teachers whose pupils scored in the upper and lower quarter of various distributions. Pupil gains in the biology scores, after covariance adjustment for IQ and pretest scores, were significantly and positively related to:

1. Science credits earned by the teacher—77 or more versus 32 or less quarter-hours.
2. The teacher's having graduated from a private college rather than a university or a teachers college.
3. The teacher's holding a master's degree.
4. The laboratory time in course—60 or more hours versus 12 or less.
5. Class size—29 or more students versus 17 or less.

Pupil gains in chemistry scores (after adjustments) were significantly and positively related to:

1. Chemistry credits earned by the teacher —35 or more quarter-hours versus 13 or less.
2. The pupils' use of laboratory manual rather than no use of a manual.
3. The pupils' election of chemistry (this occurred in 90 per cent of the schools) versus the pupils' being required to take it.
4. The laboratory time in course—74 or more hours versus 34 or less.

5. The teacher's having graduated from a university or a private college rather than a teachers college.
6. Class size—25 or more students versus 16 or less.
7. The teacher's being obliged to make fewer daily preparations—one or two versus six. (This is related to school size.)

Significant positive relations were also found between pupil gains and school size, teacher experience (10 years or more versus one year or less), teacher knowledge of the subject, and collegiate plans of the pupils. No significant relation between pupil gains and sex of the teacher was found.

A multivariate analysis would have made greater use of the data than did the procedure of using upper and lower quarters of the distributions. Anderson did not explain why he did not explore the four attributes he had initially stated. The important questions he raised are still with us. To some degree, Anderson's findings may represent the operation of gross sociological factors, such as socioeconomic status of the school district, affecting both the educational level of the teacher (e.g., amount of scientific training possessed by the teacher) and the achievement of the pupils. That is, the data permit no inference of a causal connection between the teacher's scientific background and the pupil's achievement, since these two variables may have been "caused" to covary by a third variable, such as community wealth.

Pupil Descriptions of Teachers' Behavior

Inasmuch as ratings by supervisors have been relatively unreliable and unrelated to other variables, descriptions of teacher behavior obtained from pupils have seemed a promising alternative approach. Use of such a procedure develops from an obvious argument which has face validity: Since it is the pupil who is doing the learning, his image of the teacher is the important image.

Furthermore, pupils observe substantial portions of teacher behavior, not just a few brief samples. However, as noted by Barr (1948), Mitzel and Gross (1958), and Herriott (1960), there is a dearth of studies which make use of pupil descriptions of teacher behavior. Two studies (Cogan, 1958a; Reed, 1961) have used this approach in the study of science teachers.

In accordance with the general theory of Miller and Dollard (1941), Cogan sought to describe teacher behavior under three categories: (1) "inclusive" behaviors tending to draw the pupils into the classroom process, i.e., tending to make them see in the teacher's behavior the cues for "approach"; (2) "preclusive" behaviors tending to make the pupils see in the teacher's behavior the cues for "avoidance"; and (3) "conjunctive" behaviors stemming from the teacher's ability to communicate, from his effectiveness in classroom management and command, from his creativity with the subject, and from his level of demand. The study involved 33 teachers, including four science teachers, and 987 pupils in the eighth grades of five junior high schools located in two communities of sharply differing socioeconomic characteristics. The dependent variables were (1) the amount of required work, described by the pupils on a 30-item check list, and (2) the amount of self-initiated work, described by the pupils on a 25-item check list. The independent variables describing teacher behavior as seen by the pupils comprised an 80-item check list.

Using analysis of covariance, Cogan examined the relation between each child's description of his teacher and the child's description of his required and self-initiated activities for the course. For preclusive ("avoidance") teacher behaviors, essentially no significant relations with required or self-initiated work were found. However, for conjunctive ("control and demand") and inclusive ("approach") teacher behaviors, numerous significant relations appeared. Of the 66 intraclassroom rs relating the conjunctive scale (33 teachers) to required and to self-initiated activities, half were significant and positive for both required and self-initiated work. Only three rs, none statistically significant, were negative. For inclusive behavior, 46 of the 66 rs were positive and significant; for inclusive behaviors, 21 of 33 rs with required work were positive and significant, while 25 of 33 rs with self-initiated work were positive and significant.

The results for the four science teachers appear in Table 1.

TABLE 1

CORRELATIONS BETWEEN CONJUNCTIVE OR INCLUSIVE TEACHER BEHAVIOR AND REQUIRED OR SELF-INITIATED WORK AS DESCRIBED BY PUPILS IN GENERAL SCIENCE (From Cogan, 1958a)

Teacher no.	Conj. vs. req.	Conj. vs. self-init.	Incl. vs. req.	Incl. vs. self-init.
18	.33[b]	.33[b]	.46[b]	.47[b]
25	.18[a]	.16	.33[b]	.40[b]
29	.27[a]	.38[b]	.45[b]	.46[b]
30	.35[b]	.39[b]	.49[b]	.57[b]

[a] Significant at .05 level.
[b] Significant at .01 level.

Cogan concluded that for the 33 teachers his evidence "confirm[s] the hypothesis that in the perception of the pupils, inclusive behaviors of the teacher are positively related to self-initiated work" (p. 98). For the subsample of science teachers, this conclusion is also justified. In addition, however, we may conclude that a comparable relation exists between conjunctive behaviors and pupil efforts in science.

That is, insofar as the pupils in a science class see the teacher as well organized (conjunctive), they seem to respond by doing more required and self-initiated work. Similarly, as the pupils see a science teacher as "warm or friendly" (inclusive), they seem to respond with greater effort.

The meaning of Cogan's results may be questioned, however, because both of his two kinds of variables, teacher behavior and pupil work, came from the same source, the pupils. The operation of a response set, such as consistent individual differences in tendency to make socially desirable responses (perhaps due in turn to differences in pupil achievement or docility), might produce the positive correlations Cogan found. That is, the pupil who, for autistic or veridical reasons, tended to describe himself favorably also tended to describe his teacher favorably. We must remember that it was not the teacher's actual characteristics, but rather those perceived and reported by his pupils which Cogan found to be correlated with the pupil's report of how much work he did.

Cogan in a companion paper (1958b) went on to examine the differences between teachers, schools, communities, and school subjects. In this analysis, the characteristics, or traits, of the individual teachers were a mean of the descriptions recorded by the pupils. By analysis of covariance he concluded that there were significant differences between teachers and between schools. Teachers in the two communities differed significantly, at around the .05 level, on preclusive and conjunctive behaviors, but not on inclusive behaviors. Cogan observed that the communities seemed to differ more on the amount of required work than on the amount of self-initiated work. Three of the four science teachers were in different schools within one community; as perceived by their pupils, their traits differed significantly.

Cogan obtained further evidence to support the validity of pupil descriptions of their self-initiated work. The 29 teachers rated each pupil on his involvement in required and in self-initiated work. Of 29 correlations between pupil and teacher descriptions of pupils' required work, 25 were positive and 14 were significant at the .05 level. For three science teachers in this group, only one of the rs (.27) was significant. Of the 29 rs between teacher and pupil descriptions of pupils' self-initiated work, 28 were positive and 16 were significant. Here all three science teachers had sizable and significant correlations with their pupils' reports (rs of .68, .48, and .35). Possibly the difference in these correlations on required and self-initiated work might have been expected. The required work is required of all pupils and tends to be routine. The teacher may not have an adequate knowledge of the effort that different pupils put into such required work. The self-initiated work is, however, additional. It is likely to be displayed with some pride, it is deliberately done by some pupils, and it is generally more visible.

Cogan's study raised a number of additional questions which Reed (1961) subsequently examined, using much the same technique. Studying 584 boys and 461 girls in 38 ninth-grade general science classes taught by 38 teachers in 19 public schools, Reed focused upon the pupils' interest in science and upon three teacher attributes—warmth, demand, and creation of intrinsic motivation—as perceived by the pupils. Pupil interest was measured with a 70-item Science Activity Inventory of what the pupil was voluntarily doing during that school year. As his description of manifest interest, Reed took the total number of listed activities reported by each pupil. Subsequently, a factor analysis by Cooley and Reed (1961) of the 584 male inventories revealed that the Inventory included four major factors, to which most of the 70 items could be assigned. The four major factors were: (1) a general science interest factor, including such activities as "doing extra science homework, asking questions and discussing in science class, talking about science with peers and adults, listening to talks on science"; (2) a "woodsy-birdsy" factor, including activities like "studying animal and bird life, collecting biological specimens, visiting parks and zoos"; (3) a science tinkerer factor, including activities like "investigating electric appliances, working with home chemistry sets, and devising new inventions"; (4) a wonderer, "thinking about science" dimension, including activities such as "finding out about space travel, exploring the meaning of concepts like time, gravity, space and energy" (Cooley & Reed, 1961, pp. 324–325). With this new interpretation of the Activity Inventory, a re-analysis of Reed's data may yield even more interesting results.

From check lists of what the teacher did,

the pupils' perceptions of teacher warmth (13 items), demand (14 items), and creation of intrinsic motivation (15 items) were obtained. Separate analyses were made for boys and girls. Adjustment was made by analysis of covariance for each pupil's impression of the scientific interest of his father.

Reed found that for ninth-grade boys, more than girls, there was a positive correlation between the pupil's impression of his father's interest in science and the pupil's report of his overt scientific activities: for boys, $r = .40$, for girls, $r = .27$. Boys also reported significantly more scientific activities. Significant positive within-class correlations were found between teacher warmth and pupil interest: for boys, $r = .20$, for girls, $r = .28$. No significant relation could be found between teacher demand and pupil interest. Surprisingly, on the basis of class averages, none of the teachers were seen by their classes as having "high demand." The highest correlation of any of the three teacher variables was that of the teacher's perceived intrinsic motivation: for boys, $r = .32$, for girls, $r = .42$. Furthermore, the rs for boys and girls in all 38 classes were all positive. Teacher warmth and intrinsic motivation, both as perceived by pupils, were correlated: for boys, $r = .66$, for girls, $r = .70$. The warmth scores added little to the predictive power of the motivation scores, but the converse was not true. Reed also found that the pupils perceived the 28 men teachers as warmer than the 10 women teachers; this difference was, however, not examined separately for boys and girls.

Reed's ninth-grade boys showed a relatively strong manifestation of the socially expected male interest in science and "making things." He did not try to determine how many of the boys' activities were instigated or aided by the parent. Probably his most important finding is that the pupils reported themselves as having more self-initiated or "not required" activities when they perceived the teacher more as deliberately encouraging such activities. (No data were gathered on the amount of credit toward grades allotted to such extra work.) Also, the girls seemed somewhat more responsive to this teacher behavior, perhaps because they were less likely to have taken such action if not supported by such teacher behavior. Although Reed found a sizable correlation between pupils' perceptions of warmth and of intrinsic motivation, especially for girls, they seem to be discriminable teacher traits because motivation scores had higher correlation with pupil interest in science activities than did warmth scores.

Comparable studies with younger and older pupils are needed. The Science Activity Inventory would have to be modified to fit the types of activities performed by other age groups. In a small study (unpublished) of 143 pupils in the fifth grade, Cooley found only a general interest in science rather than clusters of interest and activity.

Reed's study, in also using Cogan's technique of relying on pupils for measures of both teachers' attributes and pupils' interests, is susceptible to the same artifacts, i.e., results due to pupils' response sets. Yet, the studies by Cogan and Reed have shown that pupil descriptions of what the science teacher does are closely related to what pupils do. Possibly further factor analysis of described teacher behavior will reveal particular forms of behavior which carry most of the predictive weight.

By rather different techniques, Ryans (1960) reported three major characteristics of teachers, as rated by trained observers, which are quite similar to those investigated by Cogan and Reed. Ryans' TCS Pattern X_o (warm, understanding, friendly behavior) is similar to Reed's "warmth" and to Cogan's "inclusive." Ryans' TCS Pattern Y_o (responsible, businesslike, systematic behavior) is similar to Cogan's "conjunctive" behavior and perhaps to Reed's attribute of demand. Ryans' TCS Pattern Z_o (stimulating, imaginative, surgent behavior) seems to be similar to Reed's attribute of creation of intrinsic motivation. From his sample of 497 mathematics and science teachers, Ryans found the X_o and Y_o attributes to be correlated with

$r = .34$. That these attributes are not empirically distinct is indicated by the correlations of Ryans' TCS Pattern Z_o with Patterns X_o and Y_o; these rs generally ranged from .50 upward for various groups of secondary school teachers. Specifically, for mathematics and science teachers, $r_{xz} = .48$ and $r_{yz} = .57$. These rs indicate considerable overlap of the categories.

Other Relevant Studies

Several other studies have some relevance to the topic under discussion. Kahn (1962) investigated the use of current events as a medium for influencing attitudes toward science. Two teachers were involved for half a year. Pre- and posttests were used, but were not described in the published summary. Kahn concluded that the experimental group, which was matched to the control group, "scored significantly higher than the group which received no special training." Furthermore, more than four months later, after no further special instruction, they still excelled. Pupils of low reading ability made as large gains as did those with higher reading scores. Here, as in numerous previous studies, we are hardly surprised to learn that when a particular goal is explicitly taught for, the pupils receiving instruction achieve higher scores than do untutored controls.

Boeck (1956) investigated the effect of reading and demonstrations on pupils' scientific understandings. Three groups were formed: (1) one to read and discuss, (2) one to observe demonstrations, but not to read, (3) one to both read and observe demonstrations. Eight teachers and 16 classes of ninth-grade pupils were involved. Only four class periods were used for instruction, the topic being mirrors and mirror images; two other sessions were used for testing. The reading was done from a six-page mimeographed text prepared by Boeck; it contained no diagrams.

Locally made instruments were employed: a 50-item multiple-choice achievement test on the material taught, a 32-item performance test, and a 20-item three-choice scale on attitudes about the "conduct and social climate of the class." (None of these are published.) Each teacher used more than one method, with different groups of pupils, but no teacher used the same method twice. Apparently no pretest was used.

Analysis of variance showed that performances on the final achievement test were nearly the same for all three methods. After covariance adjustment for Otis IQs, there was no significant difference in achievement between groups, even after a delayed retest. On the attitude scale, however, Boeck found a significant difference. Those who only read about the phenomena had markedly lower interest.

Also, differences in achievement between pupils classified according to teacher exceeded the combination of all differences assignable to other factors. As Boeck put it, "teachers exerted greater influence over achievement than did methods of instruction" (1956, p. 96). While this conclusion is worthy of further study, Boeck's sample of only eight teachers hardly establishes it as a large-scale generalization.

A study of classroom "atmospheres" and the formulation of scientific hypotheses in an elementary school was made by Atkin (1958). He used two classrooms each in the first, third, and sixth grades; one of each pair was described as "more permissive" than the other, but the criteria were not specified. Ten sessions in each classroom were recorded on tape and studied for the response patterns. The factors sought were (1) accuracy of response and (2) type of response, i.e., appeal to authority, use of observation, appeal to experiment, and original explanation. There was no correlation between accuracy of response and classroom "climate." But in the "permissive" classrooms, the number of responses was significantly higher, and there was a lower frequency of appeal to authority. Atkin found an essentially zero correlation of IQ with appeal to authority, and with use of empirical evidence. He concluded that pupils are more successful and active when they participate in selecting the problems

they work on. As a pioneer study, this work raises more questions than it answers.

LABORATORY WORK

The value of laboratory work in the curriculum in science has been the subject of a large number of studies, many of which appeared in the 1920's and 1930's. In a review of the literature up to 1945, Cunningham (1946) listed 37 studies, of which 18 were master's theses, and 6 were doctor's theses; 33 dealt with junior or senior high school instruction. Cunningham found that many of the early studies suffered from inadequate statistical treatment, that the validity of their design was often dubious, and that the reliability of their results was usually undetermined. Most of the studies relied upon paper-and-pencil tests as a basis for comparing no-laboratory or demonstration groups with those having laboratory work.

Two of these early studies illustrate the inadequacies of many of them. Carpenter's study (1925) involved over a thousand pupils in 34 classes in 23 schools in 14 states. His major conclusion (but note the "if") seems to be supported by the data despite the primitive statistical treatment:

The results of this experiment point to the conclusion that the majority of students in high school laboratory chemistry classes, taught by the demonstration method, succeed as well as when they perform the experiment individually, if success is measured by instruments which measure the same abilities as are measured by these tests, namely, specific information and ability to think in terms of chemistry (Carpenter, 1925, p. 45).

The test items, which are included in his publication, were based on "ten introductory experiments as found in one of the most popular chemistry laboratory manuals: Brownlee, et al., *Laboratory Exercises,* Allyn and Bacon, (edition not cited)." As Brandwein, Watson, and Blackwood (1958, p. 276) have observed, "A perusal of these test items reveals that a competent student could answer them completely on the basis of a textbook knowledge *without either* demonstration or laboratory work." For unexplained reasons, Carpenter failed to utilize his control groups, which had no laboratory work or demonstrations, but we doubt that any significant differences would have been found.

Horton (1928) tried to probe further than Carpenter did. He devised paper-and-pencil tests that required more knowledge of "doing" or "performing." In addition, he devised a test of laboratory manipulative skills which included both written tests and direct tests in the laboratory. Horton made a series of investigations in one large high school. His experimental groups were given (1) individual laboratory work without directions; (2) individual laboratory work with generalized directions; (3) individual laboratory work from a manual of directions; or (4) demonstrations of all experiments by the teacher. He concluded that "no reliable results appear in the testing by the ordinary written examinations—neither by the Regents nor by the school test" (p. 84). This result, consistent with Carpenter's, is not surprising. With the nonwritten, or laboratory, tests he did find differences "in ability

To manipulate apparatus,

To make experimentation involving use of apparatus, and

To solve perplexities or projects involving use of chemical facts in laboratory situations" (p. 100).

No significant results from studies of laboratory work in biology were found by Frings and Hichar (1958).

Lahti (1956), in a collegiate physical science course, explored the effect of various approaches in laboratory work. The group consisted of 338 students, who seemed to be typical of those enrolled in the course during other years. All students had the same lectures, and they showed no significant differences on tests covering the lectures.

For laboratory work, about one hour per week, four approaches were used: (1) individual or small-group efforts by an induc-

tive-deductive or problem-solving approach in which the answer sought was not known; (2) a case-history approach in which the answer sought was known; (3) a "theme" approach later changed to a discussion-recitation session; and (4) a standard "get the right answer" approach. Apparently the students proceeded throughout a year by one of the four approaches. Lahti used an "incomplete block" design with replications. In the null form, his hypotheses were that (1) individual laboratory work does not lead to greater resourcefulness in (a) solving new problems, (b) designing experiments, (c) interpreting results of experiments, and (d) utilizing facts and principles; also, (2) the hour of the day at which the session met was not important. Data were gathered with tests entitled Interpretation of Data, Design an Experiment Test, and Performance Test. No description of these tests or reference to published descriptions is given. Presumably they were constructed locally.

While Lahti did not find any statistically significant differences, the group which used Approach *1*, problem-solving in the laboratory, scored highest on each of his three tests. This result might encourage similar studies with other criteria of accomplishment.

With others, Kruglak made a number of studies of the consequences of laboratory work in physics (Kruglak, 1951, 1952, 1953, 1954, 1955a, 1955b, 1958; Kruglak & Goodwin, 1955). College students in introductory courses at several institutions were the subjects. Analysis of covariance was applied to data gathered by both paper-and-pencil tests and laboratory performance tests. Kruglak concluded that "performance tests measure instructional outcomes other than those measured by conventional achievement tests . . ." (1954, p. 451) (as we might expect from common experience and the findings of Carpenter and of Horton), and *"paper-pencil* laboratory tests designed to evaluate *specific* laboratory outcomes have few elements in common with laboratory *performance* tests consisting of more comprehensive tasks" (1954, p. 462).

While Kruglak labored long on these studies, his attention, like Carpenter's and Horton's, was focused on specific skills. It is no surprise that he found, as Horton did, that students who had experience with handling apparatus subsequently could handle apparatus more competently than could those who lacked this experience. As Brandwein, Watson, and Blackwood (1958, p. 279) have suggested, the importance of laboratory work, which is expensive in student and instructor time, special rooms, and special apparatus, lies in more general aspects of learning "how the scientist works." Some examples of such aspects are "the abilities of children to select and design equipment, to predict from principles, to operate carefully and accurately, to observe closely, to appraise results, to search for improved techniques and equipmental design, to apply statistical analysis, to describe data graphically and algebraically and to interpret data . . ." (1958, p. 279). Furthermore, to justify the time and expense involved in laboratory work, we need to know how much and what type of laboratory experience leads to what student behaviors.

Kruglak (1955b) and Brown (1958) inquired into the effects of high school physics laboratory work upon subsequent collegiate performance in physics. At Minnesota, Kruglak studied a sizable group of first-year college students in physics on the basis of whether in high school they had taken physics with laboratory, without laboratory, or had not taken physics. Each sex group was studied separately. Four locally designed tests on laboratory work were used: Identification of Apparatus, Function of Apparatus, Experiments, and Miscellaneous (Kruglak, 1951).

Kruglak's pretest showed a difference by sex and no significant correlations between three of his tests. Differences in high school backgrounds seemed to have some effect on the pretests in Identification of Apparatus and Function of Apparatus. By analysis of variance of the posttests and even after covariance adjustment for pretest scores, he found the sex difference maintained on two tests. On the final examination for the college course there was a significant difference between the students who had taken physics in high school and those who had not. As might be expected, the presence or absence of high school laboratory work was not a significant predictor on the college final examination.

At the Massachusetts Institute of Technology, Brown (1958) made a similar investigation but without statistical niceties and found that students who had had physics laboratory work in high school were inept at naming or identifying the function of equipment which they were known to have handled in high school.

In this brief review of studies on the impact of laboratory work on science students, a number of poorly made studies have been omitted. The whole area seems still open for investigation. The hypotheses to be examined should come from a careful analysis of the important operations of science which can be illustrated and practiced in the laboratory, and they should be operationally explicit. Adequate statistical models exist for use in such a study. Among the variables that should be investigated are sex, career aspirations, general intelligence, prior laboratory experience, manual dexterity, and ability in solving problems in spatial relations. We suspect that the nature of the task and the motivation of the student, as well as the behavior patterns of the teacher in defining the task and motivating the student, would be worth careful examination as factors influencing results.

Careful study of the results of laboratory work, individual or in small groups, is especially important at this time. The several nationwide committees suggesting modifications in high school science courses are all stressing the importance of first-hand experience with the phenomena. With them, we agree that this experience seems essential in the study of science. Yet, to provide time, space, and materials for this laboratory work is expensive. Without clear empirical evidence of what sorts of experiences result in

what subsequent behaviors, or enhanced behaviors, in pupils, we are of necessity proceeding on faith. This is hardly the strongest
basis on which to convince school administrators and school boards that the invest-
ments needed will produce desired results.

VICARIOUS INSTRUCTION
BY FILM
AND TELEVISION

With teachers of science and mathematics
in short supply, interest in television and
filmed courses has increased greatly. Such
courses essentially use a "vicarious instructor," i.e., one who is not in a face-to-face relationship with the student. The presence of
such a vicarious instructor modifies the behavior of the classroom teacher, or may sup-
plant him entirely. Therefore, the studies
described below deal with changes in pupils
in response to behavior of the local and the
remote teachers. Most of the reports now
available are mainly descriptive, or restrict
their analysis to comparisons of scores on
course examinations or achievement tests.
Apparently they reach a common conclusion:
Students taught by the vicarious or distant
instructor score as well as those taught by an
instructor at hand. Nonetheless, this conclusion is still open to question.

Commenting upon the study of television
instruction at Miami University (Ohio)
(Macomber & Siegel, 1960), Siegel (1960,
p. 204) concluded that "the results support
the general conclusion that televised instruction does *not* lead to reduced proficiency" in
the ability to solve problems and to synthesize information. This study showed no differences in achievement as a function of
learning ability. Furthermore, after one to
two years, no variance in retention was
found between groups taught differently.

Siegel's paper is especially useful because
it points to the limited base on which numerous studies rest. "It is unlikely that
studies of relatively brief duration can attempt to utilize measures of higher level cognitive processes as dependent variables. Eval-

uative data gathered in the affective domain
are even more generally neglected" (p. 208).

The Ford Foundation
Instructional Television
Programs

The Ford Foundation, during 1957–1958,
appraised the test run of numerous educational television programs which it had sponsored (Stoddard, 1959). More than 40,000
pupils in more than 200 elementary and secondary schools were involved. Primarily, this
first report was concerned with the conditions under which televised programs were
received, especially in isolated schools. Only
rough estimates were made of the effectiveness of the programs. When the project began, no extensive or detailed plans for evaluation had been made; not until July, 1957,
was there even agreement that pre- and posttests on achievement would be desirable.
Since no particular tests were identified, each
group was free to do as it chose. Of 110 comparisons between classes seeing televised instruction (mostly in science or mathematics)
and control classes, 29 were significantly favorable to the television classes and 9 were
significantly in favor of the control classes.
In the report few details of the local appraisal programs are spelled out. However,
according to the report, the research workers in Detroit matched their experimental
and control groups in fifth-grade and eighth-
grade science on sex, intelligence, a pretest,
and a listening test. For the eighth-grade science group, the experimental (TV) group
had achievement gains significantly exceeding those of the control group.

Teaching Biology by
Television

The Cincinnati study. In Cincinnati, Jacobs and Bollenbacher (1959) studied the
results of a full year of biological instruction
by live television watched by ninth-grade
pupils. From 14 schools, three were chosen
to represent below-average, average, and

above-average academic abilities. No evidence is given to support this classification of the schools. Within each school, four classes were taught by the same teacher and used the same course outline. Two classes had television instruction and laboratory work on alternate days. Two other classes were taught by the normal procedures and had the same laboratory work. Within each school, pupils were randomized between the television and normal groups. A total of 360 pupils were involved in this study.

The Cooperative Biology Test, Form X, was used as a pretest, and Form Y was used as a posttest. After covariance adjustment for the differences in the pretest scores, only the pupils in the school rated "above average academically" showed a significantly higher gain favoring the television over the nontelevision classes. No other differences were significant. Despite the covariance adjustment, the reader must be skeptical of this result, for the television group in this school had considerably higher pretest scores than any other group. Since no standard deviations are reported, no further tests of the significance of these data are possible.

Also used as pretest and posttest was the Test of Knowledge about Science and Scientists developed in cooperation with the Educational Testing Service as part of this study. The report states that after covariance adjustment no significant relationship was found. Presumably this refers to a comparison of television and nontelevision classes within schools, but the report is not clear as to what relations were tested or what means were used to test them. The over-all score change for 360 pupils was −1.01, suggesting that neither form of instruction positively influenced scores on this test, which probes somewhat into affective results of instruction. Apparently no effort was made to examine the correlations between IQs, scores on the Test of Knowledge about Science and Scientists, and gain scores on the Cooperative Biology Test.

We should note here that on the Cooperative Biology Test, Form X (maximum raw

score, 89), the mean pretest score was 46.7, with the low-ability school averaging 43.3. The over-all posttest mean on Form Y was 58.1. The highest posttest mean was 67.5 for the television group in the high-ability school.

Stress on principles as a variable. Anderson, Montgomery, Smith, and Anderson (1956) and Smith and Anderson (1958) studied effects of showing films in biology classes. Their major effort was to determine whether stress upon 34 selected principles of biology would show in subsequent pupil performance. Sixty schools enrolling between 100 and 200 pupils were chosen for study. Most of these schools had only one section in biology. After a test for homogeneity of variation of means based on pretest scores on the Nelson Biology Test, Form Am, a number of deviant schools were dropped. Ultimately, the control group, receiving no film instruction, consisted of 22 schools; in the two experimental groups, 14 schools used films without principles stressed and 11 schools used films with principles stressed. With pretest scores and IQs of the 1,354 pupils held constant by covariance adjustment, no significant difference between the three groups appeared in the posttest scores on the Nelson Biology Test, Form Bm.

The pupils receiving each type of instruction were grouped by IQ: above 106, 106 to 86, and below 86. From each instructional group, pairs of pupils with equal IQ scores were drawn and their gain scores compared. A sign test of the differences indicated that the high-ability group shown films with principles stressed gained significantly more than the other two high-ability groups. Also the low-ability group shown films with principles stressed seemed to have a higher gain than the other two low-ability groups. Furthermore, by Lucow's (1954) argument for the increase in variance, they concluded $(p < .01)$ that both film groups had exceeded the control group, and that the films with principles stressed had led to the greatest gains.

Although raw scores are not reported in the first paper (Anderson, et al., 1956), the second paper (Smith & Anderson, 1958) gives the mean pretest score as 31.6 and the mean posttest score as 35.4. The maximum possible score on the Nelson Biology Test is 75. Comments about the small gain will be made later.

In the second paper, Smith and Anderson (1958) re-examined the same data in an effort to clarify the earlier results. Students were regrouped into a top-ability group, IQ 115 or higher, and a low-ability group, IQ 90 or lower. These two groups included, respectively, 16.2 and 18.2 per cent of the pupils in the study. Then the individual test items were examined for classification into two types: fact-type and principle-type. From the items that could be so classified with some reliability two subtests were formed, and the papers were rescored. No significant difference attributable to method of instruction appeared on the fact-type subtest. However, among students shown the films with stress on principles, both high- and low-ability groups showed significantly higher gains on the principle-type subtest. From this we may conclude that when principles are stressed by the teacher and also in the films, both high- and low-ability pupils will subsequently score higher on items involving principles. The failure to include a sample of pupils of middle ability and to examine the differences according to the sex of the pupils is regrettable.

Teaching Physics by Film and Television

The American Institute of Physics study. A study of the teaching of physics by film and television, using the Harvey White physics films (Encyclopaedia Britannica Films), was made under the auspices of the American Association of Physics Teachers and the American Institute of Physics. Gale's report (1958) on this study was based upon incomplete results. Questionnaire returns from 149 teachers, from students, and local studies plus visits to the schools provided the original data. The conclusions were:

1. On the basis of those contributions to learning measured by available testing techniques [mainly the Dunning Physics Test], the teacher-physics-film combination and conventional instruction are about equally effective.

2. Limited test results show that the physics-by-film course when presented to a class without a physics teacher is only slightly less effective, again in terms of those contributions to learning measured by existing testing devices, than instruction with a teacher or with the teacher-film combination (Gale, 1958, p. 27).

The report treats a wide variety of concerns, many of them administrative. Apparently only one group of 54 pupils in 12 schools in Oklahoma received their instruction in physics from the films and, presumably, from one or more textbooks, *without* the aid of a teacher or a correspondence course. It is on this group that the second conclusion above is based. On the Dunning Physics Test, eight schools in Pittsburgh using the films via television reported overall median scores of 48 per cent, and six schools not using the films reported a median of 62 per cent. The medians and interquartile ranges of the IQs for the two groups were essentially identical. While the schools not using TV had a higher median, the median scores of the schools varied widely. Possibly a more detailed report of these results will appear.

The Chicago study. A study of the showing of the Harvey White films by television in Chicago high schools was reported by Engelhart, Schwachtgen, and Nee (1958). Television instruction with the films began in February, 1957, with the midyear beginning class. The film groups saw five telecasts each week, while the control groups had seven periods of physics weekly including two double-periods for laboratory work.

In the first study, after the first semester of instruction 692 viewers were compared with 906 controls from 15 schools. The test consisted of 140 items drawn from Questions and Problems in Science, Test Item Folio

No. 1, compiled by Dressel and Nelson, and from the physical science examinations of the Chicago City Junior College. The means of postinstruction scores and Otis IQs of the film-by-television group were, respectively, 72.0 and 115.6; for the control group, these means were 66.7 and 108.9. Because of the large difference in mean IQ of the groups, no inferences are justified.

From 13 schools offering both regular and televised instruction, two samples of 307 students were drawn and matched on IQ. The mean postinstruction test scores of the two groups were 71.03 and 71.00. In an effort to examine pupil scores in terms of ability level, four subgroups were formed: IQ above 119, 119 to 110, 109 to 100, below 100. Although the published results suggest that the middle-ability groups gained more from televised instruction than did the groups at the two ends of the ability distribution, subsequent statistical tests by Engelhart showed that none of the differences was significant.[1] However, a second sample of 584 students matched on IQ in pairs was drawn from all the 25 schools having television instruction and the 14 schools having students taught in the usual manner. For each ability group the nontelevision students scored higher, with the largest differences occurring in the highest ($p < .02$) and lowest ability groups ($p < .05$). The scores of all nontelevision students were very significantly higher than those of the television students.

These results are interesting because they suggest a relation between method and ability. Yet they cannot be given great weight since no pretest was used for covariance adjustment. Note, however, that for the first sample, drawn from schools having both television and nontelevision instruction, no difference was found; while the second sample, with controls from schools without television instruction, showed a significant difference. This suggests contamination in schools with television instruction. This effect appeared clearly in the Wisconsin study.

The Wisconsin study. Eighty-one of the Harvey White physics films dealing with mechanics, matter, and heat were evaluated in Wisconsin during the first semester of 1957–1958 (Wisconsin Physics Film Evaluation Project, 1959). Thirty experimental schools (one 30-minute film shown per day) and 30 control schools were selected at random within Wisconsin. Just five days before the posttests, 52 additional or control-control schools not previously in the study were added, but for these schools only posttest data were available. These additional control schools were added to provide a measure of the Hawthorne effect suspected of influencing schools in which the teachers knew they were serving as controls. The primary evaluation instrument was the Wisconsin Physics Test, which included content appropriate to the films as well as to the texts used in the schools.

On the pretests there was no significant difference between film and control groups in physics. There was, however, a small significant initial difference in favor of the control group in IQ on the Henmon-Nelson Test of Mental Ability. All subsequent comparisons were adjusted for this difference in IQ. At semester's end there was no significant difference in adjusted scores on the Wisconsin Physics Test. The same result was found with the Ohio Physics Scholarship Test (1957). After three months, a retention test, adjusted for IQs and semester-end scores, showed a difference in favor of the control schools significant at the .01 level. When comparison was made of the pupil scores on the end-of-semester test, after correction for IQ and teacher differences (see below), the control group exceeded the film group and the control-control group at the .05 level.

Several relationships between teacher preparation and teacher or pupil scores were examined. When all pupil posttest scores were grouped in terms of the college-level physics credits of the teachers, pupils with teachers having 10 or less credits in physics scored significantly lower, at the .05 level, than those

---

[1] Personal communication.

with teachers having 11 to 17 or 18 or more credits. A pretest of the 60 teachers with the Cooperative College Physics Test showed no significant difference between the film and control group teachers. On a posttest of these teachers at the end of the school year, the film teachers excelled the control teachers at the .05 level of significance. While the report observes (p. 24), "it can be assumed that the difference in the means and the gains by the film teachers may be attributed to their seeing the 81 Harvey White films . . .," sizable gains were also made by the control teachers who did not see the films. The latter finding strongly suggests greater effort and insight on the part of the control teachers—evidence of the Hawthorne effect.

Teachers who had 10 or less credits in physics showed no significant gain during the year, but those with 11 to 17 credits in physics or 18 or more credits did show significant gains. Also the mean scores of the three teacher groups were significantly different on both pretest and posttest scores. Unfortunately, the numbers of teachers in the various categories are not reported. Even so, these results tend to confirm the finding of Anderson (1950) that pupils with teachers having more academic study in the subject score higher on standard tests.

The significantly high performance of the control pupils compared to both the film pupils and the control-control group, plus the year-end test score gains of the control teachers support the suspicion that the Hawthorne effect was working in this study. The authors state (p. 20), "it might be assumed that the result of the superior performance of the control group was the result of the Hawthorne effect (increased enthusiasm and effort due to a group's knowing they were the control group in an experimental situation)." Thus, as in many experimental arrangements, the "cards are stacked" against the experiment. The control-control schools were probably more typical of normal operations. Had a pretest been given in the control-control schools on some pretext, the results would have been more interesting.

The students in the control classes were reported, from analysis of a questionnaire, to have expressed a greater interest in science than did the experimental (film) students. As we shall see, a similar result was obtained by Popham and Sadnavitch (1961).

The Utah study. In Utah, a year-long study of the Harvey White films was made and reported by Noall and Winget (1959). The 20 schools, 10 experimental and 10 control, involved about 500 pupils. Because of large interschool variations, precise statistical analysis was abandoned in the study.

The first Kansas study. Effects of using 149 of the Harvey White physics films as the core of a course were investigated by Anderson and Montgomery (1959) during 1958–1959 in two large schools in eastern Kansas. Both schools used the same text and workbook. The experimental group consisted of nine physics classes in one school (225 pupils with two instructors). This group saw a film every day except when tests were given. A comparable school with seven sections of physics (176 pupils and two instructors) served as the control. Two days each week were used for lectures-discussions-demonstrations, two days were used for laboratory work, and one day was used for tests. Mental age of the pupils was derived from the Terman-McNemar Test, Form C. Student achievement gains were measured with the Dunning Physics Test (maximum score, 75), using Form Am as the pretest and Form Bm as the posttest. For each school, between-class differences were not significant, and, therefore, the data were pooled for each school. With IQ and pretest score held constant through covariance adjustment, there was no significant difference between the film group and the control group.

As in previous studies using biological films, the students were classified in three categories in terms of IQ: above 124, 124 to 113, and below 113. These IQ values were chosen from the over-all range of 80 to 154 to provide three essentially equal-sized groups. The null hypothesis was accepted inasmuch as no significant differences between the gains on test scores of experimental and control groups were found for any level of IQ. However, as might be anticipated, the variance within both groups increased as a result of their instruction. While such changes were not significant for the control group on a class-by-class basis, they were significant ($p < .05$) for four of the nine experimental classes. We are not told, however, whether these four sections were taught by the same teacher. Sex differences in achievement were not examined, perhaps because the number of girls in these classes was so small.

We must question the authors' conclusion that the increased variance in four of the experimental classes showed *"that the film method produced somewhat superior results . . ."* (italics in original) (p. 390). At least there was agreement among instructors and students that 149 films were too many to use in a single year.

The second Kansas study. A careful experiment to evaluate both the Harvey White physics films and the John Baxter chemistry films was made by Popham and Sadnavitch (1961) in Kansas. They inquired into the students' subject-matter achievement, interest in the general area of physical science, attitudes toward the school subject (physics or chemistry), and attitude toward filmed courses.

When the end-of-course results were considered, the groups were equated statistically by covariance adjustment for pretest scores, previous scholastic grades, and intellectual aptitude. To measure achievement in physics, Forms Y and Z of the Cooperative Physics Test were used for pre- and posttests, respectively. To measure achievement in chemistry, Forms Y and Z of the Cooperative Chemistry Test were used as pre- and posttests, respectively. Student interest in physical science was assessed with the Thurstone Interest Schedule. The Remmers-Silance Scale for Measuring Attitude toward Any School Subject was used to assess affective responses to the physics and chemistry courses. The Otis Quick-Scoring Mental Ability Test pro-

vided approximate IQs. Also, a locally made, 30-item, Attitude toward Film Courses Scale (included in the report) provided information on the student's general reaction to such courses on a five-point agree-disagree scale. Grade-point averages were computed to measure previous academic achievement. Teacher attitudes were elicited with a questionnaire adapted from that used by Gale (1958).

The students were enrolled in 12 secondary schools in southeastern Kansas offering both physics and chemistry. The 12 schools were grouped in six pairs, matched on organization, enrollment, tax base, community population, accreditation, and size of faculty. In one school of each pair, either the physics or the chemistry films were used. Thus each school was an experimental school for one subject and a control for the other. For the physics study, 312 pupils were involved (155 taught by film), while for chemistry, 475 pupils were involved (234 taught by film).

After day-long conferences with the teachers, the films to be used were chosen. The average number of films used in each school was 149 physics films and 131 chemistry films. Since only one set of films was available for each subject, the films were rotated once each week between schools, essentially according to a plan suggested by Encyclopaedia Britannica Films. This meant that in some schools the instruction was as much as five weeks out of phase with that elsewhere.

For physics, the posttest achievement scores correlated .68 with the pretest, .51 with IQ, and .30 with grade-point average. After adjustment by covariance for these parameters, the control group exceeded the experimental (film) group ($p < .001$). By multiple covariance analysis, evidence was sought on the interaction of instructional method and ability. The students were divided into three equal-sized groups on the intelligence scale. The cutting points were not quite identical for the experimental and control groups, but the groups were roughly those above 120, 120 to 111, and 110 to 90 in IQ.

No significant interaction between method and ability was found. However, there was a significant relationship ($p < .01$) between ability level and achievement, with the low-ability group achieving higher gains than were predicted.

Popham and Sadnavitch attributed this greater gain for the lower-ability pupils to the test-ceiling effect mentioned earlier. However, the physics test included 77 items, while the unadjusted mean raw score on the posttest was 59.4 for the control group and 56.9 for the experimental group. The highest mean posttest score cited is 63.7 for the high-ability students in the control group. There were still over 13 points of raw score between this mean and the ceiling of the test. Several hypotheses as to the cause of this gain other than the influence of test ceiling should be examined in subsequent studies. Matters dealt with in certain of the test items might not have been included in the course syllabus; that is, the test might have been partially invalid for the course. Or, the instruction may have strongly emphasized certain points and skimmed over others covered by the test. Or, the instructors may have worked especially effectively with the lower-ability pupils—a well-known characteristic of conscientious teachers. The finding may, of course, be attributable to the regression effect, mentioned on page 1036.

On interest in physical science, there was no significant difference between the control and experimental groups. Both groups showed a mean loss in interest. On attitude toward physics as a school subject, the decline in interest of the experimental (film) group was significantly greater ($p < .05$) than that of the control group. When examined in terms of ability grouping, five of the six subgroups showed significant ($p < .01$) losses in interest.

Study of the effects of the Baxter chemistry films was made in the same way as the study of physics films. The tests and student populations have already been described. For chemistry, the posttests correlated .32 with the pretest, .46 with IQ, and .38 with grade-point average. After covariance adjustment for these three factors, there was no significant difference in posttest scores between the control and experimental (film) groups.

Three ability groups were formed with approximately the same cutting points as those for physics. No significant variance in achievement was attributable to interaction between method and ability.

For the chemistry students there was no significant postcourse difference in interest in physical science between the experimental (film) and control groups. When pre- and posttest interest scores were compared, significant differences ($p < .01$) were found for the whole group and for both the high-ability and the low-ability groups. All groups showed a loss of interest.

After the course, interest in chemistry as a school subject was significantly lower in the experimental (film) group than in the control group ($p < .05$). Much of this difference may be attributed to a marked decline in interest of the low-ability students in the experimental (film) group ($p < .01$). Interest in chemistry as a school subject declined in all eight methods-ability groups (six methods-ability subgroups plus two "total" groups); all pre- to posttest declines were significant ($p < .01$). Popham and Sadnavitch suggested that such a decline in interest, found in both physics and chemistry classes, may have resulted from "reality testing." That is, such a decline in interest might be expected since these were elective courses chosen more or less freely by the students, and much of the anticipated interest change would necessarily be negative. That the use of the films created greater negative shifts in interest is particularly worrisome. We do not yet have enough evidence to attribute this shift to the use of films in general, or to these particular films. Yet when efforts are being made to provide better and more interesting courses in science through means such as these films, such greater negative interest changes in groups using the films merit careful further study.

Popham and Sadnavitch also investigated

the reaction of students to film courses. There was general agreement here, as in the Chicago study (Engelhart, Schwachtgen, & Nee, 1958), that the films proceeded too rapidly and that more time for discussion and laboratory work was desirable. As to student-teacher relations, the low-ability experimental groups in both physics and chemistry were strongly of the opinion that the films had improved their relations with their teachers. One might wonder if the converse were not more likely—that, because they were viewing a vicarious instructor, a lower demand was made upon them by the classroom teacher.

A second paper (Sadnavitch & Popham, 1962) reports on retention studies after 7 and 12 months. Of the original group of pupils, only 300 were enrolled in school as seniors in the following year. In the chemistry group, 153 pupils had seen the films, and there were 52 control pupils. In the physics group, 63 pupils had seen the films, and there were 22 control pupils. By covariance, adjustments were made for end-of-course scores, school performance, and IQ. After 7 months the control group in chemistry showed, at the .05 level of significance, higher scores on the Cooperative Chemistry Test. After 12 months this difference had disappeared. On the Cooperative Physics Test, no significant differences were found for 7- or 12-month retention.

These reports have been reviewed extensively because they might well serve as a model for subsequent studies. In some cases, the reports would have been improved if the standard deviations of the variables had been furnished. One other variable that might have been considered is sex, although the number of girls in these science courses may not have been adequate to permit reliable consideration of sex differences.

Some Tentative Conclusions

Our review of these studies, which differ in elegance, permits some tentative conclusions on persistent questions.

1. Does the use of vicarious instructors of acknowledged competence lead to significantly higher achievement test scores than those obtained by pupils taught entirely by live teachers? The Cincinnati data are inconclusive. Results in Chicago and Wisconsin suggest that the control groups perform better. The more careful studies in Kansas show no outstanding difference in favor of either form of presentation.

2. Does the use of vicarious instructors lead to significantly different achievement gain scores by pupils of different academic ability? The Cincinnati evidence suggests that the high-ability students gain more from televised instruction, but this evidence is based on a small sample. The Chicago evidence suggests that the high- and low-ability groups, among four levels formed, gained more with live teachers than did the middle-ability groups. The studies by Anderson and his associates in Kansas reveal no differences according to method by ability level. Popham and Sadnavitch also concluded that differences in gain according to ability level were not related to the instructional medium used. Over-all, the results are inconclusive.

3. Does the use of vicarious instructors of acknowledged competence significantly alter the interests of pupils in science? We infer from various comments on the Wisconsin experiment (see above) that its control groups had a higher interest, or conversely, that its film group had a greater loss of interest. Similar results were found by Popham and Sadnavitch for both their physics and their chemistry groups. While these few studies do not permit a final conclusion, they strengthen the suspicion that the *vicarious instruction increases negative attitudes toward science.*

Certainly future studies should focus more strongly upon the affective consequences of instruction in science and especially of vicarious instruction. As demonstrated in the Cincinnati study with the Test of Knowledge about Science and Scientists, or possibly with the more recent Test on Understanding Science, more stable and comparable results can be obtained, from one study to the next, by using the same instruments. Shifts of interest might also be investigated with some of the subscales of the Strong Vocational Interest Blank and the various Kuder Preference Records. We must recognize that instruction in a school subject does much more than permit the pupil to obtain a higher score on an achievement test.

4. Careful studies must be made of the effects of vicarious instruction upon the role and self-esteem of classroom teachers. That the demand for excellence among teachers may not be lessened by any vicarious instruction was apparent from a recent comment: "After the expert has discussed the subject, the pupils will ask their teachers for clarification of confusing points."

5. Finally, Anderson and Montgomery (1959) raised quite a different problem. After noting the small, even though statistically significant, score changes, they said, "average improvement . . . was of the order of 0.5 of a z-score. . . . The improvement seems meager after a year's study in biology." The present author agrees.

After examining a number of studies that report pre- and posttest scores, one is struck by the relatively high pretest scores, often 50 per cent of the test maximum. Thus, the Cincinnati biology pretest mean was 47 out of a maximum possible of 89; the Anderson biology pretest mean was 31.6 out of a maximum possible of 75; the Popham and Sadnavitch physics pretest mean was 48.0 out of 77, and the chemistry pretest mean was 45.2 out of 81. Such pretest scores severely restrict the range within which pupils can gain in their scores. Also, they indicate that if students are to show gain they will have to succeed with the more difficult items built into the tests. Yet the final mean scores for even high-ability groups are well below the maximum possible on the tests used. Earlier, attention was drawn to the variety of factors which produce this result. Yet, with Anderson and Montgomery, we must wonder how it is that after a year of instruction the gains are so meager. Certainly such results must be discouraging to the teachers.

PROGRAMED INSTRUCTION

Many research workers are currently investigating the conditions under which carefully programed instruction can be used, with little or no active involvement of a teacher, to bring about learning (Lumsdaine & Glaser, 1960; see also Ch. 12 of this Handbook). The instructional materials so programed can be presented by means of a teaching machine, or by a programed text (of either the linear or scrambled type). Certainly the possibilities of relieving teachers of many of their routine tasks and drill sessions are worthy of extensive and careful investigation; it seems that this would enable them to address themselves to more complex tasks and to guidance of individual students in independent study.

Programs dealing with science are rare at present, although it is assumed that many are now under construction. Experimental studies of programed instruction which report data concerning pupil responses to programs and to pretests and posttests are rare in any subject. This underlines the fact that programing as a science is in its early stages. M. D. Smith at Harvard (unpublished report) has developed and tested a programed sequence in hydrostatics and hydrodynamics (about 150 frames). Results point out difficulties involved in adjusting programs to student capacity at higher levels (although performance of students using the program was satisfactory on a subsequent examination). Smith also observed in his own and other programs a tendency to condition verbal responses unaccompanied by understanding of the physical phenomena and relationships which the verbal statements represent. David Klaus (unpublished report) of the American Institute of Research has programed extensive material in high school physics, but early reports deal with the use of this material only as a supplement to television presentations. Klaus used 16 classes in 15 high schools; nine of the classes were "experimental" in that they used a programed text as supplementary material instead of a workbook. He was able to conclude only that the programed text was superior to the workbook used by control groups. (The workbook had been written for the purpose of the experiment.)

Kormondy at Oberlin College and Stephenson at Earlham College (unpublished report) used a 500-frame constructed-response program in programed text form covering the subject of "Introduction to Genetics"; they compared experimental groups of undergraduates with groups using a text prepared from the program and also with groups attending lectures and studying from conventional texts. The programed text group showed superior performance when compared with conventional groups (gain from pre- to post-test with covariance adjustment), but no significant difference was found between a programed text group and the group which used a text in traditional format but prepared from the program.

Outcomes of such studies have been shown by Holland (1960) to be dependent upon the nature of the program used, and thus it is too early to form conclusions concerning the comparative effectiveness of programed instruction. While not traditionally considered under the rubric of "science," Holland's classic program in the fundamentals of psychology (operant conditioning) is now in its fourth year of use at Harvard. This is a 1500-frame constructed-response program with an error rate of about 10 per cent. There are also numerous programs which treat elementary statistics.

Most studies in programed instruction done thus far have been concerned with such variables as multiple-choice versus constructed-response (they often show differences on constructed-response tests, not on multiple-choice), overt versus covert response (results inconclusive), and allowable error rates.

The last classification reflects two major points of view: (1) low error rates are necessary (though not sufficient) and small step linear programs are desirable; (2) higher error rates can be compensated for by providing alternate sequences which give reasons why the wrong answers are wrong, then return the student to the same item to try again (items are multiple-choice). Most studies reported so far represent the first point of view. In general, one finds little replication, insufficient description of programed material and pupil responses to it, and little data concerning problems of retention, review, and reference. It often seems that the programs used have not been adequately tested and standardized before variants have been compared statistically. At present, the greatest need seems to be for research in the development of good programs—programs which yield low error rates and good performance on reasonable tests of achievement (transfer not implied); once such programs are developed, different forms can be constructed and compared. An equally important task is to construct programs which teach broad concepts rather than mere vocabulary.

Programed instruction, with or without the use of teaching machines, offers its most obvious possibilities where a systematic body of information must be known; for example, we can readily visualize such devices being used to provide practice at any type of systematic classification—in botany, in zoology, in geology and mineralogy, and in chemistry. Through research it may also be possible to extend its use to include exposure to the behaviors or reactions of things, on which much of science is based. We can visualize major parts of science courses being handled by the pupils at their individual rates. With films, at least some of the phenomena under discussion can be exhibited. With interspersed problems for laboratory investigation providing contact with reality, much of a whole course might be taught with programed materials.

One major advantage of programed instruction is that it permits the individual student to proceed at his own rate and to review lessons on which he had difficulties. As now conceived, a program exposes each pupil to the fine details of the subject and requires him to make proper responses at each step. Inasmuch as teachers, or pupils, or both, may fail to include or respond to such steps when taught en masse, programed instruction provides many opportunities for individualized teaching. Well-tested programs are intended to present material in such small steps that most pupils proceed with few or no errors.

Use of such programs may relieve teachers of many routine presentations and current duties. But what functions will the teacher still perform? Some teachers will be sufficiently competent to prepare programed materials that will be used throughout the country; at present it seems likely that these will represent collaborations between recognized experts and programer-teachers. In the classroom the science teacher's function will become more that of the diagnostician who is aware of the peculiar difficulties of certain students and can recommend alternate programs to overcome these difficulties. Also he will be responsible for a major part of the affective instruction dealing with careers, with the impact of science on society, and with the more philosophical components of instruction. In considering such possible roles, however, one should not dismiss one basic fact of programed instruction: the motivation involved is of a secondary kind; some students have been conditioned to find the type of rewards used more reinforcing than others. The inspiration provided by a teacher is yet the more basic motivating force. Perhaps programing will make it possible to bring this inspiration to bear more directly and more often upon the individual student.

As observed by Ryans (1960) and by many experienced supervisors, science teachers are quite conservative. Many hold their positions and maintain their egos by virtue of their "knowledge of the subject." They enjoy "telling and showing" their pupils. If this behavior is made unnecessary by some type of "canned" instruction, many teachers will be obliged to change in position and importance. Even for those who will recognize and welcome their new role, this change will be difficult. Those responsible for developing programed instruction or anticipating its acceptance in schools must anticipate much confusion about, and resistance to, its use.

CONCLUDING REMARKS

The papers cited above, and numerous others of a more general nature read during the preparation of this chapter, have provided only a small beginning for the description of teacher behaviors and their impact upon pupils in science. The almost universal emphasis upon gains in scores on achievement tests of limited scope is alarming. This emphasis implies that the primary function of a teacher is to develop in the pupil only the small range of academic behaviors, and usually rather minor ones, which are required by the tests used. Yet the pupil is also an emotional being who responds to stress and decision-making on the basis of how he feels as well as what he knows. He may be threatened and bullied into achieving a high test score, yet come to loathe the subject, school, and all things academic. Thus such studies as those by Atkin, Cogan, and Reed, as well as that by Ryans, which have begun to probe the "climate" of instruction and the emotional reactions of pupils, are exceedingly important.

Most of the studies have seemed to treat the teacher in terms of a narrow, stereotyped conception of his role, not as an aspiring human being in a situation rife with tensions. Even the papers of Cogan and Reed, which involve the pupil's descriptions of teacher behaviors, have not penetrated the facade to the real teacher. We suspect that observed syndromes of teacher behaviors could be predicted to a significant degree from stable personality attributes of the teachers. Boeck's comment that the variance of pupil response is primarily assignable to differences among the teachers is suggestive. Cogan found quite significant differences between the three science teachers on whom he had data. Ryans noted that science and mathematics teachers were among the most conservative teachers in our schools. All these leads are worthy of careful exploration with sophisticated instruments, which now exist, and with extensive statistical analysis. Chapter 11 of this Handbook deals with research on the personality of teachers in general; this kind of research is needed on teachers of science.

On the postulate that science teachers should have identifying attributes because strument the groups differed significantly ($p < .01$). Also, 7 of the 12 individual scales gave significant differences as shown in Table 2.

TABLE 2

DIFFERENCES BETWEEN STUDENTS PREPARING TO BECOME SCIENCE TEACHERS (TEA.) AND LIBERAL ARTS SCIENCE MAJORS (SCI.)[a]

Test and scale	Prediction	p	High group	Outcome
Guilford-Zimmerman:				
Social	Sci. < Tea.	.01	Tea.	As predicted
Emotional stability	Sci. < Tea.	.01	Tea.	As predicted
Objectivity	Sci. < Tea.	.05	Tea.	As predicted
Personal Relationships	Sci. < Tea.	.025	Tea.	As predicted
Allport-Vernon-Lindzey:				
Theoretical	Sci. > Tea.	n.s.	None	No difference
Aesthetic	Sci. < Tea.	n.s.	None	No difference
Social	Sci. < Tea.	.001	Tea.	As predicted
Strong Vocational:				
Technical worker	Sci. > Tea.	.001	Sci.	As predicted
Welfare worker	Sci. < Tea.	.001	Tea.	As predicted
Musical performer	Sci. > Tea.	n.s.	None	No difference
Business detail	Sci. < Tea.	n.s.	None	No difference
Business contact	Sci. < Tea.	n.s.	None	No difference

[a] After Lee, 1961.

they are in the category of teachers and the subcategory of science teachers, Lee (1961) initiated a study of their characteristics and career development. In his first study, he investigated the relationships between personality characteristics and career choice of prospective teachers while in college. The theory on career choice is drawn from that of Super. A group of 66 fifth-year male science majors planning to become science teachers after graduating from liberal arts colleges was compared with a group of 61 male liberal arts science majors who chose other careers in science. The following questionnaires and tests were given to all participants: four scales of the Guilford-Zimmerman Temperament Survey; three scales from the Strong Vocational Interest Blank for Men; and five scales from the Allport-Vernon-Lindzey Study of Values. Twelve explicit hypotheses were made about the direction of differences between the two groups. A two-group discriminant analysis, using all 12 variables, showed a highly significant difference ($p < .001$). On the subscales from any one in-

From this study we can conclude with considerable confidence that science majors in liberal arts colleges who chose to become science teachers differed in personality from those who chose other careers in science. Further studies should explore the stability of these personality characteristics among those who continue as teachers, the ways these attributes relate to their teaching behaviors, job aspirations, mobility, and willingness to modify instruction in content and purpose as school conditions require.

Lee's study suggests that the entire area of "teacher behavior," which was initially considered as "teacher effectiveness," be examined on a different basis. Descriptive ratings of teachers have not had much reliability and have not been significantly correlated with pupil behavior. Efforts to observe samples of a teacher's behavior have suffered from the limited amount of observation feasible. Even pupil descriptions, as employed by Cogan and Reed in science, suffer from a severe limitation: The observer, whether adult or pupil, can report only what the teacher does—but he can contribute little about what the teacher *might have done,* but did not do. A mere count of the frequency with which a teacher performs some operations may lack logical or psychological relevance to subsequent pupil behavior; one severely biting comment or word of glowing praise may override a multitude of routine responses. We may suspect then that persistent attributes of the teacher would be more useful bases on which to predict his general behavior. Perhaps a few speculations may prove stimulating.

Suppose the teacher is timid or insecure. This might be an innate characteristic of the teacher or result from his realization that he is incompetent in the subject which he has been assigned to teach. What behavior patterns might we expect? Such a teacher would, we surmise, stick closely to "the book," avoid open-ended discussions which might roam into topics of which he was ignorant, and attempt to establish a tight, authoritarian climate in his classroom. His instruction would be kept within narrow bounds, and he would play the role of the anxious authority. The pupils might do reasonably well on narrow achievement examinations, but their interest in science would be low, because the course would be dull.

Suppose the teacher is strongly authoritarian. How might he behave? If this teacher was "secure" in his knowledge of the course, we would expect him to dominate the room as the center of attention—to be a "teller" and an "exhibitor." Also, we would expect him to be relatively unsympathetic to the peculiar attributes of individual pupils unless they served to feed his self-esteem.

Suppose the teacher is a "good fellow" who "just loves children" and "wants to be liked." What sort of classroom climate would result? We anticipate bedlam. Courses and lessons will be relatively unstructured. Scattered and sporadic activities would start up and disintegrate for lack of clear purpose. Classroom control would be absent.

Suppose the teacher is highly conservative

intellectually and educationally. What behaviors might we expect? Courses would remain fixed from year to year. References to new books and current events might be rare. Efforts to modify, supposedly to "improve," the curriculum would be resisted or given only lip service. The range of experience provided for pupils would be restricted to that previously tried. The classroom climate would be secure, carefully limited, perhaps kindly, but not stimulating to pupil initiative. Rewards would be based on what the pupils knew, and little attention would be paid to how pupils had changed during the year.

Surely many other possibilities can be imagined. What is needed is a careful logical and psychological analysis of the behaviors predictable from the personal traits and value system of the teacher. These teacher traits could then be used to predict consequent classroom behaviors, or, more directly, the resulting behaviors of children taught by the person. To some extent, we are suggesting that the personality characteristics of teachers take precedence over whatever instructional techniques, or roles, they have learned. Perhaps this is a hypothesis worth investigating, among teachers of science as well as among the kinds of teachers already studied from this standpoint, as discussed in Chapter 11.

REFERENCES

Ackerman, W. I. Teacher competence and pupil change. *Harvard educ. Rev.,* 1954, 24, 273–289.

Anderson, K. E. A frontal attack on the basic problem in evaluation: The achievement of the objectives of instruction in specific areas. *J. exp. Educ.,* 1950, 18, 163–174.

Anderson, K. E., & Montgomery, F. S. An evaluation of the introductory physics course on film. *Sci. Educ.,* 1959, 43, 386–394.

Anderson, K. E., Montgomery, F. S., Smith, H. A., & Anderson, Dorothy. Toward a more effective use of sound motion pictures in high school biology. *Sci. Educ.,* 1956, 40, 43–54.

Atkin, J. M. A study of formulating and suggesting tests for hypotheses in elementary school science learning experiences. *Sci. Educ.*, 1958, 42, 414–422.

Barr, A. S. Measurement and prediction of teaching efficiency: Summary of investigations. *J. exp. Educ.*, 1948, 16, 203–283.

Bimson, O. H. Do good teachers produce good results? *North Central Quart.*, 1937, 12, 271–276.

Bloom, B. S., Engelhart, M. D., Furst, E. J., Hill, W. H., & Krathwohl, D. R. *Taxonomy of educational objectives.* New York: Longmans, Green, 1956.

Boeck, C. H. The relative efficiency of reading and demonstration methods of instruction in developing scientific understandings. *Sci. Educ.*, 1956, 40, 92–97.

Brandwein, P. F. *The gifted student as future scientist.* New York: Harcourt, Brace, 1955.

Brandwein, P. F., Watson, F. G., & Blackwood, P. E. *Teaching high school science: A book of methods.* New York: Harcourt, Brace, 1958.

Brown, S. Do college students benefit from high school laboratory courses? *Amer. J. Physics,* 1958, 26, 334–337.

Carpenter, W. W. Certain phases of the administration of high school chemistry. *Teach. Coll. Contr. Educ.,* 1925, No. 191.

Cogan, M. L. The behavior of teachers and the productive behavior of their pupils: I. "Perception" analysis. *J. exp. Educ.,* 1958, 27, 89–105. (a)

Cogan, M. L. The behavior of teachers and the productive behavior of their pupils: II. "Trait" analysis. *J. exp. Educ.,* 1958, 27, 107–124. (b)

Cole, C. C., Jr. *Encouraging scientific talent.* New York: College Entrance Examination Board, 1956.

Cooley, W. W., & Klopfer, L. E. *Manual for the Test on Understanding Science.* Princeton, N.J.: Educational Testing Service, 1961.

Cooley, W. W., & Reed, H. B., Jr. The measurement of science interests: An operational and multidimensional approach. *Sci. Educ.,* 1961, 45, 320–326.

Cunningham, H. A. Lecture method versus individual laboratory method in science teaching—A summary. *Sci. Educ.,* 1946, 30, 70–82.

Davis, H. M. The use of high school examinations as an instrument for judging the work of teachers. *Teach. Coll. Contr. Educ.,* 1934, No. 611.

Engelhart, M. D., Schwachtgen, E. C., & Nee, Mary M. Chicago public schools television instruction experiment in high school physics. *Amer. J. Physics,* 1958, 26, 347–349.

Frings, H., & Hichar, J. K. An experimental study of laboratory teaching methods in general zoology. *Sci. Educ.,* 1958, 42, 255–262.

Gale, G. O. *Teaching of physics by film and television.* New York: American Institute of Physics, 1958.

Heath, R. W., Maier, M. H., Remmers, H. H., & Rodgers, D. G. High school students look at science. *Purdue opin. panel Poll Rept.,* 1957, No. 50.

Henry, N. B. (Ed.) Science education in American schools. *Yearb. nat. Soc. Stud. Educ.,* 1947, 46, Part I.

Herriott, R. E. The influence of teacher behavior upon changes in pupil behavior: Analyses and impressions of research. Unpublished manuscript, 1960.

Holland, J. G. Design and use of a teaching machine program. Paper read at Amer. Psychol. Ass., Chicago, 1960.

Horton, R. E. Measurable outcomes of individual laboratory work in high school chemistry. *Teach. Coll. Contr. Educ.,* 1928, No. 303.

Jacobs, J. N., & Bollenbacher, Joan. Experimental study in teaching high school biology by television in the Cincinnati public schools. *Sci. Educ.,* 1959, 43, 399–405.

Jones, R. deV. The prediction of teaching efficiency from objective measures. *J. exp. Educ.,* 1946, 15, 85–99.

Kahn, P. An experimental study to determine the effect of a selected procedure for teaching the scientific attitudes to seventh and eighth grade boys through the use of current events in science. *Sci. Educ.,* 1962, 46, 115.

Knapp, R. H., & Goodrich, H. B. *Origins of American scientists.* Chicago: Univer. of Chicago Press, 1952.

Kruglak, H. Some behavior objectives for laboratory instruction. *Amer. J. Physics,* 1951, 19, 223–225.

Kruglak, H. Experimental outcomes of laboratory instruction in elementary college physics. *Amer. J. Physics,* 1952, 20, 136–141.

Kruglak, H. Achievement of physics students with and without laboratory work. *Amer. J. Physics,* 1953, 21, 14–16.

Kruglak, H. The measurement of laboratory achievement. *Amer. J. Physics,* 1954, 22, 442–462.

Kruglak, H. Measurement of laboratory achievement. *Amer. J. Physics,* 1955, 23, 82–87. (a)

Kruglak, H. The effect of high school physics and college laboratory instruction on achievement in college physics. *Sci. Educ.,* 1955, 39, 219–222. (b)

Kruglak, H. Evaluating laboratory instruction by use of objective-type tests. *Amer. J. Physics,* 1958, 26, 31–32.

Kruglak, H., & Goodwin, R. A. Laboratory achievement in relation to the number of partners. *Amer. J. Physics,* 1955, 23, 257–264.

Lahti, M. The inductive-deductive method and the physical science laboratory. *J. exp. Educ.,* 1956, 24, 149–163.

Lee, E. Career development of science teachers: Personality determinants at the exploratory stage. Unpublished doctoral dissertation, Harvard Univer., 1961.

Lins, L. J. The prediction of teaching efficiency. *J. exp. Educ.,* 1946, 15, 2–60.

Lucow, W. H. Estimating components of variation in an experimental study of learning. *J. exp. Educ.,* 1954, 22, 265–271.

Lumsdaine, A. A., & Glaser, R. (Eds.) *Teaching machines and programmed learning: A source book.* Washington, D.C.: Dept. of Audio-Visual Instruction, National Education Association, 1960.

Macomber, F. G., & Siegel, L. *Final report of the experimental study in instructional procedures.* Oxford, Ohio: Miami Univer., 1960.

Mayman, J. E. An experimental investigation of the book method, lecture method, and experimental method of teaching science in elementary schools. New York: New York City Bur. of Educ. Res., 1912. (Summary in F. D. Curtis, *Digest of investigations in the teaching of science,* I. Philadelphia: Blakiston, 1926, pp. 30–33.)

Mead, Margaret, & Metraux, Rhoda. Image of the scientist among high school students— A pilot study. *Science,* 1957, 126, 384.

Miller, N. E., & Dollard, J. *Social learning and imitation.* New Haven, Conn.: Yale Univer. Press, 1941.

Mitzel, H. E., & Gross, Cecily. Development of pupil growth criteria in studies of teacher effectiveness. *Educ. res. Bull.,* 1958, 37, 178–187, 205–215.

Morsh, J. E., & Wilder, Eleanor W. Identifying the effective instructor: A review of the quantitative studies, 1900–1952. *USAF Pers. Train. Res. Center Res. Bull.,* 1954, No. AFPTRC-TR-54-44.

Morsh, J. E., Burgess, G. C., & Smith, P. N. Student achievement as a measure of instructor effectiveness. *J. educ. Psychol.,* 1956, 47, 79–88.

Nedelsky, L. Formation of objectives of teaching in the physical sciences. *Amer. J. Physics,* 1949, 17, 345–354.

Neivert, Sylvia S. Identification of students with science potential. Unpublished doctoral dissertation, Columbia Univer., 1955.

Noall, M. F., & Winget, L. Staff utilization studies help Utah educators—The physics film project. *Nat. Ass. Sec. Sch. Principals Bull.,* 1959, 43, 183–195.

Popham, W. J., & Sadnavitch, J. M. Filmed science courses in the public schools: An experimental approach. *Sci. Educ.,* 1961, 45, 327–335.

Reed, H. B., Jr. Teacher variables of warmth, demand and utilization of intrinsic motivation related to pupils' science interests: A study illustrating several potentials of variance-covariance. *J. exp. Educ.,* 1961, 29, 205–229.

Rulon, P. J. *The sound motion picture in science teaching.* Cambridge, Mass.: Harvard Univer. Press, 1933.

Ryans, D. G. *Characteristics of teachers.* Washington, D.C.: American Council on Education, 1960.

Sadnavitch, J. M., & Popham, W. J. Retention value of filmed science courses. *Sci. Educ.,* 1962, 46, 22.

Seyfert, W. C., & Tyndal, B. S. An evaluation of differences in teaching ability. *J. educ. Res.,* 1934, 28, 10–15.

Siegel, L. The instructional Gestalt: A conceptual framework. *Teachers Coll. Rec.,* 1960, 62, 202–213.

Smith, H. A., & Anderson, K. E. An inquiry into some possible learning differentials as a result of the use of sound motion pictures in high school biology. *Sci. Educ.*, 1958, 42, 34–37.

Stoddard, A. J. (Ed.) The national program in the use of television in the public schools. *Report of the first year, 1957–58.* New York: Fund for the Advancement of Education, 1959.

Super, D., & Bachrach, P. B. *Scientific careers and vocational development.* New York: Teachers Coll., Columbia Univer., 1957.

Terman, L. M. Scientists and non-scientists in a group of 800 gifted men. *Psychol. Monogr.,* 1954, 68, No. 7.

Van Denberg, J. K. An objective rating scale for teachers of biology in high school. *Sch. & Soc.,* 1937, 46, 698–704.

Webb, W. B., & Nolan, C. Y. Student, supervisor, and self-ratings of instructor proficiency. *J. educ. Psychol.,* 1955, 46, 42–46.

Wisconsin Physics Film Evaluation Project. Madison: Univer. of Wisconsin, 1959. (Pamphlet)

CHAPTER 21 Research on Teaching Foreign Languages

JOHN B. CARROLL
Harvard University

Foreign language instruction has many attractions as an area for research. Learning a foreign language in a school setting is a process in which the learner normally starts from a natural zero point and proceeds to acquire a series of habits and response capabilities which, although they may be very numerous and complex, in theory can be listed and precisely described. A large degree of control can be exercised over the choice of stimuli presented to the student and the kinds of responses he is expected to make to them; if desired, the instruction can be programed to the last detail. Reliable and valid measures of aptitude and achievement are available to assist in the design and execution of experiments.

The appeal of these attractions, however, is in many ways deceptive. The goals of language study are diverse and lead to different conceptions of what is to be learned. The specification of the stimuli presented and the observation of the learners' responses can demand a degree of sophistication in linguistic science or a knowledge of foreign languages which is not ordinarily possessed by the casual educational researcher. The learner is not learning something totally new, for the new system for encoding meanings is parallel to another system he already knows. In a sense, the learner is being retrained. Definitive research can progress only at glacial speed, because learning a foreign language requires long periods of time even when it is pursued as intensively as possible. Teacher and method variables may be difficult to measure or control, and electromechanical aids for presenting audio-visual instruction are hard taskmasters for the experimentalist unless he is a patient and ingenious gadgeteer. Measures of achievement and proficiency are often expensive and difficult to construct and unlikely to satisfy all comers. Classroom experimentation has all its familiar drawbacks, in addition to a few which are somewhat peculiar to the foreign language field, e.g., the role of the learner's classmates in facilitating or retarding his learning.

Elsewhere the writer (1962) has presented a conceptual model of the learning process which applies with particular force to the learning of a foreign language. Briefly, the model proposes that the success of learning in an educational setting is a complex function of five kinds of elements:

(1) *The learner's aptitude,* defined as an

inverse function of the amount of time which, other things being optimal, will be required for him to attain a criterion mastery in the task to be learned (in the present case, a specified degree of skill in the use of a foreign language); aptitude in turn is regarded as a function of a number of independent basic traits or characteristics of the learner.

(2) *The learner's general intelligence,* as shown by his ability to understand the nature of the task he is to learn and/or the procedure he is to follow in the learning of the task.

(3) *The learner's perseverance,* defined as the amount of time during which the learner will (voluntarily or involuntarily) engage in active learning efforts with all other relevant factors being kept constant.

(4) *The quality of the instruction,* conceived as the degree to which the presentation, explanation, and ordering of the elements of the task to be learned approach the optimum, and

(5) *The opportunity for learning* afforded the student, defined as the amount of time allowed for learning (reflected in the pacing of the instruction relative to the student's capacity to profit from it).

The first three of these elements reside in the learner, while the last two reside in the instructional process. This review will focus attention on the last two, but the former will not be neglected. Our chief purpose, however, is to inform the reader about the kinds of variables which are probably important in research on foreign language teaching and to give the would-be researcher a better understanding of the nature of foreign language teaching and the kinds of research that are practicable and meaningful. Along the way, we will also attempt to document the state of our research-attained knowledge about foreign language learning and teaching at the various grade levels.[1]

---

[1] Birkmaier's review (1960) gives much historical information and documentation omitted from the present article.

METHODS OF INSTRUCTION

Overview

It is generally accepted that there are four chief kinds of skills which can be attained in different degrees in learning a language: understanding, speaking, reading, and writing. The mixture in which these four separate goals are weighted or brought into play in any particular program of instruction varies widely. In addition, there may be subsidiary goals such as a knowledge and appreciation of the literature of a foreign country, the ability to produce a superior written translation of foreign language texts, or the ability to be a simultaneous interpreter (rendering a running translation in one language—usually one's native language—while listening to spoken discourse in another language).

In learning the use of the spoken language, the learner has three primary kinds of things to master: the *phonology* of the language (i.e., the system of distinctive phonetic elements used in the language), the grammatical *structure* of the language (including morphology and syntax), and the *lexicon* of the language (the "vocabulary" of forms used in the language, with their "meanings"). The language may or may not be presented through the intermediary of some sort of phonetic or phonemic *transcription* of the sounds of the language, and the meanings of the lexicon and grammatical structures may be presented either by reference to the customary vernacular already familiar to the learner, or by reference to the inner logic of situations and verbal and nonverbal contexts, or some combination of all of these. In learning the written form of a language, the student may be confronted either with an alphabet with which he is already familiar but whose sound values are at variance with those of writing systems which he already knows, or with a totally unfamiliar alphabet such as the Cyrillic, the Hebrew, the Arabic, the Devanagari, or the Burmese, or with a system of characters such as the Chinese, Japanese, or Korean. Sometimes the written form of a language is stylistically very different from that of the spoken language. In some cases, notably Japanese and Indonesian, one of the major tasks of the learner is to get acquainted with the various styles of the spoken language used in different social status relationships. One should also not neglect the fact that beyond spoken and written language there is the "silent language" of gesture and action which plays a part in the total communication process (Hall, 1959). These systems may also have to be learned in some degree if the student is to function adequately as an interlocutor or participant in the culture in which the language is spoken.

The learning of a language is thus an exceedingly complex task; its difficulty will depend generally upon what aspects of language are to be learned, the degree of mastery desired, and the degree to which the target language differs from the learner's native or customary language. In addition, languages differ in inherent degree of complexity, either in their sound system, their grammatical structure, or their traditional writing systems.

Methods of instruction are correspondingly diverse, depending on the goals sought and the assumptions made as to the best means of achieving those goals. Designations of methods as "grammar-translation," "direct," or "linguistic" do not imply anything like a strict taxonomy; they simply call attention to certain major emphases that may be characteristic of a course of instruction or a teaching procedure.

Traditional procedures of language instruction in American schools in the nineteenth and early twentieth centuries often used a "grammar-translation" method in the sense that they sought primarily to teach the student to translate passages in the written language; this was to be done by teaching the student "rules" of grammar and lists of vocabulary items paired with what were indicated as their English "equivalents." But the "direct" method has an equally long history: its object is to teach the student to understand and speak the language, and its distinguishing feature is that the overt use of

the student's native language is avoided. A variant of this is the "graded direct" method developed by Richards and Gibson (1945) which places emphasis upon the careful grading of the materials to be learned and upon the presentation of these materials in meaningful contrastive contexts. Methods may be called "linguistic" to the extent that the preparation of materials has been guided by scientific analyses of the language to be learned— in particular, its phonology and grammar. Nevertheless, a teaching procedure might conceivably combine features from all these methods or from none of them. Among the more unusual methods that have come to the writer's attention is that of Curran (1961), who claims to have had success in teaching foreign languages in the context of psychotherapy—utilizing "language counselors" who help the learners to express their inner desires and motives in one or more foreign languages. Curran's method therefore may be characterized as a type of "direct" method.

It may be useful here to attempt to state some prominent characteristics of the methods of foreign language teaching toward which there seems now to be convergence. Many courses of instruction could be mentioned as illustrative of contemporary methods; insofar as a textbook can be said to constitute a course of instruction, perhaps one of the most representative is the textbook *Modern Spanish* (with associated phonograph recordings) which resulted from a project of the Modern Language Association (Bolinger, et al., 1960).[2] Four characteristics of contemporary methods are prominent; a separate

---

[2] Only a selection from the enormous bibliography on foreign language teaching can be given. A reading of materials by Brooks (1959), Ciofarri (1958), Kaulfers (1942, 1956), and McKinney and Hocking (1958) gives an impression of doctrinal developments in the language-teaching profession over the past twenty years, while works by Bloomfield (1942), Cochran (1952), Fries (1945), Lado (1957), and Nida (1957) present approaches associated with the development of linguistic science. Parker (1957) considers the place of foreign language teaching in the national interest, and Oinas (1960) has edited the proceedings of a recent symposium on language teaching methods, including the use of "language laboratories" and "teach-

paragraph will be devoted to each of them.

One characteristic is that items are normally presented and learned in their spoken form before they are presented in their written form. For this reason, contemporary teaching methods are often said to be *audiolingual* in emphasis—the confusing homophony of the phrase *aural-oral* is taking it out of favor (Brooks, 1959). The justification for this emphasis is found in the observation that a language is first of all a system of sounds for social communication; writing is a secondary derivative system for the recording of spoken language, even though written language may develop its own special status and characteristics. Children normally learn spoken language before they learn written language, and even in mature writers it may be supposed that the production of written discourse is usually preceded by a formulation in silent speech. Even if the learner's aim is only to read or write the language, it is felt that a surer mastery can be attained if he passes through a substantial stage of work with the spoken language. The amount of delay between presentation of the spoken and of the written material may vary from a short time to a very long time; the essential element is that of the priority of the spoken material. Some language teachers urge that the spoken forms are to be learned as accurately as possible, i.e., with native-like phonology and sentence patterns, although it is at least debatable whether this is necessary or desirable for all students. Nevertheless, regardless of how elevated the teacher's standards are in this matter, it seems to be rather widely agreed that it is important to provide the student with some adequate model of speech —preferably in the person of a native or near-native speaker of the language, but failing that, in the form of a faithfully recorded voice of such a speaker.

Second, contemporary teaching methods are making increasing use of the results of scientific analysis of the contrasts between the learner's language and the target language, because to a considerable extent, the typical learner's difficulties can be identified and predicted in advance on the basis of this "contrastive structure analysis." English-speakers learning German, for example, may be expected to have a certain set of difficulties which are largely different from the difficulties experienced by French-speakers learning German. Pascasio (1960) studied the difficulties of Tagalog-speakers in learning certain English patterns.

Third, contemporary doctrines stress the need for overlearning of language patterns by a special type of drill known as "pattern practice." Some language teachers have stressed the purely repetitive aspects of pattern practice, but what seems to be essential is the repetition of sentence patterns with varying elements. Pattern practice gives drill in the conscious application, variation, and transformation of structural patterns in language, with a view toward making such patterns "automatically" accessible in actual use of the language. These procedures are justified on the basis of theories and observations as to how children learn their native language and how the individual functions in using the well-practiced patterns of his native language. Grammatical descriptions of patterns are taught only after the patterns are well on their way to being mastered at a purely oral level, and then only when it is

ing machines." The intensive language programs developed in World War II in the armed forces are described and evaluated by Agard, Clements, and Hendrix (1944), Angiolillo (1947), Lind (1948), and Matthew (1947). The intensive programs employed in the Army Language School are described by Hempel and Mueller (1959) and evaluated by Moore (1957). Representative programs in colleges and universities are described by Dostert (1953), Haden (1956), Hocking (1955), Moulton (1952), and Zeydel, et al. (1946); in high school, by Huebener (1956);

and in elementary schools, by Andersson (1953), DeSauzé (1953), MacRae (1957), and Mildenberger (1954). Johnston (1958), Johnston and Remer (1959), and Johnston and Seerley (1959) have compiled bibliographies on foreign languages in the elementary school, the high school, and in the language laboratory. References to developments in Europe and in the U.S.S.R. include those by Abell (1959), Frank (1958), Hood (1958), and London (1959). The proceedings of an international seminar on language teaching help broaden one's perspective (UNESCO, 1953).

felt that such descriptions will hasten the learning process or help insure retention. One can easily appreciate the role that can be played by sound film loops, tape playback devices, and teaching machines in repetitive auditory presentation. The major problem is to gain sufficient time for the large amounts of practice that appear to be necessary.

A fourth prominent characteristic of contemporary foreign language teaching is the minimization of the use of the student's native language, and the insistence on the desirability or even the necessity of learning to make responses in situations which simulate "real-life" communication situations as closely as possible. An increasing amount of instruction is given by the "direct" method—solely in the target language, with the additional support of whatever props, pictorial materials, or pantomimic gestures may be necessary to convey contextual meaning. Even in courses where some part of the instruction is given in the form of lectures or explanations in the student's vernacular, or where translation drills are used, other substantial parts of the instruction are given with strict avoidance of the student's vernacular. As soon as students are sufficiently well prepared, they are given opportunity to converse with native informants, to watch selected films with foreign language sound tracks, and to engage in other activities where linguistic materials can gain meaning in realistic situations and contexts. Justification for these procedures is sought in the psychology of language and in studies of bilingualism, in which it is held that the speaker who has acquired a mastery of a second language does not normally "translate" from his native language into the second language; instead, his second-language verbal responses are direct responses to situations, without the intervention of native-language responses. Later in this chapter the relevant research evidence is examined.

It is not essential in contemporary language teaching that the instructor and the text materials avoid *all* use of the student's native language. There are different shades of opinion on this, but practically no directly relevant research (Politzer, 1958). Most textbooks in common use make extensive use of English to convey meanings as well as to explain structure. In almost every instructional setting, the student is eventually provided with grammars, glossaries, and dictionaries which make use of his native language. On the other hand, there are courses where special efforts are made to rule out all use of the student's native language until he has attained mastery of the foreign speech patterns.

General Comments on Research Strategy

We will make the pretense here that it is possible to decompose the various methods into elements which either have been or could be examined experimentally—e.g., the use of or the avoidance of the learner's native language, the priority assigned speech over writing, or the use of native informants as models of correctness. Such a decomposition is unrealistic. For example, if the use of the native language is disallowed in a particular course of instruction, it may be necessary to make special selections of vocabulary and grammatical content (picturable objects, demonstrable actions, etc.) whereby these meanings can be conveyed deictically. If, on the other hand, use of the native language is permitted, the optimal strategy for the selection of vocabulary content may call for the grading of the materials in terms of ease of phonological or grammatical structure. Most methods represent an artful compromise or balance among the demands and limitations imposed by the underlying set of presuppositions about language teaching which have been chosen by their creators. It is difficult, then, to vary one element of instruction experimentally without modifying the effect of other elements. The experimental control of a single variable, if carried out in connection with classroom instruction, may entail the revision of an entire textbook or series of tape recordings. Successful single-variable experiments are rare in foreign language teaching.

Some research workers have felt it wise to move in the direction of "miniature" language-learning settings in which the objectives of the instruction are limited and variables can be carefully controlled. An example of such an experiment was that performed by Dunkel (1948, pp. 114–120, 177–190), in which a short series of lessons in Persian was constructed in alternate forms so that visual and auditory presentation could be compared. The danger with such experiments is that the language teaching may become extremely artificial—i.e., dissimilar to the procedures actually used by teachers, and also probably far from optimal in terms of proper programing of the instruction. For example, Dunkel's Persian materials seem to expect the student to make a series of inductions about Persian vocabulary and grammar at a rate which is almost certainly faster than the rate at which such materials would be presented in the normal classroom.

Even further removed from the actualities of language teaching is the type of verbal learning experiment with which the psychologist feels most comfortable—usually performed with memory drums, films or filmstrip projectors, or certain types of teaching machines. Often these experiments have an almost complete lack of relevance to language teaching. An example is a study by Kale and Grosslight (1955) of the use of pictures and sound in teaching foreign language vocabulary. At the outset, it should be said that the teaching of vocabulary is not the most crucial problem faced by language teachers in the beginning phases of language instruction; the vocabulary load is usually kept small at that stage in order to devote attention to the enormous phonological and structural problems. Kale and Grosslight's study, however, seemed to be based on the assumption (which might indeed be made in an extremely outdated translation method) that language learning should start with the learning of vocabulary. In their experiments, the learner's task was to learn to write a Russian word in a specially devised transcription system in response to either an English word, a picture, or a word-picture combination. Among the variables studied were the presentation of material by still picture versus motion picture, and the provision of a pronunciation of the Russian word by a narrator on the sound film, with or without student "participation" (i.e., imitative repetition of the Russian word). Among the chief findings of this study were: "Pictures of an object or an act are an aid to learning to write foreign words.... The pictures need not be in motion.... Pronunciation of the words by the narrator or learner seems to inhibit learning *to write* foreign words" (Kale & Grosslight, 1955, Foreword).

Though we grant that pictorial presentation may be in some ways an aid to the learning of foreign language vocabulary, the conclusions concerning the negative effects of pronunciation appear ridiculous and absurdly irrelevant to actual language teaching, for no properly oriented language teacher would attempt to teach his students to *write* foreign language words, even in a transcription, without first teaching them in spoken form and teaching the properties of the sound system of the language as related to the transcription system used. Kale and Grosslight interpret the poor showing of the groups which had the sound film as compared to the groups which did not have it, as "an interference effect resulting from the difference between the way some words are spelled and the way they are pronounced." This comment reveals only a dim awareness of the relations and respective statuses of speech and writing. If this experiment were to be repeated for groups having had pretraining in Russian phonology and the characteristics of the transcription system, one would not be surprised to find quite different results.

It may be recommended, therefore, that useful experiments in foreign language teaching can be conducted by adhering fairly closely, at least initially, to patterns of teaching and types of teaching materials which have already been developed and found successful by foreign language teachers. Foreign language teachers sincerely want to know how to improve their procedures, but they are not likely to attend carefully to the results of researches which utilize radically different or unrealistic teaching methods, or which appear to be formulated in terms of outmoded conceptions of language or language teaching. This requirement does not rule out the small-scale, "miniaturized" experiment, either in a psychological laboratory or in a classroom situation; it merely attempts to guide the selection of the basic teaching method upon which the changes are to be rung in such an experiment. It may be suggested that a particularly useful context in which educational experimentation could be done is a regular language course from which a short period (a few days, say) is selected to stage special variations in instructional methods.[3]

Representative Research Studies Using Broad Comparisons

Ever since the advent of "modern" language teaching methods such as those described above, foreign language teachers have felt impelled to contrast these methods with more traditional ones with respect to student attainment of the various objectives of these courses. Rigorous experimental design has been largely absent from such studies; instead, simple group comparisons have been made at various stages of training, with hardly any use of control measurements. The results of these studies have been largely inconclusive.

The large-scale investigation conducted by Agard and Dunkel (1948) is a case in point.

---

[3] Whereas psychologists perform experiments with insufficient relevance to foreign language teaching, members of the foreign language teaching profession perform studies with insufficient experimental rigor. Numerous studies are announced as "experiments" (e.g., Ferrell, 1956–1957; Siciliano, 1959; Turner, 1958) but on examination turn out to be simply reports of new teaching procedures. Even when there is an effort to set up a true experiment (e.g., Borglum, 1958; Fotos, 1955; Hoge, 1959; McMullen, 1955), the controls are often completely inadequate. Pimsleur (1957) has set forth some requirements of research in the foreign language field.

Their study was a cooperative one in which results from a variety of high schools and colleges throughout the nation using either traditional or "new-type" methods, or both, were forwarded to a central office for statistical analysis.

These investigators had many difficulties to overcome; for example, at the time they started, they felt that no satisfactory tests of auditory comprehension and speaking proficiency in foreign languages were available, and these had to be built almost from the ground up. Furthermore, they were aware that it was difficult to describe the teaching methods used at the various schools where their tests were given, and even when descriptions were available, a surprising diversity of method was evident under the single banner of the "oral-aural" method, as it was then called. For that matter, the mean levels of proficiency in reading, writing, understanding, and speaking attained by students even under "conventional" methods varied widely, even though there might have been reason to suppose that these conventional methods, developed and standardized over a period of years, would have reasonably constant yields.

Following are the main conclusions which may be drawn from the Agard-Dunkel study: (1) Few if any students in oral-aural courses were able to attain, in one or two years' time, anything like what could be called "spontaneously fluent speech." "While many students could participate in memorized conversations speedily and effortlessly, hardly any could produce at length fluent variations from the basic material, and none could talk on unrehearsed topics without constant and painful hesitation" (p. 288). (2) Nevertheless, "despite the failure of most students to retain the excellent pronunciation observable in immediate imitation, the majority were observed to have a continuing production superior to that of conventional students who were taught to speak by rules of 'how the letters are pronounced,' and who have never heard a native speaker" (pp. 287–288). (3) "By and large, experimental students failed to understand the phono-graphically recorded utterances of an un-familiar native speaker, delivering unfamil-iar though easy material, significantly better than did conventional speakers" (p. 289). (4) "In general, . . . the experimental groups did not demonstrate so high a level of reading proficiency at the end of their first or second year as did conventional students" (p. 290), probably because the oral-aural programs did not pay much attention to reading in the first year or so. (5) "The evidence from the tests indicates that superior reading skills were developed in those programs where reading received the greatest time and emphasis. The highest levels were reached in reading-method courses which featured moderate amounts of classroom oral-aural practice directly related to the material read. . . . As to the assumption made in some quarters that oral-aural competence *automatically* creates reading ability and that consequently the latter need not be specifically taught, there is evidence *per contra* so far as the experi-ments observed are concerned . . . . low cor-relations of reading and aural test results from both experimental and conventional programs furnish conclusive evidence that (at least at subnative levels of competence) oral-aural and reading proficiency constitute separate, independent skills which do not develop one from the other but rather only from direct training in each separately" (pp. 291–292). (6) "With few exceptions lan-guage students claim to be more highly mo-tivated by oral-aural than by grammar and reading goals . . . . But as drill-sessions suc-ceed each other with relentless regularity, and as the material becomes more and more diffi-cult to assimilate, many begin to tire or to lose interest and fail to apply themselves to the extent the method demands in order to assure continuing success" (p. 292). Agard and Dunkel ended their report on a some-what pessimistic note, urging that because it was unrealistic to think that high school or college programs could yield the time neces-sary to produce anything like near-native competence in students, it was necessary to

re-examine the language requirement. In any case, they felt that more precise definitions of objectives, greater modesty of claims, bet-ter tests, and more carefully planned experi-ments were needed.

The Agard-Dunkel study should be re-garded as a comparative survey study rather than as a true experiment. Exact controls and rigorous experimental design were lacking, and few pretraining measurements were taken. Even though the investigators made special efforts to construct suitable tests of achievement, these tests appear not to have been as appropriate, reliable, and valid as might be desired. (On this point see the opinions expressed by Hamilton and Haden, 1950.) It is quite conceivable that there were real differences in achievement between con-ventional and "new-type" groups which the tests failed to detect.

On the other hand, there was much of value in this study. Above all, it provided fairly clear information on how much could be accomplished in "new-type" oral courses in high schools and colleges when these courses were conducted with energy and imagination. Evidently what could be ac-complished was largely a function of time available, and that time (typically, 100 to 200 hours of instruction) was far short of the amount of time available for language in-struction in intensive courses in the Army Specialized Training Program (a minimum of 15 hours per week for a total of 36 weeks, or 540 hours in all). The study also pre-sented reports on a variety of novel tactics in language teaching, e.g., a course in which the burden of instruction was through learn-ing to act parts in French plays (there was no strong evidence to indicate any superior-ity in this method). Along with another book by one of the investigators (Dunkel, 1948), the Agard-Dunkel report contains a wealth of information and speculation about re-search on foreign language teaching.

A few other studies involving broad com-parisons between instructional programs may be mentioned at this point. Cheydleur and Schenck (1950) and Schenck (1952) have reported a series of investigations conducted at the University of Wisconsin. In the first of these, an ASTP unit was compared with college groups on the American Council on Education German Reading Test. The attainment of the ASTP group stood at approximately that of college groups who had had *six* semesters of German. "The army group median on the whole test is *ten* points higher than the national median. These results are of particular interest inasmuch as they indicate the extent to which a reading ability was developed when speaking ability was the primary aim of instruction" (p. 30, italics added). If these results seem at variance with those reported by Agard and Dunkel, it must be remembered that they concern groups at a higher average level of training, where one could expect speaking knowledge of a language to transfer more readily to reading ability. In fact, Agard and Dunkel (1948, p. 291) predicted this sort of outcome for highly trained students. Actually, the ASTP course included some training in reading. How much transfer there was from speaking to reading could therefore not be assessed.

Other comparisons performed by Cheydleur and Schenck concerned only the civilian courses; these tended to favor classes taught by the oral-aural method. Students in traditional courses were significantly more likely to drop after one semester than students in conversational classes. Students in an advanced class who had started in a traditional class tended to get slightly lower grades than those who had started in conversational classes. The statistical significance of this trend was not tested, and no control variable measurements were mentioned in the report.

Fishman (1957, p. 58) reported that students did equally well on the College Entrance Examination Board written language examinations regardless of whether they had been taught in courses emphasizing speaking and understanding or in courses emphasizing grammar and reading skills.

In programs for teaching English to Puerto Rican children in Grades 4 and 7 of New York City schools, Morrison (1958, pp. 26–44) compared the effectiveness of three kinds of emphasis: "vocabulary," "structural," and "experiential." Pretests of ability in understanding, reading, writing, and speaking English were given to most of the children, and an analysis was made of the gains from pretest to posttest. The variant emphases were significantly different in their effectiveness in Grade 7 but not in Grade 4. In Grade 7, the "experiential" emphasis resulted in better skill in understanding spoken English, the "vocabulary" and "structural" variants aided ability to write English, the "vocabulary" variant led to significantly greater gains in ability to speak English, and none of the variants led to significant gains in reading English. These results caused Morrison to conclude: "For an integrated attack on all four areas of English—understanding, reading, writing and speaking—a combination of the three emphases together with a more direct attack on reading would seem to be most desirable" (p. 39). No explanation was offered for the differences between the Grade 4 and the Grade 7 results. Nevertheless, conferences and other exchanges among the teachers led to a series of "general agreements." For example, it was agreed that "the teaching of contrasting patterns singly and separately with later teaching of their contrast, is more effective than initial teaching by contrast" (p. 43). That is, it is more effective to teach the uses of the verbs *say* and *tell* separately than to introduce them together in contrasting patterns. (This conclusion is in accord with the results found in a controlled experiment by Ching, 1960, using Hawaiian children learning to speak standard English.)

Another of the "general agreements" reached by Morrison's teachers was that teachers' use of Spanish as the chief medium of instruction in the classroom tended to retard children's acquisition of English, although occasional use of Spanish was helpful in "teaching contrasting language forms or helping the pupil more quickly to grasp the meaning of an abstract word" (p. 44). These and other conclusions, though not supported by exact quantitative research, helped the staff to revise teaching materials in such a way as to present the best features of the three experimental "variants" in an integrated fashion. It is instructive to note, however, that the most pressing problems to be solved in the development of revised guides were not matters of general method but highly specific questions as to the selection of vocabulary, the order of introduction of structure points, and the like. In the terminology favored today, these were partly questions of curriculum and partly questions of programing.

The studies considered thus far are not so much studies of the methods of teaching as of the content in teaching. They support the rather commonplace conclusions that, by and large, students learn (if anything) precisely what they are taught, and that there are no mysterious transfers between language skills. For example, students do not learn to read unless they are taught to read, but once taught, their knowledge of grammar and lexicon acquired in oral-aural practice will aid them in reading. These studies tell us little, however, about the detailed construction of procedures in teaching foreign languages. We shall now begin to examine the research literature on specific problems in language teaching.

Pronunciation

For the person who hopes to communicate with speakers of a foreign language, a reasonably good approximation to the accepted pronunciation of the language is necessary, and for the person who hopes to be taken as "near-native" in fluency, a close approximation is absolutely essential. In fact, it has been noted (R. Brown, 1958, p. 310) that good pronunciation is often erroneously taken to be the sign of good foreign language competence. The writer has speculated (Carroll, 1960a) that the fact that young children are strikingly better than adults in acquiring a native-like accent in a second language has led to the widely held belief, which has by no means been scientifically verified, that they are equally superior in other aspects of language learning. At any rate, linguists have laid great stress on the importance of learning good pronunciation, to such an extent that it may be said that emphasis on accurate phonological learning is an essential aspect of contemporary language teaching methods. Nida (1957, pp. 86–87) gives an account of both amusing and tragic errors in communication which can occur when critical phonological distinctions in foreign languages are not observed. For all the linguist's emphasis on phonology, there is surprisingly little research on the teaching of phonology. Yet, this should be a relatively easy field in which to do fruitful and experimentally neat research; its chief demand is that the experimenter be a good phonetician.

There seems to be no empirical research on the effect of a "foreign" accent on intelligibility or on success in communication, although standard intelligibility tests similar to those discussed by Licklider and Miller (1951) should be very simple to conduct. Use could also be made of the technique of the "confusion matrix"[4] employed by Miller and Nicely (1955); that is, studies could be made of the extent to which native speakers misidentify the intended utterances of speakers with foreign accents. Lundeen, Ptacek, Starr, and Henrikson (1957) reported that the "foreign-soundingness" of a group of 54 foreigners could be rated by three speech correctionists with an over-all reliability of .90. (This was the correlation of their average ratings with those of three other raters.)

In the learning of a foreign-language phonology, at least four problems may be distinguished:

(1) the problem of *discrimination*, i.e., hearing the differences between phonemes

---

[4] If one is concerned with *n* different stimuli (e.g., a series of phonemes), each of the *n* rows of the confusion matrix displays the frequency with which *S*s identify a given stimulus either as being that stimulus itself (i.e., correctly) or as being one of the $(n - 1)$ other stimuli. In the present case, the stimuli would be utterances of speakers with foreign accents, while the *S*s would be native speakers.

which are not distinguished or used in one's native language;

(2) the problem of *articulation*, i.e., learning to make the motor movements adequate to proper production of the foreign phonemes;

(3) the problem of *integration*, i.e., learning to assemble the phonemes of a connected discourse with the proper allophonic variations and "smearing"; and

(4) the problem of *automaticity*, i.e., making correct production so habitual that it does not need to be attended to in the process of speaking.

There is some evidence (Liberman, 1957) that sound discrimination and sound production are related in a sort of regenerative feedback loop: that one learns to discriminate sounds which one can differentially produce, and vice versa. There is not enough evidence on this point, however, to allow one to decide whether teaching should assign priority to practice in discrimination or to practice in sound production alone. Most teachers treat these problems as correlative. Speculation among linguists seems to run to an almost schizoid indecision as to which of two diametrically opposed theories to accept: (1) that there is an automatic capacity to form the correct modes of sound production simply by careful and repeated listening—as if the learner is already "wired" to pronounce sounds correctly if he will only give full rein to this automatic capacity, or (2) that (except possibly for the young child) the learning of a foreign phoneme occurs as a result of conscious attention to the articulatory processes involved in its production, and that a scientific knowledge of articulatory phonetics is a positive aid. (See Nida, 1957, Ch. 6; see also the comment of Agard and Dunkel, 1948, p. 287, that to many students descriptive phonetics obviously means less than nothing.) We have here a rather neat experimental problem which urgently needs exploration. It is a special instance of the general problem of the utility of guidance and coaching in learning motor skills.

There is little research available on these questions which shows the proper degree of sophistication either in experimental design, instrumentation, or phonetics. Marckwardt (1944, 1946, 1947) did a series of rather informal classroom experiments in which he claimed to show that Spanish speakers learning English in Mexico have predictable difficulties in perceiving those phonemic distinctions of English which are nonphonemic in Spanish. He found that his students had trouble in perceiving such contrasts as /n~m~ŋ/; /s~ʃ/; /i~iy/; etc. (The Trager-Smith phonemicization of English is used here; see Trager & Smith, 1951.) The writer, however, has conducted Marckwardt's tests among *native* speakers of English under the same informal conditions that Marckwardt used (words spoken aloud by an experimenter in a nonacoustically treated classroom filled with a normal-size class) and has found about the same amount of inaccuracy in discrimination that Marckwardt found. Since they lack suitable experimental controls, the Marckwardt results are interesting but unassessable.

Carroll (1958a, p. 195), however, found distinct differences between native speakers of English and foreigners (with various native languages) just beginning to learn English, in discriminating the phonemes /s, z, Θ, ð, f, and v/ presented to all groups under comparable conditions with a high signal-to-noise ratio. The foreigners misidentified the sounds more frequently than did native speakers. Sapon and Carroll (1958) made a detailed study of confusions made by native speakers of English, Japanese, and Spanish in discriminating phonemes of various European languages; there were significant differences among these groups, and the difficulties were largely those which would be predicted on the basis of contrastive linguistics. Such research tells the teacher where the learner's difficulties are likely to be, although it does not indicate how such difficulties are to be dealt with.

Lundeen, Ptacek, Starr, and Henrikson (1957) demonstrated the effectiveness of a course in problems in English phonetics (20 class hours spread out over a period of 6 months) in reducing the "foreign-sounding-ness" of a group of 54 newly arrived foreign graduate students; the progress of the experimental group was significantly better than that of a control group from which instruction was withheld. It is impossible to tell from this study, however, whether phonetic training, sheer practice, or some other element in the course was chiefly responsible for the improvement. The study would have been enhanced by a detailed analysis of the phonetic items in which most improvement was secured.

In the experience of foreign language teachers, it is found that unless one is teaching young children (say, below the fifth grade), or unless one is very determined about withholding any kind of printed material (e.g., in a teaching procedure described by Grew, 1956), there will be a demand on the part of most students to have some means of writing the foreign language, if only as an aid to memory. One must face the question of whether this writing system should be the standard orthography of the language or some sort of phonetic or phonemic transcription.

In learning character languages like Chinese or Japanese, a phonetic transcription is a necessity; even the Chinese and the Japanese have such auxiliary systems for their own use, not necessarily using the Roman alphabet, however. In cases where the standard orthography of a language contains sound-symbol correspondences at variance with those already familiar to the learner, various kinds of interference or negative transfer will occur. The same is true of a phonetic transcription system, unless the sound-symbol values are carefully chosen. The kinds of errors made by learners of second languages suggest that negative transfer from writing systems is a strong influence in pronunciation errors. For example, German-speaking learners of English are prone to give the letter v the value it has in German, namely /f/, even though the phoneme /v/ also occurs in German, but with the spelling

w. Useful experiments could be done in investigating the properties of different kinds of writing systems in facilitating correct learning of pronunciation and in investigating the ability of students to surmount the inevitable and irreducible difficulties imposed by writing systems.

Jost's first law (Woodworth, 1938, p. 58), to the effect that *"if two associations are now of equal strength but of different ages, the older one will lose strength more slowly with the further passage of time,"* suggests that incorrect habits learned initially are hard to overcome, and underscores the importance of learning pronunciation correctly from the beginning. Agard and Dunkel (1948, p. 288) observed that "students entering an oral-aural course after previous study of the language, in high schools where English habits were tolerated, generally never succeeded in matching the pronunciation of those who were taught from the beginning to imitate native models."

The foregoing considerations are illustrated by two empirical studies. Hamilton and Haden (1950) sought to determine the relative merits of four methods of teaching pronunciation: (1) imitation of the teacher; (2) use of phonetic symbols; (3) use of regular orthography (in French and Spanish); and (4) physiological description of articulations. This experiment was performed in a series of regular college classes in beginning French and Spanish. However, the criteria used—an auditory comprehension test administered after the first four weeks, and a semester final exam—seem inappropriate for probing the merits of methods of teaching students to pronounce correctly. Their conclusions, which must be regarded with caution, were that physiological descriptions of speech articulations are helpful in teaching auditory comprehension in the case of both French and Spanish, and that the preferred system of writing for beginners should be a phonetic transcription in the case of French, and the standard orthography in the case of Spanish. S. E. Richards and Appel (1956) demonstrated that in teaching spoken Spanish, delaying the use of any writing system whatsoever resulted in better pronunciation, even after the presentation of the standard orthography, than introducing the standard orthography simultaneously with the presentation of spoken material. These experiments leave the problem of the optimal methods of teaching pronunciation practically untouched.[5]

Among questions which need explanation are the following: How much does it help the student to hear his own recorded pronunciation and to compare it with a standard? How much will individual coaching by the teacher help him to produce correct foreign sounds? Can the student learn to discriminate between correct and incorrect pronunciations of other learners, and if so, can he transfer this ability to correcting his own pronunciations? To what extent is it worth while for a student to be able to see (in a native informant or on a sound film) correct articulations? Of what use are anatomical charts or models of the vocal apparatus (Obrecht, 1956–1957)? Of what importance is immediate reinforcement of correct responses? Can correct pronunciation be best taught by "shaping"—i.e., reinforcement of successively closer approximations to the desired response? Should new sounds be taught in simple, one-syllable contexts, or in complex phrase or sentence contexts? At what speed should utterances to be imitated be pronounced for presentation to the learner—at normal speed or at slow speed? Is it more efficient to train learners to understand a variety of speakers (with different voices or even with different dialects) in the initial phases of instruction, so that the learner can more quickly build concepts of the distinctive features of phonemes, or should the initial phase of instruction present a limited number of voices, perhaps only one? How should instruction be organized to teach the learner

to make the required allophonic, conditioned variations in his pronunciations?

Grammar and Structure

It is well to remind the reader that "knowing a language" means, first of all, knowing its phonology and grammatical structure, for the common core of material which must be learned in these areas is relatively fixed in comparison with the learning of vocabulary. (The particular selection of vocabulary items which the learner acquires will vary with the texts he uses, his areas of interest, or other factors.) As has been implied above, the way in which problems of grammar are treated is one of the chief contrasts between traditional and contemporary language courses. In the former, grammar was embodied in a set of grammatical generalizations (stated as "rules") which had to be learned and deductively applied to the formation of sentences, often by translating from the native language. In "modern" courses the student is introduced to speech patterns which vary in controlled ways; by practicing these patterns he is expected to incorporate the grammatical structure of the language into his repertoire of foreign language verbal behavior in somewhat the same way that the child does in learning his native language. Much effort on the part of teachers has gone into the development of "pattern practice" exercises intended to develop skill in the learner who uses these with conscientious regularity, either in a "language laboratory" or in some other setting.

Nevertheless, hardly any empirical research can be cited either to support the use of pattern practice drills as contrasted with other methods of teaching grammar, or to indicate what variables control the success of particular types of drills. Teachers' guidebooks for pattern practice and language laboratory procedures (e.g., Marty, 1960) are being developed, apparently, solely on the basis of intuition and practical experience in the language laboratory and in the classroom. Perhaps this is enough, but the premises on which the present review is written would require that

---

[5] For the sake of completeness one should mention the speculative or descriptive writings of the linguists Hockett (1950) and Sapon (1952). Klinck (1957) believed that imitation is superior to descriptive phonetics in learning pronunciation.

we be able to support teaching procedures with empirical research. Delattre (1960) demonstrated gains after an eight-week intensive course for teachers which included large amounts of pattern practice; nevertheless, there was no control group and one cannot tell whether gains were due to pattern practice or to some other element in the situation. Cuff (1956) called for experimentation to see whether grammar should be taught by induction, by deduction, or by some combination of these methods, but he presented no data of his own. Mueller (1958) reported that students frequently fail to perceive grammatical signals in French even after intensive drill. Mueller's article, however, does little more than set forth the problem to be solved.

There being no adequate classroom experimentation, one may appeal to laboratory experimentation. Here again, however, the evidence is meager and hardly pertinent. Studies concerned with the effect of the structure of the language on learning (Horowitz, 1955; Wolfle, 1932) have shown that "consistent" language structures are easier to learn than "inconsistent" ones; they demonstrate, as we might expect, that learners have a strong tendency to make "errors" by following analogic patterns. It has long been noted that children's errors in grammar are largely due to their entirely "correct" use of analogies which happen to lead them to incorrect forms. Berko (1958) studied this tendency with a series of careful tests. The implication for teaching seems to be that one should protect the learner from deviant instances and false analogies as long as possible, but that when such instances are introduced, special note of their peculiarities should be made for the student. Such a rule is difficult to carry out, because the nature of language is such that often the most irregular and exceptional forms are among the most common.

The considerable differences between natural and artificial, or constructed, languages like Esperanto in ease of learning were demonstrated by Thorndike (1933) in a series of careful experiments; one may assume that these differences were due largely to the greater regularity and simplicity of the latter. This finding, however, is not of much consolation when one is faced with the task of learning or teaching a complex, highly irregular natural language. For that matter, the initial task in teaching is not to avert false analogies but to get the student to form the grammatical habits upon which analogies (correct or incorrect) can be built. One regrets that there is practically no research from which one can draw useful conclusions for teaching grammatical habits. An experiment by Miller (1958) was in the right direction, but did not go far enough for our purposes. Miller constructed a number of redundant strings of letters according to a finite state generator (a mathematical model in which the probability of any given state in a sequence is dependent on the preceding states); in some respects these strings were an analogue of syntactical patterns. Volunteer subjects were able to learn such strings better than random strings even though they were not aware of the rules by which the redundant strings were formed. A further question which could perhaps be answered by this type of experiment would be: What variables control the amount of time the subject would take to discover the rules of formation? Would it help if "meanings" were assigned to the stimuli?

We must content ourselves with listing a series of possible research problems in the area of teaching grammar:

How well aware are students of grammatical patterns in their native language, and to what extent does this knowledge transfer to the learning of a foreign language? Do students have special initial difficulties in recognizing grammatical concepts, and if so, how can these difficulties be minimized by appropriate teaching procedures?

What are the relative advantages of a deductive, "factual" procedure in teaching grammar in comparison with a procedure which emphasizes inductive learning of grammar by pattern practice?

In pattern practice, what is the most efficient distribution of time between (1) repeated listening to recorded materials, (2) active recall and practice of the materials, and (3) active creation of new materials based on the grammatical patterns presented in the lessons?

What is the proper order and distribution of time between (1) presentation of grammatical material from which the learner can himself develop principles inductively, and (2) grammatical explanations provided by the instructors? The answer to this question might vary with the age of the learner, his ability to develop grammatical principles inductively, and his capacity to profit from grammatical explanations.

How should the problem of error be handled? Psychological theory and research suggest that the teaching should be organized so as to minimize the likelihood that a student will make an error. This principle is said to necessitate immediate reinforcement of correct responses. Further research is needed to determine what should be done with wrong responses: Should the student be told why his response is wrong? Does informing the student about the most common wrong responses help him to avoid these responses, or does it tend to increase the likelihood of his making these wrong responses? There seems to be no research directly bearing upon this problem in foreign language teaching, although studies are available in other kinds of learning (Holodnak, 1943; McIntosh, 1944), with somewhat inconclusive results.

How can grammatical material be best organized for inductive learning? Should numerous examples of a single principle be given or should these examples be interspersed with a contrasting principle?

What is the best plan for presenting syntactical materials so that the learner will most rapidly attain facility in producing meaningful and relevant spontaneous utterance-length responses? The fundamental task which faces the learner of a foreign language is that of selecting patterns of sentence-, clause-, or phrase-length which are

suitable for given situations and "filling them in" with suitable words. It is a reasonable hypothesis that specific practice in *selecting* and transforming patterns will lead to fluency more rapidly than repetitive practice of the patterns themselves.

Vocabulary

In a sense it could be said that more research has been done on vocabulary learning than on any other aspect of foreign language learning. One has only to look at the large number of experimental researches on paired-associate learning by psychologists to conclude that here indeed is a field in which psychological research has much to offer the language teacher.

This would be a hasty conclusion. For one thing, it must be remembered that most psychological research on paired-associate learning has been conducted to test various theories and hypotheses about learning as such; the use of series of "nonsense syllables" paired with English words and meanings has been quite incidental to the purposes of the experimentation, which might equally well have used numbers, mazes, or other types of learning materials having little relevance to foreign language learning. More important is the fact that paired-associate learning as organized by psychologists in learning experiments does not necessarily have much resemblance to the kind of learning of vocabulary which is organized by foreign language teachers. To be sure, a list of paired associates resembles the list of new words and phrases, with glosses (meanings in the native language), which frequently accompanies each new lesson in a textbook; some foreign language students attack these lists much in the fashion of lists placed on a memory drum. At this point the resemblance stops.

Nonsense syllables are usually presented visually and are essentially aggregates of alphabetical letters; "pronounceability" of nonsense syllables has been used as an experimental variable (Underwood & Schulz, 1960). Foreign language words are not aggregates of literal symbols but sequences of sounds, that is, sequences of phonemes, and it is supererogatory to ask whether they are pronounceable. Further, foreign language words will often be presented first auditorily and in the context of other words which will provide clues to their meanings; many foreign language teachers are sparing in their use of English. The use of paired-associate lists tends to spread the erroneous impression that it is always possible to set up exact equivalences between the words of two languages; it must be understood that the glosses given in vocabularies and dictionaries often give nothing more than suggestions as to areas of meaning equivalence. Finally, the dimensions of foreign language vocabulary learning are usually vastly different from those of psychological experiments; whereas a psychological experiment may involve the learning of a list of 20 paired associates to a criterion in a single setting, the acquisition of a foreign language vocabulary is a question of gradual increments over a long period of time until thousands or tens of thousands of items have been mastered. Rarely has laboratory experimentation provided any reasonable simulation of the dimensions of foreign language vocabulary learning. For all these reasons it is necessary to use much caution in generalizing from paired-associate laboratory experiments to actual language teaching.

From the standpoint of the teacher, the most important problem of vocabulary is that called *vocabulary control*. The teacher (or textbook writer, or programer) wants to know at what rate vocabulary should be introduced at the various stages of instruction. In the beginning stages, a limited number of words are introduced only as pegs on which to hang teaching of phonology and elementary grammar. After the sounds and structure of the language have been reasonably well mastered, knowledge of the language grows chiefly in proportion to increasing vocabulary knowledge.

Frequency counts and other statistical compilations are available to aid in vocabulary control for most of the commonly taught languages. Frequency control for the rarely taught languages is more of a problem; research is needed on how much one can rely on the judgments of native speakers as to frequency and utility of items. It is known (Morgan & Bonham, 1944) that concrete nouns and verbs are inherently much easier for the student to learn and remember than abstract words and function words (words whose function is mainly grammatical, e.g., *of, in spite of,* and *than* and their counterparts in foreign languages); presumably the latter words should be presented with greater frequency than the former if they are to compete adequately for the learner's attention. Morgan and Oberdeck (1930) demonstrated that the ratio of the student's active vocabulary (words available for use) to his passive vocabulary (words recognized) is fairly constant over most of the elementary stages of instruction; whether this is an unalterable fact or something which teaching should endeavor to modify is an open question. Astington (1958, 1959) reported, however, that confining all teaching to a list of 1,330 words selected after the manner used in developing Basic English resulted in a degree of achievement after three years of a special French course which was significantly superior to that attained in a five-year course without this kind of vocabulary control.

No experiments designed to find maximum or optimal rates of vocabulary introduction have been made, although textbooks and courses of instruction reflect various opinions. Rate is usually measured in terms either of number of words per "lesson" or in terms of new words per running words in a text; in either case, it is difficult to translate statistics into figures that will be meaningful for a given situation. One may suggest that the number of new words per instructional hour would afford a fairly standard measure. In the case of a character language like Chinese, the rates of introduction of characters must be considered along with the introduction of the words themselves.

An extensive report by Thorndike (1908) is instructive, even though it was based on experimentation under rather uncontrolled conditions. Thorndike had 22 students learn the English meanings of 1,200 German words, divided into 12 lists of 100 words each. Subjects studied at home, using whatever method they preferred, and kept records of their time. When each student felt confident that he knew practically all the 1,200 words, he was tested with the entire list. Retention was measured one month later. On the average, students learned about 1,030 words in 30 hours of study. Individual performances ranged from 380 words learned in 42 hours to 1,046 words learned in 18 hours. Retention was about 35 per cent after 40 days. There was no evidence of improvement in learning ability (i.e., no "learning to learn"), but the subjects reported the task became more interesting as time progressed. Orbison (1944) studied the rate at which subjects could learn lists of 8, 12, and 24 paired associates and found that learning by the part method became increasingly superior to the whole method as length of list increased; presumably, one could extrapolate these results to the much longer lists involved in foreign language learning, but the study provides no direct information on the optimal rate of input of new items.

Further experimental work would be useful in determining the parameters of foreign language vocabulary learning. What is wanted are statements such as "If you want to teach a vocabulary of size n, you may expect the student to spend x hours in attaining mastery, studying in such-and-such a manner." Since foreign language vocabulary is almost always learned cumulatively, one important question to be answered is how well a given set of material should be mastered before it is wise to start the learning of new material.

Implicit in the discussion of vocabulary learning is the question of whether vocabulary is best learned in lists (paired with glosses either in the native language or in the target language) or in "contexts." Foreign language teachers favor the latter approach; for example, the Modern Language Association

textbook in Spanish (Bolinger, et al., 1960) contains no vocabulary lists in its lessons, although it does contain a glossary at the end of the book. Despite the availability of many experimental studies, this question cannot be said to have been resolved. Part of the difficulty is that of defining "context." If "context" is anything that provides more associations and greater meaningfulness in materials to be learned, we can expect context to be beneficial, for recent psychological research has emphasized the important role of meaningful associations in learning (Noble & McNeely, 1957; Underwood & Schulz, 1960).

If, on the other hand, "context" turns out to be *additional* material which must be learned along with the key stimuli and which contributes little to the learning of those key stimuli, it will probably impede learning. For example, Seibert (1930) found the learning of paired associates in lists faster than learning in "context." Her "contexts," however, in many cases may have been unfamiliar or confusing to the subjects; e.g., in *On met* LE MORS (bit) *dans la bouche du cheval,* the subject who could not properly understand the context may have assigned a wrong meaning to LE MORS. Experiments favoring context learning are those of Briones (1937), Morgan and Bailey (1943), and Morgan and Foltz (1944).

It is conceivable that "learning in context" may be a disguised term for what would be more appropriately called concept-formation. There is some evidence from research outside the language-learning field (e.g., Haslerud & Meyers, 1958) that learning by "discovery" results in better retention. If teaching is organized so that the learner must induce word meanings (through use of context, formal and thematic prompts, etc.) before his discoveries are confirmed, retention may be better because of the added effort put into this kind of learning.

Another classic problem in vocabulary learning is that of whether meanings of foreign language words should be conveyed by pairing them with glosses in the learner's native language, or with pictures of, or actual pointings to objects and movements. Most of the evidence has favored pairing with pictures and the like. Studies on this problem have included those of Braunschausen (1910), Kale and Grosslight (1955), Kopstein and Roshal (1954), Netschajeff (1910–1911), Peterson (1903), Schlüter (1914), Schmidt (1923), Schönherr (1915), and Scholtkowska (1925–1926). The lack of relevance of the Kale and Grosslight study has already been commented upon. Many of the other studies are limited in design and should be repeated. Nevertheless, a generalization directly applicable to foreign language teaching seems fairly well established: foreign words are best learned (and probably better retained) when presented in association with the objects, actions, qualities, and conditions which are their referents. Foreign language instruction should take maximal advantage of this principle, but it will obviously be impossible to carry the principle to such an extreme that foreign language words are *never* learned in verbal contexts. Obviously, as soon as the student gets at all deeply into reading matter in the foreign language, he can learn a good share of his words from the verbal context provided in such reading matter, and he is also likely to make increasing use of a glossary or a dictionary. Further, the superiority of nonverbal context over verbal context is probably not very large, and combined verbal and nonverbal context will generally produce gains over each of these separate methods. There is no evidence that use of the learner's native language inhibits learning of the foreign word or its meaning.

Progress in methods of teaching foreign language vocabulary may profit from some of the recent developments in the field of associative learning theory. One promising line of study has to do with the conditions of reinforcement. Cook and Kendler (1956) have experimental evidence to back up their theory that prompting is more effective than confirmation; subjects who are continually prompted with the correct response before they make their own correct response do better on a posttest than subjects who are required to make a response before being presented with the correct response. It should be noted, however, that Cook and Kendler's experiment did not deal with foreign language vocabulary learning; consequently, extrapolation is dangerous, particularly since there is an apparent conflict between this experiment and a considerable experimental literature on the superiority of active recall over passive learning (e.g., Forlano, 1936). Forlano and Hoffman's study (1937), however, concerned foreign language vocabulary learning and suggested that prompting is more effective than confirmation, because in this way one avoids reinforcing the incorrect guesses which learners are likely to make in the confirmation procedure.

Another line of investigation has to do with the role of "meaningfulness" in learning nonsense syllables. Noble (1952) defined meaningfulness in terms of the number of associations which subjects are likely to give in a short period of time; Noble and McNeely (1957) found that the "meaningfulness" of nonsense syllables is related to the ease with which they are learned. A much more extensive analysis of the role of meaningfulness has been made by Underwood and Schulz (1960); they incline to the belief that meaningfulness can be interpreted as a measure of the frequency with which a stimulus has been experienced or a response emitted. They view rote verbal learning as consisting of two stages: a "response-learning or response-recall phase during which the responses are learned as responses and, in a recall sense, become readily available," and an "associative or hook-up phase" in which the response is associated with its corresponding stimulus. The second stage appears to be facilitated when the stimuli and responses have many associates. None of this work was done in the context of foreign language learning, but it suggests that in the teaching of foreign language vocabulary an attempt should be made to generate as many associations as possible for the items to be learned. This, in fact, is very likely the function of what foreign language teachers call "context," but the point is that the contexts must be *diverse* in order to build up a texture of associations. Interesting experimental approaches are suggested by these theoretical developments.

Reading

Prior to 1940, the "reading method" was the predominant approach to foreign language teaching in schools and colleges. Many research studies, adequately cited and reviewed by Birkmaier (1960), were concerned with measuring achievement in courses taught by the reading method. It was established that the amount of *adequately supervised* reading experience given to students was highly correlated with their performance on tests of reading comprehension and vocabulary. Because of the relatively short time available in many courses, the levels of reading competence attained rarely approached those levels necessary for fluent, profitable, or pleasurable reading of foreign language newspapers, novels, plays, etc. At the University of Chicago, Bond (1953) has reported success with experimental courses which stressed the reading objective.

Proponents of "new-type" courses which initially emphasize audiolingual skills claim, however, that reading skills will be more fluent and facile when the teaching of reading is delayed until the student has achieved a certain degree of mastery of audiolingual skills. There is no research information, however, to indicate whether this claim is sound or how long the teaching of reading should be delayed. Some feel (e.g., Reindrop, 1957) that reading may start at any time as long as it is preceded by a "reasonable" mastery of basic sounds and structures. Others (e.g., Grew, 1956) propose to delay reading until an advanced degree of mastery of audiolingual skills has been achieved. Experimental studies (e.g., Birkmaier, 1949; Hamilton & Haden, 1950; and Hohlfeld, 1950) have thus far made only gross comparisons between "traditional" and "new-type" courses without isolating the effect of different ap-

proaches to the teaching of reading. They have established, however, that students succeed in learning to read about as well under the new-type courses as in traditional courses.

There is a similar dearth of evidence on *methods* of teaching reading in foreign languages. According to observations made by Blayne (1946) on the basis of an uncontrolled experiment with developmental reading in Spanish, simplification of textual material facilitates good silent reading habits, and oral reading should be avoided lest it produce unnecessary subvocal lip movements. Beyond this report, the literature is silent on such variations as the use of interlinear translations (Bernard, 1951), reading pacers, or any others that have long been investigated in teaching children to read English. One interesting variation that deserves investigation is the practice recommended in some foreign language readers (e.g., Fairbanks, Shadick, & Yedigar, 1951) of·requiring the student to memorize in advance of each reading lesson a series of sentences illustrating the new vocabulary, structure patterns, and idioms of the reading passage. A further variant of this method would involve practice in *listening* to such sentences in advance of reading the passage; Bovée (1948) suggested that training the ear to perceive "thought-groups" facilitates the transfer of listening ability to reading ability.

Visual versus Auditory Presentation

The question of visual as against auditory presentation has already been touched upon in connection with vocabulary learning. It is of more general significance, however. Fear has been expressed that the presentation of foreign language materials in auditory form may create difficulties for "eye-minded" students—"eye-mindedness" being conceived of as either a relatively permanent constitutional trait or a result of a predominantly visual emphasis in the individual's school experiences. A pilot experiment on this problem was performed by Dunkel (1948, Ch. IX). "Alternate forms" of lessons in Persian were prepared for either visual or auditory presentation; posttests of attainment in vocabulary and grammar were also provided. Small groups of students (at what educational level we are not told) were given one form of the lessons visually to establish a baseline of performance, and the other form one week later, either visually, audiovisually (i.e., with simultaneous auditory and visual presentation), and auditorily. The general conclusion was that vocabulary was learned equally well under all three methods, but the learning of grammar was retarded when the student had no visual stimuli. Apparently under this latter condition the students found it difficult to manipulate the grammatical materials in Persian, which is an inflected language. It could be objected, of course, that the auditory training may not have been sufficiently prolonged to enable students to surmount their initial difficulties; manipulating auditory materials without visual support is possibly a process which can be learned. It is of interest that in this experiment substantial *positive* correlations were noted between ability to handle visual material and ability to handle auditory material; this result would tend to argue against the existence of different "imagery types," but it is not conclusive by any means. The question needs to be re-examined in the light of current knowledge about foreign language aptitude.

Visual versus auditory presentation was one of three variables investigated in a study of paired-associate learning by Kessman (1959). Volunteer high school students with a minimum of one year of foreign language study learned lists of 56 English-foreign pairs to a criterion of mastery under a number of conditions. It was found that learning was very significantly better when stimulus terms were presented visually rather than auditorily, and when the learning was that of giving the English word in response to a foreign word (rather than vice versa). No measures of retention were taken. The study is limited in the fact that each experimental group had only one mode of presentation of the stimulus term, i.e., either visual or audi-

tory; there was no investigation of transfer between stimulus modalities. This study is also subject to the same comment that has been made on that of Kale and Grosslight (1955), namely, that it concerns types of response behavior which may not be relevant to foreign language teaching if the objectives of such teaching are to produce competence in active use of the foreign language.

Krawiec (1946), in a somewhat similar experiment, found reliable differences in learning rates favoring visual over auditory presentation; these differences disappeared in retention tests, however. Pimsleur and Bonkowski (1961) noted faster learning aurally than visually, and greater transfer from aural to visual learning than vice versa. There is no immediately apparent explanation for the seeming discrepancy between Pimsleur and Bonkowski's results and those of Krawiec and of Kessman; one variable that needs investigation is the influence of the orthographic characteristics of the visual stimuli in relation to their auditory counterparts. For example, negative transfer may occur when use is made of paralogs which Ss are likely to pronounce quite differently from the auditory renditions of them provided by the experimenter.

Instructional Aids: The Textbook, the Workbook, and the Film

As in other areas of educational research, it is difficult to find anything but speculative and descriptive writings concerning the proper organization and format of foreign language reading materials, textbooks, and films. The literature does not even seem to contain surveys of the opinions and the preferences of the teachers and students about such materials.

An investigation conducted by the Toronto Board of Education (1960) compared conventional teaching with a program of instruction which consisted exclusively of the presentation of a series of sound films, the "French Through Pictures" series produced by I. A. Richards and Christine Gibson. Instruction was given to Grade 7 children in four 30-minute periods per week. Over a four-month period, both teacher- and film-taught groups made substantial gains, but the teacher-taught groups were favored significantly in most comparisons, especially in oral proficiency. The slower progress of the film group was considered to be a result of the undue length of the films and their too-rapid introduction of new material. It was also pointed out that film teaching did not adequately provide for correction of pupil errors. It was nevertheless concluded that appropriately revised films could be utilized effectively if they were presented as a supplementation to conventional instruction by a "live" teacher.

Exemplary in the comprehensiveness of its methods of testing and the sophistication of its statistical analysis is the study of Creore and Hanzeli (1960) comparing results obtained with two "modern" methods of teaching spoken French at the college level. In the experimental section, Borglum's audio-visual course, *Images de France,* was used (including the basic text, the color transparencies, and the magnetic tape), while the equated control section learned from Harris and Leveque's text, *Basic Conversational French,* supplemented by readers. Both groups had two hours of language laboratory per week; the experimental group had instructor-led pattern drill while the control group had dialogues for oral drill. At the end of a year, the two groups were not significantly different when tested in listening comprehension and "grammar comprehension"; however, the experimental group was superior in speaking ability while the control group was superior in reading and writing. The investigators interpreted the results as showing that the experimental treatment should be modified to give greater practice in reading and writing. One possible criticism of the study is that the experimental treatments differed in so many respects that one is hard put to identify the source of the differences that arose.

Instructional Aids: The Tape Recorder and the Language Laboratory

The greatest boon to foreign language teaching from modern technology is the tape recorder. This device can present foreign language sounds and utterances with accuracy, fidelity, and endless patience, and do so with great flexibility and ease of handling. Hence it is assured a lasting and significant role in foreign language training. On the other hand, there have been few experimental studies addressed to the questions of (1) exactly how much and in what ways the tape recorder (often incorporated into a "language laboratory") may contribute to a course of instruction, and (2) the degree to which the tape recorder may be expected to take over some of the functions of the instructor. Most of the few studies available are poorly controlled or otherwise deficient from the standpoint of valid research methodology, even though they concern what may very well be interesting and imaginative teaching techniques. In this category are reports by Borglum (1958), Borglum and Mueller (1956), and Mueller and Borglum (1956) on the audio-visual and language laboratory program at Wayne State University, by Fotos (1955) on gains resulting from use of a language laboratory at Purdue University, and by Hoge (1959) on the utility of a language laboratory in teaching Spanish pronunciation.

Pickrel, Neidt, and Gibson (1958) made a carefully controlled study of the benefits gained from use of tape recordings in junior high school Spanish classes. One (control) class was taught by a trained teacher of Spanish, who also prepared a series of tapes. The other four (experimental) classes were taught by regular classroom teachers without prior knowledge or training in Spanish who used the tapes prepared by the Spanish teacher. In three of the four comparisons of experimental classes with the control class, the control class was superior on written tests of Spanish. Scores on a spelling placement test were substantially correlated with the criterion scores and hence were used as the control variable in the analysis of covariance which established these findings. In another comparison, however, it was found that students randomly chosen from the experimental and control classes did not differ significantly in their performance on a test of oral fluency as rated (with high reliability) by a panel of experts. The investigators concluded that "the use of tape recordings is an effective method of teaching conversational Spanish to seventh-grade students" and that "regular classroom teachers who are untrained in Spanish can teach conversational Spanish effectively when they base their teaching on tapes prepared by a Spanish specialist" (p. 93). The results from this study are too limited, however, to justify concluding that an untrained teacher provided with tape recordings can effectively replace a trained teacher.

A faculty group at Antioch College (Antioch College, 1960) conducted a well-controlled two-year experiment comparing instruction organized in the conventional way (sections of 20 students each meeting six times a week with a regular instructor) with instruction organized around a language laboratory (a section of 60 students meeting twice a week with a regular instructor for a total of three hours and four times a week with student laboratory assistants in sessions running one and one-half hours each). Each laboratory session for the experimental group was divided into three 30-minute periods: (1) presentation of audio-visual materials by overhead projection of acetate transparencies accompanied by tape-recorded sound; (2) individual work in standard language laboratory booths; and (3) drill and practice exercises in face-to-face contact with the student assistants. In each of two separate years, comparisons revealed generally nonsignificant differences between experimental and control groups in end-of-year achievement; at the same time, instructional procedures tended to be better liked in the experimental than in the control groups. It was concluded that

for the teaching of 60 students, the experimental procedures saved about 12 hours per week of the time of regular instructors without any consequent loss in quality of instruction; the new method also permitted more supervised learning time for each student.

Carroll, et al. (1959) made an analysis of covariance comparison between a high school class which had the benefit of a language laboratory and another which did not. Intelligence test scores and scores on the Modern Language Aptitude Test (Carroll & Sapon, 1959) were used as control variables. No significant differences were found between the classes in auditory comprehension skills, and the class trained with the aid of the language laboratory did slightly (and significantly) poorer on Cooperative tests of reading, vocabulary, and grammar. It appeared that the control class actually had as much experience with the spoken language, by direct contact with the teacher, as the experimental class; the work in the language laboratory may have distracted the experimental class from paying proper attention to reading assignments. The results of the study cannot be taken as casting doubt on the utility of the language laboratory, however; they merely showed how the instruction in the language laboratory needed to be strengthened.

Despite the fact that extensive foreign language courses on records and tapes are commercially available in ever increasing numbers, no experimental analysis of the effectiveness of their use has ever been reported, to my knowledge.

Teaching Machines and Programed Instruction

Lumsdaine and Glaser's source book (1960) contains information on a number of attempts to teach foreign languages, or elements of foreign languages, by methods which are more systematically programed than conventional ones and which involve the use of teaching machines or other special devices for presenting material. There is no sharp dividing line between teaching procedures which are to be found, say, in commercial phonograph record courses or in language laboratories and teaching procedures devised specially for teaching machines, since certain elements of programed instruction can be found in all of these (e.g., carefully graded order, small step size, possibility of immediate confirmation of results, self-pacing).

First let us consider reports on reasonably complete or self-contained courses in foreign languages which have been presented by programed instruction. Ferster and Sapon (1958) seem to have published the first such report; their work was actually performed in 1955. They sought to teach volunteers (mostly graduate students) to write correct German sentences when presented with English sentences; no attention was paid to spoken German except in a "practice run" in which "30 German words from the first unit were presented by the voice of a native speaker of German via tape recorder." The vocabulary and structure covered were approximately that of a first-semester college course: 522 words and standard elementary morphology and syntax. The "teaching machine" used consisted of nothing more than a mask to enable the student to expose to himself successive frames of a legal-sized form on which the stimuli had been mimeographed. Only 6 out of 28 volunteers persevered long enough to finish the course; they did so in periods ranging from 38 to 78 hours (mean 47.5). Posttests showed good mastery of the material—achievement was reported as 88.3 per cent on the average.

Ferster and Sapon felt that the high drop-out rate was due to excessive difficulty of some of the steps in the program. Among the principles which guided the construction of this program were: (1) each step was to be made as easy as possible in order to keep the rate of error low and the rate of reinforcement high; (2) introduction of vocabulary was controlled, each new word being used in a few subsequent units in order to provide practice; (3) the student was to continue to work only on items which he did not yet know; (4) structural concepts of grammar were taught inductively without explicit mention of grammatical terms or principles; (5) the level of conceptual difficulty was graded from easy to difficult (as judged by the programer); (6) only one new item was presented at a time; and (7) sufficient practice was to be given with every part of the material to assure mastery of the material presented up to that point. Brown and Hodgkinson (1958) raised questions about Ferster and Sapon's work, saying that their results were not impressive when compared with those attained in typical semester courses, particularly in view of the high drop-out rate, and complaining that such work would not lead to ready acceptance of programed instruction. It should be recognized, however, that Ferster and Sapon's report concerned only a very early stage of research on programed instruction; a more appropriate criticism might have been that their report was premature. Unfortunately, Ferster and Sapon's work has not been continued.

A much more ambitious pilot project had also been carried on at Harvard University in the fall of 1953 by Morton, but was not reported on in the literature until 1960 (Morton, 1960). Utilizing only a tape recorder, this course sought to give college students "80 per cent fluency" in Spanish at the end of a semester's time. The course was intensive, and was announced as requiring 83 one-hour classroom periods plus two to four hours of outside preparation per classroom hour, giving a total of from 249 to 415 hours. Actually, it is apparent that most of the class time was given over to individual student work with tape recorders or to simple evaluation of progress. The tape-recorded drills were of an unusual character and represented the application of distinct theoretical positions concerning the nature of language learning.

The course contained five stages: (1) *Phonematization.* In this phase the student learned to recognize 16 Spanish phonemes and to transcribe them by a system of modified Gregg shorthand; in 28 to 56 hours of this drill students were able to attain the required 95 per cent accuracy. (2) *Sound reproduction.* The student had to learn to produce the sounds he had learned to recognize, largely by sheer imitation of words containing these sounds. The instructor very rarely intruded to do evaluative or corrective work. (Morton notes that the sound reproduction drills were interlarded with the phonematization drills, but that this was probably not as effective a procedure as postponing them until after the phonematization drills.) (3) *Structural clues.* In 20 playing hours of tape recordings, the bulk of the grammar of Spanish was presented on tape in the form of exercises which required the student to recognize and respond appropriately to single structural clues. Much use was made of gesturing as a form of signaling the response; for example, the student was to use appropriate pointing movements to show his recognition of the various personal pronouns. (4) *Model patterns.* Each drill consisted of four parts: basic sentence patterns exemplifying given structure points, with approximate English translations which subjects were told not to take seriously; a short text for practice in comprehension; a dialogue; and a series of questions based on the text and dialogue which were to be answered by the student. In this phase of the instruction, 105 model patterns were presented, incorporating a vocabulary of 1,500 words and approximately 300 idiomatic expressions. (5) *Vocabulary building.* A series of tapes, including texts, dialogues, skits, and the like, presented an additional 1,000 vocabulary items.

No reading or writing of Spanish was practiced in this project, except briefly at the end of the course. In evaluating its success, several points may be made: At each stage, a high degree of accuracy was required and obtained. Fifteen out of 20 students finished the course successfully and all were given high grades; by the end of the course the group had become fairly homogeneous in achievement. Although there was no information on their basic aptitudes, the instructor judged that at the end of the semester these students had attained the "natural fluency"

of students enrolled in regular third- and fourth-year courses.

Several varieties of carefully programed language learning materials exist, along with informal reports of their success. In this category are the *Language Through Pictures* series of Richards and Gibson (e.g., I. A. Richards, Ilsley, & Gibson, 1950) in English, French, Spanish, German, Italian, and Hebrew, and the "programed textbooks" in Hebrew and Russian available from a commercial organization (Teaching Machines, Inc., 1960). Systematic research into the parameters of learning with these materials would be of great value in comparing their effectiveness with that of other types of materials.

Rocklyn and Moren (1960) have reported on a programed course for teaching a limited knowledge of spoken Russian to infantry soldiers who might have need of it for intelligence purposes. Vocabulary and grammar were confined to the minimum believed to be necessary for this highly restricted purpose. All work was done by self-instruction using a tape recorder and a form for recording the correctness of responses. Essentially, the method involved learning paired English and Russian sentence patterns by the anticipation and confirmation method.

The course was divided into three parts: (1) learning to give English equivalents of commands and questions in Russian; (2) learning to give Russian equivalents of commands and questions in English (the student evaluating the accuracy of his own response); and (3) learning to give English equivalents of likely Russian answers to the commands and questions which had been learned. Posttests established the feasibility of the course and demonstrated that a satisfactory degree of competence had been attained by all students (though in varying amounts of time); one of the posttests involved a simulated intelligence interview with a native speaker of Russian. Pronunciation ability of the students was judged satisfactory even though no special emphasis had been placed on this aspect of the work. It is difficult to evaluate this course in comparison with other courses because of its special content and objectives.

Other projects in foreign language programed instruction are known to be in operation at this writing, but as yet no detailed reports are available; most of the projects seem to be concerned chiefly with the question of feasibility and contemplate no thoroughgoing comparisons with more conventional types of instruction. Furthermore, none of these projects has as yet been concerned with testing hypotheses on detailed aspects of programing, such as the popular problem of multiple-choice versus constructed responses. A series of auxiliary experiments is needed to investigate how well the student can be taught to evaluate his own oral productions against a presented standard, and how much improvement in oral production can be expected as a result of such teaching.

A few bits of useful information may be gleaned, however, from divers reports of experimentation with teaching machines using foreign language materials. All of this work has been concerned with the learning of foreign language vocabulary by the method of paired associates. Pressey (1950) reported experiments with material of the multiple-choice type presented by means of a "punchboard" in which the student could explore until he found the correct response for each item. Russian-English vocabulary was used as an exemplar of "rote" material—"more interesting and valuable than nonsense syllables, equally unfamiliar to almost everyone, and indicative of possible values of self-instructional tests in learning a foreign vocabulary" (p. 422). In comparison with tests using the learning of hard English vocabulary and facts in general psychology, the Russian tests showed relatively slow learning. Stephens (1953), using Pressey punchboards and also a "drum tutor" whose chief advantage was its continual provision of error counts, compared three procedures in administering a self-instructional multiple-choice test of Russian vocabulary: "test-as-test"—the student makes

only one response per item on a given trial, without knowledge of its correctness at any time; "vanishing"—the same, but the student immediately learns of the correctness of his response; and "retained"—a situation in which the student can make responses to an item until he finds the correct one. As might be expected, the "retained" situation gave best results.

Severin (1955) also studied Russian vocabulary learning with a punchboard. In addition to the previous finding that this type of learning is harder than more "meaningful" learning, he found that (1) two-choice tests were more time-saving and produced fully as much learning as four-choice tests, and (2) that a specially designed two-choice test requiring the learner to indicate which of two English words goes with a designated one of two Russian words maximized the number of exposures of the words in the list to be learned.

Israel (1960) used German-English vocabulary learning in a study of the use of partial associations in prompting. Subjects who could not immediately recall the English meanings of German words were allowed to manipulate a control which would bring a blurred image of the English word more nearly into focus. There was little evidence, however, that practice enhanced the partial associations to the extent that they could be effectively used in prompting. One may remark that associationistic theories probably would not have predicted much enhancement of the visual form of a response; they would have predicted, rather, that associated stimuli (e.g., semantically related words) would have functioned more effectively as cues.

The Pacing of Instruction

One factor in instruction which was introduced at the outset of this chapter as relevant to the success of students was called "Opportunity given for learning." On the assumption that students need different amounts of time for learning, it is obvious that a fixed rate of presentation of material may not give all students suitable opportunity for learning; it may be too slow for some students and too rapid for others. One hope for programed self-instruction is that it will enable the student to pace his learning at the rate most appropriate for him. In the meantime, a useful question to ask about classroom instruction concerns the average rate at which material is covered in relation to student capabilities. Does the teacher pace instruction at a rate appropriate for the apter students, or at a rate more appropriate for slower students? That is, how much opportunity for learning does the teacher give, and what are the consequences of various rates of presentation? No research related to this question seems to have been done in the foreign language field, but it is an important question for research to answer.

Travel and Immersion in a Foreign Language Environment

Perhaps travel does not deserve to be dignified as an educational *method;* since it is, nevertheless, important in many programs of instruction, it merits empirical evaluation. The results of a summer Russian travel program were studied by Carton and Carroll (1960). Students who had studied Russian for one or for two years in college were given an intensive six weeks' summer course in that language and then sent on a tour of the Soviet Union for the remainder of the summer. A series of proficiency tests in Russian was developed as a part of the project. It was noted, incidentally, that gains made during the intensive summer language training were as large as, if not larger than, the differences between first-year and second-year students at the outset of training; that is, at the end of the summer, the students with one prior year of training showed more achievement in auditory comprehension than had been exhibited at the beginning of the summer by the two-year students. The tests also showed that the two-year students profited more from the foreign travel than the one-year students; presumably they were better pre-

pared to speak to Russians they met in the course of travel. The investigators concluded that "intensive language training can be very profitably conducted in the USA until the point is reached when students are fully able to profit from the Russian travel . . .; at the same time the results show that well-trained students *can* profit very significantly from the travel experience; the gains are particularly striking in competence in the spoken language" (p. 28).

THE PSYCHOLOGY OF BILINGUALISM

Since the object of foreign language teaching is to produce a kind of bilingualism, study of the language performances of bilinguals should be of use in understanding the process of language learning.

Speculative writings and studies, exhaustively reviewed by Weinreich (1953), have suggested that bilingualism may occur in several forms. Ervin and Osgood (1954), in presenting a formal psychological theory of bilingualism, suggested that the kind of bilingual system possessed by a bilingual individual is dependent upon whether his two languages were learned in associated or disassociated contexts. A person who learns two languages in the same context, or who learns a new language through the medium of another (usually his native language), would tend to have a *compound* system, i.e., one in which two languages constitute simply two different ways of encoding the same set of referential meanings. A person who learns two languages in quite different contexts, however, would tend to have *coordinate* systems—systems in which the referential meanings encoded in the two languages differ to a considerable extent. This theory leads to the expectation that there would be more interference between languages in the case of the compound bilingual, but that the compound bilingual would be better able to translate from one language to the other. The very process of translation, furthermore, would gradually cause the transformation of a coordinate system into a compound one instead.

The theory itself says nothing about which kind of bilingualism is "better," but the immediate inference which some writers have drawn from it is that coordinate systems are more desirable and that second language learning should be organized to produce coordinate rather than compound bilingualism. This would, then, be an argument for a "direct method" in which the use of the learner's native language would be minimized or avoided altogether.

Studies conducted by Lambert and his students have, in general, supported the notion that coordinate and compound systems of bilingualism can indeed be distinguished. It was first necessary to develop ways of identifying "balanced" bilinguals, i.e., persons whose skill in two languages was approximately equal. Lambert (1955, 1956) investigated the characteristics of several measures, e.g., the relative reaction time for response to directions in two languages, word association tests in which the subject was allowed to associate to words in either of two languages, and a test in which S's pronunciation of words was rated. These tests reliably discriminated between criterion groups (undergraduate and graduate American students majoring in French, and native speakers of French with considerable experience in English). From these results, Lambert concluded that tests relying solely on vocabulary were not as indicative of true bilingualism as tests which also relied on subtler cultural and linguistic factors.

Other tests of bilingualism were investigated by Lambert, Havelka, and Gardner (1959). Among those which correlated significantly with a criterion were tests of speed of tachistoscopic word recognition, facility in word completion, facility in detecting words in text run together without spaces, facility in oral reading, and pronunciation of words spelled alike in the two languages. A test of facility in translation, however, failed to correlate with degree of bilingualism.

Evidence for two types of bilingualism was reported by Lambert, Havelka, and Crosby (1958). Thirty-two "balanced" bilinguals were selected by the reaction time test developed earlier and separated into two groups on the basis of the manner in which they acquired their bilingualism. Twenty-three were classified as "separated" and nine as "fused"; the former had learned their two languages (English and French) in quite separate contexts, e.g., one language learned in the home, the other outside the home, or one language learned in Canada, the other in France; the latter had learned their two languages simultaneously and in the same context, e.g., when both parents used the two languages interchangeably, or when the second language had been learned in school through the medium of the first language. The authors regarded it as more than mere chance that using a standard method of selecting "balanced bilinguals," they were more readily able to find bilinguals with "separated" backgrounds than with "fused" backgrounds. From this they note: "... one may safely generalize that it is comparatively easier for bilinguals with separated acquisition contexts to attain bilingual balance" (p. 240n).

Next, three behavioral indices of bilingualism were studied. It was found that although "fused" and "separated" bilinguals were significantly different in the degree to which their semantic differential profiles in the two languages were divergent, this difference was almost wholly due to the presence in the "separated" group of 15 individuals who acquired their two languages in different cultures; for these alone, the French and English words were significantly different in semantic differential meaning. Probably the referents of the words were distinctly unlike for these people; e.g., "house" and French *"maison"* referred to different kinds of houses. In a retroactive inhibition experiment, however, "an interpolated list of French translations had about the same influence for the separated group [on relearning a series of English words] as an interpolated list of nonsense syllables," while "Ss in the fused group ... clearly benefited from the interpolated French list" (p. 242). On the other hand, bilinguals with "fused" background were not significantly better than those with "separated" background in a test of ability to translate rapidly from one language to the other. The authors speculated that both groups have reason to practice translation at one time or another. On the whole, these results tend to support the Ervin-Osgood bilingualism theory; the "fused" bilinguals are obviously the "compound" bilinguals, and those with "separated" language acquisition contexts are the "coordinate" bilinguals.

Still further support for the theory comes from studies by Lambert and Fillenbaum (1959) and Lambert and Jakobovits (1961). The first of these suggested that in bilingual patients the way in which an aphasic attack affects the two languages may depend upon whether these languages have been learned in associated or in disassociated contexts. The second study concerned the so-called "verbal satiation" effect whereby a person who is asked to repeat a word over and over again may experience a temporary decrease in the "meaningfulness" of the word. Lambert and Jakobovits found, as the theory would predict, that there was less transfer of the verbal satiation effect from language to language among coordinate bilinguals than among compound bilinguals.

Lambert's studies have made no explicit reference to the age at which bilingualism was acquired. The neurologist Wilder Penfield (Penfield & Roberts, 1959, Ch. XI) feels that there is a biological "time table of the cerebral hemispheres" (p. 237) which allows particularly rapid learning of second languages by the child up to the age of ten. Thus, he feels there are physiological as well as psychological explanations for the phenomenon that languages are most readily learned at an early age. He includes as evidence the fact that children alone seem to be able to relearn language after the loss of one cerebral hemisphere; he asserts that no cases have been reported in which adults could do so after such loss. From these and other considerations he urges that the best time to teach children second languages is when they are very young, and that the direct method should be used in this teaching. Nevertheless, it must be pointed out that these recommendations are based on logical inference rather than upon direct experimental data; some critics (e.g., Milner, 1960) find Penfield's argumentation unacceptable.

THE STUDENT AND HIS CHARACTERISTICS IN RELATION TO FOREIGN LANGUAGE INSTRUCTION

Aptitude

Individual differences in readiness to learn are important in selecting, placing, and guiding students, as well as in adapting instruction to individuals. At the outset of this paper we defined aptitude as an inverse function of the amount of time that a student would require to achieve a specified criterion of success in learning, on the assumption that the student's motivation and the quality of the instruction he is receiving are optimal. Evidence that students actually differ in aptitude, defined in this manner, is hard to obtain because language students are rarely allowed to pace themselves and because motivation and the quality of instruction are difficult to measure. On the other hand, if one is willing to use subjective judgments of these factors, and if performance after a specified period of time is accepted as indicative of the rapidity of learning, it is clear that students vary enormously in rates of learning. There are many circumstances (e.g., intensive courses for government personnel) where it can be taken for granted that motivation is uniformly high and where the instruction is of very good quality; even in these situations, success varies widely. Further, these individual differences are hard to modify; Dorcus, Mount, and Jones (1952) found high correlations between early and final examinations in the eight-month intensive courses of the Army Language School and inferred from this that "important factors do exist for the prediction of language proficiency ... on the assumption that insufficient learning has occurred in the first few weeks of training to account for the relationship to the final examination score" (p. 3).

The first major efforts to develop aptitude tests for foreign language study were made chiefly in the 1920's (Henmon, et al., 1929). The tests were generally of two sorts: (1) tests of ability and achievement in the English language—vocabulary, grammar, spelling, etc., and (2) work-sample testing involving short "lessons" or problems in the language to be studied or in an artificial language. Tests were in every case of the paper-and-pencil variety and emphasized ability to deal with the intellectual, cognitive aspects of language study, that is, in the main, with the learning of a written language. This was consonant with the emphasis on the "reading objective" current in U.S. language teaching up to World War II. Few efforts were made to study aptitude for learning spoken language until after World War II. In general, foreign language teachers shared the skepticism of Kaulfers (1939), who felt that prognosis tests for foreign languages were of little practical value and were dangerous to put in the hands of anyone but an educational psychologist.

In his survey of the psychology of second language learning, Dunkel (1948, Ch. VI) limited his remarks to a consideration of the relevance of intelligence. He felt that available evidence indicated that intelligence was not a major factor in determining success or failure in elementary language learning, but warned that a closer analysis of the criterion of performance might disclose that certain aspects of intelligence were important.

Carroll (1962) reviewed his own and other studies of the prediction of success in intensive language courses and came to the following conclusions:

1. ". . . facility in learning to speak and understand a foreign language is a fairly specialized talent (or group of talents), . . . relatively independent of those traits ordinarily included under 'intelligence' . . ." (p. 89).

2. It is possible to predict success in inten-

sive language courses with high validity by means of certain tests. These tests can be effectively supplemented by further screening procedures such as interviews and short "trial" courses.

3. Data from tables of norms and from expectancy tables showing the probabilities of success in intensive language courses for given levels of measured aptitude suggest that a relatively small fraction of the general population, perhaps one-third to one-half, has a good chance of success (achieving satisfactory grades) in these courses.

4. Language aptitude as measured by tests seems to consist of at least four identifiable abilities: (a) phonetic coding—"*the ability to 'code' auditory phonetic material* in such a way that this material can be recognized, identified, and remembered over something longer than a few seconds" (p. 128); (b) grammatical sensitivity—the ability to recognize the grammatical functions of words in sentence contexts; (c) rote memorization ability—the ability to learn a large number of associations in a relatively short time; (d) inductive language learning ability—the ability "to infer linguistic forms, rules, and patterns from new linguistic content itself with a minimum of supervision or guidance" (Carroll, 1962, p. 130; see also Carroll, 1958b).

5. The traditional "verbal" or vocabulary knowledge factor is not of great importance in predicting success in elementary language training where audio-lingual skills are stressed.

6. Phonetic discrimination ability—the ability to learn to distinguish foreign sounds—does not seem to be susceptible to reliable measurement and is probably not a useful predictor of success over and above tests of "phonetic coding" ability as described above.

7. Foreign language aptitude is not specific to particular languages or particular groups of languages; the same battery of tests predicts success in languages as diverse as German and Chinese with approximately the same degree of validity.

8. Some evidence indicates that a battery of language aptitude tests can provide informa-

tion useful in forecasting and diagnosing particular types of learning difficulties.

Carroll and Sapon (1959) and Carroll (1959) have also published results on the validity of their Modern Language Aptitude Test in predicting course grades in numerous foreign language courses in high school and college, both of the "contemporary" variety stressing audio-lingual skills and of the more "traditional" variety stressing reading and translation. Twenty-eight validity coefficients presented for high school courses ranged from .25 to .78 and had a median of .545; 25 coefficients presented for college courses ranged from .13 to .69 with a median of .44. Evidence was presented that this test was superior in predictive power to intelligence tests. On the question of the prediction of success in different types of foreign language courses, it was reported that "there was no systematic fluctuation of validity dependent on teaching methodology."

Contrary to the somewhat pessimistic conclusion cited above with respect to the fraction of the population with good chances of success in *intensive* courses, the expectancy tables presented by Carroll and Sapon for students in high school or college show that a large proportion of such students attain measured aptitude levels high enough to forecast success in foreign language study in academic settings. The difference apparently results from the lessened degree of "intensivity" in academic language courses; students with relatively low aptitude can succeed in these courses because of the slower pace of instruction. Further research is needed to indicate what relationship there may be between foreign language aptitude and the degree to which the individual is capable of coping with the pace of intensive language instruction.

Interests, Attitudes, and Motivation

When college undergraduate students are asked what they want to get from foreign language instruction, a heavy majority stress that they wish to attain competence in communication with the spoken language; learning to read is also important, but secondary (Politzer, 1953–1954). This is in accord with unpublished findings of the writer in a wide variety of schools.

There have been few studies of students' attitudes toward foreign language instruction as actually practiced. Bamberger (1955) presented a model questionnaire which teachers might use, but gave no data.

The perennial question of the role of motivation may be raised in connection with foreign language teaching. Lorge (1939) reported that adults who were paid to learn Russian in experiments on adult learning during the depression learned equally well regardless of whether they were interested in the task. Dunkel (1948, Ch. VIII) found that promise of a monetary reward did not result in significantly better performance in a miniature language learning task administered in a laboratory situation. Carroll (1962) found that whether a person likes foreign language study is not related significantly either to aptitude or to achievement. From these results one could infer that as long as learners remain cooperative and actively engage in learning, *whether they want to or not*, motivational differences will not make much difference in achievement. Motivation will be related to achievement, however, when it affects how well students will persevere in active learning efforts in a situation in which they are relatively free to lag in attention. Gardner and Lambert (1959), for example, found clear evidence for a relation between motivation and the success of eleventh-grade Montreal English-speaking high-school students in learning French. Motivation was measured by means of questionnaires completed by the students. Success was related to two measures of motivation: (1) a "motivational intensity scale," and (2) an "orientation index" measuring the degree to which the student was oriented toward "integrative" motivations (desire to be like, and to communicate with, French-Canadians) rather than merely "instrumental" motivations (desire to use French as a tool to gain personal ends). These writers stress, therefore, that the student's attitude toward language study and toward the speakers of the language he is studying can have profound influences over and above those of aptitude.

More evidence of a relation between "motivation" and performance comes from Politzer's (1960) observation of a correlation between number of hours spent in voluntary language laboratory periods and performance in course examinations. On the other hand, Politzer's data show that the amount of time spent in doing homework in a more traditional course had a curvilinear relation to grades; those getting A's tended to do least homework. Politzer's observations were made on college students.

The research literature does not throw any light on *methods* of motivating students in foreign language instruction. It has been widely claimed that the new methods of teaching languages almost invariably stimulate students during the early stages of instruction; effective means of forestalling the tedium and fatigue that often set in at later stages have not been discovered.

Prior Language Training

When a student transfers from elementary school to high school or from high school to college and yet continues language study, his new instructor may be concerned about his prior language study and its effect (positive or negative) on his success in the new course. Cheydleur and Schenck (1948) reported on the system of placement examinations used at the University of Wisconsin to section students. They claimed that the system was successful, saving many students a half-year or a year of instruction. Putter (1955) compared second-semester college freshmen who presented three types of records of high school language study: (1) none; (2) language study, with no lapse between high school and college; and (3) language study, but with a

lapse of at least two years between high school and college. It is hardly surprising that he found the second of these groups to be superior in performance. Similar results are reported by Dunkel (1948, pp. 93–96). It would seem that properly designed placement tests could practically eliminate the problem of prior background in the language to be studied.

The effect of prior background in foreign language other than the one to be studied has been extensively discussed in educational literature. Essentially, it reduces to the question of whether study of one language transfers to another. Several large-scale studies of this question have been undertaken, primarily because of its crucial relevance to general educational policy, but the results thus far are inconclusive. Dunkel (1948, pp. 97–99) interpreted research findings as showing that a year or more of training in one language does give some positive help in learning another. The studies made to date, however (e.g., Kettelkamp, 1945, 1949), have not controlled adequately for language aptitude. That is to say, they have collected data on students who elected a second foreign language; such students are likely to be those who have been successful in studying their first foreign language and have therefore *ipso facto* demonstrated a degree of aptitude which will also predict success in the second foreign language. Carefully controlled experiments on the transfer of language skills from language to language are needed.

The Age and Sex of the Learner

Henmon (1934) summarized evidence then available concerning the age at which foreign language instruction might best begin and concluded that "if it is desirable or necessary to do so, adults can acquire a foreign language as easily [in their adult years] as in earlier years." At the time this statement was written, there was little interest in the possibility of teaching foreign languages to children in the elementary school. Foreign language study was regarded as being properly placed in the high school and college years. Today there is concern with language learning both by children and by adults.

The writer has elsewhere (Carroll, 1960a) reviewed the research literature that bears on the learning of foreign languages by children in school settings. The widespread occurrence of child bilingualism acquired in "natural" situations—in the home or neighborhood—is well known, although there seem to be no careful studies of whether bilingualism appears in every case where conditions are favorable for it. When the language milieu is favorable, children will readily learn second languages in school settings, particularly when they have an opportunity to converse with children who have already mastered the language (Lorge & Mayans, 1954). These observations agree with those by Penfield cited above. Teaching foreign languages in the elementary school without the support of an appropriate language milieu must be considered as a separate and distinct problem. The evidence seems clear[6] that the earlier the child is introduced to a foreign language, the better his pronunciation will be, other things being equal; it is probable that facility in acquiring good pronunciation without special instruction is a decreasing function of age and levels off at about the age of puberty. On the other hand, there is no good evidence that children learn other aspects of language any better or faster when account is taken of the amount of time they spend on learning. Children do not, in short, learn foreign languages with miraculous ease in school settings; Dunkel and Pillet (1957–1958) observed that at the end of a second year of elementary school language instruction "the children's ability to speak spontaneously was somewhat disappointing when put to impromptu test" (p. 147). Children also vary in

aptitude; the writer's unpublished studies show considerable validity for certain predictive tests even among children already highly selected for intelligence. According to Dunkel and Pillet (1957–1958), some 10 to 20 per cent of the children who show normal or superior progress in most school subjects appear to have a distinct lack of ability in foreign languages. These children cannot readily be helped by extra drill or special attention. We do not yet know how to teach these children, and serious consideration may be given to the possibility of withdrawing them from foreign language instruction.

We do not know enough about the long-term effects of early foreign language instruction, whether or not such instruction is continued until the later school years. Research is needed to answer such questions as: How much of early-acquired language competence is forgotten with disuse, and how easily can it be reacquired? Are persons who have had early foreign language instruction better able to acquire still another language, later in life, than persons who have not had such instruction (other things being equal)?

Popular opinion seems to hold that it is increasingly difficult to learn a foreign language as an adult grows older. The writer's own studies (1962) suggest that there is a slight negative correlation between age and success in learning a foreign language; these data are for a group with a mean age of 34, standard deviation 5. Nevertheless, many older people in the sample were quite successful in learning; measured aptitude was a much more important variable than age.

No data on the relation between sex and foreign language learning have been systematically collected and examined for this purpose. Data assembled in the Manual of the Modern Language Aptitude Test (Carroll & Sapon, 1959) show that girls have higher scores on the test, and also tend to get higher marks in language courses in school, particularly in the upper grades (Grades 11–13). Insufficient data have been collected on adult women to compare them with adult males.

---

[6] However, a recent experiment by Grinder, Otomo, and Toyota (1961) found that accuracy in learning pronunciation of Japanese was positively related to grade level in a group of English-speaking Hawaiian children in Grades 2 through 4.

Adapting Instruction to the Characteristics of the Learner

Except for an early report by Tharp (1929), no published studies have been found concerning the sectioning of foreign language students according to intelligence, aptitude, or other criteria, although such sectioning is known to be practiced fairly widely (Eaton, 1958). If Carroll (1962) is correct in regarding aptitude as a matter of the time required for attaining a desired degree of competence, it should be possible to accelerate progress in high aptitude sections; "enrichment" could also be practiced, but it seems less relevant than acceleration in the case of foreign language instruction.

Aside from several studies, some cited earlier (Ching, 1960; Morrison, 1958; Pickrel, Neidt, & Gibson, 1958), there are few published investigations of methods of adapting foreign language instruction for children. Progress reports by Dunkel and Pillet (1956–1957, 1957–1958, 1958–1959) contain useful information and empirical data on the teaching of French starting at Grade 3. Important discussions of teaching methods are to be found in works by Andersson (1953), MacRae (1957), and Tireman (1948). According to Carroll (1960a), "All the reports of successful FLES [foreign language in the elementary school] teaching stress the importance of carrying on class work in the foreign language, without the use of English" (p. 15).

THE MEASUREMENT OF ACHIEVEMENT IN FOREIGN LANGUAGE TEACHING

Adequate and valid measures of achievement in foreign languages are needed both in instruction and research. For certain kinds of research, the chief requirement is that the measuring procedures validly discriminate among levels of competence so that the effects of different instructional procedures may be compared. Most standardized tests of

foreign language achievement assess competence only in relative terms; percentiles or other derived measures based upon the performance of typical groups in typical courses of instruction give no direct information concerning absolute levels of success. The fact that a college student attains, say, the 99th percentile on a test of proficiency in German after a year of study may completely conceal the fact that he can read a German newspaper only with difficulty. If we are to study the parameters of the language learning process and related aspects thereof such as retention, forgetting, and relearning, we need measures which report competence in more meaningful terms.[7] It would be desirable to be able to state, for example, how long (in terms of hours of instruction or study, say) it takes a person of a given measured degree of language aptitude to attain a specified degree of competence in a foreign language. At present we are not able to do this with a satisfactory degree of precision.

An example of a meaningful scale on which it would be desirable to report proficiency is that established by the Foreign Service Institute of the U.S. Department of State. The standards in speaking proficiency are as follows: S-0, No practical knowledge of the language; S-1, Able to use limited social expressions, numbers, and language for travel requirements; S-2, Able to satisfy routine social and limited office requirements; S-3, Sufficient control of structure and adequate vocabulary to handle representation requirements and professional discussions in one or more fields; S-4, Fluency in the foreign language; S-5, Competence equivalent to English. There is a similar series of standards for reading and writing. The Foreign Service Institute has promulgated a chart of estimated time requirements for attaining each of these standards; the time requirements vary considerably with type of language and with language aptitude (see Cleveland, Mangone, &

---

[7] Almost nothing has been reported concerning retention of skills (see Dyer, 1949; Hodgson, 1957), and there is no research evidence on the speed of relearning languages once forgotten.

Adams, 1960, pp. 250–251, for a reproduction of this chart). The chart is based on general experience and subjective opinions; a revision based on objective and meaningful measurements would be highly desirable.

The present writer (Carroll, 1954) surveyed the history of foreign language achievement testing, considered the various types of objective tests which have been developed for measuring proficiency in understanding, speaking, reading, and writing a foreign language, and listed the standardized tests available at that time. Lado (1961) has prepared a comprehensive discussion of the construction and use of language tests.

Aside from the usual problems incident to the construction of any achievement test—specification of the behaviors, skills, and knowledges to be tested, adequate sampling of the content field, clear and unambiguous item writing, provision of proper time limits, etc.—testing in foreign languages presents a few special problems, well illustrated in opinions expressed at a recent conference of foreign language teachers on language learning (Brooks, et al., 1959). It was felt that tests which expose the learner to incorrect forms of language are harmful. It was also asserted that tests which require students to make translations or do other things which are not normal in classes conducted by the direct method suffer from the standpoint of validity and are inimical to the smooth progress of such instruction. Research is needed concerning the extent to which it is possible to construct reliable and valid tests at various stages of instruction which will conform to the desiderata stated.

There has been some interest in the interrelationships of foreign language skills (e.g., Beezhold, 1956; Kamman, 1953). It may be suggested, however, that the relationships which may be observed in a given situation are a function of the degree to which each skill has been featured in the instruction. For example, skills in oral and written language may be expected to be highly correlated at the end of a course of instruction which has included the teaching of both kinds of skills;

the correlation observed at the end of a course which has underplayed either of these skills will in all probability be lower. On the other hand, interest in the interrelationship of skills is legitimate to the extent that it may indicate what kinds of measurements may be substituted for other measurements which may be more difficult to make. For example, research is needed on the extent to which measurements of auditory comprehension and discrimination—testable in large groups—may be substituted for tests of oral production skills—which must be administered to one person at a time. Despite the work of a number of investigators (e.g., Agard & Dunkel, 1948; Tharp, 1935), there is little reliable information on these points.

THE FOREIGN LANGUAGE TEACHER

It hardly needs research demonstration that the competence of the teacher in the foreign language will have an important bearing on the success of the instruction, and currently attempts are being made to raise the standards of competence through the provision of special training supported by the National Defense Education Act of 1958. The Modern Language Association is at this writing in the process of developing tests of teacher competence in French, Spanish, German, Russian, and Italian in seven areas: speaking, understanding, reading, writing, cultural knowledge, linguistic analysis, and teaching methodology (Starr, 1961).

There has been some interest in whether native- or foreign-born teachers are preferable. In her review of foreign language teaching research, Birkmaier (1960) reports that students taught by American-born instructors make higher achievement test scores, on the average, than students taught by foreign-born instructors. A similar conclusion was reached by Schenck (1952). Regardless of these findings, it would seem that whether an instructor is native- or foreign-born is hardly a proper consideration in selecting teachers. Skill in teaching and competence in the foreign language are obviously the matters of first importance.

Although Thomas (1954) reported that 69 per cent of 309 institutions preparing teachers of foreign languages offered courses in foreign language teaching methodology, no research reports seem to have been made on the utility or efficacy of such courses.

CONCLUSION

The general state of our knowledge concerning the teaching of foreign languages may be summarized by saying that although we know how to produce satisfactory or even superior levels of accomplishment in most students, this inevitably takes large amounts of time, even with careful organization of instruction. New developments in teaching methods have stemmed primarily from advances in linguistic science, rational analysis of the terminal behavior desired as a result of teaching, and the appearance of devices with language-training potentialities. Educational research has contributed very little to foreign language teaching methodology aside from general knowledge concerning the construction of achievement tests, the role of foreign language aptitude in the learning process, and the psychology of bilingualism. Psychologists who have tried to investigate elements in the foreign language teaching process have frequently failed to produce useful results because their experimental settings and materials have not been sufficiently similar to those of the actual teaching situation as it occurs in the classroom or in the language laboratory. At the same time, research undertaken by foreign language teachers has only rarely been adequate with respect to research methodology.

Thus, there remain many questions which could be profitably investigated by rigorous psychological and educational research, and it is clearly within the realm of possibility that the results of such research could make language teaching more effective and efficient. Research on teaching could make an important contribution by providing the

knowledge needed to formulate educational policy concerning the teaching of foreign languages (Carroll, 1960b). Information is desired on which to base decisions concerning who should be taught foreign languages, at what ages instruction should be started and how long it should be continued, what languages should be taught, what skills should be emphasized, and what kind of outlays of staff, space, and equipment are required to support the resulting instructional program.

REFERENCES

Abell, M. A. Foreign language teaching in the USSR. *Mod. lang. J.,* 1959, 43, 72–78.

Agard, F. B., Clements, R. J., & Hendrix, W. S. *A survey of language classes in the Army Specialized Training Program.* New York: Modern Language Association of America, Commission on Trends in Education, 1944.

Agard, F. B., & Dunkel, H. B. *An investigation of second-language teaching.* Boston: Ginn, 1948.

Andersson, T. *The teaching of foreign languages in the elementary school.* Boston: Heath, 1953.

Angiolillo, P. *Armed forces' foreign language teaching: Critical evaluation and implications.* New York: Vanni, 1947.

Antioch College. *Experiment in French language instruction; Second report, 1959–1960.* Yellow Springs, Ohio: Author, 1960.

Astington, E. Vocabulary selection in French reading. *Mod. Lang.* (*London*), 1958, 39, 102–107.

Astington, E. A basic vocabulary for French teaching. *Mod. Lang.* (*London*), 1959, 40, 9–10.

Bamberger, F. H. What about the student's point of view? *Mod. lang. J.,* 1955, 39, 240–242.

Beezhold, F. W. Factor analyses of language achievement tests. *J. nat. Inst. Personnel Res., Johannesburg,* 1956, 6, 63–73.

Berko, Jean. The child's learning of English morphology. *Word,* 1958, 14, 150–177.

Bernard, W. Psychological principles of language learning and the bilingual reading method. *Mod. lang. J.,* 1951, 35, 87–96.

Birkmaier, Emma M. An investigation of the outcomes in the eclectic, reading and modified Army method courses in the teaching of a second language. Unpublished doctoral dissertation, Univer. of Minnesota, 1949.

Birkmaier, Emma M. Modern languages. In C. W. Harris (Ed.), *Encyclopedia of educational research.* (3rd ed.) New York: Macmillan, 1960. Pp. 861–888.

Blayne, T. C. Results of developmental reading procedures in first-year Spanish. *Mod. lang. J.,* 1946, 30, 39–43.

Bloomfield, L. *Outline guide for the practical study of foreign languages.* Baltimore: Waverly Press, 1942. (Special publication of the Linguistic Society of America)

Bolinger, D. L., et al. *Modern Spanish: A project of the Modern Language Association.* New York: Harcourt, Brace, 1960.

Bond, O. *The reading method: An experiment in college French.* Chicago: Univer. of Chicago Press, 1953.

Borglum, G. Modern language audio-visual project. *Mod. lang. J.,* 1958, 42, 325–328.

Borglum, G., & Mueller, T. Addendum to language laboratory and target language. *French Rev.,* 1956, 30, 58–59.

Bovée, A. G. The relationship between audio and visual thought comprehension in French. *French Rev.,* 1948, 21, 300–305.

Braunschausen, N. Les méthodes d'enseignement des langues étrangères. *Rev. Psychol.,* 1910, 3, 298–306.

Briones, I. T. An experimental comparison of two forms of linguistic learning. *Psychol. Rec.,* 1937, 1, 205–214.

Brooks, N. *Language and language learning: Theory and practice.* New York: Harcourt, Brace, 1959.

Brooks, N., et al. Definition of language competences through testing. In F. D. Eddy (Ed.), *Reports of working Committees, 1959 Northeast Conf. on Teaching Foreign Languages.* Washington, D.C.: Georgetown Univer., 1959. Pp. 49–56.

Brown, G. I., & Hodgkinson, H. L. A note concerning "an application of recent developments in psychology to the teaching of German," by C. B. Ferster & S. M. Sapon. *Harvard educ. Rev.,* 1958, 28, 156–157.

Brown, R. *Words and things.* Glencoe, Ill.: Free Press, 1958.

Carroll, J. B. *Notes on the measurement of achievement in foreign' languages.* Cambridge, Mass.: Author, 1954. (Mimeographed)

Carroll, J. B. Process and content in psycholinguistics. In R. Glaser, et al., *Current trends in the description and analysis of behavior.* Pittsburgh: Univer. of Pittsburgh Press, 1958. Pp. 175–200. (a)

Carroll, J. B. A factor analysis of two foreign language aptitude batteries. *J. gen. Psychol.,* 1958, 59, 3–19. (b)

Carroll, J. B. Use of the Modern Language Aptitude Test in secondary schools. *Yearb. nat. counc. Meas. used in Educ.,* 1959, 16, 155–159.

Carroll, J. B. Foreign languages for children: What research says. *Nat. elem. Principal,* 1960, 39 (6), 12–15. (a)

Carroll, J. B. Wanted: A research basis for educational policy on foreign language teaching. *Harvard educ. Rev.,* 1960, 30, 128–140. (b)

Carroll, J. B. The prediction of success in intensive language training. In R. Glaser (Ed.), *Training research and education.* Pittsburgh: Univer. of Pittsburgh Press, 1962. Pp. 87–136.

Carroll, J. B., & Sapon, S. M. *Manual, Modern Language Aptitude Test.* (1959 ed.) New York: Psychological Corp., 1959.

Carroll, J. B., et al. *Annual report, Committee on Foreign Languages, School and University Program for Research and Development, Period of July 1, 1958–June 30, 1959.* Cambridge, Mass.: Graduate School of Education, Harvard Univer., 1959.

Carton, A. S., & Carroll, J. B. *The 1959 summer Russian language learning program: Final report of testing project.* Cambridge, Mass.: Graduate School of Education, Harvard Univer., 1960. (Mimeographed)

Cheydleur, F. D., & Schenck, Ethel A. Attainment examinations in foreign languages, past, present, and future: Credits vs. achievement at the University of Wisconsin 1931–1947. *Bull. Univer. Wis.,* Serial No. 2952, February, 1948.

Cheydleur, F. D., & Schenck, Ethel A. From the ASTP forward: Standardized test results in foreign languages at the University of Wisconsin 1943–1949. *Bull. Univer. Wis.,* Serial No. 3194, June, 1950.

Ching, Doris C. Evaluation of a program for the improvement of English language ability and reading achievement in Hawaiian bilingual children. Unpublished doctoral dissertation, Harvard Univer., 1960.

Ciofarri, V. Factors involved in good modern language teaching. *Peabody J. Educ.*, 1958, 36, 93–100.

Cleveland, H., Mangone, G. J., & Adams, J. C. *The overseas Americans.* New York: McGraw-Hill, 1960.

Cochran, Anne. *Modern methods of teaching English as a foreign language: A guide to modern materials with particular reference to the Far East.* New York: United Board for Christian Colleges in China, 1952. (Reprinted by Educational Services, Inc., Washington, D.C., 1958)

Cook, J. O., & Kendler, Tracy S. A theoretical model to explain some paired-associate learning data. In G. Finch & F. Cameron (Eds.), *Symposium on Air Force human engineering, personnel, and training research.* Washington, D.C.: National Academy of Sciences —National Research Council Publ. 455, 1956. Pp. 90–98.

Creore, A. E., & Hanzeli, V. E. *A comparative evaluation of two modern methods for teaching a spoken language.* Seattle: Department of Romance Languages and Literature, Univer. of Washington, 1960.

Cuff, R. P. Teaching college grammar by induction and deduction. *Mod. lang. J.*, 1956, 40, 76–79.

Curran, C. A. Counseling skills adapted to the learning of foreign languages. *Bull. Menninger Clin.*, 1961, 25, 78–93.

Delattre, P. Testing students' progress in the language laboratory. In F. Oinas (Ed.), *Language teaching today.* Bloomington: Indiana Univer. Res. Center in Anthropology, Folklore, and Linguistics, Publ. 14. 1960. Pp. 77–93.

DeSauzé, E. B. *The Cleveland plan for the teaching of modern languages, with special reference to French.* Philadelphia: Winston, 1953.

Dorcus, R. M., Mount, G. E., & Jones, Margaret H. *Construction and validation of foreign language aptitude tests.* Los Angeles: Department of Psychology, Univer. of California, 1952 (Personnel Res. Branch Res. Rept. 993, AGO, Dept. of the Army, Contract DA-49-083).

Dostert, L. The Georgetown Institute Language Program. *Publ. Mod. Lang. Ass. Amer.*, 1953, 68, 3–12.

Dunkel, H. B. *Second-language learning.* Boston: Ginn, 1948.

Dunkel, H. B., & Pillet, R. The French program in the University of Chicago elementary school. *Elem. sch. J.*, 1956–1957, 57, 17–27.

Dunkel, H. B., & Pillet, R. A second year of French in elementary school. *Elem. sch. J.*, 1957–1958, 58, 143–151.

Dunkel, H. B., & Pillet, R. A third year of French in elementary school. *Elem. sch. J.*, 1958–1959, 59, 264–266.

Dyer, H. S. The effect of recency of training on the College Board French scores. *Sch. & Soc.*, 1949, 70, 105–106.

Eaton, Esther. Foreign languages. In N. B. Henry (Ed.), *Yearb. nat. Soc. Stud. Educ.*, 1958, 57, Part II, 295–301.

Ervin, Susan M., & Osgood, C. E. Second language learning and bilingualism. In C. E. Osgood & T. A. Sebeok (Eds.), Psycholinguistics: A survey of theory and research problems. *J. abnorm. soc. Psychol.*, 1954, 49, (4, Part 2), 139–146.

Fairbanks, G. H., Shadick, Helen E., & Yedigar, Zulefa. *A Russian area reader for college classes.* New York: Ronald Press, 1951.

Ferrell, J. An experiment in the use of drill instructors in language laboratories. *Lang. Learning*, 1956–1957, 7, 59–64.

Ferster, C. B., & Sapon, S. M. An application of recent developments in psychology to the teaching of German. *Harvard educ. Rev.*, 1958, 28, 58–69.

Fishman, J. A. *1957 Supplement to College Board Scores*, No. 2. New York: College Entrance Examination Board, 1957.

Forlano, G. School learning with various methods of practice and reward. *Teach. Coll. Contr. Educ.*, 1936, No. 688.

Forlano, G., & Hoffman, M. Guessing and telling methods in learning words of a foreign language. *J. educ. Psychol.*, 1937, 28, 632–636.

Fotos, J. The Purdue Laboratory method in teaching beginning French. *Mod. lang. J.*, 1955, 39, 141–143.

Frank, J. G. Can one really learn a foreign language at school? *Mod. lang. J.*, 1958, 42, 379–381.

Fries, C. C. *Teaching and learning English as a foreign language.* Ann Arbor: Univer. of Michigan Press, 1945.

Gardner, R. C., & Lambert, W. E. Motivational variables in second-language acquisition. *Canad. J. Psychol.*, 1959, 13, 266–272.

Grew, J. H. Another experiment. *French Rev.*, 1956, 30, 41–47.

Grinder, R. E., Otomo, A., & Toyota, W. *Comparisons between 2nd, 3rd, and 4th grade children in the audio-lingual learning of Japanese as a second language.* Honolulu: Department of Psychology, Univer. of Hawaii, 1961.

Haden, E. F. The Texas language program. *Publ. Mod. Lang. Ass. Amer.,* 1956, 71, 14–20.

Hall, E. T. *The silent language.* Garden City, N.Y.: Doubleday, 1959.

Hamilton, D. L., & Haden, E. F. Three years of experimentation at the University of Texas. *Mod. lang. J.,* 1950, 34, 85–102.

Haslerud, G. M., & Meyers, Shirley. The transfer value of given and individually derived principles. *J. educ. Psychol.,* 1958, 49, 293–298.

Hempel, V., & Mueller, K. Introduction to U.S. Army Language School. *Mod. lang. J.,* 1959, 43, 62–65.

Henmon, V. A. C. Recent developments in the construction, evaluation, and use of tests in the modern foreign languages. In A. Coleman (Ed.), *Experiments and studies in modern language teaching.* Chicago: Univer. of Chicago Press, 1934. Pp. 191–218.

Henmon, V. A. C., et al. *Prognosis tests in the modern foreign languages.* New York: Macmillan, 1929. (*Publications of the American and Canadian Committees on Modern Foreign Languages,* Vol. 14)

Hockett, C. F. Learning pronunciation. *Mod. lang. J.,* 1950, 34, 261–269.

Hocking, E. The Purdue language program. *Publ. Mod. Lang. Ass. Amer.,* 1955, 70, 36–45.

Hodgson, F. M. An experiment in language learning. *Mod. Lang.* (London), 1957, 38, 107–110.

Hoge, H. W. Testing in the language laboratory: A laboratory experiment in Spanish pronunciation. *Hispania,* 1959, 42, 147–152.

Hohlfeld, J. M. An experiment employing two methods of teaching Spanish to college freshmen. Doctoral dissertation, Univer. of Pennsylvania, 1950.

Holodnak, H. B. The effect of positive and negative guidance upon maze learning in children. *J. educ. Psychol.,* 1943, 34, 341–354.

Hood, M. H. Foreign language method in Europe and America. *Mod. lang. J.,* 1958, 42, 279–283.

Horowitz, A. E. The effects of variation in linguistic structure on the learning of miniature linguistic systems. Unpublished doctoral dissertation, Harvard Univer., 1955.

Huebener, T. The new course of study in foreign languages. *High Points,* 1956, 38, 24–27.

Israel, M. L. Variably blurred prompting: I. Methodology and application to the analysis of paired-associate learning. *J. Psychol.,* 1960, 50, 43–52.

Jakobovitz, L., & Lambert, W. E. Semantic satiation among bilinguals. *J. exp. Psychol.,* 1961, 62, 576–582.

Johnston, Marjorie C. (Ed.) *Modern foreign languages in the high school.* Washington, D.C.: U.S. Government Printing Office, 1958. (U.S. Office of Education Bull. 1958, No. 16)

Johnston, Marjorie C., & Remer, I. *References on foreign languages in the elementary school.* Washington, D.C.: U.S. Office of Education, 1959. (U.S. Office of Education Circular No. 495, Rev.)

Johnston, Marjorie C., & Seerley, Catherine C. *Foreign language laboratories in schools and colleges.* Washington, D.C.: U.S. Government Printing Office, 1959. (U.S. Office of Education Bull. 1959, No. 3)

Kale, S. V., & Grosslight, J. H. *Exploratory studies in the use of pictures and sound for teaching foreign language vocabulary.* Tech. Rep. SDC 269-7-53. Port Washington, N.Y.: U.S. Navy Special Devices Center, 1955.

Kamman, J. F. A comparison of factor patterns in a native language and an auxiliary language. Unpublished doctoral dissertation, Univer. of Illinois, 1953. (*Microfilm Abstr.,* 1954, 14, 406)

Kaulfers, W. V. Prognosis and its alternatives in relation to the guidance of students. *German Quart.,* 1939, 12, 81–84.

Kaulfers, W. V. *Modern languages for modern schools.* New York: McGraw-Hill, 1942.

Kaulfers, W. V. Earmarks of a good foreign language program. *Calif. J. sec. Educ.,* 1956, 31, 4–13.

Kessman, M. Experimental comparison of writing-speaking versus speaking-writing sequences in learning paired associates. Unpublished doctoral dissertation, Indiana Univer., 1959.

Kettelkamp, G. C. Student achievement in two or more foreign languages as related to order of study. *Sch. Rev.,* 1945, 53, 610–614.

Kettelkamp, G. C. *Which step first? The relation of sequence of language achievement.* Urbana: Bur. of Res. and Service, Univer. of Illinois, 1949.

Klinck, G. A. Psychology of the direct method. *Canad. mod. lang. Rev.,* 1957, 14, 10–14.

Kopstein, F. F., & Roshal, S. M. Learning foreign vocabulary from pictures vs. words. *Amer. Psychologist,* 1954, 9, 407–408.

Krawiec, T. S. A comparison of learning and retention of materials presented visually and auditorially. *J. gen. Psychol.,* 1946, 34, 179–195.

Lado, R. *Linguistics across cultures.* Ann Arbor: Univer. of Michigan Press, 1957.

Lado, R. *Language testing: The construction and use of foreign language tests.* London and New York: Longmans, Green, 1961.

Lambert, W. E. Measurement of the linguistic dominance of bilinguals. *J. abnorm. soc. Psychol.,* 1955, 50, 197–200.

Lambert, W. E. Developmental aspects of second language acquisition. *J. soc. Psychol.,* 1956, 43, 83–89, 91–98, 99–104.

Lambert, W. E., & Fillenbaum, S. A. pilot study of aphasia among bilinguals. *Canad. J. Psychol.,* 1959, 13, 28–34.

Lambert, W. E., Havelka, J., & Crosby, C. The influence of language-acquisition contexts on bilingualism. *J. abnorm. soc. Psychol.,* 1958, 56, 239–244.

Lambert, W. E., Havelka, J., & Gardner, R. C. Linguistic manifestations of bilingualism. *Amer. J. Psychol.,* 1959, 72, 77–82.

Liberman, A. M. Some results of research on speech perception. *J. Acoust. Soc. Amer.,* 1957, 29, 117–123.

Licklider, J. C. R., & Miller, G. A. The perception of speech. In S. S. Stevens (Ed.), *Handbook of experimental psychology.* New York: Wiley, 1951. Pp. 1040–1074.

Lind, Melva. Modern language learning: The intensive course as sponsored by the United States Army, and implications for the undergraduate course of study. *Genet. Psychol. Monogr.,* 1948, 38, 3–81.

London, I. D. (Trans.) Conference on the improvement of Soviet foreign language teaching (translation of document in *Sovetskaia Pedagogika,* 1958, 22, 146–150). *Sch. & Soc.,* 1959, 87, 200–202.

Lorge, I. Psychological bases for adult learning. *Teachers Coll. Rec.,* 1939, 41, 4–12.

Lorge, I., & Mayans, F. Vestibule vs. regular classes for Puerto Rican migrant pupils. *Teachers Coll. Rec.,* 1954, 55, 231–237.

Lumsdaine, A. A., & Glaser, R. (Eds.) *Teaching machines and programmed learning: A source book.* Washington, D.C.: Department of Audio-Visual Instruction, National Education Association, 1960.

Lundeen, D. J., Ptacek, P. H., Starr, C. D., & Henrikson, E. H. The effects of a language training program on foreign soundingness. *Speech Monogr.,* 1957, 24, 74–76.

MacRae, Margit. *Teaching Spanish in the grades.* Boston: Houghton Mifflin, 1957.

Marckwardt, A. H. An experiment in aural perception. *Engl. J.,* 1944, 33, 212–214.

Marckwardt, A. H. Phonemic structure and aural perception. *Amer. Speech,* 1946, 21, 106–111.

Marckwardt, A. H. Phonemic bifurcation as an English teaching problem. *Pap. Mich. Acad. Sci. Arts Lett.,* 1947, 33, 363–371.

Marty, F. *Language laboratory learning.* Wellesley, Mass.: Audio-Visual Publications, 1960.

Matthew, R. J. *Language and area studies in the Armed Services: Their future significance.* Washington, D.C.: American Council on Education, 1947.

McIntosh, J. R. Learning by exposure to wrong forms in grammar and spelling. *Teach. Coll. Contr. Educ.,* 1944, No. 892.

McKinney, J., & Hocking, E. Modern language class. *NEA J.,* 1958, 47, 182–184.

McMullen, E. The intensive method: An experiment. *Mod. lang. J.,* 1955, 39, 293–294.

Mildenberger, K. W. The current status of the teaching of Spanish in the elementary schools. *Hispania,* 1954, 37, 63–65.

Miller, G. A. Free recall of redundant strings of letters. *J. exp. Psychol.,* 1958, 56, 485–491.

Miller, G. A., & Nicely, Patricia E. An analysis of perceptual confusions among some English consonants. *J. Acoust. Soc. Amer.,* 1955, 27, 338–352.

Milner, P. M. Review of W. Penfield & L. Roberts, "Speech and Brain Mechanisms," and R. K. Overton, "Thought and Action." *Canad. J. Psychol.,* 1960, 14, 140–143.

Moore, J. M. Army Language School: An evaluation. *Mod. lang. J.,* 1957, 41, 332–337.

Morgan, B. Q., & Oberdeck, Lydia M. Active and passive vocabulary. In E. W. Bagster-Collins, et al., *Studies in modern language teaching.* New York: Macmillan, 1930. Pp. 213–221. (*Publications of the American and Canadian Committees on Modern Foreign Languages,* Vol. 17).

Morgan, C. L., & Bailey, W. L. The effect of context on learning a vocabulary. *J. educ. Psychol.,* 1943, 34, 561–565.

Morgan, C. L., & Bonham, D. N. Difficulty of vocabulary learning as affected by parts of speech. *J. educ. Psychol.,* 1944, 35, 369–377.

Morgan, C. L., & Foltz, Mary C. The effect of context on learning a French vocabulary. *J. educ. Res.,* 1944, 38, 213–216.

Morrison, J. C. *The Puerto Rican Study, 1953–1957: A report on the education and adjustment of Puerto Rican pupils in the public schools of the City of New York.* New York: Board of Education, City of New York, 1958.

Morton, F. R. *The language laboratory as a teaching machine.* Ann Arbor: Univer. of Michigan Language Laboratory, 1960. (*Series Pre-prints and Reprints,* Vol. I)

Moulton, W. The Cornell language program. *Publ. Mod. Lang. Ass. Amer.,* 1952, 67, 38–46.

Mueller, T. Perception in foreign language learning. *Mod. lang. J.,* 1958, 42, 167–171.

Mueller, T., & Borglum, G. P. Language laboratory and target language. *French Rev.* 1956, 29, 322–331.

Netschajeff, A. Untersuchungen über die Beobachtungsfähigkeit von Schülern. *Z. angew. Psychol.,* 1910–1911, 4, 335–346.

Nida, E. A. *Learning a foreign language: A handbook prepared especially for missionaries.* New York: Friendship Press, 1957.

Noble, C. E. An analysis of meaning. *Psychol. Rev.,* 1952, 59, 421–430.

Noble, C. E., & McNeely, D. A. The role of meaningfulness (*m*) in paired-associate verbal learning. *J. exp. Psychol.,* 1957, 53, 16–22.

Obrecht, D. A. A visual aid to pronunciation. *Lang. Learning,* 1956–1957, 7, 51–58.

Oinas, F. J. *Language teaching today.* Bloomington: Indiana Univer. Res. Center in Anthropology, Folklore, and Linguistics, Publ. 14, 1960.

Orbison, W. D. The relative efficiency of whole and part methods of learning paired-associates as a function of the length of list. Unpublished doctoral dissertation, Yale Univer., 1944.

Parker, W. R. *The national interest and foreign languages: Discussion guide and work paper.* Washington, D.C.: U.S. Government Printing Office, 1957.

Pascasio, E. M. A descriptive-comparative study predicting interference and facilitation for Tagalog speakers in learning English noun-head modification patterns. Unpublished doctoral dissertation, Univer. of Michigan, 1960.

Penfield, W., & Roberts, L. *Speech and brain-mechanisms.* Princeton, N.J.: Princeton Univer. Press, 1959.

Peterson, H. A. Recall of words, objects, and movements. *Psychol. Rev. Suppl.,* 1903, No. 17, 207–233.

Pickrel, G., Neidt, C., & Gibson, R. Tape recordings are used to teach seventh grade students in Westside Junior-Senior High School, Omaha, Nebraska. *Nat. Ass. Sec. Sch. Principals Bull.,* 1958, 42 (234), 81–93.

Pimsleur, P. Experimental design in the language field. *Mod. lang. Forum,* 1957, 42, 157–163.

Pimsleur, P., & Bonkowski, R. J. Transfer of verbal material across sense modalities. *J. educ. Psychol.,* 1961, 52, 104–107.

Politzer, R. L. Student motivation and interest in elementary language courses. *Lang. Learning,* 1953–1954, 5, 15–21.

Politzer, R. L. Some reflections on the use of the native language in elementary language teaching. *Lang. Learning,* 1958, 8 (3–4), 49–56.

Politzer, R. L. Assiduity and achievement. *Mod. lang. J.,* 1960, 44, 14–16.

Pressey, S. L. Development and appraisal of devices providing immediate automatic scoring of objective tests and concomitant self-instruction. *J. Psychol.,* 1950, 29, 417–447.

Putter, I. High-school-college articulation in foreign languages. *Mod. lang. J.,* 1955, 39, 123–125.

Reindrop, R. C. The reading aim reexamined. *Mod. lang. J.,* 1957, 41, 239–243.

Richards, I. A., & Gibson, Christine. *Learning Basic English: A practical handbook for English-speaking people.* New York: Norton, 1945.

Richards, I. A., Ilsley, M. H., & Gibson, Christine. *French self-taught through pictures.* New York: Pocket Books, 1950.

Richards, S. E., & Appel, Joan E. The effects

of written words in beginning Spanish. *Mod. lang. J.*, 1956, 40, 129–133.

Rocklyn, E. H., & Moren, R. I. A feasibility study of a special machine-taught oral-aural Russian language course. *Amer. Psychologist*, 1960, 15, 423.

Sapon, S. M. An application of psychological theory to pronunciation problems in second language learning. *Mod. lang. J.*, 1952, 36, 111–114.

Sapon, S. M., & Carroll, J. B. Discriminative perception of speech sounds as a function of native language. *Gen. Linguistics*, 1958, 3, 62–72.

Schenck, Ethel A. *Studies of testing and teaching in modern foreign languages, based on materials gathered at the University of Wisconsin by the late Professor Frederic D. Cheydleur.* Madison, Wis.: Dembar Publications, 1952.

Schlüter, Luise. Experimentelle Beiträge zur Prüfung der Anschauungs- und der Übersetzungsmethode bei der Einführung in einen fremdsprachlichen Wortschatz. *Z. Psychol.*, 1914, 68, 1–114.

Schmidt, A. G. *The effect of objective presentation on the learning and retention of a Latin vocabulary.* Chicago: Loyola Univer. Press, 1923.

Schönherr, W. *Direkte und indirekte Methode im neusprachlichen Unterricht.* Leipzig: Quelle & Meyer, 1915.

Scholtkowska, Gita. Experimentelle Beiträge zur Frage der direkten und indirekten Methode im neusprachlichen Unterricht. *Z. angew. Psychol.*, 1925–1926, 25, 65–87.

Seibert, Louise C. An experiment on the relative efficiency of studying French vocabulary in associated pairs versus studying French vocabulary in context. *J. educ. Psychol.*, 1930, 21, 297–314.

Severin, D. G. Appraisal of special tests and procedures used with self-scoring instructional testing devices. *Abstr. doctoral Dissertations, Ohio State Univer.*, 1955, 66, 323–330.

Siciliano, E. A. An experiment in listening comprehension. *Mod. lang. J.*, 1959, 43, 226–227.

Starr, W. H. Competency first: New tests in foreign languages. In J. B. Carroll (Ed.), *Proc. 1960 Invitational Conf. on Testing Problems.* Princeton, N.J.: Educational Testing Service, 1961. Pp. 97–110.

Stephens, A. L. Certain special factors involved in the law of effect. *Abstr. doctoral Dissertations, Ohio State Univer.*, 1953, No. 64.

Teaching Machines, Inc. *Basic Hebrew reading: A teaching machine program.* Albuquerque, N.M.: Teaching Machines, Inc., 1960.

Tharp, J. B. How shall we section beginning foreign language classes? *Mod. lang. J.*, 1929, 13, 433–449.

Tharp, J. B. A modern language test. *J. higher Educ.*, 1935, 6, 103–104.

Thomas, J. V. Special methods in the modern language area: A report. *Mod. lang. J.*, 1954, 38, 387–393.

Thorndike, E. L. Memory for paired associates. *Psychol. Rev.*, 1908, 15, 122–138.

Thorndike, E. L. *Language learning: Summary of a report to the International Auxiliary Language Association in the United States, Incorporated.* New York: Bur. of Publs., Teachers Coll., Columbia Univer., 1933.

Tireman, L. S. *Teaching Spanish-speaking children.* Albuquerque: Univer. of New Mexico Press, 1948.

Toronto Board of Education. *Experimental study of learning French in the public schools undertaken by the Toronto Board of Education.* Rept. No. 1, 1959–1960. Toronto, Canada: Author, 1960.

Trager, G. L., & Smith, H. L., Jr. *An outline of English structure.* Norman, Okla.: Battenburg Press, 1951. ("Studies in Linguistics," Occasional Papers No. 3)

Turner, D. Deus ex machina. *Mod. lang. J.*, 1958, 42, 396–398.

Underwood, B. J., & Schulz, R. W. *Meaningfulness and verbal learning.* Chicago: Lippincott, 1960.

UNESCO. *The teaching of modern languages.* Paris: UNESCO, 1953.

Weinreich, U. *Languages in contact.* New York: Linguistic Circle of New York, 1953.

Wolfle, D. L. The relation between linguistic structure and associative interferences in artificial linguistic material. *Lang. Monogr.*, 1932, No. 11.

Woodworth, R. S. *Experimental psychology.* New York: Holt, 1938.

Zeydel, E., et al. A symposium on intensive German courses for civilians. *German Quart.*, 1946, 19, 1–94.

CHAPTER 22 Research on Teaching the Visual Arts

JEROME HAUSMAN
The Ohio State University

The field of art education, as we know it today, is a relatively new development. There is, for example, a much greater tradition for the artist-apprentice relationship. Indeed, some writers deny that a "field of art education" should exist and insist that true artistic insight cannot be "taught" by persons trained "to teach." Their point of view is that only through continuous and intensive contact with the artist himself can a person realize the deep and rich significance of art.

Despite this seeming criticism, one can look about at the many forms that "teaching" situations take in the contemporary educational scene, each with the expressed purpose of providing insight in creating, confronting, and appreciating works of art. Most elementary schools are staffed by art teachers or visited by art supervisors; most comprehensive secondary schools have required or elective art programs; museums and community centers have turned their energies to problems of adult art education; art departments in colleges and universities have grown at phenomenal rates with the recognition of art as a humanistic discipline; professional programs for the training of artists, designers, and teachers have been developed; the mass media—television, movies, the publishing industry, etc.—have devoted some of their resources to enhancing judgment and taste in the visual arts. In short, many forces have now turned toward recognition of art as a basic human discipline. For example, the report "Art Education for Scientist and Engineer" (Comm. for the Study of Visual Arts at the Massachusetts Institute of Technology, 1957) recognized that it is only recently that American educational thinking has turned to the educational potential of the visual arts. "American education has been, and still is, based on vocational convenience rather than deep-rooted values" (p. 9). The report then went on to observe that "like sound, vision is a sensory experience relating the external world to both emotion and intellect" (p. 13). A visual arts program should "draw attention to the human control of form and space and color *no matter where it occurs*" (p. 15). Logan (1955) pointed to three major areas for projecting and evaluating art education: (1) "general education in the arts in the elementary and secondary schools and in the colleges. General education is to be interpreted as education for the acquisition and growth of an art background for all citizens not expecting to be professionally engaged in art"; (2) "art education available to students hoping to practice the arts and the teaching of the arts professionally"; and (3) social influences (as evidenced in books, magazines, museums, galleries, private and institutional patronage) that shape educational theory and practice.

Despite directions of activity which seem too diverse to comprise a discipline, a conception of a field is emerging that centers in the development of theory and practice in the teaching of art. It is this field and research efforts relevant to it that are discussed in this chapter.

DEFINITIONS
OF THE FIELD

Kahler (1959) has offered the following definition: "Art is a human activity which explores, and thereby creates, new reality in a suprarational, visional manner and presents it symbolically or metaphorically, as a microcosmic whole signifying a macrocosmic whole" (p. 171). The work of art becomes the physical embodiment of the artist's resolution of his intuitive feelings and conceptions; it enables the viewer to apprehend this resolution as experience rather than as discursive language (Langer, 1948, 1953). The apprehension of art gives new meaning to "the elusive present." This is what Yeats referred to in his statement that "the noblest art will be always pure experience . . . an art that is almost silent and is overheard rather than heard" (as quoted by Parkinson, 1958).

Research on the teaching of art must be intimately related to or derived from an underlying conceptual and value system growing out of the nature of art. No study can be undertaken without consciously or unconsciously assuming some axiomatic values. Even if one adopts the point of view that basic questions involving a definition of art cannot be answered with finality, there still remains the value frame of reference within which factors are perceived as relevant to actions and their consequences. Gallie (1956)

maintained that art is an "essentially contested concept" and pointed out that philosophers are concerned with the clarification and understanding of meaning, not with the discovery of new facts. Art criticism is never in the nature of proof or demonstration in an empirical sense. He pointed out that we should be in a position to appreciate the peculiar structure of the concept of art: essentially complex and contested. This view was supported by Weitz (1956), who stated that "art, itself, is an open concept. New conditions (cases) have constantly arisen and will undoubtedly constantly arise; new art forms, new movements will emerge, which will demand decisions on the part of those interested, usually professional critics, as to whether the concept should be extended or not. Aestheticians may lay down similarity conditions but never necessary and sufficient ones for the correct application of the concept" (p. 32). Nevertheless, we do use the term *art* in a descriptive and evaluative sense. "The primary task of aesthetics is not to seek a theory but to elucidate the concept of art. Specifically, it is to describe the conditions under which we employ the concept correctly" (Weitz, 1956, p. 33).

Just as there are many ways in which works of art can be described, different points of view underlie the ideas and attitudes that accompany theorizing about the teaching of art. Persons basing their aesthetic and educational judgments on intuitive feelings, on conceptions of "significant form," or on a cultural-relativist point of view can be expected to formulate different questions regarding their teaching; moreover, their "answers" will probably be perceived as having different meaning. Herein lies one of the major problems confronting anyone attempting to formulate theory about the teaching of art; indeed, the problem exists in varying degrees in virtually every area of educational inquiry.

The primary and subjective nature of artistic experience has separated artists from those who would seek rational understandings and insights into the nature of aesthetic form and the processes involved in its creation. Shahn (1957) views the relationship between the painter and theoretician about art as suspect. He says that artists are people who work with images, and that aestheticians and critics are people who tell other people why they either like or do not like the images the artists make. He then points out that for reasons best known to themselves, artists and theoreticians rather sedulously avoid each other. Gilson (1959) reaffirmed this point, saying that while there are occasions when some art critics are able to approach the work of art in a comprehensive manner, this is more often than not an exception. At best, criticism raises many thorny problems. The "reality" of art remains in its own intrinsic form. The critic is then confronted with the problem of "explaining" something that should be "seen." Many artists have come to view with suspicion any attempts to bring clarity and understanding through rational or scientific processes. They argue that the artist is not (nor should he be) concerned with explaining his work or the ideas and feelings that he attaches to his efforts. Beyond this, they argue that an artist has no responsibility other than the creation of his art. These arguments point to the necessary and obvious limitations of inquiry and rational understanding. "A house is a house; a tree is a tree; a flower is a flower"—the immediacy of experience is contrasted with the limitations of definitions and accounts of this experience. Some draw the dichotomy even more sharply: "Either you are for art or you are for talking about it." Research workers are then characterized as one of the breed that "talk about art."

It can be contended, however, that insisting upon sharp distinctions between being a teacher of art, a practicing artist, or a researcher concerned with the nature and teaching of art does injustice to the field of art education (Hausman, 1958, 1959). Admittedly, few persons (if any) can maintain a high level of activity simultaneously in each of these kinds of work. The field of art education requires (and is defined by) individuals who appreciate and have insight into each of these areas of activity. Rather than an inclination to separate rational and intuitive understandings, there should be an awareness that each may enhance the other. The artist more than most people should appreciate that prelogical processes, so much a part of art—dreams, hallucinations, nonverbalized feelings—can also be considered a subthreshold for rational discourse. Rather than being antithetical to research, such processes should add to its potential. We need to accept and work through our human sensibilities instead of avoiding them. Tauber and Green (1959) pointed out that prelogical thinking is part of the basic endowment of man throughout life which operates continuously. "The prelogical processes build out of the innumerable subthreshold precepts the foundations of one's everyday thinking, relating man to the world about him in many subtle and elusive ways that are not given conscious, logical formulation" (p. 2).

The systems we create should be seen as tools with which to probe deeper into hidden meanings; hypotheses should be set forth with an awareness that they structure possible answers (and necessarily omit other directions for inquiry). Beittel (1957) supports this view:

We cannot think all things at once, although we can feel all things as immanent. To me it is still helpful to hang on to a pluralistic view of man and his functions, and say that art appraises and evaluates man's existence, whereas science designates and informs us about what exists. Each of these functions remains unassailable and irreplaceable . . . . There are not many different ways of laying hold on things: through our having experienced them and realized their meaning through some construction of the spirit, through our deliberately experiencing or experimenting with them, or through research. I feel most drawn to that total grasp, that "thinking in a marrow bone" that Yeats talked of. Yet I do not believe that for sharing *in the form of concepts and generalizations* there is any way like research (Beittel, 1957, p. 7).

For those carrying on research in the teaching of art, there should not be too rigid an insistence on "fixed relationships," on mathematical precision beyond the limits of the nature of the field. These limits, however, are constantly changing. Through disciplined inquiry and action we may shatter the very concepts that give definitions to the field and underlie our questions and procedures. New concepts are often difficult to grasp; more often than not, our contemporaries will try to "picture" the concept with ideas and images that existed before. The problem is not limited to new conceptions in the teaching of art; indeed, it characterizes most attempts to transcend existing systems of defining "reality." The challenge is that of being able to transcend our older systems. The researcher in the teaching of art, as in virtually all fields, must confront the seemingly paradoxical situation of giving structure to a reality that contains an infinite number of variables. He must realize that the goals of research are explanation and understanding; that the researcher seeks to reduce ambiguity and gain heightened awareness of the role of art in the education of man.

The position being presented with regard to research on teaching the visual arts is compatible with the view expressed by Popper (1959): "The empirical basis of objective science has nothing 'absolute' about it. . . . Science does not rest upon rock-bottom. The bold structure of its theories rises, as it were, above a swamp" (p. 111). We must not, according to Popper, regard science as a "body of knowledge," but rather as a system of hypotheses.

A scientist, whether theorist or experimenter, puts forward statements, or systems of statements, and tests them step by step. In the field of the empirical sciences, more particularly, he constructs hypotheses, or systems of theories, and tests them against experience by observation and experiment (Popper, 1959, p. 27).

It would be a fundamental error to assume that research in the teaching of art seeks to fix with finality a single set of procedures for the teaching of art. There can be no single theoretical base that is final and correct to the exclusion of other points of view. We need to be wary of notions of "objective" truth catering to explanations that are pleasant to believe or easy to categorize regardless of our experience. Recognizing the multiplicity of unknown possibilities for understanding an insight need not become an argument against inquiry of any kind. Quite the contrary, it places inquiry in its proper perspective—humble men seeking understanding of the intricacies and complexities of their world.

OUTLINES FOR INQUIRY

The teacher of art (and hence, researchers in the field of study) needs to be concerned with a number of major and related areas for study: (1) the art student; (2) the art student in process; and (3) the art student as revealed through his product. (See Fig. 1.) These areas must then be seen in relation to some of the other factors in the teaching transaction: the teaching environment and the teacher-student dynamic. What follows is an attempt to set forth some of the critical questions confronting research in the teaching of art in the light of theoretical and empirical analyses of these issues.

The Art Student

The generalization *art student* has little value for discussion because of the many ways in which it is used. This becomes increasingly clear when one looks at the diversity of persons and environmental factors that can be identified in a "teaching" situation. The problems of teaching art in an elementary school are obviously different from those associated with the training of advanced students. Children and mature artists each may identify with their own ideas and feelings, but the levels of identification and ensuing actions differ greatly. It

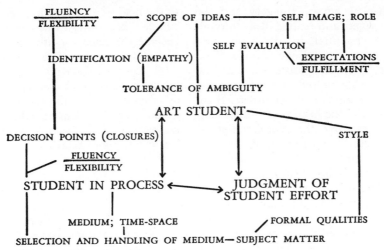

Fig. 1.   Research in Art Education—Related Aspects of Inquiry.

would be all too simple to assume a linear development from the naïve expression of children's art to the sophisticated forms of mature artistic expression. Lacking a simple assumption of linear development, we still have sufficient reason to study the development of a child's capacities to conceive and project visual form. Lowenfeld (1947) asserted that "creative expression is as differentiated as are individuals. . . . However, the child's creative expression during specific stages in his mental and emotional growth can only be understood and appreciated if the general causal interdependence between creation and growth is understood" (p. vi). Schaefer-Simmern (1948), inspired by the theories of Gustaf Britsch, presented case-study materials to support the assertion that the mind, in its striving for an orderly conception of reality, proceeds in a developmental pattern from the perceptually simple to increasingly complex patterns. Arnheim (1954) has continued this effort to analyze developmental trends. There is still, however, a need for further study of developmental factors that characterize growth in awareness and capacity to project visual and aesthetic forms. Such study would entail longitudinal research on human symbolic and expressive behavior. It would shed light on many ques-

tions regarding relationships between the development of a "language" of visual forms and thus make possible the communication of ideas and the development of aesthetic sensibilities.

Research in language formation and communication theory is directly relevant to art education. It is becoming increasingly clear that language cannot be divided into two separate spheres—conceptual and emotive. The implications of this fact for research in the teaching of the visual arts have been expressed by Werner (1955):

Many theorists have recognized the necessity of postulating a mode of apprehending language which transcends any bifurcation into cognitive and emotive—a mode of using language which involves a fusion of affective, motor and conceptual components . . . . The ubiquity of "expressive language" and its protean character imposes on those who desire to study it the acceptance of a truly interdisciplinary view, i.e., the willingness to recognize the contributions that the perspectives of other disciplines offer to one's own studies, without striving to reduce all perspectives to one's own (Werner, 1955, p. 1).

It is no longer possible to think of learning and intelligence as existing only in a verbal or mathematical syntax. Imagery and the capacity to project and realize ideas through imagery are essential in developing an awareness of oneself and one's world. Read (1955), for example, postulated that the image might well precede the idea in the development of human consciousness. If so, we must "rewrite the history of human culture" and re-examine the postulates of all our philosophies. The theory that "art is a mode of knowledge as well as a practice dependent on sensibility" suggests research into the nature of and relationships among the symbolic forms that humans use. Such research would not only delve into the nature of symbols themselves; it would also seek understanding of how and why symbols are used. As Read (1954) pointed out:

[Consciousness] arises not from the perception of space, time, size, shape, and number as discrete phenomena, but for [from?] certain significant arrangements of those phenomena which permit comparison and judgment. Those arrangements in their turn depend on the development of memory and imagination; that is to say, on the ability to store images and recall them at will. Language and conceptual thinking can only develop later, on the basis of imagination (Read, 1954, p. 147).

Hayakawa (1950) stated that the kind of language we speak largely determines the kind of thoughts we have; what is being suggested here is that how we act in relation to our symbolic world is relevant to the kind of life we live.... "no more order . . . [can] be found in the universe than we put there by ordering our observations and abstractions and generalizations into systems" (p. 5). The artist and his discipline can perform a unique educational role. "Every way of abstracting produces its own kind of truth, which, in the hands of one who orders his abstractions well, results in its own kind of beauty" (p. 5).

Many other directions are available for the study of persons in relation to artistic activity. Attention should be given to the question of artistic "talent." In many respects, the term *talent* has done great harm

to the field of art education. When seen as a simple dichotomy, talent or nontalent has become the basis for arbitrary and insensitive classifications of people. Misuse of the term has tended to place the very idea of talent in disrepute. Recently, with the surge of interest in scientific talent, questions regarding artistic talent have been raised. It is no longer sufficient to refer to talent as "gifts bestowed upon man" or a divine trust. Rather, the questions being raised concern the physical-social basis for artistic talent. Research that clarifies the role of various functional and sensory processes as they relate to artistic performances can help in developing greater awareness of teaching problems. Are there environmental factors that account for artistic talent? Are there discernible differences in sensitivity to color stimuli that would correlate with achievement in the visual arts? Is there a tactile-cutaneous sensitivity factor that would account for variance in performance?

Research has been done on questions concerning the intellectual and aesthetic traits that would account for qualitative and quantitative differences in artistic achievement. Burkhart (1958), for example, raised questions regarding the concept of intelligence as it relates to measuring creativeness. He concluded that intelligence tests currently in use are not good predictors of art ability beyond the third grade. His work suggests several different factors that would account for changes in art activity occurring between childhood and adolescence.

In general, certain assumptions seem to be emerging regarding study of artistic talent: (1) The study of talent must be approached multidimensionally; (2) a talented person possesses a high degree of sensitivity in the particular area or areas of his talent; (3) a talented person is challenged rather than frustrated by ambiguities and doubts in this area (in this sense, talent is related to a motivational function); (4) a talented person is skilled and disciplined in handling media and techniques in his field; and (5) a talented person is able to make novel adjustments to problematic situations within the field. Inevitably, asking questions about artistic talent moves the researcher to a conception of visual-tactile-aesthetic intelligence.

The use of art as a projective technique that provides some background for understanding the student has been treated in an extensive literature. For the most part, these research efforts have not confronted problems involving aesthetic considerations; what they have accomplished, however, is a greater sense of the nature of spontaneous and personal expression. Research by Bender (1938), Goodenough (1926), Machover (1952), and Naumburg (1947) provides a rich background for appreciating the basic and related aspects of visual expression as seen in drawings and paintings.

The Art Student in Process

Education in art should do more than develop technical skill or understanding. Development of such competencies is important, but it is more important that we encourage the development of the individual's creativity—his ability to discover new relations, to reformulate ideas and feelings, to devise new means and approaches to his own artistic realization. If research is to help with these problems, it must not avoid critical questions because of their complexities or because of the difficulties in arriving at research designs.

Over the years, images have developed in the professional as well as in the public mind as to what constitutes artistic process—drawing from a still life form or landscape; using a variety of materials, e.g., clay, wire, or paint. The image varies in relation to the age and experience of the person engaged in the "process"; the image also varies in relation to the intentions and skills of the "artist." Actually, the process of "making art"—that is, of creating and building artistic forms—is often an informal, illogical, and messy-looking affair. An individual's actions within the generalized notions of artistic "process" are not easy to understand rationally. A person engaged in artistic activity will often act in

ways contradictory to "accepted ideas." Successful artists provide little clarification of this phenomenon since many of the points of agreement and uniformity among them as to their processes do not seem to be critical in accounting for high-level performance. Indeed, what is impressive is the diversity of ways in which individuals go about the more creative aspects of studio work. Nevertheless, the artist should be a primary source of data as we seek greater understanding of the creative process. Ghiselin (1955) and Roe (1946) provided excellent examples of efforts to use artists as sources in this way. The difficulties in generalizing about the creative process have tended to focus attention on the more easily discerned aspects of artistic effort, such as biographical data about artists and descriptive and technical materials about works of art or situations in which art is "taught." By contrast, both Ghiselin and Roe, in very different ways, draw directly upon the more personal and unique data of artists as individual cases.

Many attempts have been made to give greater specificity to our conceptions of creative activity. These efforts have been aimed at identifying critical factors in accounting for creative behavior. In reviewing some of the research into creative behavior, it is interesting to note the similarities in concepts that have been developed, in many instances, independently. Beittel and Lowenfeld (1959) compared a listing of attributes identified in their own study with factors identified by Guilford (1950, 1954). Terms such as flexibility, closure, originality, sensitivity, and fluency were common to both of the lists. Work now underway is being directed at giving greater specificity and operational significance to such terms. For example, Guilford (1959) has sought to differentiate among terms such as associational fluency, expressional fluency, and ideational fluency. His study has been directed toward the development of a unified and enlarged theory "which organizes the known, unique or primary intellectual abilities into a single system called the 'structure of intellect' " (p. 469).

Maslow (1957, 1959) has projected what happens to cognition when it is involved in creative experience: the personality fuses into a fully functioning, idiosyncratic whole. He postulates that a person involved in creative activity experiences in a unified manner—a manner in which dichotomies, polarities, contradictions, and conflicts tend to fuse. Through such involvement, perception becomes richer and more sensitive; experience has its own intrinsic value apart from expediency and status symbols. As such, cognition acquires a special flavor of wonder, of awe, and of humility before one's creative powers.

Another major contribution toward a theoretical framework for understanding creative behavior was provided by Mooney (1953). He identified four "dimensions" for describing and accounting for creativity: (1) openness to the reception and extension of experience; (2) focusing of experience: movement toward differentiation and realization of self; (3) disciplined management and aesthetic forming; and (4) deriving significance from experience. Mooney has gone ahead to the more specific task of differentiating factors within each of the above dimensions. For example, openness to the reception and extension of experience has been further defined in terms of direct and spontaneous experiencing, openness to oneself, and openness to environment.

It is becoming increasingly clear that no single pattern will be sufficiently inclusive and specific to predict single creative acts. This limitation does not, however, lead to the abandoning of research efforts. Individual instances of creativity can be described only in relation to the conditions within which they occur: the nature of the task and the circumstances surrounding it. As we become more sensitive to the dynamics involved in individual cases, we may come closer to identifying one or more syndromes that will help teachers be more sensitive to the behaviors they observe and foster. This goal, in effect, provides a challenge to researchers to identify rationales for teaching art that would honor and encourage the vari-

ability and levels of achievement so much a part of the human creative situation.

Doubtless, study of perceptual processes will provide another resource for understanding creative thought and behavior. Basic work by researchers such as Witkin and others (1954) has led to increased awareness of perception as a key to understanding human thought and action. Ames (1950, 1955), in his study at the Hanover Institute, provided dramatic "demonstrations"—such as the rotating trapezoidal window—for showing the relevance of perceptual processes to thought and action. His findings are based on perceptions of our visual and tactile world; as such, they are relevant to research efforts in the teaching of art. Ames summarizes his findings as follows: (1) Consciousness does not have its total origin in immediate externality. "Meaning is significance which has been disclosed through prior purposeful action"; (2) "Our field of visual sensations discloses multiple possibilities for action, but only certain of these possibilities will further the organism's purpose. Therefore, it is in accordance with purpose, conscious or unconscious, that the choice is made"; (3) "Because abstractions do not include the 'point of view' or purpose of the organism, they in themselves are not identical with reality"; (4) "If it is purpose and not abstracted knowledge that underlies sensations, it is only through change in purpose that sensations and the behavior of the organism can be affected" (pp. 11–12).

Following Ames's lead, numerous other visual demonstration centers have been established. It is generally agreed that the study of vision yields insights that offer indispensable leads for the better understanding and handling of social relationships. For the art educator, there is the suggestion that heightened sensitivity to one's own actions within an artistic framework could have aesthetic implications for other areas of activity. In large part, this has become one of the key arguments for the inclusion of an art curriculum as part of general education. There are still, however, many questions regarding relationships between aesthetic sensitivity and judgment, as reflected in painting or sculpture, and aesthetic awareness, as reflected in social and personal activities. This, of course, raises the question of transfer of learning.

The Art Student and Judgments of His Efforts

There are many ways in which a student's efforts can be viewed by teachers. If the criteria refer to orderliness—whether materials are put away and whether the students go about their business with quiet efficiency—then a model of physical organization is being used in evaluation. If the criteria refer to the imagination and diversity of the works being done or to the involvement of the students with their own ideas and feelings, then a model of the creative-expressive aspects of art is being used. If criteria refer to works of art of our own and other periods and if students are made aware of the traditions of artistic expression, then a model involving a student's awareness of history and criticism is being used. Each of these models, as a basis for evaluation of a student's efforts, assumes a frame of reference within which student and teacher actions become relevant or irrelevant. Physical orderliness, creative-expressive qualities, critical-historical judgments—each is a basis on which a teacher can judge his students and their products. Obviously, such judgments vary in relation to the age, purposes, and backgrounds of the students.

Research on the teaching of art has tended to concern itself with questions regarding students and the processes in which they engage. This emphasis has resulted from needs for understanding the dynamics of expression. Activity-centered curricula have focused on the more spontaneous and expressive aspects of art activity. Critics of "progressive education," while not grasping many key ideas involved in encouraging spontaneous, creative activity, have tended to discount much of this research effort as betraying lack of understanding of art itself. Their

standard criticism is that progressive education has emphasized "process" without regard for the quality of the product involved. Such criticisms have not taken into account many other factors that moved inquiry away from problems of criticism, i.e., of making judgments about the work of art.

Among these factors have been the following: (1) Emphasis upon the highly personal and innovative aspects of present-day art and criticism has created difficulties in making judgments about the work of art. (2) There has been a decided shift in art history and its emphasis as a discipline. Whereas earlier historians conceived of their role as being closer to that of archaeologists, educators have sought a much closer and more direct tie to contemporary life. Present-day historians are, to a much greater extent, involved in contemporary criticism, connoisseurship, and iconography. Most historians no longer conceive of their discipline as that of learning long lists of names or dates or memorizing images based upon inadequate color reproductions. (It should be added that this was never substantially held to be the discipline of art history.) (3) Art education has itself undergone dramatic changes in relation to the changes in our art world. It is important to realize that there is a growing interdependence between art education and the capacity to make critical judgments about art. Thus, the trend toward separating the pedagogy of art theory from educational theory is now being reversed. Whereas the arts were once associated with limited groups and their activities, we have now an enlarged view of the educational potential of the visual arts. This view can be realized if inquiry and action in the field can draw upon the disciplines of aesthetics, art criticism, and art history. These disciplines, when related to insights derived from the behavioral sciences, will form a basis for viewing the student's efforts. If this basis can be achieved, the problem will not be one of studying process *or* product; rather it will be one of understanding the process of creating products judged to be aesthetically sound.

Munro (1956, 1958) has contributed toward the resolution of ambiguities concerning aesthetic judgments. He has not sought to establish rules of what people "ought to like" or to measure or dissect works of art in a pseudoscientific manner. His aim is that of "descriptive inquiry which seeks to find out and state the facts about works of art as a kind of observable human phenomena, in relation to other phenomena of human experience, behavior, and culture" (p. 11). Munro does not seek a substitute for subjective feelings; rather, he proposes a method which would incorporate and value those differences that exist in making aesthetic judgments. This point of view is supported by Sourian (1955). He pointed out that it is extremely difficult to substitute objective methods of appreciation for precious personal sensibility. He urged that we work through our sensibility instead of bypassing it, and make subjectivity the very object of study. The methodological procedure which developed should grow from the very object of study. Gotshalk (1959) has emphasized the need for aesthetics to achieve (in its own distinctive way) the status of science. Art educators, especially those engaged in study in the field, would do well to keep informed of efforts in this direction.

Along with an awareness of research in aesthetics, researchers in the teaching of art need to follow closely developments in the history and criticism of art. In doing so, they should distinguish between an ephemeral event, which disappears, and the affirmation about the event, which persists. In the case of the visual arts, the works are literally and bodily present for our contemplation. Ackerman (1960) states:

. . . there is no art of the past in the sense of the word as employed by the political historian, except what has been destroyed. Since what we call the art of the past really exists in the present, the chronological sequence of its production is irrelevant to its potential for communicating quality or for influencing the present and future (Ackerman, 1960, pp. 257–258).

Thus, inquiry that relates to artistic and aesthetic values can draw on the ever-present vastness of human visual formulations.

Persons doing research need a sense of history and tradition as well as a sense of the "present" of their field. Such a sense provides an enriched background for orienting inquiry to a larger context than the merely personal. The subject matter of history is human life; accordingly, the personal equation cannot be eliminated. Contrary to popular impressions, art history is not a collection of slides, reproductions, facts, and dates; these data do not "speak for themselves." The discipline of history requires engagement in the symbolic re-creating and re-enacting of the context in which the artifacts were produced. Connoisseurship and iconography have become intertwined with history to broaden and give greater depth to the discipline.

When all is said and done, it is the historian "who speaks"; he must exercise taste and judgment. In so doing, he engages in an empathic process of a synthetic and subjective character. In its richest and broadest meaning, historical training can be inculcated in researchers through visual training in viewing works of art with the spatial and temporal distance so necessary for contemplation and understanding. All of the disciplines —history, iconography, and connoisseurship —are intimately related; each provides dynamic points of reference where the dimensions vacillate, enabling the research worker to maintain aesthetic and historical distance along with the immediacy of personal involvement.

The Teaching Environment and the Teacher-Student Dynamic

Armed with a conception of artistic process and the qualitative dimensions for judging aesthetic products, one can turn to questions more closely related to the teaching process itself. Some of these questions might be stated generally: What leadership role should an art teacher play in relation to his students? What conditions are more likely to encourage creative activity? Recognition of the seemingly paradoxical aspects of accounting for creative behavior gives rise to further thought about the expectations of researchers investigating teaching processes. More than teachers in most areas of instruction, the teacher of art seeks to encourage the unique and the personal. By definition, the creative artist transcends the meaning and form of his world. Instruction in art, at whatever level it is carried on, must encourage efforts in this direction. There is, nevertheless, a tradition of art. More specifically, there are tools and materials that have become integral to the art forms themselves. Learning to use these tools and materials is a function of art instruction. There are also bases upon which judgments have been made regarding works of art. Learning to recognize such bases for judgment is another function of art instruction. Thus, the essential paradox is that of teaching within a tradition that requires expanding beyond that tradition. To the extent that teaching is an art, its paradoxical elements become resolved and composed; its logically or analytically contrasted parts are woven together in the personal and unique style of the teacher. Simple cause-and-effect relationships cannot be reconciled with the complexities and dynamics of an infinity of teaching situations.

As we view aspects of artistic process, we sense the creative act as a resolution of points at seeming polarities. During the course of such resolution, a person must embrace the seeming paradox of being involved in artistic expression and yet having sufficient aesthetic distance to make judgments of his own involvement. If this be the case, research into the teaching process needs to take into account the dynamic "tensions" that are so much a part of the process being studied. Montgomery (1959), in his report on situational factors affecting creative group work, organized his data along four continua: permitting—preventing; inviting—repelling; focusing—diffusing; and supporting—depressing. It is not that one can simply state a teacher's function as permitting *or* prevent-

ing. The function of Montgomery's research was to provide greater insight into the factors relevant to how the teacher may resolve the tensions implicit in his role. For example, Montgomery referred to "time as an element in work" and established polarities in a teacher's possible valuing of factors within the "time dimension": "There is no time pressure (external to individual) to close play, set goals, and work out"; "timing left to chance" is contrasted with "time limits are prescribed as negative boundaries" (p. 49). Another example is that of "tolerance of waste, risk" as a situational factor in which "the group can afford unlimited error, waste, or failure" as contrasted to "the group can afford no error, waste, or failure" (p. 49). Montgomery then checked the internal consistency of the behavior at varied points in group activity. He found great variety of specific strengths and weaknesses in individual work and variations toward extremes of diffusion and rigidity in certain situational factors. This suggests the extreme complexity in trying to construct theoretical models of creative behavior. In a somewhat similar fashion, Barkan and Hausman (1956) reported on their identification of a concept-bound versus percept-bound continuum. This work was part of a pilot investigation aimed at clarifying hypotheses for research into creative behavior. Factors such as the perception of self and task (private-official task), the degree and direction of involvement, and the decision-making pattern were related to a concept-percept model. Hypotheses formulated in this pilot investigation are still under investigation.

Numerous other critical questions related to the teaching of art require further study. One group of issues concerns the teacher and his impact on the student. Another revolves around the teacher's role in encouraging artistic process. A third grouping stems from questions about the art teacher's relationship to the products produced in his class.

The art teacher seeks the emergence of aesthetic forms that are symbolic of his student's ideas and feelings. In doing so, he must be sensitive to his own role in relation to the roles he asks his students to play. The tasks and values that he sets forth should enable his students to project themselves into the situation while maintaining their psychological safety and freedom. Such safety and freedom (within the context of the artistic act) are necessary if a person is to venture forth with expression of personal ideas and feelings in new form. This is especially so if such expressions are contrary to the prevailing standards. Rogers (1953) speculated that through maximizing conditions of psychological safety and freedom, we maximize the likelihood of an emergence of constructive creativity. He suggests that psychological safety may be established by three associated conditions (pp. 79–80): (1) "accepting the individual as of unconditional worth"; (2) "providing a climate in which external evaluation is absent"; (3) "understanding empathically." He then goes on to define the conditions for psychological freedom:

When a teacher, parent, therapist, or other facilitating person permits the individual a complete freedom of symbolic expression, creativity is fostered. This permissiveness gives the individual complete freedom to think, to feel, to be whatever is most inward within himself. It fosters the openness, and the playful and spontaneous juggling of percepts, concepts, and meanings, which is a part of creativity (Rogers, 1953, p. 80).

Research efforts should be directed toward clarifying the dynamics of the relationship between a student, his teacher, and the teaching environment. A teacher creates a "structure" of expectations; these can be referred to as the "official task." Students approach their artistic activities with their own perceptions, values, and expectations. These give rise to a definition of his "private task." Much more also needs to be known about relationships between a person's self-image and his expectations as to intrinsic and extrinsic rewards. Tumin (1953, p. 65) proposed three helpful categories for distinguishing loci of human satisfaction: (1) "the

extrinsic rewards received for performance"; (2) "the social relations with others while in the performance"; and (3) "the very actions which constitute the performance." While artistic activity holds great intrinsic value (indeed, the artist need only be concerned with the creation of the artifact), there are still the critical questions to be posed by the art educator concerning the nature of extrinsic rewards for intrinsically satisfying experiences. Along with further study of personal value systems operating while one is engaged in artistic activity, research should be directed at the phenomenon of self-identification as it impinges upon effectiveness in aesthetic action. Empathic involvement, as related to a student's conception and potential for action, should be studied. How do factors such as intensity, range, and direction of ideas relate to performance? To what extent can there be an internal locus for evaluation? These critical questions should be pursued to provide greater insights into the teaching of art.

Artistic media vary in terms of their resistancy and resiliency as well as their potential for use. Crayons and paint, for example, require little training before their "use" as media; by contrast, metal-forming or weaving requires backgrounds of knowledge as well as some equipment if the artist is to achieve some aesthetic satisfaction with them. The selection of media in teaching situations poses many questions. The observation that media provide opportunities for choice leads to complex questions that impinge on teaching theory. Insights into these matters are important in answering questions regarding the selection of media for children or adults at various levels of maturity, as well as questions about teaching emphasis in relation to the kind of medium being used. Certain media, for example, require a more sustained effort; others will not permit earlier decisions to be altered; still others require a greater physical investment (time, money, energy). Each of these considerations should be seen clearly as a teacher encourages the use of varied media in a classroom.

Questions of media and process soon become intertwined in any serious study of art education theory. Numerous "unanswered" questions arise regarding the concept of "transfer" as it would apply to teaching in art. Many teachers assume some transfer of learning from one medium to another. Many aspects of these "assumptions" need further study. For example, we need research into the relationships between two- and three-dimensional expression.

Another area needing study is the capacity to tolerate ambiguity as one works with artistic media. Artists often refer to the ability to "sustain" a work, to discard the immediate possibility of completing a work in order to seek greater refinement and depth (without "overworking" one's effort). This suggests a relationship between resistance and value. This capacity involves "exploring" a range of ideas as well as depth and sensitivity in seeking aesthetic "solutions." Capacity to sustain a work gives rise to greater adventure and risk; it should not be confused with the routine aspects of "polishing" something or working on an object after all essential "decisions" have been made. It is much closer to Rogers' (1953, p. 77) description, "the ability to receive much conflicting information without forcing closure upon the situation." Research efforts should seek understanding of the dynamic relationship between the need for closure and the capacity for deferring final judgments while other solutions are possible.

The teacher evaluating artistic efforts needs to be sensitive to multiple cues. Unlike the art critic, he does not judge the artifact alone. Teachers need to be aware of factors that contribute to the personal-poetic aspects of a student's work. In this sense, artistic intent becomes relevant to the judgment being made. Numerous criteria are suggested for such judgment: ideational fluency, intensity of identification, sensitivity to ideas, selection and use of the medium, willingness to express oneself, skill in handling materials, capacity to derive significance from one's actions.

Along with judgments of "behavior" there can be judgments of range, diversity, and sensitivity in the formal aspects of the work completed: its texture, line, form, and color. These provide a formal basis for describing the relating of ideas, materials, and visual form.

DISCIPLINED RESEARCH ON THE TEACHING OF ART

Most previous research in art education consists of descriptive and status studies. These would include the many studies of stated objectives in the teaching of art; of certification requirements in the various states; of current practice in the use of materials, equipment, space, etc.; of cost per pupil; and of teacher supply. It is important that we continue to make such studies. Indeed, such data are urgently needed to serve as a background for the development of new art programs. But this chapter has focused on more complex research areas confronting art educators. Our effectiveness in these areas will be crucial to the development of theory in the field.

Researchers undertaking studies in the dynamics of a teaching situation cannot do so with the so-called "distance" of objectivity. Studying communicative or symbolic intentions in relation to an aesthetic standard or studying the inner dynamics of a person as he makes aesthetic choices requires that the researcher "accept himself" as a participant in his inquiry. In so doing, he must recognize that his value judgments are functions of his concepts rather than the objects themselves. Every effort should be made to "anchor" concepts directly or by mathematical techniques in concrete operations. The "truth," however, will always be in the "middle" between a continuous searching for clarity and the intuited feelings so much a part of art.

Mooney (1951, 1953) has offered the following suggestions to the research worker: (1) "He accepts himself as creator of his inquiry"; (2) "He develops the relevance of his project to his past (and present) experience, seeking to integrate the current undertaking into the full stream of his life"; (3) "He honors his feelings as they enter into the unfolding of his work, seeking to bring them as fully into the open as he can"; (4) "He accepts his values as the major selectors of what he does"; (5) "He carefully clarifies his purpose, which is to guide him through his work, realizing that his purpose will be under continual expansion and modification as he works his way through"; (6) "He continually searches for his implicit assumptions and tries to make them explicit"; (7) "He carefully forms his hypotheses"; (8) "He clarifies the role he is taking in the total enterprise"; (9) "He specifies the points from which he expects to observe the field out there"; (10) "He makes predictions as to what he will find in the field from particular points of view"; (11) "He clarifies what he is focusing in the field out there"; (12) "He takes the field out there as 'given' "; and (13) "He reports his research in the first person" (Mooney, 1953, pp. 124–128).

From such a basis, we can learn to use ourselves as our intellectual resource: continually examining, interpreting, and reporting our inquiry and action. Through such a procedure, the self-contained aspects of our personal-professional concerns can become part of a larger professional complex where the truths we feel can be used to achieve greater clarity and insight.

REFERENCES[1]

Ackerman, J. S. Art history and the problems of criticism. *Daedalus,* 1960, 89, 253–263.

Ames, A. Sensations, their nature and origin. *Transformation,* 1950, 1, 11–12.

Ames, A. *An interpretative manual for the demonstrations in the Psychology Research Center.* Princeton, N.J.: Princeton Univer. Press, 1955.

Anderson, H. H. Creativity as personality de-

velopment. In H. H. Anderson (Ed.), *Creativity and its cultivation.* New York: Harper, 1959. Pp. 119–141.

Arnheim, R. *Art and visual perception—A psychology of the creative eye.* Berkeley: Univer. of California Press, 1954.

Arnold, J. E. *Creative seminar notes.* Cambridge, Mass.: Creative Engineering Lab., Massachusetts Institute of Technology, 1954.

Barkan, M. *A foundation for art education.* New York: Ronald Press, 1955.

Barkan, M., & Hausman, J. Two pilot studies with the purpose of clarifying hypotheses for research into creative behavior. In M. Barkan (Ed.), Research in art education. *Yearb. nat. Art Educ. Ass.,* 1956, 7, 126–141.

Barkan, M., & Mooney, R. L. (Eds.) *The Conference on Creativity: A report to the Rockefeller Foundation.* Columbus: Ohio State Univer., 1953.

Barron, F. The disposition toward originality. *J. abnorm. soc. Psychol.,* 1955, 51, 478–485.

Barron, F., & Welsh, G. S. Artistic perception as a possible factor in personality style: Its measurement by a figure preference test. *J. Psychol.,* 1952, 33, 199–203.

Beittel, K. R. Growth in appreciation. *Res. Bull., Eastern Arts Ass.,* 1953, 4, 10–15.

Beittel, K. R. Experimental studies of the aesthetic attitudes of college students. In M. Barkan (Ed.), Research in art education. *Yearb. nat. Art Educ. Ass.,* 1956, 7, 47–61.

Beittel, K. R. Some viewpoints on research. *Art Educ.,* 1957, 10, 6–7, 12–15.

Beittel, K. R. The creativity complex in the visual arts. *Stud. art Educ., Nat. Art Educ. Ass.,* 1959, 1, 26–37.

Beittel, K., & Lowenfeld, V. Interdisciplinary criteria of creativity in the arts and sciences: A progress report. In J. J. Hausman (Ed.), Research in art education. *Yearb. nat. Art Educ. Ass.,* 1959, 9, 35–44.

Bender, Lauretta A. A visual motor Gestalt test and its clinical use. *Res. Monogr., Amer. Orthopsychiat. Ass.,* 1938, No. 3.

Bostetter, E. E. The eagle and the truth: Yeats and the problem of belief. *J. Aesthet. art Crit.,* 1958, 16, 362–372.

Brittain, W. L. Can creativity be measured? *Res. Bull., Eastern Arts Ass.,* 1954, 5, 12–14.

Brittain, W. L. An experiment toward measuring creativity. In M. Barkan (Ed.), Research in art education. *Yearb. nat. Art Educ. Ass.,* 1956, 7, 39–46.

---

[1] While many of the references indicated in this listing are not cited in the chapter, it is the author's intention that they serve as a bibliography for research on teaching the visual arts.

Brunswik, E. The conceptual framework of psychology. *International encyclopedia of unified science,* Vol. 1, Part II. Chicago: Univer. of Chicago Press, 1955. Pp. 655–760.

Burkhart, R. C. An analysis of individuality of art expression at the senior high school level. Unpublished doctoral dissertation, Pennsylvania State Univer., 1957.

Burkhart, R. The relation of intelligence to art ability. *J. Aesthet. art Crit.,* 1958, 17, 230–241.

Burns, R. Some correlations of design with personality. In J. J. Hausman (Ed.), Research in art education. *Yearb. nat. Art Educ. Ass.,* 1959, 9, 125–130.

Carter, B. Artistic development and auditory sensitivity: An initial study. *Art Educ. Bull., Eastern Arts Ass.,* 1957, 14, 28–29.

Committee for the Study of the Visual Arts at the Massachusetts Institute of Technology. *Art education for scientist and engineer.* Cambridge, Mass.: Massachusetts Institute of Technology, 1957.

Committee on the Visual Arts, Harvard Univer. *Report of the* . . . . Cambridge, Mass.: Harvard Univer., 1956.

Corcoran, A. L. Children's responses to color stimuli. In M. Barkan (Ed.), Research in art education. *Yearb. nat. Art Educ. Ass.,* 1956, 7, 84–95.

Countryman, C. A test on the visualization of tactile sensations. Unpublished doctoral dissertation, Pennsylvania State Univer., 1955.

Dyson, F. J. Innovation in physics. *Scient. American,* 1958, 199, 74–82.

Edmonston, P. A pilot study involving the use of visual, literary, and dramatic materials in a core program. In J. J. Hausman (Ed.), Research in art education. *Yearb. nat. Art Educ. Ass.,* 1959, 9, 83–89.

Frank, L. K. Tactile communication. *Genet. Psychol. Monogr.,* 1957, 56, 209–255.

Gallie, W. B. Art as an essentially contested concept. *Phil. Quart.,* 1956, 6, 97–114.

Ghiselin, B. (Ed.) *The creative process.* New York: Mentor Books, 1955.

Gilson, É. *Painting and reality.* New York: Meridian Books, 1959.

Goodenough, Florence L. *Measurement of intelligence by drawings.* New York: World Book Co., 1926.

Gotshalk, D. W. The next step for aesthetics. *J. Aesthet. art Crit.,* 1959, 18, 46–54.

Granger, G. W. An experimental study of colour harmony. *J. gen. Psychol.,* 1955, 52, 21–35.

Granger, G. W. An experimental study of colour preference. *J. gen. Psychol.,* 1955, 52, 3–20.

Guilford, J. P. Creativity. *Amer. Psychologist,* 1950, 5, 444–454.

Guilford, J. P. The nature of creative thinking. *Res. Bull., Eastern Arts Ass.,* 1954, 5, 5–9.

Guilford, J. P. The structure of intellect. *Psychol. Bull.,* 1956, 53, 267–293.

Guilford, J. P. Three faces of intellect. *Amer. Psychologist,* 1959, 14, 469–479.

Guilford, J. P. Traits of creativity. In H. H. Anderson (Ed.), *Creativity and its cultivation.* New York: Harper, 1959. Pp. 142–161.

Guilford, J. P., & Smith, Patricia C. A system of color preferences. *Amer. J. Psychol.,* 1959, 72, 487–502.

Hausman, J. J. A review of research in the graphic and plastic arts. *Rev. educ. Res.,* 1958, 28, 169–179.

Hausman, J. J. Toward a discipline of research in art education. *J. Aesthet. art crit.,* 1959, 17, 354–361.

Hayakawa, S. I. Modern art and the 20th century man. *Transformation,* 1950, 1, 2–5.

Herberholz, D. W. An experimental study to determine the effect of modeling on the drawing of the human figure by second grade children. *Art Educ. Bull., Eastern Arts Ass.,* 1957, 14, 30–32.

Institute on Contemporary Art. *Conference on creativity as a process.* Boston: The Institute, 1956.

Kahler, E. What is art? In M. Weitz (Ed.), *Problems in aesthetics.* New York: Macmillan, 1959. Pp. 157–171.

Kieselbach, A. G. An experimental study in the development of an instrument to measure aesthetic perception. In M. Barkan (Ed.), Research in art education. *Yearb. nat. Art Educ. Ass.,* 1956, 7, 62–73.

Korzybski, A. *Manhood of humanity: The science and art of human engineering.* New York: Dutton, 1921.

Langer, Susanne K. *Philosophy in a new key.* New York: Mentor Books, 1948.

Langer, Susanne K. *Feeling and form.* New York: Scribner's, 1953.

Lifton, W. M. The implications of a study on empathy and aesthetic sensitivity for art education. In J. J. Hausman (Ed.), Research in art education. *Yearb. nat. Art Educ. Ass.,* 1959, 9, 52–57.

Logan, F. M. *Growth of art in American schools.* New York: Harper, 1955.

Longman, L. D. Criteria in criticism of contemporary art. *J. Aesthet. art Crit.,* 1960, 18, 285–293.

Lowenfeld, V. *Creative and mental growth.* (3rd ed.) New York: Macmillan, 1947.

Machover, Karen. Drawings of the human figure: A method of personality investigation. In H. H. Anderson & G. Anderson (Eds.), *An introduction to projective techniques.* New York: Prentice-Hall, 1952.

Maslow, A. H. Two kinds of cognition and their integration. *Gen. semantics Bull.,* 1957, 20, 21.

Maslow, A. H. (Ed.) *New knowledge in human values.* New York: Harper, 1959.

Maslow, A. H., & Mintz, N. L. Effects of esthetic surroundings: 1. Initial effects of three esthetic conditions upon perceiving "energy" and "well-being" in faces. *J. Psychol.,* 1956, 41, 247–254.

McFee, June K. A study of "perception-delineation": Its implications for art education. In J. J. Hausman (Ed.), Research in art education. *Yearb. nat. Art Educ. Ass.,* 1959, 9, 9–14.

Meer, B., & Stein, M. I. Measures of intelligence and creativity. *J. Psychol.,* 1955, 38, 117–126.

Michael, J. The effect of award, adult standard, and peer standard upon the creativeness in art of high school pupils. In J. J. Hausman (Ed.), Research in art education. *Yearb. nat. Art Educ. Ass.,* 1959, 9, 98–104.

Mills, C. W. *The sociological imagination.* New York: Oxford Univer. Press, 1959.

Mitchell, Coretta W. A study of relationships between attitudes about art experience and behavior in art activity. In J. J. Hausman (Ed.), Research in art education. *Yearb. nat. Art Educ. Ass.,* 1959, 9, 105–111.

Montgomery, C. Creative work within a group: Its situational factors. In J. J. Hausman (Ed.), Research in art education. *Yearb. nat. Art Educ. Ass.,* 1959, 9, 45–51.

Mooney, R. L. Problems in the development of research men. *Educ. res. Bull.,* 1951, 30, 141–150.

Mooney, R. L. Implications for the research worker. In M. Barkan & R. L. Mooney (Eds.), *The Conference on Creativity: A report to the Rockefeller Foundation.* Colum-

bus: Ohio State Univer., 1953. Pp. 124–128.

Morris, C. W. Comments on mysticism and its language. In S. I. Hayakawa (Ed.), *Language, meaning, and maturity.* New York: Harper, 1954. Pp. 295–302.

Morris, C. W. *Signs, language and behavior.* New York: Prentice-Hall, 1946.

Munro, T. *Toward science in aesthetics: Selected essays.* New York: Liberal Arts Press, 1956.

Munro, T. The criticism of criticism: An outline for analysis applicable to criticism of any art form. *Coll. art J.,* 1958, 17, 197–198.

Naumburg, Margaret. *Studies of the "free" art expression of behavior problem children and adolescents as a means of diagnosis and therapy.* New York: Coolidge Foundation, 1947.

Osborn, A. F. *Applied imagination: Principles and procedures of creative thinking.* (Rev. ed.) New York: Scribner's, 1957.

Parkinson, T. Intimate and impersonal: An aspect of modern poetics. *J. Aesthet. art Crit.,* 1958, 16, 373–383.

Popper, K. R. *The logic of scientific discovery.* New York: Basic Books, 1959.

Rapaport, D. (Ed.) *Organization and pathology of thought.* New York: Columbia Univer. Press, 1951.

Read, H. E. Art and the evolution of consciousness. *J. Aesthet. art Crit.,* 1954, 13, 143–155.

Read, H. E. *Icon and idea.* Cambridge, Mass.: Harvard Univer. Press, 1955.

Roe, Anne. The personality of artists. *Educ. psychol. Measmt,* 1946, 6, 401–408.

Rogers, C. Toward a theory of creativity. In M. Barkan & R. L. Mooney (Eds.), *The Conference on Creativity: A report to the Rockefeller Foundation.* Columbus: Ohio State Univer., 1953. Pp. 73–82.

Schaefer-Simmern, H. *The unfolding of artistic activity.* Berkeley: Univer. of California Press, 1948.

Shahn, B. *The shape of content.* Cambridge, Mass.: Harvard Univer. Press, 1957.

Sourian, É. A general methodology for the scientific study of aesthetic appreciation. *J. Aesthet. art Crit.,* 1955, 14, 1–18.

Stein, M. I. Creativity and culture. *J. Psychol.,* 1953, 36, 311–322.

Tauber, E. S., & Green, M. R. *Prelogical experience: An inquiry into dreams and other creative processes.* New York: Basic Books, 1959.

Taylor, C. W. *Research conference on the*

identification of creative scientific talent. Salt Lake City: Univer. of Utah Press, 1956 and 1958.

Torrance, E. P. *Effects of induced evaluative sets on the development of new ideas.* Minneapolis: Bur. of Educ. Res., Univer. of Minnesota, 1959.

Tumin, M. Creativity and society. In M. Barkan & R. L. Mooney (Eds.), *The Conference on Creativity: A report to the Rockefeller Foundation.* Columbus: Ohio State Univer., 1953. Pp. 65–72.

Weitz, M. The role of theory in aesthetics. *J. Aesthet. art Crit.,* 1956, 15, 27–35.

Weitz, M. (Ed.) *Problems in aesthetics.* New York: Macmillan, 1959.

Werner, H. (Ed.) *An expressive language.* Worcester, Mass.: Clark Univer. Press, 1955.

Werner, H., & Kaplan, Edith. The acquisition of word meanings: A developmental study. *Monogr. Soc. Res. Child Develpm.,* 1950, 15, No. 51.

Whorf, B. L. *Language, thought, and reality.* Cambridge, Mass.: Technology Press of Massachusetts Institute of Technology, 1956.

Witkin, H. A., et al. *Personality through perception.* New York: Harper, 1954.

CHAPTER 23 Research on Teaching at the College and University Level[1]

W. J. McKEACHIE
University of Michigan

The ultimate criteria of effective college teaching are changes in students toward the goals of higher education. Research on college teaching begins with consideration of institutional objectives and course goals. While it is not appropriate to discuss the goals of higher education here, it is important to note that they include attitudinal and emotional changes as well as more obvious cognitive goals such as critical thinking and broad knowledge. In evaluating the effectiveness of college instruction we need to consider not only the accumulation of knowledge but the development of problem-solving skills and desirable attitudes.

Because different professors weight different types of goals differently, some see the professor primarily as an information-giver, others as a group leader, and others as a nondirective psychotherapist. Each endeavors to fulfill the particular role he sees as most important in effecting his students' education.

But teachers seldom ask themselves "What do I contribute to the educational process?" They make assignments, lead discussions, reflect student comments, give and correct tests—all in the faith that these activities contribute to education. Is their faith justified? Is each activity important and worth while? Does it matter which methods they use?

This chapter reviews the evidence bearing on these questions. General principles of learning are relevant to our use of teaching methods, but there is little empirical evidence to guide one's choice of method.

LEARNING PRINCIPLES RELEVANT TO TEACHING METHODS[2]

Let us first review briefly some principles of learning believed to be important in effect-

[1] The author gratefully acknowledges the able assistance of Mrs. Virginia Lickey in compiling the bibliography upon which this chapter is based. Portions of the literature survey were carried out in connection with projects supported by the Lilly Endowment, the Fund for the Advancement of Education, and the U. S. Office of Education. Major portions of this chapter are also contained in the author's book, *Teaching Tips* (4th ed.; Ann Arbor, Mich.: Wahr Publishing Company, 1960), and in the author's chapter in Nevitt Sanford (Ed.), *The American College* (New York: Wiley, 1962).

[2] Portions of this section are based upon W. J. McKeachie, *How do students learn?* in R. Cooper (Ed.), *The Two Ends of the Log* (Minneapolis: Univer. of Minnesota Press, 1958), pp. 26–39.

ing the student's achievement of the objectives of education. What principles apply to how a student acquires a knowledge and understanding of chemistry? An appreciation of music? We shall consider motivation, organization, variability, verbalization, feedback, contiguity, and active learning.

Motivation

We know that student learning and memory are closely tied to *motivation*. Students usually learn what they want to learn, but they often have great difficulty learning material which does not interest them. Most of us have to recognize that not all students are deeply interested in everything we want to teach them.

One primary problem, then, is motivating students. Usually the learning psychologist stops with this point, but to be useful the principle of motivation needs to be accompanied by information about dependable motives of college students. Most students are taught by their parents to want to do well in school and hence have some motivation for school achievement.

Also, most students want to be liked. This motive may work against teachers as well as for them. The teacher's friendly approval can be an important reward for learning, but the "average-raiser" is not always well liked. Some students who seek acceptance by their classmates may avoid any conspicuous display of academic achievement. Many students suffer conflict between the need to get good grades and the need to be well liked. One symptom of the conflict is the ostentatious neglect of study by some bright students and their apparent surprise when they get good grades—a "ploy" carefully analyzed in Potter's *One-upmanship* (1955).

Many students have other conflicting motives. Conflict between desire for independence and dependence occurs often; students are likely to resent a teacher who directs their activities too closely, but they also are likely to be anxious when given too much independence. The teacher then has the problem of simultaneously satisfying both needs. As a result of this conflict, some students disagree with the teacher, not on any rational grounds but simply as a way of expressing emotions. Similarly, student apathy in a required course may be an irrational expression of resentment at being required to do anything.

Any thoughtful college teacher could list many other common student needs. The point is simply that these needs provide the tools by which teachers get learning to take place. As far as learning or retention is concerned, it matters little which motives are involved—the important thing is that motivation exists and that conflicts do not become activated.

Let us then consider the case of our most important motivational device—grades. Whatever a student's motivation for being in college, grades are important to him. If he is genuinely interested in learning, grades represent an expert's appraisal of his success; if he is interested in getting into professional school, good grades will unlock graduate school doors; if he wants to play football, grades are necessary to maintain eligibility. Most students are motivated to get passing grades, and thus grades are a powerful motivational tool for teachers.

Most college teachers are a little embarrassed by this. They regard grades as one of the necessary evils of teaching. They try to discount grades in discussing the organization of the course; they try to arrive at grades in such a way as to avoid trouble with disappointed students. But they also frequently fail to use grades to bring about the sort of learning they desire.

Because grades are important to them, students will learn whatever is necessary to get the grades they want. If teachers base their grades on memorization of details, students will memorize the text. If students believe grades are based upon their ability to integrate and apply principles, they will try to acquire such ability.

As far as speed of learning goes, it does not matter what motives are aroused. Yet this does not mean that the type of motivation used may not affect other aspects of learning. For example, a good deal of evidence has accumulated to suggest that negative and positive motives affect behavior differently. When negative motives predominate, students will work hard, but only if this is the only way to avoid undesirable consequences. If there are ways out of the situation, students will take them. The result frequently is that students do as little work as they can get away with and cannot develop a beneficial interest in the subject.

The closer the goal or threatened danger, the higher motivation is. But negative motives are not as effective outside the learning situation as are positive motives because the effectiveness of fear depends more upon the closeness of the goal than does the effectiveness of positive motives. Thus the teacher who motivates his students by fear of bad grades or of reprimands must use frequent tests if his threats are to be taken seriously by his students.

The striking difference between the behavior of a student motivated by fear and one motivated by hope is illustrated in their behavior during examinations. Atkinson and Litwin (1960) showed that male students who were high in anxiety about tests, as measured by the Mandler-Sarason Test Anxiety Questionnaire and the TAT, were among the first to complete the course examination and tended to do poorer work on the examination than they did during the course. Students with positive motivation to succeed tended to stay in the examination room longer. The fearful students tended to avoid the situation which aroused their anxiety.

Thus, motivation is important in learning. We can use student motivation for success and approval to produce learning, and grades can be important incentives for both negative and positive motivations. Thus it is important to make sure that grades are not separate from the kind of learning we want to occur. Using grades chiefly as a threat may produce avoidance rather than interest.

Organization

A teacher's job is not done when he arouses the interest of his class, for the amount students learn depends in part upon the amount he teaches. But this relationship is not so simple as it may at first appear. It may well be that the *more* we teach, the *less* our students learn.

In *The Great Didactic,* Comenius writes:

If we take a jar with a narrow mouth (for to this we may compare a boy's intellect) and attempt to pour a quantity of water into it violently, instead of allowing it to trickle in drop by drop, what will be the result? Without doubt the greater part of the liquid will flow over the side, and ultimately the jar will contain less than if the operation had taken place gradually. Quite as foolish is the action of those who try to teach their pupils, not as much as they can assimilate, but as much as they themselves wish . . . (Comenius, trans. by M. W. Keatinge, 1931, pp. 87–88).

Some years ago, several teaching fellows were arguing about how to teach about the nervous system. One group argued that since students do not remember many details, teachers might better omit them and teach only the essentials which they wanted everyone to learn. Another group argued that students forget much of what they learn. "But," they said, "if they're going to forget a large percentage, we need to teach much more than we expect them to remember. Otherwise they'll forget even the important things."

Since such an argument invited an experiment, both groups agreed to try out their ideas in their own classes and compare the results on the final examination questions covering the nervous system. The outcome was clear: students whose instructor had omitted details were clearly superior to those whose instructor had given them the whole story. This result would not have surprised Katz (1950), the German-Swedish psychologist who devised a number of experiments demonstrating that beyond a certain point adding to the elements in an intellectual task causes confusion and inefficiency. Katz called this phenomenon "mental dazzle."

Fortunately, it is possible to teach more and have it remembered better. The key factor is "Organization." As Katona (1940) demonstrated, in a series of experiments on organization and memory, we can learn and remember much more when our learning fits into an organization. If one heard a series of numbers chosen at random, like 738105477, and was asked later what the fourth number was, he would probably have difficulty remembering it. But given the numbers 248163264, along with the principle of the series, he could remember immediately what the fourth number was. Teaching which helps students find a framework within which to fit new facts is likely to be much more effective than teaching which simply communicates masses of material in which the student can see no organization. The successful teacher is one who enables students to see meaningful problems. The ideal class would begin with a problem so meaningful that the students would always be just a step ahead of the teacher in approaching a solution.

Thus *motivation* and *organization* are two key concepts which should guide efforts to help students acquire knowledge.

Variability and Verbalization

Another group of objectives stems from the traditional intellectual objectives of education. How can we help students develop principles and concepts which they can apply to a wide range of problems? Many teachers have been disheartened by having a student answer a routine problem perfectly and then fail to use the same knowledge in solving a new problem to which it is also relevant.

A number of attempts to improve this kind of learning have been made. The theory of "learning by doing" held that if one learned something in the situation where the learning was to be used, he would not have the added step of learning when to apply it. At first glance, this seems perfectly

reasonable, and it even makes sense psychologically. The only problem is that the number of situations in which one must use knowledge is infinite. Our whole civilization is based on the fact that man can use words to short-cut the long process of learning by trial and error. Direct experience may be useful at certain stages of learning. If we are to learn to apply a principle in new situations, we need to develop it from experiencing specific instances of the principle in *varying* contexts. A number of experiments have demonstrated that repetitive drill is much less effective than varying problems in developing principles which can be applied to new situations (e.g., Wolfle, 1935).

Verbalization can help the student identify the common elements in these situations and shorten the learning process. In fact, research suggests that even such a complex skill as flying an airplane can be learned in shorter air time if the learner practices the skill mentally and verbally (Flexman, Matheny, & Brown, 1950). While verbalizing principles is undoubtedly better than unresolved confusion, Kersh (1958) suggested that allowing students to discover principles for themselves may enhance motivation.

Feedback, Contiguity, and Active Learning

If students are to learn skills, they have to practice the skills, but practice alone does not make perfect. Practice works only if the learner *sees the results* of his practice, i.e., if he receives feedback (Woodworth & Schlosberg, 1954).

Feedback is most effective when it is contiguous to the response being learned. A major feature of teaching machines is that the learner finds out quickly whether his response is right or wrong.

A number of experiments have demonstrated that *active* learning is more efficient than passive learning (McGeoch & Irion, 1952). One reason for this may be that active learning provides improved opportunities for feedback. Discussion techniques may help develop critical thinking because students do the thinking and can check their thinking against that of others. But one danger of "student-centered" or "non-directive" discussion is that the *results* are not apparent. Students may make comments, express opinions, and participate actively, but their opinions may not be any more informed at the end of a semester than at the beginning. Of course not all feedback has to come from the instructor—students can learn much from other students or from books—but, in order to learn, students need to test their ideas in a situation in which they can get the results of the test.

Nevertheless, we need to go a step beyond the principle that students learn what they practice when they see the results of their practice. It is not always easy to get students to practice critical thinking in the classroom. The student who remains quiet in class avoids the risks of disagreement, criticism, and embarrassment. To develop critical thinking, the student must learn to want to think.

This brings us to another category of goals of education—developing interests, changing attitudes, creating motivation. There are many ways to do these things. To develop a student's interest in thinking, we have to make it satisfying. A smile, a nod of encouragement, an excited "Good! Let's follow that idea through"—these are the tools that teachers use, not only to provide knowledge of results, but to develop the motivation to continue intellectual activity.

To develop motivation, teachers must pose problems within the range of their students' abilities. Studies of the development of achievement motivation in children indicate that parents develop this motivation by encouraging the child to do well and setting standards which the child can achieve. Other parents orient their children toward achievement but are disappointed in their aspirations for their children because they set unreasonable goals. To motivate students first to develop the ability to think critically and then to engage in critical thinking, teachers must

give them experience in solving problems within their ken. This by no means implies that the student should never experience failure or criticism, but it does mean that the problems which he faces should, more often than not, be soluble.

One misconception of educators who have recognized the importance of motivation is that they have stopped with the motives students already have. Teachers have assumed that students will learn only those things in which they are interested so that one need only turn students loose in an environment which contains possibilities for learning. But a student's motives are not fixed; teachers can create new motives. We can teach students to enjoy learning for its own sake. Thus, while we must make use of existing motives to create initial satisfactions in learning, our efforts need not be limited by them.

METHODOLOGICAL CAUTIONS

Before turning to the research evidence on the effectiveness of teaching methods, let us review a few methodological points. Determining which of two teaching methods is more effective looks like a simple problem. Presumably, all that is necessary is to teach something by one method and then to compare the results with those obtained by teaching the same thing by another method. This is essentially the research design of many studies widely quoted as demonstrating the effectiveness of television, discussion, independent study, or other methods. Unfortunately, there are pitfalls which enthusiasts for one method or another are likely to overlook.

Suppose, for example, that students are given an opportunity to take a class taught by some method quite unusual in their college. The very fact that the method is different gives it excitement. Sometimes students react to a new method with enthusiasm, at other times, with outraged hostility. A hostile reaction seems particularly likely when students taught by a new method know that they are competing on examinations with students taught by traditional methods. In any case, it is difficult to know how much of student improvement (or loss) in learning may be accounted for by emotional reaction to a new and different method and how much we can expect when the new method is routine. This "Hawthorne effect" influences professors as well as students. How many new curricula, new courses, or new teaching methods have flowered briefly and then faded as the innovators' enthusiasm waned or as new staff members replaced the originators? Unfortunately, relatively few studies have made comparisons over a period longer than one semester. As we shall see later, students who have experienced a semester of instruction by a new method (except television) are generally more likely to choose a section taught by this method than are students without such previous experience. This difference in motivation of students as well as their added skill in a new method might result in even greater advantages for the new method after two or more semesters of trial than after a single semester.

A second problem is that of establishing a suitable control group. In some experiments a single instructor uses both teaching methods. Here it is obviously difficult for the experimenter to determine how much the instructor's own personality and skills influence the outcome. One remedy for this difficulty is to persuade several professors to use both methods. Aside from the salesmanship necessary to institute such a research design, the effort involved in trying to teach by two methods, keeping strictly to each, is tremendous. As a result, the methods either tend to coalesce or the experimenter institutes additional, artificial constraints to accentuate the differences between them.

Another problem in establishing controls may arise when the conditions of the experiment introduce special factors which interfere with normal results. For example, the experiment may require extensive testing, the presence of observers in the class, or other interferences with normal classroom routine. A class in which a "live" professor is talking to television cameras is probably not a suitable comparison group for classes watching the lesson on television receivers.

A fourth problem, biased sampling, needs only brief mention. Such a problem would arise in studies of educational television aimed at determining whether students taking the course at home learn as much as those taking it on campus. People who sign up for a television course and come to campus to take the examination are probably somewhat different in motivation and background from typical college sophomores. As Greenhill (1959) pointed out, efforts to equate such groups are rarely successful.

A fifth problem lies in the statistical methods used to analyze the results of teaching methods experiments. Ordinarily, we carefully try to avoid the type of error involved in concluding that one method is more effective than another when in reality they do not differ significantly. However, we are less likely to be sensitive to another type of error which may be just as damaging—the error of concluding that there is no difference in effectiveness when two methods are not found to differ significantly. In addition to the logical fallacy involved in accepting failure to disprove the null hypothesis as proof of no difference, there is the problem of choice of methods of analysis. The chance of obtaining such results depends upon the type of statistical analysis one uses. If one uses "weak" statistics, a difference is less likely to be detected than if one uses "strong" statistics. The true effect of a variable may be clouded if no effort is made to remove other sources of variance. As is suggested later, multivariate statistics (such as analysis of covariance) might, by taking out other sources of variance, reveal more clearly the true effects of varying methods. Further, when several tests of the same hypothesis are made with different groups, experimenters might well use combined tests of significance. For example, if 10 groups come out in the same direction, it is extremely unlikely that the methods do not differ in effectiveness even though no one difference would be statistically significant alone.

Sixth is the problem of dealing with interactions among teaching methods, student characteristics, teacher characteristics, or other variables. As we shall see in the section on student characteristics, a method which is effective for the learning of some students may be ineffective for others in the same classroom. Ordinary group comparisons between teaching methods may thus hide very important differences in the effects of the methods upon a particular type of student.

The Criterion Problem

The major problem in experimental comparisons of teaching methods is the criterion problem. Stuit and Wilson (1946) found that prediction of success in naval training improved as the criterion became increasingly well defined. Undoubtedly, one reason for the many nonsignificant differences in studies of teaching is poor criterion measures. The criterion problem is further illustrated by the experiment of Parsons, Ketcham, and Beach (1958). To determine the effectiveness of various methods, they set up groups in which students did not come to classes at all. The groups who did not come to class did *best of all* on the final examination. The examination was based entirely upon the textbook, however. As Parsons and Ketcham pointed out, their results with the other groups suggest that, as more and more new ideas and points of view are introduced, students become less and less likely to remember what the textbook says. This points to the problem of evaluation of effectiveness. If our goal is to have students remember the textbook, a test on the textbook is appropriate, but we cannot conclude that a particular method is superior in achieving all goals if we have measured only one.

Few professors complain that students are too highly motivated. Yet for purposes of research the degree of student motivation for good grades may actually make it very difficult to evaluate the effectiveness of two teaching procedures. Because passing or excellent grades are so important to students,

they may compensate for ineffective teaching by additional study in order to pass the course examination at the level to which they aspire. Thus the effects of ineffective procedures may be masked or even misinterpreted when course examinations are used as criterion measures. Nachman and Opochinsky (1958) provided a neat demonstration of this when they found differences between a small and large class on surprise quizzes but no difference on a final examination. When significant differences in achievement are found in an experiment, the difference may simply reflect the degree to which students in differing classes were able to find out the content of the examination and the degree to which it would determine their course grade.

The difficulty in arriving at an over-all index of teaching effectiveness is complicated by the probability that a teacher who is effective in achieving one course objective is not necessarily effective in achieving others. Bendig (1955), for example, found a significant interaction between instructors and tests in an introductory psychology course. Some instructors' students did particularly well on certain tests during the course but not well on other tests. Cross (1958) and McKeachie (1959) found that instructors whose students did well on an objective test in psychology were ineffective when their students' achievement was measured on an essay test designed to measure understanding and integration of the materials. Thus, in studies of teaching it is important to specify objectives and to use measures of each objective. Measures of retention after the end of a course would often add to one's confidence in reported differences.

Because achievement measures have been so insensitive to differences in teaching methods, many experimenters stress the favorable student reactions to the new method they have introduced. Although the relationship between student satisfaction and learning is low (Elliott, 1950), it certainly can be argued that, assuming equal learning between two methods, we would prefer to have students leave our classes with warm feelings about their experience. Moreover, we would expect this feeling to be related to interest in learning more, and there is some evidence to support this expectation (McKeachie & Solomon, 1958). When, however, we use student satisfaction as a criterion, we should be aware that it is highly influenced by students' role expectations of college teachers. Marked deviations from these expectations are almost inevitably rated lower than more conventional teaching behavior. Laboratory studies of problem-solving groups reveal that group members rate authoritarian leaders as more efficient than democratic leaders (Haythorn, et al., 1956). This makes sense because of our expectations for leaders and also because a leader who plays an active role almost inevitably makes a more vivid impression on a group than a leader whose behavior is more subtle. In evaluating student reactions, therefore, one needs to be conscious of these role expectations and to determine a proper base line against which to evaluate the reactions.

As an aside here, let us also note that new methods are not usually tested except by a teacher who is enthusiastic about them. Consequently, we may be comparing student reactions to a new method and an enthusiastic teacher with reactions to an old method taught unenthusiastically.

The prospective researcher also needs to be warned that even a careful definition of desirable outcomes does not solve the criterion problem. In many cases, laudable attempts to measure attitudinal or affective outcomes have led to the conclusion that neither of two teaching methods was superior in achieving this or that goal, when there is no evidence that *any* teaching could affect achievement of the goal as measured by the tests used. At the very least, the experimenter needs to report some index of reliability; even better would be some evidence that the measure is at least sufficiently sensitive to reveal significant changes which occur between the beginning and end of the semester. If there is no change on a variable over a semester, it is unlikely that two teaching methods will differ in the amount of change they yield.

Finally, let us remind ourselves that evaluation need not end with tests given to the students who are enrolled in the experimental classes. In a large university it is easy to assume that an experimental course is assimilated into the whirlpool of teaching activity without even a ripple. Seldom, however, has this assumption been tested, and in smaller colleges or with large-scale innovations, it is not a safe assumption. We might gain much useful knowledge by looking outside our experimental classrooms to other effects of the experiment. Do students taught by one method rather than another make more use of their knowledge and skills in other courses they are electing? Is superior achievement in the experimental course won at the expense of achievement in other courses? What is the impact of a particular teaching method upon other faculty members? How does the use of a new method like television change faculty perceptions of teaching and its value? How does it affect faculty-administration relationships? In short, what effects does a new method have upon the total culture of the college?[3]

With these caveats in mind, let us review some of the research on college teaching.

RESEARCH ON TEACHING METHODS

This review is organized in terms of traditional categories of teaching method—lecturing, discussion, laboratory—and also in terms of fairly recent approaches to college instruction—project methods, independent study, and automated techniques.

LECTURING

College teaching and lecturing have been so long associated that when one pictures a college professor in a classroom, he almost inevitably pictures him as lecturing. The popularity of the lecture method probably derives from a conception of the instructor's primary

---

[3] Morris Janowitz started my trains of thought along this line.

goal as that of transmitting knowledge.

Since students typically have few opportunities to make responses during lectures, they seldom receive feedback from their efforts to learn during lectures. Delay of feedback may not, however, seriously hinder the learner in acquiring knowledge if he is motivated and the material is not too difficult. We would expect lack of feedback to be a greater handicap if the lecturer's goal is to develop concepts or problem-solving skills. There is experimental evidence that, when this is the goal, active participation on the part of the learner is more effective than passive listening or observing.

Lecture Method versus Discussion Method

The effectiveness of lecture and discussion methods has often been compared. Since discussion offers the opportunity for a good deal of student activity and feedback, it could, in theory, be more effective than the lecture method in developing concepts and problem-solving skills. However, since the rate of transmission of information is slow in discussion classes, we would expect lecture classes to be superior in helping students acquire knowledge of information.

Although many studies have been made comparing the lecture method with discussion or other methods, few have used independent measures of these different types of outcome. The results of these studies are generally in line with our hypotheses but are certainly not conclusive. For example, using tests of information, Remmers (1933) found slight but nonsignificant differences favoring learning in large lecture groups as compared with that in small (35–40) recitation sections. Spence (1928) obtained similar results comparing lecture and discussion technique in classes of over a hundred students. In one of the earliest comparisons of lecture and discussion methods, Bane (1925) found little difference between the methods on measures of immediate recall but a significant supe-

riority for discussion on a measure of delayed recall. Ruja (1954), however, found that the lecture was superior to discussion as measured by a test of subject-matter mastery in a general psychology course. In the other two courses in his experiment there were no significant differences in achievement, nor were there differences in changes in adjustment in any of the courses. Eglash (1954) found no difference between a discussion class and lecture class in scores on the final examination, in scores on an achievement test administered several weeks after the course had ended, or in scores on a measure of tolerance. Husband (1951) also found no significant difference in achievement of students in large (200-student) lecture and in "small" (50-student) recitation classes, but in five out of six semesters the lecture group was nonsignificantly superior. In all these experiments, the information measured by the examination could be obtained from a textbook, and in only one was a discussion group of less than 35 used.

When we turn to measures of more complex outcomes, the results are somewhat different. Hirschman (1952), using a measure of concept learning, compared the effectiveness of presenting material by dictation with that of presenting written materials followed by discussion and rereading. The reading-discussion method resulted in superior ability to identify examples of the concepts presented. In quite a different type of experiment, Barnard (1942) compared the effectiveness of a lecture-demonstration teaching method with that of a problem-solving developmental discussion in a college science course. In this experiment the lecture-demonstration method proved superior on a test of specific information, but the discussion method proved to be superior on measures of problem solving and scientific attitude. Similarly Dawson (1956) found problem-solving recitation and lecture-demonstration methods to be equally effective in a course in elementary soil science as measured by a test of recall of specific information, but the problem-solving method was significantly superior as measured by tests of problem-solving abilities. Other evidence favoring discussion was the experiment of Elliott, who found that students in his discussion groups in elementary psychology became more interested in electing additional courses in psychology than did students in a large lecture.[4] The results of DiVesta's (1954) study of a human relations course tended to favor a discussion method over the lecture method in improving scores on a leadership test. Similarly, Casey and Weaver (1956) found no differences in knowledge of content but superiority in attitudes (as measured by the Minnesota Teacher Attitude Inventory) for small-group discussions as compared to lectures.

Despite the many findings of no significant differences in effectiveness between lecture and discussion, those studies which have found differences make surprisingly good sense. In only two studies was one method superior to the other on a measure of knowledge of subject matter; both studies favored the lecture method. In all six experiments finding significant differences favoring discussion over lecture, the measures were other than final examinations testing knowledge.

When one is asked whether lecture is better than discussion, the appropriate counter would seem to be, "For what goals?"

Distribution of Lecture and Discussion Time

Many universities and large colleges divide class meetings between lectures and discussions. This administrative arrangement is supported by a study in the teaching of physiology, in which discussion meetings were substituted for one-third of the lectures (Lifson, Rempel, & Johnson, 1956). Although there were no significant differences in achievement, as compared with all lectures, the partial discussion method resulted in more favorable student attitudes which per-

sisted in a follow-up study two years later. Warren (1954) compared the effectiveness of one lecture and four recitations with that of two lectures and three demonstrations per week. In one out of five comparisons, the one-lecture plan was superior, while the other comparisons found nonsignificant differences. Superior students tended to prefer the two-lecture plan while poorer students did not. On the other hand, in Remmers' (1933) comparison of two lectures and one recitation versus three recitations, the poorer students tended to do better in the lecture-recitation combination, although students in both groups preferred the three-recitation arrangement. In Klapper's study (1958) at New York University, most students preferred a combination lecture-discussion method to one employing all lectures or all discussions. Students at the State University of Iowa also preferred all group discussion or a combination of lecture and discussion to lectures alone (Becker, Murray, & Bechtoldt, 1958).

In a course in which the instructors wish not only to give information but also to develop concepts, the use of both lectures and discussions would thus seem to be a logical and popular choice. The lecture can effectively present new research findings; the discussion can give students opportunities to analyze the studies, find relationships, and develop generalizations. By participating actively in discussion, the students should not only learn the generalizations but should also begin developing skill in critical thinking.

The Lecturer versus Automation

Since we have hypothesized that the lecturer is particularly effective in transmitting information, it is in order to ask how the lecturer in the ordinary classroom compares with other means of transmitting information. As has already been suggested, if the learner is motivated, a good deal of communication of knowledge apparently can

[4] D. Beardslee, R. Birney, & W. J. McKeachie, *Summary of Conference on Research in Classroom Processes* (Dept. of Psychology, Univer. of Michigan, 1951) (Unpublished).

take place with relatively infrequent checks on the progress of the learner and relatively few extrinsic rewards. From Hebb (1949) it could be inferred that relatively fresh ideas would be motivating, but that experiences too far removed from the student's past experience would produce anxiety. This suggests that the organization of materials should be of great importance in learning.

Skinner and his students have recently popularized teaching machines which present course materials in well-organized step-by-step fashion with questions (Skinner, 1958). When a student misses a question on some machines, the question is later repeated, but when the correct response is made, the learner proceeds. It seems that the teaching machine should have advantages over the lecturer, for the sequence can be carefully planned to utilize research on the method of successive approximations, on concrete to abstract sequences in problem solving, and on building up generalizations from varying specifics. Lecturers, on the other hand, vary greatly in the degree to which they organize their materials systematically. Probably few lecturers use optimal sequences of presentation.

Moreover, the learner in a lecture is largely passive, while the learner using a teaching machine is continually active. Many studies of different types of learning and concept-formation demonstrate that active learning is more effective than passive learning (e.g., Ebbinghaus, 1913; Wolfle, 1935). Further, the lecturer presents material symbolically. For learning involving perceptual or motor responses, verbal descriptions should be less effective than actual sensorimotor experiences.

Because the lecture provides little feedback, does not always present material in an optimum sequence, allows the student to be passive, and provides little direct experience, lectures may be inferior to other teaching media in achieving certain goals. In fact, if instructors become extinct, they will probably first disappear from the lecture hall.

The chief competitor of the lecturer is not the teaching machine, television, or film, but a much older invention—printing. If rate of transmission of knowledge is important in teaching, a good book is hard to beat. Not only can the reader control his own rate, but the motivated, skilled reader can traverse the printed page much more rapidly than even the fastest lecturer can deliver the material. Over a generation ago, Greene (1928) demonstrated that college students learned as much from reading a passage as from hearing the same material in a lecture.

Although printed materials have been almost as popular as television and have existed for a much longer time, lectures have survived. Even the advent of picture-book textbooks did not dislodge the lecturer. If we stop to think about this, we probably should not be surprised that dozens of research studies have not had much impact upon lecturers' attitudes toward television.

Perhaps the lecturer's arguments are rationalizations, for there is little research to support them. Nevertheless, psychologists may have underestimated important factors in their usual analyses of the learning situation. To maintain good experimental controls, we carefully control rate and sequence of presentation in most of our experiments. The materials used are meaningless to the learner. The results lead us to stress the importance of feedback to the learner.

Lecturing, however, is largely devoted to communicating meaningful materials to somewhat motivated learners. Apparently such learning can take place with relatively infrequent checks on the progress of the learner. In fact, the learner can to some extent obtain feedback by himself. Our experimental controls lead us to overlook the important fact that when knowledge is presented by a teacher he is able to respond to feedback from the learners. This may be an important asset of the instructor. Films and television present material at a relatively fixed rate, but an instructor can go faster or slower when he gets cues of inattention, irritation, or confusion from his class.

The reader too can pace himself, but the

inexperienced student may not be able to separate the important from the unimportant. Even though lecturers speak more slowly than books can be read, a good lecturer may be able to give his students all they need from a book in much less time than it would take them to read it.

Textbooks, films, and teaching machines must be organized to fit average students if they are to be economically feasible. The lecturer can not only plan his lecture for his own class but he can respond to feedback from his class as he delivers it. This responsiveness to cues from the class is probably the reason that material can be covered less rapidly in "live" classes than in television classes. Because the instructor responds to feedback, his presentation may appear to be unorganized. Yet one might hypothesize that this very responsiveness makes for greater effectiveness than does a carefully organized, inflexible presentation.

Although there is little relevant research evidence on this matter, we would expect live lecturing to be most effective in situations where there is considerable variation between groups in ability, relevant background, or motivation and where flexible adjustment to the group is therefore important.

Most lecturers avow aims beyond transmission of information. College instructors often say that they provide the integration lacking in the text. Again one would expect that other means of communication could also provide integration. Probably what the instructor really does is to provide his own system of integration. Whether or not this is preferable to the integration provided by a textbook, acceptance of the frame of reference of the instructor does at least make a difference in the grade received by the student. Runkel (1956) measured the structure of instructors' and students' attitudes in beginning college courses in psychology and zoology. He found that *agreement* with the instructor's position *did not* predict students' grades, but students whose attitudes were *colinear* (i.e., who used the same dimensions) with the instructor *did* earn higher

grades. In short, students who structured the field as the instructor did tended to earn higher grades. What we do not know yet is whether or not the instructor can communicate his structure to students who do not already have it.

Probably the most careful attempts to measure attitudinal and motivational outcomes have been those comparing live instruction with television instruction in the research programs at Pennsylvania State University and Miami University. In neither case did the live instructor seem to be superior. Still, if the students' tendency to identify with the instructor has anything to do with personal interaction with the instructor, it may be ominous that students did not seek personal conferences with television instructors as much as with "live" instructors.

Methods of Lecturing

Few experiments have compared the effectiveness of classroom lectures with other teaching methods in achieving attitude change, but if we turn from classroom experiments to other research dealing with change of attitudes, we find a substantial and growing literature relevant to differing techniques of lecturing.

The research of Hovland and his associates at Yale (1953) indicates that such variables as credibility of the lecturer, order of presentation, presentation of one side of an issue versus presentation of both sides, and emotionality of argument are factors in determining the effect of a lecture. For example, the Hovland group found that a group of college students were more likely to change their opinions (at least temporarily) when they received a persuasive communication from a source which they considered highly credible than when the same communication came from a less credible source. Although we assume that students perceive their instructors as credible sources, faculty rating scales including an item such as "Knowledge of Subject Matter" have revealed that students do discriminate between professors on this dimension. It has been argued, against inclusion of this item, that students are not competent judges of the instructor's knowledge. Regardless of the validity of the student ratings, however, they may indicate the students' credence in the instructor's statements and thus his effectiveness in bringing about attitude changes.

In most of the Yale experiments comparing communication sources with differing credibilities, the actual information gained from the communication was not different for different communicators. In one study, however, a communication from a neutral source resulted in greater informational learning than did the same communication emanating from either an expert or a biased source. Should teachers try to be neutral laymen?

Sometimes even college professors try to reinforce their points by waving the flag or preaching academic hell-fire and brimstone. The Yale studies suggest that this type of teaching is ineffective, for they indicate that the greatest change in reported behavior occurred in those groups to which a minimally fear-arousing lecture was given. This difference persisted at least a year, even though all presentations resulted in equal factual learning.

In presenting controversial points the lecturer often wonders whether he should present the evidence on both sides of the issue or simply present that favoring the position he accepts. Aside from the ethical problems involved, the Yale experiments indicated the greater effectiveness of presenting both sides for (1) an intelligent audience, (2) those initially disagreeing with the lecturer's position, and (3) those who come into contact with the opposing arguments in some setting other than the lecture.

If he wishes to present two sides of an issue, the lecturer is faced with the problem of choosing the order in which to present them. An extensive series of studies has illuminated the effects of differing orders. The most relevant results have been summarized as follows:

When contradictory information is presented in a single communication, by a single communicator, there is a pronounced tendency for those items presented first to dominate the impression received (Hovland, 1957, p. 133).

The primacy effect found in presenting contradictory information in the same communication was reduced. by interpolating other activities between the two blocks of information and by warning the subjects against the fallibility of first impressions (Hovland, 1957, p. 134).

Placing communications highly desirable to the recipient first, followed by those less desirable, produces more opinion change than the reverse order (Hovland, 1957, p. 136).

When an authoritative communicator plans to mention pro arguments and also nonsalient con arguments the pro-first order is superior to the con-first order (Hovland, 1957, p. 137).

Research on organization of materials is also relevant to lecturing aimed at cognitive changes. In organizing a lecture the professor frequently is guided by the maxim "Tell them what you're going to tell them. Tell them. Then tell them what you've told them." In a classroom experiment in a course in physics (Lahti, 1956), the instructor first stated a principle and then illustrated and applied it. He compared this with a technique in which he developed principles by demonstration and analysis of application situations and then stated the principle. For students with poor backgrounds the results showed the latter (inductive) method to be superior to the former method on tests of ability to apply the principles. On the other hand, Hovland and Mandell (1952) found that opinions were more likely to change in the direction advocated by the speaker if he drew the conclusion appropriate to his argument rather than leaving it to the students. As we shall again see later in our consideration of laboratory teaching, research on this topic is not clear-cut. Probably it is important for the instructor to point out the conclusion if most students would not arrive at it by themselves. On the other hand, as we have seen, discovery of a conclusion by oneself may have considerable motivational value for a student.

Katona's (1940) classic studies of college student learning supported the importance of organization in learning and retention and also pointed toward the importance of the learner's own organization. Katona found that learning by organization results both in superior retention and in superior application when compared with learning by rote memorization. Such findings make apparent some of the ways in which lecturers are not as effective as they might be.

Size of Lecture Class

Our examination of research on class size led to the conclusion that more meaningful research on this variable must take into account the methods used in teaching classes of differing sizes. Thus, it seems illogical to treat class size separately from method; we will consider class size under the general topics of lecture and discussion.

Among the earliest and most comprehensive programs of research on college teaching were the monumental studies of class size conducted at the University of Minnesota in the 1920's. These studies pointed to the conclusion that large classes are actually superior to small classes. Fifty-nine well-controlled experiments were reported by Hudelson (1928). These experiments involved such widely varying subject matter as psychology, physics, accounting, and law. In 46 of the experiments, results favored the large classes. Although many of the differences were not statistically significant, the majority of significant differences favored large classes. In these experiments small classes averaged 25 to 30 students, but they ranged from 12 to 60 in size while large classes ranged in size from 35 to 150. Extreme differences in size were no more favorable to small groups than were small differences. Although most of the criterion measures were tests of knowledge, some experiments also attempted to measure

higher-level intellectual changes, with similar results.

More recent experiments have been less favorable to large classes. Rohrer (1957) found no significant differences. The Macomber and Siegel experiments at Miami University (1956, 1957a, 1957b, 1960) are particularly important because their measures included, in addition to conventional achievement tests, measures of critical thinking and problem solving, scales measuring stereotypy of attitudes, and tests of student attitudes toward instruction. Although the only statistically significant differences favored the smaller classes (particularly for high-ability students), most differences were very small. Significant differences favoring small classes were found on measures of change in misconceptions in psychology, on a case test of problem solving in marketing, and on measures of student attitudes toward all the courses. When retention of knowledge was measured one to two years after completion of the courses, large classes did not prove to be significantly inferior to small classes in any one course. However, in eight of the nine courses compared, differences favored the small class (Siegel, Adams, & Macomber, 1960). As we saw earlier, Nachman and Opochinsky (1958) found a small class to be superior to a large class in performance on surprise quizzes, but the two classes were not significantly different on the final examination for which students prepared.

At Grinnell College, students gave instructors higher ratings in smaller classes (Lovell & Haner, 1955); at Brooklyn (Riley, Ryan, & Lifshitz, 1950) and Purdue (Remmers, 1927), there was no significant difference in ratings of instructors by small and large classes generally, although Remmers (1933) reported that students involved in a controlled experiment at Purdue preferred a small recitation to a large lecture. The weight of the evidence seems to favor small classes if one uses student or faculty satisfaction as a criterion.

Despite the lack of conclusive experimental support for their position, most college professors still believe small classes to be superior to larger ones. For example, the Miami University professors involved in the Macomber-Siegel experiments felt that large classes were about equal to small classes in covering content but inferior in achieving other objectives. In view of the research results, is this simply academic featherbedding or are there good reasons for the professors' distrust of the research results?

Let us briefly return to theory. We have stressed the role of the lecturer as an information communicator. Insofar as information-giving is a one-way process, size of group should be limited only by the audibility of the lecturer's voice. In fact, as Hudelson suggests, a large class may have sufficient motivational value for an instructor to cause him to spend more time in preparation of his lectures and thus to produce better teaching and greater student achievement. But if, as we suggested in our discussion of automation, the effective lecture involves interaction between instructor and students, the large class may be inferior even for lectures, for laboratory experiments suggest that fewer students raise questions or interpose comments in large classes than in small (J. R. Gibb, 1951).

If there is less participation in large classes, the Minnesota research may suggest that we hark back to the criterion problem mentioned earlier. Were the achievement tests used biased against teaching which introduced varying points of view? If our tests place a premium upon exact recall of the materials presented by the teacher or textbook, the student who hears other points of view may be at a disadvantage.

To sum up: large lecture classes are not generally inferior to smaller lecture classes if one uses traditional achievement tests as a criterion. When other objectives are measured, large lectures tend to be inferior. Moreover, both students and faculty members feel that teaching is more effective in small classes. Regardless of the validity of these feelings, any move toward large classes is likely to encounter strong resistance. Probably of more significance than class size per

se is its relation to the teaching method used. For example, one would expect class size to be of minimal relevance in television teaching, of slight importance in lecturing, but of considerable significance in discussion teaching. One unplanned consequence of increasing class size may be a restriction upon the teacher's freedom to vary his methods to fit his objectives.

What is the role of the lecturer in higher education? The research results we have cited provide little basis for an answer. They do not contradict—sometimes they support—our earlier notions that the lecture is an effective way of communicating information, particularly in classes where variations in student background, ability, or interest make feedback to the lecturer important. We have also seen that the organization and presentation of lectures may influence their effectiveness in teaching students how to apply knowledge or in influencing attitudes. However, a suspicion, supported by bits of evidence, arises that other methods of teaching may be more effective than lecturing in achieving some higher cognitive and attitudinal objectives.

DISCUSSION METHODS

In our review of research comparing the effectiveness of lecture and discussion methods, we implied that discussion may be ill-suited for communicating information because the rate of communication from instructor to student is slow. However, we should point out that not all information is eagerly received. When information encounters intellectual or emotional resistance, discussion methods may be necessary to bring the source of resistance to light.

Moreover, if students are to achieve application, critical thinking, or some other higher cognitive objective, it seems reasonable to assume that they should have an opportunity to practice application and critical thinking and to receive feedback on the results. Group discussion provides an opportunity to do this. While teaching machines and mock-ups may also be designed to provide prompt and realistic feedback, a group discussion permits presentation of a variety of problems enabling a number of people to gain experience in integrating facts, formulating hypotheses, amassing relevant evidence, and evaluating conclusions. In fact, the prompt feedback provided by the teaching machine may actually be less effective than a method in which students are encouraged to discover solutions for themselves with less step-by-step guidance (Della-Piana, 1957). Since problem solving ordinarily requires information, we might expect discussion to be more effective for groups with more information than for those lacking in background. Some support for this hypothesis is provided by a study of the learning of children in visiting a museum. Melton, Feldman, and Mason (1936) found that lectures were more effective than discussions for children in Grades 5, 6, and 7, but discussions were more effective for eighth-graders.

We noted that lectures usually place the learner in a passive role and that passive learning is less efficient than active. We would expect discussions to promote more active learning, and for once we have some relevant evidence. Bloom and his colleagues (1953) at the University of Chicago used recordings of classes to stimulate students to recall their thoughts during class. As predicted, they found that discussion did stimulate more active thinking than did lecture classes. Krauskopf (1960) substituted written for oral responses to the tape recordings and found that rated relevance of thoughts was positively correlated with achievement, accounting for variance in achievement beyond that accounted for by ability.

The idea that discussion methods should help overcome resistance to learning is also difficult to verify. Essentially, the argument is that some desired learning encounters emotional barriers which prevent it from affecting behavior. For example, a psychology student may learn that distributed practice is effective, but not change his study methods because his anxiety about grades is so great that he doesn't dare try anything different. In such circumstances, experiments on attitude change suggest that the instructor must either bring about changes in underlying attitude and motivation or change the individual's perception of the instrumental relationship between his belief and his motives. Psychotherapists believe that expressing one's attitude in a nonthreatening situation is one step in the process of change. A group discussion may provide such opportunities for expression as well as give opportunities for other group members to point out other instrumental relationships.

In addition, most attitudes influencing learning have some interpersonal antecedents and are stabilized by one's perception of the attitudes of liked persons. Group discussion may facilitate a high degree of liking for the instructor and for other group members. It also permits more accurate assessment of group norms than is likely to occur in other techniques of instruction. Consequently, change may follow.

In fact, while individual instruction would be advantageous for many teaching purposes, group processes can provide a real advantage in bringing about changes in motivation and attitudes. Lewin (1952) showed in his classic experiments on group decision that it is sometimes easier to change a group than an individual.

Whether or not discussions actually are superior in these respects cannot be easily determined, for discussions range from monologues in which occasional questions are interposed to bull sessions in which the instructor is an interested (or bored) observer. Nevertheless, a good deal of research has been attempted to compare the effectiveness of differing discussion techniques.

Student-Centered versus Instructor-Centered Teaching

The theories of client-centered counseling and of Lewinian group dynamics have led to an increased interest in discussion techniques. A wide variety of teaching methods are described as "student-centered," "nondirective," "group-centered," or "democratic" discussion. Nevertheless, they have in common the desire to break away from the traditional instructor-dominated classroom and to encourage greater student participation and responsibility. In Table 1 are listed some of the ways in which the student-centered method has been supposed to differ from the traditional "instructor-centered" method.[5]

With the instructor's role as information-giver reduced, his role as source of feedback virtually eliminated, his opportunity to provide organization and structure curtailed, it is apparent that a heavy burden falls upon the group members to carry out these functions. We expect that these functions could best be assumed by groups which not only have some background in the academic discipline involved but also have had experience in carrying out these functions in "democratic" groups.

TABLE 1

DIMENSIONS UPON WHICH STUDENT-CENTERED AND INSTRUCTOR-CENTERED METHODS MAY DIFFER

Student-Centered	Instructor-Centered
Goals	
Determined by group (Faw, 1949)	Determined by instructor
Emphasis upon affective and attitudinal changes (Faw, 1949)	Emphasis upon intellectual changes
Attempts to develop group cohesiveness (Bovard, 1951b)	No attempt to develop group cohesiveness
Classroom Activities	
Much student participation (Faw, 1949)	Much instructor participation
Student-student interaction (McKeachie, 1951)	Instructor-student interaction
Instructor accepts erroneous or irrelevant student contributions (Faw, 1949)	Instructor corrects, criticizes, or rejects erroneous or irrelevant student contributions
Group decides upon own activities (McKeachie, 1951)	Instructor determines activities
Discussion of students' personal experiences encouraged (Faw, 1949)	Discussion kept on course materials
De-emphasis of tests and grades (Asch, 1951)	Traditional use of tests and grades
Students share responsibility for evaluation (Ashmus & Haigh, 1952)	
Instructor interprets feelings and ideas of class member when it is necessary for class progress (Axelrod, 1955)	Instructor avoids interpretation of feelings
Reaction reports (Asch, 1951)	No reaction reports

From the standpoint of theory, student-centered teaching in its more extreme forms might be expected to have some serious weakness, at least in achieving lower-level cognitive goals, such as knowledge of facts.

Since student-centered teaching attempts to reduce dependence upon the instructor, it would be expected to diminish his influence as a prestige figure, and possibly to reduce his power to bring about attitudinal changes. However, this may be more than compensated for by increased freedom of expression and increased potency of group norms as

[5] A good summary and critical evaluation of studies in this area may be found in R. C. Anderson (1959).

sources of influence. Participation in discussion gives students an opportunity to gain recognition and praise which should, according to learning theory, strengthen motivation. Thistlethwaite (1960) found that National Merit Scholars checked as one of the outstanding characteristics of teachers who contributed most to their desire to learn, "allowing time for classroom discussion." Other characteristics mentioned include "modifying course content to meet students' needs and interests," "treating students as colleagues," and "taking a personal interest in students." However, in line with our earlier discussion of feedback, another trait mentioned was "providing evaluations reassuring the student of his creative or productive potentialities."

The advocates of student-centered or group-centered teaching also introduced another category of objectives not usually considered in traditional classes—development of skills in group membership and leadership. The group-centered teacher might often argue that even if his method were no more effective than traditional methods in achieving the usual course objectives, it is so important that students learn to work effectively in groups that it may even be worth sacrificing some other objectives in order to promote growth in this area.

Student-centered teachers often stress group cohesiveness. Hence, a possible explanation for the contradictory results on student achievement in the experiments considered below may be found in the studies of group cohesiveness and productivity in industry (e.g., Seashore, 1954). These studies indicate that it is not safe to assume that a cohesive group will be a productive one. Cohesive groups are effective in maintaining group standards, but may set either high or low standards of productivity. Since strongly cohesive groups feel less threatened by management than do less cohesive groups, it may be more difficult to change their standards. Thus in creating "groupy" classes an instructor may sometimes help his students develop strength to set low standards of achievement

and maintain them against instructor pressures, or at least to develop group goals different from their normal academic goals.

Another factor may account for the fact that some researchers report student enthusiasm for student-centered teaching while others report hostility. Horwitz (1958) found that aggression toward the teacher increased when the teacher exercised his authority arbitrarily, i.e., refused to abide by the students' decision about teaching methods after telling them that their vote would count. The same method was not resented when the instructor indicated that he would make the final decision. This is important because the limits of student power are often ambiguous in student-centered classes. Also relevant was Horwitz's finding that the more hostility was inhibited, the less learning took place on a type-setting task.

Experiments on student-centered teaching. With this introduction, let us review experimental attempts to demonstrate the effectiveness of student-centered teaching.[6] One of the best known comparisons of student-centered and instructor-centered instruction is that made by Faw (1949). Faw's class of 102 students met two hours a week to listen to lectures and two hours a week in discussion groups of 34. One discussion group was taught by a student-centered method, one by an instructor-centered method, and one group alternated between the two methods.

As compared with the instructor-centered class, the student-centered class was characterized by more student participation, lack of correction by the instructor of inaccurate statements, lack of instructor direction, and more discussion of ideas related to personal experiences.

Faw's major measure of attainment of objectives was in the intellectual area. Scores on the objective course examination based on the textbook showed small but significant differences favoring the student-centered

[6] Much of the following material on student-centered discussion is based on Birney and McKeachie (1955) and is used with the permission of the American Psychological Association.

method. In the area of his major interest, emotional growth, Faw's method of evaluation was to ask students in the student-centered and alternating method classes to write anonymous comments about the class. Generally Faw thought that these comments indicated that the students felt that they received greater social and emotional value from the student-centered discussion groups than from an instructor-centered class.

A very similar experiment was carried out by Asch (1951). Like Faw, Asch taught all the groups in his experiment. Three sections of about 30–55 students were taught by an instructor-centered method which was half lecture and half discussion. One section of 23 students was taught by a nondirective method quite similar to that of Faw. However, there were certain differences between the two experiments. In Faw's experiment both student-centered and instructor-centered classes spent two hours a week listening to lectures. While Faw did not mention grading, one assumes that grades were determined by the instructor on the basis of the course-wide examination. In Asch's experiment, students in the student-centered class were allowed to determine their own grades.

Asch's results do not completely agree with Faw's. On the final examination in the course, students in the instructor-centered class scored significantly higher than members of the student-centered class on both the essay and objective portions of the test. Note, however, that the student-centered class was specifically told that this examination would in no way affect their grades in the course, and therefore the two groups were probably not equivalent in motivation. Haigh and Schmidt (1956), however, found no significant difference in a similar comparison.

As measured by the Bogardus Social Distance scale, attitude change in the two sections was not significantly different. Yet, in comparison with the instructor-centered class, a greater percentage of members of the student-centered class improved in adjustment as measured by the Minnesota Multiphasic Personality Inventory.

Asch's students, like Faw's, had a different perception of their achievement from that shown by the course examination. Faw's student-centered class did better on the course examination than the instructor-centered class section but thought they would have learned more if they had been in an instructor-centered class. Asch's students, however, rated the student-centered class higher than the instructor-centered class in helping them to learn the subject matter of the course even though they actually scored lower than the instructor-centered class.

Following the model of Lewin, Lippitt, and White's (1939) study of authoritarian, democratic, and laissez-faire group climates, the staff of the University of Michigan's general psychology courses set up an experiment using three styles of teaching: recitation, discussion, and group tutorial (Guetzkow, Kelly, & McKeachie, 1954). As compared to discussion and tutorial methods, the more autocratic recitation method proved not only to produce superior performance on the final examination, but also to produce greater interest in psychology, as measured by the election of advanced courses in psychology. Furthermore, students liked the recitation method better than the other methods. The greater gains in knowledge produced by the recitation method fit in with the general principle that feedback aids learning, for students in the recitation sections had weekly or semiweekly quizzes. McKeachie (1951) suggests that the popularity of this method is related to student anxiety about grades, which is most easily handled when students are in familiar, highly structured situations.

Another factor in these results may be the inexperience of the instructors involved, most of whom had had less than a year of previous teaching experience. It is possible that skillful discussion or tutorial teaching requires greater skill than do more highly structured methods.

Despite the superiority found for the recitation method in producing achievement measured immediately after the course, two results dealing with motivational outcomes favored the other methods. The discussion sections were significantly more favorable than the other groups in their attitude toward psychology; a follow-up of the students three years later revealed that seven men each from the tutorial and discussion groups majored in psychology and none of those in the recitation sections did so.

One of the most comprehensive experiments on student-centered teaching was that of Landsman (1950). He contrasted a student-centered type of teaching with a more direct type of democratic discussion organized around a syllabus. His experimental design involved eight classes in a course sequence of "Human Development," "Adjustment," and "Learning." Three instructors took part in the experiment, and each instructor used both methods. Outcome measures included the Horrocks-Troyer test (an analysis of case histories), a local case-history analysis test, the group Rorschach, the MMPI, autobiographies, and students' reactions. His results showed no significant difference between methods on any of the measures.

Other experiments have also been carried out with negative results. For example, Johnson and Smith (1953) also found no significant difference in achievement test scores between small "democratic" and large lecture classes. An interesting sidelight of their experiment was that one democratic class evaluated their procedure very favorably, while the other democratic class tended to be less satisfied than lecture classes. Bills (1952) also found no difference in achievement between psychology classes taught by lecture-discussion versus student-centered methods, but did find that the students in the student-centered class were significantly more favorable in their attitude toward psychology.

Maloney (1956) found no differences in achievement between two types of discussion groups but did find gains in group cohesiveness, participation, and other indices of effectiveness in groups in which the leader specifically tried to establish acceptance and other characteristics of the student-centered

group. In a graduate course in counseling, Slomowitz (1955) found no significant differences between nondirective and problem-oriented discussions in achievement or application to a case-study test. The nondirectively taught student did, however, change in self concept more (at the .10 level of confidence) than did students in the other group. Like Slomowitz, Deignan (1955) was concerned not only with achievement but also with emotional changes. Although there were no other significant differences between the groups on follow-up tests a semester later, the student-centered group evaluated the course more highly. Rasmussen (1956) also reported no difference in achievement but higher morale among groups of in-service teachers electing student-centered extension courses as compared with students taught by instructor-centered methods. Krumboltz and Farquhar (1957) compared student-centered, instructor-centered, and eclectic teaching methods in a how-to-study course. There were no significant differences between methods on an achievement test or on self-ratings of study habits. Burke's results (1956) are similar.

In an attempt to teach critical thinking, Lyle (1958) compared a problem-oriented approach with conventional lecture-discussion-text procedures. Apparently he found that the conventional group was superior to the problem-oriented group in achievement. Gains in critical thinking were not greater in the problem-centered classes. When students were asked to write a question for the final examination, the conventional group wrote factual questions and the problem-centered group wrote "thought" questions.

In an experiment in teaching written and spoken English, Jenkins (1952) found that a teaching role in which the instructor acted as resource person in a democratic class was not significantly superior to traditional methods on three measures of communication skills.

The Johnson and Smith study (1953) is one of the few to support our earlier suggestion that the success of student-centered teaching depends upon the previous group experience of the students. They suggest that the critical factor in the success of one democratic class was the enthusiastic participation of one student who happened to be a member of a student cooperative.

Wispé (1951) carried out an interesting variation of the student-centered versus instructor-centered experiment. Instead of attempting to control the instructor personality variable by forcing instructors to teach both instructor-centered and student-centered classes, Wispé selected instructors who were rated as naturally permissive or directive. He then compared their sections of the Harvard course in "Social Relations." He found no difference in final examination scores between students taught by the different methods. Students preferred the directive method, and the poorer students gained more in directive classes.

In a methodological aside, it is worth noting that analysis of covariance and multiple correlation were used in Wispé's study. As indicated in our introduction, one reason why statistically significant differences are so rare in this research may be that the researchers commonly use "weak" statistics in which the error estimates are inflated by failure to take account of known sources of variance such as individual differences in previous knowledge or intelligence.

As a counterpoint to Wispé's study with teachers using their preferred method, we have the Springfield College experiment (Ashmus & Haigh, 1952; Haigh & Schmidt, 1956) in which the students were given their choice of group-centered or instructor-centered teaching. Students choosing either type did not differ significantly in intelligence. The results showed no difference in the achievement of the two groups on a test not counted toward the course grade. Those in the nondirective classes were more highly satisfied with the course.

Moore and Popham (1959) reported that three student-centered interviews with students produced greater gains on the college Inventory of Academic Adjustment than did three content-centered interviews conducted outside of class in an educational psychology course. Similarly, Zeleny (1940) found not only greater gain in knowledge but also greater self-rated change in personality in a group-discussion class than in a traditional recitation-discussion class.

While scores on objective final examinations seem to be little affected by teaching method, there are, in addition to the changes in adjustment reported by Asch, Faw, Zeleny, and Moore and Popham, other indications that student behavior outside the usual testing situation may be influenced in the direction of educational goals by student-centered teaching. The classes compared by Bovard (1951a, 1951b) and McKeachie (1951) differed in the degree to which interaction between students was encouraged and in the degree to which the class made decisions about assignments, examinations, and other matters of classroom procedure. Like other experimenters, Bovard and McKeachie found that the groups did not differ in achievement measured by the final examination. However, two clinical psychologists evaluated recordings in the class discussions which followed the showing of the film, "The Feeling of Rejection." Both clinicians reported that the "group-centered" class showed much more insight and understanding of the problems of the girl in the film.

Patton (1955) felt that an important variable in group-centered classes was the students' acceptance of responsibility for learning. In his experiment he compared traditional classes with two classes in which there were no examinations, no lectures, and no assigned readings. Students in the experimental classes decided what reading they would do, what class procedure would be used, what they would hand in, and how they would be graded, so that they had even more power than had previous experimental groups. At the end of the course, these classes, as compared to the control group, felt that the course (1) was more valuable, (2) showed greater interest in psychology, and (3) tended to give more dynamic, motivational analyses of a problem of behavior.

But giving students power cannot work if they will not accept responsibility; so Patton also obtained individual measures of acceptance of responsibility within the experimental classes. As hypothesized, he found that the degree to which the student accepted responsibility was positively correlated with gain in psychological knowledge, gain in ability to apply psychology, rating of the value of the course, and interest in psychology. The effect of giving students additional responsibility seemed to depend upon the student's readiness to accept that responsibility.

Although the Bovard, McKeachie, and Patton experiments suggested that student-centered classes promoted transfer of learning, D. E. P. Smith (1954), comparing three methods varying in degree of directiveness, found no differences in their effects upon students' abilities to make "applicational transfer" of their learning.

The most impressive findings on the results of small-group discussion come from the research on the "Pyramid Plan" at Pennsylvania State University (Carpenter, 1959; Davage, 1958, 1959). The basic plan may be represented by a description of their experiments in psychology. Each "Pyramid Group" of psychology majors consisted of six freshmen, six sophomores, two juniors, who were assistant leaders, and a senior, who was group leader. The Pyramid groups met weekly for two-hour periods to discuss personal-professional goals, requirements for entering their selected professions, skills needed for academic success, the significance of their courses for their goals, issues in higher education, and the central concepts of psychology. The group leaders worked with a faculty supervisor in defining objectives, discussing small-group theory and techniques, and defining issues to be considered by the Pyramid groups. One control group consisted of students who simply took pretest measures; another control group received comparable special attention by being given a special program of lectures, films, and demonstrations equal to the time spent in discussion by the Pyramid groups. The results on such measures as attitude toward psychology, knowledge of the field of psychology, scientific thinking, use of the library for scholarly reading, intellectual orientation, and resourcefulness in problem solving were significantly favorable to the Pyramid Plan. Moreover, a follow-up study showed that more of the Pyramid students continued as majors in psychology. Such an array of positive results, little short of fantastic, testifies not only to the effectiveness of the Pyramid program but also to the resourcefulness of the Pennsylvania State research staff.

L. M. Gibb and Gibb (1952) reported that students who were taught by their "participative-action" method were significantly superior in role flexibility and self-insight to students taught by traditional lecture-discussion methods. In the participative-action method class, activities centered around "subgrouping methods designed to increase effective group participation."

The instructor, who played a constantly diminishing role in the decisions and activities of the groups, gave training in role playing, group goal setting, problem centering, distributive leadership, evaluation of individual performance by intra-group ratings, process observing, and group selection, evaluation, and revision of class activities (L. M. Gibb & Gibb, 1952, p. 247).

Gibb and Gibb also supported the assumption that group-centered teaching can facilitate development of group-membership skills. They found that in nonclassroom groups the participative-action students were rated higher than other students in leadership, likeableness, and group-membership skills. DiVesta's results tend to support this (1954), and R. P. Anderson and Kell (1954) reported that members of student-centered groups were characterized by positive attitudes toward themselves as participants in the group.

Although McKeachie (1954) reported significant changes in attitudes of students toward Negroes and toward the treatment of criminals, differences between leader-centered and group-centered classes were not significant. As predicted, however, group decision did produce more accurate perception of the group norm and more conformity to the norm than lecture or discussion without decision. While no direct attempt was made to change the group norm, the experiment suggests that the instructor who wishes to change attitudes might find the group-decision technique useful. Wieder (1954) found that a nondirectively taught psychology class tended to reduce prejudice more than did conventional classes.

One final bit of support for less directive teaching is Thistlethwaite's (1959) finding of a significant negative correlation between a college's productivity of Ph.D.'s in natural science and the directiveness of the teaching methods used.

In the Guetzkow, Kelly, and McKeachie (1954) experiment reported earlier, none of the males in the very popular highly structured recitation sections majored in psychology. At least seven males in the sections taught by each of the other two methods completed a psychology major. Since the three methods had been equated in terms of the number of students intending to major, this is a surprising finding. Such results are shocking to conventional theory. Most psychologists have thought that prompt feedback and well-structured sequences of presentation were conducive to learning. Yet the Thistlethwaite studies indicate that the top colleges in production of scholars are those where tests are infrequent and where students don't know what to expect next. If this is so, maybe we need to throw some random elements into our lectures and teaching machines. In any case, these results suggest that techniques most suitable for teaching knowledge may not be those most effective for developing motivation and high-level achievement.

The results of the spate of research on student-centered teaching methods are not conclusive, but tend to support the theory with which our discussion began. We had suggested that student-centered teaching might be ineffective in achieving lower-order cognitive objectives. Experiments reporting losses and gains in this area seem to be balanced. Students apparently can get information from textbooks as well as from the instructor.

We had also predicted that any superiority of student-centered discussion methods would be revealed in higher-level outcomes. In 11 studies, significant differences in ability to apply concepts, in attitudes, in motivation, or in group membership skills have been found between discussion techniques emphasizing freer student participation compared with discussion with greater instructor dominance. In 10 of these the differences favored the more student-centered method. The eleventh (Guetzkow, Kelly, & McKeachie, 1954) had mixed results.

In short, the choice of instructor-dominated versus student-centered discussion techniques appears to depend upon one's goals. The more highly one values outcomes going beyond acquisition of knowledge, the more likely that student-centered methods will be preferred.

Variations in Discussion Teaching

Buzz sessions. One popular technique for achieving student participation in groups is the buzz session (McKeachie, 1960). In using this procedure, classes are split into small subgroups for a brief discussion of a problem. Although many teachers feel that this technique is valuable as a change of pace or as a way of getting active thinking from students, little research has tested its effectiveness. Vinacke (1957) found that, in comparison with their performance on a pretest, students in two- and three-man groups wrote more new ideas after a five-minute discussion than did students working alone. It is possible, however, that similar changes could have been produced by a general discussion or a lecture.

Leadership. Laboratory and field studies of group processes may shed some light on factors which condition the effectiveness of groups and which thus may help account for the lack of effectiveness of many discussion classes.

For example, one problem faced by the discussion leader is the student who dominates discussion or the clique who carry the ball. In some discussion classes, the instructor's fear of exerting too much control over the class may result in failure to give minority points of view an adequate hearing. Research suggests that effectiveness of group problem solving depends upon the leader's ability to obtain a hearing for minority opinion (Maier & Solem, 1952).

Some student-centered teachers assume that all decisions should be made by the group. Hence, they feel, the instructor should not determine objectives, make assignments, or give tests, but should ask the group to make these decisions. If the group does this, can the time they lose from academic work in making decisions be compensated for by the increased motivation of the students? Democratic methods permit formation of group norms and more acute perception of group norms, but as in industry these norms may not necessarily be conducive to high productivity or learning. The general question of the areas in which the instructor should make decisions is one which different instructors have answered in different ways and one well worth further discussion and research. One hunch based on research on business conferences is that the instructor should make most procedural decisions, leaving the class time for problems related to the content of the course (Heyns, 1952).

Even in discussion of course content, however, it appears that some instructor direction may be useful if the goals are the learning of relationships and the ability to apply this learning. In comparing groups given more versus less instructor direction in discovering the basis of solutions of verbal problems, Craig (1956) found that the directed group not only learned faster but retained their learning better than the group given less help. This result is supported by Corman's research on guidance in problem solving (1957).

Studies of business conferences have also shown that one of the commonest causes of dissatisfaction is the member's failure to understand the purpose of the conference. It is little wonder that a student with a high need to achieve success may be frustrated and often aggressive in a democratic class in which he is confused about the purposes of the teacher's procedures and, at the same time, subject to the stress involved in getting a good grade. Bloom's studies (1953) of student thought processes show that on the average 30 per cent of the student's time in discussion classes is spent in thinking about himself and other people as compared with 18 per cent of the time in lectures. With members of the group thus concerned about their own needs, it is no wonder that discussion groups are not always productive.

Grading. Another important problem in conducting student-centered (or other) classes is that of grades. Not only does the instructor control the pleasantness or unpleasantness of a good many student hours, but because of his power to assign grades he can block or facilitate the achievement of many important goals. The importance of this aspect of the teacher's role is indicated by studies of supervision in industry. In one such study it was discovered that workers were most likely to ask a supervisor for help if the supervisor was not responsible for evaluating his subordinates (Ross, 1956). This suggests that as long as students are anxious about the grades the instructor will assign, they are likely to avoid exposing their own ignorance.

The student's anxiety about grades is likely to be increased if his instructor's procedures make him uncertain about what he must do to attain a good grade. Although we have already seen that a high degree of structure may not lead to better education, it is nevertheless worth noting that for many students democratic methods seem unorganized and ambiguous. In an ordinary course the student knows that he can pass by reading assignments and studying lecture notes, but in a student-centered class the instructor does not lecture, does not make assignments, and leaves the student ignorant of what the instructor is trying to do.

Some instructors have thought that the grade problem might be solved by using a cooperative system of grading. Deutsch (1949) found no differences in learning between students in groups graded cooperatively and those graded competitively, although the cooperative groups worked together more smoothly. Following up Deutsch's work, Haines (1959) also found no significant achievement advantages for students working cooperatively as compared with those working competitively for grades, but he did find marked differences in group morale. Haines's work suggests that cooperative grading in the discussion group can be successfully combined with individual grading on achievement tests.

In comparing a "teamwork" class using group incentives with a lecture class, H. C. Smith (1955) did not find differences in satisfaction comparable to those found by Haines and by Deutsch in their experiments.

Complicating the problem of grading is the probability that low grades produce different effects upon different students. Waterhouse and Child (1953) found that frustration produced deterioration in performance for subjects showing high "interference tendencies" but produced improved performance for those with low "interference tendencies." "Interference tendencies" were assessed by a questionnaire in which the subjects were asked to check on a six-point scale the degree to which 90 responses to frustration were characteristic of them.

Considering the importance of grading for both students and instructors, it is regrettable that there is so little empirical research on it. How do students learn to evaluate themselves? How do they learn to set goals for themselves? Do differing grading procedures facilitate or block such learning? Can more educational substitutes for grades be devised? To these questions we have no answers at the present time.

Size of Discussion Group

One of the earliest experimental studies on college teaching was that of Edmonson and Mulder (1924) on class size. This study was conducted in an education course in which there were two sections—one of 45 students and the other of 109. Both sections were taught by the same instructor in order to control the possible effect of instructor differences, and both sections used the same text and took the same tests. The discussion method was used in each section. Forty-three students in each class were paired on the basis of intelligence and past experience. This pioneer study led to the conclusion that size of class is not a significant variable in effecting student learning as measured by usual course achievement tests, although students preferred the small class (if 45 can be considered a small discussion group).

As in the size experiments reported in our discussion of the lecture method, there seemed to be little theoretical reason for the choice of class sizes in this experiment. There is, in fact, some doubt whether either size is optimal for discussions. However, similar results were reported by Hudelson (1928) when using classes of 20 and 113 in an education course, and by Brown (1932) in psychology classes. In fact, using special team procedures, Brown produced slightly better achievement in groups of 60 than were obtained from discussion classes of 25.

Support for small classes, however, comes from the studies on teaching French conducted by Cheydleur (1945) at the University of Wisconsin between 1919 and 1943. With hundreds of classes ranging in enrollment from 9 to 33, Cheydleur found the smaller classes to be consistently superior on departmental examinations, with reliabilities of .72 to .95. These departmental examinations correlated about .8 with standardized tests of achievement in French. The only thing unclear in Cheydleur's report is whether or not some selective factor could have been operating.

Mueller (1924) in a pioneer study also found the smaller class to be more effective in an experiment comparing elementary psychology classes of 20 and 40 students. A study by Schellenberg (1959) in a Western civilization course suggested that even the smallest groups in these studies may be above optimal sizes. Working with discussion groups of 4, 6, 8, and 10 students, he found higher satisfaction and higher instructor grading in the smaller groups. While Schellenberg recognized that grades are an unsatisfactory criterion since the instructor's judgment may shift from section to section, he referred to laboratory studies of group problem solving which point to optima in the range of 4- to 6-person groups.

From the standpoint of theory one might expect increasing size to have two effects. One of these would be an increase in the resources of the group in knowledge, different approaches to the problem, and ability to provide feedback. The second consequence of size, however, is likely to be a decreasing ability to exploit the total resources of the group because of the difficulty in obtaining contributions from everyone. Further, with increasing size, group members are likely to feel restraints against participation (J. R. Gibb, 1951). The consequence of increasing feelings of threat in larger groups is that group participation is increasingly dominated by a few people. In Princeton classes of 4 to 12 students, Stephan and Mishler (1952) reported that increasing group size was related to increasing instructor dominance. Thus group size becomes a much more relevant variable in classes taught by discussion than in those taught by lecture.

Homogeneous versus Heterogeneous Grouping

One common criticism of discussion classes is that class time is wasted either by discussion of problems raised by the able students which are beyond the ken of the other students or by problems raised by poor students which the other students feel are too elementary. One answer to such criticism is to use homogeneous groupings so that each student is discussing problems with students of his own ability.

Recently, concern about America's resources of high-level talent has resulted in the proliferation of honors programs featuring homogeneous classes for students with high academic aptitude and achievement. The logic of such programs is evident, and research evidence supports their educational value. Nevertheless, an earlier college experiment on ability grouping showed no significant advantages for homogeneous grouping by intelligence and even a trend toward the opposite result in psychology classes (Longstaff, 1932).

Briggs (1947), on the other hand, found that special intensive seminar classes meeting less often than conventional classes produced greater achievement for superior students than did the conventional class for a control group matched in ability. Unfortunately, in this study the seminar students volunteered and were selected by interview so that they probably had higher motivation than their controls.

The two earliest publications in this area (Burtt, Chassel, & Hatch, 1923; Ullrich, 1926) reported results which seem very reasonable. They both concluded that homogeneous groups were not superior to heterogeneous groups when given standard material but did superior work when the bright students were pushed. Similarly, Tharp (1930) found homogeneous grouping to be superior in foreign language classes and Taylor (1931) found it to be superior in analytic geometry. All in all, it seems safe to conclude that homogeneous grouping by ability is profitable, if teaching makes use of the known characteristics of the groups.

Homogeneous grouping by personality proved to be ineffective in Hoffman's (1959) experiment in group problem solving. Comparing groups of four students who were similar in personality profiles on the Guilford-Zimmerman Temperament Survey with groups made up of dissimilar students, he found that the *heterogeneous* groups produced *superior* solutions. Hoffman accounts for this difference by suggesting that heterogeneous groups are more likely to propose a variety of alternatives permitting inventive solutions.

On the other hand, in a study by Stern and Cope (Stern, 1960, pp. 315–316), groups of "authoritarian," "antiauthoritarian," and "rational" students in a citizenship course were segregated into homogeneous groups in which the instructor was unaware of which group he was teaching. Authoritarian students in the experimental group achieved more than comparable authoritarians did in conventional classes.

It is apparent that we need further analysis to determine what kinds of homogeneities or heterogeneities contribute to what objectives. If we omit from consideration the general adjustment problems of segregated groups, the idea that one should be able to do a better job of teaching a group with known homogeneous characteristics than a heterogeneous group seems so reasonable that it is surprising that the results of research on this idea are not uniform. It may be that the potential advantages of carefully planned grouping have not been realized simply because we have not yet learned optimal teaching procedures for such groups.

From a theoretical point of view the importance of group size and heterogeneity probably depends upon the purpose of the discussion. If, for example, one is interested in using group members as sources of information or differing points of view, the larger and more heterogeneous the group, the greater its resources. On the other hand, the degree to which a group uses its resources depends upon communication; fewer group members can participate in a large group and members are less likely to volunteer their contributions in large groups.

A final problem is that of group pressures toward consensus and conformity. As we saw in our consideration of discussion techniques, one barrier to effective group problem solving is the tendency of a group to accept the majority view without sufficient consideration of minority views. Since group members may be less likely to express divergent opinions in large groups than in small groups, we might venture the paradoxical hypothesis that the larger the group, the more effect a few outspoken members are likely to have in determining the success of discussion.

LABORATORY TEACHING

The laboratory method is now so widely accepted in scientific education that it may seem heretical to ask whether laboratory experience is an effective way to achieve educational objectives.

Laboratory teaching assumes that first-hand experience in observation and manipulation of the materials of science is superior to other methods of developing understanding and appreciation. Laboratory training is also frequently used to develop skills necessary for more advanced study or research.

From the standpoint of theory, the activity of the student, the sensorimotor nature of the experience, and the individualization of laboratory instruction should contribute positively to learning. Information cannot usually be obtained, however, by direct experience as rapidly as it can from abstractions presented orally or in print. Films or demonstrations may also short-cut some of the trial and error of the laboratory. Thus, one would not expect laboratory teaching to have an advantage over other teaching methods in amount of information learned. Rather we might expect the differences to be revealed in retention, in ability to apply learning, or in actual skill in observation or manipulation of materials. Unfortunately, little research has attempted to tease out these special types of outcomes. If these outcomes are unmeasured, a finding of no difference in effectiveness between laboratory and other methods of instruction is almost meaningless since there is little reason to expect laboratory teaching to be effective in simple communication of information.

In a course on methods of engineering,

White (1945) found that students taught by a group-laboratory method achieved more than those taught by a lecture-demonstration method. However, Balcziak (1953), comparing (1) demonstration, (2) individual laboratory, and (3) combined demonstration and laboratory in a college physical science course, found no significant differences between them as measured by tests of information, scientific attitude, or laboratory performance.

Kruglak (1952) compared the achievement of students in elementary college physics laboratories taught by two methods—the demonstration and the individual method. The individual method proved superior not only in student learning of techniques but also in solving simple laboratory problems. Another experiment on methods of laboratory instruction found that a problem-solving method was superior to traditional laboratory-manual methods in teaching students to apply principles of physics in interpreting phenomena (Bainter, 1955). Lahti (1956) also found a problem-solving method to be superior to more conventional procedures in developing ability to design an experiment. Because many laboratory teachers have been interested in teaching problem-solving methods, this may also be an appropriate place to note Burkhardt's finding (1956) that students who are taught calculus with an emphasis on the understanding of concepts learn concepts better than students taught with conventional emphasis upon solving problems. On the face of it this might appear to be in opposition to the results of Kruglak, Bainter, and Lahti. Actually all of these studies point to the importance of developing understanding rather than teaching students to solve problems by going through a routine series of steps. Whether or not laboratory is superior to lecture-demonstration in developing understanding and problem-solving skills probably depends upon the extent to which understanding of concepts and general problem-solving procedures are emphasized by the instructor in the laboratory situation.

PROJECT METHODS AND INDEPENDENT STUDY

The recent interest in independent study as a means of utilizing faculty time more efficiently has brought to the fore a teaching method which has been used in some form for many years. If one goal of education is to help the student develop the ability to continue learning after his formal education is completed, it seems reasonable that he should have supervised experience in learning independently—experience in which the instructor helps the student learn how to formulate problems, find answers, and evaluate his progress himself. One might expect the values of independent study to be greatest for students with high ability and a good deal of background in the area to be covered since such students should be less likely to be overwhelmed by difficulties.

Independent study programs frequently involve the execution of projects in which a student or group of students undertakes to gather and integrate data relative to some problem.

The results of research on the effectiveness of the project method are not particularly encouraging. One of the first "independent study" experiments was that of Seashore (1928). His course consisted primarily of guided individual study with written reports on eight projects, each of which took about a month to complete. Final examination scores, however, were no different for these students than for students taught by the usual lecture-discussion method (Scheidemann, 1929). In a college botany course, Novak (1958) found that students in conventional classes learned more facts than did those taught by the project method. The project method was particularly ineffective for students in the middle third of the group in intelligence. Similarly, Goldstein (1956) reported that students taught pharmacology by a project method did not learn more than those taught in a standard laboratory.

Unfortunately, measures of achievement such as those used in the studies just noted are probably not sufficient measures of the objectives of project instruction. Presumably the real superiority of the project method should be revealed in measures of motivation and resourcefulness. Novak's experiment was laudable in its inclusion of a measure of scientific attitude, but neither conventional nor project classes made significant gains from the beginning to the end of the semester. Similarly, in a class in mental hygiene, Timmel (1954) found no difference in the effectiveness of the lecture and project methods in changing adjustment. One morsel of support comes from Thistlethwaite's (1960) finding that National Merit Scholars checked requirement of a term paper or laboratory project as one characteristic of their most stimulating course.

With the support of the Fund for the Advancement of Education, a number of colleges have recently experimented with more elaborate programs of independent study. As with other comparisons of teaching methods, few differences have been found between achievement of students working independently and those taught in conventional classes. Moreover, the expected gains in independence have also often failed to materialize. Students taught by independent study do not always seem to develop greater ability or motivation for learning independently.

One of the most comprehensive research programs on independent study was that carried out by Antioch College (Churchill, 1957; Churchill & Baskin, 1958). The Antioch experiment involved courses with varying periods of independent study in humanities, social science, and science. A serious attempt was made not only to measure cognitive and affective achievement but also to evaluate the effect of independent study upon "learning resourcefulness." In addition, the Antioch staff, recognizing that not all students are ready to work independently, planned programs of training for independent work.

The results of the experiments, however, do not point clearly to any conclusion. For example, in one experiment, independent small groups learned more subject matter in physics than students working independently as individuals. But in art, students working individually learned more than those in independent small groups. As in most experiments on teaching methods, the predominant results were of "no significant difference." An exception to this may be found in various indices of student satisfaction in which several significant differences favor lecture-discussion over independent study and especially over independent small groups.

In the Antioch College study, however, one method of saving faculty time was found effective as measured by both student learning and student attitudes. This method, used in teaching French, increased the students' time in class from six to eleven hours a week, but eight of the instructional hours were in charge of a student assistant who used visual materials prepared by the instructor (Baskin, 1960).

In another well-controlled experiment, carried out at Oberlin College (McCollough & Van Atta, 1958), students in introductory science, psychology, and mathematics were required to work independently of the instructor in small groups. This independent work occupied one-third of the college year following several weeks of preliminary training. As in the Antioch experiment, no significant differences in learning appeared either as measured by the usual achievement tests or by a test of learning resourcefulness. Generally, the Oberlin students seem not to have been unhappy about the independent study experience although they indicated that they would have preferred several two-week periods of independent study to the single longer period.

The most favorable results on independent study were obtained at the University of Colorado by Gruber and Weitman (1960). In a course in freshman English in which the group met about 90 per cent of the regularly scheduled hours and had little formal training in grammar, the self-directed study group was significantly superior to control groups on the test of grammar. In a course in physical optics, groups of students who attended class independently of the instructor but were free to consult him learned fewer facts and simple applications but were superior to students in conventional classes in difficult applications and learning new material. Moreover, the latter difference was maintained in a retest three months later while the difference in factual knowledge disappeared (Weitman & Gruber, 1960). In a class in educational psychology an experimental class meeting once a week with the instructor and twice a week in groups of five or six students without the instructor was equal to a conventional class hearing three lectures a week in mastery of content, but tended to be superior on measures of curiosity. In another experiment, students in self-directed study paid more constant attention to a lecture than did students in conventional classes.

The experiment by McKeachie, Lin, Forrin, and Teevan (1960) also involved a fairly high degree of student-instructor contact. Students normally met with the instructor in small groups weekly or biweekly, but they were free to consult the instructor whenever they wished. The results of the experiment suggest that the "tutorial" students did not learn as much from the textbook as students taught in conventional lecture and discussion section classes, but they did develop stronger motivation both for course work and for continued learning after the course. This was indicated not only by responses to a questionnaire administered at the end of the course but also by the number of advanced psychology courses later elected.

Independent study experiments have varied greatly in the amount of assistance given students and in patterning instructional versus independent periods. For example, merely excusing students from attending class is one method of stimulating independent study. The results of such a procedure are not uniform but suggest that classroom experience is not essential for learning. However, the kinds of learning that

take place out of class may be different from those that take place in class.

Jensen (1951) compared four groups, including one in which students were completely excused from class attendance. The results showed no difference in gains among the four groups, but students who had worked independently were more willing than others to volunteer for further independent study. Wakely, Marr, Plath, and Wilkins (1960) compared performance in a traditional four-hours-a-week lecture class with that in a class which met only once a week to clear up questions on the textbook. In this experiment the traditional classes proved to be superior. Similarly, Paul (1932) found 55-minute class periods to be superior to 30-minute periods as measured by student achievement.

The results of studies in a child development course by Parsons (1957) and Parsons, Ketcham, and Beach (1958) were more favorable to independent study. In the latter experiment four teaching methods were compared—a lecture, instructor-led discussions, autonomous groups which did not come to class, and individual independent study in which each student was sent home with the syllabus and returned for the final examination. All groups were chosen randomly. In both experiments students working independently made the best scores on the final examination, which measured retention of factual material in the textbook. The instructor-led discussion groups were the lowest in performance on the final examination. There were no significant differences between groups on a measure of attitudes toward working with children. The authors explain their results on the grounds that the independent group was not distracted by the interesting examples, possible applications, or points of view opposing those in the text, all of which were presented in the other groups.

However, in the latter experiment one group of students was made up of teachers commuting to campus for a Saturday class. The results for these students were quite different from those for resident students.

In this case students in independent study performed significantly worse than other groups on the examination, perhaps because they were less committed to regular study and may also have experienced more frustration in not having class.

Although the Parsons, Ketcham, and Beach results were favorable to independent study, they are not satisfying to the advocate of this method. These results lead to the conclusion that if a student knows that he is going to be tested on the factual content of a particular book, it is more advantageous for him to read that book than participate in other educational activities. In fact, one might suggest that even better results could be obtained if the desired facts could be identified by giving the students test questions in advance. But knowledge of specific facts is not usually the major objective of an independent study program. What we are hoping for is greater integration, increased purposefulness, and more intense motivation for further study. That independent study can achieve these ends is indicated by the Colorado and Michigan experiments. But the paucity of positive results suggests that we need more research on methods of selecting and training students for independent study, arranging the independent study experience, and measuring outcomes. Note that the Colorado results came in courses in which a good deal of contact with the instructor was retained.

AUTOMATED TECHNIQUES

The impending shortage of college teachers has sparked several hotly contested skirmishes about the virtues or vices of various techniques of teaching with devices substituting for a portion of the usual face-to-face interaction between instructors and students. Since some college faculty members anxious about technological unemployment resist innovations, research has often been used as a technique of infiltration rather than as a method of developing and testing educational theory.

Along with many inconsequential studies, a few carefully executed programs of research have emerged. Representative of these are those described in the following section.

Television[7]

Before reviewing the research on teaching by television, let us consider two hypotheses that may help in analyzing the research results.

Television is not a method of instruction in the sense that discussion and lecture are methods of instruction. Rather it is a means of giving the student a clear view of the instructional situation. Therefore, we would expect that (1) the relative effectiveness of teaching via television will vary depending on the importance of being able to see clearly. For example, we would expect television to be effective when it is important for students to see demonstrations, visiting lecturers, or films, but to have little advantage when communication is primarily verbal.

Television reduces the opportunity for students to communicate with teachers and for teachers to interact with students. We would thus expect that (2) the effectiveness of television will vary inversely with the importance of two-way communication not only for feedback to the student but particularly for feedback to the teacher.

In 1954, Pennsylvania State University (Carpenter & Greenhill, 1955, 1958) received a grant from the Fund for the Advancement of Education to study the effectiveness of conventional courses taught for a full semester over closed-circuit television as compared with the same instruction given in the usual manner. With these funds, a program of research was initiated on the courses entitled General Chemistry, General Psychology, and Psychology of Marriage. In 1957 the research program was expanded to (1) extend the project to additional courses; (2) study instructional variables, and (3) work on meth-

---

[7] Some portions of this section were previously published in W. J. McKeachie, TV for college instruction, *Improving Coll. & Univer. Teaching*, 1958, 6, 84–89, and are used by permission of the publisher.

ods of improving instruction on television.

The results of this research may be used either to extol or damn television. Essentially they indicate that there is little loss in student learning in courses taught by television as compared with classes taught conventionally. For example, the first experiment dealt with the lecture portion of courses in general chemistry and general psychology. In the chemistry course the differences between methods on objective measures of information were not significant. In the psychology course the conventional class did prove to be slightly superior in knowledge to the television class.

Students learned the information needed to pass examinations, and most did not object strongly to the televised classes although they preferred live instruction. Students in psychology were asked (1) how much they liked psychology, and (2) how much it contributed to their education as compared with other courses they were taking. On both counts, ratings of the students in the television classes were lower than those of students who were in the same room as the instructor. The psychology students were also asked if they would like to take another course in psychology. About the same percentages of students signed up from lectures, television originating rooms, and television receiving rooms, but when asked if they would prefer taking it in a large class or by television, a plurality preferred television. While students at other colleges do not rebel at television either, research findings quite consistently report less favorable attitudes toward courses taught by television as compared with conventional classes (e.g., Lepore & Wilson, 1958; Macomber & Siegel, 1960).

The effectiveness of television is particularly astonishing to one who has seen the apparent inattention in many television classes. If students who are obviously inattentive learn as much as those who appear to be attentive, one might suspect that many students have developed the ability to appear attentive in conventional classes even though their minds are wandering. In the latter case, television students may simply be exposing the reactions to lectures which polite students ordinarily hide from their instructor. The New York University research staff (Klapper, 1958) used student observers to classify television students into high-, middle-, and low-attention groups. In none of their courses was attention level related to achievement, although their evidence suggested that students who had more previous knowledge of the subject paid less attention than those who had less.

Factors unimportant in using television. The heading of this section would normally be "Factors Conditioning the Effectiveness of Educational Television," but the results of the research are more clearly indicated by the title chosen. For example, recognizing that instructor-student interaction is sometimes important in learning, the Pennsylvania State group installed "two-way" microphone communication in the receiving rooms so that students in the receiving rooms could ask questions. This technique has been used even more extensively at the State University of Iowa (Stuit, et al., 1956) and at Case Institute of Technology (Martin, 1957a, 1957b). The Pennsylvania State group found that this method of instruction was not superior to simple one-way communication, although students prefer two-way communication (Carpenter & Greenhill, 1958). Similar results were found in the research on television instruction in the Army and at Case (Fritz, 1952; Martin, Adams, & Baron, 1958).

Another attempt to combine the value of interaction with that of television was an experiment in presenting a 35-minute television lesson followed by a 15-minute discussion period in each of the receiving rooms. Other students in the same course observed by means of television the 15-minute discussion conducted by the instructor with the eight students in the origination room. Still other students were allowed to leave or to study their notes. As in the other attempt to provide interaction, results showed no significant differences in test performance between students taught by each of these three methods. A poll of students indicated that they preferred two hours of lecture followed by a full period of discussion to a short discussion each period.

Size of the viewing group is not an important variable in television instruction, nor do proctors in the viewing rooms contribute to student learning. Adapting a course for television by adding supplementary visual aids also proved to be no more effective than televised lecture-blackboard presentations (Carpenter & Greenhill, 1958). In fact, both at Pennsylvania State and at New York University (Adams, Carpenter, & Smith, 1958), the "visual" productions tended to be *less* effective than "bare bones" television. This result should probably not startle us after having read the Parsons, Ketcham, and Beach results (1958) in research on independent study. Just as discussion and lecture apparently interfered with learning the textbook, so here visual materials may have distracted the students from the verbal content upon which the tests were based. Such experiments make it clear that we still have little firm evidence upon which to base selection of visual materials for television or for other types of teaching. Selecting materials on the basis of "hunch" or of student reactions may be unwise, for such materials may lull the student into a comfortable feeling that he understands when in fact he doesn't.

The Pennsylvania State research does provide some support for the idea that television's effectiveness lies in giving the student a good view. In one experiment, students who had three weeks of instruction were given their choice of whether to finish the course in television classrooms or in the originating room. Depending upon the course, one-third to two-thirds of the students chose television; these students were predominantly those who had been assigned seats toward the back of the lecture hall.

Some theorists suggest that one important outcome of education is the tendency of students to identify with teachers. Proponents of television have suggested that television increases student identification with the instructor; thus it helps him feel closer to the instructor by improving his ability to observe facial expression, eye movement, and other individual characteristics not as clearly observable in a large lecture hall. While this may be true, the television students at Pennsylvania State reportedly did not often come in to talk to the instructor outside of class. Whether this would be paralleled by the behavior of students in other classes of the same size is not known. If individual contact with an instructor is important in any sort of learning, the large class, whether taught by television or not, may be ineffective.

Television compared with large and small classes. A second major project in closed-circuit instruction was that at Miami University (Macomber & Siegel, 1956, 1957a, 1957b, 1960). This group's research is of particular interest because it compared closed-circuit television with both large lecture classes and small semidiscussion classes, and studied the possible differential effect of different types of instruction upon students of differing abilities and attitudes.

The Miami University group attempted to use each method at its best. The television courses utilized professional directors, and audio-visual assistance was available in both television and other classes. The result was that the television classes gained and held student attention as well as most good classroom lectures. (But remember the New York University and Pennsylvania State findings that visually enriched production may produce inferior achievement.)

In the first experiment at Miami University, the main measure of achievement was the final examination in each course, and the television classes were not inferior on this criterion. In fact, in a human biology course the television students scored higher than the conventional classes, although other factors might have contributed to this difference. However, in the second year of telecasting, live teaching produced achievement superior to that in television classes in the second semester of the four courses, and in economics proved to be superior in producing gains in critical thinking. Results of third-year experiments were less unfavorable to television, although television classes in zoology proved inferior to conventional classes on a test of problem solving.

Since television is usually considered as a substitute for large classes, it is worth noting that large "live" classes did not consistently produce the inferior results of television instruction in cognitive outcomes but did tend to be inferior to small conventional "live" classes in effecting changes in attitudes.

Other experiments in college teaching by closed-circuit television. Among the other experiments on television teaching, those carried out at Purdue University, the State University of Iowa, New York University, and San Francisco State College were the largest and best designed. While these experiments have already been cited in our discussion of the Pennsylvania State and Miami experiments, a few points remain. One of these relates to teaching English composition by television. Even though the Purdue experiment (Seibert, 1958) used television for only two of the three instructional periods per week, and television students apparently had a good deal of practice in theme writing, television instruction proved to be significantly inferior to conventional instruction in several comparisons. The superiority of conventional teaching was most marked for students of lower ability. At New York University (Klapper, 1958) similar ability-level differences were not found, but there was evidence of superiority of conventional methods as measured by theme writing. Similar differences favoring conventional instruction using objective tests of achievement were found during the first semester but were reversed during the second semester.

At Purdue television instruction also was found to be inferior to conventional instruction in mechanical engineering (Seibert & Honig, 1959), military science (Kasten & Seibert, 1959), and, on some tests, in calculus (Seibert, 1957).

When a course demands the demonstration of small objects or parts, the use of television or films should be advantageous. In an experiment at Rensselaer Polytechnic Institute (Throop, Assini, & Boguslavsky, 1958) in teaching Strength of Materials, television was not inferior to conventional methods in teaching instrumentation and specimen behavior, but was inferior in teaching theory and familiarity with machinery.

Student ability generally does not make a difference in the relative effectiveness of television. At Miami University, low-ability students in Foundations of Human Behavior and Government achieved more in conventional classes than in television classes, but in physiology and zoology, the opposite was true. However, student ratings of television instruction are inversely correlated with student ability. While the best television instructors are liked by all types of students, the better students ordinarily dislike television and large classes more than do the poorer students. Students feel that television hurts both the instructor's pacing of the instruction and his stimulation of interest. Attitudes toward television, however, do not greatly affect achievement. Students who dislike television achieve almost as much (or little?) as those who like it, and, interestingly, such attitudes tend to reflect those of the proctors in the viewing rooms.

In both large lectures and in television sections, students complain of lack of contact with the instructor, but Miami students disliked television less than large lectures, while New York University students tended to prefer lectures. The attitudes toward television of both groups tended to become more negative during a second semester of television. If they could have the same instructor, students generally preferred a small section to television or a large class. But they preferred television or a large class to a small class if they could be sure of having an excellent instructor in the television or large class but had to take their chances in electing a small class. This is probably a fairly realistic alternative. The student's choice may not always be wise, however, for in experimental comparisons Miami graduate assistants proved to be inferior (as measured by student achievement) to regular staff members in one course and superior in another. Moreover, students taught by graduate assistants did more outside reading.

Uses of television. From our hypothesis that television would be of most value in courses depending upon visual presentation of information, we might expect it to be more effective in science and engineering courses than in social sciences and humanities courses. From our second hypothesis that television would be of less value in classes where interaction between students and instructor is important, we might expect it to be relatively less effective in psychology, speech, and language courses than in courses usually taught by lecture. However, such comparisons are difficult to make. As we have seen, students learned as much by television as in conventional classes in chemistry at Pennsylvania State and in engineering at Purdue (Seibert & Honig, 1959), but in general psychology the television students both at Purdue and Pennsylvania State did not do as well as students in conventional classes. This evidence is in line with our hypothesis but certainly not conclusive.[8]

It was suggested above that television should be especially effective in courses requiring the use of demonstrations. If we assume that science courses are more likely to use demonstrations than are other courses, we can examine the experimental results to determine the relative effectiveness of television instruction in science and in other courses. Such an appraisal provides some support for our hypothesis, for if we simply look at the direction of the differences, about half the experiments in science classes favor tele-

vision and half favor conventional instruction. In nonscience courses well over two-thirds of the differences favor conventional teaching. Similarly, the one experiment in which television was significantly superior to conventional instruction was in a biology course, while six of seven experiments in which conventional teaching proved superior were in nonscience courses.[9]

Whether television or film should be used in a course requiring demonstrations of small phenomena seems to be largely a matter of cost. However, there seems to be a tendency to forget the possibility of reproducing diagrams and photographs as an alternative to television. While television and film seem to be clearly advantageous as methods of presenting relations between moving parts, many of the "visuals" used on television do not involve movement, and many photographs, enlargements, slides, and lithoprints can be made for the price of one television camera or film.

Insofar as student-instructor interaction is important in teaching a course, television appears to be of little help. Television does not permit more students to talk, even with two-way audio connections. The student's opportunity to participate is an inverse function of the number of students in the class. If actual participation is important, larger classes should be less effective whether they are taught in one classroom or by television. Television may permit students to gather in smaller groups (as in the Iowa experiments) but the Iowa results (Stuit, et al., 1956) suggest that students feel less free to participate in television classes than in regular classes. The 90-minute classes at Miami used television during the first part of the period to provide the stimulus for discussion; this pro-

---

[8] Few experiments have adequately evaluated the possible assets of television as a visual medium. Most achievement tests are verbal. We would expect television to reveal its unique values when outcome measures require visual recognition or discrimination. While the objectives of most college courses emphasize abstraction and verbalization, there must be some areas in which visual relationships are important.

[9] The preceding comments have been primarily concerned with closed-circuit television instruction on campus. While it is difficult to make adequately controlled studies of the educational effectiveness of broadcast television, it seems quite clear that students motivated enough to take a television course for credit at home learn well and have favorable attitudes toward television (Dreher & Beatty, 1958; Evans, Roney, & McAdams, 1954; Lepore & Wilson, 1958).

cedure seems to be successful. However, the Pennsylvania State studies did not reveal any gains from discussion or two-way communication.

Cutler, McKeachie, and McNeil (1958) compared the effectiveness of teaching equal-sized groups in face-to-face groups and by *telephone*. Both groups showed significant learning and attitude change, and there was no significant difference in the effectiveness of the two methods. Thus, if economy in instruction is desired, perhaps the expense of television cameras and receiving tubes is unnecessary. One of the few experiments comparing the effectiveness of radio and television, however, showed better learning and retention for television (Paul & Ogilvie, 1955), and experiments conducted a generation ago tended to find differences favoring face-to-face instruction over radio or printing (e.g., Wilke, 1934).

Television can, however, have certain *advantages* in promoting interaction. On any large college campus, one difficulty in education outside the classroom is that students have few common educational experiences. Since their common experiences tend to be social or athletic, these are likely to be the usual topics of conversation. Stephens College (1955) met this problem by developing a required course, "Ideas and Living Today," which consisted of brief television lectures viewed by students in small faculty-led discussion groups. The course is scheduled just before lunch so that discussions spill over into the dining halls. The course thus provides a common intellectual experience which can stimulate interstudent education outside the classroom—an element of education lacking in many colleges today.

Even if closed-circuit television were a potential answer to all our educational problems, its success would probably depend to some extent on faculty acceptance. Apparently all colleges using closed-circuit television have found that many faculty members are skeptical of its value. Polls generally indicate that faculty members are willing to teach by television if necessary but prefer traditional teaching methods (e.g., Carpenter & Greenhill, 1955).

Faculty acceptance of television seems to be greatest when the faculty has participated in planning for it. For example, the faculty of Stephens College seems to have accepted television more fully than the faculties of other institutions, and this is probably due in no small part to their involvement in planning for their television course.

A second factor in the acceptance of television at Stephens is that the course offered does not set a particular department or instructor apart from the rest of the faculty. The course offered at Stephens is interdivisional and involves almost all of the faculty. Since the course is a new one, no local professor was pushed aside to make room for a "Master Teacher."

When television enables a department to provide instruction which would otherwise be difficult or impossible, acceptance also seems to be good. Thus Pennsylvania State found no faculty objections to teaching electrical engineering by television when a large enrollment plus a staff shortage resulted in several unstaffed sections.

Finally, the support of administrative officials is also of obvious importance. Since television teaching is difficult and time-consuming, faculty members are much more likely to participate if they feel that this activity is valued not only by their colleagues but also by their administrative officials. (One evidence of such support is a reduction in teaching load for television instructors.)

Taking the results of all research on television instruction, we feel safe in concluding that television instruction for a complete course is inferior to classroom lectures in communicating information, developing critical thinking, changing attitudes, and arousing interest in a subject but that this inferiority is probably not great. This conclusion may surprise the reader who has seen publicity releases reporting no significant differences between classroom and television instruction. In our consideration of methodological issues, we noted the logical fallacy in concluding that no difference exists because the difference found was not great enough to disprove the null hypothesis. This is particularly pertinent here because a review of a number of studies of television leaves one with quite a different conclusion than he might draw from a review of just one. In 20 of the 26 well-controlled experiments reviewed, conventional classes were superior to television classes in achievement. Although few of the differences were statistically significant by themselves, simple application of the sign-test indicates that the differences were not random. In contrast with research comparing other instructional methods, the consistency of results favoring conventional instruction over television is unusual.[10] When one weighs heavily the necessity for accommodating higher education to large numbers of students, however, the differences between television and conventional instruction seem very small. It may be that researchers are reluctant to report findings contrary to the hypotheses of the foundations that support them, and their reports are thus as gentle as possible.

Films

The great mass of research on instructional films is relevant to our topic, even though most of it is not concerned with college teaching. While we cannot summarize all of the relevant studies, certain principles have emerged. (For a more complete analysis, see Chapter 12 and Miller, 1957.)

1. Students can learn from films and usually do learn at least as much as from a poor teacher (VanderMeer, 1950).

2. Such learning is not confined to details but may include concepts and attitudes (Hoban & Van Ormer, 1950; Kishler, 1950; Mertens, 1951).

3. Repeating the film increases learning (McTavish, 1949).

---

[10] Note that most research has dealt with television as a substitute for conventional instruction. The potential of television as a tool for enriching classroom teaching has not been assessed.

4. Students learn how to learn from films; i.e., students with previous experience in learning from films learn more than those with no previous experience with instructional films (VanderMeer, 1951).

5. Presenting pictures is more effective than presenting words as stimuli in rote association tasks such as learning a foreign language (Kopstein & Roshal, 1954; May & Lumsdaine, 1958).

6. Participation increases learning (Hovland, Lumsdaine, & Sheffield, 1949).

Much of the preceding discussion of instructional television is relevant to teaching by films. The chief differences seem to be that the movie camera has greater mobility than the television camera, it is more expensive to produce a film than a television lesson (assuming that the television equipment is already available), and "live" television is presumed to have greater immediacy. Unfortunately, we have little evidence on the educational importance of immediacy. Intuitively it seems that students would feel more involvement in watching a television professor on their own college's staff, knowing that they are seeing him at the actual moment of performance, than they would feel in watching a film made at some earlier time. Whether or not such differences in involvement do occur (and if they occur, whether they make any difference educationally) is still unknown.

Tests and Teaching Machines

While we usually think of testing procedures in terms of their validity as measures of student achievement, their function as instruments for promoting learning may be even more important. After dismal recitals of nonsignificant differences between differing teaching methods, it is refreshing to find positive results from variations in testing procedures.

In some of the earliest experiments in this area, Jones (1923) found that immediate testing after a psychology lecture resulted in improved retention. The good effects of testing persisted or increased over an eight-week period.

Jones's results supporting the value of immediate feedback are supported by an experiment in a government class (Fitch, Drucker, & Norton, 1951) in which students having weekly noncredit quizzes made better scores on monthly tests than a nonquizzed control group. Similarly, in a remedial English course at Purdue (Maize, 1954), students who wrote 40 themes evaluated in class made greater improvement on a test of English usage than a group which had workbook drill and wrote 14 themes, individually corrected by the instructor. Similar results were noted in the study by Guetzkow, Kelly, and McKeachie (1954). May and Lumsdaine (1958) reported that learning from film is also positively influenced by participation and feedback devices.

Tests provide knowledge of results, one of the major elements in learning, and we would expect that the more information contained in the feedback, the greater its value. In an experiment in the Air Force (Stone, 1955), performances benefited from return of multiple-choice tests together with information about why the alternative chosen was wrong and why the correct alternative was right. This technique proved superior to four other techniques which gave less complete knowledge of results ranging down to returning only a score on the total examination. Similar results were obtained by Bryan and Rigney (1956). In a related study, McKeachie and Hiler (1954) found that students required to answer study questions performed better on test questions in the same area than students not given the study questions and tended to do better than those whose answers were not required or graded. Thus the simple principle that knowledge of results facilitates learning is one of the few generalizations clearly supported by research on college teaching.

Until this point, the reader of this section may wonder why testing procedures have been classified under the general heading,

"Automated Techniques." The bridge to that general topic is found in the work of Pressey (1926, 1950; also included in Lumsdaine & Glaser, 1960), who published the results of an extensive program of research with tests which students scored for themselves by punching alternatives until they hit the correct one. Four types of studies were carried out, and Pressey concluded that (1) the self-scoring characteristics represent a tremendous saving in time; (2) test taking is transformed into self-instruction by the immediate knowledge of mistakes; (3) supplemental use of the tests improves performance on regular objective tests; and (4) even more automatic self-scoring devices can be devised. This last conclusion proved to be prophetic, for there are now many models of "teaching machines."

The term *teaching machine* now refers to a device for presenting content and questions in predetermined sequences and providing immediate knowledge of results to an active learner. Teaching machines permit the learner to proceed at his own rate. The successive questions proceed in tiny steps from the simple to the complex. If a student makes a series of correct responses, he may adjust the machine to skip some steps. If he fails items, they are repeated. The program of the lesson may include hints or other guidance. Thus teaching machines or workbooks have many theoretical advantages over lecturing or other conventional methods of instruction. Unfortunately, little experimental work has been done at the college level to determine the limits of their usefulness. At present it appears that learning is enhanced by programed presentation but that programed presentations require more time than conventional textbooks (Angell, 1949; Evans, Glaser, & Homme, 1960; Little, 1934; Stephens, 1953; Stolurow, 1960). At present, much developmental work is being directed not only at the basic problem of devising appropriate sets of items and determining optimal modes of presentation but also at development of machines flexible enough to adjust to individual differences in the background and ability of the learners. (See Galanter, 1959; Lumsdaine & Glaser, 1960; and Chapter 12 in this Handbook.)

As we pointed out earlier, one advantage of the skilled teacher is his ability to utilize feedback in adapting his teaching to individual and group differences. Moreover, the instructor often provides feedback which not only tells the learner that he is wrong but tells him why he is wrong. Experiments at the System Development Corporation (Coulson, 1959; Coulson & Silberman, 1959) suggested that teaching incorporating such human characteristics is more effective than teaching by the typical fixed-sequence machines. (In these experiments, instead of using teaching machines to simulate human teachers, the experiments used humans to simulate teaching machines.)

Printing

Books used as substitutes for the live teacher have been in existence for some time. Unlike other technological aids, printing has found wide acceptance by college faculties. Perhaps a few centuries of use will produce the same degree of acceptance of television and teaching machines.

Despite the age of printing as a technique, there is relatively little research on its use, although much of the research on independent study, of course, bears upon students' ability to learn from books. In an early study, Greene (1928) found that students learned as well from reading material themselves as from listening to the same material read aloud. The better students, however, profited more from reading than from listening. Corey (1934) found better immediate recall for reading than for a lecture, although the difference disappeared on a later test. Oral presentations, however, seem to be superior to printing in changing attitudes or opinion (Knower, 1935, 1936; Wilke, 1934). Cantril and Allport (1935) suggested that critical attitudes are favored by reading.

Becker and Dallinger (1960) compared three teaching methods in a course on Com-munication Skills. One method reduced class meetings from four to three a week and presented basic principles through assigned and optional readings. A second method used kinescope presentation of basic principles by experts, supplemented by discussion led by the classroom instructor. The third method, like the second, used four class periods a week for normal instructional procedures. An analysis of variance of achievement tests revealed significant differences between instructors but not between methods. Both students and instructors, however, preferred the normal method.

One recent development is the "programed textbook," an instructional book developed by utilizing the learning-in-small-steps sequence of the conventional teaching machine (Glaser & Homme, 1958). It seems entirely reasonable that books designed specifically to achieve certain objectives could be more effective than our present textbooks. Unfortunately, we are probably better able to devise sequences optimal for cognitive learning than for arousing and maintaining motivation. Information obtained by research on teaching-machine programs should be valuable to the textbook writer.

A recent study on the learning of college text-type materials by Ausubel, Robbins, and Blake (1957) probably will not seem significant to those who are unfamiliar with classical learning theory. Psychologists have used the concept of "retroactive inhibition" to describe the fact that in learning experiments new learning tends to interfere with memory of previous learning. Recent research (Underwood, 1957) has cast some doubt on the interpretations of this phenomenon. The experiment by Ausubel and his associates demonstrated that memory of a passage on Buddhism was not affected adversely by later study of a passage on Christianity. In fact, when passages repeated points from the earlier material, memory was actually facilitated. One critical question for the instructor, however, is still unanswered: What is the effect of giving one point of view in a lecture and assigning opposing points of view in readings? One would guess that this technique would be ineffective as measured by a test of retention but might contribute positively to ability to think creatively about a problem.

The research to date indicates that television, films, teaching machines, and books can be used to achieve educational objectives. Their usefulness depends on the objective, characteristics of the students, and the excellence of the materials. Research at present reveals no likelihood that these devices will eliminate the need for face-to-face contacts between professors and students.

STUDENT CHARACTERISTICS RELATED TO EFFECTIVE TEACHING

Most teachers are aware that differences between students are not taken into account sufficiently by our usual teaching methods. Experienced teachers have felt for years that no one teaching method succeeds with all kinds of students. One reason for the host of experimental comparisons resulting in nonsignificant differences may be simply that methods optimal for some students are detrimental to the achievement of others. When mean scores are compared, one method thus seems to be no different in its effect from any other.

It is encouraging to note that when an instructor is aware of the nature of differences among his students, his teaching is more effective. In an experiment in which teachers of physics were given increased knowledge of their students' personal backgrounds for one of their two classes, the students made significantly greater gains in achievement and rated their instructors as being more effective in the experimental (informed) classes (Sturgis, 1958).

We have already noted some analyses of teaching methods taking such individual differences into account. For example, using analysis of variance, Guetzkow, Kelly, and McKeachie (1954) found that students differing in intelligence or in preferences for teaching methods were not differently af-

fected by the three methods used in their study. Hudelson (1928) found similar results in his studies of class size. Macomber and Siegel's results (1956), although not strongly opposite, did reveal a tendency for high-ability students to gain more in course-related attitudes in small rather than large sections. They also report a small superiority in achievement in television or large classes for those who initially held favorable attitudes toward the method used. Other personality measures did not, however, predict differential achievement in large and small classes. Ward's (1956) results also suggest that the ablest students benefit most from small groups. Comparing group study and lecture-demonstration methods in a physical science course, he found that the group method resulted in better achievement on a measure of understanding and problem solving for the abler students. The poorer students, however, benefited more from lecture-demonstration.

Parsons, Ketcham, and Beach [11] (1960) reported that the abler students are less satisfied the less their responsibility for setting goals of learning. Calvin, Hoffman, and Harden (1957) found in three experiments that less intelligent students consistently did better in group problem-solving situations conducted in an authoritarian manner than in groups conducted in a permissive manner. The same difference did not occur for bright students. The experimenters suggest in a footnote that the inferior performance of dull students in permissive groups may be due to an inferior ability to adjust to a change from the usual methods of conducting groups. If this were true, we should expect brighter students to adjust more easily to new methods than less intelligent students. So far, this has not been demonstrated, although the trends reported seem to be in that direction. For example, in the Miami experiment,

---

[11] T. S. Parsons, W. A. Ketcham, & L. R. Beach. Students, teachers, and fellow students: A study of instructional interactions and outcomes. Unpublished paper, 1960. (Dittoed)

high-ability students did as well in television classes as in conventional classes although they had more negative attitudes toward television than the less able students had. On the whole, our best guess would be that face-to-face discussion teaching is more advantageous for the more intelligent students than for those with less ability.

The analysis of student characteristics in studies such as those above is worth while, but, except for the study by Calvin, Hoffman, & Harden (1957), analysis of individual differences was largely peripheral to the main purpose of the studies and was undertaken with little theoretical basis to guide it. As focus shifts to student characteristics, research designs should employ teaching method variables and dimensions of individual differences bearing some theoretical relationship to one another, as suggested by Cronbach (1957). For example, if we are going to investigate intelligence as a student characteristic affecting learning under different teaching methods, we need to develop a more specific theory about the conditions which are effective in producing learning for students of high and low intelligence.

Independence

A pioneering step in the direction of relating personality and response to teaching methods was taken by Wispé (1951), who used TAT-like measures to differentiate three types of students: the "personality-insecure" student (51 per cent of the sample), the "satisfied" student (26 per cent of the sample), and the independent student (23 per cent of the sample). The "insecure" student had unfavorable attitudes toward permissive teaching. The "satisfied" student had favorable attitudes toward instructors, fellow students, and both directive and permissive teaching methods. The "independent" student was highly verbal and wanted more permissive teaching no matter what method his instructor used. The independent student had moderately favorable attitudes toward fellow students and instructors but was

likely to direct aggression against the instructor in directive classes.

In conjunction with Wispé's results, a study of factors associated with student choice of directive or nondirective classes is of interest. In their study of Springfield College students, Ashmus and Haigh (1952) found, unlike Wispé, that almost equal numbers chose each method. Students choosing nondirective classes did not differ in intelligence or grades from students choosing directive classes, but they were more likely to have had previous experience in nondirective groups and tended to be more flexible, to be better able to cope with ambiguity, and to have more self-insight (Haigh & Schmidt, 1956).

A cluster of variables probably related to Wispé's is Patton's (1955) "acceptance of responsibility for learning." Patton found that the degree to which the student accepted responsibility was positively correlated with gain in psychological knowledge, gain in ability to apply psychology, rating of the value of the course, and interest in psychology.

But what sort of student will accept responsibility in such a course? Patton (1955) found that the students who liked his experimental class and assumed responsibility were likely to be independent of traditional authority figures and high in need for achievement. Koenig and McKeachie (1959) also found that women high in need for achievement preferred independent study to lectures. Something similar may be involved in the suggestion in the Oberlin studies (McCollough & Van Atta, 1958) that students who are less rigid and less in need of social support are likely to profit more from independent study than those students who are not as independent.

Despite the variety of measures used, the studies cited in this section show some consistency in finding that a certain type of student, characterized as independent, flexible, or in high need for achievement, likes and does well in classroom situations which give students opportunity for self-direction.

Anxiety and
Sex Differences

One of the most active intersections of experimental psychology and experimental study of personality has been the area involving the effect of anxiety upon learning. The impetus for much of this work came from deductions from Hullian theory by Spence and Taylor (1951). Essentially, this theory suggests that a high level of anxiety facilitates simple learning, but beyond an optimal point hampers complex learning. Since academic situations sometimes produce high levels of anxiety, we might expect damaging effects. Beam (1955) showed that doctoral examinations and oral reports did decrease ability to learn nonsense syllables but improved conditionability.

Since individuals obviously differ in their reactions to stress, a number of investigators have attempted to devise questionnaires which might differentiate individuals who respond differently in stressful situations. In addition to the Taylor Manifest Anxiety Scale used in the studies cited above, a number of experimenters have used the Mandler-Sarason (1952) questionnaires. Individuals who scored as highly anxious on this questionnaire responded with poorer performance after reports on their success or failure while those with low anxiety improved.

The Interfering Tendency Questionnaire (which correlates well with the Taylor scale) developed by Waterhouse and Child (1953), differentiates individuals responding differently to failure. Under neutral conditions, individuals scoring high in interfering tendencies do better than low scorers, but after failure the high scorers do worse. This result was confirmed by Williams (1955), who also found that reaction to different types of failure is affected by achievement motivation.

One of the most comprehensive studies of student personality was carried out by Gaier (1952). Using the Rorschach, Gaier determined the relationship between certain personality characteristics and students' thoughts in small discussion groups. He found that

anxiety readiness, as measured by the Rorschach, correlated negatively with scores on a reading test and a test requiring comparisons of familiar and unfamiliar materials. Rigidity predisposition correlated positively with class time spent in negative thoughts about other people and negative thoughts about ideas expressed in class.

Since anxiety is generally believed to be increased by uncertainty, we would expect the anxious person to work most effectively in a highly structured situation. This hypothesis is partially supported by the research of D. E. P. Smith and his co-workers (1956), who found that anxious students who were permeable (sensitive to stimuli, impulsive, socially oriented, and low in ego strength) made optimal progress in a remedial reading course when taught by directive methods. Impermeable anxious students, however, were unaffected by differences in teaching methods. H. C. Smith (1955), on the other hand, found that students with high anxiety and low initial achievement gained more on achievement tests and were more highly satisfied in a "teamwork" class than in a conventional lecture.

The relationship between anxiety and performance on classroom examinations administered under varying conditions has been the subject of several experiments. To test experimentally whether the aggression created by tests might be dissipated by permitting students to write comments on tests, half of the students in a University of Michigan experiment were given answer-sheets with spaces for comments and half were given standard answer-sheets. Measures of students' feelings about the tests failed to show any difference between the two groups; but the students who had the opportunity to write comments made higher scores on the test. These results held up in a series of experiments (McKeachie, Pollie, & Speisman, 1955).

It thus appeared that some students were too highly motivated—at least for performance on tests. The findings indicated that student anxiety during classroom examinations builds up to such a point that it interferes with memory and problem solving. Reducing the stress of the examination by permitting students to write comments resulted in improved performance.

This interpretation was supported by Calvin, McGuigan, and Sullivan (1957), who found that students who were given a chance to write comments on an achievement test were superior to control students in their performance on the second half of the test and that the students who made the greatest gain were the highly anxious students as measured by the Taylor Manifest Anxiety Scale. Similarly, W. F. Smith and Rockett (1958) found that instructions to write comments significantly interacted with anxiety, helping the performance of high-anxiety students but hurting the performance of students low in anxiety.

Carrier (1957) investigated the manner in which individual differences in four personality variables affected performance in more and less stressful testing situations. In the "low-stress" condition, students had answer-sheets with spaces for comments, and the test was administered in a friendly, relaxed fashion. In the "high-stress" condition, the test was taken in a strange room, was administered by an austere stranger who announced that he would answer no questions during the test, and students were told that a point would be deducted for every wrong answer but that they must answer every question.

Carrier found that one of the most important variables determining reaction in his experiment was sex. Women were much more detrimentally affected than men by his stress situation. Individual differences in need for achievement and need for affiliation failed to predict reactions to the stress situation. However, the permeable students, as measured by Smith's SA-S scale (Smith, et al., 1956), were detrimentally affected by stress.

In a later experiment (McKeachie, 1958c), half of a group of 350 students taking a test received conventional IBM answer-sheets; half received answer-sheets with space for comments. In addition, half of the students received a tranquilizing drug, meprobamate ("Miltown"), from a physician associated with the Institute of Mental Health Research, while the other half received a placebo. All of the students had taken a number of tests of anxiety and of need for achievement a week before the examination. If students tend to be too anxious, such a drug should improve test scores. The results did not confirm this hypothesis. Students who actually had the Miltown reported experiencing less anxiety during the examination than did the placebo group, but they did not make better scores.

The really interesting result of the experiment was the interactions. The sex-drug interaction was significant both in its effect on performance and on anxiety, with women benefiting from the drug more than men. Thus sex once again turned out to be an important variable. The results make sense if we assume a curvilinear relationship between anxiety and performance, with women more anxious than men. Thus, reduced anxiety should result in improved performance for women, but poorer performance for men.

An Air Force experiment on teacher-student interviews also revealed complex interactions. Although the interviews were not effective overall in influencing achievement, Hoehn and Saltz (1956) found that anxious students tended to be helped by interviews while rigid students were more likely to fail if interviewed. The results were further affected by type of interview; interviews in which students were encouraged to gripe produced the interaction noted above while interviews oriented toward the student's goals and sources of satisfaction did not. If this result can be generalized to the testing situation, we might expect the "comments" technique to be unsuccessful for rigid students.

The experimental results on interaction of anxiety and teaching variables are tantalizing enough to stimulate further work, but they are not consistent enough to lead to any stable generalizations. The fact that differences in sex and in other personality variables, such as permeability, interacted with anxiety in the experiments above suggests that multivariate designs are necessary to explore this area more fully.

Authoritarianism

One of the most intensively studied research variables of the past decade has been "authoritarianism." It is not surprising, therefore, that this variable has been studied in relation to college learning.

Watson (1956) studied the effect of permissive and restrictive teaching and testing methods upon students differing in authoritarianism and permeability (extraversion). The methods were not differentially effective as measured by achievement tests but student satisfaction was affected by testing methods. Highest satisfaction resulted when one was tested in an atmosphere appropriate for his needs, i.e., permissive for permeable, restrictive for impermeable. This finding is in line with the finding of Bendig and Hountras (1959) that authoritarian students prefer a high degree of departmental control of instruction and with the Hoehn-Saltz results reported earlier. Somewhat more complicated is the finding of Koenig and McKeachie (1959) that flexible nonauthoritarian women participate more in small groups than rigid women. For males, however, the relationship is reversed; flexible men are less likely to participate than rigid men.

Beach (1960) studied the personality variable of sociability as a predictor of achievement in lecture and small-group teaching methods. In the lecture section the nonsociable students (as measured by the Guilford Inventory of Factors STDCR) achieved significantly more than the sociable students; in the small-group sections the results were reversed.

By far the most extensive studies of personality characteristics related to college achievement are those of Stern, Stein, and Bloom (1956) and Pace and Stern (1958). These authors have developed not only a variety of methods of assessing student personality, but also a scale for assessing the pressures on students in various college environments. First,

they set up a theoretical model of the personality syndrome being studied (a sort of rigid, uncritical, authoritarian pattern), created the Inventory of Beliefs as the chief predictive instrument for the theoretical model, and then obtained extensive data over a period of one year on an incoming group at the University of Chicago. In addition, after the initial data had been analyzed, an individual was selected who seemed closest to the syndrome described, and a case study was made. Correlations were found between the personality syndrome taken from the extremes of the Inventory scores and (1) excellence in placement tests, (2) grades in subsequent courses, (3) ability to adjust to university life at Chicago, and (4) classroom behavior.

Extending the personality model to include major needs, Stern, Stein, and Bloom created the Activities Index as a measure of these needs and have used it and the Inventory of Beliefs in a number of studies in academic settings.

For example, as we saw earlier, students high on a variable akin to authoritarianism were found to gain more when taught in a homogeneous group. The instructor who taught this section found that he had to resist pressures from the students for lectures. He secured his good results by using many direct questions, encouraging student responses, and by vigorously defending absurd positions which even authoritarian students would argue against (Stern, 1962).

In addition, Pace and Stern have studied the relationship between student needs and the forces affecting students in differing colleges. Their College Characteristics Index and the Activities Index reveal great differences between colleges in such characteristics as the tendency to support the need for order or the need for achievement. Presumably, the effects of variations in teaching methods not only interact with student characteristics but also with aspects of the college's culture. Thus, apparently inconsistent results may simply reflect differences in the cultures in which the experiments have been conducted.

In summing up the studies on the interaction of personality characteristics and teaching methods as that interaction affects student learning, it is safe to say that no major break-through has occurred. The results so far do, however, appear promising. Fortunately, multivariate statistical techniques now permit precise analysis of the sorts of complex interaction involved in teaching. Although we have little data on this point (Guetzkow, Kelly, & McKeachie, 1954; Jenkins, 1952), it is probable that instructor characteristics and content characteristics also interact with teaching methods. For example, in both the Michigan State and Army studies of educational television, some instructors proved to be more effective on television than face to face while others proved to be more effective in face-to-face teaching. Similarly, the experiments of Wakely and his associates (1960) and Russell (1951) indicate that some teachers are more effective with the abler students, while others are more effective in teaching the poorer students. Such interactions pose exciting problems for investigation.

THE ROLE OF FACULTY ATTITUDES

What can we say about the work of the college teacher? Clearly it is not possible to detail in a few summary statements the "best" methods of teaching. Nevertheless, a conclusion that it does not make any difference which methods are used is clearly unjustified. Rather, recent research suggests that decisions about teaching methods do have important consequences in terms of differential achievement of the differing objectives of a course, differential effects upon different types of students, and probable differential effects depending upon other factors such as the instructor, the course content, and the over-all "climate" of the institution. To analyze such complexities would obviously be a task for an electronic computer. In the absence of the data necessary for such an analysis, we must, as in other frontier areas, depend upon expert judgment. Most of the reports of research on teaching neglect to report

the reactions of the faculty involved (except in the case of television, where they are generally negative). Yet until we gain more confidence in our evaluation tools, we are almost forced to weigh faculty judgment heavily. This writer would argue that faculty judgments of teaching methods are extremely important for the educational researcher even aside from their possible validity.

As was pointed out earlier, we seldom know how well a particular method was used in experimental studies of teaching methods, but it seems very likely that the effectiveness of a method depends upon the competence and enthusiasm of the teacher. If the teacher is important, his enjoyment of the method becomes a critical variable. Thistlethwaite (1960) reported that National Merit Scholars consider one of the critical variables influencing their choice of a field to be the instructor's enthusiasm. Such enthusiasm is not likely to be communicated if the instructor finds teaching distasteful. Thus, even though we found that a particular method when ideally used is superior to other methods, we should be dubious about urging its widespread adoption if teachers using it become bored or dissatisfied.

We have already discussed the probability that teaching effectiveness is not a direct function of the method used but rather of the interaction of teacher and method. One instructor may be an excellent lecturer, another a fine discussion leader. But so far our researchers have been unable to obtain large enough samples of instructors to be able to generalize to populations of instructors. It may be, for example, that, even though the discussion method seems potentially superior to the lecture method in achieving higher-level educational outcomes, lecturing is more effective for inexperienced teachers. Perhaps if large numbers of inexperienced teachers are to be employed, lecturing should be the method chosen.

Some administrators and foundation executives seem to be annoyed by the stubbornness of some professors in not accepting larger classes or teaching by television. But if we look at the rewards in teaching, the attitudes of faculty members toward class and institutional size become more understandable.

What are the satisfactions in teaching? Certainly one is the pleasure of seeing a student develop. Another is the pleasure of intellectual interchange with young people possessing questioning minds and fresh ideas. Perhaps a less laudable but nonetheless real satisfaction is that found in having disciples who respect and admire us. These satisfactions are difficult to secure without close, sustained personal contact with students. If we are to know students well enough to see their progress, small classes are important. Such classes permit more individual interaction with students and permit the instructor to use term papers, essay tests, and other evaluation methods which give him a greater understanding of what the student is thinking. While objective tests might also be used to give a personalized understanding of each student's strength and weaknesses, few teachers take the time to analyze the patterns of right and wrong answers that would be necessary for such understanding. Such an analysis becomes prohibitively time-consuming in a large class, whatever the testing methods used.

Many professors conscientiously attend some student teas or other social functions to promote contacts between students and faculty. In small colleges it is likely that the professor will meet at such functions some of the students he has taught and will have an opportunity to use this contact to gain greater understanding of the students and perhaps even to stimulate their thinking. But the larger the college, the less the statistical chance that he will meet students he knows at such functions; in fact, the larger the college, the less chance that he will ever meet again the student he meets at a tea. This means that even the professor who conscientiously devotes a portion of his time to such "informal" contacts with students is unlikely to have significant encounters with them. Because the professor is nearly always dealing with strangers or near-strangers, the intellectual interchange is almost perforce limited to polite inquiry about the student's academic and vocational aspirations or conversation about the current film at the campus theater. In short, any satisfaction received from observing and contributing to a student's growth must ordinarily come during the semester (or at most two semesters) that the student is enrolled in one's class. No matter how powerful one's impact, it is asking a great deal to expect it to have great, noticeable effects in 16 weeks.

Size of an educational institution has a very similar relationship to the quality of education students receive from one another. The large institution with a student body of heterogeneous background offers students an opportunity to gain breadth, tolerance, and new perspectives from their contacts with one another. But large size is likely to reduce educational values by reducing intellectual interchange between students. There is certainly no reason why a student at a large college could not discuss with another student an interesting problem raised by one of his professors. But he is probably more likely to do so if he is living near another student who is also familiar with the problem and concerned about it. In a large college the statistical chances that another student in the same class will be in the same living group are smaller than in a small college. Students in a large college with many courses, and even many sections of the same course, have few common intellectual experiences. Consequently it is difficult for them to communicate about intellectual problems outside of class, and the common concerns which become the basis of social communication are football, the student newspaper, dating, and the dormitory food. With such barriers to interstudent education, the professor misses the good feeling one experiences when he finds that his teaching has provided an intellectual stimulus reaching beyond his classroom.

Of course there are also satisfactions in teaching by television or in a large class. One can gain a very satisfying sense of power from knowing that one is communicating one's ideas to a large number of students. The roar of laughter at a joke well told is music to a lecturer's ear. The satisfaction of carrying through without interruption a well-planned lesson is satisfying to the "Master Teacher" whose performance is televised.

Although these are valid satisfactions, they seem less directly related to the goals of education than the satisfactions associated with observing student development. What would a college be like if its faculty were made up largely of teachers whose satisfactions were received primarily from being a good performer?

As colleges increase in size in order to cope with a growing student population, there is a natural tendency to routinize and automate educational processes in the interest of increased efficiency. In industry, assembly line methods have long been effective. Yet, in recent years, industry has found that workers are even more efficient if, instead of performing one specific, repetitive task, their jobs are enlarged enough to provide variety and interest (e.g., Mann & Hoffman, 1960). While there is little likelihood that college administrators will intentionally insist upon uniform teaching methods, increasing class size indirectly limits the professor's choice of teaching methods, reducing his ability to select the methods best suited for his objectives and reducing his satisfaction in teaching.

Enjoyment of teaching is important not only for the enthusiasm which the professor communicates to his students but also for his interest in continued improvement. These important values are likely to be lost if teaching becomes so routinized and depersonalized that it is no longer fun. The motivated teacher can respond to feedback from his students so as to achieve better and better approximations to optimal solutions to the problems of teaching. As additional information from research accumulates, as better conceptualizations emerge, he should be able to do an even better job.

REFERENCES

Adams, J. C., Carpenter, C. R., & Smith, Dorothy R. (Eds.) *College teaching by television*. Washington, D.C.: American Council on Education, 1958.

Anderson, R. C. Learning in discussion: A resumé of the authoritarian-democratic studies. *Harvard educ. Rev.*, 1959, 29, 201–215.

Anderson, R. P., & Kell, B. L. Student attitudes about participation in classroom groups. *J. educ. Res.*, 1954, 48, 255–267.

Angell, G. W. Effect of immediate knowledge of quiz results on final examination scores in freshman chemistry. *J. educ. Res.*, 1949, 42, 391–394.

Asch, M. J. Nondirective teaching in psychology. *Psychol. Monogr.*, 1951, 65, No. 4 (Whole No. 321).

Ashmus, Mable, & Haigh, G. Some factors which may be associated with student choice between directive and nondirective classes. *Amer. Psychologist*, 1952, 7, 247. (Abstract)

Atkinson, J. W., & Litwin, G. H. Achievement motive and test anxiety conceived as motive to approach success and motive to avoid failure. *J. abnorm. soc. Psychol.*, 1960, 60, 52–63.

Ausubel, D. P., Robbins, Lillian C., & Blake, E., Jr. Retroactive inhibition and facilitation in the learning of school materials. *J. educ. Psychol.*, 1957, 48, 334–343.

Axelrod, J. Group dynamics, nondirective therapy, and college training. *J. higher Educ.*, 1955, 26, 200–207.

Bainter, Monica E. A study of the outcomes of two types of laboratory techniques used in a course in general college physics for students planning to be teachers in the elementary grades. Unpublished doctoral dissertation, Univer. of Wisconsin, 1955. (*Dissertation Abstr.*, 1955, 15, 2485–2486)

Balcziak, L. W. The role of the laboratory and demonstration in college physical science in achieving the objectives of general education. Unpublished doctoral dissertation, Univer. of Minnesota, 1953. (*Dissertation Abstr.*, 1954, 14, 502–503)

Bane, C. L. The lecture vs. the class-discussion method of college teaching. *Sch. & Soc.*, 1925, 21, 300–302.

Barnard, J. D. The lecture-demonstration versus the problem-solving method of teaching a college science course. *Science Educ.*, 1942, 26, 121–132.

Baskin, S. Experiment in French language instruction. *Antioch Coll. Rept.*, Oct., 1960.

Beach, L. R. Sociability and academic achievement in various types of learning situations. *J. educ. Psychol.*, 1960, 51, 208–212.

Beam, J. C. Serial learning and conditioning under real-life stress. *J. abnorm. soc. Psychol.*, 1955, 51, 543–551.

Becker, S. L., & Dallinger, C. A. The effect of instructional methods upon achievement and attitudes in communication skills. *Speech Monogr.*, 1960, 27, 70–76.

Becker, S. L., Murray, J. N., & Bechtoldt, H. P. *Teaching by the discussion method.* Iowa City: State Univer. of Iowa, 1958.

Bendig, A. W. Ability and personality characteristics of introductory psychology instructors rated competent and empathic by their students. *J. educ. Res.*, 1955, 48, 705–709.

Bendig, A. W., & Hountras, P. T. Anxiety, authoritarianism, and student attitude toward departmental control of college instruction. *J. educ. Psychol.*, 1959, 50, 1–8.

Bills, R. E. Investigation of student centered teaching. *J. educ. Res.*, 1952, 46, 313–319.

Birney, R., & McKeachie, W. The teaching of psychology: A survey of research since 1942. *Psychol. Bull.*, 1955, 52, 51–68.

Bloom, B. S. Thought processes in lectures and discussions. *J. gen. Educ.*, 1953, 7, 160–169.

Bovard, E. W., Jr. Group structure and perception. *J. abnorm. soc. Psychol.*, 1951, 46, 398–405. (a)

Bovard, E. W., Jr. The experimental production of interpersonal affect. *J. abnorm. soc. Psychol.*, 1951, 46, 521–528. (b)

Briggs, L. J. Intensive classes for superior students. *J. educ. Psychol.*, 1947, 38, 207–215.

Brown, A. E. The effectiveness of large classes at the college level: An experimental study involving the size variable and the size procedure variable. *Univer. Iowa Stud. Educ.*, 1932, 7, 3.

Bryan, G. L., & Rigney, J. W. An evaluation of a method for shipboard training in operations knowledge. Tech. Rept. 18, Electronics Personnel Res. Group, Univer. of Southern California, 1956.

Burke, H. R. An experimental study of teaching methods in a college freshman orienta-

tion course. Unpublished doctoral dissertation, Boston Univer., 1955. (*Dissertation Abstr.*, 1956, 16, 77–78)

Burkhardt, Sara M. A study in concept learning in differential calculus. Unpublished doctoral dissertation, Columbia Univer., 1956.

Burtt, H. E., Chassel, L. M., & Hatch, E. M. Efficiency of instruction in unselected and selected sections of elementary psychology. *J. educ. Res.*, 1923, 14, 154–161.

Calvin, A. D., Hoffman, F. K., & Harden, E. L. The effect of intelligence and social atmosphere on group problem solving behavior. *J. soc. Psychol.*, 1957, 45, 61–74.

Calvin, A. D., McGuigan, F. J., & Sullivan, M. W. A further investigation of the relationship between anxiety and classroom examination performance. *J. educ. Psychol.*, 1957, 48, 240–244.

Cantril, H., & Allport, G. W. *The psychology of radio.* New York: Harper, 1935.

Carpenter, C. R. The Penn State Pyramid Plan: Interdependent student work study groupings for increasing motivation for academic development. Paper read at 14th Nat. Conf. on Higher Education, Chicago, March, 1959.

Carpenter, C. R., & Greenhill, L. P. An investigation of closed-circuit television for teaching university courses. Instructional Television Res. Rept., Project No. 1. University Park: Pennsylvania State Univer., 1955.

Carpenter, C. R., & Greenhill, L. P. An investigation of closed-circuit television for teaching university courses. Instructional Television Res. Rept., Project No. 2. University Park: Pennsylvania State Univer., 1958.

Carrier, N. A. The relationship of certain personality measures to examination performance under stress. *J. educ. Psychol.*, 1957, 48, 510–520.

Casey, J. E., & Weaver, B. E. An evaluation of lecture method and small group method of teaching in terms of knowledge of content, teacher attitude, and social status. *J. Colo.-Wyo. Acad. Sci.*, 1956, (4), 54.

Cheydleur, F. D. Criteria of effective teaching in basic French courses. *Bull. Univer. Wisconsin,* Serial No. 2783, August, 1945.

Churchill, Ruth. Preliminary report on reading course study. Yellow Springs, Ohio: Antioch Coll., 1957. (Mimeographed)

Churchill, Ruth, & Baskin, S. Experiment on

independent study. Yellow Springs, Ohio: Antioch Coll., 1958. (Mimeographed)

Corey, S. M. Learning from lectures vs. learning from readings. *J. educ. Psychol.*, 1934, 25, 459–470.

Corman, B. The effect of varying amounts and kinds of information as guidance in problem solving. *Psychol. Monogr.*, 1957, 71, No. 2 (Whole No. 431).

Coulson, J. E. An experimental teaching machine for research at S.D.C. Tech. Memo. 416. Santa Monica, Calif.: System Development Corp., 1959.

Coulson, J. E., & Silberman, H. F. Results of initial experiments in automated teaching. Rept. SP-73. Santa Monica, Calif.: System Development Corp., 1959.

Craig, R. C. Directed vs. independent discovery of established relations. *J. educ. Psychol.*, 1956, 47, 223–234.

Cronbach, L. J. The two disciplines of scientific psychology. *Amer. Psychologist*, 1957, 12, 671–684.

Cross, D. An investigation of the relationships between students' expressions of satisfaction with certain aspects of the college classroom situation and their achievement on final examinations. Unpublished honors thesis, Univer. of Michigan, 1958.

Cutler, R. L., McKeachie, W. J., & McNeil, E. B. Teaching psychology by telephone. *Amer. Psychologist*, 1958, 13, 551–552.

Davage, R. H. The Pyramid plan for the systematic involvement of university students in teaching-learning functions. University Park: Div. of Academic Res. and Services, Pennsylvania State Univer., 1958.

Davage, R. H. Recent data on the Pyramid project in psychology. University Park: Div. of Academic Res. and Services, Pennsylvania State Univer., 1959.

Dawson, M. D. Lectures versus problem-solving in teaching elementary soil sections. *Science Educ.*, 1956, 40, 395–404.

Deignan, F. J. A comparison of the effectiveness of two group discussion methods. Unpublished doctoral dissertation, Boston Univer., 1955. (*Dissertation Abstr.*, 1956, 16, 1110–1111)

Della-Piana, G. M. Searching orientation and concept learning. *J. educ. Psychol.*, 1957, 48, 245–253.

Deutsch, M. An experimental study of the effects of cooperation and competition upon group processes. *Human Relations*, 1949, 2, 199–232.

DiVesta, F. J. Instructor-centered and student-centered approaches in teaching a human relations course. *J. appl. Psychol.*, 1954, 38, 329–335.

Dreher, R. E., & Beatty, W. H. An experimental study of college instruction using broadcast television. *Instructional Television Res. Proj.* No. 1. San Francisco: San Francisco State Coll., 1958.

Ebbinghaus, H. *Memory: A contribution to experimental psychology*, Trans. by H. A. Ruger & C. E. Bussenius. New York: Teachers Coll., Columbia Univer., 1913.

Edmonson, J. B., & Mulder, F. J. Size of class as a factor in university instruction. *J. educ. Res.*, 1924, 9, 1–12.

Eglash, A. A group discussion method of teaching psychology. *J. educ. Psychol.*, 1954, 45, 257–267.

Elliott, P. N. Characteristics and relationships of various criteria of college and university teaching. *Purdue Univer. Stud. higher Educ.*, 1950, 70, 5–61.

Evans, J. L., Glaser, R., & Homme, L. E. A preliminary investigation of variation in the properties of verbal learning sequences of the "teaching machine" type. In A. A. Lumsdaine & R. Glaser (Eds.), *Teaching machines and programmed learning: A source book*. Washington, D.C.: Dept. of Audio-Visual Instruction, National Education Association, 1960. Pp. 446–451.

Evans, R. I., Roney, H. B., & McAdams, W. J. An evaluation of the effectiveness of instruction and audience reaction to programming on an educational television station. *Amer. Psychologist*, 1954, 9, 361–362.

Faw, V. D. A psychotherapeutic method of teaching psychology. *Amer. Psychologist*, 1949, 4, 104–109.

Fitch, M. L., Drucker, A. J., & Norton, J. A., Jr. Frequent testing as a motivating factor in large lecture classes. *J. educ. Psychol.*, 1951, 42, 1–20.

Flexman, R. E., Matheny, W. G., & Brown, E. L. Evaluation of the School Link and special methods of instruction. Urbana: Inst. of Aviation, Univer. of Illinois, 1950.

Fritz, M. F. *Survey of TV utilization in Army training*. Instr. Film Res. Rept. U.S. Naval Training Device Center, Office of Naval Research, SDC 530-01-0, December 31, 1952.

Gaier, E. L. Selected personality variables and the learning process. *Psychol. Monogr.,* 1952, 66, No. 17 (Whole No. 349).

Galanter, E. H. (Ed.) *Automatic teaching: The state of the art.* New York: Wiley, 1959.

Gibb, J. R. The effects of group size and of threat reduction upon creativity in a problem solving situation. *Amer. Psychologist,* 1951, 6, 324. (Abstract)

Gibb, Lorraine M., & Gibb, J. R. The effects of the use of "participative action" groups in a course in general psychology. *Amer. Psychologist,* 1952, 7, 247. (Abstract)

Glaser, R., & Homme, L. E. Relationships between the programmed textbook and teaching machine. Paper read at Air Force Office of Scientific Res. and Univer. of Pennsylvania Conf. on the Automatic Teaching of Verbal and Symbolic Skills, December, 1958.

Goldstein, A. A controlled comparison of the project method with standard laboratory teaching in pharmacology, *J. med. Educ.,* 1956, 31, 365–375.

Greene, E. B. Relative effectiveness of lecture and individual reading as methods of college teaching. *Genet. Psychol. Monogr.,* 1928, 4, 457–563.

Greenhill, L. P. New directions for communication research. *AV commun. Rev.,* 1959, 7, 245–253.

Gruber, H. E., & Weitman, M. Cognitive processes in higher education: Curiosity and critical thinking. Paper read at Western Psychological Ass., San Jose, Calif., April, 1960.

Guetzkow, H., Kelly, E. L., & McKeachie, W. J. An experimental comparison of recitation, discussion, and tutorial methods in college teaching. *J. educ. Psychol.,* 1954, 45, 193–209.

Haigh, G. V., & Schmidt, W. The learning of subject matter in teacher-centered and group-centered classes. *J. educ. Psychol.,* 1956, 47, 295–301.

Haines, D. B. Cooperative vs. competitive discussion methods in teaching introductory psychology. Unpublished doctoral dissertation, Univer. of Michigan, 1959.

Haythorn, W., Couch, A., Haefner, D., Langham, P., & Carter, L. The effects of varying combinations of authoritarian and equalitarian leaders and followers. *J. abnorm. soc. Psychol.,* 1956, 53, 210–219.

Hebb, D. O. *The organization of behavior.* New York: Wiley, 1949.

Heyns, R. W. Conference leadership which stimulates teamwork. *Michigan Bus. Rev.,* 1952, 4, 16–23.

Hirschman, C. S. An investigation of the small groups discussion classroom method on criteria of understanding, pleasantness, and self-confidence induced. Unpublished master's thesis, Univer. of Pittsburgh, 1952.

Hoban, C. F., Jr., & Van Ormer, E. B. *Instructional film research 1918–1950.* (Pennsylvania State Univer. Instructional Film Research Program) Port Washington, N.Y.: U.S. Naval Training Device Center, Office of Naval Research, Tech. Rept. No. SDC 269-7-19, 1950.

Hoehn, A. J., & Saltz, E. Effect of teacher-student interviews on classroom achievement. *J. educ. Psychol.,* 1956, 47, 424–435.

Hoffman, L. R. Homogeneity of member personality and its effect on group problem solving. *J. abnorm. soc. Psychol.,* 1959, 58, 27–32.

Horwitz, M. The veridicality of liking and disliking. In R. Tagiuri & L. Petrullo (Eds.), *Person perception and interpersonal behavior.* Stanford, Calif.: Stanford Univer. Press, 1958. Pp. 191–209.

Hovland, C. I., (Ed.) *The order of presentation in persuasion.* New Haven, Conn.: Yale Univer. Press, 1957.

Hovland, C. I., & Mandell, W. An experimental comparison of conclusion-drawing by the communicator and by the audience. *J. abnorm. soc. Psychol.,* 1952, 47, 581–588.

Hovland, C. I., Janis, I. L., & Kelley, H. H. *Communication and persuasion.* New Haven, Conn.: Yale Univer. Press, 1953.

Hovland, C. I., Lumsdaine, A. A., & Sheffield, F. D. *Experiments in mass communication.* Princeton, N.J.: Princeton Univer. Press, 1949.

Hudelson, E. *Class size at the college level.* Minneapolis: Univer. of Minnesota Press, 1928.

Husband, R. W. A statistical comparison of the efficacy of large lecture vs. smaller recitation sections upon achievement in general psychology. *J. Psychol.,* 1951, 31, 297–300.

Jenkins, R. L. The relative effectiveness of two methods of teaching written and spoken English. Unpublished doctoral dissertation, Michigan State Univer., 1952. (*Dissertation Abstr.,* 1952, 12, 268)

Jensen, B. T. A comparison of student achievement under conditions of class attendance and non-attendance. *Coll. & Univer.,* 1951, 26, 399–404.

Johnson, D. M., & Smith, H. C. Democratic leadership in the college classroom. *Psychol. Monogr.,* 1953, 67, No. 11 (Whole No. 361).

Jones, H. E. Experimental studies of college teaching. *Arch. Psychol., N.Y.,* 1923, 10, No. 68, 5–70.

Kasten, D. F., & Seibert, W. F. *A study of televised military science instruction.* Television Project Rept. 9. West Lafayette, Ind.: Purdue Univer., 1959.

Katona, G. *Organizing and memorizing.* New York: Columbia Univer. Press, 1940.

Katz, D. *Gestalt psychology.* New York: Ronald Press, 1950.

Keatinge, M. W. *Comenius.* New York and London: McGraw-Hill, 1931.

Kersh, B. Y. The adequacy of "meaning" as an explanation for the superiority of learning by independent discovery. *J. educ. Psychol.,* 1958, 49, 282–292.

Kishler, J. P. The effects of prestige and identification factors on attitude restructuring and learning from sound films. Port Washington, N.Y.: U.S. Naval Training Device Center, Office of Naval Research, Tech. Rept. SDC 269-7-10, 1950.

Klapper, Hope L. *Closed circuit television as a medium of instruction at New York University.* New York: New York Univer., 1958.

Knower, F. H. Experimental studies of changes of attitude. I. A study of the effect of oral argument on changes of attitude. *J. soc. Psychol.,* 1935, 6, 315–347.

Knower, F. H. Experimental studies of changes of attitude. II. A study of the effect of printed argument on changes of attitude. *J. abnorm. soc. Psychol.,* 1936, 30, 522–532.

Koenig, Kathryn, & McKeachie, W. J. Personality and independent study. *J. educ. Psychol.,* 1959, 50, 132–134.

Kopstein, F. F., & Roshal, S. M. Learning foreign vocabulary from pictures vs. words. *Amer. Psychologist,* 1954, 9, 407–408.

Krauskopf, C. J. The use of written responses in the stimulated recall method. Unpublished doctoral dissertation, Ohio State Univer., 1960. (*Dissertation Abstr.,* 1960, 21, 1953)

Kruglak, H. Experimental outcomes of laboratory instruction in elementary college physics. *Amer. J. Physics,* 1952, 20, 136–141.

Krumboltz, J. D., & Farquhar, W. W. The effect of three teaching methods on achievement and motivational outcomes in a how-to-study course. *Psychol. Monogr.,* 1957, 71, No. 14. (Whole No. 443)

Lahti, A. M. The inductive-deductive method and the physical science laboratory. *J. exp. Educ.,* 1956, 24, 149–163.

Landsman, T. An experimental study of a student-centered learning method. Unpublished doctoral dissertation, Syracuse Univer., 1950.

Lepore, A. R., & Wilson, J. D. An experimental study of college instruction using broadcast television. *Instr. Television Res. Proj.* No. 2. San Francisco: San Francisco State Coll., 1958.

Lewin, K. Group decision and social change. In G. E. Swanson, T. M. Newcomb, & E. L. Hartley (Eds.), *Readings in social psychology.* (2nd ed.) New York: Holt, 1952. Pp. 330–344.

Lewin, K., Lippitt, R., & White, R. K. Patterns of aggressive behavior in experimentally created social climates. *J. soc. Psychol.,* 1939, 10, 271–299.

Lifson, N., Rempel, P., & Johnson, J. A. A comparison between lecture and conference methods of teaching physiology. *J. med. Educ.,* 1956, 31, 376–382.

Little, J. K. Results on use of machines for testing and for drill upon learning in educational psychology. *J. exp. Educ.,* 1934, 3, 45–49.

Longstaff, H. P. Analysis of some factors conditioning learning in general psychology. *J. appl. Psychol.,* 1932, 16, 131–166.

Lovell, G. D., & Haner, C. F. Forced-choice applied to college faculty rating. *Educ. psychol. Measmt,* 1955, 15, 291–304.

Lumsdaine, A. A., & Glaser, R. (Eds.) *Teaching machines and programmed learning: A source book.* Washington, D.C.: Dept. of Audio-Visual Instruction, National Education Association, 1960.

Lyle, E. An exploration in the teaching of critical thinking in general psychology. *J. educ. Res.,* 1958, 52, 129–133.

Macomber, F. G., & Siegel, L. *Experimental study in instructional procedures. Progress Rept. No. 1.* Oxford, Ohio: Miami Univer., 1956.

Macomber, F. G., & Siegel, L. A study of large group teaching procedures. *Educ. Res.,* 1957, 38, 220–229. (a)

Macomber, F. G., & Siegel, L. *Experimental study in instructional procedures. Progress Rept. No. 2.* Oxford, Ohio: Miami Univer., 1957. (b)

Macomber, F. G., & Siegel, L. *Final report on the experimental study in instructional procedures.* Oxford, Ohio: Miami Univer., 1960.

Maier, N. R. F., & Solem, A. R. The contribution of a discussion leader to the quality of group thinking. *Human Relations,* 1952, 5, 277–288.

Maize, R. C. Two methods of teaching English composition to retarded college freshmen. *J. educ. Psychol.,* 1954, 45, 22–28.

Maloney, R. M. Group learning through group discussion: A group discussion implementation analysis. *J. soc. Psychol.,* 1956, 43, 3–9.

Mandler, G., & Sarason, S. B. A study of anxiety and learning. *J. abnorm. soc. Psychol.,* 1952, 47, 166–173.

Mann, F. C., & Hoffmann, L. R. *Automation and the worker.* New York: Holt, 1960.

Martin, J. R. Two-way closed-circuit educational television. Res. Rept. No. 941-1. Cleveland: Case Institute of Technology, 1957. (a)

Martin, J. R. Two-way closed-circuit educational television. Res. Rept. No. 941-1. Cleveland: Case Institute of Technology, 1957. (b)

Martin, J. R., Adams, R. B., & Baron, M. R. Studies in educational closed-circuit television. Res. Rept. No. 948-5. Cleveland: Case Institute of Technology, 1958.

May, M. A., & Lumsdaine, A. A. *Learning from films.* New Haven, Conn.: Yale Univer. Press, 1958.

McCollough, Celeste, & Van Atta, E. L. Experimental evaluation of teaching programs utilizing a block of independent work. Paper read at Amer. Psychol. Ass., Washington, September, 1958.

McGeoch, J. A., & Irion, A. L. *The psychology of human learning.* New York: Longmans, Green, 1952. Pp. 46 ff.

McKeachie, W. J. Anxiety in the college classroom. *J. educ. Res.,* 1951, 45, 153–160.

McKeachie, W. J. Individual conformity to attitudes of classroom groups. *J. abnorm. soc. Psychol.,* 1954, 49, 282–289.

McKeachie, W. J. How do students learn? In R. M. Cooper (Ed.), *The two ends of the log.* Minneapolis: Univer. of Minnesota Press, 1958. Pp. 26–35. (a)

McKeachie, W. J. Motivating students' interest. In R. M. Cooper (Ed.), *The two ends of the log.* Minneapolis: Univer. of Minnesota Press, 1958. Pp. 36–39. (b)

McKeachie, W. J. Students, groups, and teaching methods. *Amer. Psychologist,* 1958, 13, 580–584. (c)

McKeachie, W. J. Appraising teaching effectiveness. In W. J. McKeachie (Ed.), *The appraisal of teaching in large universities.* Ann Arbor: Univer. of Michigan, 1959. Pp. 32–36.

McKeachie, W. J. *Teaching tips.* (4th ed.) Ann Arbor: Wahr, 1960.

McKeachie, W. J., & Hiler, W. The problem oriented approach to teaching psychology. *J. educ. Psychol.,* 1954, 45, 224–232.

McKeachie, W. J., & Solomon, D. Student ratings of instructors: A validity study. *J. educ. Res.,* 1958, 51, 379–382.

McKeachie, W. J., Lin, Y. G., Forrin, B., & Teevan, R. Individualized teaching in elementary psychology. *J. educ. Psychol.,* 1960, 51, 285–291.

McKeachie, W. J., Pollie, D., & Speisman, J. Relieving anxiety in classroom examinations. *J. abnorm. soc. Psychol.,* 1955, 50, 93–98.

McTavish, C. L. *Effect of repetitive film showings on learning.* (Pennsylvania State Univer. Instructional Film Research Program) Port Washington, N.Y.: U.S. Naval Training Device Center, Office of Naval Research, Tech. Rept. No. SDC 269-7-12, November, 1949.

Melton, A. W., Feldman, N. G., & Mason, C. N. *Experimental studies of the education of children in a museum school.* Washington, D.C.: Amer. Ass. Museums, Publ. No. 15, 1936.

Mertens, Marjorie S. *The effects of mental hygiene films on self regarding attitudes.* (Pennsylvania State Univer. Instructional Film Research Program) Port Washington, N.Y.: U.S. Naval Training Device Center, Office of Naval Research, Tech. Rept. No. SDC 269-7-22, July, 1951.

Miller, N. E. Scientific principles for maximum learning from motion pictures. *AV commun. Rev.,* 1957, 5, 61–113.

Moore, Mary R., & Popham, W. J. The role of extra-class student interviews in promoting student achievement. Paper read at joint session of Amer. Ass. for the Advancement of Science and Amer. Educ. Res. Ass., Chicago, December, 1959.

Mueller, A. D. Class size as a factor in normal school instruction. *Education,* 1924, 45, 203–227.

Nachman, M., & Opochinsky, S. The effects of different teaching methods: A methodological study. *J. educ. Psychol.,* 1958, 49, 245–249.

Novak, J. D. An experimental comparison of a conventional and a project centered method of teaching a college general botany course. *J. exp. Educ.,* 1958, 26, 217–230.

Pace, C. R., & Stern, G. G. *A criterion study of college environment.* Syracuse, N.Y.: Psychol. Res. Center, Syracuse Univer., 1958.

Parsons, T. S. A comparison of instruction by kinescope, correspondence study, and customary classroom procedures. *J. educ. Psychol.,* 1957, 48, 27–40.

Parsons, T. S., Ketcham, W. A., & Beach, L. R. Effects of varying degrees of student interaction and student-teacher contact in college courses. Paper read at Amer. Sociol. Soc., Seattle, Washington, August, 1958.

Patton, J. A. A study of the effects of student acceptance of responsibility and motivation on course behavior. Unpublished doctoral dissertation, Univer. of Michigan, 1955.

Paul, J. B. The length of class periods. *Educ. Record,* 1932, 13, 68–75.

Paul, J., & Ogilvie, J. C. Mass media and retention. *Explorations,* 1955, 4, 120–123.

Potter, S. *One-upmanship.* New York: Holt, 1955.

Pressey, S. L. A simple apparatus which gives tests and scores—and teaches. *Sch. & Soc.,* 1926, 23, 373–376.

Pressey, S. L. Development and appraisal of devices providing immediate automatic scoring of objective tests and concomitant self-instruction. *J. Psychol.,* 1950, 29, 417–447.

Rasmussen, G. R. Evaluation of a student-centered and instructor-centered method of conducting a graduate course in education. *J. educ. Psychol.,* 1956, 47, 449–461.

Remmers, H. H., & Brandenberg, G. C. Experimental data on the Purdue Rating Scale for Instructors. *Educ. Admin. Superv.,* 1927, 13, 519–527.

Remmers, H. H. Learning, effort, and attitudes as affected by three methods of instruction in elementary psychology. *Purdue Univer. Stud. higher Educ.,* 1933, 21.

Riley, J. W., Ryan, B. F., & Lifshitz, Marcia. *The student looks at his teacher.* New Brunswick, N.J.: Rutgers Univer. Press, 1950.

Rohrer, J. H. Large and small sections in college classes. *J. higher Educ.,* 1957, 28, 275–279.

Ross, I. C. Role specialization in supervision. Unpublished doctoral dissertation, Columbia Univer., 1956. (*Dissertation Abstr.,* 1956, 17, 2701–2702)

Ruja, H. Outcomes of lecture and discussion procedures in three college courses. *J. exp. Educ.,* 1954, 22, 385–394.

Runkel, P. J. Cognitive similarity in facilitating communication. *Sociometry,* 1956, 19, 178–191.

Russell, H. E. Inter-relations of some indices of instructor effectiveness: An exploratory study. Unpublished doctoral dissertation, Univer. of Pittsburgh, 1951.

Sarason, S. B., & Mandler, G. Some correlates of test anxiety. *J. abnorm. soc. Psychol.,* 1952, 47, 810–817.

Scheidemann, Norma V. An experiment in teaching psychology. *J. appl. Psychol.,* 1929, 13, 188–191.

Schellenberg, J. A. Group size as a factor in success of academic discussion groups. *J. educ. Soc.,* 1959, 33, 73–79.

Seashore, C. E. Elementary psychology: An outline of a course by the project method. *Aims and Progress of Res.,* No. 153. Iowa City: Univer. of Iowa, 1928.

Seashore, S. E. Group cohesiveness in the industrial group. Ann Arbor: Survey Res. Center, Univer. of Michigan, Publ. No. 14, 1954.

Seibert, W. F. *A brief report and evaluation of closed-circuit television instruction in the first semester calculus course.* West Lafayette, Ind.: Audio-Visual Center, Purdue Univer., 1957.

Seibert, W. F. *An evaluation of televised instruction in college English composition.* Television Project Rept. 5. West Lafayette, Ind.: Purdue Univer., 1958. (Mimeographed)

Seibert, W. F., & Honig, J. M. *A brief study of televised laboratory instruction.* Television Project Rept. 8. West Lafayette, Ind.: Purdue Univer., 1959. (Mimeographed)

Siegel, L., Adams, J. F., & Macomber, F. G. Retention of subject matter as a function of large group instructional procedures. *J. educ. Psychol.*, 1960, 51, 9–13.

Skinner, B. F. Teaching machines. *Science*, 1958, 128, 969–977.

Slomowitz, M. A comparison of personality changes and content achievement gains occurring in two modes of instruction. Unpublished doctoral dissertation, New York Univer., 1955. (*Dissertation Abstr.*, 1955, 15, 1790)

Smith, D. E. P. Applicational transfer and inhibition. *J. educ. Psychol.*, 1954, 45, 169–174.

Smith, D. E. P., Wood, R. L., Downer, J. W., & Raygor, A. L. Reading improvement as a function of student personality and teaching method. *J. educ. Psychol.*, 1956, 47, 47–58.

Smith, H. C. Team work in the college class. *J. educ. Psychol.*, 1955, 46, 274–286.

Smith, W. F., & Rockett, F. C. Test performance as a function of anxiety, instructor, and instructions. *J. educ. Res.*, 1958, 52, 138–141.

Spence, R. B. Lecture and class discussion in teaching educational psychology. *J. educ. Psychol.*, 1928, 19, 454–462.

Spence, K. W., & Taylor, Janet A. Anxiety and strength of the UCS as determiners of the amount of eyelid conditioning. *J. exp. Psychol.*, 1951, 42, 183–188.

Stephan, F. F., & Mishler, E. G. The distribution of participation in small groups: An experimental approximation. *Amer. sociol. Rev.*, 1952, 17, 598–608.

Stephens, A. L. Certain special factors involved in the law of effect. *Abstr. doctoral Dissertations, Ohio State Univer.*, 1953, 64.

Stephens College. Courses to be taught over closed-circuit TV. *Stephens Coll. News Reporter*, 1955, 14, No. 4.

Stern, G. G. Congruence and dissonance in the ecology of college students. *Student Med.*, 1960, 8, 304–339.

Stern, G. G. Environments for learning. In N. Sanford (Ed.), *The American college.* New York: Wiley, 1962. Pp. 690–730.

Stern, G. G., Stein, M. I., & Bloom, B. S. *Methods in personality assessment.* Glencoe, Ill.: Free Press, 1956.

Stolurow, L. M. Teaching machines and special education. *Educ. psychol. Measmt,* 1960, 20, 429–448.

Stone, G. R. The training function of examinations: Retest performance as a function of the amount and kind of critique information. *USAF Pers. Train. Res. Cent. Res. Rept.*, 1955, No. AFPTRC-TN-55-8.

Stuit, D. B., Harshbarger, H. C., Becker, S. L., Bechtoldt, H. P., & Hall, A. E. *An experiment in teaching.* Iowa City: Dept. of Speech, State Univer. of Iowa, 1956.

Stuit, D. B., & Wilson, J. T. The effect of an increasingly well-defined criterion on the prediction of success at Naval Training School (Tactical Radar). *J. appl. Psychol.*, 1946, 30, 614–623.

Sturgis, H. W. The relationship of the teacher's knowledge of the student's background to the effectiveness of teaching. A study· of the extent to which the effectiveness of teaching is related to the teacher's knowledge of the student's personal background. Unpublished doctoral dissertation, New York Univer., 1958. (*Dissertation Abstr.*, 1959, 19, 11)

Taylor, S. Helen. An experiment in classification of students in mathematics. *Math. Teacher*, 1931, 24, 414–423.

Tharp, J. B. Sectioning in Romance language classes at the University of Illinois. In *Studies in modern language teaching.* New York: Macmillan, 1930. Pp. 367–432.

Thistlethwaite, D. L. College environments and the development of talent. *Science*, 1959, 130, 71–76.

Thistlethwaite, D. L. College press and changes in study plans of talented students. Evanston, Ill.: National Merit Scholarship Corp., 1960.

Throop, J. F., Assini, L. T., & Boguslavsky, G. W. *The effectiveness of laboratory instruction in strength of materials by closed-circuit television.* Troy, N.Y.: Rensselaer Polytechnic Inst., 1958.

Timmel, G. B. A study of the relationship between method of teaching a college course in mental hygiene and change in student adjustment status. Unpublished doctoral dissertation, Cornell Univer., 1954. (*Dissertation Abstr.*, 1955, 15, 90)

Ullrich, O. A. An experimental study in ability grouping. Unpublished doctoral dissertation, Univer. of Texas, 1926.

Underwood, B. J. Interference and forgetting. *Psychol. Rev.*, 1957, 64, 49–60.

VanderMeer, A. W. *Relative effectiveness of instruction by films exclusively, films plus study guides, and standard lecture methods.*

(Pennsylvania State Univer. Instructional Film Research Program) Port Washington, N.Y.: U.S. Naval Training Device Center, Office of Naval Research, Tech. Rept. No. SDC 269-7-13, July, 1950.

VanderMeer, A. W. *Effect of film-viewing practice on learning from instructional films.* (Pennsylvania State Univer. Instructional Film Research Program) Port Washington, N.Y.: U.S. Naval Training Device Center, Office of Naval Research, Tech. Rept. No. SDC 269-7-20, November, 1951.

Vinacke, W. E. Some variables in buzz sessions. *J. soc. Psychol.,* 1957, 45, 25–33.

Wakely, J. H., Marr, J. N., Plath, D. W., & Wilkins, D. M. Lecturing and test performance in introductory psychology. Paper read at Michigan Academy of Science, Ann Arbor, March, 1960.

Ward, J. Group-study vs. lecture-demonstration method in physical science instruction for general education college students. *J. exp. Educ.,* 1956, 24, 197–210.

Warren, R. A comparison of two plans of study in engineering physics. Unpublished doctoral dissertation, Purdue Univer., 1954. (*Dissertation Abstr.,* 1954, 14, 1648–1649)

Waterhouse, I. K., & Child, I. L. Frustration and the quality of performance. *J. Personnel,* 1953, 21, 298–311.

Watson, R. P. The relationship between selected personality variables, satisfaction, and academic achievement in defined classroom atmospheres. Unpublished doctoral dissertation, Univer. of Michigan, 1956.

Weitman, M., & Gruber, H. E. Experiments in self-instructed study: Effects on immediate achievement, performance of achievement and educational values. Paper read at Western Psychol. Ass., San Jose, Calif., April, 1960.

White, J. R. Methods in engineering laboratory instruction. *J. engng Educ.,* 1945, 36, 50–54.

Wieder, G. S. Group procedures modifying attitudes of prejudice in the college classroom. *J. educ. Psychol.,* 1954, 45, 332–344.

Wilke, W. H. An experimental comparison of the speech, the radio, and the printed page as propaganda devices. *Arch. Psychol., N.Y.,* 1934, 25, No. 169.

Williams, J. E. Mode of failure, interference tendencies, and achievement imagery. *J. abnorm. soc. Psychol.,* 1955, 51, 573–580.

Wispé, L. G. Evaluating section teaching methods in the introductory course. *J. educ. Res.,* 1951, 45, 161–186.

Wolfle, D. The relative efficiency of constant and varied stimulation during learning. *J. comp. Psychol.,* 1935, 19, 5–27.

Woodworth, R. S., & Schlosberg, H. *Experimental psychology.* (Rev. ed.) New York: Holt, 1954.

Zeleny, L. D. Experimental appraisal of a group learning plan. *J. educ. Res.,* 1940, 34, 37–42.

Name and Subject Index

Abbott, M. G., 729, 730, 805, 993

Abbott-Trabue Exercises in Judging Poetry, 993

Abelard, P.: and the rise of the universities, 4; teaching method of, 16; and the problem of universals, 18; dialectic of, 18; efforts to evoke mood or attitude in pupil, 39–40; use of logic to rationalize Church teachings, 41; mentioned, 1, 2, 17, 42

Abell, M. A., 1063, 1094

Abelson, P., 26, 42

Abrams, Barbara K., 852, 859

Absolute Idealism: and Froebel, 32–36

Abstraction Ladder, 897

Academic freedom: studies of, 936

Achievement: attempts to study behaviors related to, 286–290; in "activity" schools, 290–292; attempts to improve predictions from intelligence test scores, 400–403; relation to teacher-pupil interaction, 424–425, 569, 698–699; in "Pyramid plan" classes, 427–428, 1139; effect of teacher personality on, 533; and reflective theory of teaching, 939; in algebra, 1023; in foreign language teaching, 1092–1093

Achievement examinations: uses of, 385–386; effect on students, 392–393; effect on teachers and curriculum, 393–394; improvement of, 394–395

Achievement need: attempts to measure, 401

Achievement words versus process words, 1027–1028

Ackerman, J. S., 1110, 1114

Ackerman, W. I., 116, 139, 476, 501, 1032, 1056

Acquiescence set: characteristic of MTAI and California F Scale, 522

Active and passive review, 610–611, 615, 644

Active learning: versus passive learning, 1121–1122, 1128; promotion of by discussion methods, 1133

Active recall, 1077

Active student response: as object of experimentation, 609–610; effectiveness of, 610–611, 616–628; time as a variable in experiments on, 611–614; optimum amount of, 614–615; roles of, 615; direct-practice effects versus side effects, 615–616; form of overt response in verbal learning, 616–617; overt and covert responding, 617–619; feedback, reinforcement, and knowledge of results, 619–621; cueing or prompting, 621–623; prompting versus confirmation, 623–624; interaction of prompting and overt responses, 624–625; organizational and sequencing factors, 625–626; "size of step" experiments, 626–627; self-pacing of practice, 627; teaching machine instrumentation, 627–628; stimulus control, 628; interaction with amount of review, 644

Activities Index, 406–407, 417, 424, 1161

"Activity" schools, 290–292, 470, 693–694

Adams, Fay, 905, 928

Adams, J. A., 937, 951, 964

Adams, J. C., 1093, 1096, 1150, 1164

Adams, J. F., 1131, 1171

Adams, R. B., 1149, 1169

Adaptability: of school systems, 779

Adelson, J., 136, 138, 139, 740, 807

Adjunctive or nonprogramed materials: survey of research on, 608–609

Adkins, M., 406, 444

Adler, A., 456, 505

Administrator behavior: Halpin's paradigm for, 106–108; styles of, 781–788; autocratic and democratic, 781–785; other styles of, 785–788

Administrators: and ranking of teacher roles, 450

Adorno, T. W., 406, 423, 434, 523, 576, 751, 783, 805

Adult-Child Interaction Test (ACI), 557, 558, 565

Agard, F. B., 1063, 1066, 1067, 1068, 1070, 1071, 1093, 1094

and observed, 306–307; quantifying results of, 307–325; dimensionalizing classroom behavior, 308–309; definition of reliability coefficient, 309–310; general design for estimation of reliability, 310–312; adaptation of design to a particular study, 312–315; measuring changes in, 317–320; analyzing results of methods experiments, 320–321; analyzing results of surveys, 321–325; effect of observers' presence in classroom, 425

Observational techniques: nature of, 250–254; defined, 250; validity of, 250–253; abstractive and coding functions of observers, 251–253; reliability coefficients, 253; coefficient of observer agreement, 253–254; stability coefficient, 254

Occupational background of teachers, 720

Occupational mobility: effect on teaching-learning process, 753–756

Occupational prestige of teaching: 744–748; basis for prestige estimates, 744–746; ratings of, 746–747; consequences of, 747–748

Occupational selectivity: consequences of, 740–741

Occupations: rankings of, 746–747

Odell, W. C., 772, 811

Odenweller, A. L., 725, 811

O'Dowd, D. D., 418, 435

Oelke, M. C., 511, 558, 580

Office of Strategic Services: assessment program, 402–403

Ogilvie, J. C., 1153, 1170

O'Hara, R. P., 157, 169

Ohio Physics Scholarship Test, 1047

Ohio Social Acceptance Scale, 533, 691, 694, 705, 785

Ohio State University, University High School Class, 1938, 692, 713

Ohlsen, M. M., 417, 420, 443, 444, 529, 530, 558, 565, 580, 581

Oinas, F. J., 591, 679, 1062, 1096, 1099

Ojemann, R. H., 478, 504, 694, 695, 713, 752, 811

Oliver, W. A., 423, 443, 751, 812

Olson, Edna, 545, 559, 560, 565, 578, 853, 854, 855, 856, 861

Olson, W. C., 345, 376, 465, 497, 498, 504, 691, 692, 713, 818, 820, 833, 849, 863, 912, 925

Omnibus Personality Inventory, 431

One-group pretest-posttest design, 177–182, 217

One-shot case study, 176–177

Operational concepts, 58

Operational definitions, 49–50

Operationism, 62, 710

Opochinsky, S., 1124, 1131, 1170

Oppenheim, P., 952, 964

Oral-aural method: comparison with conventional method of teaching foreign languages, 1066–1067

Oral questioning, 1022

Oration: divisions of, 7

Oratory: as objective of education, 5

Orbison, W. D., 1076, 1099

Ordinal scales, 146

Organicism, 53

Orleans, J. S., 139, 140

O'Rourke, L. J., 977, 1004

Osborn, A. F., 1116

Osburn, W. J., 887, 925

OScAR, 268–269, 278–286, 304, 308, 321

Osgood, C. E., 139, 354, 360, 361, 362, 377, 378, 758, 759, 1085, 1087, 1096

Osgood-Suci *D* statistic, 758, 759

O'Shea, M. V., 977, 1005

OSS Assessment Staff, 402, 414, 443

Ostreicher, L. M., 417, 443, 517, 518, 562, 564, 580

Otis Group Intelligence Test, 533, 694

Otis-Pintner test, 694

Otis Quick-Scoring Mental Ability Test, 1049

Otomo, A., 1091, 1097

Otterman, L. M., 891, 925

Ottina, J. R., 473, 505

Otto, H. J., 609, 679

Overchosen: defined, 347, 354

Overt response: in verbal learning, 616–617; comparison with covert response, 617–619; interaction with prompting, 624–625

Overton, R. K., 1098

Ovid, 7

P technique, 411, 414

Pace, C. R., 406, 443, 750, 812, 1161, 1170

Page, D., 1026

Page, E. B., 191, 193, 244

Page, M. L., 842, 863

Page, Martha H., 420, 443, 446, 555, 556, 563, 565, 580, 581

Paired associates: comparison of multiple-choice and constructive responding, 616–617; comparison of methods of learning, 622–623, 624; use of pictures versus words in learning of, 636–637; varying amount of review in teaching, 644; determination of most effective practice sequence, 648–649; and foreign language vocabulary learning, 1074–1075

Palmer, J. R., 954, 964

Palmer, Josephine S., 459, 460, 504

Palos, Viola A., 875, 876, 911, 921

Pan, S., 622, 679

Panel studies, 237–238

Paradigms: nature and uses of, 95–102; representation of variables and their relationships, 95; generality of, 95–96; for Pavlovian conditioning, 95–96; explicit and implicit, 96; innovation-installation process, 97–99; usefulness of, 100–101; for statistical methods, 102–103; for psychopathologies, 103–106; for administrator behavior, 106–108; for research on group dynamics, 108–110; for small group research, 110–113; criterion-of-effectiveness paradigms, 113–120; Wisconsin studies, 115; types of criteria of effectiveness, 115–116; Domas-Tiedeman categories, 115–116; "ultimacy" of criteria of teacher effectiveness, 116–117; "career levels" and criteria of teacher effectiveness, 117–118; Mitzel's refinement of criterion-of-effectiveness paradigm, 118–120; "micro-criteria" of effectiveness, 120; teaching process paradigms, 120–129; Smith, 121–122, 127, 128, 134; Ryans, 122–125, 127, 128, 134; Stone-Leavitt, 125–128, 134; Runkel, 126–127, 128, 134; common elements in